Osborn First-Line Index

First-Line Index of English Poetry 1500–1800
in Manuscripts
of the James M. and Marie-Louise

Osborn Collection

in the Beinecke Rare Book and
Manuscript Library of Yale University

EDITED BY MANY HANDS UNDER THE DIRECTION OF

Stephen Parks, *Curator*

CONTINUED BY

Marc Greitens

COMPLETED BY

Carolyn W. Nelson

BEINECKE RARE BOOK AND MANUSCRIPT LIBRARY

Yale University · New Haven · Connecticut

To the memory of James M. Osborn,
who first dreamed of this index
more than half a century ago

Designed by Greer Allen
Typeset by Tseng Information Systems, Inc., Durham, North Carolina
Printed by Thames Printing Company, Norwich, Connecticut
Bound by Acme Bookbinding Company, Charlestown, Massachusetts

The Beinecke Rare Book & Manuscript Library
Yale University
P. O. Box 208240
New Haven, Connecticut 06520-8240
U.S.A.

Library of Congress Cataloging-in-Publication Data
Beinecke Rare Book and Manuscript Library.
First-line index of English poetry, 1500-1800, in manuscripts of the
James M. and Marie-Louise Osborn Collection in the Beinecke Rare Book
and Manuscript Library of Yale University / edited by many hands under the
direction of Stephen Parks, curator ; continued by Marc Greitens ; completed
by Carolyn W. Nelson.
p. cm.
ISBN 0-8457-3162-9 (alk. paper)
1. English poetry—Early modern, 1500-1700—Indexes. 2. Manuscripts, English—
Connecticut—New Haven—Indexes. 3. Osborn, James Marshall—Library—Indexes.
4. Osborn, Marie-Louise—Library—Indexes. 5. English poetry—18th century—Indexes.
6. Openings (Rhetoric)—Indexes. I. Parks, Stephen. II. Greitens, Marc.
III. Nelson, Carolyn W. IV. Title.
Z2014.P7B36 2005
[PR531]
016.811008—dc22
                                                          2005022944

Contents

vii   Introduction

ix   Editorial Note

1   First-Line Index

1109   Index of Osborn Manuscripts Listed by Shelf-Marks

1111   Index of Authors

1136   Index of Names Mentioned

1180   Index of Authors of Works Translated, Paraphrased, or Imitated

1188   Index of References to Composers of Settings

            and of Tunes Named or Quoted

Introduction

The Osborn Collection first-line index began in 1968 with an interleaved copy of Margaret Crum's index of poetry in the Bodleian Library, published by the Index Committee of the Modern Language Association, which had long been chaired by James Osborn. Mr Osborn and a few colleagues in the Yale English department had created the Index Committee in the late 1940s to publish works of reference without profit and to plow back any earnings into future publications. Their major success was Donald Wing's Short-title catalogue of English books published from 1640 to 1700. In 1968, before turning their assets over to the Modern Language Association of America, they published the Bodleian index.

English poetry was Mr Osborn's original focus as a collector and scholar, and from the 1930s he amassed a large gathering of English manuscripts, chiefly poetry. Some of it was autograph, but the majority were single sheets as they were circulated in the seventeenth and eighteenth centuries, much as we would circulate photocopies of political satires today, and volumes of collected verse. Mr Osborn's collection was immensely valuable to the editors of the eight volumes of *Poems on Affairs of State*, edited by various members of the Yale English department and published by Yale in the 1950s, whose editorial tasks included the comparison of many versions of certain political and satirical verses in order to establish the correct text and to explain obscure references.

Mr Osborn had long envisioned a first-line index of the poetry in the Osborn Collection, and for years he had his own research assistants, young scholars from Oxford who came for a year or two, work on indexing the poems in his collection. From 1968, with the help of Yale undergraduates who worked for me in the Beinecke Library, where the Osborn Collection was now housed, we entered references to Osborn Collection verses in our interleaved Crum and made cards for those not in Crum.

By the time of Mr Osborn's death in 1976 we had accumulated about 3,000 annotations in our interleaved volume and about 8,000 cards in our own file of English poetry in the Osborn Collection not in the Bodleian.

The first-line index was taken off the back burner by Marc Greitens, a Yale graduate student who proposed to survey our shelves and files of manuscripts and locate items not yet listed, to methodically search our acquisitions of English verse made during the period when work on the first-line index was in abeyance, and to combine entries from our interleaved Crum with those on our own cards. This task required a knowledge of early Modern English language spellings, abbreviations and forms of expression, an understanding of traditional forms of versification and, at this stage, an understanding and experience with multiple computer languages, including word processing, database entry, and on-line research.

Unfortunately, Marc Greitens left Yale when the project had not long been underway, but we were very fortunate to have the formidable technical skills and interest in the project volunteered by Carolyn Nelson, who earlier had compiled the invaluable index to *The Luttrell File*, which I had just completed with the assistance of Earle Havens. It is fair to say that the completion of this index is due primarily to the skill, tenacity, and sheer determination of Carolyn Nelson, to whom we owe immense gratitude. For my part, as I am about to retire as Curator of the James M. and Marie-Louise Osborn Collection, I am very happy indeed to see the completion of this project, which Mr Osborn had first envisioned many years ago.

STEPHEN PARKS, Curator,
James M. and Marie-Louise Osborn Collection.
December 2004

Editorial Note

The printed version of this index was compiled from three sources: from the card index prepared by research assistants under the direction of James Osborn and later under Stephen Parks; from an annotated copy of Margaret Crum's *First-Line Index of English Poetry 1500–1800 in Manuscripts of the Bodleian Library Oxford* (Oxford University Press, 1969); and from computerized index files compiled from manuscripts (for the most part new acquisitions) not included in the card index or the Bodleian index. All of the entries were keyed or rekeyed using Microsoft Word. The Word files were then exported to Excel spreadsheets and combined into one database. The Excel entries were sorted according to shelfmark reference, checked against the original manuscript, and eventually resorted alphabetically according to first line and exported back into Word files.

The arrangement of the entries follows that of Margaret Crum's index (first line, last line, author if known, title, editorial information, and shelfmark). Entries for poems also found in separately printed form include references to D. F. Foxon's *English Verse 1701–1750* and Donald Wing's *Short-Title Catalogue of Books Printed in England, Scotland, Ireland, Wales, and British America, and of English Books Printed in Other Countries, 1641–1700* in the editorial notes. Entries for poems also found in Margaret Crum's index are followed by the 'Crum number', and entries for poems printed in the Yale edition of *Poems on Affairs of State* are followed by a reference to those volumes.

The spelling of first lines, last lines, and title has been modernized, but contractions such as 'heav'n' and 'wish'd' have been retained. 'O' and 'Oh' have been interfiled in the alphabetical sequence, as have 'Thro'/'Through' and 'Tho'/'Though'.

Since the chronological scope of the indexing project includes the years 1500–1800, datable later poems from manuscripts that cross the century line have been omitted.

Of poems known to be incomplete, only those which begin with the first line of the complete poem are included in the index, and are distinguished by '(incomplete)' following the shelfmark. Extracts from longer poems which do not include the first line have generally been omitted from the index.

When a poem exists in more than one copy or version, the first shelfmark listed is that from which the text of the first line, last line, and title is taken. Versions with a different last line, or other significant differences, are distinguished by a parenthetical note such as '(var.)', following the shelfmark of the variant.

Carolyn W. Nelson

A

A0001   A bad woman! Heav'n bless us, Sirs, who dare
But prithee (reader) show me one that's good.

     'The character of a bad woman Mant[uanus]
     ecl[ogue] 3'
     fb.68, p. 103

A0002   A bag-wig of a jaunty air,
And plainness in the dress of use.

     [Christopher Smart], 'The bag-wig and the tobacco
     pipe a fable'
     c.578, p. 158

A0003   A ball of stiffen'd rain from Julia flew,
Love's madded wildfire, but an equal flame.

     c.189, p. 51

A0004   A ballad late was made
And came again in May.

     William Lakes, 'A reply unto the former song' ['It is
     not now a fortnight . . .']
     [Crum A2]
     b.197, p. 73; b.200, p. 73

A0005   A bard, dear Muse; unapt to sing
Farewell to Burnham beeches!

     Henry Luttrell, 'Burnham beeches'
     File 17071 (autogr.)

A0006   A bard on whom Phoebus a steed had bestow'd,
By this good man's art was transformed to an [ass].

     [Phanuel Bacon], 'Extempore, on reading the
     foregoing verses ['Reader, expect no flattery here . . .'],
     which are only a lengthening of a short copy of verses
     written on the same subject, at the request of the
     author of this volume'
     c.237, fol. 82v [i.e., 102v]

A0007   A basket of French nuts a lad had got
I found at the last there were 36 score and one.

     'A dialogue between a boy and his mother', with
     'Answer'
     c.115

A0008   A beau would smile to see the young divine
That choice, since 'tis for you is fully justified.

     'To Mrs. Wait of Broad-Somerford my Valentine
     1699—presenting to her Mr. Collier's essays'
     b.322, p. 4

A0009   A beauteous nymph, who long was ill at ease,
The six first letters of the six first lines.

     'A receipt' [acrostic on 'a prick']
     c.189, p. 167

A0010   A beautiful daughter lies here
And she died, at the age of fourteen.

     'An epitaph'
     c.378, p. 65

A0011   A beauty bright Dorinda is her name,
And they like these constant and just may prove.

     'Bion and Dorinda. A pastoral'
     fb.142, p. 19

A0012   A beauty comes, a heroine in her air
And fill her veins with Charles's royal blood.

     [Horace Walpole, 4th earl of Orford], 'Countess of
     Harrington'
     c.157, p. 70

A0013   A beauty not to art in debt,
I give my love, I give my life.

     Poetry Box x/73

A0014   A beauty smoother than an ivory plain
Those hearts are double slain, it shines so bright.

     [William Strode], 'On a gentlewoman injured by the
     [small]pox'
     [Crum A11]
     b.197, p. 156; b.205, fol. 33v; b.356, p. 265

A0015   A beauty without art complete
I'd give my love, I'd give my life.

     [Ambrose Philips?], 'If e'er I quit the single life | Be
     this the model of my wife . . . Free-thinker no. [ ]'
     c.549, p. 111

A0016   A beggar, a beggar, a beggar I'll be
A bonny bold jolly bold beggar to be.

     'A song to the tune of When the weather is cold and
     raw'
     b.207, p. 23

A0017   A beggar can bang a man of estate
By heaven 'tis all a joke.

     'A rencounter between a gentleman and a beggar'
     c.360/1, p. 217

A0018 A beggarman exceeding poor
Yet both of us our oaths did save.

    'A riddle'

c.356

A0019 A bishop thou art Peter's successor
Religiously—to speed this is the way.

    [Sir Philip Wodehouse], 'Episcopus anagrammata . . .
    thus Englished . . .'

b.131, back (no. 8)

A0020 A blest and happy ark be thou? Wherein
Till dear to God, and friends, I pass away.

    [Sir Philip Wodehouse], 'Upon Mrs. Betty Cradock—
    Dr. Brown's niece . . .'

b.131, back (no. 67)

A0021 A blockhead! Void of sense and prudence too!
'Oons you're too low by much—you want a head.

    [Thomas Hull]

c.528/39

A0022 A blooming flow'r my Chloe chose
Oh think how few would live!

    'Song'

c.90

A0023 A boar who had enjoy'd a happy reign,
Destroy each other, every mother's son.

    [George Granville, 1st baron] Lansdowne, 'The wild
    boar's defense'

c.186, p. 120

A0024 A book is never lik'd, till first we're told
And you, 'tis hop'd, will follow their example.

    [William O'Brian and David Garrick], 'Prologue' [for
    O'Brian's The duel]

Acquisition 92.3.1ff. (autogr.)

A0025 A book to help the young and gay
To please all sorts there is a strain.

    'A bookseller's whimsical advertisement 1751.
    Tomorrow will be published . . .'

c.360/3, no. 97

A0026 A box well fill'd is a rich store
But often lent will soon grow poor.

    [John Rose?]

b.227, p. 36

A0027 A brace of sinners, for no good,
I took the liberty to boil my peas.

    John Wolcot ('Peter Pindar'), 'The pilgrims and the
    peas. A true story (from Peter Pindar's Farewell odes)'

c.90

A0028 A British youth to an Italian dame
'Come home my dear and lie with me tonight.'

    [William] Parsons, [July 1685]
    [Crum A29]

Greatheed Box/49

A0029 A Briton I toast, whom good Britons revere
But the arts of the wicked may justice confound! |
              To Cumberland Fletcher success!

    John Lockman, 'Cumberland Fletcher's health: 2d
    Decr. 1768. A new ballad. The tune O the roast beef
    of old England &c. to be sung east, west, north and
    south'

c.267/4, p. 395

A0030 A brood of legendary saints of old
Whose rites, thy pen, did in sad time retrieve.

    [Thomas] Fuller, 'Mr Fuller on Dr Sparke's book'

b.137, p. 2

A0031 A brother died—a much-lov'd brother's bier,
The temp'rate (nay th'abstemious) life he led.

    [James Mulcaster, sr.], 'On the death of a younger by
    an elder brother'

c.118, p. 21

A0032 A bumper of good liquor
That's crabbed when he's mellow.

    'Song 42'

c.555, p. 67

A0033 A butcher with a heart as hard as stone
While all the time—good soul!—she skins live
                     eels!

    'Habit'

c.81/1, no. 252

A0034 A butcher's son judge capital
And so like a knave we leave thee.

    [Stephen College?], 'Upon Judge Scroggs about [Sir
    George] Wakeman's trial: 1679'
    [POAS II.284]

b.54, p. 1111; b.327, f. 3

A0035 A buxom widow, stories tell,
Cried she and do your worst.

    Earl of B—k, 'On Lady F—r'

c.74

A0036 A buxom young beggar was toasting of cheese
The man—not the mouse—would be caught in the
                     gin.

    'Toasted cheese'

c.241, p. 78

A0037 A buzzing fly with fervid zeal
The one is in—the other out.

    S[tephen] Simpson, 'The fly, the wasp and the bee a
    fable'

c.563

A0038 A candle always cannot stand upright
The reason is because his head is light.

    'On a candle'

b.356, p. 308

A0039 A cannon ball, one bloody day,
His leg was off, and not his head.

    [William Taylor], 'The mistake' [Dodsley Collection]

c.487, p. 140; fc.130, p. 81

A0040 A carcass vile lies here to rot
The devil's agent, John à Barnes.

    George Eyre, 'Epitaph on John Barnes . . . this man
    was an agent for the Duke of Devonshire, when the
    farm in Woodland was raised, and set value on the
    lands'

c.160, fol. 45

A0041 A carter there was, pray attend to my theme
Is fittest for Hamilton Tertio(?) or West.

    [Paul Sandly], 'Song to the tune of Derry Down'
    [1793]

File 13119

A0042 A castle fair, and reverend, I sing,
The worthy heirs of an illustrious line.

    'Tamworth castle'

Accession 97.7.40

A0043 A catalogue of curious books concerning
Give printed priced catalogues to any.

    [ ] Jackson, 'Jackson the bookseller's whimsical
    advertisement[.] This day is published . . .'

c.360/2, no. 18

A0044 A cater one time did sink in the hid
Whereby his deuce was made to stir apace.

    Sir Thomas Urquhart, 'All the parts of the dice may
    be found in this tetrastich'

fb.217, p. 332

A0045 A certain artist, I forget his name,
Resolv'd to post him for an arrant heat.

    [John Byrom, of Manchester], 'A fragment'

c.140, p. 1

A0046 A certain country gent, scarce half a man
To have at least a new one ev'ry year.

    R[obert] Shirley, 1st earl of Ferrers, 'The book. From
    the French'

c.347, p. 95

A0047 A certain great patriot whose name you may guess,
Whilst this spirit of Cha[t]h[a]m survives in his
                           son.

    'The private reflections of a patriot . . . Jan 31. 1784'

c.83/3, no. 880; File 294

A0048 A certain idle wag of late,
Was water in a freezing state.

    [Enigma/Charade/Conundrum 79c]

c.389

A0049 A certain man four children had
William and Mary, George and Anne. | Mary,
                           Mary &c.

    'The four children' [of James II]
    [Crum A43]

b.111, p. 373

A0050 A certain old cook called his dog cuckold
To call a dog after Christian's name.

    'On a cuckold'
    [Crum A46]

b.62, p. 78

A0051 A certain poetaster, not long since
Whose ushers walk before him, where he goes.

    Sir Thomas Urquhart, 'One speaks here of a
    presumptuous, yet very bad poet'

fb.217, p. 79

A0052 A certain Presbyterian pair
The parson sung a psalm.

    'The matrimonial consummation'

c.360/1, p. 223

A0053 A certain priest had hoarded up
Your God is rise[n] and gone.

    'Upon a priest that hid money'
    [Crum A47]

b.104, p. 117; c.81/1, no. 302

A0054 A certain priest once riding on the way
Since priests have learnt to bless without a cross.

b.62, p. 114

A0055 A certain rich knight | In amorous plight
And stoop to an ignoble passion.

    'On Sir Abraham Shard's kissing the girl at the coffee
    house at Tunbridge Wells 1745'

c.360/2, no. 70

A0056 A chandler, once upon a time
Your worship's wife, had managed better.

[Thomas Hamilton, 6th earl of Haddington], 'The
chandler from La Fontaine'

c.458/2, p. 72

A0057 A chandler's shop being robb'd a neighbor
Your candles, Sir, must come to light.

c.546, p. 32

A0058 A cheerful glass shall raise man to a god,
But drain the goblet, and he sinks a clod.

John Lockman, 'A hint'

c.267/1, p. 74

A0059 A cheerful peace of conscience
Exalt 'em to love's [?] sphere, the realms above.

[Edmund Wodehouse], 'Decr. 6 [1714]'

b.131, p. 106

A0060 A chief of high mettle mankind to convince
That poor hungry author's weak part is his belly.

'On the duel betwixt [Frederick Augustus] Duke of
York, and Col. Lennox [later duke of Richmond;
1789], also betwixt the Col[onel] and an author'

c.90

A0061 A child, and dead? Alas how should this come,
Surely his thread of life was but a thrum.

[Thomas Freeman], 'On an infant'

b.356, p. 249

A0062 A child so young to sweep the quivering strings,
With heavenly sounds our ravish'd ears to charm?

[John Lockman], 'Hearing Dr. Pepusch's son play on
the harpsichord'

c.268 (first part), p. 30

A0063 A choir of bright beauties in spring did appear,
When Pan, little Daphne, and Syrinx return.

[John] Dryden, 'A song made against May Day 1691'
[Crum A58]

fb.207/3, p. 38; b.111, p. 80

A0064 A choir of friends this morning on you wait,
And health and ease here guard your peaceful bed.

'To Mrs Christian Kerr of Chatto on her birthday
August 22d 1727[.] Inscribed to her cousin John Kerr
of Frogden at whose house she resided and was that
day entertained'

c.102, p. 132

A0065 A chosen privacy a cheap content
Be virtuous, is the great immortal man.

[Katherine Philips], 'A resvery [revery]'
[Crum A59]

b.118, p. 71

A0066 A Christian, Sir, is one of Adam's race,
In heav'nly mansions thither brought by grace.

[Thomas Stevens?], 'Question, what is a Christian?
Answer . . . April 22. 1780'

c.259, p. 82

A0067 A Christian slave did once obtain,
Worse than he was in double chains.

[Mrs. Christian Kerr], 'By a Christian slave to a
Turkish lady upon drawing her for a valentine'

c.102, p. 101

A0068 A cinquefoil marrying with a star does show
The flow'r must stoop, to th'spangle of the sky.

[Sir Philip Wodehouse], 'Upon Dr. Astley dean of
Norwich his arms a cinquefoil marrying with Miss
Hobarts who bears a star'

b.131, p. 3 and back (after anagram 235)

A0069 A Clement mean
That Clem's as good as John-a-Green.

[Sir Philip Wodehouse], 'Clement Green'

b.131, back (no. 208/2)

A0070 A clerk of Oxford next appear'd in sight,
And gladly would he learn, and gladly teach.

'The clerk or scholar of Oxford' [modernized from
Chaucer]

c.83/2, no. 355

A0071 A cobbler there was and he liv'd in a hall
That love brings us all to an end at the last. | Derry
down, &c.

'The cobbler's end' [on Dr. Bentham, Regius
Professor of Divinity at Oxford]
[Crum A67]

fc.61, p. 67; Accession 97.7.40, p. 26 ('stall'); see also
'There was a cobbler . . .'.

A0072 A cobbler to be hanged, on the way
Call not a halter; 'tis but a cobbler's end.

'On Walter Ree a cobbler being to be hanged'

b.104, p. 5 (end of book)

A0073 A cock within a stable pent,
We tread not upon one another.

Poetry Box II/9

A0074   A comely creature that of late was sped
We'll to it each morn for health each night for
                                  pleasure.

     'Upon a new married woman'

b.205, fol. 49r; see also 'A lady that was lately . . .', 'A
lady which had oftentimes . . .'.

A0075   A comet, blazing with a glow-worm's zeal,
The burial of (Jehorakin) an ass.

     'On a seperatist'

b.356, p. 243

A0076   A common theme a flattering muse may fire
Adieu! Till then my little saint adieu!

     'A poem sacred to the memory of a dearly beloved and
only daughter who died in the eleventh year of her
age. Written by her mourning father'

c.517, fol. 10v

A0077   A conscience clear is like a wall of brass
When guilty minds are rack'd with fearful fits.

b.234, p. 311

A0078   A countess of fame
His bed should to Bridges be common.

     'An ill song to a good old tune'

fb.70, p. 28

A0079   A country clown, while cleaving of a block,
Says he, forsooth, I do not cleave, but bore.

     Sir R[ichard] B[ulstrode], 'In rusticum epigramma
Georgii Buchanum Scot . . . Englished by Sir R. B.'

fb.88, p. 118v; see also 'A rustic . . .', 'A country
swain . . .'.

A0080   A country family for London bound
Who might as well have thought of raising rent.

     [Maurice Johnson], 'On Squire Putterkin and his
family's journey to London to buy a new coach'

c.229/2, fol. 9v

A0081   A country fellow coarser cloth'd than witted
Forsooth quoth he because you have no law.

     '[Epigrams.] 2. In causidicum'
     [Crum A74]

b.205, fol. 97r

A0082   A countryman some sweetings pull'd,
To curb his own desire.

b.53, p. 70

A0083   A country parson of great note
With a divine and am'rous fire.

     Will[iam] Steer, 'Decemb. 26th, 1738 . . . The
breeches'

c.160, fol. 38

A0084   A country swain was cleaving of a block
For then I cleaving was but now I bore.

     'On a countryman'
     [cf. Crum A259, A408]

b.62, p. 41; see also 'A country clown . . .', 'A rustic . . .'.

A0085   A courtier answer'd to some pious men,
For my thoughts only on the earth are bent.

     Sir Thomas Urquhart, 'The profane reply of a gallant
to certain devote and zealous men'

fb.217, p. 233

A0086   A courtier profess'd, much esteem'd by the great
And depend on my service to tell my Lord Bute.

     N. B—y, [To the gentlemen freeholders of the county
of Gloucester; dated '1763', i.e., 1753?]
     [Crum A79]

Poetry Box IV/138 (dated 1763)

A0087   A covetous priest did lay in store a secret nigh of
                                      gold
Wrote on *surrexit, non est hic,* your god is rose and
                                      gone.

     'A covetous priest'
     [Crum A81]

b.62, p. 77

A0088   A crabbed stump, yet silly husband's care
The thing, which never flourished, should wither.

     [George Daniel], 'Enigma'

b.121, fol. 51

A0089   A Cretan says—all Cretans liars are
And lying, must speak truth—fine sophistry.

     [Sir Philip Wodehouse], 'Ephemeridis'

b.131, p. 32

A0090   A cuckold is a horned beast
As for to know his maker.

     'On a cuckold'

b.356, p. 307

A0091   A curse on impert'nent age
Or leavings of many a whore.

     'The young gallant'

fb.107, p. 80

A0092   A custom most right for a blessing most rare—
You'd eaten your own, and I sav'd my, bacon!

     [Charles Earle], 'The flitch. A New Year's gift,
extempore to Mr. and Mrs. E[arle?]'

c.376

A0093   A dawn of hope my soul revives
She sinks into his arms.

    'A dawn of hope'

c.361

A0094   A day of sorrow, darkness, and of death
In the rich garb, of Christianity.

    'Good Friday'

fc.54, p. 52

A0095   A day's a rose's life how quickly meet
Then snatch the gifts there and hurl so swift away.

    W[illiam] Smith

Smith Papers, folder 73

A0096   A deacon write epigrams! why should he not?
A deacon shall then an archdeacon be thought.

    'On a deacon writing epigrams'

c.152, p. 75

A0097   A dean, and prebendary
And ne'er was heard on since.

    [William Pittis], 'The battle royal between
Mr. Sherlock, Dr. South and Dr. Burnet of the
Charter House' [1695]
[Crum A99; POAS V.472]

c.189, p. 187; c.150, p. 164

A0098   A diamond set in brass may be neglected
And scorn this earthly and vain habitation.

    [Mary Serjant]

fb.98, fol. 168

A0099   A doctor of divinity thou art
Chang'd with K[ing] Edward—Mary—Elizabeth.

    [Sir Philip Wodehouse], 'Dr. William Starkey I am
stark Will'

b.131, back (no. 208/1)

A0100   A doctor once; now gladiator made,
Add eight companions, and he makes a man.

    'Upon an unskillful physician's fighting a duel'

c.53, fol. 19

A0101   A dog, at hunger's urgent call,
Truth's rarely found reflected in the glass.

    'On covetousness . . . the moral'

c.93

A0102   A dog—let Trooper be his name!
The breeches—crown—and something more.

    [Phanuel Bacon], 'Trooper a tale' [differs from next]

c.237, fol. 100 [i.e., 120]

A0103   A dog (let Trooper be his name,
'Tiz how—as I'm a living zoul!

    [Phanuel Bacon], 'Distincta tunica fugiundum est ac
pede nudo ne nummi periant' [differs from previous]

c.237, fol. 67 [i.e., 87]

A0104   A' done (my friend) lay pen and paper by
Their envy that will not afford thee love.

    [Sir Aston Cokayne], 'To my very good friend Mr
Tho: Bancroft on his works'

b.275, p. 111

A0105   A dove o' snow is written in her name
Speak their own mothers and never walk astray.

    [Sir Philip Wodehouse], 'An[n] Wodehouse a dove o'
snow'

b.131, back (no. 28)

A0106   A dove this arctic(?) vast did first declare
Whole earth's discov'ry's due to Columbus.

    [Sir Thomas Urquhart], 'Of Columba, and to
Columbus the messengers of Noah and Ferdinand
from the ark [?] and the court at Madrid'

fb.217, p. 513

A0107   A dowager, beyond the Tay,
Till all mankind respect me.

    [Thomas Hamilton, 6th earl of Haddington], 'Song to
the tune of Jamaica upon the Countess of St—ne,
turning Papist'

c.458/1, p. 67

A0108   A drunkard such an one I take to be,
That it would make a sober man to spew.

    [Joseph Rigby], 'The drunkard's prospective or his
burning glass' [pr. 1656 (Wing R1473)]

b.132, p. 5

A0109   A drunkard's like a sponge, whose craving lip
{Like that plant-animal/to that zoophyte} to shrink
                      for fear.

    [John Hobart], 'The character of a drunkard'

b.108, fol. 14

A0110   A Dutchman he's a sin, a bug—or is worse
Both lie interr'd herein, God-a-mercy horse.

    'On the defunct's tomb'

c.171, p. 9

A0111   A Dutchman never to a French approaches:
The Frenchmen render this more hoggish stuff,
                       guff, guff.

    Sir Thomas Urquhart, 'Of the Germans, and
Frenches'

fb.217, p. 181

A0112 A fair one, whom her helmet veils
A beauteous head may be ill-lin'd.

John Lockman, 'The paper bonnets worn by ladies'

c.267/1, p. 243; c.268 (first part), p. 3

A0113 A faithful friend in house
For her I trow.

'Riddle'

Poetry Box VII/46

A0114 A fakir (a religious well known in the east
All tortured by choice with th' invisible nail.

Richard Owen, 'The fakir: a tale' [Dodsley Collection]

c.487, p. 130

A0115 A farmer once to London went
That whilst he bites he may be bit.

'The farmer's blunder'

c.186, p. 63

A0116 A farmer, who was blest by heav'n
To prey on innocence and maids.

'The lamb and the wolf addressed to the ladies'

c.186, p. 134

A0117 A fatal illness, hast soon conveyed,
But him much [must?] follow to eternity.

'On the death of a young woman . . . copy Judith Alsop'

c.303

A0118 A father's danger could a tongue unloose,
Our mother-church complains thy faithful ardor shew.

'Upon the death of my father'

b.322, p. 50

A0119 A favor, design'd for a bard's humble table
And prove that both parties came honestly by't.

John Lockman, 'To John Fielding esqr on his sending me a fawn'

c.267/3, front flyleaf

A0120 A favorite of hearts; oh heavn'ly state!
His Lord eternal, never to be lost.

[Edmund Wodehouse], 'Feb. 14 [1715]'

b.131, p. 167

A0121 A female bird who tends her young with care,
The Christian name of her who reads you this.

'A rebus'

c.152, p. 71

A0122 A female doctor Sirs . . . and pray why not?
And makes King John submit to grave Queen Bess.

[David] Garrick, "Epilogue to The spleen or Islington spa. Written by . . . spoke by Mr. King in the character of Dr. Anodyne'

c.68, p. 166

A0123 A fitter match could never ha' been
The flesh is married to the skin.

[William Strode?], 'On a tanner marrying a butcher's daughter'
[Crum A130]

b.62, p. 1; b.200, p. 408; c.233, p. 61; b.356, p. 309

A0124 A fizgig was given
Decorum and friendship takes wing to the skies.

[John Walker?], 'The fizgig of the descent of decorum—for the sawyers' anniversary'

fc.108, fol. 43v

A0125 A flaming shrub in wat'ry orbit, set
An humble Christian's zealous sacrifice.

[Sir Philip Wodehouse], 'An emblematic essay upon his Mockus (?) ring'

b.131, p. 4

A0126 A fleeting shadow, in the horrid vale
Joy in thy thoughts; and vanish as I came.

[George Daniel], 'Vervicensis' [elegy on Richard Neville, Earl of Warwick]

b.121, fol. 3

A0127 A fool bit by fleas straight extinguish'd the light,
Saying, 'If you can't see me, I'm sure you can't bite!'

'An epigram in the Anthologia, translated'
[cf. Crum A131]

c.94

A0128 A fool that prospers: though his enterprise
Is deem'd a fool: though he were an Apollyon.

Sir Thomas Urquhart, 'The popular judgment of everything is by the event: be it good, or bad'

fb.217, p. 67

A0129 A foreign muse, not quite unknown to fame,
Your frown condemns—save them by your
applause.

'Prologue to The birthday' [by John O'Keeffe]

c.83/3, no. 1005

A0130 A fox of far more sense and grace,
A satire 'gainst our belles, and beaux.

[J. B.], 'A fable from Phaedrus'

Poetry Box IV/155

A0131 A fox, the basest of his kind,
Less cruel the poor ass await.

'The fox, the ass and the lion . . . Nov. 1774'

fc.74, p. 15

A0132 A fox would unmolested sleep,
Possesseth naught thy bags have got.

'A fable . . . Moral'

c.578, p. 19

A0133 A friend from foe is not discerned by face,
Because the bad do mask with seemly grace.

c.339, p. 316

A0134 A friend I have who never yet
And so procure, secure our happiness.

[Edmund Wodehouse], 'July 17 [1715]'

b.131, p. 232

A0135 A friend, like to ourselves, we should seek out
Because we cannot stand long on one foot.

Sir Thomas Urquhart, 'It is requisite for everyone to
have a friend'

fb.217, p. 84

A0136 A friend of virtue, a lover of lear[n]ing
Of London late Lord Mayor and alderman of same.

'On Sr Rowland Hill Lon[don] Mayor'

fb.143, p. 10

A0137 A friend sequester'd in a land remote,
With saints be number'd and rejoin my friend.

J[ames] Gough, 'An epistle from . . . to J. Fry'

c.139, p. 451

A0138 A friend to all whom justice can defend;
Impartial justice would our rites [rights?] maintain.

'A true character of Ld. C[hief] J[ustice] Pratt' [later
earl of Camden; Whitehall evening post, 22 Dec.
1763]

c.157, p. 72

A0139 A funeral hearse with wreaths of cyprus crested
What must be done at last, as good at first.

'A prolusion upon the emblem of the third chapter'

c.189, p. 72

A0140 A future life the object is
All we shall see, all we shall hear.

[Edmund Wodehouse], 'Septr 10 [1715]'

b.131, p. 262

A0141 A gallant lady sitting in a mews,
My key can open, but not shut the lock.

[Sir John Harington], 'On a lady sitting straddling'
[Crum A151]

b.200, p. 430; see also 'A virtuous lady . . .'.

A0142 A gallant leading by the hand a Scots,
Away with thee; this flesh is for the spit.

Sir Thomas Urquhart, 'Of one, conveying a proper
handsome girl, with whom he had been formerly
familiar'

fb.217, p. 168

A0143 A gallant man you were and courtier true
A quiet soul in life or death was thee.

Lady Jane Cavendish, 'On my grandfather
Mr. [William] Basset'
[Crum A153]

b.233, p. 34

A0144 A gallant 'twixt his mistress's white thighs
And she his sacred dart.

Sir Thomas Urquhart, 'An entendtrois [triple
entendre] of countenance'

fb.217, p. 342

A0145 A gallant youth with his enamor'd lady
Said, oph [sic], if this continue long the way'll
                                        seem short.

Sir Thomas Urquhart, 'Of a courtier traveling with his
mistress in a carroach [sic]'

fb.217, p. 333

A0146 A game that is oftentimes play'd by the great
The town wherein dwelleth my elder brother.

'A rebus by Crocus'

c.360/3, no. 221

A0147 A gard'ner, once, at early day,
The gard'ner crush'd him with his toe.

'The gardener and the snail a fable'

c.578, p. 127

A0148 A garment not wore, sure, is New.
And the fields in their beauty are Green.

'Solution to the rebus no. 89' ['The name that you
give to a garment not wore . . .']

c.360/3, no. 96

A0149 A gay old man's a sight of joy
[torn]ing nut-brown maid. . . .

'On Miss Banks and Miss Howe's conversing with
Colley Cibber the Poet Laureate, at Tunbridge Wells
in Kent 1745'

c.360/2, no. 60 (incomplete)

A0150 A genius, when by heav'n inspir'd,
Then, with his rubbish, stink and die.

John Lockman, 'The Hilliad(?) hero. 9 Sept. 1757'

c.267/4, p. 361

A0151 A gentleman he is—a baronet
Honor in abstract. Others adjuncts be.

[Sir Philip Wodehouse], 'Upon Sr John Rous his honor'd kinsman'

b.131, back (no. 15)

A0152 A gentleman, one wintry day,
If he can't eat them, sure I can.

[Thomas Hamilton, 6th earl of Haddington], 'The oyster a tale'

c.458/2, p. 152

A0153 A girl entrusted to her own discretion
For empty chambers make inferior minds.

[Sir Thomas Urquhart], '[?] and solitariness are great impugners of chastity'

fb.217, p. 533

A0154 A girl new married ask'd a matron, which
I muse (says she) then, why he doth't not ofter.

Sir Thomas Urquhart, 'The discourse of a young lass with an old practitioner of her own sex'

fb.217, p. 240

A0155 A girl of fourteen, beautifully trim,
She needed not have been so sorely vexed.

Sir Thomas Urquhart, 'The fear of the loss, is greater than the loss itself, upon a maiden'

fb.217, p. 77

A0156 A girl that had follow'd the camp to the wars
But de shild, must be born den, widout e'er a shirt!

[Phanuel Bacon], 'Forte recepi est indiciis monstrare nuntibus abdita rerum'

c.237, fol. 82

A0157 A girl we long to toy with,
As Colley's annual rhymes.

[John Lockman], 'Women like books. The tune, As Cupid one day wily &c.

c.268 (first part), p. 59

A0158 A glittering gallant from a-prancing stood,
Do it yourself (quoth he) and slunk away.

'On a gallant'

c.356

A0159 A glorious angel brings the news
Emblem of grace, emblem of glory.

Henry Howard, 'Upon the Epiphany'

c.229/1, fol. 74

A0160 A glorious immortal prize
Leaving both common souls and common clay.

'A receipt for friendship'

fc.135; see also 'He who would great in science . . .'.

A0161 A glorious King doth sit in heaven,
Until his foes be trod to dust.

'A spiritual king'

c.187, p. 20

A0162 A glorious new prophetic star
But knoweth Robin Goodfellow.

'An epigram'

c.570/3, p. 84

A0163 A glorious time dear Madam
And doth our wants report.

[Mary Pluret], 'To a friend going to be married'

c.354

A0164 A glutton renowned
But of him found nothing but bone.

'Epitaph'

c.113/13

A0165 A godly preacher gave a touch,
Christ crucified, that he affects.

'Paul's determination'

c.187, p. 15

A0166 A godly sister by one of her society
She hath pulpit where a preacher may be.

'Parturiene puritana' [of a Puritan woman who wanted her son to become a preacher]
[cf. Crum A163]

b.205, fol. 43v; see also 'A holy maid . . .'.

A0167 A gold watch found on cinder whore,
Not that they're rich, but that they steal.

[Alexander Pope]

c.265, p. 12

A0168 A good repute a virtuous name,
You nevermore will find one.

[Walter Chamberlaine], 'The tale of the travellers'
[pr. 1733 (Foxon C102)]

c.83/1, no. 222

A0169 A good wife once a bed of organs set
Hogs Norton call, here pigs on organs play.

'Upon pigs discovering a bed of Pon Royal commonly called organs'

c.356

A0170   A graceful aspect, and a spotless mind,
Where goodness triumphs, and can never die.

> [John Lockman], 'Epitaph—to the memory of Jane
> Shields, born 3d Nov. 1723, died Feb. 6. 1737/8'
>
> c.268 (first part), p. 9; c.267/1, p. 172 ('where virtue
> triumphs')

A0171   A gracious God I'm sure we have,
When we betray our innocence.

> [Edmund Wodehouse], 'Decr. 2 [1714]'
>
> b.131, p. 103

A0172   A grateful sense of what's already given,
For clearing doubts to wish it more severe.

> 'To Lady H[arpu]r on Master Harpur's recovery from
> the smallpox Decbr. 1713'
>
> b.322, p. 28

A0173   A gray pate for to marry want of policy
Poor Tom thou hast a she-wolf by the ears.

> 'On the same' [Dr. Bambridge's marrying Mall Wolfe,
> a butcher's daughter]
>
> b.356, p. 148

A0174   A grazier alighting one night at the Bear
Who hash pull'd off de bootsh now, and left on
de spur.

> [Phanuel Bacon], 'Pergis pugnanti sicum frontibus
> adversis componet'
>
> c.237, fol. 78 [i.e., 98]

A0175   A great wit nature hath on you bestow'd
And virtue will both which from God did flow.

> [Sir Thomas Urquhart], 'To [blank]'
>
> fb.217, p. 520

A0176   A Grecian youth of talents rare,
To govern men and guide the State.

> [William Whitehead], 'The youth and the
> philosopher'
>
> c.140, p. 513; Poetry Box I/81

A0177   A grotto so complete, with such design,
Pleas'd to reflect the well-sung founder's praise.

> 'To Mrs. ———— on her grotto'
>
> c.83/3, no. 774

A0178   A hamper I received of wine
Oh! Let me not receive but give.

> c.546

A0179   A happy and unhappy anagram
To die, to save—a kingdom, church, and crown.

> [Sir Philip Wodehouse], 'Upon my Ld Orrery's
> anagram Sr Edmond-bury Godfrey I find murdered
> by rogues'
>
> b.131, back (no. 196)

A0180   A happy destiny: he'll be all-blest
What a blest case is he in, who shall have honor?

> [Sir Philip Wodehouse], '. . . A destiny—all blest'
>
> b.131, back (no. 129)

A0181   A harmless life, to me I think most safe
My heart for heaven's inclin'd.

> Joseph Rule, 'A divine poem composed by . . . on his
> sweet experience of his retired life in a hermitlike
> manner . . . in Wales'
>
> c.186, p. 16

A0182   A health to you Sir, to the inmost drop:
I am well pleas'd: but you must change the liquor.

> Sir Thomas Urquhart, 'A merry jovial wench in
> making water speaketh thus to a gentleman, she had
> been familiarly acquainted with'
>
> fb.217, p. 358

A0183   A heap of dust alone lies here conceal'd:
Here sculptor stop—this scene you can't portray.

> 'Upon viewing a grave in 1795'
>
> c.515, fol. 36v

A0184   A hearty giver [?] receives such pleasure
Virtue no other recompense allowing.

> [Sir Thomas Urquhart], 'A truly liberal man gives
> never any gift in hope of recompense'
>
> fb.217, p. 529

A0185   A heathen author of the first degree,
My tedious sermon here is at an end.

> 'Advice to an old bachelor resolved to take a wife'
>
> c.578, p. 49

A0186   A heathen priest and yet in Christian lawn!
As Egypt's queen to melt a future age.

> 'An epilogue intended for Lady Ca—ns who acted one
> of the priests of Isis, in All for love, etc. Perform'd
> lately at Blen[hei]m. Dressed in a white sort of
> surplice'
>
> Poetry Box VI/125

A0187   A Helen she's m[?]. A younger than
As lovely as the last, but more discreet.

> [Sir Philip Wodehouse], 'Upon his fair neighbor
> Helen Gournay (now Mrs. Long)'
>
> b.131, back (no. 62)

A0188 A hermit on the banks of Trent,
For love and and [sic] virtue joined her train.

    'Armine and Elvira: a legendary tale' [signed
    Almonza]

    c.343, p. 50

A0189 A hermit (or if chance you hold
Either too early or too late.

    [William Cowper], 'The moralizer corrected a tale'

    c.140, p. 517

A0190 A Hogg in armor is no common sign
You ne'er was lugg'd so since you suckt a sow.

    'Robin Hogg uncloaked 1680'

    b.54, p. 1200

A0191 A holy maid with one of her society
And has a pulpit wherein a preacher may be.

    'On a puritan maid'
    [cf. Crum A163]

    b.62, p. 41; see also 'A godly sister . . .'.

A0192 A hopeless shepherd in a lonely shade
Made you my heart so tender her so fair? &c.

    c.416

A0193 A husband should not upon any 'ccasion,
A patent way for reconciliation.

    Sir Thomas Urquhart, 'Why man, and wife should not
    be long at variance'

    fb.217, p. 199

A0194 A Jew, would eat such pork, as this,
'Tis Bunbury's neck, and Fanny's hair.

    David Garrick, 'By David Garrick esq.' [on Lady
    Sarah Bunbury]

    c.130, p. 16

A0195 A jockey took a horse t' th' fair
I'll always doubt a horse's eyes!

    [Phanuel Bacon], 'Is qui nil dubitat nil capit inde boni'

    c.237, fol. 69

A0196 A jolly brisk tar, but a little time since,
And sung as he reel'd, down, down with the
                      French. | Derry down

    'Song 9'

    c.555, p. 13

A0197 A jolly old tinker who work'd in a stall
Then fill me a bumper 'twill keep me as warm.

    'St. Paul and the tinker'

    c.360/3, no. 100

A0198 A jolly old toper, who could not forbear
No sooner are tapp'd but give up the ghost.

    [William Taylor], 'The dropsical man'

    c.176, p. 84

A0199 A justice walking o'er the frozen Thames,
I prithee help me over on thy back.

    'On a foolish debt'

    c.356

A0200 A king in one o' his merry moods
The stockings were the same!

    [Phanuel Bacon], 'Invant quae pluris emuntur'

    c.237, fol. 68

A0201 A king was got by candle light,
Resolve me this, my riddle's done.

    J. B., 'In eundem' [on the first Duke of Buckingham]

    b.200, p. 53

A0202 A knife, dear girl, cuts love, they say;
Save only—cut and come again.

    [Samuel Bishop], 'With a present of a knife'
    [Crum A209]

    c.82, p. 27

A0203 A knight delighted in deeds of arms,
Keep the first letters of these lines and guess.

    [John Wilmot], 2nd earl of Rochester, 'The virgin's
    desire' [acrostic on 'a prick']

    c.189, p. 3; see also 'A maiden fair . . .'.

A0204 A lady he in name—a lady in his face
As 'tis to lady which does spell the same.

    [Sir Philip Wodehouse], 'Upon Mr. Hadly, my Lady
    Doyly's brother, the fine musician'

    b.131, back (no. 170 [bis])

A0205 A lady of no shining sense
Idea's idiot's female gender.

    c.546

A0206 A lady of suspected chastity
You and your cook do in the case agree.

    Sir John Strangways

    b.304, p. 37

A0207 A lady once two suitors had
Before I go I will thee [fuck].

    [John Davies, of Hereford], 'On a lady'
    [Crum A219]

    b.62, p. 75 (incomplete?)

A0208 A lady, possess'd of a handsome estate,
To be happy fore'er, or fore'er be undone.

'To the heroes of the British nation'
c.83/2, no. 649

A0209 A lady speaking of the Jewish nation
And that piece, which endures the circumcision.

Sir Thomas Urquhart, 'Here a lady of a very free
humor, vents her opinion thus on the profession of the
Jews'
fb.217, p. 219

A0210 A lady that a kiss does take
Which you are to explain.

c.150, p. 52; see also 'He that doth a kiss receive . . .'.

A0211 A lady that was lately wed,
We'll toast all day for health, all night for pleasure.

[Crum A220, 'newly wed']
b.197, p. 39; see also 'A comely creature . . .', 'A lady
which had oftentimes . . .'.

A0212 A lady told a witty peer
Means in English plain b[u]m f[i]ddle.

c.546

A0213 A lady which had oftentimes been fed
We'll taste the morn for health, the night for
pleasure.

'On a lascivious lady'
[cf. Crum A8, A213]
b.200, p. 6; see also 'A comely creature . . .', 'A lady that
was lately . . .'.

A0214 A lady who'd long been with learning delighted,
So pray let me help you to those that remain.

'The pedant and the peas'
c.81/2, no. 556

A0215 A lady wise as well as fair,
The living luster, of your eyes?

[Patrick Delany], 'An apology to my Lady Carteret,
writ in Ireland' [pr. 1733 (Foxon S799; attr. Swift)]
[Crum A221]
c.176, p. 125

A0216 A lady wit in time of need
The filt[h] of lady fair.

Poetry Box VIII/73 (incomplete)

A0217 A lady with her paramour, both Scots
And with a foreright fugue her revert reverted.

Sir Thomas Urquhart, 'Of a lover and his mistress,
trying themselves in the art of singing descant'
fb.217, p. 37

A0218 A lady's heart on Marlb'o' Downs
To any modern man.

'An advertisement'
fc.51, p. 11

A0219 A lady's secret door I once unshut,
In time of war, when Cupid's in the field.

Sir Thomas Urquhart, 'One speaks here of a lovely
war'
fb.217, p. 151

A0220 A land tax and poll are just coming forth,
For fear of the charge of maintaining our poor.
Which nobody can deny.

'On the taxes'
[Crum A222]
b.111, p. 505; b.204, p. 54; fb.207/1, p. 14; see also 'A poll
and land-tax . . .'.

A0221 A lantern I of a pure crystal frame
The mean, denotes it, either curst or kind.

[Sir Philip Wodehouse], 'Ann Taylor a lantern'
b.131, back (no. 223)

A0222 A lass that was laden with care,
And I heavily sigh'd for him.

'A song'
c.358, p. 39

A0223 A late expedition to Oxford was made
They'd marched more nimble without their music. |
Which nobody can deny.

[John Smith, of Magdalen College, Oxford], 'The
[Lord Lovelace's] Oxford expedition' [1689]
[Crum A224; POAS v.66]
b.111, p. 585 (ll. 1–72)

A0224 A lawyer, physician and reverend divine
When wound up too high of a sudden will crack.

'Song 244'
c.555, p. 388 (incomplete)

A0225 A lawyer says of all his clients best
Because he hath so many suits in hand.

'On a tailor'
b.62, p. 55

A0226 A learned baron who did best [?]
At your election jointly now rejoice.

[Sir Thomas Urquhart], 'To my Lord Keyes'
fb.217, p. 390

A0227 A learned bishop of this land
That scruple trouble all the rest.

    [Francis Andrewes, on Archbishop Bancroft]
    [Crum A227]

b.62, p. 131; fb.138 (folder 1)

A0228 A learn'd divine, a book is of the sky,
Wherein we learn to spell eternity.

    [Sir Philip Wodehouse], 'Upon Dr. [Herbert] Astley
    liber aetherus'

b.131, back (no. 147)

A0229 A learn'der, or a better man, than you,
Or deed, none ever reach'd a higher pitch.

    Sir Thomas Urquhart, 'To Doctor [crossed out] of
    [crossed out]'

fb.217, p. 316

A0230 A letter by which a fine river's express'd
The name of a town in the western route.

    'Rebus'

c.484, p. 60

A0231 A life obscure my friend, I always lov'd,
Deplore our loss, and his just praise rehearse.

    'To Mr. Fenton'

b.322, p. 20

A0232 A light young man lay with a lighter woman
A yard of Holland, for an ell of Cotton.

    'On the marriage of Jo. Holland and Nell Cotton'
    [Crum A233]

b.62, p. 22

A0233 A like deceiving is this secret way
With that collusion(?) bewilder'd mortals stray.

    'Over the entrance to Pope's grotto Secretum iter et
    fallentis semita vitae'

c.74, p. 25

A0234 A lily, jewel, frankincense this grace,
Perfumes thy mouth, and shineth on thy face.

    'Gulielmus Thommatius. Anagramma. Tu gemma,
    thus idiem. Os. Epigramma'

b.212, p. 93

A0235 A ling'ring illness gave the silent blow,
Pitied my sighs, and kindly sent me rest.

    'Another [epitaph], which, if I remember right, is in
    [Islip] churchyard'

c.240, p. 136

A0236 A lion, emblems magnanimity;
When in their presence, all the world stood bare.

    [Sir Philip Wodehouse], 'Upon his noble neighbor Sir
    J[ohn] Holland'

b.131, back (no. 130)

A0237 A lion faint with heat, and exercise,
To show that kindness past, he don't forget.

    E[lizabeth (Shirley)] C[ompton, countess of
    Northampton], 'The lion and the mouse fable'

Accession 97.7.40

A0238 A little less reading of novels and plays
I'll tell in her ear she'll have hearts by the score.

    'A recipe to make Miss ——— irresistable'

c.53, fol. 43

A0239 A little lioness thy name denotes
With wise complaisance, that all's a-paid.

    [Sir Philip Wodehouse], 'Caroline Lea Cara Leonilla'

b.131, back (no. 120)

A0240 A little table-mushroom spread
Grac'd by his priest, the feast is ended.

    R[obert] Herrick, 'Oberon's feast'
    [Crum A239, 'mushroom table']

b.197, p. 6; b.356, p. 3 ('mushroom table')

A0241 A lofty tower and doors of brass,
'Tis our best happiness and peace.

    Abraham Oakes, '[Horace to Maecenas.] Ode XVI. B.
    2 translated'

c.50, p. 148

A0242 A long adieu to all that's bright
Since all that can be said of woman was her due.

    [Thomas Flatman?], 'To the memory of the
    incomparable Orinda'
    [cf. Crum A246]

b.115, fol. 29v

A0243 A long epistle—this, you say, and fear
By freedom's dread award, till Time himself decay.

    'An epistle to R[ichard] Brinsley [Butler] Sheridan
    esq. secretary to the right honorable Charles Fox'
    [1782]

fc.53, p. 77

A0244 A long fatigue the fam'd Ulysses bore,
She owes her riches and her learning too.

    S. Phipps, 'Merchant Taylor's School'

Poetry Box VI/102

A0245   A Lord Baron Bish,
A hierarchy not worth a louse.

     'No lord bishops'
     [Crum A248]

fb.70, p. 301

A0246   A louse I say, for when a man's distrest,
And others do fall off she sticks the best.

     'Who the best friend'

c.356

A0247   A love-sick Damon lay along
Complaining still of hopeless love.

     [ ] Jacobs, 'Damon to Philomel'

c.152, p. 38

A0248   A lovely bride obtain'd, a large domain,
Should the vane shift, O may no tempest follow!

Diggle Box: Poetry Box XI/57

A0249   A lovely lass to a friar came,
That your penance is prevailing.

     'Song 54'

c.555, p. 80

A0250   A lovely rose there grew
And gilds my pleasant shades.

c.83/2, no. 523

A0251   A lover I'm born, and a lover I'll be,
How we kiss and embrace and can never have done.

     'The resolution'
     [Crum A254]

fb.107, p. 16

A0252   A loving husband, and tender father dear,
In heav'n, I hope we all shall meet again.

     'An epitaph'

c.175, p. 11

A0253   A lowly flower, in secret bow'r
Known only by its smell.

     [George Horne, bishop of Norwich], 'The violet'
Diggle Box: Poetry Box XI/48

A0254   A lusty bon'd mortal first we must suppose,
If this portrait you like, I will you the brute!

     Joanna Southcott, 'Portrait of an informer. (B**k) . . .
     Snaith, printed for the authoress, by David Swift
     Cloughstreet'

c.81/2, no. 567

A0255   A lusty lad that past along Cheapside
To buy (quoth he) if not, shut up your shop.

     b.65, p. 135

A0256   A maid, I dare not tell her name,
O there, O there, O there, O there.

     'The drowsy girl'

fb.107, p. 48

A0257   A maid, unask'd may own a well-plac'd flame!
Not loving first, but loving ill's the shame.

     [George] L[yttelton], 1st baron Lyttelton, 'Maxims in
     love' [no. 4]

c.487, p. 28

A0258   A maiden fair I dare not wed
Some fault remains amongst them all.

     'No maid good'
     [Crum A265]

b.200, p. 24; b.205, fol. 23r

A0259   A maiden fair of the green sickness late,
Keep the first letters of these several rhymes.

     'An excellent remedy for the green sickness' [acrostic:
     a prick]
     [Crum A266]

b.200, p. 431; see also 'A knight delighted . . .'.

A0260   A maid's a pretty thing of virgin's wax
Which nothing else, but an impression lacks.

     'On a maid'

b.356, p. 307

A0261   A man as dead lay in a trance
And G. B. [Great Britain?] pays the piper.

     'A dream by Mr. Maxwell in Nithsdale 1723'

c.102, p. 128

A0262   A man, before he writes a book,
My foot, your bottom, does not greet.

     [Frederick Corfield], 'A hint'

c.381/1

A0263   A man did penance in Chelsea Church on Sunday
                                        last

In time of divine service for getting a bast- | Ard
child, for pain and shame will follow pleasures past.

     'A whim on a penance November 12 1732'

c.360/2, no. 227

A0264   A man does right who hath a woman led
First to the bed and the[n] unto the church.

     [John Mackereth? c. 1778]

b.132, insert

A0265 A man, in many a country town, we know,
Well, and what then?'—'Then, Sir, my master—
died!'

George Colman [the elder?], 'The rhyming
apothecary, a tale'

c.142, p. 487

A0266 A man inclin'd to spend his life
Than lacking half a lac[e?] in purse.

[Frederick Corfield], 'Advertisement'

c.381/1

A0267 A man lies with a wife which is his own,
Be spurious legitimate or not?

'A case to the lawyers'

c.356

A0268 A man lives forty years, before he knows
By any man well done *ex tempore*.

Sir John Strangways, '21° Aprilis: 1647'

b.304, p. 83

A0269 A man long troubled with a waking sprite,
The five first letters of the five first lines.

'A receipt' [acrostic on 'a cunt']

c.189, p. 168

A0270 A man may in a wholesome woman's lap
And spare the scabbard.

Sir Thomas Urquhart, 'That a husband may with his
wife, though never so well complexioned in body, reap
infirmities, whereof she is free herself'

fb.217, p. 48

A0271 A man of human nature vain
A black heart view'd, cures a proud eye.

Charles Atherton Allnutt, 'The man and the peacock a
fable'

c.112, p. 162

A0272 A man of late, in woeful state
But yours can life restore.

[Thomas Hamilton, 6th earl of Haddington], 'The
f[ar]t'

c.458/2, p. 13

A0273 A man of learning may disguise
Found out a cleanlier lover, to lie by her.

[William] Taylor, 'A tale'

c.176, p. 72

A0274 A man of Wales 'twixt David's day and Easter
Dost think her know not chalk from cheese.

'On a Welshman'
[Crum A275]

b.62, p. 79

A0275 A man once e'er so honest
When naught he's got to pay.

c.361

A0276 A man that is drunk is void of all care, Tol loll &c.
When dead drunk I'll be carried away. | Tol, loll
a &c.

'A spiritual hymn, integer vitae burlesqued'

File 17483

A0277 A man that is meager and wan,
I never will mind her, not I.

'A song'

c.530, p. 159

A0278 A man there is, a real man,
In that tremendous day.

[Hymn]

c.180, p. 77

A0279 A man there is well to fame
To scorn a martyr, and unknown to praise.

Miss [ ] Andrews, 'On a dancing master'

File 245/10

A0280 A man to whom fortune her favors denied
Declar'd the score paid and acquitted the guest.

[Phanuel Bacon], 'Tempus abire tibi est ne potum
largius aquo rideat'

c.237, fol. 71 [*i.e.*, 91]

A0281 A man unknown trust not, except
With guile is overthrown.

b.234, p. 97

A0282 A man, who ever is at strife,
Art sure sweet husband, you can swim?

[Thomas Hamilton, 6th earl of Haddington], 'A tale'

c.458/2, p. 158

A0283 A man without learning as Cato doth say,
May well be compar'd to an image of clay.

c.93

A0284 A married couple liv'd a happy life—
Paula was kind—and the dispute was over.

T[homas] W[arton], 'The dispute settled in an
amicable way[:] a tale—addressed to married persons'

File 15773

A0285 A master betray'd! and is Cottrell the traitor?
The master betray'd, and—pray, he is the Judas.

'Lines, on seeing an epigram on the subject of Judas
Iscariot'

Poetry Box XII/118[2]

A0286   A master tailor (as 'tis said)
There's no disgrace will screen a fool.

     'A tale, not of a tub but of tailor, or of the prodigal son
of a tailor'

     c.115

A0287   A mate that's ill to ill his mate
Which from that vice was pure.

     'Consortium. Ad mala facta . . .'

     b.234, p. 4, p. 82

A0288   A mawkish, tallowy face; a lech'rous leer;
The devil himself would have been made the jest.

     John Lockman, 'A sketch . . . May 1 1734'

     c.267/1, p. 244; c.268 (first part), p. 4

A0289   A medley of ruffians bound up in a band,
And justice and trade may revive from their sleep.

     'The Dutch troop'

     b.111, p. 593

A0290   A meeting once held at the Angel and Crown
The fighting [The matter] referred to Westminster
Hole. | Derry down

     W. R., 'Major Midnight['s] triumph or the Falstaff of
the East a new song'

     Poetry Box v/109, 110 (var.)

A0291   A merchant's crest must be a hive.
'Look after pounds; they guard themselves.'

     [Frederick Corfield], 'Arms for a merchant'

     c.381/1

A0292   A mermaid's flesh above and fish below
I pray let's taste the lower parts this Lent.

     'On a maiden'
     [Crum A285]

     b.62, p. 78

A0293   A merry maid
Thank you for this fair cure.

     [Sir Nicholas] Bacon, 'Of a maid and a painter'

     fa.8, fol. 167v

A0294   A merry man abhors a man that's sad
A sprightly person scorns a man that's slow.

     c.361

A0295   A midwife lies under this stone supprest.
No doubt, she now, doth from all travails rest.

     'On a midwife'

     b.356, p. 245

A0296   A mien whose dignity with ease combined
That rules, informs, and animates the whole.

     Miss [ ] Knight, 'A portrait of Lady Charlotte Finch'
Poetry Box IV/185

A0297   A mighty God transcendently supreme,
Till through sweet Jesus, I the heav'ns inherit.

     Sir Thomas Urquhart, 'To the everliving a prayer'
fb.217, p. 52

A0298   A mighty great fleet, the like was ne'er seen
With the loss of some ships, but in battle none
slain. | [Which nobody can deny]

     'England's triumph at sea in the year 1691' [to the tune
of The blacksmith]
[Crum A287; *POAS* V.392]

     b.111, p. 254; b.115, fol. 24; Poetry Box VII/53; see also 'I
sing the adventures . . .'.

A0299   A mighty monarch you begot
After my reign of courting.

     [Thomas Brown], 'Upon the Princes[s] of Conti'

     c.158, p. 143

A0300   A mighty pain to love it is,
Gold, alas, doth love beget.

     A[braham] C[owley], 'On gold'
     [Crum A288]

     c.258; c.549, p. 20 (incomplete?)

A0301   A mill to let of famous invention,
Of schoolmaster, shopkeeper, or country squire.

     fb.68, p. 137

A0302   A mind unmoved by every vulgar fear,
Yet better still by native prudence taught.

     [George] Lyttelton, 1st baron Lyttelton

     c.151, p. 5 (incomplete?)

A0303   A mind whose quiet conscience sets at ease,
Fears not the public's blame, nor seeks its praise.

     R[obert] Shirley, 1st earl of Ferrers, 'Nec laudem
quaerit nec culpam imet mens conscia recti Englished
by me thus'

     c.347, p. 3

A0304   A mine of gold some say is found
And yet to see some under.

     'On a mine in Scotland'
     [Crum A291]

     b.356, p. 306

A0305   A miser who had oft been told
My chest and guineas may not hop away.

     'Epigram'

     c.546

A0306 A modest carriage and a modish mean
Who would not covet in her arms to be.

    'The maiden's pattern or rule to walk by'
    fb.142, p. 18

A0307 A modest young doctor, the pride of the south,
Was only an old woman's f[art].

    [Elizabeth?] Moody, 'The sequel [to 'Gay Moody
    once . . .'] or a second singular case'
    File 7048

A0308 A Monday by noon, I invite noble Proc:—
To see out, or swim in, the bowl of the vicar.

    [Charles Earle], 'To Proctor—an invitation at dinner
    extempore'
    c.376

A0309 A mongrel bard of Anglo-Flemish breed,
Rail'd on the grapes—alas! they only hung too high.

    'From the Ipswich journal answer to The farewell to
    Norwich ['Farewell at length . . .'] . . . Norwich, Janry
    22nd [17]83'
    c.90

A0310 A monster in a course of vice grown old,
Pity a wretch like him should ever live.

    [ ] Lewis, 'The monument'
    [Crum A299]
    c.244, p. 462

A0311 A monster vile is envy sure
Is hard to find in hell.

    b.234, p. 3

A0312 A month hath roll'd its lazy hours away,
And we shall meet again, to part no more.

    R. Luyd, 'An imitation from the Spectator'
    c.83/4, no. 2007

A0313 A monument at length I've rais'd,
The laurel crown—it is my own.

    [William Popple, trans.], '[Horace] book 3rd. ode
    30th'
    fc.104/2, p. 322

A0314 A moping melancholy blade
So safe as hampered in a pound?

    'To be omitted'
    Poetry Box x/45, p. 20

A0315 A mother dead! and am I from the throne
Let Kendal at her peril mourn for thee.

    'Prince G[eor]ge's resolution' [on not going in
    mourning for the Queen; 1726]
    [Crum A304]
    c.233, p. 102; c.570/2, p. 168

A0316 A mother who vast pleasure finds,
To raise the mind, and mend the heart.

    [Mary] Barber, 'A true tale' [pr. 1728 (Foxon B77)]
    c.83/2, no. 510

A0317 A moth's a vermin, not denied
'Tis born and buried in a clout.

    [Sir Philip Wodehouse], 'Upon his barber Thomas
    Gybs is a big moth'
    b.131, back (no. 201)

A0318 A mourning bride on this auspicious day
And every day serene and glad as this.

    [William Congreve], 'Prologue [to The mourning
    bride] spoken by the King'
    File 19022

A0319 A murm'rer full of discontent,
And be to providence resign'd.

    'The resignation'
    c.83/3, no. 948

A0320 A muse, unskilled in venal praise,
While shouting nations gaze.

    [James Beattie], 'Ode on Lord [John] Hay's birthday,
    1767'
    c.139, p. 190

A0321 A muse's power tho' fate has stopp'd his breath
Tho' kind, yet chaste, tho' prodigal, discreet.

    'In praise of nobody' [1698]
    [Crum A307]
    c.392, p. 17 (incomplete?)

A0322 A myrtle-bough my sword shall shade
To Athens equal law restor'd.

    [ ] Ellison, 'A song of Callistratus'
    Greatheed Box/27

A0323 A name I thought as yet did properly
Have heard he so did seem . . . .

    'Innocent XI'
    b.216, p. 155 (incomplete)

A0324 A neat physician for a farrier sends
For nothing do we take of our own trade.

    'A farrier physician'
    c.356

A0325 A negro I, but sprung from northern climes
And then in iron cage like Bajazet I die.

    'A riddle' [on the duty on coals to build churches]
    c.392, p. 10; c.241, p. 81

A0326   A new and noble race he ran so fast,
By this example in the noble race.

> J[ohn] V[ernon], 'An anagram. Caleb Vernon. Nue
> noble race'
>
> b.228, p. 72

A0327   A niggard seldom to the heav'ns ascends;
For nothing he repents, but what he spends.

> Sir Thomas Urquhart, 'Why peevish wretches will
> hardly be saved'
>
> fb.217, p. 243

A0328   A night of slumber after life's short day
Soldiers in arms and panting in the flight.

> Charles Atherton Allnutt, 'Elegiac sonnet, by way of
> acrostic [on Alice Hopkins]'
>
> c.112, p. 167

A0329   A nightingale, in her retreat,
Selfishness is always cruel.

> 'The nightingale'
>
> c.83/3, no. 992

A0330   A nimble footman run away from death
And sent him of an errand to his grave.

> 'The footman and death'
>
> c.360/2, no. 16

A0331   A noble lord—who had—a wife!
When you've the original to show.

> [Phanuel Bacon], 'O imitatores servum pecus'
>
> c.237, fol. 73 [*i.e.*, 93]

A0332   A noble playing with a king at chess,
'When a knight moves the trumpet ought to sound.'

> 'The apology'
>
> c.81/1, no. 430

A0333   A number do deserve rebuke and shame
Who do despise the stock whereof they came.

> c.339, p. 319

A0334   A number of princes and poor ones 'tis true,
And brag of what mischief you did to our fleet! |
                Not a t[ur]d Sir [&c.]

> 'A satire on the royal confederates'
>
> fb.207/3, p. 48; b.111, p. 265

A0335   A nun there was, as primrose gay,
When we—as righteous Jane have done.

> [John Lockman], 'Dame Jane, or the penitent nun
> [imitation or translation of La Fontaine]. Set to music
> by the late Mr. Haym'
>
> c.268 (second part), p. 95; see also 'Dame Jane a
> nun . . .'.

A0336   A nymph I am told too long for a husband has
                 tarried,
So ample a dowry and so learned a wife.

> [Sir William Morice?], 'On a lady that said she would
> give a 200 £ to be married'
>
> c.174, p. 95

A0337   A nymph unequall'd! surely, Sir you sport, or
But hold—your pardon—I forgot—Miss Porter.

> c.360/3, no. 2

A0338   A painted bear a publican desires,
No bear will ever stay without a chain.

> c.53, fol. 19

A0339   A painter draws a homely coquette,
'Tis me in ev'ry feature!

> John Lockman, 'Human nature . . . 1734'
>
> c.267/1, p. 283; c.268 (first part), p. 57

A0340   A painter once, who knew the art
The dress would spoil the charity.

> [Phanuel Bacon], 'Probitas laudatur et alget'
>
> c.237, fol. 76

A0341   A painter, skillful in his trade
They can't retrieve a blasted name.

> [Thomas Hamilton, 6th earl of Haddington], 'The
> poet's complaint'
>
> c.458/2, p. 126

A0342   A papist died, as 'twas Jehovah's will
Should you come in you'd eat the Devil here.

> 'On a papist's ghost'
> [Crum A330]
>
> b.115, fol. 4v

A0343   A parish priest was of the pilgrim train
He needs no foil, but shines by his own proper
                 light.

> [John] Dryden, 'Chaucer's good parson mended by
> Dryden'
> [Crum A331]
>
> b.201, p. 172

A0344   . . . A parliament of knaves and sots
If such kings are by God appointed . . . .

> [John Wilmot, 2nd earl of Rochester, ll. 49–156 of
> 'The insipids']
>
> b.52/1 (last page)

A0345   A parson a whore led into a tavern
Who saw the gray goose trod by the black gander.

> 'Song'
>
> c.189, p. 172

A0346 A parson of the name of Black
It cannot wash a blackmoor white.

Poetry Box x/114

A0347 A parson who had the remarkable foible
But you're, ten to one knave and fool in your
practice. | Derry down &c.

'Song 78'

c.555, p. 120

A0348 A part that helps compose a wheel,
Who finds it must correctly spell.

'A rebus'

c.360/3, no. 208

A0349 A passive puppet thou to Nature's wire!
So that the devil drive no matter where.

'Pithy advice to a young friend at Ch[rist] Ch[urch]
Oxford asking me what books he should read'

fc.53, p. 20

A0350 A patient mind
That marriage is the devil.

c.546

A0351 A patriot's even course he steered,
By all who knew his heart, beloved.

[Richard] Fitzpatrick, 'On a bust of Charles Fox,
belonging to Lord Holland, are the following lines by
General Fitzpatrick'

Smith Papers, folder 74/9

A0352 A peaceful mind goes humbly clad,
Guiltless at the trumpet's sound.

T[homas] Ast[on? or Henry Phillipps?], 'Of a
contented life'

b.62, p. 136

A0353 A pensioner is a corrupted thing
And drudges his low worthless life away.

'The pensioner'

c.570/3, p. 132

A0354 A perfect virgin to bring forth a son:
Till heaven dissolve and the last trump shall blow.

[Henry Phillipps?]

b.156, p. 5

A0355 A Philip once to England came
A Mary mov'd again.

'Philip and Mary'

b.197, p. 217

A0356 A pillar of the Church some Lee did call
We'll have his room but not his company.

'On Lee a papist'
[Crum A342]

b.356, p. 305

A0357 A place of retirement, with cypress surrounded,
Causing the death of unfortunate Jockey?

'Jockey's complaint. A song'

c.530, p. 45

A0358 A pleasing form, a firm, yet cautious mind
At length enjoys that liberty he lov'd.

A[lexander] Pope, 'An epitaph written by . . . on Sir
William Trumbull one of the principal Secretaries of
State to King William the Third, who having resigned
his place, died in his retirement at Easthamsted in
Berkshire, in the year 1716'
[Crum A354]

c.360/2, no. 203

A0359 A pleasing form, where every grace combin'd,
And in that hope the pious Christian died.

[ ] Murphy, [paraphrase of Samuel Johnson's Latin
elegy on Hester Maria (Cotton) Salisbury, d. 1773]

c.504, p. 109

A0360 A pleasing subject, first with care provide;
And sure to please, altho' ten times repeated.

[Philip Dormer Stanhope, 4th] earl of Chesterfield, 'A
receipt to make an epigram'

c.152, p. 37; c.229/2, fol. 7v

A0361 A pleasing sweetness, harmless fire,
A tender something wants a name.

'Love'

c.144, p. 178

A0362 A poem now! and that a long one too!
There's some perhaps may think me overfree.

John Wolcot ('Peter Pindar'), 'The author to the
public' [1794]

Poetry Box IV/96

A0363 A poet and a traitor is such news
Poets should live by the lines, not die by the rope.

[Sir Aston Cokayne], 'Of Cornelius Gallus'

b.275, p. 97

A0364 A poet of your own, around whose tomb
Applaud ye gen'rous souls, echo ye ancient walls.

[Maurice Johnson], 'Epilogue by the same [at
Spalding]'

c.229/2, fol. 26

A0365 A poet once the Spartans led, to fight
Let Caesar live, and Carthage be subdued.

  John Dryden, 'The epilogue to [the play of]
  Amboyna'
  [Crum A356]

 b.111, p. 484

A0366 A poet once well pleased, survey'd
'Who by another's fall would rise.'

  'The poet and the rose'

 c.186, p. 79

A0367 A polish'd neatness shines thro' ev'ry part,
Fine without pomp, without aspiring, great.

  [from 'The amours of Alatheus and Eustathea']

 c.379/1, p. 62

A0368 A politician yet a fool;
No worser hell) 'tis Hamilton.

  'On D[uke] Hamilton beheaded' [1649]

 fb.143, p. 5

A0369 A poll and land-tax are now coming forth,
Like parting with our goods, and our consciences
       too; | Which nobody can deny.

  'Ballad on the poll-act'

 fb.70, p. 1; see also 'A land tax . . .'.

A0370 A poor man once a judge besought
And broke thy pot of oil!

  'Bribery'

 c.81/1, no. 319; c.578, p. 96

A0371 A poor old man who had by cleaving wood
Yet dar'd not venture on eternal rest.

  Captain Alexander Radcliffe, 'A fable from Æsop,
  Phaedrus and Avienus'

 c.229/1, fol. 53

A0372 A poor weak-grown gander, who'd goos'd all his
days,
O, Youth! How caress'd! O Age! How depress'd!

  'The constant gander's fate'

 c.94

A0373 A portly stag (they say) once stood
And still continue discontent.

  'The coward'

 c.416

A0374 A pox of the troubles men make in the world
I'll be here in a trice, I read a good trot.

  [drinking song temp. Charles II]
  [Crum A363]

 fb.106(13)

A0375 A pox of your brace of sage sisters the dice
And I'd keep my head whole 'cause I'm broke by
         the main.

  'The broken gamesters'

 Poetry Box VII/5

A0376 A pox of your pother about this or that
Where all act the scene of toll loll de roll &c.

  'Song 175'

 c.555, p. 270

A0377 A pox on the jailer, and on his fat jowl
And make our hard irons cry clink in the close.

  [William Cartwright], 'The slaves' song in the
  dungeon . . .' [from The royal slave, 1636]

 b.200, p. 156

A0378 A prating physician whose tongue never ceases
That my life is almost, and my health is quite gone.

  'On Dr. P—y's attending Miss B—n. Translated from
  the Greek'

 c.484, p. 95

A0379 A prelate hurl'd to the other world
Went hand and hand together.

  'Strange news from the dead' [on Burnet]
  [Crum A371]

 c.570/1, p. 124

A0380 A presbyter seven(?) bishop's times
Of public faults and perjury.

  James Salter, 'Calliope's cabinet opened'

 Poetry Box VIII/14

A0381 A pretty, bold, and stern compagnon strove
I swear, just now, you must be put in prison.

  Sir Thomas Urquhart, 'An amorous peer of justice'

 fb.217, p. 138

A0382 A pretty fricket [sic], to her tippling mates
Of fleshes, which he never tasted of.

  Sir Thomas Urquhart, 'An honest man's opinion of his
  own wife, whom he justly suspected to be something
  too kind'

 fb.217, p. 357

A0383 A pretty girl in brushing my apparel,
And that she gave, but to receive the like.

  Sir Thomas Urquhart, 'A gentleman, with whom a
  certain frisky chambermaid was sporting, speaks thus
  of himself'

 fb.217, p. 250

A0384 A pretty Irish boy, of mongrel breed
To Him, I shall confess and save my shilling.

    'The Irish boy and the priest'
Poetry Box v/103

A0385 A prince fatigued with living great
You had liv'd and died an humble swain.

    [Robert Cholmeley], 'A tale—Horace'
c.190, p. 130

A0386 A prince out of the north shall come
Shall take away his aged breath.

    'Maudlin's [*i.e.*, Merlin's] prophecy found long before
    King James came into England'
    [Crum A378]
fb.69, p. 229; b.197, p. 174

A0387 A printer once (a Hollander)
And know the master there.

    [Thomas Hull], 'On reading the play of Double
    falsehood, or the distressed lovers, unnecessarily said
    to be originally written by Shakespeare'
c.528/22

A0388 A proclamation from the K[ing]
We'll loyal stomachs find.

    [M.] S[harpe], 'Upon a proclamation for a fast'
c.116, p. 28

A0389 A prologue ask ye, that's indeed too hard,
Ought to plead something for our unskilled stage.

    [George Howard, 6th earl of Carlisle], 'Prologue to
    The reconciliation'
c.197, p. 9

A0390 A Protector: what's that? It is a stately thing
From whom the king of kings protect us all.

    'Of Oliver Protector'
    [cf. Crum w820]
b.52/2, p. 162; see also 'What's a Protector? . . .'.

A0391 A Protestant is such another thing
He is one that's no true subject but a slave.

    'A Protestant so will the [formalist?] of love be called'
    [cf. Crum A388]
fb.23, p. 337; see also 'A puritan . . .'.

A0392 A Protestant priest, a man of great fame
But the flesh did prevail by the help of his wife. |
Which nobody can deny . . .

    'The weasel uncased or the in and outside of a priest
    drawn to the life' [on William Sherlock; 1690]
    [*POAS* V.247]
b.111, p. 191

A0393 A prudent man in all his affairs
Make sure of Christ and come away.

    'Epitaphs (Milton Oxfordshire)'
c.546

A0394 A Puritan is such another thing
He's one that would a subject be, no slave.

    'A Puritan nicknamed but indeed the true Protestant'
    [cf. Crum A388]
fb.23, p. 336v; see also 'A Protestant . . .'.

A0395 A Puritan of late
And has turned balladmonger | For their sake.

    [on a Puritan's zeal for his sister]
b.197, p. 33; b.200, p. 363 (var.)

A0396 A Puritan sheds many tears
But oftentimes he lies.

    Sir Thomas Urquhart, 'The nature of a Puritan'
fb.217, p. 67

A0397 A quickness flowing from a deep conception,
Still bended are t'achieve the King's intentions.

    Sir Thomas Urquhart, 'To the Marquis of Hamilton'
fb.217, p. 35

A0398 A quill made into a pen,
Doth joy and grieve many men.

c.536

A0399 A rap at the door, when forth from her chair
I hope I shall see you, when you've naught else to
                       do.'

    'A modern visit'
fc.51, p. 115

A0400 A restless lover I espied to go from place to place
Like one that found no rest he cried hath Cupid no
                       physician.

b.213, p. 7; b.4, fol. 4v (damaged)

A0401 A reverend dean which had his band starch'd clean
That he handl'd it [more] than his text.

    'Upon Dr. Corbett Dean of Christ Church'
    [Crum A394]
b.356, p. 101

A0402 A rev'rend prelate stopt his coach and six
Drive on (quoth he) this man's more knave than
                       fool.

    Apulius (pseud.), 'Broughton Green August the 20'
c.166, p. 87

A0403 A rev'rend sage esteem'd for knowledge,
Sir, you ne'er heard our Jenny's clack.

    'A[n] epigram'

c.94

A0404 A rich country farmer possest of a mill
Get what you can Robin my family's large.

    'The Norfolk miller excised'

c.570/3, p. 210

A0405 A rich lord had a poor lout to his guest
And of that fowl give me my part in money.

    [Sir John Harington], 'Upon a lord and a countryman'

b.205, fol. 47r

A0406 A rich old earl in silver hairs
To die when I am growing wise.

    [Thomas Stevens?], 'Stanzas'

c.259, p. 18

A0407 A robe! For my dame: what the deuce can this
mean?
But how should I fume, had you giv'n a green-
gown?

    John Lockman, 'To a friend, who presented my wife
with a beautiful Irish shift'

c.267/1, p. 212

A0408 A robin redbreast brisk and gay
But that, my Lord, I leave to you.

    [( ) Davis], 'A fable' [addressed to the young Lord
Compton, son of the earl of Northumberland]

Accession 97.7.40

A0409 A robin who perching himself on a wall
Being heartily stung with the frog's sharp replies.

    'Honor and honesty displayed, in a dialogue between a
robin on a wall and a frog in a pool' [on Sir Robert
Walpole]

c.570/3, p. 14

A0410 A rod, surpassing all old Busby had
And make the charm of Panacea thine!

    C[harles] E[arle], 'To Mr. Drake Proctor of
Barnstaple . . . be pleased to accept the following
compliment before you receive the future reward'

c.376

A0411 A Romanist is such another thing
He is Spain's subject, and a Romish slave.

    'A papist'

fb.23, p. 340v

A0412 A rosebud overcharg'd with dew,
In pity to a rose.

    [Elizabeth (Knipe) Cobbold], 'Sensibility—a tale'

c.140, p. 169

A0413 A rose indeed sprung from so great a blood
Whom this fair rose shalt choose to be her mate.

    Francis Lenton, 'Upon that sweet and beauteous
virgin Mrs. Dorothy Seamor anagrams . . . made a
rose i' th' roe'

b.205, fol. 19v

A0414 A rose is but a flower—blows gloriously
No flow'r invok't no rose adored be.

    [Sir Philip Wodehouse], 'Edward Osborn no rose
adored be'

b.131, back (no. 145)

A0415 A rose may well be said to blush when she
Who want not eyes, or intellectual.

    [Sir Philip Wodehouse], 'Upon his noble
kinswoman . . . Elizabeth Rous'

b.131, back (no. 50)

A0416 A royal fleet is terror to the seas
Rebellious knaves their princes' wills devour.

c.158, p. 49

A0417 A rumor was spread thro' a village in Spain
She'd have wept (I'll be sworn) when I bor'd her so
deep.

    'The miraculous image'

c.241, p. 77

A0418 A Rump d'ye call't? that is too sweet a word
But say this knave that rogue one of the Rump
Parliament.

    'The Rump salted'

fb.140, p. 16

A0419 A rustic swain was cleaving of a block
For when I humm'd I clave, but now I bore.

    'On a clown'
    [Crum A408]

b.200, p. 431; b.205, fol. 49v; see also 'A country
clown/swain . . .'.

A0420 A sable curtain round his bed,
The luster of your eyes.

    [Charles Earle], 'At the chamber-door of Miss A—ds
upon a dismal dark morning. Extempore'

c.376

A0421 A sad mischance I sing alas,
Unless thy next silencing, be with a rope. | Which
nobody can deny.

[Thomas] Shadwell(?), 'Upon a late fallen poet.
Supposed to be written by . . .'
b.105, p. 328 (incomplete)

A0422 A safe retirement from the noise of towns,
We either can enjoy, or will despise.

K[atherine] Phil[ips], 'Invitation to the country'
b.118, p. 57; see also 'Be kind, my dear Rosania . . .'.

A0423 A sailor once did launch a ship of force,
And only wished he might be run aground.

'Another [rebus]'
Diggle Box: Poetry Box XI/71

A0424 A saint on earth, who can declare?
And then his mercy ne'er to doubt.

[Edmund Wodehouse], 'Aug. 9 [1715]'
b.131, p. 243

A0425 A saint on earth would vilipend a single
As much true joy, as a bridegroom can wish.

Sir Thomas Urquhart, 'To the Countess [crossed out]
of [crossed out]'
fb.217, p. 290

A0426 A scene like this, can seldom fail to please,
And praise the great Director as I ought.

'Stanzas written in a wood'
c.83/2, no. 650

A0427 A Scræan president of quires, and dences,
With cataracts of the Pimpleid well.

Sir Thomas Urquhart, 'The invocation to
Terpsichore'
fb.217, p. 194

A0428 A self-conceited country bumpkin
He prais'd his maker and went home.

'The bumpkin and the pumpkin'
c.150, p. 149

A0429 A sense of darkness did my soul affright
In this confusion I heard one say, O God it is the
King.

[Mrs. ( ) Feilding], 'On the morning the King was
taken ill my dream of him'
b.226, p. 29

A0430 A senseless ass, as Æsop tells,
For the king is the god, whoe'er be the ass.

[Thomas Hamilton, 6th earl of Haddington], 'A fable
[of Æsop] inscribed to the earl of Findlater'
c.458/2, p. 157

A0431 A sergeant and colonel with a doctor of physic
For 'tis plain who has put the doctor upon them.

[c. 1740]
Poetry Box x/95

A0432 A sergeant lo—a Roman lictor who
With much ado scarce proves a spade's a spade.

[Sir Philip Wodehouse], 'John Sergeant a Roman
priest who wrote Fiat lux no giant's he'
b.131, back (no. 184)

A0433 A servant of God, of Christ the Lord,
Those heinous sins, for which he else had died.

Sir John Strangways, 'The epistle of St. James in verse
by . . . in the 80th year of his age . . . 1665'
b.304, p. 140

A0434 A session of lovers was held t'other day
He had left being a man, she would make him a
beast.

'The lovers' session' [1687]
[Crum A424]
fb.108, p. 25

A0435 A set of phrases, learnt by rote
So holla boys, God save the King.

[Jonathan Swift], 'The furniture of a woman's mind'
[pr. 1750? (Foxon S857)]
[Crum A426]
c.570/4, p. 165

A0436 A settled mind free from distracts of cares
Be turn'd to thistles and the rest to weeds.

c.158, p. 29

A0437 A shabby fellow chanc'd, one day, to meet
When you play'd Hamlet, Sir—I play'd the cock.

[John Walcot ('Peter Pindar')], 'A true story . . . Ode
10—1786'
c.355, p. 97

A0438 A ship, by dreadful tempest tost,
To be, the lightest thing in nature.

[Thomas Hamilton, 6th earl of Haddington], 'The
storm appeased'
c.458/2, p. 154

A0439 A shirt I have on,
But the Lord knows when I shall have it.

'A song'

c.530, p. 155

A0440 A shitten king bewray'd the usurped throne,
Plenty of turd will be the nation's gain.

'The golden age' [on William III and Gilbert Burnet]

b.111, p. 372

A0441 A short time ago, my dear A—— was a ball
Record this one night to their sempitern praise.

Poetry Box x/164

A0442 A sickly wretch, both poor, and old
To lay my bundle, on my back.

[Thomas Hamilton, 6th earl of Haddington], 'A fable'
[of Æsop]

c.458/2, p. 126

A0443 A sign three painted asses grace
Of asses makes the number four.

c.53, fol. 20

A0444 A silly poor shepherd was folding his sheep
The warmer thou art the cuc-colder am I.

'Song 173'

c.555, p. 268

A0445 A simile oft I've endeavored to find
But a flash of true lightning gets once in an age.

'Burke'

c.391, p. 68

A0446 A sinner, is a sheep astray,
'The wand'ring sheep to save.'

M. S., 'A hymn'

c.156, p. 75

A0447 A sister once I had which always saw
Thus in her quiet rest, myself was crost.

Lady Jane Cavendish, 'On my sweet sister the Lady
Harpur'
[Crum A445]

b.233, p. 32

A0448 A small neat mansion, where embow'r'd in trees
And pity all that bustle thro' the throng.

'The wish'

c.142, p. 392

A0449 A small thing as you can see,
I do conclude—God save the King.

'[Enigma/Charade/Conundrum] 79'

c.389

A0450 A small world of kitchens most complete
Shine stars of gold in ruby sky.

Lord [ ] E., 'Another [riddle]'

Poetry Box VII/46

A0451 A solitary walk my steps convey'd
Belov'd by few, and yet approv'd by all.

'The rural philosopher'

c.481, p. 141

A0452 A son of the church that liv'd in the north
And will ne'er be recall'd but by great reformation.

'The doctor and vicar'

c.83/3, no. 745

A0453 A sore disease this scribbling itch is
He founded hospitals for fools.

'An epigram on Ld Orrery's remarks on the life of Dr
Swift'

Poetry Box v/127

A0454 A sot by chance hearing his father say,
Then faith 'tis plain you know not what you do.

R[obert] Shirley, 1st earl of Ferrers, 'The unsatisfied.
From the French'

c.347, p. 96

A0455 A soulful man in th'Hebrew signifies,
As if in Britain men had ne'er a soul.

Sir Thomas Urquhart, 'The Israelitish, and British
idiom'

fb.217, p. 338

A0456 A sow had farrow'd in her sty,
Self-service at your cost their end.

'The sow and the wolf'

Poetry Box IV/85

A0457 A Spanish soldier sick unto the death,
Sir, all alive, and have the world at will.

'On a Spanish soldier'

c.356

A0458 A sparing hand and often taking pain,
Are enemies to getting, and to gain.

b.234, p. 104

A0459 A speech if like to grief is like to sport,
If long 'tis trivial if grave 'tis short.

'Speech'

c.356

A0460 A sprightly gallant gentleman, and proper,
The supper is not ready.

> Sir Thomas Urquhart, 'How a certain cavalier, after
> his return from a long voyage, was welcomed by his
> wife'
>
> fb.217, p. 174

A0461 A spurious wight of empire fond
To bribe religion out of doors.

> 'Canto' on the Old Pretender]
>
> Poetry Box x/74

A0462 A stag caught young and tamely bred
For custom, conquers fear and shame.

> 'The tame stag'
>
> c.186, p. 69

A0463 A star of late was seen in Virgo's train
Then Charles, sit fast, and look unto thy wain.

> [Richard Corbett], 'On Dr Sapworth's comet, while
> Prince Charles was with the Span[ish] lady' [c. 1623]
> [Crum A467]
>
> b.200, p. 411

A0464 A star thou art, and shin'st in eminence
Bright continues (?) in wise and heav'nly care.

> [Sir Philip Wodehouse], 'Upon Sr Ralph Hare's
> second lady Elizabeth Hare'
>
> b.131, back (no. 119)

A0465 A steady mind, a friendly soul
And languishes to death.

> S[tephen] Simpson, 'Edwin'
>
> c.563

A0466 A story I'll tell you a story at large
For he's out of their debt if he ow'd them a shame.

> 'On the fall of the bed's tester on K[ing] G[eorge],
> and the D[uche]ss of M[un]st[e]r [later Duchess of
> Kendal]'
> [Crum A470]
>
> c.570/2, p. 165

A0467 A strange crew at St. James are harbor'd now,
Your arms won't save you, for your horse must fly.

> 'The English court made a Dutch b[awd]y house'
>
> c.570/1, p. 76

A0468 A strange report I've heard today
Deceiving you, deceiving me.

> 'Epistle VI. To Celia on hearing she was in love
> with me'
>
> fc.100, p. 29

A0469 A stranger gazing of the stables, cries,
Kings lodg'd as horses, and as horses, kings?

> John Lockman, 'The mistake: or St. James's Palace,
> and the stables in the mews . . . 1734'
>
> c.267/1, p. 108; c.268 (first part), p. 23

A0470 A strife arose (yet many(?) a fit(?) of love
That these receiv'd before, and these behind.

> [Sir Thomas Urquhart], 'Of two courtesans who did
> [?] together upon great wages which of them should
> be able to satisfy the desires of manyest(?) men'
>
> fb.217, p. 519

A0471 A subtle fox the story goes,
Pray tell me, Celia, where's your brains.

> 'An epigram the fox and vizard mask applied to a lady'
>
> c.578, p. 24

A0472 A summulist, t'explain a lass's mind,
To modify, by way of dilatation.

> Sir Thomas Urquhart, 'How a certain nimble-witted,
> but amorously affected boy, whilst he was learning his
> introduction to logic instructed a young wench of his
> acquaintance'
>
> fb.217, p. 47

A0473 A sunny bank in shade is seldom seen,
But they still prate, and nothing secret keep.

> 'On one Sunnybank taken in the night by Proctor
> Parret' [Oxford, 1545/6]
> [Crum A479]
>
> b.200, p. 411

A0474 A supper was in London made
And cried out mercy(?) good d[eity?].

> b.213, p. 156

A0475 A sycamore
The leaves, but words: 'tis deeds, do fruit express.

> [Sir Philip Wodehouse], 'James Cooper my musician
> poor sycamore'
>
> b.131, back (no. 198)

A0476 A table so spread and a cellar so stor'd
While Foote eats on gold, you'll be feeding on
                                    Delft.

> [David Garrick], 'Upon a certain person's remarks . . .
> upon Foote's manner of living'
>
> Acquisition 92.3.1ff. (autogr.)

A0477 A tailor, [thought] a man of an upright dealing
Of suchlike colored silk in all the flag.

> [Sir John Harington], 'Upon a precise tailor'
> [Crum A485]
>
> b.62, p. 94; b.205, fol. 47v; b.197, p. 99

A0478 A tailor's crest must always be,
'Crib and cabbage what you can.'

    [Frederick Corfield], 'Arms for a cross-legged knight'

c.381/1

A0479 A taper burning! And in broad midday!
He grudg'd the glimm'rings of a farthing light.

    John Lockman, 'A lady, who saw a candle burning, in
    the house of an egregious miser, the morning after his
    decease, spake, to her maid, in near the following
    words . . . Jany 1755'

c.267/1, p. 151

A0480 A tender tale, O Hannah, wilt thou hear;
Than dies in Mendip's shade dies on the
                       murmuring winds.

    Dr. [John?] Langhorne, 'The lost shepherdess to
    H[annah] More on her appearing in the character of a
    shepherdess of the alps in a late masquerade'

c.341, p. 18

A0481 A thief that bravely bears away his prize
Let Heer van Brush or Tyburn be his doom.

    'On the Lord Chan[cellor] [Jeffreys]'s restoring the
    charter'
    [Crum A492]

fb.108, p. 115

A0482 A thin ill-natured ghost that haunts the king,
Should e'er be thus condemn'd to counseling.

    [John Sheffield, 1st duke of Buckingham and
    Normanby], 'The nine cabinet council' [1690;
    Carmarthen (later duke of Leeds), Devonshire,
    Dorset, Bolton, Nottingham, Monmouth,
    Marlborough, Lowther, Russell]
    [Crum A493; POAS V.196]

b.111, p. 543; b.154, p. 48 (incomplete); fb.66/12

A0483 A thirsty poet void of chink
There is no trust in such a face.

    [Phanuel Bacon], 'Fronti nulla fides'

c.237, fol. [80a]

A0484 A thought has just struck me, my dearest A. D.,
Take this for want of a better.

    F[rederick] D[ickinson], 'Letter from . . . to A[nn]
    D[ickinson]'

c.391

A0485 A thousand, and a thousand times
No muse can and—no God inspire.

    [J. B.], 'To a lady'
    Poetry Box IV/155

A0486 A thousand foes prepare to war
And Antichrist fall down.

    'Hymn 6th'

c.562, p. 6

A0487 A thousand kings to me are naught
I hate all Horaces but Flaccus.

    [Robert Merry], 'Reply'

Greatheed Box/44

A0488 A thousand of both sexes may be kill'd
Of either sex, must join themselves in one.

    Sir Thomas Urquhart, 'Of life, and death'

fb.217, p. 42

A0489 A Thracian boy on frozen Hebrus play'd
That I brought forth for waters this to burn.

    [Sir Aston Cokayne], 'Epigramma de peuro Thracensi
    in Caius Germanicus Augustus'

b.275, p. 44

A0490 A threefold cord, the wisest man said true,
And threaten Sommerton if he but dare.

    'On Mr. Pr[io]r's letters to Mr. Sheph[er]d; (not
    omitting the last short one unowned)'
    [POAS V.110]

b.204, p. 74; fb.70, p. 231

A0491 A toleration spells, as with a sigh
And let Bray vicars be Bray vicars still.

    [Sir Philip Wodehouse], 'A toleration O alteration
    1672'

b.131, back (no. 85)

A0492 A tower with sounding walls erected stands
Beyond whatever can be, by my words express'd.

    [Charles Hopkins], 'The passion of Scylla for Minos
    from the eight[h] book of Ovid's Metamorphoses'

b.130, p. 107

A0493 A town of old as has been said
From a poor rhyming country cook(?).

    W[illia]m Hamilton [14 October 1730]

File 6565

A0494 A train of mourners, each a spotless maid,
And in one grave these sister beauties lay.

    'A riddle'

c.578, p. 92

A0495 A trait'rous bishop, histories record
Dares do 'gainst kings in low condition.

    Sir John Strangways, 'Of the Bishop of Hereford's
    sermon at Oxford preached before Queen Isabel . . .
    9no Decembris 1646'

b.304, p. 76

A0496 A tree, which was once a merry king's seat,
United, discover the name of a town.

'A rebus'

c.360/3, no. 205

A0497 A trifling song you shall hear,
And his song is a trifle to boot.

[George Farquhar], 'The trifle' [pr. 1714 (Foxon T480, anon.)]
[Crum A509]

fc.24, p. 20; c.570/3, p. 61

A0498 A truant so long, now I try to begin,
And become Poet Laureate instead of Will
Whitehead.

[Henry Skrine?], 'Poetical epistle to a lady at Paris'

c.509, p. 55

A0499 A truce with your proverbs 'bout taking great care
They've both drawn a prize in love's lottery.

[John Walker?], 'Jack Oddfish'

fc.108, fol. 39v

A0500 A twelvemonth last May
I love him the more since he's constant to one.

[John Walker?], 'Ciss of the grove or the mischief maker'

fc.108, fol. 21

A0501 A valentine, from some fair hand it came
Must know that epithet belongs to matchless Ann.

c.391

A0502 A verse may find him, who a sermon flies
With saints on earth shall one day with him shine.

[Crum A518a, 'take him']

b.137, p. 1; Poetry Box x/61 (incomplete)

A0503 A very skillful painter on a time
But for my children I did work by night.

'On a painter'

b.205, fol. 48v

A0504 A vintner's daughter with her paramour
For presently I'm feeling that he enters.

Sir Thomas Urquhart, 'Of a wine taverner's daughter who lay near the door not far from the bed wherein her father reposed'

fb.217, p. 189

A0505 A virgin life, altho' Eliza led
A numerous offspring of our maiden queen.

'[Several copies of verses spoken at Westminster School on the anniversary of the defeat of the Spanish Armada] 5'

c.233, p. 32; fc.24, p. 72

A0506 A virgin's like the spotless rose
What once so lovely was by all confest.

'A similitude between a virgin and a rose given me by Miss Eliza Clarke. Nov. 26. 1749'

c.360/3, no. 47

A0507 A virtue 'tis that dares all fear dissolv'd,
Who fears not God, cannot courageous be.

[Sir Philip Wodehouse], '3. That dares'

b.131, p. 16

A0508 A virtuous dame that saw a lawyer roam
To fear for want your wife should 'paid' borrow.

'[Epigrams.] 5. On a lawyer's absence'

b.205, fol. 96v

A0509 A virtuous lady, sitting in a mews
You shut it when you will you keep the keys.

[Sir John Harington], 'Vir ad dominam'
[Crum A526]

b.205, fol. 46v; see also 'A gallant lady . . .'.

A0510 A visit lately from a friend
From him renewed lives.

[ ] R., 'Riddle'

Poetry Box VII/49

A0511 A Vulcan and a Venus seldom part
Have like the watch one pulse one sympathy.

[William Strode], 'On a watch made by a blacksmith'
[Crum A532]

b.205, fol. 59r

A0512 A wandering gypsy Sirs am I,
A little treasure lodg'd in mine.

John Wolcot ('Peter Pindar'), '. . . Spoken at a masquerade in the character of a gypsy'

c.90; c.83/2, no. 277

A0513 A wanton widow here does live
This [thus?] to be us'd so drolly.

[Mrs. Christian Kerr], 'A song upon an old lady's of 66 designing to marry a young man of 40: to the tune of Dainty Davie'

c.102, p. 64, 66

A0514 A warrior made doctor thus vented his mind,
Then, not till then, may hellish powers prevail.

'The dream'

b.204, p. 150

A0515 A warrior so bold and a virgin so bright
And his consort, the false Imogene.

[Matthew Gregory Lewis], 'Alonzo the brave, and fair
Imogene a romance, from a novel, The monk'

c.83/2, no. 625; c.141, p. 297; Greatheed Oversize Box
4/124; Poetry Box XII/82

A0516 A watch in tavern lost, fie that's a crime,
Pocket your watch, and watch your pocket too.

'Upon a watch lost in a tavern'
[Crum A536]

b.104, p. 90

A0517 A watch to man does plainly show
A chain can unreluctant wear.

'On a watch'

c.143, fol. 15

A0518 A waterman, upon the Thames
Unless, you first are brib'd with gold.

[Thomas Hamilton, 6th earl of Haddington], 'The
doctor and the waterman'

c.458/2, p. 151

A0519 A wealthy island which no help desires
And surfeit great Augustus with her treasures.

'One Alfred of Beverley a poet of the middle times
saying this of Britain viz. England'
[Crum A539]

b.206, p. 119

A0520 A wedding there was, and a dance there must be,
Their marriage is good. Pray how could that be?

'A riddle' [answered by 'Old Priam the king . . .']

c.578, p. 52

A0521 A wedding's a wedding the universe over,
And Turks buy their wives like our chickens by
dozens. | And sing ballinimono oro &c.

'Merry wedding'

c.160, fol. 62

A0522 A week and a day has past and no more
To restore a poor frantic to his senses again.

'Le Brosse to the good lady abbess at Cirencester . . .
April the 24th 1762'

c.484, p. 147

A0523 A well-time[d] pregnancy her titles gain'd
A faithful clue to Rosamonda's bower.

[Horace Walpole, 4th earl of Orford], 'C[ountess] of
Rochf[ord]' [d. 1773]
[Crum A541]

c.157, p. 69

A0524 A Welshman and an Englishman disputed
Aye, quoth the other, each man toasts his cheese.

[Henry Parrot], 'Dispute'

c.81/1, no. 298

A0525 A Welshman coming late into an inn
I' th' morning he took his heels and run away.

[Crum A542]

b.65, p. 88; c.186, p. 73; fb.142, p. 63

A0526 A Welshman walking in the dark, for fear
My nose was longer then my arm till now.

'On a Welshman'

b.205, fol. 49v

A0527 A wheel, will roar, 'til it [be] greas'd about:
An advocate, 'til he be greas'd is mute.

Sir Thomas Urquhart, 'The difference between an
advocate, and a wheel'

fb.217, p. 138

A0528 A Whig and a Tory o'er a pot of good ale
'Twas not to compare to good eating and drinking.

'The argument'

c.570/2, p. 42

A0529 A while ago my cruel fate
My love shall ne'er grow less.

'Another by the same hand' [as 'Tho' in their
flame . . .']

fb.142, p. 52

A0530 A whore came to Mac-John,
Be of his mother's faction.

Sir Thomas Urquhart, 'Of an advocate called Master
John whose pater was dubii generis'

fb.217, p. 253

A0531 A wicked old peer
Will bring in the House of Hanover.

'On the death of the Bishop of Sarum [Gilbert
Burnet] and [Thomas] the Marquis of Wharton. Hell
in an uproar' [satire, 1715]
[Crum A548]

fc.58, p. 107; c.570/1, p. 12; Accession 97.7.40

A0532 A widow, who to pelf was ever prone,
The bond was cancell'd, and she found relief.

'A widow outwitted'

c.81/2, no. 582

A0533 A wife careful and silent, loves home and ne'er
                                        thwarts us,
As we learn from the keys, prest lips, dove and
                                        tortoise.

    'Distich. Wrote under the figure of a woman standing
    upon a tortoise, a bunch of keys in her right hand, the
    forefinger of her left hand upon her lips, and a dove
    upon her shoulder . . . translations [4]'

    c.81/1, no. 70

A0534 A wife I adore if either she's constant and civil
But Jove take an whore she's company fit for the
                                        devil.

    'A catch'

    b.54, p. 1157

A0535 A wife I do hate—
Have always a punk to their mother.

    [William Wycherley], 'The evening wife' [in Love in
    a wood I.2]

    fb.107, p. 50

A0536 A wife in your old age, what demon bewitches
You had proved a wise Beaver and 'scaped with
                                        your life.

    [Theophilus Hill], 'On [Mr Beavor, an aged
    schoolmaster, who married a young lady of great
    fortune]'

    c.546

A0537 A wife is like a garment worn and torn
Sold at the second hand like broken ware.

    'On wives, maids and widows'
    [Crum A555]

    b.356, p. 105

A0538 A wife should be kind, careful, calm, not rove
This the shell show, the keys, shut lips and dove.

    'Distich. Wrote under the figure of a woman standing
    upon a tortoise, a bunch of keys in her right hand, the
    forefinger of her left hand upon her lips, and a dove
    upon her shoulder . . . translations [1]'

    c.81/1, no. 70

A0539 A wife, so chaste; so tender; and so kind;
You bachelors, repent—e'er yet too late.

    Joseph Spence, 'The happiness of marriage. July 23,
    1745'

    Spence Papers, folder 148

A0540 A wife, who as our own by law we hold
And a false woman is a matchless curse.

    '[Epigram] 4, On a wife' [from Flaminius]

    c.158, p. 131

A0541 A wife you wisht and S[i]r rich, fair and young
Expect such plainly, I would wish no [more].

    'In amorosum epig:'

    b.205, fol. 40v

A0542 A wig that's full, an empty skull,
A hand that's white a ring that's right . . . .

    fc.73 (incomplete)

A0543 A wight he is whose very size
When justice angry is, she's in a passion.

    [( ) Goddard, fellow of St. John's, Cambridge, tripos
    verses on the stealing of bodies for dissection, 1731/2]

    c.489, p. 5 [bis]

A0544 A wight there was, scarce known I ween to fame
To duty's path, and useful to mankind.

    'A character, after the manner of Chaucer, from
    Mr. G—s's reveries of solitude'

    c.83/3, no. 807

A0545 A willing mind makes an industrious hand,
Ascending thus you may at last transcend.

    Poetry Box IV/107

A0546 A wily fox upon a day,
Sour grapes—than in confusion to retreat.

    R[obert] Shirley, 1st earl of Ferrers, 'The fox and the
    grapes'

    c.347, p. 54

A0547 A wise and sturdy earl was wont to say
Bring not the island to shame and misery.

    Sir H. Bourchier, '1655 A saying of . . . at the Earl of
    Bath'

    b.131, p. 43

A0548 A wit, you tell me, once allow'd
On her own head the horns she places.

    'Comparison of woman to the moon'

    Greatheed Box/67

A0549 A woe-worn heroine in me you spy!
A kind and easy passport to my grave!

    'Epilogue, spoken by Mrs. Bellamy, or rather intended
    to have been spoken by her as a fareful [farewell?] to
    the town—but she was so affected as to be unable to
    speak it—it was spoken by Miss Farrell [later
    Kennedy]'

    c.90

A0550 A wolf in sheep's clothing near twelve years ago
Let the bells ring and bonfires merrily flame, |
                                        Derry down.

    fc.61, p. 71

A0551   A wolf so far in butchery did go,
      Aesop had warn'd the dupes—as I do now.

      'The wolf reformed. A fable'

      c.578, p. 97

A0552   A woman cannot choose but be respectful
      Anticipates [?] [?] disease.

      [Sir Thomas Urquhart], 'How [?]ious that man is in
      his wife who omits not the convenient occasions of
      satisfying her matrimonial desires'

      fb.217, p. 526

A0553   A woman is a microsphere whose center
      Whom that center resteth not but moves.

      [Sir Thomas Urquhart], 'Of the center of women's
      little world and how different men are in the end of
      their apprehending(?) it from all other (either
      elements) or elementary things'

      fb.217, p. 388

A0554   A woman is of glass or weaker
      Gold shower also would be found.

      [Sir Aston Cokayne], 'Of women'

      b.275, p. 64

A0555   A woman lately fiercely did assail
      I may scratch mine one head and so may you.

      'On a woman scratching her husband'

      b.356, p. 104; b.65, p. 89

A0556   A woman may be call'd, a man's culotte
      And trifling—he who wears it, wants advice.

      [Sir Philip Wodehouse], 'Upon [his wife's] sister—
      Alice Cotton'

      b.131, back (no. 59)

A0557   A woman's love is like a Syrian flower,
      That buds, and spreads, and withers in an hour.

      'Women's love'
      [Crum A573]

      c.356

A0558   A woman's rule should be in such a fashion
      Obedient husbands or commanding wives.

      [Crum A574]

      b.197, p. 23; see also 'Ill thrives that hapless family . . .'.

A0559   A wonder that science and learning profound
      And we meet with so few that bring any away.

      'Epigram'

      c.115; see also 'No wonder that Oxford and
      Cambridge . . .'.

A0560   A word that's composed of three letters alone,
      Toils in his service, and becomes his food.

      'Enigma'

      c.389

A0561   A word that's oft used and entailed on mankind,
      Exposed to all winds, and in all sorts of weather.

      '[Enigma/Charade/Conundrum] 6'

      c.389

A0562   A world that's full of fools and madmen,
      I cry for all their ills, and laugh at all their follies.

      'A short view of some the world's contents'

      c.83/3, no. 968

A0563   A worm that creeps and crawls into the breast
      Who was before their master's now their game.

      'Oliver Cromwell anagram O cruel ill worm'

      fb.228/26

A0564   A would-be sage, of all adventure,
      The gypsy'll have you by your line.

      W[illia]m Melmoth, 'Verses occasioned by a lady's
      delivering a specimen of the author's handwriting . . .
      April 9th 1796'

      File 17460

A0565   A wretched and too solitary he
      To help to bear't away.

      c.548

A0566   A wretched cit—for there are some
      Pray let me help you to a plate.

      [Phanuel Bacon], 'Ne in penuria victus opprimiret
      maturbat'

      c.237, fol. 76 [i.e., 96]

A0567   A Yorkshire man! And hostler still!
      For damn it! Measter's Yorkshire too.

      'On a Yorkshire hostler'

      c.546, p. 2

A0568   A young beginner walking through Cheapside
      Yes you may let alone for aught I see.

      F. R.

      b.197, p. 102

A0569   A young gay lord when call'd of late
      And copy what you dare approve.

      H[enry] Skrine, 'Prize poem at Batheaston on modern
      courtship . . . Bath—Dec. 23 1779'

      c.509, p. 26

A0570 A young man, and an old together chid,
Else hadst thou not begged of me this abuse.

'Found by Ned Leycester in one of the books in the
library'

c.591

A0571 A young [man?] late as I heard say
And show me now good preacher(?).

M. P., 'Certain most beneficial meditations, etc.'

a.6, p. 118

A0572 A youth, by elegance of taste refin'd,
Late, to exchange this paradise for heav'n.

'To Mr. Gayland on his nuptials with Miss Darby of
Chiselhurst in Kent, the seat of Robert Salusbury esqr'

c.360/3, no. 252

A0573 A youth delights in something new,
Whether to reach it soon or late.

'An holiday ramble on Easter Monday March 28th
1785 . . .'

c.504, p. 70

A0574 A youth in years, but ripe in grace,
He joins the seraph's song.

'Epitaph at Bolton'

c.139, p. 445

A0575 A youth there was whose haughty pride
The wretch that sees her, surely dies.

'On Miss Howe writ by a young gentleman
passionately in love with her'

c.360/2, no. 138

A0576 A youth whose sole delight and pride
His flutt'ring pinions o'er your head.

'An idyllium from Bion imitated'

fc.85, fol. 32v

A0577 A youth, whose sprightly inclination
Prithee, honest Robin, bring my mare.

[David Garrick?], 'The reproof'

Poetry Box v/33

A0578 A youth with every virtue blest,
Or by the varying friend.

[Helen Craik], 'Lines written upon hearing a
gentleman complain of the ins[t]ability of human
friendships'

c.375, p. 80

A0579 A youth with more than manly courage bless'd
Rejoic'd—he wav'd his trembling hand—and died.

'Epitaph on a midshipman killed on board the
Antelope'

c.83/2, no. 734

A0580 A zealous locksmith died of late,
Because he means to pick the lock.

'Upon a puritanical smith'
[Crum A600]

b.200, p. 409; b.62, p. 47; fb.143, p. 15; fc.14/8

A0581 Abhorred of man, unknown to brute,
In all that time, but twice I bear.

'A riddle . . . Christmas 1774'

fc.74, p. 18

A0582 Abjuring prelates: th'articles of Perth
Some other tables will admit of you.

Sir Thomas Urquhart, 'The encouragement for a
covenanter to a certain gentleman of a lewd life, in the
interim of their great troubles'

fb.217, p. 229

A0583 About the sapless season of the year,
Then straight at Duncomb's feet resolv'd my verse
to lay.

Susanna (Carroll) Centlivre, 'A poem to the right
honorable Sr. Charles Duncomb upon his being
chosen Lord Mayor of London, 1709'

c.158, p. 108

A0584 About the time that I shall be
The fox shall ride the goose the goose the ass.

'Part of a prophecy [of Nostradamus in the year 1520]
which hath been in the L. Powys' house above 60
years' [pr. 1679? (Wing P3685)]
[Crum A607a. 'that one']

Poetry Box vi/13; 15 ('About that . . .')

A0585 Above distress a mortal pain
And weeping day . . . .

[Thomas Hull]

c.528/56 (incomplete)

A0586 Above the subtle foldings of the sky
And silence kept while its Creator spake. &c.

[Abraham] Cowley, 'Cowley's description of heaven'
[Crum A616]

fb.66/39 (incomplete)

A0587 Abraham, when severely tried,
And loss shall be eternal gain.

'Hymn 83d'

c.562, p. 109

A0588 Absalom hang'd on a tree
And put a spear in his arsie.

[Zacharie Boyd]
[Crum A619]

b.231, p. 6; b.232, p. 5

A0589 Absence, hear thou my protestation
And so enjoy her and so miss her.

    [John Hoskins], 'A poem'
    [Crum A621]

b.148, p. 63; see also 'By absence this good mean . . .'.

A0590 Absence thou bane of every social bliss
But pleasure court me to her roseate bower.

    Miss [ ] Andrews, 'On absence and hope'

File 245/17

A0591 Absent from thee I languish still
And lose my everlasting rest.

    John Wilmot, 2nd earl of Rochester, '13. Song'

b.334, p. 194

A0592 Absolute ethics; common duties fix
Yet still unto felicity we tend.

    [Daniel Baker], 'Verses out of ethics'

b.81, p. 31

A0593 Accents so sweet, so melting, so divine,
Warbled the sounds which we, enraptur'd, hear.

    John Lockman, 'To Signor Hasse: writ whilst his Salve
    regina was performing . . . April 1744'

c.267/1, p. 179

A0594 Accept a miracle, instead of wit,
See two dull lines with Stanhope's pencil writ.

    [Edward Young], 'Lord Chesterfield, and a party of
    gentlemen and ladies, were sitting after dinner one
    day, when it was proposed, that the company should
    each of them make two lines, one of the gentlemen . . .
    borrowed Lord Chesterfield's pencil . . . and wrote'

c.378, p. 75; c.360/1, p. 125 ('Except a miracle'); c.74

A0595 Accept an homely invitation
If justice weighs the *Dantis amor*.

    J. W. L[ee] to Sir George Lee

Poetry Box I/134

A0596 Accept, as most rare (for 'tis rare, if so soon
The last of your toasts—remember the vicar.

    [Charles Earle], 'To Justice S—— at Dulverton (with
    a leash of woodcocks)'

c.376 (2 copies)

A0597 Accept Boscawen! these unpolish'd lays
And, dread, yet wish to find one hero more.

    [Hannah More], 'Sensibility a poetical epistle to the
    Hon: Mrs. Boscawen'

c.130, p. 45

A0598 Accept, dear Ann, this box of scent,
Their merits as you find their excellence.

c.391

A0599 Accept dear friend this fragrant flow'r,
Ever the favor'd child of heav'n.

    'From a lady to a friend, with a rose, and a drawing of
    it—written on her daughter's birthday'

c.90

A0600 Accept dear Hetty for thy purse
From hand to hand, from heart to heart.

    W[illiam] W[arren] Porter, 'To Miss ———'

c.83/2, no. 733

A0601 Accept, dear maid, to gild thy studious hours,
Nor one Hayleyan glory shine in vain!

    [Anna Seward], 'To Miss Inge' [written in a volume of
    William Hayley's poems; Lichfield, 9 August 1785]

File 17513

A0602 Accept, Democritus! the lay
Or were thy soul in me enshrin'd.

    John Lockman, 'To Democritus [John Atkins of
    Plaistow, Essex] on his birthday (21 March 1756) from
    his friend Heraclitus'

c.267/1, p. 208

A0603 Accept, fair bride, this ripening fruit
Blest with their mother's charms!

    R[ichard] V[ernon] S[adleir], 'To Mrs. [crossed out]
    late Miss [crossed out] with a basket of fruit, on her
    wedding day 1781—impromptu. She became base and
    lewd to the grief, and wonder of all who knew her'

c.106, p. 53

A0604 Accept, fam'd Des Cageaux, without a pish,
The king of bards should eat the king of fish.

    John Lockman, 'To an illustrious French poet, with a
    Shetland pickled herring . . . Jany 1751'

c.267/1, p. 264

A0605 Accept, good Madam, if you please
Can miter'd appetites run higher?

    'To Mrs. Master'

c.484, p. 105

A0606 Accept, great God, a dying monarch's prayer,
And my last sigh—thus—dies upon thy name.

    [Richard] Daniel, dean of Armagh, 'Solomon—Psalm
    72d'

c.244, p. 369

A0607 Accept great God thy Britain's songs
And foam to feel their fury vain.

    P[hilip] Doddridge, 'A hymn on the Thanksgiving
    Day Oct. 9. 1746 from Ps. LXXVI 10 The wrath of
    man &c.'

c.493, p. 47

A0608   Accept improving Hill
For even . . . [missing last lines]

     Poetry Box v/35 (mutilated)

A0609   Accept kind guide! 'Tis all that's mine
My age shall bless thy sway.

     'An ode to my ever respected master, the Rev. Osmond
     Beauvoir [King's School, Canterbury]'

     c.169, p. 3

A0610   Accept, (kind Postlethwait!) this hasty lay,
Plans, great as thine, substantial favors claim.

     John Lockman, 'To Malachi Postlethwait esqr. after
     reading a national scheme, drawn up by him . . . May
     1758'

     c.267/1, p. 215

A0611   Accept lamented shade this mournful voice
Alike averse to avarice and pride . . . .

     [ ] Phillips

     c.416 (incomplete)

A0612   Accept, (learn'd Onslow!) from the world retir'd;
Her fame's secure, since Onslow is her friend.

     John Lockman, 'To the right honorable Arthur
     Onslow, on his resigning the chair of the House of
     Commons, Wednesday, 18 March 1761'

     c.267/2, p. 381

A0613   Accept, most gracious God, our grateful lays,
And thou'[r]t the only God whom we adore.

     'The Lord's prayer. Attempted in easy verse never, as
     yet published'

     c.487, p. 48

A0614   Accept (most worthy Lord of York's fair city)
And fame shall be the trumpet of thy praise.

     Thomas Robinson, 'To the right honorable William
     Robinson Lord Mayor of this city of York. Dedication
     of The life and death of Mary Magdalene'
     [Crum T482]

     fb.144, p. 1

A0615   Accept, much honor'd shade! these artless lays
And spend their bless'd eternity in praise.

     'On the death of Mrs. Rowe'

     fc.51, p. 170

A0616   Accept my Lord of this poor glittering thing
When the Archduke is King, you an Archduke
                         shall be.

     'On the K[ing] of Spain's giving his picture set with
     diamonds, and his sword, to the D. of Marlb[oroug]h'
     [Crum A626]

     c.111, p. 59; b.201, p. 101, 179

A0617   Accept these flowers dearest Bet,
Her fragrance still remains, when beauty's lost.

     H[annah] M[ore], 'To Miss B. More when ill in the
     smallpox sent round some flowers'

     c.341, p. 83

A0618   Accept these lines, by indignation penn'd,
Dullness conferr'd—in body, mind, and face.

     [Charles Burney, the younger], 'Parody on some lines
     signed Fidelia, addressed to Mr. Cundall, surgeon,
     Hungerford, Berkshire, which were published in the
     Reading mercury. December 1. 1777'

     c.37, p. 28

A0619   Accept this sketch of me, decreed by fate
You cannot read without a glass.

     'A riddle addressed to the honorable Mrs. B.
     Walsingham'

     c.157, p. 100

A0620   Accept this tribute of an humble muse,
The pageantry of courts and pomp.

     'An epistle to Mrs B—'

     c.116, p. 48

A0621   Accept thou shrine of my dead saint
Till we shall meet and never part.

     [Henry King], 'An exequy' [on King's wife, 1624]
     [Crum A633]

     b.205, fol. 84 v.; c.240, fol. 8; b.356, p. 126; Poetry Box
     VI/121 (ostensibly on Margareta Key)

A0622   Access to Thee O God by pray'r,
Whilst here they live and when they die.

     [Edmund Wodehouse], 'Octr. 22 [1714] so long as we
     admitted are vouchsafed'

     b.131, p. 65

A0623   Accomplish'd dames, whose soft consenting minds
The proud preeminence of noble birth.

     William Roscoe, 'The nurse, a poem. Translated from
     the Italian of Luigi Tansillo'

     c.142, p. 35

A0624   According to my skill in th'harmony,
The title of B sharp in music sets.

     Sir Thomas Urquhart, 'A musician speaks thus to a
     merrily disposed wench, who was indifferently well
     seen in the art of music'

     fb.217, p. 310

A0625   Accounts must pass of every day
Agree with what Christ's counsel is.

     [Edmund Wodehouse], 'Novr. 5 [1714]'

     b.131, p. 77

A0626 Accursed wretch, whose impious pen blasphemes
Of envy, malice, infamy, and hate.

'An answer to a vile epitaph'

c.360/1, p. 305

A0627 Acon the lad did want his worthier eye
And thou the blind god Cupid then will prove.

[translation from Girolamo Amalteo's De gemellis]
[cf. Crum A647]

b.197, p. 36

A0628 Acon unto a queen himself resign'd
And thee to virtue transubstantiate.

J[ohn] Hobart, 'Mr. J[ohn] Hobart's ritornello—a true
story'

b.131, p. 40

A0629 Across his arms while flippant Courtenay lies,
And stand the Pharos of the coming time.

'On the biographers of Dr. Saml. Johnson'

Poetry Box x/14

A0630 Acteon's dogs eat 's bones, his flesh, and skin:
His horns, at London ever since have been.

Sir Thomas Urquhart, 'Upon the relics of Acteon, at
London'
[cf. Crum A651]

fb.217, p. 240

A0631 Actions alike, alike should bear the blame
Hang but the last, the parallel's complete.

'On the D[uke] of M[arlborough]'
[Crum A652]

b.382(5); c.570/2, p. 49 ('should be their shame')

A0632 Adam alone could not be easy,
He never slept so sweet again, Sir.

[John] S[traight], 'By the Rev. Mr. S.——' [Dodsley
Collection]

c.487, p. 132; c.241, p. 83; c.81/1, no. 57

A0633 Adcock is dead, a man of merit,
Of learned sons, but learning lost deplore.

'1753. On the choosing a master for Oakham School'

c.229/1, fol. 137v

A0634 Add the half of a woman to part of your face
A market town's name as plain as your nose.

'A rebus'

c.484, p. 55

A0635 Addition of whole numbers comprehend
Which shows the total sum if right you cast.

[Mary Serjant], 'Addition'

fb.98, fol. 7

A0636 Adieu, blest spot! The fairy glades;
Then soon, from kindred ashes, rise.

John Lockman, 'The farewell to Vauxhall Gardens:
writ in one of the alcoves . . . Sept. 1745'

c.267/1, p. 180

A0637 Adieu dear nymph
To order so.

'Epitaphs Bersted'

c.546

A0638 Adieu deceitful world, thy pleasures I detest,
Now others with thy shows delude, my hope in
                                        heaven doth rest.

[Geffrey Whitney]
[Crum A669]

c.339, p. 328

A0639 Adieu each hop'd-for blessing
Is to resolve to die. | But come bright glory aid
                                        me &c.

'Song 6'

c.555, p. 8

A0640 Adieu false Britons, false to your vows adieu!
Is guilty of the ten, and breaks them all.

'His Majesty's royal farewell to England a Pindaric'

b.111, p. 1

A0641 Adieu fond love farewell you wanton powers
Find love declines if heavenly love grows higher.

[Francis Beaumont and John Fletcher]

b.213, p. 48

A0642 Adieu, kind genius! May no ill betide;
The queen of nymphs, demands your earliest care.

John Lockman, 'To the genius of Vauxhall Gardens,
on the closing of that entertainment . . . Sept. 1755'

c.267/1, p. 144

A0643 Adieu kind youth, worthy of better times
Should no[w?] had thee, and others had thy fate.

'To the memory of Mr Robert Dickson of Buchtrig
advocate and a worthy member of Parlia[men]t'

Poetry Box VIII/26

A0644 Adieu loved form! Once more adieu!
For you[r] own faithful little Warner.

L. Concannon, 'Verses to Mrs Rigby occasioned by
her departure from Sacket's Hill on the 12th of Oct:
1794 by Vere Warner esqr. . . .'

Greatheed Box/24

A0645 Adieu my friend, heaven calls, we must resign;
A friend on earth, an advocate above.

'An elegy on . . . Richd Thorton esq. Recorder of
Leeds, who died Sept. 1710'

c.160, fol. 81

A0646 Adieu my life adieu
And must I talk ever—then . . . .

[John Black]

fc.107, p. 82 (incomplete)

A0647 Adieu! Sweet bard! To each fine feeling true,
Depart in peace, and imitate the man!

W. Woty, 'Epitaph on Dr. Goldsmith'

fc.132/1, p. 121

A0648 Adieu sweet shade, complete was thy career
Nor death affright whom not a vile had soil'd.

H[orace] Walpole, 4th earl of Orford, 'Said to be
wrote by . . . on Lady Dysart'

Poetry Box III/6

A0649 Adieu the delights of the stage
And crowd to my preaching each night.

[Thomas Hull]

c.528/42

A0650 Adieu thou blest retreat, sweet peaceful shades,
The[n] farewell love, and farewell happiness.

'Absence, a pastoral'

c.175, p. 89

A0651 Adieu to the pleasures, and follies of love,
Then, then, I never will part with him more.

'Dorinda's lamentation for Amintas'

fb.107, p. 16

A0652 Adieu, vain mirth and noisy joys,
Thy steps; adieu, vain world adieu.

[William] Broome, 'An ode on melancholy . . . wrote
on the occasion of the death of an only daughter'

c.244, p. 484; c.360/2, no. 119; fc.60, p. 112

A0653 Adieu vain world thou tinsell'd toy
Creation great and fly to thee.

'The farewell'

File 13409

A0654 Adieu! Ye lovely haunts, a long adieu!
There magic fancy still shall picture thee.

c.83/2, no. 535

A0655 Adieu, ye plains! Adieu, ye verdant groves!
And ye, my friends, accept these humble songs.

[Charles Burney, the younger], 'A farewell to
Shinfield. 1778'

c.37, p. 9

A0656 Admire not, that you judge's ears are shut:
Seeing avarice hath giv'n your hands the gout.

Sir Thomas Urquhart, 'To a sparing man, who
complained, he could get no justice'

fb.217, p. 179

A0657 Admit (thou darling of mine eyes)
To blind the world, but only thine.

[Thomas Carew]

b.213, p. 21

A0658 Adore the spring which flows with nectar, all
Of crystal, for pure innocence.

[Sir Philip Wodehouse], 'Another epig[ram] referring
to Sr Christopher Calthorpe her knight'

b.131, back (no. 56)

A0659 Adultery and ravishment
You surely shall die for your sin.

Sir John Strangways, 'In adulterium et adulteres . . .
6to Octobris 1646'

b.304, p. 58

A0660 Adults in ev'ry science learn
Most men to ridicule inclin'd.

S[tephen] Simpson, 'Ridicule'

c.563

A0661 Advance George Monck, and thou St. George shalt
be,
Then all will cry God save the King.

b.104, p. 2 (end of book)

A0662 Advise no more with earth then let her be
To seek a rest where 'tis not to be sought.

[Mary Serjant]

fb.98, fol. 163

A0663 Æneas, in a surly mood,
From Virgil's mine, to Freeman's mite.

[Isaac Freeman], 'On receiving a bill from Benjamin
Barker esqr.'

fc.105

A0664 Æneas must progenitor have been
Equally dutiful, took off his mother.

'Epigram. Suetonius . . . translation'

c.81/1, no. 453

A0665 Affable, courteous, witty and discreet,
And falls a victim to her conq'ring eyes.

> 'On Miss Jane Barnard daughter of Sir John Barnard, knt. and alderman of London and Lord Mayor of the said city 1738 [the year of her marriage]. Wrote at Tunbridge Wells . . . 1733'

c.360/2, no. 148

A0666 Afflicting(?) hour of fate's most awful cast
Accept and hallow this sequester'd tear.

> [William Hayley], 'Sonnet . . . May 9 [1800]'

File 6968

A0667 After a fruitful chase, resolv'd to know,
The bolt uplifted, hangs to crush thee down.

> 'Pride and discontent silenced'

c.244, p. 627

A0668 After a pretty amorous discourse,
Y[ou]'d been more happy, had you been less fair.

> [Sir George Etherege], 'The imperfect enjoyment' [trans. from Charles Beys, 'Le jovissance imparfaite'] [Crum A715]

b.218, p. 42

A0669 After an old man's death in gold was found,
What must the widow have? And what each child?

> 'An arithmetical, poetical, law question'

c.93

A0670 After death nothing is, and nothing death,
Dreams, whimsies, and no more.

> [John Wilmot, 2nd earl of Rochester], 'Seneca's Troas. Act 2, Chor[us]' [Crum A718]

b.105, p. 106; c.189, p. 10; Poetry Box vI/68

A0671 After invoking of the muse
Ye'll be advertised by the next.

> S[amuel] C[olvill], 'Mock poem or Whigs' supplication part first' [pr. 1681 (Wing C5425)] [Crum A722]

b.231, p. 9; b.138 (incomplete); b.232, p. 7

A0672 After long penance of a nine year Lent
Whilst Bungy and his wife solace within.

> [Thomas Smith, University College, Oxford], 'Prologue to the music speech . . . [8 July] 1693' [Crum A725]

c.146, p. 46; b.115, fol. 37 (with 16 more lines)

A0673 After long storms and tempests overblown
Else would afflicted man despair.

c.358, p. 34

A0674 After our pains our pleasures make us glad,
But without sour the sweet is hardly had.

c.339, p. 320

A0675 After our rites done to the king we do
May pass for ware 'tis only judgment here.

> W[illiam] Cartwright, 'The prologue to the university in the same manner as before' [from The royal slave, 1636]

b.200, p. 151

A0676 After so long a sleep, does Shakespeare wake
The hand that equals Shakespeare's— come and write.

> 'On seeing Shakespeare's monument when first set up in Westminster Abbey without an inscription, in 1740, 124 years after his death, where his effigy points to a scroll at first left blank'

c.360/2, no. 213

A0677 After so many concurring petitions
Already you have had too much of his prose.

> [Sir John Denham], 'To the five principal members of the House of Commons the humble petition of the poets' [Crum A729]

fb.228/1

A0678 After so many in the English tongue
Of praise beseech a pardon when I'm read.

> [Sir Aston Cokayne], 'To my dear friend Mr Mar: Wivell'

b.275, p. 51

A0679 After so many sad mishaps
Full soft and fair, he made her arse lie.

> [Sir John Denham], 'To Sir W. D'Avenant' [on Gondibert] [Crum A730]

pb.53, p. 3 (autogr.)

A0680 After some threescore years of caterwauling
For she'd as soon be d[amn]'d, as be at rest.

> 'Epitaph on an old scold'

c.113/12

A0681 After the duty of a verse
If you be pleased I have my pay.

> Lady Jane Cavendish [dedication of a pastoral to the Earl of Newcastle] [Crum A732a]

b.233, p. 43

A0682 After the honey drops of pearly showers
Heaven put his hand forth and did glean.

> 'To the same. The rose'

Poetry Box v/106

A0683 After the pangs of a desperate lover
Ah what a joy to hear that again. | Ch[ange] ah
what, &c.

    [John Dryden]

b.213, p. 152; fb.107, p. 27 (var.)

A0684 After the sort of academic wit
Like mighty muses there inspiring it.

    [John] Smallwood, 'Smallwood's epilogue to the ladies
    in the Commencement House' [Cambridge, 1680?]
    [Crum A731, 'that sort']

b.115, fol. 35; fb.142, p. 57 (var.)

A0685 After the sweetest pangs of hot desire
She hugs the dart that wounded her and dies.

    [Richard Duke], 'Song, supposed to be written by my
    Lord M[ulgra]ve'

b.105, p. 400

A0686 After thinking this fortnight of Whigs and of Tory
The fools should be Whigs, none but knaves
should be Tories.

    [Charles Sackville, 6th earl of Dorset], 'My opinion or
    the ninepins'
    [Crum A734; POAS II.391]

fb.106(21); Poetry Box x/38

A0687 After thy course of various travel run
And rear Athenian domes in freedom's land.

    S[neyd] Davies, 'To Tho. Anson at Shugborough'

c.157, p. 74

A0688 After two sittings now our Lady State,
Himself the poet and the painter too.

    [Andrew Marvell], 'September 1661' [i.e., 1667; 'Last
    instructions to a painter'; envoy: 'So to his bold
    tube . . .']
    [Crum A735; POAS I.99]

Poetry Box VII/15

A0689 After venting all my spite,
I to laugh, and you grow wise.

    [Jonathan Swift], 'An epistle to a lady who desired me
    to make verses on her' [pr. 1733 (Foxon S841)]

c.570/4, p. 105, p. 165 ('on Sir R[obert] W[alpole]')

A0690 Again, at thy belov'd command
May heav'n in mercy close my date!

    [ ] Birch, 'A birthday anniversary to his wife'

c.504, p. 54

A0691 Again for war, long ceas'd, prepare!
For cruel thou, elud'st my pain.

    [William Popple, trans.], 'The odes, epodes &ca. of
    Horace translated. Book 4th. Ode 1st. To Venus'

fc.104/2, p. 328

A0692 Again I urge my wonted cry,
And happy made in Thee?

    Charles Atherton Allnutt, 'Divine aspirations'

c.112, p. 76

A0693 Again, my glowing bosom burns
Or kindly smile Lucinda to my arms.

    'Horace ode 19 book 1'

Poetry Box I/21

A0694 Again rejoicing nature sees
When nature, all is sad like me!

    [Robert Burns], 'Stanzas'

c.142, p. 278

A0695 Again the day returns of holy rest,
Glory supreme be Thine till time shall end.

    'Hymn before morning service'

c.83/3, no. 898

A0696 Again the morn I see return,
The pen that Lucy gave me.

    [( ) Smyth], 'Stanzas written with a pen given to the
    author by a lady who desired him to write verses
    with it'

c.141, p. 25

A0697 Again the sacred day returns,
Exult and spread th'obedient wing.

    'Sunday morning—detained from church'

c.515, fol. 4v

A0698 Again the wood, and long withdrawing vale,
Have power to cure all sadness—but despair.

    [Charlotte (Turner) Smith], 'By the same to spring'

c.130, p. 95

A0699 Against a covenant a parliament
The day is done and so good Tom goodnight.

    [on Thomas Bampfield; 1658 or later]

Poetry Box VII/50

A0700 Against a gate Dick had a damsel got
I only mean, said Dick, to prop-a-gate.

    'Epigrams'

c.546, p. 30; c.81/1, no. 321

A0701 Against Admiral Byng, Lo! each bard has a fling,
Sure, he ought to be kick'd for a blockhead.

    [N.] H[erbert], 'Reflections upon some dull (out of
    many) poetical scribblers against Admiral Byng'

Spence Papers, folder 91

A0702 Against our God, it is a great offence
In earthly things to put our confidence.

    c.339, p. 321

A0703 Against our peace we arm our will;
We soon create a future pain.

    c.549, p. 105

A0704 Against such odds if Edward could succeed,
And future field with that of Poictiers vie.

    [William Shirley], 'Epilogue to the same tragedy'
    [Edward the Black Prince]

    c.578, p. 117

A0705 Against the charms our ballocks have
To such a bitch as Phyllis. | Whom . . .

    [John Wilmot, 2nd earl of Rochester], 'Song'

    b.105, p. 152 (incomplete)

A0706 Against the colic nettleseed and honey
It helps him of the gout that eats it often.

    [Joshua Sylvester, trans. Guillaume de Salluste,
    seignieur Du Bartas], 'Of nettles'

    b.284, p. 52

A0707 Against unthrift Severn[u]s did provide
And wisdom still against such unthrift cries.

    b.234, p. 310

A0708 Agape her little circle stand
Such care upon a future day.

    [( ) Birch], 'The magic lantern or a press at Lilliput'

    c.504, p. 41

A0709 Age of itself puts us in mind,
Both frequently and ardently.

    [Edmund Wodehouse], 'Septr 11 [1715]'

    b.131, p. 263

A0710 Ah! beauteous nymph, whoe'er thou art
The virtuous love thee, and the world admire.

    Charles Burney, the younger, 'Sonnet written in
    Evelina, and addressed to the ladies . . . April. 1779'

    c.35, p. 29

A0711 Ah! Belidore, when you express
Life, liberty and ease.

    'Another by the same hand' [as 'Tho' in their
    flame . . .']

    fb.142, p. 50

A0712 Ah blame me not if on the mournful lyre
And to our tears our mourning parent spare!

    'On the death of a beloved father'

    c.140, p. 558

A0713 Ah! briny tears ye ceaseless flow in vain
Lo thus I hurl you to your parent main.

    fc.40

A0714 Ah! but too well, dear friend, I know
They best confer, who merit most.

    Sir W[illia]m Jones, 'Answer' [to 'Sir William you
    attempt the vain . . .']

    c.83/4, no. 2035

A0715 Ah! cease this kind persuasive strain,
Will heave one tuneful sigh, and soothe my
                       hov'ring shade.

    [William] Mason, 'Ode to melancholy a lyric poem'

    c.83/1, no. 91

A0716 Ah! cease thy shrill pipe little sweep
Alas! I only wake to weep.

    'To a chimney sweeper' [signed 'Leonora']

    Poetry Box x/46

A0717 Ah! Celia, as thou'rt fair be kind
Yet let me love or die.

    c.549, p. 4

A0718 Ah! Celia, that I were but sure,
Whole hearts and boast the happiness.

    [Sir George Etherege]

    c.549, p. 91

A0719 Ah, Celia! Where are now thy charms
Or she has not a heart like thine.

    [William Walsh], 'To Celia upon some alterations in
    her face'

    c.223, p. 78

A0720 Ah! Celia, with what anxious care,
Nor scorn the counsel of your friend.

    'The mirror addressed to a young lady'

    c.83/3, no. 742

A0721 Ah Chloris that I now could sit
With fortune they must see.

    [Sir Charles Sedley]

    b.213, p. 143

A0722 Ah Chloris, 'tis time to disarm your bright eyes,
For all maidens are mortal at fourteen.

    [Charles Sackville, 6th earl of Dorset?], 'Song to
    Chloris from The blind archer by my Ld. Buckhurst'

    c.189, p. 112

A0723 Ah! Chloris would the gods allow
Half in unkindness is misspent.

  'The wish'
  [Crum A755]
  fb.107, p. 11

A0724 Ah cried Arsenia, long in wedlock blest
But in the third—alas—became a bride.

  'Epigram'
  c.360/1, p. 127

A0725 Ah cruel bloody fate!
Then clos'd her eyes and died.

  [Nathaniel Lee], 'A song' [in Theodosius, act V]
  [Crum A756]
  b.54, p. 1137

A0726 Ah cruel death! That dost no good
What shall we do for faggots?

  'On Jno. Underwood'
  [Crum A758a]
  c.250

A0727 Ah cup of woe! Most terrible to drink,
And this weak tribute reach the awful sky.

  '[Hymns composed the week preceding the
  sacrament] 5th'
  c.515, fol. 18v

A0728 Ah! dry those tears they flow too fast
Expresses half the pangs I feel.

  'To a lady on the loss of her favorite goldfish'
  Poetry Box VII/69

A0729 Ah fading joy | How quickly art thou past,
To gentle slumbers [c]all.

  [Thomas Head], 'The careless mortal'
  [Crum A765]
  fb.107, p. 62

A0730 Ah filthy shabby Tarse!
Cried fuck I thee command.

  'A mock song to Philander. 1680'
  b.54, p. 1198

A0731 Ah! fond remembrance of my former state,
Bless our good God, and praise his glorious name.

  [Richard] Daniel, dean of Armagh, 'Absalom.
  Psalm 3d.'
  c.244, p. 340

A0732 Ah fortune! Wilt thou never smile,
And give to joy its noblest pow'r!

  'Elegy'
  c.89, p. 91

A0733 Ah, friend, forbear nor fright the fields
Their own eternal rights and Nature's injur'd reign.

  Poetry Box I/112

A0734 Ah gentle Zephyra, ah! If e'er,
But not whose eyes those tears supplied.

  'Sonnet . . . Eastern poetry'
  c.344, p. 81

A0735 Ah! hapless babe, the parent cries,
Great God thy will be done.

  [ ] Worseley, 'Epitaph on a child of four years old'
  c.391

A0736 Ah! hapless victory, what avails
And buries numbers in thy womb.

  'The Victory man of war in distress'
  c.179, p. 61

A0737 Ah happy grove, dark and secure retreat
And whilst they live, their flames can never die.

  [Wentworth Dillon, 4th earl of Roscommon, trans.,
  part of Guarini's Pastor Fido, Act II, scene v]
  [Crum A773]
  b.218, p. 18; Poetry Box IV/53

A0738 Ah! Hero, when to you my course is bent,
Sink at thy feet into eternal rest.

  'Leander's epistle to Hero: in imitation of Ovid'
  c.94

A0739 Ah, hills belov'd! where once, unhappy child,
There's no oblivion—but in Death alone!

  Charlotte (Turner) Smith, 'To the south downs'
  c.343, p. 97; c.504, p. 97

A0740 Ah! how long have I fed my desires,
But in spite of your scorn, I must love you too well.

  'The lawless lover'
  fb.107, p. 21

A0741 Ah how sweet ah how sweet it is to love
Are so made to believe—all all all all all all who &c.

  c.374

A0742 Ah! how sweetly is begun
And gazers leave behind.

  'The passage of life'
  c.83/2, no. 589

A0743 Ah, how unkind is the nymph I adore?
Than languish in lukewarm indifference.

  'The scornful lass'
  fb.107, p. 6

A0744 Ah I will storm—I find thy name is short
But will't protest against that foreign court.

    [Sir Philip Wodehouse], 'William Short a Romanist
    ah! I will storm'

    b.131, back (no. 177)

A0745 Ah, Joseph, Joseph! To my voice attend,
For all thy boasted barb'rous yard of name!

    Timothy Priestley, 'Mr. Timothy Priestley to
    Dr. Joseph [Priestley]'

    c.83/3, no. 796

A0746 Ah! kind but simple maiden you do amiss
Which druggists sell you and you to them.

    'To a kind but painted lady'

    fb.142, p. 58

A0747 Ah let no more the tear-swol'n eye
And you're most blest of human kind.

    'Consolatory verses to the Burney family on the recent
    death of Thomas Frederick Burney aged 19 years . . .
    August 1784'

    c.486, fol. 6

A0748 Ah let thy young enthusiast stray
And comfort what you cannot cure.

    c.250

A0749 Ah little think the gay licentious proud,
Repining still, the social passions work.

    [James] Thomson

    File 245/30

A0750 Ah lovely Celia, why so coy
My former face, or former mind.

    'To a young lady who refused an offer of marriage'

    c.360/1, p. 281

A0751 Ah lovely Stella, fairest of the fair
Estrang'd to passion, discord or despair.

    'Hebe's complaint to Stella composed by desire of the
    gentleman called here Hebe'

    c.91, p. 217

A0752 Ah lowly grave! What bed of down,
From what high source is flow'd.

    'Reflections on seeing a grave newly dug in ———
    churchyard.'

    c.83/1, no. 128

A0753 Ah me—how promis'd joys delude us still,
Nor spring's gay blooms flow sweeter in the lay.

    [J. M—tt], 'To Ophelia, on her long silence'

    c.140, p. 370

A0754 Ah me my friend the flatt'ring bliss is o'er,
And call our God our Father and our friend.

    'Elegy to Robert Remmett esqr.'

    c.89, p. 29

A0755 Ah me! That time should scathe with ruthless hand,
Dull wisdom cannot ken the greatness of despair.

    [Thomas] Dudley Fosbroke, 'A sketch of Nettley
    Abbey near Southampton'

    c.230

A0756 Ah me! what envious magic thins my fold?
To form the garland, elegy! for thee.

    [William Shenstone], 'The early love of poetry and its
    consequences'

    c.149, p. 5

A0757 Ah me! Where's now that mien! That face!
Now by the just revenge of time stol'n from herself
                                   should be.

    c.549, p. 75

A0758 Ah! me, will thoughtless mortals ever prize
And all, but virtue's solid pleasures, woe.

    Charles Burney, the younger, 'Elegy. On virtue . . .
    June 2d. 1779'

    c.35, p. 33

A0759 Ah, merry swain, who laugh'd along the vales,
And friends beloved—more joy than wealth can
                                   bring.

    [Ann (Ward)] Radcliffe, 'The Piedmontese'

    c.83/3, no. 743

A0760 Ah, might a tenderhearted maid,
Join Mr. D. to | Esther Fast.

    [Frederick Corfield], 'Miss Fast to Mr. D.'

    c.381/1

A0761 Ah modest shentle when her see
I pray send her word if her can love . . . .

    'The loving Welshman to his mistress . . . these verses
    her send peing rudely penned'
    [Crum A792]

    b.62, p. 43 (incomplete); see also 'Modest shentle . . .'.

A0762 Ah! mourn'd by all, by whom thou wast admir'd!
And as they vanquish cry—remember Eld.

    'ABACD in a tribute to the memory of an officer
    whose death is justly regretted by his country. He was
    killed at Valenciennes in 1793' [signed Edward]

    c.343, p. 37

A0763   Ah! my fickle Jenny while there was not any
With thee alone I'd live and die.

    [William Walsh], 'A Scotch dialogue in imitation of
    the 9th ode 3d book of Horace'

    c.223, p. 95

A0764   Ah, my sad heart! of deep and ceaseless grief
Grinning a horrid smile, and pierced my heart.

    'A sonnet. The sweetest enjoyment of friendship
    interrupted by malice' [14 April 1799]

    c.136, p. 155

A0765   Ah never say you'll love no more
And therefore I'm resolve'd to keep you low.

    'Phyllis absolute'

    fb.142, p. 45

A0766   Ah! no, 'tis all in vain, believe me, 'tis
Themselves outdone in luxury.

    [William] Congreve, 'Another paraphrase of [Horace
    book 2 ode 14]'
    [Crum A798]

    c.244, p. 80

A0767   Ah now sad muse! invoke heaven's great Apollo
Noted with pencils of eternity.

    J. R., 'In idem' [elegy on the death of Andrew
    Horsman]

    b.212, p. 246

A0768   Ah! painful thought! And must you go?
His fair one still as true to love.

    Sir Joseph Mawby, 'Absence an elegy'

    c.83/2, no. 349

A0769   Ah! pardon, Madam, if I ever thought
Is not the smallest trophy of your eyes.

    [Sir George Etherege], 'Submission'

    b.218, p. 21; Poetry Box IV/53

A0770   Ah! pardon my rashness that so abuse divinest love
I would from God as well as man receive a just
                              commission.

    Poetry Box VII/76

A0771   Ah! pass not yet, if thou didst ever know
The feeling heart alone should tarry here.

    'Inscription for the monument of Emma Corbet'

    c.83/2, no. 685

A0772   Ah pearly drops, that pouring from those eyes,
And thro' the lucid shower his living lightning flings.

    [William Roscoe], 'Sonnet from the same' ['Lorenzo
    de Medici']

    c.142, p. 93

A0773   Ah! poor Almida, never boast
He like a god is everywhere.

    'Song'

    c.189, p. 174

A0774   Ah, poor Barsanti! Hard thy fate!
Again relate the pleasing tale.

    [Charles Burney, the younger], 'Part of a letter to Miss
    Burney London Aug. 12. 1779'

    c.37, p. 43

A0775   Ah! poor Quebec:
Now thou'rt a—speck.

    John Lockman, 'Extempore. (Jocoso) Hearing the
    town guns fire, for the taking of Quebec . . . Oct.
    1759'

    c.267/1, p. 268

A0776   Ah Posthumus our years hence fly,
Far more than night, be married.

    [Robert] Herrick, 'Mr. Herrick to Mr. Weekes'
    [Crum A803]

    b.356, p. 5

A0777   Ah pretty fav'rite were thou blest with sense
Thou lack'st his reason and he lacks thy place.

    'To a lady's lapdog—wrote 1727'

    c.360/1, p. 35

A0778   Ah reign wherever man is found!
Than these of ice, and give us new.

    [William Cowper, trans.], 'Wishing for the reign of
    love. Vol. 2. Cant. 236' [of Jeanne Guion's 'Spiritual
    songs']

    c.470 (autogr.)

A0779   Ah, sacred may the vessel glide,
Thy radiance, ever bright.

    [Charles Burney, the younger], 'Ode to the ship, in
    which Mr. F. J. H. Wallaston sails from St. David's, to
    Bristol, June. 1777'

    c.37, p. 6

A0780   Ah Sally! Had you liv'd in days of old
And well supply the absent husband's place.

    'To a certain young lady wife to an old lawyer'

    c.360/2, no. 92

A0781   Ah say sweet songster, gentle nightingale,
And leads her charge to realms of endless day!

    'Ode'

    c.89, p. 50

A0782 Ah seeing I am sore wounded with affection:
Cure me, that I may live in your subjection.

> Sir Thomas Urquhart, 'All the eight parts of grammar
> are comprehended in the first line of this distich'
> fb.217, p. 71

A0783 Ah! shall my inharmonious verse aspire
Will antedate the raptures of the blest.

> Charles Burney, the younger, 'Elegy, addressed to
> Dr. Beattie, on perusing his Poems and elegies . . .
> 1779'
> c.35, p. 43

A0784 Ah silly John surpris'd with joy
Joan whiter than the lily.

> [Crum A810]
> b.148, p. 70

A0785 Ah since thou art great Marquis of Ormonia
To vindicate King Charles' bloody bane.

> 'James Ormonde admonish Rome anagr[am]'
> fb.228/31

A0786 Ah! still sad memory tends my side,
And meet my Shenstone there.

> J[ames?] Woodhouse, 'Verses wrote at the Leasowes
> after Wm Shenstone's death'
> c.139, p. 1

A0787 Ah! stormy world! Thy waves run high o'er me,
Compose my sorrows, and enerve their sting.

> 'Thoughts in affliction'
> c.515, fol. 11v

A0788 Ah! Strephon would you hope to be,
To indicate—the lack of brains.

> Poetry Box x/66

A0789 Ah! such to know, what place detains
And soothe her griefs to rest.

> 'Song'
> c.83/2, no. 318

A0790 Ah; tell me no more, my dear girl, with a sigh,
I've already forgot thou art fair.

> John Wolcot ('Peter Pindar'), 'To Cynthia'
> c.355, p. 197; c.90

A0791 Ah the charms of the beauty, disdainful and fair!
And she cures with those pleasures before she
destroyed.

> 'A song: 1676'
> b.54, p. 980

A0792 Ah treacherous Nichols! F[r]iend as thou wouldst
seem
Who've rather kill'd him by a weight of notes.

> [on John Nichols' Life and anecdotes of William
> Bowyer, published in 1778]
> Poetry Box VIII/69

A0793 Ah urge too late! From beauty's bondage free,
Or, pitying, give me hope, or bid me die!

> [James Thomson], 'Verses addressed to Miss Young'
> c.83/2, no. 384

A0794 Ah wanton Phyllis! 'Tis in vain
Or he's engag'd to her.

> R[obert] Shirley, 1st earl of Ferrers, 'A song'
> c.347, p. 15

A0795 Ah were you but more, or less kind than you are
Your business is only to burn and destroy.

> 'Song'
> Poetry Box I/111[5]

A0796 A[h] what a hero is here,
And never will after be vex'd.

> 'The answer' [to 'Good master Apollo . . .']
> c.356

A0797 Ah! what art thou, whose eyeballs roll
For dead and dark they seem, and almost chill'd to
stone.

> M[ary (Derby)] Robinson, 'The maniac'
> c.83/2, no. 518

A0798 Ah, what avails the wealth that Indus brings
Shuns his embrace, and still perversely flies.

> 'Lines on health'
> c.83/3, no. 750

A0799 Ah what is fortune? What is fame?
To guard, to guide, to bless my friend.

> 'Rhymes address'd to Mr Z. B. written soon after his
> departure March [17]73'
> c.89, p. 74

A0800 Ah! when so late I press'd this mossy sward
Ye little heed my tears, along the green sod, gay.

> [Richard Polwhele], 'Sonnet on a visit to P—— near
> Truro'
> c.141, p. 571

A0801 Ah! wherefore veil that lovely face
Unseen while you inspire.

> [John Black?], 'To a young lady who always wore a
> veil'
> fc.107, p. 34

A0802 Ah!—whither,—where,—whatever!
To fly—where Rome's victorious eagles never flew.

    William Combes, 'Ode to nonsense'

    c.341, p. 135

A0803 Ah whither wouldst thou fly, too love[l]y youth
How I might find a passage to thy heart?

    Mrs. [ ] Whittell, 'The Indian'

    c.83/2, no. 623

A0804 Ah who can tell how hard it is to climb
'Tis meet that I shall mourn:—flow forth afresh
                        my tears.

    James Beattie, 'The minstrels'
    [Crum A826b]

    c.139, p. 202 (incomplete?)

A0805 Ah! who could have thought
And hang up old Churchill their master.

    'A lampoon'

    c.570/1, p. 79

A0806 Ah! who in all those happy plains
Alas! Too well I know!

    Miss [ ] White, of Edgbaston, 'The mutual
    symptoms'

    c.532

A0807 Ah! who shall hail the saffron morn,
Fair Rosalie Chamonix's queen.

    'Lindore's sonnet on the departure of Rosalie from the
    vale of Chamonix'

    c.83/2, no. 559

A0808 Ah who that's wise accounts as vain
And on her spirit pure a throne of bliss bestow.

    'An ode to the memory of the Lady Viscountess
    Valentia formerly the Hon[ora]ble Lucy Lyttelton'

    fc.53, p. 149 (cf. p. 147)

A0809 Ah! who would believe in that creature call'd man
Should certainly form, of my life the whole plan.

    c.83/2, no. 536

A0810 Ah! why did cruel nature form my heart
Her charms can bless me and her love can save.

    'Elegy'

    Poetry Box XII/80[2]

A0811 Ah! why does Mary heave that sigh
Sigh I sigh enough for you.

    [ ] Hackett, 'To Mary ———'

    c.546

A0812 Ah why that sober air put on
You make men fall in love with grief.

    J. B., 'To the same [a lady] on seeing her in mourning'
    Poetry Box IV/155

A0813 Ah why these tears—this rising sigh,
Who flies the path of truth.

    'Credulia's complaint'

    c.83/3, no. 972

A0814 Ah why will memory with officious care,
Ah share for me—and I will not complain.

    [Charlotte (Turner) Smith], 'Sonnet 10 to Mrs. Y——'

    c.504, p. 98

A0815 Ah! why with restless, anxious search explore
And calmly yield to death whate'er can die.

    [Charlotte (Turner) Smith], 'The universal sway of
    death[.] To a friend'

    c.83/2, no. 336

A0816 Ah! wish not, mortal, with precarious breath,
And freed from flesh, our spirits soar'd to heav'n!

    'Thoughts on sudden death addressed to a person who
    used to wish for it'

    c.487, p. 50

A0817 Ah! woods forever dear! whose brambles spread
'Mid shades impervious to the beams of day.

    'Translation of one of Haller's(?) elegies'

    c.344, p. 52

A0818 Ah! wretched Israel, once bless'd and happy state,
For every life a myriad, every drop a flood.

    [John] Oldham, 'David's lamentation for the death of
    Saul and Jonathan—paraphrased by . . .'
    [Crum A834]

    c.244, p. 199

A0819 Ah! wretched me! Thus unresig'n to bear,
And 'dear Maria' sounds in ev'ry line.

    'Subsellium loquitur—Sepr. 22d. 1755'

    c.591

A0820 Ah wretched me! Unhappiest, sure, of lovers!
Dimm'd his bright torch, and half his arrows broke.

    John Lockman, 'In occasion of the new regulation
    with regard to franks'

    c.267/1, p. 385

A0821 Ah wretched wainscot to receive
My friend the dish-clout comes tomorrow.

    'Written on an iron(?) door'

    c.504, p. 5; see also 'O wretched . . .'.

A0822 Ah you that love to weep, come weep with me,
Ever my tears will gush, I'll still lament.

> S[amuel] R[aymond], 'A[n] acrostic' [on Andrew Horsman]
>
> b.212, p. 256

A0823 Ahasuerus now's invested on the throne
To no better place than the gallows for his end.

> c.158, p. 40

A0824 Aid me, great Neptune, whiles I would make way
While fear paints death most horrid to the soul.

> 'A sailor's extempory description of a storm and shipwreck'
>
> c.578, p. 44

A0825 Alas, alas, what can we wretches do
Farewell forever to our author's age.

> [George Howard, 6th earl of Carlisle], 'Epilogue to [The reconciliation]'
>
> c.197, p. 10

A0826 Alas! and did my Savior bleed!
'Tis all that I can do.

> [Isaac Watts, Hymns and spiritual songs (1707), bk. II, Hymn 9]
>
> c.180, p. 29

A0827 Alas dear friend, our time flies fast away
Is only fit, for gods, and them to drink.

> [Thomas Hamilton, 6th earl of Haddington], 'Horace book 2d ode 14th'
>
> c.458/2, p. 76

A0828 Alas! dear friend, time hastes away
Than that of consecrated prelates when they dine.

> 'Horace book 2d. ode 14th'
>
> c.244, p. 78

A0829 Alas fond child
When gain's uncertain, and the pain is sure!

> [Francis] Quarles, 'From a very old book, entitled— . . . Emblems'
> [Crum A855, 'fond man']
>
> c.90

A0830 Alas for Britain and her sons
And dying love restore.

> P[hilip] Doddridge, 'On Mat. XXIV. 12'
>
> c.493, p. 80

A0831 Alas for me! whene'er my footsteps trace
Believes th' insidious vow—and from me flies.

> [William Roscoe], 'Sonnet from Lorenzo de Medici'
>
> c.142, p. 89

A0832 Alas how barbarous are we,
Can first oblige, and then endure.

> [Katherine Philips?], 'On graving a name on a tree'
>
> c.189, p. 29

A0833 Alas! I burn! In pure and holy zeal
To see my God—to me Thy face reveal.

> [Sir Philip Wodehouse], 'Upon the eldest d[aughter] Anne Burlasy'
>
> b.131, back (no. 34)

A0834 Alas I feel my strength decay
With him is power to save.

> [Thomas Stevens?]
>
> c.259, p. 95

A0835 Alas! I hear a murm'ring throng
Through Father Son and Holy Spirit.

> [on Pope, Prior, Swift, and Gay]
>
> Poetry Box x/3, p. 1

A0836 Alas! I never meant thee ill
The dying slave that does adore thee.

> c.549, p. 31

A0837 Alas! I'm in a woeful plight,
Enroll'd amongst his happiest sons.

> 'The breeches'
>
> c.382, p. 62

A0838 Alas! in plaintive strains I fondly mourn
To make him loveliest of the feather'd kind.

> Miss [ ] Andrews, 'On the death of a favorite bullfinch'
>
> File 245/9

A0839 Alas! my friend, thus, Astrea sigh'd, and said,
It dropp'd down dead a willing sacrifice.

> [Mrs. Christian Kerr], 'A young lady's lamentation to her friend for the sudden death of a favorite linnet . . . March of 1719'
>
> c.102, p. 103

A0840 Alas! my friend, you write in vain
To bear the kiss, with added sweets, to me!

> R[ichard] V[ernon] S[adleir], 'Mr. Sotheby having written some verses (much to long to be inserted here) . . . at the foot of those verses I wrote what follows'
>
> c.106, p. 102

A0841 Alas my God, that we should be
Where all thy singers meet.

> [Thomas Stevens?], 'For communion with God. (Penitential cries.) . . . Decr. 10. 1779'
>
> c.259, p. 62

A0842 Alas! my Lord is going, oh my woe!
Comfort me quickly, or I die . . . .

   [Christopher Harvey], 'Synagogue'

   b.245 (inside back cover; incomplete)

A0843 Alas! my Postumus, the flying years
Than that at pontiffs' feasts, and proudly stain the
                                                    floor.

   [William Mills], 'Odes of Horace translated. Book II.
   Ode XIV. To Postumus'

   c.472, p. 32

A0844 Alas my son thy death is death to me
Farewell my dear son thousand times adieu.

   [( ) Pierson], 'An elegy on the much lamented death of
   my son Isaac Pierson who departed this life the 12th of
   Feby. 1736 . . . He was 13 years 3 months and 8 days
   old'

   c.328, p. 125

A0845 Alas! no more I could survive
But be as dead as any man alive.

   'Epitaph in a country churchyard'

   c.360/3, no. 125

A0846 Alas! poor Brown, thy days are done,
And die, oh die! A natural death.

   'To the memory of Mr. Saml. Brown, a Cornish
   fiddler'

   c.382, p. 49

A0847 Alas, poor Cowley, how I pity thee!
And humbly thank the God for sparing thee.

   'Copy of verse consisting of the same number of
   verses and in the same meter by way of answer to
   Mr. Cowley's The mistake'

   c.416

A0848 Alas! poor mortal man why do you grieve?
Her return, all thy past joys will double.

   'On his mistress leaving him to go into the country'

   c.158, p. 23

A0849 Alas! poor Tabby's dead who can deny,
And her lov'd memory from oblivion save.

   [Henry] Needler, 'On the death of a tabby cat'

   c.244, p. 545

A0850 Alas, poor Werther! To himself a prey,
And gives them force to bid the world adieu.

   'Elegy, written after having read The sorrows of
   Werther'

   c.344, p. 94

A0851 Alas she's gone the charming Celia's fled
Where friendship reigns and grief | Shall be no
                                                    more.

   'On the death of Lady [Elizabeth (Chomley)] Cocks,
   March 1749'

   c.181, p. 53

A0852 Alas! that even birds are doom'd to share
That from Maria I must part.

   [William Carpenter], 'To Miss Maria C—r on the
   death of a Java sparrow'

   c.247, p. 154

A0853 Alas things sort not to my will,
I am to grief alive to them as dead.

   [George] Herbert, 'Cross'
   [part of Crum w548]

   b.245 (inside back cover; incomplete)

A0854 Alas! to this we come—why why is life
Alas! So long their art, so short their day.

   [ ] Lewis, 'On [the] death of Sr. Godfrey Kneller'
   [1723]

   c.244, p. 464

A0855 Alas what blindness seiz'd our mind
Makes lasting sorrows grow.

   T[homas] S[tevens]

   c.259, p. 140

A0856 Alas! what mortal lives of bliss secure
To welcome death, and calmly pass away.

   c.83/3, no. 1022

A0857 Alas why stay'd you him if needs must go
Nor yet his grace, whose soul to heaven is gone.

   'Upon one that died having his grace denied in the
   Regent House'

   b.356, p. 145

A0858 Alas! ye fair why from cosmetic art,
In briny torrents melt upon your dust.

   A. R., 'An imitation of Dr. Akenside's style, in his
   poem entitled 'The pleasures of imagination'

   fc.51, p. 16

A0859 Alas young man, what is thy blood so staid?
And then a lower but a higher bliss.

   'On a modest youth'

   b.356, p. 306

A0860 Albanum is a city fair
Which never shall decay. | Amen

   'Another of S. Bart[ho]lemew [August 24]'

   a.30[29]

A0861 Albinus hence thy faults discern
And thou in peace thy days shall end.

    'To Albinus. On the prodigal son'

    c.570/3, p. 66

A0862 Alexis saw me and I saw him
And got the likenesss of the father.

    'Some lines out of a poem on his royal Highness
Frederick prince of Wales and Miss Vane, daughter of
Ld Barnard and maid of honor to Queen Caroline'

    c.360/1, p. 253

A0863 Alexis shunn'd his fellow swains
He bow'd obey'd and died.

    [Matthew Prior], 'Song'
    [Crum A899]

    fc.61, p. 66; Accession 97.7.40, p. 14

A0864 Algernon Sidney fills this tomb
Where Pope and Devil have naught to do.

    [Thomas Brown], 'On Colonel Algernon Sidney'
    [beheaded 7 Dec. 1683]
    [Crum A900]

    fb.143, p. 31

A0865 Alidor in's easy chair
Are not articles of faith.

    R[obert] Shirley, 1st earl of Ferrers, 'Against an atheist.
From [Boileau]'

    c.347, p. 26

A0866 Alindor liv'd in yonder grove,
Bereft of him,—I wish to die.

    [Sophia Raymond] Burrell [Clay], 'Alindor and Lubin.
A story taken from an accident which happened at
Tunbridge Wells in Sept. 1784'

    c.141, p. 519

A0867 Alius, whose high birth, we trace,
Barbecue the shot with wine.

    [William Popple, trans.], '[Horace] book 3rd. ode
17th. To Alius Lama'

    fc.104/2, p. 268

A0868 Alive I'm buried, in my grave I move
Nor wood nor earth nor marble for my grave.

    [ ] R., 'Riddle'

    Poetry Box VII/47

A0869 All actions quickly to their period tend:
Though life, and lust hath each, its proper end.

    Sir Thomas Urquhart, 'Of vital breath, and lechery'

    fb.217, p. 244

A0870 All are freeborn you say? There's no such matter
Confute new English liberty.

    [Sir Philip Wodehouse], 'My obj[ection]'

    b.131, p. 44

A0871 All are indebted much to thee,
Experience makes it ours.

    [William Cowper, trans.], 'Pure love on a principle of
gratitude. Vol. 2. Cant. 96' [of Jeanne Guion's
'Spiritual songs']

    c.470 (autogr.), p. 16

A0872 All are mistaken here on earth,
And half dead got to shore.

    R[obert] Shirley, 1st earl of Ferrers, 'The dog and his
prey—from La Fontaine'

    c.347, p. 32

A0873 All are not just, because they do no wrong,
To be, not to be thought, an honest man.

    'Justice . . . [Observer, v. 5] no. 139'

    c.355, p. 89

A0874 All attendance apart,
And do penance in shape of a wife.

    [Miss ( ) Soaper], 'Repentance or second thoughts'
    [11 July 1730]
    [Crum A904]

    fc.51, p. 29; see also 'All disguises . . .'.

A0875 All-bounteous heav'n! we own the great and wise
And this my last advice— dear friends,—farewell.

    'On parting with a friend . . . 20th Sept. 1788'

    c.91, p. 12

A0876 All buildings are but monuments of death
All curious music but our passing bell.

    'Upon death'

    b.62, p. 148

A0877 All by a silent darksome glade
The charms of every face, and every mind.

    Joseph Spence, 'The rover the best husband: a new
ballad very fit to be sung (or said) by all godly people'

    Spence Papers, folder 148

A0878 All changing time, had cancelled and supprest
So strict besieged the Samarians' towers.

    [Francis Quarles], 'On Israel's afflictions and
deliverance out of Egypt'

    b.137, p. 150

A0879 All Christian men in my behalf,
And when he came to his father's years might he
       have worn horns.

 'Epitaph the 28 made by a merry poet upon one John
 Calfe in King Henry the 3rd's time'
 [Crum A913]

 c.158, p. 106; c.81/1, no. 180; fb.143, p. 21

A0880 All Christian people being under the steeple of
       Jesus Christ's faith
And that of thy mere mercy and grace, within that
time and place, to illumine us with thine sincere
       verity.

 [ ] Gray, 'A book entitled the fantasy of idolatry . . .
 this little book made and compiled by Gray in his
 martyr's book' [early 17th century?]

 fb.138 (folder 11)

A0881 All Christians else begin their new year at
Fourscore three days before he was conceived.

 [Sir Thomas Urquhart], 'That the juridicate
 computation and epoch of England differeth full
 twelvemonths from that of other nations . . .'

 fb.217, p. 507

A0882 All creatures living have a time for rest
With thoughts of what may be, destroys what is.

 'Taken from a window at Hockrel. July 9 1749'

 c.360/2, no. 15

A0883 All cuckolds' heads must to the Paphian Dame
Is called Cerasos or the horned land.

 [Sir Thomas Urquhart], 'Why he may properly said to
 have horns, whose wife out of a Venerian disposition
 prompted to a vagrant coit, is permitted to alienate
 her [?] due to the lascivious use of other men'

 fb.217, p. 507

A0884 All dainty meats I do defy, that feeds men fat as swine,
That carry his kitchen in a box his roast meat in a
       pipe.

 'On the commendations [of] tobacco'
 [Crum A920]

 b.207, p. 16; b.62, p. 80 (attr. Richard Corbett)

A0885 All day like one that's in disgrace
Wherein I do both live and die.

 '8. Enig. Res: A candle'

 b.205, fol. 99r

A0886 All day she scolds it out, and cries,
And think'st an easy yoke, and light.

 Sir Thomas Urquhart, 'Of a gentlewoman, scoldingly
 disposed in the daytime, and amorous enough to her
 husband, at night'

 fb.217, p. 249

A0887 All day the bells, for him, in concert rung;
For the lone honors of the mold'ring tomb.

 John Lockman, 'On a young man, of Plaistow in
 Essex, who sickened and died immediately after his
 marriage'

 c.267/1, p. 160; see also 'Gaily the bells . . .'.

A0888 All delights, that can betide,
And from those blows, which leave no scars.

 'To the bridegroom and his bride'

 c.189, p. 15

A0889 All disguises apart, | I examined my heart
And do penance in shape of a wife.

 [Miss ( ) Soaper], 'A young lady's repentance of a
 promise she had made to retire into the country,
 written by way of letter'

 c.233, p. 89; see also 'All attendance . . .'.

A0890 All Dutch and English that are left
Would act fair, and stand neuter.

 'The Dutchmen's reasons for a Dutch Sunday to be
 observed once a month'
 [Crum A924]

 b.111, p. 311

A0891 All earthly glory posts away with speed,
What once was venerable now is dead.

 W. D., 'Anagram Caleb Vernon. Once venerable'

 b.228, p. 1

A0892 All fable is figure—I your bard will maintain it
Your applause will be ever the true *baume de vie*.

 'Epilogue to A peep behind the curtain. Spoken by
 Mr. King'

 c.68, p. 193

A0893 All flesh['s] like grass, and withereth like the hay,
Today man laughs, tomorrow lies in clay.

 [Crum A930 (var.)]

 c.339, p. 327

A0894 All folks who pretend to religion and grace
How happy for us, that it is not at home.

 [Jonathan Swift], 'On the place of the damned' [pr.
 1731 (Foxon S897)]

 c.570/3, p. 120

A0895 All fortune's blessings does appear
That must succeed my present pain.

 'Fortune'

 c.83/2, no. 321

A0896 All-glorious Lord! eternal God!
O Father, Son, and Holy Ghost.

'The love of God'

c.167, p. 10

A0897 All-guiding heaven that on my aged head
Faithful however [?]. . . .

[William Hayley], 'Sonnet . . . Feb 14 [1800]'
[incomplete]

File 6968

A0898 All hail bright beams that usher in the morn
Forever loving and forever lov'd.

'On Miss S—— R——'s birthday'

fc.60, p. 111; c.244, p. 622; see 'Like charity itself . . .'.

A0899 All hail great Sir in seeing whom we see
In memory preserv'd th'immortal book.

David Humphreys, 'A poem presented to Robert
Nelson esqr on his birthday June 22d [1713]'

File 7764

A0900 All hail, hallelujahs joyfully prepare
And made time run with an unequal law.

'Song of triumph or the charmer charmed'

Poetry Box VI/89

A0901 All hail! illustrious parent of the day,
Athens revive, where Cam and Isis flow.

[William Pattison], 'On light an ode'

c.244, p. 481 (attr. [ ] Taylor)

A0902 All hail mighty monarch, tho' banish'd your throne
He's a tyrant that rules by compulsion.

'On the same occasion' [the marriage of the Old
Pretender]

c.570/2, p. 36

A0903 All hail! of ages thou perpetual source,
Then gave a monitory glance and fled.

[ ] Roche, 'An ode on time'

c.244, p. 537

A0904 All hail sweet poet full of more strong fire
All the world's lion though I be thy ape.

J[ohn] D[onne], 'To Mr. T. W.'
[Crum A949]

b.148, p. 55; b.114, p. 213

A0905 All hail the zephyr, whose auspicious breeze,
Tho' unsupported by some splendid name.

John Lockman, 'On the return of his excellency the
Earl of Northumberland, and the Countess, from his
government of Ireland'

c.267/2, p. 395

A0906 All hail to Jesson and Potter of fame
With iambic and spleen marches sullen away.

Poetry Box X/109

A0907 All hail to the chief of the post
What a plague dost thou mean for to do.

'Oates greeted'

c.171, p. 6

A0908 All hail to the day, the glorious day,
To revel in bliss, and fear no decay.

'Sung when hardly sensible in the night, to [?]ly music
invented at the time'

fc.124, p. 132

A0909 All hail, ye curls, that rang'd in reverend row,
Beneath the licent(?) of a humble bob.

[ ] Warton, 'Ode to a grizzle wig'

c.83/2, no. 405

A0910 All hail, ye fields, where constant peace attends!
And sees his errors while there's time to mend.

[William] Walsh, 'The retirement'

c.351, p. 87; c.223, p. 80

A0911 All hail! ye gentle gales that play
Where endless glories shine.

Maria [Done], 'Morning—ode to spring'

c.140, p. 75

A0912 All hands up aloft, swab the couch fore and aft,
In the bowl still a calm is where'er the winds blow. |
With full double cups &c.

'Song 27'

c.555, p. 34

A0913 All health to her, in whose bright form we find
For Venus and the graces were but four.

'Drinking the Countess of Bridgewater's health'

c.360/2, no. 176

A0914 All help in man is vain, where shall I flee?
Who'll cure? None able. Lord I flee to Thee.

S. P., 'Caleb Vernon. Cure? None able'

b.228, p. 1

A0915 All human things are subject to decay,
With doubled portion of his fathers's art.

[John] Dryden, 'MacFlecknoe. A satire' [on Richard
Flecknoe and Thomas Shadwell, 1676-1677, pub.
1678]
[Crum A958; *POAS* I.378]

b.105, p. 314; Poetry Box IV/54 (in John Oldham's hand)

A0916   All in a bower by love designd
Thus sweetly passes life's dream away!

    John Lockman, 'Sylvia'

c.267/4, p. 155

A0917   All in a dale, beneath the moon's bright ray,
Glides a mere fairy, and is seen no more.

    John Lockman, 'Writ under a picture of Mr. Hayman
    (the subject given by the author) of fairies dancing by
    moonlight . . . in Vauxhall Gardens, 1743'

c.267/1, p. 5

A0918   All in a rosebud, infant pity lay:
Blooms a new grace, and Ella's person wears . . . .

    'Verses written in a lady's book of poems'

c.83/2, no. 275 (incomplete)

A0919   All in amaze at what is done I stood
Lord keep me steadfast, for my trust's in thee.

    'The layman's resolution'
    [Crum A963]

b.111, p. 73; fc.58, p. 77; c.570/2, p. 66

A0920   All in the city [of] W[estminster]
But I will save my soul.

    'The chimney sweeper in disgrace or a dialogue
    between the Bp. of Ely, Dr. Moore, and T[om]
    N[egro] . . . to the tune of Chevy Chase'
    [Crum A964a]

b.90, p. 8; Trumbull Box: Poetry Box XIII/38

A0921   All in the Downs the fleet lay moor'd
Adieu she cried adieu she cried and wav'd her lily
                                  hand.

    [John Gay], 'A song' ['Black-eyed Susan']
    [Crum A964b]

c.374; c.358, p. 37 (var.)

A0922   All in the land of Essex
When a Quaker turns Italian.

    [Sir John Denham], 'The Colchester Quaker' [on Fox,
    Naylor, and Martin Woodcock]
    [Crum A967]

Trumbull Box: Poetry Box XIII/39

A0923   All in the town of London
And thrust it further in.

    'A song 1668. B[ishop of?] Rochester [to the tune of
    the loyal tinker]'
    [Crum A968]

b.54, p. 1240; fb.140, p. 88 (incomplete)

A0924   All infants have | This discrepance with Love:
They suck receive, | But he doth only give.

    Sir Thomas Urquhart, 'The differ between Cupid, and
    other children'

fb.217, p. 41

A0925   All is not gold that glittereth to the eye,
The crab ofttimes is beautiful to see.

c.339, p. 317

A0926   All joy to great Caesar;
And not one of us boys.

    [Thomas D'Urfey], 'Song' [on Robert Harley, 1st earl
    of Oxford]

c.189, p. 157

A0927   All kings and all their favorites
To write threescore, this is the second of our reign.

    J[ohn] D[onne, 'The anniversary']
    [Crum A971]

b.148, p. 104

A0928   All languid and pale
And so sin no more.

    'A song to the tune of The Louvre'
    [Crum A974]

c.570/2, p. 60

A0929   All laud and praise to W[alpo]le be
But die in perfect health.

    'To the praise of R[obert] W[alpole]'

c.570/3, p. 130

A0930   All laud and praise with heart and voice
And in the grave to fall.

    [John Hopkins], 'The 11 psalm a thanksgiving for
    deliverance from danger' [verses from Psalms 30–31]
    [Crum A975]

a.3, fol. 79v

A0931   All lovers must approve the fashion
For some can write, and some cannot.

    [Rev. ( ) Nares], 'On the Peruvian quipos'

Diggle Box: Poetry Box XI/68 and 69

A0932   All men are gods pert Sally cries
Be devils that must live in hell.

    'Epigram. Sally and Blunt'

c.81/1, no. 222

A0933   All mortal men on fortune's wheel that climb,
Should bear in mind that they have but a time.

c.339, p. 260, p. 309

A0934   All mortal men that live must surely die
Zeal for the Lord and 'lead into all truth.'

    J. Fry, 'An alphabetical acrostic'

c.517, fol. 24r

A0935 All mortal vanities begone,
And dwell upon his father's throne.

    [Isaac Watts, Hymns and spiritual songs (1707), bk. I, Hymn 25]

    c.180, p. 24

A0936 All must submit to time's despotic power,
When Chaos shall his ancient reign resume.

    [Henry] Needler, 'A translation from Seneca'

    c.244, p. 543

A0937 All my past life is mine no more
'Tis all that heav'n allows.

    [John Wilmot, 2nd earl of Rochester], 'Love and life a song'
    [Crum A992]

    b.105, p. 148; b.334, p. 189; b.113, p. 29

A0938 All my whole, soul and body, all I am
Should pity move, ev'n none will I despise.

    [Edmund Wodehouse], 'Feb. 16 [1715]'

    b.131, p. 168

A0939 All nature bland, serenely gay,
His radiant charms withdrew.

    S[tephen] Simpson, 'The cottagers. A ballad'

    c.563

A0940 All nature's charms in Sunderland appear
Seems undiscover'd to herself alone.

    Charles Montagu, 'On the Countess of Sunderland'

    c.360/2, no. 177

A0941 All nature's works in Frederick does appear
Seems unregarded by herself alone.

    'On Miss Frederick, wrote at Tunbridge Wells—1733'

    c.360/1, p. 37

A0942 All own, my Lord, 'twas right to quit your station
And make such havoc 'mongst the horned cattle. |
                            Coloquintida

    'Lloyd's post Fri. Feb: the 2d, 1770. To the D[uke] of G[rafton] on his sudden retirement'

    Poetry Box x/102

A0943 All parties him esteem, a knowing man
As both his books and practice do aver.

    [Sir Philip Wodehouse], 'Symon Patricius Dr. Patrick'

    b.131, back (no. 156)

A0944 All people of England I pray you give ear,
Mr. Walpole replied he could find none at all. |
                     Which nobody can deny.

    'Song' [on Walpole's trial of Bolingbroke and Strafford for treason, 1715]

    fc.58, p. 40

A0945 'All people that on earth do dwell'
Remember the rebuilding vestry!

    'A brief to be read in the church of St. Margaret Westminster 1789. For repairing our vestry's well beloved vestry'

    fc.40

A0946 All praise to chaste Diana be
Which she to nations must impart.

    b.213, p. 161

A0947 All Rome was still and nations stood at gaze,
Victorious; peace returns and Albion smiles.

    Dr. [ ] Davies, 'Lines composed by . . . of Kingsland in the year 1757 in honor of Caraitacus, spoke on the 10th August 1773 at the Caraitacan meeting, before that society'

    c.481, p. 11

A0948 All Salern School thus writes to England's King;
Expects you may full often here.

    [Philemon Holland, trans., excerpt from Regimen sanitatis salernitanum by John of Milan, c. 1650]

    b.255

A0949 All scribblers poor who write to eat
That ever tries to part you.

    [Philip Dormer Stanhope, 4th earl Chesterfield], 'On Sir Robert Walpole'

    c.570/2, p. 160

A0950 All that have eyes, now wake, and weep;
James the peaceful and the just.

    Geo[rge] Morley, 'On King James his death' [1625]
    [Crum A1016, F498]

    b.200, p. 124 & 128; b.205, fol. 31v (incomplete); see also 'He that hath . . .', 'You that have . . .'.; b.356, p. 231

A0951 All that I can sing of love
Then they foreshow or figure could.

    'Song 42th'

    b.4, fol. 35v

A0952 All that I owe you, is love apostolic;
All that I credit you, is faith Catholic.

    Sir Thomas Urquhart, 'Of a Christian debtor, and creditor'

    fb.217, p. 72

A0953 All that is lovely, noble, good we see
    Myra shall still be lov'd, and still ador'd by me.

    c.549, p. 71

A0954 All that is obscure doth always give offence
    And want of decency is want of sense.

    [Wentworth Dillon, 4th earl of Roscommon, 'Essay
    on translated verse']

    c.549, p. 61 (ll. 113–114)

A0955 All that my heart on knees doth humbly crave
    This was King James his blessed deed.

    fb.9, fol. 40

A0956 All that thou hast is not too dear,
    To make it recompense the sweat.

    Sir John Strangways, '10 Septr 1646'

    b.304, p. 56

A0957 All that will good works wurch[sic]
    Pater Noster and Ave.

    'On John Brokitwell founder or new-builder of
    Leonard's Foster-Lane'

    fb.143, p. 22

A0958 All that's said to you with attention hear
    Aim not to make too much of wit appear.

    c.361

A0959 All th'autumnal scenes are past
    They can raise the drooping heart!

    F[rances] B[urney d'Arblay], 'Winter . . . F. B. aged 13
    years'

    c.486, fol. 23

A0960 All the busy cares of life
    'Twas better to lie drunk than dead.

    'Anacreon ode 25th'

    fb.142, p. 64

A0961 All the expressions man can find,
    That such excellency of love did breathe.

    [Edmund Wodehouse], 'Jan. 13 [1715]'

    b.131, p. 140

A0962 All the flatt'ries of fate,
    Be interr'd with the dirge of a desolate choir.

    'Pleasures of love'

    fb.107, p. 47

A0963 All the four elements in her are found:
    It burns it only, and the place beside it.

    Sir Thomas Urquhart, 'The description of a certain
    very lecherous woman'

    fb.217, p. 302

All the long night with cold and hollow blast
And rather seem to sink in sleep than die. A0964

  'An elegy written on a winter's day'

 c.83/2, no. 608

All the news that's stirring now
As here poor French folks do. | With a hey &c. A0965

  [on the Spanish match, 1623]
  [Crum A1026]

 b.197, p. 222; b.356, p. 292

All the world is a stage thro' every rank and station
Death shall drop the curtain. | Row dow [&c.] A0966

  [John Walker?], 'The farce of life . . . tune bow bow'

 fc.108, fol. 11v

All the world, like I, and you, know,
Were partial to the owl and dove. A0967

  [Frederick Corfield], 'To vindicate my choice . . .
  Saml. Stitch'

 c.381/1

All the world's in strife and hurry
What a whimsical world is this. A0968

 Poetry Box IV/23

All th'homage, that the humblest man can tender A0969
Which none will contradict, that's not a Stoic.

  Sir Thomas Urquhart, 'To the Earl of [crossed out]'

 fb.217, p. 107

All things adverse combine
You're not the fair belov'd. A0970

  R[obert] Shirley, 1st earl of Ferrers, 'To Climene—
  from [Boileau]'

 c.347, p. 27

All things are chang'd in church and state,
In spite of her nose of wax, Sir. A0971

  [Arthur] Mainwaring, 'A ballad' [on Harley and Mrs.
  Masham; answered by 'All things went well . . .'; 1708]
  [Crum A1304 ('court and state'); POAS VII.319]

 fc.24, p. 27

All things are gay, the blooming flow'rs appear A0972
'Tis here he condescends to keep his last.

  [ ] Bowles and [ ] Box, 'A pastoral dialogue on Doctor
  Braithwait's election'

 c.170, p. 25

All things at all times mayn't be spoke A0973
Must make his tongue to's thoughts a stranger.

  [Crum A1037]

 c.489, p. 10

A0974   All things I thought I knew, but now confess,
The more I know, I know I know the less.

     'Practical wisdom'

     c.356

A0975   All things submit themselves to your command
Foregoing sense for a fantastic name.

     John Wilmot, 2nd earl of Rochester, 'The advice'
[Crum A1043b]

     b.334, p. 172

A0976   All things went well in court and state,
But have at her head or so, Sir.

     'The answer' [to 'All things are chang'd . . .', on
Harley and Mrs. Masham]
[Crum A1045]

     fc.24, p. 27

A0977   All things were hush as when the drawers tread
And greasy cookmaid sweats in elbow chair. | No
                coach nor link was here, &c.

     'Thus burlesqued' [a parody of Dryden's description
of Night, missing from this manuscript]

     fb.108, p. 189

A0978   All those external ornaments of health
So long a space, and never discontent us.

     [Sir Thomas Urquhart], 'That we ought not to be
excessively grieved at the lack of anything that is in the
power of [blotted]'

     fb.217, p. 524

A0979   All those that have attain'd to the experience
In finding midses [sic] fitly to extol ye.

     Sir Thomas Urquhart, 'To my Lord [crossed out]'

     fb.217, p. 217

A0980   All vice O youth! resist, hate, and forsake;
To th'eye of heav'n thy secret sins reveal.

     J[ohn] R[obinson], 'Raro antecedentem scelestum
deseruit poena pede claudo'

     c.370, fol. 63v

A0981   All virgins and wives, and young widows rejoice
In reason and conscience should give double fees.

     Lord Blaney et al., 'A song made by the Lord Blaney,
Sir Charles Sidney, Mr. Estrice, and Sir Thomas
Ogle . . . 1665'

     b.207, p. 41

A0982   All wasters, avaricious men reject:
Yet wretches still the prodigal respect.

     Sir Thomas Urquhart, 'Of covetous men, and
spendthrifts'

     fb.217, p. 197

All wheresoever yet you did command
That discipline which heldeth them in awe.
             A0983

     [Sir Thomas Urquhart], 'To the Earl of Anglesey'

     fb.217, p. 390

All wise men should, when they do danger dread,
With all their force, present the same with speed.
             A0984

     c.339, p. 314

All women naturally are called Eves
Women do run until they come to the devil.
             A0985

     'Of women'

     b.197, p. 110; b.200, p. 99 (var.)

All women were by God ordain'd
Names are prophetic and our fates us teach.
             A0986

     [Sir Philip Wodehouse], 'Elizabeth Maidston'

     b.131, back (no. 102)

All ye nuns in Holywell
Pray for the soul of Sir Thomas Lowell.
             A0987

     'On Sir Thomas Lowell' [epitaph 25 May 1524, written
on a window in the old nunnery of Holywell in old
London]
[Crum A1027, 'Lovell']

     fb.143, p. 22

All ye poets of the age,
To his genius victims fall.
             A0988

     [Henry Carey], 'Namby pamby. Or a panegyric on the
new versification addressed to A[mbrose] P[hillips]
esqr. . . . by . . . author of The apology for Parson
Alberoni' [pr. 1725 (Foxon C49)]

     c.503, p. 3 (attr. Captain Gordon)

All ye that have husbands, or ye that have none,
With wives upon earth, or to lead apes in hell.
             A0989

     [Charles Earle], 'An extempore whimsical answer to a
wanton wife, who desired me to read her fortune on
the cards, and give my opinion'

     c.376

All ye who are fir'd with a genius attend;
And riches give wisdom, wit, beauty and grace.
             A0990

     John Lockman, 'The favor of the great—tune, I'll
make thee, (fair,) to follow me'

     c.267/2, p. 153; c.268 (first part), p. 103 ('All you that . . .')

All you loyal subjects both far and near
Great Britain cannot be at peace Sirs.
             A0991

     'A song'

     Poetry Box IV/64

A0992   All you my young companions pray take care
By an unhappy stroke as well as I.

'[High Wycombe, Buckinghamshire:] Epitaph 3rd
upon John Scoch died by the kick of a horse age 22
years 1707'

c.158, p. 84

A0993   All you navigation wellwishers,
And turn unto Tannaway Jock.

'Tannaway Jock, a song. Tune, Colin's complaint'

c.530, p. 223

A0994   All you that are friends to Old England's best cause,
We may lose the whole sheep for a ha'p'orth of
tar. | [Derry down, &c.]

'Song to the tune of The king and the cobbler'

Poetry Box IV/154

A0995   All you that are wise and think life worth enjoying
One moment to toy and enjoy her sweet charms. |
You'd better be singing &c.

'Song 206'

c.555, p. 333

A0996   All you that chance to hither come
The Frenchman's harms within.

'On the Fleur de luce sign to a bawdyhouse' [at
Oxford]
[cf. Crum A1070]

b.62, p. 41; see also 'All you that hither chance . . .'.

A0997   All you that come my grave to see
I in my prime was ta'en away.

'Epitaph in Kimbolton churchyard over John Lettice
aged 21 years' [paraphrased in 'John Lettice's
complaint . . .']

c.113/27; c.158, p. 85

A0998   All you that delight in a jocular song,
For why should I be in a passion.

'Song 24'

c.555, p. 28

A0999   All you that have Protestant ears to hear,
Then broke all the swords, and cried *Vive le roi*!

Jo[seph] Haines, 'A ballad of the royal regiment of the
citizens of London . . . 1691 [*i.e.*, 1689?]'
[Crum A1069; *POAS* V.95]

fb.207/3, p. 43

A1000   All you that hither chance to come
The Frenchman's harms within.

'On the Fleur de luce' [an inn at Oxford]
[Crum A1070]

b.200, p. 409; see also 'All you that chance . . .'.

A1001   All you that lovers be,
Their things are made of felt.

'A description of women'
[Crum A1071]

b.200, p. 428

A1002   All you that pass by now this pillar cast eye
Bring us all, man after man.

'On Sr John Mandeville writ upon a pillar by his tomb
in St Albans'

fb.143, p. 22

A1003   All you that take delight in play,
Tho' knaves of clubs bears all the sway.

c.160, fol. 101

A1004   All you that would no longer
On the bridge or Tower discover. | Come come
away &c.

[Thomas Weaver], 'Song 55. The tune Tom: a Bedlam'
[1642; five members and Kimbolton]
[Crum A1077]

b.4, fol. 45v; b.213, p. 77; fb.106(2)

A1005   All you which do in prison bide
To joys that ever shall remain. | Amen

'S. Symphorosa and her seven sons. July. 18'

a.30[12]

A1006   All you which for the love of Christ
With you may have a place. | Amen

'S. Felicitas and her seven sons. July. 10'

a.30[9]

A1007   All you who by this tomb shall pass,
Where sin and death shall never reign.

'An epitaph on Mr. Joshua Barton'

c.244, p. 289

A1008   All you whose cheeks my London's obsequies
More glorious by our overthrow.

[James Langham], 'London's remains, made English
and dedicated . . . to . . . Mrs Mary Langham'

b.210, p. 255

A1009   Allan thy maxims just, all must allow,
Till genius, wit, and learning are no more.

John M—r, 'On the above lines' ['Reading such
books . . .', by Allan Ramsay]

c.118, p. 73

A1010   Allelujah; praise ye the Lord,
And do them, to their endless praise.

'Psalm 111. Hallelujah'

c.264/3, p. 35

A1011 Allen the tailor's dead! 'Tis now too late
And 'prentices could not stitch up again.

'On a tailor'

c.74

A1012 All's well that ends well as old proverbs say
Continued still since Chaucer led the dance.

M[aurice] J[ohnson], 'Epilogue by . . . at the free
school play'

c.229/2, fol. 27v

A1013 Almighty Father! Myriads boast that name,
(Almighty potentate!) through boundless time.

'The Lord's prayer'

c.515, fol. 13r

A1014 Almighty Father, Son and Holy Ghost,
With him, in endless joys, unutterable.

Arthur Bransby, 'A divine poem in Miltonic verse
written upon [the death] of John Johnson of the
Hon[ora]ble Society of the Inner Temple'

c.229/2, fol. 68v

A1015 Almighty Father, who thy seat
Thine ear to Thine own prayer.

'The Lord's prayer'

c.264/3, p. 117

A1016 Almighty Father! why thus mad'st thou man,
With still devotion pure, and pensive praise.

[ ] Ellison, 'The thoughts of an evening' [1774?]
Greatheed Box/34; fc.74, p. 25

A1017 Almighty God to whom all hearts alone
Great crimes before an open enemy.

Sir John Strangways, 'The ten commandments'
b.304, p. 172

A1018 Almighty God, who art in heav'n,
And shall be to the latest hour. | Amen

'The Lord's prayer'

c.83/3, no. 820

A1019 Almighty Jove in plenteous show'rs
In bounteous streams, as rain does now.

[from 'The amours of Alatheus and Eustathea']

c.379/2, p. 175

A1020 Almighty Lord, most merciful!
In serving thee be humbly spent! | Great God [&c.]

John Lockman, 'The sincere penitent: a hymn writ
by . . . to a favorite solemn movement in the overture
to Dr. Arne's Maximus'

c.267/4, p. 396

A1021 Almighty Lord, thro' all whose ways and works
I will submit myself, and kiss his rod.

Charles Darby, of Kediton in Suffolk, 'Verses made
upon the death of his eldest son'

c.244, p. 77

A1022 Almighty, maker God!
In sweet perfumes of praise.

[Isaac] Watts, 'Sincere praise'

c.244, p. 298

A1023 Almighty maker of our feeble frame,
I fondly leave you there! Dear friends, adieu.

Peter Bell et al., 'Elegaic lines. By Peter, Jane, and
Betsy Bell'

c.91, p. 289

A1024 Aloft in air see gallant Keppel bring
The house of Hugh Palliser to tumble down.

Sarah More, 'The following very irregular ode is most
humbly inscribed to Robert Lovewell Gwatkin(?)
esqr. By a real friend of the British constitution and
sent to him with a complete model of—Admiral
Keppel armed . . . as he went forth to battle'

c.341, p. 119

A1025 Aloft, in wagons, we from far are come,
Most human acts are but a mere puppet farce.

John Lockman, 'Prologue to a puppet-show, exhibited
in a barn, at Plaistow, Essex'

c.267/3, p. 110; c.268 (first part), p. 149

A1026 Alone with books encompass'd round,
'Twere time indeed that I was dead.

[John] Aikin, 'A fireside meditation'

c.355, p. 189

A1027 Along these blushing borders, bright with dew,
And polyanthus of unnumber'd dyes.

'On the spring'

c.361; fc.85, fol. 103v

A1028 Along this road full many a pair
To have the knot untied.

[ ] Balfour, 'At Ferrybridge in Yorkshire'

File 245/21

A1029 Aloud I heard the voice of fame
And trembling own their God.

'A poem on Prince Charles' [the Young Pretender]

c.275; c.570/2, p. 100

A1030 Alpha and Omega God alone,
And thine elect rejectest never.

> 'On God the Father Son and Holy Ghost from 1: John
> 5:7: There be three that bear record in Heaven, and
> these three are one: The Father'
>
> b.137, p. 124

A1031 Already from before the sacred throne
And hov'ring souls their former mansions take.

> [Elizabeth (Singer)] Rowe, 'Revelation chapter 16th'
>
> c.487, p. 68

A1032 Alteria, proud of family, disdains
For mines of gold to quarter with a cit.

> 'Alteria, a character'
>
> Poetry Box IV/157

A1033 Although a poor dog that is bartered for gold
Then think of your dear little Pincher.

> 'Doggerel'
>
> fc.40

A1034 Although a thousand lines
Express'd by the divines.

> Sir Thomas Urquhart, 'That the earth is not the
> center of the heavens. A paradox'
>
> fb.217, p. 180

A1035 Although dear Tom, the day was cold
Who am, and while I live, shall be. | Yours &c.

> [Thomas Hamilton, 6th earl of Haddington], 'To the
> Honble Thomas Leslie'
>
> c.458/2, p. 164

A1036 Altho' soft sleep death's fell resemblance bears
Thus without life to live, thus without death to die.

> c.391, p. 77

A1037 Although the crystal orbs of heav'n still move,
For ev'ry corner may her errors show.

> Sir Thomas Urquhart, 'That more constancy may be
> found in motion, than rest'
>
> fb.217, p. 99

A1038 Although the desert's scorching gale
By mercy cheer'd, salvation led.

> 'A paraphrase of v.17.18.19. of the 3d chaptr. of
> Habakkuk'
>
> Poetry Box IV/160

A1039 Although the sweetness of your voice excel
Is but the qualit' of a beast.

> Sir Thomas Urquhart, 'To one very skillful in music
> but as he could have sung excellently well, did pride
> himself too much into it'
>
> fb.217, p. 341

A1040 Although the world the virtuous men despise
Yet up aloft in spite of them they rise.

> c.339, p. 327

A1041 Although they sit, they are at the communion
The table gesture is) put on their hats.

> Sir Thomas Urquhart, 'The puritans should either be
> covered in taking of the cene: or else admit of
> geniculation'
>
> fb.217, p. 330

A1042 Altho' this age is against crosses set
Whilst we can say the will of Heaven be done.

> [Sir Aston Cokayne], 'To my sister Pegge'
>
> b.275, p. 72

A1043 Altho' thus early from all ills remov'd,
An angel now! when but a mortal here.

> 'Andrew Millar, died at Scarboro[ugh]: 30 July 1750
> Aged: 5 years 6 mths 28 days' [epitaph composed for
> Andrew Millar Sr.]
>
> File 16819

A1044 Although thy hand, and faith, and good works too
Of music, joys, life and eternity.

> [John Donne], 'Elegia tertia'
> [Crum A1119]
>
> b.114, p. 75; b.148, p. 78

A1045 Although we be not grown but perfection,
Yet let us strive to show a good affection.

> b.234, p. 250

A1046 Although you be an ass, you've not the honor
Be Balaam's ass; for he did prattle proudly.

> Sir Thomas Urquhart, 'To a babbling coxcomb'
>
> fb.217, p. 49

A1047 Although you make two morsels of a cherry,
At no more than one bite to snatch a ———.

> Sir Thomas Urquhart, 'To one named Marie, who was
> modest at table, and in bed lascivious'
>
> fb.217, p. 342

A1048 Although your adversary have more light
Study the judges, rather than the law.

> Sir Thomas Urquhart, 'A counsel to a pleader, whose
> adverse party was well versed in the laws'
>
> fb.217, p. 46

A1049 Although your beauty, royal blood, imperial
That once you were enamor'd with our king.

> Sir Thomas Urquhart, 'To the Empress'
>
> fb.217, p. 256

A1050　Although your birth be equal to the best:
There's none more provident in this dominion.

　　Sir Thomas Urquhart, 'To my Lady [crossed out]'

　　fb.217, p. 59

A1051　Although your place in Parliament be great,
For grace, and eloquence you're our Apollyon.

　　Sir Thomas Urquhart, 'To the Earl of [crossed out]
　　High Treasurer of Scotland'

　　fb.217, p. 261

A1052　Always trusty and firm, in or out of place,
Yet, unask'd, lends his help, when the ship is in
　　　　　　　　　　　　　　　　　　danger.

　　'Court characters Ld. Granville. Old John delights in
　　his bottle and King'

　　c.186, p. 124

A1053　Am I the Lord['s] and is he mine
I seek no rest beside.

　　[Thomas Stevens?], 'Thursday exposition. Evening.'

　　c.259, p. 136

A1054　Am not I head? Are not in me combined
I'll not capitulate of old what's said.

　　'Sir John salting(?) 1620 Harry's plot: Billingsley
　　caput' [answered by 'Head from his crown . . .']

　　b.356, p. 115

A1055　Amanda beams on him that look divine
I would not change my lot o'er all the world to reign.

　　[William Sotheby], 'Oberon' [from the German of
　　Wieland]

　　c.340

A1056　Amanda say shall gentle love,
Each fleeting hour enjoy'd.

　　'Ode'

　　c.89, p. 14

A1057　Amaryllis told her swain,
For I do love thee dearly.

　　[Thomas Porter], 'Love's directory' [song in 'The
　　villain,' 1663, Act. III]
　　[Crum A1132]

　　fb.107, p. 2

A1058　Amazement seiz'd on all and shame to see,
Of Israel, his own flock, less careful be?

　　'Saul's answer'

　　b.118, p. 23

A1059　Amazing beauteous change!
Of ardent praise.

　　P[hilip] Doddridge, 'The happy effects of the gospel
　　from Is. XII. 18, 19'

　　c.493, p. 10

A1060　Amazing change, in that capacious mind,
'Tis we must cheer the honors of his way.

　　John Lockman, 'A thought: on reading a playbill, for
　　Merope, to be performed at Drury Lane Theater, on
　　Saturday, 3d Feb. 1759, for the benefit of his ingenious
　　friend, Mr. Christopher Smart'

　　c.267/1, p. 267

A1061　Amazing man, of such stupendous size
May mark how nature has o'ershot her mark.

　　'On seeing the tall man [Daniel Cajanus, d.
　　25 February 1748/9], who was shown at Charing Cross,
　　London, and was shortly going to Oxford'

　　c.360/2, no. 66

A1062　Ambition flee which often worketh shame,
But virtue love, which may extol your name.

　　c.339, p. 315

A1063　Ambition is a steed [weed?] that's always found
But he, who plucks the fruit, and tastes it, dies.

　　[Elijah Fenton; pr. 1712 (Foxon F108)]

　　fc.14/10

A1064　Ambition never me seduc'd,
And all the wild creation dies.

　　[John Lockman], 'The wish. Set by Mr. de Fosch, and
　　Mr. J. C. Smith'

　　c.268 (first part), p. 68

A1065　Ambition 'tis true too often inspires
You had surely no right to demand a translation.

　　[Phanuel Bacon], '. . . Alluding to a jack in the
　　author's ponds destroyed by tadpoles'

　　c.237, fol. 89 [i.e., 109]

A1066　Amelia, beauteous princess, deign to view
The task to abler poets I resign.

　　[Mary] Chandler, 'A description of Bath inscribed to
　　the Princess Amelia' [pr. 1733 (Foxon C108)]

　　c.351, p. 120

A1067　Amen is gone, but not a tear or sigh
No more shall vex or libel us—amen.

　　Charles Atherton Allnutt, 'Epitaph on a scribbling,
　　satirical clerk—by a parishioner in the joy of his heart'

　　c.112, p. 164

A1068   Amend your lives ye that hand Midas mint,
And be possest with heart as hard as flint.

    c.339, p. 320

A1069   Amid all the blessings we share,
Through ev'ry age be renown'd!

    John Lockman, 'Anniversary song: in honor of the
Earl of Northumberland's birthday (19 Decr) writ (by
desire) for the feast of the governors of the Middlesex
Hospital . . . set to music by Mr. Riesh'

    c.267/2, p. 176

A1070   Amid the dreary prison's awful gloom,
And hurl'd destruction flaming on mankind.

    'Reflections on the perilous and melancholy situation
of the Dauphin and on his probable enlargement by a
counter-revolution'

    c.83/3, no. 818

A1071   Amid the mounts of holiness
In thee my springs of physic be.

    'Psal: 87:'

    b.217, p. 38

A1072   Amid the terrors of this awful night,
As now; and wake to everlasting joy!

    'Written during a storm 1790'

    fc.124, p. 55

A1073   Amidst her flowers Eliza strays,
Eliza's fond regret or love.

    'To a lady remarkably fond of gardening'

    c.83/3, no. 890

A1074   Amidst the den the lions prey,
If tigers bend, and savages obey.

    [Christopher] Pitt, 'On King Geo. 2d playing with a
tiger in Kensington Gardens'

    c.244, p. 515

A1075   Amidst the discord of a factious land
The preaching and the grace alike are free.

    [J. B.], 'Anticipation' [1779]

    c.140, p. 108

A1076   Amidst the lightning's blaze, and thunder's roar,
The beast may tremble, but the brute will play!

    [Charles] Earle, 'The lines underneath were made
by . . . on having a favorite horse killed in a violent
storm of thunder and lightning amidst which some
miscreants persisted playing at cards'

    c.376

Amidst these frequent deaths and common plaints,   A1077
Though Calvin's priest: ah! this his only crime.

    S. B., 'On the . . . death of . . . William Taylor' [d.
7 September 1641]

    b.88, p. 6

Amidst those tombs, where even envy sleeps,   A1078
And spread, uncheck'd, his triumphs o'er the land.

    'Reflections on the above' ['Struck with religious
awe . . .']

    c.94

Aminda when those eyes did first impart   A1079
Withdraw but yourself, I shall perish alone.

    'The languishing shepherd'

    fb.107, p. 56

Ammonius did his own right ear put off   A1080
Of bishops in their persons and their place.

    [Sir Thomas Urquhart], 'Of Ammonius a learned
monk who being chosen to be a bishop maimed
himself of an ear thereby to make himself incapable of
the charge and of Doctor Bastwick who was so
mutilated by a decree of the Star Chamber for
publishing defamatory libels . . . bishops . . .'

    fb.217, p. 506

Among the arts which fondly soothe the breast,   A1081
This each one proves who hears the rapturous
                                strains.

    John Lockman, 'Writ under a mezzotinto, by Van
Haacken, of a lady at her harpsichord . . . May, 1738'

    c.267/1, p. 292

Among the ashes where the eye   A1082
So near the ashes if we lie.

'Braye Lute Book,' Music Ms. 13, fol. 20

Among the crowds, on this revolving day,   A1083
Where all is peace, and joy, and harmony, and love.

    'To Beliza on her birthday'

    c.547, p. 194

Among the High Church[men] I find there are   A1084
                                        several
It may be Hoadley the high and Sacheverell the low.

    [Matthew Prior?]
    [Crum A1150; POAS VII.359]

    b.90, p. 12; b.155, p. 64; b.204, p. 154; fc.24, p. 19

Among the little pages who were sent   A1085
Or mother church espouse her bully's cause.

    'Satire on Dr. [Peter] B[ir]ch' [1703]
    [Crum A1151; POAS VI.543]

    c.111, p. 76; Poetry Box IV/47

A1086 Among the many friends that I do name
I can present you but a grateful heart.

> [Sir Aston Cokayne], 'To Mr. Rob: Creitton, Dr. of Divinity'
>
> b.275, p. 97

A1087 Among the race of England's modern peers
With such a subject and a brother blest.

> 'A satire on the coffeehouse club' [answered by 'Among the writing race . . .']
>
> b.327, f. 19v

A1088 Among the spirits of the blest,
True happiness her dower!

> [William Hayley], 'Oct. 2'
>
> File 6925

A1089 Among the various arts that soothe the town,
Each day a new device attends her will.

> 'An extempore acrostic by a lady on Mrs. Alice Brace the celebrated maker of flowers in shellwork 1752'
>
> c.360/3, no. 198

A1090 Among the virtues which adorn the mind,
And industry's fair fruits in season yield.

> John Lockman, 'Prologue for The miser: acted at Covent Garden, Tuesday 19 Decr 1758, for the benefit of the asylum'
>
> c.267/3, p. 134

A1091 Among the vulgar many an ass—
Our friend here has a nose of copper.

> 'Vulgar errors exploded by Arabin's nose'
>
> fc.76.iii/214

A1092 Among the writing race of modern wit
By gentle poet, and by small commander.

> 'Ironical' [parody of 'Among the race of England's modern peers . . .']
>
> b.327, f. 21; see also 'Amongst . . .'.

A1093 Amongst these virgins fair and bright,
That so in heaven we may have place. | Amen

> 'Of S. Cicily. November. 22'
>
> a.30[55]

A1094 Among those drops of light, that so
And captivate the swains.

> 'Upon being asked which was the greatest beauty at Bristol'
>
> c.188, p. 39

A1095 Amongst all the hard names that denote reproach
A Scotchman's greatest plague, God send him
                        home.

> 'On Dr. G[ilbert] Burnet'
> [Crum A1159]
>
> b.111, p. 149

A1096 Amongst British worthies in London's pantheon
Which would they worship, the man or the horse.

> 'On the proposition for a statue designed for King W[illiam]'
>
> c.570/3, p. 114

A1097 Amongst my roses redolent,
And after pain a joyful place. | Amen

> 'Of S. Laurence. Aug. 10'
>
> a.30[24]

A1098 Amongst our sex sweet purslane pure you are
'Tis Frances Cavendish, and no other she.

> Lady Jane Cavendish, 'On my sweet sister Frances'
> [Crum A1164]
>
> b.233, p. 13

A1099 Amongst the causes of our evils, this
[?] than error which is done in woman.

> [Sir Thomas Urquhart], 'That nothing more opposeth the [?]ality of life which is proper and p[?] to wise men than to be tied to a generality of public example in all our acts'
>
> fb.217, p. 522

A1100 Amongst the darling attributes of heaven:
Bless their kind Lordships—and adore the King.

> John Lockman, 'To the honorable House of Commons, on occasion of the insolvent debtors' bill . . . Feb. 1747/8'
>
> c.267/1, p. 57

A1101 Amongst the dissembled puritans, the man,
No color give, which dips not on the Brownist.

> Sir Thomas Urquhart, 'Why puritans affect not much neither white nor black, in their church habits'
>
> fb.217, p. 90

A1102 Amongst the High Churchmen I find there are
                        several
It may be Hoadly the High and Sacheverell the
                        Low.

> [Matthew Prior?], 'On the humors of the age'
> [Crum A1150; POAS VII.359]
>
> c.171, p. 14; see also 'Among . . .'.

A1103   Amongst the ladies of our nation, few
Chaste, noble, pious, loving, good and fair.

> Sir Thomas Urquhart, 'To my Lady [crossed out] of [crossed out]'

fb.217, p. 320

A1104   Amongst the myrtles as I walk'd
Like these short sweets are knit together.

> [Robert Herrick], 'The inquiry'
> [Crum A1166]

b.52/2, p. 122; b.213, p. 16

A1105   Amongst the natives of the Scythian coast,
To ev'ry dame her own distinguish'd crack.

> 'Are sounds in sounding bodies found? No. Or is't the air that gives the sound? Yes'

c.382, p. 69

A1106   Amongst the pleasant tree himself did Adam hide
For none but God can thee forgive, who all thy
                              ways doth see.

b.234, p. 329

A1107   Amongst the race of England's modern peers
With such a subject and a brother blest.

> 'Satire' [answered by 'Amongst the writing race of modern wits . . .']

b.371, no. 9

A1108   Amongst the radiant stars to stand
Of heaven a place to bear.

> '['Digna ratis quae siet . . .'] Englished'

c.360/2, no. 270

A1109   Amongst the votaries Astrea had
My justice soon shall know.

> [Mrs. Christian Kerr], 'To Astrea the goddess of justice'

c.102, p. 92

A1110   Amongst the writing race of modern wits
By gentle poet and by small commander.

> 'An answer to a satire' ['Amongst the race of England's modern peers . . .']
> [Crum A1171]

b.371, no. 8/2; see also 'Among . . .'.

A1111   Amongst ye pure ones all,
And scoff us in every corner.

> 'The Quakers' song, sung by Mrs. Willis at the new playhouse'

c.416 (incomplete?)

A1112   Amoralizing on these Sieur Sorres writes
Whose judgment prizeth wisdom above wit.

c.189, p. 87

A1113   Amphiaraus and Eriphile
Bring many gallant men, into their ills.

> [Sir Philip Wodehouse], 'Amphiaraus and Eriphile'

b.131, p. 8

A1114   Amyntas wasted with despair
That had too much before.

> 'A song'

b.207, p. 29

A1115   An active young man, who's to labor inclin'd,
And qualities more, which I do not there mention.

> 'Wants a place . . . from a country newspaper, Mar: 1792'

c.94

A1116   An adored Lord—writ in his name
Rays of the cherub, and the seraphim.

> [Sir Philip Wodehouse], 'Upon the Lord Bishop of Norwich Edward Reynolds is an adored Lord'

b.131, back (no. 9)

A1117   An age in her embraces past
And make us blest at last.

> John Wilmot, 2nd earl of Rochester, '12. Song'

b.334, p. 192 (incomplete)

A1118   An aged couple have combin'd
The wedding seems more like a winding-sheet.

> Captain Alexander Radcliffe, 'An epithalamium on a doting pair'

c.229/1, fol. 57v

A1119   An amorous wreath of flowers by Britain's far sons,
O grant me heaven! to be no longer Merry.

> [Robert Merry], 'Sonnet [on Bertie Greatheed, William Parsons, and Hester Thrale Piozzi] . . . Aug. 1785'

Greatheed Box/44

A1120   An ancient fable tells us, how
To die is better than to live.

> Abraham Oakes, 'The universal blessing'

c.50, p. 94

A1121   An angel clear did once appear
That we with ye in heaven may reign. | Amen

> 'S. John Baptist. June. 22'

a.30[5]

A1122   An angel is contained in Glean
Let that the same denominate.

> [Sir Philip Wodehouse], 'Upon my Lady Glean'

b.131, back (no. 98)

A1123 An antiquated, batter'd, beau
I'll try my [k]nack, at poetry.

Poetry Box x/63

A1124 An ape, a lion, a fox and an ass
Then birds of ill omen and no more women.

'A song'
[Crum A1182]

c.374

A1125 An ass cloth'd in a lion's skin,
Include their chiefest wit.

R[obert] Shirley, 1st earl of Ferrers, 'The ass in the
lion's skin. From [La Fontaine]'

c.347, p. 59

A1126 An ass once left his master's home:
Pray bang him well—the pig is mine.

'The countryman and his ass—a tale'

c.487, p. 63

A1127 An ass with Popish relics stor'd,
Of gown and golden chain.

R[obert] Shirley, 1st earl of Ferrers, 'The ass laden
with relics. From [La Fontaine]'

c.347, p. 58

A1128 An easy death may justly be
But meet it with less fear, than joy.

[Edmund Wodehouse], 'Septr. 16 [1715]'

b.131, p. 265

A1129 An easy heart adorns the vale,
Right happy such a peasant.

[Anna Seward], 'The country maid a pastoral'
Poetry Box IV/1 (attr. S. Smith)

A1130 An eclipse causes people to admire
Try it or else perhaps you'll think I lie.

[Edmund Spenser, poems from 'The shepherd's
kalendar']

c.158, p. 186

A1131 An education forms the youthful mind,
As the twig is bent, the tree's inclin'd.

c.93

A1132 An elderly lady, whose bulky, squat figure
As she came with a hoop, she is gone with a hollow.

c.549, p. 27

A1133 An empire, her I gave—a meek one 'tis
All her commands come candied in a kiss.

[Sir Philip Wodehouse], 'Lady Mary Kempe a meek
empire'

b.131, back (no. 51)

A1134 An English lad long wooed a lass of Wales
Have digged already I can dig no more.

[Sir John Harington], 'Nil refert loqui dum uti liceat'
[Crum A1196]

b.148, p. 3; b.197, p. 111

A1135 An English prologue to a Latin play
Will please you better when you come again.

'Prologue to the Adelphi. 1715'

c.233, p. 69

A1136 An English sparrow pert and free
A visit from the bird of Jove.

[William] Hayley, 'Mr Hayley to Mr Gibson'
Poetry Box x/19

A1137 An envoy of the Spanish nation
That both the parties kiss and friends.

[Phanuel Bacon]

c.237, fol. 73

A1138 An epigram by a schoolboy writ
But your acrostic's worse.

c.546, p. 31

A1139 An epigram, is like a handsome woman,
Even those, who formerly did love her best.

Sir Thomas Urquhart, 'The best epigram, that is,
being made ordinary, in end breeds loathsomeness'

fb.217, p. 157

A1140 An epitaph at least we may bestow
The beauteous glories of the British isle.

'An epitaph upon Miss Blandy'

c.53, fol. 3

A1141 An Ermine see, in nature as in name
May this to th' King of kings be dear.

[Sir Philip Wodehouse], 'An epigram upon Ann
Armin before she married my son'

b.131, back (no. 27/1)

A1142 An Eton boy, who did not want for wit,
He found the rogue had not forgot the dart.

Dr. [ ] Crane, 'The pointed epigram'

c.175, p. 88

A1143 An evil thing it's to be ruled by many:
One lord, one king, if there be any.

'Not many rulers . . . English thus'

c.189, p. 31

A1144 An herb there is takes of the swallow's name
It helps young swallows' eyes when they are out.

[Joshua Sylvester, trans. Guillaume de Salluste,
seigneur Du Bartas], 'Celandine'

b.284, p. 54

A1145 An honest clothier—so says fame
St. Hurden's nun's reply—the sylph was P[ey]t[o]n.

'To Mrs. Peyton on picking my pocket of a borrowed
pamphlet entitled A guide to hell'

c.484, p. 122

A1146 An honest man
To his relations dear.

'In Cuckfield churchyard'

c.546

A1147 An honest man, and of a noble house
If poor, is no more valu'd than a louse.

c.361

A1148 An honest man, but wretched poor,
True, they are useless, I want bread.

[Thomas Hamilton, 6th earl of Haddington], 'A tale'

c.458/2, p. 116

A1149 An honest soul, dear Janus, sincere,
To hear her speak and sweetly smile.

'Horace book 1. ode 22 . . . paraphrased'

c.578, p. 129

A1150 An honest yeoman in his town one day
I cannot devise with any wit who it is.

'In cornutum'

b.205, fol. 44v

A1151 An honorable sale of Dunkirk was made
Offering a double sacrifice to my Lord Denham's
ghost.

[Crum A1208 (var.)]
Poetry Box VIII/12

A1152 An house he hath 'tis made of such good fashion,
To such a house who would not tenant be?

'An epitaph in Falkston church'

c.115

A1153 An humble muse, which but for thee had slept
Be with thy happy soul transplanted there.

Maria [Done], 'On benevolence inscribed to
Mr. Roscoe'

c.140, p. 62

A1154 An humdrum doctor of the gown
Crown'd with a diadem of horn.

[Robert Cholmeley], 'Larsander or the cuckold's tale'

c.190, p. 107

A1155 An husband's loss goes always fraught with sighs
And the petitioner shall ever pray.

R[obert] Shirley, 1st earl of Ferrers, 'The young
widow. From La Fontaine'

c.347, p. 60

A1156 An ill year, of a Goodyear us bereft
Wise, comely, learned, eloquent, and kind.

'On Sir Henry Goodyear of Polesworth'
[Crum A1215]

fb.143, p. 18

A1157 An infant form for earth too pure, too bright
To find the dream full realized in heaven.

'Epitaph on a child'
Poetry Box XII/34

A1158 An infant's fate may make a parent sad:
Reader! repent, since thou hast liv'd so long.

William Smith, 'Epitaph on an infant son of Capt.
Wm. Ridsdale, on Sleiar, in Cornwallshire, who died
1740'

c.139, p. 6

A1159 An innkeeper in Cambridge dwelling was
You'll cease to mock you are such another.

'In cornutum jocosum'

b.205, fol. 48v

A1160 An oak with spreading branches crown'd
This graces me alive and dead.

[Mary Barber], 'The oak and its branches. A fable'

fc.60, p. 51

A1161 An odd northern tyke, for no good it is like
'Gainst such no better betide.

[Samuel Ward], 'A libel against Mr. Garthwaite in
answer to the former libel ['The sturdy ram . . .'] 1621'

b.197, p. 178

A1162 An ode, in true form,
No critic will spurn it.

[Charles Burney, the elder], 'New-Year's ode for 1777.
To the Revd. Thomas Twining . . . Prologue'

c.33, p. 109

A1163 An old bridegroom did with his servants chide,
Some longer in the task you owe a lady.

Sir Thomas Urquhart, 'Of an aged man, and his bride'

fb.217, p. 135

A1164 An old dull sot, who 'ad told the clock
He look'd for, bid him put on's hat.

    'Description of a certain justice of the peace'

    c.578, p. 69

A1165 An old man, and his graceless young,
Then happy boys are we.

    'The falling-out' [pr. 1717/18, on George I and
    George II (Foxon F44)]

    fc.58, p. 156

A1166 An old musician, the first night he married,
For she by nature play'd and he by B-mol.

    Sir Thomas Urquhart, 'Of an aged man, who was
    skillful in music, and had espoused a young wanton
    lass'

    fb.217, p. 230

A1167 An old song made by an aged old pate,
And old liquor enough to make a cat speak, and a
             man dumb. | Like an old courtier, &c.

    c.391

A1168 An old trite proverb let me quote,
Nor girls can scratch nor fools can write.

    [David] Garrick, 'Prologue to The musical lady,
    written by . . . and spoken by Mr. King'

    c.68, p. 1; c.115

A1169 An one-eyed boy born of a half-blind mother
Goddess of beauty, thou the god of love.

    'Anglice' [of the Latin 'Lumine castus Acon . . .']
    [Crum A324, 'A one-eyed boy']

    b.62, p. 137; see also 'Thou one-ey'd . . .'.

A1170 An orator dismal of Nottinghamshire,
And mistakes to prevent have obtained a copy.

    [Jonathan Swift], 'The intended speech of a famous
    orator [Lord Nottingham] ag[ain]st the Peace. 1711'
    [POAS VII.526]

    b.204, p. 33; File 19405

A1171 An ox, long fed with musty hay,
And Sheridan's recanted.

    [Samuel Taylor Coleridge], 'Recantation a political
    allegory' [1798?]

    Greatheed Box/23

A1172 An ox who call'd himself the master
And sought the mead he erst had us'd.

    Charles Atherton Allnutt, 'The ox and the horse a
    fable addressed to a Baptist friend'

    c.112, p. 175

A1173 Ancient person for whom I
Ancient person of my heart.

    John Wilmot, 2nd earl of Rochester, '14. Song. A
    young lady to her ancient lover'

    b.334, p. 195

A1174 And after singing psalm the 12th
I am a rascal, that thou know'st.

    [John Wilmot, 2nd earl of] Rochester, 'Rochester ex
    tempore 1670'

    b.54, p. 1200

A1175 And all expired days and years and famed pleasures
                        past
Since happiness is ever seen best by the happy end.

    'The present fears or troubles' [from 'Cecil's
    commonwealth']

    fb.40, p. 185

A1176 And am I born to die?
To all eternity.

    'Hymn 94th'

    c.562, p. 126

A1177 And are these all the rites that must be done
Till he return i' th' resurrection.

    Robert Wild, 'An elegy upon the Earl of Essex, his
    funeral' [buried 19 October 1646]
    [Crum A1236]

    c.166, p. 236

A1178 And are ye sure the news is true?
In troth I'm like to greet.

    Poetry Box XII/78

A1179 And are you gone, O, heavens our tears abate,
Of a dear spouse, and best of human race.

    'On the departure of B—g—g from Leeds officers in
    the 39th regiment of infantry'

    c.175, p. 38

A1180 And art return'd again with all thy faults
Thy treachery, neglect, and cowardice.

    [John Heappe?], 'On the return of Buckingham from
    France' [November 1627]
    [Crum A1240]

    b.200, p. 50

A1181 And believe me, dear Bess
As full as a tart. . . .

    [Charles Burney, the elder], 'Playful epistle, to Miss
    Eliz. Allen at a boarding school in Paris, 1776. Aetat
    suae 14'

    c.33, p. 96 (incomplete; crossed out)

A1182 And can you ask detested hag,
The fribbling nerve still falls.

> [William Popple, trans.], '[Horace, ep]ode 8th. To a
> libidinous old woman'
>
> fc.104/2, p. 426

A1183 And can you sing poor birds? do you not see
Tune your loud whistles to an elegy.

> 'Hearing the birds sing after the death of Juno. At
> Hornby Castle'
>
> Poetry Box VII/46

A1184 And Cato fell,
Death being overcome, invincible.

> 'In Catonem . . . Manil:'
>
> c.81/1, no. 239

A1185 And certain shepherds in a field
Divine benignity.

> 'Song of the angels at the nativity'
>
> c.264/3, p. 126

A1186 And conquer'd all where'er his eagle flew
But Cato's mind, that nothing would subdue.

> 'In Catonem . . . Horat:'
>
> c.81/1, no. 241

A1187 And dar'st thou, after what has past,
Thou'lt soon(?) from Britain fly.

> John Lockman, 'To [Dr. Coretti] a certain Italian . . .
> impostor, who tricked many . . .'
>
> c.267/2, p. 358

A1188 And do we then believe
May now and ever be.

> [John Austin], 'Hym. 22' [Hymn xvi, Devotions in the
> ancient way of offices, 1672, p. 141]
>
> c.178, p. 20

A1189 And doth her soul fly thro' the winged air?
The least iota of her praise, farewell.

> Is. F., 'An epicidium upon the death of that grand
> exemplar of true honor, and virtue, Madam Elizabeth
> Boothy'
>
> Poetry Box IV/130

A1190 . . . And draw the battle terribler to show
Denham says this, but Waller always so.

> [ll. 111–336 of 'Second advice to a painter']
>
> Poetry Box VII/54 (incomplete)

A1191 And durst thou, then insulting youth, demand
And makes ev'n nature's dreary prospects shine.

> 'Eliza in answer to ———'
>
> c.391, p. 14

A1192 And dwells there in a female breast
A lively fancy guess!

> [William] Cowper, 'Addressed to a lady, approving
> Mrs Greville's Ode [to indifference?]'
>
> Trumbull Box: Poetry Box XIII/71

A1193 And fair Macaulay claims a Livy's right,
Who shall object to a Catherine's government.

> H[annah] M[ore], 'Six lines by . . . and published in
> her epilogue to The search after happiness it not being
> thought proper as appearing too satirical'
>
> c.341, p. 60

A1194 And first, man's ingress into the world is naked and
bare,
If I preach a whole year.

> 'A laconic sermon . . . I shall divide the discourse into,
> and consider the three following heads . . .'
>
> c.361

A1195 And has thou fix'd my doom, sweet master say?
And gently stretch me at my master's door.

> 'The address of the superannuated horse to his master'
>
> c.83/3, no. 986

A1196 And has thy gentle spirit wing'd its flight?
When thus, dear friend, our tears shall stream for
thee!

> 'On the death of B. H.'
>
> File 13409

A1197 And hast thou left old Jemmy in the lurch,
And may all Christian people say Amen to't.

> [Thomas Brown], 'A satire upon the French King
> written by a nonjuring parson and dropped out of his
> pocket at Sam's Coffee House' [after the peace was
> concluded at Ryswick, 1697]
> [Crum A1265; POAS VI.6]
>
> fb.142, p. 34

A1198 And hast thou left us then dear soul must we
In death undarkened with the night of sin.

> 'On my Lord Stanhope's son dying in Oxford'
> [Crum A1266]
>
> b.356, p. 136

A1199 And hast thou, then, in the gay spring of life,
With modest independency to dwell.

> [William Parsons], 'Verses to a friend; ere his
> resigning a place under the government, and with it all
> hopes of future promotion, to enjoy the sweets of
> private life, and independency . . . 1779'
> [Crum A1267]
>
> fc.132/1, p. 180

A1200 And have you Sir at length resolv'd to take
Your friends you've made your foes, your foes no
friends.

[Thomas Brown], 'To the late pillar of the Protestant
church'

b.111, p. 199

A1201 And is he come? and doth true honor bring
We sent a sun to cleanse their hemisphere.

'Upon the King's return out of Scotland'

b.150, p. 138

A1202 And is Miss Tabby from the world retir'd
For ev'ry muse should celebrate a life!

'On the death of a favorite cat'

c.504, p. 53

A1203 And is poor Titibone forever fled
And they with pride, shall wear thy silken chain.

Thomas Leigh, 'On a young lady [Ann Hoskins],
whose squirrel was killed by a cat'

c.53, fol. 17

A1204 And is she gone ah who like her can sing
I hope I have not written quite in vain.

'On the death of Mrs. Mary Pluret'

c.354

A1205 And is the spirit of the poet fled?
And only perish when the world's consum'd.

'An elegy on the death of Wm: Cowper esqr'

c.83/3, no. 1073

A1206 And is there a last day? and must there come
'Creation aught, but God, and my own soul.'

[Edward] Young, 'Mr Young's last day'

fc.54, p. 80

A1207 And is this she? That celebrated fair!
And then dispatch'd her as she lay conceal'd.

'On Mrs Bertie who died of the smallpox'

c.233, p. 61

A1208 And Isaac led Rebecca to her tent,
Isaac begot Esau and Jacob.

[( ) Thomson? From Zacharie Boyd]

Spence Papers, folder 148

A1209 And is't the fate still of the college walls
Tom thou mayst do, what hath been done before.

'On the same' [Dr. Bambridge's marrying Mall Wolfe,
a butcher's daughter]

b.356, p. 148

A1210 And Jacob said; my sons come hither all;
Divides his spoils in the decline of day.

[William Sandys?], 'A paraphrase upon the 49th chap:
of Genesis unto the 28 verse: being Jacob's blessing
upon his sons before his death in Egypt'

b.230, p. 7

A1211 And liest thou there, my darling child?
Since thy sweet face we ceas'd to view.

[Mary (Shackleton) Leadbeater], 'Lines written after
mournfully contemplating the remains of a deceased
child . . .'

c.142, p. 125

A1212 And lives there one by canker'd malice led
And scorns to tear the unresisting prey.

[Judith (Cowper)] Maden, 'The answer to a scurrilous
pamphlet entitled Sarah [Stout] the Quaker to
Lotharian defense of the hon[ora]ble Mr. Justice
Spencer Cowper which was published after his death'

c.229/1, fol. 29; fc.51, p. 157

A1213 And Mary then the lamp of fair Lorraine
Who [?] to us that is our true aim.

'[Rulers of Scotland] 14'

fa.4, fol. 29

A1214 And must I go and must I be no more
I'd even lose myself since I've lost Thee.

[John Norris, of Bemerton], 'The complaint of Adam
turned out of Paradise'
[Crum A1291]

c.548

A1215 And must I write in verse?—The muse obeys
Tho' kind, not soft; tho' smart, yet not severe.

[Thomas Morell], 'To the same' [Anne Barker, later
his wife]

c.395, p. 61

A1216 And must my little store of friendship priz'd
A tear—a verse, 'tis all I can, I give.

Thomas Robinson, 'On the death of Dr. Hodgson'

fc.61, p. 114

A1217 And must we, dear Belinda, bid adieu
And from their breasts, shut ev'n a glimpse of joy.

[John Lockman], 'The farewell to the spring gardens.
Supposed to be writ by a gentleman who is obliged to
leave England, and settle in a foreign country' [1739]
[Crum A1297]

c.268 (first part), p. 38; c.267/1, p. 284 ('dear Britannia')

A1218   And must you leave me now my friends?
Without reluctance or control.

'Upon the return of the books of Sir John Kaye,
knight and baronet lent me in great kindness for some
years. An elegy'

Poetry Box VI/117

A1219   And nice Mr. Duelly
But would hear and believe all she said.

'Verses on Mr. Duelly' [docket title]

File 19031

A1220   And now (my Hubart) if th[torn]
Let's kiss and friends, [torn]

[Sir Philip Wodehouse]

File 17713

A1221   And now my soul, canst you forget
May now and ever still be done.

[John Austin], 'Hym. 12' [Hymn xxiii, Devotions in
the ancient way of offices, 1672, p. 203]

c.178, p. 11

A1222   And now my soul enjoy thy rest
And endless day within a deity

Thomas Traherne, '[Meditation (third century)] 57'

b.308, p. 145

A1223   And now my soul, the day is gone,
May now and ever be.

[John Austin], 'Hym: 17' [Hymn viii, Devotions in the
ancient way of offices, 1672, p. 76]

c.178, p. 16

A1224   And now the scales have left mine eyes,
With ev'ry darling sin.

[Isaac Watts, Hymns and spiritual songs (1707), bk II,
Hymn 81]

c.180, p. 9

A1225   And now the time returns
Eternal glory be.

[John Austin], 'Hym. 36' [Hymn xxxii, Devotions in
the ancient way of offices, 1672, p. 287]

c.178, p. 35

A1226   And now they had attir'd their king,
They never can outshine.

'Translation of a Latin poem on the queen of the
fairies'

c.159, p. 213

A1227   And now 'tis fair, how shall we spend the day
Nor serene skies please with a better light.

[George Daniel]

b.121, fol. 25v

A1228   And on the cliff a hanging wood
In death's embrace do rest.

[John Black]

fc.107, p. 18

A1229   And prithee why your F—ue [?]
To say, where most, the palm is due.

[ ] Birch, 'Thalia's relation'

c.504, p. 11

A1230   And sayst thou so? Then give the devil's due
Faith 'tis all one he'll fetch you in the end.

'Michael Jones anagram I am hell's coin'

fb.228/26

A1231   And see the bright occasion dawns at last,
And one in case of need to sweep the whole away.

[George] Canning, 'Lines written by . . . on the
progress of a bill in the House of Commons'

Poetry Box v/126

A1232   And shall I pass this bright auspicious morn,
By age respected and by youth rever'd.

'To the Revd. Wm. Cornwallis on his birthday—old
style the 18th of March 1792 aged forty'

fc.124, p. 75

A1233   And shall proud mortals then mount up so high
Under his government then let us press.

[Mary Serjant]

fb.98, fol. 161

A1234   And shall then another embrace thee my fair?
And save me, O! save me! ere madness ensue.

Charles James Fox, 'The frantic lover'

Poetry Box v/36

A1235   And shall then Master Robert
Deserves a better blade.

Sir Thomas Urquhart, 'To a young gentlewoman
contracted with an old man, named Mr. Robert'

fb.217, p. 347

A1236   And since this number [1628] and thy name agree
This year shall fatal prove to th' state or thee.

'Chronogramam in eandem Villars Georgius Dux
Buckingamiae. In which year he was killed by
Lieutenant Felton . . . .'

b.200, p. 53

A1237   And so my dear Julia you're greatly admir'd
It is very seldom they take it amiss.

['Written at 15']

File 295

A1238 And thou blest Hanway! Long thy country's prayer,
Which taught the young to live, the old to die.

'Stanzas sacred to the memory of Jonas Hanway esqr.'
File 17440

A1239 And thou my Brute! cries Caesar, when by fate
Let's rise as friends, and be honest too.

Sir Ph[ilip] W[odehouse], 'Some old epistolary passes
between my friend Mr. Hobart and myself about the
year 1660 and 1662'
b.131, p. 34; File 17713 (var.)

A1240 And thus the fencer cries thus must you ward
Where thou hurt'st one I do one hundred kill.

'[Epigrams.] 3. In medicum'
b.205, fol. 97r

A1241 And we do hope as well to pass you all at last,
And that the world shall witness be ere many years
be past.

b.208, p. 71

A1242 And well th'eternal King
Through our Redeemer's name.

P[hilip] Doddridge, 'The living sacrifice. Rom. 12. 1'
c.493, p. 73

A1243 And when no other rival he could find,
Strove with himself—and left himself behind.

Knightley Chetwood, 'To Ossory [later duke of
Ormonde]. Coll[ectio]n of poems by noblemen,
Lond: 1702'
Spence Papers, folder 113

A1244 And why should I not share my tear[s] and be
Some wept, let those that know more weep the rest.

'On the death of Toby Mathew Archbishop of York'
[29 March 1628]
[Crum A1329]
b.62, p. 81; b.356, p. 21

A1245 And why so coffin'd in a vile disguise
A league with moldy bread and clouted shoes.

[John Cleveland], 'On the King's disguise'
b.93, b. 125

A1246 And why so pensive? 'cause you lov'd her? Thence
To make yourself the mother of the nine.

'To my worthy friend Mrs. Dodson on the death of
her daughter'
fc.61, p. 139

A1247 And why such sudden shouts? what news could
bring
Vivat rex Carolus Secundus.

T[homas] Q[uick], ['At the proclamation of our most
royal sovereign Charles the 2d . . .']
b.212, p. 216; see also 'The glitt'ring sun . . .'.

A1248 And why yet silent Will I trow
Or carping Momus fears.

'The second part [of a fragment beginning '. . . Belfast
then . . .'] to the same tune'
Poetry Box VII/60

A1249 And wilt thou go (great Duke) and leave us here
And we shall think't a happy victory.

'Upon the Duke [of Buckingham]'s voyage to the Isle
of Rhee. 1627'
[Crum A1338 (var.)]
b.54, p. 881

A1250 And would you fain the reason know
To fight till both be overthrown.

'Cant: 34'
b.4, fol. 28v

A1251 And you auspicious Prince, our other care,
To you return the vigor they receive.

[Thomas] Cowslade, 'To the Prince' [James Stuart,
the Old Pretender? 1702]
[Crum A1340]
fc.24, p. 57

A1252 And you, celestial Venus, power divine!
Bawd to a woman's lust and cruelty.

[Soame Jenyns, suppressed lines from his collected
works]
File 17482

A1253 Angelic regent of my tender mind
And life's last hours be like the hour of prime.

[William Hayley], 'Sonnet . . . June 9 [1800]'
File 6968

A1254 Angelic suff'rer whose existence seems
Seal'd with the seal of God his servant's eyes.

[William Hayley], 'Sonnet . . . Jan 31 [1800]'
File 6968

A1255 Angels and saints are finite, all are so,
To such idolatry man to invite.

[Edmund Wodehouse], 'Septr. 17 [1715]'
b.131, p. 266

A1256   Angels are pleas'd as Punch ('tis said)
Did they rejoice? I'm sure I did.

    'When a good man dies the angels rejoice'

c.340

A1257   Angels dwell here,
But now I know it.

    [Thomas Morell], 'A parody [of Gay's epitaph] . . .
written at Alscot'

c.395, p. 143

A1258   Angels of light, your God and King surround,
Whilst every circling year maintain the blissful
                          state.

    [Isaac] Watts, 'A sight of Christ'

c.244, p. 300

A1259   Angels shall pious souls at death convey (?)
Their rapt'rous heav'nly Alleluias.

    [Edmund Wodehouse], 'Aug. 5 1715'

b.131, p. 240

A1260   Angels! who our paths prepare,
Henry will be my own.

    [John Maxwell?], 'Emily's song . . . Royal captive'

c.83/2, no. 541

A1261   Anna, take this damask rose,
Yes you my fair, the world and I.

    Miss [ ] O., 'By Miss O to Mrs S sent with a fullblown
rose and a bud in [the] year 1754'

c.116, p. 25

A1262   Anne is an Angell, what [then] if she be
What is an angel but a lawyer's fee.

    'On Anne Angell married to a lawyer'
[Crum A1352]

b.205, fol. 26v; b.356, p. 308; File 19344

A1263   Another civil war! O! shame!
In Italy no longer live.

    [William Popple, trans.], '[Horace, ep]ode 16th: to the
Roman people'

fc.104/2, p. 456

A1264   Another wheel is wheel'd about
No treason in their hearts will keep.

    'Verses' [docket title; c. 1660]

Poetry Box VIII/9

A1265   Anxious about your doubtful fate,
Another Venus, risen from the sea.

    'To the Countess of Pembroke on her intended
journey'

Poetry Box III/35

A1266   Apart from every other set
Will soothe you with a song.

    'Shergold's bow-windows'

Poetry Box II/44

A1267   Apollo, and the tuneful nine,
But singe him first with X, his mark.

    John Lockman, 'Verses, occasioned by a certain
egregious gentleman [Eustace Budgell]'s threatening
the public with a new translation of Mr. de
Montesquieu's Considerations sur les causes de la
grandeur des Romains, &c.'

c.267/1, p. 343; c.268 (first part), p. 139, ('but brand')

A1268   Apollo, and the warbling nine,
And the bright circle rose content.

    John Lockman, 'Reading a ticket for Mr. Oldmixon's
benefit, at Hickford [Hugford]'s great room . . .
Thursday, 4 Feb. 1741/2'

c.267/1, p. 83

A1269   Apollo concern'd to see the transgressions,
Was writ by a vicar who'd forty pounds for't . . . .

    [William Pattison], 'The session of poets'
[Crum A1360]

fb.140, p. 102 (incomplete)

A1270   Apollo facetious and merry no doubt
Diana herself till found out was a prude.

    [Hester Grenville-] Temple, countess Temple,
'Apollo's rout—by a lady'

c.546, p. 12; c.83/4, no. 1082

A1271   Apollo first of laureates would
But 'tis for t'other end.

    [Phanuel Bacon], 'To Colley Cibber esqr. Poet
Laureat'

c.237, fol. 10

A1272   Apollo great, whose beams the greater world doth
                          light,
That nothing wins the Heaven, but what doth
                          earth forsake.

    [Sir Philip Sidney], 'Out of Arcadia' [Works, 1912,
p. 328]
[Crum A1361]

fb.69, p. 58

A1273   Apollo lent him lute for solace' sake
More speedy death than such me did deprive.

    G[eorge] Turberville, 'Epitaph' [printed 1567]

c.344, p. 5

A1274 Apollo, Pallas, and ye Muses all,
That stirs up truly valiant men to fight.

> I[ohn] F[avel], 'To our valiant English nation. An
> encomium on . . . Capt. John Baddison, commander
> of the Swallow . . . I. F. Printed 1671' [Wing F561A]

b.54, p. 907

A1275 Apollo! patron of the healing art,
And blast each vicious habit— *de la coeur*.

> 'Invocation to the god of physic'

Poetry Box II/40

A1276 Apollo who never his favor refuses
Has created a tenth and has made her your own.

> [Richard] Fitzpatrick, 'To [Lord Holland on his
> birthday 21 November 1799]'

c.340

A1277 Apollo's in love and the sequel will prove
On that place where the laurel first grew.

> [Thomas Hull]

c.528/21

A1278 Apollo's male the muses feminine
For full Apollo is worth all the wine.

> [Sir Thomas Urquhart], 'Of Apollo and the muses'

fb.217, p. 393

A1279 Appear O James! Approach thy native shore
And bravely laid them down for James's sake.

> 'The landing' [of the Old Pretender, 30 Jan.
> 1714/15]
> [Crum A1367]

fc.58, p. 79 (incomplete?); c.570/1, p. 9

A1280 Appearance bubbles all mankind
And piety a bawd.

> 'Wrote on a window at Bury in Suffolk'

c.360/1, p. 295

A1281 Apply thy mind such things to learn,
And raise thy state again.

> [John Rose?]

b.227, p. 78; b.234, p. 3

A1282 Approach my muse the melancholy strand
Then parents, sisters, brother—all adieu!

> 'An elegy on the death of four children'

c.91, p. 128

A1283 Approach not you dull souls that dirt and muck
And (tis no doubt) we shall arrive at Heaven.

> [Sir Aston Cokayne], 'Of a room in a tavern called the
> Minerva'

b.275, p. 93

A1284 Approach this place with rev'rence, come,
And meet the kindest smiles of God.

> 'Verses written on one of the panes of glass in a
> window in the meeting house of the people called
> Quakers in Edinburgh' [London chronicle, 5 Sept.
> 1778]

c.139, p. 318

A1285 Approach this tomb, my friend; thou needst not
fear,
The shrewd, the learn'd, th'enlighten'd Richard
Price.

> Miss [ ] Andrews, 'Epitaph for Dr. Price'

File 245, flyleaf

A1286 Approach ye wise of soul! With awe divine
And but forsook one world to know the laws of
more.

> 'Designed for the monument of Sir Isaac Newton'

c.165, p. 54

A1287 Aquarius and the Goat are Chronus' home
In th' Bull she triumphs, weeps in Scorpio.

> Henry Rantzove, 'Verses made upon the planet's
> houses, and exaltations'

b.227, p. 62

A1288 Arabia renowned is
To rest with you for aye. | Amen

> 'S. Cosmas and Damianus. Sept. 27'

a.30[39]

A1289 Arabin's laureates have great praise
Than old Ovidius Naso.

> 'The praise of the poets'

fc.76.iii/214

A1290 Arcadia's plains, where shepherds ever gay,
Turn where we will, 'tis all enchanted ground.

> John Lockman, 'Writ during the representation of the
> opera of Il cyro niono scinto . . . 17 June 1759'

c.267/1, p. 264

A1291 Ardalid nymph, and Hymenæus mother,
From th'aquaducts of the Sebetian spring.

> Sir Thomas Urquhart, 'The invocation. To Calliope'

fb.217, p. 327

A1292 Are all diseases dead, or will death say
Nor time, nor death, could ever celebrate.

> 'On the Duke of Richmond and Lennox' [Ludovic
> Stuart, d. 17 Feb. 1623/4; opening of Parliament,
> 19 February]
> [Crum A1375]

fb.143, p. 27; b.356, p. 250

A1293 Are all ye poets dumb? and is there none
And gain yourselves a crown, her crown more glory.

> 'An elegy on the . . . Lady Cavendish Countess of
> Devon . . . being above a hundred years old . . . 1674'
> b.54, p. 90

A1294 Are days of old familiar to thy mind
Lives and shall live, immortalized in song.

> Robert Southey, 'Inscription for a tablet at Penshurst'
> File 14214

A1295 Are not the ravens, great God, sustained by Thee?
Whilst lilies flourish, and the raven's fed.

> [Francis Quarles], 'On ravens and lilies'
> [Crum A1379]
> b.137, p. 194

A1296 Are only poets mad?
The poet sings, the politician's sad.

> [George Daniel?]
> b.121, fol. 83v

A1297 Are these the crowns that grace the faithful head
And leave to future times, a never-dying name.

> [William] Taylor, 'Epilogue to The siege of Damascus
> [by John Hughes]'
> c.176, p. 16

A1298 Are these the shades—are these the envied scenes;
And scenes celestial soothe my tortur'd mind.

> c.83/2, no. 300

A1299 Are thy woes, Philistia, fled
And in her courts his poor escape their wonted woes.

> 'In the year in which Ahaz the King died this oracle
> was delivered' [cf. 'Songs of joy, Philistia . . .']
> fc.53, p. 134, 135

A1300 Are we forbid our zeal in flames to show
Nor fear the black extinguisher of time.

> Sir Charles Hanbury Williams, trans., 'Verses
> occasioned by the prohibition of fireworks at
> Göttingen'
> c.157, p. 55

A1301 Are we forgotten then so soon can he
And he that bids him go, will bring him back.

> A[braham] C[owley], 'God's speech to Saul'
> fb.142, p. 40

A1302 Are we such nothings, then say he, our will
And horribly spoke out with looks the rest.

> [Abraham] Cowley, 'The Devil's speech taken out of
> Cowley's Sacred poems'
> fb.142, p. 39

A1303 Are women fair? yea wondrous fair to see to;
Or so kindhearted, any way procure them.

> [Francis Davison], 'What women are'
> [Crum A1386]
> b.200, p. 18

A1304 Are you dear Gibby, one of those
I care not, if your sisters smile.

> [Thomas Hamilton, 6th earl of Haddington], 'To Mr
> [Gilbert] Burnet epistle 2d'
> c.458/2, p. 135

A1305 Are you the judge of wit dread monarch hail
That done I prostrate all my little mine | Unto thy
doom.

> [George Daniel]
> b.121, fol. 43

A1306 Are you the only fair? false Sylvia no;
Raise better feature there, then you had ever.

> [George Daniel]
> b.121, fol. 36

A1307 Are you there with your bears? Your strength I fear
I fear (Sirreverence) bear must go to th' wall.

> 'Answer' [to 'Bear leave . . .']
> b.356, p. 110

A1308 Argo, that ship renown'd of ancient Greece,
And, its bright place, that famous buss supply.

> John Lockman, 'On the launching of the Pelham; the
> first buss, built for the Herring Fishery Society,
> established in 1750'
> c.267/1, p. 191

A1309 Ariadne one morning
So here here's to the practice of love's *baume de vie*.

> 'Song 198'
> c.555, p. 318

A1310 Arise Britannia see around thy head
Resum'd his seat, and shone more awful than before.

> 'On the King's landing in Scotland'
> [Crum A1396b]
> c.570/1, p. 134

A1311 Arise fair Naiad! from thy well,
The words of purest eloquence.

> [Lady ( ) Burrell], 'An invocation to the nymph of the
> spring at Tunbridge: written on Lord Mansfield's
> having declared an intention of leaving the place'
> Diggle Box: Poetry Box XI/47

A1312 Arise my love my Jesus said
I long I faint to be above.

    [Mary Pluret], 'A paraphrase on Canticles by way of
    dialogue between Christ and the soul'

    c.354

A1313 Arise, my muse, and to thy tuneful lyre
And glorious his return.

    [Thomas D'Urfey], 'To the Queen' [set to music by
    Henry Purcell, 30 April 1690]
    [Crum A1398, with two more stanzas]

    fb.70, p. 69

A1314 Arise, my muse, awake thy sleeping lyre,
To sing his bounteous [?] solemn praise

    [Henry] Needler, 'A vernal hymn'

    c.244, p. 555

A1315 Arise my muse that long has dormant laid
This labor has not been bestow'd in vain.

    Ann Alsop, 'To S. A. on I. G. Bevan'

    c.303

A1316 Arise my tend'rest thought arise
And turn these drops of grief to joy.

    P[hilip] Doddridge, 'Of beholding transgressions with
    grief from P. CXIX 158'

    c.493, p. 15

A1317 Arise O [George] why sleepest thou? awake,
Take heart and like the ministry resign.

    [satire addressed to George II during Walpole's
    ministry, c. 1745]
    [Crum A1400]

    c.157, p. 17; fc.135; Poetry Box I/92

A1318 Arise, O Israel, know thy Lord,
And bind the jarring world, in everlasting peace!

    [Richard] Daniel, dean of Armagh, 'The storm Psalm
    29' [pr. 1713 (Foxon P61, anon.)]

    c.244, p. 349

A1319 Arise O my soul with thy desire to heaven
To thee I die to thee I only live.

    [Sir Theodore Colladon? from Petrarch]

    b.211, p. 7

A1320 Arise, O Phosphorus! And bring the day,
'Tis barb'rous to insult on one that dies.

    [William Walsh], 'Eclogue 3d. Damon. (Taken from
    the eight[h] eclogue of Virgil)'

    c.223, p. 89

A1321 Arise our sorrows and our tears,
Confess him Lord of life and death.

    P[hilip] Doddridge, 'On the apostle's question, Lord
    is it I? Math. 26 XXVI. 22 [sic]'

    c.493, p. 66

A1322 Arise, sleepy Kate,
You take not the bulk to your bed.

    [Charles Earle], '[On a dismal dark morning] at the
    door of my L—— (supposed to be spoken by
    Mr. P[eard])'

    c.376

A1323 Arise ye sons of Greece arise
Arise ye sons of Greece arise.

    [George] H[owar]d, [6th earl of Carlisle], 'Ode on
    freedom'

    c.197, p. 46

A1324 Arithmetic nine digits and no more
How soon mischance hath made a hand of thee.

    T[homas] Randolph, 'On the loss of a finger cut off'
    [Crum A1402]

    b.54, p. 933

A1325 Arithmetic's the art of computation
As is its excellencies to compute.

    [Mary Serjant], 'Arithmetic'

    fb.98, fol. 3

A1326 Arm, arm in heaven there is a faction
To see how they can gull him.

    'The wars of the gods' [on Jove (James I) and
    Ganymede (Buckingham), 1623]
    [Crum A1403]

    b.197, p. 111; b.4, fol. 20; b.356, p. 139

A1327 Arm'd thro' the realm dread Louis! Legions wait,
Vain terms, where monarchs call the earth their
                                     own!

    John Lockman, 'A reflection on the despotic
    government of France . . . Nov. 1741'

    c.267/1, p. 88

A1328 Arm'd with full pow'rs, the champion of my sex,
And beg—for our young Bayes your kind
                                    protection.

    H[enry] F[rancis] R[obert] Soame, 'Prologue to The
    learned lady—a new farce'

    File 14024

A1329 Arm'd within with innocence,
Prattle, drive the heat away.

    [William Popple, trans.], '[Horace] book 1st. ode 22d.
    To Fuscus Aristius'

    fc.104/2, p. 64

A1330 Armies and powers know no inferior friends;
'Twas this brought England to confusion.

    Sir John Strangways, 'The mystery of war . . . 28°
    Novembris 1646'

    b.304, p. 73

A1331 Arms and the bloody field of Mars
'Tis love alone commands my lyre.

    'The lute'

    c.360/2, no. 221

A1332 Around the hill no longer howls the storm,
The night of sorrow, and the vale of tears.

    [Anna Seward], 'Elegy on the death of a young
    gentleman written April the 1st 1778'

    File 13371

A1333 Around this grave, ye types of merit spread!
Revered on earth! Rewarded on the skies!

    [William?] Hayley, 'Epitaph on Major Mercer the
    brother-in-law of Lord Glenbervie, whose death was
    occasioned by the affliction he suffered on the death of
    a most dearly beloved wife'

    c.83/4, no. 2028

A1334 Arrah! my dear joy, says a stout Irish blade
When William's first landing drove Stuarts away.

    'A dialogue between two chairmen on a report that no
    gunpowder was to be allowed in Ireland on certain
    holidays . . .' [Gazetteer and daily advertiser, 30 Oct.
    1764]

    c.157, p. 53

A1335 Array'd in all the fruits that grace
With virtue's gentle train.

    [George] H[owar]d, [6th earl of Carlisle], 'Ode to
    gratitude'

    c.197, p. 7

A1336 Art and nature too obliges
To see Bridges under Wa[l]ter.

    'Upon Mrs. Bridges and Mr. Walter O.'

    fb.66/3

A1337 Art grieved, George, at thy exalted horn?
What's no disgrace to her is none to thee.

    'Solamen guelphicum. (Kennedy.) . . . Translation'

    c.81/2, no. 533

A1338 Art rarifies the mind, and various ways
Improves dull nature to Jehovah's praise.

    [John Rose?]

    b.227, p. 76

A1339 Art thou gone in haste and will forsake me
Or for need to a reed turn if thou follow.

    [William Rowley?], 'Cant: 30' [song in Webster's The
    Thracian wonder]

    b.4, fol. 26

A1340 Art thou gone too (thou great and gallant mind)
Leave on thy stone—here lies the ministry.

    R[obert] W[ild], 'Upon the much to be lamented
    death of the reverend Mr. Vines'
    [Crum A1420]

    c.166, p. 310

A1341 Art thou grown so melancholy?
And then would I cure thee.

    'A song'

    b.62, p. 122

A1342 Art thou not dear unto my heart
'Tis loving thee too well.

    'The lover's sigh'

    c.546

A1343 Art thou revil'd, and slander'd, and yet whine
If conscience bless thee, do let Shemei curse.

    [Francis Quarles], 'On Conscio' [Divine fancies IV,
    106]

    b.137, p. 185

A1344 Art thou sick? the way to health
Till from thee I've purchased peace.

    H[enry] C[olman], 'Another' [on prayer]
    [Crum A1423]

    b.2, p. 34

A1345 Art thou supine my pretty Sue? Look up
Meanwhile my joys I will anticipate.

    [Sir Philip Wodehouse], 'Upon young
    Mr. Whitefoot's Mrs. Susanna Payne'

    b.131, back (no. 116, no. 225)

A1346 Art thou the man whose impious tongue defies
In Adam view'd, a brother I descry.

    Charles Atherton Allnutt, 'The following lines were
    written underneath a print of Dr. Priestley the
    Socinian blasphemer'

    c.112, p. 153

A1347 Artist or sage by chance or leisure led
He spurns the grave, to triumph in the skies.

    'A thought on the gravestone of Jos: Highman esqr. in
    Canterbury Cathedral. Obit 3rd March aetatis 88—
    1780'

    c.546, p. 11

A1348   Artist, that underneath my table
Ends both the spider and the poet.

     Edw[ard] Littleton, of King's College, Cambridge,
     'The spider'
     [Crum A1426]

c.233, p. 101; fb.142, p. 57; c.244, p. 280; c.360/2, no. 74;
c.487, p. 129; c.83/3, no. 1043

A1349   Artist would you my fancy please
Come try thy skill, and copy me.

c.188, p. 59

A1350   Artists! take courage, drag me out to view:
To find my name I think enough is said.

     'A riddle'

c.578, p. 137

A1351   As a cast mariner, from boist'rous seas,
Know what a store of virtues you possest.

     Michael Clancy, 'To my worthy friend Mr. John
     Lockman: on his poems on various occasions'

     c.267/1, first leaf

A1352   As a mark that I truly esteem Lady Payne,
And continue her faithful Johannes through life.

Poetry Box II/45

A1353   As a poor urchin on the ice,
With them are ruined ever more.

     'On sin a simile'

     c.179, p. 57

A1354   As a rare painter draws for pleasure, hear
That 'reft of eyes, he seems not 'reft of sight.

     [Joshua Sylvester, trans. Guillaume de Salluste,
     seignieur] Du Bartas, 'The manyfold variety of fishes
     their several natures, feeding and manner of living,
     wonderful and strange'

     b.137, p. 94

A1355   As a vast work repels the rolling tides
From the large head, too ponderous ground to
                                   bear.

     b.173 (last page)

A1356   As Actaeon's hounds, so man's affections base
Do him denounce and all his deeds deface.

     c.339, p. 310

A1357   As after noon one summer's day
I took you for your likeness Chloe.

     [Matthew] Prior, 'Cupid mistaken'

     fc.60, p. 29

A1358   As Alexander all the world subdued,
Croak'd loud disdain and [shat] upon his head.

     'Divinity of Alexander'

c.81/1, no. 112; c.115

A1359   As Alexander on a soldier,
As that the gift proceedeth from my spirit.

     Sir Thomas Urquhart, 'Why there be sundry persons,
     treated of in my epigrams, whom I extol beyond their
     worth'

fb.217, p. 49

A1360   As all things eke when Wren pisst in the sea
So are our knights augmented O Wren by thee.

     'Upon Sr. Thomas Wren. Epigr'

b.197, p. 173

A1361   As Amaryllis on the plain,
As if he felt her pain.

     'A song, &c. The disconsolate shepherd'

c.570/2, p. 59

A1362   As Amoret with Phyllis sat
Alas! 'Tis now too late.

     [Sir Carr Scroope], 'The kind nymph'

fb.107, p. 30

A1363   As an old jackdaw and a young jackdaw
With a hastiness over your clothes.

     'The rival jackdaws'

Poetry Box IV/165

A1364   As ancient Troy a tedious war maintain'd
Having such patrons, and such citizens as you.

     Pet[er] Roussignac, 'The Monument'

Poetry Box VI/105

A1365   As Anstis was trotting away from the chapter
So the King saves his money, and God save the
                                     King.

     'On the Dukes of St. Albans, Marlborough, Kingston,
     and Portland being made Knights of the Garter—
     April 1741'
     [Crum A1441]

c.360/1, p. 127; fc.135; Accession 97.7.40

A1366   As Ariadne's thread mad Theseus find
The rightest way: so faith leads human kind.

     Sir Thomas Urquhart, 'Of faith, and our life, which is
     a labyrinth'

fb.217, p. 330

A1367   As at the solemn noon of night
Who laughs at all my care.

     [( ) Jacobs], 'The foolish shepherd'

c.152, p. 40

A1368 As aw'd th' approach, and fix'd respectful love,
There fix, there shine and heighten social life.

c.153, p. 2

A1369 As Bacchus ranging at his leisure
He spread the vines of Lesbos isle.

[Thomas Parnell], 'Bacchus'
File 11383, p. 18

A1370 As, bath'd in tears, we pensive lay,
Sad trophies of our fallen state.

John Lockman, 'From the 137th Psalm'
c.267/1, p. 104

A1371 As Billy and Molly together were,
So God bless our lord and our lady.

'Interest outvying honesty'
b.111, p. 438

A1372 As bleakly seated on the naked plains
The mother's kindness, and the husband's love.

fb.66/19

A1373 As both good men, and robbers wear the sword
So heretics, and Cath'lics read God's word.

Sir Thomas Urquhart, 'Of the sacred scripture'
fb.217, p. 313

A1374 As Britain mourn'd with all a mother's pain
Envying the dead, who are so sweetly sung.

[William] Hayley, 'To Miss Seward. An impromptu'
[August 1781]
Poetry Box v/60; c.391, p. 87

A1375 As, by the rigid laws of Rome
Portend his lordship's fate is near.

'An epigram on the Lord Lovelace's being beaten'
[Crum A1460]
b.111, p. 442; fb.70, p. 257

A1376 As by the templar's holds you go,
And law without delay.

'The Inner Temple gate London being lately repaired
and curiously decorated the following inscription is
intended to be put over it'
[Crum A1462]
c.362, p. 65

A1377 As Canace the fair, near to a forest drew,
The emblem sweet of hope, and perseverance true.

[Stephen] Duck, 'The falcon'
c.83/1, no. 178

A1378 As careful nurses [mothers] do in bed soon lay
Nature my nurse laid me to bed betimes.

[Sir John Davies?], 'On the death of an infant' [Lady
Mary, daughter to King James, d. 1606?]
[Crum A1464]
b.62, p. 132; b.200, p. 219; b.205, fol. 33v, 52v; fb.143,
p. 28; b.356, p. 252

A1379 As causer of the smoke is the kindler of the fire
Flee then all occasion that belongeth thereuntil.

[Sir Nicholas] Bacon, 'Against occasion of evil'
fa.8, fol. 165v

A1380 As Celia, and fair Chloe sat
Heard and approv'd it with a smile.

T[homas] M[orell], 'On a young lady [Miss
Williams]'s saying she believed she should cuckold her
husband if he was like Sir A—— A——'
c.395, p. 12

A1381 As Celia near a fountain lay
And rifled all her charms.

'Celia a song'
[Crum A1465]
Poetry Box I/29

A1382 As charity does God most please,
Our duty and felicity.

[Edmund Wodehouse], 'Septr 8 [1715]'
b.131, p. 261

A1383 As children oft amid their random talk,
May such, in time, bless ev'ry fair one here!

John Lockman, 'Occasional prologue to The fair
penitent. Performed by young ladies and gentlemen,
at Mr. Hugford [Hickford]'s great room, Brewer
Street, 31 Decr 1753, and 2d of January following'
c.267/3, p. 130

A1384 As Chloe came into the room t'other day,
And forgot ev'ry word I design'd to have said.

[Matthew] Prior, 'A song. The fall of the rosebud'
c.94 (incomplete?)

A1385 As Chloe, with affected air
Mourn their ill conduct soon or late.

[Daniel Bellamy, the elder], 'Select Æsopian tales. The
lady and the wasp' [Fable 7]
c.186, p. 70

A1386 As Chloris in the hedgerow sat
Must oft their anguish prove!

R[ichard] V[ernon] S[adleir], 'Seeing a young lady
sitting under a quickset hedge and talking to two
gentlemen on the other side of it—she desired one to
write sometimes on the incident'
c.106, p. 85

A1387 As Chloris on her downy pillow lay
The deuce is in't, would make one almost mad.

> [George] Granville, 1st baron Lansdowne, 'A true
> account of one who lately died for a lady' [also attr.
> Lady Mary Wortley Montagu]
>
> c.229/1, fol. 50v

A1388 As cities, that to the fierce conqueror yield
Yet we'd better by far have him, than his brother.

> [Andrew Marvell], 'On the statue [of the king on
> horseback] erected by Sir Robert Viner' [in
> Woolchurch Market, London; unveiled 29 May 1672]
> [Crum A1474; POAS I.267]
>
> fb.140, p. 89; b.52/1, p. 174

A1389 As Colin drove his sheep along
Blither girls than any there.

> [Charles Sackville, 6th earl of Dorset], 'A satire . . .
> 1679' [on the Duchess of Portsmouth's place being
> exposed to sale]
> [Crum A1475; POAS II.168]
>
> b.54, p. 1143; b.105, p. 382; b.327, f. 11v; fb.106(27);
> Poetry Box VII/4 ('his hogs')

A1390 As Colin fed his sheep the other day
Just setting minded Colin to go home.

> 'A Bath lampoon . . . 1698'
>
> fb.70, p. 31

A1391 As Colin saunter'd with his bride,
O I had tasted honey sweets!

> John Lockman, 'Kiss for kiss [taken from La
> Fontaine] . . . imitated in 1731'
>
> c.267/4, p. 135; c.268 (second part), p. 115

A1392 As commonly, when blind men travel, none,
Whilst you adventure, where you cannot see.

> Sir Thomas Urquhart, 'To a certain profound lover, in
> the heat of his youth'
>
> fb.217, p. 117

A1393 As Creech swung up in a sanctifi'd twine
So see High Church hang upon such mathematics.

> [ ] Laney, 'By . . . on his hearing Sacheverell in his
> sermon [9 March 1703] compare the Whigs and
> Tories to two parallel lines . . .' [pr. c. 1709 (Foxon
> H199, anon.)]
>
> c.189, p. 181

A1394 As Cupid by his mother sat,
This seems more soft that that, and this than that
                 seems smoother.

> T[homas] M[orell], 'The glove—after Spenser'
>
> c.395, p. 3

A1395 As Cupid once, the arrant'st rogue alive,
Who tho' so little, giv'st so great a wound.

> 'The honey stealer'
>
> c.90

A1396 As Cupid was numbering his arrows one day
Are both shot together no wonder they hit.

> H[annah] More, 'On Mr. ———'
>
> c.341, p. 100

A1397 As custom guides or tender fancy
The model of material graces.

> [William Hayley], 'Cornelia'
>
> File 6973

A1398 As Cytherea, in a myrtle grove
The prize unrival'd, she shall wear in peace.

> [Thomas Hamilton, 6th earl of Haddington], 'The
> judgment of Venus' [on King George II and Queen
> Caroline]
>
> c.458/2, p. 172

A1399 As Damon late with Chloe sat
The silent flute's the sweetest.

> c.416

A1400 As death does daily its approaches make,
God never fails above death's threats to raise.

> [Edmund Wodehouse], 'Apr. 16 [1715]'
>
> b.131, p. 198

A1401 As death patroll'd the western road,
Stopp'd short, and stole this worthy man away.

> 'An epitaph in Twickenham churchyard, in the tomb'
>
> c.150, p. 139

A1402 As Dick was trudging through the wood
The casks so clear—none will remain.

> 'A query division for the author's young accountants at
> school'
>
> c.91, p. 222

A1403 As Doctor Harvey holdeth forth,
Frig'd with the cream staff brings forth butter.

> 'Doctor [William] Harvey's opinion about
> generation, etc.'
>
> b.104, p. 19

A1404 As Doctor ——— musing sat,
And I am sure to have your friends.

> D. G., 'Death and the doctor. Occasioned by a
> physician's lampooning a friend of the author'
> [Dodsley Collection]
>
> c.487, p. 166

A1405   As doctors give physic by way of prevention,
         He cares not—yet prithee be kind to his fame.

         [Matthew] Prior, 'For my own monument'

         c.90

A1406   As dogs on dogs forbear to feed
         To perish on the main.

         c.546, p. 34

A1407   As down on Banna's [Banner's] banks I stray'd one
                                        evening in May,
         Tho' thou art false may heaven on the[e] its
                            choicest blessings pour. | Ah Gra, &c.

         'Song 146 [& 147]'

         c.555, p. 202; c.555, p. 204

A1408   As down the dewy lawn, at dawn of day
         And both unite to guard the British throne.

         'The rose and the thistle'

         c.83/3, no. 1019

A1409   As down the torrent of an angry flood
         For know that you are clay, and they are brass.

         [Charles Montagu, 3rd earl of Halifax?], 'The fable of
         the pot and the kettle' [as it was told by Col. Titus the
         night before he kissed the King's hand]
         [Crum A1483; POAS IV.233]

         fb.108, p. 255

A1410   As dubious fortune often draws
         To market drove the parson's cow!

         'The parson's cow, versified from Norman tales'

         c.344, p. 6

A1411   As duteous to the place of prayer,
         And bade once more the world farewell.

         Dr. [John?] Langhorne, 'From the fables of Flora—
         the sunflower and joy'

         c.90

A1412   As erst o'er Damon's sacred bier
         More passions than you calm.

         'A song'
         Poetry Box IV/15

A1413   As ever Gladsmuir's bloodstain'd field
         The sweets of union liberty and love.

         'An ode on the victory at Gladsmuir'

         c.171, no. 18

A1414   As every poetaster uses
         With fighting, made it serve for pudding.

         [Edward?] Browne, 'Lucernis medus Acinaces immane
         quantum discrepat?' [answered by 'So spoke the
         poet . . .']

         b.115, fol. 5v

A1415   As Eve's descendant she an apple won
         From coyness unto pity: 'tis Cupid's court.

         [Sir Philip Wodehouse], 'Upon his pretty kinswoman
         Anne Walpole . . .'

         b.131, back (no. 115, no. 222)

A1416   As facts revolve by rules unfix'd—
         All study for the myrtle-bough.

         'On trifles and triflers . . . Bath January 15th 1778'
         Poetry Box 11/22

A1417   As fam'd Alcides, in a pathless wood,
         I'll find both deities united here.

         John Lockman, 'A thought, in Vauxhall Gardens,
         suggested by the judgment of Hercules'

         c.267/1, p. 135

A1418   As far beyond the gazer's eye
         Have glared(?) as stars this year or two.

         [Robert Cholmeley], 'To Mrs. Eliza Wigmore asking
         pardon for not celebrating her sooner'

         c.190, p. 159

A1419   As fashion in Bath so long has prevail'd,
         Till they meet with this idol in some other place.

         'On a gentleman whose name was Fashion having
         lately quitted Bath'

         c.83/3, no. 938

A1420   As fast as thou shalt wane, so fast thou grow'st
         Thou should'st print more, nor let that copy die.

         [William] Shakespeare [Sonnet XI]

         c.94

A1421   As fierce invaders when they sack a state
         Those gave a goddess life, and these restore.

         'To Mrs Briscoe on her coming to Tunbridge Wells in
         Kent for the recovery of her health—1713'

         c.360/1, p. 73

A1422   As flaming flakes too closely pent
         If you will yield to comfort me.

         'The 3 trial by a wary [i.e., weary?] lad' [answered by
         'Your fiery flakes . . .']

         b.205, fol. 95r

A1423   As flattery is the basest vice,
         And bring 'em to the joys above.

         [Edmund Wodehouse], 'Septr 6 [1715]'

         b.131, p. 260

A1424 As Flora's gayest blossoms disappear,
While mirthful meetings crown succeeding years.

[Charles Burney, the younger], 'A farewell epilogue. Intended to have been spoken by Mr. Woods, at Aberdeen—Nov. 7th. 1779—the last night of representation'

c.38, p. 14

A1425 As for the absent sun our clime does mourn
We only strive to seem that which you are.

'Prologue to the Duke of Ormonde spoke by Mr. Ashbury'

Poetry Box I/III[4]

A1426 As for the rest—let them alone.
Mere foils to set these diamonds forth.

[Gilbert West; incomplete?]

File 17449

A1427 As fortune good vain pleasure breeds
Better happy then to be too wise.

[Sir Nicholas] Bacon, 'Of fortune and wisdom'

fa.8, fol. 161

A1428 As Frazier one night at her post in the drawing
room stood
Go marry Carr Scroope, and your father will cure
his pox.

'To the tune of There was an old woman and she sold puddings and pies . . . in Harry Neville's style'

Spence Papers, folder 108; c.188, p. 69

A1429 As from a bramble springs the sweetest rose,
Demurest life are fruits affliction bears.

'Ex amaris dulcia'

b.205, fol. 11r

A1430 As, from a fair one, parts a swain,
To lengthen out my short-liv'd bliss.

John Lockman, 'The goodbye, to Vauxhall Gardens, on the closing of that entertainment . . . Sept. 1751'

c.267/1, p. 168

A1431 As from Eve (then the world's sole beauty) Adam
Whereby the fairest on the earth h'enjoyed.

Sir Thomas Urquhart, 'Adam, and Paris'

fb.217, p. 133

A1432 As from God's blessed love do flow
But that they all from God receive.

[Edmund Wodehouse], 'March 27 1715'

b.131, p. 188

A1433 As from his pure aerial seat
And quencht a flaming world.

[Robert Cholmeley], 'To [Eliza Wigmore]. Upon Mr Prior's two lines to Lady K. Hyde'

c.190, p. 160

A1434 As from the morning gates Cephalus' love,
Phoebus was thought the morn and Indamore the
sun.

R[obert] Shirley, 1st earl of Ferrers, 'Indamora—from the French, Des portes du matin'

c.347, p. 17

A1435 As from their wintry cells
And in sweet interchange delight awhile to rest.

[William Roscoe], 'Verses from the same' ['Lorenzo de Medici']

c.142, p. 97

A1436 As from your presence sadly I withdrew,
And only asks—to live or die with you.

[ ] Henry, 'The departure, to a lady'

c.175, p. 39

A1437 As genius, virtue, reputation
'Lost reputation's never to be found.'

'Genius virtue, and reputation'

c.578, p. 122

A1438 As gentle Carter sweeps the sounding lyre,
Her ravish'd soul shall hail her native skies!

'On Miss Carter's poems'

c.89, p. 18

A1439 As G[eo]rg[e] lays panting in his m[i]n[i]st[e]r's
arms
You rule a Virgo, I preside a Bull.

[Robert Cholmeley], 'Epig: ab incerto. in R: G[eo]rg[ia]m. imitated'

c.190, p. 151

A1440 As God his spirit does impart
Their bliss is heav'nly light, and heav'nly love.

[Edmund Wodehouse], 'Jan. 8 [1715]'

b.131, p. 135

A1441 As good, is but an abstinence from ill,
The operation in the conscience.

'Of sin'

fb.69, p. 213

A1442 As gout in age from pox in youth proceeds,
The worst disease that love and wenching breeds.

[John Rose?]

b.227, p. 77

A1443   As great Alcides in the prime of years,
        The deathless labors of his life begun.

> 'The judgment of Hercules taken from a print in the
> Earl of Shaftesbury's Characteristics'

c.481, p. 234

A1444   As happy souls in t'other life
        Had tortur'd many a stouter heart than mine.

> H[enry] Neville, 'Verses'

Spence Papers, folder 108

A1445   As harpies Graham [harpy Hopkins] thunder'd at
                                            John's door,
        For who so like, as Graham [Hopkins], and his
                                            brother?

> John Lockman, 'Beelzebub, and his brother Graham
> [Hopkins], the usurer'

c.267/1, p. 175; c.268 (first part), p. 7

A1446   As he that sees a star fall, runs apace
        Gave either eye or heart.

> 'The bridegroom's coming'

b.205, fol. 25v

A1447   As he whose body is not well in health
        Is not the end, but change of miseries.

> [Sir Thomas Urquhart], 'Riches without more can
> make no man happy'

fb.217, p. 496

A1448   As heroes, states and kingdoms, rise and fall;
        At least we're vanquish'd in a noble cause.

> 'The new occasional prologue spoken at the opening
> of Drury-Lane Theater: by Mr. Garrick'

c.578, p. 148

A1449   As his chamberlain him brought as he rose on a day,
        In this manner serve me, otherwi[se] serve me not.

b.208, p. 46

A1450   As Homer, awful bard, whose rapt'rous lays
        United, you'll th'opposing world defy.

> John Lockman, 'Prologue . . . designed for Oedipus,
> acted, at the Theater Royal in Drury Lane, for the
> benefit of the learned Dr. Clancy, a physician who has
> lost his sight . . . 4 April 1744'

c.267/3, p. 114

A1451   As I about the town do walk,
        His son brought the petition.

> 'Song of the times. June 1641'
> [Crum A1521]

fb.106(3)

A1452   As I along the Mall one evening walked
        Yourself is headlong fall'n into the snare.

> 'The snare'

Poetry Box VI/59

A1453   As I am I wish to be
        Pray'r is our sacrifice, not meat and cake.

> [Sir Philip Wodehouse], '[Thomas?] Amyas rector of
> Kimberley as I am'

b.131, back (no. 176)

A1454   As I am your friend, be willing to lend
        And hope now to purchase, girls—you must bid
                                            high—or live singly.

> 'Advice to the girls'

c.233, p. 92

A1455   As I beneath the myrtle shade lay musing,
        Then sucked the balm, and found a cure.

Spence Papers, folder 113

A1456   As I came from Lombardy
        The babe of my brain.

> [Sir John Denham], 'Song to the tune of Walsingham'
> [on Sir William D'Avenant]

pb.53, p. 12 (autogr.)

A1457   As I did stand on Houth's high top
        For who was he who dar'st deny.

> 'James Duke of Ormonde his return August 23th,
> 1677'

Poetry Box VII/20

A1458   As I from Adam did proceed
        For being born again.

> 'Regeneration John 3d except a man be born again he
> cannot see the kingdom of God'

c.362, p. 20

A1459   As I lay drowsy in my dreams
        When I am wrapt in beauty's grace.

> R. C.

'Braye Lute Book', Music Ms. 13, fol. 53v

A1460   As I lay slumb'ring in my naked bed
        To be so near, and miss so good a turn.

> 'A maiden's dream'
> [Crum A1536]

b.62, p. 79; b.197, p. 144

A1461   As I not long ago lay musing in my bed
        And I will answer him again Cuckolds all a-row.

> 'Songs [11]'

b.356, p. 288

A1462   As I on purple tapestry lay
Then strove to sleep and dream again.

    J[ohn] Hoadly, 'Anacreon ode the 8th'

    c.176, p. 173

A1463   As I once a chaplet bound,
His fluttering wings make in my heart.

    George Montagu, 'From Anacreon'

    fc.135, p. 12

A1464   As I out of a casement sent
For fear of some idolatry.

    W[illiam] Strode, 'On a strange gentlewoman passing
    by his window'
    [Crum A1540]

    b.200, p. 244

A1465   As I past o'er the river Tweed
Thou's ne'er be counted a man of Weare.

    fb.66/15

A1466   As I post forth to Aberdeen to— | Take my way,
None but you has my poor heart | Enchained.

    c.374

A1467   As I range these spacious fields
Shall forget your very name.

    [William] Pattison, 'The morning contemplation'

    c.244, p. 475

A1468   As I sat musing on affairs of state
Better the traitors fall than you should bleed.

    'To the King' [c. 1680]

    c.171, p. 1

A1469   As I saw fair Clora walk alone,
To deck her froze into a gem.

    [William Strode], 'A song'
    [Crum A1542]

    c.536; see also 'I saw fair Chloris . . .'

A1470   As I stood by yon roofless tower,
I winna' ventur't in my rhymes.

    [Robert Burns], 'A vision'

    c.142, p. 313

A1471   As I stroll the city oft I
May their god, the devil, confound 'em.

    [Jonathan] Swift, 'On the Parliament House' [1736]

    fc.135

A1472   As I walked by myself
What will, will certainly be.

    'King William musing'
    [Crum A1545]

    b.111, p. 360; b.204, p. 134

A1473   As I was a-walking down by a fair river side
Lives contented and leads a happy life.

    'The resolute maid or the jolly sailor's song'

    File 17369

A1474   As I was going last night to Whitehall
Or you should have had them the end of September.

    'News from Whitehall'

    fb.207/1, p. 41

A1475   As I was pondering one evening late
Usurp Hell's royal throne, and me should abdicate.

    'The rivals. December 8th 1690'
    [Crum A1552]

    b.111, p. 345

A1476   As I was sitting on the grass,
To sigh, and make my moan.

    'The discontented nymph'

    fb.107, p. 27

A1477   As I was, so be ye
What I left that I lost.

    'On John Orgen and Helen his wife'
    [Crum A1553]

    fb.143, p. 4; c.81/1, no. 401 (on 'Mr. Lambe')

A1478   As I was walking the other day
And when I more do hear, I more will tell ye.

    '19. Jan. 1679. The fancy, or his r[oyal] Highness['s]
    last farewell'

    b.54, p. 1220

A1479   As I went by St. James's I heard a bird sing
For she loves the clapper of Winchester bell.

    'A song, which in the singing every verse must be
    repeated twice: 1666' [on Margaret Denham, mistress
    of the Duke of York; parodied by next]

    b.54, p. 994

A1480   As I went by St. James's I heard a bird sing
There was no other way for the mending the breed.

    'The warming pan' [on the birth of the Old Pretender,
    1688; parody of previous]
    [Crum A1556; *POAS* IV.256]

    fb.108, p. 111

A1481 As I went to Luller Fair
Jolly companions every one.

    'Luller-Fair'

    c.74

A1482 As I went to Westminster Abbey
They're undone by the maids of honor.

    [Crum A1558]

    fb.66/4

A1483 As Icarus of old, so I
Tho' owing to the wounds he gives.

    'An enigma'

    Poetry Box I/14

A1484 As I'm an artist, can my skill do better
I'll copy these—next week send home your picture.

    [David] Garrick, 'Epilogue to The choleric man,
    written by . . . spoken by Mrs. Abington'

    c.68, p. 58

A1485 As in a dream our thinking monarch lay
Laughing to find himself so far outdone.

    'The vision' [of Charles II's ghost; 1691]
    [Crum A1561; POAS V.303]

    b.111, p. 351; fb.68, p. 25

A1486 As in a feast so in a comedy
Who once made all, all rules, all never pleased.

    [Phineas Fletcher], 'A comedy' [the 'epilogus' to
    Sicelides]
    [Crum A1562]

    b.205, fol. 42r

A1487 As in an enchyridion, here see
Like righteousness and peace may kiss each other.

    [Sir Philip Wodehouse], 'Upon this my niece [Anne]
    being married to Mr. Samwell'

    b.131, back (no. 31)

A1488 As in his mouth a piece of flesh a dog
Nor could so much as touch what he desired.

    'The dog and shadow, a fable, translated from
    Phaedrus'

    c.136, p. 4

A1489 As in my silent study late I sat,
That all your fame like mine, but turns to dust.

    [William] Pattison, 'The hourglass'

    c.244, p. 474

A1490 As in some rural paradise, a rose,
Her graces fade, and she untimely dies.

    John Lockman, 'The virgin and the rose, from
    Guarini's Pastor Fido, Act I scene 4'

    c.267/4, p. 123; c.268 (second part), p. 107

A1491 As in the bark's prolific wound
That now, forever makes us one.

    [Phanuel Bacon], 'To Mira inoculating'

    c.237, fol. 21

A1492 As in the days of yore was odds
He turned the parliament out of door.

    'The royal kiss, or prorogation' [1675]
    [Crum A1567; POAS I.263]

    fb.140, p. 175; fb.228/50 ('kick'd')

A1493 As in the great creation of this all,
But the next touch will silence all again.

    [Katherine] Philips, 'Out of Mrs. Philips her
    poems . . . on submission'

    b.118, p. 59

A1494 As in the groves I walk'd alone
But thanks the gods that him restore.

    'A ballad, occasioned by a report of the Queen's being
    past hope of recovery. To the tune of Zephyrs gently
    court' [Queen Anne, 1714]
    [Crum A1570]

    fc.58, p. 120; c.570/1, p. 59

A1495 As in the moral world we wond'ring see,
And happy judgment crowns its rising worth.

    'A poem'

    c.481, p. 146 (incomplete)

A1496 As in the park Ms. Celia shone
They murder men, and weep for flies.

    'On a gnat'

    c.172, p. 2

A1497 As in the woods, where leathery lichen weaves
Forgets his sorrows past, or gives them to the wind.

    [Charlotte (Turner) Smith], 'Verses, supposed to have
    been written in the New Forest, in early spring'

    c.141, p. 85

A1498 As in yon grove Myrtillo chanc'd to stray
In the [?] fancy does some pleasure find.

    'Some thoughts on love by way of a pastoral'

    c.416

A1499 As is a glorious planet in his house:
That still he moves: but whiles, I must repose.

    Sir Thomas Urquhart, 'The speeches of an amorous
    gallant, whose darling was named Theodose'

    fb.217, p. 262

A1500 As is the fire in the infernal center:
Which though it burn not, flames exceeding bright.

> Sir Thomas Urquhart, 'The speeches of one to his
> mistress, who seemed to be more profoundly
> enamored, than she was in effect: whilst he had really
> greater passion, than he was able to make show of'
>
> fb.217, p. 277

A1501 As it designs | Your folly, to think matchless every
one
So show'st your malice, to be pleas'd with none |
Of all these lines.

> Sir Thomas Urquhart, 'To critics, and flatterers'
>
> fb.217, p. 359

A1502 As it is prov'd, by scholars of great fame
Which fate has drawn upon your comely faces.

> David Garrick, 'Epilogue to the tragedy of Sethona'
>
> c.115 (incomplete?)

A1503 As I've no penetrating brain,
T'apply it to—unless the mind.

> 'Answer' [to 'Here is a thing that nothing is . . .']
>
> c.578, p. 26

A1504 As Joey Bluster, in his errand cart
To finish this business pray accept of my song.

> 'Joey Bluster'
>
> Poetry Box x/98

A1505 As justice heretofore was said to have
As chorister unto the King of kings.

> 'On Captn. Robert Whyniard who died the 30th. of
> Jan: 1671'
>
> Poetry Box VII/11

A1506 As Lambeth pray'd, so prov'd the dire event
The bishop and his clerks did say Amen.

> 'A copy of verses found on Sir Cloudsley [Shovell]'s
> tomb. 1705 [i.e., 1707]'
> [Crum A1579]
>
> b.90, p. 9; c.189, p. 12 (with two more lines); fc.24, p. 18;
> Trumbull Box: Poetry Box XIII/82 (incomplete)

A1507 As language was at Babel's Tower
Then my friend Plumpton how you'd stare.

> [( ) Huddesford], 'On Mrs. Plumpton and Mrs.
> Stephens supposing Hebrew to be the language in the
> other world . . .'
>
> c.181, p. 73

A1508 As late along Etruria's vale I stray'd
And loud proclaim his skill, and wondrous deeds.

> Edward Sneyd, 'On the navigation [in (James)
> Brindley's memory]'
>
> c.214, p. 1

A1509 As late at Comus' court I sat
That nightingales should sing alone.

> [David] Garrick, 'Mr. Garrick's answer' [to verses by
> Christopher Anstey, 1769: 'Thro' every part . . .']
>
> Poetry Box v/29; c.68, p. 107

A1510 As late Eliza on Arcadian plains
And to the solemn owl preferr'd the cooing dove.

> [Maurice Johnson], 'A rhapsody written in 1708'
>
> c.229/2, fol. 23v

A1511 As late I wove a garland
The wings of Cupid tickle.

> [ ] Ellison
>
> Greatheed Box/30

A1512 As late on Avon's willow'd banks I stray'd,
And clos'd her sorrows in the wat'ry grave.

> H[enry] Skrine, 'Prize poem at Batheaston on The use
> and abuse of cards . . . Bath—Jan: 21 1779'
>
> c.509, p. 18; File 13885

A1513 As late when fell disease and racking pain
Adored the author, and the vision blest.

> 'The vision written in a most painful and dangerous
> illness'
>
> c.89, p. 139

A1514 As lately the Picrian maids
Proceed—I'll lend it once a year.

> John Lockman, 'After reading the bill, for the benefit
> of Mr. and Mrs. Arne, at Drury Lane Theater'
>
> c.267/1, p. 131

A1515 As lately thro' the flow'ry meads I rov'd,
Left Orpheus coming from the shades below.

> [John Jacob Oakes], 'The gift of poetry: a dream. By
> [Abraham Oakes's] son, a junior sophister, of T[rinity]
> C[ollege] Cambridge. 1742'
>
> c.50, p. 31

A1516 As learned doctors can give proof,
Were nothing to the sense.

> Sir Thomas Urquhart, 'Of wickedness, and the
> torments it deserveth'
>
> fb.217, p. 196

A1517 As Lesbia mourn'd her sparrow dear,
When daws and magpies live.

> T[homas] M[orell], 'To Miss Athelina Goodrick, on
> the death of her bullfinch'
>
> c.395, p. 93

A1518   As light and heat, from the great form does flow
         And in heav'n's court its vigor ever bend.

> 'In cene dominiae receptionem 5 Julij 1691 in euch a
> sci Dunstani'

b.127, p. 19

A1519   As long as I live shall my fiddlestick move
         Let it be with my girl in my arms.

> John Wolcot ('Peter Pindar'), 'Song'

c.344, p. 33

A1520   As long as my heart and my Myra's are one
         I'd love, live, and die, and be ever with you.

> Ed. Thompson

c.157, p. 99

A1521   As long as tea is in repute,
         That as our vows, your censure is but wind.

> T[homas] Holland, of Jesus College, Oxford, 'Tea and
> scandal inseparable companions'

c.233, p. 42

A1522   As love in life conjoin'd us once
         And God in joy join us again.

> 'Epitaph no. 5'

c.158, p. 47

A1523   As love requireth and the faithful heart
         Your loving friend to my life's end.

> R. K.

'Braye Lute Book,' Music Ms. 13, fol. 48v

A1524   As Lucifer doth far excel
         Where Sunday ever shall endure. | Amen

> 'Trinity Sunday'

a.30[1]

A1525   As lusty Will and jolly Jack
         They'll never keep us here.

> [John Walker?], 'On Messrs. Turner and Stevens'
> breaking down with their weight each about 17 stone'

fc.108, fol. 75

A1526   As Madam wills I will: such complaisance
         With the great world, too much idolatry.

> [Sir Philip Wodehouse], 'Anagram Sr William Adams
> a Madam will'

b.131, back (no. 132)

A1527   As manly exercises raise
         Heightens a Titian-color'd face.

> John Lockman, 'Suppressed in my Lyrical epistle to
> Lord Warkworth [later duke of Northumberland]'

c.267/3, opposite p. 1

A1528   As Mars, by Venus: so by whores, are soldiers
                                              charmed
         She sets to sail the naked bodies: Mars, the armed.

> Sir Thomas Urquhart, 'That soldiers, cannot goodly
> lack courtesans in their company: whether in a
> leaguer, garrison, or march'

fb.217, p. 265

A1529   As Martial's life was grave and sad,
         Whate'er we want, our book has nose.

> [Sir John Denham], 'Upon the preface of [Sir William
> D'Avenant's] Gondibert' [Martial, epigrams, 'Lasciva
> est nobis pagina . . .']
> [Crum A1595]

pb.53, p. 3 (autogr.)

A1530   As mastiff dogs in modern phrase are,
         Whether this ben't a salamander!

> [Jonathan Swift], 'The description of a salamander.
> Out of Pliny's Nat. hist. Lib. 10. C. 7 & l. 29. c. 4
> anno 1705'

c.265

A1531   As men of Athens thought it fit
         But soft, I did but dream—Hum Ba!

> 'To the young lady that subscribes herself Hum-Ba a
> cant word for dullness'

fc.51, p. 81

A1532   As men with stones do break the smoothest glass,
         So want of stones doth break the finest lass.

b.52/1, p. 120

A1533   As Mira once, and I, were laid
         Far quicker eyes have been deceiv'd.

> John Lockman, 'The lovely mistake, imitated from
> Marot . . . in 1734'

c.267/4, p. 143; c.268 (second part), p. 111

A1534   As mire in walls: so's Satan in our minds;
         Some secret way, he either makes, or finds.

> Sir Thomas Urquhart, 'The temptation of the devil'

fb.217, p. 58

A1535   As moody Job in shirtless case
         'Twill ease thee of thy anguish.

> [Thomas Brown, on William Sherlock]
> [Crum A1598]

b.111, p. 207; Poetry Box VII/5

A1536   As moon round-faced, complexion white,
         And, now, pray ladies what's my name.

> 'An enigma'

c.152, p. 72

A1537 As Moses taught the world's true genesis:
That some would show its exodus, I wish.

> Sir Thomas Urquhart, 'Genesis and Exodus'
> fb.217, p. 332

A1538 As most corrupt, who leads the van?
To witness bear 'gainst S[herida]n.

> 'Poet's corner . . . on R[ichard] B[rinsley] Sheridan'
> [1794]
> Poetry Box IV/75

A1539 As musing fancy guides me o'er the lawn
Thy fame shall live, when thou art sunk away.

> 'The desolated abbey'
> c.83/2, no. 561

A1540 As musing I rang'd in the meads all alone,
My darling is gone, and a fig for them all.

> 'Mocking is catching or a pastoral lamentation for the
> loss of a man and no man'
> [Crum A1604]
> c.503, p. 6 (incomplete?)

A1541 As musing in my bed I lay,
I only could in dreams be blest.

> 'A dream'
> c.360/3, no. 181

A1542 As my days pass away, in course I go down,
And rebuild the like cottage, ne'er to decay.

> J. N., 'The old man's wish . . . Novr. 1790'
> c.94

A1543 As my health is so queer
In return I'll find whip, spurs, and boots.

> John Lockman, 'To all and sundry his acquaintance,
> who the present what-d'ye-call-it may suit, the author
> sends greeting . . . June 1740'
> c.267/1, p. 288; c.268 (first part), p. 14

A1544 As my young master after crawling
And only wish to be with you.

> Edward Rolle
> Spence Papers (various essays, 'The pendant')

A1545 As naked almost and more fair you appear
We're not barely contented with viewing.

> 'Song 201'
> c.555, p. 324

A1546 As naked Eve, in tasting of an apple's
Infect man first with the Venerian pox.

> Sir Thomas Urquhart, 'The parallel of Eva, and the
> Indian woman, whose lechery with French men
> advanced the Neapolitan disease'
> fb.217, p. 91

A1547 As Nature's beauteous form, which lately bow'd
Approving wait, and plenty ever smile!

> Eliza W——, 'On the recovery of George the 3rd,
> King of Great Britain'
> c.343, p. 102

A1548 As nature's works is what you most admire
Fit for the muses, and great Strathmore's seat.

> 'To the right honorable the Countess of Strathmore
> on her passion for shells, stones, &c. &c. &c. . . .
> Kensington Octr. 3d. 1794'
> fc.40

A1549 As near Portobello lying
And for England sham'd in me.

> [Richard Glover], 'Admiral Hosier's ghost' [parodied
> by next]
> [Crum A1609]
> c.358, p. 73

A1550 As near Portsmouth harbor lying
And lament its fate with me.

> Lord Sandwich and Lord Halifax, 'Britannia's ghost'
> [parody of previous]
> fc.135; c.358, p. 97

A1551 As needy gallants in the scriveners' hands
As much improper, as would honesty

> [John Dryden], 'Prologue to . . . Amboyna'
> [Crum A1610]
> b.111, p. 483

A1552 As Neptune with his watery train
But ne'er come errandless again.

> Poetry Box IV/63

A1553 As Nero laughing saw fierce fires consume
And call K[in]g J[ame]s our rightful m[onarc]h
home.

> 'Nero II' [on George I and a fire in Thames street,
> 13 Jan. 1714/15]
> [Crum A1611]
> fc.58, p. 103; c.570/1, p. 33 (incomplete?)

A1554 As N. . . . . le late retreating
Make 'em free you'll find them brave.

> 'The wonder of Surrey or the genuine speech of an old
> British oak [to] a certain great minister. To the tune of
> Hosier's ghost or As near Portobello lying'
> Poetry Box V/106

A1555 As o'er the airy Alps you pass
And leave the year behind.

> 'To a lady with Mr. Thomson's poem upon summer,
> written in December'
> c.172, p. 18

A1556   As o'er the heath amid his still-clad thanes
Murder'd king, adieu! Adieu!

     'Duncan's warning'

     c.140, p. 222

A1557   As o'er the smooth expanse of summer's sky
And bid their memory live to future days.

     [William Roscoe], 'Sonnet to Dr. C——'

     c.142, p. 514

A1558   As o'er the swelling ocean's tide
And dares or truly speak, or bravely die.

     Philip Wharton, 1st duke of Wharton(?), 'On the
banishment of Bishop Atterbury in 1723'

     c.468

A1559   As o'er the varied meads I stray
And pleasure to devotion turns.

     [( ) Webb], 'A thought on a walk'
     [Crum A1615]

     fc.51, p. 174

A1560   As o'er these hills I take my silent rounds,
Will fly as faithless and as fleet as they.

     [William Lisle] Bowles, 'Sonnet 22'

     c.83/2, no. 308

A1561   As oft as in thy glass thou view'st thy face,
Th'art frail, though beautiful yet like thy glass.

     'To Carolina'

     c.356

A1562   As often as I please it changeth form,
Unto its death, a giant it doth die.

     'Enigma'

     c.356

A1563   As on a calm bespangled night
My bow's unhurt—and so adieu.

     John Belfour, 'To the printer of the Ledger no. 31 The
3d. ode of Anacreon translated . . . Stratford the 14th
Augt. 1767'

     c.217, p. 195

A1564   As on a lovely summer's day
And thus his case bemoan'd.

     [Thomas Hamilton, 6th earl of Haddington], 'Song to
the tune of Down the burn Davie'

     c.458/1, p. 52

A1565   As on a sultry summer day
When you transfix his heart.

     'Cupid and the bee a cantata'

     c.186, p. 77

A1566   As on a summer's day
What is all the world besides?

     Lady [Frances] Burgoyne, 'A song'

     c.358, p. 66

A1567   As on flowers I lay reclin'd,
With ethereal music's sound.

     John Lockman, 'The enchanter: writ under a
beautifully engraved ticket, for Farinelli's benefit . . .
in King's Theater in the Haymarket'

     c.267/1, p. 291; c.268 (first part), p. 21

A1568   As on her bed the gay Corinna lay
By sighs and silent eloquence the rest.

     [Robert Cholmeley], 'An agreeable surprise, or the
dumb orator'

     c.190, p. 194

A1569   As on his deathbed Strephon gasping lay
Live not like Strephon, but like Strephon die.

     [Thomas Flatman], 'A poem on the Earl of
Rochester . . . Sept. 1680'
     [Crum A1621]

     b.54, p. 1126

A1570   As on his mother's lap, one day
To so much real excellence.

     [Thomas Hamilton, 6th earl of Haddington], 'To
Florella, from the Greek'

     c.458/1, p. 44

A1571   As on Septimia's panting breast
Bow'd and blest the augury.

     'A sonnet set by Doctor Blow'

     fb.142, p. 43

A1572   As on the brink of a deep well,
Ill fortune's still his lot!

     R[obert] Shirley, 1st earl of Ferrers, 'Fortune and a
child. From La Fontaine'

     c.347, p. 57

A1573   As on the river bank, a workman stood
He answers yes; this hatchet mine must be.

     E[lizabeth (Shirley)] C[ompton, countess of
Northampton], 'Mercury and the woodman'

     Accession 97.7.40

A1574   As once a satyr o'er the forest rang'd
My honest cave, no longer thee shall hold

     E[lizabeth (Shirley)] C[ompton, countess of
Northampton], 'The satyr and the traveler fable . . .
1722'

     Accession 97.7.40

A1575   As once in black I disrespected walk
Nor maid, nor honor, sure no modesty.

     [Thomas Randolph], 'On a maid of honor in Somerset
     Garden'

     b.356, p. 89

A1576   As Orpheus' bolder notes affect the plains
The tuneful air that to her orb aspires.

     [Abraham Cowley?], 'On hearing Mr. Bowman and his
     wife sing one night in the vineyard'

     File 3782/3

A1577   As our saint patron with his eagle's eye,
While all your Worcester angels clap their wings.

     [Edward Villiers, earl of Jersey], 'Verses spoken to the
     King in St. John's College Library in Cambridge'
     [4 Oct. 1671]
     [Crum A1631]

     fb.140, p. 139

A1578   As over Gladsmuir's blood-stain'd field,
The sweets of liberty and love.

     'An ode on the victory at Gladsmuir, Sept. 21. 1745'

     fc.59, p. 129; Poetry Box IV/37

A1579   As Ovid sings a beau of old admir'd
Gay as a flower, but empty as a shade.

     [William Jackson], 'The transmutation of a beau
     by . . . called the Beau new-modelled'

     c.229/1, fol. 96v; c.81/1, no. 277

A1580   As paradoxes abound
And I shall think you very keen.

     John Belfour, 'Read and admire' [Wapping,
     23 October 1766]

     c.217, p. 23

A1581   As Peyton's person and more lovely mind
Who are not proud to wear her pleasing chains.

     'Answer to the foregoing' ['Did Peyton's lovely
     person . . .']

     c.360/1, p. 35

A1582   As Phoebe thou seest the cloud on my eye
The groves are all cheerful, and burst into song.

     [John Wolcot ('Peter Pindar')], 'Song'

     File 16343

A1583   As Phoebus, when his palfreys have outrac'd
Itself at last in tears of sad contrition.

     Sir Thomas Urquhart, 'A counsel to an ancient
     courtesan, wishing her to dree repentance for her
     bygone sins'

     fb.217, p. 133

A1584   As plaintive, in a shady grove,
The shafts of envy you'll defy.

     John Lockman, 'To Serafina and Visconti; on their
     singing a favorite duet in the opera of Ataserfe(?),
     composed by Signor Hasse'

     c.267/1, p. 61

A1585   As plants, whilst tender, bend which way we please
'Tis, then, hard labor to reform the mind.

     'Ill habits are hard to be removed, or, the prejudice of
     education a simile'

     c.186, p. 104

A1586   As pray'r and acts of charity well meant
Ye friends of Job these did learn at last | From God
                             Himself.

     [Edmund Wodehouse], 'Novr. 15 [1714]'

     b.131, p. 84

A1587   As Prior I'll gain bright renown:
The charms of divine Peggy Ha[ys].

     S. T. T. and John Lockman, 'Peggy Ha[ys] a song'

     c.268 (first part), p. 89

A1588   As prostrate on the banks we lay
Who neither vows can save nor cries.

     Thomas Cook, 'Psalm 137'

     c.244, p. 578

A1589   As queen, where nature's mother, reason reigns;
For reason should command all nat'ral things.

     Sir Thomas Urquhart, 'Of reason's legally authorized
     sovereignty'

     fb.217, p. 56

A1590   As Quin and Foote
Your debts you pay, | One shilling in the pound.

     [Crum A1640]

     c.391, p. 100; c.81/1, no. 412

A1591   As raised aloft in windy weather,
He droops, and downwards steers his flight.

     P[eregrine] G[reatheed]

     Greatheed Box/39

A1592   As Ralph and Nick i' th' field were plowing
There'll be two los[s]es for one winner.

     'The ploughman' [November 1688]
     [POAS IV.299]

     fb.108, p. 155

A1593   As rapt in thought the musing mind survey'd
Now rest in peace she said, and soar'd to heav'n.

     [James Ogilvie], 'To the memory of Jas. Hervey'

     c.140, p. 116

A1594   As reason, fairest daughter of the skies,
       Oped to his fainting eyes eternity of pain!

       M[ary (Derby)] Robinson, 'The cavern of woe'
       c.83/2, no. 500

A1595   As rival archers who contend for fame
       Our only last request is you'll—excuse.

       [John Hoadly], 'Prologue to his play of Constancy
       approved or love in disguise'
       c.176, p. 178

A1596   As Rochefoucault his maxims drew
       Methinks you may forgive his ashes.

       [Jonathan] Swift, 'Verses on the death of Doctor Swift
       [written by himself; Nov. 1731 the third edition]'
       Poetry Box x/4, x/5

A1597   As Roger was pulling, and towsing of Nan,
       When the swains shall all know what a vixen you
                                         are.

       'Answer to [enigmas in The ladies' diary for 1747]'
       c.241, p. 116

A1598   As roll the clouds in fleet aerial tides
       Embalm my memory with a duteous tear.

       W[illiam] Shepherd, 'Written in Miss Johnes's garden'
       Poetry Box IV/164

A1599   As round the Christmas fire were sat—
       But this in hand my heart.

       [Robert Cholmeley], 'The Christmas night'
       c.190, p. 111

A1600   As rov'd a fly with wanton haste,
       Your sins the pot of honey.

       Charles Atherton Allnutt, 'The fly and pot of honey a
       fable'
       c.112, p. 170

A1601   As safely, Pyrrhus, you may bear,
       The fairest of the Grecian host!

       [William Popple, trans.], '[Horace] book 3rd.
       ode 20th. To Pyrrhus'
       fc.104/2, p. 278

A1602   As sage Sowgelder roves the country round,
       That here at leisure they may all forget.

       [on Dr. Mander, master of Balliol; 1703]
       fc.24, p. 6

A1603   As Samson's lion honey gave
       That mighty state till now had stood.

       [Edmund Waller], 'Of the Lady Mary' [on her
       marriage to William of Orange, 1677]
       [Crum A1649]
       fb.106(15)

A1604   As Satan o'er Lincoln was looking one day,
       He'd be glad to come off half as well at Cambray. |
                                   Derry [down], &c.

       'A dialogue between the gent that looks over Lincoln
       and the gent [George I] on Bloomsbury steeple'
       [Crum A1651]
       c.233, p. 114; fc.58, p. 126; c.570/2, p. 120

A1605   As saucy as idle, of youth disgrace,
       He can without arms, get his living the faster.

       [Sir Henry William Bunbury], 'Charade—1'
       File 17066

A1606   As Sawney had long been disorder'd in town
       That I from that instant grew perfectly well.

       [Phanuel Bacon]
       c.237, fol. 73 [i.e., 93]

A1607   As scholars of the learning, they acquire
       Infused liquors, but a great deal faster.

       Sir Thomas Urquhart, 'Of schools, and shoals a
       paranomasia'
       fb.217, p. 73

A1608   As seated on some mountain's side
       Dispel the low'ring dark.

       [Robert Cholmeley], 'To the King upon his accession
       to the throne written from Cambridge. An ode'
       c.190, p. 179

A1609   As Sh— was pleading for bribes, and for pensions,
       The man like the boy souses o'er head and ears.

       'Epigram'
       c.570/4, p. 107

A1610   As she is glad each man to weigh
       To that side, she gets most.

       Sir Thomas Urquhart, 'Of a covetous whore'
       fb.217, p. 58

A1611   As she was once, few of her sex you'll see
       To the most fair, for fairest Digby died.

       'Epitaph on Mrs M. Digby' [d. 1729]
       Poetry Box XIV/194 (attr. A. Pope); c.53, fol. 64

A1612   As shipwrecked sailors on the Greenland coast
       But Mira's promise clears the clouds within.

       'To Mira on her promise of making a visit to me at
       Oxford, Oct. 19th 1740'
       Poetry Box I/69

A1613 As sin makes gross the soul, and thickens it
Asleep in dust dream of eternity.

> [William Strode], 'An epitaph on Mris Eliz:
> Needham'
> [Crum A1655]
> b.205, fol. 6or

A1614 As singing grasshoppers, a fond youth revels
Of their young years, i'th' winter of their age.

> Sir Thomas Urquhart, 'The different fruits of
> idleness, and virtue in young men'
> fb.217, p. 72

A1615 As some brave admiral in former war,
And being good for nothing else, be wise.

> [John Wilmot], 2nd E[arl] of R[ochester], 'Upon his
> lying in and could not drink'
> [Crum A1660]
> b.105, p. 71; fb.140, p. 178

A1616 As some fair flower which grows in secret pride
Dear to the nymphs, or pleasing to the swains.

> Rev. [ ] Evelyn, 'Catullus Carmen nupt: 63'
> fc.51, p. 271

A1617 As some fair plant, that's in a garden rear'd,
By none she's courted, is belov'd by none.

> c.549, p. 38

A1618 As some friends round a table were sitting at ease
For a little of this will go a great way.

> N. Herbert, 'The maggotty cheese'
> c.157, p. 65

A1619 As some poor mariner, if chance a rock
And launch anew on love's tempestuous main.

> William Parsons, 'To a lady who advised me to marry'
> [Crum A1664]
> Greatheed Box/12

A1620 As some sweet flower, fenced round, in secret grows,
The men forsake, the blushing maids abhor.

> fb.66/19

A1621 As some too timid traveller whose way
Hopeless I live, nor can to peace return.

> William Parsons, 'Sonnet, on the strict Italian model'
> [of Gioseffo Corsi]
> [Crum A1666a]
> Greatheed Box/12

A1622 As some two woodbines round each other grow
Bid him a fond, a sad, a last farewell.

> J[oseph] Lovell, 'To my dearest friend Charles
> Dudley'
> Poetry Box v/5

A1623 As soon a little, little ant
Ere these affections die.

> [James Howell], 'Constant affection'
> b.104, p. 30

A1624 As soon as bright Miranda's charms
And blasted let them die.

> 'To Miranda on her recovery'
> Poetry Box I/41

A1625 As soon as customers begin to stir,
And then, sometimes the brewer pays for all.

> 'Of the ale draper' [Poor Robin's almanac]
> c.186, p. 139

A1626 As soon as the wind, it came kindly about
For the devil won't take ye if I turn ye away. Derry
down.

> 'A new ballad to the tune of King John and the Abbot
> of Canterbury' [on George I; May 1719]
> [Crum A1670]
> Poetry Box I/128; Poetry Box IV/66; c.570/2, p. 70

A1627 As sprightly sunbeams gild the face of day,
And prove her heiress of—the public favor!

> Richard Fitzpatrick, 'Prologue to The comedy of the
> heiress. Written by . . . and spoken by Mr. King'
> c.504, p. 90

A1628 As spring in showers make fading flowers smile,
Born both to guide the war and rule the peace.

> [William] Wycherley(?)
> c.548

A1629 As still a greater [?] doth man possess
Laborious to give benefits than owe them.

> [Sir Thomas Urquhart], 'That a generous mind had
> rather give a [?] than to be [?] [?] after the presented
> opportunity to repay it'
> fb.217, p. 520

A1630 As strange a wonder as black swans from geese
But you are and are honest; so more rare.

> [Sir Aston Cokayne], 'To Isabel Manifold to come
> after the former to her'
> b.275, p. 86

A1631 As Strephon in a wither'd cypress shade
Vow'd endless truth and everlasting love.

> [John] Pomfret, 'The fortunate complaint'
> fc.60, p. 88; Poetry Box v/108 (attr. Josiah Walker;
> incomplete)

A1632   As Strephon to his room repairs,
The cloak had been as short again.

    'The short cloak'
c.241, p. 79

A1633   As such we lov'd, admir'd, almost ador'd,
The charming cause is justly snatcht away.

    'On a child 4 years and 9 months old' [in Birchington churchyard in the Isle of Thanet, Kent]
c.240, p. 138

A1634   As summer's torrid beam destroys
She fears Alexis fell in war!

    'Verses extempore on the late report from India'
c.142, p. 399

A1635   As sweetly tun'd once on a bough
And his above to sing.

    N. Herbert, 'A fable[:] the nightingale and drake'
Spence Papers, folder 91

A1636   As sweets are abated, and wine is clear,
To your faithful sincere and affectionate friend.

    [Charles Earle], 'To an apothecary in Crediton, extempore for a friend by his request'
c.376; see also 'Not long after twelve . . .'.

A1637   As sylvan swains exalt the poet's fire;
The shades receive new beauties from his lyre.

    John Lockman, 'On Epping Forest'
c.267/1, p. 163

A1638   As Syrinx was sat by the glen's crystal stream,
And makes me thy vassal both body and soul.

    M[aurice] J[ohnson], '1740. A fen ditty by . . . set to music by Dr. Musgrave Heighington'
c.229/2, fol. 48

A1639   As Teague was looking in a glass—
How mine eyesh look when I wash sleeping.

    [Phanuel Bacon], 'Ludit imago vana que porta fugiens eburna somnium ducit' [Horace, ode iii.27]
c.237, fol. 77 [i.e., 97]

A1640   As tender lambs with wolves agree
Is best at cutting purses.

    Sir James Baker, 'Horace [ep]ode 4th imitated . . . to Lord Cadogan'
[Crum A1673]
b.155, p. 75; fc.58, p. 143

A1641   As Terry on the sofa lay,
Ah where is William gone!

    'The canine lamentation, on the departure of the L[or]d William [Gordon]'
Poetry Box III/23

A1642   As that will ne'er be white, which once was black:
So from the hells, there's no returning back.

    Sir Thomas Urquhart, 'Of everlasting darkness'
fb.217, p. 77

A1643   As the bark, when it parts from the shore,
Till we founder at length in the main.

    [Allan Ramsay]
c.163, p. 5

A1644   As the best porcelain the fired clay
May change that pale to red.

    'On Miss Beal leaving the card table, sick'
c.74

A1645   As the bird to whom great Jove,
War, and danger, they command.

    [William Popple, trans.], '[Horace] book 4th. Ode 4th. In praise of Drusus'
fc.104/2, p. 342

A1646   As the bold Phoenix that invades the skies
And tell the world, ye fair ones, tell my name.

    [Robert Cholmeley], 'An enigma upon glass'
c.190, p. 152

A1647   As the Chaldean swain
Each lovely in itself and lovely in the whole.

    Joseph Spence, 'Simile on criticism in poetry &c.'
Spence Papers, folder 148

A1648   As the chameleon who is known
And he lies with those he never saw.

    [Matthew] Prior, 'The chameleon'
fc.60, p. 83; Trumbull Box: Poetry Box XIII/59

A1649   As the chas'd deer, whose weary steps
His truth and love shall sing.

    [Sir William Trumbull], 'Ps[alm] 42. 1 Janry 1689/90'
b.177, p. 31; Trumbull Box: Poetry Box XIII/7

A1650   As the claim is admitted from both
And bring off a similar flitch.

    Charlotte Ann Broome, [answer to 'Charlotte said to her husband . . .']
c.486, fol. 40

A1651   As the devil was walking o'er England's fair isle
For the devil can't find such a race, when you're
gone.

    [before 1751]
Poetry Box X/103

A1652   As the earth the earth doth cover
So under this stone lies another.

> 'Epitaph at St. Mary's at Rotherhithe on Capt.
> Thomas Stone'

c.360/3, no. 133

A1653   As the first matter hath no form at all
Not to have liberty in prostitution.

> [Sir Thomas Urquhart], 'Why courtesans ought not to
> be married'

fb.217, p. 541

A1654   As the grammaticaster Poll proves, we
But you still follow t'orthograph his horns.

> Sir Thomas Urquhart, 'To Kerodotes, of Poll the
> grammarian, and his wife, whose affection was so
> inordinately bent towards him, that by him only, and
> none else, she cornuted her husband'

fb.217, p. 314

A1655   As the great sons of war, that are rais'd high
Long time mention'd by the dull people sin.

> [Sir William D'Avenant]

fb.66/35

A1656   As the hart panteth for the rill,
In his benignity.

> 'Psalm 42'

c.264/1, p. 185

A1657   As the heat of the fire the cold outdrives,
So by repentance drive vice from your lives.

b.234, p. 257

A1658   As the nine warbling maids, and their chieftain,
                             Apollo,
Alone the god fix'd it, by pointing to Boyce.

> John Lockman, 'The musical patronage . . . Decr.
> 1754'

c.267/1, p. 1

A1659   As the pale moon the sun's bright beams o'erspreads
So let the cuckold to the king give way.

> 'Found in the King's Bench walks just after the eclipse'
> [22 Apr. 1715]
> [Crum A1679]

fc.58, p. 13; c.570/1, p. 5 ('bright orb')

A1660   As the poor hart doth pant and bray
The cause that others mock at thee.

> [John Black], 'Psalm XLII paraphrased'

fc.107, before p. 55

A1661   As the premises are two propositions,
The marrow of the matter.

> Sir Thomas Urquhart, 'Of Cupid's didymi, and the
> premises of a syllogism'

fb.217, p. 336

A1662   As the sun's early beams attract and warm,
Meridian heat, and scorch the fools away.

c.549, p. 13

A1663   As the sweet sweat of roses in a still
She and comparisons are odious.

> [John Donne], 'Elegia duodecima' [The comparison]
> [Crum A1684]

b.114, p. 113; b.148, p. 73

A1664   As the wing'd minister of thund'ring Jove,
Thro' all the rocks and shoals of doubtful war?

> [George Lyttelton, 1st baron Lyttelton], 'A trans[lation]
> of the 4th ode of the 4th book of Horace'

c.368, p. 113

A1665   As these are three blue beans in a blue bladder,
There are three universities.

> 'A propereous parison'

c.356

A1666   As thine own heart, if all things there are right?
Like baleful meteors rise, and stink, and die.

> John Lockman, 'To a very eminent citizen [Slingsby
> Bethell], most vilely calumniated . . . Feb. 1758'

c.267/1, p. 115

A1667   As those that only on the bye
From that reflection I may prove a poet.

> John Gainsford [22 December 1670]

Poetry Box VI/71

A1668   As those we love decay, we die in part,
Till dying, all he can resign is breath.

> [James Thomson], 'Verses occasioned by the death of
> a particular friend of the author'
> [Crum A1688]

c.163, p. 22; Poetry Box IV/183

A1669   As threat'ning storms insult the skies,
Return triumphant to our hemisphere.

> 'On my Lord Bolingbroke's going over into France'
> [Crum A1693]

c.570/1, p. 67

A1670   As through St. Edmund's streets I past
Should winking choose their country's knight.

> 'Blind man's buff. Or the new Suffolk way of choosing
> a knight for the shire . . .'

Poetry Box VI/72

A1671   As through the fields I chanced to stray
       Of Willy of the dale.

         'Willy of the dale'

       Poetry Box IV/62

A1672   As thro' the temple gate I late did pass,
       And that the rascals both had hand i' th' plot.

         'A quarrel between two rats, one belonging to the
         Temple, and the other to Clement's Inn. 1679'

       b.54, p. 1238

A1673   As thus in calm domestic leisure blest,
       And soothe thy latest hours to soft repose.

         William Roscoe, 'Sonnet. To ——' [prefatory to 'The
         nurse']

       c.142, p. 33

A1674   As time does by a daily progress nourish
       You are express'd to be a hopeful youth.

         Sir Thomas Urquhart, 'To the Earl of [crossed out]'

       fb.217, p. 312

A1675   As 'tis the soul that has access
       All right true wisdom flows from his.

         [Edmund Wodehouse], 'March 12 [1715]'

       b.131, p. 180

A1676   As to Sebastian, let them search the field
       Which his good sword had digg'd.

       Diggle Box: Poetry Box XI/5

A1677   As to the world I naked came
       So naked stripp'd I leave the same.

         'Epitaph'

       c.360/3, no. 61

A1678   As Tom and Paul together sat
       Translated what he could not read.

         'Equidem credo quici [aqui] sit divinitus illis ingenium
         Virg.' [imitation of Matthew Prior's 'Alma']

       Poetry Box x/161; Poetry Box x/162, 163 (var.)

A1679   As Tommy was sitting, one day in a shade
       Poor Tom, I'll soon fall a prey to despair.

         [Thomas Hamilton, 6th earl of Haddington], 'A song
         to a Yorkshire tune'

       c.458/2, p. 64

A1680   As t'other day in harmless chat
       To such a charming creature?

         'Song 183'

       c.555, p. 284

A1681   As t'other day in saunt'ring mood
       Be sentenc'd apes to lead to hell.

         'A tale to Miss W—n May 29th 1737'

       Poetry Box I/53; Poetry Box IV/126 (incomplete)

A1682   As t'other night in bed I thinking lay
       'Tis ten to one, but we shall dream again.

         'The gambol or a dream of the grand Cabal' [Clifford,
         Ashley, Buckingham, Arlington, Lauderdale; 1672/3]
         [Crum A1703]

       b.52/2, p. 145; fb.68, p. 71; Poetry Box IV/126
       (incomplete)

A1683   As t'other night, my body drown'd in sleep,
       But I was wakt, Tom opening the door.

         'A dream'

       b.216, p. 162

A1684   As tree by fruit and gold by fire
       By use of these let men it see.

         [Sir Nicholas] Bacon, 'Of talk and fellowship'

       fa.8, fol. 161v

A1685   As 'twixt the sun, and moon, the earthly mass is:
       So betwixt God, and us, stand our trespasses.

         Sir Thomas Urquhart, 'The eclipse of the soul'

       fb.217, p. 108

A1686   As tyrants dread each person, and are still
       And being most good, not one's afraid of you.

         Sir Thomas Urquhart, 'To any gracious, and mighty
         prince'

       fb.217, p. 280

A1687   As unthrifts grieve in straw for their pawn'd beds
       Dead, all her faults are on her forehead writ.

         [Francis Beaumont, 'An elegy on the death of the lady
         Markham'; 1609]
         [Crum A1708]

       b.148, p. 146; b.197, p. 49 ('unthrifts mourn')

A1688   As usual having naught to go,
       Sterree, sturre, starum.

         [John Lockman], 'Song (in the person of a
         nobleman)[.] The words and tune proposed as a model
         for our opera bard, and musical performers. Tune,
         Robin had a horse, and Jenny had a mare'

       c.268 (first part), p. 96

A1689   As various fancies strike each whimsied bard,
       Which Addison him has deign'd to grace.

         [William] Shenstone(?)

       c.528/15

A1690 As Venus with her son one day,
You'd look just like the widow Licet.

> J. B., 'To Mrs. Licet of Mallow in the kingdom of Ireland'
> Poetry Box IV/155

A1691 As virtuous men pass mildly away
And makes me end where I begun.

> J[ohn] D[onne], 'An elegy' ['Valediction forbidding mourning']
> [Crum A1711]
> b.148, p. 58

A1692 As walking forth to view the plain
Or I die for Kath'rine Ogie.

> 'A song'
> [Crum A1712]
> fc.61, p. 67

A1693 As we by swift Euphrates' side
Finish th' accursed race.

> [Sit William Trumbull], 'Psalm the 137' [December 1688]
> Trumbull Box: Poetry Box XIII/25

A1694 As we can take unfeign'd delight
When we reflect that thou dost of them allow.

> [Edmund Wodehouse], 'Iterum [22 April 1715, on the sun's eclipse]'
> b.131, p. 203

A1695 As we th'Euphrates' banks lay near
And throws them 'gainst the stones.

> 'The same [Psalm 137], another meter'
> c.264/3, p. 88

A1696 As when a bully draws his sword
Mongrels will serve to keep him down,

> E[dmund] A[shton], 'On the same author [Edward Howard] upon his British princess [princes; 1669–1671]'
> [Crum A1721; POAS I.339]
> b.105, p. 192

A1697 As when a constable invades
A cordial to his friends affords.

> 'A simile (on Æneas' satisfaction in putting an end to the war by the death of Turnus)'
> c.555, p. 57

A1698 As when a furious tempest from on high,
But unto none, than to myself, more dear.

> W[illia]m Stukeley, 'A meditation in the fields, on seeing the hearse of . . . the Duke of Montagu . . . July 18 . . . 1749'
> c.229/1, fol. 101; c.371, fol. 66

A1699 As when a mighty monarch with renown
The Day of Judgment shall oft mercy prove.

> [Edward] Sparke, 'Poem 2: upon Advent Sunday' [Crum A1725]
> b.137, p. 8

A1700 As when a panting traveller, quite spent,
Contemplate glad the haven of thy rest.

> 'Wrote fifteen years after the author's safe arrival in England from America. In imitation of Dr. Young' [1795]
> c.515, fol. 5v

A1701 As when blithe lambs their vernal revels keep,
Lest they should swerve from virtue in their play.

> 'The governess, or innocence secured a simile'
> c.186, p. 92

A1702 As when by laboring stars new kingdoms rise
Eternity is the good writer's share.

> Knightley Chetwood, 'To the Earl of Roscommon on his excellent poem'
> b.86, p. 49

A1703 As when high Jove, with Hermes, left the skies;
To soothe a mistress, joy of ev'ry lyre.

> John Lockman, 'To the Duchess of Buckingham, on her grace's sending my wife a basket of fruit, from her garden . . . Sept. 1742'
> c.267/2, p. 337

A1704 As when, on sylvan holiday, the swain
Man's footsteps dark to guide through life's entangled maze.

> 'To the author of the poetical translation of Isaiah'
> fc.53, p. 148

A1705 As when our eyes fix'd on some royal seat
To make thee Queen of Rivers as before.

> 'To Mrs Brookes at Tunbridge Wells —1713'
> c.360/1, p. 77

A1706 As when proud Lucifer aim'd at the throne;
For tho' his pride's as great, his cunning less.

> 'The parallel'
> [Crum A1731]
> fb.228/54

A1707 As when some beauteous nymph with virgin shame
A train of beauteous colors ere it die.

> 'On the snow drop'
> fc.132/1, p. 79

A1708   As, when some great and gracious monarch dies
For thou shalt make it live, because it sings of thee.

     [John Dryden], 'Eleonora, a panegyrical poem'

     c.164, p. 1 (attr. K. Bridgeman)

A1709   As when some tempest rages in the air,
A grief that equals our unhappiness.

     Anthony Spinage, of Jesus College, Cambridge, 'On
the death of the Reverend Dr. John Sherman
Archdeacon of Salisbury and late fellow of Jesus
Coll[ege] Camb[ridge] [d. 1 May 1667] 1671'
[Crum A1728, 'when a tempest']

     b.63, p. 67

A1710   As when t'a coupl'of passengers, both willing
Both wit, or valor may receive (?) his charges.

     Sir Thomas Urquhart, 'How different the prejudices
of men, and women are in matters of incontinency'

     fb.217, p. 125

A1711   As when the dusk of some tempestuous night
Bear the long winter, and expect his spring.

     E[dmund] B[urke], 'On Dr. Taylor'

     File 2233

A1712   As when the generous man's drawn off and gone
As tailors do by turning upside down.

     'To the advocates who stay behind' [docket title:
'Verses on the advocates and ministers '74']

     Poetry Box VIII/27; see also 'Whenas . . .'

A1713   As when the glorious magazine of light
And firmly stands when crowns and scepters fall.

     K[atherine] Philips, 'On the 3d of September 1651'

     b.118, p. 41

A1714   As when the illustrious offices of day
Each violet lifts up the pensive head.

     [Sir William D'Avenant]

     fb.66/35

A1715   As when the King of peace, and Lord of love
And ask the certain way to rise as high.

     [William] Broome, 'On the death of a friend'

     c.244, p. 486

A1716   As when the silkworm, erst the tender care
Chanting his peerless praise in never-dying strains.

     T[homas] M[orell], 'To my friend Mr [James]
Thomson on his unfinished plan of a poem, called
The castle of indolence—in imitation of Spenser'

     c.395, p. 63

A1717   As when the storms of horrid war doth cease
To thee in endless praises may aspire.

     [Edward] Sparke, 'Poem 15th, on Whitsunday'

     b.137, p. 38

A1718   As when the wearied mariners have tried
He fill'd thy heart and then employ'd thy tongue.

     [Thomas Gurney], 'To myself after recovered from
the smallpox'

     c.213

A1719   As when, the years of manly vigor past
And sickly manhood hopes for lengthen'd age.

     'In the London evening post July 23d. 1748: Flattering
uncertainty'

     Poetry Box I/127

A1720   As when those sisters rent their golden hair,
In all her plaints, and answer all her cries.

     Tho[mas] Quick, 'A prosopopeia of England,
lamenting the sad effects of civil discord'

     b.212, p. 236

A1721   As when wild fancies some enchantments raise
He fir'd their navy and their camp alarms.

     'On the King of France his statue brought over by the
Duke of Marl[borough] and placed before Blenheim
House'

     c.170, p. 11

A1722   As whirls around the chariot wheel,
(None live exclusive of the urn.)

     'Memento mori . . . Anacreon'

     c.94

A1723   As, whom Penelope made lose their pains
His lower understanding.

     Sir Thomas Urquhart, 'Of a gentlewoman, curious to
learn philosophy from a certain gentleman, who
though he taught her not the science he got her
nevertheless with child'

     fb.217, p. 136

A1724   As wicked vice and mortal sin
May win a worthy place. | Amen

     'Of S. Simon and Jude. Octo. 28'

     a.30[45]

A1725   As Wild broke in for hopes of prey,
Steal what thou canst by night.

     [Robert Cholmeley (trans.)]

     c.190, p. 45

A1726 As Willy once assay'd
Which never till death was paid.

 [Robert Markham], 'Cant: 16'
 [cf. Crum A1736]
 b.4, fol. 11 (damaged)

A1727 As wise as Pallas, fair without design;
Tho' more inviting than the Cyprian Queen.

 [Horace Walpole, 4th earl of Orford?], 'Countess of
 Plymouth' [d. 1790]
 [Crum A1738]
 c.157, p. 69

A1728 As wise Ulysses came to his chaste wife,
Death steals on us: whilst like her web's our life.

 Sir Thomas Urquhart, 'How death surpriseth mortals'
 fb.217, p. 79

A1729 As wise Ulysses, long to ills inur'd,
To make us valiant, and to keep us free.

 [Francis Fawkes], 'On the peace' [1748]
 fc.21, p. 11

A1730 As wishing will neither procure nor prevent
Is the state I would choose and the state I enjoy.

 J. Fry, 'A resolution . . . Sutton Benjam[in], 1762'
 c.517, fol. 22v

A1731 As wolves and lambs each other hate,
When such a tribune goes.

 [William Popple, trans.], '[Horace, ep]ode 4th. To
 Menas—Pompey's freed man'
 fc.104/2, p. 406

A1732 As words can't express or fancy e'er frame
May the fair miss our passion approve.

 Lord [ ] Sunbury
 fc.135

A1733 As words express'd are of the heart,
And gratitude enforces this.

 [Edmund Wodehouse], 'March 24 [1715]'
 b.131, p. 187

A1734 As wrapp'd in death-like sleep Xanthippe lay,
Nor make a toil of that which gives us pleasure.

 'Xanthippe, (Socrates's wife) a peevish one'
 [Crum A1740]
 c.94

A1735 As yet unfit to bear the yoke,
With flowing hair and doubtful face.

 [William Popple, trans.], '[Horace] book 2nd. Ode
 5th. On Lalage'
 fc.104/2, p. 128

A1736 As you came from the holy land | Of Walsingham
O joys all delusions are | And an empty name.

 [cf. Thomas Deloney, in A garland of good will, part 3
 (1631)]
 [cf. Crum A1742]
 b.213, p. 34

A1737 As you did [?] here to make election
A happier lady nowhere should we find.

 [Sir Thomas Urquhart], 'To L[ord?] Dum[.]'
 fb.217, p. 389

A1738 As you my loving sister are
That's the man that crowns your days.

 [Thomas Gurney], 'An extempory poem written in a
 book he accidentally took in his hand, of his maiden
 sister's'
 c.213

A1739 As your behavior is surpassing comely
Cannot be wanting to your prime deserts.

 Sir Thomas Urquhart, 'To my Lady Fleming'
 fb.217, p. 332

A1740 As you're a man of great estate
I'll pray that you may live forever.

 G[eorge] Eyre
 c.160, fol. 49

A1741 As you're both willing to do well, and able
With greater skill in the affairs of state.

 [Sir Thomas Urquhart], 'To Secretary Windebank'
 fb.217, p. 391

A1742 As you're the child, the grandchild, and the near
Fair queens t'your sisters, and a king t'each
                                        brother.

 Sir Thomas Urquhart, 'The first epigram to the
 princess'
 fb.217, p. 131

A1743 Ascend three thrones great captain and divine,
And all bare-headed cry God save the king.

 ''Tis I' [inscribed under General Cromwell's picture
 upon one of the pillars of the Exchange, 1653]
 [Crum A1747]
 Poetry Box VII/34

A1744 Asham'd so long to be your debtor,
The understanding is beshit.

 Edward Sneyd, 'An epistle 8th: my answer to my Lady
 Birmingham Copperface by desire of the curate sent
 to her, in his own name'
 c.214, p. 25

A1745 Ashton found guilty? Surely 't cannot be
Ashton a crown, a crown of glory gains.

'On Mr [John] Ashton's being condemned' [1690]

b.III, p. 87

A1746 Ask him no more sweet girl w[h]ere stray,
And in your beauteous bosom dies.

'Lines to a young lady, who proposed some questions
on natural history' [imitation of Carew's 'Ask me no
more . . .']

c.344, p. 10

A1747 Ask me no more whither do stray
Be too, and we shall ne'er agree.

[answer to Carew's 'Ask me no more . . . And in your
fragrant bosom dies']
[Crum A1755]

b.197, p. 234; b.356, p. 273

A1748 Ask me no more whither do stray
And in your fragrant bosom dies.

[Thomas Carew], 'A song' [answered by 'Ask me no
more whither do stray . . . Be too, and we shall ne'er
agree']
[Crum A1754]

b.62, p. 126; b.200, p. 110 (with another stanza); b.356,
p. 272

A1749 Ask me not how calmly I
Woman woman woman brings.

'A favorite song'

Greatheed Box/75

A1750 Ask me why I send you here
What doubts and years are in a lover.

[Robert Herrick], 'The primrose'
[Crum A1757]

c.94 (attr. Carew)

A1751 Ask not fair maid the fates to know
Thou'lt find it in the sky.

'Response of a Scotch wizard to Lady Harriet
Hamilton, inquiring his opinion of her features and
her fortune'

Poetry Box XII/40

A1752 Ask not, vain wand'rer, whence yon distant bell
Unerring wisdom is the cause of all.

H. F. D., 'An elegy on the death of Mr. [Thomas]
Cholmondeley of Vale Royal' [d. 1702]

c.139, p. 502

A1753 Ask what my falt'ring tongue would own
This this indeed is love.

'L'amour timide'

c.546

A1754 Ask when the birds delight to build and breed
And made Duke Hamilton take Betty Gunning.

'Epigram'

Poetry Box x/22

A1755 Ask ye companions of my infant years,
Sadly, dear Eton, take a long farewell.

'From the microcosm—by an Eton boy'

c.90

A1756 Ask you what's friendship 'tis the link which binds,
And heav'n is all reflected by the mind.

'Definition of friendship'

c.83/2, no. 338

A1757 Ask'st thou what cause consign'd to early fate
Who Phoebus and the Muse to envy mov'd.

[William Roscoe], trans., 'On the same subject' [the
death of Politiano, from 'Lorenzo de Medici']

c.142, p. 111

A1758 Asleep the gen'rous lion lay,
Bravely they join to crush the foe.

John Lockman, 'Fables. The lion and the cock. Writ
during the rumor of an invasion, from France; and
addressed to the good people of England'

c.267/3, p. 81

A1759 Aspasia, blest with ev'ry charm
Will draw all Olympus down.

John Lockman, 'Aspasia's birthday'

c.267/2, p. 197

A1760 Aspasia come! The favorite grove
Haste, my Aspasia! Haste away.

John Lockman, 'To Aspasia: inviting her to Vauxhall
Gardens . . . May, 1740'

c.267/1, p. 156; c.267/2, p. 354; c.268 (first part), p. 26

A1761 Aspasia, Laura, lovely pair
Whom pomp and vanity surround.

[ ] Bayley, 'Verses occasioned by a comparison made
between Lady Pembroke, and Miss Lawrence of the
Pump Room—Bath'

Poetry Box v/15; c.83/1, no. 153

A1762 Aspasia! Let thy gen'rous soul,
And show forth thine, as Phoebus might.

John Lockman, 'To a lady of Salisbury (Mrs. Knight)
most villainously aspers'd in the rebellion of 1745'

c.267/2, p. 361

A1763 Aspersions, which base people viciously
Where he that is undermined, doth undermine.

   [Sir Thomas Urquhart], 'We ought not to regard the
   [?] and calumnies of profane lying men'
   fb.217, p. 528

A1764 Aspire the god of wit—divine aspire!
Cry out the tyrant's dead we will rejoice.

   'Paraphrased out of scripture for the good of England'
   fc.58, p. 3

A1765 Assassin-like, who lurks and stabs his frined
Avoid him Roman! He's as black as hell.

   'On a false friend'
   c.361

A1766 Asses' milk half a pint take at seven or before
And those you may end, when you please to prove
                                                   kind.

   [Philip Dormer Stanhope], 4th earl of Chesterfield,
   'Lord Chesterfield's prescription to Lady Frances
   Shirley or a receipt for a consumption'
   [Crum A1767]
   c.83/1, no. 188; fc.51, p. 69; c.578, p. 99 ('at six'); Poetry
   Box VI/11 (with six more lines); Spence Papers, folder 113
   (with two more lines)

A1767 Assist me Muse, that in a glorious strain,
And send it to the folks, that sent them up to town.

   'A postscript to The golden age'
   fb.70, p. 3

A1768 Assist me now good Polyhymny
Who has not heard of chimney money.

   [ ] Eyers, 'The chimney sweeper turned poet'
   c.170, p. 23

A1769 Assist me, some auspicious muse, to tell
The wretched beadle sinking on his knees . . . .

   'Upon the beadle' [Peter Vernell, who died in a fight
   with the Dukes of Albemarle, Somerset, and
   Monmouth, 1670/1]
   [Crum A1773; POAS I.174]
   fb.140, p. 145 (incomplete)

A1770 Assist me, some good sprite with a hey with a hey
And like ravens cry, York, York, | With a hey
                                      tronny, nonny, nonny, no.

   Aaron Smyth, 'A ballad sung by . . . before the D[uke]
   of B[uckingham] and those . . . who were for passing
   the bill, against the Duke of York's inheriting . . .' [i.e.,
   the Exclusion Bill, November 1680]
   [Crum A1774]
   b.54, p. 1208

A1771 Assist my doubtful Muse, propitious love
And high descent for God Himself is love.

   'An ode on love inscribed to the Honorable Mrs.
   Finch' [Lady Charlotte Finch, daughter of the Earl of
   Nottingham?]
   Poetry Box x/10(10)

A1772 Astrologers say Venus the selfsame star
With every year a new Epiphany.

   [John Cleveland], 'Upon Princess Elizabeth born the
   night before New Year's Day' [daughter of Charles I,
   born 28 Dec. 1635]
   [Crum A1785]
   b.93, p. 47

A1773 At a mixed club a French marquis
By our addition of a shirt.

   [Phanuel Bacon]
   c.237, fol. 74 [i.e., 94]

A1774 At a rude epigram ne'er vex dear Miss
For what you buy—must surely be your own.

   'To the same [kind but painted] lady by another hand'
   fb.142, p. 58

A1775 At a table where travelers met to regale,
I would answer I thank you, I'm well,—how do
                                                   you?'

   'The Irish echo'
   c.94 (incomplete?)

A1776 At all the diverse times, you were employed
He did you ne'er the good, that doth repent him.

   Sir Thomas Urquhart, 'To the Earl of [crossed out]'
   fb.217, p. 164

A1777 At arse of cart poor I must pack
All this is true, for he has been serv'd so.

   'On one being sentenced to be whipped'
   c.361

A1778 At B—n liv'd the happy three
The phantom slunk to hell again.

   [Phanuel Bacon], 'A tale'
   c.237, fol. 90 [i.e., 110]

A1779 At benefits each play'r's a privateer,
Corrupted freemen are the worst of slaves . . .

   [David Garrick], 'Epilogue' [to John Home's Alfred;
   incomplete draft]
   Acquisition 92.3.1ff. (autogr.)

A1780   At Christ Church marriage made before the King
He offered twice, or thrice to go away.

'The epigram on the play' [Barten Holiday's
Technogamia, or the marriage of the arts]

b.200, p. 34; see also 'Christ Church a marriage . . .'.

A1781   At close of the day when the hamlet is still,
Oh when shall it dawn on the night of the grave!

[James] Beattie, 'The hermit'

c.83/1, no. 44 (stanzas 1–4); see also 'At the close . . .'.

A1782   At court you'll find Ulysses, to surprise
To make you of them all, as blind's a stone.

Sir Thomas Urquhart, 'Who resides at court hath
great reason to be circumspect: how wise, or of what
condition soever he be: whether a Polyphemus, or an
Argus'

fb.217, p. 71

A1783   At Covent Garden playhouse t'other night
Aurora dawn'd, and link boys ran away.

'A link omitted in the above chain'

fc.76.iii/214

A1784   At dead at night, after an evening ball,
Leaving the trembling princess drown'd in tears.

'The Duchess of York's ghost' [1690/1]
[Crum A1800; POAS v.298]

fb.68, p. 115; b.111, p. 427; fb.207/3, p. 39

A1785   At dead of night imperial reason sleeps,
For sleep, like death, its image, equals all.

George Stepney, 'Poems . . . The nature of dreams'

c.351, p. 73; c.360/3, no. 182 (var.)

A1786   At dead of night, the hour when courts
See joys that Rosline never gave.

'Rosline Castle'

c.142, p. 370

A1787   At dead of night, when stars appear
Safe is my bow, but sick thy heart.

[Matthew Prior], 'The third ode of Anacreon
translated . . . Miscellany poems'

c.186, p. 115 (attr. Dryden)

A1788   At death the soul this world will slight,
Is man's entire felicity.

[Edmund Wodehouse], 'Feb. 9 [1715]'

b.131, p. 162

A1789   At Delphos' shrine, one did a doubt propound,
While Spenser is alive, it is no question.

'Dr. Edm. Spencero poetarum opt. max.'
[Crum A1801]

b.197, p. 39; fb.143, p. 1

A1790   At dinner-time, the pamper'd glutton ate
And, through pure envy, waste away by inches.

'Ver-vert the parrot belonging to the nuns'

c.83/2, no. 393

A1791   At Emmaus when Christ our Lord appear'd,
Another Raphael may we find in you.

Philip Wharton, 1st duke of Wharton(?), 'Upon the
(late) Bishop of Rochester preaching (written in 1723)'

c.468

A1792   At Ephesus a temple stood,
You'll kiss me and be friends.

'To Cloac[i]na upon erecting a new temple to her'
Spence Papers, folder 113

A1793   At every time, in what thou dost assay,
Let reason rule, and do the things thou may.

c.339, p. 313

A1794   At famous Rome the other day
When truly know will turn out apes.

[George] H[owar]d, [6th earl of Carlisle], 'Fable'

c.197, p. 22

A1795   At first both sexes near in man combined
And makes them both but one hermaphrodite.

'On marriage'

b.356, p. 144

A1796   At first occasionally good for fear
They'd damn themselves but they'd throw out the
                            bill.

W. B.
Poetry Box xiv/181

A1797   At first sight ne'er commend a man, lest thou
Thereafter blush for him thou praisest now.

c.361

A1798   At first view lovely Zachary
For hogs be crazy pain.

'To Zacharias Bogan'

c.189, p. 48

A1799   At five this morn when Phoebus rais'd his head
Did seem to me by much the wiser creature.

[John Wilmot], 2nd earl of Rochester, 'A satire upon
Tunbridge Wells . . . 1673'
[Crum A1808]

b.52/2, p. 164; b.105, p. 251; b.113, p. 17

A1800   At five years old the lovely dying child
So with it all the pains of life are past.

Trumbull Box: Poetry Box xiii/83

A1801 At Hardenberg, which late
As Burgomaster for the year.

'Curious Ballol [*sic*] . . . vid: Huett's Journ: by
Duncombe'

c.81/1, no. 196

A1802 At his reproachful words do not [?]
Is like a scabbed sheep not worth the marking.

[Sir Thomas Urquhart], 'An advice to a gentleman,
who was extremely offended at the defaminate
speeches of a base detracter'

fb.217, p. 540

A1803 At Jacob's wall Messiah sought,
Come drink and thirst no more.

'The spiritual invitation'

c.361

A1804 At James's house is a fearful rout
Instead of a child to have got nothing at all.

'To him Towzer on the court scuffle' [on Prince
George William]

fc.58, p. 91; c.570/2, p. 7

A1805 At James's of late
That you'd pull an old house on your head.

'The bed-tester plot, to the tune of The Commons
and peers' [on George I]

fc.58, p. 147

A1806 At Kensington there was a wedding
But believe not too much for the bride.

'Fanny and Brooky a ballad'

Poetry Box x/27

A1807 At last I find | 'Tis vain to believe
That woman's deceiv'd that believes any more.

'The libertine'

fb.107, p. 75

A1808 At last, my fair Florella, I've transcrib'd
Thy faithful friend, and most obedient slave.

[Thomas Hamilton, 6th earl of Haddington], 'The
conclusion to Florella'

c.458/1, p. 81

A1809 At last old winter op'd its frozen arms
And for him own a warm and ardent fire.

'Ode 4th Lib 1st of Horace'

c.233, p. 12

A1810 At last sad proof of a degenerate age
And think of love and politics no more.

'On the Hermitage at Richmond'

fc.135; see also 'When York . . .', 'When Young . . .'.

A1811 At Leith fortifications, ev'ry woman
Seeing ladies bore the stones, which lords laid on.

Sir Thomas Urquhart, 'Upon the fortifications of
Leith, where ladies carried the wheelbarrow'

fb.217, p. 205

A1812 At length, blest shade, thy soul has wing'd her flight,
And truth and nature mark'd thee for their own.

H[enry] Skrine, 'Elegy on the death of an old
woodman of Warley'

c.509, p. 6

A1813 At length by so much importunity prest
We harden like trees and like rivers are cold.

[Lady Mary Wortley Montagu], 'The lover, a ballad
addressed to Miss S[kerret]t [later Countess of
Orford] by the same'

fc.51, p. 53; Poetry Box x/149 (as from Miss Skerrett to
Sir Robert Walpole)

A1814 At length by work of wondrous fate,
As for the great rapping and oft coming in.

'On Winchester porter'
[Crum A1816]

b.356, p. 241

A1815 At length, Catalio, gentle swain
For all is rapture, truth, and love.

[Charles Burney, the younger], 'The shepherd's
return. A song'

c.38, p. 7

A1816 At length dearest Freddy the moment is nigh
Good Lord! How St. Stephen will ring with his
                                        crowing.

'Letter from ——— to ———' [from George, prince
of Wales, to Frederick Augustus, duke of York and
Albany?]

Greatheed Box/77

A1817 At length escap'd from every human eye,
There yield up all his power e'er to divide you more.

George Lyttelton, 1st baron Lyttelton, 'A monody to
the memory of Lady Lucy Lyttelton'

fc.132/1, p. 193

A1818 At length from scepter'd care and deadly state,
And blame th'oppresser, as they blam'd the opprest.

[Helen Craik], 'Lines written at sea by the late Queen
of Denmark during her passage to Stade—1772'

c.375, p. 3

A1819 At length I feel the power of love
I never, never lov'd till now.

'Maria's conquest'

c.360/2, no. 48

A1820 At length, my dreams of virtue past,
By our own folly she's unkind.

G[eorge] Granville, [1st baron Lansdowne], 'Song'
fb.70, p. 45

A1821 At length my golden dream is past
And of his heart the key.

Poetry Box II/54

A1822 At length our sanguine hopes arise—
To love—to friendship—and to me.

'On a beautiful young lady recovering from a violent
fever, and going to bathe in the sea'
c.83/4, no. 1078

A1823 At length the heroine's crown'd: her numerous foes,
Nor fear lest age should e'er destroy her bliss.

'An ode to the memory of the Lady Mary['s] page'
c.244, p. 637

A1824 At length the morn unfolds its purple ray,
'Tis that alone confers superior worth.

'Morning an elegy'
c.83/3, no. 756

A1825 At length the pompous yacht is come
Thy fleets from ev'ry land can bring.

Rev. [ ] Brown, 'Verses on his Majesty King George
the first's safe arrival in England after having been to
visit his German dominions in the year 1723'
c.360/1, p. 183

A1826 At length this oak all canker'd round
Thou shalt submit to mine.

[Nicholas Amhurst], 'A sequel to the fable of the oak
and the dunghill. In imitation of Sternhold and
Hopkins addressed to a certain pretended senator,
lately preferred for his political writings'
c.570/3, p. 44

A1827 At length to complete my life and my glory
For betraying the church, and enslaving the land.

'On the E. of Marlborough'
b.III, p. 530; see also 'Deserted, and scorn'd . . .'.

A1828 At Mary's tomb (sad sacred place)
And thou sustain'st the orb below.

[Matthew] Prior, 'An ode presented to King William
on his arrival in Holland after the Queen's death, anno
1695'
c.144, p. 80

A1829 At midnight's hour, when nature fosters rest;
From its broad basement fill the map of stone. . . .

'Opening of Nashomah attempted in poetry' [rough
draft]
c.311

A1830 At morn, at night, and intermediate noon,
May burn more brightly, and invercase [sic] with
time.

'A mid-day hymn'
c.515, fol. 22v

A1831 At my command, when 'Peace, be still,' I say,
To reign in life with me.

Job Scott, 'Continuation of a passage in Job. Scott's
journal. . . . 1791'
c.141, p. 313

A1832 At night where shepherds from their fleecy care
For wisdom much, for virtue more renown'd.

[one of] 'Two rebuses' [on chess]
Trumbull Box: Poetry Box XIII/100

A1833 At noon one sultry summer's day
You shall no more be lull'd asleep | By me mistaken
maid.

[Charles Sackville, 6th earl of Dorset]
c.416

A1834 At noon when dear Hebe I meet,
Shall banish your fears of a sigh.

'To Hebe . . . her answer—by Fiddo [Fido?]'
c.83/3, no. 882

A1835 At noon's approach, with toils of study tir'd
'Forever contemplate th' eternal Mind.'

E[dmund] Rack, 'The cell of contemplation, a vision'
c.141, p. 178

A1836 At once from hence my lines, and I do part
Merit of love, bestow that love on me.

[John Donne, 'An old letter']
[Crum A1835]
b.148, p. 4

A1837 At once to raise our rev'rence and delight
And his tribunal see whose cross they paint so well.

[Robert Lowth], 'The genealogy of Christ as it is
represented on the east window in Winchester
Chapel'
Poetry Box I/84

A1838 At others' wealth an envious man doth fret,
Sicilian kings, then envy never yet—

b.53, p. 67 (incomplete?)

A1839   At our creation but the word was [said]
How slight is man at what an easy [cost he's made
and lost].

[Francis Quarles, 'On man']
[Crum A1837]

b.156, p. 41 (damaged)

A1840   At Oxford there arose of late
In the clear convex of the sky.

'The contest on choosing a lady-patroness for the
High-Borlace club for the year 1730'

c.233, p. 100

A1841   At Portsmouth (Duke) I will no longer stay,
Adieu, I have no title, not a tittle.

'A dialogue between Charon, and G: Villiers, Duke of
Buckingham' [1628]
[Crum A1839]

b.200, p. 54

A1842   At Rome a time of license and of sin
What we must first give thanks and then repent.

'Upon the thanksgiving of King J[ame]s' accession
appointed at Dublin upon Shrove Tuesday'
[Crum A1840a]

fc.58, p. 106

A1843   At Saint James's yesterday,
'Tis ev'ry leaf i' th' shop.

R[obert] Shirley, 1st earl of Ferrers, 'From Boileau'

c.347, p. 88

A1844   At Saint Osyth by the mill
And grant it all in her.

[Sir Charles Hanbury Williams], 'A song' [on 'the lass
of Saint Osyth']
[Crum A1841]

c.358, p. 72

A1845   At Se'noak so famed for virginity old,
The justice desisted, and here ends my tale.

[Elizabeth Amherst], 'Sevenoaks Nunnery; to the
tune of Packington's pound' [1745]
[Crum A1844]

fc.51, p. 262

A1846   At setting day and rising morn
A heart which cannot wander.

[Allan Ramsay, in The gentle shepherd]

c.358, p. 171

A1847   At setting sun as the sweet nightingale
And constellations mark his way.

[Phanuel Bacon], 'Cantata[.] The hermit's meditation
at setting sun'

c.237, fol. 83 [i.e., 103]

A1848   At sight of me deep blush'd the lovely maid
Nor meanly joy'd to lie so ill conceal'd.

'Extract . . . Corn[elius] Gall[us] et vidi Virg: Ecl:
3:64.65'

c.81/1, no. 108

A1849   At the brow of a hill a fair shepherdess dwelt
But remember the lass of the brow of the hill.

'The lass of the hill'
[Crum A1850]

c.358, p. 106

A1850   At the clear light, which sparkleth from each taper
And lovely cadence of your charming voice.

Sir Thomas Urquhart, 'To the incomparable Aura'

fb.217, p. 105

A1851   At the close of the day, when the hamlet is still
And beauty immortal awakes from the tomb.

[James] Beattie, 'The hermit'
[Crum A1853]

fc.14/2; c.116, p. 53 (stanzas 1–4); see also 'At close . . .'.

A1852   At the corner of Wood Street when daylight
appears,
Mayst hear the thrush sing from a tree of its own.

'Poor Susan'

c.142, p. 427

A1853   At the foot of this hill,
Make the air ring with all their wild notes.

'The hermit'

Poetry Box IV/69

A1854   At the football she is so choice a wench,
To make the founding have the greater force.

Sir Thomas Urquhart, 'Of a very handsome woman's
dexterity at the football'

fb.217, p. 125

A1855   At the head of Bugg and Bunn
Ireland was lost and won.

b.208, p. 154

A1856   At the large foot of a fair hollow tree,
With peace, let tares and acorns be my food.

[Abraham Cowley], 'The country-mouse' [Horace,
satire ii.6]
[Crum A1857]

b.135, f.113v; fc.60, p. 77

A1857   At the last day, from every part the just
But one eternal holy day go on.

'Friends known in heaven'

c.244, p. 427

A1858 At the night raven's dismal voice
To the echoes from a hollow hill.

   'Chorus [2, with musical score for tenor and bass,
   from Macbeth]'
Music MS. 534

A1859 At the pastoral staff
Like the new second wife Paniarty(?).

fb.70, p. 215

A1860 At the pleasing approach of the spring,
In health, in mirth, and pleasure! | Long may she
                                                    live &c.

   'Ode on Lady Ann Hamilton's birthday'
c.241, p. 112; Poetry Box I/75

A1861 At the same time two Spartan kings were fear'd
We've now two Horaces on Arno's side.

   [Robert Merry], 'Epigram'
Greatheed Box/44

A1862 At the sheiling in the glen,
All the lads contending keen | Long have I been
                                                    lonely.

   'Perthshire airs no. 91 . . . Translation, Long have I
   been lonely to the same air'
Poetry Box VIII/70

A1863 At the silence of twilight's contemplative hour
To bear, is to conquer our fate.

   [ ] Campbell, 'On visiting a scene in Argyleshire'
c.364

A1864 At thieves I bark'd, at lovers wagg'd my tail
And thus I pleas'd both lord, and lady frail.

   'Lady's lapdog' [translation]
c.81/1, no. 208

A1865 At this glad season of the smiling year,
In glorious triumph to the realms of day.

   George Brown, 'Farewell lines addressed to Mrs.
   Garrick'
File 1927

A1866 At this sad scene, which blood must quickly stain,
For a whole hecatomb of rebels, calls.

   'On viewing the scaffold for the execution of the two
   rebel lords, viz, William Earl of Kilmarnock and
   Arthur Lord Balmerino, who were beheaded on the
   Tower Hill London on Monday August the 18 1746'
c.360/2, no. 207

At thy approach my avarice does own   A1867
Whose wealth, not love, my liberty disarms.

   'Aliter' [on Miss Delme at Tunbridge Wells 1730;
   parody of 'At thy approach my quick'ning pace . . .']
c.360/2, no. 141

At thy approach my quick'ning pulse does own   A1868
With pleasure I resign my liberty.

   'To Miss Delme writ at Tunbridge Wells 1730'
   [parodied by 'At thy approach my avarice . . .']
c.360/2, no. 140

At Thy command, our dearest Lord,   A1869
And we are waiting till he come.

   [Isaac Watts, Hymns and spiritual songs (1707),
   bk. III, Hymn 19]
c.180, p. 50

At Thy command the waters peopled were   A1870
Faultless in shape, naked, yet free from shame.

Poetry Box VI/112

At Trumpington, not far from Cambridge, stood   A1871
And learn'd in that choice school, the nunnery.

   [Thomas Betterton], 'The miller of Trumpington: or
   The reeve's tale from Chaucer'
fc.61, p. 129

At Tunbridge Wells a new England apostle   A1872
And putteth sacred shams on all but Titus.

   Sir Robert Howard, 'On Mr Hawes at Tunbridge,
   1680' [answered by 'On Tunbridge walks . . .']
b.54, p. 1133

At two afternoon for our Psyche enquire   A1873
She saves half her victuals, by feasting your ears.

   [Jonathan] Swift, 'On Psyche'
Poetry Box X/133

At Westminster warehouse are now to be sold   A1874
Be pleased to enquire of Zach'ry and Co.

   'Advertisement' [satire on Zachary Pearce, dean of
   Westminster]
   [Crum A1878]
c.150, p. 1

At Whitehall sits a High Commission   A1875
Led a much better king than you, to France.

   'On the judges going to Bristol'
   [Crum A1881]
c.570/1, p. 68

At will while fortune turns her wheel,   A1876
Content, makes any lot a prize.

   'Content'
c.83/1, no. 205; c.186, p. 46

A1877 Attempting once Eunica to salute
But die an unlamented spotless maid!

George Montagu, 'Translation of an idyllium of
Theocritus at Eton School'

fc.135, p. 13

A1878 Attend and prepare for a cargo from Dover
Whores, cuckolds and fools, bawds, bullies and
beaux, | Which nobody can deny.

'The merchants a-la-mode. To the tune of The
Com[mon]s and Peers'
[Crum A1889]

b.382(1)

A1879 Attend and you shall hear
Till the tailors were almost undone.

'Of the seven tailors'

c.158, p. vi

A1880 Attend good people, lay by scoffs and scorns
Mine only Strange-Lee and his Le-Strange.

[Robert Wild], 'The recantation of a penitent Proteus
or the changeling [as it was acted with good applause
in St. Marie's in Cambridge and St. Paul's in London,
1663] to the tune of Doctor Faustus'
[Crum A1895]

Poetry Box VIII (oversize), no. 3

A1881 Attend, my child, the mortal lay:
As others, at their mid-day height.

[Stephen Barrett], 'To my daughter on her 11th
birthday'

c.193, p. 106

A1882 Attend my soul, the early birds inspire,
As infants sleep upon their mother's breast.

'The lark'

c.244, p. 132; Poetry Box IV/28

A1883 Attend my soul the voice divine
Till heav'n complete the rapturous scene.

P[hilip] Doddridge, 'A hymn on Exod. XXXIV 6, 8
The Lord passed by before him I proclaimed the Lord
the Lord God merciful and gracious &c'

c.493, p. 37

A1884 Attend thee bold Britain, I sing of a battle
For whenever they die, they will ne'er leave their
peers.

fb.68, p. 135

A1885 Attend thou sun, be watchful ev'ry star,
The orb of beauty where you shone before.

'Amanda's birthday'

c.241, p. 111

A1886 Attend ye ever tuneful swains,
And that is Polly Willes.

c.358, p. 9

A1887 Attend, ye glad Britons, attend to my strain,
We give up at the end of the year fifty-nine.

[James Mulcaster, sr.], 'The year [17]fifty-nine. A
song'

c.118, p. 31

A1888 Attend ye nymphs and am'rous swains,
And that is Polly Spencer.

Poetry Box IV/67

A1889 Attention paid the living may have aim
Thy short-lived merits mourn, until it cease to beat.

'Miss Bel'

Diggle Box: Poetry Box XI/18

A1890 Attracted by Mattei's fame,
The muses, ten; or graces, four.

John Lockman, 'Seeing Seignora Mattei perform in
the opera of Zenobia, at the King's Theater in the
Haymarket . . . June 1758'

c.267/1, p. 111

A1891 Attune your harps to your immortal strains
She laid her burden down and smil'd and died.

William Combes, '. . . And now for the verses—I
mean lines'

c.341, p. 138

A1892 August master of the globe,
Will answer me in kind, as you did Hanger.

'Epistle from Yartie to Fr. Wollaston esqr.'

fc.51, p. 207

A1893 Aurora fair and fresh of hue
Come thou ad vitae limina. | Amen

'Of S. Mary Magdalen. July. 22'

a.30[14]

A1894 Auspicious day! the best in all the year!
But drink a jolly health to good old Puss.

'On the 30th of January' [1687]
[Crum A1921]

fb.70, p. 213

A1895 Auspicious day too long with clouds o'ercast
With cheerful rays adorn the tenth of June.

[Mrs. Christian Kerr], 'On the 10 of June. 1718'

c.102, p. 104

A1896 Auspicious genii, who reside
But cannot lull my soul to rest.

c.83/2, no. 591

A1897   Auspicious health appear'd divinely bright
Find ease in chains, or anguish in a crown.

    'On health'

c.360/1, p. 181

A1898   Auspicious sun gild the enliven'd earth
But till the sun itself that gives the day.

    [Robert Cholmeley], 'The twenty ninth of May King
    Charles' birth and return 1724'

c.190, p. 33

A1899   Author of being, source of light,
May his fame and glory last.

    S[amuel] Wesley, the elder, 'Eupolis's hymn to the
    Creator'

c.229/1, fol. 80

A1900   Autumn gives fruit, and corn makes summer fair
Spring shows us gays, fire helps cold winter's air.

b.65, p. 133

A1901   Autumn! wooed by every swain
Pleasure to the stately hall!

    F[rances] B[urney d'Arblay], 'Autumn'

c.486, fol. 22v

A1902   Av ah fait' he has taken my money away
Than if I have been seen with a blick on my face.

    'Air in a Quaker opera'

c.503, p. 54

A1903   Avaunt ye smooth-tongued flatterers of the age;
That these black patches stick upon her face.

    Lewis Griffin(?), 'A supplement to the ass's complaint:
    or the cry of [the country against ingnorant and
    scandalous ministers]' [printed 1661? (Wing G1984)]
    [Crum A1925]

b.63, p. 51

A1904   Avaunt you empiric and quacksalving gull
For men would live were they but cur'd of you.

    'To Madam Baker living at Mr Huntington's
    apothecary in Aldersgate Street' [posting address]

b.216, p. 2

A1905   Averse to all my love or muse inspir'd,
Pity my fate, but still my judgment own.

    'To Miss Sally P—s, inviting her to Cheltenham,
    where her beauty had been reflected upon'

c.221, p. 27

A1906   Awake, Æolian lyre, awake
Beneath the good how far—but far above the
great.

    [Thomas] Gray, 'Ode'

c.481, p. 304

Awake all ye dead with oh with oh
Lie two in a grave and to bed to bed.   A1907

b.213, p. 126

Awake, arise! The hour is come
And eating all that's nice, Sir.   A1908

    'A radical ballad to be sung at all radical clubs'

File 17461

Awake, awake, fair goddess of this place,
But alas! 'tis cold comfort to be lov'd in a dream.   A1909

    'A song'

b.54, p. 1162

Awake, awake see through thy curtains spread
A time, which even the God, would emulate.   A1910

    [George Daniel], 'To my muse'

b.121, fol. 51v

Awake drowsy Britons and prevent your doom
To advance her cause and the Pretender's claim.   A1911

Poetry Box x/38

Awake dull eyes, and let me see,
Be evermore adored.   A1912

    M[ary] Cornwallis, 'Hymn altered from one of
    Dorrington's meditations . . . August 12th 1795'

fc.124, p. 114

Awake from silence ev'ry voice,
And time itself shall be no more.   A1913

    'On the nativity of Christ'

c.83/1, no. 134

Awake from sleep secure, when peril doth appear,   A1914
No wisdom then to take our ease, and not the
                                   worst to fear.

c.339, p. 326

Awake my drowsy soul awake,
From these deluded eyes.   A1915

    P[hilip] Doddridge, 'Christian watchfulness in
    resisting spiritual enemies and discharging the duties
    of life. Mark XIII. 37'

c.493, p. 70

Awake my genius, view this universe
And live with him to all eternity.   A1916

    'On the proof of a God by his works of creation'

c.181, p. 49

A1917 Awake my heart, arise my tongue,
Let all thy pow'rs agree.

 [Isaac Watts, Hymns and spiritual songs (1707), bk. I, Hymn 20]

c.180, p. 41

A1918 Awake my muse and hail this blissful day
A stronger cement of their mutual love.

 J. B. D[ickinson], 'To M[artha] D[ickinson] 4. March 1788'

c.391

A1919 Awake, my muse! And strike the tuneful lyre:
And he's too bright to be beheld by thee.

 [John Jacob Oakes], 'An ode, on gunpowder treason: composed by [Abraham Oakes's] son, and given up in T[rinity] C[ollege] C[ambridge] as an exercise, 1743'

c.50, p. 66

A1920 Awake my muse, awake and sing,
Let that O God, my exit be.

 'In festum pentecostae 31e May 1691 dno die commemorati blessi mei dni Jesu mortem salva sci Dunstani'

b.127, p. 17

A1921 Awake, my St. John! Leave all meaner things
And bid self-love and social be the same.

 [Alexander] Pope, 'Amusements 1768' ['Essay on man', epistles 1–3]

c.156, p. 1

A1922 Awake (my soul) and in that incestuous bed
Conscience thy company and heaven thy end.

 [Crum A1947]

b.197, p. 217

A1923 Awake my soul, and with the sun
Praise Father, Son, and Holy Ghost.

 [Thomas Ken], 'Morning hymn'
 [Crum A1948]

c.259, p. 66; c.91, p. 344 (var.)

A1924 Awake my soul, cast off the dregs of sin,
But be presented as the purest wheat.

 'Fuge peccatum'

c.146, p. 40

A1925 Awake my soul, chase from thine eyes
In one eternal thankful song.

 [John Austin], 'Hym: 33. F[ea]st. of S[ain]ts' [Hymn xxxvi, Devotions in the ancient way of offices, 1672, p. 321]

c.178, p. 31

A1926 Awake my soul, from sleepy dreams,
Bless'd whilst you live, and happy when you die.

 'Another by the same hand' [as 'Grim death . . .']
fb.142, p. 56

A1927 Awake my soul! In hallow'd raptures raise
And sing to him who gave her first to sing.

 [Walter] Harte, 'Psalm 104'

c.244, p. 492

A1928 Awake, my soul! Lift up thine eyes,
Why should his faithful followers fear?

 [Anna Laetitia (Aikin) Barbauld], 'Hymn'

c.141, p. 154

A1929 Awake, my soul! my glory rise and sing,
Complete the bold design, and close th'
        advent'rous song.

 'Paraphrase on Mr. Crashaw's hymn to the name of Jesus'

c.167, p. 27; c.244, p. 585

A1930 Awake my soul, rise from the bed
May now and ever be.

 [John Austin], 'Hym. 15' [Hymn ii, Devotions in the ancient way of offices, 1672, p. 20]

c.178, p. 14

A1931 Awake my soul, the morning wakes,
And that to die is immense gain.

 'Morning hymn'
c.515, fol. 21v

A1932 Awake my soul your hallelujahs sing
My soul may fly, where reigns eternal day.

 'On Christmas morn'
c.186, p. 62

A1933 Awake, my verse-resounding lyre!
And shield thy country from disgrace.

 John Lockman, 'Odes. To His Grace the Duke of Buckingham, (in the country,) a little before his embarking for France . . . anno 1730'

c.267/2, p. 205; c.268 (first part), p. 115

A1934 Awake O muse; a noble theme
'Tis all that I desire.

 'Ode in praise of friendship'
c.135, p. 22

A1935 Awake O muse thy softest lyre
Happy darling boy be thine.

 [Judith (Cowper)] Madan, 'On Lysander's birthday July 1, 1724'

c.152, p. 48

A1936 Awake, poor youth, ah! Sleep not here,
The soul with guilt deform.

'To a young gentleman sleeping in church'

c.83/1, no. 23

A1937 Awake sad muse the trembling strain
And Roslin's Castle never known!

Miss [ ] Bradford, 'Song to the tune of Roslin's castle'

c.504, p. 52

A1938 Awake, sweet babe, the sun's emerging ray
A saint on earth, an angel in the sky.

[William] Broome, 'On the birthday of one 3 years old'

c.244, p. 490

A1939 Awake, ye nymphs of Avon's stream
A wreath immortal and divine.

J. Wander, 'On reading the tragedy of The regent [by Bertie Greatheed]'

File 17481

A1940 Awake ye that sleep, arise, to judgment come,
Waiting their dreadful fate, and never die.

'A dialogue between an angel and a man at his resurrection'

c.244, p. 221

A1941 Awake you fairest thing in nature
You are fit for some lover's arms.

'A song'

c.374

A1942 Away, away,
Have not disdain'd to wear the horn.

[Henry Carey], 'Song 130'
[Crum A1961]

c.555, p. 185 (stanzas 1–2)

A1943 Away dark thoughts. Awake my joys
My Christ is all in all.

'A song of praise for the birth of Christ'

a.3, fol. 67

A1944 Away; | Fond man, thy brain is sick, thy quill doth stray;
And yet retain, the liberty, thy muse would choose.

[George Daniel]

b.121, fol. 74

A1945 Away; let naught to love displeasing,
And I'll go wooing wi' my boys.

'A translation of a poem wrote in the ancient British tongue' [sometimes attr. Thomas Percy or John Gilbert Cooper]

c.244, p. 189 (attr. [ ] Lewis); c.83/1, no. 182; c.90; fc.132/1, p. 175; Poetry Box I/97

A1946 Away officious flutt'ring string,
Fiend transform'd to a seraphim.

'Meditations for a lady at her looking glass'

c.83/2, no. 292

A1947 Away those airy thoughts no more come here
As John or Joseph thou mayst die.

[Thomas Gurney], 'An elegiac poem on the death of his intimate friend Mr. Tho: Davis late of Newport—Pagnal who died anno. 1733. Sep. 23d. Aged 35 years . . . John died 1721 . . . Joseph—1739'

c.213

A1948 Away thou changeling motley humorist
And constantly awhile must keep his bed.

[John Donne], 'Satira prima'
[Crum A1969]

b.114, p. 1; b.148, p. 10

A1949 Away with all those fruitless tears
And warm his hands contented by their flame.

[Robert Cholmeley], 'Casimire ode 2: libs. Ad Aurelium lycum'

c.190, p. 100

A1950 Away with jealousy, and strife:
Must have to do with ev'rybody.

Sir Thomas Urquhart, 'A friendly advice to a suspicious merchant not to be offended at his wife's licentiousness'

fb.217, p. 199

A1951 Away with the causes of riches, and cares,
And makes ev'ry day both happy, and long.

'The merry prince'

fb.107, p. 24

A1952 Away, ye ballad singers!
Shall we then aid this stroller? | Hiss away.

John Lockman, 'No Italian strollers: a new British chorus—the tune, A very pretty fancy, a [ ] gallant show . . . Nov. 1749'

c.267/2, p. 161

A1953   Aw'd and confounded I approach you here,
        We skulk beneath them in security.

    Master Soame, 'An epilogue written and spoke by . . .
    after a play performed by the gentlemen of the
    Grammar School at the Assembly Room in Christmas
    1789'

    c.130, p. 66

A1954   Awful hero, Marlb'ro', rise:
        Half an angel; man no more.

    [Leonard Welsted], 'The genius. An ode written in
    1717, on occasion of the Duke of Marlborough's
    lethargy' [enclosed in a letter to William Cowper, 1st
    earl of Cowper, 5 Aug. 1718]

    File 17190 (attr. John Hughes)

A1955   Awhile O! linger sacred shade!
        Respects the son, it soothes in vain.

    Horace Walpole, 4th earl of Orford, [elegy on Lady
    Mary (Lepell) Hervey, widow of John Lord Hervey,
    d. 2 Sept. 1768]

    File 4043

Awoke to being by the vig'rous ray,   A1956
Bedropt with sapphire, emerald and gold.

    'The summer day'

c.83/3, no. 947

Ay me (distressed wight) what shall I do: A1957
Than to be proud in mind and haughty-hearted.

    'Conscience her complaint'

c.339, p. 295

Ayliffe and Fox when called in days of old,   A1958
And like to Bute in all a first-rate patriot shines.

    [John?] Wilkes

Spence Papers, folder 113

B

B0001 Bacchus and the queen of love,
Gentler Venus will incline.

[William Popple, trans.], '[Horace] book 1st. ode 19th.
On Glycera'
fc.104/2, p. 58

B0002 Bacchus assist us to sing thy great glory
And sober souls at our joys be amazed.

'Song 226'
c.555, p. 357

B0003 Bacchus deity, deity divine,
Bacchus rules the human frame.

'Song 113'
c.555, p. 165

B0004 Bacchus, god of mortal pleasure,
After death no drinking's found.

'Song 56'
c.555, p. 84

B0005 Bacchus god of pleasing drinking:
Whom this fox will soon remove.

[Phanuel Bacon], 'A song'
c.237, fol. 37

B0006 Bacchus Iacchus fill our brains
'Tis wine pure wine | Therefore fill us.

[Aurelian Townshend], 'Songs [8]'
[Crum B6, anon.]
b.356, p. 281

B0007 Bacchus one day gaily striding,
He who drinks not, lives in vain!

'Song 150'
c.555, p. 208

B0008 Bacchus to give the toping world surprise,
Pray copy Bob in measure and attendance.

'Universal spectator: on a table[t] in the churchyard,
behind the Boar's Head Tavern in Eastcheap. Here
lieth the body of Robert Preston, late drawer at
the . . . tavern . . . who departed this life March 16.
anno dom. 1730. aged 27 years'
fc.24, p. 76; c.111, p. 167

B0009 Backed with confederate force the Austrian goes,
You're king of Spain as A[nne] is Q[ueen] of
France.

'On the King of Spain' [on Queen Anne's sending
assistance to the Archduke, later Charles III of Spain,
1703–4]
[Crum B8; *POAS* VI.611]
c.111, p. 79; Poetry Box IV/119

B0010 Bad dreams are good: good dreams are bad;
therefore,
Their ills I love: their goodness I deplore.

Sir Thomas Urquhart, 'One's opinion of dreams'
fb.217, p. 94

B0011 Bad friendship must be eschewed [?] [?] lest we
Both lose a friend, and gain an enemy.

[Sir Thomas Urquhart], 'The great wariness that is to
be used in shaking of an unworthy friend'
fb.217, p. 526

B0012 Bad verse, that vile excrescence of the head,
So dull an animal's a dun.

[Isaac Freeman], 'Extempore verses on my having no
money'
fc.105

B0013 Badger, around thy humble cot,
With pleasure be obey'd.

[Charles Burney, the younger], 'To Mr. Badger'
c.37, p. 12

B0014 Ballooe my boy, lie still and sleep,
And sleep securely, heart, alone. | Ballooe, ballooe,
&c.

'Ballooe'
b.200, p. 363

B0015 Barbados sugar is most pleasant tasted
Which spirit leads them to the marriage bed.

Jeremy Cliff, 'The nature and virtues of each
ingredient is prescribed . . . in the aforegoing sack
posset' ['From famed Barbados . . .']
c.158, p. 360

B0016 Barbarian—dost not see
You wish to see me die.

[John Black]

fc.107, p. 80, p. 81 (var.)

B0017 Bards say, that when the Phoenix dies,
Mortals can wish, or gods bestow.

John Lockman, 'Writ under the new orchestra, in
Vauxhall Gardens . . . July 1754'

c.267/1, p. 136

B0018 Base-born child of pale-ey'd want,
None but jollity, and me.

'Ode to avarice'

c.241, p. 20

B0019 Base metal hanger by thy master's thigh,
Or I'll ne'er draw thee but against a post.

'A poor prick cursed' [attr. John Wilmot, 2nd earl of
Rochester]
[Crum B32]

b.54, p. 1199

B0020 Basil Fitzherbert did Jane Cotton wed
By all your actions confirm it true.

[Sir Aston Cokayne], 'To Mr Basil Fitzherbert of
Norbury'

b.275, p. 88

B0021 Batter'd with wear in many a hard campaign,
None can be happy but the good and wise.

'Spoken by Mr. Havard on leaving the stage'

c.83/3, no. 953

B0022 Bavius attacks my verse, with foul dispraise,
Proceed, and thou'lt a new Longinus rise.

John Lockman, 'To one Horse-Tail, (a pretended
friend,) who permitted my ode, on the crushing of the
rebellion in 1745, to be lampooned, and, at the same
time, applauded some very contemptible lines . . .
1747'

c.267/1, p. 17

B0023 Bawds, fiddlers, whores, buffoons of the age
Smirk Darnell shall be judge in this.

H[enry] H[igden], 'The second satire of the first book
of Horace made English'
[Crum B35]

File 17462

B0024 Be amiabl' if you'd be lov'd b'each one
But love all, if you would be lov'd by none.

Sir Thomas Urquhart, 'A secret concerning love and
hatred'

fb.217, p. 234

B0025 Be calm, my Delius, and serene,
Never!—never more!

[John Howe?], 'Horace. B. 2. Ode 3'

c.94

B0026 Be careful still to guard thy soul from wrong,
And let thy thought prevent thy hand and tongue.

c.549, p. 32

B0027 Be cautious always of a friend's pretense;
Or he's a rival, who was once a friend.

[Charles Earle?], 'Prudent advice'

c.376

B0028 Be cautious Madam, how you thus provoke
The fate may be your own another day.

'The caution' [to the Duchess of Marlborough, who
cut down an oak planted by Charles II]

c.570/1, p. 63

B0029 Be dumb ye beggars of the rhyming trade
And makes the world but her periphrasis.

[John Cleveland], 'The hecatomb'

b.93, p. 37

B0030 Be dumb ye infant chimes; thump not the metal
We'll all be glad (great Tom) to see thee hang'd.

[Richard Corbett], 'On the great bell of Christ
Church'
[Crum B43]

b.62, p. 55; b.200, p. 16 (attr. Jer. Terrent); b.205, fol. 32r

B0031 Be frugal ye wives, live in silence, and love,
And the tortoise, she's dwelling at home.

'Distich. Wrote under the figure of a woman standing
upon a tortoise, a bunch of keys in her right hand, the
forefinger of her left hand upon her lips, and a dove
upon her shoulder . . . translations [5]'

c.81/1, no. 70

B0032 Be hush'd, my griefs, 'tis His almighty will,
Just are thy ways, thou King of saints, and true.

'On the divine veracity'

c.83/2, no. 568; c.163, p. 23

B0033 Be hush[ed] my soul! For heaven prepare,
When distant climes shall hear our woe.

'The captive[.] Supposed to be written by the queen of
France, in the Temple, after the execution of the 16'

c.83/2, no. 375

B0034 Be Isr'el's God exalted high,
To peace and righteousness.

'The same [the Song of Zacharias]—another meter'

c.264/3, p. 125

B0035 Be it O science! Radiant maid,
And justly boast the glorious name.

[John Lockman], 'Stanzas'
c.268 (first part), p. 40

B0036 Be kind my dear Chloe, let's kiss and let's—love
When he had no shame, and his Eve had no—fear.

Lady [Catherine] Walpole and Sir William Young,
'Bouts-rimes given to Sir William Young by Lady
Walpole' [and filled up by him]
c.176, p. 39; c.360/1, p. 149

B0037 Be kind my dear Rosania, though 'tis fain
We either can enjoy, or will despise.

[Katherine Philips], 'Invitation to the country'
b.118, p. 78; see also 'A safe retirement . . .'.

B0038 Be kind to my remains and O defend,
And whom it most afflicts, it most rewards.

'Epitaph'
c.481, p. 275

B0039 Be mine, only mine; take care
They're serpents all, and thou the tempted Eve.

c.549, p. 15

B0040 Be mine simplicity; to know
Derives its source from her alone.

c.532

B0041 Be not curious, to amaze
To have lived well, or done amiss.

'Relatory to the third emblem'
c.189, p. 83

B0042 Be not deceiv'd dull world he is not dead
Recant; or else 'tis you, not he is dead.

[George Daniel], 'Upon Ben: Jonson's book'
b.121, fol. 51

B0043 Be not deceived; I know it by my own;
I could lie warmer, in a lesser room.

[George Daniel]
b.121, fol. 82

B0044 Be not from death by any means a stranger
The course of all your life will be the sweeter.

[Sir Thomas Urquhart], 'That to employ our thoughts
on the study of mortality, and frailty of our nature is a
profitable and necessary speculation'
fb.217, p. 511

Be not impos'd upon by fashion's roar,
—Judge by other people's eyes.   B0045

John Wolcot ('Peter Pindar'), 'Fashion . . . 11th ode
([17]82)'
c.355, p. 93

Be not in haste to handle pen and ink!
Before you write, be sure you learn to think.   B0046

[Charles Earle?], 'Boileau's advice to scribblers'
c.376

Be not proud pretty one, for I must love thee,
Sits Cupid now enthron'd by pains deriding.   B0047

[William Lawes], 'The proud pretty one' [a glee]
[Crum B67a]
fb.107, p. 33

Be not puff'd up with knighthood, friend of mine,
Thou that are now King Phyz, was't once King Ush.   B0048

[Thomas Brown], 'On Sr. R—d Bl—— being
knighted'
fc.24, p. 24

Be not too forward, but do wisely frame
With their fair game, know fortune ever strays.   B0049

[Francis] Quarles(?), 'Backgammon—Quarles'
emblems'
c.360/3, no. 177

Be not too soon a friend, too kind too coy,
The less will be your grief the more your joy.   B0050

b.197, p. 38

Be not too zealous; I ere this have seen
Who builds on sands, has no safe residence.   B0051

[George Daniel]
b.121, fol. 71

'Be quiet—don't Sir', cried a prude,
She meant to say 'Sir, don't be quiet.'   B0052

'Epigram'
c.81/2, no. 562

Be quiet or I'll straight be gone
Speak low, if you'd enjoy.   B0053

L[ord] E., 'Another [riddle]'
Poetry Box VII/47

Be quiet Sir! begone I pray!
But—are you sure you shut the door.   B0054

'The struggle'
c.81/1, no. 177

B0055 Be richly glad since God has blest thee lo
And fate has in thy name inscrib'd it so.

> [Sir Philip Wodehouse], 'Upon [Sir Hugh Windham's]
> second daughter [Rachel Digby] married to Ld.
> Digby'
>
> b.131, back (no. 39)

B0056 Be silent ye still music of the spheres
To die with such an anthem o'er my tomb.

> [William Strode], 'On a gentlewoman that played on a
> lute'
> [Crum B79]
>
> b.205, fol. 34r; b.200, p. 246

B0057 Be soft ye winds be calm ye seas
Your eyes bring day your absence night.

> Poetry Box VII/39, p. 6

B0058 Be still, my fears, suggest no false alarms;
And lends the quick'ning beam to cheer the arts of
peace.

> Dr. [ ] Hurd, 'Ode to peace'
>
> c.83/3, no. 752

B0059 Be still my soul, let not these nations' storms
Who can my actions as well guide as see.

> [Sir Richard Bulstrode?], 'Good thoughts in bad
> times'
>
> fb.88, p. 114

B0060 Be still nor anxious thoughts employ,
And leaves deception to her fools.

> 'Obedience'
>
> c.83/2, no. 326

B0061 Be still O ye winds and attentive ye swains,
And learn to be happy from Colin and me.

> 'Colin and Phoebe'
> [Crum B80]
>
> c.358, p. 178

B0062 Be still, ye throbs that agitate my breast
Unfeigned happiness to taste with you.

> [Frederick Dickinson? or Frances Milner?], 'By the
> same in answer' [to 'Haste, my lov'd Frances . . .']
>
> c.391, p. 37

B0063 Be sure if any know our town
Soon as Will brought him to't he died.

> 'A tale'
>
> c.172, p. 12

B0064 Be 't spoke with all submission
And thou shalt be, my best-lov'd spouse.

> 'The husband's advice to his learned wife. Imitated
> from Molière'
>
> fc.51, p. 255

B0065 Be this my guide thro' life's uncertain round
In everlasting triumph to the skies.

> 'Written by a young lady on a blank leaf the beginning
> of her Bible'
>
> c.83/2, no. 617

B0066 Be this your leading law, to worship God,
Where wisdom joys eternally with love.

> 'The golden verses of Pythagoras modernized'
>
> fc.53, p. 49

B0067 Be thou, O Lord, my refuge in distress,
The God of Jacob thy retreat and guard.

> [Thomas Hull], 'For a Saturday's paper in the
> Middlesex journal. Paraphrase on Psalm 46'
>
> c.528/29

B0068 Be thou to others kind and true,
Whate'er you would not take again.

> 'Our Savior's golden rule . . . Lyncup Hill 25th Aug.
> [17]82'
>
> c.93

B0069 Be wise as Somerset, as Somers brave
Will make thee for an able statesman fit.

> [Joseph Browne], 'The country parson's advice to the
> Lord Keeper [William] Cowper' [Browne was
> pilloried for this; 1706]
> [Crum B94; POAS VII.156]
>
> b.90, p. 2; c.171, p. 13; fc.24, p. 19; fc.73

B0070 Be wise, fair toasts, nor overrate the charms,
Must condescend to bless a groom at last.

> [David Stokes], 'On Belinda marrying Mr. Knapp'
>
> c.233, p. 43

B0071 Be with me Lord where'er I go
Be spent and ended to thy praise.

> 'Hymn 4th'
>
> c.562, p. 4

B0072 Bear leave my master's room for Charles his wain
Above all nectar Jove delights in bear.

> 'Ursa major' [answered by 'Are you there with your
> bears . . .']
>
> b.356, p. 109

B0073 Bear me, Faunus, gentle god,
Let me never wake again.

    'Song'

c.241, p. 33

B0074 Bear me hence, ye pitying pow'rs,
How, alas! I lov'd too well.

    'The wish'

c.83/1, no. 93

B0075 Bear me, ye friendly powers, to gentle scenes
And peaceful olives flourish'd from the wound.

    [William] Broome, 'On solitude'

c.244, p. 488; c.83/3, no. 981 (var.)

B0076 Bear me, ye propitious powers,
Avernus, Styx, and Phlegathon. | Give. . . .

    B[eaupré] Bell, 'Verses imitated from Aratus'

c.229/1, fol. 54v (incomplete)

B0077 Bear patiently with Master Bel's | Miscarriage;
The moon descended to the hells | Of marriage.

    Sir Thomas Urquhart, 'A counsel to the wife of one
    Master Bel, who was a very bad husband'

fb.217, p. 308

B0078 Bear up Sarissa thro' the ruffling storms
All join'd by pow'r divine and every link is love.

    [Isaac] Watts, 'An epistle to Sarissa'

c.244, p. 305

B0079 Beasts spoke of old and in the golden time,
And then shall kindly re-embrace each other.

    [Sir Thomas Urquhart], 'Of Master Fox and Mistress
    Lamb a pair of sincerely constant mutual lovers'

fb.217, p. 388

B0080 Beat on proud billows, Boreas blow,
My King can only captivate my mind.

    [Sir Roger L'Estrange], 'Loyalty confined'
    [Crum B100]

b.63, p. 72 (attr. Hamon L'Estrange); b.104, p. 102 (var.);
b.111, p. 69 (with two more stanzas); c.223, p. 97 ('Great
[sic] on . . .'); fb.108, p. 311 (with seven more stanzas);
Poetry Box VII/40 (with two more stanzas)

B0081 Beat up a drum
Frolic for a new.

    'A Christmas carol'
    [Crum B101]

b.356, p. 121

B0082 Beaufront a fair extensive view commands,
Till on the 'gulfing German ocean toss'd.

    [Thomas] Oliver, 'On Beaufront Hall'

c.93

B0083 Beauteous handmaid of the spring,
Thy sweets, most worthy of Jove's cup.

    George Montagu, 'On a violet an anacreontic'

fc.135, p. 5

B0084 Beautiful Venus, come, descend from thy throne,
With Chloe the nights are fine days!

    J. C., 'Zelis in the bath. A poem in four songs. 1789'

c.168, p. 1

B0085 Beauty alone, can make a sovereign
Love is a powerful scepter of command.

    [Sir Philip Wodehouse], 'Helen Gournay O Helen
    reign'

b.131, back (no. 63)

B0086 Beauty and humor are great names and they
Humor may stick upon her innocent.

    [Sir Aston Cokayne], 'Of beauty, and humor'

b.275, p. 28 (incomplete)

B0087 Beauty at length resigns her charms
May he be vig'rous still and she be fair.

    T[homas] H[olland], of Jesus College, Oxford

c.233, p. 65

B0088 Beauty complete, and majesty divine
Thou, in an infinite degree dost claim.

    [Elizabeth (Singer) Rowe], 'On the works of creation'

c.83/2, no. 593; fc.132/1, p. 46 (var.)

B0089 Beauty divine in nature's heav'nly charms
And puts it out o'th' lover's pow'r to miss—tho'— |
                       Love be blind.

    [Maurice Johnson], 'Three triplets from the French of
    Mons. Voiture'

c.229/2, fol. 8v

B0090 Beauty is subject unto age
May not be young again.

    'Roman hand'

b.234, p. 5

B0091 Beauty itself entire results from all
When from a brooch of stars springs forth thy light.

    [Sir Philip Wodehouse], 'Upon Pulchritudo et ex
    plurium . . .'

b.131, p. 6

B0092 Beauty itself lies here, in whom alone
Nature despairs, because her pattern's gone.

    T[homas] Randolph, 'Her epitaph' [Lady Venetia
    Digby]

b.54, p. 932

B0093 Beauty—let ornaments, and arts of dress
Waving, the sport of every idle wind.

'Ode to an accomplished beauty'
c.136, p. 30

B0094 Beauty like ice our footing doth betray
Who can tread safe on this most slippery way.

'On beauty'
[Crum B115]
Poetry Box VII/5 (incomplete)

B0095 Beauty no longer shall suffer eclipse,
And a vizard excommunication.

'The law hater'
fb.107, p. 18

B0096 Beauty of celestial frame
But of beauty had its birth.

'The beauties of nature an ode'
c.83/3, no. 1029

B0097 Beauty thou art but sand-dust sprinkled over
Whose walls are paper whose foundation sand!

b.208, p. 58

B0098 Beauty, thou wild fantastic ape,
Than murth'rer which hast kill'd, and devil which
would damn me.

A[braham] C[owley], 'On beauty'
c.258

B0099 Beauty was wont to dazzle and surprise,
He spoke: and light once more from chaos sprung.

'To Sir Harry Beaumont [i.e., Joseph Spence] on his
dialogue on beauty'
c.360/3, no. 197

B0100 Beauty when blest with wit was form'd to please
Said Betty Careless, and he answered, she.

[Robert Cholmeley], 'Wit and beauty. to Betty
Careless. An acrostic'
c.190, p. 154

B0101 Beauty when it's loose desires
Not our love, but our compassion.

c.549, p. 88

B0102 Beauty's a thief—though parties robb'd, I guess,
A sober one, in her mild influence.

[Sir Philip Wodehouse], 'Sarah Roberts (wife to the
Ld Roberts' son . . .)'
b.131, back (no. 46)

B0103 Beauty's a throne true gallants may adore
Not to adorn thy head, but joy thy heart.

[Sir Philip Wodehouse], 'Upon my fair kinswoman
Dorothy Heron . . .'
b.131, back (no. 109)

B0104 Beauty's but bare opinion white and red
[And] what would fright [ ] [her] [they] count
[her] fair.

'De forma'
b.205, fol. 16r

B0105 Beauty's mirror, nature's boast,
Exactly tun'd in unison.

[Robert Cholmeley], 'Nanny jealous'
c.190, p. 189

B0106 Because by them I have offended Thee
Then grant me Lord a place in heav'n with Thee.

Sir John Strangways
b.304, p. 47

B0107 Because excess sometimes gives spoil and pain,
The mean prefer before immoderate gain.

c.339, p. 311

B0108 Because I fear my fate is not so good
Whilst here you live in the right road to Heaven.

[Sir Aston Cokayne], 'To my daughter Mary'
b.275, p. 89

B0109 Because I have no better gift, therefore,
You gave m' yourself: yourself I render, adieu.

Sir Thomas Urquhart, 'A self-lover on New Year's
Day propines a friend of his, thus'
fb.217, p. 330

B0110 Because one lovely boy your eyes did enter:
Another issu'd at a lower center.

Sir Thomas Urquhart, 'To a certain gentlewoman,
concerning Cupid, and a newborn babe of hers'
fb.217, p. 42

B0111 Because she cannot number thousands, even
Resist my way, or make me love her less.

[Sir Aston Cokayne], 'To be added before one of my
love elegies'
b.275, p. 109

B0112 Because she disesteems
T'enjoy the choicest beauties.

Sir Thomas Urquhart, 'The most expedient way in
some men's opinion, that can be made use of, for the
gaining of a gentlewoman's favor to a certain
freshwater wooer'
fb.217, p. 106

B0113 Because the sun, the fourth day was created:
Amongst the planets he's so situated.

> Sir Thomas Urquhart, 'Of the sun concerning his
> origin, and place'

fb.217, p. 305

B0114 Before a circle let appear,
You'll quickly see what conquers men.

> 'Rebus'

Diggle Box: Poetry Box XI/71

B0115 Before ambition touch'd the poison'd heart
Of beau and bigot a promiscuous share.

> Charles Tooke, 'The state of nature'

fc.60, p. 71

B0116 Before an organ rais'd this church's fame,
Some think 'tis heaven: but most conclude—the ear.

> John Lockman, 'On the first setting up of an organ in
> Covent Garden church . . . 1728'

c.267/1, p. 319

B0117 Before creating nature will'd
Read and you have me for your pains.

> 'A riddle [on nothing] by a young lady'
> [Crum B139]

c.116, p. 39; c.360/1, p. 45; Diggle Box: Poetry Box XI/71

B0118 Before his Lordship Caius bows
Who knelt a deacon, rose a priest!

> Charles Atherton Allnutt, 'Ordination—a satire'

c.112, p. 178

B0119 Before I leave these sweet, these charming bow'rs
And recommends these verses to the fire.

fc.40

B0120 Before I sigh my last gasp let me breathe
T'invent and practice this one way to annihilate all
three.

> J[ohn] D[onne], 'The will'
> [Crum B143]

b.148, p. 52; b.114, p. 200 ('breathe my last gasp'); b.150,
p. 197

B0121 Before the city, boys, and blooming youth
Launch the tough javelin, with the dart and shaft.

> [Joseph] Trapp

fc.14/10

B0122 Before the conquest many years revolved
Lancaster's marches Arundel and Westmorland.

> William Peeris, [metrical history of the Percy family]

fa.19, fol. 42

B0123 Before the end of Jason's reign
And Anjou shall to Gaul again.

> 'Another [prophecy]' [dated 1704]

c.111, p. 80

B0124 Before the fountains did with water flow
And as the sinner justice shock him down.

> [Thomas Gurney], 'On the person of the mediator'

c.213

B0125 Before the noose what deities you are
Ande good as angels when they succor bring.

> 'What woman is before matrimony'

Poetry Box VI/53

B0126 Before the starry threshold of Jove's court
Heav'n itself would stoop to her.

> John Milton, 'A masque [Comus] presented at Ludlow
> Castle, 1634 before the Earl of Bridgewater then
> president of Wales . . . 1658'

b.63, p. 197

B0127 Before the urchin well could go
And let her prison be my arms!

> [Charles Windham, 2nd earl of Egremont], 'The fair
> thief'

c.546, p. 5; see also 'I tell with equal truth . . .'.

B0128 Before Thy awful throne
Fat hecatombs shall slay.

> [Sir William Trumbull], 'Ps[alm] 51'

Trumbull Box: Poetry Box XIII/8, 9

B0129 Before we poll the town I wish to sound
Bright as the phoenix, from his burning bed.

> [Frederick] Pilon, 'Prologue to The humors of an
> election written by Pilon and spoken by Mr. Wilson'

c.115

B0130 Before your eyes Duns Scotus see,
Nor leave your food for learning's sake.

> 'Duns Scotus his hibernaculum'

fc.124, p. 53

B0131 Begin, my lyre, the great Creator's praise,
Th'harmonious discourse which it strives to praise.

> [Joseph] Trapp, 'Psalm 104th. Paraphrased by . . .'

c.244, p. 124

B0132 Begin, my muse! the grateful lay,
A friend to virtue, and to me.

> 'To Athenia. 1753'

c.238, p. 59

B0133 Begin my muse the soft-inspiring song,
With whom I'd choose to live, with whom to die.

    'In praise of the amiable Miss M[ar]y Sh[e]lt[o]n'

c.93

B0134 Begin sweet muse, inspire a tuneful swain,
Lest the horn'd he-goat spoil your wanton play.

    [ ] C., 'The philosopher no. 1 A continuation and
    conclusion of the idyllium [of Theocritus]'

c.368, p. 42; see also 'Thro' the tall pine . . .'.

B0135 Begin the nine immortally rehearse
No beauties never resigned with greater sway.

    'A copy of verses on the beauties of Stepney and Mile
    End' [cf. 'From Troy Novant's . . .' and 'Who in this
    frantic strain . . .']

    c.162, p. 14

B0136 Begone, dull care! without delay,
These are the blessings from above.

    'Song 138'

c.555, p. 190

B0137 Begone thou fatal fiery fever
Do never wake again.

    [Crum B183]

Poetry Box VI/20

B0138 Begone, vain Muse, thy fruitless plaints give o'er,
Too true, thou say'st, then must I bid farewell!

    'On the much lamented death of a father, by his very
    mournful and only daughter in the seventeenth year of
    her age'

    c.139, p. 417

B0139 Begone vain world my heart resign,
To find my all my heaven in thee.

    'Hymn 7th'

c.562, p. 8

B0140 Begone, ye critics, and restrain your spite;
Since 'tis enough we find it so in you.

    [Alexander Pope], 'To the author of a poem entitled
    Successio'

    c.531

B0141 Begone, ye sighs! Begone, ye tears!
While you with all your wisdom live in pain.

    [William Walsh], 'The reconcilement'

    c.223, p. 67

B0142 Begone you slaves, you idle vermin go,
A convert free from malice and from pride.

    [Wentworth Dillon], 4th earl of Roscommon, 'On
    Mr. Dryden's Religio laici'

    c.351, p. 54

B0143 Begot by butchers but by bishops bred
How high his honor holds his haughty head.

    'On Cardinal Wolsey'

c.113/2

B0144 Behavior is the garment of the mind
And o'er deformity to cast a blind.

    [Sir Philip Wodehouse], 'Behavior—a sally according
    to Fr. Bacon'

b.131, p. 23

B0145 Behind an unfrequented glade
And knaves and prudes are six times married.

    Matthew Prior, 'The turtle and sparrow'

c.150, p. 79

B0146 Behind this brazen plate these ashes lie
Their rays shall burn without comsumption.

    'An epitaph'

b.205, fol. 59v

B0147 Behold a bird's nest!
Could compass such another?

    'Bird's nest'

c.81/2, no. 578

B0148 Behold a wonder such as hath not been
For I'm resolved that mine shall teach me wit.

    'A wonder'
    [Crum B196]

b.114, p. 230; b.197, p. 33

B0149 Behold, and look away your low despair!
Nor is their music, nor their plaint in vain.

    'On birds'

c.83/2, no. 507

B0150 Behold! behold! What wondrous love
Even most unspottedly.

c.124, no. 5

B0151 Behold, by undiscerning fate,
The roses fade, the lilies die.

    Jos[eph] Thurston, 'On a lady dangerously sick'

c.244, p. 570

B0152 Behold delightful spring resumes her reign
And views with heartfelt joy the verdant scene.

    F[rances] B[urney d'Arblay], 'Pastoral poetry. Spring'

c.486, fol. 21v

B0153 Behold great Timbertoe—illustrious name,
More with one foot, than others can with two.

    'On a dancer who had but one leg—1752'

c.360/3, no. 209

B0154   Behold, he comes to make thy people groan,
To stem by force, his madness and despair.

> 'Pasquin to the Queen [Anne]'s statue at St. Pauls,
> during the procession' [20 Jan. 1714/15]
> [Crum B202; *POAS* VII.619]
>
> fc.58, p. 118; b.382(3) (incomplete); c.570/1, p. 66

B0155   Behold, his age of sorrow past,
Forget the pangs they bade thee feel.

> 'Written on the grave of a beggar'
>
> c.83/3, no. 838

B0156   Behold his tomb, who bravely helpt to save
Forgot, or cloth'd with general infamy.

> 'An epitaph on Mr. William Bedloe'
>
> c.244, p. 284

B0157   Behold how papal Wright with lordly pride
At once to charm the ear and mend the heart.

> [Sir James Baker?], 'Some verses made on the
> dissenting ministers' [1736]
> [Crum B211]
>
> c.186, p. 84

B0158   Behold in less than half a span
Truth's champion, and the c[h]urch's glory.

> 'On the death of Doctor John Reignolds'
>
> c.548

B0159   Behold my Edward's form confest
And raise to thee my song.

> Charles Burney, the younger, 'Ode, written on the
> back of a friend's picture [painted by himself] . . .
> June 21. 1778'
>
> c.35, p. 23

B0160   Behold, my fair, whene'er we rove,
And screen me from the ills of life.

> S[amuel] Johnson, 'The first of November or the
> winter's walk'
>
> c.83/1, no. 162; c.90

B0161   Behold my soul with awe profound
Come death and bear our souls away.

> T[homas] S[tevens]
>
> c.259, p. 143

B0162   Behold now give heed such as be
His blessing, mercy, and favor.

> 'An exhortation unto the praise of God to be sung
> before evening prayer . . .'
> [Crum B216]
>
> a.3, fol. 151

B0163   Behold (O Lord) thy servant offers thee
The precious incense to be cast away.

> H[enry] C[olman], [poem in shape of an altar]
> [Crum B221]
>
> b.2, p. 2

B0164   Behold, O Lord, with pitying eye
And thro' his blood we hope relief.

> Charles Atherton Allnutt, 'Collect for the fourth
> Sunday in Advent'
>
> c.112, p. 55

B0165   Behold our crimes, ye foreign shores and see
God may with thunder strike the usurper down.

> 'A hymn on the 20. of Jan.' [anniversary of Charles I's
> trial]
> [Crum B223]
>
> c.570/1, p. 50

B0166   Behold our don in all his sprightly airs
With [?] empty drawers and gilded words.

> [Thomas Gurney], 'The reading don'
>
> c.213

B0167   Behold our God! He owns the name
Thine empire and thy name shall cease.

> P[hilip] Doddridge, 'Rejoicing in God as our salvation
> from Is: XXV. 9'
>
> c.493, p. 51

B0168   Behold, our God with anxious care
Shall shout with Tommy Yerrow.

> Charles Atherton Allnutt, 'The subject of the
> following lines (Tommy Yerrow) was born a shapeless
> mass of human nature, afflicted with violent
> contortions of his limbs &c. but he possessed the
> grace of God in a miraculous degree'
>
> c.112, p. 172

B0169   Behold our sov'reign lord completely blest
What must the loss of such a princess be.

> [epitaph on Queen Caroline, d. 20 Nov. 1737]
>
> fb.142, p. 65

B0170   Behold proud, tawdry antic drama tread;
And cry—oh never was distress so deep!

> John Lockman, 'The stage wonders: a poem . . . These
> lines, writ in 1732, endeavored to point out one of the
> great improvements then naturally expected to be
> made, in dramatic competitions; from the laudable
> encouragement given to pantomime entertainments'
>
> c.267/3, p. 385; c.268 (first part), p. 153

B0171 Behold! Round Johnson's honor'd urn
Heav'n claim'd him, and he ceas'd to live.

> Will[ia]m Jackson, 'On Maur[ice] Johnson esq: who
> died aged 86 merely by a decay of nature'

c.229/1, fol. 100

B0172 Behold saith Jesus at the door
And will your grief redress.

> [Mary Pluret], 'Another [poem written on waste
> paper]'

c.354

B0173 Behold Soracte cover'd o'er with snow,
Or what her yielding fingers scarcely hold.

> [William Mills], 'Odes of Horace translated. Book I.
> Ode IX. To Thaliarchus'

c.472, p. 22

B0174 Behold; strong signs, sad tokens shall forerun
They prosper not, their labor is in vain.

> [William Sandys?], 'Signs of the time to come Esdras
> 2: chap: 5: to ver. 13'

b.230, p. 89

B0175 Behold that tree, in autumn's dim decay,
Shivering they cling to life, and fear to fall!

> [Anna] Seward, 'Sonnet'

c.83/3, no. 1067

B0176 Behold the amazing sight!
To thy triumphant throne.

> P[hilip] Doddridge, 'The soul attracted to a crucified
> Savior from Jer. XII 32'

c.493, p. 28

B0177 Behold the awful scene and tell
And with thy train at last appear.

> T[homas] S[tevens], 'Rev[elatio]n 21.8'

c.259, p. 138

B0178 Behold the blind their sight receive!
Which bear credentials so divine.

> [Isaac Watts, Hymns and spiritual songs (1707), bk. II,
> Hymn 137]

c.180, p. 14

B0179 Behold the end ere thou began
And life shall spring where death hath mowers.

fb.9, fol. 30v

B0180 Behold the father is the daughter's son
Et memor mortis.

> [Robert Southwell], 'Of Christ'
> [Crum B232 (var.)]

b.284, p. 76

B0181 Behold the genuine bard whose hallow'd lyre
And moral softness to the glowing heart.

> [William Hayley], 'New inscription for the portrait of
> Cowper'

File 6954

B0182 Behold the glass the gospel leaves
To all the glare of noon.

> P[hilip] Doddridge, 'Of looking in the perfect law of
> liberty and continuing in it from Jam: I.25'

c.493, p. 26

B0183 Behold the glories of the lamb
And bring the promis'd hour!

> [Isaac Watts, Hymns and spiritual songs (1707), bk. I,
> Hymn 1]

c.180, p. 22

B0184 Behold, the grace appears,
And loud repeat their songs.

> [Isaac Watts, Hymns and spiritual songs (1707), bk. I,
> Hymn 2]

c.180, p. 1

B0185 Behold! The green fields yellowing into corny gold,
The circling summons to a cool repast.

> [William] Pattison, 'A harvest scene'

c.244, p. 482

B0186 Behold the infant budding rose,
We all must wish her beauty still!

> '1774'

Poetry Box III/53

B0187 Behold the Lamb of God lift up on high
Love to the death, for him, lov'd us no less.

> H[enry] C[olman], 'I.N.R.I.' [written in the shape of
> an altar]
> [Crum B237]

b.2, p. 108

B0188 Behold the Lilliputian throng
They mount, and as they mount, they sing.

> 'A riddle, on the jacks of a harpsichord or spinet'

c.360/1, p. 9

B0189 Behold the man whose blood was rudely spilt,
For none lived better, none so bravely fell.

> 'Written under Mr [John] Ashton's picture'

b.111, p. 100; b.204, p. 6, p. 88 (incomplete)

B0190 Behold the measurer of the sea and land!
Three handfuls only, and in peace begone!

> [William Popple, trans.], '[Horace] book 1st. ode 28th.
> Dialogue between Horace and Archytas'

fc.104/2, p. 78

B0191   Behold the muse, devoted to your shrine
And yet despair thy flattery to pay.

      Frederick Corfield, 'The poet's prayer'

      c.381/2

B0192   Behold the parent flower decline,
Joint themes to late posterity.

      'From the Whitehall evening post June the 8th 1773
On the death of Lady Caroline Seymour'

      c.152, p. 70

B0193   Behold the path that mortals tread
Secure I shall return no more.

      P[hilip] Doddridge, 'The great journey from
Job: XVI. 22'

      c.493, p. 30

B0194   Behold the place, whence England's woes proceed
The villain's refuge and the woman's lust.

      'On a conventicle'
[Crum B241]

      b.111, p. 494

B0195   Behold the rose of Sharon here,
Nor stir, nor wake, nor grieve my love.

      [Isaac Watts, Hymns and spiritual songs (1707), bk. I,
Hymn 68]

      c.180, p. 64

B0196   Behold the shades of ev'ning close,
And welcome immortality.

      'Rhymes written in a winter evening. To T. S. esqr.'

      c.89, p. 65

B0197   Behold the woman's promis'd seed!
And own thee as the promis'd seed.

      [Isaac Watts, Hymns and spiritual songs (1707), bk. II,
Hymn 135]

      c.180, p. 14

B0198   Behold the wonder of her sex and time
The force of nature could no further go.

      [Horace Walpole, 4th earl of Orford], 'Count[es]s of
Coventry'
[Crum B248]

      c.157, p. 70

B0199   Behold these armies here in rank, and file
Brings up the rear, and stops my muse's breath.

      'Snaith [parish] register. Anno 1657 [1]'

      c.81/1, no. 150

Behold these woods, and mark my sweet   B0200
Unless you'll meet again tomorrow.

      T[homas] R[andolph], 'A pastoral courtship' [with
'Her reply']
[Crum B250]

      b.200, p. 138; b.62, p. 139

Behold, this emblem of our fleeting years,   B0201
And heavenly-minded, long to be with God.

      Richard Lely, 'On an hourglass sent to a religious
lady'

      c.244, p. 517; c.547, p. 207

Behold this feeble taper light,   B0202
Extinguisher of all.

      'Verses on a candle'

      c.91, p. 300

Behold this little volume here enroll'd   B0203
The legible and written Deity.

      [William Strode], 'On the Bible'
[Crum B251]

      b.205, fol. 61r

Behold this lock, which deck'd my face,   B0204
Has age bestow'd with tresses hoar.

      'From Madame la Marechale de Mirepoix, to
Mons[ieu]r le Duc de Nivernois, with a lock of her
hair . . . imitated'

      c.90

Behold this nosegay, beauteous maid,   B0205
Send little Cupid with a kiss.

      'To a young lady with a bow-pot of flowers'

      c.487, p. 107

Behold this valiant admiral,   B0206
His heart and sails are never down.

      'Upon Admiral [Maarten] Tromp's picture concerning
his overthrowing the Spaniards. 1639'

      b.197, p. 241

Behold this world, full of crooked streets   B0207
They all would live, and none but poor must die.

      'An epitaph in Farnborough Churchyard'

      c.341, p. 43

Behold today the month complete   B0208
And chronicle her joy!

      [William Hayley], 'Conclusion' [October 1800]

      File 6968

B0209 Behold we come dear Lord to thee;
Till time itself be done.

> [John Austin], 'Hymn 1' [Devotions in the ancient
> way of offices, 1672, p. 3]
> [Crum B253]

c.178, p. 1

B0210 Behold where Britannia points joyful her lance!
All hail George the Second, what glory is thine!

> John Lockman, 'Admiral Hawke's welcome to old
> England, on his completing the ruin of the French
> navy. The tune, O the roast beef &c.'

c.267/2, p. 41

B0211 Behold with fondest love, and pious care
Certes he'll give to ev'ry wight his meed.

> Miss [ ] White, of Edgbaston, 'Translated from
> the . . . original sonnet of Vincenzio—the mother, in
> imitation of Spenser'

c.532

B0212 Behold with hallow'd weight these brothers bend
Wide ruin was the price of infinite renown.

> [William Hayley], 'A translation of Claudian's verses
> on the statues of two brothers at Catina'

File 6979

B0213 Behold with pleasing ecstasy
Or call me to thy realms above.

> P[hilip] Doddridge, 'A prayer for the speedy
> propogation of the gospel from Is. LXVI. 8'

c.493, p. 33

B0214 Behold (with solemn stupor! There!—behold
Whilst being, and eternity, endure. Amen.

> [Thomas Stevens?], 'The rainbow and covenant. &c.
> A poem in blank verse'

c.259, p. 83

B0215 Behold, yon newborn infant griev'd
What ill, though ask'd deny.

> J[ames] Merrick, 'The ignorance of man'

c.83/4, no. 2006

B0216 Behold you dull mortals heaven gives you a sign
The scene of this action stands still undefaced.

> 'Another [satire]'

Poetry Box VII/75

B0217 Being amorous himself into a swan
Is no more man when he begins to love.

> Sir Thomas Urquhart, 'That lovers are devoid of
> reason. A paradox'

fb.217, p. 156

B0218 Being ask'd which of the bigamies implied
For else how should therein one flesh be two.

> Sir Thomas Urquhart, 'Here a woman affirms, that it
> is more lawful for one of her sex to have two
> husbands, than for a man to have two wives'

fb.217, p. 143

B0219 Being defil'd and sin-contaminate
Will make admission into Paradise.

> [Sir Philip Wodehouse], 'Upon Mr. Christopher
> Bedingfield being defiled, offer Christ'

b.131, back (no. 191)

B0220 Being great, you may be greater
By time: not greater.

> Sir Thomas Urquhart, 'The power that time hath of
> an increasing, and intensive progress in quantity, and
> quality'

fb.217, p. 331

B0221 Being man, and wife, you're discrepant in name:
You diverse sexes are: yet you're but one.

> Sir Thomas Urquhart, 'To a married couple, who
> loved others entirely'

fb.217, p. 142

B0222 Being married pair of [?]gian why
And Capricorn the member geniture.

> [Sir Thomas Urquhart], 'A conference betwixt
> Philogynes and Astrea the wife of a mathematician,
> wherein both of them from the practicing of logic
> deduce fixed [?] he for adultery, she for pudicity'

fb.217, p. 391

B0223 Being of beings God of love,
And be with Christ in God.

> 'Hymn 44th'

c.562, p. 52

B0224 Being poor thyself, and cannot feast at all,
Thank God for such as thee to feasting call.

c.93

B0225 Being stript herself and [?] [?] desire
Till she did burn like charcoal without smoke.

> [Sir Thomas Urquhart], 'To one who was so intime
> with her sweetheart that she would not entrust the
> service of their mutual dalliance with one thread of
> her [?]'

fb.217, p. 536

B0226 Being wise, you are a fool, that doth not speak:
But being a fool, you're wise, no speech to make.

> Sir Thomas Urquhart, 'An antistasis, or contradiction
> in adjecto'

fb.217, p. 102

B0227 Believe it or not, as you choose,
How soon I can make her a mother.

    [William Cowper], 'To Catharina on her marriage
    with Geo: Courtenay esq.'

    File 17707

B0228 Believe me Chloe those perfumes that last
Thou smell'st not of thy sweets they stink of thee.

    [George Granville, 1st baron] Lansdowne, 'On Chloe
    perfuming herself'

    fc.60, p. 49

B0229 Believe me dear Aunt,
Than in hell be a leader of apes.

    'Song 44'

    c.555, p. 69

B0230 Believe me, dear Cleveland, with pleasure I write,
Nem contradicent yours till death Jemmy Byng.

    'Admiral Byng's letter to Secretary Cleveland versified'
    [c. 1756]

    File 17487

B0231 Believe me fair one, was it not for you,
And be to mankind, a reproach, and shame.

    [Thomas Hamilton, 6th earl of Haddington], 'To
    Florella epistle the ninth'

    c.458/1, p. 23

B0232 Believe me ladies, I'm no cheat
Rich only in simplicity.

    [Phanuel Bacon], 'A riddle'
    [Crum B269]

    c.237, fol. 22 (incomplete?)

B0233 Believe me, Sir, 'twas sad, 'twas shocking news,
Nor worldly charms or cares your heavenly zeal
                       alloy.

    J[oshua] W[illiams, of Kidderminster], 'Verses to a
    friend recovered from illness, his friend has been
    afflicted with exquisite pain and brought very nigh to
    the grave'

    c.259, p. 119

B0234 Believe not always those that seem
There are the deepest fords.

    b.234, p. 6, p. 171 ('oft are')

B0235 Believe not each aspersing tongue
Which ought not to be true.

    [Richard Brinsley Butler Sheridan]
    Poetry Box XII/95

B0236 Believe thou sweet, tho' cruel fair,
One pitying glance will save.

    [John Lockman], 'The languishing lover'

    c.268 (first part), p. 73

B0237 Believe us dread Sir,
Such princely things govern this Helen.

    'Totnes address versified' [pr. 1727 (Foxon A50)]

    c.172, p. 24

B0238 Believing on my Lord I find,
Where faith in sight shall end.

    'Hymn 43d'

    c.562, p. 51

B0239 Belinda see from yonder flow'rs
Which you inhumanly would starve.

    'Excuse for stealing a kiss . . . Spec[tator] 473'
    [Crum B277]

    c.144, p. 66; c.546 (stanzas 1–2); c.549, p. 107

B0240 Belinda with affected mien
Her sister frowns in vain.

    'The rival sisters'

    c.176, p. 152

B0241 Belira bella! The particle between
May move us to admire, and not to sin.

    [Sir Philip Wodehouse], 'Isabella Bedel Belira! Deh
    bella'

    b.131, back (no. 112)

B0242 Bell's wife is of good mettle—besides she's very
                         dapper,
Yet hath he work to hark of horns that are on
              Ferbert [*i.e.*, Herbert?] headed.

    'On the beadles' wives: Oxon: 1630'

    b.200, p. 427

B0243 Belov'd associate of my inmost soul
The lawyer scholar gentleman and friend.

    [William Hayley], 'Sonnet . . . Jan 15 [1800]'
    File 6968

B0244 Beloved Chloe ask you why
And she became his lovely bride.

    N. B[urney], 'Corilas and Chloe a pastoral dialogue'
    c.486, fol. 28v

B0245 Beloved this word rod does not only signet
In a morter(?) he will not forsake his folly says |
                     Solomon(?). . . .

    'The rod is made for the back of fools'

    b.356, p. 333 (incomplete)

B0246 Below good Barwise, clos'd in body lies
Shall them survive till they revive again.

'A memorative epitaph for . . . Richard Barwise late of
Islekirk esqr. He died the 13th of February 1648, in the
47th year of his age'

c.547, p. 328

B0247 Below, in bed
Correct it in thyself.

T. M——, 'An epitaph for Mr. Shuter when it may
please God to call him' [6 April 1765]

c.116, p. 51

B0248 Below this marble monument is laid
In sickness patient and in death resign'd.

[John Dryden], 'The monument of a fair maiden lady
who died at Bath and was there interred'

fc.60, p. 57

B0249 Below this stone here generous Grimstone lies
Think with thyself that thou thyself must die.

'In Arthurst church . . . who had eight sons and eight
daughters and died July 14 aged 57 years A. D. 1671'

c.547, p. 334

B0250 Ben Block was a veteran of naval renown,
'That to see me quick scalp'd were no wonder.'

'The naval subaltern'

c.82, p. 7

B0251 Ben Hoadley, Julian Johnson, Titus Oates
When thou mayst be impeacht and he preferr'd.

'Jan: 1 1709–10'
[Crum B286]

b.90, p. 10

B0252 Beneath a beech's bowery shade
Beams on the mind, and makes all nature gay.

[Francis Fawkes], 'An irregular ode . . . a parody on a
passage in Milton's Paradise lost, book the 4th ver.
641'

fc.21, p. 19

B0253 Beneath a bush unseen
And nevermore was shy.

'Song'

c.530, p. 37

B0254 Beneath a craggy mountain's awful brow,
While thou, and time, shall all the pains I feel
assuage.

'Verses on melancholy'

c.83/3, no. 924

B0255 Beneath a laurel's shade the youth reclin'd,
And great designs his raptur'd fancy warm'd.

'Silius Italicus. Book XV'

c.368, p. 174

B0256 Beneath a myrtle's verdant shade
Gives grief or pleasure spares or stills.

[Matthew Prior], 'Love disarmed'

fc.60, p. 12

B0257 Beneath a neck, so dazzling white,
That stings the melting soul with bliss.

'Translation of the description of Agnes in the first
canto of Voltaire's Maid of Orleans'

c.487, p. 124

B0258 Beneath a shady willow, near
Ah! Celadon thou now art come too late.

'The sleeping shepherdess'

fb.107, p. 50

B0259 Beneath a sleeping infant lies,
Had been as short as thine.

[Samuel Wesley, the elder], 'Epitaph on an infant in
Wisbech churchyard'
[Crum B294]

c.355, p. 36; c.360/2, no. 220; c.82, p. 26 (var.); c.221, p. 40
('an infant sleeping')

B0260 Beneath a soul with genius fraught,
And leave me dead to ev'ry art.

William Jackson, 'The muse's elegy to Dr. Jn.
Green . . . June 1745. by . . . being removed from
Spalding to Boston . . .'

c.229/1, fol. 92

B0261 Beneath a tyrant thistle, grew
Will still that little give.

'The thistle and the daisy'

c.83/3, no. 865

B0262 Beneath Aurelia's foot I sat,
I then may pity what I now deride.

'The cruel nymph'

fb.107, p. 40

B0263 Beneath in the dust, the earthmade old crust,
In hopes that her crust will be rais'd.

'An epitaph on Elinor Batchellor, an old pie-woman'

c.94; see also 'Beneath the dust . . .', 'Here lies Dick . . .',
'Under this dust . . .'.

B0264 Beneath lie the bones of a worm-eaten dame
Hypocrisy's branded above and below.

> 'A whimsical epitaph on Mrs. Maria Muggot, spinster'
> [d. 6 November 1743]
>
> c.360/2, no. 219

B0265 Beneath lies in turd the remains of a bird,
But she'll always leave something behind her.

> 'Epitaph on a parrot, that Betty the servant threw
> down the necessary'
>
> c.481, p. 222

B0266 Beneath the beech, whose branches bare
'To pluck from God's right hand his instruments
of death.'

> Thomas Warton, 'The suicide'
>
> c.142, p. 323

B0267 Beneath the branches of yon sacred yew,
How fatal death's devouring dart to me.

> 'The yew tree—by a lady'
>
> c.83/2, no. 409

B0268 Beneath the cloudy canopy
Demand my highest praise.

> T[homas] S[tevens], 'March 16. 1780'
>
> c.259, p. 79

B0269 Beneath the cov'ring of this little stone
Its pride when living, and its grief when dead.

> [John] Hervey, baron Hervey of Ickworth, 'By the late
> . . . upon Ldy B[ett]y Mansell'
>
> fc.51, p. 223

B0270 Beneath the dust,
In hopes that her crust will be rais'd.

> Herbert Beaver, 'To the pie-house memory of Moll
> Batchelor, late a pie-woman in Oxford by . . . C. C. C.'
>
> c.241, p. 18; see also 'Here lies Dick . . .', 'Under this
> dust . . .', 'Beneath in the dust'

B0271 Beneath the gloom of Hendon's chequer'd shade
Far nobler were the tears that grac'd his fate.

> H[enry] S[krine], 'To Mrs. Aislabie on the fall of her
> great cedar at Hendon Place planted by Queen
> Elizabeth . . . London—May 26 1779'
>
> c.509, p. 24

B0272 Beneath the heavens a creature once did dwell
Suffer in hell, or reign among the just.

> 'Another [riddle]'
>
> Diggle Box: Poetry Box xi/71

B0273 Beneath the hedge or near the stream
And boasts its splendor too.

> [William Cowper], 'The glow-worm'
>
> Poetry Box x/136

B0274 Beneath the honors of a tomb,
And aids the triumphs of the day.

> [Isaac] Watts, 'An epitaph on King William 3d who
> died March the 8th 1701[2]'
>
> c.244, p. 327

B0275 Beneath the shade of Spence's pleasing grove
If Spence approves,—his approbation's fame.

> [ ] Harding, 'Florella an eclogue'
>
> Spence Papers, folder 113

B0276 Beneath the spreading oak thus stretch'd along,
On humble pipe, I'll tune my sylvan song.

> [Thomas Hull, translation of Virgil]
>
> c.20/5; c.21

B0277 Beneath these moss-grown roots this rustic cell
What drawing room can boast so fair a train!

> [Gilbert West], 'Over the door, the inside of the
> hermitage' [at Meresworth, seat of the earl of
> Westmorland]
> [Crum B304]
>
> fc.51, p. 42; c.360/1, p. 259 (attr. G. Lyttelton)

B0278 Beneath this gravel and these stones,
And he replied, 'All flesh is grass!'

> 'Epitaph on [John] Tissey the punster'
>
> c.81/1, no. 279; c.360/1, p. 51

B0279 Beneath this green turf put to bed with a spade
Shall quit this clay mansion and flourish above.

> William Davis, 'Epitaph on Mary Davis wife of
> William Davis gardener to I. Fane esqr. Written by
> himself'
>
> fc.14/8

B0280 Beneath this grot, and Ketton Stones
Tears of the tankard o'er his hearse.

> J. E., 'Epitaph on my living friend [Samuel Tryon]'
>
> b.204, p. 64

B0281 Beneath this hallowed shrine there peaceful lies,
Or greet her mem'ry with a sigh sincere.

> S. C., 'Lines to the memory of an amiable lady'
>
> c.343, p. 49

B0282 Beneath this humble stone, now rests enshrin'd,
Heav'n wond'ring snatch'd her to the joys above.

> Dr. [ ] Templeman, 'Epitaph on a lady who died in
> childbirth'
>
> c.83/1, no. 103

B0283 Beneath this little stone interr'd
So stranger, weep a little thou.

'Epitaph on the late goldfinch of Lady Charlotte
Herbert'
Poetry Box III/5

B0284 Beneath this marble stone does lie,
Her Savior waits once more to see.

'An epitaph on the old Lady Vere'
[cf. Crum B307]
c.244, p. 283

B0285 Beneath this poor remembrancer
Nor, what thou feel'st not, dare decry.

c.528/7

B0286 Beneath this rough and rustic stone
And as your pass it cry oh dear.

D. R., 'Epitaph on Dancer'
c.150, p. 126

B0287 Beneath this rugged stone doth lie
And send me anywhere but there.

'Epitaph on a termagant wife written by her husband'
c.150, p. 156

B0288 Beneath this sculptur'd stone, a lovely maid
Be from this spot by no rude hands remov'd!

'An epitaph'
Poetry Box IV/147

B0289 Beneath this sculpture's arch with roses spread
In aught save beauty, do resemble mine.

[Martha] Peckard, 'On a monument of Mary Queen
of Scots, removed from the cathedral of Peterborough
into the deanery garden, and placed in an arbor of
roses . . . addressed to the Dean's wife before she was
married'
c.504, p. 17

B0290 Beneath this silent stone is laid
Because she hates a place of rest.

'An epitaph on a talkative old maid'
[Crum B313]
c.360/3, no. 34

B0291 Beneath this sod, depriv'd of breath
In dawn of early youth.

[epitaph in Cheltenham]
c.546

B0292 Beneath this stone a lump of clay
Began to hold her tongue.

'Epitaph' [on a scold]
[Crum B314]
c.546

B0293 Beneath this stone Biberio's dust is laid,
For there's a dreadful reck'ning still to pay.

'On the death of one very remarkable for his excess in
drinking'
[Crum B316]
c.186, p. 48

B0294 Beneath this stone by the bone of his bone
And now that he's dead he lies still.

'Epitaph on one Adam Gill, attorney'
c.81/1, no. 386

B0295 Beneath this stone fair ladies lies [sic],
But savor in the dust.

'Another [epitaph]'
fc.60, p. 116

B0296 Beneath this stone lies Katherine Gray,
She in her shop may be again.

'An epitaph written on a tomb in a country
churchyard, on an old woman who sold earthenware'
[Crum B319]
fc.130, p. 50; Poetry Box x/90, x/92; see also 'Under this
stone . . .'.

B0297 Beneath this stone lies our dear child
But him can ne'er go back again to we.

'Epitaph in a churchyard in Wiltshire'
c.360/3, no. 124

B0298 Beneath this stone obscurely laid
His landlord, Death—this grave his home.

H[enry] Skrine, 'Epitaph to the immortal memory of
John Thompson near 50 years waiter at the King's
Head Inn at Derby . . . March 20. 1783'
c.509, p. 54

B0299 Beneath this stone, reader, there lieth flat
He'll say, where shall I wait upon you Sir.

'On Mr. Jo Sprat late Steward of Grays-Inn'
fb.143, p. 30

B0300 Beneath this stone, the man of feeling lies,
No kind relation clos'd his clay-cold eyes.

'Epitaph of the Revd. Mr. Eccles'
c.83/3, no. 903

B0301 Beneath this stone there lies a hapless youth,
And all his virtues find reward in heav'n.

'Epitaph'
c.175, p. 84

B0302 Beneath this stony roof reclin'd,
Prefer the blameless hermitage.

[Thomas Warton], 'Inscription in a hermitage at
Ansley Hall in Warwickshire'

c.90

B0303 Beneath this tomb, in sacred sleep,
A good man never dies.

[Edmund?] Burke, 'Epitaph on Sir Joshua Reynolds'

fc.132/1, p. 221

B0304 Beneath this turf two tender infants sleep
And strive fond parents strive | To meet her there.

[( ) Huddesford], 'On my three girls in Leamington
churchyard'

c.181, p. 71

B0305 Beneath this verdant hillock lies
Will think his better half alive.

'Epitaph on a miser'

fb.142, p. 8 (second series)

B0306 Beneath thy place,
Here lies Henry Duke of Grafton!

'On the death of the Duke of Grafton killed at the
siege of Cork &c.'

fb.207/1, p. 9

B0307 Benevolence meek pity's darling child
He speaks, and pity listens to his prayer.

'Benevolence'

Diggle Box: Poetry Box XI/7

B0308 Benevolence of heart, all hail!
But with thy wonted smiles bestow.

John Lockman, 'Extempore after hearing a sermon, in
the asylum, near Westminster Bridge . . . Decr. 1761'

c.267/1, p. 315

B0309 Ben's wife having beat him: his friend Will cries Nan
I'll swear I've not seen one this hour or more.

c.546, p. 28

B0310 Bentinck the goblet holds, Carmarthen fills,
But none regards the writing on the wall.

'Mene, mene tekel, upharsin'
[Crum B321]

b.111, p. 418

B0311 Bereft of faith's effulgent light,
Can succor yield in a distressing hour.

Charles Atherton Allnutt, 'The soul's relief in
spiritual distress'

c.112, p. 69

B0312 Bermuda's wall'd with rocks who does not know
I'd make the listening savages grow tame.

[Edmund] Waller, 'A description of Bermudas or the
Summer Isles'

c.244, p. 193

B0313 Beside a gentle murm'ring brook
To distant climates, untried, unknown.

'The angler and philosopher'

c.83/2, no. 646

B0314 Besides, that all of your acquaintance know ye,
When I'd least skill to know the good, you did me.

Sir Thomas Urquhart, 'To the lady [crossed out]
baronetess'

fb.217, p. 46

B0315 Besides the beauteous bloom of face,
And equal joys attend the marriage state.

T[homas] M[orell], 'To Miss Anne Paxton (of Kew)
on the choice of a husband'

c.395, p. 91

B0316 Besides the most apparent dignities,
How many trillion grains of sand there be.

Sir Thomas Urquhart, 'To the Duchess of [crossed
out]'

fb.217, p. 66

B0317 Bess being sick, Burnett prescribes a vomit,
Burnet best fits the mouth, and Birch the tail.

[William Barrett, epigram on Elizabeth H. and
Dr. Burnett]
[Crum B328]

c.233, p. 55

B0318 Bess never goes abroad, lest she should lose
Who not to lose it, carries none at all.

Sir Thomas Urquhart, 'Of Bess, and Mistress Rose'

fb.217, p. 204

B0319 Bessy Bum-bee, let a thud flee
An' they—aw'—ran Gowlan home.

c.155, fol. 23

B0320 Best entertainment doth not still appear
For cheerful looks will make one dish a feast.

[Sir Thomas Urquhart], 'Welcome with four or five is
better than the most certain delight with a harsh
acceptance'

fb.217, p. 535

B0321 Best object of the passion most divine,
At length o'erwhelm'd in beauty's boundless sea.

[John] N[orris, of Bemerton], 'Beauty'

c.258

B0322 Bet,—receive my gratulation—
Sea-born Ma'am of heavenly kind.

'A congratulatory ode to Miss Surflen, the ladies' fair
guide at Margate, on her marriage with a son of
Vulcan'

c.116, p. 42

B0323 [Bethell], I write, nor frown upon my plan
Rancor its father, and its mother, spleen.

Charles Atherton Allnutt, 'The following lines were
written intentionally to be sent to a clergyman of the
establishment [W. Bethell], on his refusing to suffer a
hymn to be sung over the corpse of a righteous
woman, at her interment in his churchyard'

c.112, p. 141

B0324 Better it is a poor house to hold,
Than to lie in prison with fetters of gold.

b.234, p. 258

B0325 Betty who yet had look'd on man
Fair Proserpine away.

'The fatal marriage' [of Joseph Smith and Elizabeth
Bourchier of Long Hanborough]
[Crum B342]

c.241, p. 25

B0326 Between Bluster, and Jarvise there arose a dispute
Let the judge and the jury determine the rest. |
                                              Derry down

'Song'
Poetry Box x/98

B0327 Between extremities on either side
That Sylvia's neck is not the whitest place.

'On the new passing-house at Tunbridge Wells, 1713'
c.360/1, p. 85

B0328 Between two suitors sat a lady fair
She doth most honor, she most love doth bear.

'Quaestio' [rhymed conundrum]
[Crum B346]

b.197, p. 212; c.83/3, no. 920

B0329 Betwixt Father Patrick and his Highness of late
He managed this business, as he did the sea-fight.

'A debate betwixt the D[uke] of Y[ork] and Father
Patrick' [1673; on the Duke's changing his religion]
[Crum B348; POAS I.211]

fb.140, p. 166; fb.70, p. 235

B0330 Betwixt her breasts there is a trink,
Of Cupid's center.

Sir Thomas Urquhart, 'The paths of love'
fb.217, p. 267

B0331 Betwixt two vices, there's one virtue plac'd:
Though I had rather vice, that place possess'd.

Sir Thomas Urquhart, 'Of vice, and virtue a paradox'
fb.217, p. 155

B0332 Beware fair maids of musky courtiers' oaths
Break ice in one place, yet will crack in more.

[Joshua Sylvester], 'To young gentlewomen at court'
[cf. Crum B357]

b.148, p. 23

B0333 Beware incautious maid beware,
And when too late—be wise.

'Advice to a young lady, too apt to visit the camp in
Hyde Park'

c.83/3, no. 1008

B0334 Beware let not the sluggish sleep
And ask for mercy's sake.

Richard Lullay, 'A godly meditation to be had in mind
at our going to bed . . . 1612'

fb.29, fol. 1

B0335 Beware Madam B—ss—t
When physic'd must stick to his stool!

R[ichard] V[ernon] S[adleir], 'On a certain bishop
who treated a lady uncivilly though he knew her
rank—not rising from his chair when she entered the
room &c. &c. and disputing about the number of days
he was to stay in the lodging'

c.106, p. 83

B0336 Beware ye swimmers of all checks, for naught
Must soon expire. Sad spectacle, sad thought.

c.519

B0337 Beware you Christian doctrines all,
Was anti-Christian self-denial.

fb.207/1, p. 1; see also 'Certain, and sure . . .'; 'In hopes
of speedy resurrection . . .'.

B0338 Beyond the malice of abusive fate
For sweet Amintor's dead, who was my dear.

'Farewell to Amintor'
fb.107, p. 23

B0339 Beyond the rage of time or fortune's power,
Secure to feel no second loss like thine!

Thomas Day, 'Epitaph on Dr. Small'
File 14205

B0340 Beyond the seas there is a place
Than live at home a freeborn slave.

fb.234, p. 118

B0341 Beyond this, in the roadway as we went,
Ofttimes write verses, some say, such as these.

[Richard] Corbett, 'In an old poem by . . . entitled,
Iter boreale'

Greatheed Box/107 (ll. 377-380)

B0342 Beyond those walks where first did grow
Which waits on innocence and Bell.

J[ohn] T[weddell], 'Fragment of a legendary tale.
found in the vicinity of Holland House . . . April 1792'

Smith Papers, folder 75/2

B0343 Bid me not, Maecenas, sing,
Which by force 'twas thine to take.

[William Popple, trans.], '[Horace] book 2nd. Ode
12th. To Maecenas'

fc.104/2, p. 150

B0344 Bid reason, Pollio, number those delights
To bloom again in heav'n's eternal clime.

'To Pollio—an epistle'

fc.53, p. 170

B0345 Bird of May,
Chloe smiles, my soul's all gay.

John Lockman, 'The request: to the nightingales.
Made to a favorite movement in the opera of Alcina'

c.267/2, p. 110; c.268 (first part), p. 67

B0346 Bird of Pallas! Reverend fowl!
Fond to disturb ignoble ease.

Dr. [ ] Faulconer, 'An Oxonian to his owl'

c.229/1, fol. 30

B0347 Birds fly away when stones are at them cast
And for such things a friend will soon depart.

Sir John Strangways, 'Of friendship's break-bonds . . .
17mo Decembris 1646'

b.304, p. 80

B0348 Bird's wings are clipt Potter is turn'd to clay
Wentworth wants worth and Snow is melt away.

'Upon the city's overthrow by the university'

b.208, p. 60

B0349 Births weddings burials do divide this book
Into three parts. Therefore in order look!

'Snaith [parish] register. Anno 1657' [3]

c.81/1, no. 150

B0350 Black eye in the dark orbs do lie
By bane or bliss my paradise or hell.

b.213, p. 113

B0351 Black girl, complain not that I fly,
And I'll bequeath myself to thee.

Henry King, 'The answer' [to 'Fair boy, alas! . . .']
[Crum B379]

b.200, p. 7; b.62, p. 25; b.205, fol. 50r

B0352 Black grisly Death did nick his arrow right
When leaving covers, he did hit the White.

'On one White'
[Crum B380]

b.356, p. 249

B0353 Blackbourne will be dean 'tis certain,
But he's Cornelius Tacitus.

'On Blackbourne late Archbishop of York upon its
being surmised he would be made Dean of Exeter, at
which time he was supposed to be intimate with the
wife of one Cornelius Martin'

c.74; see also 'Nigrellus/Nigrinus leads a merry life . . .'.

B0354 Blackburman would a wencher seem and would but
                                                    seem
He's both a liar, and a lecher too.

[Sir Philip Wodehouse], 'An imitation of Martial's
Pauper videm . . .'

b.131, p. 32

B0355 Blake whose pure thoughts the patient 'graver guide
Correctly beautiful and mildly grand.

[William Hayley], 'Sonnet . . . July 12 [1800]'

File 6968

B0356 Blame not my cheeks though pale with love they be
Poor Cupid sits and blows his nails for cold.

[Thomas Campion], 'Song 43'

b.4, fol. 36

B0357 Blame not sweet mistress my so near approaching,
Upon your goods, I came to close the door.

Sir Thomas Urquhart, 'The speeches of a proper
gallant youth, to a comely, handsome young
gentlewoman, to whose bedside, he had come about
midnight, without any former appointment'

fb.217, p. 117

B0358 Blame not these lines, so bad the letters stand,
She who hath stabb'd, the heart hath kill'd the hand.

Littleton Brown, 'Another [fragment]'

c.221, p. 34

B0359 Blame not your fate, ye hawkers shrill
By pamphlet proclamations.

'On the proclamations'
[Crum B391a]

c.570/1, p. 85

B0360 Blaspheme not love with any other name
We'll hoist up sail and touch the wished shores.

[John] Cleveland, 'Platonic love'

b.225, p. 129

B0361 Blast me! What crowds of heretics I see:
Each Briton shall a patriot Phocian rise.

[John Lockman], '21 April 1746. Prologue to The siege of Damascus acted at Mr. [blank]'

c.268 (first part), at front

B0362 Blasted with sighs and surrounded with tears
Who's therefore true, because her truth kills me.

[John Donne], 'Of Twickenham garden'
[Crum B392]

b.114, p. 258; b.148, p. 56

B0363 Blazon thy youthful and ingenious fire
And vast returns of fame and honor bring.

[Mary Serjant?]

fb.98, fol. 148; b.227, p. 73

B0364 Bleak are thy hills, oh North! and wild thy plains;
Art may be forc'd: but art alone, beguiles.

A. H., 'June 3. 1728'

Spence Papers, folder 113

B0365 Bleak roar'd the blast, and horror's giant form
To seal a tyrant's doom.

[Richard] Archdall, 'Verses by . . .' [on Danaë and Perseus her infant son]

c.130, p. 8

B0366 Bless me what dreaming mortals now are seen
Nor Flatus wants the health he never lost.

'Quae mentem insomnia ferrent?'

c.546, p. 6

B0367 Bless me! What glory's yon that gilds the air,
The whole vast choir with sacred anthems rung.

J[ohn] R[obinson], 'Ascension day'

c.370, fol. 19v

B0368 Bless thou the Lord that giveth bliss
And listened not unto their cries.

b.27, fol. 41

B0369 Bless'd above women, virgin, bless'd,
That on His truth rely.

'The same [the Song of Elizabeth]—another meter'

c.264/3, p. 123

B0370 Blessed are [they] that perfect are
Thy commandments to keep.

[William Whittingham], 'For a godly life to be led according to his word. Psal: 51' [verses from Psalm 119]
[Crum B403]

a.3, fol. 130v

B0371 Bless'd are the heav'nly troops, which bodies lack:
We are far more with reason cross'd, than rul'd.

Sir Thomas Urquhart, 'Of angels, men, and beasts'

fb.217, p. 124

B0372 Bless'd are the humble souls, that see
Glory and joy are their reward.

'St. Matthew 5. ver. 3 to 12'

c.83/3, no. 817

B0373 Blessed art thou that fearest God,
Forevermore the same.

[Thomas Sternhold, Thomas Norton, William Whittingham, and William Kethe], 'Against affliction and tyrannous persecution. Psal. 56' [verses from Psalms 128–130, 134]
[Crum B404]

a.3, fol. 140

B0374 Blessed Creator, who before the birth
After this vision, any sight but Thee.

'A paraphase on Simeon's song'

b.49, p. 19

B0375 Blessed is he that is sincere,
Preserve thy heav'nly lore.

'Psalm 119. Evening prayer [24th–26th days]'

c.264/3, p. 47

B0376 Bless'd is the maid, and worthy to be bless'd,
And gratitude forbids desire to range . .

'In conjugal felicity'

c.94 (incomplete?)

B0377 Bless'd is the man who to the poor,
And loud Hosannas sing.

'Psalm 41 Evening prayer'

c.264/1, p. 181

B0378 Bless'd is the man whose pardon'd sin
And to his courts with joy draw near.

'Psalm 32 Evening prayer'

c.264/1, p. 135

B0379 Blessed oh blessed are the poor in mind
Yea such hath made his child, his son, his heir.

'A Christian's character Matthew 5th verse 3[–9]'

b.216, p. 234

B0380 Blessed O Lord be thy wise grace,
Belov'd, obey'd, ador'd.

    [John Austin], 'Hym: 20' [Hymn xii, Devotions in the
    ancient way of offices, 1672, p. 107]

c.178, p. 19

B0381 Blessed Redeemer, we do not meet this day
First in his virgin Mother, then in thee.

    'Christmas Day, 1661'

b.49, p. 16

B0382 Blest are the souls that hear and know
Thy God forever lives.

    'Hymn 37th'

c.562, p. 43

B0383 Blest, as the first of mortals were!
And put it out again next day.

    [William Popple, trans.], '[Horace, ep]ode 2nd. In
    praise of a country life'

fc.104/2, p. 396

B0384 Blest as th' immortal gods is he
I fainted, sunk, and died away

    [Ambrose Philips], 'Sappho ad Lesbiam' [from the
    Spectator, 1711]
    [Crum B423]

c.144, p. 67; c.186, p. 3; c.358, p. 146; c.549, p. 95
(incomplete)

B0385 Blest bard whose sacred pen has writ
Who would not die to have been Prior?

    [Robert Cholmeley], 'Written in Mr. Prior's Poems,
    under his lines upon Mezeray's history of France'

c.190, p. 220

B0386 Blest be my friend with all that sweetens life
This year, and every year, dear friend, be thine!

    [Charles Earle], 'An extempore New Year's gift to my
    friend—a fragment'

c.376

B0387 Blest be the characters so kindly traced
To life to joy to glory and to love.

    [William Hayley], 'Sonnet . . . Feb 1 [1800]'

File 6968

B0388 Blest be the God that's Israel's Lord
From Jesse's root to spring.

c.187, p. 26

B0389 Blest be the hand that lends the power to feel
The social powers of pity and of love.

    'Sympathy'

c.355, p. 222

B0390 Blest be the man (and blest he is) whome'er
Let my life sleep, and learn to love her end.

    A[braham] C[owley], 'The country life'
    [Crum B427]

b.118, p. 19

B0391 Blest be the man! His memory at least,
And ask an art to help us to embrace.

    [Anne Finch, countess of Winchilsea], 'Copy [of]
    verses on the invention of writing. Written by a lady,
    part of which was published in the 172 Guardian in
    1713 . . . Pasquin no. 97'
    [Crum B428]

c.360/2, no. 159; c.83/2, no. 596 (ll. 1–26); c.163, p. 4 (ll.
1–10); File 13409 (ll. 1–6)

B0392 Blest be the man, who rescues from foul shame,
Unto a poet, and that poet you.

    'To Mr. Fenton—on his Herod and Mariamne'

b.322, p. 40

B0393 Blest be the memory of this happy day,
And prove the comforts of our latter day.

    [ ] Murray, 'On the birthday of Eliza Anne Murray
    three years old Jan. 7. 23rd [sic] 1789'

Poetry Box XII/16

B0394 Blest be the princes, who have fought
That happiness is but opinion.

    [Matthew] Prior, 'Written in a book called Nouveaux
    interets de princes de Europe'

c.189, p. 139

B0395 Blest be the youth (if such there can be found)
And every Joseph meets a Joseph's fate.

    'Joseph and Potiphar's wife. By a young lad at Oakham
    School, set him by his master'
    [Crum B429]

c.94

B0396 Blest be those glorious rays of light divine,
And bear in mind thy poor unworthy friend.

    J. Henderson, 'Verses sent to Mabel Wigham by a
    parson of the Church of England' [Bristol, 1777]

c.139, p. 319, p. 450 ('Bless'd')

B0397 Blest Father! Who with brave disdain
Forget the woes of age!

    [William] Hayley, 'To Mr. Seward' [Eartham, 15 Sept.
    1781]

Poetry Box V/61

B0398 Blest genius, hail! Propitious smile!
They think—to rise no more.

[Charles Burney, the younger], 'The 12 Pythian ode of Pindar. In praise of Midas, who gained a victory on the flute. To the tutelary nymph of the city Agrigentum'

c.37, p. 65 (incomplete)

B0399 Blest gift, that heav'n's indulgence could bestow,
And they are still the noblest, we possess below!

[Elizabeth] (Singer) [Rowe], 'On memory'

c.244, p. 424; c.83/3, no. 945 ('Bless'd')

B0400 Blest he! that with a mighty hand,
Contentedly enjoy'd, a mistress and a muse.

'Content. Dryden Miscel[lany] V[olume] 2d.'

c.244, p. 293

B0401 Blest health! Once more I share a blissful ease,
With heav'nly harmony fill your native plains.

T[homas] Liddiard, 'Written after my recovery. To health'

c.344, p. 125

B0402 Blest husbandman whose frugal hands have till'd
At home, who rests contented, life enjoys.

'Claudian's Old man of Verona'

c.244, p. 623

B0403 Blest in thy rank, and in each winning grace
Where ev'ry creature, who resists him, dies.

John Lockman, 'To a lady of quality [the Duchess of Marlborough] insulted by the rabble of writers . . . anno 1741'

c.267/2, p. 321

B0404 Blest is the loyal man whose steps,
With joy for those behind.

John Hopkins, 'The loyal man's psalter or some select psalms [4, 12, 37, 73, 94, 97] fit for the time of the persecution . . . turned into meter by . . .'

fb.207/5, p. 26

B0405 Blest is the man, supremely blest indeed!
Thou universal friend, to humankind.

'Friendship'

c.391, p. 6

B0406 Blest is the righteous man, who ne'er has trod
Shall wing your fate, and triumph in your fall.

[Richard] Daniel, dean of Armagh, 'Blessedness. Psalm the first'

c.244, p. 338

B0407 Blest leaf, whose aromatic gales dispense
And let me taste thee unexcised by k[ing]s.

[Isaac Hawkins Browne, 'In praise of tobacco'; imitation of Pope]
[Crum B446]

Poetry Box I/139

B0408 Blest nature from thy kindred sky(?)
And warm the blossoms at thy sight| To come and glad thy stay.

Georgiana [Spencer Cavendish, Duchess of] Devonshire

File 17988

B0409 Blest pair! Since Hyman first your wishes crown'd,
With all the luster of their mother's eyes!

John Lockman, 'To a gentleman, and his lady, at Breteuil, on their wedding day . . . May 1641'

c.267/1, p. 62

B0410 Blest pair the prologue now is done
To earth, may all that knew you for you mourn.

[Sir Aston Cokayne], 'To Mr N. H. and his wife on their marriage'

b.275, p. 32

B0411 Blest providence! By whose auspicious care,
And everyone, as lord of Boughton, lives.

W[illiam] Stukeley, 'A month's entertainment at Boughton'

c.229/1, fol. 102v; c.371, fol. 58

B0412 Blest temple, hail where the chaste altar stands
That courteous fate decrees Castara mine.

[William Habington], 'To Seymors. The house in which Castara lived'

b.150, p. 262

B0413 Blest, who far from all mankind,
Spare the sleep a God bestows.

[William Cowper, trans.], 'Repose in God. Vol. 2. Son: 17' [of Jeanne Guion's 'Spiritual songs']

c.470 (autogr.)

B0414 Blind atheist! Could a giddy dame
Th'amazing soul to be!

'By [ ] student of physic'

c.171

B0415 Blind beauty if it be a loss
Tho' bright as day within.

[John Grange]

b.213, p. 46; b.4, fol. 53v

B0416 Blind Cupid lay aside thy bow,
He'll kiss, not curse, thy dart.

'Cupid's cruelty'

fb.107, p. 23

B0417 Blind fortune no dominion has
Then to the finest gold.

[Mrs. Christian Kerr], 'The gentleman's answer' [to 'Tho' fortune frowns . . .']

c.102, p. 94

B0418 Blind love to this hour,
But more blest be those eyes that caus'd my desire.

[John Dryden], 'Love's fire'
[Crum B454]

fb.107, p. 39; b.213, p. 140

B0419 Bliss which one receives,
Nor grief, nor misfortune come nigh.

[John M—r], 'An elegiac epithalamion'

c.118, p. 74

B0420 Blissful time! Propitious seats!
True riches in content we find.

John Lockman, 'Yarico: an American pastoral drama. Set to music by Mr. John Christopher Smith: and writ for Buckingham House . . . 1742'

c.267/3, p. 178; c.268 (second part), p. 189 (var.; 'blissful clime')

B0421 Blithe Bacchus ask'd, by a bold devotee,
Pointed his Thyrsis to a pickled herring.

John Lockman, 'Extempore, in Fishmonger's Hall, at Mr. [?] Boswell's entertainment there'

c.267/1, p. 176

B0422 Blood has a voice to pierce the skies,
And, for our pardon, pleads his blood.

[Isaac Watts, Hymns and spiritual songs (1707), bk. II, Hymn 118]

c.180, p. 35

B0423 Blood! Underneath the holy coat, this was
In the next world, we wish you hang'd in this.

'The answer' [to 'When daring Blood . . .']
[Crum B457]

fb.140, p. 136

B0424 Blooming beauty, brilliant wit,
Death forever shall remove.

Lady [Catherine Rebecca] Manners, 'On virtue'

c.83/2, no. 335

B0425 Blot out the day, blot out th'accursed day;
And make me quite forget the ills of life.

'Job. Chapter. 3d. part'

c.244, p. 620

B0426 Blow, blow, thou winter wind
As friend remember'd not.

[William Shakespeare]

Diggle Box: Poetry Box XI/37

B0427 Blow cruel blast, and from the forest tear
The sorrowing pilgrims' thorny path can cheer.

S[arah] Herd, 'Sonnet to the north wind'

c.141, p. 382

B0428 Blow high blow low let the tempest tear the
mainmast by the board
In hopes on shore to be once more safe moor'd
with thee.

'Song 190'
[cf. B462]

c.555, p. 305

B0429 Blown on the rolling surface of the deep,
And heaven, indulgent bless'd their nuptial bands.

S[tephen] Duck, 'Felix and Constance'

c.83/1, no. 191

B0430 Blown up by faction, by guilt spurr'd on
Wedg'd in that timber which he strove to rend.

[Sir William Trumbull], 'On Ld Somers' [1700]
[POAS VI.198]

Trumbull Box: Poetry Box XIII/57

B0431 Blush not, fair maid, amidst [?] laugh to own
You but lament the mischief of your eye.

'Occasioned by Miss Sally P—s's blushing upon her sister's telling her she would not walk out with a design to stay at home with Mr. Brown who was sick. June 8th 1741'

c.221, p. 24

B0432 Blush not, ye fair, to own me, but be wise,
And even, lend mortality a charm.

'Lady's [skull]' [inscription in an alcove in the garden of Mr. Tyer's at Denbigh, Surrey]
[Crum B470]

c.156, p. 60; c.83/1, no. 96

B0433 Blush Phidias blush to see your rivall'd art
Thy art thy manner no one can attain.

[George] H[owar]d, [6th earl of Carlisle], 'On Mrs. Darner(?)'

c.197, p. 41

B0434 Boast not a gold rain, O Jove behold
Cupid descends in show'rs more rich than gold.

'Love tears'

c.360/3, no. 50

B0435 Boast not mistaken swain thy art
Whom love has render'd blind.

A. B., 'A copy of verses sent to Ensign William Farrell
of the Second Regiment of Foot Guards, on Friday
August 15—1740 when encamped on Hounslow
Heath—by a lady unknown'

c.360/1, p. 67; c.358, p. 96 (attr. Lady F. Burgoyne);
c.549, p. 58 ('mistaken maid')

B0436 Boast not of Bolingbroke's retreat
All smiling join in chorus.

'Song' ['The new toast,' June 1715]
[Crum B472]

fc.58, p. 67; c.570/1, p. 23

B0437 Boast not, ye few, your better fate,
Free air and sunshine are for all.

'On a fine day'

c.83/4, no. 2000

B0438 Boats (flat-bottom'd,) sold here.
By a jilt now betray'd.

John Lockman, 'Verses said to be stuck up, at
Versailles [Oct. 1759]'

c.267/4, p. 171

B0439 Bob Sandford call'd here, yesterday
No matter, whether girls or boys.

'To Saml. Sheppard esqr. On the birth of a daughter'

c.484, p. 99

B0440 Bold, foul-mouth'd Crab, by vice brought low,
I buried thee a twelvemonth since.

John Lockman, 'Sir Robert Walpole, and Crab the
poet a true story . . . July 1754'

c.267/1, p. 171

B0441 Bold infidelity, turn pale and die
It died for Adam sinn'd, it lives for Jesus died.

[Thomas Stevens?], 'An epitaph in the churchyard at
Whitser [Whittlesey?] in Cambridgeshire'

c.259, p. 109

B0442 Bold is the man, and *compos mentis* scarce
If you would save Old Nick, you'll never damn
poor me.

'Prologue to A peep behind the curtain. Spoken by
Mr. King'

c.68, p. 188

B0443 Bold poetry durst never feign a change
May prove a penitent or preaching Paul.

[Edward] Sparke, 'Poem 21st—on the conversion of
St. Paul'

b.137, p. 50

B0444 Bold Tallard yields, brave Marsin dies,
Forget the tyrant, and a monarch reign.

'Upon the Duke of Marlborough's repeated victories'
Poetry Box IV/53

B0445 Bold was the man as ancient poets say
Secured from envy's blast or faction's rage.

[William Boscawen], 'The progress of satire'
fc.106, p. 69

B0446 Boldly, my muse, on stronger pinions soar,
What muse refrain her tributary verse.

[preface to 'By agonizing pain . . .']
c.591

B0447 Bone and Skin, two millers thin
That flesh and blood, won't bear it.

[John Byrom, of Manchester], 'Made extempore by
Mad Byron [*sic*] on two millers of Manchester (who
were both very thin men) being tried and punished by
the mayor (a very fat man) for ingrossing all the corn
in a time of scarcity'

c.360/1, p. 157; c.81/1, no. 320; see also 'Two millers
thin . . .'.

B0448 Born at the first to bring another forth
Dying myself renews it in my seed.

[Richard Brathwaite], 'Upon a gentlewoman dying in
childbed her child living'
[Crum B495]

b.62, p. 115

B0449 Born of ancient Tuscan kings,
Pleas'd, above the stars, to rise.

[William Popple, trans.], 'Horace book 1st. ode 1st. To
Maecenas'

fc.104/2, p. 2

B0450 Born to a triple empire, I submit
Than all the wonders of her prosp'rous reign.

'On the King' [The Old Pretender (James Edward
Stuart) on a sight of his own and his sister's (Queen
Anne's) picture]
[Crum B497]

fc.58, p. 104; Poetry Box VII/63 ('triple kingdom');
c.570/1, p. 41

B0451 Born to command to conquer and to spare
In provinces preserv'd and cities saved.

H[annah] More, 'An epitaph on Gen: Lawrance'

c.341, p. 30

B0452 Born to engage all hearts, and charm all eyes
Her mind, was virtue by the graces drest.

[George] Lyttelton, 1st baron Lyttelton, 'On Mrs.
Lyttelton; by her husband'
[Crum B499]

Spence Papers, folder 101; see also 'Made to engage . . .'.

B0453 Born(?) to the treasures of the spring,
And bright as they, her lays shall rise.

John Lockman, 'To the Countess of Middlesex: with a
most splendid nosegay of flowers . . . Spring Gardens,
Vauxhall . . . 1748'

c.267/1, p. 283

B0454 Born under a cloud of misfortune and sorrow,
Come buy my sweet cowslips come buy.

'The cowslip girl'

c.83/3, no. 759

B0455 Born when stars propitious shone,
In the ocean when he lies.

[William Popple, trans.], '[Horace] book 4th. Ode
5th. To Augustus'

fc.104/2, p. 348

B0456 Borne aloft on zephyr's wing
Bellowing for unhallow'd joys.

R[ichard] V[ernon] S[adleir], 'My niece Mrs. M:
having written to me from the country, and elegantly
described the beauties of the spring, I wrote the
following contrast to create mirth'

c.106, p. 86

B0457 Borne on the wings of zephyrs bland,
The glad creation smiles around.

[William Mills], 'Ode to spring'

c.472, p. 7

B0458 Borne with a strong unusual wing
Nor give you reason to complain.

Abraham Oakes, '[Horace to Maecenas.] Ode XX. B.
2. translated'

c.50, p. 158

B0459 Both from your love, and loyalty, I gather
A truer subject, nor sincerer friend.

Sir Thomas Urquhart, 'To the [crossed out]'

fb.217, p. 266

B0460 Both my first and my second are often denied
Yet *tête-à-tête* found, no terrible deed.

[Four charades (4)]

Poetry Box II/42/4

B0461 Both robb'd of air we both lie in one ground
Both whom one fire burnt one water drown'd.

[John Donne], '[Epigrams.] 6. Hero et Leander'

b.205, fol. 96v

B0462 Both stout, and prudent Marquis, your successors
Their merit in your greater worth's compacted.

Sir Thomas Urquhart, 'To the Marquis of Donglay'

fb.217, p. 329

B0463 Both th'author, and work's of such esteem,
That he renowns the word, and the work him.

Sir Thomas Urquhart, 'Of a worthy gentleman, who
wrote an excellent good book'

fb.217, p. 218

B0464 Both Tuscans, and Castilians answer each
The Spaniards more the truth, than man affect.

Sir Thomas Urquhart, 'Of signorsi, and so senor'

fb.217, p. 73

B0465 Both wives, and widows, maids, and whores entice
From only what is lawful you refrain.

Sir Thomas Urquhart, 'To a lecherous man, and bad
husband'

fb.217, p. 177

B0466 Bothmer acts Father Peters in disguise
Who sent a greater King than you to France.

'The caution' [on George I's first ministry, 1714–17]
[Crum B511]

fc.58, p. 111

B0467 Bound for Sarum's distant plains
Endless peace and endless love.

H[enry] Skrine, 'Ode on the marriage of a sister . . .
Salisbury—Dec. 8 1777'

c.509, p. 7

B0468 Bounding billow, cease thy motion,
Now we part—to meet no more!

'Stanzas written between Dover and Calais July 24th.
1792'

c.250

B0469 Bow Albion thy inglorious head in dust
Than those that freed themselves, and righted
J[ame]s.

'To England'
[Crum B514]

c.570/1, p. 149

B0470 Bow the head thou lily fair,
That with such ease and grace did move.

T[homas] H[amly] Butler, 'Dirge. To the memory of
Mrs. Sheridan'

c.142, p. 415

B0471 Bowman; amongst those whom kinder stars yet
                                                    spare
Enthron'd our King, and all their factions broke.

[Thomas Stanley], 'Bowman' [in 'A register of
friends']

b.153, p. 13

B0472 Boy, take away my gown, I hate those shows
About with it, while a catch we sing.

'To a serv[an]t'

c.361

B0473 Bra' Ormonde now is o' the main
Will bless this happy nation.

'A song to the tune of Catherine Mogey'

c.570/2, p. 54

B0474 Brabus of late hath often said
He wanted money, and he needs must sell it.

'On Brabus'

b.200, p. 407

B0475 Brag not thereof, when thou good deeds hast done,
For with his grace to good God makes thee run.

c.339, p. 328

B0476 Brag on proud Christ Church, neither fret, nor
                                                    grieve
Which made the Sabbath worse than Holiday.

'Art Holiday' [on Barten Holiday's Technogamia, or
the marriage of the arts, acted 26 August 1621;
answered by 'I could forgive . . .', 'More trouble
yet . . .' and ''Tis not my person . . .']
[Crum B520]

b.200, p. 35

B0477 Brave boys come on no longer servile things
With cheerfulness to serve our gracious king.

[Sir Philip Wodehouse], 'An ironical preverication
between a Royalist and a republican 1660'

b.131, p. 45

B0478 Brave English lads, beat up your drums:
                                        dubadubadub,
And here's to thee good fellow.

'On the rumors of the Spaniards' coming towards
England. 1608'

b.200, p. 367

B0479 Brave Englishmen once, now base cowards
                                                esteem'd,
We'll have nothing to do with rotten Orange's
snout, | But we'll bring back King James again.

'A loyal Jacobean song'

b.111, p. 48

B0480 Brave gallant Duke do not lament
With beauty wit and treasure.

'The answer' [of the Princess Royal to the Duke of
Lorraine's courtship, 'Fair princess let me not
complain . . .']
[second part of Crum F86]

c.536

B0481 Brave lads take your nets; heave them into the
main;
In the meantime all Europe will ring with their
                                sound. | O pickled herring, &c.

John Lockman, 'The superintendant's exhortation to
the crews of the Society's busses, fishing off
Yarmouth, in Nov. 1751 the tune, O the roast beef of
old England; and sung by Mr. Leveridge &c. in
Stationer's Hall, in Lord Mayor's Day of the same
year; (after a dessert of Shetland pickled herrings)'

c.267/2, p. 78

B0482 Brave loyal souls be not cast down,
Who we hope will enjoy his own again.

'A song on the 10th of June' [birthday of the Old
Pretender]

fc.58, p. 135

B0483 Brave Oakum Mainbrace honest Jack
To my messmates out [at] sea.

'Messmates at sea'

c.160, fol. 61

B0484 Brave Walworth, knight, lord mayor that slew
A dagger to the city arms.

'Wrote under the effigy of Sir Wm Walworth Knt in
Fishmonger's Hall London'

c.360/1, p. 165

B0485 Brave youth, to whom fate in one hour
I'll die thy valor's sacrifice.

[Thomas Carew], 'For a picture where the Queen
laments over the tomb of a slain knight'

b.150, p. 228

B0486 Break off thy slumber, gentle god,
And bring th'idea of the saint I love.

[John Norris], 'To sleep'

Diggle Box: Poetry Box XI/35

B0487   Break they their fast on Friday, who refresh
And fasts are only for mortification.

> Sir Thomas Urquhart, 'A question to a Roman
> Catholic'
>
> fb.217, p. 329

B0488   Breathe breathe the flute and tune the lyre,
His name to Britons dear!

> 'Song for Nov. 4th 1767'
>
> c.89, p. 23

B0489   Breathe soft, ye winds! ye numbers gently flow!
And make me worthy of the name of friend!

> [cf. Crum B548]
>
> Greatheed Box/64

B0490   Breathe soft ye zephyrs smile Aurora bright
And join the joyful feast. | We'll be [blithesome
and gay] &c.

> 'An ode for Mira's birthday Feb. 14'
>
> Poetry Box I/59

B0491   Breathless and pale! Would heaven no longer lend
And tell—the young, the learn'd, the good, must die.

> 'To the memory of a friend writ 1724'
>
> c.360/2, no. 100

B0492   Bred up in solitude and gloomy shades,
Nor wish for freedom, while such slav'ry's mine.

> Poetry Box III/4

B0493   Brethren, by this my mind you'll know
Will soon fill up their proper places.

> [John Byrom, of Manchester], 'Rules for preaching
> from a bishop to his clergy' [pr. General evening post,
> 25 March 1749]
> [Crum B549]
>
> c.186, p. 117; c.83/1, no. 220; c.229/1, fol. 66 ('this comes
> to let you know'); Spence Papers, folder 113

B0494   Brethren, let us praise our L[ord]
Their G[od] and guide till death.

> [Hymn]
>
> c.180, p. 85

B0495   Bretons! My slipp'ry contr'mans are come
He's Louisbourg:—so you may kiss ———.

> John Lockman, 'Prologue, supposed to be spoke by a
> Frenchman, the great shadow of a poet; at the opening
> of the little theater in the Haymarket, by French
> strollers'
>
> c.267/3, p. 142

B0496   Bridle your will, let reason be your guide:
So may you stand while others down do slide.

> c.339, p. 260; see also 'That man who hath . . .'.

B0497   Bright Amphitrite, goddess of the sea,
Ready to tune that lyre her votaries strung.

> M[aurice] J[ohnson], '1705. In imitation of
> Saumazarius . . . an invocation to Amphitrite. Set and
> sung by Mr. [Henry?] Holcombe'
>
> c.229/2, fol. 11v

B0498   Bright are the tints that paint th'ethereal bow
And still more swift her dear deceptions fly.

> 'From the novel of Delia'
>
> Diggle Box: Poetry Box XI/14

B0499   Bright as Diana, as sweet Hebe gay,
Turn to a sight like this, and then be proud.

> John Lockman, 'The contrast. Looking on his dear
> mother's picture, as she lay in her coffin . . . May 1742'
>
> c.267/1, p. 10

B0500   Bright as the day and as the morning fair
Such Chloe is—and common as the air.

> [George Granville, 1st baron] Lansdowne, 'On Chloe'
>
> fc.60, p. 40; c.360/1, p. 89

B0501   Bright charming fair in whose resplendent mind
If thy disdain permit it long to burn.

> [Mrs. Christian Kerr], 'Sent with a present of nuts on
> Hallow Eve 1720'
>
> c.102, p. 121

B0502   Bright dawns the day with rosy face
Shrill horns wind his knell and he dies.

> 'Song 186'
>
> c.555, p. 296

B0503   Bright ethereals! Matchless pair,
E'en ancient maids, the truth confess.

> 'On the two celebrated beauties of Ireland, the two
> Miss Gunnings, at London 1751'
>
> c.360/3, no. 174

B0504   Bright god of day, whose genial power
And make his people great, and happy by his sway.

> [Francis Fawkes], 'A vernal ode. Sent to his grace the
> Lord Archbishop, March 14, 1754'
>
> fc.21, p. 17

B0505   Bright Mariana who can see
And court their new-made choice.

> 'A song'
>
> Poetry Box X/87

B0506 Bright shone the morn, in all its orient pride,
Slept 'twixt the sheets, and married upon tick.

> John Lockman, 'The extempore wedding, solemnized
> surreptitiously, not many hundred miles from
> Salisbury . . . Sept. 1746'
>
> c.267/1, p. 139

B0507 Bright shone the taper's sparkling blaze,
The issues of our heart.

> 'The allurements of vice, exemplified in the fable of
> the fly and the candle'
>
> c.83/1, no. 105

B0508 Bright star! by Venus fix'd above,
Who lately stole my heart away.

> George Stepney, 'To the evening star. Englished from
> a Greek Idyllium'
>
> b.150, p. 217; c.351, p. 78

B0509 Bright Stella, object of my constant love,
I'd seek some friendly shade, and silent die.

> 'Epistle III. To Stella, written soon after her leaving
> the island'
>
> fc.100, p. 11

B0510 Bright Venus, who of late, as sages say,
And there with undiminish'd luster, shines.

> 'On the mar[riage] of Roger Pocklington, esq. To
> Miss Thoe(?) of Winthorpe Kents . . . Oxoniensis'
>
> fc.85, fol. 103

B0511 Brighter than Phoebus in his fine career
Borrows all nature, and is nature's right.

> [Horace Walpole, 4th earl of Orford], 'Countess of
> Wal[de]gr[a]ve' [d. 1807]
> [Crum B568]
>
> c.157, p. 70

B0512 Bring a bowl! I'll toast a health,
Him back again that's blawn awa'.

> 'A ballad to a Scotch tune'
>
> c.570/1, p. 54

B0513 Bring forth the pris'ner, Just[ice]: thy commands
Th'offended dies, to set the offender free.

> [Francis Quarles], 'A dialogue Christ justice sinner'
> [Crum B573]
>
> b.49, p. 24

B0514 Bring me flowers, and bring me wine!
When we live but for a day!

> [Georgiana Spencer Cavendish], duchess of
> Devonshire(?), 'Sonnet—said to have been written by
> Her Grace . . .'
>
> c.90

B0515 Bring me quoth one a trowel quickly quick
Scatter their stuff and rumble down their tools.

> 'On the confusion of Babel'
> [Crum B577]
>
> c.158, p. 51; see also 'God well perceiving . . .'.

B0516 Bring to the Lord, the mighty, to your King
The Lord shall shower his blessing down of peace.

> George Montagu, 'Psalm the 29th paraphrased'
>
> fc.135, p. 5

B0517 Brisk and airy, blithe and gay
Such the nymph that I admire.

> 'Second acrostic on Miss Banks'
>
> c.360/2, no. 45

B0518 Brisk as a bee on summer's day
Speaks the perfect beauty born.

> 'Acrostic on Miss Banks Tunbridge Wells 1745'
>
> c.360/2, no. 44

B0519 Brisk god of love assist a maid
Too little if 'tis *tout de bon*.

> [Horace] Walpole, [4th earl of Orford], 'Translation
> of a French song applied to Lady Caroline Fitzroy and
> Mr. Conway'
>
> fc.135

B0520 Bristol! To worth any genius ever just,
All else a bubble or an empty name.

> G[eorge] Colman [the elder?], 'Epitaph on
> Mr. Powell'
>
> c.341, p. 159

B0521 Britain at length may boast a finish'd piece,
And heav'n and earth in one great chorus join.

> 'To Sr. Richard Blackmore, upon his poem called
> Creation'
>
> c.73, p. 11

B0522 Britain, attend the warning voice,
Be guilty, unreprov'd.

> 'On the two earthquakes which happened at London
> on Thursday February the 8th and Thursday March
> the 8th'
> [Crum B583]
>
> c.360/3, no. 73

B0523 Britain. Expect from heaven no happy fate,
Still more deprav'd than that we see.

> 'In imitation of Horace . . . lib. 3 ode 6'
>
> b.111, p. 507

B0524 Britain once famed through many a distant region
If you again restore the Stuarts' name.

'The advice' [c. 1715–16]
[Crum B589]
fc.58, p. 49

B0525 Britain's hope and illustrious seven
Everlasting glory gain.

'On the new ministry appointed 1783 composed of
seven cabinet councillors'
fc.53, p. 145

B0526 Britannia mourn, lament thy sinking state,
Long live King James our true, and lawful king.

'Advice to Britain' [on George I]
[Crum B592]
c.570/1, p. 105

B0527 Britannia, to the god who sounds the lyre,
What need of aliens? See my fav'rite—Arne!

John Lockman, 'After hearing Dr. Arne's opera of
Artaxerxes . . . March 1762'
c.267/1, p. 321

B0528 Britannia when by heaven inspired
Deathless and great shall be her fame. | Choose
Britannia—

[Claude Champion de] Crespigny, 'A parody upon
Rule Britannia'
File 17394

B0529 Briton! If thou would'st sure destruction shun,
Fatal to all who dare approach too nigh.

John Lockman, 'Chalked on the shutters of a gin shop'
c.267/1, p. 195

B0530 Britons behold the glory of the isle!
Nor old Rome boast more virtue than within.

[David Garrick], 'Inscription for Stowe'
Acquisition 92.3.1ff. (autogr.)

B0531 Britons behold the product of your isle
Then judge the vicious growth, and guess the men.

'[preface to] A collection of state flowers'
c.570/4, p. 23

B0532 Britons! Draw the shining steel:
Till time's no more!

John Lockman, 'The exhortation, to Britons;
(extempore) on the threatened invasion of the French
[June 1756]. The tune, Let ambition fill thy mind, &c.'
c.267/2, p. 14

B0533 Britons in me you may behold of late
I'm without female aid, the product of the male.

'A riddle on a man's beard'
c.360/1, p. 3

B0534 Britons now retrieve your glory
Or you never can be blest.

'A song'
c.570/2, p. 156

B0535 Britons rejoice your pray'rs are heard,
No longer shall command.

'An ode on his Majesty's happy recovery'
c.139, p. 356

B0536 Britons! Shall France a fleet to India send?
Swift let her navies rise, and [?] the deep.

John Lockman, 'To my countrymen . . . Decr. 1751'
c.267/1, p. 232

B0537 Britons tonight in native pomp we come,
Or kinder censure him forbear.

[William Whitehead], 'Prologue to The Roman
father'
c.578, p. 124

B0538 Bromfield's pastor here entomb'd
An anthem to the King of Kings.

'Bromfield on the north side of the communion table
there lies a late vicar under the following epitaph . . .
1673'
c.547, p. 327

B0539 Brood not too much over anxious themes
So kindly name next week some day.

'Horat. lib. 2 ode 11 imitated. Putney Septem. 16. 1747'
Poetry Box I/126

B0540 Brothers and sisters dry up your tears, and weep no
more,
For I am only gone a little before.

c.378, p. 32; see also 'Friends dry up . . .'.

B0541 Brought forth in solitude, my infant muse
How blind their hearts on the inglorious plain!

John Lockman, 'David's lamentation over Saul and
Jonathan. A lyric poem. Set to music by Mr. Boyce:
and performed in the Apollo Society . . . in 1736'
c.267/3, p. 306; c.268 (second part), p. 37

B0542 Brute beasts which of right reason want the use,
Which ill requital, causeth in the heart.

Sir John Strangways, '3tio Novembris 1646'
b.304, p. 67

B0543   B—t to give each word its proper grace
Betwixt each drop stops half a minute.

     c.188, p. 34

B0544   Buckingham swears and drinks,
Wharton prays and talks.

     b.54, p. 866

B0545   Buda and Rhodes' proud Solyman had torn
A title to be call'd, the son of heav'n.

     [Edmund Waller], 'To his Majesty upon his motto
     Beata pacifici'

     fb.228/39

B0546   Buford in spite of all detractions
Straight on the banks of Cam go fie. . . .

     'Epigram on the Duke of Newcastle'

     c.74 (incomplete)

B0547   Build me my mansion in a cypress grove
On the soft mossy floor finds calm repose.

     fb.66/25

B0548   Building of castles did commence,
In castles of eternal rest.

     'On building of castles'

     c.83/3, no. 976

B0549   Burgundia sometimes did breed
And come to heaven the perfect way. | Amen

     'Of S. Barnard. Aug. 20'

     a.30[27]

B0550   Buried I am and yet not dead
E'er lived in death in such a tomb or place.

     '1 Enigmata: resol: Jonas'

     b.205, fol. 99v

B0551   Buried in darkness, and oppress'd with care,
And place my sure, my lasting hopes in them.

     [Richard] Daniel, dean of Armagh, 'The supplication.
     Psal: 130'

     c.244, p. 389

B0552   Burleigh and Walsingham in former days
Unite them—how—to hate and scorn the knight.

     'An epigram in praise of modern unity'

     c.570/4, p. 9

B0553   Burnet forever has the Whigs forsook
There won't be such another congregation.

     'On Sarum [Burnet] and Wharton' [Jacobite verse,
     1715]
     [Crum B619]

     fc.58, p. 105; c.570/1, p. 29

B0554   Burney, beneath the venerable roof
In sweet Cecilia's smile, on Evelina's love.

     John Walters, 'Ode to the master of Newton House
     [St. Martin's Lane] . . . 1783'

     c.486, fol. 29v

B0555   Burst forth in tears thou heart of adamant
She liv'd, she died, the mirror of the youth.

     'A funeral elegy upon the most Christian death of
     Mrs. Bridget Philipps' [d. 29 April 1634]

     b.52/2, p. 160

B0556   Bursting with pride, the loath'd impostume swells,
This knight o'th' burning pestle make us sport.

     [John Wilmot, 2nd earl of Rochester], 'My Lord All-
     Pride' [John Sheffield, duke of Buckingham and
     Normanby]

     b.105, p. 350; b.54, p. 1183

B0557   Bus'ness thou plague and pleasure of my life,
I cannot with thee, nor without thee live.

     'A conflict upon business'

     c.111, p. 131

B0558   Busy, curious, thirsty fly
Will appear as short as one.

     [William Oldys], 'The fly'
     [Crum B624]

     c.360/1, p. 275; c.358, p. 158

B0559   Busy old fool, unruly sun
This bed thy center is, these walls thy sphere.

     [John Donne], 'Ad solem. A song'
     [Crum B626]

     b.114, p. 312; b.148, p. 85

B0560   But ah! what wish can prosper, or what pray'r,
That has a heart and life in it, be free!

     William Cowper, 'On slavery and the slave trade'

     c.139, p. 486

B0561   But all our subtle actions seem
Shall take it out in kisses.

     [Robert Cholmeley], 'Harlot's love sent to a young
     gentleman that was very fond of one'

     c.190, p. 161

B0562   But am I sure he's dead, whom yet I see
Write this: Gray's Inn's interr'd beneath this stone.

     [William Lewes, of Oriel College], 'An elegy on the
     death of Dr Fenton of Gray's Inn' [d. Jan. 1615/16]
     [Crum B629]

     b.200, p. 221; b.356, p. 36

B0563　But are my riches gone?
　　　　Or else, as got or sought.

　　　　　[George Wither], 'A hymn'
　　　　c.139, p. 156

B0564　But art thou come, dear Savior, hath thy love
　　　　Will make a stall a court, a cratch [creche], a
　　　　　　　　　　　　　　　　　　　　　　throne.

　　　　　[Sir Matthew Hale], 'Christmas Day 1665'
　　　　　[Crum B631]
　　　　b.49, p. 16; see also 'When I begin sadly . . .'.

B0565　But being found out heir of greater worth
　　　　Than all the virtues that the earth brings forth.

　　　　　[Sir Thomas Urquhart], 'Ep. 1. 4'
　　　　fb.217, p. 535

B0566　But gypsy fortune now began to grudge
　　　　Sweet meat with dash of sour sauce.

　　　　c.519

B0567　But if you can make right elucid
　　　　For tediousness oft gives abuse.

　　　　　R[icha]rd Farnham, 'Writ at Radburne near Baxby
　　　　　June the 14. 1655, for . . . Lady Anne . . . Poole'
　　　　Poetry Box VII/29

B0568　'But life creeps on, and wastes away'—
　　　　Nor let a selfish heart be blest.

　　　　　'To Stella. 1752. Novr. 2. N. S.'
　　　　c.238, p. 15

B0569　But lo! The sons of genius stand,
　　　　While rapture lifts her voice, and goodness smiles
　　　　　　　　　　　　　　　　　　　　　　around.

　　　　　'Part of an ode to science'
　　　　Diggle Box: Poetry Box XI/26

B0570　But now alas! far other views disclose
　　　　And the rent rock unbraids, man's stubborn heart.

　　　　　[Robert] Lowth, 'On the death of Christ'
　　　　c.391

B0571　But now far other cares my mind engage,
　　　　And as thy converse, shall thy numbers please.

　　　　　[Charles Burney, the younger], 'October 18. 1778'
　　　　c.37, p. 20

B0572　But now, I saw a work that nature framed,
　　　　Which planted at once and on a sudden rotteth.

　　　　　'Felice tanto, nessuno, maj.'
　　　　Poetry Box VI/31

B0573　But oh the curse of wishing to be great
　　　　And wonted happiness returns no more.

　　　　　[John] Dryde[n], 'Juv[enal] 9—Lat[in] Dryde[n]
　　　　　trans[ation] fo[lio] 178'
　　　　Trumbull Box: Poetry Box XIII/35

B0574　But oh! what arms shall I now find
　　　　Take all exemptions you would have.

　　　　　[Mrs. Christian Kerr], 'The answer' [to 'Within this
　　　　　breast . . .']
　　　　c.102, p. 96

B0575　But oh! What wretched scenes of grief appear
　　　　Attend ambition and a courtly life.

　　　　c.416

B0576　But our great Turks in wit must reign alone
　　　　They praise no works but what are like their own.

　　　　　[Alexander] Pope, 'Lines copied from Mr. Pope's
　　　　　handwriting on a scrap of paper'
　　　　Poetry Box X/148

B0577　But painter cease, here draw your largest bayle(?)
　　　　The rare effects of art's bold industry.

　　　　　Edm[und] Borlase, 'Elegies on Sr. Horatio Vere'
　　　　b.52/2, p. 126

B0578　But persuade Caesar that his heart may prove
　　　　Not utterly unworthy of your love.

　　　　　'Alexander to Cleopatra his sister'
　　　　c.189, p. 24

B0579　But reader be content to stay
　　　　Whether saint devil, witch, man, maid, or whore.

　　　　　'On Joan of Arc'
　　　　c.189, p. 45; see also 'Here lies Joan of Arc . . .'.

B0580　But say (thou very woman) why to me
　　　　I shall have ten as fair, ten times more true.

　　　　　[Henry King], 'To a gentlewoman who promising him
　　　　　marriage, married another'
　　　　　[Crum B661]
　　　　b.200, p. 144

B0581　But should all my endeavors prosper ill,
　　　　What I can't do, sure Cleopatra will.

　　　　　'Caesar'
　　　　c.189, p. 24

B0582　But since on knavish models G[eor]ge is split,
　　　　To stem by force his madness, and despair.

　　　　　'Pighburgh and Kilmanseck [Kielmansegge]. The
　　　　　modest toast | We'll soon have pensions at the nation's
　　　　　cost | Beyond what Portland, or what Orkney boast'
　　　　c.570/1, p. 67

B0583 But soft—the muse enraptur'd sings,
Thus blest let him live, thus blest let him die.

[Charles Burney, the younger]

c.37, p. 15; see also 'Tell William . . .'.

B0584 But stay! Is God like one of us? Can he,
God turns his hand but alters not his will.

[Thomas Stevens?], 'Pious thoughts and
contemplations extracted from Wilcox['s] Guide to
eternal glory'

c.259, inserted after p. 16

B0585 But suppose not that the earth doth yield
But 'gainst the shooter do the shaft [re?l]

[Joshua Sylvester, trans. Guillaume de Salluste,
seigneur] Du Bartas, 'Of dittany'

b.284, p. 54

B0586 But that thou art my wisdom, Lord,
Do not so well agree . . . .

[George] Herbert, 'Submission'
[Crum B670]

b.245 (inside back cover; incomplete)

B0587 But the false fox most kindly played his part
That to give hugely to the box refus'd.

'Mother Hubbard's tale, where the fox is always
represented as the emblem of craft and baseness is
raised to be first minister of the kingdom of beasts'

c.570/3, p. 55

B0588 But to defend the injured peer
Hosts will support him, and with spirit.

[docket: 'Burns']

Poetry Box XIV/199

B0589 But to his eldest son his house, and lands he assigns,
O the King's young courtier.

'The King's young courtier'

fb.107, p. 70

B0590 But vainly we resist the gods who will
Their just decrees on guilty men fulfil.

'Pompey'

c.189, p. 24

B0591 But what are these to great At[os]sa's mind
Or wanders Heav'n-directed to the poor.

[Alexander Pope(?), lines on the Duchess of
Marlborough, supposedly omitted from his Satire on
women in expectation of a reward]

Poetry Box I/102

B0592 But what vast rising bulwarks' mighty row,
War, and footsteps of destruction here.

'Upon the sight of a demolished castle. Gent.
magazine'

c.160, fol. 73

B0593 But what will those increasing beauties do,
As cheers the soul, yet still maintains your height.

[Thomas Creech], 'To the Lady Anne [spoken] by
Mr. [Philip] Bertie' [Oxford, 21 May 1683]

fb.142, p. 24

B0594 But who climbs above the mean
And nearer his decay.

fb.9, fol. 30v

B0595 But why this fury[?] All that e'er was writ
Houses blown up have stopt a fire's course.

'A satire ignis ignibus extinguitur' [1682]
[Crum B687]

b.113, p. 151

B0596 But will you now to peace incline
We'll have or spoil, at last.

[Sir John Denham], 'Mr. Hampden's speech
occasioned upon the Londoners' petition for peace'
[23 March 1643]
[Crum B688]

fb.106(8)

B0597 But wrapt in error is the human mind
Know we how long the present shall endure?

[Gilbert Weston, 'The seventh olympick ode',
translated from Pindar]

fc.156

B0598 But you are overblest plainly this day
A century to this heart.

'Feasts and revels'

b.205, fol. 26r

B0599 But you lie like a rascal, God's hookers pork and
spitchcock,
Pass in the humble(?) pie, Peg Waniford fills in a
blackpot.

'Tom Redman's humor'

b.356, p. 43

B0600 Buxton, whom manners rough and storms renown,
Adieu forever to thy hated town.

'Wrote upon the wall of Buxton Well August 14th
1741 . . . imitated from Caesar by Mary Queen of
Scots'

c.221, p. 26

B0601 Buxton, whose fame thy baths shall ever tell,
Whom I, perhaps, shan't see again, farewell.

'The celebrated beauty, Mary Queen of Scots, took
her leave of Buxton Wells in Derbyshire with the
following distich [from Caesar's verses upon Feltria,
translated]'

c.360/2, no. 241

B0602 By a bold people's stubborn arms opprest
And on an open stage unburied lie.

[Abraham Cowley], 'The sortes Virgiliana dipped into
by K[in]g Charles the 1st at Oxford anno 1640 . . . At
bello audacis: Virgil: l[ib]: 4 v: 615'
[Crum B694]

c.229/1, fol. 41

B0603 By a cool fountain's flowing side
To share a death like thine.

[Hester Grenville] Pitt, countess of Chatham, 'The
bee. a song'
[Crum B695]

c.233, p. 85; c.536 ('By a clear crystal fountain's side . . .')

B0604 By a (God help ye) when the poor sue them
Being frozen in the point of granting alms.

Sir Thomas Urquhart, 'Of certain puritans' lack of
charity'

fb.217, p. 265

B0605 By absence this good mean I gain
And so enjoy her, and so miss her.

'Upon absence'

c.102, p. 26 (incomplete?); see also 'Absence, hear my
protestation . . .'.

B0606 By agonizing pain long time opprest,
Nor ever want that help he gave to me.

Lady [ ] Grogan, 'Paraphrase' [imitated by 'Teased
with a rotten tooth . . .']

c.591

B0607 By all the pow'rs, whoe'er they be,
In mem'ry of thy vow.

[William Popple, trans.], '[Horace, ep]ode 5th. On
Canidia'

fc.104/2, p. 410

B0608 By any means with all your might endeavor
The fault is in the [?] and not in you.

[Sir Thomas Urquhart], 'That no [?] adventure should
hinder us from being good, though we be [?] if the
reward [?]'

fb.217, p. 526

B0609 By Avon's stream the artless poet sung,
Triumphant rescu'd Shakespeare's injur'd name.

[David Garrick], 'Sonnet'

Poetry Box v/30

B0610 By Babylon's waters we sat down,
They'll snatch, and dash against the stones.

'Psalm 137'

c.264/3, p. 87

B0611 By beastly birth into the world I slipt
Makes a firm cement for the artist's use.

'Riddle'

c.111, p. 159

B0612 By birth 'tis a bastard, incestuous in love
'Tis a priest, that fears neither God nor the devil.

'A true account of a monster called a Yahoo'

c.360/1, p. 265

B0613 By Britain's true monarchs, great William and Mary
Usurpers and rebels may ne'er get the day.

'The proclamation for a general fast in the nation. To
the tune of . . . Packington's pound'
[Crum B713]

b.111, p. 225; fb.70, p. 221

B0614 By Calvin's doctrine now you must die
Was King was Church and fine religion.

'My Lord . . .'

Poetry Box viii/44

B0615 By civil government of God ordain'd
Is regular, and subjects in obeying.

[Daniel Baker], 'Of politics'

b.81, p. 125

B0616 By critic storms how many vessels lost,
A hiss would drive him out to sea again.

'Prologue to The female captain spoken by
Mr. Palmer'

c.115

B0617 By custom doom'd to folly, sloth and ease,
And vie in fame with ancient Greece and Rome.

[Isabella (Machell) Ingram, viscountess Irwin?], 'On
Mr. Pope's characters of women by a lady of quality'

c.83/3, no. 967

B0618 By death my ills had ended long ago
Shall see his ends with good success fulfilled.

Sir John Strangways

b.304, p. 34

B0619 By Dian's crescent on her front display'd
And solve the knot that puzzles Warburton.

'Epigram on Mrs. Warburton who appeared with
Dian's crescent'

c.74

B0620 By doxies ruin'd, oft in panic fright,
My shop, in open daylight, fled from me!

John Lockman, 'The above fellow [in 'Had
Hogarth . . .'] having opened a little shop, adjoining
the house of one, who had done him great service: he,
in return, libeled that person who thereupon threw up
a blind, in the night, before his shop, which quite hid
it'

c.267/1, p. 30

B0621 By envious wits abus'd so long,
And study, e'er they close with,—man.

[Stephen Barrett], 'To Miss Harriet Hussey in a set of
Pope's works—Bp. Warburton's edition. Instead of a
copy of verse on her birthday'

c.193, p. 105

B0622 By evil in the city we suppose,
But smites him justly as he went astray.

[Thomas Gurney], 'Answer to the 1 . . . to the 2d . . .
to the 3d [question by Mrs. M. B—y]'

c.213

B0623 By faith to God have we access,
Of a more close, more constant sight of Thee.

[Edmund Wodehouse], 'Novr. 23 [1714]'

b.131, p. 94

B0624 By fits, or by some random view
And kings, supreme in whoredom, reign.

[Robert Cholmeley], 'A passage in the chorus of the
3rd act of Seneca's Hippolytus imitated'

c.190, p. v

B0625 By force h'unmaiden'd me, alas
For weakness ne'er had done it.

Sir Thomas Urquhart, 'The complaint of a young
wanton girl, to the chief justice, on him, that had
depucelated her'

fb.217, p. 191

B0626 By fortune led
Could I but call her mine.

'Number 1' [in a three-volume collection of verse]

c.360/3, no. 1

B0627 By fraud, by ignorance, by pride,
And e'en vile rats the ruin fly.

John Lockman, 'The fair warning . . . Feb. 1757'

c.267/1, p. 211

B0628 By hapless youths, who pomp of war admire,
Of splendors fond, by which itself must die.

'To Miss Sally P—s from Cheltenham March 17. 1741'

c.221, p. 25

B0629 By heaven a hellish tribe so curst a crew
And make their final exit in a string.

'Another on the same picture [of the Queen and King
and seven new bishops]'

b.111, p. 409

B0630 By heav'n I'll tell her boldly, that 'tis she,
To an undeserving beggar than a thief.

'The discovery . . . Harl. 3991. P. 139b 17c anon.'
[docket]

Poetry Box vi/47; fb.107, p. 34

B0631 By heaven! She's hard, and melts no more
They are doubtless by nature, as forward as we.

'Amintor's fate'

fb.107, p. 33

B0632 By holy writ, I heard it prov'd at large,
Make strong my faith like to the dying thief.

'Holy advice'

c.187, p. 32

B0633 By impoliteness if you mean,
Shall study to deserve your hate.

[Isaac Freeman], 'To a lady who taxed me with
impoliteness'

fc.105

B0634 By Jove I think my wits are shrunk with wetting
I am thy friend as true as steel.

M. P., 'To his friend from a tavern'

b.205, fol. 45r

B0635 By knocking down of churches, Knox gave edge
If some new knocks came not, and knock them out.

Sir Thomas Urquhart, 'A non-covenanter's opinion of
the violent, and impetuous dissolution of some of our
Puritans in Scotland'

fb.217, p. 35

B0636 By land let them travel, as many as please
Where on earth can you find such a lodging.

'The balloon traveller'

c.179, p. 45

B0637 By lawless power and secret woes oppress'd,
When proud oppression ne'er shall part us more.

[William Boscawen], 'Elgira to Ediry'

fc.106, p. 4

B0638 By love betray'd I woo'd a belle,
Or else behold more kind.

    [Robert Cholmeley], 'The hard-hearted fair one'

c.190, p. 7

B0639 By lovely Mira's art alone
No art can e'er excel.

    [Phanuel Bacon], 'To Mira painting flowers, her own picture being ill-drawn'

c.237, fol. 53

B0640 By magic art I can discover,
Frederick is nam'd your favorite lover.

c.391

B0641 By Middleton we're told,—which thing Whiston
                    denies:
Has made the sly serpent to cuckold poor Adam.

    Abraham Oakes, 'The controversy: an epigram'

c.50, p. 140

B0642 By miracles exceeding power of man
Moist with one drop of thy blood, my dry soul.

    [John Donne], '[Holy sonnets. La Corona] 5th'
    [Crum B731]

b.114, p. 158

B0643 By mortal hands fram'd, yet I came from the skies
But perhaps when you know me, you'll grant me a
                    smile.

    [Thomas Hull]

c.528/38

B0644 By nature faith is fiery and it tends
In proper motion, mixt of faith and love.

    'Faith, love, and charity'

b.118, p. 230

B0645 By nature form'd to tread the stage,
An Oldfield I may rise.

    John Lockman, 'On a ticket, for the benefit of Miss Flamand, a Lilliputian player . . . Jan. 1745'

c.267/1, p. 29

B0646 By nature in my first estate
How to amend its way.

    A. C., 'From his own friend, and his father's friend. Caleb Vernon. Anagram. Bor'e[sic] unclean. Nue clean robe'

b.228, p. 76

B0647 By nature lord[s], men worse than nothing be;
Where is that something thou so boasts, proud
                    man.

    [Francis Quarles], 'On man'
    [Crum B733]

b.118, p. 233

B0648 By numbers known by few revered
Perhaps you'll find us at a stand.

    [Enigma/Charade/Conundrum 77e]

c.389

B0649 By our baptismal covenant
And Christ their Lord obey.

c.124, no. 10

B0650 By our first strange and fatal interview
Think it enough for me, to have had my [thy] love.

    [John Donne], 'Elegia nona' [On his mistress]
    [Crum B740]

b.114, p. 93; b.148, p. 121

B0651 By Prior well it has been said,
That all was full, and round, and fair.

    Cha[rle]s Burney, the elder

File 17448

B0652 By pronouncing my first you a blackguard may
                    please
Sure a Frenchman would make or a polecat.

    [Sir Henry William Bunbury], 'Charade—3'

File 17066

B0653 By purchas'd experience this maxim I'll prove,
That life is not life when divided from love.

    'On life, and love'

c.361; see also 'Come give your attention . . .'.

B0654 By sin came death, death brought us to the grave
By Christ came life our sinful souls to save.

c.240, p. 136

B0655 By sin came death—each sin's a moth
Thine are but little ones, each sin's a moth.

    [Sir Philip Wodehouse], 'Upon Thomasin Neech each sin's a moth'

b.131, back (no. 105)

B0656 By sounds like these Cecilia heavn'ly maid,
Like thee she drew another angel down.

    [J. B.], 'Extempore; a young lady coming downstairs half dressed upon hearing her cousin play one of Handel's anthems on the harpsichord'

Poetry Box IV/155

B0657 By sure artificers my husband Jean
Pusht to the third and to the fourth by mine.

> [Sir Thomas Urquhart], 'The expression of a [?] wife concerning the many variously introduced fashions upon her husband by sundry divers and [?] [?] efficient causes'
>
> fb.217, p. 540

B0658 By that which hinders kinds to perish,
The individual most miscarries.

> Sir Thomas Urquhart, 'That a frequent copulation is prejudiciable [sic] to the person'
>
> fb.217, p. 70

B0659 By the blue taper's trembling light,
And mingle with the blaze of day.

> [Thomas] Parnell, 'A night piece on death'
>
> c.244, p. 270; c.83/2, no. 284

B0660 By the chance of the die,
And is with us again in a trice.

> 'Epitaph on Mr. Thomas Hammond, a parish clerk, and an excellent backgammon player . . . succeeded . . . by Mr. Trice'
>
> c.113/31

B0661 By the coach, I have sent you a hare;
My service to you and likewise to Madam.

> 'A letter sent with a hare' [answered by 'Your present, dear Sir, came duly to hand']
>
> c.487, p. 90

B0662 By the colors we wear, we proclaim what we are!
Are the men for their country and me.

> [Phanuel Bacon], 'Quisquis erit vitae scribam color'
>
> c.237, fol. 85

B0663 By the gaily-circling glass
Sons of care, 'twas made for you.

> 'Song 18'
>
> c.555, p. 25

B0664 By the hills of Combe Martin so steep
Which shall cheat and perplex me the most.

> '. . . The parson's lamentation—an excellent new ballad—to the tune of Despairing beside a clear stream'
>
> c.74

B0665 By the keys in the picture, the lips, and the dove,
That wives should at home be contented to dwell.

> 'Distich. Wrote under the figure of a woman standing upon a tortoise, a bunch of keys in her right hand, the forefinger of her left hand upon her lips, and a dove upon her shoulder . . . translations [7]'
>
> c.81/1, no. 70

B0666 By the Lord Bishop of St. David's the Revd. Mr.
John Gwin
Was lately presented to the vicarage of
Lanvihgenel(?) Glynn.

> 'A whim'
>
> c.360/2, no. 228

B0667 By the side of a maund'ring (?) stream
No [?] music is sweeter than this.

> fb.228/[62a]

B0668 By the use of my first is the difference shown
Each love and each grace are Dian's own.

> J. B. D[ickinson], 'Charade'
>
> c.391

B0669 By this grave Latin motto, of honor the boast
That you boast on your head, what you've lost by
your tail.

> 'Virtus tutissima cassis—Mr. B.'
>
> c.546, p. 35

B0670 By those eyes which power is wanting
To be honest then, be frail.

> [ ] Jephson, 'To a lady'
>
> Poetry Box v/4

B0671 By thought, and meditation, time's improv'd
And warms her wishes, for fruition.

> 'Divine meditation'
>
> fc.54, p. 72

B0672 By thy full-branch'd ivy twine,
Never let it want for wine.

> 'The debauchee. (St. Amard[?] to Bacchus)'
>
> c.81/2, no. 564

B0673 By two black eyes my heart was won
With two black eyes.

> 'Rondeau'
>
> c.546

B0674 By vain science hurried on,
Low'ring those of nobler clay.

> [William Popple, trans.], '[Horace] book 1st. ode 34th. To himself'
>
> fc.104/2, p. 94

B0675 By Venus' self beneath this stone
While she lies close to captain Pory.

> 'On the E[arl] of Holland beheaded' [1649]
>
> fb.143, p. 5

B0676   By virtue rais'd this goodly pile shall last
Nor shall a wretch complain—he wants a friend.

     C[harles] E[arle], 'On the Devon and Exeter Hospital
     founded August 27 1741'

     c.376

B0677   By wand'ring up and down, I now have found
Verses, like wine, always run low at last.

     [Sir Richard Bulstrode], 'Upon myself, the farewell'

     fb.88, p. 117v

B0678   By warding injury on a thankless man
Which was the willingness in giving it.

     [Sir Thomas Urquhart]

     fb.217, p. 386

B0679   By warmth of the fancy a friend may suppose
The hand that presents it may offer a heart!

     R[ichard] V[ernon] S[adleir], 'To Miss Rob—ts on
     delivering her a mourning ring from Mrs Fon—r—can
     in memory of a deceased friend, the device an urn &c.'

     c.106, p. 107

B0680   By your honor's command
O! Save me from that which has nine.

     [Thomas Brown?], 'A sailor in his Majesty's sloop the
     Tartar, being sentenc'd to the cat-o'-nine-tails, spoke
     the following lines to his commander'

     c.382, p. 36; c.233, p. 114; c.536; c.578, p. 21

C

C0001 Cadwallo, late a hearty cit
Attend the dying misanthrope.

> H[enry] Skrine, 'Prize poem at Batheaston on Old
> bachelors and their joys . . . Bath—Jan: 12. 1779'

c.509, p. 15

C0002 Caesar and Jove suppose should me invite,
Secure in greater Caesar's company.

> R[obert] Shirley, 1st earl of Ferrers, 'Martialis
> epigramma'

c.347, p. 16

C0003 Caesar on earth the scepter sways,
That to them appertains.

b.234, p. 90

C0004 Cain 'tis true it was and did appear!
Or found more able shoulders to have borne it.

> [Henry Phillipps?]

b.156, p. 17

C0005 Calais, lovely youth and I
My life for hers resign.

> J. E., 'Horace. Od. III.29'

Poetry Box IV/78

C0006 Caleb hath now attain'd the promis'd land
Nor couldst thou conquer, but by it wast foil'd.

> S. P., 'From another schoolfellow. An acrostic [on
> Caleb Vernon]'

b.228, p. 1

C0007 Call for the master, O! this is fine,
Tell the constable this, and let him come.

> 'The Hectors of Holborn'

fb.107, p. 21

C0008 Call not a muse—invoke no fabled name,
Those now present an angel, to her God.

> 'Epitaph on Mrs. Barnard widow of the Bp. of Derry
> and mother of the present bishop of Killaloe'

c.504, p. 12

C0009 Call not that title small which friendship gives
Firm and unbroken, till one of us should die.

> [George Howard, 6th earl of Carlisle], 'To [George
> Canning] upon his having sent me the world'

c.197, p. 4

C0010 Call to my burial my acquaintance young,
Unto Him should my soul subjection pay.

> J[ohn] V[ernon], 'By his near relation. An acrostic [on
> Caleb Vernon]'

b.228, p. 71

C0011 Call'd by a heroine from our isle,
Too proud to flatter, even kings.

> John Lockman, 'An ode to His Eminence Cardinal
> Fleury . . . presented to His Eminence, in his cabinet
> at Versailles . . . printed . . . 1741'

c.267/2, p. 269

C0012 Calling to mind mine eyes [went long] about
I loved myself because myself loved you.

> [Sir Walter Raleigh], 'A fancy'
> [Crum C21]

b.205, fol. 27v; b.356, p. 132

C0013 Calm contemplation O! descend,
All was not vanity below.

> 'Contemplation'

c.83/1, no. 25

C0014 Calm was the evening and clear was the sky
He burst out with a ha ha ha ha.

> [John Dryden, song in An evening's love, IV.i.]
> [Crum C26]

b.213, p. 153; fb.107, p. 41

C0015 Calmness is great advantage; he that lets,
As cunning fowlers suffer heat (?) to tire.

> [George] Herbert, 'Calmness'

c.356

C0016 Cambray whilst of seraphic love you set
The execrable phantom disappear'd.

> [William Cavendish], 1st duke of Devonshire, 'An
> allusion to [Fénelon] the [arch]bishop of Cambray's
> supplement of Homer'

fb.66/34

C0017 Cambridge one doth commend, Oxford another
May leave to trouble me and ask another.

> [Sir Aston Cokayne, 'Of Cambridge and Oxford']

b.275, p. 74

C0018 Camden's description of Great Britain here
From white cliffs Albion, from Brute Britain came.

[Mildmay Fane], 2nd earl of Westmorland, 'To
Mr. William Camden the best chorographer of this
island . . . autograph poem of [the] Earl of
Westmorland'

fb.106(29)

C0019 Camilla glories in the jovial chase,
And shouts and follows with the babbling hounds.

'Female characters. 1. Camilla, or the huntress'

Poetry Box IV/148

C0020 Camilla-like in gentle disposition
Seek till you find, then by yourself the same.

Ralph Broome, 'An acrostic on Charlotte Francis'

c.486, fol. 40

C0021 Can any man's condition then be worse
The rich poor man's emphatically poor.

b.118, p. 5

C0022 Can Banks appear and How be here
And ne'er write odes again.

'To Colley Cibber esqr. Poet Laureat, Tunbridge Well
1745'

c.360/2, no. 22

C0023 Can Caleb stay when God will have him go
Now to the Lord alone be praise therefore.

W. A., 'From a very dear relation. An acrostic [on
Caleb Vernon]'

b.228, p. 74

C0024 Can Christendom's great champion sink away
And see the new sun rising in the east.

[William Strode?], 'Upon K[ing] James [I] elegy'
[Crum c41]

b.62, p. 99; b.356, p. 251 ('Upon the king of Sweden')

C0025 Can common madness find a thing that's more
Oh what are men, how more than beasts are we.

[Francis Quarles], 'On idolatry' [Divine
Fancies III, 30]

b.137, p. 176; b.156, p. 9

C0026 Can fair Florella, think so ill of me,
Then all my wishes, and my fears shall end.

[Thomas Hamilton, 6th earl of Haddington], 'To
Florella epistle the fifth'

c.458/1, p. 15

C0027 Can forms like yours want ornament of dress,
You put off nothing, but what veil'd a charm.

'To a pretty lady, on dress'

c.360/3, no. 48

C0028 Can Gloriana, whom I long have known
But 'tis not proper, to be nam'd by me.

[Thomas Hamilton, 6th earl of Haddington], 'Copy
of an epistle to a lady, who wrote me she was coming
to Scotland, then said she was sorry she had told
me so . . .'

c.458/1, p. 38

C0029 Can I, all-gracious providence!
And better ev'ry day.

'A birthday thought'

c.83/3, no. 1042

C0030 Can it be any sign of wisdom to
Was one of the sev'n sages died for gladness.

[Sir Thomas Urquhart], 'Against such as to be
accounted the more judicious every way affect a
severity of gesture, believing that to have a sullen
countenance deeply ingrained with melancholy is the
most senator-like behavior'

fb.217, p. 502

C0031 Can it be love which the rude action
Two ways at once.

[George Daniel]

b.121, fol. 75v

C0032 Can it be thought ye wives this scribbling fool
Wives won't be taught—be it the school for maids.

'Epilogue to The school for wives spoken by Mrs.
Abington'

c.68, p. 71

C0033 Can joy be where there doth dwell
Where's all true joy.

H[enry] C[olman], 'On joy'
[Crum c47]

b.2, p. 70

C0034 Can Kezia, then, without a sigh, forego
How oft affliction flows from him we love.

[William] Sotheby, 'Oberon from the German of
Wieland'

c.340

C0035 Can love be controll'd by advice?
We may always find time to grow old.

[John Gay], 'The modest question. A song' [answered
by 'Dire love should be check'd . . .']
[Crum c48]

c.94; c.193, p. 40

C0036 Can man sustain a greater curse
And not enjoy the power to taste.

[J. M.], 'On an empty purse'
[Crum c50, 'possess a greater']

c.391, p. 12; c.94

C0037 Can power happiness bestow,
And leave the rest [to] heaven.

    M. S.

c.156, p. 107

C0038 Can real beauties move the lyre
And you eclipse his Venus and his Hyde.

    [Robert Cholmeley], 'To the two Miss Nuttings upon
    a poem called The four real beauties'

c.190, p. 24

C0039 Can Southwell ask, or Carrington apply
So vile an act is foreign to the Muses.

    'On Miss Carrington and Miss Southwell desiring
    Mr. Jones to lampoon at Tunbridge Wells 1745'

c.360/2, no. 36

C0040 Can the Almighty greater mercy show
No prayer if duly made was ever lost.

    [John Hobart] 'Prayer'

b.108, fol. 2v

C0041 Can the fates so cruel be, as for to give
Anthems of joy unto the King of kings.

    Gil[es] Hayward, 'On the death of Mr. John Haines of
    Magd. Hall. Who died on Easter morning early'

b.62, p. 112

C0042 Can this be he!—could Charles the good, the great,
And one destroy'd, a thousand kings defend.

    Thomas Tickell, 'Thoughts—occasioned by the sight
    of an original picture of King Charles I. taken at the
    time of his trial'

c.351, p. 90

C0043 Can we believe it is enough to wear
Shall share with him in his eternity.

    H[enry] C[olman], 'Another' [acrostic on 'Christians']

b.2, p. 107

C0044 Can you leave ranging, ne'er think of changing,
                         and constant grow,
I would deceive you, your fate to know. | You'd
                         wish to leave me &c.

    'Media. Sung by Ms. Lindsey in the opera of
    Thamysis'

c.160, fol. 83

C0045 Canonical black-coats, like birds of a feather,
Yet not find so much brain as in Oliver's porter.

    'Vox clero, lil-ly bur-le-ro, or the second part of a
    merry new ballad to be sung in the Jerusalem
    Chamber, January 24, 1689'
    [Crum c72; POAS V.130]

b.111, p. 127

C0046 Canst be idle? canst thou play,
Neither sin, nor Savior feels.

    [George] Herbert, 'Business'
    [Crum c73]

c.139, p. 130

C0047 Canst grip a whirlwind in thy hand
Thy grief and women's faults who'll end.

    'Cant: 39. To the tune of The damask rose'

b.4, fol. 33

C0048 Canst thou insensible, Elisa, prove
And make thy burden'd heart again rejoice.

    R[ichard] V[ernon] S[adleir], 'The farewell [cut away]
    desire of some of hers and my intimate friends Augt.
    1784'

c.106, p. 57

C0049 Canst thou my muse, such desolation view:
And learn that virtue is the cause of God.

    'On a late defeat . . . On Culloden battle'

c.171

C0050 Canst thou send me thy mare for a mile
Money will make my mare to go.

    'Catches [2]'

b.356, p. 71

C0051 Canst thou, vain man! in riches think to find
Yet need not fortune court, nor dread her frown.

    'On hearing a gentleman say, he would never marry
    any but a great fortune and beauty'

c.156, p. 63

C0052 Canst thou, vain man, provide the lion meat,
Resolves into its naught from whence it came.

    'Part of the book of Job paraphrased 38 chap. 39 v.
    Written in the year 1720'

c.221, p. 28

C0053 Can't three sevens' years then expiate
Try try to quit thy jail[?] at any rate.

    [Mrs. ( ) Feilding]

b.226, p. 11

C0054 Caparison once more fleet Hippogriff of the Nine;
To list, and all in just progression hear.

    J. S., 'Oberon'

Poetry Box v/106

C0055 Care in love is perfect pleasure
Poorly counterfeiting thee.

b.197, p. 153

C0056   Care, torturing care! Is felt by all
Will ev'n in heaven, new transports give.

     James Waker, 'On care . . . Feb. 19th. 1725'

     c.94

C0057   Careful observers may foretell the hour,
Dead cats and turnip-tops come tumbling down
                           the flood.

     [Jonathan Swift], 'A description of a city shower. Oct. 1710'

     c.265, p. 5; c.116, p. 2; c.83/1, no. 244 (ll. 1–46)

C0058   Careless how ill I with myself agree;
Long as the night to her whose love's away.

     c.148, p. 3 (incomplete?)

C0059   Careless of wealth of fortune's fickle smiles
Might claim a sov'reign's more immediate care.

     S[tephen] Simpson, 'On the Duke of Grafton's quitting his place in government'

     c.563

C0060   Carlie(?) with happy skill could trace
All hail'd her a new Cyprian queen.

     John Lockman, 'The lovely four . . . 31 Decr. 1762'

     c.267/1, p. 320

C0061   Carmarthen, misconceive not that the mind
From, my dear Doctor, to, my Lord your Grace.

     'An epistle to the Marquess of Carmarthen' [1783]

     fc.53, p. 87

C0062   Carnarvon! See a muse attend
She may have leave to join the voice.

     John Lockman, 'To the most noble the Marquis of Carnarvon [later Duke of Chandos]; an epistle: humbly requesting his lordship to present to the author, and his verses to the king'

     c.267/4, p. 1

C0063   Castara! O you are too prodigal
Thy tears, by hind'ring its return, work more.

     [William] Habington, 'To Castara, weeping'

     b.150, p. 266

C0064   Casting my eyes around, I smiling cry,
Those who have power, immov'd could see me starve.

     John Lockman, 'A comfortable reflection . . . Decr. 1749'

     c.267/1, p. 42

C0065   Catch me a star that's fallen from the sky
And then find faith with a woman's mind.

     'On the faith of a woman'
     [Crum C104]

     b.62, p. 38; b.200, p. 3

C0066   'Cause a knave play'd his tricks, where vile sharpers
                           abound,
Is those pickpockets nabbing a brother.

     John Lockman, 'On seeing a diver hurried out of a noted coffeehouse, when tickets were at 40 premium . . . Nov. 1751'

     c.267/1, p. 139

C0067   Cease anxious sorrows, hence no more appear
That never enter'd in a mortal breast.

     [Thomas Gurney], 'On the glory and employment of glorified saints faintly attempted. Occasioned by Mr. Gill's declaring his satisfaction as touching the blessed state of his departed daughter . . . 1738'

     c.213

C0068   Cease, beauteous nymph! Oh cease to weep;
Of endless sleep, her heav'n! possess'd.

     [Stephen Barrett?], 'The dead dormouse to its sorrowing mistress' [Gentleman's magazine, November 1747]

     c.193, p. 130

C0069   Cease boist'rous winds! Ye softer zephyrs blow!
But that my eyes too well their Chloe knew.

     Peregrine Greatheed, 'Chloe sleeping. Written . . . at the age of 13'

     Greatheed Box/39 (3 copies)

C0070   Cease, cease in epic strains to sing
Has pierced my soft and yielding heart | From
                           Aurelia's eyes.

     J[ohn] H[oadly], 'Anacreon ode the 16'

     c.176, p. 124

C0071   Cease, cease, my friend I now implore
The small remains of life my friend.

     [Mrs. Christian Kerr], 'A young gentlewoman to her friend who was persuading her to marry' [answered by 'Thou dear'st . . .']

     c.102, p. 95

C0072   Cease charming fair
Who has so many ways to kill.

     c.416

C0073   Cease Chloris cease to wonder why
You'll cheat the world, yourself, and me.

     'The female physician'

     fb.107, p. 60

C0074   Cease Damon, cease to court the fair,
To steal the dog, and leave the bitch behind.

     [Robert Cholmeley], 'To Mr. Will: Powell of St Johns Coll: Camb: upon stealing the lap dog of Mrs. Ann. Baker a Cambridge lady'

     c.190, p. 22

C0075 Cease, faithless mirror, to persuade
To shine distinguish'd in the rolls of fame!

> R[ichard] V[ernon] S[adleir], 'Palemon's
> expostulation to his looking glass, inscribed to Miss
> Spilsbury who drew his picture in the 76th year of his
> age'
>
> c.106, p. 147

C0076 Cease, fools, of birds and four-legg'd cattle,
Up to the moon—I know not where.

> John Blyth, 'The fairies' [for the Lent Probation at
> the Merchant Taylor's School, 1700]
> [Crum C115]
>
> Poetry Box VI/75

C0077 Cease Galatea cease to grieve
Thro' verdant plains to roll his urn.

> [John Gay, Alexander Pope, and/or John Hughes], '5
> chorus [in Handel's Acis and Galatea]' [with musical
> score for tenor]
>
> Music MS. 534

C0078 Cease, generous bard, to waste thy noble fire
What thanks are due to thy protecting Muse.

> 'To an anonymous poet, who undertook the defense of
> a person of distinction, unjustly attacked'
>
> c.360/1, p. 177

C0079 Cease lovely mourner, if thou canst, to weep,
Whatever is, is right.

> F[rederick] D[ickinson], 'Verses by . . . written
> immediately upon his hearing of the sudden death of
> Mr B. supposed to be written to his wife'
>
> c.391, p. 38

C0080 Cease lovely nymph give over
The godlike creature man.

> 'A song'
>
> c.374

C0081 Cease not sad reader here to find
To find a king so far above a tomb.

> Sir Tho[mas] Roe, 'Upon the glorious king of Sweden'
> [Gustavus Adolphus]
>
> Poetry Box VI/30; see also 'Seek not reader . . .'.

C0082 Cease, O Pindar, cease the strain
And reign, sweet fancy's fav'rite child.

> 'To Peter Pindar on reading his sonnet to a glowworm
> by a lady'
>
> c.373, p. 57

C0083 Cease, poets, cease each unavailing tear
More worth than all your incense o'er the dead.

> R. W., 'Another [epitaph on Dancer]'
>
> c.150, p. 125

C0084 Cease, rude Boreas, blust'ring railer!
None,—our danger's drowned in wine.

> [George Stevens], 'Song 31'
>
> c.555, p. 48

C0085 Cease rural conquests and set free your swains
Tho' each a goddess, or a Sunderland.

> [Sir Samuel Garth], 'To the Duchess of Bolton'
>
> c.111, p. 96

C0086 Cease to beauty to be suing
Still be conqu'ring not complaining.

> [John Gay, Alexander Pope, and/or John Hughes],
> '[chorus] in [Handel's] Acis and Galatea' [with musical
> score for bass]
>
> Music MS. 534

C0087 Cease to demand the cause why I,
Shall my black thoughts renew.

> [William] Pattison, 'An ode to Iris'
>
> c.244, p. 523

C0088 Cease to lament for Oxburgh's sudden fall,
Whee'er our king or honor claims our breath.

> 'On Count Oxburghs [Oxborough]'
>
> c.570/1, p. 162

C0089 Cease ye vain scribblers, boast no more
Is she not something more than woman!

> R[ichard] V[ernon] S[adleir], 'Portrait of a celebrated
> beauty'
>
> c.106, p. 125

C0090 Cease, Hirpinus to inquire,
Loose her hair like Spartan dame.

> [William Popple, trans.], '[Horace] book 2nd. Ode
> 11th. To Quintius Hirpinus'
>
> fc.104/2, p. 146

C0091 Celadon says Matt. Prior came
I'm Celia's slave, Melissa's friend.

> 'To Melissa, an epistle'
>
> Poetry Box I/32

C0092 Celemena of my heart
When we come together.

> [John Dryden], 'Damon and Celemena' [from An
> evening's love]
>
> fb.107, p. 18; b.213, p. 154

C0093 Celestial child, fair hope! descend,
Oh shed, dear hope! thy pow'r divine.

> 'Verses to hope'
>
> c.142, p. 400

C0094 Celestial maid receive this prayer,
Whose laws they kept below.

'A hymn to prosperity'

c.83/1, no. 72

C0095 Celestial natures, since yourselves do pray
Worship to them's a double violence.

[Edward] Sparke, 'Poem 33th—on St Michael [and All Angels]'

b.137, p. 68

C0096 Celestial spirit! Heavenly dove
The world and vanity control.

'[Hymns composed the week preceding the sacrament] 4th Whitsunday'

c.515, fol. 18r

C0097 Celestial spring! To nature's fav'rites given
When warm religion lifts the thought on high.

[ ] Turningham, 'Sensibility'

c.344, p. 6; c.139, p. 409

C0098 Celestial was her language, every phrase
That flesh-veil'd sun, her mental majesty.

Rob[ert] Davenport, 'Description of piety'

b.52/2, p. 191

C0099 Celia adorn'd with ev'ry grace,
And Esau's where it should be.

[Philip Dormer Stanhope, 4th earl of Chesterfield], 'Orig[inal]' [of 'Celia fairest work of nature . . .']

c.591; see also 'In Flavia's eyes . . .', 'Chudleigh has . . .'.

C0100 Celia and I the other day
I with thee, or without thee die.

[Matthew] Prior, 'The lady's looking-glass'

c.144, p. 79

C0101 Celia, dear nymph, than whom no fairer toast
And hide its beauties in obscurity.

'Verses on Miss D——n of D——r'

fb.142, p. 10 (second series)

C0102 Celia fairest work of nature,
The changes of tomorrow.

'Celia paraphrased. Made 1754, on seeing the original' ['Celia adorn'd with ev'ry grace . . .']

c.591

C0103 Celia is all made up of art
Whene'er she leaves off paint and sin.

R[obert] Shirley, 1st earl of Ferrers, 'To painted Celia from the French—Cette femme &c.'

c.347, p. 28

C0104 Celia that faithful servant you disown,
Since dying I must be no more your slave.

John Wilmot, 2nd earl of Rochester, 'The discovery'

b.334, p. 174

C0105 Celia 'tis done my passion I dismiss
A generous scorn shall from thy hate protect me.

R[obert] Shirley, 1st earl of Ferrers, 'Sonnet from [Malherbe]'

c.347, p. 82

C0106 Celia, too late you would repent,
Before our loves is gone?

[William Walsh], 'Upon a favor offered'

c.223, p. 66

C0107 Celia when thou wast young and fair,
But now I'm tied to Chloris' chain.

R[obert] Shirley, 1st earl of Ferrers, 'From Martial'

c.347, p. 93

C0108 Celia whilst you on earth no pity show
Ere from above you can expect the same.

R[obert] Shirley, 1st earl of Ferrers, 'From [Malherbe]. Upon Celia's devotion'

c.347, p. 84

C0109 Celia your tricks will now no longer pass,
That boasts her favors, and proclaims my wrong.

[William Walsh], 'Elegy. To his false mistress'

c.223, p. 62

C0110 Celia's importunate with me,
Equally to serve all men's turn.

R[obert] Shirley, 1st earl of Ferrers, 'Celia. From the French cette femme n'importune &c.'

c.347, p. 14

C0111 Censorio takes in hand, by sharp reproof
[The] temple's snuffers must be pure gold.

[Francis Quarles], 'On Censorio'
[Crum c147]

b.137, p. 190

C0112 Censure not sharply then but me advise
Her fury; though no friendship he betray.

B[en] J[onson, 'An epistle to a friend']
[Crum c148]

b.148, p. 5

C0113 Cerona, Xanth, and Cephisus, do make
Th'Arabian fountain maketh crimson sheep.

'Upon waters changing color in cattle'

c.158, p. 118

C0114   Certain, and sure under this stone
Was anti-Christian self-denial.

     'An epitaph on passive obedience' [1689]
     [Crum c149]

     b.382(23v)

C0115   Chance, my old dog, ah! alas! he is gone
Thus died a good servant, to yours, J. Moore.

     J. Moore, 'An epitaph on a favorite dog'

     c.94

C0116   Change now the scene,—see that man's way
And tastes the sweets of ease.

     'The virtuous man. The only road to happiness is
     virtue. Juv[enal]'

     c.487, p. 55

C0117   Changes on towers, as well as mortals wait.
Yet man's reserv'd to fall where Dilston stood.

     [Thomas Oliver?]

     c.93

C0118   Chaotic pile of barren stone,
With legal toils to drag me to my fate!

     [Charlette (Turner) Smith], 'A descriptive ode . . .'

     c.141, p. 78

C0119   Chappel, I praise
That form the river wide.

     'To the same [Rev. John Chappel Woodhouse] 1780'

     fc.53, p. 12

C0120   Chappel, thy friend with sorrow worn, and care
Youth at the glittering helm, and hope sublime.

     'To the Revd. Mr. [John Chappel] Woodhouse 1781. A
     sonnet'

     fc.53, p. 11

C0121   Charge all a bumper to the Queen
And then be as they were.

     'A loyal health to the Queen and royal family'

     fb.142, p. 45

C0122   Charity and pride both feed the poor in the den
Increase men's states decrease no man's living.

     'Charity' [poem in the shape of a heart]

     c.189, p. 40

C0123   Charles at this time, having no need
Thanks you as much as if he did.

     [answer to 'In all humility we crave . . .'; written
     c. 1642, here applied to Charles II]
     [Crum c161, 'Charles at present']

     c.189, p. 5 (attr. Rochester)

C0124   Charles Berkeley talks aloud.
Coxcombs for th' whole family.

     'On the Duke's servants'

     fb.140, p. 19

C0125   Charles reasons well—the tax upon receipts,
For he can pay no tax who pays no bill.

     R[ichard] V[ernon] S[adleir], 'Epigram on the stamp
     receipt tax'

     c.106, p. 81

C0126   Charley the big the booby esquire
To grace the seat of Cambria's king.

     Poetry Box x/118

C0127   Charlotte said to her husband one day
And our best thanks and wishes shall attend it.

     Ralph Broome, 'The flitch of bacon'

     c.486, fol. 39v

C0128   Charm of the solitude I love,
Alas! I vanish into naught.

     'On a pipe of tobacco'

     c.83/1, no. 203

C0129   Charm'd, into silence, by some magic spell,
For now I must be gone adieu adieu.

     [Mrs. Christian Kerr], 'A farewell'

     c.102, p. 128

C0130   Charm'd with its happy and experience'd ease,
And dies a stranger to himself alone.

     'In praise of a country life'

     c.481, p. 97; see also 'No, I shan't envy . . .'.

C0131   Charm'd with thy truth, and with thy learning fir'd,
The noblest things of earth, alas! how vain.

     John Lockman, 'Meeting the corpse of Monsieur
     Rollin, when going to visit him in Paris . . . Sept. 1741'

     c.267/1, p. 74

C0132   Charming Chloe look with pity,
Chloe might not Strephon smile.

     [cf. Crum c167]

     c.358, p. 164

C0133   Charming Florella, could I think that you
Than all the sorrows, I have known before.

     [Thomas Hamilton, 6th earl of Haddington], 'To
     Florella, epistle the tenth'

     c.458/1, p. 26

C0134 Charming in infancy! What hope appears!
Engaging carriage be your chiefest view.

[William Boscawen], 'Acrostic on Lady Caroline
Spencer, then four years old; written at the age of
fourteen'

fc.106, p. 1

C0135 Charon come hither Charon
Proud of her new society.

'Charon and Hobson's ghost'
[Crum c170]

b.356, p. 35

C0136 Charon, O Charon, | The wafter of all souls to
bliss or bane:
Then come aboard and pass till then be wise.

[John Fletcher], 'Cant: 14' [song in The mad lover,
iv. i.]
[Crum c172]

b.4, fol. 10 (damaged)

C0137 Charon! O gentle Charon, let me woo thee
Who else with tears will doubtless drown our ferry.

[Robert Herrick], 'Philomel and Charon'
[Crum c173]

fb.107, p. 58; b.71, p. 25

C0138 Chas'd by the hounds, which thirst for blood,
Whilst He his glorious arm for thee displays.

'Psalm 42d. paraphrased'

b.322, p. 11

C0139 Chaste Arethusa from Alpheus flies,
Men oft dissemble, and words are but air.

John Lockman, 'Writ under a mezzotinto, by
Mr. Faber, of Alpheus attempting to seize
Arethusa . . . 1754'

c.267/1, p. 54

C0140 Chaste as an aged hermit, at his death
All women are so, or at least should be.

[George Daniel]

b.121, fol. 17v

C0141 Chaste Hippolyte, and Paris fair, Ulysses wise and sly,
Æneas kind, fierce Hector, here jointly entomb'd lie.

'An epitaph at Tunbridge on Richard de Clare, Earl of
Gloucester, who deceased July the 14 A:D. 1262 . . .
Englished'

c.360/1, p. 217

C0142 Chaste, my friend, from madding crowds retire
Blest with kind health, soft pleasures and a friend!

'Epistle to Thomas Landen'

c.89, p. 56

C0143 Chaste Phyllis 'twixt enfolded arms
Perpetual looking glass.

H[enry] D[rummond] of B[alloch], 'Phyllis in two
sections first age and life second virtue and fortune'

b.92, p. 3; b.377; c.591, p. 1

C0144 Chaste, pious, prudent Charles the second
Is wretched, king'd, by storks, or logs.

[John Freke?], 'The chronicle of the history of the
insipids' [usually attr. Rochester]
[Crum c177; POAS I.243]

fb.140, p. 130; b.52/2, p. 170

C0145 Chaste without pride; tho' gentle, yet not soft,
Not always cruel, nor yet kind too oft.

c.549, p. 130

C0146 Cheer up my grieved soul! and do not fear,
And raise thy courage higher then thy fear. | Fiat
voluntas tua

Eliz[abeth] Cellier(?), 'Verses upon her sentence to
stand in the pillory. 1680'

b.54, p. 1201

C0147 Cheer up sad soul and banish now all fear,
That together, we may pay you your due.

'Upon a lady's return from the country'

c.158, p. 24

C0148 Cheer up, suff'ring matrons, you cannot want
friends
You get not[.] Do it by the miter you wear.

'On reading an advertisement . . . containing the
Bishop of Wor[cester]'s generous recommendation of
an unfortunate lady and family to the charitable
people of Bath' [General advertiser, 18 Feb. 1780]

c.157, p. 117

C0149 Cherub of heaven! that from thy secret stand
That glistens in the eye uprais'd to heaven.

[Richard Brinsley Butler Sheridan], 'By Mr. Sheridan'

Poetry Box III/28

C0150 Chetwood as fame reports, thus spoke to Kate,
I ne'er ask'd aught of God, and why should God
of me.

'An epigram on Mrs. Clive the actress—late Miss
Rafter—1740' [answered by 'Thou that hast neither
shame . . .']

c.360/1, p. 57

C0151 Chide not thy sprouting lip, nor kill
The root below cannot be dry.

[William Strode?], 'On a blistered lip'
[Crum c188]

b.197, p. 156; b.200, p. 210; b.205, fol. 60v

CO152 Chief of writer's comforts, fire,
Warm from the bottom of my soul.

>[Charles Burney, the elder], 'New-Year's ode for 1777.
>To the Revd. Thomas Twining . . . Ode'
>
>c.33, p. 110

CO153 Child of my heart! Whose ever gentle mind
And of his honest heart has crowned thee queen.

>[Charles] Burney, the elder, 'Verses on the marriage of
>Miss Susan Burney [Mrs. Phillips]'
>
>c.486, fol. 2

CO154 Child of the light, fair morning hour,
The muse's modest gifts, her tribute to a friend.

>'Ode to the morning'
>
>c.83/2, no. 385

CO155 Child of the melancholy song!
To taste, to fancy, and to virtue dear!

>[Ann (Ward)] Radcliffe, 'To the nightingale'
>
>c.83/3, no. 854

CO156 Child of the summer, charming rose,
To fan thy bosom, as they play.

>'The rose'
>
>c.83/2, no. 732

CO157 Children are given to man
It's God that giveth them.

>fb.151/3

CO158 Children like tender osiers take the bow,
In age we are by second nature prone.

>[John] Dryden
>
>c.93

CO159 Children of fancy whither are ye fled?
And folly wonders that her dream was vain.

>John Langhorne, 'The visions of fancy, in four elegies'
>
>c.139, p. 530

CO160 Children of wrath conceiv'd in sin,
But Christ hath bruis'd his head.

>Charles Atherton Allnutt, 'On 3d. Gen[esis] 15 v.—
>Composed to be sung at the meeting of a Christian
>society'
>
>c.112, p. 133

CO161 Children's duty to parents should proceed
To reverence them and help them if they need.

>c.339, p. 314

CO162 Chill blows the blast, and twilight's dewy hand
Ah! where shall hapless man repose in peace.

>[Robert Merry] (Della Crusca, pseud.), 'Elegy written
>on the plain of Fountenoy'
>
>c.140, p. 160

CO163 Chilled by rough gales, while yet reluctant May
Sure none will say—it ought to be diminish'd.

>[Richard Brinsley Butler] Sheridan, 'Prologue to Lady
>Craven's comedy of The miniature picture written
>by . . . and spoken by Mr. King'
>
>c.115

CO164 Chill'd by the northern winds, the muse complains
Both are dead, forever live their fame.

>'A full and true account of the tragical end of
>Diamond and Jolly who were condemned to a cruel
>and ignominious death by the Revd Wm Barker their
>master showing how many miseries they endured and
>how they prevented their aforesaid master's cruelty by
>wisely dying of themselves, by Mrs. —— late of
>Belsham'
>
>c.116, p. 20

CO165 Chloe a coquette in fashion
The De'il take me if e'er I do.

Poetry Box x/44 (incomplete; first part: Poetry Box
x/122)

CO166 Chloe a rebel to love's power
That Joshua was the son of Nun.

>[Phanuel Bacon], 'To [a young lady going into a
>nunnery]'
>
>c.237, fol. 51

CO167 Chloe at church with looks divine
And loudly cried, 'Amen'.

>'Old maid's prayer'
>
>c.81/1, no. 306

CO168 Chloe be wise, no more perplex me,
Throw off those frowns, and love obey.

>'The entreaty'
>
>fc.61, p. 65

CO169 Chloe, by your command in verse I write
But you are tired, and so am I—farewell.

>[John Wilmot], 2nd E[arl] of R[ochester], 'A letter
>fancied from Artemisa in the town to Chloe in the
>country'
>[Crum c198]
>
>b.105, p. 45; b.334, p. 196 ('Chloe in verse by your
>command . . .')

C0170   Chloe coquette and debon—air
Curse, but cannot break the—snares.

     Molly Jones, 'Matrimony, a tale [in bouts-rimes] for
     Mr. [G.] Phillip's use'

     c.233, p. 90

C0171   Chloe delights us, when the rich brocade,
Till, lost in rapture, we could wish to die.

     John Lockman, 'Writ under a mezzotinto, by
     Mr. Faber, of a nymph bathing'

     c.267/1, p. 61

C0172   Chloe detests the name of wife,
I'll be not such a sinner.

     'Epigram on a young lady, who vowed never to marry'

     c.94

C0173   Chloe new-married looks on men no more
Why then 'tis plain for what she lookt before.

     [William Walsh], 'Epigram. Chloe'

     c.223, p. 76

C0174   Chloe no more I'll love, I swear,
Then patient I'll adore the while.

     [Charles Burney, the elder], 'Song. From the French'

     c.33, p. 107

C0175   Chloe survey'd the tiger's cage
I'd only broach—that same.

     [John Winter], 'A tale. In imitation of Horace'

     c.74

C0176   Chloe with smiles receives my present flame;
Time changes thought, and flatt'ry conquers truth.

     c.549, p. 99

C0177   Chloe, you write to me for coin,
Enjoy'd god Bacchus, and became a star.

     [Thomas Brown], 'An epigram of Flaminius. To his
     drinking mistress'

     c.158, p. 130

C0178   Chloe's the wonder of her sex
A boundless will to ease us.

     [George Granville, 1st baron Lansdowne], 'La[dy]
     Kingston'
     [Crum C200]

     Trumbull Box: Poetry Box XIII/62 (attr. Dorset)

C0179   Chloris enough! I've seen the deep
When I beheld my Chloris overcast.

     [Robert Cholmeley], 'To Chloris angry. A song'

     c.190, p. 178

C0180   Chloris farewell I now must go
But make my constant meals at home.

     [Edmund Waller]
     [Crum C203]

     b.213, p. 12

C0181   Chloris forbear awhile, do not o'erjoy me,
And buckle now, and then, and that's enough.

     [Henry Bold], 'The amorous gallant'
     [Crum C204]

     fb.107, p. 76

C0182   Chloris I dare not say your eyes
I cannot deny what I know would undo me.

     [Sir Charles Sedley, 'To Chloris . . . the entire lover']
     [Crum C205]

     b.213, p. 141

C0183   Chloris sat, and sitting slept
O Amyntas and so died.

     [Crum C211]

     b.197, p. 237

C0184   Chloris 'twill be for either's rest
'Tis too much to lose time and you.

     b.213, p. 118

C0185   Chloris we see th'offended gods,
To look as if I lov'd thee not.

     [Edmund] Waller

     Poetry Box IV/102

C0186   Chloris, you live ador'd by all,
And when't can speak, unruly grows.

     'To Chloris'

     b.218, p. 20

C0187   Chloris yourself you so excel
For of his voice the boy had mourn'd.

     [Edmund Waller, 'To a lady singing a song of his
     composing']
     [Crum C216]

     fb.66/27

C0188   Choice! Doubly grateful to our envied isle,
A Marlborough's sword must be the dread of Gaul.

     John Lockman, 'Hearing that Charles, Duke of
     Marlborough, was appointed general of all his
     Majesty's foot forces, and going against the French'
     [1738]

     c.267/1, p. 219

C0189   Christ bore the cross: the cross bore Christ: but
           thus,

     That it bore him: and he bore it for us.

       Sir Thomas Urquhart, 'Of Christ and his cross'

   fb.217, p. 360

C0190   Christ came in winter: John the Baptist in
     For fire doth purge, and water washeth sin.

       Sir Thomas Urquhart, 'Of our Savior Christ, and
       John the Baptist'

   fb.217, p. 157

C0191   Christ Church a Marriage made before the King
     He offer'd twice or thrice to go away.

       [William Meredith?], 'On [Barten] Holiday's
       Marriage [of the arts], acted before the King' [at
       Woodstock, 1621; answered by 'What more trouble
       yet? . . .']
       [Crum c229]

   b.62, p. 3; b.197, p. 162 ('presents a Marriage'); see also
   'At Christ Church . . .'.

C0192   Christ come into this world saw mortal men,
     And o'ercame death: then went to heav'n again.

       Sir Thomas Urquhart, 'Veni, vidi, vici'

   fb.217, p. 280

C0193   Christ conquered death, death hath me slain
     Yet I by Christ shall live again.

       'Epitaph the 2nd'

   c.158, p. 85

C0194   Christ crucified on the cross,
     Christ crucified for me.

       'Paul's desire'

   c.187, p. 18

C0195   Christ here cur'd at diseases, and was a
     Theolog, there he'll judge conform to law.

       Sir Thomas Urquhart, 'Of our Savior's skill in this,
       and in the world to come: in being a jurist, divine, and
       physician'

   fb.217, p. 154

C0196   Christ honored marriage with His deity,
     He would have cried the water better wine.

       'John 2.10'

   c.160, fol. 51 [bis]

C0197   Christ is our high anoint', in glorious state
     Let's serve and praise—O spare not any hour.

       [Sir Philip Wodehouse], 'Upon our present bishop
       some years after Bp. Ray [Reynolds?] of Norwich
       Anthony Sparrow . . . O spare not any hour'

   b.131, back (no. 10/1)

C0198   Christ is the anchor, which our hope doth tie:
     Ship of our faith, and sea of charity.

       Sir Thomas Urquhart, 'Of Christ, concerning faith,
       hope, and charity'

   fb.217, p. 210

C0199   Christ Jacob's ladder stood at Jacob's wells
     That she should let the upper spring alone.

       'John 4.5.4'

   c.160, fol. 51 [bis]

C0200   Christ the Lord is risen today
     Thus to sing—and thus to love!

       'On Easter Day'

   Poetry Box v/92

C0201   Christ (the word) he spake it
     That I believe and take it.

       Elizabeth I, queen of England(?), 'Elizabeth . . . when
       persecuted [by Mary I] to the Papists'

   c.189, p. 59; see also 'It was the word . . .'.

C0202   Christians in name, and not in nature strange,
     Strive in my heart to be a true Christian.

       H[enry] C[olman], 'On the name, Christians.
       Anacrostica'

   b.2, p. 106

C0203   Christians they died submissive to their fate,
     Also are men, with resolution great.

       [Thomas Oliver?]

   c.93

C0204   Christmas gambols to make, being valiant and stout
     Kill'd wounded and taken—the rest away fled! |
            Derry down

       'Song 81'

   c.555, p. 128

C0205   Christ's kingdom is not of this world we are taught
            it
     Says Gideon 'tis true for I by God have bought it.

       'An epigram'

   c.154, p. 29

C0206   Christ's picture humbly worship thou, which by
            the same doth pass;
     When life was death upon that cross, where Christ
            himself was spread.

   a.19, fol. 5v

C0207   Christ's was a life of trouble, from his birth
     Strive to be like him in integrity.

       H[enry] C[olman], 'Another' [acrostic on 'Christians']

   b.2, p. 106

C0208 Christ's wounds are rather salves, than wounds; for
                                                      sure,
His wounds have virtue our plagued souls to cure.

>   Sir Thomas Urquhart, 'The five wounds of our Savior'
>   fb.217, p. 272

C0209 Chronicles and annual books of kings
I before your good Lordship to attempt the good
                              will and ponder the true heart.

>   William Peeris, 'Here beginneth the prologue of this
>   little treatise following which is the descent of the
>   Lord Percy . . .'
>   [Crum c299]
>   fa.19, fol. 41v

C0210 Chudleigh has every charm, and grace,
And Esau's where they should be.

>   'On Miss [Elizabeth] Chudleigh Duchess of Kingston
>   now, who appeared at a masquerade in a robe of lawn,
>   neck, arms, legs &c. bare' [last line borrowed from
>   Chesterfield's 'In Flavia's eyes . . .']
>   c.81/1, no. 286

C0211 Churchmen of old were chaste, with no fair faces,
Now having other wives to care for, she's neglected.

>   Sir Thomas Urquhart, 'Of the puritan church now,
>   and as Christ's church was in former times'
>   fb.217, p. 235

C0212 Chyndonax with officious care
The brighter lightning of her eyes.

>   'Presented with a hand-firescreen. 16 Dec. 1754'
>   c.371, fol. 83

C0213 Cibber, fair Banks's charms you justly sing
Act but like her, they never need despair.

>   [ ] Snook, 'To Mr. Cibber, on Miss Peckham, by . . .
>   Tunbridge Wells 1745' [answered by 'Cibber, you
>   say . . .']
>   c.360/2, no. 24

C0214 Cibber, you say too high aspir'd
Whose theme, has every grace.

>   [Samuel Howard], 'To Mr. Snook on his verses
>   ['Cibber, fair Banks's charms . . .] on Miss Peckham,
>   written by Leumas Drawoh esqr.'
>   c.360/2, no. 25

C0215 Circles are prais'd not that abound
Not in much time but acting well.

>   [Edmund] Waller, 'On long and short life'
>   fc.60, p. 47

C0216 Cislianus when of me you sought
No earthly piece would half so lovely be.

>   R[obert] Shirley, 1st earl of Ferrers, 'Upon Antony's
>   picture. From [Martial]'
>   c.347, p. 33

C0217 Citizens of London call you to remembrance
Unto the city of giving liberally &c.

>   'On John Rainwell fishmonger Ld. Mayor'
>   fb.143, p. 8

C0218 Civil commotions strongly carried on,
And through all ways to certain ruin steer.

>   fb.234, p. 61

C0219 Civil wars your subject make!
Caean numbers suit thee best.

>   [William Popple, trans.], 'The odes, epodes &c. of
>   Horace translated. Book 2nd. Ode 1st. To Caius
>   Asinius Pollio'
>   fc.104/2, p. 114

C0220 Civility enforceth me to anchor
May challenge from a gen'rous inclination.

>   Sir Thomas Urquhart, 'To the Earl of Ancrum'
>   fb.217, p. 227

C0221 Clara was blest with ev'ry grace
Regard the lay; remember Time.

>   'The coquette and Time'
>   c.83/2, no. 317

C0222 Clarendon had law and sense
And all for sleeves of lawn.

>   [Charles Sackville, 6th earl of Dorset],
>   'Dr. Stillingfleet his sermon on the mischief of
>   separation—2 May 1680'
>   [Crum c309; POAS II.339]
>   b.52/1, p. 135 (with six extra lines); fb.228/44 (ll. 1–10)

C0223 Clarinda bids me now invoke
May death itself not part.

>   [On Martha Blount]
>   Poetry Box x/86

C0224 Clarinda vows my hopes are vain,
And virtue is no pain.

>   [ ] Nash, 'On virtue'
>   fc.73

C0225 Clarissa blest with ev'ry grace,
The sequel must remain untold.

>   'The rival nymphs'
>   c.83/2, no. 377

C0226 Clean hyssop is an herb to purge and cleanse
Are killed, purged and driven away by mint.

    [Joshua Sylvester, trans. Guillaume de Salluste,
    seigneur Du Bartas], 'Of hyssop'

    b.284, p. 53

C0227 Cleanse then thy thoughts let thy desires flee
'Tis he when this life end must thy new life begin.

    [Mary Serjant]

    fb.98, fol. 158

C0228 Clear, as untroubled waters, from their spring
Author of truth; such be my poesie.

    [George Daniel]

    b.121, fol. 57

C0229 Clear is the air and the morning fair,
Those whom I trust do now my trust betray. |
                          Dead, dead, a[h] dead.

    'The huntsman's song'
    [Crum c316]

    b.197, p. 235

C0230 Clear was the night, and o'er the dusky plain
A lovely form may ev'ry vice conceal.

    'Night a pastoral'

    c.89, p. 47

C0231 Clearer than transparent glass,
Vocal waters, tinkling ring.

    [William Popple, trans.], '[Horace] book 3rd. ode
    13th. To the fountain Blandusia'

    fc.104/2, p. 254

C0232 Cleora has her wish, she weds a peer,
They cannot make me wretched, blessing her.

    George Granville, [1st baron Lansdowne], 'By the
    honorable Mr. George Granville'

    c.189, p. 118

C0233 Cleveland was doubtless to blame
So many butter'd buns.

    [on the Duchess of Cleveland]
    [Crum c318]

    fb.66/5; fb.70, p. 27 ('much to blame')

C0234 Clients before a thief run singing home
For from the city moneyless they come.

    'Of clients'

    c.356

C0235 Clio, behold this charming day
To comfort English widows.

    [Sir Charles Hanbury Williams], 'On her Grace [the]
    Duchess of Cleveland [i.e., Manchester]'s marriage
    with Mr. Hussey an Irish fortune-teller to Henry Fox
    esqr.'
    [Crum c322]

    c.360/2, no. 237; c.241, p. 47

C0236 Clive's blameless life this tablet shall proclaim,
And heav'nly plaudits hail the virtuous deed.

    'Epitaph on Mrs. C. Clive'

    c.83/2, no. 280

C0237 Cloak (if I so may call thee) though thou art
Tell him, his wits are gone a wool-gathering.

    [Thomas Jordan], 'A poet's farewell to his threadbare
    cloak' [answered by 'Will you be guilty . . .']
    [Crum c323]

    b.65, p. 196

C0238 Cloaks for the senate are they say decreed,
'Twill raise a tax the nation cannot bear.

    'On the House of Commons'
    [Crum c324]

    fb.207/1, p. 11

C0239 Clodio retiring to his room
We've fairly got in tail.

    'On a lawyer who was shot in his posteriors while he
    was exposing them in Lincoln's Inn Gardens'

    c.360/1, p. 307

C0240 Cloncorry Cloncorry come here in a hurry
A blanket has toss'd you much higher.

    Poetry Box IV/25

C0241 Clorinda does at fifty-six
She must lead apes to Hell.

    'Song 208'

    c.555, p. 335

C0242 Clorinda's likeness, here, complete I see,
The portrait is insensible as she.

    c.549, p. 10

C0243 Close by a stream whose flowery bank might give
And arms my tortur'd soul to bear my pains.

    [Sir Carr Scroope, trans.], 'The parting between
    Sireno and Diana'
    [Crum c328]

    b.327, f. 27; b.105, p. 401

C0244 Close hugg'd in Portsmouth's smock thy senses are
Exalts his whore, and calls her Mazarin.

'An acrostic' [On 'Charles Stewart Rex', c. 1679]

b.371, no. 15; b.327, f. 22 (var.); b.52/2, p. 179
(incomplete); b.54, p. 1154 (incomplete)

C0245 Close in her hallowed grot, where mildly bright
And pleas'd prefer oblivion to disgrace.

[William Mason], 'Isis an elegy' [1747-1750]
[Crum c330]

Poetry Box I/86; see also 'Far from her hallow'd
grot . . .'.

C0246 Close link'd in friendship's tender ties,
Lost reputation none retrieve.

'A fable'

fc.85, fol. 116v

C0247 Close up the sluice, and spare the rill—
The meadows now have drunk their fill.

T[homas] H[ull], [translation of William Shenstone]

c.20/8

C0248 Clouds, gold and purple, o'er the western ray
Tho' poor and plunder'd, he absolves his fate!

[Charlotte (Turner) Smith], 'Sonnet written at
[Exmouth] on seeing a seaman return who had been
imprisoned at Rochfort'

c.141, p. 114

C0249 Cloy'd with the city, and the fears that it brings
I spent my five guineas and so return'd home.

Thomas D'Urfey, 'A satire on Epsom: summer: 1679'

b.54, p. 1120

C0250 Cold blows the wind upon the mountain's brow
Save the sweet converse of the friend I love.

'Laura to Leonardo'

c.344, p. 115

C0251 Cold chills, heat scorches, what must mortals do?
But know you barter health for temporary ease.

[James Mulcaster, sr.], 'Written in a frost'

c.118, p. 5

C0252 Cold-natur'd Chronus, pond'rous moving light
That's own'd by virtue of *probatum est*.

[John Rose?], 'On the seven planets, and their
significations'

b.227, p. 169

C0253 Colley has tun'd again his fife
Not yet; ——'s death.

'On the New Year's ode for the first of January 1735/6
composed by Colley Cibber poet laureate a pastoral'
[satire]

c.360/1, p. 103

C0254 Colinus Jobson has a wife,
Instead of bleeding she had p[issed].

Abraham Oakes, 'The groaning, or Colin and Mopsa:
a tale'

c.50, p. 112

C0255 Come Alecto and lend me thy torch
Therefore, gentlemen be merry in prose.

'On old Thomas Churchyard the poor court poet'
[Crum c351]

fb.143, p. 33

C0256 Come, all harmonious tongues,
To everlasting days.

[Isaac Watts, Hymns and spiritual songs (1707), bk. II,
Hymn 84]

c.180, p. 11

C0257 Come all ye Douffs, that Douffs are true
And every Douff his mate may see.

[Mrs. Christian Kerr], 'A circular advertisement for
the Douffs in Kelso district, to the consecration of the
yew at Sunlaws'

c.102, p. 133

C0258 Come all ye nymphs and shepherds
The happy, happy, happy, happy charms of love.

'4th song'

Accession 97.7.40, p. 7

C0259 Come all [ye] young lovers who wan with despair
For in spite of grave lessons by Jove I'll be free.

'Song 222'
[Crum c371]

c.555, p. 351

C0260 Come all you muses and rejoice
At your Apollo's happy choice.

[Jeremiah Terrent], 'On Dr Corbett's marriage day'
[Crum c365, 'all ye']

b.205, fol. 56v

C0261 Come all you pale lovers, that sigh, and complain,
No rival can lessen, nor envy destroy.

'The jolly lover'
[Crum c368, 'all ye']

fb.107, p. 57

C0262 Come all you that love treason and listen I beg
Is as plain as the first he was maul'd for alive. |
Which nobody can deny.

'The posthumous plot'

c.154, p. 23

C0263 Come all you whores and bawds that are in this
nation,
He's an ass that says that thou weren't with an
whore boys.

'Upon the Rump's act of Parliament for fornication
and adultery'

fb.140, p. 8

C0264 Come, Amarillis, come, and with me share
While contemplation wafts you to the sky.

'Country invitation—Letters moral'

c.244, p. 587

C0265 Come and behold, good brother Hugh!
E'en this will be their life.

'Marriage for interest. Illustrated by a simile'

c.94

C0266 Come and let us love my dear
That they mock, the envious sky.

[Richard Crashaw], 'Catullus ad Lesbiam'
[cf. Crum c368, 'let us live']

b.356, p. 224

C0267 Come and listen to my ditty
Since in yours I cannot be.

[Crum c396]

c.188, p. 9

C0268 Come Apollo with the muses
'Twould spoil all to tell you now.

'A pastoral ballad . . . (to the tune of Fairest isle &c)'

c.341, p. 9

C0269 Come Aurelia, come and see,
'Tis so hid with jessamy.

J[ohn] Dyer

Spence Papers, folder 148

C0270 Come away make up th'account
All good keep out all good keep out.

'Come away in Macbeth' [with musical score for bass
and tenor]

Music MS. 534

C0271 Come away prince o'th' sea, come Neptune,
This third will make to rue for't.

'3 song'

fb.228/60

C0272 Come away to the skies!
And fly up to acknowledge him there.

'Hymn 104th'

c.562, p. 141

C0273 Come away, t'other glass,
In a jolly brave soul that's a stranger to care.

'The heir'

fb.107, p. 39

C0274 Come beaux, virtuosos, heirs and musicians
That your heirs will do so just a hundred years
hence-a.

[Henry Hall, of Hereford], 'Song 227'

c.555, p. 358

C0275 Come blooming goddess fair Hygeia light,
Which, like the morning sun, each vapor clear'd.

'Sonnet'

c.135, p. 28

C0276 Come boys and before the old vessel unmoors
And drink reformation to Commodore Gale. |
Sing, drink and remember, &c.

'Song 160'

c.555, p. 243

C0277 Come boys let's crown our joys with bumpers of
the best;
We singing, drinking, never thinking, please the
mighty Jove.

'Song'

c.189, p. 159

C0278 Come brave boys and let us sing
In spite of usurpation.

'Song to the tune of How now comes on &c.' [c. 1716]

fc.58, p. 61; see also next.

C0279 Come brave boys, now let us sing,
To the joy of all the nation.

'A health to the King's restoration' [James II]

b.111, p. 37; fb.207/2, p. 45; see also previous.

C0280 Come bright Urania nay come all the nine
Ever thrice blessed be the three in one.

[Edward] Sparke, 'Poem 16th, upon Trinity Sunday'

b.137, p. 41

C0281 Come Britons your case forget to implore
Attend on the glorious two hundred and four.

'The British merchants' toast'

c.570/3, p. 206

C0282   Come brothers of the water!
Lest Essex calves want water.

     'The complaint of the pouts . . . occasioned by the
     undertaking of the lords and other gentlemen for
     draining the Levels from a MS. copy of Mr. Martin
     Johnson's in 1546'

     c.229/1, fol. 27

C0283   Come bustle bustle drink about
Thus sailors pass their lives. | And a-sailing &c.

     'Song 199'

     c.555, p. 320

C0284   Come buy my fine wares,
They'll make a sweet bishop when gentlefolks sup.

     [Jonathan Swift], 'Verses made for women who cry
     apples &c.'

     c.83/1, no. 53

C0285   Come cease all your pother about this or that;
May justly be reckoned a Man.

     'Song 143'

     c.555, p. 196

C0286   Come cheer up my hearts, come cheer up again
And cheer up our evening with 'God save the King!'

     [William] Smith, 'Song written and sung by . . . at a
     [Naval] ball given at Bury St. Edmunds Nov. 1st
     [1797] in honor of Nelson's victories'

     Smith Papers, folder 56

C0287   Come, children young and lovely,
The everlasting king.

     'Hymn III'

     c.91, p. 338

C0288   Come Chloe view with curious eye
Be something more than butterfly.

     'To Chloe, on a butterfly'

     fc.51, p. 175

C0289   Come, come Astatia come away
If it move slowest at the last.

     'The tedious bridegroom'

     fb.107, p. 80

C0290   Come come follow follow me
And we too late repent tomorrow.

     'A song' [pr. 1715? (Foxon R172)]
     [Crum c430]

     b.62, p. 14

C0291   Come come great monarch come away
Except to dance a Tyburn jig. | Couragio &c.

     'Revolution upon revolution. An old song made the
     the year 1688. revised in the year 1715'

     c.570/1, p. 109

C0292   Come come I faint thy heavy stay
If living thus, I live, or dead I be.

     [William Strode], 'On a friend's absence. Song 3.'
     [Crum c431]

     b.205, fol. 68v

C0293   Come, come, let's mourn, all eyes that see this day
A god on earth, more than a saint in heaven.

     'An elegy upon the death of our dread sovereign lord
     King Charles the martyr'

     b.54, p. 1227

C0294   Come come my dear shepherd our flocks we must
                                    shear
And leave to fine folk to deceive and betray.

     'Song 246'

     c.555, p. 396

C0295   Come, come, my friends! no more delay:
Because you neither drink nor eat.

     [Stephen Barrett], 'An invitation to two abstemious
     friends (Dr. Johnson and Mr. Cave) to Bush[e]y in
     Herts. in the true modern strain of sinking in poetry'

     c.193, p. 115

C0296   Come come O blessed Bar'lemew,
Which never shall decay. | Amen

     'Of S. Bart[ho]lemew. Aug. 24'

     a.30[28]

C0297   Come come ye sons of art,
Our songs to Apollo whose ear is divine.

     'Song on King George's birthday'

     c.160, fol. 86

C0298   Come cut again the game's not done
For they the dole will make.

     'The new game at one and forty to the tune of I'll tell
     ye Dick' [c. 1680]

     c.171, p. 2

C0299   Come darling muse, who lov'st to sing
But as the spring, it glows anew.

     [ ] Matthews, 'The groves of Llanelthy'

     c.83/4, no. 2018

C0300   Come dear religion, heavenly maid,
On P[ilkingto]n and H[a]y.

     'An ode to Miss Pilkington and Hay, sometime before
     marriage'

     c.91, p. 159

C0301   Come death, make haste and waft my soul
To fetch my soul away.

     [( ) Pierson]

     c.328, p. 29

C0302 Come, Delia, come, let's shun the heat,
But seize the present hour.

'J. Spr—g C——— February 27 1783'

c.74

C0303 Come doctor, use thy roughest art,
That I should hope 'twould almost quench my fire.

A[braham] C[owley], 'The cure'
[Crum c443

c.258

C0304 Come drawer, come, come come and draw good
wine,
We grow, we grow together more divine.

'A catch for 4 voices'
[cf. Crum c445]

Music ms. 16, p. 421

C0305 Come Echo I thee summon
If not belov'd she cares not.

[William Barlowe?], 'A song'
[Crum c449]

b.205, fol. 77v; c.356 (var.)

C0306 Come, elves, and fairies, all a-row
With growling bass, shall bear a part. | Ban, ban,
cacaly ban.

[Thomas Morell], 'A glee as performed at the jubilee
at Stratford'

c.395, p. 142

C0307 Come fair Astara let us for awhile
The further 'tis removed from joys of sense.

[Lady Mary Chudleigh], 'A dialogue between Alexis
and Astara'

c.548

C0308 Come, fair one, be kind
If after I drink water-gruel.

'Song'

c.189, p. 223

C0309 Come fancy from the mottl'd sky,
Thy power can raise to life again.

'Ode to fancy'

c.83/3, no. 951

C0310 Come fates I fear you not, all whom I owe
But for the clearness from a lump of snow.

[Sir John Roe], 'Elegia 16ta' [attr. John Donne]
[Crum c450]

b.114, p. 125; b.148, p. 74

C0311 Come fill a glass I'll toast a health
What's that to him that's far away, over the hills &c.

'Song'

fc.58, p. 55

C0312 Come fill us up the widest bowl,
Drink most is the best warrior.

'[The good fellow.] A song'
[Crum c455]

Poetry Box VII/67

C0313 Come follow, follow me,
By our exploits, where we have been.

John Lockman, 'The Bacchanals, or mock fairies. Set
by Mr. Arnold . . . 1730'

c.267/2, p. 133; c.268 (first part), p. 63

C0314 Come follow, follow me | Ye fairy elves that be
The glow-worm lights us home to bed.

[Edward Phillips], 'The fairy ballad' [printed in
Percy's Reliques, 1767]
[Crum c460]

Trumbull Box: Poetry Box XIII/102 (ll. 1–42); b.356,
p. 69; Accession 97.7.40

C0315 Come friends and lend your help let's now inter
To wrong his ashes by a proud compare.

'His epitaph' [on John Reignolds]

c.548

C0316 Come from the dungeon to the throne
First they are crowned, and then they bleed.

[William Cartwright], 'The priests' song, while the
royal slave was putting on the robes' [from The royal
slave, 1636]
[Crum c467]

b.200, p. 156

C0317 Come from your groves each goddess,
Lies until Jove is jealous . . . [cropped].

'A song'

b.197, p. 249 (incomplete)

C0318 Come full of days and rich in works benign
This blessed(?) love and truth may grace your tomb.

[William Hayley], 'In the adjoining vault lie the
remains of Thomas Steele esqr. Epitaph . . . May 14
[1799]'

File 6937

C0319 Come gard'ner come weed me the banks around,
Hear—and your brethren of the dust forgive!

[Thomas Hull], 'Irregular ode written in a garden, on
contemplating the number of unhappy wretches who
are executed in this country'

c.528/33

C0320   Come genial spring! Resume thy reign,
Feel ev'ry youthful flame reviv'd.

     [Charles Burney, the elder], 'Spring'

     c.33, p. 87

C0321   Come gentle Chloris! let us rove
Partake my lot—and be my mate.

     [Sophia Raymond] Burrell [Clay], 'The shepherd's
     courtship'

     c.141, p. 540

C0322   Come gentle god of soft desire!
Put on Amanda's winning form.

     [James] Thomson, 'A song'

     c.152, p. 33

C0323   Come gentle god of soft repose
Let life be all a dream!

     Miss [ ] Ramsey, 'The dream an ode'

     fc.51, p. 20

C0324   Come gentle Morpheus, with thy magic pow'rs,
And bid within his soul new pleasures rise.

     'Address to Morpheus'

     c.83/3, no. 921

C0325   Come gentle muse, and sweep the string,
And sensibility delight no more!

     C[harles] Burney, 'Ode. Addressed to Alexander
     Burnet esqr. of Seaton House—January 1. 1780'

     c.38, p. 31

C0326   Come gentle muse my soul's desire,
To leave this earthly clay.

     'Ode on retirement'

     c.83/1, no. 109

C0327   Come, gentle peace, departed guest,
Ye gracious pow'rs make resignation mine!

     [ ] C——, 'Ode to peace'

     c.83/3, no. 840

C0328   Come gentle Sylvia and with pleasure view
Then will her Strephon be supremely blest!

     F[rances] B[urney d'Arblay], 'Summer'

     c.486, fol. 22

C0329   Come give your attention to what I unfold
That life is not life when divided from love.

     [Theodosius Forrest?], 'Song 165'

     c.555, p. 251; see also 'By purchas'd experience . . .'.

C0330   Come grant come lend me your list'ning ear
Imagine all vices were buried in graves. | Then
        there were a golden age, O then there etc.

     b.197, p. 181

C0331   Come heaven-born gratitude my muse inspire
In them each grace each virtue is combined.

     Miss [ ] Andrews, 'To the house in general—Mrs.
     Caley's boarding school'

     File 245/1

C0332   Come here and view this face ye proudest lasses
Nothing recalls it but th'resurrection.

     'On a death's head thought to be a virgin's when 'twas
     taken out of the grave'

     b.205, fol. 40v

C0333   Come here my Bentinck and indulge thy charms
To horse great Sir, and let's away to Loo.

     'Actus quintus. Enter K. Phys. in his nightgown, and
     Bentinck with his breeches down'

     b.111, p. 371

C0334   Come here's to thee in my horn
That cannot bear a high horn.

     'To the tune of A health to Betty'

     b.213, p. 96

C0335   Come hither Apollo's bouncing girl
G'if ever I have a man square cap for me.

     [John Cleveland], 'Songs [6]'
     [Crum c481]

     b.356, p. 276

C0336   Come hither, come hither, ye languishing swains,
For 'tis Comus invites; to his temple away.

     'Song 53'

     c.555, p. 78

C0337   Come hither melancholy
And so farewell faithless woman.

     'Song 47'

     b.4, fol. 37v

C0338   Come hither, painter, thou that art
And presently the paint will talk.

     George Montagu, 'Advice to a painter from Anacreon'

     fc.135, p. 2

C0339   Come hither read my gentle friend
The man that made him soles at will.

     'On a cobbler'
     [Crum c485]

     b.208, p. 59; see also 'O mighty death . . .'.

C0340 Come hither Sir George, my picture is here,
Tho' I think it will soon, 'tis so like you.

'On a lady, who used to bang her husband, showing him a picture of her—which she had just been sitting for'

Poetry Box v/18

C0341 Come hither to me and I'll tell you some news
He got from the P[arliamen]t.

[Henry d'Auverquerque, Lord Grantham, 'Naked truth. An excellent new ballad on the maids of honor's washerwoman being robbed of their smocks in May 1729, to the tune of Under the greenwood tree']

Poetry Box VII/88; see also 'Come listen to me . . .'.

C0342 Come hither women leave your vanities
Of air and sun might in the grave be laid.

'Epitaph no. 9'
[Crum c488]

c.158, p. 48

C0343 Come hither, ye jolly and jocund and gay,
And make us divine as great Jove.

'Song 92'

c.555, p. 141

C0344 Come Holy Ghost eternal God
Our souls and bodies frame.

'A hymn' [Veni Creator Spiritus]
[cf. Crum c493]

c.124, no. 2

C0345 Come Holy Ghost send down those heav'nly beams
That we at last may endless joy inherit.

[Sir Richard Bulstrode?], 'Upon the Holy Ghost'

fb.88, p. 117v

C0346 Come Holy Spirit, come and breathe
Belov'd and prais'd, fear'd and ador'd.

[John Austin], 'Hym. 31' [Hymn xxxiii, Devotions in the ancient way of offices, 1672, p. 290]

c.178, p. 29

C0347 Come Holy Spirit, send down those beams,
While time does last, when time decays.

[John Austin], 'Hym: 37. H[oly] G[host]' [Hymn xxxv, Devotions in the ancient way of offices, 1672, p. 317]

c.178, p. 36

C0348 Come honest sexton take thy spade,
Farewell my loving friends, farewell!

[Nahum] Tate, 'The passing bell'

c.244, p. 148; fb.142, p. 62; c.328, p. 49

C0349 Come Hymen! Rosy god! Appear;
And bless us with the sweets of peace.

John Lockman, 'Translations, and imitations from Metastasio, and other Italian opera poets [20, by Signor Botarelli]. Epithalamium'

c.267/4, p. 115

C0350 Come Jack come tipple off you[r] wine
A lark is better than a kite.

'Another by the same hand' [as 'Grim death . . .']

fb.142, p. 56

C0351 Come Jesus come my heart inspire
The way of truth and righteousness.

'Hymn 58th'

c.562, p. 70

C0352 Come jolly Bacchus god of wine,
Live and die with pleasure.

'Song 73'

c.555, p. 111

C0353 Come, kindly welcome little friend
Each winter come again.

'An address to the Robin-Red-Breast in the beginning of winter'

c.91, p. 171

C0354 Come kiss my Muse and spread thy flutt'ring wings
Their God their Savior by them glorified.

b.216, p. 153

C0355 Come ladies, ye that would appear
Go learn of her humility.

'On Dame Rebecca Berry the wife of Tho: Elton of Stratford-Bow gent. Apr. 26. 1696. Aged 52' [Stepney Churchyard]
[Crum c503]

fb.143, p. 26; c.244, p. 86

C0356 Come lay aside your murmuring
When they had none at all.

'A song on the present times' [c. 1689]
[Crum c506]

b.111, p. 358; fb.207/1, p. 13

C0357 Come lay these foolish niceties aside
While youth and beauty give you leave to choose.

c.549, p. 59

C0358 Come leave the city's strife
Center my joys, in a poor country life.

[George Daniel], 'A pastoral ode'

b.121, fol. 49

C0359 Come let us drink, and drown all sorrow,
This is to all men the best of physic.

    'Song 131'

c.555, p. 185

C0360 Come let us join a joyful tune
To raise and heal the dead.

    [Isaac Watts, Hymns and spiritual songs (1707),
    bk. III, Hymn 8]

c.180, p. 45

C0361 Come, let us join our God to bless,
Hath plac'd us in the way.

    [Thomas Stevens?], 'Hymn the 4th'

c.259

C0362 Come let us lift our voices high,
Exceed our noblest songs.

    [Isaac Watts, Hymns and spiritual songs (1707),
    bk. III, Hymn 21]

c.180, p. 55

C0363 Come let us rejoice, merry boys at his fall
For sure, if he'd liv'd, he had buried us all.

    'Epitaph in a country churchyard on the parson of the
    parish'

c.360/3, no. 39; c.113/15

C0364 Come let's adore the gracious hand,
Till time itself be done.

    [John Austin], 'Hym. 5' [Hymn ix, Devotions in the
    ancient way of offices, 1672, p. 80]

c.178, p. 4

C0365 Come let's adore the king of love
Now, and forever be.

    [John Austin], Hym: 11' [Hymn xxi, Devotions in the
    ancient way of offices, 1672, p. 178]
    [Crum c518]

c.178, p. 10

C0366 Come let's drink the time invites
And that's our only treason.

    'Song 203'

c.555, p. 326

C0367 Come Liberty, damme boys, but we'll be free,
Because while we're drinking we live. | My brave boys.

    'Song 70'

c.555, p. 105

C0368 Come life come death
As warm'd by those delightful beams.

    [Mary Pluret], 'All things shall work together for good
    Rom. Chap. [ ] Verse [ ]'

c.354

C0369 Come listen awhile, and I'll tell you a tale
And a dean or a bishop you quickly shall be.

    'The parson of Walton de Dale. Tune: the Abbot of
    Canterbury'

b.382(2); c.171, no. 9 (incomplete?)

C0370 Come listen brave boys to a story so merry,
And since Melville's got justice the devil take
          Law. | Derry down, down down derry down.

    'The lawyer and the bishop to the tune of King John
    and the Abbot of Canterbury'

c.340

C0371 Come listen, good folks, and a tale I'll relate,
And down with Sedition and Paine.

    [William Boscawen], 'The reformer of England. A
    song written in Dec[ember] 1792. Tune—The roast
    beef of Old England'

fc.106, p. 14

C0372 Come, listen, good people, to what I shall say
To the shame and confusion of Perkin Warbeck.

    'A ballad to the tune of Packington's pound made on
    the day of the Duke of York's return' [on the Duke of
    Monmouth; September 1679]
    [Crum c526]

b.54, p. 1122

C0373 Come listen, my friends and I'll sing you a song
And his favor is what they most prize. | Hey brave
                                boys

File 17398

C0374 Come listen, my friends, to a story so new
Oh no: quoth the Duke—I'd be robbing myself. |
                            Derry &c.

    'Robin Hood and the Duke of Lancaster. To the tune
    of the abbot of Canterbury' [pr. 1727 (Foxon R232)]

c.570/3, p. 11

C0375 Come listen to me, and I'll tell you some news
He got of his Parliament.

    [Henry d'Auverquerque, Lord Grantham], 'Naked
    truth. An excellent new ballad [the maids of honor's
    washerwoman being robbed of their smocks in May
    1729] to, the tune of Under the greenwood tree'
    [Crum c528]

Poetry Box x/28; see also 'Come hither to me . . .'.

C0376 Come, listen, ye Tories and Jacobites now,
And whoe'er disbelieves it, is one of the plot. |
                    [Which nobody can deny,] &c.

    [Samuel Wesley, the younger], 'Another on [Francis
    Atterbury, Bishop of Rochester's] plot in 1723'
    [Crum c529]

c.233, p. 112; Poetry Box IV/100, 123; Poetry Box IV/100

C0377   Come listen you freemen awhile to my song
        Confutation to those that oppose hearts of oak. |
                                    . . . Steady boys steady

        Poetry Box x/80

C0378   Come live with me and be my love
        Alas is wiser far than I.

        [John Donne, 'The bait'; parody of next]
        [Crum c531]
        b.148, p. 100; b.150, p. 195

C0379   Come live with me and be my love
        Then live with me and be my love.

        [Christopher Marlowe], 'Sir Walter Raleigh [sic] to
        Q. Elizabeth' [parodied by previous]
        [Crum c530]
        b.356, p. 329; see also 'Live with me . . .'.

C0380   Come Lord come love and that long day
        Then for thy 'vail give me thy face.

        [Lady Ursula (Darcy) Wyvill], 'Aug: the 22 1672'
        b.222, p. 113

C0381   Come Lord to a sinner's relief
        And safely conduct me away.

        'Hymn 26th'
        c.562, p. 30

C0382   Come lovely fancy, bright-ey'd maid,
        To warm Belinda's broth, and gruel.

        G[eorge] Dyer, 'A recipe for a lady's cold'
        c.83/2, no. 614

C0383   Come, lovely gentle peace of mind,
        The pledge of heaven, shall make me blest.

        'To peace . . . Bombay 1774'
        fc.132/1, p. 93; c.83/4, no. 2008

C0384   Come lovely vision do not stay
        Keeps cares on laws yet daily covets more.

        c.416

C0385   Come lovers all to me and cease your mourning
        H' has lost a thousand servants to kill one.

        [Crum c538]
        b.213, p. 6

C0386   Come Madam, come, all rest my powers defy
        What needst you have more covering than a man.

        [John Donne], 'Elegia prima' [Elegie XIX: Going to
        bed]
        [Crum c543]
        b.114, p. 69; b.148, p. 79; b.200, p. 208; b.62, p. 97

C0387   Come Margaret O virgin rare
        In heaven forevermore. | Amen

        'S. Margaret. July 20'
        a.30[13]

C0388   Come melancholy! Silent pow'r
        Of active life and bliss.

        [Elizabeth Carter], 'Ode to melancholy'
        c.83/1, no. 99

C0389   Come mild and holy dove,
        One equal glory be.

        [John Austin], 'Hym: 32' [Hymn xxxiv, Devotions in
        the ancient way of offices, 1672, p. 308]
        [Crum c545]
        c.178, p. 30

C0390   Come Mira! Idol of the swains;
        Thy graces claim unrivall'd sway.

        John Lockman, 'The invitation to Mira: requesting
        her company at Vauxhall Gardens, before she went
        abroad . . . May 1740'
        c.267/1, p. 272; c.268 (first part), p. 55

C0391   Come mortals then o'er time adore
        And a new courage raise.

        [Sir William Trumbull, rough draft of Psalm 4]
        Trumbull Box: Poetry Box XIII/3

C0392   Come mournful muses, weep the saddest tears,
        Submit—and not the will of heaven to blame.

        'To the memory of Prince Lee Boo'
        c.91, p. 278

C0393   Come, Muse and assist me a duel to sing
        My muse is too humble; so God bless the king.

        T[homas] M[orell], 'The lord and the 'squire. A
        ballad. 1731'
        c.395, p. 24

C0394   Come Muses all great joys of spring
        Then she with ivy will him reward.

        'Virgil's commendation of a garden translated out of
        Latin iambic verse'
        Poetry Box VI/8

C0395   Come my bonny love
        While my love's away.

        Miss [ ] White, of Edgbaston, 'Rural group'
        c.532

C0396   Come my buskin'd hunter, come,
        This beating heart's the token.

        'Sylvia'
        c.344, p. 69

C0397 Come my Celia let us prove
Those have crimes accounted been.

[Ben Jonson], 'To Celia'
[Crum c551]

b.356, p. 231

C0398 Come my Cynthia, gladly fix
The faculties, unstained with desire.

[George Daniel]

b.121, fol. 75

C0399 Come, my dear girl, let's sit in this valley:
There's my good maid.

'To remember the Dijon minuet tune by'

Spence Papers, folder 113

C0400 Come my dear goddesses
With us forever and for aye.

'The paraphrase' [of French verses by the Prince of
Wales addressed to Lady Middlesex (later duchess of
Dorset), Lady Catherine Hanmer, and Lady Faulcon
who represented Venus, Juno and Minerva in
Congreve's masque The judgment of Pano, 1755]

fc.135; Poetry Box IV/191

C0401 Come my Nicotiana, we'll renew
Careless, who see, fearless who know our love.

[George Daniel]

b.121, fol. 18

C0402 Come my sweet Phyllis
Of love's desire.

'A sonnet'

b.356, p. 73

C0403 Come my sweet, while every stream
Scorning the forgetful lake.

[William Cartwright], 'A treacherous song by the
Persian nobles . . .' [in The royal slave, 1636]

b.200, p. 156

C0404 Come my vain thoughts that wand'ring fly
Eternal homage shall be done.

[John Austin], 'Hym: 38' [Hymn xx, Devotions in the
ancient way of offices, 1672, p.175]

c.178, p. 37

C0405 Come my way, my truth, my life:
Such a heart as joys in love.

[George] Herbert, 'Call'
[Crum c560]

b.245 (inside back cover); c.139, p. 137

C0406 Come near ye saints and I will tell
And make a war with sin.

[Mary Pluret], 'First awakenings'

c.354

C0407 Come not ye curious fools so far
Hoh hoh (quoth the devil) in great Oliver.

b.52/1, p. 114

C0408 Come now all ye social pow'rs,
And never mind tomorrow. | Bring the flask &c.

'Song 25'

c.555, p. 31

C0409 Come nymph with all thy smiling train
All heaven's artillery roar'd and thunder'd as he
rode.

J[ohn] W[ilson], 'Ode to fancy'

Poetry Box IV/143

C0410 Come, O come, I brook no stay,
But spriteful kisses strikes the hours.

W[illiam] C[artwright, a song in The ordinary III.iii]
[Crum c567]

b.200, p. 432

C0411 Come on, come on, brave Irish boys
That the king shall enjoy his own again.

'The Irish resolution'

b.111, p. 57

C0412 Come on ye critics find one fault who dare
Did ever libel yet so sharply bite.

[Charles Sackville], Lord B[uckhurst, later 6th earl of
Dorset], 'On Mr. Edw[ard] Howard upon his British
princess' [i.e., princes; 1669–71]
[Crum c569; POAS I.338]

b.105, p. 186

C0413 Come painter take a prospect from the hill,
Kneel to this image, and pour out their prayers |
And then die by suffocation.

[John Phillips], 'The hieroglyphic, being a synopsis of
the whole year by way of conclusion . . . 1688' [on
John Gadbury]

Poetry Box VI/85 (attr. H. H.); fb.155, p. 537

C0414 Come, pretty birds, fly to this verdant shade,
Nor shall the song be mortal, where's the songs
divine.

[Isaac Watts], 'The sacred concert of praise'

c.259, p. 70

C0415 Come prithee Cupid play with me
And flout thee e'en to death.

    'Song 41th'

    b.4, fol. 34v

C0416 Come roseate health, my temples bind
Death snatch my soul away.

    'Wisdom and health . . . Anjengo, 1772'

    fc.132/1, p. 81

C0417 Come, rosy health, celestial maid,
And Harold's beauties yield to thine.

    'Ode to health'
    [Crum c584]

    fc.51, p. 160

C0418 Come rouse brother tars! hark the seamen all cry;
And pleas'd, thus we make the reprisals, long due.

    'Song 16'

    c.555, p. 22

C0419 Come royal Sion come and sing,
Convictors all of thy full cup.

    [John Austin], 'Hym. 10' [Hymn xvii, Devotions in
    the ancient way of offices, 1672, p. 144]

    c.178, p. 9 (incomplete)

C0420 Come Savior, Jesu, from above!
And freely give up all the rest.

    [John Byrom?], 'Hymn 82d'

    c.562, p. 108; see also 'O let the sacred presence . . .'.

C0421 Come shepherds, happy shepherds, leave awhile
                       your rural toils,
Prone to bless, itself be blest, | Oh! Anna &c.

    [Thomas Hull]

    c.528/48

C0422 Come, shepherds, we'll follow the hearse,
And thus—let me break it in twain.

    [John Cunningham], 'Corydon: a pastoral to the
    memory of W. Shenstone esq.'

    c.149, p. 1; c.83/1, no. 197; c.83/2, no. 327; fc.132/1, p. 191;
    Poetry Box V/88

C0423 Come sing round my favorite tree,
And the nightingale fill'd up the pause.

    'Song 117'

    c.555, p. 169

C0424 Come spade ill and dig a hole,
Behold, here lies the beast.

    Alexander Pope(?), 'Epitaph on a favorite dog, call'd
    Basto' [docket attribution]

    Poetry Box IV/7

C0425 Come spread my muse and mount upon the wing
A joyful welcome to our gracious king.

    b.216, p. 169

C0426 Come sweet companion of each mournful hour!
In peace indulge its griefs, or lessen all its woes.

    [Frances Burney d'Arblay], 'Sonnet. To melancholy'

    c.486, fol. 14v

C0427 Come sweet repose, and calm my breast,
Indifferent then to me to sleep or die.

    A. L., 'On sleep'

    c.116, p. 7

C0428 Come tak' your glass the Northern lass
But sunshine at the rest.

    c.188, p .2

C0429 Come take my advice now, Willy my son
An[d] it's Wogin[?] you'll be lordly &c.

    'Willy be lordly a ballad'

    Trumbull Box: Poetry Box XIII/94

C0430 Come taste and see how good is he
Of Adam since the world had place.

    [Mary Pluret], 'Another [poem written on waste
    paper]'

    c.354

C0431 Come then, Dione, let us range the grove,
And thus I construed the mellifluent strain.

    [William Shenstone], 'To a lady on the language of
    birds'

    c.149, p. 4

C0432 Come then, my friend thy sylvan task display
The care of other strains and turn thy own.

    [William Shenstone], 'Dodsley's bower—Faunus'

    c.21; c.20/2

C0433 Come, Thomas, give me t'other sonnet;
Your most obliged humble servant.

    Capt. [ ] Thomas, 'Capt. Thomas of Batereau's [62nd]
    Regt . . . to Capt. Price at Fort Augustus. Upon
    reading the news of the treaty of peace signed at
    Aix-la-Chapelle' [1748]

    fc.51, p. 281

C0434 Come thou queen of pensive air,
And grottos the wild notes resound.

    'Ode to contemplation'

    c.83/3, no. 906

C0435　Come thou soft and sacred favor,
　　　　Still embosom'd will we lie.

　　　　　[James Hammond], 'Address to a locket with a braid
　　　　　of Emma [Dashwood]'s hair'
　　　　c.83/1, no. 33; no. 87 (var.)

C0436　Come thou universal blessing
　　　　Christ is God and God is love.

　　　　　'Hymn 61th'
　　　　c.562, p. 74

C0437　Come to Jehovah let us shout
　　　　My holy rest t'invade.

　　　　　'Psal: 95'
　　　　b.217, p. 61

C0438　Come trowl it away,
　　　　But small beer would make us all asses.

　　　　　'The worth of wine'
　　　　fb.107, p. 11

C0439　Come view the grave—come drop the tender tear,
　　　　Nor chang'd her form, since 'twas angelic here.

　　　　　'Lines on the death of Mrs. George Byron'
　　　　c.83/3, no. 810

C0440　Come weavers, come butchers, come cobblers,
　　　　　　　　　　　　　　　　　　　　　come all,
　　　　With hunger and cold. God-a-mercy good Scot.

　　　　　'God-a-mercy good Scot' [on Parliament, 1640]
　　　　　[Crum c650]
　　　　fb.106(6); see also 'You wily projectors . . .'.

C0441　Come White prepare to 'grave that man once more
　　　　Who's been of ev'ry side, but true to none.

　　　　　'Advice to Mr. [Robert] White [who engraved the
　　　　　seven bishops] June 4th.1691'
　　　　　[Crum c651]
　　　　b.111, p. 112

C0442　Come ye beautiful virgins and youths most refin'd,
　　　　Then descend to the grave, just like husband and
　　　　　　　　　　　　　　　　　　　　　　　　　wife.

　　　　　'Damon and Daphne a poem . . . 28th August 1788'
　　　　c.91, p. 32

C0443　Come, ye fair, ambrosial flowers,
　　　　Sweetly dying in her breast.

　　　　　[Francis Fawkes], 'Nosegay for Laura'
　　　　fc.21, p. 8

C0444　Come ye lads who wish to shine,
　　　　And see your country righted.

　　　　　'Song 13'
　　　　c.555, p. 18

C0445　Come ye lovers of peace, who are said to have sold
　　　　And her navies in port are the terror of Spain.

　　　　　'England's glory. Being an excellent ballad on the
　　　　　Fleet at Spithead. To the tune of Cutpurse' [pr. 1729
　　　　　(Foxon G257)]
　　　　　[Crum c657]
　　　　c.416

C0446　Come ye sinners, poor and wretched
　　　　Sinners here may sing the same.

　　　　　[Mary (Shackleton)] Leadbeater, 'A hymn'
　　　　File 13409; c.562, p. 16 (attr. Ann Clapham)

C0447　Come, ye sons of glory, come
　　　　To hail the man who dared to fight.

　　　　　'Rodney's welcome or all alive at Bristol to the tune of
　　　　　Away to the downs &c'
　　　　c.341, p. 124

C0448　Come you young gallants, you that have the name,
　　　　I yield, and give to Wisbech cock the day.

　　　　　[Robert Wild], 'A terrible, true, tragical relation of a
　　　　　duel June 17: 1637'
　　　　b.200, p. 196; see also 'Go you young gallants . . .'.

C0449　Comedians laugh at us, as Democrit,
　　　　To whom, our faults being weigh'd, we wretched
　　　　　　　　　　　　　　　　　　　　　　　　seem.

　　　　　Sir Thomas Urquhart, 'Of preachers, and comedians'
　　　　fb.217, p. 118

C0450　Comets meteors blazing stars
　　　　Let us be loyal to the end.

　　　　　'Upon the burning of the Pope in effigy at Ex[ete]r(?)
　　　　　upon Christmas Day December 25, 1680'
　　　　Poetry Box VIII/38

C0451　Coming a tender girl from school,
　　　　Contract my stomach or enlarge my diet.

　　　　　[Thomas Brown], 'Epigram 2d on a young lady
　　　　　married too young' [from Flaminius]
　　　　c.158, p. 130; see also 'When I was younger . . .'.

C0452　Coming by chance into St. Laurence-Kirk
　　　　Call home the King, and then rebel no more.

　　　　　'To the Reverand Dr. Beveridge an eucharisticon.
　　　　　Occasioned by his seasonable and excellent sermon
　　　　　about restitution, on St. Luke 19.8 preached at St.
　　　　　Laurence's London, Tuesday, March 17, 1690'
　　　　　[Crum c666 (incomplete?)]
　　　　b.111, p. 211; fb.207/1, p. 21

C0453　Commanding beauty, smooth'd by cheerful grace,
　　　　And drank his bottle, tho' he miss'd the world.

　　　　　[Horace] Walpole, [4th earl of Orford], 'Portrait of
　　　　　John Earl Granville'
　　　　Poetry Box V/26

C0454 Commit the ship unto the wind
To make a good thing of a bad.

    'Of women'
    [Crum c669. 'thy ship']
    c.356; c.158, p. 133 (var.)

C0455 Common good manners should not let us show
Them from us, once committed to our breast.

    'Arcana. Hor[ace] . . . [translation]'
    c.81/1, no. 432

C0456 Compar'd with Clorinda the sun's but a star,
Yet I'll cherish my flame were it equall'd by hers.

    'Beauty in its prime'
    fb.107, p. 52

C0457 Compassion checks my spleen, yet scorn denies
Man claims from God, than what in God he fears.

    [Thomas] Parnell, 'The third satire of Dr. John
    Donne [paraphrased] by Dr. Parnell'
    File 11383, p. 2

C0458 Comus that sups so duly at the Rose
Catsup the reckoning truly e'er he goes.

    'A choice spirit'
    c.74

C0459 Conceal thy beams, meek regent of the night,
The light of all my joy was lost when Edmund died.

    'Sonnet to the moon'
    c.344, p. 31

C0460 Concord doth bloody broils abhor
And let their armor rust.

    b.234, p. 6; c.339, pp. 260, 314

C0461 Condemn not rashly, all that looks like ill,
That leads to life, and enter, tho' 'tis strait.

    '[St. Matthew] c[h]apter the 7.'
    c.83/1, no. 185

C0462 Condemn'd to hope's delusive mine,
And freed his soul the nearest way.

    [Samuel] Johnson, 'On the death of Mr. Robert Levet;
    a practicer in physic. By his intimate friend . . .'
    [Crum c686]
    fc.132/1, p. 204; c.504, p. 3 ('life's delusive mine'); c.83/3,
    no. 782

C0463 Condole, ye lapdogs, and her fate deplore,
Chloe, the beauteous Chloe, is no more.

    [William Carpenter], 'An elegy on a lapdog that died
    in puppying May 11th 1756'
    c.247, p. 120

C0464 Conduct me Hermes to the grot
So Virga rules below.

    'On a rod'
    c.157, p. 18

C0465 Conductors, come away,
As served so many masters, | For nothing.

    'A ballad from the English camp in the north. 1640'
    [Crum c687]
    b.54, p. 886

C0466 Confess good folks—has not Miss Rusport given
You all rejoice with me you're living now.

    [David] Garrick, 'Epilogue to the comedy of The
    West Indian written by . . . and spoken by Mrs.
    Abington'
    c.115; c.68, p. 116

C0467 Confin'd to fools, and damn'd to sots
For ribs of steak or hoops of brass.

    [Robert Cholmeley], 'A ballad'
    c.190, p. 117

C0468 Conflanu, De la Clu, and such great men as those,
We think it's sufficient to send only boys.

    'An epigram on Thurot's squadron' [1760]
    c.186, p. 79

C0469 Conquer'd with soft and pleasing charms
Shall lie like us despis'd.

    [Wentworth Dillon, 4th earl of Roscommon], 'The
    fourth ode of the 1st book of Horace'
    b.201, p. 114

C0470 Conscience doth in my first reside,
And am a [?] amongst the fair.

    '[Enigma/Charade/Conundrum] 49'
    c.389

C0471 Conscious of guilt thy smoke is well applied,
A fruitless passion recompens'd with wind.

    [Abraham Cowley?], 'On sight of London'
    File 3782/4

C0472 Conscious that I no pow'rs possess
Thus wretched is too much for me!

    R[ichard] V[ernon] S[adleir], 'To an inconstant fair'
    c.106, p. 117

C0473 Consent of crowds exceeding credit brings,
Things their dishonest bosoms never knew.

    [Katherine Philips]
    b.118, p. 52

C0474   Consider always what thou art,
Dominion over thee.

     b.234, p. 112

C0475   Consider, fair Sylvia, e'er wedlock you choose
I'll marry and joyfully rattle my chains.

     'Song 52'

     c.555, p. 77

C0476   Consider well and try and prove thy deeds,
For oft self-love reproach and shame proceeds.

     c.339, p. 318

C0477   Consider well my soul, why hast thou breath
Disdain not such as are to good inclined.

     Anne Watkins

     c.165, p. 31

C0478   Consider well some bypast days,
Abound eternally.

     [Thomas Stevens?], 'A remembrancer'

     c.259

C0479   Consider your affairs, peruse and read, and often
                               mark:
The man that softly sets his steps, goes safest in the
                                 dark.

     c.339, p. 323

C0480   Constant companion let our hearts now join
To seek his name, can he require less.

     Poetry Box VI/129

C0481   Constant thrice happy pair by Hymen join'd;
Nor aught disturb ye till old time shall end.

     'To Richard Wallin esq. Spalding Thursday August 15.
     1751' [on Ann Alethea's wedding]

     c.229/2, fol. 74

C0482   Constraint in all things makes the pleasure less:
Sweet is the love that comes with willingness.

     c.93

C0483   Consuming time Neotis' flesh
More famous than before.

     'St. Neots. Cornwall'

     c.81/2, no. 536

C0484   Contagious air engendering pestilence
Angelica that happy counterbane.

     [Joshua Sylvester, trans. Guillaume de Salluste,
     seigneur Du Bartas], 'Of angelica'

     b.284, p. 53, 54

C0485   Contemplating of late with softest woe,
Mercy! O mercy! Still the heart receive.

     '[Hymns composed the week preceding the
     sacrament] 3rd Easter Sunday'

     c.515, fol. 16v

C0486   Contemplation genial pow'r,
To realms of bliss beyond the skies.

     'Ode to contemplation'

     c.89, p. 32

C0487   Contemplation, lovely fair,
Teach me to live, and teach to die.

     'Contemplation an ode'

     c.83/4, no. 2001

C0488   Content is all we aim at with our store,
If that be had with little, what needs more.

     'On content'

     b.118, p. 228

C0489   Content is wealth, the riches of the mind,
And happy he who can this treasure find.

     c.93

C0490   Content, the false world's best disguise,
Enjoy content, or else the world hath none.

     [Katherine Philips], 'Content [to my dearest friend]'
     [Crum c704]

     b.118, p. 62

C0491   Content who lives with competent estate
While some in midst of store contentless strive.

     [Mary Serjant]

     fb.98, fol. 148

C0492   Content! who oft art wont to dwell
Oh deign with me to take thy way.

     J. C.(?), 'Ode to content'

     Spence Papers, folder 113

C0493   Contented I am and contented I'll be,
And say that his drinking is done, | My brave boys.

     'Song 68'

     c.555, p. 101

C0494   Contented I to frame a rural ode
Which her to every creature doth dispense.

     [George Daniel]

     b.121, fol. 28

C0495   Contentment gracious lady you impart
Unless I have it by the first four letters.

     Sir Thomas Urquhart, 'On the word contentment'

     fb.217, p. 78

C0496 Contentment, placid as the summer's day
Thus round your happy heart may every grace
entwine.

Charles Atherton Allnutt, 'Double acrostic' [on Charles Allnutt]

c.112, p. 135

C0497 Contentment, rosy dimpled fair
I ask but competence and thee.

Lady [Catherine Rebecca] Manners, 'Address to contentment'

c.83/3, no. 748

C0498 Continual toil and labor is not best,
The day to work, the night was made to rest.

[Crum c707]

c.339, p. 316

C0499 Continual war I wage without expense:
Search these five lines, my name you'll find with
ease.

'Acrostic. Cards'

c.81/1, no. 188

C0500 Contraries do not others still oppose;
For here the nimblest action is repose.

Sir Thomas Urquhart, 'Contrarieties are found in the art of love'

fb.217, p. 241

C0501 Contrite, and humble minds, though they delight
The rite, that's usual at so sweet a feeling.

Sir Thomas Urquhart, 'A tmesis on contrite to a certain jovial gentlewoman'

fb.217, p. 147

C0502 Cook Lorell would needs have the devil his guest
From whence it was called the devil's arse.

Ben Jonson, 'The devil's banquet' [from The metamorphosed gypsies]
[Crum c712]

b.197, p. 180; b.200, p. 360; b.62, p. 127; b.213, p. 75a;
b.356, p. 278

C0503 Cooper designs, Sawpit dares not oppose,
The third's a great atheist, the fourth a great fool.

'Upon the Duke of Bucks Lord Shaftesbury Lord Salisbury and Lord Wharton when sent to the Tower by the Parliament'

fb.140, p. 129

C0504 Coquetta rings; 'twas now past ten;
Above the study of a face.

[William Carpenter], 'Discite inter mensas lancesq' nitentes'

c.247, p. 128

C0505 Cordelia slumb'ring in a grove,
Fam'd Britain is, itself, a world.

John Lockman, 'Cordelia, or the British heroine: on occasion of the menaced invasion from France [June 1759]. Set to music by Mr. Worgan; and sung by Miss Stevenson, in Vauxhall Gardens'

c.267/2, p. 29

C0506 Corelli's are good compositions,
You only raise the vapors.

'Cedite Romani scriptores cedite Graii'

c.111, p. 58

C0507 Corinna, in the country bred.
And cured of all their rustic fears.

[Soame Jenyns], 'A simile'

Poetry Box I/72

C0508 Cornaro Padua's learned wench
And Blackhood's elocution.

W[illiam] S[mith]

Smith Papers, folder 73

C0509 Cornet Fitzherbert who in many a fight
Will glorious rise, and live among the just.

[Sir Aston Cokayne, 'An epitaph on Mr Ralph Fitzherbert who died at Ashby de la Zouch about the 22nd year of his age, and lies there buried']

b.275, p. 69

C0510 Cornus proclaims aloud his wife's a whore,
But being so, we cannot make thee none.

[William Walsh], 'Epigram. Cornus'

c.223, p. 77

C0511 Cornwall! Had pow'r been to my wishes lent,
Not tusk, but splendid salmon had been sent.

John Lockman, 'To a most revered friend . . .
15 March 1764'

c.267/1, p. 385

C0512 Cornwall! Who dear to ev'ry muse,
And will no more inspire.

John Lockman, 'An epistle to Velters Cornwall esqr. member of Parliament; on this gentleman's hinting that I should address a poem to the right honble William Dowdeswell, Chancellor of the Exchequer'

c.267/4, p. 379

C0513 Coroner Willy t'other day
Don't hollo till you are in the wood.

'Epigram'

Poetry Box x/24

C0514   Corruption and brib'ry were fatal to Rome;
Give patriot Beckford your votes.

> John Lockman, 'Alderman Beckford's health: or no
> bribery and corruption . . . the tune, The roast beef of
> old England. 1768'
>
> c.267/2, p. 167

C0515   Corycian maid, pale Cynthia's divine soul,
That they may still in new conceptions flourish.

> Sir Thomas Urquhart, 'The invocation to Thalia'
>
> fb.217, p. 130

C0516   Corydon, arise my Corydon,
Heaven keep our love alway.

> [Allan Ramsey], 'A dialogue between G[i.e.,
> C(orydon)] and P[hyllida]'
> [Crum c718]
>
> b.197, p. 97

C0517   Cosmelia's charms inspire my lays
Like Thisbe through the wall.

> [Christoper Pitt?], 'A copy of verses delivered to a lady
> (who painted) waking at Tunbridge'
>
> c.176, p. 6

C0518   Could amiable qualities but save
Whether we're heav'n on earth, or earth in heav'n.

> 'An elegy upon Frederick Prince of Wales introduced
> by an address to an head of a college in the University
> of Oxford from a foundationer of the same'
>
> c.53, fol. 8

C0519   Could any show where Pliny's people dwell,
My armor proof is incredulity.

> Will[iam] Strode, 'On a dissembler'
> [Crum c721]
>
> b.200, p. 202; b.205, fol. 56r

C0520   Could but our tempers move like this machine
And endless joy when time shall be no more.

> [John Byrom], 'On a watch'
> [Crum c723]
>
> c.186, p. 59; c.360/1, p. 121; c.83/2, no. 704; c.93

C0521   Could Daphne fly Apollo's arms
Nor Daphne half so fair.

> [Robert Cholmeley], 'The inhuman or advice to
> Chloe'
>
> c.190, p. 123

C0522   Could exemplary worth, and virtue save,
Expecting crowns less troublesome than theirs.

> 'Epitaph on a woman in the churchyard of Cumner in
> Berkshire'
>
> c.240, p. 133

C0523   Could eyes weep epitaphs, or grief sigh verse,
Tho' widow'd here of all felicity.

> Poetry Box VIII/52

C0524   Could gold immortalize a man,
Call over wine, and love the night and day.

> 'Imitated from Anacreon'
>
> c.229/1, fol. 40v

C0525   Could heaps of wealth prolong our state,
We that best know how to live.

> 'On gold to a miser'
>
> b.218, p. 23

C0526   Could heaven be jealous that so pure a mind
That such perfection cannot dwell below.

> [William] Smith, 'Lines . . . on Lucy Michals'
>
> Smith Papers, folder 73

C0527   Could I arrive to the most perfect rise
Triumphant sister of the three shall reign.

> [ ] Porter, 'On charity'
>
> c.83/3, no. 1033

C0528   Could I command the sweet Ausonian lyre,
Under the sweet and hallow'd name of friend.

> [John Bowden], 'Stanzas to a friend' [1800]
>
> c.142, p. 459

C0529   Could I her faults remember
And sees—while Reason's blind.

> [Richard Brinsley Butler Sheridan], 'Song 237' [from
> The duenna]
>
> c.555, p. 381

C0530   Could I like this your sleeve attend
Unless you made this sleeve a breast-knot.

> G. B., 'An impromptu to Miss Traine's sleeve-knot'
>
> c.150, p. 147

C0531   Could marble know what virtue's buried here,
She seem'd a copy of the saints in heaven.

> [Francis Fawkes], 'On a very good woman'
>
> fc.21, p. 25

C0532   Could men see virtues naked, it would plenish
And vitiated them with small ado.

> Sir Thomas Urquhart, 'Concerning Plato's opinion of
> virtue: and how Venetian courtesans are so bold as to
> ascribe to themselves the names of Prudentia,
> Temperantia, Clementia, and so forth'
>
> fb.217, p. 317

C0533 Could Milton be restor'd to sight
The paradise his Adam lost.

[Phanuel Bacon], 'Upon seeing Milton's bust in Ld. Newnham's garden'

c.237, fol. 71v

C0534 Could my soft voice but heal my soul
But bless the voice that gave the wound.

[Robert Cholmeley], 'To Mrs. Catherine Om—ch after having heard her sing written at Epping upon the road from London to Cambridge'

c.190, p. 44

C0535 Could nature then no other woman grace
Such grace in motion and such sharp replies.

fb.66/28

C0536 Could old Palemon once again
Like those which torture me!

R[ichard] V[ernon] S[adleir], 'To two beautiful young ladies who visited me in sickness Miss Wom[ ] and Miss D—y—1792'

c.106, p. 131

C0537 Could Orpheus leave the shades, and reappear,
What Orpheus was, Geminiani's now.

John Lockman, 'Reading the bill for his friend Signor Geminiani's concert, at the little theater, in the Haymarket . . . 22 April 1742'

c.267/1, p. 10

C0538 Could piety and virtue aught avail,
Beyond what thought can frame, or tongue describe.

[Henry] Needler, 'To the memory of Favonia'

c.244, p. 561

C0539 Could pray'rs and tears this precious dust
Nor heav'n so soon an angel gain'd.

'Epitaph on a young lady at Pembroke'

c.142, p. 542

C0540 Could Prior's eye behold this sparkling fair
A Muse, a Grace, a Venus live in you.

[Robert Cholmeley], 'To Mrs. Peggy Horseman'

c.190, p. 73

C0541 Could Sylvia from my numbers know
Return'd into the Ark.

[Robert Cholmeley], 'To Sylvia after having gone to another mistress returned to her again'

c.190, p. 156

C0542 Could then the babes from yond' unshelter'd cot
Shall gild their passage to eternal rest.

[Thomas] Russell, 'Sonnet'

c.83/3, no. 751

C0543 Could we with ink the ocean fill,
Tho' stretch'd from sky to sky.

'Lines written by a person at Cirencester who was called an idiot'

c.250; c.391

C0544 Counsel which afterward is sought
When heat hath parch'd the flowers.

'Dourte [Dort?] hand'
[Crum c748]

b.234, p. 7

C0545 Count all as doing for Christ whose name ye bear,
Shall please to clothe with his own purity.

H[enry] C[olman], 'Another' [acrostic on 'Christians']

b.2, p. 107

C0546 Count that in youth no slavery
Or in winter of age live poor and in want.

[James Rhodes?]

b.206, p. 150

C0547 Courage friend Phoebus be n't dismay'd
Whose years for love await an end.

'Horace Lib. 2. Od. 4'

c.416

C0548 Courage majestic Queen, the hero goes
Shall bring him safe to you their sovereign.

'To the Queen's Majesty'

b.204, p. 85

C0549 Courage my boys! Up and be doing
Peace will bring plenty, after all your plowing.

J[ohn] R[obinson]

c.370, fol. 5

C0550 Courageous Joshua sword and prayer did fight
Attended one whole day on victory.

'Joshua 10.13'

c.160, fol. 53

C0551 Court city and country too
That something has some savor(?).

'Song: something'
Poetry Box VI/97

C0552 Courtier if thou needs wilt wive
Gain her servants, and thee honor.

'The courtier'

fb.107, p. 42

Co553 Courtiers and heralds, by your leave
Let Bourbon, or Nassau go higher.

[Matthew] Prior, 'Prior's epitaph' [made on himself]
[Crum c756, first part]

c.81/1, no. 352; fb.142, p. 69; fc.60, p. 117; see also
'Heralds and courtiers . . .', 'Nobles and heralds . . .',
Statesmen and courtiers . . .'.

Co554 Cousins, be careful now of your affairs
Your city-widows have not hearts of stone.

[Sir Aston Cokayne], 'To Mr John and Mr Ferdinand
Stanhope, brothers, my cousin germans'

b.275, p. 104

Co555 *Couvre le feu*, ye Huguenots
Short time will show you what's behind.

'By the Papists after that dreadful conflagration at
London' [1666]

b.52/1, p. 150; fb.140, p. 141; Poetry Box VI/16

Co556 Cowper! Delight of all who justly prize
His harp of highest tone, his sanctity of song.

[William] Hayley, 'Sonnet addressed to Mr. Cowper'

Poetry Box III/12

Co557 Coyness becomes her, as she is a maid
Calmness becomes her, as by reason sway'd.

[Sir Philip Wodehouse], 'Upon Madam [Thomasina]
Clench Sr. J. Holland's niece'

b.131, back (no. 64)

Co558 Crabbed age and youth cannot live together;
For, methinks, thou stay'st too long.

[William] Shakespeare, 'Ancient antipathy'

c.94

Co559 Cramp, the barber, lives here; step in if you please,
And I'll endeavor to please you, while on this side
the grave.

'Lines pasted up in the window of a young hair-
dresser just begun business at Kinchley in
Lancastershire'

c.83/2, no. 727

Co560 Creation's God! with thought elate,
Thee, Thee, my God, I trace!

H[elen] M[aria] Williams, 'A hymn written among the
alps'

c.141, p. 459

Co561 Creator source of genial day,
To live in my paternal song.

[Leonard Welsted], 'A hymn to the Creator by a
gentleman wrote on the occasion of the death of his
only daughter' [pr. 1727 (Foxon W295)]

c.244, p. 428

Co562 Creator Spirit, by whose aid
Eternal Paraclete to Thee!

[John] Dryden, 'Veni creator spiritus'
[Crum c769]

c.244, p. 426; b.201, p. 138

Co563 Creatures of every name farewell
When creatures bid me die.

T[homas] S[tevens]

c.259, p. 125

Co564 Cries Celia to a reverend Dean,
They cannot find a priest.

'Epigram'

c.152, p. 44; c.360/1, p. 61; c.546, p. 28

Co565 Cries logical Bobby to Ned, will you dare
A mare has but four legs, and no more has five.

'Epigram'

c.344

Co566 Cries Ned to his neighbors as onwards they prest
For why should we thus make a toil of a pleasure.

'Epigram'

c.546, p. 24

Co567 Critics, avaunt, tobacco is my theme
For which we drink, eat, sleep, smoke, everything.

[Isaac Hawkins Browne, 'In praise of tobacco';
imitation of Young]
[Crum c776]

Poetry Box I/139

Co568 Critics, whene'er I write, in ev'ry scene
But if well made, I wish you health to wear it.

[George Colman the elder], 'Prologue'

File 3561

Co569 Croesus being rich, with care turmoil'd his life:
And you are griev'd, by reason you have none.

Sir Thomas Urquhart, 'To one, who did vex himself
beyond all measure, for that he was not married'

fb.217, p. 264

Co570 Crown'd with flowers
Turn'd all her faith and sand away together.

'Woman's love'
[Crum c781]

b.356, p. 104

Co571 Crusht by that just contempt his follies bring
Than what thy very friends have said before.

[John Wilmot, 2nd earl of Rochester], 'On poet
Ninny' [Sir Carr Scroope; 1677]
[POAS I.374]

b.105, p. 348; b.54, p. 1182

C0572 Cry ye pretty Muses cry
Do nothing but lament *heu! heu!*

Hen[ry] Reade, of Queens College, Cambridge, 'An imitation of Catullus's ode on the death of a sparrow burlesqued'

c.157, p. 11

C0573 Cuckoo, the spring's swift-winged messenger,
Their youthful wings, and serenade the sky.

Dr. [ ] Thompson, 'Ode to the cuckoo'

c.141, p. 347

C0574 Cudd's life and precious coals
Are graves become Button holes?

'On Master Button'
[cf. Crum H847]

fb.143, p. 36; see also 'Here lies John Button . . .', 'O heavens, O poles . . .'.

C0575 Cundall, accept these lines, by friendship penn'd,
Lest a new Duncida celebrate thy race.

[Charles Burney, the younger], 'To Mr. Cundall'
[Reading mercury, Dec. 14, 1777]

c.37, p. 28

C0576 Cunt whose strong charms the world bewitches
The tired tinker's ease and pleasure.

fb.66/30

C0577 Cupid and Hymen, foes no more
And pleasing thee form all my joy.

John Lockman, 'Cupid and Hymen, or the blissful union . . . anno 1754'

c.267/2, p. 193; see also 'Thyrsis lamenting . . .'.

C0578 Cupid and my Campaspe play'd,
What shall alas! become of me?

[John Lyly, song in Alexander and Campaspe]

c.391, p. 78; fc.132/1, p. 188

C0579 Cupid by accident mislaid
'For here I see my quiver!'

'The discovery'

c.175, p. 86

C0580 Cupid by chance one day had stray'd
And with the muses join'd remains.

'Anacreon ode the 30th'

c.368, p. 25

C0581 Cupid is an affection,
Whence she's perverse, if she obey not nature.

Sir Thomas Urquhart, 'A description of love'

fb.217, p. 238

C0582 Cupid is careless and doth shoot at random
The marriage bed is surgeon and physician.

[Sir Aston Cokayne], 'Of Cupid and marriage'

b.275, p. 91

C0583 Cupid no more shall conquest boast,
Nor idly dream of conquest more.

[John Lockman], 'Cupid disarmed. A song'

c.268 (first part), p. 95

C0584 Cupid o'er human breasts resistless reigns,
Oh blind to truth! The brilliant forms it all.

W[illia]m Shenstone, 'The diamond. A poem written by . . . about the year 1734. Not inserted in his works'

c.364, p. 1

C0585 Cupid of all the heavenly host
The bee by stinging others, dies.

[ ] Warner, 'Cupid stung by a bee' [Theocritus, Idyll 19]

c.170, p. 13

C0586 Cupid once in search of prey
Never will I use you more.

'Song 228'

c.555, p. 360

C0587 Cupid that sly that artful boy
And thence the urchin learnt to pity men.

N. B[urney], 'Cidalia a pastoral . . . N. B. aged 13'

c.486, fol. 30

C0588 Cupid, the slyest rogue alive,
And yet how wide, how deep the wound!

'Cupid, stung by a bee' [Theocritus, Idyll 19]
[Crum c808]

c.94

C0589 Curious, the bookish man surveying
And the pale bookworms may be right.

John Lockman, 'On the first view of Tunbridge Wells, in Kent . . . July 1739'

c.267/1, p. 159

C0590 Curse on such representatives
And then it runs full spout.

[George Villiers, 2nd duke of Buckingham], 'On Kg. Ch. 2d's pension Parlt.' [1675; copied from British Library MS Harl. 7316, fol. 27, 60]
[*POAS* I.261]

Poetry Box IV/120 (2 copies, both ll. 1–12 only); see also 'I'll tell thee Dick . . .'.

C0591 Curse on those critics ignorant and vain
To make way for the son to bring a whore.

'Satire'

b.371, no. 36

C0592 Cursed be her that ever shall defend
Unless it be some knowledge how to kill.

'Against physicians'

b.62, p. 31

C0593 Curs'd be the star, which did ordain
Prove that 'mongst us, and curse me too!

'Ash-Wednesday' [answered by 'Curst be the stars . . .
God bless King James . . .']
[Crum c823]

fb.70, p. 269; Poetry Box VII/28; Poetry Box VI/57

C0594 Cursed be the timorous fool, whose feeble mind
And stems the fury of the foaming tides.

'The true Englishman'
[Crum c824 (with eleven more lines)]

Poetry Box VI/57

C0595 Curs'd be the wretched hapless hour,
Yet know no reason why.

'Another by the same hand' [as 'Charge all a
bumper . . .']

fb.142, p. 46

C0596 Curst as the devil himself is he,
I rise—take breath—and run away.

'Travesty of Sappho's ode'

c.81/1, no. 338

C0597 Curst be the stars which did ordain
God bless King James and so farewell.

'The anti-curse, September 1690' [answer to 'Curs'd
be the star . . . Prove that 'mongst us . . .']

b.111, p. 472

C0598 Curst be the wretch whose rebel muse,
Shall crown my wishes with eternal life.

R[obert] Shirley, 1st earl of Ferrers, 'Against profane
poetry. A Pindaric ode'

c.347, p. 37

C0599 Curst be those dull unpointed doggerel rhymes
As when old Hyde was catch'd with Rem in Re.

[Charles Sackville, 6th earl of Dorset?], 'A faithful
catalogue of our most eminent ninnies' [1688]
[Crum c825; POAS IV.191]

fb.70, p. 173; fb.108, p. 209 ('unpitied rhymes')

C0600 Curst Curll, besieg'd by duns, to raise the cash,
Imprint the monarch's image on their dross.

John Lockman, 'On a modest bookseller [Curll]
setting up, by way of sign, the head of a famous
English poet [Pope]'

c.267/1, p. 239; c.268 (first part), p. 6

C0601 Custom alas! does partial prove
Or give to mankind less.

'The female complaint'

c.83/2, no. 703; Poetry Box x/99

C0602 Custom our native loyalty doth awe
And doubl'd by their love, their piety.

c.189, p. 74

C0603 Cut off all your delays when dangers are begun,
For if beginnings we withstand the conquest soon
                                    is won.

c.339, p. 326

C0604 Cymon a poor, but happy wight;
It's manly never to despair.

'The self-taught philosopher'

c.83/2, no. 342

C0605 Cynthia adorn'd with hundred fumes and flames,
And more, the more Lucina waxeth round.

[John Rose?]

b.227, p. 165

C0606 Cynthia frowns whene'er I woo her
To be past, yet wish fruition!

'Song'

c.189, p. 221

C0607 Cypress, coffins, bays, with sundry flowers
All teach us how they fade, and pass away.

'1629'

fb.69, p. 75

C0608 Cyprus must now two Venus's adore;
She's a new muse, a Venus, and a grace.

'On Stella'

c.241, p. 46

C0609 Cytheriad astrologian damosel,
Till it be purg'd in the Permessian River.

Sir Thomas Urquhart, 'The invocation to Urania'

fb.217, p. 294

D

D0001 Daily disgracer of our English satire
The body's half abortive like the wit.

    [Robert Wolseley], 'A second familiar epistle [to
    William Wharton]'
    [Crum D6]

b.219, p. 14

D0002 Dame Briton of the grange once fam'd
Myself a beggar, and a fool.

    'A fable of an old woman and her doctor' [sometimes
    attrib. Matthew Prior]
    [Crum D9b]

c.570/2, p. 33

D0003 Dame Fortune doth an equibalance bear
She fills the poor with hopes the rich with cares.

    'Fortune's apology'

c.356

D0004 Dame Jane a nun, as lilies fair;
When we, as righteous Jane, have done.

    John Lockman, 'Dame Jane, or the penitent nun, a
    tale, from La Fontaine'

c.267/4, p. 139; see also next, and 'A nun there was . . .'.

D0005 Dame Jane, a sprightly nun, and gay,
But first let's do as she has done.

    'Dame Jane' [from La Fontaine]

c.233, p. 117; see also previous, and 'A nun there was . . .'.;
c.503, p. 20

D0006 Dame Jean Cockburne here she doth lie
I [?] his say you the rest.

    Poetry Box VIII/51

D0007 Dame Law to maintain a more flourishing state
And fourteen new sergeants step out at the call.

    'On the call of new sergeants' [1736]
    [Crum D11]

fb.142, p. 62

D0008 D[am]n your epilogue: and hold your tongue
A farce or two—and Woodward's pantomimes.

    [David] Garrick, 'Prologue written and spoken by . . .
    in the character of a fine gentleman'

c.115

D0009 Damned to a set of philosophic fools
Then you shall love, and I will write no more.

    [Robert Cholmeley], 'To Mrs. Ellen Robinson at
    London, just after an excursion to her'

c.190, p. 67

D0010 Damon and Sylvia; Florimond and Chloris,
Careless of what a snarling world might say.

    John Lockman, 'Writ under a mezzotinto by
    Mr. Faber, from a picture of Mr Mercier, representing
    nymphs and swains drinking . . . 1741'

c.267/1, p. 17

D0011 Damon be ruled and don't yourself expose,
And may his glories with his hours increase.

    'Damon paraphrased'
    [Crum D21]

fb.207/2, p. 75

D0012 Damon fond of his peaceful retirement, free from
                  the town
But O. how happy am I, who I'm sure, hath a
               bottle and Chloris is mine.

c.171, no. 16

D0013 Damon, forbear and don't disturb your Muse,
Jove's great vicegerent and the tyrant's rod.

    'Another satire called Damon' [on King William's
    court, c. 1701]
    [POAS VI.251]

fb.207/2, p. 73

D0014 Damon, if thou wilt believe me,
Much more gentle, not so kind.

    [Charles Sackville], 6th earl of Dorset, 'The answer
    by . . .' [to 'Die wretched Damon']
    [Crum D22]

b.204, p. 82

D0015 Damon O Damon tell me how
Angels like these do marry beasts like them.

    'Pythias and Damon'

b.63, p. 69

D0016 Damon that author of so great renown
To find a better patron of the pope.

    'The renegade poet, or a satire upon poetry' [on John
    Dryden]

fb.70, p. 139

D0017 Damon took Phyllis by the hand,
To celebrate this joyful day.

[Thomas Morell], 'A pastoral. On the birthday of
J[?ohn] Rich esq. set by Mr. Vincent'

c.395, p. 140

D0018 Damon, who lov'd his flocks to feed;
She'll roam, and glad thine eyes!

John Lockman, 'Damon: on occasion of a great lady's
leaving London, for the recovery of her health'

c.267/2, p. 190

D0019 Dancer the fav'rite of the fair
For lovely Catherina dropt a tear.

Miss A. C., 'Epitaph on Dancer'

c.150, p. 125

D0020 Daphnis and St[r]ephon to the shades retir'd
And the low sun had lengthen'd every shade.

c.83/3, no. 1024

D0021 Dapper, neat, compact, and strong,
Blame the painter, not thyself.

[Charles Burney, the elder], 'A miniature picture
drawn 1786'

c.33, p. 189

D0022 Dark air the desert waste the low'ring clouds
Sees lightnings flash far wide—as horrors deepen
round.

F[rances] B[urney d'Arblay], 'A descriptive sonnet'
c.486, fol. 15v

D0023 Dark and conceal'd art thou, soft evening's queen,
And shine for beings less accurst than I.

[Charlotte (Turner) Smith], 'Sonnet to the invisible
moon'

c.141, p. 134

D0024 Dark is the state of things below!
Death takes us out, to make us live!

[Charles Earle?], 'An allusion to that ambiguous
monumental inscription Quod fuit &c. in the
Gentleman's magazine March 1746'

c.376

D0025 Dark was the dawn! and o'er the deep
And with her heart's true love, plung'd in a wat'ry
grave!

[Mary (Derby)] Robinson, 'The storm'
c.83/2, no. 579

D0026 Dark was the night, and lightnings glar'd around
And crowding fools invade the weak'ning tide.

'Belial a mad philippic—'
fc.53, p. 184

D0027 Dark were the days, and gloomy were the skies,
And thus, as I did dream, declar'd her state.

'A consult of physicians or the church not in danger'
b.204, p. 150

D0028 Darkness and death! Oh dismal day!
For truth, God's honor, and your own renown.

'An elegy upon the death of King Charles the 2nd'
Poetry Box VII/12

D0029 Darkness! Thou first kind parent of us all,
And fate confirm thy kingdom, evermore thy own.

[Thomas] Yalden, 'On darkness'

c.244, p. 82

D0030 Dashing bards of their critics will often complain,
And, 'with harmonious fire,' blaze out another day.

Mary Knowles, 'The Vauclusiad'

c.142, p. 431

D0031 Daughter of beauty, who enraptur'd hail
With rival ardor catch'd the instructive theme.

Dr. [ ] Wheeler, 'Ode, at the encaenia held at Oxford
July 1773 for the reception of the Rt. Honable
Frederick Lord North Chancellor of the University
[later earl of Guilford], the words by . . . set to music
by Dr. Hayes'

c.481, p. 14

D0032 Daughter of Colla! thou art low—
We sing; and raise Darthula's tomb.

[ ] Ellison, 'The bards of Cairbar'

Greatheed Box/33

D0033 Daughter of fancy, fickle maid,
And Steavens shall command.

[Isaac Freeman], 'Hymn to novelty'

fc.105

D0034 Daughter of Jove, relentless power,
What others are, to feel, and know myself a man.

[Thomas Gray], 'Hymn to adversity'
[Crum D41]

c.156, p. 110; fc.132/1, p. 147

D0035 Daughter of liberty, whose knife
Death and the devil, and Tom Paine.

[John Walcot ('Peter Pindar')], 'Hymn to the
guillotine'

c.83/2, no. 529

D0036 Daughter of spring, sweet child of solitude,
Catch the fair ray, sweet daughter of the spring.

'The solitary rose-tree'

c.83/3, no. 912, no. 1066

D0037 Daughters of Sion, come, behold
With all his Father's glories on.

> [Isaac Watts, hymn]

c.180, p. 61

D0038 D'Avila, Bentivoglio, Guicciardine
Bestow a benefit, then receive a favour.

> [Sir Aston Cokayne], 'To Mr Charles Cotton Junior'

b.275, p. 88

D0039 Dawson the butler's dead, although I think
My life for his John Dawson had been here.

> [Richard Corbett], 'On John Dawson butler of Ch:
> Church' [d. 1622]
> [Crum D49]

b.205, fol. 80r

D0040 Day of delight thro' many a year
In rapturous ascension.

> [William Hayley], 'The matin song of Oct. 5 1800'

File 6951

D0041 Day walks at length his golden road
Where is thine house—the tomb.

fc.124, p. 87

D0042 Dead is Dick Dumbelow
His stout heart had not broken.

> 'On Mr. [Richard] Dumbelow, that died of the colic'

c.74

D0043 Deaf giddy helpless left alone
I scarce can hear a woman's clack.

> [Jonathan] Swift, 'On Doctor Swift's deafness by
> himself . . . the English'

Poetry Box XIV/197

D0044 Deaf to the bar, the pulpit and the throne
Than lies, alack, in twenty of their swords.

> 'Prologue to the duelist—a new play'

c.115 (incomplete?)

D0045 Dean Swift, first in vogue
That thy heart was the stone of the mill.

> 'A song' ['The lass of Isleworth Mill']
> [Crum D57]

c.392, p. 11

D0046 Dear and honor'd Lady Strath
At her lov'd feet resign thy breath.

> [on Lady Strathmore]

fc.40

D0047 Dear Ann when I look at the date of your letter,
From hence may your nose ever wear a carbuncle.

> Edward Sneyd, 'An epistle 4th to my niece Ann. April
> the 7th 1773'

c.214, p. 18

D0048 Dear anxious parent widow of the friend
To see in wedded love thy song serenely(?) blest!

> [William Hayley], 'Sonnet . . . Jan 6 [1800]'

File 6968

D0049 Dear Bertie! In whose youthful veins
But now I know far more than he!

> W[illiam] P[arsons]

Greatheed Box/11

D0050 Dear Bess this wise rule I shall ever lay down,
And has promis'd to carry my poem to Keel.

> Edward Sneyd, 'An epistle 6th. To my niece Elizabeth.
> April the 11th 1773'

c.214, p. 22

D0051 Dear Betsy, to hit your gay fancy
Is my having together three tongues.

> [William Carpenter], 'To Miss R—dd'

c.247, p. 156

D0052 Dear Betty leave your nasty pages
It instructs the mind, and charms the sight.

> 'On seeing the foregoing verses ['The muse this
> morn . . .', addressed to Betty Jeffreys]

c.360/1, p. 31

D0053 Dear Castadoris let me rise
What bliss our pleasure yields.

> 'A song by way of dialogue'

b.104, p. 117

D0054 Dear Catholic sister, thou son of great Mars
The devil shall be after taking Teague his pains.

> 'Teague's ramble to London'

fc.61, p. 57

D0055 Dear Celadon, to me your friend reveal,
That one so good, and fair, can never err.

> [Thomas Hamilton, 6th earl of Haddington], 'To
> Florella a dialogue explaining my seal of an old man
> on crutches'

c.458/1, p. 59

D0056 Dear Charles I've seen a charming creature
The world must cease to be.

> T[homas] D[udley] F[osbroke], 'On Miss [Mary]
> A—— 2nd d[aughte]r of the Bish[op] of Norwich
> addressed to a friend'

c.230

D0057 Dear Charles this comes to give you warning
I rest your faithful F. Boscawen.

> F[rances Glanville] Boscawen, 'A Letter from . . . to
> Charles Frederick esqr. Oxford Sep. 17th 1748'
>
> fc.51, p. 316

D0058 Dear Charles | Two months scarce have pass'd
since 'twas said without reason,
I hate to be grave when I'm writing to you.

> 'From a resident at Bath to his friend in the country'
>
> c.83/4, no. 1084

D0059 Dear child these words which briefly I declare,
Lock them up safe that the[y] may ne'er depart.

> T. P., 'T. P. to M[ary] (S[hackleton) Leadbeater], the 1
> of 11 month 1776'
>
> File 13409

D0060 Dear children pledges of my love
In grandeur more sublime.

> 'Father's address to his children epitre de S. Paul aux
> Ephesians chap. VI'
>
> c.91, p. 229

D0061 Dear Chloe, how blubber'd is that pretty face?
As he was a poet sublimer than me.

> [Matthew] Prior, 'A better answer' [copy dated
> 10 December 1770]
>
> Poetry Box x/145

D0062 Dear Chloe, while the busy crowd,
And smooth, the bed of death.

> [Nathaniel] Cotton, 'The fireside'
> [Crum D72]
>
> c.156, p. 67; c.391, p. 17; c.487, p. 146; c.82, p. 2; fc.132/1,
> p. 171; c.83/1, no. 132

D0063 Dear Chloe, while thus beyond measure
Which decrepit old age cannot freeze.

> Poetry Box XII/41

D0064 Dear Chloris hearken to my true advice,
'Tis sought by many, but by few is found.

> 'A poem by Horatio Dactyl [pseud.], addressed to a
> young lady at Dover . . .'
>
> c.166, p. 61

D0065 Dear clyster-pipe! You're much too hard
Sickness return'd with your long bill.

> John Lockman, 'To a skillful country apothecary, who
> sent me in a most extravagant bill . . . Oct. 1743'
>
> c.267/1, p. 6

D0066 Dear Colin, prevent my warm blushes,
What I in my bosom confine.

> Lady Mary] W[ortley Montagu], 'Lady Mary
> W[ortley Montagu], to Sir W[illiam?] Y[oung?]'
> [answered by 'Good Madam, when ladies are
> willing . . .']
> [Crum D73]
>
> c.487, p. 125; c.152, p. 22

D0067 Dear contemplation my divinest joy,
Forget not to attend their charge below.

> [John Norris], 'The return'
>
> c.547, p. 167

D0068 Dear Cos and Councillor I greet ye,
Sheds out its specimen within.

> 'An apology to my friend, occasioned by his
> misconstructing of my compliment to his learned heel
> in the foregoing poem'
>
> c.176, p. 52

D0069 Dear cousin, didst thou never hear
While some fair goblin leads the dance.

> 'A simile: in imitation of Prior'
>
> c.94

D0070 Dear cousin, or holiness, or whate'er is your will,
To his eyes, their soft beams, to his breast, a warm
heart.

> 'Czar to Tinker . . . Ayot St. Lawrence Jan. 5th 1795'
>
> fc.40

D0071 Dear Cynthia shall I swim in tears
In love's sacred fires.

> 'Faustus and Cynthia'
>
> b.356, p. 96

D0072 Dear Daniel, as the other day
And I'll ne'er plague you more with hobbling verse.

> P. A.
>
> Poetry Box IV/65

D0073 Dear Davy, give me leave to join
He sought, and gain'd esteem.

> [Thomas Morell], 'To Mr. Garrick, on the death of
> Mr. Holland'
>
> c.395, p. 126

D0074 Dear! Dear! Departed soul farewell!
Is, that they're good, and that they're fair.

> [Charles Earle], 'An extempore epitaph on
> Miss ———'
>
> c.376

D0075 Dear do not your fair beauty wrong
And flies away from aged things.

'On one's mistress thinking her life too young'
[Crum D78]

b.62, p. 28; see also 'Dear love do not . . .'.

D0076 Dear Doctor—I prithee discover,
And so bid adieu to cold Vise.

[John] Winter, 'Ballad—by . . . Odi imitatorem . . .'
[on Mrs. Vise]

c.74

D0077 Dear Doctor this comes from your flock at Byfleet
Will come to eat us till we've eaten them.

[N.] Herbert

Spence Papers, folder 91

D0078 Dear Doctor—'tis not every friend
By the directions of Kinnier.

'Native air. To Surgeon Paul at the request of Miss
Coole'

c.484, p. 51

D0079 Dear Doctor, when I heard the news
Can never long thy charms inherit.

[1769?]
c.136, p. 81

D0080 Dear Dyer, did thou never see
Should Dyer then be forc'd to blame?

[Isaac Freeman], 'To Mr. Samuel Dyer on his
importuning me to publish my poems'

fc.105

D0081 Dear dying image of my child a sight
Lead me to hear that you by seraphs sing.

[William Hayley], 'Sonnet . . . Sept. 5 [1800]'
File 6968

D0082 Dear Elveston that art a grace
Till the world to chaos doth return.

[Sir Aston Cokayne], 'To Elveston'
b.275, p. 66

D0083 Dear Fanny, in your last you jok'd
Sincere, and ever yours.

Mrs.[L.] Frederick, 'Epistle from . . . to Mrs.
Boscawen at Englefield Green . . . 15th Aug 1748'

fc.51, p. 272

D0084 Dear filial angel since to heaven you rise
To our sweet maid fix the sanctifying seal.

[William Hayley], 'Sonnet . . . May 19 [1800]'
File 6968

D0085 Dear friend, I hear this town does so abound,
From the innocent reproach of infamy?

[John Wilmot, 2nd earl of R[ochester], 'An epistolary
essay very delightful and solid from . . . to the Ld.
M[ulgrave?] upon their mutual poems' [1675]
[Crum D82b; POAS I.349]

b.105, p. 1 (ll. 1–98); see also 'Dear friend, | It seems . . .'.

D0086 Dear friend, I send this to present my love
To subscribe myself your friend. | T. B.

Thomas Bittleston, 'An invitation to Neal Dickson's
wedding, sent by . . . to Stephen Smith, the wedding
being held on a Shrove Tuesday'

c.530, p. 56

D0087 Dear friend I'll help thy burial too, and must
Is born in death to life's eternity.

'On the death of W. R.'
b.150, p. 136

D0088 Dear friend, I'm sorry from my very heart,
That would to God it had befall'n to me.

Sir Thomas Urquhart, 'How a gentleman, that had an
exceeding bad one of his own, condoles the death of
his friend's wife'

fb.217, p. 304

D0089 Dear friend, | It seems this town does so abound
Of idle rumor, keep at home and write.

John Wilmot, 2nd earl of Rochester, 'An epistolary
essay very delightful and solid from M. G. to O. B.
Upon their mutual poems'

b.334, p. 163; see also 'Dear friend, I hear . . .'.

D0090 Dear friend! thy soaring muse admits no guard
And with a loud huzza—proclaim it all thy own.

'An address to a friend a poet, who was afraid to
publish'

c.91, p. 79

D0091 Dear friend when those we love are in distress
The thoughtful traitor 'tis offends the king.

'A consolatory epistle to Mr. [Robert] Julian in his
confinement'
[Crum D87]

b.113, p. 243; Poetry Box IV/52

D0092 Dear friends attend yon solemn awful bell!
My blessing with you rest— dear friends farewell.

'Elegy on Miss A. Haslam of Moses-Gate'
c.91, p. 291

D0093 Dear friends! We're highly pleas'd to see you here,
Come Fanny here,—and Dicky—both come in.

'[Prologue to] The maternal conference. In two parts,
for a public speaking'

c.91, p. 309

D0094 Dear friends—you're welcome all,
The wish to please you all.

'An introductory poem, for some young pupil at a public speaking'

c.91, p. 299

D0095 Dear gentle animal how blest
Ever yet could need it more.

fc.40

D0096 Dear gentle shade, sweet little saint attend!
And asks if heav'n too soon could claim the saint.

H[annah] M[ore], 'Elegy on Miss Gwatkin(?)'

c.341, p. 79

D0097 Dear girl be not dismayed, that you days
Whose mother had no stallion, but an ass.

Sir Thomas Urquhart, 'To a young handsome lass, who was affianced to a very arrant blockhead'

fb.217, p. 174

D0098 Dear good sir Mr. Boole I have sent you in here
My spouse to your lady sends compliments due.

'Observe a friend send me the following letter Novr. 17th 1797'

c.115

D0099 Dear Gordon, by thy pleasing strain
And so, dear Gordon, yours I rest.

W[alte]r Titley, 'A poetical letter from . . . to Gn Gordon'

c.233, p. 50

D0100 Dear Hal, with you I disagree,
To yield no rhyme or reason.

N. H[erbert], 'Poetry and law are two extremes'

Spence Papers, folder 91

D0101 Dear Hayley! Chill no more the blood
It bursts and makes the valley sing!

R[ichard] V[ernon] S[adleir], 'To Wm. Hayley esqr. author of an essay on old maids The triumph of temper &c. &c.'

c.106, p. 76

D0102 Dear health, belov'd by men and gods
'Without thee dwells no happiness.'

'On health—from Aripheon'

Poetry Box x/107

D0103 Dear if you change I'll never choose again
And on my faith, my faith shall never break.

'To his mistress'
[Crum D95 (var.)]

b.356, p. 97

D0104 Dear is the mem'ry, Vyse, of thy desert
May feeling friendship remember me.

'To the memory of Archdeacon Vyse buried in Lichfield Cathedral'

fc.53, p. 4

D0105 Dear Jack in deepest contemplation lost
Write in thy own defense and write to me.

[Robert Cholmeley], 'To Mr Taylor at Shrewsbury in answer to his letter from Birmingham'

c.190, p. 1

D0106 Dear Jane, two godmothers contend,
Is fairly worth the other ten.

[Stephen Barrett], 'Sent with a little baby house bed, bought by one godmother, and worked by the other, to Miss Jenny Jacob'

c.193, p. 102

D0107 Dear Jesu! when, when shall it be
And every age thy glory sing.

[John Austin], 'Hym: 16' [Hymn iv, Devotions in the ancient way of offices, 1672, p. 40]

c.178, p. 15

D0108 Dear Jesus let me see
When I shall be above.

[Mary Pluret], 'Canticles'

c.354

D0109 Dear Jesus when, when shall it be
But thou shalt live and die no more.

'An hymn, or divine song'

c.481, p. 241

D0110 Dear Joy was dispatch'd to fetch home her new
stays—
Dat by Chreesh and Shaint Pawtrick, I got up
behind!

[Phanuel Bacon], 'Est locus uni cuiqu suus—by a lady on one of her visiting days'

c.237, fol. [80a]

D0111 Dear Julian twice or thrice a year
From some of th'authors nam'd above.

'To [Robert] Julian'

b.113, p. 275

D0112 Dear ladies and gentleman, customers pop
Yet back in the hay poor as Job we'll soon send ye. |
Then Ma'am &c.

'The Margate toy shop'

Poetry Box iv/62

DO113 Dear, little, pretty, favorite ore
Though he should keep me out of heaven.

> [Henry Fielding], 'Verses addressed to a half-penny,
> which was given to a beggar by a lady and a gentleman
> [the author] who saw it gave him sixpence for it'
> [Crum D104]

c.360/1, p. 211

DO114 Dear Lloyd, they say you're Walpole's ferret
And you, how ill he paid his pimp.

> Philip Wharton, 1st duke of Wharton(?), 'The Duke's
> letter to Mr. Lloyd'

c.468

DO115 Dear loss, to tell the world I grieve, were true
Which thy frail flesh denied, and her disease.

> [Richard] Corbett, 'An epitaph on the Lady
> Haddington' [who died of the smallpox, 6 Dec. 1618]
> [Crum D106]

b.197, p. 163; b.356, p. 13

DO116 Dear love continue nice and chaste
My love [y]our sport you[r] godhead end.

> [Sir John Roe]
> [Crum D107]

b.148, p. 134

DO117 Dear love do not your fair beauty wrong,
And flies away from aged things.

> [Thomas Randolph], 'Love's prime'
> [Crum D108]

c.356; see also 'Dear do not . . .'.

DO118 Dear love, for nothing less than thee
Will dream that hope again or else would die.

> [John Donne], 'A dream'
> [Crum D109]

b.148, p. 81

DO119 Dear lovely rose, that in the morn,
With cold and chilling snows?

> 'The rose'

c.83/3, no. 1002

DO120 Dear lyrist Powell, since you rightly know
And die soft-warbling with my latest breath.

> 'To that excellent player on the harp Mr. [George]
> Powell junior' [d. 1714?]

Poetry Box x/10(6)

DO121 Dear Macdougal, say,
Like hearty M[adam] V[aughan].

Accession 97.7.40

DO122 Dear Madam, did none never gaze
Were only form'd to please their eyes.

> 'Rotten cheese—a simile an imitation of Prior to a
> lady'

c.360/3, no. 237

DO123 Dear Madam, forgive that so long I delay
Of your ever devout humble servant and friend.

> H[enry] Skrine, 'Familiar epistle from an Oxonian to
> Lady Miller on A college life . . . Oxford—Nov: 24.
> 1780'

c.509, p. 39

DO124 Dear Madam, I promised when I saw you last
And make her sing Jemmy is never but clean.

> 'To Mrs. Kirkby of Bartlet's Buildings London 1757'

c.484, p. 121

DO125 Dear Madam—this thirteenth of August I thought
That this French Gasconade is—Le Compte's
floating tree.

> 'To Mrs. Pettat on her resolution to atten Captain
> Pettat in his march with the Gloucestershire militia'

c.484, p. 132

DO126 Dear Madam when you next think fitting
Th'impatience so urgent as mine.

> 'To Mira an epistle'

Poetry Box I/56

DO127 Dear Madam, good morrow much joy you attends
For sure such a poet there never was heard. |
Which nobody can deny.

> 'To the Right Honble the Lady Charlotte Compton'

Accession 97.7.40

DO128 Dear maid who canst with so much ease
And thy sure meed shall be respect and love!

> R[ichard] V[ernon] S[adleir], 'To Miss Bird on her
> presenting a wrought-iron firescreen'

c.106, p. 67

DO129 Dear Maria, the things I have both heard and seen!
Are enough I protest, to make lovers despair.

> Edward Sneyd, 'Epistle. Supposed to be dated from
> London. Against the fashionable deformities of
> hairdressing and cork-rumps which were introduced
> in the country some time after. To a lady of low
> stature'

c.214, p. 84

DO130 Dear Marquis! Methinks I've some cause to
complain
And for which you alone express any regret.

Poetry Box II/46

D0131 Dear Martin Folkes, dear scholar brother friend
I'm your humble servant and grand master.

> [John Byrom, of Manchester], 'A full and true account of a horrid and barbarous murder committed on Epping Forest on . . . the 10th Jan 1728 on the body of the Cam[bridge] coach'
>
> c.176, p. 97

D0132 Dear Mary attend, sad news from your friend,
Unless I could write something better.

> 'From a country lady who had lost her portmanteau to her friend in London'
>
> c.83/1, no. 47; Poetry Box x/112

D0133 Dear Molly! Fair in feature
To taste delights like these.

> John Lockman, 'Greenwood Hall: or Colin's description, to his wife Marian, of the pleasures of Vauxhall Gardens. Made to a favorite gavotte, in an organ concerto, composed by the late Mr. Gladwin . . . May 1740'
>
> c.267/2, p. 121

D0134 Dear Molly, why so oft in tears?
Discharge the jordan at him.

> George Stepney, 'The 7th ode of the 3d: book of Horace imitated'
>
> c.351, p. 74

D0135 Dear mother, my time has been wretchedly spent
Can cure all distempers that ever were known.

> [Christopher Anstey], 'Consultation of Bath physicians'
> [Crum D128]
>
> c.83/4, no. 1094

D0136 Dear Nelly, did you never see,
But close my ditty with a sonnet.

> J. N., 'Gloucester Sept. 20.'
>
> Poetry Box x/26

D0137 Dear nymph, inspir'd by saints above
In sublunary bliss!

> [William Hayley]
>
> File 6930

D0138 Dear object of my late and early pray'r!
And sweeter breathe their little lives away!

> [John] Langhorne, 'To *** wrapped round a nosegay of violets'
> [Crum D133]
>
> c.139, p. 567

D0139 Dear offspring of my thoughtless years,
Would sorrowing send him to the grave!

> [Charles Burney, the elder], 'To my daughter Esther, on her recovery from a long illness, and dangerous childbirth . . . Septr. 28th. 1789'
>
> c.33, p. 210; c.486, fol. 2v

D0140 Dear Peggy no female need boast of her senses
But pollute not your pen with the name of a man.

> [Edward Sneyd?], 'An epistle 10th from Mrs. Deborah [Prude (pseud.)] my lady's maid to Miss Peggy an Abigail'
>
> c.214, p. 31

D0141 Dear Peggy, since the single state
And blushing, throw the pen aside.

> 'Advice to a young lady lately married'
> [Crum D137]
>
> c.391, p. 49; c.83/3, no. 1013

D0142 Dear Phil, I protest what you say in your letter,
Tell C. E. the vicar your uncle and friend.

> C[harles] E[arle], 'A letter from . . . to his niece [Philadelphia Earle]'
>
> c.376

D0143 Dear Pompeius, first with whom,
For a friend so lost and won.

> [William Popple, trans.], '[Horace] book 2d. ode 7th. To Pompeius Varus'
>
> fc.104/2, p. 134

D0144 Dear Pratt! To that incurious age
What love did first inspire.

> [ ] Powys, 'To the Hon. Mr. Pratt, on his marriage with Miss Molesworth . . . 1786'
>
> c.504, p. 85

D0145 Dear Psyche, come, with cheerful face,
And conquer ev'n the tyrant's pain.

> [Mary?] Barber, 'To a friend'
>
> c.83/3, no. 1074

D0146 Dear Ram | Some time ago a month or two
So I conclude | Dear Ram | Adieu.

> [John Walker?], 'Poetical epistle to Abraham Ramsbottom on hearing his father had enlisted for a soldier'
>
> fc.108, fol. 51

D0147 Dear relic hallow'd by paternal grief
But let thy tenderness adorn my life!

> [William Hayley], 'Sonnet . . . July 31 [1800]'
>
> File 6968

D0148 Dear ribbon, you or none can tell
Upon the fairer heaven of her breast.

> [Robert Cholmeley], 'Queries proposed to a lady's breastknot'

> c.190, p. 176

D0149 Dear Robin 'tis pity
Which a Venus would grace.

> 'On Miss Banks written at Tunbridge 1745'

> c.360/2, no. 26 (incomplete?)

D0150 Dear royal youth I'll ne'er repent
To see a restoration.

> 'The loyal resolution' [Jacobite poem, addressed to James Edward Stuart, the Old Pretender]

> fc.58, p. 152; c.570/2, p. 151

D0151 Dear sacred plant! Supremely blest thy fate;
For Hannah's pen lies in your hallowed breast.

> 'On seeing Miss Hannah More's inkstand which was made out of the mulberry tree which Shakespeare planted'

> c.341, p. 168

D0152 Dear saint on earth, the angels cannot choose,
Than all the treasures, and the pomp of Croesus.

> Sir Thomas Urquhart, 'To Master Thomas young person at Kirkmichel'

> fb.217, p. 183

D0153 Dear Sally, emblem of thy chop-house ware
Shrink, and become an undistinguish'd coal.

> 'To pretty Sally at the Lamb . . . 1732'

> c.360/1, p. 109

D0154 Dear seat of rural beauty lovely hill
And by his death your charms to me are dead.

> [William Hayley], 'Sonnet . . . August 8 [1800] begun on Earlton(?) Hill'

> File 6968

D0155 Dear sensibility—'tis thou, and thou alone
A tender generous sympathizing heart.

> Maria [Done], 'A paraphrase on that justly admired soliloquy to sensibility in Sterne's Sentimental journey vol: 2. Page 182'

> c.140, p. 78

D0156 Dear Septimus soon with me
Of the poet and the friends.

> [William Popple, trans.], '[Horace] book 2nd. Ode 6th. To Septimus'

> fc.104/2, p. 130

D0157 Dear shade! Some tribute from thy sons receive
Whose youth was godly, and whose age was wise!

> [Charles Earle], 'An epitaph designed for Justice B—ns—n on a monument, erected by his two sons'

> c.376; see also 'What praise, dear parent . . .'

D0158 Dear ship, who in thy hollow sides
And angry billows roll.

> [Thomas Hamilton, 6th earl of Haddington], 'The beginning of the 3rd ode book 1st of Horace'

> c.458/2, p. 134

D0159 Dear sinless babe, whose peaceful room
And then you'll never want a friend.

> 'A mother to her child before its birth'

> c.83/3, no. 982

D0160 Dear Sir as you told me to stir up your mind
To plate fork and knife, at the vicar's poor table.

> Charles Earle, 'To Mr. Sydenham Barnstaple'

> c.376

D0161 Dear Sir lately hearing a cry about wood
He easily gets, whom the parish maintains.

> [Charles Earle], 'To my friend Mr. S[y]d[e]nh[a]m in Barnstaple extempore'

> c.376

D0162 Dear Sir—next Wednesday—turkey fat
I am your most oblig'd C. E.

> C[harles] E[arle], 'To Mr. Sydenham—most able— | Most honest counsel—in Barnstable . . . March 1th, 1765 West-down'

> c.376

D0163 Dear Sir the physicians pronounce an histeric
I have hit on't at once, I have harass'd my muse.

> Edward Sneyd, 'An epistle 9th. To Mr. Wedgwood Decbr. The 15th: 1774'

> c.214, p. 28

D0164 Dear Sir 'tis with pleasure the following I write,
And in all things (but fighting) believe me | Yours | Byng.

> 'To Mr. C[leveland, secretary of the Admiralty]. The better part of valor is discretion . . .' [satirizing Admiral John Byng's letter, printed in the London Gazette, written 25 May 1756]

> Poetry Box v/122

D0165 Dear Sir, what strange hard-hearted fate,
Send cards about if they think fit.

> 'A poetical epistle to the Revd. Mr. ———'

> c.83/1, no. 102

DO166   Dear Sister, accept (all my tenement yields)
(As 'tis said) 'Take the will, for the deed', of your
                                           brother.

     [Charles Earle], 'To Sister [Philadelphia] Earle with
     three little artichokes, and one little hare'

     c.376

DO167   Dear Sister Ann the source of Cowper's lay
Long to enjoy the blessings you possess.

     [William Hayley], 'London Dec. 2 1800'

     File 6931

DO168   Dear Sister, I send (in compliance with you)
In Indian might worship instead of a god.

     [Charles Earle], 'To Mrs. [Catharine] Peard desiring a
     copy of the above ['Long have I thought . . .']

     c.376

DO169   Dear Sister when these lines you read
I had not wept alone.

     [Charlotte (Turner)] Smith, 'The gudgeons an elegy'

     c.504, p. 200

DO170   Dear Smed, I read thy brilliant lines
For then your horns shall be your pride.

     [Jonathan] Swift, 'His Grace [the Duke of Grafton]'s
     answer' [to 'It was my Lord . . .', by Jonathan
     Smedley]

     c.176, p. 116

DO171   Dear soul! art gone from church militant?
Of known and unknown saints a company.

     G. C., 'Upon the removal of Mr. William Taylor . . .'
     [d. 7 September 1641]

     b.88, p. 6

DO172   Dear Sylvia let not thy Thyrsis know
When fortunes not affections equal are.

     [Thomas Weaver]

     b.213, p. 131

DO173   Dear Thomas didst thou never pop
Always aspiring always low.

     [Matthew] Prior, 'A simile'

     fc.60, p. 40; c.179, p. 53 (ll. 1–12); see also 'Dear
     William . . .'.

DO174   Dear, thoughtless, Clara, to my verse attend,
And live for Him who more then died for you.

     Poetry Box I/22, 104

DO175   Dear Titus think it no reproach—
Who rode behind before.

     'Mrs. Titus of Watford who loved music had a servant
     John Smith who was a good performer—she put him
     out of livery and made sort of a companion of him.
     Verses wrote by some wag of her acquaintance . . .
     altered by another wag'

     c.74

DO176   Dear to themselves alone, two miscreants lie,
'Tis boundless.—else they plunge to fiery woe.

     [John Lockman], 'Sepulchral verses on a Catholic
     v[iscount?] and his son, late tenants of a castle.
     Written for a friend'

     c.268 (first part), p. 145

DO177   Dear Tom, both your letters from camp I received;
Then consign'd his campaign to thy pitiful muse.

     [Frederick Corfield], 'The campaign'

     c.381/1

DO178   Dear Tom let us taste the true pleasures of wine,
But fail not to meet thy kind friend at the George.

     'Song 4'

     c.555, p. 3

DO179   Dear Tom, this brown jug, that now foams with
                                    mild ale
So here's to my lovely sweet Nan of the vale.

     [Francis Fawkes], 'The metamorphosis or Toby
     reduced'

     fc.21, p. 24; c.555, p. 159 (var.)

DO180   Dear Tom, to thee myself addressing
And put it in my Latinea.

     [ ] Pooly, [address to Tom 'Kill(egrew?)']

     fb.228/56

DO181   Dear Tom, you wish me to send down
She runs most monstrously to belly.

     c.344

DO182   Dear tuneful friend, I'm sick of noise,
Apollo, and the tuneful nine.

     John Lockman, 'To Signor Pandalfo Collins [brother
     to the Countess of Abingdon] after hearing him play
     on the lute . . . this epistle was writ in 1757'

     c.267/2, p. 329

DO183   Dear, why do you say you love
Prove true, and say thou canst not love.

     [Sir Robert Ayton], 'Cant: 28' ['On his mistress']
     [Crum D163]

     b.4, fol. 24v; b.200, p. 148 ('Speak true')

D0184 Dear Will I frankly must the truth confess
And tho' I spare none else, I'll honor her.

R[obert] Shirley, 1st earl of Ferrers, 'The ninth satire
of Boileau'

c.347, p. 112

D0185 Dear William didst thou never pop
Always aspiring, always low.

[Matthew Prior], 'A simile'

c.111, p. 125; see also 'Dear Thomas . . .'.

D0186 Dear Wye what [. . .] suns thy waves behold
And mix my being summer in your turn.

Poetry Box IV/139

D0187 Dear youth! This is thy natal day,
Which gives thy laurel's bloom!

'Lines addressed to a friend whose birthday falls on
the 12 of April. By a lady'

c.83/2, no. 580

D0188 Dearer than daughter, rivaled by few
'O come to my paternal arms again.'

'Epitaph . . . Bishop Lowth . . . translation'

c.81/1, no. 40

D0189 Dearest Amanda! Why so obdurate?
Save a lover, who for you dies!

John Lockman, 'The despairing shepherd'

c.267/4, p. 304

D0190 Dearest do, you easily may,
And not to reap a bliss.

'The hasty bridegroom'

fb.107, p. 58

D0191 Dearest Mrs. Belle Pearce
When I hobble on crutches.

Sarah More, 'A note from . . . to Miss Pearce'

c.341, at front

D0192 Dearest of all the names above,
And there I fix my trust.

[Isaac Watts, Hymns and spiritual songs (1707), bk. II,
Hymn 148]

c.180, p. 16

D0193 Dearest of guides whose counsel and whose love
Social and sweet as Cowper's sacred muse.

[William Hayley], 'Sonnet'

File 6968

D0194 Dearest thy tresses are not threads of gold
So be within as fair, as good, as true.

[Thomas] Carew, 'The comparison'
[Crum D173]

b.225, p. 134; b.205, fol. 88v (var.); see also 'Fairest . . .'.

D0195 Death and the cobbler were long at a stand
And ript his soul from the upper leather.

'On a cobbler'
[Crum D175]

b.356, p. 243

D0196 Death art thou mad? or having lost thine eyes
Whilst we do write your epitaph in tears.

b.197, p. 159

D0197 Death, as a friendly foe, that sorrow hath
Destroyed, which procur'd their mutual death.

Sir Thomas Urquhart, 'The epitaph of Pyramus, and
Thisbe'

fb.217, p. 314

D0198 Death at a cobbler's door, oft made a stand
The cobbler call'd for's awl.—Death brought his
last.

[Richard Brathwaite], 'Epitaph on a cobbler'
[Crum D177]

c.113/6; c.360/1, p. 135; c.81/1, no. 175

D0199 Death at the length both old and young doth strike,
And into dust doth turn to all alike.

c.339, p. 328

D0200 Death be not proud, thy hand gives not this blow
The grave no conquest gets, death hath no sting.

L[ucy Harington], C[ountess] of B[edford?], ['Elegy
on the Lady Markham']
[Crum D179]

b.148, p. 118

D0201 Death being but sleep, and sleep a sort of death:
The more he sleeps, the less of life he hath.

Sir Thomas Urquhart, 'Of a long sleeper'

fb.217, p. 49

D0202 Death common is to all, to rich to poor
A requiem to her soul, where joys are mo[r]e.

Samuel Lightfoote, 'In obitum . . . magistrae Okenor
carmen funebre' [20 March 1626]

Poetry Box VI/50

D0203 Death does the virtuous to heaven lead,
Who would not die? could they their footsteps
tread.

fb.142, p. 59

D0204 Death duly thought on must awake
As to triumph o'er all assault.

    [Edmund Wodehouse], 'June 29 [1715] I. More's death'

    b.131, p. 227

D0205 Death envies all my happiness and lays
Watch to surprise me in my common ways.

    [Petrarch]

    b.211, p. 62

D0206 Death frights not him who does believe,
These may exalt our happiness.

    [Edmund Wodehouse], 'Octr. 28 [1714] Simon and Jude'

    b.131, p. 71

D0207 Death I recant, and say, unsaid by me
Because the chain is broke, though no link lost.

    [John Donne], 'Elegia 18ua. A funeral elegy on Mrs. Boulstrede'
    [Crum D187]

    b.114, p. 134; b.148, p. 117

D0208 Death is a debt it must by all be paid;
As to believe 'twill bring to him more high.

    [Edmund Wodehouse], 'Septr 24 [1715]'

    b.131, p. 273

D0209 Death is a fisherman, the world we see,
And all is fish with him that comes to net.

    'Death's trade'

    b.197, p. 234; c.158, p. 84; c.356

D0210 Death is a pursuant with eagle's wings
And as she leaves thee, so will judgment find thee.

    'To the covetous person'

    c.189, p. 103

D0211 Death is eternal sleep—a fine long nap
Pray is this sleep, to be exempt from dreams.

    'Epigram on a late metaphysical decree of the French convention'

    c.344

D0212 Death is invisible not seen but felt
Eternal life for mortal life unsure.

    Elizabeth Jekyll, 'Upon death . . . 1652 a year of great mortality'

    b.221, p. 31

D0213 Death is life's solstice: the sun stands not, but
Seems to stand: so man seems to die, dies not.

    Sir Thomas Urquhart, 'That man dieth not'

    fb.217, p. 142

D0214 Death is the certain lot of all
So my opinion's shown to you.

    Thomas Tipping, 'On death'

    c.213

D0215 Death is the common lot impos'd on all,
From it they come, return to it they must.

    'An elegy on the much lamented death of Sir Walter Blackett'

    c.93

D0216 Death is the road to everlasting life,
Who enters once, must ne'er return again.

    Henry Baker, 'On death'

    c.244, p. 400

D0217 Death, judgment, heav'n, and hell, think Christian think
Hear me at least, O hear me from my grave.

    Dr. [ ] Trap, 'The following is Doctor Trap's epitaph—composed by himself, and in his will expressly desired to be engraved upon his tomb'

    c.53, fol. 7

D0218 Death, look it in his empty skull
Sharp in the bosom of her friends.

    'On the death of Miss E[liza] Parker at Farnham Jan. 16. 1793'

    c.391, p. 117

D0219 Death lov'd pease porridge, and for this intent
He took away the King of peace in Lent.

    'On K[ing] J[ames]'

    b.356, p. 249

D0220 Death must forever to Christ's death succumb;
His death being death's sole death: his cross the tomb.

    Sir Thomas Urquhart, 'Death's epitaph'

    fb.217, p. 181

D0221 Death passing by, and hearing Parsons play
For Parsons rests, his service being done.

    [Thomas Randolph], 'On Mr. Parsons organist at Westminster [Abbey; buried 3 Aug. 1623]
    [Crum D197]

    fb.143, p. 43

D0222 Death thou hast turn'd to cold inactive clay
How mild thy hours were how sweet thy voice.

    [William Hayley], 'Sonnet . . . August 7 [1800]'

    File 6968

D0223 Death threatens me with a lifted-up arm
I fly and shake but must at length obey.

    Petrarch

b.211, p. 61

D0224 Death to this wrestler gave a final fall
That trip up his heels, and took no hold at all.

    'On a wrestler'
    [Crum D209]

fb.143, p. 9

D0225 Death varies oft, no certain rule can be,
He strikes old age, youth, manhood, infancy.

    S. P., 'Caleb Vernon. No rule can be'

b.228, p. 1

D0226 Death who'll not change prerogatives with thee,
I cannot write but I will weep her one.

    T[homas] Randolph, 'An elegy on the Lady Venetia
    Digby' [followed by 'Beauty itself lies here . . .']
    [Crum D215a]

b.54, p. 932

D0227 Death will the certain entrance prove,
Entitled man to heav'nly bliss.

    [Edmund Wodehouse], 'Novr. 1 1714'

b.131, p. 74

D0228 Death with his besom came to Babram
And beat him down to Beelzebub.

    'On Sir Horatio Polivicini'

b.356, p. 249

D0229 Death with the good a better life begins
And as death leaves thee so will judgment find thee.

    [Mary Serjant]

fb.98, fol. 148

D0230 Death without warning was as bold as brief
When he kill'd two in one a miller and a thief.

    'On a miller'
    [Crum D217]

fb.143, p. 19

D0231 Death's steps to some are many, t'others few,
Who in each case O God thy love do see!

    [Edmund Wodehouse], 'Iterum [10 April 1715]'

b.131, p. 195

D0232 Deem not amiss, if all too weak,
Maria's good, and Tom is blest.

    T[homas] H[ull], 'June 9th 1765'

c.528/54

D0233 Deep-immers'd the Squire Clay in his countrified
                                air
And then breakfast with lords at your *grande dejeuner*.

    'The grande dejeuner'

fc.53, p. 23

D0234 Deep in a dangerous hateful gloom,
And try the force of pray'r.

    Charles Atherton Allnutt, 'An obvious conclusion
    from the circumstances of Peter's imprisonment and
    release—12 Acts'

c.112, p. 50

D0235 Deep in a wood! And solemn silence round!
How great his art, to thus illude our eyes!

    John Lockman, 'Viewing the transparent scenes, in
    Vauxhall Gardens . . . May 1754'

c.267/1, p. 140

D0236 Deep in the fame(?) where monarchs breathless lie,
Beauty is best distinguished by her foil.

    John Lockman, 'Prologue (spoke by Mr. Hale) to The
    miser, acted at Covent Garden Theater, Decr. 1743,
    for the benefit of the widow and four small children,
    of the late unfortunate Mr. Henry Carey'

c.267/3, p. 118

D0237 Deep in the forest's gloom I dwell
Betray the spot where Edwin lies.

    R[ichard] V[ernon] S[adleir], 'The despairing lover to
    his friend'

c.106, p. 52

D0238 Deep in the shades of death
And win them to his love.

    T[homas] S[tevens]

c.259, p. 139

D0239 Deep in the vale old Liffey rolls his tides,
And, loudly roaring, smoke, and foam below.

    James Ward, 'Mr. Pope's Miscellany vol. 2. Poem,
    Phoenix Park by . . . page 192'

c.160, fol. 76 (incomplete)

D0240 Defend, O sacred spirit, th'ethereal height,
When I resign, grant I may live with thee.

    'A philosophical poem or hymn for Whitsunday 1740'

c.371, fol. 34

D0241 Deft ambition's idle call
And trace thy footsteps o'er the green.

    [Thomas Hull]

c.528/32

D0242   Degenerate times! When scandal lifts her head,
Then squat a toad, nor dare to face the sun.

> John Lockman, 'Occasioned by reading some
> scurrilous verses, against a patriot nobleman . . . Nov.
> 1756'
> c.267/1, p. 168

D0243   Deign at my hands this crown of prayer and praise
Salvation to all that will is nigh.

> [John Donne], '[Holy sonnets.] La Corona [1]'
> [Crum D233]
> b.114, p. 152

D0244   Deign heavenly muses, to assist my song:
His powerful works, his daily praise renew.

> [Stephen] Duck, 'The Shunamite'
> c.165, p. 1

D0245   Deign now O Lord! thy servant to release,
And take me with thee to thy blest abode!

> 'A prayer for the pious, at the approach of death'
> c.487, p. 74

D0246   Deign (Sir) in your perusal of these lines
Our purse as full, as were of charity.

> [Richard?] Brathwaite, 'Mr. Brathwaite's address in
> poetry to Charl. Howard . . . upon his demand of the
> tenth part of his estate, as being private to the last
> plot. anno 1655'
> c.160, fol. 98

D0247   Deign to accept, (benignant King!)
Thy poet cannot be forgot.

> John Lockman, 'Aug. 1765. To the King's most
> excellent Majesty: with a present of Shetland herrings,
> from the Free British Fishery Society'
> c.267/1, p. 388

D0248   De'il faw mine eyen
As the stoot bonny Scot takes the Tarker.

> 'Song'
> b.204, p. 42; b.111, p. 81

D0249   Delbo, a soldier old and brave,
And laughs at the luxurious cully.

> 'An old soldier turned young husband a tale'
> c.503, p. 25

D0250   Delia, in whose form to trace
This sweet spot fell from the skies.

> John Lockman, 'To Delia: made to a favorite musette,
> in Mr. Howard's overture of The amorous
> goddesses . . . June 1740'
> c.267/2, p. 125

D0251   Delia you praise, and much even prize
The living luster of a nose.

> 'To Arabin'
> fc.76.iii/214

D0252   Delia's affection for the brute creation
Storms at her trifling taste, and swears her d—d
absurd.

> '[Female characters.] 6. Delia, or the lover of animals'
> Poetry Box IV/148

D0253   Delia's good sense condems thy strains
Such neither hurt nor please.

> 'An acrostic [Dallas]'
> Poetry Box x/69

D0254   Delightful Hampstead! Hill renown'd!
Next morn [?] more pleasures rise.

> John Lockman, '14 July 1765. The pleasures of
> Hampstead a cantata. Set to music'
> c.267/2, p. 203

D0255   Delights which are in virtue found
Of sorrows are the spring.

> 'Chancery hand'
> [Crum D242]
> b.234, p. 9

D0256   Delos, to you, and you the sov'reign dame
That now I from your graces take my leave, | And
rest your humble servant.

> Sir Thomas Urquhart, 'The adieu to Apollo and the
> muses'
> fb.217, p. 364

D0257   Deluded fly, that thus presum'd
And stoops to any prey.

> 'On a fly drowned in a lady's eye'
> c.360/2, no. 99

D0258   Deluded men these holds forego,
The jockeys that will ride you.

> 'Written in answer' [to 'As by the templar's holds
> you go . . .']
> c.362, p. 66

D0259   Deluder fair! where art thou fled?
And I no longer be misled.

> 'Stanzas to fancy written in the West Indies'
> c.140, p. 545

D0260 Democritus, his sensual eyes ejected
Save only that you laugh as much as he.

> [Sir Thomas Urquhart], 'To one who for that he
> deservedly obtained with Democritus the title of
> Jelasino [*sic*] affected to have the repute of such
> another man as he was'

fb.217, p. 505

D0261 Democritus not finding truth, did gauge,
Dutches will find it, if they have not found it.

> Sir Thomas Urquhart, 'Where germana veritas may
> be found'

fb.217, p. 250

D0262 Democritus still laugh'd: with mournful moan
Or weep at th'other most.

> Sir Thomas Urquhart, 'Democrit[us], and Heraclitus'

fb.217, p. 143

D0263 Denham, come help to laugh | At old Daph . . .
Had advis'd thee to scribble no more.

> [Sir John Denham], 'Ld. Crofte' [on Sir William
> D'Avenant]
> [Crum D247]

pb.53, p. 11 (autogr.)

D0264 Denham is dead and Cleveland is fled
And Portsmouth, that's younger is rotten.

> 'On my Lady Denham, &c.'

fb.140, p. 161

D0265 Depart from me! How strange the word!
From thee our blessings flow.

> T[homas] S[tevens], 'St. Luke 5. 8.9.10.11 . . . March 2.
> [17]80'

c.259, p. 78

D0266 Departing summer, trips it o'er the meads,
Till do the fount of bliss immortal ye ascend.

> [Miss ( ) Bradford], 'St. John in the wilderness the
> parochial church of Widdicombe and part of
> Exmouth'

c.504, p. 33

D0267 Deposited within this silent tomb doth lie
Seam all perfections up, and fix to Blackett's name.

> 'Another on Sir William Blackett bart.'

c.530, p. 197

D0268 Derwent! what scenes thy wandering waves behold,
And mix my briny sorrows in your urn.

> [Erasmus Darwin], 'Ode to the River Derwent,
> written near its source, in the wilds of the peak in
> Derbyshire'
> [Crum D252]

c.142, p. 532

D0269 Descend bright Venus! Leave yon shadowing cloud;
Is blest, when crown'd by mutual love.

> John Lockman, 'The loves of Eginhart and Imma. A
> musical tale . . . writ in 1736'

c.267/3, p. 58; c.268 (second part), p. 19

D0270 Descend, celestial spirit, from above,
In soft responses sing from rosy bowers.

> 'A hymn to the Holy Ghost'

c.167, p. 30

D0271 Descend, O muse, and strike the lyre;
But cease the melting song.

> 'Guy an epic poem'

c.224, p. 1

D0272 Descend, ye Nine! Descend and sing
Hers lifts the soul to heav'n.

> [Alexander] Pope, 'Ode on St. Cecelia's Day'

fc.132/1, p. 133

D0273 Descend ye rajahs and ye nabob kings
Brunswick the bench and India have thrice rung.

> [George Howard, 6th earl of Carlisle], 'Ode on Major
> Scott parody of Pope's ode on St. Cecilia'

c.197, p. 32

D0274 Descend, descend, great god of wine!
And fashion'd by the gods above.

> John Lettice, 'Achilles [an opera], from Metastasio'
> [1766]

c.551

D0275 Describe the Roman clergy who can do't?
As to eat God, in hell will eat the devil.

> H[enry] Care, 'A New Year's gift for English papists.
> A true description of the Roman clergy. By R. S.
> 1673 . . . made by H. Care'

b.54, p. 940

D0276 Desdemona *la divina*
Venga a Queen Ch[arlo]tte Row.

> 'Ma cara mia Charlottina' [in English and Italian]

c.486, fol. 34v

D0277 Deserted, and scorn'd the proud Marlb[orough] sat,
For betraying the church, and enslaving the land.

> 'The false favorite's downfall. To a merry tune called,
> Packington's Pound' [1692]
> [Crum D260b; *POAS* v.330]

fb.70, p. 151; see also 'At length to complete . . .'.

D0278 Desist, rash youth, for young thou seem'st to be,
Will ever stoop her lot with thine to share.

'To the author of the foregoing verses' ['Maria's charms . . .', on Miss Mary Turner]

c.360/1, p. 285

D0279 Despair of nothing, that you would attain,
Unwearied diligence your point will gain.

c.93

D0280 Despairing beside a clear stream
His ghost shall glide over the plain.

[Nicholas Rowe], 'Colin's complaint'
[Crum D268, 'over the green']

c.392, p. 19; Accession 97.7.40, p. 40 (with a separate copy)

D0281 Despise all pleasures vain, hold virtue by the hand
As steadfastly in the rage of seas, the work doth
firmly stand.

c.339, p. 315

D0282 Desponding artist, talk no more
Which Emily, might yield to Evelyn's eyes.

[Horace Walpole, 4th earl of Orford], 'Advice to Eckardt the painter' [printed 1746 (Foxon W31)]

fc.51, p. 186

D0283 Destined by fate to guard the crown,
I instant fly to arms.

'[Enigma/Charade/Conundrum] 8' [hat]

c.389

D0284 Destruction northward tends. Then haste to Kent
Reason rules both—let this by [sic] criticis'd.

'On fourteen couple of English hounds being sent to Scotland as a present to the Duke of Hamilton 1722'

c.360/2, no. 84

D0285 Detested sin thro' thee
Nor let the sinner die.

T[homas] S[tevens]

c.259, p. 147

D0286 Devil confound each senseless loon
Who pulls down the father to set up the son.

'A Scotch song' [on James II]

b.111, p. 82

D0287 Devil thou know'st we're thine
To see great Lucifer tonight.

Lady Jane Cavendish, 'The song' [of witches in a pastoral]
[Crum D274]

b.233, p. 48

D0288 Devoid of all care was my morning of life,
But to hide his despair and to die?

'The insolvent debtor'

c.175, p. 71

D0289 Devout composer of the stormy breast
O might they live to soothe all similar distress!

[William Hayley], 'Sonnet . . . Sept. 7 [1800]'

File 6968

D0290 Diana and Hymen encounter'd one day
For I joy to have found what you weep to have lost.

'Diana ad Hyman an extempore epigram to Mrs. Brickenden on her marriage March 1767'

c.341, p. 134

D0291 Dick, after drunk, when crop-sick gravely swore
Himself but says he breathes not whilst he drinks.

'Epigram'

c.115

D0292 Dick get me a poipe
That our little Sal shall fright all the town foalk.

'The farmer's return from London. An interlude as performed at Drury Lane'

c.68, p. 196

D0293 Dick Norris of old, nor modern Dick neither
That, shall ever live in the records of fame.

'Verses on the late inimitable Tom Weston in Scrub'

c.68, p. 219

D0294 Dick [Star] and Sis. Moon together art wed
This Star will be turn'd to the man in the Moon.

'Of Richard Star and Sisly Moon's marriage'
[Crum D286]

b.197, p. 39

D0295 Dick tell me, and you shall be mine Apollyon:
Till he was cuckolded in ev'ry point.

Sir Thomas Urquhart, 'A conference, concerning a very kind-hearted woman, whose husband being the corrector of a press, was exceeding well versed in all the points, that ordinarily serve to distinguish members, by their several sense in the close of a speech'

fb.217, p. 348

D0296 Dick where hast thou been all the while
Foil(?) his who tells the story.

b.213, p. 99

D0297 Dick with his dogs to such an outrage grew
Nay up thou goest quote Dick, and 'twere my
father.

'On Dick the huntsman'
[Crum D287]

b.356, p. 103

D0298 Did Celia's person and her mind agree
Enrich'd the image, but defac'd the mind.

[Alexander] Pope, 'Spoken by . . . to the Duchess of
Queensborough' [Queensberry]
[Crum D290]

Poetry Box v/89

D0299 Did ever judge more equally proceed
That men may easily know the one, by th'other.

[Francis Quarles], 'On Dives and Lazarus' [Divine
Fancies III, 44]

b.137, p. 171; b.156, p. 11

D0300 Did ever nature prodigal appear,
'Tis rude in us his ashes to molest.

Jos[eph] Rawson, 'On the death of Mr. Thomas
Coker, Bachelor of Arts of Christ's College
Cambridge'

fb.108, p. 279

D0301 Did he give leave to lie beneath
When I am wholly thine.

T[homas] S[tevens], 'Feb. 13. [17]80'

c.259, p. 76

D0302 Did he who thus inscrib'd this wall
That house is not a House of Lords.

[ ] Barrington, 'In Chichester Cathedral is a family
vault built for the interment of the Dukes of
Richmond [and Lennox] . . . inscribed—Domus
ultima. On this the following epigram was written . . .'
[Crum D292]

c.373, p. 62; c.546, p. 29; c.82, p. 28

D0303 Did ladies now as we are told
A forest scarce could find them leaves!

'Modern Eves'

c.81/1, no. 512

D0304 Did not my sorrow sigh into a verse
Without forefathers thine own pedigree.

[John] Earles, 'In obitum Gulielmi Pembrocensis
Cancellarii Oxonii' [on William Herbert, Earl of
Pembroke, d. 10 April 1630]
[Crum D295]

b.62, p. 56

D0305 Did Peyton's lovely person and her mind agree
Has grac'd the image, but defac'd the mind.

'On Miss Peyton—wrote at Tunbridge Wells—1733'
[answered by 'As Peyton's person . . .']

c.360/1, p. 35

D0306 Did sweeter sounds adorn my flowing tongue,
Forever blessing, and forever blest.

[Matthew] Prior, 'Charity' [paraphrase of I
Corinthians xiii]
[Crum D296b]

c.144, p. 53; c.176, p. 135; c.360/3, no. 251

D0307 Did ye see Simeon on the hill today
Then hide their love—or then conceal their pain.

[John Black]

fc.107, p. 79

D0308 Did you but know what pains I feel,
Yourself will need much more than I.

'Timely love, by the same hand' [as 'Tho' in their
flame . . .']

fb.142, p. 53

D0309 Did you but know, when bath'd in dew,
If once you let them go!

'Lines sent to a young lady addicted to fashionable
hours, with a violet'

c.83/3, no. 1062

D0310 Did you ever see the day
So let our heavenly angel rest.

Sir Rob[ert] A[y]ton, 'Upon the Prince his death to
the King' [Prince Henry, 1612]
[Crum D298]

b.197, p. 25

D0311 Did you hear of the news an invisible fleet
For a Parliament sunk, and six regiments rais'd.

'The invasion' [1688]
[Crum D299]

fb.108, p. 113

D0312 Did you not hear of a newfound dance
Farewell all deserve a hope.

'The devil and the excise man. A song'

c.530, p. 51

D0313 Didst thou but know thy destin'd race,
And thou mayst die tomorrow.

[Jonathan] Swift(?), 'An inscription on the house
called the Golden Cross near Sutton Colefield, said to
be originally written on a pane of glass there by Dean
Swift'

c.481, p. 134

D0314 Die Ben Jonson cross not our religion so
With thee began all art, with thee it ends.

[Nicholas Oldisworth], 'A letter to Ben Jonson'
[Crum D313, 'Die Jonson']

b.356, p. 316

D0315 Die envy, die—for now great Pope is dead
No other's verse with envy will be read.

'On the death of Alexander Pope esqr. 1744'

c.360/2, no. 253

D0316 Die Townshend, die, thy odious life resign
Make some atonement for the guilty land.

'On the Lord Townshend's being turned out from
being Secretary of State'

c.570/1, p. 170

D0317 Die wretched Damon, die quickly to ease her
Never of love so true her complain.

[John How], 'A song by Mr. Wolseley' [false
attribution? answered by 'Damon, if thou wilt
believe me . . .']
[Crum D317]

b.204, p. 81

D0318 Diodorus is in suit, and has the gout
Sure, Flaccus, h'has the gout too in his hands.

'Litigat et podagra Diodorus . . .'

b.207, p. 10

D0319 Diogenes, in Cypric guise,
Which is a king's or common's head.

c.189, p. 75

D0320 Diogenes inky and proud
We ne'er should have had philosophers poets or
kings.

[Edward Ward], 'The tippling philosophers' [printed
c. 1710 (Foxon W183)]

fc.61, p. 66; c.555, p. 171 ('Diogenes surly . . .'; var.)

D0321 Diogenes, the famous cynic,
The asp, and viper—changing venom.

c.94

D0322 Diogenes was richer in his tun
Than were some kings that many lands had won.

[John Playford, in The musical companion, 1667]

c.339, p. 325

D0323 Dire is the passion, that our scenes unfold,
And hail the blessings of domestic peace.

c.340

D0324 Dire love should be check'd by advice,
And soon make thee wrinkled and old.

'An excellent answer [to 'Can love be controll'd . . .']
by a fair moralist of quality'

c.94

D0325 Discourteous death that wouldst not once confer
He would have spar'd a life to gain a bribe.

'On [Lord] Treasurer Buckhurst in K. James the 1st
time'
[cf. Crum U10]

fb.143, p. 43; see also 'Uncivil death . . .'.

D0326 Discreet and prudent, of good sense,
With these virtues, who could hate her.

'The agreeable wife'

c.341, p. 98

D0327 Discreet? What means this word discreet?
When they are bound naked to the stake.

A[braham] C[owley], 'Discretion'
[Crum D325]

c.258

D0328 Disgrac'd, undone, forlorn, made Fortune's sport
Next after you by God I will be k[ing].

'The Du[ke] of Monmouth's letter to the K[ing]'
[1680]
[Crum D332; POAS II.254]

b.113, p. 109; b.327, f. 15; b.371, no. 11; b.52/2, p. 179; c.171,
p. 1; fb.106(26); Poetry Box VI/61

D0329 Dishevell'd still like Asia's bleeding queen,
And pity—greet her—with a sister's love.

R[ichard] B[rinsley Butler] Sheridan, 'Epilogue to the
tragedy of Semiramis. Written by . . . spoken by Mrs.
Yates'
[Crum D333]

c.391

D0330 Disloyal Sylvia see
Is fair and chaste, and though still changing, true.

[George Daniel]

b.121, fol. 36

D0331 Dispel, auspicious queen of night,
In thy bright progress through the sky.

'On the evening entertainments in Vauxhall Gardens
finishing this even[ing] Friday September the 7 1750'

c.360/3, no. 76; c.267/1, pp. 99, 124

D0332 Distinction fails, and in the darkening west,
And name and place are here forever lost!

[David] Mallet

c.240, fol. 28

DO333　Distracted with care,
To his cottage again.

　　[William] Walsh, 'The despairing lover'

c.351, p. 88; c.189, p. 8

DO334　Distrust and darkness of a future state,
To be we know not what, we know not where.

c.189, p. 103

DO335　Diversity of bodies that true is
Which it invests as a thin fine-spun veil.

　　[Edmund Wodehouse], 'March 17 [1715]'

b.131, p. 183

DO336　Dives on this terrestial sphere was great
Like Lazarus rise and not like Dives fall.

　　'Dives and Lazarus. Being a paraphrase on part of the
　　16 chapter of Luke . . .'

c.143, fol. 3

DO337　Divide thy woes and give me my sad part
And well can suffer to give you relief.

　　'Bro. book'

c.549, p. 43

DO338　Divine contentment circles round
The son, who died, adore.

　　[G. Routh], 'Verses to J.and M. R[outh]'

c.139, p. 268

DO339　Divine Florella, 'tis with grief I see
And own he was, too honest to deceive.

　　[Thomas Hamilton, 6th earl of Haddington], 'To
　　Florella epistle the fifteenth'

c.458/1, p. 50

DO340　Divinity and justice hand in hand,
Abjured their king and Barabbas did choose.

　　'On Mr. [William] Paul and John Hall esq. who were
　　murdered the 13th of July 1716 for the love of God and
　　justice'

fc.58, p. 42; c.570/1, p. 171

DO341　Division that soever you do intend
Then only do even as thou didst before.

　　[Mary Serjant], 'Division'

fb.98, fol. 29

DO342　Do as you say, or say, Sir, as you do:
But never do you any of those two

　　Sir Thomas Urquhart, 'To one, whose speeches still
　　varied from his actions'

fb.217, p. 233

DO343　Do but consider this small dust
That lovers' ashes take no rest.

　　[Ben Jonson], 'The hourglass'
　　[Crum D353]

b.205, fol. 73v; b.197, p. 59

DO344　Do cuckolds wear horns says Tom? Marry, cries
　　　　　　　　　　　　　　　　　　　　　　　　　　Ned
You need go no farther to know than your head.

c.546, p. 28

DO345　Do I not venture much? The point is nice
I'll hear their censure, and will hear with ease.

　　'Epistle V. To Lucius advising him against vanity'

fc.100, p. 23

DO346　Do I resolve an easy life
By an endless eternity.

　　[John Austin], 'Hym: 24' [Hymn xix, Devotions in
　　the ancient way of offices, 1672, p. 169]

c.178, p. 22

DO347　Do not ask me, charming Phyllis,
Let but yours my passion meet.

　　M[aurice] J[ohnson], 'Pinks and lilies . . . a love song
　　with rhapsodies from the poets'
　　[cf. Crum D361]

c.229/1, fol. 75v

DO348　Do not at his inconstancy repine:
And yet he never doth from thence remove.

　　Sir Thomas Urquhart, 'To a gentlewoman, wishing
　　her not to esteem the less of her servant, that he is
　　something changeable'

fb.217, p. 240

DO349　Do not belief in everyone repose
And most deceit is clad in flattery.

c.549, p. 64

DO350　Do not most fragrant Earl disclaim
Am turn'd of five and forty.

　　[Nicholas Rowe], 'The 4th ode of the 2nd book of
　　Horace—by [i.e., for] my Lord Granville inscribed to
　　the E. of Scars[da]le' [on Scarsdale's supposed
　　attachment to Mrs. Bracegirdle]
　　[Crum D366]

c.111, p. 126; Poetry Box IV/72 (attr. Granville)

DO351　Do not profane the Sabbath for gain
Has hanged himself.

　　'On one Munday that hanged himself'

b.356, p. 244

D0352 Do not thine alms defer, when need doth bid thee
　　　　　　　　　　　　　　　　　　　　haste,
　　For why, one gift is double thought, that in due time
　　　　　　　　　　　　　　　　　　　　is plac'd.

　　　c.339, p. 324; b.234, p. 9

D0353 Do nothing timorously and yet beware
　　What's to be shunn'd who shuns what's to be fear'd.

　　　[Sir Thomas Urquhart], 'We ought to be wary and
　　　circumspect in all our actions without the meanest
　　　share of timorousness, or temerity'

　　　fb.217, p. 512

D0354 Do pious marble, let thy readers know
　　An everlasting monument to thee.

　　　[Francis Quarles], 'On Mr. Michael Drayton a
　　　memorable poet of this age who died . . . 1631'
　　　[Crum D375]

　　　fb.143, p. 9

D0355 Do put some money in the plate,
　　Keeps a cook's shop to feed the trade.

　　　'A Methodist sermon . . .'

　　　c.555, p. 39

D0356 Do what he will, she's ever at his sleeve,
　　I told him all my secrets long ago.

　　　'Nature the oracle of Mr. Garrick'

　　　c.83/3, no. 741

D0357 Do what thou wilt, ill nature will prevail,
　　And ev'ry elf has skill enough to rail.

　　　c.189, p. 87

D0358 Do you not mark my child
　　Which offers to thy hopes a glorious prize.

　　　'To Miss Caroline Frances Cornwallis upon her
　　　birthday the 12th of July 1797'

　　　fc.124, p. 42

D0359 Do you said Fanny, t'other day
　　And cried you've sworn—now kiss the book.

　　　'Epigram'

　　　fc.130, p. 50

D0360 Dobbin careless how he goes
　　Prize its virtues know its uses.

　　　'[Enigma/Charade/Conundrum] 42' [lodestone]

　　　c.389

D0361 Doctor as you with artful skill
　　Else she's a drug, you'll never sell.

　　　'Advice to ———— [an apothecary]'
　　　[Crum D387a]

　　　c.546, p. 32

D0362 Doctor, my system's all my own,
　　That you yourself may live.

　　　[George] Cheyne, 'Dr. Cheyne to Dr. Winter' [answer
　　　to 'Tell me from whence . . .']
　　　[Crum D390]

　　　Poetry Box x/94; c.233, p. 98; see also 'My system,
　　　Doctor 's . . .'

D0363 Doctor Peirse before his dying day
　　He could else to Jesus cleanly go.

　　　'Another [upon Dr. Peirse of Caius College in
　　　Cambridge]'

　　　b.197, p. 219

D0364 Doe is my name, and here I lie
　　My grammar taught me, *do fit di*.

　　　'Upon J. Do[e]'
　　　[Crum D393]

　　　b.197, p. 205; c.74 ('On Martin Do[e]')

D0365 Does Bear presume to go before the Cup?
　　Here's a health to you, drink this potion.

　　　'Crater' [answered by 'We pledge you . . .']

　　　b.356, p. 110

D0366 Does Cr[eator?] sp[iri]ts awe
　　They fill Eternity's vast space.

　　　[Sir William Trumbull; rough draft]

　　　Trumbull Box: Poetry Box XIII/28

D0367 Does Halsted wear its native face?
　　Oh! Quick return no more to part.

　　　C[ecilia] B[urney], 'Verses occasioned by Mrs.
　　　Sandford's leaving Halsted . . . C. B. aged 11 years'

　　　c.486, fol. 36

D0368 Does Sh—y then affect the prude
　　That he's a common wencher!

　　　R[ichard] V[ernon] S[adleir], 'Lady Th—g's character
　　　brought to light—she complained of the aspect of her
　　　bedchamber being to the east and heated by the rising
　　　sun'

　　　c.106, p. 103

D0369 Does the pious Theophron
　　Who redeem'd her by his blood.

　　　T[homas] S[tevens], 'To Placentia . . . March 6. 1781'

　　　c.259, p. 132

D0370 Does then she feel for me the lambent flame
　　And each in blessing is more amply blessed.

　　　[Summer (July) 1764]

　　　c.136, p. 75

D0371 Does thy corrected frailty still complain
Grains of allowance and pardon must be had.

'On the memory'
b.118, p. 227

D0372 Dog's very choleric himself he feigns
Whate'er the cost he cares not he will bite.

'Answer' [to What? Ye great Syrius . . .']
b.356, p. 113

D0373 Domestic anguish drops o'er virtue's bier;
And write Prepare to die, on every heart.

H[annah] More, 'Epitaph on Mrs. Stonehouse . . .
December 18th 1788'
c.341, p. 36

D0374 Don Burgess the second,
To finish 'em now in November.

C[harles] E[arle], 'To a boot maker'
c.376

D0375 Dona in qualms, sent Abb her drab for ease
You'se understand ere lang.

'High church loyalty or a tale of Tory rebellion (To
the tune of Windsor Tarras)'
Poetry Box IV/80

D0376 Don't you know who I am
I'll make them look fair with my whitewash brush.

[John Walker?], 'The whitewash brush'
fc.108, fol. 29

D0377 Dorinda cheerful, young and gay,
Be warn'd, shun gaming and be wise.

'The effect of a passion for gaming'
c.83/1, no. 104

D0378 Dorinda's sparkling wit and eyes
She took up with the blind and lame.

[Charles Sackville, 6th earl of Dorset], 'On a lady [i.e.,
Catherine Sedley, countess of Dorchester] who
fancied herself a beauty' [1694]
[Crum D406; POAS V.384]
c.189, p. 1 (attr. Thomas Brown); fb.207/3, p. 37;
Trumbull Box: Poetry Box XIII/63 ('wit and sparkling
eyes; ll. 1-8)

D0379 Dorset, the grace of courts, the muses' pride,
And patriots still, or poets, deck the line.

A[lexander] Pope, 'An epitaph in the church of
Witheyam in Sussex, written by . . . on Charles Earl
of Dorset'
c.360/2, no. 204

D0380 Dorsetshire stream's insignificant . . . Wey,
And waters a fine fertile . . . land.

'Rebus no. 160 vol. 4th solved'
c.360/3, no. 82

D0381 Dost hear the bells ring, and the great cannons roar?
He's ne'er like more to have one hot meal.

'A dialogue on the campaign 1692'
b.111, p. 305

D0382 Dost see how unregarded now, that piece of beauty
passes
Have certain periods set, and hidden fates.

[Sir John Suckling]
[Crum D411]
b.213, p. 18

D0383 Dost stand? Go safely on—thy warrant's writ
A lion guards thee, from the Papal paws.

[Sir Philip Wodehouse], 'Upon Titus Oates . . .'
b.131, back (no. 197)

D0384 Dost thou, the important question ask
Tho' it discovers lurking sin.

[Thomas Stevens?], 'A hymn'
c.259, p. 61

D0385 Dost thou to live at Rome desire,
Is sure the way the good of life to find.

J[ohn] R[obinson], 'Quid Romae faciam? Mentiri
nescio'
c.370, fol. 68v

D0386 Doth the prosperity of a pardon, still
Cropt, branded, flit, and neck-stockt, go, y'ave
stript.

Ben Jonson(?), 'Ben: Jonson's reply' [to 'Is this your
lodestone . . .']
b.200, p. 15

D0387 Doth their bulls roar, why stop thy frighted ear
Will frustrate make them, spite of Innocent.

[on Innocent XI]
b.216, p. 157

D0388 Doth William Cole lie here, henceforth be stale
Burned up the coal; and turn'd it into ashes.

'On Wm. Cole an alehousekeeper at Caton near
Cambridge'
[Crum D423]
b.197, p. 45

D0389 Doubtless such frame, such temper of the mind
As my reviving hopes of bliss suggest.

[Edmund Wodehouse], 'June 24 [1715] John Baptist'
b.131, p. 226

D0390 Down came grave ancient S[ergean]t [Sir] Jo[hn]
Crooke
He'll 'scape out of prison without payment of fee.

[John Hoskins, 'The Parliament fart,' 1607]
[Crum D435 (var.)]
Poetry Box VII/38; see also 'Puffing comes down . . .'.

D0391 Down, down a thousand fathom deep,
There, in cool seas, I love to lave.

[Ann (Ward)] Radcliffe, 'The sea-nymph . . .
Udolpho'
c.83/2, no. 509

D0392 Down in the meadows were violets blue
Saying oh! that the war was all over.

[Mary (Shackleton) Leadbeater?], 'Polly's complaint
for her lover's absence, who is now a soldier in
America'
File 13409

D0393 'Down rebel crew'—the mitered Horsley cries,
'Hear me—ye thrones! dominions! princedoms!
powers!'

[William Parsons], 'On the Bishop of Rochester's late
speech . . . 3 Janry 1796'
Greatheed Box/54

D0394 Down rush the skies, and with impetuous rain,
Now with vast winds, the woods, now lashes he the
shores.

'Some passages from Virgil[.] The description of a
thunderstorm Geo: I v. 324'
File 13832

D0395 Down to the vale of life I tend,
And make them happy in their state.

'An old bachelor's reflections on matrimony'
c.130, p. 89; c.341, p. 51; c.391, p. 21; fc.132/1, p. 122

D0396 Down with this love that hath made such a pother,
We'll change no more gold, and good stones for
your glass.

'A defiance to beauty'
fb.107, p. 65

D0397 Downing, O Downing hear a wretch opprest
If not no penny dry: no penny wet.

'A dialogue between a scholar and an alehouse keeper:
to the same tune [Caron]'
b.197, p. 62

D0398 Doctor Pratier for an excellent physician,
A jester the Duke, the King a politician.

Poetry Box VII/5; see also 'Monmouth the witty . . .'.

D0399 Drake Howard, th'impudent'st bawd in town,
I could say more, but let that pass.

'Upon my Lord Salisbury, and his sisters'
[Crum D454]
fb.70, p. 65

D0400 Draulus who carries in his face
No.—He can play, and prate.

Abraham Oakes, 'An epigram. On the Revd.
Mr. A——'
c.50, p. 132

D0401 Draw England ruin'd by what was giv'n before,
Which most the Dutch or Parliament they fear.

'The fourth advice to a painter, for carrying on his
piece from London's conflagration to the burning of
our ships at Chatham by the Dutch . . . 1667'
[Crum D455; POAS I.141]
fb.140, p. 79; Poetry Box VII/37, 56; fb.70, p. 203; b.136,
p. 33 (ll. 1–132); c.160, fol. 16v (attr. Denham; ll. 1–132)

D0402 Draw him on his mercy seat
While endless life shall last.

T[homas] S[tevens], 'Experience Meeting . . .
March 14. [17]80'
c.259, p. 79

D0403 Draw me a lord standing in separation
Draw him, if possible thou canst, to fight.

'Directions to a painter, July 1679. Lord Roberts'
b.54, p. 1226

D0404 Draw near me brave boys I'll tell ye a story
And show the poor rogues they've at last caught a
tartar.

'A new ballad inscribed to the lawful voters of the
town of Northampton by Legal Freeman' [on the
disputed election of 1734]
Accession 97.7.40

D0405 Draw not too near unless you drop a tear
For she is dead, her soul is fled | Unto a place more
rare.

'Clora's epitaph' [sometimes attr. William Strode]
[Crum D462]
b.197, p. 30

D0406 Drawn by the countless charms of these retreats,
But hush! For o'er the lyre his fingers fly.

John Lockman, 'On the same occasion' [on Handel's
statue, carved by Roubiliac, in Vauxhall Gardens]
c.267/1, p. 161; c.268 (first part), p. 16 ('by the fame of
these embower'd retreats')

D0407 Dread dream! that hovering in the midnight air,
And steep my pillow with unpitied tears.

    [Erasmus] Darwin, 'The dream in a dangerous illness'

    c.142, p. 530

D0408 Dread is a thing—from love and honor springs
Turn'd from your loyalty—for gain or fear.

    [Sir Philip Wodehouse], 'Upon Sr Edward Turner no truer dread'

    b.131, back (no. 162)

D0409 Dread Madam if you'll rule this land in peace,
For poets dare at all adventures speak.

    'To the Queen'

    b.90, p. 14

D0410 Dread winter rules, and o'er the ravag'd plain—
Gilds every hope with pleasures yet to come.

    Maria [Done], 'A winter piece—to friendship'

    c.140, p. 71

D0411 Dreams are the shadows of this life, as this
Of Thee, who only wretched us canst save.

    [Edmund Wodehouse], 'Jan. 7 [1715]'

    b.131, p. 134

D0412 Dreams which in sleep their various scenes display,
And images of things confus'd awake.

    [Henry] Needler, 'Dreams'

    c.244, p. 544; c.83/2, no. 341

D0413 Drest in the charms of wit, and fancy long
Confess himself subdu'd, and wisely quit the field.

    [Henry] Needler, 'On Blackmore's creation'

    c.244, p. 552

D0414 Drink, drink, drink, all you that think
This cup of Apollo's nectar.

    'A song on the praise of drinking'
    [Crum D469]

    b.200, p. 126

D0415 Drink says old sophist, and then fear no evil
And so keep whetting wheresoever they go.

    'In socios seniores Coll: Oxon: [6]'

    c.81/1, no. 24

D0416 Drink we now, and beat the ground,
Great when living—great when dead.

    [William Popple, trans.], '[Horace] book 1st. ode 37th. To his companions'

    fc.104/2, p. 104

D0417 Drive slander, ye monarchs, far, far from your gate,
That a king's the true image of God.

    'An imitation of the stanzas in the chorus at the end of the fourth act of Racine's tragedy of Esther'

    c.360/3, no. 250

D0418 Drooping soul shake off thy fears
Thou art greater than my heart.

    'Hymn 38th'

    c.562, p. 44

D0419 Drop mournful eyes, your pearly trickling tears
Ne'er nonesuch near her corpse interred lie.

    [Joseph Sparrow?], 'On Dr. Hackett's wife'

    fb.143, p. 4

D0420 Drummond, while Phoebus shall with annual ray
Drummond, deserving of more noble lays.

    'On the birthday of John Drummond esqr by his ever devoted and faithful'

    Poetry Box XII/77

D0421 Drunk I was last night, that's poss'
And by degrees, I should have ease, having the pot
                           to sp[ew].

    c.160, fol. 84v

D0422 Drunk with excessive joy for victory
Who loves the father cannot hate the child.

    'On Dr. [William] Sherlock's sermons May 29th and Octob: 27th. 1692'

    b.111, p. 203

D0423 Dry barren arguments whereby we strive
Again an angel, king and priest appear.

    Thomas Traherne, '[Meditation (first century)] 90'

    b.308, p. 51

D0424 Dubius thy ears are two, thy tongue but one
Hear God and priest, confess to God alone.

    [Francis Quarles], 'On confession'

    b.137, p. 179

D0425 Duchess, to France I on thy steps did wait,
Enough, ambition! Thou canst grant no more.

    John Lockman, 'Presented to the Duchess of Buckingham, the evening of our return to Paris . . . 2d Decr. 1741'

    c.267/1, p. 74

D0426 Duck cackled verse on Richmond Green,
As bad a poet, and as great a goose.

    fb.68, p. 133

D0427 Ducus keeps house and it with reason stands
The he keeps house yet sold away his lands.

'On Ducus'

b.356, p. 103

D0428 Dudley methinks 'tis blessedness to full
Who made, who governs, and directs all things.

Joseph Lovell, 'Joined to the friend of my bosom . . . 4
mo 6. 1799'

Poetry Box v/2

D0429 Duke Lauderdale that lump of grease
Then our faith, freedom, and our pence.

[lampoon, 1674/5]
[Crum D487]

b.52/2, p. 133

D0430 Dull business hence, avoid the sacred round,
And Phoebus in her eyes.

c.358, p. 166

D0431 Dull fool; to mock a flame
That face of virtue, to the act of sin.

[George Daniel], 'To the Platonic pretender'

b.121, fol. 75v

D0432 Dull mortals measure by th'external hue
Outside, and inside strive to make alike.

H[enry] C[olman], 'On deformity'
[Crum D492]

b.2, p. 55

D0433 Dull sonnet-writing now runs dry
Must sentries thus your chamber clear.

'An acrostic [DIMPLE BELINGHAM] for Mrs.
Catherine [Villiers]'
[Crum D495]

b.113, p. 261

D0434 Dullness, to thee I consecrate my lays,
And Io paeans rend the vaulted skies.

'An address to dullness'

c.570/4, p. 112

D0435 Dumb with surprise when first the stroke was given,
Nor dear dispute what providence thinks fit.

Diggle Box: Poetry Box XI/53

D0436 Duns Scotus most dark, or Aquinas most dull,
Prove equally pow'rs and preacher divine!

[Charles Earle], 'Returned with a wretched sermon
(the author had sent me to peruse) on the powers
that be'

c.376 (2 copies)

D0437 During our youth let us provide for age,
For ere we think she stealeth on the stage.

c.339, p. 322

D0438 Dust, earth, and ashes is our strength,
We must return again.

b.234, p. 9 and 10

D0439 Dust is lighter than a feather,
Lighter than feather, dust, or wind.

'Quaestio . . . answer'

c.81/1, no. 268

E

E0001 Each art has one consistent settled rule,
The nymph consenting crowns the untuned lays.

> [George] H[owar]d, [6th earl of Carlisle], 'The art of courting'

c.197, p. 38

E0002 Each beau and belle,
Forever, and for aye.

> John Lockman, 'The happy downfall of French cambrics . . . March 1749'

c.267/1, p. 143

E0003 Each closing period thro' life's dubious maze,
While truth still lives and England has a name.

> [ ] Whittington, 'Vocat labor ultimus'

Diggle Box: Poetry Box XI/22

E0004 Each coxcomb first intent to kill
By scintillation of the nose.

> 'The difference'

fc.76.iii/214

E0005 Each day another man, another mind;
I am not blind; to my deformities.

> [George Daniel]

b.121, fol. 69v

E0006 Each day by Celia's request
The rest in tattling ends.

> R[obert] Shirley, 1st earl of Ferrers, 'From the French'

c.347, p. 92

E0007 Each day does death exert its pow'r
As on this stage it well or ill did act.

> [Edmund Wodehouse], 'Septr 26 [1715]'

b.131, p. 274

E0008 Each day Sir Minim does some dirty deed,
Goes oft to church, but never reads his Bible.

> 'On Sir Minim'

fc.53, p. 146

E0009 Each day we break the bond of human laws
The sweeping deluge love comes ere and conquers all.

> [Eliza (Fowler) Haywood?], 'Tit: pa: to 2d part of Love in excess'

c.549, p. 40

E0010 Each day's today, tomorrow and yesterday,
That future liest down present than bypast.

> [Sir Thomas Urquhart], 'Of today, tomorrow, and yesterday'

fb.217, p. 513

E0011 Each girl is a table book where men
Can blot out maidenhead and make her woman.

> [Sir Thomas Urquhart], 'How a virgin is to the impression of man'

fb.217, p. 395

E0012 Each grace of life retired.—these shine alone,
The favor'd few that share the sacred hour.

c.391, p. 72

E0013 Each grace of yours, men's fancy doth so tickle
As it obeys their several affections.

> Sir Thomas Urquhart, 'To Lady [crossed out]'

fb.217, p. 146

E0014 Each has his faults, we readily allow,
The heartfelt blessings of domestic peace.

> 'Epilogue to [Everyone has his faults, a comedy]'

c.83/3, no. 809

E0015 Each in your face this truly now doth see,
They read you right by heart, without the book.

> Lady Jane Cavendish, 'On an acquaintance' [Crum E8]

b.233, p. 19

E0016 Each little village yields his short and homely fare
And melancholy cures by sovereign hellebore.

> 'On a hermit's life'

c.158, p. 43

E0017 Each living corpse must yield at last to death
And is an image of eternity.

> 'Pindarus'

b.208, p. 67

E0018 Each man hath his own sense, and apprehension,
For that all men agree, there lacks, but will.

> Sir Thomas Urquhart, 'Why the world is at variance'

fb.217, p. 81

E0019 Each novice in philology know this
Thou dar'st be good in spite of names and times.

b.212, p. 73

E0020 Each of the twelve apostles being a sign
Christ is our sun, and faith th'ecliptic line.

Sir Thomas Urquhart, 'The Christian zodiac'

fb.217, p. 246

E0021 Each one in France has his own drinking glass
They would not need to have so many glasses.

[Sir Thomas Urquhart], 'Why in France and many other places the drinking each in his own several [c]up is so commonly receiv'd: and universally approven'

fb.217, p. 515

E0022 Each opportunity embrace,
To pry into their mysteries.

Sir Thomas Urquhart, 'How to purchase the affection of a gentlewoman'

fb.217, p. 142

E0023 Each 'parel of her body she hath sold,
There's none but Satan will give monies for it.

Sir Thomas Urquhart, 'On a bycast courtesan'

fb.217, p. 184

E0024 Each place some wonder can produce
And hearts to feed their friends with presents.

[Charles Burney, the elder], 'On the culinary productions of Norfolk'

c.33, p. 228

E0025 Each pocket in coat and in waistcoat I've sought
And happiness restore?

'To Miss Betty Coxe—on her parting with Miss Guise'

c.484, p. 57

E0026 Each shuns his brother, and each fears his friend!
Till nature, faint with anguish, sinks in sleep!

'Descriptive of the miseries of France'

c.83/2, no. 515

E0027 Each sweet attraction warmed with gentle fires
With raptures gaze, and call the graces four.

[Horace Walpole, 4th earl of Orford], 'Countess of Essex' [d. 1759]
[Crum E14]

c.157, p. 69

E0028 Each tree (so righteous providence has fixt)
Dame Nature's jury brings him in a cuckold.

R[obert] Shirley, 1st earl of Ferrers, 'Upon cuckoldom'

c.347, p. 74

E0029 Each wand'ring planet hath a heaven alone:
The fixed stars have 'mongst them all but one.

Sir Thomas Urquhart, 'The glory of inconstancy'

fb.217, p. 42

E0030 Each wight the baker with the pillory rallies,
Transferr'd the proverb to a blacker rogue.

John Lockman, 'On the unaccountable rise in the price of coals . . . April 1744'

c.267/1, p. 2

E0031 Each youth, who friendship's joys has prov'd
And friendship love their very shade.

'Lines written in a book of shades'

c.504, p. 213

E0032 Earl Walter winds his bugle horn;
Th'infernal cry of holla, ho!

'The chase, a poem from the German of Gottfried Augustus Bürger'

c.141, p. 479

E0033 Early remov'd from bleak misfortune's pow'r
Hath to eternal summer chang'd thy spring.

'Epitaph on a child'

c.83/3, no. 1021

E0034 Earth air and fire were with the water mixt
I do my [blank] my love my life adore.

[Robert Cottesford?]

b.144, p. 3

E0035 Earth has too long detain'd my feet
And saints with joy embrace.

T[homas] S[tevens], 'Hymn by . . . sung December the 1st. 1779. at Colchester'

c.259

E0036 Earth thou art a barren field
Darts at us to brandish.

'To earth a sonnet'

b.205, fol. 38r

E0037 Earth upon earth, consider may,
Earth shall from earth, pass poor away.

'An epitaph on Florence Caldwell'

c.244, p. 213

E0038 Earth's entertainments are like that of jail,
Her left hand brings me milk, her right a nail.

'The world's welcome'

b.118, p. 229

E0039 Echo I thee summon
If not lain with she's snappish.

'An echo'

c.356; see also 'Come Echo I thee summon . . .'.

E0040 Eclipsed from your sight, all joys I hate,
None can dissolve a true love's knot (once tied).

Thomas Rich, 'Thomas Rich gent. to Mrs. Ellen Bogan'

c.189, p. 49

E0041 Edina! Scotia's darling seat!
I shelter in thy honor'd shade.

R[obert] Burns, 'Address to Edinburgh'

c.142, p. 224

E0042 E'er since our blessed Savior was betrayed
To kiss his other end I mean his toe.

[Francis Quarles], 'On a kiss' [Divine Fancies III, 22]

b.137, p. 175; b.156, p. 13

E0043 E'er since the morning of the day,
And pardon its delaying wings.

[Isaac Watts], 'In a letter to Mother'

c.349, fol. 8

E0044 Egbert a young and valiant hero
And ev'ry joy on them bestow'd.

S. E. B[urney], 'Egbert and Ellen a legendary tale'

c.486, fol. 25

E0045 Egregious Wright of thy right hand bereft
Wright, should have had another left by right.

'On one Wright a writing master losing his hand by accident'

c.74

E0046 Egypt long time had to Israel's men
And with no fewer they shall it receive.

Sir John Strangways, 'The affliction of Israel translated by . . . out of Doctor Hall bishop of Exeter into verse: during his imprisonment in the Tower whither he was committed by the Parliament the 29th of November 1645 and continued to the 15th of May 1648'

b.304, p. 127

E0047 Elijah's example declares,
And leave all my cares in his hand.

[Thomas Stevens?], 'Every creature at God's command'

c.259, p. 60

E0048 Elisa, while your curious hand
And let me wish the portrait mine!

R[ichard] V[ernon] S[adleir], 'To a lady painting flowers and fruits'

c.106, p. 96

E0049 Eliza is a name of majesty
No misbecoming levity admit.

[Sir Philip Wodehouse], 'Upon an honorable lady my daughter Wodehouse's neighbor the Lady Elizabeth Musgrove'

b.131, back (no. 232)

E0050 Eliza that great maiden queen lies here,
Subjects her good deeds, princes her imitation.

Char[les] Best, 'An epitaph on Queen Elizabeth' [Crum E44]

b.197, p. 218

E0051 Eliza thou art just sixteen
I recommend myself.

[John Wolcot ('Peter Pindar')], 'To Eliza on her birthday'

File 16343

E0052 Eliza was beyond compare
And mournfully expir'd.

'A ballad founded on fact'

c.83/1, no. 69

E0053 Ella, like some inferior creature,
To warm your wits, sweet Sirs, I'm yours!

R[ichard] V[ernon] S[adleir], 'On an incident happening where I was'

c.106, p. 97

E0054 Emblem of him, in whom no stain
Are not array'd like me.

[George Horne, bishop of Norwich], 'The lily'

Diggle Box: Poetry Box XI/48

E0055 Emblem of purity! Thyself less pure
He chang'd thy nature, he transforms their soul.

Charles Atherton Allnutt, 'Sonnet on Christ's changing water into wine'

c.112, p. 148

E0056 Embrace a sunbeam, and on it
More than a Delphian deity.

'Impossibilities'
[Crum E50a]

c.158, p. 103

E0057 *Emula campana* strengthens each inward part
Great help to these that have their belly broken.

    [Joshua Sylvester, trans. Guillaume de Salluste,
    seigneur Du Bartas], 'Of emula campana'

b.284, p. 53

E0058 Enamel'd rock! adieu: I see
Survive the worst her fire could do.

    'To Celia proving unfaithful'

b.104, p. 20

E0059 Enchanting sight! A poet thus to bless,
Soft pity touch'd him, and he dropt a tear.

    John Lockman, 'Seeing my table covered with silver
    sent me by a great lady, who honors me with her
    patronage . . . Novr. 1740'

c.267/1, p. 247

E0060 Enchanting smiler gentle be thy rest,
Their parent dies, and saddens all the shade.

    'To an infant sleeping in the arms of its mother'

c.83/1, no. 74

E0061 Enclos'd within this silent tomb
To join the rapt'rous song.

    'Epitaph on Mr. Pope'
    [Crum E54]

c.360/2, no. 267

E0062 Encompast with troubles and shatter'd by grief
To see their fond mother exult in the sight.

    [William Hayley], 'Song'

File 6963

E0063 Encounter then my soul with harder things
To bring his soldiers home he never miss'd.

    [Mary Serjant]

fb.98, fol. 164

E0064 Encouraged by Thy word
But God receives a sinner's pray'r.

    [Thomas Stevens?], 'The beggar . . . December the 18.
    1779. Omieron'

c.259, p. 63

E0065 End here; and O! remember ere too late,
By Pallas, when she finds herself outdone.

    [J. B.], 'To Miss Ward of Dublin, on seeing her
    picture of Sir Kenelm Digby in needlework
    unfinished'

Poetry Box IV/155

E0066 Endow'd with all that fortune could bestow;
In silence falls—while spring is blooming round.

    [Edward Jerningham], 'To the memory of a young
    lady'

c.90

E0067 Endu'd with all that could adorn,
At once the lover and the friend.

    'The lover and the friend'

c.364, p. 21

E0068 Engaging people! Form'd for social joys,
So sky-born Hebe o'er your feasts preside.

    John Lockman, 'On the French: in return for civilities
    received, when among them . . . 1741'

c.267/1, p. 17

E0069 England beware for the people are come,
Sure none but the devil himself can come after.

    ['The Hanover crew', 1714]
    [Crum E63]

fc.58, p. 64

E0070 England by all thought beauty's natural soil,
I give good counsel which I ne'er can take.

    [Thomas?] Skipwith, 'A satire—on Tunbridge Wells
    1680'

b.54, p. 1128

E0071 England hath his one fate peculiar to her,
Never to want a party to undo her.

    'On England'

c.189, p. 24

E0072 England, Netherland, the heavens and the arts
All soldiers his grief, the world his good name.

    'An epitaph in old St. Paul's church in London over
    the grave of the Honorable Sir Philip Sidney'
    [Crum E67]

c.360/2, no. 55; fb.143, p. 21; fb.69, p. 208

E0073 England proud, as I came through't
For there's nae fending alive without her.

    'A Scots song'

c.530, p. 42

E0074 England unknown as yet unpeopl'd lay
And so have left the king and them together.

c.158, p. 54

E0075 Enjoin'd by my fair one to write one song more,
To be true to the charms of *le je ne sais quoi*.

    W. Buller, 'Le je ne sais quoi'

c.341, p. 13

E0076 Enjoy and use your goods, your houses and your
lands,
Because the Lord unto that end, commits them to
your hands.

c.339, p. 325

E0077 Enjoy the present time, be thankful for the past,
And neither wish, nor fear th'approaches of the
last.

b.155, p. 63; c.549, p. 34 ('present minute')

E0078 Enjoy thy bondage, make thy prison know
Stout Felton, England's ransom, here doth lie.

Z[ouch] Towneley, 'To Felton in the tower for killing
Villiers Duke of Buckingham' [1628]
[Crum E74]

b.200, p. 120; b.62, p. 37; b.356, p. 138

E0079 Enlight'ning grace hath from your mind abolish'd
To th'holy progress of your soul's instruction.

Sir Thomas Urquhart, 'To my Lord [crossed out]'

fb.217, p. 168

E0080 Enough—and leave the rest to fame,
'Twas more significant, that she's dead!

'An epitaph on Mrs. Elizabeth Hampton'

c.244, p. 283

E0081 Enough! Enough! My soul of worldly noise,
No fortune can exalt, but death will climb as high.

[George Granville, 1st baron] Lansdowne, 'On death'

c.244, p. 153

E0082 Enough, keen satirist! enough thy pen
And leaves no room for thy satiric rage.

'To Mr. [Alexander] Pope upon sending the Dunciad
to V. C.'

c.116, p. 38

E0083 Enough, my Muse, of earthly things,
That he will still require some waters to his blood.

[Abraham Cowley, trans.], 'Christ's passion taken out
of a Greek ode, written by Mr. Masters of New
College in Oxford'
[Crum E81]

b.118, p. 33

E0084 Enough to glory and his country given
To cheer the darkling horrors of the night.

'Verses on the retirement of some great man. From
Jack's papers'

Spence Papers, folder 113

E0085 Enough to sorrow my indulgent fire
To love the living and revere the dead.

[William Hayley], 'Sonnet . . . Sept. 23 [1800]'
File 6968

E0086 Enter, chaste nymph! As op'ning lilies fair,
But be what wisdom, and just heaven ordain.

John Lockman, 'On reviewing, from his most
ingenious friend Mr. Christopher Smart, No I, of a
periodical pamphlet, entitled The universal visitor . . .
Feb. 1756'

c.267/1, p. 103

E0087 Enter O see this tomb (Sirs) do not fear
A speedy resurrection from the grave.

R[obert] W[ild], 'Upon some bottles of wine laid in
sand and covered with a sheet'
[Crum E89]

c.166, p. 325

E0088 Enthron'd above the spangled sky,
Who fain would change his heaven for thine.

'A lap dog'

c.172, p. 39

E0089 Enthusiasts, Lutherans, and monks,
Kindly forgives them all.

'Toleration'

c.81/1, no. 264

E0090 Entomb'd with kings though Gay's cold ashes lie
Belov'd in life, in bemoan'd in death by Pope.

[John Boyle], 5th earl of Orrery, 'Verses by . . .
occasioned by seeing Mr. Pope's epitaph on Mr. Gay'
[Crum E94]

c.144, p. 147

E0091 Entreat me not Stella to go
Remember his Mira was true.

Mrs. [ ] West, 'A pastoral poem'

c.83/2, no. 302

E0092 Envious grown to share the gain
Promis'd, for your age's store.

[William Popple, trans.], '[Horace] Book 1st. ode
29th. To Iccius'

fc.104/2, p. 82

E0093 Envious men, when neighbor's house doth flame,
It is not ours, let others care that will.

b.234, p. 11

E0094 Envy by self oppressed, one day to Love thus taunting said
Envy turned pale, and shrunk behind as they approach'd Ware Park.

J. B. D[ickinson], 'Acrostic' [Eleanor Byde]

c.391

E0095 Envy I'm told my gentle friend
And to thy purer mind.

[William Hayley], 'To Eliza on learning that her translation of Madam Lambert was said to be mine'

Poetry Box x/19

E0096 Envy so much men's virtues doth deface,
It makes them foes, to them they should embrace.

c.339, p. 309

E0097 Envy, that loves not merit, ne'er will spare
And spare thy glorious father's honor'd name.

'To Lady Tyrconnel'

c.130, p. 30; c.150, p. 53

E0098 Envy the praise of the [?] with gore
As worms the bodies of the dead devour.

[Sir Thomas Urquhart], 'Envy not greatness for thou makest envy is a [?] worm thereby thyself the worse and so thou distance greatness'

fb.217, p. 393

E0099 Equal alike to joy and sorrow
The rough Ægean, when it roars.

b.154, p. 5

E0100 Erasmus did The praise of folly write,
Which folly of his express'd his pregnant wit.

Sir Thomas Urquhart, 'Upon Erasmus his encomium of foolishness'
[cf. Crum E101]

fb.217, p. 235

E0101 Ere epilogue or prologue did begin;
If Satire did not grin, and growl, and guard the coast.

'An epilogue'

b.204, p. 36

E0102 Ere foreign deleterious drugs were known,
And thou, O Melville! Art my butt entire.

'Brewariana'

c.340

E0103 Ere I go hence and be no more
Nourish in's breast, a tree of life.

R[obert] Herrick, 'R. Herrick's daughter's dowry'
[Crum E105]

b.197, p. 11

E0104 Ere I lov'd I could frolic and play,
And teach me my anguish to heal.

'Song 19'

c.555, p. 25

E0105 Ere I saw Sylvia, I with ease,
And were no longer what they were.

c.549, p. 25

E0106 Ere in court favors further you advance,
A regent, a young king and D'Ancre's fate.

[on Louis XIII, his mother Marie de Medici, and Marquis d'Ancre]

Poetry Box I/137

E0107 Ere manhood is reach'd, the fond youth tells his tale,
Who in courtship are honest, or mean to deceive.

'A caution to unthinking females'

c.116, p. 49

E0108 Ere old Rome's city could corrupted be
These civic honors give a real fame.

'On Admiral Vernon's being presented with the freedom of the city of London'

c.360/2, no. 67

E0109 Ere sin could blight or sorrow fade
And bid it blossom there.

'Epitaph on an infant'

Poetry Box IV/43

E0110 Ere the blue heav'ns were stretch'd abroad
The glories of Emanuel!

[Isaac Watts, Hymns and spiritual songs (1707), bk. I, Hymn 2]

c.180, p. 2

E0111 Ere the foundations of the world were laid,
Ten thousand thousand rolling years are naught.

John Gay, 'A thought on eternity'

c.139, p. 101

E0112 Ere the Red Sea had Israel cross'd
And ever since, the Jews are thieves.

[John Walker?], 'Historical facts a hymn tune St. Martin's Lane'

fc.108, fol. 77v

E0113 Ere the sun rise, light shines to ev'ry nation;
Because the light, was first in the creation.

Sir Thomas Urquhart, 'Of the aurore'

fb.217, p. 329

E0114 Ere this firm hand procures eternal rest,
Let stern parental duty speak the rest.

[Helen Craik], 'The right honorable the Earl of
Caithness to Miss D——'

c.375, p. 47

E0115 Ere to the real groves I go,
Enjoy these pleasures in a dream.

John Lockman, 'Flavia's wish for one more Italian
opera, this season . . . May 1755'

c.267/1, p. 148

E0116 Ere yet affliction's tears, have ceas'd to flow,
A sister's love, may claim protection here!

c.340

E0117 Ere yet commenc'd the wondrous day
A race accepted in thy sight.

Charles Atherton Allnutt, 'Collect for the third
Sunday in Advent'

c.112, p. 54

E0118 Ere you read this you'll suppose that some now
listed lover
But those would better hold a string than here let
monkeys rule us.

'A song' [to the tune of Sally &c.]

c.374; Trumbull Box: Poetry Box XIII/95

E0119 Esau goes forth strives with his own disquiet
'Twill please my father, and procure my blessing.

[Francis Quarles], 'On Esau and Jacob' [Divine
fancies III, 41]

b.137, p. 171

E0120 Escap'd from storms, and tempests, wrecks and ills,
Hoping for rest, after the ills I've past.

'Epitaph on a Jack Tar who had sailed round the
world. Written by his shipmate'

c.360/3, no. 180

E0121 Essex prays
And Cromwell quaffs.

[cf. Crum E122]

fb.69, p. 150

E0122 Esteem't not incivility;
The clock could not but sound the hour.

Sir Thomas Urquhart, 'Here one excuseth a certain
aged gentleman, who as he was ready to pay his
matrimonial debt, to his bedfellow so carried that she
affectionately reaching her hand to his Venerian cane,
no sooner had touched it: but out of too much
fervency. . . . he did let a 'scape'

fb.217, p. 352

E0123 Eteocles and Polinyes, brethren were
Then kindred, country God and all—goodbye.

[Sir Philip Wodehouse], 'The Oedipolis'

b.131, p. 9

E0124 Eternal and immortal King!
As only portion and delight.

P[hilip] Doddridge, 'The invisible God. From
Heb. XI.27 he endured as seeing him who is invisible'

c.493, p. 39

E0125 Eternal God, at thy command
To be dispos'd by Thee.

[Tho[ma]s Gibbons, 'Recovery from sickness [from]
Juvenile poems'

c.186, p. 29

E0126 Eternal God! Creator good and wise,
To God which was, which is, and is to come.

H[annah] M[ore], 'A paraphrase attempted on the 8th
psalm'

c.341, p. 58

E0127 Eternal happiness is gained in time
In time to gain a blessed eternity.

[Mary Serjant]

fb.98, fol. 49

E0128 Eternal joy will best befit,
For him that lived and died for thee.

H[enry] C[olman], 'On his birthday'
[Crum E130]

b.2, p. 69

E0129 Eternal King is there one hour
Or set the prisoners free.

[Mary Barber], 'Written in the conclusion of a letter
to Mr. Tickell recommending Mrs. Gordon's petition'

Poetry Box IV/132

E0130 Eternal mind by whose most just commands,
That I may to thy wonted freedom thee restore.

'King James' sufferings described by himself. A
Pindaric'

b.111, p. 9

E0131 Eternal Power, whose high abode
And praise sits silent on our tongues.

[Isaac Watts], 'The conclusion; God exalted above all
praise'

c.186, p. 43

E0132 Eternal slave and mistress of quadrille
But where's my lord to dote, my lord to pay?

   [Horace Walpole, 4th earl of Orford], 'Countess of
   Carl[isl]e'

   c.157, p. 69

E0133 Eternal sleep! Ye monsters none deny it,
To men once human, now transform'd to brutes.

   Charles Atherton Allnutt, 'Epigram on the French
   doctrine of eternal sleep'

   c.112, p. 149

E0134 Eternal source of ev'ry joy
When days and years revolve no more.

   P[hilip] Doddridge, 'God crowning the year with his
   goodness Ps. LXVII for New Year's Day'

   c.493, p. 14

E0135 Eternal Sovereign, we confess
But then they'll be forever mine.

   T[homas] S[tevens], 'God's right to assert his
   sovereignty over his creatures. Job. Ch. 9. 12 verse'

   c.259, inserted after p. 16

E0136 Eternal wisdom arm'd with might
My conscience (which is thine) expend.

   [Thomas Stanley], 'Meditat: XI. Upon the
   propositions sent to the King'

   b.152, p. 34

E0137 Ethereal source of cheerful light!
Or can I ask, or can you give?

   [Isaac Freeman], 'Hymn to the morning'

   fc.105

E0138 Europe gives Lin[col]n's happy shape due praise,
She stoutly once refused her husband's bed.

   [Horace Walpole, 4th earl of Orford], 'Count[es]s of
   Lincoln' [d. 1760]
   [Crum E141]

   c.157, p. 68

E0139 European vain, mock not my hue
And death a tyrant then.

   'Epitaph on a Negro servant'

   fc.132/1, p. 177

E0140 Europia fair love's chiefest care
Curl'd kissing pressing you will save the world.

   'Jupiter and Europia'

   c.503, p. 59

E0141 Euterpe, fairest of the virgin nine
For lovely Delia, in Miss Betty Chowne.

   'Verses on Miss Betty Chowne by the name of Delia
   1741'

   c.360/2, no. 168

E0142 Evank is a word of great fame,
Spell it backwards, it is your name.

   [John Rose?]

   b.227, p. 70

E0143 Eve was a wife as soon's she was a woman,
To try that, which they ought not [?] marry.

   [Sir Thomas Urquhart], 'Eve compared to many of
   her sex, more [?] that are marriageable'

   fb.217, p. 538

E0144 Eve was debarr'd from th'only fruit of one,
Because she had more liberty than you.

   Sir Thomas Urquhart, 'To a gentlewoman, whose
   neglect in cuckolding her husband is compared to
   Evah's tasting of the forbidden fruit'

   fb.217, p. 197

E0145 Even as a flower, or like unto the grass:
So is our fate: now here, now hence we pass.

   c.339, p. 328

E0146 Even as the tree doth flourish fine,
Where we his praise may ever sing. | Amen

   'Of S. Luke. Octo. 18'

   a.30[44]

E0147 Ev'n ev'ry sense has some delight,
That is, to sound our Maker's praise.

   [Edmund Wodehouse], 'Octr. 23 [1714]'

   b.131, p. 66

E0148 Ev'n here on earth her happiest,
Our souls must soar to His throne above.

   [Edmund Wodehouse], 'Octr. 9 [1714]'

   b.131, p. 56

E0149 Even hidden manna that our souls may see
But thou Commander of eternal light.

   [Mary Serjant]

   fb.98, fol. 166

E0150 Ev'n so dead Hector thrice was triumpht on
So vile a Price ne'er ransom'd such a prince.

   R[ichard] Corbett, 'An antianniversary' [on Daniel
   Price's anniversary sermon on the death of Prince
   Henry; answered by 'So to dead Hector . . .']
   [Crum E157]

   b.200, p. 211

E0151 Even such is time which takes in trust
The Lord will raise me up I trust.

Sir Walter Raleigh, 'Sir Walter Raleigh's epitaph on
himself'
[Crum E159]

fb.143, p. 14; fb.69, p. 208; b.356, p. 250; c.547, p. 332
(epitaph used for Wilfred Lawson); Poetry Box VI/107

E0152 Ever let him want a hopeful happy end
Which by the issue, doth the art commend.

fb.151/3

E0153 Every bird was made for use;
Jove chose a swan—I like a goose.

[Frederick Corfield], 'The motto which I intend to
have gilded on the carriage when finished'

c.381/1

E0154 Every Christian heart seeketh to extol
Directing her faith to Christ the only mark.

'On one Eliz. the wife of Emanuel Lucar' [d. 29 Oct.
1537, aged 27]

fb.143, p. 8; see also 'She wrought all needlework . . .'.

E0155 Ev'ry man take a glass in his hand,
Here's a health to all honest men.

[Thomas D'Urfey?], 'A health to all honest men'
Poetry Box IV/33; see also 'Nine tripled and two . . .'.

E0156 Ev'ry man tho' his son's but a booby
An archbishop he'll be, and charm the whole nation.

[John Lockman], 'The wisdom of parents'
c.268 (first part), p. 85

E0157 Ev'ry man to King James drink a health
To the honor of James our King.

'The King's health' [c. 1715]
fc.58, p. 34

E0158 Every mortal some favorite pleasure pursues,
And my pleasures confine to my dogs and my gun.

'Song 66'
c.555, p. 94

E0159 Evil by custom, as by nature frail
To raise me hence and seek my rest above?

'From Petrarch'
fb.66/20

E0160 Exactly here, thy awful form we trace;
Form'd to rule mighty states, and charm mankind.

John Lockman, 'Writ under a print of Cardinal
Fleury, given by Monsieur Barjac, to the author, at
Versailles . . . 1741'

c.267/1, p. 14

E0161 Exalted genius! To whose skill we owe
And tipp'd thy pencil with his glorious fire.

John Lockman, 'Seeing, at Lord Folkestone's gallery
at Longford, near Salisbury, two capital pictures of
clouds [?], representing morning and evening . . . Aug.
1757'

c.267/1, p. 116

E0162 Excel, and emulate thy parent's praise;
Never forsake, deep rooted in thy heart.

Ann Murry
c.248

E0163 Excellent Brutus! Of all human race
A[nd] show'd thee a God crucified.

[Abraham] Cowley, 'Brutus'
c.244, p. 225

E0164 Excellent mistress fairer than the moon
As I hope to be saved I love you dearly.

[Crum E182]

b.197, p. 163

E0165 Excellent prince! To kingdoms heir,
This scheme will all her wants supply.

John Lockman, 'Stanzas, on the depravity of mankind.
On occasion of some most iniquitous practices, in the
undertaking of the Herring Fishery. To his royal
highness the Prince of Wales, governor . . . Aug. 1754'

c.267/1, p. 323

E0166 Except that wisdom evermore ensue,
We lose our time and books in vain do view.

c.339, p. 321

E0167 Except the Lord do give success,
Or in the courts must plead best.

'Psalm 127'
c.264/3, p. 73

E0168 Except the Lord sustain the pile
His foes repel, his age support.

'The same [Psalm 127], another meter'
c.264/3, p. 74

E0169 Excuse fair Belinda, and deign to attend
I'll secure you the game by the gift of a heart.

'To Belinda a young lady passionately fond of gaming'
c.83/3, no. 959

E0170 Excuse me Sirs I pray—I can't yet speak—
Pronounce him regular or dub him quack.

[David] Garrick, 'Prologue to She stoops to conquer
or the mistakes of a night. Written by . . . spoken by
Mr. Woodward'

c.68, p. 150

E0171 Excuse the verse that strives to show
Only to rise again more fair.

'To Mira'

Poetry Box I/44

E0172 Exhausted by her painful throes,
Those virtues, I adore in thee.

[Jeffrey Ekins], 'On going into his wife [Anna]'s room
and finding her asleep, after she was brought to bed'

c.157, p. 110; c.391, p. 25

E0173 Exil'd by fate's severe decrees
Confess contentment beams around.

[Helen Craik], 'To Mr. D—— from Goat Whey
quarters'

c.375, p. 20

E0174 Expect not, reader, to misspend thy time
In pity veil their splendors from our eyes.

'Designed for myself'

c.221, p. 22

E0175 Expedients have in vain been tried
Can fix it in the air.

R[obert] Shirley, 1st earl of Ferrers, 'A passion for
politics in church and state deduced from the stand in
the tree, and the menagerie'

c.347, p. 111

E0176 Experience tells no places may compare
Unto our homes, where no commanders are.

c.339, p. 315

E0177 Experience tells that agues are about
Confession profits not unless we mend.

[Francis Quarles], 'On confession' [Divine
fancies III, 51]

b.137, p. 192

E0178 Exposed to every snare we stand
Where all shall own the reign of grace.

T[homas] S[tevens]

c.259, p. 139

E0179 Extinguish the candles Phoebus fair play
Here's the girl that we love and the friends we can
trust.

'Song 171'

c.555, p. 266

E0180 Exult, young Perkin! With your farcic clan,
(Mad Highlanders!) And after in your king.

John Lockman, 'After reading the list of persons, who
formed the Young Pretender's council . . . Oct. 1745'

c.267/1, p. 152

E0181 Eye-flattering fortune look then ne'er so fair,
Then after thy calm look I for a storm.

[William Roper, in The life of Sir Thomas More,
knight]

a.25, p. 104

E0182 Eye no more yon blooming fair
Her aim is ruin—ah, *mon Dieu.*

[Frederick Corfield], 'An acrostic [Elizabeth]'

c.381/1

E0183 Eye-service is the common guise
As what is done most openly.

[Edmund Wodehouse], 'Aug. 23 [1715]'

b.131, p. 251

E0184 Eyes that improve the luster of the day
Envy itself must her bright name revere.

'Acrostic on Miss [Elizabeth] Vere [later Howard],
daughter of Thomas Vere of the city of Norwich,
esqr: written at Bury 1734'

c.360/1, p. 61

E0185 Ezekiel's mystical vision doth afford
Let all true Christian eagles(?) thither fly.

[Edward] Sparke, 'Poem 14th, on the ascension'

b.137, p. 36

F

F0001   Fade beauteous flow'r nor mourn thy transient date
Flavia would scorn one, as she now does you.

     'On seeing a flower in a lady's bosom'
     c.83/1, no. 206

F0002   Fade flowers fade nature will have it so
That none for them can when they perish grieve.

     [Edmund] Waller, 'From the French'
     fc.60, p. 52

F0003   Fain I would if I could by any means obtain,
You'd pluck him from his throne, and make that
                         too your own.

     'King Charles 1st song'
     [Crum F2]
     fb.140, p. 14

F0004   Fain I'd comply with what you're pleas'd to ask;
Can raise the luster of the radiant stone.

     'Carolina's answer' [to 'Madam, tho' oft . . .']
     c.83/1, no. 253

F0005   Fain would I dare a lover's grief relate
Dear Bessie Bell, I'll o'er Kale water swim.

     J[ohn] K[err] of F[ro]g[de]n, 'To Mrs. B[ess]y
     B[?enne]t'
     c.102, p. 119

F0006   Fain would I sing the pow'r supreme,
'Tis thine to wonder and adore.

     [ ] Lewis, 'An ode to God'
     c.244, p. 186

F0007   Fain would my thoughts fly up to thee,
Now and forever be. | Amen

     [John Austin], 'Hym. 6' [Hymn xi, Devotions in the
     ancient way of offices, 1672, p. 102]
     c.178, p. 5

F0008   Fair Albion of the world the fairest isle,
Enclose as due my body in her earth.

     [George Daniel]
     b.121, fol. 34v

F0009   Fair Amarinta if thy eyes
Such and as great as feeds my flame.

     b.213, p. 56

F0010   Fair as creation in its pride
Stop muse and wonder, at untainted youth.

     'Acrostic on Miss Frances Jeffreys—Bath 1736'
     c.360/1, p. 17

F0011   Fair as unshaded light; or as the day
Then in their sleeps forgiven hermits are.

     [Sir William D'Avenant], 'D'Avenant to the Queen'
     fb.66/34

F0012   Fair author of my hopeless flame,
A spaniel's loss, by which men daily die.

     R[obert] Shirley, 1st earl of Ferrers, 'Stanza. From
     Voiture. To a lady grieving the loss of her lapdog'
     c.347, p. 90

F0013   Fair Beatrice tuckt her coats up somewhat high
And yet between them both a man was born.

     [John Taylor], 'On Beatrice'
     [Crum F28]
     b.200, p. 81; b.62, p. 3 ('used to tuck')

F0014   Fair blew the winds, the vessel sails:
Unrivall'd in her Sidney's breast.

     [ ] Pearson, 'Pearson's Medallion'
     c.83/2, no. 542

F0015   Fair blossom of the snowy vest,
Disport it in thy praise.

     Dr. [ ] Thompson, 'The snowdrop. An ode'
     c.141, p. 351

F0016   Fair boy, alas! why fliest thou me,
So thou shouldst need no shade, but I.

     [Henry Rainolds], 'The black maid to the fair boy'
     [answered by 'Black girl, complain not . . .']
     [Crum F30, with Crum G379]
     b.200, p. 6

F0017   Fair Caroline, most lovely maid,
And shines an angel there.

     'On the death of Miss C[aroline] Fisher'
     c.83/3, no. 783

F0018   Fair Celia adieu!
And the birds shall sit over, and weep.

     'The resolute lover'
     fb.107, p. 20

F0019 Fair Celia walking in the plain
When Phoebus doth his f[l]ames disclose.

'On his mistress walking in the rain'
b.356, p. 75

F0020 Fair charity! 'tis thine to wipe away
And weeping friend the tear unbidden shed.

'To charity'
c.83/4, no. 1093

F0021 Fair charmer see how various poets meet
And gild it with a beam from your bright eye.

'To a fair lady sent with a miscellany of poems'
Poetry Box VI/38

F0022 Fair Chloris I will praise so high
Do after any christ'ning feast | So much as me.

R[obert] Shirley, 1st earl of Ferrers, 'A song from
Voiture'
c.347, p. 35

F0023 Fair Chloris in a pigsty lay
She innocent, and pleas'd.

[John Wilmot, 2nd earl of Rochester], 'Song to
Chloris'
b.105, p. 133; Poetry Box VI/88 (incomplete)

F0024 Fair Chloris you ne'er can
Prove ever fatal to the proud, and great.

'Song'
Poetry Box I/111[1]

F0025 Fair copy of my Celia's face,
Only because you are her coin.

[Thomas Carew, 'Of one like his Celia . . . song']
[Crum F36]
b.197, p. 143; b.225, p. 131 (stanzas 1–5); b.356, p. 78

F0026 Fair copy of the fairest flower
How much I wish the trial mine.

[Henry Fox, 1st baron Holland], 'To L[ad]y Pembroke
with an artificial flower, 1725'
Poetry Box II/16

F0027 Fair dream of my slumber and thoughts of my
                                                    waking
When the web we have burst can be woven no more.

W. Reader, jr., 'Indian melodies, arranged by C: E
Horn the poetry by. . . .'
Diggle Box: Poetry Box XI/24

F0028 Fair Eve, by Satan's guileful speeches won,
Spread rosy health thro' Stella's aching heart.

Dr. [ ] Thompson, 'His daughter Sally recovered from
a violent fever . . . Feb. 1753'
c.267/1, p. 74

F0029 Fair fall their wits whoever first did frame
Better . . . [torn]

Poetry Box IV/106 (damaged)

F0030 Fair flower, be wise, nor fruitless bloom in vain
And crown thy pleasure with a mother's joy.

'To Paloria on a single life . . . Tunbridge Wells—1727'
c.360/1, p. 31

F0031 Fair hand that can on virgin paper write,
So much the [?] goes beyond the pen.

[Edmund Waller], 'Of a fair lady that cut free in
paper'
[Crum F54]
fb.228/58

F0032 Fair Hebe, lovely Hebe's gone—
Bedew'd from Colin's eyes.

'The death of Hebe'
Poetry Box XII/98

F0033 Fair Helen, that Paris long fought for,
To get quit of bewitching Lepell.

[Elizabeth (Shirley) Compton, countess of
Northampton], '4 verses added to The praise of
Lepell'
Accession 97.7.40

F0034 Fair Herbert, while with wild theatrical rage,
Or teach the way to keep him, in his seat.

'To the hon[orable] Mrs. Hobart [i.e., Herbert?]'
c.90

F0035 Fair innocen[ce] the muses' loveliest theme,
Beauty is but your second excellence.

[Mary Barber], 'To the Honble Miss Carteret' [later
countess of Dysart; supposedly by the widow Mary
Gordon. Pr. 1725 (Foxon B80)]
File 13409; Poetry Box IV/133

F0036 Fair is the face of earth, when cheerful spring
Who dying sleep, to wake in endless bliss.

'An elegy on the death of my nephew Henry Bates,
who died in December 1774 of a consumption illness,
at the age of nine years . . . January 1775'
fc.74, p. 29

F0037 Fair kind and true, a treasure each alone
So loved when living and when dead so mourn'd.

[John Dryden], 'Taken out of Twickenham church
July 25 1734'
c.547, p. 232

F0038 Fair ladies three whose playful lays
If Walcot I forget or race of Clive.

Poetry Box II/20

F0039 Fair maid whose wand'ring footsteps stray
Our constancy shall own.

    'Strephon to Delia'

c.89, p. 25

F0040 Fair marble, tell to future days,
That death mistook them both for one.

    'Epitaph on two twin sisters, who died at the same
    time, and were buried in one grave'

c.360/3, no. 53

F0041 Fair mistress of the moving art,
He's little else to recommend him.

    J. M., 'The answer to Carolina' [*i.e.*, to 'Your verses,
    complaisant . . .']

c.83/1, no. 255

F0042 Fair, modest, wise, let my beloved be,
And let me live deserving such as she.

    [John Rose?]

b.227, p. 75

F0043 Fair Narcissa when you left me
Till thou charming spring return.

b.71, p. 24

F0044 Fair nymph! In pride of beauty drest,
Which ev'n unkindness can't destroy.

    John Lockman, 'Translations, and imitations from
    Metastasio, and other Italian opera poets [4]'

c.267/4, p. 95

F0045 Fair nymph, whose verses sweet and free
Thy present, which will ever live.

    [William?] Hayley, 'Verses from . . . to Miss
    Williams, upon her wishing to see his house'

c.83/4, no. 1092

F0046 Fair on thee may Venus shine!
Wicked man his pow'r defies.

    [William Popple, trans.], '[Horace] book 1st. ode 3rd.
    To the ship on which Virgil embarked when going to
    Athens'

fc.104/2, p. 10

F0047 Fair opening spring in lovely blossoms dress'd
And whilst we live, we'll never cease to love.

    'Pastoral Pyramus and Sylvia'

c.91, p. 205

F0048 Fair Phyllis dances through the streets in white,
Or make amends by giving one that's green.

c.53, fol. 21

F0049 Fair Phyllis, last night in a jocular vein,
And sweetly revenge thy whole sex by a kiss!

    R[ichard] V[ernon] S[adleir], 'On a young lady who
    complained of a weakness of eyes and borrowed
    spectacles in jest and fell asleep in company and being
    called to the card table scarce found her way'

c.106, p. 59

F0050 Fair praise is sterling gold—all should desire it.
Nay, court the smiling harlot's very kisses.

    John Wolcot ('Peter Pindar'), 'Praise and flattery'

c.355, p. 196

F0051 Fair princess let me not complain,
Then princess don't disdain me.

    'The Duke of Lorraine's courtship to the Princess
    Royal tune of Princess royal'
    [first part of Crum F86]

c.536

F0052 Fair Psyche yield to Cupid's sway:
All pleasures are in love combin'd.

    John Lockman, 'The charms of loving [translated
    from La Fontaine] . . . set to music by Dr. Boyce'

c.267/4, p. 203

F0053 Fair rose, to thee all other flowers must yield
Not from the red, nor white, but the black rose.

    'The rose written 1716'

c.360/2, no. 216

F0054 Fair shone thy dawn, each muse thy bosom fir'd,
And, to the ear, the subtlest(?) sounds convey'd.

    John Lockman, 'To Lord Middlesex [later duke of
    Dorset] 30 July 1760. on reading his ode on the death
    of Frederick Prince of Wales'

c.267/4, p. 394

F0055 Fair soul, which wast not only as all souls be,
That testimony of love unto the dead. . . .

    [John Donne], 'Obsequies on the Ld [John]
    Harington brother to the count[ess] of Bedford' [d.
    1614]
    [Crum F93]

b.114, p. 318 (ll. 1–248)

F0056 Fair-spoken Mendax: on the least occasion
For wares so poor, to leave so great a pawn.

    [Francis Quarles], 'On Mendax' [Divine
    Fancies IV, 96]

b.137, p. 183

F0057 Fair spring appear'd, and hush'd was ev'ry wind,
With down, more soft than the fam'd insect weaves.

    John Lockman, 'The willow and the peach tree; from
    a Chinese poem'

c.267/4, p. 83; see also 'The spring appear'd . . .'.

F0058 Fair Susan did her wifehood well maintain,
Full marvelous, I wot, were such denials.

> [Matthew Prior], 'Susanna and the elders'
>
> c.81/1, no. 243

F0059 Fair sweet and young receive this friendly strain
Bath is the touchstone of a lady's sense.

> 'To Amanda going to Bath'
>
> fc.60, p. 119; c.189, p. 9; c.233, p. 86

F0060 Fair Tivy, how sweet are thy waves gently flowing,
Love can alone make it blissful to live.

> Sir William Jones, 'The damsels of Cardigan'
>
> c.90

F0061 Fair Valentine since once your welcome hand
A weak edge turn'd, meeting a softer touch.

> [William Strode], 'To his Valentine'
> [Crum F100]
>
> b.200, p. 124; b.205, fol. 33v (ll. 1–4)

F0062 Fair Venus grant me my desire and I'll obey thy
sovereignty
That I to thee do now return, O fire fire fierce I
burn.

> Poetry Box VII/76

F0063 Fair Venus long with envious eyes,
That thousands may adore, and die.

> [Soame Jenyns], 'On the right honble the Marchioness
> of Carmarthen's recovery from the smallpox'
>
> c.147, p. 31

F0064 Fair was her form, more fair her gentle mind,
Oh stay and drop the tender tribute here.

> 'Epitaph on Mrs. Moody who died at Bristol'
>
> c.116, p. 60

F0065 Fair was the graceful form Prometheus made
As touch'd by heav'n and all the picture liv'd.

> 'Verses written on Garrick and Shakespeare'
>
> c.68, p. 126

F0066 Fair wav'ring object of my constant flame
'Tis you, that promise love and never prove it.

> R[obert] Shirley, 1st earl of Ferrers, 'To a changing
> lady. From [Malherbe]'
>
> c.347, p. 85

F0067 Fair wench, I cannot court thy sprite-like eyes
Hark in thine ear: zounds, I can ——— thee
soundly.

> 'A rustic gallant's wooing'
> [Crum F104]
>
> b.200, p. 128; b.205, fol. 28r

F0068 Fair words persuade not without money; for
He that gives most, is the best orator.

> Sir Thomas Urquhart, 'The rhetoric, that is to be
> used before a bribing judge'
>
> fb.217, p. 76

F0069 Fair young folly tho' you were
This is pretty sport.

> b.213, p. 61

F0070 Fair Zara on a cloudy day
In thy remembrance claim an envied place!

> R[ichard] V[ernon] S[adleir], 'Written at Eastham'
>
> c.106, p. 40

F0071 Fairer than thy mother fair,
I renounce the odious strain.

> [William Popple, trans.], '[Horace] book 1st. ode 16th.
> To Tyndaris. A palinody'
>
> fc.104/2, p. 48

F0072 Fairest flower, all flowers excelling
Evergreens, that ne'er decay.

> 'To a child of five years old'
>
> c.391, p. 20; c.83/1, no. 174

F0073 Fairest needs I must confess
For to have a servant's place.

> 'To his mistress'
>
> b.356, p. 147

F0074 Fairest nymph my delay
Ripen'd it better.

> 'The amorist'
>
> fb.107, p. 3

F0075 Fairest Octavia, you are much to blame,
A freer gift, than is my love to thee.

> 'The platonic'
>
> c.549, p. 50

F0076 Fairest of the fair creation
Still gentle sigh for sigh return?

> 'A song'
>
> c.358, p. 5

F0077 Fairest, thy tresses are not threads of gold,
Be goddess-like dispos'd, be good, be true.

> [Thomas Carew], 'On a virgin's complexion, and
> p[er]fection'
> [Crum F115]
>
> b.200, p. 131 (attr. John Grange); see also 'Dearest . . .'.

F0078   Fairfax! the valiant! and the only he!
A man so great in war, in peace so just as he.

'An epitaph. Under this stone doth lie one born for
victory'

b.105, p. 245; see also 'Under this stone doth lie . . .'.

F0079   Faith and respect are seldom found
That by good proof I find this true.

Sir John Strangways, '12mo Octobris 1646'

b.304, p. 59

F0080   Faith gentlemen I do not blame your wit
With your dull advocate, or ignorant.

'Unto the comedians of Cambridge . . . John of a
Stiles student . . . wisheth a sounder judgment, and a
more reverent opinion of their betters' [On
G. Ruggle's Ignoramus, acted 1615 before James I,
satirizing lawyers; answered by 'Reverend John
Stiles . . .']
[Crum F117]

b.197, p. 79

F0081   Faith, if it be not certain, is not faith:
But hope's not hope, whilst it assurance hath.

Sir Thomas Urquhart, 'Faith, and hope'

fb.217, p. 198

F0082   Faith must be joined to works, Rhemus I wonder
What God has joined, thou darest presume to sunder.

[Francis Quarles], 'On faith and works'

b.137, p. 179

F0083   Faith must perform the office of invention
Of wit to learn, much more of art to teach.

[Christopher Harvey?], 'Trinity Sunday'

b.245 (inside back cover)

F0084   Fall, dews of heav'n, upon my burning breast,
To hearts o'erwhelm'd with grief, to eyes suffus'd
with tears.

[Charlotte (Turner) Smith], 'Sonnet written at
Exmouth, midsummer 1795'

c.141, p. 112

F0085   Fall down, fond saints, as you begun,
The jailer, thief, and Gregory.

fb.234, p. 33

F0086   Fall smooth ye streams, and gently wave ye trees,
And the free soul looks down to pity kings.

fb.68, p. 134

F0087   Fallaral-laral, let us sing,
Shall captivate me more.

'The whimsical love of T. W. and comical reception it
found from that imperious beauty Anne Dobson' [in
prose and verse]

c.530, p. 268

F0088   'False are all mankind!' cried Chloe,
You, above the world, I prize.

John Lockman, 'Writ to a favorite air in Signor Bach's
Carattaco. Damon and Chloe. 20 March 1767'

c.267/1, p. 394

F0089   False honor court, or lying scandal fear,
This the bad only, that the insincere.

'Horace Ep. I. xvi l.39 translated' [15 March 1794]

c.136, p. 149

F0090   False man whose best religion hath been
He died for treason, I for martyrdom.

[Thomas Randolph], '[A wronged mistress] to a false
servant'
[Crum F134-5]

b.197, p. 242

F0091   False moral doctrines, are the worst of lies
And but against sin to never sin less bent.

[Sir Philip Wodehouse], 'Daniel Scargill a Hobbesian
lies danger call'

b.131, back (no. 179)

F0092   False on his deanery! Nay more I'll say
Should raise itself by ballads more than merit.

'An apologetic rhyme vindicating Dr. [Richard]
Corbett concerning the verses sent by him to Marquis
Buckingham 1618' [satire]
[Crum F136]

b.200, p. 29; b.208, p. 255

F0093   False Robin the little that lately was great
Found traps for his foes, and base tricks for his
friends.

'A state riddle'

c.570/1, p. 1

F0094   False rumps—false teeth—false hair—false faces—
To clasp cork—gums—wool—varnish—in thy arms.

'Man's misfortune, or the modern, fine lady. An
epigram' [Gentleman's evening post]

c.487, p. 101

F0095   False world, thy malice I espy
And holy hallelujahs.

[George Wither], 'The contented man's morris'

c.139, p. 169

F0096 Falsehood—plague—my steps pursuing
Tho' friendship law, and duty fail.

    [Thomas Hull]

    c.528/46

F0097 Falsely we think that change of place
Her presence makes it constant spring.

    'Stanzas on content'

    c.83/1, no. 41

F0098 Fame heard with pleasure—straight replied
A friend of yours—'tis Lyttelton!

    [Philip Yorke] 2nd earl of H[ardwicke], 'Addition
    extempore' [to 'Virtue and fame . . .']

    c.83/1, no. 24

F0099 Fame like deserted jilt does still belie men,
For he knows best of any, how to try men.

    c.549, p. 12

F0100 Fame loud proclaims it and to mortals sings
The act may please you, not our idle prating.

    b.197, p. 121

F0101 Fame who does over the universe scatter,
There are no more subjects left for my rhymes.

    'Epsom Wells. A dialogue between Critic and Fame'

    b.111, p. 568

F0102 Fam'd Father Adams, learn'd to high degree
A top divine, card-and-inal was he.

    'An epitaph in St. Caecilia's church at Rome . . .
    Englished'

    c.360/3, no. 112

F0103 Fam'd for his justice, our late monarch shone;
Dread foes to Rome, and arbitrary sway.

    John Lockman, 'Verses most humbly addressed to the
    King'

    c.267/4, p. 2

F0104 Fam'd for his memory, ingenious, kind;
For [?], O [?] charity, atone!

    John Lockman, 'Writ under a mezzotinto of John
    James Heidegger esqr.'

    c.267/1, p. 173

F0105 Fam'd for the cure of each disease
At least to write good sense.

    [Robert Cholmeley], '['Derbensi inter sopulos . . .' by
    ( ) Saul, A. M.] burlesqued'

    c.190, p. 37

F0106 Fam'd for the social life, humane, discreet;
Be Symons such—for Cornwall recommends.

    John Lockman, 'On reading an advertisement
    presenting Richard Symons esqr. as a candidate, to
    represent the city of Hereford in Parliament . . . 1758'

    c.267/1, p. 395

F0107 Fam'd mistress of the siren choir!
For who would her own fame destroy?

    John Lockman, 'To Signora Mingotti, writ whilst she
    was performing . . . Feb. 1757'

    c.267/1, p. 127

F0108 Fam'd Orpheus drew the Thracians with his lyre:
You'll think the tributary marble due.

    John Lockman, 'Writ for the statue of Mr. Handel,
    (by Mr. Roubiliac) in Vauxhall Gardens'

    c.267/1, p. 160; c.268 (first part), p. 17

F0109 Fam'd stream, by whose restrictive force we're
                                         taught,
Great is the running, and from weakness too.

    'Epigram on a prating young lady at the hot well in
    Bristol' [Universal spectator]
    [Crum F142]

    fc.24, p. 77

F0110 Fam'd Zamparini left our isle:
Re-tread the stage, and sweetly touch the heart.

    John Lockman, '16 May 1768. Sung, at the exhibition
    in Spring Gardens, the portrait (by Mr. Home) of
    Zamparini, in the character of La Cecilina(?)'

    c.267/4, p. 385

F0111 Fame's a strange good and a strange evil that
Else each have's due after his funeral.

    [Sir Aston Cokayne], 'Of fame'

    b.275, p. 72

F0112 Famous men's art, if writers did not save,
Their fame had ceas'd and gone with them to the
                                           grave.

    c.339, p. 317

F0113 Fanatic's idol-bearer—bears her name,
They leave the church they but this idol bear.

    [Sir Philip Wodehouse]

    b.131, back (no. 75/2, 90/2)

F0114 Fancaelia's heart is still the same,
Beauty takes delight in killing.

    'Love's labyrinth'

    fb.107, p. 29

F0115 Fancy, a bashful nymph, had fixed her seat
And shake at ev'ry trembling spray.

    'Fancy'
c.83/2, no. 504

F0116 Fancy itself ev'n in enjoyment, is
But a dumb judge, and cannot prove its bliss.

c.189, p. 36

F0117 Fancy still loves to guard her vot'ry's tomb,
While heaven approv'd and virtue led the way!

    'Lines in memory of T. Linley esqr and his two
    daughters Mrs. [Elizabeth] Sheridan and Mrs. [Mary]
    Tickell'
c.83/2, no. 627

F0118 Fanny sweet nymph whom in a few short years
Folds in [?] presence—his departed child.

    [William Hayley], 'Sonnet—Fanny'
File 6968

F0119 Far as the world can stretch its bound,
Whose pow'r controls the war.

    [Christopher] Pitt, 'Psalm 24'
c.244, p. 502

F0120 Far from her hallow'd grot where mildly bright
And pleas'd, prefer, oblivion to disgrace.

    [William] Mason, 'Isis: an elegy written by . . . 1748'
c.481, p. 260; see also 'Close in her hallowed grot . . .'.

F0121 Far from mankind, my weary soul, retire,
Look up on high, and thank thy God for all.

    [Walter] Harte, 'To my soul—from Chaucer'
c.244, p. 497

F0122 Far from our pleasant native Palestine,
And fill thy glutted channels, with their scatter'd
                     brains and gore.

    [John] Oldham, 'Psalm 137. paraphrased by . . .'
c.244, p. 196

F0123 Far from the city's noise, as far from fame
Either to might, or to the multitude.

    [George Daniel]
b.121, fol. 34

F0124 Far from the crowded world Cornelia dwells
How much she suffers, and how much she grieves.

    '[Female characters.] 5. Cornelia; or the melancholy
    Methodist'
Poetry Box IV/148

F0125 Far from the gaudy scenes of life remov'd,
Her worth so matchless, and so few her days.

    'On the death of a young lady'
c.83/1, no. 234

F0126 Far from the noise of pomp and pride
That such a pastor came.

    'The country parson'
c.91, p. 95

F0127 Far from the reach of mortal grief,
And gave them Hannah More.

    [David] Garrick
c.341, p. 33

F0128 Far from the town's tumultuous noise,
Ye seats of peace and virtue hail!

    [J. M—tt], 'Novistne locum potiarem nire beato'
c.140, p. 507

F0129 Far hence remov'd beyond life's busy scene,
To climates most remote, Britannia's trade.

    Edward Sneyd, 'Epitaph upon Mr. James Brindley
    engineer'
c.214, p. 71

F0130 Far hence, ye careless, light and vain!
Who chang'd the beauty to the bird.

    H[annah] M[ore], 'Written in the Apollo at
    Belmont . . . Saturday April 1767'
c.341, p. 77

F0131 Far hence ye light and transitory joys,
A few pulsations more—and all is past!

    'Reflections occasioned by the death of Miss C. and
    Mr. C.'
c.89, p. 134

F0132 Far in a vale a peaceful dwelling lay,
Move the vain wish, and force the tender tear.

    [ ] I., 'Thyrsis an eclogue'
c.368, p. 204

F0133 Far in a vale adorn'd with fairest flow'rs
And leave this world to join the heav'nly choir.

    C. C. B[urney], 'Colin and Sylvia a pastoral tale . . .
    C. C. B. aged 13 years'
c.486, fol. 23v

F0134 Far in a wild, unknown to public view,
And pass'd a life of piety and peace.

    [Thomas] Parnell, 'The hermit'
c.244, p. 274; c.139, p. 16

F0135 Far in the forest of Arden
Was ever half so blest.

    'A pastoral'

b.197, p. 126

F0136 Far in the windings of a vale
She shivering sigh'd and died.

    David Mallet, 'Edwin and Emma a true story'

c.362, p. 11; c.83/1, no. 194

F0137 Far north in the Atlantic seas,
As if they'd each their rival slain.

    'The horses of fashion a tale'

c.503, p. 27

F0138 Far on the road that upward lies,
And fill up the celestial choir.

    'To the memory of Charles Rogers of Stamford, an
    excellent musician, who died 20 November 1746, was
    buried in S. George's churchyard on 22. S. Cecilia's
    evening'

c.371, fol. 55

F0139 Fare ever well, go over wishes he
Who is more thine, than he can seem to be.

    [John Rose?]

b.227, p. 74

F0140 Farewell, a long farewell, my son, my son,
The bliss that knows no change resides in God alone.

    'An elegy on the death of the Rev. Mr. Samuel Love,
    Fellow of Balliol Collge, Oxford, and minor canon of
    the Cathedral, Bristol'

c.341, p. 145

F0141 Farewell at length the proud insulting spot,
To taste the sweets of wisdom and of love.

    'For the Ipswich journal. Farewell to Norwich. (Made
    on the road to Bury)'

c.90

F0142 Farewell Aurora, welcome sable night
The sting of love, but he that loves as I.

    'A lover's passion debarred from his mistress'

b.356, p. 92

F0143 Farewell, auspicious spot! Where health resides;
Will fire my muse, while on your heights I sing.

    John Lockman, 'The adieu to Islington: after
    receiving great benefit from the air . . . Oct. 1758'

c.267/1, p. 235

F0144 Farewell awhile to mortal things—
Shall ev'ry grief defy.

    [Mary] Chandler, 'To the Revd. Mr. Sam. Chandler—
    On wisdom'

c.351, p. 134

F0145 Farewell Craigie Wallace the cause of our grief
And bid you appeal to your Parliament.

    'The n[ew] Armida'

Poetry Box VIII/33 (2 copies, one incomplete)

F0146 Farewell damn'd Stygian juice! That dost bewitch,
And not let brandy be physician!

    [Joseph Haines], 'A satire on brandy' [printed 1683
    (Wing H197)]

fb.207/4, p. 35

F0147 Farewell dear friends—ah! Cease to weep!
Till then we kindly bid adieu.

    'Epitaph on Mrs. Dearden and her daughter interred
    together at Bolton le Moors intended to cut on the
    gravestone'

c.91, p. 242

F0148 Farewell, dear friends, whom tender love
                                   constrains
And solid peace in every silent thought.

    'To Mary Weston and Mary Peaseley'

c.365, p. 25

F0149 Farewell dear servant since thy heavenly Lord
Truth's tender praise and tears of grateful love.

Poetry Box XII/68

F0150 Farewell, dear spirit, with the blest above,
I'll tread her virtuous steps, and put my trust on
                                     God.

    'On the death of a beloved wife'

c.83/3, no. 1054

F0151 Farewell divine instructor, we no more,
And learn like him to live, like him to die.

    'On the death of Samuel Fothergill'

c.517, fol. 34v

F0152 Farewell Duke and Duchess the cause of our grief
And bid your ambassador snuff when we piss.

    'Farewell to Lauderdale [16]74' [docket title]

Poetry Box VIII/23

F0153 Farewell, fair Anrik's flowery banks,
Once more, to visit you.

    [Thomas Hamilton, 6th earl of Haddington], 'A trifle
    of a song tune The broom of Cowden knows made in
    the ceach [catch?] called The farewell to Buchanan'

c.458/1, p. 55

F0154 Farewell fair Armida my joy and my grief
You'd say with a sigh, 'twas given by me.

> [John Dryden], 'To Armida his farewell before he
> went to sea'
> [Crum F165]

Poetry Box VII/77

F0155 Farewell fair saint, may not the sea nor wind
Whilst each contribute to their own undoing.

> [Thomas Cary, 'On his mistress going to sea']
> [Crum F166]

fb.66/31; b.201, cover (ll. 1-16; attr. Edmund Waller);
Poetry Box VII/77

F0156 Farewell, farewell! Illustrious friend!
Forgot thy pencil's magic power—

> [Charles Burney, the elder], 'Elegy on the death of Sir
> Joshua Reynolds, 1792'
> [Crum F170]

c.33, p. 229 (incomplete); fc.14/11

F0157 Farewell, fond love, under whose childish whip
The hollow echo will reply, 'twas I.

> Henry King, 'The farewell'
> [Crum F172]

b.150, p. 207

F0158 Farewell, for clearer ken design'd,
To rove thy sceneful world with this!

> [William] Collins, 'The manners—an ode'

c.363, p. 168

F0159 Farewell forever he! around whose urn
'Tis needless now to say—that Cockman died.

> 'Epitaph on Dr. Cockman. Master of University Coll.
> Oxon'

fc.51, p. 67

F0160 Farewell great painter of mankind,
For Hogarth's honor'd dust lies here.

> David Garrick, 'Epitaph by . . . on Hogarth'

c.504, p. 49; fc.14/12; c.94

F0161 Farewell, Ianthe, faithless maid
Can never taste of rest.

> 'Song 164'

c.555, p. 250

F0162 Farewell, just Bowes! O name we all revere!
Whilst his works live, the good man never dies.

> John Lockman, 'To the memory of George Bowes
> esqr, of Gipside, in the county of Durham . . . 10 Sept.
> 1760'

c.267/1, p. 295

F0163 Farewell lov'd L——; since 'twas the will of
Heaven
Known but by death, which ev'ry doubt resolves.

fc.61, p. 115

F0164 Farewell, lov'd mansion of my earlier days,
And never fail to go contented home.

> 'The adieu'

c.83/1, no. 86

F0165 Farewell meek Mary: so thy kindred earth
And thy short spotless spans extreme old age.

> R. D., 'In memory of Miss Moore only daughter of his
> Grace the Archbishop of Canterbury'

Poetry Box XII/51

F0166 Farewell, my best lov'd, whose heavenly mind,
My guide, my friend, my best belov'd, farewell.

> Miss [ ] Andrews(?), 'Epitaph by a gentleman to the
> memory of his lady'

File 245/23

F0167 Farewell my bonny, bonny, pretty, witty, Moggy
With our general's health in Flanders.

> 'Song'

c.189, p. 164

F0168 Farewell my dog, companion, and my friend,
Heaving a sigh—poor Tom, poor Tom's a-cold.

> W[illiam] Smith, 'Written by 1786 . . . on a beautiful
> dog who was killed by a fall from Beachy Head near
> Eastbourne Sussex'

Smith Papers, folder 62

F0169 Farewell my friends the tide abideth no man
That shedst thy blood for my redemption.

> 'On John Shrow stockfish-monger 1589'
> [Crum F185]

fb.143, p. 8

F0170 Farewell my hopes, farewell my happy days;
Welcome sweet grief th' subject of my lays.

> Sir F[rancis] C[astillion]

fb.69, p. 192

F0171 Farewell old year, for thou canst ne'er return,
Farewell old England thou hast lost thy glory.

> 'On the old year' [1714]
> [Crum F193]

c.570/1, p. 51

F0172 Farewell poor world I must be gone
In leaving thee my Lord I meet.

> 'The pilgrim's farewell to the world'
> [Crum F194]

c.548

F0173 Farewell the muses and Apollo
And laugh, and sing, drink, dance, and eat.

Poetry Box III/55

F0174 Farewell the world, the mortal cares,
And be each other's tomb.

'The ravished shepherd'

fb.107, p. 52

F0175 Farewell thou best of kings, and human race
Destroy the mortal, but the saint adore.

'Verses made upon King Charles the First['s] death'

fb.88, p. 120

F0176 Farewell thou best of Scots, who didst maintain
And didst not fall, but with thy country's fate.

[John] Dryden, 'Translation by Dryden' [epitaph on
John Graham of Claverhouse, Viscount Dundee,
translated from the Latin of Dr. Pitcairne]

b.204, p. 134; see also 'O last . . .'.

F0177 Farewell thou thing time past so true and dear,
Shall smell hereafter of the lamp not thee.

R[obert] Herrick, 'Mr. Herrick's farewell to sack/ In
praise of sack'
[Crum F210]

b.197, p. 150; b.356, p. 318

F0178 Farewell to all my shady bowers,
And never never ask for more.

'A song. To the tune of I'll range around the shady
bowers &c.'

c.570/1, p. 181

F0179 Farewell to earthly joys, no more
'Tis ten to one, I bring another song.

T[homas] M[orel]l, 'To Dr Brown on the death of his
second wife. At the request of M[atthew?]
Humberstone esq. Lincolnshire. 1729'

c.395, p. 29

F0180 Farewell to Lochaber and farewell my Jean
Then I'll ne'er leave thee nor Lochaber no more.

[Allan Ramsay], 'Farewell to Lochaber' [answered by
'Syne Jockey has bidden . . .']

Poetry Box VII/66, p. 1

F0181 Farew[ell] to Newmarket, and farewell the course
Behold he is gone and Newmarket's no more.

W[illiam] S[mith], 'Song . . . Newmarket'

Smith Papers, folder 69

F0182 Farewell vain world! and thou its vainest part
Of which the noisy babbling [world] complains.

[Benjamin Ibbot], 'A fit of the spleen. In imitation of
Shakespeare' [finished by Pope: 'What are the falling
rills . . .']

Poetry Box I/5; c.360/1, p. 153; fc.51, p. 13

F0183 Farewell vain world, I've had enough of thee,
And look at home, enough is to be done.

'Epitaph in a churchyard near Gillingham in Kent'
[Crum F214, 'known enough']

c.360/3, no. 233

F0184 Farewell ye gilded follies, pleasing troubles,
I'll never look for't but in heaven, again.

[Sir Henry Wotton], 'On a hermit in a grove with a
prayerbook in his hands'
[Crum F216]

b.200, p. 110; b.62, p. 20 (attr. Donne)

F0185 Farewell, ye lawns, by fond remembrance blest
Bless the dear Lord—of this regretted scene.

C[harlotte(Turner]) Smith, 'Lines by . . .'

c.83/2, no. 574

F0186 Farewell ye orient horror, ye Syrenian airs,
I will attend it at my fatal bier.

'A penitentiary passing from the temple to his cell,
with his Bible in his right hand, and a palm in his
other, whereon is written on both sides: Flens video,
dum Patmom video'

b.356, p. 234

F0187 Farewell ye rarities!
The joys of Heaven, by their influence

Thomas Traherne, [Meditation (fourth century)] 65'

b.308, p. 216

F0188 Farewell, poor Ti! I'll ne'er complain,
In fond attachment equal thee.

Lady F[rances] (S[cott]) Douglas, baroness Douglas]

Poetry Box III/folder 51-61

F0189 Farmo one afternoon was drunk extremely
They come not from my heart but from my drink.

[Sir Aston Cokayne], 'Of Farmo'

b.275, p. 39

F0190 Fashion in ev'ry age bears sov'reign sway
I will be Bon Ton to see 'em and like 'em.

Geo[rge] Colman [the elder], 'Prologue to Bon Ton
or high life above stairs. Written by . . . spoken by
Mr. King'

c.68, p. 11

F0191 Fashion, thou tyrant of despotic sway,
And ev'ry requisite for belle and beau!

'Lines on fashion'

c.83/1, no. 27

F0192 Fashion'd by thine almighty hand
And be the objects of thy care.

Charles Atherton Allnutt, 'The potter and the clay'

c.112, p. 14

F0193 Fatal Culloden in whose hated field
If the great prince and chieftains are no more.

'On the battle of Culloden'

c.171

F0194 Fatal wood! Pernicious tree!
Lynx or lion on the plain.

[William Popple, trans.], '[Horace] book 2nd. Ode
13th. To the tree by whose fall Horace had like to have
been crushed in his Sabine field'

fc.104/2, p. 154

F0195 Fate did our souls, goods, bodies b'Adam's fall
To divines', lawyers', and physicians' thrall.

Sir Thomas Urquhart, 'The triumvirate of theologs
lawyers, and physicians'

fb.217, p. 114

F0196 Fate first ordain'd, that Satan, here should dwell
But sent in mercy, to that milder hell.

'Lines written on a window at Tynearum in the
Highlands [with an answer]'

Poetry Box v/11

F0197 Fate governs fools, the wise more sublimate,
Themselves by wisdom govern not by fate.

'The wise' [translation from John Owen]

c.356

F0198 Fate so ordain'd who knew best how compunct
And from a soldier came the printing art.

[Sir Thomas Urquhart], 'Comparing John
Jerthudenberg [Gutenberg] his invention of printing,
and Bartholdur Swart [Schwarz] à Fraunstan
[Frauenstein?] his inventing of gunpowder'

fb.217, p. 388

F0199 Fate to the soul most honor whilst allows
And wealth (like venom) fals on the weaker parts.

[Sir Thomas Urquhart], 'Why wise men have not
always most wealth and preferment'

fb.217, p. 533

F0200 Fates guide us: unto fates yield we;
The first prescribeth the last day.

G[eorge] Sandys, 'G. Sandys' translation' [of a passage
from Seneca's Oedipus, 'Fatis agimur . . .']
[Crum F228b]

c.240, fol. 1v

F0201 Father and King of Heav'n, my footsteps guide!
What must be borne and done, resign'd or no.

[ ] Toplady, 'Toplady's translation' [of a passage from
Seneca's Cleanthes, 'Duc me, parens . . .']

c.240, fol. 1v

F0202 Father! methinks, in wondrous state
Was drawing pictures to the life.

Dr. [ ] Denn, of Trinity College, 'An pictoribus atque
poetis quidlibet audendi semper fuit aqua potestas'

b.115, fol. 41v

F0203 Father of all! In every age
All nature's incense rise.

[Alexander] Pope, 'Pope's universal prayer'
[Crum F235]

fc.61, p. 119; c.362, p. 87; c.391; fc.132/1, p. 129

F0204 Father of all! Whose throne illumines Heaven,
Thy pow'r, thy glory is forevermore.

[Francis Fawkes], 'The Lord's Prayer'

fc.21, p. 28; c.81/1, no. 214

F0205 Father of Britain (late restor'd) awhile
Ask thy own Britain—she confims my voice.

[Sneyd Davies], 'To old Camden's picture at Ld.
Camden's in Kent'

c.157, p. 80

F0206 Father of heaven and Him by whom
And [i.e., as] sin is nothing, let it nowhere be.

[John Donne], 'The litany'
[Crum F237]

b.148, p. 126; b.114, p. 163 ('Father of him . . .')

F0207 Father of Jesus Christ my Lord
Which shall in glory end.

'Hymn 51st'

c.562, p. 60

F0208 Father of light O cleanse my stains
Where sin shall be no more.

'Anthony Spier of Scarlett in the county of Berks . . .'

fb.69, p. 170, 253; cf. p. 222

F0209 Father of light we sing thy name
And the heavenly Eden end.

> P[hilip] Doddridge, 'God's providential bounties
> surveyed and impressed from Math. V. 45'

c.493, p. 32

F0210 Father of mercies God of love
With sacred joy we say amen!

> T[homas] S[tevens]

c.259, p. 143

F0211 Father of peace and God of love,
And fix us near thy throne.

> P[hilip] Doddridge, 'The Christian perfected by the
> grace of God from Hebr. XIII. 20, 24'

c.493, p. 64

F0212 Father of souls, for thy bright flame
With liquid odors we bedew.

> [Simon] Patrick, 'A funeral hymn upon the obsequies
> of a friend. From Prudentius'

c.352, p. 66

F0213 Father supply my every need
And feel that Christ is all in all.

> 'Hymn 42d'

c.562, p. 50

F0214 Father, we wait to feel thy Grace
More than the wine we taste.

> [Isaac Watts, Hymns and spiritual songs (1707), bk. II,
> Hymn 68]

c.180, p. 58

F0215 Father why this on me d'ye think this face
These are our wits; and faith I pity jesting.

> 'Quid est jocus?'

b.115, fol. 21

F0216 Fatigu'd with illness, sick with pain
I hope—I am resign'd.

> Mrs. [ ] D—e, 'Hymn to resignation'

c.83/2, no. 609

F0217 Fatigu'd with *priés* half the week—
To sense, to virtue, and to you.

> A. R., 'An invitation to the Honble Mrs. Boscawen.
> April 1745'

fc.51, p. 9

F0218 Faunus ever fond to chase
Pleas'd, to thee, respect to show.

> [William Popple, trans.], '[Horace] book 3rd. ode
> 18th. To Faunus'

fc.104/2, p. 272

F0219 Favonius, come!
And all Elysium open there.

> John Lockman, 'To Favonius: set by Mr. John
> Christopher Smith . . . April 1740'

c.267/2, p. 118

F0220 Favor them much that goodness learn in youth,
And love them well that learn and write the truth.

c.339, p. 317

F0221 Fav'rite of Venus, and the tuneful nine,
But to be a country gentleman, at heart!

> George Lyttelton, 1st baron Lyttelton, 'To Lord
> Hervey. In the year 1730 from Worcestershire'

Poetry Box IV/159

F0222 Fear chills our hearts, what heart can fear dissuade
'Twas not, that man should think his heaven's here.

> 'Upon an earthquake'

c.158, p. 118

F0223 Fear Him who soul and body made,
Proceed, yet never sep'rated.

> [Edmund Wodehouse], 'June 18 [1715]'

b.131, p. 223

F0224 Fear not (my son) if that we be made poor
To thee that good thou didst enjoy before.

> Sir John Strangways, '17° Octobris 1646'

b.304, p. 65

F0225 Fear not (dear love) that I'll reveal
The world will find thy picture there.

> [Thomas Carew], 'To his mistress' secrecy protested'
> [Crum F262]

b.200, p. 115 (114); b.197, p. 152; see also 'Think not dear
love . . .'.

F0226 Fear not, my dear, a flame can never die,
Love but again, and 'twill a heaven be.

> [Sir Charles Sedley], 'Constancy'
> [Crum F263, with four more lines]

b.218, p. 17; Poetry Box IV/53 (attr. Etherege); c.549,
p. 101

F0227 Fear not my soul! thy hope with joy pursue
And for perfection, wait eternity.

fc.54, p. 42

F0228 Fear not that the rest of the nine will condemn ye,
'Tis as well done at mass as in Conventicle. |
                              Which nobody can deny

> '20th song on Dame Church's going to mass'

Accession 97.7.40, p. 35 (with a separate copy)

F0229 Fear not to pray to God pray not cease
Except thou shun acts custom by control.

   Elizabeth Jekyll, 'Upon prayer' [1652]

b.221, p. 35

F0230 Fear not, ye sons of men, (ye angels sing)
And for our pattern was His meekness meant.

   'Another copy on the incarnation or birth of Christ'

c.167, p. 39

F0231 Fear of an after-clap makes many store
Happy for me thou hast afflicted me.

   H[enry] C[olman], 'On affliction'
   [Crum F267]

b.2, p. 88

F0232 Fear of too slight, too faint a sense
Are infinite as are their days.

   [Edmund Wodehouse], 'June 17 [1715]'

b.131, p. 223

F0233 Fear to offend forbids my tongue to speak
And yields no fruit to recompense my love.

   'Cant: 18'

b.4, fol. 15 (damaged)

F0234 Fearing to break thou break'st the glass, offence
Proceeds from care as well as negligence.

   [John Cleveland?]

b.93, p. 1, also 2

F0235 Fearless, too cautious maid, thou may'st invoke
Poets may sweetly sing, untaught by love.

   'Delia's answer to Harriet'

Poetry Box III/13

F0236 Feddy's recov'ring? What else can be?
The former virtues had so well deserv'd.

   R[obert] Shirley, 1st earl of Ferrers, 'To my brother
   upon his recovery of the jaundice'

c.347, p. 41

F0237 Feign to yourself the scene reluctance meets
Know then your friend and read his feelings there.

   'Another'

Diggle Box: Poetry Box XI/64

F0238 Fell weapon, that in ruthless hand
We crown the Prince of Peace, He reigns th'eternal
                    King.

   [ ] Williams, 'Ode on converting a sword into a
   pruning hook'

c.83/2, no. 521

F0239 Fellows and scholars mourn awhile,
Now let him raise a tear.

   'An extempore epitaph on the Revd. Dr. Hugh
   Grafton professor of history and oratory in Trinity
   College, Dublin decd. in November 1743'

c.360/2, no. 245

F0240 Few boast their age, many it plead,
His mercy from its terror saves.

   [Edmund Wodehouse], 'July 3d. [1715]'

b.131, p. 228

F0241 Few days here pass but t'advise to us
Of true celestial joy, the antepast.

   [Edmund Wodehouse], 'Novr. 28 [1714]'

b.131, p. 98

F0242 Few dishes well-dressed and welcome withal
Sweet sauce, is as crafty, as ever was friar.

   [Sir Francis Castillion?]

fb.69, p. 185

F0243 Few, from their own discernment, praise or blame
Observe them glitter, and believe them gold.

   [Anna Seward], 'On the commendations with which
   Miss Seward's ingenious friends have honored her
   manuscript collection of rhyming trifles'

File 13376

F0244 Few in so tender years have been endow'd
Upon the will, might breed the soul's corruption.

   Sir Thomas Urquhart, 'Upon my Lord [crossed out]'

fb.217, p. 282

F0245 Few judges take rewards for justice' sake,
But are, like fishes, taken, when they take.

   Sir Thomas Urquhart, 'Of bribing judges'

fb.217, p. 105

F0246 Few men in each respect as blest,
Without woe do not live.

b.234, p. 101

F0247 Few words are best; I wish you well
Want nothing else, except your wife!

   [Alexander] Pope, 'To Mr. C. St. James' Place . . .
   London October 22 . . . Edinb[urgh] mag[azine]'

fc.85, fol. 117v

F0248 Fickle as fair, my mistress slights her vows,
Her heart should still be mine and only mine.

   [Petit Andrews], 'Song, from Ovid'

c.90

F0249 Fickle goddess! Great at court,
And let Getes and Arabs feel.

    [William Popple, trans.], '[Horace] book 1st. ode 35th.
    To fortune'

    fc.104/2, p. 96

F0250 Fiddlers and singers ('tis a truth well known)
Private felicity, is all in all.

    [William Popple, trans.], 'Horace book 1st satire 3rd
    imitated. Inscribed to Thomas Bladen esq.'

    fc.104/1, p. 57

F0251 Fidelia blest with ev'ry charm
Can draw all Olympus down.

    [John Lockman], 'Beauty and music. Fidelia's (Mrs.
    Smith's) birthday. Set to music by J. Ch. Smith Jr.'

    c.268 (first part), p. 110

F0252 Fie Bobby fie—your spiteful verse decline
To heaven and the offender of the beauteous race.

    Rebecca Truth, pseud., 'To Mr. Say Grace'

    c.391

F0253 Fie, Chloris, 'tis silly to sigh thus in vain,
As you now laugh at me, I will then laugh at you.

    'The scornful lady'

    fb.107, p. 3

F0254 Fie Cupid you defraud
The old the whore.

    Sir Thomas Urquhart, 'Of a stripling girl, who was
    bawd to her mother. To Cupid'

    fb.217, p. 304

F0255 Fie false scout do you grow mad,
Those that know not, whither else to go.

    Lady Jane Cavendish, 'On a false report of your
    Lordship's landing'
    [Crum F283]

    b.233, p. 10

F0256 Fie fie Montgomery, fie fie
And looks like any sucking calf.

    [on William Pulteney, earl of Bath, and others]
    [Crum F286]

    Accession 97.7.40

F0257 Fie, fie, my Lord! Attack a saint-like past!
So come, come eat thy beef at Lowther Hall.

    John Wolcot ('Peter Pindar'), 'Ode to Lord Lonsdale'

    c.83/2, no. 306

F0258 Fie for a herald to decide the place
As a ring'd tournor does a sh[?] tam.

    'There was a play about place betwixt Lady Hatton
    and Lady Lochermaker on which the following satire
    was made' [1674]

    Poetry Box VIII/28

F0259 Fie Lolly fie—thou giv'n to lie
None else do see—thy foolery.

    [Sir Philip Wodehouse], 'An extempore dithyrambic
    against lying'

    b.131, p. 31

F0260 Fie on this courtly life full of displeasure
And rest ourselves till the next sun rising.

    'Cant: 22'

    b.4, fol. 18v (damaged)

F0261 Fie! Poor and proud—a match as odious
Do scornful pity, or much laughter find.

    [Sir Philip Wodehouse], 'Essay of poor and proud'

    b.131, p. 24

F0262 Fie Rome's abus'd, can any thought be able
To move her suit by a collateral saint.

    [Francis Quarles], 'On merits'
    [Crum F292]

    b.137, p. 176

F0263 Fie, scholars, fie! have you such thirsty souls
Cut doth the deed, and Longtail bears the blame.

    Benjamin Stone, 'On Samburne, Sheriff of Oxford'
    [Crum F293]

    b.208, p. 58; b.200, p. 84 (var.)

F0264 Fie, that I so for thy sake
I'll do so, and with thee change.

    'Resolute love'
    [Crum F295]

    b.200, p. 84

F0265 Fierce lions roaring for their prey: and then
Had I but only Daniel's [lion] there.

    [Francis Quarles], 'On Daniel in the den'
    [Crum F299]

    b.137, p. 166; see also 'It was Daniel's faith . . .'.

F0266 Fill, fill to the brim, for the sun does go round,
And ripens our joys to delight.

    'The jovial crew'

    fb.107, p. 5

F0267 Fill the bowl with rosy wine,
To the gods belongs tomorrow.

> [Abraham Cowley], 'A song [The epicure]'
> [Crum F305, 'easy wine']

Poetry Box VII/74

F0268 Fill the pot no more
For this is right traindedaddod.

> 'To the virtuous and ever honored lady Mrs. Jane
> Lottisham these humble present'

File 19017

F0269 Fill your glasses, banish grief,
Of a bad bargain make the best.

> 'Song 8'

c.555, p. 11

F0270 Fill'd with the noisome folly of the age
Unthinking Charles rul'd by unthinking thee.

> [Charles Sackville, 6th earl of Dorset?], 'Rochester's
> farewell'
> [cf. Crum T2722]

b.371, no. 28; fb.106(31); Poetry Box VIII (oversize), no. 5;
see also 'Tir'd with . . .'.

F0271 Find me an end out of a ring,
And teach a woman constancy.

> 'On women'
> [Crum F308]

c.356

F0272 Find you fault either with my style, or matter,
Which you have not the skill to imitate.

> Sir Thomas Urquhart, 'To any that will take upon him
> to dispraise, and undervalue my epigrams'

fb.217, p. 220

F0273 Finding these verses in the street
And hunted where there was no deer.

> 'An answer to them' [Mr. Street's verses about the
> draining of Slappen Ley: 'The reformers and
> drainers . . .']

b.104, p. 1/1 (end of book)

F0274 Finish me one task more for critic muse
Thou only to be his, he to be thine is fit.

> [Robert Wolseley], 'A postscript' [to William
> Wharton]
> [Crum F315]

b.219, p. 22

F0275 Finish'd Tartuffe! Vile excrement of pride!
Thy trait'rous heart, and thy outside agree.

> John Lockman, 'Seeing one of the executors of a great
> lady, in colors in Vauxhall Gardens, a month after her
> interment . . . May 1743'

c.267/1, p. 62

F0276 Fire water woman are man's ruin
And great thy wisdom Vander Bruin.

> [Matthew Prior], 'A Dutch proverb'
> [Crum F319]

Diggle Box: Poetry Box XI/62; c.536; Trumbull Box:
Poetry Box XIII/59

F0277 Fir'd by his muse, the poet thinks he sees
Now up in air, now sinking towards the ground.

> John Lockman, 'The mistaken bard . . . 1740'

c.267/1, p. 59

F0278 Fir'd with like hopes, and banish'd every tear,
Their farce and prologue are—quite of a piece.

> John Lockman, 'Prologues and epilogues. Prologue to
> The wheedler, from the French of the celebrated
> avocat Pat[h]elin'

c.267/3, p. 109; see also 'Flush'd . . .'.

F0279 Firm as the bass when thund'ring tempest roar
Those shocks of chance which make the vulgar fret.

> [Allan Ramsay], 'The constancy of a gentleman
> showed in a great storm at sea, gave occasion to the
> translation of . . . lines in Virgil'

c.360/2, no. 135

F0280 Firm I believe in that almighty Mind
In everlasting life beyond the skies.

> 'Apostle's creed'

c.81/1, no. 213

F0281 First draw an arrant fop, from top to toe
Has made them woeful ministers of state.

> [George Villiers, 2nd duke of Buckingham], 'Advice to
> a painter, to draw the delineaments of a statesman
> [and his underlings]' [on the Earl of Arlington,
> 11 Sept. 1674]
> [Crum F325]

fb.140, p. 174

F0282 First draw the sea, that portion which between
His valor, conduct, and his country's love.

> Ed[mund] Waller, 'Instructions to a painter for the
> drawing of the posture and progress of his Majesty's
> forces [under the Duke of York] at sea . . . with the
> battle, and victory obtained over the Dutch. June 3.
> 1665' [followed by envoy: 'Great Sir, disdain not . . .'
> [POAS I.21]

fb.140, p. 42

F0283 First for a strong savor stinking a leek may be taken
A rose, or else nothing that drafty informity cureth.

> 'Sr Thomas More his receipt for a strong breath
> translated out of his Latin epigrams'

b.207, p. 6

F0284 First, for the arms, you know full well,
I rest your humble slave Dan Bellamy.

T[homas] M[orell], 'Mr. Bellamy's dedication of his
sermons to Mr. Comer, versified'

c.395, p. 75

F0285 First heaven resolv'd William should reign, and
then
There should be one good king, | And this is he.

[Charles Sackville, 6th earl of Dorset], 'Under the
King's picture. Vox populi vox Dei'

fb.108, p. 83

F0286 First holy and happy, | Was the estate of man,
Of sinners we shall be: | Holy and happy men.

Arnold Webb [1671]

b.20, fol. 1v

F0287 First I was small and round like a pearl
And now like a rogue in the wide world I dwell.

'6 Enig. Res: a silkworm'

b.205, fol. 99r

F0288 First in procession of the pompous day,
Could they but view the picture of thy mind.

'On the women strewing flowers before the
coronation'

c.83/2, no. 719

F0289 First in the frontispiece, an angel shows,
The soul is foster'd by the pastor's care.

'Description of a frontispiece to a Bible'

c.83/1, no. 233

F0290 First in these lines shall young Britannia stand
My mistress kinder, or as old as thee.

'Remarks on the ladies at Holt in Wiltshire—1731'

c.360/1, p. 63

F0291 First Nestor suck'd and Homer first was taught,
Both famous once, yet both to dust are brought.

c.339, p. 320

F0292 First principles denying—why dispute?
Through ages blast the hopes of all mankind.

'On the denial of self-evid[ent] propositions'

fc.53, p. 133

F0293 First read, then mark, then practice what is good
For without use we drink but oblivion's flood.

c.339, p. 321

F0294 First take thy call thankfully be it in wealth or
poverty
Fast, watch, and pray continually, sin makes to
work thee injury.

'Certain godly admonitions directing a man how he
should govern his life'
[cf. Crum F336]

b.234, p. 307

F0295 First take what does for half a hundred stand
Which will a famous city soon disclose.

H[annah] More, 'London a rebus'

c.341, at front

F0296 First to the gods thy humble homage pay
And scorn the dark dominion of the grave.

N[icholas] Rowe, 'The golden verses of Pythagoras
translated from the Greek'
[Crum F338]

fc.60, p. 5; c.481, p. 226 (var.)

F0297 First try then trust: like gold the copper shows:
And Nero oft in Numa's clothing goes.

c.339, p. 318

F0298 First try then trust: so mayst thou live in rest,
But chiefly see thou trust thyself the best.

c.339, p. 318

F0299 First, with spring water and unwearied pain,
You'll see the coxcomb shine in ev'ry limb.

[Mary Leapor], 'Proper ingredients for the head of a
beau found among the rules of Prometheus'
[Gentleman's evening post, Sept. 1776]

c.487, p. 100

F0300 First you must know true honor is not won
And have no generous virtues, is a scorn.

'Honor'

b.62, p. 118

F0301 Firstborn of Chaos, who so fair didst come
From thence took first their wish, thither at last
must flow.

[Abraham Cowley], 'Hymn to the light'
[Crum F323]

b.135, fol. 112; c.244, p. 238

F0302 Firstborn of Erebus! and g[l]oomy care,
Gladness comes after grief, and sadness follows joy.

[William] Pattison, 'On melancholy'

c.244, p. 521

F0303 Five and five and fifty-five
And makes the world go mad.

    'A riddle'
    [Crum F344]

    fc.73

F0304 Five deep politicians once met to debate,
So she snivels—but roars herself quiet again.

    [Robert Cholmeley], 'To a lady who though a great
    talker seldom spoke without tears. A song to the tune
    Which nobody can deny'

    c.190, p. 9

F0305 Five fav'rite performers from the muses' bright
                       choir,
'Tis there: 'tis at Hugford's: hark! Hark! Hays's
                        bow.

    John Lockman, '. . . Extempore—writ after coming
    home from Mr. Hay's Friday concerts at the great
    room in Brewer Street. 28 March 1767'

    c.267/1, p. 395

F0306 Five hundred begins,
Are properly placed between.

    '[Enigma/Charade/Conundrum] 94' [David]

    c.389

F0307 Five hundred in a week in one poor city
But rather wonder there were men to die.

    [Francis Quarles], 'Upon the sight of a plague bill'
    [Crum F348, 'Five thousand']

    b.356, p. 157

F0308 Five hundred pounds; too small a boon
It would not buy the paper.

    [Allan Ramsay], 'An epigram, occasioned by a report,
    that five hundred pounds was offered by the Dowager
    Duchess of Marlborough to any poet who should exert
    his genius best in honor of the Duke her husband'
    [Old Whig, 16 Sept. 1736]
    [Crum F347]

    Poetry Box x/141

F0309 Five males amongst the wand'ring stars we find:
But only two of all the female kind.

    Sir Thomas Urquhart, 'That women are not so
    inconstant as men'

    fb.217, p. 176

F0310 Five roses grew, upon the selfsame stem
Gave charter, to such innocence.

    [George Daniel]

    b.121, fol. 64

F0311 Five years ago (says story) I lov'd you,
Beauty and color stay not when we die.

    A[braham] C[owley], 'Inconstancy'

    c.258

F0312 Fix not your mind on features, lips or eyes,
But only love the virtuous, and wise.

    [John Rose?]

    b.227, p. 75

F0313 Fix'd in his center as the sun
In a like planetary scheme.

    [Phanuel Bacon], 'Regis ad exemplum totus
    componitur orbis'

    c.237, fol. 51

F0314 Flattery's the turnpike road to fortune's door—
That river got a sixpence by her speeches!

    [John Walcot(?) ('Peter Pindar')], 'Flattery . . . Ode 9
    (1785)'

    c.355, p. 95

F0315 Flavia for my numbers, sues,
Tho' Pope should write, or Kneller paint.

    J[ohn] Wolcot ('Peter Pindar'), 'A sketch of Miss
    P[hilippa] Chubb'

    File 18072

F0316 Flavia the least and slightest toy
To ev'ry other breast a flame.

    [Francis] Atterbury, bishop of Rochester, 'Flavia's fan
    an epigram'
    [Crum F352]

    c.360/2, no. 258; b.201, p. 142; Poetry Box IV/53

F0317 Flavia's a name by much too free
And Chesterfield, the elder.

    'An answer to the foregoing' [on Eleanor Ambrose: 'In
    Flavia's eyes . . .']

    c.360/2, no. 150

F0318 Flaxman kind partner in the hallow'd task
And as ye grac'd his life adorn his grave.

    [William Hayley], 'Sonnet . . . Sept. 25 [1800]'

    File 6968

F0319 Flee idleness, which beggar's state doth give,
If thou be born with laboring hand to live.

    c.339, p. 315

F0320 Flee those that haunt too much the alewives' can,
For like a beast this doth transform a man.

    c.339, p. 323

F0321 Fleet! spread thy canvas wing:
And humble France.

> John Lockman, 'Admiral Hawkin's [*i.e.*, Edward
> Hawke's?] health, or success to his expedition. The
> tune, O the roast beef of old England, &c . . . writ in
> the Salisbury coach, 24 Aug. 1757'
>
> c.267/2, p. 21

F0322 Fling off your silks; for freezing winter's come!
And by a cheerful fire, like other females—talk.

> 'Verses under the pictures of the four seasons; for
> Miss Herbert . . . winter'
>
> Spence Papers, folder 113

F0323 Flocks are sporting.
Ye swains and nymphs so fair.

> [Henry Carey], 'A pastoral'
>
> c.160, fol. 85v; c.244, p. 105 (var.)

F0324 Flora and Zephyrus from Tempe's vale
And thousands of thy sex, shall [ ] sing.

> John Lockman, 'Zephyrus and Flora 15 Octr. 1766. On
> seeing flowers drawn and worked, for the cradle of the
> royal infant by Mrs. Wright of Newport Street'
>
> c.267/1, p. 390

F0325 Flora! Goddess sweetly blooming,
Bless'd by love, and wound with flow'rs.

> John Lockman, 'Vauxhall songs. Rural pleasures, or
> Vauxhall Gardens. Set by Dr. Boyes [William
> Boyce] . . . anno 1733'
>
> c.267/2, p. 113; c.268 (first part), p. 49

F0326 Flora plain rural beaux content on,
Without God-damn-me's aid.

> [William Carpenter], 'An attempt to assign a reason
> why ladies are fond of officers, addressed to a lady,
> that is not'
>
> c.247, p. 118

F0327 Flora to Ida's top withdrew,
Beauteous as those which paint the field.

> John Lockman, 'Flora to the graces. Writ after
> viewing pattens, of Christian's painted silk
> manufactury, in [?] Street, Longacre . . . March 21
> 1765'
>
> c.267/1, p. 386

F0328 Flora, who led by jocund hours,
Tho' months or years have roll'd between.

> 'To Miss Jellicoe on her presenting me with a
> firescreen of her own painting Decr: 1776'
>
> c.89, p. 130

F0329 Florio had drunk five pints of wine
I ate a piece of orange peel.

> Greatheed Box/102

F0330 Flourish George! Long live the king!
Kings thus reigning seem divine.

> John Lockman, 'Translations, and imitations from
> Metastasio, and other Italian opera poets [18] . . . by
> Signor Bottarelli'
>
> c.267/4, p. 111

F0331 Flow Welsted flow! Like thine inspirer beer,
Heady, not strong, and foaming, tho' not full.

> [Alexander] Pope, 'To Mr. Welsted. A parody on the
> foregoing [lines from Denham's Cooper's Hill]'
>
> c.360/2, no. 130

F0332 Flow, gentle grief, in melting numbers flow,
And what we lost by death, by death regain.

> Katharine Compton and Charlotte Ferrers(?), 'On the
> death of the right honorable and much lamented Lady
> Jane Compton' [daughter of the earl of
> Northumberland; d. 1749]
>
> Accession 97.7.40

F0333 Flown are those roses that illum'd thy cheek;
Till it had plac'd the olive in thy breast.

> 'To my lovely friend'
>
> c.83/2, no. 364

F0334 Flush'd with gay hopes, how did I think to reign
Should clasp me in thy arms and hug me on thy
breast.

> [Mrs. Christian Kerr], 'By a young gentlewoman, to a
> young lady, on their being disappointed of meeting in
> the country'
>
> c.102, p. 116

F0335 Flush'd with his conquest, and with youth elate,
She sunk in silent raptures on his breast.

> [William Hayley], 'Tigranes and Arbacia a tale'
>
> File 6972

F0336 Flush'd with like hopes, and banish'd ev'ry fear,
This farce and prologue are—quite of a piece.

> [John Lockman], 'Prologue, by the author'
>
> File 9162; see also 'Fir'd . . .'.

F0337 Flushed with the pride of this auspicious day
And hails and fosters, learning's honored choice.

> Lord [ ] Morpeth, 'Written by . . .'
>
> c.340

F0338 Fluttering busy insect go
She's Damon's only pleasure.

> 'To a fly'
>
> Poetry Box I/43

F0339   Fly care, and dull spite,
And a pox of our college's foe.

    'The scholars' carouse'
    fb.107, p. 19

F0340   Fly careless nymph from thy pursuer fly
Plant anything but laurels on his brow.

    'Advice to Miss R[a]dc[li]ff[e] to avoid
    Dr. Ashenhurst, who was fond of her'
    c.176, p. 110; c.360/1, p. 151

F0341   Fly fly my heart unto the place of rest
In Him is found true rest and peace alone.

    [Mary Serjant]
    fb.98, fol. 163

F0342   Fly, fly, those fond deluding eyes
And the man wisely thinks she smiles for more.

    [Joseph] Spence
    Spence Papers, folder 113

F0343   Fly foul soul to some forsaken hill
To rest, unblest because I slew a maid.

    'Upon one that killed a virgin with his false love, his
    one repentance'
    b.62, p. 111

F0344   Fly fro' the press, and dwell with soothfastness
And troth thee shall deliver, it is no dread.

    [Geoffrey] Chaucer, 'Good counsel of Chaucer. Urry,
    p. 548' [pr. 1721]
    b.150, p. 151

F0345   Fly from Olinda young and fair
'Tis for the blessings they bestow.

    [Crum F375]
    fb.66/14

F0346   Fly from the crowd, and be to virtue true,
So truth shall shield thee, or from hurt or fear.

    'C[h]aucer's last advice. Attempted in modern
    English'
    c.83/2, no. 353

F0347   Fly hence, grim Melancholy's train
For 'tis pleasure's golden reign.

    'Song 166'
    c.555, p. 253

F0348   Fly not so fast, delicious May
Thy bloom to every month I live.

    'To May'
    c.83/3, no. 891

F0349   Fly swift, ye tardy, mournful hours,
That rest which passion never knows.

    c.83/2, no. 553

F0350   Fly to the altar (sacred souls) with me,
But to rejoice, obey, and to admire.

    fb.234, p. 30

F0351   Fly up my fair soul unto that blessed place!
Where angels sing, life's here but a breathing
                       space.

    [Sir Francis Castillion]
    fb.69, p. 192

F0352   Fly youthful lust with all thy might,
And in God's laws get thy delight.

    John Rose
    b.227, p. 36

F0353   Flying years still glide away—
Priests, less sumptuous feasts, shall know.

    [William Popple, trans.], '[Horace] book 2nd. Ode
    14th. To Posthumus'
    fc.104/2, p. 158

F0354   Foe to restraint—sworn friend to womankind;
Who gave one woman, what I seek in all!

    'To a lady after marriage'
    c.94 (incomplete?)

F0355   Folks talk of supplies
He'll drive all such monsters to Hell. | Horse foot
                   and dragoons. . . .

    'Britain excised. Part the first' [pr. 1733 (Foxon B459]
    c.570/3, p. 145

F0356   Folly and vice of every sort and kind,
A satire's smiles are sharper than its frown.

    'On satire'
    c.83/2, no. 636

F0357   Folly to ridicule, and vice upbraid,
Foote gives the picture as he treads the stage.

    John Lockman, 'The three satirists . . . Nov. 1750'
    c.267/1, p. 371

F0358   Fond atheist! Could a giddy dance
And hung it in the skies.

    'The mechanism of the human body'
    fc.132/1, p. 225

F0359 Fond busy thoughts be still! Torment me not
Our friendship to renew, and part no more.

'Eliza's farewell with Amelia who was leaving the
country to go along with her parents, to another part
of the world'

c.91, p. 84

F0360 Fond Celadon no more complain
Might she but always smile.

[Robert Cholmeley], 'The constant. A song'

c.190, p. 48

F0361 Fond love why dost thou dally
And thou of all cruelty go quit and clear.

'Cant: 11'
[Crum F410]

b.4, fol. 7 (damaged)

F0362 Fond man, how false thy dreams, thy hope now vain!
Friendship, or love, controlled, or ill returned.

'A sonnet. Injured friendship' [30 May 1799]

c.136, p. 161

F0363 Fond man! retire to this lone cell
Who made these peaceful minutes thine.

J. C.(?), 'Inscription for an hermitage'

Spence Papers, folder 113

F0364 Fond man, that canst believe her blood
Shed all the blood, felt all the smart.

[Thomas Carew], 'To the surgeon, on Celia bleeding'
[Crum F412]

b.200, p. 115

F0365 Fond of the woods, but wanting human aid,
The noblest mistress, and the sweetest grove.

John Lockman, 'Supposed as spoke by a robin red-
breast, in Buckingham House gardens . . . June 1742.
The Duchess, after reading the above lines, ordered
one of her women to throw bread, every morning, on
the ledges of the window'

c.267/1, p. 10

F0366 Fond self purest love's never to permit
For when we think we're wise we're nothing less.

[Sir Thomas Urquhart], 'That overweening
oftentimes impeacheth the perfectioning of the
quality we are proudest of'

fb.217, p. 510

F0367 Fond wanton youth makes love a god,
Our woe to woe to wed our grief.

'A song against marriage'

b.197, p. 60

F0368 Fond woman which wouldst have thy husband die,
Do London's mayor, or Germans the Pope's pride.

[John Donne], 'Elegia 2da' [Jealousy]
[Crum F419]

b.114, p. 72; b.148, p. 83

F0369 Fond youths in days of yore, 'tis said,
A wig that's made of dead men's hair.

Poetry Box III/3

F0370 Fool man would cry if sure to die
Which is perhaps his last.

'Epigram'

c.115

F0371 Foolish love begone said I
O love my conqueror pity me.

[George Granville, 1st baron Lansdowne], 'Song 210'

c.555, p. 338

F0372 Fools! at the other House go try the priest!
You that can make a king can make the lords.

'To the House of Commons' [in reference to the
impeachment of Sacheverell, December 1709]
[Crum F427]

c.171, p. 13; b.90, p. 10 ('Fools! At a foreign bar . . .')

F0373 Fools strain, but prudent more restrain their voice
Which hath least labor silence or a noise?

'Tattling'

c.356

F0374 Fools tell the truth the English proverb says
To tell the truth then there is foolishness.

Sir Thomas Urquhart, 'An English proverb'

fb.217, p. 274

F0375 For a few moments lovely nymph attend
Till both together sink in endless rest.

'To Miss [blank]'

c.504, p. 163

F0376 For a seat in this house when the candidates start
When the house is dissolv'd and the members
adjourn.

[ ] Wastell, 'From . . . to Mr. Smith . . . written on a
signal flag [on a privy]: When down you sit take me
down too | And hook me up before you go'

Smith Papers, folder 74/14

F0377 For Adam's sin we, and our predecessors
In criticism, is till this hour reproach'd.

Sir Thomas Urquhart, 'Of the different case of Adam,
and Zoil'

fb.217, p. 76

F0378   For all our slips in memory or tongue
Year after year our talents will increase.

> Ralph Broome, 'A[n] epilogue for juvenile actors'
> c.486, fol. 34

F0379   For all the mischief you have done us,
By G[od] next Parliament have at you.

> [on Louis XIV]
> fb.68, p. 22 (incomplete)

F0380   For all thy mercies O my God
In heart in mind in thought.

> [( ) Huddesford], 'On my brother J[oh]n
> Huddesford's breaking his thigh at Coleshill, 1754'
> c.181, p. 67

F0381   For an apple of gold
At a dish of our coffee, or tea.

> 'The coffee women turned courtiers. To the tune of Ye
> Commons and Peers'
> [Crum F436]
> c.570/1, p. 98; fc.58, p. 50

F0382   For beauty Pyramus and Thisbe were
The lovers' ashes in one urn repose.

> [William Mills], 'The story of Pyramus and Thisbe
> translated from the fourth book of Ovid's
> Metamorphoses'
> c.472, p. 49

F0383   For beauty state; and virtuous inclination,
Than formerly the fates on them bestowed.

> Sir Thomas Urquhart, 'To the Countess of [crossed
> out]'
> fb.217, p. 135

F0384   For critic's feet are devilish sharp they say
And then I'll ask your censures on this play.

> b.216, p. 201

F0385   For ease, the harassed seaman prays,
Health, leisure, peace, and ease.

> Warren Hastings, 'Horace, ode 16, book 2 . . . imitated
> by . . . at sea, an. 1785'
> Poetry Box v/125

F0386   For England when with favoring gale
And to the watchful pilot sing quarter less five.

> [William Pearce], 'The heaving of the lead'
> Poetry Box IV/50

F0387   For every hour that thou wilt spare me now
One that loves me.

> [John Donne]
> [Crum F444]
> b.114, p. 259; b.148, p. 89

F0388   For every lady, now a billet
For Newburgh was the name I drew.

> 'Verses sent by a young lady to her valentine'
> c.360/2, no. 40

F0389   For every prince that hit my fancy
Have mercy on a garter'd sinner.

> 'The Duke of Buckingham's epitaph' [1721?]
> File 17710

F0390   For figures and numbers I ne'er was design'd
One and one maketh two and thrice two maketh
four.

> Miss [ ] Andrews, 'On a young lady's first beginning
> arithmetic'
> File 245/4

F0391   For further preface look and see
And don't the author stigmatize.

> [prefaced to 'The poor man's meditations and
> contemplations . . . by a wellwisher of Zion's welfare']
> b.91, p. 5

F0392   For gentle case for downy ease,
Has kindly rais'd above the crowd.

> [ ] Lewis, trans., 'Horace Ode 16. Book 2d'
> c.244, p. 447

F0393   For Gloucester's death which sadly you deplore,
And to preserve the man destroy'd the boy.

> [Charles Sackville, 6th earl of Dorset], 'On the D[uke]
> of Gloucester's death' [1700]
> [Crum F449]
> c.111, p. 60; Poetry Box VII/73

F0394   For God's sake come away and land
Then joy in my companion's total sum.

> Lady Jane Cavendish, 'Passion's invitation'
> [Crum F452]
> b.233, p. 17

F0395   For God's sake hold your tongue, and let me love
A pattern of your love.

> [John Donne], 'Canzone [The canonization]'
> [Crum F453]
> b.114, p. 299; b.148, p. 97

F0396   For haughty Phyllis, Thyrsis pines;
The fair one had not been displeas'd.

> [John Lockman], 'Vous cachez avec soin vos
> peines . . . imitated. The tattling shepherd'
> c.268 (first part), p. 100

F0397　For her what slaves in rhyme and prose have died?
The thing that covers Manch[ester]'s delight.

> [Horace Walpole, 4th earl of Orford], 'D[uchess] of
> Manch[este]r'
c.157, p. 68

F0398　For his gray hairs, Madam, reject him not;
When on the mountains so much snow is seen.

> Sir Thomas Urquhart, 'To a widow lady, whom a
> certain aged nobleman was suiting for in marriage'
fb.217, p. 282

F0399　For his paying of your grateful action
And not the noble arts of a free mind.

> [Sir Thomas Urquhart]
fb.217, p. 386

F0400　For if a watery cloud shall sidelong sit,
To see at once more shining moons, than one.

> 'To show how the sun being reflected may seem to be
> three suns'
c.158, p. 117

F0401　For impious Sodom's guilty land
Like heav'n may you forgive.

> [Robert Cholmeley], 'To the Reverend Dr. Baker
> STP: Senior Dean of St. Johns Coll Camb: made by
> way of punishment'
c.190, p. 27

F0402　For infant's hand the water is unfit
And fools unmeet in wisdom's seat to sit.

c.339, p. 315

F0403　For lack of rest, the field doth barren grow,
And daily bent doth weak the strongest bow.

c.339, p. 316

F0404　For liberty so long we fought in vain,
While they are punish'd for a sprig of oak.

> 'A collect for the Restoration Day. May the 29'
c.570/2, p. 9

F0405　For loss of things much lov'd 'tis hard, but best
Lay them aside, and me pardon.

> 'Mistress: verses have in them melody, which sweetens
> comforts; therefore give mine in verse'
Poetry Box VI/124

F0406　For love's sake kiss me once again
Or wish us death.

> Ben J[onson], 'Claiming another kiss on color of
> mending the former'
> [Crum F462]
b.104, p. 115

F0407　For man, and wife then can be nothing more
Two helping other[s] bear the weight of four.

> [Sir Thomas Urquhart], 'Concord union and [?]
> providence(?) are profitable for a [?] [?]'
fb.217, p. 535

F0408　For me deceased grieve not my dear,
Make no delay, but follow I.

> 'Epitaph in a country churchyard' [answered by 'I am
> not grieved . . .'/'I do not grieve . . .']
c.113/16; Greatheed Box/73

F0409　For me no lofty turrets rise
That check, all mis'ry that retreat.

> 'An imitation of Horace. lib. 2. ode 18 . . . To the Earl
> of Bath'
Poetry Box x/119

F0410　For men's estates, I know not which is worse,
And force, the good suppresseth, as by law.

> Sir Thomas Urquhart, 'The object and effects of law
> and force'
fb.217, p. 150

F0411　For most unhappy is that state
As if we never meant to have our senses again.

> 'Troy town'
Poetry Box VII/76

F0412　For my first twenty years since yesterday
Am (by being dead) immortal. Can ghosts die?

> [John Donne], 'Canzonets [The computation]'
b.114, p. 251; b.148, p. 109 (at end of 'So so leave off . . .'
without separation); b.114, p. 251

F0413　For my irreverence be not too critic,
And still begins at *nobis notiora*.

> Sir Thomas Urquhart, 'The apology of a gentleman,
> to one Leonora . . . for the kissing of another
> gentlewoman before her, who was inferior in quality'
fb.217, p. 74

F0414　For my zeal and loyalty
Rocket in my eye.

> 'Another [tombstone inscription] at Woodstock'
c.74

F0415　For myself I sigh often, without knowing why,
And when absent from Phyllis, methinks I could die.

c.549, p. 62

F0416　For of all ages ever known,
I fear you'll see the right on't.

c.115

F0417 For oft when sleep enwraps my wearied frame
The fairy landscape gently glides away.

[William Roscoe], 'To Maria'

c.141, p. 52

F0418 For once in our lives,
And thus we get rid of them all.

'The following glee among others, was sung with
uncommon glee, a few evenings since, at the house of
a man of quality' [Gentleman's evening post, 1776]

c.487, p. 99

F0419 For one soft moment, courtly scenes resign;
And, in these groves, a new Diana shine.

John Lockman, 'To Lady Augusta, with the author's
sketch of the Spring Gardens Vauxhall, a pamphlet . . .
1756'

c.267/1, p. 112

F0420 For our instructions, gracious Lord
Which is thy gift thro' Jesus' love.

Charles Atherton Allnutt, 'Collect for the second
Sunday in Advent'

c.112, p. 54

F0421 For physic and farces,
His physic a farce is.

'On Dr. Hill jr.'

c.74; c.546, p. 24

F0422 For plainness hated, and for truth revil'd;
Which, as the more he knew, the less he lov'd.

[Charles Earle], 'Another [epitaph]'

c.376

F0423 For private loss the lenient tear may flow,
Cover'd by laurels, when a Granby dies!

[John] Cunningham, 'On Lord Granby's decease'
[1770]

c.90

F0424 For prudence, zeal, and knowledge in all arts:
The ruling of the hearts of kings is due.

Sir Thomas Urquhart, 'To the Archbishop of
Canterbury'

fb.217, p. 98

F0425 For public service grateful nations raise
With leaf unfading under happier skies.

'To the memory of John Martins gardener a native of
Portugal who cultivated here with industry and
success, the same ground under three masters, forty
years'

c.150, p. 62

F0426 For quiet, Yorke, the sailor cries
I mean that a'nt freeholders.

[Soame] Jenyns, 'Ode 26th of the 2nd book of Horace:
imitated by . . . of Cambridgeshire the day after the
general elections' [addressed to Philip Yorke, 2nd earl
of Hardwicke, 1747; also attr. C. H. Williams]

fc.51, p. 224; c.229/1, fol. 74v

F0427 For shame! Deny, that thou bear'st love to any
That beauty still may live in thine or thee.

[William] Shakespeare [Sonnet x]

c.94

F0428 For shame ye doting fools, for shame be wise
Of your own ruin, and your sovereign's doom.

['On the bishops,' referring to Sacheverell, 1710]
[Crum F477]

Poetry Box x/40

F0429 For shooting stars, these some do fondly call;
As if those heavenly lamps from heaven could fall.

'Upon an exhalation shooting in the air'

c.158, p. 115

F0430 For such the bounteous providence of heav'n,
Each trembling heart with grateful terrors quell'd.

'On the love of novelty'

c.156, p. 86

F0431 For temperance and other qualities
For virtue a more large and spacious field.

[Sir Thomas Urquhart], 'That riches afford more
matter than poverty to virtue to work upon'

fb.217, p. 523

F0432 For the few hours of life allotted me,
I'll thank for this, and go away content.

[Abraham Cowley]
[Crum F480]

b.118, p. 11

F0433 For the King some days
Therefore being of being whatever you be | Have
mercy on me.

'[The Duke of Buckinghamshire's epitaph, made by
himself . . . Englished thus] Or thus'

fc.24, p. 60

F0434 For the love of the smock
Then we shall live more at our ease.

'A satire 1679'

b.54, p. 1213

F0435 For the miracles done | This year ninety and one
If religion proves worth one year's purchase.

[ballad on James II, 1691]
[Crum F484; *POAS* V.312]
Poetry Box VII/39 (ll. 1–18); see also 'The miracles done . . .'.

F0436 For the word you're to guess, it has ever been
                                                                reckon'd,
That I don't afford milk, tho' I do afford cream.

'Charade'
Diggle Box: Poetry Box XI/68

F0437 For thee (dear Sir) we moan with doleful cries,
To die: there rest (dear soul) I'll leave thee now.

J. R., 'In idem' [elegy on the death of Andrew Horsman]
b.212, p. 244

F0438 For thee industrious France with living praise
Doth with his summer robes the plains adorn.

b.212, p. 128

F0439 For thee my first what risks are run,
I am a beauty and her guide.

'[Enigma/Charade/Conundrum] 21' [gold watch]
c.389

F0440 For thee my thoughts all pleasures shall forego,
Join thee at death—and be forever thine.

'Epitaph on a lady by her husband'
Poetry Box XII/67; c.344, p. 61

F0441 For thee, O amiable as mustard sweet!
If you can't walk, I'll take you pick-a-pack.

John Lockman, 'The fond lover: a mock song, extracted from a ballad opera of the author's. The tune, Fair lady lay your costly robes aside . . . 1731'
c.267/2, p. 101; c.268 (first part), p. 93

F0442 For thee, O friend, my garden's pride I've chose
This wreath, devoted to fair friendship's shrine.

'To a lady with some of the author's verses'
c.135, p. 37

F0443 For thee, the firstlings of the year shall blow,
The dew of pity on its leaves may rest.

'Verses presented to a young lady with a nosegay, on the 3rd of January 1797'
Diggle Box: Poetry Box XI/42

F0444 For these few hours of life allotted me
I'll thank for that and go away content.

[Abraham Cowley]
c.548

F0445 For thinly odd tho' Laïs pass,
How scorching was her noon?

W[illiam] Diaper, 'Plato's epigram upon Laïs'
Poetry Box V/90

F0446 For this additional declaration
By the next synod of the nation.

'Anthem to be sung in the Lord Mayor's chapel at the reading of the new Declaration' [1688]
[Crum F492; *POAS* IV.219]
fb.108, p. 109

F0447 For this illustrious lord they oft have seen
And felt, that he their patron best hath been.

[couplet used as an exercise in penmanship]
Poetry Box VIII/6

F0448 For this, my God, my humblest praises wait;
Seems to demand a tribute from the skies.

'[Soliloquies] (6)'
c.153, p. 161

F0449 For to defend our country dear from harm,
For war or work, ought ourselves to arm.

c.339, p. 313

F0450 For Tunbridge Wells, when first I left the town,
And prostrate lays each Briton at her feet.

'Directions for drinking Tunbridge waters. 1728'
c.221, p. 22

F0451 For two and twenty year's long care,
James the peaceful and the just.

[George Morley], 'Another [epitaph] on K[ing] J[ames I]'
[Crum F498]
fb.143, p. 25; see also 'All that have eyes . . .'.

F0452 For underneath Oebalia's lofty tow'rs,
To those who drink beneath its spreading leaves.

[William Mills], 'Virgil's description of the old Corycian, translated from his fourth Georgic'
c.472, p. 117

F0453 For universal sway design'd,
No more unconquer'd worlds remain.

[Soame Jenyns], 'To a young lady, on her intended voyage to the West Indies'
c.147, p. 21

F0454 For us and for our trials three
We beg your reading pati-ent-ly.

[Richard Brinsley Butler Sheridan], 'A third by way of Wotton' [to William Hayley on his 'incomparably long' poem entitled The triumphs of temper, c. 1781]
File 13565

F0455 For various purposes serves the fan,
Are govern'd by a toy.

‘On the use of the fan’

c.83/1, no. 145

F0456 For virtue's sake now in your youthful prime
And gives them favor with the best of kings.

[Mary Serjant]

fb.98, fol. 149

F0457 For want of good carrier all on foot did jog on
Since he died for a cart you're balked of your
wagon.

fc.24, p. 7

F0458 For Warwick, she keeps two stallions in pay,
Who from his high throne was unpitied flung
down. | Which [nobody can deny]

‘Lampoon on several ladies’

fb.70, p. 9

F0459 For weighty reasons to himself best known
For fear some rogue should swear my ears are horns.

‘A paraphrase out of the Centum Tabula’

fb.142, p. 36

F0460 For what sad season, when the hapless belle
Whose vows in private are with favor heard.

Mrs. [ ] Fitzpatrick, ‘Dorinda an elegy’

Poetry Box XII/7

F0461 For which thy matchless beauties call
Each kindles to a golden ball.

[William Harrison], ‘To Miss Mears [daughter of
Dr. Mears, principal of Brasenose], with an orange’

Spence Papers, folder 113

F0462 For whom are now your airs put on?
Who snatch'd from ruin, sav'd me at the last.

[Lady Mary Wortley Montagu], ‘The 5th ode of
Horace imitated by the same’

fc.51, p. 51

F0463 For wit, for youth, for merit fam'd
Long may he live, this blooming fair to bless.

‘On Lady Payne’

Poetry Box II/13

F0464 For your dear sake I court again
You'd ask—the poet take.

[William Carpenter], ‘Ode on a lady's birthday’

c.247, p. 149

F0465 For your lascivious pranks, you husband Dick,
His forehead is, you're rather a Diana.

Sir Thomas Urquhart, ‘To one Susanna, whose
husband named Richard, esteemed her to be a little
too licentiously disposed’

fb.217, p. 155

F0466 Forbear, and at another's cost be wise,
Why shouldst thou lose thy mistress and thy labor
too.

c.549, p. 8

F0467 Forbear dear muse and curb thy ranting quill
I've yet more work t'employ thy lab'ring brain.

R[obert] Shirley, 1st earl of Ferrers, ‘The seventh
satire of Boileau imitated’

c.347, p. 18

F0468 Forbear dearest . . . . with a fruitless desire
And take, not expect, what hereafter'll bestow.

[John Hervey, baron Hervey of Ickworth], ‘To a lady
upon her asking the author where he thought he
should be that time twelvemonth’

Poetry Box v/12

F0469 Forbear Eliza press me not
In Andrews' fancy all combine.

Miss [ ] Andrews, ‘On Miss Howard pressing her for a
scrap of poetry’

File 245/14

F0470 Forbear, my dear Leuconoe,
Then seize on this, nor trust a future day.

[William Mills], ‘Odes of Horace translated. Book I.
Ode XI. To Leuconoe’

c.472, p. 24

F0471 Forbear my dear Stephen, with a fruitless desire
And receive, not expect, what hereafters bestow.

[John] Hervey, baron Hervey of Ickworth, ‘The late
Lord Hervey to Mr. Fox’

c.138, p. 29

F0472 Forbear, my friend, forbear and ask no more
Sophron, she waits above for thee.

J. W., ‘An elegy on Sophronia, who died of the
smallpox 1711 . . . Feby. 19. 1780’

c.259, p. 71

F0473 Forbear my outside friend to squeeze my hand
And fresh affronts deserve a smarter stroke.

‘A gentle reproof to a deceitful friend’

fc.61, p. 111

F0474 Forbear—no scatter'd flowers are wanted here
Fair Kitty's, Fanny's Polly's tender tear.

　　J. K., 'Another [epitaph on Dancer]'

　　c.150, p. 125

F0475 Forbear, nor more deride the key,
Is by love and duty, lock'd from thee.

　　'Apology for the present fashion of the ladies' wearing
　　keys on their breasts'

　　c.83/1, no. 139

F0476 Forbear thy rude approach bold passenger:
The top of all his glories to his tomb.

　　[Sir Aston Cokayne], 'Of Henry the 4th of France'

　　b.275, p. 70

F0477 Forbearance makes men more offend,
To thrust their sovereign out of place.

　　'Indulgentia malum . . . English thus'

　　c.189, p. 32

F0478 Forc'd from home, and all its pleasures,
Ere you proudly question ours.

　　[William] Cowper, 'The Negro's complaint'
　　[Crum F526]

　　fc.132/1, p. 213; Poetry Box V/106

F0479 'Fore two, or three, friends—let me see—am I able
Whose lot make a church, and whose chimney a
　　　　　　　　　　　　　　　steeple!

　　[Charles Earle], 'Sent (with an hare) to Mr. Collector
　　Pater; who, with two friends beside, had praised my
　　mutton-pasty for buck of high taste. Decr. 10th 1754'

　　c.376

F0480 Foreign, untutor'd jades! Had you but known,
The measure of your power, is their base fear.

　　'An elegy written on the unhappy accident which
　　befell the Lord Protector'

　　fb.228/28

F0481 Forever, Crito, will you thus complain
Concent'ring all the fire of all the tuneful train!

　　'An epistle to Crito'

　　fc.53, p. 39 (damaged)

F0482 Forever Fortune wilt thou prove
Make but the dear Amanda mine.

　　[James Thomson], 'Song'

　　c.358, p. 123

F0483 Forever, O merciless fair,
If you ever resolve not to love.

　　Lord G——, 'The expostulation to Delia' [General
　　evening post, 13 November 1779; answered by 'O cease
　　to mourn . . .']

　　c.157, p. 112

F0484 Forgive, dread Sir, an honest untaught muse
Not vain of knowledge, tho' by Clarke admir'd.

　　Thomas [Hamilton], 7th earl of Haddington, 'On the
　　death of Queen Caroline . . . November—20—1737 to
　　the King'

　　c.360/1, p. 93

F0485 Forgive fair creature form'd to please
But he that loves you not, is blind.

　　[David] Lewis

　　c.157, p. 48

F0486 Forgive me dear friend, for I own 'tis a crime,
Some in hopes a good fire, or their coach to obtain.

　　'A letter from Miss T. to Miss R.'

　　c.83/3, no. 998

F0487 Forgive me friends if I conceal
To use me well, or let me quite alone.

　　'An enigma'

　　c.153, p. 89

F0488 Forgive me, worthy Sir, if I
My dearest friend, sincerely—yours.

　　'An epistle to the worshipful gent [Henry Clarke] who
　　designed to stand candidate for a worshipful place [at
　　Trinity College, Dublin]' [pr. 1727 (Foxon E189)]

　　c.503, p. 21

F0489 Forgive my Canning this ill-timed delay
You'll ne'er be wanting at blest friendship's shrine.

　　[George Howard, 6th earl of Carlisle], 'To [George
　　Canning]'

　　c.197, p. 2

F0490 Forgive my coming thus, our griefs to utter,
Nor Ronan and Rivina die in vain.

　　David Garrick, 'Epilogue [to John Home's Fatal
　　discovery] spoken by Mrs. Abington'

　　File 5611

F0491 Forgive the muse who in unhallowed strains
And glad all heav'n with millions thou hast sav'd.

　　[Matthew] Prior, 'To Dr. Sherlock, on his Discourse
　　concerning death'
　　[Crum F536]

　　c.160, fol. 96

F0492 Forgive the muse, who, touch'd with neighb'ring grief
While William lives—to conquer—and revenge the slain.

[Thomas Morell], 'To Mrs Cathcart, and Mrs Sabine, sisters . . . who lost their husbands at the Battle of Fontenoy'

c.395, p. 98

F0493 Forgive this humble effort of a grateful friend,
Verses that please the ear delight the heart.

'To Clifford'

c.528/13

F0494 Forgive, ye fair, wrong'd innocence!
Immortal tea! 'tis all deriv'd from thee.

[Thomas Holland], of Jesus College, Oxford, 'The recant[at]ion'

c.233, p. 43

F0495 Forlorn upon the lofty mount I rove,
And to her memory drop a pensive tear.

[William Marriott], 'Elegy on the death of Dorothy Leaver'

c.140, p. 363

F0496 Form'd for a state of varied good, and ill
'Here we forever bathe in overflowing bliss.'

'An elegy to a friend on the premature death of her beloved sister Alicia in her prime at Bordeaux, in her way home from America after an absence of several years' [30 Nov. 1787]

c.136, p. 139

F0497 Form'd for the studious and the cheerful hour,
These dues of friendship to thy hallow'd dust.

[William Hayley], 'The remains of Edward Gibbon esqr. who was born in 1731 [i.e.; 1737] and died in London in his 57th year were deposited in this monument January 1794'

File 6943

F0498 Formed long ago, made every day,
And none would wish to keep.

'[Enigma/Charade/Conundrum] 9' [bed]
[Crum F539]

c.389

F0499 Form'd of the sweetest notes, this tender air
And glows with beauty unperceiv'd before.

John Lockman, 'Hearing the minuet, in the overture of Ariadne, played by Mr. Jackson on the violin'

c.267/1, p. 167; c.268 (first part), p. 12

F0500 Form'd with each grace, to captivate the eye,
Wept; breath'd a groan; then clos'd his eyes in night.

John Lockman, 'On his son Jonathan, who lived but a few days [d. 13 June 1736]'

c.267/1, p. 171; c.268 (first part), p. 8

F0501 Forsake with me the earth, my fair
Why should not we, by purer love?

[William] Habington, 'To Castara by the same'

b.150, p. 265

F0502 Forster! had I thy eloquence; and art
And risks his liberty to gaze on thee.

'On Mr. Forster having desired that some verses might be written on the subject of a robin redbreast having twice come to the communion table on a Christmas Day during the time that he administered the sacrament'

Diggle Box: Poetry Box XI/45

F0503 Forth from my cage and darksome cell
Will fire the bush at his back.

'Tom of Bedlam's song'
[Crum F544]

b.197, p. 36; c.555, p. 339; b.200, p. 344 ('sad and darksome')

F0504 Forth from my den, where my mad merry men
And so there's an end of my medley.

'Junes [sic] 1st. the hunter's career(?)'
[Crum F545]

b.213, p. 92; Poetry Box VII/76 (incomplete)

F0505 Forth from my first sprung Medecean grace
Look in the glass, and ten to one you see it.

[Four charades (3)]

Poetry Box II/42/3

F0506 Forth of thy mind throw down the world with speed,
First look for heaven, after worldly need.

c.339, p. 328

F0507 Fortune could not bless thee more
A nut had been the richer prize.

[Anna Laetitia (Aikin)] Barbauld, 'Sentiments by . . . given in walnuts after dinner on the wedding day of Dr. Parry to Miss Rigby'

c.364, p. 74

F0508 Fortune hath failed alas why so
Always in one Forto endure.

'Braye Lute Book', Music Ms. 13, fol. 47v

F0509 Fortune her gifts may variously dispose
But future views of better, or of worse.

c.83/2, no. 322

F0510 Fortune! How vain thy flatt'ring voice,
Which soothes all sorrow, and contents the mind.

'Sonnet'

c.83/3, no. 869

F0511 Fortune is now my foe
Some win and some lose all.

'Braye Lute Book,' Music Ms. 13, fol. 27v (incomplete?)

F0512 Fortune made up of toys and impudence
Rather than follow such a dull, blind whore.

[George Villiers], 2nd d[uke] of Buckingham, 'On fortune being part of the 29th ode lib. 3 of Horace' [Crum F554]

fc.60, p. 76

F0513 Fortune since thou art grown so kind
And all my foes away may find, | I ask no more.

'I ask no more. The Spanish wish'

b.200, p. 358; see also 'Since fortune thou . . .'.

F0514 Fortune that blind supposed goddess is
You make the fault, and call your saint unkind.

[Francis Quarles, 4 lines from the 9th 'Pious meditation', from A feast for worms, 1620] [Crum F557]

c.158, p. 34

F0515 Fortune we sooner may that woman trust
Who to her tongue and eyes most credit gives.

c.549, p. 93

F0516 Fortune, who often prove obdurate,
But let us save the tenement.

'The compromise. A tale'

c.94

F0517 Fortune with wealth and honor at her feet
That by their means the good are brought all under.

[Sir Thomas Urquhart], 'How blind fortune is [?] bestowing of her favors without having regard of merit'

fb.217, p. 541

F0518 Fortune's thought blind who doth to fools allow
Her gifts on foolish men so constantly.

[Sir Thomas Urquhart], 'That fortune is not blind'

fb.217, p. 539

F0519 Forty-eight years, exalt, this genial day,
Oh may this freedom thro' all time endure!

John Lockman, 'On the birth of the Duke of Cornwall [later George IV], 12 Aug. 1762'

c.267/1, p. 301

F0520 Foul I am, and cannot tell
Lest by his blood in vain w'have purged been.

H[enry] C[olman], 'On the Lord's Supper' [Crum F566]

b.2, p. 75

F0521 Founded upon the holy hills
As a fresh spring, shall them prolong.

'Psalm 87'

c.264/2, p. 82

F0522 Fount of comfort, heav'nly bright,
Virtue and content's the same.

'To contentment'

c.83/3, no. 946; see also 'Sweet contentment . . .'.

F0523 Four brothers and a sister such I had
They were most His so sav'd amongst the few.

Lady Jane Cavendish, 'On my dear brothers and sisters' [Crum F576]

b.233, p. 31

F0524 Four clerks of Oxford, doctors two and two
As Raleigh from his voyage, and no more.

[Richard] Corbett, 'Corbett's Iter boreale' [Crum F578]

b.356, p. 49

F0525 Four impudent cits, stockjobbers I mean,
This once she would pardon, 'cause 'twas midsummer moon.

[on the visit of Sir Gilbert Heathcote etc., representing the Bank, to Queen Anne on the dismissal of Sunderland, June 1710] [Crum F581]

b.90, p. 20

F0526 Four Irish Dearshoys—who had walk'd a great
waish
Among ush ah four, is but two milesh a pricet.

[Phanuel Bacon], 'Duo milia non piget in'

c.237, fol. 71 [i.e., 91]

F0527 Four kings in one place
And all ye warriors went to rest.

c.188, p. 27

F0528 Four ladies of engaging parts
To Foote—ambassador at large.

'The alliance an apologue. Inscribed to Samuel Foote esqr.'

c.68, p. 133

F0529 Four merry fiddlers play'd all night
And each receiv'd a guinea.

'Solution' [to 'Four people sat down . . .']

c.81/1, no. 423

F0530 Four modish dames, not prone to ill,
Who best should know my spouse's knock?

[John Lockman], 'The experienced matron'

c.268 (first part), p. 24

F0531 Four mongrel teachers lately ran a race
Young Orthodox stepp'd forth and got the day.

'On [the] late elect[ion] of an ordinary of Newgate'

fc.85, fol. 81

F0532 Four people sat down in one evening to play,
Tho' none of 'em lost, to the amount of a penny.

'Paradox' [answered by 'Four merry fiddlers . . .']

c.81/1, no. 422

F0533 Four sorts of men discourage me to crave
Yet none of these men shall relieve my want.

Sir John Strangways, '21° Decembris 1646'

b.304, p. 82

F0534 Four winter months, our senate sits
To squander it away.

'Written in the reign of King Charles the 2nd'

c.360/1, p. 59; c.94

F0535 Four wives I have had and believe me my friends
After so much ill luck, I would marry no more.

'Matrimonial experience'

c.115

F0536 Four yearly sessions are for saints design'd
He is not able to abide their terms.

[Sir Thomas Urquhart], 'That lingering in suits of law perplexeth even those who share(?) the best cause'

fb.217, p. 532 (two drafts)

F0537 Fox, Sheridan, and Burke, sweet trio!
And in a puff the whole goes out.

'Hasting's trial' [1788]

c.81/1, no. 210

F0538 Frag[r]ant the rose, but it fades in time,
Which time, or sickness speedily destroys.

'On youth'

fc.130, p. 81

F0539 Frail daughter to my words attend,
And confessors, confess to thee!

'Answer to the confession'

Poetry Box XII/120

F0540 Frail things' first matter, is like Isabel;
It covets ev'ry form: she, ev'ry male.

Sir Thomas Urquhart, 'An analogy betwixt the material prima, and a courtesan named Isabel'

fb.217, p. 337

F0541 Fram'd to give joy, the lovely sex are seen:
Gives him a title to untainted bliss!

'On woman'

c.81/1, no. 315

F0542 France aims at all
Or else the devil would overrun all.

'The powers of Europe engaged all at all'

c.111, p. 106

F0543 France pours her legions ov'r the rapid main:
Always thus fight, thus heat, and shine in story.

Abraham Oakes, 'The contrast: an epigrammatic description of the late war. 1748'

c.50, p. 138

F0544 France totters under these three royal names
For William fate reserves both name, and thing.

[translation of libel fixed on 'the king of France's statue in the Place of Victory,' for which the libellers were tried 8 August 1689]
[Crum F595]

Poetry Box VII/40, p. 4

F0545 Frances but clay—though of the purest mold
Whilst young and brisk in a frank gaiety.

[Sir Philip Wodehouse], 'Upon [Lucia Repps'] maiden sister Mrs. Frances Calybut'

b.131, back (no. 228)

F0546 Frank in regard thou's art and fair respect
Was a brave senator of Rome—be't so.

[Sir Philip Wodehouse], 'Upon Mr Francis Gardiner of Norwich—alderman'

b.131, back (no. 192)

F0547 Frantic love to what extremes
Alas! alas! what shall I do.

    William Cleggate, 'A song or poem made by . . . upon
    Mrs. Thomasin North . . 1675'

b.54, p. 1036

F0548 Fraud, levity, lechery, pride and high disdain;
Say, is't not known these in the Louvre reign?

    W. F., '[In Gallicas perignot] The [English] version'

Poetry Box VI/43

F0549 Free from all thoughts of guilt, all acts of shame
And every wife and sister drop a tear.

fc.14/10

F0550 Free from confinement and strife,
But rot in the harbor at home.

    'Song 60'

c.555, p. 88

F0551 Free from the din of waters bawl'd around;
And raise them, lovelier, to thy mental eye.

    John Lockman, 'To the Duchess of Buckingham;
    humbly requesting her Grace to leave her retirement,
    and remove to Versailles . . . Aug. 1741'

c.267/2, p. 369

F0552 Free you from the roughness then
To God's glory and bright day.

    'Votum'

Poetry Box VI/118

F0553 Freedom of will, which is the world's contest,
Husbands have lost but wives have it possest.

    'Free will'

c.356

F0554 Freedom's charms alike engage
Bliss is born of liberty.

    'On freedom'

fc.85, fol. 115v

F0555 Frenchmen tenacious of the rights of men
Deserves our worship—'tis the right of God.

    Charles Atherton Allnutt, 'On the French decade'

c.112, p. 175

F0556 Frequent along the pebbly beach I pace,
And role in flaming billows to the shore.

    [John] Aikin, 'Description of the seashore'

c.83/2, no. 571

F0557 Freron, a candidate for fame,
What would be left for poor Freron.

    'On Freron'

c.83/2, no. 689

F0558 Fresh and surprising scenes of grief appear
Great as her worth and lasting as her fame.

    'Another elegy on her late Majesty Queen Caroline'
    [d. 20 Nov. 1737]

fb.142, p. 67

F0559 Fresh from the skies, the other day,
And each did diff'rent paths pursue.

    'Hymen Plutus and Cupid a fable on the marriage of
    W. C. esqr. and Miss T.'

c.89, p. 80

F0560 Fresh streams, run to the sea, as life to death;
'Tis sour to die: but sweet's our vital breath.

    Sir Thomas Urquhart, 'Of death, and the sea'

fb.217, p. 334

F0561 Fret not, dear Tom that thou hast lost the race
Till warmth shall both erect their stings and
                               crest[s].

    [William Plaxton], 'An epistle from J[emmy]
    Singleton to his friend Tom Pullam about the
    [Yorkshire] election race' [1708; pr. 1709 (Foxon
    P481)]
    [Crum F606, with 76 more lines]

Poetry Box VII/14; c.160, fol. 24

F0562 Friend, as we both in confidence complain,
Have stray'd, and now we stray farther than before!

    [from Petrarch]

fb.66/20

F0563 Friend Boulton! take these ingots fine,
Whose heav'n-wrought statue charms the world.

    [Erasmus] Darwin, 'Directions for a tea vase'

c.142, p. 507

F0564 Friend for Jesus' sake forbear
And curst be he that moves my bones.

    [William] Shakespeare, 'Shakespeare's epitaph by
    himself'

b.54, p. 1157; see also 'Good friends . . .'.

F0565 Friend Isaac, 'tis strange, you that live so near Bray
It must needs be a sign of good liquor.

    'Epigram' [answered by 'Indeed master poet . . .']

c.81/1, no. 344

F0566 Friend let thy mind an even temper know,
And hurls 'em headlong to eternal night.

'Ode 3d lib 2nd imitated Horace'

c.233, p. 11

F0567 Friend! o'er this sepulcher forbear,
In life, in death, supremely blest.

G. Wakefield, 'Epitaph from the Greek anthologia'

c.240, p. 140

F0568 Friend of my heart, consider, ere thou wed
And antedate the wish'd-for joys above.

[Charles Burney, the younger], 'Answer to all the
enigmas in The ladies' diary, 1778'

c.37, p. 25

F0569 Friend of my heart! Whose pen, like magic wand
Can long subsist, were Erebus the room.

[Charles Burney, the elder], 'To the Revd. Thomas
Twining'

c.33, p. 105

F0570 Friend of the arts, and virtue's friend
No ages could destroy.

Dr. [ ] King, 'Ode inscribed to Sr. Abraham Hume
bart. On his painting two pictures of views near his
seat at Worsley(?) Herts—1783'

c.504, p. 18

F0571 Friend of those days when round our brows
Domestic concord's happiest power.

[ ] Simcoe, general, 'Answer to the foregoing'
[[William Boscawen], 'You, whom so oft . . .']

fc.106, p. 46

F0572 Friend Oldmixon, I needs must praise
Is turning to Oldmixon.

John Dennis, 'An epistle from . . . to John Oldmixon'

File 16887 (annotated)

F0573 Friend Palo may boast of true orthodox merit
What he wants in the flesh, he makes up in the
                                                spirit.

'On a bad dinner with excellent punch'

c.546

F0574 Friend, sister partner of that gentle heart
To teach that prudence which itself admires.

[John] Langhorne, 'Precepts of conjugal happiness
addressed to a young lady on her marriage'
[Crum F620]

c.139, p. 489

F0575 Friend to the drooping heart, still whisp'ring peace
Which calm the sorrowing soul thro' each sad
                                                scene below.

'Religion'

c.83/3, no. 866

F0576 Friend William North, the dial's gone
Be claim'd by him that gave it.

Tho[mas] Harding, '6 mo. 16th. 1790'

File 13409

F0577 Friendless—alone—with ev'ry woe opprest
Well-pleas'd to find some pity still below.

[Helen Craik], 'The maid of Enterkin'

c.375, p. 65

F0578 Friends are like melons, of which sort of food
We'll taste a hundred, ere we find one good.

Sir Thomas Urquhart, 'That it is a difficult matter to
chance upon a man of real, and sincere friendship'

fb.217, p. 35

F0579 Friends dry up your tears, and weep no more,
For I am only gone a little before.

c.378, p. 7; see also 'Brothers and sisters . . .'.

F0580 Friends ought to be with us in such esteem
To harm oneself for any other creature.

[Sir Thomas Urquhart], 'To one who desired a [?] for
a friend which tended too much [illeg.]'

fb.217, p. 511

F0581 Friendship, adieu! Thou dear deceitful good!
And find ourselves deserted—and undone.

[Samuel Boyse], 'On friendship . . . General evening
post, August 6th 1776'

c.157, p. 103

F0582 Friendship best of human things,
A friend and husband both in God.

T[homas] Scott, jr., 'Verses addressed to the widow
gentlewoman on her loss of a special friend'

c.244, p. 131

F0583 Friendship hath honey and hath oil
Just as the muse reveal'd I send it.

'To Athenia. 1752. Novr. 8 N. S.'

c.238, p. 51

F0584 Friendship, how sweet! How comely dost thou
                                                seem
A wretch, as he who only wakes, to mourn.

'On the changes of friendship'

c.83/2, no. 340

F0585 Friendship is an empty name made to deceive,
Can hope for here is faint neutrality.

Mary Armyns, 'Written in the glass window of the
dining room at Mr. Master's in Bath'

b.52/2, p. 129

F0586 Friendship is the bond of reason
Or sacrilege to love and her.

'Song 239'

c.555, p. 382

F0587 Friendship is the joy of reason,
Friend[ship] without bound delights.

'On friendship'

fc.85, fol. 115v

F0588 Friendship is to the dual number tied:
Love to the plural scarce being multiplied.

Sir Thomas Urquhart, 'How rare a thing it is to have
friends'

fb.217, p. 323

F0589 Friendship: peculiar boon of heav'n,
Shall aid our happiness above.

[Samuel] Johnson, 'On friendship'
[Crum F634]

c.341, p. 144; c.83/4, no. 2022; fc.132/1, p. 203

F0590 Friendship that antidote of woe,
But dare to act the friend.

'Ode on friendship'

fc.51, p. 5; Poetry Box I/11 ('thou antidote')

F0591 Friendship the heavenly theme, I sing,
As light we haste away.

[Mary Chandler], 'Friendship'

c.244, p. 631; c.351, p. 137

F0592 Friendship! Thou powerful sovereign of the mind,
Who leads us thro' the maze of life, and kindly
fix'd us there.

'Sent in the beginning of a letter to Aurelia'

c.153, p. 83

F0593 Friendship! Thou soft propitious pow'r,
He dares be honest, tho' he dies.

'Friendship'

c.83/2, no. 325

F0594 Friendship true delight bestows,
It will with greater splendor shine.

'On friendship'

c.156, p. 235

F0595 Friendship! Which so like true love art
And let it be, till death, confin'd.

[Phanuel Bacon], 'A song'

c.237, fol. 75

F0596 Friendship's a name to few confin'd,
And leave you to your foes a prey.

'Friendship'

c.83/3, no. 1006

F0597 From a bundle of lies, and a fardel of nonsense,
From men whose religion lies in a romance, |
Libera nos Domine.

'A new litany'

b.111, p. 237

F0598 From a kind hand there came t'enrich a place
Made both your Rose and Crown to flourish still.

R[obert] W[ild, on a bookseller's shop]

c.166, p. 301

F0599 From a proud, sensual, atheistical life,
From making our heirs to be Morris, and Clayton. |
Libera nos [Domine]

'The D[uke] of B[uckingham's] litany' [on George
Villiers, second Duke of Buckingham; printed c. 1680,
Wing L2536]
[Crum F643, 'sensual, proud'; POAS II.192]

b.105, p. 377; Poetry Box IV/120

F0600 From a thick wood's embow'ring glade,
Can daunt his soul, or tempt his stay.

John Lockman, 'The scholar and the bee . . . 1733'

c.267/1, p. 327; c.268 (first part), p. 31

F0601 From a vain world to us replete with woe
For heav'n nor earth has pity left for me.

[Helen Craik], 'Written by Charlotte at Werther's
grave'

c.375, p. 30

F0602 From a woman that fifty long winters has seen
And is ever commanding instead of obeying. |
Libera me.

'The bachelor's litany'

Poetry Box X/15, p. 25

F0603 From Abram's bosom full of lice
And bid the nitty cur good night.

[Thomas Brown], 'Epitaph on Sarah, wife to one
Abram, a tailor'

c.360/2, no. 19

F0604 From all decanal cares at last set free,
Heav'n is the gold refin'd, earth but the drop. |
Amen

> M[ary] C[ornwallis], 'The wish 1768 by Dr. Zachary
> Pearce when he resigned the deanery of Westminster'
> fc.124, p. 133

F0605 From all the busy scenes of life,
What man can't give nor man destroy.

> 'The wish'
> c.156, p. 73; c.83/3, no. 819

F0606 From all the giddy whirls of fate
Name the day and fix on me.

> [Robert Cholmeley], 'To a young lady desiring her to
> leave the town for a country retirement'
> c.190, p. 173

F0607 From all the women we have whor'd
And never see Breda again. | *Quaesimus te audire nos
Domine*

> 'A litany for the holy time of Lent' [1688]
> [Crum F650]
> b.52/2, p. 206; fb.108, p. 271; fb.68, p. 127; Poetry Box
> vi/80 (satirically subscribed 'O[badiah] Walker')

F0608 From all uneasy passions free,
'Tis worth a life to die within your arms.

> [John Sheffield], 1st duke of Buckingham and
> Normanby, 'Song'
> Poetry Box iv/53

F0609 From all your cogitations, deeds, and speech
T'adorn your outward parts more pure, than coral.

> Sir Thomas Urquhart, 'To the Countess of [crossed
> out]'
> fb.217, p. 296

F0610 From alpine heights where clad in snow
Could all partake the common right!

> 'Ode to the lake of Geneva after a tour of the glaciers
> of Chamonix and through the lower Valais' [signed
> 'Adolphus']
> c.343, p. 4

F0611 From an old inquisition, and new declaration
The finding it all Ignoramus at last. | Forever [good
Lord deliver me].

> 'A short litany on the acquitting the Lord [ ]' [1688]
> [Crum F652]
> fb.108, p. 181

F0612 From atoms, in confusion hurl'd,
If thou no more canst mend than make.

> [Thomas] S[e]w[ar]d, 'By the Revd. Mr. S—w—d'
> Poetry Box v/48

F0613 From bad health and bad weather and parties' dull
strife,
And I ask for no more within the four seas.

> 'The true Englishman's wish'
> c.570/4, p. 40

F0614 From barb'rous heathen's cruel yoke
Till time it shall end.

> [Sir William Trumbull], 'P[salm] 106 v. 47'
> Trumbull Box: Poetry Box xiii/21

F0615 From beauty did the brave Æneas spring,
With a more num'rous race, or more divine.

> [ ] Hicks, of Christ Church, Oxford, 'On my Lady
> Monthermer's brave boy'
> c.189, p. 184; c.241, p. 40

F0616 From Bristol there came
By the frowns of a barbarous dame.

> 'A song on Ld Wm Hamilton and Miss Dolly Haws, a
> Bath toast'
> c.233, p. 91

F0617 From Britain's isle to China's distant land,
Yet none so precious as himself we have.

> R[obert] Shirley, 1st earl of Ferrers, 'Boileau's verses
> upon Tavernier, applied to my honorable uncle Lewis
> Shirley, esq.'
> c.347, p. 27

F0618 From Britain's isle to Cyprian groves
A short-liv'd minion's deathless fame.

> Nicholas Harding, 'Upon the death of Mr. Page's
> dove'
> c.152, p. 26

F0619 From Cephalus's tragic story, read
That drowns my hopes, and drives me to despair.

> [Charles Hopkins], 'The story of Cephalus and
> Procris'
> c.94; b.130, p. 30 ('Chephalus')

F0620 From chaos wrapt in drear repose,
Nor question, but obey.

> 'Creation. An ode'
> c.83/2, no. 590

F0621 From Charter House College, I beg leave to send,
When he handled and view'd them, with joy and
surprise.

> C[harles] B[urney], 'To my little friend Charles
> Wollaston, on his being put into breeches'
> c.37, before p. 53

F0622　Entry cancelled. 'From Chephalus' tragic story . . .'
See 'From Cephalus's . . .'.

F0623　From cloister's cell where pedantry and pride
All my ambition gratified in thee.

　　'To M. Lyttelton at Soissons from Oxford . . .
　　holograph by Gray—CB'
　　Poetry Box x/2

F0624　From Compton low in Warwickshire,
And now subscribe myself your friend.

　　E[lizabeth (Shirley)] C[ompton, countess of
　　Northampton], 'A letter to the lady A[nne] C[ompton]
　　in ciphers from . . . dated [ ]'
　　Accession 97.7.40

F0625　From Coram learn: wealth rarely is consign'd
Such is the will of man, not that of heaven.

　　John Lockman, 'A reflection, at Capt. Coram's
　　funeral, in the chapel of the Foundling Hospital'
　　c.267/1, p. 231

F0626　From councils of six where treason prevails
From Franky's lame jests and Sir Roger's lampoons |
　　　　　　　　　For ever good Lord deliver me.

　　'A new litany appointed for this Lent . . . To an
　　excellent old tune called Cavallilly man'
　　b.113, p. 271

F0627　From Cynthia's swearing,
To die like us mortals below.

　　[Robert Cholmeley], 'The happy change. A song'
　　c.190, p. 39

F0628　From death we rose to life: 'tis but the same
And to be long a-dying only pray.

　　[ ] Howard
　　c.240, p. 119

F0629　From deepest dungeon of eternal night
If you believe seducers more than me.

　　[Wentworth Dillon, 4th earl of Roscommon], 'The
　　ghost of the last House of Commons at London. 1680.
　　appearing to the new one at Oxford' [1681]
　　[*POAS* II.407]
　　File 17951; b.210, p. 122; c.171, p. 4

F0630　From Delia oft I strove in vain
When lip to lip is join'd.

　　'Sonnet. On hearing a young lady play the flute'
　　c.361

F0631　From deposing of kings as a damn'd popish tenet
But James may drive 'em both away. | *Quaesimus te*
　　　　　　　　　　　　　　　　　　　　&c.

　　'A litany for the monthly fast, April 7th, 1692'
　　[*POAS* V.324]
　　b.111, p. 241

F0632　From dirt I came; and unto dirt I go:
That those yet private never may be known.

　　[Catherine Dering], 'Verses made by a young lady of
　　thirteen'
　　Spence Papers, folder 113

F0633　From dirt to save yon page uptook
At their dull poesy.

　　[N.] Herbert, 'Epigram upon the book of Oxford
　　verses being unpaged'
　　Spence Papers, folder 91

F0634　From distant climes, o'er widespread seas we come,
Thus, in an honest way, still pick your pockets.

　　[George Barrington?], 'Prologue spoken by the
　　celebrated Mr. Barrington opening the Theater at
　　Sydney, Botany Bay' [1800?]
　　Poetry Box x/152

F0635　From distant climes, where virtue never dies,
I go to regions where the happy dwell.

　　J. G., 'Taken out of the Leeds mercury, 1780. William
　　Penn's ghost'
　　c.365, p. 257

F0636　From dreary realms where cold and famine reign,
The land that made you monarch worship me.

　　'A speech deliver'd by the High German-speaking dog
　　when he had his audience at Kensington introduced by
　　his grace the Duke of Newcastle to G[eor]ge' [1718]
　　c.102, p. 106; fc.58, p. 139; c.570/2, p. 3

F0637　From earth and all its fading vanities
Saints, eternally to hymn his praise!

　　[Thomas Stevens?], 'An elegiac poem on the death of
　　Mr. Edwards, late of Ipswich, in Suffolk'
　　c.259, p. 65

F0638　From earth we come, to earth we must return
But from this earth to heaven Earth's soul is gone.

　　'An epitaph in Dinton church Wilts. Roger Earth, ob.
　　5 April 1634'
　　c.150, p. 144

F0639　From easing females in pain
The first . . . . knight as e'er was seen.

　　'The midnight knight' [Sir David Hamilton]
　　[Crum F674]
　　fb.70, p. 17

F0640 From education all our ills arise,
And pleasures found not in the breast of kings.

'On education'
c.83/2, no. 379

F0641 From ev'ry muse, and ev'ry art, thy own
And long, and lovely, as thy walks, thy days.

'An address, from the statues at Stowe, to Lord
Cobham, on his return to his garden'
c.536

F0642 From ev'ry quarter of the sky,
Your choral voices gladly join.

Jabez Hughes [enclosed in a letter to William
Duncombe, London 1718]
File 16982 (autogr.)

F0643 From fairest creatures we desire increase,
To eat the world's due, by the grave and thee.

[William] Shakespeare [Sonnet 1]
c.94

F0644 From famed Barbados on the Western main
And fall on fiercely like a starved dragoon.

Sir Fleetwood Sheppard, 'Receipt for a sack posset'
[answered by 'Barbados sugar . . .']
[Crum F683a]
c.158, p. 359

F0645 From Father Adam's first and best-spent hours
Demand, and ever have, our grateful prayers.

'An epilogue spoken at the Freemason's play acted in
the town hall at Spalding in January 1739 by Thomas
Lewood Freemason an eminent comedian'
c.229/2, fol. 48v

F0646 From flower to flower his joys to change
And who's the longest free.

'Song'
Poetry Box x/153

F0647 From foreign reigns hither come
But always make my court in white.

[ ] R., 'Riddle'
Poetry Box VII/49

F0648 From forth the Elysian fields,
And we will be blithe together.

'Songs [5]'
b.356, p. 274

F0649 From friends, divisions, and quarrels intestine,
Causing fools to admire, and wise men to wonder. |
[*Libera nos domine*] &c.

'October 1700'
c.189, p. 16

F0650 From frozen climes, and endless tracts of snow
And as he goes the transient vision mourns.

[Ambrose] Philips, 'A winter piece addressed to the
Duke of Dorset' [Copenhagen, 1709]
c.140, p. 156; c.83/3, no. 776

F0651 From Gotha, fair Augusta full of charms
A present princess, and a future queen.

'Extempore verses on the arrival of Princess Augusta'
[25 April 1736]
c.360/1, p. 141

F0652 From grace to grace by love my mind so fast
And of m'enamored thoughts the nimbleness.

[Sir Thomas Urquhart]
fb.217, p. 508

F0653 From grave lessons and restraint,
If he's false I'll fit him too.

'Song set by John Weldon, sung by Mrs. Bradpeace'
[Crum F690]
c.160, fol. 83

F0654 From guiltless dreams prepared to pray,
And in each stitch some mortals read.

'Eudosia, or the accomplished virgin'
c.186, p. 94

F0655 From H[a]gl[e]y's gay bowers, where L[u]cy has
strayed,
Give place to slaves—Parnassus repair.

'Court characters. Ld. Ly[ttelto]n'
c.186, p. 123

F0656 From happy climes where virtue never dies,
Then find the generous labor is not lost.

[William Meston], 'Cato's ghost,' [Jacobite verses on
Addison's play, pr. 1715 (Foxon M209)]
[Crum F693]
c.570/1, p. 116; fc.58, p. 109

F0657 From hate, fear, hope, anger, and envy free,
Call in the States of Holland to their aid.

A[braham] C[owley], 'The passions'
c.258

F0658 From haunts of men, from day's obtrusive glance,
Twilight thy love—thy guide her beaming star.

'To the bat'
c.83/3, no. 744

F0659 From heaven a voice majestic sounds
To find the dear communion sweet.

T[homas] S[tevens], 'March 18. 1781 Lord's day'
c.259, p. 134

F0660 From heav'n, Prometheus stole some sparks away,
Freedom he brought, as well as fire from heav'n.

> 'The modern Prometheus . . . alluding to the doctor
> [Benjamin Franklin]'s electrical experiment'
> c.160, fol. 50

F0661 From her, alas, whose smile was love,
And only flutter at her name.

> [John Walcot ('Peter Pindar')], 'A song (to Cynthia)'
> c.355, p. 97

F0662 From her fair limbs the last their veil she drew
The spot where Cynthia bathes at noon beware.

> 'Sonnet. From the Italian . . . Annual register [17]89'
> c.344, p. 116

F0663 From her whose hands these airy nets enweave,
Of faithful friendship, and of filial love!

> Anna Seward, 'To Mrs. Eliot . . . March 1st 1792'
> File 13377

F0664 From Isis' banks which, near the Muse's seats,
Flow backwards to thy spring, and I shall cease to
love.

> [J. Jones, of Balliol], 'On Nancy Brickenden's going to
> Newnham by water' [answered by 'Whilst you my
> charming Nancy . . .']
> [Crum F704]
> Poetry Box IV/127

F0665 From Italy's enchanting scenes
The muse and genius absent too.

> [Helen Craik], 'To a gentleman—written after riding
> through a mountainous part of the country'
> c.375, p. 42

F0666 From Julia's cheek the rose is fled
When love depends on Julia's mind.

> 'To Julia'
> c.546

F0667 From kings that would sell us to pay their own
scores,
When all is as false as the saving of Flanders. |
Libera nos Domine.

> ['A new litany' 1680]
> [Crum F709]
> Poetry Box VI/44

F0668 From lasting and unclouded day,
Nor shall Cornelia shed a tear.

> [Katherine Philips], 'Pompey's ghost to his wife
> Cornelia' [from The tragedy of Pompey, act iii]
> [Crum F710]
> c.83/1, no. 13

F0669 From life's first moment to its longest date
Defer not till tomorrow to be wise.

> 'On life death judgment, Heaven, and Hell 1735'
> c.181, p. 43

F0670 From life's superfluous cares enlarg'd
While yet with life his ashes glow.

> [Abraham] Cowley, 'Epitaph on himself'
> c.83/3, no. 775

F0671 From ling'ring pain thy patience bore
For heav'n! if not to bless mankind.

> D[avid] Garrick, 'To the memory of Master Barnard
> Hale on a marble stone in the parish church of Abbots
> Langley the following lines by the late . . . are
> inscribed'
> c.373, p. 47

F0672 From London, Paul the carrier, coming down
I warrant I'll find mouth, if they'll find men.

> [William King, D. C. L.], 'Little mouths'
> c.578, p. 102

F0673 From Louis's battles we never could know
And to find an old whore make an excellent wife.

> [Matthew] Prior, 'Sr Evremont's verses on [the]
> Fr[ench] K[ing]. Translated by Mr. Prior. Aug [16]96'
> Trumbull Box: Poetry Box XIII/60

F0674 From love's fruition let no man divert us
For both of them aim only at the mids[t].

> Sir Thomas Urquhart, 'That in the art of venery can
> be no great sin a paradox'
> fb.217, p. 112

F0675 From low and abject themes the grov'ling muse
From such a chief to fight and bard to sing.

> [John Philips], 'A poem upon the battle at
> Blenheim . . . 1705' [pr. 1705 (Foxon P226)]
> c.553

F0676 From lowest depth of heart
He's merciful as just.

> 'Psalm 130. 6th penitential'
> c.264/3, p. 76

F0677 From me dear Charles, inspir'd with ale,
The cart would drive, and I be hang'd. | With a fa
&c.

> [William Tunstall], 'A ballad from a prisoner in the
> Marshallsea, to another at Newgate' [Sir Charles
> Wogan; pr. 1716 (Foxon T546)]
> [Crum F713]
> c.570/1, p. 148

F0678 From mercy's throne, where Jesus sits above
Since thus thou bidst me live.

> 'Words fitted to be sung to a song of Mr. H. Purcell
> called From rosy bowers'
>
> c.167, p. 23

F0679 From misinforming of our state
And [?] dooms(?) that does much ill | *Libera*
[*me*]. . . .

> 'The Westland litany'
> Poetry Box VIII/32 (incomplete)

F0680 From morn to eve
Find nothing else that's worth professing. | Ho my
bonny ditto

> Accession 97.7.40

F0681 From mundane cares, and each delusive toy
The retribution of her suff'rings here.

> 'Verses sacred to the memory of a deceased friend
> Witney June the 7 1746'
>
> c.360/2, no. 163

F0682 From my devotion[s] yonder am I come,
You come both th' entertainer, and the guest.

> W[illiam] Cartwright, 'The prologue to the King, and
> Queen's Majesty on Cartwright's . . . Royal slave'
> [1636]
> [Crum F715]
>
> b.200, p. 150

F0683 From my good God do I request,
Such is my present, my eternal bliss.

> [Edmund Wodehouse], 'Jan. 26 [1715]'
> b.131, p. 148

F0684 From my happy seat above,
Should you neglect her at your own.

> [William Carpenter], 'An ode on the 5th November
> 1755. in imitation of the chorus at the end of the first
> act'
>
> c.247, p. 106

F0685 From my sad cradle to my sable chest
Because I am not lost but sent before.

> 'On Mary the wife of Jo. Merrion who died Nov. 25
> 1693 in the 26th year of her age' [also inscribed at
> Long Ashton to Joseph Crossman, d. 20 Jan. 1671]
> [Crum F717]
>
> fb.143, p. 24

F0686 From Needless-Hall I took a trip
And grateful did persuade me.

> 'The ramble'
> c.530, p. 189

From neighboring seas, th'echoing report,   F0687
Come in sea nymphs, for sadness were a sin.

> 'A Triton of the sea with his three-forked mace to
> make the speech'
>
> fb.69, p. 235

From noise, from folly, fraud and strife,   F0688
Their world, let vice and folly keep.

> W[illia]m Jackson, 'To the Revd. Mr. Bay Ray M. A.
> vic[a]r of Surfleet and perpetual curate of Cowbitt in
> the parish of Spalding Elloe Holland Lincolnshire . . .
> on his hermitage composed of willows and reeds
> 20 Aug. 1747'
>
> c.229/1, fol. 95v

From ocean's bosom an enormous pile   F0689
How Alyra shines with beauties all her own.

> 'St. Helena a poem wrote in the year 1742'
> Poetry Box I/95

From one that languisheth in discontent   F0690
Rest you in much content, I in despair.

> Sir George Radney, 'Sr George Radney to the
> Countess of Hertford' [December 1600]
> [Crum F723]
>
> b.197, p. 206

From others' folly wisdom learn,   F0691
If lurking there he hides.

> [N. Herbert], 'Reflections on the great Scotch ram
> with two curling horns and one straight one in the
> middle presented to the Prince of Wales or Duke of
> Cumberland'
>
> Spence Papers, folder 91

From parching summers and boisterous winters;   F0692
From the wiles of the purser, the d[evi]l, and
steward, | May we be delivered.

> 'Song 97. The sailor's litany'
> c.555, p. 147

From parley-making in the Parliament,   F0693
'Twas never known that they could cure a knave.

> 'Some lines fixed upon a pillar at the Bath when J[ac]k
> H[o]w[e] was there'
>
> c.111, p. 25

From peace with the French and war with the   F0694
Dutch
And if e'er it be dissolv'd will die in a jail. | *Libera
nos Domine.*

> 'These were writ in Lincoln's Inn boghouse 1672'
> [*POAS* I.190]
> fb.140, p. 161

F0695 From pensioner, papist, and rusty dragoons,
That would bring us all to pay Peter pence. | *Libera*
nos &c.

'The new litany. 1672 . . . G[ilbert Sheldon,
Archbishop of] Canterbury'
[Crum F730]
b.54, p. 1215

F0696 From place to place forlorn I go,
Why speaks not he who may?

[Sir Richard Steele], 'A song'
c.152, p. 16

F0697 From pleasantness the left hand hath its name,
An idle hand and in all labor lame.

'The left hand'
c.356

F0698 From public noise, and factious strife
Mayst thou be false, and I be great.

[Matthew] Prior, 'Lines by Prior'
fc.132/1, p. 190

F0699 From realm to realm with cross or crescent
crown'd,
And murmuring demons hate him—and admire.

'On the death of Jo[h]n Howard esq.' [1790]
c.140, p. 82

F0700 From regions far remote, and lands that lie
And life's calm ev'ning set without a shade.

'Cynthia to Leonora . . . an epistle from the Cape of
Good Hope'
c.139, p. 471

F0701 From restless faction, calumny, and noise
Th' effect is love, but Sylvia is the cause.

H[annah] M[ore], 'Henrique to Sylvia'
c.341, p. 86

F0702 From rosy fingers morning shook the dew,
With guiltless mirth to crown the happy day.

'The accident, a pastoral elegy' [pr. 1747 (Foxon A5)]
c.139, p. 430

F0703 From Satan's guile
Of Jesu Christ our Lord. | Amen

'A prayer to our blessed Savior Jesu'
a.6, p. 31

F0704 From scenes of tumult, noise, and strife,
Her sober hue and light serene.

[John] Aikin, 'Horatian philosophy'
c.355, p. 192

F0705 From scheming, fretting, famine, and despair,
But judgment govern, and the stage obey.

'Mr. Macklin's prologue 1744'
fc.85, fol. 34

F0706 From scourging rebellion, and baffling proud
France,
And bind those in chains who would Britons
enthrall. | Your glasses &c.

John Lockman, 'The victory at Culloden: gained by
his royal Highness, the Duke of Cumberland, over the
rebels'
[Crum F745]
c.267/2, p. 5

F0707 From shamming three nations by new-coin'd
inventions,
From ten thousand things more that make you sick
and me sick | Deliver us good Lord deliver us.

'A new litany, for the General Fast Day'
b.111, p. 231

F0708 From Sinai's lofty palaces on high,
Obtain the bright reward, and reign in bliss with me.

[Richard] Daniel, dean of Armagh, 'The sinner
sentenced—Psalm 50'
c.244, p. 362

F0709 From storms and eastern blasts secure,
Her eyes their fury had disarm'd.

'On Mrs. Gisborne of Stavely with child'
b.322, p. 34

F0710 From stormy winter's cold domain
Of 'I was chairman all night long.'

John Belfour, 'To the printer of the Ledger ode the
4th 1st. book of Horace, liberally translated . . . to a
friend no. 25 . . . Wapping 29th April 1767'
c.217, p. 148

F0711 From strenuous sires bold sons proceed
Beget a weak and timorous dove.

'A translation of . . . lines in Horace'
c.360/2, no. 136

F0712 From stronger proofs, if I aright divine,
You'll find them false and brittle as the glass.

'Written on a window with a diamond'
c.570/3, p. 135

F0713 From such a face whose excellence
Heaven bless our King and all his senses.

[William Drummond, of Hawthornden?], 'A prayer
for the King's five senses'
[Crum F751]
b.54, p. 877

F0714 From sunset to daybreak whilst folks are asleep,
But who will secure it from morning till night.

Philip Wharton, 1st duke of Wharton(?), 'On robbing
the Exchequer'

c.468

F0715 From Swedish wolf see you yourself secure
And of his detestable perfidy.

'In memoriale L. S. imperatoris exhibitum. Simulata
pietas duplex iniquitas'

b.54, p. 1237

F0716 From Telamon when gen'rous Teucer fled
Today, my friends, and hoist up sail tomorrow.

'Ex Hor: ode 7a lib: 1°. Translated'

Poetry Box VII/44

F0717 From that dire era, bane to Sarum's pride,
How much you'd suffer, if religion fell.

[Thomas Parnell], 'On Bishop Burnet's being set on
fire in his closet'

File 11383, p. 13

F0718 From that vast circle of my Paphian fires,
To your accomplishments concentric are.

Sir Thomas Urquhart, 'To the never too much to be
admired the divine Aura'

fb.217, p. 141

F0719 From the black regions of eternal night
And may'st thou ne'er experience woes like mine!

F[rances] B[urney d'Arblay], 'Poetical epistles from
the dead to the living by F. B. aged 16 years. Sappho to
Phaon'

c.486, fol. 16

F0720 From the bright regions of eternal day
Shall like old Ely's son unpitied fall . . . .

'Lord Lucas his ghost'
[Crum F755]

b.52/2, p. 141 (incomplete)

F0721 From the court to the cottage convey me away
But retire from the world as I would to my rest.

fc.51, p. 109

F0722 From the crimes your sires have done,
Worse than us, our wives shall bear.

[William Popple, trans.], '[Horace] book 3rd. ode 6th.
To the Roman people'

fc.104/2, p. 226

F0723 From the dark dungeon, from the lonely cell,
While willing worlds bow down, and own your
dread command.

[Richard] Daniel, dean of Armagh, 'The captive.
Psalm 102'

c.244, p. 372

F0724 From the dark Stygian lake I come
Th' Assyrians' palace to his urn.

[John Ayloffe?], 'Andrew Marvell's ghost' [1678]
[Crum F762; POAS I.285]

b.54, p. 1089; b.371, no. 17 (ll. 1–43)

F0725 From the deep-vaulted den of endless night
Souls doom'd to night must never view the day.

'Rochester's ghost—addressing himself to [Robert
Julian] the Secretary of the Muses'

b.113, p. 167

F0726 From the Dutch coast when you set sail,
If you design to live one happy hour.

'A familiar advice [supposedly from Dr. Richard
Lower] to King William' [on Thomas Osborne,
Marquis of Carmarthen, 1690]
[Crum F766; POAS V.174]

b.111, p. 383; fb.207/1, p. 51 (var.); fb.66/7

F0727 From the gaze of lost Alcanzor
Still he weeps o'er Layda's tomb.

F[rances] B[urney d'Arblay], 'Alcanzor and Zayda [by
Mr. Percy] continued by F. B. aged 15 years'

c.486, fol. 10

F0728 From the lewd city to your country stage
Afford, or else we starv'd must quit the place.

M[aurice] J[ohnson], 'A prologue by . . . spoken by
Mr. Maddox at the playhouse in Spalding 1705, a
company of strolling comedians succeeding a show
and a magic lantern'

c.229/2, fol. 11

F0729 From the long silence of an hundred years
Upon the injur'd ghost of Reresford.

[Robert Cholmeley], 'Reresford's ghost. To Wm Baker
STP fellow of St John's Coll Cant. upon the election
of a gentleman into a fellowship founded by him for
his relations'

c.190, p. 162

F0730 From the lov'd hermitage remov'd,
When that approaches, haste away.

John Lockman, 'To Stella, bathing at Scarborough.
8 July 1762'

c.267/2, p. 398

F0731 From the most admirable faculties
Accomplishments, to be, but what you are.

    Sir Thomas Urquhart, 'To my Lord [crossed out]'

fb.217, p. 231

F0732 From the pure regions of a happier shore
Had fate on earth a Burns for her decreed.

    [Helen Craik], 'The ghost of Queen Mary—
    occasioned by a beautiful poem written and sent me,
    by Mr. Burns'

c.375, p. 92

F0733 From the sad place where sorrow ever reigns,
And yet while you have power, my wrongs redress.

    [Edward Moore?], 'Yarico to Inkle' [pr. 1736 (Foxon
    M434)]

c.382, p. 1

F0734 From the Spanish king the Dutch we freed long
                                 since
For which and gold we're sold to slavery.

    'Cambium Anglo-Batavum . . . Englished'

b.111, p. 268; see also 'From the Dutch coast . . .'.

F0735 From the tail of session when causes go throng
We beseech and request ho[no]r(?) at that dear
                           rate. | [*Libera nos Domine*]

    'Verses' [docket title]

Poetry Box VIII/10

F0736 From the third Henry's reign I my pedigree trace
We all of us stand before we can sit.

    'Another [rebus]'

Diggle Box: Poetry Box XI/71

F0737 From the top of ane my thraust
I am thrown into the dust.

    Mary [Stuart], queen of Scots, 'By Mary Queen of
    Scotland writ in her window when imprisoned by
    Queen Eliz: with a diamond'

fb.140, p. 141

F0738 From the top of Pindus hill,
Pirithous groan in chains.

    [William Popple, trans.], '[Horace] book 3rd. ode 4th.
    To Calliope'

fc.104/2, p. 208

F0739 From the white-blossom'd sloe my dear Chloe
                                  requested
I plant in that bosom a thorn.

    R[obert] Burns, 'The thorn'

c.391

F0740 From the womb of the earth
What a whimsical creature am I. | A minc'd pie.

    'A riddle'
    [Crum F776]

c.172, p. 11

F0741 From these blest realms, how pleasing to my eyes,
For O! their case may be your own.

    John Lockman, 'Charity (from the skies,) to those
    who relieved the unhappy sufferers, by the fire in King
    Street, Covent Garden . . . 23 Decr. 1759'

c.267/1, p. 287

F0742 From these drear cells, where horror silent reigns,
Those bounties to dispense, which flow from heav'n.

    'The confined debtor'

c.175, p. 6

F0743 From this auspicious night shall rise a star,
Shall be compell'd to happiness, by need.

    'On the birth of St. George'

c.570/1, p. 38

F0744 From thorny wilds a monster came,
And this poor heart from which it came.

    [William Cowper, trans.], 'Self-love and truth
    incompatable. Vol. 2. Son: 21' [of Jeanne Guion's
    'Spiritual songs']

c.470 (autogr.)

F0745 From those gay meads where Avon leads her train
Nor hurl me on the rock of cold disdain.

    [ ] Schone, 'An imperfect copy of Mr. Schone's verses
    wrote by him when abroad to a friend in England
    written in the year 1769 or 1770'

c.341, p. 126

F0746 From those lone walls, where gloomy silence
                                  reigns,
And bear my spirit to your happier sphere.

    [Helen Craik], 'The monk of La Frappe—a tale—
    written by himself, and found in his cell'

c.375, p. 141

F0747 From thy simplicity and truth
And check the rising tear.

    'In [St. Michael's churchyard, Oxford] on a child'

c.240, p. 134

F0748 From thy waves stormy Lannow I go,
Will delight and repay all my care.

    [Anna Seward?], 'The adieu to Lannow'

c.83/4, no. 2024 (attr. S. Fiddes)

F0749 From too alert a disposition,
And genius in a garret died.

'The death of genius'
c.83/2, no. 652

F0750 From Troy Novant's northeastern gate
And Milton his immortal fire.

[( ) B—y], 'Paphos Britannica a panegyric on the
l[adie]s of St[epne]y and M[ile En]d' [answered by
'Who in this frantic strain . . .'; see also 'Begin the
nine . . .']
c.162, p. 1

F0751 From unnatural rebellion that devilish curse
And desert the dull craven cornuted Stadtholder |
We beseech thee to hear us good Lord.

'A litany for the reducing of Ireland'
[Crum F785; POAS V.219]
b.111, p. 233

F0752 From villainy dressed in a doublet of zeal
From the plagues that are kept for a rebel in store. |
Libera nos Domine

'A new litany'
[Crum F788]
Poetry Box VI/18, 65

F0753 From visions of disastrous love
'And heav'n relenting take thy soul!'

W[illiam] R[obert] Spencer, trans., 'Leonora,
translated from the same author [Bürger]'
c.141, p. 479

F0754 From weight of sordid venal cares
Of beauty and of sense.

'On Miss Talbot's conversing with a lawyer at Bath—
1736'
c.360/1, p. 21

F0755 From what strange motive springs this gen'ral cry,
I've done: nor will I add a couplet more.

[Stephen Barrett], 'The first satire of the first Book of
Horace, paraphrased. A college exercise'
c.193, p. 79

F0756 From whence old Weaver's sandy tides my friends
With seraphs mix and tread her native skies.

'Epistle to a friend J. Williamson of Balliol Col. Oxon'
Poetry Box I/55

F0757 From whence these dire portents around,
Nor bleed, nor die in vain.

[ ] Lewis, 'On Christ's sufferings'
c.244, p. 457

F0758 From whence why so much impudence
Our destin'd quarters see.

'Cromwell arrives at Saint James's from the infernal
shades, the evening of the battle of Culloden; being
sent by the Elector and Nassau; and enters George's
presence abruptly'
c.171, no. 15

F0759 From Whimple [Wimpole?] there came half a
buck to Clarehall.
They shall e'en have the Pasly but we'll have the
haunch.

c.116, p. 44

F0760 From whom, or how did I begin?
The secret stands reveal'd.

'Accidental reflections'
c.83/3, no. 990

F0761 From William's ambition, his pride and vainglory,
From scolding and whining and women's fain'd
fears, | *Libera nos Domine*.

'A litany'
b.111, p. 245

F0762 From Winchester to you dear friend,
E'en take your horse and thither go.

John Shackleton, 'A journey to Studland in a letter to a
friend'
c.241, p. 62

F0763 From witty men and mad
A witty man, or one that's out of's wits.

[Thomas Randolph], 'On poetry'
[cf. Crum F793]
b.104, p. 114/1

F0764 From worldly cares and wanton love's conceit
To gain thee life, where love can never end.

'Introduction' [to 'The path to paradise']
a.5, fol. IV

F0765 From York to London town we come
And traitors all to justice bring | Amen Amen Amen.

'The following verses were spoken at the burning of
the Pope at Temple Bar Nov: 1679'
[Crum F794]
b.54, p. 1164

F0766 From your minority, your prudence hath
Deserves th'unfeigned love of all men's hearts.

Sir Thomas Urquhart, 'To mine [crossed out] my
Lord [crossed out]'
fb.217, p. 112

F0767 From your letters to Nell, to Kit, Peg, and Bess,
For the passion's to thee, tho' they fixt the name.

[Robert Cholmeley], 'To Mrs. Robinson having seen
several of the foregoing copies of verses'

c.190, p. 74

F0768 From youth to age all men have rattles,
The acts, vile death shuts up the scene.

'Human life'

Poetry Box IV/147

F0769 From Zembla's ever icy plain
For a youth of brave toil, an age in repose.

'Song sung at Stepney Feast'

c.360/1, p. 291

F0770 Froze January, leader of the year:
To do God honor, makes himself a beast.

'Calandar months with allusions to Popish and
provincial customs'

c.81/1, no. 300

F0771 Frugality, with av'rice not allied;
Fair charity, her crown to justice owes.

'To the same [Rev. John Chappel Woodhouse] a
sonnet on frugality. 1781'

fc.53, p. 11

F0772 Fruitless the task his virtues to rehearse,
Then not in dust, nor e'en his grave survive.

'On the death of Mr. Shovell'

c.591, p. 3

F0773 Fuca, thou quot'st the scriptures on thy side
Can stoop to what Rebecca did beside.

[Henry Phillipps? 1655]

b.156, p. 13

F0774 Fucksters, you that will be happy
What can mortal wish for more!

'Advice to a c—— and monger'

b.105, p. 394; fb.70, p. 27

F0775 Full as a bee with thyme and red
He'll do't no doubt, till his yarn be spun.

[Robert] Herrick, 'Oberon's palace'
[Crum F797]

b.197, p. 2

F0776 Full fifty years it shall be
Then feed the fish.

'Lilly's prophecy'

c.570/1, p. 43

F0777 Full forty years old England complain'd
For want of a halfpenny light.

'An historical ballad, humbly inscribed to the
duumviri' [pr. 1730? (Foxon H252)]

c.570/3, p. 105 (crossed out; incomplete?)

F0778 Full jovial round the board were sat
Pardie, poor bard, I'll give thee two.

[Robert Cholmeley], 'The bard, in Chaucer's style.
Imitated from Erle Robert's Mice [by Matthew Prior]'

c.190, p. 228

F0779 Full many a chance, or dire mishap
Excuses them, and falls on puppies!

Charles Atherton Allnutt, 'Epigram on the hair
powder license tax at a time when general expectation
looked for a tax on dogs'

c.112, p. 156

F0780 Full many a year had swiftly roll'd away,
For we may pity, though we cannot love.

[Charles Burney, the younger], 'Altamira. A town
dialogue . . . Jan. 23d. 1780'

c.38, p. 1

F0781 Full many dear girl of these days may you see,
And your friendship for me, with your life only
end.

J. B. D[ickinson], 'April 4—[17]91 to A[nn] Dickinson'

c.391, p. 118

F0782 Full of the spirit, righteous shell
The secret of thy body.

[Robert Cholmeley], 'The fair Quaker answered'

c.190, p. 60

F0783 Full oft from our first setting out,
The harvest reap of peace?

'Psalm 129'

c.264/3, p. 75

F0784 Full well by learned clerkis it is said
Pardie! He, fearing it, away doth hie.

'Emblem of wedlock. Modo Chaucer'

c.81/1, no. 272; Poetry Box I/96

F0785 Full well you know, that France was always restless
and ambitious;
Who frighten all the world with a bugaboo
invasion.

'A loyal song sung by the Chiswick Association, 1798
To the tune of Ally Croaker in slow time'

Poetry Box IV/71

F0786 Fulvia with a thousand charms,
To all the same, to you and me.

  Abraham Oakes, 'Fulvia: a young lady described'
c.50, p. 8

F0787 Fungus by a peculiar knack,
When fame had dubb'd poor Fung a poet.

  John Lockman, 'To an impertinent would-be poet,
  who had used the author ill . . . Sept. 1730'
c.267/1, p. 26; c.268 (first part), p. 36

F0788 Furio, will not forgive, Furio, beware,
Furio, will curse himself in the Lord's prayer.

  [Francis Quarles], 'On Furio' [Divine fancies I, 46]
b.137, p. 184

F0789 Fyndall the reporter for reporting evil
With the report of a pistol was sent to the devil.

  'Upon Fyndall killed with a pistol'
b.208, p. 60

G

G0001
G. P. with eager eye survey'd
By rage and disappointment fix'd.

> R[ichard] V[ernon] S[adleir], 'To G. F. P. a young surgeon'
>
> c.106, p. 78

G0002
Gad not ye wives, be frugal, silent love,
Taught by this tortoise, keys, close lips, and dove.

> 'Distich. Wrote under the figure of a woman standing upon a tortoise, a bunch of keys in her right hand, the forefinger of her left hand upon her lips, and a dove upon her shoulder . . . translations [2]'
>
> c.81/1, no. 70

G0003
Gaffer Grubb, full of cares a good trade for his son
That noddle of thine will ne'er do for a forge.

> 'The hiss. A tale'
>
> c.570/3, p. 72

G0004
Gaily I liv'd at ease and nature taught,
Should think of me, who never thought of him.

> 'Epitaph'
>
> c.81/1, no. 235

G0005
Gaily the bells (for him) in concert rung,
For the lone horrors of the mold'ring tomb.

> [John Lockman], 'On a young man (of Plaistow in Essex) who sickened, and died soon after his marriage'
>
> c.268 (first part), p. 18; see also 'All day the bells . . .'.

G0006
Gain greedy fathers nowadays turmoil
Naked the while, in wet and cold to starve.

> 'Avaritia parentum'
>
> b.205, fol. 12r

G0007
'Gainst faithless Harry, why exclaim,
And his seraglio's the whole town.

> John Lockman, 'The weathercock. Set to music by Lewis Granom esqr.'
>
> c.267/2, p. 144

G0008
'Gainst love, fond nature struggles still in vain
O! let her sleep in unmolested peace.

> 'Elegy on Mary Blandy'
>
> c.140, p. 358

G0009
'Gainst misadventures being resolv'd to fight
Hath shot against m' and break them in her face.

> [Sir Thomas Urquhart], 'How a man should oppose himself to adversity'
>
> fb.217, p. 499

G0010
'Gainst the destructive wiles of man,
For men are wondrous sly.

> John Lockman, 'A hint to the fair sex: in answer to the very ingenious Mr. Christopher Smart's song, The blind catch many a fly &c . . . July 1746'
>
> c.267/2, p. 154

G0011
'Gainst transmigration we'll no more exclaim,
In him you'll see immortal Caesar rise.

> John Lockman, 'Extempore: whilst the King of Prussia's health was drinking . . . May 1757'
>
> c.267/1, p. 208

G0012
Galatea dry thy tears
Mourning still thy gentle love.

> [John Gay, Alexander Pope, and/or John Hughes], 'Galatea dry thy tears 6th chorus [in Handel's] Acis and Galatea' [with musical score for tenor and bass]
>
> Music MS. 534

G0013
Gallants, you're welcome—that's my foremost care,
And hope that shape for all these changes will
                                                    atone.

> 'Prologue' [spoken by Davies; after 1695]
>
> Trumbull Box: Poetry Box XIII/97

G0014
Gallia bent down beneath the yoke
Thus martyr'd Louis fell.

> [John Walker?], 'The fall of Louis 16. A Pindaric ode'
>
> fc.108, fol. 67v

G0015
Garrick! My fav'rite son! It glads my shade
This friendly deed proclaims a gentle heart.

> John Lockman, 'On reading a paragraph, hinting at the kind concern, which a manager of Drury Lane Theater showed, for the unhappy Mr. Christopher Smart. Shakespeare to Mr. Garrick . . . 2d Feb. 1759'
>
> c.267/1, p. 267

G0016 Garrick, no voice nor powers but thine, can tell
And gain thee plaudits in the realms divine.

> [E. C.], 'Addressed to David Garrick and sent to him
> on his quitting the stage'

c.150, p. 122

G0017 Gay, blooming Chloe, form'd to please,
Than gate, wall, padlock, bolt or bar.

> [John Lockman], 'The Italian padlock. Imitated from
> M[onsieur] de Voltaire'

c.268 (second part), p. 143

G0018 Gay Celia's is a happy case
And Esau's on her tail.

> 'On Miss Chudleigh maid of honor to her royal
> highness Augusta Princess of Wales written in 1746—
> the same thought as ['In Flavia's eyes . . .']'

c.360/2, no. 151

G0019 Gay happy youth the muses' darling care
Lest what's your jest, turn to a serious truth.

> [Mrs. Christian Kerr], 'An advice to the young
> gentleman'

c.102, p. 121

G0020 Gay Moody once lost all his spirit and pith;
The pain in his liver, instead of her belly.

> [Elizabeth?] Moody, 'A singular case or the doctor
> mistaken'

File 7048

G0021 Gay were the notes in yonder vale,
Conclude Palemon's harvest home.

> 'The harvest-home'

c.139, p. 83

G0022 Gaze not on swans on whose soft breast,
Sunk in their sockets and decay'd.

> [William Strode?]
> [Crum G15]

c.223, p. 93

G0023 Geld not this book, and it may furnish wit,
Will serve t'engender others out of it.

> Sir Thomas Urquhart, 'To the austere readers'

fb.217, p. 333

G0024 Gellius is ever building, one while he's
I'm building now, excuse me Sir I pray.

> 'Gellius aedificat . . .'

b.207, p. 10

G0025 Gem of this lone and silent vale,
Observed by few, or but by one.

> Capel Lofft, 'To the glow-worm from the Morning
> chron: Dec. 7. 1796 . . . 11 Dec. 1796'

Poetry Box v/116

G0026 Generosity divine,
Felt but only felt by thine.

> 'On generosity. An ode'

fc.53, p. 36

G0027 Generous gay and gallant nation
Happy soil adieu adieu.

> [John Arbuthnot], 'The following lines were sung by
> Durastanti when she took her leave of the English
> stage. The words were in haste put together by
> Mr. Pope [*sic*] at the earnest request of the earl of
> Peterborough' [Harl. 7316]

c.468; c.166, p. 48

G0028 Generous social love and sounds
We're in friendship more strong.

> M[aurice] J[ohnson], '1738. An ode for the celebration
> of the anniversary of the institution of the
> Gentlemen's Society in Spalding Lincolnshire
> composed by . . . founder and first secretary . . .'

c.229/2, fol. 42

G0029 Genius of Blodud's healthful spring!
And long preserve his valued life to bless mankind.

> 'Verses presented to the Duke of Northumberland on
> his arrival at Bath for the recovery of his health'

c.391, p. 40

G0030 Genius of Britain! Was it thou
When freemen join'd the league of courts against
                                                    mankind.

> 'Verses written on reading the account of the battle of
> St. Amand'

c.140, p. 540

G0031 Genius of Hagley from thy sacred cell
Extinguish'd by the brighter light of heav'n.

> Anna Snelling, 'To Miss F—— Fanshawe verses begun
> at Hagley and concluded at Birmingham in July
> 1776 . . .'

c.504, p. 143

G0032 Genius of this calm retreat:
Distant lands shall sing thy fame.

> [ ] Sandford, 'Written in a hermitage'

Greatheed Box/57

G0033 Genius of this verdant bank,
Do thou regale the heart.

> Charles Atherton Allnutt, 'Lines on a rural bower'

c.112, p. 115

G0034 Genteel in personage
But ever true.

c.188, p. 73

G0035 Genteel is my Damon, engaging his air
Since the picture I've drawn is exactly the man.

'The following copy of verse said to be the production of a very great personage' [Queen Charlotte, 1765] [Crum G26]

c.116, p. 50

G0036 Gentility and sweetness here combine
Then think how truly Ancaster is blest.

[Horace Walpole, 4th earl of Orford], 'D[uchess] of Ancaster'
[Crum G27]

c.157, p. 68

G0037 Gentle herald of the spring,
Gentle herald of the spring!

'Ode to the swallow'

c.83/3, no. 867

G0038 Gentle Jesus lovely lamb,
Still thou giv'st me all in love.

'Hymn 40th'

c.562, p. 48

G0039 Gentle love propitious shine
Keep his years a mystery.

[Phanuel Bacon], 'To Doctor Cummings on his birthday Feb. 14'

c.237, fol. 42

G0040 Gentle muses aid my pen
And then sweet maid you cannot err.

'On Miss Smyth'

c.341, p. 92

G0041 Gentle reproofs have long been tried in vain
To fright away the vermin of the age.

'Prologue. To the noisy crew and disturbers of the House'

Trumbull Box: Poetry Box XIII/78

G0042 Gentle stream on thy banks let me pensively rove
A requiem to breathe to the days that are gone.

'Lines written on the banks of a river . . . Emma. The world'

c.344, p. 111

G0043 Gentle swallow stay and twitter
Twitter F—r still to B—m!

R[ichard] V[ernon] S[adleir], 'To [Miss Fitter], in badinage, personating Mr. B—m one of the E[ast] I[ndia] directors living in the neighborhood'

c.106, p. 69

G0044 Gentlemen of England; this I let you understand,
For my part he may go fast and pray.

[on the restoration of St. Paul's Cathedral, c. 1620–23] [Crum G35]

fb.106(14); b.197, p. 183 (incomplete?)

G0045 Gentlest air, thou breath of lovers
Ev'ry nymph may read thee here.

[Anne] Finch, countess of Winchilsea, 'A sigh'
[parodied by 'Gentlest blast . . .']

fb.70, p. 191

G0046 Gentlest blast of ill concoction,
The amusement of the maids at court.

['A fart'; parody of 'Gentlest air . . .']

fb.70, p. 193

G0047 Gentlest of angels who with filial care
My thoughts my feelings and my conduct thine.

[William Hayley], 'Sonnet . . . June 5 and 6 [1800]'

File 6968

G0048 Gentlest of rivers as thou flow'st along
To Gertrude sacred and connubial love.

'To the river Mole'

Poetry Box III/30

G0049 Gently, ah gently, Madam, touch
Rather than be part of it.

A[braham] C[owley], 'Counsel'

c.258

G0050 Gently stir and blow the fire,
O ye gods how we shall dine.

'A song'

fb.68, p. 142

G0051 Gently touch the warbling lyre
And indulging whisper sounds.

A. Bradley, 'Song'
[Crum G39]

c.503, p. 59

G0052 George came to the crown without striking a blow
Ah! quoth the Pretender, would I could do so.

[Ambrose Philips]

c.360/1, p. 91

G0053 George Davis grieves and swears by mighty Dis,
But in his purse, one angel dares not venture.

    T. R., 'An epigram . . . Bucks'
c.326, p. 168

G0054 George Harrison gentleman lieth here
And in the faith of Jesus Christ they both assuredly
                              died.

    'Epitaph no. 6'
c.158, p. 47

G0055 George has, 'tis true, vouchsaf'd to mention
I wish you'd get a better lover.

    'Prince Edward'
c.578, p. 63

G0056 George Lewis now usurps the British throne,
Our lawful monarch's from their throne is forc'd.

    'A remembrance to Great Britain'
c.570/1, p. 71; fc.58, p. 106

G0057 George Woodd and his rib their best compliments
                                 send
Which have oft been the lot of dean, bishop, and
                                 priest.

    George Woodd, 'The answer' [to 'Rev'rend whom
    lately . . .']
c.74

G0058 Germania late by Britain's aid could boast
And Colt perform what Marlbro' left undone.

    'To Mrs Colt—on her being born in Germany—wrote
    in 1713'
c.360/1, p. 79

G0059 Germanicus was Drusus son o'th high
Unto our times but this one epigram.

    [Sir Aston Cokayne], 'Of Caius Germanicus
    Augustus'
b.275, p. 45

G0060 G—h, list'ning to his tatter'd choir,
To ours, begrim'd with soot and grease.

    [John Lockman], 'Vauxhall and Marylebone Gardens.
    A Hogarthian comparison'
c.268 (first part), p. 10

G0061 Gibson from sorrow rests beneath this stone,
And heav'n applauded when the curtain fell.

    [David Garrick], 'Epitaph' [on William Gibson, d.
    1771]
Acquisition 92.3.1ff. (autogr.)

G0062 Gibson of London to hell is gone,
The devil will ride in a chaise and pair.

    'Wrote in a window at Crown Inn—Reading'
c.74

G0063 Gifts are love's glasses which do represent
The mind that sendeth in the thing that's sent.

b.62, p. 116

G0064 Giles Jolt as sleeping in his cart he lay,
If not, oddsbodikins, I've found a cart.

    'Giles Jolt'
    [Crum G52a]
c.81/1, no. 490

G0065 Gill Morice was an earl's son
In bow'r where she went brain.

    'Gill Morice'
Spence Papers, folder 113

G0066 Girded with dreadful wrath, let God arise
They triumph in thy power—forever God be blest!

    [Nathaniel Hamby], 'Psalm 68—by the transcriber'
c.244, p. 416

G0067 Girls now are such that they take more offence
Silence with action being a maid's delight.

    [Sir Thomas Urquhart]
fb.217, p. 540

G0068 Give Celia but to me alone
Since judge who will the odds are mine.

    'On kissing &c.'
    [Crum G57]
c.229/1, fol. 43

G0069 Give Chloe a bushel horse-hair and and wool
You will find you have lost half your wife.

    'The lady's dress. A receipt' [General evening post,
    14 June 1777]
c.157, p. 104; c.487, p. 112

G0070 Give credit, but first well beware
Before thou trust them, who they are.

    'Caution'
c.360/1, p. 263

G0071 Give ear and a comical story I'll tell,
Supported by pillars notable to stand. | Tol de rol,
                                  lol &c.

    'Song 116'
c.555, p. 168

G0072 Give ear fair creature to my hapless—love
'Tis joy to think thou art no other's—lot.

  [John Hoadly], 'A *bouts-rimes*, in imit[ation] of
  Thyrsis a youth'

  c.176, p. 160

G0073 Give ear my people to my law
In holy order guide.

  'Psal: 78'

  b.217, p. 13

G0074 Give ear to my wonderful ditty,
As they did in the year forty-one. | With a &c.

  'A ballad. &c.

  c.570/2, p. 74

G0075 Give ear to us who long have cried
Thy face let shine and safe are we.

  'Psal 80'

  b.217, p. 24

G0076 Give God the great Creator homage due,
And dread to be a slave to common fame.

  'The following maxims were found in French verse in
  the strongbox of the D[uke] of Burgundy, the French
  king's father, at his death'

  Poetry Box IV/136

G0077 Give Isaac the nymph who no beauty can boast,
But I only desire—she mayn't have a beard.

  [Richard Brinsley Butler Sheridan], 'Song 112' [from
  Act II of The duenna]

  c.555, p. 164

G0078 Give laud unto the Lord, from heaven that is so high
His word fulfil and Him obey.

  [John Hopkins, 'A praise of God for the defense of his
  church . . . Psal. 65' [verses from Psalm 148]
  [Crum G67]

  a.3, fol. 149v

G0079 Give law[?]tye be in love
I take less feast of others for her sake.

  'Braye Lute Book,' Music Ms. 13, fol. 51v

G0080 Give leave to me, here is a man of mark
Ear is best seen whenas it hath a ring.

  'Cade auris' [answered by 'In ears (son) . . .']

  b.356, p. 118

G0081 Give light to th'nations increase this birth
But look to heaven from which their wishes flow.

  Poetry Box VI/92

G0082 Give me a fiery muse to sublimate
Then let Rome read them in his calander.

  'Upon the powder treason Novemb: 5'

  b.197, p. 146

G0083 Give me a form, give me a face
They please the eyes, but these your heart.

  'On beauty'

  b.200, p. 410

G0084 Give me a little respite that I may
Little I have; against my own conceit.

  [George Daniel]

  b.121, fol. 42v

G0085 Give me a soul so great, so high,
Nothing of self, but a bare name.

  'True greatness'

  c.244, p. 124

G0086 Give me ambrosia in a kiss!
And as to kissing—kiss my ass.

  [Joseph Spence], 'Three greyhounds at
  Burroughsbridge'

  Spence Papers, folder 119

G0087 Give me an odd, or an exotic face
I cannot make a Mercury, you see. | Sweet cousin,
                                                    pardon me

  [Sir Philip Wodehouse], 'An ata-lountida (?) of an odd
  face being put upon of a sudden by my coz—Mary
  Carey'

  b.131, p. 43

G0088 Give me but a wife; I expect not to find
Each fair can make happy, if woman we prize, |
  And he that seeks more is more curious than wise.

  'Song 43'

  c.555, p. 68

G0089 Give me great God a soul to feel the smart
To that bless'd world devoid of care and strife.

  Charles Atherton Allnutt, 'A prayer'

  c.112, p. 37

G0090 Give me great God (said I) a little farm
Who dares have virtue in a vicious age.

  [Lady Mary Wortley Montagu], 'Constantinople by
  the same'

  fc.51, p. 126

G0091 Give me joy, my brave peers, says the monarch of
hell
And Beelzebub blame if the business don't do.

'Diabolical advice'

fc.53, p. 18

G0092 Give me leave to rail at you,
And makes the slave grow pleas'd and vain.

[John Wilmot, 2nd earl of Rochester], 'Song'
[answered by 'Nothing adds to your fond fire . . .']

b.105, p. 136; see also 'Kindness has resistless
charms . . .'.

G0093 Give me my chains replied the swain,
And captive gods attend thy car.

'*Omnia vincit amor* was her meed. Chaucer . . . the
subject the triumph of love is masterly represented by
Seignior Varrio in the Grand Sal of Burleigh'

c.229/1, fol. 55

G0094 Give me my scallop shell of quiet
To tread those paths of which I writ.

Sir W[alter] Raleigh, 'Sir W. Raleigh's pilgrimage'
[Crum G78]

b.197, p. 25

G0095 Give me O God, (for all things come of Thee)
To look for't where it is in a contented mind.

Henry Baker, 'Content'

c.244, p. 400

G0096 Give me the enlarged desire,
My soul forever fill.

c.562, p. 73

G0097 Give me the kindling eye from whence
Thy magic and thy sweetness blend.

'To sensibility'

c.546

G0098 Give me the sober muse, and simple thought
Let others sing of love, and loose delights.

[George Daniel]

b.121, fol. 20v

G0099 Give me thro' life to love one virtuous maid—
And hand in hand go gently to the grave.

J. Wilkinson, 'A fragment'

c.139, p. 511

G0100 Give me trembling hands and feet
E'en on a cross, I life would choose.

'Maecenas's wish'

c.360/2, no. 133

G0101 Give me, ye fates, the verdant meads and flowers,
And mirth and wit keep an eternal round.

'In answer to a letter from the Duke of Montagu. 8.
Jan. 1744/5'

c.371, fol. 54

G0102 Give Midas gold, and let him pine with shame,
Use ye your goods to live and die with fame.

c.339, p. 325

G0103 Give o'er ye poor players depend not on wit
Shall turn all my liquor to champagne and Nantes.

'The Epsom ballad. [Robert] Julian's farewell to the
family of the coquettes. A new ballad to the tune of
An old man is a bedful of bones'
[Crum G89]

fb.108, p. 73

G0104 Give over love, or love as reason will,
For lovers lewd do vainly languish still.

c.339, p. 323

G0105 Give peace in this our time, O Lord,
The guilty nations would forget Thee God.

Charles Atherton Allnutt, 'Give peace in our time, O
Lord'

c.112, p. 144

G0106 Give praises unto God the Lord
Praise ye the Lord therefore.

[Thomas Norton], 'He praiseth God for His
providence in governing the church. Psal: 45' [verses
from Psalms 105–106]
[Crum G95]

a.3, fol. 123

G0107 Give sorrow words the grief that does not speak
Her last and only refuge is the tomb!

[Frances Burney d'Arblay], 'Sonnet. To despondency'

c.486, fol. 14v

G0108 Give thanks unto the Lord,
Be highest praises giv'n | For His mercy.

'Psalm 136. Evening prayer'

c.264/3, p. 84

G0109 Give thanks unto the Lord our God
Condemn his soul to die.

[William Kethe, John Hopkins, and Thomas Norton],
'An exhortation to praise God for his mercy. Psalm.
46' [verses from Psalms 107–109]

a.3, fol. 124v

G0110 Give us glasses, my wench, give us wine and we'll quench
And she never remember'd him more.

   'Song 46'

c.555, p. 71

G0111 Glad designs are over the way
Mine! For the public good!

   'The rival bakers of Longacre or the triumphant
   baker. On one's raising the price of bread'

c.361

G0112 Glad Mary I'm in heav'n—this anagram
Of that to come, which shall forever last.

   [Sir Philip Wodehouse], 'Lady Mary Heveningham'

b.131, back (no. 101)

G0113 Gladly the call of friendship I obey,
Not only both must love, but both obey.

   'A nuptial verse sent to a young couple on their
   wedding day'
   [Crum G107]

c.391, p. 39

G0114 Gladsome spring brings on the year,
And animates the glorious grape.

   [ ] Lewis, 'The spring'

c.244, p. 189

G0115 Glide gently on, thou murm'ring brook,
Yet broke his faith with me.

   [Elizabeth (Singer) Rowe], 'A sonnet'

c.83/2, no. 729

G0116 Glorious, all-forming pow'r, thy works on high!
O'er lands remote her influence displays!

   [Thomas Hull], 'Evening from the 104th [Psalm]'

c.528/10

G0117 Glorious design! To send to France,
Lend her brave hawks, and half our fleet.

   John Lockman, 'On the proposed exportation of corn
   to our enemies . . . Jany 1747/8'

c.267/1, p. 18

G0118 Glorious thou art, old Snowdon, with thy head
Firm on its solid base remains unmoved.

   John Howson

Poetry Box x/30

G0119 Glory to do—'tis action gives renown
And to all noble ends it adds the crown.

   [Sir Philip Wodehouse], 'Dorothy Ogle glory to do'

b.131, back (no. 79)

G0120 Glory to Thee, my God this night
I'm still secure, for still with Thee.

   [Thomas Stevens?], 'The evening hymn'

c.259, p. 67

G0121 Go-add this verse unto Goad's hearse
And death's goad draws him thither.

   [Matthew Wren?], 'On one [Dr. Thomas] Goad'
   [Crum G117]

b.356, p. 245

G0122 Go and be free. Put thy bonnet on
Thy nature speaks thy liberality.

   [Sir Philip Wodehouse], 'Upon Mrs. Biarley—her
   Christian name is unknown'

b.131, back (no. 125)

G0123 Go and bestride the Southern wind
Then will her heart and thine be one.

b.213, p. 59

G0124 Go and catch a falling star;
False, ere I come, to two, or three.

   John Donne, 'Woman's inconstancy'
   [Crum G118]

b.200, p. 92; see also 'Go catch . . .'.

G0125 Go and count her better hours
Fair sun, that governs thee and me.

   W[illiam] S[trode], 'A watch sent home to Mrs. E. K.'
   [Crum G120]

b.200, p. 175; b.205, fol. 34v; b.62, p. 43

G0126 Go: and with this parting kiss
Know virtue taught thee, not thy self.

   Rob[ert] Herrick, 'His charge to his [supposed] wife'
   [Crum G124]

b.197, p. 8

G0127 Go, bards by heaven inform'd, attend
The patriot, poet, and the friend.

   Charles Burney, the younger, 'Written in the works of
   Anacreon, Sappho, and Alceus, and presented to
   Percival Stockdale . . . Oct. 21. 1779'

c.35, p. 39

G0128 Go bold aspiring muse,
Good as his father is, but far more fortunate.

   'On the birth of the princess [Louisa Mary]. A
   Pindaric' [15 July 1692]

b.111, p. 22

G0129 Go catch a falling star
False ere I come to two or three.

    [John Donne]
    [Crum G136]
    b.148, p. 66; see also 'Go and catch . . .'.

G0130 Go dainty worms' meat, if such things as they
Without a sculpture laid, yet there I lay.

    'On one drowned in the snow'
    b.356, p. 262

G0131 Go daughters of fashion for pleasure repine
And our names, and our virtues, survive in our son.

    Mrs Pebham, 'A song'
    c.83/3, no. 1065

G0132 Go doth fond lover, seek
And raise a character in her great name.

    [George Daniel]
    b.121, fol. 27

G0133 Go empty joys
And blend us both in our dead night.

    'Ode 1' [1640; answered by 'Welcome sad night . . .']
    [Crum G142, first part]
    fb.106(10)

G0134 Go! fair example of untainted youth
'Tis all a father, all a friend can give.

    A[lexander] Pope, 'The epitaph on the monument of
    the Hon. Robert Digby esqr. and of his sister Mary,
    erected by their father, the Lord Digby, in the church
    of Sherborne in Dorsetshire. 1727' [i.e., 1729?]
    [Crum G143]
    c.360/2, no. 199

G0135 Go, favored fruit, and to Alicia bear,—
Revive the languid head, and raise the failing heart.

    'A sonnet with a basket of strawberries to Alicia who
    was sick, and could relish little else' [23 June 1786]
    c.136, p. 137

G0136 Go favorite casket, once the joy
And all embellish'd by celestial bliss!

    [William Hayley, 1797 or later]
    File 6941

G0137 Go garter, happiest of thy kind!
Thou'll henceforth make her think of me.

    'Presented to a young lady with a pair of garters'
    c.578, p. 7

G0138 Go, gentle songster, and repeat
To snatch her favorite from the grave!

    Charles Burney, the younger, 'Ode, on the death of a
    favorite bird . . . May. 1780'
    c.35, p. 53

G0139 Go go O you most deceitful man
Then all my griefs will have an end.

    'The deceitful lover'
    c.374

G0140 Go, hapless Sidney! Let thy page
If anguish mourn, or grief complain.

    C[harles] B[urney],' Ode, sent with The memoirs of
    Miss Sidney Bidulph [by Frances Sheridan], to the
    Miss Wilcoxes . . . Dec. 14. 1779'
    c.38, p. 40

G0141 Go happier friend, in Barton's rural seat
And want no son to mourn thy sacred bier.

    [Jeffrey] Ekins, 'To a friend who succeeded his father
    in the living of Barton'
    c.504, p. 48; see also 'You happier friend . . .'.

G0142 Go happy paper by command,
Even thought to her is gross, is dull.

    [William Strode], 'On a letter to his m[ist]r[es]s'
    [Crum G159]
    b.200, p. 125; b.62, p. 4

G0143 Go happy spirits freed from sin and care
And God himself the judge award the prize.

    'Epitaphs (Milton Oxfordshire)'
    c.546

G0144 Go happy Sydney to Belisa go
None but a lover could so warmly write.

    c.416

G0145 Go happy veil, possess, but not enjoy
And Celia crowns it with a bridal kiss.

    'To a young lady, with a present of a net handkerchief'
    fc.132/1, p. 47

G0146 Go heaving sigh and go then flowing tear
I think of heaven when I think of thee . . . .

    [John Black: rough draft]
    fc.107, p. 56 (incomplete)

G0147 Go hunt the whiter ermine and present
Give what is oftener heard of than received.

    [Sir William D'Avenant], 'To the wife of
    Mr. Endymion Porter'
    [Crum G161]
    b.197, p. 23 (attr. Tho. Carew); b.356, p. 79

G0148 Go, ingenious artists, to her,
Gentle agent be sincere.

    [James] Hammond, 'Verses from . . . to Emma. With
    a present of some pins, given at parting'

    c.83/1, no. 34

G0149 Go keep that hand
From Hymen's band.

    [William Strode], in 'Posies for bracelets'
    [Crum G164]

    b.205, fol. 55v

G0150 Go, let the fatted calf be kill'd,
Would ne'er return, had not the flood been out.

    A[braham] C[owley], 'The welcome'
    [Crum G165 (var.)]

    c.258

G0151 Go little book, and to the world impart
What's built upon esteem can ne'er decay.

    [William Walsh], 'To his book'

    c.223, p. 51

G0152 Go little brat respected by the just,
Go grace a gallows and hang under it.

    'The farewell to the Church of Eng[lan]d'

    fb.108, p. 65

G0153 Go little jest | undepuced of speech
In this my labor | I might it not intend.

    'L'envoy [to 'Ipomydon'] of Robert C. the printer'

    fc.179

G0154 Go little painted butterfly
And clipt each nimble wing.

    [Petit Andrews], 'Song from a Spanish poet'

    c.90

G0155 Go, lovely boy! To yonder tow'r,
And calls its angel home to rest.

    Major [ ] Mordaunt, 'A poem said to have been
    written by . . . during the last German war'

    c.142, p. 379

G0156 Go lovely fragrant blossom! Go
And unregretted die.

    'To Miss Hy. B—m with a rose'

    c.186, p. 54

G0157 Go lovely rose
Who are so wondrous sweet and fair.

    [Edmund Waller], 'Beauty's a fair but fading flower or
    the rose'
    [Crum G175]

    c.186, p. 101; c.83/1, no. 30

G0158 Go make a rape of fancy; and bring down
Knows how to do? What wit knows what to say.

    [George Daniel]

    b.121, fol. 69

G0159 Go now, ingenuous youth!—the trying hour
Mayst die, as Hampden or as Sidney died.

    [Charlotte (Turner) Smith], 'Sonnet to a young man
    entering the world'

    c.141, p. 128

G0160 Go on brave Sirs in your immense design
Hang but the latter: the parallel's complete.

    'The Tories' advice to the secret cabal'

    c.570/2, p. 140

G0161 Go on dear youth, deep learning's path pursue,
And dedicate to God, the temple—man.

    Ann Murry, 'I shall subjoin an exhortation . . . which I
    sent some time ago to an amiable youth at Eton'

    c.248

G0162 Go on little Cap: stick close to Sir Bob
Are sure in Destruction to end.

    'On reading a certain speech [by Sir Abraham Elton]
    which ended with the terrible word Destruction' [pr.
    1715? (Foxon O184)]

    c.570/4, p. 1

G0163 Go on Lorenzo, thou the muse's pride,
And doves, the pride of Venus, throng thy woods.

    [William Roscoe], trans., 'Conclusion of the 'Ambra'
    of Politian's' [from 'Lorenzo di Medici']

    c.142, p. 100

G0164 Go on—prepare my bounty for my friends
The proverb change—be merry but not wise.

    'Prologue to The Christmas tale . . . Mr. Palmer in the
    character of Christmas'

    c.115

G0165 Go passenger, within this hollow vault
Lies nothing but a body and a fault.

    'On Sir Walter Raleigh'

    b.356, p. 250

G0166 Go patter to lubbers and swabs, d'ye see,
Will look out a good berth for—poor Jack.

    [Charles] Dibdin, the younger, 'Poor Jack! A song'
    [Crum G188]

    c.94

G0167 Go perjur'd man, and if thou dost return
Might blow my ashes up, and strike thee blind.

[Robert Herrick], 'To a false lover'
[Crum G189]

b.54, p. 931; b.197, p. 10; b.205, fol. 74r; fb.142, p. 33

G0168 Go perjur'd man, to your new mistress tell
Is not how great, but how well known they are.

'Another by the same hand' [as 'Charge all a
bumper . . .']

fb.142, p. 46

G0169 Go, pretty bird, to Sylvia fly,
Or bribe me to forego her chain.

'Song—presenting a goldfinch to Sylvia'

c.241, p. 86

G0170 Go pretty birds that sit and sing
Return with pleasant warbling.

'A sonnet'

b.356, p. 97

G0171 Go, rose! my [Chloe's] bosom grace
You die with envy, I with love.

[John] Gay, 'The rose'
[Crum G196]

c.186, p. 111

G0172 Go, said old Lyce, senseless lover. Go,
And that which most enrag'd me, was 'twas true.

[William Walsh], 'Lyce'

c.223, p. 70

G0173 Go search the world collect its scatter'd worth
Her solitary journey thro' the gloomy path.

c.148, p. 12

G0174 Go seek new conquests, go, you have my leave
Is now to prove more constant in your hate.

c.549, p. 7

G0175 Go serve asking to make one's self a slave,
He that would have a place must do all that.

R[obert] Shirley, 1st earl of Ferrers, 'The court life.
From the French'

c.347, p. 94

G0176 Go sigh! Go, viewless herald of my breast,
And live the silent tenant of my breast.

M[ary (Derby)] Robinson, 'A sigh'

c.83/2, no. 517

G0177 Go silly paper and present,
My true love, and her cruelty.

'To my paper'

b.197, p. 229

G0178 Go soft desires, love's gentle progeny,
Then take your flight, and visit me no more.

[Katherine Philips], 'A lover'

c.189, p. 29

G0179 Go sordid earth and hope not to bewitch
I might perchance get riches and be poor.

Tho[mas] Rand[olph], 'Of the inestimable content he
hath in poetry to those that dissuade him'
[Crum G203]

b.62, p. 9

G0180 Go soul the body's guest
No stab the soul can kill.

Sir Walter R[aleigh], 'The lie written by . . . before he
was beheaded'
[Crum G205]

c.341, p. 7; b.356, p. 133

G0181 Go, spotless honor and unsullied truth,
A friend inscribes thy tomb, whose tears bedew'd
thy hearse.

'Inscribed on the tomb of a young lady, by her lover'

c.83/2, no. 279

G0182 Go, spotless innocence thy heaven receive
To them their guardian angel from above.

Dr. [ ] Yates, 'An epitaph on Miss Ann Crayle who
died Jan 21 1754'

c.157, p. 66

G0183 Go straight address'd, my honest lay!
That peace which virtue gives our own.

'To Stella. 1751'

c.238, p. 7

G0184 Go thou gentle whispering wind
Or else quite extinguish mine.

[Thomas Carew], 'A sigh'
[Crum G215]

b.205, fol. 75r

G0185 Go Time and tell the little boy
Remember I am Time.

'On time'

c.546

G0186 Go to some tomb hid in a dreadful vault
And then return, and I will love again.

[Robert] Herrick, 'Herrick to his coy mistress'

b.356, p. 74

G0187 Go, tuneful bird, that glad'st the skies,
Who sings her praise, and sings forlorn.

[William] Shenstone, 'The skylark'

fc.132/1, p. 162

G0188 Go virgin kid with lambent kiss,
Than ever yet I've done.

'Verses written by a gentleman on a lady's glove'

c.83/4, no. 1088

G0189 Go ye who think reason your own,
While they fought not for her, but for pride.

[Summer 1766]

c.136, p. 79

G0190 Go you tame gallants you that have the name,
I yield and give to Wisbech cock the day.

[Robert Wild], 'A description of the battle fought
between the unparalleled cocks Norfolk and Wisbech
[17 June 1637]'
[Crum G235]

b.104, p. 6; b.356, p. 311; c.166, p. 293 ('Go ye . . .'); see
also 'Come you young gallants . . .'.

G0191 Go, Zephyr, and whisper the maid,
And her cot is the seat of the loves.

[John] Walcot [('Peter Pindar')], 'To Cynthia'

c.83/3, no. 765

G0192 God all things made, because he thought it very
Expedient, not to be solitary.

Sir Thomas Urquhart, 'Why the Lord created the
world'

fb.217, p. 250

G0193 God be thanked
But God be prais'd for all.

[Petit] Andrews, 'An extemporal grace on returning
thanks after a scant supper of buttered wheat'

c.360/1, p. 65

G0194 God bless our gracious sovereign Anne
On t'other side o' th' main.

[Arthur Mainwaring], 'The history of the fall of the
Conformity Bill being an excellent new song to the
tune of The lady's fall' [1703]
[Crum G242; POAS VII.6, with four more lines]

c.111, p. 48; Poetry Box IV/76; Poetry Box IV/117

G0195 God bless our Prince, and endow him with grace,
And send him instructors, no worse than the last.

'On his royal highness George Prince of Wales, eldest
son of his late royal highness Frederick Prince of
Wales. 1752'

c.360/3, no. 244; Poetry Box I/129 ('our young
prince . . .')

G0196 God bless the King.—God bless the faith's
                              defender.
God bless us all!—that's quite another thing.

[John] Byrom, of Manchester, 'The Manchester
blessing. 1745'

c.82, p. 5; Spence Papers, folder 113 (var.)

G0197 God bless the lives
And so w' are rid of all. Amen.

[Sir Francis Castillion?], 'A grace . . . 1620'

fb.69, p. 191

G0198 God could not suffer death, nor man o'ercome it
But Christ being God, and man, did both
                              consummate.

Sir Thomas Urquhart, 'Of Christ, God, and man'

fb.217, p. 52

G0199 God Cupid's for certain as foolish, as blind,
Love will fly the pursuer, the flyer pursue.

'Cupid's folly'

fb.107, p. 73

G0200 God did appoint my time and days
And brought me here where now I lays.

'Epitaph in Woodstock churchyard'

c.360/3, no. 145

G0201 God first the man created, all alone:
May man in greater numbers multiply.

Sir Thomas Urquhart, 'Of man, and woman's
creation, and marriage'

fb.217, p. 202

G0202 God freely gives, as freely we receive
It is not, do: but, ask, and thou shalt have.

[Francis Quarles], 'On God's bounty'
[Crum G249]

b.137, p. 193; b.118, p. 220

G0203 God gie me wisdom and contentful state
Love and a clear repute—honor I bate.

[Sir Philip Wodehouse], 'Upon my old friend John
Hobart honor I bate'

b.131, back (no. 149)

G0204 God give me grace, that I may Thee desire!
And leaving sin, may ne'er relapse. Amen.

[Sir Philip Wodehouse], 'St. Austin's climax. Domine
Deus meus'

b.131, p. 25

G0205　God give[s] us wealth, and craves but honor for it:
Let honor then to riches be preferred.

Sir Thomas Urquhart, 'Of reputation, and means'

fb.217, p. 205

G0206　God grant the grandchild such a race may run
As thou throughout thy life hast nobly done.

fb.151/3

G0207　God grant us all such race to run
To end in Christ, as she hath done.

fb.151/3

G0208　God grants ev'n ev'ry thing that's good
It there becomes a temple sanctified.

[Edmund Wodehouse], 'Jan. 30 [1715]'

b.131, p. 153

G0209　God grants us all things that are truly good,
For all the good they do; God's to be praised.

[Edmund Wodehouse], 'July 29 1715'

b.131, p. 237

G0210　God hath created unto man
And speak less than he hears.

b.234, p. 169

G0211　God in all cases is without all [?]
Yet ev'rywhere he's sought to be found out.

[Sir Thomas Urquhart], 'That God holds that man thus in greatest price God is everywhere though nowhere to diligently search after'

fb.217, p. 515

G0212　God in his own assembly stands
All nations are thine own.

'Psal: 82'

b.217, p. 28

G0213　God in the nature of each being, founds,
That ease, for which we labor, and we die.

c.83/3, no. 1025

G0214　God is a gracious God to me,
For every past defect, every offence.

[Edmund Wodehouse], 'Apr. 19 [1715]'

b.131, p. 199

G0215　God is a light all infinite
The love that never turns to hate.

[Robert Cottesford?]

b.144, p. 250

G0216　God is almighty, gracious, wise,
With all his pow'r to the most wise.

[Edmund Wodehouse], 'Novr. 3 1714'

b.131, p. 76

G0217　God is my God; he's pleas'd t'admit
We may no farther pay, than this.

[Edmund Wodehouse], 'Octr. 15 1714'

b.131, p. 59

G0218　God is our strength and certain hope,
To Jacob's late posterities.

'Psalm 46'

c.264/1, p. 199

G0219　God is the Lord most justly prais'd
Unto our latest hour.

'Psalm 48'

c.264/1, p. 205

G0220　God loves the adverb better than the noun:
And hates the good, if it be not well done.

Sir Thomas Urquhart, 'Of the adverb and the noun'

fb.217, p. 307

G0221　God made man and man made money;
God made a dungeon to put Satan in.

'Lyncup Hill May 2nd 1783'

c.93

G0222　God may being Alpha, and Omega crave
The first fruits, and the tithes of all we have.

Sir Thomas Urquhart, 'Why tithes are due to the church'

fb.217, p. 204

G0223　God measures all; and so's unmeasurable:
And being but one, he is innumerable.

Sir Thomas Urquhart, 'Of God'

fb.217, p. 213

G0224　God never fails them to embrace,
[?] and shall be till Eternity.

[Edmund Wodehouse], 'Octr. 21 [1714]'

b.131, p. 64

G0225　God of almighty love
The will by all be done.

'Hymn 47th'

c.562, p. 55

G0226　God of love that hearest the prayer,
Find our happy all in thee.

'Hymn 98th'

c.562, p. 133

G0227 God of my health! whose bounteous care
That stamp'd his image there.

> [James] Merrick, 'An hymn to the Creator'
> [cf. Crum F282]
>
> c.487, p. 23; c.83/1, no. 237; fc.132/1, p. 26 ('tender care';
> attr. John Lewis)

G0228 God of my life! and author of my days!
And having lived to thee, in thee to die.

> [Anna Laetitia] (Aikin) [Barbauld], 'An address to the
> Diety'
>
> c.487, p. 1

G0229 God of my life, in thee I trust,
Upon the speaking chord.

> 'Psalm 7'
>
> c.264/1, p. 17

G0230 God of my life, whose daily care
Which lift the soul to heav'n.

> 'Psalm 23'
>
> c.264/1, p. 91

G0231 God only is to be ador'd
None but the All-wise, All-good | Can fathom this.

> [Edmund Wodehouse], 'Octr. 30 1714'
>
> b.131, p. 73

G0232 God prosper long from being broke
Lately did befall.

> Philip Wharton, 1st duke of Wharton(?), 'A true and
> lamentable ballad called The Earl's defeat'
>
> c.468 (first stanza only)

G0233 God prosper long great Chesterfield,
In genteel carriage lies!!!

> 'Song 80. A warning piece to clowns: or the
> Chesterfield miracle.'
>
> c.555, p. 125

G0234 God prosper long our gracious King.
Descend from f[oo]l to f[oo]l.

> 'An ode for the New-Year by Colley Cibber poet
> laureate' [satire; after 1730. Printed 1731? (Foxon
> C195)]
> [Crum G294]
>
> c.188, p. 79; c.392, p. 14; Poetry Box IV/170; c.570/3,
> p. 102

G0235 God prosper long our gracious Will;
We ne'er shall see such, more.

> 'A song to the tune to Chevy Chase'
> [Crum G296 (var.)]
>
> c.570/2, p. 130

G0236 God prosper long our learned court,
At leisure all sneak'd in.

> H[enry] Skrine, 'The Westminster fracas. A ballad in
> imitation of John Gilpin . . . Nov. 10 1785'
>
> c.509, p. 79

G0237 God prosper long our manor's lord,
To conquer first—must yield.

> 'Verses by ———'
>
> c.83/4, no. 1083

G0238 God prosper long our noble king,
'Twixt noblemen may cease.

> 'Chevy Chase' [with Latin translation by Henry Bold,
> of New College]
>
> b.372, p. 1

G0239 God prosper long our noble king
For this tranquility.

> 'Safety and tranquility an excellent new ballad to [the]
> tune of Chevy Chase'
>
> c.570/2, p. 145

G0240 God prosper long our noble king
Which God grant may be soon!

> 'The Belgic boar [William III] or Chevy Chase
> revived' [pr. 1695 (Wing B1784)]
> [Crum G300]
>
> fb.207/3, p. 13

G0241 God prosper long our noble king,
Till they are at Hanover.

> 'The christening [of George William, son of
> George II]. To the tune of Chevy Chase' [pr. 1718
> (Foxon E560)]
> [Crum G299]
>
> fc.58, p. 144; Poetry Box XIV/184

G0242 God prosper long our noble king
And all the people laugh.

> 'An excellent new and long historical ballad upon the
> times' [1755]
> [Crum G301]
>
> Poetry Box I/108

G0243 God prosper long our noble king
May such be ever free.

> 'The lord [the Duke of Bedford]'s lamentation or the
> Whittington defeat' [at the Lichfield races; pr. 1747
> (Foxon L265)]
>
> Poetry Box X/150

G0244 God save me for thy holy name,
Withal my heart and lust.

> [John Hopkins], 'The 21 psalm. Against the falsehood
> of his familiar acquaintance' [verses from Psalms
> 54–55]
> [Crum G307]

a.3, fol. 96v

G0245 God save our noble King,
Rebellious Scots to crush. | God save the King

> 'Song on the rebellion in Scotland 1745'

c.358, p. 7

G0246 'God save the Queen!' cries a motley rout,
As woman, there is hope for all in heaven.

> 'God save the Queen!!!'

Poetry Box II/29

G0247 God send us peace, and free from open wars,
We'll never heed some small domestic jars.

c.93

G0248 God shield me from those friends I trust and be
My sure defense from such, as trust not thee.

> [Francis Quarles], 'On friends'
> [Crum G311]

b.137, p. 191; b.118, p. 222

G0249 God sits where he doth see and hear
Sing therefore hallelujah.

> G[eorge] Wither, 'A hymn'

c.139, p. 178; c.158, p. 51 (incomplete?)

G0250 God that made both earth and heaven
For now and evermore. Amen.

> 'Isumbras'

fc.179

G0251 God well perceiving how that man combin'd
Scatter their stuff and tumble down their tools.

> 'On the building of Babel and the confounding their
> language'

b.137, p. 120; see also 'Bring me quoth one . . .'.

G0252 God works wonders now and then
Here lies a lawyer was an honest man.

> [Sir John Harington], 'On a lawyer' [Justice Randal,
> of Surrey?]
> [Crum G326]

b.62, p. 42; c.360/1, p. 159 (attr. B. Jonson)

G0253 God! whose arrows overthrew
Which the poet did compose.

> [William Popple, trans.], '[Horace] book 4th. Ode
> 6th. To Apollo'

fc.104/2, p. 352

G0254 Goddess! In various hues attir'd;
How would it glad his patriot shade!

> John Lockman, 'To fortune, (a portrait.) On Myra's
> purchasing a ticket in the state lottery, 1769'

c.267/4, p. 363

G0255 Goddess! O'er me diffuse thy influence,
I'll quaff the bowl of joy, or drain the cup of woe!

> 'Ode to memory'

c.83/3, no. 904

G0256 Goddess of golden dreams, whose magic pow'r
And snatch a bliss beyond the reach of fate.

> 'An elegy'
> [Crum G331]

c.83/1, no. 236

G0257 Goddess, whose dire, terrific power
And let each 'scutcheon pierce some loyal Briton's
heart!

> [William Boscawen], 'Ode to anarchy'

fc.106, p. 50

G0258 Godolphin's easy and unpractic'd air,
Who 'scape their arms, are captives to her eyes.

> 'On the Lady Harriet Godolphin [later Duchess of
> Newcastle] daughter of Francis Earl of Godolphin by
> his countess, daughter of the great Duke of
> Marlborough'

c.360/2, no. 178

G0259 God's blessed spirit, His dear Son
By solemner, more frequent pray'r.

> [Edmund Wodehouse], 'Feb. 1 [1715]'

b.131, p. 154

G0260 God's boundless goodness, boundless mercy may,
Whilst thousand rubric-martyrs want a place.

> 'On the possibility of the salvation of the heathens'

c.186, p. 107

G0261 God's favor daily I profess,
May kindle my faint weak desire.

> [Edmund Wodehouse], 'March 23 [1715]'

b.131, p. 186

G0262 God's favor the whole man o'erspread;
Desires their happiness to the whole.

> [Edmund Wodehouse], 'Feb. 23 [1715]'

b.131, p. 171

G0263 God's grace it was—she made a noble choice
Her graciousness—to love him, and rejoice.

> [Sir Philip Wodehouse], 'Upon his dear mother the
> Lady [Blanche] Wodehouse'

b.131, back (no. 19)

G0264 God's holy spirit is God here
The saints and angels join in this.

    [Edmund Wodehouse], 'Decr. 22 [1714]'

b.131, p. 121

G0265 Gods! Life's your gift, you season't with such fate
But make life what I ask, or take't away.

    c.188, p. 15

G0266 God's love, God's favor: oh what bliss
But say to exalt their rank they ought.

    [Edmund Wodehouse], 'Apr. 13 [1715]'

b.131, p. 197

G0267 God's mercy and his justice is the same
'Tis but the object, that divides the name.

    [Francis Quarles], 'On mercy and justice'

b.137, p. 195

G0268 God's mercy how should we adore,
By which he should right judgment make.

    [Edmund Wodehouse], 'Decr. 10 [1714]'

b.131, p. 110

G0269 God's name be prais'd my heart and voice
With cheerful lips and lives the same.

    [Edmund Wodehouse], 'Feb. 6 [1715]'

b.131, p. 160

G0270 God's niggs, here liggs
Here stir(?), the earl of Exeter.

    'On the earl of Exeter'

b.356, p. 247

G0271 God's presence to the soul of man,
And by our prayer, kindles, enflames its fire.

    [Edmund Wodehouse], 'Novr. 9 [1714]'

b.131, p. 80

G0272 God's rest implies not that He e'er
Others will judge, so as they please.

    [Edmund Wodehouse], 'May 28 [1715]'

b.131, p. 218

G0273 God's sacred word, is like the lamp of day,
The bees will bring in wax and honey too.

    'On man'

b.118, p. 233; b.156, p. 15

G0274 God's spirit can't be seen ('tis true)
Than what did then those Jews possess.

    [Edmund Wodehouse], 'May 25 [1715]'

b.131, p. 216

G0275 God's spirit is his viceroy here,
And ever when he swerves from that, most deeply
                                grieves.

    [Edmund Wodehouse], 'Decr. 31 [1714]'

b.131, p. 128

G0276 God's spirit only's infinite
Their light, their love, their life, their bliss.

    [Edmund Wodehouse], 'May 22 [1715]'

b.131, p. 216

G0277 God's spouse: her father's mother: her son's child:
A maid man-tied: and mother undefil'd.

    Sir Thomas Urquhart, 'The Virgin Mary in Joseph's
    day was styled'

fb.217, p. 310

G0278 God's the beginning was in the beginning
From which beginning all things had beginning.

    [Sir Thomas Urquhart], 'A Jove principia'

fb.217, p. 515

G0279 God's vast existence ne'er decays,
In one eternal day.

    'On the deity. By a dissenting clergyman in Bristol'

c.94

G0280 God's wisdom perfect is and infinite
Our safety, or relief from His assize.

    [Edmund Wodehouse], 'Decr. 10 [1714]'

b.131, p. 111

G0281 God's wisdom's infinite, man's hearts he knows
And with devoted souls ever t'adore.

    [Edmund Wodehouse], 'Feb. 20 [1715]'

b.131, p. 170

G0282 Going downstairs he met a scullion
They scold on, or wright [write?] at one another.

    'The doctor and the cook'

fb.68, p. 47

G0283 Gold is restorative, how can I then
If I should separate what so is knit.

    W[illiam] S[trode], 'To Sir John [*i.e.*, Thomas?]
    Ferrers'
    [Crum G362]

b.205, fol. 53v; b.150, p. 139 (incomplete?)

G0284 Gold-pippin first in fruit (like text)
But, much like you a nonpareil.

    [Charles Earle], 'West-down. Sent to [Miss Harris of
    Pickwell] with some apples'

c.376

G0285 Goldsmith I yield. Restrain thy rage
Has wounded thee and fled.

    [Thomas Barnard]

    fc.14/13

G0286 Good, bad, rich, poor, the foolish and the sage,
Present displeasure makes us sad or fret.

    [Robert Hayman], 'Most men mistaken'

    c.356

G0287 Good bearer of thy cross, great spring of light,
Them to this starry mansion calls, and says My
                followers come.

    [Simon] Patrick, 'A hymn before meat. From
    Prudentius'
    [Crum G373]

    c.352, p. 11

G0288 Good children are God's gifts. Mortality
May grant thy suit his gracious face to see.

    [Sir Philip Wodehouse], 'Upon his son-in-law Sir
    Jacob Astley . . .'

    b.131, back (no. 18)

G0289 Good Christian people, all draw near
Who sees her, loves, and dies.

    'A lamentable new ballad called The destructive
    damsel. To the tune of Old stories tell how
    Heracles &c.'

    Trumbull Box: Poetry Box XIII/95

G0290 Good Christians all compose the scrape
In winter with the other.

    [on the Bangorian controversy]
    [Crum G406, 'Good people']

    c.233, p. 43

G0291 Good counsels those that loving friends enjoy,
Try not them oft with every foolish toy.

    c.339, p. 324

G0292 Good day, Myrtillo. And to you no less
We'll bless his face, then to our country pleasures.

    [Robert Herrick], 'Upon the birth of the prince
    eclogue'
    [Crum G377]

    b.356, p. 202

G0293 Good folk for gold or hire
Or send it home to me.

    [Michael Drayton, 'The crier']
    [Crum G384]

    b.213, p. 10; b.4, fol. 54v; b.148, p. 23; b.197, p. 37 ('love
    or hire'); c.356 ('love or hire')

G0294 Good Friday should sad Friday be;
We must at once give thanks and grieve.

    [Edmund Wodehouse], 'Apr. 15 [1715] Good Friday'

    b.131, p. 198

G0295 Good friend inform us if you can
For you perchance may lose yourselves | As well as
                        Joe and I.

    [John Walker?], 'Joe and I a song'

    fc.108, fol. 49

G0296 Good friends, for Jesus' sake forbear
And curs'd be he that moves my bones.

    [William Shakespeare], 'The epitaph on the stone
    over the grave of Mr. William Shakespeare . . . at
    Stratford upon Avon . . .'
    [Crum G385, 'friend']

    c.360/2, no. 162; see also 'Friend for Jesus' sake . . .'

G0297 Good gentlemen all, who love to regale
Observe, near Clare Market is Blackamoor Street.

    'A whimsical advertisement of an ale-house man'

    c.360/2, no. 81

G0298 Good God! And am I still alive!
That I am spar'd another year.

    'A New Year's meditation'

    c.83/1, no. 122

G0299 Good God, what a house is this!
Nothing but fish-guts to handle!

    [ ] Thomson(?), 'From Zacharie Boyd . . . who
    transl[ated] all the Bible in 7 years'

    Spence Papers, folder 148

G0300 Good Halifax and pious Wharton cry
First stop her mouth, and then deflower the dame.

    'On the L[ord]'s votes that the Church is not in
    danger'
    [Crum G389-390]

    c.171, p. 11; b.90, p. 10

G0301 Good Hilary bids thee fancy briskly so
May thy conceit, the with(?) of wine o'erflow.

    [Sir Philip Wodehouse], 'Upon Sr Francis Bickley'

    b.131, back (no. 218)

G0302 Good is the church's mighty King
To everlasting day!

    T[homas] S[tevens], 'God's goodness discovered in his
    being a stronghold to them who trust in him . . . Decr.
    10. 1779'

    c.259, p. 61

G0303 Good life true wisdom is, ev'n howsoe'er
Grief without end, grief without all relief.

> [Edmund Wodehouse], 'June 26 [1715] Mr. George's
> text 37 Ps. 3rd verse'
>
> b.131, p. 226

G0304 Good Lord what a life of misfortune I've led
Till then Johnny Bull will go wrong. | All in the
wrong &c.

> [John Walker?], 'All in the wrong'
>
> fc.108, fol. 67

G0305 Good Madam Fowler do not trouble me
Against herself conceiv'd an epigram.

> Francis Beaumont, 'On Madam Fowler desiring to
> have a sonnet written on her'
> [Crum G395]
>
> b.200, p. 218; b.148, p. 133

G0306 Good Madam, when ladies are willing,
Indeed is too mellow for me.

> Sir W[illiam] Y[oung? or Lady Mary (Wortley)
> Montagu?], 'Sir W—— Y——'s answer' [to 'Dear
> Colin, prevent my warm blushes . . .', by Lady Mary
> (Wortley) Montagu' [Dodsley Collection]
>
> c.487, p. 125

G0307 Good Maevius without scruple courting gain
The doctor's merit and the poet's fame.

> [John Sheffield? or George Villiers?], duke of
> B[uckingham?], 'On Dr G[arth] by the D[uke] of
> B[uckingham?] . . . The dispensary is said to be most
> of it a translation of the Lutrin [by Boileau]'
>
> Trumbull Box: Poetry Box XIII/66

G0308 Good master Apollo,
To cure the grin and the shaking.

> 'Apollo' [answered by 'A(h) what a hero is here . . .']
>
> c.356

G0309 Good master Doctor, can you tell?
Oh! 'Tis a favor, drink or die.

> 'Song'
>
> c.189, p. 117

G0310 Good Master Dolben, you did very well
And so Master Dolben I wish you a good morning.

> 'These verses the bellman spoke at Mr. Dolben's upon
> that morning Dr. Sacheverell gave his answer'
>
> b.90, p. 11

G0311 Good men suffer wise men grieve
Or knaves and fools will quite undo us.

> [Thomas Stevens?]
>
> c.259, p. 18; see also 'Wise men wonder/ Suffer . . .'.

G0312 Good Mister Moody
While Whittell's my name.

> [ ] Whittell, 'Verses to Mr. Moody with a razor which
> I sent to him to grind for me'
>
> c.530, p. 252

G0313 Good morning sweet Nelly how charming you look,
And both in each other confide. | Dearest John
pretty Nell [&c.]

> [John Walker?], 'John and Nell'
>
> fc.108, fol. 20

G0314 Good morrow Mr. P. may your coach
Gold hast the sodden(?) while ye get the rest.

> 'A dialogue by an accidental rencounter between Mr
> Patrick Gillespie and ane country gentleman of his
> own and a [?] [?]'
>
> Poetry Box VIII/50

G0315 Good morrow Sir! I wish you joy:
I may obtain the joy I want.

> 'Soliloquy, on being wished joy on a birthday'
>
> c.360/2, no. 13

G0316 Good mother, if you please, you may,
Instead of watching—you may sleep.

> 'To my mother'
>
> c.83/1, no. 216

G0317 Good Mister Kingham
You'll find me your trusty Bob Dormer.

> Robert Dormer, 'Lincoln's Inn 19 Febr. 1704'
>
> Poetry Box I/135

G0318 Good Mister Speaker—some are glad
Two kings and one Protector.

> 'Some lines to Mr. Speaker'
>
> Poetry Box VIII/8

G0319 Good-natur'd Hermes for his care and aid,
Whether my flocks devour'd by wolves or gods.

> Francis Lockyer, dean of Peterborough, 'From the
> Greek on the sacrifices paid Mercury and Hercules'
>
> c.229/1, fol. 44

G0320 Good news Mr. Tart,
So adieu, from your friend: Thomas Tart.

> Henry Abbotts, of Gloucester, 'A true copy of verses
> found among the papers of . . . in answer to a dunning
> letter sent to him by Mr. Tart of Birmingham'
>
> c.83/1, no. 143

G0321 Good passenger, here lies one here,
That living did lie everywhere.

> 'On a liar'
>
> c.74

G0322 Good people come buy
And his juggling Eve, may by chance lose his own |
                                                    By an Orange.

'Buy my Oranges, or a new ballad to an excellent old
tune of A pudding'

fb.108, p. 239

G0323 Good people do but lend an ear,
Do take the helm, and better sway.

'The sea-martyrs or, the seamen's sad lamentation for
their faithful service, bad pay, and cruel usage'

b.111, p. 515

G0324 Good people draw near
Of what a pox wad ye be at.

'Song 169'

c.555, p. 258

G0325 Good people draw near, if a ballad you'll hear,
Level coil with a prince and a player.

'A ballad' [on Lord Arlington, Sir Thomas Clifford,
and others]
[Crum G408]

fb.140, p. 84; Trumbull Box: Poetry Box XIII/33

G0326 Good people draw near I'll tell you a tale
That had any hand from Holland to bring, | Us
                                                    this Orange.

'An Orange'

b.111, p. 337

G0327 Good people fast,
We're full as bad as they.

'An admonition against the Fast Day' [1690]

b.111, p. 248; fb.207/1, p. 40 (var.); see also 'O God we
pray . . .', 'Good people pray . . .'.

G0328 Good people give ear, and I'll tell you a story,
So the scheme for the public is very well laid. |
Which &c.

'The Pacific fleet'

c.570/3, p. 69; Poetry Box X/49

G0329 Good people give ear to the fateless duel
And let her make a kirk, and a mill of the breaks.

'Sawney Ogilby's duel with his wife. To the tune of
The world's past'

c.530, p. 198

G0330 Good people, I pray ye come hither
We never shall see any Moor. | Sing hey ding ding a
                                                    ding ding

'On the picture of the King and Queen and seven new
bishops, January 3, 1691'
[Crum G409]

b.111, p. 405

G0331 Good people pray for what is past
Were e'en as bad as they.

c.570/3, p. 122; see also 'Good people fast . . .', 'O God
we pray . . .'.

G0332 Good people what will you of all be bereft
Why the devil, why should we be kept in the dark?

[Edward Ward?], 'On the taxes. K[ing] W[illia]m's
reign' [1696]
[Crum G412; POAS V.499]

Poetry Box VII/5; fb.207/3, p. 10; Trumbull Box: Poetry
Box XIII/80

G0333 Good Robert king, we humbly pray
That all they say are lies.

'The countryman's petition' [to Walpole]
[Crum G414]

c.570/3, p. 131

G0334 Good sentences who keepeth in his breast,
By proof shall find he harbors happy guest.

c.339, p. 308; see also 'Wise sentences . . .'.

G0335 Good Sir altho' I am inclined
The lady's most obedient servant.

Dr. T. Stamper, 'An epistle in verse from . . . to his
uncle at Oxford 10th September. 1717 . . .'

b.155, p. 71

G0336 Good Sir had it been in my power
And justly acknowledge 'twas right.

'Her [Mira's] answer'

Poetry Box I/57

G0337 Good Sir, this comes to let you know
To die by Ketch as mutton monger.

'Stateley. to Saml. Sheppard esqr.'

c.484, p. 103

G0338 Good so transcends: no limits it include;
Therefore, within this world, there is none good.

Sir Thomas Urquhart, 'Transcendent good, a
property of being'

fb.217, p. 110

G0339 Good springs from union: from division evil;
For there's one only God: but many a devil.

Sir Thomas Urquhart, 'Concord, and discord'

fb.217, p. 273

G0340 Good we must love and must hate ill
Who doth not fling away the shell.

J[ohn] D[onne]
[Crum G420]

b.148, p. 106; b.114, p. 254

G0341 Good wrestler he will not close in
Her in turn—whence he could not him unloose.

[Sir Philip Wodehouse], 'Nicolas Wilton my kinsman
will not close in'

b.131, back (no. 178)

G0342 Goodness, that guides you, guard you; and may
sooth
Clear fame renown you, true loves crown you.

'The much honored George Lane esquire secretary to
the right honorable James Marquess and Earl of
Ormonde and Ossery'

fb.228/[49a]

G0343 Gorg'd is the ravenous throat of war,
And the wide pinion'd eagle cease his flight.

T[homas] Warton, 'Speech of a Druid after the
Romans had taken Mona'

c.149, p. 9

G0344 Gough, list'ning to his tatter'd choir,
To ours begrim'd with soot and grease?

John Lockman, 'Vauxhall and Marylebone Gardens: a
comparison . . . 1738, before the present handsome
orchestra was erected'

c.267/1, p. 236

G0345 Gout! I conjure thee by the powerful names
Their herring trade is brought unto its last.

[Robert Wild], 'An essay upon the late victory
obtained by his royal highness the Duke of York
against the Dutch upon June 3rd 1665. by the author of
Iter boreale'
[Crum G429]

c.166, p. 276

G0346 Grace as the sun, incessantly its light
Then blame thyself if not regenerate.

'Grace compared to the sun'
Poetry Box v/106

G0347 Grace will and art assist me for to see
Thrice blessed one in three, and three in one.

[Sir Richard Bulstrode?], 'On Trinity Sunday'
fb.88, p. 118

G0348 Gracious disposer of all worldly things
Whole nations by her life will joy receive.

[ ] P., 'Mr P. on the Queen's sickness'
fb.142, p. 64

G0349 Gracious is God to offer means of grace
With ever-blessed souls at Christ['s] right hand.

[Mary Serjant]
fb.98, fol. 149

G0350 Gracious pow'rs convey me where
Join to grace my charmer's mind.

'On retirement'
c.83/1, no. 176

G0351 Grandfather, father, and son lies here interr'd,
At Norwich city born, but liv'd at Bixley.

'Epitaph on the three Edward Wards of Bixley near
Norwich b[aronet]s'
c.360/3, no. 118

G0352 Grant me an heart O God flaming with love,
Yes believes such, as now no heart conceives.

[Edmund Wodehouse], 'July 25 1715'
b.131, p. 235

G0353 Grant me gentle love said I,
For love, love, himself's no more.

[William Congreve], 'Peti[ti]on'
c.176, p. 38

G0354 Grant me good God I pray a life
Peru and Mexico be theirs.

'A wish'
Poetry Box vii/5

G0355 Grant me O God an heart on thee so set,
As I shall slight or prize 'em for thy sake.

[Edmund Wodehouse], 'July 16 [1715]'
b.131, p. 232

G0356 Grant me O God so right a sense
My days, my nights, delight, employ.

[Edmund Wodehouse], 'May 11 [1715]'
b.131, p. 211

G0357 Grant me O God to address to thee
Make all these worldly things to me all one.

[Edmund Wodehouse], 'Aug. 29 1715'
b.131, p. 255

G0358 Grant me, ye gods, a calm and safe retreat
In chanting hymns to my Creator's praise.

'The wish . . . Nottingham—Dec. 28: 1747'
c.326, p. 169

G0359 Grant me, ye gods, before I die
Still I shall praise you, and be well content.

Henry Baker, 'The petition'
c.244, p. 395

G0360 Grant me your secret favor, I request ye,
For labor best befits so ripe a soil.

> Sir Thomas Urquhart, 'The words of a gentleman to
> his mistress, who was of a most pleasingly merry, and
> jovial humor'
>
> fb.217, p. 309

G0361 Grant O my God, O grant to me,
Thy right and our felicity.

> [Edmund Wodehouse], 'Jan. 2 [1715]'
>
> b.131, p. 130

G0362 Grant that thy love O God may ever be
If 'get his laws his love we ben't rebellious.

> [Edmund Wodehouse], 'Apr. 5 [1715]'
>
> b.131, p. 192

G0363 Granta! too soon thy happy awful scenes
And thought, and spoke the soul of truth.

> [William] Mason, 'Ode to independency'
>
> Poetry Box v/75; Poetry Box I/17 (5 Oct 1745)

G0364 Granting he did unchristian priest
For ribald wit, to the profoundest hell.

> 'To Dean Swift, occasioned by the following lines
> ['Thus Steele, who own'd . . .'] in his satire on
> Doctor D.'
>
> c.360/1, p. 279

G0365 Grass, smoke, a flower, vapor, shade, a span,
The certainty of death; of life the vanity.

> 'An epitaph on Mr. Francis Bretton gentleman'
>
> c.244, p. 211

G0366 Grateful (O muse!) thy services I own,
Thou not procuring,—win a pair of shoes.

> John Lockman, 'To his muse . . . July 1761'
>
> c.267/1, p. 279

G0367 Grateful's to me, the fire, the wound, the chain,
That burns, that binds, that hurts, I must desire.

> [on Prince Charles addressing himself to the Infanta,
> translated from the Latin]
> [Crum G447]
>
> b.104, p. 31

G0368 Gratitude is rare! Most, after favors
Excites my wonder and transcends my praise.

> 'On gratitude'
>
> c.156, p. 172

G0369 Grave aged Nestor since the fates decree
And in Elysium slumbers e'er be blest.

> 'Upon the death of Dr. Whaly'
>
> b.197, p. 155

G0370 Grave Milton says, old Eve soon as brought forth
possess'd me
All but my name—and that's your task to tell.

> 'A riddle'
>
> c.578, p. 94

G0371 Grave Pythian knight, seeing that to crown the
hopes
To eternize the off'ring of my vein.

> Sir Thomas Urquhart, 'The invocation to Apollo and
> the muses' [preceding Urquhart's epigrams]
>
> fb.217, p. 30

G0372 Grave Socrates, that sage of old
Was more than Socrates could do.

> c.536

G0373 Grave Vaughan's dead, Frank North appears,
Were most egregious servitors.

> 'Upon Sr. Francis North being made Lord Chief
> Justice'
>
> fb.140, p. 137

G0374 Grave, yet not prudish, modest yet polite
If free, not forward, if sedate not sad.

> 'A character of a young lady'
>
> c.360/1, p. 119

G0375 Graves are lodgings for the best
In this hope they here reside.

> 'On Sr. Wm. Knight in Banbury church Oxfordshire'
> [Crum G453]
>
> c.240, p. 135

G0376 Gray hairs are honorable when they are crown'd
Do seek in shades of ivy bowers to shun.

> [John Hobart], 'Against periwigs'
>
> b.108, fol. 5v

G0377 Great Alexander's thoughts the world embrac'd,
Your lines had made him choose you for his poet.

> Sir Thomas Urquhart, 'To a certain well-traveled
> gentleman, who withal was a good poet'
>
> fb.217, p. 267

G0378 Great, and poor thus steep in sorrow,
Only we enjoy a peace.

> 'The airy spirits'
>
> fb.107, p. 43

G0379 Great, and proud, if she deride me,
'Tis but, O unconstant man.

> 'De eodem subto'
>
> b.200, p. 85

G0380 Great are thy mercies Lord and manyfold
When we would seek to sound thy praises forth.

    [Mary Serjant]

fb.98, fol. 158

G0381 Great Atlas of religion since thy fate
The crozier fell in Laud, the church in thee.

    'On the Reverend Dr Prideaux Bishop of Worcester'

b.137, p. 202

G0382 Great awful structure whose celestial view
And that joy lost all others lose their taste.

    R[obert] Shirley, 1st earl of Ferrers, 'Upon Versailles.
    From Malherbe'

c.347, p. 4

G0383 Great bounteous Author of the day
With comfort, peace and joy!

c.250

G0384 Great Britain now may well regret
Reduc'd again to anarchy | By Coningsmark's
                        pretenders.

    'Old England's resentment. To the tune of Britain's
    new health'

c.570/1, p. 88

G0385 Great Britain's King, rare puissant, opulent,
That if I liv'd, would now your grave adore.

    [Thomas Rogers], 'The Earl of Leicester's ghost. The
    ghost's speech, dedicatory to King James's most
    excellent Majesty' [dedication to 'I that sometime
    shin'd . . .']

fb.206, p. 207

G0386 Great Charles we do lament thy fate
Of monarchy and all its friends.

Poetry Box VII/32

G0387 Great Charles, who full of mercy didst command
Till the stroke's struck which they can ne'er retrieve.

    [Henry Savile], 'To the King' [1673; envoy to 'Spread
    a large canvas . . .']
    [Crum G468]

fb.70, p. 144; Poetry Box VIII/22; fb.140, p. 171; b.52/2 (as
part of 'Spread a large canvas . . .')

G0388 Great Cincinnatus, for his country's good
His heart unblemish'd, and his hands unstain'd.

    'The dictator' [on Sir Robert Walpole]

Poetry Box X/34

G0389 Great Curius that thrice triumphed in Rome
Left here by you to be dispos'd by me.

    Sir John Strangways, 'In Decium Curium'

b.304, p. 43

G0390 Great deities! To whose impartial sway
In his calm breast, who rules the upper skies.

    John Lockman, 'Psyche's speech to Pluto and
    Proserpine' [translated from La Fontaine]

c.267/4, p. 263

G0391 Great Drake! My physician
The King's patent-letter.

    [Charles Earle]

c.376

G0392 Great Earl of B[ath] your reign is o'er
With now and then an ode.

    [Sir Charles Hanbury Williams], 'An ode to the Earl
    of B[at]h'

Poetry Box XIV/195

G0393 Great Edmund hoarse, you say the reason clear;
For Attic lungs respire Boeotian air.

    [Anna Laetitia (Aikin)] Barbauld, 'An epigram by . . .
    on Mr. Burke's being seized with a hoarseness when he
    was first elected member for Bristol'

c.341, p. 43

G0394 Great Elliot fills the trumps of fame,
On the rack's top, his beaver show.

    'An imitation of Dean Swift's Mordanto— the first
    triplet is Swift's. On General [George Augustus]
    Elliot Governor of Gibraltar [later Lord Heathfield]
    during the famous siege from April 1781 to Feb 1783'

Poetry Box III/16

G0395 Great flame of English poets gone; how shall
Ben Jonson, cannot choose but make a verse.

    [George Daniel], 'To the memory of the best dramatic
    English poet Ben: Jonson'

b.121, fol. 50

G0396 Great Fred'rick! emulous of Gustavus' fame;
O fix thine eagle in the heart of France!

    [ ] Wolthers, 'Verses, to the King of Prussia, by . . .
    agent to His Britannic Majesty, at Rotterdam [3 April
    1758]'

c.267/4, p. 171

G0397 Great God! A worm would sing thy praise,
And mingle praise with saints above.

    Charles Atherton Allnutt, 'A prayer and confession'

c.112, p. 15

G0398 Great God I beg assist me all the days
Thy mercy nor my duty ne'er omit.

    [Mrs. ( ) Feilding]

b.226, p. 25

G0399 Great God, in awful majesty arise,
His love is wondrous all, and cannot be express'd.

   [Richard] Daniel, dean of Armagh, 'Goliath. Psalm 8'

   c.244, p. 343

G0400 Great God of mercies! condescend,
May ev'ry pray'r combine.

   'Hymn on the fast day 1793'

   c.91, p. 243

G0401 Great God that dost inspire the hearts of thine
And present help, may future hope afford.

   [John Taylor], 'The invocation' [from 'The world turned upside down']

   fb.40, p. 376

G0402 Great God, when my weak, trembling steps
Into the path of day.

   [Thomas Stevens?], 'November the 1st. 1779'

   c.259, p. 37

G0403 Great God whom heav'nly host revere
And in the Lord rejoice.

   Rev. [ ] Brown, 'By the Rev. Mr. Brown'

   c.360/1, p. 193

G0404 Great God! Whose pow'r o'er earth and heav'n
                        presides
My wealth contentment, silence—peace my lot.

   'Wrote by a person in distress'

   c.481, p. 224

G0405 Great God, with conscious blushes lo! I come
And future worlds like me shall bless the Lord.

   [Richard] Daniel, dean of Armagh, 'Uriah—Psalm 51'

   c.244, p. 365

G0406 Great, good, and just, could I but rate
And write thy epitaph in blood and wounds.

   [James Graham, marquis of] Montrose, 'Another [poem] on King Charles the first . . . writ with the point of his sword (Scotland's glory)'
   [Crum G501]

   b.137, p. 199; b.169, p. 255; b.204, p. 60; c.189, p. 58; fb.143, p. 5

G0407 Great heart, who taught thee so to die?
We died thou only livedst that day.

   [Henry King], 'On Sir Walter Raleigh at the time of his execution'
   [Crum G504]

   b.197, p. 47 (attr. [ ] Cecil); b.54, p. 877; Poetry Box VI/107

G0408 Great in belly, but small in sense
Men will betray their want of head.

   L. S. [or Frederick Corfield?], [acrostic on Graham]

   c.381/2

G0409 Great in thy self, of womankind
Be still to Chyndonax a friend.

   'Presented with an almanac for 1755 . . . 30 Dec. 1754'

   c.371, fol. 84

G0410 Great is th'amazement of encircling fog
Than this attends a parlous length of chase.

   c.519

G0411 Great is that jewel which thy name employs
Even Christ the giver no it cannot be.

   [Mary Serjant]

   fb.98, fol. 157

G0412 Great is the force that him adorns:
Why may he not, he hath more horns.

   Sir Thomas Urquhart, 'Of a very strong man, whose wife was something kind'

   fb.217, p. 222

G0413 Great is the mercy of the Lord,
We may assure our souls of bliss.

   [Edmund Wodehouse], 'Novr. 7 [1714]'

   b.131, p. 79

G0414 Great is the merit to retrieve from sin,
But greater, to prevent our plunging in.

   John Lockman, 'On occasion of the asylum, and the Magdalen House . . . Decr. 1758'

   c.267/1, p. 179

G0415 Great Jove! Look down on us poor Whigs
Or have no god at all.

   'Semper idem. Or the Whig's litany 1713'
   [Crum G511, '1735']

   c.570/3, p. 80

G0416 Great Jupiter being at a solemn feast
Their lungs yield idle breath: their noses smoke.

   'In tobacco nistas'
   [Crum G513, 'tongues']

   b.197, p. 85

G0417 Great king of hearts, in arms transcending fame!
With those fierce wars which heaven hath thus
                          decreed?

   'Upon a king of Sweden whose name was Gustavus Adolphus about the year 1632'

   c.158, p. 116

G0418 Great king to bid you welcome here so I
Ere you say any more let our recorder speak.

    Geo[rge] Bostock, of Churton, 'Mr . . . .made this
    droll on Mr. Button mayor of Chester'

fc.61, p. 135

G0419 Great Lord Frog and Lady Mouse
Must have tails as well as pates. | Tweedle come
                         tweedle twee

    [Thomas D'Urfey], '19th song the court frog or love
    in miniature'

Accession 97.7.40, p. 33 (with a separate copy)

G0420 Great Lord, in mercy from thy throne
Through heav'n and earth display.

    [Sir William Trumbull], 'Ps. 57'

b.177, p. 35; Trumbull Box: Poetry Box XIII/12

G0421 Great luminaries of the sky,
Our rites perform'd, return we home.

    [William Popple, trans.], 'The secular poem' [Horace]

fc.104/2, p. 476

G0422 Great majesty? Oh heavens thou noddy pole
Hedge dance it plays because it's full of stakes.

    'Answer' [to 'Stella polaris']

b.356, p. 114

G0423 Great men are envied always by the small,
Let each impert'nent fool say what he list.

    R[obert] Shirley, 1st earl of Ferrers, 'To the D. of
    Marlborough in tempore'

c.347, p. 7

G0424 Great monarch, hasten to thy native shore
And willing nations, own their rightful king.

    'England's most humble address to her lawful
    sovereign, of all princes the most accomplished and
    eminently endowed with all manner of virtues, yet
    exiled' [pr. 1718? (Foxon E323)]
    [Crum G528]

c.570/1, p. 123

G0425 Great monarch of the world from whom power
                            springs
I fear they'll force me to make bread of stones . . . .

    'Majesty in misery, or an imploration of the King of
    Kings written by his Majesty King Charles the First,
    during his captivity in Carisbrook Castle . . . 1648'
    [Crum G529]

fb.68, p. 139 (incomplete)

G0426 Great monarch, since the world's nativity,
Then the bright sun transcends terrestrial things.

    Sir Thomas Urquhart, 'The first epigram to the King'

fb.217, p. 34

G0427 Great Monarch whose fear'd hand the thunder fling
With painful throes brings forth a wretched death.

    [Thomas Stanley], 'A paraphrase upon Psalm
    CXXXIX'

b.152, p. 97

G0428 Great nature, then, thro' all her diff'rent works,
Eternal glories, and enchanting beauties!

    [Elizabeth (Singer)] Rowe, 'And time shall be no
    more'

fc.132/1, p. 80

G0429 Great nature's God whose lib'ral hand appears
Who thro' eternity, is still the same.

    'On God'

c.83/2, no. 330

G0430 Great news we lately heard from court—
I may speak what I have seen | Save treason

Poetry Box VIII/46

G0431 Great object of thine Israel's hope
Shall bloom beyond the grave.

    P[hilip] Doddridge, 'Jer. XVIII: 13, 14. Sept. 11. 1750'

c.493, p. 81

G0432 Great patron of th'apostate sons of wit
As when the words were bad to make the letters
                            good.

    [Robert Cholmeley], 'To Mr C. Crownfied upon
    printing the Tripos verses: AD: 1725/6 in a neater
    letter then any of the former'

c.190, p. 147

G0433 Great poverty with heavy clog of care,
Pulls some men down when they ascending are.

c.339, p. 318

G0434 Great prince! and so much greater as more wise
To woods and groves what once the painter sings.

    [Andrew Marvell?], 'To the King' [envoy to
    'Sandwich in Spain now . . .']
    [Crum G540, POAS I.87]

b.136, p. 33; c.160, fol. 16; fb.140, p. 78

G0435 Great princess! Model of the fair;
If rightly we our plan pursue!

    John Lockman, 'To their royal highnesses the Prince
    and Princess of Wales: on waiting upon them with
    early Shetland pickled herrings: from the Council of
    the Free British Fishery . . . July 1757'

c.267/2, p. 305

G0436 Great Queen, the sum of this great little book,
And though detraction bark, she dares not bite.

'To Queen Anne of Great Britain' [1616]

fb.69, p. 121

G0437 Great Queen! Who sit'st on Peter's throne conceal'd,
And Hell, once beautified, become a heaven.

John Lockman, 'Sonnet, imitated from the Italian'

c.267/1, p. 72

G0438 Great royal dreamer where is now that thing,
Perchance as well as they, God save the king.

c.158, p. 35

G0439 Great Ruler of the heav'n and earth
Crown us with good success.

[Sir William Trumbull], 'Ps. 90'

b.177, p. 25; Trumbull Box: Poetry Box XIII/15

G0440 Great Schomberg say what's due unto thy name?
Thou cam'st, thou saw'st, and overcam'st by flight.

'Upon Duke Schomberg's conquest in Ireland'

b.111, p. 259

G0441 Great sinners have been though more blessed than
For he that tumbling falls not mends his pace.

[Sir Thomas Urquhart], 'Experience of evil is a great furtherance to good'

fb.217, p. 533

G0442 Great Sir, belov'd of God and man, admit
And, like a Jove, fighting in clouds and thunder.

[Robert Wild], 'To the King' [envoy to 'Gout! I conjure thee . . .'; licensed 16 June 1665]
[Crum G546]

c.166, p. 279

G0443 Great Sir, disdain not in this peace to stand
And in Great Britain thought the thunderer born.

'To the King' [envoy to 'First draw the sea . . .']

fb.140, p. 52

G0444 Great Sir, our poor hearts were ready to burst
That sign not this address.

'The humble address [to King James] of the loyal professors of divinity and law' [May 1685]
[POAS IV.12]

fb.68, p. 13

G0445 Great Sir the man his humble tribute pays
Declare what's truth and truth will them confound.

[Thomas Gurney], 'To Mr. G[eorge] Whitefield minister of the gospel' [acrostic]

c.213

G0446 Great Sir, whose majesty doth fill a throne
(Once two) will be but one, like them and you.

fb.234, verso of tp

G0447 Great son of night come from thy ebon cell
And charm them gently with thy silver wands.

'To sleep'

b.356, p. 105

G0448 Great sorrows, yea death's pangs do compass me,
Not only I, but both, and yet but one.

'A lover on his sick love'
[Crum G553]

b.200, p. 112

G0449 Great-soul'd Achilles was a noble friend
You in you have the virtues of all these.

[Sir Aston Cokayne], 'To my noble friend Colonel Edward Stamford'

b.275, p. 42

G0450 Great source of being and of love
To him who all thy virtues gave.

P[hilip] Doddridge, 'The statutory and essence of effects of the gospel from Ezek. XLVII. 89'

c.493, p. 38

G0451 Great source of bliss, inspire my soul,
And raise him from the grave.

'Ode to charity'

c.83/3, no. 950

G0452 Great source of life our souls confess
To souls of nobler life above.

P[hilip] Doddridge, 'Of walking before the Lord in the land of living Ps. CXVI. 9'

c.493, p. 69

G0453 Great Sovereign of the world, thy glorious name
Thy perfect laws, and worship at thy throne.

[Henry] Needler, 'Psalm 92d'

c.244, p. 548

G0454 Great Steele the friend is dead; oh empty name
How just and warm his zeal, how like your own.

'To the memory of Sir Richard Steele knt. who deceas'd in September 1729. Inscribed to the right honorable Sir Robert Walpole'

c.360/1, p. 275

G0455 Great Strafford! worthy of that name, though all
Our nation's glory, and our nation's hate.

[Sir John Denham, elegy on the Earl of Strafford]
[Crum G555]

b.200, p. 279; b.54, p. 887; fb.106(9)

G0456 Great things you promist, greater you have done us,
You promist but a prince, and palm'd a king upon us.

    b.204, p. 132

G0457 Great Tycho's labors also do foreshow
What destinies on kingdoms God directs.

    'Upon the new supposed star in 1632' [the year of
    Gustavus Adolphus' death]

    c.158, p. 116

G0458 Great tyrant of eternal night
She scorns his sting and triumphs o'er the chains of
                              fate.

    [Robert Cholmeley], 'O death! where is thy sting? O
    grave! where is thy victory? 1 Epist: to the Corinthians
    Chap: 15—Verse 55th'

    c.190, p. 77

G0459 Great was his soul, and nobly descended
Heaven his soul praising God's holy name.

    'An epitaph on the worthy and good Lord of Altyre
    who died the 20th day of February 1748'

    Poetry Box VIII/61

G0460 Greatly to your progenitors you owe,
Hence, in each deed, yourself a Perry show.

    John Lockman, '16 Nov. 1765. Writ under a
    mezzotinto, representing Lord Warkworth [later duke
    of Northumberland]'

    c.267/1, p. 385; c.267/4, p. 394

G0461 Greatness, with thy modest eye
Where such rare perfection found.

    [part of the epitaph of Simeon Cufand in Basingstoke
    churchyard, d. 1638]

    c.150, p. 5

G0462 Green is the heart which guards this flow'r,
And deadly poison lurks beneath.

    'On one young person's giving another a sprig of
    briony for a nosegay'

    c.504, p. 206

G0463 Green o'er the copses spring's soft hues are spreading,
Rejoice to bid a world like this, adieu!

    [Charlotte (Turner) Smith], 'April'

    c.141, p. 95

G0464 Green were the trees, with flowers the meads were
                           crown'd,
And long, may blooming(?) George, the psalms adorn!

    John Lockman, 'Truth: a vision. Most humbly
    addressed to the Prince of Wales: on his royal
    highness's birthday, June 4, 1758. Presented to his
    royal highness at Savile House'

    c.267/4, p. 10

G0465 Grief brings on death: but death is its relief;
Death is a great deal better then, than grief.

    Sir Thomas Urquhart, 'Of death, and love'

    fb.217, p. 302

G0466 Grief, deep as mine, cannot be known:
How Christian ministers should live!

    Mrs. [ ] K—lly, 'Another [epitaph] on [W. K—lly]'

    c.376

G0467 Grief makes me poet, I who ne'er made verse
I have my wish, my verse is pitiful.

    'On the death of a friend'
    [Crum G587]

    b.62, p. 33

G0468 Grief sadness sounds what shall she take,
Mixed, he is landed safe, and then she'll live.

    Lady Jane Cavendish, 'Passion's debate'
    [Crum G588a]

    b.233, p. 9

G0469 Grief thou hast luxuries to mirth unknown
Conviction of his bliss each selfish pang repays.

    [William Hayley], 'Sonnet . . . Sept. 10 [1800]'

    File 6968

G0470 Grief's passion child this night had died
Until good new itself, joy doth proclaim.

    Lady Jane Cavendish, 'The revive'
    [Crum G588b]

    b.233, p. 10

G0471 Grieve not fond man, nor let one tear
If not increas'd by gentle fire.

    'Dissuasives from love'

    fb.107, p. 47

G0472 Grieve not for me, for I'm at rest at last
Froward, capricious, insolent and old.

    'Epitaph'

    c.360/3, no. 153

G0473 Grieve not for me, for why my race is run
With what just reason can you then complain.

    'Epitaph on John Russell he decd March—22—1735—
    aetatis 45'

    c.360/1, p. 325

G0474 Grieve not for me, my dearest dear
And in short time you'll come to I.

    'Inscription on a woman's tombstone in Herts
    supposed to be addressed to her husband' [answered
    by 'I am not grieved . . .']

    c.150, p. 114; see also 'For me deceased . . .'.

G0475 Grieve not friend, in mournful song?
Doted on a vixen's charms.

> [William Popple, trans.], '[Horace] book 1st. ode 33rd.
> To Albius Tibullus'
>
> fc.104/2, p. 92

G0476 Griev'd and dishonor'd with licentious strains,
A perfect pattern to each master's hand.

> [Thomas] Fitzg[eral]d, 'The muses' complaint:
> humbly addressed to the right honorable the Earl of
> Middlesex'
>
> Spence Papers, folder 113

G0477 Grim death came to me t'other day,
Or take the living or restore the slain.

> 'Mori praestat quam vivere'
>
> fb.142, p. 55

G0478 Grown old, and grown stupid, you just think me
fit,
The nectar your sister presents to the gods.

> 'A receipt, to make l'eau de vie'
>
> c.83/1, no. 135

G0479 Grows up to mourn indeed! And every nerve
Nor ever be of parricide accurs'd.

> T[homas] S[tevens], 'Man grows up to mourn . . .
> [Isaac] Watts'
>
> c.259, p. 130

G0480 Grudge not to see the wicked men,
Thou sav'st both man and beast.

> [John Hopkins and William Whittingham], 'The 16
> psalm for consolation in the time of the prosperity of
> the wicked, and affliction' [verses from Psalms 36–37]
> [Crum G603]
>
> a.3, fol. 86

G0481 Guard well your hearts postillions, post boys,
grooms,
His guide, his shield, his currycomb for life.

> [Horace Walpole, 4th earl of Orford], 'D[uchess] of
> Chandos' [d. 1759]
> [Crum G604]
>
> c.157, p. 69

G0482 Guardian angels, now protect me
Shall I never see him more?

> 'A song'
>
> c.358, p. 61

G0483 Guardian of Israel, heavenly King!
And Israel's sons thy name, forever will adore.

> [Richard] Daniel, dean of Armagh, 'Sion preserv'd.
> Psalm 48'
> [Crum G605]
>
> c.244, p. 358

G0484 Guided by truth, how could'st thou hope to please,
The center of each well-conducted line.

> John Lockman, 'To David Mallet esqr, after reading
> his Life of Lord [i.e., Francis] Bacon . . . March 1741'
>
> c.267/2, p. 353

G0485 Guiltless of thought, each blockhead may compose
By schoolboys quoted and by girls admir'd.

> 'Verses; agst Mr Pope'
>
> Spence Papers, folder 113

G0486 Gustillo, with a noodle face,
Settle on woods with ordure fraught.

> John Lockman, 'To one Price, an attorney, who
> inveighed against everything tolerable, in a musical
> drama of mine; but applauded every trifling touch in
> that of another writer . . . May 1731'
>
> c.267/1, p. 248; c.268 (first part), p. 35 ('witless face')

H

H0001 Ha! What art thou, whose voice unknown
Each rocky cave, and vocal hill.

Miss [ ] White, of Edgbaston, 'Verses to Echo—
occasioned by one found in my parsonage-garden'

c.532

H0002 Had Alexander your bright form survey'd
For one, and too mean a sacrifice to you.

'An epigram made on sight of the Countess of
Sunderland at Tunbridge Wells, in the year 1705'

c.189, p. 186

H0003 Had all the modern doctors such a sound
Your judgment is so orthodox and polish'd.

[Sir Thomas Urquhart], 'To Doctor John Gauden'

fb.217, p. 391

H0004 Had Cain been Scot, God would have chang'd his
                                                  doom,
Not let him wander, but confin'd him home.

c.233, p. 31

H0005 Had Eve in Paradise possess'd that look
And adoration been the first offense.

'On a beautiful lady'

c.150, p. 120

H0006 Had fate propitious made it mine
Against reproach is innocence.

[John Kidgell], 'Verses occasioned by the advice of
the dwarf [Thomas Loggan, fan-painter] at Tunbridge
Wells' [pr. 1748 (Foxon K46)]

Poetry Box I/103

H0007 Had he to law become a drudge?
But still his muse did him trepan.

[Sir John Denham]

pb.53, p. 25 (autogr.)

H0008 Had Hogarth, or had Hayman sketch'd the draught,
By such an ass as thee, quite makes me sick.

John Lockman, 'To a fellow, who after the author had
done him some service, [?] to ridicule him in a stupid
print . . . 1744'

c.267/1, p. 29

H0009 Had I a heart for falsehood fram'd
And brothers in the young.

'Song 241'

c.555, p. 384

H0010 Had I a wish I knew it would be giv'n
Let avarice ambition take the rest.

'The wish'

File 13409

H0011 Had I been deaf: or if you had been mute,
Nor with unclosed eyes, esteem you old.

Sir Thomas Urquhart, 'To a gallant young gentleman
extremely eloquent, and wise'

fb.217, p. 147

H0012 Had I been U
Far better lines on D.

'Addressed to the author of some bad lines on the
River Dee'

Diggle Box: Poetry Box XI/21

H0013 Had I Ben Jonson's brain, Diogen's gall;
Lest in his wrath we find Gomorrah's fate.

'On the new nocturnal assemblies'

c.530, p. 90

H0014 Had I, Pygmalion-like, the pow'r,
And make her more, than womankind.

[Soame Jenyns], 'The choice'

c.147, p. 17

H0015 Had I the art to win your charms,
Or die this very hour.

[Frederick Corfield]

c.381/1

H0016 Had I the most capacious mind
But love to endless years shall last.

John Author, 'Charity from 1. Cor. 13th. Ch.'

c.244, p. 563

H0017 Had I those wings that soars above the sky
But heavenly treasures doth transcend it far.

[Mary Serjant]

fb.98, fol. 155

H0018 Had I with Plato's eloquence been fill'd,
And in the temple, we anoint you His.

'To his sacred majesty King James the Third' [Foxon
S110]
[Crum H19]
c.570/1, p. 117

H0019 Had Juno and Pallas invited
And adhere to my own Charlotte Anne.

Ralph Broome, 'Lines on the marriage of Mrs.
Broome'
c.486, fol. 31v

H0020 Had Mahomet, who wine forbid,
And charg'd thy goblet high.

John Lockman, 'Arising in Vauxhall Gardens . . . June
1745'
c.267/1, p. 152

H0021 Had my past life been so improv'd,
Observes, and yet imputes them not.

[M. S.], 'A thought on sickness'
c.156, p. 79

H0022 Had nature giv'n you horns, I could transplant
them,
But seeing the gift's your wife's, you'll never want
them.

Sir Thomas Urquhart, 'To a cuckold of the
impossibility to be at any time rid of his horns'
fb.217, p. 67

H0023 Had not the L[ord] been on our side
Both now and evermore.

[Henry Blaxton]
[cf. Crum H23]
a.28, s. 2V8

H0024 Had not the Lord (may Israel now say)
And ever shall of both sole monarch reign.

J. B. [or Thomas Fairfax?], 'Psalm 124 . . . Dec. 23,
1702'
[Crum H24]
b.63, p. 102, 107

H0025 Had not the Lord, may Isr'el say,
Be not His saints afraid.

'Psalm 124'
c.264/3, p. 71

H0026 Had not your gentle heart a cause to mourn
All are but shadows borrow'd from the sun.

'On a beautiful woman dressed in black'
c.391, p. 53

H0027 Had Pallas, Juno, or fair Venus, been alive to see
This golden ball is yours, sweet nymph, none else
can have it.

Sir F[rancis] C[astillion]
fb.69, p. 191

H0028 Had parts and merit gained the chair,
Do this, and then the chair's thy own.

'Advice' [Tory verses addressed to William Bromley,
standing for Speaker, on the election of John Smith,
24 Oct. 1705]
[Crum H26]
c.111, p. 122

H0029 Had R[i]d[e]ll liv'd in sweet Anacreon's days
In brighter odes he'd celebrate her worth!

R[ichard] V[ernon] S[adleir], 'To Lady Rid[de]ll who
desired my opinion of translation of Anacreon's
odes—impromptu'
c.106, p. 101

H0030 Had she but liv'd in Cleopatra's age
That all the world for love had well been lost.

'On the Duch[es]s of Portsmouth's picture'
b.371, no. 27

H0031 Had she liv'd so long, so much she was admir'd,
Heav'n dash'd the idol to create the saint.

'On the death of Queen Mary'
c.233, p. 90

H0032 Had Solomon wish'd wealth, he had been wiser:
He wished wisdom; for he was not wise.

Sir Thomas Urquhart, 'Of King Solomon his wish'
fb.217, p. 69

H0033 Had the breath of dewy morning
Lovely nature will restore.

'The country, written by a rich young heiress'
c.344, p. 26

H0034 Had the earth's drawing center (so her unto
Subjects to be the murderers of their king.

William Smyth, 'On the unnatural murder of my
king'
fb.228/23

H0035 Had [?] then be estrang'd from death,
He had not died so soon.

[Sir Thomas Urquhart], 'Of a dyer who died in dying'
fb.217, p. 538

H0036 Had thy spouse Dr. Douglas been ta'en from thy side
Thou with truth might'st have said, 'Thou art bone
of my bone.'

[William Lort Mansel], 'Epigram'
[Crum H32]

c.116, p. 55

H0037 Had women wit, methinks they should not boast
I'm sure we thrust them from us all we can.

'How men love women'
[Crum H34]

b.200, p. 413

H0038 Had you but felt an equal flame
Nor gentle pity touch your mind.

[Frederick Corfield], 'The retort'

c.381/1

H0039 Had you then liv'd, your port had grac'd th'old Roman
Your Lordship, for their Mars, and their Apollo.

Sir Thomas Urquhart, 'To the Earl of Arundel'

fb.217, p. 62

H0040 Hadst thou abroad found safety in thy flight
What more could Brutus or just Cato do.

'On Sr. Thomas Armstrong'

fb.143, p. 31

H0041 Hadst thou like other sirs and knights of worth
What life of man is worth by valuing thine.

[Richard Corbett], 'On Sir Thomas Overbury'
[Crum H35, 'knights and sirs']

b.356, p. 29

H0042 Hadst thou Pandora, but receiv'd
And Nell's the world by night.

[Robert Cholmeley], 'Upon a tobacco box given me
by Mr Ralph Creak. and a snuffbox by Mrs Ellen
Ro[binson] upon which was engraved a love story'

c.190, p. 26

H0043 Hail! Albion's daughters! Virtuous fair!
Art racks her power to supply.

'To the British ladies'

c.115

H0044 Hail ancient book! most venerable code,
And at thy handle hang my crutches up.

[Thomas Tickell], 'The hornbook' [pr. Dublin 1728
(Foxon T300)]

c.176, p. 167

H0045 Hail Arathusa! Wherefore meet we thus,
Forget the passions which they cannot prove.

John Hoole, 'Calypso a dramatic masque'

c.551 (autogr.)

H0046 Hail artless simplicity, beautiful maid,
When without it we purchase both pleasure and
health.

[Hannah More], 'Simplicity'

c.83/3, no. 768; fc.132/1, p. 118; fc.85, fol. 102v

H0047 Hail, beauteous stranger of the wood,
Companions of the spring.

'Ode: to the cuckoo'

c.391; c.83/3, no. 824

H0048 Hail Bishop Valentine whose day this is
Till which hour all thy day enlarge O Valentine.

J[ohn] D[onne], 'Upon the marriage of the Prince
Palatine [later Frederick V, king of Bohemia] and the
Princess [Elizabeth] on St. Valentine's Day' [1613]
[Crum H40]

b.148, p. 122; b.197, p. 27

H0049 Hail! blessed day, on which the tidings came
And wallows with more glaring infamy.

'The first day of the week . . . April 5: 1761'

c.136, p. 22

H0050 Hail Blessed Virgin, full of heavenly grace
The weed not being, I may adore the wearer.

[Francis Quarles], 'On the infancy of our Savior'
[Divine fancies I, 4]

b.137, p. 194

H0051 Hail, blushing goddess, beauteous spring,
And waft sweet odors to the skies.

[Esther Vanhomrigh], 'An ode to spring'

c.83/2, no. 722

H0052 Hail bright invention! By whose friendly aid,
But seems fol-lol, and comfortably clean.

'Reflections on a clean shirt'

c.83/1, no. 213

H0053 Hail bright religion! Best support
And faultless charms display.

'On true religion'

c.94

H0054 Hail celestial harmony
From every distant part respond.

'An ode St. on [sic] Cecilia's Day'

c.172, p. 31

H0055 Hail Chesterfield hail on whose reverend head,
And mounting to heaven leave your mantle behind.

'Court characters Ld Ch[este]rf[iel]d'

c.186, p. 124

H0056 Hail conscious virtue! Sacred guest,
Secure is virtue's frame.

    'Ode to virtue . . . [by] Lavinia'

c.83/3, no. 940

H0057 Hail! daughters of the generous house
That skim, like wind, along the course.

    'Greek metaphor . . . the above was wrote by the
Greek poet Simonides, who was offered money to
celebrate certain mules which had won a race . . .'

c.81/1, no. 271

H0058 Hail early morning of that awful day
And ever be this day by his devotion blest!

    [William Hayley], 'Sonnet . . . Jan 9 [1800]'

File 6968

H0059 Hail! empress of the star-bespangled sky!
To plunge into that sea of sun—a bustling world.

    W. Woty, 'The moonlight night'

c.487, p. 84

H0060 Hail evening, the skies how calm how bright!
To unutterable bliss, and everlasting light.

    'An evening thought'

c.578, p. 83

H0061 Hail ever-pleasing solitude!
A Lycidas or Lycon be.

    [James Thomson], 'An ode on solitude'

c.244, p. 636

H0062 Hail! ever-wakeful son of sleep,
Avert the terrors of the night.

    [Isaac Freeman], 'Hymn to the god of dreams. Prague'

fc.105

H0063 Hail everlasting Spring!
Thy praise may speak.

    P[hilip] Doddridge, 'The living fountain Zech. XIII
as 148 Ps.'

c.493, p. 6

H0064 Hail! excellent young man! Hail noble youth!
To dwell with Him immortally in heaven!

    F[rances] B[urney d'Arblay], 'To the right honorable
[William] Pitt'

c.486, fol. 19

H0065 Hail, fair Aurora! Hail thrice welcome day!
And wears a life of innocence away.

    N. B. Halked, 'Epithalamium inscribed to Mr
Hodgson and Miss Ranger. Oct: 23rd 1764 . . .
aetatis 19'

Diggle Box: Poetry Box XI/34

H0066 Hail fairest female in whose cheek I see
For one so worthy and I wish no more.

    'An epithalamium'

Poetry Box VI/87

H0067 Hail, fancy, hail, thou airy pow'r,
Such is the will of the Supreme, and such his great
                      design.

    'Ode to fancy'

c.224, p. 151

H0068 Hail first companion of a thoughtful hour,
Blew out his pipe and ended was his song.

    'Ex fumo dare lucem. [Ars poetica V.43] Horat. 1 Jan.
1736/7'

c.371, fol. 12

H0069 Hail fortune! Darling object of mankind;
Bewilder'd, lost, where millions miss their way.

    John Lockman, 'The indigent poet's invocation to
fortune . . . 1740'

c.267/1, p. 85

H0070 Hail freedom hail thou lovely maid
A victim to wild lawless liberty.

    [John Walker?], 'Freedom'

fc.108, fol. 62

H0071 Hail friendly Muse! whose soothing lay
And reign forever there!

    L[ady] F[rances] S[cott Douglas, baroness Douglas],
'To L. B.'

Poetry Box III/17

H0072 Hail friendly plant, beneath the shade
My verse which cannot thee survive.

    [Henry] Needler, 'Verses made under an oak'

c.244, p. 548

H0073 Hail generous Catharine, honored nymph attend
And in harmonious raptures pass away.

    J. H[owell], 'To C[atharine] B.'

c.303

H0074 Hail! gentle charmer of the mind,
And cure my love-distracted breast.

    [Isaac Freeman], 'Hymn to sleep'

fc.105

H0075 Hail gentle Clio! Form the verse,
Friendship and truth with grace combine.

    Ann Murry, 'I shall repeat a few lines from a letter . . .
in which I invoked the muse Clio . . .'

c.248

H0076 Hail, gentle love and soft desire,
And make the cruel tyrant bleed!

Colonel [ ] Cutts, 'Song'
[Crum H48]
fb.70, p. 85

H0077 Hail! gentle nurse of sorrow solitude!
The peace which flows from rectitude of mind.

[Frances Burney d'Arblay], 'Sonnet. To solitude'
c.486, fol. 14

H0078 Hail! gentle piety! unmingled joy
As thy accesses to a shipwreck'd mind.

'The young lady's address to piety'
c.186, p. 105

H0079 Hail gentle youth! Whom merit owns for me
And ev'ry grace unite in thy renown.

'The silver pen in the year 1788 to be won by that
pupil who improved the most in writing in one month'
c.91, p. 29

H0080 Hail! goddess of the lonely fields and groves,
And bow'd submissive with a lowly nod.

[ ] Roche, 'An ode to melancholy'
c.244, p. 531

H0081 Hail gracious monarch whose extensive sway
Adorn my song with thy illustrious name.

'The two following poems [sic; only one present] were
presented to the King with a petition in May 1775'
Poetry Box IV/145

H0082 Hail gratitude divine of heav'nly birth,
Let her thy silken bands forever wear!

Ann Murry, 'I will repeat an invocation to gratitude,
which I wrote some days ago'
c.248

H0083 Hail great Diana thou that over
May never be distinguishable.

c.519

H0084 Hail great Sir old Albion's treasure
Themselves in a Parliament next do create.

Poetry Box VI/37

H0085 Hail guardian goddess, ever bless'd,
Still hoping to be bless'd.

'Ode to hope'
c.83/3, no. 927

H0086 Hail happy Albion! Thou art strangely blest;
Thou has the will but thou want'st the touch.

'On Thanksgiving Day' [20 Jan. 1714/15]
[Crum H58a]
fc.58, p. 47; c.570/1, p. 4

H0087 Hail happy bride, for thou art truly blest
With fellow angels you enjoy it now.

[Lady Mary Wortley Montagu], 'Upon Mrs. [George]
Bowes' [who died after three month's marriage; Mist's
journal 25 Dec. 1724]
[Crum H58b]
c.188, p. 21; c.360/2, no. 77; c.468

H0088 Hail happy day forever blest!
And fond desire with mutual love be crown'd.

T[homas] H[olland], of Jesus College, Oxford, 'On
Valentine Day'
c.233, p. 64

H0089 Hail, happy day! When ev'ry swain
And dries up all my tears.

Paul Tanner, 'On Valentine's Day'
c.233, p. 102

H0090 Hail happy hour in which I heard
I chose at first, and choosing still. . . .

T[homas] S[tevens]
c.259, p. 142 (incomplete)

H0091 Hail, happy Pope, whose gen'rous mind
Despising slaves that cringe for bread.

[Jonathan] Swift, 'Eulogium of A. Pope' [excerpt
from 'A libel on Dr. Delany']
c.144, p. 153

H0092 Hail happy saint on thine immortal throne
Till life divine reanimates his dust.

Phyllis Wheatley, 'On the death of the revd.
Mr. George Whitefield. 1770 by . . . a Moor'
c.259, p. 96

H0093 Hail happy Scotland bless the long'd-for day
They came, they saw, and conquered at the sight.

'A poem to his Royal Highness Charles Prince Regent
after the battle fought near Gladsmuir' [1745]
c.275

H0094 Hail happy seat of holy rest,
To seek the shades below.

Henry Man, 'The consecration of the temple'
File 17392

H0095 Hail, happy shores! And hail ye wanton waves,
On charms such as in heav'n he never saw!

'Royal bathing. A manuscript poem under this title has
been handed about . . . at Weymouth, and read with
much applause. The author is not clearly ascertained,
some who pretend to be in the secret naming Miss
[Anna] Seward, others Mr. [William] Hayley'

c.382, p. 52

H0096 Hail happy walls within your ample space
A little heaven of harmony and love.

Poetry Box v/59

H0097 Hail health! Auspicious heav'nborn guest,
And fix thy dwelling with my friend.

H[annah] M[ore], 'To health'

c.341, p. 83

H0098 Hail heaven-born pleasure! Without thee
Thirty would seem as none.

John Lockman, 'Hymn to pleasure' [translated from
La Fontaine]

c.267/4, p. 271

H0099 Hail heav'nly guardian of the virtuous dead!
I perish in th'enjoyment of my pray'r!

R[ichard] V[ernon] S[adleir], 'Lines written on a visit
to the monument of Mrs. Sadleir at St. Mary's
Southampton who died 5th Apl. 1793'

c.106, p. 137

H0100 Hail holy, heavenly convert! Bower cries,
To cheat the world become each other's bail.

Spence Papers, folder 113

H0101 Hail, holy mother of the Christian band
In spite of all the blows your foes can give.

H[enry] C[olman], 'To the church'
[Crum H71]

b.2, p. 77

H0102 Hail Indian plant to ancient times unknown
In smoke thou'rt wisdom—and in s[?] thou'rt wit.

'On tobacco'

c.481, p. 223

H0103 Hail Jordan! Fam'd Britannia's brightest boast!
On Britain's honored theater appear.

F[rances] B[urney d'Arblay], 'Ode addressed to the
celebrated Mrs. Jordan'

c.486, fol. 19v

H0104 Hail Lady Mary, with thine awful looks,
And let my subjects cry, vive Carl' teraro.

'King Charles 3d. his dedication of his sword to the
Virgin Mary at Montserrat . . . imitation in English'

c.111, p. 165

H0105 Hail London noblest mart on earth
Let him touch me if he dare.

'The romp' [with musical score for tenor]

Music MS. 534

H0106 Hail love! Divinity supreme!
And all adore the son of beauty's queen.

'True love an ode. By a gentleman'

c.361

H0107 Hail! lovely babe, pure as thy natal morn,
And with his tears bedew'd the sad untimely grave.

'A little elegy to the memory of a natural child, which
died in a few days after it was born, upon the 13 of
Oct. 1772'

c.229/2, fol. 74v

H0108 Hail man belov'd, whose shining form declare,
To him who gave the muse the pow'r to sing.

'God's goodness display'd, in his creation and
presentation'

c.83/3, no. 1039

H0109 'Hail Master!' Judas said; and in one word
Soon hang'd himself—good Colonel do so too.

'Epigram, on a certain character dining at the County
Meeting, and drinking the candidate's health on the
day of nomination'

Poetry Box XII/118[1]

H0110 Hail, meek-ey'd maiden, clad in sober gray,
That fills with farewell songs the dark'ning plain.

[Joseph Warton], 'Ode to evening'

Poetry Box IV/18

H0111 Hail (melons) hail! Fit for a king or queen!
Unto a cooling banquet of delight.

W. F., '[Galen's Melo romanus] the English
translation'

Poetry Box VI/40

H0112 Hail mighty gold! Hail potent clay!
To dim their envious eyes, and still their snarling
tongues.

'On gold'

c.244, p. 606

H0113 Hail mighty monarch at whose happy birth,
Since heav'n your triumphs by its smiles does own.

'To his sacred Majesty [Charles II] on his coronation'
fc.135

H0114 Hail mighty nothing! Whose tremendous form
All ends, by which we may deserve thee too.

R[obert] Shirley, 1st earl of Ferrers, 'To nothing.
Upon the change of the ministry. By a club of Tories'
c.347, p. 65

H0115 Hail! Minister by paradoxes great
Thy stars, or genius, never match'd before.

'A panegyrick on Card[inal] W[alpole]'
c.570/3, p. 57

H0116 Hail mossy cot! sequester'd seat,
What wisdom thinks, you best can tell.

'Soliloquy in a thatched house in a retired part of
W—y gardens'
Poetry Box IV/95

H0117 Hail most renowned sacrament
Come cure our souls forevermore. | Amen

'Of the blessed sacrament'
a.30[2]

H0118 Hail music sweet enchantment hail!
Love, beauty, friendship, ev'ry joy is thine!

[David Garrick], 'Ode to music'
Acquisition 92.3.1ff. (autogr.)

H0119 Hail! old patrician trees, so great and good,
A solitude almost.

[Abraham] Cowley, 'Solitude'
[Crum H91]
c.244, p. 241

H0120 Hail opening dawn, approach of spreading light
And what thou know'st I want still constantly
                                        impart.

'Reflections in a morning's walk'
c.91, p. 185

H0121 Hail peaceful friend! thrice welcome here
The dew shall drop on thee.

'Cherry's reception enlarged from the other canary,
by desire, for a particular friend'
c.91, p. 24

H0122 Hail, pensive Fairfax, learning's hermitage,
Though born on earth, souls are in heav'n begot.

[Thomas Stanley], 'Fairfax' [in 'A register of friends']
b.153, p. 2

H0123 Hail pensive virgin! ever hail!
Sweet nun, I long to visit thee!

'Ode to solitude'
c.139, p. 361

H0124 Hail pious bird! Dear friend to sacred lays,
You sing alone for pure respect and love.

[Robert Cholmeley], 'Thus translated'
c.190, p. 134

H0125 Hail pity sweet dejected maid!
A balm to heal the wound.

F[rances] B[urney d'Arblay], 'Elegiac poems by F. B.
aged 15 years. Ode to pity'
c.486, fol. 13

H0126 Hail, poesy, seraphic maid,
And still my joy, my chief delight, | And
                                        consolation.

'Poesy, an ode'
c.224, p. 157

H0127 Hail Poet Laureate of this barren isle
As church ones are and better understood.

'An answer to the satire on St. Giles Church' ['To St.
Giles's I went']
b.113, p. 211

H0128 Hail, poetess, for thou art truly bless'd,
But gods themselves are only fit for you.

Philip Wharton, 1st duke of Wharton(?), 'The answer.
By the Duke of Wharton' [to 'Hail, happy bride . . .',
on Mrs. Bowes (d. 1724)]
c.468

H0129 Hail pretty warbler! Peaceful friend
In softest notes expire.

'The canary bird extempore on the author receiving
one 12th Sept. 1788'
c.91, p. 22

H0130 Hail Q[ueen] of Hearts! to whose true English
                                        praise
For yours, what shall we not have cause to do?

'The 8th of March 1703/4'
[POAS VI.614]
c.111, p. 73

H0131 Hail, queen of thought sublime! propitious power,
Pour the warm gush of sympathetic tears!

'Ode to melancholy' [signed Orlando]
c.343, p. 24

H0132 Hail Reverend Salmon, whose sweet candid mind
The love of the most learned and the best.

> [Thomas Stanley], 'Salmon' [in 'A register of friends']

b.153, p. 18

H0133 Hail Rex and Regina the King and the Queen
Then my present too little can never be thought.

> [George Howard, 6th earl of Carlisle], 'Upon a certain great personage who should not pay for his Microcosmus'

c.197, p. 24

H0134 Hail! roseate morn, returning light,
And mourn them when too late.

> Miss [ ] Pennington, of Huntingdon, 'Ode to the morning'

Poetry Box IV/35

H0135 Hail sacred art! Bright beauty's powerful shield
But gave new life to crown her parent's joy.

> John Lockman, 'On inoculation: occasioned by Miss Kitty Cornwall's successful experience of that practice . . . April 1757'

c.267/1, p. 204

H0136 Hail sacred envoy of th'eternal king
Of gratitude to my Creator sent.

> [Sir William Trumbull]

Trumbull Box: Poetry Box XIII/28

H0137 Hail sacred haunt, fit to receive
Or death dissolve this tyrant's sway.

> 'Verses written with a pencil in a grove, at ———, near Lewes, October 8. 1764. Inscribed to Miss B——'

c.83/1, no. 117

H0138 Hail sacred island! Whom no threat or art
The interests of his faith, country and king.

> 'To Ireland'

fb.228/14

H0139 Hail sacred light! Thy quick'ning glance
For the full glories of thy face.

> 'A morning hymn'

c.244, p. 632

H0140 Hail sacred muse and vocal shell
Kinder thine, than Cupid's dart.

> William Harrison, 'Sappho' [pr. 1711 (Foxon H50)]

Poetry Box X/10(14)

H0141 Hail sacred solitude! From this calm bay,
With ease convey me to a better shade.

> [Anthony Hammond?], 'On solitude' [pr. 1709 (Foxon S801)]

c.244, p. 171 (attr. Roscommon); c.351, p. 50; see also next.

H0142 Hail sacred solitude, hail bless'd retreat
And thus convey me to a better shade.

> 'On solitude'

c.83/3, no. 1031; see also previous.

H0143 Hail sacred subject of my slender wit
That night once past may come a happy day.

> 'Cant: 40'

b.4, fol. 34

H0144 Hail! sober queen of darkness, hail!
Those evils which I cannot cure.

> [Isaac Freeman], 'Hymn to night'

fc.105

H0145 Hail solitude divine! Wherever dwells,
And trusts to greet you in the realms of light.

> [ ] Parsons, 'Elegy on the convent at ———'

c.83/2, no. 533

H0146 Hail source of transport, ever new!
And make me wholly thine.

> 'Hymn to benevolence'

c.83/3, no. 1050

H0147 Hail spring of all our joy auspicious morn
To horrid shades of night and everlasting woe.

> 'On Christmas Day'

c.416

H0148 Hail the beauteous spring appearing
The golden harvest of the year.

> 'Anacreon ode 36th'

Poetry Box I/115[1]

H0149 Hail the day that sees him rise,
Find our Heav'n of Heav'n in Thee!

> 'On the ascension'

Poetry Box V/92

H0150 Hail the happy peaceful morn,
Of a smiling deity.

> 'Ode to a friend on his birthday . . . Rosina'

c.83/2, no. 573

H0151 Hail! thou dear cot, in which my tranquil days
Thro' life's perplexing and deceitful ways.

'The cottage'

fc.124, p. 98

H0152 Hail thou pale moon! and all ye host of night!
And tell me we shall meet, no more to part.

'An elegy on seeing the chapel of La Hague built by
the widow of a noble Norman who was murdered on
the place from Normandy' [signed Helena, Chateau
Mont Orgueil]

c.343, p. 75

H0153 Hail thou returning year, for ne'er
Like love, like skill, like friendship meet.

[Mary (Shackleton) Leadbeater], 'On William
Leadbeater's recovery from a fever New Year's Day'
[1798]

c.142, p. 121

H0154 Hail thou, whose muse contemning grandeur's bow'rs
And gentle souls unborn my useful zeal commend.

'To Dr. Beattie'

c.139, p. 265

H0155 Hail to election loveliest time
And we the living fellas not the dead.

[George Howard, 6th earl of Carlisle], 'The turtle
feast. Irregular ode'

c.197, p. 20

H0156 Hail to Emanuel ever-honored name
And with heav'n's hierarchy conspiring.

P[hilip] Doddridge, 'Christ the Lord of angels and
men from Col. II. 10'

c.493, p. 45

H0157 Hail to the day that gave Maria birth,
May He, who made her, seat her with the blest.

F[rederick] D[ickinson senior], 'To Maria Stow—on
11th Septr. 1797'

c.391, inserted at front

H0158 Hail to the conscious muse of eagle wings,
Each mountebank, or Quixote of the state

'To the author of the epistle to Sr. W. Chambers and
of the postscript'

fc.14/6

H0159 Hail to the morn! May each bright ray
Or only render home more dear!

'On a rainy [blank] of April [17]77 the birthday of
Miss M. Myrtilla Jesser'

c.89, p. 116

H0160 Hail to the opening of the thirteenth year!
'Hail! The return of Charlotte's natal day!'

Ralph Broome, 'Lines addressed to Miss Frances on
her birthday'

c.486, fol. 31

H0161 Hail to thee Britain! hail! delightful land
This noble Nestor of th'historic field.

W[illia]m Hayley, 'Characters of Clarendon,
Burnet[,] Rapin, Hume, and Lyttelton'

Poetry Box XIV/180

H0162 Hail to thee, gloomy specter, death!
And lead me to my God!

[William Hayley], 'Ode to death' [28 August 1779]

File 7048

H0163 Hail, to this auspicious morn,
The day, on which my girl was born.

'Address to Miss Cornwallis—on her birthday July the
28th 1791'

fc.124, p. 5

H0164 Hail to thy brightness glorious sun,
That never will decay.

'On the sun's rising'

c.362, p. 46

H0165 Hail to thy golden light propitious star!
Of love, of peace, and mild content possest.

'To the pole star'

c.83/2, no. 544

H0166 Hail tricking monarch! more successful far
Led her himself unto the royal bed.

'[The British ambassadress's (the Duchess of
Shrewsbury's) speech to the] French King' [1713]
[Crum H131; POAS VII.592]

Poetry Box VI/12; c.111, p. 55; b.382(27 and 28)

H0167 Hail tuneful pair, say by what wondrous charms,
To her shrub hedges, and tall Nottingham.

[Charles Montagu, 3rd earl of] Halifax(?), 'Orpheus
[Jacob Greber] and Margareta L'Epine' [c. 1702]
[Crum H132]

Music Ms. 16, p. 419; c.111, p. 55

H0168 Hail! Venerable shades, where oft I've play'd,
A wish for immortality inspires.

'The moralist, a poem'

c.94 (incomplete?)

HO169 Hail venerable symbol of the law,
The humbler circle of my frowsy shop!

> R[ichard] V[ernon] S[adleir], 'Soliloquy—written before the Common Council of London had changed their gowns both black and scarlet for the present blue silk spoke by a citizen to whom two gowns were left by a relation'

c.106, p. 141

HO170 Hail Windle, rural seat of sweet delight,
And more engage our gratitude and love.

> M. B[irkett], 'On Windle' [aged 14]

c.139, p. 9

HO171 Hail winter healthiest season of the year,
Men, athiests, deists [crossed out] and rakes.

Poetry Box IV/104

HO172 Hail! wish'd-for scion, from a gen'rous root:
And add a vista to fam'd Golden Grove.

> John Lockman, 'To the newborn son, after hearing the lady of Richard Vaughan esqr, is lately delivered, at Golden Grove in Carmarthenshire . . . June 18, 1762'

c.267/1, p. 319

HO173 Hail ye mighty seven our church's chief glory,
Who the impudence had to call themselves
Christians.

> 'On the seven bishops'

b.111, p. 105

HO174 Hail! ye sacred horrors hail!
Twice nerve the hero's arm, and make the coward
brave.

> W[illiam] Shepherd, 'The negro incantation'

c.141, p. 543

HO175 Hail ye, whom wedlock's twisting cord
I'll try no more, Ma'am,—till the next.

> 'Epithalamium'

c.169, p. 11

HO176 Hail Zion city of our God
Are both the seats of Jesu's love.

> [Thomas Stevens?]

c.259, p. 97

HO177 Half burnt alive, beneath this dunghill lies
Whilst each dread start of frenzy governs you.

> John Lockman, 'Epitaph on a gin-drinker'

c.267/1, p. 196

HO178 Half dead the Church of England lies,
The banner of Christ crucified.

> 'An epitaph on the Church of England . . . 1690' [translation from Latin, 'Epitaphium ecclesia anglicanae']

b.111, p. 121

HO179 Half of your book is to an index grown;
You give your book contents, your reader none.

> [John Pyne], 'On Dr. H——'

c.74

HO180 Half out of this place, and half in
Let's me enjoy half-consecration.

> H[enry] Neville, 'Epitaph; in his sham-story to Mrs. Ewen's mother'

Spence Papers, folder 108

HO181 Hallelujah: praise ye
Now and always.

> 'Psalm 148'

c.264/3, p. 111

HO182 H'along'd a boot, that she might have the proof
She countergripp'd, and past below his rapier.

> Sir Thomas Urquhart, 'The expression of a single combat, betwixt a gentleman, and his mistress'

fb.217, p. 167

HO183 Hammond, dear uncle, of so sweet a frame!
That all who read thee might my sorrows share.

> [Thomas Stanley], 'Hammond' [in 'A register of friends']

b.153, p. 4

HO184 Hang a small bugle cap on as big as a crown
A-la-mode de françois, you're a bit for His Grace.

> 'A receipt for modern dress'

Poetry Box x/108

HO185 Hang up those dull and envious fools
To love one man, he'd leave her first.

> Ben J[onson], 'In defense of women's inconstancy'

b.104, p. 116

HO186 Hannah, by zeal in prayer, obtain'd a son
And exalt the horn of his anointed king.

> [William Sandys?], 'Hannah's song when she brought Samuel to Shiloh, 1 Sam: chap 2 unto ver: 11'

b.230, p. 35

H0187 Hans Carvel impotent and old,
You've thrust your finger G[o]d knows where.

    Mat[thew] Prior, 'Monsieur de la Fontaine's Hans
    Carvel imitated'
    [Crum H151]

c.189, p. 140; c.111, p. 1

H0188 Happen what will in fortune's spite
You and your pretty family.

    [John Walker?], 'Poetical epistle to Mrs. Rook who
    had left the country to reside in London'

fc.108, fol. 50

H0189 Happily hous'd these Lares are
Then might the mighty Lares sing.

    [Sir Richard] Steele, 'By . . . on Sic siti laetantur lares
    one of the mottoes on the Duke of Buckingham's
    house in St. James's Park'
    [Crum H152]

c.189, p. 12; c.111, p. 75; see also 'How happily . . .'.

H0190 Happ'ning the other morning to peruse,
The latent devil in the seeming saint.

    William Harris

c.233, p. 9

H0191 Happy a man may pass his life
To spend is what all women hate.

    Diggle Box: Poetry Box XI/33

H0192 Happy am I when I feel
There again to sing thy grace.

    [Thomas Stevens?], 'Another [hymn]'

c.259, p. 69

H0193 Happy are they who when alone
And much more, pleas'd with bubbles, than with
                           solid joy.

    Lady [Mary] C[hudleigh], 'Solitude'

c.258

H0194 Happy are you, whom Quantock overlooks,
For though the world be burn'd, this never will be
                                  Brent.

    W[illia]m D[iape]r, 'Brent, a poem. To Thomas
    Palmer, esq. East-Brent, lying at the foot of Mendip
    Hills in Somersetshire . . . 1709'

Poetry Box v/90

H0195 Happy art thou whom God does bless,
To thank the gods, and to be thought myself
                             almost a god.

    [Abraham] Cowley, 'The garden. An epistle to John
    Evelyn esquire'

c.244, p. 231

H0196 Happy beauteous fugitive!
One tongue ineffectual proves.

    George Montagu, 'On a swallow from Anacreon
    [Ode 10]'

fc.135, p. 1

H0197 Happy, happy grasshopper,
Faith thou art almost a god.

    'Turned from Farnaby's epigram. July 21st. 1755'

c.591

H0198 Happy he and happy he alone
Tomorrow do thy worst, for I have lived today.

c.163, p. 18 (incomplete?)

H0199 Happy his state above the fate of kings
That truly could but know the cause of things.

    [John Rose?]
    [Crum H167]

b.227, p. 35

H0200 Happy hours all hours excelling
Griefs when told soon disappear.

    ['A song . . . the pleasures of solitude']
    [Crum H169]

Poetry Box IV/32

H0201 Happy insect ever blest,
Thou art starv'd, and so am I.

    Walter Harte, 'The grasshopper'

c.244, p. 491

H0202 Happy is he, who with prudence and care,
Avoid the ways, that brought them to distress.

    J[ohn] R[obinson], 'Optimum est aliena frui insania'

c.370, fol. 23

H0203 Happy is that soul whose sole desires are fixt
Vanquishing all that would his life deface.

    [Mary Serjant]

fb.98, fol. 156

H0204 Happy man, whom God doth aid,
Take the everlasting praise.

    'Hymn 90th'

c.562, p. 119

H0205 Happy now youth thy tender bosom warms,
Th'attendant vot'ry at Apollo's shrine.

    'To a young lady occasioned by her fondness for
    novels'

c.83/2, no. 599

H0206 Happy place! Serenely sweet,
Peace and harmony abound.

'Mountpleasant boarding school'

c.91, p. 272

H0207 Happy soul, that free from harms,
Enter in by thee to heaven!

'Hymn 91st'

c.562, p. 120

H0208 Happy teaspoon, which can hit
Doctor Hill's unequall'd wit.

'The teaspoon. Occasioned by Dr. Hill's prescribing a
teaspoonful of every medicine to every patient
indiscriminately'

c.487, p. 27; c.83/1, no. 264

H0209 Happy that author, whose correct essay
Which none knows better and none comes so near.

[Wentworth Dillon], 4th earl of Roscommon, 'An
essay on translated verse'

b.86, p. 1

H0210 Happy that man! Do so prepare
I certain pledge of happiness give.

[Edmund Wodehouse], 'Oct. 31 [1714]'

b.131, p. 74

H0211 Happy that man must pass/spend his life
Keep reason always in their sight.

'Eulogium on women'

Poetry Box XII/38, 46

H0212 Happy the Briton whom indulgent fate
In sweet oblivion of solicitude.

[Francis Fawkes], 'To William Brooke, M.D. at
Fieldhead in Yorkshire—Cambridge, 1740'

fc.21, p. 9

H0213 Happy the day, the year, the month, the place
But thy first look was causer of my death.

'To his love'

b.205, fol. 42v

H0214 Happy the fair, who here retired
One supernumerary steak!

George Canning, 'Verses written in the album at
Crewe Hall on leaving the place Oct. 1789'

Poetry Box III/54

H0215 Happy the glorious fields and blest the bowers,
That you should always be compell'd to love.

'To Gloriana in the country'

fb.142, p. 29

H0216 Happy the great, who, by experience know
Much to God's honor and his own content.

'Lines on Waller'

c.83/3, no. 1049

H0217 Happy the man of mortals happiest he,
Thro' sev'ral paths, and none are in the right.

'Contentment—given me by Miss Eliza Clarke. They
cannot want, who wish not to have more | Whoever
said an anchorite was poor'

c.360/3, no. 43 (incomplete?); c.549, p. 77 (var.)

H0218 Happy the man that from the city free
He can't below a greater bliss possess.

'Laus ruris'

c.146, p. 38

H0219 Happy the man that has *per annum*
This being for another.

'A wish a la mode'

c.186, p. 68

H0220 Happy the man who far from fear's alarms
And scorn the bliss that only smiles and dies.

c.378, p. 63

H0221 Happy the man who free from care
And dies, lamented by his friends.

'The country retirement—written extempore on
reading the second epode in Horace'
[cf. Crum H188]

c.360/1, p. 269

H0222 Happy the man who free from cares
Tell where I lie.

[Alexander] Pope, 'An ode on solitude. Writ by . . .
before he was twelve years old'
[Crum H188]

c.176, p. 1

H0223 Happy the man who from disturbance free
And he lives happy who is't can do more?

'Epod. 2'

c.416

H0224 Happy the man who, from the busy town,
Nor once remorse with misspent hours reproach.

[Leicester, 15 Oct. 1763]

c.136, p. 57

H0225 Happy the man, who his whole time doth bound,
The voyage life is longest made at home.

    Abraham Cowley, trans., 'Claudian's Old man of
    Verona' ['The health and security of a country life',
    Carm. Min. xx.]
    [Crum H190]

    b.150, p. 204

H0226 Happy the man, who in his pot contains
He enjoys as full content, without his cares.

    'The suet dumpling. A poem'

    c.94

H0227 Happy the man, who sees Celinda's eyes,
Who sighs for her sake, whilst she sighs for his.

    c.549, p. 149

H0228 Happy the man, who to the cell
And ev'ry joy be mine.

    John Lockman, 'Rural songs. Sam. Russell, on the
    pleasures of Chigwell Row, Essex . . . May 1743'

    c.267/2, p. 165

H0229 Happy the man, who void of cares and strife,
The ship sinks foundering in the vast abyss.

    [John] Philips, 'The splendid shilling' [in imitation of
    Milton]

    c.244, p. 149; c.166, p. 106; b.201, p. 75; c.146, p. 42
    (incomplete)

H0230 Happy the man, who with indignant brow
Would chew vile husks, or starve on viler leaven?

    Charles Atherton Allnutt, 'Sonnet to faith'

    c.112, p. 146

H0231 Happy the man! who's free from anxious care
Tho' they were kindly check't, awakened thrice.

    [Sir Philip Wodehouse], 'Apr: 29 going to the sessions'

    b.131, p. 1

H0232 Happy the man whose peaceful mind,
And never, never cease.

    Thomas Parsons, 'On affliction'

    c.259

H0233 Happy the man, whose pious mind
Shall sink in endless moan.

    [Sir William Trumbull], 'Ps[alm] 1'
    Trumbull Box: Poetry Box XIII/1

H0234 Happy the man, with pious fear
And pine with fruitless spite.

    [Sir William Trumbull], 'Ps[alm] 112'
    Trumbull Box: Poetry Box XIII/22

H0235 Happy the man with prudence blest,
To worlds beyond our view.

    [William Mills], 'Retirement an ode'

    c.472, p. 15

H0236 Happy the men who fear
To dwell above.

    T[homas] S[tevens], 'God showing his covenant to
    those who fear him . . . Psalm the 25th and the 14
    verse . . . sung the 4th of March [1781]'

    c.259, p. 130

H0237 Happy the senate worthy of applause
The traitor St. John's that vile informer.

    'A panegyric on the Sanhedrim'

    c.570/2, p. 123

H0238 Happy the soul whom God delights
And swallow up our souls in thee.

    'Hymn 81st'

    c.562, p. 107

H0239 Happy the world, in that blest age
You're poor—he flings the door at you.

    John Lockman, 'Modern venality . . . anno 1729'
    [Crum H195]

    c.267/2, p. 97; c.268 (first part), p. 72

H0240 Happy the worms, who spun their lives away,
And burnt their web, their curious art had made.

    [William Taylor?], 'A very gallant copy of verses . . .
    upon the fine ladies and their fine clothes, at a ball'

    c.176, p. 81

H0241 Happy the youth, who are betimes set right
He who gilds o'er his precepts best succeeds.

    c.186, p. 114

H0242 Happy those men, whose hearts do lie
At some time will compassion show.

    'Song'

    fb.70, p. 87

H0243 Happy! Thrice happy he alone
And 'tis undoubtedly our bliss.

    [Edmund Wodehouse], 'Decr. 29 [1714]'

    b.131, p. 127

H0244 Happy! Thrice happy is his fate
And crush at once th'inglorious line.

    'Damocles' [on Walpole? pr. 1720? (Foxon D19)]

    c.570/2, p. 1

H0245 Happy thy lot! Who in a consort find
A son—and now felicity's thy own.

 John Lockman, 'To Richard Vaughan esqr. on the
 birth of his son . . . 7 April 1757'

c.267/1, p. 236

H0246 Happy was man, when first by nature made
But never never think on womankind.

 'The folly of love or a satire against women'

Poetry Box x/15, p. 1

H0247 Happy were he could finish forth his fate,
Where harmless robin dwells with gentle thrush.

 [Robert Devereux, 2nd] earl of Essex, 'Verses made by
 the Earl of Essex'
 [Crum H202]

b.197, p. 213; Poetry Box VI/31

H0248 Happy, who thy charms possessing,
Peace shall crown the sliding year.

 John Lockman, 'A little epithalamium . . . Nov. 1746'

c.267/1, p. 260

H0249 Hard by a crystal spring, as I my lambs sat keeping
[last line missing]

 'Cant: 1'

b.4, fol. 1 (damaged)

H0250 Hard by lies one, belov'd of some
I knew it well—it lay be[hin]d.

 'On the death of I—s L—de late singing man at
 C[an]t[erbur]y'

File 17323

H0251 Hard fate that I sh'd banish'd be
Whate'er becomes of me &c.

 'An excellent ballad, to the tune of The broom' [on the
 Old Pretender; pr. Edinburgh 1716? (Foxon E586)]

fc.58, p. 138

H0252 Hard, hard, O Sawney is thy lot
The French may e'en boast like the frog in the fable. |
          Oh the roast beef &c.

 'Air (the broom of Sowden [i.e., Cowden] knows)'

Poetry Box IV/62

H0253 Hard is the touch, in love or grief to feign;
And finds a passage to the heart.

c.549, p. 5

H0254 Hard is your lot, if hither e'er you come
Raving they can't do all the ill they would.

 'To the Pretender—[acrostic on Hanover]'

Trumbull Box: Poetry Box XIII/89; c.570/2, p. 49

H0255 Hard tale of Israel! Slave to Egypt's king!
That suff'ring Israel's his own.

 John Lockman, 'Moses: an oratorio . . . writ about
 1742'

c.267/3, p. 321

H0256 Hard was my lot! Once banish'd from your sight,
Yet still, I languish'd pined and died for you.

 'Poll's elegiac epistle to his absent mistress'

c.74

H0257 Hard was thy fate! Alas unhappy maid!
Her only blemish was, she lov'd too well.

 'Epitaph on a young lady who died for love'

c.83/1, no. 209

H0258 Hark! A voice divides the sky,
Rise ye dead, to judgment come.

 [Thomas Stevens?], 'Hymn the 1st'

c.259

H0259 Hark Damon, hark, what music's this I hear
Orpheus himself's not so merry so merry as we.

 'A pastoral'

fb.142, p. 33

H0260 Hark dying mortals if the sonnets prove
Be explicated in the following way.

 Ralph Erskine, 'Gospel sonnets or spiritual songs . . .
 A poem upon Isaiah 54 and 5V [sic]'

c.186, p. 4

H0261 Hark forward cries the squire: his hounds
I don't mind running through my own.

c.546

H0262 Hark, from the tombs, I hear a doleful sound
Where shortly you must lie.

 'An epitaph in Beaconsfield churchyard, in Bucks'

c.360/1, p. 151

H0263 Hark, hark jolly sportsmen awhile to my tale,
So Luna took care in conducting us home.

 'Song 76'

c.555, p. 115

H0264 Hark! hark! the joy-inspiring horn
Till echo rends the skies.

 'Song 105'

c.555, p. 157

H0265 Hark hark 'tis a voice from the tomb,
She hung on his tombstone and died.

 'The tombstone'

c.362, p. 8

H0266 Hark! Hark! What news the angels bring,
Shall join to sing redeeming love.

    'Hymn for Christmas day'

    c.139, p. 505

H0267 Hark, hark when I my warbling cantos sing
I'll eternize your never dying praise.

    'Lyra' [answered by 'Oh sweet how handsomely . . .']

    b.356, p. 106

H0268 Hark, hark ye how echoes the horn in the vale,
Led on by the horn and the cry of the hounds.

    'Song 163'

    c.555, p. 249

H0269 Hark! Heard ye not that piercing cry,
For others' woe down virtue's manly cheeks.

    'Slavery'

    c.140, p. 525

H0270 Hark how my Celia with the choice
The idol proves idolator.

    Tho[mas] Carew, 'On the same' [Celia singing in the vault at York House]
    [Crum H238]

    b.62, p. 70 (first stanza); see also 'Mark how . . .'.

H0271 Hark, how the birds on every spray,
From thee, thou charming maid.

    T[homas] M[orell], 'To Miss M. R—ds of Cambridge on Valentine's day 1722'

    c.395, p. 1

H0272 Hark! how the church-bell's thund'ring harmony
Her comforter, who art the widow's friend.

    'A war poem, on the late Mr. Blythe, a midshipman on board the Mars'

    c.141, p. 475

H0273 Hark! How the op'ning hand, and cheerful horn
Prevent his flight and end in death his woes.

    [ ] Hay, 'The chase'

    c.152, p. 35

H0274 Hark how the raging tempests rend the skies and
                              roar,
That I may ever live with thee in thy calm bay.

    J. W., 'On the day of judgment'

    c.258

H0275 Hark how the sacred thunder rends the skies
Since but one Lord, one faith, one baptism saves.

    M. M****'s answer to Parson ———' [answer to 'Hear how the sacred thunder . . .']

    c.517, fol. 21r

H0276 Hark how the trumpet sounds to battle
While I have caress'd her. | My Celia divine

    'Princes[s] Sobieski's minuet'

    Poetry Box VII/57

H0277 Hark how the trumpets
We may always find time to grow old.

    'A song'

    c.358, p. 49

H0278 Hark Is'bel Barker Is'bel Hood: but hold
That you (of men) have lain with Manifold.

    [Sir Aston Cokayne], 'To Isabel Manifold of the Black Swan in Ashburn'

    b.275, p. 84

H0279 Hark Israel, O Jacob hear my law
His place, his house, or aught that is not thine.

    'The decalogue'

    b.137, p. 122

H0280 Hark, my gay friend, that solemn toll
Let it my God, be happy too.

    [Laurenc]e St[er]n[e]?, 'The unknown world[:] verses occasioned by hearing a pass-bell'

    c.83/1, no. 147; c.83/3, no. 836 (stanzas 1–11); c.362, p. 72; c.259 (stanzas 1–11); c.186, p. 80; c.175, p. 45 (stanzas 1–8)

H0281 Hark my gay friends! Why tolls yon solemn bell
To perfect freedom, and her native skies.

    [Thomas Stevens, Baptist minister], 'On the death of a boy a pupil of the author's till his death'

    c.91, p. 73 (incomplete?)

H0282 Hark! She bids her friends adieu,
And all her dreams of joy to come.

    [Isaac] Watts, 'On the sudden death of Mrs. Mary Peacock'

    c.244, p. 324

H0283 Hark sisters hark! that bursting sigh
Recorded in the book of heaven.

    'Sung by the pupils in the blind asylum Liverpool'

    Poetry Box XII/95

H0284 Hark! The bonny Christ-Church bells
And the verger troops before the dean. . . .

    'Song 102'

    c.555, p. 154 (incomplete)

H0285 Hark, the glad sound! The Savior comes
With thy beloved name.

    P[hilip] Doddridge, 'Christ's message. Luke IV. 18, 19'

    c.493, p. 72

H0286 Hark, the horn calls away;
And renew the chase over the bowl.

'Song 47'

c.555, p. 72

H0287 Hark! The loud drum;
Will win a deathless name.

John Lockman, 'Great Britain forever! A ballad for
the new militia: on the rumored invasion from France,
anno 1759: set to music by Mr. Worgan; and sung, by
Mr. Laws, in Vauxhall Gardens, accompanied by
drums, trumpets, hautboys &c.'

c.267/2, p. 33

H0288 Hark! The loud thunder rattles thro' the sky:
The righteous own, and tremble and rejoice.

'Storm'

c.81/1, no. 333

H0289 Hark! the redeemer from on high
My love, my Savior, from my side!

[Isaac Watts, Hymns and spiritual songs (1707), bk. I,
Hymn 70]

c.180, p. 68

H0290 Hark the sweet melody! Inspiring strains!
Eternal praise be given then to God.

Charles Atherton Allnutt, 'Reflections on spriing'

c.112, p. 66

H0291 Hark the trumpet sounds to arms, O fatal noise!
But can never change my vows.

'The Prince of Wales' round'

c.160, fol. 86v; c.360/1, p. 189

H0292 Hark! 'tis lov'd Philomela's song
In fancy verdant scenes arise.

John Lockman, 'Writ in Vauxhall—after hearing Miss
Burchell sing, in a room there, at Christmas 1751'

c.267/1, p. 192

H0293 Hark! 'tis our heav'nly sender's voice
To rush and seize the prize.

P[hilip] Doddridge, 'A hymn on Rev. II.10, by D. D.
on the death of Col: Gardiner'

c.493, p. 19

H0294 Hark to the village bells, that soft to bear
Resign'd to part with these—nor shrinks appall'd
                                                with those.

'Sonnet'

c.344, p. 49

H0295 Hark!—what a mournful solemn sound
And hail him victor thro' the sky.

J. G., 'Some reflections upon hearing the bell toll for
the death of a friend' [Dodsley Collection]

c.487, p. 136

H0296 Harley, (once call'd) the nation's great support,
He does with insolence, at least with pride.

[Jonathan Swift, imitation of Horace, bk. I, epistle vii]

File 16945

H0297 Harms flying [?] but keep away which still
Comes in by yards, and giveth out by inches.

[Sir Thomas Urquhart], 'Evils swiftly [?] as swallows
but departure like snails'

fb.217, p. 535

H0298 Harps others praise, a scepter his doth sing
Of crowned poets and of Laureat king.

[ ] Nevil, 'On Sir Philip Sidney'

c.360/2, no. 46

H0299 Harry the bailiff, a rare stick of wood,
Such a fellow should ne'er cross his fancy no more. |
                                                With &c.

'A morning adventure. A song'

c.530, p. 46

H0300 Harry whate'er thou dost (by day or night)
And all thy reckonings be as thou art Right.

[Sir Aston Cokayne], 'To Henry Right of the Cock in
Poulesworth'

b.275, p. 86

H0301 Harshly I strike the lyre and sorrowing lead
And die a lesson to succeeding times.

[Henry Howard], earl of Suffolk [and Berkshire],
'Verses spoken at Oxford by the Earl of Suffolk . . . at
the installation of the Earl of Westmorland
[Chancellor of the University of Oxford July 3.] 1759'
[Crum H270]

Poetry Box IV/198

H0302 Has Bourbon sent his tool to waste our land
'Tis number not fine clothes must quell the foe.

[Thomas Gurney], 'To the committee meeting at
Bla[ckwel]l's Coffee House 1745'

c.213

H0303 Has freedom's flame thy breast illum'd?
With me for Kosciuszko mourn.

[( ) Smyth], 'Stanzas written at the close of the year
1794'

c.141, p. 11

H0304 Has he these qualities? Does he eat well?
'Gainst all the powers of man, and devil, stands
free.

[Sir Philip Wodehouse], 'A satirical hash the
modesman's catholicism'
b.131, p. 29

H0305 Has heaven smil'd, and shall my muse be mute,
May seraphs wing him to the realms of day.

Charles Atherton Allnutt, 'The following familiar
epistle I sent to my sister from Bristol Hot Wells on
her delivery of another boy—written 60 years ago'
c.112, p. 7

H0306 Has not kind heaven regarding human woe
And my last breath shall bless thee for my peace.

'The VII chapter of Job paraphrased'
fc.60, p. 104; c.244, p. 618

H0307 Has not my friend transported run,
And calls eternity its own.

Cuthbert Wilson, 'To my friend the Reverend
Mr. Barrett with a paper book'
c.193, p. 1

H0308 Has not the fair one charms to move,
And melt e'en frozen age to love.

Poetry Box x/66

H0309 Haste, O haste hither you ungrateful eyes
Must only be supplied with sighs and groans.

'Upon the death of Sr. Robert Philipps'
b.52/2, p. 160

H0310 Hast thou at last that mother church too quitted
And have no hope of heaven but his word.

[Robert Wolseley], 'A new address to Mr. Bayes
[Dryden] on his late conversion to the Church of
Rome'
[Crum H273]
fb.70, p. 241

H0311 Hast thou been lost a month, and can I be
I'll come a pilgrim to weep o'er thy tomb.

'An elegy upon the death of Mr. Thomas Washington
one of Prince Charles his pages who died in Spain . . .
1623'
[Crum H274]
b.197, p. 190

H0312 Hast thou for mold'ring dust one pitying tear
Weep o'er this grave, and sigh she is no more.

'Epitaph on a lady'
c.83/1, no. 78

H0313 Hast thou forsaken all thy sins but one.
Believe it, Partio, th' hast forsaken none.

[Francis Quarles], 'On Partio'
[Crum H276-7]
b.137, p. 184

H0314 Hast thou observ'd how the curious hand
And lighter: 'tis but lighter by the dross.

[Francis Quarles], 'On the refining of gold'
[Crum H281]
b.118, p. 231

H0315 Haste (fair one!) to the favorite shade,
For such a beauteous scene as this?

John Lockman, 'Hearing that the entertainments of
Vauxhall Gardens were going to end . . . Aug. 1750'
c.267/1, p. 104

H0316 Haste generous youth, a foreign world explore
And sighing goddesses pursu'd his love.

'The oracle adapted to the modern times—epigram
8th' [of Flaminius]
c.158, p. 133

H0317 Haste gentle Charon haste, I prithee come
As gentle as if the great Pluto were here.

'Sonnet set by Mr. Hen. Purcell'
fb.142, p. 44

H0318 Haste gentle friends nor to the sacred cell
Bring lenient tidings to parental woes.

[William Hayley], 'Evening sonnet May 9 [1800]'
File 6968

H0319 Haste, haste, Amanda to restore
And I will strive to dream the rest.

R[ichard] V[ernon] S[adleir], 'To [blank]'
c.106, p. 56

H0320 Haste, haste, Phyllis, haste, 'tis the first of the May,
You must wear the soft chain, then they'll go where
you will.

'A pastoral dialogue'
c.578, p. 136

H0321 Haste, murky cloud, to pour your fleecy load
And we, with kindred tears, our loss proclaim!

R[ichard] V[ernon] S[adleir], 'On a lady intending to
return from a visit to her friend in the winter when
snow was hourly expected'
c.106, p. 116

H0322 Haste, my lov'd Frances, to an anxious friend
And let these arms embrace my dearest friend.

Frederick [Dickinson], 'Verses written by . . .
supposed to [his sister's] friend [Frances] Milner'

c.391, p. 36

H0323 Haste night unto thy center, are thy wings
No rival shall him of his life deprive.

[Henry Arscall], 'A lover's verses before he killed
himself'
[Crum H287]

b.62, p. 86

H0324 Haste royal James, and quickly come over
Would you but bless us with your return.

'Song'

fc.58, p. 39

H0325 Haste thee to blow, thou lovely rose,
Will light thee to thy fate.

Petit Andrews, 'Canzonette from a Latin epigram'

c.90

H0326 Haste Thee to help me, gracious Lord,
That death, whereof I am afraid.

'Psalm 70'

c.264/2, p. 40

H0327 Haste ye muses haste ye all
That's how to live and how to love.

Nat. Weston, 'On the marriage of John Wingfield of
Tickencote Rutl[and] esqr. with Eliz. youngest
daughter of Sir John Oldfield baronet epithalamium'

c.229/1, fol. 50

H0328 Hasten, Euphrosyne! away,
'Athenia was not born in vain.'

'To Athenia. 1751'

c.238, p. 43

H0329 Hasty love lasts not it is a flower, which
To happy therefore love't as blind's a whelp.

[Sir Thomas Urquhart], 'The opinion of some who
thinking Cupid be the son of lust, by a very homely
comparison distinguish him from a [?], and [?] [?]'

fb.217, p. 393

H0330 Hate and debate Rome o'er the world hath spread
Since from all backward love, all hate doth grow.

[Sir John Harington], 'Of Rome'

b.52/1, p. 120

H0331 Hate me dear soul, and say no more you love
Bestow it freely whilst it is your own.

'To his mistress denying him to lie with her'

b.104, p. 119; b.62, p. 27

H0332 Hate none, yet to yourself shall kindest prove
Your neighbors will but break not down your hedge.

[Sir Thomas Urquhart], 'Let our actions oblige others
to respect us, yet so look to ourselves as if they were to
hate us'

fb.217, p. 534

H0333 Hath Christmas furr'd your chimneys
Soon out of town, will whip them. | Then will I
rush. &c.

Will[iam] Strode, 'The chimney-sweeper's song'
[Crum H301]

b.200, p. 193

H0334 Hath death seiz'd on thee could not virtue keep
Or thou and thy name in one tomb shall lie.

'An [i.e., On] the death of King James'

b.62, p. 85

H0335 Hath this late year effac'd one single crime?
Short is the journey, and the end is bliss.

'The New Year'

c.153, p. 77

H0336 Hats are for use and ornament but why
Men put their heads there where their tails
should be.

'Steeple-crowned hats and rochets'
[Crum H306]

fb.106(5)

H0337 Have angels sinn'd, and shall not man beware?
His joys are joys of conquest, not of peace.

'Watch—'

fc.132/1, p. 166

H0338 Have fitly join'd the lawyer and his wife!
He moves at bar, and she at home, the strife.

'The lawyer and his wife'

c.487, p. 58

H0339 Have I a corner in your memory,
Will beautify the soul that thinks thereon.

[William Strode], 'A reply to a friend'
[Crum H310]

b.205, fol. 6or

H0340 Have I renounc'd my faith, or basely sold
At once to bid the devil, and her farewell.

Rich[ard] Corbett, 'On Mris Mallet'
[Crum H315]

b.200, p. 173; b.356, p. 29

H0341 Have I then no tears for thee, my father?
Be noble wretched—but her father happy.

    Miss [ ] Andrews(?), 'Filial piety'

File 245/22

H0342 Have mercy Lord on me I pray
With such as live in light.

    [John Hopkins], 'For succor against our enemies and
that we may praise in his church. The 22 psalm' [verses
from Psalm 56]
[Crum H317]

a.3, fol. 98

H0343 Have mercy Lord on me poor wretch,
Sheweth forth his pleasant face.

    [Thomas Sternhold], 'The 4 psalm' [verses from
Psalms 9, 11]

a.3, fol. 70v

H0344 Have mercy on me, Lord,
Shall from thine altar rise.

    'Psalm 51'

c.264/2, p. 1

H0345 Have mercy on us Lord, us Lord
Praised be God therefore.

    [Thomas Sternhold and John Hopkins], 'The 26
psalm. For the obtaining of God's favor and for the
abiding in his thoughts' [verses from Psalms 67–68]
[Crum H320]

a.3, fol. 104v

H0346 Have you ever been in love,
At once you both my love and virtue wrong.

    'A dialogue betwixt two ladies'

c.158, p. 28

H0347 Have you heard of a plot to destroy the poor
                                K[in]g
As much in the pistols, as was in the plot. |
                                Which &c.

    'The masquerade plot'

c.570/3, p. 1

H0348 Have you heard what an elegy lately was writ,
For writing—so fine an elogium on shoes.

    Poetry Box x/65

H0349 Have you not heard how our sovereign of late
Meet if she dare, and fairly with the swine.

    'A satire'

fb.140, p. 173

H0350 Have you not heard of an army complete,
What they intended to do.

    'Song. To the tune of The king of France with forty
thousand men, &c.'

fb.70, p. 185

H0351 Have you not in a chimney seen
Cracks and rejoiceth in the flame.

    'A droll upon a green faggot'

b.104, p. 90; fb.66/38

H0352 Have you not seen at country wake,
Old England must the piper pay.

    'To Caleb D'anvers esqr. [*i.e.*, Nicholas Amhurst] a
simile'

c.570/3, p. 107

H0353 Have you seen a blackheaded maggot
Oh so black oh so rough, oh so sour | So sour is she!

    'Contrary' [parody of 'Have you seen the white lily
grow . . .']
[Crum H331]

b.205, fol. 73r

H0354 Have you seen the raging stormy main
If you have seen all this then kiss mine a[rse].

    'To all curious critics and admirers of meter'

b.105, p. 249

H0355 Have you seen the white lily grow
Oh so sweet, oh so soft, oh so sweet | So sweet is
she.

    [Ben Jonson], 'A song' [The Underwood, 4, 'See the
chariot at hand . . . ,' verse 3; parodied by 'Have you
seen a blackheaded maggot . . .']
[Crum H334]

b.205, fol. 73r; b.213, p. 65a

H0356 Have you the ears of princes, with an aim,
Be patient, civil, painful, and importune.

    Sir Thomas Urquhart, 'To grand courtiers, of the
fittest way, how to advance their honorable projects'

fb.217, p. 36

H0357 Having lived among you many years
And with these words he bid the world adieu.

    [John Nixson], 'The righteous man's exhortation the
last dying words of Doctr S: to his parishioners to
forsake the sins that reign in this present age: as pride
envy hatred malice drunk[e]ness and
Sabbath-breaking'

b.215, p. 32

H0358 Having madden'd the land and himself with his
tricks
To join with such hell-hounds in glorious
convention.

'An impromptu on a supposed event'
Poetry Box III/58

H0359 Having no friend from whom I might
Will oblige your friends the muses.

[ ] Barwick, sr., 'A complaint from Parnassus or an
annual epistolary commerce between Oxford and
Winton College'

c.170, p. 6

H0360 Having thank'd me so much for the news in my last
For they'll mind their own business whether I will
or no.

[conference between King William and the Earl of
Sunderland, 1700]
[cf. Crum H 338; *POAS* VI.214]
Trumbull Box: Poetry Box XIII/54; Poetry Box X/54, p. 13
(incomplete?)

H0361 Hay! Nobly glad may well be said by thee
And only they—'tis thence true honor springs.

[Sir Philip Wodehouse], 'Another on the former
Abigail Holland'

b.131, back (no. 81)

H0362 He a good wife did pencil to the life,
She'd got a husband, far beyond her worth.

Sir Thomas Urquhart, 'In praise of Sir Thomas
Overbury'

fb.217, p. 178

H0363 He best provides, for the last day,
Transcend the knowledge of man's mind.

[Edmund Wodehouse], 'March 29 [1715]'

b.131, p. 189

H0364 He can make people here all think as he will
To the wish of your true | Your affectionate friend.

Poetry Box XII/127

H0365 He comes, he comes, the hero comes,
And Britons shall be slaves no more. | And Britons
&c. &c.

[on the Old Pretender, c. 1715]
[Crum H349]
fc.58, p. 99; c.555, p. 341 (incomplete?)

H0366 He comes, he comes, the judge severe
Forever, and forever reigns.

[Thomas Stevens?]

c.259, p. 59

H0367 He comes the royal conqueror comes
Which sweetly conquer'd thee.

P[hilip] Doddridge, 'A hymn on Luk. XIX. 27 But
those my enemies that would not that I should reign
over ye'

c.493, p. 41

H0368 He craves enough who does his master please:
Who diligently serves, may hold his peace.

[Sir Philip Wodehouse], 'Francis Carver once my
servant'

b.131, back (no. 205)

H0369 He deserves not at all a lover's name
Shall like an hollowed taper burn.

'The constancy of true love'

b.356, p. 76

H0370 He did not lose his wits though he was mad;
For lose he could not what he never had.

[Sir Thomas Urquhart], 'Of a fool turned mad'

fb.217, p. 539

H0371 He died, as if dead no life there were,
As if there were no death he lived here.

'The atheist's epithet'

c.356

H0372 He died of a quinsy
And was buried at Binsy.

'Epitaph on a doctor of divinity buried at Binsy near
Oxford'

c.360/3, no. 129

H0373 He dwells secure, who puts his trust
And bear thee to the skies.

[Sir William Trumbull], 'Meditation, out of the 91st
Psalm . . .' [1688]

b.177, p. 21; Trumbull Box: Poetry Box XIII/16 and 17 (2
copies)

H0374 He forthwith shut the northern wind
How great God's wonders of the waters be.

'Upon the fiction of Æolus god of the winds'

c.158, p. 117

H0375 He gave his heart to God first, then his King
How perfectly he could, who gave by 'hart'.

W. C., 'To the right wor[shipful] Sr. Harvey Bagot
Kt. Anagramma . . . O gave by hart'

Poetry Box VI/24

H0376 He gives to take: to give he never takes;
To give's the dart: to take, the butt he makes.

> Sir Thomas Urquhart, 'The nature of a covetous
> wretch' [translation of an epigram by John Owen]
>
> fb.217, p. 228

H0377 He hopeth not for what's to come: nor proves
Things past by faith: yet present times he loves.

> Sir Thomas Urquhart, 'Of an atheist'
>
> fb.217, p. 284

H0378 He is a God of sov'reign love
My Savior and my God.

> 'Hymn 30th'
>
> c.562, p. 35

H0379 He is beyond the reach of common men
Th'inferior dangers of a boist'rous storm.

> [Sir Thomas Urquhart], 'How a valiant man behaveth
> himself towards such as offend him'
>
> fb.217, p. 497

H0380 He is inflam'd with love and the remoter
The fire, that burns him is, he is the hotter.

> Sir Thomas Urquhart, 'Of a lover in his mistress'
> absence'
>
> fb.217, p. 340

H0381 He is gone gone like a springing rose,
That heaven is true, that all men sinners be.

> 'An epitaph on Sr. Charles Mackland'
>
> c.244, p. 287

H0382 He is interr'd whose soul (now fled away)
And now, tho' worms dwell in't, doth not lament.

> S. P., 'From a schoolfellow, an epitaph [on Caleb
> Vernon]'
>
> b.228, p. 2

H0383 He is no Fleming; for he cannot swill
Shall make him all, or which of all you will.

> [Francis Quarles], 'On the independent/On Morus'
> [Divine Fancies I, 22]
>
> b.137, p. 181 and 183

H0384 He is so liberal, that lest he should
Give but his own, he takes his neighbor's gold.

> Sir Thomas Urquhart, 'Of a prodigal robber'
>
> fb.217, p. 87

H0385 He is stark mad who ever says
But after one such love, can ne'er love more.

> [John Donne], 'Canzone'
> [Crum H369]
>
> b.114, p. 303; b.148, p. 62; b.205, fol. 26r

H0386 He is the happy man whose constant mind
Lies smiling down and bids mankind adieu.

> Lady [Mary] C[hudleigh], 'The happy man'
>
> c.258; c.83/2, no. 351

H0387 He keeps still fools with him, to spy the errors
Of his own folly 'n them: they being his mirrors.

> Sir Thomas Urquhart, 'The reason, why there was a
> weak-witted gentleman, who never lacked in his
> company a rabble of fools, wheresoever he went'
>
> fb.217, p. 119

H0388 He liv'd, as if he could not die: and died,
As if he could not be revivified.

> Sir Thomas Urquhart, 'The epitaph of an atheist'
>
> fb.217, p. 296

H0389 He lives with God none can deny,
That while he lived to the world did dye.

> [John Ashmore], 'On a dyer'
>
> c.74

H0390 He loves, admires, adores himself alone:
And save himself, who loves him, there is none.

> Sir Thomas Urquhart, 'Of a glorious fool'
>
> fb.217, p. 175

H0391 He made a pun: and to his friend he cried
While puns are puns, or punning men have breath.

> 'Elegy on Mr John Tissey. a not-able punster 1732'
>
> c.360/1, p. 49

H0392 He makes himself a servile wretch,
As knew them not before.

> 'No man ever repented of having kept silence, but
> many wish that they had not done so . . .'
>
> c.93; c.549, p. 80

H0393 He may be envied, who with tranquil breast
By friendship hallow'd—rural happiness!

> [Charlotte (Turner) Smith],'Sonnet'
>
> c.141, p. 136

H0394 He now lies low, but high his fame does rise
Adding a branch to his eternal crown.

> [Sir Richard Bulstrode?], 'Upon the death of
> Mr. Dryden the poet' [c. 1700]
>
> fb.88, p. 119v

H0395 He, of all others is the noblest wight
That intermixeth profit with delight.

> fb.151/3

H0396 He only is happy, and cannot miscarry
He in the conclusion is certain to win.

'The happy man' [Gentleman's evening post, June 1776]

c.487, p. 98

H0397 He opens mysteries, and to read men's
Who can deny the deity of Bacchus.

Sir Thomas Urquhart, 'Upon the deity of Bacchus and that he is aged'

fb.217, p. 219

H0398 He proffers you but mere discourse,
May put him to the horn.

Sir Thomas Urquhart, 'To a Scots gentlewoman, whose husband being something old, did not pay to her, as he ought, the conjugal debt . . .'

fb.217, p. 279

H0399 He said; and join'd the choir. Now left alone
Fragments of broken light, that gild the horrors
round.

[Gloster Ridley], 'Melampus; or the religious groves . . . Canto, 1st: 61, & 62'

Spence Papers, folder 127

H0400 He set forth books, unworthy of the light:
Yet worthy of the fire in all men's sight.

Sir Thomas Urquhart, 'Of an impertinent author'

fb.217, p. 252

H0401 He should be for the statue, which he made
You would believe, he saw the goddess naked.

Sir Thomas Urquhart, 'Of a cuckold, who being a statuary, had represented to the very life, in stone, the massive image of Diana'

fb.217, p. 82

H0402 He speaks so stoutl' his valor must b'unfeigned:
Mercure talks well: and yet his heels are winged.

Sir Thomas Urquhart, 'That the proudest, and most eloquent prattlers have not always the greatest courage'

fb.217, p. 302

H0403 He spoke—I sat in silent wonder
His voice was thunder and his aspect lightning.

'On Arabin's speech in James versus Smith at the Sheriff's Council London'

fc.76.iii/214

H0404 He sung of God, the mighty source,
Replied, O Lord, Thou art.

C[hristophe]r Smart, 'Lines written by the late . . . whilst confined in a madhouse . . .'

Smith Papers, folder 74/6

H0405 He that a good thing doth to a bad end,
He makes the devil thereby to act God's will.

Sir John Strangways, '10 Septr 1646'

b.304, p. 56

H0406 He that a watch would wear this he must do
Pocket his watch, and watch his pocket too.

'On hearing of a gentleman's pocket being picked of his watch'

Diggle Box: Poetry Box xi/68, 69; see also 'He that would wear a watch . . .'.

H0407 He that accord by wrong would alter'd see,
He in a cord by right should halter'd be.

[Crum H389, 'by might . . . by weight']

b.356, p. 305

H0408 He that acts with his heart and helps with his hand
Whose health I do wish, and whose friendship I own.

Hugh Smithson, duke of Northumberland, 'The honest wish'

b.90, p. 1; see also 'He that owns . . .'.

H0409 He that admits aught that is here,
As a limb torn off from his head.

[Edmund Wodehouse], 'Aug. 25 [1715]'

b.131, p. 252

H0410 He that agreeth with his poverty
If wealth in new desires employs his heart.

[Sir Thomas Urquhart], 'Who are really rich and who poor'

fb.217, p. 499

H0411 He that at secrets shall compose his aim
Once scorcht, he'll venture at the flame again.

[Henry Phillipps?]

b.156, p. 15

H0412 He that buys land, buys many stones,
Shall want money, as well as I.

[Crum H393]

c.160, fol. 48

H0413 He that can now so far improve
Of the chief good being there possest.

[Edmund Wodehouse], 'Octr. 16 [1714]'

b.131, p. 59

H0414 He that can read a sigh, or spell a tear,
By blessing them once more against their will.

[William] Lewes, of Oriel College, 'To the memory of my lord [1st] Duke of Buckingham' [Crum H396]

b.54, p. 874

H0415 He that can throw [?] of kind with the foresaid
                                                    mold
Of the [?] he shall not miss for to make [ ]d potable.

fa.16, p. 38

H0416 He that dyed so oft in sport
Died at last no color for't.

'On a dyer'
[Crum H403]
fb.143, p. 7

H0417 He that does lips or hands adore,
Who can express what 'tis he likes.

c.549, p. 63

H0418 He that does most his will submit
Blindness and misery affect.

[Edmund Wodehouse], 'Septr 19 [1715]'
b.131, p. 267

H0419 He that does so to God apply
No more that that, ever be learn'd that late.

[Edmund Wodehouse], 'Octr. 17 1714'
b.131, p. 61

H0420 He that doth a kiss receive,
Which you are to explain.

c.389; see also 'A lady that a kiss doth take . . .'.

H0421 He that for doing well, seeks recompense;
Knows not the worth of a good conscience.

Sir John Strangways, 'Virtus ipsa, sibi praemium . . .
22do Januarii 1646[/7]'
b.304, p. 70

H0422 He that for money weds preposterous shapes,
And curse you with a race of monkey sons.

'Concerning our choice in marriage'
c.158, p. 141

H0423 He that gets a groat a day and in that [?] sturdily(?)
Shall [?] a better by the care no haste ere was [h]is
                                                    pain.

'Be light and glad in God [?] which is your strength
and stay'
a.6, p. 39

H0424 He that has mix'd the useful with the sweet,
Has cobbler-like made both his ends to meet.

'Motto . . . Hor[ace] . . . translation'
c.81/1, no. 405

H0425 He that [hath] [all] [the] world [hath] but thus much
Which farther still [ ] health [ ] [ ] I find.

'In mundi felicitatem'
b.205, fol. 13v

H0426 He that hath eyes now wake and weep;
Rake in their graves to prove them men.

[George Morley], 'On King James the 1st'
[Crum H421; cf. Crum A1016]
fb.143, p. 25; see also 'All that have eyes . . .'.

H0427 He that his heart to God now gives
He the celestial life begins.

[Edmund Wodehouse], 'Iterum [29 November 1714]'
b.131, p. 99

H0428 He that in inmost holy place
Of my salvation raise.

'Psal: 91'
b.217, p. 50

H0429 He that intends a house to build
The actors of it well commend.

Sir John Strangways, 'Begin well, and end well . . . 2do
Novembris 1646'
b.304, p. 68

H0430 He that is near, he that is dear
Whats'e'er he sees, whats'e'er he hears.

[Edmund Wodehouse], 'Septr 5 1715'
b.131, p. 259

H0431 He that is proud of fancied piety
Thus taught and liv'd, and thus for us did die.

[Edmund Wodehouse], 'Aug. 5 [1715]'
b.131, p. 241

H0432 He that largely subscribes, has a true loyal heart,
Who have nothing to fear, or nothing to lose.

Abraham Oakes, 'On the subscription against the
rebels. 1745. An epigram'
c.50, p. 111

H0433 He that lets anything to vie
Whatever man's opinion is.

[Edmund Wodehouse], 'Decr. 1 1714'
b.131, p. 101

H0434 He that lets aught within his breast,
So peace, so bliss, so God true reigns.

[Edmund Wodehouse], 'Feb. 17 [1715]'
b.131, p. 169

H0435 He that lives best, does God most please,
Great share of the celestial bliss.

> [Edmund Wodehouse], 'March 7 [1715]'

b.131, p. 175

H0436 He that loves a rosy cheek
Can disdain as much as thou.

> [Thomas Carew, 'An invective against his mistress']
> [Crum H444]

b.213, p. 4 (ll. 1–12); fc.132/1, p. 189 (ll. 1–18)

H0437 He that loves glass without a G
Take away L and that is he.

b.52/1, p. 120

H0438 He that many learned authors reads,
And in the room their ignorance they advance.

> 'Advice to seek knowledge'

c.158, p. 154

H0439 He that marry a merry lass
He had better be without her.

> 'Song 6th'

c.503, p. 61

H0440 He that needs five thousand pounds to live
Is full as poor as he that needs but five.

> 'Prodigality'

c.356

H0441 He that on heav'n his heart can set,
Be blest thou to eternity.

> [Edmund Wodehouse], 'Octr. 7 1714'

b.131, p. 55

H0442 He that once sins, like him that slides on ice,
He slides on smoothly, and looks back no more.

> [Thomas] Creech, 'The contrast or vice and virtue
> beautifully exemplified in a paraphrastical version of
> the first Psalm'

c.487, p. 54

H0443 He that out of another's eye
The beam without delay.

b.234, p. 164

H0444 He that owns in his heart, and helps with his hand,
Whose health I now drink, and whose friendship I
own.

> 'Hic est quem legis, ille quem requiris' ['The Welsh
> health,' against occasional conformity; pr. 1704/5
> (Foxon H124)]
> [Crum H446]

c.111, p. 128; b.382(11); see also 'He that acts . . .'.

H0445 He that selleth ware and lives by the last(?)
Will quickly give over his fund to his creditor's cost.

a.6, p. 92

H0446 He that shall find how often I
As in my life to be exprest.

> [Edmund Wodehouse], 'July 19 [1715]'

b.131, p. 233

H0447 He that shall seek lost credit to regain,
That on my sufferings I may sit and smile.

> Sir John Strangways, 'When I was taken up by the
> soldiers and kept at Dorchester and Weymouth by
> them: June 19th 1645. Upon a private and retired life'

b.304, p. 138

H0448 He that things' causes knows, with times complies,
Calms his affects, orders his acts is wise.

> 'The temperate'

c.356

H0449 He that thinks God at death will him prefer
Folly and fond self-love in such man's mind.

> [Edmund Wodehouse], 'Novr 28 1715'

b.131, p. 49

H0450 He that this day doth gold or silver send,
To draw from thee a better new year's gift.

> P. Lumley, 'P. Lumley to Dr. Randolph'

b.197, p. 173

H0451 He that to anger and wrath is thrall,
Over his will hath no power at all.

b.234, p. 258

H0452 He that to our dear Lord is join'd,
And never lose its force.

> James Hutton, 'To my dear Br[other] Trancker on his
> birthday Oct. 6 1771'

File 7846

H0453 He that trusts before he try,
May repent before he die.

> [couplet, with Latin; an 'old saying']
> [Crum H459]

fb.88, p. 119

H0454 He that wants faith, and apprehends a grief
What grace is absent, where true faith abides.

> [Francis Quarles], 'On faith'
> [Crum H461]

b.118, p. 229

H0455 He that will give my Grace but what is hers,
But virtue, worth and sweetness, widowers.

'On Grace the wife of Thomas Scot'

c.546, p. 23

H0456 He that will win a widow's heart,
And hates the formal wooer.

c.549, p. 146

H0457 He that within the secret place,
And drink at joy—celestial's spring.

'Psalm 91'

c.264/2, p. 95

H0458 He that would have his heart quite free
Ne'er vex, ne'er tremble, faint nor feign.

[Edmund Wodehouse], 'July 18 [1715]'

b.131, p. 233

H0459 He that would wear a watch, this must he do,
Pocket his watch, and watch his pocket too.

'On hearing that a pocket had been picked of a watch'

c.152, p. 75; see also 'He that a watch would wear . . .'.

H0460 He that's a blockhead call'd let it not grieve him;
Twenty to one but he dies—with a pension. | Titles
are honors . . .

'Song 144'

c.555, p. 198

H0461 He that's imprisoned in this narrow room
Whose virtue must outlive his epitaph.

'Berkeley's epitaph' [on Sir Robert Berkeley, d. 1616,
tablet in Canterbury Cathedral]
[Crum H493]

b.62, p. 51; b.356, p. 258

H0462 He that's of pure and upright life,
With gratitude—addresses!

Abraham Oakes, 'An ode: on long life and happiness'

c.50, p. 128

H0463 He thought betwixt Imperia's thighs t'have trac'd
It was the broad way brought him to perdition.

Sir Thomas Urquhart, 'Of one who could not fancy to
himself a greater happiness, than to enjoy his mistress'

fb.217, p. 48

H0464 He to true honor lays best claim,
To love itself becoming dear.

[Edmund Wodehouse], 'March 18 [1715]'

b.131, p. 183

H0465 He used to rise while it was dark
Will never get to Troy.

Poetry Box II/55

H0466 He was an humble obsequious son
Hath scarce been found, or left behind his fellow.

'An inscription in Thame church in Oxfordshire on
Robert Crews who died Jan 7—1731—aetatis 60'

c.360/1, p. 171

H0467 He was, but words are wanting to say what;
Say all that's good and brave, and he was that.

'An epigram on Capt. Grenville buried May 22nd.
1747'

c.94

H0468 He was for curing of the young girl's eye,
To vitiate the pupil.

Sir Thomas Urquhart, 'Of a certain very skillful
chirurgeon, who heal'd a virgin of an exceeding sore
eye, but rul'd the flower of his virginity'

fb.217, p. 181

H0469 He was not hidden, neither was he unseen
Or else be noticed I know how.

fc.156

H0470 He who by choice, or kinder influence led,
Tell but her deeds and they'll declare her fame.

Robert Pauncefort, 'The character of a good wife,
from the 31st chap. of Proverbs, verse the 10th to the
end'

c.152, p. 8

H0471 He who by principle is sway'd
Nor sing the mighty theme with low unequal lays.

'Ode 3. of the 3 book' [of Horace]

Poetry Box X/75

H0472 He who commits a fault shall quickly find,
'Twill prove acceptable, when 'tis once worn.

J[ohn] R[obinson], 'Conscia mens recti, famae
mendacia ridet'

c.370, fol. 67v

H0473 He who could first two gentle hearts unbind,
The loving still who died not of despair.

[James] Hammond, 'Eleg. 9th' [translation of Tibellus
book 3, elegy 2nd]

c.240, fol. 10

H0474 He who disturbs his house, shall reap the wind,
A little college of humanity.

[Sir Philip Wodehouse], 'Solomon's prov. Qui
conturbat domum . . .'

b.131, p. 21

H0475 He who does walk in paths of life may call
And bids thee be aware of and refell. | Farewell

    [Sir Philip Wodehouse], 'Andrew Hatley they wander all'

    b.131, back (no. 171)

H0476 He who first taught the grape to strain
An universal prayer.

    [Charles James Fox], 'To the god of eating'

    Diggle Box: Poetry Box xi/69 (attr. William McLaren); Poetry Box iii/folder 21–30

H0477 He who in scandalizing pleasure takes,
Speak ill of none, and none 'gainst thee will rail.

    J[ohn] R[obinson], 'Qui ex maledicendo voluptatem capiat; male audiendo amittat'

    c.370, fol. 71v

H0478 He, who in war, so great a figure made
And full of years, and full of fame he died.

    'An epitaph on Lieutenant Genl. Wood—who died 1712'

    c.244, p. 208

H0479 He who sits from day to day
Make us learn that we must die!

    William Cowper(?), 'The following lines are said to be a production of . . . for the bellman'

    c.140, p. 211

H0480 He who unlawful means advance to gain,
Take but your due, and never covet more.

    'Of dealing unjustly'

    c.160, fol. 71

H0481 He who willfully breaketh the fifth command,
And will scour the nation of all their foul rust. |
                Which none but great rogues will deny.

    'The reformers'

    b.111, p. 455

H0482 He who would great in science grow
Leaving both common souls and common clay.

    [Walter] Titley, 'The 2nd. ode of the 3rd. book of Horace imitated by . . . to Dr. Bentley' [answered by 'Who strives to mount . . .']

    fc.135; c.416 (attr. G. Lyttelton); Poetry Box x/74; see also 'A glorious immortal prize . . .'.

H0483 He who would learn to fence for his life,
The third a d—— atheist, the fourth is a fool.

    'The statesman's academy . . . Buckingham, Salisbury, Shaftesbury, Wharton . . .' [1677]

    Poetry Box vii/8; b.54, p. 873; see also 'He who would learn how to fence . . .'.

H0484 He who would write an epitaph
Here underneath lies Isabel.

    'An epitaph on Isabella'

    c.74; see also 'The way to write an epitaph . . .'.

H0485 He who's magnanimous, does truly know
At length a burden of the earth, will be.

    [Sir Philip Wodehouse], 'Magnanimity according to Aristotle . . .' [Nichomachian ethics, IV.3]

    b.131, p. 13

H0486 He whose delights are filthy vile and base
And rather likes with reprobates to live.

    b.234, p. 310

H0487 He will trust none; therefore, no faith he hath:
All men trust him; therefore he must have faith.

    Sir Thomas Urquhart, 'Of a wealthy precise usurer'

    fb.217, p. 149

H0488 Head from his crown would fain a king be call'd
By men nay women in the forefront plac'd.

    'Answer' [to 'Am not I head . . .']

    b.356, p. 115

H0489 Health from the lover of the country, me;
The horse doth with the horseman run away.

    [Abraham Cowley, trans., 'Horace to Fuscus Aristius' [Horace, Epistles I.x.] [Crum H510]

    b.118, p. 16

H0490 Health good supreme! Offspring of heaven! Divine
Heart-gnawing care, and lighten human woe.

    Henry Baker, 'An invitation to health' [pr. 1723 (Foxon B10)]

    c.244, p. 405

H0491 Health to great Glo'ster—from a man unknown,
How low, how mean, and full as poor as I.

    Charles Churchill, 'The dedication [to William Warburton, bishop of Gloucester] prefixed to the sermons of the late . . .'

    c.83/3, no. 1072

H0492 Health to my friend, and long unbroken years,
And hides her head in the green lap of spring.

    [Anna Laetitia] (Aikin) [Barbauld], 'The invitation; to a young lady'

    fc.132/1, p. 109

H0493 Health to my friend, and many a cheerful day,
'To let suspicion intermix a tear.'

    [William Shenstone], 'To a friend on some slight occasion estranged from him'

    c.149, p. 7

H0494 Health to my sister, to my brother health!
Their welcomes loud and wishes high as mine.

'Kensington, Aug. 30, 1788' [Frederick Dickinson to Martha Dickinson]

c.391

H0495 Health to my sweet! And wheresoe'er she stray,
And end, as it began, in perfect love!

Thomas Hull [verse epistle to his wife, 29 June 1771]

File 7714

H0496 Health to our king—may Jacob's God give ear,
O prosper thou his arms, and bless our King.

[Richard] Daniel, dean of Armagh, 'The triumph of faith—Psa: 20'

c.244, p. 348

H0497 Health to the king, whose touch our ills can cure
Then all would love their prince, and all obey.

'A Worcester health'

fc.58, p. 142

H0498 Health to the myrtle shades
Phyllis that makes the day young . . . .

'A song 1680'

b.54, p. 1134 (incomplete)

H0499 Health to the royal Dane,
Say, that philanthropy | Adorns a throne.

John Lockman, 'The King of Denmark's health. A volunteer toast: writ for the banquet given, Oct: 7th 1768, at Sion House to his Danish Majesty, by his grace the Duke of Northumberland'

c.267/4, p. 307

H0500 Hear, all ye friends of knighthood
Whereon depend your glory.

[Philip Dormer Stanhope, 4th earl of Chesterfield], 'On Sir Wm Morgan's losing his ribbon. To the tune Of noble race was Shinkin' [William Morgan of Tredegar, knighted 1725, among George I's first Knights of Bath when he revived the order] [Crum H524]

c.233, p. 39; c.360/1, p. 171; c.176, p. 4

H0501 Hear Cornlay lies in cold clay clad
Who died for want of what he had.

c.360/3, no. 37

H0502 Hear from Thy throne of grace and pray'r
In presence of Thy sight.

'Morning prayer 20 day Psalm 102. 5th penitential'

c.264/3, p. 1

H0503 Hear, hear the morning bell the usher cries
May but we leave our sexton in his rope.

c.53, fol. 22

H0504 Hear how the nightingale on ev'ry spray,
Be gay: too soon the flow'r of spring will fade.

[Sir William] Jones, 'A Turkish ode of Mesihi'

c.90

H0505 Hear how the sacred thunder rends the skies
And Christ by figure only saved mankind.

'From Parson ——— to Mrs. M****' [answered by 'Hark how the sacred thunder . . .']

c.517, fol. 20r

H0506 Hear Jesus hear thou virgin's son
And take my everlasting place.

'Hymn'

c.562, p. 166

H0507 Hear me, great empress of my heart, or I
I beg the best pretensions, or a grave.

fb.70, p. 161

H0508 Hear me ye nymphs and every swain,
To lonely wilds I'll wander.

[W. Crawford], '14th song the bush o' boon Traquair' [Crum H536, 'you nymphs']

Accession 97.7.40, p. 25; fc.61, p. 63

H0509 Hear, mighty God, the humble suppliants cry,
From God who keeps his vengeance for my foes.

[Richard] Daniel, dean of Armagh, 'The penitent pardoned. Psalm 6'

c.244, p. 342

H0510 Hear much but little speak a wise man fears
Do let in wit the tongue do let out folly.

[Thomas Randolph]

fb.98, fol. 150

H0511 Hear much, but little speak and flee from that is
                                                    naught,
These are three lessons brief and good to each one
                                                    to be taught.

c.339, p. 324

H0512 Hear my fond wish on Cornwall's natal day—
Its deeds enroll'd in time's immortal page.

John Lockman, 'The birthday of Velters Cornwall esq. 22 February 1766'

c.267/2, after p. 134

H0513 Hear my tale out—'tis which I think
The piece had neither head nor tail.

[Phanuel Bacon], 'Tenet insanabile multos scribendi caiorthes(?)'

c.237, fol. 71

H0514 Hear, O ye heav'ns, and O thou earth, give ear
And who shall turn it from its destin'd end?

'1 C[hapter] [-14 Chapter] Isaiah' [various drafts]

fc.53, p. 44 (i); p. 55 (iv); p. 73 (ix); p. 98 (vi–xiv); p. 138 (xiii–xiv); p. 152 (i–v)

H0515 Hear, see, and hold your peace, if you be married
T' a wicked wife: else all will be miscarried.

Sir Thomas Urquhart, 'To Joan Thomson's man'

fb.217, p. 53

H0516 Hear sweet spirit hear the spell;
Miserere domine.

[Samuel Taylor] Coleridge, 'From the tragedy of [Osorio]' [Act III. Scene i]

c.364

H0517 Hear this, and tremble all
'I know no heaven but fair Wentworth's eyes.'

[Thomas] Carew, 'Upon my Lord Chief Justice [Finch] his election of my Lady A. W[entworth] for his mistress' [c. 1635]

b.150, p. 225

H0518 Hear Thou my pray'r, O Lord, perpend
To Thee devoted whole.

'Psalm 143 7th penitential'

c.264/3, p. 100

H0519 Hear when I call, my God! Defend
Thou dost me safely keep.

'Psalm 4'

c.264/1, p. 9

H0520 Hear with joy you rival train,
Still succeeding, ever new.

'A song on the Ld Scudamore's marriage wth Ms Digby'

Poetry Box VII/80

H0521 Hear ye the solemn notes that awful bell
'Tis love 'tis friendship pays an honest tear.

[Enesor Heathcote], 'Elegy on the untimely death of Mr. J[ohn] Bent'

Poetry Box X/160

H0522 Heard ye not the solemn bell
Peace to thy deserving shade.

[on Eliza Huddesford, d. 2 May 1768]

c.156, p. 99

H0523 Heard ye not the solemn strain?
The orphan's grateful voice shall fill the choir.

Hugh Boyd, 'Ode on the performance of selected sacred music for the benefit of the male asylum'

c.141, p. 575

H0524 Heardst thou the tolling of yon fun'ral bell?
Shall weeping kneel around their Garrick's tomb.

Charles [John] Fielding, 'An elegy to the memory of David Garrick esq'

c.341, p. 148

H0525 Hearing a woman cry out fish,
The sense of honor's scarcely known.

'Use of the word Honor'

c.94

H0526 Hearken, and I will tell to thee,
Sing Ceurialin with A.

'Johnny Breckin's wedding. A song'

c.530, p. 227

H0527 Heart fly to Christ—he must thy refuge be
Up to his kingdom art. Pray and obey.

[Sir Philip Wodehouse], 'Upon old Mr [Christopher] Hatley'

b.131, back (no. 158)

H0528 Heart to be robb'd? How can that be? I pray?
Ta'en up—'tis petty—larceny at most.

[Sir Philip Wodehouse], 'Deborah Barrett heart to be robb'd'

b.131, back (no. 107)

H0529 Heav'n and earth, both angel, man, and beast
Such two engend'ring and destroying words.

[Sir Thomas Urquhart], 'The last words will be come ye blessed, go ye cursed'

fb.217, p. 527

H0530 Heaven approves
The conquering cause, the conquer'd Cato loves.

'In Catonem . . . Lucan'

c.81/1, no. 240

H0531 Heaven bless King James our joy
You must be this witty.

'1623' ['The Duke of Buckingham's kindred'] [Crum H552]

b.197, p. 187 (incomplete?)

H0532 Heav'n-born charity one day,
When charity and pleasure join.

> John Lockman, 'Charity and pleasure: on occasion of the assembly and ball, at Ranelagh house, Tuesday, 9 June, 1761'
>
> c.267/3, p. 101

H0533 Heav'n first taught letters for some wretch's aid
And waft a sign from Indus to the Pole.

> [Alexander] Pope, 'Eloisa to Abelard—on writing letters'
>
> c.360/2, no. 160; c.186, p. 90

H0534 Heaven knows! I never would repine,
Ah! Let me die, and feel no more.

> [Mary (Derby)] Robinson, 'Lines from Mrs. Robinson's novel of Angelina'
>
> c.83/2, no. 604; File 245/29 (attr. Miss Andrews)

H0535 Heaven! My native home I meditate,
That I may cheerfully resign my breath.

> 'A meditation on heaven'
>
> c.515, fol. 23v

H0536 Heaven once was in an uproar when the gods
Neptune, trident, Jove lightning could not brook.

> J. R.
>
> b.197, p. 117

H0537 Heav'n seems to smile on the solemnity;
Heav'n's doctrine wrought to the purposes of Hell.

> [Edmund Wodehouse], 'The same day as the Coronation Day [21 October 1714], being bright sunshine'
>
> b.131, p. 63

H0538 Heav'n what an age is this what race
And thinks him happy when he is.

> [Charles Cotton], 'Contentation, directed to my dear father, and most worthy friend, Mr Isaak Walton'
>
> fb.64

H0539 Heaven with its glories we receive
Its basis is eternal love.

> T[homas] S[tevens]
>
> c.259, p. 138

H0540 Heavenly Father Creator of all things
Thou seest good for us, but grant | Us. . . .

> Poetry Box x/13 (incomplete)

H0541 Heaven's {blazing star/wonder late}, but now earth's
          glorious ray
Day obscur'd that, this makes the day more bright.

> 'Anagram/ Anne Gawdy. New and gay'
>
> b.197, p. 211

H0542 Heavens are we all asleep, all for our ease
But by God, there is cold lodging in a trench.

> 'A lampoon: 1678 upon the English not opposing the French in their unjust progress in Flanders'
>
> b.54, p. 1062 (incomplete?)

H0543 Heavy on me, O Lord, thy judgments lie,
Thou that art the God of love!

> [Matthew] Prior, 'Psalm 88'
>
> c.244, p. 147

H0544 Hebe, with charms and charms by dozens,
They're merely rails without a hook.

> '[Greek] . . . Antholog. Lib. VII . . . imitated'
>
> c.221, p. 41

H0545 Hector, though warn'd by an approaching cry
Does his own part, and leaves the rest to fate.

> 'The parting of Hector with his princess Andro[mache] and his son Astyanax when he went out and was slain [by] Achilles' [cf. Iliad vi, 406]
>
> b.218, p. 13

H0546 Heedless creature whither hasting
Which the most destruction be!

> 'On a scale the device of which was a mousetrap and the motto—Prenez garde!'
>
> c.504, p. 14

H0547 Heedless wanderer, come not here
Than nature and simplicity.

> 'Inscription for a rural arbor'
>
> c.142, p. 376

H0548 Helen high favor'd by the inspiring Nine
And all the powers of sympathy combine.

> R. R., 'R. R. 1790'
>
> c.375, in front

H0549 He'll be not sav'd; he hath no sp'rit but which,
Which is the place of beasts.

> Sir Thomas Urquhart, 'Of a devote gull'
>
> fb.217, p. 278

H0550 Help! Help! O help divinity of love,
And forever constant prove.

> [Henry Hughes], 'The tempest' [1655]
> [Crum H577]
>
> fb.107, p. 52

H0551 Help me O blessed Lord to die
Welcome my happy death.

> [( ) Pierson]
>
> c.328, p. 35

H0552 Hence all ye vain delights
There's nothing truly sweet, save melancholy.

[John Fletcher], 'On the praise of melancholy' [from
The nice valor, III.I]
[Crum H593]

b.200, p. 46 (another stanza beginning 'My woeful
monument . . .' on p. 109); b.213, p. 49; b.205, fol. 76r
('Hence, hence . . .')

H0553 Hence, base inglorious passions! Hence
But waft the virtuous soul to realms of endless day.

[William Boscawen], 'For the anniversary of the
subscribers to the Literary Fund. May 1796.'

fc.106, p. 24

H0554 Hence Cupid with your cheating toys
And is not much transported, but still pleas'd.

[Katherine Philips], 'Against love'
[Crum H596]

b.118, p. 80

H0555 Hence, hence vain illusions, fond visions of joy,
Soft act and live but to love and admire.

'The resolution'

c.83/2, no. 622

H0556 Hence, let me haste, from life's fantastic shows,
Forever triumph, and forever reign.

'The tender sister. An elegy'

c.83/1, no. 76

H0557 Hence London dames into the country run
And schoolboy Beaufort clasps her in his arms.

'On Mrs. Digby's coming to town who was the Duke
of Beaufort's wife'

fc.73; c.111, p. 163

H0558 Hence melancholy! hence! with all thy train
And safe conduct thee to celestial day.

'Elegy on the search of happiness, addressed to a
friend'

c.139, p. 393

H0559 Hence, motley mirth and wanton song
This wreath for pity wove, and brighten'd with a
tear.

G[eorge] Dyer, 'On pity'

c.83/3, no. 747

H0560 Hence pond'rous first to where the artist's hand
Ne'er let this monster your affection share.

'[Enigma/Charade/Conundrum] 39'

c.389

H0561 Hence, sorrow, luckless sprite,
Hail the glad approach of pleasure.

H[enry] Skrine, 'Ode to pleasure in imitation of the
Allegro of Milton addressed to Mrs. Aislabie on her
fête at Hendon place . . . London—May 24. 1780'

c.509, p. 31; File 13884

H0562 Hence stoic apathy! To breasts of stone,
The Christian yields an angel to his God.

[William] Mason, 'On the death of Miss Drummond
daughter to the Archb[isho]p of York'

c.391, p. 24; see also 'Here sleeps what once . . .'.

H0563 Hence superstition hide thy daring head,
In chains thou shalt appear to grace her state!

Ann Murry

c.248

H0564 Hence to some convent's gloomy aisles,
From noisy mirth, and business free!

[Joseph Warton], 'Ode to superstition'

Poetry Box x/79

H0565 Hence wanton suitors all, Mall your delight
Lest thou perchance a Vulcan's nightcap wear.

'On Dr. Bambridge marrying Mall Wolfe a butcher's
daughter'

b.356, p. 147

H0566 Hence with cares, complaint and frowning
May they long in triumph reign.

'Song 37'

c.555, p. 59

H0567 Hence, with thy frowns, penurious solitude!
Our moments to gild and our tempers refine.

[Thomas Hull], 'Ode to solitude'

c.528/60

H0568 Hence ye profane; I hate you all;
Much will be missing still, and much will be amiss.

[Abraham Cowley], 'Horace lib. 3 ode 1'
[Crum H612]

b.118, p. 25

H0569 Hence ye vulgar and profane!
Wealth but ill the toil repays.

[William Popple, trans.], 'The odes epodes &ca. of
Horace translated. Book 3rd. ode 1st. To Asinius
Pollio'

fc.104/2, p. 190

H0570 Henceforth, be every tender tear suppress'd,
And on the eleventh winter, died a man.

> [Christopher Smart], 'Epitaph on Master Newbury'
> [Crum H616]
>
> c.83/2, no. 705; c.157, p. 107 ('nineteenth winter')

H0571 Henceforth my pen, unforward to indite,
Expose it to my view, and censure then.

> Charles Atherton Allnutt, 'Answer to a friend who on
> my showing him the foregoing poem, taxed me with a
> plagiary from Thomson's Season[s]'
>
> c.112, p. 65

H0572 Henceforth no more great prince your sacred breast
He's stronger far than I, my God than his.

> 'David's speech to Saul'
>
> b.118, p. 22

H0573 Henceforth ye learned sots, henceforth forbear
And we forget we ever were undone.

> 'On Miss Fanny Robinson written on a window at
> Hockrel'
>
> c.360/1, p. 295

H0574 Henry a youth by nature form'd to please
For the bright mansion of eternal day.

> 'The pursuit of pleasure'
>
> c.143, fol. 8

H0575 Her action, Sir, you say
That she's well grounded.

> Sir Thomas Urquhart, 'To an advocate, on the suit of
> a very lovely-disposed gentlewoman'
>
> fb.217, p. 61

H0576 Her awful sword, when sacred justice rears,
May he stern justice weigh in mercy's scale!

> 'Lines on the melancholy situation of a certain
> unfortunate divine'
>
> c.83/1, no. 141

H0577 Her best conceptions are her vein being tactile
Where after one long measure two shorter follow.

> Sir Thomas Urquhart, 'Upon a poetess of a very
> amorous disposition'
>
> fb.217, p. 70

H0578 Her bleating flock the young Cleonia drove
Desperately wicked and deceitful too.

> 'By Melania an allegory'
>
> Poetry Box x/10(17)

H0579 Her charming eyes inflame the nation,
And cause a general conflagration.

> 'On the same' [Miss M.]
>
> c.93

H0580 Her dreadful navy o'er the ocean flies,
Dig thou the mine while we enjoy the ore.

> '[Several copies of verses spoken at Westminster
> School on the anniversary of the defeat of the Spanish
> Armada] 7'
>
> fc.24, p. 72

H0581 Her even lines her steady temper show;
That form her manners and her footsteps guide.

> [Anna Laetitia] (Aikin) [Barbauld], 'On a lady's
> writing'
>
> c.487, p. 10

H0582 Her eyes are so divine, that from my heart
For all her body's in a restless motion.

> Sir Thomas Urquhart, 'The praises of a certain
> gentlewoman, counterchecked by the hearer for her
> lasciviousness'
>
> fb.217, p. 146

H0583 Her eyes like diamonds without a flaw
Enough to pierce a thousand thousand hearts.

> [Sir William Trumbull]
>
> Trumbull Box: Poetry Box XIII/31

H0584 Her eyes victorious as great Marlb'rough's arms
Good nature weeps. Behold a mourning bride.

> [Horace Walpole, 4th earl of Orford], 'C[ountess] of
> Pembr[oke]' [d. 1794]
> [Crum H626]
>
> c.157, p. 68

H0585 Her fair aspects give hope to fair desire
To God's anoint' the loyal pope adore.

> [Sir Philip Wodehouse], 'Upon his fair neighbor the
> Lady Dorothea Yallop'
>
> b.131, back (no. 54)

H0586 Her father gave her dildoes six
And swears by God she'll frig no more.

> 'Upon Betty Frazer 1677 . . . Rochester'
>
> b.54, p. 1094

H0587 Her feet express in dancing the love vites
(Her tongue being silent) which her heart endites.

> [Sir Thomas Urquhart], 'Of an [?] girl practicing [?]
> [?] of lascivious dancing'
>
> fb.217, p. 520

H0588 Her for a mistress fain would I enjoy
Then she shall be my bedfellow but not my wife.

> [William Strode, trans.], 'Choice of mistress' [from
> Ausonius, Epigram 78, Qualis velit habere amicam]
> [Crum H630]
>
> b.205, fol. 22v

H0589   Her hair's not hair: but plaits of precious gold,
No wit, nor valor's able to prevail.

> Sir Thomas Urquhart, 'In praise of fair Aura's hair'
> fb.217, p. 359

H0590   Her handmaids, the graces, wherever she roves
Till the air of a goddess they give her.

> [N.] Herbert
> Spence Papers, folder 91

H0591   Her hassit locks were waving o'er her cheek,
And O her mows like any honey-pear!

> Al[lan] Ramsay
> Spence Papers, folder 148

H0592   Her heav'nly wit and beauty join
E'en Venus cannot her outshine.

> 'Acrostic on Miss Howe Tunbridge Wells 1745'
> c.360/2, no. 47

H0593   Her kisses, are but favors in retail:
Have seen an object worthy to behold.

> Sir Thomas Urquhart, 'Of kisses, and embraces. On Isabel'
> fb.217, p. 298

H0594   Her life alone is greatly blest
Wears her remains of life away.

> 'Felicia or the happy virgin'
> c.186, p. 110

H0595   Her looks import such virtue, that th'effects
Yet truly 'r eyes speak rather of a male.

> Sir Thomas Urquhart, 'Of a very majestic, and lovely gentlewoman'
> fb.217, p. 170

H0596   Her lust was Cupid's priest, her body his
Upon the altar of her husband's belly.

> [Sir Thomas Urquhart]
> fb.217, p. 387

H0597   Her matter being inform'd by the privation
She lov'd *de anima* but for the touch.

> Sir Thomas Urquhart, 'Of a certain gentlewoman how she preached her skill in the science of natural philosophy'
> fb.217, p. 101

H0598   Her mien so constrain'd and her paces so sure
You would scarcely suspect that it all is concerted.

> Miss [ ] Rogers, 'Bout[s] rimes'
> c.364, p. 66

H0599   Her nakedness their mother church Geneva
Did once abash.

> Sir Thomas Urquhart, 'Here the profession of Geneva, for being stripped of all ceremonies, is compared to Eva, immediately after her fall'
> fb.217, p. 244

H0600   Her name an army well doth represent
Since here the Lord of Hosts did pitch his tent.

> [George Herbert], 'Anagram Mary, army'
> fb.88, p. 114v; see 'How well/ill an army . . .'

H0601   Her name in Latian language drest
Into her epitaph, an epithet.

> [Sir Philip Wodehouse], 'Upon Sr Ed: Bacon's Lady of Redgrave Elizabaetha Bacona'
> b.131, back (no. 49)

H0602   Her noble guests well pleas'd let Cambria hail
Grant that indulgence which you gave tonight.

> [William] Clever, [bishop of St. Asaph], 'Prologue to Chronon holen theologos' [Aug. 1773]
> Poetry Box IV/162

H0603   Her picture her resembleth not, thought she
Be as like it, as anything can be.

> Sir Thomas Urquhart, 'Of a certain lady, accustomed to farding, whose portrait, the limner drew to represent her face, as it was painted'
> fb.217, p. 127

H0604   Her policy taught ancient Rome to save
And like Deucalion raises men from stones.

> [Phanuel Bacon], 'Fortus creantur fortibus'
> c.237, fol. 69

H0605   Her sp'rits in liquor are not always sunk,
Why may it not be so with Mistress Rose.

> Sir Thomas Urquhart, 'Of one gossip, or . . . Rose, who never went to evening prayers, but half tipsy, after a cup of sack'
> fb.217, p. 184

H0606   Her tender age, her form divinely fair,
Her moving softness and majestic grace.

> 'Woman'
> c.360/3, no. 225

H0607   Her true encomium is well set forth
In this her anagram—grave modest worth.

> [Sir Philip Wodehouse], 'Margaret Wodehouse'
> b.131, back (no. 26)

H0608 Her virtue keeps her beauty unallur'd
Thus is she—in a gallant form secur'd.

> [Sir Philip Wodehouse], 'Upon my cousin her
> daughter Magdalein Ravenscroft'
> b.131, back (no. 44)

H0609 Her wit, her sense, her virtues were her own;
When those who now lament her are no more.

> c.391, p. 62; see also 'Here shall our ling'ring
> footsteps . . .'.

H0610 Her works are catholic in ev'ry place,
And noways will believe, unless she touch.

> Sir Thomas Urquhart, 'Of a certain woman, exceeding
> free of her body, who seemed nevertheless to be very
> religiously set'
> fb.217, p. 106

H0611 Heralds and courtiers, by your leave
Let Bourbon or Nassau go higher.

> [Matthew Prior], 'An epitaph said to be made by a late
> ingenious poet, is an instance that men of merit, don't
> want a family to support their credit'
> [Foxon E369]
> c.489, p. 16; see also 'Courtiers and heralds . . .', 'Nobles
> and heralds . . .', 'Statesmen and courtiers . . .'.

H0612 Hercule, Orland', and Amadis kill'd dread,
The greatest beast, that ever was to die.

> Sir Thomas Urquhart, 'Master Loggerhead's epitaph'
> fb.217, p. 85

H0613 Here a bad angel is not understood;
For you were man's reserver; therefore good.

> Sir Thomas Urquhart, 'To Galen. His anagram'
> fb.217, p. 265

H0614 Here a queer hulk lies poor Tom Bowline
Her lodging in the loft.

> [John Walker?], 'Tom Bowline a parody' [of Crum
> H652, on Tom Bowling]
> fc.108, fol. 77

H0615 Here Abbot, virtue's great example lies,
To heaven, than that it stay'd so long below.

> 'An epitaph on Mordecai Abbot esquire'
> c.244, p. 88

H0616 Here am I great Dermot Monaghan as great as any
lord
To kill and cut the throats of all the foes. | Whack
fal &c. of old Hibernia

> [John Walker?], 'The Irish recruit'
> fc.108, fol. 24

H0617 Here an old volume lies,
'A neat new, corrected edition!'

> 'Mr. James Leah, an eminent bookseller of Bath,
> desired a gentleman, in 1750, to writh an epitaph upon
> him, and presented him with an elegant Greek
> testament for the following impromptu'
> c.82, p. 22

H0618 Here Andrew lies yet vexed with a wife
Did 'cause his brother Peter shut her out.

> 'On Andrew Leigh'
> fb.143, p. 36

H0619 Here Antoninus spells thy Latin name
He'd nick't myself in my design.

> [Sir Philip Wodehouse], 'Antoninus Nicke my
> chaplain'
> b.131, back (no. 200)

H0620 Here Aretine interr'd doth lie
His God, he said, he did not know.

> 'Epitaph on Peter Aretine'
> Poetry Box VIII/68

H0621 Here Aretine lies reduc'd to earthly clod
But his excuse was this he did not know Him.

> 'On Peter Aretine a satirist in the fifteen[th] century'
> fb.143, p. 4

H0622 Here Aretine sincerely sets to view
Nor would, tho' to show wit, from wisdom stray.

> R[obert] Shirley, 1st earl of Ferrers, 'Written in
> Aretine's book'
> c.347, p. 67

H0623 Here as John came, here so he went;
And fairly snor'd away the other.

> John Lockman, 'La Fontaine's epitaph: writ by
> himself'
> c.267/4, p. 183

H0624 Here Bateman's hand first bade my waters flow,
So great a blessing were my fountain dry.

> 'Designed for a fountain in Lord Bateman's park at
> Totteridge, Hertfordshire. 1730'
> c.221, p. 24

H0625 Here biting Aretine lies buried
His reason was, because he knew Him not.

> 'On the arch-atheist Aretine the Italian'
> [Crum H661]
> b.200, p. 221

H0626 Here Blacow lies
That long they may rob and confound us.

   'Here lies the odious remains of Richard Blacow . . . .'
Poetry Box x/93

H0627 Here Britain's statesmen oft the fall foredoom
With singing laughing ogling and all that.

   Alexand[e]r Pope(?), 'On Hampton Court'
b.155, p. 68

H0628 Here buried lies within this hallow'd ground
And thereby hindered him to go his round.

   [Sir Aston Cokayne], 'An epitaph on Mr Peter
   Allibond'
b.275, p. 81

H0629 Here Car'line rests and round this tomb
That brother's love and constant woe.

   [Robert] Merry, 'A[n] epitaph for Lady Caroline
   Seymour written by . . . for Lord Cowper her brother'
Greatheed Box/9

H0630 Here Charles the best of monarchs butcher'd lies
The world ne'er saw but one, nor can again.

   'An epitaph on King Charles I'
b.137, p. 200

H0631 Here, child, thy own bright mother is the toast!
As nothing could repair—but such a son.

   [Charles Montagu, 3rd earl of] Halifax, 'Hannibal's
   good genius. Livy 21 and 22, spoke extempore by . . .
   to the present Duke of Grafton . . .'
Spence Papers, folder 113

H0632 Here Chloe lies | Whose once bright eyes
Ungrateful, she | Did all the world admire.

   'Epitaph'
c.115; c.360/3, no. 10

H0633 Here Cumberland lies, having acted his parts,
He grew lazy at last, and drew from himself.

   [Oliver] Goldsmith, 'Character of Mr. Cumberland'
c.83/3, no. 739

H0634 Here Dr. Lamb the conjuror lies
Among the goats to see a Lamb.

   'On Dr. Lamb the conjuror'
b.356, p. 244; fb.140, p. 8 ('Lamb the comicer')

H0635 Here Dr. Richard Prichard lies,
Here's nothing here but his bare stones.

   'On one who built his monum[en]t before his death'
c.233, p. 67

H0636 Here does the shadow of a shadow stand:
There once was such a wretched thing as me.

   Henry Graham, 'Mr Henry Graham on his own
   picture'
b.204, p. 55

H0637 Here doth lie the good old knight Sir Harry
He doth lie and she is kneeling.

   'On old Sir Harry [Leigh]'
fb.143, p. 34; see also 'Here lies the good old knight . . .'.

H0638 Here ends a jolly woodman's course,
And clove his block asunder.

   H[enry] Skrine, 'Epitaph . . . Warley Sep. 26. 1777'
c.509, p. 7

H0639 Here ends notwithstanding her specious pretenses
She was too bad a daughter and too good a wife.

   'The royal epitaph' [on Mary II, d. 1694]
   [Crum H680]
fb.207/1, p. 11; see also 'Here lies . . .'.

H0640 Here fast asleep, full six feet deep
And the first that found the way.

   [Crum H681]
c.233, p. 118; see also 'Here five foot deep . . .'.

H0641 Here Ferdinando Earle of Huntington
Courtesy and good nature here do lie.

   [Sir Aston Cokayne], 'An epitaph on Ferdinando Earle
   of Huntington'
b.275, p. 85

H0642 Here festering rest a quondam plague of earth
Printed and sold by Simpson next the Fleet.

   'Epitaph'
Poetry Box xii/24

H0643 Here five foot deep
And first that found that way.

b.200, p. 379; see also 'Here fast asleep . . .'.

H0644 Here from the restless bed of lingering pain
And whose sad inmate—is a broken heart?

   [Charlotte (Turner) Smith], 'Sonnet written at Bristol
   in the summer of 1794'
c.141, p. 104

H0645 Here Gascoigne lies that brave heroic he,
Their utmost malice cannot reach thee, there.

   'An epitaph on Mr. Gascoigne'
c.570/1, p. 160

H0646 Here Grubbinol lies
A friend, yet was dead long before him.

> [Lionel Cranfield Sackville, 1st duke of Dorset], 'On the Duke of Bolton's dying from too large a dose of cathartics'
>
> fc.135

H0647 Here, hail thou melancholy beam
Hail to thy silver soft inspiring beam!

> 'Address to the moon'
>
> c.344, p. 47

H0648 Here, Hermes says Jove, who with nectar was mellow,
Your Hermes, shall fetch him, to make him sport here.

> [David] Garrick, 'Jupiter and Mercury a fable'
> [Crum H694]
>
> c.83/3, no. 737; c.90

H0649 Here Hobbinoll lies, our shepherd while'er
In spite of his tar-box, he died of the scab.

> Sir Walter Raleigh, 'Upon Sr Robert Cecil, earl of Salisbury and Ld. Treasurer'
> [Crum H695]
>
> b.54, p. 880; see also 'Here lies Hobbinoll . . .'.

H0650 Here Hobson lies amongst his many betters,
And supreme wagoner, next Charles his wain.

> '[Thomas] Hobson's epitaph the Cambridge carrier'
> [doubtfully attrib. John Milton]
> [Crum H696]
>
> b.200, p. 225

H0651 Here Hobson the merry Londoner doth lie
He thereupon took pot and so did die.

> 'On Hobson the merry Londoner'
>
> fb.143, p. 33

H0652 Here Hocus lies with his tricks and his knocks
While death play'd the hocus and brought him to
th' pot.

> 'On a hocus-pocus'
>
> fb.143, p. 31

H0653 Here honest Micoe lies who never knew
Sat vigilati bonus nachios Micoe.

> 'On the worthy and truly vigilant Sam. Micoe esq.'
>
> fb.143, p. 30

H0654 Here I am | Riding upon a black ram,
Therefore, good master steward, let me have my
lands again.

> 'Curious villenage tenure'
>
> c.81/1, no. 497; c.360/3, no. 149

H0655 Here I lie entomb'd at my master's expense
To show all my virtues, and his want of sense.

> 'The dog's answer' [to 'The female who within this tomb . . .']
>
> c.150, p. 39

H0656 Here I lies, no wonder I'm dead
For a broad wheel wagon went over my head.

> 'Epitaph'
>
> fc.14/8

H0657 Here I sit half the day, here I weep
Of grim death sends my corpse to the tomb.

> 'The dumps' [second of 'Two pastoral ballads']
>
> Poetry Box IV/69

H0658 Here I stand with all my might,
And serve thy God, as I serve thee.

> 'On a clock May 1st 1783'
>
> c.93

H0659 Here if my spotless fair one look bestows
To hers what Marcia was the same to me.

> 'To Sylvia wrote in the first leaf of Addison's Campaign Cato and Rosamond bound up together and presented to her'
>
> Poetry Box I/35

H0660 Here in cool grot, and mossy cell,
Who dares our hallow'd haunts profane!

> [William Shenstone], 'Preparing your entrance to the Priory Walk'
>
> c.20/1; c.21

H0661 Here in the bow'r of beauty newly shorn
And tender pity softens into tears.

> 'The birth of Cupid'
>
> c.546

H0662 Here in the consecrated earth enshrin'd,
Maria lives—and is—herself again.

> 'To the memory of Miss Maria Carr'
>
> c.83/3, no. 1003

H0663 Here in the Tower's to be seen
A Yorkshire wolf without a screen.

> 'Fixed on the walls of the Tower of London in April 1721'
>
> c.360/2, no. 94

H0664 Here in this shady lonely grove
Calm as those seats above, which know no storm
nor wind.

> c.549, p. 3

H0665   Here innocence and beauty lies—whose breath
Is the next blessing to a life well-spent.

c.163, p. 20; see also 'Here sweetness . . .'.

H0666   Here is a thing that nothing is,
Doth feed on nothing but itself.

'A riddle' [answered by 'As I've no penetrating
brain . . .']
c.578, p. 25

H0667   Here is an old song made by an old ancient pate
That good housekeeping is nowadays grown so cold. |
Alteration &c.

'Song 155'
c.555, p. 216; see also 'With an old song . . .'.

H0668   Here is Elderton lying in dust
For who knew him standing all his life long.

'Epitaph the 21 upon a liar [William Elderton, a
drunken ballad maker]'
[Crum H713]
c.158, p. 105; fb.143, p. 11

H0669   Here is much lov'd Celia laid
And to the ears of all her neighbors.

'Epitaph'
c.546

H0670   Here is [no] more news then virtue; I may as well
At court; though from court were the better style.

[John Donne], 'From the court'
b.114, p. 215; see also 'Here's no more news . . .'.

H0671   Here is recorded many names
Dwelling with him in peace and rest.

[on Foxe's Martyrs; written on a fly-leaf extracted
from a copy of that work.]
Poetry Box IV/14

H0672   Here lays Joan Kent, who when her glass was spent
Kick'd up her heels, and away she went.

'An epitaph in the churchyard at Bury'
c.360/2, no. 39

H0673   Here lays the actress Mrs. Clive
No more she'll play, no more she'll swive.

Captain [ ] Sheldon, 'Epitaph by . . . on the false
report of Mrs Clive's death'
c.360/1, p. 325

H0674   Here let me rest; where spreads this hallow'd shade
And, after life, your ashes honor'd rest.

'A rhapsody written at the tomb of Rousseau, Augt.
31th 1788'
c.344, p. 38

H0675   Here lie Father Mother and I who all died in one
year
Father and Mother were buried at Water Eaton,
but I am buried here.

'Another [tombstone inscription] in St. Giles Oxon'
c.74

H0676   Here lie I, Martin Ellenbrode,
And you were Martin Ellenbrode.

'Epitaph in Edinburgh churchyard'
c.113/11; see also 'Here lig I . . .'.

H0677   Here lie I quiet, now transform'd to dust,
Sleeping in death, as other mortals must.

[Sir Francis Castillion], 'Finis coronat'
fb.69, p. 192

H0678   Here lie I | Who did die
By a sky | Rocket in my eye.

'A country epitaph'
c.360/2, no. 233

H0679   Here lie three knights, grandfather, father and son,
Sir Edward, Sir Edward, and Sir Edward Littleton.

'Epitaph on the three Sir Edward Littletons'
c.360/3, no. 119

H0680   Here lies a blessed virgin
Nor e'er will have another.

'An epitaph on . . . Mrs. Anne Luther . . .' [d.
16 October 1680]
b.54, p. 1134

H0681   Here lies a body that gave lodging to
The joy of mankind living, now the grief.

[Sir Aston Cokayne], 'An epitaph on Colonel Ralph
Sneyde'
b.275, p. 65

H0682   Here lies a branch of Christ the vine
And praise Him to eternal day.

J. Turner(?)
c.487, p. 106

H0683   Here lies a captain that seldom drew sword
Here lies Buckingham, all the world's hate.

'On the D[uke] of B[uckingham]'
b.356, p. 248

H0684   Here lies a chandler dead I need not tell it
He could make many weeks [wicks] but not one day.

'On a chandler'
[Crum H733]
b.62, p. 53; see also 'Here lies a tallow chandler . . .'.

H0685 Here lies a child of high renown,
The workmanship of half the town.

'An epitaph on a bastard'

b.200, p. 413

H0686 Here lies a creature of indulgent fate,
By his preposterous translation.

'The epitaph' [to 'The youth was belov'd . . .'; satire
on Laurence Hyde, 3rd earl of Rochester; answered by
'Here lives a peer . . .'.]
[Crum H737; POAS IV.98]

fb.70, p. 195; b.204, p. 44; fb.108, p. 95

H0687 Here lies a dog yclept honest Pincher
His life was ended by suspension.

'Pincher'

c.81/1, no. 225

H0688 Here lies a gallant, a gentleman of note
Who living could never change a groat.

'Epitaph 7th [on a spendthrift]'
[Crum H741]

c.158, p. 104; fb.143, p. 7

H0689 Here lies a good woman to speak but the truth
That she cried a *peccavi* for all her lewd courses.

[Sir Aston Cokayne], 'Of a penitent bawd'

b.275, p. 63

H0690 Here lies a horse that died, cut
Should make him go that made him lame.

'On a horse'

fb.143, p. 36

H0691 Here lies a John, a burning shining light
Whose name, life, actions, all alike were White.

'On John White esq'

fb.143, p. 24

H0692 Here lies a juggler under this stone
To whom Death said presto begone.

'On a juggler'

b.356, p. 244; File 19344

H0693 Here lies a knight in London born
Twice seven and six times ten.

'On Sr Tho: Blank Ld. Mayor' [d. 28 Oct. 1588]

fb.143, p. 8

H0694 Here lies a lord that wenching thought no sin
As he did rob the country, with the city.

'Another' [on Thomas Buckhurst, Lord Treasurer in
King James I's time; see also 'Uncivil death . . .']

fb.143, p. 43

H0695 Here lies a man as God shall me save,
For if he gapes—y'are gone by G[o]d.

'The following lines were written on a man of
Coleshill Warwickshire who was remarkable for
having the largest mouth in the parish, and actually
engraved on his tombstone'

c.391

H0696 Here lies a man, nor pagan, Turk nor Jew
'Tis Strange indeed, but not so Strange as true.

'On one Strange'

b.356, p. 247

H0697 Here lies a man who lov'd his horse
In honor to his name.

'On a tombstone in the churchyard at T[h]ame in
Oxfordshire on Joseph Rigby . . .'

c.360/1, p. 161

H0698 Here lies a mouse that on a winter's day
As *ne plus ult*—in love, is *ne plus ult*—in life.

R[obert] Shirley, 1st earl of Ferrers, 'To the beaux. An
epitaph upon a lady's mouse that died in the seat of
love'

c.347, p. 68

H0699 Here lies a pattern for the human race,
Is all the duty beast or man can pay.

c.94 (incomplete?)

H0700 Here lies a Peck! Which some men say,
And here he lies, a Peck of dust.

'Epitaph on Mr. Peck'

c.81/1, no. 347

H0701 Here lies a peer, beneath this place
That shot him. | I'll say no more.

[Sir Fleetwood Sheppard?], 'An epitaph on the Duke
of Grafton, who was killed at the siege of Cork in
Ireland' [1690]
[Crum H761a; POAS V.223]

b.111, p. 143; b.204, p. 8; fb.143, p. 29

H0702 Here lies a peer; whose look was form'd to move
And bid thee welcome to the world unknown.

[Joseph Spence?], 'A heathenish copy of verses,
designed to be addressed to the E. of Middlesex [later
Charles Sackville, 2nd duke of Dorset], whenever he
pleases to die'

Spence Papers, folder 149

H0703 Here lies a piece of Christ, a star in dust,
Be used in heaven, when Christ shall feast the just.

Robert Wild, 'For a godly man's tomb'
[Crum H761b]

c.166, p. 312; see also next.; c.360/3, no. 126 ('on Anne
Green a Quaker')

H0704 Here lies a piece of Christ, a star in dust,
Though young like fruit when ripe she fell.

'. . . Epitaph, on a rail erected to the memory of Mrs.
Mugridge, who died in 1755, aged 36 years, wife of
Emanuel Mugridge, and two children who died
infants, and a grandchild in 1776, aged four years'
c.487, p. 105; see also previous.; c.547, p. 86

H0705 Here lies a piece of heaven, and heav'n one day,
Earth shall give up her part, and heaven take all.

'On the death of a young lady'
c.378, p. 68

H0706 Here lies a pinner O thou cruel death!
Made better dust than thou canst make of him.

'On a pinner'
b.356, p. 249

H0707 Here lies a proof that wit can never be
Defense enough against mortality.

'Another [epitaph] on the famous Mrs. [Aphra] Behn'
[1689, Westminster Abbey]
[Crum H762]
fc.60, p. 119 (first two lines)

H0708 Here lies a smith that died of late
Meaning I think to pick the lock.

'On a smith'
b.356, p. 246; see also 'A zealous locksmith . . .'.

H0709 Here lies a tallow chandler, I need not tell it
He that made many weeks [wicks], can't make one day.

'On a tallow chandler'
[Crum H766]
fb.143, p. 36; see also 'Here lies a chandler . . .'.

H0710 Here lies a virgin, sacrific'd to death,
Weep reader, and show virtue in your eyes.

[( ) Brockhurst], 'Epitaph by a gentleman that courted
a lady, which lady died for love of another'
c.83/1, no. 210

H0711 Here lies a woman good without pretense
The saint sustain'd it, but the woman died.

[Alexander Pope]
File 13409; see also 'Here rests . . .'.

H0712 Here lies a woman, no one can deny it,
You gently tread for if she wake she'll talk.

'Epitaph' [on Dr. Fuller's wife]
[Crum H769]
fb.207/2, p. 100; b.62, p. 42; fb.143, p. 19; b.356, p. 249

H0713 Here lies a woman that died for want of breath
Who when alive would talk a dog to death.

fb.143, p. 9

Here lies a woman under this marble stone
Who when alive lay under more than one.

fb.143, p. 9

H0714

Here lies an honest cobbler whom curst fate
Honest John Cobbler lies here underlaid.

'Upon the death of a cobbler'
[Crum H774]
b.62, p. 52; fb.143, p. 27; b.356, p. 246

H0715

Here lies an old bawd (whom the grave should have
gotten
The more we stir in it the more it will stink.

[Sir Aston Cokayne], 'Of an old bawd'
b.275, p. 63

H0716

Here lies an old woman,
She got there before seven.

T[homas] Holland, of Jesus College, Oxford, 'Epitaph
on a person [Old Mother Allen] famous for ticking at
Oxford dying before 6'
[Crum H776]
c.233, p. 9

H0717

Here lies antiquity involv'd in dust
Young men may die, but old men must.

'On an old man'
b.356, p. 243

H0718

Here lies at least a fathom deep
And reach the port of heav'n at last.

'Epitaph on a sailor'
c.150, p. 144

H0719

Here lies at least ten in the hundred
'Tis a hundred to ten, he's scarce gone to heaven.

'On an usurer'
[Crum H778]
fb.143, p. 15; see also 'Here lies ten . . .'.

H0720

Here lies buried father, mother, sister and I,
But I was buried here.

'An epitaph'
c.378, p. 42

H0721

Here lies by we
Our children three.

c.74

H0722

Here lies Captain Wildbore
Betwixt two rogues and a whore.

'On Captain Wildbore'
fb.143, p. 28

H0723

H0724 Here lies Catherine, Anne and Mary Riggs
And honest Andrew who h—m'd all their gigs.

'An epitaph in a churchyard in Bedfordshire . . .
Englished'

c.360/3, no. 114; c.81/1, no. 502

H0725 Here lies Charles the First, the great
The honest man, the righteous king.

[Crum H786]

c.160, fol. 103

H0726 Here lies crafty Joan deny it who can,
Whilst one leg stood still the other was running.

'An epithet on Joan Trueman who had an issue in her
leg'
[Crum H788]

c.356; see also 'Here lies Joan . . .'.

H0727 Here lies David Garrick, describe him who can,
And Beaumonts and Bens be his K[el]lys above.

[Oliver] Gold[smith], 'Retaliation a poem'

fc.85, fol. 107v (incomplete); c.83/3, no. 738 (incomplete)

H0728 Here lies Dick! A baker by trade
In hopes that his bread may be raised.

'Epitaph on a baker'

c.113/5; see also 'Beneath the dust . . .', 'Under this
dust . . .'.

H0729 Here lies Dick Primer, O most envious death!
Make better dust, than thou canst make of him.

[Thomas Bastard], 'On Dick Primer'
[Crum H794, 'Dick Pinner']

fb.143, p. 34

H0730 Here lies Doctor Evans
Who died as he liv'd, at sixes and sevens.

[on Dr. Evans of Oxford]

c.360/3, no. 8

H0731 Here lies Doctor Tindal
Who ne'er pray'd on his own.

Dr. [ ] W—n, 'An epitaph on Dr. [Matthew] Tindal
fell[ow] of All Souls, who turned Roman Cat[holic] In
King James' reign'
[Crum H797b]

c.233, p. 61

H0732 Here lies dry eyes, read not this epitaph
Heroic Henry, Atlas of our hope.

'Lachrymæ lachrymarum a funeral elegy' [on Henry,
prince of Wales, d. 1612]
[Crum H797c]

b.205, fol. 6r

H0733 Here lies Du Vall. Reader if male thou art
Du Vall the ladies' joy Du Vall the ladies' grief.

'On Monsieur Du Vall'
[Crum H799]

fb.143, p. 34

H0734 Here lies Dumbelowe
His heart had not broke.

Ben Jonson, 'Mr. [Richard] Dumbelow who died of
the wind colic'
[Crum H798]

b.197, p. 47

H0735 Here lies Elizabeth Thomas Reynolds his wife
Two died before her, and three she left alive.

'Upon a fair tomb is this inscription'

Poetry Box VII/55

H0736 Here lies enshrined in a marble veil,
A saint's installed in the courts of day.

[Thomas Robinson?], 'An elegiacal epitaph upon the
death of the most gracious Queen Ann'

fb.144, end

H0737 Here lies entrenched a veteran brave
And death resign his captive prize.

'Epitaph on a soldier'

c.113/10

H0738 Here lies exposed beneath this sculptured stone
And hails the shade of Douglas with a sigh.

[ ] Dunlop, 'Epitaph on Douglas Duke of Hamilton
dec. written by . . . of Glasgow'

Poetry Box XII/14

H0739 Here lies fair and virtuous dust
And death made grave her marriage bed.

'Found in Stanwick churchyard in 1500 and odd'

c.547, p. 232

H0740 Here lies fair Luce, that pick't hatch't drab
Of the great whore of Babylon.

'An epitaph on Luce Morgan'

b.197, p. 68

H0741 Here lies father mother sister and I
And I be buried here.

[John Godfrey], 'Epitaph'

c.150, p. 128

H0742 Here lies Grashen an honest blackamoor
In Tutbury died, and here lies buried.

[Sir Aston Cokayne], 'An epitaph of Grashen, a
servant of mine'

b.275, p. 112

H0743 Here lies he underneath this stone
There's none that knows, nor none that cares.

'On a usurer'
[Crum H815]

fb.143, p. 1

H0744 Here lies he where no man sees
Less sums his reckoning would have paid.

'On a courtier'

fb.143, p. 36

H0745 Here lies he who was born and cried
Told threescore years, fell sick and died.

'Epitaph the 10' [pr. Camden's Remaines, 1605]

c.158, p. 104; see also 'Here lieth he/one . . .'.

H0746 Here lies her type, who was of late
That she still lives in loyal hearts.

'In the p[arish] c[hurch] of St. Katherine
Christchurch' [on Queen Elizabeth]

fb.143, p. 23

H0747 Here lies his parents' hopes and fears
You'll say he's best that's first at home.

[Brian Duppa?], 'On a young infant'
[cf. Crum H760, H964]

b.356, p. 258; see also 'Here lies the . . .'.

H0748 Here lies Hobbinall, our shepherd while'er
In spite of his tarbox he died of the scab.

[Sir Walter Raleigh, 'Upon Sir Robert Cecil Lord
Treasurer']
[Crum H822]

Poetry Box VI/84; see also 'Here Hobbinoll lies . . .'.

H0749 Here lies honest Ned, | Because he is dead;
But since 'tis honest Ned | There is no more to be
said.

'The following droll epitaph is on a monument at
Chippenham iin Norfolk'

c.115; see also 'Here lies Ned Hyde . . .'.

H0750 Here lies honest Stephen, with Mary his bride
'Twill one day be ashes, and molder away.

'Epitaph on Stephen and Mary'

c.360/3, no. 35

H0751 Here lies Humphrey Gosling of London vintner
God send more Goslings to be such.

'Epitaph at St. John Baptist's at Westminster on
Humphrey Gosling a vintner'

c.360/3, no. 140; see also 'Here lieth . . .'.

H0752 Here lies Humphrey Salter
Than did from the builders of Babel.

'On the death of Mr. Humphrey Salter'

c.166, p. 182; c.536

H0753 Here lies in a dyke
One good office merits another.

'Translation of no. 18 [missing]'

c.360/3, no. 20; c.81/1, no. 483

H0754 Here lies interr'd the royal Caroline
Give loose to grief till we can weep no more.

'Epitaph' [on Queen Caroline]

fb.142, p. 67

H0755 Here lies interr'd this turtle Dove,
And bids this wicked world goodnight.

'An epitaph on Mrs. Mary Dove'

c.244, p. 211

H0756 Here lies interr'd under this tomb
Martha's cure and Mary's better part.

'Mr. [Anthony] Cumber's wife's epitaph'

c.158, p. ix; see also 'This silent grave . . .', 'She/The
dame that takes . . .', 'She who here . . .'.

H0757 Here lies Jack Careless
And died at length in the street.

'On a spendthrift'
[Crum H837]

fb.143, p. 36

H0758 Here lies Joan Trueman (deny it who can)
While one leg stood still the other was running.

'Upon Joan Trueman who died of an issue in her leg.
Epitaph'

b.197, p. 173; see also 'Here lies crafty Joan . . .', and
next.

H0759 Here lies Joan Goodman, deny it who can,
Th' one leg was standing whilst th' other was
running.

'On Joan Goodman having an issue in her leg'

b.65, p. 88; see also 'Here lies crafty Joan . . .', and
previous.

H0760 Here lies Joan of Arc, the which
Whether saint, witch, man, maid, or whore!

'Epitaph on Joan de Arc'
[Crum H844]

c.81/1, no. 384; b.65, p. 229; fb.143, p. 1; see also 'But
reader be content . . .'.

H0761 Here lies John Baker enrolled in mold
As undid the barber and starv'd up the lice.

> 'Upon one that was bald'
> [Crum H845]
>
> fb.143, p. 19

H0762 Here lies John Brown a man of but few words
He might have liv'd all the days of his life.

> 'Epitaph'
>
> c.360/3, no. 4

H0763 Here lies John Button, heaven and poles
Are graves become but Button-holes?

> 'An epitaph on John Button'
> [Crum H847]
>
> Poetry Box VII/5; c.360/1, p. 69; see also 'Cudd's life . . .',
> 'O heavens, O poles . . .'.

H0764 Here lies John Crooker a maker of bellows
He that made bellows could not make breath.

> 'Upon a bellows maker of Oxford'
> [Crum H848]
>
> c.158, p. 105; fb.143, p. 15; see also 'Here lies old
> Craker . . .'.

H0765 Here lies John Death, the very same
That went away with a cousin of his name.

> 'On one John Death'
> [Crum H849]
>
> fb.143, p. 35

H0766 Here lies John Duke of Marlborough
Died at St. James, buried at Westminster.

> Dr. [ ] Evans, 'A humorous epitaph on the great Duke
> of Marlborough by . . . of Oxford'
>
> c.360/3, no. 7; Poetry Box VIII/68

H0767 Here lies John Hall the university cap
That liv'd by the bell, and died by the clap.

> 'On one John Hall knocked down with the clap of a
> bell, and supposed dead'
> [cf. Crum H854]
>
> b.356, p. 247

H0768 Here lies John Hubberton
Hey for brave John Hubberton.

> 'On one Hubberton'
> [Crum H857]
>
> fb.143, p. 17

H0769 Here lies John Jones
What young John Jones? Aye.

> c.150, p. 77

H0770 Here lies John Trott, by trade a bum,
When he died, the devil cried, | Come, John, come.

> 'Epitaph on a bailiff—bum bailiff'
>
> c.360/3, no. 40

H0771 Here lies John Waugh of Barrow Hill
For what he was his good life did declare.

> 'An epitaph'
>
> c.360/2, no. 80

H0772 Here lies Jonson
His name was Benjamin.

> 'On Ben Jonson by himself' [misattributed?]
>
> b.356, p. 247

H0773 Here lies Julius Mazarin
This tomb is a robber's den.

> [R. W., trans.], 'The epitaph of Cardinal Mazarin'
> [Crum H864]
>
> Stair Papers, folder 19

H0774 Here lies lamented both by church and state
And unforgiven the forgiving died.

> 'Reply' [to 'An epitaph' on Queen Caroline by Lord
> Chesterfield: 'Here lies unpitied . . .']
>
> Poetry Box V/123

H0775 Here lies lamented much, and much belov'd,
They'll dwell in bliss to all eternity.

> 'Her epitaph' [Queen Caroline, d. 20 Nov. 1737]
>
> fb.142, p. 66

H0776 Here lies learning loyalty
Call it his shade for all his worth lies here.

> 'An epitaph on the late pious and learned
> Dr. [William] Sherlock'
>
> b.111, p. 208

H0777 Here lies lechery treachery pride,
Who swore God's wounds and so he died.

> 'In eundum' [Buckingham]
> [Crum H866]
>
> b.356, p. 242

H0778 Here lies little Lundy, a yard deep and more
Contribute some tears to water her grave.

> [Matthew Prior], 'Mrs. Lundy's epitaph' [docket title]
>
> fb.68, p. 123

H0779 Here lies Lycisca that was full of evil,
Her husband may walk in the road to Haven.

> [Sir Aston Cokayne], 'Of Lycisca who forc'd her
> husband to counterfeit his religion'
>
> b.275, p. 78

H0780 Here lies M. F. the son of a bearward
Three crookt Apostles, and six arrant whores.

'On [M. F.] one of a base condition and a notorious
liar, yet would have claimed kindred of a most noble
family'
[Crum H871]

fb.143, p. 17

H0781 Here lies Madam Wagg, and we hope she's at rest
She discreetly withdrew with a pack in her hand.

'Epitaph on Mad[am] Wagg who died playing at cards
with a pack in hand'

c.115; c.150, p. 51

H0782 Here lies Mary Beach, as by this stone appears
Since he lugg'd and he tugg'd at her bubby so long.

'Under the tombstone of Mary Beach, who nursed
A[lexander] P[ope] 38 years'

c.74

H0783 Here lies Mirandola, enough is done
His reputation travels with the sun.

[Robert Cholmeley], '[Johannes hic jacet . . . , on
Giovanni Pico della Mirandola] translated'

c.190, p. 45

H0784 Here lies Mr. Overton and here lies his wife
And hi, ho, for Mr. Overton.

'On one Mr. Overton'

b.356, p. 242

H0785 Here lies mother and babe both without sins,
Next birth will make her and her infant twins.

'On a gentlewoman and her child dying in childbed'

fb.143, p. 24

H0786 Here lies murder, treason, and ambition,
Dost thou not pay for murd'ring of the king.

'An epitaph upon Oliver Cromwell Protector'

fb.140, p. 10

H0787 Here lies my poor wife, without bed or blanket
But dead as a doornail, God be thanked.

'Epitaph'

c.360/2, no. 69

H0788 Here lies my wife,—Ah! that is fine,
As well for her repose—as mine.

'An epitaph'

c.94

H0789 Here lies my wife and great's my sorrow
Till so be as her I follow.

'Epitaph in Newport churchyard Isle of Wight'

fc.14/8

H0790 Here lies my wife in earthly mold
She had, but now I have my will.

'An epitaph'

c.536

H0791 Here lies my wife!—reader enough is said
Good only must be spoken of the dead.

'Epitaph'

c.115

H0792 Here lies N. a man of fame
The first of his house and last of his name.

'Epitaph 3' ['on N . . . . a mushroom']
[Crum H877]

c.158, p. 103

H0793 Here lies Ned Hyde,
So no more's to be said.

'Ep[itaph] on Chanr: Hyde's son'
[Crum H879]

b.155, p. 64; fb.143, p. 29; see also 'Here lies honest
Ned . . .'.

H0794 Here lies Ned West, of men the best,
And let him live again.

'On Mr West'

fb.143, p. 24

H0795 Here lies, notwithstanding all specious pretenses
Too bad a daughter and too good a wife.

[on Mary II, d. 1694]
[Crum H880]

Poetry Box VII/45; see also 'Here ends . . .'.

H0796 Here lies ———. Oh, what a pity!
The bones of Robert Newcity.

'N. B. his proper name was Newtown, but that would
not rhyme'

c.113/3

H0797 Here lies old Craker a maker of bellows,
He who made bellows, could not make breath.

'Epitaph (on a bellows maker)'

c.81/1, no. 168; see also 'Here lies John Crooker . . .'.

H0798 Here lies one dead under this marble stone
Who in her life lay under more than one.

'In eundem' [on the Lady Penelope Rich]
[Crum H888]

b.62, p. 80

H0799 Here lies one deep underground
That died on the pose, and yet was Sound.

'On one Sound'

b.356, p. 245

H0800 Here lies one enclosed under this brick
To pull out your p—— and piss upon her.

'An epitaph on a lascivious woman'
[Crum H890]
b.200, p. 412

H0801 Here lies one Foot, whose death may thousands save
For death himself has now one Foot i' th' grave.

'Epitaph on Mr. Foot'
c.360/1, p. 251

H0802 Here lies one in flower of youth
Ere long thy ruin and the end of me.

'On Master Kitchen'
fb.143, p. 36

H0803 Here lies one who for medicines would not give
Could he but think how much his fun'ral cost.

'Epitaph on a miser'
Poetry Box VII/5

H0804 Here lies one with his head full bare
Who with catching of conies left many a hare.

'In calvum'
b.205, fol. 44r; b.356, p. 247 ('skull quite')

H0805 Here lies our little baby Nancy
Both daughters of Thomas and Mary Rivers.

'Epitaph on Anne Rivers a child'
c.360/3, no. 132

H0806 Here lies our sovereign the king
Nor never did a wise one.

[John Wilmot, 2nd] earl of Rochester(?), 'King
Charles's epitaph'
c.176, p. 180; see also 'Here lives a great and might
monarch . . .'.

H0807 Here lies Penelope or the Lady Rich
Her that in life, was not content with two.

'On the Lady [Penelope] Rich'
[Crum H898]
b.62, p. 80; see also 'One stone sufficeth . . .'; 'She's dead,
who . . .'.

H0808 Here lies poor Dancer peace to her departed shade
And o'er her grave let fall one pitying tear.

G. B., 'Another [epitaph on Dancer]'
c.150, p. 126

H0809 Here lies poor Dick, devein'd (?) of breath
For now he's gone to pot.

'Epitaph on a drunkard'
c.113/1

H0810 Here lies poor duck; that Samuel Johnson trod on
For it would have been an odd one.

[Samuel] Johnson, 'Epitaph by . . . when five years old,
upon a duck, which he trod on and killed'
c.378, p. 65

H0811 Here lies poor Johnson, reader have a care,
Will tell you how he wrote, and talk'd, and
                                    cough'd— and spit.

Soame Jenyns, 'Epitaph on Dr. Johnson'
c.504, p. 100; c.90

H0812 Here lies puried under these stones
Her went to Cot by a fery mischance. | Law now.

'These verses were found written on a Welshman['s]
grave'
[Crum H785]
b.207, p. 15

H0813 Here lies Queen Anne Bullen,
Before in his leman.

'Upon Queen Anne Bullen [Boleyn]'
fb.140, p. 3

H0814 Here lies Randal Peter
Of Peter Randal of Oriel.

[ ] Bramston, 'Epitaph on Peter Randal of Oriel
College a remarkable glutton'
[Crum H903, 'Randolph']
c.74

H0815 Here lies, retir'd from busy scenes
He rises not till further orders.

'Epitaph on a marine officer'
Diggle Box: Poetry Box XI/32

H0816 Here lies Rich Hewett a gentleman of note,
He was wise because Rich and now you know all.

'On Rich Hewett'
fb.143, p. 33

H0817 Here lies Richard à Preen
And he that will die after him may.

'Epitaph the 11th'
[Crum H906]
c.158, p. 104; fb.143, p. 11; see also 'Here lies the body of
John . . .'.

H0818 Here lies Richard Hobbs
On whose soul Jesus have mercy amen.

'On one Hobbs' [buried in St. Martin's in the Fields,
19 Feb. 1561]
[Crum H907]
fb.143, p. 33

H0819   Here lies Richard Howkins who out of his store
        Until the appearing of our dearly beloved.

    'On Rich[ar]d Howkins'

    fb.143, p. 24

H0820   Here lies she, deny it who can?
        Who lived an old woman, and died a Newman.

    'On old Goody Newman'
    [Crum H911]

    c.233, p. 28; see also 'Here lieth . . .'.

H0821   Here lies she whom death befriended
        In Tower died born princess free.

    [epitaph on Lady Arabella Seymour, 1615, following
    epicedium, 'Too soon alas . . .']
    [Crum H914]

    b.197, p. 205

H0822   Here lies she whose spotless fame
        This grave is but a cabinet.

    'On Anne Littleton wife of Edwd. Littleton son and
    heir of Sr Tho: Littleton'

    fb.143, p. 10

H0823   Here lies Sir John Calfe of high renown
        Who was thrice mayor of this our town. | Honor
                                        honor honor

    'Epitaph' [on Sir John Calfe; answered by 'O cruel
    death . . .']

    c.150, p. 128

H0824   Here lies Sir John Shipsquire, an ell underground
        For he had no issue but one in his leg.

    'On Sir John Shipsquire'
    [Crum H916]

    b.356, p. 247

H0825   Here lies Sir Richard Salkeld that knight
        For as they are so we must be.

    'In Wetheral church in old characters almost
    obliterated'
    [Crum H921]

    c.547, p. 330

H0826   Here lies Sir Roger Nevison
        Cope, who did his sister marry.

    'On Sir Roger Nevison'

    b.356, p. 242

H0827   Here lies Sir Steven Somes with his head full low
        To whom death swore, before God you shall go.

    'On Sr Steven Somes' [who said 'Before God you
    shall go']
    [Crum H922]

    fb.143, p. 36

H0828   Here lies Sir Thomas Scott by name, O happy
                                        Kempe who bore him
        He spent and lookt for no reward he could not play
                                        the beggar.

    'An epitaph upon the death of the noble and famous
    knight Sir Thos. Scott of Scott Hall in the county of
    Kent, who died on the 30th day of December 1594'

    b.382(30)

H0829   Here lies sweet E. . . . n whose merit was such
        And the tear of affliction in torrents descend.

    [Helen Craik], 'Epitaph—upon the honorable Mrs.
    S——'

    c.375, p. 122

H0830   Here lies sweet Robin, gentle bird,
        In doing what he ought.

    'Epitaph on a Robin Redbreast'

    c.83/2, no. 519

H0831   Here lies ten in the hundred
        But his soul is damn'd.

    'Upon an old usurer'
    [Crum H923]

    c.158, p. 105; fb.143, p. 33; b.62, p. 42; see also 'Here lies
    at least . . .'.

H0832   Here lies the best and worst of fate
        The great man's volume, all time's story.

    [James] Shirley, 'Epitaph on George Villiers, Duke of
    Buckingham'
    [Crum H927]

    c.360/2, no. 53; Poetry Box VI/28

H0833   Here lies the best of men, whose life is at an end,
        Happy with him to all eternity.

    'An epitaph on Mr. John Hensham'

    c.244, p. 206

H0834   Here lies the body of a beauteous maid,
        And fear'd they would disturb her in the grave.

    'Epitaph on an old virgin'

    c.81/1, no. 385

H0835   Here lies the body of Anthony Baker
        Where just men's spirits perfect move.

    'Epitaph on a bellows maker'

    c.113/21

H0836   Here lies the body of Captain Tully,
        So shall the tenth when she doth die.

    'Epitaph on Capt. Tully mayor of Exeter'

    c.360/3, no. 109; c.360/2, no. 56

H0837 Here lies the body of Daniel Saul
Spitalfields weaver, and that is all.

'Epitaphs in Stepney churchyard [2]'
[Crum H931]

c.487, p. 89; Poetry Box VII/55

H0838 Here lies the body of John à Preen
And he that will die after him may.

c.360/3, no. 128; see also 'Here lies Richard . . .'.

H0839 Here lies the body of John Dry
His very ghost will go with you to law.

[Crum H932]

fb.143, p. 28

H0840 Here lies the body of Martha Dias,
Then gave to the worms which she refus'd men.

'Epitaph on an old maid'

c.360/3, no. 185

H0841 Here lies the body of Mrs. Power
Who delighted in doing good ever hour.

'Epitaph in Sutton Coldfield churchyard in
Warwickshire'

c.487, p. 71

H0842 Here lies the body of Sarah Sexton
I can't say that for her at the next stone.

John Sexton, 'By Jno. Sexton on his second wife's
tomb which adjoin'd that of his first wife'
[Crum H934, 'Mary Sexton']

c.250

H0843 Here lies the body of the golden maid
Of whom some gentle things will hence be said.

'The celebrated Miss Aurea Punto a beauty aetatis 19
died on Friday August the 8th 1746 . . . with this
epitaph . . . Englished'

c.360/2, no. 234

H0844 Here lies the brief of badness, vice's nurse;
All these, and more, lies here the Lady L[ake].

'An [ironic] epitaph on the Lady [Lake, widow of Sir
Thomas; buried 25 February 1642/3, but the verses
were probably written 1619–20]
[Crum H939]

b.200, p. 101

H0845 Here lies the carcass of a cursed sinner,
Doom'd to be roasted for the devil's dinner.

Robert Wild, 'For a wicked man's tomb'

c.166, p. 312; fb.143, p. 32

Here lies the carcass of a happy spirit,
Buried in a morning cloud.   H0846

'An epitaph for a youth'

c.189, p. 23

Here lies the collier John of Nashes
And being dead he is no more.   H0847

[Samuel Pick], 'On a collier'
[Crum H941]

fb.143, p. 21

Here lies the corpse of William Prynne,
Death crops the remnant of his lugs.   H0848

[d. 24 October 1669]
[Crum H943]

fb.140, p. 3

Here lies the day that darkness could not blind,
Set up this tomb, herself turn'd to a stone. H0849

'Upon brass plate in little Bradley church'

c.116, p. 37

Here lies the decoy-man, who liv'd like the otter,
And here he lies mold'ring, as you and I must. H0850

'Lately died at Whittington in Shropshire, Andrew
Williams aged 84. He served as decoy-man under the
Aston family . . . in the Blackmoor above 60 years, and
had retired of late upon a freehold at Whittington,
which he had purchased with the perquisites of his
place . . . [Northampton mercury, 1776]'

c.487, p. 97

Here lies the good old knight Sir Harry
He lies along, and she is kneeling.   H0851

'An epitaph on the monument of Sir Harry Leigh and
his paramour, on which were their effigies. His laying
at length, and hers kneeling'

c.360/1, p. 159; see also 'Here doth lie . . .'.

Here lies the governor of kings,
The vice of Italy, and faith of Rome.   H0852

'E[arl] of S[underland's] epitaph' [1702]

fb.70, p. 313

Here lies the great, the loyal, wise, Dundee
Thou brave, thou noble, thou divine, Dundee! H0853

'Dundee's epitaph' [1689]
[Crum H951]

fb.70, p. 237

Here lies the leg of Master Conder
The famousest surgeon of the nation.   H0854

'A gentleman in the north of England, having lost his
leg by amputation, caused a monument to be erected
over it in the churchyard where it was buried with this
inscription . . . 1725'

c.489, p. 19

H0855 Here lies, the Lord have mercy upon her
She died a maid the more the pity.

'Epitaph the 8th [upon one of the maids of honor to
Queen Elizabeth]'
[Crum H956]

c.158, p. 104; fb.143, p. 7

H0856 Here lies the man Richard
And the wife wore the breeches.

'On a tombstone in Essex'

c.113/33

H0857 Here lies the man that madly slain
One life to lose, another to live.

'On Anonymus'
[Crum H958]

fb.143, p. 18

H0858 Here lies the man who in life
Pray for his soul's health gentle brother.

'Upon a contentious man'
[Crum H959]

c.158, p. 104; fb.143, p. 11

H0859 Here lies the man whose horse did gain,
You or your horse rather to read it.

'Epitaph'
[Crum H961]

c.158, p. 104

H0860 Here lies the parents' hopes and fears
You'd say he's best that's soon'st at home.

[Brian Duppa?], 'On the death of a child'
[Crum H964]

b.62, p. 23; see also 'Here lies his . . .'.

H0861 Here lies the pattern of good men;
Was wrapt up in the Commonwealth.

'Epitaph on Sir R. D.'

Poetry Box v/106

H0862 Here lies the physician that never was doctor
That died in the year when the devil was proctor.

'On Dr. Butler'

b.356, p. 249

H0863 Here lies the relics of a martyr'd knight
To cut off Holland's head from England's
shoulders.

[Henry Hall, of Hereford], 'Epitaph on Sir John
Fenwick'

fb.207/1, p. 49; c.171, p. 9 ('injur'd knight')

Here lies the relics of a murder'd Earl   H0864
To join three nations, and their head together.

'An epitaph on the Earl of Derwentwater'
[Crum H968]

c.570/1, p. 161

Here lies the ruins of a lowly tent;   H0865
Heir to the double portion of his mind?

J. W., 'To the pious memory of the Revd. Mr. Samuel
Harvey, who died April the 17. 1729. aetat. 30 . . . an
epitaph'

c.259, p. 71; c.244, p. 664 ('lovely tent')

Here lies the ruins (who can but lament?)   H0866
The fate, and ruin of a rotten state.

Poetry Box vii/30, p. 4

Here lies the sacred bones   H0867
The Dutchman's *templum pacis*.

[Andrew Marvell], 'Upon [Clarendon's] house' [c.
1665]
[Crum H971]

b.136, p. 47

Here lies the son, here lies the mother   H0868
All but three bodies on my life.

'At Alincourt near Paris on the tomb of a mother and
her children'

fb.143, p. 2; c.81/1, no. 21

Here lies the worthy warrior   H0869
Whom earth and heaven hates.

[epitaph on Robert Dudley, earl of Leicester (d. 1588)
from 'Cecil's commonwealth']
[Crum H978]

fb.40, p. 224

Here lies Thom Dashe that notable railer   H0870
That in his life ne'er paid shoemaker nor tailor.

'On Thom Dashe'
[Crum H982]

fb.143, p. 18; c.158, p. 104

Here lies Thomas Cole   H0871
With his crimes undigested,—poor sinner.

'Epitaph'

c.113/7

Here lies thy urn, O what a little blow   H0872
How much thou wronged thy maker, how mankind.

[William Hemings], 'A contemplation over the Duke
[of Buckingham]'s grave' [1628]
[Crum H980]

Poetry Box vi/27

H0873 Here lies Tom Nicksbody
Whether fools' souls goes to heaven or hell.

    'On Tho: Nicksbody'
    [Crum H983]
    fb.143, p. 18; c.158, p. 105

H0874 Here lies two loving brothers side by side,
In one buried and in one day died.

    'On another'
    fb.143, p. 26

H0875 Here lies unpitied both by church and state,
And unforgiving, unforgiven died.

    [Philip Dormer Stanhope, 4th earl of Chesterfield],
    'An epitaph [on Queen Caroline, 1737]
    [Crum H984]
    c.154, p. 3; fc.135; Poetry Box v/123

H0876 Here lies Will Satter, honest man!
And leaves to other hands the reins.

    Rev. [ ] Loddington, 'Haddinoc . . . by the late . . .'
    Smith Papers, folder 74/12

H0877 Here lies William Banknot and Anne his wife
Say a Pater-Noster and an Ave.

    'On Wm. Banknot and Anne his wife . . . 1400'
    fb.143, p. 22; see also 'Pray for the soul of Maud
    Davy . . .', 'Such as ye are . . .'.

H0878 Here lies William Emerson
Who lived and died an honest man.

    [couplet in church of St. Mary Overy or St. Mary
    Savior's]
    [Crum H988]
    fb.143, p. 24

H0879 Here lies William Goodman
He d[ied?] a Good-man.

    'Upon William Goodman. Epit[aph]'
    b.208, p. 62

H0880 Here lies wise and valiant dust
Speechless still, and never cry.

    [John Cleveland? or Clement Paman?], 'Upon the
    Earl of Strafford's death which was 12 May 1641'
    [Crum H989]
    b.101, p. 113; b.137, p. 200; fb.143, p. 3; pb.47, endpaper

H0881 Here lies wrapt up within this bed of clay,
With his Redeemer, forever to be blest.

    'An epitaph' [on Dr Thomson, d. 11 March 1677;
    follows 'Must good men still die first . . .']
    b.54, p. 900

H0882 Here lieth C. underground,
Drink was his life, and drink was his end.

    'Epitaph the 5th [on a hard drinker]'
    [Crum H1002]
    c.158, p. 104; fb.143, p. 18

H0883 Here lieth Catherine Prettyman
And she shall be my wife.

    'Epitaph at St. Bennet's Sherehoy(?) in London. On
    Catherine Prettyman'
    c.360/3, no. 130

H0884 Here lieth Father Sparges
That died to save charges.

    'Epitaph 17' [pr. Camden's Remaines, 1605]
    c.158, p. 105

H0885 Here lieth Francis Benson, a citizen was he
Of other worthy Christians who evermore are blest.

    'AD 1570. primo Feb: on Francis Benson Merch[an]t
    Adven[turer]'
    fb.143, p. 6

H0886 Here lieth graven under this stone
Christ have their souls to heaven['s] bliss.

    'On Thomas Knowles [grocer and alderman] and Joan
    his wife of St. Anthony's'
    [Crum H1007]
    fb.143, p. 22

H0887 Here lieth he that lov'd well a wench
For carrying nothing hence but his good name.

    'On a lecher'
    b.356, p. 241

H0888 Here lieth he who was born and cried,
Told threescore years, fell sick and died.

    'On Anonymus'
    [Crum H1011]
    fb.143, p. 24; see also 'Here lieth one . . .', 'Here
    lies he . . .'.

H0889 Here lieth he whose rest if it be bad
It is because he wanted, yet he had.

    'On a bishop'
    b.356, p. 241

H0890 Here lieth Humphrey Gosling of London vintner
God send more Goslings to be such.

    'On Humphrey Gosling'
    fb.143, p. 22; see also 'Here lies . . .'.

H0891 Here lieth Menalcas, as dead as a log,
Without either book, candle, or bell.

'Epitaph: on Walter Milles'
[Crum H1030]

c.81/1, no. 148; c.158, p. 105; fb.143, p. 19

H0892 Here lieth now dead which once was quick
In heaven with Christ in joy and bliss.

'In another tomb'
[Crum H1033]

c.158, p. 42

H0893 Here lieth old Henry, no friend to mischievous
envy,
Henry place in kingdom, that is also named
Abingdon.

'An epitaph written [in Latin] by Sr Thomas More
upon . . . Henry Abingdon'
[Crum H1037]

b.207, p. 13

H0894 Here lieth one quite blown out of breath
Who liv'd a merry life and died a Meredith.

'On Mr Meredith the organ-blower'

c.233, p. 36

H0895 Here lieth one that was born and cried
Liv'd several years and then he died.

'Epitaph from Camden'
[Crum H1038]

c.360/1, p. 51; see also 'Here lieth/lies he . . .'.

H0896 Here lieth she deny it who can
The liv'd an old woman, and died a Newman.

'On one [Mrs.] Newman'

b.356, p. 243; see also 'Here lies she . . .'.

H0897 Here lieth Swift that swiftly fled
Yet here he lieth still if the worms have not eat him.

'Upon a melancholy man'

b.208, p. 57

H0898 Here lieth the body of Daniel Knight
To trust a canting false dissenter.

'In Luton church Bedfordshire . . . who died June the
11th in the 61st year of his age 1756'

c.74

H0899 Here lieth the body of Jo. Ball
Weaver of Spittlefields—that's all.

'On Jo. Ball'
[cf. Crum H931]

fb.143, p. 28

H0900 Here lieth the body of Roger Hog
They'd start up nimble on his trotters.

'Epitaph in Pork-Arlington churchyard'

c.113/23

H0901 Here lieth Walter Garden, come out of the west,
Pray for me, for I am gone.

'Epitaph at Saint John Baptist's in Westminster'

c.360/3, no. 134

H0902 Here lieth willing Wills
With his head full of windmills.

[epitaph on the whimsical Doctor Wills, who died at
Vienna c. 1630]
[Crum H1060]

c.158, p. 104

H0903 Here lieth wrapt in clay
I have no more to say.

'Epitaph [in] St. Michael's, in old London [on
William Wray]'

c.360/1, p. 167; fb.143, p. 22

H0904 Here lig I Martin Eltinbrode
And ye were Martin Eltinbrode.

'A Scotch epitaph' [Edinburgh churchyard]
[Crum H727]

c.360/1, p. 69; Poetry Box VII/5; c.361 ('Here liv'd Martin
Elden Brogue'); see also 'Here lie I . . .'.

H0905 Here ligs Mess Andrew Gray
For which God dom'd him when he dee'd.

'Epitaph in Glasgow churchyard in Scotland on
Andrew Gray'

c.360/3, no. 36

H0906 Here, like a Persian, prostrate laid,
Let me—kiss your pretty face.

[Charles Earle], 'Occasioned at a Christmas feast;
where it was proposed that every man, in turn, should
kneel at some woman's feet, and make verses, sing a
song or tell a tale. Extempore'

c.376

H0907 Here (like Leander [in the] Hellespont)
Past help, past hope, if now you fail I fall.

M. P., 'Ad amicam'

b.205, fol. 10r

H0908 Here lives a great and mighty monarch
Nor ever did a wise one.

[John Wilmot, 2nd earl of Rochester(?), 'Posted on
Whitehall Gate by my Lord Rochester'

c.189, p. 1; see also 'Here lies our sovereign the king . . .'.

H0909 Here lives a painter, a delightful thief,
He'll give a peep, and steal away your face.

John Lockman, 'Writ in chalk on Mr. Whood's door, in Bloomsbury Square'

c.267/1, p. 163; c.268 (first part), p. 12

H0910 Here lives a peer raised by indulgent fate
True to his God, and faithful to his trust.

'Panegyric on [Laurence Hyde, 3rd] E[arl of] R[ochester]' [1687; answer to 'Here lies a creature . . .']
[Crum H1063; POAS IV.99]

b.204, p. 44; fb.108, p. 89

H0911 Here lives the wolf justice that butcherly knave
We'll die at our door ere at Smithfield we'll burn.

'A lampoon on Lord Scroggs put on his door. Nov: 1679'

b.54, p. 1138

H0912 . . . Here love's divine (since all divinity
But to mark them [i.e., when], and where the dark
eclipses be.

[John Donne], 'Canzone [Valediction of the book]' [Crum H1125]

b.114, p. 290 (incomplete)

H0913 Here M. reposes whose merit was great
In calmness and credit she ended her days.

[Helen Craik], 'An epitaph on a friend'

c.375, p. 139

H0914 Here, Madam see in youth, in age, in prime
Think what a moment is—to him that dies.

'For Mrs. C—x's watch'

c.484, p. 60

H0915 Here malice, rapine, accident conspire,
And here a female atheist talks you dead.

'A fragment'

c.81/1, no. 305

H0916 Here may B—n read and choose
'Hope' shall point thee to the skies!

R[ichard] V[ernon] S[adleir], 'To Miss B—n with two copies of verses in different styles which she requested copies of—impromptu'

c.106, p. 114

H0917 Here may the eyes of an attentive mind
Yet never shall the gates of hell prevail.

[Edward] Sparke, 'Poem 29th—upon the feast of St. Peter'

b.137, p. 62

H0918 Here meanly clad in common clay are laid
The urn, the pyramid can do no more.

[ ] Brown, 'From a ms. of . . . written with a black lead pencil upon a gravestone near Oxford 1720'

c.221, p. 21

H0919 Here 'midst the friends he loved, the man behold
Uphold his greatness, and confirm his fame.

Georgiana [Spencer Cavendish], duchess of Devonshire, 'Inscription on the pedestal of Charles Fox's bust'

Smith Papers, folder 74/9

H0920 Here Mrs Brigit Allibond doth buried lie;
May see how maids belov'd can love again.

[Sir Aston Cokayne], 'An epitaph on Mrs Bridget Allibond'

b.275, p. 77

H0921 Here native genius gay, unique, and strong
But pow'rs like thine can only come from heav'n.

[Helen Craik], 'Lines written upon a blank leaf of Mr. Burn's poems'

c.375, p. 53

H0922 Here Newton lies, to whose all-piercing view,
Where, without end, he might new worlds explore.

'An epitaph on Sir Isaac Newton'

c.360/2, no. 202

H0923 Here night and Day conspire a secret flight
Tho' it was ne'er so dark, Day would be light.

'On John Day the poet, running away and bilking his landlord'

c.360/3, no. 157; c.170, p. 15 (var.)

H0924 Here now into this grave a man is thrust
Who is by drinking drunk as dry as dust.

'On a drunkard'

fb.143, p. 1

H0925 Here old Motteaux-al lies
His friend who was dead long before him.

'An epitaph on Mr. Peter Motteaux a dramatic poet who died by taking cantharides, and he was found dead in a common bawdy-house. This accident happened in the year 1718 and on his birthday when he entered the 58 year of his age'

c.360/3, no. 9

H0926 Here on a mount a ruin'd tower I spy,
And, as their sums increase, distend their hill.

James Ward, 'Mr. Pope's Miscellany vol. 2. Poem, Phoenix Park . . . page 193'

c.160, fol. 76 (incomplete)

H0927 Here once my princess, when we first did meet
So rare a gem should not be set in lead.

> [George Goad], 'On the print of his lady's foot, cut in
> King's College Chapel leads where before she had
> slipped and fallen'
> [Crum H1077]

b.356, p. 85

H0928 Here or elsewhere (all's one to you, to me)
Not how you end, but how you spend your days.

> Henry Marten, 'Harry Marten, when imprisoned in
> Chepstow Castle, some time before he died made this
> epitaph by way of acrostic on himself . . . aged 78'
> [1680]
> [Crum H1078]

c.240, p. 137

H0929 Here Parsons lies—oft on life's busy stage,
Respected knew to live;—lamented die.

> [epitaph on William Parsons, died 3 Feb 1795, aged 59]

Poetry Box v/9

H0930 Here pause fair fancy in thy flow'ry way
And scap'd that worst of labyrinths the world.

> 'Epistle 1 . . . written immediately after an imitation of
> Milton's three juvenile poems . . .' [28 Dec. 1744]

Poetry Box I/16

H0931 Here peaceful lies, beneath this marble tomb
But patterns leave, for ages that succeed.

> 'Epitaph on Lord Tamworth's tomb in Stanton
> Church, Leicestershire'

fc.51, p. 135

H0932 Here phoenix Butler lies whose precious mold
Than the whole kingly race of Ptolemies can boast.

> [John] Smith, 'An epitaph on [Samuel] Butler, the
> incomparable author of Hudibras'

fc.60, p. 58

H0933 Here Raphael lies by whose untimely end
Nature has lost a rival, and a friend.

> [ ] Pitt, of New College, 'Raphael's epitaph'

c.229/1, fol. 36

H0934 Here, Reader, mayst thou read for little cost,
Thou here mayst read, and see in little space.

> 'To the reader'

fb.69, p. 115

H0935 Here rests a woman good without pretense,
The saint sustain'd it, but the woman died.

> A[lexander] Pope, 'Epitaph on Miss [Elizabeth]
> Corbett who died of a cancer in her breast'

c.360/2, no. 187; c.83/2, no. 699; see also 'Here lies . . .'.

H0936 Here rest[s] a youth meant good without pretense
Or gave her parents grief but when she died.

> 'Epitaphs Bersted' [imitation of Pope's epitaph, 'Here
> rests a woman . . .']

c.546

H0937 Here rests his head upon the lap of earth
The bosom of his father and his God.

> [Thomas] Gray, 'An epitaph' [last lines of 'Elegy in a
> country churchyard']

c.156, p. 145

H0938 Here rests his head upon the lap of earth,
Nor dread the horrors of a tailor's hell.

> [parody of the epitaph in Thomas Gray's 'Elegy in a
> country churchyard']

c.362, p. 64

H0939 Here rests Lycisus, undisturb'd and freed
Poor Irus, of his guardian, and his guide.

> 'An epitaph on a blind man's dog'

c.83/1, no. 219

H0940 Here rests the gentlest of the gentle kind
All meet alike the inevitable grave.

> 'An epitaph'

c.341, p. 60

H0941 Here rests the musical Kit Shrider,
The loss of tuneful Kit bemoan.

> 'An extempore epitaph on the celebrated
> Mr. Christopher Shrider'

c.360/3, no. 108

H0942 Here rests, what once had ev'ry charm,
The gentle maid, despair'd and died.

> 'An epitaph on an unfortunate lady'

c.83/1, no. 199

H0943 Here Rogers sat, and here forever dwell,
To me, those pleasures that he sings so well.

> Henry Luttrell(?), 'Distich'

File 17071 (autogr.)

H0944 Here Sarum lies, of late as wise
For Marlborough and his Duchess.

> [Edward Ward], 'The Bishop of Sarum's epitaph'
> [Gilbert Burnet, 1715 (printed, Foxon W112)]
> [Crum H1093]

fc.58, p. 117; c.233, p. 55; see also 'Here Scotus lies . . .'.;
c.570/1, p. 5 ('Here Scotus')

H0945 Here shall our ling'ring footsteps oft be found,
When those who now lament her are no more.

W[illiam] Whitehead, 'In Lord Harcourt's gardens
Newenham S. N. of Frances Vis[countes]s
Palmerston'

c.391, p. 26; see also 'Her wit, her sense . . .'.

H0946 Here she lies, whose spotless fame
The grave is but a cabinet.

'Epitaph' [in the temple church in London, for Mrs.
Anne Littleton]
[Crum H1097]

fc.51, p. 80

H0947 Here silence with her hallow'd wand
Resigning life, I'll cheerfully obey.

R[ichard] S[impson], 'One my solitude an ode . . .
anno aetatis. 16'

File 13832

H0948 Here six foot deep in his last sleep
And the last that found that way.

'On the L[or]d of Lampasse'
[Crum H1101, 'Lamport']

fb.143, p. 34; see also 'Here fast asleep . . .', 'Here five
foot deep . . .'.

H0949 Here sleep the brave, who sink to rest,
To dwell a weeping hermit there.

[William] Collins, 'Ode on Westminster Abbey'

c.141, p. 303; see also 'How sleep the brave . . .'.

H0950 Here sleeps a man, who ne'er a friend deceiv'd;
Though born to die—we die to live again.

'Epitaph'

c.83/2, no. 270

H0951 Here sleeps, what once was beauty, once was grace,
The Christian yields an angel to his God.

[William Mason], 'Epitaph on Miss Drummond
aged 17'

c.221; c.130, p. 22; fc.132/1, p. 186; see also 'Hence! Stoic
apathy . . .'.

H0952 Here sleeps what was innocence once, but its snows
And the lily will bloom on her sod.

[John] Walcot [('Peter Pindar')], 'Corinna's epitaph'

c.141, p. 573

H0953 Here stands the monarch of a British throne
None but his whores e'er found him flesh and blood.

'Fixed on King George's statue'
[cf. Crum H1108, 'Here stands a thing usurps . . .']

c.570/2, p. 15

H0954 Here Stitch the tailor in his grave doth lie
Who by a stitch did live and by it die.

'On a tailor who died of a stitch'

fb.143, p. 35

H0955 Here (strangers) lies proud Sam of Oxon
But was at his own weapon beat . . . .

'Epitaphium. N. S. Samuel Oxon' [Samuel Parker,
bishop of Oxford, d. 1688]
[Crum H1110]

fb.108, p. 283 (incomplete)

H0956 Here Stuarts once in triumph reigned
And blast thy hopes of future fame.

[Robert Burns], 'On a window at Stirling'

Poetry Box v/65

H0957 Here sweetness lies and innocence, whose breath
Is the next blessing, to a life well spent.

'An epitaph on an infant'

c.244, p. 87; see also 'Here innocence . . .'.

H0958 Here take my picture, though I bid farewell
To feed on that which to disused tastes seems tough.

[John Donne], 'Elegia quinta' ['His picture']
[Crum H1112]

b.114, p. 83; b.148, p. 93

H0959 Here th'earthly parts of William Benson lies,
As is the robe, wherein his soul is dight.

'Epitaph at St. Olave's Church London on Mr. Benson
a linen draper'

c.360/3, no. 115

H0960 Here Thomas Saffin lies interr'd, ah! why
Who was the joy and comfort of his life.

'Stepney churchyard . . . [on Thomas Saffin]'

Poetry Box VII/55; fb.143, p. 26

H0961 Here those precious relics lie
God paid the loans with interest.

[Richard] Owen, of Oriel College, Oxford, 'An
epitaph on a gentlewoman'

b.62, p. 62

H0962 Here thoughtless Bromley lies: God rest his soul,
Who, of things mortal, left us but his pole.

John Lockman, 'Epitaph for a tippling barber, of
Plaistow, in Essex . . . this was literally true; he having
made away with everything else'

c.267/1, p. 9

H0963 Here, thrown by time, old Parkyns' laid;
As soon as he gets up again.

'April 1741. Died . . . at Bunny, in Nottinghamshire,
Sir Tho. Parkyns, bart. . . . His statue . . . on which
was wrote'
[Crum H1118]

c.94

H0964 Here, to man's honor and to man's disgrace,
Were God not mercy, when his creature's dust.

'An epitaph on that extraordinary character, John
Elwes esqre of Berkshire'

fc.132/1, p. 222; c.83/2, no. 401

H0965 Here to prevent this youth's approaching crimes
Nature his nurse led him to bed betimes.

'Another' [on the death of a child; last two lines of 'As
careful mothers . . .']

b.62, p. 24

H0966 Here two young Danish soldiers lie,
By sword was sever'd by a blow.

'Epitaph. St. Mary's, Beverley'

c.81/1, no. 263

H0967 Here unconstrain'd we both might live
No life so blest as ours.

Poetry Box x/88

H0968 Here under this stone is laid Mr. Lacke,
But now he is dead I will all to beshit him.

Mrs. [ ] Lacke, 'Mrs Lacke's epitaph on her husband
being dead with whom she lived an unquiet life
standing upon the stone'

b.197, p. 103

H0969 Here, underneath this lieth slain,
Will England never see again.

'Robin Hood' [epitaph]

c.81/1, no. 55

H0970 Here uninterred suspends (though not to save
Contend, to reach his body to his soul.

[Sir Henry Cholmley], 'Upon [John] Felton that
stabbed the Duke of Buckingham and was hanged in
chains'
[Crum H1129]

b.197, p. 27; b.200, p. 130; b.62, p. 19; c.160, fol. 104;
Poetry Box VI/27

H0971 Here view a man who lov'd the can
Here hangs the tankard, not the man.

'On a man who was a great drinker—but hanged
himself'

c.361

H0972 Here virtue, valor, charity call
Capel lies here loyalty's choicest glory.

'On the Ld. Capel beheaded' [1649]

fb.143, p. 5

H0973 Here we must rest: and where else should we rest?
Sepulcrum enim domus mea est.

[William] Austin, 'Mr. Austin's Sepulcrum domus mea
est. Job 17.13'
[Crum H1132]

b.65, p. 65

H0974 Here, when with unwithdrawing hand
Requites a timely friend.

[Thomas Hull], 'Occasional stanzas written in
retirement. To Maria'

c.528/31

H0975 Here, where I wander, and indulge in thought,
We darkly read, that superstition was,

[ ] Ellison, 'Finckale Abbey'

Greatheed Box/36; fc.74, p. 13 ('wander wrapped in
pleasing thought . . . 1766')

H0976 Here, where the Scottish muse immortal lives,
And heaven-born piety her sanction seals.

[Robert Burns], 'Written on the blank side of the
titlepage of a book presented to —'

c.142, p. 289

H0977 Here whereby all saints invoked are,
He that believes himself, doth never lie.

J[ohn] D[onne], 'A letter to the Lady Carey, and her
sister Mrs. Essex Rich from Amiens']
[Crum H1133]

b.148, p. 91

H0978 Here will I stop my progress, and restrain
Accordingly, now I believe are ended.

Sir Thomas Urquhart, 'The epilogue' [to 'Apollo and
the muses']

fb.217, p. 361

H0979 Here wisdom, quickt with inoffensive wit
O'er all religion stood, which speaks him best.

'Another [epitaph]'

b.104, p. 2

H0980 Here Withers rest! Thou bravest, gentlest mind,
The last true Briton lies beneath this stone.

A[lexander] Pope, 'An epitaph in Westminster Abbey
written by . . . 1729. on General Henry Withers'
[Crum H1138]

c.360/2, no. 197

H0981 Here, without martial prelude, am I come,
The sole return my present power can give.

> 'An epilogue spoken by one Morgan, a child of five years old after acting the mock tragedy of Tom Thumb, at the theater in the city of York, on Saturday February the 22 1752'
>
> c.360/3, no. 196

H0982 Here, worthy of a better chest,
This stone's too good to be engrav'd.

> R[ichard] Zouch, 'To the memory of Ben Stone of New Coll[ege]'
> [Crum H1140]
>
> b.200, p. 226

H0983 Here York's great Metropolitan is laid,
Who God's anointed and his Church betray'd.

> [John] Cleveland, '. . . That Eboracan Archbishop [John Williams] on whom Cleveland wrote this epitaph'
>
> fc.78, fol. 3

H0984 Here youthful innocence of humble birth
Each modest virtue that becomes thy state!

> [on Frances Kent, d. 1777, Eartham churchyard, Sussex]
> [Crum H1141]
>
> Diggle Box: Poetry Box XI/49

H0985 Hereafter my affection to the wise,
The other lifts too soon her petticoat.

> Sir Thomas Urquhart, 'A certain gentleman's resolution, to be no more inflamed with the passion of love'
>
> fb.217, p. 256

H0986 Hereby I naked, so th'anatomy
And in my soul, thy sacred laws engrave.

> 'The remedy for all our sins'
>
> b.137, p. 123

H0987 Here's a health to the glorious twenty-four,
Than the mystical sum of two hundred and four.

> 'On the number of members who voted against the late bill of excise being the same with the amount of the first eight square numbers in arithmetic . . .'
>
> c.570/4, p. 106

H0988 Here's a health to the jolly print cutter,
The merrier we shall be.

> 'Song 50'
>
> c.555, p. 76

H0989 Here's a health to the King about let it pass
And he's but a fop who asks which king I mean.

> 'A health to the King in dialogue' [Jacobite song]
> [Crum H1147]
>
> b.111, p. 38

H0990 Here's a health to the King and his royal successors,
To the downfall of Whigs and fanatical Rumpers.

> 'A loyal health on the marriage of the king [the Old Pretender]'
>
> c.570/2, p. 35

H0991 Here's a health to the King, to the King that
            prevails
They'll over a bottle compose new thanksgivings.

> 'A true swearing parson's health'
> [Crum H1149]
>
> b.111, p. 39; fb.68, p. 97

H0992 Here's a health to the king whom the crown does
            belong to,
And then 'twill be better for me and for you, boys.

> 'The loyal bumper being a health to the King, etc.'
> [Crum H1150a]
>
> b.111, p. 33; c.570/1, p. 70

H0993 Here's a health to the king, whom the people have
            chose,
May they still be betray'd, boys!

> 'Song'
>
> fb.70, p. 145

H0994 Here's a health to the man, that will wrong do to
            no man,
But here's his good health, and God save the true
            king.

> 'A health [to the Old Pretender]'
>
> fc.58, p. 168

H0995 Here's a House to be let for the Stuart [steward]
            hath swore
Kept it shut many years, but he paid for it at last.

> 'Fixed on the Parliament House door Febr. [16]79[/80]'
>
> b.52/2, p. 179; b.371, no. 16; Poetry Box VII/35; see also 'There is a House . . .'.

H0996 Here's a thing whose brain is sick
To be plac't in paradise.

> 'Song 51'
>
> b.4, fol. 41

H0997 Here's a tobacco shop and in the seller [i.e., cellar?]
Too bad almost for English imitation.

> Poetry Box VI/107

H0998 Here's an health to the tackers, my boys,
Will be surely a rogue on occasion.

'The health' [Tory rhyme before the general election, 1705]
[Crum H1155]
c.111, p. 116

H0999 Here's Evans the barber
If you open your lips.

'Written over the door of a sadler at St. Ives in Huntingdonshire'
c.361

H1000 Here's joy upon joy and bell upon bell
And for opening M—y's p[acke]t.

R[obert] Shirley, 1st earl of Ferrers, 'Spoken extempore upon the B—y of M—d and D—y of M—y'
c.347, p. 36

H1001 Here's Mother Bunch's little house under the hill
And tarts and cheese-cakes are their fare.

'Mother Bunch's house'
c.179, p. 62

H1002 Here's no more news then virtue; I may as well
At court; though from court were the better style.

[John Donne], 'From court'
[Crum H1158]
b.148, p. 71; see also 'Here is . . .'.

H1003 Here's Stiffy's picture, alias Stumpy;
It's so like nothing, nothing's like him.

'One one whose name was Stiffy, who refused to sit while his picture was drawing'
c.530, p. 181

H1004 Here's the doctor who opens your eyes;
And your consciences— of his own size.

[on Sacheverell's picture]
Poetry Box XIV/173

H1005 Here's three sure epithets which [in] her name
To be a lady nor too cold nor hot.

Fra[ncis] Lenton, 'Upon the model of modesty the truly virtuous virgin Mrs. Siceley Croftes / Anagram / Is yce, frost, cley'
b.205, fol. 17v

H1006 Here's to him and to't, and to him that shall do't,
And to him that would do't, if he could come to't.

'A health'
b.54, p. 1133

H1007 Here's to the maiden of bashful fifteen,
And e'en let us toast them together. | Let the toast
pass &c.

'Song 1'
c.555, p. 1

H1008 Here's to thee Dick; this whining love despise
None double see like men in love.

[Abraham Cowley], 'Ode'
b.135, p. 111

H1009 Here's your pure love, thus should true lovers woo
Scarce worth a fart; and so I owe you naught.

'Upon an escape straining for a compliment to his mistress'
b.104, p. 94

H1010 Hereunder lieth a man of fame
Thirteen hundred, fourscore and three odd.

'The epitaph on Sr W: Walworth, in St Michael's church in Crooked Lane, in old London'
c.360/1, p. 165

H1011 Hereunder rests an eunuch friend to no man
They should keep down and never raise his flesh.

'On an eunuch'
b.356, p. 245

H1012 Hermaphrodite in show, indeed a monster,
For wisest women sure have written none.

[Edward] Denny, 1st earl of Norwich, 'To the Lady Mary Wroth for writing The Countess of Montgomery's Urania'
b.197, p. 117

H1013 Hermes appear'd, not long ago,
And Algarotti equal Pope.

[Isaac Freeman], 'To Seignor Algarotti on his poem upon trade. Extempore Dryden'
fc.105, p. 1

H1014 Hermes the gamester of the skies
And let her fill it full of verses.

Poetry Box I/81

H1015 Hermit hoar, in solemn cell,
'Come, my lad, and drink some beer.'

[Samuel Johnson], 'Extracts from Hester Lynch Piozzi's memoirs of Dr. Johnson' [Johnson's parody of a contemporary poet]
c.504, p. 109

H1016 Herod, here mad as Hercules with rage
To see their choir so fill'd with cherubims.

    [Edward] Sparke, 'Poem 6th, upon the Feast of
    Innocents'

    b.137, p. 15

H1017 Heroic acts of Jacob's God we sing,
Egypt did haste to meet; but would avoid too late.

    [William Sandys?], 'The song of Moses, after the
    perishing of Pharaoh and his army in the Red Sea.
    Exodus Chap 15 to ver: 20'

    b.230, p. 15

H1018 He's all pedantical, and is his prose
Ab urbe condita our computation.

    Sir Thomas Urquhart, 'Of an affected school orator'

    fb.217, p. 110

H1019 He's bald without; because he lacketh hair:
But bald within, for lack of brains, you are.

    Sir Thomas Urquhart, 'To a foolish sot, who did
    deride an honest man, by reason of his baldness'

    fb.217, p. 317

H1020 He's bound for all he hath t'his predecessors:
But so will not to him be his successors.

    Sir Thomas Urquhart, 'On the virtuous son of
    virtuous parents'

    fb.217, p. 185

H1021 He's call'd your patient: though he be (I'm sure)
Doth more, than any sickness him misease.

    Sir Thomas Urquhart, 'To a bad physician on the
    virtue of whose recipes a certain infirm gentleman
    reposed the hopes of his convalescence'

    fb.217, p. 239

H1022 He's dead! The beauty of our see is fled,
That all our blooming sweets with him may die.

    'On the death of Doctor Jos. Butler bishop of Durham
    who died on [blank]'

    c.360/3, no. 240

H1023 He's done with all those transitory things
Nor doubt his wisdom or his faithfulness.

    [Thomas Gurney], 'The conclusion of a letter sent to
    my honored father on the death of my eldest son . . .
    departed in 1741. May the 1'

    c.213

H1024 He's duly thron'd and fits a chair of state
Three silver lions in an azure sky.

    [Sir Philip Wodehouse], 'Upon his noble kinsman Ld
    North Dudley North duly thron'd'

    b.131, back (no. 6)

H1025 He's fairly honor'd, who by fair ways
As well as birth, has sued his title forth.

    [Sir Philip Wodehouse], 'Upon his honored Uncle the
    old Earl of Dover H. Carey—Henry Earl of Dover
    fairly honor'd'

    b.131, back (no. 7/1)

H1026 He's fairly rec[eiv]'d in honor. For he knows
Keeping fit state, with fair complaisance.

    [Sir Philip Wodehouse], 'Henry Earl of Dover in
    honor fairly rec[eiv]'d'

    b.131, back (no. 7/2)

H1027 He's gone alas! The mighty man is dead
Who fell thy king and country's sacrifice.

    'A funer[c]al Pindaric ode to the memory of the truly
    loyal Mr. John Ashton' [1690]

    b.111, p. 93

H1028 He's hers alone and is all hers she is
Not his alone, nor yet is she all his.

    [Sir Thomas Urquhart], 'Of a chaste husband and
    unchaste wife'

    fb.217, p. 511

H1029 He's like a lusty soil, whose moisture feeds
If not a world of corn, a world of weeds.

    [Francis Quarles], 'On the knowing man' [Divine
    Fancies III, 58]

    b.137, p. 193

H1030 He's more a brute than any beast,
Not in reality, but name.

    [Edmund Wodehouse], 'Jan. 22 [1715]'

    b.131, p. 149

H1031 He's more [than] witless yet his willful throes
In toilful fears will [his] own death procure.

    'Temeritas in malum'

    b.205, fol. 13r

H1032 He's not the happy man, to whom is given
Thine is the fortune, and the mind is thine.

    [James Thomson], 'The happy man'

    c.244, p. 635

H1033 He's rich who craving nothing else doth find
Not to desire and have is all but one.

    [Sir Thomas Urquhart], 'A contented man is rich'

    fb.217, p. 500

H1034 Hey-day! Angelica cries out
But as a sister, let it live!

    [ ] Birch, 'Angelica Kauffman alarmed. To a lady'

    c.504, p. 40

H1035 *Hic jacet ille, qui centies et mille* did scold to his wife
Her name was Nan, who lov'd well a man | Then
gentlemen *vale.*

[macaronic epitaph]
[Crum H1192]

b.207, p. 14

H1036 *Hic jacet* John Shorthose
Sine cloak *sine* shirt, *sine* breeches.

'Epitaph 27 upon [Sir] John Woodcock mercer and
mayor of London 1405 buried in St. Albans in
Woodstreet'
[Crum H1193]

c.158, p. 106; c.360/3, no. 42; c.487, p. 89

H1037 '*Hic victor caestus artemque repono.*'
So here on his back lies the famous Broughton.

'Epitaph on Broughton. He was a noted pugilist and
died soon after he gave up his profession of boxing'

c.81/1, no. 197

H1038 Hicaulia travell'd to see Solomon
One in the body th'other by the mind.

[Sir Thomas Urquhart]

fb.217, p. 386

H1039 Hid within the hollow mine,
Such her crown and scepter hold.

[William Popple, trans.], '[Horace] book 2nd. Ode
2nd. To C. Crispus Sallustius'

fc.104/2, p. 118

H1040 Hide O hide, that charming creature
Let all the world besides be his.

fb.66/17

H1041 Hierusalem a city bright
That we may dwell with ye in heaven. | Amen

'The invention of S. Stephen. Au. 3'

a.30[20]

H1042 Higgledy piggledy here we lie
Pull'd and pick'd and put in a pie.

'Charade'

c.504, p. 205

H1043 High are the thoughts, whose buskin'd mistress sings
May ev'ry injur'd prince have such a day.

Charles Cotton, 'The battle of Yvry' [March 1590]

b.139, p. 1

H1044 High as thy genius, on the wings of fame
Lending such helps, your better part can give.

J. A. Hesse, 'Acrostic on Handel—1738'

c.360/1, p. 93

H1045 High drinkers are high sons of scorn
Which men misguide, flash out, and die.

[Sir Philip Wodehouse], 'Vino letus violantus'

b.131, back (no. 84)

H1046 High in midair the towering eagle bears
I seek the nightingale's and poet's lay!

William Parsons, 'Sonnet on going into the
country . . .'

Greatheed Box/12

H1047 High let us swell our tuneful notes,
Their own immortal strains!

P[hilip] Doddridge, 'The angels' song at Christ's birth
Luke II.14'

c.493, p. 68

H1048 High o'er Tintagel's echoing tow'rs
And join the murmur of the restless wave.

'The castle of Tintagel'

c.141, p. 163

H1049 High swells the ocean, when the moon's at [full]
And with her frown as basely counterbuft.

'Ignobilis natura'

b.205, fol. 10r

H1050 High tow'ring pride, is like the windy purse,
Empty flesh, fill'd with airy wind, heav'n's curse.

'Pride'

c.189, p. 41

H1051 Hip music! Music! Have you more to play
Yes, I'll lie snug till you have fix'd its fate.

[Arthur Murphy], 'Prologue to The Grecian daughter.
Spoken by Mr. Weston'

c.68, p. 91

H1052 Hippolyta greets Castalion—in this sign
And grateful'st praises for thy safe return.

'An epistle from the Lady Hyppolyta Taurella
Castalion di Mantua to his excellency the right
honorable Sr. Balthazar Castalion her husband . . .'

c.229/2, fol. 58

H1053 Hippomanes alone with hope inspir'd
But if you love keep him you love conceal'd.

[Charles Hopkins], 'The story of Hippomanes and
Atalanta in imitation of part of that in the tenth book
of Ovid's Metamorphoses'

b.130, p. 20

H1054 His absence makes me think I am
The winter of a summer's colder year.

   Lady Jane Cavendish, 'A song' [in a pastoral]
   [Crum H1215]

   b.233, p. 59

H1055 His angle-rod was made of sturdy oak,
He sat upon a rock, and bobb'd for whales.

   [John] Dryden(?), 'A giant angling'

   c.360/2, no. 125; c.81/1, no. 144

H1056 His arguments who money wants are sick,
Gifts now not words, are the new rhetoric.

   'New rhetoric'

   c.356

H1057 His armor is his honest thought
Secure in this thy tortoise-shell.

   [Sir Philip Wodehouse], 'Upon his kinsman . . .
   Maurice Barrow brave armor is'

   b.131, back (no. 167)

H1058 His being was for her alone
That tombs the two is justly one.

   Sir Philip Sidney, 'Epitaph from Sir Philip Sidney's
   Arcadia on Pamedorus and Musimela'
   [Crum H1216]

   c.391, p. 29

H1059 His black hairs, turning white, made a compact
With's mind, whose candor changeth daily in black.

   Sir Thomas Urquhart, 'Of an aged man, who, as his
   gray hairs multiplied, did proportionably increase in
   wickedness'

   fb.217, p. 311

H1060 His card is cut—long days he shuffled through
When the last trump is play'd his tricks will count.

   'Epitaph on a card maker'

   c.82, p. 26

H1061 His chimney smokes, it is some omen dire
His neighbors are alarm'd and cry out fire.

   'The miser's feast'

   c.546, p. 20

H1062 His Chloe's breast the bard of old
Is turn'd to yielding wax.

   'Waxen bosoms—an epigram'

   c.83/3, no. 1053

H1063 His commentar['s] a circle, whereof the
But in the centric point they never enter.

   [Sir Thomas Urquhart], 'Concerning a book written
   by a neoteric stoliast, the gloss whereof did not [?]
   with the meaning of the text'

   fb.217, p. 520

H1064 His course of glory finish'd here
And mounts exalting to the skies.

   [Phanuel Bacon], 'Epitaph on a lady of quality'

   c.237, fol. 80

H1065 His critic power thro' darkness, deep and dense
He turn'd depression into grateful pride.

   [William Hayley]

   File 6947

H1066 His disease was unknown, his grief was hid,
He cried, I die and so he did.

   'On one dying suddenly'

   fb.143, p. 36; b.356, p. 104

H1067 His eloquence persuades you so,
A wand'ring star, and hath no stay.

   Sir Thomas Urquhart, 'They that say most to it, prove
   not oftentimes the best lovers to a credulous lady'

   fb.217, p. 277

H1068 His enemies, her husband needs not fear
And by the same means they were got preserves
                                          them.

   [Sir Thomas Urquhart], 'Of a certain gentleman at
   out with many, and of his wife with whom many were
   at in, whose constitution of body was such, though she
   was too often versed in the secrets of the procreating
   faculty, that she would have no issue'

   fb.217, p. 514

H1069 His enemies, my husband should not dread,
With horns, for the defense.

   Sir Thomas Urquhart, 'The speeches of a certain kind
   woman whose husband had many illwillers'

   fb.217, p. 245

H1070 His first house was the Blessed Virgin's womb,
The next a cratch [crêche], the third a cross, the
                                          fourth a tomb.

   [Francis Quarles], 'On Christ's four houses' [Divine
   Fancies I, 8]

   b.137, p. 194; fb.69, p. 199

H1071 His grace declares he has no hopes and dies,
Who then can say the reverend prelate lied.

   'On the duke and bishop who buried [the Bishop of
   Rochester]'

   fc.24, p. 61

H1072 His heart's but care, his life's a carcass, and
Sickness his birth, his life at death command.

    'Man'

    c.356

H1073 His house being good why should you say, that he
As to 'ware changes on a man to keep it.

    Sir Thomas Urquhart, 'A good face put upon the
    parsimony of a certain aged gentleman . . .'

    fb.217, p. 83

H1074 His last great debt is paid. Tom is no more.
Last debt? Tom never paid a debt before.

    Diggle Box: Poetry Box xi/69

H1075 His last steak done, his fire rak'd out and dead,
'Oh! At your feet, dear masters, let me die!'

    Captain [Thomas] Morris, 'Epitaph on Edwd.
    Handson, thirty years cook to the Beefsteak Society'

    c.82, p. 1

H1076 His life is short who present times neglects
A base abode in time but liveth not.

    [Sir Thomas Urquhart], 'A wise man only enjoyeth
    life'

    fb.217, p. 500

H1077 His life the Christian's character display'd
The Christian faith the debt of death he paid.

    'In Twickenham churchyard. Beneath this tomb lies
    interred the remains of William Pritchard who died
    on the 2d of January 1763 aged 55'

    c.74

H1078 His little heart o'erwhelm'd with woe,
And Venus please, and Cupid kill.

    'Venus and Cupid occasioned by the foregoing'
    ['What do scholars and bards . . .']

    c.233, p. 81

H1079 His look, a book, wherein seem'd to be writ
It still consorted person, time, and place.

    Rob[ert] Davenport, 'Description of policy'

    b.52/2, p. 190

H1080 His love-sword's not so ready for offence,
As is her Cyprian buckler for defense.

    Sir Thomas Urquhart, 'An unequal conflict betwixt a
    strong woman, and a weak man'

    fb.217, p. 113

H1081 His love t'his mistress, when h'had gain'd the purse
Him, who can put in in so dext'rously.

    Sir Thomas Urquhart, 'Of a gentlewoman, who with a
    most fervent courtesy accepted the amorous offer of a
    Cavalier, whom she saw run at the ring'

    fb.217, p. 286

H1082 His master's words could not avail
For death has caught a Tartar.

    'Epitaph on Tartar, a terrier of Sr. S. Northcote's'

    Diggle Box: Poetry Box xi/3, 69

H1083 His mem'ry bless, whose pious care
And left a pattern to mankind.

    John Lockman, 'A hymn: on the death of Mr. Jackson,
    treasurer to the charity children of St. Amis(?)
    Westminster. Set to music by Mr. Arnold. 10 June
    1766'

    c.267/1, p. 391; c.267/2, p. 171

H1084 His mind might be abased by [ ]
For blessed are the poor in spirit.

    Sir Thomas Urquhart, 'That it is a sort of ambition to
    strive to be ignorant. Of a presumptuous sot'

    fb.217, p. 268

H1085 His mother gives to each child she begets
For he alone may represent them all.

    Sir Thomas Urquhart, 'Of one, who was the son of a
    very common woman'

    fb.217, p. 283

H1086 His name does in the sacred language say
And pious souls who in their Savior trust.

    [Sir Philip Wodehouse], 'Matthew Hales'

    b.131, back (no. 139)

H1087 His name, his office speaks—and quality
There's no such neatness, as is honesty.

    [Sir Philip Wodehouse], 'Thomas Green—my heart
    groans'

    b.131, back (no. 181)

H1088 His oft-tried prowess in his country's cause
That calls, whate'er is mortal, to eternity!

    [Charles Burney, the elder], '. . . Epitaph on Captain
    John Frodsham in Buford Church, Oxfordshire [who
    died aged 54 on 7 June 1783]'

    c.33, p. 226

H1089 His painful, skillful travels reach'd as far
Is hous'd in heaven, a haven never fading.

    'Epitaph at St. Stephen's Church at Bristol on
    Mr. Martin Pringe, a merchant'

    c.360/3, no. 130

H1090 His prodigality flows from devotion,
That rich men hardly reach eternal glory.

>Sir Thomas Urquhart, 'A waster favorably censured'
>fb.217, p. 273

H1091 His servants God preserves though they in danger
fall;
Then as from viper's deadly bite he kept th'apostle
Paul.

>c.339, p. 320

H1092 His stomach so much liquor can retain
But he three thousand acres swallowed up.

>[Sir Thomas Urquhart], 'Of one who had spent his estate on wine'
>fb.217, p. 503

H1093 His string, is hope: faith, th'arrow: the bow, love:
God is the mark: the butt, the heav'ns above.

>Sir Thomas Urquhart, 'A heavenly archer'
>fb.217, p. 356

H1094 His sword, Saint Peter to our Savior shew,
Did throw away the keys, to snatch the sword.

>Sir Thomas Urquhart, 'To Pope Julius the second'
>fb.217, p. 187

H1095 His time was short, his touch was neat,
To change his notes for cash.

>'On a runaway musician'
>c.82, p. 23; Diggle Box: Poetry Box XI/68, 69

H1096 His tongue required a sign, which might afford
Hers was the voice of wonder, his of doubt.

>[Francis Quarles], 'On Zacharias and the Blessed Virgin' [Divine Fancies III, 2]
>b.137, p. 170

H1097 His vein at her entreaty was so ready,
Did quickly turn the letters of her name.

>Sir Thomas Urquhart, 'Of a gallant poet, enamored with a certain dame'
>fb.217, p. 178

H1098 His will's no ill this by just consequence:
Is prudent innocence—his will's no ill.

>[Sir Philip Wodehouse], 'Upon John Willis son to Sr Thom[as]'
>b.131, back (no. 137)

H1099 His wit's infirm, that think we can
'Gainst him that burns and's scarce lukewarm. |
Then hang him &c.

>'The answer' [to 'I am confirm'd . . .']
>b.197, p. 240

H1100 His worthy office very well
To heaven we may ascend. | Amen

>'Of S. Triphone. Nov. 10'
>a.30[50]

H1101 Historic muse awake!—and from the shade,
Preserv'd by time, from dark oblivion's shade.

>'The fatal conquest occasioned by the death of the brave Sir Richard Greenville, in the year 1595, after sustaining in the Revenge, an English man-of-war a fight of fifteen hours against the Spanish armada of 53 sail'
>c.382, p. 19

H1102 Histories of all ages do declare
Had sealed her love t' her country with her blood.

>[Sir Aston Cokayne], 'Of high spirited women'
>b.275, p. 98

H1103 Historiographers of old did boldly
That they lie boldly and dare not tell the truth.

>[Sir Thomas Urquhart], 'How dissonant the smooth passing over of men [?] in this age would have been to the present integrity of writers in former times'
>fb.217, p. 516

H1104 History speaks of kings of great fame
If I trust them again I'll hang on a bough. | Karo,
[karo, etc.]

>[see Cambridge U. Lib. MS Ee.6.46]
>Poetry Box VII/65

H1105 Hither, ev'ry dying lover,
'Tis ten to one, things never mend.

>'The rape of the clog. A tale'
>Poetry Box X/25

H1106 Hither, O Melibeus, haste,
Beneath this shady bow'r.

>[( ) Masser, translation of Virgil]
>c.20/2

H1107 Hither quick the victim bring,
Round the lusty oak, than she.

>[William Popple, trans.], '[Horace] book 1st. ode 36th. On the return to Rome of Plotius Numida'
>fc.104/2, p. 100

H1108 Hither we're bound: avast! Enchanting spot!
Round the vast globe our native rights maintain.

>John Lockman, 'Epilogue to The miser, acted at Covent Garden Theater, for the benefit of the boys put out by the Marine Society . . . 1757'
>c.267/3, p. 129

H1109 Ho, behold each sinful wight,
If preparation you bring hither.

> H[enry] C[olman], 'The invitation'
> [Crum H1248]
>
> b.2, p. 73

H1110 Ho brother Teague dost hear de decree
Be Christ and St. Patrick de nation's our own. |
                    Lero, lero, Lilliburlero, etc.

> [Thomas Wharton, 1st marquis of Wharton,
> 'Lilliburlero'; autumn 1688]
> [Crum H1249; POAS IV.311]
>
> Poetry Box VII/65, p. 2

H1111 Ho, (publicans!) if you are wise,
And drink your cellars dry.

> John Lockman, 'A friendly hint to the publicans, in
> and about London; on the arrival of Shetland
> herrings, by the British busses . . . Aug. 1751'
>
> c.267/1, p. 223; c.360/3, no. 171

H1112 Ho! Who lies here?
What we left, that we lost.

> 'Epitaph' [on the old earl of Devonshire and Maud his
> wife]
>
> c.81/1, no. 372

H1113 Hoarse winter had resign'd his reign,
Like Flora meet a hapless doom.

> Charles Atherton Allnutt, 'A sharp frost in May
> improved by applying it to the case of an apostatizing
> friend'
>
> c.112, p. 131

H1114 Hob bit in the hand, by his pest of a wife,
Than that one runs on two legs, the other on four.

> John Lockman, 'After seeing a man's hand (which his
> wife had tore with her teeth,) dressed by Mr. Freke, in
> St. Bartholomew's Hospital . . . 1743'
>
> c.267/1, p. 18

H1115 Hobnelia, seated in a dreary vale,
Oh dear! I fall adown, adown, adown.

> [John] Gay, 'The spell' [in 'Thursday' in The
> shepherd's week]
>
> c.250

H1116 Hobson, O Hobson, thou master of the weary
                             traveller?
For now you shall not go I tell you plain.

> 'A dialogue between a scholar of Cambridge and
> Hobson the carrier to the tune of Caron'
>
> b.197, p. 61

H1117 Hobson—what's out of sight is out of mind,
Is now, alas! content with a single sheet.

> 'On Hobson the carrier'
>
> c.74

H1118 Hold brother Cob: let us once more engage,
Till two such coxcombs shall meet here again.

> [ ] Boles, of New College, Oxford, 'Verses spoken
> by . . . on Monday in answer to [Jacob] Allestry's
> reply to the former' [prologue to the music speech at
> the Music School, Oxford, in 1682: 'The ladies he
> endeavors . . .']
>
> fb.142, p. 22

H1119 Hold ere I part I humbly do beseech
I'll boast 'twas I Jo. Haines reform'd the age.

> Jo[seph] Haines
>
> b.204, p. 37

H1120 Hold fast thy sword and scepter Charles
And raising civil war.

> [John Wilmot], 2nd earl of Rochester(?), 'Made
> by . . . a little before his death' [docket title:
> 'Rochester's verses to the king 1680']
> [Crum H1263]
>
> Poetry Box VIII/36; b.327, f. 1; b.54, p. 1154; fb.106(22)

H1121 Hold, hold, and no further advance
But I thought at the first when.

> 'Song'
>
> c.189, p. 11

H1122 Hold hold my worthy friends—why this applause?
To all your health's and mine—vain glass of ink.

> Edward Sneyd, 'An epilogue Novbr. The 3d 1775. The
> play The English merchant by George Colman esqr:'
>
> c.214, p. 78

H1123 Hold! Softly tread my friend—awhile
A friend and comrade mourn.

> [Thomas Hull]
>
> c.528/24

H1124 Hold stay who lies here
We lived sixty and five year.

> 'On an E of Devonshire'
>
> fb.143, p. 27

H1125 Hold! 'Tis too much for thought! decide no more:
That he who knows God right, must, first, be he.

> 'A short answer to the solemn question what is God?'
>
> c.487, p. 49

H1126　Hold ye carbuncled fools! Ye're quite mistaken;
　　　　Where ran the devil, when he drove the swine.

　　　　'In socios seniores Coll: Oxon: [7]'
　　　　c.81/1, no. 24

H1127　Homage, fair Seward! is thy due
　　　　Immortalize the hero's fire.

　　　　'To Miss Seward with Dillon's Spanish poets'
　　　　Poetry Box v/57

H1128　Homer his goddesses array'd
　　　　Ambrosia would be there!

　　　　R[ichard] V[ernon] S[adleir], 'The seven following
　　　　bagatelles were written almost impromptu when at
　　　　General Mocher's on a visit of some weeks—Miss
　　　　F—t—r and the Moodys being of the company'
　　　　c.106, p. 68

H1129　Honest and poor, faithful in word and thought.
　　　　Is vexatious to the wise and pious.

　　　　[Abraham Cowley], 'Martial's advice to Fabian, upon
　　　　his arrival at Rome'
　　　　b.118, p. 40

H1130　Honest Jack and his wife once to sea took a trip
　　　　'Tis a bad wind indeed! that blows nobody good.

　　　　'Fortunate sailor'
　　　　c.81/1, no. 290

H1131　Honest lover whosoever
　　　　Thou must begin again and love anew.

　　　　[Sir John Suckling]
　　　　b.213, p. 31

H1132　Honest praise you may parry as much as you will
　　　　I'd like Marsyas be flay'd by Apollo.

　　　　[Charles Burney, the elder], 'To Mrs. Thrale, on her
　　　　accusing me of flattery in some verses of thanks for a
　　　　gold pen'
　　　　c.33, p. 118

H1133　Honest Teague when return'd from a trip to the
　　　　　　　　　　　　　　　　　　　　　　　　north
　　　　But I never saw it rain deer.

　　　　'The simple truth most simply told'
　　　　c.546

H1134　Honest William an easy and goodnatur'd fellow
　　　　That enable you brewers to ride in your coaches.

　　　　[William Taylor?], 'Written by a brewer's daughter on
　　　　her father's discharging his coachman for getting in
　　　　liquor'
　　　　c.487, p. 64; c.83/1, no. 259; fc.130, p. 59

H1135　Honor all day assails our car[e]s
　　　　And knaves without, and knaves with ears.

　　　　'Modern honor'
　　　　c.83/3, no. 934

H1136　Honor and peace! Ye guardians kindly just!
　　　　And from the mind of Cowper—call'd the task!

　　　　William Hayley, 'Epitaph on a lady'
　　　　c.142, p. 583

H1137　Honor becomes the best, I would fain write
　　　　Less to our castle's powder, than thy dust.

　　　　F[rancis] Palmer, 'Elegies on Sr. Horatio Vere'
　　　　b.52/2, p. 126

H1138　Honor, dear Jack, gets in the world applause,
　　　　True honor's only to be found in God.

　　　　R[obert] Shirley, 1st earl of Ferrers, 'Upon honor.
　　　　From Boileau'
　　　　c.347, p. 101

H1139　Honor had rather be with danger driven
　　　　Than stay with virtue on the hand of heaven.

　　　　'On honor'
　　　　c.189, p. 34

H1140　Hope follows faith; when man is most opprest
　　　　Yet, will never leave us, if we leave not it.

　　　　'Hope' [poem in the shape of an anchor]
　　　　c.189, p. 39

H1141　Hope, fortune's cheering lottery!
　　　　More ways and turns then hunted nature knows.

　　　　[Richard Crashaw, answer to 'Hope, whose weak
　　　　being ruin'd is . . .']
　　　　[Crum H1294, second part]
　　　　b.209, p. 85

H1142　Hope is a friendly passion of the mind
　　　　And in the midst of pain, does still some pleasure
　　　　　　　　　　　　　　　　　　　　　　　　　　give.

　　　　'Bri: Apollo: fo. 34'
　　　　c.549, p. 40

H1143　Hope never entered heav'n; what can be wish'd,
　　　　Triun' God, th'object of saints' love hath been.

　　　　Sir Thomas Urquhart, 'That no theological virtue
　　　　save charity, affects the inhabitants of the celestial
　　　　paradise'
　　　　fb.217, p. 206

H1144　Hope, of all ills that men endure
　　　　To which all soon return that travel out.

　　　　[Abraham Cowley], 'Of hope'
　　　　[Crum H1292]
　　　　b.209, p. 87; c.258

H1145 Hope, whose weak being ruined is
If it take air before, his spirits waste.

> [Abraham Cowley], 'Against hope' [answered by
> 'Hope, fortune's cheering lottery . . .']
> [Crum H1294]
>
> b.209, p. 85; c.244, p. 214

H1146 Hopeless, abandon'd, aimless and oppressed
And when she pities, who can be distress'd.

> Aaron Hill, 'Verses by . . . on the cruel treatment of
> Mr. Richard Savage from his mother, Anne Countess
> of Macclesfield'
>
> c.360/2, no. 20; c.83/1, no. 187

H1147 Hopeless and silent I must still adore
Her heart's more hard than stone whom I'd implore.

> [Eliza (Fowler) Haywood], '[lines from] Love in
> excess'
>
> c.549, p. 45

H1148 Hopeless I languish out my days
Confirms the conquest of her eyes.

> Sir G[eorge] Etherege, 'Voiture's Urania'
> [Crum 1240]
>
> Poetry Box IV/53

H1149 Hopeless we own is thy distress
The maid whom every man must love.

> [ ] Nugent, 'To Lady Lucy Manners, grieved at being
> censured by some of her own sex'
>
> c.360/1, p. 59

H1150 Horace I think prescribes thy rule,
And rolling thunders fly and fate is in the blow.

> [William] Pattison, 'The case stated'
>
> c.244, p. 526

H1151 Horace while I alone was beauteous in your eye
And gladly chose with thee to live and die.

> [Robert Cholmeley], 'Hor[ace]: ode the [9th] book
> the [3rd] Donec gratus [eram] tibi . . .'
>
> c.190, p. 36

H1152 Horses and hounds, their care, their various race,
And his pale master flies the dang'rous ground.

> Thomas Tickell, 'A fragment—of a poem on hunting'
>
> c.351, p. 93

H1153 Hosanna to the prince of light
Sound our Emmanuel's praise.

> [Isaac Watts, Hymns and spiritual songs (1707), bk. II,
> Hymn 70]
>
> c.180, p. 6

H1154 Hosanna to the royal son
Thus silence into songs.

> [Isaac Watts, Hymns and spiritual songs (1707), bk. I,
> Hymn 16]
>
> c.180, p. 3

H1155 Hostess whether you lodge woman or man
Even so in this chimney, I have rhymed to it.

> 'On lying in an inn and being forced in the night to
> rise, not finding anything convenient for his purpose,
> made use of the chimney: over which at his parting he
> writ thus'
>
> b.197, p. 59

H1156 Hot-livered Gallus, could not long forbear,
That to the mare I should straight married be.

> 'Omnia Roma venalia'
> [Crum H1300]
>
> b.197, p. 106

H1157 Houses, churches, mix'd together,
This is London—how d'ye like it.

> [J. Bankes], 'A description of London'
>
> c.83/2, no. 697; c.81/2, no. 545

H1158 How Ahab longs, Ahab must be possest
Should (being priest) afford more blood then wine.

> [Francis Quarles], 'On Ahab getting Naboth's
> vineyard' [Divine Fancies II, 35]
>
> b.137, p. 169

H1159 How all unsettled am I? Toss'd betwixt
Resign, and thus uncumbered calm pursue my way.

> T[homas] S[tevens], 'Setting out on a journey.
> August 19. 1780 . . . August 25. 1780'
>
> c.259, p. 108

H1160 How am I lost? Though some are pleas'd to say
Me glory truth, the better part's behind.

> [George Daniel]
>
> b.121, fol. 57v

H1161 How an analysis? This name's the text
Go spell her well into her mother tongue.

> [Sir Philip Wodehouse], 'Upon one Mrs. Anne Lewis
> my friend (my chaplain) Mr. Neech's mistress'
>
> b.131, back (no. 82/1)

H1162 How anxious is the pensive parent's thought!
Go, cater, where you list.

> H[orace] Walpole, [4th earl of Orford], 'The magpie
> and her brood a fable, from the tales of Bonaventure
> Despériers, valet de chambre to the Queen of
> Navarre; addressed to Miss Hotham'
> [Crum H1306]
>
> c.74

H1163 How apt are men to lie! How dare they say
Who where she is, first learn'd to hold her tongue.

'Epitaph on a talkative lady'

c.360/3, no. 33

H1164 How aptly man's life is compar'd to the ocean,
Mild, placid, and cheerful, reflective and free!

'Written at Hastings May 1789'

c.140, p. 555

H1165 How are deluded humankind
But everywhere a shade?

Christopher Pitt, 'On a shadow'

c.244, p. 500

H1166 How are thy glories here display'd,
And ev'ry tear be dry.

[Isaac Watts, Hymns and spiritual songs (1707),
bk. III, Hymn 25]

c.180, p. 59

H1167 How are thy servants blest, O Lord!
Shall join my soul to thee.

[Joseph Addison], 'A divine ode. Per a gentleman upon
the conclusion of his travels' [Spectator 489, 20 Sept.
1712]
[Crum H1313]

c.186, p. 34; c.244, p. 6; c.547, p. 158; c.83/3, no. 777;
fc.132/1, p. 39; File 13409

H1168 How artful was Corydon's praise
And a Hebe be heard in each vale. | Phillida sigh—
and a mourner be new—

[John Wolcot ('Peter Pindar')], 'Phillida—for Ferrari'
Poetry Box v/102

H1169 How arts improve in this degenerate age
Our follies sanction first and then our bliss.

[Richard Brinsley Butler Sheridan]
Poetry Box xII/53; see also 'To ready Scotland . . .'.

H1170 How awful is the scene, while here we tread
Nor till tomorrow the great work adjourn.

'On Sarah Meadows, aged 73' [in Birchington
churchyard in the Isle of Thanet, Kent]

c.240, p. 138

H1171 How beauteous is the glist'ning dew
And blunt the barbed shaft of fate.

'To Miss A. F.'
Diggle Box: Poetry Box xI/7

How beautiful is night! H1172
The now unequall'd palace, from its height | Dash'd
on the pavement down &c.

[Robert Southey, 'Thalaba the destroyer', stanzas
1-13]
Diggle Box: Poetry Box xI/61

How blest a life! How short its date H1173
The victim of too fierce a flame.

'On the death of Mrs. Bowes a beautiful young lady
not fifteen years old. Wife to George Bowes of the
bishopric of Durham esq. Whose tender age making
her incapable of enduring his vigorous love, occasion[ed]
her death' [d. 14 December 1724; in Reading Mercury]
[Crum H1316c]

c.360/2, no. 76

How blest are the charms of a country life H1174
Enjoy the charms of a country life.

'Written at 15'
File 295

How blest could I in Chloe's heart H1175
Another fool might do the same.

'Writ in a lady's pocketbook'
c.360/1, p. 295

How blest has my time been what days have I H1176
known,
To hold it for life you must find it at home.

c.358, p. 12

How blest the days of Saturn's golden reign H1177
And Jack the advice to learn did not dispair.

'Golden age'
c.570/3, p. 149

How blest the race of that Saturnian reign H1178
It is not for boys to prate of states and kings.

'Upon Queen Elizabeth'
Poetry Box v/68

How blest the sacred tie that binds H1179
A heav'n of joy because of love.

[Anna Laetitia (Aikin)] Barbauld, 'Hymn . . . sung
after the Revd. Mr. Barbauld's sermons on occasion of
Dr. Parry's marriage [24 September 1778]'

c.364, p. 72

How blest was I when I was free H1180
Since I'm so worthless she so fair.

Charles Cotton, 'Upon my Lady Mary Fitzherbert'
File 3744

H1181 How blest was I when thou wert true,
Thou should'st alone employ my care.

'9th ode of Horace lib. 3. Universal spectator. A dialogue between Horace and Lydia'

fc.24, p. 75

H1182 How blest was the created state
You love me for a frailer part.

John Wilmot, 2nd earl of Rochester, '10. Song. The fall'

b.334, p. 190; b.105, p. 149

H1183 How blithe was I each morn to see
While heaven preserves my Highland laddy. | O my bonny—

'A song'

c.358, p. 117

H1184 How bold is George to venture o'er,
And leave you to obey your fate. | March Brunswick.

'On the King' [1714]
[Crum H1325]

c.570/1, p. 14

H1185 How bonny, and brisk, how pleasant, and sweet,
For beauty enjoy'd but does turn to disdain.

'The joys of Jenny'

fb.107, p. 68

H1186 How bravely the topers the devil defy,
For it stands upon record, he walks in the dry.

'In socios seniores Coll: Oxon: [3]'

c.81/1, no. 24

H1187 How brimful of nothing's the life of a beau
Such, such is the life of a beau.

'The life of a beau, a song. Sung by Mrs. Clive at the Theater-Royal in Drury Lane'
[Crum H1329]

c.360/1, p. 71; see also 'What life is so happy . . .'.

H1188 How can a man o'erload with drinking stop
That what is in the bottom is cast up.

[Sir Thomas Urquhart], 'Why men given to cups are apt to reveal anything'

fb.217, p. 496

H1189 How can I at aught repine
In pain and richness I am blest.

Poetry Box XIV/172

H1190 How can I sink with such a prop
My cheerful heart resign.

'Hymn 56'

c.562, p. 67

H1191 How can it be? 'tis strange to understand
So soft a face, should own so hard an hand.

[Charles Earle?], 'To Miss Morgan with hard pens'

c.376

H1192 How can the age of time be measur'd by
The sun; who's three nights younger than the day.

Sir Thomas Urquhart, 'That the ordinary calculation of time, made by the anniversary circumvolution of the sun, may fail. A problem'

fb.217, p. 62

H1193 How can the emblem of mortality
Arm'd with our strong affection scorn'd to break.

[William Strode], 'On a glass falling on the stones without breaking'
[Crum H1339]

b.205, fol. 65v

H1194 How can these lines be trifling called
For your own luster hers.

'To Mira'

Poetry Box I/66

H1195 How can we measure hours by a sand glass:
Where time makes th'open greater, the sand less.

Sir Thomas Urquhart, 'That a sand glass cannot always measure alike'

fb.217, p. 253

H1196 How can you, (beauteous Nancy!) thus cruelly slight
Since I'm constant as your sex, be not fickle as ours.

John Lockman, 'Shinkin's complaint, on the inconstant fair one. Writ to a favorite air of Mr. John Festing . . . Jn 1730'

c.267/2, p. 99

H1197 How can you lovely Nanny
Or not fickle as ours.

'A song'
[Crum H1342, 'Nancy']

c.358, p. 77

H1198 How capricious were nature and art to poor Nell,
She was painting her cheeks at the time her nose fell.

[Matthew] Prior, 'Critical moment'
[Crum H1343]

c.144, p. 178

H1199 How chang'd my state! Thrice blissful was the day,
I'll call it heav'n, and worship at thy feet.

John Lockman, 'The ruined Margaritta's soliloquy, in her garret, Drury Lane; after reading a proposal, for saving deserted and prostitute girls, in the plan for a police . . . 1757'

c.267/1, p. 203

H1200 How charm th'exertions of thy matchless art,
Which yet draw luster from thy social heart!

  John Lockman, 'To Mr. Hogarth, with my Lives of
  Cupid and Psyche, from La Fontaine'

c.267/1, p. 279

H1201 How charming are the pleasures and how sweet,
He does but ask your love that will be true.

c.549, p. 1

H1202 How charming is this little spot,
And ev'ry action guides.

  [Mary] Chandler, 'To Mrs. Boteler. A description of
  her garden'

c.351, p. 131

H1203 How charmingly the wool our fair becomes!
Our ladies wear them on their heads.

  'On the ladies' woolly headdress'

c.487, p. 77

H1204 How cheer you, captain, with just going to sail
To brew—and bottle—ere you go to Cork.

  [Phanuel Bacon], '[Greek:] Useron protoron A
  dialogue'

c.237, fol. 65

H1205 How cheerful along the gay mead,
My soul shall be wrapt in my God!

  'Hymn in the oratorio of Abel' ['A hymn of Eve', pr.
  c. 1685]

c.140, p. 111; Poetry Box IV/26

H1206 How cheerful I pass the long day;
And hold thee, the first of my joys.

  'A pastoral'

c.83/3, no. 915

H1207 How Christian trot! with heavy heart
To lay a squawking creature at one's door.

  'On a whore that was whipped at the cart's-arse
  through Camb[ridge]'

b.115, fol. 3v

H1208 How condescending and how kind
Mourn that we pier[c]ed the Lord.

  [Isaac Watts, Hymns and spiritual songs (1707),
  bk. III, Hymn 4]

c.180, p. 17

H1209 How could thy soul fond woman be assur'd
Thy faith, and not his garments wrought the cure.

  [Francis Quarles], 'On the woman with the issue'
  [Divine Fancies IV, 45]

b.137, p. 173

H1210 How could you friend forget that I
With devote heart on bended knee.

  [Mrs. Christian Kerr], 'To a young gentleman that
  had made an escape'

c.102, p. 134

H1211 How could you—M—let my muse descend
Which thou alas! know naught of, but the name.

  Marjorie Trim, pseud., 'To the Revd. Defamer'

c.391

H1212 How cruel dost prove
In a tavern I'll sing, and I'll roar.

  'A farewell to Cupid'

fb.107, p. 13

H1213 How dark has the day been! How veiled the sun,
Gives prospects of glory at evening-tide.

  T[homas] S[tevens], 'Light at eventide . . . Colchester
  Augt. 10. [17]79' [on the death of Mrs. M. H.]

c.259, p. 6

H1214 How dark is the hour while my love is away;
Who brought them all hither and led them away.

  [John Walcot ('Peter Pindar')], 'The disconsolate—a
  song'

c.83/3, no. 1075

H1215 How dar'st thou thus disturb that surly shade
That cost thy heir at least four hundred pound.

  'A dialogue between Col: Birch's ghost and the Bishop
  of Hereford'

Poetry Box XIV/178 (incomplete)

H1216 How dearly I love you, bear witness my heart!
But tell my John—how many smacks make a buss?

  John Lockman, 'Peggy to John: on his setting out for
  the Herring Fishery . . . May 1750'

c.267/1, p. 46

H1217 How dearly mortals love to laugh and grin!
Be thou my soft companion and my friend.

  [John Walcot(?) ('Peter Pindar')], 'Laughter, wit and
  candor'

c.355, p. 96

H1218 How deep the silence, whilst the warbling sound
How will she strike in her meridian charms!

  John Lockman, 'Hearing Mr Chalran play, at Misses
  Steward's benefit, at the great room, Dean Street,
  Soho'

c.267/1, p. 292

H1219　How did I love my dear Great-Uncle Joe!
No matter, I shall cry myself to sleep.

　　'To my great-Uncle Joseph Wiggins esqr.'
　　Diggle Box: Poetry Box xi/69

H1220　How diff'rent thou, from the blithe race
Soon all was life, and all was joy.

　　John Lockman, 'To the Duchess of Buckingham: on
　　her Grace's sending my sick mother a present of
　　mineral water . . . April 1742'

　　c.267/2, p. 217

H1221　How dismal's the abode in mansions where
For he in love would soon a bankrupt grow.

　　[Mrs. Christian Kerr], 'By a young gentlewoman on
　　an old bachelor who teased a young lady with
　　importunities of courtship encouraged by a lady
　　friend of hers in the same house'

　　c.102, p. 115

H1222　How do I pity that proud wealthy clown
You own the cage, I in it sit and sing.

　　[John Norris], 'My estate'

　　c.547, p. 175

H1223　How do I spin my time away
Its cover off, grant it a crown.

　　H[enry] C[olman], 'On the spirit adulterated by the
　　flesh'

　　b.2, p. 19

H1224　How do I thank thee death, and bless thy power
And what my birthright claimed, my death's right
　　　　　　　　　　　　　　　　　　　paid.

　　[Richard Corbett], 'The Lady Arabella [Stuart]'s
　　epitaph' [d. Sept. 27 1615; attrib. Sir Walter Raleigh]
　　[Crum H1360]

　　b.197, p. 39

H1225　How do men's wand'ring thoughts mistake their way,
Before the joys, to which heaven invites.

　　J[ohn] Robinson, 'Nullus vel magni sceleris labor'

　　c.370, fol. 39v

H1226　How do, ye do, ye heirs of grace
And he'll be found a gracious Lord.

　　T[homas] S[tevens], 'Spiritual health inquired after'

　　c.259, p. 17

H1227　How does this morn our life's vain scene set forth,
Upon the rock of ages, God's his hold.

　　[Edmund Wodehouse], 'Septr 2 [1715] On the sudden
　　change of bright to clouds, and then again sunshine'

　　b.131, p. 257

H1228　How doth the city solitary sit,
Thy just provoked wrath for me assign'd.

　　[William Sandys?], 'Israel deploreth her captivity
　　complaineth of grief. Lament[ion]s of Jeremiah:
　　chap: 1'
　　[cf. Crum H1367]

　　b.230, p. 79

H1229　How doth the mournful widow'd city bow?
My sighs are many, and my heart is faint.

　　'The lamentations of Jeremiah [1–25]'

　　b.218, p. 52

H1230　How drear the remnant of my days must seem
[?] nature and befriends mankind.

　　[William Hayley], 'Sonnet . . . Sept. 1 [1800]'

　　File 6968

H1231　How dull and how insensible a beast
Learn to write well or not to write at all.

　　[John Sheffield, 1st duke of Buckingham and
　　Normanby], 'An essay upon satire' [1679]
　　[Crum H1370; POAS I.401]

　　b.327, f. 5; b.113, p. 59; fb.108, p. 327; Trumbull Box:
　　Poetry Box XIII/50; see also 'Now the reformer . . .'.

H1232　How eager are our vain pursuits
Or undermin'd by time, we fall to dust.

　　Robert Veel, 'Vanity of worldly happiness'

　　b.150, p. 221

H1233　How easy our minutes whilst our conscience is clear,
Thrice blest be this day and thrice happy our king.

　　'The Jacobite Club'
　　[Crum H1377]

　　b.111, p. 56

H1234　How easy pleasant life were thus,
And we adore below.

　　[John Austin], 'Hym. 14' [Hymn xxvii, Devotions in
　　the ancient way of offices, 1672, p. 240]

　　c.178, p. 13

H1235　How everything will this mild rain
Thank God, she's deaf and dumb!

　　'Exclamations caused by the welcome appearance of
　　rain . . . Answer'

　　c.83/3, no. 1011

H1236　How faint the scene how dim the day
And I am completely clean.

　　[Mary Pluret], 'I had a glorious manifestation beyond
　　all words, then these words'

　　c.354

H1237 How fair and sweet the planted rose
Leaves art to polish and refine.

    'Art improves nature or the force of education'

    c.186, p. 93

H1238 How fair is the scene and in grandeur transcendent
Hark! The silence of night rolls the tide of His praise!

    'An evening scene at sea'

    c.58

H1239 How fair the fair! Each amiable grace
Ev'n heav'n sings with joy, who join'd this
                            matchless pair.

    'Published at London in the Daily advertiser of
    Thursday April the 24 1746 on Theophilus
    Ecclestone . . . and Miss Jacomb . . . this day married
    at Mortlack in Surrey'

    c.360/2, no. 146

H1240 How far are they deceiv'd, who hope in vain
Before your pity, I would choose your hate.

    [Sir George Etherege], 'Ephelia [a deserted lover] to
    Bajazet' [*i.e.*, the Earl of Mulgrave; 1675. A caveat to
    women; answered by 'If you're deceiv'd . . .']
    [Crum H1381; *POAS* I.342]

    b.54, p. 1180; b.105, p. 340

H1241 How fast my tears, my cause is great
To feel the risen Savior's power.

    [Thomas Stevens?], 'A hymn'

    c.259, p. 69

H1242 How fast the minutes fly away
Then all our life to curse that hour and wish it
                              ne'er had been.

    [Mrs. ( ) Feilding]

    b.226, p. 31

H1243 How few and short to humankind
Amid the horrors of decay!

    [Charles Burney, the elder], 'Life' (first part crossed
    out)

    c.33, p. 135

H1244 How few are those who teach while they delight
The duty to be—happy for our pains.

    'To the Marquis de Villette'

    c.83/2, no. 694

H1245 How few can please one side; both sides how few
Below 'twas no less to the devil (his son).

    c.340

H1246 How fond of metaphor was I when young
Engender'd by the putrid fogs of night.

    [John Wolcot ('Peter Pindar')], 'Hymn to simplicity'
    [November 1797]

    File 17287 (including several verse fragments)

H1247 How fondly (dearest Hugford!) slide thy hours,
But shine the jocund mortal, as before.

    John Lockman, 'To James Hugford esqr, at West
    Drayton, Middlesex . . . Aug. 1756'

    c.267/2, p. 357

H1248 How foolish is the spark to trust the lass,
To borrow English coin, but pay in French.

    'The town jilt'

    c.578, p. 9

H1249 How frail is life! How soon 'twill end
And wishes are no more.

    c.153, p. 73

H1250 How frail is man, how short his breath,
And full of misery.

    J[ohn] R[obinson], 'Felix dicique beatus ante obitum
    nemo supremaqur funera possit'
    [cf. Crum H1390]

    c.370, fol. 53v

H1251 How frail O England are thy natives' mind?
To send King James a restoration day.

    'Britain's inconstancy'

    b.111, p. 501

H1252 How frail's [the] [ ] [of] a woman's will
A woman's reason is measur'd [by] her list.

    'In foeminam'

    b.205, fol. 15r

H1253 How frames it with your sober looks
In secret love breed open smart.

    'Her answer' [to "What you suspect']

    b.205, fol. 93v

H1254 How full of savor is the name
Are only lumberers of the ground.

    T[homas] S[tevens], 'Hymn upon Matt. 5.13'

    c.259, p. 94

H1255 How gaily it at first begun
Leave following crowds behind.

    [Anne Finch, countess of Winchilsea], 'The progress
    of life'

    c.244, p. 182 (attr. Mrs. Manley); c.258

H1256 How giveth this upstart arms I pray
Use upon use did work out arms and all.

    'The usurer's arms'

    b.208, p. 60

H1257 How glorious Lord art Thou
To thee be all the praise.

    P[hilip] Doddridge, 'The excellency of the righteous
    with respect to their temper from Prov. XII. 26'

    c.493, p. 23

H1258 How goes it brother Jack?
To Pitt, Hawke and Boscawen. | Jolly Buck

    'Messmate Tom and Brother Jack. Song 29'

    c.555, p. 41

H1259 How good a God thou art how great and free
Perpetual praise to thee th'Almighty king.

    H[enry] C[olman], 'On God's mercy'
    [Crum H1397]

    b.2, p. 3

H1260 How good, how wise, thus to instruct mankind,
You should be lov'd, esteem'd by all mankind.

    'To the author of The morning walk a poem'

    c.360/3, no. 175

H1261 How gracious and how wise
Still more completely thine.

    P[hilip] Doddridge, 'Afflictions useful to bring us near
    to God from Ezek: XX 37'

    c.493, p. 54

H1262 How gracious is my God who grants
Or whilst we live, or when we die.

    [Edmund Wodehouse], 'Septr 29 [1715]'

    b.131, p. 275

H1263 How gracious is our God t'admit
Who rightly pray, ne'er fail of bliss.

    [Edmund Wodehouse], 'Decr. 18 [1714]'

    b.131, p. 117

H1264 How grateful does the incense rise
To live, and to be lov'd, like thee.

    W[illiam] W[arren] Porter, 'On the death of a young
    lady'

    c.83/2, no. 578

H1265 How great his faith was this doth prove
That he a Mountain could remove.

    'On my Lord Mountain put out of his place by the
    King'

    b.356, p. 306

H1266 How great is our God who by his Son
By which it here begins heav'n to possess.

    [Edmund Wodehouse], 'Feb. 7 [1715]'

    b.131, p. 161

H1267 How great my pleasure at the play,
Religious joys will last, when call'd to die.

    'The contrasted joys. A fact'

    c.83/2, no. 554

H1268 How great your art!—for while we view'd
And saw their woes—without a tear!

    'Spoken extempore at the first representation of a
    tragedy'

    Diggle Box: Poetry Box XI/69

H1269 How great's the glory (Sir) that you have gain'd
Peace be your coat, till glory be your crest.

    'Jo[?shua]: Bowes late Lieut.'

    Trumbull Box: Poetry Box XIII/68

H1270 How happily housed those Lares are,
Then might the happy Lares sing.

    [Sir Richard Steele], 'The transcription on the Duke
    of Buckingham's house'

    fc.24, p. 37; see also 'Happily housed . . .'.

H1271 How happily seated those men are
And walk their suppertime away?

    [Joseph Spence], 'Mr. Davison's at Ferry Hill'

    Spence Papers, folder 119

H1272 How happy a sailor's life passes
Scribere cum dasho hem [sic].

    c.188, p. 75

H1273 How happy a state does the miller possess
If so happy a miller then who'd be a king.

    'A song of the miller of Mansfield' [printed 173-?
    (Foxon M232)]

    c.536; Accession 97.7.40, p. 13

H1274 How happy and blest
Tho' somebody else hath been with her.

    Sir Jedd[?] Corwallis, 'A ballad in the year 1644 when
    the Prince of Wales, who was after King Charles the
    2d, was in the west of England, with the army
    commanded by General Goring'

    fb.88, p. 118v

H1275 How happy, and free is the plunder,
And make long addresses, but never prevail.

    'The soldier's delight'

    fb.107, p. 36

H1276 How happy and free is the resolute swain,
To be checkt in the womb, or o'erlaid by the nurse.

'The country life'
fb.107, p. 48

H1277 How happy and how wise is he?
And from this woeful delusion save.

[Edmund Wodehouse], 'Jan. 4 [1715]'
b.131, p. 131

H1278 How happy are the newborn race,
In sacred, sure repose.

[William Cowper, trans.], 'The testimony of divine
adoption. Vol. 2. Sonnet 78' [of Jeanne Guion's
'Spiritual songs']
c.470 (autogr.)

H1279 How happy are the saints above
To dwell with thee above.

'Hymn 67th'
c.562, p. 80

H1280 How happy are the times to what they were
By their own folly punishes mankind.

'Occasioned by the repealing of the Habeas Corpus
Act'
fc.58, p. 1

H1281 How happy are we,
For a bawd always dies in her drink.

'Song'
c.189, p. 179

H1282 How happy are we,
In a rapture of heavenly love.

'Hymn 103d'
c.562, p. 139

H1283 How happy are we that are roaring
And that is acquired by drinking.

W[illiam] Aliffe, 'A drinking catch'
fb.207/4, p. 24

H1284 How happy Chloris (were they free)
The lusty juice of men.

[John Wilmot, 2nd earl of Rochester], 'Song'
b.105, p. 146; b.334, p. 188 (incomplete)

H1285 How happy is a woman's fate!
When reason bids, obey.

T[homas] M[orell], '['How wretched is a woman's
fate . . .'] answered . . . Gent. mag.iii. p. 371'
c.395, p. 6

H1286 How happy is he born or taught
And having nothing yet hath all.

Sir Hen[ry] Wotton
[Crum H1407]
b.197, p. 49; c.487, p. 51; b.356, p. 135

H1287 How happy is the humble cell
To death's untroubled shore.

[J. B.], 'Song'
Poetry Box IV/155

H1288 How happy is the man! How calm his breast!
Bless your good God, and clap your hands for joy.

[Richard] Daniel, dean of Armagh, 'The instructor—
Psalm 32'
c.244, p. 351

H1289 How happy is the man, O Lord,
In harmony believe.

[Mrs. Christian Kerr], 'An ode of thanks'
c.102, p. 131

H1290 How happy is the pilgrim's lot
Receive me to thy breast.

'Hymn 80th'
c.562, p. 103

H1291 How happy lives the man, how run to charm,
For women choose their men, like silks for show.

'The happy beau, or the ladies' favorite'
c.186, p. 100

H1292 How happy the sorrowful man
And glory obtain in a crown.

'Hymn 27th'
c.562, p. 32

H1293 How happy the souls whom Jesus unites
Triumphantly sitting in glory with Thee.

'Hymn 59th'
c.562, p. 71

H1294 How happy they,
Unmixt with gall.

John Lockman, 'Translations, and imitations from
Metastasio, and other Italian opera poets [14]'
c.267/4, p. 107

H1295 How happy you! who varied joys pursue,
Deep (tho' unseen) remains the secret wound.

Lady M[ary] W[ortley Montagu], 'An epistle to Ld.
Bat[hurs]t'
fc.51, p. 45

H1296 How happy's the prisoner who conquers his fate
Who hath nothing to lose may cry, God bless our
King, | . . . [For man's the world's epitome.]

    'The prisoner'
    [Crum H1418]

    fb.107, p. 54

H1297 How happy's the silly poor innocent swain,
Shall heighten our pleasures, and banish despair.

    'Country content'

    fb.107, p. 13

H1298 How hard dear Delia is the fate
When most for mercy he implores.

    [Charles] B[urney, the elder], 'Song by Dr. B.'

    c.486, fol. 5

H1299 How hard I strive, and sorely grin,
Thy temple's glory and thy praise!

    Abraham Oakes, 'To Cloacina: a libation'

    c.50, p. 6

H1300 How hard is the fortune of all womankind
We're sham'd if we're kind, we're blam'd if we're coy.

    '7th song'

    Accession 97.7.40, p. 12

H1301 How hard 'twill be to go school again
We'll teach our childen, what we learn'd from you.

    Sir Richard Steele, 'Epilogue to Tamarlane . . .'

    c.176, p. 14

H1302 How hath God wrapp'd up Zion in a cloud
Now mercy show: sheathe thy avenging sword.

    [William Sandys?], 'The prophet lamenteth her
misery in the 2d chapter unto ver: the 17th'

    b.230, p. 83

H1303 How hath th' oppressor ceas'd before our eyes!
Hath sworn, 'As I've decreed it shall remain.'

    'The fall and death of the king of Babylon: taken from
the 14th chapter of Bishop Lowth's Isaiah'

    c.515, fol. 30

H1304 How have you been since last we met
And she submit to his command.

    T[homas] S[tevens], 'To Miss M. R. D. by . . .
Believers excited to relate their spiritual experiences'

    c.259, p. 4

H1305 How heaven and earth and light and sky
Created was of God and when.

    'The [blank]'

    a.6, p. 95

H1306 How heav'n in scorn of human arrogance
And whelms the swelling architect beneath.

    [signed 'H.']

    c.156, p. 233

H1307 How heavy glide the tardy hours by
My unavailing grief shall never add to thine.

    'To Eliza June 1792'

    c.344

H1308 How I wish that my wife would not practice all day
I'm a wretched—unfortunate man. | O! Beware ye
young men &c.

    'The musical wife'

    Poetry Box XII/92

H1309 How ill alas is fix'd by ruthless fate,
If this you quit you must remove to heav'n!

    Edmund Burke and Richard Shackleton, 'Panegyric
on Ballitore . . . 1746'

    Files 2234, 4316 [2 copies, attr. William Dennis]

H1310 How ill an army does thy name present
In whom the lord of hosts did pitch his tent.

    [Sir Richard Bulstrode?], 'Anna Mary Gram' [Army]

    fb.88, p. 118; see also 'How well an army . . .' 'Her name
an army . . .'.

H1311 How ill doth he deserve the name of man
In what in beasts doth detestation breed.

    H[enry] C[olman], 'On drunkenness'
    [Crum H1434]

    b.2, p. 38

H1312 How ill the motion with the music suits
So Orpheus fiddled, and so danc'd the brutes.

    [Ambrose Philips], 'On a company of bad dancers to
excellent music'

    c.176, p. 54

H1313 How ill the rostrum with the sound accords
Mount not that pulpit, but O mount—a stool.

    Charles Atherton Allnutt, 'On a very plain preacher in
a very fine pulpit'

    c.112, p. 181

H1314 How inconsistent with the lover!
Until his lovely damsel made a—pair of shoes.

    'Answer to a panegyric written by a gentleman on a
lady's making a pair of shoes'

    Poetry Box X/67

H1315 How irresistibly we find
To such a [?] flame.

S[tephen] Simpson, 'The imperfect description to
T. Eyre in whose presence an amiable young lady was
pleased to distinguish the author by the appellation of
irresistible eyes'

c.563

H1316 How is he able now, his brains being dull,
Where he rode post before, he now may fly.

Sir Thomas Urquhart, 'Of a post rider altogether
besotted'

fb.217, p. 141

H1317 How is it in this chilling time
Or men and plants in town must die.

[Anne Finch, countess of Winchilsea]

Poetry Box I/89

H1318 How is it with your loving spouse?
Lov'd mistress of your heart and house?

[Charles Earle, postscript to 'Dear Sir—next
Wednesday . . .']

c.376

H1319 How is the heart lift up with joy
And faithlessness eschew?

'Psalm 92'

c.264/2, p. 99

H1320 How is the world deceived by noise and show!
Silently strong, and its deep bottom hides.

'A simile'

c.487, p. 45

H1321 How is thy love['s] creative power display'd,
Till at the case he numbers with the dead.

S[tephen] Simpson, 'Phaon. An elegy'

c.563

H1322 How is't that I i'th' second place do stand
On earth the king of birds, in heaven king's bird.

'Aquila' [answered by 'I you're a jovial chicken . . .']

b.356, p. 107

H1323 How joyous birds frequent the silent grove
The sun and Thyrsis set, we mourn the double night.

[Robert Cholmeley], 'A pastoral essay upon the death
of Mr. Alexander Popham. Corydon and Damon'

c.190, p. 93

H1324 How joys my soul that long forlorn
In these dear shades I love.

Miss [ ] White, of Edgbaston, 'Ode'

c.532

H1325 How just is then the tribute of our eyes,
And bathe with tears (of joy) each bishop's hearse.

'Upon the sickness of the A[rch] B[isho]p of
C[anterbury, William Sancroft, 1689? or 1691?]'
[Crum H1441; POAS V.278]

File 19019

H1326 How! Justices seiz'd, and dragg'd before their
betters!
The Lord have mercy on this wicked town!

John Lockman, 'On an infamous report concerning a
very able magistrate . . . July 1755'

c.267/1, p. 207

H1327 How like Erasmus' ghost in Scottish mist
Death to himself when poison to his king.

'On Monck's approach out of Scotland'

fb.140, p. 15

H1328 How like to Yorick 's Chesterfield?
Alike the knight and peer.

'Yorick and Chesterfield of the unlike likeness a song'

Spence Papers, folder 113

H1329 How little cause we have for mirth
So that my after may be crown'd.

H[enry] C[olman], 'On mourning'
[Crum H1449]

b.2, p. 71

H1330 How little do the landmen know,
And the royal family.

'Song 11'
[Crum H1450]

c.555, p. 16

H1331 How little nature's greatest artist knew
Produc'd his son!—and died.

'Shakespeare outdone' [on Richard Sheridan]

Poetry Box IV/74

H1332 How long, Amintor, faithless haughty swain
Because you fear, you own a future state.

'The immortality of the soul in answer to
Mr. Glanville's translation from Seneca, Troas, Act 2'

b.382(16)

H1333 How long, dear Thyrsis, shall thy generous heart
Through all his veins, and pants for instant foes.

'To Thyrsis on his amours 1724'

c.360/2, no. 104

H1334 How long great God, how must I
But fly and love on all the way.

[John] N[orris, of Bemerton], 'The aspiration'

c.258

H1335 How long my God how long how long
And dwell in flesh no more.

'39 Psalm'

c.124, no. 3

H1336 How long provok'd shall I conceal my rage,
And then to play the hypocrite no more.

Abraham Oakes, 'Hypocrisy: a satirical essay'

c.50, p. 75

H1337 How long shall I bite on the bit
Which thine it is, a [?] wherein no favor is.

'Braye Lute Book,' Music Ms. 13, fol. 38

H1338 How long wilt Thou forget me Lord,
And power forevermore.

[Thomas Sternhold], 'The 5 psalm for help in
afflictions' [verses from Psalms 13, 16]
[cf. Crum H1463–64]

a.3, fol. 71v; see also next.

H1339 How long wilt Thou forget me Lord,
I will glad hymns prepare.

'Psalm 13' [first line from Sternhold]

c.264/1, p. 41; see also previous.

H1340 How look'st I should a gift to thee commend,
I but myself have nothing else to lend.

'Ph: to P: calendar January' [see 'Thou nothing
sent'st . . .']

c.356

H1341 How lovely thy pavilions are
Thee trusts, with courage bold.

'Psal: 84'

b.217, p. 32

H1342 How lovely's a woman before she's enjoy'd
Wine and music for you, and a woman for me.

'Song'

fb.70, p. 47

H1343 How many a heart is happy at this hour
Of welcome shall that sorrow overpay.

'Christmas Day'

Poetry Box II/11

H1344 How many accidents mankind befall?
On him alone, not our own care rely.

[Edmund Wodehouse], 'May 4 [1715]'

b.131, p. 208

H1345 How many days in one whole year there be,
Strange tales to tell, yet not so strange as true.

[Peter] Heylyn, 'Salisbury Cathedral . . .
paraphrased by . . .'
[Crum H1470]

c.81/1, no. 127

H1346 How many foolish, paltry, painted things,
And still survive in my immortal song.

[Michael] Drayton, 'Drayton's sixth sonnet.
Addressed to a lady'

c.83/3, no. 844

H1347 How many fools at court bawl out aloud,
And therefore 'tis high time to make an end.

'Satire. Aug. [16]91 . . . Tunbridge lampoon'
[POAS v.348]

fb.70, p. 97; b.111, p. 561

H1348 How many hardships do the poor attend
That only money makes the mare to go.

J[ohn] R[obinson], 'Omnia Romae cum pretio'

c.370, fol. 71

H1349 How many hardships must each man oppose,
A due reward, which he did surely gain.

J[ohn] [Robinson], 'Per varios casus, per tot
discrimina rerum tendimus in latium'

c.370, fol. 79v

H1350 How many hearts with silent grief attend,
To imitate the actions we admire.

[Francis Drummond], 'Epitaph on the late Sir Henry
Drummond'

c.343, p. 100

H1351 How many O my God the warnings are
These heav'nly qualities endow'd his mind.

[Edmund Wodehouse], 'Aug. 19 [1715] on hearing my
nep[hew] Ham's death'

b.131, p. 249

H1352 How many souls require, sweep 'em clean, sweep
'em clean,
A filthy broom! Not I; mine's swept clean, mine's
swept clean.

[John Lockman], 'Chimney sweepers turned
preachers. (Supposed to be sung on the stage by six
chimney-sweepers.) Tune, A young man and a maid'

c.268 (first part), p. 97; c.267/2, p. 150

H1353 How many stories, have been heard
And teach, even Satan to be civil.

[Thomas Hamilton, 6th earl of Haddington], 'The
ghost from Boccace'

c.458/2, p. 60

H1354 How many with industrious malice dare
Tho' chance surprise you with a man of sense.

'Against lampooning'

c.188, p. 29

H1355 How many years have I now past?
And make our wills to his blest will resign'd.

[Edmund Wodehouse], 'Apr. 27 [1715]'

b.131, p. 205

H1356 How merry the sailor's life passes
Then merrily live till we die. | Then why should we
quarrel &c.

c.160, fol. 86v

H1357 How mournful feeble nature's tone,
And mourn eternal Ratcliffe's tragic fate.

Thomas Oliver, 'On Dilston Hall, once the seat of
James earl of Derwentwater'

c.93

H1358 How much a verse deceives
A verse too strong for envy or for age.

[George Daniel]

b.121, fol. 18v

H1359 How much do ev'ry heart regard
Compar'd to time's [un]ending store.

[Edmund Wodehouse], 'Decr. 12 [1714]'

b.131, p. 112

H1360 How much, egregious Moore are we,
Which maggots was before.

[Alexander Pope], 'On the famous Mr. Moore's
worm-powder' [1716]
[Crum H1477]

c.172, p. 1; fb.7, fol. 8

H1361 How much O God does ev'n the least
A mote compar'd to what's immense.

[Edmund Wodehouse], 'Aug. 18 [1715] upon my Lord
of Oxford's commitment to the Tower'

b.131, p. 249

H1362 How much the more hard usage I
A bliss from that which some think hard t'endure.

[Edmund Wodehouse], 'Iterum [10 February 1715]'

b.131, p. 163

H1363 How much the stronger, hopes on life rely,
So much the weaker is my faith, to die.

'On faith, and hope'
[Crum H1480]

b.118, p. 230

How my soul struggles pants for liberty,   H1364
O, could I soar above them.

'[Soliloquies] (5)'

c.153, p. 157

How now my John what is't the care?   H1365
Thou hast lost thy friends, amongst them I.

Sir Jo[hn] Mennes, 'The invitation of . . . to Mr. John
Weekes to return to London'

fb.140, p. 1

How oft Louisa hast thou said   H1366
And I'll take kingdoms back from thine.

'Song 242'

c.555, p. 385

How oft the just man falls, the scripture shows: H1367
But how oft the just woman falls, who knows.

Sir Thomas Urquhart, 'Of the just man, and just
woman'

fb.217, p. 174

How oft the thing that gives delight   H1368
Possession is the bane of bliss.

[Thomas Stevens?]

c.259, p. 16

How oft the warblings of thy plaintive lyre   H1369
And each proud rock repeat it to the vale.

'To Lorenzo'

c.344, p. 62

How oft when Cupid's fires decline   H1370
The other in goodbyeing.

Poetry Box XII/84

How often pride produces cares,   H1371
Nor by our wrangling copy man.

'The tinderbox'

c.83/4, no. 1096

How often those we think our friends,   H1372
To share my griefs, and taste my bliss.

'The true friend'

c.487, p. 49

How ominous are names? His name does show,   H1373
Or else the parallel, as just allow.

[Edmund Wodehouse], 'Doctor Hicks is heterodox'
[14 May 1715]

b.131, p. 213

H1374 How, pensive Bavius, tippling ale,
Should'st thou, long as patriarchs live.

[John Lockman], 'The opera-bard's invocation to
nonsense'

c.268 (first part), p. 112

H1375 How pleasant a sailor's life passes;
Who merrily live till we die. | Then why should &c.

'Song 64'
[cf. Crum H1496]

c.555, p. 91

H1376 How pleasant is the green wood's deep-matted
shade,
If I, with my pale light, came not near.

[Ann (Ward)] Radcliffe, 'The glow-worm'

c.83/3, no. 870

H1377 How pleasant! See! How good and right
Exist, when faith and hope shall cease.

'Psalm 133'

c.264/3, p. 80

H1378 How pleasing are the paths to sin!
He raves, despairs, and dies.

'The hardened sinner'

c.487, p. 54

H1379 How poor, how rich, how abject, how august,
And hold communion with my God on high.

'A hymn after receiving the Holy Communion'

c.515, fol. 20

H1380 How poor was Jacob's motion and how strange
For toys we often sell our heaven our crown.

[Francis Quarles], 'On Jacob's purchase' [Divine
Fancies I, 58]

b.137, p. 167

H1381 How prodigious is my fate
That I through absence died not scorn'd.

[Katherine Philips]
[Crum H1503]

Trumbull Box: Poetry Box XIII/41

H1382 How prone the bosom is to sigh!
And then, 'tis all the sighing tear.

'The tear'

c.83/1, no. 60

H1383 How? Providence, and yet a Scottish crew
Drops into Styx, and turns a Solon-goose.

[John Cleveland], 'The rebel Scots'
[cf. Crum W653, 'What Providence']

b.93, p. 87

H1384 How pure was Catharine, Christ made her so,
To star-pav'd mansions, and a gem-blazed crown.

'Mrs. Cath. Bretterg's epitaph paraphrased'

c.58

H1385 How quick, alas! time slides away,
And everlasting day.

'A young gentleman on his sister's birthday'

c.83/3, no. 960

H1386 How rich are thy provisions, Lord!
The vast expense our lives would cost.

[Isaac Watts, Hymns and spiritual songs (1707),
bk. III, Hymn 12]

c.180, p. 47

H1387 How rich the wave, in front imprest
By virtue's holiest powers attended.

'Lines written near Richmond, upon the Thames, at
evening'

c.142, p. 363

H1388 How rich thy favors God of grace
To joys that never end.

P[hilip] Doddridge, 'The grace of God displayed in
making the Christian perfect through sufferings from
[I] Pet. V 10'

c.493, p. 56

H1389 How sacred and how innocent
But chose to spend my life.

[Katherine Philips], 'A country life'
[Crum H1507]

b.118, p. 75; c.189, p. 27 (ll. 1–32)

H1390 How sad a bargain does he make?
O God to serve, praise, honor Thee.

[Edmund Wodehouse], 'March 10 [1715]'

b.131, p. 178

H1391 How sad our state by nature is!
My Jesus, and my all.

[Isaac Watts, Hymns and spiritual songs (1707), bk. II,
Hymn 90]

c.180, p. 33

H1392 How sad the day when thou proud ship
The parent, and the muse.

'To the Rochfort and ocean'

Poetry Box II/51

H1393 How sadly solemn is the dawn of birth
Of sorrow looking back on better days.

W. Wright, 'Infancy . . . 1798'

c.364

H1394 How seldom I see you, dear neighbor of late,
So it is not my fault it is clear.

'Note from an Irishman, to his neighbor'
Diggle Box: Poetry Box XI/69

H1395 How seldom poor mortals a blessing obtain
And death, only death, put an end to your love.

[Charles Burney, the elder], 'Epithalamium. The
marriage of the Revd. Mr. Spelman, with Miss Harwin
after a long and almost hopeless courtship . . .
London, 1760'
c.33, p. 49

H1396 How severe is forgetful old age,
And breathe out my life in hey-ho.

'Love sighs'
fb.107, p. 31

H1397 How shall a crazy bark survive
To Canaan's lands.

Charles Atherton Allnutt, 'The Christian's voyage
through the sea of life—27 acts'
c.112, p. 20

H1398 How shall a youth condemn'd by early fate,
Nor deem the tribute paid my verse, too dear.

[Frederick Corfield], 'To Miss Eliza S.'
c.381/1

H1399 How shall I begin? for in vain 'tis to write
That Mary of Burfield be chosen my second.

[ ] B., 'The following lines were wrote in consequence
of a young lady's expressing a wish that she might be
Mr. B's second wife'
fc.57, p. 34

H1400 How shall I now the nine invoke
Lest it should into atoms fly.

[Laurence Whyte], 'The broken mug' [attr. Jonathan
Swift]
c.176, p. 27

H1401 How shall I paint the miseries I feel
The poignard strikes me, and the harlot dies.

'An epistle from Eliza to Henry, on the tomb of her
sister Constantia, who died of grief on perceiving an
improper intimacy between Henry her husband, and
Eliza'
c.391, p. 30

H1402 How shall I speak my Savior's worth
His name forbids your hearts to fear.

'Hymn 16th'
c.562, p. 18

H1403 How short is life's uncertain space
Be center'd in a friend.

'The wish'
c.83/2, no. 343

H1404 How short the joys that happiest mortals find,
Nor murmur since he lives amongst the blest.

'On the death of a lovely boy, addressed to his
disconsolate friends'
c.83/3, no. 958

H1405 How short's man's life compar'd with [other] lives
To live well so to die well and live ever.

'Humanae vitae brevitas quae sit tamen quam profusi
temporis homines'
b.205, fol. 35r

H1406 How should we strive our God to please?
This caus'd him t'pay so dear to redeem.

[Edmund Wodehouse], 'Jan. 12 [1715]'
b.131, p. 139

H1407 How sickness summons us unto one dome
To greatest prince who in the world doth live.

M. P., 'Certain most beneficial meditations . . . the
argument of the first part'
a.6, p. 1

H1408 How sits this city lately most populous
And to be utterly enrag'd at us.

J[ohn] D[onne], 'The lamentation of Jeremy'
[according to Tremellius and others]
b.148, p. 26

H1409 How sleep the brave, who sink to rest
To dwell a weeping hermit there.

[William Collins, new year's ode 1746]
[Crum H1522]
c.53, fol. 63; see also 'Here sleep the brave . . .'.

H1410 How slight a thing is man, how frail, how brittle,
How seeming great is he, how truly little.

'More on man'
c.189, p. 104

H1411 How slight a toy is offer'd here by me!
High in midair, with double sweetness sings.

John Lockman, 'To abbé Dubos; on his giving me the
fourth edition (most elegantly bound) of his
Reflexions critiques sur la poesie et la peinture; and
my presenting him with some verses of mine'
c.267/2, p. 342

H1412 How slight, how shallow is his sense
As to deliver him e'en from Hades.

    [Edmund Wodehouse], 'Idem [8 September 1715]'

    b.131, p. 261

H1413 . . . How small of all that human hearts endure
Leave reason, faith, and conscience, all our own . . . .

    [Samuel] Johnson, 'Lines from Goldsmith's poem of
    The traveller, written by Johnson'

    Diggle Box: Poetry Box XI/1

H1414 How smooth that lake expands its ample breast
And fancy all her loveliest dreams impart.

    [Ann (Ward)] Radcliffe, 'Stanzas'

    c.83/3, no. 857

H1415 How sour a thing is love
Than crosslines in a globe.

    [answer to 'How sweet a thing . . .']

    b.213, p. 69

H1416 How still is the evening! The vessel's white sail
'Tis done—and I follow an—ass!

    John Tebbit, 'Adventure at Netley Abbey'

    Poetry Box X/156

H1417 How strange it is, that Cupid should decree,
The bee flies always to the sweetest flowers.

    Dr. [ ] Farmer, 'An epigram made extempore by . . .
    upon a gentleman observing that every toast begun
    with B'

    c.378, p. 33; see also 'Is it not strange that fortune . . .'.

H1418 How strangely doth the power of custom rule
Thus to convert, their old clothes into food.

    [William Taylor], 'Another of the same' [on fine ladies
    and their clothes]

    c.176, p. 82

H1419 How strong's the venal thirst of gold!
Speaks thee a seraph from the skies.

    John Lockman, 'To Mr. Freke [one of the surgeons of
    St. Bartholomew's Hospital], on his constantly
    resisting a fee . . . May 1754'

    c.267/2, p. 245

H1420 How subtle a thing 'tis to love,
That our pretty love-fainting is done.

    'The sickly lovers'

    fb.107, p. 6

H1421 How sweet a thing is love
Is not to have her will.

    [answered by 'How sour a thing . . .']

    b.213, p. 68

H1422 How sweet her face! How elegant her air!
Who fix'd the graces to the number three.

    John Lockman, 'Stella dancing at Mr. Hugford's
    ball . . . April 1757'

    c.267/1, p. 100

H1423 How sweet is love's first gentle sway,
Relentless frowns, and wings th'envenom'd dark.

    [Ann (Ward)] Radcliffe, 'Sonnet'

    c.83/3, no. 853

H1424 How sweet my first when stormy nights appear,
And thus to be my second well deserves.

    '[Enigma/Charade/Conundrum] 20' [housewife]

    c.389

H1425 How sweet the air! how fair each scene!
My God is nature's king.

    'Soliloquy on a spring morning'

    c.487, p. 67

H1426 How sweet the calm of this sequester'd shore,
The social virtues, and the absent friend.

    [Elizabeth] Carter, 'The calm evening'

    c.83/2, no. 610

H1427 How sweet the moon's resplendent light,
Nor wish to break her sweet repose.

    'Thoughts by moonlight'

    fc.124, p. 3

H1428 How sweet the scene! How gaily drest!
And let it be like this.

    'The landscape'

    c.382, p. 40

H1429 How sweet the sound when Celia sings
While youth and beauty join.

    'Occasioned by a certain young lady playing on an
    harpsichord'

    Poetry Box IV/99

H1430 How sweet to gaze on Sylvia's eyes!
Can credit those who deal in rhymes?

    John Lockman, 'Sylvia' [translated from La Fontaine]

    c.267/4, p. 183

H1431 How sweet to the hearts is the thought of tomorrow
That his joys and his will expire with today.

    'Tomorrow'

    Poetry Box XII/72

H1432 How sweet to wind the forest's tangled shade,
Here spread her blush, and bid the parent live.

[Ann (Ward)] Radcliffe, 'The first hour of morning'
c.83/3, no. 868

H1433 How sweetly that harmonious music strikes mine ear,
Dissolve to flesh in teary water.

H[enry] C[olman], 'On prayer'
[Crum H1539]
b.2, p. 32

H1434 How sweet's that feast where Jesu's friends
And all the feast is love.

[Thomas Stevens?], 'Delightful repast . . . sung at the
Exp[erience] meet[in]g August 17 1779'
c.259, p. 1 (incomplete), p. 15

H1435 How swift, we cry, the restless years roll on
Strew it with flowers to obstruct thy way.

'Life'
c.244, p. 631

H1436 How Tallboy, Killprick, Suckprick did contend
Contrived by turns how each might rub her arse on.

[John Wilmot, 2nd earl of Rochester?], 'Argument'
[of 'Say heav'n-born muse . . .']
b.105, p. 76

H1437 How thick the shades of evening close!
Which none but friends and lovers know.

[Mark Akenside], 'Hymn to cheerfulness'
Diggle Box: Poetry Box XI/70

H1438 How thou art envied; let Pygmalion prove
Or how at first hope any more than me.

[Charles Hopkins], 'The story of Pygmalion—
imitated from the tenth book of Ovid's
Metamorphoses'
b.130, p. 14

H1439 How time doth pass away by stealth
Will grant to God for Jesu Christ his sake.

M. H., 'A survey of time . . . Finis. M. H. Anno 1595'
a.6, p. 32

H1440 How transient is the sinner's breath?
O'er the remains of that which late was envy lust
                                        and pride.

Barnaby Gouche, 'A second Pindaric by . . . a worthy
and ingenious member of the Gent[lemen's] Soc[iety]
in Spalding . . . 1728'
c.229/1, fol. 31v

H1441 How true the tale which Stella does relate,
Be mine these charms which never will decay.

'Deceitfulness of human friendship'
c.83/3, no. 979

H1442 How uneasy are we here,
That we may live eternally.

[( ) Pierson]
c.328, p. 5

H1443 How unhappy a lover am I
And esteems all her sufferings your own.

[John] Dryden, 'A song [from Dryden's Conquest of
Granada, Act IV]. 1674'
[Crum H1544]
b.54, p. 965

H1444 How vain a thing is man, how soon made earth!
And as Christ taught us say, God's will be done.

Joseph Kempt, 'An elegy or mournful song on the
death of Mr. John Neale, son and heir to Mr. Thomas
Neale'
c.181, p. 1

H1445 How vain a thought is bliss below!
To her eternal home.

'On pleasure'
c.83/3, no. 933

H1446 How vain are mortal man's endeavors,
Runs the same track it did before.

[John Arbuthnot], 'Quid nunc . . . said to be
Mr. Pope's' [on the death of the Duke of Orleans]
c.176, p. 24; Spence Papers, folder 153 (attr. Swift)

H1447 How vain are riches, honors, titles, birth!
'Tis only virtue yields immortal fame.

'Epitaph for the Earl and Countess of Sutherland'
c.53, fol. 47

H1448 How vain is all our life 'tis but deceit
Adored by them like to a deity.

[Mrs. ( ) Feilding]
b.226, p. 18

H1449 How vain is man, how fluttering are his joys
Or never hope to meet with happy days.

'On the uncertainty of worldly enjoyments'
[Crum H1551]
c.83/3, no. 1034; c.360/3, no. 163

H1450 How vain is man! How foolish all his ways!
Man's born, knows cares, looks round, laments and
                                        dies.

Henry Baker, 'A reflection on human life'
c.244, p. 397

H1451 How vain is our hope of pleasure below
And shows me the virtue of pardoning blood.

> T[homas] S[tevens], 'The snail . . . occasioned by the snail's eating the author's Africanus, and other flowers to which he had paid great attention. Copied April 1st. 1780'

c.259, p. 75

H1452 How vain man's power is, unless God command
In peaceful tunes t'adore the God of peace.

> [Sir William Trumbull]
> Trumbull Box: Poetry Box XIII/29

H1453 How vain Sir Knight is thy affected rage,
Thy charity begins and ends at home.

> [Nicholas Amhurst], 'To a certain gentleman who takes the character of Cardinal Woolsey, to himself. An epigram'

c.570/3, p. 62

H1454 How vain the joys that human pride elate
And yield the spotless off'ring to the skies.

> [Elizabeth] Carter, 'Epitaph on Master Quested, aged seven years'

fc.51, p. 168

H1455 How varied lies the chequer'd scene!
The hawthorn left to bloom.

> Hector Macneill, 'Grandeur: an ode'

c.142, p. 142

H1456 How vast his fancy; how sublime his skill;
And, in a vision, give the grand design.

> John Lockman, 'Thoughts suggested on seeing a perspective drawing (by Mr. Jackson) of Salisbury Cathedral . . . Aug. 1757'

c.267/1, p. 123

H1457 How vile a wretch is man when reason is drown'd
A man in form, in all things else a beast.

> 'On a drunken man'

c.186, p. 47

H1458 How was Aminta, sprightly as the morn
With just such dignity of virtue joined.

c.152, p. 168 (incomplete?)

H1459 How weak a star doth rule mankind
Shall die, as infants go to sleep.

> K[atherine] Phil[ips], ['Death']
> [Crum H1556]

b.118, p. 43

H1460 How weak alas! is all the power of man
And will afflict or bless us in its own way.

c.186, p. 61

H1461 How weak must be the spark who trusts a lass,
To borrow English coin, and pay in French.

> 'A memento written on a tavern window'

c.360/3, no. 254

H1462 How well great things with small can fodge!
For heaven's become a Porter's lodge.

> 'On Dr. Porter'

b.356, p. 243

H1463 How well her name an army doth present
In whom the Lord of hosts did pitch his tent.

> [George Herbert], 'An anagram on the blessed Virgin {Mary/Army}'
> [Crum H1558]

b.137, p. 201; c.189, p. 46; see also 'How ill . . .' and 'Her name an army . . .'.

H1464 How well our Savior and that landed youth
Will lick their scalded lips, and run away.

> [Francis Quarles], 'On the young man in the gospel' [Divine Fancies I, 54; 'sneak' for 'run']

b.137, p. 166

H1465 How well this war's prolong'd, when him to fight
Nothing to do was best [?] for them by far.

> [Sir Richard Bulstrode, translation from a Latin poem, c. August 1696]

fb.88, p. 118

H1466 How well thy name and nature here agree
For grace, and glory, Barnaby the bright.

> [Edward] Sparke, 'Poem 27th—On St Barnabas'

b.137, p. 59

H1467 How wise are you to throw off earthly cares,
Before this seventy years of yours expire.

> [Mrs. Christian Kerr], 'To Mr. Kerr of Chatto Senior on his birthday entering 70 March 25, 1719'

c.102, p. 110

H1468 How wondrous are the works of G[od]
The greatest glories G[od] can show.

> [Hymn]

c.180, p. 83

H1469 How wretched is a woman's fate!
That cheerfully I may your will obey.

> [Katherine Thurston], 'Woman born to be controlled. Sent [to Thomas Morell], by Miss Kitty Thurston. 1725' [answered by 'How happy is a woman's fate . . .']

c.395, p. 5

H1470　How wretched, who ne'er taste of love,
The boar, that hides for fear.

　　[William Popple, trans.], '[Horace] book 3rd. ode
　　12th. To Neobule'

　　fc.104/2, p. 250

H1471　How you thus Atlas-like sustain
I beg the Delta t'wards a cock'd hat.

　　'Verses addressed to Major General the Earl of Cavan,
　　on the ridiculous absurdity of attempting to take
　　Cleopatra's Needle from Egypt to England. By an
　　officer' [c. 1802]

　　Poetry Box x/124

H1472　How! How! Who is here | I Robin of Doncaster.
Threescore years and seven, yet liv'd not one.

　　'An epitaph at Doncaster in Yorkshire on Robert
　　Byrkes and Margaret his wife 1579 [1597?]'
　　[Crum H1431]

　　c.360/3, no. 107

H1473　Howe'er the cause, fantastic may appear
The effect is real, and the pain sincere.

　　'On love'

　　c.360/1, p. 191

H1474　Howe'er the papists may perplex
And smiling said, go sin no more.

　　[Thomas Hamilton, 6th earl of Haddington], 'The
　　talents'

　　c.458/2, p. 159

H1475　However former ages, this we know
I'll covet for no wealth, wish for no more.

　　H[enry] C[olman], 'On poverty'
　　[Crum H1574]

　　b.2, p. 86

H1476　However it be, yet God is good
Amen, amen say I.

　　[Thomas Sternhold and John Hopkins], 'That we be
　　not discouraged with the prosperity of the wicked nor
　　with the affliction of the godly. Psalm 29' [verses from
　　Psalms 72–73]
　　[cf. Crum H1575]

　　a.3, fol. 109

H1477　However short of other's art and wit
In the vessel to be all embarkt.

　　[on Henry, prince of Wales, d. 1612]
　　[cf. Crum H797c]

　　b.205, fol. 6r

H1478　Howlit thy matchless pride throughout is seen
They're not worth reading, that's the reason why.

　　T[homas] Gurney, 'Written in a book I borrowed
　　written by Mr Howlit against the Baptist inquisition'

　　c.213

H1479　Howsoe'er they be, thus they do seem to me,
They be and seem not, seem what least they be.

　　'Women'
　　[Crum H1580]

　　c.356

H1480　H—t conceives himself elected,
'Tis odds but they are both becapon'd.

　　'Epigrammatic'

　　fc.130, p. 47

H1481　Huge gluttonies, unfathom'd gulf doth waste
Great Croesus unknown wealth though ne'er so vast.

　　'Gluttony'

　　c.189, p. 41

H1482　Huge weight, of earth, and sin!
From utter death, and the devouring wave.

　　[George Daniel]

　　b.121, fol. 60

H1483　Hugh ap Rees, built a colleese(?)
There he lees Hugh ap Rees.

　　'Upon Hugh ap Rees a Welshman'

　　b.356, p. 157

H1484　Humane, just, vigilant; quite free from stain,
Enough, that rectitude of soul is thine.

　　John Lockman, 'To a real patriot: on the expiration of
　　his mayoralty . . . Nov. 1756'

　　c.267/1, p. 115

H1485　Humbly behold, I bow myself to Thee,
And only hope forgiveness in the grave.

　　'Jane Shore's prayer. O thou most righteous judge!'

　　c.83/2, no. 714

H1486　Humid seat of soft affection,
Of a tender, parting kiss.

　　[Robert Burns? or Richard Sheridan?], 'The kiss'

　　c.344, p. 32; c.82, p. 13

H1487　Humility who art heaven's welcom'st guest
Foundations of the loftiest towers lie deep.

　　[John Hobart], 'Humility'

　　b.108, fol. 1v

H1488 Humility's a vine, whose root through earth
Only to heaven, and thee may fructify.

> H[enry] C[olman], 'On humility'
> [Crum H1587]

b.2, p. 60

H1489 Hungry, and poor, despairing, and forlorn
Where penitence may hope and gain relief!

> [William Parsons], 'Elegy on a girl of the town
> meeting with a gentleman who resembled her seducer'

Greatheed Box/50

H1490 Hush! hush! my dearest lovely boy!
Thy father's darling mother's joy.

> M. S[harpe, on his infant son sleeping upon his arm.
> Oct 21, 1730]

c.116, p. 26

H1491 Hush there with your ballads! Let mine first be
                                            heard,
You may sing fifty-nine, now I've sung fifty-eight.

> [James Mulcaster, sr.], 'The year [17]fifty-eight. A
> song'

c.118, p. 42

H1492 Hush'd be the voice of joy, nor let the lyre,
Wing'd her quick passage to the realms of light.

> 'Elegy on the death of Miss Eliza Price'

c.83/3, no. 923

H1493 Hymen, god of pure desire,
His poor petitioner must die a maid.

> 'The maiden's wish'
> [Crum H1603]

c.233, p. 94

H1494 Hymen! God of virtuous pleasures,
More than gems each other prize!

> John Lockman, 'On the marriage of two friends of the
> author (set to music by the late Signor Palma)
> Christmas 1751'

c.267/1, p. 287; c.267/2, p. 94

H1495 Hymen light thy purest flame
Bless your ever-peaceful nights. Amen.

> 'An epithalamium on the marriage of the Hon[ora]ble,
> William Lee esqr. and the Hon[ora]ble Miss Dyke
> 1757'

Poetry Box I/93

H1496 Hymen, my Martha, here his wreath may see
Prepare his tints again, and paint from you.

> 'To my wife, a sonnet, 1779'

fc.53, p. 9

H1497 Hymen of highest bliss, or deepest woe,
Attune in feeling concert to thy praise.

> 'A petition to Hymen'

c.136, p. 34

H1498 Hymns of transport, hymns of praise, Hallelujah!
Guards our steps, and points our way. [Hallelujah!]

> [Thomas Hull], 'Anthem from the two first verses of
> the hundredth psalm'

c.528/8

H1499 Hypocrisy that cursed sin
To deserts far from human race.

> [William Stukeley], 'Bruin vs. Bantam, a fable'

File 17839

H1500 Hypocrisy usurps the chair,
'Whatever is, is right!'

> Abraham Oakes, 'A sarcastic ode: on Mr. P[ope]'s
> morality'

c.50, p. 13

I

10001 I A. B. do truly swear
If God won't help me, I'll help myself.

'The parson's oath'
[Crum I1]

b.111, p. 133

10002 I admire you should write to me for a cloak
And yet I mean to keep the cloak.

W. B., 'On one that made a cloak' [Thomas Rabbets]
[Crum I4]

b.200, p. 49

10003 I always Flora lov'd. The Hovillian rose
That this might come—Well may Lilly love.

[Sir Philip Wodehouse], 'Upon Sr William Hovill who
married Miss Lilly, who repaired his fortune William
Hovill well may Lilly love'

b.131, back (no. 16)

10004 I always shall him for my friend approve
When by reproof we better grow, not worse.

Sir John Strangways, 'Of reproof and of the right use
thereof . . . 5 Sept: 1646'

b.304, p. 54

10005 I am a jolly scribbler
While he keeps open door. | And a begging we may
go . . .

[Philip Dormer Stanhope, 4th] earl of Chesterfield(?),
'A song to the tune of Begging we will go. This was
right on the bench, on the Mount at Kensington
supposed by . . .'

Poetry Box IV/163; see also 'I am a saucy . . .'.

10006 I am a lover, and 'tis true.
O show not, lest you strike me blind.

'To his m[ist]r[es]s'
[Crum I15]

b.200, p. 91

10007 I am a pad swift safe and good
Except I chance lie down.

[Lord E.], 'Riddle [A ship]'

Poetry Box VII/47

10008 I am a painful plowman
Twisted(?) frig[h]t and leadeth ram by [?]

'The ploughman's pains and pleasures'

a.6, p. 126

10009 I am a saucy scribbler
And a-begging we may go &c.

[Philip Dormer Stanhope, 4th earl of Chesterfield?],
'Tune of The jovial beggar'

Poetry Box IV/91; see also 'I am a jolly . . .'.; c.570/3,
p. 137

10010 I am a sensual thing with a hey | Men call me a
King with a ho.
I must run away | With a Hey trolley lolley lo.

'The King's confession' [1679]
[Crum I18, 'senseless thing'; POAS II.176]

fb.140, p. 172

10011 I am a sturdy beggar
No ribbon but a halter. | And to Tyburn they
would go. . . .

'The London merchants' triumph' [pr. 1733 (Foxon
L239)]

c.570/3, p. 219

10012 I am a swan you plainly see
Because John Harvey sells good beer.

'Country poetry on a sign at a place Tittensor near
Trentham in Staffordshire was written under the sign
of a swan chained to a tree, this stanza'

c.361

10013 I am a turnip-hoer
So I can have my hoe.

[Thomas Wharton?], 'A new song, to the tune of
A-begging we will go' [Jacobite satire on George I]

fc.58, p. 133

10014 I am a weary pilgrim,
Hope says they're happy pains.

'The weary pilgrim'

c.83/3, no. 1012; c.578, p. 163

10015 I am always out of fashion,
Yet I'm here, before your eyes!

'A riddle'

fc.40

10016 I am an Englishman, and naked I stand here
Now I will wear, I cannot tell what.

'Fickleness of the English'
[Crum I22]

c.81/1, no. 160

10017 I am both to the farmer and doctor a friend,
And covered with sackcloth and mourning I cry.

    '[Enigma/Charade/Conundrum] 62'

c.389

10018 I am but a woodman and live on yon hill
When she has given content for our lot. | Their
                          days are thus &c.

    [John Walker?], 'The woodman or the country cot'

fc.108, fol. 45

10019 I am Christ's spouse: and each of you's his brother:
I'm your good sister then, and not your mother.

    Sir Thomas Urquhart, 'The church of Jesus speaks
    thus to the Christians'

fb.217, p. 290

10020 I am confirm'd a woman can
If e'er I dote upon you more.

    [Owen Felltham?], 'On the dispraise of women'
    [answered by 'His wit's infirm . . .']

b.197, p. 239

10021 I am fond of the swallow—I learn from her flight,
That leads to the day-spring appearing above.

    [William Cowper, trans.], 'The swallow—Vol. 2.
    Cant. 54' [of Jeanne Guion's 'Spiritual songs']

c.470 (autogr.)

10022 I am found in the earth but how I came there
And am made the most scandalous slave in the
                          nation.

    [riddle, accompanied by a copy of 'The gentleman's
    letter that first solved this enigma' dated 22 January
    1707/8]

Poetry Box IV/34

10023 I am just two of two—I am warm, I am cold,
And yielded with pleasure when taken by force.

    William Cowper, 'Riddle by . . . author of The task'

Smith Papers, folder 74/9

10024 I am like Archimedes for science and skill,
I am like a young lady just bringing to bed.

    'Fragment of an oration'

c.340; Poetry Box III/26 (var.)

10025 I am [Mercury] the mighty *flos florum* alone
For in all other things ye find [?] naught.

    [Brown-Robbins 1276]

fa.16, p. 41

10026 I am monarch of all I survey,
And reconciles man to his lot.

    [William Cowper], 'Verses written by Alexander
    Selkirk in the year 1707 when on the island of Juan
    Fernandez'

c.391, p. 79; c.83/2, no. 728

10027 I am neither High-Church nor Low Church, nor
                         Tory, nor Whig;
I submit to the will of a merciful God.

    'To all whom it may concern to know me'

c.157, p. 4; see also 'I'm neither . . .', 'I'm not . . .'.

10028 I am not as I seem
I must be as I may.

    [John Rose?]

b.227, p. 37

10029 I am not common mourner; neither crowd
Glorious to time; and equal in their names.

    [George Daniel], 'To the memory of . . . Sr William
    Alford . . . obit. 1642'

b.121, fol. 72v

10030 I am not concerned to know
She might ever live alone.

    Isaac Watts, 'True riches'

c.139, p. 88; Diggle Box: Poetry Box XI/32, 70

10031 I am not grieved my dearest life
For I must go to bed to she.

    'The husband marrying about a month after his wife's
    death . . .' [answer to 'For me deceased . . .', 'Grieve
    not for me . . .']

c.113/17; c.150, p. 114; see also 'I do not grieve . . .'.

10032 I am not indefil'd nor think I am
Set-meditated words—lip-offerings.

    [Sir Philip Wodehouse], 'Upon Sr Henry Bedingfield'

b.131, back (no. 143)

10033 I am not limited to a precise
Within the region, of a noble wit.

    [George Daniel]

b.121, fol. 79v

10034 I am not what I was but the very reverse
Because I am not what I was yet.

    '[Enigma/Charade/Conundrum] 30' [old maid]

c.389

10035 I am now at a modern school
For night the welcome night we pray.

    Miss [ ] Andrews, 'On a school'

File 245/5

10036 I am now very ill and ready to faint,
I believe—no bones broke!—but d[ou]bly bruis'd.

> [ ] Springthorpe, '. . . The underwritten. Impromptu'
>
> c.361

10037 I am old D'Avenant | With my fustian quill,
O gentle knight | Thou writ'st for those who shite.

> [Sir John Denham], 'Song' [the author (Sir William
> D'Avenant) upon himself]
> [Crum 134]
>
> pb.53, p. 14 (autogr.)

10038 I am only sent, and as it were a patent given,
To learn little children how to go to heaven.

> 'Epitaph in Haines churchyard'
>
> c.378, p. 7

10039 I am Paston—I've had of life my fill
Each minute myriads—frail world farewell.

> [Sir Philip Wodehouse], 'Some ana/epigrammatical
> conceits upon Sr W. Paston . . . 1661/2'
> [cf. Crum 135]
>
> b.131, back (no. 11/1)

10040 I am resolv'd I will not break my troth
Upon the rules of law and conscience?

> Sir John Strangways, 'Concerning the negative
> oath . . . 6to Augusti: 1647'
>
> b.304, p. 112

10041 I am Saint Paul the patron of my church,
We of Paul's sword that smote the schism's ear.

> 'Sr H: Edwin Lord Mayor'
>
> b.90, p. 5

10042 I am so fallen in love
I should be cured.

> 'An amorous catch' [answered by 'The devil take your
> love . . .']
>
> b.104, p. 12

10043 I am that faithful deputy
And what you hear soon teach again.

> [William Strode], 'A register for a Bible' [followed by
> 'I am your memory's recorder . . .']
> [Crum 143]
>
> b.205, fol. 55r

10044 I am that Savior that vouchsafed to die
Happy in death, than you in happiness.

> H[enry] C[olman], 'Jesus of Nazareth, king of the
> Jews' [acrostic and telestich spellings]
> [Crum 144]
>
> b.2, p. 92

10045 I am the D[uke] of Norfolk, lately come out of
Suffolk,
Thou shalt drink of another cup, cup, cup.

> [cf. Crum 146]
>
> c.416

10046 I am the evening dark as night,
Pond water shall wet their whistles.

> 'Evening, and boy a dialogue'
>
> fb.107, p. 59

10047 I am the king, and the prince of drunkards
When we can neither go nor stand.

> 'A song made by some scholars of Cambridge, in
> imitation of I am the king and the prince of fairies:
> 1675'
>
> b.54, p. 1027

10048 I am the same whom men call deaf and blind
Any content, I like myself them make.

> Petrarch
>
> b.211, p. 61

10049 I am the winged messenger of love
Where I may sleep within thy sepulcher.

> W[illiam] S[andys?], 'The tragady of Jeptha's
> daughter. Or Jeptha's vow. A foul first draft not to be
> read by any'
>
> b.230, p. 117

10050 I am tho' small yet when entire
I once contain'd all humankind.

> c.150, p. 52

10051 I am two fools I know
Who are a little wise, the best fools be.

> [John Donne], 'Canzone'
> [Crum 150]
>
> b.114, p. 305; b.148, p. 81

10052 I am unable yonder beggar cries
To stand or go, if he say true he lies.

> [John Donne, 'On a cripple']
> [Crum 151]
>
> b.148, p. 68; b.205, fol. 96v; b.356, p. 308; b.205, fol. 96v;
> c.546, p. 29; see also 'I cannot go or stand . . .'.

10053 I am very much concern'd to find
And love King George, of kings the best.

> 'The Duke of Marlborough's speech to the First
> Regiment of Foot Guards, June the 2nd. 1715' [satire;
> pr. 1715 (Foxon S627)]
> [Crum 152]
>
> c.570/1, p. 120

10054   I am well pleas'd to see my commands done,
To appease Buckingham's enraged ghost.

     'A dialogue between the Duke of Buckingham and his
     father's ghost appearing with Felton's knife in his
     wounded body'

     fb.140, p. 97

10055   I ask not to be rich or great—
They'll ope with sweet surprise.

     'A thought'

     c.83/3, no. 1038

10056   I ask not wealth ye gods, nor power nor fame,
To please my Emma, and attune my lyre.

     [ ] Edwin, 'The lover's petition or the pleasures of
     love in retirement preferable to the noise and bustle of
     a gay life, an elegy' [Chard-Somerset, 17 July 1796]

     Poetry Box IV/142

10057   I ask your pardon, ladies—but indeed
We thank you all, and wish you all goodnight.

     'Epilogue to The orphan [by Thomas Otway]'

     Poetry Box I/73 (cf. i/77)

10058   I asked Fabulus why he had no wife?
(Quoth he) 'cause I'd live a quiet life.

     [Edward May], 'On Fabulus'

     c.356

10059   I B. take thee C. | To be my dear wife,
Three persons above!

     [Charles Earle], 'Matrimony rhymed when a boy
     [man]'

     c.376

10060   I bend my knees O God before thy throne,
When it shall hear that voice, prepare to die.

     [Edmund Wodehouse], 'July 9 [1715]'

     b.131, p. 229

10061   I bless my God for every sense,
O God, is with the song of men.

     [ ] Grove, 'Sight—a hymn'

     c.244, p. 136

10062   I bless my stars I envy none
To the result be harmony, what part I bear.

     [John Norris], 'Content'

     c.547, p. 174; c.258

10063   I bring thee O! thou charming fair,
A heart that's free, a heart that's free from care!

     'The free gift'

     fb.107, p. 45

10064   I burn'd, and languish'd, sigh'd and swore,
To have and hold your soul forever.

     [Isaac Freeman], 'On Miss S. B. Hamburg'

     fc.105, p. 3

10065   I. C. take thee B. | To be my dear man
Were publish'd by me.

     [Charles Earle], 'Matrimony rhymed when a boy
     [woman]'

     c.376

10066   I call thyself my own self's better part,
Thou hast no husband, nor I any wife.

     'To his love'

     b.200, p. 410

10067   I call'd on Cotta for an evening's chat
For deathly-dull am I when you are madly vain.

     'The vain poet'

     fc.53, p. 46

10068   I came from England into France,
Who's thought ne'er did the same.

     [Thomas Goodwyn]
     [Crum 180]

     Poetry Box VI/36; b.356, p. 210; see also 'I went . . .'.

10069   I came I saw and was undone;
Employ me, mighty love, to dig the mine.

     A[braham] C[owley], 'Thralldom'

     c.258

10070   I came in with Adam, and outlived his fall,
Remember I strictly am charged not to tell.

     'A riddle'

     Poetry Box IV/55

10071   I can! I dare! But what? All what I may
But God, who gives me magnanimity.

     [Sir Philip Wodehouse], 'Upon his kinswoman the
     Lady [Jane] Darey'

     b.131, back (no. 52)

10072   I can love both fair and brown,
You shall be true to them who are false to you.

     [John Donne, 'The indifferent']
     [Crum 183]

     b.114, p. 252; b.148, p. 69; b.205, fol. 27r (stanzas 1–2)

10073   I can no other way be safe in the evils I have done,
Take me, but let the English be for their rebellion
                             curs'd.

     'King William's complaint'

     b.111, p. 363

10074 I cannot bend the bow, wherein I shout [*i.e.*, shoot]
I show
This shaft must have a notch, whereat my lady
laught.

    [Sir Walter] Raleigh, 'Raleigh to the Lady Bendbow'
    [Crum 187, 'wherein to shoot I sue']

    b.200, p. 412

10075 I cannot blame the fates thus for to fear
His life, since great Gustavus lies in grave.

    'On the death of the King of Sweden'

    b.62, p. 59

10076 I cannot change as others do,
Can never break, can never break, in vain.

    Sir Carr Scr[oope], 'Song' [answered by 'I swive as
    well as others do . . .']

    b.105, p. 159; fb.107, p. 46

10077 I cannot charm your souls with magic verse,
And tankards do begin to illuminate.

    'Ale, a copy of verses spoke by Brasenose butler before
    the whole society'

    fc.24, p. 36

10078 I cannot dwell in sorrow, neither please
So prevent fortune, ere she be aware.

    [George Daniel]

    b.121, fol. 67v

10079 I cannot go nor stand the cripple cries
What does he then? If he says true he lies.

    [John Donne], 'On a cripple'
    [Crum 192]

    b.62, p. 3; b.197, p. 103; see also 'I am unable . . .'.

10080 I cannot! I adorn thy sable hearse
And make his life and death your precedent.

    John Symonds Sr., 'By an old and honorable disciple of
    Christ (in the same congregation) who dearly loved
    [Caleb Vernon], and is since also himself fallen asleep
    in Jesus, and in the hope of the resurrection to glory
    by Him'

    b.228, p. 80

10081 I cannot like the swine that sluggish be
And first fruits of my English poetry.

    G[iles] H[ayward], 'Ximis'

    b.62, p. 102

10082 I cannot love and if I could
Nor die like a condemn'd mechanic slave.

    [Mrs. ( ) Feilding], 'To one that O if I could love him'

    b.226, p. 35

10083 I cannot meet the lambkin's asking eye,
The cry of murder shall not damn my dome.

    [John Walcot ('Peter Pindar')]

    c.83/2, no. 311

10084 I cannot send you back my heart
Perhaps may prove your net.

    Lady Jane Cavendish, 'An answer to my Lady Alice
    Egerton's song of I prithee send me back my heart'
    [Crum 198]

    b.233, p. 18

10085 I cannot speak, nor look, nor nothing say,
For if you will not come I'll make a hermit's vow.

    Lady Jane Cavendish
    [Crum 1101]

    b.233, p. 41

10086 I cannot yet believe but am content
And make their way known by my weeping eyes.

    [Mrs. ( ) Feilding]

    b.226, p. 33

10087 I can't for my life learn the cause of this strife
To [C.] in a bumper wherever she goes.

    'To C. in a bumper' [docket title]

    Poetry Box VIII/66

10088 I care not so in virtue she abound
And sweetest luster in the hardest shell.

    [Sir Thomas Urquhart], 'In choice of a wife'

    fb.217, p. 387

10089 I cared last night amidst our glee
To grieve I never can before.

    'On a friend visiting Dr. Altham'

    Smith Papers, folder 74/20

10090 I chanced my Lesbia's voice to hear
Or strike her dumb or strike me blind.

    [Thomas Randolph], 'On a very deformed creature
    having a voice incomparably sweet' [a Frenchwoman
    attending the Queen]
    [Crum 1108]

    b.62, p. 6

10091 I come I come my God to Thee
An everlasting one.

    c.124, no. 4

10092 I come! I come! Ye dead, you have
Know, and be known again of, mine!

    [Charles Earle], 'An epitaph on ——— desiring to be
    buried with ——— in hope to rise with them'

    c.376

10093 I come not to ye for that, I love you not:
But that for love of you, I'm like to dote.

> Sir Thomas Urquhart, 'The excuse that one makes
> here to a gentlewoman, for not repairing ofter to the
> the place, where she resides to visit her'

fb.217, p. 222

10094 I could forgive thy macaronic rhymes
When we intend to rail, but when we pray.

> 'The answer' [to 'Brag on proud Christ Church . . .']

b.200, p. 35

10095 I could have wish'd you, Sir, to stand
Seeing you may mount upon her.

> Sir Thomas Urquhart, 'To a gentleman, who had
> convoyed on the street a woman of a Catholic life, and
> too familiar carriage'

fb.217, p. 354

10096 I counted o'er
You will die tomorrow.

> Nicholas Rowe, 'On the late Lady Hervey'

Poetry Box x/128

10097 I dare not judge those judgments ill-advis'd
Moses was sav'd, I read that none was drown'd.

> [Francis Quarles], 'On baptized infants' [Divine
> Fancies I, 85]

b.137, p. 189 and 187 (incomplete)

10098 I dare not stir a coal—this to apply
Which makes addresses daily to the sky.

> [Sir Philip Wodehouse], 'Elizabeth Coke the coal is
> black'

b.131, back (no. 111)

10099 I dare not (were't to save my ransom)
And you begin where others end.

> 'Upon Madam Maintenon, Louis the 14th's mistress'

c.158, p. 143

10100 I dare not yet begin to write on love;
Lov'd by my father and my sisters too.

> Miss [ ] Clark, 'By a child, that was desired to write
> some verses on love . . . of Red Lion Square, 10 yrs
> old'

Spence Papers, folder 113

10101 I demand satisfaction in a rage cries Sir John
Then fast, as he could hopt away.

> 'Epigram'

c.546, p. 2

10102 I descend from a string so 'tis sure a strange thing
Tho' again very often you may.

> [Enigma/Charade/Conundrum 77f]

c.389

10103 I die whenas I do not see
Both when I see and when I see her not.

> 'A despairing lover to his cruel mistress'
> [Crum 1134]

b.62, p. 46

10104 I died to live and yet tho' strange most true
By dying lost my life and business too.

> 'On a dyer'

c.546

10105 I do confess great God my sins are great
I may be thine, and saved by thy death.

> Lady Jane Cavendish, 'To heaven or a confession to
> God'
> [Crum 1137]

b.233, p. 36

10106 I do desire to live
A gallant man for fame.

> Lady Jane Cavendish, 'A song'
> [Crum 1143]

b.233, p. 23

10107 I do in public here protest
From being judg'd as fools or knaves.

> Sir John Strangways, 'Against false and pretended
> friends and friendship . . . 31° Octob: 1646'

b.304, p. 66

10108 I do not ask thee fate to give
And bound to no set laws, but humorsomely rove.

> [John Norris], 'Freedom'

c.547, p. 168

10109 I do not feel the storm
The muse's bower, under the living bay.

> [George Daniel]

b.121, fol. 46v

10110 I do not glory in my fate
That image, 'tis my glory, my disgrace.

> [George Daniel]

b.121, fol. 68v

10111 I do not grieve my dearest life
For I must go to bed to, she.

> 'He married soon after and wrote the following
> answer' [to 'For me deceased . . .']

Greatheed Box/73; see also 'I am not grieved . . .'.

10112 I do not love thee, Sabidus, but for what
Know not; I only know I love thee not.

   'De Sabido'

c.189, p. 22

10113 I do remember an apothecary
What ho, apothecary.

   'Parody on Romeo's apothecary'

fc.14/7

10114 I do not touch ye, and yet you give th'alarm;
Sir, not to touch me, is to do me harm.

   Sir Thomas Urquhart, 'A parley betwixt an old man, and his bride, the first night of their marriage'

fb.217, p. 207

10115 I do not utter this t'exalt the worth
Endowments, that a mortal can refine.

   Sir Thomas Urquhart, 'The author's apology for the presumption, that happily will be laid upon him by sinester interpretations of the last line of the nearest preceding epigram' ['As Alexander on a soldier']

fb.217, p. 50

10116 I do not wish thee to bestow
Dismay'd beholds thy colors fly.

   M[aria] Logan, 'Address to health'

c.83/2, no. 398

10117 I Doctor Staines | With wondrous pains
That are not past redemption.

   'Inscription placed over a cobbler's stall in the flask walk Hampstead'

c.115

10118 I dote, I dote, yet am a sot to show't
And that's the short and the long on't.

   [William Cavendish, 1st duke of Newcastle?] [Crum 1149]

b.213, p. 134

10119 I doubt not, but that as your years increase
As ever had a mother in this nation.

   Sir Thomas Urquhart, 'To the Earl of [crossed out]'

fb.217, p. 245

10120 I dreamt my dear, quoth Ralph to Joan
A dream before that happened true.

   'A true dream'

c.546, p. 24

10121 I dreamt that buried in my fellow clay
This is my [i.e., thy] rotting place and that is mine.

   'Epitaph on a nobleman's tombstone at Woodford Wells'
[Crum 1151]

c.360/3, no. 6

10122 I—e L—l C—e and I sat out,
Who brought us to our journey's end.

   [William Popple, trans.], 'Horace book 1st satire 5th imitated. A journey through York to Edinburgh'

fc.104/1, p. 99

10123 I 'dmire, Maecenas, how it comes to pass,
The old plain way, ye gods, let me be poor.

   [Abraham Cowley, trans.], 'Of avarice' [translation of Horace, Satires I.i.]
[cf. Crum 13]

b.118, p. 1

10124 I envy none their pageantry and show
In every rill a sweet instruction flows.

   'Young love of fame'

Diggle Box: Poetry Box XI/12

10125 I envy not the proud their wealth
And crown with peace my hours.

   'By a young lady . . . Grubstreet journal, June 7th 1733'

c.157, p. 102; c.157, p. 3; c.536; fc.132/1, p. 24 (incomplete?); fc.51, p. 167

10126 I envy not your large domain
Of great men in and great men out.

   'The cot to the neighboring mansion'

Poetry Box IV/57

10127 I Eye should be next to face, but let Tongue be
'Tis plain they are beholden unto me.

   'Spinke oculus' [answered by ''Tis not your great look . . .']

b.356, p. 117

10128 I fain would court the lady, that should be
The fruits of my reciprocal affection.

   Sir Thomas Urquhart, 'Here a certain gentleman discovers how void of trifling ceremony, he could wish her to be, whom he would make choice of, to be his wife'

fb.217, p. 172

10129 I fare you well Lady Hounsibell,
And buried them both in a grave. | As of
               Marlborough

   'Lord Lovel and the Lady Hounsibell'

c.358, p. 30

10130 I fear an oath before I swear, to take it;
   But farewell London; farewell corporation.

    [Robert Wild], 'The loyal nonconformist'

    c.578, p. 6

10131 I feed/feel a flame within that so torments me
   Nor can I fall more low, mounting no higher.

    [John Dryden], 'A song'
    [Crum 1159]

    b.207, p. 26; b.213, p. 134; fb.107, p. 9

10132 I fill not the glasses
   And foes, long contending, are friends.

    John Lockman, 'The downfall of Montreal, or
    General Amherst's health. Set to music by
    Mr. Worgan'

    c.267/2, p. 45

10133 I find no peace, and want wherewith to war
   Sweet mistress you are cause of my disease.

    Sir F[rancis] C[astillion], '1620'

    fb.69, p. 212

10134 I first of Romans stoop'd to rural strains
   And to prevailing shades, the murmuring which
                resign'd.

    [Wentworth Dillon], 4th earl of Roscommon,
    '[Virgil] sixth eclogue/Silenus Englished by . . .'

    b.201, p. 117

10135 I, first: you, second: he, third man implies;
   Yet ev'ry man is I, in his own eyes.

    Sir Thomas Urquhart, 'Of Philoty'

    fb.217, p. 92

10136 I fix mine eye on thine and there
   Being in thine one heart from all malice free.

    J[ohn] D[onne], 'The picture'
    [Crum 1166]

    b.148, p. 54

10137 I flatter thee not tho' I love thee dear Ann
   For a sweet bosom friend to the bard.

    [William Hayley], 'Song'

    File 6961

10138 I flung my tuneful lyre away,
   Apollo's lavish hand adorns.

    S[arah] Herd, 'Fragment'

    c.141, p. 384

10139 I found my Celia one night undrest,
   Nor the critical minute refuse no more.

    [Thomas D'Urfey], 'The apparition' [from The fool
    turned critic, 1676]

    fb.107, p. 22

10140 I from a famous race am sprung,
   Brandy perhaps may save me.

    Mrs. [ ] Walsingham, 'By Mrs. Walsingham'

    Diggle Box: Poetry Box XI/71

10141 I from earth my being boast,
   On yours, Castalio.

    'Another [riddle]'

    c.578, p. 59

10142 I from henceforth do protest
   Then laughs to think how soon you are undone.

    'A song'

    c.374

10143 I from the earth my being boast
   Inspired by flowing bowls.

    'Riddle . . . a leek'

    c.391

10144 I give and bequeath,
   This my true act, the deed of—Will Jackett.

    Will[iam] Jackett, 'Authentic copy of a will . . .
    Mr. Jackett was 30 years clerk to Messrs. Fuller and
    Vaughan, barristers, London'

    c.81/1, no. 43; fc.130, p. 52

10145 I greatest am and likest reign,
   The thunder's Jove's and mine.

    [translation of Latin verse:] 'Ad Regem
    Christianissimum Ludovicum'

    b.111, p. 264

10146 I grieve, yet dare not show my discontent;
   Or die, and so forget what love e'er meant.

    Elizabeth I, queen of England(?), 'The regal muse . . .
    Ashm. Mss.6969'
    [Crum 1173]

    c.94

10147 I grovel still, and cannot gain
   An equal man, an earthborn slave.

    [George Daniel]

    b.121, fol. 70v

10148 I grow in days, I grow in years,
   And be my all in all.

    T[homas] S[tevens], 'Growing taller . . . Feb. 28, 1780'

    c.259, p. 78

10149 I had a little stunted vine,
   Alas! what should we do without a friend?

    'To the Abbé de Voisenon'

    c.83/2, no. 695

10150 I had a mother which to speak was such
And now sweet saint, thy happy soul's at rest.

    Lady Jane Cavendish, 'On my dear mother the
    Countess of Newcastle' [d. 17 April 1643]
    [Crum 1177]

b.233, p. 31

10151 I had a vision yesternight,
Had not she stopt the sallie port.

    [John Cleveland, 'The seat of love, or the senses'
    festival']
    [Crum 1179]

b.209, p. 79

10152 I had no king in '41 when prelacy went down
Till another revolution.

Poetry Box VII/5

10153 I had of late a housemaid curst,
Tho' very seldom find sincere.

    '[Enigma/Charade/Conundrum] 46' [patriot]

c.389

10154 I hate a lie and yet a lie did run
'Tis ten times better than it had been true.

    'Upon the report of the death of the Earl of
    Kensington and Sir George Goring' [falsely rumored
    at the siege of Breda, 1637]
    [Crum 1185]

b.197, p. 130

10155 I hate my breakfast and I love to dose
So get my tea prepar'd without delay.

Poetry Box III/1

10156 I hate old Aristotle's rules
Night fell, the moon arose, and yet no Selim came.

    'Bermeddin, a poem in various meters and on various
    subjects'

c.402

10157 I hate the man, whate'er his name
Tho[u] mayst securely lie abed.

    'To an officer who wrote some very severe verses on a
    young lady'

Poetry Box X/69

10158 I have a mighty part within
Both rejoice when there we meet.

    Isaac Watts(?), 'Miss M.B. sampler'

c.186, p. 25

10159 I have a silent sorrow here,
Unpardon[ed], love, by thee.

    [Richard Brinsley Butler Sheridan], 'Song in The
    stranger' [by Benjamin Thompson; pr. 1798?]
    [Crum 1191]

c.83/3, no. 937

10160 I have a state design into my head
I must to court and see all things you cite.

    'The new policy 1670'

Poetry Box VIII/19

10161 I have a wife offers her love, so rather,
So birds for others not themselves do build.

    'An husband and an adulterer'

c.356

10162 I have been of late to London
You shall keep your places still.

    'A song'

c.570/2, p. 148

10163 I have before the time prescrib'd by you,
And be propitious to your humble slave.

    Stephen Duck, 'A letter from . . . to Mr. Clark . . .
    aged 25'

c.165, p. 27

10164 I have beheld two lovers in a night
Doing's the fruit of doing well: farewell.

    R[obert] Herrick, 'R. Herrick's farewell unto poetry'
    [Crum 1198]

b.197, p. 20

10165 I have cross'd this earth's equator just sixteen times,
I hope we'll meet in another world and a better.

    'On Harriet wife of Lieut. Alexander Davidson
    (Putney)'

c.546

10166 I have done one braver thing
Which is, to keep that hid.

    [John Donne], 'Canzone'
    [Crum 1200]

b.114, p. 269; b.148, p. 109

10167 I have droop'd long beneath this slow disease,
Doubly afflict and irritate my pain.

    [Daniel King?], 'Lines written during a long
    confinement'

Greatheed Box/78

10168 I have heard of one Jup'ter who in a swan's shape
But again in my arms I might press[?] my dear Bob.

Poetry Box XII/39

10169 I have languish'd too long for one who I find,
But the pleasure to think, how others may smart.

'The recovery'

fb.107, p. 35

10170 I have lost my milch cow
And our purses they are empty.

[Elizabeth (Cavendish) Brackley], 'The song' [in a
pastoral]
[Crum 1203]

b.233, p. 55

10171 I have loved twice two year
Contempt can never kill me kindness may.

b.213, p. 120

10172 I have married a wife of late
Their damned and unruly tongue.

'The scolding wife'

c.374

10173 I have my piety too, which could
I feel, I am rather dead than he.

Ben Jonson, ['An epitaph on Master Vincent Corbet']

fb.230

10174 I have no flesh nor skin for cover
Tell me who, or what I am.

[ ] R., 'Riddle [a fire grate]'

Poetry Box VII/49

10175 I have no vein in verse, but if I could
Whilst other muses write mine only cries.

[Richard] Senhouse, 'Upon the death of Prince
Henry' [1612]
[Crum 1210]

b.197, p. 210; b.200, p. 124 (attr. Dr. Juxon)

10176 I have now received thy sacrament, so find
Thy father's landed safe, hath sent for thee.

Lady Jane Cavendish
[Crum 1211]

b.233, p. 41

10177 I have of lands, nor moneys no large portion:
They must be all of them alike in fullness.

[Sir Thomas Urquhart], 'That men may be alike rich,
though they share not alike qualities'

fb.217, p. 528

10178 I have of late been where we were as free
First to the King, the next to little Joan.

Arth[ur?] Swayne, 'On his entertainment being
distressed at a mitt'

b.200, p. 383

10179 I have often admir'd what should be the cause,
In spite of the devil and the word abdicate.

'Pandora's box or the mischievous effects of the word
abdicate'
[Crum 1213]

b.111, p. 443

10180 I have seriously weigh'd it and find it but just,
This, this and this only's the maid to my mind.

'Song 110'

c.555, p. 162

10181 I have tasted all the pleasure here
And guilt and grief be chang'd for endless joy and
bliss.

c.148, p. 7

10182 I have too long endur'd her guilty scorn,
That down love's current drives me fast away.

[John Oldham], 'Upon an undeserving and ungrateful
mistress, whom he could not help loving or the second
part of Phyllis' [Ovid, Amores III.xi, paraphrastically
translated]
[Crum 1221]

Poetry Box VI/67

10183 I having heard of a fair lady's fame,
Long may she live, fair lady so adieu.

[Sir William Trumbull, anagram on Jane Cottrell]

Trumbull Box: Poetry Box XIII/31

10184 I hear my friend is gone to college
No one can then his conduct blame.

Joseph Sillion, 'An acrostic upon my brother Jack
[John Sillion]'s going to college'

c.391

10185 I hear of late this town doth so abound
Of idle rumor keep at home and write.

[John Wilmot], 2nd earl of Rochester, 'A letter
from . . . to the Earl of M[ulgrave]'

Poetry Box VI/58

10186 I hear the midnight hours nor passing speak
[?] us where no grief no parting pangs are known.

[William Hayley], 'Sonnet . . . Jan 24 [1800]'

File 6968

10187 I hear you take a world of pride
Your brisk warm love does but seize his own.

'To his unkind mistress. By the same hand' [as 'Charge
all a bumper . . .']

fb.142, p. 48

10188 I heard much talk of Oxford town
And little sister Joan.

'Song 156'
[Crum 1228]
c.555, p. 220

10189 I heard the virgins sigh I saw the sleek
Thus even by rivals to be deified.

[Thomas Carew], 'On the death of the earl of
Carlisle's daughter' [the Lady Anne Hay]
[Crum 1230]
b.62, p. 87

10190 I heard two neighbors talk the other night,
As when in health, and driv'n to it by art.

[John Byrom of Manchester], 'On inoculation when it
first began to be practiced in England'
c.140, p. 53

10191 I help'd him credit being bad
O gratitude profound!

R[obert] Shirley, 1st earl of Ferrers, 'The grateful
creditor. From [Boileau]'
c.347, p. 31

10192 I here insert amongst mine epigrams
Of Israel was rul'd, one is a psalm.

Sir Thomas Urquhart, 'How in this tractate, to some
enigmas, sentences, epitaphs, and so forth, for the
point of their conception, deservingly is ascribed the
title of epigram'
fb.217, p. 55

10193 I here record a noble wife
When you are told [And sorrowing tell], fair
Leeds lies here!

'Epitaph on Mary Duchess of Leeds'
Poetry Box v/84 and 85

10194 I hest off my clogs—hung th' belt cwoat on a pin
To meet you next year—and for twenty years
more. Derry down [&c.].

P. [or E.] Clark, 'A satirical ballad in the Cumberland
dialect'
c.179, p. 41

10195 I hold for faith—what England's church allows,
Who shuns the Mass—is Catholic and wise.

[William Strode?], 'The Jesuits' creed' [equivocal
verses]
[Crum 1231]
b.155, p. 62; b.205, fol. 97v, 98r; c.362, p. 84; c.81/1,
no. 141; c.83/1, no. 215

10196 I Homer's Samian hosts' work so relate
Could good Creophilus himself aspire?

[Maurice Johnson], 'Callimachus's epigr[am] on the
destruction of Oechalia . . .'
c.229/2, fol. 14v

10197 I honor draw by the attractive force
To make it good true nobleness my end.

[Sir Philip Wodehouse], 'Henry Howard now duke [of
Norfolk]'
b.131, back (no. 144)

10198 I hope it is no treason when I own,
Are very oft mistaken for each other.

[Enigma/Charade/Conundrum 77d]
c.389

10199 I hope my pardon's seal'd and I resign
My precious, and immortal soul's now thine.

Mary Ambler, 'In a paper sealed up all of the
handwriting of [Maurice Johnson's] dear wife's
mother . . .'
c.229/2, fol. 22

10200 I hope so little to transgress the law
For fortune's frowns, so that my deeds be good.

[Sir Thomas Urquhart], 'The wish of a proficient in
virtue'
fb.217, p. 497

10201 I hope this morning lecture's to your mind
Full fraught with scandal for the ensuing year.

[ ] Smith, of University College, Oxford, 'The
epilogue' [to the Music Speech, Oxford 8 July 1693]
[Crum 1238]
b.115, fol. 39

10202 I invocate no nymph, no grace, no muse
And ev'ry leaf may celebrate thy praise.

H[enry] C[olman], 'The invocation [to] Divine
meditations'
[Crum 1245]
b.2, p. 1

10203 I invoke you, ye muses, now I sing the law scheme
That none but dear Hardwick may muster our
troop. | Derry down, down, down, derry down.

'The lawyers disbanded, or the Temple in an uproar'
Poetry Box xiv/196

10204 I John Criegton had ne mickle
And now lig here in filthy pickle.

c.360/3, no. 160

10205　I judge the muse of lewd desire,
Broke down the timber, and dug up the stone.

　　[Isaac] Watts, 'On his burning several lewd poems of
　　Ovid Martial Oldham Dryden &c.'
　　[Crum 1253]

　　c.244, p. 310

10206　I kindness will and judgment sing
Ill workers I may cut.

　　'Psal: 101'

　　b.217, p. 71

10207　I kiss not where I wish to kill
I feel no want nor have too much.

　　b.150, p. 192[insert]

10208　I knew him here alive whose every breath
He lives here, pleased more, dies, troubled less.

　　[George Daniel]

　　b.121, fol. 53

10209　I know a man, an abject slave,
I shall not care when he's in hell.

　　[Robert Merry], 'A character'
　　Greatheed Box/44

10210　I know a thing that's most uncommon;
The woman's deaf, and does not hear.

　　'On a certain lady at court [Mrs. Howard]'
　　c.229/1, fol. 69v

10211　I know, Celinda, I have borne too long,
Resign the heart so hardly freed from you.

　　[William Walsh], 'Elegy. Upon quitting his mistress'

　　c.223, p. 74

10212　I know I'm no poet, my song it will show it,
And there is an end of poor Nancy.

　　'Song 65'

　　c.555, p. 92

10213　I know more than Apollo
That now she's fit for no man.

　　'Song 7'

　　c.503, p. 62

10214　I know my dear cuz you'll rejoice when I tell ye
Subscribing myself your affectionate friend.

　　'A letter from Miss Feathertop Fashion in town to her
　　friend Miss Cherry Beanblossom in ——shire'

　　c.150, p. 106

10215　I know my Jesus doth me love,
My Jesus is my advocate.

　　[( ) Pierson]

　　c.328, p. 16

10216　I know no paint of poetry
Might be his own evangelist.

　　W[illiam] Strode, 'On the same' [on Fairford
　　windows]
　　[Crum 1264]

　　b.200, p. 204

10217　I know not by what virtue Rome deposes
Then Rome hath color to depose a king.

　　[Francis Quarles], 'O[n] disposing [*i.e.,* deposing]
　　princes' [Divine Fancies I, 90]

　　b.137, p. 175

10218　I know O God he's frail and weak,
From God the thus enamor'd heart.

　　[Edmund Wodehouse], 'March 9 [1715]'

　　b.131, p. 177

10219　I know, O Lord, when thou dost speak,
One glorious God, in Persons three.

　　'Upon a crack of thunder'

　　c.187, p. 14

10220　I know that all beneath the moon decays,
But that, O me! I both must write and love.

　　[William] Drummond, of Hawthornden, 'Sonnet . . .
　　1616'

　　c.142, p. 401

10221　I know, that anagrams are counted but
Æquivers, contrepets—let's leave to boys.

　　[Sir Philip Wodehouse], 'A pretty preface apologetical
　　to the following anagrams'

　　b.131, back flyleaf

10222　I know that you are wont to be
And recommend it unto you.

　　S[tephen] Simpson, 'To R[obert] L. R. written at
　　school'

　　c.563

10223　I know the elder, and the younger, too
A reason, therefore I despair to know.

　　[Francis Quarles], 'On the younger brother' [Divine
　　Fancies I, 61]

　　b.137, p. 186

10224 I know the kindred mind, 'tis she! 'tis she!
Dress it with chains of gold, to hang upon my heart.

> [Isaac] Watts, 'On the death of an aged honored
> relative Mrs. M. Watts who died July 13. 1693'

c.244, p. 325

10225 I know thee sorrow with thy downcast eye
To mourn upon the brink of dark despair.

> [ ] Oram, 'Sonnets by . . . on sorrow'

c.341, p. 61

10226 I know we're resolved each shall see
For than shall think the sea is condens'd me.

> Lady Jane Cavendish, 'The song' [in a pastoral]
> [Crum 1276a]

b.233, p. 61

10227 I laid me down and sweetly slept,
Nor think ye call too soon.

> 'A morning hymn . . . by Aurelia'

c.153, p. 57

10228 I Laïs to whom Greece her homage paid,
I won't see, what I am; I can't see, what I was.

> Francis Lockyer, dean of Peterborough, 'Illa ego
> famosa . . . thus excellently Englished'

c.229/1, fol. 44v

10229 I languish no more at the glance of your eye;
Let me, unpitied feel again my old pain.

c.549, p. 39

10230 I lately dream'd I was fast bound
And what is only fancied so.

> 'Fancy and enjoyment. By the same hand' [as 'Tho' in
> their flame . . .']

fb.142, p. 53

10231 I leave mortality, and things below,
And mount herself, like him, t'eternity in fire.

> [Abraham] Cowley, 'The ecstasy'

c.244, p. 225

10232 I lift mine heart to Thee,
From all their pain and grief.

> [Thomas Sternhold], 'Another of the same' [for
> assurance of God's protection and guidance; verses
> from Psalm 25]
> [Crum 1282]

a.3, fol. 76

10233 I like and see but yet I cannot find
The likt and seen. O love with error blind.

b.205, fol. 22v

10234 I like not tears in tune, nor will I prize
We floating islands living Hebrides.

> [John Cleveland], 'Upon the death of Mr. King'
> [drowned in the Irish seas 1637]
> [Crum 1287]

b.93, p. 21

10235 I like not to possess too little of
Riches, nor yet too much; enough's enough.

> Sir Thomas Urquhart, 'David's wish concerning
> wealth'

fb.217, p. 316

10236 I little thought (my Damon) once that you
Is now to prove more constant in your hate.

> [John] N[orris, of Bemerton], 'The irreconcilable'

c.258

10237 I live no more since you my dear are dead,
And animate mine ashes in your urn.

> [Samuel] Johnson, 'Non ego nunc vivo . . . which
> Dr. Johnson thus rendered into English'

c.229/2, fol. 65

10238 I liv'd in just proportion as I knew,
These were the charms. . . .

> 'A fragment found amongst some manuscripts'

c.373, p. 57

10239 I long observ'd disturbance in your face,
Is the people's freedom: and the tyrant's doom.

> 'Verses fixed on King James the Second's statue in the
> Privy Garden on the 22. of April 1715. in the midst of
> the eclipse'
> [Crum 1295, 'disquiet']

c.570/1, p. 25

10240 I long to talk with some old lover's ghost
If she whom I love, should love me.

> [John Donne], 'Love's deity'
> [Crum 1298]

b.114, p. 262; b.148, p. 69

10241 I look not at once in a female to find
And I'll love her forever—I mean if I can. | And &c.

> 'Song 207'

c.555, p. 334; see also 'I seek not at once . . .'.

10242 I lost not the field, tho' for it I fought
And sav'd my brave army—by winning the race.

> 'Marshall Noailles' answer' [to 'Prenez le roi . . .']

c.360/2, no. 90

10243 I love because it comes to me by kind,
By kind, mind, heart, desert and all in one.

'To his mistress' [answered by 'Thou lovest not . . .']

b.197, p. 62; c.356; see also 'That if I do love . . .'.

10244 I love her only best; of whom I get
And love's all fire.

Sir Thomas Urquhart, 'That enjoying increaseth affection'

fb.217, p. 209

10245 I love it but I love so
Gives fuel to my fire.

'A song'

b.207, p. 27

10246 I love my Laura, sweetest lass
What Laura keeps for me.

[( ) Waldo], 'Laura' [address: 'For the editor of the European magazine']

Poetry Box IV/81

10247 I love my Savior Christ
And let me ever love.

'Hymn 22d'

c.562, p. 25

10248 I love the fair who freely gives her heart,
And is too modest for a hypocrite.

c.549, p. 95

10249 I love the fat [jet], I love the fair
All that is woman, and will do.

[William Cavendish, 1st duke of Newcastle], 'A song' [Crum 1311]

b.207, p. 34

10250 I love the labyrinth the silent glade,
That seeks for solitude, and sighs for rest.

[Mary (Derby)] Robinson, 'Solitude'

c.83/2, no. 552

10251 I love the Lord because my voice
Praise ye the Lord I say.

[Thomas Norton], 'A thanksgiving for deliverance from afflictions. Psal. 49' [verses from Psalms 116–117] [Crum 1312]

a.3, fol. 128v

10252 I love the Lord, how can I less,
The Lord our God praise ye. Allelujah.

'Morning prayer 24 day Psalm 116. Hallelujah'

c.264/3, p. 41

10253 I love the modes of ancient days
And in her bliss forget thy sorrows past!

Poetry Box III/36

10254 I love thee by heaven I cannot say more
Before men sit down to their dinners.

'A love song'

fc.61, p. 65

10255 I love thee, mournful sober-suited night,
May reach, tho' lost on earth, the ear of heav'n.

[Charlotte (Turner) Smith], 'To night. A sonnet' [Crum 1315]

c.142, p. 374

10256 I love those weapons (says Leontia) which
May give our children breath.

Sir Thomas Urquhart, 'Of swords, and the out[f]its of affection'

fb.217, p. 61

10257 I love to rise ere breaks the tardy light
From drear decays of age outlive the old.

A[nna] Seward, 'Morning scene from a window in the west front of the Bishop's Palace Lichfield sonnet by . . .'

Poetry Box IV/1

10258 I love with all my heart | The Stuart's party here
Tho' none should take my part | Resolves to live
and die.

[equivocal verses, Whig and Tory, 1714/15] [Crum 1320]

c.160, fol. 78; b.52/2, p. 128; c.570/1, p. 117; fc.58, p. 121; c.158, p. 7; b.111, p. 527

10259 I love you Chloe, it is true,
I'll wear your favors, not your chains.

'Written on a window in Wales'

c.90

10260 I love you for your squinting eyes,
And save-alls for your nose.

'Song 32'

c.555, p. 51

10261 I lov'd a sweet maid and was married and blest
I was then more than bless'd—was transported.

'Going to Botany Bay'

fc.14/8

10262   I lov'd thee once I'll love no more,
       A-begging, to a beggar's door.

> [Sir Robert Ayton], 'A sonnet' [answered by 'Thou that loved'st once . . .']
> [Crum 1325]
>
> b.197, p. 175; b.213, p. 24

10263   I march'd four mile thro' scorching sand
       What mortal else, could e'er go through it.

> [Jonathan] Swift, 'Dean Swift upon his curate Robin Hewit'
>
> fc.51, p. 193; c.150, p. 78 ('three miles' and ff.); c.81/1, no. 98; fc.135; c.362, p. 85; c.94 ('three miles')

10264   I marvel not the tuneful tribe that sing
       Shall come I trust as welcome as this goes.

> Job Scott, 'Joseph Nicholson's, Bavaria(?) near Charlemont. My dear fr[ien]d 3th of 8th mo. 1793 Mary Leadbeater'
>
> c.303

10265   I may as well to take in hand
       No loss at all.

> 'Braye Lute Book,' Music Ms. 13, fol. 36v

10266   I may forget to eat, to drink, to sleep
       By longer looking on her quiet grave.

> Francis Beaumont(?), 'An elegy on the death of the Countess of Rutland' [1612]
> [Crum 1337]
>
> b.197, p. 65; b.148, p. 136 (attr. J. D[onne])

10267   I may not war is written in my name
       Yet I'll not yield to them. My God's my shield.

> [Sir Philip Wodehouse], 'Upon my honorable cousin—the Lady Mary Wharton'
>
> b.131, back (no. 106)

10268   I met my heart's fond idol in the palace,
       The day blots out the promise made at night.

> [John Lockman], 'From the Arabic'
>
> c.268 (second part), p. 140

10269   I muse by what hypocrisy, you can
       Hate books for that, which you love best in man.

> Sir Thomas Urquhart, 'To a puritanical gentlewoman of a kind enough disposition other ways: who seemed to be offended at the word pr . . . in some of mine epigrams'
>
> fb.217, p. 344

10270   I muse not, why you fickle are;
       Seeing Venus is a wand'ring star.

> Sir Thomas Urquhart, 'To a fair inconstant woman'
>
> fb.217, p. 73

10271   I muse what water 'tis, doth fret so sore
       Which springs out of the jawbone of an ass.

> Sir Thomas Urquhart, 'To one, who for being grievously troubled with a toothache to ease himself a little of his pain did hold down his head, the better to distill the acrimonious humor'
>
> fb.217, p. 114

10272   I must confess, to me it odd appears,
       There's time enough, for sleeping after death.

> [Thomas Hamilton, 6th earl of Haddington], 'To Florella that all old maxims are not true'
>
> c.458/1, p. 69

10273   I must, I will have gin! That skillet take:
       I was born naked, and will naked die.

> John Lockman, 'Strip-me-naked, or royal gin forever: a picture'
>
> c.267/1, p. 195

10274   I Nan fear God is written in my name
       I'll make it good with an unspotted fame.

> [Sir Philip Wodehouse], 'Upon his kinswoman Mrs. Anna Godfrey'
>
> b.131, back (no. 94)

10275   I need invoke no sabled muse to mourn
       And in the raptur'd chorus joyful join.

> 'To the memory of my much esteemed friend Daniel Stanton who departed this life the 28th of the 6th month 1770 . . . [by] a female friend'
>
> c.517, fol. 37v

10276   I need no muse to give my passion vent
       'Tis height makes Grantham steeple stand awry.

> [John Cleveland], 'An elegy upon the right reverend father in God William L[au]d, Archbishop of Canterbury'
>
> b.93, p. 121; b.137, p. 200

10277   I need no trophies to adorn my hearse
       That horns him first and then cuts off his head?

> 'Epitaphium' [on the Lord of Castlehaven (Mervyn, 2nd earl, executed 1631) and his lady]
> [Crum 1354]
>
> b.125, fol. 38; b.126, fol. 23; b.200, p. 226; b.62, p. 28; Poetry Box VIII/5

10278   I ne'er could any luster see
       That heaving bosom sigh for me.

> [Richard Brinsley Butler Sheridan], 'Song 238' [from The duenna]
>
> c.555, p. 381

10279 I never din'd with Dennis or with Pope,
Go home and dine, and then pick up a wench.

'Perseus Scaramouche. By way of dialogue betwixt
Mr. D'anvers [Nicholas Ámhurst], and orator [John]
Henley, by Griffith Morgan D'anvers M. A. formerly
of Tr. College . . . in imitation of the first satire of
Perseus' [pr. 1734 (Foxon D42)]

c.570/4, p. 53

10280 I never having yet espied a youth,
I'm your Melissa; and you my Chrysippus.

Sir Thomas Urquhart, 'The words of a certain
lascivious woman to a philosopher, who was her
paramour'

fb.217, p. 276

10281 I never heard of any [?] yet
They purchase virtue from your conversation.

[Sir Thomas Urquhart], 'To her. Ger.'

fb.217, p. 389

10282 I never knew a Winifred but good
And so, all Winifreds will that in imitate you.

[Sir Aston Cokayne], 'To [Henry Hardman's] wife'

b.275, p. 104

10283 I never meddl'd with intrigues,
I never will do so no more.

'A true touchstone of the times. The freethinker's
confession' [pr. 1719 (Foxon T533)]

c.570/2, p. 81

10284 I never think on God, but I conceive
Preserving it, so many years and ages.

'On God's providence, power, and goodness and
wisdom'

b.137, p. 114

10285 I now dear Jemmy now at last perceive
And think myself, as I'm indeed, more blest.

M[aurice] J[ohnson], 'Ariosto's 5th satire imitated
from the Italian . . . to Mr. James Ravenscroft'

c.229/2, fol. 8

10286 I now, brother freemen take up my pen
Then, the leaders of your reforming tribe.

[John Wolcot ('Peter Pindar')], 'Dedication to the
freemen at large'

Poetry Box IV/96

10287 I oblig'd you, when coin I you did lend:
Now oblige me, and give me mine again.

Sir Thomas Urquhart, 'To a bad debtor'

fb.217, p. 89

10288 I oft dear Spence, thou man of sense,
You'll soon forget you had 'em.

[N. Herbert], 'The request. To Mr. Joseph Spence
famous (by his own confession) for a bad memory'

Spence Papers, folder 91

10289 I oft have wonder'd whence that horrid thought
Sin deeper dyed than can be found in hell.

[John Hobart], 'Of atheism'

b.108, fol. 13

10290 I often for my King have stood,
And so I pray excuse me Sir.

'[The Duke of Buckinghamshire's epitaph, made by
himself . . . Englished thus] Or thus'

fc.24, p. 60

10291 I often read your riddle o'er,
And so the grist came out.

'Answer' [to 'Whene'er I work . . .']

c.578, p. 90

10292 I often tried in vain, to find
That one may go, for t'other's name.

[Thomas Sheridan], 'A simile for the ladies' [pr. 1737
(Foxon 409)]

c.83/1, no. 192

10293 I once had a cabin a horse and a cow
Whilst in horror I brood o'er my crimes.

'The united Irishman or Paddy's lamentation. 1798 . . .
[by] Posthumus'

c.250

10294 I, only I, great God thy law do spurn,
For others' fortune malcontent with mine.

'A confession of our breach of the whole law'

b.137, p. 122

10295 I own, Gil Blas, 'tis strange to me,
So full of devil and not damn'd.

'On the same on the frequent repetition of the words,
devil and devilish' [in Gil Blas, by Edward Moore,
acted for nine nights at Drury Lane in Feb. 1750/1]

c.360/3, no. 88

10296 I own, I own thy mighty pow'r,
Thy linen wears the vouching red.

[William Popple, trans.], '[Horace, ep]ode 17. To the
sorceress Canidia a palinody'

fc.104/2, p. 464

10297 I pass all the night in a shady old grove,
Like the pleasures, the pleasures of love.

'The disconsolate shepherd' [sometimes attr.
Charles II]
[Crum I383, 'all my hours']
fb.107, p. 14

10298 I pity crave since 'tis my fate
I gave her thanks, and so I took my leave.

'The convert'
fb.107, p. 4

10299 I place an off'ring at thy shrine,
And ever in thy power!

[William Cowper, trans.], 'The perfect sacrifice.
Vol. 4. Son. 74' [of Jeanne Guion's 'Spiritual songs']
c.470 (autogr.)

10300 I 'plain'd me to my friends of mine unrest
For I must still be sick, or else must die.

'Lovesickness'
b.356, p. 95

10301 I play'd upon the flute; my mornings all
Ignorant as dirt!

'[Parody] from Macbeth'
Poetry Box II/57

10302 I pluck'd the sweet rose when just wash'd by a show'r,
May be follow'd perhaps with a smile.

'The shaken rose'
c.391, p. 74; see also 'The rose had been wash'd . . .'.

10303 I pray the Christian man that hast eye to see this
On whose soul, Almighty God have mercy. Amen.

'On the pulling down the old church at Islington in
the year 1751, they found a plated stone with the
following inscription'
c.360/3, no. 167

10304 I pray thee leave, love me no more,
I cannot live without thee.

[Michael] Drayton, 'From Drayton's works. To his
coy love, a canzonet'
[Crum I391]
c.193, p. 36

10305 I pray thee Protestant leave with me
Who is the Son of God most true.

'The Papist's rhyme'
b.209, p. 99

10306 I pray thee, this one thing me show,
Show me in reason how this may be.

'A picture representing three young gent[lemen]
coming from a castle adjoining a wood; on the side of
it sits a lady with an elderly gentleman whose head is
laying in her lap. A gentleman passing that way thus
addressed the lady . . . to whom the lady replies'
fc.85, fol. 34v

10307 I pray you, in your anecdotes,
And smote him down the stairs.

'Parody from Othello'
Poetry Box II/57

10308 I pray you my countrymen, lend me an ear,
And wish you well crampt in a strong wooden
shoe. | Derry down—

T[homas] M[orell], 'A new ballad, to an old tune'
c.395, p. 22

10309 I pray you Sir impale your woods that we
A pleasant grace unto your Amington.

[Sir Aston Cokayne], 'To my honest kinsman Sir
J[ohn] Rep[pington]'
b.275, p. 57

10310 I pray you tell me my sweet darling, why
Can with his lancet strike me in the vein.

Sir Thomas Urquhart, 'The reason why a pretty
handsome lass married a barber, by way of dialogue'
fb.217, p. 204

10311 I pray you tell me was not this man kind
That rid before and kist his wife behind.

'On one kissing his wife on horseback'
b.356, p. 307

10312 I prithee book when I am gone
To be at his commandment.

'Her answer' [to 'I prithee lute . . .']
b.62, p. 79; b.356, p. 305 ('I prithee lute . . .')

10313 I prithee Death tell me the reason why
I took her up to cheat the devil with.

'On Joan Hog a question to Death'
fb.143, p. 36

10314 I prithee, good Tommy, stay at home with thy wife,
To hazard our lives where nothing is got.

'Tommy and Peggy. Or a dialogue between a seaman
of the navy and his wife'
b.111, p. 511

10315   I prithee leave this peevish fashion,
And your pride may make you so.

     Alexander Brome, 'Song. To a coy lady'

     b.150, p. 224

10316   I prithee lute when I am gone
To play upon her instrument.

     [Richard Corbett], 'Upon a lute' [answered by 'I
     prithee book (lute) . . . tell your writer . . .']
     [Crum 1407]

     b.356, p. 305; b.62, p. 79

10317   I prithee send me back my heart
As much as she hath mine.

     [Sir John Suckling? or Henry Hughes?]
     [Crum 1408]

     b.213, p. 104

10318   I rage I melt I burn
Sweet Galatea's beauty and my love.

     [John Gay, Alexander Pope, and/or John Hughes], 'I
     rage I melt I burn in [Handel's] Acis and Galatea'
     [with musical score for bass]

     Music MS. 534

10319   I raise my soul to Thee,
Through Sinai's wilderness.

     'Psalm 25'

     c.264/1, p. 97

10320   I ransack'd for a theme of song
Who is belov'd where never seen.

     [William Cowper], 'Annus memorabilis 1789 in
     commemoration of His Majesty's happy recovery' [in
     the handwriting of Lady Harriet (Cowper) Hesketh]

     File 17727

10321   I rather would virtue than children have,
Convincing them with shame unto their face.

     Sir John Strangways, 'The fourth chapter of the Book
     of Wisdom'

     b.304, p. 51

10322   I read it in her eye before she spoke
She rallies prettily—Jane Coke can joke.

     [Sir Philip Wodehouse], 'My cousin her sister Jane
     Coke . . .'

     b.131, back (no. 110)

10323   I read the meaning of the gift you send,
Clear as the stream of charity in you.

     W. Parker [27 Sept. 1756]

     Poetry Box x/57

10324   I read your riddle till 'twas night,
And then I cried, Ay that's the thing.

     'Answer' [to 'The vernal sun . . .']

     c.578, p. 139

10325   I reap by baldness, in my younger years
This good: that I will never have gray hairs.

     Sir Thomas Urquhart, 'A very thin haired gentleman
     speaketh thus in favors of baldness, of himself'

     fb.217, p. 350

10326   I said dear Lord that I would sin no more
Perform thy vows when thou thinken on them
                           laid(?).

     [Sir Richard Bulstrode], 'Broken vows renewed'

     fb.88, p. 114v

10327   I said I lov'd V best of any letter,
Now if you will I'll make but one of you.

     'On one that asked his mistress what letter she loved
     best'

     b.62, p. 53

10328   I said that Clairien would adorn the stage;
And, in return, is by that goddess crown'd.

     John Lockman, 'The prophecy [by David Garrick]
     fulfilled'

     c.267/4, p. 301

10329   I said to my heart between sleeping and waking
Give the eye any joys, or the heart any sorrows. |
                     [Derry down, &c.]

     Charles Mordaunt, 3rd earl of Peterborough, 'A
     rhapsody on the beautiful Mrs. Howard of
     Twickenham afterward Countess of Suffolk . . .
     reprinted in the Aviary [or magazine of British
     melody; to the tune of King John], p. 252'
     [Crum 1426]

     c.229/1, fol. 68v; fc.135 (var.)

10330   I sail'd in the good ship the Kitty
[torn] and anchor yo yea.

     'Yo yea'

     Poetry Box iv/62

10331   I saw a man who unprovok'd with ire,
Stuck brass upon another's head with fire.

     'Greek enigma'

     c.81/1, no. 73; b.207, p. 20

10332   I saw a peacock, with a fiery tail
I saw the man that saw that dreadful sight.

     [Richard Gough], 'A prodigy anno Dom: 1665'
     [Crum 1428]

     b.207, p. 20; see also 'I saw the east and west . . .'.

10333 I saw fair Chloris walk alone
To deck her froze into a gem.

[William Strode, 'Song']
[Crum 1430]
b.209, p. 56; b.62, p. 138; b.62, p. 24 (attr. Corbett); b.200, p. 12; see also 'As I saw fair Clora . . .'.

10334 I saw him rising in the east,
In greater splendor than he rose.

[William Thomas] Lewis, 'On Garrick. By . . . a comedian . . .'
Diggle Box: Poetry Box XI/69

10335 I saw Sylvester, that celestial wench,
I bade her kiss my a[r]se, and so we parted.

'Epigram'
c.326, p. 171

10336 I saw the east and west meet both together
I saw a man that saw this wondrous sight.

'A vision'
b.63, p. 25; see also 'I saw a peacock . . .'.

10337 I saw the world, and wondered at the sight
His ruin, and his reparation make.

[George Daniel]
b.121, fol. 65v

10338 I saw thine offer generous V[ere]
The title of Lord Mayor.

John Belfour, 'Ode to Mr. Chas. Vere of Fleet Street on his late proposal of 500 £. to be distributed among the poor inhabitants of Cripplegate Ward provided the city of London would choose him alderman thereof . . . Wapping 12th Feb. 1767'
c.217, p. 43

10339 I scarce believe my love to be so pure
No winter shall abate this spring's increase.

[John Donne], 'Spring'
[Crum 1435]
b.114, p. 293; b.148, p. 82

10340 I scarce know what's to live: no wonder I,
Then know not what 'tis to be born or die.

'Man's ignorance'
c.356

10341 I see, I see approach these wish'd-for days,
And all be joy prosperity and peace.

'The triumph of freedom'
c.83/2, no. 392

10342 I see the beast—O thou of monstrous size,
He'll rise, revenge himself, and crush thee into
                                                        atoms.

Abraham Oakes, 'The pedicule: on seeing him in a microscope'
c.50, p. 50

10343 I see you view me with the stoniest eyes
And take the penance of the virtuous wife.

'A prologue spoken by Punch'
c.188, p. 52

10344 I seek for truth in vain
Witness what Hippocrates holds | Who says &c.

R[obert] Shirley, 1st earl of Ferrers, 'Upon wine. From the French'
c.347, p. 97

10345 I seek not at once in a female to find
And I'll love her forever—I mean if I can.

'The reasonable lover'
c.487, p. 44; see also 'I look not at once . . .'.

10346 I sell good ale and I sell good gin
I give you *gratis* for nothing bread and cheese.

'Written on a sign in a little country village down in the west'
c.361

10347 I serve thee here, with all my might
To serve thy God, as I serve thee.

'An inscription on a clock'
c.186, p. 51

10348 I set myself down to obey your command.
And keep within its teeth.

c.157, p. 101

10349 I shall be thought upon! When? How? How long?
And when you're gone, your honor shall survive.

[Sir Philip Wodehouse], 'Upo his kinswoman [Elizabeth Houghton] Lady Catlin'
b.131, back (no. 65)

10350 I shall not ask Jean Jacques Rousseau
But proper time to marry.

[William] Cowper, 'Pairing time anticipated a fable'
c.140, p. 564; File 15773

10351 I shall not mount my subject to the spheres,
Plague 'em with verse until they hang themselves.

'Essay on poetry'
fb.68, p. 17

10352 I sigh and lament me in vain,
My blood it runs cold at the sound.

　[Anne (Home) Hunter], 'Mary Queen of Scot's
　lamentation'

c.83/1, no. 133

10353 I sigh fair injur'd stranger! For thy fate
Like two bright dew-drops meeting in a flower.

　'On a late connubial rupture in high life'

c.83/2, no. 628

10354 I sight [sigh] not Sir nor yet complain
Or pity on your sex I'll have.

　Elizabeth Kennedy, 'These verses composed by the
　famous and eminant hand of Mrs. Elizabeth Kennedy'

fb.68, p. 142

10355 I sigh'd, and I writ,
They will cry for their bauble again.

　'The proud nymph'

fb.107, p. 78

10356 I sing a supper Cuthbert eat
Of Killam Hall with squire Stevens.

　'A supper given by Henry Hivers of Killam Hall to
　three persons and himself'

fb.68, p. 138

10357 I sing a woeful ditty
How the bullets will whistle, and the cannons will
roar.

　'Haymarket Hector' [on the slitting of Sir John
　Coventry's nose by Monmouth and others, November
　1670]
　[Crum 1455; POAS I.169]

Poetry Box VI/63; fb.106(24)

10358 I sing my Savior's wondrous death;
He pass'd to reach the crown.

　[Isaac Watts, Hymns and spiritual songs (1707), bk. II,
　Hymn 114]

c.180, p. 13

10359 I sing not of Priam nor the siege of Troy
I cannot live with nor without myself.

b.64, p. 38

10360 I sing of a meeting that happen'd of late
Yet he cares not a fig for his prerogative. | Which &c.

　'On the peerage bill' [24 June 1719]
　[Crum 1463]

c.570/2, p. 57

10361 I sing of a whistle, a whi[st]le of worth—
The field thou hath won by yon bright god of day!

　[Robert] Burns, 'The whistle'

c.344, p. 28

10362 I sing of Jesus as the angels sing
The dead arise and graves be open found.

　C[harles] E[arle], 'On the nativity of Christ'

c.376

10363 I sing of sad discords, that happen'd of late,
And so farewell to Bravo, farewell to Encore. |
　　　　　Derry down down hey derry down.

　'The Italian opera's downfall'

fc.135

10364 I sing of the days that are gone,
Ah why do I sorrow in vain,

　[Probably incomplete.]

c.517, fol. 23v

10365 I sing the adventures this year did befall
With many a ship lost, but not a man slain. |
　　　　　Which [nobody can deny]

　'England's triumph at sea, the year 1691—to the tune
　of The blacksmith'

fb.70, p. 181; see also 'A mighty great fleet . . .'.

10366 I sing the boy who gagg'd and bound
And cork'd thee but to make thee quicker.

　'On a dumb boy very beautiful, and of great quickness
　of parts'

c.391, p. 101; c.83/1, no. 173

10367 I sing the certain fate of humankind
And joyful meets the cold embrace of death.

　'A poem on life, death, judgment, Heaven and Hell'

Poetry Box x/165

10368 I sing the church of Armthorpe town,
On bells that only tingle.

　J[ohn] C[arter], 'Armthorpe bells—a ballad'

c.488, p. 1

10369 I sing the funeral of an earl's grandmother
While the power is in French brandy.

　'An elegy upon old Madam Gwyn' [mother of Nell
　Gwyn?]

b.327, f. 10v

10370 I sing the man read it who list,
Virtue will be its own reward.

　Edward Sneyd, 'Quo teneam vultus mutantem protea
　rodo? . . .'

c.214, p. 47

10371   I sing the man that rais'd a shirtless band,
And orphan's curses all your steps attend.

     [Arthur Mainwaring], 'The king of hearts [Lord
     Delamere, later earl of Warrington] 1689'
     [Crum 1475; *POAS* v.84]

     fb.207/1, p. 36; b.111, p. 569; fb.68, p. 107

10372   I sing the man, whose wit abounds,
They give this blund'ring politician.

     'A satire'

     c.530, p. 113

10373   I sing the men, by whose facetious wile
And tunes her strains to peace, and
                             all-commanding love.

     Aquila Rose, 'Zorobabel's conquest, or, the triple
     contention; a poem'

     c.346

10374   I sing the praise of heroes brave,
'Tis very strange 'tween you and I.

     'A hymn. To the victory in Scotland' [25 June 1719]
     [Crum 1480]

     c.570/2, p. 77

10375   I sing the praises of a fart;
If not I do not care a fart.

     'A paradox. The best perfume. Or a paradox in praise
     of farting' [pr. Dublin 1723 (Foxon P49)]

     c.503, p. 8

10376   I sing the praises of a worthy wight
For his father was ruin'd by the best of the kind. |
                            With a [fa, la, la, la].

     'A new ballad to an old tune called Sage leaf [satire on
     George Villiers, 2d Duke of Buckingham] from
     L. Oxford's collection of mss. in the Museum,
     no. 7315, fol. 46'
     [Crum 1479]

     Poetry Box IV/120; b.105, p. 369; Trumbull Box: Poetry
     Box XIII/64 ('doughty')

10377   I sing the source of life divine
To tell the world that I am thine.

     T[homas] S[tevens], 'O: D: Sabbath morning Psalm
     2.7.1'

     c.259, p. 102

10378   I sing the Welshman, whose ingenious hand
And with the fragrant leek adorn their joyful brow.

     'The mouse trap . . . the slice of toasted cheese'

     Poetry Box X/43

10379   I sing thy sad disaster, fatal king
And tell the world that all the world is vain.

     [Sir Francis Hubert, 'The life and death of King
     Edward II']
     [Crum 1484]

     b.12 (581 stanzas); b.9 (503 stanzas); fb.7, fol. 9 (576
     stanzas); b.373 (556 stanzas)

10380   I sleep each night with my books all around
Proceeds from naught else but my spelling and
                                 grammar.

     Miss [ ] Andrews, 'On a young lady sleeping with her
     books under her bed'

     File 245/7

10381   I soon shall run distracted mad
So rid myself of shewfolk.

     [John Walker?], 'Song the shewfolk'

     fc.108, fol. 68v

10382   I spend the time in trifles and in folly,
Thus lest my time be lost, I lose it wholly.

     'Of himself'

     c.356

10383   I start a candidate for grace,
I'll humbly take my place.

     Charles Atherton Allnutt, 'An improvement on
     elections'

     c.112, p. 59

10384   I swear (Eugenio!) scarce without a tear,
Retrieves thy credit or thou art undone.

     John Lockman, 'The memento: to a greatly valued
     friend . . . Feb. 1753'

     c.267/1, p. 74

10385   I swive as well as others do,
Deserves not to be scorn'd. | Why . . .

     [John Wilmot, 2nd earl of Rochester], 'The mock
     song' [answer to 'I cannot change as others do . . .']

     b.105, p. 160 (incomplete)

10386   I tell with equal truth and grief
And let her prison be my arms.

     'The thief 1746'
     [Crum 1507]

     c.360/2, no. 247; c.391, p. 82; see also 'Before the
     urchin . . .'

10387   I' th' ev'ning of one summer's day,
Awoke me, and dissolv'd the charm.

     'The last day' [8 March 1790]

     c.136, p. 8

10388   I' th' middle state all pious souls are blest,
His present as his endless plague pursues.

     [Edmund Wodehouse], 'Octr 2 [1715]'

     b.131, p. 278

10389   I' th' midst o' the land of Vanna Gloria,
Nor huff and ding(?) and draw the dagger.

     'Ponsonthonsoncausticon'

     c.93

10390   I' th' world's no constancy, all's circular:
What wonder then no rectitude is there?

     'The world'

     c.356

10391   I thank you for your pretty fable
It is not worth a pot of ale.

     [Elizabeth (Shirley) Compton, countess of
Northampton], 'To Mr. Davis . . . [1728/9]' [in the
name of her son Lord Compton]

     Accession 97.7.40 (two copies)

10392   I that had carried a hundred bodies brave
May I be porter to the gates of heaven.

     'An epitaph on a sexton at St. Edmundsbury'

     c.360/1, p. 231

10393   I that have robb'd so oft, am now bid stand,
His mercy is beyond severity.

     [John] Clavell [of Brasenose College, Oxford,
condemned 30 January 1625/6]
[Crum 1516]

     b.197, p. 47; b.200, p. 4

10394   I that my country did betray
Expect my spotted soul among the just.

     ['On the Duke of Buckingham', 1628]
[Crum 1517a]

     b.200, p. 54 (following 'At Portsmouth, duke . . .'); b.54,
p. 880

10395   I that sometime shin'd like the Orient sun
He both in vice and virtue did excel.

     [Thomas Rogers], 'Leicester's ghost'
[Crum 1520]

     fb.40, p. 325; fb.206, p. 213

10396   I that was once a humble log
Got in my box, and went to rest.

     'A true and full account of a late conference, between
a wonderful speaking head and Father Gauden . . .
related by the head's own mouth to Dr. Frazier'
[Crum 1522]

     fb.70, p. 167; fb.108, p. 185; Poetry Box VI/64; see also 'I
who was once . . .'.

10397   I think I shall never despair
Till justice is tack'd with a halter | To the 134.

     [John Tutchin], 'The French King's cordial' [on
Louis XIV's support of the Old Pretender]
[Crum 1525; *POAS* VII.46]

     c.111, p. 93; c.356; Poetry Box VII/39, p. 3; File 19034

10398   I think our people will discover soon,
That wings, and feathers do portend their flying.

     Sir Thomas Urquhart, 'Of the fashion of winged
coats, and the wearing of plumes in our hats'

     fb.217, p. 338

10399   I think there's none that in our court can tell
With their old authors are forgot at last.

     [Sir Richard Bulstrode?], 'Upon the same subject' [the
court at St. Germain's]

     fb.88, p. 116

10400   I think you are a thief you shall not fail
Seeing none are form'd such but these have wealth.

     [Sir Thomas Urquhart], 'The aim of a certain thief
declared to a bailiff who speaks to him thus in the
[?]ing and [?]ing him'

     fb.217, p. 394

10401   I thirst for thirstiness I weep for tears
For those that rest not here, there's rest behind.

     [Thomas Gataker, 'The zealous penitent']
[Crum 1529]

     b.222, p. 104; Poetry Box V/37

10402   I those black letters, on white paper sign'd:
That this, may 'xpress your body: these, your mind.

     Sir Thomas Urquhart, 'A missive to a beautiful, but
inconstant lady'

     fb.217, p. 341

10403   I thought by mingling with the gay,
From the full heart the conscious tear will flow.

     'Reflection'

     c.83/2, no. 637

10404   I thought I might upon your promise build—
Have emptied one and fill'd the other two.

     [Phanuel Bacon], 'To obviate the ladies' objections for
not coming to see ———'s house upon the score of a
certain place being built upon the moat'

     c.237, fol. 45

10405   I thought if too much pleasure me would kill
I envy not but much good do their pain.

     [Sir Aston Cokayne], 'The old man's wife translated
forth of the twenty second canto of Orlando
Inamorato'

     b.275, p. 50

10406   I thought the graces were but three,
To those three gives a thousand.

'Epigram on seeing the pict[ure]s of L[ord]
Townshend and sister painted by M. Josh.
Reyn[ol]ds . . . they toasted in Dub[lin] by the graces'
fc.85, fol. 88

10407   I to refulgent Phoebus owe my birth,
And bless the fair ones with superior joy.

[Mary] Leapor, 'A riddle: by the same hand'
Spence Papers, folder 113

10408   I, to the muses dear, to mirth inclin'd,
And with new songs and music consecrate his fame.

[Robert Cholmeley], 'Horace ode VI: lib 1. Musis
amicus &c'
c.190, p. 182

10409   I too, says Chloe, would to love
Of my sincere and melting kiss.

'The forced Berero'
Poetry Box II/33

10410   I took up my lyre and struck on the string,
Attend, whilst I sing of my love.

[N. Herbert], 'Anacreon ode the 1st imitated'
Spence Papers, folder 91

10411   I touched her hand, in touching it she trembled
Love deeply grounded can hardly be dissembled.

[John Mackereth? c. 1778]
b.132, insert

10412   I trap all men
Part il[l] amen.

'Anagram vizt. Parliament'
b.115, fol. 40v; see also 'My clergy's from me rent . . .'.

10413   I understand and sor[row] for
And you safe home restore.

'To his Grace the Duke of Ormonde'
fb.228/38

10414   I wail Adonis, nymphs in Pindus' shade,
And yearly keep a jubilee of woe.

[Isaac Freeman], 'The epitaph of Adonis imitated
from Bion Idyll 5. London'
fc.105, p. 27

10415   I wait O blessed Lord to see
Dissolved by Thy almighty love.

[Mary Pluret], 'Another [poem written on waste
paper]'
c.354

10416   I waited long and sought the Lord
And shall be sent no more.

[John Hopkins], 'The 18 psalm a thanksgiving for
deliverance from trouble and a praising of God's
providence' [verses from Psalms 39–40]
[cf. Crum 1554]
a.3, fol. 91

10417   I want but a monarch to play for the vole
I tremble to lose all my capital stock.

'Quadrille, as now played at Soissons'
fc.135; Accession 97.7.40

10418   I wanted a couplet or two t'other day,
With his whole Heliconian throng.

Spence Papers, folder 113

10419   I was long in doubt,
Which from Bacchus and Venus oft lurks.

'Answer' [to 'Silence, ye Tories . . .']
c.578, p. 88

10420   I was till now much overseen
And bake her if I bake her not.

b.213, p. 125

10421   I was told, one was charg'd, and had up *coram
no[bis]*,
And so, Sir your servant| Says, old Jingle Bo[bus].

'Epigram'
c.81/1, no. 369

10422   I was yesterday ask'd to a fine turtle feast
Tho' we really have eat till we're ready to burst!

Mrs. [ ] Noel, 'The turtle feast'
c.504, p. 55

10423   I weep not those who life's sweet light have lost,
But those, in constant fear of dying tost.

George Montagu, 'Another [translation of Greek
epigrams]'
fc.135, p. 11

10424   I weeping wonder that thou shouldst regard
Thee my God.

[Mary Pluret], 'Another [poem written on waste
paper]'
c.354

10425   I went from England into France
Who 'twas thought ne'er did the same.

[Thomas Goodwyn, 'Journey into France', 1618]
[Crum 1572]
b.197, p. 113; b.200, p. 176 ('J. Goodwyn'); see also 'I
came . . .'.

10426 I went in order Sir to your command
When bearded men in floating castles land &c.

> [John] Dryden, 'Guyomar's description of the Spanish navy to his father Montezuma emperor of Mexico'
>
> fb.66/40

10427 I went to church on Sabbath even,
Since now our desks can pray, and pulpits talk.

> 'On Mr. I—d'
>
> c.382, p. 54

10428 I went to St. Clement's with an honest design
Or a creature so bright create us no more.

> [Robert Cholmeley], 'To Mrs Eliz Nutting written extempore at the sight of her in St Clement's Church in Cambridge—The idolatrous'
>
> c.190, p. 29

10429 I—when winter comes desire,
We know but darkly since or not at all.

> 'Lyncup Hill Ingoe Township'
>
> c.93

10430 I who am Dolobian on fair Vernevia's stream sited [?]
Who was sure of me yet me lost.

> [30 November 1753]
>
> Poetry Box x/118

10431 I who am now a vet'ran of the stage
May every joy you give be tenfold yours.

> [David] Garrick, 'Epilogue spoken by . . . on the night of performance for benefit of the Theatrical Fund'
>
> c.68, p. 221

10432 I who beneath croft's solitary shade
And health adorn the widow, wife, and maid.

> 'The triumphs of the whiskey humbly dedicated to Miss Harley afterwards Mrs. G. Drummond'
>
> Poetry Box xii/58

10433 I who by nature was design'd
Diversify each rolling year.

> 'Madam du Bocage to her sister'
>
> c.83/2, no. 644

10434 I who of divers villains sung before
To taste their sweetness drops with pleasure dead.

> 'A supplement to the foregoing satire—ille ego qui quondam . . .'
>
> b.113, p. 131

10435 I who sang of Jack-a-Dandy,
Hey ding! Ho ding! Ding a ding!

> [prefaced to 'Mocking is catching or a pastoral lamentation for the loss of a man and no man']
>
> c.503, p. 6

10436 I who was late concern'd to hear
May recompense a mother's woe.

> [ ] Lewis, 'Recovery from sickness'
>
> c.244, p. 462

10437 I who was once an humble log
Got in my box and went to rest.

> 'A true and full account of a conference between the late wondrous speaking head and Father Gauden as it was related by the head's own mouth to Dr. Fr[azie]r'
>
> b.115, fol. 16; see also 'I that was once . . .'.

10438 I will call that a paradox, which may
I honor the endowments of that sex.

> Sir Thomas Urquhart, 'Why I term that a paradox, which encroacheth never so little upon the disadvantage of ladies and gentlewomen'
>
> fb.217, p. 41

10439 I will give laud and honor both,
Nothing shall them confound.

> [Thomas Sternhold], 'The 14 psalm a thanksgiving for deliverance from trouble' [verses from Psalm 34] [Crum 1585]
>
> a.3, fol. 82v

10440 I will not if this victory be glorious
Your fortune only is o'ercome by mine.

> [Sir Thomas Urquhart], 'A wise man cannot be overcome, though he be overthrown in body'
>
> fb.217, p. 531

10441 I will not praise you, lest my praises puff
You up with greater pride; being proud enough.

> Sir Thomas Urquhart, 'To a presumptuous coxcomb'
>
> fb.217, p. 229

10442 I will not think it longer wonderful
Is wounded with th'affection of an ass.

> Sir Thomas Urquhart, 'Of a young girl, who was over the ears in love with a homely gentleman, of no great moment'
>
> fb.217, p. 207

10443 I will not trust thy tempting graces
Than love or beauty could before.

> [Thomas Stanley]
> [Crum 1593]
>
> b.213, p. 62

10444 I will to God lift up my voice,
Through deserts and the deep.

> 'Psalm 77'
>
> c.264/2, p. 55

10445 I William King, the third year of my reign
And my third son Henry.

'Title deed granted by William the Conqueror to an
ancestor of the present Ld. Moira copied verbatim
from the original'

Diggle Box: Poetry Box XI/69

10446 I Willoughby Dixie of Bosworth Park
And all the store of swine and grains.

Willoughby Dixie, 'Copy of the will of . . . of
Bosworth field'

Smith Papers, folder 75/25

10447 I wish all cuckolds were in Thames, quoth Cim;
I'm glad, quoth's wife, that you have learn'd to swim.

Sir Thomas Urquhart, 'A parley betwixt the cuckold
Cim, and his bedfellow' [translation of an epigram by
John Owen]

fb.217, p. 136

10448 I wish for death yet loath to die
The soul shall live in spite of death.

'A conflict between the flesh and the spirit'

a.6, p. 23

10449 I wish I was where Anna lies
A long, a last, a sad adieu.

Poetry Box III/24

10450 I wish I were a book, by transformation:
That I might change you for another yearly.

Sir Thomas Urquhart, 'The speeches of a
gentlewoman, whose husband was . . . seriously
addicted to reading . . . being otherwise, somewhat
variable and inconstant'

fb.217, p. 88

10451 I wish my language could impart
I'd sing thy praise and worship thee.

[Mrs. Christian Kerr], 'The answer' [to 'Such
language from my friend . . .']

c.102, p. 96

10452 I wish no more thou shouldst love me
No murder but a sacrifice.

[Crum I602]

b.213, p. 15

10453 I wish not Sophy to offend,
Glorious eternal hymns of praise.

'Verses address'd to Miss [Sophia] Apthorp on her
return from school'

c.175, p. 64

10454 I wish to sing Macaulay's fame
'The good alone are great.'

'An ode to Mrs. Macaulay' [Leicester, 19 May 1777]

c.136, p. 111

10455 I wish you joy on this important day
'Twill make him dance, without Desnoyer's fiddle.

'On the birthday of the Rt Honble the Lady Charlotte
Compton'

Accession 97.7.40

10456 I wish you old age, but not death: s'in strictness,
I wish you not the physic but the sickness.

Sir Thomas Urquhart, 'To a very good young man,
who was of a tender, and weak complexion'

fb.217, p. 188

10457 I with a sharp tho' cloven dart,
Will sure my language understand.

'A riddle by a young lady'

c.578, p. 140

10458 I with my voice to God do cry
Thou didst them safely guide.

[John Hopkins], 'Against affliction and grievous
temptations. Psal: 31' [verses from Psalm 77]
[Crum I608]

a.3, fol. 112

10459 I wonder at those people that do think,
It shall not stick with them as a disease.

Lady Jane Cavendish, 'The cautious man, or wit's
wonder'
[Crum I611]

b.233, p. 27

10460 I wonder, by my troth, what thou, and I
Love just alike in all, none of these loves can die.

[John Donne], 'Canzone'
[Crum I613]

b.114, p. 276; b.148, p. 105

10461 I wonder quoth Dame as he[r] spouse she embraces
And the breach there was clos'd the same way it was
made.

'Song 193'

c.555, p. 310

10462 I wonder what's the cause our hearts do prove
That of all evils are the upper springs.

b.216, p. 152

10463 I wonder why men lay their head
Though's bed be flock so his wench be down.

'On a featherbed'

b.356, p. 103

10464 I wonder, why that having sail'd the deep,
Upon a bed of sands.

    Sir Thomas Urquhart, 'Of a traveled gentleman, who
    was in suit of one Mistress Sands'

    fb.217, p. 75

10465 I would be thine thou know'st I would
Let all I am be God.

    'Hymn 64th'

    c.562, p. 77

10466 I would believe Thy word
And all thy bounties prove.

    T[homas] S[tevens], 'Aft[e]rn[oo]n s[a]m[e] d[a]y
    Mattw. 28.16.17.18'

    c.259, p. 102

10467 I would breathe my life with joy, your royal
To cause you die an everlasting death.

    Sir Thomas Urquhart, 'To mine own self'

    fb.217, p. 202

10468 I would have mercy too but cannot ask
And God, the hearing of my cause I crave.

    H[enry] C[olman], 'The unregenerate sinner's plea'
    [Crum I626]

    b.2, p. 26

10469 I would love's language tell but so
And this each one, will, whispering speak.

    Lady Jane Cavendish, 'A song'
    [Crum I630]

    b.233, p. 26

10470 I would not alway wish to breathe
Would sing forever to His praise.

    Charles Atherton Allnutt, '7 Job 16 v.—I would not
    live alway'

    c.112, p. 79

10471 I would not have my mistress be so coy
Within a short while after puts me to it.

    Sir Thomas Urquhart, 'How a gentlewoman should
    behave herself towards him she loves'

    fb.217, p. 152

10472 I would not have my throat cut for a bushel of gold,
I assure you gentlemen, it's true what I've told.

    c.93

10473 I would not have you take such pains at all,
In your best favors, doth not see a stime [sic].

    Sir Thomas Urquhart, 'That too curious primping
    and pinning is not very necessary for the purchase of
    affection, seeing Cupid is blind. To a bride'

    fb.217, p. 298

10474 I would on my friends bestow
Bacchus hear the vows we pay.

    [William Popple, trans.], '[Horace] book 4th. Ode 8.
    To Marcus Censorinus'

    fc.104/2, p. 360

10475 I would rather keep more strings that one t'a bow
When I divide them 'twixt two mistresses.

    [Sir Thomas Urquhart], 'His reason why he would not
    content himself with one mistress'

    fb.217, p. 386

10476 I wys I am too weak a clerk
With my shape.

    'Braye Lute Book,' Music Ms. 13, fol. 23v

10477 I your memory's recorder
Unlock Heaven so soon as these.

    [William Strode], 'Another' [on a register for a Bible;
    following 'I am that faithful deputy . . .']
    [Crum I638]

    b.205, fol. 55r

10478 I[:] you're a jovial chicken yet who feels
On Thursday we shall keep Good Friday's feast.

    'Answer' [to 'How is't that I . . .']

    b.356, p. 107

10479 I'd knows [sic] why the devil I should keep a coach
                           in the town
And be at the Parliament at their next seating.

    Spence Papers, folder 113

10480 I'd not presume to beg a kiss,
Do but believe I love you, and I ask no more.

    c.549, p. 9

10481 Idly some think, that Almack's is a scene
If deeds portray, [?] is their name.

    John Lockman, 'Verses supposed to be writ, at the
    grand concert and ball, tomorrow, (Friday 18th
    instant,) at Almack's, for the benefit of the Middlesex
    Hospital, in order to add a wing to it'

    c.267/1, p. 389

10482 I'd be a favorite—not mortal I
But blessed favor seek, sent from on high.

    [Sir Philip Wodehouse], 'Upon the second of the
    d[aughters] Elizabeth Fortescue'

    b.131, back (no. 35)

10483 I'd give a limb with all my heart,
This author wrote by inspiration.

    Edward Sneyd, 'An extempore on reading a copy of
    verses written by Miss A. F.'

    c.214, p. 68

10484 I'd have her merry laugh and smile
Then merry for thy sake.

    b.213, p. 50

10485 I'd have her reason all her passions sway,
She goes the least of womankind astray.

    'Description of a woman's perfections'

    c.83/2, no. 378

10486 I'd have you quoth he,
So do I Sir.

    'Country courtship'

    fb.107, p. 74

10487 I'd rather see a hare encatch'd still run
To taste them with than touch them casually.

    [Sir Thomas Urquhart], 'That there is a great pleasure
    in courting of a lady that in the enjoying of her'

    fb.217, p. 386

10488 If a body put a body in the speaker's chair,
Yet all the day I'm blithe and gay, and drunk at
                            night am I.

    'A quintetto, supposed to be sung at one of
    Mr. Addington's late dinners—to the tune of If a body
    see a body'

    c.340

10489 If a daughter you have and she's the plague of your
                                 life
Oh! what a plague is an obstinate daughter.

    'Song 240'

    c.555, p. 383

10490 If a man in contrition for sins that are past
May live upon hope and not fear condemnation!

    R[ichard] V[ernon] S[adleir], 'To Mrs. Mocher
    Gen[era]l M's lady'

    c.106, p. 70

10491 If a more near access to Thee
I should not fear to die, nor long to live.

    [Edmund Wodehouse], 'Jan. 16 [1715]'

    b.131, p. 142

10492 If a truth may be ask'd Sir, pray what it mean,
Poor Charles is forgotten—to make you the martyr.

    'Samuel Croxall clerk; of Hampton to Sr. Robert
    Walpole, Knight of the Garter' [satire on Croxall's
    sermon of 30 January 1730]

    Poetry Box v/128, 129

10493 If a wretch in tatters, a poor shilling
Tyburn hangs not th'illustrious villain.

    John Lockman, 'The rich and poor rogue: the tune,
    Profitez bien jeunes fillettes'

    c.267/2, p. 145; c.268 (first part), p. 81

10494 If abdicate James
And they have for their money their jest.

    'A new ballad . . . by Cool[ing] and [Fleetwood]
    Shep[pard] to the tune of God prosper long our noble
    King . . .' [1690]
    [Crum 1649; *POAS* v.104]

    fb.70, p. 251

10495 If after all endeavors made
Shall be while He doth reign.

    Thomas Traherne, '[Meditation (first century)] 89'

    b.308, p. 51

10496 If after death souls can appear,
And place the souls in glee?

    'To make hid the notion of souls appearing after death
    one thus writes'

    c.158, p. 116

10497 If age, and sickness, poverty and pain
If a star fell to set their thatch on flame.

    Lady Mary Wortley Montagu, 'By . . . on her
    daughter's marriage' [ll. 5–6 not in printed version]

    fc.51, p. 125

10498 If all be true, that I do think,
Or any other reason why.

    [Henry Aldrich], 'Reasons for drinking'
    [Crum 1652]

    c.233, p. 68

10499 If all I say, if all I write,
Continue perfect grow, all alone within.

    [Edmund Wodehouse], 'Jan. 9 [1715]'

    b.131, p. 136

10500 If all the graces dress'd in all their ease
But to define it—is impossible.

    H[annah] More, 'Written extempore after hearing
    Mrs. Powell perform in tragedy'

    c.341, p. 65

10501 If all the hair upon the head of men
That to be drunk is scarce accounted since.

    'In ebrietatem'

    b.205, fol. 49v

10502 If all those ancient fathers did embrace
Let all the saints from hence attend His praise.

[Thomas Gurney], 'To Mr. John Gill on his last part of The cause of God and truth' [acrostic]

c.213

10503 If angels on that happy morn the Savior of the
world was born
All the powers of death and hell before his
sov'reign sway.

[John Savidge]
Music Ms. 8

10504 If any ask me what would satisfy
They who ask more are covetous, not wise.

'Moderate contentment'
c.360/2, no. 41

10505 If any be so curious, as to know,
Their zeal's so fiery, they cannot affect it.

Sir Thomas Urquhart, 'Why puritans admit no rites, wherewith to apparel their devotion'
fb.217, p. 103

10506 If any ever merited to be
And save from the effects of forty-one.

'To B[ishop Benjamin] Hoadley'
b.90, p. 13

10507 If any has his father kill'd,
And at the bed's foot lie.

[William Popple, trans.], '[Horace, ep]ode 3d. To Maecenas'
fc.104/2, p. 404

10508 If any man call you a hart,
And far more horns.

Sir Thomas Urquhart, 'To one, that was both a cuckold, and a coward'
fb.217, p. 205

10509 If any thoughts worth memory
That I good matter can't refuse.

[Edmund Wodehouse], 'Decr. 17 [1714]'
b.131, p. 116

10510 If any wanton lines have issu'd from
Enwrapp'd before the reader in a sheet.

[Sir Thomas Urquhart], 'The penance of lascivious verse'
fb.217, p. 536

10511 If anyone wants to know who lies within,
Look you d' you see me, 'tis Edward Gwynn.

H. H., 'On a councillor famous for leading with a, look you do you see me, at every sentence. Who so seen of a another more noble family of his took an epit[het] for that person and ordered it to be put on his own and on which was writ . . . this epithet'

c.233, p. 8

10512 If Aphra's worth were needful to be shown
And what thou canst not comprehend admire.

'The female laureat'
[Crum A682]

b.113, p. 285

10513 If ardent wishes can prevail
And fly from such a court.

[Isabella (Machell) Ingram], viscountess Irwin, 'Verses on the King by . . . wrote at the request of the Lady Augusta'

Poetry Box x/9

10514 If, as in Æsop's days, when brutes could speak,
And, from your Lordship's horse, embrace your
feet.

[Alexander] Pope, 'Epistle to the e[arl] of Burlington—versified. V.7.L.10. p. 336'

c.395, p. 43

10515 If as it ought the only end
Which we believe may it increase.

[Edmund Wodehouse], 'Aug. 28 [1715]'
b.131, p. 254

10516 If as my numerous [?] increase
And above all for their address | I shall above all &c.

[Edmund Wodehouse], 'Feb. 24 [1715]'
b.131, p. 172

10517 If as the ancient poets sing
That glory's due to Dover's coast.

'1729'
Trumbull Box: Poetry Box xiii/103, p. 1

10518 If, as the psalmist says, the age of man
The sage's life can never be too long.

John Lockman, 'To [John Atkins, of Plaistow, Essex] on his birthday [21 March] 1757'

c.267/1, p. 208

10519 If asked I should be which life doth please me best?
I like the golden liberty, let golden bondage rest.

c.339, p. 325

10520 If aught could soothe to peace the wounded breast,
To fan Aurora's burning breast.

  Mary [(Derby)] Robinson, 'Ode to the harp of the
  late Louisa Hanway'

c.83/2, no. 387

10521 If aught of oaten stop, or pastoral song
And love thy favorite name!

  [William] Collins, 'Ode to evening'

c.351, p. 167

10522 If, beauteous nymph! thro' yonder bowers
And lull his pangs to balmy rest.

  John Lockman, 'Translations, and imitations from
  Metastasio, and other Italian opera poets [1]'

c.267/4, p. 91

10523 If beauty innocence and truth,
'Tis yours to rail, 'tis mine to shine.

  [John Gay], 'The owls, the bats, and the sun, a fable
  inscribed to the right honorable Lady Mary Tufton'

Poetry Box I/101

10524 If birth and titles, if a graceful frame;
O'errun with luxury, and party rage.

  John Lockman, 'To the nymph of the springs of Passy
  (now Paris) when the Duchess of Buckingham was
  there, drinking the waters . . . Aug. 1741'

c.267/1, p. 80

10525 If bleeding hearts, dejected souls find grace
More life to those that now desire to live.

  'To the most high and mightiest . . . chancellor of
  heaven, and judge of earth [the petitions of the
  commons of England' [1623/24; answered by 'Your
  bold petition . . .']
  [Crum 1697]

b.197, p. 86

10526 If blest the marriage state as some agree,
Kind heavens, O! give me him—or give me none.

  'A spinster's choice of a husband'

fb.142, p. 62

10527 If bounteous Thrale could then transfer
Let this example tell.

  C[harles] B[urney, the elder], 'To Mrs. Thrale on
  receiving from her a gold pen'

c.33, p. 117 (crossed out)

10528 If butchers kill'd not lambs, and death young men:
The world could not her fools, and sheep sustain.

  Sir Thomas Urquhart, 'Of death, and fleshers'

fb.217, p. 254

10529 If by myself, my self were to be tried,
I for my sins may truly mourn and grieve.

  Sir John Strangways, 'A private meditation'

b.304, p. 46

10530 If by our preachers parents are led
And not be in a stude(?).

  [Thomas Gurney], 'On a independent minister
  ordering a infant out of the meeting for crying and
  reproving the parent for bringing it there'

c.213

10531 If by plus minus, I express
Quod erat demonstrandum.

  'Epigram'

Poetry Box VIII/72

10532 If by the necessary use of things
Our minds of what might otherwise molest us.

  [Sir Thomas Urquhart], 'That if we [?] not here for
  substance than for what is needful we would not [?]
  much humbled'

fb.217, p. 523

10533 If by the want of things their worth is known,
I know the worth of wealth for none's my own.

  'To a rich friend'

c.356

10534 If Caporali charm'd the list'ning ear,
From the superior magic of thy bow?

  John Lockman, 'To Signor Loneretti: on his
  performing at the great room . . . for Miss Sheward's
  benefit . . . 26 Feb. 1754'

c.267/1, p. 54

10535 If care do cause men cry
Full well declare my smart.

  [cf. Crum 1705]

'Braye Lute Book,' Music Ms. 13, fol. 22

10536 If casually your virtue be empestred [*sic*]
You're better'd by how much the more, they're
                                          worse.

  Sir Thomas Urquhart, 'To my Lord [crossed out]'

fb.217, p. 209

10537 If Charles thou wouldst but grow so kind,
When you please to resign your crown. | We'll ask
                                          no more.

  'Another libel. The humble petition of the Lords and
  Commons in Parliament'
  [Crum 1708]

b.101, p. 127; b.4, fol. 48v; fb.140, p. 5; b.213, p. 72

10538 If Chloe would only do my first with me, tonight
I can but just make it out myself, pray can you?

[Sir Henry William Bunbury], 'Charade—2'
File 17066

10539 If Christ Church lads were sad, they spent their
breath
Breda is lost your bargain you maintain.

[William Strode], 'An answer to a copy of verses
['Why how now . . .'] on the striving of Christ
Church. &c.'
[Crum 1712]
b.200, p. 132

10540 If comeliness I want,
Will still run fresh in thee.

[ ] Chares [on Caleb Vernon]
b.228, p. 56

10541 If Cupid in sport,
And make shift with an old-fashioned beau.

'A lady's resolution'
c.83/2, no. 701

10542 If Cupid were not blind,
That he doth venture.

Sir Thomas Urquhart, 'Love is the bolder, that he sees
not'
fb.217, p. 211

10543 If Cupid wound thy lovesick heart,
Such is the magic power of wine!

Charles Burney, the younger, 'On wine, from the same
author [Bacchylides]'
c.35, p. 51

10544 If Damon loves I love him to excess
That in thy absence I shall feel no pain.

[Mrs. ( ) Feilding]
b.226, p. 16

10545 If daring man his God blasphemes,
He deprecates th'almighty Pow'r.

Mary Cornwallis, 'St. Evremond sur l'existence de
Dieu . . . translated by . . . 1790'
fc.124, p. 69

10546 If days of absence gives such pain
'Tis thou must cure, a broken heart.

[Thomas Hamilton, 6th earl of Haddington], 'A song'
c.458/2, p. 71

10547 If dearest friend, it my good fate might be
Knows a man how to live, and does he stay?

A[braham] C[owley], 'In imitation of Martial's
epigrams'
c.258

10548 If death doth come as breath departs
Then death's a fart, and so a fart for death.

'Epigram on death'
Poetry Box VII/5

10549 If death my friend and me divide,
In that eternal day.

c.562, p. 149

10550 If e'er again Eliza's heart
In thee find endless peace.

Eliza[beth Ann (Linley) Sheridan], 'Eliza's choice'
Poetry Box III/29

10551 If e'er ambition did my fancy cheat
The humble blessings of that life I love.

[Mrs. Christian Kerr]
c.102, p. 88; see also 'If ever I more riches . . .'.

10552 If e'er I quit the single life, be this the model of my
wife
To such a virgin such a wife, I give my love I give
my life.

'The bachelor's choice'
c.115; c.487, p. 123

10553 If e'er I'm doom'd the marriage bands to wear,
Or, keep me happy in a single life.

I[saac] W[at]t[s](?), 'The maiden's choice . . .
Norwich Feb. 20. 1758'
c.94

10554 If e'er on earth true happiness were found
That not on earth true happiness is found.

[William] Mason, 'Epitaph'
Poetry Box XII/112

10555 If e'er sincerity inscribed the stone
The living monument of Spencer's fame.

'To the memory of John [Spencer, 1st] earl Spencer [d.
31 Oct. 1783]'
Poetry Box X/97

10556 If e'er thou'dst be happy, make haste, and remove,
And much of love to know.

'True enjoyment'
fb.107, p. 34

10557 If e'er thy bosom swell'd with grief sincere,
Fair branches budding from the lifeless tree.

[Francis Fawkes], 'On that most accomplished lady,
Mrs. Fontayne, daughter of Thos. Whichcot esq. and
wife to the Dean of York . . . she died in childbed July
1750, aetat 19'

fc.21, p. 27

10558 If e'er you leave us in a lasting peace
Shall crown your heads, and we shall sing your praise.

[George Wither], 'Postscript' [to 'Vox et lacrimae
Anglorum']
[Crum 1735]

File 16328

10559 If e'er you see a rambling pile
You won't mistake to call it Prague.

[Isaac Freeman], 'The picture of Prague. To Thomas
Steavens esqr.'

fc.105, after p. 35

10560 If eighty-eight be past then thrive
A Spaniard protestant to be.

'A prophecy found in the abbey of St. Benedict near
the city of Norwich in Norfolk. Anno 24 Hen: octavi'
[Crum 1736]

b.101, p. 57; b.197, p. 189; fb.7, fol. 5

10561 If ever I more riches did desire
The humble blessings of that life I love.

A[braham] C[owley]

b.118, p. 21; see also 'If e'er ambition . . .'.

10562 If ever I so chance to meet
Such a girl might kiss my ass.

[Joseph Spence], 'Sung at Biggleswade'

Spence Papers, folder 119; c.176, p. 2 ('ever I should . . .')

10563 If ever tears could perfect grief improve,
Where he is gone, and we all wish to come.

'On the death of the right worshipful Sr. Wm. Blackett
bart.'

c.530, p. 193

10564 If fair one, you your suit would gain,
My suit to you, I must obtain.

'Female client and magistrate'

c.81/1, no. 434

10565 If fair Serena yet retains
Prevail on her to read your poem.

[Richard Brinsley Butler Sheridan], 'A fourth' [to
William Hayley on his incomparably long poem
entitled The triumphs of temper, c. 1781]

File 13565

10566 If fate go right, where'er this stone is pight
The regal race of Scots shall rule that place.

b.208, p. 191

10567 If favor, wisdom, and beauty be given unto thee
One thing, that's pride will mar all these if it
adjoined be.

b.234, p. 71

10568 If fell corruption in each scene appears
Forgive Lord Noel, when she says, 'tis you.

'The man of measure' [pr. 1737 (Foxon M63)]

Poetry Box v/120

10569 If filial duty, if fraternal love,
But learn from his example how to live.

H[annah] More, 'Epitaph on T. B[lan]df[or]d . . .
1771'

c.341, p. 35

10570 If first with compliments you entertain her
To cross a lady, is the way to please her.

Sir Thomas Urquhart, 'How to court a gentlewoman'

fb.217, p. 271

10571 If five to one you join with care,
More than beauty, lips, and eyes.

Diggle Box: Poetry Box XI/71

10572 If for a grace, or if for some dislike,
Your glove's perfumed, your lips, and cheeks are
painted.

'On a gentlewoman, who painted her face'
[Crum 1754]

b.200, p. 18

10573 If for despairing love, a balm be found
Nor dare to cast the mangled limb away.

Charles [James] Fox, 'To the late Ld. Holland'

c.504, p. 9

10574 If for four terms four terms there were
Th' one takes whole angels, t'other crackt crowns.

'Cedant arma togæ'
[Crum 1755]

b.205, fol. 43v

10575 If for the good effects they have produc'd
Which is the hearty pray'r and wish of | Yours, &c.

Samuel Phillips, of St. John's College Oxford, 'To
Mr. and Mrs. Green daughter of Martin Johnson esq.
on her birthday'

c.229/1, fol. 42

10576 If fortune favor'd you, as nature did
Despis'd the gifts, to have enjoy'd your face.

> Sir Thomas Urquhart, 'To Lady Elizabeth [crossed out]'

fb.217, p. 275

10577 If friend, a wife you mean to wed,
Worthy of your board and bed.

> [ ] Lewis, 'A choice of a wife'

c.244, p. 450

10578 If friendship, charity, zeal, virtue die,
Equal she fell, but shall not equal rise.

> 'Epitaph in a churchyard in Gloucester'

c.83/2, no. 698

10579 If from the word glove
And that won't do for me.

> '[Enigma/Charade/Conundrum] 66'
> [cf. Crum 1764, 1766]

c.389

10580 If gay Calista in the flow'ry road
'The path of virtue is a thorny way.'

> 'Epigram'

c.81/1, no. 116

10581 If gentleness could tame the fates, or wit
Ought to be buried, as he would.

> [Richard] Corbett, 'Dr. Corbett upon Henry Boline'
> [Crum 1773 (var.)]

b.356, p. 142

10582 If giants of old, as poets have told
Shall flourish with unfading bays.

> [ ] M., 'On [the capture of de Winter the Dutch admiral 11 October 1797]'

c.546, p. 18

10583 If gifts and words you equally esteem
In the same habit, thy own gifts are drest.

> R[obert] Shirley, 1st earl of Ferrers, 'To a profuse promiser, but frugal giver. From [Martial]'

c.347, p. 33

10584 If God from heaven, should send an angel down
And Britain be the happiest of isles.

> [Thomas Hamilton, 6th earl of Haddington], 'A prologue to the next new play'

c.458/2, p. 64

10585 If God's blest love deep root had ta'en
Of which that love the fountain is.

> [Edmund Wodehouse], 'Jan. 15 [1715]'

b.131, p. 141

10586 If good ladies, you will make a trial of skill,
Then a treat it shall cost me and mine.

> 'Ænigma . . . Ostrea'

b.63, p. 127

10587 If great men wrong me, I will spare myself
If good like gods, the naught are so like devils.

> [Sir John Roe], 'Epistola secunda to Mr. Ben. Jonson' [attr. John Donne; dated 9 Nov. 1603]
> [Crum 1782]

b.114, p. 147

10588 If greatest griefs be dumb, then this to speak
There's nothing of this world, him thence can steal.

> [Edward] Sparke, 'Upon the passion of Christ—poem 12th'

b.137, p. 27

10589 If happy be the man,
Plead causes at the bar.

> Sir Thomas Urquhart, 'Of a good advocate'

fb.217, p. 228

10590 If he cannot live chaste,
Be she [?], be she [?], [?] late repent.

> 'A merry admonition to all those that wants wives'

Poetry Box VIII/4

10591 If, heated to excess by sport or toil,
At once, forever, all those feelings kill!

Poetry Box III/56

10592 If heaven be pleased, when man do cease from sin
Then all is pleased, thy father's in his grave.

> 'Epitaphium'
> [Crum 1790]

b.197, p. 229; b.220, p. 1 (applied to Burnet); b.356, p. 248 (applied to Dr. Lamb); fb.143, p. 28; c.360/3, no. 41 (applied to [ ] Coleman); b.209, p. 73 (applied to Samuel Parker); see also 'If hell be pleas'd . . .'.

10593 If heaven the grateful liberty would give,
A permanent sincere substantial bliss.

> [John] Pomfret, 'The choice' [pr. 1700 (Wing P2794)]
> [Crum 1792]

c.244, p. 242; c.326, p. 150

10594 If heaven would please to purge thy soul as well
As Rome thy purse thou needst not fear a hell.

> [Francis Quarles], 'On Rhemus' [i.e., 'On Purgatory'; Divine Fancies IV, 5]

b.137, p. 179

10595 If hell be pleas'd when sinners sin
Then all are pleas'd that Burnet's in his grave.

'The Bishop of Sarum's epitaph' [Gilbert Burnet, 1715]

fc.58, p. 104; see also 'If heaven be pleased . . .'.

10596 If help of any man you would implore,
To mischief, that they can do good to none.

c.549, p. 37

10597 If her disdain in you least change can move
Except self-love seek private end.

'Earl of Pembroke' [answered by ''Tis love breeds love . . .']
[Crum 1798]

b.148, p. 132

10598 If Hercules' tall stature might be guess'd
If but to kiss your face I should aspire.

[William Strode], 'On a good leg and foot'
[Crum 1799]

b.205, fol. 66r

10599 If hitherto thou shot'st without a mark,
For heavenly glory still comes after grace.

John Cusacke, 'The author to the reader' [preface to Adam's paradise, 1621]

b.141, p. 5

10600 If 'honor in the breech is lodg'd',
Sir Peter's honor's gone!

'Distich upon Sir Peter Parker's wound off Sullivan's Island'

c.81/1, no. 463

10601 If honor to an ancient name be due
Lest her own captive else should her subdue.

K[atherine] Phil[ips], 'On the British language'
[Crum 1806]

b.118, p. 53

10602 If hundred *pois* you do extract
From eight your drams must still extracted be.

[Mary Serjant], 'Subtraction [of weight]'

fb.98, fol. 20

10603 If Hymen e'er my liberty restrain
To love, my pride, my pleasure to obey.

Lady F. T—n, 'The choice, by a lady'

c.157, p. 2

10604 If I am doom'd the marriage chain to wear
Or keep me happy in a single life.

'The choice . . . wrote by a young lady at Chester'
[1 January 1746/7]
[Crum 1809]

fc.51, p. 159

10605 If I could ever write a lasting verse,
From the prevailing language of thy eyes.

[Katherine Philips], 'On Mary Morris 1695 aged 3 quarter of a year and nine days'
[Crum 1813]

fb.143, p. 24

10606 If I could recollect a song
In rowing out one chorus. | Sing fallal &c.

[John Walker?], 'A chorus for the dull part of a convivial evening without a song'

fc.108, fol. 74

10607 If I dear Madam, thought you not my friend,
No farther search, but think on Celadon.

[Thomas Hamilton, 6th earl of Haddington], 'The dedication'

c.458/1, p. i

10608 If I do love, the fault is in your eyes,
That form divine, and not be made to taste.

c.549, p. 30

10609 If I freely may discover
Nor her peevishness annoy me.

[Ben Jonson, song in Poetaster II.ii.]
[Crum 1820]

b.114, p. 310 (attr. John Donne); b.148, p. 4

10610 If I have any other end
They joy in all they do, for love and duty's sake.

[Edmund Wodehouse], 'Novr. 10 [1714]'

b.131, p. 81

10611 If I live to be old, for I find I go down,
(Without gout or stone) by a gentle decay.

W[alter] Pope, 'A wish, written by . . . fellow of the Royal Society'
[Crum 1828]

c.189, p. 94; c.555, p. 89 ('live to grow' and ff.); fb.142, p. 63; b.155, p. 67; see also 'Since I find I'm grown old'

10612 If I may say, one attribute divine,
And neither end, decrease, nor interruption know.

fc.54, p. 27

10613 If I my Celia could persuade
As well as beauty charms the heart.

[Sir George Etherege], 'To a lady who fled the sight of him'

b.218, p. 21

10614 If I remember Ælia you had four (teeth)
There's nothing for another cough to do.

'An epigram out of Martial to Ælia thus translated'

fb.142, p. 26

10615 If I stranger may presume to mourn
And let him live although he die.

'In idem' [elegy on the death of Andrew Horsman]

b.212, p. 242

10616 If I urge my kind desires
Never liv'd or lov'd to die.

[Thomas Campion], 'Cant: 36'

b.4, fol. 31

10617 If I was young as I have been
His makes you die yet mine still lets you live.

'Riddle'

Poetry Box VII/47

10618 If I were as rich as Job
What may you [?] doth think.

'A man'

a.6, p. 102

10619 If I were not my first, or my second were now
Who have tried it is no very easy condition.

'Answer' [to 'O make me your first . . .']

Diggle Box: Poetry Box XI/71

10620 If idle passengers ask who lieth here
Ambition, treason, murder, pride and lust.

'On the D[uke] of B[uckingham]'
[Crum I841, 'idle travellers', (var.)]

b.356, p. 248

10621 If in his study Haman hath such care
To hang all old strange things, let's wife beware.

[John Donne], couplet in 'The antiquary'
[Crum I845]

b.148, p. 56

10622 If in love disappointed your spirits keep up
You run a good risk of your doubling Cape Horn.

[Phanuel Bacon], 'Sperat infestis—metuit secundis
bene praeparatum pictus'

c.237, fol. 78

10623 If in the day the Devil doth walk,
He'll ne'er possess our fellows.

'In socios seniores Coll: Oxon: [I]'

c.81/I, no. 24

10624 If in the following tale you trace
O'erturn their health and constitution.

[William Smith], 'Ephesian matron from Petronius'

Smith Papers, folder 59

10625 If in the morning sky or sun be red,
Soon after look for tempest, or for rain.

[John Rose?], 'Infallible signs of rain'

b.227, p. 174

10626 If in the spring of early life
And reason first our choice approve.

c.549, p. 69

10627 If in this scroll you find yourself admir'd
But if despised is dead forevermore.

[Sir Francis Castillion, 'Of Mrs. Lucy [Elizabeth?] St.
John [Castillion] . . . Verses in commendation of his
beloved saint'

fb.69, p. 205

10628 If in those plains, where all is bright and clear,
You'll scorn the sullied dull embrace of mortals
here below.

'Letters from an unfortunate lady. British Apollo'

c.244, p. 612

10629 If in your favors, fortune equaled
Deservingly the title of a king.

Sir Thomas Urquhart, 'The first epigram. To the
Palsgrave'

fb.217, p. 227

10630 If injur'd monarch may his cause explore,
Which heaven approv'd of by a cheerful voice.

[Charles Blount?], 'A dialogue betwixt King James and
King W[illia]m'
[cf. Crum I853; POAS V.235]

fb.207/4, p. 25 (ll. I–50); b.III, p. 355 ('cause deplore';
ll. I–50); c.570/2, p. 167; see also 'If vanquished
monarchs . . .'.

10631 If it be true as Welshmen say,
I die by resurrection.

'Riddle 2nd' [i.e., 56; bedfellow]

c.389; c.504, p. 113

10632 If it be true, that many men have said,
At least I am assur'd some told me so.

Sir Thomas Urquhart, 'A certain wench, who
remembered not on the time she was depucelated [sic]
in: or whether she had parted from her virginity, or
not, spoke thus'

fb.217, p. 301

10633 If it should suit your inclination
Good Mr. Lowman there's an end.

James Eckersall [10 Aug. 1741]

Poetry Box X/59

10634 If it's true as you say, that I've injure[d] a letter
And that I may be never mistaken for U.

> [David] Garrick, 'Epigram by . . . on being accused of
> altering the letter U to the letter I' [answer to a
> pamphlet by Dr. Hill, 1759]
> [Crum 1861]

Diggle Box: Poetry Box xi/69; c.81/1, no. 96; see also 'If
'tis true . . .'.

10635 If Jupiter from heaven should pour down gold;
For golden showers, I would hold up my smock.

> 'Honesty is sold for money'
> [Crum 1866]

b.200, p. 95

10636 If kisses did not to the taste belong
That th'only mouth can interchange a kiss.

> [Sir Thomas Urquhart], 'Why kisses are most
> conveniently applied to the mouth'

fb.217, p. 513

10637 If kisses to the taste bring nothing sweet,
Why kiss we with our mouths when friends we meet.

> 'A problem to naturalists of kisses'

c.356

10638 If late the muse essay'd to sing
England deceiv'd th'infallible.

> [ ] Newton, 'The fifth of November. 1726'

c.190, p. 94

10639 If legacies be worth, but to be rent,
Seeing he that made it, cannot suffer death.

> Sir Thomas Urquhart, 'Of the Old Testament a
> problem'

fb.217, p. 123

10640 If liberty of conscience e'er was good
Thus kindness gains, where arguments do fail.

> [Thomas Brown], 'Written in a boghouse in Gray's
> Inn'
> [Crum 1872]

b.209, p. 97; c.189, p. 171; fb.108, p. 319

10641 If lies; if slanders; if debate
That they may sovereign in the new.

> 'In Puritanos'

b.197, p. 144

10642 If liquorish and disobedient Eve
There had been Flora, and there had not been
Floyd.

> H[enry] Neville, 'On Flora, countess of Clarendon's
> garden'

Spence Papers, folder 108

10643 If love be a fault or in me thought a crime
The cause of my death was for loving too well.

> 'A song'

c.358, p. 121

10644 If love's a sweet passion, why does it torment?
For 'tis beauty that conquers and keeps the fair field.

> [Elkanah Settle], 'Song 87' [from The fairy queen]
> [Crum 1881]

c.555, p. 137

10645 If Madam you cannot divine
Existence in a future state.

> R[alph] Broome

c.486, fol. 39

10646 If marriage ever be my lot in life,
Pleas'd I'll admire, and strive to make them mine.

> 'A choice supposed to be written by a young lady . . .
> Liverpool . . . Aleanor'

c.175, p. 16; c.487, p. 72

10647 If married women, go astray,
And brought him twins, at nine months' end.

> [Thomas Hamilton, 6th earl of Haddington], 'The
> crib from Boccace'

c.458/2, p. 36

10648 If men are deem'd for loyalty
Were led in pomp by him.

> 'Song' [pr. 1715? (Foxon F221)]

fc.58, p. 56; c.570/1, p. 61

10649 If mighty god what poets say be true—
Like second thoughts we'll prove our second time.

> [Maurice Johnson], 'To M. T., Cupid. An invocation.
> By . . . in imitation of I. Second[u]s Eleg.'

c.229/2, fol. 9

10650 If mighty wealth that gives the rules
The circle made by Celia's arms.

> 'Song'

Poetry Box vi/48

10651 If mirth alone to thee be dear,
And made thy sorrows all its own.

> 'Lines written in a garden seat'

c.141, p. 6

10652 If modest merit ever claim'd thy tear,
And melt in visions of seraphic love.

> [Francis Fawkes], 'On Mr. Laycock, a hopeful young
> gentleman, who (as it is said) died for love. In the
> church of Doncaster'

fc.21, p. 27

10653 If monsters, painter, thou hast skill to draw,
With mighty reverence style the old does own.

'Advice to a painter' [on William Lloyd, bishop of St. Asaph]

b.111, p. 215

10654 If mortals aren't thankful for what they receive,
When advice they despise and imprudently rake.

Edward Sneyd, 'Epistle to Miss [Grace] Smith of Great Fenton. Janry. the 24th: 1781'

c.214, p. 131

10655 If mourn I may in time so glad
Why Watt where art O here below.

Poetry Box VI/7

10656 If mournful eyes could but prevent
A valiant patience with dry eyes.

Gorstello Snow, 'To M[aurice] Johnson by . . . of the Middle Temple esqr recorder of Stamf[or]d 4 Aug 1703'

c.229/1, fol. 79

10657 If music's charms can soften rocks
Here rocks dissolve like dew.

'On hearing that certain musical ladies had determined on making the rocky shores of Stonehouse their future residence'

Poetry Box XII/123

10658 If music's charms can soothe the savage breast,
Whilst candor crowns him with Apollo['s] lays.

H[annah] M[ore], 'Written extempore after hearing Mr. Sheridan's first lecture on oratory'

c.341, p. 68

10659 If my advice you will receive, dear friend,
You with delight life's short remains will spend.

'Hor: l. 2. Od. 10'

b.322, p. 5

10660 If my master keeps hounds I can double the pack
And the riches I boast, I bear at my back.

[Phanuel Bacon], 'A riddle'

c.237, fol. 15

10661 If my sight offensive be
I should joy to lose my breath.

T[homas?] H[eywood?], 'One to his love being angry'

b.62, p. 108

10662 If Narcissus foolish boy
Wound as many hearts as they . . . .

'Cant: 25'
[Crum I900]

b.4, fol. 22 (incomplete)

10663 If nature never acts her part in vain
And left such darkness in a coxcomb's head.

c.546

10664 If Ne[crossed out]n spirits here should rise
Lament their folly in so vile a thing.

[Thomas Gurney], 'To Mr. John Gill on his second part of The cause of God and truth' [acrostic]

c.213

10665 If none be offended with the s[c]ent
Hell is the rump and no more to be set out. |
Which [nobody can deny]

'The resurrection of the Rump or rebellion and tyranny revived'

Poetry Box VI/19

10666 If not alone her pretty airs,
To fly the killing dart.

T[homas] M[orell], 'On her wearing a feather in her cap'

c.395, p. 7

10667 If not convinc'd, learned Penny, by the schools,
And can there be an argument more fair?

[John] Harvey, capt., 'To the Rev. Doctor Penny, Dean of Lichfield, on his elegant discourse of a God and attributes proved'

c.152, p. 6

10668 If now with me you'll run, in the first place,
And thus I end with you, and you with me.

J. F., 'Verses on the names of the Holy Bible . . . written . . . 1707'

c.356

10669 If of good breeding he hath guess'd the laws
Which when it burns it rakes(?).

[Sir Thomas Urquhart], 'One excuseth a gentleman to his mistress in whose presence he had let a [?] thus'

fb.217, p. 393

10670 If old Nick in dry places forever will stray
He'll be nick'd by our fellows who drink night and day.

'In socios seniores Coll: Oxon: [2]'

c.81/1, no. 24

10671 If on my theme I rightly think
But if good liquor can't be got.

'Quinque causae bibendi'

c.81/1, no. 80

10672 If on this roof, high heav'n should send,
Whate'er becomes of mine.

    'An ode on affliction'

c.156, p. 65; c.83/1, no. 214

10673 If once thy honor have one minute's stain,
An hundred years scant can it cleanse again.

fb.69, p. 239

10674 If one foot down then th'other is above
Thus one man's fall, another's rise doth prove.

    'The state of man'

c.356

10675 If our desires whate'er they be
Nothing but this can make us blest.

    [Edmund Wodehouse], 'Octr. 23 [1714]'

b.131, p. 67

10676 If pagan papists tell us they brought in
If, when they took the pair, they'd ta'en the seven.

    'On stealing the candlesticks in Westminster Abbey'
    [1689/90; against the bishops]
    [Crum 1911]

fb.70, p. 247

10677 If pagan princes, for their Olympian sports
Run forth thy race, be patient, do not fear.

    'Cherish no sin'

c.187, p. 42

10678 If papist, Jew, or infidel, would buy a place at court,
She took his footman to her bed, to do what he
                  omitted.

    'A new ballad . . . fixed on the Ld. Dorset's door at the
    Cockpit' [1689]
    [Crum 1912; POAS v.102]

fb.70, p. 229

10679 If Phidyle with pious hands,
As if an hecatomb you kill.

    [William Popple, trans.], '[Horace] book 3rd. ode
    23rd. To Phidyle'

fc.104/2, p. 286

10680 If Plutus smiles, and riches 'round you flow,
And use each guinea, as tho' 'twas your last.

    John Lockman, 'Advice to his daughters 18 Decr. 1765'

c.267/1, p. 388

10681 If poet's credit does not weaken fame
Since neither truly is, and neither should be, blind.

    [ ] Gardiner, 'Westminster Hall'

c.170, p. 1

10682 If pray'rs, and tears, the shields, the church of
                  England only bears,
And now the crown is fall'n, is fall'n from our
                  Josiah's head.

    'Sighs! for our late sovereign' [Charles II]

fb.108, p. 175

10683 If private men (whose otious care
Some Cupid's honey be not mixt between.

b.205, fol. 13v

10684 If prone to scribbling pause, nor dare presume
If not to virtue yield at least to shame.

    [ ] Balfour, 'At Spital near Lincoln'

File 245/20

10685 If pure of hand and pure of heart,
Not crowns nor miters offer more!

    [John] Aikin, 'Horace Ode 23. book 3d. imitated. To
    the poor'

c.355, p. 195

10686 If purest virtue, sense refin'd in youth,
And Harriet, O my Harriet, had not died.

    'The Earl of Comber to the memory of his lady'

c.83/2, no. 586

10687 If reason, is the proper stamp of man
Its God, in beatific vision.

    'From a reflection upon the uncertainty of life'

fc.54, p. 49

10688 If rhyme e'er spoke the language of the heart,
When the last curtain shall have dropt on me.

    Richard Cumberland [1797]

File 4050

10689 If righteous souls in their blest mansions knew
In thee and in thy virtuous fair, I live.

    [ ] Talbot, 'The dream—occasioned by the death of
    the Lady Seymour addressed to her son the D[uke] of
    Somerset'

c.244, p. 145

10690 If rip'ning virtue of a spotless name
Tho' nature's may not shall my wishes flow.

    [George Howard, 6th earl of Carlisle], 'To George
    Canning esq.'

c.197, p. 1

10691 If Roman geese could cackle Gauls away,
Their harlequin's a Jesuit in disguise.

    John Lockman, 'On certain strollers . . . Nov. 1749'

c.267/1, p. 184

10692   If Rome can pardon sins, as Romans hold
      To gull 'em of their souls and money too.

      [John Wilmot, 2nd earl of Rochester], 'On Rome's
      pardon' [parody of 'If Rome can pardon . . . We'll
      search no scriptures . . .']
      [Crum 1935]

      c.158, p. ix; c.188, p. 68; fb.142, p. 25

10693   If Rome could pardon sins, as Romans hold
      We'll search no scriptures, but the mines for gold.

      [Francis Quarles], 'On Rome's pardons' [Divine
      Fancies III, 86; parodied by 'If Rome . . . To gull 'em
      of their souls . . .']
      [cf. Crum 1935]

      b.137, p. 176

10694   If Romulus, as ancient poets sing,
      Who were originally sons of whores.

      'On viewing that noble structure the Foundling
      Hospital. August 22d: 1753'

      c.266, p. 82

10695   If royal virtues ever crown'd a crown
      Lives still admir'd, ador'd Elizabeth.

      'On Q. Elizabeth in Great All-hallows before the fire'

      fb.143, p. 21

10696   If rules of life Christ['s] life doth comprehend
      Meditate on the immense omnipotence.

      [Mary Serjant]

      fb.98, fol. 148

10697   If saints in heaven, can either see or hear
      And give it to his hands that can relieve us.

      'To the blessed Elizabeth . . . the humble petition
      of . . . the poor commons of England' [prologue to 'If
      bleeding hearts . . .']
      [Crum 1937]

      b.197, p. 96

10698   If Samson, with the jawbone of an ass,
      What may you do | Then, that have two.

      Sir Thomas Urquhart, 'To an able man of body, but
      weak in judgment'

      fb.217, p. 212

10699   If scenes of civil rage awake our fear,
      Made Charles the sire, a saint; and Charles, the
                                     son, a king.

      [Robert Cholmeley], 'The Restoration'

      c.190, p. 160

10700   If Scylla's ghost made bloody Cat'line start
      Send Doctor Burnett to me or I die.

      [Sir George Etherege], 'Mrs. Nelly's complaint' [on
      Mall Knight]
      [Crum 1960]

      b.113, p. 35

10701   If services perform'd require returns,
      Will call forth Mister(?) Bly, and make his their
                                    choice.

      John Lockman, 'A thought. 16 March 1768 submitted
      to the various consideration of the worthy electors of
      the borough of Southwark'

      c.267/2, p. 396

10702   If shadows be a picture's excellence
      The black mark would I hit, and not the white.

      Walton Poole(?), 'On a gentlewoman [Beatrice
      Brydges, Mrs. Henry Poole?] with black eyes'
      [Crum 1945]

      b.200, p. 427; b.62, p. 35 (incomplete); b.205, fol. 24r
      (incomplete?)

10703   If Shakespeare err'd, to Richard's form unkind,
      Was half so mangled, agoniz'd and tortur'd.

      R[ichard] V[ernon] S[adleir], 'On seeing ———
      attempt the character of Richard the 3'

      c.106, p. 59

10704   If sharp and flat in music fit,
      Mon, change the theme; and choose a text.

      [Charles Earle?], 'Odd whimsical reflections on an
      odd monumental inscription'

      c.376

10705   If she do not some dalliance feel
      Will roar, till she be greased.

      Sir Thomas Urquhart, 'Of a well-complexioned, but
      so lecherously disposed woman, that she used always
      to scold her husband, when at any time she happened
      to be frustrate of her matrimonial disport'

      fb.217, p. 315

10706   If she doth chide, she would not have you gone,
      If with his tongue he cannot win a woman.

      'Get you gone'

      b.200, p. 408

10707   If she hath love engendered, it is sure:
      The mother of her son must be a whore.

      Sir Thomas Urquhart, 'Of a gentlewoman, whose free
      carriage bred love in the hearts of many'
      fb.217, p. 306

10708   If she prove constant obliging and kind,
      I'd have her to know I'm above her.

      c.549, p. 16

10709 If Shelley's charms can life restore
And you may profit by her charms!

R[ichard] V[ernon] S[adleir], 'Reply to ['Near no
churchyard . . .']'
c.106, p. 101

10710 If sighs and tears thy pity move
We should wish for 't again.

'Another by the same hand' [as 'Tho' in their
flame . . .']
fb.142, p. 53

10711 If sighs, my friend, could banish grief,
But never make your burden less.

c.94

10712 If silent sepulcher, my Calvius, know
Now mourn her early death, when wept by thee.

Catullus
fc.14/10

10713 If so in ev'ry man, the flesh would dwell
The universal world would be at peace.

Sir Thomas Urquhart, 'How to make all the world
peaceable'
fb.217, p. 123

10714 If so the midst ought to be most extoll'd:
Exalt the earth above the heav'ns we should.

Sir Thomas Urquhart, 'In medio virtus'
fb.217, p. 231

10715 If some of you chance to remain,
Then do as you see men do things.

b.234, p. 83

10716 If sorrow claims compassion's meed, a tear,
And snatch each Negro out of slavery.

[ ] Eyers, 'The poor Negro—a tale . . . Poetic essays'
c.83/3, no. 863

10717 If sorrows that are deep
Dart greater luster than the sun's bright rays.

'Incitements to rest'
fb.107, p. 53

10718 If spite be pleas'd whenas its object's dead
And strike the two first blind, the other dumb.

'On Sir Walter Raleigh'
[Crum 1958]
b.356, p. 29

10719 If still she'll keep the star
Dismal effects of war.

[Sir Philip Wodehouse]
b.131, p. 3

10720 If storms of persecution do appear
Prove what you seem and you shall peace possess.

b.216, p. 152

10721 If stubborn heat of eager youth
'To err is human, to forgive divine.'

[Robert Cholmeley], 'The recantation [to Thomas
Baker, senior dean of St. John's College Cambridge]'
c.190, p. 146

10722 If Sylvia aught a faithful muse can move
If aught on earth this Sylvia must be heaven.

'To Sylvia in the country an epistle'
Poetry Box I/54

10723 If Taylor's muse awake the tuneful lyre
And love shall the defect of verse supply.

[Robert Cholmeley], 'To Mr. Pinsent of St Johns Coll
upon desiring to see some verses of my composing
after having read Mr Taylor's inimitable
performances'
c.190, p. 31

10724 If that Apelles now did reign
Unto the gods I her betake.

'Braye Lute Book,' Music Ms. 13, fol. 57

10725 If that four terms there were in war
The one takes good angels the other cracks crowns.

'On soldiers and lawyers'
b.356, p. 307

10726 If that from glove, you take the letter G,
Then glove is love, and that I give to thee.

[William Strode], 'A lover, when he presented a pair
of gloves to his lady'
[Crum 1965]
c.189, p. 64

10727 If that, I wis, she not beneath thy eyne
So Venus's charms, if they with thine compare.

[Joseph Spence], 'Whilst reading Chaucer'
Spence Papers, folder 150

10728 If that my laziness you disapprove,
And you shall see how I will go.

Sir Thomas Urquhart, 'Of a poet to his Maecenas'
fb.217, p. 323

10729 If that one moment short suspense can be,
More true a people, or more lov'd a queen.

'On the death of her sacred Majesty Queen Caroline'
[20 Nov. 1737]
[Crum 1971]

fb.142, p. 66

10730 If that same little painter too,
As lively, strong, and durable as they.

[from 'The amours of Alatheus and Eustathea']

c.379/1, p. 29

10731 If that the world and love were young,
To live with thee and be thy love.

'The nymph's reply' [to 'Live with me and be my
love . . .']
[Crum 1978]

c.362, p. 7

10732 If that you care within the path
Why, how, and when you talk.

'Dourte [Dort?] hand'

b.234, p. 35; see also 'If you regard . . .'.

10733 If that you love me, come to me, my deary,
Here lies a point open, you never can hit it. |
Tom &c.

'Song'

c.189, p. 182

10734 If the all-ruling fates be as propitious—
That never better were set down in story.

Sir Thomas Urquhart, 'The first epigram to Prince
Rupert of Palatine'

fb.217, p. 295

10735 If the day of St. Paul be clear
Both neat and fowl this year shall die.

b.234, p. 176

10736 If the decreas'd desire you be thus vexed
Give over your unprofitable grief.

[Sir Thomas Urquhart], 'Not to be excessively sorry at
the death of a friend'

fb.217, p. 531

10737 If the doctrine be sound, that 'mongst lovers and
friends
That at more than a tester you appreciate her love.

[Frances (Kolbel) Payne, baroness Lavington], 'The
box's reply' [addressed to Ralph Payne, baron
Lavington]

Poetry Box II/6

If the false fox geese and the greedy wolf sheep   10738
Since thou seest education change nature.

[Sir Nicholas] Bacon, 'The strength of education'

fa.8, fol. 165v

If the great benefaction you'd rightly apply   10739
To cure the crack'd earth but to moisten the clay.

[Phanuel Bacon], 'A catch'

c.237, fol. 79

If the just may seven times each day   10740
Keep me O Lord for thy son's sake.

[Sir Nicholas] Bacon, 'A prayer of a penitent'

fa.8, fol. 160v & 166

If the rough masters of the sea   10741
Remember there's a laureat's place.

[Robert Cholmeley], 'The poet's address to his most
excellent Majesty George 2d'

c.190, p. 165

If the sister of Rose be a whore for anointed,   10742
The bullets must whistle and cannons must roar.

Poetry Box VII/36

If the treasur'd gold could give   10743
Friend sincere, and beauty kind.

'The vanity of riches. Anacreon Ode 13'

c.142, p. 395; c.555, p. 295

If th'emperor require his eagle: Rome   10744
Her keys: by law, what will your arms become.

Sir Thomas Urquhart, 'To Geneva concerning her
arms, which are the eagle, and the keys'

fb.217, p. 183

If there be any gem on earth excelling   10745
To the most quintessenced inspirations.

Sir Thomas Urquhart, 'To my Lord [crossed out]'

fb.217, p. 299

If there be lady that this name doth own   10746
And thus much said I hope w' are free from blame.

[Sir Aston Cokayne], 'Of Nann Colt, to the World'

b.275, p. 47

If there be nothing new, but that which is,   10747
To subjects worse, have given admiring praise.

[William] Shakespeare

c.94

If therefore all must quit the stage,   10748
To make our peace with heav'n, or to return again.

c.549, p. 13

10749 If there's a man, who doth in life delight,
While I in quiet, in the grave shall rest.

[Thomas Hamilton, 6th earl of Haddington], 'To
Florella epistle the sixteenth'

c.458/1, p. 63

10750 If there's a muse among the tuneful nine
All that thy Soph can sing, or muse can give.

[Robert Cholmeley], 'The rise of Soph, or the
ceremonies of Staincoat Hole. Canto the first'

c.190, p. 136

10751 If there's delight in love, 'tis when I see
That heart which others bleed for, bleed for me.

c.360/1, p. 181

10752 If things' true worth be best known by their want,
Of wit, and virtue, you're not ignorant.

Sir Thomas Urquhart, 'To a vicious fool'

fb.217, p. 184

10753 If this fair rose offend thy sight
And turn Lancastrians there.

[William Somervile], 'A gentleman of the House of
York sent a present of a white rose with the following
lines to a lady of the House of Lancaster'

c.378, p. 3; c.546; see also next.

10754 If this pale rose offends your sight
And with despair turn white.

[William Somervile], 'On offering Miss Molly Green
a white and red rose on the tenth day of June'
[Crum 11001]

c.229/1, fol. 36v; see also previous.

10755 If this strange drink, so like the Stygian lake,
What store of dregs must needs remain within.

'Barley wine: vulg: ale . . . Translation' [of Henry of
Avranches]

c.81/1, no. 117

10756 If th'oracle, of Socrates spoke true:
You're wise, who knows, that you know nothing,
                                                    Hugh.

Sir Thomas Urquhart, 'To a very ignorant man, whose
name was Hugh'

fb.217, p. 143

10757 If those sweet shades could, unadorn'd, invite,
Has rais'd rich bounties in that Eden land!

John Lockman, 'On the introducing a concert &c. in
Vauxhall Gardens'

c.267/1, p. 103

10758 If thou Barine, fair, as frail,
Ere clasp'd within their arms.

[William Popple, trans.], '[Horace] book 2nd. Ode
8th. To Barine'

fc.104/2, p. 138

10759 If thou cannot like a friend
Of a stiff Quaker.

'Phillida flouts me'

c.503, p. 55

10760 If thou Craterus art Hephaestion I?
As did Craterus and Hephaestion do.

[Sir Philip Wodehouse], 'My reply to the former'

b.131, p. 38

10761 If thou dost find
My labor is not lost.

'A clergyman who built a house on his parsonage, had
these verses written or engraven on it'
[Crum 11015]

c.189, p. 46

10762 If thou Florella, couldst but see my breast,
To be the first, in poetry, and wit.

[Thomas Hamilton, 6th earl of Haddington], 'To
Florella epistle the fourth'

c.458/1, p. 11

10763 If thou hast given me wealth, great God I crave
If not thine alm'ner, yet thy bedesman here.

[Francis Quarles], 'A resolution'

b.137, p. 193

10764 If thou learn to know Christ, it may suffice,
In other things, thy knowledge is but vain.

b.234, p. 67

10765 If thou, so young, when most can scarcely spell
And thou shine forth, the Phoenix of our age!

John Lockman, 'To Miss Bowes hearing her repeat,
and afterwards read a great number of lines out of
Paradise lost . . . March 1757'

c.267/1, p. 216

10766 If thou to liars wouldst not lend thine ear,
None with a lie before thee durst appear.

'On Procillus a nobleman'

c.356

10767 If thou wilt in the Lord confide,
With my salvation will Him crown.

'The same in other words, same meter. Psalm 91'

c.264/2, p. 97

10768   If thou would have the nuptial union last
       Let virtue be the bond that ties it fast.

       c.391

10769   If thou wouldst learn, not knowing to pray
       At all times ore tenus, not by saints.

       [Francis Quarles], 'A form of prayer'
       [Crum 11026]

       b.137, p. 189

10770   If 'tis true as you say that I've injur'd a letter
       And that I may be never mistaken for U.

       David Garrick, 'In answer to a gentleman [Dr. John
       Hill] who accused him of a wrong pronunciation at
       times of the letters I and U'

       c.504, p. 199; Diggle Box: Poetry Box XI/31; see also 'If
       it's true . . .'.

10771   If 'tis true what Apollo of Socrates said,
       Is that in truth thou nothing dost know.

       R[obert] Shirley, 1st earl of Ferrers, 'Ep: Audoeni'

       c.347, p. 35

10772   If to be born or not, our selves could choose
       From all this noisy and empty pageantry.

       'Timon in town to Strephon in the country'

       fb.68, p. 79

10773   If to bear children shows a fertile belly,
       How much less barren's she that bears men daily?

       Sir Thomas Urquhart, 'That some sort of women
       should not be called barren, though they have no issue'

       fb.217, p. 166

10774   If to construe correctly you really aspire
       So accept with my love the old Eton grammar.

       [on the Eton Latin grammar]

       File 5080

10775   If to defend my king and country be
       Say how I pious helped, in their need.

       J[ohn] Hobart], 'Philip Wodehouse How I pious help'

       b.131, p. 37; File 17713

10776   If to hear a droll song then it is your intention
       As nobody's injur'd when nobody's nam'd. | I
                    mention'd no nobody. No nobody

       'The song of nobody'
       [Crum 11036]

       File 19035

10777   If to love sweetness in alluring eyes,
       As hopeless to enjoy, as to remove.

       'W[ha]t it is to be in love'
       [Crum 11037]

       b.200, p. 77

10778   If to perfection these plantations rise
       Who for posterity perfom'd the same.

       [Charles Howard, 3rd earl of Carlisle, inscription at
       Castle Howard 1731]

       Poetry Box 11/48

10779   If to prelatic order you'd ascend
       Exper'ence shows 'tis the best way to rise.

       'The way to church preferment'

       c.360/2, no. 143

10780   If to relieve the wants of humankind,
       Springs up afresh and lives a longer day.

       'Prologue'

       fc.135

10781   If to see an old friend
       But if proud, pop to town like a prig.

       John Lockman, 'Writ in an unknown hand, to
       Mr. Hogarth, when in an inn at Salisbury . . . Oct.
       1737'

       c.267/1, p. 82, p.107; c.268 (first part), p. 2

10782   If traveller, good treatment be thy care,
       The girls, oh frowzy frights, here with the mistress
                                     vie.

       'Epigram wrote at an inn at Stockport—Cheshire . . .
       translation'

       c.81/1, no. 495

10783   If true good sense without a spark of pride
       And Perry chose by ev'ry patriot vote.

       'On Micajah Perry—alderman of London—wrote 1741
       before the election of the 9th Parliament of Great
       Britain'

       c.360/1, p. 179

10784   If truth can fix thy wav'ring heart
       May gather ev'ry flower.

       [David] Garrick, 'A song to Delia'

       fc.51, p. 315

10785   If universal use can plead
       Each liquor under heaven.

       'Tobacco'

       c.360/3, no. 161

10786   If useful knowledge, sense devoid of art,
       Their best inheritance, a spotless name.

       [William Boscawen], 'Epitaph'

       fc.106, p. 31

10787   If Valvine, (says the jolly Dean,)
       As Norris, or his leaner wife.

       c.193, p. 95

10788 If vanquished monarchs may their cause explore,
Which heav'n approved of by the people's voice.

  'Dialogue between K. W[illiam] and K. James'
  [Crum 11045]

  Poetry Box x/168; see also 'If injur'd monarch . . .'.

10789 If Venus' pupils have such fiery holes
Their only net of the powt[sic] fro[?] forth(?).

  [Sir Thomas Urquhart], 'Of the incendiary courtesans
  of the time, and the deplorable case of the gallants
  who are unveiled by them'

  fb.217, p. 388

10790 If virtue, honor, truth, and fame,
Renew the letters with his tears.

  [Thomas Randolph?], 'On Mr. [Thomas] Harrison'
  [vice-master of Trinity College]
  [Crum 11047]

  b.356, p. 252

10791 If void of art my languid verse appears,
Whose actions soon shall better speak thy worth.

  Stephen Duck, 'To Dr. Friend on quitting the
  mastership of Westminster School'

  Poetry Box v/86

10792 If warm'd by beauty's radiant beam
Beauty may win, but merit reaps(?) the heart.

  'Verses occasioned by a late conversation'

  c.53, fol. 43

10793 If we cease from devotion 'cause our actions are evil,
And we without prayers, can never be better.

  Sir T[homas] B[rand]

  Spence Papers, folder 74

10794 If we have reason and the scriptures too
Let reason spead, and reason will deny thee.

  [Thomas Gurney], 'To Mr. John Gill on his third part
  of The causes of God and truth' [acrostic]

  c.213

10795 If we lack virtue, and good deeds to hold
For he liv'd not that lives not after death.

  [Sir Thomas Urquhart], 'That no man liveth but he
  that is wise and virtuous'

  fb.217, p. 535

10796 If we may call them Christians, who contest
They stop the current of our protestations.

  Sir Thomas Urquhart, 'The puritans' countercheck'
  [to 'We may hold them Christians . . .']

  fb.217, p. 45

10797 If we to God once humbly fly,
Are happily gather'd to their head.

  [Edmund Wodehouse], 'Feb. 15 [1715]'

  b.131, p. 167

10798 If we would be both divine, and human:
And then repent being old.

  Sir Thomas Urquhart, 'A lascivious woman vents
  herself thus'

  fb.217, p. 264

10799 If wealth produc'd content, if heaps of gold,
Or beauty shines, or gratitude inspires.

  Henry Baker, 'The meditation'

  c.244, p. 398

10800 If what is rare's preclare [sic], and of account
A good man doth all rarities surmount.

  'A good man'

  c.356

10801 If when at noon the sun displays
Both light and darkness, night and day.

  [Thomas Carew], 'To his mistress'
  [Crum 11054, 'the sun at noon']

  b.356, p. 146

10802 If when Don Cupid's dart
And others doth offend when 'tis let loose.

  b.213, p. 5; see also 'Love then the fart . . .'.

10803 If when I die in hell's eternal shade
Thou shall be there condemn'd as well as I.

  [William Fowler?], 'To his cruel mistress'
  [Crum 11053]

  b.356, p. 97

10804 If when the Latin tongue gain'd greatest praise,
And gone beyond the eloquence of Tully.

  Sir Thomas Urquhart, 'To Doctor Arthur Johnston a
  laureate poet, and one of his Majesty's physicians in
  ordinary'

  fb.217, p. 272

10805 If when the tender sympathizing sigh,
Where darkness, grief and pain, and dangers cease.

  'To a friend in trouble'

  c.156, p. 139

10806 If when you only tread the stage,
By sweetly answering—thou art he.

  [John Lockman], 'To the new Imoinda (the charming
  Miss B.)

  c.268 (first part), p. 39

10807 If, while the streams of Cam no more inspire
And beam, my friend, from every thought of thine.

> F[rederick] Montagu, 'To George Montagu esqr.'
> fc.135

10808 If wine and music have the pow'r
And all the day be thine alone.

> [Matthew Prior], 'Song 248'
> c.555, p. 399

10809 If wine be a cordial, why does it torment?
And am wrapt in such pleasures as still want a name.

> 'Song 88. A burlesque on the foregoing' ['If love's a
> sweet passion . . .']
> c.555, p. 137

10810 If wisdom, wit, religion, chastity
Grim death had not her life so soon assail'd.

> 'On Elizabeth Langham who died 1639'
> c.547, p. 333

10811 If wishing, asking, praying, might prevail
If wishing, asking, praying, may prevail.

> 'To Mrs. Juliana Moore'
> b.35, p. 33

10812 If with just grief, and a concern but due
Or merchants, who dare death (if gainful) meet.

> W. R., 'To the happy memory of that incomparable
> person Mr [Thomas] Clifford, who died at Florence'
> [1671]
> File 17635

10813 If with the Almighty he prevailed so
I would not be afraid of martyrdom.

> [Robert Wild], 'On [Jeremy Whitaker's] preaching'
> c.166, p. 317

10814 If with thee beneath the shade,
When he tunes to thee his lays.

> [William Popple, trans.], '[Horace] book 1st. ode
> 32nd. To his lyre'
> fc.104/2, p. 88

10815 If within your capacity the sense
Will surely think, that you are misconceived.

> Sir Thomas Urquhart, 'To certain ladies, who had
> mistaken the meaning of many of my epigrams by the
> sinister, and wrong interpretation of some ignorant
> men'
> fb.217, p. 284

10816 If without virtue blood could dignify
Some fleas might boast of their gentility.

> [Sir Thomas Urquhart], 'That true nobility is not only
> by heritage'
> fb.217, p. 535

10817 If words alone can make a man of sense
Then to the title, you have just pretense.

> 'On Mr. J.'
> c.546, p. 19

10818 If worth departed still to you be dear,
True to his king, his country, and his God.

> 'On the death of Sr. Clement Trafford, knight, late of
> Stoke Ferry, Norfolk. Addressed to his friends . . .
> Norfolk chronicle February 25th 1786'
> fc.130, p. 45

10819 If worthy causes call for his address
He'll soon appear: in valiant readiness.

> [Sir Philip Wodehouse], 'Upon honest Valentine
> Saunders in valiant readiness'
> b.131, back (no. 188)

10820 If yet I have not all your love,
Be one, and [one] another's all.

> J[ohn] D[onne]
> [Crum 11074]
> b.148, p. 111

10821 If yet, perfidious girl, a blush is thine,
It scents the canker'd bud, its beauty gone.

> R. H., 'To a false mistress'
> c.373, p. 43

10822 If you approve, what task can be too hard,
And, when you judge the actor, spare the friend.

> [William Smith], 'Lines spoken by Mr. Smith who
> performed Charles in The school for scandal, for the
> benefit of Mr. King, 18th May 1798'
> Poetry Box IV/73; Smith Papers, folder 50 (2 copies)

10823 If you are a sailor, or a sailor's friend,
Pray conduct these letters to their journey's end.

> 'A quart-bottle mail'
> c.94

10824 If you are dry, you thirst, if so, thirst still
Until your soul is from your corpse put out.

> G[iles] H[ayward], 'Anagramma: MARY DAYE—I
> AM A DRY. G.H.'
> b.62, p. 102

10825 If you ask why th'eleventh of June I remember
Mine recorded on journals, his blazon'd on signs.

> c.340

10826 If you at Westow-Lodge do live, I there
I talked of those things, but would these enjoy.

[Sir Aston Cokayne], 'To Mrs Elizabeth Nevill'
b.275, p. 74

10827 If you b'a soldier searching fortune,
That she's a common whore.

Sir Thomas Urquhart, 'An encouragement to a soldier
concerning Lady Fortune'
fb.217, p. 146

10828 If you desire for to be wise,
Why, how you speak, and when.

b.234, p. 35

10829 If you expect to be of toil, and care
'Gainst fortune's most elaborate mischiefs.

[Sir Thomas Urquhart], 'That men have remedies
within themselves against the [?]est accidents that can
befall them'
fb.217, p. 530

10830 If you fair Sylvia, hope the gods will hear,
And none but you, can quench the amorous fire.

'Written in a lady's prayerbook'
c.186, p. 58

10831 If you from discontents hath a desire
Your riches from yourself, and not from fortune.

[Sir Thomas Urquhart], 'The truest wealth man hath
is from himself'
fb.217, p. 523

10832 If you have poverty you have no sumptious
Of thieves, which may [?] to those have wealth.

[Sir Thomas Urquhart], 'The advantages of those that
have poverty'
fb.217, p. 525

10833 If you have sense at least of feeling
Since whole ones are such wretched lumber.

'On half a crown'
fc.60, p. 108

10834 If you join to five six, with one eighth of sixteen,
You will know what in blockheads was never yet
seen.

Diggle Box: Poetry Box XI/71

10835 If you my actions truly scan,
Proves that I'm true to all.

'The inconstant by the same hand' [as 'Tho' in their
flame . . .']
fb.142, p. 51

10836 If you, my lord, a leisure hour can spare
Yet raising him's the glory of his reign.

W[illiam] D[ennis], 'On the right honble Robert
Jocelyn, &c. 1747'
File 4315

10837 If you my son, should e'er incline
And bid thee fly to her relief.

'To my child, if a son'
c.83/3, no. 983

10838 If you refuse me once and think again
Then let our souls go on where they did end.

[Edward Herbert, lord Herbert of Cherbury]
b.213, p. 106 (with extra lines?)

10839 If you regard within the path
Why, how, and when you talk.

b.234, p. 170; see also 'If that you care . . .'.

10840 If you should ask who's here, take this reply
For why should Vertue all defame us so.

[Thomas Gurney], 'Extempory poem on seeing
Mr. Gill's picture badly engraved by Vertue'
c.213

10841 If you should meet a matchless dame,
She'll seen be lull'd asleep.

C. H. C., 'Extempore on Julian's asserting that all the
ladies who knew him, fell in love with him—1775'
c.37, p. 67

10842 If you son hath afforded you no pleasure
Their dying should not make their fathers sad.

[Sir Thomas Urquhart], 'That no man should be
excessively grieved at the death of his son'
fb.217, p. 496

10843 If you the wretches' fate bemoan,
Their coldness all, and all their fires.

[J. B.], 'On hearing a lady say she pitied those people
who inhabited under the extremes of heat and cold'
Poetry Box IV/155

10844 If you, who often entertain
To papers, causes, fees and clients.

J. Wd., 'Putney. June 24, 1746'
Poetry Box I/125

10845 If you will my surname and Christian name know
The other in short is not good, till I die.

[Phanuel Bacon], 'To Mr. Wil[liam] Jackson, a rebus'
c.237, fol. 84v

10846   If you would know my name and trade,
      A fiddler and shoemaker.

      'Written over the door of a country cottage in the
      west'

      c.361

10847   If you would know whose dust lies here
      They liv'd a sober life amongst the Dutch.

      R[ichard West], 'Elegies on Sr. Horatio Vere'

      b.52/2, p. 126

10848   If you would learn in folly's school,
      Let Milton, Pope, and Young be read.

      'Written in a lady's Ovid's Art of love'

      c.487, p. 30; c.94

10849   If you would rightly multiply to learn
      Which added will the product signify.

      [Mary Serjant], 'Multiplication'

      fb.98, fol. 23

10850   If you'd be wise and learn to know
      Whate'er contrary winds disturb the main.

      'Poetical remarks. He that is desirous is, his wens
      should not offend his friend, must wink at pimples of
      his friend'

      c.361

10851   If you'd have a good pudding, pray mind what
                               you're taught,
      And then dish it up, with some verjuice, and butter.

      'Mother Eve's recipe for a pudding'

      c.378, p. 70

10852   If you're a clever guesser and discreet
      But a plain simple honest artless story.

      'Riddle'

      c.150, p. 2

10853   If you're deceiv'd, it is not by [my] cheat
      Disturb'd with swords, like Damocles his feast.

      [John Wilmot, 2nd earl of Rochester], 'A very heroical
      epistle in answer to Ephelia' [by the Earl of Mulgrave:
      'How far are they deceiv'd'; 1675]
      [Crum 11089; POAS I.346]

      b.54, p. 1181; b.105, p. 344

10854   If youth and innocence with beauty join'd
      His happy state, whom Howe shall deign to bless.

      'Another copy of verses on the same lady [Miss Mary
      Howe] written 1723'

      c.360/2, no. 96

10855   If zeal, can be of ignorance begot:
      You may be first 'mongst such, as are devote.

      Sir Thomas Urquhart, 'To an unlearned hypocrite'

      fb.217, p. 261

10856   I'll be reproach'd condemn'd and slighted
      And I thy pleasure shall with joy endure.

      [Mary Pluret], 'Another at a time of trial'

      c.354

10857   I'll bid the hyacinth to blow,
      And thou shalt be my ruling star.

      [ ] Campbell, 'Caroline'

      c.364

10858   Ill-busied man; why shouldst thou take such care
      Are but as tears shed for thy funeral.

      [Henry King], 'On man's life' [attr. Dr. John King]
      [Crum 11095]

      b.200, p. 122

10859   I'll cut it down I swear by this same hand
      For in so doing he did make it well.

      'Upon a pump stopt with stones'
      [Crum 11096]

      b.205, fol. 45r

10860   I'll do't, by heav'n I will—pray get you gone,
      But let the contest be who most shall please ye.

      'An epilogue spoken by Mrs. Clive'

      c.578, p. 154

10861   I'll dote on nothing here below,
      O God! Who adore aught else but Thee.

      [Edmund Wodehouse], 'Jan. 11 [1715]'

      b.131, p. 138

10862   Ill-fated France thro' every age
      And wide the conflict burn in memory of his woe.

      [William Hayley?], 'On the death of Capt. Wright
      cruelly murdered in a French prison'

      File 6922

10863   Ill-fated friend! whose presence cheer'd the day,
      Adieu dear friend! forevermore farewell.

      'A tear at Cherry's grave'

      c.91, p. 199

10864   Ill-fated wretch his [?] cost him dear
      Should such a Priap land upon thy shore.

      [Thomas Orby] Hunter, lord Croyland, 'On a
      Scotsman hang'd for cuckolding one Pringles an
      advocate'

      c.229/1, fol. 29v

10865   Ill-fated youth! says erring Fame,
        Immortalized in death!

     [William Boscawen], 'To a lady who lamented the fate
     of the unfortunate Major André'

     fc.106, p. 9

10866   I'll form a wreath of artless verse,
        For 'neath this turf she rests in peace.

     M[artha] Roberts, 'Epitaph on Duchess a favorite dog
     who died Oct. 13 1794'

     c.391, p. 113

10867   I'll gaze no more on her bewitching face
        I surfeit with excess of joy, and die.

     [Thomas Carew], 'On a mistress'
     [Crum 11099]

     b.62, p. 132; b.213, p. 66; b.356, p. 82

10868   I'll give you five shillings you ask'd me but four
        This pain I have gotten by straddling so wide.

     'A song'

     b.207, p. 27

10869   I'll give you, Sir, one kiss in sign of love:
        And to declare, that I will constant prove.

     Sir Thomas Urquhart, 'All the six cases of grammar,
     are in the first line of this distich. One speaks here to
     her sweetheart'

     fb.217, p. 168

10870   I'll go to my love, where he lies in the deep,
        To ring, to ring out his knell!

     'The watery tomb'

     fb.107, p. 11

10871   I'll have a new test, which neither shall own
        And France is encumbered by politic Paul. |
                          Which nobody can deny.

     'A new nothing' [1692]
     [Crum 11104]

     b.111, p. 361

10872   I'll love while I live, though for love I must die,
        Was love ever, ever, like mine.

     'The constant lover'

     fb.107, p. 48

10873   I'll no more to shady courts
        What to do I do not know.

     'Jockey a song' [docket title]

     File 19030

10874   Ill-omen'd bird! whose cries portentous float
        When from ideal ill, th'enfeebled spirit fails!

     [Charlotte (Turner) Smith], 'Sonnet supposed to have
     been written in America'

     c.141, p. 100

10875   I'll own that you write better than I do,
        Must none but civet cats, have leave to shit?

     c.239

10876   I'll prove by a paradox soon if you will
        When highly improper that I should be there.

     'On a lady using the word I for me'

     Diggle Box: Poetry Box XI/50

10877   I'll sing of mercy's boundless source,
        The holy city of the Lord.

     'Psalm 101. 19 day'

     c.264/2, p. 1

10878   I'll sing unto the Lord my God,
        But Jacob pass'd thro' on dry ground.

     'The song of Moses' [24 Nov. 1759]

     c.136, p. 5

10879   I'll sing you a sonnet that ne'er was in print
        When the vintner shall tell you there's nothing to
                                 pray.

     'A song'

     b.207, p. 23

10880   I'll sing you the praise if you'll lend but an ear
        They broke all their swords, and cried *Vive le roi.*

     Jo[seph] Haines, 'Jo. Haines's ballad upon the
     disbanding the Royal Regiment'
     [Crum 11121]

     b.111, p. 589

10881   Ill suits that froward scorn
        To inspire men, beyond all character.

     [George Daniel]

     b.121, fol. 81v

10882   Ill suits the tragic muse my instant years,
        But kill or cuckold every spouse we can.

     [Robert Cholmeley], 'An occasional epilogue to be
     spoken by a child in widow's weeds'

     c.190, p. 62

10883   I'll tell thee dear love what thou shalt do
        But to mark when, and where the dark eclipses be.

     J[ohn] D[onne], 'The book'
     [Crum 11122]

     b.148, p. 101; see also 'I'll tell thee now . . .'.

10884 I'll tell thee Dick where I have been
Then thou and I have done before | With Bridget,
and with Nell.

Sir John Suckling, 'On the Lord [*i.e.,* Richard?]
Lovelace his marriage'
[Crum 11123]

b.200, p. 373; see also next.

10885 I'll tell thee, Dick, where I have been
And I for them be s[h]ent.

[Andrew Marvell], 'The Exchequer Inn of the supper
made by Thomas Earl of Danby . . . 1675 Made in
imitation of Sr John Suckling's ballad'
[Crum 11124; *POAS* I.253]

b.54, p. 1113; b.52/2, p. 173; Poetry Box VI/124 (with
answer, 'Curse on such representatives . . .'); see also
previous.

10886 I'll tell thee now (dear love) what thou shalt do
Schools might learn sciences, spheres music, angels
verse.

[John Donne], 'A valediction: the book'

b.114, p. 255 (incomplete); see also 'I'll tell thee dear
love . . .'.

10887 I'll tell thee what's the cure of jealousy
Prithee, why then a cuckold not to be.

Lady Jane Cavendish, 'The cure'
[Crum 11127]

b.233, p. 8

10888 I'll tell you a story, a story most true
You might have been sweet, had you been in his
coat.

[Matthew] Prior(?), 'A tale wrote by . . . but not
printed with his works' [spurious?]

fc.51, p. 103; c.237, fol. 38; see also 'I'll tell you a story, a
story that's true . . .'.

10889 I'll tell you a story a story so merry
He could ne'er make amends but by this cavalcade. |
Derry down &c.

S[amuel] W[esley, the younger], 'A song made on the
funeral of J[ohn] Duke of Marlborough' [9 Aug. 1722]
[Crum 11128]

c.154, p. 57; fc.135 (var.)

10890 I'll tell you a story, a story that new is
You think him not yours, but the son of a whore. |
Derry &c.

'On the bishop of Rochester. To the tune of the
Archbishop of Canterbury'
[Crum 11130 (var.)]

c.570/2, p. 111

10891 I'll tell you a story, a story that's true,
That you might have been sweet, had you been in
his coat. | Derry down. . . .

[Matthew Prior?], 'The snipe by a gentleman of
Magdelen College, Oxford'

Accession 97.7.40; c.555, p. 80; Poetry Box IV/111

10892 I'll tell you a tale of two boobies of note;
As they fell out like fools; so like fools they'll fall
in. | Sing hey ding, ho, ding. . . .

'A song. To the tune of 'twas early one morning &c.'
[on 'Cornutus' [Whig] and 'Noddy' (Tory)]

c.570/2, p. 10

10893 I'll tell you a wonderful riddle
Yet without it no mortal can live.

'A riddle'

c.150, p. 36

10894 I'll tell you how the rose [at first] grew red
And flourish only in your livery.

[William Strode? or William Baker?], 'One to his
mistress'
[Crum 11141]

b.62, p. 92

10895 I'll tell you news will make you curse
The king comes back again.

[dialogue between a courtier and a patriot, on
George I]

Spence Papers, folder 113

10896 I'll tell you why I love my love:
And makes her mine secure.

'A song'

c.83/1, no. 124

10897 Ill thrives that hapless family that shows,
Obeying husbands, or commanding wives.

[Francis Quarles], 'On men and women'
[Crum 11142]

c.356; see also 'A woman's rule . . .'.

10898 Illustrious lords, and ladies, I have chosen
Which hath by nature sprung from blood
connection.

Sir Thomas Urquhart, 'To some of those nobles and
dames, mentioned in this treatise, whom having the
honor to be in consanguinity with, I have adjoined to
ther names, in the superscription of their praises, this
sign following'

fb.217, p. 47

10899 Illustrious muse! on thee we call
When we have don't . . . .

'Groans from Newgate; or an elegy on the suspension
of . . . Tho: Sad[l]er . . . March 16. 1677'

b.54, p. 901 (incomplete)

10900 Illustrious prince! A tribute here behold,
Thou king of freemen, Louis king of slaves!

John Lockman, 'To the King's most excellent Majesty:
with a present of Shetland herrings from the Council
of the Free British [Herring] Fishery . . . Sept. 1761'

c.267/1, p. 307

10901 Illustrious prince! whom far above
The Iliad's hero not so great as thine!

[Stephen Barrett?], 'Extract of a Pindaric ode, upon
the late action in Flanders; inscribed to his r[oyal]
H[ighness] William Duke of Cumberland'
[Gentleman's magazine, May 1745]

c.193, p. 117

10902 Illustrious princess, had thy chance not been
Had we not first been slaves w'had ne'er been kings.

[Francis Quarles], 'On Queen Hester' [Divine
Fancies II, 54]

b.137, p. 170

10903 Illustrious Sorrell shall the Zodiac grace
O'er all the planetary signs to reign.

[William Meston], 'On the horse that threw K[ing]
W[illiam]'
[Crum 11155, 'Illustrious steed'; POAS VI.366]

c.171, p. 9

10904 I'm a cold insipid creature,
Useful both in will and deed.

'Another [rebus]'
Diggle Box: Poetry Box XI/71; see also next.

10905 I'm a cold unfeeling creature,
I my slender substance waste.

'A riddle'
fc.40; see also previous.

10906 I'm a devil, so please you—and must hoof
Whene'er the devil pleads against damnation.

'Prologue to The fashionable lover spoken by
Mr. Weston in the character of a printer's devil'

c.68, p. 86

10907 I'm angry,—Sirrah,—not a little,
Nor Whitefield lend—the last relief.

[John] Winter, 'Anathema on my tailor a follower of
Whitefield, for putting me to the expenses of . . .
pockets . . .'

c.74

10908 I'm blam'd by many,
(On my soul) be cover'd.

Sir Thomas Urquhart, 'The words of a frolic damsel,
who always went to the streets unmasked, and
unveiled'

fb.217, p. 274

10909 I'm born a poor unhappy prince
A mortal worthy praise.

'The fatal journey. A ballad'
Poetry Box II/24

10910 I'm by two masters to such slav'ry brought,
That th'one hath nothing: th'other gives me naught.

Sir Thomas Urquhart, 'The regret of a servant who
had two masters'

fb.217, p. 141

10911 I'm called you must know an odd fellow,
While both sexes love a good shag.

[John Walker?], 'The shag weaver'
fc.108, fol. 47

10912 I'm confined in a case of wonderful make
But that no man can see me till my owner is dead.

'Riddle'
c.150, p. 8

10913 I'm double, I'm single I'm good, and I'm bad,
I ne'er without honor am known.

'[Enigma/Charade/Conundrum] 12' [game at whist]
c.389

10914 I'm foe to none: twice friend t'one I was never;
For whose I'm once, his friend I'll be forever.

Sir Thomas Urquhart, 'Of amity, and foed [sic]'
fb.217, p. 200

10915 I'm friend to the harmonious choir,
The winds shall bear them to the Cretic sea.

c.346

10916 I'm glad with all my heart, I've 'scap'd my
                                    wedding—
And leaves behind—ten thousand madmen like
                                            him.

'Epilogue'
c.578, p. 75

10917 I'm glad you hear such news of me
But now that's past, a happy year.

[Elizabeth (Shirley) Compton, countess of
Northampton], 'To Mr. Davis . . . [1728/9]' [in the
name of her daughter Lady Anne Compton]

Accession 97.7.40

10918 I'm handled by the rich and great
You always find in me a knave.

 '[Enigma/Charade/Conundrum] 3' [pack of cards]
c.389

10919 I'm just now four and twenty
Why go to Bath for Neddy.

 [John Walker?], 'Squire Neddy (tune The oak stick)'
fc.108, fol. 74v

10920 I'm neither High Church, nor Low Church, nor
           Tory, nor Whig,
I submit to the will of a merciful God.

 'To all whom it may concern to know me'
File 17396; see also 'I am neither . . .' 'I'm not . . .'.

10921 I'm not a statue I—that is a stone
Lest Cynthia pull thee by the ear.

 [Sir Philip Wodehouse], 'Mathew Stanton (my
 musician) I'm not a statue'
b.131, back (no. 209)

10922 I'm not High Church, nor Low Church, nor Tory
            nor Whig,
I submit to the will of a merciful God.

 A. H——, 'Honble Mr. A. H——'s answer to the
 question put to him What art thou'
c.116, p. 29; fc.24, p. 76 (var.; attr. H. S.); c.578, p. 15;
fc.51, p. 31; see also 'I am/I'm neither . . .'.

10923 I'm often drawn to make a stop,
And peace and joy at once an entrance find.

 [Charles Rich], 'Religion—a simile'
 [Crum I1170]
c.351, p. 146 (attr. R. Dodsley)

10924 I'm old mad Tom behold me,
Then let the nation judge it.

 'Song 59'
c.555, p. 87

10925 I'm plagu'd with my friends and my neighbors to
               boot,
But jovial and merry will a-take a good drink.

 'Song 178'
c.555, p. 274

10926 I'm rent in twain, that horses turning thus
Let thine your counterpane go south with me.

 [John Cleveland], 'Parting with a friend upon the
 road'
b.93, p. 53

10927 I'm rough I'm smooth, I'm wet, I'm dry,
I'm used by all, tho' only his.

 'Another [rebus]'
Diggle Box: Poetry Box XI/71

10928 I'm seen in the fire, but not in the flame
I'm seen in the cream, but not in the milk.

 'Riddle . . . the letter R'
c.391

10929 I'm sore from my heart good father freer
Should lie; for ev'rybody calls me father.

 Sir Thomas Urquhart, 'To a Cordelier for having
 devirgined a young lass, whose name was Anne'
fb.217, p. 68

10930 I'm sure of glory in this bold essay,
How gain you glory then?—I've err'd with Spence.

 [N.] Herbert
Spence Papers, folder 91

10931 I'm told good people that your tragic folks
We may be cheerful and yet decent too.

 J[ohn] Hoadly, 'Epilogue to Measure for measure
 spoken by Isabella'
Poetry Box I/79 (2 copies)

10932 I'm very sorry, poor Canterbury | At thy ill state,
God give you grace in this small space | Your soul
              to save.

b.229, fol. 122

10933 I'm wealthy and poor,
And toast Mrs. ———.

 [Jonathan Swift], 'A riddle' [a beau]
c.578, p. 106

10934 I'm wearin' awa' John
In the land o' the leal.

 'The auld wife's lament'
c.364

10935 Image of death, my wishes give
Thus without death to die.

 'Translation' [of an epigram 'Ad somnum', Leicester,
 30 Nov. 1774]
c.136, p. 127

10936 Image of her whom I love more than she
Mad with much love, rather than fool with none.

 J[ohn] D[onne]
 [Crum I1177]
b.148, p. 113

10937 Image (O reader!) in thy pensive mind,
Then drop the tender tear, for such was she.

John Lockman, 'For the tombstone of Mrs. Gordon,
wife of Thomas Gordon esq . . . June 1744'

c.267/1, p. 29

10938 Imagination in the flight
For praise, may never sink to scorn.

C[hristopher] Smart, 'Reason and imagination'

c.83/2, no. 648

10939 Immensity cloistered in thy dear womb
With his kind mother, who partakes thy woe.

[John Donne], '[Holy sonnets. La Corona] 3'
[Crum I1180]

b.114, p. 154

10940 Immortal bard whose truly noble lays
A glorious sample—of a glorious pate.

[Frederick Corfield], 'Epigram upon epitaph'

c.381/1

10941 Immortal Gabriel, hail, immortal son
Long live John Gabriel on the banks of Thame.

'Acrostic to Mr. John Gabriel on his treatise entitled,
The state of the nation'

c.360/2, no. 194

10942 Immortal Newton, never spoke
But folly['s] at full length.

[Philip Dormer Stanhope, 4th earl of Chesterfield?],
'On Mr. Nash's present of his own portrait, at full
length, placed between the bustoes of—Mr. Pope, and
Sir Isaac Newton, in the Long Room, Bath—(from
the Gent[le]m[an']s mag[azine]'
[part of Crum T1101?]

c.90; Spence Papers, folder 113 (attr. Mrs. Aldworth); see
also 'The old Egyptians . . .'.

10943 Immortal Quixote fraught with martial fire,
And knows no wraths but those with safety won.

'Occasioned by reading Hudibras . . . Translated'

c.591

10944 Immortal were we in this world below
Which conscious virtue tells him is his own.

'On the fear of death'

fc.53, p. 5

10945 Impeachments, prosecutions,
Now poverty and tears.

'King George his annals. 1714 . . . 1721'

c.570/2, p. 93

10946 Imperial Jove commands his heav'n alone
Earth she has freed by arms and vanquish'd heav'n
by pray'rs.

[ ] Bradford, 'On the present reign [of Queen Anne]'

c.170, p. 19

10947 Imperial prince! King of the seas and isles
Kings are but cards in war, they're gods in peace.

[Andrew Marvell?], 'To the King' [envoy to 'Nay
painter if thou dar'st . . .']
[Crum I1198]

b.136, p. 15; c.160, fol. 7v; fb.140, p. 63 (last line: l. 336
from 'Nay painter . . .')

10948 Impetuous sigh
And deluges of tears resistless flow?

[Robert Cholmeley], 'Love's philosophy to
Zephilinda. A Pindaric ode'

c.190, p. 169

10949 Impressive truth by splendid fiction drest
When round the bark the swelling surges sweep.

'On Rasselas'

Diggle Box: Poetry Box XI/2, 3 (2 copies)

10950 Imprimis—my departed shade I trust
In body healthy, and compos'd in mind.

[Mary Leapor], 'Mira's will'

c.83/3, no. 1041

10951 Imprison'd Philomela melts in tears
Tho' mute her tongue; expressive was her hand.

c.53, fol. 17

10952 In a barn or a cottage I often appear,
We are tortur'd, abus'd nay and trampled on too.

'[Enigma/Charade/Conundrum] 17' [cobweb]

c.389

10953 In a brisk evening when the sun was set,
But hills and valleys it resound again.

J[ohn] Rutherford(?), 'To my countrymen, and all my
readers'

c.93

10954 In a cottage, embosom'd within a deep shade,
And lo! her blue eyes are now seal'd up in death!

E[dward] Rushton, 'Blue-eyed Mary'

c.141, p. 471

10955 In a council of state
Nor for all you can do to secure you.

'A song' [temp. coronation of George I, 1714]

fc.58, p. 125; c.570/2, p. 126

10956 In a craz'd age at which our sons will smile,
And beam, while Hottentots exert their grin.

> John Lockman, 'The Italian burletta singers, (under Dr. Croza,) and the French strollers . . . Nov. 1749'

c.267/1, p. 372

10957 In a craz'd age, which south sea projects sham'd,
Me sat to Pumpkin, and so crown'd the jest.

> John Lockman, 'Three and one . . . 1738'

c.267/1, p. 372; c.268 (first part), p. 15

10958 In a dish came fish
Because there was no beer.

> [Thomas Shadwell], 'Ben Jonson, when the Archbishop [of Canterbury] sent him a dish of fish, but no drink, said . . .'
> [Crum I1208]

c.189, p. 63

10959 In a dull stream, which moving slow,
Fools, fops, and rakes, for chaff and straws.

> 'The inconstant a simile'

c.186, p. 98

10960 In a fair cottage, on a daisied mead,
And rest assur'd thou hast a friend on high.

> Dr. [ ] Wilkinson, 'Elegy on a grandmother'

c.142, p. 494

10961 In a fair island in the southern main,
Would prove, no doubt, as perjur'd as before.

> [Laetitia] Pilkington, 'The statues, or the trial of constancy. A tale for the ladies'

c.360/3, no. 104

10962 In a famous street near Whetstone's park
Or 'tis forty to one but they'll catch a fall. | With a
fa la la la la la

> 'A ballad to the tune of An old man with a bed full of bones'
> [Crum I1209]

b.113, p. 115; b.113, p. 115; b.327, f. 25v (var.)

10963 In a glen, far sequester'd, where innocence reigns,
And Jessy, the pride of the green.

> 'Elwyn and Jessy'

Poetry Box IV/178

10964 In a little dark room at the back of his shop
'Tis virtue alone can design as a Swift.

> [Sir Walter Scott], 'On Faulkner's edition of Swift'

fc.76.ii/164

10965 In a lone corner, almost hid in shade,
Forgot his mournful wreath, and dropp'd a pitying
tear.

> M[ary (Derby)] Robinson, 'Unhappy love'

c.83/2, no. 501

10966 In a melancholy fancy out of myself
Or else what is the light[n]ing at which we gaze
and wonder. Hello my fancy

> 'All the world surveying'

c.189, p. 105

10967 In a moldering cave, where the wretched retreat
Should induce him again to return.

> 'On the death of General Wolfe, said to [be] written by General Washington'

c.391, p. 91

10968 In a morn when I rise, I open my eyes
I fear you would easily guess me.

> 'A riddle'

c.150, p. 23

10969 In a neat little village, remote from all strife,
Where like a true blood I am scribbling my tale.

> G. W. L., jr., 'The life of a blood by . . . tune the high-mettled racer, Feb. 20th 1790'

fc.130, p. 53

10970 In a neighborly way with an honest man's fame,
And practice the precepts I give.

> [George] Alex[ande]r Stevens, 'Mediocrity. A song'

c.94

10971 In a room big enough for work, or for play,
For they ev'ry one danc'd with their necks in a
string.

> 'Enigma'

c.241, p. 129

10972 In a strait path one day I walked a mile,
So how I walked that mile pray ladies say.

> 'Conundrum [77c]'

c.389

10973 In actions, manners, thoughts and lives
'Tis dev'lish odd ye can't agree.

> [Isaac Freeman], 'Cum sitis similes . . . Martial: Lib: 8. Epigr. 95'

fc.105, before p. 27

10974 In acts of goodness I do light;
Whatever be my lot.

> John Lockman, 'A reflection . . . July 1761'

c.267/1, p. 299

10975 In Æsop's days, when beasts, and birds,
And with our murmurs, fill the plain.

[Thomas Hamilton, 6th earl of Haddington], 'A fable'
[pr. 1716 (Foxon P756)]

c.458/2, p. 115

10976 In Æsop's tales an honest wretch we find
He without hairs and thou without a crown.

[Sir Charles Sedley? or Matthew Prior?], 'Mr. Tho:
Brown's [sic] fable' [from Æsop]
[Crum 11229]

fb.207/4, p. 38; c.111, p. 12 (first part); Poetry Box
XIV/179; Trumbull Box: Poetry Box XIII/73; Spence
Papers, folder 153 (attr. Swift); see also 'The parties,
henpeck'd William . . .'.

10977 In age most oft women know not now
To deck themselves or court a looking glass.

'Pride'

b.62, p. 119

10978 In Aire the nimble deer shall leaner(?) graze
Or gratitude desert my faithful heart.

c.540

10979 In Albion's isle shall rise a Monck
When lions three shall mount the throne.

'A prophecy 1654'

b.54, p. 1160

10980 In all her bloom the graceful fair,
Unmindful of our fruitless sighs and tears.

[Allan] Ramsay, 'To the memory of Lady Margaret
Anstruther'

c.83/1, no. 246

10981 In all his troubles, Lord, defend,
In Thee, our strength and stay.

'Psalm 20'

c.264/1, p. 75

10982 In all humility we crave
Thanks them as much as if they did.

'A libel written in the name of a petition from the
Lords and Commons in Parliament to His Majesty'
[verse 5 of 'Justice is here made up of might . . .' (not
in Osborn collection); 1642]
[Crum 11230]

b.101, p. 126; b.113, p. 177; c.189, p. 5 (var.; applied to
Charles II)

10983 In all I did I most miscarried
For they that are in it fain would b'out on't.

Thomas D'Urfey, 'Tom Durfey's character of
matrimony'

b.155, p. 66

10984 In all men's fancies to consider truly
Owes homage to endowments so sublime.

Sir Thomas Urquhart, 'To the Viscount of Aboyne'

fb.217, p. 227

10985 In all my soul, there's not one place,
Ere I shall cease to love her.

'A beautiful passage from a Scotch song'

c.378, p. 4

10986 In all our prayers th' Almighty does regard
To buy his wares by weight, and not by measure.

[Francis Quarles], 'On prayer'
[Crum 11233]

b.137, p. 191

10987 In all that was, or is, we see
Before and at and in the grave.

'Upon Sr. Wal. Raleigh against Sr. Lewis Stuk[ele]y's
book'

Poetry Box VI/107

10988 In all thy humors whether grave or mellow,
There is no living with thee, nor without thee.

'Ditto parody on ['Epigramma . . . translation']'

c.81/1, no. 231; c.536

10989 In an old author once I found
They starve midst fancied pow'r and gold.

'The longitude discovered. A tale by the author of
The deluge and The bottomless tub' [pr. 1726 (Foxon
L251)]

c.503, p. 10

10990 In ancient days I've heard with horns
They're cuckolds all a-row.

'Song 213'

c.555, p. 341

10991 In ancient days of superstition
None 'scape the flames—but by good works.

[Charles Burney, the elder], 'On Sir John Hawkins
giving his collection of old musical books to the
British Museum'

c.33, p. 131

10992 In ancient days, we read that patient youth,
The weak presumption with unfeign'd remorse.

'Lines written on the reading the poetic composition
of a young Westminster scholar—which discovered
strong indications of genius but a deficiency of
judgment'

fc.124, p. 104

10993 In ancient days, when Romans sigh'd for fame,
For suffering France—O heave one mournful sigh.

> Frederick Corfield, 'Prologue' [to 'The patriots a
> tragic farce in two acts']
>
> c.381/2

10994 In ancient Rome, 'tis said, and ancient Greece,
If they are pleas'd—these still are lucky days.

> H[annah] More, 'A prologue wrote by . . . and spoke
> at Mr. Lee's school by one of the young gentlemen'
>
> c.341, p. 107

10995 In ancient times a god of wood
For still his wooden head's the same.

> 'Origin of an alderman'
>
> c.115

10996 In ancient times (as poets sing)
And wedlock's grown a Smithfield bargain.

> 'An idea of wedlock ancient and modern'
> [Crum I1241a]
>
> c.186, p. 102

10997 In ancient times as story tells
So the next parson took and burnt it.

> [Jonathan] Swift, 'Baucis and Philemon. Imitated
> from the 8th book of Ovid' [pr. 1709 (Foxon S800)]
>
> fc.60, p. 33

10998 In ancient times, before a pulpit-throne
Belov'd of all, but those, whom all despise.

> J. M., 'To Sir Richard Steele on the successful
> representation of his excellent comedy The conscious
> lovers' [16 Nov. 1722]
>
> Poetry Box x/10(3)

10999 In ancient times, from history we find
To guard their queen, their property and hive.

> 'The two hives of bees, a fable' [Dec. 1798]
>
> Poetry Box IV/174

11000 In ancient times in Britain's isle
'My love'—and so she died.

> 'Henry and Catherine'
>
> c.83/2, no. 313; Poetry Box VII/82

11001 In ancient times, some hundred winters past,
And boldly prints and publishes her shame.

> 'The heroines written on reading the memoirs of the
> three famous modern courtesans 1750 viz. Mrs.
> Constantia Phillips, Mrs. Laetitia Pilkington, and
> Lady Vane'
> [Crum I1242]
>
> c.360/3, no. 90; c.83/3, no. 1028

11002 In ancient times, when sages able
He only writ what I inspir'd.

> 'Squerries Park in Kent, flower into Surrey'
>
> fc.51, p. 112

11003 In April when primroses paint the sweet plain
The witty, sweet Susie his mistress might be.

> [Allan Ramsay], 'A song'
>
> c.358, p. 114

11004 In Aristotle's spite and of his musty club
And who lives without snuff does not merit to live.

> R[obert] Shirley, 1st earl of Ferrers, 'Upon snuff. From
> the French'
>
> c.347, p. 92

11005 In *bakesh shalom verod fehu*, which
The year wherein the covenant did reign.

> Sir Thomas Urquhart, 'A chronogram, taken from an
> Hebrew passage, in the 34 Psalm, and 14 verse: and
> applied to the treaty of peace condescended upon at
> Barwick in the year 1639'
>
> fb.217, p. 218

11006 In beauty dwells no bitterness—no gall
The bridle more than spur, prevents a fall.

> [Sir Philip Wodehouse], 'Upon [my cousin Newton's]
> lady, Abigail Newton'
>
> b.131, back (no. 216)

11007 In bed we laugh, in bed we cry,
Of human bliss to human woe.

> [Samuel] Johnson, 'On a bed, improviso translation
> from the French, by . . .'
>
> fc.132/1, p. 205

11008 In Bedlington liveth a damsel gay,
And 'tis a great pity he should have either.

> 'The indifferent lovers, a song'
>
> c.530, p. 263

11009 In Bess's reign, e'en dames of rank could make
She joins Eliza's reign with George's polish'd days.

> 'The little cake'
>
> c.83/2, no. 545

11010 In Bishopsgate Street on last Saturday
A woman expir'd run o'er by a dray.

> 'A whip on a poor woman killed by a dray Nov. 18 1732'
>
> c.360/2, no. 225

11011 In [?] book I am if you will know
Look underneath and there it is.

> a.6, p. 96

11012 In Britain's isle no matter where,
And still the nymph be deem'd divine.

   [ ] Spatter(?), 'Addressed to a young lady by . . . on
   Cousin Porter'

c.83/1, no. 61; see also next.

11013 In Britain's isle no matter where
He ne'er was for a conjurer taken.

   [Thomas] Gray, 'Lady Schaub and Miss Harriet Speed
   went one morning . . . to find Gray the poet and
   missing of him left a card . . . to whom he sent these
   verses'

Poetry Box v/38; see also previous.

11014 In Broome so neat, in Broome so clean,
Can with her eyes compare.

   [William] Shenstone, 'Ballad written at Broome, by
   the late . . . on his cousin Miss Dalmon, taking some
   verses left upon his table. (Not published in his
   works.)'

c.83/2, no. 274

11015 In Callrly [sic] dwells an honest man,
In three, or four, and twenty weeks.

   'Willy Lang's mare. Tune, Eckey's mare'

c.530, p. 216

11016 In Celia's face a question once did rise,
Weeping, or smiling pearls to Celia's face.

   [Thomas Carew], 'A contention between lips, and
   eyes'
   [Crum 11258]

b.200, p. 113; c.391, p. 110

11017 In Charles the Second's golden days
I will be vicar of Bray Sir.

   'The vicar of Bray' [Jacobite song; pr. c. 1714
   (Foxon V84)]

fc.61, p. 69; c.570/4, p. 51; see also next, and 'In good
King Charles's . . .'.

11018 In Charles the Second's merry days
I'll drink my gallon a day Sir.

   'A new song in imitation of The vicar of Bray'
   [Crum 11259]

c.157, p. 122; c.555, p. 19 (incomplete); see also previous,
and 'In good King Charles's . . .'.

11019 In Cheshire dwelleth a good squire
With verse like this to tire your patience.

   [George Ellis], 'From the album at Crewe Hall—1787'
   [verses addressed to Lady Frances Crewe]

File 3945; Poetry Box II/26

11020 In childhood, and in earliest youth,
Is birthday of new love.

   'A song in praise of matrimony in answer to the one
   abusing it to the same tune'

Accession 97.7.40

11021 In coffeehouse begot, the short-liv'd brat,
And on paternal mountain dies at last.

   [Thomas Brown], 'Upon a pipe, lighted with a leaf of
   K. Arthur'

fc.24, p. 24

11022 In Constantius' happy time
And 'scape eternal pain. | Amen

   'Another for S. Stephen' [August 3]

a.30[21]

11023 In cottages and lonely cells,
And call the mountains to their aid.

   [William] Somervile, 'An husbandman's epitaph' [on
   Hugh Lumber]

c.244, p. 465

11024 In cruelty you greater are
And let me have my three days' reign.

   'The sacrifice'

fb.107, p. 64

11025 In days of old there was a town,
And fight and love again.

Poetry Box IV/83

11026 In days of yore as poets tell
A mouse may be a good gallant!

   R[obert] Shirley, 1st earl of Ferrers, 'The dormouse'

c.347, p. 75

11027 In days of yore as sages sing
To Jove addres'd her guilty pray'r.

   'The progress of envy. A fragment'

Poetry Box IV/141

11028 In days of yore, as we are told
To see you on your feet.

   [ ] North, 'A trick upon travellers'

fc.85, fol. 23

11029 In days of yore, Dame Prudence shed
A lurking folly smiles.

   'Folly triumphant addressed to the ladies' [London
   magazine, March 1776]

c.487, p. 92

11030 In days of yore St. Dunstan thought
For if you won't, the devil will.

    [Robert Cholmeley], 'St Dunstan taking the Devil by
    the nose. A tale in imitation of Mr. Prior'

    c.190, p. 223

11031 In days of yore, when Edward fill'd the throne,
Thrown from his horse, with numbers at his side.

    'William the Conquer[or] . . . written in March 1796
    for the use of the verse writers'

    c.91, p. 246

11032 In days of yore, when errant knights
Each one returned to his home.

    [ ] R., 'Riddle [venison (or rather hare) pie]'

    Poetry Box VII/48

11033 In days of yore, when mother time,
Fresh girls, backgammon, and the vicar.

    [Soame Jenyns], 'An epistle to the right honble the
    Lord Lovelace'

    c.147, p. 38

11034 In days of yore, when statesmen bore
Thou'rt damn'd when thou art dead.

    'A few lines lately dropped out of the British Pasquin's
    mouth near a wall between the poles Arctic and
    Antarctic' [against Walpole; pr. 1741? (Foxon G124)]

    fb.142, p. 68; Poetry Box IV/70

11035 In days of yore, when truth was fled,
But that he enter'd heaven's gate.

    J. R., 'The right of tithes asserted or, the knight of
    Oxfordshire a tale from a Popish legend'

    c.326, p. 158

11036 In days when good King Stephen reign'd,
And they pull'd her out by the tail.

    'Song 75'

    c.555, p. 114

11037 In de dark wood no Indian nigh,
Me pray hear two times more.

    'An Indian hymn'

    c.91, p. 340

11038 In different passions, for relief
More pleasure in your tail.

    'On Mrs. Collier's mid[dle] finger, one of the maids of
    honor to Queen Anne'

    c.189, p. 174

11039 In dismal scenes of solitude and woe,
Still panting for perfection, heav'n, and thee.

    Tho[mas] Scott, jr., 'Breathings towards God'

    c.244, p. 409

11040 In distant Ceylon's spicy isle
Awake—a bird of paradise.

    [Helen Craik], 'To Lady W. M. Constable, with a bird
    of paradise'

    c.375, p. 11

11041 In distinct hours she did divide the day
As worthy as Ulysses was of praise.

    'Devotion and chastity'

    b.62, p. 118

11042 In doubt I live, in doubt I die
And undismayed expect eternity.

    [Laurence Shirley], 4th earl of Ferrers, 'Written by
    late . . . previous to his being hanged for the murder
    of his steward [Johnston]'

    Smith Papers, folder 74/4

11043 In dread and devotion, I implore by this scroll
Thus prays thy sad suppliant, poor sinner, and
                               servant.

    [Charles Earle], 'To neighbor Pope at Woolsery in my
    confinement by the colic'

    c.376

11044 In duty bound I must comply,
And now, sweet girl—adieu!

    'The soldier's adieu, on the morning of battle'

    c.94

11045 In each ambitious measure crost
As shamefully as they came in.

    [Soame Jenyns?], 'Horace Lib. II Ode XVI . . .
    imitated inscribed to the Earl of Bath' [pr. Dublin
    1747, in Foxon J65]

    fc.135

11046 In earliest times, ere men had learn'd
Inspir'd by fair Lucinda's charms.

    'Stanzas in the manner of Waller: occasioned by a
    receipt to make ink, given to the author by a lady'

    c.90

11047 In early affection how blest is the hour
The kind asylum of a hermit's arms.

    [William Hayley], 'Song Oct 7[-8] composed on
    horseback in returning from [?]'

    File 6968

11048 In early life's unclouded scene,
That leads from thirty e'en to thirty-eight!

    Charlotte (Turner) Smith, 'Thirty-eight to Mrs.
    H—y'

    c.83/3, no. 754

11049 In early times ere nature's genuine laws
Beauty and wit in laurel wreaths conferr'd.

'Sonnet to Dr. Sanden on his viewing a white favor
with this motto We'll deck him with laurel from the
Misses Page'

c.89, p. 111

11050 In ears (son) 'tis no glory to surpass
But I will bar and keep ye under lock.

'Answer' [to 'Give leave to me . . .']

b.356, p. 119

11051 In earth we lie; till God on high
Feet, hands, ears, eyes, nor tongue.

'On a tombstone in Rosse churchyard'

b.137, p. 203

11052 In easy numbers softly flowing,
In hopes to join her in the heav'nly choir.

Henry Howard, '3 Febr. 1725. An elegy on the much
lamented death of that excellent good wife mother
mistress and friend [Mary Ambler]'

c.229/2, fol. 22

11053 In Eden's garden no such creature
Cuckolds are of women's making.

'On a cuckold'

b.62, p. 18

11054 In Edlingham there dwelleth
Bore the wench away.

'Valiant Edward Steel. Tune Scotch haymakers'

c.530, p. 204

11055 In 'eighty-eight ere I was born, as I do well
                                                remember
As they did, they know when-a.

b.197, p. 218

11056 In elder times, ere shepherds were so great
At the bemoanings of the bleating sheep.

Josh[ua] Carleton(?), '1709 . . . The bleating sheep or
the sheep's complaint of their shepherds'

File 2763

11057 In elder times the ancient custom was
Mass, faith and troth outworn, they find damnation.

[Henry Fitzsimon, S. J.? or Sir John Harington?], 'On
swearing'
[Crum 11296]

b.200, p. 23; b.62, p. 22; see also 'In older times . . .'.

In England born my inclination,   11058
More cheerfully obey'd by me.

'Prince Edward' [son of Frederick Louis, prince of
Wales; spoken at a performance of Cato at Leicester
House, 1749]

c.578, p. 65

In every age, love's smiling god,   11059
To crown the glories he had won.

[John Lockman], '[La Fontaine] imitated'

c.268 (second part), p. 139; c.267/4, p. 175 ('potent god')

In every cast and color of my thought   11060
Each act of goodness is a step to thee.

[William Hayley], 'Sonnet . . . August 28 [1800]'

File 6968

In every matter, and each thing,   11061
Before all men's reason.

b.234, p. 85

In every varied posture, place, and hour,   11062
Save in my heart—they left no wreck behind!

'Elegy by a gentleman on the death of his wife'

c.139, p. 405

In evil hour and with unhallowed voice   11063
Such as the wise and good might love to share.

[William] Crowe, [verses intended for the installation
of the Duke of Portland as Chancellor of Oxford
University, 4 July 1793]
[Crum 11306]

Poetry Box v/80

In fables all things hold discourse,   11064
And fight, e'er since, for pay, like Swisses.

Philip Wharton, 1st duke of Wharton [? or John
Gay?], 'The triple alliance'

c.468; see also 'Once on a time, near Channel Row . . .'.

In fabulous pages where grave tutors train us   11065
You're a strumpet you slut and that I know and you
                                                know.

'Song 221'

c.555, p. 349

In fair Circassia, where, to love inclin'd,   11066
Wide o'er the moon-light hills renew'd their flight.

William Collins, 'Eclogue fourth. Agib and Secander;
or, the fugitives'

c.140, p. 141

In faith and patience I will wait   11067
Ascribing praise to Thee.

[Mary Pluret], 'Another [song]'

c.354

11068 In faith I cannot keep my sheep
Since first in love in love I chanc'd to fall.

'Song 45'
b.4, fol. 37

11069 In faith I waited for the Lord,
And my redemption not delay.

'Psalm 40'
c.264/1, p. 177

11070 In faith O Tom now thy garlic nature's seen
Why let'st thou in, a wolf among the sheep.

'On the same' [Dr. Bambridge's marrying Mall Wolfe,
a butcher's daughter]
b.356, p. 148

11071 In families both great and small (or more or less)
That half a dozen only make a pair.

'Enigma [76b]'
c.389

11072 In fennel seed this virtue you shall find
For pleasure these, for medicine those are fit.

[Joshua Sylvester, trans. Guillaume de Salluste,
seigneur Du Bartas], 'Of fennel'
b.284, p. 51

11073 In fifteen hundred thirty-one,
And next with solemn steps his father trod.

'[Enigma/Charade/Conundrum] 67'
c.389

11074 In flames forever envy's entrails fry
To see another man's felicity.

'Envy'
c.189, p. 42

11075 In Flavia's eyes is ev'ry grace
And Esau's where it should be.

Philip [Dormer Stanhope], 4th earl of Chesterfield,
'On Miss Eleanor Ambrose a celebrated beauty at
Dublin'
c.360/2, no. 149

11076 In Florence once, there lived a gentle youth
One tomb contains their bones, one fame their
memory.

[Thomas Hamilton, 6th earl of Haddington], 'The
faithful, the unfortunate lovers from Boccace'
c.458/2, p. 77

11077 In flower of mine age you see
Tho' Honor lie in grave.

'An epitaph on Ms. Honor Rich'
c.189, p. 59

11078 In foreign climes I oft am seen to roam
My spirit they to other realms translate.

Diggle Box: Poetry Box XI/71

11079 In foreign parts, there was no just occasion
Of your unfeigned loyalty, and stoutness.

Sir Thomas Urquhart, 'To Colonel [crossed out]'
fb.217, p. 137

11080 In form in manners and in mind a queen
Thou model, judge, and patroness of art.

[William Hayley], 'Sonnet . . . Jan 23 [1800]'
File 6968

11081 In former days good manners made a man
Let it thy mind to good deservings raise.

[Mary Serjant]
fb.98, fol. 150

11082 In former days when wit and mirth took place,
She found a court of justice left in you.

R[obert] Shirley, 1st earl of Ferrers, 'Prologue. To the
fall of Hannibal. 1710'
c.347, p. 63

11083 In former time, no matter where for,
Goodbye, and now depart in rest.

R[obert] Shirley, 1st earl of Ferrers, 'The travellers
and the oyster. From Boileau'
c.347, p. 55

11084 In French, or in Latin my first's often found,
Which too frequently with it abound.

[Four charades (1)]
Poetry Box II/42/1

11085 In friendly part a well-meant gift receive
Who ne'er saw Devon's cliffs nor Calais' sands.

[ ] Lewis, 'A letter to a traveller'
c.244, p. 436

11086 In friendship's sober garb array'd
In ev'ry form his pow'r the same!

Poetry Box III/52

11087 In fruitful Lombardy, of yore,
That ev'ry woman comes from Eve.

'Woman'
c.189, p. 189

11088 In gallant fruit, the core is oft decay'd,
Yea poison oft in cup of gold assay'd.

c.339, p. 327

11089 In gardens and meads, Flora's treasures delight;
Who brightens the ball, as she darts round her eyes.

John Lockman, 'A peep at Mr. Hugford's elegant ball, in Brewer's Street, Golden Square . . . April 1755'

c.267/1, p. 151

11090 In Georgia's land, where Teflis' towers are seen
And ev'ry Georgian maid like Abra lov'd!

William Collins, 'Eclogue third. Abra; or, the Georgian sultana'

c.140, p. 136; c.83/2, no. 290

11091 In God th'Almighty Father I believe
Remain with him in endless joy and bliss.

Sir John Strangways, 'The apostle's creed'

b.304, p. 170

11092 In God the Father, great in pow'r
And to their, latest, seed.

'The apostle's creed'

c.264/3, p. 118

11093 In God the Father I believe,
And the soul's everlasting doom.

'The creed'

c.83/3, no. 821

11094 In God the Lord will I confide:
Of's countenance's light.

'Psalm 11'

c.264/1, p. 37

11095 In golden cars the monarch, and his court,
True genius, which such splendid works could raise.

John Lockman, 'The beauties of Versailles' [translated from La Fontaine]

c.267/4, p. 223

11096 In good king Charles's golden days
I will be vicar of Bray Sir.

'Song 158' ['The vicar of Bray'; pr. c. 1714 (Foxon V87)]

c.555, p. 239; see also 'In Charles the Second's golden/merry days . . .'.

11097 In Goodwood's grove, with beech o'ergrown,
But always shut the door.

'The foolish virgins'

c.241, p. 44

11098 In gray-hair'd Celia's wither'd arms
Te deum sing in quiet.

[Charles Sackville, 6th earl of Dorset], 'A paraphrase on the French'
[Crum 11341]

b.201, p. 144

11099 In happier hours, ere yet so keenly blew
The unfading amaranth of gratitude.

[Charlotte (Turner) Smith], 'Sonnet to Dr. Parry of Bath, with some botanic drawings which had been made some years'

c.141, p. 106

11100 In happy days was Sacharissa's reign
In Kneller's oil, or Halifax's song.

'Upon the same subject [seeing Van Dyck's picture of Lady Sunderland] by a boy of 15 at Westminster School'

c.111, p. 30

11101 In harsh grating stanzas by Tom Sternhold penn'd,
Thy noise and his nonsense can never be praise.

'On a country parish clerk'

c.487, p. 24

11102 In haste towards Ireland two fierce princes go,
May George and William, O heavens the like obtain.

'The Irish expedition'

b.111, p. 260; see also 'Towards Ireland in haste . . .'.

11103 In heaps confus'd the letters lie
She is indeed a wonder.

'Lines occasioned by a lady's giving the word Necromancy as a puzzle'

c.504, p. 57

11104 In heav'n, bright maid that bliss receive
Thou goddess art below.

'Ode to humanity'
[Crum 11350]

c.83/2, no. 638; c.83/3, no. 901

11105 In heaven only is there bliss
All that I have, all that I live.

Poetry Box x/61

11106 In heav'n there is none bad: none good in hell
That heav'n and hell shall [?]ed be with guests (?).

[Sir Thomas Urquhart], 'Of heaven, earth, and hell'

fb.217, p. 514

11107 In heaven we higher joys shall find,
Shows 'tis mere madness, some think wit.

[Edmund Wodehouse], 'Iterum [3 August 1715]'

b.131, p. 239

11108 In heavenly choirs a question rose
And vain delights, adieu.

Ralph Erskine, 'The believer's principles concerning heaven and earth' [Gospel sonnets]

c.186, p. 6

11109 In hell of late there fell a great disorder
If he were pleased, to bring his clerk unto him.

    'On the death of [Sir Anthony] Benn Recorder of
    London [and his clerk]' [1618]
    [Crum 11356]

    b.200, p. 227; Poetry Box VI/107

11110 In high Olympus' sacred shade
Man is for his country born.

    John Lockman, 'On the Earl of Middlesex's birthday;
    Feby 6. (O. S.) 1761 . . . Set to music by Mr. Dupuis'

    c.267/2, p. 196

11111 In his religion, credit me,
And therefore is an atheist.

    Sir Thomas Urquhart, 'Of one who got no license, to
    be a Roman Catholic, and determined never to be a
    Calvinist'

    fb.217, p. 176

11112 In history we ever find,
Must to all conquering time submit.

    'Reflections on reading history'
    Poetry Box IV/146

11113 In hoary age with youthful raptures fir'd
But bless that being which your beauty gave.

    'Sent to Miss Dolly Anguish, with Dryden's Fables'
    c.360/1, p. 299

11114 In hopes of lucrous gains
'Twas not worth a fiddle.

    'To the publisher of the riddle on nothing.
    No. 48 vol. 2d with some few variations, which
    concluded with the following line 1751. Solve me, and
    have me for your pains . . . Bridget Lovegain'

    c.360/3, no. 162

11115 In hopes of speedy resurrection,
Condemned and sentenced thus she died.

    'An epitaph on passive obedience. Executed for high
    treason . . . by . . . a sentence from the bishops and
    inferior clergy' [1688]
    [Crum 11366]

    b.111, p. 119; Poetry Box VII/87 (with last line of
    'Certain, and sure . . .'); fb.207/1, p. 1

11116 In how few years have you raised up an high
So high to shadow all that are below.

    [Sir Aston Cokayne], 'To my cousin Mr Charles
    Cotton the younger'

    b.275, p. 56

11117 In Indian climes, while injur'd Britons rot
Repair our loss, and fill our isle again.

    'To the author of the poem, entitled Consummation—
    1741'

    c.360/1, p. 231

11118 In Islington, bless'd with salubrious air,
Form'd a third garden from the other two.

    John Lockman, 'Three gardens in Islington . . . June
    1758'

    c.267/1, p. 371

11119 In Italy there is a town,
Sweet Kitty, she was ne'er alone. . . .

    'Kitty. A tale'
    c.360/2, no. 229 (incomplete)

11120 In jerkin short and brown coat I live,
Black is my face, and blubber is my lip.

    '[Enigma/Charade/Conundrum] 13'
    c.389; see also next.

11121 In jerkin short and nutbrown will I live
Sleeping I wake, and waking sleep.

    'Riddle'
    Smith Papers, folder 74; see also previous.

11122 In joyful June's late month befell
And th'wonder died on the ninth day.

    W. F., 'Balivamachia. A battle with bailiffs; being a
    wondrous rencontre and contest, between threescore
    bailiffs, and five Gray's Inn gent[lemen] happening on
    Monday 16th of June an. [16]73 in that Midsummer
    term'

    Poetry Box VI/42

11123 In Judah God is known, his name
With terror overtops.

    'Psal: 76'
    [cf. Crum 1376–77]

    b.217, p. 9

11124 In Judah men do know the Lord,
By all the kings on earth rever'd.

    'Psalm 76'
    c.264/2, p. 54

11125 In kitchens oft a meddling fool you'll find
To form a mortal's face and shape divine.

    [one of] 'Two rebuses'
    Trumbull Box: Poetry Box XIII/100

11126 In lady's writ All Die and daily too.
Here mortify your pride, before you go.

[Sir Philip Wodehouse], 'Upon the general word Lady now too common'

b.131, back (no. 53)

11127 In larg's, and longs they fair, and softly broke
She tim'd it faster, than the semiquaver.

Sir Thomas Urquhart, 'How a gallant, and his mistress did sing together a plain song'

fb.217, p. 263

11128 In Latin Barbara sounds barbarous
A sweet preserve will thee become much better.

[Sir Philip Wodehouse], 'A conceit upon her name'

b.131, p. 4

11129 In Leister fields a goodly fabric stands
Deliver us from so vile a generation.

'A poem. &c.'

c.570/2, p. 98

11130 In life most valued, and in death most dear
He died an exile from his sovereign's ear.

Mrs. [ ] Walsingham, 'On the much lamented death of William duke of Devonshire'

Poetry Box v/22

11131 In life's gay morn young Mary's eye,
To meet my angel in the skies.

[ ] Pearson, 'Song'

c.83/2, no. 543

11132 In life's great drama parts of various kind,
To you—and you—to each—to all of you.

[ ] Walker, 'The occasional address spoken by Mrs. Simpson, on the night of her benefit, written by the Revd. [ ] Walker'

fc.130, p. 46

11133 In Linden when the sun was low
Since lifeless to my heart ye prove.

[Thomas Campbell], 'Hohenlinden'

c.364 (attrib. William Robert Spencer); see also 'When midnight o'er . . .'.

11134 In Liquorpond Street, as is well known to many,
And the bride entertain him with pilchards and gin.

'The barber's nuptials'

Greatheed Box/63

11135 In loftiest strains my tuneful voice I'll raise,
And guide me safely with a shepherd's care.

[ ] Atwood, 'The CXIX Psalm paraphrased in English verse'

Poetry Box x/69

11136 In London houses are of late become
And for herself keeps but the back to lie on.

Sir Thomas Urquhart, 'Why Mistress Nyon became a courtesan'

fb.217, p. 216

11137 In London I never know what to be at
O! give me the sweet, shady side of Pall Mall. |
[Derry down . . .]

[Captain Thomas Morris, 'The country life']
Poetry Box IV/151; c.340; Poetry Box II/18; c.83/3, no. 1037 (var.)

11138 In London I receiv'd my birth
You would my name explore.

'A riddle'

c.578, p. 110

11139 In London stands a famous pile
Consists in scraps of paper.

[Edward Ward], 'On the remarkable rise of the South Sea and other stocks in the year 1720'

c.360/1, p. 199

11140 In lonesome cave,
All hermits in the grave.

'A hermit's meditation'

c.138, p. 39

11141 In love I'm prodigal, and sparing too:
Free of myself: and covetous of you.

Sir Thomas Urquhart, 'The disposition of a lover, to the gentlewoman, who he beloved'

fb.217, p. 278

11142 In marble hard our harms we always grave,
In dust we write the benefits we have.

c.339, p. 323

11143 In March 1588 was buried in this place
A stream that swiftly slid down from their springs.

'On one Alexander Every merchant'

fb.143, p. 6

11144 In marriage are two happy things allow'd
Since the last day's as happy as the first.

[Thomas Brown?]

c.536; c.549, p. 15

11145 In melting strains that sweetly flow,
For ah! his absence ne'er can cease.

'An elegy. By Mary queen of Scots. On the death of her husband Francis 2nd of France.'

c.343, p. 1; c.83/2, no. 572

11146 In mercy, Lord, now me release,
And Isr'el's sun, is ris'n.

'Song of Simeon, another meter'
c.264/3, facing p. 117

11147 In merry, musty chronicles we read,
When half of them should be transform'd to swine.

'To the gin drinkers David's sow'
c.360/3, no. 84; c.267/1, p. 196

11148 In merry old England it once was a rule
That Cibber doth serve both for fool and for poet.

[Alexander Pope], 'On Colley Cibber, Poet Laureate'
fc.60, p. 46

11149 In metamorphosis, as poets tell,
Freethinker turn'd, and there he stands confess'd.

[ ] Lewis, 'A prologue to Ignoramus [originally written
in Latin, by George Ruggle] acted 1711'
c.244, p. 446; Poetry Box x/10(9)

11150 In military feats you dread no danger
Were you a native of The Hague, or Delft.

Sir Thomas Urquhart, 'To my Lord A[crossed out]'
fb.217, p. 151

11151 In mine, alas! good Sirs, you see
I make of him an ass.

[Charles Earle], 'An extempore thought on a
punch-ladle'
c.376

11152 In Mira's cheek the damask rose
The present's in thy power.

'To Mira'
Poetry Box 1/40

11153 In mists, and darkness, long my soul has dwelt
By strict obedience; and my joy, by praise.

'Whitsunday'
fc.54, p. 2

11154 In moral arts it is in use to say
Each man may swear inducing earn'd her good.

Francis Lenton, 'Upon that provident and virtuous
maiden Mrs. Goodith [Judith] Arden/ Anagram /
Earn'd thy good'
b.205, fol. 20v

11155 In morn when Sol from the celestial skies
Near some such place I'd choose to live and die.

'The angler's choice'
c.578, p. 80

11156 In mournful strains such as befitteth woe
And on thy fun'ral rites with solemn steps attend.

'On the same [the death of Samuel Fothergill]'
c.139, p. 448

11157 In mutual happiness twice twenty years
And tells him she is bless'd with endless peace.

'In Twickenham churchyard—in memory of Mrs
Francis Francklin . . .'
c.74

11158 In my beginning God be my good speed
In grace and virtue long to proceed.

[John Rose?]
b.227, p. 36

11159 In my dark cell, low prostrate on the ground
And your racked soul be calmly hushed to peace.

[Judith (Cowper)] Madan, 'Abelard to Eloisa' [answer
to 'In these deep solitudes . . .'; also attrib. Susanna
Centlivre]
[Crum 11410]
c.138, p. 19

11160 In my most bushy grounds,
Until they break my sleep.

Poetry Box x/6

11161 In nature Lord men worse then nothing be
Where is that something, thou so boasts proud
man.

[Henry Phillipps? 1655]
b.156, p. 7

11162 In nature why doth emptiness deny,
Sith in thy head's so much vacuity.

'On Marcus'
c.356

11163 In nature's pieces shall I see
You gods send her some more humanity.

[Thomas Carew], 'On his mistress's perfections'
[Crum 11419, 'still I see']
b.356, p. 77

11164 In no part of the scripture is it seen,
Was by Zipporah boldly circumcised.

Sir Thomas Urquhart, 'Why no woman should be
blamed for loving the member of man's circumcision
better, that that, which is modified by baptism'
fb.217, p. 153

11165 In northern climes there stands a town,
From stupidness to sense.

'The rape of the garter'
c.530, p. 161

11166 In northern country, as says story
Others may, if they please, relate.

[ ] R., 'Riddle'
Poetry Box VII/47–48

11167 In older times an ancient custom 'twas
Having lost mass, and faith they find damnation.

[Henry Fitzsimon, S. J.? or Sir John Harington?],
'Upon swearing'
[Crum 11426]
b.205, fol. 47r; see also 'In elder times . . .'.

11168 In others, sorrow beauty's force disarms
And prove you grief victorious as your joy.

'Martilla weeping'
c.244, p. 622

11169 In our own fancies we appropriate
What came from others must to others go.

[Sir Thomas Urquhart], 'Some seem to be so assured
of what they have [?] from them and [?] it were never
to be alienated'
fb.217, p. 534

11170 In Pannomie a worthy imp
Eternal joy may have. | Amen

'S. Martin. November. 11'
a.30[51]

11171 In paper case
Repent of yours in time.

[Richard Gough], 'Epitaph on a dormouse' [c. 1747]
[Crum 11435]
c.179, p. 55

11172 In paradise a woman caused all
When w'are more weak and they perhaps as fair?

[Sir Aston Cokayne], 'To the same'
b.275, p. 67

11173 In [Paris], there's a race of animals
And in her sleep the nuptial knot was tied.

[John] Gay, 'A true description of a fribble out of . . .'
Accession 97.7.40

11174 In pensive melancholy clad
In thee a friend I found.

S[tephen] Simpson, 'A letter to T. Eyre'
c.563

11175 In pensive numbers let the muse rehearse
And mourn her death your friendship could not
                                                    save.

'A pastoral elegy on the death of a young lady'
c.341, p. 90

11176 In pious hymns, and consecrated lays,
And rivers to the thirsty ocean flow.

[Henry] Needler, 'Psalm 146'
c.244, p. 549

11177 In pious peace when spotless worth expires
And bless the hour that knell'd him to the tomb.

E. Brisco, 'An elegy on the death of Dr. H[odgson?]'
fc.61, p. 113

11178 In pity, Lord I pray,
Throughout rever'd, and own'd.

'Psalm 67 12 day'
c.264/2, p. 30

11179 In plaintive sounds that tun'd to woe
Shall harmonize his lyre.

[Elizabeth Carter], 'To Dr [Walwyn] Preb[enda]ry of
Canterbury. When he designed cutting down the trees
in his garden'
fc.51, p. 172

11180 In planning expeditions 'gainst the fire
Slow to depart and sure—to be too late.

'Slow and sure'
Poetry Box XII/32

11181 In Pluto's dark abodes, the sisters three
Requires an abler pen, and stronger pow'rs than
                                                    mine.

'To the King of Prussia on his recovery . . . Voltaire'
c.83/2, no. 692

11182 In points of faith some undetermined jars
And yet both mourn'd because both won the day.

[Peter Heylyn, trans. of Latin verses on John
Reynolds and William his brother, by W. Alabaster]
[Crum 11444]
b.206, p. 118

11183 In praise of patience H[ay]l[e]y's muse
Where every reader shares the praise.

[Richard Brinsley Butler Sheridan], 'A sixth' [to
William Hayley on his incomparably long poem
entitled The triumphs of temper, c. 1781]
File 13565

11184 In purple vest array'd (as poets say)
Lucina smil'd, and said, let Shirley rise.

[James] Compton, [earl of Northampton], 'On the
19th of August' [to his countess Elizabeth, née
Shirley]
Accession 97.7.40

11185   In Randolph's curse a pox confound ye all
      I love to keep my night though not my day.

      T[homas] H[eywood?], 'T. H. to his creditors in
      imitation of Ra[ndolph]'

      b.62, p. 109

11186   In raptures let our hearts ascend
      To wing its airy way.

      P[hilip] Doddridge, 'Christ ascending to his Father
      and ours from John: XX. 17'

      c.493, p. 34

11187   In reading of the sacred writ, beware
      Thou climb not style, whenas the gap stands fair.

      [Francis Quarles?], 'On reading the scriptures'

      b.137, p. 166

11188   In riches, titles, honors, see her soar
      Her pastry lasting, as a chanc'ry suit.

      [Horace Walpole, 4th earl of Orford], 'C[ountes]s of
      Hardw[ic]ke' [d. 1761]
      [Crum 11457]

      c.157, p. 70

11189   In ridicule's enchanting glass
      But you may scalp my neighbor.

      c.90

11190   In Rome of old, as ancient poets sing,
      But thy indiff'rence makes a thousand blest.

      'Epistle to Sophia'

      c.83/2, no. 688

11191   In Rome when Lucius bore the sway,
      As from examples may be shown.

      'A tale of Gower's modernized'

      c.83/2, no. 350

11192   In Rome's great senate there was such a strife,
      The church's glory, but the senate's hate.

      J. S., 'Ad Caesarem Dec 19. 1705'

      b.90, p. 2

11193   In Russia's frozen clime some ages since
      And everything on earth submits to time.

      [Thomas Lisle], 'The history of Porsenna, King of
      Russia' [Dodsley collection]

      c.83/4, no. 1090

11194   In sable weeds I saw a matron clad;
      We'll sweetly sound it to our God. Amen.

      C. A., 'Protestantism revived or the persecuted church
      triumphing . . . by C. A. gent. Oxon. Anno 1688'

      fb.207/5, p. 23

In sable weeds, the beaux and belles appear   11195
Had Sorrell stumbled thirteen years ago.

      [Bevil Higgons?], 'The mourners' [1702]
      [Crum 11460; POAS VI.362]

c.171, p. 11; b.204, p. 15

In sacred sheets of either testament   11196
And in my mouth, my fainting word be mute.

      [Joshua Sylvester, trans. Guillaume de Salluste,
      seigneur] Du Bartas, 'On the mystery of the Holy
      Trinity'

b.137, p. 85

In sacred writ 'tis a divine command   11197
Translate th'example of this golden prayer.

      [Edward] Sparke, 'Poem 35th—upon St Simon and St
      Jude'

b.137, p. 72

In sad and ashy weeds   11198
Let mine entomb his woe.

      [Anne Howard], 'A poem on the death of Prince
      Henry' [1612]
      [Crum 11461]

b.197, p. 129; b.356, p. 32

In satire toil, who will, to raise his name   11199
Then shalt thou blaze, 'tis then thy noontide day.

      'Gratulatory verses, design'd to have been prefixed to
      the second edition of Mr. Welsted's poems 1724/5'

c.360/2, no. 131

In Saurin's heavenly page we find   11200
His mantle and his spirit.

      [ ] Lesley, 'To the Revd. Dr. Stonehouse on the
      sermons of Monsr. Saurin translated from the French
      of Miss H. More by . . .'

c.341, p. 117

In Scotland a strict creditor first gets   11201
Best goods distrain, and serve them with a caption.

      Sir Thomas Urquhart, 'How conjugal, and civil debts
      admit different executions, by Cupid's law, and the
      municipal of Scotland'

fb.217, p. 251

In Scotland's realm, where trees are few,   11202
And may his hope be true!

      [William Cowper], 'A tale . . . 1793'

Poetry Box v/100

11203 In scripture, Sir, 'tis said, we must,
I took a deal of pains to make it.

> [Mary] L[epipre], 'Miss L—— to Cornet F—— on
> his falling down and breaking his nose, sent with a
> nose of clay . . . Reading Jan. 2d.'
> [Crum 11466]

c.83/1, no. 150

11204 In search of some lambs from my flock that had
stray'd

And no more let my labor be vain.

> [Thomas Hull]

c.528/37

11205 In search of wisdom far from wit I fly,
And, wed to wisdom, lead a happy life.

> [Ambrose Philips], 'Wisdom preferable to wit'
> [Crum 11467]

Poetry Box XIV/169

11206 In secret place this handres nicht
Ye break my heart my bonny yene.

> [William Dunbar? (in first-line index at the British
> Library, with variant last line)]

'Braye Lute Book,' Music Ms. 13, fol. 50v

11207 In serpent's share the devil spake,
And tempts him with a plum.

> 'Written some years ago, on the report that C: F:
> offered to obtain a hundred thousand pounds a year
> for the prince'

Diggle Box: Poetry Box XI/69

11208 In serving others half my life has past,
If you are false, I give up all mankind.

> John Lockman, 'To **** . . . Dec. 1755'

c.267/1, p. 220

11209 In Sevenoak, into the world my mother brought me
Now laid in grave oblivion covereth me.

> 'On one Tho: Scot'

fb.143, p. 10

11210 In Shrovetide various pleasant games are us'd
Becomes an ornament to pot or spit.

> J[ohn] R[obinson], 'De alectryomachia on the
> cock-fightings'

c.370, fol. 58v

11211 In silence of | A winter's night
That I may live | With thee for aye.

> 'St. Bernard's vision, taken out of an ancient
> manuscript'

b.35, p. 34

11212 In silent dust beneath the humble tomb,
Adieu, dear Hayward, till the last great day.

> [Thomas Stevens?], 'Sacred to the memory of the
> Revd. Mr. Hayward who died July 23d. 1757'

c.259, p. 58

11213 In silent horror o'er the boundless waste
When back to Shiraz' walls he bent his way.

> William Collins, 'Eclogue second. Hassan; or, the
> camel driver'

c.140, p. 131; c.83/2, no. 635 (ll. 1–68)

11214 In silent night now I have wept
By the bright star that leads the day.

> [ ] Prigher, 'On the same' [on the death of Sidney
> Montagu, killed in battle 28 May 1672]

fb.68, p. 85

11215 In situation high or low,
Who would not wish for Lilling Hall?

> Thomas Plumer, 'Lilling Hall . . . A rhapsody . . .
> January 1774'

c.323

11216 In slumbers of midnight, the sailor boy lay
Oh! sailor boy! sailor boy! peace to thy soul.

> E. F., 'The mariner's dream'

Poetry Box XII/17

11217 In slumbers soft my eyes were seal'd
Myself will Steven's form assume.

> John Lockman, 'On Miss Bincks's attempting the part
> of Imsinda, at Covent Garden Theater; on which
> occasion Mr. Stevens was to act Oroonoko, for the
> first time . . . May 1735'

c.267/1, p. 243; c.268 (first part), p. 5

11218 In softest hours I'm handl'd by the fair,
But fools for want of reason use me ill.

> 'A riddle'

c.578, p. 107

11219 In sounds of joy your tuneful voices raise
But thank the Almighty, that you are not damn'd.

> 'The thanksgiving' [1709]
> [Crum 11487; POAS VII.374]

b.90, p. 12; c.171, p. 13; fc.24, p. 20; File 17422; Poetry
Box X/37

11220 In spite of all the virtue we can boast,
The woman that deliberates is lost.

c.549, p. 104

11221 In spite of the Dutch,
I wish he may never drink wine.

   'A loyal health'

b.111, p. 41

11222 In spring we had a summer blow,
And winter sweeps us quite away.

   'A sketch of human life'

c.115

11223 In stately marble tombs, what were our peers
To be interr'd, but th'art intomb'd in tears.

   G[iles] H[ayward], 'G. H. on the death of one'

b.62, p. 62

11224 In stately Rome sometimes did stand
That we with you might have our place. | Amen

   'For All Saints' Day. Nov. 1'

a.30[47]

11225 In sterner studies, enemies to wit
Their names when dead whom living I revere.

   W[illia]m Dennis, 'To Sir George Macartney knight
   of the silver eagle, and late envoy extraordinary to her
   imperial majesty of Russia on his return to
   England . . . Aug. 15th 1767'

File 4328

11226 In storms when clouds the moon do hide,
Shunning the knaves, and fools I scorn.

   Thomas Otway, 'The sixteenth ode of the second
   book of Horace'
   [Crum 11492]

b.150, p. 215; fc.60, p. 48

11227 In such green shades, have kings and monarchs slept,
Here we do wisdom, health and pleasure gain.

   'The rural shade'

c.91, p. 63

11228 In sure and steadfast hope to rise,
And lamblike as her Lord she died.

   'On Mrs. Wesley'

c.362, p. 62

11229 In tender Otway's moving scenes we find
Nor reason ever disagree with love.

   [George Lyttelton, 1st baron Lyttelton], 'To a young
   lady with Venice preserved'

fc.51, p. 23

11230 In th'act of sin, do but religion cry
Says Tereus you as holy are as I.

   J[ohn] R[obinson]

c.370, fol. 3

11231 In that black year which fill'd our wat'ry eyes
As once my prayers did to come too late.

fb.234, p. 47

11232 In that blest month when, nursed by kindly rain
Fancy, not reason, rules the lovesick mind.

   [William Boscawen], 'Verses occasioned by a dispute
   which of two lovers received the highest compliment,
   he from whom his mistress took a nosegay, or he to
   whom she gave her own. Written at Eton School'

fc.106, p. 2

11233 In that Elysian region of the blest
Attunes his harp to join the muse's son.

   'Dialogue in the Elysian shades between Horace, and
   Addison'

fc.53, p. 175

11234 In that fam'd region which the Indus laves,
O snatch me back, (ye fates)—I dread his spear!

   John Lockman, 'Alexander again in India, or the
   victorious Colonel Clive . . . Feb. 1758'

c.267/1, p. 124

11235 In that O Queen of Queens thy birth may free
Who had your God for father, spouse for son.

   [Henry Constable?], 'A sonnet on the blessed Virgin
   Mary'

b.114, p. 161

11236 In that roguish face one sees
Witcheries that wait on love.

   [Hester Lynch Thrale] Piozzi, 'Female fascination'

c.83/2, no. 607

11237 In the barn, the tenant cock,
Bid the setting sun adieu.

   [John Cunningham], 'A pastoral. The morning . . .
   noon . . . evening' [c. 1761]
   [Crum 11516]

c.83/1, no. 196

11238 In the beginning God the world produc'd
Then God survey'd his works, and did pronounce
                            them good.

   'A paraphrase on Moses's account of the creation'
   [16 Oct. 1759]

c.136, p. 1

11239 In the beginning I was not
The church and King's defender.

   'A riddle. Mr. Poole's'

c.484, p. 93

11240   In the black noxious fens that to Lincoln pertain
When shrieking away they all fly.

     'The three levelers or, impiety punished'
     c.546

11241   In the bride's sorrow, this I did remark
And lose the sooner her Virginia wares.

     Sir Thomas Urquhart, 'Of a certain bride, who wept
     and sighed extremely the first day of her marriage'
     fb.217, p. 261

11242   In the county of Norfolk that paradise land,
As may glare in the eyes of the whole British
                     nation. | Which &c.

     'The Norfolk lantern'
     c.570/3, p. 16

11243   In the days of Dean Jon if you came here to dine
Instead of the deans make the deanery double.

     [Patrick] Delany, 'Wrote on Swift's window'
     fc.135

11244   In the days of George and Nanny
Allows him a snack of the shame.

     fb.108, p. 310

11245   In the days of my youth I was sensibly crazy,
If you will consent your condition to alter. | Sing
                    Larry hi ho, &c.

     'Song 28'
     c.555, p. 39

11246   In the days of our sires, strange sights and wild fires
'Twas Simon's great dog and a flea.

     'Song 79'
     c.555, p. 123

11247   In the days of Q[ueen] A[nne] | Deny it who can
Her parts had improv'd by cutting her phlegm. |
                   [Harley, Harley, &c.]

     'Song to the tune of Lillebullero'
     c.111, p. 161

11248   In the days of yore, when statesmen bore
To have your head fix'd on a pole Sir.

     'A song'
     c.570/4, p. 55

11249   In the downhill of life when I find I'm declining
May become everlasting tomorrow.

     'Tomorrow'
     Poetry Box IV/61

11250   In the fever of youth, ev'ry pulse in a flame,
Though tir'd of living, yet dreading to die.

     'The dying rake a soliloquy'
     c.83/3, no. 941

11251   In the fields, in frost and snows,
Here a bah, there a bah, everywhere a bah. | We
                   defy all care, &c.

     'Song 119'
     c.555, p. 172

11252   In the first dawning of dramatic art
And meet loud plaudits in their grateful peal.

     'Epilogue'
     Greatheed Box/72

11253   In the first ruder age, when love was wild
Itself for its own proper object melt.

     [Thomas Carew], 'Love's force'
     [Crum 11525]
     b.150, p. 227

11254   In the gardens of Kew,
Shall have his head bustoed without, Sir.

     T[homas] M[orell], 'The hermitage. A dainty new
     ballad. 1732'
     c.395, p. 81; c.489, p. 3

11255   In the island of Britain, I sing of a knight
For no rope yet was made that could tie up a plum.

     'The knight and the prelate' [pr. 1734 (Foxon K97)]
     c.570/4, p. 79

11256   In the isle of great Britain long since famous grown
From the Hector of France to the cully of Britain.

     [John Wilmot, 2nd earl of Rochester, 'a base copy' on
     Charles II]
     [Crum 11528; *POAS* I.424]
     fb.70, p. 28

11257   In the last age how mighty bards did shine,
And claims by due desert, the never-dying bays.

     'A question and answer about Milton and Waller'
     c.244, p. 282

11258   In the lovely months of spring
So very nice are nice plum cakes.

     C[ecilia] B[urney], 'On the four seasons of the
     year . . . C. B. nine years'
     c.486, fol. 35

11259   In the midseason of this mortal strife
My mortal senses in a trance were drown'd.

     [William Hayley, specimen of translation from
     Dante's Inferno, Canto 1]
     File 7050

11260 In the midst of the sea like a tough man of war,
What do you think of the land in the ocean.

    'Land in the ocean'

    c.160, fol. 60

11261 In the morn comes a sprite, by whom authors are
                                            hunted,
'You and I, friend, were born but to plague one
                                         another!'

    'More copy?' [parody of Shenstone's 'Poet and dun']

    Poetry Box v/42

11262 In the morn when I rise I open my eyes,
I fear you will easily guess me.

    'Enigma 78'

    c.389

11263 In the name of my good friend the D. Amen,
To sign, spike(?), and deliver, as my act exceeds(?).

    'The will of a Macaroni'

    fc.85, fol. 119

11264 In the preamble of your proclamation,
Worthy your noble patrons the convention.

    'To the Queen on her proclamation concerning
    passes'

    b.III, p. 435

11265 In the royal exchange as I walked
The hangman leaves them at the gallows.

    'A song'

    b.197, p. 42

11266 In the same age, three first-rate scoundrels born,
To form a third, she join'd the other two.

    John Lockman, 'Imitations of Dryden's famous
    epigram, viz. The poets in three different ages born
    &c . . . Nov. 1748'

    c.267/1, p. 371

11267 In the sightless air I dwell,
To die along the gales of eve.

    [Ann (Ward)] Radcliffe, 'Song of a spirit . . . from . . .
    Romance of the forest'

    c.83/3, no. 786

11268 In the summer's sweet prime, as alert as Aurora,
And my hand seiz'd a pen, which their kindness
                                           inspir'd.

    [William Hayley], 'Hymen and Felicity from the
    French of Mr. [blank]'

    File 6942

11269 In the sweet days of honeymoon
I fear she has nine lives.

    'A matrimonial thought'

    c.546

11270 In the time of the Rump, by a rumor that spread
But not without taking his bond for appearance.

    [Phanuel Bacon], 'Datis vadibus'

    c.237, fol. 76 [i.e., 96]

11271 In the times of the Bourbons a man was rewarded
Men are honor'd for running away.

    [John Wolcot ('Peter Pindar')], 'On Admiral Linois
    receiving a reward from Bonaparte, on his escape
    from Sir J. Saumarez' [1801?]

    File 18072

11272 In the winding recess of a vale
In those haunts I'll no longer be seen.

    Miss [ ] White, of Edgbaston, 'Pastoral'

    c.532

11273 In the worst inn's worst room, with mat half-hung
That life of pleasure and that soul of whim.

    [Alexander] Pope, 'Pope's description to Lord
    Bathurst of the death of the Duke of Buckingham'

    c.148, p. 12 (incomplete); see also 'In yonder room . . .'.

11274 In Thee, O Lord my trust,
And ye new strength shall find.

    'The same [Psalm 31] another meter'

    c.264/1, p. 127

11275 In these cold climates, where the sun appears
If, spite of thee, 'tis possible to die.

    [John Sheffield, 1st duke of Buckingham and
    Normanby, trans.], 'The temple of death a poem' [pr.
    1709 (Foxon S390)]

    b.71, p. 15; see also 'In those . . .'.

11276 In these deep solitudes and awful cells,
He best can paint 'em, who shall feel 'em most.

    [Alexander Pope], 'Eloisa to Abelard' [pr. 1720 (Foxon
    P801); answered by 'In my dark cell . . .']
    [Crum 11557]

    c.138, p. 1

11277 In these gay times, when pleasure swells her sail,
Warren and Co. would soon leave off their trade.

    'On fashions'

    c.83/3, no. 1001

11278 In these sad moments of severe distress,
His faith unshaken; and unchanged his love!

    [William] Dodd, 'Lines by . . .'

    c.341, p. 40

11279 In these sweet shades where Health with smile
                                          serene
      The soul of truth, of honor, and of love.

          'An elegy wrote in the year 1781'
      Diggle Box: Poetry Box XI/38

11280 In thickest wood I hunt with beagles ten
      And what take not, only that keep I.

          '4 Enig. Res. One scratching his head'
      b.205, fol. 99v

11281 In this address what grateful eye but sees
      Over her Son, but in her Savior.

          [Edward] Sparke, 'Poem 24th—on the annunciation'
      b.137, p. 55

11282 In this at least he hopes you'll all agree,
      The friend who strives to make your pleasures less.

          Diggle Box: Poetry Box XI/25

11283 In this bright scene with matchless skill display'd,
      Jove form'd the world, but Homer form'd a Jove.

          'Upon a lady's picture'
      c.73, p. 15

11284 In this cold tomb his silent body rest,
      And a good husband, to a virtuous wife.

          'An epitaph on Captn. Francis Maynard'
      c.244, p. 207

11285 In this dark glass to your eyes
      Let him be wise.

          b.284, p. 54

11286 In this, dear George, we both agree,
      A washing every week.

          'The washing week'
      c.83/2, no. 358

11287 In this dear place parent of all my joys
      But raise my worth by imitating thine.

          'Epistle by a gentleman of a narrow fortune in Ireland
          to his wife some years after marriage occasioned by his
          being at the place where he first saw her . . .'
      fc.51, p. 177

11288 In this fair season, when the whispering gales
      And, ye bright realms, receive my fleeting shade!

          Henry Jones, bricklayer, 'Laura an elegy, from
          Petrarch'
      c.139, p. 116; c.90

In this her Latin name, here is portray'd   11289
And sing sweet lays of love in concord met.

    [Sir Philip Wodehouse], 'Upon Mrs. B[arbara]
    B[rown] my neighbor'
b.131, back (no. 99)

In this little scope   11290
In his cost and his pains Broom can tell.

    'An epitaph, Billingsgate Fishmarket day' [verse satire
    on the death of Alexander Pope]
File 12118

In this metropolis, the present year,   11291
She fram'd a third hum, from the other two.

    John Lockman, 'The three hummers . . . July 1758'
c.267/1, p. 372

In this most solemn mournful hour   11292
To guard the place where Lambert lies.

    'On the death of Dr. Lambert. Master of St. John's
    Coll—Cambridge'
c.360/1, p. 227; fc.135

In this my rural seat how matters go   11293
An honest man! and only held by fear?

    [Thomas] Fitzgerald, of Wotton, trans., 'The 16th
    epistle of the first book of Horace translated'
fc.51, p. 297

In this repose the secrets of your mind   11294
Our vows are perjur'd, and our sighs a jest.

    'Verses wrote by a young gentleman on a pocket-book
    which he gave to his sister'
c.360/1, p. 299

In this small fort, besieged by snow,   11295
And keep false friends away.

    W[illiam] S[henstone?], 'Written when confined to
    the house, by a deep snow'
c.378, p. 76

In this, that tempers after all agree,   11296
And all shake hands, as brethren first or last.

    'The epilogue to The Adelphi. 1736'
Poetry Box I/78

In this thy metagram I see   11297
With joy and swear 'mas will, I'm well.

    [Sir Philip Wodehouse], 'Upon my nephew William
    Samwell—married my niece Strutt'
b.131, back (no. 175)

In this tumultuous sphere, for the unfit,   11298
Repent no more—that misery has been mine?

    [Charlotte (Turner)] Smith, 'Sonnet to tranquillity'
File 245/25

11299   In this vile wicked world (meek Mawworm said)
Now reverend Sir pray which of these are you.

     [John Walker?], 'Epigram'

fc.108, fol. 77

11300   In this world of grimace,
And his actions detest.

     John Lockman, 'This, to be printed among the catches
or songs. Wholesome advice. A catch'

c.267/3, opposite p. 1

11301   In those blest shades, those verdant groves
Its horrors shed in vain.

     H[enry] Skrine, 'Presented to Miss W—— with a pair
of Woodstock gloves . . . Oxford July 16 1785'

c.509, p. 51

11302   In those cold climates where the sun appears
If spite of thee, 'tis possible to die.

     [John Sheffield, 1st duke of Buckingham and
Normanby, trans.], 'The temple of death' [pr. 1709
(Foxon S390)]
[cf. Crum 11582]

b.218, p. 1; see also 'In these . . .'.

11303   In those commandments (great God) direct me,
By the unspotted virtue of Christ's merit.

     Sir Thomas Urquhart, 'A supplication to almighty
God'

fb.217, p. 360

11304   In those more dull and more censorious days
When few dare give and fewer merit praise.

     'Ad laubellam'

c.189, p. 20

11305   In th' universal list, of all the spirits,
And best statesman, that ever was a poet.

     Sir Thomas Urquhart, 'To the Earl of Sterling, a little
before he died'

fb.217, p. 132

11306   In thy requests importunateness flee,
For overmuch doth tire the courser free.

c.339, p. 324

11307   In thy stern beauty I can see
When ice itself heats others' hands.

     [William Strode], 'To his m[ist]r[es]s'
[Crum 11657]

b.205, fol. 75v

11308   In time of need, thy neighbor lend,
When others' wants I do relieve.

     Sir John Strangways, 'Concerning alms and
suretiship . . . 17° Octobris 1646'

b.304, p. 62

11309   In time of yore, when Berwick was Scotch land,
That spectacle, which without grief or shame
                             cannot be told.

     Sir John Strangways, 'Upon the Lord Seaton [Ii.e, Sir
Andrew Seton] refusing to deliver Berwick to Edward
the Third King of England . . . 15to Decembris 1646'

b.304, p. 77

11310   In times like these when to St. Stephen's walls
And thou and Wingerworth ne'er thought of more!

     [ ] A., 'A's reply [to Lady Holland] . . . Chatsworth
Decr. 1800'

c.340

11311   In times long since gone
Since they're such as can never be cur'd.

     'Upon touching for the King's evil'

c.570/4, p. 12

11312   In times of old, at war's imperious call,
Has Peter robb'd—but Paul will never pay.

     'Occasioned by the conduct of the French towards the
Pope in the year 1794'

Poetry Box v/34

11313   In times of old, when time was young,
They from the ruins build their own.

     [Jonathan Swift], 'Vanbrugh's house built from the
ruins of Whitehall that was burnt written 1703'

c.265, p. 14

11314   In times of sultry heat it is no wonder
He stands secure, no devil can come near him.

     'L[yncup] H[ill] Augt. 7th 1782'

c.93

11315   In times remote (as reverend sages say)
And holds the honor of a demigod.

     'The choice of Hercules from Xenophon'

c.503, p. 33

11316   In times, when mean self-interest sways,
This grateful nation saw.

     John Lockman, 'An ode. On occasion of the tour
made by his excellency the Lord Viscount Townshend,
in Ireland'

c.267/4, p. 304

11317 In times when princes cancelled nature's law
Stands still recorded in the books of fame.

> [Arthur Mainwaring], 'Tarquin and Tullia' [1689]
> [Crum 11590; *POAS* v.47]
>
> b.111, p. 421; fb.70, p. 279; fb.207/3, p. 31

11318 In trifling works of fancy, wits agree
If with your hands you'll but hold up my chin.

> [David] Garrick, 'Prologue to The cozeners. Written
> by . . . spoken by Mr. Foote'
>
> c.68, p. 211

11319 In truce, although all other Scots surcease
The highland men make bloody wars in truce.

> Sir Thomas Urquhart, 'A difference betwixt
> highlanders and other Scotsmen'
>
> fb.217, p. 171

11320 In Trumpington | Not far from Cambridge
But he ne swore he should [anon] abedge.

> Geoffrey Chaucer, 'The reeve's tale from the works
> of . . . printed at London by Thomas Godfrey . . .
> Mdxxxii'
>
> c.160, fol. 44 (ll. 1–84)

11321 In truth friend Crocus, I think it is plain,
So Chesham's the town where your brother doth
dwell.

> 'Solution to the rebus' ['A game that is oftentime . . .']
>
> c.360/3, no. 227

11322 In twice twelve years, this honest horse a steady
course maintained;
A shrew's a fiend, that's conjured up, to double all
his woes.

> J. B. D[ickinson], 'Epitaph on [his horse] Dismal who
> died Dec. 11 1792'
>
> c.391, p. 111, p.?

11323 In vain are the smiles the gods diffuse,
And 'bide the shocks of misery and scorn.

> [Thomas Hull], 'Triton to Harlequin in prison.
> For W. Fisher. Dec. 31st: 1772'
>
> c.528/43

11324 In vain, bright nymphs ye would disguise
And all the inmost soul displays.

> [John Lockman], 'The sweet betrayers. Set by Mr. R.
> Vincent' [1738]
>
> c.268 (first part), p. 54; c.267/1, p. 259

11325 In vain brisk god of love, in vain have I
I've lost a heart that never went astray.

> 'The yielding heart'
>
> fb.142, p. 36

11326 In vain could malice aim a dart
And a new life inspire.

> [1781]
>
> fc.53, p. 2

11327 In vain dear Chloe you suggest
But Chloe is my home.

> [Crook Thomas]
>
> Poetry Box iv/186; see also 'In vain, my Chloe . . .'.

11328 In vain fond youth, thy tears give o'er,
And all that I inflict endure.

> 'A song'
>
> c.358, p. 114

11329 In vain for me does silence spread
Time will relieve me of my pains.

> T[homas] Liddiard, 'Written in illness . . . May 2nd
> [17]93'
>
> c.344, p. 119

11330 In vain I ev'ry art assay,
And fiercer make the smart.

> 'Song 41'
>
> c.555, p. 67

11331 In vain I go to bed, or close my eyes—
That scarce the dead, can in their churchyards sleep.

> 'Oldham'
>
> c.239 (incomplete?)

11332 In vain I struggle now to hide
Why should we struggle heaven to obey.

> [Mrs. Christian Kerr], 'Upon a supposition of being
> in love written in banter'
>
> c.102, p. 89

11333 In vain I try with ev'ry soothing art
For her—whose ill-plac'd love hath laid her here.

> Eliza[beth Ann (Linley) Sheridan], 'Eliza to Pollio—
> by Mrs. Sheridan [to Mr. M——]'
>
> Greatheed Box/59; Poetry Box iii/18

11334 In vain I write, in vain I rail,
And left the husband, with his dear-bought horse.

> [Thomas Hamilton, 6th earl of Haddington], 'The
> bargain from Boccace'
>
> c.458/2, p. 85

11335 In vain in vain thy pencil strives
The beauties of that face.

> 'Upon seeing Sylvia's picture'
>
> Poetry Box i/52

11336 In vain long parchment-pedigrees adorn
How comes a lion by an ass's ear.

   'On quality'

c.570/3, p. 134

11337 In vain, my Chloe, you suggest
But Chloe is my home.

   Crook Thomas, 'A song to his mistress being jealous
of him' [answered by 'With artful verse . . .']

c.233, p. 22; see also 'In vain dear Chloe . . .'.

11338 In vain my enemies would try
And puts my name to his.

   R[obert] Shirley, 1st earl of Ferrers, 'From Boileau'

c.347, p. 89

11339 In vain, my fair one, I design'd
Each time you look, you'll find some more!

   [Joseph Spence], 'The retraction. June 3, 1745'

Spence Papers, folder 151

11340 In vain, poor sable son of woe,
The last will do't alive.

   Colonel Diggs, 'Verses wrote by . . . on the statue of a
negro slave with tears in his eyes, that supports the
dial in Lincoln's Inn . . .' [pr. Whitehall evening post
7 March 1737/8]
[Crum 11623]

fc.51, p. 140; c.546

11341 In vain the boist'rous ocean,
And ever grumbling, murm'ring he is seen.

   Mary Cornwallis, 'St Evremond . . . translated by . . .
1791'

fc.124, p. 70

11342 In vain the Bourbon and Plantagenet
The devil's nature has the devil's fate.

   'On the two sisters' [Queen Mary, Princess Anne;
c. 1690]
[Crum 11625]

b.111, p. 431; fb.207/1, p. 49

11343 In vain the fulsome errors of the age
Thou yet hast stock enough thy self to trade.

   'A satire' [1683]
[Crum 11628]

b.113, p. 221

11344 In vain the gods benign impart
And eternize the lay.

   A. R., 'Ode on the Hon[or]ble Mrs. Frances Boscawen
and Miss Julia Evelyn collecting and transcribing the
following poems' [July 1746]

fc.51, p. 1

11345 In vain the stately monument you raise,
This sheaf, the tribute of the field receive.

   Elizabeth Tollett, 'Verses by . . .'

c.139, p. 415

11346 In vain the triflers of the times
Perhaps she'll change her name!

   R[ichard] V[ernon] S[adleir], 'Charades were much
the labors of poetasters and many very trifling lines
were written as such, but none on Miss Mackett fit to
be shown'

c.106, p. 84

11347 In vain thro' all the world I roam,
To true content, and endless rest.

   'Acon to Lavinia'

fc.51, p. 17

11348 In vain we know that free-will'd man has pow'r
Imperious death directs his ebon lance.

c.549, p. 73

11349 In vain we strive to cure our grief by art
Lord, and th' anointed ointment of our bliss.

   H[enry] C[olman], 'On the names Jesus, Christ,
Emanuel' [with acrostics on the names]
[Crum 11634]

b.2, p. 47

11350 In vain with plaintive voice, and weeping eyes,
Which time cannot deface, nor death destroy.

   'On the much lamented death of Miss B.' [*i.e.*, Mrs.
Fontayne, wife of the Dean of York?]
[Crum 11638]

c.175, p. 52 (incomplete?)

11351 In vain with riches you would try,
All other bribes are vain.

   [Lionel Cranfield Sackville, 1st duke of Dorset], 'To
one who endeavored to persuade me to marry a lady of
great fortune'

Poetry Box v/11; fc.135

11352 In vain ye woo me to your harmless joys,
Heartless and hopeless, life and love, all gone!

   [William Cowper, trans.], 'Love faithful in the
absence of the beloved. Vol. 4. Son. 49' [of Jeanne
Guion's 'Spiritual songs']

c.470 (autogr.)

11353 In vain you show a happy nation
The waters turn their hearts to steel.

   [Mary Barber], 'To Dr. Lynch on his excellent sermon
for the support of the charity children of Tunbridge
where there was a very small collection considering
the audience'

Poetry Box IV/133

11354 In vain you tell your parting lover,
Of slighted vows and cold disdain.

    Lt. Col. Edward Montagu, 'Wrote by . . .'

c.358, p. 155; Poetry Box x/123 (2 copies)

11355 In valor you were equal t'Alexander,
A king of more incomparable worth.

    Sir Thomas Urquhart, 'Of [the King of] Sweden'

fb.217, p. 158

11356 In various ways designing mortals move,
Adding no griefs to those we can't avoid.

    [Nahum] Tate, 'Simonides on human life'

c.244, p. 419

11357 In verse we'll therefore tell, that Neptune's train
The smiling goddess, and to kiss her feet.

    John Lockman, 'The triumphal procession of Venus'
    [translated from La Fontaine]

c.267/4, p. 203

11358 In virtue parents should their children train,
For if they spare the rod, they spoil the child.

    J[ohn] R[obinson], 'Patrio pater esse mehi probor'

c.370, fol. 32v

11359 In virtue's cause to draw a daring pen;
The most ill-natur'd man alive,— is you.

    Robert Dodsley, 'To Mr. Pope— on good and
    ill-nature'

c.351, p. 145

11360 In Wales full many a grave divine,
They learn to practice there.

    'Vindication of the Welsh parson'

c.83/2, no. 581

11361 In Wales, they say, a mine is found
And yet to find it under.

    'Upon a mine in Wales'

b.200, p. 408

11362 In warbling notes your matchless worth we'll sing
To crown this day, and end the glorious night.

    'On the birthday of his Grace the Duke of Leeds'

Poetry Box v/83

11363 In wedlock when the sen[s]es(?) meet,
And taught the tongue to wrong the heart.

    Dr. [ ] Colton, 'Marriage'

c.83/2, no. 324

11364 In what desperate earnest, said I,
Or in love, and enjoyment can die.

    'Lucatia slighted'

fb.107, p. 37

11365 In what soft language shall my thoughts get free,
My spotless faith, shall be, forever thine.

    Eliz[abeth] Singer [Rowe], 'On the death of [a]
    husband' [Thomas Rowe, d. 13 May 1715]
    [Crum 11644]

c.244, p. 178

11366 In wicked times when wanton wives
When Rose and Brindle fight the bull.

    [Edward Ward], 'Fortune's bounty or an everlasting
    purse for the greatest cuckold in the kingdom' [pr.
    1705? (Foxon W72)]

c.158, p. 74; c.503, p. 40 (var.)

11367 In wild Northumbria's bleak domain
The dull fireside and gouty chair.

    H[enry] Skrine, 'Prize poem at Batheaston on A
    chimney corner, and a gouty chair . . . Bath Dec. 30
    1778'

c.509, p. 12

11368 In Windsor Forest before war destroyed
Time or ambition is supplied by love.

    Sir Robert Howard, 'The duel of the stags' [pr. 1668
    (Wing H2991)]

fc.60, p. 61; Poetry Box VIII/18 (missing last four lines)

11369 In year six hundred eighty two,
We all subscribe our names thereto.

    'On Beveridge paid for a new suit of clothes. By the
    same hand' [as 'Charge all a bumper . . .']

fb.142, p. 47

11370 In yonder dust unmark'd for public fame,
May guardian angels thy sad story tell.

    'On Luisa a poor lunatic who died in Bedlam Hospital
    in 1800. She had some years before been found in a
    distressed state under a haystack— and was by some
    persons supposed to be a foreigner of illustrious birth,
    but her history could never be ascertained'

c.373, p. 83

11371 In yonder room, with ragged mat half hung
'Oh shield me from the thought'— he groan'd and
                          died.

    [Alexander Pope], 'Death of Villiers duke of
    Buckingham'

c.504, p. 45 (attr. Miss Bradford); see also 'In the worst
inn's . . .'.

11372 In you, in you we nature's art adore,
Orb—the orb of her bright eye.

[John] Weldon, 'A song to Brunetta on her complexion'

c.160, fol. 83v

11373 In young man love is pleasant to behold
But is ridiculous in one that's old.

fb.151/3

11374 In your addition broken sums observe
Do this in every one without omission.

[Mary Serjant], 'Addition broken'

fb.98, fol. 10

11375 In your bed, O Queen, I'd lie this night
Thus, that the poor lies everywhere, you're right.

'Queen Elizabeth and beggar . . . July 1572' [translation]

c.81/1, no. 514

11376 In your fair cheeks two pits do lie
Being dead can live, and living die.

[Thomas Carew]
[Crum 11655]

b.200, p. 147

11377 In your reduction weight you must be sure
By it divide if it be differing.

[Mary Serjant], 'Reduction of weight'

fb.98, fol. 36

11378 In youth, blest season of ecstatic joy!
And happier prospects chase these ills away.

'Elegy'

c.89, p. 62

11379 In youth, by hope remov'd to distant days,
My hand shall beckon, and my wish shall meet.

'Thoughts on death'

c.83/2, no. 344

11380 In youth, how blithe, and sweet and gay,
Which gilds 'the end of all'.

'The end of all'

c.142, p. 388

11381 In youth ungoverned—to the sacred calls
—Servant of God well done.

'To the memory of Samuel Fothergill'

c.517, fol. 33r

11382 In youth's first blush in beauty's freshest bloom
And joins existence with each kindred soul.

[Robert Southey?]

File 14205

11383 Incline thine ear unto my words
Defend him from all ill.

[Thomas Sternhold], 'The 2 psalm against the wicked that vex the godly' [verses from Psalm 5] [Crum 11666]

a.3, fol. 68v

11384 Inconstant man! Of doubts and creeds the sport!
Be such thy works—thy faith no more shall waver!

W[illiam] P[arsons]

Greatheed Box/12

11385 Inconstant Molly at fifteen
A painted butterfly.

[Robert Cholmeley], 'The silkworm. A simile'

c.190, p. 200

11386 Increase our toil and labor doth requite,
And after pain comes pleasure and delight.

c.339, p. 319

11387 Increase this flame O Lord within my breast
It is my pleasure that you here should stay.

[Mary Pluret], 'Another [poem written on waste paper]'

c.354

11388 Indeed, Euphemia, my command
Such pleasures as will never cloy.

C[harles] B[urney], 'To Miss Mitchell, with her picture, which the author had borrowed; and at her earnest request returned'

c.38, p. 26

11389 Indeed master poet, your reason's but poor,
'Twere a sign 'twas bad liquor within.

'Answer' [to 'Friend Isaac . . .']

c.81/1, no. 345

11390 Indeed Mister C——, it seems very odd,
How happy 'twill be for the devil and you.

'To a certain atheist'

c.360/3, no. 105

11391 Indignant, will I treat the foe,
And weave a wreath, t'adorn his brow.

Poetry Box x/64

11392 Indulgence, thunder clap, Medusa's head
Indulgeo seldom has the accusative.

'On the fanatic indulgence[.] To the King'
Poetry Box VIII/21

11393 Indulgent Hymen, to reward your truth,
The sweetest gift his bounty could bestow.

John Lockman, 'To Peter Shaw esqr, on his marriage
with Miss Spooner, New Year's Day 1757'
c.267/1, p. 215

11394 Indulgent nature to each kind bestows
And bears the like antipathy to trees.

'Epigram wrote by a young student of Oxford on the
bursar of St John's College, cutting down a fine row of
elm trees'
[Crum I1675, 'on all things bestows']
c.360/1, p. 37; c.176, p. 63

11395 Indulgent quiet, power serene,
How can the vile malignant crowd disdain.

[John] Hughes, 'A paraphrase on Horace book 2d.
od. 16'
c.244, p. 133

11396 Indulgent to the thoughtful muse
Not overwise nor yet a fool.

'Ode on mediocrity'
Poetry Box I/20

11397 Industrious, unfatigu'd in faction's cause,
Abhorr'd by Heaven and long since due to hell.

[William Shippen?], 'The Lord Wharton's
character . . . printed in the year 1712' [Foxon C119]
[Crum I1676; *POAS* VII.537]
b.204, p. 89

11398 Industrious Whigs! What have you now to boast
Of Presbyterian tubs to make a fire.

[1710]
[*POAS* VII.393]
b.90, p. 13; c.160, fol. 110; see also 'Invidious Whigs . . .'.

11399 Infamous priest that dar'st profane the place,
Near'st him suff'ring, and next him in bliss.

'An acrostic on John Tillotson'
b.111, p. 116; fb.207/1, p. 2

11400 Infinite beauty, everlasting love
A seraph here on earth, let man to heaven aspire.

I[saac] W[atts], 'The world a stranger to God . . .
Jany. 20. 1783'
c.259, p. 70

11401 Infinite guilt! amazing woe!
In undissembled woe.

[Isaac Watts, Hymns and spiritual songs (1707), bk. II,
Hymn 95, with 'grief' for 'guilt']
c.180, p. 12

11402 Infirmus snoring by his spousey's side
'Ah me! Felicity is but a dream!'

'The dream'
c.81/1, no. 358

11403 Inflamed with love and led by blind desires,
He'll love no longer, and she'll fear no more.

[Charles Sackville, 6th earl of Dorset, trans. from
Latin, 'The maiden conjugates']
[Crum E59, I1680]
Trumbull Box: Poetry Box XIII/42

11404 Ingenious friend, prais'd by thee
He gives to thee the vine thy praise inspires.

'The answer' [to 'I had a little stunted vine . . .']
c.83/2, no. 696

11405 Ingenious youth—whose manners form and mind
For all who heard all lov'd him and admired.

[William Hayley], 'Sonnet . . . Sept. 3 [1800]'
File 6968

11406 Ingrateful muse awake, and silence break
In Chomley's name until the world do end.

Thomas Lytler, 'Lachrimae et vota' [upon the Lady
Mary Cholmondeley, d. 15 Aug. 1625; written 1628]
b.203, p. 15

11407 Ingratitude—how deadly is thy smart,
Drags the loose knee, and intermitting step.

[Anna Seward], 'Sonnet'
c.141, p. 267

11408 Ingratitude—thou sin accurst,
Art only equall'd, by the devil.

'On ingratitude'
c.83/3, no. 969

11409 Injurious charmer of my vanquisht heart
Together both expire.

John Wilmot, 2nd earl of Rochester, 'Dialogue[:]
nymph . . . shepherd'
b.334, p. 176

11410 Inscribed on many a learned page
And she jogs after if she can.

[Hester Lynch Thrale Piozzi]
c.389; c.504, p. 192

11411 Insensible as clay deaf dumb, and blind
Sometimes the comfort then, the curse of life.

    'Another [enigma]'

Diggle Box: Poetry Box XI/71

11412 Insipid folk I thought to temporise,
To bear a double heart but single tongue.

    [( ) Hilton, of Gloucestershire?], 'An answer to the foregoing verses' ['O temporizing wretch . . .']

    b.111, p. 210

11413 Inspire me heaven, nor in me leave a thought
Since Allah calls throughout a virtuous land.

    c.83/2, no. 588

11414 Inspire me truth whilst I the praises sing
Has had the luck to bring it back again.

    [satire on women at court, temp. Charles II] [Crum 11691]

    fb.106(28)

11415 Inspiring power! By heaven assign'd
Who liv'd but to relieve the miseries of man!

    [William] Hayley, 'Ode in honor of [John] Howard esqr. author of The inquiry into the state of the various prisons in Europe'

    c.345

11416 Instead of a puzzle by changing each letter
And wit keen as yours will quickly unfold it.

    W[illia]m Smith, 'Dear ladies . . . Bury, January 28 1799'

    File 17474

11417 Instruct me, fame, why British Addison
Which every heart must honor ev'rywhere.

    'Why hath not Addison a tomb in Poet's Corner, W[estminster] Ab[bey]?'

    fc.53, p. 56

11418 Insult not too much on thy fading success,
Poor lovers tormented, and cast on the sea.

    'The rival'

    fb.107, p. 72

11419 Insulting Gaul, and her blind pupil, Spain
Return and triumph in thy country's peace.

    'On the march of Duke William [of Cumberland] against the rebels in November and December 1745' [Crum 11697]

    c.360/2, no. 114

11420 Interred beneath this marble stone
And so they lived; and so they died.

    [Matthew] Prior, 'Epitaph on sauntering Jack and idle Joan' [Crum 11700]

    c.179, p. 11

11421 Interval of grateful shade
Shall regale my mental eye.

    [Philip Doddridge], 'Hymn 35th'

    c.562, p. 41

11422 Into such wickedness the aims are hurl'd
So bless me God that I be none of them.

    [Sir Philip Wodehouse], 'Upon my son Edmund'

    b.131, back (no. 146)

11423 Into the world we nothing brought,
Eternally employ'd.

    Poetry Box VII/33

11424 Into this world, as strangers to an inn
He only broke his fast, and went his way.

    'On the same' [an infant; the son of Sir Ralph Winwood?] [Crum 11708]

    b.356, p. 252

11425 Invading William did at first pretend
Will soon shriek Master tho' they go to hell.

    [Sir Richard Bulstrode?], 'Upon the Prince of Orange's invasion'

    fb.88, p. 119v; see also 'Usurping William . . .'.

11426 Invidious Whigs since you've made your boast
With Presbyterian tubs to light the fire.

    'Two distichs writ over Dr. Burgess' meeting house' [1710] [POAS VII.393]

    Poetry Box VI/2; see also 'Industrious Whigs . . .'.

11427 Invited to visit a friend out of town,
I had much rather tramp it on foot, by the L[or]d.

    'The stagecoach; or, a trip to York' [Gentleman's evening post, July 1776]

    c.487, p. 99

11428 Involv'd in flame and suffocating breath
Is writ by sorrow on the finest heart.

    [Edward Jerningham], 'On the death of two favorite birds'

    c.90

11429 Inward and outward graces met,
Will fan my flame, and keep it in.

[from 'The amours of Alatheus and Eustathea']
c.379/1, p. 98

11430 Ireland's Saturn, England's sun I am
The Mars of France, and Norman's Mercury.

b.208, p. 177

11431 Iris I'd praise you: 'tis the easiest theme;
And honey sucks from ev'ry flower.

John Lockman, 'Iris . . . Madame de la Sabliere, a very
ingenious lady, and a noble patroness of La Fontaine'
[translated from La Fontaine]

c.267/4, p. 175

11432 Iris you ask me how to write
Whene'er we look on you.

'To a lady that asked how to write love letters'
fc.51, p. 141

11433 Is any church more Catholic than we?
Hell would be hard put to't to match the crew.

'A character of the church of Chichester [and its
bishop Peter Gunning], 1673'
[POAS 1.312]

b.54, p. 873

11434 Is any heart so hard as not to mourn
Let now our tears increase, and sighs still flow.

Ab[raham] Sherwill, 'In idem' [elegy on the death of
Andrew Horsman]

b.212, p. 252

11435 Is Cupid not a fezard [sic],
To hide him in a cleft.

Sir Thomas Urquhart, 'That Cupid is not stout'
fb.217, p. 275

11436 Is death so cunning now that all her blow
As mine will hide the truth, which others feign.

[William Strode], 'On one that died of an impostume
in the head' [Sir John Portman, Wadham College, d.
10 December 1624]
[Crum 11719]

b.205, fol. 61v

11437 Is Duck ordain'd?—Why not? great Tully shows,
His plain account best taught by plainest men.

T[homas] M[orell], 'An epigram'

c.395, p. 71

11438 Is it a sport is it a place
Then turtles suffer when they bill.

'Leave Chloris leave'
[cf. Crum L106]

b.213, p. 132

11439 Is it because he died, or that his years
To wish him long life then, had been a curse.

'To the same. The reasons'
Poetry Box v/106

11440 Is it birth puffs up thy mind,
That made me much more proud than fair.

'To a proud lady'
[Crum 11732, with six more lines]

b.197, p. 241

11441 Is it for fear to wet a widow's eye,
That on himself such murd'rous shame commits.

[William] Shakespeare [Sonnet IX]

c.94

11442 Is it for love, then, to pronounce your fate?
Must speak my doom; must guide me, or mislead.

John Lockman, 'Conclusion of the last scene of Act II
of Adelaide, a tragedy by Mr de Voltaire'

c.267/4, p. 295; c.268 (second part), p. 119

11443 Is it for us thy charms are spread?
To blush unknown or vainly waste.

[ ] Bidlake, 'Ode to the rose'
c.83/2, no. 506

11444 Is it not strange presumption that once more
In real life to copy what we feign.

Charles Yorke, 'Prologue to Shakespeare's Measure
for measure'

Poetry Box I/79 (2 copies)

11445 Is it not strange that fortune should decree
The bee flies always to the sweetest flowers.

Dr. [ ] M., 'By . . . of Emmanuel College
[Cambridge], the company having all drank their
favorite ladies, and finding that every name began
with B'

Diggle Box: Poetry Box XI/69; see also 'How strange it
is, that Cupid . . .'.

11446 Is it not strange that such a thing as this is,
Who gives to dogs what nature meant for man.

'Inscription for the collar of a young lady's lap dog'

c.115

11447 Is it thy sprightly nature that aspires
Light on her breast and true love kindle there.

   [Phanuel Bacon], 'To Mira occasioned by a spark of
   fire hitting her in the eyes'

   c.237, fol. 18

11448 Is it to me this sad lamenting strain!
And all the terror's doubled in their breast.

   [Lady Mary Wortley Montagu], 'An answer to a love
   letter in verse. From Mrs J. . . . n'

   fc.51, p. 62

11449 Is it true I am derided
When I can love and can disdain.

   b.213, p. 32; b.4, fol. 38v

11450 Is John departed, and is Lilburne gone?
For if they ever meet they will fall out.

   'John Lilburne's epitaph'
   [Crum 11735b]

   b.54, p. 1232

11451 Is not a mansion totally divine
And Venus a bright planet.

   Sir Thomas Urquhart, 'A question with the solution
   thereof concerning a cuckold and his wife, who were
   supposed (both of them being dead) to have gone to
   heaven'

   fb.217, p. 228

11452 Is not Christ's church a glorious faithful vine
Since Goodwin's sent for to a heavenly feast.

   'On Dr Goodwin's death' [William Goodwin, Dean
   of Christ Church, Oxford, d. 1620]
   [Crum 11743, 'fruitful vine']

   b.200, p. 226

11453 Is not each of these writers a very sad dog
Truth was hid in a Mist, now she's lost in a Fog.

   'On the writings of Mist and Fog'

   c.546, p. 31

11454 Is not my measter here among you pray?
But pack up all and whistle whoame again.

   [David] Garrick, 'Prologue to Barbarossa, written
   by . . . and spoken by him in the character of a
   country boy'

   c.546, p. 26; c.68, p. 28

11455 Is not that riches that's eternal gain'd
But doth the just with lasting honor crown.

   [Mary Serjant]

   fb.98, fol. 169

11456 Is not thy sacred hunger of science
Except confirmed and bishoped by thee.

   [John] Donne, 'To Mr B. B.'

   b.150, p. 201

11457 Is she a puritan, that doth accomplish
And hugs so willingly geniculation [*sic*].

   Sir Thomas Urquhart, 'Of a covenanting wench who
   was a catholic in her love'

   fb.217, p. 261

11458 Is she, at last, restor'd to my fond wishes,
O heav'ns! Here Guzman: Here's his father! O!

   John Lockman, 'Alzira, by Mr de Voltaire, act III,
   scene IV'

   c.267/4, p. 279; c.268 (second part), p. 125

11459 Is she black-brown! Oh no! her name says nay
So let her love her lambkins and her kid.

   [Sir Philip Wodehouse], 'Upon his fair neighbor
   An[n] Blackbourn . . .'

   b.131, back (no. 91)

11460 Is she not wondrous fair? but oh I see
As now it freezeth, now again it burns.

   [Thomas Carew], 'The lover's passion'
   [Crum 11750]

   b.200, p. 47; b.205, fol. 34r

11461 Is then your time so ill bestow'd?
Till you are loud proclaim'd by heav'n.

   'To Athenia. 1754'

   c.238, p. 65

11462 Is there a charm ye powers above,
Then grasps the snake and dies.

   'The power of beauty'
   [Crum 11756]

   c.358, p. 139

11463 Is there a daughter of so hard an heart,
How hard the task would be to bear my own.

   Charles John Fielding, 'A farewell epilogue spoken by
   Mrs Wheeler at the Theater Royal in Bath'

   c.130, p. 25

11464 Is there a man whom folly calls her slave,
And let him be high steward to the devil.

   [Thomas Hull], 'The candidate'

   c.528/44

11465 Is there a pious pleasure that proceeds,
Cure for my wounds, and from my labors rest.

   [William Walsh], 'Elegy. The petition. (In imitation
   of Catullus)'

   c.223, p. 73

11466 Is there a sanctity in love begun,
Where softer kisses are the only darts.

[William Cartwright], 'Upon a gentlewoman's silk
hood'
[Crum 11759]
b.197, p. 238

11467 Is there a scourge is there a rod for me
Who doth thy children still in safety keep.

[Mary Serjant]
fb.98, fol. 160

11468 Is there a solitary wretch who lies
The depth or the duration of his woe.

[Charlotte (Turner) Smith], 'Sonnet on being
cautioned against walking on a headland overlooking
the sea, because it was frequented by a lunatic'
c.141, p. 116

11469 Is there a whim-inspired fool,
Is wisdom's root.

[Robert Burns], 'A bard's epitaph'
c.139, p. 354; Poetry Box xiv/189

11470 Is there God, and shall this tribe
A glorious constellation.

'A poem'
c.570/2, p. 14

11471 Is there in heav'n a pow'r we dare invoke,
Proves language is but gaud on sorrow's sable train.

[ ] Yearsley, 'On the death of Mr. Smyth surgeon of
Bristol . . . Clifton June 29 1791'
c.341, p. 105

11472 Is there no peace on earth not without him
Till she's assured of life's eternal state.

[Mary Serjant]
fb.98, fol. 163

11473 Is this the day, is this the sacred morn,
Forbid it gratitude—forbid it love.

'Hymn wrote on the morning of Christmas Day 1778'
[Northampton mercury]
c.487, p. 159

11474 Is this the heavenly crown, are these the joys
Opprest with triumphs of their victory.

'Stafford's ghost'
Poetry Box vi/55

11475 Is this thy bravery man is this thy pride
Whom the red river cannot mend the Red Sea
                                        must destroy.

[Abraham Cowley, 'The plagues of Egypt']
[Crum 11771]
c.548

11476 Is this thy crystal rock, we clearly see
Has all his worth epitomiz'd.

[Sir Philip Wodehouse], 'Sr Christopher Calthorp i'th'
crystal rock repose'
b.131, back (no. 160)

11477 Is this your liberty, ye men of Rhode,
Claiming a right of lording over Rome.

'To the Assembly of Rhode Island, North America on
their proceedings against Mr. Ro—e'
fc.85, fol. 81

11478 Is this your lodestone Ben, that must attract
The loathed stage; for thou hast made it such.

Alexander Gill, the younger, 'Upon Ben: Jonson's
magneti[c] lady' [1632; answered by 'Doth the
prosperity . . .']
[Crum 11772a]
b.200, p. 13; b.356, p. 206

11479 Is virtue set so thick in our thin court,
By placing in his trust, his second care.

'The death of his dear friend Sr. George Radcliff'
fb.228/49

11480 Is Wolly's wife now dead and gone?
A thousand thanks then thou shalt have.

'The loyal Scot on the death of our late Queen Mary'
[1695]
[Crum 11777; POAS v.447]
fb.207/1, p. 9

11481 Isaac is gone to everlasting rest
Now all my honey's mix'd with bitter gall.

[( ) Pierson], 'An acrostic on the death of Isaac
Pierson'
c.328, p. 131

11482 Isaac was courteous pleasant brisk and free
No doubt he's happy why should I lament.

[( ) Pierson], 'An acrostic on the death of Isaac
Pierson'
c.328, p. 133

11483 Isaac where are those dear obedient hands?
No joys below can be of any worth.

[( ) Pierson], 'An acrostic on the death of Isaac
Pierson by way of dialogue betwixt his father and him'
c.328, p. 130

11484 Isaac would sweetly play, Isaac would sweetly sing
None more devout, nor musical inclin'd.

[( ) Pierson], 'An acrostic on the death of Isaac
Pierson'

c.328, p. 132

11485 Iseham, thy kind ascendant did compose
All that I lost, and more, themselves to me.

[Thomas Stanley], 'Iseham' [in 'A register of friends']

b.153, p. 12

11486 Israel's once favor'd race
Pursu'd by vengeance down.

T[homas] S[tevens], 'January the 18 Exposition from
Mattw. 19. 30 ver.'

c.259, p. 113

11487 Is't true that souls their bodies do survive?
Death will no more the soul than body save.

'The immortality of the soul in answer to
Mr. Glanville's translation from Seneca, Troas, Act 2'
[Crum 11788]

b.382(15)

11488 It acts and suffers—indisturbedly
Determines there can be no majesty.

[Sir Philip Wodehouse], '5. Indisturb[ed]'

b.131, p. 18

11489 It appear'd just at first like a great ball of fire
May all their schemes vanish like castles in air.

'An impromptu, on the ball of fire which appeared in
the air 1783'

c.504, p. 19

11490 It being the law of nations to restore
Who will not lose his debt, I must needs die.

[Sir Thomas Urquhart], 'Why I must die'

fb.217, p. 496

11491 It better is (we say,) a cottage poor to hold,
Than for to lie in prison strong, with fetters made
of gold.

c.339, p. 325

11492 It blew an hard storm, and in utmost confusion
They toss'd the poor parson souse into the ocean.

W[illiam] Taylor, 'Epigram' ['Absolution'; Dodsley
Collection]

c.487, p. 129; c.81/1, no. 155; c.115; fc.130, p. 59

11493 It cannot move thy friend, firm Ben! that he
Cast malefactors are made jurymen.

[Zouch Towneley], 'Iucertus author to Ben Jonson'
[verses against those sent to him by Alexander Gill on
his 'Magnetic lady': 'Is this your lodestone . . .';
c. 1632]
[Crum 11793]

b.200, p. 15 (incomplete?)

11494 It chanc'd, by some mistake or other,
And all the while were thrashing me!

'Translation [Le bon caractere]'

Diggle Box: Poetry Box xi/68, 69

11495 It chanc'd that Phoebus having supp'd with Jove,
Your labors shall succeed, and books be drest.

'Good news for poets, or the metamorphosis of
Dublin University printing house into a cook's shop'

c.172, p. 9

11496 It dares both do, and suffer—for both these
Than Anacharsus' tongue, which he spit forth |
I' th' tyrant's face.

[Sir Philip Wodehouse], '4. Both do and suffer'

b.131, p. 17

11497 It did prognostic Cupid's inundation
To which he gliding slunk into a fountain.

[Sir Thomas Urquhart]

fb.217, p. 540

11498 It eases not my mind, you can't restore
May well content and please him all his life.

[Mrs. Christian Kerr], 'The gentleman's answer' [to
'To ease my mind . . .']

c.102, p. 95

11499 It falls—great gods prevent the stroke!
At Treves, and detest his name.

[Isaac Freeman], 'On the breaking of my snuff box.
To T. Steavens esqr. At Venice'

fc.105

11500 It fell about the Martinmas time,
Get up and bar the door.

'Song 77'

c.555, p. 118

11501 It fell on the day (as good people say)
And his last will be from a cart. (Amen)

'The mistake: September the 29th [16]54. To the tune
of a Reverend Dean' [Satire on Cromwell]
[Crum 11798]

Poetry Box VII/30, p. 1

11502 It fills me much with admiration
To show these gentry to their lodging.

   'Mercury'

c.172, p. 47

11503 It grieves me Lord, it grieves me sore
And live without that impious string or show my
                    zeal in death.

   [Isaac] Watts, 'Self-consecration . . . Dr. Watts' Lyric'

c.259

11504 It grieves me that due thanks I thus retain
Who nothing pays, pays all of what he can.

   [William Strode], 'To the same [Sir John? or Thomas?
   Ferrars]'
   [Crum 11800]

b.205, fol. 53v

11505 It grieves my heart, and yet I can't but smile
And [blank] us with the grievance of the nation.

   'A dialogue between the Duchess of Portsmouth, a
   Frenchwoman, and Madam Elinor Gwyn, both
   mis[tres]ses to Carolus II Rex . . . at the former's
   departure from England to France'

c.189, p. 88

11506 It happened in the twilight of the day
Starts from his couch and bids the dame draw near.

   'Sr E[dmond]b[ury] Godfrey's ghost'
   [Crum 11802; POAS II.7]

b.371, no. 18; see also 'There happened . . .'.

11507 It happen'd on a certain time,
The devil could not read his hand.

   'Rome's pardon—a tale'

Poetry Box IV/9; see also 'It happen'd once upon a
time . . .'.

11508 It happen'd once Dame Dobson slept so fast
For should she wake again t'would be the de'il and all.

   [Robert Cholmeley], 'Carm. quad. page the 100th . . .
   [translation of Latin poem, 'Xantippe quandam . . .']'

c.190, p. 148

11509 It happen'd once upon a day
He had the honor to end the ball.

   'A ballad to the tune of the beggar wench of Hull'

Accession 97.7.40

11510 It happen'd once upon a time,
The d[evi]l could not read his hand.

   'Rome's pardon'

c.115; see also 'It happen'd on a certain time . . .', and
next.

11511 It happen'd once upon a time
But whom I leave, I leave forever.

   'Fame and his companions a fable'

c.241, p. 98; see also previous.

11512 It happen'd one day that Tom took a ride out
We'll leave him—perhaps he may sometime return.

   'Tom riding too far'

c.91, p. 168

11513 It helps the teeth it gives the bald man hair
Do water make which will the sight renew.

   [Joshua Sylvester, trans. Guillaume de Salluste,
   seigneur Du Bartas], 'Of cresses'

b.284, p. 53

11514 It is a common observation
But frame their minds to what they've got.

   'Ardua quam res opibus non tradere mores'

c.176, p. 111

11515 It is a false and common way by friendship to
                    deceive,
But false and common though it be, 'tis knavery by
                    your leave.

fb.151/3

11516 It is a good sign when a man affecteth
The same good things which he would fully savor.

b.234, p. 250

11517 It is a motion, whereby the heart doth crave
But of his wealth his wishes still increase.

   'What's love'

c.158, p. 28

11518 It is a punishment to love,
Whose wills, whose minds, whose hearts, are none
                    our own.

   [Abraham] Cowley, 'On love'
   [Crum 11811]

c.356

11519 It is a snare, to him that shall, devour what holy is
To prosper to the third descent; nor shall we now
                    need be.

   Sir John Strangways, 'In sacriligos . . . 29° Novembris
   1646'

b.304, p. 73

11520 It is a truth so certain and so clear
The coronation day is more than a thousand years.

   A[braham] C[owley], 'Taken out of A. C[owley's]
   Government of Oliver Cromwell'

fb.142, p. 39

11521   It is an easy thing with God a rich man's wealth to
                                                    slake:

    It easy is, with God also, a poor man rich to make.

        c.339, p. 329

11522   It is an error ev'n as foul to call
    Our sins too great for pardon as too small.

        [Francis Quarles], 'On our sins'
        [Crum 11820]

        b.137, p. 191; b.118, p. 221

11523   It is enough to me
    Inferior objects; weak, and partial.

        [George Daniel]

        b.121, fol. 62v

11524   It is envy, not love (as I suppone [sic])
    That each of them would have her all alone.

        Sir Thomas Urquhart, 'Of many co-rivals, who did so
        strive together for a certain lady, that none of them
        could suffer any one of the rest to be a partner in her
        favor'

        fb.217, p. 152

11525   It is for yourself, or him that you are sorry
    And not being so to mourn is frenzy.

        [Sir Thomas Urquhart], 'The reason why we should
        not excessively lament the death of any friend'

        fb.217, p. 529

11526   It is I vow an admirable matter,
    The hardest she can get, being her best diet.

        Sir Thomas Urquhart, 'Of a lady very amorously
        disposed, and withal much given to feasting'

        fb.217, p. 187

11527   It is impossible, to gather from
    Upon the earth, for our edification.

        Sir Thomas Urquhart, 'To Sir Robert [crossed out]'

        fb.217, p. 334

11528   It is most certain, the Thrice-Sacred One,
    Sin's, death's, and hell's eternal taming king.

        'On certain places in scripture beginning with God's
        appearing to Abraham Gen: 15:'

        b.137, p. 125

11529   It is no coranto news I undertake
    The tollingman Barnaby strikes them good luck, |
                        And so the commencement grows [new].

        [John Cleveland], 'Upon the commencement'

        b.93, p. 13

11530   It is no derogation by(?) the vogue(?)
    This dog was slain—we'd all beware of that.

        'Upon the fatal death of the Earl of Tweeddale's dog
        most valiantly slain by the Lord Commissioner at one
        sheriff'

    Poetry Box VIII/34

11531   It is no wonder you shed tears; for when
    A sign of heaven.

        Sir Thomas Urquhart, 'To Mistress Craven's waiting
        maid, whilst she was weeping the first night, that her
        mistress was married'

    fb.217, p. 218

11532   It is not always folly that engages
    Did challenge Phryno to the single combat.

        [Sir Thomas Urquhart], 'That to shun the hazard of
        entering in duel is not to be preferred to the saving of
        one's reputation'

    fb.217, p. 506

11533   It is not, Celia, in our power
    To live, because w' are sure to die?

        Sir G[eorge] Etherege, 'To a lady, asking him how
        long he could love her'
        [Crum 11842]

    Poetry Box IV/53; c.549, p. 70

11534   It is not every day, | A genius does arise;
    As good and great a poet, | A Cicero,—or me?

        Abraham Oakes, 'The comparison: an humorous
        epigram'

    c.50, p. 64

11535   It is not now a fortnight since
    The sale of Rex Platonicus.

        [Richard Corbett], 'A certain grave poem . . . styled
        liber novus de adventu regis ad Cantabrigiam . . .
        faithfully translated into English with some few
        additions . . . to the tune of Bonny Nell' [March
        1614/15; answered by 'A ballad late was made . . .']

    b.197, p. 69; see also 'It is not yet . . .'.

11536   It is not to be wonder'd at,
    More favorably us'd than he!

        [from 'The amours of Alatheus and Eustathea']

    c.379/1, p. 46

11537   It is not worth your care;
    As high, as full, as fair.

        [George Daniel]

    b.121, fol. 59

11538 It is not yet a fortnight since
I'th' sale of Rex platonicus.

[Richard Corbett], 'A grave poem as it was
presented . . . before His Majesty in Cambridge'
[March 1614/15]
[Crum 11853]

Poetry Box VI/108; b.200, p. 346; see also 'It is not
now . . .'.

11539 It is so difficult a task
Fixt principles her rule.

'On Miss ———'s character'

c.546

11540 It is the Lord that rules the world, which he
We strove, at least, our gratitude to pay.

George Montagu, 'Psalm the 97th paraphrased'

fc.135, p. 8

11541 It is the nature of the fates
They weave and make our winding sheet.

'Upon the three fatal sisters'

b.356, p. 132

11542 It is thought Mr. Sandys had small reason to boast
As if God had sent meat, and the devil sent cooks.

W[illiam] Taylor, 'On the motion in the House of
Commons against Sir Robert Walpole—Friday
February 13—1740/1'

c.360/1, p. 91

11543 It is to dive in women's kind embraces
In th'knowledge of the subject, which it touches.

Sir Thomas Urquhart, 'A woman, is a knowledge
theoretic'

fb.217, p. 51

11544 It is true that our eyes do not feed in its cheek
May that soul lovely Ann be united to mine!

[William Hayley], 'Song ballad Sept. 17th'

File 6962

11545 It is unjust to blame or praise,
Thy courage has been tried.

[N. Herbert], 'Upon Admiral Byng and Genl.
Blakeney'

Spence Papers, folder 91

11546 It is with pleasure, I observe
To praise the great and famed three.

'To Mrs. Bucks and Hardcastle on their charity in
school for poor girls and clothing them plain and neat'

Poetry Box IV/179

11547 It is your prayer (I hope) these words enfold
If God's love draw us not, his rod should beat.

W. C., 'To the wor[shipful] Edward Bagot Esq.
Anagramma . . . God draw, beat'

Poetry Box VI/25

11548 [It] lies beyond [the] power [of] [this] to smother
It's evenly poised betwixt hope and fear.

b.205, fol. IV

11549 It matters not, good folks, say what you will,
Would warm you[r] beauty, and adorn our youth.

[Robert Hitchcock], 'Epilogue to The macaroni'

c.115

11550 It must be done my soul but 'tis a strange
With horror they resign'd to the untried abyss.

[John] Norris, of Bemerton, 'On death'

c.244, p. 75; c. 258; c. 548; c.156, p. 57 (var.); c.547, p. 179
(var.)

11551 It must be so—the bubble soon must break
Which leads to the bright realm of ever-during day.

'The dying wish'

b.322, p. 37

11552 It must be so—thou gen'rous youth, farewell.
Flourish in summer suns, and genial air.

[John Bunce], 'To the memory of Mr Lewis
Duncombe, late of Merton College, Oxon. obiit 26
Decembr 1730 ætatis 19' [enclosed in a letter to his
uncle William Duncombe, Brensett, 9 Feb. 1730/1]

File 16983 (autogr.)

11553 It oft has been agreed, you know,
Where death no more shall intervene.

'Written by a gentleman to his wife on the tenth
anniversary of their marriage'

c.391, p. 103

11554 It oft my puzzl'd pericranium racks
A waxen candle and bronz'd candlestick.

'The double resolver'

fc.76.iii/214

11555 It seems that masks do women much disgrace,
Sith when they wear them they do hide their face.

[Samuel Pick], 'On women's masks'

c.356

11556 It seems that prologues are so much of course
And bid anew forgotten manners live.

Charles Yorke, 'Prologue to the Adelphi of Terence'

Poetry Box I/109

11557 It seems the lions now are not so wild
Which he begot not in the lion's den.

[Sir Thomas Urquhart], 'Of one John Bunce who had six children with his wife Jean Lyon'

fb.217, p. 388

11558 It should not have been set down as a fable,
Being of such metamorphosises full.

Sir Thomas Urquhart, 'That in all ages there have been cuckolds'

fb.217, p. 122

11559 It wakes thy wonder young and gentle friend
Soul to thy shadow to thy portrait grace.

[William Hayley], 'Sonnet . . . Sept. 8 [1800]'

File 6968

11560 It wants an epithet, ingratitude,
A mighty monarch here, a saint above.

'An essay to the King on the late transactions by the Dutch upon our coasts'

fb.108, p. 303

11561 It was a dismal and a fearful night,
When grief and misery can be join'd with verse.

[Abraham] Cowley, 'On the death of Mr. William Harvey'

c.244, p. 213

11562 It was a lover and his lass
How that life is but a flower | In spring time—&c.

[William Shakespeare], 'Rondeau. Words (with alt[ernative?]s from Sh[akespeare])'

c.528/52 (stanzas 1–3)

11563 It was a most unfriendly part
Steals to her sleeping spouse to bed.

[Jonathan] Swift, 'The journal of a modern lady' [pr. 1729? (Foxon S863)]

fc.60, p. 14

11564 It was a squire of low degree
Amen amen for charity.

'The squire of low degree'

fc.179

11565 It was a summer evening,
But 'twas a famous victory.

Robert Southey, 'The battle of Blenheim'

File 14207

11566 It was a winter's evening, and fast fell down the
                                                    snow
Then raised her eyes, to heaven, then closed them
                                                    slow and died.

J[ohn] Aikin, 'A ballad'

c.341, p. 49; c.83/1, no. 43

11567 It was Daniel's faith that stopt the lion's rage
Had I but only Daniel's lions there.

'Daniel 6.23'

c.160, fol. 51v [bis]; see also 'Fierce lions roaring . . .'.

11568 It was decreed that I should die
Which soon brought me to my long home.

'Epitaph at Woodstock on one killed by a rocket. 1714'

c.360/3, no. 146

11569 It was in the sweet month of May
My shepherd's holiday . . . .

'A new song called fair Clemency' [Bridlington, 29 Dec. 1776]

Poetry Box IV/167 (incomplete)

11570 It was my Lord the dext'rous shift,
To save my own and other souls.

[Jonathan Smedley], 'A petition to his Grace the Duke of Grafton' [answered by Swift's 'Dear Smed . . .' pr. Dublin, 1724 (Foxon S498)]

c.176, p. 115

11571 It was no flea on blanket playing
He rose a critical reviewer.

'A palinodical fable for the reviewers published in the St James' chronicle 1770'

Poetry Box IV/87

11572 It was not thou my Brutus. Caesar cried
And this Craterus, that Hephestion be.

J[ohn] Hobart], 'The same day I sent the last I sent this his own answer to the first'

b.131, p. 36

11573 It was on a certain Sunday
Let him go farewell him.

'A song'

c.536

11574 It was said by the courtiers of Louis's nation
She only regretted their queen was a woman.

'Epigram'

c.90

11575 It was that month in which the righteous maid
But have the gospel of free liberty . . . .

   [Edmund Spenser], 'Prosopopæia [or Mother
   Hubbard's tale]'
   [Crum 11888]
   b.65, p. 53 (ll. 1–478)

11576 It was that time when fiery Cancer's heat
Until this, that, and these, do prove them to your
                                              pain.

   [R. M.]
   Poetry Box VI/4

11577 It was the hour of midnight
'But thou at heart shalt sicken.'

   [ ] Ellison, 'From Anacreon 3d . . . 1780'
   Greatheed Box/30

11578 It was the spring, and flowers were in contest
Methinks looks whiter than it was before.

   Rob[er]t Wild, 'In memory of Mrs. E. T., who died
   April 7, 1659'
   c.166, p. 280

11579 It was the time when silly bees could speak
'Twas not tobacco stupefied my brain.

   [Robert Devereux, 2nd earl of Essex], 'The complaint
   of the bee'
   [Crum 11876, 'was a time']
   File 19020

11580 It was the word that spake it
That I believe and take it.

   Eliz[abeth I, queen of England?], 'The answer of the
   Lady Eliz: when she was asked in her sister's reign
   (Queen Mary's) what her thoughts were of the
   sacrament'
   b.209, p. 138; see also 'Christ (the word) . . .'.

11581 It was when the dark lantern of the night
I found my belly wet and slept again.

   'The E. of R[ochester's] dream'
   [Crum 11895, 'mantle of the night']
   fb.70, p. 50

11582 It were more fit that you relics should strow
Therefore we should as soon's we can desist.

   [Sir Thomas Urquhart], 'Too much bewailing and
   grief is to be avoided at funerals'
   fb.217, p. 529

11583 It would not be an universal case
It is but justice by the talion law.

   [Sir Thomas Urquhart], 'Ingratitude is such a [?] vice
   that even those who incline most against it are not
   most free of it'
   fb.217, p. 521

11584 Italian hearts mun be as hard as stan
To ken or to prolong death's fatal hour.

   'An elegy occasioned by the death of the Revd. [?]
   Alexander Sinclair who departed the world the first
   day of April 1721' [docket title: 'Sawney Sinclair's
   elegy']
   File 13409

11585 It's found in most countries, yet not in earth, nor
                                              sea
And always in its proper place, where you may it
                                              find.

   'A riddle on the letter M'
   c.360/1, p. 1

11586 It's hey for th'lads of our town eyne!
And hey for sick anither!

   M[ichael] L[ort?], 'The upshot or Orton merry night
   a rhyming narrative attempted in the Cumberland
   dialect . . .'
   c.155, fol. 1

11587 It's more than time (good Lady) for to end
In gloria cum excelsis Deo. Amen.

   a.6, p. 34

11588 It's not at court 'mongst grandees and renown'd
Because they in too perfect channels flow.

   [Mrs. Christian Kerr], 'On Astrea and Damon's
   friendship a poem presented for a New Year's gift
   1720'
   c.102, p. 97

11589 It's not (dear love) that amber twist
No liberty can make me free.

   [Mrs. Christian Kerr?], 'Upon receiving a present of
   hair'
   c.102, p. 26

11590 It's now my part to choose, yours to advise,
What you believe to be most safe and wise.

   'Orondatus to Statira (both in danger)'
   c.189, p. 18

11591 It's now since I began to reign
For Ryswick, and partition.

   'The lamentation of the French King for the death of
   K[ing] William—a ballad to the tune of, The dragon
   of Wantley'
   c.111, p. 85

11592 It's only wealth prevails, let him be base,
That can with money, both his pockets fill.

   'On riches . . . January 2nd anno Domini 1784'
   c.93

11593 It's true, you need no trophies to your hearse;
That you that lived so, should die a monster.

   'Respontio' [to 'I need no trophies . . .']
   b.126, p. 23

11594 I've a cask of Alban wine
Like a rush-light, go out on, a save-all.

   [William Popple, trans.], '[Horace] book 4th: ode
   11th: to Phyllis'
   fc.104/2, p. 372 [bis]

11595 I've been importun'd by some friends to tell
Will please the Christians and amaze the Turks.

   [Sir Aston Cokayne], 'To Captain Mouther'
   b.275, p. 76

11596 I've been where so many Puritans dwell,
Too long with them; and so much for today.

   Abraham Cowley, 'A Puritan lecture described by . . .'
   fb.108, p. 5

11597 I've but one wife, (quo' Hodge,) and she
When each was plagu'd with half a score?

   John Lockman, 'Hen-pecked Hodge . . . 1731'
   c.267/1, p. 108; c.268 (first part), p. 92

11598 I've dared our Cestrian patriots and Maecenas
That men is only blest who thinks he is.

   Samuel Edwards, 'To my much honored master and
   benefactor Charles Cholmondeley esq . . . .poor
   Pilgaric's case'
   Poetry Box VII/23

11599 I've gravely trac'd that C. B. S.
Nor place was e'er from pride quite free.

   'An answer to the riddle on page [ ]'
   c.578, p. 106

11600 I've heard of Afric monsters strangely rare,
Derive your own religion from Joan's placket.

   'On Pope Joan by a gentleman of Christ Church in
   Oxford'
   fb.142, p. 24

11601 I've heard of islands floating, and removed,
In all your greatness, whatsoe'er you are.

   [Richard] Corbett, '1618 [i.e., 1623]. Dr. Corbett to
   Marquis Buckingham' [on the Spanish match, 1623]
   b.200, p. 24; see also 'I've read . . .'.

11602 I've heard the muses were still soft and kind
Blast great Apollo with perpetual shame.

   'Advice to Apollo'
   [Crum 11916; POAS I.393]
   b.327, f. 24; b.371, no. 2

11603 I've heard, tho' plac'd at humble distance
To help the family of York.

   Rev. [ ] Arden, 'To the nobility and gentry at Althorp
   [seat of Lord Spencer], after a Christmas country
   dance; John York fiddler and blacksmith sendeth
   greeting' [c. 1799]
   Smith Papers, folder 74/22, folder 75/23

11604 I've lost my love, I know not where,
'Tis she, have mercy; for I die.

   [Robert Merry], 'Madness'
   Greatheed Box/9

11605 I've lost my mistress, horse, and wife,
I'm sorry for my horse.

   'A gentleman losing his mistress, his horse, and his
   wife all at the same time, made the following lines'
   c.378, p. 24; c.115

11606 I've oft been ask'd by plodding souls
To fill my glass again.

   Poetry Box XII/111[1]

11607 I've often heard for poets used to tell't
There dwells Apollo(?), with the happy Spence.

   Mrs. [ ] Hynard ('teacher of a school of young ladies,
   in Old Palace Yard')
   Spence Papers, folder 113

11608 I've often heard, yet ne'er believed
Imagination fade!

   'Answer from Delia to L[or]d W[illia]m G[ordon] on
   his leaving Dalkeith' [1755]
   Poetry Box III/15

11609 I've read of islands floating and remov'd
In all your greatness whatsoe'er you are.

   [Richard] Corbett, 'Dr. Corbett's letter to the Duke
   of Buckingham being in Spain' [1623]
   [Crum 11920]
   b.197, p. 119; b.208, p. 253; see also 'I've heard . . .'.

11610 I've search'd the fair quite round and round
Can doom to death, no cat devour.

   John Johnson, 'Given with a toy, a dove, a fairing to a
   little boy'
   c.229/2, fol. 26v

11611 I've seen, what very few have seen beside,
And, in his gayest altitudes, John Far.

   John Lockman, 'Seven wonders seen in Salisbury . . .
   June 1730'
   c.267/1, p. 244; c.268 (first part), p. 1

11612 I've strove in vain–here take my heart,
Unable to dislodge th' imper'ous guest.

    Mary Lepipre, 'The concession . . . 1711. To Strephon'
c.360/3, no. 258

11613 I've strove long time but strove in vain,
Grateful to live, prepared to die.

    M. Dickinson, 'From a simple poet on a watch.
From . . . to A[nn] Dickinson'

c.391

I've that within which baffles all their art,   11614
A burning fever and a sunken heart.

    'By a youth who refused advice from a physician'
c.93

I've thought, the fair Clarissa cries   11615
'Tis like a doctor—like a whale.

    [Phanuel Bacon], 'Conundrums [1]' [answered by
'Why are my eyes, Sir . . .']
[Crum 11929]

Poetry Box XIV/188; c.74 ('To raise up something like a
whale' and following); c.237, fol. 43

J

J0001 Jack an acrostic made on Celia's name,
Why, like for like, a stick across his back.

   'An epigram'

c.578, p. 23

J0002 Jack and Joan's twa queer fellaws
And Jacky was put in the stove(?) at the door.

   'Jack and Joan a comic song . . . written . . . 1796'

c.179, p. 63

J0003 Jack eating rotten cheese did say
And with the selfsame weapon too.

c.546, p. 33

J0004 Jack Gospel's married to a Jewish fool
Maybe produc'd a Turk.

   'On a Protestant marrying a Jew'

c.546, p. 32

J0005 Jack of Norfolk, be not too bold
For Dicken thy master is bought and sold.

   'Wrote on the Duke of Norfolk's gate, the even[ing]
   before the battle of Bosworth Field—1485'

c.360/2, no. 259

J0006 Jack Plow, your wife: Dick sows her till she breer
                           [sic]:
Yet you the harvest reap from both, each year.

   Sir Thomas Urquhart, 'To a certain cuckold, whose
   wife was yearly with child'

fb.217, p. 304

J0007 Jack prov'd an alibi when late arraign'd
Should be so very like an errant knave!

   R[ichard] V[ernon] S[adleir], 'Epigram occasioned by
   a late trial for felony'

c.106, p. 81

J0008 Jack Tar from his wife had been absent some years
There's nothing the matter (disclosing her pad).

   'Extempore'

c.344

J0009 Jack Vainlove, to show his most exquisite taste,
Which alas, before morning, produced a fine lad.

   'Another'

c.344

J0010 James the first in marriage did yet
This James the first short while possest the throne.

   '[Rulers of Scotland] 9'

fa.4, fol. 28v

J0011 James the second that noble famous king
Unto his wife which was a lusty queen.

   '[Rulers of Scotland] 10'

fa.4, fol. 28v

J0012 James the third of noble memory
The same King James the fourth to him she bore.

   '[Rulers of Scotland] 11'

fa.4, fol. 28v

J0013 Janus did ever to thy wond'ring eyes
And governs but to bless.

   [Edmund Smith], 'Upon the victory at Blenheim'
   [New Year's ode, 1705 (Foxon S514)]
   [Crum J16]

fc.24, p. 17 (attr. F. S.)

J0014 Japlow once more to thy lov'd shades I come,
And undivulg'd my pious sorrows flow.

   [Daniel King?], 'Lines written under the tulip tree in
   the garden upon his revisiting Japlow'

Greatheed Box/78

J0015 Jar! Who born with me, dost hold
Stars, and rise to light us home.

   [William Popple, trans.], '[Horace] book 3rd. ode 21st.
   To his jar'

fc.104/2, p. 280

J0016 Jealous and with love o'erflowing
In the trials he ordains.

   [William Cowper, trans.], 'Love pure and fervent.
   Vol. 4. Son. 31' [of Jeanne Guion's 'Spiritual songs']

c.470 (autogr.)

J0017 Jean loveth James, whose humer is so Gothic,
And both in other's arms revive together.

   Sir Thomas Urquhart, 'The severally inflicted wounds
   of Cupid's darts, love being whiles reciprocal, whiles
   not'

fb.217, p. 205

J0018 Jehovah bow thine ear and hear
Dost help and comfort me.

    'Psal: 86'

    b.217, p. 35

J0019 Jehovah gives the high command
'Tis full, 'tis all perfection there.

    T[homas] S[tevens], 'Composed for a harvest sermon
    Lord's day evening August the 6 1780'

    c.259, p. 98

J0020 Jehovah God, that dost me save
All those I knew, in darkness live.

    'Psal: 88'

    b.217, p. 39

J0021 Jehovah hear my pray'r and let
Shall stand forever sure.

    'Psal: 102'

    b.217, p. 72

J0022 Jehovah here, of nothing, all things makes,
To place them by themselves, from holy writ.

    [verses on the books of the Old Testament; pr.
    Dublin, 1726? (Foxon H259)]

    fb.69, p. 121

J0023 Jehovah preserve and restore to his own
And to thee what is thine.

    'A song to the tune of Ianthe the lovely &c.' [on the
    Old Pretender]
    [Crum J28, 'to his throne']

    c.570/1, p. 156

J0024 Jehovah reigneth, cloth'd
Thy house to length of days.

    'Psal: 93'

    b.217, p. 57

J0025 Jehovah reigneth let the earth
Of his true holiness.

    'Psal: 97'

    b.217, p. 65

J0026 Jehovah reigns, let every nation hear,
And deep within your inmost hearts adore him.

    [Anna Laetitia] (Aikin) [Barbauld], 'A hymn'

    c.487, p. 11

J0027 Jehovah reigns! Messiah King,
Thy church forever holy be.

    'Psalm 93. Evening prayer'

    c.264/2, p. 101

J0028 Jehovah reigns; the people much
Our God is holiness.

    'Psal: 99'

    b.217, p. 68

J0029 Jehovah thou hast been our place
Confirm'd be they by thee.

    'Psal: 90'

    b.217, p. 48

J0030 Jehovah to his prophet gives command:
Yea onward march, and know no weariness.

    'Blessings temporal and spiritual, promised to the
    royal house of David, and the tribe of Judah. Isaiah
    chap 40 from [Bishop Lowth's version]'

    c.515, fol. 33v

J0031 Jehovah's kindnesses in songs
And aye Amen Amen.

    'Psal 89'

    b.217, p. 40

J0032 Jehu's crown'd king, Jehu the king must fall
Princes like Jehu, would but worship Baal.

    [Francis Quarles], 'On Baal's priests' [Divine
    fancies II, 41]

    b.137, p. 169

J0033 Jenny being caught
If ever we punished any.

    Poetry Box VI/21

J0034 Jenny Bull the other day,
If that be liberty.

    'On liberty'

    c.83/2, no. 526

J0035 Jenny came the other day
And serv'd her—as I mount(?) the cask.

    [John] Winter, 'An epigram'

    c.74

J0036 Jenny the wanton'st slut alive
Sh'as wept herself into a stone.

    [Robert Cholmeley], 'A reasonable affliction, or: the
    modern Pict'

    c.190, p. 192

J0037 Jerusalem's curse shall never light on me
For here a stone upon a stone we see.

    Ben[jamin] Stone, 'Ben Stone upon himself'
    [Crum J41]

    b.208, p. 59; b.62, p. 77; b.356, p. 244

J0038 Jesu Christ of heaven king
That never shall have end.

'Eglamour of Artas'

fc.179

J0039 Jesu is in my ear, his sacred name
Confirmed with joy by heaven's eternal King.

George Herbert, 'A poem of . . . in his Temple on the
picture of Jesus'
[Crum J44, 'in my heart']

b.202, p. 97 (with six more lines)

J0040 Jesu Lord of myztes most
Sayeth amen for charity.

'Tundale' [eighteenth-century copy of a
fifteenth-century poem]

fc.179

J0041 Jesu! sweet beyond expressing!
Thus to praise thee, God most high.

'An hymn to Jesus'

c.167, p. 1

J0042 Jesu, that suffer'd bitter passion and pain
One thousand, four hundred, fourscore and seven.

'Epitaph in All Hallows the less in Thames Street
London–on John Chamberlain and his wives'

c.360/3, no. 142

J0043 Jesu! who from thy Father's throne,
By all ador'd, belov'd, obey'd.

[John Austin], 'Hym: 29' [Hymn xxix, Devotions in
the ancient way of offices, 1672, p. 249]

c.178, p. 27

J0044 Jesu! whose grace directs thy priests
Its own eternal glorious rays.

[John Austin], 'Hym: 30' [Hymn xxxi, Devotions in
the ancient way of offices, 1672, p. 280]

c.178, p. 28

J0045 Jesuits! Your bark so many thousands saves;
Whether ye are of God, or of the devil.

John Lockman, 'The doubt'

c.267/1, p. 172; c.268 (first part), p. 11

J0046 Jesus, accept the praise
Adorned with Christ and meet for God.

'Hymn 106'

c.562, p. 145

J0047 Jesus appears, and in him shines
Still show the righteousness of God.

[Thomas Stevens?], 'Lord's day morning Matt:
5.17 &c.'

c.259, p. 106

J0048 Jesus Christ both God and man
Save thy servant Jernegan.

'On an ancient knight Sir Jernegan buried crosslegged
at Somerby in Suffolk some hundred years since'
[Crum J59]

fb.143, p. 19; c.158, p. 105

J0049 Jesus Christ is risen today
Where the angels ever cry. Hallelujah

[Thomas Stevens?], 'A hymn for Easter Sunday'

c.259, p. 67

J0050 Jesus drinks the bitter cup,
Th' immortal King of Heaven!

'On the crucifixion'

Poetry Box v/92

J0051 Jesus friend of sinners hear,
And bid me sin no more.

'Hymn 95th'

c.562, p. 128

J0052 Jesus from whom all blessings flow,
Shall with thy people live, and die.

'Hymn 73d'

c.562, p. 91

J0053 Jesus gives us true repentance
Come to us thro' J[esus'] blood.

[Hymn]

c.180, p. 82

J0054 Jesus God of my salvation,
Burn with a pure seraphic flame.

'Hymn 13th'

c.562, p. 15

J0055 Jesus God of my salvation
Save me who for me have died.

'Hymn 21st'

c.562, p. 24

J0056 Jesus, I lift mine eyes
For his redeeming love?

[Thomas Stevens?], 'Hymn the 3rd'

c.259

J0057 Jesus I love thy charming name,
The antidote of death.

P[hilip] Doddridge, 'Christ precious to the believer
Pet: II. 7'

c.493, p. 12; c.259, p. 62; c.562, p. 17

J0058 Jesus invites his saints
And ev'ry voice be praise.

    [Isaac Watts, Hymns and spiritual songs (1707),
    bk. III, Hymn 2]

c.180, p. 42

J0059 Jesus is gone above the skies
To fetch our longing spirits home.

    [Isaac Watts. Hymns and spiritual songs (1707),
    bk. III, Hymn 6]

c.180, p. 44

J0060 Jesus is holy and he calls
Do honor to his word.

    T[homas] S[tevens], 'Another [hymn sung after
    Mr. Jabez Brown's sermon]'

c.259, p. 94

J0061 Jesus is the chiefest good,
Jesus' blood has bought us heav'n.

    [Hymn]

c.180, p. 79

J0062 Jesus Lord we look to thee
Show how true believers die.

    'Hymn 32d'

c.562, p. 37

J0063 Jesus must bear the curse
To make salvation mine.

    [Thomas Stevens?]

c.259, p. 106

J0064 Jesus my all to heaven is gone
And say, 'Behold the way to God.'

    'Hymn 50th'

c.562, p. 59

J0065 Jesus, my life, thyself apply,
A temple built by God.

    'Hymn 84th'

c.562, p. 111

J0066 Jesus my Lord shall have my praise
Must be admired and be ador'd.

    T[homas] S[tevens]

c.259, p. 129

J0067 Jesus my truth, my way,
This fainting soul of mine.

    'Hymn 2d'

c.562, p. 2

J0068 Jesus of Naz'reth, humble Beth'lem's light,
The pious usurer reaps at least a hundredfold.

    [Simon] Patrick, 'The fasters' hymn. From
    Prudentius'

c.352, p. 26

J0069 Jesus our soul's delightful choice
As shades despair'd by opening light.

    P[hilip] Doddridge, 'On the struggle between faith
    and unbelief from Mark IX. 24'

c.493, p. 63

J0070 Jesus, shall I never be
Jesus is a perfect mind.

    'Hymn 93d'

c.562, p. 123

J0071 Jesus soft harmonious name,
Only sing and praise and love.

    'Hymn 79th'

c.562, p. 102

J0072 Jesus that suffer'd bitter passion and pain
A thousand four hundred fourscore and seven.

    'All Hallows the Less'

fb.68, p. 130

J0073 Jesus, the God, invites us here,
For 'tis immortal food!

    [Isaac Watts, Hymn]

c.180, p. 54

J0074 Jesus the shepherd long foretold
But shuts itself against his sin.

    [Thomas Stevens?]

c.259, p. 99

J0075 Jesus thou art my righteousness
And all my soul be love.

    'Hymn 25th'

c.562, p. 29

J0076 Jesus thy saints attend thy voice
Thro' all thy Zion's happy ground.

    T[homas] S[tevens]

c.259, p. 144

J0077 Jesus! we bow before thy feet!
A loud hosanna 'round the place!

    [Isaac Watts, Hymns and spiritual songs (1707),
    bk. III, Hymn 18]

c.180, p. 53

J0078 Jesus we hail thy bride, and thee
Is guided by thine eye.

T[homas] S[tevens], 'Evening same day exposition
from Ruth 4.11.12'

c.259, p. 102

J0079 Jesus, with all thy saints above,
Our saints to feel his grace.

[Isaac Watts, Hymns and spiritual songs (1707), bk. II,
Hymn 29]

c.180, p. 4

J0080 Jewels being lost are found again this never
This lost but once, and once lost, lost forever.

'Of virginity'
[Crum J104]

b.205, fol. 24v

J0081 Joan vows to hearten timorous youth
Joan does believe she saw the Devil.

c.546, p. 32

J0082 Job silent stood, when from a thick'ning cloud
Firm peace recovered soon, and wonted calm.

W[illia]m Thompson, Trinity College Dublin, 'Job
chapters 38. 39. 40. 41. paraphrased in blank verse
by . . .' [in imitation of Milton; pr. Dublin 1726
(Foxon T168)]

c.244, p. 110

J0083 Job somewhere says that man's a worm
Where'er her steps shall range!

R[ichard] V[ernon] S[adleir], 'To Catan [Tanket],
who killed an earwig on her neck—after a
conversation on transmigration'

c.106, p. 39

J0084 Jockey was a lively(?) lad and Jamie's swarth and
tawny

But I love only Sawney.

[Thomas D'Urfey]

b.226, p. 72

J0085 Joe hates a sycophant; it shows
Self-love is not a fault of Joe's.

'Epigram'

Diggle Box: Poetry Box XI/69

J0086 John a suit'ring when [went] to Joan
And give me the gay gold ring.

'23d song John's courtship to Joan'

Accession 97.7.40, p. 42

J0087 John Balliol King of the Scots
Built this college for a parcel of sots.

'On Balliol Coll[ege] Oxon'

c.74

J0088 John Bell broken-brow
Without mickle strife.

'Epitaph the 2nd at Farlam on the west marches
toward Scotland, near Naworth Castle'
[Crum J114]

c.158, p. 103; fb.143, p. 15; c.229/1, fol. 48v (var.; 'John
Bell of Brekenbow')

J0089 John Bonsar blue hen
No more let every idle ass . . . .

'[from] Poor Robin. Or a collection of poems . . .
for . . . 1798' [Poor Robin's almanac, 1798]

c.179, p. 27 (incomplete)

J0090 John call'd for candles at approach of night
But Arabin came in and all was light.

'An incident that occurred at the Old Bailey where the
uncommon Serjeant was presiding'

fc.76.iii/214

J0091 John Chambers, till death brought him here
For liberal hospitality.

'Abbey-Holme Feb. VII: 1655'

c.547, p. 326

J0092 John Claxton lies here,
Who knows?—He may serve them again!

'The following lines were intended to commend John
Claxton (a glover) late of East Dereham, who died
Feby. 21th 1790 aged 50 years . . .'

c.94

J0093 John come kiss me now
And make no more ado.

'Calvinistical hymn'

c.81/1, no. 354

J0094 John Gilpin was a citizen
May I be there to see!

[William Cowper], 'The facetious history of John
Gilpin, to the tune of Chevy Chase'

c.150, p. 168; c.488, p. 18 (attr. J. C[arter])

J0095 John Hall still lives, and yet in hope
To live by the bell when you die by the rope.

'His answer' [to 'Here lies John Hall']
[Crum J118, 'Hall is alive']

b.356, p. 247

J0096 John Lettice's complaint, and indeed with some
                                                    reason
And grant that in future each Lettice may cabbage.

> 'Paraphrase [of 'All you that come my grave to
> see . . .'] . . . Nov. 28th 1797'
>
> c.113/28

J0097 John Palfreyman which lieth here
Also his father when he dies.

> 'Epitaph [on a basket maker] in Grantham
> churchyard'
> [Crum J121]
>
> c.360/1, p. 231

J0098 John Presbyter and the sons of the pope
By the moans of Loyola and Calvin the fox. |
                                Which nobody can deny

> 'Geneva and Rome. Or the zeal of both boiling over in
> an earnest dispute . . .'
>
> b.111, p. 464

J0099 John rests below. A man more infamous
For they must bear the burthen of thy crime.

> Robert Southey, 'Epitaph on K. John'
>
> File 14215

J0100 John run so long, and run so fast,
He distanc'd all—and run away.

> 'An epigram on a gentleman who expended his whole
> fortune in horse racing'
>
> c.487, p. 77

J0101 John Rutherford is my name,
But do not think it worth my while.

> John Rutherford
>
> c.93

J0102 John Thompson lieth here, bachelor in divinity,
To God's glory, who grant that we his godly heart
                                                    pursue.

> 'An epitaph in the royal chapel of St. George in
> Windsor Castle, near the ascent to the choir. 1571'
>
> c.360/3, no. 64

J0103 John Townsend lies here,
This heavy odd lump of a stone.

> 'An epitaph on Mr. J[oh]n Townsend of Oxon . . . thus
> Englished'
>
> c.233, p. 120

J0104 Johnny Carnegie lies here
I'll willingly give him leave.

> 'An epitaph on a tombstone at [ ] in Scotland an
> imitation of Mr. Prior's celebrated epitaph for
> himself'
>
> c.360/3, no. 5

J0105 Join all you sweet fair graces leave today
Even you I wish may all these blessings share.

> 'An epithalamy presented on the names and nuptials of
> the much honored James Fortery esq. And the most
> truly virtuous-minded lady Mary Fortery his most
> endeared consort' [c. 1650?]
>
> File 17867

J0106 Join Hadleigh to lament your loss, your sexton old
                                                John Hilles
Who never joy'd since Bowtell broke his head.

> 'Epitaphium de vita et morte Johannes Hilles [d.
> 5 March 1625]'
>
> b.197, p. 227

J0107 Join morals to your physic that you may
Leaarn both your bod', and soul's anatomy.

> Sir Thomas Urquhart, 'How a man shall come to
> know himself'
>
> fb.217, p. 117

J0108 Join thy lips, breathing soul to mine,
Taste we what fruit the country yields.

> 'A lover to his mistress'
> [cf. Crum J127]
>
> c.189, p. 29

J0109 Jolly Roger Twangdillo of Plowden Hill
'Twas she that brought down Twangdillo.

> [Elizabeth Amherst]
> [Crum J130]
>
> Poetry Box I/117

J0110 Jonah, imprisoned within the womb
Jonah was vomited upon the land.

> [William Sandys?], 'Jonah the prophet in the whale's
> belly chap: 2d'
>
> b.230, p. 87

J0111 Jove heavily in clouds brings on the day,
The old world he destroy'd, she built a new.

> c.53, fol. 23

J0112 Jove, issu'd Latonid, endow'd with cunning
What will give most contentment to the reader.

> Sir Thomas Urquhart, 'The invocation to Apollo'
> [preceding Urquhart's epigrams]
>
> fb.217, p. 33

J0113 Jove said—let there be light. And lo!
The venal herd obey'd his nod!!

> 'Candle and windows tax'
>
> c.81/1, no. 233

JO114 Jove summon'd a committee lately on high,
And pronounce they consist in war, love and wine.

> [Helen Craik], 'The soldiers' joy. A song'
>
> c.375, p. 40

JO115 Jove's brain-babe Pallas kept her maidenhead,
Whilst springs of virtue in the brains reside.

> Sir Thomas Urquhart, 'Of Eva, and Minerva'
>
> fb.217, p. 166

JO116 Joy in the gates of Jerusalem
Pace be in Sion.

> 'Catches [4]'
>
> b.356, p. 72

JO117 Joy is a serious thing, nay ev'n severe,
Exalts the soul to a seraphic state.

> [Sir Philip Wodehouse], 'Upon Seneca's Res
> severa . . .'
>
> b.131, p. 6

JO118 Joy is life's [in the] world's vast round
[Yet when] drain'd fullest—freshest is.

> 'Vera voluptas'
>
> b.205, fol. 14r

JO119 Joy single known is only known in part
Smiles at the idle impotence of power.

> 'Poetry; by a Quaker'
>
> c.344, p. 7

JO120 Joy to my col'nel, for the Twentieth's thine,
Succeeding both the friends [?] [?].

> D[avid] G[arrick], 'On Coll. [Bernard] Hale's
> promotion'
>
> Acquisition 92.3.1ff.

JO121 Joy ushers grief: and after grief comes joy:
Thus all our life in fear, or hope we 'mploy.

> Sir Thomas Urquhart, 'The vicissitude of human
> passions'
>
> fb.217, p. 116

JO122 Judge and revenge my cause O Lord
Even so be it therefore.

> [Thomas Sternhold and John Hopkins], 'The 19
> psalm for deliverance from enemies and that he may
> praise God freely' [verses from Psalms 41–43]
> [cf. Crum J157]
>
> a.3, fol. 93

JO123 Judge not, and so you shall not judged be,
As do the scribes, but with authority.

> Sir John Strangways, 'The seventh chapter of St.
> Matthew . . . 1665'
>
> b.304, p. 167

JO124 Judge not in haste, but wait and see
If not, why then's the time to hiss.

> 'On the suspicion of the late Great Commoner
> [William Pitt the elder]'
>
> c.157, p. 89

JO125 Judge not that field, because 'tis stubble
Judge not: their treasure is within.

> [Francis Quarles, 'On outward show']
> [Crum J161]
>
> b.156, p. 17

JO126 Judge not too fast: this tree that doth appear
A Saul today, may prove a Paul the next.

> [Francis Quarles], 'On rash judgment'
> [Crum J162]
>
> b.137, p. 182

JO127 Judge then, did record ever round thine ear
Have, with their issue died for want of food.

> c.158, p. 29

JO128 Judges being gods; it ought to be the fashion,
To deal with them by angel's mediation.

> Sir Thomas Urquhart, 'Bribery by a Roman Catholic
> warranted from the scripture a paradox'
>
> fb.217, p. 82

JO129 Judicious man we offer willingly
Lay(?) all the building flat as thou'st begun.

> [Thomas Gurney], 'To Mr. John Gill on his first part
> of The cause of God and truth' [acrostic]
>
> c.213

JO130 Juggins had all the various powers of art,
With equal skill to dress the feasts of gods.

> [Phanuel Bacon], 'A poem in praise of Tho. Juggins an
> Oxford cook' [d. 1719]
> [Crum J169]
>
> c.172, p. 14

JO131 Julia of all the village fair,
Her soul to Edward flew.

> [ ] Farrell, 'Julia a ballad'
>
> c.83/2, no. 673

JO132 Julian how comes it that of late we see
The whores, rogues, bawds and rake-hells of
Whitehall.

> 'To [Robert] Julian'
> [Crum J173]
>
> fb.68, p. 131

JO133 Julian, in verse to ease thy wants I write
And villain Frank f—— Mazarine no more.

'To [Robert] Julian'

b.113, p. 53; b.54, p. 1187 ('to ease thy wants in verse')

JO134 Juno and Jupiter, Tinsier(?) and Troller,
Tarquin and Tamarlane, Thunder and Thumper.

'Pack of hounds. Last century'

c.81/1, no. 283

JO135 Juno, Pallas, and Venus, resolv'd once to hie
For what can compare with his wit, and his lyre?

John Lockman, 'Juno, Pallas, and Venus: on the
progress to Earth'

c.267/1, p. 230

JO136 Just at these words, came in the man
You honest Dick, shall preach in Lent.

'Upon Mr. [Richard] Hill's going to court'

Trumbull Box: Poetry Box XIII/72

JO137 Just broke from school, pert, impudent, and raw;
And, groaning for the bets he loses by't, he dies.

[Soame Jenyns], 'The modern fine gentleman'
[Dodsley Collection]

c.487, p. 149

JO138 Just emblem of our station here,
Shall sweeten life while life doth last.

'A moral'

c.83/2, no. 332

JO139 Just like the candles on his shelves
The later ranks 'twixt them and sixes.

Charles Atherton Allnutt, 'Another [epigram on a
poem entitled The receding volunteers] on the
unequal measure of Mr. Charles's lines'

c.112, p. 161

JO140 Just now from our repast we came,
Still may we bear thy cross! Still may we follow
thee!

[Simon] Patrick, 'A hymn after meat. From
Prudentius'

c.352, p. 20

JO141 Just on the borders of a pleasant wood
And with two worthy only sons was blest. | In
comely features. . . .

[Elizabeth (Shirley) Compton, countess of
Northampton]

Accession 97.7.40 (incomplete)

JO142 Just taking coach—our author press'd my stay
They've power to lay the devils which they raise.

'Epilogue to Edwin [by George Jeffreys], a tragedy
acted at the Theater Royal in Lincoln's Inn Fields
1723/4'

c.360/2, no. 126

JO143 Justice is drawn impartial, dauntless, blind:
See Fielding there! She has not fled mankind.

John Lockman, 'Seeing Justice Fielding pass along . . .
March 1757'

c.267/1, p. 180

JO144 Justly the tribute unto thee I owe,
I do not vie; I only imitate.

[John Newson Farnham], 'Revd. Sir . . .' [to John
Milford]

File 5154

JO145 Justly to copy beauty's magic queen,
Can ne'er be drawn but by a hand divine.

'To a young lady at Bath who complained that her
painter had not drawn her likeness . . . General
evening post, Octr. 10. 1776'

c.157, p. 103; see also 'What artist's hand . . .'.

K

K0001 Kate in the sweet of a Venerian knowt
You wear them all before, and I behind.

> Sir Thomas Urquhart, 'The suit of a lovely wench
> whose name was Kate to her dear heart'

fb.217, p. 270

K0002 Kate with her husband, whilst she cross'd a ferry,
Being sure that peer would never reach the ground.

> Sir Thomas Urquhart, 'The refuge, that a certain
> honest woman named Kate had recourse into, to save
> herself from drowning'

fb.217, p. 59

K0003 Katherine, a kitchen wench, merrily said
They that have legs defective love to ride.

> [Sir Aston Cokayne], 'Of a kitchen wench'

b.275, p. 34

K0004 Keen blaws the wind o'er Donocht-head,
'I wander thro' a wreath o' snow.'

> [Robert Burns], 'Stanzas'

c.142, p. 320

K0005 Keen was the blast, and black the morn
She slept, to wake no more.

> [Christopher Anstey], 'The farmer's daughter[.] A
> tale'

c.83/2, no. 562

K0006 Keep a pure diet to bear down the flesh,
To quench the hottest of your fire.

> Sir Thomas Urquhart, 'A counsel to a young man,
> whose flesh did rebel against the spirit'

fb.217, p. 344

K0007 Keep far from him that hath the power to kill,
Without all doubt then instantly shall die.

> Sir John Strangways, 'Good counsel and safe for these
> times . . . 13° Octobris 1646'

b.304, p. 61

K0008 Keep friends with care and friendly them do treat,
Press not them down when causes be too great.

c.339, p. 324

K0009 Keep not still silence, nor behold
God blessed over all.

> 'Psalm 83'

c.264/2, p. 75

K0010 Keep on your mask, and hide your eye
When life is done where shall I go?

> Will[iam] Strode, 'On being in despair to his
> m[ist]r[es]s'
> [Crum K8]

b.200, p. 122; b.205, fol. 67v; b.62, p. 19; b.150, p. 274
('veil')

K0011 Keep silence, all created things
Beneath my Lord the Lamb.

> Isaac Watts, 'God's dominion and decrees . . . Lyric
> poems'

c.186, p. 40; c.259, p. 126, and back flyleaf

K0012 Keep to the true Church whilst you may
You may forever vary.

> 'Song. To the tune of Gather your rosebuds'
> [Crum K13]

fb.108, p. 69, p. 285

K0013 Keep your thoughts close
And your countenance loose.

> 'The witty Spaniard to Sr. Harry Wotton / Distrust or
> beg'

b.155, p. 63

K0014 Keeping his waves from working on that day,
In our days, waters, of more wondrous kind.

> 'Upon waters that rest or stop their course every
> seventh day and other wonders'

c.158, p. 118

K0015 Kelynge, my friend, you hope in vain to raise,
He's read by all, and is by all admir'd.

> Colonel Brett, on John Lockman

c.268 (second part), inserted before p. 113

K0016 Kendal is dead, and Cambridge riding post
What fitter sacrifice for Denham's ghost.

> [Andrew Marvell], 'Upon [Clarendon's]
> grandchildren' [the children of James II and his first
> wife Anne née Hyde, May–June 1667]
> [Crum K17]

b.136, p. 48

K0017   Kill me not with asking why
Phryne will have more than one.

> [William Popple, trans.], '[Horace, ep]ode 14th. To
> Maecenas'
>
> fc.104/2, p. 452

K0018   Kind Ariadne drown'd in tears
Flies to the bottle for relief.

> 'Song 132'
>
> c.555, p. 186

K0019   Kind Barnes adorn'd by ev'ry muse
That ever trod on English ground.

> [on Joshua Barnes of Emanuel College, Cambridge, d.
> 1712]
>
> c.157, p. 88, 94

K0020   Kind be the added hours
Be but fair as today.

> Rev. [ ] Mills, 'Addressed to W. Smith'
>
> Smith Papers, folder 74/13

K0021   Kind charmer of my solitude,
To lose myself just like to thee.

> 'On tobacco'
>
> c.94

K0022   Kind friend whose pencil can assure
Transparencies of joy.

> [William Hayley], 'To Miss Chetwynd in return for a
> transparent lamp'
>
> File 6974

K0023   Kind god of sleep, since it must be
Who would not be deluded so.

> 'Song 45'
>
> c.555, p. 70

K0024   Kind god of sleep! Thy aid impart,
And sweeten my repose.

> 'To sleep'
>
> c.83/3, no. 771

K0025   Kind guardian of the font, (sagacious Barrett!)
And suck thy subterranean cellar dry.

> John Lockman, 'To Mr. Barrett, at the Hot Well,
> Bristol . . . 1747'
>
> c.267/1, p. 69

K0026   Kind heaven that lets presumptious sinners know
The monarch's crown's as glorious as before.

> [Phanuel Bacon], 'Occasioned by a report of a
> diamond's dropping out of the crown upon the day of
> coronation'
>
> c.237, fol. 99 [*i.e.*, 119]

K0027   Kind heavens who to my life's decline
Of exemplary love.

> [William Hayley], 'Stanzas . . . Oct 15 [1800]'
>
> File 6968

K0028   Kind is the speech of Christ our Lord,
When Christ invites my soul away.

> [Isaac Watts, Hymns and spiritual songs (1707), bk. I,
> Hymn 73]
>
> c.180, p. 63

K0029   Kind Jesuits you have but justly done
(As anciently they were) of noble race.

> 'A satire against the Inns of Court'
>
> b.54, p. 1169

K0030   Kind messmates all, these children come before ye,
Nelson is gone to keep a birth for Jack!

> 'Lines spoken in the character of a British sailor, at a
> play for the benefit of the orphan children of a seaman
> who was killed at the Battle of Trafalgar'
>
> Smith Papers, folder 75/27

K0031   Kind nature in P[i]tt, hath an active soul wrought,
The rights F[ox?] attack'd, here lives P[itt] who
                     has sav'd.

> [on 'characters of the age', written in 1757]
>
> c.186, p. 122

K0032   Kind neighbor and countrymen, listen, I pray
I might be in danger of losing my nose.

> 'On the slitting Sr John Coventry's nose [by
> Monmouth and others] . . . to the tune of Jama both
> ragged and bound' [1670]
> [Crum κ31]
>
> Poetry Box VII/64

K0033   Kind pity chokes my spleen; brave scorn forbids
Power from God claim'd, than God himself to trust.

> [John Donne], 'Satira tertia'
> [Crum κ32]
>
> b.114, p. 17; b.148, p. 12; File 11383, p. 1

K0034   Kind Sirs, you would set me a-singing,
There's always diversion for you. | Tol lol de
rol, &c.

> 'Song 84'
>
> c.555, p. 132

K0035   Kindness has resistless charms
And makes the slave grow pleas'd and vain.

> John Wilmot, 2nd earl of Rochester, '3. Song'
>
> b.334, p. 183; see also 'Give me leave to rail at you . . .'.

K0036   King Arthur's sword both broad and sharp yclept
                          Excalibur
   And eke the stout Saint George eftsoon he made
           the dragon follow. | Saint George he was &c.

> 'Song 233'
> c.555, p. 364

K0037   King David's body did for coldness tremble
   In your old age you chose a spriteful bride.

> Sir Thomas Urquhart, 'To a certain nobleman, who in
> his decaying age did marry a young handsome lady'
> fb.217, p. 354

K0038   King George in a fright
   Which his conduct exhibits at home.

> Charles James Fox, 'Lines said to be wrote in
> Mr. Gibbon's History of the fall of Rome'
> c.504, p. 130; c.150, p. 123; File 5385; Poetry Box v/78;
> Poetry Box III/folder 21-30

K0039   King Hezekiah lay diseas'd
   And turn'd the mind of God.

> [Thomas Stevens?], 'The effect of King Hezekiah's
> fervent prayer. A hymn'
> c.259, p. 80

K0040   King James the fifth the flower of flowers all
   Named and called Holyrood House.

> '[Rulers of Scotland] 13'
> fa.4, fol. 29

K0041   King James the fourth the flower of policy (?)
   With great honor and worship he [?] did marry.

> '[Rulers of Scotland] 12'
> fa.4, fol. 29

K0042   King Midas' touch to gold did each thing turn
   Or have but that, without which we must sterve.

> [Sir Thomas Urquhart], 'Of Midas the king of
> Phrygia, and Clais one of the three sons of Amy, and
> grandchild of Apollo, and Rhaea'
> fb.217, p. 506

K0043   King of floods! Whom friendly stars ordain,
   Till time nor more renews its date—and Thames
                          forget to flow.

> 'An ode to the Thames for New Year's Day 1720'
> c.244, p. 625

K0044   King of glory, King of peace
   To discharge what is behind.

> George Herbert, 'L'envoy'
> [Crum K44a]
> c.139, p. 142

K0045   King Ptolomy with Cleopatra had
   That stol'n embraces further procreation.

> [Sir Thomas Urquhart], 'That the depraved nature of
> man contributes more to the engendering of bastards
> than of lawful children'
> fb.217, p. 504

K0046   King, Queen, Prince, potentate, I ne'er yet saw
   Say all that's great and good, and he was that.

> 'Character of his most sacred majesty King William
> the third, of glorious and immortal memory'
> c.360/2, no. 179

K0047   King William's cause shall thrive When the sea
                                 burns,
   And rebels shall perish This prophecy's true.

> 'Another ambidexter'
> b.111, p. 528

K0048   Kings are the adored fountains here below,
   Join saints and angels Alleluia.

> [Edmund Wodehouse], 'Feb. 10 [1715]'
> b.131, p. 163

K0049   Kings', queens', men's, judgment's eyes
   To show she was a woman.

> [Nicholas Burghe], 'Another on Q[ueen] E[lizabeth]'
> [Crum K56]
> fb.143, p. 23; b.356, p. 253 ('virgin's eyes')

K0050   Kiss me, lovely Mirabell,
   And at last be nothing.

> [Henry] Neville, 'Mrs. Belle Heydon daughter of Sr.
> John Heydon and sister to Col: N[eville]'s wife'
> Spence Papers, folder 108 (2 copies)

K0051   Kiss me sweetest, with the kisses
   So great a guest, is greatest gain.

> [Edward Manisty, trans.], 'The song of songs'
> [Crum K62]
> b.224, p. 1

K0052   Kisses the subject of debate
   Proclaim the battle—I'm your man.

> 'On some young ladies expressing a surprise what
> pleasure there could be in kisses'
> c.487, p. 70

K0053   Kitchen lies here, for so his name I found,
   Devour their Kitchen now for want of meat.

> 'On Mr. Kitchen'
> c.74

K0054 Kitty a fair tho' frozen maid,
I'll kiss you if you guess.

[David Garrick], 'Enigma 72' [chimney sweeper]
[Crum K66]

c.389

K0055 Kitty affronted, t'other day
But de'il a bit to swallow.

[Thomas Morell], 'The revenge'

c.395, p. 8

K0056 Kneller, by heav'n, and not a master, taught
Her works, and dying, fears herself may die.

A[lexander] Pope, 'The epitaph on the monument for
Sir Godfrey Kneller . . . principal painter to King
George the first . . . he died on Saturday the 26.
October 1723'
[Crum K74]

c.360/2, no. 157

K0057 Kneller thy pencil take with shame
You drew a G[eorg]e, a Cromwell he.

'Verses occasioned by Mr. Addison's poem on
G[eorge]'s picture' ['Kneller, with silence . . .']

c.570/2, p. 138

K0058 Kneller, with silence and surprise
Had drawn a George, or carved a Jove?

Joseph Addison, 'To Sir Godfrey Kneller, on his
picture of King George' [pr. 1716 (Foxon A41);
answered by 'Kneller, thy pencil take . . .']
[Crum K75]

c.139, p. 111; c.244, p. 143

K0059 Knew e'er three days old the marriage bed
And what['s] more strange, ere she was born, was
dead.

[Eve] 'Translated' [from the French]

Poetry Box VII/46

K0060 Knew'st thou whose these ashes were
Renew the letters with his tears.

[William Lewes, of Oriel College], 'Epitaph' [upon
the death of Mr. Thomas Washington who died in
Spain 1623]
[Crum K77]

b.197, p. 192; b.54, p. 879

K0061 Knighthood, at first, was the reward
In thee bid ancient knighthood shine.

John Lockman, 'To Mr. Fielding: on the honor
conferred upon him by the King . . . Oct. 1761'

c.267/1, p. 311

K0062 Know all men by these presents once again,
That Grogan died, but Grogan's gone to bed.

'An elegy on the death of Patrick Grogan esqr. of
Wexford in Ireland a noted miser and recluse. He died
on Wednesday January the 11th 1720/21'

c.360/2, no. 205

K0063 Know, Celia, since thou art so proud,
Know her themselves through all her veils.

Tho[mas] Carew, 'A lover that had sent many verses to
his mistress that cares not for him'
[Crum K79]

b.200, p. 246; b.205, fol. 81r

K0064 Know every Christian man alive
I hereunto subscribe my name.

[J. Free], 'The following receipt was occasioned by a
quarrel between Esquire [Hastings] Ingram of Great
Woodford in Warwickshire and the curate [who]
wrote the following'
[Crum K81]

Poetry Box X/41

K0065 Know gentle reader here a priest is laid
Their thoughts were more on Christ then on the
Pope.

'On Mr Drury the Jesuit who was slain by the fall of a
house in the Blackfriars. [26 October] 1623'

b.197, p. 103

K0066 Know happy prince the mirror of thy birth,
Of thy birth, was the birthday of our joy.

Tho[mas] Warmestry, 'Upon the birth of Prince
Charles now King. 1634'

b.200, p. 10

K0067 Know then my brethren, heaven is clear; and all
the clouds are gone,
We'll make the wanton sisters fall, | And hey then
up go we.

[Francis Quarles], 'The Roundheads' race. 1641'
[Crum K86]

b.54, p. 889; b.4, fol. 43v; b.213, p. 74; Poetry Box VI/35

K0068 Know you what He is you scorn,
Scorn, and bethorn eternity.

H[enry] C[olman], 'On Christ crowned with thorns'
[Crum K93]

b.2, p. 18

K0069 Knowledge and truth lay hid in darkest night:
God said let printing be! And there was light.

'Ditto. Parody on [Pope's epitaph on Isaac Newton]'

c.81/1, no. 191

K0070 Knowledge impart born for themselves none are
Such as love learning well shall be well-learned.

    [Mary Serjant]
    fb.98, fol. 150

Known good divided into three
Pleasure so ill bringeth long shame.

    [Sir Nicholas] Bacon, 'Of the kinds and fruits of good
    and ill'
    fa.8, fol. 161

K0071

L

L0001　La! What a sight is here! A special show!
What decency of manners still prevails.

'Epilogue in the character of a baker's man spoken by
Mr. Dance'

c.115

L0002　Labor in youth to get what you can,
For age is a burden to a laboring man.

[James Rhodes?]

b.206, p. 4

L0003　Laden with years, by sickness press'd,
Her upright life did end in peace.

'An epitaph on Mrs. Audrey Warren'

c.244, p. 85

L0004　Ladies although the conquests of your eyes
So long as we behold th'horizon clear.

'Prologue to Alcamenes and Menalippas spoke by
Mr. Richards'

Poetry Box I/111[8]

L0005　Ladies and gentlemen my claims are such,
The more I'll visit you.

'Riddle'

Diggle Box: Poetry Box XI/68

L0006　Ladies and gentlemen—our tales are told,
For which, we thank you all—and bid good night.

'[Epilogue to] The maternal conference. In two parts,
for a public speaking'

c.91, p. 330

L0007　Ladies fly from love's smooth tale
Conquer love that run away.

[Thomas] Carew, 'Conquest by flight'
[Crum L9]

b.225, p. 130; b.213, p. 1 (first stanza); see also 'Young
men fly . . . '(second stanza), presented as a separate
poem.

L0008　Ladies, I come your favors to implore:—
We reap the profit;—but the pleasure you.

'A prologue, spoken by Mrs. Fisher, at the opening of
their theater at the Bath Gardens. Monday Sept. 8
1777'

c.136, p. 115

L0009　Ladies in good Queen Bess's sober age
With British candor—for I need it all.

'Prologue spoken by Miss Ibbott in the character of
H. Milet'

c.115

L0010　Ladies now glad ye, here comes Dr Paddy
And so farewell bawdy doctors.

'On the physicians of London'
[Crum L14]

b.200, p. 86

L0011　Ladies of old, 'twas understood
She fears not what vain man can do.

'On the present loose drapery of the fair'

c.83/2, no. 528 (bis)

L0012　Ladies take care of your reputation
How the ladies would frig themselves which would
be pure.

'Song'

c.189, p. 164

L0013　Ladies that wear black cypress veils
Which lady's censured, which is free.

[Richard Corbett], 'Upon the ladies of the new dress'
[Crum L18]

b.62, p. 101

L0014　Ladies there is a lovely creature
Run to the south and there you'll find it.

'[Enigma/Charade/Conundrum] 7'

c.389

L0015　Ladies to you we women make complaints
We have as little doings in the dark.

'Prologue spoken by Peggy'

Poetry Box I/111[3]

L0016　Ladies tonight an unexperienced train
Spare censure, we expect not panegyric.

H[annah] M[ore], 'An introductory address'

c.341, p. 87

L0017 Ladies who chance to frisk this way,
May you, like her, have peace in death.

[ ] Lackington, 'An epitaph on the tombstone of Mrs.
Lackington'

c.83/3, no. 760

L0018 Ladies, whose dress, wit, sprightliness, and air
Had the fam'd painter, Bunyan sweet, been there.

John Lockman, 'A caricature of Paris, in 1741'

c.267/1, p. 263

L0019 Ladies, why doth love torment you?
And warms me with a pleasing ray.

'Consent at last'

c.416

L0020 Ladies, your wits to exercise,
I'm still surviving, tho' oft dy'd.

'A riddle'

c.241, p. 91

L0021 Lads! (quo' the Scotch captain)—yon soldiers you
see,
Else 'twill eat up your flesh, and scarce leave you
the skin.

John Lockman, 'Memento: to our countrymen'

c.267/1, p. 195

L0022 Lady Di: being gone this morning to Glyne
I'll be sure to return him safe and sound at eleven.

M. S.

Poetry Box II/52

L0023 Lady Dorothy Drum sends her compliments
My Lord (she knows whose works) and the shells
for the grot.

'Universal business—a banter on the ladies' custom of
writing their messages on cards'
[Crum L25]

c.360/2, no. 192

L0024 Lady I entreat you wear
Turns the beholders into stone.

Robert Herrick, 'Upon a cherrystone sent to the tip of
Mrs Jemmonia Waldgrave's ear [on the one side a
delicate face; on the other side a death's head]'
[Crum L26a]

b.197, p. 7; b.205, fol. 76r

L0025 Lady, mistake me not for one,
For dirty company and kitchen.

'A letter' [in prose and verse]

c.530, p. 342

L0026 Lady muse shall chant anon,
If such is life, and such are men.

'Life; an anacreontic ode. From Rural philosophers'

c.83/1, no. 59

L0027 Lady, thy book will never fill
Present I do but gaze!

'To her who desired the author to write something in a
volume of manuscript poetry as a punishment of
having looked unbidden into it. In imitation of Sir J.
Suckling'

Poetry Box IV/139

L0028 Laïs being old, once looking in a glass
My youth restor'd and I will rest content.

J. R.

b.197, p. 116

L0029 Lamb's dead, the devil he is how could it be
They eat a Paschal rascal Lamb in Hell.

'On Dr. Lamb'

b.356, p. 241

L0030 Lament—for Fothergill is dead
'That virtue is its own reward.'

'On the death of S[amuel] F[othergill]'

c.139, p. 446

L0031 Lament, lament, you scholars all
But now we'll drink like doctors!

[Thomas Randolph], 'On the fall of the Miter Tavern
in Cambridge'
[Crum L40]

b.200, p. 354; b.205, fol. 50v

L0032 Lamented babe! How early hast thou fled?
And to thy shade, celestial anthems sing.

'To the memory . . . Edin[burgh] 4th April'

Poetry Box VIII/67

L0033 Langhorne! Whose sweetly varying muse has pow'r
This letter'd shore has smooth'd my toilsome way.

H[annah] More, 'The following lines were wrote
by . . . on her seeing some lines wrote on the sand by
Dr. [John?] Langhorne'

c.341, p. 113

L0034 Language thou art too narrow and too weak
Of grief; for all would waste a stoic's heart.

[John Donne, 'An elegy on the death of Mrs
Boulstrede']
[Crum L43]

b.114, p. 140; b.148, p. 77

L0035 Lascivious words they harshly hear:
When it doth enter at the ear.

> Sir Thomas Urquhart, 'Of such women to whom,
> though in matters of love practice be most acceptable,
> take nevertheless great exceptions at the freedom of a
> licentious discourse'
>
> fb.217, p. 167

L0036 Last New Year's Day I heard one say
So he took his nag and he rode away. | Hoy fal
                                        lal &c.

> 'A song'
>
> Accession 97.7.40

L0037 Last New Year's Day was din enough,
Than them to eat the pie Sir.

> 'A Scots song'
>
> c.530, p. 130

L0038 Last night a dream came into my head
Let body now with soul agree.

> 'The comical dreamer'
>
> c.188, p. 87

L0039 Last night as on my couch I lay
I fell, and broke my dream.

> Frederick Corfield, 'A vision'
>
> c.381/2

L0040 Last night as resting on my bed I lay
And ask the Eton-conj'rers what I mean?

> R[obert] Shirley, 1st earl of Ferrers, 'The dream. To
> Lory the plagiary'
>
> c.347, p. 43

L0041 Last night by chance conducted or by choice
Nor let the rigor part what nature join'd.

> R[obert] Shirley, 1st earl of Ferrers, 'Stanza. From
> Voiture'
>
> c.347, p. 86

L0042 Last night when I to sleep myself had laid
They all concluded with an Ave Mary.

> 'The vision of toleration' [1687]
> [Crum L51]
>
> fb.108, p. 167

L0043 Last of the hours, that track the fading day,
Down the deep west I fly from midnight's shroud.

> [Ann (Ward)] Radcliffe, 'Song of the evening hour'
>
> c.83/3, no. 877

L0044 Last Saturday night when the warrants were out
Here's damnation to the Lord Mayor and a
                        reformation of manners. |
                With my chip chow [&c.]

> 'Reformation of manners'
>
> Poetry Box IV/42

L0045 Last week in Lent I came to town
Has such a fair in his dominion.

> 'Song 236'
>
> c.555, p. 373

L0046 Last week in this town was a furious debate
Since the voice of the people on both sides declares.

> [Nicholas Amhurst], 'Occasioned by a dispute against
> the national debts between Sr R. W[alpole] and
> Mr. P[ultene]y'
>
> c.233, p. 58

L0047 Last year in the spring,
For a prince who has never offended.

> [John Grubham Howe?], 'A new ballad to a scurvy
> new tune'
> [POAS V.507]
>
> fb.207/3, p. 5

L0048 Last year, just before that my harvest begun,
He maybe may leave off his joking. | His
                thinking—and blinking [&c.]

> [John Walker?], 'Robin and Fanny'
>
> fc.108, fol. 18v

L0049 Last year our English travellers would be
With all men's plans of that great league soon sever.

> [Sir Richard Bulstrode?], 'Upon our young King's
> embarkation at Dunkirk, with Monsr. Fourbin
> admiral' [1708]
>
> fb.88, p. 116v

L0050 Last year when this convivial meeting began
May for one night let us have one at a time. |
                The evening we'll spend [&c.]

> [John Walker?], 'Song on the reopening of the
> Convivials'
>
> fc.108, fol. 78v

L0051 Late as I on my bed reposing lay,
I'd wink forever, be forever blind.

> [John Oldham], 'The dream'
> [Crum L54]
>
> b.209, p. 37

L0052 Late as I, slumb'ring, on my bed were laid,
To show me heav'n, and yet in hell to leave me.

> 'A dream'
>
> c.189, p. 14

L0053 Late from those radiant orbs her eyes
And from her mouth breaks half the thunder.

    J. B., 'An epigram on a handsome termagent'
Poetry Box IV/155

L0054 Late in the Graces' annals have I read—
And Hervey only has exchang'd her throne.

    'Lines upon the same lady [Lady Hervey] fifty years
    after'
Poetry Box X/128

L0055 Late in the solemn silence of the night,
And paid his tears of grief, with tears of ale.

    [Robert Cholmeley], 'Wm. Of Wickham's ghost to
    the fellows of New Coll: Oxon. in their common
    room'
c.190, p. 5

L0056 Lately I wrote Honora on the sand,
But will on lasting tablets write thy name.

    [Anna Seward], 'Elegy written at Bridlington Quay in
    Yorkshire, July 1777—addressed to Mrs. Edgeworth'
Poetry Box V/53

L0057 Launcy, how shall I be easy,
The more they cry, the less they'll piss.

    'A dialogue between the K[ing] and the
    A[rch]b[isho]p of Y[o]rk'
Spence Papers, folder 113

L0058 Laura, canst thou forsake the town,
Both love and charms more true.

    'To Laura'
c.83/2, no. 551

L0059 Laura today your fever burns
In seeing Laura well.

    [Robert Cholmeley], 'Galen to his mistress Laura ill
    of an ague and fever'
c.190, p. 180

L0060 Law, and religion made a covenant,
To rule men's spirits: and therefore to daunt.

    Sir Thomas Urquhart, 'Of law, and religion'
fb.217, p. 282

L0061 Law was ordain'd to plague mankind,
'Tis nothing but retaliation.

    'Retaliation—for Batheaston'
fc.53, p. 15

L0062 Laws were establish'd for no other end,
Direct our hearts to loyalty and love.

    J[ohn] [Robinson], 'Melius vivitur ubi nihil licet,
    quam ubi omnia'
c.370, fol. 77

L0063 Law's your religion faith over this you
Will not believe the noblest [?] you do.

    [Sir Thomas Urquhart], 'To the [?]'
fb.217, p. 520

L0064 Lawyers get wrong: theologs go to hell:
And oft physicians are in health not well.

    Sir Thomas Urquhart, 'How incident error is to
    human frailty'
fb.217, p. 166

L0065 Lawyers themselves uphold, The common weal,
And love, they want, Not keeping amity.

    'In the praise and dispraise of lawyers' [equivocal
    verse]
    [Crum L85]
b.62, p. 60

L0066 Lay by the books—and come dear Jack
Than to appeal t'you—come and see.

    Dr. [ ] Balon, 'Dr. Balon's compliments to
    Mr. Loveday Messrs. Huddesford and Brine'
c.237, fol. 109 [i.e., 129]

L0067 Lay by your reason,
For either you must take the swear, or starve, and
                             quit your station.

    'The reformation. April 5th 1693'
b.111, p. 467

L0068 Lay that sullen garland by thee
Sleep will come and that's as good.

    [Crum L89]
b.213, p. 52

L0069 Lazar solicits but one single pence
That's more, my friend than you ought to receive.

c.546, p. 34

L0070 Lazarus come forth: why could not Lazarus plead,
The voice that calls, gives, and gives then the power.

    [Francis Quarles], 'On Lazarus, the damosel, and a
    sinner'
    [Crum L91]
b.137, p. 171

L0071 Lead on, my muse, while trembling, I essay
But these best show, what thou art sure to be.

    [John Dart], 'A poem called Westminster Abbey'
c.547, p. 160

L0072 Lead on swift herald Aurora away
With a luster more bright than he darts upon thine.

    [William Hayley], 'Apollo's address to Aurora'
File 6926

L0073 Leader of faithful souls and guide
And meet our captain in the skies.

'Hymn 75th'
c.562, p. 94

L0074 Learn, pretty trifler, from that fair undone,
Let silence save the conquest of your eyes.

'To Miss M[in]u[na(?) Godfrey] by a major quartered
at Peterborough'
c.229/1, fol. 73

L0075 Learn, learn, nobility, th'important truth!
What of nobility remains? The name.

'An epigram occasioned by the trials of Ld. G. S. and
Earl Ferrers, the first disobeying orders in Germany
Novr. 59 the latter killed his steward in cold blood'
c.372; see also 'Sure man says . . .'.

L0076 Learn, my fair one, to be wise;
And by conduct show perfection.

c.549, p. 67

L0077 Learned Saint Paul the slothful [?] doth threat,
Who worketh not, let not meat that [?] eat.

c.339, p. 315

L0078 Learn'd Sir, you're right for all engag'd in sin,
This doctrine to refute, and strike me dumb.

'On the love of God'
Poetry Box IV/4

L0079 Learned thyself, and having such for friends,
Choose while thou mayst, none ever had them both.

[Sir Charles] Sedley, 'Character of L[or]d Leicester'
fb.68, p. 75

L0080 Learning doth live and virtue still doth shine,
When folly dies and ignorance doth pine.

c.339, p. 327

L0081 Learning hath fed me, yet I know no letter
What student this is I pray you rehearse.

'5 Enig. Res. A worm fed in a book'
b.205, fol. 99r

L0082 Learning, whose forces did dispersed lie
Truth in their van, and triumph in their rear.

[Robert Wild], 'Aliud' [upon Ed. Reynolds, D. D.]
c.166, p. 303

L0083 Learning, worship, credit, patrimony,
But that some go before, and some come after.

'On Tho: Penistone of an ancient family' [clerk of the
Council to Queen Elizabeth, at Rochester]
[Crum L104]
fb.143, p. 33

L0084 Learning would I desire and crave,
And all by virtue of my knell.

'Learning'
[cf. Crum L105, 'and knowledge crave']
b.284, p. 82

L0085 Leave Clorinda, leave the town,
And turn the forest to a town.

[Thomas] Rymer
Poetry Box VI/100

L0086 Leave, Garrick, the rich landscape, proudly gay,
Who, rich in rural peace, ne'er thought of pomp,
                                                  or gold.

William Pitt, 1st earl of Chatham, 'To Mr. Garrick in
answer to his verses from Mount Edgecombe' ['The
gods on thrones . . .', actually by Lyttelton; 3 April
1772]
File 17579; Poetry Box V/32

L0087 Leave, leave all you adulterers of verse
Will seem Apocrypha to scriptures next.

'[To the right hon. Sir Thomas Wotton] on the death
of the Lady Dacres'
Poetry Box VI/81

L0088 Leave martial deeds, to martial men, and let the
                                          priests go pray:
Such devilish counsel worse received wrought
                                          Europe's great decay.

'On the priests, their going to war'
c.189, p. 32

L0089 Leave off unhappy wretch, and drudge no more,
Live miserably mean, and starve like me.

'A satire upon schoolmasters supposed to be spoken by
the ghost of Dionysius to a master instructing youth'
fb.142, p. 26

L0090 Leave off your ogling Francis
And servant | Roger Martin.

'Advice or an heroic epistle to Mr. Francis Villiers to
an excellent new tune called A health to Betty' [1683]
[Crum L123]
b.113, p. 249 (with two more stanzas)

L0091 Leave (teasing principle!) my breast,
Nor, witless, steer'd for fairy land.

John Lockman, 'The complaint, to his genius, a lyric
rhapsody . . . 1727' [satire on Stephen Duck; pr.
Dublin c. 1730 (Foxon D423)]
c.267/1, p. xiv

L0092 Leave trade with but one hundred pounds a year,
Or by this time, of half on't I'd been plunder'd.

    C. M., 'On quitting books'

fc.85, fol. 107v

L0093 Leaves sing their love, each complemental tree
Their arms, the plane infettereth the places.

    'Verses unknown'

b.197, p. 250

L0094 Led by a wrong scent—where the ladies call wind
You will pardon this urgent intrusion.

    [Phanuel Bacon], 'Occasioned by Sr. John ———'s
    retiring to the place appropriated to the ladies—at—
    Waters to be set to music'

c.237, fol. 35v

L0095 Led by the meditating muse I strayed,
And [?] now no more fair science grac'd.

    'Beginning of [17]55. on the improvements made in
    Eton' [unfinished]

c.591 (incomplete?)

L0096 Led on by love,
I kiss, and keep it up.

    'Song 96'

c.555, p. 145

L0097 Led on by pensive thought I left erewhile
In private studies and in public toils.

Diggle Box: Poetry Box XI/41

L0098 Left to herself she would not muse,
'Tis ten to one she'll dance with thee.

    [Frederick Corfield], 'The spirit of contradiction'

c.381/1

L0099 Legs I have some but unlike you,
And make on me a merry meal.

    '[Enigma/Charade/Conundrum] 14' [table]

c.389

L0100 Lemona was daughter of Hudda the brave
Lord ha' mercy they cried—what a bug!

    'A German tale'

c.250

L0101 Lent all the year! faith that's too much,
For his damn'd roguery to the Harwich crew.

    George Alsop, 'A lampoon upon the purser of the
    Harwich frigate'

b.54, p. 1207

L0102 Lent signifies the spring a spring of grace
Th'observing this same treble good of Lent.

    [Edward] Sparke, 'Poem 10th, on the feast of Lent'

b.137, p. 24

L0103 Lesbia let's live and love and never weigh
Knowing that we have had so many kisses.

    'Catullus. Ep. 5'
    [Crum L130]

b.197, p. 39

L0104 Lesbia the fair, the gay, the young,
Then women will be women still.

    'Lesbia a tale in two cantos'

c.382, p. 12

L0105 Less shall proud Rome her ancient trophies boast,
And Anson's spoils are from a tribute world.

    John Lockman, 'Seeing the wagon loaded with
    treasure, from on board Acapulco ship, pass through
    London . . . July 1744'

c.267/1, p. 25

L0106 Lest ill thou see'st, or hear'st thy windows close,
Lest ill thou speakest locks on thy lips impose.

    'A threefold continency of the eyes ears and tongue'

c.356

L0107 Lest time seem long they lie, they snort, they sit
They're not asham'd to say, their life is short.

    Sir Thomas Urquhart, 'Concerning such as complain
    on the brevity of man's age, and yet cannot make good
    use of the little time, that is bestowed upon them'

fb.217, p. 87

L0108 Lest you should think me—*levis*,
From, my Lord, your humble servant—Juvenis'

    'To L[or]d North' [later earl of Guilford]

fc.85, fol. 84v

L0109 L'Estrange the fop, that arbitrary tool,
As makes him vote for Marylebone and Pope.

    'Upon Roger L'Estrange.1680'

b.54, p. 1200

L0110 Let all degrees of men appear,
('Tis not the trade that forms the man.)

    'Let everyone practice that which he is acquainted
    with'

c.175, p. 63

L0111 Let all in heav'n and earth combine,
To praise the great eternal King.

    'Hymn'

c.153, p. 95

L0112 Let all my sins lie dead within this mournful chest.
Then shall my joyful soul forever be at rest.

[Sir Francis Castillion]
fb.69, p. 192

L0113 Let all our tongues be one
And witness to my heart!

[Isaac Watts, Hymns and spiritual songs (1707),
bk. III, Hymn 9]
c.180, p. 19

L0114 Let all that purified sect
Keep both itself, and state secure.

'Cant: 17' ['A proper new ballad called The summons
to New England to the tune of The townsmen's cap']
[Crum L143]
b.4, fol. 13 (damaged)

L0115 Let all the choice surveyors of the earth,
Few other wits reach your peregrination.

Sir Thomas Urquhart, 'To one, who had set down
very accurately the history of his own travels'
fb.217, p. 306

L0116 Let all the muses now assist my quill
He wears a crown of immortality.

'On Mr. [John] Ashton' [1690]
b.111, p. 92

L0117 Let all the pris'ners stand forth to the bar
With Satan in Hell's ever-burning fire.

H[enry] C[olman], 'The sentence'
[Crum L150]
b.2, p. 29

L0118 Let all ye orthodox sons of Holy Church
Will have its crown when he's above.

'An elegy on the Reverend Mr. Ab. Sellar'
Poetry Box IV/115

L0119 Let amorous coxcombs in a whining way
And quit their lechery, or leave the town.

[William Harrison], 'On the ladies of Winton'
Spence Papers, folder 113

L0120 Let ancients boast no more
Whilst her great name confronts eternity.

'Pindaric'
b.371, no. 31

L0121 Let Britons now a grateful homage pay,
And bind with Ormonde's laurels James's crown.

'The birthday [of the Old Pretender] June 10th 1715'
[Crum L158]
fc.58, p. 35; c.570/1, p. 104

L0122 Let bumpers go round,
Huzza drink it round.

'A song'
c.570/1, p. 150

L0123 Let burgandy flow,
With a number so small.

Tho[ma]s D'Urfey, 'Joy after sorrow'
[cf. Crum L160]
Poetry Box IV/33; c.570/1, p. 82

L0124 Let business and care
And sweet Jessy be mine.

[Charles Burney, the younger], 'Verses sent in a letter
to Ensign Simon Macdonald . . . Feb. 25. 1779'
c.37, p. 49

L0125 Let busy rumor, and fantastic fame
But makes herself a witness to thy charms.

'To a lady on her complaint that she was censured'
c.360/1, p. 81

L0126 Let but my God my self regard,
Till we by them may b'happy made.

[Edmund Wodehouse], 'Octr. 5 [1714]'
b.131, p. 53

L0127 Let but my heart O God be giv'n to thee,
'Tis fit to leave to Him the rest.

[Edmund Wodehouse], 'Octr. 27 [1714]'
b.131, p. 70

L0128 Let Cato's fame
Whilst he shall live, eclipse great Caesar's name.

'In Catonem . . . Mart:'
c.81/1, no. 238

L0129 Let common mistresses complain,
Cry loudly, one and all.

'Another by the same hand' [as 'Charge all a
bumper . . .']
fb.142, p. 49

L0130 Let coward guilt with pallid fear,
Of everlasting day.

[Elizabeth Carter], 'Written at midnight in a
thunder-storm'
[Crum L165]
fc.132/1, p. 11

L0131 Let cynics bark, and the stern Stagyrite
Props of the church and pillars of the throne.

'The paradox upon the confinement of the Lords' [on
the seven bishops, May 1688]
[Crum L166; POAS IV.225]
fb.108, p. 299 (incomplete)

LO132   Let Damon weep, rejoice, stand, sit, or walk
        I am my lovely Sylvia ever thine.

           c.549, p. 131

LO133   Let debauchees call matrimony dull
        As the glad father shall be proud to own.

           [( ) C., of Kings College, Cambridge], 'On
           matrimony'
           [Crum L167]

        Poetry Box IV/53; fb.142, p. 35

LO134   Let desperate wights and ruffians thirst for blood,
        Win foes with love and think your conquest good.

           c.339, p. 326

LO135   Let each man mark the frailty of his kind
        For here his term is like a puff of wind.

           c.339, p. 327

LO136   Let each man to whatsoever house
        And when to loose his tongue.

           b.234, p. 169

LO137   Let each youth of riotousness,
        Many deprived are.

           b.234, p. 91

LO138   Let earth and heaven agree,
        The life of heaven on earth I live.

           'Hymn 92d'

           c.562, p. 121

LO139   Let earth occasion teach you how to do:
        Omit no time, that all times may serve you.

           Sir Thomas Urquhart, 'A politic counsel'

        fb.217, p. 51

LO140   Let earthly minds court what they please,
        Beyond the end of days.

           [John Austin], 'Hym: 8' [Hymn xv, Devotions in the
           ancient way of offices, 1672, p. 136]

        c.178, p. 7

LO141   Let England bewail
        Till once more, till once more, in his throne we've
                                                  replaced him.

           'The wish'

        b.111, p. 64

LO142   Let England glory in Sir Francis Drakes,
        Then territories are more worth, than seas.

           Sir Thomas Urquhart, 'In praise of [crossed out] the
           traveller'

        fb.217, p. 49

LO143   Let England rejoice with heart and with voice,
        Since crowds now come over with William and
                                                  Mary.

           'England's congratulation, for its true-happy
           condition, under . . . King William and Queen
           Mary . . . To the tune of Packington's Pound'
           [Crum L169]

        fb.70, p. 261; parodied by next.

LO144   Let England rejoice, with heart and with voice
        For they show they do love neither William nor
                                                  Mary.

           'A new Protestant ballad called England's
           congratulation'
           [Crum L169]

        b.111, p. 249; parody of previous.

LO145   Let England's Church her sinking state deplore
        Give laws at will, and by the sword command.

           'To the King's most excellent Ma[jes]ty . . . The
           humble address of the tower of London presented by
           the secret committee June 10th introduced by his
           Grace the Duke of Marlborough' [1715]
           [Crum L171]

        fc.58, p. 12; c.570/2, p. 142

LO146   Let Englishmen sit and consult at their ease
        If we leave it again, then hang up the Scot.

           'A Scottish man's protestation' [satire on the Long
           Parliament, 1640; answer to 'You wily projectors . . .']
           [Crum L172]

        b.101, p. 111; fb.106(7)

LO147   Let every freeholder and burgher rejoice
        And wish they had been wiser, a hundred years
                                                  hence.

           'Herefordshire's happiness or Wye made navigable
           wherein is showed the benefit that will accrue to the
           city and county by the demolishing of the weirs. A
           new ballad to the tune of Packington's Pound'

        Poetry Box VI/45

LO148   Let ev'ry nation, tongue, and speech,
        The heav'n and earth shall end.

           'Psalm 117'

        c.264/3, p. 43

LO149   Let fam'd Descartes, or Newton tell,
        Like the first happy pair.

           'The friendship between two ladies'

        c.83/1, no. 17

L0150   Let fawning poets, if they choose
By name, state and title of Benedick—

R[ichard] V[ernon] S[adleir], 'To a gentleman on his
approaching marriage with a lady born in Africa and
partly educated there 177[ ]'

c.106, p. 5

L0151   Let fools great Cupid's yoke disdain
And wounds from Helius have made discourse.

[Thomas Carew], 'The heavens and earth and all you
see | Dispersed collected is but she'

b.213, p. 1

L0152   Let fortune, and Phyllis frown if they please
To love if I please, or to let it alone.

'The careless lover'

fb.107, p. 46

L0153   Let Fulsome eat, drink do whate'er he will
He who smells always well, is never sweet.

'To the same [kind but painted lady] by another hand'

fb.142, p. 58

L0154   Let gay ones and great,
But health and diversion unite.

'Song 106'

c.555, p. 158

L0155   Let gloomy skeptics in their spleen compose
Show where his spirit dwells and fix me there!

[William Hayley], 'Sonnet . . . August 28 [1800] on
horseback'

File 6968

L0156   Let great men loll ingloriously in state
And this made Sidrophel secure you his.

'The state weather-cocks' [pr. 1734 (Foxon S728)]

c.570/4, p. 39

L0157   Let H—— no letter be 'tis plain
First letter of his name, with pain.

[Sir Philip Wodehouse], 'Upon Mr. Hungate being
thrown in prison'

b.131, back (no. 199)

L0158   Let here the fair Chariclea in whom strove
She shall appear true Ethiopian.

'A superscription on the fair Ethiopian sent for a
token to a gentlewoman'

b.356, p. 69

L0159   Let heroes join, and hearts combine,
And in eternity.

'The wish or advice another poem to his Royal
Highness Charles Prince Regent, and his army, by a
private hand'

c.275

L0160   Let Him embrace my soul, and prove
Raise us to nobler seats above.

[Isaac Watts, Hymns and spiritual songs (1707), bk. I,
Hymn 66]

c.180, p. 60

L0161   Let him retire, who will for me
Who, having done no harm, has done no good.

[Thomas Morell], '['Well; let him climb . . .']
reversed'

c.395, p. 35

L0162   Let him that will ascend the tottering seat
But unacquainted with himself, doth fall.

[Sir Matthew Hale], 'Paraphrase on Seneca's Thyestes'
[391–403]
[Crum L201]

b.49, p. 22; b.54, p. 1214; b.63, p. 110; fb.124, fol. 5v;
fb.142, p. 40; see also next, and 'Let them that will . . .'.

L0163   Let him that will to the tottering seat
Excepting to himself, that's known to all.

[Sir Richard Bulstrode, translation from Seneca's
Thyestes]
[cf. Crum L203]

fb.88, p. 118v; see also previous.

L0164   Let him to whom we now belong,
To all eternity.

'Hymn 102d'

c.562, p. 138

L0165   Let history record
You grand cock—

[in later handwriting, inserted in a Jacobite volume,
early 18th century]

c.570/2, p. 109

L0166   Let it be now my case and duty
Virtue's so finish'd—long to spare.

[Phanuel Bacon], 'To Miss Nichol upon the foregoing
occasion three years afterward'

c.237, fol. 47

L0167   Let joy flourish round Anacreon's urn,
If any pleasure reaches to the grave.

George Montagu, 'On Anacreon'

fc.135, p. 12

LO168   Let knaves dispute the rights of kings,
And drank good claret still.

> 'A Bacchanalian health'
> [Crum L213]

b.111, p. 40

LO169   Let ladies, born to high estate,
Your bosom let it warn.

> 'Rhymes with some ribbons to Betsy Thomas at
> Helston'

c.89, p. 95

LO170   Let lawyers, divines, and physicians
Dissemble not with either of those three.

> Sir Thomas Urquhart, 'Our three ghostly fathers'

fb.217, p. 89

LO171   Let lazy hermits strangers to the day
And ev'ry soft illusion melts away.

> William De Grey, [baron of Walsingham], 'On
> leaving the Merton hunt'

fc.51, p. 121

LO172   Let loftier bards the hero's act relate
And to the trophied relics points on high.

> [Samuel Bowden], 'The fate of the mouse. A
> tragicomic poem, occasioned by a mouse that was
> caught and killed by an oyster'

c.326, p. 163

LO173   Let lovely Mira from the muse
When you gave me but one.

> [Phanuel Bacon], 'At Mira's request upon three
> feathers and a broomstaff'

c.237, fol. 20

LO174   Let low'ring clouds descend in floods of rain
Or wreak their vengeance on a second Jove.

> [ ] Robinson, 'The 5th of November. Gunpowder
> treason'

c.190, p. 89

LO175   Let Mary live long,
With loud acclamations, | With loud acclamations, |
His Majesty greet.

> 'The loyal subject's wish'

b.111, p. 51

LO176   Let me but to my God still pay
Enjoy eternal heav'nly life.

> [Edmund Wodehouse], 'Novr. 25 [1714]'

b.131, p. 97

LO177   Let me pour forth
Whoe'er sighs most is cruellest, and hastes the
                 other's death.

> J[ohn] D[onne], ['A valediction']
> [Crum L231]

b.148, p. 7; b.148, p. 104 (ll. 1-3)

LO178   Let me wander not unseen
Under the hawthorn in the dale.

> 'Song'

c.358, p. 143

LO179   Let men beware lest friendly looks be like
The lure, to which the soaring hawk doth strike.

c.339, p. 324

LO180   Let misers tremble o'er their wealth
The royal house of Stuarts.

> 'A song to the tune of Katryn Moggie'

c.171, no. 12; c.570/2, p. 121 ('o'er their gold')

LO181   Let misses, and gallants
When your lives, and estates, are both sunk.

> 'A drinking catch'

fb.107, p. 20

LO182   Let mortal men that are but earth and dust
Consider of the place whereto they must.

c.339, p. 314

LO183   Let much mistaken young recall
In private—on her back.

> 'On a lady's falling on her face as she was dancing in a
> public assembly—1741'

c.360/1, p. 225

LO184   Let neither gold nor gems nor crowns entice
Your minds to commendable works inflame.

> [Mary Serjant]

fb.98, fol. 150

LO185   Let never want of money vex your brain
Than to the hierarchies of angelkind | T'abase your
                 spirits . . .

> [Sir Thomas Urquhart], 'To one who seemed to be
> grievously discontented with his poverty'

fb.217, p. 511 (incomplete)

LO186   Let never wisdom be of you forsaken,
Jove suffer'd most.

> Sir Thomas Urquhart, 'His friend's answer to the
> former paradox' ['You would fain have me . . .']

fb.217, p. 92

LO187 Let no man know thy secret deeds,
He once may be thy foe.

'Cloven hand'

b.234, p. 13

LO188 Let no man make his vaunt of his desert
For it is God that worketh in his heart.

c.339, p. 328

LO189 Let no man's will hold up his head for fame,
When inward want may not support the same.

c.339, p. 312

LO190 Let no one think Lucina's labors vain
And his great actions speak the emblem true.

[Phanuel Bacon], 'To Mrs. Carson midwife to the
Princess of Wales upon her collection of medals,
corals, &c.'

c.237, fol. 36

LO191 Let no profane ignoble foot tread near
And want a mourner at his funeral.

[Henry King], 'On [Richard Sackville, 3rd] earl of
Dorset' [an epitaph, attr. Richard Corbett]
[Crum L239]

b.200, p. 220; b.356, p. 259

LO192 Let no sad tear upon his tomb be shed,
With godlike envy, sigh for such a grave.

'Under the bust of General Wolfe, at General
Conway's'

c.378, p. 7

LO193 Let no vain alarms deceive thee
In a nutshell may be love.

'To Mira enclosed in a walnut shell'

Poetry Box I/45

LO194 Let noble Sir Positive lead up the van
That His Majesty lives at the Rose and Crown.
                                        [Which nobody can deny]

['The club men of the House of Commons' 1694]
[Crum L240; POAS V.430]

fb.70, p. 187

LO195 Let none admire why thus I sit lamenting
And cold as stone immovable as lead.

'Upon the death of his mistress'

b.356, p. 145

LO196 Let none ambition in his mind possess
For nothing's so contemptible as vice.

[Sir Thomas Urquhart], 'Pride is vile and
ignominious'

fb.217, p. 500

LO197 Let none despair of providence,
What seems impossible to view.

c.83/1, no. 108

LO198 Let none despair that truth is hidden oft
Because at length it shall be set aloft.

b.234, p. 259; c.339, p. 309

LO199 Let not Alicia slight an old man's praise
Views the pure gold that in the casket lies!

[Richard Vernon Sadleir?], 'To Miss Hamilton
daughter of the Revd. Mr. H. of Ireland, a young lady
of ten years old remarkably sensible and accomplished,
1786'

c.106, p. 76

LO200 Let not my sister tho' a wife,
And providential care.

'Hereto wrote by a parson to a new married sister'

c.303

LO201 Let not the fair my offer'd verse refuse
And rescue hallow'd passion from the grave.

[Sir Richard Steele]

File 14451

LO202 Let not the gaudy toys that strike the eye
So that ye all the vice of gaming flee.

'Answer to the riddles on pages [ ]'

c.578, p. 141

LO203 Let not the gay Florella grieve
'Tis racy, rich and fine.

Philip Wharton, 1st duke of Wharton(?), 'Song. To
the tune of When fair Aurelia, &c.'

c.468

LO204 Let not the Roman animosity
To make themselves a hydra-headed c[rew].

[Sir Philip Wodehouse], 'Rebellion is as the sin of
witchcraft'

File 17713

LO205 Let not the splendor of high birth
And beam them with eternal light.

'Relating to the fourth being the last emblem'

c.189, p. 85

LO206 Let not the sun go down upon your ire,
Let friendship's force subdue your rash desire.

c.339, p. 326

L0207 Let not the vice of gaming please your mind: |
                                                    2nd [riddle] solved
But learn to be content with what you find. |
                                                    1st [riddle] solved.

    'Answer to the riddles on pages [ ]'

c.578, p. 140

L0208 Let not thine eyes the sweets of slumber taste
The way will lead you to a life divine.

    'Pythagoras's golden verses'

c.391

L0209 Let not thy beauty make thee proud,
Thy virtue with a story.

    [Aurelian Townshend]

b.213, p. 14

L0210 Let not thy blackness move thee to despair
Thy face is comely, though thy brow be black.

    Henry Phillipps

b.156, p. 19

L0211 Let not thy wife command give, if she crave
Make not thy wife thy master nor thy slave.

    'To an uxorious man'

c.356

L0212 Let not your dame's inconstancy withhold
Are for their lightness 'bove the earth extoll'd.

    Sir Thomas Urquhart, 'A counsel not to be sorry, that
    a certain lady is something fickle'

fb.217, p. 170

L0213 Let Ormonde for the knaves provide
The last I'm sure will prove the best.

    'The advice'

fb.140, p. 86

L0214 Let other bards a spirit claim
And eat and drink and live together.

    [ ] Webb, 'By . . . at Bristol 1744, upon the ladies'
    refusing to be present at Ld. Euston's breakfast'

Poetry Box I/123

L0215 Let other bards implore Apollo's aid
May leave us still a race of men like him.

    'On East Shaftoe, a poem'

c.530, p. 1

L0216 Let others boast of an unlawful flame,
And her own works shall praise her in the dust.

    'A good wife in allusion to Prov. 31. by a lady'

c.244, p. 173

L0217 Let others boast Palladian skill
And wings the conscious hours with gladness as
                                                    they fly.

    James Woodhouse, 'Benevolence an ode by . . . a
    journeyman shoemaker, inscribed to his friend'

c.83/2, no. 352

L0218 Let others boast their heaps of shining gold,
While pitying maids our wondrous loves relate.

    [James] Hammond, 'The thoughts of Tibellus are not
    more closely copied than his elegance and simplicity,
    in the following imitation by . . .'

c.240, fol. 7

L0219 Let others boast with matchless skill to raise
And shepherd girls adorn our lowly grave.

    'Love-elegy'

c.89, p. 36

L0220 Let others glory in their hawks and hounds
The Heavens (without a cloud) would think in view.

    [Sir Aston Cokayne], 'To my son Mr Tho: Cokayne'

b.275, p. 96

L0221 Let others hail the rising sun
They know they've lost their friend.

    'To the honorable memory of a general friend. An
    elegy'

c.517, fol. 8r

L0222 Let others hope of wealth a shining store,
This hour be love's, be fortune's all the rest.

    'The 1st elegy of Tibullus'

c.368, p. 106

L0223 Let others, if they will, in lofty lays
So innocent his life, his conscience was so clear.

    'On the death of a poor, but very inoffensive fellow,
    who died suddenly. By a schoolboy'

c.578, p. 143

L0224 Let others live a court for me,
Who all things, but himself, had known.

    'On a private life'

b.371, no. 41

L0225 Let others' lives be in what blood, they list
My life is only in the blood of Christ.

    Sir Thomas Urquhart, 'The life of all flesh is blood.
    Levit. 17.14'

fb.217, p. 109

LO226 Let others paint the tragic scenes
Exists but in the art of teasing.

> H[enry] Skrine, 'On fun—or the modern art of
> tormenting . . . Bath—Jan. 4 1781'

c.509, p. 44

LO227 Let others praise as fancy leads,
Tomorrow put to sea again.

> [William Popple, trans.], '[Horace] book 1st. ode 7th.
> To Munatius Plancus'

fc.104/2, p. 22

LO228 Let others praise in pompous rhyme,
Smiles at the follies of the age.

> 'A description of a cottage, lately rebuilt by the Earl of
> Orrery, in his garden at Marston in memory of the
> Revd. Mr. Asberry, who liv'd there in the year,
> 1649 . . . inscribed to His Lordship 1752. Frome
> April 30'

c.360/3, no. 223

LO229 Let others praise the martial song,
The story of the wood.

> 'On the author of the ballad called The children in the
> wood'

c.343, p. 90

LO230 Let others reckless be, and not prepare
A care in abstract—too oft but tender were.

> [Sir Philip Wodehouse], 'Upon my virtuous cousin
> german Mary Carey'

b.131, back (no. 22)

LO231 Let others round the world and wand'ring roam
Me forth abroad. With it I'll stand or fall.

> [Sir Philip Wodehouse], 'Upon the Honorable
> Thomas Howard son to my Ld Marshall A sword at
> home'

b.131, back (no. 182)

LO232 Let others seek for trenchant mirth
I'll serve no other gods but thee.

Poetry Box IV/27

LO233 Let others seek the lying aids of art,
May thus Constantia look, Constantia smile.

> [John Langhorne], 'Theodosius to Constantia'

c.139, p. 552

LO234 Let others sing of heads and some of caps,
And Scaliger did thus outbrave his gout.

> [Henry Vintner], 'Upon a boil'
> [Crum L270]

b.356, p. 120

LO235 Let others take their course
Sing hymns of praise to thee.

> [John Austin], 'Hym. 18' [Hymn x, Devotions in the
> ancient way of offices, 1672, p. 95]

c.178, p. 17

LO236 Let others tempt your youth with praise not due,
But think what creatures swarm on Nile's too
fertile shore.

> 'Human life an epistle'

b.322, p. 15

LO237 Let others the all-bounteous Pow'r entreat
And proves a bright example to mankind.

> 'On friendship by a lady' [1734?]

File 274

LO238 Let others toil ambition's heights to scale:
Adieu to greatness, I renounce the whole.

> 'Retirement. A sonnet' [27 July 1799; pub.
> Gentleman's magazine, May 1800]

c.136, p. 163 (two versions); c.142, p. 503

LO239 Let others warm'd by fortune's fav'ring ray,
Nor quench with life's last sparks her Damon's fire!

> 'Elegy'

c.89, p. 99

LO240 Let others, whose ambitious hopes
They're lost forlorn to grope your last.

> R[obert] Dobyns, 'Seneca ex Thyestes. Act. 2 Cho.'

b.154, p. 71

LO241 Let pageant trophies heroes' urns adorn,
And stand recorded at the throne of grace.

> 'On the death of Joseph Rathbone of Liverpool—who
> died the 29th of 8th mo. 1790'

c.141, p. 557

LO242 Let prayer and faith thy practice be
If faith doth fail then for a supply call.

> Elizabeth Jekyll, 'Upon: prayer'

b.221, p. 33

LO243 Let proud blaspheming France defy
These ploughshares once were swords.

> Charles Atherton Allnutt, 'Hymn sung at St. Mary's
> church, the dissenting meeting house in the
> marketplace on Thursday 28th Nov. 1798 being set
> apart for a thanksgiving day'

c.112, p. 173

LO244 Let rigid famales boast of virtue's charms
Still be the sympathetic sorrows mine.

> 'On reading Rousseau's Nouvelle Heloise'

c.504, p. 50

LO245 Let Rome no more of relics sing
Some other form for fashion['s] sake.

   'Upon an antiquated closestool pan melted into a
   spoon'

   b.90, p. 6

LO246 Let sacred songs of praises be sung
And prove the world by righteousness and truth.

   [Robert Cholmeley], 'Psalm XCVI parap[hrase]d'

   c.190, p. i

LO247 Let sages, with superfluous pains,
Ye cannot fail to please.

   'Instructions from flowers'

   c.83/3, no. 828

LO248 Let servile Mavius scrawl his spiteful lays,
I'll let the fair alone, and you the quill.

   [Robert Cholmeley], 'An excuse to a gentleman for
   not answering his lampoon against me upon
   supposition that I had railed against the Cambridge
   ladies among whom was the mistress of his affections'

   c.190, p. 23

LO249 Let shining charity adorn your zeal,
O faithless man! Who yet distrusts him too.

   '[St. Matthew] chapter the 6.'

   c.83/1, no. 184

LO250 Let skeptics assert it they will
Unless from my being bewitch'd?

   [Charles Burney, the elder], 'The witch'

   c.33, p. 53

LO251 Let slander with her many tattling tongues,
They rend it not, but spread its odor.

   'Slander'

   c.344, p. 4

LO252 Let social mirth with gentle manners join;
We'll neither wish, nor fear, our final day.

   [Philip Dormer Stanhope, 4th earl of] Chesterfield

   Spence Papers, folder 76

LO253 Let some at ease consult their mind,
If you so good a judge approve.

   'On amusements'

   c.83/3, no. 939

LO254 Let some with rolling chimes
Than the lass of F—sh—m Mill.

   'The lass of F—sh—m Mill'

   Poetry Box I/58

LO255 Let still the pink, the lily and the rose
Pledge of a friendship not unworthy thine.

   Poetry Box III/34

LO256 Let stoics boast the cold relentless heart,
Her precepts make my neighbor's int'rest mine.

   'On sympathy'

   c.83/2, no. 339

LO257 Let that flat soul whose mercenary pen
The worst of poets but the best of men.

   'To his mistress'

   b.356, p. 218

LO258 Let that majestic pen that writes
That it could scarce be quench'd without a jury.

   [Robert Speed], 'A true . . . delineation of a great
   tumult . . . at the Counter at Woodstock called the
   counterscuffle' [pr. 1647 (Wing S4890A)]
   [Crum L283]

   b.200, p. 101 (incomplete)

LO259 Let the Act against vagabonds chase the Pretender:
Which none will refuse, but a Whig, or a Rumper.

   'On the act of Parliament [against vagabonds]'
   [Crum L284]

   c.570/1, p. 26

LO260 Let the Commons hunt after plots, With a hey &c.
After the old English way with a hey— | Nonny,
                     nonny, nonny, no.

   [Stephen College], 'A song. Whitehall. Feb. 28, 1679'
   [Crum L287]

   b.54, p. 1161; b.371, no. 39 (var.)

LO261 Let the critics adore
If my Celia were there.

   'Venus condemned'

   fb.107, p. 59

LO262 Let the discourse be serious you impart
It must be idle, frivolous, and vain.

   [Sir Thomas Urquhart], 'What the subject of our
   discourse ought to be with men of judgment and
   account'

   fb.217, p. 524

LO263 Let the dull merchant curse his angry fate,
And reap no fruit, no favor, no reward.

   [William] Walsh, 'Elegy—the unrewarded lover'

   c.351, p. 82; c.223, p. 52

LO264   Let the French stop and sing and a cage ye list(?)
                                             best
      Till liberty strung them and tun'd them again.

        [Phanuel Bacon], 'A song'

      c.237, fol. 72

LO265   Let the gay with pompous bowers
      Woods and verdant meads resound.

        H[enry] Skrine, 'Dedication of a Chinese temple at
        Ancoats in L—shire . . . Ancoats Augt. 10 1785'

      c.509, p. 76

LO266   Let the grave and the gay,
      Come here's to our friend and our glass.

        'Song 48'

      c.555, p. 75

LO267   Let the grounds lie high or low,
      Caesar rais'd to quell their pride.

        [William Popple, trans.], '[Horace] book 2nd. Ode
        9th. To Valgius'

      fc.104/2, p. 140

LO268   Let the little Welsh parson, I pray, ne'er offend,
      H stands for humility, hangman, and halter.

        [Charles Burney, the younger], 'On Mr. Jane—curate
        of Shinfield'

      c.37, p. 56

LO269   Let the mob rage, and all the Whiggish crew
      And all, great Anne, that love the church and you.

        'Semper idem, or the honor of self-consistency
        displayed in imitation of the third book [*i.e.*, book II
        ode 11?] of Horace. Humbly inscribed to the right
        honorable William Bromley esq: Speaker of the
        Honorable House of Commons'

      b.382(7)

LO270   Let the night perish, cursed be the morn
      Within the silent chambers of the grave.

        'A paraphrase on the 3d chapter of Job'

      fb.142, p. 33

LO271   Let the old heathens tune their song
      Round the wide earth, and wider heaven.

        [Isaac Watts, Hymns and spiritual songs (1707), bk. II,
        Hymn 21]

      c.180, p. 3

LO272   Let the Parnassian immortal choir
      And save our England precious blood, and
                             precious money too.

        'A Pindaric ode by way of panegyric upon the glorious
        conquests of magnanimous K[ing] William in the
        campaign 1692'

      b.111, p. 287

LO273   Let the soft shepherd tune his oaten reed
      And shake the dewdrop from the lion's mane!

        W[illiam] P[arsons], 'To a friend in love'
        [Crum L294]

      Greatheed Box/12

LO274   Let the soldiers rejoice
      Give the devil his due, they'll do better than Parker.

        'A new ballad' [parody of a song with the same first
        line in Thomas Betterton's The prophetess; last line
        refers to Thomas Parker, 1st earl of Macclesfield]
        [cf. Crum L295]

      fc.58, p. 149

LO275   Let the tempest of war
      To sully our measures of bliss.

        'Song 93'

      c.555, p. 141, p. 271

LO276   Let the Tories look big,
      Yet trade it does flourish amain. | Brave &c.

        'A song on K[ing] G[eorge II]'s speech to the
        Parliament'

      c.570/2, p. 105, p. 95 ('Let Tories . . .')

LO277   Let the wicked, conscience-wrung
      Half the globe shall bear thy name.

        [William Popple, trans.], '[Horace] book 3rd. ode
        27th. To Galatea on a voyage'

      fc.104/2, p. 300

LO278   Let the woman be damn'd (a moderate fate)
      That her lover refuses for want of estate.

        [Thomas Brown]

      c.549, p. 117

LO279   Let them neglect thy glory, Lord,
      In one eternal round.

        [Isaac Watts, Hymns and spiritual songs (1707), bk. II,
        Hymn 35]

      c.180, p. 31

LO280   Let them read Tully and Plato
      Will be study enough for me.

        [John Black]

      fc.107, p. 80

LO281   Let them that stand aloft on fortune's wheel,
      And always look for fear their footing slide.

      b.234, p. 312

LO282   Let them that unto choler much incline
      That gout's great pain is cured by pennyroyal.

        [Joshua Sylvester, trans. Guillaume de Salluste,
        seigneur Du Bartas], 'Of pennyroyal'

      b.284, p. 53

L0283 Let them that will ascend the tottering seat
But unacquainted with himself doth fall.

Sir Matthew Hale, 'On retirement . . . from a Latin
translation [of Seneca]'

fc.60, p. 60; see also 'Let him that will . . .'.

L0284 Let them turn satires 'gainst impartial death
Bear the eternal victory of death.

[ ] Nourse

b.197, p. 159

L0285 Let this book have for patrons such as sue
The book to them.

Sir Thomas Urquhart, 'The speeches of an observant
author to the patron of his treatise'

fb.217, p. 208

L0286 Let those who love the silent cell,
And what I share, I learn to prize.

Lady [ ] Burrell, 'The anchorite's invitation'

c.83/2, no. 406

L0287 Let thy tears no longer flow
Faithful servant enter here. | Though unpitied &c.

Miss [ ] White, of Edgbaston, 'Consolatory hymn to
the slow air in Berenice'

c.532; c.83/2, no. 333

L0288 Let Tories now no more repine,
Whilst angels smiling see the curst usurper's fall.

'A song to the tune of One evening having lost'

fc.58, p. 166

L0289 Let truth and love your thoughts secure,
A sure instruction sends.

'Importuning a very young lady to write'

c.83/1, no. 88

L0290 Let us adore th'eternal word,
Our bodies from the tomb.

[Isaac Watts, Hymns and spiritual songs (1707),
bk. III, Hymn 5]

c.180, p. 43

L0291 Let us drink and be merry dance joke and rejoice
Have broods to succeed us a hundred years hence.

[Thomas Jordan], 'Song 223'

c.555, p. 352

L0292 Let us drink disappointment to restless fanatics
And he's a false brother who'll not drink the same.

'Another health'

Poetry Box VI/2; see also 'Long life to the Queen . . .'.

L0293 Let us friends, our children rear,
Wicked men where'er they are.

[William Popple, trans.], '[Horace] book 3rd. ode 2nd'

fc.104/2, p. 196

L0294 Let us not doubt, that art may nature help,
Think how the bear doth form his ugly whelp.

c.339, p. 315

L0295 Let us still wash, our hands from every crime
That God may bless and here prolong our time.

c.339, p. 317

L0296 Let Varius in heroic verse,
And pare her nails to scratch.

[William Popple, trans.], '[Horace] book 1st. ode 6th.
To Agrippa'

fc.104/2, p. 20

L0297 Let venal bards their homage pay,
Vie with a birthday morn.

'To a lady on her birthday'

c.89, p. 119

L0298 Let vulgar souls endure a length of days,
And point the way to happiness, and thee.

[ ] Whitehead, 'An elegy on the death of
Mr. Sunderland student of Clare Hall in Cambr[idge]'

c.229/1, fol. 63v, fol. 83; c.116, p. 62 (on the death of
Samuel Forlow); Poetry Box IV/79

L0299 Let Whigs remember | The fourth of November,
Yet we barter the Church we own.

'Song', [1715; on the birthday and wedding day of
William III, the birthday of James the Old Pretender,
and the birthday and restoration of Charles II]
[Crum L318]

fc.58, p. 54; c.570/1, p. 70

L0300 Let wolves and bears be cruel in their kinds
But women meek, and have relenting minds.

'Kindness in women'
[Crum L322]

b.62, p. 119

L0301 Let wreaths of laurel deck the victor's tomb,
And her own radiance, light thee to mankind!

S[arah] Herd, 'Written under a print of Dr. Fothergill'

c.141, p. 390

L0302 Let your [ ] be a butterfly slightly hung on;
And you'll shine in the park, for 'tis taste-a-la-
mode.

'A LA MODE, or, a modern young lady' [Morning
herald, 17 Nov. 1781]

c.157, p. 124

L0303 Let's be jovial, fill our glasses,
Drinking souls can never die.

'Song 121'
[cf. Crum L1326]

c.555, p. 175

L0304 Let's charm some poet from his grave
'Tis ten to one she bears a child. | So old so cold &c.

[John Cleveland?], 'On an alderman who married a
very young wife'

b.93, p. 19

L0305 Let's go then, and those needless scruples quit
Showing my heart to her that wounded it.

'Caesar [in love with Cleopatra] to one of his
followers'

c.189, p. 19

L0306 Let's imitate the elephants, who enter
To say, it is; because they are but beasts.

Sir Thomas Urquhart, 'The speeches of a husband, to
his wife, with her answer'

fb.217, p. 57

L0307 Let's laugh and let's kiss, let's dance and let's sing
But none are so happy, so happy as we.

[Thomas Duffett], 'The shepherd' [from Beauties
triumph, 1676]

b.54, p. 1161

L0308 Let's live good honest lads [lives]
The devil the devil the devil the devil the devil and
all his works.

'Set to tune [by] Mr. Burrell'

c.160, fol. 85v

L0309 Let's love and let's laugh, let's dance, and let's sing
With spite and contempt on the ashes they gaze.

Poetry Box VII/72

L0310 Let's sing and be merry
A hundred years hence.

'A song on a hundred years hence'
Poetry Box VII/68

L0311 Let's take impatience, sickness, banishment,
As tributes which we pay into this life.

[Sir Thomas Urquhart], 'We should not be troubled at
the accidents of fortune nor those things which cannot
be evited'

fb.217, p. 525

L0312 Let's toss up our bonnets my Sawney
May Jemmy enjoy all | His kingdoms again.

'A loyal Scotch song'

b.111, p. 62

L0313 Let's use our time, and let us still suppose
No greater loss, that time that we do lose.

c.339, p. 325

L0314 Let's view my little atlas over now,
As Nelson lately did—Britons huzza!

'The pocket atlas intended for a speaking'

c.91, p. 302

L0315 Levina chaste as matron chaste may be
She went forth honest but return'd a queen.

'In Levinam'

b.197, p. 161

L0316 Lewes de Granado doth relate
Go Socrates unto my grave.

Sir John Strangways

b.304, p. 36

L0317 Lewis is well—if he well thinks him so,
Then be content, and thou art well.

[Sir Philip Wodehouse], 'Lewis is well'

b.131, back (no. 131)

L0318 Liberality in nobles in lawyers' eloquence
Thus to each of these belong such a quality.

[Sir Nicholas] Bacon, 'Qualities belonging to certain
persons'

fa.8, fol. 160

L0319 Licinus, know that safer way
Them fill'd with too prosperous wind.

[G. T.], 'Mediocrity so used in either fortune'
[translation of Horace book II ode 10]

Trumbull Box: Poetry Box XIII/85

L0320 Lie heavy on him, Earth, for he
Laid many a heavy load on thee.

[Abel Evans], 'Epitaph on Sir J. Vanbrugh, archite[ct]'

c.113/4; c.233, p. 100 ('Lie heavy, Earth, on him . . .');
c.193, p. 132 (on Sir Christopher Wren); c.360/3, no. 28;
see also 'Reader beneath this stone', 'Under this stone,
reader . . .'.

L0321 Lie still if you are Wise
You'll be damn'd if you rise.

'Written with chalk upon a tombstone of one
[Alderman] Wise'

c.360/2, no. 232; c.74, p. 26

LO322   Lie still sweet maid, and wait the Almighty's will!
Then rise, unchang'd, and be an angel still.

'On a beautiful lady who died at 18. The following
couplet was written with chalk on her tombstone by a
stranger who was told her character, and lamented the
want of an epitaph'

c.74; see also 'Lie sweet in dust . . .', 'Sleep soft in
dust . . .', 'Sleep on blest angel . . .' 'Soft rest thy
dust . . .'.

LO323   Lie sweet in dust, and wait the almighty Will,
Then rise unchang'd, and be an angel still.

'Epitaphs'

c.378, p. 32; see also 'Lie still sweet maid . . .', 'Sleep soft
in dust . . .', 'Soft rest thy dust . . .', 'Sleep on blest
angel . . .'.

LO324   Lie thus (the fencer cries) thus must you guard
W[h]ere thou kill but one a thousand I do kill.

'The fencer and physic doctor'

c.356; see also 'And thus . . .'.

LO325   Life how uncertain! how precarious!
But what were children then, are angels now!

'Epitaph on Dorothy, Sarah and Ann Soosly in
Chesham churchyard Buckinghamshire'

c.487, p. 66

LO326   Life is a jest and all things show it
I thought so once, but now I know it.

[John] Gay, 'Epitaph on Gay's monument in
Westminster Abbey, wrote by himself'

c.360/1, p. 161; c.360/2, no. 156; fb.142, p. 66; fc.53, p. 164

LO327   Life is a journey from our mothers' wombs
Eternal death will be our journey's end.

[Sir Richard Bulstrode?], 'The journey'

fb.88, p. 115

LO328   Life is but a mixture of profit and pleasure
Who would not in love's happy dominion forever
live.

'A song upon love'

b.54, p. 1160

LO329   Life is chequer'd toil and pleasure
Let them lose or win. | On the deck is heard no
other sound, &c.

'Song 151'

c.555, p. 210

LO330   Life is fleeting, feed not sorrow,
And bliss there reigns without allay.

'On hope'

c.83/1, no. 5

LO331   Life is uncertain, death is sure;
Sin is the wound, Christ is the cure.

'An epitaph in St. Michael's churchyard Oxford'

c.240, p. 134; c.186, p. 114

LO332   Life ne'er exulted in so rich a prize,
So from it ravish'd, leaves it bleak and bare.

[Robert] Burns, 'Elegy on [the late] Miss Burnett
daughter of Lord Monboddo . . . .'

Poetry Box XII/60; c.142, p. 238 (stanzas 1-6)

LO333   Life never grudge to God to lend,
It makes his great goodness known.

[Edmund Wodehouse], 'May 10 [1715]'

b.131, p. 210

LO334   Life recounting all its gains,
Than your siren arts can bring.

'Life'

c.360/2, no. 248

LO335   Life seems my greatest comfort but at best
It proves the hindrance to my joys and rest.

[Petrarch]

b.211, p. 60

LO336   Life the dear precarious boon!
Awful period! Who can tell.

'Life an ode'

c.83/3, no. 834

LO337   Life, thou prime source of all that's good and fair,
To live on earth, that I in heaven may live.

'Life. A sonnet' [24 Sept. 1799]

c.136, p. 167

LO338   Life's a long tragedy: this globe the stage
Thus angels mix their flames, and more divinely
glow.

[Isaac] Watts, 'A poem to Mitio soon after his
marriage addressed to him by . . .'

c.244, p. 328

LO339   Life's a vapor up it flies
Cuts a caper, then it dies.

'On Mr. Noverre the dancing master's marriage'

c.74

LO340   Life's a varied, bright illusion,
Catch the pleasures ere they fade.

[Ann (Ward)] Radcliffe, 'Song'

c.83/3, no. 849

LO341 Life's business ended, and each task complete,
Now hard to feel the loss, and not repine.

'On the death of Henrietta youngest daughter of the
Revd. Mr. Archer Leigh who died at the age of fifteen
on April 12th 1793'

c.82, p. 14

LO342 Life's journey half was o'er, when far away
A nimble panther with a speckled hide.

[William Parsons]

Greatheed Box/52

LO343 Life's like a flow'r the gard'ner plants
Borne down with many years.

'Life an ode'

c.83/3, no. 1046

LO344 Life's ocean slept— the liquid gale
Where far from me you deign to dwell.

Diggle Box: Poetry Box XI/17

LO345 Lift high, my soul, thy praises to the Lord
And heav'n, and earth, and seas in the loud consort
join.

Tho[mas] Scott, jr., 'Psalm 104'

c.244, p. 258

LO346 Lift up your hearts to things above,
Go on! We'll meet you there!

'Hymn 105th'

c.562, p. 143

LO347 Lifted t'our leader his divining wand
God by a straw a rush will push thee down.

Poetry Box VI/95

LO348 Light-fingered Catch to keep their [i.e., his] hands
in ure,
To steal such things, as need must come to light.

'Upon one that stole a pound of candles'
[Crum L374, 'wretch', 'his hands']

b.200, p. 408

LO349 Light of life seraphic fire,
Still we all enjoy in love.

'Hymn 45th'

c.562, p. 53

LO350 Light of my life whose cheering rays are fled
There to whose height thy spotless soul is sped.

[William Hayley], 'Sonnet . . . May 11 [1800]'

File 6968

LO351 Light trips the spring in sandals shod
And wraps thee in the pictur'd robe.

E. S. J., 'Ode to spring'

Poetry Box x/55

LO352 Light-heel'd Faunus fond to range,
Cut thy robe or tear thy hair.

[William Popple, trans.], '[Horace] book 1st. ode 17th.
To the same [Tyndaris]'

fc.104/2, p. 52

LO353 Lightning and love have cross-complexion'd power
Each is, and each eats up, what pois'nous is.

[Sir Philip Wodehouse], 'Italian proverbial import: est
flumen venenum'

b.131, p. 28

LO354 Like a cold fatal sweat which ushers death
Whose influence may crown thy glorious war.

Hen[ry] King, [elegy on Gustavus Adolphus]
[Crum L379]

File 16934

LO355 Like a flourishing young gallant, newly come to his
land
But in the ensuing ditty you shall hear how he was
inclin'd. | Like a young courtier of the king's |
And the king's young courtier.

c.391

LO356 Like a good-natured fingerpost, showing the way
You're just like a turnpike, with no trust is here.

Diggle Box: Poetry Box XI/11

LO357 Like a long snake, my slender body moves
But leave 'em when his absence brings on night.

'Riddle on a lace'

c.360/1, p. 115

LO358 Like a poor ghost the night I seek;
My Harriet!—may like thine be cold!

[Charlotte (Turner) Smith], 'Verses on the death of a
lady, written in 1794'

c.141, p. 91

LO359 Like a poor tree whose shelter's gone
I am even ready to despair and die.

[Mrs. ( ) Feilding]

b.226, p. 45

LO360 Like a prompt sculler one physician plies
Conduct you soonest to the Stygian shores.

c.546, p. 31

LO361 Like a soft flow'r, on some deserted plain,
That we this truth may learn—whatever is, is right.

'From the Norfolk chronicle on the death of Miss
Lucy Howes—of Thorpe'

c.90

LO362 Like Æsop's fellow slave: O Mercury
Mercury in stealing, but liest like a Greek.

[John Donne], 'Upon Mercurius Gallobelgicus'

b.114, p. 68

LO363 Like as I found you
Therefore I refrain.

'Braye Lute Book,' Music Ms. 13, fol. 22v

LO364 Like as the day his course doth consume
So full of change, is of this world the glory.

'On Robt Fabian Alderm[an] writer of a chronicle of
England and France 1511' [d. 1513]

fb.143, p. 6

LO365 Like as the hand which hath been us'd to play
That something more than bodies us combine.

[Thomas Carew?], 'To a friend in absence' [also attr.
W. Strode]
[Crum L387]

c.102, p. 25

LO366 Like as the hart explores with curious eyes
Light of my countenance, my joy and endless peace!

George Montagu, 'Psalm the 42d: paraphrased'

fc.135, p. 9

LO367 Like as the sun returning doth disperse,
Will spend our night in wishes day to see.

b.216, p. 169

LO368 Like as the tree of fruit most pure
To save for the one and despise the other.

[Sir Nicholas] Bacon, 'Perils following fortune by
envy and malice'

fa.8, fol. 161v

LO369 Like birds of prey death snatcht away
In heaven above.

'Epitaph 4th [High Wycombe, Buckinghamshire]

c.158, p. 84

LO370 Like charity itself no ill she thought
Forever loving, and forever lov'd.

'In memory of Martha, the wife of Henry Whitfield,
M. A. vicar of this parish . . . who died April the 1st:
1753. Aged 56'

c.241, p. 101; see also 'All hail bright beams . . .'.

LO371 Like gold, she still corrupts those who adore,
Free, as the sun, and boundless as the air.

[Horace Walpole, 4th earl of Orford],
'Vi[s]c[ountes]s Vane' [d. 1788]
[Crum L398]

c.157, p. 71

LO372 Like heaven, who oft with secrecy bestows,
The manner speaks her, and is self-reveal'd.

John Lockman, 'Extempore: on receiving, (privately,)
a considerable present from a great lady . . . May 1739'

c.267/1, p. 167; c.268 (first part), p. 9

LO373 Like hermit poor in pensive place obscure
The flames may serve which from my heart arise.

[Sir Walter Raleigh]
[Crum L407, 'Like to an hermit']

b.213, p. 65 (ll. 1–16); fb.69, p. 236 (ll. 1–16); b.4, fol. 2v
(damaged; ll. 1–16)

LO374 Like jolly sons of Bacchus
We'll chuck him in the bowl.

'The sons of Bacchus by a gentleman'

c.361

LO375 Like leaves on trees, the race of man is found.
So flourish these, when those are past away.

'Metaphor'

c.81/1, no. 152

LO376 Like Milo whilst her husband was a calf
To bear him now that he's become an ox.

[Sir Thomas Urquhart], 'Of the trouble which a
certain gentlewoman of too [?] a carriage was
supposed to have by satisfying as oft [?] by did the
matrimonial desires of her bedfellow who had waxed
of late very grown fat and corpulant'

fb.217, p. 387

LO377 Like one who in her third widowhood doth profess
But to know, that I love thee, and would be loved.

[John Donne], 'Dalla corte' [to Sir Rowland
Woodward]
[Crum L401]

b.114, p. 217; b.148, p. 94

LO378 Like raging tempests, which aloft
As avarice had digg'd for it before.

[Edmund] Waller

Trumbull Box: Poetry Box XIII/91

LO379 Like sharpers, who a livelihood,
To the game away!

John Lockman, 'The cajolers: a catch or glee'

c.267/2, p. 154

LO380 Like some sweet flow'r, that scents the ambient air,
Mortality may weep, but must resign.

  S[arah] Herd, 'On the death of a lovely girl (Sarah
  Jepson) who died at the age of 9'

  c.141, p. 388

LO381 Like that poor callow bird, scarce fledg'd doth hop
Sprightly, beyond the reach, of calumny.

  [George Daniel], 'An apology'

  b.121, fol. 16v

LO382 Like the fawn, whose dam it seeks,
Ripe, as now you are for man?

  [William Popple, trans.], '[Horace] book 1st. Ode 23d.
  To Chloe'

  fc.104/2, p. 66

LO383 Like the ridolto, Mira shines,
And, clasp'd by thee, I'm doubly blest.

  John Lockman, 'Mira and Flirtilla, or the ridolto and
  the masquerade . . . March 1749'

  c.267/2, p. 93

LO384 Like the soft gladd'ning dawn of light
That feels another's woe.

  'Friendship an ode'

  c.130, p. 24; c.83/1, no. 157

LO385 Like those points of Cupid's lovely strain,
Quick by dark proofs my zealous thoughts explain.

  Sir Thomas Urquhart, 'In the second line of this
  distich are inserted all the letters of the alphabet'

  fb.217, p. 136

LO386 Like to a light fast lock[ed] in lantern dark
I may enjoy my hopes, the best at last.

  'The joy in sweet harmony of praise that never shall
  have an end'

  b.202, p. 95

LO387 Like to a ship that is by tempest ta'en
And to destruction are thy foes resolv'd.

  b.216, p. 154

LO388 Like to a silent tone of unspoke speeches
To see such strange lines wrote on's epitaph.

  [Richard] Corbett(?), 'Pure nonsense'
  [Crum L406]

  b.62, p. 54

LO389 *Man's life is* | Like to the bubble in the brook
The water glides man's life is done.

  [James Rhodes?]

  b.206, p. 145

LO390 Like to the damask rose you see,
The gourd consumes—and man he dies.

  [Francis Quarles], 'Epitaph. On Richard Humble. St.
  Mary Ovarie'
  [Crum L409-411]

  c.81/1, no. 244 (ll. 1–12); c.189, p. 52 (var.); b.4, fol. 5
  (var.; damaged)

LO391 Like to the eye which sleep doth chain,
The news renew'd, and man new-liv'd.

  [William Strode], 'On resurrection'

  b.200, p. 228

LO392 Like to the falling of a star
The flight is past and man forgot.

  [Henry King, 'Sic vita']
  [Crum L412]

  b.213, p. 63

LO393 Like to the rolling of an eye,
The news disprov'd, man's life expir'd.

  [William Strode?], 'On mortality'
  [Crum L415]

  b.200, p. 228

LO394 Like to the seed put in earth's womb;
So man that dies shall live again.

  'On man's resurrection'
  [part of Crum L409-411]

  c.189, p. 57

LO395 Like to the self-inhabiting snail
So doth my mistress's beauty in a taffata gin.

  'A comparison'

  b.197, p. 229

LO396 Like Venus smiles, like Juno walks,
Confess her beauty deity.

  [ ] Nash, 'On Celia'

  fc.73

LO397 Like you all I first sprung from our mother the
              earth,
And I promise next winter I'll surely befriend.

  '[Enigma/Charade/Conundrum] 61 [skates]'

  c.389

LO398 Linkt was in wedlock a lofty thrasonical huff snuff:
This my blade in thy body should have been with
              speediness hasted.

  'Of a craking cutter extracted out of Sir Thomas More
  his Latin epig[rams]'

  b.207, p. 6

L0399 Linus replied being ask'd which was the best
Himself h'had rather to the shrew'd one wed.

  [Sir Thomas Urquhart], 'The preposterous and [?]
  opinion of [?] brains affecting a [?] [?] to the stain and
  universal reproach of the deservedly illustrious
  feminine sex'

  fb.217, p. 518

L0400 Listen dear Mira, to the voice of truth,
That pall the heart and banish calm repose.

  'To Mira a prey to discontent'

  c.83/3, no. 746

L0401 Listen gallants to my words,
See them, when the sky doth fall.

  [James Shirley], 'The commonwealth of birds'
  [Crum L427]

  b.356, p. 301

L0402 Listen, my fair one, whilst you hear
Will make me think the more on you.

  'At parting'

  c.416

L0403 Listen ye Douffs beneath this yew,
You might [have] been blest, and happy here.

  [Mrs. Christian Kerr], 'Advice to the Douffs, of the
  district of Kelso, under the yew tree at Sunlaws—
  inscribed to my Lady Chatto, 1727'

  c.102, p. 133

L0404 Listen, ye sons of Israel, to my voice,
And with the father sleeps the good-for-nothing son.

  [Richard] Daniel, dean of Armagh, 'The rich not
  always happy. Psalm 49'

  c.244, p. 360

L0405 Little bird with bosom red,
Eat thee bones and all my boy.

  [John?] Langhorne, 'To a redbreast'

  c.83/1, no. 247

L0406 Little Cupid I find
Then he like other blind puppies | Shall drown—

  c.188, p. 86

L0407 Little Cupid one day
Sunt cetera, De.

  John Hoadly, 'Anacreon ode the 40th burlesqued'

  c.176, p. 40

L0408 Little girl in swaddling clothes,
Till she's in her bridal bed.

  [Edward Young? or William Pattison?], 'On Lord
  Hervey's daughter, a month old, in imitation of
  [Ambrose] Phillips'

  c.176, p. 69

L0409 Little hinderer of my rest
Safe shall sleep and cease to bleed.

  'Verses on a flea'

  c.546, p. 8

L0410 Little, magic, Tunbridge fairy,
Ysca's banks with those of Thames.

  H[enry] Skrine, 'To a lady in Brecknockshire with a
  small Tunbridge writing box . . . Tunbridge Wells
  Augt 9 1797'

  c.509, p. 90

L0411 Little Mary has from nature
Little Mary has no art.

  [Richard Brinsley Butler] Sheridan, 'On Miss Linley'

  Poetry Box IV/195

L0412 Little pretty girls and boys,
Is good friends with Mast', or Miss.

  [Elizabeth (Shirley) Compton, countess of
  Northampton]

  Accession 97.7.40

L0413 Little queen of infant treasure
To lull thy waxen babe asleep.

  'Lines addressed to a child of four years old sitting at
  her baby house surrounded by her playthings by a lady'

  c.504, p. 161

L0414 Little siren of the stage
Leave the Britons, rough and free.

  [Ambrose Philips], 'To Signiora Cuzzoni'

  c.360/1, p. 181

L0415 Little Tom Hodman lies underneath this sod
And now it's his turn to be turn'd into earth.

  [Barnaby Gouche], 'An epitaph in Croyland churchyard'

  c.229/1, fol. 34v

L0416 Little Tommy Timperan had an old yoww
And Cat by the fire, jingling keys!

  c.155, fol. 22

L0417 Little tube of mighty pow'r
Happiest he of happy men.

  [Isaac Hawkins Browne, 'A pipe of tobacco'; imitation
  of Ambrose Philips]
  [cf. Crum B446, C776, O868]

  Poetry Box I/139; c.344, p. 78

LO418 Live and destroy
Th' interruptions of thy joy.

    Jane Halford, 1666

    b.52/2, p. 129

LO419 Live and love enjoy the fair
Careless, airy, gay and free.

    'Song 172'

    c.555, p. 268

LO420 Live, and love, you peevish harlot,
With the loss of all miscarry.

    'Beauty's decay'

    fb.107, p. 43

LO421 Live happy great William,
Good Lord of thy mercy defend me.

    'On the Duke of Berwick's plot'

    c.530, p. 171

LO422 Live, my dear Hartop, live today,
And grow for future years.

    [Isaac] Watts, 'To John Hartop esquire'

    c.244, p. 320

LO423 'Live while you live,' the epicure would say
I live in pleasure, when I live to Thee.

    [Philip] Doddridge, 'Dum vivimus, vivamus. This was
    the motto of Dr. Doddridge's family arms, and he
    wrote under it the following lines, very expressive of
    his general temper'

    c.240, fol. 1; c.83/1, no. 3

LO424 Live with me and be my love
Then live with me and be my love.

    [Christopher Marlowe], 'The passionate shepherd to
    his love'

    c.362, p. 6; see also 'Come live . . .'.

LO425 Lives there a friend sincere as we are told
Let me be hang'd, if Gascoyne is not he.

    T[homas] M[orell], 'Martial l.1 ep. 40' [imitated in
    'Lives there a girl . . .']

    c.395, p. 60

LO426 Lives there a girl so chaste as we are told,
Whom all admire and Barker is her name.

    [Thomas Morell], '[Martial bk. 1, ep. 40: 'Lives there
    a friend'] imitated' [On Anne Barker, later his wife]

    c.395, p. 60

LO427 Lives there a man, not awed by servile fear,
And snatch'd from chains and death the happy
                               maid.

    [Thomas Morell], 'The patriot. 1731' [on the earl of
    Bath]

    c.395, p. 26

LO428 Lives there a man who turns from pity's sighs
A friendship fly from anguish with neglect.

    'Verses to a gentleman who often expressed his dislike
    of being pitied'

    c.504, p. 141

LO429 Lives there a wretch that with unmelting eye
And claim the tear she shed for other's woe!

    R[ichard] V[ernon] S[adleir], 'Written at Miss Gore's
    desire for a drawing from the picture of Sterne's
    Maria by Angelica—see The sentimental journey
    vol. 2'

    c.106, p. 94

LO430 Lives there compos'd of earthly frame
To lurk accountable to none?

    [Samuel Wesley, the younger], 'Reflections on the two
    following lines in Oldham: Lord of myself
    accountable to none | But to my conscience and my
    God alone'

    c.244, p. 440

LO431 Lives yet unsung this blooming fair?
And finds the third in you.

    [Robert Cholmeley], 'To Miss Merrill: Day having
    seen the foregoing copy of verses upon [a poem called
    The four real beauties]'

    c.190, p. 25

LO432 Lizzy, who innocent would toy;
Shield them heav'n! I glide to bliss!

    John Lockman, 'The father, to his dying child . . . Feb.
    1741/2'

    c.267/2, p. 189

LO433 Lo Amyrillis—now have I found out
For his thy pipe, is blessed from above.

    [Sir Philip Wodehouse], 'Upon my son Savage's sister
    an excellent poetess Maria Willis'

    b.131, back (no. 70)

LO434 Lo contemplation, best companion; here
Be humble, and be just.

    'Over the door, on the inside' [at Pensoroso]

    fc.51, p. 101

LO435 Lo death invested in a robe of ermine,
As runs the gliding sand i' 'th' hour-glass.

    'On a skeleton sitting on a pile of dead mens' bones'

    c.189, p. 64

LO436 Lo! Direct thy wand'ring eye
To bring home Charles, and give the world a king.

　[ ] Robinson, 'May the 29th. King Charles' return'

　c.190, p. 81

LO437 Lo! Discord from her hideous cavern springs,
And ev'ning, with its dew embalms the dead.

　'On war'

　c.83/3, no. 789

LO438 Lo He cometh, countless trumpets,
Come to judgment; stand before the Son of Man!

　'Hymn on the day of judgment'

　Poetry Box v/92

LO439 Lo he that all our tubs was wont to mend
The lords that hath, will bring in open sight.

　[John Taylor], 'The search' [from 'The world turned upside down']

　fb.40, p. 381

LO440 Lo, hear the blessed son of God and man,
And how all people must abide his doom.

　[verses on the books of the New Testament]

　fb.69, p. 115

LO441 Lo! Here a general metropolitan
Who God's anointed, and his church betray'd.

　'On [John] Williams Abp. of York' [d. 25 March 1650]
　[Crum L464]

　b.137, p. 201

LO442 Lo! Here a tatter'd slip of blue,
Red, fall to view as winter cherry.

　[Thomas Hull]

　c.528/45

LO443 Lo here she lies that was and was Not
Was in her life, Not honest, not a whore.

　'On Peg Not'

　b.208, p. 62

LO444 Lo here, the Christian's great artillery,
And in the end, thy God, become thy law.

　'To a lady with St. Austin's meditations. 1703'

　c.239

LO445 Lo, I can argue laws
Wherewith I will their *summum jus*, divide.

　[Sir Philip Wodehouse], 'Nicolas Walgrave (a noble soldier with the King) Lo I can argue laws'

　b.131, back (no. 183)

LO446 Lo I who erst at break of day
And I am thine with all my heart.

　F. N. B. Mundy, 'The harehunter a burlesque imitation of various parts of Milton's L'allegro and Il penseroso written in 1765'

　Poetry Box x/140

LO447 Lo! In the orient when the gracious light
Unlook'd on diest,—unless you get a son.

　[William] Shakespeare, 'Quick prevention'
　[Sonnet VII]

　c.94

LO448 Lo, in yon silent grave are left,
And join'd them in the realms of day.

　'On the funeral of Mr. [ ] whose wife and child and himself died within a short time of each other'

　c.83/2, no. 619

LO449 Lo! Kneeling at yon rail with pensive air
The move to sympathy the feeling breast.

　[Edward Jerningham], 'The Magdalens'

　c.130, p. 10

LO450 Lo! My fair, the morning lazy,
Christmas comes but once a year.

　'The year'

　c.382, p. 64

LO451 Lo! O'er the earth the kindling spirits pour
Ethereal dew to glad the earth in showers.

　[William Hayley]

　File 6950

LO452 Lo on my neck this twist I bind
Both by the gem and by the place.

　[William Strode], 'Idem'
　[Crum L496]

　b.205, fol. 32r

LO453 Lo paleface death doth in his chariot ride
The rich, the poor, either by sea or land.

　J[ohn] R[obinson], 'Pallida mors aequo pede pulsat pauperum tabernas regum et turres' [Horace book I ode 4]

　c.370, fol. 70

LO454 Lo Phoebus! From the southern hemisphere,
Whose object is the welfare of mankind.

　John Lockman, 'A simile: presented to His Majesty at St James's, New Year's Day 1761'

　c.267/1, p. 300

LO455   Lo, the destroying angel flies
And God's avenging sword.

     [Isaac Watts, Hymn]

c.180, p. 38

LO456   Lo! The sun with splendor shining
And gives the heart a—fairer spring.

     Charles Atherton Allnutt, 'Spring . . . wrote this when
at the Hot Wells and inserted it in a Bristol paper . . .'

c.112, p. 1

LO457   Lo! Walbrook's church thy pride O Wren, of late,
Squats his broad, bulky, brawny, breech before her.

     [N.] H[erbert], 'Epigram upon the Mansion House
built so as to hide the famous church of Walford'

Spence Papers, folder 91

LO458   Lo! What a pleasing form is there
Eternal horrors on thy soul.

     [Thomas?] Scott, jr., 'Ecclesiastes II. Verse last'

c.244, p. 408

LO459   Lo where he comes, the monarch of the earth
My newborn soul, in an immortal verse.

     [George Daniel]

b.121, fol. 23v

LO460   Lo! Where in yonder glory-fringed sky
A death as placid! A reward as sure!

     Dr. [ ] Cooper, 'An elegy'

c.83/2, no. 606

LO461   Lo yonder sails th'unlucky gaudy yacht
And winds and tempest should these victims share.

     'Epode the 10th imitated. Hor.'

c.233, p. 11

LO462   Loaded with wood and wet with water too,
And strait I call'd for you to have it tied.

     R[obert] Shirley, 1st earl of Ferrers, 'Death and the
carpenter. From Boileau'

c.347, p. 26

LO463   Loaden with cares, oppressed with woe,
Shalt 'venge, and answer Lord for me.

     H[enry] C[olman], 'On my enemies' unjust malice'
[Crum L513]

b.2, p. 4

LO464   Lock'd are the golden gates of day
Beyond the pow'r of human reach.

     Christopher Jones, 'Midnight thoughts by . . . a
journeyman weaver, who makes verses while writing at
his loom'

c.83/1, no. 14

LO465   Lock'd in the arms of downy sleep
That flash that melts the world.

     Rev. [ ] Conyers(?), 'Stanzas by . . . on being waked
out of his sleep by a violent storm of thunder and
lightning'
[Crum L515, 'balmy sleep']

c.504, p. 66; c.391, p. 27 (incomplete?)

LO466   Lockman a bard, a merry sinner,
Come, and we'll fancy Virgil there.

     John Lockman, 'A card, sent to Monsieur de Voltaire,
in Paris . . . Nov. 1741'

c.267/1, p. 74

LO467   Lodg'd in the Northern Pole, the wise
And veers about no more.

     [ ] Kennick, 'The political magnet, a simile'

c.53, fol. 49

LO468   Logicians should define and argue matters
Are wholly employ'd in making of divisions.

     [Sir Thomas Urquhart], 'Against seditious persons,
alluding to the homonymy of the word division'

fb.217, p. 516

LO469   Lolling at ease in elbow chair,
Or any view to praise.

     Abraham Oakes, 'The introduction' [to 'Poetical
essays']

c.50, p. 1

LO470   London awake! Behold Pitt's gen'rous friend,
Secure his voice, and freedom is your own.

     John Lockman, 'A memento to the citizens during the
election for members . . . 20 March 1761'

c.267/1, p. 307

LO471   London bred me, Westminster fed me,
Earth did crave me, and heaven would have me.

     'Epitaph. On Revd. R[alph] Tyrer at Kendal'

c.81/1, no. 273; c.241, p. 109

LO472   London was a noble place O hone O [hone]
As much in English as O hone O hone.

b.213, p. 44

LO473   Lone bird of Eve whose liquid throat
Of sweetest peace to thee.

     [John Wolcot ('Peter Pindar')], 'Invocation to a robin
red-breast'

File 16344

LO474   Lone minstrel of the moonlight hour,
I hear my sorrows mix with mine [thine?].

     [John Walcot ('Peter Pindar')], 'The nightingale'

c.83/2, no. 583

LO475   Lone to the night I pour my plaintive sighs
Thy love-attesting eye, and hush'd repose were
                                                made.

   'Sonnet'

c.344, p. 22

LO476   Long, ah! too long soft Farinelli reign'd
And will maintain their right and liberty.

   'On the French players' coming to England'

fb.142, p. 9 (second series)

LO477   Long as on earth by faith I live
My glorious heavenly Lord.

   'Hymn 57th'

c.562, p. 68

LO478   Long at receipt of custom, Matthew sits
That we (howe'er began) may like him end.

   [Edward] Sparke, 'Poem 32—on St. Matthew'

b.137, p. 67

LO479   Long bound in ice, and horrid hills of snow
Runs, to thy shame, and argues thy own guilt.

   [George Daniel]

b.121, fol. 54v

LO480   Long by the madness of a guilty age
And all the willing would their power united own.

   Joseph Dobbins, 'To Sir Richard Steele on his comedy
   of The conscious lovers' [22 Nov. 1722]

Poetry Box x/10(1)

LO481   Long detain'd by winds contrary,
Who, now, the palm will claim | For arts and arms.

   John Lockman, 'The invocation, to Neptune. Writ
   extempore, at Calais, when returning, with the
   Duchess of Buckingham to England. The tune, What
   is greater joy and pleasure. Set to music by Dr. Boyes'

c.267/2, p. 84

LO482   Long did the fair Camilla sigh
And teach disease itself to smile.

   'On a young lady in an intermitting fever, who tried
   the Jesuit's bark without success, and was cured by the
   new remedy. 1752'

c.360/3, no. 246

LO483   Long exercise my friend
We pleasing find.

c.156, p. 197

LO484   Long flourish the Orange and the rose,
Or to hell with our Protestant king.

   'The Protestant king'

b.111, p. 390

LO485   Long grass in valleys short on mountains grows,
Each top is bare, and type is like unt' it.

   'Humility'

c.356

LO486   Long had Britannia's sons, in wealth, and ease,
But, to the blessings of your glorious reign.

   [Abraham Cowley?]

File 3783

LO487   Long had I sought in vain to find,
Denote the rage with which he writes.

   'A simile in the manner of Swift'

c.83/3, no. 999

LO488   Long had Melpomene beheld with pain
With what success, each aching bosom ask?

   [ ] Birch, 'On hearing a lady read tragedy'

c.504, p. 11

LO489   Long had our isle by ignorance been led
Nor call him friend, who is our country's foe.

   J. Walker, of Eton, 'Prologue to Julius Caesar'

c.591

LO490   Long had the French navy, with that of proud
                                                Spain,
Ye angels fly round, and direct William's lance!

   John Lockman, 'Anson and Warren. On their signal
   victory, over the French, 3d May 1747, off Cape
   Finesterre. Set to music by Lewis Granom esqr: and
   sung very joyously, by Mr. Sullivan; many nights
   together, at Ranelagh'

c.267/2, p. 6

LO491   Long had the rose, in vernal pomp array'd,
Will vie in charms with Berenice's hair.

   John Lockman, 'To the author of The carnation, a
   poem, addressed to the honorable Miss Grace
   Pulham . . . April 1753'

c.267/1, p. 70

LO492   Long had the shepherds unadorn'd
That gave us back our queen.

   'Eliza's return'

c.241, p. 84

LO493   Long had the world in gloomy shades
As time his course shall run.

   [John Austin?], 'Hym. 9'

c.178, p. 8

L0494 Long had young Damon sought, and sought in vain,
But faintly paint the melancholy darkness of his soul.

'The discovery' [Edinburgh, March 1763; Leicester,
14 Oct. 1763]

c.136, p. 49

L0495 Long has great Louis form'd the vast design
When keeping faith betrays thee.

'Upon the D[uke] of Savoy's coming into the
Confederacy. 1703'

c.111, p. 31

L0496 Long has it been the critic's poor delight,
Take it, ye critics, it belongs to you.

[Mary] Masters, 'Mrs. Masters' commendatory verses
on Mr. [Thomas] Scott's poems . . .'

c.244, p. 254

L0497 Long has the bard hung up his broken lyre
By heaven ordained, to cheer your happiest hour.

F[rederick] D[ickinson], '30th Aug. [17]85 by my dear
F. D.'

c.391, p. 66

L0498 Long has the poet his just license wa[i]v'd
As thou art now unto all other men.

'Simkin'
[POAS V.373]

fb.70, p. 61a

L0499 Long has the stage been practic'd to the sin
On all things, and be most [?] [?]

[Sir Richard Steele?], 'Prologue'

File 14451

L0500 Long have I felt the awful heat
See grace and wisdom shine.

[Thomas Stevens?], 'The same evening [Tuesday
night at the conference following] from Psalm 66.10.
Believers refined like silver'

c.259, p. 107

L0501 Long have I labor'd with a manly pride
And save me from the storm.

M[aurice] J[ohnson], 'To Miss E. A. his mistress'
billet'

c.229/2, fol. 16

L0502 Long have I sought my Lord in vain
Lifts his high throne above.

T[homas] S[tevens], 'St. John 20.14.15.16 . . . Feb. 13th
[17]80'

c.259, p. 75

L0503 Long have I sought that peace
And that shall fit me for the chase.

Charles Atherton Allnutt, 'The weight of sin the
obstacle to our overtaking peace'

c.112, p. 71

L0504 Long have I sought, the wish of all,
Which nothing can destroy.

[Owen Felltham], 'On true happiness'
[Crum L542 (var.)]

c.94

L0505 Long have I thought (or had sent somewhat quicker)
Too gross for a saint, but too good for a sinner.

[Charles Earle], 'To Miss Su: P[eard] with a pig'

c.376

L0506 Long have I view'd, long have I thought,
Nor beg thy angel to sheath up his sword.

[John] N[orris, of Bemerton], 'The resignation'
[Crum L545]

c.258

L0507 Long have my eyes gaz'd with delight
My doubtful hopes like winds do move.

[Thomas Campion], 'Cant: 38'

b.4, fol. 32

L0508 Long have the busy instruments of hell
Ruins the world and triumphs in his spite.

[ ] Eyers, 'On Hobbes stole out of the library'

c.170, p. 16

L0509 Long have the fair, to softer arts confin'd,
Which thus your colors blazon with refulgent fame.

[James Compton, earl of Northampton], 'To the Rt.
Honble the Countess of Northampton on her
pedigree of the Compton and Shirley family'

Accession 97.7.40

L0510 Long have you seen the Greek and Roman name
And 'tis your virtue swells into your eyes.

'Prologue to Busiris'

c.176, p. 62

L0511 Long idly sauntering in Parnassian shades
May all thy latter days, as his be blest.

[Miss ( ) Bradford], 'To Mrs. M—be . . . from Bath
1782'

c.504, p. 26

L0512 Long in a country town and free from guilt
And learn betimes to seek all blessings from above.

R[obert] Shirley, 1st earl of Ferrers, 'To J—— C——
esq., upon his election 1710'

c.347, p. 28

L0513 Long in the sacred lists of fame
Me and my offering.

    R[obert] Shirley, 1st earl of Ferrers, 'A song'

  c.347, p. 6

L0514 Long I've lov'd my charming Molly,
I'm resolv'd, at once to die.

    [Thomas Hamilton, 6th earl of Haddington], 'A song'

  c.458/2, p. 66

L0515 Long life to the Queen and a prosperous reign,
And he's a false brother, that won't pledge the same.

    'The new health' [for the fair ladies at tea or the
    gentleman at wine, 1710; in praise of Sacheverell]
    [Crum L549]

  b.90, p. 20; see also 'Let us drink disappointment . . .'.

L0516 Long! long! condemn'd in foreign climes to roam,
I'll ask no blessings but my charming maid.

    James Potter, 'On the prospect of England, wrote at
    sea' [15 Oct. 1769]

  c.139, p. 419

L0517 Long, long, had Phyllis Strephon lov'd,
Believe me dearest so is mine.

    'Another by the same hand' [as 'Charge all a
    bumper . . .']

  fb.142, p. 45

L0518 Long, long I have Florella lov'd
To purchase thy esteem.

    [Thomas Hamilton, 6th earl of Haddington], 'A song'

  c.458/1, p. 14

L0519 Long lookt for comes at last, long lookt for things
Might be more welcome to you by their stay.

    M. P., 'To Mr. J. M. with verses'

  b.205, fol. 4v

L0520 Long may the well-concerted union last
A virtuous race may still adorn mankind.

    E. J., 'E. J. priest to M[artha?] Dickinson'

  c.391

L0521 Long may we live, and happy may we be,
Bless'd with contentment and from misfortune free.

  c.93

L0522 Long since fair Clarinda my passion did move
You will owe so much as you never can pay.

    'Passionate love'
    [Crum L554, 'fair Lucinda']

  fb.107, p. 36

L0523 Long since I warn'd you, Sylvia, long since,
But flies, like death, thy monumental arms.

    'On Sylvia, from Greek epigrams'

  c.591

L0524 Long since on Findhorn's rocky shore
And many a sister grace besides.

    [Henry] Mackenzie, [on Foreman's mistaking
    Burdsyards for The man of feeling]

  File 9519

L0525 Long take the crown for it belongs to thee
And pray fair goddess, whose are more than thine.

    'On Miss Long'

  c.360/1, p. 305

L0526 Long the social knot shall last
Bade unanimity bind it fast.

    [Thomas Hull]

  c.528/41

L0527 Long, thro' domestic feuds and party rage
And o'er the spacious mead, triumphant reign.

    'Verses occasioned by the united address of both
    Houses of Parliament to the King—November—21—
    1739'

  c.360/1, p. 255

L0528 Long time ago, a rake I knew,
But will revenge, wrong'd womankind.

    [Thomas Hamilton, 6th earl of Haddington], 'The
    rake outwitted'

  c.458/2, p. 94

L0529 Long time ago ('tis wondrous strange
If they in church, such notes could hear.

    [Thomas Hamilton, 6th earl of Haddington], 'The
    famous preacher'

  c.458/2, p. 99

L0530 Long time death strove me to arrest
And brought me to my grave.

    'Crosby Ravensworth churchyard . . . Feb. 2 1693 Wm.
    Thwaites'

  c.547, p. 332

L0531 Long time had Israel been disus'd from rest
And let them know what Jewish nobles are.

    [John Tutchin], "The foreigners' [1700]
    [POAS VI.230]

  fb.142, p. 1

L0532 Long time, I err'd, uncertain of my way,
Secure, and it is my fault, if I fall.

    'From [Giovanni della] Casa'

  fb.66/22

LO533 Long time I lived a single life
Had Becky not a Bible back. | You jealous mortals
be [&c.]

[John Walker?], 'Humpbacked virtue or Bible-back
Becky'

fc.108, fol. 23v

LO534 Look above; and see thy wonder
Nature contracted, in her store.

[George Daniel]

b.121, fol. 61

LO535 Look back ye foreign shores and see
Were never crown'd but in Oudenarde.

'During the 20th of January'

Poetry Box IV/90

LO536 Look cheerfully in company; for he
Let me alone to get a quiet mind.

'To keep company'

c.361

LO537 Look down blest soul,
And leave our feelings, to rejoice in thine.

[ ] Web, 'Epitaph by . . . on his wife'

c.504, p. 193

LO538 Look forth, and take a last adieu!
And here in each spectator's heart she's found.

[Richard] Cumberland, 'Epilogue by . . . to the play
for the advantage of the noble plan for relieving
debtors for small sums from the sufferings of common
felons, Decr. 23. 1773. Spoken by Mrs. Mattocks, and
Mr. Hull'

c.528/55

LO539 Look gently down, almighty Grace
And let thy power my love confine.

c.152, p. 113

LO540 Look how the russet morn exceeds the night
The eye of all the world loves to be grey.

[William Strode], 'Commendation of grey eyes'
[Crum L575]

b.205, fol. 58v

LO541 Look in thy glass, and tell the face thou viewest,
Die single,—and thy image dies with thee.

[William] Shakespeare [Sonnet III]

c.94

LO542 Look learned Doctor—here's the bird
H'as eat your cellar key.

[John] Winter, 'Reply of a Trinity divine to Lord
——— on my Lord's showing him an ostrich'

c.74

LO543 Look man before thee how thy death hasteth
Look man beneath thee, the pains without rest.

'On one that suppressed his name'
[Crum L576]

fb.143, p. 19; b.208, p. 56 (incomplete); c.81/1, no. 88

LO544 Look not too high and with puffed worldly pride,
Neither delight the poorest to deride.

c.339, p. 314

LO545 Look on this picture where you'll see,
For such a one, was ne'er before.

Lady Jane Cavendish, 'On my sister Brackley's
picture'
[Crum L583]

b.233, p. 24

LO546 Look out bright eyes and bless the air
Even the fetters which you wear.

[John Fletcher, from The false one]
[Crum L584, 'clear the air']

b.213, p. 9

LO547 Look round the habitable world, how few
What their unerring wisdom sees the want.

[John Dryden], 'Juvenal's 10 satire'
[Crum L586]

b.155, p. 70

LO548 Look sensibility on this,
To lead me to my home.

'A father's reflection on viewing the body of his only
boy in his coffin who died under five years'

c.362, p. 58

LO549 Look up dear shade, look up and see,
Dear brothers, once more, give the kiss.

Frederick Corfield, 'The dirge' [from 'The patriots a
tragic farce in two acts']

c.381/2

LO550 Look well to thy house in every degree,
And as thy getting is, so let thy spending be.

b.234, p. 257

LO551 Look wisely (friend) thou seldom seest such men
Would dare to adore, we justly may admire.

[Robert Wild], 'Another' [upon Ed. Reynolds D. D.]

c.166, p. 303

LO552 Look! You're a judge this essay to command
He reads it not, for fear it should be—good.

C. B., 'The author's complaint'

c.74, p. 26

LO553 Loquacia was so wondrous odd,
Your earthly, prating station?

   [William Carpenter], 'An epitaph on an almsgiving
   shrew from St. Evremond'

   c.247, p. 116

LO554 Lord be my judge and Thou shalt see,
That they may never swerve.

   [Thomas Sternhold and John Hopkins], 'The 10
   psalm for aid against our enemies with praise and
   thanksgiving' [verses from Psalms 26–28]
   [Crum L605]

   a.3, fol. 77v

LO555 Lord Belville can his generous soul confine
A stratagem in war is no defeat.

   c.229/1, fol. 38

LO556 Lord, by Thy holy name me save,
Thou hast calt [sic] to my toes.

   'Psalm 54'

   c.264/2, p. 6

LO557 Lord for my sleep and rest this night
I me to Thee wholly commit.

   [Sir Nicholas] Bacon, 'An English hymn. Morning
   prayer'

   fa.8, fol. 166v

LO558 Lord for thy grace give[n] me this day
Both when I sleep and when I wake.

   [Sir Nicholas] Bacon, 'An English hymn. Evening
   prayer'

   fa.8, fol. 167

LO559 Lord, from this mournful Egypt here below,
Boasting indeed, yet boasting of thy praise.

   'From Torqu[ato] Tasso'

   fb.66/23

LO560 Lord, give us grace to cast away
And govern with Him in the skies.

   Charles Atherton Allnutt, 'Collect for the first Sunday
   in Advent'

   c.112, p. 53

LO561 Lord go Thou with me or may I not go
Though Satan in them should to me appear.

   [Mary Pluret], 'The following verses were written on
   the back of one of the foregoing papers a little before
   she appeared before the church'

   c.354

LO562 Lord God of my salvation, I
Thou'st broke, and not a friend remains.

   'Psalm 88'

   c.264/2, p. 83

LO563 Lord grant me such a firm belief
Where saints and angels dwell.

   [( ) Pierson]

   c.328, p. 25

LO564 Lord Henry informs is he'll tax us no more,
He'd too mettlesome grow for Lord Harry to ride.

   'On the new plan of finance proposed by L[ord]
   H[enry] Petty by means of a supplementary loan . . .
   fr[om] St. James' chronicle Feb. 7'

   c.373, p. 85

LO565 Lord how are we from snarling come to bite
To them that sow them in the fields of peace.

   Sir John Strangways

   b.304, p. 35

LO566 Lord how divine thy comforts are!
Eternal as his days!

   [Isaac Watts, Hymns and spiritual songs (1707),
   bk. III, Hymn 11]

   c.180, p. 46

LO567 Lord how he swells as if he had at least
He has a leash of churches in his belly.

   [Francis Quarles], 'On a impropriator'
   [Crum L646]

   b.137, p. 184

LO568 Lord! How immense thy being is!
And give the nobler praise.

   John Author, 'Universal praise'

   c.244, p. 564

LO569 Lord I believe a rest remains,
Let all be lost in God.

   'Hymn 97th'

   c.562, p. 131

LO570 Lord I to thee direct my cries
But in my clearness succor me.

   [Thomas Stanley], 'Meditat: XIIII. Upon the
   covenant'

   b.152, p. 44

LO571 Lord, I vile creature, weak, and blind,
Their great and sure reward.

   [Sir William Trumbull], 'Ps. 131'

   b.177, p. 29; Trumbull Box: Poetry Box XIII/24

LO572 Lord I would spread my sore distress
And turn to God again.

    'Hymn 10th'

    c.562, p. 11

LO573 Lord, if my griefs were not oppos'd with joy,
The more my heaven's affections are at rest.

    [Francis Quarles], 'On joy and grief'
    [Crum L659]

    b.118, p. 228

LO574 Lord if our days be few, why do we spend
Great God we make them evil, Thou mak'st them
                        few.

    [Francis Quarles], 'On the days of man'
    [Crum L660]

    b.137, p. 190

LO575 Lord if thou the grace impart,
Trust him praise him evermore.

    'Hymn 49th'

    c.562, p. 57

LO576 Lord in the strength of grace,
To serve my God alone.

    c.562, p. 87

LO577 Lord! In thine anger ne'er inspect me,
Nor in thy furious wrath correct me!

    '. . . Psalm 6.1 . . .'

    c.346

LO578 Lord in Thy mercy give me rest,
Thou giv'st in Thy precepts?

    'Psalm 56 Morning prayer 11. day'

    c.264/2, p. 10

LO579 Lord in Thy mighty pow'r arise,
'Mongst whom thy praise shall never cease.

    'Psalm 68 Morning prayer 13 day'

    c.264/2, p. 31

LO580 Lord in thy wrath reprove me not
Of Him that is most high.

    [Thomas Sternhold], 'The 3 psalm for remission of sin
    against the horror of death everlasting' [verses from
    Psalms 6–7]
    [cf. Crum L678]

    a.3, fol. 69v

LO581 Lord join my heart so close to thee
Thy worthy praise. Amen.

    [Lady Ursula (Darcy) Wyvill?]

    b.222, p. 105

LO582 Lord keep me from a conscience free from grief
He shall be sav'd, though he do not entreat.

    'A conscience quiet, not good'

    c.187, p. 35

LO583 Lord keep not silence long, but clear
Hard-sentenc'd to reprieve.

    'Psalm 109'

    c.264/3, p. 31

LO584 Lord, let my crying pierce Thine ear,
The Holocaust prepare.

    'Psalm 61'

    c.264/2, p. 19

LO585 Lord let the tuneful trumpet sound
Which thro' eternal years shall run.

    P[hilip] Doddridge, 'The gospel jubilee from Ps.
    LXXXIX. 15'

    c.493, p. 53

LO586 Lord look upon a soul that sighs for sin,
And so at length, obtains his wished end.

    'A conscience never quiet, yet good'

    c.187, p. 35

LO587 Lord look upon my leprosy
I will; then thou be clean.

    'The leper's complaint'

    c.187, p. 9

LO588 Lord look with mercy down on human race,
Death, judgment, heaven, and hell—think on these
                        four.

    'A prayer for the conversion of swearers'

    c.360/3, no. 95

LO589 Lord make me what thou shall delight
To Thee although but small.

    [Mary Pluret], 'Another [poem written on waste
    paper]'

    c.354

LO590 Lord of all pow'r and might, thine arm
Joys shall to joy succeed.

    'Psalm 16'

    c.264/1, p. 47

L0591 Lord Pam in the church (could you think it)
                                                    kneel'd down
Since God had no hand in his Lordship's
                                                    promotion.

[Jonathan Swift], 'An epigram on seeing a worthy
prelate [Josiah Hort, Bishop of Kilmore] go out [of]
Church . . . to wait on his Grace the D[uke] of
D[orset]'
[Crum L714]
fc.60, p. 46

L0592 Lord plead my cause against my foes,
Sing laud, and thanks always.

[John Hopkins], 'The 15 psalm. That God would
defend the innocency of the right' [verses from
Psalm 35]
[Crum L715]
a.3, fol. 84

L0593 Lord save me from the evil man,
Thy servant am and shall.

[Thomas Norton], 'Against the falsehood cruelty and
injury of enemies. Psal. 60' [verses from Psalms
140–143]
[Crum L721]
a.3, fol. 144v

L0594 Lord, teach me patiently to follow thee,
Teach us to suffer, till we reign with Thee.

[Thomas Stevens?], 'A meditation'
c.259

L0595 Lord those whom thou in vows hast tied
Which time shall never waste.

[Thomas Stanley], 'Meditat. VII. Upon the Queen's
departure and absence'
b.152, p. 21

L0596 Lord, Thou art mine, and I am Thine,
Or rather make no Thine and mine.

George Herbert, 'Clasping of hands'
[Crum L728]
c.139, p. 135

L0597 Lord, Thou from dust didst raise me,
(To praise thee) meet me there.

George Wither, 'A hymn of confession and praise'
c.139, p. 143

L0598 Lord Thou hast been from all times past,
The blessing makes it Thine.

'Psalm 90. Common meter'
c.264/2, p. 93

L0599 Lord Thou in heaven and in my heart
And joy in thy salvation send me.

[Thomas Stanley], 'Medit: III upon his Ma[jes]ty's
going to the House of Commons'
b.152, p. 11

L0600 Lord Thou sacred unity
Than thy justice or men's hate.

[Thomas Stanley], 'Meditat: XXVI. Upon the army's
surprisal of the King at Holmeby, and the ensuing
distractions in the two Houses the army and the city'
b.152, p. 84

L0601 Lord Thou who beauty canst return
Of inward virtue outward peace.

[Thomas Stanley], 'Meditat: XX. Upon the
reformation of the times'
b.152, p. 63

L0602 Lord tho' exalted high,
And to eternity.

'Psalm 131'
c.264/3, p. 77

L0603 Lord to thy land in former times
Justice shall go before.

'Psal: 85'
b.217, p. 34

L0604 Lord, we adore thy bounteous hand,
And reach where Jesus is.

[Isaac Watts, Hymns and spiritual songs (1707),
bk. III, Hymn 20]
c.180, p. 52

L0605 Lord we adore thy wond'rous name
And ev'ry frailty cease.

P[hilip] Doddridge, 'The frailty of human nature and
God['s] gracious regard to it—Ps. CIII. 4'
c.493, p. 65

L0606 Lord we again lift up our eyes,
Who reign one God above.

[John Austin], 'Hym. 13' [Hymn xxv, Devotions in the
ancient way of offices, 1672, p. 215]
c.178, p. 12

L0607 Lord what a monstrous age is this
Such a bitter fading pleasure.
b.216, p. 147

L0608 Lord what a place is the camp
Why how is my new mutton pies.

'Bagshot Heath camp sung by Johannot at Ashley's'
Poetry Box IV/61

L0609 Lord what am I? a worm, daft, vapor, nothing;
Present me to thy blessed throne.

    [ ] Hall, 'An anthem made by Dr. Hall'

    b.356, p. 233

L0610 Lord! What is time? Much less the life of man?
There's no repentance in the life to come.

    'Epitaph'

    c.81/1, no. 408

L0611 Lord when I hear thy children talk
Give me that frame which thou lik'st best.

    [Thomas Stevens?], 'Blessed by the poor. Luke 6. 20.
    Hart.(?)'

    c.259, p. 136

L0612 Lord when my soul shall leave this house of clay
Where I shall meet thee in the air.

    [Lady Ursula (Darcy) Wyvill?]

    b.222, p. 107

L0613 Lord, when on Thee I call, me hear
His ways and works proclaim.

    'Psalm 64'

    c.264/2, p. 24

L0614 Lord, when the sense of thy sweet grace
Dead to myself I live in Thee.

    R[ichard] C[rashaw], 'A song'
    [Crum L754]

    b.259, p. 82

L0615 Lord when thou dost call on me
I may not lose my soul withal.

    [Lady Ursula (Darcy) Wyvill?]

    b.222, p. 100

L0616 Lord! Who hast pow'r to cure or kill,
Keep us from Doctor Ignoramus.

    'Parish prayer'

    c.81/1, no. 216

L0617 Lord who shall dwell above with thee
Who reign one God above.

    [John Austin], 'Hym. 4' [Hymn vii, Devotions in the
    ancient way of offices, 1672, p. 72]

    c.178, p. 3

L0618 Lord, who's the happy man that may
Beneath thy long delay.

    [Thomas Stevens?], 'Hymn the 2nd'

    c.259

L0619 Lord will thou keep me in thy way
And seeing sing thy love and grace.

    [Mary Pluret], 'What follows were found after her
    death written on bits of waste paper . . .'

    c.354

L0620 Lords! Ladies! A burletta here behold,
De gustibus non esse disputandum.

    John Lockman, 'Imitation of the sonnet, by way of
    prologue [to La famiglia in scompiglio]. Here end the
    pieces writ by Signor Botarelli'

    c.267/4, p. 119

L0621 Lords! Ladies! (Calzo!) see mine phiz of brass!
Il diavol shall seize, if here ye find me more.

    John Lockman, 'Prologue, for the Italian actors, at
    their opening of the little theater in the Haymarket.
    Supposed to be spoke by Don John Francesco
    Charlatano, the raree-show doctor . . . 1749'

    c.267/3, p. 138

L0622 Lorn tenant of the peaceful glade
Blest hope to an eternal May.

    'To the primrose'

    c.83/3, no. 1010

L0623 Lost to the world, alone I pine;
Which calls me to the tomb.

    Charles I(?), 'Supposed to be written by . . . during his
    imprisonment in Carisbrook, and intended for his
    queen, Henrietta Maria'

    c.83/2, no. 539

L0624 Lot's wife, we read, in days ofold,
A maiden turn'd to Mudd.

    'A wedding.—July 14th, 1790, a few days since was
    married Mr. Richard Mudd, surgeon, to Miss
    Catherine Wheeler St. James's Street London.
    Impromptu'

    c.94

L0625 Love, a strong designing foe,
While a greater holds the place.

    'The advice'

    c.83/3, no. 773

L0626 Love and beauty young and gay
Nor think of love and beauty more.

    'Song 229'

    c.555, p. 361

L0627 Love and folly were at play
And wretched when wise.

    Accession 97.7.40

Lo628 Love and obey thy parents in thy heart
And brings the child into the way of life.

    'An admonition for children'

    c.187, p. 25

Lo629 Love and the world together had their birth,
And yet he dwells in fair Clarinda's eyes.

    R[obert] Shirley, 1st earl of Ferrers, 'Love. From the
    French, l'amour est un enfant &c'

    c.347, p. 14

Lo630 Love any devil else but you
Rackt carcasses make ill anatomies.

    J[ohn] D[onne]
    [Crum L792]

    b.148, p. 105

Lo631 Love bade me hope and I obey'd
In women mean mistrustful shame.

    John Wilmot, 2nd earl of Rochester, '6. Woman's
    honor[:] song'

    b.334, p. 171; b.105, p. 142

Lo632 Love bred of glances, 'twixt amorous eyes
[Angels] are guests and dance at this blest wedding.

    'Cant. 20'
    [Crum L797]

    b.148, p. 1

Lo633 Love by the art of steganography [*sic*]
By all the remnant of the alphabet.

    [Sir Thomas Urquhart], 'Tom Cretio to his Majesty
    studying the art of shortwriting and initiated in the
    practice thereof'

    fb.217, p. 507

Lo634 Love calls the muses, and the tuneful choir,
Sweet song! No med'cine's pleasanter than thee!

    c.346

Lo635 Love controls the greatest souls
But gen'rous souls can love.

    c.416

Lo636 Love God, and love thy neighbor as thyself
Hates his own soul, who loves iniquity.

    [Sir Philip Wodehouse], 'St. Augustine's Ep. 52—
    Diligamus proximos . . .'

    b.131, p. 10

Lo637 Love, hope, and joy,—fair pleasure's smiling train,
Gives all the strength and color of our life.

    [Alexander] Pope(?), 'On the passions of love, &c.'

    c.94

Lo638 Love if a god thou art, then evermore thou must
Heal me like her, or else wound her like me.

    [Francis Davison]
    [Crum L813]

    b.197, p. 229

Lo639 Love! If thy destined sacrifice am I,
As pleased when shipwreck'd as when safe on shore.

    [William Cowper, trans.], 'The acquiescence of pure
    love. Vol. 2. Son: 135' [of Jeanne Guion's 'Spiritual
    songs']

    c.470 (autogr.)

Lo640 Love in this age from deeds to words is fled
Religion being not in this heart but bane.

    [Sir Thomas Urquhart], 'How much at this time faith,
    love, and religion are decayed in the world'

    fb.217, p. 518

Lo641 Love into Chloe's chamber came
Chloe will never die a maid.

    [Phanuel Bacon], 'To [Chloe]'
    [Crum L816]

    c.237, fol. 34

Lo642 Love is a babble no man is able
Or if it is I cannot tell what.

    'On love'

    b.62, p. 45

Lo643 Love is a burden which two hearts,
Alas, can bear it long alone.

    c.549, p. 122

Lo644 Love is a constant will of doing good
Cheers, and illuminates mortality.

    [Sir Philip Wodehouse], 'An essay upon Aristotle's
    Amara est vella . . .'

    b.131, p. 5

Lo645 Love is a golden bubble full of dreams,
That waking breaks and fills us with extremes.

    [John Rose?]

    b.227, p. 73

Lo646 Love is a jest, and vows are wind,
By sad experience will find.

    c.549, p. 10

Lo647 Love is a labor I have my labor lost
Or else our instant joys will perish.

    b.197, p. 154

Lo648 Love is a noble passion of the heart;
But an offensive subject of our loathing.

    c.158, p. 21

L0649 Love is a toy, a nothing, it is worse
Fr(?) gy(?) and heat, gr(?) I will love commend.

Poetry Box VIII/3

L0650 Love is in us, as fire within a block;
Thus we're but ashes, and our love mere fume.

Sir Thomas Urquhart, 'The speeches of a devote couple of mutual lovers'

fb.217, p. 182

L0651 Love is inconstant: sometimes glad,
And is not plac'd amongst the fixed stars.

Sir Thomas Urquhart, 'Why love is both fickle, and fugitive'

fb.217, p. 132

L0652 Love is like a game at tables where the die
Do what you can they will be bearing men.

[Sir Robert Ayton? or William Strode?], 'Of love'

b.205, fol. 24; see also 'Love's like . . .'.

L0653 Love is like drunkenness; th'one maketh blind
Th'eyes of the body: th'other of the mind.

Sir Thomas Urquhart, 'Of love, and drunkenness'

fb.217, p. 269

L0654 Love is the fart | Of every heart
And others doth offend when 'tis let loose.

[Sir John Suckling]

fb.66/38; see also 'Love then . . .', 'If when Don Cupid's dart . . .'.

L0655 Love is the greatest of the ethnic gods
To reach no higher than the midst.

Sir Thomas Urquhart, 'Why Cupid is always drawn little'

fb.217, p. 189

L0656 Love is the life of friendship letters are,
Or else all commerce and all love would die.

'Valentine's Day'

c.481, p. 272

L0657 Love is the Lord whom I obey,
And will not dwell with so despised a guest.

[William Cowper, trans.], 'Love endures no rival. Vol. 2. Sonnet 155' [of Jeanne Guion's 'Spiritual songs']

c.470 (autogr.)

L0658 Love is the noblest frailty of the mind,
For love like fortune does not always please.

J. W., 'On love'

c.258

L0659 Love is the only victor of our hearts
To see that through him all the world runs mad.

'Of the power of love'

b.197, p. 243

L0660 Love is the purest spirit, that the soul,
Since in eternity, all time is lost.

'Divine love'

fc.54, p. 40

L0661 Love is the sire, dam, nurse and seed
Who love what most deserves their love.

'Of love sonnet'

b.205, fol. 41v

L0662 Love is, we own it, but a name
Her nicest claims for you.

'To Eliza [Bernard] on receiving from her a heart cut in card-paper'

Poetry Box X/45, p. 11

L0663 Love like the sea doth flow, doth ebb again:
Among the planets not the fixed stars.

'Venus'

c.356

L0664 Love never more shall give me pain,
I'm lost, if Peggy die.

c.358, p. 1

L0665 Love not me for lovely grace
To dote upon me ever.

[Crum L847]

b.213, p. 9

L0666 Love, seeing the fire ascends,
The lowest mark is his desire.

Sir Thomas Urquhart, 'That Cupid is not so fiery, as he is given out to be'

fb.217, p. 229

L0667 Love shot his darts at random,
The rest will be no better.

'Jenny Whinney, a song'

c.530, p. 337

L0668 Love, soft intruder, penetrates my heart,
And be propitious to my earnest prayer.

'Horace's 19th ode imitated, lib: 1'

c.233, p. 13

L0669 Love sounds the alarm,
For life is a pain.

[John Gay], 'Song 21'

c.555, p. 26

L0670 Love take pity on me,
And so must die.

'Lucinda's conquest'

fb.107, p. 45

L0671 Love then the fart | Of every heart,
And others doth offend when 'tis let loose.

[Sir John Suckling, last four lines of] 'A catch on love'

b.54, p. 1157; see also 'Love is . . .'., 'If when Don
Cupid's dart . . .'.

L0672 Love thy country wish it well
Full perfection shall begin.

George Bubb Doddington, lord Melcombe, 'Lines
addressed [by] the late . . . to the late Doctor Young'
[Crum L864]

File 17397

L0673 Love? what's love? It's a noble fire
Where joy and torment, pain, and bliss do dwell.

'Upon his being asked what love was'

c.158, p. 27

L0674 Love when 'tis true needs not the aid
To strife to show what none can hide.

Sir George Etherege(?), 'Indifference excused' [also
attr. Sir Charles Sedley]

Poetry Box IV/53; c.549, p. 43 (first stanza)

L0675 Love, without hope; and hope, without fruition:
And without you, all three work my perdition.

Sir Thomas Urquhart, 'A passionate lover to his
peremptory mistress'

fb.217, p. 99

L0676 Love ye the scenes of rural life—
For solid bliss on Champion Hill.

'Champion Hill near Camberwell'

c.83/2, no. 615

L0677 Lovelace, I must to fame for pardon plead
Was with both laurels by just Pallas crown'd.

[Thomas Stanley], 'Lovelace' [in 'A register of
friends']

b.153, p. 10

L0678 Lovell was of the doubtful gender
He's now the common of two.

[Robert Cholmeley], '[An epigram upon Edward
Lovell, 'Whilst nature did herself perplex . . .'] thus
answered upon his lying with two bedfellows'

c.190, p. 22

L0679 Lovely, blooming, fragrant May,
Then enjoy serenity.

[William Mills], 'Ode to May'

c.472, p. 9

L0680 Lovely charmer, dearest creature
None could e'er be more beloved.

[Peter Motteux], 'Song' [in The island princess
(1699), p. 12]
[Crum L870]

c.189, p. 221

L0681 Lovely courier of the sky,
Tell me, tell me, gentle dove.

[Samuel Johnson, trans., Anacreon ode ix]

c.391, p. 110

L0682 Lovely flow'r! That smiling rose,
And leave it,—more than half-divine.

[Stephen Barrett], 'To Miss Harriet Hussey (on her
birthday the 7th of June 1762) three years old, who had
adopted me some time before, for her father'

c.193, p. 96

L0683 Lovely is her shape and air
None can give so sweet a zest.

'Acrostic on Miss Lamborn of Hackney—1741'

c.360/1, p. 315

L0684 Lovely lasting peace of mind—sweet delight of
                                            humankind,
And find a life of equal bliss—or own the next
                                            begun in this.

[Thomas] Parnell, 'A hymn to contentment'

c.244, p. 273; c.163, p. 5; c.83/2, no. 370

L0685 Lovely Lydia, prithee say,
He's forc'd to war's alarms.

'The eight[h] ode of the first book of Horace
imitated'

Poetry Box I/113[1]

L0686 Lovely matron all whose breast
You alone can explain who alone are the cause.

[William Hayley], 'Song'

File 6963

L0687 Lovers behold the monster Polypheme
See how the thund'ring giant roars.

[John Gay, Alexander Pope, and/or John Hughes],
[chorus from Handel's Acis and Galatea, with musical
score for bass; see also 'Wretched lovers . . .']

Music MS. 534

L0688 Lovers of one same thing are apt to hate
You so, which no rivals have in love.

> [Sir Thomas Urquhart], 'To one who loved none but
> himself, whom none else beloved'
>
> fb.217, p. 536

L0689 Lovers so 'ware now on their mistresses
Each fair and virtuous lady, hath two hearts.

> [Sir Thomas Urquhart], 'Concerning those who being
> loved are said to possess the hearts of such as are
> enamored with them'
>
> fb.217, p. 502

L0690 Love's a dream of mighty treasure
Changing happy to be wise.

> [Thomas Cheek]
> [Crum L873]
>
> c.358, p. 165

L0691 Love's a gentle, generous passion
Of the blissful state above!

> Betty Moore, 'A song'
> [Crum L874]
>
> c.358, p. 150

L0692 Love's a sweet and soft musician,
Tweedledum and Tweedledee.

> 'Song 89'
>
> c.555, p. 138

L0693 Love's a sweet grief: short pleasure: constant fear:
Sad joy: uncertain hope: and idle care.

> Sir Thomas Urquhart, 'An antistasis of love'
>
> fb.217, p. 201

L0694 Love's a true, and lasting treasure,
And both happy be, and wise.

> [Thomas Hamilton, 6th earl of Haddington], 'Answer
> to a song of the late Ld Dorset's'
>
> c.458/2, p. 77

L0695 Love's crisis in the happy minute lies;
Hit, but that minute and you gain the prize.

> c.186, p. 61

L0696 Love's fine: but he's frozen, so, that he
Wherewith to light his candle.

> Sir Thomas Urquhart, 'The dissuading of a well-
> complexioned young woman, from the marrying of an
> aged man, whom she carried great affection to'
>
> fb.217, p. 84

L0697 Love's like a game at tables, where the die
Do what you can they will be bearing men.

> [Sir Robert Ayton? or William Strode?], 'Love's like a
> game of tables'
> [Crum L880]
>
> b.200, p. 46; b.62, p. 28; see also 'Love is like . . .'.

L0698 Love's queen, sat in majestic pow . . .
When Mars his tilting ended.

> 'Cant: 13'
>
> b.4, fol. 9 (damaged); b.197, p. 179 (first four words
> missing)

L0699 Love's smiling queen, whose tender aid
Left to thy choice this fairer tree.

> 'To the same [Miss Mears, daughter of Dr. Mcars,
> principal of Brasenose]'
>
> Spence Papers, folder 113

L0700 Lov'st thee the King? His page will then thee love,
As shadows bodies when the sun's gone down.

> 'Courtship to his friend a courtier'
>
> c.356

L0701 Lucetta's charms our hearts surprise,
And in her voice his thunder.

> [Thomas Warton], 'On a lady with fine eyes and a bad
> voice'
>
> Diggle Box: Poetry Box XI/69

L0702 Lucia has charms that would excite desire,
But soon retreat from a forbidding glance.

> '[Female characters.] 2. Lucia, or the insensible'
>
> Poetry Box IV/148

L0703 Lucia the bright, who takes her name from light
Is totally compos'd of melody.

> [Sir Philip Wodehouse], 'Upon Mrs. Lucy Suckling
> daughter to Charles'
>
> b.131, back (no. 113, no. 221)

L0704 Lucro it is believ'd thy conscience either
So far from wide, I fear th'hast none at all.

> [Francis Quarles], 'On Lucro' [Divine fancies IV, 75]
>
> b.137, p. 185

L0705 Lucy, in a primrose dale,
How he gave you a green-gown.

> John Lockman, 'Seeing a young lady, who was running
> in a field near Denby's, fall down . . . July 1740'
>
> c.267/1, p. 164

L0706 Lucy, while resting in this verdant shade
Beguile the tedious hours with farther talk.

> 'Henry and Lucy, a pastoral'
>
> c.83/2, no. 567

LO707 Lud! What's come to the ladies,
Or but peep at me thro' your fans.

> John Lockman, 'The coxcomb—tune, Lud what's
> come to my mother'

c.267/2, p. 153; c.268 (first part), p. 71

LO708 Luke deliberating long
Nothing Luke will ever be.

> [Charles Burney, the elder], 'Indecision'

c.33, p. 139

LO709 Lust is the cause of earthly love,
Without which life's a death.

> Sir Thomas Urquhart, 'The speeches of a very
> lascivious whore'

fb.217, p. 231

LO710 Lust taking pleasure in its own delight,
Rejoiceth at the sorrow of a brother.

> [Sir Thomas Urquhart], 'Of lust, and anger'

fb.217, p. 495

LO711 Luxuriant vale, thy country's early boast,
Llangollen's vanish'd pair, and wreath, their sacred
urn.

> Anna Seward, 'Llangollen Vale'

c.141, p. 237

LO712 Luxuriant with perennial green
And know a myrtle from a bramble.

> [Henry James Pye], 'The myrtle and bramble. A fable'
> [1778]
> [Crum L896]

c.53, fol. 41

LO713 Lyce at last the gods have heard my prayer
Neglected live and unregretted die.

> [George Howard, 6th earl of Carlisle], 'Translation of
> the [IV.xiii ode of Horace]'

c.197, p. 16

LO714 Lyddal! Who constant to life's proper end,
Nor strive to pass you—when you lead the way.

> [William Popple, trans.], 'Horace book 1st epistle 2nd
> imitated. Inscribed to Henry Lyddal esq.'

fc.104/1, p. 377

LO715 Lysander whom you know the gay
And spotless as thy whitest dove.

> [Judith (Cowper) Madan], 'The theft of Lysander'
> [1724]

c.152, p. 50

M

M0001 Machaon sick! In ev'ry face we find
And by preserving Ga[r]th, preserves mankind.

> [George Granville, 1st baron of Lansdowne], 'Verses sent to Doct. [Samuel] Ga[r]th in his sickness'

c.189, p. 128

M0002 Mad lust (alas) makes blind the witless will,
'Tis pleasing care, and joy, or luscious ill.

> 'Lust'

c.189, p. 41

M0003 Mad paper stay and grudge not here to burn
Would fain love him that shall be loved of her.

> J[ohn] D[onne]
> [Crum M4]

b.148, p. 114

M0004 Mad was our mother Eva, when she came
She could not be but fitly term'd a Madam.

> [Sir Thomas Urquhart], 'That Eve was properly called Madam'

fb.217, p. 532

M0005 Madam—a stranger purpose in these lays
And draught on all the drooping herbs around.

> [William Cowper], 'An epistle to a Protestant lady in France [Jeanne Guion], by the translator of the foregoing pieces' [Guion's 'Spiritual songs']

c.470 (autogr.)

M0006 Madam—all know your virtue, honor, birth
And say—I am a lady true in worth.

> [Sir Philip Wodehouse], 'Upon his wife's noble aunt . . . the Lady Mary Wintour'

b.131, back (no. 32)

M0007 Madam although your face and form despise
As the Italian dame her negro doth.

> 'A paradox in praise of a painted face, the preface dedicated to a worthy lady' [sometimes attr. Donne]

b.205, fol. 29v

M0008 Madam, and friend, for truth must call you so,
If look on virtue, truth, then look, on you.

> Lady Jane Cavendish, 'On a noble lady'
> [Crum M7b]

b.233, p. 20

M0009 Madam at first I scarcely could believe
That you should want an equal match t'were pity.

> 'Upon the right honorable the Lady Jane Cavendish her book of verses'

b.233, p. 77

M0010 Madam be cover'd why stand you bare
Take up your smock, and hide your breasts.

> 'A song against women that wear their breasts bare' [Crum M9]

b.197, p. 45

M0011 Madam before your feet I lay,
That every line was wrote by me. | Cupid

> 'Hymen to Eliza'

c.83/4, no. 1080

M0012 Madam enrag'd bawls in her husband's ear
You be both w[hor]e and a d[amn']d dog's wife.

c.546, p. 30

M0013 Madam! Forbear to smile and cease to grin
So much you show, to think there's night within.

> 'On Mrs. J.'

c.546, p. 19

M0014 Madam forgive this bold and rash attempt
And what I can't express shall e'er admire.

> Henry Biddle, 'On the recovery of Miss Humfreys'

Accession 97.7.40

M0015 Madam give leave to praise you though you are,
And so as prisoner, you are kept I swear.

> Lady Jane Cavendish, 'On an honorable lady' [Crum G68]

b.233, p. 28

M0016 Madam I hear to my great sorrow
Who always kept the field he won.

> [Mary Barber], 'The humble petition of little Jemmy Penn to her Grace the Duchess of Manchester and Lady Diana Spencer'

Poetry Box v/99; Poetry Box iv/134 ('I hear and hear with sorrow . . .')

M0017　Madam— | I heard (and surely fame
To grant a pardon to my muse.

　　　Joshua Barnes, 'To the Honble. Madam Bridget Noel'

　b.204, p. 62

M0018　Madam, I here intend to write
But—first say grace and then fall on.

　　　'To Mrs. Sheppard at the rectory . . . 1738'

　c.484, p. 61

M0019　Madam, I hope you'll think it's true,
Or else this very moment dies.

　　　[Mary Leapor], 'A modern love letter'

　c.83/3, no. 970

M0020　Madam, I loathe the censurers of the town
Is what knaves invent, the fools believe.

　　　'A letter to the Lady Osborne' [1688]
　　　[Crum M19-20; POAS V.76]

　fb.108, p. 163

M0021　Madam, I much rejoice to hear,
With the same case they wound to cure.

　　　[Thomas Brown], 'By a young vestal to a lady that
　　　loved the pastime'

　c.158, p. 144

M0022　Madam I pray give leave in this
Take him whose eyes speaks him not weak.

　　　Lady Jane Cavendish, 'On a noble lady'
　　　[Crum M22]

　b.233, p. 20

M0023　Madam, if mourning, if excess of grief,
Leave the sweet image of herself behind.

　　　Thomas Cook, 'On the death of her only son, to Mrs.
　　　Colston'

　c.244, p. 571; c.156, p. 146 (var.)

M0024　Madam, in vain you strive to cheat our sight,
And easier lay than represent the devil.

　　　H[enry] Hall, organist of Hereford Cathedral, 'To a
　　　lady, dressed like a ghost to fright her lover'
　　　[Crum M25]

　c.233, p. 99

M0025　Madam, I've heard how sullen knight,
I'll make the peeping knight of Coventry look
　　　　　　　　　　　　　　　　　　　　bluely.

　　　'From Captain Carlton [Charleton?] to Madam
　　　Palavicini upon her being whipped by Sr Chr. Haly'
　　　[Crum M27]

　c.111, p. 72

M0026　Madam look out, your title is arraign'd
I wish it be not the sad consequence.

　　　'Fair warning' [to the Queen; 1710]
　　　[Crum M28; POAS VII.409]

　Poetry Box VI/2

M0027　Madam, obsequious to your high commands
If Herring deign to read, and you to praise.

　　　[Francis Fawkes], 'To Mrs. Herring'

　fc.21, p. 3

M0028　Madam, once more, th'obsequious muse,
Kind, as the blessings you bestow.

　　　[William] Pulteney, earl of Bath, 'To the Queen going
　　　to bed' [26 August 1702]

　fc.24, p. 58

M0029　Madam, persuade me tears are good
The hardest fight is highest crown'd.

　　　I[saac] W[atts?], 'To Mrs. Bendish (against tears)'

　c.259, p. 127

M0030　Madam the greatest ladies of the past times
If you forgive this toy I've sent to you.

　　　[Sir Aston Cokayne], 'To the Lady Elizabeth Darcy'

　b.275, p. 40

M0031　Madam. This verse to Welby's muse is due
And from the court of Venus win the bays.

　　　[Robert Cholmeley], 'Dedication to Mrs Selina
　　　Welby'

　c.190, ix

M0032　Madam, tho' oft I've begg'd of you
Some pretty things in verse to say.

　　　'To Carolina. By a lady of fifteen . . . Stella'

　c.83/1, no. 252

M0033　Madam 'tis fit I now make even
I find your mercy does transcend.

　　　[Sir William] D'Avenant, 'New Year's gift to the
　　　Queen in the year 1643'

　fb.66/36

M0034　Madam to you these tuneless lines I send
And in the lambent flames as just expire.

　　　'Sent to a young lady'

　c.360/1, p. 19

M0035　Madam—tomorrow I must ride
Miss Coxe Miss Fortune and Miss Paul.

　　　'To Mrs. Paul Southfields Brook on receiving a
　　　present of cauliflower'

　c.484, p. 153

M0036 Madam we owe to your great lord, and you
By making ours a mighty looking-glass.

'Epilogue to my lady Duchess [of Ormonde] spoke by
Mrs. Richards'

Poetry Box I/111[6]

M0037 Madam, what your pleasure is but say
Or cryer-like, God save the king.

[Charles Earle], 'Whimsical articles of boarding with
——— who seemed shy of taking a boarder'

c.376

M0038 Madam, when you Rome's noble story read,
How will you praise, not thinking it your own?

John Lockman, 'To Mr. Alderman Jansson's lady, with
the Roman and English histories, compiled by the
author, and presented on New Year's Day, 1752'

c.267/1, p. 58

M0039 Madam! Wrapt up with this you'll see
Our friends with ev'ry happiness.

'Southfields Decr. 10th 1757. To Mrs. Paul'

c.484, p. 109

M0040 Madam you are so truly noble and so good,
So makes of objects, subjects, and yourself a king.

Lady Jane Cavendish, 'On a noble lady'
[Crum M50]

b.233, p. 21

M0041 Madam: your beauty hang me like an elf
Until anon I see you: I conclude.

'Poets and poetry'

c.503, p. 60 [bis]

M0042 Madam, your hand I humbly kiss,
Who carries hell within his breast.

'A dialogue between a gentleman and a lady'

c.83/1, no. 121

M0043 Madam your pious ways and matchless worth
For all the good that you may do me here.

Nehemiah Barnett [on Dame Ursula Harvey]

Poetry Box VI/110

M0044 Madam, trust not to cooks, they'll cheat you,
Sinks him, or lifts him, to a demigod!

[David Garrick], 'Prologue to introduce [Willoughby]
Lacy in Alexander'

Acquisition 92.3.1ff. (autogr.)

M0045 Made heir apparent at the hour of birth
From imperfection hath perfection brought.

[Mary Pluret], 'The following was on one that died in
the house where she lived who she had faith to believe
was newborn on his deathbed'

c.354

M0046 Made to engage all hearts, and charm all eyes,
Her mind was virtue by the graces drest.

[George] Lyttelton, 1st baron Lyttelton, 'To the
memory of Lucy Lyttelton—daughter of Hugh
Fortescue . . . who departed this life the 19 of January
1756 aged 29'

c.547, p. 238; c.487, p. 91 (applied to the Marchioness of
Granby); Poetry Box X/85; Poetry Box IV/171; fc.51,
p. 222; Trumbull Box: Poetry Box XIII/67; see also 'Born
to engage . . .'.

M0047 Maecenas, offspring of a royal race,
And its tumult'ous waves.

[William Mills], 'Odes of Horace translated.
Book III. Ode XXIX. To Maecenas'

c.472, p. 38

M0048 Maecenas smil'd and Horace rais'd the strain
When gracious Temple condescends to hear.

[J. Griffith], 'Verses to the Earl Temple'

Poetry Box IV/162

M0049 Maecenas, sprung from ancient kings!
My head shall tow'r above the sky.

Edward Sneyd, 'The first ode of Horace. To
Maecenas'

c.214, p. 72

M0050 Maecenas! Who canst justly trace
With poets of the lyric vein.

Abraham Oakes, 'Horace to Maecenas. Od. 1. B. 1
translated'

c.50, p. 145

M0051 Maecenas, whose descent we trace
My lofty head shall strike the stars.

[William Mills], 'Odes of Horace translated. Book I.
Ode I. To Maecenas'

c.472, p. 18

M0052 Maid, wife or widow, which bears the grave style,
O tell me, where is he, why doth he not come.

Lady Jane Cavendish, 'A song'
[Crum M67]

b.233, p. 15

M0053 Maidens of your sex so dear,
Yours 'tis only to refuse.

[Miss ( ) Bradford?], 'A song in imitation of Shall I
wasting in despair Die because a woman's fair'

c.504, p. 31

M0054 Maids lack sense; for no touch of man they've got:
Women have sense: but reason have they not.

Sir Thomas Urquhart, 'Of virgins and wives a
paradox'

fb.217, p. 215

M0055 Maids need no more their silver piss-pots scour,
As that which has so oft pass'd into thee.

[Thomas Brown], 'Melting down the plate or the
pisspot's farewell'

fb.66/1

M0056 Majestic bird, who lov'st to glide
A form—without a kindred mind.

Diggle Box: Poetry Box XI/27

M0057 Majestic is my look, and tho' my name
That he who dares but imitate me, dies.

'A riddle made extempore by a gentleman on a piece of
money'

c.360/1, p. 113

M0058 Make a bed in the deep,
Abandon her bosom, but tarry forever.

'The desperate lover'

fb.107, p. 8

M0059 Make Derbyshire by your most able pen
Your country's [illegible]; other country's stain.

[Sir Aston Cokayne], 'To Colonel Samuel Roper'

b.275, p. 90

M0060 Make good thy anagram—spell happily
Of chastity and liveliness.

[Sir Philip Wodehouse], 'Upon [Lucy Wodehouse's]
daughter Blanche Astley'

b.131, back (no. 25)

M0061 Make it the chief employment of thy days,
Shall triumph oe'r the power of sin and death.

'Pythagoras's golden verses made Christian'

c.547, p. 86

M0062 Make me then Lord one of these soldiers and
Possest of that true rest that's found in Thee.

[Mary Serjant]

fb.98, fol. 164

M0063 Make much of every moment of your time
In wisdom's school this lesson is the prime.

[John Rose?]
[cf. Crum M77]

b.227, p. 72

M0064 Make room for a rover,
Must all yield to Stumpy.

'Stiffy. A song. Tune Lady lie near me'

c.530, p. 201

M0065 Make the extended skies your tomb,
Greatly triumphant live.

'The Christian's wish'

fc.132/1, p. 24

M0066 Make trial ere ye trust the outward show
For Sinon false in Damon's shape doth go.

c.339, p. 317

M0067 Make way make way ye neighbors all
I sit whole hours—and then—walk back again.

'Twelfth night'

c.504, p. 167

M0068 Make your honors Miss throll, loll, loll,
Then I will give you my Poll, throll, la.

'A song dance'

c.416

M0069 Malicious bard suppose His Highness lies,
Whom truth, for no one virtue will commend?

'Answer to the above' ['To Norfolk House; lords,
knights . . .']

c.154, p. 11

M0070 Mallius in sleep both day and night employs
That Pharius may ever drowsy be!

R[obert] Shirley, 1st earl of Ferrers, 'Claudian
epigrammata'

c.347, p. 13

M0071 Man and wife are all one
And you see him no more till supper.

[Sir Fleetwood Sheppard?], 'Hampton court life'
[1689]
[Crum M89; POAS V.56]

b.204, p. 135

M0072 Man as head his horns bewail
To have a beastly head.

Sir Thomas Urquhart, 'The reason why the husband
wears the horns for the woman's fault'

fb.217, p. 37

M0073 Man beareth God and mammon in his mind
But mammon first, and God doth come behind.

c.339, p. 328

M0074 Man being God's image should be loath to burn
That meeteth not sometime with sacrilege.

[Sir Thomas Urquhart], 'A Christian consolation to
such as have been affronted with a personal wrong'
fb.217, p. 531

M0075 Man bows one knee; for once he's subject made
T'her father: then t'her husband, if she marry.

Sir Thomas Urquhart, 'Why a woman becks with
both her knees and a man but with one'
fb.217, p. 231

M0076 Man, fearful, credulous and vain,
And spread, to latest times, thy fame.

John Lockman, 'The cat. The following tale is
founded on a true incident, which happened in 1741, at
the author's house . . .'
c.267/3, p. 37; File 9162 (var.)

M0077 Man framed arts, by artless nature made;
Thus man's the work of his own work, and wit.

Sir Thomas Urquhart, 'Man, art, and nature'
fb.217, p. 219

M0078 Man, in the first Elysian garden placed
I'm ruin'd and undone—you dog, you've made me
wise.

[Joseph Spence], 'Ode against knowledge'
Spence Papers, folder 152

M0079 Man is a glass, life is as water
So runs the water out.

'On man's life'
[cf. Crum M104]
fb.143, p. 28 and 41; see also 'Man is as . . .'.

M0080 Man is a lump, where all beast[s] kneaded be
Your friends find every day a mart of new.

[John Donne], 'Satira octava' [To Sr Edward Herbert
at Julyers]
[Crum M101]
b.114, p. 64; b.148, p. 110; b.150, p. 199

M0081 Man is as a glass, life is as water
So runs the water out.

'On man's mortality'
[Crum M104]
b.200, p. 224; see also 'Man is a glass . . .'.

M0082 Man is no star, but a quick coal,—of mortal fire
Lets his own ashes cloak his soul.

[George] Herbert, 'On man'
c.356

M0083 Man is the world, and death the ocean
Of such a prey, and to his triumphs add.

[John Donne], 'Elegia 17ta. A funeral elegy on the
Lady Markham'
[Crum M106]
b.114, p. 129; b.148, p. 119

M0084 Man like a bubble in the water rises
And closes up the day with this: Here lies.

[Thomas Gurney], 'On the life of man'
c.213

M0085 Man, love your wife; for she your heart is made:
Wife, serve your husband; for he is your head.

Sir Thomas Urquhart, 'To man, and wife'
fb.217, p. 132

M0086 Man may (quoth Moses) reach to sixscore yeares:
For both, to th'age they spoke of did attain.

Sir Thomas Urquhart, 'Of Moses, and David'
fb.217, p. 186

M0087 Man newly born is at full age to die,
Now heaven thee pulls, thou it with violence.

[William Strode], 'An epitaph'
[Crum M114]
b.205, fol. 60v

M0088 Man of himself to goodness weak doth live,
But God gives power, to whom all glory give.

c.339, p. 328

M0089 Man of precarious science vain,
The squire sneaks home and beats his wife.

'The officious messenger a tale'
c.73, p. 1; Trumbull Box: Poetry Box XIII/101

M0090 Man ought his future happiness to fear,
The virtue and the force of these, are sure of
victory.

b.118, p. 15

M0091 Man (screen'd by flesh and blood) and wrapt within
Some creatures creep, as well as others flee.

[George Daniel]
b.121, fol. 64v

M0092 Man should for no unfortunate event
Can nothing else possess that's worth to lose.

[Sir Thomas Urquhart], 'The settled quiet of our
mind should not be moved at sinister accidents'
fb.217, p. 530

M0093 Man, should rather adorn the house of prayer,
Or gold of all things on earth is most unblest.

fb.69, p. 213

M0094 Man sinn'd against his life, 'cause of action
In future generations, though he's dead.

'On the death of Mr Rich: Withye an attorney of
Worcester, dying at Uxbridge'
b.137, p. 203

M0095 Man, thee behooveth oft to have this in mind,
So God me help and Holidom, he died a poor man.

'Written in black letter characters on a wall in St.
Edmund's church, Lombard Street'
c.240, p. 137

M0096 Man, when he first was made, by perfect love
And hug fresh joys, for those divine, are ever new.

'Use [of] this world, is not abusing it'
fc.54, p. 56

M0097 Man whilst alone in Eden mourn'd his state
Eve only could content the happy man.

'Acrostic, in praise of marriage'
c.360/1, p. 33

M0098 Man, whom the serpent's envious mind destroy'd
By Christ again the bliss of heaven enjoy'd.

'St. Olave's Hart Street [1]'
c.81/1, no. 51

M0099 Man! Woman! Thing! For somewhat sure thou art!
Go, wretch, to those like thee, and there repeat thy
tale.

'A dialogue between death and a Macaroni'
c.150, p. 105

M0100 Mankind delights in what is new
Divert, and lead my thoughts astray?

[Edmund Wodehouse], 'Decr. 7 [1714]'
b.131, p. 107

M0101 Mankind from Adam have been women's fools
No[t] left us women or not threatcn'd hell.

'Epigram'
c.360/1, p. 211

M0102 Mankind may walk unvex'd by strife
'I'd never live,—or quickly die?'

'For life, from the Greek of Metredorus . . . Moschus'
c.94 (incomplete?)

M0103 Mankind one day serene and free appear
And what we like at noon we leave at night.

c.549, p. 59

M0104 Manners with fortunes, humors turn with chimes,
Tenets with books and principles with times.

'Observations on manners'
c.361

M0105 Man's a poor deluded bubble,
Lost in error, lives and dies.

Robert Dodsley, 'Song'
c.351, p. 148

M0106 Man's all contradiction a medley machine
Here's a bumper to prove ourselves right.

'Song 194'
c.555, p. 312

M0107 Man's breast's the temple, and the spirit, the sayer
On a clean heart, which is the book of prayer.

Sir Thomas Urquhart, 'Of saying prayers'
fb.217, p. 85

M0108 Man's flesh is humbled by no better way
For death proceeds to threat thee night and day.

b.234, p. 136

M0109 Man's heart and body present grief doth grieve
But fear of future pain doth it disease.

'Grief and pleasure'
c.356

M0110 Man's heart's like Ahaz' dial, if it flees
Not forward; it goes backward ten degrees.

'On Ahaz' dial'
b.118, p. 222

M0111 Man's ingress into the world, is naked and bare,
I can tell you no more, if I preach a whole year.

'A sermon—the text was, Man is born to sorrow, as the
sparks fly upward'
c.378, p. 48

M0112 Man's jail's the earth, whole walls, are th'azurplains
[sic]
The keeper's sin: but woman is the chains.

Sir Thomas Urquhart, 'The world is a prison'
fb.217, p. 220

MO113   Man's life is like a winter's day
The longest life but sups and goes to bed.

    'Another [epitaph]'
    [cf. Crum M138]

    c.150, p. 77; see also 'The longest life . . .'.

MO114   Man's life is like an hour-glass, wherein
Our sins are finished, as our lives are done.

    [Francis Quarles], 'On a hourglass'
    [Crum M139]

    b.118, p. 229; b.156, p. 19

MO115   Man's life is short, and like a shade,
Whilest it doth seem to stay.

    b.234, p. 179

MO116   Man's life, like any weaver's shuttle flies,
Let us be ready, come death when he will.

    'Life is short!'

    c.487, p. 75

MO117   Man's life was once a span; now one of those
Since through a double mean naught right appears.

    'To the same. Man's life'

    Poetry Box v/106

MO118   Man's spittle kills the scorpion, therefore Anne,
To kill the scorpion of her concupiscence.

    Sir Thomas Urquhart, 'Of the too ardent, and
    exorbitant desire, that one named Anna had to be
    married'

    fb.217, p. 357

MO119   Man's wrath shall sing Jehovah's praise
Whom outward evil cannot harm.

    [Mary Pluret], 'Another [poem written on waste
    paper]'

    c.354

MO120   Man's yard is not unlike (if you would know it)
It will renew in her, her Cyprian madness.

    Sir Thomas Urquhart, 'Of the service tree, and the
    staff of generation, how nearly they sympathize'

    fb.217, p. 345

MO121   Many aspiring fellows you may see
Because a thrifty garment they have spun . . . .

    'Essay 2. Of cowardliness'

    b.150, p. 278 (incomplete)

MO122   Many men of many minds,
Many birds of many kinds.

    c.93

MO123   Many there be which now abroad do live
That promise much, and yet will nothing give.

    c.339, p. 319

MO124   Many too many men there be,
Faith plants, hope waters, love, love gives the
                        increase.

    [Edmund Wodehouse], 'Jan. 25 [1715]'

    b.131, p. 147

MO125   Many will ask the bellman why
Reply, the sun expels the Dew.

    'On Mrs Dew dying for grief of her son's death'
    [Crum M165]

    b.200, p. 137

MO126   Marble—the pillar against which he stood,
My hope's last conflict, and its last reward.

    'On our Savior's being bound to a pillar before Pilate.
    An Italian epigram'

    c.83/1, no. 249

MO127   Marcella now grown old hath broke her glass
Should show good countenance that receiveth none.

    [Henry Parrot, 'Forma bonum fragile']
    [Crum M171]

    b.148, p. 3

MO128   March forth, with ev'ry wish that can attend
Rewarding, throw a glory round your toils.

    John Lockman, 'The adieu, to our soldiers: those
    particularly who returned from Flanders; on their
    setting out, from London, against the rebels . . . 4
    Decr. 1745'

    c.267/1, p. 225

MO129   March on, march on my merry merry mates
Wassail, jolly wassail and joy go with our King.

    'Catches [3]'

    b.356, p. 72

MO130   March with his wind hath struck a cedar tall,
And yet sad May, must lose the flower of flowers.

    'Upon Queen Anne who died in March, was kept all
    April, and buried in May' [1619]
    [Crum M175]

    b.200, p. 220; fb.143, p. 24; b.62, p. 76

MO131   Marcus, around thy humble cot,
With pleasure be obey'd.

    Charles Burney, the younger, 'Ode, addressed to a
    friend . . . October. 1778'

    c.35, p. 31

MO132 Maria mistress of my song,
But death must aid his power.

'An ode . . . 1759'
fc.74, p. 1

MO133 Maria sets no value on her skin
Which closely clings to academic fools.

'[Female characters.] 7. Maria: or the pattern'
Poetry Box IV/148

MO134 Maria's charms have won my heart
Her easy chains to wear Sir.

'On Miss Mary Turner of Devonshire Square without
Bishopsgate—London—1741/2 rara avis in terra'
[answered by 'Desist, rash youth . . .']
c.360/1, p. 283

MO135 Mark but this flea, and mark but this
Will waste as this flea's death took life from thee.

[John Donne], 'The flea'
[Crum M181]
b.114, p. 282; b.148, p. 50; fb.66/38; fb.88, p. 120 (stanzas
2 and 3 reversed)

MO136 Mark how, ere eve, the morning honors fade!
And life beginning teems with seeds of death!

'Epitaph on a young lady'
fc.132/1, p. 166

MO137 Mark how her coral lips her beauty grace
And reign each one beyond superlative.

'Upon his mistress'
b.62, p. 92

MO138 Mark how it snows! how fast the valley fills
To sell the gaudy hour for ages of renown.

[Isaac] Watts, 'Ode to a friend translated from the
Latin of Leibniz'
Poetry Box V/52

MO139 Mark how my Celia with the choice
Are all turn'd into stones again.

Tho[mas] Carew, 'On his m[ist]r[es]s singing to her
lute in a gallery at York House'
[Crum H238]
b.200, p. 118; b.356, p. 77; see also 'Hark how my
Celia . . .'.

MO140 Mark how the drops do trickle down his face,
Could have made God in such a case have been.

H[enry] C[olman], 'On his sweat on Mount Olivet'
[Crum M185]
b.2, p. 17

MO141 Mark how this polish'd eastern sheet
To fold up silks, may wrap up wit.

[Thomas Carew], 'A fancy'
[Crum M188]
b.150, p. 227

MO142 Mark how young David with a sting
And cause the strong man to depart.

[Mary Pluret], 'Another on David and Goliath'
c.354

MO143 Mark the soft falling snow
Consenting nod.

P[hilip] Doddridge, 'Fruitful shores &c. Emblems of
the salutary effects of the gospel from Is. IV 10–12'
c.493, p. 52

MO144 Mark well you tree, that shades the neighb'ring
                                                    plain,
As conscious of the sacred deed I vow'd.

[Edward Jerningham], 'The oak'
c.90

MO145 Mark when the good man prospers with his plot
How canst thou Fido, look t'have peace with men.

[Francis Quarles], 'On the righteous man' [Divine
fancies III, 34]
b.137, p. 192

MO146 Mark, where the silver Thames, in beauty's pride,
That fixed as fate may scorn power of time.

[William Boscawen], 'Address to the committee of the
Literary Fund at their annual meeting at Greenwich.
5 July 1797.'
fc.106, p. 42

MO147 Mark'd you her eye of heavenly blue
The other blushing at the wound.

[Richard Brinsley Butler] Sheridan[? or Percival
Stockdale?], 'Lines by . . . Sheridan' [parodied by
'Mark'd you that wit . . .']
c.546, p. 19; c.391, p. 106 (var.; last line from Cowper's
The task)

MO148 Mark'd you that wit of jealous hue;
The other—mean excuses makes.

[Frederick Corfield], 'A parody' [of 'Mark'd you her
eye . . .']
c.381/1

MO149 Marlborough is dead! and in the word is lost
And wait upon their master to the ground.

'An elegy on the death of his grace John Duke of
Marlborough' [d. 1722]
c.166, p. 207

M0150 Marlborough, who, next to Jove, Great Britain sav'd
E'en hate his race, 'cause exquisitely fair.

'Acrostic on the Duchess of Montagu, youngest
daughter of the great Duke of Marlborough—
Tunbridge 1719'

c.360/2, no. 175

M0151 Marriage as old men not[e] hath liken'd been,
And those that are within would fain get out.

'Upon marriage'

c.356; see also next.

M0152 Marriage hath well compared been
And those within would fain get out.

'On marriage'
[Crum M197]

b.62, p. 75; see also previous.

M0153 Marriage is a country dance,
And conclude with back to back.

'On marriage'
[Crum M198]

fb.142, p. 62

M0154 Marriage is that sacred tie
Need a separation fear.

H[enry] C[olman], 'On marriage'
[Crum M200]

b.2, p. 41

M0155 Marriage it seems is for better or worse
Consider it well there's none happier can be.

'Song 214'
[cf. Crum M201]

c.555, p. 342

M0156 Marriage the happiest bond of love might be
If hands were only join'd when hearts agree.

c.549, p. 21

M0157 Marriage they say's a tie sure I think not
But if it be then 'tis a riding knot.

'On marriage'

b.356, p. 308

M0158 Marriage thou curse of love, and snare of life
But that which sick men have (of life) their pains.

'An invective against marriage 1667'

b.54, p. 1197

M0159 Married, and I not dead, it cannot be,
I'll give the priest the lie and say thou'rt mine.

A[lexander] Brome, 'To his mistress married to
another'

b.104, p. 120

M0160 Marry a Turk! A haughty tyrant king,
Receives his full reward in beauty's arms.

'Epilogue to Irene a tragedy acted at Drury Lane
Theater 1748/9 spoken by Mrs. Cibber late Miss Arne'

c.360/3, no. 151

M0161 Marry and love thy Flavia for she
For things in fashion every man will wear.

J[ohn] D[onne], 'In Flaviam' [Elegy II]
[Crum M207]

b.148, p. 115; b.205, fol. 32v

M0162 Marry in French importeth to be sad:
Then that in marriage is both joy, and grief.

Sir Thomas Urquhart, 'That wedlock is a mixed sort
of life'

fb.217, p. 248

M0163 Marry late my dear friend—you ask me what then
Kill your wife by a quack, and ne'er marry again.

'Epigram'

c.115

M0164 Mars successful in love as victorious in arms
And rush into the field my boys when drums shall
beat to arms.

[John Walker?], 'The loyal sons of Mars'

fc.108, fol. 54

M0165 Martha, a farmer's joy, and care,
And still keep virtue in their view.

[Thomas Hamilton, 6th earl of Haddington], 'No
nearer'

c.458/2, p. 137

M0166 Martin is fled, Farewell my friend,
Muskets discharge and War at an end.

[John] Hoskins, 'Mr. Hoskins a lawyer in the Middle
Temple made these two verses of four gentlemen of
the Temple (Mr. Martin Mr. Farwell Mr. Musket
Mr. Warre)'

fb.69, p. 200

M0167 Marvel not (friend) that oftentimes I write
Which is the cause I sometimes write of drink.

[Sir Aston Cokayne], 'To [Mr Henry Longville]'

b.275, p. 95

M0168 Mary deriv'd is sharp, sharp things you see
Of th'sweetest birds whom hearing all admire.

b.62, p. 93

M0169 Mary! I want a lyre with other strings;
And since thou own'st that praise, I spare thee mine.

[William] Cowper, 'Sonnet. To Mary [Unwin]'
[Crum M213]

c.142, p. 579

M0170 Mary, I've heard of many names
I'd write the name of Jesus there!

Poetry Box v/37

M0171 Mary, my child—O no, I must forbear
And heav'n, as I do, pity—and forgive!

'Written on the elopement of L[ad]y Mary Singleton,
daughter to the late Lord Cornwallis 1785' [copied
from a magazine c.1805]

Smith Papers, folder 75/24

M0172 Mary the wonder of her sex,
A boundless boundless pride to ease us.

'A satirical song on the Queen'

b.111, p. 436

M0173 Mary, a chambermaid, a brown-eyed lass
Surely at night then you'll be brought to bed.

[Sir Aston Cokayne], 'Of a chambermaid'

b.275, p. 34

M0174 Master, I own thy lawful claim,
And let our all be lost in thee.

'Hymn 77th'

c.562, p. 98

M0175 Master Kent being desir'd for the speaker to plan
And call'd all his trees back—to order.

'On Kent the surveyor laying out the gardens of
Arthur Onslow esqr—Speaker of the House of
Commons'

c.360/1, p. 249

M0176 Master of eloquence, of pow'r to please
Words are inadequate to what we feel.

[Anna] Seward, 'On Col. F. P. E.'s acting the part of
Edward at Lichfield Theater'

File 13372

M0177 Mat Lewis was little, Mat Lewis was young
Should write not at all or should write common
sense.

[George Watson-Taylor],'The old hag in a red cloak
inscribed to the author of The grim white woman
[Matthew Gregory Lewis]'
[Crum M216]

Poetry Box III/49 (post-1800?)

M0178 Matchless as when Venus, heav'n's blooming rose
Know you must the remedy yield.

'Acrostic' [on Miss Mary Kirk]

c.360/2, no. 158

M0179 Matchless in virtue, and a beauteous mind
Employ your sighs elsewhere, for here they're vain.

'Acrostic' [on Miss Betty Chowne]

c.360/2, no. 169

M0180 Matthew Parker lived sober and wise,
He liv'd to God, to God he made his end.

'On Archbp. Parker'

fb.143, p. 20

M0181 Maxentius a mighty state,
And purchase heaven withouten end. | Amen

'Of S. Katherine. No[vember] 25'

a.30[57]

M0182 May all new years, and happiness, be so
Happy again, in your dear friends to see.

Lady Jane Cavendish, 'On my sister Brackley'
[Crum M227]

b.233, p. 28

M0183 May angels guard thee with distinguish'd care,
To rise and flourish in immortal bloom.

'The wish'

c.83/2, no. 328

M0184 May England see her errors ere too late?
And end their lives by halter's suffocation.

'A loyal wish'

b.111, p. 49; fb.207/1, p. 41

M0185 May heaven in mercy blessings pour,
God cannot be unjust.

C. E. Stewart, 'To Mr. [Edmund] Burke on the loss of
his son [Richard, d. 1794] . . . 1797'

c.82, p. 25

M0186 May heavenly dews most plenteously distill
That walks with Christ, while you are sinking down.

[Thomas Gurney], 'To his woman Mrs. Martha Hunt
at his hearing she had joined herself to the church of
Christ, under the religious care of that faithful servant
of Jesus Christ Mr. Fra: Walker' [acrostic]

c.213

M0187 May I not fear nore wish for death
By our dear Lord and Sovereign.

[Edmund Wodehouse], 'Novr. 24 [1714]'

b.131, p. 96

M0188   May I presume in humble lays,
Then one may say the ball is ended.

> William Pulteney, earl of Bath, 'On Kellom
> Tomlinson's Book of dancing'
> [Crum M242]

Poetry Box v/81; c.487, p. 113 (attr. 'Judge Burnet'); File
17383

M0189   May Jemmy remain
Make the darling complain.

> [Charles Burney, the younger], 'To Master James
> Francis'

c.37, p. 19

M0190   May not our God whose gracious care
Thy will be done O God.

> Charles Atherton Allnutt, 'On the adverse
> dispensations of Providence'

c.112, p. 87

M0191   May plagues, like those which abdicated kings
May they live slaves to kings enslav'd by priests!

> 'A curse on King William's enemies'

fb.70, p. 217

M0192   May Pollio's health forever shine
Aspasia still delight his eyes.

> John Lockman, 'A toast, for the Earl of Middlesex's
> birthday. 6 Feb. (O. S.) 1746'

c.267/1, p. 217

M0193   May she be damn'd, nay doubly damn'd the first
And none supply her lust, when she turns whore.

> 'By a certain young lady, a little loosely inclined,
> whose friend (for interest) had married a rich old man'

c.360/2, no. 93

M0194   May spits of double-heated brass
Omnipotence can do no worse.

> [Robert Cholmeley], 'To Crassus Sen: Fellow of St
> Johns Coll: in Cambridge'

c.190, p. 181

M0195   May that just and grateful thing,
The rest from God himself receive.

b.204, p. 132

M0196   May the act against vagabonds reach the Pretender,
Which none will refuse but a Whig or a Rumper.

> 'Upon the act against vagrants' [1713; Jacobite verse]
> [Crum M250]

fc.58, p. 128

M0197   May the ambitious ever [favor] find
Her arms much softer nights.

> [Charles Sackville, 6th earl of Dorset], 'Songs'

c.189, p. 113

M0198   May the girl that I love
And her hair be as black as the devil.

> 'The wish'

c.360/1, p. 213

M0199   May the youth none of life's dire vicissitudes prove
May remembrance shed tears of esteem o'er his urn.

> [Helen Craik], 'Lines written in a summer house,
> under the initial letters of a gentleman's name'

c.375, p. 60

M0200   May two parts of my first be forever united!
'Tis a blessing we ask for in prayer.

> 'Charade'

c.389

M0201   May wine and wisdom never fail
And wit and beauty e'er prevail.

c.361

M0202   May you live ever blest in your favorite state
Too much to the cellar Tom Greedy-guts shall go.

> [William Hayley], 'Hidalgio the lover to Mouse the
> sedate'

File 6948

M0203   May you my dear be daily seen,
And ever blooming—evergreen.

> 'From a gentleman to his niece, on sending her a pot
> of myrtle'

c.83/1, no. 245

M0204   May you to whom each close intrigue lies bare
A brawny pamper'd priest can at the altar snore.

> M[aurice] J[ohnson], 'To Mrs. Manley authoress of
> the Atalantis the Moysia Signa of this age written
> 15 November 1709'

c.229/2, fol. 16v

M0205   May your care ye sweet Floras be amply repaid,
They'll shoot out again, and bloom fresh in the
             skies.

> J. B. Dickinson, 'To his nieces A. and M. R. with
> paling for their garden 1713'

c.391, p. 94, p.?

M0206   May'st please Her Majesty to condescend
Fail not to come—we'll feast on tea-like things.

> 'A triple invitation to sea'

c.91, p. 225

M0207　Me tho' mistaken kindness doom'd
　　　　Are wisdom's lot alone.

　　　　　W[illiam] P[arsons], 'To Bertie Greatheed, at Eton
　　　　　School'

　　　　Greatheed Box/11

M0208　Me who have lived so long among the great
　　　　The place's bounty there shall give me more.

　　　　　[Abraham Cowley, trans.], 'Martial book 10. Epigram
　　　　　96' ['Preferring a country life as many ways more
　　　　　commodious than that of the city']
　　　　　[Crum M266]

　　　　b.135, fol. 116.

M0209　Me, whom each poet woos in various strains,
　　　　With softer violence might thy guests detain!

　　　　　'To Mr. W. P. on verses of his to Æolus supplicating a
　　　　　tempest to detain some lady friends from going to the
　　　　　Isle of Wight—spring [17]78 . . . Favonius'
　　　　　[cf. Crum M267]

　　　　c.89, p. 123

M0210　Meare, since unmixt, unmarried and a maid
　　　　Pray let me taste your nether parts this Lent.

　　　　　'To Mary Meare'

　　　　b.197, p. 125

M0211　Medea, as old bards have sung,
　　　　The sorceress, you northwards send.

　　　　　[Thomas Hamilton, 6th earl of Haddington], 'To the
　　　　　Honble Mr Johnston an epistle'

　　　　c.458/2, p. 163

M0212　Meek animal, whose simple mien
　　　　Is to murmur I obey.

　　　　　W[illiam] C[rowe], 'Written under the print of an
　　　　　ass . . . 1775'
　　　　　[Crum M273]

　　　　c.373, p. 44

M0213　Meek Franco lies here friend without stop or stay.
　　　　On a single surmise that the owner is dead.

　　　　　[Matthew Prior], '[Mock-] Epitaph on [Francis
　　　　　Atterbury] Bp. Rochester'

　　　　fc.24, p. 61; c.229/1, fol. 35v ('Francis'; with extra lines?
　　　　attr. Henry Johnson)

M0214　Meek modest and mild
　　　　And it pleas'd God to take her.

　　　　　'Epitaph'

　　　　c.150, p. 127

M0215　Meek shade, farewell! Go seek that quiet shore
　　　　The vision promis'd to the pure in heart.

　　　　　H[annah] More, 'Epitaph on E. B[lan]df[or]d . . .
　　　　　1788'

　　　　c.341, p. 36

M0216　Meekest of angels in whose potent eye
　　　　As fields desert the disenchanted wood.

　　　　　[William Hayley], 'Sonnet . . . May 9 [1800]

　　　　File 6968

M0217　Melancholic looks, and whining,
　　　　Are the bless'd efforts of love.

　　　　　'Song'

　　　　c.189, p. 7

M0218　Melodious lark go sport and sing
　　　　Beware I leave worse foes behind.

　　　　　'From the Arabic composed by Tarfat Jo'n al Abad . . .'

　　　　Poetry Box I/37

M0219　Melpomene! In sable ever clad,
　　　　Nor envy who o'erhear a city's loud huzzas.

　　　　　[James Mulcaster, sr.], 'The complaint'

　　　　c.118, p. 7

M0220　Members prepare yourselves both Whig and Tory
　　　　Grim death at last, has caught him in his trap.

　　　　　'On Topham's departure Serjeant to the House of
　　　　　Commons'

　　　　File 19032

M0221　Men for the loss of gold no tears do feign;
　　　　They fret no more, no more their deaths bemoan.

　　　　　J[ohn] R[obinson], 'Planguntur nummi, quam funera,
　　　　　nemo doler fingit in hoc casu'

　　　　c.370, fol. 38v

M0222　Men for the wars shall frugally be bred
　　　　Are the improvements of more modern times.

　　　　　'On warfare from a Swedish bard'

　　　　c.229/2, fol. 36

M0223　Men have become by studying knowledge wood;
　　　　But none have made that studier to be good.

　　　　　[Sir Thomas Urquhart], 'Goodness is better than
　　　　　knowledge'

　　　　fb.217, p. 393

M0224　Men if you love us play no more
　　　　To make anew and hang that by.

　　　　　[Ben Jonson]

　　　　b.213, p. 51

M0225　Men look on poems, but they do not read
　　　　The poet made 'em such; and that's his own.

　　　　　[George Daniel], 'Protrepticon'

　　　　b.121, fol. 16

MO226 Men mortal do not flourish long
I may them well compare.

    b.234, p. 111

MO227 Men now to earthly dross are so much given
The number weight and measure of fine gold.

    [Sir Thomas Urquhart], 'Of people's exorbitant desire
    to become wealthy'

    fb.217, p. 388

MO228 Men should court mistresses advisedly
To woo some women breedeth double woe.

    [Sir Thomas Urquhart], 'Of wooers and women'

    fb.217, p. 538

MO229 Men to their lawyers go; because they are
That last, which should be first, and first, what last.

    Sir Thomas Urquhart, 'The different respect the
    world carries to theologs, lawyers, and physicians'

    fb.217, p. 216

MO230 Men whilst they live, like rivers in a motion
As men are equal in the bonds of death.

    Sir Thomas Urquhart, 'The difference betwixt men,
    whilst they are alive, and after that they are dead'

    fb.217, p. 102

MO231 Men without love, have often so cunning grown
As all but thou appear to me.

    'Love's visibility'

    Poetry Box VI/47

MO232 Men writ[e], that love and reason disagree
'Tis virtue to be chaste, which she'll make thee.

    [Sir John Roe], 'Satyra septima' [attr. John Donne]

    b.114, p. 60

MO233 Men's fancies vary strangely, like their faces,
Sometimes in high, sometimes in low estate.

    c.93

MO234 Mercury, from Atlas sprung,
Grateful thou to gods below!

    [William Popple, trans.], 'Hymn to Mercury.
    [Horace] book 1st. ode 10th'

    fc.104/2, p. 32

MO235 Merely to breathe, howe'er enrich'd with wealth,
This toast, health 'tis with thee I wish to live.

    'On the recovery of a most valued friend . . . Otranto
    Castle Nov: 2 [17]86'

    c.83/1, no. 16

MO236 Meridian glory of the plains
Deign but a smile, and Strephon lives.

    'Acrostic' [on Miss Betty Crawford]

    c.360/2, no. 215

MO237 Merit like yours, invites each Muse to sing
Laughing at mortals whom we lov'd before.

    'Acrostic' [on Mary Powell]

    c.360/2, no. 209

MO238 Merit's a plant so delicate in bloom,
Evelyn, the pride of Thornley's lone retreats.

    'The village monitor'

    c.83/2, no. 558

MO239 Merry Mumpey the smell-feast, like Gratho the
                             great,
This,—the only sure way to be happy and wise.

    Abraham Oakes, 'Mumpeius parasitus'

    c.50, p. 95

MO240 Merry was he for whom we now are sad,
Whilst puns are puns, on punning men have breath.

    'Punning lines on a punster' [John Tissey]

    c.81/1, no. 400

MO241 Metellus I have heard by one of late,
And the loud censures of the world defy.

    Edward Sneyd, 'An epistle 11th:—vivendi recte qui
    prorogat horam . . .'

    c.214, p. 34

MO242 Methinks a line we might employ
And punch had been the drink of Jove.

    'Honos euit huic giroque succo'

    c.546, p. 4

MO243 Methinks death like one laughing lies
Showing his teeth shutting his eyes | Only . . . .

    [Edward Herbert, lord Herbert of Cherbury], 'On
    Mrs. Boulstred' [July 1609]
    [Crum M338a]

    b.148, p. 150 (incomplete)

MO244 Methinks I hear, when I do hear it thunder
Preposterously into disorder strange.

    [Joshua Sylvester, trans. Guillaume de Salluste,
    seigneur] Du Bartas, 'A Christian use of the changes
    of the weather'

    b.137, p. 91

MO245 Methinks I see great Dioclesian walk
The garden's greatest hero lodges here.

    'Upon the Lord Dover's Cheveley'

    b.63, p. 94

M0246   Methinks I see with what a busy haste
From earth to the tree, and from the tree to heaven.

    [Francis Quarles], 'On Zaccheus' [Divine fancies I,
    66, with two more lines]

    b.137, p. 167

M0247   Methinks I see you newly risen
The reins of government will break.

    'The looking glass'
    [Crum M343]

    b.371, no. 35

M0248   Methinks, O! vain ill-judging book,
Go, my delight! Dear book, adieu!

    'A preface'

    c.83/3, no. 883

M0249   Methinks she hath not lost her maidenhead
And purchas'd since above a dozen for it.

    [Sir Thomas Urquhart], 'That all those that are not
    maids, and never were married have not lost their
    maidenheads'

    fb.217, p. 538

M0250   Methinks the entry of your room
I made it patent for ye.

    Sir Thomas Urquhart, 'The respective answer of a
    bride to her husband's very homely question'

    fb.217, p. 247

M0251   Methinks the god dwells on Cassandra's hands
The God informs her body, and her mind.

    Poetry Box IV/102

M0252   Methinks the Vicar General bears the keys
The vicar got so rich, the Lord so poor.

    [Francis Quarles], 'On Christ and his vicar' [Divine
    fancies III, 28]

    b.137, p. 174

M0253   Methinks 'tis very strange that the devil
I'll laugh in my sleeve, and cry a pox on the devil.

    'A pox on the devil. By the same hand' [as 'Tho' in
    their flame . . .']

    fb.142, p. 52

M0254   Methinks when I behold your verdant yew
Who'd think the name, should give the truth the lie.

    William Yates, of Clarely, 'A copy of verses on
    Mr. Wilton's yew tree'

    c.148, p. 12

Methought I saw before my feet,
Virtue would think her best reward!   M0255

    [George] L[yttelton, 1st baron Lyttelton], 'Letter to
    Earl H——, occasioned by ['Fame heard with
    pleasure']'

    c.83/1, no. 24

Methought I wander'd in that pleasant globe   M0256
Climb'd up the hill while the spangled robe
                    sky-made.

    [Benjamin Strutt]

    fc.156

Methought one night, I went unto my dear   M0257
And vext and storm'd because 'twas but a dream.

    [Richard Corbett?], 'A dream' ['Dr Corbett to his
    mistress']

    b.62, p. 103

Mickle she is—ye in humble bee   M0258
Yet 'gainst her pilferers, she wears a sting.

    [Sir Philip Wodehouse], 'Upon Sr Francis Bickley's
    daughter Mary Bickley'

    b.131, back (no. 229)

Midas we read with wondrous art of old   M0259
Touch them with gold they'll change to what you
                    please.

    [Charles Earle?], 'An epigram'

    c.376; c.115

'Midst barren rocks the heedless poet plays,   M0260
And laugh at all the little crowd below.

    'Mr. Voltaire's answer to the Duke of Bouillon who
    had written a letter in verse on the edition of
    Corneille'

    c.83/2, no. 687

Might I but choose a wife unto my mind,   M0261
To hug so dear an armful of content.

    'How to choose a wife'
    [Crum M368]

    b.200, p. 146

Might we ascend to excellence sublime   M0262
Above the reach of every dunce and drone.

    [Mary Serjant?]
    [Crum M369]

    fb.98, fol. 151

Mighty Pan! With tender care   M0263
From the bridegroom and the bride.

    'The happy pair'

    c.83/1, no. 231

M0264   Mild as mercy, sweet as lovers' joys
Succeed thy ev'ry wish, and crown thy latter end.

     'Acrostic' [on Miss Mary Anne Eyres]

     c.360/2, no. 170

M0265   Mild as the lamb, harmless as the dove
True as the turtle, is the maid I love.

     'Written on a window'

     c.360/1, p. 9

M0266   Mild as the opening morn's serenest ray,
To lose at once, the sister, and the friend.

     William Whitehead, 'On the death of Miss Vernon
     addressed to Lady Nuneham'

     Poetry Box x/132

M0267   Mild looks beguile the simple man
Beguilers lie in wait.

     b.234, p. 329

M0268   Mildest of mortals whose angelic mind
Tenderly brave heroically mild.

     [William Hayley], 'Sonnet . . . August 27 [1800]'
     File 6968

M0269   Millions unborn shall bless the hand
That brought deliverance on the land.

     c.358, p. 28

M0270   Mine be a cot beside the hill;
And point with taper spire to heaven.

     [Samuel Rogers], 'A wish' [1786]
     [Crum M381]

     c.355, p. 267; c.343, p. 34 (var.)

M0271   Mine eyes are dim, mine ears do heavy grow,
Thou shalt united to the Godhead rest.

     [John Hobart], '[Præludia mortis.] Æt. 70. The
     supply'

     b.108, fol. 9

M0272   Mine eyes were once bless'd with the sight
He'll die, and so turn shade again.

     [Jasper Mayne], 'On Mris Anne King's table-book of
     pictures'
     [Crum M390]

     b.205, fol. 78r; b.200, p. 186

M0273   Minerva has vow'd since the bishops do slight her,
And the first law of nature is self-preservation.

     'On wisdom's defeat in a learned debate' [sometimes
     attr. Jonathan Swift; pr. 1725 (Foxon O230)]

     c.570/2, p. 152

M0274   Minerva's image once defended Troy
But both in George, in real life appear.

     [ ] Spence, 'On the same [the battle of Dettingen]
     by . . . prenez le roi—paulo majora canamus'

     c.360/2, no. 91

M0275   Mira, take this painted fan;
Virtue may exist unseen.

     'To a lady, with a painted fan; on one side an old
     woman reading with spectacles her crutch standing by
     her; on the reverse, Virtue in a rich-wrought but loose
     robe looking upward, and giving alms, in an inclining
     posture, to a beggar on the ground'

     c.83/3, no. 837

M0276   Mira, this machine, you'll find,
Wins the Christian's crown on high.

     'To Mira with a repeating watch'

     c.83/2, no. 283

M0277   Mira, while on earth our stay,
Claim a mansion in the sky.

     'To Mira. On our removal from P. to B[at]h'

     c.83/1, no. 29

M0278   Mira would twice in colors live
Attempt to draw you o'er again.

     [Phanuel Bacon], 'To Mira setting twice for her
     picture. To the tune of The play of love, &c.'
     [Crum M394]

     c.237, fol. 7

M0279   Miro to prove his mission loud will bawl
Now brainless prophets claim a right to guide us?

     Charles Atherton Allnutt, 'Epigram on an ignorant
     self-ordained preacher [Jos. Eyre]'

     c.112, p. 171

M0280   Miscall that then his funeral 'scutcheon
His tomb (ominous syllable) it is his tent.

     [R[ichard] Painter, 'Elegies on Sr. Horatio Vere'

     b.52/2, p. 126

M0281   Miser! attend that sound, to thee it spoke
That earthly power must fall, and beauty fade.

     'On the moments of the Monitor . . . a bell in the
     Pensoroso which strikes every minute'

     fc.51, p. 99

M0282   Misguided zealots won't our church regard,
And smiling bids you welcome to the feast.

     'To Mrs. Dod, presenting to her—Common Prayer
     the best companion'

     b.322, p. 10

M0283 Miss Molly, a fam'd toast, was fair, and young,
Sir John, without a med'cine, will be kind.

[William Harrison?], 'The medicine' [pr. Dublin 1737 (Foxon A158.5)]

c.310

M0284 Miss Nanny, I've sent you a basket of stuff,
And I beg you'll remember to send back the basket.

[Francis Fawkes], 'To a young lady with a present of books, partridges and snuff'

fc.21, p. 7

M0285 Miss Nanny that grew so [?], and fit for no man
With boasting soon became a gentlewoman!

'A receipt to make a lady'

c.74

M0286 Miss Peggy at church on the conjugal day,
E'er this business be done, I will make her cry O.

'Peggy's marriage'

c.81/1, no. 125

M0287 Mistake me not I am as cold as hot
What hope, what hope, what hope has thine to stay.

[Alexander Brome; answered by 'Wrong not my mold . . .' and 'Sir I care not . . .']

b.213, p. 19; b.4, fol. 45

M0288 Mistake not nymph pray don't compare
To set your greens a-springing.

[Mrs. Christian Kerr], 'By a Tiviotdale lad to a Tweeddale lass upon comparing countries to the tune of Last time I came o'er the moor'

c.102, p. 118

M0289 Mistaken fair lay Sherlock by
'Tis I must live [i.e., learn] to die.

[Philip Dormer Stanhope, 4th] earl of Chesterfield, 'On the right honble Countess of Walsingham's reading Sherlock upon death'

c.152, p. 31; c.157, p. 7 (applied to Lady Tankerville); c.241, p. 14

M0290 Mistaken man! Is this the fancied all
Content, the celebrated Sabbath of the mind.

'From a poem against sensual pleasures'

c.186, p. 83

M0291 Mister Crockett—pray take notice,
Strains his poor eyes to sign it. | G. Instry

[G. Instry], 'Stourfield Oct: 28th. 1795'

fc.40

M0292 Mistress for abuses offer'd me | Meet me soon at
6 o' clock
Look to yourself keep close your guard | And so
farewell till six.

'A challenge to one's mistress'

b.62, p. 52, p. 78

M0293 Mrs. Holt, that lusty colt, hath ofttimes play'd the
mare,
Then Mrs. Holt might keep the colt by letter of
attorney.

[on Sir Francis Prince, knighted 1611, and one Mrs. Holt] [Crum M412]

b.200, p. 413

M0294 Mrs. Montagu tells me and in her own house,
For a woman will talk of what runs in her head.

C[harles James] Fox, 'Epigram said to be by C. Fox' [Crum 1569]

Diggle Box: Poetry Box XI/69; c.391, p. 120

M0295 Mrs. Morris (with the Peterborough blood in each
vein)
For the gov'nor and his lady will be back by July.

[Mrs. ( ) Morris to Lady Payne]

Poetry Box II/38

M0296 Mistress since you so much desire
I climb to crown my chaste desire.

'Cant: 35'

b.4, fol. 29v

M0297 Mixed with the dead, great artist, dost thou lie,
You only prick'd the arm, he strikes the heart.

T[homas] H[olland], of Jesus College, Oxford, 'On the death of John Symonds the phlebotomist'

c.233, p. 105

M0298 Mixt angels, man being the sublimest wight
Of sin, than which, no heavier thing can be.

Sir Thomas Urquhart, 'Why mankind is tied to the earth'

fb.217, p. 107

M0299 Mneme, begin; inspire, ye sacred Nine!
Improve the refuge from the wrath divine.

Phyllis Wheatley, 'Recollection—a poem—wrote by . . . at Boston, an African Negro, who did not leave her own country until she was ten years of age—and wrote this at eighteen'

fc.132/1, p. 178

M0300 Model of fortitude my martyred son
And they reflected virtue make me calm.

[William Hayley], 'Sonnet . . . Sept. 4 [1800]'

File 6968

M0301 Modest, humble, godly, wise,
Such she was, that now lies here.

   'An epitaph on Mrs. Reynolds'
   [Crum M421]

   c.244, p. 212

M0302 Modest shentle, when her see
Pray send her word if her can love.

   'A Welshman's love letter'
   [Crum M420]

   b.356, p. 326; see also 'Ah modest shentle . . .'.

M0303 Moist with one drop of thy blood, my dry soul
Salute the last, and everlasting day.

   [John Donne], '[Holy sonnets.] La Corona [6]'
   [Crum M424]

   b.114, p. 160

M0304 Moll once in pleasant company by chance,
That some impurity doth not pollute.

   '[Last two lines] taken out of Burton's Abstract upon
   melancholy'

   fb.142, p. 32

M0305 Moments there are when skill forsakes the skill'd
To deck with filial love his father's lonely bower.

   [William Hayley], 'Sonnet . . . August 1 [1800]'
   File 6968

M0306 Momus doth carp that I do write so few
And worth so many (for your worths) are you.

   [Sir Aston Cokayne], 'To Mr. [ ] Millicent'
   b.275, p. 97

M0307 Momus thou hast no cause to bark at me
Bark while th'art blind, 'gainst glorious light of sun.

   [John Taylor], 'To Momus' [from 'The world turned
   upside down']

   fb.40, p. 375

M0308 Monarchs are gods on earth allowed so;
Makes subjects earthly Hallelujahs sing.

   [William Sandys?], 'Monarchs gods on earth'
   b.230, p. 104

M0309 Monday is a jovial day:
Monday is a jovial day.

   Abraham Oakes, 'The feast, or country-wakes: an
   invitation'

   c.50, p. 3

M0310 'Mongst all the churches of the earth, there's none
That Christ would have more wives, than Solomon.

   Sir Thomas Urquhart, 'Of the several religions in the
   world'

   fb.217, p. 54

M0311 'Mongst all the goods that man hath made,
Subduing our iniquity.

   Charles Atherton Allnutt, '7th Micah 18 and 19 vs.'

   c.112, p. 75

M0312 'Mongst all the rites that nature can pretend
That drawing near to death we are all equal.

   [Sir Thomas Urquhart], 'Death makes us all alike'

   fb.217, p. 531

M0313 Monmouth the witty, and Lauderdale the pretty,
But above all the rest the Duke for a jest, | And the
                       King for a politician.

   ['A lampoon upon the English grandees, 1676']
   [Crum M447]

   fb.140, p. 129; b.54, p. 873; see also 'Dr. Pratier . . .'.

M0314 Monsieur Peter Birdee,
Finish off; and then send | To your servant and
                              friend.

   C[harles] E[arle], 'Extempore to my shoemaker'

   c.376

M0315 Monsieur was dead, and laid in ground
Like the poor frogs he used to pounce.

   'Lines on a French decree'

   c.344

M0316 Monster of monsters sure I should appear
That every change but serves to make me worse.

   'Enigma [77b]'

   c.389

M0317 Montanus, fam'd for ample paunch,
They star'd, obey'd, he eat, and died.

   [Isaac Freeman], 'The glutton from La Fontaine.
   Prague'

   fc.105, p. 3

M0318 Mopsa whipping her scarf on, scuds away to the
                              park,
Since her face would sink down, if brought forth to
                              the light.

   John Lockman, 'The arch one'

   c.267/1, p. 108; c.268 (first part), p. 27

M0319 Mopsus stretch'd at full length; breeches off; in a
                              funk,
Samson-like, thus to throw a bold youth on his
                              back.

   John Lockman, 'Mopsus's debauch in Paris . . . Oct.
   1741'

   c.267/1, p. 76

M0320 More constancy, and courage in a woman
Your fertile issue, were all kings, and queens.

> Sir Thomas Urquhart, 'The first epigram to Lady
> Elizabeth, the King's only sister'

fb.217, p. 195

M0321 More constant than the turtle-dove,
Will, instantly, unriddle this.

> 'A riddle'

Spence Papers, folder 113

M0322 More pleasing were these sweet delights
By keeping you asunder.

> 'Gray's Inn masque at the Palsgrave's marriage'

b.356, p. 130

M0323 More stateliness: yet affability:
By better actions, both of body 'nd wit.

> Sir Thomas Urquhart, 'To the Countess of [crossed
> out]'

fb.217, p. 260

M0324 More than content with what my labors gain
Or wear the cap and mask on any stage.

> [David] Garrick, 'Reply to a noble' [1761]
> [Crum M461]

fc.85, fol. 86v, fol. 118

M0325 More than his name, were less, 'twould seem to fear,
And time and Newton's name together die.

> 'An epitaph recommended in the year 1731. for
> monument in Westminster Abbey, in memory of Sir
> Isaac Newton [d. 20 March 1726]'

c.360/3, no. 192; c.547, p. 231

M0326 More trouble yet? 'twas but an organist
Such idle jigs, upon an Holiday.

> [William Meredith?], 'The organist [Meredith] of
> New Coll[ege]: supposed author. The answer' [to
> 'Brag on proud Christ Church', on Barten Holiday's
> Technogamia: or the marriage of the arts, 1621]
> [Crum M462]

b.200, p. 35; see also 'What more trouble . . .'.

M0327 More virtue that there be there's more envy
Were there more virtue, there would be less vice.

> [Sir Thomas Urquhart], 'A paradox concerning envy
> or contradiction'

fb.217, p. 517

M0328 Morn's beaming eyes at length unclose,
Eve's pensive shades more soothe her meek distress.

> [Ann (Ward)] Radcliffe, 'Sonnet'

c.83/3, no. 851

M0329 Morosa being chaste forsooth is proud
If as imperious, as Andromache.

> [Sir Philip Wodehouse], 'Essay. Casta sed superba'

b.131, p. 24

M0330 Mortal Dellius in each state,
Passage o'er the Stygian lake.

> [William Popple, trans.], '[Horace] book 2nd. Ode 3d.
> To Q. Dellius'

fc.104/2, p. 122

M0331 Mortal, from your lower sphere,
Sown in virtue reap'd in joy.

> [William Roscoe], 'Edward Rogers of Everton,
> merchant, departed this life 1795 aged 45 years'

c.140, p. 578

M0332 Mortal wouldst thou woo a feature
A thousand honors to your name.

> [George Daniel]

b.121, fol. 19v

M0333 Mortality behold and fear
To this shape all must be brought.

> [Francis Beaumont], 'A gentleman at seeing the tombs
> at Westminster made these following verses'
> [Crum M465]

b.226, p. 90 (with extra lines?); c.244, p. 87; c.362, p. 39

M0334 Mortals lament! for [ ] now and fate
Since these likewise [for] hidden ends were fram'd.

> 'Upon the death of Sr William Candish'

b.205, fol. 37r

M0335 Mortals, rejoice! With raptures introduce
Who meekly bore indignity and woe.

> [Walter] Harte, 'Psalm 107'

c.244, p. 494

M0336 Mortals who honor with devout regard
The sweetness of his love surpast his song.

> [William Hayley], 'Epitaph [on William Cowper] . . .
> Sunday eve June 8 [1800]'

File 6935

M0337 Mortals wisely learn to measure
And leave sorrow to the wind.

> 'Song 133'

c.555, p. 187

M0338 Moses conducts the Jews, their tents to strew
His feast be kept in such a fruitful season.

> [Edward] Sparke, 'Poem 31th on Saint Bartholomew'

b.137, p. 65

M0339 Moses espies a bush amazed at sight
His people were in danger safe and grew.

'Exodus 3.2'
c.160, fol. 57

M0340 Moses held up his hand, his troop prevail'd
When from his hand alone his forces live.

'On Sir R[ober]t W[al]p[o]le's gout'
c.570/2, p. 168

M0341 Moss will not cleave to Sis'phus' rolling stone
More common than the rod 'twixt [?] and this.

[Sir Thomas Urquhart], 'Why the [?] Aulinda[?] can
[?] in children'
fb.217, p. 387

M0342 Most divine lady, for I well may guess,
Your irresistable charms that all hearts move.

'Upon a lady'
c.158, p. 26

M0343 Most eloquent of the Pierian troup,
With rivulets of the Castalian font.

Sir Thomas Urquhart, 'The invocation to
Melpomene'
fb.217, p. 163

M0344 Most excellent the [?] of human kind
And feels too much to pay the tribute due.

E[dward?] Y[oung?], 'On [Miss Sally Tagg] inscribed
on her monument, at Chartham church near
Canterbury [?]—having died at the age of 18 within
the twelvemonth after her marriage with W[illiam]
Young'
File 16592

M0345 Most fitly poets unto time apply
On earth must labor to live righteously.

H[enry] C[olman], 'On time'
[Crum H1388]
b.2, p. 53

M0346 Most glorious and omnipotent,
O heavenly reformation.

Poetry Box VII/30 p. 3

M0347 Most glorious Majesty, supreme above
Incessant praises to my God and King.

'A hymn to the Creator'
Poetry Box X/10(16)

M0348 Most gracious Sir, see here before you
And prove a chip off the right block.

'The city address'
c.570/4, p. 45

M0349 Most gracious sovereign Lord, our King
We're Orford's crew,—and that's enough.

'A humorous address to King George the 2d. on his
accession to the throne of Great Britain June the 11—
1727 written by the chaplain of the Orford man of war'
[printed: Foxon S13]
c.360/1, p. 269; c.166, p. 128

M0350 Most grievous is the case if him, delights
He feeds them they therefore can devour.

[Sir Thomas Urquhart], 'How deplorable the estate is
of that man who taketh pleasure to be [?] in his [?]
and [?] of his goods by the lying report of
[?]-placebos'
fb.217, p. 525

M0351 Most happy is that mortal wight
May make a blessed end. | Amen

'St. Cyprian and Justina. Sept. 26'
a.30[38]

M0352 Most happy times are now foretold
And Wolston pray to Jesus.

'A prophecy'
c.570/3, p. 100

M0353 Most maids resemble Eve now in their lives
These have their fruit ere they their husbands know.

[John Davies, of Hereford], 'In festinantes puellas'
[Crum M489]
b.205, fol. 44v; b.62, p. 131

M0354 Most mighty Sir, the sovereign king
To George our sovereign lord and king.

William Plaistow, 'The humble petition of . . . chapel
warden of Kew in behalf of himself . . . to the King'
fc.51, p. 37

M0355 Most of our civil broils may date their spring
Purge but your household then your crown's your
own.

'The household'
fb.70, p. 199

M0356 Most of these are too long and naught 'tis true
And to my self acquire some little fame.

[Sir Aston Cokayne], 'To Mr Henry Turville'
b.275, p. 91

M0357 Most parsons 'tis said love the church and strong
beer,
A fiddlestick on him, he's not worth a song.

[David] Garrick, 'Verses written by . . . when
Mr. Allott stayed at York two days to hear Giordeni,
&c., instead of returning back to Louderburgh 1750'
c.160, fol. 42v

M0358 Most people call me January cold
The time there's none can tell; it is too deep.

    c.158, p. 163

M0359 Most reverend lords, the church's joy and wonder
The Squire of Newgate rock them on a sledge.

    [George Sacheverell], 'Hudibras on Calamy's imprisonment, and Wild's poetry. To the bishops' [Crum M497; *POAS* I.295]

    Poetry Box VIII (oversize), no. 2

M0360 Most sacred Sir and best of human race
And this all tongues may justly speak of thee.

    Lady Jane Cavendish, 'On his most sacred Majesty' [Charles I]
    [Crum M500]

    b.233, p. 11

M0361 Most true it is I dare to say
He then might show his own.

    [Alexander Pope and William Pulteney, earl of Bath], 'A ballad. The discovery: or The squire turned ferret' [on Mary Toft; pr. 1727 (Foxon D328)]
    [Crum M504]

    c.176, p. 18; Poetry Box IV/137; Poetry Box X/16

M0362 Most truly generous, and noble lords:
In th'Empyrian paradise farewell.

    Sir Thomas Urquhart, 'The farewell to the patrons'
    fb.217, p. 362

M0363 Most women as appears b'each lovely vision
In their right vein: bear ofter fruit they will.

    Sir Thomas Urquhart, 'Some women compared to the walnut tree'
    fb.217, p. 311

M0364 Most wondrous Sir we admire thy wit
That triumph's uncertain that jars in the sound.

    [Thomas Gurney], 'To Dr. Abraham Taylor, on his late performance entitled An address to young students in divinity &c . . . 1738'
    c.213

M0365 Most worthy of estimation
Will be an ample gratification.

    ['A proposal of marriage' and 'Answer'] [Crum M506, 'of admiration']

    Poetry Box III/44

M0366 Most wrongfully of my first love
They say 'tis only wind.

    [Lord E.], 'Another [riddle]'

    Poetry Box VII/47

M0367 Most youths, the shortness of Venerian strife
Our pleasure hath: who cares for neither's wife.

    Sir Thomas Urquhart, 'Of the brevity, both of man's contentment, and life'

    fb.217, p. 188

M0368 Mother Breedwell presented her husband each year
How safe should I be, had I both of them on?

    W[illiam] Taylor, 'Female caution' [Dodsley Collection]

    c.487, p. 139

M0369 Mother earth drink the rain
If I too love to drink.

    b.207, p. 9

M0370 Mother of wisdom; thou whose sway
And hail'd the master while he clasp'd the friend.

    [William Mason], 'Ode to memory'

    Poetry Box I/18

M0371 Mothers thro' too much pride or love
Yet little have to give 'em.

    'Wrong education'

    c.360/3, no. 243

M0372 Mourn all ye epicures and city fops:
For all the world has been in Dolly's beef.

    'On the death of Dolly who kept a beefsteak house'

    c.115

M0373 Mourn all ye muses weep all ye swains
The gentle Acis is no more.

    [John Gay, Alexander Pope, and/or John Hughes], '4 chorus in [Handel's] Acis and Galatea' [with musical score for tenor and bass]

    Music MS. 534

M0374 Mourn all you mortals in the mews
No comfort left but skin and shoes.

    'On his horse'

    fb.66/3

M0375 Mourn, Britons! Mourn, great Caroline is dead
Holy, holy, holy, Lord God of Sabaoth.

    'Her elegy' [Queen Caroline, d. 20 Nov. 1737]

    fb.142, p. 65

M0376 Mourn! Justice, liberty, religion, peace,
And friendless nations, weep his obsequies!

    [on William III]

    c.360/2, no. 179

MO377 Mourn mortal man in dolor of thy heart,
Thy promise Lord doth make me bold.

   'An article of our faith'
   c.187, p. 46

MO378 Mourn, mourn, that poor England is torn
For to thirst after blood.

   b.62, p. 117

MO379 Mourn not (my dear) nor do not take
Even like a pelican to die.

   'Charissimae conjugis responsum'
   Poetry Box VI/122

MO380 Mourning in music's out of season
Them from the danger to defend.

   [John Taylor], 'The dedication. To all that mourn in
   Sion' [from 'The world turned upside down']
   fb.40, p. 374

MO381 Much happy are those men who spend their
                              blessed days
In serving God, their prince, their land, unto their
                              endless praise.

   c.339, p. 325

MO382 Much has been said of strumpets of yore
Which I am certain she cannot deny.

   'An historical ballad'
   b.113, p. 217

MO383 Much has been said of Winton's Close
Nor willows seem to weep!

   R[ichard] V[ernon] S[adleir], 'Badinage'
   c.106, p. 135

MO384 Much honor'd mistress, take with gentle mind,
To you that's come, by you that hopes to live.

   'To the right worthy and virtuous Mistress Frances
   Venables, wife unto the worthy and most anciently-
   ennobled gentleman Peter Venables esquire, Baron of
   Kinderton, my singular good mistress'
   b.203, p. 13

MO385 Much meat doth gluttony procure
His stomach in a pipe.

   'On a tobacconist'
   [Crum M536]
   b.205, fol. 46v

MO386 Much suspected by me
Nothing proved can be.

   'Elizabeth prisoner'
   fb.69, p. 52

MO387 Much waters cannot quench that love
Amen amen forever.

   [Mary Pluret], 'Many waters cannot quench love
   neither can the floods drown it. Cant. Chap. 8 verse 7'
   c.354

MO388 Much we talk of J[esus]'s blood
Jes[us] died for sinner's sake.

   [Hymn]
   c.180, p. 87

MO389 Much wine had past, with grave discourse,
For they relate how heretofore . . .

   [John Wilmot], 2nd earl of R[ochester](?), 'A ramble
   in St James's Park'
   [Crum M541]
   b.105, p. 34 (incomplete)

MO390 Much wine will make dead drunk, but 'twas thy lot
If others be disposed to weep they may.

   'On the death of the King's jester [Archibald
   Armstrong] who was reported to have been slain with
   a blow on the head with a black pot'
   File 19344

MO391 Multiplication in her progress tends
Multiplication downwards whence ex gathers (?)

   [Sir Thomas Urquhart], 'A moral reason for the
   different sorts of working in arithmetical
   multiplication and division'
   fb.217, p. 515

MO392 Mundungus scar'd, lest London should come down,
Thy kindred dirt had surely suck'd thee in.

   John Lockman, 'The odd fellow, (a Londoner) who
   dreading the imaginary earthquake, got in all his
   money; and then shut himself up heroically with it, in
   his bedchamber, dreading the event . . . 17 April 1750'
   c.267/1, p. 224

MO393 Munster in a great chagrin,
The next who will have a regard. | To my la la &c.

   'An new English song, to an old French tune' [on
   George I and his mistress the Duchess of Munster,
   later Duchess of Kendal]
   c.570/2, p. 103(bis)

MO394 Muse impart all thy art,
All their lays to resound | Half their praise.

   'An ode to Delia'
   c.83/1, no. 207

MO395 Muse not so much
Their lives restore again.

   'On B. Bonner's picture'
   c.189, p. 47

M0396 Muse see thy favorite darling child
And rise the mirror of her age.

    'On Miss Betty Jeffreys on seeing her dance wrote in
    the ballroom at Bath 1736' [answered by 'The muse
    this morn . . .']

    c.360/1, p. 27

M0397 Muse! Sing in numbers real and trim,
When bald, or grown with age quite grizzle.

    'The barber'

    c.382, p. 67

M0398 Muses nine there were of yore,
But Kennicott has shown us More.

    Geo[rge] Horne, bishop of Norwich [on Benjamin
    Kennicott and Hannah More]

    File 17452

M0399 Muses sitting on Parnassus
Save a low and labor'd sigh.

    Edward Sneyd(?), 'Wagham—a tale'

    c.214, p. 121

M0400 Music can charm the human heart
One only in an age.

    'On Miss Davies, a child singing and playing on the
    harpsichord 1752'

    c.360/3, no. 212

M0401 'Music has charms to soothe a savage breast'
And strive to be more dutiful than they.

    Frederick Corfield, 'Adulation for value received' [first
    line from Congreve]

    c.381/2

M0402 Music has charms to soothe the lover's breast
Gently inwov'd the name and own'd the conq'ring
                      maid.

    Sir William Young, 'An acrostic' [on Miss Sally Tagg]

    File 16592; see also next.

M0403 Music the cordial of a troubled breast
And calms the ruffling passions of the mind.

    c.53, fol. 62

M0404 Music, thou queen of souls get up and string
Strike a sad note, and fix them trees again.

    [Thomas] Randolph, 'Mr. Randolph in commendation
    of music')
    [Crum M558]

    b.213, p. 125

M0405 Music to hear, why hear'st thou music sadly?
Sings this to thee—thou single will prove none.

    [William] Shakespeare, 'An invitation to marriage'
    [Sonnet VIII]

    c.94

M0406 Musician and logician John Jener lieth here
Who made the organs speak or else as if it were.

    'On Jo Jener'

    fb.143, p. 28

M0407 Musician prick'st thou thy best lesson here
'Twill lessen thy best prick to tune her gere.

    R. K. C. P., 'An anagram of Ruth Green | Tune her
    gere'

    b.209, p. 74

M0408 Musing on the roaring ocean,
Talk of him that's far awa'.

    [Robert Burns], 'Stanzas'

    c.142, p. 301

M0409 Must good men still die first, and is there gone
That leave such works for others' imitation.

    'An elegy upon the death of the much lamented, able,
    and learned physician Dr Thomson who died
    March 11. 1677' [followed by 'Here lies wrapt up . . .']

    b.54, p. 899

M0410 Must he be ever dead? cannot we add
Which being his can therefore never die.

    [Edward Herbert, lord Herbert of Cherbury], 'An
    elegy upon the Prince's [Henry's] death' [1612]
    [Crum M568]

    b.54, p. 882

M0411 Must I ever sigh in vain?
Let your pity once prevail.

    'Song'

    c.189, p. 116

M0412 Must I needs go must I alone
O come, Lord Jesus, quickly.

    'A dialogue between soul and body'

    c.244, p. 221

M0413 Must I with patience ever silent sit
Or who'd be safe and senseless like Tom Thynne.

    [John Wilmot, 2nd earl of Rochester], 'Semper ego
    auditor tantum' [Juvenal, Satire I, imitated; 1680]
    [Crum M573 (var.); POAS II.205]

    b.113, p. 31; b.327, f. 13v; b.371, no. 3; b.54, p. 1239;
    fb.106(20) (with six more lines)

MO414   Must murder then, O, Rome! Must fate and blood
And Rome in tears of blood her rashness mourn.

> T. R., 'Conjuratio papistica . . . Bucks'
>
> c.326, p. 168

MO415   Must she then languish, and we sorry thus;
Convey into his hand thy golden dart.

> [Thomas Carew], 'On the sickness of Ch. S.'
> [Crum M574]
>
> b.200, p. 117

MO416   Must thou depart thou firm and fervent friend
Woman's soft feelings with a manly mind.

> [William Hayley], 'Sonnet . . . Jan 27 [1800]'
>
> File 6968

MO417   Must you alone then, happy flow'rs,
To taste one dear, transporting kiss.

> [Soame Jenyns], 'To a nosegay in Pancharilla's breast.
> From Bonefonius Bas. XI'
>
> c.147, p. 52

MO418   Must your fair enflaming eye
That I must your martyr be.

> 'A sonnet [to his mistress]'
> [Crum M578]
>
> b.62, p. 120

MO419   Mute is thy wild harp, now, O bard sublime!
Enjoys with them 'the liberty it lov'd'.

> [Charlotte (Turner) Smith], 'Sonnet to the shade of
> Burns'
>
> c.141, p. 138

MO420   Mute lies this tongue which once was ever wagging
So here she lies in peace for once at home.

> 'Epitaph on a very talkative and visiting old maid . . .
> Nov. 18th 1797'
>
> c.113/29

MO421   My acts and conquests from a heptarchy
Wonder of all I lived, died a maid.

> [couplets on the kings and queens of England, Egbert
> to Queen Elizabeth]
> [Crum M581]
>
> Poetry Box VI/5

MO422   My age is not a moment's stay:
I fade the instant that I blow.

> [Jonathan Smedley?], 'Imitation [of Ambrose Philip's
> 'The rose'; on a fart]
>
> c.81/1, no. 326 (attr. Swift)

MO423   My artless muse in inharmonious lays
So make her happy, as she's good and fair.

> 'Acrostic' [on Miss Dela Williams]
>
> c.360/2, no. 172

MO424   My art's my death, I build my tomb of state
Spin life away, and draw the claw of fate.

> [Robert Cholmeley], 'A silkworm'
>
> c.190, p. 39

MO425   My beds are all furnish'd with fleas,
Who could rob a poor mite of his cheese.

> 'Burlesque on Shenstone' ['My banks they are
> furnish'd with bees . . .' (second part of 'Ye shepherds
> so cheerful . . .')]
>
> c.83/3, no. 794

MO426   My bed's my grave, my grave's my bed,
Presents death to my meditation.

> H[enry] C[olman], 'Another' [on death]
> [Crum M583]
>
> b.2, p. 36

MO427   My better self, my heaven, my joy!
Your meaning? Pray, Sir, take my wife.

> [Elijah] Fenton, 'A la mode'
>
> c.166, p. 140

MO428   My birth and time of grown all men agree
'Tis I sit paramount each monthly session.

> 'A riddle'
>
> c.484, p. 67

MO429   My birth's N'apolitan: my parents Frenches.
What country then I'm of, judge you fair wenches.

> Sir Thomas Urquhart, 'The Venerian pox, to the
> whores of Tomble-street'
>
> fb.217, p. 180

MO430   My brave city friends
You'll wish him, when once, to be always Lord
                                             Mayor.

> John Lockman, 'Sheriff Jansson's health: writ for the
> Stationer's Company; and sung, by Mr. Leveridge, in
> their hall, Lord Mayor's Day, 1749—the tune, Bumper
> Squire Jones'
>
> c.267/2, p. 89

MO431   My bulk being but my matter, I'm defin'd
I lack the skill to tell you, what I am.

> Sir Thomas Urquhart, 'A certain gentleman's answer
> to one, who was too curious to know, what he was'
>
> fb.217, p. 135

M0432 My calling is divine
We'll make a loving pair.

> 'A parson to his mistress' [answered by 'Your calling is
> divine . . .']
> [Crum M600 (var.)]
>
> b.356, p. 308

M0433 My captive soul, itself bemoans
I'm coffin'd, in, sad garrison of rest.

> Lady Jane Cavendish, 'The captive burial'
> [Crum M601]
>
> b.233, p. 22

M0434 My Caroline demands a song,
Remember what I sing.

> Mary Cornwallis, 'Written on the afternoon of
> Caroline's birthday 12th July'
>
> fc.124, p. 105

M0435 My Celia's neck, less white than snow,
An unison of soul.

> [Stephen Barrett?], 'On a young lady of Cant[erbur]y'
> [Gentleman's magazine, April 1746]
>
> c.193, p. 123

M0436 My charming friend I many a time
But am your friend sincere | J. W.

> J[ohn] W[alker], 'An epistle to my young pupil Miss
> Eliza Young'
>
> fc.108, fol. 54v; see also 'There is a jest . . .'.

M0437 My cheeks, and lips, a deadly pale put on,
Of wicked women, the most wicked deed.

> [Thomas Hamilton, 6th earl of Haddington], 'To
> Florella, epistle the second'
>
> c.458/1, p. 3

M0438 My chief, intense, ardent desire
Their worth is as to that they tend.

> [Edmund Wodehouse], 'Decr. 13 [1714]'
>
> b.131, p. 113

M0439 My child! And must I far from thee
Thy mother one embrace for thee!

> Maria Williams, 'Lines by a gentleman, during a long
> confinement in Paris, and addressed to his son only
> four years of age who had lost his mother a few
> months after his birth. Imitation from the French'
>
> c.83/2, no. 624

M0440 My children, I would you remind
A trick of youth they went awry.

> Henry Snoade, '1675'
>
> c.158, p. 59

M0441 My children promising; my conscience clear;
Tho' wicked men oppose, what need I fear?

> John Lockman, 'A reflection in Salisbury . . . Aug.
> 1757'
>
> c.267/1, p. 236

M0442 My Chloris, mark how green the groves,
But 'tis na love like mine.

> [Robert Burns], 'Pastoral stanzas'
>
> c.142, p. 291

M0443 My clergy's from me rent
Part ill. Amen.

> 'Verses upon the same' [anagrams on 'Parliament']
>
> b.101, p. 126; see also 'I trap all men . . .'.

M0444 My comforter, my advocate
To arm me against pain and fear.

> [Edmund Wodehouse], 'March 2 [1715]'
>
> b.131, p. 175

M0445 My commons and peers, I once hop'd but in vain
That their money's all safe—betwixt me and the
                                        Queen. | Which &c.

> 'G[eor]ge the 2nd's speech to his Parliament'
> [Crum M608, 'commons and lords']
>
> c.570/2, p. 170

M0446 My composition what, or how
I first was made, I do not know.

> 'Riddle 3rd. For Miss Taylor'
>
> c.484, p. 69

M0447 My counsel is you marry for your credit:
So that you be not to your husband wedded.

> Sir Thomas Urquhart, 'The subtle advice of a bawd to
> a young wench'
>
> fb.217, p. 238

M0448 My country dear I have forsook,
And we have got our ends.

> [( )Weever], 'A court ballad to the tune of The
> children in the wood' [upon the word Grudge, and the
> last part of George I's first speech to his Parliament
> 20 March 1714/15; printed: Foxon N124]
> [Crum M610]
>
> fc.58, p. 43

M0449 My course of life on earth, is smooth and ev'n
My hope in Christ props up my grov'ling age.

> [Sir Philip Wodehouse], 'Upon Sr John Potts the
> elder'
>
> b.131, back (no. 168)

M0450 My cutting board's to pieces split
And now I'm on the tramp for heav'n.

  Gregory Oldnow, 'Gregory Oldnow's epitaph of
  Illson in Derbyshire'

c.361

M0451 My dad was a joiner a jolly old blade
'Bout London carry my stools. | A horse for your
                                          clothes [&c.]

  [John Walker?], 'Stools or the travelling carpenter'

fc.108, fol. 59v

M0452 My dear and much beloved wife
And be your sure defense.

  [Job Scott], 'A farewell salutation on leaving home to
  visit the southern States in 1789'

c.141, p. 323

M0453 My dear! Cried Baucis half awake,
On every thing that is done.

  Abraham Oakes, 'The midnight colloquy: a song'

c.50, p. 30

M0454 My dear gracious Madam
Or at best like a poor silly gander.

fc.40

M0455 My dear, in merry mood cries Jack to Nan
Quoth Nan, I cannot think upon my life.

  [Crum M625]

c.546, p. 33

M0456 My dear King Charles, I see with bleeding eyes
Be thou the goddess, I'll be king of Spain.

  'The lady's [i.e., the Virgin Mary's] answer [to
  Charles III]'

c.111, p. 166

M0457 My dear Kitty,
Preserve your slave.

  'An epistle of Robin the butler to Kitty the cook's
  daughter'

c.536

M0458 My dear Lady Payne!
George William Payne.

  George William Payne [addressed to Frances Payne,
  later Lady Lavington]

Poetry Box II/8

M0459 My dear Mr. Bate, I'm a bard of this city,
The debt which you owe to fair W—r—t—n to pay.

  'Prologue to a new Bath guide for the year 1781'

c.83/4, no. 1085

M0460 My dear Pall Mall I hear you've got in favor
It's he can tell it, who has felt it most.

  [Sir Charles Hanbury Williams], 'G[iles] Earle and
  B[ubb] Dodington [baron Melcombe]' [pr. 1748
  (Foxon W478)]

Poetry Box v/74; Accession 97.7.40

M0461 My dear Pudora though the greedy flame
My verse eterniz'd, in Pudora's name.

  [George Daniel]

b.121, fol. 66

M0462 My dear Rosania sometimes to be kind,
The kindest thought is that of quick return.

  [Katherine Philips], 'A farewell to Rosania'

c.189, p. 27

M0463 My dear sister, Ann, nine or ten months are past,
To your health, my dear Ann, in a bumper of wine.

  Edward Sneyd, 'An epistle 13th. To my sister Ann
  Cannock. March the 10th. 1776'

c.214, p. 82

M0464 My dearest friend, tho' from thee far away
And humbly hope that we shall faithful be.

  J. C.(?), 'North Grove 21st of 3 mo. 1799'

File 13409

M0465 My dearest Miss Neal
Which you may contract in a minute.

  H[annah] More

c.341, at front

M0466 My dearest niece Charlotte I'm quite happy to find
In a new pair of pumps I'll bow down to your feet.

  Edward Sneyd, 'An epistle 3d. to my niece Charlotte
  soon after her arrival from Oxford April the 19th 1773'

c.214, p. 16

M0467 My dearest placemaster you know how dismally
                                          our matters go
With heaven's even [?]ing bolt the lightning of the
                                          Lord.

pc.55, endpapers

M0468 My dearest wife I still adore thy charms
Each coming hour, and happy be thy days.

  H. P[rice], 'An acrostic by . . . of Poole, to his wife
  [Mary], 1744'

c.360/2, no. 251

M0469 My dears, 'tis said in days of old,
The wicked wanton sparrow died.

   Nat[hanie]l Cotton, 'Fable of the bee, the ant, and
   sparrow. By . . . M. D. of St. Albans, addressed to his
   daughters, Phoebe and Kitty, at Stony Stratford
   boarding school'
   c.83/4, no. 1095

M0470 My Ella is in the cold grave!
She may breathe out her last on thy tomb.

   Mrs. [ ] Trell, 'On the death of her daughter'
   c.130, p. 65

M0471 My existence from nature and art I receive
Yet I can't prevent death tho' I weaken his blow.

   c.389

M0472 My face is smooth and wond'rous bright,
Then in return my name declare.

   'Another [rebus]'
   Diggle Box: Poetry Box XI/71

M0473 My fair one, like the blushing rose,
When all the blooming beauties fade.

   'December 11th anno 1783 . . . Jo[hn] Rutherford'
   c.93

M0474 My fairest is unkind, and I have lost my pains,
And therefore is wing'd Cupid painted blind.

   [Sir Robert Ayton]
   b.197, p. 154

M0475 My faithful Rattler now grows old,
We'll place thee in a quiet grave.

   W. Welce, 'Stanzas on an old dog, by Revd . . .'
   fc.130, p. 57

M0476 My father and mother and I, died all in one year,
They are buried at Water Eaton, and I am buried
                                              here.

   'Epitaph at Heddington'
   c.360/3, no. 127

M0477 My Father calls me to his arms,
I will obey the call.

   Ann Olding, 'Verses composed by . . . in the night of
   December the 9th, 1770, and written from her mouth
   by her eldest sister, as she was watching by her'
   c.259, p. 64

M0478 My Father, my God, I long for thy love,
I go on to conquer till sin is no more!

   'Hymn 89th'
   c.562, p. 117

M0479 My father now knows where I am
Stay there and be d—d with your eye out.

   [John Walker?], 'A song I wish you may get it'
   fc.108, fol. 78

M0480 My filial angel by our maker call'd
Prepare me to embrace my blissful son.

   [William Hayley], 'Sonnet . . . June 24 and 25 [1800]'
   File 6968

M0481 My first (bar accidents) you'll find
In various shapes and sizes wear.

   Poetry Box III/folder 21-30

M0482 My first adorns the fairest frame
Of future change in you and me.

   c.389

M0483 My first and second is the lot,
We must pronounce at last.

   '[Enigma/Charade/Conundrum] 24' [farewell]
   c.389

M0484 My first brings joy to all around
It may be yours tomorrow.

   '[Enigma/Charade/Conundrum] 29' [birthday]
   c.389

M0485 My first by lovers are exchanged,
Who virtue's laws observe.

   [Enigma]
   c.389

M0486 My first does affliction denote,
That affliction to heal and to cure.

   '[Enigma/Charade/Conundrum] 32' [woman]
   c.389

M0487 My first has been ever called honest and brave,
The catcher(?) to shame and division is brought.

   Poetry Box III/folder 21-30

M0488 My first has once been powerful, weak and wise
But laugh and make your game of it—'tis neither.

   'Charade'
   Diggle Box: Poetry Box XI/68

M0489 My first heaven's ministers below
It lifts to heaven or sinks to hell.

   'A charade'
   Poetry Box IV/177

M0490 My first, however here abused,
And has been an archbishop.

    'Charades' [herring]

c.382, p. 34; c.389

M0491 My first if lost is a disgrace
It makes its bed within the rose.

    '[Enigma/Charade/Conundrum] 31 [earwig]'

c.389

M0492 My first if well employ'd will prove your friend
But chiefly to my first whose name I bear.

    '[Enigma/Charade/Conundrum] 18' [bookcase]

c.389

M0493 My first if you do, you will always increase,
Is seldomer taken than given.

    'Charade'

c.389

M0494 My first is a carriage of war—
Tho' it don't to their credit redound.

c.389

M0495 My first is a liar, a cheat, a deceiver
That no other can comfort afford.

Poetry Box III/folder 21–30

M0496 My first is a preposition,
And the whole an acquisition.

    '[Enigma/Charade/Conundrum] 25' [fortune]

c.389

M0497 My first is a tree, and 'tis also a word
And my whole in all numbers you'll find.

    'Charade [3]'

Greatheed Box/65

M0498 My first is called or bad or good,
With tears may often blind one.

    '[Charade] 2nd' [farewell]

c.382, p. 35; c.389

M0499 My first is equal, second grave,
My third most sinners wish to have.

    'Charade [2]'

Diggle Box: Poetry Box XI/71

M0500 My first is equality—
My whole superiority.

c.389

M0501 My first is going every day
My whole I hope you'll freely pay.

    'Charade 81' [postage]

c.389

M0502 My first is in winter the warmth we desire
And its nature has puzzled men much.

    '[Enigma/Charade/Conundrum] 27' [glowworm]

c.389

M0503 My first is quite hideous excepting his eye
And cunning is he who can say how we come.

    'Toadstool [Charade]'

Greatheed Box/79

M0504 My first is seen array'd in purest white
Ye fair this seeming mystery resolve.

c.389

M0505 My first is sure the greatest boon
The absence of my first.

    [Enigma/Charade/Conundrum 79a]

c.389

M0506 My first is the choicest of human blessings,
My third I bestow on you.

    '[Enigma/Charade/Conundrum] 37' [friendship]

c.389

M0507 My first is the last stage of a widow's dress,
My third's a grateful being.

    '[Enigma/Charade/Conundrum] 36' [greyhound]

c.389

M0508 My first is used both day and night
To give a light to all around.

    '[Enigma/Charade/Conundrum] 48' [candlestick]

c.389

M0509 My first makes all nature appear with one face,
I think that the whole should be thrown at your
                      head.

    '[Enigma/Charade/Conundrum] 19' [snowball]

c.389; Diggle Box: Poetry Box XI/68

M0510 My first may delight you
As my first and my second, no wise man e'er on its
                    promises reckon'd.

    '[Enigma/Charade/Conundrum] 54'

c.389

M0511 My first nor life nor feeling blesses,
The greatest nuisance that I know.

    [charade]

c.389

MO512   My first of a question the negative side,
And drawn out the thorns from the roses.

    c.389

MO513   My first precedes a request
My third is the prelude to happiness.

    '[Enigma/Charade/Conundrum] 38'
    c.389

MO514   My first the sailor longs to see,
As avarice sways the human mind.

    '[Enigma/Charade/Conundrum] 53'
    c.389

MO515   My first the sensation of anguish implies
Which varies the same as the wind or the weather.

    'Charades [2]'
    Diggle Box: Poetry Box xi/68

MO516   My first there are, some men will take
Who both together well can bear.

    '[Charade] 88' [misfortune]
    c.389

MO517   My first to the fair warmth and comfort imparts
Tho' to the eyes of the fair it gently be press'd.

    'Charade'
    Poetry Box ii/41

MO518   My first when you do you increase
Is seldom taken than given.

    'Charades [1]'
    Diggle Box: Poetry Box xi/68

MO519   My first with gold and silver is array'd
My parts are friends—my whole a deadly foe.

    '[Enigma/Charade/Conundrum] 52'
    c.389

MO520   My first's a female gay and smart,
What else can two such gypsies do?

    '[Charade] 91' [misfortune]
    c.389; Diggle Box: Poetry Box xi/68

MO521   My first's a little habitation
That is to housewives of great use.

    'Charade 93' [cotton]
    c.389

MO522   My fleet, my castles, and my towns
And drest in ruins; it ascend.

    'The soliloquy upon the K[ing]'s departure'
    fb.108, p. 131

MO523   'My flesh is meat indeed!' Lord, I believe:
And serve thee faithfully while here below.

    '[Hymns composed the week preceding the
    sacrament] 6th'
    c.515, fol. 19r

MO524   My foes, you have your hearts' desire,
Sing care and life away.

    [George Wither], 'A meditation'
    c.139, p. 165

MO525   My form, dear Cooly, is uncouth
And to the fair my service lend.

    'Riddles.—for Miss Coole [1]'
    c.484, p. 68

MO526   My fortnight is o'er, and heigho!—I must fly—
Every creature's for living as long as he can.

    [Edward Rolle], 'To my friend Mr S[pence] on his
    obligingly desiring me to stay on longer with him at
    Byfleet'
    Spence Papers, folder 128

MO527   My friend judge not me
Mercy I askt, mercy I found.

    'Upon a gentleman that broke his neck from his horse'
    [Crum M674]
    c.158, p. 105; fb.143, p. 21

MO528   My friend, my Posthumus, alas,
In raptures, at a Christmas feast.

    'The fourteenth ode of the first book of Horace
    imitated'
    Poetry Box i/113[2]

MO529   My friend, preserve an equal mind,
However great or good.

    [William Mills], 'Odes of Horace translated. Book II.
    Ode III. To Delius'
    c.472, p. 35

MO530   My friend requests that like the dying swan,
Where all is love, and joy, and happiness.

    'To a lady who desired some verses on my leaving
    Bath'
    c.83/1, no. 81

MO531   My friend whoso this place of mine thou be that
                          shalt behold
And unto him commend my soul my friend I crave
                              no more.

    'Epitaph 7th'
    c.158, p. 48

MO532 My friends (forsooth) grow godly and precise
'Tis evil jesting with edge[d] tools . . . .

> Edward Crosse, 'A poem made upon Mrs. Eliz. Davis;
> by her great admirer and humble servant'
>
> b.54, p. 1022 (incomplete)

MO533 My friends—whilst in this merry age,
Some other time my muse.

> 'Keep in your quarters'
>
> c.91, p. 282

MO534 My furrow'd brow, and shrivell'd hide
In embonpoint est charmant!

> [Charles Burney, the elder], 'To [Thomas Twining] on
> Sir Thomas Robinson making reparation for a breach
> of promise'
>
> c.33, p. 106

MO535 My gentle Susan! Who in early state
For my dear Susan's welfare ardent pray!

> [Charles Burney, the elder], 'On the transportation of
> my daughter Susan (Mrs. Phillips) to Iceland. 1796'
>
> c.33, p. 267

MO536 My glass is false, for were it true to thee,
You'd look no more, for you yourself would see.

> George Montagu, 'Another [translation of Greek
> epigrams]'
>
> fc.135, p. 11

MO537 My God and gold cannot possess one heart;
My God and I, on gold and I must part.

> 'On God and gold'
> [Crum M688]
>
> b.118, p. 220

MO538 My God deliver me I pray,
To Thee, dear God, all praise.

> 'Psalm 59'
>
> c.264/2, p. 15

MO539 My God did pious Abraham pray
Where baneful poisons o'errot the ground.

> P[hilip] Doddridge, 'Abraham's intercession for
> Sodom from Gen. XVIII 32'
>
> c.493, p. 20

MO540 My God had I my breath from thee
Is now, and e'er shall be.

> [John Austin], 'Hym: 21' [Hymn xiv, Devotions in the
> ancient way of offices, 1672, p. 128]
>
> c.178, p. 20

MO541 My God I hope shall ever be
Well to see truth, is to be wise.

> [Edmund Wodehouse], 'March 22 [1715] on notice of
> his blank in the lottery 1714[/15]'
>
> b.131, p. 185

MO542 My God I wait to know thy mind
And by thy power me enclose.

> [Mary Pluret], 'The following song with a melodious
> tune with it was given about Michaelmas the year 1739'
>
> c.354

MO543 My God I'll love, my God loves me,
We thus with the saints and angels heav'n partake.

> [Edmund Wodehouse], 'Iterum [21 November 1714]'
>
> b.131, p. 91

MO544 My God I'll praise whilst I have breath,
And tune to music what most jar.

> [Edmund Wodehouse], 'March 11 [1715]'
>
> b.131, p. 179

MO545 My God (I'm sure) will pardon all
And make right use of what they have.

> [Edmund Wodehouse], 'July 24 [1715]'
>
> b.131, p. 234

MO546 My God, my God, with gracious eye
To children yet unborn.

> 'Psalm 22. Evening prayer'
>
> c.264/1, p. 81

MO547 My God my King incline thine ear
At least without, if not by me.

> [Thomas Stanley], 'Meditat: XXV. Penitential
> meditations and vows in the King's solitude at
> Holmeby'
>
> b.152, p. 78

MO548 My God my only help and hope
Amen my Lord I cry.

> 'Hymn 60th: for the evening'
>
> c.562, p. 72

MO549 My God, my Savior, tell me why
With songs the tuneful air.

> [Thomas?] Scott, jr., 'The absence of Christ
> lamented'
>
> c.244, p. 410

MO550 My God oh could I call Him mine
That I'm indeed redeem'd from hell.

> [Thomas Stevens?], 'January the 4th 1781. Thursday
> night exposition. Matt. 19. 37 to the end'
>
> c.259, p. 110

M0551 My God permit me not to be
My heaven and there my God I find.

    'Hymn 63d'

c.562, p. 76

M0552 My God so gracious I believe,
Those damps and qualms might else there move.

    [Edmund Wodehouse], 'Feb. 8 [1715]'

b.131, p. 161

M0553 My God! the Father of mankind,
My trembling soul convey.

    'A supplication to the supreme Being' [Gentleman's
    magazine, July 1754]

c.157, p. 50

M0554 My God to thee ourselves we owe
May now, and still forever be.

    [John Austin], 'Hym: 27' [Hymn xxvi, Devotions in
    the ancient way of offices, 1672, p. 231]

c.178, p. 25

M0555 My God, whence comes it that the human soul,
So heaven alone can satisfy the soul.

    Henry Baker, 'A soliloquy'

c.244, p. 402

M0556 My God, with sad perplexing straits
Will, what I trust, defend.

    [Sir William Trumbull], 'Ps[alm] 31'

Trumbull Box: Poetry Box XIII/4

M0557 My goddess Lydia, heav'nly fair!
Oh take me dying, to thy arms.

    [Wentworth Dillon], 4th earl of R[oscommon],
    'Cornelius Gallus imitated . . . A lyric'

b.201, p. 156; c.555, p. 343

M0558 My God's good is so warm I overbrew
Buys at the cost of everlasting night.

    [Sir Philip Wodehouse], 'Upon Mr. Wa[lte]r
    Overbury'

b.131, back (no. 204)

M0559 My golden locks time hath to silver turn'd,
To be your bedesman now, that was your knight!

    Sir Henry Lea, 'The following verses were wrote
    by . . . the brave ancestor of the present Lichfield
    family . . .' [1590]
    [Crum M716]

fc.132/1, p. 120

M0560 My good friend, Mr. Green,
And we parsons shall now be maltreated.

    T[homas] M[orell], '['Our first lady Eve . . .']
    Answered'

c.395, p. 143

M0561 My good masters give ear, and a story you'll hear,
So 'tis proper that here we should leave 'em.

    'A ballad'

c.176, p. 184

M0562 My good old friend accept from me,
Truth and sincerity reward.

    'A receipt for an asthma' [answered by 'My good old
    friend I'm glad . . .']

c.83/1, no. 189

M0563 My good old friend I'm glad to see,
Nor care a fig for Monsieur Bing.

    'The answer' [to 'My good old friend accept
    from me . . .']

c.83/1, no. 190

M0564 My good Squire Gray
And gin will destroy understanding.

    [John Walker?], 'On Mr. Gray giving the word Stripes
    to be transposed into a word of two syllables and also
    a word from red nuts and gin sent the next morning'

fc.108, fol. 75v

M0565 My grandmother the only piece of good
Then in his life her nephews God should bless.

    Lady Jane Cavendish, 'On the Lady Ogle my dear
    grandmother'
    [Crum M718]

b.233, p. 30

M0566 My grateful song shall glorious triumphs tell,
And endless is the fame of that triumphant day.

    [Robert] Moss, 'A brief and easy paraphrase, upon the
    triumphant song of Moses. Exod. Ch. XVth from vs.
    1st to 28 20th'

File 10577

M0567 My greater crimes I will confess
The poets' dull and common way.

    [Sir William D'Avenant], 'New year's gift to the
    Queen 1643'

fb.66/35

M0568 My grief was ne'er so high when you
If nothing can bind more so nothing less.

b.213, p. 123

M0569 My growth is strange! At first, I only knew
That made the greatness much more infinite.

    Thomas Traherne, [Meditation (third century)] 99'

b.308, p. 174

M0570 My hairs are so many I cannot them count,
And thine are so too friend, for thou hast not any.

    R[obert] Shirley, 1st earl of Ferrers, 'Audoeni ep.
    Against a baldpate man'

c.347, p. 56

M0571 My hairs I cannot number they're so many:
Nor reckon yours; because you have not any.

    Sir Thomas Urquhart, 'To a bald man' [translation of
    an epigram by John Owen]

fb.217, p. 91

M0572 My heart inditeth matters high,
Shall live till time shall be no more.

    'Psalm 45'

c.264/1, p. 195

M0573 My heart is easy and my burden light,
And hunt their ruin with a zeal to die.

    [William Cowper, trans.], 'Spring water. Vol. 4. Cant.
    81' [of Jeanne Guion's 'Spiritual songs']

c.470 (autogr.)

M0574 My heart is God's, by all undoubted right,
Would far exalted be 'bove its control.

    [Edmund Wodehouse], 'Octr. 13 [1714]'

b.131, p. 57

M0575 My heart is heavy, when my purse is light:
The [?] [?] that my purse contain.

    Sir Thomas Urquhart, 'One speaks here of an
    alternatively opposite vicissitude, betwixt his heart,
    and his purse'

fb.217, p. 185

M0576 My heart is ravish'd and my mind
And thy obedient servant be.

    [Mary Pluret], 'Another [poem written on waste
    paper]'

c.354 (2 var.)

M0577 My heart shall ne'er too dear a love environ
A cheap to me is dearer than a dear one.

    Sir Thomas Urquhart, 'The words of one who liked
    not to spend too much upon the courting of a
    mistress'

fb.217, p. 311

M0578 My heart to thee too poor an offering
It is the own thing which of thee I crave.

    [Lady Ursula (Darcy) Wyvill]

b.222, p. 122

M0579 My honest, lewd, insipid, dull,
I'm weary of them, and desert you.

    'On Mr. Bowmer and his ninepenny cans. A song'

c.530, p. 255

M0580 My hope was fair of hue
That married my hope.

'Braye Lute Book,' Music Ms. 13, fol. 21

M0581 My husband may be canoniz'd at Rome
That nothing humbler is than he.

    Sir Thomas Urquhart, 'The speeches of a
    gentlewoman, whose husband was an old decrepit
    man'

fb.217, p. 179

M0582 My husband's my uncle my father's my brother
The churchwardens of Bucks can assure you is true.

    [N.] Herbert, 'A riddle; on Mrs [Robert] H[ill, wife of
    the learned tailor of Bucks; c. 1759]'

Spence Papers, folder 91

M0583 My income's just one hundred pounds a year,
Should I be friendless, while to all a friend.

    John Lockman, 'Writ on a card. To my right
    honorable and honorable patrons . . . June 1765'

c.267/1, p. 386

M0584 My innocence environs me
No forces I attend without.

    [Sir Philip Wodehouse], 'Joannes Crofts Dicanus'

b.131, back (no. 148)

M0585 My Jesus doth forever live
Do what Thou please with it.

    [( ) Pierson]

c.328, p. 45

M0586 My Jesus while in mortal flesh
Where heaven itself is found.

    'Hymn 71st'

c.562, p. 86

M0587 My joy shall be my God to pledge
Chiefly for any Christian.

    [Edmund Wodehouse], 'Octr. 2d 1714'

b.131, p. 51

M0588 My joy's low ebbing when you do depart
Only because to love thee it presum'd.

b.197, p. 151

M0589 My kind 'squire Tom Sir Harry's eldest son
The man who cheats himself prove true to me.

[Robert Cholmeley], 'A common case. Imitated from the Greek'

c.190, p. 91

M0590 My kingdom is not of this world, so saith
But their reward to have where Satan reigns.

'St. John c: 18 v: 36'

c.81/1, no. 171

M0591 My lads, your Colonel I fear
With coming, gem'men, coming.

'On the drummers of the Westminster militia beating a long time before the colonel's quarters'

c.546, p. 2

M0592 My language is rude and uncouth,
Then melted illusive in air.

Mrs. [ ] West, 'A pastoral supposed to be in the Highlands'

c.83/2, no. 304

M0593 My life, my love;
And send relief.

'The labyrinth. A love-letter in petit-putian verse [with a] P.S.' [1736]

c.94

M0594 My life! My soul! My all that heav'n can give!
Death, and life with thee: without thee death to live.

c.189, p. 75; c.549, p. 12

M0595 My life's best joy, and pleasure of my eye
While life remains, the day that made thee mine.

'To my dearest wife on the anniversary of our nuptials'

c.148, p. 11

M0596 My limbs being weary and my head opprest
Methought I lay contented, though not at rest.

[George Morley], 'On a nightingale'
[Crum M769]

b.62, p. 29; b.200, p. 129; b.205, fol. 52r

M0597 My little Laud [Lord], methinks 'tis strange
For churches good be raised high | When such as
yours fall down.

'Upon the commitment of [William Laud] Archbishop [of Canterbury]'
[Crum M772]

Poetry Box VIII/6; b.229, fol. 119

M0598 My locks, tho' silver'd o'er by time;
Which juntoes would destroy.

John Lockman, 'Ode: 4th May 1768. On the administration of Ireland, under his excellency the Lord Viscount Townshend'

c.267/4, p. 374

M0599 My lodging is on the cold ground
The cause of my misery.

[Sir William D'Avenant, song in The rivals, Act V]
[Crum M773]

b.213, p. 128

M0600 My lord a share y'ave given me in a grove
Yet I may boast that there your love I found.

[Sir Aston Cokayne], 'To my Lord of Arglass'

b.275, p. 90

M0601 My Lord amid the mortal strife
You'll marvel who the devil sent you here.

[John Wolcot ('Peter Pindar')], 'To Lord C——'

Poetry Box V/94

M0602 My lord, I found a precious cabinet,
Prostrate it, and myself, before your feet.

John Watson, 'To the excellent and most noble lord the Lord Marquis of Ormonde. James Butler . . .'

fb.228/16

M0603 My lord—I just receiv'd I own
Your b[isho]ps L[or]ds and Commons.

'The liverymen's answer to a letter dated at Whitehall, Jan. the 22. 1727/8' [pr. 1728 (Foxon L202)]

c.570/2, p. 172

M0604 My lord, I just receiv'd, I own,
Your Bishops, Lords, and Commons.

'Occasioned by a letter [22 January 1728] from my Ld T[ownshen]d to the citizens of London desiring their [ ] from Mr Trench against Mr. Robinson' [printed: Foxon L202]

c.233, p. 59

M0605 My lord it is your absence makes each see
And as I hope for happiness 'tis true.

Lady Jane Cavendish, 'Passion's letter to my Lord my father'
[Crum M780]

b.233, p. 3, p. 75 (var.)

M0606 My Lord, my gracious Judge, acquit
Whose love bestows, compassion spares.

'Psalm 43'

c.264/1, p. 189

M0607 My lord, the conquest is my own,
Learn ladies! How to pass your time!

[Alexander Pope], 'Epistle of Lady B[urlington] to her lord'

File 12108

M0608 My lord, 'tis a christening, the verger said—
Go lock up the font—let the infant be damn'd.

[Matthew Prior?], 'An epigram on an occurrence at Westm[inster] Abbey'

c.229/1, fol. 6

M0609 My lord, whose high extraction springs
Lord of himself does rule and sway.

b.154, p. 2

M0610 My lord you live in so remote a place
Of one a kin to such a personage.

[Sir Aston Cokayne], 'To Warwick. the Lord Mohun'

b.275, p. 113

M0611 My lord your absence makes I cannot own
Then am I crown'd with height of bliss.

E[lizabeth (Cavendish)] B[rackley, to the Earl of Newcastle]
[Crum M787]

b.233, p. 76

M0612 My lord your husband cannot frame desires,
In the felicity of your embraces.

Sir Thomas Urquhart, 'To the Countess of [crossed out; Home?]'

fb.217, p. 195

M0613 My lord your picture speaks you this, to be,
That 'tis no fiction but a truth of thee.

Lady Jane Cavendish, 'The truth of pencil'
[Crum M788]

b.233, p. 6

M0614 My lords and fair ladies, I'm like Archimedes
And my fame, as my beer, shall spread wide.

S. W., 'A song of similes said or sung by S. W. esqr.'

c.340

M0615 My lords and gentlemen to laugh and dine
Nan like Queen Bess disdains a successor.

'Several copies of verses spoken at Westminster School on the anniversary [of the defeat of the Spanish Armada]. 1'

fc.24, p. 71; c.233, p. 35 (var.); see also 'What to Queen Bess . . .'.

M0616 My lords and gentlemen to you
Justice restor'd; and then—good night.

'G[eorge]'s speech to his myrmidons' [pr. 1719? (Foxon H249)]

c.570/2, p. 29

M0617 My Lords and my Commons, 'tis my resolution
By sending to old Nicholas their second Savior.

'His Majesty's speech to his Parliament [before his going to Ireland, 1690] . . . to the tune of Packington's Pound'
[Crum M791]

fb.70, p. 315; b.111, p. 315

M0618 My lords, the commons of the realm,
Beneath the glow of this sublime and beautiful.

'Burke's reply; first day—taken in shorthand'

Poetry Box V/17; Poetry Box II/57

M0619 My love and I for kisses play'd
Give me my stakes take you your stakes again.

[William Strode], 'Lusus amatorius'
[Crum M793]

b.205, fol. 44r

M0620 My love I seek but seek in vain
One thought for her who died for thee.

'The parting sigh'

c.546

M0621 My love is made of nature's freshest mold
It makes me blush to think what is below.

'In praise of his love'
[Crum M800, 'purest mold']

b.205, fol. 23v

M0622 My lov'd my honor'd, much respected friend!
In bright succession raise, her ornament and guard!

[Robert Burns], 'The cotter's Saturday night. Inscribed to R. A[iken] esq.'

c.139, p. 569

M0623 My lovely Chich' that takes delight
Like the twin gods, meet once a year.

Henry Bosseville, 'To John Chichely esqr. at his chambers in Middle Temple'

c.229/1, fol. 61

M0624 My love's ne mortal and it must be fed
A toothless midwife than have one of those.

'Resolute lines, to a scornful lady'

b.356, p. 331

M0625 My lute, be as thou wast, when thou didst grow
Like widow's turtle still her loss complain.

William Drummond, of Hawthornden, 'Sonnet to his lute'

b.150, p. 218

M0626 My madness alas I too plainly discover,
So live sober all day, and chaste all the night.

'Song'

c.189, p. 7

M0627 My maidenhead, I never will resign;
Because the virgin is a heavenly sign.

Sir Thomas Urquhart, 'The resolution of a chaste maid'

fb.217, p. 44

M0628 My Martha views with partial eyes, an action of my youth
And, at the thrones, where 'twas received, my pleasing task resign.

J. B. Dickinson, 'In return for the above ['That speech was worth all wealth . . .'] wrote the following lines to Martha Roberts'

c.391, p. 95, p.?

M0629 My master did leave me at home without doubt
And tho' I can't walk he found me gone out.

'[Enigma/Charade/Conundrum] 45' [fire]

c.389

M0630 My masters and friends and good people draw near,
To encourage she-traders and lusty young fellows.

'A poem on the monument on Fish Street Hill. A ballad to the tune of Packington's pound. 1677' [first line by Ben Jonson, song from Bartholomew Fair]

b.54, p. 939

M0631 My masters give ear, and a story you'll hear
So for decency there we will leave 'em.

'On the Knights of the Bath'

c.570/2, p. 157

M0632 My mind to love is securely bent
Of me always you may be bold.

T. W.

'Braye Lute Book,' Music Ms. 13, fol. 44v

M0633 My mind to me a kingdom is,
Would all do so, as well as I.

[Sir Edward Dyer], 'An old ballad' [to the tune of In Crete day]
[Crum M817]

c.83/1, no. 195; Poetry Box IV/77 (stanzas 1–7)

M0634 My mistress, and I both, being sick, were glad
By maniples of the satyrian root.

Sir Thomas Urquhart, 'One speaks here of himself, and his mistress, how each of them proved a physician to either's several disease'

fb.217, p. 230

M0635 My mistress loves no woodcock
And yet she loves my master.

'A servant to his mistress on his master'
[Crum M833]

b.62, p. 32

M0636 My mother brought me forth, and what of that
I bring my mother forth, there's tit for tat.

R[ichard] V[ernon] S[adleir], 'Enig. Hudfieldius—mater me peperit . . .'

c.106, p. 58

M0637 My mournful story will no more avail
Herself distress'd till she relieve their pain.

Poetry Box IV/134

M0638 My much loved Charlottine
In heav'n among the blest.

C[harles] B[urney, the elder], 'Verses by . . . addressed to his granddaughter C[harlottine] F[rancis] on receiving her first letter May 19th 1795'

c.486, fol. 28

M0639 My muse and I are drunk tonight
With here and there a pawn.

[Charles Sackville, 6th earl of Dorset], 'The chess'
[cf. Crum M839]

b.371, no. 33

M0640 My muse, that moves but slowly . . . | On,
Here's *bon repos*, and so good night.

T[homas] Lisle, 'A tale by . . . [aged] 14 to my Lady Phillips'

c.176, p. 9

M0641 My muse thus ventures to open her war
To sell you spectacles, these strange sights to see.

[on Parliament, c. 1645]

b.52/2, p. 128

M0642 My name engraved herein
For dying men talk often so.

J[ohn] D[onne], 'Valediction of glass'
[Crum M849]

b.148, p. 102; b.114, p. 296 (stanzas 1–7)

M0643　My name transpos'd, spells real Raph
Thy guardian angel be high Raphael.

　　[Sir Philip Wodehouse], 'Ralph Earl real Raph or
　　Raph real'

　　b.131, back (no. 163)

M0644　My nature fa[i]nts unless supplies
The vale shall echo with thy praise.

　　T[homas] S[tevens], 'At the ordinance . . . sung Feb. 4
　　1781'

　　c.259, p. 123

M0645　My next acquaintance, in that near degree
Repentant, loyal, pious, at thy death.

　　[Thomas Stanley], '[John] Hall' [in 'A register of
　　friends']

　　b.153, p. 8

M0646　My next address, Shirley, to thee is due,
Went'st off the stage, loaden with years and bay.

　　[Thomas Stanley], 'Shirley' [in 'A register of friends']

　　b.153, p. 6

M0647　My noble lords and gentlemen,
Till we triumph at the summer's end.

　　'His Majesty's gracious speech to both Houses at his
　　going to Ireland'

　　b.111, p. 321

M0648　My num'rous years may well suffice
And willing be to end my race.

　　[Edmund Wodehouse], 'Aug. 7 [1715]'

　　b.131, p. 241

M0649　My nuncle calls I cannot stay
And be [blank] to Adam's commonweal . . . .

　　b.216, p. 232 (incomplete)

M0650　My nymph possesses every grace
Tho' she's so cursed lousy.

　　[John Walker?], 'The cleanly fair one'

　　fc.108, fol. 13

M0651　My only piercing grief shall be,
Integrity is Thy delight.

　　[Edmund Wodehouse], 'Novr. 11 [1714]'

　　b.131, p. 82

M0652　My only wife that in her life
My Savior God most high.

　　'A flat stone raised from the ground about a yard at the
　　end of the place near Bunhill fields'

　　Poetry Box VII/55

M0653　My parent was an ox or bee—
And in a mausoleum sleep.

　　[Phanuel Bacon], 'A riddle'

　　c.237, fol. 106 [i.e., 126]

M0654　My part is done, and you'll (I hope) excuse,
To visit for the sins of lewd mankind.

　　[John Oldham], 'Apology for the foregoing verses'
　　['Now curses on you all . . .']
　　[Crum M856]

　　b.105, p. 284; b.54, p. 1008; File 17375

M0655　My people hearken to my speech,
To rule, defend, and lead.

　　'Psalm 78 Evening prayer'

　　c.264/2, p. 58

M0656　My person's seized, my house, my goods, my land
I care not what from evil tongues I hear.

　　Sir John Strangways

　　b.304, p. 45

M0657　My play is work enough, my work is play
Well may my play begin now yours is done.

　　'Ludus uxorius'

　　b.205, fol. 42r

M0658　My pray'rs to Heaven I never sent
W—d swinging on a willow tree.

　　[Thomas Morell], 'Martial. L.IV. ep. 77'

　　c.395, p. 34

M0659　My pray'rs too formal are I fear,
Only devotion reaches this.

　　[Edmund Wodehouse], 'Iterum [5 August 1715]'

　　b.131, p. 240

M0660　My priest a priest hath made of me
And much grace and favor.

　　[Mary Pluret], 'Views by faith in the promises'

　　c.354

M0661　My prime of youth is but a frost of cares
And now I live and now my life is done.

　　[Chidiock] Tichborne, 'Elegy written by himself
　　before he died'
　　[Crum M863]

　　fb.9, fol. 30

M0662　My prostrate soul the Lord of lords doth bless:
To God shall everlasting trophies raise.

　　[William Sandys?], 'The order of providence with the
　　power and glory of God described—Psal. 104'

　　b.230, p. 105

M0663　My proud H[owar]d told you a marvelous tale
Many asses assembled one ass to preclude.

　　[George Howard, 6th earl of Carlisle], 'Upon a
　　strange alarm at Boxheath'

　　c.197, p. 28

M0664　My queen of hearts
So up the cards well throw.

　　'Yours x y z'

　　Smith Papers, folder 75/26

M0665　My ravisht soul, a pious ardor fires
Carried of Jacob safe.

　　[Sir Allen Apsley], 'Order and disorder . . . being
　　meditations on the creation and fall . . .' [first five
　　cantos pr. 1679 (Wing A3594)]

　　fb.100, p. 3

M0666　My return gives in gross, what you could get,
If for the lack of one peer, I should borrow.

　　Sir Thomas Urquhart, 'A gentleman after long
　　absence speaks thus to his bedfellow of his conjugal
　　due'

　　fb.217, p. 345

M0667　My rev'rend friend, too plain I see
'Twas yours, the freedom first to court.

　　'An epistle to a divine on the united merits of the pen
　　and needle'

　　c.83/1, no. 18

M0668　My rum is out! My spirits die!
I wish my keg of rum was tight.

　　'Sung by a young tar, on the deck with a can in his
　　hand . . . Royal captive'

　　c.83/2, no. 540

M0669　My Savior calls, and I'll obey,
I make no other suit than this.

　　'[Hymns composed the week preceding the
　　sacrament] 2nd'

　　c.515, fol. 15v

M0670　My Savior God, my Sov'reign Prince,
Exceeds the figure still.

　　[Isaac Watts, Hymns and spiritual songs (1707), bk. II,
　　Hymn 41]

　　c.180, p. 40

M0671　My Savior my almighty Friend
Nor think the season long.

　　'Hymn 55th'

　　c.562, p. 66

M0672　My second has often been brought to my first
The other's quite steady and still.

　　[charade]

　　Greatheed Box/102

M0673　My second owes it[s] birth to May,
And is the pride of March.

　　'[Enigma/Charade/Conundrum] 28' [primrose]

　　c.389

M0674　My shape, nor I nor any can reveal
I tho' untaught, can talk of all your arts.

　　'Riddle on echo'

　　c.360/1, p. 119

M0675　My sickly spouse, with many a sigh,
'Twas heav'n's wile to spare my life.

　　'Epigram'
　　[Crum M877, 'heaven's will']

　　c.81/1, no. 297

M0676　My sins are like the hairs upon my head
Heaven make me bald, before that day begins.

　　[Francis Quarles], 'On sins' [Divine fancies II, 66]
　　[Crum M879]

　　b.137, p. 190

M0677　My sledge and hammer lie declin'd,
My soul, smokelike, is soaring to be blest.

　　[Alexander Pennicuik], 'Epitaph on a blacksmith
　　Gen[tleman's] mag[azine]'
　　[Crum M880]

　　c.546, p. 21; c.113/8; c.81/1, no. 120

M0678　My son attend receive the words of truth,
The soul uprising, wings its way to God.

　　[Francis Fawkes], 'Picture of old age Eccles. 12. chap.
　　[verses 1–7]'
　　[Crum M881]

　　c.156, p. 136

M0679　My son, th'instruction that my words impart,
And fall, where many mightier have been slain.

　　'Bombay 1769' [Proverbs, ch. 7]
　　[Crum M885]

　　fc.132/1, p. 45

M0680　My son thy flesh is turn'd to dust,
To Father Son and Holy Ghost.

　　[( ) Pierson], 'The following lines were made on
　　Saturday evening May: 18: 1745 occasioned by
　　reflecting on the death of my son [Isaac Pierson] who
　　had now been dead 8 years and 3 months'

　　c.328, p. 134

M0681 My song by grateful praise inspir'd
And all things shall be giv'n.

Miss [ ] White, of Edgbaston, 'An hymn—to the
supreme Being'

c.532

M0682 My soul bless thou the Lord
His name with heart and voice.

'Psalm 104 Evening prayer 20 day'

c.264/3, p. 10

M0683 My soul, come let us go,
Our stay, will always be.

[George Wither], 'A hymn'

c.139, p. 183

M0684 My soul, dost thou resolve an easy life,
Then we at last may endless joys inherit.

[Sir Richard Bulstrode], 'Pious resolutions to submit
ourselves to God's will in all our afflictions'

fb.88, p. 114v

M0685 My soul, from envious thoughts refrain
Who make him their support.

[Sir William Trumbull], 'Ps[alm] 37'
Trumbull Box: Poetry Box XIII/5 and 6 (2 copies)

M0686 My soul give laud unto the Lord
Praise ye also the same.

[Thomas Sternhold], 'A thanksgiving unto God for
remission of sins. Psal: 44' [verses from Psalm 103]
[Crum M894]

a.3, fol. 121v

M0687 My soul, in raptures rise to bless the Lord,
Who claim the God of Israel for their own.

[Christopher] Pitt, 'Psalm 144'

c.244, p. 510

M0688 My soul is arm'd with so much patience
Comfort in heaven above, on earth below.

'On patience'

c.189, p. 109

M0689 My soul is sad and much dismay'd;
That I am foil'd, and thou art griev'd!

[William Cowper], 'The valley of the shadow of
death'

c.141, p. 585

M0690 My soul Jehovah bless; my God
With praises J'ah adore.

[Lady Amy Touchet], 'Psal: 104 by the Lady Amy
daughter of the E[arl] of Castlehaven'

b.217, p. 79

M0691 My soul let not thine anger rise
As they in Him full trust repose.

'Psalm 37. Evening prayer'

c.264/1, p. 159

M0692 My soul let the true God be thine
In keeping them great gain I got.

c.124, no. 7

M0693 My soul Lord from sin's burden ease
That I thy praise may ever sing. | Alleluia, etc.

[John Hobart]

b.108, fol. 13

M0694 My soul must rule my body reign o'er it
In spite of Satan, and all worldly might.

[Sir Thomas Urquhart], 'The noble resolution of a
wise courageous and devout spirit towards the
damning of these irregular affections and [?]
perturbations . . .'

fb.217, p. 510

M0695 My soul praise thou Jehovah's name,
The noblest praise! Bless God my soul.

'Psalm 103'

c.264/3, p. 5

M0696 My soul praise thou the Lord always,
Forever to remain.

[John Hopkins], 'For sure trust in God. Psal. 63'
[verses from Psalm 146]
[Crum M909]

a.3, fol. 148

M0697 My soul praise Thou the Lord, and all
Fit off'rings; praise the Lord, my soul.

'The same [Psalm 103] same meter'

c.264/3, p. 7

M0698 My soul, the fullness of thy joy impart
Heaven, earth, my soul, my all, adore his glorious
name.

[Richard] Daniel, dean of Armagh, 'The recovery.
Psalm 103'

c.244, p. 376

M0699 My soul through my redeemer's care
And all within me shout his praise.

c.562, p. 59

M0700 My soul to praise thy God begin,
In thy eternal choir.

[Sir William Trumbull], 'The 103 Psalm translated . . .'

b.177, p. 15; Trumbull Box: Poetry Box XIII/20

M0701 My soul to thee too poor an offering
The praises of the great eternal king.

  [Lady Ursula (Darcy) Wyvill]

b.222, p. 134, p. 135

M0702 My soul trust thou upon the Lord
To him thy wants relate.

  [Mary Pluret], 'Another [poem written on waste paper]'

c.354

M0703 My soul! what's all this world to thee?
Now and forever be.

  [John Austin], 'Hym: 28' [Hymn xxviii, Devotions in the ancient way of offices, 1672, p. 246]

c.178, p. 26

M0704 My soul, with all thy strength contend
All ages to outlast. | *Laus Deo*

  [Sir William Trumbull], 'Ps.146'

b.177, p. 38; Trumbull Box: Poetry Box XIII/26 and 27

M0705 My spirit has no rest
To everlasting night.

  'A passion of anger'

c.356

M0706 My spirit mourns her awful want
From my desiring eyes.

  T[homas] S[tevens], 'Tuesday following Ex[perience] M[ee]ting, Agst 29'

c.259, p. 103

M0707 My spirits are all assembled to extol
That your perfections are to me so costic.

  Sir Thomas Urquhart, 'To the pattern of all goodness the virtuous Aura'

fb.217, p. 246

M0708 My spouse in whose presence I live,
Am happy whenever I sing.

  [William Cowper, trans.], 'Aspirations of a soul sick of love. Vol. 2. Cant. 95' [of Jeanne Guion's 'Spiritual songs']

c.470 (autogr.), p. 14

M0709 My station once was high in fairyland,
Small is the space true happiness requires.

  [ ] Pixell, 'On an urn in the parsonage house at Edgbaston, which was removed from the Leasowes'

c.528/6

M0710 My Steavens, can this frozen clime
And glories in his gloomy reign.

  [Isaac Freeman], 'Epistle to Thomas Steavens esqr: from the Hague'

fc.105

M0711 My sword about me I do always wear
Pray tell thou if you can of what 'tis made.

  'Another [riddle]'

Poetry Box VII/46

M0712 My sword's spiritual—my sword's the word
Are pray'rs sent up, through Christ, to Paradise.

  [Sir Philip Wodehouse], 'Upon his neighbor Thomas Ward a divine and a schoolmaster to his son'

b.131, back (no. 153)

M0713 My system Doctor 's all my own
That you yourself may live.

  [George] Cheyne, 'Dr. Cheyne's replication' [to 'Tell me from whom . . .']

Poetry Box XIV/197; c.152, p. 15; see also 'Doctor, my system's . . .'

M0714 My task is perform'd and now Leaper adieu
Be merit encouraged—my Simpson is well.

  S[tephen] Simpson, '[T.] Eyre July 25th, 1773'

c.563

M0715 My tears attend thee to the shades below,
Her sacred ashes unpolluted keep.

  'Epitaph on a wife'

c.83/2, no. 329

M0716 My temples with clusters of grapes I'll entwine,
'Tis the thirst of a lover—and plead me who dare.

  'Song 136'

c.555, p. 189

M0717 My term of life God only knows;
As we make Him our Sovereign.

  [Edmund Wodehouse], 'May 17 [1715]'

b.131, p. 215

M0718 My thoughts on contemplation's wing,
And usher in eternity!

fc.124, p. 9

M0719 My tides of blood now languid run,
An unmixt state of peace and love.

  [Anne (Capell) Ingram Douglas], 'By Lady [Isabella (Machell)] Irwin' [false attribution]

Spence Papers, folder 113

MO720 My time! O ye muses! was happily spent,
I thought it was spring, but, alas! It was she.

[John] Byrom, of Manchester, 'The following song,
inserted in the Spectator, was written by . . . on Miss
Betty one of the daughters of the great Dr. Bentley'
[Crum M941]

c.193, p. 146; c.358, p. 135; c.83/1, no. 154

MO721 My title O my Lord did you but know
And all your racks and torments are my own.

'Translation of Mirtillo Mirtillo anima mea of Pastor
fido'

fc.135

MO722 My tomb asks not the passing stranger's tear,
And gently laid me in the grave's repose.

'Epitaph by Carphyllides, in the Greek anthology'

c.240, p. 120

MO723 My troubles Lord are multiplied
From her perplexed state.

[Thomas Stanley], 'Meditat: XIII. Upon the calling in
of the Scots and their coming'

b.152, p. 42

MO724 My trust is in my God alone,
By faith to live, as well as know. | These truths to
live, &c.

[Edmund Wodehouse], 'Octr. 29 [1714]'

b.131, p. 72

MO725 My very good Dean, there are few that come here
But have something to ask, or something to fear.

[Sir William Fownes], [reply (attr. John Carteret, 1st
earl of Granville) to verses by Swift: 'My very good
lord . . .']

c.176, p. 3; c.229/1, fol. 43v

MO726 My very good Lord, 'tis a very hard task
For a man to wait here who has nothing to ask.

Jonathan Swift, 'Written in a window of Dublin
Castle by . . . the right honorable the Lord Carteret
then Lord Lieutenant of Ireland and there residing'
[answered by 'My very good Dean']

c.229/1, fol. 43v; c.176, p. 3

MO727 My virtuous companion my bosom's dear guest
But in waking my terror turn'd into delight.

[William Hayley], 'My dream addressed to his wife on
her birthday June 13 1798 from the French of Mr. [ ]'

File 6952

MO728 My vow was raised unto God
They like a flock did tread.

'Psal: 77'

b.217, p. 10

MO729 My vows to thee most gladly blessed maid
And the restorer of all men's decay.

[Sir Richard Bulstrode]

fb.88, p. 118

MO730 My wand'ring soul like dying tapers plays
Ere Iris came to cut the fatal string.

Poetry Box VI/90

MO731 My Westminster friends,
Then all give your votes to Percy and Sandys.

John Lockman, 'Percy and Sandys a ballad. For the
Westminster election, 1768 the tune, Bumper, Squire
Jones'

c.267/2, p. 160

MO732 My whole, by one mistake my first here brought,
His joy by day, his solace in the night.

Jonathan Dickinson, 'Charade'

c.391

MO733 My whole (in this once tho' begin from the rear)
That Venus but laughs, and Jove scarcely can scold.

[charade]

Greatheed Box/102

MO734 My whole is that stripper: for such and their work
And the d[evi]l himself as a host.

'Charade'

Greatheed Box/65

MO735 My wife and her friend were sat at their tea
And the case will be alter'd, next turn, never fear it.

'To Mrs. Parry of Easton Grey. On the birth of a
daughter Aug. 6th 1759'

c.484, p. 128

MO736 My wife she died last Saturday night,
And tomorrow, the week will be ended.

'Song 15'

c.555, p. 21

MO737 My wife's so very bad (quoth Emil)
The jade has just now sold it!!!

[John Walker?], 'Epigram sent to The wits' magazine'

fc.108, fol. 59

MO738 My woeful monument shall be a cell,
The hollow echo shall reply, 'tis I.

b.200, p. 109 (intended to follow 'Hence all ye vain
delights . . .', p. 46)

MO739 My years I spent in sickness and in pain
Desiring death that I may live again.

'High Wycombe June the 24 1707, Epitaph 2'
c.158, p. 84

MO740 My youth and middle times are past,
Scarce seem to serve to vegetate.

[John Hobart], 'Præludia mortis. Æt. 50. The wish'
b.108, fol. 6v

MO741 Mylo, forbear to call him blest
The mind's the standard of the man.

[Isaac Watts], 'False greatness'
c.139, p. 86; see also 'Were I so tall . . .'.

MO742 Myra, dear maid, in whom we find
Shalt rule, though never seem to rule.

'To Myra'
Poetry Box x/45, p. 1

MO743 Myself between Venus and Bacchus I'll poise
I'll love and I'll drink and be pleasing to both.

'Song 167'
c.555, p. 256

MO744 Myself dear Lord I'll give to thee
And I shall him possess.

[Mary Pluret], 'Prayer and praise'
c.354

MO745 Mysterious passion, dearest pain
Thou mak'st us wise, yet ruin'st our philosophy.

[John] N[orris, of Bemerton], 'To melancholy'
c.258; c.547, p. 177

MO746 Mysterious riddle of the state,
High misdemeanor, but no treason.

'The riddle' [on the Earl of Clarendon]
[Crum M982]
fb.140, p. 86

MO747 Mysterious stranger! Dark skin fare thee well!
Till he who form'd, shall call thee to thy rest.

'To Ian D'hu on his departure from Banff'
Poetry Box VIII/71

MO748 Mystic sign of magic power,
Wake at thy birth, and at thy bidding flow.

'A blush'
c.83/3, no. 944

N

N0001 N—— raving aloud on his services past,
She, weighing your merits, decrees you this halter.

>John Lockman, 'In answer to a wretch, who, after
>plundering a society, insisted upon being rewarded . . .
>Sept. 1755'
>c.267/1, p. 147

N0002 Naked she lay, clasped in my longing arms,
Hangs hov'ring o'er her balmy limbs of bliss.

>[John Wilmot], 2nd E[arl] of R[ochester], 'The
>imperfect enjoyment'
>[Crum N3]
>b.105, p. 62 (incomplete)

N0003 Namby Pamby aid my verse
Or make him some two inches higher.

>[Lionel Cranfield Sackville, 1st duke of Dorset],
>'Jack-a-Dandy a satire on Lord [ ] Raymond'
>fc.135

N0004 Names are the notes of things, and sometimes signs
Mixt wine sweet modesty, dwell in her spirit.

>[Sir Philip Wodehouse], 'Upon Mrs. An[n] Anguish'
>b.131, back (no. 92)

N0005 Nan and Frank two quondam friends
Betwixt the white staff k[night], and lady of th' red
nose.

>'The combat' [between Frank (Lord Newport, later
>earl of Bradford) and Nan (Capell), the
>orange-woman, 1681]
>[Crum N6]
>b.113, p. 95

N0006 Nancy an arrant thief thou art
More than you stole—a better self.

>[William Hayley], 'Song . . . Oct 16 [1800]'
>File 6968

N0007 Nancy, at my love you us'd to laugh,
My heart's again my own.

>Music Ms. 16, p. 408

N0008 Nancy this star's assign'd to thee
Will find it pleasant to obey him.

>[William Hayley], 'Song . . . Oct 6. 1800'
>File 6968

N0009 Nanny I must leave thee
Singing love's a treasure.

>c.358, p. 69

N0010 Nan's well for she's content, she's pure, she's free
Your paradox refutes, and speaks for me.

>[Sir Philip Wodehouse], 'An argumentation between
>[Anne Lewis] and . . . Mr. Neech'
>b.131, back (no. 82/2)

N0011 Nanty panty Jack-a-Dandy
And away did hoppy leap.

>[prefaced to 'Namby pamby. Or a panegyric on the
>new versification addressed to A(mbrose) P(hillips)
>esqr.']
>c.503, p. 3

N0012 Nash had a head, and in that head
Derrick hath none at all.

>'Mr. Derrick when he succeeded Mr. Nash, as Master
>of the ceremonies at Bath, put on a white hat which
>was the occasion of the following lines'
>c.391, p. 13

N0013 Nasus is very rich as I suppose
Can he be poor yet hath a ruby nose.

>'On a carbuncle nose'
>b.356, p. 307

N0014 Nasus was ever highly esteem'd of,
The head is cleansed by this air inspir'd.

>'Whitehead nasus'
>b.356, p. 119

N0015 Nat am'rous slave, one night being caught in net
And so, gnat, net, night, knot, nut, knit Nat's death.

>'Alliteratio . . . translation'
>c.81/1, no. 253; c.546, p. 21

N0016 Natural religion does indeed display
Whom vice, not wit, engag'd clear truth t'oppose.

>Robert Boyle, '['Natural religion, easy . . .'] answered
>by . . . author of the excellent treatise of the style of
>holy scripture'
>c.229/1, fol. 48

N0017 Natural religion, easy first and plain:
The priests eat roast meat, and the people star'd.

'A flam(?) on the p[riesthoo]d by Laureate L—n'
c.229/1, fol. 48

N0018 Nature affords us flesh, and there
May grow in virtue, and abhor all ill.

H[enry] C[olman], 'On baptism'
b.2, p. 94

N0019 Nature alas! is partial quite,
Or other men with less.

M[aurice] J[ohnson], 'Song[.] Mrs. Behn's Custom
alas burlesqued'
c.229/2, fol. 19

N0020 Nature and art long time had strove
And Gayton is Pomona's seat.

'Gayton-Garden or the triumph of nature'
c.241, p. 22

N0021 Nature and fortune gaily join today
That Cowper's spirits blest her natal hour.

[William Hayley]
File 6953

N0022 Nature and nature's laws lay hid in night:
God said let Newton be! And there was light.

[Alexander] Pope, 'Epitaph on Newton'
c.81/1, no. 189; c.360/2, no. 190; fc.60, p. 24; c.233, p. 86

N0023 Nature bids you on this picture view
The world, and no such other to be found.

Lady Jane Cavendish, 'On my sister Frances' picture'
[Crum N18]
b.233, p. 24

N0024 Nature cannot be changed but bread
Apish toys they will not leave.

'[Backwards] hand'
b.234, p. 15

N0025 Nature courts happiness although it be
And all God's will can bear, can do, can choose.

[Katherine Philips], 'Happiness'
[Crum N22]
b.118, p. 68

N0026 Nature did well in giving poor men wit,
That fools well monified may pay for it.

'Of nature'
[Crum N23]
c.356; b.62, p. 114

N0027 Nature does strangely female gifts dispense
Since every Skipworth brags he has success.

'An essay' [1683]
[Crum N24]
b.113, p. 253

N0028 Nature for defense affords
Beauty triumphs over all!

'Beauty's power'
c.487, p. 101

N0029 Nature gives all creatures arms,
Man himself to beauty yields.

'The power of beauty'
c.83/2, no. 702

N0030 Nature has arm'd with horny force
All fire is weak to that of love.

'On the beauty of women'
c.360/2, no. 222

N0031 Nature has blest the bits o' brutes,
Against both sword and fire.

'Anacreon: od: 2. In Scotch idiom'
c.81/1, no. 145

N0032 Nature has done her part, do thou but thine;
A witty sinner, is the worst of fools.

'To a young gentleman of good parts, and made a bad
use of 'em'
[Crum N27]
c.94

N0033 Nature has fram'd thee good. Give pray[er]s—
                                              rejoice
Thy care of conscience, and brave honesty.

[Sir Philip Wodehouse], 'Joannes Hobartus 1681'
b.131, back (no. 195)

N0034 Nature hath fram'd a ring beyond compare
The world's the ring and you the jewel are.

'On a ring sent to a gentlewoman'
[Crum N28, 'hath found a gem']
b.356, p. 103

N0035 Nature in this small volume was about
Threw dust upon 't, and shut up the book.

[William Browne of Tavistock?], 'On a gentlewoman's
death' [Anne Prideaux, daughter of John Prideaux,
Regius Professor at Oxford]
[Crum N32]
b.205, fol. 33v; b.62, p. 132; b.356, p. 250

N0036 Nature long doubting whether [?] should share
The work was finish'd, but the [?] mistook.

'Cum dubetet natura . . . Englished'

c.221, p. 24

N0037 Nature made all her children save this one
A stone should speak, then none no tears express.

'On K. James' tombstone'
[Crum N33, 'all her creatures but this stone']

b.356, p. 255

N0038 Nature meeting Time one day
And long preserve the happy pair.

[Phanuel Bacon], 'To Miss Anne Chamberlain on her
birthday 19 Feb. 1759 who then came of age'

c.237, fol. 85 [i.e., 105]

N0039 Nature ordains while here we dwell below,
From wisdom oft, and well-pois'd judgment springs.

[Henry] Needler, 'Learned ignorance from Grotius'

c.244, p. 543

N0040 Nature spins life, as spiders do their cauls:
The work of both is long, which made soon falls.

Sir Thomas Urquhart, 'Of man's frailty'

fb.217, p. 172

N0041 Nature, t'eschew voids in the universe,
To fill the vacuum of her microcosms.

Sir Thomas Urquhart, 'That nothing is more natural,
than to a woman, to lose her maidenhead'

fb.217, p. 61

N0042 Nature, to show she did resent
Love arm'd the thunderer's breast with down.

[Phanuel Bacon], 'A tale'

c.237, fol. 55

N0043 Nature to show what she could do
First singer in the house of Lords!

E. F. B[urney], 'An attempt at portrait painting'

c.486, fol. 20v

N0044 Nature was sure in love, or brib'd, or blind
That it transforms each student to a lover.

'On women'

b.200, p. 45; b.356, p. 105

N0045 Nature whom little serveth we extol:
For nature's pleas'd with little: he with nothing.

Sir Thomas Urquhart, 'Of the covetous man a
paradox'

fb.217, p. 99

N0046 Nature with open volume stands
And worship at his sacred throne.

[Isaac Watts, Hymns and spiritual songs (1707),
bk. III, Hymn 10]

c.180, p. 21

N0047 Nature yields as the moon but obscure light:
Whilst grace, like the meridian sun, shines bright.

Sir Thomas Urquhart, 'Of grace, and nature'

fb.217, p. 324

N0048 Nature your form has to perfection wrought,
Virtue, and learning, and the muse shall weep.

Thomas Cook, 'To the Ld. George Johnston, an
address'

c.244, p. 574

N0049 Nature's confectioner the bee
The bee committed parricide.

[John Cleveland], 'Fuscara stung or the bee errant'
[Crum N46]

b.93, p. 3

N0050 Nature's idea, virtue's rare perfection,
The heavens by this time had been turn'd to black.

'On the praise of tobacco'
[Crum N48]

b.200, p. 409

N0051 Nature's lay idiot, I taught thee to love
And leave him then, being made a ready horse.

[John Donne], 'Elegia octava' [Elegy VII]
[Crum N49]

b.114, p. 90; b.148, p. 125

N0052 Naught but affliction thund'ring out of heaven
Than any heaven holds any thunderer.

'Man's obstinacy'

c.189, p. 34

N0053 Naught does the soul so raise on high
Which is at once our duty, honor, bliss.

[Edmund Wodehouse], 'Septr 1 [1715]'

b.131, p. 256

N0054 Naught Tadcaster, can thou to fame bequeath
But a proud bridge with ne'er a stream beneath.

'Tadcaster Bridge in summer'

c.81/1, no. 157

N0055 Nay . . . but I must, I must indeed Papa . . .
Miss in her teens shall thank them for their care.

'Epilogue spoken at the Theater Royal in Drury Lane,
April 30th 1765 by Miss Hopkins, a child of six years
old, at the benefit of Mr. Hopkins, prompter and Mrs.
Hopkins, her father and mother'

c.68, p. 57

N0056 Nay, but I will tho'—sure you won't deny me,
I trust you'll not withhold your kind applause.

[Thomas] Baker, 'Lines intended to be recited by a
gentleman at his first appearance on the stage'

Poetry Box IV/6

N0057 Nay do not smile; my lips shall rather dwell
Then read to you and cannot keep you waking.

[George Daniel]

b.121, fol. 43v

N0058 Nay, hold, friend Battie, quit the press,
Yet, prithee, spare the dead.

[Thomas Morell], 'Noverint universi an epigram'

c.395, p. 33

N0059 Nay! Never blush for't, tho' we know,
Can age like mine give fear?

[William Popple, trans.], '[Horace] book 2nd. Ode
4th. To Xanthus Phoceus'

fc.104/2, p. 124

N0060 Nay now forbear, for pity sake give o'er
What can we call this loss than ecstasy?

Robert Wild, 'To the memory of Mr. Jeremy
Whitaker . . .' [d. 1654]

c.166, p. 315

N0061 Nay painter if thou dar'st design that fight,
In Petty's double-keel'd Experiment.

[Andrew Marvell?], 'Directions to a painter for
describing our naval business in imitation of
Mr. Waller' [followed by envoy, 'Imperial prince . . .']
[Crum N67; POAS I.36]

b.136, p. 1; fb.140, p. 53; c.160, fol. 1; fc.61, p. 1(ll.1–174)

N0062 Nay pish, nay aphew, nay faith, but will you, fie;
We'll go to cards, I hope we shall agree.

'A gentlewoman to a gentleman busy with her [ ]'
[Crum N69]

b.62, p. 97; b.200, p. 430; see also 'Not kiss, by Jove . . .'.

N0063 Nay prithee don't fly me
And that man has no worth that won't sometimes
be mellow.

[Alexander Brome, 'The leveller']
[Crum N71]

b.213, p. 86

N0064 Nay start not at that skeleton
Well done and enter into the rest.

N[ahum] Tate, 'Upon the sight of an anatomy'

fc.60, p. 85; File 13409

N0065 Ne gay attire, ne marble hall,
My house shall prove an hermitage.

[Gilbert West], 'Verses, wrote on a hermitage at
Mereworth the seat of the earl of Westmorland
behind the shrine of St. Agnes'
[Crum N78]

fc.51, p. 40; c.360/1, p. 259 (attr. G. Lyttelton)

N0066 Near Avon's sedgy bank there grows
'Tis spring, sweet nymph—but Delia is not here.

[Richard Brinsley Butler] Sheridan, 'Discontent'

Poetry Box III/27

N0067 Near fertile Rutland's much-frequented lawns
Who till he ceas'd to live, ne'er ceas'd to love.

[Robert Cholmeley], 'Philander to Amoret'

c.190, p. 49

N0068 Near half an age with ev'ry good man's praise
He had no foe, and Camden was his friend.

[David Garrick], 'On the late Revd Doctr Beighton of
Edgham'

fc.14/12; c.94

N0069 Near Holborn lies a park of great renown,
If such turd-flies shall break thro' cobweb laws.

'A true, and perfect relation how a bold, and saucy
beadle [Peter Vernell], being upon the watch . . . was
killed very fairly by three Dukes, Monmouth,
Albemarle, Somerset' [26 February 1670/1]
[Crum N83; POAS I.172]

b.54, p. 1230; fb.70, p. 23; see also 'Nigh Holborn . . .'.

N0070 Near no churchyard let Shelley dwell
The same effect on you.

Dr. [ ] Ogle, dean of Winchester, 'Epigram on ['Why
will dear Amanda dwell . . .']'

c.106, p. 101

N0071 Near Severn's streams the pensive Damon sat,
To calm the tumult of the troubled breast.

'No real happiness below'

c.148, p. 13

N0072 Near Thames' green banks, a love-born nymph
reclin'd,
I've but one life, and there's a choice of swains.

John Lockman, 'Well-judging Phyllis: a sonnet—set
to music by Dr. Boyce'

c.267/4, p. 155

N0073 Near that fam'd place, whose waters spontaneously
                          flow
She grants to the head, what she denied at the tail.

    Sir William Morice(?), 'A new ballad to the tune of
    The forsaken maid'

  c.174, p. 94

N0074 Near the brook in yonder dale
And heal'd, when thought to wound.

    'The wood nymph, from Love in a cottage'

  c.83/1, no. 35

N0075 Near the mad mansions of Moorfields I'll bawl
And (if I please) I'll give it to the poor.

    'Epilogue to The minor, spoken by Mr. Foote, in the
    character of Dr. Squintum'

  c.68, p. 173

N0076 Near the slow Cherwell's sullen stream,
Goes home a calm repose to find.

    [William Carpenter], 'A moral essay on human life'

  c.247, p. 137

N0077 Near the vast bulk of that stupendous frame,
Like other monarchs of her ancient line.

    'On Queen Anne's statue in Paul's churchyard'

  c.244, p. 633

N0078 Near to a stately column mounted high
Old Furio reel'd Juvenio blunder'd home.

    'Cabal at M—r—n's Coffee House in Coventry'

  b.382(24)

N0079 Near to an ancient house of prayer,
If ever I come t'ye to be confirm'd.

    'The weasels a satirical fable. Giving an account of
    some argumental passages happening in the Lions'
    Court about weaselions taking the oaths'

  b.111, p. 175

N0080 Near to Northampton's ancient town
The example of a goodly mother.

    'A tale'

  fc.135

N0081 Near twelve o'clock one dreary night
She dropp'd and died on Henry's tomb.

    [John Walker?], 'The vision . . . by desire of Miss
    Betty H.'

  fc.108, fol. 1

N0082 Necessity constrains us Lord
Till well supplied with good.

    T[homas] S[tevens]

  c.259, p. 145

N0083 Needwood! If e'er with early voice
Is worth the whole that schools have taught.

    J. W. Mundy, 'By J. W. Mundy'

  c.364, p. 43

N0084 Ne'er grip a thorn—'twill prick thy hand
A smooth and gentle mind command.

    [Sir Philip Wodehouse], 'Upon Mrs. Peregrine
    North . . .'

  b.131, back (no. 73)

N0085 Ne'er think, one room will hold
Thou gifts to Heaven, yet less will Earth appear.

    'On Mundano'

  b.118, p. 226

N0086 Ne'er vaunt Glorioso, that thou oft reliev'st
Thy own applause, hath op'd thy own again.

    [Francis Quarles], 'On Glorioso' [Divine
    fancies IV, 71]

  b.137, p. 184

N0087 Ne'er yet was a name so branded by fame
Shall rob us of Abraham Newland.

  Poetry Box IV/41

N0088 Neither do husbands here nor Heaven above
And Heaven itself affects the humble mind.

    [Sir Aston Cokayne], 'Of high spirited women'

  b.275, p. 87

N0089 Nell just deliver'd of a brat
When each has her gallant.

    R[obert] Shirley, 1st earl of Ferrers, 'Nelly's case.
    From La Fontaine'

  c.347, p. 36

N0090 Nell tried for stealing linen, answers swift
Compell'd thro' want she did it for a shift.

  c.546, p. 31

N0091 Nero of Æneas came, th'one made a way
T'er's father, th'other made his mother away.

  b.207, p. 5

N0092 Never head succeedeth one that's called face
Face says enough although the tongue lies still.

    'Elforde facies' [answered by 'The face declares . . .']

  b.356, p. 116

N0093 Never more loyal did under marble lie,
Full heavens call'd her to her crown long due.

    [Sir William Trumbull, epitaph for the Countess of
    Stirling (his mother-in-law)]

  Trumbull Box: Poetry Box XIII/34

N0094 Never seek Leuconoe,
Come tomorrow, when it will!

    [William Popple, trans.], '[Horace] book 1st. ode 11th.
    To Leuconoe'

    fc.104/2, p. 34

N0095 Never to be at ease, never to rest
Nearest perfection, who his own restrains.

    [George Daniel]

    b.121, fol. 67

N0096 Never weather-beaten sail more willing bent to
                         shore,
Oh how do I long to see that place of rest.

    [Thomas Campion], 'The black hymn'
    [Crum N118]

    c.481, p. 273; c.328, p. 33

N0097 Neville in this foolish satire
And strike them with her slipper dead.

    Christ[opher] Neville, 'On Capt Caldwell leaving
    Lincoln several verses were written and amongst
    other[s] the following lines'

    Spence Papers, folder 113

N0098 New care is come into thy house, by such
Carve Nan is best—'till death I'm in her debt.

    [Sir Philip Wodehouse], 'Upon Ann Crew late Lady
    Wodehouse—my cousin'

    b.131, back (no. 103)

N0099 New commissions are come o'er
And that way prevent our fall.

    'To all protestants in England Scotland and Ireland'

    fb.228/[44a]

N0100 New forms of prayers are sent the realms throughout
And when they're heard we'll all keep holy-day.

    'The dutiful son and daughter' [answered by 'Without
    your form . . .']

    b.111, p. 375

N0101 New horns a hart once in the year suffice:
But ev'ry day, your husband changeth his.

    Sir Thomas Urquhart, 'To one, who did daily cuckold
    her husband'

    fb.217, p. 124

N0102 New intellectual worlds, like thee, to find
'Tis to gain wisdom, at Knowl-Hills to see.

    'Under Mr. Sanderson's picture at Knowl-Hills'

    b.322, p. 43

N0103 New, is the garment which hath not been on
What color so charming as is the gay Green.

    'Another solution to rebus no. 89' ['The name that
    you give to a garment not wore . . .']

    c.360/3, no. 101

N0104 New seals are made, old styles forsaken
Down laid the blade. Scepter uptaken.

    b.208, p. 187

N0105 New Year's may well expect to find
Whilst her glad waves came leaping to the shore.

    [Edmund Waller], 'To my Lady Morton on New
    Year's Day'

    Poetry Box VII/27 (incomplete)

N0106 Newport, the sixteenth day of June—
What 'tis to love and be beloved.

    Lady Frances (Scott) [Douglas, baroness Douglas],
    'To Lady Courtown . . . Dalkeith House, June 30th
    1781' [verse journal of a tour of the Lakes, 1781]

    Poetry Box III/48 (2 copies)

N0107 News—news my friends, pray have you seen the
                               Act?
You'll curse the time, when first this Act begun.

    'Taken from the church door . . . this was given to me
    March 25 1766, by Mr. King . . .'

    c.74

N0108 News news news is come from the north
Themselves on the stool of repentence.

    [John Cleveland?], 'Juvenilia not entered'

    b.93, p. 12

N0109 Newton brought nature's secret laws to light
But Pope now thou are dead, once more 'tis night.

    [Henry Price], 'On the death of that incomparable
    poet, Alexander Pope . . . in imitation of his celebrated
    epitaph on Sir Isaac Newton'

    c.360/2, no. 244

N0110 Newton with open mouth demands his stray,
Till Carter speaks, or Newton holds his tongue.

    'On Dr. Newton and Carter [provost of Oriel, who
    admitted a gentleman from Hart Hall without a
    discessit from the former]'
    [Crum N125]

    c.233, p. 16

N0111 Newton's no more—by silence grief's exprest
Lo, here he lies—his works proclaim the rest.

    'Another' [on Sir Isaac Newton]

    c.547, p. 231

N0112 Next Monday, good Sir, will yourself and your
                                          second
Do you smile? All must come to the conjurer's call.

    C[harles] E[arle], 'Invitation to a friend and his wife
    for a day in Christmas'

    c.376

N0113 Next Sunday by 10 ('tis but stick a pin quicker,
The grace of a saint, to the meal of a sinner.

    [Charles] Earle, 'Mr. Earle's thanks and compliments
    to Miss Smith and Miss Morgan, and (after reminding
    that they are mortal) request they will observe what
    follows'

    c.376; see also 'The gods, we are told . . .'.

N0114 Next there a monk appears in place,
His horse was sleek, and as the berry brown.

    'The monk modernized from Chaucer'

    c.83/2, no. 354

N0115 Next Thursday, by noon with what am I able
A Pratt-patriot in and a Pitt-patriot out!

    [Charles Earle], 'To Mr. Sydenham Barnstaple'

    c.376

N0116 Next to that famous day of June
He tells him at the Devil.

    [Phanuel Bacon], 'Vide Oxford almanac 1736.
    thrusting out St. Barnabas from his place to insert a
    state holiday'

    c.237, fol. 32

N0117 Next to Venerian disport, to be well
May cover all your body.

    Sir Thomas Urquhart, 'A furtherance by way of advice
    for the satisfaction of her most ardent desires: to a
    courtesan whose splendid humor was inordinately
    fixed upon the gallantry of brave clothes'

    fb.217, p. 354

N0118 Nigh(?) art [?] sad in sense and loath (alas) to leave
No more the dying pilgrim spoke but rendered up
                                          his spirit.

    'A dying pilgrim's speech' [after 1627]
    Poetry Box VIII/1

N0119 Nigh Holborn lies a park of great renown,
If such t[urd-] flies break through cobweb laws.

    [cf. Crum N83; POAS I.172]
    Poetry Box VII/36; see also 'Near Holborn . . .'.

N0120 Nigh where old Don with interrupted waves
On realms above and gaz'd upon the skies.

    'The British burgomasters'
    fc.61, p. 99

N0121 Night and darkness round us close,
Unconscious of this awful roar.

    'A sonnet'
    c.83/2, no. 534

N0122 Night came, and with it came indulgent rest
And dashing waves an anxious bosom tire.

    'Nox erat &c in the 4th book of Virgil Aeneids'
    b.322, p. 9

N0123 Night, expecting the dread morrow,
Lovely Delia, fare thee well!

    'The soldier's farewell on the eve of battle'
    c.139, p. 412; c.90 ('Lovely Alice . . .')

N0124 Nigrellus leads a merry life
But he's Cornelius Tacitus.

    'The variation' [on 'Blackbourne will be dean . . .']
    c.74; c.233, p. 19 ('Nigrinus')

N0125 Nine days' folly, nine weeks' belly
Nine days blind, is the dog's kind.

    b.197, p. 149

N0126 Nine lives in sin and sorrow spent
Death had a stomach for them all.

    [David] Garrick, 'Epitaph by . . . on Miss Wilmot's
    cat who eat all her own offspring . . .'
    c.160, fol. 42

N0127 Nine tripled and two are the years,
Here's a health to such honest men.

    'The history of the first 29 years' rebellion and
    usurpation' [1688–1710]
    fc.58, p. 158; see also 'Ev'ry man take . . .'.

N0128 Nip-weight, a grocer of the chosen few,
And like good Christians let us go to prayer.

    'The pious Methodist'
    c.81/1, no. 329

N0129 No aid of fancy here I ask
Swill'd—belch'd—and went away.

    'On Doctor O—n of ——— College Cambridge . . .'
    c.169, p. 7

N0130 No bait be sweet as beauty to the eye,
Yet oft it hath a worse sting than the bee.

    c.339, p. 318

N0131 No beauty distinguish'd Ulysses, yet he
Yet you trust it, abandoning me!

    [ ] Horsley, 'A translation from part of Ovid's Art of
    love'
    c.504, p. 64

N0132 No Ciceronian figure,
B'an union hypostatic.

> Sir Thomas Urquhart, 'To a certain proper, and
> eloquent gentleman, whose mistress carried the less
> respect to him that he was not forward enough in her
> pursuit . . .'
>
> fb.217, p. 150

N0133 No city is so strong as is a constant mind
Thy life shall be the only glass heroic minds shall
have.

> 'El[izabeth?] R[egina?] fecit'
>
> Poetry Box VIII/45

N0134 No civil, and ecclesiastic function
You rule the treasure, and your diocese.

> Sir Thomas Urquhart, 'To [William Juxon] bishop of
> London, High Treasurer of England'
>
> fb.217, p. 295

N0135 No clime such men, no men have such a town,
Nor town a court, or king of such renown.

> W. F., 'Thus better varied (sans price) in Latin and
> English in more just honor to our K[ing] Ch[arles],
> his court and city'
>
> Poetry Box VI/43

N0136 No cloud whate'er can virtue's light obscure,
Whilst hell's black sins, their punishment endure.

> c.549, p. 36

N0137 No council at your scrictiaries [sic],
See that yourselves escape the scouring.

> 'To the liveryman of London a Christmas box'
>
> fc.85, fol. 34v

N0138 No courage will I e'er desire,
That chief of all true blessings, thy blest love.

> [Edmund Wodehouse], 'Iterum [23 November 1714]'
>
> b.131, p. 95

N0139 No craft will serve nor politic devise,
When wavering fortune only throws the dice.

> c.339, p. 310

N0140 No day without some line Apelles said
May make him all its batteries outface.

> [Edmund Wodehouse], 'Novr. 16 [1714]'
>
> b.131, p. 85

N0141 No doctor in the church hath lived since
You syllogistically prove laconic.

> Sir Thomas Urquhart, 'To the Bishop of [crossed out]'
>
> fb.217, p. 176

N0142 No doubtful fears shall more disturb my rest
Convinc'd, 'all things are ordered for the best.'

> 'Extempore on disappointment'
>
> c.81/1, no. 172

N0143 No epitaph need make the just man fam'd
The good are prais'd when they are only nam'd.

> 'Epitaph on Mr. [Thomas] Allen of Bath'
> [Crum N160]
>
> c.74; c.244, p. 212

N0144 No fancied muse, nor Heliconian stream
When Spence approves, and Caroline rewards.

> T[homas] M[orell], '1735' [verse and parody
> interlined]
>
> c.395, p. 68

N0145 No farther go this night, but stay,
And I'll go on with Thee.

> [Thomas Stevens?], 'Another [hymn]'
>
> c.259, p. 69

N0146 No fault in Sherlock can I spy
There you may learn to live and die.

> [Lady ( ) Tankerville], 'The answer extempore to
> [Chesterfield's 'Mistaken fair! lay Sherlock by . . .'] by
> a young lady'
>
> c.157, p. 8

N0147 No favorite of thy fickle pow'r,
To heaven, ascends my pious pray'r.

> Sarah Herd, 'To fortune'
>
> c.141, p. 357

N0148 No fewer countries, Christ than nature's hath;
Being born at Beth'lem, got in Nazareth.

> Sir Thomas Urquhart, 'Of our Savior'
>
> fb.217, p. 104

N0149 No fiend in hell can such a fury prove,
As a wrong'd woman, one that's wrong'd in love.

> c.549, p. 138

N0150 No fine or filed tongue can tell
And joy which ever shall endure. | Amen

> 'Of S. Michael. Sep. 29'
>
> a.30[41]

N0151 No foe so fell (as Bion's voice declares);
As man to man, when mischief he prepares.

> c.339, p. 316

N0152 No foe so fell, nor yet so hard to 'scape,
As is the foe that fawns with friendly shape.

> c.339, p. 311

N0153 No foreign instance need of this be shown,
Of what effects attend credulity.

'Despair'

c.94

N0154 No garish form misrob'd on Catt'ry's coin
You bade the world farewell, and slept in death.

'On the death of the Revd. Dr. Sharpe of Ch[rist] Ch[urch], Greek professor' [1782]

fc.53, p. 192

N0155 No glory I covet no riches I want
Is what all if they will may enjoy.

[Thomas Fitzgerald], 'Song 216'
[Crum N165]

c.555, p. 344; c.163, p. 9 (with another stanza)

N0156 No God thou shalt adore but me,
Or anything that he may have.

'The ten commandments'

c.83/3, no. 822

N0157 No great exploit can be expected from
When pleasure over him no power have.

[Sir Thomas Urquhart], 'How generous a thing it is not to succumb to sensuality, and pleasure'

fb.217, p. 510

N0158 No grief disturbs, no cares nor fears molest,
From heav'n alone we must expect relief.

'A country elegy of the death of Mr. John Wright who departed this life Lord's Day July 13. 1721'

c.244, p. 153

N0159 No grief, or cross
For pass'd, too late.

Sir Thomas Urquhart, 'Of sorrow'

fb.217, p. 39

N0160 No grief should any way betake him:
Was circumcised for his Mistress Dina.

Sir Thomas Urquhart, 'Of a gentleman, who took it very heavily, that he was infected of a Venerian cancer, by being too intime with a courtesan named Despina'

fb.217, p. 340

N0161 No hero ever met success
Fair Artis makes the cockades.

'On Mrs Artis (late Miss Pearse of Enfield) making the cockades for all the officers of Colonel Cholmondeley's regiment, against a review—1741'

c.360/1, p. 169

N0162 No hubbub surnam'd hue and cry
The goose of *non plus* come in's mouth.

[John Cleveland?], 'Juvenilia not entered'

b.93, p. 15

N0163 No human reason can amend this sense
Though they be great, if they be not held so.

Sir John Strangways, '22do Januarii 1646[/7]'

b.304, p. 71

N0164 No husband's bygone favors will restrain
For mills grind not with water that is past.

[Sir Thomas Urquhart], 'One courtesy hoped for is more respected of, than three already past'

fb.217, p. 534

N0165 No hydromancer's better skill'd, than she,
Commixion of erotic inundations.

Sir Thomas Urquhart, 'Of a certain prophetess, who did prognostic things to come by water'

fb.217, p. 112

N0166 No I shan't envy him whoe'er he be
But died a stranger to himself alone.

J[oh]n Norris, of Bemerton

b.63, p. 111; c.94; c.547, p. 173; see also 'Charm'd with its happy . . .'.

N0167 No I'll resist whate'er they'd have me do,
Rather than they be curs'd will live alone.

R[obert] Shirley, 1st earl of Ferrers, 'A satire against marriage—from Boileau'

c.347, p. 8

N0168 No joys of virtue like conscious goodness, please,
A life of rapture, from the wound of death.

'On virtue'
[cf. Crum N170]

c.83/1, no. 48; c.83/3, no. 881 (var.; 'No joys of sense')

N0169 No king whose minister resigns
Till nature call you to your urn.

Charles Burney, the elder, 'To my daughter Charlotte on her marriage with Clement Francis esqr. February 11th 1786'
[cf. Crum N170]

c.486, fol. 40v

N0170 No lack of thanks should hinder goodness, nor
Though punishment be lame it comes in end.

[Sir Thomas Urquhart], 'Neither want of reward or impunity should prompt us to vice or discourage us from virtue'

fb.217, p. 535

N0171 No lamps fix'd here, when ev'ry street's so bright,
And ne'er regard the dupes who plod without.

[John Lockman], 'On seeing no lights out at the
Ch—— H—— on Michaelmas night 1736. the night
when the city was illuminated'

c.268 (first part), p. 14

N0172 No liquor stirs call for a cup of wine
'Tis blood we drink we pledge thee Catiline.

[John Cleveland?]

b.93, p. 8

N0173 No living creature lives so long, but once must
needs give place
God grant them living so to do, that they in him
may die.

'On John Rogers of the company of clothworkers' [d.
5 Aug. 1676]

fb.143, p. 8

N0174 No longer blame those on the banks of Nile
If you ne'er seek me out, I'll count you wise.

'A riddle'
[Crum N174]

b.113, p. 257; fb.70, p. 51

N0175 No longer could good David quiet bear
Small streaming clouds he does for wings dis[?]. . . .

c.548 (incomplete)

N0176 No longer Cynthia; have I spent
Warm'd with the best ('bove late Platonic) fires.

[George Daniel]

b.121, fol. 74

N0177 No longer did the bell with solemn sound,
The grateful tribute of a pitying tear.

'Elegy on the death Dr. Aiken plays(?) . . . Etonensis'
fc.85, fol. 88v

N0178 No longer doubt we not
And heaven spreads all around.

'A compliment, paid the author by a friend upon his
happy situation at Toot Balden'

c.237, fol. 111 [i.e., 131]

N0179 No longer let whimsical songsters compare
And I'll sing of the ladies as long as I can.

'Song 161'

c.555, p. 245

N0180 No longer, Orpheus, shall the oaks obey,
A goddess, could not alter fate's decree.

George Montagu, 'On Orpheus'

fc.135, p. 12

N0181 No longer quacks disparage
To all that's great lays claim Sir.

'The empiric'

c.570/3, p. 119

N0182 No longer seek the needless aid
To wave around her neck, and wanton in the wind.

[William Duncombe], 'To a young lady curling her
hair . . . North Luffenham'

c.136, p. 31

N0183 No longer talk of Orpheus and Orion
But all talk'd out as womankind are used.

'On the music club at Norwich'

c.360/2, no. 34

N0184 No longer torture me, in dreams
Men, with equal heat, and haste.

[George Daniel], 'Anti-Platonic'

b.121, fol. 77

N0185 No love compar'd to God's is worth a thought,
Thou never will reject, thou still invitest me.

[Edmund Wodehouse], 'Aug. 21 [1715]'

b.131, p. 250

N0186 No man can hope for heav'n, that fears not hell:
Thus fear makes hope in prudent men to dwell.

Sir Thomas Urquhart, 'Fear is the beginning of
wisdom'

fb.217, p. 48

N0187 No man e'er liv'd (on earth) nor ever shall
That did all well, and had no fault at all.

[John Rose?]

b.227, p. 167

N0188 No man gives counsel in a clamorous voice
Outsound a hundred ayes, thro' noise impose (?).

[Sir Philip Wodehouse], 'Nemo clamor . . .'

b.131, p. 33

N0189 No man love's fiery passion can approve
His courage is as little as his wit.

[Sir Robert Ayton, stanzas 3–10 from 'There is no
worldly pleasure here below']
[Crum N179]

b.4, fol. 51; b.213, p. 60

N0190 No man of resolution will endure
But over whom she hath no pow'r at all.

[Sir Thomas Urquhart], 'A brave spirit disdaineth
fortune'

fb.217, p. 497

N0191 No man remaining in one stay may be
But healing time his birth and death may see.

c.339, p. 320

N0192 No man so poor, but God can bless his days
Who patient Job, did from the dunghill raise.

c.339, p. 312

N0193 No man's condition is so bad as his
If we are wax or tallow by the smell.

[Francis Quarles], 'On the hypocrite' [Divine
fancies I, 23; II, 96; III, 13]
[Crum N182, with additional verses]

b.137, p. 182

N0194 No marble pillar; no proud statues here
And thou wilt rear thy self a pyramid.

[Richard] Owen(?), 'An epitaph on a gentlewoman'

b.62, p. 62

N0195 No marvel if the sun's bright eye
I think he was an angel rather.

[William Strode], 'To a gentlewoman for a friend'
[cf. Crum N184]

b.205, fol. 70v

N0196 No marvel that our shamefast maids
He had rather have, then hear on't.

'Songs: on saying nay, and taking it'

b.200, p. 341

N0197 No marvel thou great monarch, didst complain,
H'as grief enough, that finds no world but this.

[Francis Quarles], 'On Alexander'
[Crum N187]

b.118, p. 224; see also 'O marvel . . .'.

N0198 No matter whether (some there be that say)
And feast at court, to say I've meat at home.

[Francis Quarles], 'On chamber-Christians' [Divine
fancies II, 38]

b.137, p. 181

N0199 No money, pox on you!
Or if out of the treaty should leave you.

'An angry message to the city anno 1696'
[Crum N189]

fb.207/4, p. 22

N0200 No monument of me remain,
Grow in my vows even part of thee.

[William] Habington, 'Domine labia mea aperies.
David'

b.150, p. 268

N0201 No more against marriage let old cynics rail,
That life's *summum bonum* is dear wedlock still.

'For W. Bannister . . . Joh[n] Rutherford March 13th
1782'

c.93

N0202 No more, as fiction we'll arraign the song,
And graceful dance, instructed by thy art!

John Lockman, 'To Mr. Hugford: on seeing a scholar
of his, naturally very awkward, dance genteelly . . .
May 1742'

c.267/1, p. 6

N0203 No more blind boy foresee my heart
Wound her for 'tis for her I die.

[Thomas Carew]

b.213, p. 63

N0204 No more earthly subjects sing,
Nor drop a tear for him, who pours his blood for
thee.

[Christopher] Pitt, 'On Christ's passion an ode'

c.244, p. 497

N0205 No more expect th'immediate aid of heav'n,
And never never know his sins forgiv'n.

'Ecclesiasticus Chapt. 38—verses 15'

c.244, p. 600

N0206 No more fond isle, no more thyself combine
Let bloody French king have proud Hammond's
end.

Anthony Cumber, sr., of Tenterden, 'A poem of . . .
Tenterden July the 28 1704'

c.158, p. 87

N0207 No more her darling liberty can boast—
For all her pleasure pride and charms are lost.

c.549, p. 17

N0208 No more I heed the muffin's zest,
The wondrous work consign.

Major [ ] Drew, of Exeter, 'Receipt to make a
Sally-Lunn (a well-known cake at Bath)'

c.83/2, no. 629

N0209 No more let Europe boast of arts refin'd
Vain is the boast of learning's hallow'd dream!

R[ichard] V[ernon] S[adleir], 'To Geo: Keate esqr on
his account of the Peters(?) Islands'

c.106, p. 139

N0210 No more, | Let me awhile be free
Go seek an orphan, I am yours no more.

[George Daniel]

b.121, fol. 22v

N0211 No more, let's part dear muses, high in mirth
In peace secure, the fears which we now bring.

    [George Daniel]

b.121, fol. 37v

N0212 No more, my friend! of vain applause,
And sing about the times.

    'The present age'

c.115

N0213 No more my Muse of lawless fop, or fool,
Close up the text or we shall ne'er 'a' done.

    'The hero' [William III, 1693]
    [Crum N207]

fb.207/1, p. 15

N0214 No more that feeling heart with friendship glows
Peace to her gentle spirit! Endless peace!

    F[rances Burney] d'A[rblay], 'In memory of Susan
    Elizabeth [Burney] Phillips'

c.486, fol. 5v

N0215 No more these things dear swain believe
And if you weep I mourn.

    [Robert Cholmeley], 'The reply. A song'

c.190, p. 48

N0216 No more th'Italian squalling tribe admit
Not what Italians sing, but Romans writ.

    'On the Italian operas'

c.360/2, no. 127

N0217 No more thyself, fair nymph perplex
That art may wonder, tho' not grant you more.

    [Robert Cholmeley], 'Written in a young lady's
    dictionary' [answered by 'Use dunce . . .']

c.190, p. 27

N0218 No more we prize the Greek and Roman lay,
All nations in sagacity excel.

    John Lockman, 'Taste' [translated from La Fontaine]

c.267/4, p. 179

N0219 No more with fruitless cares and cheated strife,
Who virtuous deeds and harmless words oppose.

    J[ohn] R[obinson], 'Nescit vox missa reverti'

c.370, fol. 74

N0220 No new year's gift, this year (as custom was)
I'm sure, Faustinus, he has made me so.

    'Tristis Athenagoras . . .'

b.207, p. 9

N0221 No, no, for my virginity
Rose, were you not extremely sick.

    [Matthew] Prior, 'A true maid'

c.176, p. 181; c.81/1, no. 4 ('Phyl, were . . .')

N0222 No, no, I'll rather suffer all the brand
His own affections, how shall I be tried?

    [George Daniel]

b.121, fol. 43

N0223 No, no 'tis in vain
Still the bloody dart sticks in my side.

    [Thomas Fitzgerald], 'Wounded love'

fb.107, p. 28

N0224 No not a quash sad poets doubt you
God makes a saint, not kills a queen.

    [Richard] Corbett, 'An epitaph on Q[ueen] Anne' [in
    exhortation to the university concerning their printed
    poetry at the Queen's death, 1618]
    [Crum N237a]

b.197, p. 165; b.200, p. 236; b.356, p. 27

N0225 No, not one word can I of this strange deed
To put her children out, to [?] to nurse.

    'An answer to Dr. Wild [touching (?) upon the liberty
    (?) in the worship of God]'

File 19024

N0226 No nymph with half thy beauties blest,
No one ever died so fond of you.

    [Robert Cholmeley], 'An acrostic to Mrs. Nelly
    Robinson'

c.190, p. 72

N0227 No old man lives hath reason to be curious:
Lest he by secret prying prove injurious.

    Sir Thomas Urquhart, 'In the first line of this distich,
    are of the five predicables of Porphyre'

fb.217, p. 103

N0228 No other goddess I adore
Attend upon my love.

    'An ode'

Poetry Box I/24

N0229 No other wares are bought unseen: but such
The more profoundly they apply the touch.

    Sir Thomas Urquhart, 'The reason why no other
    merchandise, commonly, is vented, or gets sale
    without ocular inspection: save only the commodities,
    that are most necessarily requisite for the practice of
    love . . .'

fb.217, p. 347

N0230　No pedigrees or prodigies
　　　　And coin the commonwealth.

　　　　　[Thomas Weaver, 'The generation of vipers'; c. 1642]
　　　　　[Crum N243]

　　　　b.213, p. 70; b.4, fol. 47

N0231　No place (dear Lord) unless thy goodness please
　　　　Lamenting thus a wretched deed undone.

　　　　Poetry Box VII/6

N0232　No place is dark enough for our offence and sin,
　　　　For that's watch't, by our conscience that's within.

　　　　fb.69, p. 213

N0233　No poet's tragical rage that must inspire
　　　　My flesh, my ribs had started from my chin.

　　　　　[Sir William D'Avenant], 'On George Duke of
　　　　　Buckingham his general'

　　　　b.356, p. 10

N0234　No polyp nor chameleon changeth hue
　　　　Than Prote' did transform himself in shapes.

　　　　　[Sir Thomas Urquhart], 'Concerning the temporizers
　　　　　of this age whose pliable souls receive the impression
　　　　　of several faiths conform to the external discrepance
　　　　　or alteration in sects amongst those on whom they
　　　　　imagine their secular felicity to depend'

　　　　fb.217, p. 503

N0235　No praise arises from the wealth
　　　　Still greedy longs for more.

　　　　　[George] H[owar]d, [6th earl of Carlisle],
　　　　　'Translation of the 2 ode 2 book [of Horace]'

　　　　c.197, p. 19

N0236　No pupil shall admit to me
　　　　But who from thee credentials can obtain.

　　　　　[Sir Philip Wodehouse], 'Joannes Burtonus . . .'

　　　　b.131, back (no. 154)

N0237　No question [here] is askt and yet we spy
　　　　Gives a true virgin Sir then no ill liver.

　　　　　Francis Lenton, 'Upon that unspotted virgin Mrs.
　　　　　Elinor Villiers / Anagram / No ill liver Sir'

　　　　b.205, fol. 19r

N0238　No riches may with life of man compare,
　　　　They are but dross and fortune's brittle ware.

　　　　c.339, p. 312

N0239　No salting here these many years was seen
　　　　But five brave predicables in a mess.

　　　　　Thom[as] Randolph, 'Thom. Randolph's Salting'

　　　　b.65, p. 138

N0240　No! scornful beauty e'er shall boast
　　　　Tho' I ne'er enjoy your love.

　　　　　Charles II(?), 'A song composed by his present
　　　　　Majesty Charles the Second and set by Monsieur Le
　　　　　Grange . . . 1677'

　　　　b.54, p. 970

N0241　No sculptur'd marble here, nor pompous lay,
　　　　To pour her sorrows o'er her poet's dust.

　　　　　[Robert Burns], 'Inscription over the grave of Robert
　　　　　Ferguson' [d. 16 December 1774]

　　　　c.142, p. 235

N0242　No selfish motive fires my breast,
　　　　Who knows no bliss unshar'd by thee.

　　　　　[William Roscoe], 'To the same [Maria]'

　　　　c.141, p. 54

N0243　No; she shall ne'er escape if gods there be,
　　　　And so be damn'd of mere necessity.

　　　　　[John Oldham], 'Upon a certain woman, who by her
　　　　　falsehood and scorn was the death of my friend' [1678]
　　　　　[Crum N257]

　　　　b.105, p. 289

N0244　No soldier here on earth can serve
　　　　Forevermore may reign. | Amen

　　　　　'S. Theodore. November. 9'

　　　　a.30[49]

N0245　No son of sloth e'er wore a laurel-crown,
　　　　And all the joys which from abundance flow!

　　　　　'Rest and labor'

　　　　Poetry Box IV/147

N0246　No sooner did I hear of your commission
　　　　Which shall do best, Carlisle or Corby Castle.

　　　　　Dr. [ ] Nichols, chancellor of Carlisle, 'A gratulatory
　　　　　poem to the right hon[ora]ble Francis Howard upon
　　　　　his coming to be Governor of Carlisle'

　　　　Poetry Box VII/7

N0247　No sooner had a piper on a day
　　　　But trembled on the cadences exactly.

　　　　　Sir Thomas Urquhart, 'Of a piper, and his sweetheart'

　　　　fb.217, p. 303

N0248　No sooner had the news resounded in my ears
　　　　I wish your happiness a thousand times adieu.

　　　　　'Upon the departure of one of the sisters'

　　　　b.205, fol. 43r

N0249 No sooner had the royal senate met,
The crown the bridegroom and the church the
bride.

[Charles Blount], 'A supplement to the opening of the
sessions' [of the House of Commons, 1691]
[Crum N261; POAS V.268]

fb.68, p. 9; Poetry Box XIV/182

N0250 No sooner old Dennis
That so he may 'scape the gallows.

'Upon the canvassing for Dennis [Edwards] his place
the vergerer' [Oxford University, 1642-43]
[Crum N263]

b.200, p. 351

N0251 No sooner out but grumble; is the brick
Will wag their tails and fawn, but snarl if none.

[Francis Quarles], 'On the grumbling Israelites'
[Divine fancies I, 86]
[cf. Crum N264]

b.137, p. 167

N0252 No spring nor summer beauty hath such grace
I shall ebb out with them who homeward go.

[John Donne], 'Canzone [Elegy autumnal]'
[Crum N267]

b.114, p. 238; b.148, p. 57

N0253 No stars again shall hurt you from above,
But all your days shall pass in peace and love.

'Chorus [4, with musical score for tenor and bass,
from Purcell's The tempest]'

Music MS. 534

N0254 No state is sure nor seat within this life,
For fawning foes and feigned friends are rife.

[Crum N268]

c.339, p. 318 (first two lines)

N0255 No state of life's from troubles free,
Into oblivion's everlasting night.

Lady [Mary] C[hudleigh], 'The observation'

c.258

N0256 No thicker are the stars i'th'milky way
For it damns more and therefore must be worst.

'The survey'

b.113, p. 189

N0257 No; to what purpose should I speak?
'Twas only love destroyed the gentle youth.

A[braham] C[owley], 'The concealment'

c.258

N0258 No tongue of man, nor angel, can
With bowing heads, Thee honoring.

'Psalm 65. Evening prayer'

c.264/2, p. 18

N0259 No triumph of the gospel's light but truth that
shineth clear
And let the vices that abound confirm the present
prayer.

'The vaunt of the pretended gospel' [from 'Cecil's
commonwealth']

fb.40, p. 185

N0260 No Tuscan will a gentlewoman kiss,
The form of game to touch the dame, and play her.

Sir Thomas Urquhart, 'Why Italians kiss seldom,
without enjoying'

fb.217, p. 43

N0261 No venal praise shall prostitute my muse
Lives unbelov'd and unlamented dies.

H[annah] M[ore], 'The critic'

c.341, p. 75

N0262 No woman should her reputation baffle,
To let none mount her, but an Alexander.

Sir Thomas Urquhart, 'That ladies ought neither to
be too kind, nor too coy'

fb.217, p. 101

N0263 No wonder Madam you should die a maid,
Dress'd up in rotten chastity and pride.

[Mrs. Christian Kerr], 'To a maiden lady entering her
forty [i.e., fortieth year?], born 40 days before the
time, a satire made upon her own design'

c.102, p. 98

N0264 No wonder, Homer former was of lies,
His ears were but informers not his eyes.

'Homer'

c.356

N0265 No wonder O an angel in thy name
Angel signifies an ambassador.

[Sir Philip Wodehouse], 'Upon a fair lady sister to my
cousin John Winch Anna Ogle'

b.131, back (no. 42)

N0266 No wonder Pliny catch'd at praise,
Nor need we mind what others say.

[John Boyle], 5th earl of Orrery, 'On reading Pliny's
epistles'

c.50, p. 142

No267 No wonder Powis, Finch and Shore,
Or else that thou are mad.

    'A satire' [1701]

    fb.207/4, p. 39

No268 No wonder that man's mind so oft doth change
Of hot, cold, moist and dry, things changeable.

    c.158, p. 183

No269 No wonder that Oxford and Cambridge profound
And we meet with so few who bring any away.

    'Epigrams'

    c.546, p. 20; see also 'A wonder that science and
learning . . .'.

No270 No wonder, though the churches you o'erthrew;
Such odds: your fabrics b'ing invisible.

    Sir Thomas Urquhart, 'To those puritans, who
occasioned the downpulling of the churches of
Scotland'

    fb.217, p. 306

No271 No wonder wind[s] more dreadful are by far
Burn but the witch and all things will do well.

    'On the great storm' [26 November 1703; against the
Duchess of Marlborough]
[Crum N287]

    c.111, p. 54; c.189, p. 12

No272 No worldly pleasure can be truly sound,
Or earthly joy without allay be found.

    [from 'The amours of Alatheus and Eustathea']

    c.379/2, p. 149

No273 No youthful blood, nor blushing vein
At resurrection of the flesh. | So old, &c.

    'On an old man's wedding dying day' [upon Fleming
of Stanmore, 82, who married and died 12 October
1635]
[Crum N295]

    b.62, p. 124

No274 Nobility! Thou courtier's aim,
The pleasure,—glory of mankind.

    'On true nobility'

    c.94

No275 Noble Hephaestion see; Craterus flies
We both Craterus, and Hephaestion be.

    J[ohn] Hobart, 'Mr. Hob[art']s rejoinder'

    b.131, p. 39

No276 Nobles and heralds by your leave
Can Bourbon or Nassau go higher.

    Matthew Prior, 'Epitaph on . . . by himself'
[Crum N301a, 'Nobles and poets']

    fc.24, p. 61; see also 'Courtiers and heralds . . .', 'Heralds
and courtiers . . .'.

No277 Noble's the subject but yet hard to tell,
The world in flames had been again undone.

    'On the death of a young lady. Mrs. Susannah Layton'

    c.116, p. 1

No278 Nolms dips his brush in soot, and filth, and gall,
But the strong likeness proves—that 'tis his own.

    John Lockman, 'On reading a dirty libel published
against me, as Secretary of the Herring Fishery'

    c.267/1, p. 46

No279 None being esteem'd accomplished by rarer
Above the common styles of good, and fair.

    Sir Thomas Urquhart, 'Upon my Lady [crossed out]'

    fb.217, p. 355

No280 None can God's goodness e'er deny,
Man but returns, what he receives.

    [Edmund Wodehouse], 'Novr. 18 [1714]'

    b.131, p. 87

No281 None can how long and may how well none will
Live well will you live long Sir how well still.

    [Sir Thomas Urquhart], 'Of a long and good life'

    fb.217, p. 392

No282 None dieth more willingly than those that live
                                most honestly,
The coming of the Lord is nigh go reader go
                                prepare to die.

    'Epitaph no. 4'

    c.158, p. 47

No283 None from amongst all mankind, can be picked,
And being a fool, you are not for this world.

    Sir Thomas Urquhart, 'Neither in this world, nor in
the world to come. To a profane fool'

    fb.217, p. 271

No284 None in a greater measure doth procure
Can change your mind, where once you did affect.

    Sir Thomas Urquhart, 'To the Earl of [crossed out]'

    fb.217, p. 196

No285 None lives in this tumultuous state of things
Relieves the anguish or rewards the pain.

    [John] Pomfret, 'To a friend under affliction'

    fc.60, p. 42; c.244, p. 245 (var.)

N0286   None merit meat, who tasteth not the sour,
Who fears to climb deserves no fruit nor flower.

    c.339, p. 319

N0287   None of his wife but Adam was secure
And comfort is in's wife t'have confidence.

    'To the lawyers'

    c.356

N0288   None should debar their wives from liberty:
She that may do him wrong, and doth it not.

    Sir Thomas Urquhart, 'Why married women should
at all times have license to go where they please, and
yet not be suspected of unchastity'

    fb.217, p. 109

N0289   None truly love, but who are wise—the rest
Which chokes the father's love, son's piety.

    [Sir Philip Wodehouse], 'Paradoxon Arriani Epicteti
cum paraphrastica excursus solius sapientis et amare'

    b.131, p. 7

N0290   None will demand of matters, which are certain:
But I enquir'd not, if you be a whore.

    Sir Thomas Urquhart, 'One speaks here to a woman
who was so foolish, as to augment the stain of her
reputation, with impertinent, and frivolous questions'

    fb.217, p. 236

N0291   None, without hope, e'er lov'd the brightest fair
But love can hope when reason would despair.

    [George] L[yttelton], 1st baron Lyttelton, 'Maxims in
love' [no. 1]
    [Crum N313]

    c.487, p. 28

N0292   Nonsense made vocal, charms th'illit'rate mind,
Enchants the skillful head, and gen'rous heart.

    John Lockman, 'After reading an insipid Italian opera'

    c.267/1, p. 210

N0293   Nor Bath, nor Tunbridge can my lays inspire
I weep a father but I've lost a friend.

    [John Boyle], 5th earl of Orrery [or Mary Barber?],
'The answer by the earl of Orrery'

    Poetry Box x/76

N0294   Nor boist'rous will, nor fancies big apprise
Debell these rebels which art bold, but blind.

    [Sir Philip Wodehouse], 'Francis Gybon nor fancy's
big'

    b.131, back (no. 189)

N0295   Nor can fair Iris hide her silver streams
Angels divide, and saints the descant close.

    'Upon the death of Queen Anne'

    b.356, p. 158

N0296   Nor can your sex's easiness excuse
They're comets in the troubled air appear.

    'To the same. The excuse'

    Poetry Box v/106

N0297   Nor cease to aim but always strive to be
The queen and pride of women, as was she.

    'Mary AIRES anagramma I AYME SARA'

    b.62, p. 93

N0298   Nor Celia that I am more just
'Tis easy to be true.

    'Song'

    Poetry Box IV/53

N0299   Nor Cupid's darts, nor rural plains,
Thy loveliness in heaven expand.

    Charles Burney, the younger, 'The rose . . . July 26.
1780. Addressed to Mrs. Rose, of Mountcoster(?),
Banff'

    c.35, p. 55

N0300   Nor did heaven's chorister, the day's great star
As they seem'd glorious in the masque of night.

    'On the solemn triumphs of the gentlemen of the Inns
of Court . . . the masque presented before his Majesty'

    b.200, p. 119

N0301   Nor form nor talents reach beyond the grave
'My God does bless me,' and she smil'd at death.

    [ ] Kingsman, 'Verses written by . . . on the death of
Miss Kingsman Sepr. 26—1800'

    c.373, p. 82

N0302   Nor heaps of gold, nor monuments as high,
And nature reverences his supreme command.

    [William] Pattison, 'On poetry . . . addressed to Esq.
Tufton'

    c.244, p. 472

N0303   Nor is it griev'd (grave youth) the memory
Bring better notes, or choose another text.

    R[ichard] Corbett, 'The answer to Dr [Daniel] Price'
['So too dead Hector . . .']
    [Crum N323]

    b.200, p. 213

N0304   Nor length of time, nor multitude of men,
In restless pains 'mongst damned souls forever.

    Sir John Strangways, '8° Septr. 1646'

    b.304, p. 55

N0305 Nor love nor fate dare I accuse
For which alas I fall I die.

> [Richard Brome], 'Cant: 31' ['A song' in The northern lass, II.VI, 1632; answered by 'Should I the fates relentless move . . .']
> [Crum N325]
>
> b.4, fol. 27; b.62, p. 33 (incomplete); fb.69, p. 40

N0306 Nor must you, honored Madam, be forgot,
Forever yield a governor to the garrison.

> Dr. [ ] Nichols, chancellor of Carlisle, 'A gratulatory address to the Governor's lady [Dorothy Howard]'
>
> Poetry Box VII/7

N0307 Nor organist, nor fiddler, nor yet fool
Were never chanted by Will. Meredith.

> 'An answer to the scandal laid on Mr. [William] Meredith' [on Barten Holiday's Technogamia: or the marriage of the arts, 1621]
> [Crum N237b, 'No organist']
>
> b.200, p. 36

N0308 Nor 'scapes he so, our dinner was so good
He would have liv'd only to save his meat.

> [John Cleveland], 'Upon a miree [i.e., miser] that made a great feast, and died the next day for grief' [Crum N331]
>
> b.93, p. 5

N0309 Nor wings, nor feet, unto my share have fell,
That well performed, I've nothing left to ask.

> 'A riddle' [answered by 'She needs no wings . . .']
>
> c.578, p. 29

N0310 Nor wise, nor fool, need go to school
For *omnia vincit amor*.

> [Maurice Johnson], 'Epigram' [Virgil, Eclogue 10:69]
>
> c.229/2, fol. 18

N0311 Nor with less awe, in scenes of humble life
The boatswain whistles in a softer tone.

> Poetry Box XII/34

N0312 Norfolk sprang thee, Lambeth holds thee dead,
Heaven had not won, nor earth so timely lost.

> 'On Tho: Cleve esq. buried at Lambeth 1545'
>
> fb.143, p. 18

N0313 Northumberland! Fam'd patron of the arts,
The viceroy imitates the best of kings.

> John Lockman, 'To the right honorable the Earl of Northumberland: on his being appointed Lord Lieutenant of Ireland, 20 April 1763. Presented to him at Northumberland House, 22 Apr.'
>
> c.267/2, p. 399

N0314 Northumberland! Whose patriot deeds,
For truth and Percy are the same.

> John Lockman, 'Verses to his excellency the Earl of Northumberland: on hearing that his Majesty had graciously inquired, of one of the pages, last summer why I was not seen at court as usual. Writ at the Hermitage, in 1765'
>
> c.267/4, p. 388

N0315 Not all that are accounted great
And grasp true goodness there!

> 'On true and false nobility'
>
> c.83/2, no. 643

N0316 Not all the blood of beasts
And sing his bleeding love.

> [Isaac Watts, Hymns and spiritual songs (1707), bk. II, Hymn 142]
>
> c.180, p. 15

N0317 Not all the threats or favors of a crown
Who love fierce drivers, and a looser rein.

> [Charles Montagu, 3rd earl of Halifax], 'The man of honor' [occasioned by the postcript of Penn's letter, 1687]
> [Crum N345; *POAS* IV.159]
>
> b.115, fol. 10; c.244, p. 294; fb.108, p. 291; Poetry Box VI/62; Trumbull Box: Poetry Box XIII/93; Poetry Box X/146

N0318 Not brazen bars and tower
Since she regards my pain.

> 'The return'
>
> Poetry Box I/23

N0319 Not by his lands nor goods should we esteem
That covets much, than that possesseth little.

> [Sir Thomas Urquhart], 'Wherein true wealth [?] what truly rich we ought not to'
>
> fb.217, p. 525

N0320 Not Caesar when in Senate house
More parlous, and dead-doing blows.

> c.519

N0321 Not creature merit will I sing
The crucified name.

> [Thomas Stevens?], '1 Corinthians 1.23. Mr. Stevens Wedn[esda]y'
>
> c.259, p. 101

N0322 Not dead, not born, not christened, not begot
Which when thou dost untie, thou untiest Not.

> 'On one Mrs. Not'
> [Crum N356, 'which whilst thou readest']
>
> b.356, p. 245

N0323   Not destinies did thee sustain, nor fate
Am very sorry I have told a lie.

     'And answer to this contrary report' ['Much wine will
     make dead drunk . . .', on the death of the King's jester
     Archibald Armstrong]

     File 19344

N0324   Not far from Christ-Church, as you pass the street
I'd choose to walk afoot, or ride an Oxford hack.

     T[homas] H[olland, of Jesus College, Oxford, on the
     soldiers' wooden horse; 1715]
     [Crum N359]

     c.233, p. 67

N0325   Not fir-crown'd hill, and daisied mead,
The noblest bliss that life can give!

     'The visit in winter to ** *** esqr'

     c.89, p. 79

N0326   Not five hours ere the sun, the world's great eye,
Till the world blazes at the day of doom.

     'On the burning of London Bridge: 1633'

     b.200, p. 41

N0327   Not fonder joy the wand'ring Indian feels,
Sent to improve, delight, amaze the world.

     John Lockman, 'Prologue to The conscious lovers,
     acted in Covent Garden Theater, for the benefit of the
     lying-in hospital, Aldersgate Street; writ at the request
     of Slingsby Bethell esqr. (president), and the
     committee . . . 1757'

     c.267/3, p. 122 (with alternate ending of six lines: 'And,
     thro' the empire, desolation spread.')

N0328   Not for her sake, but for our own we grieve,
And make it fragrant, when the world's a flame.

     'An epitaph on Mrs. Margaret Fitz-herbert'
     [cf. Crum N360]

     c.244, p. 210

N0329   Not for the promise of the labor'd field,
Burst these terrestrial bonds, and other regions try.

     [Henrietta O'Neill], 'Ode to the poppy in Mrs. C.
     Smith's last volume . . .'

     Poetry Box III/50; c.83/3, no. 846 (attr. 'Geraldine
     Verney' [character in C. Smith's Desmond]); Poetry Box
     XII/10

N0330   Not from the stars do I my judgment pluck,
Thy end is truth's and beauty's doom and date.

     [William] Shakespeare [Sonnet XIV]

     c.94

N0331   Not from the verdant garden's cultur'd bound
Have been our gales, and lovers' tears our dew.

     [William Roscoe], 'Sonnet from the same' ['Lorenzo
     de Medici']

     c.142, p. 95

N0332   Not giddy lawless rabbles shall control
The radiant senate of the skies addrest.

     'Horace's 3d ode in his 3d book'

     Poetry Box I/25

N0333   Not Giornovich nor Cramer's softest note
Shall rank with glorious name—my faithful
                             Warner.

     L. Concannon, 'Mrs Rigby's answer to Vere Warner
     esqr'

     Greatheed Box/24

N0334   Not gold or pearl, or shining earth,
To reach the native skies.

     'Epitaph'

     c.113/26

N0335   Not high estate can give a [?] life
But God it is that blesseth man and wife.

     c.339, p. 315

N0336   Not how to pay your debt, you careful are:
But how you may not pay's your chiefest care.

     Sir Thomas Urquhart, 'To a bad debtor'

     fb.217, p. 268

N0337   Not kiss, by Jove I must and make impression
And then at cards we better shall agree.

     'The paradox'
     [cf. Crum N372]

     b.205, fol. 30r; see also 'Nay pish . . .'

N0338   Not lands but learning makes a man complete
Virtue not honor makes him fortunate.

     [John Rose?]

     b.227, p. 76; c.83/1, no. 138

N0339   Not like a flame by force extinguish'd,
But o'er her beauteous face e'en death had
                             semblance feign[ed].

     J. W. B., '[Written on the tomb of the Baroness de
     Schomberg in the English burial ground at Leghorn]
     translation [from Petrarch]'

     Diggle Box: Poetry Box XI/40

N0340   Not long after twelve—the minute no matter—
To your faithful sincere and affectionate friend.

     [Charles Earle], 'To ——— apothecary at Witheridge
     Ash Wednesday extempore'

     c.376; see also 'As sweets are abated . . .'.

N0341 Not long ago as you shall hear tell
That fain would thrust in but I said nay.

   a.6, p. 128

N0342 Not long ago, at Aberdeen
I'll show you, thrice as deep a pool.

   [Thomas Hamilton, 6th earl of Haddington], 'The careful wife'

   c.458/2, p. 153

N0343 Not many miles from Tunbridge town,
To be excluded a lampoon.

   [William Oldisworth]

   fb.66/10

N0344 Not mirth nor care alone, but interwreathed,
Care gets mirth stomach, mirth makes care long
                                                     breathed.

   'Mirth, and care intermixed'

   c.356

N0345 Not more the hungry, pilfering wretch
And silence prating gratitude.

   [Charles Burney, the elder], 'To [Mrs. Thrale] on her munificence'

   c.33, p. 120

N0346 Not nature's richest colors can
Is full of love, is full of grace.

   T[homas] S[tevens], 'Hymn by . . . Tuesday August 7th after prayers evening'

   c.259, p. 98

N0347 Not one of the wisemen though ever so knowing
But here's to the mouth that makes no words
                                                     about it.

   'Song 188'

   c.555, p. 299

N0348 Not only are they good who virtuously
That one is good if it so hides no evil.

   [Sir Thomas Urquhart], 'Of negative and positive good'

   fb.217, p. 521

N0349 Not only blessed in herself alone
Be blest, who shall be the next maid of honor.

   Francis Lenton, 'Upon the virtuous unchosen virgin Mrs. She that shall be / Anagram / All blest she hath'

   b.205, fol. 21v

N0350 Not pray to saints, is not the warrant ample
'Tis true, but tell me what was he that did it.

   [Francis Quarles], 'On praying to saints'

   b.137, p. 176

N0351 Not Rome in all its splendor could compare
And Mrs. Staffords [Strafford?] yield to Ballock
                                                     Hall.

   'Nobilitas sola atque unica virtus' [1680]
   [Crum N384; POAS II.200]

   b.371, no. 8/1

N0352 Not roses join'd with lilies, make
This is pure Platonic love.

   [George Daniel], 'Pure Platonic'

   b.121, fol. 76

N0353 Not Shakespeare's style! O fie for shame
The love of Dido for a man of Troy.

   John Belfour, 'To the author of the Rosciad [Charles Churchill] occasioned by his remark on the tragedy of Dido for Mr. Holland's benefit . . . the 13th April 1767'

   c.217, p. 137

N0354 Not sick in body but in mind most free
Of this my will I make executor.

   H[enry] C[olman], 'My last will, and testament'
   [Crum N386]

   b.2, p. 50

N0355 Not so majestic in thy chair of state
Thy collar's head, and soul are all in oil.

   'Upon the picture of his sacred Majesty (Charles the first) sitting before the court of injustice'

   b.137, p. 198

N0356 Not splendor influence or birth,
But men of sense, are men of worth.

   c.163, p. 10

N0357 Not streams of lightning with destructive glare,
To sound thy notes, and answer to thy voice.

   'To cousin Storges on her poem—The voyage—1718'

   b.322, p. 32

N0358 Not sweeter force the orator bestows,
Charming the eye, they slide into the heart.

   John Lockman, 'Writ under the picture of Mr. Champion, a celebrated writing-master'

   c.267/1, p. 244

N0359 Not that in color it was like thy hair
Because 'tis cordial, would 'twere at thy heart.

   [John Donne, 'Elegia decima . . . Satira una catena' [Elegy XI. The bracelet]
   [Crum N397]

   b.114, p. 97; b.148, p. 64; see also 'Thee I forgive . . .'.

N0360 Not that it is not made my fate
Is one perpetual round of vanity.

    [John] N[orris, of Bemerton], 'The discontent'

c.258

N0361 Not that there need a monument of stone
Her dust is precious, as her love was true.

    'Epitaphs (Milton Oxfordshire)'

c.546

N0362 Not that you need a caveat write I
You are advised, of lords and lads, beware.

    Francis Lenton, 'Upon that lovely nymph and
    attractive piece of nature Mrs. Elizabeth Howard /
    Anagram / Oh beware thy lads'

b.205, fol. 18r

N0363 Not the blithe shepherd, the consenting maid,
Paint their effects— but never feel their rage!

    W[illiam] P[arsons]

Greatheed Box/11

N0364 Not thy beauty with grief my heart fills,
Ah, how shall I learn to forget!

    'Sonnet on leaving Bath'

c.83/1, no. 240

N0365 Not to Phoebus, the muses, or any such aid
Or a dog, pretty Tinker, like you.

    'Ex trumpery ex tempore'

fc.40

N0366 Not to record thy worth lamented shade
Graced with the tribute of a sister's love.

    'An inscription on an urn in the hermitage wood at
    Stoke in Gloucestershire erected to the memory of
    Lord Botetourt'

c.341, p. 42

N0367 Not unto us Lord not unto us
Praise ye the Lord I say.

    [Thomas Norton], 'For defense from God in time of
    persecution. Psal. 48' [verses from Psalm 115]
    [Crum N410]

a.3, fol. 127v; c.264/3, p. 39

N0368 Not unto us, Lord, not to us
Through ages yet to come.

    'Psalm 115'

c.264/3, p. 39

N0369 Not who, but what, in men's discourse I'd know:
But in divine, I ask not what, but who.

    Sir Thomas Urquhart, 'Authority, and reason'

fb.217, p. 251

N0370 Not winds to voyagers at sea
Harmon's worlds on high.

    'Resurrection'

Poetry Box x/1

N0371 Not with more transport on the genial bed,
Convince the world, that all you seek's your own.

    'To a maiden lady [Mrs. Christian Kerr] on her
    birthday August 22, 1721 entering the fortieth first year
    of her age'

c.102, p. 129

N0372 Not yet the crude materials of the earth,
Shall be the lofty theme of my aspiring muse.

    [Elizabeth] (Singer) [Rowe], 'The creation'

c.244, p. 421

N0373 Nothing adds to your fond fire
And sell the rebel in your arms.

    [Elizabeth Wilmot, countess of Rochester], 'The
    answer' [to 'Give me leave to rail at you']

b.105, p. 137

N0374 Nothing I am, yet to all things belong,
And by myself, I ne'er appear alone.

    'A riddle'

c.578, p. 108

N0375 Nothing in earth so good I find
Shrewd life and short through her joys rare.

    [Sir Nicholas] Bacon, 'Against a mind not contented'

fa.8, fol. 164

N0376 Nothing in nature can be certain fixt
Of better verse, to sing his wonders o'er.

    [George Daniel]

b.121, fol. 31

N0377 Nothing is wanting on the world's great stage,
And think each day you live, you live to die.

    Thomas Cook, 'Simonides on human life'

c.244, p. 579; c.156, p. 178 ('Nothing is lasting . . .')

N0378 Nothing lies hid from radiant eyes,
The hearts you get return no more.

    [Edmund Waller], 'A song' [to Mary (Villiers) Stuart,
    Duchess of Richmond, upon her returning a lost
    letter]
    [Crum N424]

b.207, p. 28

N0379 Nothing on this side heav'n does so
The joys are of eternity.

    [Edmund Wodehouse], 'Aug. 3d [1715]'

b.131, p. 239

N0380 Nothing so much intoxicates the brain
Tho' praise to venom turns, if wrong applied.

  'The magic of flattery, or the agreeable imposition'
 c.186, p. 109

N0381 Nothing so rare in this vain world we find
Without the vast ring of eternity.

  [Mary Serjant]
 fb.98, fol. 151

N0382 Nothing so true as what you once let fall,
To you gave sense, good humor and a poet.

  [Alexander Pope], 'Characters of women. An epistle
  to a lady' [pr. 1735 (Foxon P917)]
 c.570/4, p. 162

N0383 Nothing thou elder brother even to a shade,
Flow swiftly into thee, and in thee ever end.

  [John Wilmot, 2nd earl of Rochester, 'Upon nothing
  [or somewhat of nothing]'
  [Crum N430]
 fb.142, p. 25; b.52/2, p. 173; b.369, p. 43; c.160, fol. 95;
 c.244, p. 95; b.105, p. 108; b.327, f. 9v; b.369

N0384 Nothing to travel can some men provoke,
Beyond the smell of native country's smoke.

 c.339, p. 312, p. 326

N0385 Nothing's so dear: yet vices common are:
But virtue's cheap: of all things the most rare.

  Sir Thomas Urquhart, 'That the rarest things
  according to the ordinary tenet, are not always the
  dearest'
 fb.217, p. 287

N0386 Nott as a maid, Nott a wife, Nott a widow, Nott a
              whore,
She was Nott these and yet all four.

  'On Mrs. Nott'
 c.81/1, no. 183

N0387 Nott born Nott died, Nott christened, Nott begot,
That whilst thou seems't to read, thou readest Nott.

  'Ditto [on Mrs. Nott]'
  [Crum N352]
 c.81/1, no. 184

N0388 November's chill blast on the rough beach is
              howling,
I can warm the cold heart of the wretched no more!

  [Charlotte (Turner) Smith], 'The female exile.
  Written at Brighthelmstone in 1792'
 c.141, p. 60

Now all is hush'd; the solemn chime   N0389
As pure as when it first was mine.

  M[atthew] G[regory] Lewis, 'Midnight hymn'
 Poetry Box XII/1; c.83/3, no. 889

Now all things seem to show a mien of war N0390
Where all are actors and none lookers-on.

  'Prologue to Alcamenes and Menelippa [by William
  Philips?] spoke by Menalippas' ma[torn]'
 Poetry Box I/111[11]

[Now] all you brave boys and high churchmen N0391
              draw near,
We know who'd enjoy axes, halters and carts. |
         Which nobody can deny.

 Poetry Box VI/39

Now at moonlight's fairy hour   N0392
Call on Echo to rejoice.

  [Ann (Ward)] Radcliffe, 'Air'
 c.83/3, no. 856

Now Aurora is up the sweet goddess of day, N0393
Fill your glasses, and toast to the King.

  'Song 12'
 c.555, p. 17

Now begin the heavenly theme,   N0394
Join to praise redeeming love.

  'Hymn 29th'
 c.562, p. 34

Now bitter cold winter comes on,   N0395
To see I'm a friend to myself.

  Gregory Oldnow, 'The way to keep a friend written
  by the late . . . a facetious singing shoemaker of
  Elkiston in Derbyshire . . .'
 c.361

Now [blot] righ[t]ed is my fate   N0396
And from that one, I fear I love.

  [Mrs. ( ) Feilding], 'May the 5, 1684. I was in danger
  of being killed with a coach, had not God's providence
  prevented it'
 b.226 (inside cover)

Now boasts Prince Pinery the game he breeds N0397
He must not shoot—not even shoot at—crows.

  'On a descendant'
 c.81/1, no. 475

Now Britain, now hold up thy head   N0398
We'll give them Brunswick mum.

  'An excellent new ballad' [pr. 1714 (Foxon E537)]
 Poetry Box IV/118

N0399 Now by your Jacob's staff may you desire one
When you apply it to the feeling sense.

> [Sir Thomas Urquhart], 'To one Mistress Lyon married to a gentleman whose name was Lamb'
>
> fb.217, p. 501

N0400 Now Cambridge is a merry town,
Fool for fool to change.

> ['A . . . ballad of Cambridge'; on Ruggle's Ignoramus]
> [Crum N452, with four more lines]
>
> b.197, p. 76

N0401 Now changes the transporting verdant scene
And with sweet voice proclaims that spring is nigh.

> Charles Atherton Allnutt, 'Winter. A descriptive poem my first attempt at verse'
>
> c.112, p. 63

N0402 Now comes mild Eve, but not its former charms,
Those pangs, which time, and time alone can cure.

> Tho[mas] Liddiard, 'Sonnet written in my illness . . . May 1793'
>
> c.344, p. 124

N0403 Now comes the Prince, for to convince
O wherry Whigs a woman.

> 'The battle of Gladsmuir to the tune of Wherry Whigs a woman'
>
> c.275

N0404 Now curses on you all! ye virtuous fools,
And acted somewhat, which might merit more
than Hell.

> [John] Oldham, 'A satire [against virtue] . . . written July 77'
> [Crum N463]
>
> b.105, p. 264; b.54, p. 986

N0405 Now did the rosy morn with blushes spread
I see the Lord in pity of mankind.

> Joseph Strutt, 'Abraham. A poem in blank verse by . . . author of the Dictionary of epigrams'
>
> c.342

N0406 Now did the saffron morn her beams display
Ending the fun'ral with a solemn feast.

> [William] Congreve, 'The lamentations of Hecuba, Andromache, and Helen over the dead body of Hector . . . from the Greek of Homer'
> [Crum N466]
>
> b.201, p. 131

N0407 Now down the steep of heav'n the source of day
And heav'n enjoy, when number'd with the dead.

> 'An evening thought'
>
> c.83/2, no. 642

N0408 Now early shepherds o'er the meadows pass,
When the next comes, I'll charm thee thus again.

> [Thomas] Parnell, 'An eclogue on health'
>
> c.244, p. 267

N0409 Now echo, on what's religion grounded? |
Roundhead.
Then God keep King and state from those same
men. | Amen.

> 'The echo'
> [Crum N470]
>
> fb.106(1); see also 'Say echo . . .'.

N0410 Now fair, and clear, the heavens are pleas'd to smile
My God, my glory, I have my desire.

> [George Daniel]
>
> b.121, fol. 33

N0411 Now farewell to Cupid's power,
I forever now am thine.

> [Helen Craik], 'To indifference'
>
> c.375, p. 59

N0412 Now, fie upon't quoth Flattery
Said everything I meant to say.

> [Philip Dormer Stanhope, 4th earl of Chesterfield?], 'Truth at court, written in 1761'
> [Crum N478]
>
> fc.51, p. 260; Spence Papers, folder 76

N0413 Now for a tune of lofty praise
And echoes thro' the heav'nly plains.

> [Isaac Watts, Hymns and spiritual songs (1707), bk. II, Hymn 42]
>
> c.180, p. 5

N0414 Now for some ages had the pride of Spain
With laurel in his hand, and half Peru.

> E[dmund] W[aller], 'On the victory over the Spaniards at St. Lugar. 1656'
> [Crum N484]
>
> b.63, p. 17

N0415 Now for some time the angry pow'rs above
Our fair ghost vanish'd—and my Muse withered
[too].

> 'The ghost sacred to the memory of the late Mrs. M—— and inscribed to J. C. esqr of the Middle Temple'
>
> Poetry Box v/99

N0416 Now from a slaughtered monarch's hearse I come
Whilst he bewail thy head he lose his own.

> [Robert Wild], 'The tragedy of Mr. Christopher
> Love, a preacher of the word at Lawrence-Jury who
> was beheaded at Tower Hill the 22nd of August 1651'
>
> b.104, p. 105; c.166, p. 217

N0417 Now frowning winter from the gladsome world
At Flavia's feet, and bled from every vein anew.

> 'Fruitless repentance. Timon and Flavia'
>
> c.244, p. 639

N0418 Now, gallants, have ye all spectators been
'Twas fit th'effect should finish with the cause.

> R[obert] Shirley, 1st earl of Ferrers, 'Epilogue. To the
> fall of Hannibal [1710]'
>
> c.347, p. 64

N0419 Now gath'ring clouds obscures the azure skies,
So gave consent at last to be his bride.

> I. W., 'The lucky shower. A pastoral tale'
>
> c.118, p. 58

N0420 Now genial spring a living warmth bestows,
Remend his tackle, and his rod retie.

> 'Spring'
>
> c.83/3, no. 917

N0421 Now God preserve, as you well do deserve,
Oh but log was too heavy to dance it.

> Ben Jonson, 'Ben Jonson's masque before the King'
> [extract from The masque of Christmas, 1616]
> [Crum N490]
>
> b.197, p. 132

N0422 Now great Hyperion to decline began,
But art in art's one dialect returns.

> 'Upon a nightingale'
>
> b.356, p. 66

N0423 Now had Britannia's sun, whose splendid rays
Might soar to heights, as yet unknown to fame.

> [William Dennis], 'On his grace the Duke of Dorset
> coming to Ireland in the year 1751'
>
> File 4314

N0424 Now had fair Cynthia, with her borrowed light,
And she requite my due obedience.

> 'For a masque fit for a wedding'
>
> fb.69, p. 235

N0425 Now had the son of Jove mature, attain'd
Crown'd with eternal youth: among the gods, a god.

> [Robert Lowth], 'The choice of Hercules'
>
> fc.132/1, p. 14

N0426 Now had the sun sunk to his liquid bed,
They all awakened in St. James's Square.

> 'The taking of Namur by Lieutenant General [Henry
> Sidney, earl of] Romney' [satire on a fireworks
> display, 1695]
> [Crum N496; POAS v.460]
>
> Poetry Box VII/22; fb.70, p. 163

N0427 Now happy England most, where justice is
embraced,
And eke so many famous men within her chair are
placed.

> c.339, p. 316

N0428 Now hardly here and there a hackney coach,
And schoolboys lag with satchels in their hand.

> [Jonathan Swift], 'A description of the town.
> Morning'
>
> c.83/1, no. 243; c.265, p. 4

N0429 Now hark now here my heart my dear
Which is a wondering sight to see.

> 'Braye Lute Book,' Music Ms. 13, fol. 26

N0430 Now has th'almighty Father seated high
By guile and force, and sway'd with lawless rage.

> [Elijah] Fenton, 'Isaiah 14th, part of it
> paraphrased by . . .'
>
> c.244, p. 520

N0431 Now have I run my race; and what though death
My soul takes sweet possession of a crown.

> 'In juvenem defunctum'
>
> b.205, fol. 49r

N0432 Now have our seas resign'd unto the shore
The best lieutenant to the best of kings.

> 'To his Grace James Duke of Ormonde Lord
> Lieutenant of Ireland upon his return to this kingdom
> and government'
>
> fb.228/36

N0433 Now hear me, O Molly, no longer I'm dying
Come drink about one two three—and three. |
Come drink &c.

> 'A new song'
>
> c.116, loose page inserted in front

N0434 Now hear the bell proclaim the farce is done
Good morrow masters all—I wish ye well.

> 'The epilogue to the bellman's paper'
>
> fc.130, p. 52

N0435 Now heaven be prais'd that I'm once more arrived
Thank your forgetfulness and . . . .

> b.216, p. 227 (incomplete)

N0436 Now Hoadley long had serv'd the good old cause,
But raise the teacher fifty cubits high.

b.90, p. 11

N0437 Now Hymen rivets his ungalling chain
Cherish the fond remembrance of your friend.

J. Taylor, of Norwich, 'To Miss Rigby on her marriage
with Dr. Parry 24th Septr. 1778'

c.364, p. 69

N0438 Now I am caught I must confess
How hard it is to enter.

'An amorous catch'

b.104, p. 15

N0439 Now I confess I am in love
No women should be fit for me.

b.213, p. 118

N0440 Now, I presume our moralizing knight,
On you it rest—to make your profit your delight.

[Sir Richard Steele?], 'Epilogue to The conscious
lovers (a comedy written by . . . and acted at the
theater in Drury Lane 1722) spoken by the celebrated
Mrs. Oldfield—but omitted in the printed play'

c.360/2, no. 88

N0441 Now I reflect, we have made a gross mistake
You have had much patience and we thank you for't.

'Epilogue [to The mourning bride, by William
Congreve] spoken by Zara'

File 19022

N0442 Now I you pray (sweet heart) an't may you please,
Will purchase both their hearts and breasts
together.

'On the French fashion'

b.356, p. 43

N0443 Now I'm prepared against my Lord doth come
Lord I'm ready call me then away.

Lady Jane Cavendish, 'Hope's preparation'
[Crum N508]

b.233, p. 39

N0444 Now I'm resolv'd the crazy universe
And all as you, become untimely gray.

'To the same. Thursday'

Poetry Box v/106

N0445 Now in a song of grateful praise
My Jesus has done all things well.

'Hymn 78th'

c.562, p. 100

N0446 Now in the gall'ries of his grace
Over the hills where spices grow!

[Isaac Watts, Hymns and spiritual songs (1707), bk. I,
Hymn 77]

c.180, p. 70

N0447 Now is majestic Sol in's highest clime,
When all things that are mortal must consume.

[John Rose?], 'Of the summer quarter'

b.227, p. 166

N0448 Now is the welcome night addrest
For so true love is tried.

'Sic elige uxorem amore more ore re'
[Crum N514]

b.62, p. 100

N0449 Now is your time, the vintage to prepare;
And prudence in the fair has room to shine.

'Verses under the pictures of the four seasons; for
Miss Herbert . . . autumn'

Spence Papers, folder 113

N0450 Now ladies glad be ye
If that he have a beard.

'In quosdam doctores medicos'

b.356, p. 268

N0451 Now, land, and sea with wars are gall'd so sore,
To which, this only is the introduction.

Sir Thomas Urquhart, 'The isagogue, or introduction
[to Urquhart's epigrams] whereby some reasons
therein being deduced for the several dedications, the
specified number of my epigrams . . .'

fb.217, p. 20

N0452 Now let me sit and feast mine eyes
On thee that art my paradise.

b.62, p. 120

N0453 Now let me tell before I make an end
Unto my grave, harp sing my dying song.

[envoy to a series of verses about the stars]

b.356, p. 114

N0454 Now let my cares all buried lie
To hide me in my grave.

[Isaac Watts], 'Upon the diurnal narrative of the
afflictions of a friend'

c.349, fol. 4v

N0455 Now let our drooping hearts revive
When we are cold in dust.

'A hymn. Ministers die, but Christ and his church live'

c.148, p. 10

N0456 Now let our pain be all forgot
And all our lives be praise.

    [Isaac Watts, Hymns and spiritual songs (1707),
    bk. III, Hymn 16]

    c.180, p. 51

N0457 Now let proud Albion cease to mourn
Nor shall when these rebels are dead.

    'Albion's glory reversed'

    b.111, p. 43

N0458 Now let the feeble all be strong
And still in him let Israel trust.

    [Philip Doddridge], 'Hymn 65th'

    c.562, p. 78

N0459 Now let the sons of Belial hear
Which sleep the sleep of death.

    P[hilip] Doddridge, 'The obstinate sinner alarmed
    Prov: XXI. 1'

    c.493, p. 67

N0460 Now let us all rejoice sing paeans all
Where none dare doubt but things are carried even.

    'Poems made by the King's Maj[es]ty' [translated
    from the Latin of James I; on Buckingham's being
    made admiral]

    Poetry Box VI/107

N0461 Now let's dance agreed agreed
We should rejoice we should rejoice.

    'Chorus' [with musical score for bass]

    Music MS. 534

N0462 Now listen good friends and I'll tell you how 'twas
And so he march'd out of the town-a.

    'A proper new balled, concerning the reception of . . .
    the Duke of Buckingham, by . . . the mayor of . . .
    Oxon [William Morrell]: 1677 to the tune of
    Cuckolds all a row or Tom Tyler'
    [POAS I.430]

    b.54, p. 1056

N0463 Now Lord have mercy on us all, a strange thing
                            I'm to tell
See that your wicked [ ] declines which else will
                          bring you smart.

    'To the tune of Help Lords and Commons &c.'

    b.54, p. 913 (incomplete)

N0464 Now Lord I beg of Thee before I pray
That in Christ's blood, to bathe me purely white.

    Lady Jane Cavendish
    [Crum N530]

    b.233, p. 40

N0465 Now may the God of love appear
The goodness of the Lord.

    T[homas] S[tevens]

    c.259, p. 77

N0466 Now meek-eyed evening sheds her balmy dews,
Soft sleep the dust of the deserving shade.

    G[eorge] Huddesford, 'Elegy' [on Eliza Huddesford,
    d. 2 May 1768]

    c.156, p. 94

N0467 Now 'mid thy vistas (sweet Vauxhall!) I'm found:
Charm'd with the world, collected in our isle.

    John Lockman, 'After viewing a representation, of the
    ruins of Palmyra, in Vauxhall Gardens . . . June 1754'

    c.267/1, p. 147

N0468 Now, my boys let's dance and sing
No grog—and little wind, boys.

    'Song 3'

    c.555, p. 2

N0469 Now nature smiles in youthful beauty gay,
A passion more exalted and refined.

    [ ] A., 'Pastor fido sc. 1. a. 1'

    c.368, p. 207

N0470 Now night had spread her spangled canopy
Sweeten'd their hearts, and lull'd their cares away.

    'Night'

    c.83/1, no. 6

N0471 Now now Lucatia, now make haste
And now they call away away. | . . . And now, oh
                              now, am dead.

    [Sir John Birkenhead], 'Lucatia admired'
    [Crum N539]

    fb.107, p. 37

N0472 Now, now, resolve th'authentical record
This late began he left unended thus.

    [Francis Quarles], 'On Joseph and his service in Egypt
    and his advancement'

    b.137, p. 142

N0473 Now now the sun is fled
And warming us with a better fire than he.

    [William Cartwright], 'A song the slaves called for
    being merrily drinking . . .' [from The royal slave,
    1636]

    b.200, p. 157

N0474 Now only wealth prevails, let him be base
Each quarter gives account of war and trade.

    ''Tis money makes a man'

    c.578, p. 10

N0475　Now Patrick genius of Hibernia's isle
　　　　And then return to their original.

　　　　　'Narraghmore Fair March 17. 1747'
　　　　File 13409

N0476　Now peace and her sweets are come once more
　　　　Let us smile and hope all for the best.

　　　　　[Thomas Hull]
　　　　c.528/51

N0477　Now Phoebus did with frowns the world survey
　　　　And Mashamites supprest the Churchill-race.

　　　　　[William Walsh], 'Mrs Masham's lamentation an
　　　　　imitation of Homer' [pr. 1708 (Foxon A3)]
　　　　　[Crum N545, with two more lines; POAS VII.302]
　　　　Trumbull Box: Poetry Box XIII/77; Poetry Box IV/110
　　　　('with groans'; as in Crum)

N0478　Now Phoebus sinketh in the west,
　　　　With their grave saws in slumber lie.

　　　　　'Song 122'
　　　　c.555, p. 176

N0479　Now Phoebus slacks his summer-burning rays
　　　　Do still repine, possess they ne'er so much.

　　　　　[John Rose?], 'Of the autumn quarter'
　　　　b.227, p. 167

N0480　Now popish Jemmy is gone into France
　　　　We'll forfeit in earnest and take it in jest.

　　　　c.160, fol. 108

N0481　Now precious lovers ladies all
　　　　Be precious or else say nay for shame.

　　　　　'Braye Lute Book,' Music Ms. 13, fol. 52v

N0482　Now priests whose sacred office is to bring
　　　　But they the breath that makes the flame, inspire.

　　　　　Sir John Denham, 'Pretenses to religion'
　　　　c.244, p. 425

N0483　Now reigns aloft the glorious sun,
　　　　And lovely havoc strews the plains.

　　　　　'Summer'
　　　　c.83/3, no. 918

N0484　Now rhymes are sanctified, and purg'd
　　　　Our poets' fundamental laws.

　　　　　'On Mr Prynne's admirable poems concerning rocks,
　　　　　and seas, called Mount Orguiel'
　　　　b.200, p. 288

N0485　Now sets golden beams we their influence own
　　　　Don't let an old servant stand last on the poll.

　　　　　'Prologue spoken by Mr. Quick the first night of his
　　　　　performance at the Liverpool Theater'
　　　　c.115

N0486　Now shall I never more dread death's grim frown
　　　　With our Creator, and our fears are laid.

　　　　　[Petrarch]
　　　　b.211, p. 63

N0487　Now sharpen your wits, for you'll not be well
　　　　　　　　　　　　　　　　　　　　　　　　pleas'd
　　　　Is less airy and light than a feather.

　　　　　[charade]
　　　　Greatheed Box/102

N0488　Now show and sound their charms dispense,
　　　　But all have eyes and ears.

　　　　　'An epigram on the present state of the stage. 1792'
　　　　c.94

N0489　Now Sol, descending from his midday blaze,
　　　　Upon the victor's lyre she falls, she dies!

　　　　　'Fidicinis et Philomela certamen (from Strada)'
　　　　c.250

N0490　Now spare your censures, sons of earth;
　　　　Pursue the path that leads you to the dead!

　　　　　Charles Atherton Allnutt, 'A Michaelmas satire on a
　　　　　Christmas box being a book of musical notes,
　　　　　containing (amongst other childish bagatelles) Goosy,
　　　　　goosy gander—See saw saccaradaw &c.'
　　　　c.112, p. 168

N0491　Now stood Eliza, on the wood-crown'd height,
　　　　And clasp'd them sobbing to his aching breast.

　　　　　[Erasmus] Darwin, 'Eliza'
　　　　c.82, p. 16

N0492　Now Strephon the poet has safely brought forth,
　　　　As his verses are twins on the subject of shoes.

　　　　Poetry Box X/66

N0493　Now sweet is this nosegay how charming it blows
　　　　And adore my kind Father above.

　　　　　'In a nosegay'
　　　　c.83/2, no. 285

N0494　Now thank[s] to fate no more I rove
　　　　For she kind girl loves me.

　　　　c.549, p. 127

N0495 Now that, dire shootings in my brain,
Did ever mortal boast such friends?

    John Lockman, 'The review: writ in sickness; my wife
    and eldest little girl being ill, in the same bed . . .
    April, 1744'

    c.267/1, p. 95

N0496 Now that, Doctor Dick, I have some time
O now I have it—I'm your friend | N. Herbert

    N[ewcomen] Herbert, 'Dublin, Decbr. 3. 1743' [to
    Richard Shackleton]

    File 7202

N0497 Now that my years so numerous are,
So the bliss my faith takes f[l]ight of here.

    [Edmund Wodehouse], 'Dccr. 8 [1714]'

    b.131, p. 108

N0498 Now that rebellion's almost at an end,
'The use of the broadsword—for broad-bottom's use.'

    [N.] Herbert, 'Epigram on the use of the broad-sword
    by T. Page'

    Spence Papers, folder 91

N0499 Now that summer's ripen'd bloom
Closing in an azure sky.

    John Cunningham, 'A landscape'

    c.139, p. 46

N0500 Now, that the heat of youth inflames my brain
For your offences.

    Sir Thomas Urquhart, 'Time prevaileth so over the
    fancies of men, that ordinarily it will make them
    disgust what formerly they relished with greatest
    delight'

    fb.217, p. 360

N0501 Now that the wings of adverse fate are spread,
As reason dictates, and as God imparts.

    Charles Atherton Allnutt, 'Familiar epistle to the
    Revd. Mr. Pentycross. Written at a time of great
    dejection of soul on account of sin'

    c.112, p. 127

N0502 Now that the winter's gone, the earth hath lost
June in her eyes, in her heart, January.

    [Thomas Carew], 'The spring'
    [Crum N563]

    b.200, p. 113

N0503 Now the blush of the morn streaks with gold the
                           grey East,
To show how much joy they feel, cry.

    'Verses on the morning'

    Poetry Box IV/69

N0504 Now the bottles are come
Sweet peace, and long life crown the King. |
                        Now the bottles &c.

    '1 song'
    fb.228/60

N0505 Now, the dear, long expected moment's nigh,
Draw the verdant curtains round.

    John Lockman, 'The enraptured nymph. Set by Lewis
    Granom esqr . . . anno 1729'

    c.267/2, p. 98

N0506 Now the declining sun 'gan downward bend
Struck with a virtuous emulation.

    Will[iam] Strode, 'A translation of the nightingale out
    of Strada'
    [Crum N568]

    b.200, p. 169

N0507 Now the golden morn aloft
To him are opening paradise.

    T[homas] Gray, 'Ode on the pleasure arising from
    vicissitude'

    c.142, p. 384

N0508 Now the leaden year is done.
England thy guidance will forever rue.

    'Farewell to the year 1772' [Owen's weekly chronicle,
    2 January 1773]

    c.157, p. 97

N0509 Now the reformer of the court and stage
Learn to write well, or not to write at all.

    'The club' [on John Dryden]
    [POAS II.328]

    b.371, no. 1, with last line of 'How dull and how
    insensible . . .'.

N0510 Now the spring enters, now the sun doth cheer
Notes with the lark, be sportive with the lamb.

    [George Daniel]

    b.121, fol. 54

N0511 Now the sun hath left the skies,
Soars to hail the rising sun.

    E. W., 'Night, a pastoral, in the manner of
    Cunningham'

    c.142, p. 134

N0512 Now the veil is pulled off and this pitiful nation
Are turned into pious committees.

    'Barefaced villainy'
    [Crum N573]

    b.111, p. 463

N0513 Now the weather is warm,
And our wenches shall sew on the changes.

　　'The merry match'
　　fb.107, p. 74

N0514 Now the woodland chorists sing
Where ambition droops and dies.

　　'Song 177'
　　c.555, p. 273

N0515 Now things wax old and old things are renewed
Thus men are pleas'd with a vicissitude.

　　'Garments'
　　c.356

N0516 Now thou hast seen aspiring Dudley's son,
Rise upon him; and all his bastard brood.

　　'Epilogue to The Lady Jane Grey addressed to the
　　Prince'
　　c.570/1, p. 24

N0517 Now thou hast starved me one whole day
For by tomorrow I may think so too.

　　J[ohn] D[onne]
　　[Crum N577]
　　b.148, p. 108

N0518 Now thy servant Lord release
God incarnate, God of love.

　　'Song of Simeon, or Nunc dimittis'
　　c.264/3, p. 116

N0519 Now 'tis the King's health
Confusion to them, that would set it up again. |
　　　　　　　　　　　　　　　Huzza huzza huzza.

　　'Song' [Jacobite poem, c. 1715]
　　fc.58, p. 25

N0520 Now to the Lord a noble song!
And sing His name to harps of gold!

　　[Isaac Watts, Hymns and spiritual songs (1707), bk. II,
　　Hymn 47]
　　c.180, p. 32

N0521 Now uninspir'd the artless poet sings,
With warmer transports and diviner fires.

　　R. Barford, 'Occasioned by [Mrs. Mary Jones'] snuff'
　　[answered by 'When poets uninspir'd . . .']
　　c.233, p. 88

N0522 Now we are met in a knot,
For the Church nor the farmers' purses.

　　[Alexander Brome?], 'The charm' [on the new
　　Protector]
　　fb.140, p. 10; see also 'Now we're met . . .'.

N0523 Now we're free from college rules
That *nunc tempus est bibendum*.

　　'Song 157'
　　c.555, p. 236

N0524 Now we're met in a knot
And here's a good health to Rowland.

　　[Alexander Brome? on the new Protector]
　　b.213, p. 80; see also 'Now we are met . . .'.

N0525 Now when a limb is lopt away,
To cut away, the useless testes.

　　'On quackery'
　　c.481, p. 108

N0526 Now when stern winter giveth place to spring
Then get a noble case and even the [?] man.

　　[John Black]
　　fc.107, after p. 85

N0527 Now while from life's meridian heights I gaze,
From every faithless joy I follow thee.

　　[Thomas Wilkinson], 'Life an elegy'
　　c.139, p. 278

N0528 Now whilst Whitehall wears black and men do fear
Grief shall dissolve them, no Protector need.

　　Robert Wild, 'Upon the death of Dennis Bond esqr.
　　who died at Westminster four days before the Lord
　　Protector' [30 Aug. 1658]
　　[Crum N598]
　　b.186 (end); b.52/1, p. 112

N0529 Now worn with years, and yet in folly strong
I pipe no longer than you care to dance.

　　Colley Cibber, 'An epilogue made and spoken by . . .
　　in The old bachelor [by William Congreve] . . .'
　　fb.142, p. 70

N0530 Now you who love riddles and guess them so well,
It has often been said I'm as handsome as you.

　　'Enigma [76a]'
　　c.389

N0531 Now, young-eyed spring, on gentle breezes borne,
And gild existence in her dim decline.

　　Anna Seward, 'Sonnet' [1787]
　　[Crum N604]
　　c.141, p. 271

N0532 Numbers of foolish youths so strive to fill
On his own self gives nothing to the poor.

　　[Sir Thomas Urquhart], 'The greatest wasters are
　　greatest niggards a paradox'
　　fb.217, p. 533

No533 Nurs'd in the navel of thy native land,
Yet o'er the dread confusion, order reigns.

William Parsons, 'Epistle from Naples to Bertie
Greatheed esq. At Rome'

Greatheed Box/51

No534 Nymph of the groves, who erst on land's plains,
And peaceful glide through life's sequestered vale.

[William Boscawen], 'Inscription for an arbor in
Whichwood Forest. Written when the author was at
Eton School.'

fc.106, p. 1

No535 Nymph of the rock! Whose dauntless spirit braves
Thou and mild hope, shall teach me how to die.

[Charlotte (Turner) Smith], 'Sonnet to fortitude'

c.504, p. 97

Nymph of the stream where Chalford spreads, No536
That heart—too hard before.

c.83/2, no. 272

Nymph of this sacred place I guard its stream No537
To break my rest; drink, or bathe, silent here.

M[aurice] J[ohnson], 'Hujus nympha loci sacri . . .
Englished'

c.229/2, fol. 14v

Nymph! that flies the crowded street, No538
Come and make all nature gay.

J. C., 'Ode to health'

Spence Papers, folder 113

Nymph the fount from whose auspicious urn No539
Glide gently on; and imitate thy spring.

Poetry Box I/110

O

00001 Oaken leaves and in the wood so wide
Lullaby mayst thou sing.

'Catches [1]'
b.356, p. 71

00002 Obedient he flew at her smiling command
Though he came for her foot, but she gave him her
hand.

'On a young lady marrying a surgeon whom she sent
for, on account of a sprained foot'
Diggle Box: Poetry Box xi/68, 69

00003 Obedient to fate's tyrant call,
As pledges lie, until redeem'd.

'Epitaph on a pawnbroker'
c.113/18

00004 Obey her dictates, at her altar bend,
For all the righteous in the realms above.

Ann Murry [on virtue]
c.248

00005 Obscurest night involv'd the sky,
And whelm'd in deeper gulfs than he.

[William] Cowper, 'The castaway'
c.142, p. 573

00006 Observe my soul how everything
May all things bow to thee alone.

[John Austin], 'Hym. 19' [Hymn vi, Devotions in the
ancient way of offices, 1672, p. 65]
c.178, p. 18

00007 Observe the weary birds ere night be done
And not restore my life, but close my eyes.

K[atherine] P[hilips], 'On a friend's absence'
b.118, p. 56

00008 Obsess'd religion, heavenly fair,
And soften ev'ry grief.

'On religion'
c.83/1, no. 65

00009 Och I'm just now arrived from the ocean
'Twould never do for Larry O'Brien.

[John Walker?], 'Larry O'Brien'
fc.108, fol. 1v

00010 'Od's dickens, Maro, why dost look so sad?
I'll kill him dead, and throw him in the brook.

'To the Revd. Mr. John Johnson M. A. Maro and
Daphnis a pastoral on the death of Maurice Johnson
senr. esqr. his grandfather'
c.229/1, fol. 97

00011 'Od's fish! what wicked rhyming's here
Why not; as well as other's paper?

Rupert Barnesley, 'Billingsgate'
Poetry Box vi/106

00012 'Od's life we are undone
Turn which way we will, we are undone.

'The royal cuddens [cousins?] a poem being a dialogue
between the King and the Duke: wrote in July 1678'
b.54, p. 1091

00013 O'er crackling ice, o'er gulfs profound,
Thus lightly skim, and haste away.

[Samuel] Johnson, [translation of a French poem]
c.504, p. 89

00014 O'er distant lands and seas I swiftly roam
Sense and fidelity I ne'er forsake.

'[Enigma/Charade/Conundrum] 2' [thought]
c.389; c.153, p. 81

00015 O'er faded heath-flow'rs spun, or thorny furze
Leave but the wither'd heath, and barren thorn!

[Charlotte (Turner) Smith], 'Sonnet. The gossamer'
c.141, p. 102

00016 O'er half the convex world the ocean spreads,
I love the placid stream, the silent shore.

William Parsons, 'Sonnet'
Greatheed Box/12

00017 O'er hills and thro' forests Sir Olaf he wends
For there lay Sir Olaf, pale breathless and dead.

'The Erlking's daughter'
[Crum O11, 'through valleys . . . sped']
Poetry Box iv/51

00018 O'er ice the rapid skater flies,
Thus lightly touch and quickly go.

[Samuel] Johnson, [translation of a French poem]
c.504, p. 88

00019 O'er Ilion's plains, where once the warrior bled,
His children, wife, and happy home shall see.

    [Ann (Ward)] Radcliffe, 'Stanzas'

c.83/3, no. 872

00020 O'er life's clear stream, no cloud of sorrow brood,
No more of this—nor can I write for tears.

    'Fragment . . . Turk's Head Tavern Strand 1792'

c.344, p. 84

00021 O'er man man's fall to death the victory gave
Which makes our life short, our death doth bring.

    'Crosby Ravensworth churchyard . . . Christopher
Jaques Feb. 6. 1699'

c.547, p. 332

00022 O'er moorlands and mountains, rude, barren and
                               bare,

And shepherds have nam'd her Content.

    J[ohn] Cunningham, 'Content—a pastoral'

fc.132/1, p. 96

00023 O'er Pindus late, devoid of care!
Their son's, their poets' health went round.

    [Stephen Barrett], 'To my much-honored friend
Mr. Cuthbert Wilson upon his recovery from a fever
and rheumatism in the head: under the care of Dr. Pit.
at Oxford'

c.193, p. 9

00024 O'er sea and land I take my flight
Your heart has oft gone pit-a-pat.

    'Another [riddle]'

Diggle Box: Poetry Box XI/71

00025 O'er the dim breast of ocean's wave
Thy low winds breathe the distant shores along!

    'Night'

c.83/3, no. 860

00026 O'er the ice, as o'er pleasure you lightly should glide,
Both have gulfs which their flattering surfaces hide.

    Sir [ ] Lucas, [translation of a French poem]

c.504, p. 89

00027 O'er the mountain's airy height,
Soaring, close the distant view.

    'Crummock Water'

c.142, p. 332

00028 O'er the vine-cover'd hills, and gay regions of
                             France,

May he bind the decree on his heart!

    'A song on the French revolution. 1791'

fc.132/1, p. 217

00029 O'er the wide heath the whist'ling northeast blows
And like this barren waste, the world to me!

    [Frances Burney d'Arblay], 'Sonnet. Written at
midnight'

c.486, fol. 15

00030 O'er the wild heath, at early dawn,
And, blessing her, preserve me blest.

    [William Boscawen], 'Ode to contentment'

fc.106, p. 12

00031 O'er this lov'd tomb affliction drops her tear
And crown thy virtues with an angel's name.

    'An epitaph on ———'

c.341, p. 37

00032 O'er this marble drop a tear
And she with all mankind.

    [Mary (Molesworth) Monck], 'Epitaph on Rosalinde'
[Crum 015]

c.360/3, no. 32

00033 O'er Windsor's turrets pour'd th'impetuous show'r,
Raise to his kindred skies my Pinchy's name.

    H[enry] Skrine, 'Elegy on the death of Mr. Pinchbeck
mechanic, electrician, artist, and philosopher, the
friend, instructor, and adviser of George the 3rd . . .
London April 4 1783'

c.509, p. 60

00034 O'erjoy'd my artless lyre I strung,
Some future muse shall these proclaim.

    John Lockman, 'On the birthday of his royal highness,
George Prince of Wales, 4th June 1760. Presented to
his royal highness at Savile House'

c.267/2, p. 309

00035 Of a doctor turned patient a story I tell,
Thus far I can tell you—the doctor's at college.

    T[homas] H[olland], of Jesus College, Oxford, 'A
journey to Oystermouth, a ballad'

c.233, p. 62

00036 Of a late wedding's celebration
Soon get a husband, or a wife.

    [Elizabeth (Shirley) Compton, countess of
Northampton], 'A ballad, to the tune of The beggar of
Hull . . . on Sally Johnson's and Dicky Adcock's
wedding'

Accession 97.7.40 (2 copies)

00037 Of all ill poets by their lumber known
Might without Indian gowns keep th'author warm.

    [Sir John Denham], 'To the tune of Fortune my foe'
[on Sir William D'Avenant]
[Crum 027]

pb.53, p. 16 (incomplete, autogr.)

00038 Of all kinds of life were I but to choose
He's as good a Christian as ever he was.

> b.209, p. 69

00039 Of all men usurers are not least accurst
Which makes the lab'rers lean the idle fat.

> [Francis Quarles?], 'On usurers'
> b.137, p. 189

00040 Of all my cares and all my pains,
Let me forever be forgot.

> 'Epitaph on myself 20th May 1742'
> fb.142, p. 10 (second series)

00041 Of all our bards, there's none deserve renown
Will be accepted, for the giver's sake.

> [Thomas Hamilton, 6th earl of Haddington], 'To
> Gloriana, with The beggar's opera'
> c.458/2, p. 174

00042 Of all quality whores modest Betty for me
Sweet Cavendish in c—t and bold Frank at her a—.

> 'A ballad'
> b.113, p. 203

00043 Of all that pray in church, you are the couple,
Who may say, abba father, with least scruple.

> Sir Thomas Urquhart, 'To the two bastard sons of an
> abbot'
> fb.217, p. 262

00044 Of all the animals in earth or sea,
I'd change my shape, and be a man again.

> c.189, p. 180

00045 Of all the arts that soothe the human breast,
This, each one proves, who hears thy heavenly
strains.

> [John Lockman], 'Written under the print signed by
> Mr. Van Haacken, representing a lady playing on the
> harpsichord'
> c.268 (first part), p. 16

00046 Of all the authors that have wrote on hope
Wit, judgment, eloquence, all Pope are thine.

> 'On reading Pope's works'
> c.341, p. 101

00047 Of all the causes which conspire to blind
Truth breaks upon us with resistless day.

> [Alexander] Pope, 'Pope's picture of pride, the vice
> exposed, and from whence it flows'
> c.94 (ll. 201–212 of Essay on Criticism)

00048 Of all the crimes, to which mankind
Get nothing but an empty mortar.

> [Thomas Hamilton, 6th earl of Haddington], 'The
> mortar from Boccace'
> c.458/2, p. 30

00049 Of all the delicates which Britons try
To give a softness to the tartar juice.

> [Leonard] Welsted, 'Apple pie a poem'
> fb.142, p. 63

00050 Of all the dull, unthinking, would-be wits,
And bid that wakeful dragon, fierce resentment
sleep.

> 'On M—— C—y. A satire'
> c.530, p. 181

00051 Of all the dunces in the town
Take warning! Dr. Squintum.

> 'The wolf in sheep's clothing or advice to the
> Methodist tune of Nancy Dawson'
> Poetry Box x/48, 80 (incomplete)

00052 Of all the factions in the town,
Nor traitor like Jack Presbyter.

> 'The Geneva ballad' [1674; sometimes attr. Samuel
> Butler]
> [Crum 038; POAS 1.313]
> fb.207/3, p. 1; Poetry Box VII/71

00053 Of all the fools that pride can boast,
And vanity besots 'em all.

> [John] Gay
> c.391

00054 Of all the gods, that rule in heaven above,
Come Eginard, receive your royal bride.

> [Thomas Hamilton, 6th earl of Haddington], 'Omnia
> vincit amor, et nos cedamus amori' [Virgil, Eclogue
> 10:69]
> c.458/2, p. 167

00055 Of all the Grecian worthies most renown'd,
In hallow'd transports of paternal joy.

> [William Hayley], 'Sonnet . . . Feb 11 [1800]'
> File 6968

00056 Of all the handsome ladies
Does bear away the bell.

> [c. 1713]
> Poetry Box x/89

00057 Of all the Kirkharte bonny lasses,
Were I in bed with the lass.

'The insipids, or the mistress with her multitude of
manservants. A song'

c.530, p. 57

00058 Of all the lands of God's creation,
Should make attempts, for liberty.

[Thomas Hamilton, 6th earl of Haddington], 'The
consequence of jealousy from Boccace'

c.458/2, p. 20

00059 Of all the mortal enemies that take part
Against my peace, to keep me from my heart.

'On man's greatest enemy'

b.118, p. 222

00060 Of all the prophets that divinely wrote
And haughty maid whoe'er resembles thee.

[Thomas] Rymer, 'Why Antonia is afraid of a mouse'
Poetry Box VI/99

00061 Of all the race of animals, alone,
And to their own congenial planets fly.

'On the bees'

c.83/2, no. 594

00062 Of all the rare inventions
Platonics never do.

'Song 50'

b.4, fol. 39v

00063 Of all the sots with which the nation's curs'd
'Tis better live a fop than die a fool.

'The present state of matrimony'
[Crum 062]

b.113, p. 179

00064 Of all the spectacles to mend the sight
Must carry in their heads, and in their pockets eyes.

[Francis Fawkes], 'A pair of spectacles'

fc.21, p. 23

00065 Of all the taxes laid on human pride,
Is comprehended in the verb—obey.

[Frederick Corfield], 'Precedence'

c.381/1

00066 Of all the things beneath the sun,
No soul can wish him worse.

'Song 127'

c.555, p. 181

00067 Of all the thousands, Sodom once contain'd
One fair in twenty could not save the rest.

'Verses sent to Miss Vere, she being one of the ladies
present at the concert, mentioned in the above verses'

c.360/2, no. 35

00068 Of all the torments all the cares
But not another's hope.

[Sir John Vanbrugh], 'The rival' [1698]
[Crum 063]

c.229/1, fol. 49

00069 Of all the trades in England
Attend them ever more; | and a-begging we will
go &c.

'The sturdy beggar a poem' [1733; against Walpole's
excise bill]

File 13409; c.570/3, p. 209 ('in London')

00070 Of all the twelve St. Andrew leads the van
As thee t'attend may quit our mortal bark.

[Edward] Sparke, 'Poem 19—on St Andrew'

b.137, p. 47

00071 Of all the various wonders wit can do,
Your candor—no—your judgment be his fame.

Colley Cibber, 'Epilogue to Eugenia. Written by . . .
Poet Laureat—spoken by Mrs. Pritchard'

c.360/3, no. 194

00072 Of all the wonders since the world began
When all fools write: to think no more of rhyme.

'Barbara piramidum sileat miracula Memphis . . . the
answer to Essay on satire' [pr. 1680 (Wing E3299)]

b.327, f. 16v; b.113, p. 1; b.371, no. 7

00073 Of all the writers of the Roman part
Thy confutation, if we drink up all.

[Sir Aston Cokayne], 'Of Cardinal Bellarmine'
b.275, p. 96

00074 Of Arab's nose let's hear no more,
For on that point he's rather sore.

'Arabin now waxes warm upon which a friendly poet
exclaims—'

fc.76.iii/214

00075 Of arts I sing, to advance a spirit,
Chang'd shield of man for that of woman.

'The progress of that species of discretion mentioned
by Swift, exemplified in the life and character of
Mr. F—h Fellow of ——'s College'

Poetry Box IV/8

00076 Of blessings, dear Mother, since health is the best
Oh, trust me, dear Mums, I'll ne'er hunt again.

'The forest hunt'
c.83/2, no. 357

00077 Of Carthage great I was a stone,
Buried in the dust.

'On a stone adjoining to Stepney Church'
[Crum 077]
fb.143, p. 24

00078 Of Clineus and Dametus sharper fight
For giant Bob like Will's a dwarf in sense.

[Charles Sackville, 6th earl of Dorset], 'The quarrel'
[William Wharton and Robert Wolseley, 1697]
[Crum 084]
b.219, p. 33

00079 Of cobbler's tenements involv'd in smoke
Black blood and clotted gore, their galligaskins
                                                    stains.

[ ] Needham, 'On the Mohawks'
c.170, p. 21

00080 Of different sex the human kind was made,
But man if he deliberate—is sav'd.

[William Parsons]
Greatheed Box/53

00081 Of doubtful race was Georgy,
What does her here, pox on her!

'A new ballad' [pr. 1718? (Foxon E565)]
fc.58, p. 141

00082 Of earls for dignity, and ancient rare,
That all your faculties seem most divine.

Sir Thomas Urquhart, 'To the Earl of [crossed out]'
fb.217, p. 43

00083 Of envy you'll own that most men have a tint
When I'm dead on my tomb—just to follow *Hic jacet*.

J. Johnson, 'An ironical epistle to the Revd. Mr. Pigott
in answer to the above' ['Whilst cities and
boroughs . . .']
Poetry Box IV/153

00084 Of ev'ry day, ev'n ev'ry hour we live,
Justice binds them, whose pride scorns to repent.

[Edmund Wodehouse], 'Aug. 13 [1715]'
b.131, p. 245

00085 Of falseness Fame my mistress doth accuse
Why dost thou vex me? Cruel rumor, peace.

[Sir Aston Cokayne], 'Of the infamy of his mistress'
b.275, p. 34

00086 Of famous battles many I have read,
And Blakeney, tho' submitting Britain's glory.

[N.] H[erbert], 'Epigram on the gallant Genl.
Blakeney'
Spence Papers, folder 91

00087 Of flattering speech with sugared words beware
And few there be can 'scape these vipers vile.

[Geffrey Whitney]
[Crum 097]
b.234, p. 311

00088 Of fleeting years thrice eight are fled
Or let the present be my last.

'A birthday exclamation extempore'
c.186, p. 51

00089 Of flesh and blood I was both born and bred
The poorer sort to wail.

c.536

00090 Of fowls and fish and other dainty store
Give hunger to the rich and lo (?) the poor man
                                                    meat.

c.416

00091 Of gallantry I've the invention
A more immortal scent.

[Lord E.], 'Riddle'
Poetry Box VII/47

00092 Of gender, number, case or time,
Howe'er she smile or low'r.

[Helen Craik], 'A charade'
c.375, p. 57

00093 Of generals don't tell me of —— and such boys
If the war should continue, is general complaint.

'Epigram'
Diggle Box: Poetry Box XI/2

00094 Of gentle blood, his parents' only treasure,
He leap'd o'er age, and took the shortest way.

[John] Dryden, 'Upon young Mr Rogers of
Gloucestershire'
Poetry Box IV/54; c.360/3, no. 59

00095 Of gentle manners, and of taste refin'd,
The generous transports of a fond excess.

[Anna Laetitia (Aikin) Barbauld]
c.487, p. 22

00096 Of gentle Philips will I ever sing,
And from all wits that have a knack—God save ye.

[Alexander Pope], 'The three gentle shepherds'

c.74, p. 25

00097 Of gentlest manners, ever form'd to please
Stay gentle passenger and shed it here.

[Baptist] Noel, [4th earl of Gainsborough?], 'Epitaph on Miss Colleton'

fc.51, p. 136

00098 Of heaven ask virtue, wisdom, health,
To raptures and eternal day.

Dr. [ ] Colton, 'On virtue'

c.83/2, no. 319

00099 Of Helicon let others sing
Time to have done and so goodbye.

'For the butler of Brazen Nose' [Brasenose College, Oxford; Feb. 1735/6]

Poetry Box I/51

00100 Of him who did salvation bring
That none but God such love could show.

'Hymn 34th'

c.562, p. 39

00101 Of history, romance, tales, poems, plays
Fam'd Bayard was a *chevalier de motte*.

c.340

00102 Of humble birth, but of most humble mind,
In bliss without alloy, and without end.

[William] Somervile, 'On the death of the Revd. Mr. [John] Moore'

c.244, p. 466; c.73, p. 15

00103 Of islands England was the greatest isle,
Bless word and sword our foes for to convince.

'Of the several conquests of England'

b.104, p. 11 (end of book)

00104 Of Jack and Gill the marriage is as fine
So might their flames their house to p[er]il turn.

[Sir Nicholas] Bacon, 'Of Jack and Gill'

fa.8, fol. 167

00105 Of kings and princes great to concord join the
                                                    hand,
And knits their subjects' hearts in one, and wealthy
                                        makes the land.

c.339, p. 314; b.234, p. 18

00106 Of late as they say
As fixt as the northern star. | With a &c.

'A song. To the tune of Dursley's [Durfey's?] f[ar]t' [pr. 1720? (Foxon E563)]
[Crum O118]

c.570/1, p. 155

00107 Of late in the park, a fine fancy was seen,
And in the conclusion the bawds got the field.

'The humors of the park'

fb.107, p. 56

00108 Of late the urchin god of love
For they are cork,—and so's their heart.

'Venus and Cupid. An epigram . . . [by] Impartialist'

c.487, p. 109

00109 Of letters few my name's composed,
If I was far away.

'[Enigma/Charade/Conundrum] 68' [wax]

c.389

00110 Of love you make so much parade
At home there's not much fuss.

'On an amorous couple'

c.546, p. 22

00111 Of low, inglorious, reptile race
Explain ye connoisseurs my name.

Miss [ ] Doughty, 'A riddle on a louse'

c.360/1, p. 215

00112 Of manners engaging and virtue possess'd,
That Britain has conquer'd and France has expired.

'Court characters; Mr. L[ ]ge'

c.186, p. 122

00113 Of manners gentle, of affections mild
Striking their pensive bosoms—here lies Gay.

A[lexander] Pope, 'The epitaphs in Westminster Abbey on the monument sacred to the memory of Mr. Gay the celebrated poet'
[Crum O124]

c.360/2, no. 156; fc.60, p. 117

00114 Of mean extract and low degree,
My spirits flag, I droop and die.

Abraham Oakes, 'A riddle: to Mr. S.'

c.50, p. 15

00115 Of mercy's inexhausted store,
Till I destroy all the profane.

'101 psalm'

c.515, fol. 27

00116 Of monuments that here they show
That gratitude's duets(?) a beast.

'Legend'
fc.85, fol. 88

00117 Of mortal foes see thou not gift do take,
Although a while, a truce with them thou make.

c.339, p. 312

00118 Of mortal man how equal is the date
Which now defray his funeral expenses.

'Occasional epilogue on the departure of Mr. Colman,
the manager of the Theater Royal, Covent Garden,
spoken by Miss Barsanti'
c.68, p. 76

00119 Of my supper so lately in Cheshire trick'd
And we saw ev'ry soldier embark'd before night.

'On the embarking of British soldiers to the continent
Febry. 1793'
c.143, fol. 17

00120 Of natural parts there can no other be
Ev'n so their . . . .

'On a gentleman's and his wife's hair in a locket'
b.216, p. 189 (incomplete)

00121 Of nine pretty lasses that poets assist
In my tale that the parson's damn'd tail makes a
                                    stink. | Derry down . . .

Poetry Box IV/59

00122 Of no distemper of no blast he died
The wheels of weary life at last stood still.

'Dying of old age'
c.362, p. 86

00123 Of old in poet's land the substantive
And o'er us still her god old Homer reign.

'On the importance of the epithet to modern poets'
fc.53, pp. 17, 25, 150, 183

00124 Of old the quarrel had begun,
So let's be friends again.

'The pen, and ink'
c.83/3, no. 928

00125 Of old the Romans acted comic plays
We'll crown our master's exit with applause.

[Samuel Wesley, the younger?], 'Epilogue spoken at
West[minster] School'
c.154, p. 11

00126 Of old when Scarron his companions invited,
He shifted his trumpet—and only took snuff.

[Oliver] Goldsmith, 'The retaliation; a poem'
c.90

00127 Of old, when Terence tun'd Menander's lays,
Where British judgment blends with Gallic fire.

John Lockman, 'To Monsieur Dromgold, on his
French imitation of Dodsley's The toy-shop'
c.267/1, p. 79, p. 320

00128 Of open foes we always may beware,
Yea, though they smile, yet let us have a care.

[Geffrey Whitney]
[Crum 0143]
c.339, p. 316

00129 Of our late poets—few has nature made,
Sermons are not so much esteem'd as plays.

'An estimate of the times'
c.83/3, no. 897

00130 Of our three tempters Satan's a logician:
The world, and flesh are each a rhetorician.

Sir Thomas Urquhart, 'The world, the devil, and the
flesh'
fb.217, p. 251

00131 Of patient suff'ring, and the man I sing
Alike, in what it gives, and what denies.

'Job. A poem in blank verse in three cantos'
c.264/3, p. 1 [second series]

00132 Of peace and reason Lord
With peace which Christ hath brought.

[Thomas Stanley], 'Meditat. XVIII. Upon Uxbridge
treaty and other offers made by the King'
b.152, p. 59

00133 Of playing all the [?] I think
When John and Jean a [?] while had drink.

[Sir Thomas Urquhart], 'Of the act of love to when
they both [?] thus'
fb.217, p. 393

00134 Of Pope and of Swift
Have found out something like Horace.

'Wrote with a pencil on wainscot in the College parlor
at the Windmill at Slough near Eton, and Windsor'
c.265

00135 Of practice long experience doth proceed,
The print in mind what ye in print do read.

c.339, p. 321

00136 Of preterite, and future times, let the
Grammarians talk: the present time serves me.

Sir Thomas Urquhart, 'Of the bypast to come, and
instant time'

fb.217, p. 245

00137 Of priests he lies the model, and reproach,
For having well-preferr'd that world to this.

'Epitaph on the revd. and learned Mr. William
Whiston who died August the 22 1752. O. S. aetatis 86
born 1667'

c.360/3, no. 235

00138 Of ramblings and follies you oft have been told
The Dutch to their brandy and czar to his punk.

[( ) Kynaston], 'The royal folly'

c.111, p. 21

00139 Of Romans first Julius treads our shores
Fresh wreaths entwine our second George's brows.

'History of England—before the conquest[.] Dated
from Hume'

Poetry Box VIII (oversize), no. 6

00140 Of royal race, a British Queen shall rise,
And with eternal union bless her British isle.

'Spoken by a British bard; in The royal convert'

fc.24, p. 37

00141 Of sense and good nature as much as you please
And Hymen himself shall pronounce it a heat.

Dorothea Harris, sr., 'A receipt for a good husband . . .
1778'

fc.124, p. 39

00142 Of seven islands nature made,
Of all is little Lesbos plac'd.

'Sheringham's seven islands'

c.361

00143 Of simony all bought whores guilty prove;
For they sell sp'ritual things, in selling love.

Sir Thomas Urquhart, 'That mercenary courtesans
are simoniac'

fb.217, p. 124

00144 Of stout quotations, such a lengthy score,
And each in various course returns to sea again.

Charles Atherton Allnutt, 'Epistle 2nd to [Robert
Lovegrove], in answer to his reply'

c.112, p. 119

00145 Of strange events I sing, and portents dire;
And the air vibrates with the silver sound.

[Anna Laetitia] (Aikin) [Barbauld], 'The groans of the
tankard'

c.487, p. 17

00146 Of Studley vales let others sing,
And nature's God adore.

J. H., 'To Mr. Aislebie occasioned by a view of Studley
Park and Hackfall . . . Harrowgate 3d. Sept.1768'

c.160, fol. 40

00147 Of Tadcaster, I sang not long ago,
And seas thro' its wide arches make their way.

'Tadcaster Bridge in winter'

c.81/1, no. 158

00148 Of the Maenad girls the most solatious [sic],
In what to vulgar faculties is hid.

Sir Thomas Urquhart, 'The invocation to Euterpe'

fb.217, p. 97

00149 Of the most perfect form and what's [?] to a tittle
But they're certainly villains when beneath me
they die.

'Enigma [77a]'

c.389

00150 Of the object, family end, happiness
When a good husband, and good housewife meet.

[Daniel Baker], 'Of economics'

b.81, p. 167

00151 Of the old heroes when the warlike shades
Metempsychos'd to some Scotch Presbyter.

[Andrew Marvell], 'The loyal Scot . . . by Cleveland's
ghost' [on the death of Captain Douglas, 1667]
[Crum 0154]

fb.106(17)

00152 Of the proud Austrian line, the last is laid here
No treasure, no council, no army, no friend.

'An epitaph on the late emperor of Germany Charles
the VI, who deceased, October the 20—1740
translated from the French'

c.360/1, p. 219

00153 Of the rich legacies the dying leave
And still to be enjoy'd in truth's eternal sphere.

[William Hayley], 'Sonnet . . . August 25 [1800]'

File 6968

00154 Of thirty years' acquaintance, my dear friend
Whose friendship was as dear as of a brother.

> Henry Wilkinson, 'Upon the death . . . William
> Taylor . . . pastor of Stephen's Coleman Street' [d.
> 7 September 1641]
>
> b.88, p. 2

00155 Of this matter to you most clear
To soul's health us to move.

> [alchemical verses on the exposition of earth from
> earth; Brown Robbins 2666, copied c. 1570]
>
> fa.16, p. 37

00156 Of those the wit, and candor God approves,
Who're wise as serpents: innocent like doves.

> Sir Thomas Urquhart, 'In the proverbs of Solomon'
>
> fb.217, p. 281

00157 Of thy betters say nothing ill,
For as it will it will go.

> 'Monkish adage . . . translation'
>
> c.81/1, no. 237

00158 Of truths involv'd we vainly wish to know,
Then join'd the hymn, and their first work was
praise.

> 'An essay on the weakness of human knowledge'
>
> c.481, p. 154

00159 Of villains, rebels, cuckolds, pimps and spies
Nor Nell too much inverted nature spew'd.

> 'An heroic poem' [1681]
> [Crum 0167; POAS II.228]
>
> Poetry Box VII/3; b.113, p. 121; Poetry Box VI/22

00160 Of wasteful havoc, and destructive fate
And plung'd the Pharos in the vast abyss.

> 'On the fall of a p[i]ss-pot' [pr. 1713 (Foxon P627)]
>
> c.241, p. 35

00161 Of what I now am going to write,
That by Jove they'll ruin the nation.

> 'A character of K[ing] William'
>
> b.111, p. 364

00162 Of women some are foul and some are fair
Give me a glass of sack and choose you wenches.

> [Sir Aston Cokayne], 'To my cousin Mr John
> Milward'
>
> b.275, p. 80

00163 Of Women, Uxor, Donna th'anagrams
Afford us Orcus, Danno, Wo' to man.

> Sir Thomas Urquhart, 'Of women. A paradox'
>
> fb.217, p. 352

00164 Of woods, of plains, of hills and dales,
I need no more. I have no less.

> [Sir Edward Lewkenor], 'On a rich country
> gentleman'
> [Crum 0174]
>
> fb.143, p. 41

00165 Of you I boast, of you alone complain
Banished from thee punishment lies there.

> Poetry Box VI/34

00166 Of your court and your nurture
That died on a cross for great and small.

> 'Ipomydon'/
>
> fc.179

00167 Of your great promises, such is the pay,
Who, though they nothing give, say recipe.

> Sir Thomas Urquhart, 'To one who promised much,
> and performed nothing'
>
> fb.217, p. 285

00168 Of your harlequin fops
Of coxcomb butterflies.

> John Lockman, 'Modern prigs: the tune, Trip to
> Marylebone'
>
> c.267/2, p. 142; c.268 (first part), p. 80

00169 Of your rare parts such is the ample field
The prime's your goodness, wisdom, and
expression.

> [Sir Thomas Urquhart], 'To [blank]'
>
> fb.217, p. 526

00170 Offended justice in this court's the crier
The sentence pass to send the soul to hell.

> H[enry] C[olman], 'An appendix'
> [Crum 0177]
>
> b.2, p. 31

00171 Officious zeal defeats its ends
Injures a cause, disgusts its friends.

> [prologue to] 'The robin and the canary birds a fable'
>
> Poetry Box X/45, p. 17

00172 Offspring of heaven, celestial flame,
Which burns within my heart, and never shall
expire.

> [Richard] Daniel, dean of Armagh, 'God the creator
> and preserver. Psalm 104'
>
> c.244, p. 379

00173 Offspring of love divine, humanity!
Of truth, and justice, and unbounded love.

> [William Roscoe], 'The wrongs of Africa'
>
> c.140, p. 254

00174 Offspring of nature, yet the work of art,
And grow too young, by living to be old.

Brook Boothby, 'A riddle by Rousseau and translated by . . .' [a picture]

c.378, p. 10; c.391

00175 Oft am I by the women told,
And manage wisely the last stake.

A[braham] C[owley], 'Age'

c.258

00176 Oft as we read the royal maid's distress,
And Rosalind like Rosamonda charms.

John Lockman, 'To Mrs. Arne: on hearing her perform in the character of Rosalinda [a musical drama by the author]'

c.267/1, p. 128; c.268 (second part), p. 68

00177 Oft, at meek twilight's calm reflecting hour,
And teach your hearts to tremble and adore.

[William Boscawen], 'Meditation—an elegy'

fc.106, p. 32

00178 Oft at the solitary rock, whose brow
As to the seaman's ear the melting murmur died.

[Richard Polwhele], 'The monastery at St. Michael's Mount'

c.141, p. 567

00179 Oft by fantastic poets we are told,
Nor ever men such perfect faggots grown.

'The wooden age'

c.172, p. 30

00180 Oft dost thou ask me to thy friendly seat,
With her no lower title than your wife.

'Epistle I. To John Walter esqr. advising him to marry a young lady with whom he was in love'

fc.100, p. 3

00181 Oft for the court
May spare a poor offender.

'The Duke of Buckinghamshire's epitaph, made by himself . . . Englished thus'

fc.24, p. 59

00182 Oft hast thou told me Dick, in friendly part
Then will I own that you sincerely love.

[Nicholas Amhurst], 'The test of love to a friend who fancied himself in love'

c.83/4, no. 1080

00183 Oft have I heard of impious sons before,
O'er the dead body of thy mangled sire.

'To the Queen—1690'
[Crum O190; POAS v.157]

fb.207/1, p. 50; see also 'Oft we have heard . . .'.

00184 Oft have I heard thee, gentle friend complain
And holy hope each conscious thought beguiles.

'The instability of human happiness'

Poetry Box xii/64

00185 Oft have I rang'd from shore to shore
My sailing's done, thou art my—port.

'A song on the anniversary of a friend's marriage'

c.374

00186 Oft have I sat by limpid streams
To live in peace, in unity, and love.

T[homas] L[iddiard], 'Fragment. By T. L. Jan. 12. [17]92'

c.344, p. 68

00187 Oft have I sigh'd O! Nancy dear,
And save him lest he fall.

'To Miss W—— Doncaster—Augustus'

c.175, p. 12

00188 Oft have I tried to pay the debt I owe,
And Britain stand the mistress of the main.

'On the death of the Rt. Honble. the Lord Compton' [son of the earl of Northampton; d. 1739]
[Crum O207]

Accession 97.7.40

00189 Oft have I wish'd some artless lines to send
Not many trusts, but these sincerely loves.

[Ellis Cornelia Knight], 'To Mrs. Maurice Moseley, Rome, June 14, 1794'

File 19415

00190 Oft have you ask'd me, Granville, why
Who's lost a lord to gain a m[iste]r.

[John Parker, 2nd lord] Boringdon, 'Epistle from . . . to his friend Ld. Granville Leveson-Gower on the marriage of Lady Elizabeth Spencer . . . at Christ Church [Oxford] 1790'
[Crum O211]

Poetry Box ii/19

00191 Oft I retire in hope to find
An honor to myself, and thee.

'Hymn'

c.153, p. 93

00192   Oft it has been my lot to mark
Prefers your eyesight to his own.

     [James Merrick], 'The chameleon'

     c.140, p. 574

00193   Oft I've implored the gods in vain
Content but half to please.

     [Frances Anne] (Greville) [Crewe], 'On indifference,
from . . . to Lady Carlisle'
[Crum 0216a]

     c.163, p. 15; c.130, p. 3; c.83/1, no. 63; fc.132/1, p. 94 (var.);
fc.51, p. 306; fc.57, p. 47; Poetry Box v/64; Spence
Papers, folder 113

00194   Oft I've invok'd th'Aonian choir
Contented let me live.

     [Christopher Anstey], 'Lady Elizabeth Modeless to
Miss Jenny Wander—(from the new Bath guide)' [cf.
'Oft I've implored the gods . . .']

     c.140, p. 99

00195   Oft let me wander at the break of day,
With sparkling health, and joy, and fancy's fairy
                                   wiles.

     [Ann (Ward)] Radcliffe, 'Sunrise a sonnet'

     c.83/3, no. 852

00196   Oft on the god, who wings the amorous dart,
Their fondest joys are intermixt with woe.

     John Lockman, 'Writ under a mezzotinto, by the same
hand [Mr. Faber], of Venus scourging Cupid with
roses'

     c.267/1, p. 54

00197   Oft religion drawn with brow severe,
Sermons would charm, and news please no more.

     John Lockman, 'After reading [James Fordyce's]
sermons to young women, in 2 vols. 12mo. 23d July
1766'

     c.267/1, p. 393

00198   Oft the voracious hornet, born for spoils,
Sucks the rich produce of the bee's sweet toils.

     John Lockman, 'Seeing a work of Mr. de Voltaire
pirated . . . 1744'

     c.267/1, p. 25

00199   Oft to my calm retreat I pleased retire
And oft to thee I'll tune my votive strain.

     'Lines written in the year 1791'

     Poetry Box XII/117

00200   Oft to the fields as health my footsteps draws
Beheld the feats by namesake Peter done.

     [John Walcot ('Peter Pindar')], 'Elegy on my dying
ass'

     c.83/2, no. 312

00201   Oft virtuous men below yourself you place:
The world put in, the virtuous man above me.

     Sir Thomas Urquhart, 'The speech of a certain
courtesan, to a man of worth, who had reprehended
her for her licentious life'

     fb.217, p. 84

00202   Oft we have heard of impious sons before
O'er the dead body of thy mangled sire.

     'The female parricide' [Mary II]
[Crum 0210]

     b.111, p. 432; see also 'Oft have I heard . . .'.

00203   Oft when some languid flow'r declines its head,
Each grace retouch, reanimate each charm.

     'To Celestiana[.] Stanzas'

     c.83/2, no. 549

00204   Often burlesq'd in verse-like strains,
Than boils, the devil, wife, and all.

     T[homas] M[orell], 'On Mr Bellamy's prose
translation of Job'

     c.395, p. 75

00205   Often 'tis said, and not in jest
And no more curses paid to thee.

     'To the east wind—April 1736' [on Princess Augusta's
landing at Greenwich]

     c.360/1, p. 137; c.150, p. 12

00206   Ofttimes it haps that we our bane do brew,
When friends suppos'd do prove themselves not
                                     true.

     c.339, p. 317

00207   Oh a rare posy view wherein we find
To show, that in the heart repose resounds.

     [Sir Philip Wodehouse], 'Upon his cousin [Sarah]
Hooper once Ashton'

     b.131, back (no. 104)

00208   O Absalom, O Absalom my son
O hadst thou wore a wig thou'dst ne'er been hung.

     'Written under a periwig maker's sign in Norfolk,
which was Absalom hanging by his hair in a tree'

     c.360/3, no. 77

00209   O! all ye good people of England, give ear,
Mr. Chairman replied, they could find none at all. |
                           [Which nobody can deny,] &c.

     'A ballad on the report of the committee of heresy or,
treason and no treason' [on the Atterbury plot, 1723]

     c.233, p. 111

00210 O all ye hearers, and ye standers-by,
And so we stand adjourn'd. | God save the Queen.

'Epilogue by Ignoramus and Dullman'

c.233, p. 68

00211 O! all ye horrors of eternal night,
He must, and shall, be passive there below.

'On the Bishop of Salisbury' [Gilbert Burnet]
[Crum O236]

c.570/1, p. 52

00212 O, all ye nations, in the Lord
And shall from age to age remain.

'Psalm 100'

c.264/2, p. 111

00213 O all ye nations of the earth,
Infallible His word.

'Psalm 100 an eucharistic psalm'

c.264/2, facing p. 111

00214 O all ye nations of the earth,
Unworthy of His care.

'Psalm 66'

c.264/2, p. 27

00215 O all ye nations of the earth,
Stand fast: praise ye the Lord.

'The same [Psalm 117]'

c.264/3, p. 43

00216 O all ye people of this land
One thousand six hundred ninety one.

Sir Fleetwood Sheppard, 'Sir Fleetwood Sheppard's
inscription [in a prayer-book presented to the Earl of
Dorset's Chapel] Englished'
[Crum O240]

b.111, p. 538

00217 O Anna! See the prelude is begun
At him they strike, but thou'rt the sacrifice.

'A copy of verses laid under the Queen's toilet'
[impeachment of Sacheverell]
[Crum O248; POAS VII.385]

b.382(14); b.90, p. 11; c.171, p. 13; c.160, fol. 109 (with
four more lines); fc.24, p. 19; File 17422 (with last line of
'Among the High Churchmen . . .')

00218 O Anna! Thy new friends and prick-ear'd court
My ears I hazard to secure thy head.

'On the late promotion to the Queen 1705'
[Crum O249a; POAS VII.144]

b.90, p. 3; c.171, p. 11

O azure vault! O crystal sky!
And with His glory, recompense the praise.   00219

[Wentworth Dillon, 4th earl of Roscommon], 'A
paraphrase on the CXLVIII. psalm [at 12 years of
age]'

b.218, p. 56; c.186, p. 147; c.244, p. 92; c.351, p. 47;
Trumbull Box: Poetry Box XIII/45,46

O balmy sleep! Beneath thy wing,
For ages would I wish to live.   00220

John Wolcot ('Peter Pindar'), 'By . . . during his
residence in Jamaica'

c.90

O Barnaby O beam of grace
In heaven we may have place. | Amen   00221

'S. Barnaby. June 11'

a.30[3]

O be free, as equal air
Were treason, and I will not tell.   00222

[George Daniel], 'Court Platonic'

b.121, fol. 76v

O be it so! Ye powers above!
Not less than fifty cubits high.   00223

[quatrain appended to 'You tell me the nation . . .';
10 June 1756]

File 17486

O! Be thou blest with all that heaven can send
And be thy latest gasp a sigh of love.   00224

[Alexander Pope], 'The wish. To a young lady on her
birthday . . . sent to the author of the British journal
dated November the 6 1724. Signed G. [S.] L.'

c.360/2, no. 111 (attr. G. S. L.); c.188, p. 5; c.481, p. 33;
fc.132/1, p. 79

O Bean! whose fond connubial days
And wets it with a willing tear.   00225

'Petherton Bridge. An elegy'

c.141, p. 146

O! bear me to some lonely cell
Nor wish for heaven below the skies.   00226

c.153, p. 75

O! Bessy [Bell] and Mary Gray
And be with ane contented.   00227

[Allan Ramsay]
[Crum O257]

fc.61, p. 63

[575]

00228 O Betty! Betty! Quick as thought,
Had women boundless sway.

> John Lockman, 'The teatable song: addressed to two
> ladies in West Drayton . . . set by Mr. Arnold . . . 1758'

c.267/2, p. 157

00229 O bland Contentment, who with pilgrim feet,
And blest with thee, forgot a world unkind.

> W[illiam] L[isle] Bowles, 'Stanzas'

c.83/3, no. 895

00230 O bless the Lord my soul and all
His blessedness express.

> 'Psal: 103'

b.217, p. 76

00231 Oh blessed are all they,
Shall time outrun.

> 'Psalm 128 27 day'

c.264/3, p. 75

00232 O blessed be the Lord, my might,
Doth take and challenge for his own.

> 'Psalm 144. Morning prayer 30 day'

c.264/3, p. 102

00233 O blessed sacred spirit thee I adore!
Us thither, there to sing eternal songs of praise.

> [Edmund Wodehouse], 'June 5 1715 Whitsunday'

b.131, p. 221

00234 O blest with temper, whose unclouded ray,
And mistress of herself tho' China fall.

> 'On temper'

c.83/3, no. 893

00235 O blithe Aglaia—woven in thy name!
Both in our gifts to men and Him above.

> [Sir Philip Wodehouse], 'Abigail Holland oh Aglaia
> blanda'

b.131, back (no. 80)

00236 O bondage vile, the worthy man's deface,
Be far from those, that learning do embrace.

c.339, p. 316

00237 Oh bonny was yon rosy briar,
Its joys and grief alike resign.

> [Robert Burns], 'Scottish song'

c.142, p. 294

00238 O born for nations, Britain's joy confest!
And gives not simply one, but all perfumes.

> [Leonard Welsted], 'Of the princess' [of Wales,
> Caroline of Ansbach; pr. 1716 (Foxon W296)]

Poetry Box x/10(13)

00239 O born in liberal studies to excel
Thro' life contented, and in death resign'd.

> [Francis Fawkes], 'On a worthy friend who was
> accomplished in the sister arts of music and painting'

fc.21, p. 26

00240 O! born to soothe distress, and lighten care;
And love must owe its origin to love.

> [Anna Laetitia] (Aikin) [Barbauld], 'Characters'

c.487, p. 21

00241 O breathe in gentle strains my lyre
And envy mine.

> 'Serenade chorus'

Poetry Box XII/119; see also 'Whoe'er thou art . . .'.

00242 O! brighter than the vermeil bloom
Ye hills, ye shady bowers, adieu!

> J[ohn] W[ilson], 'An ode to health'

Poetry Box IV/143

00243 O Britons, Britons, now rejoice
Because our King is crown'd.

> 'Britain's joy on the restoration'

c.275

00244 O Caroline, thy form recalls,
And fondly hop'd, to call you mine.

> [Laurence] Sterne(?), 'To Caroline, supposed to be
> Sterne's written to his mistress after the early part of
> his life'

c.83/3, no. 832

00245 O cease, accomplish'd youth! To sweep
Are preludes to the brightest day.

> P[eter] L[ionel] Courtier, 'To Mr. R. Davenport . . .
> July 26th 1796'

File 18061

00246 O cease to mourn, unhappy youth,
Who quite have lost my own?

> Lady Mary S——, 'The reply [to 'Forever, O
> merciless fair'; General evening post, 16 November
> 1779]

c.157, p. 112

00247 O Charles in absence hear a friend complain
For they are nature's heirs and all her works their
own.

Poetry Box I/74

00248 O Christian men give care to me,
That thy sweet death our souls may save. | Amen

    'A miracle of the Cross. Sep. 14'

a.30[34]

00249 O: Cloacina! Goddess of this place
Not rudely swift nor obstinately slow.

    Abraham Oakes(?)

c.50, p. 7

00250 O come let us lift up our voice
To enter to my rest.

    [John Hopkins], 'A praise of God for the world and of
    his clemency. Psalm 40' [verses from Psalm 95]
    [Crum 0295]

a.3, fol. 116

00251 O, come, let us our voices raise
Nor there find rest with me.

    'Psalm 95. Morning prayer 19 day'

c.264/2, p. 104

00252 O, come let us our voices raise
Nor enter Sion's rest with me.

    "The same [Psalm 95] long meter as the 100th
    Sternhold"

c.264/2, p. 105

00253 O come to me with leaden hand,
And lull awhile my sense.

    T. Siddons, 'To Morpheus'

c.344, p. 37

00254 O! confidence, inspire my breast,
And never doubt my constant love.

    'Inscription to confidence'

c.83/2, no. 276

00255 O could I flow like thee, and make thy stream
Strong without rage, without o'erflowing full.

    Sir John Denham, 'From Cooper's Hill'

fb.66/26

00256 Oh could I sing like the bright train
I'll never cease to sing.

    'Hymn 70th'

c.562, p. 84

00257 Oh! could these lines console
For all the bless'd design'd.

    M. P., 'On the death of a child of the smallpox from a
    lady to her friend'

fc.85, fol. 116

00258 Oh! could this verse her bright example spread
Till God's own plaudit shall her worth attest.

    H[annah] More, 'Epitaph on Mrs. Little'

c.341, p. 37

00259 O cousin, said Eliza, dear
The promise of the Lord is sure.

    'The song of Elizabeth'

c.264/3, p. 123

00260 O cruel death more subtle than a fox
And wear among his brethren | Horns! Horns!
                                 Horns!

    [Richard Tarlton], 'On Sir John Calfe who was three
    times Lord Mayor of York'
    [Crum 0312]

c.113/22; c.150, p. 128

00261 O cruel death, O wounds most deep
Myself I wholly offer up.

    'Christo crucifixo'

a.6, p. 29

00262 O cruel death thou haste and pallid
For thou hast cropp'd our Lettice to make thee a
                                 salad.

    'In Winchester Cathedral on a Miss Lettice'

fc.14/8; see also next.

00263 O cruel death! To please his dainty palate
Has taken my Lettice; to make him a salad.

    'A sailor's epitaph on his wife Letitia'

c.378, p. 65; see also previous.

00264 O cruel death, why wert thou so unkind
Which would have been more grateful to me the
                                survivor.

    'Epitaph in Willingham churchyard in
    Cambridgeshire'

c.150, p. 120

00265 O cruel tyrant death thou hast cut down
Never let blisters be applied to a lying-in woman's
                                 back.

    Dr. [ ] Greenwood, 'Epitaph by . . . on his wife'

c.150, p. 112

00266 O Cyrus, Alexander, Julius, all
Mixt with yourselves, in the same mass of clay.

    [ ] Hughes, 'Mortality'

c.244, p. 558

00267 O dearest, best beloved! Permit the muse
And hearts by sympathy united here.

    'August the 20th, 1791'

fc.124, p. 13

00268 O dearest Lord give me an heart
Around the festal board.

    'Hymn 9th'

c.562, p. 10

00269 O death what causeth thee to make such haste
That saw her time but now alas she's gone.

    Josiah Lightfoote, 'In obitum . . . magistrae Okenor
    carmen funebre. March 20. 1626'

Poetry Box vi/51

00270 O death! What pow'r is thine, that distant thus
And all things wear a deep and heavy gloom.

    [ ] Grove, 'On death'

c.244, p. 135; c.259, inserted after p. 16

00271 O! deign to smile once more, illustrious Britons!
Which call'd us first to sing. | Lowly the lark &c.
                      da capo.

    John Lockman, 'Musical prologue, set by Seignor
    Cocchi, and sung by Seignora Mattei, at the King's
    Theater in the Haymarket, Nov. 22, 1760, at the
    opening for that season'

c.267/3, p. 145

00272 Oh did my genius like my friendship burn
Be ev'ry pang of mine bestow'd on me.

    Hannah More, 'An extempore sacred to friendship—
    to Miss Blandford on her birthday July 13th 1767
    written by . . . when very ill'

c.341, p. 62

00273 O disembodied soul most rudely driv'n,
Thy loss thy hapless countrymen deplore.

    'Proverbs 25.5 Take away the wicked from before the
    King and his throne shall be establish'd in
    righteousness'

c.362, p. 40

00274 O do not breathe too loud, though grief sometimes
Was, when I laid the plot, or rais'd the frame.

    [George Daniel]

b.121, fol. 61v

00275 O do not die for I shall hate
Of thee one hour than all else ever.

    [John Donne], 'The fever'
    [Crum 0334]

b.148, p. 87

00276 O do not wanton with those eyes
Mine own enough betray me.

    [Ben Jonson]

b.213, p. 33

00277 O do not warrant sin, in your applause
Custom, will make her errors, impudence.

    [George Daniel]

b.121, fol. 80v

00278 O d'open the door sweet Betty
And was not this honestly done?

    'Ballad'

fb.70, p. 77

00279 O dread Jehovah! Thy all-piercing eyes
That guides my feet, to thy own heav'n, and thee.

    [Christopher] Pitt, 'Psalm 139'

c.244, p. 507

00280 O dream not man that it will serve thy turn
To those that puts it off until they die.

    [Mary Serjant]

fb.98, fol. 151

00281 O Dulwich hills auspicious to the sight,
In other worlds to look forth fate of this.

    [Abraham Cowley?], 'The back aspect of Camberwell'

File 3782/5

00282 O earthly flesh and frail mankind,
The obtaining of endless bliss.

b.234, p. 145

00283 O! Edwin, what avail thy pray'r,
Shall Edwin be no more.

    Charles Burney, the younger, 'The shepherd's
    complaint. A song . . . Nov. 20. 1779'

c.35, p. 17

00284 O Elphlede! mighty both in strength and mind
So sleep in peace, virago-maid farewell.

    'On Elphlede [Ethelfleda] sister to K. Edward (before
    the conquest) the 4th'

fb.143, p. 4

00285 O! England beware for the people are come
Sure none but the devil himself can come after.

    'The Hanover crew'

c.570/1, p. 168

00286 O England's martyr, Britain's sacrifice
More power for his tyranny to reign.

    'On King Charles his death'

b.216, p. 181

00287 O! ever in my bosom live,
Shall bind our hearts the closer.

    'Mutual affection'

c.83/3, no. 989

00288 O! fair as Eve, and pure as was her heart,
Who wilt thy Moccas, in Millenium see.

    John Lockman, 'To Miss Kitty Cornwall, on
    presenting her with a description of Millenium
    House . . . 3d April 1763'

c.267/1, p. 210

00289 O fair inspirers of an humble muse,
All worldly blame, or glory I defy.

    C[harles] B[urney], 'Sonnet, addressed to Miss Rachel
    and Miss Jessy Wilcox. Prefixed to the epistles from
    Euphrasia to Castalio; and from Edwin to
    Angelina . . . July 17. 1779'

c.38, p. 17

00290 O fairest pattern to a failing age,
In death by friendship, honor, virtue mourn'd.

    [Alexander Pope], 'An inscription on the monument of
    John Knight esq.'

Poetry Box XIV/190

00291 O faithless love and broken vows,
He gave his heart for thine.

    'Selem to Irene'

c.83/1, no. 170

00292 O faithless world, and the most faithless part
Is but a guest.

    [Sir Henry Wotton]
    [Crum O362]

b.148, p. 142

00293 O Falkland offspring of a generous race
Let Blenheim speak and witness Gibraltar.

    [George Granville, 1st baron] Lansdowne, 'An ode on
    the corruption of mankind inscribed to Lord
    Falkland'

fc.60, p. 53

00294 O! fallen greenhouse thou art now forgotten
Are now quite gone and can be seen no more.

    Cecelia Burney, 'On an old greenhouse by . . . aged
    eight years. 1796'

c.486, fol. 35

00295 O fancy, whither wouldst thou fly
His precepts remedy affords.

    [Heavily corrected]

Poetry Box VI/91

00296 Oh, far from fortune's tinsel state,
Of dear domestic pleasures mine.

    'Seclusion. Adapted to the tender adagio of the
    memorable David Rizzio'

c.344, p. 104

00297 O! fatal language that calls vice polite,
Her pleasing hours glide on without a stain.

    'Reason superior to fashion'

c.515, fol. 3r

00298 O Father when thy spirit I implore,
Transcend all intellects, except Thy own.

    [Edmund Wodehouse], 'Christmas [1714]'

b.131, p. 123

00299 O! fit with elephants alone,
From wolves, and lions, fly.

    [William Popple, trans.], '[Horace, ep]ode 12th. To an
    old woman'

fc.104/2, p. 444

00300 O! fly me not bright creature stay
Preserves gay youth, and makes the aged strong.

    'The old man's address'

Poetry Box IV/53

00301 O! fly with me to distant air
And I will make them all thine own.

    [Ann (Ward)] Radcliffe, 'Titania to her love'

c.83/3, no. 858

00302 O fond of arts! The muses' friend!
How justly all thy truth revere!

    John Lockman, 'To Sir William Irby, with a poem, on
    the Prince of Wales's birthday . . . Nov. 1757'

c.267/1, p. 219

00303 O for a heart to praise my God
Thy new best name of love.

    'Hymn 87th'

c.562, p. 114

00304 O for a muse thy wondrous charms to tell,
That which remains imperfect in my verse.

    R[obert] Shirley, 1st earl of Ferrers, 'Upon seeing Mrs.
    Lewis'

c.347, p. 34

00305 O for an overcoming faith
In the decisive hour.

    [( ) Pierson]

c.328, p. 21

00306   Oh for an Ovid, or a Homer now,
But at the next flight, Sir, expect a bow.

'Upon the prince's return from Spain'
b.356, p. 149

00307   O, for that sweet Lethean pleasure,
Or look with tearless eye its everlasting leave.

'Drink of the stream and forget'
c.83/2, no. 547

00308   O for the dear domestic hour,
Save on our old acquainted bed.

'A wish'
c.83/1, no. 36

00309   O! form'd by nature, and refin'd by art,
And all be white the fates intend to spin.

[Thomas Tickell], 'To Delia'
[Crum 0381, with forty more lines]
c.139, p. 436

00310   O fortitude on me exert thy power
And ease this filial heart that beats with anxious
                                     pain.

Miss [ ] Andrews, 'On fortitude'
File 245/15

00311   O, fortune! How thy restless wavering state
So God send to my foes all they have thought.

Elizabeth I, queen of England, 'Verses . . . when a
prisoner at Woodstock in 1555'
fc.132/1, p. 188

00312   Oh! fortune like her foe is wisely coy,
And deals us sorrow but to raise our joy.

c.189, p. 75

00313   O! fram'd for love, yet stranger to its joy,
Or why thus thinking, will not youth renew?

[William Popple, trans.], '[Horace] book 4th. Ode
10th. To Ligurinus'
fc.104/2, p. 372 [bis]

00314   O fraught with nerves, acute to feel
While hov'ring angels catch his parting breath.

'To Eliza . . . Alphonzo'
c.344, p. 74

00315   O, friend of humankind, benignant sage,
As musing mid thy favorite plants he roves.

J[ohn] Aikin, 'Lines by . . . subscribed on a stone, in
the garden of Mr. White; near the plant named by
Linnaeus, Fothergalia. To the memory of John
Fothergill, M. D. F. R. S.'
fc.132/1, p. 201, p. 210

00316   O friend of nature! linger here,
Diffusing plenty where it flows!

'Inscription for a seat at Guy's Cliff'
Greatheed Box/76

00317   O genial muse that smil'st on friendship's bands,
My muse is well requited for her pains.

Charles Atherton Allnutt, 'An invocation to
friendship. Addressed to an intimate acquaintance'
c.112, p. 10

00318   O, genius of this hallow'd place
Some pitying port in vain implore.

'Imitation of the Latin ode written by [Thomas] Gray
in the album of the Grande Chartreuse'
c.142, p. 130

00319   O genius! What a wretch art thou,
And Sundays sport a strumpet and a whiskey.

[John Walcot ('Peter Pindar')?], 'Genius . . . Ode 1st,
1783'
c.355, p. 93

00320   O! gentle health, thy vot'ry tell
To lure thee back again.

'Ode to health'
c.83/3, no. 753

00321   O gentle love, do not forsake the guide
In the deep flood she drowned her beamy face.

[Thomas] Carew, 'Upon some alterations in his
mistress after his departure into France'
b.225, p. 131

00322   O George George George 'tis such rakes as you
And London prove the market of the world.

'Epilogue to The citizen, spoken by Mr. Shuter and
Mr. Woodward, in the characters of old Philpot and
young Philpot'
c.68, p. 5

00323   O Girard, blest with every grace
The golden apple had been thine.

[Charles Burney, the younger], 'On Miss Girard'
c.37, p. 71

00324   O give thee to Jehovah thanks
His laws: praise ye the Lord.

'Psal: 105'
b.217, p. 83

00325   O give ye thanks unto the Lord
Forever towards Thee.

     [John Marckant?], 'A praising of God for his mercy.
     Psalm 50' [verses from Psalm 118]
     [Crom O397]

     a.3, fol. 129v

00326   O Gloriana, charming fair
And be forever mine.

     [Thomas Hamilton, 6th earl of Haddington], 'A song'

     c.458/2, p. 174

00327   O glorious arch by wisdom rais'd!
Demonstrably, a deity.

     '19th psalm'

     c.515, fol. 27v

00328   O glorious Creator of the skies!
And boldly sing it my remaining days!

     F[rances] B[urney d'Arblay], 'Thanksgiving for his
     Majesty's happy recovery. February 28th . . . F. B.
     aged 13 years'

     c.486, fol. 18v

00329   O glorious hope of perfect love!
Give me a lot of love.

     'Hymn 99th'

     c.562, p. 132

00330   O God from whom all blessings flow
Admire the giver more.

     [Thomas Stevens?], 'Evening meeting of prayer . . .
     August 16. 1780. Tuesday night'

     c.259, p. 100

00331   O God how endless is thy love
Demand perpetual songs of praise.

     'Hymn 28th'

     c.562, p. 33

00332   O God I beg of thee thy grace
Does thee most please, else utmost bliss.

     [Edmund Wodehouse], 'Apr. 1 [1715]

     b.131, p. 191

00333   O God, in my decline of age,
My dear Redeemer's name.

     'A hymn to the Deity'

     c.83/1, no. 70

00334   O God Jehovah unto whom
Will cut them down to naught.

     'Psal: 94'

     b.217, p. 58

00335   O God, my God, give grace and might,
The God of gods grant my desire.

     'A zealous desire'

     c.187, p. 11

00336   O God my God I watch betime
Which I do never find.

     [Thomas Sternhold and John Hopkins], 'The 25
     psalm. A thanksgiving for our deliverance out of peril'
     [verses from Psalms 63-66]
     [Cf. Crum 0416]

     a.3, fol. 103

00337   O God my God! Thee oft I name,
But their full sense to know, for this beg leave.

     [Edmund Wodehouse], 'Octr. 3d [1714]'

     b.131, p. 52

00338   O God my God wherefore dost thou
From dogs that would devour.

     [Thomas Sternhold], 'The 8 psalm against all manner
     of temptations' [verses from Psalm 22]
     [cf. Crum 0418]

     a.3, fol. 74

00339   O God my heart is fix'd, 'tis bent
Till thou art here, as there obey'd.

     'The invocation or the morning sacrifice'

     c.186, p. 113

00340   O God my heart prepared is,
And victory obtain.

     'Psalm 108. Evening prayer'

     c.264/3, p. 29

00341   O God my hope I'll wholly place,
Our title to the crown above.

     [Edmund Wodehouse], 'Decr. 21 [1714]'

     b.131, p. 120

00342   O God my strength and fortitude
Praised be he always.

     [Thomas Sternhold], 'The 7 psalm a thanksgiving for
     deliverance out of trouble' [verses from Psalm 18]
     [cf. Crum 0420]

     a.3, fol. 73; c.528/9 (var.)

00343   O God no longer silence keep
Surmountest every one.

     'Psal: 83'

     b.217, p. 30

00344   O God of grace, and God of truth,
A separation more.

      T. Green, 'The prayer of a dying youth . . . the
      foregoing prayer was made by . . . in the year 1766'

      c.391

00345   O God of life and love permit
Can give true pleasure to my heart.

      T[homas] S[tevens], 'Lord's [d]ay February the 11th.
      afternoon Psalm. the 63.3'

      c.259, p. 124

00346   O God of love, how great's thy power?
And in his arms expir'd.

      [Thomas Hamilton, 6th earl of Haddington], 'A
      ballad'

      c.458/2, p. 97

00347   O God of Sabbath hear our vows,
And close my eyes and wake with God.

      P[hilip] Doddridge, 'The eternal Sabbath from
      Heb.IV.9'

      c.493, p. 25

00348   O God on Thine own heritage,
Sent to prepare his way.

      'Psalm 85'

      c.264/2, p. 79

00349   O God, our ears have heard, our lives
And mercy still abound.

      'Psalm 44 Morning prayer 9 day'

      c.264/1, p. 189

00350   O God that art my righteousness,
Thy blessing and Thy love.

      [Thomas Sternhold], 'For the sinner in distress'
      [verses from Psalms 3–4]
      [cf. Crum 0433]

      a.3, fol. 68

00351   O God the heathen fill the land
What we declare, unto thy praise.

      'Psal: 79'

      b.217, p. 22

00352   O God, Thou art my God, I'll seek,
And stop their utterance with shame.

      'Psalm 63. 12 day'

      c.264/2, p. 22

00353   O God | Thy nature and Thy property
So Christ shall be my All in All.

      Sir John Strangways

      b.304, p. 38

00354   O God thy wisdom teaches us
We shall at death a crown receive.

      [Edmund Wodehouse], 'Octr. 25 [1714]'

      b.131, p. 68

00355   O God to me take heed, take heed
O who is like to Thee.

      [John Hopkins], 'Psalm 28. For comfort and aid from
      the Lord against enemies' [verses from Psalms 70–71]
      [cf. Crum 0442]

      a.3, fol. 107

00356   O God, to whom of right belongs
And mischief recompense.

      'Psalm 94'

      c.264/2, p. 101

00357   O God we pray,
And breath also.

      'A psalm for the Fast Day'

      b.111, p. 247; see also 'Good people fast . . .'.

00358   O God! What eloquence of mortal sound
I seem to antedate the joys above.

      [Henry] Needler, 'An ejaculation'

      c.244, p. 555

00359   O God! When I resolve in mind,
Ye saints and angels own it is their bliss.

      [Edmund Wodehouse], 'Jan. 24 [1715]'

      b.131, p. 150

00360   O God who guides the golden heavens
In heaven a resting place. | Amen

      'S. Euphemia' [September 16]

      a.30[35]

00361   O God who through each various stage,
But guide me to my tomb! | Amen.

      [Sir William Trumbull], '12. Aug[u]st'

      b.177, p. 12

00362   O goddess of the soul refin'd
Soft guard from female ill.

      [Miss ( ) Bradford], 'Ode to female decorum'

      c.504, p. 24

00363   O goddess, on whose steps attend
Long as the surge shall lash thy sea-encircled land!

      [Joseph Warton], 'Ode to liberty'

      Poetry Box IV/18

00364 Oh! gold! Attractive gold in vain,
To bask in thy refulgent ray.

   [William] Somervile, 'On gold'
   c.244, p. 465

00365 O golden heavens rejoice rejoice
In joys forever may remain. | Amen

   'Of the assumption of our B[lessed] L[ord]. Aug. 15'
   a.30[25]

00366 O good and great; O infinite supreme!
In wedding garment of a welcome guest.

   'A philosophical poem or hymn on Easter 1740'
   c.371, fol. 44

00367 O Granville with the load of life opprest
The tyrant's minions and our masters are.

   'To the Lord Lansdowne whilst he was in the Tower.
   From Catullus'
   c.570/1, p. 170

00368 O gratitude celestial fair!
Nor blame the muse for want of fire.

   'Gratitude . . . humbly addressed to her Grace the
   Duchess of Bedford'
   fc.51, p. 300

00369 O, Greatheed, great and 'good as George of Green',
Gentle in grain, but, grieved;—grim as griffin.

   Greatheed Box/82

00370 O greedy Midas I've been told,
And style me only God of wine.

   'Song 62'
   c.555, p. 89

00371 Oh! had I courage but to meet my fate;
That something, or that nothing after death.

   c.189, p. 26

00372 O! had you Keate in early days,
For we a palinode must sing!

   R[ichard] V[ernon] S[adleir], 'To George Keate esqr
   who presented me his poems 1781'
   c.106, p. 138

00373 O! Haly, task me not too hard,
Be silent and admire!

   R[ichard] V[ernon] S[adleir], 'Being desired one
   morning to write some lines on Miss Hale'
   c.106, p. 42

00374 O happiness, celestial fair,
And there forever reigns!

   [Hannah] More, 'To happiness'
   fc.132/1, p. 119; c.83/3, no. 770

00375 O! happy day thrice happy hour
For His Son's sake a recompense.

   [Mary Pluret], 'Another [poem written on waste
   paper]'
   c.354

00376 O happy day wherein those bonds are broke
Now will this day ever know darkness more.

   Petrarch
   b.211, p. 70

00377 O! happy George two wives adorn thy brows;
In fertile soil she plants the gilded horn.

   [Horace Walpole, 4th earl of Orford], 'Lady
   Lyttelt[o]n' [Elizabeth, Lady George Lyttelton, d.
   1795]
   [Crum 0464]
   c.157, p. 71

00378 O happy he, to whom a sacred wedding
To crown your mutual hopes with mixed pleasure.

   Sir Thomas Urquhart, 'To my Lady Dowager of
   [crossed out] Viscountess'
   fb.217, p. 302

00379 Oh! happy he, whom freed from care,
Is thence exalted and refin'd.

   [Thomas Hull], 'Inscription for a rest house'
   c.528/34-35

00380 Oh happy he, whose conscience telleth him,
For sinner's feet stand oft on tott'ring balls.

   'A conscience, quiet and good'
   c.187, p. 36

00381 O happy hour! When the unshackled soul,
Leaving my sins and sorrows in the grave.

   [Ambrose Philips], 'The ascent of a separate soul'
   c.244, p. 88

00382 Oh happy, if they knew their happy state,
'Tis time the smoking coursers to unyoke.

   [William Mills], 'A panegyric on a country life, being
   the conclusion of Virgil's second Georgic translated'
   [cf. Crum 0467]
   c.472, p. 105

00383   O happy morn! Smile on the auspicious pair,
Forgive us if we lose our joyful smile.

     'Verses wrote on the marriage day of the Princess
     Royal and the Prince of Orange'

     Poetry Box xiv/191

00384   O happy nymph! A friendly sign
And glide to heav'nly rest.

     'To an infant—by a lady'

     c.244, p. 633

00385   O happy people you must thrive
Will more than it surround.

     Poetry Box vi/113; Trumbull Box: Poetry Box xiii/86

00386   O happy resignation
That is, when it is not.

     [John Byrom], 'On resignation'

     c.83/1, no. 250

00387   Oh happy she that can sincerely say
My fame is clear, I have not sinn'd today.

     'A clear conscience'

     c.360/3, no. 69

00388   O! happy swains! Did they their bliss but know!
The last impressions of her steps behind.

     [Edmund Burke], 'The pleasures of a country life'
     [from Virgil]
     [cf. Crum 0470]

     File 13832

00389   O, happy times, when no such thing as coin
But av'rice and excess devours the root.

     c.189, p. 6

00390   O hated war! tyrannic, cruel, blind,
And 'mid the stars inscribe thy name.

     John Lockman, 'Elfrida: an opera. Set to music by
     Mr. John Christopher Smith . . . writ at Islington, the
     summer of 1748 . . .'

     c.267/3, p. 238

00391   O have you not heard of the errors and blunders
Where she could gabble English, to—never talk
                            French.

     'English lady in France'

     c.81/2, no. 581

00392   O! have you seen bath'd in the morning dew,
Felt the fond pang, and droop'd with passion weak.

     [Ann (Ward)] Radcliffe, 'Adeline'

     c.83/3, no. 850

00393   O Hay! How often, when my pulse beat slow,
Confirms the miracles of music told!

     John Lockman, 'To Mr. Hay, in Dublin . . . Jany 19th.
     1764'

     c.267/1, p. 374

00394   O health, capricious maid!
That ever sought thine ear.

     [William Shenstone], 'Ode to health occasioned by
     the illness of Miss ———'

     c.89, p. 121

00395   O health! Thou balmy nymph of race divine,
And calls forth all my gratitude and love.

     Miss [ ] White, of Edgbaston, 'To Hygeia, and after
     illness'

     c.532

00396   O health! Thou friend of nature! Goddess blithe,
And teach the ills I may not shun to bear.

     'Ode to health'

     c.528/4

00397   O! hear a pensive captive's prayer,
And break the hidden snare.

     [Anna Laetitia] (Aikin) [Barbauld], 'The mouse's
     petition, to Dr. Bristley [Priestley], found in the trap
     where he had been confined all night'

     c.487, p. 14; fc.132/1, p. 113; c.481, p. 9; c.156, p. 156

00398   O hear my prayer Lord and let,
Forever shall stand sure.

     [Thomas Norton], 'A lamentation of an afflicted
     sinner. Psalm 43' [verses from Psalm 102]
     [Crum 0480]

     a.3, fol. 120

00399   O hear ye this my people all
With very brutes, he dies.

     'Psalm 49'

     c.264/1, p. 209

00400   O heaven, thy awful judgments I adore,
One thunder-stroke may lead to joys divine.

     'Meditations and reflections on a storm of thunder
     and lightning; June the 24th 1756'

     c.135, p. 30

00401   O heaven were she but mine, or mine alone!
But what we most desire to keep, has none.

     'Nelly's epilogue or Nelly dressed. 1671' [on Nell
     Gwyn?]

     b.54, p. 1198

00402   O heavenly God, O father dear
In heaven a dwelling place.

     [Francis Kinwelmarsh], 'The song of . . . W[alter
     Devereux], Earl of Essex sung the night before his
     death [1575] . . . Harl. MSS. No. 293 fo. 120' [attr.
     Francis Kinwelmarsh in The paradise of dainty
     devises, 1576]
     [Crum 0485]

     Poetry Box VII/79

00403   O heavenly pow'rs, why did you bring to light?
The Devil, and be damning of us all.

     'A satire on women'
     [Crum 0486]

     c.189, p. 168 (incomplete?); b.200, p. 100 (6 lines only)

00404   O heavens, O poles!
Are graves become Button-holes.

     'On one Button'

     b.356, p. 246; see also 'Here lies John Button . . .',
     'Cudd's life . . .'.

00405   O heavens! we now have signs below
Good Lord, deliver this poor realm.

     'The dissolution'
     [Crum 0490]

     b.54, p. 1105

00406   O heavy words, which once from lips of rose,
He asks submission, confidence, and prayer.

     'No more shall meet Achilles and his friend [a line
     often repeated by her son] . . . this poem was written
     by my dearest mother upon the death of her eldest son
     [on his ninth birthday] . . . Sept. 25th 1767'

     Poetry Box III/22

00407   O! Hellespont deliver me my love
His death will make me put an end to life.

     C[ecilia] B[urney], 'The lamentation of Hero on
     Leander's being drowned . . . C. B. aged 12 years'

     c.486, fol. 36

00408   O Hol[kha]m! best, belov'd abode!
Do what you will with H[orace].

     [William] P[ulteney, earl of Bath], 'An epistle from
     Lord L[ovel]l [Thomas Coke, later earl of Leicester]
     to Lord C[hesterfiel]d by Mr. P.' [pr. 1740 (Foxon
     P1160)]

     Poetry Box IV/11

00409   O holy Jesus which hath made me sue
Possessing nothing but what's from above.

     [Mary Serjant]

     fb.98, fol. 156

00410   O Holy Spirit who dost ne'er deny
O holy lamb! O holy dove! O God.

     [Edmund Wodehouse], 'Christmas Eve [1714]'

     b.131, p. 122

00411   O Holy Spirit! who inspires
I rather shall desire, than fear.

     [Edmund Wodehouse], 'Ascension May 26 [1715]'

     b.131, p. 217

00412   O hone a rie! O hone a rie!
We ne'er shall see Lord Ronald more.

     [Sir Walter] Scott, 'Glenfinlas or Lord Ronald's
     coronach . . . not printed—Sept. 1799'

     c.364, p. 77

00413   O honor'd England how art thou disgrac'd
And like another Scipio he'll sack Spain.

     'Of the Duke of Buckingham, whose head Gondomar
     requested of K. James' [1623/4]
     [Crum 0499]

     b.197, p. 225

00414   O, hope! Thou soother sweet of human woes!
And I will bless thee, who tho' slow art sure.

     [Charlotte (Turner) Smith], 'By the same to hope'

     c.130, p. 94

00415   Oh how blissful was the day
What more soothing than thy lyre?

     John Lockman, 'Octavia: (the Duchess of
     Buckingham ill) . . . 1742'

     c.267/2, p. 218

00416   Oh how chang'd is the gay scene,
Clos'd, in thee, his far-spread name.

     John Lockman, 'To the memory of His Grace the
     Duke of Buckingham . . . anno 1735' [pr. 1736 (Foxon
     L220)]

     c.267/2, p. 209; c.268 (first part), p. 119

00417   Oh! how cruel's the deed,
Still by a bull his pardon's seal'd.

     'A remonstrance'

     fc.85, fol. 29

00418   Oh how delicious as one sips the tea
Counts for a cock, the god of war.

     'Britannicus to Gallicia'

     fc.53, p. 30

00419   Oh! how does ev'ry trifle seize my heart
Be straight transported to the full possession.

     'Soliloquies [1]'

     c.153, p. 147

00420 Oh how great William's name,
And he'll conquer, he'll conquer, the world and the
                                                         devil.

    'King William ludibriated'

b.111, p. 400

00421 O how happy am I here
Take me to my Savior's breast.

    'Hymn 76th'

c.562, p. 96

00422 Oh, how I hate the sound!—it is the knell,
And Roman rites retain'd tho' Roman faith be flown!

    'A collegiate address to the chapel bell'

Poetry Box XII/36

00423 Oh! how I long my country vill[e] to see,
And days like these who would not wish to see?

    W. W., 'Gent. magazine, April 1745'

c.160, fol. 75

00424 Oh! how I long'd to give the parting kiss
Lockt in the charming Annabella's mind.

    'The lover's farewell, or upon parting with a lover
    upon the day of her nativity'

c.53, fol. 36

00425 Oh how I tremble for thy virgin heart
His household guardian, and commodious wife.

    'To a lady'

fc.51, p. 164

00426 Oh how I wander! oh where shall at last
To seek that upon earth which is nowhere | But
                                                         only there.

    [George Daniel]

b.121, fol. 24v

00427 Oh how my spirits dance, how I could fly
Might still be blest with such sweet melody.

    'On a lover hearing his mistress sing to the lute'

b.62, p. 70

00428 Oh how past scenes of bliss employ
Forc'd from her soul-delighting eyes!

    John Lockman, 'Psyche's lamentation [translated from
    La Fontaine] . . . set to music by Dr. Boyce'

c.267/4, p. 239

00429 Oh how perverse is flesh and blood in whom
Bow to strange gods till Israel was forbid.

    [Francis Quarles?], 'On man's rebellion'

b.137, p. 189; b.156, p. 21

00430 Oh how prepost'rous our affections burn!
We serve the world, love God, to serve our turn.

    [Francis Quarles], 'On our affections' [pr. Divine
    fancies, 1632, iv.102]
    [Crum 0520]

b.118, p. 220

00431 O how pretty's
Live and die.

    John Lockman, 'A Lilliputian sketch, or ode, of a very
    noble object. Drawn upon the spot . . . 6 Aug. 1762'

c.267/2, p. 240

00432 Oh how raging is the smart
Tort'ring woes, and rankling chains.

    John Lockman, 'Translations, and imitations from
    Metastasio, and other Italian opera poets [2]'

c.267/4, p. 91

00433 O how ye charm, illustrious pair!
Sweet music warbling from the sky.

    John Lockman, 'Odes. To their royal highnesses the
    Prince and Princess of Wales, after seeing them in
    Vauxhall Gardens . . . 16 Aug. 1740'

c.267/2, p. 229

00434 Oh, I am cold, the womb of earth may thaw
In griefs unpitied as though in the center | And yet
                                                         I cannot die.

    [George Daniel]

b.121, fol. 20

00435 O if compassion dwells within your breast
And follow him to the realms of endless day.

    [signed Mary]

c.343, p. 39

00436 Oh! if my mind
Great King! Do thou fulfil.

    [Thomas Stevens?], 'Another meditation'

c.259

00437 O! if such beaming luster in art's face,
O who begin t'admire thee ne'er shall end!

    [John Rose?]

b.227, p. 74

00438 O! if the foolish race of man who find
And study nature well, and nature's laws.

    'A translation from Lucretius'

c.83/4, no. 1091

00439 Oh if the muse's song could aught bestow,
Celestial product of immortal skies!

[Mary (Shackleton) Leadbeater], 'On the death of Capt. John St. Clair'

c.140, p. 86; File 13409

00440 Oh, I'll have a husband! aye marry
Than die an old maid undone.

[Henry] Carey, 'The romp's song: sung by Mrs. Cibber in The provoked husband. The words and music by . . .'

fc.61, p. 63

00441 O intermixture sweet of hill and dale!
Laughs o'er the ruins of his lost estate.

John Lockman, 'On viewing Knowle Park in Kent 24 Octr 1768, belonging to his grace the Duke of Dorset'

c.267/4, p. 394

00442 O Israel thou art blest
Among thy saints a race.

P[hilip] Doddridge, 'The saints' excellency with respect to their relation employments, pleasures and hopes. Rev. XII [?]'

c.493, p. 75

00443 O Isr'el hear: the Lord thy God
And Isr'el greatly fear'd.

'The same [the Decalogue]—another meter'

c.264/3, p. 121

00444 O Jansson! Bothell! Friends to Britain dear:
My heart was with you, tho' restrain'd my hand.

John Lockman, 'A thought: suggested whilst the names of the several candidates, to represent the city of London in Parliament, were putting up in Guildhall, 30 June 1747'

c.267/1, p. 35

00445 O Jenyns worthy brother knight
Ne'er lets him wait too long for rhyme.

[Philip Yorke, 2nd earl of Hardwicke]

Poetry Box I/118

00446 O Jesu, Jesu, [st-i-h] on [?]
If for serenity, in his kingdom.

[William Pulley?]

b.134, p. 94

00447 Oh joyful news and art thou come
Was ever love like thine.

[Mary Pluret], 'On Canticles'

c.354

00448 Oh joyful news: for Buckingham is now
In government Jove's imitator be.

[on Buckingham's being created admiral]

Poetry Box VI/29

00449 O Jupiter arise, send us good mutton pies,
And the ken, of the cellar door; that we may |
Drink.

'An additional new verse to God save the King 1786'

c.378, p. 63

00450 O Jupiter! what cause of thy so cruel hate,
Have lived in peace, from female fury free.

'Hippolytus, in Euripides, expostulates with Jupiter against the female sex'

c.189, p. 111

00451 O King eternal and divine,
Thy deeds from pole to pole.

[Christopher] Pitt, 'Psalm 8th'

c.244, p. 501

00452 O King! Forever live! Says Holy Writ:
Then wilt thou live, forever! Gracious King.

John Lockman, 'Verses (writ 6th August 1762,) presented at St James's to the King's most excellent Majesty'

c.267/1, p. 301

00453 O King supreme! All-gracious Father hear!
Then, reigning virtue will again be seen.

F[rances] B[urney d'Arblay], 'Juvenile poems. A prayer for his Majesty's recovery written during his dangerous illness . . . F. B. aged 12 years'

c.486, fol. 18

00454 O King! To mercy be thy soul inclin'd,
'Tis thine to merit, mine is to record.

'A bard introduced by Homer deprecates the wrath of Ulysses in these emphatic terms'

c.83/3, no. 790

00455 O Kneller, could our verse present so true
The gallery will a gallery appear.

'Their Majesties' pictures drawn to the life by Mr. Kneller'

Poetry Box VI/46

00456 O last and best of Scots who did'st maintain
And could not fall but with thy country's fate.

[John] Dryden, 'Upon the death of [John Graham of Claverhouse] the earl of Dundee' [27 July 1689] [Crum 0544]

Poetry Box IV/54; c.360/3, no. 57; see also 'Farewell thou best . . .'.

00457 O! lead me to some peaceful room
To rule in the house, where he's a slave.

'Song'

c.189, p. 221

00458 O lead me where my darling lies,
I'll dig my way to thee.

'Verses made by a father on the death of his
dau[ghter]'

c.244, p. 570

00459 Oh leeze me on my spinning wheel,
Of Bessy at her spinning wheel!

[Robert Burns], 'Bess and her spinning wheel'

c.142, p. 307

00460 O let me haunt the peaceful shade,
Whose latent course resembles thine.

[William] Shenstone

c.20/7; c.21; c.344, p. 93

00461 O let me learn to be a saint on earth
And angels sung the news when Christ came down.

[William Strode], 'The divine's commendation of a
good voice'
[Crum 0556]

b.205, fol. 59v

00462 Oh let me not serve so, as those men serve
What hurts it me, to be excommunicate.

[John Donne], 'Elegia [septima]' [Elegy VI]
[Crum 0557]

b.114, p. 87; b.148, p. 67

00463 O, let me seize thy pen sublime
In apathy's cold arms to die.

'Ode to the Muse. By Laura'

c.344, p. 105

00464 O let me strike my boldest lyre!
His stem secures us halcyon days. | O may it ever
bloom!

John Lockman, 'An ode, on the crushing of the
rebellion, anno 1746, humbly inscrib'd to his royal
highness the Duke [of Cumberland?]; and presented
to His Majesty at Kensington' [pr. 1746 (Foxon L218)]

c.267/2, p. 285

00465 O let me weep in English who'll deny
To wring a language from our blubbered eyes.

G[iles] H[ayward], 'G. H. on the death of the King of
Sweden'
[cf. Crum 0559]

b.62, p. 18

00466 O let the rickety and dwarfish soul
Too just to sicken at a sister's praise.

[William] Hayley, 'On Miss Seward's complaining he
had left a little soreness in her spirit'

File 6924

00467 O let the sacred presence fill
And freely give up all the rest.

'Hymn 46th'

c.562, p. 54; see also 'Come Savior, Jesu . . .'.

00468 O let thy favor, bounty, liberality,
O never leave us to our foes.

[Sir William Trumbull], 'Old hymn of St Ambrose'

Trumbull Box: Poetry Box XIII/28

00469 O let your once-lov'd friend inscribe the stone
And with domestic sorrows mix his own.

[Francis Fawkes], 'Epitaph'

fc.21, p. 25

00470 O life thou nothing's younger brother!
For all old Homer's life e'er since he died, till now.

[Abraham Cowley], 'Life and fame'
[Crum 0567b]

b.118, p. 37; c.244, p. 230

00471 O Lindore, canst thou doubt my love,
Which Lindore's fond affection blest.

Charles Burney, the younger, 'Lindore. A song,
written in answer to The fairest of the fair . . .
July 5th. 1779'

c.35, p. 19

00472 O, Logan, sweetly didst thou glide
And Willie hame, to Logan braes.

[Robert Burns], 'Sonnet'

c.142, p. 286

00473 O! London city,
For money sterling, | Adieu, farewell.

'. . . As I was resolved to leave London for awhile, I
took my farewell of it in the following song, set to the
tune of Ye beaux of pleasure'

fc.78, fol. 4

00474 O long remember'd and esteem'd as long
For the close countinghouse and smoky street.

[J. M—tt], 'To Palemon on a prospect of quitting the
country'

c.140, p. 500

00475 O Lord, a refuge and defense
So shall it thrive! The praise be Thine.

'Psalm 90. 18th day Morning prayer'

c.264/2, p. 90

00476   O Lord give ear to my just cause
And with the sword him smite.

     [Thomas Sternhold], 'The 6 psalm for the defense of
     man's innocency' [verses from Psalm 17]
     [cf. Crum 0581]

     a.3, fol. 72v

00477   O Lord how great the favor
As none below can tell.

     'Hymn 39th'

     c.562, p. 46

00478   O Lord, how well in thee
Good Joseph died beneath them both.

     [Sir Richard Bulstrode], 'Upon Christ's life and death'

     fb.88, p. 115v

00479   O Lord, I have repos'd full trust
And ye new strength confide.

     'Psalm 31'

     c.264/1, p. 121

00480   O Lord, I lift mine eyes to Thee
Erect, and pride lifts up its horn.

     'Psalm 123'

     c.264/3, p. 70

00481   O Lord, if I Thy grace obtain
God will me safely keep.

     [Sir William Trumbull], 'P[salm] 4' [rough draft]
     Trumbull Box: Poetry Box XIII/3; see also 'O righteous
     Judge . . .'.

00482   O Lord, I've trusted in Thy name,
My tongue shall praise Thee, Lord.

     'Psalm 71 Morning prayer 14 day'

     c.264/2, p. 41

00483   O Lord, let not thine anger rise,
And shame their faces fill.

     'Psalm 6. Evening prayer'

     c.264/1, p. 15

00484   O Lord my God, give grace to guide my pen,
Confess you are, no way, no truth, no light.

     'A friendly admonition to the Quakers'

     c.187, p. 54

00485   O Lord my mind is not elate
And He shall lift thee up.

     'The same [Psalm 131], another meter'

     c.264/3, p. 78

00486   O Lord, my strength, to Thee my pray'r
And crown it with success.

     'Psalm 28'

     c.264/1, p. 111

00487   O Lord of hosts hear England's cry,
Shall still rewarded be.

     'A psalm in satire on the times written by a fair lady'

     fb.207/3, p. 6; Poetry Box x/36 (ll. 1–12)

00488   O Lord of hosts, how amiable
His joys shall never cease.

     'Psalm 84'

     c.264/2, p. 77

00489   O Lord, of thy compassion hear,
My trust shall be always.

     'Psalm 55'

     c.264/2, p. 7

00490   O Lord our God and King how high
Through all this earthly frame.

     'Psalm 8'

     c.264/1, p. 23

00491   O Lord rebuke me not in wrath,
From my salvation go.

     'Psalm 38 Morning prayer 8 day'

     c.264/1, p. 169

00492   O Lord remember Jesse's son,
His foes shall clothe, and blot their name.

     'Psalm 132. Morning prayer 28 day'

     c.264/3, p. 78

00493   O Lord set thou my heart upright,
Give me, my God, my daily bread.

     'Prayers, or meditations'

     c.187, p. 39

00494   O Lord, since sinful dust may dare,
Unknown to mortals here below.

     'Hymn'

     c.153, p. 49

00495   O Lord that heaven dost possess
Forevermore shall dwell.

     [William Whittingham, Thomas Sternhold, and
     William Kethe], 'For the prosperity of the church.
     Psalm 55' [verses from Psalms 120–121, 123–125]
     [cf. Crum 0634]

     a.3, fol. 138

00496   O Lord the gentiles do invade,
For the like praise in store.

     [John Hopkins], 'Psal: 32. Against a general calamity'
[verses from Psalm 79]

     a.3, fol. 113v

00497   O Lord, the heathen do invade
And give Thee thanks always.

     'Psalm 79 Morning prayer 16th day'

     c.264/2, p. 67

00498   O Lord Thou didst us clear forsake
According to their deed.

     [John Hopkins], 'The 24 psalm. For constancy and
perseverance' [verses from Psalms 60–62]

     a.3, fol. 101

00499   O Lord Thou hast me tried and known,
Forever lead thou me.

     [Thomas Norton], 'A confession of our sins to God
the 59 psalm' [verses from Psalm 139]

     a.3, fol. 143

00500   O Lord Thou hast me tried and known,
And guide me to eternal bliss.

     'Psalm 139. Morning prayer 29 day'

     c.264/3, p. 91

00501   O Lord, Thou hast me tried and known,
And train me up to bliss.

     'The same [Psalm 139], another meter'

     c.264/3, p. 93

00502   O Lord, Thou hast perus'd me thro'
That leads to everlasting day.

     Tho[mas] Scott, jr., 'Psalm 139'

     c.244, p. 256

00503   O Lord, Thou seest my wrongs abound
From their invective power.

     [Thomas Stanley], 'Meditat.XV. Upon the many
jealousies raised and scandals cast upon the King'

     b.152, p. 48

00504   O Lord Thou'st cast thy people down,
Effect, O, speed our arms again.

     'Psalm 60'

     c.264/2, p. 18

00505   O Lord, to my complaint give ear
And my sure comforts prove.

     'Psalm 86 Morning prayer. 17 day'

     c.264/2, p. 80

00506   O Lord, to whom the heart of man
And who with him contend.

     'Psalm 5'

     c.264/1, p. 13

00507   O Lord what is such a world as this
Then for pure sorrow shall not die.

     'Braye Lute Book,' Music Ms. 13, fol. 37v

00508   O Lord what thing is man that him
Of guile and subtlety.

     [Thomas Norton], 'A thanks to God for his mercy.
Psal: 61' [verses from Psalm 144]

     a.3, fol. 146v

00509   O Lord, when I do summon up my sins,
And shine like saints before his glorious face.

     'The soul's complaint'

     c.187, p. 51

00510   O Lord with speed and gracious ear
Be caught in his own trap.

     'Psalm 141'

     c.264/3, p. 97

00511   O love, a plague, though grac'd with gallant gloss,
For in thy seats, a snake is in the moss.

     c.339, p. 327

00512   O! love! how cold and slow to take my part!
The vassal world is then thy own.

     [John Wilmot], 2nd E[arl] of R[ochester], trans.,
'[Ovid. Amores II.ix.] To love'
[Crum 0665]

     b.105, p. 67; b.334, p. 169

00513   O love how many thy weeks
A girl insists again.

     [John Wolcot ('Peter Pindar')], 'Apostrophe to love'

     Poetry Box v/101

00514   O love, of pure and heav'nly birth,
To give you room; come, reign in mine.

     [William Cowper, trans.], 'The rejection or reception
of truth and pure love. Vol. 2. Cant. 22' [of Jeanne
Guion's 'Spiritual songs']

     c.470 (autogr.)

00515   O love whose power and might
Nay then the devil take me.

     [John Hoskins?], 'To his mistress ' [Lady Jacobs?
Answered by 'Your letter I received . . .']
[Crum 0669]

     b.148, p. 6; b.200, p. 129

00516 O loved, but not enough—though deeper far
Then thou hast crown'd him and he reigns indeed.

    [William Cowper, trans.], 'Glory to God alone. Vol. 2.
    Son: 15' [of Jeanne Guion's 'Spiritual songs']

    c.470 (autogr.)

00517 O lov'd October! Still my vacant day
Far from the quiet of the rural bower.

    'October (a sonnet)'

    c.355, p. 271

00518 O lovely Richmond, lovely though in vain
Swoll'n are those eyes that shone with sweet excess.

    [Horace Walpole, 4th earl of Orford], 'Verses on
    ladies of quality. Duchess of Richmond' [d. 1796]
    [Crum 0671]

    c.157, p. 67

00519 O lovely Tam, this knot I send, of love to you that
hath no end.
And now my dear I vow to you, to love you still
and so adieu.

    c.93

00520 O make me still submit unto thy will
And then I am sure they will be conquer'd never.

    [Mary Serjant]

    fb.98, fol. 160

00521 O make me your first 'tis a natural prayer
That both for my first I would give up tomorrow.

    'Charade'

    Diggle Box: Poetry Box XI/71

00522 O man! By fate condemn'd to know
Lest, by desertion, we should fly our woes!

    'Ode to death'

    c.83/3, no. 823

00523 O man no more thy self deceive
Make us to know . . . .

    Poetry Box VI/89 (incomplete)

00524 O man what art thou till the hour of birth
And all thy age, thou spend'st in melancholy.

    b.118, p. 39

00525 O Marian! fair as op'ning May;
As down Thames' silver stream we glide.

    John Lockman, 'To Marian: (the scene Vauxhall
    Gardens) set to music by Dr. Boyes [William
    Boyce] . . . Aug. 1743'

    c.267/2, p. 129

00526 O! mark his pale shallow cheek, and mark his
eyeball's glare!
Had fixed my heart, assured my faith, and heaven
had gained a soul.

    M[atthew] G[regory] Lewis, 'The felon'

    Poetry Box X/17

00527 O marriage! Happiest, easiest, safest state
And all our senses without guilt enjoy.

    'Some lines on marriage which the Revd.
    Mr. Humphreys introduced in his sermon [18 January
    1736/7] on . . . the marriage of Gabriel Hanger esqr. to
    Miss Elizabeth Bond, an heiress. See Tatler no. 49'

    c.360/2, no. 128

00528 O marvel thou great monarch, didst complain
Has grief enough that finds no world but this.

    [Henry Phillipps?]

    b.156, p. 21; see also 'No marvel . . .'.

00529 O, Mary, heave a sigh for me,
Accept a Tony true.

    'Tony's address to Mary' [with a dog-Latin address to
    the sea, 'Tonis ad resta mare']

    File 13409

00530 O matched blessing and unheard-of thing
Was there whose coming we must celebrate.

    'Luke 1.41'

    c.160, fol. 57

00531 O! matchless circle! since thou dost contain
That twice twelve farthings would have made me
blest.

    [Ralph Payne, 1st baron Lavington], 'Addressed to my
    box' [Lady Payne, baroness Lavington]

    Poetry Box II/5

00532 O matchless eloquence, to wisdom join'd!
With jealous hand she crush'd the heav'nly mold.

    'On Mr [William] Pitt, from ministerial portraits'

    Diggle Box: Poetry Box XI/6

00533 Oh may I place in God my happiness!
Which will exalt us to the joys above.

    [Edmund Wodehouse], 'July 10 [1715]'

    b.131, p. 230

00534 Oh may my soul be giv'n to Thee
O'er our own lusts the victory.

    [Edmund Wodehouse], 'Apr. 28 [1715]'

    b.131, p. 206

00535 Oh! May no virgin be o'ercome by love;
For man, should he strive, can never constant prove.

c.549, p. 134

00536 Oh may these pencill'd tablets long remain
Whence the fair labors of the muses thrive.

'To the Rev. Mr. Gouch on reviewing on a winter
night his drawings. A sonnet. 1780'

fc.53, p. 10

00537 Oh may you walk, as years advance,
Death with his dart—but not his sting!

'Lines to the Duchess of R—— on seeing her dance'

c.83/1, no. 148

00538 O may your host, that honor'd sire,
The charms of his poetic dream!

[William Hayley]

File 7052

00539 O memory! Celestial maid!
But ah! For pleasure yields us pain.

[William] Shenstone, 'Ode to memory'

fc.132/1, p. 160

00540 O memory! thou fond deceiver,
In thee must ever find a foe.

[Oliver Goldsmith]

Poetry Box XII/96

00541 O merciful Jesu
Have mercy on the soul of Sir John Dew.

'On Sr John Dew priest'

fb.143, p. 22

00542 O might I see Thee everywhere
I'll weep till I'm with Thee.

'From a M.S. of B.' [hymn]

c.180, p. 71

00543 O might I this moment cease
With all the life of love!

'Hymn 96th'

c.562, p. 130

00544 O mighty death, whose dart can kill
The man that made him souls at will.

'Epitaph on a cobbler'

c.74; see also 'Come hither read . . .'.

00545 O modesty thou shy and bashful maid,
And give a goddess to my cell.

[Dr. ( ) Walcot (Peter Pindar?)], 'Hymn to modesty'

c.90

00546 O moonwort tell us where thou hidst the smith
So sure but thou with speed canst it undo.

[Joshua Sylvester, trans. Guillaume de Salluste,
seigneur] Du Bartas, 'Of moonwort'

b.284, p. 54

00547 O more than ecstasy! O strains divine!
Death's grisly train, and crush'd the serpent's head.

John Lockman, 'Hearing Mr. Handel's Messiah . . .
April 1759'

c.267/1, p. 271

00548 O! more than friends: O! more that father, thou
A griev'd and broken heart alone can tell.

Diggle Box: Poetry Box XI/58

00549 O! More, whose unaffected praise,
Shine with imperishable rays!

[Richard] Polwhele, 'Lines said to have been addressed
to Miss Hannah More'

c.83/3, no. 911

00550 O mortal man and worms' meat
Thy sinful life for to amend.

b.234, p. 304

00551 O mortal men have me in mind,
For Jesus' sake that died on tree. | Amen

'Of All Souls' Day. Nov. 2'

a.30[48]

00552 O muse, to whom the glory does belong
And heaven's grand chorus makes Olympus ring.

[Wentworth Dillon], 4th earl of R[oscommon], 'A
paean, or a song of triumph on the translation, and
apotheosis of King Charles the Second'

b.201, p. 124

00553 O my dearest I shall grieve thee
But would you know sweet love? For all.

[Thomas Carew], 'To his mistress'
[Crum 0713]

b.356, p. 221

00554 O my fair, my doting heart
Shows my faith, and proves thy sway.

c.549, p. 8

00555 O, my fickle Jenny,
With thee alone, I'd beg to die.

Peggy Trevor

c.358, p. 169

00556 O my God to thee I fly
Which in fullness wait on thee.

[Thomas Stanley], 'Meditat: X. Upon their seizing the King's magazines forts navy and militia'

b.152, p. 31

00557 O my good God grant thou to me
My faith to Thee forego.

[Edmund Wodehouse], 'Jan. 5 [1715]'.

b.131, p. 132

00558 O! my Nassau did you know how I languish
For if envious they prove, they may kiss my
Nassau. | Kiss my Nass, kiss my Nassau.

'The maiden's garland or fair Nanny's complaint for the absence of her true love to an excellent new tune' [Crum 0719]

File 17395

00559 O my pretty Sally how beauteous thou art
It's just like a rose that is going to fade.

Henry Williams, 'Verses on my sister Sally Williams'
Greatheed Box/61

00560 O! my treasure crown my pleasure
For all its smart.

'The bliss'
fc.61, p. 66

00561 Oh! Nan, bad news! The King have sent
Till joy comes back with Madam Ellis!

'Impromptu to Mrs. Ellis—written at Paulton's Christmas 1781. The village lamentation'
c.106, p. 44

00562 O never let a virtuous mind despair,
For constant hearts are love's peculiar care.

c.93

00563 O! Never let me see that shape again
'Tis other's happiness that gnaws my heart.

'Envy . . . Observer v. 5. no. 130'
c.355, p. 88

00564 O night! dark night! Wrapt round with Stygian
gloom.
Fools spare not heav'n itself, O Y[oung], nor thee.

[William] Whitehead, 'More night thoughts a fragment'
Poetry Box I/85 (2 copies)

00565 O night, O day, whilst nights and days shall last,
Amen, Amen, Amen, say we.

S[amuel] W[ard], 'Upon the fifth of November' [1605]
[Crum 0727]

b.197, p. 203

00566 O night thou tak'st the robe and mask away
For night's black mantle covers all alike.

[Robert Cottesford]

b.144, p. 3

00567 O Nigrocella! don't despise
Take heed you burn not to a coal.

'The fair lover and his black mistress'
fb.108, p. 205

00568 Oh! not by men, for that I could have borne,
For [?] bugs had been all plagues in one.

John Lockman, 'The exclamation of a Londoner, on his being bit, in a village near Salisbury . . . Sept. 1744'
c.267/1, p. 112

00569 Oh now I see 'tis naught but fate
Lest I should more distracted be.

[Henry Hughes]

b.213, p. 115

00570 O now the certain cause I know,
This from your cheeks, that from your eyes.

b.200, p. 433

00571 O nymph! Who loves to float on the green wave,
O nymph! From out thy pearly cave—arise!

[Ann (Ward)] Radcliffe, 'To the sea nymph'
c.83/3, no. 874

00572 O nymph whose powerful charms his heart could
gain
Must ne'er confess his heart attach'd to thee!

Faustina Marratti Zappi, 'Sonnet of . . . to a lady with whom she supposed her husband to have been formerly in love: written at the Turk's Head Tavern Strand London . . . July 1792'
c.344, p. 80

00573 Oh! of the royal martyr's sacred race!
For none could ever yet his successor destroy.

Samuel Wesley, the elder, 'The history of the Old Testament in verse by . . . chaplain to his grace John Duke of Buckingham: author of The life of Christ an heroic poem . . . here ends the first volume Decr. 31st 1729'
c.372

00574 O—O—lead me, lead me to some peaceful gloom,
Yet, you be still, yet, yet, be still, yet, yet, be still,
still a slave.

[George Powell], 'A song in The tragedy of Bonduca.
set by Mr. Henry Purcell'

c.160, fol. 83v

00575 O Pallas! queen of ev'ry art,
Are vanity and woe.

'Ode to wisdom'

c.83/2, no. 645

00576 O parent of each lovely muse
O bid Britannia rival Greece.

Joseph Warton, 'An ode to fancy'
[Crum 0735]

c.139, p. 103

00577 O people of England! when will you grow wise,
And the nation is curst 'till great J[ame]s is call'd in.

fc.58, p. 105; c.570/1, p. 43

00578 O Petersham! Delightful spot,
Will soon, alas! behold me die.

John Lockman, 'Verses, from Abbé Chaulieu'

c.267/4, p. 151; see also 'Woodford! . . .'.

00579 O Pitt thy country's hope, her steadfast friend,
He glorious rose—and sat with endless fame.

'Brittania, a poem'

c.151, p. 7

00580 O! place me where the burning noon
That faithful heart still burns for thee!

Charlotte (Turner) Smith, 'Sonnet from Petrarch'

c.343, p. 84

00581 Oh! pleasing thought it gives relief
Nor let my languid comforts die.

T[homas] S[tevens], 'Mourners for the dead carrying
their grief to Jesus'

c.259, p. 17

00582 O pleasure in successive maze!
Faint me, compar'd to these I sing.

John Lockman, 'The enchantments, or the opera of
Antigone . . . May 1746'

c.267/1, p. 41

00583 O Pollio! Hear an honest prayer:
Whose love embraces all mankind.

John Lockman, 'To the Earl of Middlesex: for New
Year's Day, 1759'

c.267/1, p. 263

00584 O ponder well be not severe
Depends poor Polly['s] life.

[John Gay], 'Air in The beggar's opera'

c.503, p. 55

00585 O popularity, thou giddy thing!
You've serv'd my turn, and vagabonds, adieu!

R[ichard] Cumberland, 'Ode to popularity'

c.83/2, no. 605

00586 O poverty! of pale consumptive hue,
And dress in smiles the tyrant hour of death.

[Charles James Fox], 'An invocation to poverty'

c.481, p. 294; c.90 ('frail consumptive')

00587 O praise the Lord, exalt Him high,
His laws: praise ye the Lord.

'Evening prayer Psalm 147. Hallelujah'

c.264/3, p. 108

00588 O praise the Lord, for He is good,
Let all the people say, Amen.

'Psalm 106. Evening prayer'

c.264/3, p. 20

00589 O praise the Lord, praise Him, praise Him,
Praise him with one accord.

[John Marckant], 'A praise of God for his mercy. Psal.
57' [verses from Psalm 135]
[Crum 0747]

a.3, fol. 141v; see also next.

00590 O praise the Lord praise Him praise Him
Which is forevermore.

'A song of praise for the Lord's Supper'

a.3, fol. 67; see also previous.

00591 O praise ye the Lord,
Such honor obtain.

'The same [Psalm 149], another meter'

c.264/3, p. 114

00592 O, pray my Lord Wharton how came it about
A health to Sacheverell—God bless our Queen.

'A health'

Poetry Box VI/2

00593 O quench the flame, the miserable fate
Grant that no day may ever us divide.

'The passionate lover'

fb.142, p. 37

00594 O rare Mr. Nott
For without it you're Nott a true blue.

    [ ] Pounceforth, 'On Randolph Nott, the man famous for flannel nine times dipped in blue'

c.373, p. 62

00595 O reeged[*sic*] thoughts pursue me not
He those He loves chastises with this rod.

    [Mrs. ( ) Feilding]

b.226, p. 28

00596 O render thanks to God, and praise,
His loving-kindness and his truth.

    'Psalm 107. Hallelujah Morning prayer 22 day'

c.264/3, p. 25

00597 O righteous Judge, who grant'st [hear'st] the
                        prayer[s]
Resolve on what is right.

    [Sir William Trumbull], 'Psalm 4' [rough draft, two versions]

Trumbull Box: Poetry Box XIII/2, 3; see also 'O Lord, if I Thy grace . . .'.

00598 O Roger hear me what I say
I wish both them and thee good night.

    'A rural panegrig on the Lady Southcott's wedding day to the tune of Gilding of the devil'

b.4, fol. 51v

00599 O royal King, if you'll these faults forgive
To royal gin and brandy show the way.

c.360/1, p. 53

00600 O ruddier than the cherry
And fierce as storms that bluster.

    [John Gay, Alexander Pope, and/or John Hughes], [chorus from Handel's Acis and Galatea, with musical score for bass]

Music MS. 534

00601 O sacred act! Religion hails thee chief
In mem'ry of thy love thy saints repair.

    'Hymns composed the week preceding the sacrament, 1st'

c.515, fol. 15r

00602 O! sacred may the vessel glide,
Which friendship can inspire.

    Charles Burney, the younger, 'Ode, addressed to the vessel, in which Mr. W—— sailed from St. David's to Bristol, June 1777 . . . June 5. 1777'

c.35, p. 25

00603 O sacred stream we hail thy source
And gospel grace is growing too.

    T[homas] S[tevens], 'Sung Jany. 14 1781 (night)'

c.259, p. 113

00604 O sacred Time how soon thou'rt gone!
And prove we're candidates for heaven.

    'A midnight thought addressed to a friend'

c.83/3, no. 830

00605 O sacred tutors of the saints you guard,
But that I fear to faint—here then, | An end.

    'A poem on the first day of the week'

b.202, p. 96

00606 O sad vicissitude that seventy-nine
They throw monarchic government quite down.

    [Sir Philip Wodehouse], 'An epigram of anno 1679'

b.131, p. 46

00607 O Sal'sbury people give ear to my song,
And make it as good as the Thames.

    Walter Pope, 'The Salisbury ballad with the learned commentaries of a friend to the author's memory. London. Printed 1676' [Wing P2915A]

b.54, p. 943; c.113/14

00608 O say my soul how greatly thou art blest,
Where truth and innocence have naught to fear.

    'Elegy—written the 28th of Decr. 1791'

fc.124, p. 73

00609 O say thou dear possessor of my breast,
Like me—with passion founded on esteem.

    [James] Hammond, 'Elegy to Miss [Emma] Dashwood' [pr. 1733 (Foxon H21]

c.130, p. 81; c.175, p. 54 (attr. E. C.; var.); c.83/1, no. 113

00610 O say! what is that thing call'd light
Altho' a poor blind boy.

    [Colley Cibber], 'The blind boy'
    [Crum O773]

Poetry Box IV/24

00611 O say what transports equal those
Fly to each other's arms.

    John Lockman, 'Songs on love and marriage. The rapturous meeting: set by Lewis Granom esq.'

c.267/2, p. 86; c.268 (first part), p. 58

00612 O Scotland lament the loss of thy friend,
Cause great Dundee is safe underground.

    'Bonny Dundee'

b.111, p. 83

00613　O serpent's seed, each bird and savage brute
　　　Will those condemn that tender not their fruit.

　　　c.339, p. 312

00614　O sex by grace and nature blest:
　　　Of my encomiums chose in female rhymes.

　　　Sir Thomas Urquhart, 'The reason, why I do not
　　　always keep in my verses (as English poets for the
　　　most parts do) a masculine rhyme: to wit where the
　　　accent falls on the last syllable of the line To
　　　womankind'

　　　fb.217, p. 52

00615　O shade of Hanb'ry, from thy seat bestow
　　　Thou shall be styl'd the little queen of May.

　　　[Edward Jerningham], 'May the 9th 1779 Miss Boyle's
　　　birthday'

　　　c.90

00616　O, share my cottage, dearest maid,
　　　Shall still be spent in pleasing thee.

　　　[Anna Seward], 'A pastoral ballad'

　　　c.83/2, no. 616

00617　O shield me from his rage celestial powers,
　　　The intemp'rate sinner's never-failing curse.

　　　[Esther Johnson], 'Jealousy by Stella, the amiable and
　　　much injured wife of Dr. Swift'

　　　c.83/2, no. 597 (attr. [Mary] Chandler)

00618　O shun ye fair, to you this verse is due,
　　　And you, perhaps, have sorrows of your own.

　　　Tho[ma]s Crop, jr., 'A rhapsody . . . Octo. 12. 1786'

　　　c.83/1, no. 11

00619　Oh! since before we cast forth sweets in love,
　　　How great? How vast? Must be our joys above.

　　　c.189, p. 36

00620　O sing, O soar, O faint, O pant and breathe!
　　　O the eternal friends they all are mine.

　　　Thomas Traherne, [Meditation (fourth century)] 15'

　　　b.308, p. 187

00621　O sing ye now unto the Lord
　　　And shall from age to age endure.

　　　[John Hopkins], 'A praise of God's mercy and fidelity
　　　unto us in Christ. Psalm 42' [verses from Psalms
　　　98-100]

　　　a.3, fol. 118v

00622　O Sir we all upstairs are mad
　　　You know Sir that a coach you brought.

　　　Miss [ ] Andrews, 'Presented to some gentlemen who
　　　spent the day at Mrs. Caley's'

　　　File 245/3

00623　O, sleep! Assuaging balm! Why not detain
　　　And let me ever bid the world—'Good night!'

　　　'Sonnet—despair . . . June 1792 City Coffee House'

　　　c.344, p. 77; c.83/3, no. 788

00624　O sleep! Thou flatterer of happy minds
　　　The wretch by fortune, or by love undone.

　　　[William Congreve], 'Address to sleep'

　　　c.360/1, p. 319

00625　O soon I must quit this house of clay,
　　　Shall soar above the sky.

　　　'Hymn 107'

　　　c.562, p. 148

00626　O span thy arrow. Measure breadth and length
　　　And at their squadrons gallantly let fly.

　　　[Sir Philip Wodehouse], 'Anthony Sparrow O span thy
　　　arrow'

　　　b.131, back (no. 10/2)

00627　O Spence, thou bugbear to the scribbling race,
　　　None e'er found faults in thee.

　　　[N.] H[erbert], 'On the same [Mr Joseph Spence the
　　　critic]'

　　　Spence Papers, folder 91

00628　O spotless paper, fair and white
　　　That which destroys, shall make thee live.

　　　[Laetitia (Van Lewen) Pilkington], 'Verses by Miss
　　　Talbot . . . a young lady of 12 years of age' [disowned,
　　　and attributed to 'Miss Van Lewen', by Catherine
　　　Talbot]

　　　c.360/1, p. 19; Diggle Box: Poetry Box XI/29

00629　O Stanley give ear to a husband's petition
　　　And pass my life—and think with Crewe.

　　　'Petition of David Garrick to the Secretary of the
　　　Customs requesting him to solicit the commissioners
　　　on behalf of his afflicted wife' [satire]

　　　c.150, p. 61

00630　O stay! And take me with you; when you go
　　　There's nothing now worth living for below.

　　　c.189, p. 58

00631　O stay your tears you who complain,
　　　To drive such busybodies home.

　　　[James I?], 'The wiper of the people's tears, The
　　　dryer-up of doubts and fears'
　　　[Crum 0803]

　　　fb.23, p. 321

00632 Oh strange! what is't I hear? the man
Would have been lost thus in a fog.

    'Another lampoon against Scroggs 1679'

    b.54, p. 1138

00633 O stranger mourn not him beneath:
In the mild regions of the bless'd.

    [ ] Ellison, 'An old man's epitaph from the Greek of
    Carphyllides'

    Greatheed Box/35

00634 O! stranger softly lightly tread
And by a friend's voice his virtues are sung.

    'Epitaph'

    Poetry Box XII/62

00635 O stretch under this stone is laid,
Rise higher if you can.

    'Epitaph at Frome in Somerset on Christopher
    Thumb'

    c.113/20

00636 Oh! sure the greedy wretch is spent
Than the first roses of the year shall blow.

    'A panagyric on salt water'

    c.481, p. 18

00637 Oh sweet how handsomely my Lyra sings
These gloves do hinder me from playing on thee.

    'Answer' [to 'Hark hark when I . . .']

    b.356, p. 106

00638 O sweetest spot, which my bright eye,
Alas! we've no such liquor here.

    John Lockman, 'The man in the moon, to the genius
    of Vauxhall Gardens . . . Aug. 1749'

    c.267/1, p. 132

00639 O talk not thus of 'tresses hoar,'
But ah! I could not feel it more!

    'Answer of the Duke de Nivernais [to 'Behold this
    lock . . .'] . . . imitated'

    c.90

00640 O, tell me Chloris, tell me why
Tho' with despair opprest and sure of no return.

    'Upon a lady going in to the country'

    Poetry Box VI/38

00641 O tell me Concord why with hasty stride
And all the glory and the praise be thine.

    Charles Atherton Allnutt, 'An invitation to Concord—
    having a retrospect to the altercation in religious
    concerns now prevailing in Wallingford'

    c.112, p. 30

00642 Oh! Tell me, tell me, Celia, why
An endless torment share.

    [Elizabeth (Shirley) Compton, countess of
    Northampton], 'A song in dialogue, to the tune of
    Alexis shunned his [fellow swains]'

    Accession 97.7.40

00643 O tell me, tell thou god of wind
One body shall our souls combine. | Go wind then
                             blow &c.

    [William Strode], 'Song on a sigh'
    [Crum O816]

    b.205, fol. 69v

00644 O temporising wretch thus to abuse,
And so you whited wall adieu farewell.

    'To Mr. Hilton of St. Nicholas's in Gloucester[shire],
    on his sermon May 29th 1692' [answered by 'Insipid
    folk . . .']

    b.III, p. 209

00645 O thank the Lord, His goodness praise,
Whose mercy lasts always.

    'Psalm 118 24 day'

    c.264/3, p. 44

00646 Oh! that folk wad weel consider
Stream'd in silence down his cheek!

    [Hector Macneill], 'The waes o' war: or the upshot o'
    the history o' Will and Jean'

    c.142, p. 177

00647 Oh that I could but vote myself a poet
Kimbolton's but a rumbling wheelbarrow.

    [John Cleveland], 'Rupertismus'

    b.93, p. 133

00648 Oh that I could by some chemic art
Then boldly f—— my passage back again.

    'Votum'

    b.105, p. 397

00649 Oh that I could my heart devote
How whilst I live, or when I die.

    [Edmund Wodehouse], 'Novr. 29 1714'

    b.131, p. 99

00650 Oh that I could so well attend
And that th'are such, as his most gracious mercy
                             does allow.

    [Edmund Wodehouse], 'Decr. 3 [1714]'

    b.131, p. 103

00651 O! that I now my dear, my charming fair,
That I of all your sex, can love but you alone.

M[aurice] J[ohnson], 'An epistle from . . . to Miss A.
his mistress and happily afterward his beloved wife'
c.229/2, fol. 20; see also 'O thou whom all . . .'.

00652 Oh that mine eyes were springs, and could transform
For this poor stream of brine shed for thy sake.

Tho[mas] Cross, 'Upon the death of Samuel Jope the
son of John Jope, who died the fifteenth of August in
the year 1660'
[cf. Crum O832]

b.212, p. 226

00653 Oh that mine eyes would melt into a flood,
To mourn for him, for whom alone he died.

'A hymn upon our Savior's passion'
[Crum O833, with last line of O830–31]

c.547, p. 164

00654 Oh! that my friend would venture forth,
Believe the muse no more.

Charles Atherton Allnutt, 'To a friend Mr. Edw[ar]d
Wells junr.'

c.112, p. 109

00655 Oh that my God would me conform
True knowledge and eternal gain.

Charles Atherton Allnutt, '8th Romans 29 v.—
predestinated to be conformed to the image of his son'

c.112, p. 42

00656 Oh that my heart did so repose
Our Savior calls it a new birth.

[Edmund Wodehouse], 'Aug. 10 [1715]'

b.131, p. 244

00657 Oh that my heart were sacrifice[d]
To love and to adore eternally.

[Edmund Wodehouse], 'Octr. 1 1714'

b.131, p. 50

00658 Oh that my soul could spread its case
Access to his indulgent ear.

T[homas] S[tevens], 'Psalm 102.1.2 . . . sung Feby. 1.
1781'

c.259, p. 122

00659 Oh that my soul soar'd so to thee
As makes us, whilst on earth, to heav'n paraise.

[Edmund Wodehouse], 'Octr. 24 [1714]'

b.131, p. 67

00660 Oh! that the chemist's magic art
And guides the planets in their course.

'On a tear . . . Florio'

c.344, p. 97; c.355, p. 266; c.504, p. 197; c.83/2, no. 406
(var.)

00661 O that the fates, who tore thee in thy bloom,
Dispel the shades of night.

[ ] Ellison, 'An epitaph written by Dr. Jortin, and
published among his Lusus poetici, as a fragment of
an ancient inscription . . . translation'

Greatheed Box/29

00662 Oh that the happy hour were come
The appearance of His Son.

[( ) Pierson]

c.328, p. 39

00663 Oh! that the muse might call without offence,
But for the King of kings' sake do not swear.

[John Byrom], 'On hearing a soldier swear'

c.83/3, no. 1018; see also 'Soldier, so tender . . .'.

00664 Oh that those lips had language! Life has pass'd
Thyself remov'd, thy power to soothe me left.

[William] Cowper, 'On the receipt of my mother's
picture . . .'

Poetry Box III/51

00665 Oh that thy love O God bore so full sway
Tho' an impartial judge to all mankind.

[Edmund Wodehouse], 'Novr. 12 [1714]'

b.131, p. 83

00666 Oh that Thy love O God had ta'en
It would enamor here my heart.

[Edmund Wodehouse], 'May 27 [1715]'

b.131, p. 218

00667 O that you were yourself! But, love, you are
You had a father,—let your son say so.

[William] Shakespeare, 'Youthful glory' [Sonnet XIII]

c.94

00668 Oh the days when I was young!
Glows a spark of youthful fire. | O the days &c.

'Song 148'

c.555, p. 205

00669 Oh! the delights, the heav'nly joys,
To fetch our souls away.

[Isaac Watts, Hymns and spiritual songs (1707), bk. II,
Hymn 91]

c.180, p. 34

00670 Oh the fickle state of lovers!
Very heaven or very hell.

[Crum 0843]

b.200, p. 432

00671 Oh the hideous chances that attend
Some obvious mischief still disturbs the course.

'In amore miseriae'

b.205, fol. 14v

00672 Oh the mighty fishery!
Doubly charming to behold.

John Lockman, 'Flourish the herring fishery! The tune, O the charming month of May &c. . . . 1750' [printed: Foxon L211–212]

c.267/2, p. 79

00673 Oh! the nightingale I hear:
Glitt'ring round the Cyprian Queen.

John Lockman, 'Hearing Miss Turner sing, at Mr. Hugford's . . . Feb. 1743/4'

c.267/1, p. 295

00674 O the pleasure of the plains,
Dance and sport the hours away.

[John Gay, Alexander Pope, and/or John Hughes], 'Chorus [9, with musical score for tenor, from Handel's Acis and Galatea]'

Music MS. 534

00675 Oh! the sad day
Persuade the world to trouble me no more.

[Thomas Flatman], 'Scena antepenultima' [Crum 0846, last line as O819]

c.81/1, no. 66; see also 'When friends shall shake . . .'.

00676 Oh the sweet comfort! Settled heav'nly joy!
Make them but cleave more close to the Lord high!

[Edmund Wodehouse], 'Apr. 26 [1715]'

b.131, p. 204

00677 O then great Power in whom we move
Call our life our strength, our joy our all.

'B. S. and H. W.'

b.62, p. 115

00678 Oh there's none there's none but I
Must either be a fool or blind.

'Song 52'

b.4, fol. 43

00679 O Theseus hark, but yet in vain
O 'tis my Theseus, or some god.

'Ariadne deserted by Theseus in the island Nepos sitting upon a rock thus complaining'

b.356, p. 122

00680 O! think no more that life's delusive joys
And cheer with hope the terrors of the tomb.

E. C., 'To a friend'

Poetry Box II/21

00681 O thirst of gold what not? but thou canst do,
And make men's heart for to content thereto.

c.339, p. 322

00682 Oh this strange drink so like the Stygian lake,
To the world's treasure pay their sundry tributes.

'It was the pleasure of a poet in the time of Henry the 3rd thus to discant on English ale'

b.206, p. 117

00683 O thou almighty Being, just and wise!
But Christ's diffusive blood must quench the
flaming ball!

Miss [ ] White, of Edgbaston, 'French hymn paraphrased in 1743'

c.532

00684 O thou, ambition's only aim and end,
Greatness to goodness join'd can bliss bestow.

'Sonnet to greatness'

c.135, p. 26

00685 O thou blest native of celestial joy
To expel the fury of resistless love.

'Of love'

b.202, p. 93

00686 O thou, by long experience tried,
And peace and safety thy reward.

[William Cowper, trans.], 'The soul that loves God finds him everywhere. Vol. 2. Son: 108' [of Jeanne Guion's 'Spiritual songs']

c.470 (autogr.)

00687 O thou by nature taught,
And all thy sons, O nature, learn my tale.

[William] Collins, 'Ode on simplicity'

c.351, p. 164

00688 O thou deep tragic genius—deep indeed!
The author's murder'd sense—so bleed and shave him.

C. B., 'To Mr. Dodsley on his tragedy of Cleone'

c.74

00689 O thou genius of rhymes give me thy might
To use splice and proceed with the long-lost cable.

Poetry Box V/7

00690 O thou God of my salvation,
In a nobler strain above.

'Hymn 12th'

c.562, p. 14

00691 O thou! In ev'ry science skill'd,
Will charm the zephyrs with your praise.

John Lockman, 'To the Earl and Countess of
Middlesex: humbly requesting them to encourage my
English imitation, in verse, of Bonarelli's Filio di sciro'
[pr. 1746 (Foxon L225)]

c.267/2, p. 241

00692 O thou in whom complacence dear I find,
And I be ever ravish'd with thy love.

[Joshua Williams, of Kidderminster], 'Mercator to his
Amanda'

c.259, p. 114; fb.142, p. 9 (second series)

00693 O thou lov'd country, where my youth was spent,
The other ever may enshrined be.

'Translation of a sonnet by Mary, Queen of Scots, in
her passage from France to Scotland'

c.240, p. 43

00694 O thou matur'd by glad Hesperian suns
Burst forth all oracle and mystic song.

[Isaac Hawkins Browne, 'In praise of tobacco';
imitation of Thomson's Seasons]
[Crum o868]

Poetry Box I/139

00695 O thou most pensive of the Aonian(?) throng
And made the widow's heart to sing for joy.

'On the death of Joseph Thompson'

File 13409

00696 O thou of tyranny and pride the scourge
Shall curse the day that e'er you robb'd us of him.

'In praise of King William'

Poetry Box I/114

00697 O thou, or friend, or stranger who shall tread
Life has no length, eternity no end!

H[annah] More, 'An epitaph by . . . on Dicey esqr.
1776'

c.341, p. 35

00698 O thou our husband, brother, friend,
And to thy heaven of heavens receive.

'Hymn 72d'

c.562, p. 89

00699 O! thou pale moon, who lead'st the shining throng,
Roll in the course of heaven's eternal day.

M[ary (Shackleton) Leadbeater], 'On the shipwreck of
Edith Lovell, and Joseph Sparrow, who perished in
their passage from Cork to Bristol in the night the 31st
of the 12th month of [17]81. Addressed to Ann
Sparrow sister of the above Joseph from her friend'

c.303; File 13409

00700 O thou pale orb, that silent shines,
A faithless woman's broken vow.

[Robert Burns], 'The lament occasioned by the
unfortunate issue of a friend's amour'

c.139, p. 580

00701 O thou source of joy! the spring
His Caledonian lyre.

Sir Thomas Brand, 'A Sabbath night's prayer for the
King . . . January 1736/7 . . . after our wonderful
deliverance from the great storm'

Spence Papers, folder 74

00702 O Thou supreme enthron'd above,
Will be our blest eternal theme!

'A sacred ode'

c.89, p. 6

00703 O! Thou supreme! Thou author of all good
And be our God, our Savior and our friend.

Poetry Box x/62

00704 O thou sweet Muse from whence there flows
Till night beguiles my woes with sleep.

'Cant: 33'

b.4, fol. 28

00705 O thou sweet smiling power whose gentle sway
But let me live beneath thy gentle sway!

[Frances Burney d'Arblay], 'Sonnet. To hope'

c.486, fol. 13v

00706 O thou that canst, to fate severe,
All heav'n transports the soul.

'Hope, an ode'

c.83/1, no. 94

00707 O thou that glad'st my lonesome hours
And solace all his woes with social sympathy.

'Ode to a singing bird'

c.139, p. 397

00708 O thou that labor'st in this rugged mine
When tenants in fee-simple, stuff thy coffers.

[Judith (Cowper) [Madan], 'Wrote by . . . in her
brother's Coke upon Littleton'

c.360/1, p. 157; see also 'O thou who laborest . . .'.

00709   O thou! that on the moss-clad wall
        The melting tale prolong.

       [J. M—tt], 'Ode to a redbreast'

       c.140, p. 382

00710   O Thou that says all souls are mine
        For Thee to gather it.

       c.124, no. 8

00711   O Thou that wert the king of heav'n and earth,
        To make us kings, that were but slaves before.

       [Francis Quarles], 'On our Blessed Savior'
       [Crum 0883]

       b.118, p. 219/1; b.137, p. 173

00712   O thou, the choicest boon of heav'n!
        The Venus of the graces reign!

       'Ode to friendship'

       c.89, p. 84

00713   O thou the friend by fate assign'd,
        Usurp, with lawless pow'r, her throne.

       'The bachelor's ode to his cat'

       c.89, p. 132

00714   O thou, the friend of man assign'd
        To hear a British shell!

       [William] Collins, 'Ode to pity'

       c.351, p. 160

00715   O thou, the nymph with placid eye!
        Low whisp'ring thro' the shades.

       [Anna Laetitia] (Aikin) [Barbauld], 'Ode to content'
       [Crum 0890]

       fc.132/1, p. 115; c.371, fol. 3; c.140, p. 570

00716   O Thou, to whom all knees do rightly bow,
        The heavenly festival, that has no end.

       [William Stukeley], 'A philosophical meditation, or
       hymn for Christmas 1736'
       [Crum 0890]

       c.371, fol. 3

00717   O thou! to whom these lines belong,
        Let others reason and repine.

       [Richard] Hole, 'Ode to stupidity'

       Diggle Box: Poetry Box xi/28

00718   O thou, to whose all-searching sight
        Where all is calm, and joy, and peace.

       'Hymn 86th'

       c.562, p. 113

00719   O thou unknown almighty cause,
        Delighteth to forgive.

       [Robert Burns], 'A prayer in the prospect of death'

       c.83/2, no. 618

00720   O thou, which to search out the secret parts
        With these articulate blasts to blow the fire.

       [John] Donne, 'To Mr S .B.'

       b.150, p. 201

00721   O thou who art all ear to hear
        Praise God, my God most dear.

       'Prayer for the King by an old curate of Deddington in
       Oxfordshire aged eighty . . . the above was written in
       the year 1789 when George the 3d lay dangerously ill'

       c.341, p. 46

00722   O thou who dost provide for all
        With all their might to cram(?) and thrive!

       R[ichard] V[ernon] S[adleir], 'The humble petition of
       Gruntadella and her family to Madam Mocher'

       c.106, p. 73

00723   O thou! who first attun'd my trembling lyre
        And shew'd me peace and pensive joy were tenants
                           of the shade.

       Sarah Herd, 'Sonnet to the muse'

       c.141, p. 361

00724   O thou who hear'st the present aid
        Ne'er walks but twice a night at most.

       'The ghost'

       c.148, p. 5

00725   O thou who know'st a lenient balm to lay
        That hopes from thee and thee alone a cure.

       'To time'

       c.344, p. 16

00726   O thou! who lab'rest in this rugged mine
        When tenants in fee simple stuff thy coffers.

       [Judith (Cowper)] Madan, 'Wrote by . . . in her
       brother's Coke on Littleton'

       fc.51, p. 158; c.176, p. 55; see also 'O thou that
       laborest . . .'.

00727   O Thou, who once did children bless,
        My friends fled long before.

       'An hymn for a child who had lost a parent'

       c.83/3, no. 974

00728   O Thou who once didst come, in tongues of fire,
        And soft responses sing, from rosy bow'rs.

       'An hymn to the Holy Ghost'

       c.167, p. 43

00729 O! thou who ridest in a foreign flood!
Nor longer, what the Queen commands, oppose.

> Maurice Johnson, 'To his excellency the right
> reverend Lord John Lord Bishop of Bristol . . . a
> congratulatory poem upon his Lordship's reception
> into the river Mars the first of January 1712 . . .'
>
> c.229/2, fol. 66v

00730 O thou who rival wits conspire to praise
Than regions vast of barren climes command.

> [ ] Melmurth, 'On Miss Fanny Jeffreys . . . written
> by . . . at Bath—1736'
>
> c.360/1, p. 25

00731 O thou, who sit'st a smiling bride
Thou, then shall rule our queen, and share our
monarch's throne.

> [William] Collins, 'Ode to mercy'
>
> c.363, p. 175

00732 O Thou! Who with surpassing glory crown'd
Who leaves no growing print of morning bliss.

> [Benjamin?] Stillingfleet, 'A rant on sleep, by . . . note
> the first six lines are Milton's'
>
> c.360/2, no. 75

00733 O thou whom all my inmost soul adores
That I of all thy sex will love but thee alone.

> 'To the same [Mira] written on the first leaf of her
> Prior's Works in the beginning of the year 1738 at
> Trodsham in Cheshire'
>
> Poetry Box I/60; see also 'O! that I now my dear . . .'.

00734 O thou! whom love and fancy lead
Because thou lov'st simplicity.

> 'Verses written in a cottage garden at a village in
> Lorraine, and occasioned by a tradition concerning a
> tree of rosemary'
>
> c.139, p. 606; Poetry Box XII/69

00735 O! thou whose aid I oft implore
And all the glory mine alone!

> [Phanuel Bacon], 'To Miss Nichol (at her own
> request) upon her birthday, being then going into the
> eighth year'
>
> c.237, fol. 46

00736 O thou, whose all-consoling pow'r
Be proud to own your sway.

> [George Tierney], 'Ode to the genius of scandal'
> [docket attribution; also 'printed as by Sheridan at one
> time']
>
> Poetry Box IV/20

00737 O thou! whose awful spirit o'er the gloom
May gently sink to rest.

> 'Translation of the lines written by Mr. Gray, at la
> Grande Chartreuse'
>
> File 17461

00738 O thou, whose charms emphatic fir'd the soul
In happy foretaste of eternal day.

> Charles Atherton Allnutt, 'Sonnet to divine wisdom'
>
> c.112, p. 144

00739 O thou, whose charms so radiant are,
With sweet returns of love.

> T[homas] M[orell], 'To the same' [Anne Barker, later
> his wife]
>
> c.395, p. 62

00740 O thou, whose eyes were clos'd in death's long
night,
Honor, in spite of love pronounc'd thy death.

> John Lockman, 'The abortion: a sonnet [translated
> from Sieur D. Henault]'
> [Crum 0905]
>
> c.267/4, p. 159; c.268 (second part), p. 89; c.94 ('death's
> pale light')

00741 O thou whose friendship is my joy and pride,
That happiness is near allied to love.

> [George Lyttelton, 1st baron Lyttelton], 'To Stephen
> Poyntz esq. at Paris in the year 1728'
>
> c.152, p. 17

00742 O thou whose glory ne'er decays
Will I wait till my change come.

> [Lady Ursula (Darcy) Wyvill]
>
> b.222, p. 106

00743 O Thou whose goodness ev'ry want supplies
The bad opprest shall fall, the good triumphant rise.

> Miss [ ] Andrews, 'An hymn'
>
> File 245/18

00744 O thou whose image here portray'd
Shall yield to everlasting spring.

> [James Gregory], 'On seeing a picture of the once
> celebrated May Drummond (a preacher among the
> Quakers) in the character of Winter'
>
> Poetry Box IV/19

00745 O thou! Whose love-inspiring air
In love with innocence and thee.

> John Wolcot ('Peter Pindar'), 'To Cynthia . . . Odes
> 1785'
> [Crum 0906]
>
> c.355, p. 268

00746 O thou whose penetrating mind,
Nor great Machaon's rival thine.

    [William] Somervile, 'To Dr Mackenzie'

c.244, p. 467 (ll. 1–63)

00747 O thou! whose shade presiding here,
And life's expiring fancy warm.

    Joseph Gilpin, 'Verses written at the fountain of
    Vaucluse in May 1798'

c.142, p. 339

00748 O thou whose tender serious eyes
And let me Myra die of thee.

    James Thomson, 'Lines written from the Song of
    Solomon'

c.344, p. 63

00749 O thou whose viewless form slow stealing time
She grants a glorious meed—'tis immortality!

    'Ode to time inscribed to Miss Seward'

Poetry Box v/54

00750 O thrice and four times happy souls
Do live eternally.

    'Curled hand'

b.234, p. 17

00751 Oh! thrice thrice happy he that shuns the cares
Free from griping lawyers' and soldiers' harm.

c.158, p. 31

00752 O, Time! What ravages thy hand hath made!
And conquer death—by thus securing thee!

    'Time' [signed Adelina]

c.343, p. 83

00753 Oh 'tis not courage, whatsoe'er men say
Doth both thy body, and thy soul confound.

    [Francis Quarles], 'Upon self-murder'

b.137, p. 197

00754 O to Jehovah sing a song
With truth and equal right.

    'Psal: 96'

b.217, p. 63

00755 O tradesmen, careless of your shops,
Mind—fools make feasts, and wise men eat 'em.

    [John Wolcot ('Peter Pindar')], 'For the rats'
    [5 February 1796]

File 16343

00756 O trouble not this sacred rest
Doth lie the peace of Christendom.

    'On K. James'

b.356, p. 255

00757 O truth! From whom soft numbers [?],
For only thou wilt tell.

    John Lockman, 'Writ on occasion of the declaration
    of the two candidates, of members for Surrey, Decr.
    1768'

c.267/4, p. 396

00758 Oh 'twas a joyful sound
Lov'd Isr'el's God vouchsafes to dwell.

    J. B., 'Psalm 122 . . . Dec 16, 1702'

b.63, p. 100, 106

00759 O Tweed! a stranger that with wandering feet
To muse upon thy banks at eventide.

    [William Lisle] Bowles, 'Sonnet'

Diggle Box: Poetry Box XI/71

00760 O Tyburn! couldst thou reason and dispute?
A little bearing towards the milder side.

    'On Tyburn'
    [Crum 0921]

c.189, p. 114

00761 O under various sacred names ador'd!
The subject may transport a breast divine.

    Gilbert West, 'To Jove—a hymn of Cleanthes—
    translated by . . .'
    [Crum 0924]

c.351, p. 31

00762 O, venerable Sparta! Glorious place!
Leave thee to fate, and wipe the crystal eye.

    'Sparta'

c.91, p. 259

00763 O Venus, beauty of the skies,
And give me all my heart desires.

    [Ambrose Philips], 'The hymn to Venus' [Spectator,
    vol. 3]

c.186, p. 143

00764 O Venus heavenly queen of love,
Warm envied Glycera's breast.

    [George] H[owar]d, [6th earl of Carlisle],
    'Translation of [blank]'

c.197, p. 37

00765 O Venus joy of men and gods
       Let Mercury come with thee.

   [Sir Charles Hanbury Williams], 'General
   Churchill['s] address to Venus in imitation of the 30th
   ode in H[orace]'
   [Crum 0925]

   c.154, p. 47; c.148, p. 1

00766 O Venus! lovely evening star!
       Where ends the wanderer's earthly way.

   'The evening star. An ode'

   c.140, p. 552

00767 O waft me, fancy, when you fly
       And left me on Tweedside to stray.

   'Ode to fancy'

   c.142, p. 404

00768 O wanton England why has thou forgot
       From this digression turn we to our theme.

   [Robert Cottesford?]

   b.144, p. 6

00769 Oh! was the hand which owns this muff but mine,
       Thus bless'd by Venus, and the god of love.

   'To Miss S—nore. An impromptu in the Assembly
   Room at Lechlade clasping a lady's muff'

   c.487, p. 88

00770 O welcome to my soul congenial power!
       The deluge of thy tears.

   [Robert Merry], 'Ode to winter'

   Greatheed Box/9

00771 Oh were I seated by some pitying pow'r
       And flow'rs shall rise where'er Hyella treads.

   'Acon, a pastoral, imitated from the original Latin of
   John Baptist Amaltheus, and humbly inscribed to
   these from Hopehall'

   Poetry Box IV/3

00772 Oh we're undone, since death has at one stroke
       Though young in years, yet old in good: and just.

   'On the deplorable death of Mr. Robert Dickson of
   Buchtrig advocate who died the 10 Jany 1674'

   Poetry Box VIII/26

00773 Oh what a condition is mine,
       A covert from every storm.

   Charles Atherton Allnutt, 'The pious resolution'

   c.112, p. 18

00774 Oh, what a cruel wicked thing,
       That I with Thee may mercy find.

   'A poem for a child against cruelty'

   c.83/3, no. 975

00775 Oh what a dreadful wintry eve
       But check my sobs and—drink my beer.

   [John Walker?], 'On Bryant's removing to Banbury in
   Oxfordshire, a letter to Mrs. Bryant'

   fc.108, fol. 75v

00776 Oh what a farce on all these turns of state:
       How little Soame(?), since rank'd among the great.

   John Lockman, 'On some late exaltations . . . 1740'

   c.267/1, p. 2

00777 Oh what a gracious mercy 'tis
       How is our sight, but not our faith here lost.

   [Edmund Wodehouse], 'Decr. 20 [1714]'

   b.131, p. 119

00778 Oh! what a holy champion Bowyer cries!
       To check the world, become each other's bail.

   Edward Moore(?), 'On the friendship between
   A. Bowyer and Sir George, now Lord Lyttelton'

   c.74

00779 Oh! what a number ([of] false Ephramites)
       Then Julian yerst or Celsus or Porphyrius.

   'Hypocrisis'

   b.205, fol. 11v

00780 Oh what a plague is love!
       Yet, all the world may see, | Phillida flouts me.

   'Song'

   c.358, p. 101; see also next.

00781 Oh! what a plague is love I cannot bear it
       Barnaby doubts me.

   [parody of] 'Phillida flouts me'

   fc.61, p. 63; Accession 97.7.40, p. 19; see also previous.

00782 Oh, what am I, who have the power
       And loathe the bliss of every hour.

   'A riddle'

   Diggle Box: Poetry Box XI/71

00783 Oh what an honor? What an height
       All those rejects, who merit boasts.

   [Edmund Wodehouse], 'Apr. 12 [1715]'

   b.131, p. 196

00784 Oh! what bosom but must yield
       Mend the hole that's in my heart.

   'On seeing a beautiful lady working with her needle'

   c.186, p. 73

00785 Oh what can mean that eager joy,
That loves without measure.

   'A dialogue between Phyllis and Strephon'

   fb.142, p. 54

00786 Oh what disgrace unto my highness 'tis
The greater majesty the slower pace.

   'Stella polaris' [answered by 'Great Majesty? Oh
heavens . . .']

   b.356, p. 113

00787 Oh what do I hear my Nassau had been fighting
Had the bully by chance stuck it in my Nassau.

   'Song on the Prince of Orange serving a volunteer on
the Rhine'

   fc.135

00788 Oh when from life's tempestuous scenes withdrawn
Ne'er shall retirement wake the smile of joy.

   'To Mr H——'

   c.140, p. 192

00789 Oh when my righteous judge shall come
The riches of Thy grace.

   'Hymn 66th'

   c.562, p. 79

00790 O when our clergy at the dreadful day
Durst ye not stoop to play the fools for him.

   [Francis Quarles], 'On those that deserve it' [Divine
fancies I, 23]

   b.137, p. 180

00791 O! when shall I behold thee as thou art?
To mount and spend eternity in praise.

   c.153, p. 55

00792 Oh, when will content find this bosom again,
And the lyre you oft prais'd will now warble no

                              more.

   'On content, inscribed to a lady at Philadelphia'

   c.83/1, no. 125

00793 O where are all the winds! O who will seize
This painful heat with transport would I [ ]n.

   [Henry Fox, 1st baron Holland], 'Written at Nice
August 1734'

   Poetry Box II/16

00794 Oh! where are thou Lord Taffy?
And so retrieve your glory.

   'A ballad to the tune of Noble race was Shankin
&c . . . on the first of March, vulgarly called the
Pr[ince']s birthday' [on the accession of George I; pr.
1715 (Foxon N55)]
[Crum O955]

   fc.58, p. 123; c.570/1, p. 54 ('St. Taffy'; 'tune of Owen
Tudor')

00795 Oh! Where's the plague in love
Since this quite breaks my peace. | Barnaby
                             doubts [me]

   'Answer' [to 'Oh what a plague is love . . .']

   c.358, p. 104

00796 O while thy beauties fire my head,
My passion he'll improve!

   [Charles Burney, the younger], 'To Miss J[essy]
Wilcox'

   c.37, p. 71

00797 Oh whither dost thou fly? Cannot my vow
Ten of his fellow moments fled away.

   [William] Habington, 'To the moment last past'

   b.150, p. 267

00798 Oh who can tell what is within man's heart,
His only rest, its only center is.

   b.118, p. 285

00799 O who would boast himself of royal birth,
You've lost a patron fit to imitate.

   'An elegy on the King of Sweden'

   c.570/2, p. 85

00800 O why did fame my heart to love betray,
So that she knew that for her sake I died.

   'Sonnet, upon his mistress' good fame'

   Poetry Box VIII/2

00801 Oh why is man so thoughtless grown;
Drops in the trench despairs and dies.

   [Isaac Watts], 'The rash soldier at the siege of Namur'

   c.349, fol. 7

00802 O why, Melpomene! these strains of woe,
Go live as Lockman did, and be admir'd.

   R. G., 'Verses on the death of Mr. John Lockman' [d.
1771]

   c.83/1, no. 248

00803 O! why should old age so much wound us? O,
And our bairns and our oys all around us, O.

   J[ohn] Skinner, 'The old man's song'

   c.142, p. 241

00804   O! why, thou lily pale,
And find thee tears to feed thy sorrowing.

     W[illiam] Roscoe, 'To a lily flowering by moonlight'
     c.142, p. 535

00805   Oh! why to hapless, helpless, humankind
And though th'unfeeling pain nor grief can know.

     'An elegy written under an agony of distress . . .'
     c.136, p. 123

00806   O wights immortaliz'd! whose happy fames
Choice flower of learning is from age to age.

     'Upon the lives of Plutarch. A poem'
     File 16683

00807   Oh! with what guilt the chimney-sweeper eyes
And, in her pride of soul, enjoys his smart.

     John Lockman, 'Writ under the print of a
     chimney-sweeper squeezing a cat . . . 1748'
     c.267/1, p. 35

00808   Oh with what transport would my bosom glow,
A wreath of brightest flowers shall crown thee now.

     John Lockman, 'To Signor Geminiani: on occasion of
     the concerto spirituale (sacred concert) to be
     performed, for his benefit, at the Theater Royal in
     Drury Lane . . . 9 April 1750'
     c.267/1, p. 187

00809   Oh with whom my heart was wont to share
The inspiring voice of innocence and truth.

     Samuel Rogers, 'On the death of his brother' [from
     'Pleasures of memory']

     c.343, p. 33

00810   Oh woe to those whose wily waxen mind
Out of his mouth, his mouth hath spoke it true.

     [Francis Quarles], 'An invective against schismatics
     and temporizers'
     b.137, p. 197

00811   O woeful wretch, whose soul is never quiet,
When will it end? A voice doth answer, never.

     'A conscience neither good, nor quiet'
     c.187, p. 36

00812   O woman, lovely woman,
Eternal joy, and everlasting love.

     [Frederick Corfield], 'This elegant rhapsody, as far as
     it regards the general nature of the sex, is very
     descriptive of their original designation . . .'
     c.381/1

00813   O wondrous power of colors, shows, and light!
If all is nature, or her rival, art?

     John Lockman, 'A thought, viewing the pictures at
     Leicester House . . . April 1758'
     c.267/1, p. 116

00814   O wond'rous sight! Five hundred heads on high,
And future miscreants dread a people's ire.

     John Lockman, 'Count Gordon newly decorated'
     c.267/1, p. 232

00815   O worthy to be sung, thro' endless time,
Unless when some curs'd rheum offends his brain.

     [William Popple, trans.], '[Horace] book 1st epistle 1st
     imitated. Inscribed to Richard [I?]nce esq.'
     fc.104/1, p. 361

00816   Oh! would it not provoke a maid,
But search'd and tried all human kind.

     [Thomas Brown], 'Upon the bitches of [La] Fontaine
     being rivall'd by Madam Maintenon'
     c.158, p. 145

00817   Oh would it please the gods to split
With half your wit, your years, and size.

     [Jonathan Swift, 'Stella's birthday' (1718/19)]
     Diggle Box: Poetry Box XI/56

00818   Oh would some muse propitious deign t'inspire,
And safe to port his deep-fraught bark convey.

     'A poem on Westow by a lady'
     c.116, p. 17

00819   O would ye ken the bonny slight [*i.e.*, sight?]
O sport for bairds and fiddlers.

     'On Moynas and his drunken lordship'
     Poetry Box VIII/49

00820   O wound us not with this sad tale; forbear
Fight to revenge thee than our land before.

     John Earles, 'An elegy upon the death of Sr John
     Burrows [Burroughs], who was slain in the Isle of Ree
     [in the night with a bullet, 1627]
     [Crum 0975]
     b.197, p. 40; b.200, p. 248; b.356, p. 17

00821   O wretched man which lovest earthly things
When time is past and wailing comes too late.

     [Philip Howard, 23rd earl of Arundel], 'The path to
     paradise'
     [Crum 0978, 'earthly life']
     a.5, fol. 7v; a.6, p. 1; see also next.

00822 O wretched man! why lov'st thou earthly things?
Then loathe that life which causeth such laments.

[Crum 0979]

fb.69, p. 199; see also previous.

00823 O wretched state of awful guilt,
The heart too hard, too proud to bow.

T[homas] S[tevens], '1. Kings. Ch. 22. ver. 21'

c.259, p. 77

00824 O wretched wainscot bound t'receive
My friend the dishclout comes tomorrow.

'Written on the wainscot at the Blue Posts at
Whitham'

c.186, p. 121; c.83/1, no. 175; see also 'Ah wretched . . .'.

00825 O ye commons and peers, who are bound by your
                                                    pay
When I have nothing to ask, and you've nothing to
                                                    spend, &c.

'The King's speech Englished a new ballad' [1734; pr.
1735 (Foxon S624)]
[Crum 0984]

fc.58, p. 131; c.570/4, p. 153; Poetry Box IV/82; Poetry
Box V/44

00826 O ye immortal throng,
Perform thy part.

P[hilip] Doddridge, 'Christ seen of angels 1.
Tim. III. 16'

c.493, p. 7

00827 O! ye Newtonians sure your wits were gone,
They lowly bend and bid you all adieu.

'Occasional prologue spoken by C. Preyo esqr. at
Newton Abbot on the 27 March 1786 to the first part
of Henry the 4th . . .'

c.382, p. 30

00828 O ye rovers, beware
If you rashly approach near the sound.

'Song'

c.358, p. 89; see also 'When the bright god of day . . .'.

00829 O ye sons of man, be wise:
And your souls shall bless the L[or]d.

[Hymn]

c.180, p. 85

00830 O ye that careless pass along this way
Build there and dwell and never more remove.

[William] Austin, 'Parasceve'
[Crum 0990]

b.197, p. 55; b.35, p. 31 (var.)

00831 O ye, who meet stern winter's frown,
On them that have the heart to give.

'Winter'

c.83/2, no. 656

00832 O! year renown'd! triumphant fifty-nine!
Their lenity extend to all mankind.

John Lockman, 'Verses, suggested by two grand
national subscriptions set on foot in 1759 . . . for . . .
the British troops abroad, and for the widows and
orphans of such . . . for clothing the French prisoners.
Addressed to the subscribers . . . April 1760'

c.267/1, p. 303

00833 Oh, yes I will search through the garden with care
For still may her breast be a mansion of peace.

'Edmund Swift esq. in Polyanthea'

Poetry Box XII/111[2]

00834 Oh yet a moment to this pensive tale
But oh! Reflect that Lyttelton is dead.

'Elegy on the death of the Lord Lyttelton A. D. 1773'

c.481, p. 54

00835 O you, that bathe in courtly bliss,
From which these peaceful glens are free.

[William] Shenstone

c.20/4; c.21; c.344, p. 91; fc.132/1, p. 179

00836 O! Zion how thy beauty fades away,
An holy song upon the holy ground.

W. L. jr., 'A lamentation over Zion on the declension
of the church'

c.517, fol. 28r

00837 Old age and this vain world are well agreed;
He thus becomes degenerate and low.

[Edmund Wodehouse], 'Septr 14 [1715]'

b.131, p. 272

00838 Old age does by the course of nature show,
Exprest in constant pray'r and practic'd piety.

[Edmund Wodehouse], 'Septr. 30 [1715]'

b.131, p. 276

00839 Old age is deem'd a venerable estate,
Or gloomy; it foretells our future plight.

[Sir Philip Wodehouse], 'Sen. mortum, non annorum
canicies'

b.131, p. 27

00840 Old and abandon'd by each venal friend,
And foxes stunk and litter'd in St. Paul's!

[Thomas Gray], 'On the seat of a decayed nobleman
[Lord Holland] in the Isle of Thanet' [1766]
[Crum 01000]

File 17399

00841 Old Bayard take care, and look well to your hits,
Despise all Dutch treachery; and damn your black
oats.

'Capiat qui capere potest'
b.iii, p. 509

00842 Old care with industry and art,
Nor wishes to be free from care.

[Christopher] Smart, 'Care and generosity'

c.90

00843 Old Charon thus preached to his pupil Achilles;
You'll ne'er go the sooner to the Stygian ferry.

'Song 61'
[Crum 01004]

c.555, p. 88

00844 Old Chaucer, like the morning star,
Nor death's dark veil their day o'ercast.

[Sir John Denham], 'On Mr. Abraham Cowley'

b.86, p. 41

00845 Old Clerus informed his curate should say
Indeed Sir you err, your living I want.

c.546, p. 33

00846 Old Cornute feels his head in pain
If my plants sprout not in season.

c.546, p. 30

00847 Old Doll Pentreath, one hundred age and two,
But in the churchyard doth old Dolly lie!

'Cornish language (last remains). The village of
Mousehole, on the western side of Mount's Bay,
became famous among antiquarians from having been
the residence of old Dolly Pentreath, one of the last
persons known to speak the Cornish language . . .
[translation of her epitaph]'

c.81/1, no. 509

00848 Old English kings were wont to speak
Proximity of blood.

'The proxy' [on George I]
[Crum 01013]

c.570/1, p. 86

00849 Old folks then take my horse that I may brag.
I'm free from clap, I have lost my running nag.

b.104, p. 15

00850 Old friend, farewell—with whom full many a day,
Men turn to dust—and broadcloth turns to rags.

'On throwing by an old black coat'

c.83/1, no. 260

00851 Old Hodge one day, on errand sent
When I survey the monument and thee!

Diggle Box: Poetry Box xi/5

00852 Old Homer! But what have we with him to do?
To Liberty Hall is an Englishman's heart.

Geo[rge] Alex[ande]r Stevens, 'Composed by . . .
music by Dr. Boyce'

Poetry Box v/115

00853 Old Homer's fancied face a form unknown,
With patriot virtue to inspire the stage!

Elizabeth Tollett, 'On Shakespeare's monument by . . .
daughter of Geo: Tollett who as a commissioner of the
navy had a house in the Tower in the reigns of
William and Anne; her works published after her
death in 1754 . . .'

c.481, p. 300

00854 Old Horace says, a man who us'd to expose
After this ample petticoat, and hoop.

Sir Richard Steele, 'Prologue for Tamarlane acted by
Mr. Newcome's school . . .'

c.176, p. 13

00855 Old Ireland looks out
They'll scamper their necks for to save.

'A ballad on the times 1716'

b.333

00856 Old Isla[y] to show his fine delicate taste
With a clump of Scotch firs by way of a screen.

[Philip Dormer Stanhope], 4th earl of Chesterfield,
'Hit or miss luck's all' [on Archibald Campbell, Lord
Islay and 3rd duke of Argyll, and his improvements
near Hounslow Heath; also attr. James Bramston]

c.229/2, fol. 25, fol. 75; fc.135; Poetry Box I/82 ('Old
Hay'); see also 'When Islay . . .'.

00857 Old James the 1st of Scottish race,
And knight's a thing—not worth a [fart].

'Knighthood'

c.81/1, no. 166

00858 Old Janus wills thee keep thy body warm,
Thy body's heat doth challenge to a duel.

'Observations out of the alma[na]c . . . 1631'

fb.69, p. 176

00859 Old Jemmy is a lad,
Old Jemmy'll come again.

'Old Jemmy. January 5th. 1692'

b.111, p. 59

00860 Old J[oh]n White
And that stands all awry.

'A reason why J[oh]n White never went right'

c.233, p. 68

00861 Old Jove in a passion to find Zara gone
Till hid in the mason she found lusty Jove!

R[ichard] V[ernon] S[adleir], 'While Zara was on this visit her mother was gone to Durham on a visit to Mrs. [blank] her daughter—these lines were written on being awakened by workman making a new skylight'

c.106, p. 41

00862 Old Nick engag'd on British grounds
He hallo'd, hark to Bowman.

'Fog's journal. Oct. 16: 1731. Epigram on [William] Bowman [vicar of Dewsbury; his visitation sermon]' [Crum O1022]

c.233, p. 117

00863 Old Oliver's dead and rotten
By my troth they may kiss my a[rs]e.

'The credulous robber cheated by treacherous favorites'

c.570/1, p. 78

00864 Old poets Hippocrene admire,
Die he with thirst that doth repine.

['Aurum potabile verum']
[Crum O1028]

Poetry Box VI/128; c.83/2, no. 307

00865 Old Priam the king with Hecuba wed;
Former husband, and wife to Menelaus.

'Answer' [to 'A wedding there was . . .']

c.578, p. 54

00866 Old Satan, mankind's inveterate foe,
Leave Paris to me—your own Robespierre.

'Equality'

c.83/2, no. 307

00867 Old stories of a Tyler sing
To learn to swear with a *bon grace*.

'Tom [Cooper,] tiler [husband of] the nurse' [on the birth of the Old Pretender]
[Crum O1034; *POAS* IV.257]

fb.108, p. 127

00868 Old stories tell how Hercules
So groan'd kick'd sh—— and died!

'Song 184' [pr. 1712, as Stoppage no payment; or a tale upon Dunkirk (Foxon S769)]

c.555, p. 285

00869 Old Walpole, Newcastle and Pelham of late
By taking (what none has too much of) our time.

'1760. Extempore—on a paragraph in the newspaper relating to a proposal for laying a tax on clocks and watches'

c.484, p. 66

00870 Old women sometimes can raise his desire,
No need sure of penance for the life you have spent.

'Letitia's character of her lover, Feb: 1785'

Poetry Box IV/30

00871 Old Young and young Young, both men of renown
One makes, t'other plays, the best fiddle in town.

'On John Young the musical instrument maker and his son Talbot Young'

c.360/2, no. 139

00872 Old Zoilus the sourest Dame Critice bore
For his edicts declare much spite and no wit.

'The session of critics' [pr. 1737 (Foxon S225)]

c.176, p. 106

00873 Omnipresent God whose aid
Change and bid me die in peace.

'Hymn 36th for the evening'

c.562, p. 42

00874 Omniscient Jove the universe survey'd
And each doth seem to have seal'd him for their own.

fc.14/4

00875 On a fair mead, a dunghill lay,
Worthless to mix with dung despis'd.

'The oak, and dunghill. A fable . . . the dunghill's answer' [pr. 1728 (Foxon B499)]

c.570/3, p. 40

00876 On a summer's day
God bless our royal J[ame]s.

'A song'

c.570/2, p. 103

00877 On a sunshiny day
But alas! Who can guess at the rest?

R[obert] Shirley, 1st earl of Ferrers, 'A song'

c.347, p. 24

00878 On Afric's wide plain, where the lion now roaring
And the soul of the Ethiop prove whiter than snow.

> [William] Collins, 'The despondent Negro'
> Poetry Box IV/61

00879 On Albion's austral bounds, on Sussex stand,
And pygmy-like seem unto them below.

> 'Beachy Head, Sussex'
> c.83/2, no. 725

00880 On beds of roses Pyrrha say,
Thy lover will to sea no more.

> [William Popple, trans.], '[Horace] book 1st. ode 5th.
> To Pyrrha'
> fc.104/2, p. 18

00881 On Belvidera's bosom lying,
You quickly would forget to love.

> [Crum 01057]
> c.549, p. 19

00882 On British stage when Roman Portia shines,
Your smile is glory—and your frown is fate.

> [Anna Seward], 'Prologue to the Duke of Braganza by
> the [ ]' [1778?]
> File 13371

00883 On duty cheerful and in battle brave
And fell a victim to a foaming wave.

> 'On Robt. White 11th light dragoons'
> c.546

00884 On earth, are weddings: but small lovely carriage;
In heav'n, there is much love: and yet no marriage.

> Sir Thomas Urquhart, 'Love, and marriage'
> fb.217, p. 112

00885 On earth could our first parents reappear,
Would wish his culture form'd their darling care.

> John Lockman, 'Walking in the gardens of Richard
> Warner esqr, at Woodford, Essex . . . Sept. 1760'
> c.267/1, p. 299

00886 On Emma's fair bosom a rose in full blossom
And found on her bosom an elegant tomb.

> J. M., 'The rose'
> Poetry Box IV/84

00887 On fair Arcadia's happy plain
Beware Corinna's hapless end.

> 'A pastoral tale'
> c.135, p. 1

00888 On fam'd Cayster's banks, foreboding death,
Complains of India heat, and loss of you.

> Anthony Fahie, 'Anthony Fahie to Tobias Wall
> esquire'
> Poetry Box V/70

00889 On foreign shores, whose flowery banks might give,
And arms my tortur'd soul, to bear its pains.

> [Mrs. Christian Kerr], 'The complaint of a
> melancholy shepherd'
> c.102, p. 124

00890 On former joys I sometimes muse,
Prepares the joy, to meet again!

> 'On recollection . . . Marseilles 20 March 1791'
> Poetry Box II/31

00891 On Friday last was fought at Ashf—t
Down dropp'd alas! the independent Whig.

> 'For the Canterbury journal Septr. 10. 1778—we insert
> the following to oblige a correspondent . . . Lest you
> our tale in prose refuse, Here take it from the
> bellman's muse'
> c.373, p. 76

00892 On Gallia's shore, we sat and wept
As Scotland had from thee.

> 'An [imita]tion of the 137 [p]sa[lm]' [pr. Edinburgh?
> 1747? (Foxon H16)]
> c.171, no. 13

00893 On God alone I'll trust for this
So a ne'er-failing Savior o'er death and hell more
than a conqueror.

> [Edmund Wodehouse], 'Septr 1 1715'
> b.131, p. 257

00894 On God supreme our hope depends,
And Jacob's God our guide.

> [ ] Lewis, 'Psalm 46'
> c.244, p. 458

00895 On God we build our sure defense,
Our succor and support.

> Christopher Pitt, 'Psalm 46'
> c.244, p. 504

00896 On God's blest love our happiness depends
Which never fails to bring us to that place.

> [Edmund Wodehouse], 'Novr. 30 [1714]'
> b.131, p. 100

00897 On her fair face, the colors we survey
Not for the British crown, but Lady Bab.

'On Lady Barbara Villiers, daughter to William earl of
Jersey written about the year 1723'

c.360/2, no. 218

00898 On her own hills, is Israel's glory lost,
And all the furniture of battle lost.

[Thomas?] Scott, jr., 'David's lamentation over Saul
and Jonathan'

c.244, p. 412

00899 On Hercules' pillars, Drake, thou may'st
Great Hercules excel.

'The English of ['Plus ultra Herculeis . . .', on Sir
Francis Drake's return after his voyage around the
world]'

c.360/2, no. 268

00900 On Ida's lofty top the thund'rer sat
Melts in her arms, and sinks to pleasing rest.

'In this poem is described the contrivance of Ju[no] to
lull Jupiter to sleep, that Neptune the mea[n]time
might assist the Grecians'

b.218, p. 27

00901 On infant's wings, for distant heights o'erspread,
Blends with immortal Plato's warranty divine.

'A visionary ode'

c.481, p. 161

00902 On Itchin's fringed bank as Warton stray'd
Nor gild with empty praise such sterling worth!

R[ichard] V[ernon] S[adleir], 'Ode on the Rev[eren]d
Thos. Warton's escape after falling into the river
between Winchester and St. Cross. 1781'

c.106, p. 48

00903 On Leslie's conversion of the Lord knows who
As was thy good old cause, to be for no good.

'On Leslie' [docket title; ?Charles Leslie, d. 1722]

Poetry Box x/10(8)

00904 On March the one and twentieth day,
In coach or cock-horse ride.

'A ballad to the tune of Chevy Chase' [on George I's
first speech to Parliament, 1715]
[Crum 01077]

c.570/1, p. 57

00905 On Monday it rain'd a great part of the day,
And this is the humor and wit of the age.

'Tunbridge epistle. From Lady Margaret to the
Countess of Bxxx'

c.150, p. 50

00906 On Monday the chamberlain made a long speech
But they lost their design, and that's best of all.

'The transactions of six days, beginning Sept: 8 1679'

b.54, p. 1124

00907 On Monimia's snowy breast,
The dear thought transports my soul! | On
                    Monimia's snowy breast &c.

[John Lockman], 'Charming Monimia. Made to the
celebrated air, in the overture of Ariadne'

c.268 (first part), p. 66

00908 On mountains' hoary tops no snow is seen,
And break the chains of hell and th'adamantine gate.

'[Horace] Ode 7. Book 4'

Accession 97.7.40

00909 On my true friend I all that love bestow
Adverse or prosperous both must have one lot.

[Mrs. Christian Kerr], 'A female friend to a male
friend'

c.102, p. 88

00910 On Newgate steps Jack Chance was found
And when tuck'd [trick'd?] up—was just the thing.

Poetry Box x/31

00911 On no weak wing thro' liquid skies,
Whose fame shall ever live.

[William Popple, trans.], '[Horace] book 2nd ode
20th. To Maecenas'

fc.104/2, p. 182

00912 On old England's best shore
We are ready to conquer again.

'Song 174'

c.555, p. 269

00913 On old Sarum Hill,
And treat such like those who bid Shinkin rebel.

John Lockman, 'A libation: on the summit of Old
Castle, near Salisbury, 18 Sept. 1749, in honor of the
Earl of Middlesex, one of its representatives. The
tune, Bumper Squire Jones'

c.267/2, p. 85

00914 On parent knees, a naked newborn child
Calm thou mayst smile when all around thee weep.

[Sir William Jones], 'From the Persian'

Poetry Box XII/114

00915 On Saturday last Miss Empson was found
With her head in a washing-tub unfortunately
                                                    drown'd.

'A whim on the death of Miss Empson' [d.
18 November 1732]

c.360/2, no. 223

00916 On Saturday night we sat late at the Rose
Perhaps there had hung our new envoy.

'A view of the religion of the town or a Sunday
morning's ramble'
[Crum o1082]

fb.108, p. 315

00917 On Saturday night my wife she died
Whether this wasn't a pretty week's work.

'A week's work'

c.361

00918 On, shepherds, on, we'll sacrifice,
We cannot pay the tithe of what we owe.

'The shepherd's sacrifice'

fb.107, p. 24

00919 On silver Thames I've daily row'd,
It surely is my lady's.

c.362, p. 33

00920 On slight-built ships, with tow'rs rais'd high,
Or like a spendthrift waste?

[William Popple, trans.], 'The book of epodes of
Horace translated. Horace [ep]ode 1st. To Maecenas'

fc.104/2, p. 390

00921 On Solway's banks a humble Muse
Nor rise above the heart.

[Helen Craik], 'To Captain Riddell'

c.375, p. 1

00922 On some bank while Phoebus shineth
Of some shepherd and some maid.

[John Black]

fc.107, p. 81

00923 On Somnus' downy bosom let me rest
To sing his praise, in bright eternal day.

'A night thought'

c.487, p. 83

00924 On Thanet's rock, beneath whose steep,
And torn from Anna—William dies.

[Elizabeth?] Moody, 'Anna's complaint'

c.83/2, no. 575

00925 On the bank of a brook, as I sat fishing.
And a whole world to each other we'll be.

'The kind couple'

fb.107, p. 5

00926 On the bank of a river
But the roses smell sweet when put in the still.

fb.228/59

00927 On the banks of that crystalline stream,
And his Ella could still be so true.

'Ella and Allen'

c.83/1, no. 75

00928 On the beautiful banks of this classical stream
And incessant their power to tease.

[Hester Lynch Thrale] Piozzi, 'July 1785'
Greatheed Box/16

00929 On the cool ground I saw thee lately laid,
The stars are rising, and advise to rest.

Abraham Oakes, trans., 'An eclogue: of [John Jacob
Oakes] . . . translated'

c.50, p. 39

00930 On the fair banks of gentle Thames
And my devotion rise on her seraphic wings.

'On the sight of some divine poems done by Mrs
[Elizabeth] (Singer) [Rowe]'

c.360/1, p. 187

00931 On the high place, in a fatal hour,
Fall'n is the boast of war, and Israel's flow'r!

Thomas Cook, 'David's lamentation for Saul and
Jonathan'

c.244, p. 576

00932 On the obedience passive still to dote
And sacrifice for us the ram of Rome.

'To the clergy of the Church of England who are
dignified and distinguished for preaching up passive
obedience'
[Crum o1092]

fb.108, p. 318

00933 On thee, blest youth, a father's hand confers
Gild the calm current of domestic hours!

[Samuel Rogers], 'To a friend on his marriage'

c.141, p. 456

00934 On Thee, each morning, O my God,
Alone all praise is due.

> [George Gwyn], 'A beautiful morning hymn,
> composed by an ingenious, though unknown author, in
> imitation of Mr. Addison's in the Spectator' [in
> Gentleman's magazine, 1732]
> [Crum 01098]

c.487, p. 46; c.547, p. 191

00935 On this fair ground with ravish'd eyes
He came, saw, vanquish'd, wept, return'd, and died.

> [Christopher Pitt], 'Epigram on the same [a flowered
> carpet worked by the Misses Pitt at Kingston]'

File 11956-57

00936 On those bright locks, which all admire,
Guiltless, they shouldn't feel your rage.

> John Lockman, 'To a beautiful widow, who tore her
> hair'

c.267/4, p. 151

00937 On Thursday morning higglers several
By three footpads were robb'd of money and all.

> 'A whim on a robbery November the 16 1732'

c.360/2, no. 226

00938 On Tiber's banks (as Strada sweetly sings)
And fairly own'd his harmony outdone.

> 'On Miss Burchell who first sang in public at Vauxhall
> Gardens, in the year 1751'

c.360/3, no. 176

00939 On tresses whiten'd o'er by time
Could never bind my heart more fast.

> 'Response du Duc de Nivernais [to 'This hair by long
> time blanch'd . . .', by the Maréchale de Mirepoix,
> translated by a lady]'

c.141, p. 538

00940 On Tunbridge walks two *bona robas* jostle,
I could say more but that I fear they'll fight us.

> [( ) Hawes the younger], 'A reply by ( ) Hawes his son'
> [to 'At Tunbridge Wells . . .']

b.54, p. 1133

00941 On unities of place and time
The fifth may be—in all the four!

> [ ] Webb, 'Observations on dramatic unities, p. 103'

Greatheed Box/12

00942 On Wednesday next (as I remember)
Come freely welcome to my all.

> C[harles] E[arle], 'An invitation to a friend who was
> about to sell some wood in West-down'

c.376

00943 On whether side soe'er I am
I still appear to be the same.

> 'A cube'

c.360/1, p. 263

00944 On Wittersham's retir'd plains,
Thy breath's to me contagious!

> Sarah Cornwallis, 'The oak and the bramble—by . . .
> aged twelve years'

fc.124, p. 70

00945 On wretched man, what ills unnumber'd wait,
Till fate asunder cut the trembling strings!

> [Charles Burney, the elder], 'To Fulke Greville esqr.
> upon the termination of a long contested difference'

c.33, p. 143

00946 On yon fair brook's enamell'd side,
Love finds out one for you.

> [Soame Jenyns], 'To Chloe angling'

c.147, p. 12

00947 On yon green bed of moss there lies my child,
Unconscious that eternal night | Veils his forever!

c.83/3, no. 1060

00948 On your soft cheeks sits blooming youth,
Pray, ladies, let me try.

> 'Spoken extempore to a couple of young ladies, the
> one remarkable for a fine complexion, the other for
> very lively eyes'

c.233, p. 89

00949 On youthful flames, nor no such trivial thing
And for her dear Adonis yet doth burn.

> [Mrs. Christian Kerr], 'Upon an old amorous lady's
> disappointment of being married to a young cavalier'

c.102, p. 66

00950 Once, all impatient for this festive day,
That leads us, not reluctant, to the tomb!

> R[ichard] V[ernon] S[adleir], 'To Mrs. Sadleir on the
> anniversary of her wedding day'

c.106, p. 120

00951 Once and but once found in thy company
T'embalm thy father's corpse, what will he die?

> J[ohn] D[onne], 'Elegy'
> [Crum 01112]

b.148, p. 95

00952 Once and twenty and six pence not three weeks ago
For fear 't should be seized by the Swede or
     Muscover, | Which nobody can deny.

> 'An excellent new ballad on the fall of guineas'

fc.58, p. 93

00953 Once born the best must die. Why (therefore) then
Shall fill Posterity's mouths with their foul crimes.

[Sir Aston Cokayne], 'Of death'

b.275, p. 71

00954 Once Flora designing a pretty parterre
At what hour we shall call to proceed to the play.

H[annah] More, 'To Mrs. Powell on her having an
apron which she was working in Miss More's parlor'

c.341, p. 62

00955 Once fondly lov'd, and still remember'd dear,
Or haply lies beneath th'Atlantic roar.

[Robert] Burns, ['Written on the blank leaf']

Poetry Box XII/66

00956 Once for my love I pluckt a marigold
Be you the sun, I'll be the marigold.

'A sonnet'
[Crum O1120a]

b.200, p. 190

00957 Once free from passions I thought love at best
And will his Susan call when death stops half the
                                                    word.

[Frederick Corfield], 'To Miss Susannah S.'

c.381/1

00958 Once happy church no longer censure Rome,
What mercy canst thou hope this second time.

'Utrum horum'

b.111, p. 216

00959 Once I found a fair lady a-rapping her box
You'll produce spears sufficient to arm their militia.

[N.] H[erbert], 'An epigram' [on some glass found in
Scottish snuff]

Spence Papers, folder 91

00960 Once I resolv'd no more in rhyme to write
Good [?] pray choose a better poet.

[verse satire against Alan Brodrick, later Viscount
Middleton, Irish judge]

File 17421

00961 Once I was lusty, fit for love
Since I can't love the jilting jade again.

'Horace—book 3—ode 26th: imitated'

c.241, p. 90

00962 Once I was nothing: but with pain and strife
I am but my first nothing once again.

[Robert Cholmeley], 'For my own tombstone'

c.190, p. 231

00963 Once in a hundred years the Phoenix died,
'He's happiest that's alone.'

'An extempore epigram in praise of Shakespeare'

c.74

00964 Once in a lone and secret hour of night
Within her rising bosom all was calm . . . .

'Lothario's triumph o'er Calista'

c.360/1, p. 247 (incomplete)

00965 Once in a ship, at ruin's brink,
But to the fisher let him go.

C[harles] D[arby?], 'On the dismissing King James
from France upon the peace' [1697]
[Crum O1127]

b.63, p. 89; see also 'Whatever in this . . .'.

00966 Once in our lives
And drink, drink, till he fall.

'Song'
[Crum O1128]

c.189, p. 222; c.555, p. 188

00967 Once in sheep's clothing as fables relate,
And can make him skip out of his skin.

[N. Herbert], 'Upon the same [the great Scottish ram
with three horns]'

Spence Papers, folder 91

00968 Once in the peaceful quarry deep I lay,
And our eighth Henry claims it as his own.

[William Popple, trans.], 'Horace book 1st satire
VIIIth imitated.'

fc.104/1, p. 149

00969 Once it fell out as poets say,
And held of all the virtues—queen.

'Prudence and truth'

c.83/1, no. 181

00970 Once Lucifer after a grand debate
And so much for lott'ries and rags. Tolderol.

John Lockman, 'A new lottery song—tune, The
yeoman of Kent'

c.267/2, p. 141; c.268 (first part), p. 77

00971 Once more his yearly course has Phoebus run,
Glad Io pæans to our church and king.

William Man, 'To all my bounteous customers, this
copy of verses is humbly dedicated by their faithful
mercury and most obedient servant . . .'

c.166, p. 32

00972 Once more I call each gentle muse
Await you on your native shore!

[Mary (Shackleton) Leadbeater], 'On the marriage of
Morris Birkbeck and Sarah Hall and their departure
from Ireland' [1776]

c.139, p. 499; File 13409

00973 Once more I hail the day decreed,
See truth and mercy reconcile.

'On Christmas Day 1795'

c.515, fol. 29

00974 Once more I'll tune the vocal shell
Is not so sweet as Peggy.

[Crum 01132]

c.358, p. 22

00975 Once more love's mighty charms are broke
At length they're sure to be betray'd.

[John Sheffield], 1st duke of Buckingham and
Normanby, 'A farewell to love'

Poetry Box IV/53

00976 Once more my muse, thy kind assistance bring,
Who liv'd thy slave, thy faithful slave did die.

[Thomas Hamilton, 6th earl of Haddington], 'To
Florella epistle the twelvth'

c.458/1, p. 30

00977 Once more the constant sun
Forevermore.

[Hymn]

c.180, p. 80

00978 Once more the ever-circling sun
Maternal charms of softer kind.

[Colley] Cibber, 'Ode [to the King] for New Year's
Day' [printed in Gentleman's magazine, January 1731]

c.165, p. 29 (ll. 1–34)

00979 Once more ye tuneful nine assist your bard
May seraphs waft her to her native heaven.

Poetry Box IV/101 (with corrections)

00980 Once on a time
Nor th' squire the name of Sh[i]tt[e]n Dick.

[John Walker?], 'The learned dog—a tale'

fc.108, fol. 14v

00981 Once on a time a mother fly,
Are sure reveng'd some time or other.

'A fable by a young gentleman in his tenth year'

c.150, p. 145

00982 Once on a time a wealthy swain,
Offer'd his person for the place.

'The wolf, the fox and the dog. A fable on
government'

File 16346

00983 Once on a time, as old stories rehearse,
You may know by the hand it had no cloven foot. |
Let censuring &c.

[Jonathan Swift], 'Lady B[etty] B[erkeley] finding in
the author's room some verses unfinished under writ a
stanza of her own, with raillery upon him, which gave
occasion to this ballad to the tune of The cutpurse
Augt. 1702'

c.265, p. 2

00984 Once on a time at Argos as they say
I've lost the pleasure of imagination.

c.361

00985 Once on a time fierce war did much engage
That honesty is the best policy.

E[lizabeth (Shirley)] C[ompton, countess of
Northampton], 'The birds the beasts and the bat'

Accession 97.7.40

00986 Once on a time I fair Dorinda kiss'd
Where there's no nose to intercept thy bliss.

c.53, fol. 51

00987 Once on a time in sunshine weather
Hath gone stark naked ever since.

[Matthew Prior], 'Truth and falsehood. A fable'

c.570/3, p. 51

00988 Once on a time near Channel Row
And fight, e'er since, for payless Swisses.

[John Gay?], 'The triple alliance . . . In fables all
things hold discourse | Then words, no doubt, must
talk, of course' [pr. 1725? (Foxon T498)]
[Crum 01141]

b.382(25); c.468 (attr. Philip, duke of Wharton)

00989 Once on a time (so goes the tale)
Go gently—or the jade will stumble.

P. N. Shuttleworth, 'The story of Phaeton or advice to
poets'

c.495, p. 6

00990 Once on Mount Edgecombe's craggy side
The yielding goddess gave her charms.

George Lyttelton, 1st baron Lyttelton, 'Verses wrote
by . . . at Mount Edgecombe'

Poetry Box V/119

00991 Once resolv'd on what is right,
Lyre, resound heav'n's high decrees.

    [William Popple, trans.], '[Horace] book 3rd. ode 3rd'
fc.104/2, p. 200

00992 Once ruddy and plump,
And triumph o'er death and the devil!

    'Epitaph M Corsley churchyard Wilts.'
c.81/2, no. 524

00993 Once Socrates as ancient tales relate,
But a tried friend—some miracle appears.

    'Parole de Socrate from Fontaine'
c.89, p. 115

00994 Once some Italians, long renown'd for shams,
They'll, for soprani, send us croaking basses.

    John Lockman, 'Writ on occasion of one of the
    performers, in Dr. Croza's company of Italians, not
    being qualified, pursuant to contract . . . May 1748'
c.267/1, p. 34

00995 Once the gods of the Greeks at ambrosial feast
And return it untainted to heav'n.

    'Song 170'
c.555, p. 262

00996 Once the gods on Olympus was merrily bent
But stick to our hammer and saw.

    [John Walker?], 'Tellmah an anniversary song'
fc.108, fol. 42

00997 Once 'tis said a prince lay dozing
Shun the former Charles's fate.

    'The royal vision'
Greatheed Box/87

00998 Once with success unclouded reason strove
By the indulgency of lib'ral heav'n.

    J[ohn] R[obinson], 'Ipsa utilitas justi prope mater et
    aequi'
c.370, fol. 56v

00999 One afternoon he taught his wife the way
And be dispos'd the sooner for our supper.

    Sir Thomas Urquhart, 'How a painter on a day
    instructed his bedfellow in the art of painting'
fb.217, p. 298

01000 One April ev'ning when the sun
Inhuman, take thy way.

    [Thomas Hull], 'Ballad 2nd referred to in the
    foregoing letter'
c.528/30; c.364, p. 21

01001 One being askt, what's best to learn? said this
For sense proves nonsense spoke but of season.

    Robert Huntington
b.52/2, p. 177 and 195

01002 One brave Maecenas in times past was wont to
                      nourish many
But now amongst a million scarce one left to
                      comfort any.

Poetry Box VI/120

01003 One day a justice much enlarged
You, won't let me pursue it.

    'Repartee'
Diggle Box: Poetry Box XI/69

01004 One day an honest cavalier
To meet set form! in such a place.

    [Phanuel Bacon], 'Pergis pugnantia sicum frontibus
    adversus componet'
c.237, fol. 75 [i.e., 95]

01005 One day at a tavern a squabble ensued
They only call'd villain—and rascal—and rogue.

    [Phanuel Bacon]
c.237, fol. 75 [i.e., 95]

01006 One day at her toilet as Venus began
Of the union 'twixt beauty and wine.

    'Song 187'
c.555, p. 298

01007 One day Goodbye met How d'ye do
Goodbye reveals the passion!

    ['How d'ye do and Goodbye']
    [Crum 01160]
Poetry Box XII/84

01008 One day in Chelsea gardens walking
And point it at the end.

    'An epigram, on an epigram'
c.90

01009 One day when the gods were engaged in chat,
When patience has rendered them worthy of
                      heaven.

    [Thomas Wilson], 'The search for content'
c.82, p. 8

01010 One evening Aminta and Phyllis
Who even our friends do betray?

    c.160, fol. 85

O1011 One evening as cold as cold might be
And died that night all in a sweat.

'A riddle on a pound of candles'

c.356

O1012 One evening Good Humor with Wit as his guest
Since we're sure that our drinking is always well tim'd.

[George Alexander Stevens, 'The killing of time']

Poetry Box v/73

O1013 One evening strolling, as I chanc'd to drop,
Make airy nothings look like flesh and blood.

'To Sir Harry Beaumont [*i.e.*, Joseph Spence] on his
dialogue on beauty'

c.360/3, no. 200

O1014 One favor, Chloe, let me see
No Chloe no you love me not.

Horace Walpole, [4th earl of Orford], 'Translation of
a French song by . . . 1739'

fc.135

O1015 One female companion, to soften my cares,
And a passport to Heav'n, when from earth I retire.

'The bachelor's wish'

Poetry Box XIV/192

O1016 One God there is, him only shall thou serve,
Nor madly covet, what's the neighbor's share.

'Decalogue in 10 lines'

c.81/1, no. 169

O1017 One hasty sketch painter on B. bestow
Is markt for where and never taste[?] the joy.

[Sir William Trumbull]

Trumbull Box: Poetry Box XIII/43

O1018 One is no number women are nothing then
So neither please yet one must needs befall.

b.205, fol. 24v

O1019 One join'd to naught, makes naught, but one, alone:
But you'll have ten, by joining naught to one.

Sir Thomas Urquhart, 'Something of nothing, an
arithmetical riddle to philomaths'

fb.217, p. 43

O1020 One limb of Sir John Cotton, and one of Corelli
Make up a whole lady, whose name pray now tell me.

[Sir William Trumbull, riddle on Cottrell]

Trumbull Box: Poetry Box XIII/44

O1021 One look;—enough;—for, look we more,
May ever live on Elwes' honor'd name.

T[homas] M[orell], 'On seeing the bride, Mrs Elwes
(sister to Mr Ewer of Richmond) come into Chiswick
Church. 1742'

c.395, p. 53

O1022 One love, one hope, twelve [?], one faith
Ten precepts, seven petitions our law hath.

[Sir Thomas Urquhart], 'Of the three theological
virtues [?] with the belief the dialogue and the Lord's
prayer'

fb.217, p. 520

O1023 One minute, fortune, thou hast let me live,
But be as rough, and angry as before.

[Sir Richard Steele], 'Upon having Mrs. Selwyn, by
lot, my Valentine'

Poetry Box X/10(12)

O1024 One moment yet renown'd Tiresias stay,
Adieu, farewell—I dare not disobey.

[William Popple, trans.], 'Horace book 2nd satire 5th
imitated. Interlocutors. Ulysses, Tiresias.'

fc.104/1, p. 289

O1025 One morning in May,
And as brittle as dame's breakfast teapot.

'Enigmas in The ladies' diary for the year 1741
answered'

c.241, p. 119

O1026 One morning more we may indulge delight
When How departs all pleasure's at an end.

'On Miss How's leaving Tunbridge'

c.360/1, p. 289

O1027 One newly practiced in astronomy
And taught his wife skill in the moon's eclipse.

'On an astronomer'

b.62, p. 80

O1028 One night I started in my bed,
And with a bang shut the back door.

'Internal dispute'

c.81/1, no. 140

O1029 One night immerg'd [*sic*] in sleep I lay,
Where lo! The baseless fabric fled.

Edward Sneyd, 'A vision'

c.214, p. 125

O1030 One of those talkers who themselves admire
To shame a liar, tell a greater lie.

'The story tellers a true anecdote'

c.115

01031　One part cast forth for rent out of hand
　　　And praise the donor for sending you a crop.

　　　　'Corn harvest devided in ten parts'

　　　c.158, p. 43

01032　One pit contains him now, who could not die
　　　Cause on his soul sin fastened almost none.

　　　　[William Strode], 'Another' [on one that died of
　　　　smallpox; epitaph on Mr. Bridgman]
　　　　[Crum 01198]

　　　b.205, fol. 65r

01033　One said the snow was black; another sad;
　　　How many foxes in this age have we.

　　　　'Backbiters and flatterers'

　　　c.356

01034　One saint with equal and impartial ears,
　　　Nor ever pray'd to any saint but you.

　　　　'The complainant'

　　　fb.107, p. 53

01035　One stone sufficeth, lo what death can do
　　　Her that in life was not content with two.

　　　　[Crum 01202]

　　　fb.143, p. 7; b.356, p. 247 ('One stone now serves'); see
　　　also 'Here lies Penelope . . .'; 'She's dead, who . . .'.

01036　One Sunday morn
　　　And grow vastly sober vastly sober.

　　　　'A song' [temp. coronation of George I, 1714]

　　　fc.57, p. 40

01037　One thing kind Sir of you I crave,
　　　You'll give it me without delay.

　　　　'[Enigma/Charade/Conundrum] 16' [husband]

　　　c.389; Poetry Box x/60

01038　One time a duke who did not lands possess
　　　Within your dukedom does my abbey lie.

　　　　R[obert] Shirley, 1st earl of Ferrers, 'From the French'

　　　c.347, p. 96

01039　One time as the prelate lay on his down bed,
　　　Strange tale to tell, yet not more strange than true!

　　　　'Lines relative to the building of Salisbury Cathedral'

　　　c.83/3, no. 908

01040　One time Xanthippe slept so long so fast,
　　　For fear a second soul, or second life succeed.

　　　c.53, fol. 21

01041　One while I think, and then I am in part
　　　O'erput by [?], and stoops to [?] up peace.

　　　　[Sir Richard Bulstrode], 'Confusion'

　　　fb.88, p. 114

01042　One who call'd himself Linch
　　　And he'll soon take an ell.

　　　　'Epigram'

　　　Diggle Box: Poetry Box xi/69

01043　One whore is dead
　　　We are all undone like the bankers.

　　　　'A song'

　　　b.105, p. 397

01044　One wish'd all cuckolds cast i' th' sea; but to him
　　　His wife thus said, learn (husband) first to swim.

　　　　'Of Pontia' [translation of an epigram of John Owen]

　　　c.356

01045　One with admiration told me
　　　None can judge who want their sight.

　　　　[William Herbert], 'To his mistress dispraised of
　　　　another'

　　　b.356, p. 90

01046　One with his wife, believing that she was
　　　Or lawful child, I know not. Tell me whether.

　　　　Sir Thomas Urquhart, 'A case to lawyers'

　　　fb.217, p. 244

01047　One woman said (and who'll gainsay?)
　　　May never live to run away!

　　　Greatheed Box/93

01048　Only tell her that I love
　　　Lovers on their stars must wait.

　　　　[cf. Crum 01217, by John Cutts, baron Cutts of
　　　　Gowran, pr. 1687]

　　　c.549, p. 46

01049　Only the bank of a brook
　　　In each other we'll be.

　　　b.213, p. 160

01050　Only three sons—(our second father's care)
　　　It goes down! Write or wrong 'tis all the same.

　　　　'The physicians. A satire'

　　　c.115

01051　Onslow, like Theown(?), th'intention only views:
　　　That good, he'll not the smallest gift refuse.

　　　　John Lockman, 'To the right honorable the late
　　　　speaker, with a tusk'

　　　c.267/1, p. 385

01052 Onwards and upwards let us away!
Hope on our banner, love for our guide.

Poetry Box XII/104

01053 Open all doors let in the polisht mob
Gallants, no other murder is confest.

[Horace Walpole, 4th earl of Orford], 'D[uchess] of
Bedford' [d. 1794]
[Crum 01220]

c.157, p. 67

01054 Open mine eyes O Lord that I may see
Must their foundations lay, both broad, and deep.

Sir John Strangways, 'A motive to humility upon the
consideration of what thou first was: 2ly of what thou
now art. 3ly what after death thou shalt be . . . 6 Maii
1647'

b.304, p. 84

01055 Open, open lovely breast,
Into raptures waken rest.

[Philip] Doddridge, 'On his wife's bosom'

c.364, p. 24; c.81/1, no. 115

01056 Open thine eyes my soul and see
May now and ever still be done.

[John Austin], 'Hym. 7' [Hymn xiii, Devotions in the
ancient way of offices, 1672, p.110]
[Crum 01221b]

c.178, p. 6 (incomplete?)

01057 Oppress'd with sin an heavy load
And find access to God.

[Thomas Stevens?], 'Confined by a fever the 3
Sabbaths following . . . sung'

c.259, p. 109

01058 Opprest with pain, a slave to woe,
Only restore, the shoes I've lost.

[Thomas Hamilton, 6th earl of Haddington], 'The
old shoe'

c.458/2, p. 10

01059 Opprest, with bold, unruly wives,
In hopes, my rib, may dangle there.

[Thomas Hamilton, 6th earl of Haddington], 'The
willow'

c.458/2, p. 133

01060 Or ere bright Sol display'd his genial flame
I straight grew tiresome to th'ungrateful bride.

'A riddle' [answered by 'Though young in
riddling . . .']

c.578, p. 27

01061 Or twice
(In all the world below.)

T[homas] M[orell], 'An epitaph . . . on the wife of the
Rev: J. Mickleborough . . . translated in monometers'

c.395, p. 125

01062 Order being kept the world is kept, but when
That is neglected, all the word's gone then.

'On order . . . English thus'

c.189, p. 33

01063 Order by which all things are made,
But one harmonious constant bliss.

[Katherine] P[hilips], ['L'accord du bien']
[Crum 01231]

b.118, p. 47

01064 Order thy park—this must mean morally,
Forests of vanity—sin's champian field.

[Sir Philip Wodehouse], 'Upon Mrs. Dorothy Parker
sister to my(?) first wife'

b.131, back (no. 76)

01065 Orinda, blooming fair and young,
And kindly still remember me.

'Love and knowledge to Orinda'

c.244, p. 598

01066 Orphe' from hell brought back his wife again:
But ne'er was woman, yet, so kind to man.

Sir Thomas Urquhart, 'That a husband hath done
more for his wife, then ever any wife did for her
husband'

fb.217, p. 120

01067 Orpheus, as learned poets tell,
Most surely concord hate!

Charles Burney, the younger, 'On the quarrels of the
Pantheon Committee, in London—April—1778'

c.35, p. 27; c.37, p. 22

01068 Orpheus of old (as poets tell)
Has most prodigious luck,—indeed.

'The unfashionable husband. A tale'

c.94

01069 Others as fair, and may as worthy prove,
May from my eyes, but not my heart remov'd.

c.549, p. 143

01070 Others far greater care may take
We shall admire, shall love, adore.

[Edmund Wodehouse], 'Jan. 28 [1715]'

b.131, p. 152

01071 Others may set their hits upon
What his rich mercy prompts, our souls that we
would save.

[Edmund Wodehouse], 'Decr. 9 [1714]'

b.131, p. 109

01072 Our author who accuses great and small,
And let all those write comedies, who can.

Rev. [ ] Nares, 'Everyone has his faults a comedy[.]
Prologue by . . .'

c.83/3, no. 808

01073 Our blessed Savior, by his sacred power divine,
Was at a marriage, to his eternal glory.

Sir F[rancis] C[astillion], 'The first miracle that
Christ did, was at a marriage in Canan [Cana] . . .
1632'

fb.69, p. 229

01074 Our blessed Savior promises,
Present and to eternity.

[Edmund Wodehouse], 'New Year['s] day [1715]'

b.131, p. 129

01075 Our brangl' of three, some take their pleasure
Must needs three things imply.

Sir Thomas Urquhart, 'Of our Scots louse dance, or
bra[n]gle of three, which the English call a gig'

fb.217, p. 283

01076 Our Canterbury's great cathedral bell
And have our church purg'd from new-fangled toys.

'Upon Archbishop Laud, prisoner in the Tower 1641'
[Crum 01246]

b.54, p. 888

01077 Our case in nothing is more desperate
We change our vices still in other vices.

[Sir Thomas Urquhart], 'So miserable is the case of
man that in the diversity of sin he repeats(?) himself'

fb.217, p. 532

01078 Our civil law is like a royal thing,
In getting, like the pope, so many a crown.

[Richard Zouch], 'On the civil, and common law'
[epigram from 'The sophister a comedy' I.iv, 1639]
[Crum 01249]

b.200, p. 410

01079 Our Clapham Club to all their friends
And bids him at a quibble aim.

[Dr. T. Stamper], 'A poetical salutation from the Club
held at the Plough in Clapham to the Club at
Tuddington'

b.155, p. 77

01080 Our councils are govern'd by Hugo Boscawen,
Sad news! but yet worth for all Englishmen's
knowing.

[Sir Fleetwood Sheppard], 'A lampoon in 1692' [verses
on the French successes]
[Crum 01250]

c.189, p. 183; File 17711; b.204, p. 10

01081 Our days are in God's hands; oh that each day
All these rejects, who merits boast.

[Edmund Wodehouse], 'Apr. 11 [1715]'

b.131, p. 196

01082 Our days until our life doth end
In labors and in hopes we spend.

'A motto'

c.360/1, p. 251, p. 315

01083 Our eagle is yet flown to a place unknown
Of the southern inferior bear.

'[Tune of:] Whoop do me no harm' [on Prince
Charles's journey to Spain, 1622]
[Crum 01254]

b.197, p. 10

01084 Our enemies we ought not to contemn,
Is able to eclipse the sun's bright rays.

Sir Thomas Urquhart, 'That we despise nobody'

fb.217, p. 56

01085 Our eyes are fixed looking on thee,
Make haste I pray thee, make our day.

Lady Jane Cavendish, 'A song'
[Crum 01258]

b.233, p. 12

01086 Our fashionable belles and beaux
To everything one sees.

'Epigrams'

c.546

01087 Our first lady Eve
Has the serpent entirely defeated.

Rev. [ ] Green, 'On Miss West's killing a snake'
[answered by 'My good friend, Mr. Green . . .'

c.395, p. 143

01088 Our glad hosannas, Prince of Peace
With thy beloved name.

P[hilip] Doddridge, '[Psalm?] VII'

c.493, p. 6

01089 Our God and king (whom God forever bless
At both they grumble, and at both repine.

[Francis Quarles], 'On God and the king' [Divine fancies II, 78]

b.137, p. 190

01090 Our God and soldiers we alike adore;
Our God's forgotten and our soldiers slighted.

[Francis Quarles]
[Crum 01271]

b.118, p. 225; c.360/3, no. 158 (attr. T. Jordan)

01091 Our God gives leave to us by pray'r,
This, if not blind, we must perceive.

[Edmund Wodehouse], 'Octr. 14 [1714]'

b.131, p. 58

01092 Our God is love! He himself says this,
Mere toys, mere traps, its treasures are.

[Edmund Wodehouse], 'March 21 [1715]'

b.131, p. 184

01093 Our good old Chaucer some despise: and why?
Not at these years your native language know.

[Sir Aston Cokayne], 'Of Chaucer'

b.275, p. 36

01094 Our gracious sovereign condescends
The devil's in't if this be n't free.

'His Majesty's request' [the proclamation for calling a Parliament, 1714/15; printed (Foxon H250)]
[Crum 01274]

fc.58, p. 124

01095 Our grandfathers were Papists
By getting Presbyterians.

[Thomas Wharton], 1st marquis of Wharton, 'Another' [verse on 'Every age grows worse and worse']

c.229/1, fol. 45; b.204, p. 2; see also 'Our grandsires . . .'.

01096 Our grandsire Adam, ere of Eve possess'd,
Woman, the best, the last reserv'd of God.

[Thomas] Otw[ay], 'O woman, lovely woman'

c.360/3, no. 224

01097 Our grandsires they were Papists,
Ours must be cursed queer ones!

Dr. [ ] South, 'Every age grows worse and worse'

c.229/1, fol. 45; Poetry Box VII/5; see also 'Our grandfathers . . .'.

01098 Our great forefathers, did the top produce
Since fortune plays with him, and he himself's a top.

'The castle top written by a lad at Winchester School' [Whitehall evening post Jan. 28. 1737/8] [Crum 01279]

c.138, p. 45

01099 Our guidman came home at e'en
But maidens wi' long beards never saw I none.

'Song 98'

c.555, p. 148

01100 Our hearts unequal to the pain
Lest age or sickness find us.

'And why do preachers of the age imagine a vain thing'

c.360/1, p. 225

01101 Our heavenly King this blessed day
Where joys and pleasures do abound. | Amen

'The transfiguration of Our Lord. Au. 6'

a.30[22]

01102 Our Hercules, who from us went
E'en let her stay—I'm cool as she.

'Horat: lib: III, od: 14. Translated by Colley Cibber esq, Poet Laureate. Upon His Majesty's happy return from his electoral dominions in company with the Countess of Yarmouth . . . Sept. 20, 1741' [satire on Cibber, King George, and others]

File 3245 (incomplete?)

01103 Our high rank and station is very well known,
No treasure can purchase, no money can buy!

'A riddle'

fc.40

01104 Our Holt, alas! has stint his hold
With Christ is better plac'd.

'Epitaph at All Hallows Staining in Mark Lane London, on Christopher Holt'

c.360/3, no. 141; fb.143, p. 6 (var.)

01105 Our Jesus was the man despis'd
And live upon his grace.

T[homas] S[tevens], 'Sabbath afternoon March 11th. 1781'

c.259, p. 134

01106 Our joys are fleeting, not our sorrows so,
Rejoicing in his joys should with the angels join.

'On Master Crew Harpur's death 1724/5'

b.322, p. 44

01107 Our ladies, fond of love's soft joys,
This living satire's Harry Colt.

'Tunbridge lampoon. 1690'
fb.70, p. 73; b.111, p. 559

01108 Our life hangs on the shore of death, being as
So life, and death all to it pertain.

[Sir Thomas Urquhart], 'That it is as natural for men to die, as to live'
fb.217, p. 514

01109 Our life is but a winter's day
Who goes the soonest has the least to pay.

[William Coyte?], 'Epitaph in Bath' [based on 'Our life's a journey . . .' by Francis Quarles]
[Crum 01297]
c.362, p. 31

01110 Our life is ever on the wing
To hurry mortals home.

[( ) Pierson]
c.328, p. 8

01111 Our life's a journey in a winter's day:
Who dies betimes, has less and less to pay.

[Francis Quarles], 'Journey through life'
[Crum 01299]
c.81/1, no. 291; see also 'Our life is but a winter's day . . .'.

01112 Our Lord Almighty, this great holy day
Be't vile or honest honored or base.

'On the seventh day, with meditations from the creatures fit for it'
b.137, p. 115

01113 Our Lord is risen indeed! How did their news
His hand stretch'd out to lead us unto bliss.

[Edmund Wodehouse], 'Easter Day Apr. 17 [1715]'
b.131, p. 199

01114 Our love of God indeed's expresst
Compar'd to this all else is flight.

[Edmund Wodehouse], 'Iterum [22 March 1715]'
b.131, p. 186

01115 Our merchants and tars a great pother have made,
On his personal credit he'll borrow you more.

'The negotiation, or Don Diego [Sir Thomas Fitzgerald, Spanish envoy] brought to reason. An excellent new ballad, [to the] tune of Packington's Pound' [on Sir Robert and Horace Walpole; pr. Gentleman's magazine May 1738]
[Crum 01305]
Poetry Box x/51

01116 Our merry men feasted, 'twas all that they did,
Is sail'd in as safe as e'er it sail'd out.

'On the fleet's being gone from Spithead'
c.570/3, p. 70

01117 Our morning's duty paid,
The glorious fifty nine, | Forevermore.

John Lockman, 'Chorus (extempore) for the Thanksgiving Night, Thursday, 29 Novr. 1759'
c.267/2, p. 41

01118 Our muses not exiled, with sober feet
In a distracted verse.

[George Daniel]
b.121, fol. 23

01119 Our native freedom Lord preserve
But they at last shall crown my peace.

[Thomas Stanley], 'Meditat: VI. Upon his Ma[jes]ty's retirement from Westminster'
b.152, p. 18

01120 Our neighbor lass, and I, in one same hour
She lost: and I, by closing mine too soon.

Sir Thomas Urquhart, 'The speeches of a certain girl, that had lost her maidenhead; concerning herself, and another wench, who happened about the same time, to have some monies stolen from her'
fb.217, p. 285

01121 Our noble king was there ever such a thing
That will not let so brave a work decay.

'Upon King James his coming to Paul's to the tune of Rise up Randall'
b.197, p. 185

01122 Our only God made up the first of men:
But man hath forg'd a hundred gods since then.

Sir Thomas Urquhart, 'Of God, and man'
fb.217, p. 174

01123 Our Parliament | Had a shrewd intent
A health unto the King.

b.104, p. 25 (end of book)

01124 Our politics, like oarsmen, whilst they row
To you go you to it—y'are molehills.

[Sir Philip Wodehouse], 'An Italian proverb . . . another of '79'
b.131, p. 47

01125 Our prelates oft pose us to know who they are,
He writes in his own proper name I hope(?), Cant.

'A nursery for politics on His Grace of Cant:'
c.74

01126 Our proper gallant youths,
That one knock spoils them.

Sir Thomas Urquhart, 'Of pretty young gentlemen,
and handsome maids'

fb.217, p. 232

01127 Our proverb calls truth-tellers fools, what then,
Is't folly to tell truth in Englishmen?

'Children and fools tell truth'

c.356

01128 Our rebel party of late
And Whigs shall it merrily sing.

'A new ballad in answer to Old Rowley the king' [on
Monmouth; 1683]
[POAS III.484]

b.113, p. 263

01129 Our resident Tom from Venice is come,
The good fellow is nowhere a stranger.

[Sir John Denham], 'To the tune First came my Lord
Scroope, he did hallo, and hoop, &c.'

fb.228/55 (attr. [ ] Pooly)

01130 Our Savior came not with a gaudy show,
Are not his sons, but those of Zebedee.

c.83/3, no. 815

01131 Our Savior's feet were kist, the people do
Upon thy lips our Savior had on his.

[Francis Quarles], 'On the great prelate' [Divine
fancies III, 29]

b.137, p. 175

01132 Our Savior's love to human race,
His wisdom and his love gainsay.

[Edmund Wodehouse], 'Octr. 19 [1714]'

b.131, p. 62

01133 Our ships are all taken our merchants all stript
What signify then more money and men.

Edward Dow[ett?], 'July the 30 1695'
Trumbull Box: Poetry Box XIII/87

01134 Our sickness makes physicians rich and healthy:
Our foolishness makes lawyers wise, and wealthy.

Sir Thomas Urquhart, 'Of lawyers and physicians'
fb.217, p. 68

01135 Our souls with pleasing wonder view
Eternal songs we'll raise.

P[hilip] Doddridge, 'The goodness which God has
laid up and wrought for his people. Ps. XXXI. 19'

c.493, p. 76

01136 Our sovereign lady that now rings in this hour
That we his lieges may ring in peace and rest.

'[Rulers of Scotland] 15'
fa.4, fol. 29

01137 Our Spenser was a prodigy of wit
Phoebus himself with all his learned throng.

[Sir Aston Cokayne], 'Of Edmund Spenser'
b.275, p. 36

01138 Our spirits join t'adore the Lamb:
A thousand lives shall be all thine.

[Isaac Watts, Hymns and spiritual songs (1707),
bk. III, Hymn 22]

c.180, p. 56

01139 Our squire of his peculiar grace
That comes to stay a day or two.

[Phanuel Bacon], 'Written in Mr. Dalby's necessary
house at Hurst 1752'

c.237, fol. 76

01140 Our storm is past: and that storm's tyrannous rage
I should not then thus feel this misery.

[John Donne], 'The calm'
[Crum O1339]

b.114, p. 226; b.148, p. 60

01141 Our talent well let so strive to bestow,
And not it hid whereby no good may grow.

c.339, p. 321

01142 Our talents we ofttimes mistake
And most egregious errors make.

Poetry Box x/63

01143 Our [?] the heart's interpreter, and should still
The legate speaks, the [?] man holds his peace.

[Sir Thomas Urquhart], 'We ought always to think
upon what we are to say, before we utter anything the
speeches and talk of solid wits being still premeditated
and never using to forerun the mind'

fb.217, p. 514

01144 Our theme is hope—but of a diff'rent kind,
Makes toil seem pleasant, and afflictions calm.

'On hope'
c.83/2, no. 347

01145 Our trust in God for riches never must
Exclude our care: nor care exceed our trust.

[Francis Quarles], 'On trust and care'
[Crum O1347]

b.137, p. 193

01146 Our tutor hath no zeal nor safety found
Where old Apollyon hath encampt his host.

c.160, fol. 46

01147 Our western colonies concerning
The lesser [?] is still our own.

[Phanuel Bacon], 'Of the American dispute'

c.237, fol. 84v

01148 Our will sometime may bubble up and swill
Of mind, unto thyself dost vindicate.

[Sir Philip Wodehouse], 'Dr William Hawkins awe
may sink will'

b.131, back (no. 155)

01149 Our wise reformers wise and gay,
To tamper with a crown.

'Whigs no changelings'

b.111, p. 476

01150 Our wit till Cowley did its luster raise
For that part buried than for all above.

[Roger Boyle, 1st earl of Orrery], 'On the death of
Mr. Abraham Cowley and his burial in Westminster
Abbey'

fc.60, p. 73

01151 Our writing in the dust cannot endure a blast,
Yet oft the dull do bear in mind what first therein
was set.

b.234, p. 322

01152 Our yesterday's tomorrow now is gone,
Today itself's too late, the wise lived yesterday.

[Isaac Watts], 'Iam Hesternum consumpsimus . . .'
['On the morrow']
[Crum 01351a]

fb.142, p. 37

01153 Our zealous sons of mother Church,
Damn his Whig soul, and there's an end.

'The Tory creed' [1690]
[Crum 01353]

fb.70, p. 275

01154 Out hideous ghastly gloomy fiend
And frenzy's loud resounding storms.

[George Howard, 6th earl of Carlisle], 'Ode on
madness'

c.197, p. 5

01155 Out upon it I have loved | Three whole days
together
There had been long time ere thee | And dozen
dozen in her place.

[Sir John Suckling. Answered by 'Say but did you love
so long . . .']

b.213, p. 54

01156 Owen's praise demands my song,
Despair, and honorable death.

[Thomas Gray], 'The triumphs of Owen Gwynedd a
fragment'

c.481, p. 45

01157 Oxford! The seat of learning, arts and wit,
Till fleeting time and death shall be no more.

'. . . I put the following lines into one of the
gentleman's coat pockets'

fc.78, fol. 7

01158 *Oyez*, from henceforth *sit omnibus notum*
And Bracciano's cheap mistress makes Charles a
dear wife.

'Upon the Duke of Shrewsbury marrying a w[hore]'
[Crum 01377a]

b.90, p. 2; c.111, p. 122 ('Bracksilio's')

01159 *Oyez*! Hereby is notice given
I'll send the shell, to Nonny's o'er.

Mrs. [ ] Morgan, 'Mrs. Morgan to Mrs. Bentley with
Henry's duty Stourfield Oct. 30, 1795'

fc.40

01160 *Oyez*! If any one can tidings tell,
And you shall be sure of a swinging reward.

'Hue and cry to the crier of Tunbridge Wells . . . 1680'

b.54, p. 1130

01161 *Oyez*, my good people, draw near;
From the charms you bring me, a kiss.

'The hue and cry by the village curate'

c.391, p. 109; c.344, p. 34

01162 *Oyez, oyez*, all men take notice,
He'll stories tell shall make ye wonder!

R[ichard] V[ernon] S[adleir], 'To some friends at a
distance who desired to know when Mr. Walker
renewed his philosophical lectures &c. . . . never sent'

c.106, p. 98

01163 *Oyez! Oyez! Oyez!*—be it known,
Then what would ye give, were blithe Comus but
nigh?

John Lockman, 'A proclamation by Comus, previous
to the shutting up of Vauxhall Gardens . . . Aug. 1750'

c.267/1, p. 128

01164 *Oyez! Oyez! Oyez!* Come nigher
And so God save our noble King!

Mrs. [ ] Bentley, 'Mrs. Bentley to Capn. Bentley. Hue
and cry &c. &c. November the 28th 1794'

fc.40

Oyez, sinful flesh come here
For this session general.

H[enry] C[olman], 'The summons'
[Crum 01382]

b.2, p. 21

01165

P

P0001 Padling, the duck goes quack, quack, quack,
Till fortune turns her wheels.

> John Lockman, '. . . On my Lord *** kindly asking me
> at St James's, whether I had not heard, with regard to
> my humble memorial, presented to the King, the
> resolution . . . 17 May 1761'

c.267/1, p. 300

P0002 Painful source, of many a sorrow,
I need not fear thy moment, Last.

> 'On the word Last'

c.83/3, no. 1068

P0003 Painter attend with awe:
Let every bow, and every part of . . . .

> 'The passion, an ode'

b.154, p. 9 (incomplete)

P0004 Painter, once more thy pencil reassume
'Tis by afflictions passive men grow great.

> [Andrew Marvell], 'On the Parliament' [1671?]
> [Crum P7; POAS I.164]

b.52/1, p. 161; fb.70, p. 155 (ll. 1–27); fb.140, p. 143 ('thy
pencil once more'; ll. 1–51).

P0005 Painter, where was't thy former work did cease,
Poets and painters are licentious youths.

> 'Fifth advice to a painter, Aug–Oct. 1667'
> [Crum P10; POAS I.146]

b.136, p. 38; c.160, fol. 19v (attr. Denham)

P0006 Painting and poetry are twins:
Will share in Edward's deathless fame.

> John Lockman, 'The Shetland herring, and Peruvian
> gold mine. Most humbly inscribed to his royal
> highness, Frederick Prince of Wales: on his graciously
> condescending to be governor of the Society of the
> Free British Fishery . . . 1751'

c.267/3, p. 85

P0007 Painting and poetry you know
Spares the proud Prince of Eloquence.

> [Peter Pinnell(?), 'Address to the dwarf fan-painter at
> Tunbridge Wells' (Thomas Loggan); pr. 1748 (Foxon
> A83)]
> [Crum P16]

Poetry Box I/120

P0008 Pale death who walks, incessant walks his round
Thou common fame? but common breath.

> 'Opposite the Monitor' [a bell at Pensoroso]

fc.51, p. 100

P0009 Pale planet of the night, whose silvery beam,
And tranquil nature sinks in soft repose!

> Sarah Herd, 'Sonnet to the moon'

c.141, p. 359

P0010 Pale wither'd wand'rer, seek not here
To seek in vain for nature and rest.

> 'On the falling of a dead leaf into the bosom of a
> distressed lady'
> [Crum P21]

c.83/3, no. 779

P0011 Pallas, destructive to the Trojan line,
Fell by Eliza—and by Anna rose.

> [Sir Samuel Garth], 'On the King of Spain'
> [Crum P22]

c.189, p. 163; c.111, p. 47 (var.; 'Pallas long fatal')

P0012 Pallas was born of Jove her father's brain,
And he that Bacchus loves, must break his shins.

> 'On learning, and drunkenness'
> [Crum P26]

b.200, p. 410

P0013 Palmers all our fathers were
And took my journey hence to Heaven.

> 'On Palmer of Oxford'
> [Crum P29]

fb.143, p. 22

P0014 Pamela still admire—for this is she,
As in her name, and noble grace you see.

> [Sir Philip Wodehouse], 'Upon the Lady Mary Palmes
> half sister to my Ld. [?]'

b.131, back (no. 45)

P0015 Pan assist my homely song
And by thee mankind increases.

> 'On a cow t[ur]d'

c.176, p. 85

P0016 Pan first taught swains, the rural pipe
And cures the sheeps's masser.

    [Thomas Hull], 'In the gothic style'

c.20/6; c.21

P0017 Panthe the lovely the joy of her swain
That they still might be kind, that they still might
                                    be true.

    [on Queen Anne]

Poetry Box v/11

P0018 Paper—the trial is of ink
Into the draught cast both away.

    C[harles] E[arle], 'To a person who sold ink'

c.376

P0019 Paplus was married all in haste,
He hath himself undone.

    'Fast and loose'

c.356

P0020 Pardon (great Saul) if duty grounded on
'Tis making anthems in the heavenly choir.

    'On the death of my much honored uncle Mr. G.
    Sandys'

Poetry Box v/106

P0021 Pardon my boldness (cousin) that defames
For in my eclogues you are Tityrus.

    [Sir Aston Cokayne], 'To my cousin Mr. Charles
    Cotton'

b.275, p. 36

P0022 Pardon, O shade divine, the officious verse
Which cannot greater be—till you are there.

    'Verses by . . . on the death of . . . Henrietta (Butler)
    Countess of Grantham . . . October the 11 1724'

c.360/2, no. 118

P0023 Pardon the muse that only begs to prove,
Find its reward, in all that heav'n can give.

    R[obert] Shirley, 1st earl of Ferrers, 'To my friend, the
    Revd. Mr. La Boneille rector of Brailsford in
    Derbyshire'

c.347, p. 69

P0024 Pardon the muse, who with inferior strains
To join hands here, go hand in hand to heaven.

c.53, fol. 28

P0025 Parent of all created things,
For we by solemn vows are thine.

    'Te Deum—poetical essays'

c.244, p. 566

P0026 Parent of arts, whose skillful hand first taught
And other Blenheims, shall adorn the land.

    [George Lyttelton, 1st baron Lyttelton], 'Blenheim'
    [pr. 1728 (Foxon L330)]

c.176, p. 88; Poetry Box I/98

P0027 Parent of dullness, genuine son of night,
Just at the closing of the bellman's rhyme.

    Dr. [ ] Sewal, 'Written by . . . on the titlepage of a bad
    play'

c.360/3, no. 159

P0028 Parent of ease! Hail sweet delusive sleep!
The everlasting spring of peace and ease.

    'On sleep'

c.591

P0029 Parent of genius! At thy shrine I bend
Real mis'ry soften and false hopes refine!

    S[arah] H[arriet] B[urney], 'A sonnet to imagination
    in answer to that of indifference 1793'

c.486, fol. 43, 54v

P0030 Parent of health to Thee I aweful sue
Preserve her then O God I ask no more.

    'These wrote by a gentleman at Bath with his sick wife
    on his wedding day 30 years after marriage'

c.148, p. 15

P0031 Parent of virtue, if thine ear
Indulge my votive strain, O sweet humanity!

    [John Langhorne], 'Hymn. To humanity'
    [Crum P42]

c.140, p. 150; c.83/1, no. 37

P0032 Parents and children both attend
To vindicate His injur'd name.

    [Thomas Stevens?], 'Evening of the same day
    [7 January 1781]. A sermon to young people, sung as
    follows'

c.259, p. 111

P0033 Parnassian butterfly; and like the bees
Fickle, alike in glory and in love.

    John Lockman, 'His muse' [translated from La
    Fontaine]

c.267/4, p. 179

P0034 Parson, these things in thy possessing
And shake his head at Doctor S[wif]t.

    [Alexander Pope], 'The happy life of a country parson
    Dean Swif't's works'

fb.142, p. 8 (second series)

P0035 P[arson]s whose candor to my humble lays,
Less gay than G[re]gg and far less learn'd than
N[are]s.

[William Boscawen], 'Horace epist. 4. lib. 1 imitated.
1796 . . . To William P[arso]ns, esq. (who had retired
in disgust to Hampstead)'
[Crum P51]

fc.106, p. 23

P0036 Part, part from thee! Nor heav'n nor earth
And give her riches rank and fame.

'Upon a painting of a flower by a young lady
fortunately falling into the hands of a gentleman and
its being asked of him again'

fc.40

P0037 Particular accounts extending hither,
Then this same blest communion of All Saints.

[Edward] Sparke, 'Poem 36—on All Saints'

b.137, p. 73

P0038 Parties in turn do make us all court slaves,
Fools ruin fools, both help t'enrich the knave.

[on the House of Commons, 1708]

c.189, p. 163

P0039 Pasiphae was enamor'd with a bull
Of horns than theirs t'obtain your mistress' love?

[Sir Thomas Urquhart], 'To a gentleman who married
to a lascivious wife doted upon the [?] being [?]'

fb.217, p. 387

P0040 'Pass but a few short fleeting years'
Secure from malice, chance or blame.

[Helen Craik], 'Lines—occasioned by a reperusal of
the foregoing epistle ['Say G. . . . is an empty
shade . . .'] to Sir W. G. baronet—written some years
afterwards'

c.375, p. 114; imitation of next.

P0041 Pass but a few short fleeting years
And the sons' sons will catch the glorious flame.

W[illia]m Whitehead, 'Ode for the new year 1774'
[Crum P59]

fc.85, fol. 79v; see also previous.

P0042 Pass to Mount Edgecombe, Chatham, there you'll
find
Look up with awe, with wonder and delight.

David Garrick, 'Mr. Garrick's invitation to Ld.
Chatham to visit Mount Edgecombe in his way to
Cornwall'

Poetry Box V/119

P0043 Passions best likened are to floods and streams
That he is poor in that which makes a lover.

[Sir Walter Raleigh?], 'On a passionate lover'
[Crum P67]

b.205, fol. 31r

P0044 Passions, too oft, are feign'd by flatt'ring art:
These artless touches from the life I draw.

John Lockman

c.267/4, p. 2

P0045 Passive obedience and non-
They that swear not, are rogues in grain.

'On Dr. Sherlock's taking the oaths' [1690]
[Crum P68; POAS V.254]

Poetry Box VII/5

P0046 Passive obedience is now out of door
Lloyd, Sancroft, Trelawny, Lake, Turner, Ken,
White. | Jeffreys, Jeffreys, &c.

Poetry Box VII/62

P0047 Past fifty now, and near threescore,
Lord! In what year shall I grow wise?

Abraham Oakes, 'On myself. 1744'

c.50, p. 92

P0048 Past is the day my friend which gave the birth
They shed their balmy influence o'er mankind.

Miss [ ] Andrews, 'On Miss Caley's birthday'

File 245/16

P0049 Past overnight while thou dost ply the pot
That the morning thou shouldst take thy drink.

'Martial lib. 12.12'

b.197, p. 38

P0050 Paternal spirit by whose power alone
I set no true [illegible]. . . .

[William Hayley], 'Sonnet . . . Jan 14 [1800]'

File 6968 (incomplete)

P0051 Patience my friend, a virtue rare I grant,
To check our pride and make the balance even.

'On patience: to a friend'

c.83/2, no. 348; see also next.

P0052 Patience my Lord, a virtue rare I grant;
Your Lordship is the patient'st man alive.

'Of patience, an epistle to Lord Masham' [husband of
Abigail, favorite of Queen Anne]

fc.51, p. 235; see also previous.

P0053 Patriots we have as thick as hail,
Whose choicest talent is to rail.

> Abraham Oakes, 'The modern patriots: in the year
> 1742'
>
> c.50, p. 29

P0054 Patron of all those luckless brains,
With equal grace below.

> [William] Cowper, 'Ode to Apollo. On an ink-glass
> almost dried in the sun'
>
> File 15773

P0055 Patron of honest worth! Whose bounteous mind,
'Tis common-place and has been said before.

> [William Popple, trans.], 'Horace book 1st satire 1
> imitated. Inscribed to the late John Selwyn esq.'
>
> fc.104/1, p. 25

P0056 Patrons, as now, in days of yore
The panegyric will be thine.

> 'To Mrs B[ernard?] on receiving an ink stand'
>
> Poetry Box x/45, p. 36

P0057 Pattern of patience, creature meekly dumb,
Shall I that day stand recompens'd.

> 'Lines written upon an ass; on Christmas Day'
>
> Poetry Box 11/34

P0058 Pattern of patience, gravity, devotion
Faithful to th'end, now heir to heav'n's promotion.

> 'Epitaph at Windsor'
>
> c.360/3, no. 65

P0059 Paul only mention'd man, whilst he pray'd for
That it was good, save when he made the woman.

> Sir Thomas Urquhart, 'Of womankind. A paradox'
>
> fb.217, p. 297

P0060 Paula in labor of her firstborn son,
But think, who shall be gossips to the next.

> 'Epigram. Primogenitum in Paula parientem . . .'
>
> fb.142, p. 37

P0061 Pause, reader, e'er you pass this sacred bier,
In lamentation for her dearest friend.

> F. B., 'On the death of the Revd. Peter Mayson'
>
> c.83/3, no. 1052

P0062 'Pay through the nose', the vulgar say,
'Twill be so hot—'twill burn the fingers.

> 'To Arabin, who boasted that he was paid in one
> instance excessively—though not beyond his deserts'
>
> fc.76.iii/214

P0063 Peace babbling muse
Torn all in pieces if he cries.

> [Edmund Waller]
> [Crum P83]
>
> b.213, p. 21

P0064 Peace beldame Eve, surcease thy suit,
An aged chronicles new cover.

> [John Cleveland], 'A young man to an old woman
> courting him'
> [Crum P84]
>
> b.93, p. 9

P0065 Peace has explor'd this sylvan scene;
Be rev'renc'd in decay!

> J[ohn] Cunningham, 'An inscription on the house at
> Mavis Bank, near Edinburgh, situated in a grove . . .
> Imitated by . . .'
>
> c.139, p. 54

P0066 Peace has unveil'd her smiling face
My path till I go home to God.

> [William Cowper, trans.], 'The entire surrender.
> Vol. 4. Son: 77' [of Jeanne Guion's 'Spiritual songs']
>
> c.470 (autogr.)

P0067 Peace mourning friend! Forbear to weep for him
Than all the instances of grief before.

> 'An elegy on the death of Dr. John Lake late lord
> Bishop of Chichester who departed this life.
> August 30th. 1689'
>
> b.111, p. 101

P0068 Peace rebel thoughts: dost thou not know my King
                  my God is here
Exact others' company; a while sit still or part
                     again.

> b.245 (inside back cover)

P0069 Peace restless soul! let not those various storms,
Renders thy loss thy gain; improves thy bliss.

> [Sir Matthew] Hale, 'Upon changes and troubles'
>
> fb.142, p. 41

P0070 Peace(?) sweet and sour
And softer than the graces.

> [William Hayley], 'Inscription for a female portrait'
>
> File 6947

P0071 Peace to the groves, the Druid's calm recess
And to your beauty add each manly grace.

> [William Stukeley], 'To Hebe retired in the country
> 1754 . . . Chyndonax. Aug. 3. 1754'
> [Crum P96]
>
> c.371, fol. 78

P0072 Peace to the noblest, most ingenuous mind
Lov'd mercy, and walked humbly with his God.

[Francis Fawkes], 'On James Fox, esqr., on a
monument under a fine marble bust erected in the
churchyard of East Horsley in Surrey, 1754'

fc.21, p. 28

P0073 Peace to the spirit which inform'd this dust,
A soul more active, yet more blameless too.

H[annah] More, Epitaph on S. B—df—d . . . 1782'

c.341, p. 36

P0074 Peace to these relics! Once the bright attire
Careless of fate, confiding in his God!

[William Hayley], 'Near this tablet lie the remains of
George Steevens esqr, who, after having cheerfully
employed a considerable portion of his life and
fortune to the illustration of Shakespeare, expired at
Hampstead in his 64th year. 1800'

File 6956

P0075 Peace, to thy placid reign belong
In nuptial hymns, and Cupid's praise.

Charles Burney, the younger, 'On peace, translated
from the Greek of Bacchylides'

c.35, p. 49

P0076 Peace wayward soul! let not those various storms
Renders thy loss, thy gain; improves thy bliss.

'Changes and troubles'
[Crum P98]

b.49, p. 20 and 26

P0077 Peaceful is he, and most secure,
And with an easy sigh give up his breath.

[Thomas] Flatman, 'The happy man'
[Crum P99]

c.244, p. 123

P0078 Peculiar therefore is her way
Bespeaks a noble mind.

[William] Congreve, 'Character of a jilt . . .
Congreve's Doris'

c.144, p. 110

P0079 Peggy in devotion
And forgot his text.

'Song 123'

c.555, p. 176

P0080 Pelham 'twill do—or charity
Is sent to Berlin with one Leg.

[Phanuel Bacon], 'To Henry Pelham upon Mr. Leg's
going envoy to Prussia'

c.237, fol. 64

P0081 Penelope sound chaste lamb, innocent
That's innocent, this bringeth shame.

[Sir Philip Wodehouse], 'Upon Mrs. Penelope Lamb'

b.131, back (no. 95)

P0082 Penelope the fair and chaste
For such a chaste Penelope.

[William Strode], 'A soldier to Penelope'
[Crum P104]

b.205, fol. 65r

P0083 Pengrowze, a lad in many a science blest,
And I to Yealstone for my master's backy.

'A western eclogue'

c.382, p. 45

P0084 Pepper is black—'tis true, a constant hue
As do her black-brown looks, believe't.

[Sir Philip Wodehouse], 'Mrs. Ann Repps Nan's
pepper'

b.131, back (no. 100)

P0085 Pepper, salt, do not fail
Put butter and water.

[Charles Earle], 'A short extempore recipe for a
piggy-tail pie'

c.376

P0086 Per sheet, two shillings, for huge Boyer's dic!
With thee, and fiddling, eke a living out.

John Lockman, 'To the reverend Mr. ———— editor of
a new edition of Boyer's dictionary, and who had
abused the author . . . 1747'

c.267/1, p. 46

P0087 Perfection comes in time and form and fashion
gives,
And ever rashness yields repent, and most despised
lives.

c.339, p. 323

P0088 Perfection stampt upon thy breast, and mark'd
thee for her own,
One only vice thou didst possess—and now that
vice is gone.

[Thomas] Parnell, 'Lady Appleby was going to net,
one day, when Dr. Parnell was in the room, but she
could not find her vice. The Doctor looked at her and
said'

c.378, p. 46

P0089 Perfection, who that rich, eye-dazzling gem,
exquire [sic],
Must by examples, kindle their ingenious fire.

[John Rose?]

b.227, p. 72

P0090 Perform some brave exploits swell the loud cheeks
                                      of fame
And by magnifique works immortalize thy name.

    [John Rose?]

b.227, p. 76

P0091 Perhaps our English may appear
At Westminster they'll learn it.

    '[Several copies of verses spoken at Westminster
    School on the anniversary of the defeat of the Spanish
    Armada] 8'

fc.24, p. 72; c.233, p. 30

P0092 Permit dear sister, this address
That your dear sister do remain.

    E[lizabeth (Shirley)] C[ompton, countess of
    Northampton], 'Oct: 26, 1726 [to Lady Anne
    Compton]'

Accession 97.7.40

P0093 Permit us Sir, your humble slaves
Better than hitherto you've done the playhouse.

    'The poet's address to King George [I]'
    [Crum P129]

fc.58, p. 163

P0094 Permit your female poet to commend
But hold here ends the epilogue to the play.

    Mrs. [ ] Thompson, 'The epilogue by a lady on the
    occasion [of a play acted at Spalding by Herbert's
    company] . . . spoken by Mrs. Herbert'

c.229/1, fol. 89

P0095 Perplex'd with duns from morn to night,
Could when alive do for themselves.

    [Isaac Freeman], 'On the pawning of my library.
    Leiden'

fc.105

P0096 Perplex'd with engagements for ten days to come
And I've a rare plaster for but[toc]ks that chafe.

    R[ichard] V[ernon] S[adleir], 'Invitation to Mrs. [ ]
    and family 1769—impromptu'

c.106, p. 30

P0097 Perplext with cares, with grief opprest
And she commands the main.

    [Robert Cholmeley], 'To Mrs. Minny Fermor from
    Cambridge'

c.190, p. 73

P0098 *Personne*, in French nobody signifies
That a dissembled churchman was worth aught.

    Sir Thomas Urquhart, 'The homonymy of the word
    person'

fb.217, p. 122

P0099 Pert angel spells his name—pert I confess
Who to the spiritual lords, their rights denies?

    [Sir Philip Wodehouse], 'Upon Sr Peter Glean being
    chosen knight 1679'

b.131, back (no. 161)

P0100 Peruse my leaves thro' ev'ry part,
He's a golden pencil tipt with lead.

    [Jonathan Swift], 'Verses wrote on a lady's ivory
    table-book by the same hand' [as 'Parson, these
    things . . .']

fb.142, p. 9 (second series); c.265, p. 1

P0101 Peter a washbasin hath made
Could not be done with less.

    'On Peter Fermin's fishpond at Dedham'

pc.97, back flyleaf

P0102 Peter, come take your boy and go to plow
Always thank God for his ordaining care.

    'A short direction to the plowman'

c.158, p. 153

P0103 Peter complains that God hath given
'Tis good to have a friend at court.

    [Alexander Pope], 'Epigram'

fc.60, p. 50 (attr. Swift)

P0104 Peter the guardian saint who keeps heaven's gate
Ever to gain the bliss you vainly seek.

    'A copy of verses made by an Italian poet . . .'

c.158, p. 8

P0105 Phaeton's sister though 'twas thy desire
Can change your own conditions when they please.

    'On a waiting gentlewoman a Nonconformist's
    daughter who would match to none under the degree
    of knight . . .'
    [Crum P142]

b.104, p. 111

P0106 Pharaoh with his goggle eyes did stare on
Into the wilderness, to heat their yearly Paschal?

    [( ) Thomson? From Zacharie Boyd]

Spence Papers, folder 148

P0107 Philander, and Sylvia, a gentle young pair,
Which he bore still about him, to cure those that
                                         die.

    'The young couple'

fb.107, p. 35

P0108 Philautos' charity is like a mouse
The mouse in time will eat up thy estate.

[Francis Quarles], 'On Philautos' [Divine fancies IV, 92]

b.137, p. 182

P0109 Philip, the King of Macedon,
His mausoleum sepulcher.

'Paragraphs'

c.189, p. 25

P0110 Philip your son when first he shone in arms;
Aspiring you disown e'en Jove your sire.

'Ambition knows no bounds'

c.53, fol. 20

P0111 Philips whose touch harmonious could remove
Till angels wake thee, with a note like thine.

[Samuel] Johnson, [extempore, 1740, on Claude Philips, musician who died very poor; 1732] [Crum P151]

Poetry Box IV/199

P0112 Phillida fly care—live nobly free
My destiny | A field o' care I fly.

[Sir Philip Wodehouse], 'Upon his noble cousin german the Lady Ph[iladelphia] Carey'

b.131, back (no. 23)

P0113 *Philoi tuo psychy mia* hold all so true
By making good this truth, two friends, one soul.

[Sir Philip Wodehouse], 'Sir Philip Wodehouse— Thomas Aldrich his anag[ram] my epig[ram]'

b.131, back (no. 235)

P0114 Philosophers consume much time and pain
And pleasures, which alone make life a blessing.

'Peace . . . [Observer, v. 5] no. 139'

c.355, p. 90

P0115 Philosophers, throw aside your tubes, and your glasses,
The transit of Venus is when Grafton leaves us.

[Horace] Walpole, 4th earl of Orford, 'Written by . . . upon the Duchess of Grafton while at his house, and during the time of the transit of Venus'

c.378, p. 8

P0116 Phoebe, thank thy false heart it has fixt my repose,
I can easily meet with a fair as unkind.

R[ichard] Roderick, 'La Libertà. translated from an Italian ode [by Metastasio]'

Poetry Box I/121 (two versions); c.157, p. 36

P0117 Phoebus, farewell! thy absence we bemoan
And re-behold us with thy lovely face.

[John Rose?], 'Of the winter quarter'

b.227, p. 167

P0118 Phoebus obliquely shot his feeble ray,
And Colinet pursued the beauteous maid.

'A pastoral dialogue address'd to Miss [blank]'

c.382, p. 38

P0119 Phoebus, of rapid, not of wild career
By increasing prudence with increase of charms?

Ralph Broome, 'On Miss Frances'

c.486, fol. 34

P0120 Phoebus thy bow and arrows hide, for she
Thy weapons fears but doth not fly from thee.

[Sir Aston Cokayne], 'To Apollo'

b.275, p. 35

P0121 Phryx has but one eye, and that's sore,
Drinks wine his poor eye poison licks.

b.207, p. 7

P0122 Phyllis as her wine she sipp'd in,
Filled for her cold disdain.

'Song 58'

c.555, p. 86

P0123 Phyllis, be gentler I advise,
And never know the joy.

[John Wilmot, 2nd earl of Rochester], 'Song' [Crum P165]

b.105, p. 139; b.334, p. 184

P0124 Phyllis despise not thy faithful lover
With thee in a cottage I'd think myself blest.

'A song'

c.374

P0125 Phyllis, for shame let us improve
Most miserably wise.

[Charles Sackville, 6th earl of Dorset], 'A song' [Crum P169]

Poetry Box V/9 (attr. Sir Charles Hanbury Williams)

P0126 Phyllis hath such charming graces,
I must love her; tho' I die.

c.189, p. 117

P0127 Phyllis I pray,
Than talking to displease you.

[Charles Sackville, 6th earl of Dorset], 'The bashful lover'

fb.107, p. 17

P0128 Phyllis, men say that all my vows
I'm richer than before.

    [Sir Charles Sedley], 'Song'

    fb.70, p. 57

P0129 Phyllis, the darling muse's friend, retir'd
And shoot, through the thick gloom, a feeble ray.

    [Stephen Barrett?], 'Phyllis a pastoral. A school exercise'

    c.193, p. 67

P0130 Phyllis the fairest of love's foes
As would neither kiss nor spin.

    [Charles Sackville, 6th earl of Dorset], 'Song' [Crum P178, 'love's fair']

    c.189, p. 222

P0131 Phyllis when you was in your prime,
My love grew less and you less fair.

    R[obert] Shirley, 1st earl of Ferrers, 'To a decayed and cruel beauty'

    c.347, p. 5

P0132 Phyllis you're lovely you're charming and wise
Tho' fixt in a cottage a— | Happy young swain.

    'Song'

    c.374

P0133 Physicians and lawyers in their trade
Their helping hand, but help themselves thereby.

    'The alliance of physicians and lawyers'

    c.356

P0134 Physicians are imposters, for they give
To sick men physic that themselves may live.

    "A distich'

    File 19344; b.356, p. 306

P0135 Physicians must be rash, and lawyers cunning:
Else both may beg their meat for all their winning.

    Sir Thomas Urquhart, 'Of jurists, and mediciners'

    fb.217, p. 147

P0136 Physicians take gold but seldom give,
Give gold, each other thus supply support.

    'A physician'

    c.356

P0137 Pierian nine! Your kindest influence bring
See none more virtuous, none more blest than she.

    H[annah] More, 'To Miss Cave'

    c.341, p. 74

P0138 Pimps, poets, wits, Lord Fanny, Lady Mary,
This fourth, let L—l Jeffrys, Onslow tell.

    [Alexander Pope], 'Sober advice from Horace'

    c.570/4, p. 130

P0139 Pious Belinda goes to prayers
Or I of her a sinner.

    [William Congreve], 'Song'

    c.176, p. 38; see also 'Pious Selinda . . .'.

P0140 Pious in soul, benevolent in mind:
In friendship faithful, and in manners kind.

    [Charles Earle]

    c.376

P0141 Pious Selinda goes to prayers,
Or I of her a sinner.

    [William] Congreve, 'Song'

    c.189, p. 2; see also 'Pious Belinda . . .'.

P0142 Piss, spew, and spit
Issue, and clyster.

    'The doctor's decade or the ten articles of his trade'

    c.81/1, no. 341

P0143 Pity my ignorance; I must confess
Me, and the world, to clear it in each page.

    [George Daniel], 'Upon a late printed book'

    b.121, fol. 84v

P0144 Pity the sorrows of a poor old maid,
My mind forever could pursue the theme.

    'The old maid's petition'

    c.83/2, no. 641

P0145 Pity the sorrows of a poor old man,
Oh! Give relief, and heaven will bless your store.

    'The beggar's petition'

    c.83/1, no. 127; fc.132/1, p. 102 ('sorrow'); c.481, p. 34 ('poor blind man'); c.156, p. 203 (var.)

P0146 Pity the sorrows of a wretch forlorn,
And continence to honor leads the way.

    'On reading in the papers that the lady of a member of Parliament who had eloped with her servant was seen begging in the streets of Brussels' [signed Euphemia]

    c.343, p. 36

P0147 Plac'd on the verge of youth, my mind
And curbs the headlong tide.

    'The trials of virtue'

    c.139, p. 421

P0148 Plague of all cowards say I! Why bless my eyes!
Is't fit we lose our benefit of clergy?

'An epilogue designed to have been spoke by Mrs. Woffington after The castle of Falkirk' [pr. 1746 (Foxon F102)]

fc.135

P0149 Plain humble port is all you'll meet,
When Welcome crowns the gourd.

[William Boscawen], 'Horace ode 20 lib:1 imitated 1796 . . . To Henry Gregg esq.'

fc.106, p. 22

P0150 Plain in his form
Meek and kind.

'Epitaphs Bersted'

c.546

P0151 Plant by which both glass and flagon
Respect the nose[?] of Chloris.

[Lord E.], 'Another [riddle]'

Poetry Box VII/46

P0152 Plausus has built a church, and lest his glory
Thou either seekst God's glory, or thy own.

[Francis Quarles, 'On Plausus,' Divine fancies IV, 41]

b.156, p. 23; b.137, p. 183

P0153 Playing at Irish I have seen
He that is the fairest for the game may doubt.

'Of Irish at tables'
[Crum P208]

b.197, p. 161

P0154 Plays are like mirrors, made for men to see
And the soft hand reveal the softer heart.

[Charles Earle?], 'Written on a playbill'

c.376

P0155 Plead Thou my cause, with them that plead
From early dawn to night.

'Psalm 35. Morning prayer 7 day'

c.264/1, p. 149

P0156 Pleas'd with the calm bewitching hour,
Still shalt thou sing—to solace me.

'Shrine of Bertha'

c.83/2, no. 538

P0157 Pleas'd with the empty toys of life,
And court him as a friend.

Charles Atherton Allnutt, 'Homely conceptions of the vain life and miserable death of an ungodly man'

c.112, p. 2

P0158 Pleas'd with the music of my lay,
Fulfill the promise love has made.

'To Miss ———.'

c.382, p. 57

P0159 Pleasure but cheats us with an empty name,
Discern those evils which he cannot shun.

[Thomas Catesby Paget, baron Paget], 'On pleasure'

c.83/1, no. 120

P0160 Pleasures are bitter when abus'd;
At first a dupe, at last a knave.

[Sir Charles] Sedley, 'Upon gaming'

c.93

P0161 Pleasures are often enticing to youth,
And now must take his chance.

'On the folly of an idle life'

Poetry Box IV/29

P0162 Pleasures prove commonly serpents with stings,
But virtue's voice offspring affect better things.

[John Rose?]

b.227, p. 72

P0163 Plenty and pleasure had o'erwhelm'd this while
With such an ink as nothing can deface.

[Francis Quarles], 'The sacred founder of man's sovereign bliss world's peace, world's ransom, and world's righteousness. On the sins of Sodom and Gomorrah . . .'

b.137, p. 128

P0164 Plots true or false are necessary things
He had his jest and they had his estate.

'On the Duke of Monmouth'

c.158, p. 50

P0165 Plung'd in a gulf of dark despair
His love can ne'er be told.

[Isaac Watts, Hymns and spiritual songs (1707), bk. II, Hymn 79]

c.180, p. 8

P0166 Pluralities abhorr'd of old
H—— re cries, for my part, I commend them.

'An epigram'

fb.142, p. 62

P0167 Pluto did frown, but Proserpine did smile,
No fear my Lord for he has lost his stones.

'On the Lord Argyll's death'

fc.24, p. 18

PO168   Pluto prince of shades infernal,
Fall a-laughing great and small.

> 'On one Rabelais a monk, a man of a pleasant humor who died at Paris in 1553'
>
> fb.143, p. 2

PO169   Plutus for mortal men procures
For present praise and honor not for Lifes.

> [John Pattison, translation of Greek poem by Bacchylides into Latin and English]
>
> fc.156

PO170   Poet and pot differ but in a letter,
Which makes the poet love the pot the better.

> 'Pot-poet'
> [Crum P228]
>
> c.356; b.356, p. 306

PO171   Poet 'tis true I must confess
For it ne'er gave a moment's pain.

> 'On seeing the two following lines . . . Condemn me fate to the eternal pain | To see share, ride, and dance and prate in vain'
>
> c.360/1, p. 13

PO172   Poet was in early times a glorious name,
For some deluding blasts of barren fame.

> 'Upon Mr. Gould's design to print his poems more correct' [?Robert Gould, d. 1709]
>
> b.322, p. 6

PO173   Poet we see thro' your design
That you stand fairest to be blest.

> 'Answer to the author of ['O thou who rival wits . . .'] by a lady'
>
> c.360/1, p. 25

PO174   Poets angry rail at Zoil, tho'
Be punish'd for his whole posterity.

> [Sir Thomas Urquhart], 'Of Zoil Homeromastix and at such as foolish rail at the writings of others'
>
> fb.217, p. 514

PO175   Poets are apt to censure those
The spider on his web withdrawn.

> S[tephen] Simpson, 'The spider and fly. A fable'
>
> c.563

PO176   Poets are prodigies so greatly rare
And bless implicit the supported name.

> 'The importance of a poet'
>
> fc.51, p. 8

PO177   Poets behold Miss Tabby there
No more than just their skins.

> 'A cat'
>
> c.172, p. 35

PO178   Poets had formerly not only bread
Honor dead bards, and let the living starve.

> 'On seeing many monuments in Westminster Abbey to famous poets'
> [Crum P240]
>
> c.360/2, no. 214; c.267/1, p. 9

PO179   Poets have license, and that license use
Lest in the search of good I find thee worse.

> 'Epistle VII to C—— Marinus'
>
> fc.100, p. 31

PO180   Poets, like lovers, should be bold and dare,
As by the Painter they designed were.

> J. E., 'Amoris effigies . . . from the original Latin prose of Mr. Robert Waring of Christ Church Oxford . . .'
>
> Poetry Box VII/19

PO181   Poets of old, e'er law restrain'd the stage
Compell'd each stubborn heathen in the Pale.

> [William Popple, trans.], 'Horace book 1st satire 4th imitated. Inscribed to the R[ight] Honorable the Earl of Chesterfield'
>
> fc.104/1, p. 75

PO182   Point of that pyramid, whose solid base
Might soar to times unborn thy purer, nobler name.

> [John] Aikin, 'Sonnet to his excellency George Washington, President of the United States of America'
>
> c.355, p. 192

PO183   Poll, when he wak'd, at ease, survey'd
Is—keep this silent as the grave.

> John Lockman, 'The parrot in the nunnery'
>
> c.267/4, p. 163

PO184   Pollio! My patron, and my pride,
To whom I fortune ow'd, and fame.

> John Lockman, 'To the Earl of Middlesex: on being honored with an important commission by his lordship . . . anno 1752'
>
> c.267/2, p. 230

PO185   Poltroons oft find it an easy task,
The world's one great masquerade.

> John Lockman, 'The mock heroes. The tune, Come buy my greens, and flowers fine'
>
> c.267/2, p. 146; c.268 (first part), p. 83 (var.)

P0186 Pomposo still boasts of his lack of rupees;
Vast lacks of good breeding, discernment and wit!

    [ ] Parsons, 'Epigram'

Diggle Box: Poetry Box xi/69

P0187 Pond'ring with admiration,
That sheds their blood like Steven.

    'Meditations of Saint Steven'

c.187, p. 27

P0188 Pontius said to his wife, my dear, come and see,
I'll go for the parson—but first—can you swim?

    R[obert] Shirley, 1st earl of Ferrers, 'Audoeni [John
    Owen's] epigramma'

c.347, p. 23

P0189 Poor Aminta look and see
Since I can ne'er return to thee.

    [Mrs. ( ) Feilding]

b.226, p. 85

P0190 Poor are the arts which vain coquettes employ
Each charm of person and each grace of mind.

    'Acrostic on Miss Paine'

c.89, p. 105

P0191 Poor bird! By what hard fortune cross'd,
That you have learned from me.

    'To a red-breast written in the frost'

c.83/3, no. 925

P0192 Poor bird I do not envy thee
What I would speak.

    [George Daniel]

b.121, fol. 72

P0193 Poor Canterbury, in a tottering state
If so it be, you'll fall the lighter.

b.229, fol. 116

P0194 Poor citizen if thou wilt be
Where such a citizen doth dwell.

    'The citizens'
    [Crum P253]

fb.107, p. 42

P0195 Poor clod of earth, despise
Truth, only meets humility.

    [George Daniel]

b.121, fol. 59v

P0196 Poor Corydon thy flames remove,
There soon would be nothing but trees.

    'The slighted swain'

fb.107, p. 19

P0197 Poor envious soul! what could'st thou see
Th'heart bankrupt at antiquity.

    [John] Cleveland, 'Upon a fly that flew into a lady's
    eye and there lay buried in a tear'

b.225, p. 129

P0198 Poor fellow! Short has been thy date
In fancy still thy urn.

    [Helen Craik], 'Lines written upon the death of T. H.
    in the East Indies'

c.375, p. 89

P0199 Poor Grogan lies below this clay
The dev'l a bit of bread tomorrow.

    'The epitaph' [on Patrick Grogan, d. 1721, a noted
    miser and recluse. See 'Know all men by these
    presents . . .']

c.360/2, no. 205

P0200 Poor harmless Tom Tudway
Shall make of new anthems a score.

    'Petition in behalf of Tom Tudway, who was degraded
    etc. at Cambridge for a pun'

c.111, p. 103

P0201 Poor heart, lament.
—Glad heart rejoice.

    George Herbert, 'The method'
    [Crum P256]

c.139, p. 133

P0202 Poor Herring Fishery! Now completely curs'd,
Since Nolms the second reigns like Nolms the first.

    John Lockman, 'The finished varlet . . . Feb. 1757'

c.267/1, p. 216

P0203 Poor I, toss'd up and down from shore to shore,
I will glad the father, tho' the schemist fails.

    'Mr. Macklin's farewell-epilogue'

c.115

P0204 Poor in ev'ry perfection of art and of nature,
His friend may be careless, his counsel a baker.

    'Epigram. The lectureship of Richmond being vacant,
    the churchwarden declared, the poorest man should
    succeed to it, meaning by that declaration to serve his
    friend La[ughton] . . .'

c.74

P0205 Poor Irus still was careful, why? Poor.
Because thou hast a wife are vex'd now.

    'To Pontilion'

c.356

P0206 Poor is the best that man can pay,
Keep you my heart—and grant your own.

'In a snuffbox with the picture of the author's heart'
c.83/1, no. 208

P0207 Poor Jenny am'rous, young, and gay,
If we had seen as much.

[Soame Jenyns], 'The way to be wise. Imitated from
La Fontaine'
c.147, p. 54; c.81/1, no. 357

P0208 Poor Job alas! You will not find
But pity Job and me that suffer more.

R[obert] Shirley, 1st earl of Ferrers, 'To Clarinda.
From the French. Job se lasse &c'.
c.347, p. 53

P0209 Poor Laïs sinn'd with her anterior parts:
T'ensue upon trespasses of that kind.

Sir Thomas Urquhart, 'Of Laïs whipped'
fb.217, p. 183

P0210 Poor Lilliput! 'tis thine to fast encore,
Whip on my team and then I'll hear thy cries.

'On the 3d feast held by the Lilliputians since their
war with Iberia or to speak more properly Iberia's war
with them. 1742. November' [Based on debates in
Gentleman's magazine, but these verses not printed
there]
Poetry Box IV/16

P0211 Poor little, pretty, fluttering thing,
Should dread that and hope that thou knowst not
what.

Mat[thew] Prior, '[Verses in French by Bernard le
Bovier de Fontanelle, from the Latin of Hadrian]
translated—or rather imitated'
c.189, p. 127; c.81/1, no. 218 (attr. Pope); see also 'Thou
pretty, wand'ring . . .'.

P0212 Poor Lofty's gone no more at Nimney Bourne nor
Culverside you'll find him,
May I as placid view my friends as calmly seek the
tomb.

J. B. Dickinson, 'Epitaph on [his horse] Lofty'
c.391, p. 112

P0213 Poor man; I am as dull, as dull, can be,
Myself, in my own heart, and all in thee.

[George Daniel]
b.121, fol. 85

P0214 Poor melancholy bird, that all night long,
So sigh to sing at liberty—like thee!

Charlotte (Turner) Smith, 'To a nightingale'
c.343, p. 96; c.130, p. 92

P0215 Poor men, have little: beggars, nothing; many
Rich men, too much. Who hath enough? Not any.

Sir Thomas Urquhart, 'Of little, nothing, too much,
and enough'
fb.217, p. 60

P0216 Poor merry men of Enfield Chase
You'll look like fools and come again. | With a
fa la la

[Sir Charles] Hanbury Williams, 'An answer to Col.
Grimes's song that he wrote to the dowager Duchess
of Marlborough'
Accession 97.7.40

P0217 Poor Methodists: the envy of the times
Such Methodists as these O may they still increase.

[Thomas Gurney], 'On the Methodists by a
Methodist'
c.213

P0218 Poor Nurse is sent to bid you all goodbye
If you applaud me, Nurse is old no more.

S[amuel] Wesley, the younger, 'Epilogue ad Adolphos
canthara loqr—1724 and thus Englished'
c.233, p. 70

P0219 Poor Ophelia couldst thou be
I have I think in it the greatest part.

[Mrs. ( ) Feilding]
b.226, p. 17

P0220 Poor Ora, tink on Yanko dear
Good deal and dat relieve me.

'By a Negro girl' [in Jamaica]
[Crum P272]
c.344, p. 3

P0221 Poor Phyllis wrapt in clouds of grief
And offer at thy shrine.

'The sick shepherdess'
fb.107, p. 65

P0222 Poor spiteful Cupid, keep your wish,
Shalt die, a good, old, virtuous wife.

[Thomas Morell], 'The recantation'
c.395, p. 10

P0223 Poor Strafford worthy of no name at all
The nation's shame and so the nation's hate.

'Wentworth's fatal fall' [parody of 'Great
Strafford . . .' by Sir John Denham]
[Crum P288]
fb.106(9)

P0224 Poor stream held captive by the frost,
You're bound by cold, and I by love.

    Lady [ ] Hertford, 'On the stream at Marlborough
    Mount in Wilts the seat of the right honorable
    Algernoon Percy Seymour earl of Hertford . . . being
    frozen up in 1727'

    c.229/1, fol. 41v

P0225 Poor the wine thou'lt drink with me,
Nor Falernian grapes to squeeze.

    [William Popple, trans.], '[Horace] book 1st. ode
    20th. To Maecenas'

    fc.104/2, p. 60

P0226 Poor worldly care a noble heart defies
One heav'nly one it is her edifies.

    [Sir Philip Wodehouse], 'Upon Lady Fr[ances]
    Hobart'

    b.131, back (no. 75/1, 90/1)

P0227 Pope Innocent chief of the Roman rout
Answers his name but how if in was out.

    'On Pope Innocent'

    b.356, p. 308

P0228 Pope Quin who damns all churches but his own
It is not heresy but reformation.

    [David] Garrick [on the actor James Quin?]

    Poetry Box IV/196

P0229 Populous cities please us then
To win her grace while all commend.

    [John Milton], 'Chorus [1, with musical score for
    tenor, from Handel's L'Allegro]'

    Music MS. 534

P0230 Ports are the places where ships may reside
The name of the place is Portsmouth.

    'Ditto' [solution to a rebus, 'To places where
    ships . . .']

    c.360/3, no. 219

P0231 Possess'd I, Petrarch, thy mellifluous vein,
My brow, let faith's conspicuous helmet grace.

    'An elegy on the death of Lady Viscountess Deerhurst'

    fc.53, p. 187

P0232 Possessor of your charms
I hold it in my arms.

    'To Chloe'

    c.360/3, no. 228

P0233 *Possum ludere*—I could play
Curaque dulcis—and sweet care.

    'Latino-English song'

    c.81/1, no. 349

P0234 Pound's subtle weight to add it is no more
'Twill perform thy desire to perfection bring.

    [Mary Serjant], 'Addition of weight'

    fb.98, fol. 13

P0235 Powerful beauty, lovely creature
Each lovely dart she doth shoot | From her eyes.

    'Beauty's advocate or the charms of beauty. The
    Bellasyse minuet'

    c.374

P0236 Pow'r shows we may an endless wish subjoin,
For greatest kings do most at want repine.

    Sir Thomas Urquhart, 'In this first line of this distich
    all the moods of a verb are subjoin'd'

    fb.217, p. 300

P0237 Pow'r, wealth and fame, the world pursue,
Nor could possession dull thy charms.

    'Another [acrostic], on [Miss Paine]'

    c.89, p. 105

P0238 Pox o' the fooling and plotting of late
This is the profession that never will alter.

    [John Oldham], 'A ballad' [1680]
    [Crum A364, 'A pox']

    b.371, no. 34

P0239 Pox on the rhyming fops that plague the town
And calls the best of kings a senseless log.

    'The visit'

    b.327, f. 23; b.371, no. 14

P0240 Pox take ye all from you my sorrows swell
May they more debtors have but all like me.

    [Thomas] Randolph, 'Randolph's dun on his petition
    to his creditors'
    [Crum P306]

    b.62, p. 47; b.200, p. 37

P0241 Practice will make thy tow'ring muse *experto*,
Thy next task be the praises of Roberto.

    'To Hurlothrumbo'

    c.570/3, p. 32

P0242 Praise for our God in Sion waits
And bring forth precious heavenly fruit.

    [Mary Pluret], 'In confessing the name of Jesus I saw
    there was a glory ascribed to him which was due and I
    was for having others experience what I did in a
    church of Christ'

    c.354

P0243 Praise makes the bad men, worse: the foolish greater
Fools the crafty, subtler: the good men, better.

    Sir Thomas Urquhart, 'The fruits of encomiums'
fb.217, p. 316

P0244 Praise some desire when they dispraise deserve
Signifies nothing if not crowned within.

    [Mary Serjant]
fb.98, fol. 152

P0245 Praise the Lord in sanctity,
Ev'ry creature, God, above.

    'The same [Psalm 150], another meter'
c.264/3, facing p. 116

P0246 Praise the Lord my soul,
And world without end.

    'Psalm 146. O Hallelujah. Or [:]'
c.264/3, p. 106

P0247 Praise thou the Lord my soul whilst breath
Incessant praises sing.

    'The same [Psalm 146], another meter'
c.264/3, p. 107

P0248 Praise thou the Lord O thou my soul
Eternal praises give.

    c.124, no. 9

P0249 Praise to God, immortal praise
Crown'd with gen'ral happiness.

    [Anna Laetitia (Aikin)] Barbauld, 'Britain's
    thanksgiving an ode . . . 22 October 1798'
c.83/3, no. 987; c.141, p. 159

P0250 Praise to that love whence we receive
Thy wondrous love and sov'reign grace.

    [Thomas Stevens?], 'Afternoon [Lord's] day'
c.259, p. 106

P0251 Praise us and ours is written in my name:
If this my piety may seem too large.

    [Sir Philip Wodehouse], 'Upon my Lord Bishop's
    daughter Susan Sparrow . . .'
b.131, back (no. 121)

P0252 Praise ye the Lord, confess ye to
And bitterly he spake.

    'Psal: 106'
b.217, p. 89 (incomplete)

P0253 Praise ye the Lord, for it is good
Praise ye the Lord above.

    [Thomas Norton], 'For sure trust in God. Psalm 64'
    [verses from Psalm 147]
a.3, fol. 148v

P0254 Praise ye the Lord ye Gentiles all,
Now and at every season.

    [T. B.], 'An exhortation unto the praise of God to be
    sung before morning prayer'
a.3, fol. 151

P0255 Praise ye the Lord: devoutly wait
And all that breathe, swell up the sound.

    'Psalm 150'
c.264/3, p. 115

P0256 Praise ye the Lord: sing to His name,
They shall His praises sing.

    'Psalm 149'
c.264/3, p. 113

P0257 Praised be the God of love
Who hath made of two folds one.

    George Herbert, 'Antiphon'
    [Crum P333]
c.139, p. 128

P0258 Prais'd by the grandsires of the present age
And liv'd thus long, but to behold it die.

    'On the death of Thomas Southerne esqr. a celebrated
    poet. Author of Oroonoko a tragedy . . . on Monday
    May the 26 1746 aged near 90 years'
c.360/2, no. 154

P0259 Pray ask you why I a rich wife refuse?
The match would be unequal else than so.

    R[obert] Shirley, 1st earl of Ferrers, 'To one advising
    him to wed a rich woman'
c.347, p. 34

P0260 Pray believe me, my dear Hetty,
To a better planet lead.

    [Charles Burney, the elder], 'To my daughter Esther
    on the birth of her fifth child, Septr. 26th. 1777'
c.33, p. 127 (first part crossed out)

P0261 Pray by what right pretends your king to be
Who have but one short step of life to make.

    'A conference, between Montezuma emperor of
    Mexico, an Indian priest; and Cortez the Spanish
    General, and a Jesuit, concerning some chief points,
    in popery'
b.77, p. 15

P0262 Pray for the soul of Maud Davy,
Say a Pater Noster and an Ave.

'On Richd Davy master of the Jewel House and Maud his wife'

fb.143, p. 22; see also 'Here lies William Banknot . . .', 'Such as ye are . . .'.

P0263 Pray gentlemens come now and see my fine show
It's to drink a good health to the noble King Jemmy.

'A new ballad to the tune of Dear Catholic brother'
[Jacobite; pr. 1715? (Foxon N89)]
[Crum P335]

fc.58, p. 37; c.570/1, p. 111

P0264 Pray ladies who in seeming wit delight
Say what's invisible, yet ne'er out of sight?

Diggle Box: Poetry Box XI/71

P0265 Pray listen all unto our tale
To be, a halter take them, &c.

'A godly new ballad' [on the election of the Long Parliament, Nov. 1640]
[Crum P338]

fb.106(12)

P0266 Pray listen awhile and a Lord I'll describe,
What set of my beauty alas! Are lost all. | Which nobody can deny

'A satire or, a new ballad on Ld. Ranelagh to the tune, Which nobody can deny'

fb.207/2, p. 96

P0267 Pray neighbors give ear, and soon you shall hear
Why what the pox would you be at.

'A whimsical ballad'

c.360/3, no. 204

P0268 Pray pardon Mr. John Bayes for I beg your excuse,
Draw out fair conquering men and guard the crown.

'The assembly of moderate divines' [Barlow, Stillingfleet, Burnet]

b.111, p. 123

P0269 Pray Sir what news,
Have got the devil and all.

'The novelist'

c.570/3, p. 99

P0270 Pray take an house and so continue on
To noble minds each country is their own.

[Sir Aston Cokayne], 'To Mr Gilbert Knyveton, and Mr Tho: Knyveton, my wife's brothers'

b.275, p. 79

P0271 Pray tell for what reason we're call'd on so late
In small talk, little wit, bow, shrug, simper and grin.

H[enry] Skrine, 'Impromptu on [modern courtship]'

c.509, p. 31

P0272 Pray tell me what that is which dances and skips,
But if money can buy it it's not worth a groat.

'Enigma: 1' [heart]

c.389; see also 'The riddle of riddles . . .'.

P0273 Pray that thy name and heart agree
Whose aims on honesty to mak't their prey.

[Sir Philip Wodehouse], 'Upon Sr James Johnston aims on honesty'

b.131, back (no. 187)

P0274 Prayer ardent opens heaven; lets down a stream
The praise, glory and righteousness to Him.

[Thomas Stevens?], 'On the spirit of prayer in believers a poem, in blank verse . . . April 22. 1780'

c.259, p. 80

P0275 Prayeth for the soul in way of charity
A thousand four hundred fifty and nine.

'On Richd Bonevant in the stone church in Rochester's diocese'

fb.143, p. 22

P0276 Preacher or poet choose you whether
'The doctor liv'd and died a Tory.'

[ ] Harper, of Shorage(?), 'Lent from an unknown hand to Dr. Savage. July, 1760 supposed to be wrote by . . .'

Poetry Box IV/135

P0277 Precluded from singing the acts so divine
With Brutus' virtue, and Burleigh's cares.

[James Mulcaster, sr.?], 'The year [17]fifty-seven. A song'

c.118, p. 46

P0278 Prefac'd with holy zeal the page begins
His own, in flatt'ring men's esteem.

T[homas] S[tevens], 'Modern religious disputation . . . Septembr. 5th 1780 . . .'

c.259, p. 108

P0279 Preferment, like a game at bowls,
Whose own true bias cuts the way.

W[illiam] Strode, 'A parallel betwixt bowling and preferment'
[Crum P353]

b.200, p. 214; b.205, fol. 68r

P0280 Preferment so long sought at last is found
The more he shows his a-s.

'On Ld Chief J[usti]ce P[ar]ker'

Poetry Box x/101

P0281 *Prenez le roi!* Cries Grand Marshall Noailles
He lost only—his army, the field, and the day.

'On the battle of Dettingen, fought Thursday June 26.
1743 the French parole—*prenez le Roi*'

c.360/2, no. 89

P0282 Entry cancelled. Prepar'd to rail resolv'd to
part . . . . *See* P0287.

P0283 Prepare, great sons of Mars, prepare,
Yet does defend our cause.

'Verses'

b.197, p. 247

P0284 Prepare me Lord for an immortal state
The holy ever-blessed Trinity.

[( ) Pierson]

c.328, p. 12

P0285 Prepare my soul to meet the day,
And spend eternity in praise.

[Thomas Stevens?], 'Lines written by a young lady at
the hot well at Bristol a week before her death June
1771'

c.259, p. 12

P0286 Prepare, prepare, prepare,
He'll serve to guard your Hanoverian crew.

'Song to the tune of Britons strike home'

fc.58, p. 46; c.189, p. 157 (var.); c.570/1, p. 133

P0287 Prepar'd to rail resolv'd to part
Nor dares her slave repine [complain].

[George Granville, 1st baron Lansdowne], 'Song'

c.549, p. 72; Poetry Box IV/53 (attr. Etherege)

P0288 Preserve O Lord this our inconstant nation,
Bring David back, and place him on his throne.

'Two short prayers [second prayer]'

b.111, p. 378

P0289 Pretender in the Isle of Egg?
To crush it in the shell.

[N.] H[erbert], 'Epigram upon the Pretender's
landing in the Isle of Egg in 1745'

Spence Papers, folder 91

P0290 Pretty, little, rural scene,
Of all the splendors of a court.

John Head, 'Tibbs' farm'

c.341, p. 3

P0291 Pretty miss whose beauteous face
Make her fair and good as she.

'To Miss D—n—ll on her birthday Feb. 12th 1737/8'

Poetry Box I/61

P0292 Pretty pigeon, white and fair
And the saucy jay outprating.

'Anacreon ode the 9th'

c.368, p. 23

P0293 Pretty Polly, may joys,
The joys of true love.

[Charles Burney, the younger], 'To Miss Polly Francis'

c.37, p. 17

P0294 Pretty rebel why that rose
England's glory, Scotland's pride.

W[illia]m Smith, 'Copy of lines written by . . . whilst
at Eton School . . . 1745' [on Jenny Cameron]

Smith Papers, folder 73

P0295 Pretty, sweet one! though it grieve me,
Do you cry still—thy will be done.

Francis Standish, 'A respective admonit[ion to] the
mistress of the late . . . Henry Lord Hasting[s] . . .'

Poetry Box VI/69

P0296 Pretus that late had office borne in London
Replied incontinent '*adieu* knave *semper*'.

[Henry Parrot, 'Levi responsio levis']
[Crum P385]

b.148, p. 4

P0297 Prevailing vice still fattens sordid souls,
Who seeks a crown must gen'rous toils endure.

'A poem on youth'

c.481, p. 145 (incomplete)

P0298 Prick also being a place of small account:
Take you one end, and I shall snatch the other.

Sir Thomas Urquhart, 'A debording [*sic*] youth here
by a double tmesis discovereth his desire to his
mistress'

fb.217, p. 358

P0299 Pride keeps me oft, but nature smooths my way;
For what her tongue would hide, her eyes betray.

c.549, p. 121

P0300 Pride, lust, ambition, and the people's hate
His sacrilege, ambition, lust and pride.

'On the Earl of Clarendon's downfall' [1667]
[Crum P395, 'lust, avarice'; *POAS* I.158]

b.52/1, p. 158; fb.140, p. 87; Poetry Box IV/135; Poetry
Box VIII/16 (2 copies)

P0301 Pride of my heart—my true my filial friend
The mind's true wealth the treasure of my choice.

    [William Hayley], 'Sonnet . . . July 29 [1800]'
File 6968

P0302 Pride still presumes how foul soe'er it be,
This pride shall God himself to heaven exalt.

    H[enry] C[olman], 'On pride'
    [Crum P397]
    b.2, p. 57

P0303 Priest in the popish sense a jest,
Of mercy and of judgment sing!

    'P litera infausta. Priest, prelate, primate, patriarch, pope'
    b.214

P0304 Priests make Christ's soul, and body you must not
                          doubt
And though he's mortal, we'll not think him so.

    [John Seares], 'On Sir Thomas Hobbey [Thomas Hobbes?] against transubstantiation'
    b.356, p. 66; Poetry Box VI/107; b.197, p. 58; b.62, p. 133

P0305 Priest's sons are not so forward now, to drive
Their being from their parents' fornication.

    Sir Thomas Urquhart, 'That few sons of Roman priests, nowadays would have behaved themselves, as the son of Eleazar did, in the trespass of Zimri; and Cosbi'
    fb.217, p. 74

P0306 Prince of dissentients from erroneous ways,
And starves, and writhes, and breathes upon the
                           ground.

    Charles Atherton Allnutt, 'Epistle to Mr. Rob[er]t Lovegrove'
    c.112, p. 116

P0307 Princes and kings cries Beckford I defy,
But which good Signor can't be got.

    c.362, back cover

P0308 Princess! For goodness long renown'd,
And find his fortune in your smile.

    John Lockman, 'Verses: most humbly inscribed to the Princess of Wales: requesting her . . . graciously to patronize a subscription, for printing Poems on several occasions, in 2 volumes, 4°, by John Lockman . . . June 1757'
    c.267/1, p. iii

P0309 Printer, make haste and set the frame
Themselves an immortality.

    [Phanuel Bacon], 'Verses printed off while the author was showing some ladies the Printing House at Oxford'
    [Crum P413]
    c.237, fol. 4

P0310 Prior, sweet bard! in Anna's genial days,
Then(?) shall fam'd Prior's heroine yield to mine.

    John Lockman, 'To Mrs. Caesar, of Hertfordshire, after seeing her at Buckingham House . . . May 1741'
    c.267/2, p. 338

P0311 Prior's inimitable ease
You mockt a Jove, and I a Prior.

    [Robert Cholmeley], 'An excuse for the former imitation of Prior'
    c.190, p. 227

P0312 Priscilla always calls her husband dear
That she may live to see her dear a buck.

    'An epigram'
    [Crum P414]
    b.62, p. 72

P0313 Priscus was weeping when his wife did die,
Had I but his dead wife for mine alive.

    'Of an ill wife'
    c.356

P0314 Pris'ners of hope arise
The bounty of a God.

    T[homas] S[tevens], 'Zechariah 9.12. Turn ye to the stronghold of the prisoners of hope &c.'
    [Crum P415]
    c.259, p. 100

P0315 Prithee boy at once forbear,
Drinking in this place with thee.

    [William Popple, trans.], 'To his boy' [Horace]
    fc.104/2, p. 108

P0316 Prithee dear friend no longer stay
Shall my most faithful friendship sever.

    E[lizabeth (Shirley) Compton, countess of] N[orthampton], 'A letter intended to be sent to Lady Anne Compton when she was in France from . . . 1728'
    Accession 97.7.40

P0317 Prithee, little buzzing fly,
Flies are weak, and man's a fly.

    [N. A. Northcote], 'The fly'
    c.83/4, no. 2002; Poetry Box VI/10

P0318 Prithee now fond fool give o'er,
Making fools than keeping lovers.

> John Wilmot, 2nd earl of Rochester, '1. Song[:]
> Strephon. Daphnis'

b.334, p. 178

P0319 Prithee Phyllis say
For you 'tis now too late.

> 'Chloe, to Phyllis, desiring her to tell her her fortune
> by the cards, the tune, Pretty parrot say'

Accession 97.7.40

P0320 Prithee Sammy reflect, can there be such a thing
So round about R—n, the play is the same.

> 'To Dr. C—l, on his sermon Jan. 30th'

c.570/3, p. 91

P0321 Prithee Somnus prithee stay
So wretched now, so blest before!

> 'Just wakened from dreaming of her'

c.416

P0322 Prithee tease me no longer dear troublesome friend,
And lord of all nature beside.

> G[eorge] Whitehead, 'To a friend'

c.139, p. 459

P0323 Prithee, tell me, gentle swain,
You never can recover.

> [Sir Charles Sedley]

c.358, p. 177; see also 'Tell me prithee . . .'.

P0324 Prithee Tom Fool, why will thou meddling be
Thou dost at home, neglect thy own affairs.

> 'July 17. anno Domini [17]83'

c.93

P0325 Priz'd by kind Frederick, to his country dear;
Such is our wish; to heav'n we leave the rest.

> John Lockman, 'A toast for the birthday (Feb. 6. 1747.
> O. S.) [of the Earl of Middlesex]'

c.267/1, p. 217

P0326 Problem of sexes must thou likewise be
So shall it be thy son and yet my daughter.

> [John Cleveland?], 'The author to his Hermaphrodite
> made after Mr. Randolph's death yet inserted in his
> poems'
> [Crum P432]

b.93, p. 49

P0327 Problems of old likeness and figures
With supportation of his benignity.

> 'Here beginneth The churl and the bird. This title
> over a woodcut of a schoolmaster on his throne with a
> rod in his left hand and three youths sitting on a
> bench before his . . . Imprinted at Westminster in
> [William] Caxton's house by Wynken de Worde'

c.369, p. 1

P0328 Professions of friendship in these modern days,
So we breakfast, and dine, we sup, and we sleep.

> 'From a lady in the country to her friend in town'

c.83/3, no. 949

P0329 Profuse of woe, and harass'd out with care,
Charm'd with the task of raptur'd love and praise.

> Richard Lely, 'Self-resignation'

c.244, p. 516

P0330 Promiscuous shafts of random fate
To 'ave lived like that, or like thee, died.

> [Robert Cholmeley], 'Inscribed upon a column raised
> over the grave of a gentleman struck dead by a flash of
> lightning 1727'

c.190, p. 235

P0331 Promise is debt: And debt implies a payment
How can the righteous then want food, and raiment.

> [Francis Quarles], 'On the righteous man'
> [Crum P442]

b.137, p. 186; b.118, p. 222

P0332 Promis'd blessing of the year
Darling native of our isle.

> [Ambrose Philips], 'A lyric ejaculation written in
> January 1722[3], for the speedy and safe deliverance of
> her Royal Highness, Caroline Princess of Wales, then
> big with child [Princess Mary, married in 1740 to
> Prince Frederick, later Frederick II, king of Prussia]'

c.360/2, no. 73

P0333 Promote a fool, his folly soon is heard,
Then keep him down, let wise men be preferr'd.

c.339, p. 324

P0334 Prompted by friendship's undiminish'd fire,
Sitting with genius calmly in the shade.

> [Richard] Cumberland, 'Address'

c.83/2, no. 408

P0335 Promus since that thy maintenance is all
Sleep to serve God, but watch to serve ourselves.

> [Crum P444]

b.197, p. 32

P0336 Prophets at home, are in no reputation:
Nor have kings power in a foreign nation.

> Sir Thomas Urquhart, 'Of kings and prophets'
> fb.217, p. 84

P0337 Propitious boy! How didst thou dare to wound
That brow, which thou so justly might'st have
crown'd?

> W[illiam] B[enson] E[arle, on Garrick being struck
> on the temple with the bough of a bay tree]
> Acquisition 92.3.1ff.

P0338 Propitious chance led Perseus once to view
Desire, hope, jealousy and endless train.

> [Charles Hopkins], 'The story of Perseus and
> Andromeda in imitation of part of that in the tenth
> book of Ovid's Metamorphoses'
> b.130, p. 9

P0339 Propitious heav'n regard my humble prayer
Make me an happy bridegroom her an happy bride.

> S[tephen] Simpson, 'The following was written on the
> 26th. June 1776 the day preceding my marriage with
> my dear [Sarah] Leaper'
> c.563

P0340 Propitious pow'r! no wretched mortals kind,
O'er the green meadow and enchanted grove.

> [Henry] Needler, 'To sleep'
> c.244, p. 544

P0341 Prorogued on prorogation, damn'd rogues and
whores,
Next wish if not, tha[t] we may all be free.

> 'Upon the prorogation of the Parliament twice' [1671]
> [Crum P448; POAS I.179]
> fb.140, p. 93; b.52/2, p. 117; Poetry Box VII/5 ('on
> proroguer'; ll. 1–138)

P0342 Protect (great Lady) servant from control
A theme more great (long hence) to poet's pen to
give.

> 'To the right h[onora]ble the Lady Catherine
> Viscountess Cholm[ond]eley'
> b.203, p. 10

P0343 Protectress of our rural shades
Of what you labor to conceal!

> [Robert Cholmeley], 'Verses inscribed upon an
> hunting horn'
> c.190, p. 233

P0344 Proud of her ancient race, Britannia shows
And genius wakes thy Randal's harp divine.

> [Anna Seward], 'Verses on Wrexham and the
> inhabitants of its environs'
> c.141, p. 254

P0345 Proud Protantinus boasting of his yard
As e'er was Paul's before the top was fired.

> 'On Protantinus'
> b.200, p. 407

P0346 Proud women I scorn, the brisk wine's my delight,
I'm a king when I grasp thee, much more, when I
kiss.

> 'Song'
> c.189, p. 158

P0347 Provide in harvest with the ant,
Old age thy joints will numb.

> 'Chained hand'
> [Crum P464]
> b.234, p. 19

P0348 Prudence a virtue banished from this age
Deserve enjoy supremest happiness.

> H[annah] More, 'An acrostic on the amiable Miss
> [Pritchard]'
> c.341, p. 99

P0349 Prudence nor valor never yet was seen
Is hardly parallel'd, but in Utopia.

> Sir Thomas Urquhart, 'To the Earl of [crossed out]'
> fb.217, p. 143

P0350 Prudence, Sir William, is a jewel—
She left them with her pattens—at the door.

> [John Walcot(?) ('Peter Pindar')], 'Prudence . . . Ode
> 4th 1785'
> c.355, p. 94

P0351 Prussia will be obdurate still
For sending such a Leg as he.

> [Phanuel Bacon], 'An answer to ['Pelham
> 'twill do . . .']'
> c.237, fol. 64v

P0352 Puffing comes down grave ancient Sir John Crooke
Yet not a close prisoner but at large in the tower.

> [John Hoskins], 'A fart censured in the lower House
> of Parliament'
> [Crum P470]
> b.197, p. 99; see also 'Down came . . .'.

PO353 Puissant Prince the object of our fears,
God prosper long and bless our rightful King.

    'The congratulation'

    b.111, p. 387

PO354 Pupil, wouldst thou wish t'impart
Follow Bond—and seek no more.

    [Thomas Hull], 'Parody. On Mr. Shenstone's
    inscription at the Leasowes: Shepherd, wouldst thou
    here obtain, &c. written on receiving a picture of that
    excellent man, painted by W. Daniel Bond of
    Birmingham'

    c.528/23a

PO355 Puppies whom I now am leaving
Bubbles all adieu adieu.

    Philip Wharton, 1st duke of Wharton(?), 'A burlesque
    of the lines on the other side made by Dr. Arbuthnot'
    [Harl. 7316]

    c.468

PO356 Pure are her virtues as the unsullied snows
And pity weep when mem'ry breathes her name.

    'On Rosalia . . . M. Cot.'

    c.83/2, no. 557

PO357 Pure goodness not uncertain chance virtue
Obscure death take the hateful but live forever.

    'In ducem Buckinghamia . . . Englished'

    b.197, p. 40

PO358 Pursue her [?]ly and be bountiful(?)
And dwells in the burgh of Eden.

    [Sir Thomas Urquhart], 'That an indigent maid
    wisheth(?) still her residence in Edinburgh may lastly
    be [?] to apprehend'

    fb.217, p. 394

PO359 Push the bottle about, drink my toast, and away,
While I bumper the last of my bottle.

    'Song 101'

    c.555, p. 153

PO360 Pusillus can be jocund, never whines,
To pipe no more, if thou give one to dance.

    'On Pusillus'

    b.118, p. 223

PO361 Put me not to rebuke O Lord,
My safety and my stay.

    [John Hopkins], 'The 17 psalm for the turning away of
    God's wrath for sin' [verses from Psalm 38]
    [Crum P481]

    a.3, fol. 90

PO362 Put not thy trust in any worldly things
For [?] are ofttimes the mighty kings.

    c.339, p. 313

PO363 Puzzled I Apollo pray
None but she thy pains appease.

    'Acrostic' [on Pretty Sally Mason]

    c.360/2, no. 171

PO364 Pythagoras did gladly sacrifice
And more than was to him a [?].

    [Sir Thomas Urquhart], 'To a certain shallow
    mathematician who most studiously employed his
    fruits in the contemplation and searching out of such
    [?] propositions as that of the 47 of the first book of
    the elements of Euclid the finding out whereof made
    Pythagoras . . . cry out aloud eureka . . .'

    fb.217, p. 519

PO365 Pythagoras, whose genius books refin'd,
A new one springs from the creative fire.

    John Lockman, 'To his much esteemed friend
    Mr. Robert Strange after viewing his drawings, in
    colors and chalks, from Raphael, Guido &c. . . . 7 July
    1765'

    c.267/1, p. 392

Q

Q0001   Quakers' harangue all harangues doth surpass
I should say—your obedient—oblig'd—humble
servant.

     Cha[rles] Earle, 'To Barum's mayor (with great
respect) | This superscription I direct . . .'

     c.376

Q0002   Queen, and huntress, chaste, and fair,
Goddess excellently bright.

     B[en] Jonson, 'Hymn to the moon'

     c.83/3, no. 825

Q0003   Queen Dido, and Lucretia were renown'd,
Had they not left their maidenheads behind them.

     Sir Thomas Urquhart, 'To a very comely lady, who lay
heavily diseased of the pale colors'

     fb.217, p. 253

Q0004   Queen in your chamber I should lie by night
If a poor man lies everywhere were right.

     [Sir Aston Cokayne], 'A translation'

     b.275, p. 87

Q0005   Queen of beauty, queen of love,
Queen of beauty queen of love.

     c.549, p. 6

Q0006   Queen of Cyprus, Venus come
Wit and youth to love allied.

     [William Popple, trans.], '[Horace] book 1st. ode 30th.
To Venus'

     fc.104/2, p. 84

Q0007   Queen of soft fraud and kind deceit
Yet thy soft comforts make me blest.

     'Lady Hertford'

     Poetry Box VII/85

Q0008   Queen of the garden, see the rose appear,
Hers is the dying, thine the living rose.

     J. H., 'To Chloe attempting a rose in needlework'

     c.368, p. 209

Q0009   Queen of the rapt'rous hour!
Thou e'er shall rule great sovereign of the whole!

     'To Venus'

     c.344, p. 17

Q0010   Queen of the silver bow!—by thy pale beam,
Poor wearied pilgrim—in this toiling scene!

     [Charlotte (Turner) Smith], 'By the same to the moon'

     c.130, p. 93; File 245/24

Q0011   Queens fought of old: but since th'invention of
Which 'bide the push of pick, but not the pistol.

     Sir Thomas Urquhart, 'How it is that women are not
so warlike now, as they were in ancient times'

     fb.217, p. 274

Q0012   Quench wanton Venus fond delights
If thou return at last.

     [Crum Q8]

     b.234, p. 21

Q0013   Quick from my mem'ry let me blot
A genuine heartsease I have paid.

     'Upon a flower called the heartsease painted by a
young lady'

     fc.40

Q0014   Quick from the sight thine eyes remove
Each bud contains a snare.

     'Upon seeing a most beautiful drawing of flowers by a
lady'

     fc.40

Q0015   Quickly run, boy, bring the wine,
Till the winter's rage is o'er?

     'Anacreontic'

     c.391

Q0016   Quickness of thought hath made and unmade kings,
And in the race give conquest to the slow.

     'A few lines providentially fallen from the mouth of a
youth that caused a revolution in the kingdom of
Abyssinia'

     c.139, p. 320

Q0017   Quietness love hate all hate and strife
The best companions in this mundane sphere.

     [Mary Serjant?]

     fb.98, fol. 152; c.549, p. 29 (first two lines)

Q0018 Quintilius with pace of snail proceeded to his pen,
And very rare is that attempt, that is not harm'd
with haste.

b.234, p. 323

Q0019 Quit for awhile the soldier's trade,
Bring Rigby, all in one.

[David Garrick], 'Bayes at Hampton to Coll.
[Bernard] Hale at London; the hint from the 30th ode
of the first book of Horace'

Acquisition 92.3.1ff. (autogr.)

Q0020 Quo' John! What makes Dame Urban scowl?
'Cause she's fall'n out with common sense.

John Lockman, 'Supposed to be writ by a person who
seemed surprised at the author's being threatened with
an attack, from Sylvanus Urban [in Gentleman's
magazine], who pretended a great friendship with him'

c.267/1, p. 172

Q0021 Quoth Bede when the Provost of Crell
Then farewell farewell Albion's glory.

'The nobster's (?) prophecy'

Poetry Box VIII/32

Q0022 Quoth Dick to Tom, the other day,
His grace the Duke is dead.

'An epigram'

fc.85, fol. 37

Q0023 Quoth George to John, 'tis said, your private life
But don't you live with one that's not your wife.

'Epigram'

c.81/1, no. 323

Q0024 Quoth Harry to his friend one day
Gadzooks I could not read 'em.

'Dialogue between Harry who had a large library and
Dick who had more understanding than books'

c.546

Q0025 Quoth John to his teacher good Sir if you please
But a sourheaded saint will be ever vexation.

[William Taylor], 'Quoth John to his teacher'

c.176, p. 159

Q0026 Quoth King Robin my ribbons I find are too few
For as fast as they rob, they will fill it again.

[Jonathan Swift], 'On the Knights of the Bath' [1725]
[Crum Q20]

c.570/2, p. 117

Q0027 Quoth Mead, that his Lordship is better, is true,
If Garnier writes *gratis*, and cares when he pleases.

[David Garrick], 'The sequel' [to 'The physician']

File 5612

Q0028 Quoth old Charon, in wrath, what monsters I carry,
What strength can bear up against Churchill and
H[arle]y.

'Charon's complaint' [deaths of Burnet and Wharton,
1715]
[Crum Q22]

fc.58, p. 101; c.188, p. 61; c.570/1, p. 7 ('old Charon')

Q0029 Quoth Sir Harry Poole it was a bold trick
Was better than the blast of the powder Catholic.

[John Hoskins], 'On a fart let in Parliament'

b.356, p. 295

Q0030 Quoth the Duchess of Cleveland to fair Mrs.
Knight,
To some cellar in London your Grace must . . . .

[John Wilmot, 2nd earl of Rochester], 'A dialogue
between Mall Knight and the Duc[hess] of Cleveland'

fb.140, p. 108 (incomplete)

Q0031 Quoth the Duke to his Countess, how like you my
farce
Half so well, as I like the hole next your arsehole.

[on the Duke of Buckingham's 'The rehearsal' and his
mistress, the Countess of Shrewsbury]

fb.140, p. 171

Q0032 Quoth the fox—when I got my neck out of the
noose
Whilst will binds the state 'tis an ill card for you.

'An epigram on the new ministry. An: Do: 1783'

fc.53, p. 137

Q0033 Quoth the King to the Parliament,
If once again we're beat at Sole Bay.

'The King's speech to both Houses, October 19th.
1689' [referring to the English encounter with the
Dutch at Sole (Southwold) Bay, 1672]

b.111, p. 319

Q0034 Quoth the King to the Queen
That one is scarce better than none.

'On a medal of the King and Queen'

fc.135

Q0035 Quoth the screw to the cork, what misfortunes
accrue
Thus we all are reliev'd by a hair of the same dog.

'The cork and the screw. An epigram'

c.152, p. 7

Q0036 Quoth the shrieve to the judge, since on you my
                                                    dependence
For there your good Lordship can have no
                                                    commission.

>   [ ] Whaley, 'On James Mackerel esqr . . . desiring Sir
>   Laurence Carter . . . to excuse his attendance, who
>   answered in a pet, that he did not care if he did not see
>   him till the last grand assize'

c.360/1, p. 227

Q0037 Quoth the sons of fire of fury
And bid you all farewell Sir.

>   'A needless journey to London or I would if I could. A
>   ballad. To the tune of A noble race of Shinkin'

Poetry Box VII/51

Q0038 Quoth Thomas to William that numbskull behold,
A mind is a balance for a thousand a year.

>   'Equality'

c.83/4, no. 1098

Q0039 Quoth Wild unto Walpole, make me undertaker,
For what I have emptied, they'll soon fill again.

>   Philip Wharton, 1st duke of Wharton(?), 'Another'
>   [on robbing the Exchequer; 'Wild' is Jonathan Wild]

c.468; see also 'This Wi[ld] . . .'.

R

R0001 R. H., they say is gone to sea
The plot is still a-driving.

'A psalm . . . to be sung . . . upon Friday, the 11th of
April 1679 . . . in relation to the horrid and damnable
popish plot, lately discovered . . . to the tune of the
fourth Psalm'
[*POAS* II.120]

b.54, p. 1095

R0002 Rage on, ye proud Philistines of the land,
That dog that bites an ass will worry sheep.

Lewis Griffin, 'The apology of the author of the ass's
complaint against Balaam' ['Ye miter'd members . . .']

b.63, p. 59

R0003 Rail no more ye learned asses,
With applause we'll quit the stage.

'Song 20'

c.555, p. 26

R0004 Rail on poor feeble scribbler speak of me,
Thy pen is full as harmless as thy sword.

[Sir Carr Scroope], 'The author's reply' [to 'To rack
and torture . . .'; 1677]
[*POAS* I.373]

b.54, p. 1022; b.105, p. 105

R0005 Raise veiny marble from its bed below,
It may do good—at least will do no harm.

'A receipt for a running frush in a horse's foot'

c.176, p. 138

R0006 Raised by a prince of Lombard blood
Free from old Roman melancholy.

[Sir John Denham, on Sir William D'Avenant's
Gondibert]
[Crum R3]

pb.53, p. 7 (autogr.)

R0007 Rais'd by his [?], aloft great Milton flies;
Must have no heart, or else his heart be steel.

John Lockman, 'Hearing Mr. Handel's oratorio of
Samson . . . Feb. 1756'

c.267/1, p. 65

R0008 Rally again boys; rally again boys
To rub, and dub, and dub; God save the Queen.

'Song'

c.189, p. 166

R0009 Rancliffe, farewell—if e'er good temper shone
Let reason tell them, they shall vanish too.

'To the memory of the right hon. Lady Rancliffe,
daughter of the late Sr Wm James'

c.83/3, no. 862

R0010 Randolph, thou often dost my thoughts require,
And shame and reason luxury restrain.

[John] Glanvill, trans., 'The choice of a king' [from
the Latin of Buchanan]

c.244, p. 469

R0011 Rapt by my better genius beyond
Of the great light, put out in me.

[George Daniel]

b.121, fol. 63v

R0012 Rare Eve—for few her parallels we find
Is rightly one, in graceful chastity.

[Sir Philip Wodehouse], 'Upon Sir L. Hare's lady
sister to my Ld Townsend Vere Hare'

b.131, back (no. 41)

R0013 Rare excellent lady! She makes good her name
Wherein does shine the Schichinah of light.

[Sir Philip Wodehouse], 'Epigram upon the honorable
Lady Sophia . . . Chaworth'

b.131, back (no. 230)

R0014 Rare Fox (well [con]ferr'd with patience) lived a life
Most thrives the Fox that most of all is cursed.

'On the death of W. Fox'

c.548

R0015 Rare genius hers who thus could join the three,
In Blagdon's leafless shades to her a poet chide.

Dr. [John?] Langhorne, 'The underwritten was sent
me by the Bard of Blagden . . . Dr. Langhorne's thanks
to Miss S[arah] More for her acid favor . . . for her
sweet favor . . . for her civil favor'

c.341, p. 16

R0016 Rare mirror of the age; who dost present
Upon your labors, to my use, and ease.

[George Daniel]

b.121, fol. 47v

R0017　Rare piece of angel's gold that art yet hot
Of miser's gold, and are entomb'd in ground.

　　'On an infant'

　b.356, p. 262

R0018　Rash fool! that happy in a private sphere,
To my first station may they guide my foot.

　　'The English' [of 'Epigramma de aulico servitio per
　　amicum suum Johannem Gibbon']

　b.54, p. 1232

R0019　Rash hasty words sometimes thy grief may breed,
Then while thou may'st square out thy speech with
　　　　　　　　　　　　　　　　　　　　heed.

　c.339, p. 323

R0020　Rash mortals ere you take a wife
Shall never but with life expire.

　c.481, p. 60

R0021　Rat too, rat too, rat too, rat tat too, rat tat too
So tho' these liv'd in oaths, yet they die with a Psalm. |
　　　　　　　　　　　　　　　　　Farewell guard, etc.

　　[Captain Alexander Radcliffe], 'A call to the guard by a
　　drum' [pr. 1725 (Foxon C3)]

　b.105, p. 303

R0022　Rather than gold will I unfold the tenor of my hart
I [ ] would not miss . . . .

　　'Braye Lute Book,' Music Ms. 13, fol. 33v (incomplete)

R0023　Raving winds around her blowing,
'And to dark oblivion join thee!'

　　[Robert Burns], 'Isabella'

　c.142, p. 299

R0024　Rawlet's remains lodge in this humble cave,
He rests with greater honor, but less cost.

　　'An epitaph on the reverend Mr. John Rawlet'

　c.244, p. 209

R0025　Read but her reign, the princess might have been
Such was unparallel'd Elizabeth.

　　'Another [epitaph on Queen Elizabeth] in the parish
　　c[hurch] of Allhallows'

　fb.143, p. 21

R0026　'Read in one(?) island in an age forgot!'
To [?] the growing world and win its just regard.

　　[William Hayley], 'Sonnet . . . Feb 12 [1800]'

　File 6968

R0027　Read in the progress of this blessed story
And in the flames he seal'd it with his blood.

　　'A poem on the death of Bishop Ridley who was burnt
　　Oct. 16 1555 to ashes in the reign of Queen Mary'

　c.548

R0028　Read it right and you will find
There much such canters left behind.

　c.570/1, p. 6

R0029　Read lovely nymph and tremble not to read,
You pay my pangs—nor have I died in vain.

　　[Lady Mary Wortley Montagu], 'Epistle from Arthur
　　Grey to Mrs. M[urra]y'

　fc.51, p. 57; c.175, p. 41

R0030　Read o'er these lines the records of my shame,
Before my fancy, the furious queen appears.

　　'Fair Rosamond to King Henry the 2d' [cf. Foxon
　　A178, 'of my woes']

　c.83/1, no. 169

R0031　Read the commandments Mills—translate no
　　　　　　　　　　　　　　　　　　further,
For there it is written—thou shalt do no murder.

　　'Reviewers once speaking of Virgil's Georgics
　　translated by [William] Mills' [pr. 1780]

　c.378, p. 37

R0032　Read them bright lady, with a tear
From eyes that style can charm.

　　'To the Lady Lavington'

　Poetry Box II/10

R0033　Read this and then look on the maid
That yields to none, but Cupid's conquering dart.

　　'Annabella English. I am an English belle' [anagram]

　fc.24, p. 69

R0034　Read this yet be not troubled when you read
Sink at thy foot into eternal rest.

　　[Charles Hopkins], 'Leander's epistle to Hero in
　　imitation of part of that of Ovid'

　b.130, p. 69

R0035　Reader, a soldier lies here dead
Tho' dead, he'll rise and hit the ground.

　　'Epitaph on a cowardly officer . . . Nov. 30th, 1797'

　c.113/25

R0036　Reader attend, ambition is my theme,
Then this thy rule, be honest and be just.

　　'Ambition a poem'

　c.116, p. 45

R0037 Reader attend! And if thou hast a tear
And flowing eyes behold thee laid in dust.

> [Thomas Hull], 'Epitaph on Wm. Gibson'

c.528/61

R0038 Reader behold a genuine son of earth
Leap o'er time's narrow bounds and reach the skies.

> M[artin] M[adan], 'Epitaph on a fox hunter' [William
> Abbey, huntsman at Cottesmore]
> [Crum R28]

c.150, p. 76; c.546, p. 9; Poetry Box x/117

R0039 Reader, behold, one stone keeps Kitty down,
Who when alive mov'd half the stones in town.

c.233, p. 38

R0040 Reader beneath this marble lies
And thou shalt see this flower in heaven.

> 'Monumental inscription on a beautiful child'

c.391, p. 29

R0041 Reader beneath this marble stone
He caught a cold so cough'd and died.

> 'On Mr Bennet procurer extraordinary'

fb.143, p. 30

R0042 Reader beneath this modest marble lies
The bishop's palace is his monument.

> 'Dr. Waddington, Bp. Of Chichester his epitaph, he
> lies buried at Chichester'

c.547, p. 238

R0043 Reader beneath this stone survey
Laid many a heavy load on thee.

> [Abel Evans], ''Tis said of some architects, that they
> build light and clean, and of others that they build
> heavy and clumsy. The following epitaph seems to
> have some reference to that observation'

c.489, p. 16; see also 'Underneath this stone . . .', 'Lie
heavy on him . . .'.

R0044 Reader cease thy pace and stay
To come godly unto your grave.

> 'On a man and his wife buried together'

fb.143, p. 31

R0045 Reader consider well how poor a span,
Two stabs at heart the stoutest captain slay.

> [on Capt. Thomas Chevers, Anne his wife, and John
> their child]
> [Crum R35]

fb.143, p. 26; Poetry Box VII/55

R0046 Reader didst thou but know what sacred dust
Earth shall give up her share, and heav'n have all.

> [Robert] Wild, 'An epitaph upon [Mrs.] E. T.' [d.
> 7 April 1659]

c.166, p. 281

R0047 Reader, expect no flattery here
Which leads to everlasting day.

> [Phanuel Bacon], 'Epitaph for Mrs. ———'

c.237, fol. 82 [i.e., 102]

R0048 Reader forbear nor seek to know
And very dust has pow'r to charm.

c.391, p. 107

R0049 Reader here lies beneath this stone,
For all that's pox'd lies buried here.

> 'An epitaph'

fb.142, p. 53

R0050 Reader here underneath this place I am,
You may believe two kings before one slave.

> 'On the same D[uke of] B[uckingham]'

b.356, p. 248; see also 'Reader stand still and look . . .'.

R0051 Reader I was born and cried
I left the commonwealth mine heir.

> [John Hoskins], 'Epitaph' [to 'On a fart let in
> Parliament']
> [Crum R43]

b.356, p. 299; b.62, p. 24; b.200, p. 218; see also
'Reader it . . .'

R0052 Reader, if thou canst read at all thou'lt find
That for her species' sake thus greatly fell?

> 'Epitaph on a lady's lap-dog'
> [Crum R46]

fc.51, p. 85

R0053 Reader if thou desirest to know
To God that gave thee sight who dwells in heaven.

> S[amuel] J[effery], 'To the inquisitive reader'

b.195, f.1v

R0054 Reader if Whig thou art thou'lt laugh
The learn'd say to Achitophel.

> 'Epitaph on Algernon Sidney' [d. 1683]
> [Crum R49]

b.111, p. 140

R0055 Reader if you'd not spend your time in vain
Read Wright and only what is right maintain.

> [Thomas Gurney], 'Written in Mr. John Wright's
> hymns'

c.213

R0056   Reader it was born and cried
I left the commonwealth mine heir.

     [John Hoskins], 'The fart's epitaph in the Parliament House'
     [Crum R52, with last line of Crum R43]

   b.197, p. 58; see also 'Reader, I . . .'.

R0057   Reader, know whoe'er thou be
Its only hope is underground.

     'On Baptist Ld Visct. Campden'

   fb.143, p. 10

R0058   Reader look to't
Buried in Westminster.

     'On one John Foot'
     [cf. Crum R55]

   fb.143, p. 11

R0059   Reader pass on ne'er idly waste your time
And what I was, is no affair of yours.

     'In Guildford churchyard'
     [Crum R58]

   fc.14/8; c.546

R0060   Reader pay thy tribute here
And learn from her to live and die.

     'The following lines are intended for an urn to be erected at Hilton to the memory of my dear wife if ever my circumstances will admit of it'

   c.203

R0061   Reader! Remember, in this vault does lie
In glory bright—and as an angel there.

     'An epitaph of Queen Caroline' [d. 20 Nov. 1737]
     [Crum R61]

   c.360/1, p. 101

R0062   Reader, search the world around,
'Tis the virtues of the mind.

   c.83/1, no. 106

R0063   Reader stand still and look lo here I am
You will believe two kings before one slave.

     'The epitaph' [on the Duke of Buckingham, 1628; followed by 'Yet were bidentals sacred . . .']
     [Crum R63]

   Poetry Box VI/28; see also 'Reader here underneath . . .'.

R0064   Reader the author of these following lines
Before the steps into eternity.

     [Thomas Gurney], 'To the reader'

   c.213

R0065   Reader, the title of this solemn day
A debt, in the observance of this day.

   b.49, p. 8

R0066   Reader, this rude or humble spot contains
And virtues to remotest ages told.

     [Charles] B[urney, the elder], 'Epitaph on Samuel Crisp esqr.'

   c.486, fol. 5v

R0067   Reader, whoe'er thou art, here thou mayst find
That our neglect should cause our light to die.

     [Robert Wild], 'Upon the learned works of his reverend divine, Ed. Reynolds, D. D.'

   c.166, p. 302

R0068   Reader, whoe'er thou art, let some tears fall
A severe conduct, in a gentle mind.

     'An epitaph on Mrs. Bretton'

   c.244, p. 207

R0069   Reader, wonder think it none
Melt themselves to tears and die.

     [Giles Fletcher?], 'Epitaph on Prince Henry' [1612]
     [Crum R76]

   b.197, p. 205; fb.143, p. 23 (with four more lines from 'Within this marble casket . . .'); c.360/3, no. 62

R0070   Reader, wouldst know what goodness lieth here,
Surer in tears, than ink, in eyes than book.

     'An epitaph on Thomas Hesketh esquire'

   c.244, p. 285

R0071   Reading an author that I will not name,
The world to scorn, in heaven to have a share.

     'A heaven on earth'

   c.187, p. 50

R0072   Reading Descartes I perceive a thing,
Hereunto whom this diagram's devote.

     [Sir Philip Wodehouse], 'A whimsical anagram referring to the star of sight points beneath being the Hobart 'scutcheon Barbara Hobart . . .'

   b.131, back (no. 88)

R0073   Reading the gospel by our Lord, we find
Among twice twelve that seems an honest man.

     'Occasioned by the bishops' having all but one voted against the proceedings of the South Sea directors'

   c.570/3, p. 207

R0074   Reading thy verse, we cannot but admire
Tho' young discreet, and modest tho' she's fair.

     W. N., of Exeter College, Oxford

   c.233, p. 4

R0075 Realms of this globe, that ever circling run,
No longer murmur, and no longer wave!

    [John Langhorne], 'Written in a collection of maps, 1765'

c.139, p. 560

R0076 Rear high thy bleak majestic hills,
That ever breath'd the soothing strain.

    W[illiam] Roscoe, 'On the death of Robt. Burns . . . from the first volume of Burns' works by Currier'

c.142, p. 214

R0077 Reason holds it criminal,
A female must so stint her inward flames.

    Sir Thomas Urquhart, 'That reason is not a competent judge in matters of love'

fb.217, p. 89

R0078 Reason! thou vain impertinence!
To set to show, what none can hide.

Poetry Box II/7

R0079 Reasons to value pelf tho' shrewd men seek
Than teach you to be wretched, and be poor.

    'Juvenal's satires'

c.156, p. 190

R0080 Rebecca, we have read, was young and fair
And all these nymphs had soon unstitch'd the
                          sheets.

Poetry Box x/84

R0081 Rebel to me unto thy kindred curst
Thy dust-born body turn to earth again.

    [Robert Cottesford]

b.144, p. 8

R0082 Rebels Whigs and traitors that long have plagued
                         the nation
Heaven sure will burn the rods.

    'Forty-one revived'

b.111, p. 474

R0083 Rebuke for faults one that is wise,
And hate thee very sore.

b.234, p. 173

R0084 Receive and write, write when you pay,
'Tis gain'd by many actions lost by one.

b.155, p. 63

R0085 Receive, thou blessed partner of my soul,
Adieu, farewell, peruse, what I impart.

    [ ] W., of Eton, 'Verses on the birthday of Mr. [ ]'

c.591

R0086 Receiv'd this genial day, with thanks profound,
And think of an ungrateful world no more.

    John Lockman, 'A poetical acquittance, for an annual New Year's gift, Jany 1748/9'

c.267/1, p. 45

R0087 Redeem'd by blood, the price how great
May honor much my Savior God.

    [Thomas Stevens?]

c.259, p. 138

R0088 Redoubled stroke, how down the tallest(?) arbor
May I [?] pierce ye and o'erthrow ye too.

    [Sir Thomas Urquhart], 'An amorous and diffident gentleman speaks thus to his coy mistress'

fb.217, p. 387

R0089 Reflect fair maid, before it be too late,
In pity veil their splendors from our eyes.

    'A fragment'

c.221, p. 34

R0090 Reflect that life and death affecting sound,
And virtue cheaply sav'd with loss of life.

    [ ] Johnson

c.156, p. 234

R0091 Reflecting on life's num'rous griefs below,
With them be happy and their glory share.

    'Lines of sympathetic consolation on the death of infants' [Bradford, 1773]

c.139, p. 442

R0092 Reform dark Queen, the errors of thy youth
We dance for joy, that you are danc'd away.

    'On the Queen's dancing' [1670]
    [Crum R91, 'dear Queen'; POAS I.421]

fb.140, p. 142

R0093 Regard not, with contempt, the muses' train,
The god of arts, and so divide his care.

    [Charles Burney, the younger], 'Translation of part of Milton's poem, Ad patrem, from the Latin. From 56th to 66th verse . . . Nov. 8. 1779'

c.37, p. 60

R0094 Regard O Lord for I complain
I cry to thee O God.

    [John Hopkins, Psalm lxi]
    [cf. Crum R95]

b.156, p. 25

R0095 Regard the world with cautious eye,
Eludes the fury of the gale.

    Dr. [ ] Colton

c.83/2, no. 320

R0096 Regardful to improve each nat'ral part
Yielding to all when reason thinks it due.

    [Robert Cholmeley], 'An acrostic upon Mrs Rebecca
    Cholmeley'

    c.190, p. 32

R0097 Regardless of the pangs I feel,
For flint and steel will soon strike fire.

    'Flint and steel an epigram'

    c.83/1, no. 31

R0098 Regrets for past, and fears of future crimes
Live, whilst they live: and when they die, they die.

    Sir Thomas Urquhart, 'That the unreasonable
    creatures in this world, have as much pleasure as men'

    fb.217, p. 94

R0099 Rehearse to me ye sacred sisters nine
The rest untold no living tongue can speak.

    [Edmund Spenser], 'Musarum lachrymae'
    [Crum R100]

    b.65, p. 24

R0100 Rejoice rejoice rejoice
But for his lies, O let him loose his tongue.

    'On Cupid'
    [Crum R108]

    b.356, p. 102

R0101 Rejoice that now arm'd Mary with proud high looks
All goodness quite out of them, while they quake.

    'Learning's excellency'

    b.284, p. 54

R0102 Rejoice ye good writers, your pens are set free,
One good verdict more might secure all our laws.

    [William Pulteney, earl of Bath], 'The honest jury, or
    Caleb [D'anvers, i.e., Nicholas Amhurst] triumphant.
    To the tune of Packington's pound' [pr. 1729 (Foxon
    P1161)]

    c.570/3, p. 84

R0103 Rejoice ye Whigs, your idol's come again.
Ring not the bells you fools, but wring your hands.

    'On the Duke of Marlborough' [1715]
    [cf. Crum R110, 'ye fops', 1692]

    c.570/1, p. 3; fc.58, p. 48 ('you Whigs')

R0104 Releas'd from pain my darling guest
Or watchful heaven's peculiar grace.

    [William Hayley], 'Serious stanzas Oct 14'

    File 6960

R0105 Relentless death!—ah, why so soon
Ah, wherefore droop'd the flower so soon!

    [Hector Macneill], 'An elegy on the sudden death of a
    beautiful young boy in Jamaica'

    c.142, p. 483

R0106 Relentless time, destroying power,
In health 'tis only ease.

    [Thomas] Parnell, 'An imitation of some French lines'

    c.244, p. 269

R0107 Religion and law conjoin, combine,
That curbs men's heart, their hands this doth
                             confine.

    'The commonwealth's eyes'

    c.356

R0108 Religion is a generous lively flame
From the wild frenzies of a feverish brain.

    [Judith (Cowper)] Madan, 'On religion'

    fc.51, p. 156

R0109 Religion mitigates each painful loss
More useful than the pedantry of schools.

    H[annah] M[ore], 'Of religion'

    c.341, p. 101

R0110 Religion stands on tiptoe in our land,
They have their time of gospel ev'n as we.

    [George Herbert?]

    c.158, p. 41

R0111 Religion! Vast, most interesting thought,
Ten thousand praises to our gracious God.

    Charles Atherton Allnutt, 'Progressive regeneration'

    c.112, p. 39

R0112 Religion was her compass truth her star
To sleep with her among the blessed dead.

    'Epitaph no. 10'

    c.158, p. 49

R0113 Religion's a politic law;
And then let us fight for the best.

    'The deist, moderator between the Roman Catholic
    and Lutheran churches, a satirical ballad'
    [Crum R127]

    fb.70, p. 147; c.555, p. 306 (var.)

R0114 Remember as thou art a man
Wherefore take heed live not secure.

    b.27, fol. 40v

R0115   Remember at sun setting death thine urn,
And at sun rising mind thy thence return.

    'Of sun rising and setting'

c.356

R0116   Remember brave Britons, the canons and the oath
To the devil for all his devices and fraud.

    'A memento to the Parliament'

b.101, p. 87

R0117   Remember, Britons this happy day;
Our hopes are still the stronger.

Poetry Box IV/94

R0118   Remember, dear Chloe, I told you awhile,
And save this precaution, a fig for my song.

    'Advice to Chloe'

c.83/3, no. 878

R0119   Remember, Delius, to control
In father Charon's leaky wherry.

    'The third ode of the second book of Horace imitated'

Poetry Box I/113[4]

R0120   Remember for to shun a double-tongued mate:
Let such not sup, nor dine with thee, nor come
                        within thy gate.

c.339, p. 319

R0121   Remember man and do thou scan
Thy Savior for to be.

b.234, p. 23

R0122   Remember man that die thou must,
And after death return to dust.

c.93

R0123   Remember man that thou art made of clay:
And in this world thou hast not long to stay.

    [John Rose?]

b.227, p. 36

R0124   Remember me and bear in mind
A faithful friend is ill to find.

    'Jo[hn] Rutherford Saville Row Newcastle upon Tyne North Newcastle'

c.93

R0125   Remember still there is no greater cross,
Than of a true friend to sustain the loss.

c.339, p. 318

R0126   Remonstrate good Masjames how comes to pass
The lads avow they'll go to school no more.

    'To ———' [docket title: 'Verses on the advocates and ministers '74', addressed to President Stair]

Poetry Box VIII/27, 32 ('remonstrant'; 'against President [James Dalrymple, 1st viscount] Stairs')

R0127   Remote from cities lived a swain
To make men moral good and wise.

    [John] Gay, 'One of Gay's fables'

c.163, p. 26

R0128   Remote from city smoke and rumbling cars
Remember— these advices came from me.

    'An epistle from the country to my son Thomas Gibbons'

c.148, p. 17

R0129   Remote from hurry, care and strife,
To endless light eternal day.

    'Retirement'

fc.130, p. 49

R0130   Remote from liberty and truth
Shall tell the patriot's name.

    [Robert] Nugent, 'Ode [to William Pulteney, later earl of Bath] by . . . on his conversion to the Protestant religion' [pr. 1739 (Foxon N339)] [Crum R143]

c.241, p. 15; File 11955; Poetry Box I/3

R0131   Remote from men with God he pass'd the day,
Banks, trees and skies in thick disorder run.

    [Thomas] Parnell, 'The hermit from Parnell's poems (a simile)'

c.250

R0132   Remove, enchanting nymph! Each fear:
And sweetly captivate thy eyes.

    John Lockman, 'Translations, and imitations from Metastasio, and other Italian opera poets [13]'

c.267/4, p. 107

R0133   Renowned patriots, open your eyes,
You'll also share with those you have turn'd about.

    [George Wither], 'Vox et lacrimae Anglorum' [printed 1668 (Wing W3208)] [Crum R153, with postscript]

File 16328

R0134   Renowned Spenser, lie a thought more nigh
Honor hereafter to be laid by thee.

    [William Basse], 'On Will[ia]m Shakespeare buried at Stratford upon Avon, his town of nativity' [Crum R154]

fb.143, p. 20; b.197, p. 48

R0135 Renowned twins most fitly termed savers,
Whe you receive them in your sanctuary.

Sir Thomas Urquhart, 'To the [laird?] of Cromarty'
fb.217, p. 184

R0136 Repine not, dear girl, that the gods in their ire
Except that your form is too small for your mind.

[Charles Burney, the elder], 'On a diminutive female'
c.33, p. 62

R0137 Report's a bell—which on her silver wings
Fair Isabella's fame, resounds and sings.

[Sir Philip Wodehouse], 'Upon his fair kinswoman
Isabella Porter . . .'
b.131, back (no. 74)

R0138 Repose heroic dust, thy better part
Ev'n till thy own name, can no more be sung.

[George Daniel], 'To the memory of Richard Neville,
the great Earl of Warwick'
b.121, fol. 14v

R0139 Reposing in a settled state,
A vision of felicity.

'Wrote 10 years after the author's great deliverance at
sea'
c.515, fol. 3v

R0140 Reproach me not if heretofore
Is better than elsewhere success.

['A song']
[Crum R161]
b.213, p. 116; b.207, p. 31 (var.)

R0141 Resist me not; by Jove I must enjoy ye?
(That you may save your oath) to let y'enjoin.

Sir Thomas Urquhart, 'The amorous success of a
certain cavalier, who having the opportunity of time,
and place for the obtaining of his mistress' favor and
finding that neither by charming promises, not
insinuating assaults, he was able to prevail . . .'
fb.217, p. 237

R0142 Resolv'd to touch the lyre for thee,
Of Venus and her race.

[William Popple, trans.], '[Horace] book 4th. Ode
15th. The praises of Augustus'
fc.104/2, p. 384

R0143 Resolved to rescue Newton's bust
That decorate her wondrous bow.

'On seeing the head of Sr. Isaac Newton, richly gilt,
and placed by a celebrated optician upon the top of a
certain temple . . .'
Poetry Box v/34

R0144 Respect to Dryden justly Sheffield paid
The city printer, and the city bard.

'On [Samuel] Butler's monument being erected by
Alderman Barber'
c.360/2, no. 211

R0145 Respected swain who mak'st thy lyre
And trust me 'tis no crime to gaze.

'To Richard Sadler esqr. In answer to some verses
lately written by him'
c.53, fol. 39

R0146 Rest awhile you cruel cares
Be as dark as hell to me.

'Cant: 37'
[Crum R167]
b.4, fol. 31v

R0147 Rest in soft peace, and ask'd, say how doth lie
[Ben Jonson], Ben Jonson his best piece of poetry.

[Ben Jonson], 'On Ben: Jonson's son dying an infant'
fb.143, p. 3 (ll. 9-10)

R0148 Rest now my soul, have care to kill
That gives me grace in faith to pray.

'A watch over the soul'
c.187, p. 12

R0149 Rest thou, whose rest gives me a restless life
A final leave until thy ashes wake.

'On Mary wife of Capt. Malachi Simons 1677
Aged 50'
fb.143, p. 26; c.74 (var.)

R0150 Rest undisturb'd ye much lamented pair,
Swift fled their youth—they knew not age's care.

'Epitaph on two brothers'
c.83/2, no. 721

R0151 Rest ye by fit amongst your great affairs,
But not too much, lest sloth do set her snares.

c.339, p. 316

R0152 Rethink, ye heedless youths, in time
And joys that ever last.

fc.132/1, p. 28

R0153 Retir'd from noise, from earthborn joys retir'd,
Gloriously bright all peaceful and serene.

M[aria] Done, 'Meditations in a churchyard'
c.139, p. 425

R0154   Retired some distance from the seat
That each future annal may celebrate thy fame.

     'An ode'

     c.515, fol. 1r

R0155   Retir'd to solitude, oppress'd with grief,
Should not these gloomy shades afford her meat.

     'The following lines were fixed to a tree near the
     mineral spring in the grove at Hyde Park, under it sat
     a young woman with an infant lying in her lap'

     c.360/3, no. 173

R0156   Retreat base Monck into some loathsome jail
Thou may'st be damn'd, but God will own the king.

     'Upon General Monck's pulling down the city gates'

     fb.140, p. 17

R0157   Return lovely nymph, while you hear who 'tis
                              woos ye,
Might have worn the dull bays, but have whoop'd
                             for the laurel.

     [Anna Seward], 'Daphne's coyness accounted for'

     File 13370

R0158   Return, my child, O soon return
All happiness restor'd.

     [Stephen Barrett], 'To Miss Barrett gone to Faversham
     for one night; an epigram, in imitation of the Greeks.
     1787'

     c.193, p. 133

R0159   Return my heart homeward again
Tho' find a crop(?) of mine so false.

     'Braye Lute Book,' Music Ms. 13, fol. 45v

R0160   Return my joys, and hither bring
To be more wretched, than we must, is folly.

     [William Strode], 'An opposite to melancholy'
     [Crum R177]

     b.200, p. 48; b.205, fol. 70v

R0161   Return, return thou wand'ring guest
Than to thy own thou must retire.

     'A song'

     Poetry Box IV/53

R0162   Return'd from the opera as lately I sat
Tho' shortest the day is— the night is the longest.

     'On a lady's wedding being on the 21st of December'

     c.115; c.175, p. 81; c.81/1, no. 199

R0163   Return'd? I'll ne'er believe't, first prove him hence
Now he the counterpane comes south to us.

     [John Cleveland], 'On the King's return from
     Scotland'
     [Crum R180]

     b.93, p. 131

R0164   Reveal not secrets hate vain tales and songs
Enricht by virtue and from vice refin'd.

     [Mary Serjant]

     fb.98, fol. 152

R0165   Revenge, although a great pernicious sin
If thou of God forgiveness would receive.

     J[ohn] R[obinson], 'Infirmi est animi exiguique
     voluptas ultio'

     c.370, fol. 61v

R0166   Revenge inspire my angry breast
But shall bewail in vain.

     'An answer to the foregoing verses ['Some surly
     goddess . . .'] made by a young lady'

     fc.85, fol. 79

R0167   Revenge thou godlike attribute inspire,
The sacred signet of a wondrous fool.

     Captain Guyon, 'Captain Guyon the person that
     wrote the above satire and was took by a young lady
     for a stage play[er]' [upon some reflections cast upon
     him at Sheffield Assembly, 1757, because he danced
     better than the rest of the company]

     fc.61, p. 91, p. 103

R0168   Revere these relics, that with genius glow'd!
A fonder parent, or a firmer friend.

     [William Hayley], 'Epitaph' [on Jeremiah Meyer, d.
     1789]

     File 6936

R0169   Reverend John Stiles (for style we will not jar)
And looks for an answer in the next vacation.

     W[illiam] Lakes, 'Dullman the clerk to John of Stile
     of Gray's Inn sends greeting' [on George Ruggle's
     Ignoramus, acted before James I, 1615; answer to
     'Faith gentlemen . . .']
     [Crum R181]

     b.197, p. 81

R0170   Reverend Sir I fain would know
Then you're all damn'd infallibly.

     'A letter sent to Dr. Pelling' [on his apostasy from his
     doctrine of nonresistance]
     [Crum R182]

     b.111, p. 214; b.371, no. 46; fb.207/1, p. 2

RO171 Revolving in my mind,
To live in bliss for aye. | Amen

    'Of S. Christen [Christina]. July. 24'

  a.30[15]

RO172 Revolving years add, Mira, to your charms,
All day with Armstrong, and all night with you.

    'To Mira; on New-Year's Day'

  Spence Papers, folder 113

RO173 Rev'rend whom lately you dar'd to the fight,
Or rashly escaping—your own be the deed.

    Miss [ ] P., 'An invitation to Richmond Assembly held
    at the Castle Tavern. By . . . to Mr. [George] Woodd'
    [answered by 'George Woodd and his rib . . .']

  c.74

RO174 Rewards and punishment being needful for
Of penal statutes: none for recompense.

    Sir Thomas Urquhart, 'Of penal statutes'

  fb.217, p. 48

RO175 Rex and Grex hath both one sound
That Dux bears Crux, and Crux not Dux again.

    'On the old Duke of Buck[ingham] George Villiers'
    [motto: Fidei coticula crux]
    [Crum R185]

  b.52/2, p. 179; b.200, p. 55; see also 'Where only one . . .'.

RO176 Rhemus upon a time I heard thee tell,
How dare you be so bold to die so rich.

    [Francis Quarles], 'On Purgatory' [i.e., 'On Rhemus';
    Divine fancies IV, 17]

  b.137, p. 179

RO177 Rhubarb, a doctor of renown,
Since you, have fifty slain, by God.

    [Thomas Hamilton, 6th earl of Haddington], 'Honest
    Teague'

  c.458/2, p. 136

RO178 Rich Gripe does all his thoughts and cunning bend,
And of two wretches make one happy man.

    [William] Walsh, 'Epigram—Gripe and Shifter'
    [Crum R189]

  c.351, p. 86; c.223, p. 76

RO179 Rich hurt the poor, poor cannot hurt again,
Then like to like, or both alone remain.

  c.339, p. 319

RO180 Rich in good works, oh happy he!
To whom, all that is good, we owe.

    [Edmund Wodehouse], 'May 2d [1715]'

  b.131, p. 207

RO181 Rich men their wealth, as children rattles keep;
Which play'd awhile with't then they fall asleep.

    'On rich men'

  c.356

RO182 Riches and power by gracious heaven,
And still more glorious rise.

    John Lockman, 'To the Earl of Middlesex, with some
    of my poems . . . 1750'

  c.267/1, p. 79

RO183 Riches are fair inducements to deceive us,
Repent sincerely e'er your years be done.

  c.93

RO184 Riches chance may take or give,
And beauty, mirth, and pleasure fail.

    'The retrospect of life, or the one thing needful'

  fc.132/1, p. 23

RO185 Riches have wings and often fly away
But true love never will decay.

  c.93

RO186 Riddle riddle, neighbor John, with a late ha' boa?
Do take in great indudgeon.

    [William Strode], 'A western humor'
    [Crum R207]

  b.104, p. 12 (end of book); see also 'Thou ne'er woot
  riddle . . .'.

RO187 Right heir to Flutter Fop o' th' last edition,
A merry blockhead treacherous and vain.

    [Robert] Wolseley, 'Mr. Wolseley's familiar epistle to
    Sir Frivolous Insipid alias Sir Hen. H—d [Sir Harry
    Hubert]'
    [Crum R214]

  fb.108, p. 243; b.218, p. 1

RO188 Right noble earl I humbly here present
Aught pleasing [in this] way my stare [than] kind.

    [Francis Lenton], 'To the right honorable and truly
    noble the Earl of Dorset'

  b.205, fol. 17r

RO189 Right well to the life in line and feature
Your humble servant, Thomas Brittain.

    Thomas Brittain, 'Mr. Brittain's answer' [to 'While
    the mongrel Calvinist . . .']

  c.213

R0190 Rightly these names are join'd when both agree
Are his, who is no more his own; but yours, |
Richard Daniel

Richard Daniel, 'Anagram Richardus Daniel Elizabeth
Durant'

b.52/2, p. 200

R0191 Ring the bells backward! Lusty bonfires make!
Good fortune scorns him, all his glory spurns.

'Another satire &c.' [on the bombing of St. Malo,
5 June 1695]
[Crum R223]

fb.207/3, p. 7

R0192 Ripe sober fancy—spells the name
Of a most pretty, virtuous dame.

[Sir Philip Wodehouse], 'Upon my wife's half sister
Frances Proby: lady to Sr Thomas Proby'

b.131, back (no. 58)

R0193 Rise Britons rise defend your injur'd cause,
Is, a German's absence and a Stuart's reign.

'To the Britons'

c.570/2, p. 5

R0194 Rise distracted land, rouse thee, and bring
Disclaims in interest and disdains to rest.

fb.228/4

R0195 Rise Faery's Queen, awake my rueful rhyme
That she naught worth is, or worthy pity.

Sir F[rancis] C[astillion], 'Threnodia. A mourning
song like unto old Chaucer's English, and much
imitating Spenser. To the tune of The widow's song.
1630'

fb.69, p. 184

R0196 Rise, for a serene morn brings on the day,
Summon our wand'ring souls to heaven, or hell.

'A morning call'

c.189, p. 66; b.209, p. 83 (incomplete)

R0197 Rise from your lurking holes, each dastard fool!
A birchen rod to runaways, like you.

John Lockman, 'A word more: to otherwise only . . .
6 April 1750'
[Crum R228]

c.267/1, p. 224

R0198 Rise lovely Celia, and be kind
Oh let me hear thee gently cry | I yield.

'A love sonnet'

b.62, p. 1

R0199 Rise noble dust
Here leave him, and posterity to weep the rest.

'An epitaph on the Earl of Strafford'

b.63, p. 77

R0200 Rise, O my soul, with thy desires to Heaven
To thee I die, to thee I only live.

attr. Sir Henry Wotton
[Crum R234]

b.150, p. 263

R0201 Rise, universal nature, rise,
O'er nature's wreck they will prevail.

'100 psalm'

c.515, fol. 26v

R0202 Rise up great William your call's now to France,
That whene'er you complain I will set you free.

'King William's invitation to France'
[Crum R240]

fb.207/3, p. 25

R0203 Rise, winds of night! relentless tempests rise!
Again! their vengeful look—and now a speechless
glance.

[Helen Maria Williams], 'Part of an irregular
fragment found in a dark passage of the tower'

c.140, p. 343

R0204 Rise with the morn, and gather up the dew
Rests in ourselves, not seeking any more.

[George Daniel]

b.121, fol. 73

R0205 Rise youths, the evening's come, and her bright star
Thy sacred influence on the nuptial bed.

'An epithalamium from Catallus'

b.218, p. 24

R0206 Robber with pistol at my throat,
And when I can by G[o]d I'll shoot thee.

'On the oath'

c.570/1, p. 145

R0207 Robe, rocket, blade found in his name him dight
Which from its eminence produc'd the rest.

[Sir Philip Wodehouse], 'Upon Sr Robert Baldock
robe, rocket, blade'

b.131, back (no. 136)

R0208 Robin the father has lost it most truly,
For the enemy's fairly beat out of your trenches.

'On the colonel's being chosen Chamberlain'

c.233, p. 59

RO209 Roger! If with thy magic glasses
The filth they leave—still points out where they
crawl!

'Lines occasioned by the intended demolition of Friar
Bacon's study in Oxford'
[Crum R252]

c.382, p. 33

RO210 Roger told his brother clown
For pimping and procuring . . . .

'Upon the court ladies a lampoon'

fb.140, p. 22 (incomplete)

RO211 Romans, to show thy living worth and prize,
First carve the bust, then bid the artist starve.

John Lockman, 'Reading Mr. Handel's address (after
his being neglected by the town,) printed in the Daily
advertiser . . . 17 Jany 1744/5'

c.267/1, p. 83

RO212 Rome, that the conquer'd world so long had sway'd
Forever lost, and past recalling.

'On ancient Rome, from the Latin[.] Lond. Mag.
March 1733'

c.160, fol. 74

RO213 Rome thou art tainted with the martyrs' blood,
Whom zeal inflames, do barefooted resort.

Captain Henry Bell, 'A description of the cities in
Italy'

fb.139, p. 5

RO214 Rome's worst Philenes and Pasiphae's lust
Since there's a higher king can pardon it.

[upon the conviction of Mervyn Lord Audley, earl of
Castlehaven April 1631]
[Crum R259, 'Pasiphae's dust']

b.125, fol. 38v

RO215 Romney! expert infallible to trace,
While I was Hayley's guest, and sat to thee?

[William Cowper], 'To George Romney esq.'

c.142, p. 581

RO216 Romulus long to shady ba[n?]ks confin'd,
At which repeated cry owl—like he tumbl'd down.

R[obert] Shirley, 1st earl of Ferrers, 'Rome's seven
kings burlesqued and enlarged from the four Latin
verses, Romule savus eras &c'

c.347, p. 79

RO217 Room for a pedant, with those forms of speech,
But Monsieur's coin will always heavier weigh.

'The comparison' [1690]
[Crum R260]

b.204, p. 79

RO218 Room for our lawyers in villages and towns
And lawyers now have much ado to [?] within the
town.

'[torn] Duk[e] [torn] to my march sung to the tune of
[torn . . . Du]ke of Lorraine's [?]'

Poetry Box VIII/32

RO219 Room for the Bedlam Commons hell's fury
Present you pretty babes which you ne'er got.

'A charge to the grand inquest of England' [c. 1674]
[Crum R261; POAS I.221]

File 17952

RO220 Room for the merry rhymer who appears
Not to cause mourning or raise your fears.

Poetry Box VII/60

RO221 Room, room for the best of poets heroic
With thirty-two slaves to plant mundungus.

[Sir John Denham], 'On Gondibert: the preface,
being published before the book was written'
[Crum R266]

pb.53, p. 2 (autogr.)

RO222 Room room room for a man of the town,
And there's an end of bully.

[Thomas D'Urfey], 'The town shift' [in The fool
turned critic]
[Crum R265, 'blade of the town']

fb.107, p. 12

RO223 Rose of the world, not rose the pure fresh flower,
Which erst was wont to savor passing well.

'Fair Rosamond . . . translation'

c.81/1, no. 260

RO224 Roses till ripe and ready to be blown
Of early flourishing the bashful bride.

[Sir William D'Avenant]

fb.66/34

RO225 Round as a hoop the bumpers flow
And mute as any fish.

[Jonathan] Swift(?), 'A new song of old similes. To the
tune of Chevy Chase'

Spence Papers, folder 153

RO226 'Round Flavia's glass, unnumber'd message cards
In nightly routs, or morning visits end.

'Fashionable friends'

c.83/2, no. 309

RO227 'Round Hughes' humble tho' distinguish'd urn,
And leaves behind, gay tracts of beamy light.

    [Judith (Cowper) Madan], 'On the death of Mr. John
    Hughes [d. 1720]. By a lady'

    c.244, p. 615

RO228 'Round with the health—Ophelia is the toast
To drown, at once, despair.

    'The toast an ode'

    c.360/2, no. 109

RO229 Rouse Britons rouse let ancient valor shine
Condemn his passive laws and wooden shoe.

    [Thomas Gurney], 'Designed for the public paper in
    Sep. 1745. To the public'

    c.213

RO230 Rouse, genius, rouse! something that's lofty say,
Tho' but mortals we are, yet we feast like the gods.

    'An ode; Sung at the Kentish feast. 1696'

    fb.108, p. 11

RO231 Rouse, rouse jolly sportsmen the hounds are all out,
Next morning return to the chase. | Next
                       morning, &c.

    'Song 114'

    c.555, p. 165

RO232 Rous'd by necessity to arms,
And conquer gloriously, or die!

    John Lockman, 'Translations, and imitations from
    Metastasio, and other Italian opera poets [11]'

    c.267/4, p. 103

RO233 Royal-born William, flower of earls lies here
A sheath thus short doth Longsword serve to bear.

    [on William Longsword, earl of Salisbury]

    b.208, p. 178

RO234 Ruddy miss Pru with golden hair,
That travellers must go.

    [Robert Cholmeley], 'The learned relations'

    c.190, p. 60

RO235 Rude, shoeless children, mumbling Ave's o'er,
'Tis one pert, tricking, tawdry masquerade.

    John Lockman, 'A sketch of Popish worship, drawn
    from the life, in France . . . 1741'

    c.267/1, p. 87

RO236 Rue is a noble herb to give it right,
With honey, rew and onions make a plaster.

    [Joshua Sylvester, trans. Guillaume de Salluste,
    seigneur Du Bartas], 'Of rue'

    b.284, p. 52

RO237 Rufus the pedant at a nuptial feast
Some feminine, some of the neuter gender.

    'Epithalamium grande . . . translation'

    c.81/1, no. 132

RO238 Ruin seize thee, ruthless king!
Deep in the roaring tide he plung'd to endless
                       night.

    [Thomas] Gray, 'The bard; a Pindaric ode, by . . .
    founded on a tradition current in Wales that Edward
    the 1st ordered all the bards that fell into his hands to
    be put to death'

    c.481, p. 36

RO239 Run round my lines, while I as roundly show
Mine O was round, and I have made it long.

    [Edward Lapworth?], 'Upon the letter O'
    [Crum R281]

    b.197, p. 223 (attr. Donne)

S

S0001 Sackville! Munificent, enlighten'd, kind,
For Middlesex and Dorset are the same.

> John Lockman, 'Compliment paid to the Duke of
> Dorset, the first time of waiting on his grace, after the
> death of his father . . . Decr. 1765 (I think)'

c.267/4, p. 394

S0002 Sacred to freedom be this night,
But Gallia weep, and rebels bleed.

> John Lockman, 'Writ in a vast lantern, hung out in
> Salisbury, the night of the thanksgiving, for the
> victory at Culloden . . . 15 Oct. 1746'

c.267/1, p. 223

S0003 Sacred to science where the solemn domes
And ev'ry blissful faculty restore.

> [Miss ( ) Bradford], 'On madness'

c.504, p. 37

S0004 Sacred to thee and to eternal fame,
Accept their duty, and enjoy their love.

> Abraham Oakes, 'A poem: on the battle of Dettingen,
> 1743'

c.50, p. 53

S0005 Sacred urn, with whom we trust
Till he shall die, with her and live.

> 'An epitaph on Mrs. Elizabeth Dunton'

c.244, p. 284

S0006 Sad and fearful is the story
Wherefore left he me alive?

> 'Durandarte and Belerma'

c.83/3, no. 886

S0007 Sad and heavy should I part,
Than hers that came so far away.

> [Thomas] Rymer, 'Jaufre Rudel a noble Provençal
> poet and commander under K[in]g R[ichard] I in the
> holy wars'

c.229/1, fol. 94v

S0008 Sad notes be heard thro' the sky,
Demands a monument of tears.

> [Isaac Watts?], 'Mourning for the death of K.
> [William] the 3 of glorious memory' [1702]

c.349, fol. 4

S0009 Sad relic of a blessed soul, whose trust
The resurrection for his epitaph.

> [Henry King], 'On John King bp. of London, buried
> in St. Pauls . . .'
> [Crum s15]

fb.143, p. 12

S0010 Sad! Sad disaster! Whence arose the quarrel?
For to repent of our iniquity.

> 'A confused drunken quarrel repented of'

b.104, p. 22 (end of book)

S0011 Safe from the browsing flocks or plowshare's wound
She lives neglected, unlamented dies.

> [William Dennis]

File 4317

S0012 Safe in this spreading elm, I hence survey
One wish I have—that I may never die!

> John Lockman, 'Speech of the dryad, or nymph, of
> the lofty elm, in he garden of William Jansson esqr: at
> the Nunnery, Chesthurst, Hartfordshire . . . 1754'

c.267/1, p. 49

S0013 Safe on the fair one's arm my first may rest,
And where I'm most admired, I suffer most.

> 'Charade'

c.389; Diggle Box: Poetry Box XI/71

S0014 Safety gives insolence to ev'ry slave;
Which those, unless protected, durst not give.

Music Ms. 16, p. 398

S0015 Sagacious Smyth, whose practice was to save,
Surpass'd he ne'er was yet, or ever will.

> 'On the death of the late Mark Smyth M. D. of Wells,
> by a medicinal friend—March 25th 1786'

fc.130, p. 46

S0016 Sage Corydon, fam'd for the play of his knife,
And our latest sons fancy they hear his wild splutter.

> John Lockman, 'Corydon, or the Salisbury Bacchanal.
> As exhibited, not many centuries since, from High
> Street, in that city . . . Sept. 1744'

c.267/1, p. 363

S0017 Sage strengths the sinews, fierce heat doth 'suage,
Or if this breed not help, then look for none.

    [Joshua Sylvester, trans. Guillaume de Salluste,
    seigneur Du Bartas], 'Of sage'
    b.284, p. 51

S0018 Sage were thy counsels and as well applied
His head to us and to our foes his heart.

    [Francis Quarles], 'On Achitophel' [Divine
    fancies II, 21]
    b.137, p. 168

S0019 Said Balsompiere one day to Louis
Your Majesty I represented. . . .

    [Charles Burney, the elder], 'Epigram, from the
    French'
    c.33, p. 62 (incomplete; crossed out)

S0020 Said Scott to Squire White are carp now in season?
With all their dull see-saw of animal pleasure.

    'Carp in season on April 28'
    Poetry Box v/43

S0021 Saint Ambrose slumbering in the night
O plain us grace this blessed day. | Amen

    'Of S. Gervatius and Prothasius. Jun. 19'
    a.30[4]

S0022 Saint Austin Plutarch Cicero express
That threats of war return to peace in fine.

    Sir Thomas Urquhart, 'Seven chronograms, upon the
    treaty of pacification made at Barwick, in the year of
    God 1639'
    fb.217, p. 254

S0023 Saint Clement was a Roman born
To heaven may find the way. | Amen

    'Of S. Clement. No[vember] 23'
    a.30[56]

S0024 Saint Francis to his father had
In joys withouten end. | Amen

    'S. Francis. October. 4'
    a.30[43]

S0025 Saint George and for a maid a dragon slew
There is no dragon; pray God there be a maid.

    'An extemporary to a company of young and confident
    ladies, who . . . forced a . . . modest scholar to answer
    their unseasonable desires, upon the subject of St.
    George'
    [Crum s23, 'to save a maid']
    b.104, p. 19; Poetry Box x/19 (bis)('there's no St.
    George'); see also 'To save a maid . . .'.

S0026 Saint George for England here doth rest
Cuius contrarium venens est.

    'On the Duke of Buckingham'
    b.356, p. 242

S0027 Saint George's little knight by sea
You may shake off your crown.

    'An epigram' [temp. George II]
    c.154, p. 3

S0028 Saint James says ask and you shall never want,
Would God, King James to me the like would grant.

    Sir Thomas Urquhart, 'Owen's wish'
    fb.217, p. 118

S0029 Saint John a quondam statesman out of place,
He never used one drop of English spirit.

    fc.135

S0030 Saint John came poor, had neither gold nor money,
Betray'd poor John and made him lose his head.

    'The glory of the Trinity'
    c.187, p. 28

S0031 Saint John's is governed by a P.
The vice in President's room by statu[t]e is.

    'On the president [Richard Bailey] of St. John's
    [College, Oxford] being nonresident'
    [Crum s24]
    b.62, p. 78; b.200, p. 407

S0032 Saint Martha born of noble line
To live in bliss withouten end. | Amen

    'Of St. Martha. July. 29'
    a.30[17]

S0033 Saint Paul was call'd the Gentiles for to call,
With angel's food, in signs of wine and bread.

    'Paul's counsel to the Gentiles'
    c.187, p. 31

S0034 Saint Paul's deep bell from stately tow'r,
To sleep in Poet's Corner.

    S[amuel] Johnson(?), 'A posthumous work of . . .'
    Poetry Box v/124

S0035 Saint Paul's proclaims the solemn midnight hour,
His epitaph in th'ordinary account.

    'A parody on Gray's Elegy in a country churchyard'
    Poetry Box XII/24

S0036　Saint Peter's seat | Is in a sweat
Must hang, or run away, O hone! O hone!

'The mass priest's lamentation, for the strange
alteration begun in this nation . . . the tune is Poor
Shon . . . printed by Richard Burton in Smithfield'
[1641; Wing M948N]

b.101, p. 114

S0037　Saint Thomas' Day (among the festivals)
When Christian faith to such perfection came.

[Edward] Sparke, 'Poem 20th—on the feast of Saint
Thomas'

b.137, p. 47

S0038　Sally, as the chops you turn
Oh the thought is ecstasy.

'An anacreontic to pretty Sally at the Lamb 1732'

c.360/1, p. 111

S0039　Sally be a virtuous child
None better, happiness shall be found.

R[ichard] S[hackleton], 'Lines addressed to Sarah
Shackleton when a little girl'

File 13409

S0040　Sally Sally don't deny
That once lively youth Carlisle.

'To Lady Sarah Bunbury [later Lennox], in imitation
of Lydia dic per omnes' [Horace ode I, 8]

Poetry Box II/16

S0041　Sally Williams lost her pocket,
Out of two they have made three. | Yankee doodle,
doodle do with a yankey doodle dandy.

'June 1775 burlesque poetry a Yankee song'

Poetry Box IV/22

S0042　Salonian fountain and thou Andrian spring,
In Bacchus' trade and Pallas art thou found?

'Upon waters that intoxicate'

c.158, p. 118

S0043　Salute the last, and everlasting day
Deign at my hands this crown of prayer and praise.

[John Donne], '[Holy Sonnets.] La Corona [7]'
[Crum s37]

b.114, p. 161

S0044　Salvation to all that will is nigh
Immensity cloistered in thy dear tomb.

[John Donne], '[Holy sonnets. La Corona] 2d'
[Crum s38]

b.114, p. 154

S0045　Sam Whitbread the brewer for many a year
Inspire him good angels to drink his own porter.

c.340

S0046　S[and]f[ord] once so fam'd for riot
Kitty shines the livelong day.

'The inside of the mansion modernized S[and]f[or]d
Oct 10, 1760'

Poetry Box x/71 (2 versions)

S0047　Sandwich in Spain now, and the Duke in love,
Truth is, thou'st drawn her in effigy.

[Andrew Marvell?], 'Directions to a painter [Richard
Gibson]' [followed by 'Great prince! . . .']
[Crum s41; POAS I.68]

b.136, p. 17 (attr. Denham); fb.140, p. 65; c.81/2, no. 555

S0048　Sandy, my boy, indulge your itch!
Get rich; by any means, get rich!

'Sandy'

c.81/2, no. 555

S0049　Sangrado, of gold-headed cane mighty vain
But the meaning's reversed when the cane is in
your hand, Sir.

Dr. [ ] Peterson, 'By . . . on Dr. Farquharson's
gold-headed staff'

b.389 (mutilated; stanzas 1–130 complete)

S0050　Sarah Frowd | Don't laugh out loud
And liked by Mr. B[uller].

H[annah] More

c.341, at front

S0051　Sat were the gen'rals, and the vulgar band
And thence we hear the deity complain.

[Robert Cholmeley], 'The speeches of Ajax and
Ulysses for the armor of Achilles from the XIII book
of Ovid's Metamorphoses'

c.190, p. 202

S0052　Satan's the great Goliah, that so boasts
And I will meet Goliah, when he please.

'On David and Goliah'

b.118, p. 232

S0053　Satire ascend, with good intention fir'd,
Is worthy, wise, and right; and challenges applause.

'The fair thinker or reason asserted: in a dissection of
bigotry and devotion. A satire' [pr. 1740 (Foxon F35)]

c.161, p. 4

S0054 Satire, be bold, make some attempt in verse
Expect a place in Tutchin's Observator.

> [ ] Wright, 'Lydia sic, per omnes te Deos oro Sybarin cur properes amando'

b.90, p. 4

S0055 Satire I thank you for your declaration
But let their honor free go.

> Lady Jane Cavendish, 'A song in answer to your Lordship's satire'
> [Crum S135]

b.233, p. 7

S0056 Saucy swallow, cease to twitter
In my ears the name of F[i]tter!

> R[ichard] V[ernon] S[adleir], 'Recantation address to a swallow occasioned by the marriage of a gentleman mentioned by a former address' ['Gentle swallow, stay and twitter . . .']

c.106, p. 111

S0057 Savage and Wodehouse are more fitly joined
With cank'ring spleen, but each the other trust.

> [Sir Philip Wodehouse], 'Upon Savage whose crest is a bear's paw a coronet marrying Marg[are]t Wodehouse, whose crest is hands club with frappe fort'

b.131, p. 2 and back (var.) (after anagram 235)

S0058 Save, Lord, and help in my distress,
And scarce know where to fly.

> 'Psalm 12. Evening prayer'

c.264/1, p. 39

S0059 Save me O God and that with speed
A dwelling place shall find.

> [John Hopkins], 'The 27 psalm. Against anguish of mind' [verses from Psalm 69]
> [Crum S62]

a.3, fol. 105v

S0060 Save me, O God, immers'd in grief
Ev'n Abram's late posterity.

> 'Psalm 69 Evening prayer 13 day'

c.264/2, p. 36

S0061 Savior, canst thou love a traitor?
I will magnify Thy name.

> [Thomas Stevens?], 'A hymn'

c.259, p. 69

S0062 Savior I do feel thy merit
They are freely justified.

> 'Hymn 3d'

c.562, p. 3

S0063 Savior on dear Miss Flower,
For me, and dear Miss Jane.

> J[ohn] Newton, 'To Miss Flower on her birthday'
> File 10820

S0064 Say are they fled the instructors of our age
I'll e'er [?] [?] friends his name.

> [George Howard, 6th earl of Carlisle], 'On the departure of the Microcosmus politans'

c.197, p. 30

S0065 Say, bearers, whence that solemn lead,
Relaxes at Eliza's name.

> [Thomas Hull], 'On seeing the Marchioness of Tavistock's coffin brought ashore' [1768]

c.528/28

S0066 Say, bold licentious muse
And calm the relics of his grief, with hymns divine.

> [John] Norris, of Bemerton, 'The passion of Christ'

c.244, p. 58

S0067 Say but did you love so long? | In sooth I needs must blame you
Prest each moment such as you | A dozen dozen to disgrace.

> [Sir Tobie Matthew], 'An answer' [to 'Out upon it I have loved . . .']

b.213, p. 55

S0068 Say, canst thou, soul enchanting nymph refuse
And then to celebrate thy charms is fame!

> C[harles] B[urney], 'To Miss Nancy Gordon, Letmoir . . . Feb. 21. 1779'

c.38, p. 11

S0069 Say, Chloe, where must the swains stray,
You ne'er was so pressing before.

> 'A song'

c.591

S0070 Say, cruel fair then, would you that my flame
And for your sake do anything but die.

c.549, p. 41

S0071 Say, dearest object of my virgin love,
E'er riot in Euphrasia's heart again!

> [Charles Burney, the younger], 'An epistle from Euphrasia to Castalio'

c.38, p. 19

S0072 Say dearest Villiers poor departed friend
And equal rites perform to that which once was thee.

[Matthew] Prior, 'An ode inscribed to the memory of
the Honble. Col. George Villiers, drowned in the river
Piava, in the country of Friuli [1703] . . . wrote in
imitation of Horace ode 28. lib. 1'
[Crum s79]

fc.60, p. 25; c.111, p. 81 (var.)

S0073 Say Delia, say, from whence this downcast eye?
And peace, sweet peace, shall crown each day.

'Written on a journey from London to a convent'

Diggle Box: Poetry Box XI/39

S0074 Say Echo who this now religion grounded? |
Roundhead.
Then God keep our church and state from the
same men, | Amen.

'The echo'

fb.140, p. 5; see also 'Now echo . . .'.

S0075 Say fair maid in every feature
Cries God help thee crazy Jane.

M[atthew] G[regory] Lewis, 'Crazy Jane'

Poetry Box XII/2

S0076 Say fair one, didst thou never see
Be thou the Duck, and I the Drake.

[Stephen?] Duck, 'A simile, written by . . . who was in
love with Miss Drake'

c.83/1, no. 67

S0077 Say—foul-mouth'd cur why all this rage?
And blubber like a boy?

[William Popple, trans.], '[Horace ep]ode 6th. To
Caspius Severus, an orator and informer'

fc.104/2, p. 422

S0078 Say G. . . . , is an empty shade
Esteem superior far to love.

[Helen Craik], 'To Sir W. G. baronet—written upon
his sending me his profile some years ago'

c.375, p. 109

S0079 Say, gentle breeze, what music charms the plains
Soothe every sense, and ravish all the heart.

[Francis Fawkes], 'Bella singing'

fc.21, p. 7

S0080 Say, gentle herdsman, why so drear
And close in peace his lengthen'd day.

[Henry Erskine], 'Lines written on the tomb of two
lovers buried by the fall of a hill . . .'

c.142, p. 523

Say, gentle youth, that tread'st, untouch'd with care, S0081
Earth's flatt'ring dainties prove but sweet distress.

'The hermit's address to youth—written in the
gardens of the Vauxhall at Bath'

fc.132/1, p. 101

Say, gossip muse, who lov'st to prattle, S0082
To gather nosegays in the air.

[David] Garrick, 'Fribbleriad'

c.83/3, no. 735

Say heav'n-born muse, for only thou canst tell, S0083
Those things with them, are trifles out of fashion. |
Great . . .

[John Wilmot, 2nd earl of Rochester?], 'The
argument. How Tallboy, Killprick, Suckprick did
contend . . .'

b.105, p. 76 (incomplete)

Say, laurell'd leader of this little troop, S0084
Pray Heav'n to keep me from cold.

'1783'

Poetry Box XII/83

Say, lonely maid, with downcast eye— S0085
Whose guilt could force a pang from thine.

[John Walcot ('Peter Pindar')], 'Song. To Delia . . .
Ode 12. 1786'

c.355, p. 98

Say, love, for what good end design'd S0086
Should I disturb the rest.

'On the government of the passions'
[Crum s94]

c.83/3, no. 1045

Say love (tho' the world's not able S0087
All you see and love 's but color.

'The priture' [picture?]

b.213, p. 65a

Say lovely Lowther how didst thou conceal S0088
Treading those paths blessings do us attend.

Poetry Box VI/96

Say lovely maid, who dost thou mock so great a woe, S0089
And shine more bright a Venus dress'd in jet.

'On Miss D— T— of Cecil Street in the Strand
appear[ing] in mourning . . . Sunday March 31 1751
for . . . Frederick Prince of Wales'

c.360/3, no. 92

S0090   Say mighty love and teach my song,
And Cupid yokes the doves.

>> [Isaac] Watts, 'Few happy matches'
[Crum s96]

>> c.244, p. 311; c.349, fol. 1; c.362, p. 82

S0091   Say mourner say! Can naught they spirits cheer?
Heav'n spare thee long, a bright example here.

>> 'To the honble Miss S—ter on the lost of her brother'

>> c.83/1, no. 212

S0092   Say mournful muse! how o'er the weeping world
And meek-eyed pity sighs for virtue gone.

>> 'Elegy on the death of a young lady'

>> Poetry Box XII/116

S0093   Say much incensed maid! can anger swell
And Sylvia's bosom swell with naught but love.

>> [Samuel Bowden], 'To an ingenious young lady,
discomposed with passion, who grew calm on reading
some lines in Epictetus . . . Frome April 20. 1750'

>> Poetry Box IV/56

S0094   Say Muse, how court | And Elton sport
Tho' I do't without my smocks.

>> 'The unlucky accidents which befell Miss Elton at
shuttlecock. A tale by a lady'

>> c.233, p. 119

S0095   Say, my best friend, if aught you know,
In such a restless world as this.

>> 'No happiness below'

>> c.244, p. 124

S0096   Say not because no more you see
To grow in his own paradise not ours.

>> 'Upon the funeral of Mrs. Pawley's daughter'

>> b.4, fol. 50v

S0097   Say not that Charlotte wastes her days
And thus becomes more fair!

>> R[ichard] V[ernon] S[adleir], 'On Miss W——'

>> c.106, p. 88

S0098   Say not the marble's hard, not those seas cold
Quench my dim taper, and conclude my verse.

>> [George Daniel], 'To the memory of . . . the Lady
Alford [d. 1636], an elegy'

>> b.121, fol. 52

S0099   Say not you love unless you do
And will not lie unless with you.

>> [Sir Walter Raleigh?], 'A dialogue' [answered by 'You
say I lie . . .']
[Crum s103]

>> b.62, p. 16; b.205, fol. 98r

S0100   Say Puritan, [if] it came to pass
Who loves whores painted else all paint doth slight.

>> Ben Jonson(?), 'A Puritan his catechism'
[Crum s108]

>> b.200, p. 342 (incomplete?)

S0101   Say Sacharissa! Tell us fair distrest!
And curs'd the very hands that did the deed.

>> Robert Blair, 'To Sacharissa weeping'

>> fc.109.i/29

S0102   Say shall the man who knows her worth,
Secure since sovereign pow'r obtains.

>> 'On the soul'

>> c.83/2, no. 334

S0103   Say shall the past alone receive our praise?
By reason led, we gaze, admire, and love!

>> 'Verses in answer to some poetical aspersions on the
ladies of Chichester'

>> c.89, p. 70

S0104   Say, should the emblem of my love,
Were all as fair as you.

>> [Robert Cholmeley], 'To Chloe having been driven
from her a second time by his friends'

>> c.190, p. 167

S0105   Say, Sire we've crippled the poor people's backs,
Your Majesty must lend me H—ry's face.

>> [John Walcot ('Peter Pindar')], 'More money'

>> c.83/2, no. 310

S0106   Say, sov'reign queen of awful night,
And with consenting waves and mingl'd tides
                    forever flow the same.

>> Philip Wharton, 1st duke of Wharton, 'The fear of
death. An ode' [pr. 1739 (Foxon W379)]

>> c.468

S0107   Say sweet confessor, is not art
'Tis his alone to feel.

>> 'To Celia author of verses styled Self-examination in
Hants Chron[icle]'

>> c.89, p. 106

S0108   Say Sylvia whence these cares arise,
The will of heav'n is right, is best.

>> 'To a friend'

>> c.83/2, no. 382

SO109 Say thou almighty Pow'r who rul'st above—
Where morning stars together sing and angels
                                    shout for joy.

    M. K., 'The following verses were composed by . . .
    when in extreme pain'

c.139, p. 467

SO110 Say, Tunbridge, shall thy royal guest
And grav'd thy name shall flourish by his bride's.

    'Presented by the Lord Percival [later earl of Egmont]
    to the Princess Amelia, at Tunbridge Wells 1728'

c.221, p. 32

SO111 Say was my vision false or did I spy
In man's head, breast, limbs, liver, spleen, and gall.

    W[illiam] S[mith], 'Copy of lines by . . . to Sr. Wm.
    Dolben'

Smith Papers, folder 67

SO112 Say, what is beauty? Ah, declare,
What no expression can reveal.

    'Beauty . . . Albert'

c.83/3, no. 787

SO113 Say what is life, and wherefore was it given?
The fair result, the congregate of all.

    'On life and the proper employment of it'

c.83/3, no. 1044

SO114 Say what you will, 'tis not safe for the state,
'Twill us and ours bring to confusion.

    Sir John Strangways, 'Concerning the ending of our
    unhappy differences by peace . . . 23° Novembris 1646'

b.304, p. 72

SO115 Say whence the motions which I feel
Which waits the saints above.

    T[homas] S[tevens]

c.259, p. 140

SO116 Say, where were your politics, dear patriot Pitt,
To thrive in this world you must run with the Fox.

    John Lockman, 'A query, and its answer . . . March
    1757'

c.267/1, p. 216

SO117 Say, while you press, with growing love,
To make us fully bless'd.

    'To the mother'

c.83/3, no. 935

SO118 Say who are ye that with unhallow'd feet,
Shall find sweet peace and heaven-inspir'd rest.

    'The genius of the rocks. Addressing a party at Roach
    Abbey, a venerable ruin near Sheffield' [1794]

c.175, p. 91

SO119 Say, who art thou, grim upstart of the plain,
And break thy numbskull, as thou'd'st crack a
                                    louse.

    John Lockman, 'A colloquy: (not from Corderius,)
    between the hill and vale giants'

c.267/1, p. 251

SO120 Say, who art thou O specter pale
I only trace her by her sighs!

    [John Wolcot ('Peter Pindar')], 'Song'

Poetry Box V/93a

SO121 Say, will Maria much lov'd fair, excuse
A kind acceptance from Maria's hands.

    'To Miss ———'

c.391, p. 4

SO122 Say, will no white-rob'd son of light
Thus the Almighty spake; he spake and call'd me
                                    Truth.

    [William] Mason, 'Ode to truth'

fc.132/1, p. 151; c.140, p. 146

SO123 Say, ye Ephesian elders, since I came
With lingering looks they bid a sad adieu.

    Charles Atherton Allnutt, 'Saint Paul's address to the
    elders of Ephesus when about to depart from them 20
    Acts 17 ver.'

c.112, p. 33

SO124 Say ye, who through the round of fourscore years,
To bow the head, and say, 'Thy will be done'.

    [Anna Laetitia (Aikin)] Barbauld, 'Written by . . . in
    her 30th year'

Poetry Box V/72

SO125 Say you the nymph which I adore
I must still love you tho' I die.

c.374

SO126 Say youthful mourner, blooming maiden say,
A calm succeed thy troubled state of mind.

    'To Monimia'

c.83/1, no. 217

SO127 Says a reverend priest to his less reverend friend
That saints heretofore should be now cannonized.

    'On the French melting down the images of their
    saints to make artillery'

Diggle Box: Poetry Box XI/10, 69

SO128 Says a thief to Jack Ketch, who was tying the noose
Beg therefore to trouble you just with one line.

    'Epigram'

fc.130, p. 50

S0129 Says Apollo to Albion: my best thanks, (at last,)
That's in Rome; you're in London; O charming
mistake!

John Lockman, 'Apollo and Albion, whilst supposed to
be visiting the exhibition of pictures, sculptures &c in
the Society's great room, opposite Branford buildings,
in the Strand . . . April 1761'

c.267/1, p. 272

S0130 Says Apollo to Bacchus: for a frolic let's fly
They open'd the same, and enchanted mankind.

John Lockman, 'Apollo and Bacchus, in Vauxhall
Gardens . . . 1740'

c.267/1, p. 283; c.268 (first part), p. 42; c.360/1, p. 163

S0131 Says Beauty to Fashion, as they set at the toilette
And even your ladyship, die an old maid.

'Beauty and fashion a repartee'

c.130, p. 27

S0132 Says Celia to a rev'rend dean,
They cannot find a priest!

'Celia and Swift'

c.81/1, no. 440; c.391, p. 86

S0133 Says Dick to his comrade—'Pray, Tom, do you
know

Till the French are prepared and quite ready to
fight us.

'Epigram—on Lord Moira's expedition'

c.344

S0134 Says Dicky to Sal, how happens it thus
For it mostly happens all about you.

'Epigram. The retort'

c.546, p. 35

S0135 Says Dolly to Nell, why sure the girl's mad
In return for my true love to him.

'Epigram'

c.344

S0136 Says fierce Maloch to Satan: so loud Henley roars,
His grim phiz would outbronze all the fiends here
in Hell.

John Lockman, 'The orator' [John Henley]

c.267/1, p. 175; c.268 (first part), p. 7

S0137 Says Giles my wife and I are two
She's one, and you're a cipher.

'Epigram'

Diggle Box: Poetry Box XI/2, 3, 69

S0138 Says Habbakuk, 'The walls shall cry
And future Greens shall laud the name of West.

[Thomas Morell], 'On seeing Preston Church pewed
with the timber purchased by James West esqu from
the Jubilee Booth at Stratford'

c.395, p. 144

S0139 Says Heraclitus: woe to England now!
As evident, as—two and two make eight.

John Lockman, 'After the sudden changes, 11 of July
1766. Heraclitus, and Democritus, and Momus'

c.267/1, p. 385

S0140 Says His Grace to Will Green whom he found at
his stall
The squire will outpoll us, and peach you again.

'Death and the cobbler: being a full and true account
of the late conference between a meager D[eath] and
Will Green cordwainer of St. James Westminster' [on
Thomas Osborne, marquis of Carmarthen and duke
of Leeds]
[POAS V.463]

fb.68, p. 41

S0141 Says Hodge my wife in an ill-fated hour
And hope ere long 'twill bear for me such fruit.

c.546, p. 30

S0142 Says kind Mrs. Thrale my dear tell me now
In heroics I'll answer—why let 'em!

[Frances] B[urney] d'Arblay], 'A letter from Miss B. to
her sister Mrs. B[urney]'

c.486, fol. 3v

S0143 Says lovely Laura frank and free
This is true philosophy.

'A bagatelle. True philosophy'

c.81/1, no. 229

S0144 Says my Lord to the vicar of Tud—h—m one day,
Keeps close to the dunghill, and follows the stink.

'The honest vicar of T—d—h—m'

Poetry Box IV/36

S0145 Says my uncle I pray you discover
And so I shall lose Molly Mog.

[John Gay], 'Molly Mog' [pr. 1726 (Foxon G59)]
[Crum S128]

fc.61, p. 63; Accession 97.7.40

S0146 Says Nan one day to her husband Dick
Or you'd been somewhere else by this time.

'Epigram'

c.81/1, no. 425

S0147 Says 1 to 2, I'll lay you—3
Four letters make each name.

    Frederick Corfield

c.381/2

S0148 Says Peter to Paul, I will have his body
For he ever robb'd Peter to pay his dear Paul.

    'On application for the body of the Earl of Chatham'

c.361

S0149 Says Phyl to Damon, pray explain
Were you transported o'er the sea?

    'The reply'

c.546

S0150 Says Quibus to Lockman; (they both were in
                 France),
I'm the first of my race; and of thine thou'rt the
                 last.

    John Lockman, 'A dialogue . . . Oct. 1741'

c.267/1, p. 92

S0151 Says Richard to Thomas (and seem'd half afraid)
And ere night had inform'd her what Thomas had
                 said.

    [William Shenstone], 'The progress of advice. A
    common case' [Dodsley Collection]

c.487, p. 133

S0152 Says Richard to Tim I can't think what you're at,
For the reason I drink is to make my head swim.

    'Epigram'

c.115

S0153 Says Roger to his wife, my dear!
Surpriz'd! pray ha'n't you learn'd to swim?

    'Epigram'

c.326, p. 183

S0154 Says Sharper to Cornus, I'll set you amain
I fancy this way, you your fortune might make.

c.546, p. 33

S0155 Says the mother: ah! (Kitty)—these frolics, I said,
Sure of liars, the L. Almanac(?) folks are the worst.

    John Lockman, 'Kitty, and her mamma: on the new
    style, 14 Sept. 1752'

c.267/1, p. 267

S0156 Says the pert Gallic cock, clapping strongly his
                 wings;
Give me once to range, and I'll soon stop your
                 crowing.

    John Lockman, 'The British lion and the Gallic
    cock . . . Aug. 1756'

c.267/1, p. 211; c.267/3, p. 82

S0157 Says truth to falsehood: what's thy aim
A more conspicuous mark.

    John Lockman, 'On the [?] darted at a very worthy
    baronet . . . 5th Jany. 1768'

c.267/4, p. 396

S0158 Says Watkin to Colin I thought my lord Gower
Pray where's the broad bottom? Says Colin, My
                 a[s]s.

    'Epigram'
    [Crum s134, 'to Cotton']

c.81/1, no. 485

S0159 Scandal a busy fiend in truth's disguise
Sweetness to soothe the pain and smiles to cure.

Poetry Box IV/89

S0160 Scarce had Aurora harbinger of day
Accept the offering which it brings to you.

    [Henry] Neville(?), 'An ep[ithalamium] . . . finis
    Mr. Nevill'

c.548

S0161 Scarce had the tender hand of time
Which heav'n first breath'd into her infant breast.

    Bryan Edwards, 'On the death of a very young lady'

Poetry Box XII/11

S0162 Scarce hush'd the sigh, scarce dried the ling'ring
                 tear
'Tis friendship's sigh, and gentle beauty's tear.

    [Richard Brinsley Butler Sheridan]

Diggle Box: Poetry Box XI/55

S0163 Scarce patient now, the Virgin tries
I die because I live. | Aspiring &c.

    'A hymn of the Holy Mother Teresa . . .' [translated]

b.259, p. 35

S0164 Scarce worth an epitaph from Tate or Quarles
Two such to form a R—t and a G[eorge].

    'On the finding and opening the coffins of Charles 1st
    and Henry 8th'

c.546

S0165 Scarce would an age suffice to tell
The love of nature and of art.

> W[illiam] W[arren] Porter, 'Lines by . . . sent to a
> lady with a drawing of a gentleman's face well known
> to each party'
>
> c.83/4, no. 2026

S0166 Scenes of my youth ye once were dear,
I must remember such things were.

> 'Scenes of my youth by Mr. ———'
>
> c.83/2, no. 297

S0167 Schools are the nurs'ries of illustrious arts
No rest, no peace, no ease he can procure.

> J[ohn] [Robinson], 'Occidit miseros crambe repetita
> magistros'
>
> c.370, fol. 79

S0168 Science! thou fair effusive ray
And sit at peace with thee.

> [Mark Akenside], 'A hymn to science'
>
> c.157, p. 61

S0169 Science, thou friend, and hand-maid unto her,
Perfect my duty here; my happiness above.

> 'Knowledge'
>
> fc.54, p. 83

S0170 Scorn popular applause 'tis but a blast
Neither from judgment springs nor long doth last.

> [John Hobart]
>
> b.108, fol. 4

S0171 Scotland and England now's to be
The cursed revolution.

> 'Upon the union and act of settlement'
>
> fc.58, p. 137

S0172 Scotland thy weather's like a modish wife
And when she can no longer scold—she cries.

> [Aaron Hill], 'Epigram'
>
> c.113/34

S0173 Scots are no rebels who like conquerors
Being almost now triumph'd on twice by bastards.

> [Sir Thomas Urquhart], 'That the Scots covenanters'
> entering so boldly into England under the conduct of
> General Leslie is a reproach to the English nation'
>
> fb.217, p. 503; see also next.

S0174 Scots are no rebels, why? th'are conquerors;
Now bastard Leslie, or else your own knavery.

> 'The Scottish invasion. 1640'
> [Crum S159]
>
> b.54, p. 883; see also previous.

S0175 Sea nymphs hourly ring his knell,
Hark now I hear them ding dong bell.

> [William Shakespeare], 'Chorus [3, with musical score
> for tenor, from Purcell's The tempest]'
>
> Music MS. 534

S0176 Seal up the book, all vision's at an end
His works are the apocalypse of verse.

> 'On the death of poet Pope 1744'
>
> c.360/2, no. 266

S0177 Search all the earth, you ev'rywhere shall see
To murder mortals, by a slipp'ry snare.

> 'The devil'
>
> c.189, p. 43

S0178 Search, and consult dark registers of old,
And praise His holy name forevermore.

> J[ohn] [Robinson], 'On the Powder Plot, November
> the 5th 1605'
>
> c.370, fol. 75v

S0179 Search the world o'er, and ev'ry distant state,
Where flowing Isis waves her curling stream.

> P[eter] Roussignac, 'Insects' [written for the Lent
> Probation at the Merchant Taylor's School, 1700]
> [Crum S165]
>
> Poetry Box VI/78

S0180 Search thou, O Lord, my heart at ground,
To sing, and see the Trinity.

> 'A holy desire'
>
> c.187, p. 34

S0181 Searching the garden for the richest fruit,
An humble tribute, Boston! paid to you.

> John Lockman, 'To the right honorable Lady Boston:
> with a large pineapple . . . Oct. 1761'
>
> c.267/1, p. 308

S0182 Seas circle th'earth: from th'earth all rivers burst;
Lest waters hunger: and the dry land thirst.

> Sir Thomas Urquhart, 'Of sea, and land'
>
> fb.217, p. 306

S0183 Seated beneath a spreading tree,
And so all's well again.

> W[illiam] A[liffe], 'A song by the same hand'
>
> fb.207/4, p. 24

S0184 Seated on Parnassus Hill,
Vive Bon'cini! Shouts proclaim.

> John Lockman, 'Seeing Seignor Bon[on]cini, in the
> character of Merope king of Egypt, in the opera of Il
> fetente . . . Feb. 1746/7'
>
> c.267/1, p. 37

S0185 Seats of my childhood! yon low roofs impart
That sweet employment to the virtuous mind.

[Edward Hamley], 'Sonnet'

c.142, p. 149

S0186 Secluded from domestic strife,
Jack finds his wife a perfect beauty.

'The double transformation—a tale'

c.83/3, no. 996

S0187 Secret shall be her ever dearest name
Gently enwove the name and own'd the conq'ring
maid!

Sir William Young, 'An acrostic by [on Sally Tagg]
1746' [see also 'Music has charms to soothe the lover's
breast . . .']

File 16592; see also previous.

S0188 Secure in Christ I dwell
And see Him face to face.

'Hymn 54th'

c.562, p. 64

S0189 Secur'd by mounds of everlas[ting] [torn]
Shows where my labors ended where begun.

[Edmund Burke]

fc.46/4

S0190 Sedition [?] lies and tyranny
Speak first [?] and he's done.

'Argyll's epitaph'
Poetry Box VIII/11

S0191 Seduc'd by winning airs and wiles,
And kindly love for love return'd.

'The linnet and the goldfinches, to a jilt. From
Sentimental fables'

c.83/1, no. 131

S0192 See a new progeny descends
My pride shall be to sing them.

[Sir Charles Hanbury Williams], '1742 a new ode to a
great number of great men' [i.e., the ministry which
succeeded Walpole's, 1742]
[Crum S177]

fc.135 (attr. [Robert] Nugent); Poetry Box XIV/196

S0193 See a poor knight, a poorer squire,
One lame, and t'other blind.

John Lockman, 'Sir John Fielding and Mr. John
Lockman, walking arm in arm, in the royal
apartments, St. James's'

c.267/4, p. 396

S0194 See Albion see! Thy monarch comes,
To have made all Europe friends and given France
a law.

'An ode on King William's public entry after the peace
at Ryswick' [November 1697]

fb.207/2, p. 39

S0195 See all things here their old appearance show
And while the old one nods the new one sleeps.

'[Several copies of verses spoken at Westminster
School on the anniversary of the defeat of the Spanish
Armada] 3'

fc.24, p. 71; c.233, p. 47 ('Ad [John] Friend M. D.')

S0196 See, amongst you venal throng,
Perjur'd souls for slaves were made.

'Vice versa' [to 'See the legal member comes . . .']

fc.85, fol. 28

S0197 See Aurora quit her bed
Forgive me heaven and seal me thine.

H[annah] More, 'The recluse penitant'

c.341, p. 97

S0198 See Austria's daughter, Gallia's queen,
Amidst this sad captivity!

'Captivity[.] Supposed to be sung by the unfortunate
queen of France confined in Temple'

c.83/2, no. 376

S0199 See Belinda! Fair as morning,
Kings might envy such a prize.

John Lockman, 'Belinda. Writ to a favorite minuet of
Mr. Dupuy's . . . Jany 1758'

c.267/2, p. 109

S0200 See black despair with scowling brow,
And wipe the tear from sorrow's eye.

'Sonnet to patience'

c.83/3, no. 988

S0201 See, bright Apollo, and the nine,
Their fainter beams, and less'ning die.

[John Lockman], 'An ode for St. Cecilia's Day. Set by
Mr. Boyce composer to His Majesty'

c.268 (first part), p. 125

S0202 See! charming Sylvia, with compassion, see!
Hurl all your thunder at my breast or waft me to
my joy.

'To charming Sylvia'
Poetry Box VII/25

S0203 See, Clelia! In this shatter'd glass,
Forever lost and past recalling.

Abraham Oakes, 'To Clelia: on her breaking a
drinking glass'

c.50, p. 5; see also 'See sister . . .'.

S0204 See C. . . . y rise! With horrid grin,
For the worm rankles there, which never will die.

J[ames] Northcote(?), 'On a recent motion in the
Royal Academy, to expel a late publication . . . Feby
11th 1794'

File 11119

S0205 See fam'd Apollo, and the nine,
And draw down blessings from the skies.

John Lockman, 'Love and music: a Cecilian ode; in
two acts, writ for the Academy of Music, held in the
Apollo, Devil Tavern, Temple bar . . . anno 1733' [pr.
1739 (Foxon L216)]
[Crum S188]

c.267/2, p. 254

S0206 See friends, how sweetly temperance looks and
smiles,
And soothe the conscience, as we pass along.

'On temperance'

c.91, p. 308

S0207 See from his wat'ry tropic how the sun
Born to our flesh, into his spirit one.

'Upon the nativity of our Savior and sacrament then
received'

Poetry Box v/106

S0208 See! from the giddy crowd a sinner flies
And ev'n in troubles give me rest.

'Words fitted to be sung w[ith] Dr. Pepusch's cantata
called See from the silent groves'

c.167, p. 21

S0209 See Gawkee and Pitt how they sue for a place
That shall hang the vile Duke if he leaves the good
K[ing].

Poetry Box x/116

S0210 See generous Marlb[orough] nobly mourn
Find comfort in th'embraces of her son.

[Horace Walpole, 4th earl of Orford], 'D[uchess] of
Marlborough' [d. 1761]
[Crum S191]

c.157, p. 67

S0211 See gentle reader, see in me
For every cup of water given.

[Phanuel Bacon], 'Inscription for a spring at Mr. Lee's
in the Isle of Wight, catched in a marble cistern and
flowing through an arched drain underground to his
canals'

c.237, fol. 86 [i.e., 106]

S0212 See here all hale [pale?] and dead she lies
Fly nuptial bliss and chaste desires.

'On Sarah wife of John Pring'

c.546

S0213 See here the fair and humble Lucifer
Can speak us better life when murder'd dead.

[Edward] Sparke, 'Poem 28th—on St John Baptist'
[Crum S201]

b.137, p. 60

S0214 See here! When either way you turn your eye,
I, and my flock, with pleasure meet our Lord!

'A contemplative walk in a churchyard'

Poetry Box XII/80

S0215 See here, who does in one both beauties
comprimize [sic]:
Of mind and body she Castabella is.

[Sir Philip Wodehouse], 'Upon my niece . . . Elizabeth
Castle'

b.131, back (no. 36)

S0216 See here's the bride, and here's the tree,
The woman's worse drive on the cart.

'On a man whose choice was to be hanged or married'

c.356

S0217 See him returning to his turnip soil
The grin of monkey, from the laugh of man.

'Pasquin, the 2d. July the 7th. 1716'

c.570/1, p. 164

S0218 See how a crafty vile projector picks
And daily courts the silly dame for more.

'The projector'

c.570/4, p. 106

S0219 See how he scuds and treads with nimble pace
And roast the world as thou didst meat below.

'A turnspit dog'

c.172, p. 37

S0220   See how my goddess, from her well-stor'd quiver
Pines, languishes, and now is dead, ere he knew
what ail'd.

    [George Daniel]

b.121, fol. 42v

S0221   See! how the globe heavy with convulsive throes!
He'll raise thy ruin'd frame more beauteous than
before.

    [Henry] Needler, 'On the prodigies at Christ's birth'

c.244, p. 554

S0222   See how the hills stand thick with snow!
'Tis only varied harmony.

    'The seasons of life'

c.83/3, no. 930

S0223   See how the Lord of mercy spreads
In agony and shame.

    P[hilip] Doddridge, 'Christ's tenderness to sinners
and his readiness to receive them illustrated from
Math: XXIII 37, 38'

c.493, p. 50

S0224   See how the panes, where'er we go
Alone can read you there.

    'Written on a glass window at an inn'

fc.51, p. 66

S0225   See how the rainbow in the sky
The pill our taste: man God as well.

    [William Strode], 'On justification'
    [Crum s215]

b.200, p. 229

S0226   See how the virgin rose with modest eyes
A thousand nymphs, with grief, who thousand
swains admired.

    George Montagu, 'The rose from Tasso'

fc.135, p. 16

S0227   See! how this beaten road is throng'd
Climb'd only by the penitent.

    'The broad way'

c.487, p. 118

S0228   See, how those flocks beneath us rush so fast
And robb'd of genial grass, they browse on weed.

    Spence Papers, folder 148

S0229   See how white the hills with snow!
Force enough—for an excuse.

    [William Popple, trans.], '[Horace] book 1st. ode 9th.
To Thaliarchus'

fc.104/2, p. 28

S0230   See! How yon phantom wondrous forms assumes
And with a dash, expunge it from the scene.

    [John Lockman], 'The following piece was writ in
1732 . . . The pantomimes—a rhapsody'

c.268 (first part), p. 157

S0231   See, how yon lilies bend their heads,
Confess'd her claim, and his.

    [Thomas Morell], 'On the death of Master Maddox,
only son to the Bp of Worcester'

c.395, p. 118

S0232   See Hymen the gay bridegroom lead!
Till Jove can grant no more.

    John Lockman, 'On the marriage of Sir Bourchier
Wrey, bart. With Miss Thresher'

c.267/2, p. 226

S0233   See innocence with various cares distress'd,
They walk contented through the vale of grief.

    'Cruelty frequently practiced on strangers'

c.83/1, no. 20

S0234   See Lockman, with unwearied zeal,
And the kind scaffoldings thrown down.

    John Lockman, 'Modern gratitude, or the free British
fishery . . . Feb. 1757'

c.267/1, p. 216

S0235   See my own Eden, dress'd in verdant charms!
And image Pindus, rising in a dream.

    John Lockman, 'The goddess of the spring, to the
muses: on the opening of Vauxhall Gardens . . . May
1755'

c.267/1, p. 151

S0236   See Nancy comes, like Beauty's queen,
And draw admirers from the sky.

    [Charles Burney, the younger], '. . . The subsequent
ode' [to Nancy Gordon. See 'Say, canst thou . . .']

c.38, p. 12

S0237   See! Now, my fair, the goddess lies!
As much as Juno does in charms so thee.

    'On the mount of a fan in which Jupiter was described
embracing of Juno'

c.233, p. 92

S0238   See O see | How every tree
When the mind has lost all measure.

b.213, p. 127

S0239   See pale submissive Cowley bend,
And hope her sovereign long to know.

> M. Dickinson, 'Verses written by . . . on the King's illness'
>
> c.391

S0240   See Rome discover'd, Italy made plain,
That love the truth, and look for Babel's fall.

> [William Lithgow], 'A brief poetical description of his whole travels in ten parts'
>
> c.158, p. 327

S0241   See royal Charlotte come!
With lasting peace.

> John Lockman, 'A loyal chorus, for all the good people of this land. Sung in Vauxhall Gardens by Mr. Low, accompanied by many gentlemen of the King's Chapel, the boys &c.'
>
> c.267/2, p. 50

S0242   See sage Minerva smile,
No man by talents rare | Lost to mankind!

> John Lockman, 'Anniversary ballad for the meeting of the Society of Arts, Manufacture, and Commerce . . . 6 March 1759 . . . the tune, God save our noble King &c.'
>
> c.267/2, p. 82

S0243   See St. Lucas' distant isle
Trust and serve him all my days.

> 'Sorrows of Yambo'
>
> c.91, p. 332

S0244   See Sally how those roses bloom
Receiv'd a third and turn'd out me.

> [Robert Cholmeley], 'To Miss Sally Newby [Kewby?] after having been forsaken by her first lover received a second, but soon turned him off, and accepted a third—supposed to have been writ by the second'
>
> c.190, p. 155

S0245   See, see, Chloris, my Chloris, comes in yonder bark,
The earth expects thee for a greeting kiss.

> [Henry Hughes], 'The nymph's return'
>
> fb.107, p. 66

S0246   See, see fair nymph, if you can find,
Who art so much more bright than he.

> 'Another by the same hand' [as 'Grim death . . .']
>
> fb.142, p. 56

S0247   See, see! I am now what I was not before
If oft be to be wondered at, 'tis she.

> 'One whose mistress charging him that he had not, as other lovers in his courtships presented her with any poetry he sat down and taking his pen said he would amend that neglect and hastily wrote as followeth'
>
> b.104, p. 16

S0248   See! See! My Seraphina comes:
As she whom Strephon loves.

> [Edward Worlidge?], 'Song'
>
> c.464, end

S0249   See sinful soul, thy Savior's suff'rings see
One cleansing drop with grace to sin no more.

> [Isaac Blackwell?], 'An anthem for Good Friday' [Crum s240]
>
> b.155, p. 62

S0250   See sister in this shatter'd glass,
Forever lost, and past recalling.

> [Abraham Oakes], 'To a young lady on her breaking a glass'
>
> c.115; c.578, p. 59; c.50, p. 163; see also 'See, Clelia! . . .'.

S0251   See Strafford's fate, who therefore stood awry
Like Granta [Grantham?]'s steeple, 'cause he was too high.

> [John Cleveland?]
>
> b.93, p. 2

S0252   See the buildings, which when my mistress laid in
When she abed with Mars by all the gods were seen.

> [James I, on the death of Queen Anne, 1619] [cf. Crum s245]
>
> fb.69, p. 236 (incomplete?)

S0253   See the chariot attend here of love
Oh so sweet is she.

> [Ben Jonson]
>
> b.197, p. 186

S0254   See the close-fisted knight in form display,
With his friends Osborne and Squire Walsingham.

> 'On the fable of the ass in the lion's skin'
>
> c.570/3, p. 121

S0255   See the grand emblem of Messiah rise
He was declar'd, the only son of God.

> 'The passion flower'
>
> c.91, p. 57

S0256 See! The great leader L—dl—w comes!
So down, my brave boys, with them, down!

R[ichard] V[ernon] S[adleir], 'An election eulogy
found among the papers of an ancient widow and set
to music by a Spanish transposer'

c.106, p. 109

S0257 See the leaves around us falling,
Bears those leaves that never fade.

'The fall of the leaf'

c.83/2, no. 367; c.83/3, no. 826; c.139, p. 401

S0258 See, the legal member comes!
Of those who dread no tyrant power.

'Worcester[.] The voters provided a chair, with a
triumphal arch . . . a b[and] of mus[ic] play[ed] a tune
to the following song'

fc.85, fol. 28

S0259 See the lov'd matron, whose unclouded brow
Sweet remembrance of thy friend!

R[ichard] V[ernon] S[adleir], 'A trio.—Mrs. S . . .
Mrs. Hayley . . . Mademoiselle Catan Tanket'

c.106, p. 37

S0260 See the old dragon from his throne
Shall lay their laurels at thy feet.

P[hilip] Doddridge, 'The victory of the saints over the
devil by the blood of the lamb from Rev. XII 11'

c.493, p. 46

S0261 See the seraphic spirit soaring high
Such was the woman—can the saint be more?

'On the death of Mrs. E. Blount. Lond[on]
Magaz[ine] March 1754'

c.157, p. 49

S0262 See the sky glows! how fierce the beams of noon,
Fame and the summer morn shall gild his passage
there.

A[nna] Seward, 'Written July 22, 1782. And addressed
to a young gentleman'

Poetry Box v/51

S0263 See the source of all light darts his rays from above,
For he lays up a treasure in heaven.

'On the Society of Universal Goodwill dispensing
their charities last year to 199 persons in distress . . .
Decr. 2nd. 1788'

c.94

S0264 See the star, that leads the day,
Who thy sacred spirit love.

[Thomas Parnell], 'Hymn to the morning'

c.83/2, no. 511

See the strange fate of seditious preachers and
writers
Whilst Burnet harangues 'em from Salisbury
steeple. S0265

Dr. [ ] Barker, 'Epigramma Sam. Wesley M. [i.e., A.?]
M. . . . Englished'

c.229/1, fol. 52v

See the welcome fleet appears S0266
Has vouchsaf'd to hear our prayer.

'A song &c.'

c.570/2, p. 53

See the wild waste of all-devouring years! S0267
And prais'd, unenvied, by the muse he loved.

[Alexander Pope], 'Verses occasioned by Mr. Addison's
treatise of medals'
[Crum s248]

fc.61, p. 123, p. 125; c.160, fol. 77

See there he goes into the nation's joy S0268
May James then reign in peace and long I pray.

'The procession to Hanover, July 1716'

fc.58, p. 70

See this little mistress here, S0269
No sure she's Pope Innocent or none.

'K. James 1st came in his progress to Sir [William]
Pope's house Kt. when his lady [Elizabeth] was lately
delivered of a daughter [Anne] . . .'
[Crum s250]

fb.143, p. 2

See Thyrsis see! beneath yon spreading thorn S0270
Coos in her face and smiles at all her tears.

[Susanna (Carroll)] Centlivre, 'A pastoral to the
honored memory of Mr. [Nicholas] Rowe'

fc.60, p. 1

See what is written on the outward skin, S0271
Where nature writes her best they make a blot.

c.115

See where Aurora does with brightness rise, S0272
I'll shake my icy chains, and in a torrent flow.

[Mrs. Christian Kerr], 'To a young lady upon her
birthday Ap[ri]l 4 1700 addressed by her lover'

c.102, p. 112

See, where love advances unreprov'd, S0273
Of husband, parent, children, brother, friend.

'Marriage'

c.250

S0274 See where Phyllis, ever sprightly,
Be theirs the world, so I've her heart.

> John Lockman, 'Phyllis: writ to a favorite minuet by
> Mr. James Hugford junior . . . Jny 1759'
>
> c.267/2, p. 106

S0275 See! where she lies, in baleful weeds array'd,
And see! He wafts thee to eternal rest

> John Lockman, 'Looking at his daughter Molly, an
> infant, in her coffin . . . 1731'
>
> c.267/1, p. 256; c.268 (first part), p. 28

S0276 See where she sits in mourning robes array'd
And never wish to be at ease again.

> Poetry Box VI/38

S0277 See where the falling day
They're sisters all | And all deceive.

> [Anna Laetitia (Aikin) Barbauld], 'Tomorrow'
>
> Diggle Box: Poetry Box XI/20

S0278 See whom late yours fears [sic] decreed
Were, what most with Horace took.

> [William Popple, trans.], '[Horace] book 3rd. ode
> 14th. To the Roman people on the return of Augustus
> from Spain'
>
> fc.104/2, p. 256

S0279 See ye not where our harps are hung
To Jacob's gracious God and sacred Sion's praise!

> [Thomas Hull], 'Hymn 3d, from the 137th psalm'
>
> c.528/11–12

S0280 See ye who make your boasts
Who th'heav'n and earth did make and frame.

> 'Psalm 134'
>
> c.264/3, p. 81

S0281 See yon gilt coach! how things revers'd we find!
Why good for ill, and ill for good, bestow?

> John Lockman, 'Mutatis mutandis . . . Feb. 1758'
>
> c.267/1, p. 268

S0282 See yonder eaglet swift ascend,
Acquire, if possible, his fame.

> John Lockman, 'To the honorable Master Percy
> Seward, son to His Excellency, the Lord Lieutenant of
> Ireland. A simile'
>
> c.267/1, p. 319

S0283 See yonder storms subvert the troubled waves,
Because not crusht by bigger drops of rain.

> J. W., 'The vanity of man in the similitude of a bubble'
>
> c.258

S0284 See yonder sun proclaims approaching night,
Their stings we suffer, yet their justice own.

> 'An ode'
>
> c.83/2, no. 584

S0285 Seeing a scrivener's shop, a country clown
Since you have sold them all except your own.

> Poetry Box XIV/169 (2 copies; alternate last line: 'For all
> are sold I see, excepting one')

S0286 Seeing Adam, we the noblest man esteem;
We are the nobler, and to God the nearer.

> Sir Thomas Urquhart, 'Against the tenet of some that
> the younger brother is the gentlest man'
>
> fb.217, p. 138

S0287 Seeing all of the elements do scarce refresh
(As best part is) a monster he must be.

> Sir Thomas Urquhart, 'Of man pantophagus a
> paradox'
>
> fb.217, p. 331

S0288 Seeing at your birth you wept to testify
Your sorrow, should not you be glad to die.

> Sir Thomas Urquhart, 'To an old diseased man who
> was loath to depart from this world'
>
> fb.217, p. 111

S0289 Seeing by the multitude of these, offend
That vice may be suppressed and virtue flourish.

> [Sir Thomas Urquhart], 'How necessary a thing the
> administration of justice is for the government of a
> commonwealth'
>
> fb.217, p. 509

S0290 Seeing crosses cannot be evited, I'll
Till all her rage be spent sustain the fight.

> [Sir Thomas Urquhart], 'The firm and determinate
> resolution of a courageous spirit in the deepest
> calamities inflicted by sinister fate'
>
> fb.217, p. 531

S0291 Seeing ev'ry man's a liar, it is plain,
He says, you lie, who says, you are a man.

> Sir Thomas Urquhart, 'To one who cited the passage
> of Paul to the Romans, and of the king and prophet
> David'
>
> fb.217, p. 109

S0292 Seeing God sees ev'ry one,
Each where latent.

> Sir Thomas Urquhart, 'Of the allseeing, and invisible
> God'
>
> fb.217, p. 136

S0293 Seeing he who after weariness, but hath
Be though so sour, its image being so sweet.

> Sir Thomas Urquhart, 'That we need not be
> affrighted at the terrors of death'
>
> fb.217, p. 91

S0294 Seeing health, and riches make you haughty Dick:
You never will be well, till you be sick.

> Sir Thomas Urquhart, 'To a proud man whose name
> was Richard'
>
> fb.217, p. 167

S0295 Seeing Iol' and Omphale by a strange
With which we're tied to imitate our betters.

> [Sir Thomas Urquhart], 'Why a brace of gallant
> gentlemen who in former occasions had given evident
> testimonies of unfeigned valor inveigled by the
> charming beauty of two incomparable ladies resolvedly
> surceased from . . . military adventures . . .'
>
> fb.217, p. 505

S0296 Seeing man's first matter's nothing: his form, but
But think upon my end, and my efficient.

> Sir Thomas Urquhart, 'Of the four several causes of
> mankind'
>
> fb.217, p. 165

S0297 Seeing nature entered me on this condition
To die being th'end of all you ought to do.

> [Sir Thomas Urquhart], 'A courageous resolution'
>
> fb.217, p. 496

S0298 Seeing none condignly can his praise set forth
When he shall reign in everlasting glory.

> Sir Thomas Urquhart, 'On the Archbishop of [crossed
> out]'
>
> fb.217, p. 40

S0299 Seeing of the golden Ind the sov'reign is
It is no order: but a prophesy.

> Sir Thomas Urquhart, 'El tuson d'or'
>
> fb.217, p. 55

S0300 Seeing of this county you're the only pearl
'Tis fitting you be threaded by an earl.

> Sir Thomas Urquhart, 'To a young, and very proper
> gentlewoman whom an earl was enamored with'
>
> fb.217, p. 312

S0301 Seeing of your breasts, and lips the fruits I reap:
And be debarr'd from ent'ring in the land.

> Sir Thomas Urquhart, 'To a comely gentlewoman,
> who was prodigal of all the parts of her body: save
> only the center of love's fruition'
>
> fb.217, p. 200

S0302 Seeing steel out of the hardest flint for the fire
[?]er than heat and softer than the flint.

> [Sir Thomas Urquhart], 'Cleander here expresseth her
> wonder how her master hath been able so long to
> assist [?]ing of his answer(?)'
>
> fb.217, p. 387

S0303 Seeing that to me, Jehovah, you deny
The pow'r to live: grant me the will to die.

> Sir Thomas Urquhart, 'The spiritual ejaculation of a
> heavily diseased man upon his deathbed'
>
> fb.217, p. 68

S0304 Seeing use makes brass to shine, and wealth unus'd
Is to no use, should usurers b'accused?

> Sir Thomas Urquhart, 'That none ought for usury, to
> be brought under the compass of the law. A paradox'
>
> fb.217, p. 71

S0305 Seeing venery is sold, as oft as wine,
Why have not stews, as well as inns a sign?

> Sir Thomas Urquhart, 'Of Venus, and Bacchus'
>
> fb.217, p. 350

S0306 Seeing we aim both at heav'nly knowledge Rafe
Let me use Jacob's ladder: you, his staff.

> Sir Thomas Urquhart, 'To the astronomer Rodolphus'
>
> fb.217, p. 202

S0307 Seeing when I kiss'd you, you kiss'd me, bestow
Receive your own again, or give me mine.

> Sir Thomas Urquhart, 'The speeches of a certain
> cavalier, to a proper young gentlewoman, whose lips
> he had very affectionately savored'
>
> fb.217, p. 320

S0308 Seeing you see not your eyes, nor know your mind,
Why are you to selflove so much inclin'd?

> Sir Thomas Urquhart, 'A dissuasion from philoty, to
> one that was too much enamored with himself'
>
> fb.217, p. 141

S0309 Seek he who will in grandeur to be blest,
Ah gentle thoughts! Soon lost the city cares among.

> [William Roscoe], 'Sonnet from the same' ['Lorenzo
> de Medici']
>
> c.142, p. 91

S0310 Seek not by guile thy stock to augment
For goods evil-gotten are seldom well spent.

> b.234, p. 257

S0311 Seek not, reader, how to find
To find a king so far above a tomb.

[Sir Thomas Roe], 'On the King of Sweden'
[Crum s275]

fb.143, p. 14; see also 'Cease not sad reader . . .'. .

S0312 Seek not the [?] chaplet's toy
And such the garland of my boy.

[George] H[owar]d, [6th earl of Carlisle],
'Translation of the 30th ode 1 book [of Horace]'

c.197, p. 18

S0313 Seek not to know our sorrow's doom;
So all our life is but one instant Now.

c.549, p. 90

S0314 Seek not to know tomorrow's doom
Then this will be no more.

[William] Congreve(?), 'On tomorrow'

c.362, p. 86

S0315 Seek not to know what must not be reveal'd
I am forbid by fate to tell the rest.

c.53, fol. 52

S0316 Seek ye to know what keeps the mind
These make the balm we call content.

'The ingredients of contentment'

fc.130, p. 51; c.83/3, no. 829 ('seek you . . .'); c.578, p. 35
('Seek you')

S0317 Seems she so cold,
A sign of summer.

Sir Thomas Urquhart, 'How to court a coy maid'

fb.217, p. 92

S0318 Seems to me, that dalliance nourisheth
The better still, the more, that it is fouted [sic].

Sir Thomas Urquhart, 'Of the courtisan Clorinda,
who was never well that day, she tasted not of some
Venerian chip'

fb.217, p. 43

S0319 Seest thou that form slow gliding by,
Beyond her sable clouds, a dawn of endless light.

'Disappointment an ode'

c.83/1, no. 241

S0320 Seest thou those jewels which she wears?
She that will wear thy tears, would wear thine eyes.

R[obert] H[errick], 'A song' [on his mistress adorned
with jewels]
[Crum s286]

b.197, p. 8; b.205, fol. 74r (var.)

S0321 Seest thou yon sunny spot of rising ground?
He stamps the beauteous colors which he shows.

'Life made agreeable'

c.244, p. 629

S0322 Seeing th'Amazonian beautiful virago
The glory of inconstancy.

Sir Thomas Urquhart, 'That any gentlewoman (how
gallant soever) may break off her affection to a
cavalier, without the meanest blemish of disreputation'

fb.217, p. 42

S0323 Seldom but yet sometimes the wise give way
Who all his sacred summons must attend.

M[aurice] J[ohnson], 'In imitation of Seneca's
Serenus, or ag[ainst] immoderate grief. De vita beata.
Lib. II. Cap. 23 addressed to ———[.] To Mrs. Green
on occasion of her husband's death'

c.229/2, fol. 54

S0324 Self a little dirty creature,
Make it nothing but a name.

'Self'

c.172, p. 21

S0325 Self-love doth guide
And thus self-love each one betrays.

J[ohn] R[obinson], 'Amor sui caecus'

c.370, fol. 36v

S0326 Selinda sure's the brightest thing
Dull and insipid to the smell.

Diggle Box: Poetry Box xi/59

S0327 Senators with plebeians lost their breath
To cut the infant's new-spun thread of life.

Tho[mas] May, 'A translation from Lucan'

c.360/1, p. 167

S0328 Send forth dear Julian all thy books
And all the night I'll sit and write | Then hey boys
up go we.

'To [Robert] Julian' [1680]
[Crum s293]

b.113, p. 291

S0329 Send forth, O sacred spirit, thy light divine,
In worthy strains, to all eternity.

[William Stukeley], 'The vision. A poem written at
Grimsthorp, in August 1736'

c.371, fol. 20

S0330 Send home my long stray'd eyes to me
Or prove as false as thou art now.

[John Donne], 'Sonnet'
[Crum s295]

b.148, p. 70; b.114, p. 314; b.356, p. 156

S0331 Send me, dear saint! On whom my vow attends
I'll have 'em quit the nymphs of Drury Lane.

M[aurice] J[ohnson], 'Mr. [John] Hedges' letter from
Germany to Dr.[Noel] Broxholme translated and
inscribed to the ladies of Spalding Assembly . . .'

c.229/2, fol. 32

S0332 Send me some tokens that my hopes may live
But swear thou think'st I love thee and no more.

[John Donne], 'Elegy'
[Crum s296]

b.148, p. 67

S0333 Sensibility how charming,
Thrill the deepest notes of woe.

[Robert Burns], 'On sensibility to a friend'

c.142, p. 316

S0334 Sentenc'd to die, the curst portmanteau nabber,
High hung long Giles(?), as the most dangerous
vermin.

John Lockman, 'The thief, and the attorney, after
losing my portmanteau from the Salisbury coach'

c.267/1, p. 240

S0335 Sepulchral stones our sense deceive,
'No cheat is here—there's naught within!'

Charles Atherton Allnutt, 'Epigram'

c.112, p. 156

S0336 Sequester'd in a lonely vale
And ev'ry flame but love allay.

'From [obliterated] R. M.'

c.344, p. 66

S0337 Sequestered spot whose mossy bower
To love or to revere her more.

[William Hayley], 'Inscription for a moss seat'
File 6948

S0338 Serene and calm the evening hastens on
And leave the busy world calm as this sacred night.

'Reflections in an evening's walk'

c.91, p. 192

S0339 Serene as evening in the pride of spring
Softness and all the beauties of the mind.

[Horace Walpole, 4th earl of Orford], 'Lady
Fortescue' [d. 1812]
[Crum s306]

c.157, p. 71

S0340 Serene as light is Myron's soul,
And give my slaves the rest.

[Isaac] Watts, 'The happy man'

c.244, p. 318

S0341 Serene the morn, the season fine
Nor courage let him fight.

'The review[.] On the King reviewing his troops, with
the Countess of Yarmouth'
[Crum s307. 'Nor cowardice']

c.360/2, no. 37; c.154, p. 1; fc.135

S0342 Serene the zephyrean breeze
The will of God be done.

'The summer evening'

c.83/3, no. 902

S0343 Servant companion friend and guard
That [?] you more than ever.

[William Hayley], 'The character of Jago'
File 6929

S0344 Servant, no[,] friend thou wert and truly so
Thus in thy death you're placed near him to lie.

Lady Jane Cavendish, 'On my good and true friend
Mr Henry Ogle'
[Crum s309]

b.233, p. 32

S0345 Servio serves God, Servio has bare relation
Servio may find the cooler place in hell.

'On Servio'

b.118, p. 225

S0346 Set to the sun a dial that doth pass
Love is the lodestone, my beloved the pole.

[Simon Ives]
[Crum s311b]

b.104, p. 90

S0347 Set Zion's watchmen all awake
That we may watch for Thee.

P[hilip] Doddridge, 'Of watching for souls in the view
of the great account from Heb. XIII. 17'

c.493, p. 24

S0348 Seven and eleven was Sr. Harry's play,
Two damn'd unlucky sixes threw him out.

'The colt dismembered, or Sr. H. D. C.'s miscarriage
in the Westminster election'

fc.24, p. 31

S0349 Seven hours to law, to soothing slumber seven,
Ten to the world allot, and all to heaven.

Sir W[illia]m Jones

c.83/4, no. 2033

S0350 Seven planets they do grace the skies,
Perhaps may have them all again.

'The seven wise men of England. To the tune of To all
ye ladies &c.' [Oxford, Sunderland, Townshend,
Cowper, Robert and Horace Walpole, Edgcumbe; pr.
1719 (Foxon S352)]
[Crum s315]

c.570/2, p. 91

S0351 Seven sages in our happy isle are seen,
Tho' they like Samson in the ruin fall.

'The seven wise men' [Somerset, Devonshire,
Sunderland, Scarborough, Townshend, Wharton,
Somers, a committee to inquire into the Scottish plot;
pr. 1704 (Foxon S350)]
[POAS VI.624]

c.111, p. 68

S0352 Seven sleepless nights have pass'd away,
I taste of bliss without allay.

'The spendthrift's enlargement and reformation'

c.83/2, no. 528

S0353 Seven years childless, marriage past,
Yet in less than six weeks dead.

'A parent on the death of a child'

c.189, p. 21

S0354 Sev'n years have roll'd round, since we saw
Cornwall here,
The nation were blest, and themselves more
respected. | Derry down [&c.]

John Lockman, 'Velters Cornwall: a new ballad: on
occasion of the election of representatives for the
county of Hereford. Wednesday 6th April anno 1768.
The tune, Down derry down &c.'

c.267/4, p. 383

S0355 Sexton be mute! I know thy ill-taught tongue
Then lead them forth, lest they grow blind with
weeping.

'On the earl of Dorset'

b.356, p. 265

S0356 Sextus upon a spleen did rashly swear,
He wore the old, until the old was new.

'On Sextus'
[Crum s318]

b.200, p. 408; b.356, p. 305

S0357 Shadrach lies here, who made both sexes happy
The women with love-toys, the men with nappy.

'Epitaph on Shadrach Johnson . . . noted for being the
father of many children and also for brewing good
beer'

c.360/1, p. 249

S0358 Shake England shake! Thy grand upholder's down,
T'enclose him with the crown of martyrdom.

J[ohn] R[obinson], 'Verses upon the martyrdom of
King Charles the First of ever blessed memory,
murdered publicly by his subjects, on the 30th of
January 1648[/9]'

c.370, fol. 49

S0359 Shakespeare your Wincote ale hath much renown'd
Did put Kit Sly into such lordly trances.

[Sir Aston Cokayne], 'To Mr Clement Fisher of
Wincote'

b.275, p. 76

S0360 Shall birthday odes, to pleasure kings
And care dissolves in mirth.

'On the birthday of a dear friend'

c.90

S0361 Shall Chatham's bones in Paul's grand dome
On ev'ry British heart.

'On the city's late request to have Lord Chatham
interred in St. Paul's Cathedral'

c.139, p. 363

S0362 Shall dullness triumph in these realms of wit?
Be thou our boast at home, as Titley is abroad.

[Robert Cholmeley], 'A satire addressed to Mr Titley
AM: of Trin: Coll: Camb upon his being made
Secretary to Mr. Hedges—and to Mr Taylor AB: upon
his being elected Fellow of St Johns Coll: Camb.
designed as an answer to The session of poets written
by Mr. Pattison . . . in imitation of Juvenal's sixth
satire'

c.190, p. 11

S0363 Shall each vile scribbler publish William's fame
And by his virtue propt a falling state.

'On the twenty-ninth of May—1746'

c.171, no. 11

S0364 Shall fish not in the water swim?
And in the heavens with you have place. | Amen

'Of All Saints' Day. November. 1'

a.30[46]

S0365 Shall furious man lead on a desp'rate mob,
Who states would overturn, and worlds destroy.

Abraham Oakes, 'On the sentence against the rebels
1746'

c.50, p. 133 (bis)

S0366 Shall gay attire forever charm the fair
The silk is on her tongue, the brilliant's in her mind.

Poetry Box I/70

S0367 Shall George who fills a Christian throne
To carve a head to match his heart.

H. Young, 'Inscription for a marble bust of Gibbon
when the same shall be erected in His Majesty's royal
Library . . . to Lady Payne'

Poetry Box II/23

S0368 Shall heaths and snow-topt mountains dare
The happiness of pleasing you.

Charles Burney, the younger, 'Epistle to a lady, with a
present of moor fowl . . . Mar Lodge. Aug. 24. 1780'

c.35, p. 62

S0369 Shall I be only heretic in wit?
And please them in a Canterbury Tale.

[George Daniel]

b.121, fol. 38v

S0370 Shall I be silent, 'cause I am not heard
I ever value, come it soon, or late.

[George Daniel]

b.121, fol. 55v

S0371 Shall I be slave unto a woman's will
Because I know a woman was my mother.

'A hater of women'
[Crum S328]

b.205, fol. 23r

S0372 Shall I be stopt? Oh no? Virtue's my race
No 'luring devils can stop a zealous soul.

[Sir Philip Wodehouse], 'Elizabeth Potts shall I be
stopt?'

b.131, back (no. 97)

S0373 Shall I die, shall I fly
In such a case causeth repenting.

[attr. William Shakespeare in Oxford copy]
[Crum S333]

b.197, p. 135

S0374 Shall I express to thee the woe
This care-full life I soon shall end.

[R. M.]

Poetry Box VI/4

S0375 Shall I go force an elegy, abuse
Keep you my lines, as secret as my love.

[Sir John Roe], 'Elegia decima tertia' [Elegy to Mrs.
Boulstrede; attr. John Donne]
[Crum S337]

b.114, p. 118

S0376 Shall I grieve or pine with sorrow
Such a love will I prove, or I vow to lie alone.

'I former fucator [sic]'

b.62, p. 17

S0377 Shall I read my mistress over,
'Tis my mistress' heart, or none.

b.200, p. 149

S0378 Shall I wasting in despair
What care I for whom she be.

[George Wither], 'Song 126'

c.555, p. 180; b.197, p. 174

S0379 Shall I weep, or shall I sing?
Because that man no faith can keep.

'Love lamenting'
[Crum S346]

b.200, p. 81

S0380 Shall I when glitt'ring knaves deride,
That e'er for man on earth was meant.

'On virtue'

c.94

S0381 Shall I who oft have woo'd the muse
The ladies of the lake.

[George] Crabbe, 'Written upon two ladies who were
fond of going on the water'

c.90

S0382 Shall mimic kings long fill the British throne,
And Nature smile on the propitious day.

'The queries. Post nubila Phoebus'
[Crum S349]

c.570/1, p. 50; fc.58, p. 111

S0383 Shall mortals yield subjection to earth's king
Towards him whose love being gained will last
forever.

[Mary Serjant]

fb.98, fol. 155

S0384 Shall not Rogation Week, a blessing crave
That keeps a harmless helpful liturgy.

    [Edward] Sparke, 'Poem 18th, on Rogation Week'

  b.137, p. 45

S0385 Shall Orford die, and every muse be dumb,
And rule the world with undisputed reign.

    'On the death of the right hon. Edward, Earl of
    Orford'

  c.166, p. 179

S0386 Shall riches tempt thee no for they have wings
For I am still for that that last forever.

    [Mary Serjant]

  fb.98, fol. 158

S0387 Shall Scug the blooming nymphs' peculiar care,
What brandy could not Helicon should give.

    'On the death of a lady's squirrel'

  c.172, p. 27

S0388 Shall she whose charms inspir'd each sprightly lay;
Think on thy beauty and forget thy shame.

    William Pitt, [1st earl of Chatham? or Lady Mary
    Wortley Montagu?], 'Elegy on the Lady Abergavenny
    by Mr. William Pitt'

  Poetry Box v/87; Poetry Box iv/169 (applied to 'Miss
  Howe of Somerset House')

S0389 Shall Stockdale die whose subtle spirit
And brood o'er noxious weeds for more.

    R[ichard] V[ernon] S[adleir], 'Written in Percival
    Stockdale's Inquiry into the nature of poetry, with a
    defense of Pope, London 1778'

  c.106, inserted after p. 149

S0390 Shall such a champion of the nine decay?
A citizen he is above enroll'd.

    [J. R.and G. B.], 'In idem' [elegy on the death of
    Andrew Horsman]

  b.212, p. 250

S0391 Shall then so bright a day forgotten be
For's restoration and his birthday too.

    'On the 10 of June' [the birthday of the Old
    Pretender]
    [Crum s354, 'forgotten lie']

  c.570/1, p. 112

S0392 Shall there be nothing left me, but a grave?
Sepulchrum mihi solum super est.

    [William Austin], 'Sepulchrum mihi solum super est'
    [Crum s355]

  b.65, p. 67

S0393 Shall vice then triumph? shall her impious hand
While malice, baffled, meets its awful doom.

    'A sonnet. Mon. May 15 1799'

  c.136, p. 159

S0394 Shall virtue thus unnotic'd pass along,
Where smiling happiness forever reigns.

    'Elegy on the death of Miss Anna Norman'

  c.89, p. 20

S0395 Shall we all die?
Die all we shall.

    'Epitaph taken from a tombstone at Gunwallow near
    Helstone, Cornwall'

  c.487, p. 88

S0396 Shall we stand tamely mute and see our England
                                           sunk
[cropped] and let all the people say amen.

    'The ploughman's complaint, the freeholder's
    proposition, and the high shoes' resolution. From the
    heart of England the 1. March called St. Taffy's Day'
    [1678/9]

  b.54, p. 1231

S0397 Shall we the streams and not the fountain sing
That we may once his endless rest enjoy.

    [Edward] Sparke, 'Poem 17th, upon the Lord's Day'

  b.137, p. 43

S0398 Shall words of women me disgrace
You know they will still say nay.

    [John Mackereth? c. 1778]

  b.132, insert

S0399 Shame is the proper fruit of sin,
As it in Magdalene did prove.

    [Edmund Wodehouse], 'Decr. 1 [1714]'

  b.131, p. 102

S0400 Shame of my life, disturber of my tomb
Like him your angry father kicked you down.

    [Wentworth Dillon, 4th earl of Roscommon], '[Tom]
    Ross his ghost' [to the Duke of Monmouth, autumn
    1679]
    [Crum s356; *POAS* II.251]

  b.113, p. 165; b.327, f. 4v; b.371, no. 5; fb.106(20)

S0401 Shameful my sin if e'er I have seen
And will rule us and rid us at pleasure.

    'Introduction to the character'

  c.171, no. 10

S0402 Shameful that shame is that prevents
That which is meant for our abuse.

    [Edmund Wodehouse], 'Decr. 5 [1714]'

b.131, p. 105

S0403 Sharp is the conflict of the just,
But thou shall follow still.

    Charles Atherton Allnutt, 'Faint, yet pursuing'

c.112, p. 124

S0404 Sharpe, whilst true doctrine from his lips proceeds,
Takes care to sanctify it by his deeds.

    John Lockman, 'On his excellent friend, the reverend
    and learned Dr. Gregory Sharpe . . . 1750'

c.267/1, p. 112

S0405 She all her lifetime thought it most expedient,
Felicity forerun eternal glory.

    Sir Thomas Urquhart, 'Upon the Countess of [crossed
    out] Dowager lately deceased'

fb.217, p. 315

S0406 She came—she is gone—we have met—
Might we view her enjoying it here.

    William Cowper, 'Cathrina addressed to Miss
    Stapleton [later Mrs. Courtenay]'

c.140, p. 521; Poetry Box III/50

S0407 She can with charms release the lovesick mind
And whom she will in amorous fetters bind.

    'On a lady'

c.360/1, p. 301

S0408 She chose one to be her husband, who's
Her limbic with most matter.

    Sir Thomas Urquhart, 'Why a certain gentlewoman
    preferred a very arrant lubbard, to many wise, and
    gallant gentlemen'

fb.217, p. 311

S0409 She daily thought on—ev'n by all which have known
Pure souls alone, see immortality.

    [Sir Philip Wodehouse], 'Upon my cousin her sister
    Lydia Houghton . . .'

b.131, back (no. 66)

S0410 She dropp'd a tear, and sighing seem'd to say—
Young maidens marry, marry while you may.

c.549, p. 148

S0411 She first deceas'd, he for a little tried
To live without her, lik'd it not, and died.

    [Sir Henry Wotton?], 'On two lovers who died before
    they were married'
    [Crum s366]

fb.143, p. 43; c.360/1, p. 33 ('departed'); see also 'The
first deceased . . .'.

S0412 She gives m'a kiss, when I her bed would leave:
Whence I know that, who gives, would fain receive.

    Sir Thomas Urquhart, 'One speaks here of his
    mistress'

fb.217, p. 303

S0413 She in the common first of two or three
Still to the best constructions had an eye.

    Sir Thomas Urquhart, 'Of a she-grammarian'

fb.217, p. 353

S0414 She is a monture, whereupon to ride
Till she have glutted up the best of man.

    [Sir Thomas Urquhart], 'The character of a whore'

fb.217, p. 389

S0415 She is all wine—the vine's most generous blood
Whence witty solace springs, and chaste delight.

    [Sir Philip Wodehouse], 'Upon Madam Jane Willis is
    all wine'

b.131, back (nos. 71, 89)

S0416 She is faithless—am I then undone?
But, I lov'd her, for what she had not.

    Sir John Cullum, 'The recovery . . . Decr. 10. 1763'

c.90

S0417 She is gone. Heaven's great will must be obey'd
And let your friendship live e'en after death.

Poetry Box IV/112

S0418 She is so proud in th'actions of her will,
Had I not whiles the care to close the door.

    Sir Thomas Urquhart, 'One speaks here of an
    ambitious woman, with whom he was most
    intrinsically familiar'

fb.217, p. 217

S0419 She Jacob's beauties modishly reveals
But Esau's beauties modestly conceals.

    'On the same [Eleanor Ambrose, in 'In Flavia's
    eyes . . .'] being fond of showing her breast'

c.360/2, no. 153

S0420   She knows man's constitution well,
Practiseth day and night.

     Sir Thomas Urquhart, 'That a whore is a good
     physician'

     fb.217, p. 60

S0421   She lay all naked in her bed
But a pox on't 'twas but a dream I waked and lay
                         without her.

     ['The dream']
     [Crum s372]

     b.209, p. 82

S0422   She lives in vain who lives a maid
With apes in hell, the brawls (?) to tread.

     [Sir Philip Wodehouse], 'An extempore crambo of the
     form Anne Lewys lives in vain'

     b.131, back (no.82/3)

S0423   She loved like Pyramus, like Thisbe he,
And in one peaceful urn the lovers' ashes rest.

     'Ovid. 4.B.'

     c.94

S0424   She may take other men each night:
The ship must brangl', and be unstayed.

     Sir Thomas Urquhart, 'The reason why, in some
     men's opinion, the wife of an old skipper, may
     prostitute herself to another man'

     fb.217, p. 85

S0425   She needs no wings, she makes but too much haste,
A cursed fiend! And scandal is her name.

     'Answer' [to 'Nor wings, nor feet . . .']

     c.578, p. 30

S0426   She pierc'd his heart, till he was like to die:
She lived ever since more glad.

     Sir Thomas Urquhart, 'Of a gentleman, and his
     mistress'

     fb.217, p. 300

S0427   She said t'excuse her wenching disposition
Because the man was never born, she hated.

     Sir Thomas Urquhart, 'Of a certain girl, who was too
     amorously affected'

     fb.217, p. 203

S0428   She scorns to let her thighs
To lie as under.

     Sir Thomas Urquhart, 'Of a lady, whom mere
     arrogancy kept chaste'

     fb.217, p. 246

S0429   She should not be esteem'd the less,
To be the mother of a god.

     Sir Thomas Urquhart, 'That women ought not to be
     blamed for making love to men. Of Pamphila'

     fb.217, p. 269

S0430   She shriek'd and wept, and both became her face:
No gesture could that heavenly form disgrace.

     c.189, p. 125

S0431   She takes a kiss: but gives to none, that lives;
Because she knows, who taketh that way gives.

     Sir Thomas Urquhart, 'Of a scrupulous gentlewoman,
     who though she would not bestow a kiss on any, made
     nevertheless no great ceremony to receive one'

     fb.217, p. 256

S0432   She talks, but nothing does she say
But never see the flour [flower?].

     [Hester Lynch Thrale] Piozzi, 'Principessa
     Lambertini . . . August 1785'

     Greatheed Box/16

S0433   She tells me with claret she ne'er can agree
Let her go to the devil there's no more to be said.

     c.188, p. 85

S0434   She that takes her rest within this tomb
Martha's case and Mary's better part.

     'Epitaph on Mary New in the abbey of St. Alban's'

     fc.24, p. 69; see also 'Here lies interr'd . . .', 'This silent
     grave . . .', 'She who here . . .', The dame that takes . . .'.

S0435   She, that was married yesterday, appears
A horse came, and enjoy'd her in one night.

     Sir Thomas Urquhart, 'Of a gentlewoman that refused
     many brave cavaliers who were in suit of her, to match
     with a loggerhead'

     fb.217, p. 221

S0436   She was, but I want words to tell you what
Ask, what a wife sh'd be, and she was that.

     'Epitaph'

     c.150, p. 77

S0437   She was descended of right noble blood
Her life in death and bliss when world is done.

     'Epitaph no. 2'

     c.158, p. 45

S0438   She was so mad to counterfeit for me,
But now we both are well and both are free.

     c.549, p. 11

S0439 She wears the feather, as a martial badge,
That Venus cannot be to Mars but kind.

> Sir Thomas Urquhart, 'Why a certain courtesan went never abroad, without a feather to set forth the more gracefully the rest of her head attire'
>
> fb.217, p. 142

S0440 She well might say it. Clear Diana I!
All say—she well deserv'd—this eulogy.

> [Sir Philip Wodehouse], 'Upon his noble cousin german the Lady A[nne] C[arey]'
>
> b.131, back (no. 20)

S0441 She who here takes her rest beneath this tomb,
With Martha's care and Mary's better part.

> 'In memory of Anne the late dear wife of John Smith tailor in Islip church in Oxfordshire'
>
> c.229/1, fol. 44; see also 'Here lies interr'd . . .', 'She/The dame that takes . . .', 'This silent grave . . .'.

S0442 She whose unblemish'd life her husband blest
But she, I trust, hath gain'd eternal life.

> B[arnaby] Gouche, 'Another [epitaph in Croyland churchyard] on Mary Derby'
>
> c.229/1, fol. 35

S0443 She wrought all needlework that women exercise
Directing her faith to Christ her only mark.

> 'Elizabeth wife of Mr. Lucer had it thus upon her tomb 1577'
>
> c.158, p. 46; see also 'Every Christian heart . . .'.

S0444 Sh'enamors him by coyness, and denying:
And, like the Parthian archers, wounds in flying.

> Sir Thomas Urquhart, 'Of one who gained the affection of a gentleman by her niceness, and precise carriage'
>
> fb.217, p. 59

S0445 Shepherd divine, our wants supply,
And prayer in endless praise.

> 'Hymn 85th'
>
> c.562, p. 112

S0446 Shepherd of Isr'el, lend thine ear
Made whole, them placidly behold.

> [Philip Doddridge], 'Psalm 80'
>
> c.264/2, p. 69

S0447 Shepherd! seek not wealth nor pow'r
Nor exchange thy peace for gold.

> 'To a shepherd'
>
> c.141, p. 157

S0448 Shepherd, what is love I pray thee tell
And went(?) away his sheep to fold.

> [Sir Walter Raleigh?], 'The forsaken lass'
>
> a.6, p. 125

S0449 Shepherd, when you see me, fly—
That has my vows, but you my heart.

> Lady F[rances] Burgoyne, 'A song'
>
> c.358, p. 60; c.374

S0450 Shepherd wouldst thou here obtain
Close thy wish and seek no more.

> [William Shenstone], 'Shepherd's bush. Exterior prospect'
>
> c.21; c.20/3; c.344, p. 89; c.83/1, no. 46; c.83/3, no. 835

S0451 Shepherds I have lost my waist,
For cheese, tart, cake, or jelly.

> 'A parody on Shepherds I have lost my love'
> Poetry Box III/10 (2 copies)

S0452 Shepherds, rejoice, lift up your eyes,
For there's a Savior born!

> [Isaac] Watts, 'The nativity of Christ . . . Watts's Lyric poems' [Northampton mercury, Dec. 1776]
>
> c.487, p. 104

S0453 Shepherds, whither are you bound?
This holy Babe, this Savior's praise.

> H[enry] C[olman], 'On [Christ's] birth. A pastoral'
> b.2, p. 66

S0454 Sheppard is now secur'd at last
The loose their chains, and break the jail.

> 'Verses to Sir James Thornhill the great painter on a report that he had painted the picture of John Sheppard the noted robber and jail-breaker 1724'
>
> c.360/2, no. 110

S0455 Sherburne, I greet thee next, nor can decide,
Congratulate th'accession of thy name.

> [Thomas Stanley], 'Sherburne' [in 'A register of friends']
>
> b.153, p. 14

S0456 She's dead, the beauteous Anna's dead
And meet thy saint above.

> Allan Ramsay, 'Copy of verses by . . . to the memory of Anne [(Cochran)] Duchess of Hamilton who died [14 August 1724] at the age of seventeen, leaving one son an infant of about six weeks old'
>
> c.360/2, no. 79

S0457 She's dead, who living no man e'er could please
Who in her life-time wasn't content with two.

    'On a lustful woman'

    fb.143, p. 28; see also 'Here lies Penelope . . .'; 'One stone sufficeth . . .'.

S0458 She's gone, her soul is fled! from earth's abode
And endless pleasures which will never cloy.

    'Mrs. Ann Stephens granddaughter to [Ann Neale], died 11 Janr . . . 1740/1'

    c.181, p. 40

S0459 She's such a lustful dangerous virago
With Cyprian paroxysms she daily trembles.

    [Sir Thomas Urquhart], 'Clorinda's description'

    fb.217, p. 386

S0460 Shine on our souls, eternal God,
With everlasting peace.

    [Thomas Stevens?], 'Hymn the 6th'

    c.259

S0461 Ship must have a steersman
They'll frown and look grimly.

    'Ship loaded of waggery'

    c.503, p. 66

S0462 Sho! Pox o' this nonsense, I prithee give o'er,
Boys, fill up a bumper and let it go round.

    'Song 139'

    c.555, p. 191

S0463 Shoeless Scriblerus, from his cell,
And bellow: 'I'll squirt out the sun!'

    John Lockman, 'In answer to a slovenly epigram, against a noble peer . . . Lord Carteret [earl of Granville], 1743'

    c.267/1, p. 34

S0464 Short and uncertain is the life of man,
Where bliss ineffable knows no decrease.

    c.175, p. 3

S0465 Short anger should not man to rage transport:
But anger's rage; therefore, it should be short.

    Sir Thomas Urquhart, 'Anger is a short fury'

    fb.217, p. 213

S0466 Short is the sentence of the greatest doom
I may be call'd to come, not bid to go.

    Sir John Strangways

    b.304, p. 41

S0467 Short-liv'd delight of every friend,
T'instruct each rival youth.

    'Epitaph on Lord Carteret [earl of Granville]'s youngest son (who died in his nineteenth year) . . . translation of the above'

    Poetry Box VIII/69

S0468 Short was my life if live I ever
Go reader go prepare to die.

    'A very old epitaph in Stoke Church G[l]ou[cester]shi[re]'

    c.341, p. 41

S0469 Should Cupid, god of love, with many a dart,
Completes his caricature of Tunbridge-Walk.

    Sir W[illiam] Browne, 'Remarks, on a copy of verses, entitled: A sketch of Tunbridge-Wells'

    File 1965

S0470 Should curious readers wish to know
He liv'd but seven short years.

    'Epitaph on a gentleman who retir'd late from the world'

    c.360/3, no. 60

S0471 Should ev'ry grace your face adorn
Lest sad experience make you wise.

    'To my child if a daughter'

    c.83/3, no. 984

S0472 Should he who launch'd an idle bark to glide
Contend for honor as a volunteer.

    [William Hayley], 'Prologue to Marcella'

    File 6958, 6959

S0473 Should I the fates relentless move
But that I lov'd and loving died.

    [Richard Brome], 'Cant: 32' [answer to 'Nor love nor fate . . .' in The northern lass, II.VI, 1632]

    b.4, fol. 27v; b.62, p. 76

S0474 Should now the subjects of a certain prince,
But Christians now no honesty retain.

    'The receiver, as bad as the thief' [on George I] [Crum s440, 'German prince']

    c.570/1, p. 84

S0475 Should our old honor be forgot?
As Charles long syne.

    'A song to the tune of Old long syne[:] To those whose honor is sound | That cannot be named and must not be found'

    c.171, no. 17

S0476 Should Providence present a man of parts,
And with a pleasure know, no will but his.

'Picture of a good husband'

c.186, p. 52

S0477 Should smiling joys on all thy steps attend,
While vast destruction raves beneath his feet.

'To a young friend'

c.244, p. 626

S0478 Should some mild traveller o'er this marble bend
But endless blessings crown the good and just.

'To the memory of a friend'

c.83/4, no. 2031

S0479 Should the lone wanderer, fainting on his way
Where the pale specter can pursue no more.

Charlotte (Turner) Smith, 'Sonnet'

c.504, p. 95

S0480 Should the whole earth of growing numbers stand,
More worth in them, than what I left behind.

'Father's advice to his son on the important subject of
eternity'

c.578, p. 133

S0481 Should twenty people out of twenty-five
How readily a man may be foresworn.

Edward Sneyd, 'An extempore upon a gent[lema]n
who was apt to fall asleep in company'

c.214, p. 129

S0482 Should woman's fault obscure a man's renown:
Seeing Venus never yet eclips'd the sun.

Sir Thomas Urquhart, 'Man should not be the less
thought of, for the fault of a woman'

fb.217, p. 214

S0483 Should you learn anything by what is penn'd
'He may in some particulars miscarry.'

'To the reader'

c.143, fol. 2

S0484 Should you order Tom Brown
And your petitioner shall ever pray.

[Charles Sackville, 6th earl of Dorset], 'Tom Brown
the poet being ordered by the Parliament to be
whipped for satire against the King, a friend saves him
by this apology' [1697]
[Crum s444]

b.115, fol. 36v

S0485 Shout Sion and rejoice,
As if already won!

'Epinicion'

b.214

S0486 Show mercy Lord to my sad soul
A spirit holy and upright.

'Jan. 13. 1702. Psalm 51'

c.124, no. 1

S0487 Show mercy, mercy Lord
His so exalted power.

c.124, no. 6

S0488 Show my sin O Lord no favor,
And sin's inspirers bring to naught.

Charles Atherton Allnutt, 'Prayer and imprecation
against the spiritual enemies of the soul'

c.112, p. 28

S0489 Show your flames you brag of, you that be
'Twill make a new account from the second flood.

William Cartwright, 'Upon the great frost, and snow:
1634'
[Crum s451]

b.200, p. 7

S0490 Shun the rude sort that brag of drinking much,
Seek other friends, and join not hand with such.

c.339, p. 324

S0491 Shut, shut your door, good Jack! Fatigu'd I said,
Thus far was right, the rest belongs to heav'n.

[Alexander] Pope, 'An epistle from . . . to
Dr. Arbuthnot' [pr. 1734 (Foxon P802)]

c.570/4, p. 151

S0492 Shut within a brazen tow'r,
Just enough, with sparing hand.

[William Popple, trans.], '[Horace] Book 3rd. ode
16th. To Maecenas'

fc.104/2, p. 262

S0493 Sicilian goddess whose prophetic tongue
The poet's envy, and the critic's pain.

'The Golden Age reversed'
[Crum s460; POAS VI.519]

b.382(18); b.204, p. 22; Poetry Box VI/54

S0494 Sicilian muse begin a loftier flight
Honest George Churchill will supply the place.

[William Walsh], 'The Golden Age restored or the
fourth eclogue of Virgil translated, supposed to have
been taken from a Sybil's prophecy' [1703]
[Crum s461; POAS VI.91]

b.204, p. 18; fb.108, p. 307; Poetry Box VI/53; Poetry Box
VII/86

S0495 Sicilian muse, my humble voice inspire,
Grief stops my tongue, and tears o'erflow my eyes.

   [William Walsh], 'Pastoral eclogues. Eclogue 1st'

c.223, p. 82

S0496 Sick to the death, diseas'd past human art
And happy had I been thus arm'd, thus dress'd.

   H[enry] C[olman], 'A dream'
   [Crum s463]

b.2, p. 81

S0497 Sickness and death shook hands and vow'd to kill
The King and Judge eternal sits upon.

   'Epitaph in Lewkner Church on Sir Thomas
   Fleetwood 1625'

c.360/3, no. 137

S0498 Sickness! I yield to thy subduing sway,
And smiling bear me to the throne of grace.

   [Henry] Headley, 'The following lines were written
   by . . . a scholar of Trinity College in Oxford, who
   died of rapid consumption at Norwich'

c.140, p. 206

S0499 Sickness intending my love to betray,
How matchless would it be if she were well?

   'Sonnet of his own and of his mistress' sickness at one
   time'

Poetry Box VIII/2

S0500 Sickness the racking trial is
Whom He at no time will chastise.

   [Edmund Wodehouse], 'Novr. 20 [1714]'

b.131, p. 90

S0501 Siddons accept the counsels of a friend
Discord produce instead of harmony.

   W[illiam] S[mith]

Smith Papers, folder 68

S0502 Siddons! When first commenced thy ardent course,
'Her radiant science and her spotless life!'

   [Anna] Seward, 'To Mrs. Siddons'

Poetry Box V/55

S0503 Sidneyan's hardest dogs alive
Say it cost him more in spits than mutton.

   'Upon the members of Sidney College'

Poetry Box I/8

S0504 Sift ye the good and well discern their deeds,
And [?] the bad no better than the weeds.

c.339, p. 314

S0505 Sigh, O my soul, sigh till thy loins do swell
The lovel'est hallelujahs to their King. Amen.

   'A parallel between Jerusalem and England'

b.52/2, p. 111

S0506 Sigh, shepherd, sigh!
The only life is to be dead.

   'The shepherd's loss'

fb.107, p. 44

S0507 Silence! Coeval with eternity!
All rest in peace at last, and sleep eternally.

   [Alexander] Pope, 'On silence by . . . in imitation of
   Rochester's poem about nothing'

c.244, p. 23

S0508 Silence! Name of mental peace—
Must from a frequent silence flow.

   Lydia Hawkesworth, 'Verses by . . .'

c.139, p. 469

S0509 Silence, thou gentle nurse to thought,
And only hear and learn.

   'An address to silence'

c.83/2, no. 288

S0510 Silence would best become me and I fear
Now swaggers in his color'd gallantry.

   Thomas Hickes, 'In idem . . . 1661 [In victorem
   laudes]'

b.212, p. 121

S0511 Silence ye prating ignorant mortals all
As near akin as empty sons and mothers.

   'A satire on a neighboring schoolmaster who sent into
   the school a very simple question (by one of the
   author's pupils) wrong stated and very
   ingrammatically penned'

c.91, p. 177

S0512 Silence, ye Tories, lofty Whigs, attend,
Whiles life, and pleasing hope of liberty remains.

   'A riddle' [answered by 'I was long in doubt . . .']

c.578, p. 87

S0513 Silence, ye warblers, still your pretty throats,
'Tis choice esteem, persuasion, friendship, taste.

   H[annah] More, 'Enrique and Aminta a pastoral
   dialogue written by . . . 1765'

c.341, p. 162

S0514 Silent and lonesome while I lie
And where, O death, thy sting?

   [ ] Lewis, 'The penitent'

c.244, p. 435

S0515 Silent as yielding maids consent,
Tho' all should countermand them.

    'Lysander lamenting the departure of Chloe. A song'

c.530, p. 69

S0516 Silent grave to thee I trust
Till his widow asks for room.

    'Epitaphs Bersted'

c.546

S0517 Silent my voice, my lute unstrung
To crown a monarch's hopes a nation's ardent
                               pray'rs.

    'Ode'

Poetry Box IV/144

S0518 Silent nymph, with curious eye!
With the groves of Grongar Hill.

    [John Dyer], 'Grongar Hill' [1727]
    [Crum s478]

c.139, p. 92; c.244, p. 452 (attr. [ ] Lewis)

S0519 Silent, opprest by sympathetic pain
Some trifling conquest first, thence mightier
                           conquests grew.

    'Acrostic' [on Sandys]

c.591

S0520 Silk though thou be
That weareth thee.

    [William Strode], 'Idem' [following 'Another'
    following 'Posies for bracelets']
    [Crum s479]

b.205, fol. 56r

S0521 Simon bring gold enough and I will tell thee
They will not give what Peter would not sell.

    [Francis Quarles], 'On the Pope and the Church of
    Rome on Simon-Magus and the Pope' [Divine
    fancies IV, 19]

b.137, p. 174

S0522 Simon excepted then restor'd to grace
And take again thy prostituted dame.

    'An epistle to the Lord Guilford'

c.570/2, p. 115

S0523 Simple I am 'tis own'd and e'en my name
And more than once preserv'd a nation's glory.

    'Riddle'

c.150, p. 113

S0524 Sin cannot be exposed to the sense
It is accomplish'd or the deed is acted.

    [Sir Thomas Urquhart], 'That sin is in the intention'

fb.217, p. 524

S0525 Sin fly, for sharp revenge doth follow sin,
Though long he stay, at last he striketh sure.

fb.69, p. 235

S0526 Since all mankind to happiness
The self-same distance keeps.

    [ ] Lewis, 'Life contented'

c.244, p. 435

S0527 Since all men that I come among
To sin by precedent.

    [John Grange], 'Cant: 21'

b.4, fol. 17v

S0528 Since all must certainly to death resign,
To reach the haven of eternal light.

    Sir Rob[er]t Howard, 'Against the fear of death'
    [Crum s499]

c.94

S0529 Since all the actions of the far-fam'd men
But must cry, Jack, what have you stole today?

    'On Capt. S[utherland] and Bedloe' [1679]
    [Crum s502]

Poetry Box VI/56; b.371, no. 19

S0530 Since all the downward tracts of time,
Are blessings in disguise.

    [John Hervey, baron Hervey of Ickworth], 'On
    resignation'
    [Crum s503]

c.83/1, no. 71

S0531 Since all the mighty monuments of fame,
For nothing Eve decays that you create.

    Mrs. [ ] Petty, 'To the order of Toast . . . petition to
    the Toast'

fb.70, p. 43

S0532 Since all the world is distracted with wars,
For I have all that was e'er worth desiring.

    'Another song'

fb.207/3, p. 11

S0533 Since am'rous cupids on their northern wing,
For still a Scot, and still a Stuart reigns.

    'On a late promotion to the Privy Council'

Poetry Box IV/166

S0534 Since at the tavern I can't meet you,
The feet confinement is of sense.

[Dr. ( ) Waldron, of All Souls], 'Browne's baralipton.
Sent to Dr. [ ] Crossy [Crosthwait] of Queen's
College in Oxford' [about taking the oath, 1690]
[Crum s507]

b.111, p. 173; fb.207/4, p. 11 (var.)

S0535 Since bishops first began to ride,
That was our gracious king.

'A copy of a printed ballad called The bishops' bridles:
lent by Will. Buxton of Wakefield. Oct. 1639'

b.101, p. 65

S0536 Since by just flames the guilty piece is lost
And makes us while we pity him forget our loyalty.

[Matthew Prior], 'Advice to the painter upon the
defeat of [Monmouth's] rebels in the west' [1685]
[Crum s510; POAS IV.44]

fb.228/43

S0537 Since by your cruel hatred I
Yet none will put him out of pain.

'The lovesick petition'

fb.107, p. 63

S0538 Since Celia, 'tis not in our power
In vain you part what nature join'd.

'Song'

c.189, p. 42

S0539 Since Celia's my foe,
For loving but one.

[Thomas Duffett], 'The wanderer' [1674?]

fb.107, p. 10; b.54, p. 971 (var.)

S0540 Since celibacy is understood
Amongst the jolly friars.

[John Walker?], 'The friary'

fc.108, fol. 47v

S0541 Since Chloe you ask me what like I would choose
That this may be your wish as much as 'tis mine.

Diggle Box: Poetry Box XI/23, 41 (var.)

S0542 Since Christ embrac'd the cross himself dare I
That cross's children, which our crosses are.

[John Donne], 'The cross'
[Crum s514]

b.148, p. 86

S0543 Since Colin first honor'd these plains
As hitherto we have been swains.

[Robert Cholmeley], 'To Mr. Rudd upon his
admission into St Johns Coll: Camb: under the tuition
of Mr. Williams BD'

c.190, p. 47

S0544 Since dark December shrouds the transient day,
Nor count the heavy eve-drops as they fall!

Anna Seward, 'Invitation to a friend. Sonnet'
[Crum s518]

c.141, p. 273

S0545 Since, dearest friend, I oft am told,
To render up thy mortgage tenement.

R[obert] Dobyns, 'Mart[ial] 10.l. 47.ep.'

b.154, p. 68

S0546 Since, dearest friend, 'tis your desire to see
And neither fear nor wish th'approaches of the last.

[Abraham Cowley, trans.], 'Martial, lib. 10, epist. 47'
[Crum s519]

b.118, p. 12; b.135, fol. 115v; c.356

S0547 Since, dearest Harry, you will needs request
And so at once dear friend, and muse farewell.

Joseph Addison, 'An account of the greatest English
poets To Mr. H. S[acheverell]. Ap. 3. 1699'
[Crum s520]

b.201, p. 159; c.244, p. 138

S0548 Since, dearest Martial, you of me inquire,
To relish life tho' not afraid of fate.

[Henry] Needler, 'Martial—Epigram 47. Book 10th'

c.244, p. 542

S0549 Since death on all lays his impartial hand,
Since One, by Heav'n inspired, left Heaven to
                                                          follow them.

[Sir George Etherege], 'Song'
[Crum s523]

fb.70, p. 89

S0550 Since distant far on wild Arabia's shores
In pupil, soldier and precepter shone.

M. F., 'On the lamented death of Lt. Col. George
Procter late superintendant of studies at the Royal
College . . .'

Poetry Box III/folder 11/20

S0551 Since Dorset's grown dull
To kick 'em, confound 'em, and damn all.

'The revolution' [1692]
[POAS V.334]

b.111, p. 539

So552 Since dreg[s] and clay, and substance vile,
To earth return we shall.

b.234, p. 111

So553 Since England was England, none ever yet knew
But the heavens themselves are adorned with blue.

'A song occasioned by one composed for Burford Race'

c.154, p. 51

So554 Since England was England there never was seen
We can't keep our pence, and the Protestant line.

'On G[eor]ge and C[aroli]na'

c.570/2, p. 171; Poetry Box IV/48; c.570/3, p. 6

So555 Since fancy of itself is loose and vain
Degenerate manners and ill past suggest.

'Part of a prologue' [docket title]

Poetry Box x/10(15)

So556 Since farce, and tongueless pantomimes can charm
So shall my brethren live, and eke Tom Thumb.

T[homas] M[orell], 'An epigram on the death of Mrs Oldfield 1731'

c.395, p. 32

So557 Since fasts and Lenten sermons do no good
And must by claps and fluxes be reclaim'd.

'Omnia sponte sua reddit justissima Tellus . . . 1691' [POAS V.356]

fb.70, p. 37

So558 Since fortune thou art become so kind
I may have heaven when I am dead, | I ask no more.

b.197, p. 152; see also 'Fortune since thou . . .'.

So559 Since freedom's in fashion my friends let me tell you all
We now have demolish'd both him and his idol.

'The Northampton garland for the month of April 1734 part the IV'

Accession 97.7.40

So560 Since George has abused our good common prayer,
Is but shameful dissembling with God at the best.

'A reason for a nonjuror absenting from the Church' [on George II]

c.154, p. 7

So561 Since good Master Prior
Can't know a c—t from a cart wheel.

'On Mr. [Thomas] Prior's treatise on tar water' [pr. 1747 (Foxon T39)]
[Crum s537]

c.481, p. 264

So562 Since Hanover is come
Now's the time for a restoration.

'[Jacobite] song'

fc.58, p. 28

So563 Since happy years with splendid lush smile
And I'll be Prior Sir! with all my heart.

[Robert Cholmeley], 'Mart: Epig: 29: lib: 4. imitated. Honos alit artes'

c.190, p. 90

So564 Since he is dead report it thou my muse
The mother weeps and all the children cries.

'On Dr. John Huit [Hewit]'

fb.143, p. 5

So565 Since here we are set in array round the table,
And drink Melville forever as long as we live.

'A health to Lord Melville being an excellent new song'

c.340

So566 Since holier, better, wiser, did increase
The whole world of irregularity.

Sir John Strangways

b.304, p. 33

So567 Since honest men are, in this world, so rare;
How sad a loss to cut off Cornwall's days!

John Lockman, 'To old time: writ (extempore) on the birthday of Velters Cornwall esq., 22 Feb. 1767'

c.267/1, p. 394

So568 Since honey whistle not but rather sing
And let thy ditty be—God save the King.

[Sir Philip Wodehouse], 'John Twistleton—honey whistle not'

b.131, back (no. 220)

So569 Since I came last, I've seen a lampoon here,
She's willing to disown the matter.

'The second Tunbridge lampoon. 1690'

fb.70, p. 81

So570 Since I find I'm grown old and apace going down
Let me die in my bed, and heaven obtain.

'Poor Robin's wish, or choice, or prayer: | Call't what you please, it follows here' [imitation of Walter Pope's The old man's wish]

Poetry Box x/77; see also 'If I live to be old . . .'.

So571 Since I have freed myself, from Cupid's ark
Which he to save his cot, was forc't to sink.

[Sir Philip Wodehouse], 'Upon his noble kinsman Sr. Charles Barkeley'

b.131, back (no. 135)

S0572 Since in this dome, the muses' hallowed shrine,
Whilst mighty he protects, and worthy you adorn.

N[athaniel] Saltier, 'Woman' [verses for the Lent
Probation at the Merchant Taylor's School, 1700]
[Crum s553]

Poetry Box VI/74

S0573 Since it came in my mind of late to turn poet,
That regain'd our lost freedom, and cur'd all our
woes.

'The complaint and conclusion'

fb.70, p. 209

S0574 Since I've wrote a poetical letter to Nan,
And when time will permit, write me out a new
tune.

Edward Sneyd, 'An epistle. 5th. To my niece Barbara.
April the 9th. 1773'

c.214, p. 21

S0575 Since judges high graced with learning and taste
So push round the can to—Judge Thumb. | Toll de
roll &c.

'Song 180'

c.555, p. 281

S0576 Since knaves are captious, and since fools are dull,
Guides our frail barks, and points to wisdom's
shores.

'Poem on stupidity'

c.481, p. 165

S0577 Since ladies were ladies, I dare boldly say
And a Protestant prince should prove an Italian.

'The ladies' complaint'
[Crum s559]

b.111, p. 369

S0578 Since language never can describe my pain
'Tis all I ask—eternally adieu.

[John] Hervey, baron Hervey of Ickworth, 'Monimia
to Philocles. Miss [Sophia] Howe to Mr [Anthony]
Lowther' [pr. 1726 (Foxon H157.5)]

c.392, p. 3; fc.51, p. 146

S0579 Since lengthening days their genial force renew
And stones to form the wall harmoniously
conspired.

'To Celia a New Year's epistle'

Poetry Box I/28

S0580 Since life in sorrow must be spent,
Spent O Lord, in pleasing Thee!

[William Cowper, trans.], 'Live to love. Vol. 2. Son.
165' [of Jeanne Guion's 'Spiritual songs']

c.470 (autogr.)

S0581 Since life is a span let us drive away care
We may be in our own coffins tomorrow.

T[homas] Liddiard, 'Anacreontic extempore'

c.344, p. 121

S0582 Since life's a rough path as all sages have said:
And strew it with roses of pleasure between.

'The roses of pleasure'

c.344, p. 1

S0583 Since love and verse as well as wine,
When kiss'd and press'd in foreign arms.

Sir George Etherege, 'To my Lord Middleton . . .
Ratisbon May the 10th 1686'
[Crum s562]

fb.68, p. 99; fb.70, p. 53

S0584 Since love intrigues are out of date
If we shall do ourselves the reason.

'The lady's address to the Q[ueen]' [c. 1692–1694]

fb.108, p. 79

S0585 Since Marylebone no longer can delight,
Each prove himself the true . . . .

[Charles Burney, the younger], 'Occasional prologue
to The goodnatured man, a comedy, when acted by
ladies and gentlemen, for their diversion. Autumn.
1775'

c.37, p. 40 (incomplete)

S0586 Since mighty realms have left, a lonely waste,
One endless bliss king, words, and commons gain.

James Gough, 'Britannia—a poem—with historical
notes'

c.139, p. 286

S0587 Since moderation is so much in vogue
And show the face of truth you've wrong'd before.

c.160, fol. 112

S0588 Since my good friends, tho' late are pleas'd at last
To find the secret to deserve your favors.

[David Garrick], 'Mr. Garrick's address to the town in
the character of Marplot, in [Mrs. Centlivre's] The
busybody'

c.68, p. 23; c.115

S0589 Since nature's so form'd us why should we complain
I'd rather have none than possess | Such a nose,
such a carbuncle &c.

[John Walker?], 'Nosey—a song'

fc.108, fol. 48v

S0590 Since, noble Fronto, you to know desire,
And spend his days in hurry noise and strife.

[Henry] Needler, 'Martial Epigr. 56. Book 1'

c.244, p. 541

S0591 Since noon? Have you been solitary still?
But now, that you are come, I am alone.

Sir Thomas Urquhart, 'The answer of a learned
gentleman, to an importunate lubbard, who by a rude
intrusion interrupted the pleasure, he purposed, for an
hour or two, to have enjoyed with the tickling vivacity
of his own cogitations'

fb.217, p. 127

S0592 Since now Florella, I with sorrow see
If I was sure, that thou wert truly blest.

[Thomas Hamilton, 6th earl of Haddington], 'To
Florella epistle the nineteenth'

c.458/1, p. 80

S0593 Since now my Sylvia is as kind as fair,
Love fill'd our hearts, there was no room for fear. |
Now . . . .

[John Sheffield, 1st duke of Buckingham and
Normanby], 'On the enjoyment of his mistress'
[Crum s578]

b.105, p. 194 (incomplete)

S0594 Since oaths are solemn serious things,
I can't well suffer in a better cause.

'The new oath examined and found guilty'
[Crum s580]

b.111, p. 165

S0595 Since of our quarters you, a view desire,
I shall more fools for thy diversion find.

[Captain B——], 'A Canterbury story'

Poetry Box IV/12

S0596 Since oft, fair infidel! we wish'd to prove
Constant, melodious, and even blest in death.

[Stephen Barrett], 'Male constancy exemplified in the
story of Stellus: a peacock. To Mrs. M——'

c.193, p. 98

S0597 Since one thing needful is to be desired
So shall our souls enjoy a lasting peace.

[Mary Serjant]

fb.98, fol. 157

S0598 Since our first parents' fall,
But in a mighty circle, round forever goes.

[cf. Crum s584]

fc.54, p. 75

S0599 Since Phyllis we find,
By force of your wit, and your beauty.

'The free willer'

fb.107, p. 14

S0600 Since Phyllis you resolve to hate,
Nor absolutely kill, nor spare.

'Another by the same hand' [as 'Tho' in their
flame . . .']

fb.142, p. 52

S0601 Since pigs were invented, grains, porridge, and oats
Like a dog, that's stark mad at the sight of salt water.

J[ohn] C[arter], 'Truro pork to the tune of The roast
beef of old England [by Peter Pindar]'

c.488, p. 35

S0602 Since pleasure's in fashion and life's but a jest
Swell round the gay chorus of ha ha ha ha.

'Song 168'

c.555, p. 257

S0603 Since popery's the plot
Under Bloody Jamy.

'The loyal healths' [c. 1680]
[Crum s592]

fb.106(23)

S0604 Since printers with such pleasing nature write,
Let printers write, and let your writers print.

John Lockman, 'Advice to the booksellers: after
reading Pamela . . . March 1740/1'

c.267/1, p. 33

S0605 Since promotion seems that one thing
Still keeps his eyes on Durham bent.

c.546

S0606 Since prose is turn'd quite out of door,
From your obedient, humble servant.

C[harles] B[urney], 'Extempore answer' [to Miss Jessy
Miller's verses: 'Since you're so fond of writing
rhyme . . .']

c.37, p. 69

S0607 Since prose won't move we'll try what verse can do
To come like Salisbury a convert home.

'The friendly advice to the Prot[estant] peers'

Poetry Box VII/2

S0608 Since she is purely ice—she is as cold
The other bids her pierce with lively sprite.

[Sir Philip Wodehouse], 'Lucy Pierce is purely ice'

b.131, back (no. 114, no. 224)

S0609 Since she must go and I must mourn, come night
As I will never look for more in you.

    [John Donne]
    [Crum s599]

b.148, p. 148; b.205, fol. 88r ('must stay')

S0610 Since that the name betokens wise and saving
And by its help no ague long endures.

    'Upon sage an herb'

c.158, p. 120

S0611 Since the court is gone from you, which made you
                  so gay
I have great esteem and shall have while I've
                 breath.

    '1746 Nov. 11'

Poetry Box x/68

S0612 Since the dean went away
And a full yard long, and yet longer.

    [Frances (Kolbel)] Payne, baroness Lavington, 'From
    Lady Payne to Lord Binning'

Poetry Box II/14

S0613 Since the fate of most poets is toil and disgrace;
So make me (good Lord!) in thy house a
                 doorkeeper.

    John Lockman, 'To the right honorable patron of the
    Italian opera . . . April 1747'

c.267/1, p. 35

S0614 Since the impartial fates did so conspire
And breath'd her last but straight she was enthron'd.

    T[homas] H[eywood?], 'T. H. on the lady
    Fleetwood's death'

b.62, p. 110

S0615 Since the marriage act's pass'd—by which fortune's
                 protected—
Go to Sussex! Or Wilts—any borough—but this.

    [Phanuel Bacon], 'In amori haec sunt mala—spoken at
    Abingdon after Mr. Moreton's election'

c.237, fol. 83

S0616 Since the pox is so rife in the town
And a buggerer by Wade.

fb.66/16

S0617 Since the professor's life's the rule, whereby
Then vindicate the once wrong'd innocent.

    [John Hobart]

b.108, fol. 5v

S0618 Since the scum of these three nations
His own good subjects ne'er may want.

    'To the King's most excellent Majesty, the humble
    address of the mayor, aldermen . . . and loyal hundreds
    of Drury'

fc.58, p. 150

S0619 Since the sons of the muses grow clam'rous and loud
For he had writ plays yet ne'er came in print.

    [John Wilmot, 2nd earl of Rochester?], 'A sessions of
    the poets' [imitation of Boileau; 1675]
    [Crum s613; POAS I.352]

b.105, p. 238 (attr. E. Settle); b.54, p. 1038 (ll. 1–82)

S0620 Since, then, o'er the admiring world,
Which echo to far distant lands.

    John Lockman, 'Stanzas, on the progress of poetry,
    and the polite arts, among the Greeks and Romans:
    their decay, and revival . . . this rhapsody was struck
    out in 1727, being one of the author's first essays in
    verse'

c.267/1, p. 375

S0621 Since there's so small difference 'twixt drowning
                 and drinking
And plentiful store of good Burgundy send us.

    'Song 152'

c.555, p. 211

S0622 Since these gay thoughts your fair obliging friend
For married ladies not so good as you.

    [Mrs. Christian Kerr], 'To a married lady upon giving
    her back some of her letters of friendship lest they
    should be seen and taken for gallantry'

c.102, p. 99

S0623 Since they are blind, who do not wealth admire,
And gold in virtue's cause does with true luster
                 shine.

    'Wealth'

b.322, p. 27

S0624 Since thine illustrious ancestors thee own,
Be Tully, Mars and Ormonde all in one.

    'James Butler be Tully, Mars anagr[am]'

fb.228/31

S0625 Since thine's the only power on earth we know
To the true husband send the spotless wife.

    'To the Pope, on a lady abroad 1774'

c.546, p. 4

S0626 Since those soft lips which just begin
Then startled views the pointed flash.

> [Robert Cholmeley], 'To Flavia. Upon singing a song
> of my composing'
>
> c.190, p. 150

S0627 Since thou art dead Clifton the world may see
Shall pass by thee to her, but not so fast.

> Fra[ncis] Beaumont, 'An elegy upon the death of
> Penelope the late Lady Clifton'
> [Crum s621]
>
> b.197, p. 208

S0628 Since thou into rebellion fell
God sendeth meat, the devil finds a cook.

> 'Charles Coote anagram art Hell's cook'
>
> fb.228/26

S0629 Since thou my fair Florella bids me write,
Heaven grant, my maxims be approv'd by thee.

> [Thomas Hamilton, 6th earl of Haddington], 'To
> Florella epistle the seventh'
>
> c.458/1, p. 19

S0630 Since thou, relentless maid, canst daily hear
Consider how much more you owe to true.

> [Soame Jenyns], 'Written in a lady's volume of
> tragedies'
>
> c.147, p. 51 (attr. G. M.)

S0631 Since thou to blare thine own worth hast a face,
Lingua doth spit defiance in his face.

> 'Cubit lingua' [answered by 'Tongue your shape . . .']
>
> b.356, p. 117

S0632 Since thus you urge me to declare
Be chang'd to gentle smiles of love!

> R[ichard] V[ernon] S[adleir], 'To [blank]'
>
> c.106, p. 134

S0633 Since time with gliding fame(?) has gone
As polish gives—the diamond's blaze.

> Mrs. E. M. B., 'March the 20—1785. From a lady to
> her son, on his birthday, being then twenty-one years
> of age'
>
> c.90

S0634 Since 'tis my doom love's undershrieve | Why this
reprieve?
I feel you are consenting ript | By that soft grip . . . .

> [John Cleveland], 'To Julia to expedite her 'gainst a
> lyric poem'
> [Crum s631]
>
> b.93, p. 41 (incomplete)

S0635 Since 'tis Neptune's high festival, say,
Night—night—my dear girl, is the thing.

> [William Popple, trans.], '[Horace] book 3rd. ode
> 28th. To Lyde'
>
> fc.104/2, p. 310

S0636 Since 'tis the will of all-disposing heav'n
When they enjoy the good and patient bear the ill.

> General [ ] Conway, 'Elegy on the death of Miss
> Caroline Campbell'
>
> c.373, p. 48; c.391, p. 84

S0637 Since 'tis to thee I undergo
Since thou hast made my sorrows thine.

> T[homas] Liddiard, 'Lorenzo to Sylvia . . . Cold
> Harbor 1793'
>
> c.344, p. 117

S0638 Since to be chaste and fair
Or playing of the whore.

> G. M., 'On a deformed mistress'
>
> b.115, fol. 28v

S0639 Since to the will of all-disposing heaven,
When they enjoy the good and patient bear the ill.

> General [ ] Conway, 'Elegy on the death of Miss
> Caroline Campbell, daughter of the right hon. Lord
> William Campbell'
>
> c.391, p. 84

S0640 Since truth has left the shepherd's tongue
Is all that will remember me.

> 'Maria's complaint'
>
> c.83/2, no. 524

S0641 Since Valentine again appears
Be only good men's memory!

> [Phanuel Bacon], 'To Doctor Cummings on his
> birthday Feb. 14'
>
> c.237, fol. 35

S0642 Since various subjects various pens employ
Than all the conquests he had gain'd before.

> 'The court monkeys' [printed 1734 (Foxon C468)]
>
> c.570/4, p. 23

S0643 Since we can die but once and after death,
Which no cessation knows.

> [John] Pomfret, 'A prospect of death' [pr. 1704 (Foxon
> P733)]
> [Crum s642, attr. Roscommon]
>
> c.244, p. 68; b.218, p. 33; c.549, p. 76

S0644 Since we poor slavish women know
Is but a lawful whore for gain.

[William Wycherley], 'The opportunity' [in The
gentleman dancing-master, II.ii, 1672]

fb.107, p. 42

S0645 Since what's above written some years have expir'd
From all sorrows here to enjoy endless peace.

J. F[ry], 'Postscript [to 'As wishing will neither . . .']
written in the year 1769'

c.517, fol. 23r

S0646 Since you are fair, you to be false are free,
The judge is easy, though your cause is bad.

'To his mistress desiring her if she will be false to be
private too'

fb.142, p. 32

S0647 Since you, dear doctor, sav'd my life,
To do, as has done yours, C: H.

[Thomas Hearne], 'Letter from C. [i.e, T.] H. to Dr:
L.' [actually to Sir Hans Sloane; satire. Printed 1729
(Foxon E437)]

c.241, p. 125; c.116, p. 31 (var.); c.360/2, no. 196 (attr. Mrs.
E. H.); fc.51, p. 132; Poetry Box I/87; Spence Papers,
folder 113

S0648 Since you fair friend, have given me leave to write,
Till then my fair, and valued friend adieu.

[Thomas Hamilton, 6th earl of Haddington], 'To
Florella, epistle the first'

c.458/1, p. 1

S0649 Since you have pronounc'd my doom
Will there a wat'ry star appear.

'Song'

Poetry Box I/111[9]

S0650 Since you resigned your dear commission
Good-nature, modesty, and breeding.

'A familiar epistle to the king of hearts' [Lord
Delamere, later earl of Warrington; 1691]
[Crum s655; POAS v.179]

b.111, p. 575

S0651 Since you so earnestly some lines demand
The sweet Maria long has this possess'd.

Cecelia B[urney], 'Epithalamium inscribed to
Mr. Bourdois . . . aged 12'

c.486, fol. 42

S0652 Since you the lady of this day is known,
Like the high steeple bells his numbers chime.

'To Mrs Christian Kerr of Chatto on her birthday
Agst 22 1725 after Doc: Rutherford had presented her
with a poem at an entertainment in Lady Helen
Scott's by a young gentleman'

c.102, p. 130

S0653 Since you, who oft have prisoner made
Depriv'd of liberty.

'On Sir John Fielding's marriage . . . Benedick'

fc.85, fol. 116

S0654 Since you will needs my heart possess,
Will prove just such another.

'Inconstancy'
[Crum s658]

fb.107, p. 32

S0655 Since your campaign of 70 now is gone,
Of invalids, about your easy chair.

[Mrs. Christian Kerr], 'To Mr. Kerr of Chatto
March 25 1720 being his birthday entering 71 year few
of the company with him being in perfect health'

c.102, p. 113

S0656 Since your curiosity led you so far
Is the only favor your Lordship can hope. | Which
nobody [can deny]

[Philip Wharton, 1st duke of Wharton], 'A letter from
Jack Sheppard to Tho. E[arl] of Mac[c]l[e]s[field]'
[who sent him to Chancery Bar to see him after he
was tried, 1724. Printed 1725 (Foxon E369)]
[Crum s659]

c.489, p. 11; Poetry Box x/147; see also 'When your
curiosity . . .'.; c.570/2, p. 113

S0657 Since you're alike in sense and life
A pair so matcht cannot agree.

[Robert Cholmeley], '[Martial's epigram In pessimos
conjuges] translated'

c.190, p. 66

S0658 Since you're so fond of writing rhyme,
And thank you for your fruit, you Brute.

Jessy Miller, 'Verses by . . . to thank C[harles]
B[urney] for a present of fruit. July 22, 1779'

c.37, p. 69

S0659 Sincerest critic of my prose or rhyme,
And oh the golden age is but a dream.

[William] Congreve, 'Albi, nostrorum sermonum
candide index. Hor. Ep. 3 . . . Mr. Congreve's letter to
Ld. Cobham' [pr. 1729 (Foxon C375)]

fc.135

S0660　Sincerity what are thy views,
They know your value there.

　　[Mary Barber], 'Sincerity'

　c.83/1, no. 172

S0661　Sinful soul, come forth and stand
But first th'indictment shall be read to you.

　　H[enry] C[olman], 'The arraignment'
　　[Crum s662]

　b.2, p. 22

S0662　Sing all ye nations! Your hands clap around,
Forever tasting there the bliss at God's right hand.

　c.167, p. 34

S0663　Sing Heliconian muse, strange deeds untold
Unwearied, all must wonder, and applaud.

　　'Annals of staghunting'

　c.519

S0664　Sing, Muse, how rebel Titans rose,
And bid with peace the skies be blest.

　　[Stephen Barrett], 'The battle of the giants: an
　　allegorical poem on the suppression of the rebellion in
　　1745 by the Duke of Cumberland' [pr. 1746 (Foxon
　　B87)]

　c.193, p. 107

S0665　Sing Muse the torch, witness of stol'n delight
In Hero's eyes, ten thousand graces shine.

　　'Hero and Leander from Musaeus. 1729'
　　Trumbull Box: Poetry Box XIII/103, p. 6

S0666　Sing on sweet thrush, upon the leafless bough,
The mite high heaven bestowed, that mite with
　　　　　　　　　　　　　　　　　　　thee I'll share.

　　[Robert Burns], 'Sonnet written in 1793 on the
　　birthday of the author on hearing a thrush sing in a
　　morning walk'

　c.142, p. 318

S0667　Sing to the Lord a song new made
Therein his righteousness.

　　'Psal: 98'

　b.217, p. 67

S0668　Sing to the Lord in new-made songs
In equity and right.

　　'Psalm 98'

　c.264/2, p. 109

S0669　Sing to the Lord new songs of praise,
In truth announce the gen'ral doom.

　　'Psalm 96'

　c.264/2, p. 106

S0670　Sing to the Lord ye loud proclaim
For God will guard, where God has led.

　　P[hilip] Doddridge, 'God's name the encouragement
　　of our faith Ps. IX 10'

　c.493, p. 74

S0671　Sing ye redeem'd of the Lord
While lab'ring up the hill.

　　P[hilip] Doddridge, 'The way of salvation plain pure
　　and safe from Is. XXXV 8-10 And a highway shall be
　　there &c.'

　c.493, p. 60

S0672　Sing ye unto the Lord our God,
Agree with one accord.

　　[Thomas Norton], 'The 66 psalm' [verses from
　　Psalms 149-150]
　　[cf. Crum s686]

　a.3, fol. 150

S0673　Sing ye with praise unto the Lord
And mindful of the same.

　　[John Hopkins], 'The 41 psalm. A praise to God for
　　his mercies' [verses from Psalms 96-97]
　　[cf. Crum s687]

　a.3, fol. 116v

S0674　Sinister accidents so propagate
Evil should be welcome if it come alone.

　　[Sir Thomas Urquhart], 'One [?] still follows upon
　　another'

　fb.217, p. 534

S0675　Sinners obey your heavenly call
When wash'd from all our sins in blood.

　　'Hymn 33d'

　c.562, p. 38

S0676　Sinners with sinners can agree
Who feast on manifested love.

　　[Thomas Stevens?], 'The 3. chapr. of Amos 3 verse
　　Can two walk together except they be agreed'

　c.259, p. 131

S0677　Sins, in respect of man, all mortal be
All venial, Jesu, in respect of thee.

　　[Francis Quarles], 'On sins'
　　[Crum s692]

　b.137, p. 179

S0678　Sin's popery of late
For the second part of my ditty.

　　'The Catholic ballad'

　b.226, p. 58

S0679   Sir Bartolph Testy and his wayward dame
A wonder they can always disagree.

     'An epigram'

     c.115

S0680   Sir be advis'd, she's not your daughter now
That's more than canonizing by a pope.

     Rob[er]t Wild, 'To the father of a very virtuous
     virgin, who desired an obscure person to make an
     elegy'

     c.166, p. 286

S0681   Sir Boswell to thee blest honors rise!
A proof that justice is not fled to skies.

     John Lockman, 'Extempore: when the city members
     were declared from the hustings'

     c.267/1, p. 5

S0682   Sir call me not receiveress
In sadness, nothing I receive.

     Sir Thomas Urquhart, 'The moan of a receiver of the
     taxation's wife, her husband being an aged man to a
     friend of her own'

     fb.217, p. 267

S0683   Sir Charles the witling of the town,
They give one crack and then they die.

     [Robert Cholmeley], 'The fop'

     c.190, p. 201

S0684   Sir Circumspect! whose either eye
The other blind, both strive to blink.

     'On Sr. Jn. Tr[e]v[o]r M[aste]r of the R[o]lls'
     Poetry Box IV/5

S0685   Sir Drake, whom well the world's end knows
His fellow-traveller.

     ['Drace penerrati . . .'] Englished'

     c.360/2, no. 269

S0686   Sir Herod's house in Christ his time
That we in heaven may plant our place. | Amen

     'Of St. James. July. 25'

     a.30[16]

S0687   Sir I admit your general rule
That every fool is not a poet.

     [Alexander Pope?], 'Another [epigram] from the
     French' [sometimes attrib. Jonathan Swift]

     fc.60, p. 50

S0688   Sir I applaud your enterprise and say
Art fit to sit with Phoebus in his throne.

     [Sir Aston Cokayne], 'To my friend Mr Humph
     [C—ford] on his love's hawking bag'

     b.275, p. 60

S0689   Sir I care not | When you be cold or hot
What hope what hope that should bake it.

     'Another answer to Mistake me not'

     b.213, p. 22

S0690   Sir I do here present unto your view
In such a pace it stands not at a stay!

     Sir John Strangways, 'Another motive to humility
     upon consideration of these three times. Viz: 1. What
     man was before he was born. 2. What he is all his life
     long, after he is born. 3. What he shall be after his life
     is ended . . . In the Tower of London . . . 10 June 1647'

     b.304, p. 97

S0691   Sir I had writ in Latin but I fear
Nor never want whereby to cause a wish.

     [William Strode], 'To Sr Edmund Lingo'
     [Crum S714]

     b.205, fol. 54r

S0692   Sir, I have list'ned long, yet fear'd to speak—
Who'd keep a servant better taught than he?

     [William Popple, trans.], 'Horace book 2nd satire 7th
     imitated. Or, a dialogue between a man of fashion and
     his valet.'

     fc.104/1, p. 323

S0693   Sir, if a curious tomb, you would erect,
Write here below lies my sweet mistress Jean.

     Sir Thomas Urquhart, 'An instruction to a certain
     cavalier, how to rear a monument in honor of his
     mistress, whose name was Jean'

     fb.217, p. 278

S0694   Sir if two hundred crowns so much conduce
Let me live and enjoy the blessings I foresaw.

     R[obert] Shirley, 1st earl of Ferrers, 'Mlle Bernard's
     father having for his services obtained a pension from
     the King she makes this petition to his Majesty for
     continuance of it after her father's death'

     c.347, p. 91

S0695   Sir in your epigrams you did me grace
Freely enjoy with me my utmost fame.

     [Sir Aston Cokayne], 'To Mr Tho: Bancroft'

     b.275, p. 40

S0696   Sir, I've a pupil—Well, draw near
Be sure you don't forget the crown.

     [Chester Perne], 'A dialogue between Dr. Barnwell
     and Mr. Johnson'
     [Crum S724]

     c.489, p. 22

S0697   Sir John at this place
But made me a daddy.

     'From a window at Spinhamland'

     c.81/1, no. 373

S0698   Sir John got him an ambling nag
But his lost honor must still live the last | At
                    Barwick away it went a.

     [Sir John Mennes?], 'Upon Sr Jo: Suckling's most
     warlike preparations for the Scottish war' [1639]
     [Crum S726, 'bought him']

     b.65, p. 193

S0699   Sir John's a good old knight—'tis true
It first runs strong—and then small beer.

     [Phanuel Bacon], 'Fortis non creantur fortibus'

     c.237, fol. 69

S0700   Sir many years ago when you and I
Pray laugh at them again now in this book.

     [Sir Aston Cokayne], 'To my very good friend Mr
     Francis Lenton'

     b.275, p. 46

S0701   Sir marry ere you burn; the care is fresh,
In your wife's lap to mortify the flesh.

     Sir Thomas Urquhart, 'A counsel to marry'

     fb.217, p. 158

S0702   Sir may it please you but to hear
Your said petitioner shall pray.

     'The humble petition of his Grace Philip Duke of
     Wharton, to a great man in London, wrote in 1728'
     [satire; pr. 1730 (Foxon H396)]

     c.468

S0703   Sir Monday—my trumps will be cock'rel or capon,
With your poor poetaster—but poet divine.

     [Charles Earle], 'To Mr. Rogers—Pilton—gent | This
     rhyming compliment is sent . . .'

     c.376

S0704   Sir more than kisses, letters mingle souls
To know my rules: I have, and you have, | Donne.

     [John Donne], 'To Sr. Hen. Wotton'
     [Crum S731a]

     b.114, p. 233; b.148, p. 71

S0705   Sir Nice, thou art a finisht beau,
He's a mere trifle, and an empty show.

     [Robert Cholmeley], '[Martial] thus translated'

     c.190, p. 28

S0706   Sir Numps (in Old Nol's time) Lord Mayor—
The pasty seiz'd on was his own.

     [Phanuel Bacon], 'Qui capit ille facit'

     c.237, fol. 65

S0707   Sir or Madam choose you whither
Coining thee a Philip and Mary.

     [John Cleveland], 'Upon an hermaphrodite' [also attr.
     Thomas Randolph]
     [Crum S734]

     b.93, p. 31

S0708   Sir Philip Sidney did present your mother
Surmounts th'abstract ide' of a romance.

     Sir Thomas Urquhart, 'To the Countess of Pembroke'

     fb.217, p. 99

S0709   Sir Ralph a simple rural knight
And lies with every man she meets.

     [Nicholas Amhurst], 'The progress of patriotism'

     c.570/3, p. 25

S0710   Sir Robert at the late parade,
Which crowds were ready there to kiss.

     [Samuel Wesley, the younger], 'On the string of Sr
     Robt. Walpole's breeches being broke' [during a
     procession in 1725]
     [Crum S739]

     c.233, p. 56

S0711   Sir Robert brags that he has sunk
As tinkers mend a kettle.

     'On Sir Robert Walpole'

     c.570/2, p. 171

S0712   Sir Robert, close pursued by foes,
And plays aloft, in the rebound.

     John Lockman, 'The now peer: a simile . . . 1742'

     c.267/1, p. 14

S0713   Sir R[obert] his merit and interest to show
Odd numbers are lucky, he looks for a third.

     'On Sr. R. W[alpol]e being made Knight of the
     Garter' [26 May 1726]
     [Crum S738]

     c.176, p. 7; c.360/1, p. 177; c.489, p. 23; c.233, p. 29; see
     also 'Sir Robert to show . . .'.

S0714   Sir Robert in a late parade
That crowds were ready there to kiss.

     'On Mr. Walpole on the day of his installment'

     c.570/2, p. 149

S0715 Sir Robert to show what to merit is due
Odd numbers are lucky, may he soon have the third.

    'Mr. Walpole's blue garter'

c.570/2, p. 159; see also 'Sir Robert his merit . . .'.

S0716 Sir Roger from a zealous piece of frieze
That they and theirs were all *et cetera*.

    [John Cleveland], 'A dialogue between two zealots
    concerning the new oath'
    [Crum s740]

b.200, p. 268; b.93, p. 43 (incomplete)

S0717 Sir since you have prepared tea
If bread and butter is granted.

c.341, p. 101

S0718 Sir! That grand monarch whom you boast of,
Who 'scapes his rage, nor hears his voice.

    E. G., 'A solution of the universal monarch
    enigmatically described. Addressed to the author by E.
    G. esq.'

c.50, p. 73

S0719 Sir that I do expose these trifles to
Once more to make us laugh at them again.

    [Sir Aston Cokayne], 'To my very good friend Mr
    Tho: Lightwood'

b.275, p. 48

S0720 Sir Thomas de Veil thinks it proper to tell
As witness his writing Sir Thomas de Veil.

    'On Sir Thomas De Veil, when first knighted signing
    his name Sir Thomas De Veil'

c.360/1, p. 319

S0721 Sir though (I thank God for it) I do hate
Within the vast reach of the statutes laws.

    [John Donne], 'Satira secunda' [Satire III]
    [Crum s752]

b.114, p. 9; b.148, p. 138

S0722 Sir 'tis Apollo's pleasure and the will,
Keep it for them that hath acquired praise.

b.216, p. 160

S0723 Sir Titus Vernon, since you have betray'd
That of thy office seats I well shall earn one?

Trumbull Box: Poetry Box XIII/79

S0724 Sir whiles you pity my affected state
To all observance faithful to my end.

    Sir John Strangways, 'The free prisoner: or the
    comfort of restraint: written some while since in the
    Tower by Dr. Joseph Hall the bishop of Norwich: and
    translated by . . . knight and prisoner in the same
    place . . . 1646'

b.304, p. 3

S0725 Sir, whilst you seem to court a muse,
By these the reader dies.

    'To the unknown author of a lampoon'

c.146, p. 37

S0726 Sir, will you please to walk before?
Go forward, friends—or he'll surprise ye.

    William Shenstone, 'The ceremonial'

c.487, p. 135

S0727 Sir William Paston 'tis, who here does lie
None past on braver, thro' this pilgrimage.

    [Sir Philip Wodehouse], 'A more solemn epitaph'

b.131, back (no. 11/2)

S0728 Sir William proves no man can be
From death, that tyrant's clutches free.

    'Sr. Wm. Blacket's epitaph'

c.530, p. 196

S0729 Sir William you attempt the vain,
You're ignorant of yourself alone.

    Tho[mas] Law, 'The following lines were sent to Sir
    Wm Jones by . . . in consequence of a
    conversation . . .'

c.83/4, no. 2034

S0730 Sir William's no more a poet
He wants(?) no more verse to repeat. | For the
                           honor [&c.]

    [Sir John Denham], 'To the tune of Arthur of Bradley'
    [on Sir William D'Avenant]

pb.53, p. 15 (autogr.)

S0731 Sir you are heir unto a fine estate
One thing is wanting still, and that, a wife.

    [Sir Aston Cokayne], 'To my worthy Cousin Mr
    [Seabright?] Reppington'

b.275, p. 102

S0732 Sir, you, being old, should court for other men
An ass of twenty.

    Sir Thomas Urquhart, 'The speeches of a young
    coxcomb, to a very proper aged man, entertaining a
    pretty, handsome maid'

fb.217, p. 137

S0733 Sir, your lines I receiv'd, with a cry for a wood—
Your friend—now a curate—who once was a vicar.

    C[harles] E[arle], 'To one, who sent me a cry for a
    wood, omitting the growth, mistaking the day and
    forgetting the place. Novr. 5th'

c.376

S0734 Sir your looks a conqueror doth presage
Then you for monarch's pattern stand alone.

Lady Jane Cavendish, 'On his Highness the Prince of
Wales' [afterwards Charles II]
[Crum s759]

b.233, p. 11

S0735 Sire gin your honor would vouchsafe to take
Where's muckle thronging, there'll be muckle stink.

Allan Ramsay, 'Horace's [?] invitation—sipotes
archaices . . . Epist. 5'

c.229/1, fol. 37

S0736 Sister! So proud you've grown, such scorn you dart,
And thenceforth be proclaim'd, joint Queen of
Hearts.

John Lockman, 'The Opera—Tuesday's complaint to
her sister Saturday . . . March 1759'

c.267/1, p. 275

S0737 Sit still ye cowards and lament in vain,
And at the name of Britain, be no more.

'The remonstrance, occasioned by the murder of the
Revd. Mr. Paul, and H. Hall esqr.'

c.570/1, p. 174

S0738 Sith th'harp's discording strings, concording be
It's not a shame for men to disagree.

'An harp'

c.356

S0739 Sitting and ready to be drawn
Next sitting we will draw her mind.

[Ben Jonson], 'On a gentlewoman [Venetia Stanley,
lady Digby] sitting in a chair to have her picture
drawn'
[Crum s774]

b.205, fol. 87r

S0740 Sitting and shitting I read your letter
I took your letter, and wip'd my arse.

[Crum s775]

fb.66/2

S0741 Sitting around our father's board,
Or equal thanks repay.

[Isaac Watts, Hymns and spiritual songs (1707),
bk. III, Hymn 23]

c.180, p. 56

S0742 Sitting beyond a river's side
But like unconstant wretches live again.

'A song: 1678'

b.54, p. 1102

S0743 Sitting late in sorrow's keeping
For I have lost my dearest friend. | O hone
honononus . . .

[c. 1590]
[cf. Crum s778]

File 19009

S0744 Six days has man in duteous toil employ'd:
In his full court, the universal King.

[Moses] Browne, 'Browne's Sunday thoughts part 1
page 116'

c.148, p. 7

S0745 Six foots [sic] of ground hold a dead man, which
was both strong and tall;
Though in his life he had many acres, and dwelt in
a brave hall.

c.339, p. 307

S0746 Six holy sisters of the purest sect,
They all like sitting well but standing best.

[Sir John Harington], 'The holy sisters'
[cf. Crum s779]

fb.207/1, p. 8

S0747 Six hours in sleep, in law's grave study six
Four spent in prayer, the rest on nature fix.

Sir Edward Coke(?)

c.83/4, no. 2032

S0748 Six London squires one morning rose,
And so they walk'd to town.

'The Sunday ride'

c.116, p. 56; c.175, p. 77

S0749 Skill'd in the globe and spheres, he gravely stands,
A whole night's vigor, to repair his shame.

[John] Dryden, [prefaced to 'The longitude
discovered. A tale by the author of the deluge . . .';
Dryden's lines taken from Juvenal, satires 6 and 9]

c.503, p. 9

S0750 Slacken thy hearty steps, too thoughtless youth!
The friuit shall ripen in eternity.

[ ] Porter, 'On the death of a young lady'

c.83/1, no. 62

S0751 Sleep close at home the tortoise says,
The turtle—love and peace.

'Distich. Wrote under the figure of a woman standing
upon a tortoise, a bunch of keys in her right hand, the
forefinger of her left hand upon her lips, and a dove
upon her shoulder . . . translations [6]'

c.81/1, no. 70

S0752 Sleep for that soul must surely want relief
And give the transports quite unknown before.

　　Miss [ ] Andrews, 'On seeing Miss Howard asleep'
File 245/8

S0753 Sleep is the body's rest, the soul takes none
Mercy and pity when his servants cry.

　　[Edmund Wodehouse], 'Jan. 3 [1715]'
b.131, p. 130

S0754 Sleep lovely babe, sleep on from dangers free
Which past the bloom of youth shall still remain.

　　C[harles James] F[ox], 'On a child sleeping to Lady
M——Fox'
File 5380

S0755 Sleep next society, and true friendship
Things worth the truth, reading dear Nick, good
night.

　　[Sir John Roe], 'Satira sexta. To Sr. Nicholas Smith
[1602?]' [attr. John Donne]
[Crum s796]
b.114, p. 51

S0756 Sleep on blest angel, till thy Maker's will
Then rise unchang'd and be an angel still.

　　'Another [epitaph on a child]'
c.83/3, no. 1021; c.83/4, no. 2021; see also 'Sleep soft in
dust . . .', 'Lie sweet in dust . . .', 'Lie still sweet maid . . .',
'Soft rest thy dust . . .'.

S0757 Sleep on, sleep on, sweet babe, beguile
Which thou dost imitate so near.

　　'The babe asleep'
c.83/3, no. 929

S0758 Sleep silence['s] child, sweet father of soft rest,
I long to kiss the image of my death.

　　William Drummond, of Hawthornden, 'Sonnet to
sleep' [1616]
[Crum s804]
b.150, p. 218

S0759 Sleep soft in dust, wait th'Almighty's will,
Then rise unchang'd, and be an angel still.

　　'Epitaph on a very beautiful and virtuous young lady'
Poetry Box XII/97[2]; see also 'Soft rest thy dust . . .', Lie
sweet in dust . . .', 'Lie still sweet maid . . .','Sleep on
blest angel . . .'.

S0760 'Sleep, that knits up the ravell'd sleeve of care'
I shall be laid, and feel that loss no more!

　　[Charlotte (Turner) Smith], 'Sonnet. The winter
night'
c.141, p. 124

S0761 Sleep, that once [?] his poppies o'er my couch,
That I may meet their just reward in Heaven!

　　'Midnight reflections on the departed year 1793'
[signed Anna]
c.343, p. 8

S0762 Sleep! Though death thou dost resemble,
Life, without its load of care.

　　'Address to sleep'
c.83/3, no. 1059

S0763 Sleepless eyelids dim with tears,
The blest insensibility.

　　[ ] Kendel, 'A song'
c.83/2, no. 394

S0764 Slight not the following lines
Let devil do his worst.

　　'An advertisement to the grand inquest or the
Parliament. 2 Sept 1680. Forewarned, forearmed'
b.54, p. 1127

S0765 Slip on, sad infants, of a groaning time
Not man to stop one foot, in his own way.

　　[George Daniel]
b.121, fol. 82v

S0766 Slow o'er the Apennine, with bleeding feet,
But, dying, for his murderer breath'd—a sainted
prayer!

　　'The pilgrim'
c.83/3, no. 873

S0767 Slow, pensive Bavius, tippling ale,
Show'st thou long as patriarchs live.

　　John Lockman, 'The opera bard's invocation to the
goddess of nonsense: a mock cantata . . . 1735'
c.267/2, p. 202

S0768 Slow spreads the gloom my soul desires,
From that dear stream which flows to Clyde.

　　[Robert Burns], 'Evan banks'
c.142, p. 310

S0769 Small are the trophies of the boasted bays,
And cherishing that muse, whose fatal curse he
bears.

　　'Poets seldom rewarded'
c.244, p. 147

S0770 Small force of wit in man there is
If God against him be.

　　'Running secretary [hand]'
b.234, p. 25

S0771 Small fragile weed, while thus I view
That those I love 'forget me not'.

pc.97, back fly-leaf

S0772 Small I'd have her, and incline
Let her be of ———— race.

'The bachelor's wish'
[Crum s818]

c.233, p. 95

S0773 Small store of beauty, is requir'd
My long dead heart has won.

[Thomas Hamilton, 6th earl of Haddington], 'A song'

c.458/2, p. 171

S0774 Small, viewless aeronaut, that by the line
Ah! soon at sorrow's touch the radiant dreams
dissolve!

[Charlotte (Turner) Smith], 'Sonnet to the insect of
the gossamer'

c.141, p. 130

S0775 Smectymnuus? the goblin makes me start
And stretch her patent to your leather ears.

[John Cleveland], 'Smectymnuus or the club divine'
[Crum s820]

b.93, p. 115

S0776 Smile, smile, blest isle.
Of George and Caroline.

[Henry Carey], 'Lilliputian verses or a stanza on King
George the 2nd's coming to the crown' [pr. 1727
(Foxon C45)]

c.158, p. 7, p. 354; c.83/2, no. 712; c.536 (incomplete)

S0777 Smiles from a pauper's honest heart,
Are worth a king's if forc'd by art.

John Lockman, 'A truth'

c.267/1, p. 9

S0778 Smiling freedom! lovely guest,
Lay her haughty tyrants low.

'Addition to a duet in the oratorio of Deborah'
Poetry Box IV/161

S0779 Smite with debility my trembling frame,
I'll bless thee still, if life—dear life—remains.

[Seneca, Ep. 101]
Greatheed Box/90

S0780 Smooth Jacob's beauties Celia's face doth show,
And Esau's beauties, she conceals below.

'On the same' [Eleanor Ambrose, in 'In Flavia's
eyes . . .']

c.360/2, no. 152

S0781 Smug the smith for ale and spice
Sold all his tools yet kept his vice.

'On a smith'
b.356, p. 308

S0782 Snatch me, some god, from Baia's desert seats
And art and nature all in ruin lies.

[James Thomson], 'Verse extempore'
Spence Papers, folder 153 (attr. William Drummond of
Hawthornden)

S0783 Snatch'd from oblivion, see time's annals stand
Irradiated by Sharpe's superior light.

John Lockman, 'Writ in a blank leaf, of Dr. Gregory
Sharpe's translation with large notes, of Baron
Holberg's Introduction to universal history . . . June
1755'

c.267/1, p. 152

S0784 Snatch'd hence in early bloom, forbear to mourn,
And scorn that dust which once they were below.

'An epitaph on two beautiful children, viz a boy and
girl who were buried in the same grave at the same
time'

c.360/2, no. 200

S0785 So Abraham at the Lord's command
How great Emanuel's beauties be.

T[homas] S[tevens], 'January the 7th 1781 Lord's day
morning'

c.259, p. 111

S0786 So am I 'slav'd by time,
My weight of cares, to linger out the day | In lyric
rhyme.

[George Daniel]
b.121, fol. 78v

S0787 So boar and sow when any storm is nigh
And snore and gruntle to each other's moan.

[George] Villiers, 2nd duke of Buckingham, '[John
Dryden's 'So too kind turtles . . .'] ridiculed thus'

c.229/1, fol. 41v

S0788 So bright the pretty widow's eyes
She levels at a heart?

'A poem on a certain young widow'
c.503, p. 18

S0789 So chaste a woman hitherto with men
To find a wife, that makes her husband cuckold.

Sir Thomas Urquhart, 'The praise of a gentlewoman
lately buried, carped at'

fb.217, p. 154

So0790 So dress'd Lucretia was by Tarquin seen,
That be a second, fairer, Helen might enjoy.

    M[aurice] J[ohnson], 'On a lady surprised in dishabille
    in imitation of Waller'

    c.229/2, fol. 14

So0791 So easy a couple sure never was seen
She with his statesman spends the whole day.

    [on George II and Caroline]

    Trumbull Box: Poetry Box XIII/81

So0792 So fair in pureness th'elemental flame
Gross, thick, and smoky enemy to sight.

    [Robert Cottesford]

    b.144, p. 7

So0793 So fair, so young, so innocent, so sweet,
Now she is gone, the world is of a piece.

    [John Dryden], 'An epitaph on Mrs. Margaret Paston'
    [Crum s839]

    c.244, p. 207

So0794 So falls a cedar, some by some rude blast
When canst thou now, find such another tree?

    fb.228/47

So0795 So falls that stately cedar; while it stood
It was thy glory, but the kingdom's shame.

    J[oseph] H[all], bp. of Norwich, 'On K. Charles the
    martyr'
    [Crum s840]

    fb.143, p. 37; b.137, p. 198

So0796 So firm the saint's foundation stand;
While such a fountain flows.

    P[hilip] Doddridge, 'The impovered [*sic*] saints
    rejoicing in God Heb. III 17'

    c.493, p. 64

So0797 So generous, so prodigal of hair
Or else, to touch a single lock, despair.

    Poetry Box III/2

So0798 So great a hate I bear not to the father
But that I love the son of him much rather.

    b.208, p. 123

So0799 So green the fields, the sun so bright,
So strongly place affects the thoughts.

    John Lockman, 'Hearing sheep-bells in a delightful
    solitude, near Denbies . . . house, opposite to Box Hill,
    in Surrey, belonging to Mr. [Jonathan] Tyers of
    Vauxhall'

    c.267/1, p. 239

So0800 So grieves the adven'trous merchant, when he
                      throws
Bid her but send me hers, and we are friends.

    Tho[mas] Carew, 'To his m[ist]r[es]s desiring back
    her letters'
    [Crum s847]

    b.200, p. 234

So0801 So hard is now your suppliant's case
You must the Venus be.

    [Robert Cholmeley], 'The fair rivals or Bonfoy's
    complaint to Lovell'

    c.190, p. 29

So0802 So hath it been that of all other books
The which their parents cannot bring them forth.

    [Sir Thomas Urquhart], 'The wits of men as well as
    the bodies of women after long continuance of time
    become so barren, that it hath been almost ever held
    no less extraordinary in a man anything [?] in years
    and set forth above, as to a woman . . .'

    fb.217, p. 508

So0803 So have I seen a cunning rook at play,
Lost when he won, because the dice run true.

    'On the dissolution of Parliament and calling a new
    one 1695'

    fb.207/2, p. 77

So0804 So have I seen, but not at Stratham,
'Tis Hobson's choice—the maim'd or none.

    [Charles Burney, the elder], 'Extract of a letter to Mrs.
    Thrale, who had complained of the fading honors of
    Brighthelmstone; where the whole company was
    reduced, one by one, to a lame Lord'

    c.33, p. 123

So0805 So here a virgin doth her sex excel
Sincerely offer'd, purify our sins.

    [Edward] Sparke, 'Poem 22th on the purification'

    b.137, p. 51

So0806 So here I sing the happy rustic's weal
Fearless, and sings but what his heart indites.

    'A commendation of the country life, above other
    employments'

    b.137, p. 113

So0807 So here she comes, sure heaven will joy today,
What eye could weep, what bosom feel distress.

    'Written on the death of a young lady who had been
    ill some time, and was found dead one morning in her
    bed; by way of dialogue, between her departed spirit,
    and an angel'

    c.83/4, no. 1097

So808 So here the man who stirr'd Rome's common shore
His life was death his death eternal life.

   'On the death of Bale'

   c.548

So809 So high a tide, so low an ebb
Whose fancy comes and goes by fits.

   'To his unconstant mistress' [answered by 'The
   highest tides . . .']

   b.356, p. 102

So810 So his bold tube man to the sun applied
Give us this court, and rule without a guard.

   [Andrew Marvell], 'To the King' [envoy to 'After two
   sittings . . .']

   Poetry Box VII/15

So811 So in a running stream one wave we see
Still the same brook, but different waater still.

   'Metaphor on a river'

   c.81/1, no. 212

So812 So in old times; the mournful Orpheus stood
Oft gaz'd and sigh'd, and murmur'd out adieu.

   [Charles Hopkins], 'The story of Orpheus and
   Euridice imitated from the tenth book of Ovid's
   Metamorphoses'

   b.130, p. 47

So813 So in the zodiac of our Christian sky
He chang'd his martyr for a martyr's crown.

   [Edward] Sparke, 'Poem 26th—on St Philip and
   James'

   b.137, p. 57

So814 So Lernae's snake; already greatest fame,
Horace his patron to be less than mine.

   'The same ['Gratia ad Drm. Glm.'] translated into
   English'

   b.150, p. 143

So815 So like the chances are of love and war
They fly that wound and they pursue that die.

   fb.66/28

So816 So little given at chapel door
Not as you give, but as you game.

   [Mary Barber], 'An epigram on the same [Dr. Lynch's
   sermon]'

   Poetry Box IV/133

So817 So live with ev'ry man as in God's eyes:
So speak to God as if men heard your cries.

   [Sir Thomas Urquhart], 'How one should behave
   himself both before God, and man'

   fb.217, p. 500

So818 So long degraded to a meaner theme
Since faith and works must save, whom
                        Godhead would redeem.

   W[illia]m Dennis, 'On the redemption an ode . . .
   Clonmell July 12th 1757'

   File 4322

So819 So long's he lives, it is not crumblike mommacks
                                    [*sic*]
If they adventure t'eat him without mustard.

   Sir Thomas Urquhart, 'Of a certain gross, and fat
   man, who had a surpassing good appetite for his meat'

   fb.217, p. 248

So820 So lov'd the two Alcides as you two
Grant us a life immortal in my lines.

   [Sir Aston Cokayne], 'To my friends the two Colonel
   Will Bales'

   b.275, p. 49

So821 So many royal qualities' renown
Before, you could not pass, but for a queen.

   Sir Thomas Urquhart, 'The first epigram to the
   Queen'

   fb.217, p. 66

So822 So many thousands for a house
Your house and hospitality.

   'On a nobleman's house which cost 1000 £.'

   c.81/1, no. 441; c.115; Poetry Box X/70

So823 So many yards of curious ribbons she
The more profoundly measur'd by the yard.

   [Sir Thomas Urquhart], 'To a gentleman whose
   mistress in a [?] [?] tied to his hat some five or six
   yards of ribbons'

   fb.217, p. 391

So824 So may I, | Ascend th'ethereal sky
With these, the eternal host, are ever fraught.

   'On Good Friday 18 April 1690'

   b.127, p. 3

So825 So may my unbelief suggest
Because the promise of a God.

   T[homas] S[tevens]

   c.259, p. 112

So826 So may the Cyprian goddess steer
Nor can he lay his thunder down.

   'In imitation of the 3d. ode of the 1st book of Horace'

   Poetry Box VI/33

So827 So mild thy look, so soft thine air
To bear about a double heart.

 [Petit Andrews], 'Song, from a thought in a very old
 English poet'

c.90

So828 So much dear Pope, thy English Iliad charms
Who 'twas translated Homer into Greek.

 'On Pope's translation of Homer'

c.360/1, p. 219

So829 So much oblig'd, and in the kindest way!
'And be most bless'd, because you bless the most.'

 'By [a gentleman of narrow fortune in Ireland] to his
 Grace the Duke of Dorset on his giving him a living'

fc.51, p. 181

So830 So mysterious a being is Cupid
To our sightless poor brother god Love.

 [William Carpenter], 'Love, and folly a fable'

c.247, p. 158

So831 So neighbors, how do ye? ye sit in a row,
May we live thus, and die thus, amen, boys, amen.

 George Alexander Stevens, 'The cutler's song' [From
 an entertainment at Sheffield, 1761, for the benefit of
 Mr. and Mrs. Herbert]

fc.61, p. 105

So832 So nice a maid requires a tricking time
To make them all their choicest sweets impart.

 'Anna Christiana English. Anagram: Gain her in the
 orifice'

fc.24, p. 70

So833 So noted for learning was Tom Fortinbras
And his body and name both perish'd together.

 'November 13th. 1796'

c.115

So834 So oft I've seen a mimic thing
Whate'er the enchanting spirit muttered.

 'Upon the King's speech a simile to an echo in St.
 James' Park'

fc.58, p. 7

So835 So oft my soul shrinks from the worlds selfish plan
Thou hast given me all for thou givest me Nancy.

 [William Hayley], 'Song . . . Oct 9 [1800]'

File 6968

So836 So often jilted, and so oft diseas'd;
Read this, old bachelors, and mourn too late.

 [Joseph Spence], 'The miseries of celibacy. July 26
 [1745]'

Spence Papers, folder 154

So837 So old an Orpheus he may both vie years,
Were fools, became strange prophets at their death.

 'Upon a very old man playing excellent well upon the
 lute'

b.104, p. 94

So838 So pert Mistress Prate-apace how came you here
You're proud and ill-natured—go | Hussy go home.

 'To a bad girl'

c.179, p. 60

So839 So Polly Daldy can't forget
In the pure mansions of the blest.

 [Thomas Stevens?]

c.259, p. 4

So840 So powerful nature doth in things appear
From the first flame, which gave it first entire.

 [George Daniel]

b.121, fol. 29

So841 So pretty Miss Prudence, you're come to the fair
Nay have what she pleases—your | Servant Miss
              Prue.

 'To a good girl'

c.179, p. 59

So842 So ripe for honor, and so full of worth
That you deserve well, and the king is just.

 'Carmen acrostichum on the name of the most truly
 noble-minded Sir John Key [Kaye] knight'

Poetry Box VI/116

So843 So Roscius spake, with such an air he mov'd,
Which with new beauty grac'd, as yours, the poets
              sing.

 M[aurice] J[ohnson], 'To Mr. Philipps of St. John's
 Coll. Oxford on his acting . . . 1706'

c.229/2, fol. 13

So844 So sad as since she got a man, I vow,
She lies at under.

 Sir Thomas Urquhart, 'Why a certain young lady
 happened to be melancholious after her marriage'

fb.217, p. 303

So845 So shall the chequer'd scenes of life delight
As morning bright appears proceeded still by night.

c.391

So846 So should you have my picture; would it change
So may you see me here.

 [George Daniel]

b.121, fol. 58

so847   So sick of self-conceit, as h'had the gift
More fool, than ignorant, who will advise.

    [Sir Philip Wodehouse], 'Upon a self-conceited groom
    of his Robert Swift . . .'

    b.131, back (no. 202)

so848   So skill'd in music had this boy appear'd
Returning to our world, when the lov'd boy
                            return'd.

    'On the young Irish musician at E. Ferrer's'

    b.322, p. 42

so849   So smil'd the charming golden fruit,
Whilst thou a goddess deck'st, I fleeting clouds
                            embrace.

    M[aurice] J[ohnson], 'To his mistress A. occasioned
    by a sprig of oranges embroidered on her stomacher'

    c.229/2, fol. 12v

so850   So smooth and so serene but now
And leaves the laborer to renew his toils.

    George Granville, [1st baron Lansdowne], 'Song'
    Poetry Box IV/53; c.549, p. 74 (var.)

so851   So, so, leave off this last lamenting kiss
Being double dead, going and bid me go.

    [John Donne], 'Valedictio amoris'
    [Crum s885]

    b.114, p. 311; b.148, p. 109

so852   So soft streams meet, so springs with gladder smiles
May ne'er prophetic Daphne crown my brow.

    [Robert] Herrick, 'Mr. Herrick's welcome to sack'
    [Crum s886]

    b.356, p. 322; see also 'So swift streams . . .'.

so853   So spake the god and heav'nward took his flight
Till sorrow seemed to wear one common face.

    [William] Congreve, 'Priam's lamentation, and
    petition to Achilles for the body of his son Hector . . .
    from the Greek of Homer'
    [Crum s889]

    b.201, p. 127

so854   So speak to God, as if men heard you talk;
When thou art old, to die well then contrive.

    'An epitaph on Sr. Edwin Rich who died 1675'

    c.244, p. 211

so855   So spoke the poet: for he best could tell
What Soph pull'd down, now let the poet build.

    'Vino et lucernis medus Acinaces immane quantum
    discrepat?' [answer to 'As every poetaster uses . . .']

    b.115, fol. 19v

so856   So sweet and so pathetic are thy strains,
And thus fair Venus, sing for lost Adonis.

    'To the concealed authoress of the elegiac pastoral on
    the death of . . . Frederick Prince of Wales 1750/51
    intitled Britannia in tears'

    c.360/3, no. 99

so857   So sweet was her breath so dying her eyes
Life—life—now you kill me—I faint—and she died.

    'Song'
    Poetry Box I/111[12]

so858   So swift streams meet, so meet with gladder smiles,
To thee-wards died in th'embers, and no fire . . . .

    [Robert] Herrick, 'Mr. Herrick's welcome to sack'
    b.200, p. 252 (ll. 1-36); see also 'So soft streams . . .'.

so859   So that desire, and fear may never jar
Nor misadventure can disturb your quiet.

    [Sir Thomas Urquhart], 'How to be always in repose'
    fb.217, p. 500

so860   So the first man from paradise was driv'n,
His Eve went with him,—mine is left behind.

    [Sir William Young], 'Impromptu on being sent out of
    a room for affronting a lady'

    c.150, p. 121; see also 'Thus Adam look'd . . .'.

so861   So time but turns his glass, and the same sand
Of a sad life; incessantly, all toil.

    [George Daniel]
    b.121, fol. 56v

so862   So to dead Hector boys may do disgrace,
Thy works among the best will be of Price.

    [Daniel] Price, 'An answer to Dr Corbett's
    Antianniversary' ['Ev'n so dead Hector . . .']
    [Crum s900]

    b.200, p. 212

so863   So too kind turtles when a storm is nigh
And coo and hearken to each other's moan.

    John Dryden, 'A simile by . . . poet laureate' [for
    parody see 'So boar and sow when any storm is nigh']

    c.229/1, fol. 41v

so864   So two rude waves, by storms together thrown
As yours, when you thank'd God for being beat.

    [Abraham Cowley], 'Satire[.] The puritan and the
    papist'

    File 19025

so865   So (?) vulgar souls in whom they love will see
Next kindred to their soul, by heav'nly birth.

    [Sir Philip Wodehouse], 'An occasional. The 18'
    b.131, p. 14

so866 So when a generous bull for clown's delight
And proudly owns(?) the spoils about him spread.

   'Upon a bull-baiting'

b.197, p. 245

so867 So when a wife's abused and husband horn'd,
The woman's pitied, but the cuckold's scorn'd.

   'On the [faded] and the [faded] we favor still the
   weaker sex's faults'

c.189, p. 18

so868 So when the ravenous hawk with gentle pace,
Is ignorance at best, and often worse.

   Richard Lely, 'A simile'

c.244, p. 517

so869 So whilom thro' the ancient wood and grove
Our ravish'd grandsires saw, and woo'd the
                          charming maids.

Spence Papers, folder 113

so870 So wind in hypochondrium pent
Inspires new light, and prophecy.

   'Hudibras'

b.204, p. 38

so871 So zealously why will my friend
—A man should think on't all his life.

c.546

so872 Social bird, by fate defeated,
Copy him, and mend thy own.

   H[enry] Skrine, 'Elegy on the death of a lady's
   favorite starling . . . Salisbury 20 Dec. 1785'

c.509, p. 88

so873 Social virtue's liberal plan,
The golden band of social love!

   Anne (Christian) Penny, 'Ode sung in
   commemoration of the institution of the Marine
   Society, at their anniversary meeting at the Crown and
   Anchor Tavern the 22d of Febry 1773'

File 11696

so874 Soft as evening closed round us
With thy presence still be blest.

   Miss [ ] Smith, 'An evening hymn'

c.91, back cover

so875 Soft as the downy plumage of the dove
Keep still united, innocent and pure.

   'Acrostic on two young ladies' [Susanna and Anne]

c.360/2, no. 252

so876 Soft as the wearied babe's repose,
And brightest hopes the bosom fill.

   'Fragment ext: . . . L.'

c.344, p. 36

so877 Soft breathing the zephyrs [blotted] the grove—
Such such are the glory and pride of the grove!

   [Thomas Hull], 'Wrote for and sung by Mrs. Pinto at
   Vauxhall—1768'

c.528/25

so878 Soft came the breath of spring smooth flow'd the
                                 tide
For lovers' spirits guard the holy shade!

   [Ann (Ward)] Radcliffe, 'The mariner'

c.83/3, no. 876

so879 Soft flowed the lay, when late, with downcast eye,
And o'er each meaner care exalt the heart.

   [William Boscawen], 'Elegy. On the death of Dr
   Joseph Warton. 1800'

fc.106, p. 87

so880 Soft god of shadows, gentle sleep,
To mimic, with their sports, the graver cares of
                                 man.

   [ ] Whitehouse, 'Stanzas to sleep'

c.83/2, no. 508

so881 Soft god of sleep when thou dost seal
By finding it a dream.

c.53, fol. 56; fc.73

so882 Soft o'er the mountain's purple brow
Set to this world—and rise in future day.

   [Ann (Ward)] Radcliffe, 'Sunset'

c.83/3, no. 861

so883 Soft pity is the fairest flow'r,
Can e'en to Godhead raise mankind.

   'On pity'

c.83/1, no. 232

so884 Soft rest thy dust! and wait th'Almighty's will;
Then rise unchang'd, and be an angel still.

   'Wrote extempore. In the tomb of a beautiful and very
   young lady'

fc.51, p. 68; see also 'Sleep soft in dust . . .', Lie sweet in
dust . . .', 'Lie still sweet maid . . .', 'Sleep on blest
angel . . .'.

so885 Soft silken flow'r that in the dewy vale
And sorrow fly before joy's living morn.

   [Ann (Ward)] Radcliffe, 'The lily'

c.83/3, no. 848

so886 Soft slumbers now mine eyes forsake,
Creation's Lord to praise.

    Hannah More, 'A morning soliloquy . . . Matt. 13: 46'

c.487, p. 110; c.341, p. 28

so887 Soft smiling hope thou anchor of the mind!
Pass but this instant, storm and tempests cease |
                           [last line trimmed]

    'On hope'

c.83/2, no. 730

so888 Soft sweetest warbler! 'tis for thee
And soothe the storm to melody.

    [Phanuel Bacon], 'The Æolian harp'

c.237, fol. 72

so889 Soft Venus, love's too anxious queen,
The nymph a finish'd teapot stands.

    [Ambrose Philips?], 'The lady's transformation into teapot' [pr. Dublin, 1725–30 (Foxon P218]

c.172, p. 6

so890 Soft virgins you whose gentle hearts are prone
Content then acts of a suburran(?) whore.

    [Sir Aston Cokayne], 'To maids'

b.275, p. 52

so891 Soft was her voice, and musically sweet,
Return to stay, or save me, with those eyes!

    [Richard] Cumberland, 'The maid of Snowdon'

c.83/2, no. 407

so892 Softest persuasion sat upon his tongue
That forc'd its way, and left its sting behind.

    'Eupolis on Pericles'

fc.14/12

so893 Softly blow the evening breezes
Gracious Allah be thy guide!

    [Thomas] Percy, 'Alcanzor and Layda a Moorish tale'

c.486, fol. 8

so894 Sol seem'd in his mild, evening glories drest,
The various charms of this enchanting place.

    John Lockman, 'The grotto in Versailles Gardens' [translated from La Fontaine]

c.267/4, p. 183

so895 Soldier, so tender of thy prince's fame,
But for the King of King's sake, do not swear.

    [John] B[yrom], 'Spoken extempore by . . . to a gentleman of the army, on the latter's swearing much'

fc.132/1, p. 81; see also 'Oh! that the muse . . .'.

so896 Soldier think before you marry,
What is of no use to you.

    [John Gay]

c.358, p. 161

so897 Soldiers by peace; and churchmen lose by wars
Surgeons gain both by Venus, and by Mars.

    Sir Thomas Urquhart, 'Of soldiers, ecclesiastical persons, and chirurgeons'

fb.217, p. 278

so898 Solon was granted rich, as he was wise
He always kept a sort of scabs about him.

    'On the Athenian Solon'
    [Crum s940]

b.200, p. 411

so899 Some air, some shape, some humor seek
For he that's dazzl'd by the sun to other things is
                              blind.

    'To Jo[h]n Wingfield esq. of Tickencote in Rutlandsh[ir]e'

c.229/1, fol. 51

so900 Some bald without, thou bald within, 'tis plain,
They want their hair, thou want'st as much of brain.

    'On Fabianus'

c.356

so901 Some beauty's blaze may be extinguish'd quite
But virtue's hue still keeps fair, clear and bright.

    [John Rose?]

b.227, p. 72

so902 Some boys went out to drown a cat
And make the application.

    [Thomas Gurney], 'A fable . . . [by] a Protestant dissenter'

c.213

so903 Some by experience vainly some
For wives to imitate.

    'To the memory of my beloved Portia'

File 13409

so904 Some called him Garrot, but that was too high
Whereof grocers there is many more.

    'On one Jarrot a grocer' [in St. Mary Overy, Southwark]
    [Crum s946]

fb.143, p. 35

S0905 'Some certain good from every evil springs:'
May love inspire, and rapture be their source!

> Anna Seward(?), 'To Mrs. Heywood of Liverpool, on
> her conjugal virtues'

c.391, p. 105

S0906 Some Colinaeus praise, some Bleau
For some folks read but all folks sh[i]t.

> [Alexander Pope], 'Verses designed to be prefixed to
> [Bernard] Lintot's Miscellany'

c.531; c.265, p. 23

S0907 Some counties vaunt themselves in dyes,
There's room enough for you!

> 'The Norfolk turnpike. An ancient tale'

c.90

S0908 Some courtiers, if the king but smile on you
As shades evanish [sic], when the sun is cloudish.

> Sir Thomas Urquhart, 'The character of courtiers'

fb.217, p. 299

S0909 Some dare not live for fear of death and some
Where streams of glory mix with light and love.

> [Mary Serjant]

fb.98, fol. 153

S0910 Some do bestow upon a friend a thing
A [?] bounty and a[?] hatred.

> [Sir Thomas Urquhart], 'Gifts ought to be such, as
> that by their once [?] the receiver may not be called
> the [?]'

fb.217, p. 529

S0911 Some eat much: but digest not: he likewise
Knows many things: but is in nothing wise.

> Sir Thomas Urquhart, 'Of a profound scholar, whose
> prudence was but shallow'

fb.217, p. 211

S0912 Some English dames in Cupid's parliaments
Whilst ours but kiss, they vote more inwardly.

> Sir Thomas Urquhart, 'Of the upper, and the lower
> House'

fb.217, p. 81

S0913 Some fair ones are so very kind.
They'd own, they love a kiss.

> [Charles Burney, the younger], 'Answer to the prize
> enigma, in The gentlemen's diary. 1778'

c.37, p. 24

S0914 Some faithless folks have been so bold
He that says yes, deserves a rope.

> 'On the peace'

c.570/3, p. 95

S0915 Some faiths are like those mills that cannot grind
Their corn unless they worked against the wind.

> [Francis Quarles], 'On contentious spirits' [Divine
> fancies II, 93]

b.137, p. 191; see also next.

S0916 Some faults are like those mills that cannot grind
So is my love unto my friend.

> [Henry Phillipps]

b.156, p. 41; see also previous.

S0917 Some fond youth by Mother Matthews led
Resign'd up to Lord Townshend [?] fate.

> [Maurice Johnson], 'The Doctor [Noel Broxholme]'s
> answer [to John Hedges' letter from Germany,
> translated]'

c.229/2, fol. 33

S0918 Some have no ears to hear the loudest noise:
That serves the individual: this the kind.

> Sir Thomas Urquhart, 'That all the senses may be
> spared, save the touch, and the gust'

fb.217, p. 107

S0919 Some him a pillar of the church do call,
We love his room, but hate his company.

> 'On a Papist'
> [Crum s961]

b.200, p. 412

S0920 Some husbands, on a winter day,
And that you'll find the safest way.

> [Samuel Wesley, the younger], 'The pig: a tale' [pr.
> 1725 (Foxon W347)]

c.83/2, no. 356

S0921 Some imperfection doth (no doubt) proceed
Within a while, some man to labor at her.

> Sir Thomas Urquhart, 'What Phyllis still for the most
> part stood in need of'

fb.217, p. 335

S0922 Some maids are maids without their maidenhead
Fathers although they never had a child.

> [Sir Thomas Urquhart], 'The names of maid and
> father are not always taken in the same sense. Some
> make their use but ground of a relation gives things
> names related but [?] enliven'

fb.217, p. 538

S0923 Some man unworthy to be possessor
But doth waste by greediness.

> J[ohn] D[onne], 'To the worthiest of all my love my
> virtuous mistress'
> [Crum s969]

b.148, p. 54

S0924 Some marry twice,
Now lives alone.

   T[homas] M[orell], 'An epitaph . . . on the wife of the
   Rev: J. Mickleborough . . . translated in bimeters'

   c.395, p. 124

S0925 Some matters have been long impending
Tomorrow I design for Dover.

   [ ] Cranley and [ ] Gardiner, jr., 'A dialogue between
   John Bull and Nicholas Frog'

   c.170, p. 9

S0926 Some may expect, what justly we explode
And from the culture, ev'ry bliss insult find.

   [John Lockman], 'Epilogue [to The siege of
   Damascus] by Eudocia'

   c.268 (first part), at front

S0927 Some may so full assurance have,
He surely guides our feet to bliss.

   [Edmund Wodehouse], 'Aug. 17 [1715]'

   b.131, p. 248

S0928 Some men being born t'a huge, and free estate
They fill their brains with mere imagination.

   Sir Thomas Urquhart, 'The nature of lavishing
   wasters'

   fb.217, p. 105

S0929 Some men children spoil and bring them unto
                                                    naught,
When foolish love forbids them to be taught.

   c.339, p. 324

S0930 Some men live in such awe, as if it were offense,
Now being fall'n, none help them for to rise.

   b.234, p. 326

S0931 Some men no sooner are advanc'd to have
Had rais'd; could prudence too on them bestow.

   [John Hobart]

   b.108, fol. 4

S0932 Some men that hunt for that they long have miss'd,
Will make their boast that they might if they list.

   c.339, p. 316

S0933 Some men there are that swear, and whore and rant
And only has one fault, he's too too kind.

   'The royalist'

   b.111, p. 76

S0934 Some men to those they should most friendship
                                                    show,
Do lie in wait to work their overthrow.

   c.339, p. 311

S0935 Some mirthful lass the other day
He'd never be an angel more.

   'The fallen angel'

   c.326, p. 157

S0936 Some oracles of old to cause more wonder
Yet still you've all his lightning in your eye.

   'Epigram to a young lady who pretended to tell
   fortunes'

   c.360/3, no. 44

S0937 Some others may with safety tell
Twenty to one but I shall live again.

   A[braham] C[owley], 'Love undiscovered'

   c.258

S0938 Some people ask what has this Haddock done
He cruises, takes their ships—how many—one.

   'On Admiral Haddock's tak[ing] one ship when
   cruising in the Mediterranean sea—against the
   Spaniards. 1739'

   c.360/1, p. 59

S0939 Some people say and others sing
And only wish to—done.

   R[ichard] V[ernon] S[adleir], 'To Mrs. Ellis with a
   basket of pears—1781'

   c.106, p. 32

S0940 Some people's senses wealth doth so bereave
The ague, when 'tis the ague that hath them.

   [Sir Thomas Urquhart], 'That riches is a sickness to
   those that do not possess insomuch as they are
   possessed by it'

   fb.217, p. 522

S0941 Some poison strong a sugar'd taste doth keep,
The adder fell amongst the flowers doth creep.

   c.339, p. 317

S0942 Some potentates prime poets so abase,
Those fain would cherish't, but they quite mistake it.

   Sir Thomas Urquhart, 'That poets are not always
   reputed of according to their merit'

   fb.217, p. 171

S0943 Some question it much,—if the story be true,
So I shall believe, tho' you doubt, the story.

   Abraham Oakes, 'On the duke at Culloden. 1746. An
   epigram.'

   c.50, p. 131

S0944 Some say by drinking, that I'll lose my sight:
But from my drinking I will not leave off.

> Sir Thomas Urquhart, 'A drunkard speaks here of his
> own invincible determination of carousing'
>
> fb.217, p. 144

S0945 Some say, it is not lawful: but it vexes
Have one 'gainst th'other, by the law of Cupid.

> Sir Thomas Urquhart, 'Of venery practiced by such,
> as are not married together a paradox'
>
> fb.217, p. 45

S0946 Some say money makes dukes and earls,
For when you've no money you're reckon'd no man.

> 'January 25th. 1784 Jane Clasper'
>
> c.93

S0947 Some say Peg J—ys has wit
And looks as if she melt [meant?] it.

> 'Wrote in Richmond Gardens'
>
> c.74

S0948 Some say that Seignior Bononcini
'Twixt Tweedledum and Tweedledee.

> [John Byrom], of Manchester, 'By the author of that
> celebrated pastoral, My time and the muses, &c.'
>
> c.233, p. 10; c.176, p. 3

S0949 Some say women are like the waves
In this are near of kin.

> 'A song' [1668]
>
> b.207, p. 35

S0950 Some scorn the cross, whilst others fall before it
Fools act a sin, whilst they decline a vice.

> [Francis Quarles], 'On fools of both kinds' [Divine
> fancies IV, 43]
> [Crum s996]
>
> b.137, p. 179

S0951 Some serious ask, and some in joke,
Starts Gulliver, and squirts it out.

> John Lockman, 'To a friend, most falsely reported to
> be a bankrupt . . . Aug. 1742'
>
> c.267/1, p. 127

S0952 Some simple men do simply judge of things,
And do not weigh that time perfection brings.

> c.339, p. 325

S0953 Some sins are brisk and fierce—some sins are tame
Bred out of delicacy, or wanton gust.

> [Sir Philip Wodehouse], 'Tomasin Lovet Love not
> tame sins'
>
> b.131, back (no. 118)

S0954 Some skillful limner help me, if not so
'Tis England's Roscius, Burbage that I keep.

> 'On Mr Burbage his death' [13 March 1618/19]
>
> b.62, p. 89

S0955 Some strollers invited by Warwick's great Earl,
But a plague on your family dinner.

> [David] Garrick, 'Verses written by . . . on going with
> his wife to Warwick Castle . . . being dismissed
> immediately after breakfast' [1766]
> [Crum s999]
>
> c.160, fol. 41; c.150, p. 30; Poetry Box IV/194

S0956 Some study men—some read fair fashion
Whose name I bear, this theme to me has sent.

> [Sir Philip Wodehouse], 'John Covel of Christ College
> I con love'
>
> b.131, back (no. 173)

S0957 Some surly goddess give me aid
And fix upon their members.

> 'A copy of verses on the Bedfordshire ladies . . . 1749'
>
> fc.85, fol. 78

S0958 Some that have deeper digg'd love's mine, than I
Sweetness, and wit, they are but money
            [i.e., mummy] possest.

> [John Donne], 'Money' [i.e., Mummy]
> [Crum s1001]
>
> b.114, p. 267; b.148, p. 62

S0959 Some that their wives may neat and cleanly go,
Makes her perhaps a wagtail all her life.

> [John Davies], 'On fine apparel'
>
> c.356

S0960 Some there be delight in hounds,
I'll early scold tomorrow.

> Dr. [ ] Fuller, 'An elegy made by . . . on [the] death of
> his wife'
>
> fb.207/2, p. 99

S0961 Some thieves by ill hap, with an honest man met,
And all that thence follows, hangs on the same
                          string.

> 'On the word abdicate' [on William III and James II]
> [Crum s1003]
>
> b.111, p. 449

S0962 Some think that learning will impede their fortune
That Mercure never yet eclips'd the sun.

> Sir Thomas Urquhart, 'That it derogates nothing
> from the splendor of noblemen, to be grand scholars'
>
> fb.217, p. 236

S0963 Some through the world do pass by land and sea,
So all their life, at home some others stay.

    c.339, p. 326

S0964 Some time for you, sprung from Uranian kings!
And the two brothers that ov'r shipping reign.

    Abraham Oakes, '[Horace to Maecenas.] Ode XXIX.
    B. 3. translated'

    c.50, p. 153

S0965 Some time thy speech may turn unto thy smart,
As that thy mate do bear a Judas' heart.

    c.339, p. 318

S0966 Some time was wit esteem'd of greater price than
                              gold,
But wisdom poor may now go beg and starve
                            without for cold.

    c.339, p. 320; b.234, p. 25 ('art esteem'd')

S0967 Some touches do but please: there is that tickles;
Old men have th'one: young gallants, th'other
                              prickles.

    Sir Thomas Urquhart, 'Of the sense of touching'

    fb.217, p. 314

S0968 Some wept for Anguish, but for anger I
That ignorance should live, and art should die.

    'Epitaph upon Mr. Anguish of Corpus Christi College
    in Oxford'

    b.197, p. 211

S0969 Some were reproach'd alive, who're prais'd being
                              dead:
Whence more account of death, than life is made.

    Sir Thomas Urquhart, 'Putations, are put upon
    sundries out of season'

    fb.217, p. 339

S0970 Some when their minds do mount unto the skies,
Their fall is wrought by things which they despise.

    c.339, p. 314

S0971 Some when through drink on feet they cannot stand,
Yet as they lie they'll have their bowls in hand.

    c.339, p. 316

S0972 Some when to know the stars they take in hand
Of dangers near they do not understand.

    c.339, p. 314

S0973 Some when we trust would work our overthrow,
And undermine the ground whereon we go.

    c.339, p. 318

S0974 Some, whom a savage fierceness blinds
'For human softness fills my eyes.'

    'A fable being an exercise at Canterbury School . . .'
    c.169, p. 1

S0975 Some wicked persons lewdly do bestow
Such things as should unto good uses go.

    c.339, p. 313

S0976 Some will not let their daughters learn to write
And show their children how to use it right.

    [Sir Thomas Urquhart], 'Against such as do not think
    it fitting that young gentlewomen should be instructed
    in writing'

    fb.217, p. 539

S0977 Some wise and learned men in former ages
Was of the Druids taught by word of mouth.

    [Sir Thomas Urquhart], 'It hath been held by many
    judicious and expert scholars in ancient times an
    indirect and altogether unprofitable way for obtaining
    the knowledge of arts to publish anything by write
    [sic]'

    fb.217, p. 501

S0978 Some women kindly bruis'd
But to assuage men's swellings.

    Sir Thomas Urquhart, 'A crush sometimes is able to
    make a soft apple rotten'

    fb.217, p. 242

S0979 Some write the ass's praises nowadays:
And further I read verses in your praise.

    Sir Thomas Urquhart, 'To a loggerhead, whom a
    certain poet had extolled above his worth'

    fb.217, p. 309

S0980 Some Yarborough's beauty praise and say,
Release the captives of her eyes.

    'On Mrs. Yarborough'

    fc.73

S0981 Something I am, but what I scarcely know
All know they love me, tho' they can't tell why.

    '[Enigma/Charade/Conundrum] 47'

    c.389

S0982 Something substantial I would have of you
In your own time soon as you can.

    Mrs. M. B—y, 'Some questions, as part of a letter
    from . . .'

    c.213

S0983 Sometimes a fiery circle doth appear
Whereof that people made them store of bread.

'Upon a bright circle seen round the sun or moon'
c.158, p. 117

S0984 Sometimes there's dirty work to do,
But so he stinks it's thought he'll not receive him.

'Sir Jona[tha]n Simple's journey to London'
fc.55, p. 1

S0985 Son of social mirth and glee,
To the music of the spheres.

J. S., 'Social converse a new song by . . . sung by
Mr. Hawke'
fc.85, fol. 85

S0986 Songs of joy, Philistia, sing
And lay the needy down in holy peace secure.

[cf. 'Are thy woes, Philistia . . .']
fc.53, p. 136 (2 copies)

S0987 Sonorous brass of changeful pow'r,
Alike in thee, 'tis innocence.

'Stanzas to a church bell'
c.83/3, no. 1056

S0988 Sons of genius, droop, and languish,
Science weeps for Rozier dead.

'An ode on the death of M. Pilatre de Rozier' [9 July
1785; pub. Gentleman's magazine, March 1800]
c.136, p. 129

S0989 Sons of God by blest adoption,
Cheerful hope, and godly fear.

J. Hart, 'A funeral hymn'
c.240, p. 125

S0990 Soon as Aurora from the blushing skies
Where frisking lambs now crop the verdant green.

[Edmund Burke]
fc.46/2

S0991 Soon as Gaby possession had got of the Hall
For if Gaby don't like 'em, he'll pick out their I's. |
Which nobody can deny

[Herbert Beaver], 'The cushion plot' [Dr. Thomas
Shaw Principal 1740–51 of St. Edmund Hall Oxon
and Sr. Jemmet Raymond, formerly of the same Hall]
[Crum S1032]
Poetry Box x/47

S0992 Soon as my Jesus came to show
Though joined to a cross.

[Mary Pluret], 'Another [poem written on waste
paper]'
c.354

S0993 Soon as pale Cynthia, queen of night,
We will pass it in dancing and singing and mirth.

M[ary] C[ornwallis], 'Written for Caroline
Cornwallis's birthday aged 7 years . . . supposed scene
in the Midsummer night's dream'
fc.124, p. 108

S0994 Soon as the beauteous queen of love
Love conquers, and all yield to love.

[Thomas Hamilton, 6th earl of Haddington], 'The
hourglass from the French'
c.458/2, p. 116

S0995 Soon as the blushing morn on Peter rose
Nor e'er forgives the lapse her virtue made?

H[annah] More, 'A passage from The tear of St. Peter
translated from the Spanish by . . .'
c.341, p. 116

S0996 Soon as the morning from her eastern bed,
But if she scorn me—love and life farewell.

Miss [ ] White, of Edgbaston, 'Pastoral'
c.532

S0997 Soon as young Jotham saw his brethren's fate,
And th'oak with sullen anger, shook his head.

'Jotham's prophecy. Judges the 9. and 47th and the
following verses . . . The parable'
[Crum S1039]
c.570/2, p. 47

S0998 Soon beneath the brightest skies,
That the lot of nature's thine.

'Moral reflection'
c.83/2, no. 363

S0999 Soon will the trees (dear friend) around
To dare the curious light.

[J. Crane], 'An imitation from Horace'
c.83/2, no. 630

S1000 Soon will the waning star, with silver ray,
Glory supreme be thine, till time shall end.

'Hymn before evening service'
c.83/3, no. 898

S1001 Sophronia marrying did chance to cry:
And each day since, does tell him why.

[Sir Philip Wodehouse], 'An occasional epigram'
b.131, p. 4

S1002 Sophronia to be thought a scholar aims,
Th' Italian modes, with those of Greece confounds.

'[Female characters.] 3. Sophronia: or, the pedant'
Poetry Box IV/148

S1003 Sore sick a lady late did lie
That call'd for a physician.

'The lady's fall' [the Church in danger, Dec. 1705]
[Crum s1049]

c.111, p. 123; c.171, p. 12

S1004 Sore wept the nine, when dire disease
Did thro' the storm, his steps attend.

John Lockman, 'To the Earl of Middlesex, on his
birthday: 6 Feb. (O.S.) 1759: after his lordship's
recovery from a grievous fit of sickness'

c.267/2, p. 237

S1005 Sorrell transform'd to Pegasus we see,
Gave the last stroke and made number ten.

'In praise of the author' [Dr. Stephen Hales of
Cambridge; on William III's death, 1702]
[Crum s1050]

fc.24, p. 35

S1006 Sorrow hath shut my silly soul up
For else I must die how can I choose.

'Cant: 23'

b.4, fol. 19

S1007 Sorrow, who to this house scarce knew the way
He, and about him, his, are turn'd to stone.

[John Donne], 'Elegia sexta' ['On the L. C. (Lord
Chancellor Ellesmere?)']
[Crum s1056]

b.114, p. 85; b.148, p. 135

S1008 Sotus hates wise men for himself is none
And fools he hates because himself is one.

'Sotus'

c.356

S1009 Soul-moving Hervey, in whose smiling eyes
And pour their mother's sweetness round the isle.

'To Lady Hervey on a conversation concerning names
by Miranda'

Poetry Box x/127; Accession 97.7.40

S1010 Sound out his pow'r in notes divine,
Praise him with mirth high cheer and wine.

'Chorus [7, with musical score for tenor and bass,
from Handel's Samson]'

Music MS. 534

S1011 Sound, sound the trumpets, wind the cheerful horn
Old Fame bids her trumpet blow.

'Written on the birthday of Miss E. K. . . . D. C.
19 March 1791 G. H.'

c.373, p. 81

S1012 Sour wages issue from the sweetest sin,
Upon my midnight cries.

c.158, p. 33

S1013 Source of love and light of day,
Cast the children's bread away!

[William Cowper, trans.], 'Self-diffidence. Vol. 2. Son:
125' [of Jeanne Guion's 'Spiritual songs']

c.470 (autogr.)

S1014 Source to me of all that's dear;
Shall with blood faun's altar drain.

[William Popple, trans.], '[Horace] book 2nd. Ode
17th. To Maecenas, recovering from a long illness'

fc.104/2, p. 190

S1015 Sovereign of angels we adore
And half thus heav'n shall here be known.

P[hilip] Doddridge, 'Society of ministers with angels
in the courts below and above. From Zech. III. 6, 7
And the angel &c.'

c.493, p. 49

S1016 Sowden is gone, he is no more
And our exalted Sowden on the heav'nly shore.

Miss M. H., 'Verses composed by a young woman
occasioned by the death of the Revd. Samuel Sowden
Baptist minister at Wolverstone'

c.259, p. 122

S1017 Spain is the cause of all
The devil will take all.

'On the Congress. 1728'

c.570/3, p. 26

S1018 Spalding the envy of each neighboring town
And none like yours can recompense his toil.

M[aurice] J[ohnson], 'Prologue by . . . to The
recruiting officer'

c.229/2, fol. 31

S1019 Spare not, nor spend too much, be this thy care
But he spends best, that spares to spend again.

[Thomas Randolph]
[Crum s1078]

b.206, p. 150

S1020 Speak but of bawdry and my mistress spits
Her teeth do water for to think of it.

'On his mistress'

b.356, p. 307; see also 'Take but . . .'

S1021 Speak satire, for there's none can tell like thee
'Tis personal virtue only makes us great.

[Daniel Defoe], 'The trueborn Englishman, a satire'
[pr.1700 (Wing D849)]
[*POAS* VI.265]

c.158, p. 88; fb.142, p. 3; see also 'Then let us boast of ancestors . . .'.

S1022 Speak sister speak is the deed done
Worse to make his title good.

[Sir William D'Avenant], 'Speak sister in Macbeth'
[with musical score for tenor (incomplete) and bass]

Music MS. 534

S1023 Speak, who beneath this stone does lie?
And farewell you; let me alone.

[Joseph Spence], 'White Lion, at Hatfield'

Spence Papers, folder 119

S1024 Speech but reality no virt' affords
Faith hope, and charity being things, not words.

Sir Thomas Urquhart, 'That lip religion edifies not, without one be exemplarly material'

fb.217, p. 93

S1025 Speech fitly is compar'd to grief, and sport;
Because the long is light: the weighty, short.

Sir Thomas Urquhart, 'Of succinct and prolix discourse'

fb.217, p. 210

S1026 Spirit and life His words are found
That I might love the lame.

T[homas] S[tevens], 'John 6.63'

c.259, p. 124

S1027 Spirit of him who wing'd his daring flight
Reflects his genius, and partakes his fame.

[William Roscoe], 'To Henry Fuseli esq. On his series of pictures from the poetical works of Milton'

c.142, p. 82

S1028 Spirit of love and sorrow—hail!
O'er foaming seas and distant sail.

A[nn (Ward)] Radcliffe, 'To melancholy'

c.83/2, no. 404

S1029 Spirit rever'd! if aught beneath the sky
Monarch and slave to praise their God conspire!

R[ichard] V[ernon] S[adleir], 'Lines written on a visit to the monument of Sir Ralph Sadleir Knt. Banneret at Standon in Hertfordshire who died in the year [blank] being at that time the last banneret in England'

c.106, p. 145

S1030 Spirits, list, unhallow'd eyes
Then with you dissolve in air!

[ ] Kendel, 'The cavern and dreams'

c.83/2, no. 395

S1031 Spirits of peace, O! whither are ye fled!
And sacred be the turf that wraps my head.

[signed Caroline]

c.343, p. 32

S1032 Spirus would wed but he would have a wench,
He hath enough; if two she 'as two too many.

'Spirus his choice'

c.356

S1033 Sportive Zephyrus! Gently blowing;
Sighing, dying in my arms.

John Lockman, 'To Zephyrus: writ to the allegro part of [Mr. Howard's overture of The amorous goddesses, June 1740]'

c.267/2, p. 125

S1034 Spread a large canvas painter to contain
This crowd of traitors hang in effigy.

[Henry Savile], 'Sixth advice to a painter to draw the Duke of Y[ork]' [1673]
[Crum s1099; *POAS* I.214]

fb.140, p. 168; b.136, p. 48 (ll. 1–59); b.52/2, p. 123 (includes envoy as part of poem); fb.70, p. 143; Poetry Box VIII/22

S1035 Sprightly airs and songs of pleasure
And seraphs hail thee to their choir.

[ ] Irye(?), 'Elegy on the death of Richard Gustavus Burney Novr. 18th 1791'

c.486, fol. 6v

S1036 Sprightly as birds who wing from spray to spray,
In this sweet nymph are all perfections join'd.

John Lockman, 'Aspasia at Mr. Hugford's ball . . . April 1759'

c.267/1, p. 268

S1037 Spring comes! Again the blossom'd hedge is seen
This night may seize, and snatch thy soul away.

'Return of spring'
[Crum s1101]

c.546, p. 14

S1038 Spring, summer and autumn had once a dispute,
No amusements like mine are at present in season.

'The contrast of the seasons or winter triumphant'

c.83/3, no. 1070

S1039 Sprung from men of royal line,
And the twins together shone.

[William Popple, trans.], '[Horace book 3rd. ode 29th.
To Maecenas'

fc.104/2, p. 312

S1040 Sprung from the noblest meanest race
And give my motley form a name.

'Another [rebus]'

Diggle Box: Poetry Box XI/71

S1041 Squab puppy who can bark but never bite
To all a jest, the natural white Bulkear.

[Sir Harry Hubert], 'A short answer to [a] laborious
trifle [by Robert Wolseley]'
[Crum S1107]

b.219, p. 13; fb.108, p. 253

S1042 Squeeze me that cloud to ink and be my light
What his age owes you, that, his youth will pay.

'A copy on the execrable murder of our King'
[Charles I]

fb.228/22

S1043 St silence bodes: yet is't the only word,
Which can without a vowel, a sound afford.

Sir Thomas Urquhart, 'Of st the interjection of
silence'

fb.217, p. 349

S1044 Stain of thy country and thy ancient name
Eclipse those glories you for us have won.

'On the Earl of Torrington' [1690]
[Crum S1110; POAS V.228]

fb.70, p. 245

S1045 Stand fast thou shaking quaking keeper,
And hang it in the smoke.

'In eadem'

b.197, p. 182

S1046 Stand forth thou grand impostor of our time
Recant thy book and then go hang thyself.

'The observator. Le Strang[e] or the history of Hodge
as reported by some | From his fiddling to Nol, to his
scribbling for Rome' [Sir Roger L'Estrange]
[Crum S1115]

b.209, p. 57; fb.108, p. 21

S1047 Stand forth, vile wretch! I'll hang thee in thy twine,
Hang then in verse, till come the Tyburn cart.

John Lockman, 'To a certain twine-spinner, who had
sold vile goods to the Herring Fishery Society . . .
[by] John Rogue-Stretcher . . . May 1751, when [the
lines] were printed in the London evening post . . .'

c.267/1, p. 172

S1048 Stand off and let me take the air
Than wash an Ethiopian skin.

[John Cleveland], 'A dialogue betwixt a black boy and
a fair wench, he courting her'
[Crum S1116]

b.93, p. 29

S1049 Stand off, ye scoundrels, puny fellows
(Good people) at the point of hanging.

J[ohn] Blyth, 'Newgate'

Poetry Box VI/104

S1050 Stand passers-by here's good news come to town
We'll stop their mouths and arselicks without cork.

fb.228/32

S1051 Stand round my brave boys
And bless the brave youth in her arms.

c.358, p. 13

S1052 Stand stand says the watchman
May hell be your coffin and grave.

c.503, p. 68

S1053 Stand still and I will read to thee.
And his first minute, after noon is night.

J[ohn] D[onne], 'The shadow'
[Crum S1119]

b.148, p. 107; b.114, p. 287

S1054 Stand your glass 'round, about ye have a care my
boys,
A bottle and kind landlady cures all again.

'Song'

c.189, p. 160

S1055 Stanley and Graham, you that liv'd and died
With lighted tapers that shall ever burn.

'On the much lamented death of James earl of
Derwentwater who was beheaded Feb: the 14: 1715'

c.570/3, p. 3

S1056 Stately Belira be—thyself revere
This lesson's taught thee, in thy anagram.

[Sir Philip Wodehouse], 'Upon Madam Elizabeth
Astley, Sr Jacob's mother'

b.131, back (no. 93)

S1057 Stately dames extending wide,
Which, for gods, law bid them build.

[William Popple, trans.], '[Horace] book 2nd. Ode
15th'

fc.104/2, p. 162

S1058 Statesman, yet friend to truth, of soul sincere
Prais'd, wept, and honor'd by the muse he lov'd.

> A[lexander] Pope, 'An epitaph in Westminster Abbey
> on the monument for James Craggs esqr. who died of
> the smallpox on Thursday February the 16 1720/1'

c.360/2, no. 164; c.244, p. 468; fc.60, p. 118

S1059 S[t]atesmen, and courtiers! by your leave,
Let Bourbon or Nassau go higher.

> [Matthew] Prior, 'Prior's epitaph on himself'

c.193, p. 59; see also 'Courtiers and heralds . . .', 'Heralds
and courtiers . . .', 'Nobles and heralds . . .'.

S1060 Statues of brass may waste with rust
And virtue shed a tear.

> 'Occasioned by an elegy written by a young lady on an
> unfortunate though favorite chick'

Poetry Box IV/99

S1061 Staunch friend to your trade he has smoked ev'ry day
As waste paper to light all the pipes he shall smoke.

> [Phanuel Bacon], 'The petition of Rich[ar]d Poulter
> day-laborer at Balden near Oxford to the worshipful
> company of merchants trading to Virginia humbly
> sheweth that . . .'

c.237, fol. 88 [*i.e.*, 108]

S1062 Stay, ah stay, ah turn, ah whither would you fly,
No not one, no not one, not one pitying, pitying,
pitying look behind.

> [Nicholas Rowe], 'A song in The fair penitent'

c.160, fol. 84

S1063 Stay and spend a wonder; Here's
And 'gainst their nature, force them kind.

> 'On a gent: that died of the smallpox'

b.200, p. 209

S1064 Stay bachelor! If you have wit
Unless you die unmarried.

> 'Another epitaph on a man and his wife'

c.360/3, no. 26; c.487, p. 58

S1065 Stay, Christian, stay—let not thy pride disdain
But celebrate an endless nuptial day.

> [Thomas Hull], 'For the Middlesex journal epitaph on
> a young bride'

c.528/29

S1066 Stay Christian stay, nor let thy haste profane
And op'ning heaven the newborn angel hails.

> [John Paterson], 'An epitaph on a young lady [Mrs.
> R. P.]'
> [Crum S1133]

c.360/1, p. 123 (incomplete)

S1067 Stay Cupid whither a[r]t thou flying
That now, now, would be billing.

> 'A petition to Cupid'

fb.107, p. 26

S1068 Stay lady! Stay, for pity's sake,
Your happy, happy orphan boy!

> Mrs. [ ] Opie, 'The orphan boy's tale'

c.82, p. 30

S1069 Stay lusty blood where canst thou seek
White lilies to a ruddy rose.

> [William Strode], 'A blush'
> [Crum S1146]

b.205, fol. 74v

S1070 Stay, mortal, stay, remove not from this tomb
The grave that next is opened, may be thine.

> 'On one &c.'

b.356, p. 254

S1071 Stay not the eye whose gaze is for delight
And would in no wise be persuaded thence.

> [John Speed], 'David's harp'

b.89, p. 1

S1072 Stay O sweet and do not rise
And perish in their infancy.

> [John Donne], 'Break of day' [preceding ''Tis
> true . . .']
> [Crum S1149]

fb.88, p. 120; b.148, p. 5

S1073 Stay passenger and lend a tear,
Then like this youth embalm thy dust.

> 'A epitaph on an hopeful youth'
> [cf. Crum S1150]

c.481, p. 226; see also 'Stay passenger, and shed . . .'.

S1074 Stay passenger and read under this stone
Tell him the angels trumpet shall awake.

> [Sir Aston Cokayne], 'An epitaph on my father'

b.275, p. 83

S1075 Stay passenger, and shed a tear,
Have her with bliss and glory crown'd.

> 'An epitaph on Mrs. Jane Smith'
> [cf. Crum S1150]

c.244, p. 211; see also 'Stay passenger and lend . . .'.

S1076 Stay passenger and though within
Has fix'd her mansion here.

[James Merrick?], 'On a thatched house window [on
the grounds at Berwick] extempore'
[Crum S1154]

fc.51, p. 84; c.229/1, fol. 52v; c.90 (attr. [ ] Ponis); see
also 'Stay/Stop traveller . . .'.

S1077 Stay passenger awhile and light
Here's usage good and reckonings right.

[Sir Aston Cokayne], 'To be added into the third book
of epigrams'

b.275, p. 99

S1078 Stay passenger for there bold Barwick lies
And, dying colonel, lives crowned sure.

'On the choir at Wigton Cumberland a memorative
epitaph for the worthy and loving Colonel Thomas
Barwick who died the 15th day of December 1648
[aged] 27'

c.547, p. 325

S1079 Stay, passenger, until my life you read,
An end to all perfection I have seen.

'Curious epitaph from a monument in Dunkeld Abbey
Scotland Marion Scott [d. 28 November 1727]'

c.152, p. 76; see also 'Stop, passenger . . .'.

S1080 Stay rare relicts, and sweet goal
Sure of change and alteration.

Ja[mes] Frasert, 'On the virtuous and right worshipful
Dam[e] Elizabeth Farq[u]har my lady Gordonstoun
younger . . . [d.] November 1663'

Poetry Box VIII (oversize), no. 1

S1081 Stay (reader) and bewail his end
His 'scutcheon is his/was but's character.

'Another [epitaph]'

b.104, p. 2

S1082 Stay reader and herewith leave one groan
Then heaven is thine. Reader farewell.

'One Thomas Cook gardener who died at 24 years of
age'

c.547, p. 331

S1083 Stay reader and own before you go past her
Let her be entomb'd and he lie in a ditch.

'Written on the back side of the tomb by a lady'
[comment on 'Here I lie entomb'd . . .']

c.150, p. 39

S1084 Stay reader it is vain to fly death's universal
                                    monarchy
It is enough this tragedy to tell. This is the prince
                                    for whom Gustavus fell.

Sir Tho[mas] Roe, 'Upon the death of the king of
Bohemia'

Poetry Box VI/30

S1085 Stay, should I answer lady then
Intends to speak the rest by signs.

[John Cleveland], 'To Mrs. Katherine Thorold who
when she had kissed him, he not speaking asked him if
he was dumb'
[Crum S1167]

b.93, p. 83

S1086 Stay silly soul and do not break
My epitaph that I died for love.

'Cant: 20'
[Crum S1169, 'silly heart']

b.4, fol. 17 (damaged)

S1087 Stay, stay Æneas, for thine own sake stay,
I'll answer make, for thee thus, thus I die.

'Dido her last speech to Æneas'

Poetry Box VI/8

S1088 Stay sweet enchanter of the grove,
Sooth'd sorrow's self shall list to thee.

'To the wood-robin'

c.83/2, no. 612

S1089 Stay traveller; and tho' within,
Has fixt her mansions there.

[James Merrick?], 'Wrote by a traveller on the window
of a thatched cot'

fc.132/1, p. 25; see also 'Stay passenger . . .', 'Stop
traveller . . .'.

S1090 Stay traveller—for all you want is near,
When death here treads on all that man can be.

'Epitaph on Cardinal Richelieu'

c.360/3, no. 56

S1091 Stay traveller guess who lies here:
To whom late Archy was a drone. | *Stultorum plena*
                                    sunt omnia.

'On Wm. Summers King Hen: the 8th jester'

fb.143, p. 13

S1092 Stay, traveller, thy hasty tread,
Till faithful recollection dies.

'An epitaph'

c.83/3, no. 943

S1093 Stay view this stone if that thou beest not such
Would make the fables of good women true.

   [Ben Jonson], 'Upon one Mrs. Boulstred'
   [Crum s1178]

b.356, p. 99

S1094 Stay wretched swain, lie here and here lament
Adieu to poetry, adieu to love.

   [Charles Hopkins], 'A pastoral elegy on the death of
   Delia Daphnis and Thyrsis'

b.130, p. 116; c.360/1, p. 287 (incomplete?)

S1095 Stebbing and Warburton contest
Punch intercepts and lets a fart.

   'Epigram on Jo: Edwards of Magdalen College'

c.74

S1096 Stella and Flavia ev'ry hour
Each hour gives Stella more.

   [Laetitia (Van Lewen) Pilkington?], 'Autre' [on the
   Duchesses of Newcastle and Queensberry]
   [Crum s1182]

c.358, p. 122

S1097 Stella! Be cheerful. 'Tis the day
And oh! How blest if I were he!

   'To Stella. 1753'

c.238, p. 23

S1098 Stella grown jealous, and half mad to know,
For I had never been perceiv'd before.

   ['Stella growing jealous']

fb.142, p. 38

S1099 Stella to whom I long in vain
I would not for the world return.

   Mrs. [ ] Walsingham, 'Riddle'
Diggle Box: Poetry Box XI/71

S1100 Stella! Whose face enchants the eye;
She soars aloft on golden wings.

   John Lockman, 'On the opening of Vauxhall Gardens
   To Stella. 20 May 1766'

c.267/4, p. 303

S1101 Stephen and time are now got even
Time's beat Stephen.

   'In Suffolk on blind Stephen the fiddler'
   [Crum s1185]

c.74

S1102 Sterling sense, and true genius will ever incite,
But few, very few, have a talent to write.

Poetry Box x/65

S1103 Stern Æol raves, the rigid king
And hold forever back the spring.

   [W. Gibson], 'Ode to Delia'

c.90

S1104 Stern Fortune's frown I own 'tis hard to bear,
Outlive the storm, and still unmov'd remain.

   'Reflections on fortune'

c.156, p. 208; c.83/3, no. 1047 (var.)

S1105 Stern winter, frowning now, recedes
Point up to nature's God.

   'The invitation' [23 Jan. 1786, pub. Monthly magazine
   Jan. 1799, p. 43]

c.136, p. 133

S1106 Stern winter is come, with his cold chilling breath,
And the rich should remember the poor.

   'On the season for remembering the poor'

c.83/4, no. 2019

S1107 Sterne, rest forever, and no longer fear,
Great were his faults, but glorious was his flame.

   'Epitaph for the Revd. Laurence Sterne's tombstone
   by a lady'

c.341, p. 158

S1108 Still am I doom'd to bear this slavish chain
Resound thy griefs thou soon wilt be no more.

   'The complaint'
Poetry Box I/27

S1109 Still as I live the longer here
So does heav'n's light more int' it shine.

   [Edmund Wodehouse], 'Aug. 15 [1715]'

b.131, p. 246

S1110 Still by your weakness
Your only strength will know.

   [Mary Pluret], 'Under great bodily weakness I had
   these words which I have found good'

c.354

S1111 Still constant stand, abiding sweet or sour
Until the Lord appoint an happy hour.

c.339, p. 316

S1112 Still have regard to banish idle fits,
And in your youth with skill adorn your wits.

c.339, p. 321

S1113 Still hovering o'er the fair at fifty-four
A teasing ghost of the departed man.

> Lady Mary Wortley Montagu, 'Wrote under General
> Churchill's picture at Vanloos'

fc.135; Poetry Box v/12; Poetry Box x/142

S1114 Still in our ears Andromache complains;
Who made the world his country by his fame.

> George Montagu, 'On Homer'

fc.135, p. 11

S1115 Still in the hopes to get the better
And confess myself a slave.

> 'Song 51'

c.555, p. 76

S1116 Still let thy wisdom be my guide
And glory end what grace begun.

> 'Hymn 41st'

c.562, p. 49

S1117 Still, like his Savior, known by breaking bread,
And learn each grace his pulpit taught before.

> 'An epitaph' [on Richard Mason, parson of Morborn,
> d. 1723]

c.244, p. 624; fc.60, p. 115

S1118 Still may this morn with fairest luster rise,
And point it to that heav'n from whence it came.

> [Elizabeth Carter], 'To a lady on her birthday'

fc.132/1, p. 5

S1119 Still, my dear Lord, do fair Italia's shores
Your Lordship might be happy even at Derry.

> [ ] Stone, dean, 'Horace Ep. 11 Lib. 1mo . . . Imitated
> by . . . to Lord Middlesex [later duke of Dorset]'

fc.135

S1120 Still restless still chopping and changing about
What a pity it is he don't alter himself.

> 'On a dissatisfied ill-tempered man'

c.546

S1121 Still shall the sun through B—ks—n's curtains peep
Stretch thy dear limbs and to new conquests rise!

> R[ichard] V[ernon] S[adleir], 'On a lady who said she
> usually slept on her face'

c.106, p. 111

S1122 Still shall unthinking man substantial deem
In silence shed the sympathetic tear.

> 'An elegy'

c.139, p. 196

S1123 Still to be neat, still to be drest,
They strike mine eyes, but not my heart.

> [Ben Jonson], 'The sweet neglect—written in 1609'
> [Crum S1203]

fc.132/1, p. 189; b.213, p. 7

S1124 Still was the night, and scarce the sighing breeze
Vengeance demand it—'tis resolved—'tis done.

> G. Baker, 'Medea . . . 1793'

c.495, p. 1

S1125 Still we do find, black cloth wears out the first,
Must wash his marble too, before she go.

> Rob[ert] Wild, 'Upon the death of many reverend
> ministers of late'
> [Crum S1206]

c.166, p. 323

S1126 Still weeping work! and must our burning lights
Bemoan his death, let us translate his life.

> John Wells, 'On the . . . death of . . . William Taylor'
> [d. 7 September 1641]

b.88, p. 5

S1127 Still ye old heathen gods in number dwell
Ah that our greatest faults were in belief.

> 'On Mr. Crashaw's death'

Poetry Box x/1

S1128 Still'd is the tempest's blust'ring roar;
I'll ne'er burn harp again for thee!

> [Hector Macneill], 'The harp, a legendary tale in two
> parts'

c.142, p. 463

S1129 Stop birds—bestow one pious tear
The monarch of the grave, and sov'reign of the
night.

> [Robert Cholmeley], 'Upon the death of Mrs.
> Katherine Lee's parrot'

c.190, p. 172

S1130 Stop gardener here, nor dig too deep,
For thee no brighter joys, no heav'nly crown.

> Martha Dickinson, 'On a favorite horse and dog
> buried under a cypress in our garden'

c.391

S1131 Stop noses gentlemen: this Rump methinks
May have your pay, disband, and so adieu.

> 'The Rump. Together with a (hopeless) address to the
> army for the redress of this grievance'

Poetry Box vi/115

S1132 Stop passenger, and drop one pitying tear,
Where none will wish to part the man and wife.

> James Soame, 'To the sacred memory of Stephen
> Soame esqr . . . who departed this life the 11th of
> August 1771 aged 34'
>
> c.90

S1133 Stop, passenger, until my life you read,
I have an end of all perfection seen.

> 'Inscription on Margaret Scot her tomb in the
> churchyard of Dunkeld who died the sixth day of
> January 1728' [pr. 1729 (Foxon E442)]
> [Crum S1218]
>
> Poetry Box IV/175; c.83/2, no. 613; see also 'Stay,
> passenger . . .'.

S1134 Stop passenger (your own race may still be run)
That to the good the grave's the way to bliss.

> [Phanuel Bacon], 'The verses referred to [in the title
> of 'A bard on whom Phoebus . . .'] are these'
>
> c.237, fol. 82v [*i.e.*, 102v]; see also 'Those tufted
> hillocks . . .'.

S1135 Stop, stop my steed! Hail Cambria, hail,
I'll come again to London.

> [Sir Charles Hanbury Williams], '[Edward] Hussey to
> Sr Cha: Hanbury Williams: or the rural reflection of a
> Welsh poet' [satire; pr. 1746 (Foxon H346)]
> [Crum S1222]
>
> c.241, p. 52

S1136 Stop thoughtless youth, see here I lie
Your morn is not insur'd till noon.

> '[Epitaphs] Lyme'
>
> c.546

S1137 Stop, traveler, and drop a tear:
Then weep thy inauspicious lot.

> [Charles Burney, the elder], 'Epitaph, from the
> French'
>
> c.33, p. 228

S1138 Stop traveller, and gravely muse on,
The early fate of lovely Sue.

> 'Epitaph on a village maiden—April 26 1786'
> fc.130, p. 47

S1139 Stop, traveller, for though within
Has fix'd her mansion here.

> 'Written on the window of a thatched cot'
>
> c.139, p. 396; see also 'Stay passenger/traveller . . .'.

S1140 Stop, traveller! For underneath this stone
The epicures repose their bodies here.

> [Charles Burney, the younger], 'Epitaph on the
> departing magistrands, of King's Coll. Aberdeen; who
> voted in favor of a feast, and against a ball, at the
> graduation 1779'
>
> c.37, p. 5

S1141 Stout Hannibal before he came to age
Appointed at Newstead(?) for that effect.

> 'A satire against Monmouth[.] The Oxford alderman's
> speech to the Duke of Monmouth' [1680?]
> [Crum S1225]
>
> Poetry Box VIII/40

S1142 Straight my green gown into breeches I'll make
Ding, dong bell, ding, dong bell.

> 'The frenzy'
>
> fb.107, p. 20

S1143 Strain not at things that are beyond thy length:
Nor were revealed since the world hath been.

> Sir John Strangways,.'Noli altum sapere . . . 16to
> Decembris 1646'
>
> b.304, p. 79

S1144 Strange creature man! By spirits lifted high,
He groans in sackcloth, and he limps, a goose.

> [John Lockman], 'Homo'
> c.268 (first part), p. 15

S1145 Strange! (cries Tom Tinkle,) that my flowing lines,
Mead's words gave health: thy nonsense made him
sick.

> John Lockman, 'The physician and the bard'
> c.267/1, p. 163; c.268 (first part), p. 11 ('Jack Tinkle')

S1146 Strange fate is ours! | Thus to be mock'd by every
saucy billow
And plunders equally both friends and foes.

> [John Lockman], 'The shipwrecked sailors. A tragic
> scene. Written in 1731'
> c.268 (second part), p. 167

S1147 Strange is our nature, wondrous is our power!
Where is our blest abode, and what we are?

> '[Enigma/Charade/Conundrum] 69'
> c.389

S1148 Strange is thy power, Love! What numerous veins,
And pain had never found 'em!

> [Isaac] Watts, 'Dr. Watts' Lyric'
> c.259

S1149 Strange it is the human mind,
Where satisfaction lies.

    'Ode to satisfaction'

    c.83/3, no. 961

S1150 Strange! my friend are women now grown so scarce,
And so deprive you, of your lookt-for bliss.

    'On a young man between 20 and 30 marrying an old
    woman almost fourscore'

    c.158, p. 25

S1151 Strange news from Barbary learn'd Digby tells
Things baser far then solid stones and rocks.

    'Of the news of a town near Tripoli in Barbary turned
    with all the things in it to stone' [c. 1658]

    b.52/1, p. 105

S1152 Strange revolutions, mighty storms,
On who sit propp'd behind the scenes.

    John Lockman, 'Utrum horum . . . Decr. 1744, about
    which time there had been great revolutions, both in
    the ministry and the stage'

    c.267/1, p. 33

S1153 Strange time when fruits so ripe, yet early fall
On some of worth who may thy place supply.

    'Elegy on the untimely death of Mr. Robert Dickson
    of Boughtrig advocate'

    Poetry Box VIII/26

S1154 Stranger! Behold this little beechen grove!
And the Five Happy Sisters be their name.

    'Verses on the planting of five trees, on an eminence at
    Barrington Castle, in Herefordshire; the seat of the
    right honorable Thomas Harley—1st November 1775'

    fc.132/1, p. 219

S1155 Stranger, or guest, whome'er this hallow'd grove
And hails thee welcome to his friendly grove.

    [Thomas Edwards], 'Verses in an hermitage' [at Wrest
    in Bedfordshire, seat of the earl of Hardwicke]

    fc.85, fol. 118v

S1156 Stranger pause—for thee the day
Give thine alms—thou canst not heal.

    [( ) Smyth], 'For the blind asylum, Liverpool'

    c.141, p. 8; c.83/3, no. 1020

S1157 Stranger, should thou approach this awful shrine
From earth to heav'n, from blessing to be blest.

    'Epitaphs (Milton Oxfordshire)'

    c.546; see also 'What worthless grandeur . . .'.

S1158 Stranger! whoe'er thou art? shall tread
Such gifts, united in a Queen.

    [Stephen Box], 'On the Queen's grotto at Richmond
    in which are placed the busts of Mr. Locke Sir Isaac
    Newton Dr. Clarke Mr. Wollaston'

    Poetry Box IV/173

S1159 Stranger whoe'er thou art whose wand'ring jut
And let thy heaven-born soul aspire to heaven.

    [Hugh Hutton]

    Greatheed Box/40

S1160 Stranger wouldst thou Albion know?
Such is her equality.

    'On the benevolence of England'

    c.83/2, no. 525

S1161 Stray we from virtue? Peace? Then wings her flight,
And leaves the soul in everlasting night.

    'Virtue'

    c.93

S1162 Strephon and Phoebe toy below,
Nothing, cries Phoebe, nothing's here.

    'Printed in the London magazine for July 1751 as a
    solution of the celebrated riddle on nothing'

    c.360/3, no. 166

S1163 Strephon, at last, th'unhappy veils remov'd,
While her back door admits them all at night.

    'To Strephon'

    c.189, p. 4

S1164 Strephon by his Flora lying,
Kisses o'er and o'er again.

    'Song 2'

    c.555, p. 2

S1165 Strephon hath fashion, wit, and youth
Returns into my breast.

    'Written by a lady' [on 'the heart at rest at home']
    [Crum S1242]

    b.201, p. 143

S1166 Strephon there sighs not on this plain
When love is at an end.

    John Wilmot, 2nd earl of Rochester, 'Dialogue[:]
    Alexis and Strephon'

    b.334, p. 215 (incomplete)

S1167 Strephon why that cloudy forehead?
Wine's the weapon conquers love.

    'Song 38'

    c.555, p. 59

S1168 Stretched as I lie on bed of state
And Britain's still more hard to reign.

'Supposed to be thought of in a bed where two kings of the Stuart blood had lain'

fc.58, p. 169

S1169 Stretch'd on his bed of straw the maniac groans
Still shall I reign and still a monarch die.

Edward Walford, 'The maniac composed by . . . of Berkhamsted school'

c.504, p. 189

S1170 Stretch'd on his homely bed, the wearied hind
Had fall'n, and earth design'd with heaven to vie.

[Henry] Needler, 'On a country summer's night'

c.244, p. 550

S1171 Stretch'd on the grass, in a thick shady grove
The prosecutions of *et cetera*.

'Upon *et cetera*'

fb.66/41

S1172 Stretched on the thorny bed of pain
The guardian genius of this isle.

William Stewart Ross, 'On the receiving of the ring . . . March. 1789'

File 17441

S1173 Strike up ye instruments of joy and war,
Nor ever think of trifles past.

Lady Dorothea du Bois, 'An ode on the King of Prussia'

File 13832

S1174 Strive to do good, and not to sink in sin,
For after guiltiness must grief begin.

c.339, p. 312

S1175 Strong Samson's love despoil'd his head of hair:
Such Delilahs, are nowadays not rare.

Sir Thomas Urquhart, 'Of Delilah'

fb.217, p. 122

S1176 Strong sense from nature, by sweet art refin'd
Adorn her words, and dignifies her face!

'Miss [ ] Wale'

Poetry Box x/12

S1177 Struck by the beauties form'd by blended dyes,
The magic pencil, and the heav'nly lyre.

John Lockman, 'Writ after the rehearsal, in the Banquetting House of Mr. Handel's anthem, composed for Queen Caroline's funeral . . . March 1742/3'

c.267/1, p. 160; c.268 (first part), p. 20 ('Struck with')

S1178 Struck with a reverential awe,
There is no night, till those eyes close.

'Miriam's bedchamber. 13. Novr. 1754'

c.371, fol. 82

S1179 Struck with religious awe, and solemn dread,
And all the horrors of the grave defy.

Rev. [ ] Moore, of Cornwall, 'A soliloquy written in a country churchyard'
[Crum s1259]

c.94

S1180 Studious of peace, he hated strife;
Before both God and man.

'An epitaph'

c.341, p. 159

S1181 Studious, the busy moments to deceive
Be now cut off betwixt the grave and thee.

[Matthew Prior, trans.], 'The reflection[:] Quid sit futurum cras fuge quaerere? Horat.' [from the Latin of Alexander Pitcairne; pr. Edinburgh, 1710? (Foxon P366)]
[Crum s1265]

c.326, p. 166

S1182 Study thyself, and read where she hath writ
God and himself, needeth no further go.

[Sir Richard Bulstrode], 'Travels at home'

fb.88, p. 115v

S1183 Studying as I stood I was moved in my mind
So the melody was marr'd the mean was too high.

'Braye Lute Book,' Music Ms. 13, fol. 49v

S1184 Subdu'd by death, here death's great herald lies,
Made it his business to look out for death.

'Epitaph on an undertaker'

c.360/3, no. 183

S1185 Sublime sensations thrill within the soul
And gladden every heart with nature's mirth.

Charles Atherton Allnutt, 'Sketch of a rural situation, Lockinge'

c.112, p. 23

S1186 Submit thy fate to heav'n's indulgent care
So dies, and so dissolves in supernatural light.

c.83/3, no. 816

S1187 Subtraction broken what remains to find
It will proportion every man his due.

[Mary Serjant], 'Subtraction [broken]'

fb.98, fol. 17

S1188   Subtraction whole are sums that are entire
Remember this rule never to forsake.

     [Mary Serjant], 'Subtraction'

     fb.98, fol. 15

S1189   Success and plenty to the Kentish plains,
And who not own, that Montagu was he.

     F[rederick] M[ontagu], 'To George Montagu esqr. at
     Hawkhurst in Kent'

     fc.135

S1190   Successful o'er the course the race-horse flies
For ever yours—for who shall you excel.

     Rev. [ ] Mills, 'Bury, Angel Hill June 3rd 1791'

     Smith Papers, folder 74/11

S1191   Such a fuss, and an uproar about your Gil Blas
Sing ribaldry, scribbledry Moore.

     'On the comedy call'd Gil Blas, written by
     Mr. [Edward] Moore, and acted for nine nights at
     Drury Lane in Feb. 1750/1'

     c.360/3, no. 85

S1192   Such a sad tale prepare to hear
No dildoes from his ashes rise.

     [Samuel Butler? or Sir Charles Sedley?], 'Dildoides'
     [1672]
     [Crum s1276]

     fb.70, p. 49

S1193   Such as are honored with your acquaintance,
As much as any, that they ever knew.

     Sir Thomas Urquhart, 'To my Lord [crossed out]'

     fb.217, p. 349

S1194   Such as for ready coin their place have bought,
Should not bestow their suffrages for naught.

     Sir Thomas Urquhart, 'An apology for bribery'

     fb.217, p. 229

S1195   Such as I am, such shall ye be,
A thousand four hundred just his was.

     'On Simon Street and Agnes his wife'

     fb.143, p. 22

S1196   Such as I have to my own heart propounded,
Friend I do hear, you have her to the life.

     'A wife'
     [Crum s1279]

     b.197, p. 210

S1197   Such as in God the Lord confide
Thy peace in Israel.

     'Psalm 125'

     c.264/3, p. 72

S1198   Such as ye are, such were we
Say a paternoster and an ave.

     'The following epitaph was on a brass plate in the
     middle aisle of Brill church in Bucks; it was in
     blackletter characters and scarce legible'

     c.240, p. 135; see also 'Pray for the soul of Maud
     Davy . . .', 'Here lies William Banknot . . .'.

S1199   Such has been this ill-natur'd nation's fate
Nothing can make us greater than a queen.

     [Daniel Defoe], 'The mock mourners. A satire by way
     of elegy on King William; the fifth edition [Foxon
     D138] corrected by the author of The true-born
     Englishman 1702'
     [POAS VI.376]

     c.158, p. 134

S1200   Such Helen was and who can blame the boy
That in so bright a flame consumed his toy.

     [Edmund Waller], 'On the amiable Miss W——'
     [Crum s1284]

     c.546, p. 22

S1201   Such is her virtue, such her modesty
As in a court—she well may ruler be.

     [Sir Philip Wodehouse], 'Upon Mrs. Mary Burwell.
     Now married to my cousin Walpole'

     b.131, back (no. 68)

S1202   Such is her virtue, that you have no shift,
For when you're idle, she's best occupied.

     Sir Thomas Urquhart, 'Of a certain gentlewoman's
     virtue expressed to her husband, who had just reason
     to be jealous of her carriage'

     fb.217, p. 275

S1203   Such is the folly, such the fate
The ways of vice—to death.

     'On villainy'

     c.361

S1204   Such is the frailness of our mortal state
But with a valiant mind, endure each frown.

     J[ohn] R[obinson], 'Grata superveniet, quae non
     sperabitur, hora'

     c.370, fol. 49v

S1205   Such is the mode of these censorious days
To save herself was forced to let him die!

     [John Sheffield, duke of Buckinghamshire and
     Normanby], 'On Mr. Hobbes' [1691]
     [Crum s1286]

     fb.70, p. 319

S1206 Such is the nature of most humankind,
Ungrateful people, and deal not with them.

    J[ohn] R[obinson], 'Ingratos ante omnia pone sodales'

c.370, fol. 26v

S1207 Such is the posies Love composes
A stinging nettle mixt with roses.

    'On a nosegay with a nettle in it'

b.356, p. 103

S1208 Such is the thin and ragged mask of vice
[?] [?] this good for what's commodious.

    [Sir Thomas Urquhart], 'That the most solid gain is in the action of virtue, all other emoluments how lucrative they soever appear to the [?] mind, being the chiefest [?] [?] of human f[r]ailty to an inevitable [?]'

fb.217, p. 517

S1209 Such language from my friend I cannot bear
I'm yours entire and ever will remain.

    [Mrs. Christian Kerr], 'To the same friend' [answer to 'But oh! what arms . . .'; answered in turn by 'I wish my language . . .']

c.102, p. 96

S1210 Such looks as those gave Adam his fall
I to the rough war with my Nanny will go.

    'A song'

b.207, p. 26

S1211 Such maltsters as ill measured sell for gain
Are not more knaves, but also knaves in grain.

    'On maltsters'

c.74

S1212 Such men are like to owls; they take delight
But they shall howl, when day-birds be at rest.

    [Francis Quarles], 'On corner-sinners' [Divine fancies II, 85]

b.137, p. 191; b.156, p. 25

S1213 Such novel innocence dwells in her breast
True blue they've always been in loyalty.

    [Sir Philip Wodehouse], 'Upon Martha Shelton late Appleton married to his kinsman Shelton'

b.131, back (no. 78)

S1214 Such odds, as betwixt use and nature be:
Are found 'twixt love, and consanguinity.

    Sir Thomas Urquhart, 'The difference betwixt friends and kinsmen'

fb.217, p. 152

S1215 Such passions, as may possible disturb
To daunt your will, and purge your mind, of sin.

    Sir Thomas Urquhart, 'To my Lady Dowager of [crossed out]'

fb.217, p. 123

S1216 Such people should not be traducers, nor
He that barefooted goes must not plant thorns.

    [Sir Thomas Urquhart], 'He that mocks a cripple ought to be whole'

fb.217, p. 534

S1217 Such pity hovers round the gentle heart,
Still clings compassion round this mourning breath.

    'Eliza'

c.344, p. 67

S1218 Such points of noble courage I have found
Of knowing good, and doing't dex'trously.

    [Sir Thomas Urquhart], 'To my Lord Willoughby [later earl Lindsey]'

fb.217, p. 389

S1219 Such powerful charms in wit with beauty move
They take the yielding heart of all mankind.

    [Sir William Trumbull], 'On a lady of great beauty and wit'

Trumbull Box: Poetry Box XIII/75

S1220 Such royal qualities did her adorn,
To the catastroph' of a sov'reign martyr.

    Sir Thomas Urquhart, 'Upon Queen Mary of Scotland'

fb.217, p. 127

S1221 Such sentinels, such brazen towers,
Who's only blest with just sufficiency.

    'In imitation of Horaces 10th ode. lib: 3'

c.233, p. 9

S1222 Such strains might grace an angel's song,
In Rowe's harmonious numbers are combin'd.

    'Extempore on reading Mrs. Rowe's poems'

c.89, p. 13

S1223 Such such were his noble ancestors and yet
Inspired by him still flourish on his hearse.

    'A funeral poem sacred of the honorable and most accomplished gentleman Sr. Warham St. Leger' [c. 1631]

File 17712

S1224 Such virtue scorn'd on cowards' terms to please
And when Jove told the truth, he told us all.

    'Lucan's great character of Cato'

c.481, p. 232

S1225 Such war and wrong way ever saw
And they[?] die aim for our behoof.

'Verses made in Scotland 20. years past and now come to pass'
fb.9, fol. 27v

S1226 Such was my charity, that tho' I knew
And found her false, yet I would think her true.

c.549, p. 3

S1227 Such was the man, and such his ev'ry grace
That virtue wing'd with thee, to heav'n is fled.

'Wrote on the left hand of Lord Petre's tomb in the Pensoroso'
fc.51, p. 94

S1228 Such was the second Drelincourt, a name
Transmit his image, or extend his praise.

[George Jeffreys?], 'Mr. Drelincourt [Dean of Armagh]'s epitaph'
c.244, p. 624

S1229 Such were the author's parts, thy judgment such
To see his works, when such a saint could read.

[Robert Cholmeley], 'To a young lady upon reading the works of the Revd. Mr. Kettlewell'
c.190, p. 61

S1230 Such were the hopes that Israel's prophet fir'd
'Through ways of comfort, and thro' paths of peace.'

'Although the fig tree shall not blossom . . .'
Poetry Box iv/105

S1231 Such were the notes thy once-lov'd poet sung,
Nor fears to tell, that Mortimer is he.

[Alexander] Pope, 'Lines of . . . to [Robert Harley] Earl [of] Mortimer' [and Oxford; c. 1721] [Crum s1305]
c.83/3, no. 1048

S1232 Suckling, Randolph, Donne, Drayton, Massinger
And you to me are all of them in one.

[Sir Aston Cokayne], 'To Mr Charles Cotton Junior'
b.275, p. 92

S1233 Sue thought herself the only wife,
'Twas buzz'd about he'd laid a score.

Edward Sneyd, 'Simon and Susan, a tale'
c.214, p. 57

S1234 Sue's nose hangs down so low, one would suppose
Whene'er she gapes that Sue would cut her nose.

'On the beautiful Miss S——'
c.74

S1235 Suffer me not to sleep in shades of night
Is such they are content to part with never.

[Mary Serjant]
fb.98, fol. 167

S1236 Superfluous is this shield, in sable state,
All, all proclaim, Octavia is no more.

John Lockman, 'Seeing an achievement over the door of a great lady . . . July 1743'
c.267/1, p. 2

S1237 Superfluous wealth and pomp I don't desire
With pleasure would I sail down the swift stream
of life.

'Juvenal 9 Satire'
b.155, p. 70

S1238 Superior beings when of late they saw
And show'd a Newton as we show an ape.

'On Newton'
c.81/1, no. 192

S1239 Superior far to India's boasted gold,
Follow their light, and you'll not go astray.

John Lockman, 'Writ in the blank leaf of Sir John Fielding's Universal mentor (a collection of important examples, observations, &c.) given to a young gentleman going to Bombay . . . 28 July 1769'
c.267/4, p. 314

S1240 Support me: O! I faint, I fall, I die.
Was ever skit so fine!

John Lockman, 'The coalition; or Lady Revenue, and Madam Gin: a ballad opera intermixed with the humorous pranks, of Harlequin Smuggler . . .'
c.267/1, p. 199

S1241 Suppose a damsel, like our princess, blind,
Which give at once joy, gratitude and love.

[David Garrick], 'Epilogue for [Emmeline in Dryden's] Arthur'
File 5610 (autogr.)

S1242 Suppose a picture be design'd
Painting's the offspring of man's fancy.

'Answer' [to 'When first I . . .']
c.578, p. 51

S1243 Suppose bright beauty should invade my breast,
And value beauty much: but freedom more.

[Charles] Dibdin, the younger(?)
c.94

S1244 Suppose yourself, as well you may
Between the faithful and the fair.

'To a lady who inquired the cause of the moon's
eclipse'
[Crum S1320]

c.360/1, p. 73

S1245 Supreme and righteous judge, descend
Vanish with short success.

[Sir William Trumbull], 'Ps[alm] 55'

Trumbull Box: Poetry Box XIII/10, 11 (2 copies)

S1246 Supreme chronologist of all the muses,
Your highness with the like my mind t'enrich.

Sir Thomas Urquhart, 'The invocation to Polymnia'

fb.217, p. 259

S1247 Sure as our earth around the sun
Think on the shortest day.

'The shortest day'

c.83/2, no. 603

S1248 Sure as the dazzling orb of day
Would raise her to that height she longs to know.

Charles Atherton Allnutt, 'Breathings of the soul'

c.112, p. 73

S1249 Sure as ye live, who Arthur's fate deplore,
Thunder begins and wonder ends the year.

'Merlin's prophecy on the year 1690' [in Latin and
English]
[Crum S1323]

fb.70, p. 260

S1250 Sure, at cross purposes Dame Nature play'd,
Hand him the trowel, and snatch thou the lyre.

John Lockman, 'To Mr. Jones, a bricklayer in Dublin,
on his presenting his excellency the Earl of
Chesterfield with a good poem'

c.267/1, p. 240

S1251 Sure Cerberus a lawyer first must be,
Instead of coin, the growling puppy's fee.

'That Cerberus the dog of Hell was a lawyer'

c.158, p. 141

S1252 Sure feebly guarded are those hearts
To your wise judgment lo I bow.

[Mrs. Christian Kerr], 'The same person's true
sentiments of love written on a stormy night'

c.102, p. 90

S1253 Sure, he, who in his youth, for glory strove,
Should recompense his age with ease and love.

c.189, p. 102

S1254 Sure it is so, | Then let it go
This is a mad world my masters.

'The mad world'

fb.107, p. 78

S1255 Sure man says S—l, never shared such fate!
What of nobility remain? The name.

C. B.

c.74; see also 'Learn, learn, nobility . . .'.

S1256 Sure nature never did design
Then to live a young widow or to die an old maid.

'A song'

b.54, p. 1162

S1257 Sure naught but disappointment could engage
She's far too bright for thee, thou empty man.

'To the author of the verses on Miss Reade' ['When
Hobert's air . . .']

c.360/1, p. 263

S1258 Sure never pain such beauty wore,
We angels rise, who mortals died.

William Broome, 'On Belinda's recovery'

c.244, p. 483

S1259 Sure not to life's short span confin'd,
Still pant for brighter day.

'Friendship'

c.83/3, no. 1077

S1260 Sure the pen may be employed to relate
And so farewell—I now conclude. The end.

M[ary (Shackleton)] L[eadbeater], 'Upon a walk to
Lackington'

c.303

S1261 Sure the vessel bound to bear,
Lamb to still the tempest slay.

[William Popple, trans.], '[Horace, ep]ode 10th.
Against the poet Maevius'

fc.104/2, p. 436

S1262 Sure there are hours of ill that wait us all
Who carelessly resign our trusted fame.

c.53, fol. 57

S1263 Sure there are poets which did never dream
And knows no bound, but makes his power his
shores.

Sir John Denham, 'Coopers Hill a poem by . . .'

b.86, p. 26 (ll. 1–342)

S1264 Sure there are some that see with me the state
If Legg, or Armstrong shall be absolute.

    'The impartial trimmer' [1679–80]
    [Crum s1333]

fb.70, p. 159

S1265 Sure these are Gallia's southern plains,
And whose proud summits wave in skies.

    John Lockman, 'The greenhouse at Versailles'
    [translated from La Fontaine]

c.267/4, p. 267

S1266 Sure when I enter'd on this mortal state,
May heal the wound of your distemper'd mind.

    'Advice about scandal in a question to the British
    Apollo'

c.244, p. 313

S1267 Sure with the Papists all the devils agreed
An universal king can ever be.

    J[ohn] R[obinson], 'On the happy discovery of the
    Powder Plot. November the 5th 1605 . . . 1715'

c.370, fol. 29v

S1268 Surely I wrong you not, if my fate
Is chang'd to a glorious and happy state.

    Petrarch

b.211, p. 72

S1269 Surely the eternal eye of Providence
And fell the earth with James his noble story.

    'Libre . . . Duca d. York'

fb.66/18

S1270 Surpassing all the joys of Jove above
Is consummation in the act of love.

    'The motto to consummation a poem'

c.360/1, p. 221

S1271 Surpris'd by grief and sickness, here I lie
With those that have endur'd the heat of day.

    'On a youth dying with grief'
    [Crum s1349]

fb.143, p. 28

S1272 Surprising being! Which we nature call,
And on the great Creator fix thine eyes.

    'Nature'

c.244, p. 630

S1273 Surprising genius! How we stand amaz'd,
Ill-fated fools, when hastily provok'd.

    Abraham Oakes, 'The universal monarch,
    enigmatically described'

c.50, p. 69

S1274 Survey the conduct of mankind,
If they go to heav'n by proxy.

    'The proxy'

c.83/2, no. 383

S1275 Susanna wedded to Spendthrift
When num'rous shifts we daily make.

c.546, p. 32

S1276 Swains I scorn who nice and fair
He is. . . .

    Miss [ ] Roper(?), 'Song'
    [Crum s1359]

c.358, p. 145 (incomplete)

S1277 Swallowing too greedy down tobacco's smoke,
Pray then in what doth Peleia's spear excel.

c.53, fol. 23

S1278 Sweet Amaryllis! Blooming fair,
To tell her lovesick swain—she dies.

    John Lockman, 'The jealous shepherdess: a hint from
    La Fontaine'

c.267/1, p. 256; c.268 (first part), p. 94

S1279 Sweet are my thoughts and sweet my cares
There's something kind and pleasing still.

    [Thomas Stevens?]

c.259, p. 18

S1280 Sweet are the charms of her I love
Love only knows perpetual springs.

    [Barton Booth], 'A song'
    [Crum s1360]

c.374

S1281 Sweet are the joys that flow from moderate use
And as he liv'd a fool, he dies a knave.

    'On the abuse of cards'

c.83/3, no. 991

S1282 Sweet are those pains which lovers long endure;
He is half cured who wishes for a cure.

    [George] L[yttelton], 1st baron Lyttelton, 'Maxims in
    love' [no. 6]

c.487, p. 28

S1283 Sweet as the shepherd's tuneful reed
And waits to claim thee for her own.

    'An hymn'

c.83/3, no. 841

S1284 Sweet autumn! How thy melancholy grace
Thus joy succeeds to grief—thus smiles the varied
man.

    [Ann (Ward)] Radcliffe, 'To autumn . . . mysteries of
Udolpho'

c.83/2, no. 374 (bis); Poetry Box XII/6

S1285 Sweet babe and hast thou took thy flight
Nor sigh nor tear nor grief nor pain.

    [Mary Pluret], 'Another on the death of a very
desirable child about seven or eight years old in the
family where she then was'

c.354

S1286 Sweet babe, thrice welcome stranger! final fruit
And weep sad requiems o'er thy honor'd tomb.

    [Stephen Barrett], 'To Miss Mary Barrett; an infant.
By her father'

c.193, p. 103

S1287 Sweet Benjamin, while thou art young,
Imprison it, or it will thee.

    [John Hoskins], 'Ben Jonson to his son Ben' [actually
Hoskins to his son, written during his imprisonment,
July 1614–July 1615?]
    [Crum S1365]

b.200, p. 412

S1288 Sweet bird of night, whose honey'd throat
A songster should a songster spare.

    'To the nightingale from the Greek . . . May 17 1792'

c.344, p. 13

S1289 Sweet bird of night with plaintive strain
Thy notes—fair Cynthia's character.

    'Address to the nightingale'

c.83/2, no. 611

S1290 Sweet bird! that kindly perching near,
And pay my pensive muse the tribute of a tear.

    [Cuthbert Shaw], 'An evening address to a nightingale'

c.139, p. 513

S1291 Sweet bird that sing'st on yonder spray
In solitude itself is blest.

    [Gilbert West], 'On one side' [of the Hermitage at
Mereworth, seat of the earl of Westmorland]
    [Crum S1366]

fc.51, p. 41; c.360/1, p. 261

S1292 Sweet bird whom cruel fate's relentless doom,
Nor will they bring thee to thy friends again.

    'On the death of a canary bird, by a lady of fourteen'

c.83/1, no. 49

S1293 Sweet blooms in June's fair month the damask rose,
An emblem of the flower that decks thy nose.

    'Delia to Arabin'

fc.76.iii/214

S1294 Sweet blossoms of the vernal year
Sweet comfort yet is found.

    'To Eliza Shackleton and Marg[are]t Harvey . . . 31/5
mo:/1800'

File 13409

S1295 Sweet bud! to Laura's bosom go,
One rose without a thorn.

    'The rosebud. To a lady of fifteen years of age'

c.487, p. 124

S1296 Sweet bud, whose forward bloom displays,
Shall bow in homage to its queen.

    'The rosebud. To a young lady;— descriptive of
herself'

fc.132/1, p. 163

S1297 Sweet child of reason! maid serene!
Time journeys thro' the roughest day.

    'To meditation'

Diggle Box: Poetry Box XI/15

S1298 Sweet content, that wont'st to dwell,
And make with us thy residence.

    'Content'

c.83/1, no. 211, no. 239

S1299 Sweet contentment! heavenly bright
Virtue and content's the same.

    'Contentment'

Poetry Box II/36; see also 'Fount of comfort . . .'.

S1300 Sweet daughter of a rough and stormy sire,
With softest influence breathes.

    [Anna Laetitia (Aikin) Barbauld], 'Ode to spring'

c.140, p. 536

S1301 Sweet Echo, sweetest nymph, that liv'st unseen
And give resounding grace to all heav'n's
harmonies.

    [John Milton, 'Echo, a song . . . Comus'

c.94

S1302 Sweet Echo, vocal nymph, whose mimic tongue
Whose voice is music and whose looks are love.

    [Elizabeth Carter], 'Ld Chancellor Thurlow to Miss
Lynch'

Greatheed Box/60

S1303 Sweet flow'r, thou well deserv'st the praise
What eyes alone can e'er reveal.

    'Upon [a flower called the heartsease, painted by a
    young lady]'

fc.40

S1304 Sweet girl! tho' far below the age
To stay till you can cure us.

    'To a girl, seven years of age'

Poetry Box II/3

S1305 Sweet harbinger of spring, thou bird of joy,
But quit their blossoms as they fade away.

    E. Gardner, 'The cuckoo'

c.83/3, no. 1016

S1306 Sweet harmonist! And beautiful as sweet!
That hideous sight, a naked human heart.

    [Edward] Young, 'Picture of Narcissa. Description of
    her funeral and a reflection upon men'

c.343, p. 16

S1307 Sweet harmonist! Whose little throat
Be reason empress of the day.

    'Ode to the nightingale'

c.241, p. 95

S1308 Sweet hope the sov'reign comfort of our life,
Our joy in sorrow, and our peace in strife.

c.93

S1309 Sweet hope thou pleasing inmate of the breast!
Save me, O save me—from the ills of life.

    William Combes, 'On hope'

c.341, p. 39

S1310 Sweet Hyacinth, my life! My joy!
Of the fair boy, for whom so much he burn'd.

    [Wentworth Dillon], 4th earl of R[oscommon],
    'Apollo's grief for having killed Hyacinth by accident
    in imitation of Ovid'

b.201, p. 158

S1311 Sweet I am not come too soon. | None espies us
                              but the moon
What we act but only we.

    'Cant: 19'

b.4, fol. 16

S1312 Sweet innocence and constant love
For peace is ever virtue's guest.

    'On the dove'

c.179, p. 24

S1313 Sweet instrument of him for whom I mourn,
With thee alone it liv'd, with thee shall die.

    [Elizabeth Ann (Linley)] Sheridan, 'On my dear
    brother [Linley]'s violin'

c.250; c.373, p. 60; c.83/3, no. 916; c.343, p. 93

S1314 Sweet is the gracious task that heaven
Which swell the aching breast of woe!

    M[ary (S[hackleton) Leadbeater], 'To Anne
    Strangman of Leek'

File 13409

S1315 Sweet is the joy to haunt each various scene
Read them by day, and read again by night!

    William Parsons, 'Vos exemplaria Graeca'

Greatheed Box/12

S1316 Sweet is the voice of praise! From eve to morn,
And gives her clouded eye a golden hour.

    [John Walcot(?) ('Peter Pindar')], 'Praise . . . Ode 8th
    (1785)'

c.355, p. 95

S1317 Sweet Jesu Christ who didst vouchsafe to die
To [?] not them, sweet Jesu same Amen.

    'Five petitions to our blessed Savior Jesus upon the
    five former meditations'

a.6, p. 22

S1318 Sweet Jesu! Why why dost you love
Now and forever be.

    [John Austin], 'Hym. 35' [Hymn xxx, Devotions in the
    ancient way of offices, 1672, p. 269]

c.178, p. 34

S1319 Sweet Jesus is the name
With cheerful voice.

    [Mary Pluret], 'A hymn on the name of Jesus'

c.354

S1320 Sweet Jesus tune my heart to sing
And I must change abode.

    [Mary Pluret], 'In the year 1731 under great
    manifestations of the love of God'

c.354

S1321 Sweet ladies accept with compliments of the season
Are all set to rights and all end in a farce.

    W[illiam] Smith, 'Copied from some lines written and
    sent to the young ladies Fitzroy at Euston at Xmas'

Smith Papers, folder 58, 73

S1322 Sweet love how long shall I despairing sit
Or that my love had never been begun.

    'To his cruel mistress'

b.356, p. 96

S1323 Sweet lovely youth, let not a woman's crime
And still love on, till death proclaims— | Adieu.

'A billet to a young gentleman from a lady who hurt his lips with a stroke of her fan'

c.229/1, fol. 47

S1324 Sweet maid, if thou wouldst charm the sight,
The nymph for whom these notes are sung.

[Sir William] Jones, 'A translation of a Persian song of Hafia'

c.90

S1325 Sweet maid, is thy soft, snowy head
His viewless, but eternal chain!

[Anna Seward], 'Lichfield Sept. 5th 1800 Lydia Lettercase'

File 13375

S1326 Sweet minstrel the pride of the choir,
With rapture till music expire!

J[ohn] Wolcot ('Peter Pindar'), 'Epitaph [torn] Ranzini'

Poetry Box v/95

S1327 Sweet moralist! whose moving truths impart
Where time, and death, and sickness are no more.

[John] Langhorne, 'To the same [a lady] on the moral reflections contained in her answers to the above verses' ['Dear object of my late . . .'] [Crum s1394]

c.139, p. 568

S1328 Sweet muse! That soft in Euston's bow'rs
Will show you, speculation.

'Verses for the vase. Subject, speculation'

Poetry Box v/46

S1329 Sweet Naiad in the crystal wave
Who found these friendly shades for thee.

R[obert] Dodsley

c.21; c.20/7

S1330 Sweet nymph, accept, with spirit kind,
To soothe afflicted age.

[William Hayley], 'To Sophia with the triumphs of temper—Jan. 1800'

File 6977

S1331 Sweet nymph, I woo thee from thy lone retreat,
To soothe (what time it may) my dying hour.

[E.] Gardner, 'Sonnet to poetry'

c.83/3, no. 1017

S1332 Sweet nymph! The brightest of the woodland train;
Enraptur'd with the charms of op'ning May.

John Lockman, 'Cynthia: to the genius of Vauxhall Gardens . . . May 1757'

c.267/1, p. 84

S1333 Sweet nymph, tho' far remov'd, I start
And all the pleasures join thy train.

[John Wolcot] ('P[eter] P[indar]'), 'Song' [c. 1780]

File 17923

S1334 Sweet nymph! whose matchless virtues void of art,
He stands of love's best paradise, the heir.

[Stephen Barrett?], 'A love epistle' [Gentleman's magazine, November 1746]

c.193, p. 126

S1335 Sweet object of the zephyr's kiss,
What is he but a wither'd rose?

[John] Cunningham, 'The withered rose. The last composition . . . written a little before his death; as a true image of himself'

fc.132/1, p. 116; fc.85, fol. 73v

S1336 Sweet offspring of a stormy hour,
Thou pale first emblem of the year.

J[ohn] Bowden, 'To the snowdrop'

c.142, p. 455

S1337 Sweet pair of virgin-cousins I one day
So I to be allied unto your story.

[Sir Aston Cokayne], 'To my dear cousins Mrs Marie and Mrs Lettie Reppington, sisters'

b.275, p. 105

S1338 Sweet peace! That lov'd in placid scenes to dwell,
And peace, sweet peace, best happiness bestow.

'Verses inscribed on a tablet close to a mausoleum at North Court in the Isle of Wight, the seat of ——— Bull, esqr.'

c.373, p. 84

S1339 Sweet peace, that lov'st the silent hour,
And love and joy are in thy train.

[John Langhorne], 'Inscription in a sequester'd grotto'

c.139, p. 561

S1340 Sweet Phillida be not so coy,
And both will the pleasure approve.

'Advice to the fair one'

fb.107, p. 38

S1341 Sweet Philomel beneath the poplar shade
Of melancholy joy and elegant desire.

> Capel Lofft, 'Written in a cold and showery summer
> in the year 1788 the nightingale'

Poetry Box v/107

S1342 Sweet pleasure, daughter of the sky,
And smiling, in Vauxhall alight.

> John Lockman, 'Cupid's search after pleasure . . . July
> 1744'

c.267/1, p. 107

S1343 Sweet poet of the woods—a long adieu!
And still be dear to sorrow, and to love!

> [Charlotte (Turner) Smith], 'By the same on the
> departure of the nightingale'

c.130, p. 94

S1344 Sweet power! Long stranger to my breast,
Blot, from my soul, all hopes of love.

> John Lockman, 'Translations, and imitations from
> Metastasio, and other Italian opera poets [5]'

c.267/4, p. 95

S1345 Sweet pow'r that lovest the lone recess,
And raise the downcast eye.

> 'Ode to pity'

c.83/2, no. 514

S1346 Sweet, rosy cherub, on thy wond'ring eyes
On earth of every sorrow is beguil'd.

> 'A sonnet to my little boy Martin, 1779'

fc.53, p. 9

S1347 Sweet sister of the tuneful nine,
You wish me what I am.

> William Hayley, to Anna Seward

c.391, p. 88

S1348 Sweet, sleepy doctor! Dear pacific soul,
The fields all thunder, and they bound away.

> [James Thomson], 'The soporific doctor'

c.244, p. 635

S1349 Sweet social bird! Whose soft harmonious lays
Each tongue with music, and each heart with fire.

> [ ] Love, 'On a robin red-breast, which had taken up
> his residence in the cathedral at Bristol, and
> accompanied the organ with his singing. By . . . one of
> the minor canons of that cathedral'

c.341, p. 56; c.83/1, no. 261

S1350 Sweet solitude, thou placid queen,
And angels point the way to peace.

> [Hannah] More, 'Solitude'

c.83/3, no. 767; fc.132/1, p. 117

S1351 Sweet solitude! When life's gay hours are past,
Trust future ages, and contented die.

> [Elizabeth (Singer)] Rowe, 'Soliloquies from Rowe's
> letters'

fc.132/1, p. 80

S1352 Sweet soother of life's cares, when the rude storm
And wounded seeks the medicine which can heal.

> 'Address to Hope—Gent[leman's] Mag[azine]'

fc.124, p. 131

S1353 Sweet sung the birds on ev'ry spray;
Which the scythe of time defies.

> John Lockman, 'Cupid and Hymen. On occasion of
> the marriage of the reverend Mr. du Missy, with Mrs.
> Amproux . . . 3d Nov. 1754'

c.267/2, p. 198

S1354 Sweet tyrant love but hear me now!
And make the bashful lover known.

> [James Thomson?], 'A song by the same'
> [Crum s1411, attr. Betty Archer]

c.152, p. 34

S1355 Sweet valley, say where pensive lying
For love will feel no sorrows but its own.

> [James Thomson], 'A song'

c.83/1, no. 123

S1356 Sweet were once the joys I tasted
Shall alone thy torments feel.

> 'A song'

c.358, p. 81

S1357 Sweet were the hours when once I stray'd
Is cheerless as the wintry blast.

> [Sir Henry William Bunbury], 'Mrs [Dorothea]
> Jordan's song'

File 17066

S1358 Sweet words are honey, to some fools, which they
In all the parts of life a Christian.

> [Sir Philip Wodehouse], 'Captain John Anguish gives
> he honey? Na.'

b.131, back (no. 190)

S1359 Sweet wrecks of beauty! Though with aspic eye,
Too fondly trusting, falls the simple maid!

> John Wolcot ('Peter Pindar'), 'On that unhappy class
> of females, women of the town'

c.82, p. 23

S1360 Sweet youth why is thy blood so staid
And then a [blank] but a higher bliss.

> 'On a bashful young man'

b.205, fol. 24v

S1361 Sweeter than Hybla thyme, than swans more white,
(Can Thyrsis please?) here speed, at Thyrsis' call.

    [Thomas Hull]

c.20/5; c.21

S1362 Sweetest bud of beauty, may
When thou shalt to thy noon arise.

    [Sir George Etherege], 'To a very young lady'

b.218, p. 23; Poetry Box IV/53

S1363 Sweetest isle, of lake or main,
Exult, and laugh, to meet your friend.

    'Ode xxix of Catullus. To the peninsula of Sirmis'

c.136, p. 151

S1364 Sweetest love, I do not go
Alive, ne'er parted be.

    [John Donne], 'Sonnet'
    [Crum S1420]

b.148, p. 89; b.114, p. 307 ('Sweet love')

S1365 Sweetest nymph, of heav'nly birth,
Tender, generous, kind and dear.

    'Ode to content'

Poetry Box IV/187

S1366 Sweetest Savior, if my soul
Ah! no more: thou break'st my heart.

    George Herbert, 'A dialogue'
    [Crum S1423]

c.139, p. 126

S1367 Sweetly encircled with eternal green,
Resolv'd, no more, to trifle life away.

    John Lockman, 'Wit in an elegant summer-house, not
    far from London . . . July 1756'

c.267/1, p. 207

S1368 Swell on unbounded spirits, whose vast hope,
With greatest luster doth advance his glory.

    'A prolusion on the emblem of the second chapter'

c.189, p. 69

S1369 Swift as the sun revolves the day,
The baseness or the joy.

    [Isaac] Watts, 'The life of souls addressed to Dr. Tho.
    Gibson'

c.244, p. 304

S1370 Swift fleet the billowy clouds along the sky
Black as my fate, or cold as my despair.

    [Charlotte (Turner) Smith], 'Sonnet on passing a
    dreary tract of country, and near the ruins of a
    deserted chapel, during a tempest'

c.141, p. 110

S1371 Swift fly the hours, and speed that happy day
And when arrived, for ages let it stay.

    'Bro. Book'

c.549, p. 35

S1372 Swift-flying birds their bodies bear
Death's swift (alas!) on leaden wings.

    'Epigram on a bullet. Made while at school'

c.169, p. 6

S1373 Swift o'er the level how the skaters slide;
But pause not, press not on the gulf below.

    [translation of a French poem]

c.504, p. 89

S1374 Swift-winged time doth fly away so fast,
That whilst we ask, what time it is, 'tis past.

    Sir Thomas Urquhart, 'Of time'

fb.217, p. 188

S1375 Swifter than lightning's winged force,
And joy through solid walls to break.

    'On gold. From Horace'

c.94

S1376 Swiftly see each moment flies
Know to live, and learn to die.

    'On time'

c.83/2, no. 331

S1377 Swinging his scythe about the common mow'r
So early went to such felicity.

    'On the death of a child . . . copy J[udith] A[lsop]'

c.303

S1378 Swiving a filthy pleasure is, and short
Can this decay; but is beginning ever.

b.197, p. 109

S1379 Sylvanus wav'd, (as Barnard waves his rod)
Stand thou third giant in the Hall of Guild.

    [N. Herbert], 'Epigram on Mr Spence's bringing a
    present of trees to the author'

Spence Papers, folder 91

S1380 Sylvia be rul'd by me, nor me despise
To merit thy regard and gain a Cato's praise.

    'Advice to Sylvia 1721'

c.360/2, no. 87

S1381 Sylvia beware of love for all its joys,
As in it we ne'er find the lake Oblivion.

    R[obert] Shirley, 1st earl of Ferrers, 'Against love.
    From the French'

c.347, p. 94

S1382 Sylvia, bright nymph, who long had frown'd,
I wak'd! for oh! 'twas all a dream.

[John Lockman], 'The fond disappointment'

c.268 (first part), p. 57

S1383 Sylvia, Delia, sweetest pair
That there was her equal left.

'To the agreeable memory of two sisters who lived and
died together—written in the year 1724'

c.360/2, no. 101

S1384 Sylvia on her arm inclining,
Tales of love with Sylvia straight.

'Song 57'

c.555, p. 85

S1385 Sylvia the pride and glory of the well
A set of water-drinking souls to love.

'A copy of verses, wrote at Bristol Hot Well—1736 on
Miss Woodward'

c.360/1, p. 15

S1386 Sylvia, with this wheel I send,
Bliss of body and of mind.

'To a young lady with a spinning wheel'

c.83/3, no. 831

S1387 Sylvius thy art does claim more noble lays
And Van Dyck own himself by thee outdone.

[Wriothsley Russell, 3rd] duke of Bedford(?), 'Verses
writ by the present duke of Bedford, at 13 years of age,
on Mr. Whood's drawing Mr. Taylor's picture very
like'

c.176, p. 162

S1388 Symia once most damn'dly swore
He never would breathe more whilst he did drink.

'On Symia'

b.356, p. 308

S1389 Symons! Thrice welcome here:
Come forth: our member shine. | God save the King.

John Lockman, 'Symon's health a new chorus [?]
(extempore) to be sung at the election of members for
the city of Hereford anno 1768 tune, God save great
George our King &c.'

c.267/2, p. 167

S1390 Syne Jockey has bidden farewell to his Jean
Jockey'll ne'er leave his Jeany nor Lochaber no more.

[William Shenstone], 'Farewell to Lochaber [by Allan
Ramsay] answered'

Poetry Box VII/66, p. 2

T

T0001   T'accuse a lovely face, were calumny
Yet to steal hearts, is but smart robbery.

> [Sir Philip Wodehouse], 'Mary Roberts my cousin
> M[ary] C[arey's] fair friend'
> b.131, back (no. 47)

T0002   'Tain't on full chests that I rely,
And in these duties pass my days.

> [Edmund Wodehouse], 'Feb. 22 [1715]'
> b.131, p. 171

T0003   'Tain't possible too much to prize
So will Christian love, our happiness.

> [Edmund Wodehouse], 'St. Vincent's (?) [1714]'
> b.131, p. 126

T0004   'Tain't pride to disregard or slight
His spirit works, to him all's due.

> [Edmund Wodehouse], 'March 8 [1715]'
> b.131, p. 176

T0005   'Tain't they that most pretend God's name,
Of this the true importance is.

> [Edmund Wodehouse], 'July 12 [1715]'
> b.131, p. 230

T0006   Take a knuckle of veal
Will it fill Dean and Chapter.

> [Alexander] Pope, 'Pope entertaining Dean Swift with
> a knuckle of veal who desires a recipe' [pr. 1726
> (Foxon P952)]
> c.489, p. 17

T0007   Take a man who by nature's a true son of earth
And that thing strut a peer which before was an ass.

> 'A r[ecei]pt to make a l[or]d . . . These verses were
> wrote upon the report of Horace Walpole being
> created an earl'
> Poetry Box I/82; File 17484; Poetry Box IV/116

T0008   Take a syllable often repeated in laughter
The name of a city, to England most dear.

> 'A rebus'
> c.360/3, no. 222

T0009   Take a turd, upon my word
Into five commissioners | And Guy.

> Lady [Anne (Montagu)] Harvey(?), 'Upon the King's
> making five commissioners of the Treasury: the Lady
> Harvey makes this following recipe for the kingdom'
> [POAS II.113]
> b.54, p. 1103

T0010   Take back I pray thee dearest Jane,
The emblem of a heart of stone.

> 'A lady being remarkably fond of greengage plums a
> gentleman sent her one, which she eat, and out of joke
> returned the stone in a bit of paper; the gentleman
> presently sent the stone back to her, with the
> following lines'
> c.378, p. 14

T0011   Take [talk?] but of bawd[r]y Christiana spits and
spauls
Her teeth do water for to think on it.

> 'An epigram on a puritan'
> b.62, p. 17; see also 'Speak but . . .'.

T0012   Take, Chloe what you cannot keep,
You teach us to forget it.

> 'To Chloe with an almanac'
> c.90

T0013   Take courage, noble Charles, and cease to muse,
Forces us shadows to make haste away.

> 'Quintus Arbelius's ghost, to Charles Lord Halifax'
> [Crum T10]
> fb.70, p. 21

T0014   Take Devon's polish'd brows and auburn hair
O steal the rose from beauteous Aylesford's cheek.

> 'Receipt to make a perfect beauty 1783'
> c.391, p. 64

T0015   Take earth out of earth earth's own brother
The beginning and ending all is one.

> [on the elixir, ascribed to Pearce the Black Monk;
> Brown-Robbins 3249, copied c. 1570]
> fa.16, p. 37

T0016   Take for example of your love
And all the wedlock is in two.

> 'Propertius Lib. 1 Eleg. 15'
> c.489, p. 10

T0017 Take G from glove, and there remains love,
Which never will do for me.

    'The refusal . . . to Florilla . . . Florilla's answer'

    c.94

T0018 Take greedy death a body here entombed
When Death itself is dead shall be a star.

    [William Strode], 'On one that died of the smallpox'
    [Sir Thomas Saville]
    [Crum T12]

    b.205, fol. 64v

T0019 Take hard heat and dry
Though he have the same thing.

    [cf. Crum T13]

    fa.16, p. 39

T0020 Take heart, thou lover of true piety!
Nor shall thine honor know a shorter date.

    [Maurice Johnson], 'From the Latin'

    c.229/2, fol. 14

T0021 Take heed, fair Celia, how you slight
When age approaches or when beauty's gone.

    c.549, p. 126

T0022 Take heed fair Chloris how you tame
So bright as in these arms of mine.

    [Henry Hughes]
    [Crum T14]

    b.213, p. 122

T0023 Take heed of loving me
To let me live, O love and hate me too.

    [John Donne, 'The prohibition']
    [Crum T19]

    b.148, p. 83

T0024 Take heed of man, and while you may,
And love those that slight them the best.

    c.549, p. 1

T0025 Take heed, ye elders, let your guide be truth
Be good old boy, and do so no more.

    'Advice to an old man'

    c.570/1, p. 1

T0026 Take heed you give not your alms before men,
Sufficient is the evil of the day.

    Sir John Strangways, 'The sixth chapter of St.
    Matthew . . . 1665'

    b.304, p. 154

T0027 Take hold of time: for it doth haste away
Enrich your minds with some good thing each day.

    c.339, p. 321

T0028 Take, holy earth, all that my soul holds dear,
And bids the pure in heart behold their God.

    William Mason, 'Sacred to the memory of Mary . . .
    Sherman . . . Mason' [d. 27 March 1767]
    [Crum T22]

c.156, p. 206; c.341, p. 38; fc.132/1, p. 186; Poetry Box
IV/182; Poetry Box XII/42

T0029 Take man from woman, all that she can show
Of her own proper is naught else but woe.

    Sir Thomas Urquhart, 'On the word woman a
    paradox'

    fb.217, p. 41

T0030 Take me alone death, let my babe still move
Shall be to heaven, where with Christ abide.

    'On a woman dying in childbirth. To death'
    [Crum T26]

    b.200, p. 229

T0031 Take my poor heart just as it is
Who lived and died for me.

    'Hymn 5th'

    c.562, p. 5

T0032 Take not the first refusal ill
If you don't ask her, she'll ask you.

    'Song'

    c.189, p. 222

T0033 Take of beauty and wit what you happen to have,
Candied o'er with good sense, and I'll warrant it
                             lasts.

    'A receipt for the ladies to preserve love in the
    marriage state'

c.175, p. 82; c.391, p. 48; c.83/2, no. 293

T0034 Take of flattery enough,
Make the dose,—*probatum est.*

    'The Bury post Wednesday June 30th 1790—recipe to
    make an election'

    fc.130, p. 54

T0035 Take oft the cene, and wash but once: and you'll
Observe a sacred diet for the soul.

    Sir Thomas Urquhart, 'To an Anabaptist, how to
    become an orthodox Christian'

    fb.217, p. 169

T0036 Take one of the brights
We'll hope he's been | Mov'd(?) and here.

    'Receipt to make a beau'

Spence Papers, folder 113

T0037 Take one third of the mansions where angels reside
Place them right, and an amiable nymph will appear.

'Two rebuses[.] On Miss H[a]y . . . another on Miss
P[ilkingto]n'

c.91, p. 241

T0038 Take out a letter from the Christ-cross row
And that's the town in which I choose to live.

'A rebus riddle'

c.360/3, no. 3

T0039 Take pity for thy promise' sake
O Lord I sing to Thee.

[John Hopkins], 'The 23 psalm. That God would take
our cause in hand against our enemies' [verses from
Psalms 57, 59]
[cf. Crum T30]

a.3, fol. 99

T0040 Take, take my dry books, for I'll study no more
In thee, all her charms united, we find.

'On the celebrated Miss Betty Tatton [later
Viscountess Ashbrook], written 1739'

c.360/1, p. 55

T0041 Take the blood of the green lion
Lost the virtues of thy stone.

fa.16, p. 38

T0042 Take the gift that I bestow
To teeth of time 'twill fall a prey.

'Translation of a little sonnet wrote by Plato, in his
younger time of life, and preserved by Diogenes
Laertius'
[Crum T32]

c.361

T0043 Take then a pint of milk, and spill it
Will please a taste that's less sublime.

[William Hayley], 'As Sunday . . . is the day of
pudding, allow me to set before you the millet you
requested' [17 October 1779]

File 7049

T0044 Take time before, for he is bald behind,
Do thou the like, and then he died for thee.

'A true faith'

c.187, p. 33

T0045 Take wind water white and green
Till all come that you desire.

[Brown-Robbins 3257]

fa.16, p. 39

T0046 Take wing (my soul) and upwards bend thy flight
Nor can thy now-rais'd palate ever relish less.

[John] N[orris, of Bemerton], 'The elevation'
[Crum T37]

c.258

T0047 Take youth that's genteel, no matter for face,
Which harden'd by virtue, will ne'er reach the heart.

'A recipe to soften the hardest female heart'

c.481, p. 223

T0048 Taking of snuff is a mode in court
To a place where he is more able.

[Crum T38]

fb.66/29 (incomplete)

T0049 Tale-bearing chance! By thee is shown
Shows better how you fought and lov'd.

[Phanuel Bacon], 'The patch misplaced'

c.237, fol. 6

T0050 Talk no more of the wars or the Polander's king,
That we ne'er could endure to be led by the nose. |
Derry &c.

'The merry patriot. A ballad'

c.570/4, p. 11

T0051 Talk not to me of your exalted worth
'Tis no disgraceful lot to rival France.

'Mr. Voltaire to Mr. Diodati'

c.83/2, no. 691

T0052 Talking with Delia I did perceive
All other things and feede upon that air.

[Sir Aston Cokayne], 'Of Delia'

b.275, p. 44

T0053 Tall grew the tree and every leaf
A growing, fruitful tree.

T[homas] S[tevens]

c.259, p. 126

T0054 Tame (?) your wife's darkwardness no more: but
trow it,
What any man will put her to, she'll do it.

Sir Thomas Urquhart, 'An excuse for a certain
woman's froward, and discontented humor to her
husband'

fb.217, p. 38

T0055 Tamely frail body, abstain today, today
And in my life retail it every day.

> J[ohn] D[onne], 'The annunciation and passion'
> [falling on one day, 1608]
> [Crum T44]

b.148, p. 133; b.114, p. 149 ('Family [*sic*] frail')

T0056 T'an honest man, it is a grievous trouble
We by continual prayers imperate.

> [Sir Thomas Urquhart], 'It is the part of a generous
> mind to prevent the need of the suppliant before his
> necessity ensure him to demand'

fb.217, p. 528

T0057 Target to Mars thy name does spell mak'd good
Dismal achievements in his derring-do.

> [Sir Philip Wodehouse], 'Upon Sr Th[omas] Garrett a
> Dep[uty] Lieut. and captain'

b.131, back (no. 217)

T0058 Taste all my sweets, come here and freely sip
I may be tired but never satisfied.

> 'A maid to her lover'

b.62, p. 23

T0059 T'astronomy, and geography the reign
Of heav'n, and earth divided doth pertain.

> Sir Thomas Urquhart, 'Of geography, and astronomy'

fb.217, p. 342

T0060 Teach me Florella, teach me how to show
If I could call, the dear Florella mine.

> [Thomas Hamilton, 6th earl of Haddington], 'To
> Florella epistle the eighteenth'

c.458/1, p. 73

T0061 Teach me, my God and King,
Cannot for less be told.

> George Herbert, 'The elixir'
> [Crum T54]

c.139, p. 140

T0062 Teach me to love? Go teach thyself more wit;
Hereafter fame, here martyrdom.

> A[braham] C[owley], 'The prophet'

c.258

T0063 Teague saw, as one night with his comrades he laid
And sho now by Chresh I did tink 'em mine own.

> [Phanuel Bacon], 'Ex pede Herculem'

c.237, fol. 66 [i.e, 86]

T0064 Tears, are the orphans, of distressed care;
Of fame, takes from me here, his life his death.

> [George Daniel]

b.121, fol. 78

T0065 Tears flow no more from my swollen eyes
And she as I am burning.

> 'Song 44'

b.4, fol. 36v

T0066 Tears should wash out those faults, which this not
keeping
Because from them spring th'origin of sin.

> [Sir Thomas Urquhart], 'Why in the eyes is the
> fountain of tears'

fb.217, p. 512

T0067 Teased with a rotten tooth I wake all night,
Nor ever want that rest he gave to me.

> 'A translation of the above' ['By agonizing pain']

c.591

T0068 Tedious have been our fasts, and long our prayers
Lock up the lips of men and charm the ear . . . .

> [John Phillips, trans.], 'A satire against hypocrites'
> [from the Latin of John Milton]
> [Crum T65]

b.220, p. 3 (incomplete)

T0069 Tell her if she to hired servants show
Willing, than those that die and not confess.

> [Sir John Roe], 'Elegia 14ta. to Sr. Thomas Roe' [attr.
> John Donne]

b.114, p. 121

T0070 Tell her with fruitless care I've sought
Such is the lot of beauty.

> 'Oberon's answer to the fair writer [of 'Oft I've
> implor'd the gods in vain . . .']'

c.83/1, no. 63; c.130, p. 7

T0071 Tell me, abandon'd miscreant, prithee tell,
And so the book itself turns sodomite.

> [John Oldham], 'Upon the author of the play called
> Sodom'
> [Crum T72 (with five more lines)]

b.105, p. 299

T0072 Tell me Arminda tell me why
And stop at neither pox nor flowers.

> 'A farewell to his mistress'

b.113, p. 269

T0073 Tell me, Aurelia, tell me pray
That makes me sure of you.

c.549, p. 58

T0074 Tell me content where dost thou dwell
But never could I fancy yet that I content have seen.

> [Mrs. ( ) Feilding]

b.226, p. 27

T0075   Tell me dear Ben how came thy wife to die?
She needs must live that is Ben Jonson's wife.

    'On Ben Jonson's wife'

b.356, p. 104

T0076   Tell me, dear, delightful dove,
You make me chatter like a jay.

    [Francis Fawkes], 'The dove' [1737]

fc.21, p. 4

T0077   Tell me dear Foote, for I was told you went,
Than if some witch or fiend, had turn'd the spit.

    [William Popple, trans.], 'Horace book 2nd satire
    VIIIth . Interlocutors. Poet, and Mr. Foote.'

fc.104/1, p. 345

T0078   Tell me, dear George, have you, by chance, e'er seen
And ever most affectionate Ricciardo.

    R[ichard] S[hackleton], 'A morning's wonder.
    (extracted from R. S.'s correspondence)'

File 13409

T0079   Tell me dear Selwyn—for tho' young 'tis thine,
Such C—— has found—but found also too late!

    [William Popple, trans.], 'Horace book 1st satire 2nd
    imitated. Inscribed to George Augustus Selwyn esq.'

fc.104/1, p. 37

T0080   Tell me dog whose tomb is this?
Because no honesty he could see.

    'On Diogenes' tomb with a dog standing over it'

fb.143, p. 11

T0081   Tell me Dorinda why so gay?
At once both stink and shine.

    [Charles Sackville], 6th earl of Dorset, 'A satire
    Dorset on Dorchester' [Catherine Sedley, King James'
    mistress; 1696]
    [Crum T81; POAS V.385]

fb.207/2, p. 38; fb.88, p. 119v

T0082   Tell me fair maiden tell me why
The worms and you my relics share.

    'A dialogue betwixt an old man and a young girl'

fb.207/4, p. 27

T0083   Tell me freely, friendly Tony,
And blast you in the fire.

    'To Anthony Williams of Farnham esqr. in Surrey; if
    there; if not; a post higher: not there? Say you so?
    Why then for the money send down to old Nick; he'll
    pay for his crony. Salt Hill 23th Sepr. 1787'

c.546, p. 13

T0084   Tell me from whence, fatheaded Scot,
And let your patients live.

    [John Winter], 'Doctor [Winter] upon Doctor
    [Cheyne]' [probably in reference to Essay of health
    and long life (1724); answered by 'Doctor, my system's
    all my own . . .']
    [Crum T84]

c.233, p. 98; Poetry Box x/94; c.152, p. 14; Poetry Box
XIV/197

T0085   Tell me gentle Strephon why
To fill our breasts, and veins with fire.

    [Sir George Etherege], 'Love tricks'

fb.107, p. 29

T0086   Tell me impartial fates, did you agree
Melodious anthems to his royal king.

    'Cornwall: CT.'

b.197, p. 158

T0087   Tell me James Stuart is this town yours,
A rough coat is better nor one bare.

    'To James elector of Edinburgh Jacobus Stewartus'

Poetry Box VIII/48

T0088   Tell me lovely charming friends
Only fit for those that can't.

fc.73

T0089   Tell me, Lydia, tell me why,
Troy fell with his sex reveal'd.

    [William Popple, trans.], '[Horace] book 1st. ode 8th.
    To Lydia'

fc.104/2, p. 26

T0090   Tell me my friend, who would a favorite be
Made many thousands to Rome's altar go.

    'The remarks'

fb.108, p. 159

T0091   Tell me my heart if thou dost love the Lord?
I love the Lord, he me for everlasting.

    'The soul's desire'

c.187, p. 6

T0092   Tell me, my Steavens, (for you can,
And still should always write to you?

    [Isaac Freeman], 'Epistle to Thomas Steavens esqr.'

fc.105

T0093   Tell me no more how fair she is
In that it falls her sacrifice.

    [Henry King]
    [Crum T95]

b.213, p. 66

T0094   Tell me no more of the Arcadian plains
At least it must be into Mahomet's heav'n.

     [Thomas Morell], 'To Vincent Grantham esq
     Lincolnshire 1729'

     c.395, p. 19

T0095   Tell me no more of youth this glass shall boast
England shall pledge me when I Marlb'ro' name.

     [Christian Murray], 'On the old Duchess of
     Marlborough'

     Poetry Box IV/184

T0096   Tell me not I my time misspend
And sing of Chloris' eyes.

     [Sir Robert Ayton]
     [Crum T103]

     b.213, p. 23

T0097   Tell me not of joy—there's none,
Cease to sing, and learn to moan.

     W[illiam] Cartwright, 'Lesbia's lamentation for the
     death of her sparrow: translated above 100 years [ago]
     (from Catullus) by . . . but with some late alterations
     in The weekly miscellany, May 5, 1733'

     Accession 97.7.40

T0098   Tell me not of lords or laws,
'Cause those do judge that sold 'em.

     'Knavery unmasked'

     b.111, p. 458

T0099   Tell me, O tell me, if thou canst what rage,
Then stoutly bear each frown, each ache, each pain.

     J[ohn] [Robinson], 'Dic mihi quis furor est ne
     moriare, mori?'

     c.370, fol. 80v

T0100   Tell me O tell me some powers that are kind,
The love of Amintor shall never decay.

     'A song'

     b.54, p. 1163; fb.107, p. 23 (incomplete)

T0101   Tell me once dear how does it prove
You what I am I what you were before.

     b.213, p. 57

T0102   Tell me prithee faithless swain
Should always be suspected.

     [Sir Charles Sedley], 'A song'

     b.207, p. 45 (with another stanza); b.213, p. 144; see also
     'Prithee, tell me . . .'.

T0103   Tell me, sage Will, thou that the town around
That thing's a beau. | Why then that beau's a beast.

     'A dialogue between Will the coffeeman at Covent
     Garden, and Fleet Sheppard, esq. gentleman-usher at
     court'

     fb.70, p. 227

T0104   Tell me, says Cato, where you found
Shall sure be crown'd above.

     T[homas] M[orell], 'To Samuel Bever esq on the
     death of his son Col. Bever killed in the engagement at
     Ticonderoga. 1758'

     c.395, p. 120

T0105   Tell me sweet Jug how spell thy Joan?
When you and I must part asunder.

     'On spelling Joan'
     [Crum T111]

     b.200, p. 359; b.4, fol. 1v (damaged); b.197, p. 213 ('Tell
me sweetheart')

T0106   Tell me, tell me charming creature
Such a one as mine for you.

     Poetry Box II/53 (incomplete?)

T0107   Tell me the cause, my Phyllis why
Your very self shall force you to forgive.

     'The quarrel. By the same hand' [as 'Charge all a
     bumper . . .']
     [Crum T112]

     fb.142, p. 47

T0108   Tell me thou dear departed shade,
How soothing then is sleep to me.

     'On the death of a much-esteemed friend'

     c.83/1, no. 112

T0109   Tell me thou, my heart's kind ruler,
Did I e'er in fancy stray?

     [Thomas Hull], 'Air for Miss Harper'

     c.528/50; see also 'Witness thou . . .'

T0110   Tell me thou treasury of spite
Stink t'other to unfaithfulness.

     'A new letter to [Robert] Julian'

     fb.108, p. 105

T0111   Tell me ver a fat priest had best live
I was not reckon joli en France.

     E. F. B[urney], 'A French emigrant priest's
     lamentation'

     c.486, fol. 21v

T0112 Tell me, what genius did the art invent,
He make that lasting reason permanent?

[( ) Stennet], 'On letters'
[Crum T121]

c.244, p. 281

T0113 Tell me, where art thou, whom I die to see!
And ask the winds, where I may find my God.

'On a celestial synod and the virtue of virginity'

c.83/2, no. 655

T0114 Tell me where is fancy bred,
I'll begin it, ding-dong-bell.

[William Shakespeare], 'On fancy' [Merchant of
Venice, III.2]

c.81/1, no. 329

T0115 Tell me why my sorry fair
Buff is ever beauty's armor.

[John] Tweddell, 'To a lady with an orange ribbon in
her cap and a fan tied with buff and blue, Miss
Hutchinson'

Smith Papers, folder 74/8

T0116 Tell me, ye brooks! Where does my darling hide?
Thus what I dote on, I must never see.

John Lockman, 'Psyche's search after Cupid
[translated from La Fontaine] . . . set most agreeably
to music, in the cantata form, by Dr. Boyce'

c.267/4, p. 211

T0117 Tell me ye glorious stars that shine
May all men praise and all obey.

[John Austin], 'Hym. 34' [Hymn xxxviii, Devotions in
the ancient way of offices, 1672, p. 348]

c.178, p. 32

T0118 Tell me ye learned, if you can,
And pray, as she has done.

[Thomas Hamilton, 6th earl of Haddington], 'Sister
Jean a tale from La Fontaine'

c.458/2, p. 67

T0119 Tell me ye prim adepts in scandal's school
Thee my inspirer—and my model—crew.

[Richard Brinsley Butler Sheridan], 'A portrait
addressed to a lady [Mrs. Crewe] with The school for
scandal'

c.130, p. 74

T0120 Tell me, ye sons of Phoebus, what is this
For none can envy him whom all must love.

[George] Lyttelton, 1st baron Lyttelton, 'On good
humor'

c.391, p. 3

T0121 Tell me you anti-saints why glass
The inside dross, the outside saints.

R[ichard] Corbett, 'On Fairford windows'
[Crum T129]

b.200, p. 203; b.205, fol. 54v

T0122 Tell me, you pow'rs that rule our fate;
They never can attain.

c.549, p. 43

T0123 Tell me you stars that our affections move
Bind up all love within my frozen veins.

[Henry King], 'Upon his cruel mistress'
[Crum T132]

b.356, p. 132

T0124 Tell William, I wish him, without any measure,
Thus blest let him live, thus blest let him die.

[Charles Burney, the younger], 'To Master William
Francis'

c.37, p. 17; see also 'But soft—the muse . . .'.

T0125 Tempests now contract the sky,
Wine alone, can soften grief.

[William Popple, trans.], '[Horace, ep]ode 13th. To his
friends'

fc.104/2, p. 448

T0126 Tempt me no more, penurious solitude
But I'll live, and I'll love, and I'll laugh while I can.

[Thomas Hull], 'Address to solitude, a cantata'

c.528/23 (incomplete?)

T0127 Tempt me no more ye sensual sweets
Its happiness shall share.

T[homas] S[tevens]

c.259, p. 142

T0128 Temptation bred those love-achieving hours
Nay one half hour, I would gladly die.

'In the praise of his mistress'
[Crum T143]

b.62, p. 72

T0129 Tempting toys and earthly pleasure
To sing adore and praise and love.

'Hymn 24th'

c.562, p. 28

T0130 Ten crowns at once and to one man and he
Show but such metal, though you never fight.

[Robert] Wild, 'The grateful nonconformist, to Sr
John Baber Knt and Doctor of Physic, who sent the
poet (Dr. Wild) fifty shillings' [1665]
[Crum T144]

b.52/1, p. 136

T0131 Ten in the hundred lies here false ramm'd
An hundred to ten, but his soul is damn'd.

'On an userer'

b.356, p. 245

T0132 Ten in the hundred, lies here ingrav'd,
Oh! Ho! Quoth the devil, 'tis my John-a-Combe.

[William] Shakespeare(?), 'An extempore epitaph
by . . . on Mr. Combe of Warwickshire a rich usurer'

c.360/2, no. 243; see also next.

T0133 Ten in the hundred lies under this hearse
Ho, ho, (quoth the devil) that's my Dr. Peirse.

'Upon Dr. Peirse of Caius College In Cambridge'
[cf. Crum T147, T148]

b.197, p. 219; see also previous.

T0134 Ten lepers at Christ do prostrate lie
Were lepers still in their unthankfulness.

'Luke 17.17.18'

c.160, fol. 55

T0135 Ten lepers cleansed, and but one of ten
Receive or sue yet oft deny it thee.

[Francis Quarles], 'On the ten lepers' [Divine
fancies III, 24]

b.137, p. 171; b.156, p. 41

T0136 1066 the Conq'ror came
And still become each day more prosperous and
more free.

'Memorial verses from the conquest'

c.487, p. 61

T0137 Ten years are swiftly fled away,
While contentment strews our path with flow'rs.

'Lucy. A poem'

c.83/3, no. 907

T0138 Ten yokes of oxen were convoy'd from Rob:
She knew her tack might be occupied without them.

Sir Thomas Urquhart, 'Of one, from whose husband
named Robert, the clan Gregor had robbed ten yokes
of oxen'

fb.217, p. 301

T0139 Tender-handed stroke a nettle,
And the rogues obey you well.

'A picture too true'

c.142, p. 403; c.487, p. 45

T0140 Tender tremors touch the bosom
Shall revive the bloom again.

[James] Hammond, 'Verses written by . . . in the
moments of writing an interview with Emma'

c.83/1, no. 32

T0141 Tender virgins touch the string,
Or to distant Britain roam.

[William Popple, trans.], '[Horace] book 1st. ode 21st.
In praise of Diana and Apollo'

fc.104/2, p. 62

T0142 T'engrave the faint resemblance of a face
Express the outward and the inward man.

[Robert Cholmeley], 'Upon the image of
Mr. Shadwell with his works in his hand, being cast in
lead'

c.190, p. 63

T0143 Terrific name who'll come near ye
I'll board no ship where there's no grog.

'Epigram written on passing under the stern of the
Gorgon [?] gun ship'

c.344

T0144 Th'advent'rous mariner by tempests tost
Which (oh too soon!) dire [?] will destroy.

John Lockman, 'To Aspasia: writ after the return of
fine weather . . . June 1744'

c.267/2, p. 362

T0145 Thalia thou the joyful'st of the nine
Anthems of praise unto the King of kings.

[Sam[uel] Raymond, 'An elegy on the death of Mr:
Andrew Horsman M. A. and sometimes moderator of
the school of Plymouth'

b.212, p. 262

T0146 Th'Almighty Father thus bespake
And there at God's right hand be plac'd.

'Psalm 110. Morning prayer 23 day'

c.264/3, p. 34

T0147 Th'almighty Power who rules the skies,
Unvex'd with storms, is there.

'An ode' [Leicester, 31 July 1763]

c.136, p. 41

T0148 Th'ambassadors of England once, and Spain
Who is th'anointed of Jerusalem.

Sir Thomas Urquhart, 'The mutual taunts of an
English, and Spanish ambassador'

fb.217, p. 279

T0149 Th'amorous wind by love inflam'd
Her charms expos'd to view.

'On a young lady being blown down by a high wind'

fc.51, p. 286

T0150 Thank God I've got
And cheerfully submit.

[( ) Pierson]

c.328, p. 28

T0151 Thank you kind Bowden, whose goodnatur'd lays
We hope to hear your halcyon notes on peace.

[Peter] Lovel, 'Thanks to Mr. [Samuel] Bowden for
his ingenious poem on the new-built Vicarage House
at Frome' ['Thanks to kind Lovel . . .'; October 1747]

Poetry Box x/144

T0152 Thanks, fair Urania to your scorn
The sun on happier does not shine.

[Sir Charles Sedley, 'Indifference']
[Crum T160]

b.213, p. 138; Poetry Box IV/53 (attr. Etherege); c.549,
p. 114

T0153 Thanks for that best, that flattering way
I still shall have to learn it.

[William] Cowper, 'Verses occasioned by a lady's
refusing to give the author a copy of some lines he
asked her for, but consenting to his learning them by
heart from her repeating of them'

c.504, p. 131

T0154 Thanks gentle bard—we know not which stand
higher
That we have read it o'er—and o'er again.

James H——

c.497, inserted before text

T0155 Thanks little bird with sleek red breast
And spring invites my guest away.

'Invitation to a robin'

fc.51, p. 155

T0156 Thanks lovely and deceitful fair
Can any day be found.

[Miss ( ) Craven], 'Liberty'

Greatheed Box/25

T0157 Thanks to indulgent heav'n, our pray'rs are heard,
May thee to realms of bliss eternal go!

R. Sone, 'To the right honble Lady Charlotte
Compton, Baroness Ferrers of Chartley, the following
lines on her Ladyship's happy recovery is . . .
dedicated by her Ladyship's . . . servant'

Accession 97.7.40

T0158 Thanks to kind Lovel! whose goodnatur'd lays
A cavern glorious, or a cottage great.

[Samuel] Bowden, 'To [Peter] Lovel esq. occasioned
by his verses in praise of the author's poem on the
Vicarage House at Frome' ['Thank you kind Bowden';
October 1747]

Poetry Box x/143

T0159 Thanks to my friend when men like you admire,
The damn'd are those alone who nothing love.

'To Mr. Blin author of the heroic epistle of Gabrielle
d'Estrées mistress of Henri IV . . . Voltaire'

c.83/2, no. 687

T0160 Thanks to my God, I'm not so poor,
How, when and what I am to be.

'Augur's wish paraphrased[:] give me neither poverty
nor riches'

c.83/2, no. 368

T0161 Thanks to our good King William,
And their leaders are afraid.

'A new song on the campaign 1692'
[Crum T168]

b.111, p. 285

T0162 Thanks to that gracious God who hears my prayer,
Till you can give, and I can wish no more.

'Pedro to Alphonso, on his recovery from sickness'

c.83/3, no. 914

T0163 Thanks to the gay, the well-made suit,
The proud, the vain, the great caress.

[Charles Burney, the elder (?), translation of part of
Sidaine, Epistle]

c.194/1, p. 42

T0164 Thanks to the God who rules the deep;
To crown the wishes of the land. | O for one
universal smile &c.

John Lockman, 'On the auspicious arrival, and
nuptials, of the Princess Charlotte of Mecklenburg
Strelitz, with His Majesty King George III'

c.267/2, p. 53

T0165 Thanks to the gods! Our cheerful steps at last
Arcadia's only in the mind.

'The monument in Arcadia. A dramatic poem'

c.245

T0166 Thanks to the gods, whose favoring care
Where I unaw'd can eat.

> Charles Burney, the younger, 'The cat's thanksgiving.
> A cat, which the author had received from a lady, and
> which he was obliged to return, is supposed on her
> arrival at home, to chant the following
> thanksgiving . . . 1779'
>
> c.35, p. 47

T0167 Thanks to you, friend, for presents past,
May trace out God, and thank Him too.

> R. B., 'The answer' [to 'To thee, my truest . . .']
>
> c.90

T0168 Th'archive of fame cannot immure a relic
That honors its conceptions with your merit.

> Sir Thomas Urquhart, 'To the Earl of [crossed out]'
>
> fb.217, p. 318

T0169 Tharso picks quarrels when he's drunk at night
Drinks both at night and in the morning too.

> [William Walsh], 'Epigram'
>
> c.115; see also 'Thraso . . .'.

T0170 Th'art fair, th'art rich, th'art young—yet do not tarry
As 'tis express'd in David's sacred lays.

> [Sir Philip Wodehouse], '1. Elizabeth Maynard 2.
> Mary Maynard'
>
> b.131, back (no. 123)

T0171 Th'art, which both sexes hath so oft combin'd,
T'increase, and multiply.

> Sir Thomas Urquhart, 'The reason why the casual
> union of man, and woman is called venery'
>
> fb.217, p. 100

T0172 Th'Assembly's lawful, that was held at Glasgow;
And fleshers there, had votes in points of faith.

> Sir Thomas Urquhart, 'A non-covenanter's ironical
> opinion of the Assembly of Glasgow'
>
> fb.217, p. 53

T0173 That after thrice eight married years, a male
That Salic laws cannot prejudge your issue.

> Sir Thomas Urquhart, 'To the French queen'
>
> fb.217, p. 324

T0174 That aged man we should without all doubt
The number of the years that he is old.

> [Sir Thomas Urquhart], 'How abject a thing it is for a
> man to have been long in the world without giving any
> proof by either virtue or learning that he hath lived at
> all'
>
> fb.217, p. 500

T0175 That all should live, indulgent nature meant;
And, e'en to monarchs, riches are but lent.

> John Lockman, 'Writ under a playbill, for the benefit
> of the asylum'
>
> c.267/1, p. 271

T0176 That ancient name whose chief you are, owes this
Which by your tutors was o'erthrown of late.

> Sir Thomas Urquhart, 'To my Lord Salton'
>
> fb.217, p. 57

T0177 That angry Cupid smit thy heart
Will make a lover enter.

> 'Consolation to a fainting lover, or a cordial to my
> lovesick brother'
>
> b.104, p. 17

T0178 That approbation, which upon the solid
Have with the cords of contestation fettered.

> Sir Thomas Urquhart, 'To my Lord [crossed out]'
>
> fb.217, p. 344

T0179 That author sure must take great pains
To save his country run away.

> 'On K[ing] William's last two campaigns'
> [Crum T178]
>
> b.111, p. 304

T0180 That Bacchus is a god we must admit;
H'exalts the humble, and deserts the proud.

> Sir Thomas Urquhart, 'Of the divinity of Bacchus'
>
> fb.217, p. 111

T0181 That beauteous creature of whom I am a lover
She'll make one in love that was ne'er so before |
But I'll say no more.

> 'A song'
>
> b.207, p. 29

T0182 That beauteous face is finely wrought,
What pity folly spoilt it?

> 'On a beautiful but silly woman'
>
> c.233, p. 93

T0183 That bodies daily are begot,
Mention'd as done on the sixth day.

> [Edmund Wodehouse], 'March 31 [1715]'
>
> b.131, p. 190

T0184 That bounteous hand, which tongues unnumber'd
                                                 bless,
His pencil Bentley drop, and Gray his pen.

> Ed[ward] Bedingfield, 'On receiving from the
> Countess of Burlington Mr. Gray's poems with
> drawings by Mr. Bentley'
>
> File 1040

T0185 That Britain's isle has chang'd its clime
Whereat her sons rejoice.

> [ ] M., 'On the capture of de Winter the Dutch
> admiral October 11th 1797'
>
> c.546, p. 18

T0186 That crime cannot be capital,
More than the head.

> Sir Thomas Urquhart, 'Of lechery a paradox'
>
> fb.217, p. 108

T0187 That Crowder would from White's abstain
And Creed would leave the town.

> 'The wish' [1699]
>
> fb.70, p. 207

T0188 That Day spells aid is manifest the sense—
To him, who in his name and wit, writes Day.

> [Sir Philip Wodehouse], 'Upon his good neighbor
> Mr. Ro: Day'
>
> b.131, back (no. 164)

T0189 That deadly wound, which Hell to man had given
Was heal'd by Christ's dread sacrifice, in heaven.

> 'St. Olave's Hart Street [2]'
>
> c.81/1, no. 51

T0190 That death should thus from hence our butler catch
The butler's gone, the keys are left behind.

> [Benjamin Stone? or Henry Parrot?, 'Epitaph upon
> the death of Mr. Owen, butler of Christ Church in
> Oxford']
> [cf.Crum T189, 'That death so soon . . .']
>
> b.148, p. 4; see also 'Why cruel death . . .'.

T0191 That death that now so oft I around me see,
Thou will'st O God from these or in these, save.

> [Edmund Wodehouse], 'Septr 25 [1715]'
>
> b.131, p. 273

T0192 That disagrees with Thy most holy will
Old will not serve Thou gives us new from heaven.

> [Mary Serjant]
>
> fb.98, fol. 166

T0193 That drop by drop we pass, the young, the old,
The wretch on th' cross becomes a saint in bliss.

> [Edmund Wodehouse], 'Septr 18 [1715] on the death
> of old Shoringham'
>
> b.131, p. 266

T0194 That eagles yet sav'd Rome 'twas never known
Then why do thankless Rome the goose forget?

> 'In aquila romano'
>
> b.62, p. 119

T0195 That eye which views mankind, ere they
Which folded in the blossom lies.

> [Phanuel Bacon], 'Epitaph on a youth nine years old'
> [Crum T193]
>
> c.237, fol. 9

T0196 That famous edifice, which at the period
So far the public good excels the private.

> Sir Thomas Urquhart, 'On Master Heriot, and his
> work'
>
> fb.217, p. 116

T0197 That faulty men w[?] of [?] [?]ation
Wherein express your wi[?] i' a friend.

> [Sir Thomas Urquhart], 'To [blank]'
>
> fb.217, p. 394

T0198 That flattering glass whose smooth face wears
And melt that ice, to floods of joy.

> [Thomas] Carew, 'A looking-glass'
> [Crum T195]
>
> b.225, p. 134

T0199 That fortune favors fools, if you will not
Believe me Sir, believe your own good lot.

> Sir Thomas Urquhart, 'To a fortunate man who was
> not very wise'
>
> fb.217, p. 275

T0200 That fortune is not corporal,
That doth exalt so many sots.

> Sir Thomas Urquhart, 'What fortune is not'
>
> fb.217, p. 38

T0201 That genius in thy sculptor lit the flame
That almost made his skill eclipse thy fame.

> 'Spoken impromptu at the sight of Mr. Townley's
> Homer, as addressed to Homer'
>
> fc.53, p. 164

T0202 That God blest favor does comprise
The highest pitch of heav'nly bliss.

> [Edmund Wodehouse], 'May 10 [1715]'
>
> b.131, p. 211

T0203 That God who once mankind did make
Where we may dwell. | Amen

    'Of a miracle. Aug. 15'

    a.30[26]

T0204 That he crav'd not to see y': yet knew your merit,
And so invisible.

    Sir Thomas Urquhart, 'To a poet, who wrote verses in
    the favor of a nobleman, that though he received
    them, was nevertheless, not curious to meet with the
    composer'

    fb.217, p. 210

T0205 That he must needs be bad, there is some likeness
Of him, whose actions merit imitation.

    [Sir Thomas Urquhart], 'That the fellowship of
    virtuous or vicious people contributes much to the
    bettering or depraving of the mind'

    fb.217, p. 510

T0206 That he of two ladies right courteous and fair
And how tedious, alas! is the reign of vitation!

    [Charles Burney, the elder], 'To two ladies, who had
    done the author the honor to permit him to escort
    them to several public places, and who insisted on
    remunerating him for the expense incurred. The
    humble petition of the squire of dames sheweth . . .'

    c.33, p. 56 (crossed out; incomplete?)

T0207 That heart can never be at rest,
He died in bitter anguish.

    Edward Sneyd, 'Cymon in love'

    c.214, p. 69

T0208 That Henry Sacheverell that High Church defender
We'll first burn the doctor, and then burn the Bible.

    'The minutes'

    b.90, p. 16

T0209 That Herod who Saint James had slain
Where we may dwell for aye. | Amen

    'Of S. Peter aduncula, August. 1'

    a.30[18]

T0210 That he's a cuckold, ev'rybody says:
Though his own wife lie nightly in his arms.

    Sir Thomas Urquhart, 'Of a man, whose wife, was of
    too amorous a disposition'

    fb.217, p. 286

T0211 That he's a gentleman, I now perceive;
Been made a gentleman, as soon's a carle.

    Sir Thomas Urquhart, 'Of a man, whose gentry is
    questioned'

    fb.217, p. 80

T0212 That he's all fire, shows much
For fire brings nothing forth.

    Sir Thomas Urquhart, 'Of a fiery ticklish hasty man,
    who otherwise, was endow'd with very good parts'

    fb.217, p. 297

T0213 That holy angel, who with pleasure came
When polish'd by wise hands may it attract all eyes.

    'Upon Mr Harpur's birthday June 24th'

    b.322, p. 25

T0214 That house the wife whereof is always babbling
They are unhappy, wretch'd, and miserable.

    [Sir Thomas Urquhart], 'The misery of a disordered
    family'

    fb.217, p. 526

T0215 That I am at the period of mine age
When we have travell'd long we must return.

    [Sir Thomas Urquhart], 'An old man's expression
    before his death'

    fb.217, p. 496

T0216 That I cannot express all I wish I am grieved,
But that czar is the Pope's, true devoted, forever.

    'Czar to His Holiness . . . Ayot St. Lawrence Jan. 18th
    1795'

    fc.40

T0217 That I did not the other day salute ye,
Made me all love, and so o'erveil'd my eyes.

    Sir Thomas Urquhart, 'The excuse of a gentleman for
    not hailing of a lady, whom he had encountered with
    upon the streets, to herself'

    fb.217, p. 233

T0218 That I, dread Sir, have been so free
With your infernal majesty.

    'A card of apology to the Devil'

    fc.53, p. 22

T0219 That I have call'd y'a mother, do not care;
For beaut' engend'reth love: and you are fair.

    Sir Thomas Urquhart, 'One excuseth himself thus to a
    young, and very comely gentlewoman, whom he said
    had borne a child'

    fb.217, p. 209

T0220 That I have given the goose her worthy style
So take my goose amongst you gentlemen.

    ['Taylor's goose']

    c.158, p. i

T0221 That I see you with humble bows no more,
Believe it, thou no master need'st to have.

    b.118, p. 11

T0222 That I went to warm myself in Lady Betty's
                                  chamber, because I was cold,
Or the chaplain (for 'tis his trade) as in duty
                                  bound, shall ever pray.

[Jonathan Swift], 'To their excellencies the Lords
Justices of Ireland the humble petition of Frances
Harris, who must starve, and die a maid if it
miscarries'

c.265, p. 8

T0223 That if I do love it comes to me by kind
By kind, mind, heart, desert, and all in one.

'To one's love'
[Crum T205b]

b.62, p. 55; see also 'I love because . . .', 'Thou lovest
not . . .'.

T0224 That I'm not covetous in all my land
That all the kings on earth, can have no more.

[Sir Thomas Urquhart], 'The expression of a
contented man in poverty'

fb.217, p. 509

T0225 That Jenny's my friend, my delight, and my pride,
And let me deserve her! Or still I say, no.

[ ] Moore, 'Song'
Spence Papers, folder 113

T0226 That kingdom, and none other happy is
Where Moses and his Aaron meet and kiss.

[Francis Quarles], 'On a happy kingdom' [Divine
fancies I, 77]

b.137, pp. 187, 189; b.118, p. 223

T0227 That kings should from their thrones be rudely torn
And damn themselves, and lead their flocks astray.

'The apostasy'
[Crum T213]

b.111, p. 122; b.204, p. 4

T0228 That lewd tetrastic in a railing nonsense,
I could have done't, as fain, as I would live.

Sir Thomas Urquhart, 'Here a certain licentious poet
purgeth himself of making some satiric lines upon a
very handsome woman by way of homonomy [sic] to
herself'

fb.217, p. 346

T0229 That life at best is but a jest
And it shall be your sole reward.

[Helen Craik], 'A charade—to Mr. D——'

c.375, p. 36

T0230 That life is short which measur'd by the span
And then twenty [?]s of an ignorant.

[Sir Thomas Urquhart], 'Not time but our actions are
the measure of our life'

fb.217, p. 500

T0231 That live you cannot thus still live you would
You may wish [?] you'll wish you could.

[Sir Thomas Urquhart], 'To an old miserable man
whose mind was so much alienated from thinking
upon death'

fb.217, p. 520

T0232 That living's a joke, Johnny Gay has express'd
A tete-à-tete feast, call'd the Lex Talionis. | Fal de
                                  rol, &c.

'Song 71'
[Crum T215]

c.555, p. 107

T0233 That love grows daily weaker by possession
Than all the flatteries vanity can hear.

R[alph] Broome, 'Three weeks after marriage'

c.486, fol. 38v

T0234 That lust is a more brutish passion in
Transform herself for love of any male.

[Sir Thomas Urquhart], 'Why excessive lechery
betokeneth greater brutality in man than woman'

fb.217, p. 527

T0235 That man, in whom the grace of God begins
Christ being his guide, and Christian faith his
                                  shield.

[Sir Thomas Urquhart], 'An uprightly zealous, and
truly devout man is strong enough against all
temptations'

fb.217, p. 502

T0236 That man shall happy be, and shall escape much
                                  care,
Whom others harms and dangers great do cause
                                  for to bear.

c.339, p. 318

T0237 That man who for life
But whores are eternally craving. | But &c.

'Song 217' [answered by 'That man who for life . . . He
is harass'd . . .']

c.555, p. 344

T0238   That man who for life
He is harass'd and plagu'd beyong measure. | Poor
cur &c.

'Song 218' [reply to 'That man who for life . . . But
whores . . .']

c.555, p. 345

T0239   That man, who hath affections foul untam'd
So mayst thou stand when many down do slide.

b.234, p. 309; see also 'Bridle your will . . .'.

T0240   That man, whose tongue before his wit doth run,
Oft speaks too soon, and grieves when he hath done.

c.339, p. 323

T0241   That marble which thy monarch was denied
Had he been blest in all things on thy pen.

Roger [Boyle, 1st earl of Orrery], 'To the Ld Herbert
and upon his History of Henry the Eight' [pr. 1649
(Wing H1504)]

fpb.27, inside front cover

T0242   That Mary was a fiery star
The more *estrema dure*.

'Charles and Mary'

b.197, p. 217

T0243   That mere neglect your cuckoldry doth nourish,
The better that the ground's ill husbanded.

Sir Thomas Urquhart, 'The only true cause, that did
occasion his horns, to one who was supposed to have
them'

fb.217, p. 144

T0244   That monster custom who all sense doth eat
That aptly is put on.

[William Shakespeare, from Hamlet]

fc.156

T0245   That morning too will dawn, when I shall rise
Fast I shall sleep and dream of life no more.

'A waking thought'

c.244, p. 629

T0246   That my good God should give me leave,
That ev'n by death shall never cease.

[Edmund Wodehouse], 'May 15 [1715]'

b.131, p. 214

T0247   That Niobe to stone was chang'd
Still to be trod upon by you.

'From Anacreon'

c.189, p. 116

T0248   That no man yet could in the Bible find
When [there] is now no certain man he said.

[Lady ( ) Checke], 'An answer by . . .' [to 'There was a
time . . .']

b.205, fol. 48r

T0249   That of late his address your petition is made
If any are left unconsum'd by the flames.

[Phanuel Bacon], 'Rich[ar]d Poulter's (day laborer)
second petition to the Virginia merchants sent after
the repeal of the stamps'

c.237, fol. 96 [i.e., 116]

T0250   That of the clients come, none sees the stamp |
That is the cramp:
But that the lawyer stirs for him no foot, | That is
the gout.

Sir Thomas Urquhart, 'Of a wretched client, and a
lazy lawyer'

fb.217, p. 312

T0251   That one may not a microcosm engender,
The hidd[en]est corner being by woman shown.

Sir Thomas Urquhart, 'Why man, and woman are
called microcosms'

fb.217, p. 207

T0252   That Orpheus drew a grove, a rock, a stream
Fam'd Handel breathing, tho' transform'd to stone.

[John Lockman], 'Seeing the marble statue (carved by
Mr. Roubiliac) representing Mr. Handel in
Spring-Gardens, Vauxhall'

c.268 (first part), p. 17

T0253   That other nymphs may be belov'd
E'er to disown I love thee still | Can never, never be.

R[obert] Shirley, 1st earl of Ferrers, 'A song. From
[Malherbe]'

c.347, p. 83

T0254   That our loves may never alter
To tie them fast I've sent a halter.

'On one sending a rope to his sweetheart' [answered
by 'The rope is old . . .']
[Crum T239]

b.356, p. 305; c.356; see also 'That your love . . .'.

T0255   That passage, where our Savior saith,
He did not follow Christ.

Sir Thomas Urquhart, 'Of a foolish spendthrift'

fb.217, p. 81

T0256 That path which leads our souls to God
And faith rejoices in the sight.

   T[homas] S[tevens], 'Same evening' [Tuesday
   following Experience Meeting, 29 August]

c.259, p. 103

T0257 That plan accomplish'd, friendless boys no more
Thrice happy with an Argus in thy mind!

   John Lockman, 'To Sir John Fielding: after his
   supplying our merchant ships with distressed boys'

c.267/4, p. 370

T0258 That pretty little gaudy fly,
Whose torment and his truth deserve it all.

   'A poem to a widow upon a fly getting into her eye'
   [pr. Dublin 1726 (Foxon P659)]

c.503, p. 17

T0259 That rich man's poorer than the poor who's glad
If a loaf be [?] to content him.

   [Sir Thomas Urquhart], 'How wealth cannot make a
   [?] man rich'

fb.217, p. 517

T0260 That Scots, and English are become one nation,
T'unite, being better, than to multiply.

   Sir Thomas Urquhart, 'To Queen Elizabeth'

fb.217, p. 62

T0261 That she's a gentlewoman born, hereby
But she for nothing freely lends her own.

   Sir Thomas Urquhart, 'Of a banker's wife, whose
   gentry was put in question'

fb.217, p. 223

T0262 That ship's sure reduc'd to a pitiful case,
That as met, they parted asses.

   'The Co[n]gr[e]ss of asses'

c.570/3, p. 91

T0263 That should Your Honor some surprise express
And your petitioners as bound, shall pray.

   [Helen Craik], 'To R. O. esqr—the humble petition of
   Margaret and Helen who wish that their arguments
   may be prevailing'

c.375, p. 8

T0264 That so much rhyme you in one month have writ
And bring up two tall footmen of his own.

   [Sir Harry Hubert], 'A final answer . . .' [to Robert
   Wolseley's 'Right heir to Flutter Fop . . .']
   [Crum T255]

b.219, p. 29

T0265 That solemn day the world's great Savior died
Peep'd in the cock-pit and then hid his light.

   'On the great eclipse which happened during the
   sitting of the Select Committee, who began their
   sessions on Good Friday; and sat all Easter Sunday'
   [22 April 1715]
   [Crum T256]

c.570/1, p. 91

T0266 That some souls draw to God more nigh
Their God to praise, love and adore.

   [Edmund Wodehouse], 'Aug. 26 [1715]'

b.131, p. 253

T0267 That soul enam'ring glorious hieroglyphic,
Than all the China figures can set forth.

   Sir Thomas Urquhart, 'To the Earl of [crossed out]'

fb.217, p. 126

T0268 That soul is blest that in the love
Forever may endure. | Amen

   'Of St. Thecla. Sep. 23'

a.30[37]

T0269 That speech was worth all wealth below,
Upon that heaven most high.

   Martha Roberts, [on her uncle J. Baron Dickinson
   drinking his father's health after having his hair
   pulled]

c.391, p. 95

T0270 That 'states and emperors have their rise and fall,'
The glory of that brave enlight'ning age.

   'The G[r]ecian history—versified'

c.91, p. 253

T0271 That such a wound Sir, could not kill ye
Whereof she was no whit the worse.

   Sir Thomas Urquhart, 'To one who received at the
   single combat a stroke in the belly which was not
   mortal'

fb.217, p. 358

T0272 That the chief business of my day
Thy caution (I hope) effectual is.

   [Edmund Wodehouse], 'Apr. 7 [1715]'

b.131, p. 194

T0273 That the excise laws may not be extended
And the authors of the new scheme may be
                                    suspended.

   'The city's toast'

c.570/3, p. 149

T0274 That the eyes' pow'r could shake the heart I knew,
You came not—and it prov'd a day of pain.

> A[aron] Hill, 'To a lady who was expected in vain on a Sunday'
>
> c.83/1, no. 179

T0275 That the main business of my days
His high perfections amaze.

> [Edmund Wodehouse], 'Aug. 16 1715'
>
> b.131, p. 247

T0276 That the unwise may learn to understand,
He is a Spanish subject, and a Roman slave.

> [John Cowell?], 'The interpreter. Wherein three principal points of state much mistaken in the vulgar are clearly unfolded . . .' [1622]
> [Crum T260]
>
> b.197, p. 192; fb.23, p. 336

T0277 That thou'rt a pander,
Your wife might hold her peace.

> Sir Thomas Urquhart, 'Being called a pimp, he indirectly reveals him cuckold'
>
> fb.217, p. 340

T0278 That threefold toil which the three shares did trace
These thrice eight threes to you, in thrice five lines
I'mpart.

> Sir Thomas Urquhart, 'To a traveller, who had thrice surveyed the three parts of the half globe of the world, Europe, Asia, and Afric'
>
> fb.217, p. 111

T0279 That tongue which set the table on a roar
To his complexion must come at last.

> [David] Garrick, 'Epitaph on the late Mr. [James] Quin'
> [Crum T271]
>
> c.68, p. 186

T0280 That trifling, gaudy toy whose only care
Deceiving them she is herself deceiv'd.

> New[comen] Herbert, 'Dr. Dick [Richard Shackleton] . . . Dublin, Novbr. 15th 1743' [on a coquette]
>
> File 7201

T0281 That unripe side of earth that heavy clime
Is that love is them all contract in one.

> Walter Aston, baron Aston, 'Sr. Walter Aston to the Countess of Huntington'
> [Crum T273]
>
> b.148, p. 143

T0282 That veal and ember cakes are nobler meat
Of [?] after them they were Abram's [?].

> [Sir Thomas Urquhart], 'Which meat of any was most honored is known by the dinner made in M[?] valley to the [?]'
>
> fb.217, p. 542

T0283 That warmth divine, that holy eloquence,
His cloak and spirit left, then wing'd to heav'n his
way.

> 'The following literal translation of the above verses [in French] are by the Dean of Gloucester'
>
> c.341, p. 116

T0284 That we should more bewail the hap of kings,
His faith, heaven, Christ, and pardon for His sin.

> 'An epitaph upon Henry the Fourth, the last King of France'
>
> b.197, p. 218

T0285 That we together may for love contend,
But with the rest will satisfy my grinning.

> Sir Thomas Urquhart, 'The tmesis of contend to a gentlewoman'
>
> fb.217, p. 245

T0286 That we your Majesty's poor slaves
The overplus of the saints' merit.

> 'To the K[ing]. The humble address of your Majesty's Poet Laureate' [satire on John Dryden and others]
> [Crum T281]
>
> fb.108, p. 123; b.209, p. 51; Poetry Box VII/2

T0287 That we your petitioners, peaceable fogs,
And bright be the sunshine that glows in your sky.

> H[enry] Skrine, 'The humble petition of the association of London fogs presented to Mrs. C—— and Miss L—— . . . Cranford Bridge Dec. 3 1782'
>
> c.509, p. 53

T0288 That which her slender waist confin'd
Take all the rest the sun goes round.

> [Edmund Waller], 'On a girdle' [written at age 23]
> [Crum T285]
>
> b.197, p. 246

T0289 That wisdom which to God does lead,
Not worth our study, cast or care.

> [Edmund Wodehouse], 'May 14 [1715]'
>
> b.131, p. 212

T0290 That with much wealth, and large increase, my
Lord,
He repartee'd, nor mine perhaps to write.

> [Matthew Prior], 'To my Lord of Dorset'
>
> fb.70, p. 13

T0291 That women from the men have their perfection
The member, which they wanted.

    Sir Thomas Urquhart, 'The reason why Aristotle said,
    that womankind receiveth their accomplishment from
    the man'

    fb.217, p. 50

T0292 That year and day did blessed Paul
In heaven a resting place. | Amen

    'S. Paul. June. 31 [i.e., 29]'

    a.30[7]

T0293 That you disgorge it in a public hall,
Who renders what I get.

    Sir Thomas Urquhart, 'A drunken man's answer to
    some bad debtors, who tax him for his immoderate
    diet'

    fb.217, p. 182

T0294 That you fear nothing, and of all b'aware:
Hope for all stoutl' and wisel' of all despair.

    Sir Thomas Urquhart, 'A counsel concerning fear,
    hope and despair'

    fb.217, p. 334

T0295 That you I hail'd not on the street,
To make account of whores, but in the stews.

    Sir Thomas Urquhart, 'The words of a satiric
    gentleman, to a courtesan, who had blamed him for
    not saluting her'

    fb.217, p. 175

T0296 That your love may never alter,
I take the rope, and the rope take you.

    'One that sent a rope to his friend' [including answer,
    'The rope is old . . .']
    [Crum s746]

    b.200, p. 413; see also 'That our loves . . .'.

T0297 That you of lands and moneys are deficient
While poverty to a rich mind is pleasing.

    [Sir Thomas Urquhart], 'No man is poor that hath a
    good mind'

    fb.217, p. 527

T0298 That you traduce me still, whilst I
As I have done, till now.

    Sir Thomas Urquhart, 'To one, that spoke ill of him,
    by whom he was praised'

    fb.217, p. 198

T0299 That your honor's petitioners (dealers in rhymes
And your honor's petitioners ever shall pray.

    [Edward] Moore, 'To the right hon: Henry Pelham
    esq. the humble petition of the Worshipful Company
    of Poets and Newswriters'

    Spence Papers, folder 113

T0300 That you're descended both of earls, and lords
Being all of them superlatively good.

    Sir Thomas Urquhart, 'To Sir John [crossed out]'
    fb.217, p. 310

T0301 That you're no more a maid should it disheart ye
By that which lose you will not [?] pleasure.

    [Sir Thomas Urquhart]
    fb.217, p. 386

T0302 That you're so pain'd in childbirth, I am sorry:
The Lord therefore enlarge ye, what's fit for ye.

    Sir Thomas Urquhart, 'To a woman in travailing,
    apertinent and devote ejaculation by way of
    homonymy'

    fb.217, p. 140

T0303 That's the best physic which doth cure our ills
Without the charge of 'pothecaries' bills.

    'Upon the curiosities of common water'

    c.489, p. 17

T0304 Th'attendant nymph who thus unveils the fair,
Such beauties as no mortal ever saw.

    John Lockman, 'Writ under the picture of a lady,
    undressing in order to bathe'

    c.267/1, p. 175; c.268 (first part), p. 8

T0305 Th'advice a maid too lovely wrote
'Tis her humility to love.

    [Phanuel Bacon], 'Occasioned by Mira's writing in a
    window Pride hath ruined many—make thyself
    stumble. Mira'

    c.237, fol. 9

T0306 The accurs'd Philistine stands on th'other side
Wretch! 'tis the only good, which thou canst do.

    'Goliah'

    b.118, p. 24

T0307 The action gone, the money spent,
Will none then read me? Zounds, Sir, none will buy.

    'Bookseller B*****, and H*****'

    c.74

T0308 The admiral prudently comes up to town
And her navy in Portsmouth, is the terror of Spain.

    'On the fleet'

    c.570/3, p. 69

T0309 The air grew ruck, we boisterous thrids
Until the storm was past.

    'Extract from an old Scotch poem'

    c.81/1, no. 411

T0310   The air is hushed—save where the weak-ey'd bat
Against the pilgrim's borne in heedless hum.

     [John Pattison?]

fc.156

T0311   The air of truth we often find
Make glorious all his own.

     'A declaration of love to a lady of the house of
Bradenburg—by Voltaire'

c.391, p. 119

T0312   The air was stereometric, as did show
Flow'd in the Euoue, it was hydraulic.

     Sir Thomas Urquhart, 'That the music, which a
certain gentleman entertained his mistress with, was
stereometric, pneumatic, and hydraulic'

fb.217, p. 241

T0313   The ancient columns are so fine,
Is only a tobacco stopper.

     'Epigram in praise of the ancients'

c.481, p. 225

T0314   The ancient epigrammatist Catullus
And now th' are dead th' are bound up in leather.

     [Sir Aston Cokayne], 'Of the poets following'
[Catullus, Tibullus, Propertius]

b.275, p. 95

T0315   The ancient prime of the year take you may
So home, unlooked for does upon us steal.

c.158, p. 166

T0316   The ancient proverb came: soon ripe soon rotten
                               turns,
Provide for age, that claims her right at length.

b.234, p. 322

T0317   The angelic spirits all obey
Our rock for refuge, orb of bliss.

     [Edmund Wodehouse], 'Iterum [17 January 1715]'

b.131, p. 144

T0318   The angels call, they call me from above,
Breaks in, and God's eternal day is mine.

     'Dying transports—Letters moral'

c.244, p. 584

T0319   The angels, Lord, who kept their first estate,
Our earth to heav'n, our hearts to you in praise.

     'On Christmas Day, imitated from Judge Hale'

c.167, p. 38; see also next.

T0320   The angels, whose pure nature had no spot
Our earth to heaven, our hearts to Thee in praise.

     'Christmas Day 1655'

b.49, p. 10; see also previous.

T0321   The annual day, once more with joy returns,
All, all applaud the enliv'ning sound.

     'An ode to be sung on the annual feast time (the early
hour)'

c.481, p. 69

T0322   The ant within its little bulk, contains
What's good or bad, is, or is not, its foe.

     'On the ant'

c.83/2, no. 592

T0323   The ark is such a pretty toy,
Had kill'd a goose.

     Miss [Caroline?] Dawkins, 'Miss Dawkins to Captain
Ramsay, on having received a present of Noah's ark'

Greatheed Box/26

T0324   The art of complimenting got first passage
Admires expense, wit, pomp, and curious fashions.

     Sir Thomas Urquhart, 'Upon the Earl of Carlisle'

fb.217, p. 280

T0325   The art of love, fond foolish youth
And stare in Betty's face.

     [Robert Cholmeley], 'Look one way, and row another.
To a friend'

c.190, p. iii

T0326   The art of love interiorly discloses
The soul of man being in the woman's body.

     Sir Thomas Urquhart, 'Man's soul being tota in
qualibit parte, confirms Pythagoras his transmigration
of souls'

fb.217, p. 216

T0327   The art of rhetoric admits no phrases
Transcend all hyperbolical vexation.

     [Sir Thomas Urquhart], 'To [blank]'

fb.217, p. 392

T0328   The assemblies meet with eager mind
And grace to rest upon his wife.

     J. P., 'July 15. 1779 Mr. Hornblow's ordination'

c.259, p. 63

T0329   The author's name is sure a bribe,
He is contented to be bound.

     Dr. [ ] Bacon, 'The following verses were written
by . . . on being asked to subsribe to a book printed in
sheets, by S. Husband's'

c.94

T0330 The authors of late bribe the printers for puffing
But the author of this, I think does mean [bribes
for] nothing.

'Solution to the riddle no. 48 vol. the 2nd'

c.360/3, no. 103

T0331 The bard who dares write verses after supper
Breaks forth in clouds and dazzles all the plain.

Poetry Box VII/69

T0332 The bashful courter of a gallant lady,
The bearer, Madam, will declare the rest.

Sir Thomas Urquhart, 'Of a young wooer, who
supplied his lack of discourse with a more expressive
action'

fb.217, p. 308

T0333 The bath 'tis said gives brass a hue
Oh! That I leave to all the nation.

'Epigram in the London evening post August 1742'

c.360/2, no. 57

T0334 The beard thick or thin
Yet his land is well manur'd.

Ger[vase] Warmestry, 'The beards'
[Crum T322]

b.200, p. 183

T0335 The beauteous flow'rs you lately sent
Say—what could you yourself do more?

[Helen Craik], 'To a lady—sent with a few flowers, in
return for some beautiful artificial ones'

c.375, p. 54

T0336 The beauteous one of Israel,
They and their arms like ruin share.

[Nathaniel Hamby], 'David's lamentation over Saul
and Jonathan—in elegiac meter, by the transcriber'

c.244, p. 413

T0337 The beauties of fair Galatea undrest
Until like a hero I died on the spot.

'Song'

Poetry Box I/111[2]

T0338 The bed was earth, the raised pillow stones
With Jacob's pillow give me Jacob's dream.

[Francis Quarles], 'On Jacob's pillow'
[Crum T326]

b.137, p. 167

T0339 The beggar that doth silent stand,
Imagine what he'd have.

[ ] Nash, 'On Celia'

fc.73

T0340 The beginning of eternity,
And the end of every place.

c.389

T0341 The Belgians hate all but themselves: wherefore?
For aid received the[y] have been so ingrate.

[Sir Aston Cokayne], 'Of the low Dutch'

b.275, p. 84

T0342 The Belgic frog, out of the bog,
You both became a prey.

'Upon the English quarrel with the Dutch'
[Crum T330]

b.197, p. 220

T0343 The bell struck one—no longer whirl'd along
And he alone lament his fancied woes!

William Parsons, 'Venit et ingenti violenta tragoedia
passu—Ovid'

Greatheed Box/58

T0344 The bells they sang all in the morn
Take heed, ye come not there.

[Thomas Hull], 'Ballad 1st referred to in the former
letter'

c.528/30

T0345 The best, and brightest color in the dying,
Corrupt; thus, who's not fickle is a sot.

Sir Thomas Urquhart, 'In praise of inconstancy a
paradox'

fb.217, p. 126

T0346 The best of his artillery was prayer
Nor did he kill, but when 'twas sin to spare.

Colonel Nane, 'Elegies on Sr. Horatio Vere'

b.52/2, p. 126

T0347 The best of poets writ of frogs
That having done we scarce could stand | For
laughter.

'A company of gentlemen being at Goosefair at
Bowe . . . were committed . . . to the Counter . . .
whereupon this song was made'

b.197, p. 161

T0348 The best of prelates in a factious age
And with the church expir'd the regal state.

b.90, p. 13

T0349 The best of's wit is drown'd; an inundation
Of Yorkshire cloth, which shrinks in the wetting.

Sir Thomas Urquhart, 'The sottish care of a certain
drunken man'

fb.217, p. 318

T0350 The best siz'd pillar of the fairest pile
Like summer's sun, O let me go, I'll die.

    [Sir William Petty], 'Upon the Earl of Ossory's dying
    of a fever' [1680]

fb.228/45

T0351 The bill, and proofs on either side
Us, and the cause, to th' bench, and justicer.

    H[enry] C[olman], 'The verdict'
    [Crum T334]

b.2, p. 28

T0352 The bird first peeping at the world,
With all the pleasures of fourteen!

    [Charles Burney, the elder], 'To Sally Burney, on her
    [fourteenth] birthday, Augt. 29th. 1786'

c.33, p. 183

T0353 The bird in hand we may at will restrain,
But being flown, we call him back in vain.

c.339, p. 323

T0354 The bird of Jove his offspring leads on high;
To please and to improve is all my aim.

    'Prologue'

Poetry Box IV/98

T0355 The bird thy self has taught to sing
From judgment— to the heart appealing!

    Lady [ ] Morgan, 'To the Marchioness of Abercorn—
    who asked me to lend a trifle I had written to the
    author of The essay on taste'

c.340

T0356 The birds put off their ev'ry hue
Both poet saves, and plume from fading.

    [William Cowper], 'On [Lady Harriet (Cowper)
    Hesketh's] describing to Mr. Cowper, a room
    ornamented by Mrs. Montagu with a suite of hangings
    made entirely of the most beautiful feathers'

File 17727; File 3793

T0357 The birth of him that no beginning know
Enjoying but one joy but one of all joys best.

b.64, p. 63

T0358 The bishop being angry looked grum,
'Od's blood says the bishop what do you swear.

    '1673' [on Bishop Sheldon and the Duke of York]

b.54, p. 1200

T0359 The Bishop of Durham has chose one to spur him,
With a c—— quite as wide as his conscience.

    'Epithalamium' [on Nathaniel Crewe, bishop of
    Durham]

b.III, p. 224

T0360 The blackest ink of fate sure was my lot;
And when she writ my name she made a blot.

b.52/2, p. 129

T0361 The blanketed poem from tempests protected
You'll ne'er vanquish till virulence virtue disarms.

    H[annah] More, '. . . Be pleased to read the following
    lines as inattentively as they were written . . . [The
    prophet]'

c.341, p. 93

T0362 The blazing comet, and the monstrous whale,
Did go to Betty Bewly's for a whore.

    'Six observations for the year 1677'
    [Crum T342]

b.54, p. 940

T0363 The blessed Virgin this day Jesus brought
Then by the Lord of life to find his end.

    [Sir Richard Bulstrode], 'Upon our blessed Lady's
    purification'

fb.88, p. 115v

T0364 The blood o' the just London's doom shall fix
And pray to Jove to take him back again.

    [Andrew Marvell], 'An old prophecy of Nostradamus
    written originally in French, now turned into English
    [January 1671/2] . . . Poet Bayes [John Dryden?]'
    [Crum T351]

b.52/1, p. 178 (ll. 1-34)

T0365 The blund'ring ancients doted when they feigned
When o'er she smiles a thousand graces wanton.

    'From Musaeus'

Poetry Box I/63

T0366 The body of Joanna Jones lies here
It matters naught since both ends are even.

    'Epitaph'

c.360/3, no. 144

T0367 The body which within this earth is laid,
For still she hopes once to be chang'd again.

    'Epitaph'

c.360/3, no. 51

T0368 The boist'rous winds and waves
Our Admiral Christ to meet.

    'On a mariner named Sacket, in Margate churchyard'

c.240, p. 139; see also 'Though Boreas' blasts . . .'.

T0369 The Book of Common Prayer excels the rest
For prayers that are most common are the best.

    [Francis Quarles], 'On the book of common prayer'
    [Crum T362]

b.137, p. 191; fb.69, p. 207

T0370   The books of yore
Without the hag contented.

     'To a gentleman commoner of Ch[rist] Ch[urch],
     Oxford'

     fc.53, p. 26

T0371   The bordel doctors hold him but a dunce
A town in Spain was undermin'd by coneys.

     Sir Thomas Urquhart, 'Of Venerian casualities'

     fb.217, p. 232

T0372   The bow'r of innocence and bliss
You'll find an Eden here.

     [George Horne, bishop of Norwich], 'The garden'

     Diggle Box: Poetry Box XI/48; see also 'Through all the
     changes . . .'.

T0373   The brave Sir George Toulouse did beat,
The quite contrary way.

     'The best account yet published of a sea fight'
     [between Sir George Rooke and Comte de Toulouse]
     [POAS VII.18]

     c.111, p. 89

T0374   The brave, the fair, whose bosoms oft have known
Much honor'd, lov'd–depart–and oft return.

     'An epilogue spoke by Mrs. Woffington, before the
     Duke and Duchess of Dorset at Dublin, on their
     return to England May 1752'

     c.360/3, no. 211

T0375   The bravest tomb hath stinking bones within,
So fawning mates have often faithless been.

     c.339, p. 317

T0376   The breath of time shall blast the flow'ry spring,
Thou hadst reviv'd to triumph o'er my hearse.

     [William Habington], 'To Castara. Upon thought of
     age or death'

     b.150, p. 273

T0377   The breath which this resigns, while that receives
He kills in birth, and she in bearing dies.

     W. G., jr., 'Epitaph on a lady who died in childbirth'
     [Crum T369]

     c.175, p. 79

T0378   The breathers, too black now to gang out of doors,
She'll say it is rather too warm than too cold.

     c.188, p. 13

T0379   The bridge the height of thy ambition shows
The stream an emblem of thy bounty flows.

     'Upon the bridge and river at Blenheim'

     Poetry Box I/9

T0380   The brightest of the graces three
'Tis Hamilton! Oh sweet disguise!

     John Lockman, 'The Clifton Queen: or the views
     round Bristol. A poem . . . writ at Bristol in 1747'

     c.267/4, p. 34

T0381   The brightest symbol of atoning grace
The office key—the pick-tooth of a place.

     [Thomas Warton?]

     File 15773

T0382   The business of women, dear Chloe, is pleasure
Only take care your heart don't get into your head.

     [Horace] Walpole, [4th earl of Orford], 'The advice
     to Miss Pelham'

     Poetry Box V/25

T0383   The busy town grew still, and city fops
Shall cure him both of wit and honesty.

     'Animadversions on a paper entitled The 'prentice's
     feast . . . Aug 9: 1682'

     b.216, p. 220

T0384   The buzzing bee that sings in autumn's field,
Inflaming wax, dissolv'd, in folly's fire.

     'Wednesday 7. Augt. [17]82. J[ohn] R[utherford]'

     c.93

T0385   The card invites in crowds we fly
Tomorrow's welcome will obey | And vow . . . .

     Poetry Box VIII/64 (incomplete)

T0386   The cards was sent the muses came
Olympus join'd and hail'd true blue.

     'Song 224'

     c.555, p. 355

T0387   The case was sad of that poor woman who
Touching whose clothes, she found a remedy.

     'Mat. 9.20'

     c.160, fol. 53v

T0388   The cause however bad if such
With Jove's dread lightning aimed.

     'To Mrs. F—kes on her silencing a deistical gentleman
     in a religious dispute'

     Poetry Box I/67

T0389   The cause of love can never be assign'd
'Tis in no face but in the lover's mind.

     c.549, p. 68

T0390 The cause why to a friend we do not eat
It seems our veins must needs more love possess.

> [Sir Thomas Urquhart], 'The reason why we drink
> and eat not health one to another'

fb.217, p. 523

T0391 The cause why woman reaps the art of love
But th'art must have th'assistance of a second.

> Sir Thomas Urquhart, 'Of women's longings, and
> enjoyings'

fb.217, p. 40

T0392 The characters by which my parents were
Who finds my parents' names, can't miss of mine.

> J. B., 'Ænigma' [glacier]

b.63, p. 128

T0393 The charms of bright beauty so powerful are
And combat for her even death and despair.

> 'A song' [docket title]

File 19033

T0394 The charms of contentment we mortals in vain
Offspring of soft-plum'd peace serenity.

> S[tephen] Simpson, 'The charms of contentment'

c.563

T0395 The charnel mounted on the w[all]
In hopes to rise spiritu[al].

> 'Inscription in Hadleigh Ch. Co. Suffolk'

c.81/1, no. 151

T0396 The cherubims to guard the tree of life,
To search in her another paradise.

> Sir Thomas Urquhart, 'Why immediately after the
> passage where it is set down that man was cast out of
> the garden of Eden, it is said, that he knew Eve'

fb.217, p. 120

T0397 The chief parts of a goddess to husbandmen kind,
Pride and folly adore, love and friendship detest.

> '[Charade] 90' [ceremony]

c.389

T0398 The chill waves whiten in the sharp northeast;
All that gave me delight—ah! never to return!

> [Charlotte (Turner) Smith], 'Sonnet written at
> Weymouth in winter'

c.141, p. 118

T0399 The choicest wines make the best vinegar:
So the more wit you have, the worse you are.

> Sir Thomas Urquhart, 'To one who employed the
> quickness of his spirit in profaneness'

fb.217, p. 219

T0400 The christening was not yet begun
By foreign bears o'errun.

> 'A ballad' [on the christening of George William,
> infant son of George II, and the quarrel between his
> father and George I; pr. 1717/8? (Foxon E541]

fc.58, p. 86; c.154, p. 31

T0401 The church in her militant state
And witness an heaven below.

> 'Hymn 18th'

c.562, p. 20

T0402 The church is rising, the Queen is glad,
The Lords are sorry, the Commons mad.

> 'Dropped in the Painte[d] Chamber'

b.90, p. 10

T0403 The Church of Rome on our reprisals makes,
The monarch's rump become the seat of war.

> [Sir William Trumbull]

Trumbull Box: Poetry Box XIII/42

T0404 The church was never in our Albion['s] climate
With no less fame, than e'er was due to Livy.

> Sir Thomas Urquhart, 'To the Archbishop of Saint
> Andrews lately deceased'

fb.217, p. 252

T0405 The church with gratitude of highest rate
As he was St. Paul's convert, Mark is his.

> [Edward] Sparke, 'Poem 34th—on St Luke'

b.137, p. 70

T0406 The circumcision wounds: but baptism washeth;
For the law blots, the gospel water dasheth.

> Sir Thomas Urquhart, 'Of circumcision, and baptism'

fb.217, p. 310

T0407 The classic authors must for once give way,
The means to please are wanting—not the will.

> 'Prologue to Macbeth'

Poetry Box I/119[1]

T0408 The clock still points its moral to the heart.
Th'inspiring voice of innocence and truth.

Diggle Box: Poetry Box XI/31

T0409 The clock strikes eight, the knell of parting day,
Nor cast a longing lingering look behind.

> [George Howard, 6th earl of Carlisle], 'Thoughts on
> an evening at Eton'

c.197, p. 48

T0410 The clock strikes nine, when all around,
'Tis done, the bustle's at an end.

    'A descriptive piece. The Pump Room at Bath'

c.74

T0411 The cloth remov'd, the dinner done,
Age can't regain what youth has lost.

    [Thomas Warton?], 'A warning: a fable'

File 15773

T0412 The cloud that frowns on what we prize
Had give him double praise.

    W[illiam] C[owper], 'Lines written impromptu in
    August 1786 on . . . the happy escape of our excellent
    and beloved sovereign from assassination'
    [Crum T409]

File 17706

T0413 The cock crowed once, and Peter's careless ear
Till he shall give us tears we cannot cry.

    [Francis Quarles], 'On Peter's denial'
    [Crum T412]

b.137, p. 170

T0414 The college now thy secret's out
We'll ever take thy powder.

    'Upon Ward's pill in The craftsman'

fc.135

T0415 The comforter ayt(?) uncreate, unmade, unborn
                        ungenerate
And, let thy mercy's sovereign balm salve all my
                  sins my conscience and my soul.

    '[On God the Father Son and Holy Ghost from
    1: John 5:7: There be three that bear record in
    Heaven, and these three are one:] The Holy Ghost'

b.137, p. 125

T0416 The comforter God's spirit is,
Enlighten me by Thy life-giving word.

    [Edmund Wodehouse], 'Decr. 4 [1714]'

b.131, p. 104

T0417 The complaisant, through sweet sincerity
Wants wit, or manners, as a rude buffoon.

    [Sir Philip Wodehouse], 'Urbanity or affability'

b.131, p. 13

T0418 The confidence in God I place,
And from all vexing passions free.

    [Edmund Wodehouse], 'Aug. 2d [1715]'

b.131, p. 238

T0419 The contract is it call'd I cannot say
But you're the House of Peers—and may reverse it.

    'Prologue to The contract intended to have been
    spoken by Mr. Foote'

c.68, p. 128

T0420 The cooped lion, has broke through his grate;
That you are fall'n, to be judg'd in fame.

    [George Daniel]

b.121, fol. 81

T0421 The cosy puritans move at the people's
From this our Caladonian dominion.

    Sir Thomas Urquhart, 'Why episcopacy is hated in
    Scotland'

fb.217, p. 268

T0422 The council by committing four,
And Chute is ignorantly wise.

    [on John Hoskins and three others (Chute, Neville,
    Strafford), committed to the tower June 1614]
    [Crum T426]

b.197, p. 202

T0423 The counsels of a friend Belinda hear,
The rules of pleasing, which to you I give.

    [George Lyttelton, 1st baron Lyttelton], 'Advice to a
    young lady'
    [Crum T429]

fc.51, p. 197; c.391; Spence Papers, folder 101; c.152, p. 1

T0424 The countenance of fortune, like
In one stay to remain.

b.234, p. 102

T0425 The country, and the town,
I would open my throat. | And no more gentle
                  reader be dumb &c.

    'A song, to the tune of Dumb &c.'

c.570/3, p. 116

T0426 The courier replied, when ask'd about news
Too bold were the Greys, too bashful the Blues.

    'Dettingen Echo—1743'

c.360/2, no. 38

T0427 The court is summon'd in the ample space;
Which universal nature does maintain.

    [John Lockman], 'The witness'

File 9162

T0428 The court of France is much perplexed
Whose empire's doom'd to fall.

    'A ballad on the French king's marriage to Mad[a]m
    Maintenon, 1708'

b.382(19)

T0429 The court of St. Germain's is serv'd up in state
And all the high-flyers say to it—amen.

    c.III, p. 59

T0430 The covenant, whose narrative begins
To war; and instruments of wickedness.

    Sir Thomas Urquhart, 'How like the covenant of the
    tables is to such a courtesan, as being appareled with a
    white waistcoat, and red gown, seems to have a body
    promising innocence whilst her inferior parts portend
    war'

    fb.217, p. 75

T0431 The covetous hath all himself not giving,
He nothing hath himself, but wants while living.

    'To a covetous friend'

    c.356

T0432 The covetous man, though he abound with store,
Is not content, but covets more and more.

    c.339, p. 310

T0433 The coxcomb bird, who talks by rote,
By strict obedience—not by wit.

    'Rhymes to some ladies who wished to see my verses'

    c.89, p. 89

T0434 The cradle which the tender muse
The fav'rite of the vocal nine.

    Th[omas] Gowland, 'The 3d ode of Horace 4th book,
    imitated by . . . wine merchant of Bryanston Street'

    Poetry Box IV/156

T0435 The creed beyond the ten commands hath two;
Because 'tis easier to believe, than do.

    Sir Thomas Urquhart, 'Of the Decalogue, and the
    twelve articles of faith'

    fb.217, p. 37

T0436 The crescents shine Northumb[erlan]d is near
Peace in her breast, and plenty in her face.

    [Horace Walpole, 4th earl of Orford], 'C[ountes]s of
    Northumb[erlan]d' [d. 1777]
    [Crum T442]

    c.157, p. 70

T0437 The crests of clerks of all degrees,
'As gecho(?) damme, that's your kick.

    [Frederick Corfield], 'Arms for clerks'

    c.381/1

T0438 The crowds which thy Elysium drew,
His form, his action, speak him Pug.

    John Lockman, 'To the master of Vauxhall Gardens,
    on some [?] imitations of his entertainment . . . Jan.
    1740'

    c.267/1, p. 6

T0439 The crowing of a cock doth oft foreshow
We'll die for Christ: but 'tis as hard to do.

    [Francis Quarles], 'On the crowing of the cock'
    [Crum T446]

    b.137, p. 165

T0440 The cup of life just to her lips she prest,
She softly sighed her little soul away.

    'On a child who died a few hours after her birth'

    Poetry Box XII/48

T0441 The curfew tolls the knell of parting day,
The bosom of his father, and his God.

    [Thomas] Gray, 'An elegy, written in a country
    churchyard . . . 1751. In print'

    c.221, p. 9; c.391; c.481, p. 47; c.83/3, no. 910, no. 1000;
    fc.132/1, p. 30; fc.51, p. 291; File 13409; File 245/27

T0442 The curtain dropped, the mimic scene is o'er
And while he moves our laughter, mends the heart.

    'An epilogue to The distressed mother . . .'

    c.136, p. 89

T0443 The curtain drops—the tragic scene is o'er
Not life he begs—but quick release from pain.

    [Helen Craik], 'The following lines are supposed to be
    written by Mr. Hackman when under sentence of
    death for the murder of Miss Reay—1779'

    c.375, p. 15

T0444 The curtain dropt—my mimic life is past,
Words are too weak—my tear must speak the rest.

    Mrs. [ ] Pritchard, 'Farewell epilogue'

    c.83/1, no. 262

T0445 The curtains of the night are drawn
And shining g[?]ds sent from above.

    'Evening hymn'

    c.515, fol. 22

T0446 The cuttlefish, in brooks 'tis said
For tho' it shows him it conceals him.

    [William Carpenter], 'The anonymous writer in
    answer to a scurrilous ballad published in the General
    evening post'

    c.247, p. 161

T0447 The cynic whom chagrin inspired
So find the graces in a tub.

'Sent by the general post author unknown'

c.74

T0448 The Cyprian queen and goddess stern of war
Can what I caus'd to fall again make stand.

'Venus and Pallas' contention'

b.197, p. 190

T0449 The dam of Dun brought forth a hopeful lad,
For all thy steps thou shalt account at last.

'A satire the devil upon Dun [Sir Charles Duncombe]
newly arrived from India'
[Crum T462]

fb.207/2, p. 71

T0450 The dame that takes her rest
And Mary's better part.

'1729'

c.536 see also 'Here lies interr'd . . .', 'She that takes . . .',
'This silent grave . . .', 'She who here . . .'.

T0451 The dangler is of neither sex
Yield you, and he'll cry out—a rape.

'The dangler written in 1724'

c.360/2, no. 105; c.188, p. 53

T0452 The dawning light scarce hover'd in the east
While from its trunk a blooming virgin starts.

'The enchanted forest'

c.481, p. 275

T0453 The day is broke! Melpomene, be gone;
To scratch where it did itch; so might not we.

[Robert Wild], 'Iter boreale . . . upon the successful
march of . . . Monck from Scotland to London . . .
1659'
[POAS I.4]

b.209, p. 89 (ll. 1–86)

T0454 The day! is come, now show yourselves like men
They're all court cards the worst kn[av]e is a Hart.

'Stuck upon the church door January the 20th 1766
the day Mr. Lewis's party met to oppose the bill for
lighting and the streets' [answered by ''Twas L[ewi]s
writ them . . .']

c.74

T0455 The day is come, the mystic knot is tied
And where the poet fails accept the friend.

[Mary] Masters, 'A poem on a wedding—by . . . a
maidservant'

c.244, p. 314

T0456 The day of wrath, that dreadful day
Let guilty man compassion find.

[Wentworth Dillon], 4th earl of Roscommon, 'On the
last judgment' [trans. of Dies irae]
[Crum T469]

c.186, p. 151; c.351, p. 58; c.362, p. 54; Poetry Box x/151;
Trumbull Box: Poetry Box XIII/47, 48, 49 (3 copies)

T0457 The day was dark, and heaven his clear face shrouds
Time has no joy, nor heaven's bright flames no light.

[George Daniel]

b.121, fol. 25

T0458 The day was so dreary, the wind from the east,
And learn from a dog to be true.

Dr. [ ] Trotter, 'The snowstorm and elegy—by . . .
physician to the Fleet'

c.504, p. 207

T0459 The day was turned to starlight and was run
And Pallas, and the Muses took their flight.

'Epithalamion' [on the Spanish match, 1623; glossed by
'This poem is no Sybil . . .']
[cf. Crum T472, which includes gloss]

b.62, p. 63

T0460 The day you wish'd 's arriv'd at last,
And now despairing shuts her eyes.

'Love's nuptial'

fb.107, p. 2

T0461 The day's grown old, the fainting sun
Shall lead the world the way to rest.

'Evening quatrains'

c.83/2, no. 502

T0462 The deaf see best of any, 'nd blind men hear;
For those hear with their eyes: those see by th'ear.

Sir Thomas Urquhart, 'Of the deaf and blind'

fb.217, p. 177

T0463 The Dean must die with idiots to maintain
Perish the idiots—and long live the Dean.

'On Dean Swift's leaving his fortune to build an
hospital for idiots'

c.360/1, p. 301

T0464 The Dean to idiots, leaves his boundless store
Be wise the rich,—consider thus the poor.

'On the same' [Swift's leaving his fortune to build an
hospital for idiots]

c.360/1, p. 301

T0465 The dear domestic joys of life
They find a peaceful grave.

'Rustic simplicity, or happy peasantry' [Northampton mercury, 20 May 1776]

c.487, p. 94

T0466 The dearest friend I ever prov'd,
His happiness to mine.

'Ode to candor'

c.83/2, no. 359

T0467 The death of fair Clorinda's son
But thought, he was the father of the brat.

Sir Thomas Urquhart, 'Upon the dead child of the famous courtesan Clorinda'

fb.217, p. 254

T0468 The death of her, that was but newly born:
So end I with their joy, ne'er may that joy have end.

Thomas Robinson, 'The life and death of Mary Magdalene. Or her life in sin and death to sin' [dedicated to William Robinson, Lord Mayor of York] [Crum T483]

fb.144

T0469 The debt we all to nature owe,
Regard and value.

'An epitaph'

c.174, p. 57

T0470 The deep'ning shadows were withdrawn;
Clarinda will bring on the day.

John Lockman, 'Clarinda: a sonnet, by Mr de Mallevile'

c.267/4, p. 167

T0471 The delight of the men and the pride of the fair
And a babe may play in it and do it no harm.

'Riddle'

Poetry Box x/60

T0472 The delights of the bottle, and the charms of good wine,
Nor would kings rule the world, but for love, and good drinking.

[Thomas Shadwell], 'Charms of the bottle'

fb.107, p. 39

T0473 The desperate lover must hope no redress,
Who loves her must die.

'The extremes'

fb.107, p. 33

T0474 The devil did make a bargain with a Jew
And by his haste defrauded of his due.

[Sir Thomas Urquhart], 'How a certain Jew did deceive the devil'

fb.217, p. 537

T0475 The devil take me, if I can tell what
Long winter makes, a summer fine appear.

Lady Jane Cavendish, 'Misfortune's weatherglass' [Crum T492]

b.233, p. 27

T0476 The devil take your love
Prithee love a woman.

'The answer' [to 'I am so fallen in love . . .']

b.104, p. 13

T0477 The devil walks through places dry, and ease the devil finds not.
The doctor sits at ease and whets, and so the devil minds not.

'In socios seniores Coll: Oxon: [4]'

c.81/1, no. 25

T0478 The devil was sick, the devil a monk would be,
The devil was well, the devil a monk was he.

'Daemon languebat monachus . . .' [Crum T494]

b.356, p. 120

T0479 The devils were brawling, when Burnet descending
Great G[eorge] live forever, Amen cried all Hell.

'The d[evil] and Dr. Burnet' [1715] [Crum T496]

fc.58, p. 167; c.570/1, p. 8

T0480 The diamond's and the ruby's blaze
More beauteous than the ruby seems.

[ ] Fordyce, 'Real beauty'

fc.132/1, p. 106

T0481 The diamonds shine brighter than Jenny's bright eyes
And I love her—aye, that's what I do.

'A song'

c.163, p. 10

T0482 The differ between do, and speak
And loquor the active part.

Sir Thomas Urquhart, 'Why some talk well, who have no dexterity to put in performance: and that others again, go exceeding well about any business, that are no orators'

fb.217, p. 38

T0483 The differ some betwixt them make
The strumpet in the belly.

    Sir Thomas Urquhart, 'Of a coney and a whore'

fb.217, p. 247

T0484 The difference (spite of common rumor)
Of drollery and imitation.

    'The difference between wit and humor' [poetical
    amusements at a villa near Bath]

c.487, p. 92

T0485 The dire mischance dear sister Ann
Which fled(?) her [?] on deputed(?) [?].

    [William Hayley], 'To sister Ann on our escaping in
    the same day from two alarming accidents London
    Dec. 1 1800'

File 6975

T0486 The discontented were glad
More grievous than nothing

fc.156

T0487 The dizzy dome be his, who will;
Yet to himself a stranger dies!

    [Richard Polwhele], 'Lines from Seneca'

c.141, p. 563

T0488 The dock, though trodden grow, as it is daily seen,
So virtue, though it long be hid, with wounding
                         waxeth green.

c.339, p. 316

T0489 The doctor puts the case so odd
But oh! the Church has none.

    'Epigram occasioned by the dispute between
    Dr. Stebbing and Mr Foster on the subject of heresy'

c.360/1, p. 241; c.546, p. 21

T0490 The doctor reel'd from side to side—
'Tis better sure to stand than fall.

    'Epigram. Doctor and Polly'

c.81/1, no. 175

T0491 The doctors and surgeons all calls me a quack
So I cures 'em of all diseases.

    [John Walker?], 'The Cockney quack'

fc.108, fol. 22v

T0492 The doctrine taught us by the Samian sage,
Sweet antepast of harmony in heaven!

    John Lockman, 'After hearing Mr. Handel's oratorio
    of Judas Maccabeus . . . March 1743/4'

c.267/1, p. 22

T0493 The dog hunts on the ground, fish swim in seas,
Proud men soar birdlike, covetous hunt like hound.

    'Man an hunter fisher fowler'

c.356

T0494 The dog o'erruns the earth: the fishes keep
The greedy men are dogs: the proud men fowls.

    Sir Thomas Urquhart, 'Of wisdom, pride, and
    covetousness'

fb.217, p. 296

T0495 The Dorsetshire stream's diminutive . . . Wey
And runs thro' a fair fertile . . . land.

    'The same' ['Rebus no. 160 vol. 4th solved']

c.360/3, no. 83

T0496 The doughty Arthur's laws
And his mother [Mary]. Amen.

    'Launfal Miles'

fc.179

T0497 The dreams that own thy soft control,
Expose it, and like me, it dies!

    [( ) Smyth], 'Stanzas to fancy'

c.141, p. 3

T0498 The drum is unbrac'd, and the trumpet no more
And the birds their trim sonnets repeat.

    'Song 91'

c.555, p. 140

T0499 The duke had been dead but a week
A port—more convenient than Leeds.

    'On the Duchess of Leeds marrying Lord Portmore a
    week after the Duke's death'

Greatheed Box/85

T0500 The dusky night rides down the sky,
Then a-drinking we will go.

    'Song 124'

c.555, p. 178

T0501 The eager blast
While keenest lightnings play'd midst wind and
                         rain.

    [Robert Cholmeley], 'The solution. To Damon'

c.190, p. 170

T0502 The eagle was the bird of the heathen false god
He at on[e] stoop shall fetch the eagle down.

Poetry Box vi/92

T0503 The earth, and all that dwell therein
His praise to sing.

'Psalm 24 5 day Morning prayer'

c.264/1, p. 93

T0504 The earth and all the heaven by frame
The Father he, and friend of all.

'To God the preserver. An hymn'

c.487, p. 29

T0505 The earth did tremble, and heaven's closed eye
Till you have pierced this heart of mine, this stone.

[Francis Quarles], 'On our Savior's passion'
[Crum T514]

b.137, p. 173

T0506 The earth doth firmamental dross imbue
As what is heavy, to its center tends.

[Sir Thomas Urquhart], 'Of heaven, earth, and hell,
the recepta[c]le(?) of that worst [?] [?] the former has'

fb.217, p. 516

T0507 The earth in her best verdure, and the spring
The sun in June, conquered the storm in May.

[George Daniel]

b.121, fol. 63

T0508 The earth is pallid, ask not why?
For to do penance in a sheet.

'On a gentlewoman that died in the night snow falling
the next morning'

b.104, p. 18

T0509 The earth not only the ocean's debtor is
That works these wonders on the watery sand.

[Joshua Sylvester, trans. Guillaume de Salluste,
seigneur] Du Bartas, 'A catalogue of the most famous
rivers and the wonderful effects of them and many
fountains'

b.137, p. 91

T0510 The earth receives man, when he first is born
And still green laurel, shall be still thy lot.

[Joshua Sylvester, trans. Guillaume de Salluste,
seigneur] Du Bartas, 'Of the earth that she is mother
nurse and hostess of mankind of her trees, fruits and
herbs, their excellencies, and virtues &c.'

b.137, p. 106

T0511 The earth, round Sol, has run her annual race
And freedom bids the meanest peasant smile.

John Lockman, '. . . To his excellency the Earl of
Northumberland, Lord Lieutenant of Ireland. New
Year's Day, 1765'

c.267/2, p. 400

T0512 The earth's bones are stones, skin her face, metal
nerve,
The grass for hair, for blood the water serve.

'Earth's body'

c.356

T0513 The echo, save the voice, hath naught, that's *vive*:
The mirror, lacks but voice, to make it live.

Sir Thomas Urquhart, 'The echo, and the mirror
glass'

fb.217, p. 52

T0514 The echoing horn calls the sportsmen abroad,
Let's strew the way over with flow'rs.

[Isaac Bickerstaffe], 'Song 137'

c.555, p. 190

T0515 The edge of my inveterate affection
Of you, is stamped in my rags of heart.

Sir Thomas Urquhart, 'To the masterpiece [of] nature
the sublime Aura'

fb.217, p. 176

T0516 The eleventh of April is come about
Our gracious good King again.

'A diabolical Jacobite satiric song on the coronation of
K. Wm.' [11 Apr. 1689]
[Crum T526; *POAS* v.40]

b.111, p. 331

T0517 The emblems good, the cross I see
Seal them from the courts above.

Edward Godwin, 'I composed in my dream these
lines . . .'

c.259, p. 137

T0518 The end of marriage now is liberty,
And two are bound to set each other free.

c.549, p. 24

T0519 The English are rich, valiant, wise, devote,
Of a more sweetly relish'd conversation.

Sir Thomas Urquhart, 'In praise of the people of
England'

fb.217, p. 273

T0520 The English king account must give
Nor aught of succor to them lend.

[Thomas Rymer], 'The same noble poet Jaufre Rudel
on King Richard's raising monies for the defraying the
vast expenses of his descent upon Palestine . . .'

c.229/1, fol. 95

T0521 The English kings were wont to speak | Their mind
in P[ar]l[iamen]t
Tho' himself be a j[?] who must be spar'd.

'The proxy'
Poetry Box XIV/198

T0522 The entertainment we present today,
You see we are but men—and men may err.

[William Taylor], 'Prologue to Tamarlane [at
Mr. Newcombe's school]'

c.176, p. 79

T0523 The error in discerning groweth most of this
And in *bonis* you know *voluisse sat est*.

[Sir Nicholas] Bacon, 'The recreations of his age'

fa.8, fol. 160

T0524 The [?] espied with curious eye
Shall prove examples both to Church and State.

'Lines on the 2d comet which appeared in Scotland
anno 1666'

Poetry Box VIII/15

T0525 The evening shines in May's luxuriant pride,
Poetic minds to life, with all her ills.

[Anna Seward], 'Sonnet written on rising ground near
Lichfield'

c.141, p. 269

T0526 The expert pilot is not more precise
From heat but slowly and its heat doth last.

'Descriptio chastae virginis'

b.205, fol. 12r

T0527 The eye that can a pitying tear refuse
To thy cold marble, is that stone it views.

'On Miss Barbara Bartlet who died of the smallpox in
November—1741—aetatis 19'

c.360/1, p. 247 and p. 323

T0528 The face declares the mind no this I find
Let it be said that he dare show his face.

'Answer' [to 'Never head succeedeth . . .']

b.356, p. 116

T0529 The fair Alcmaena had such pow'rful charms
For her gallant, poor man was kept eleven.

'On a lady who married on the 2d of September 1752,
being the last day of the old style'

c.360/3, no. 234

T0530 The fair Armida (so was call'd the maid)
And inly, big with future prey, she smiles.

'From Tasso's Recovery of Jerusalem . . .canto 4.
stanza 27'

Poetry Box X/10(7)

T0531 The fair Galantis was by Sofit(?) courted
And without more so hardly puts it to her.

[Sir Thomas Urquhart]

fb.217, p. 519

T0532 The fair one is false to her word,
Alas! 'tis the nightingale's song.

[John Walcot ('Peter Pindar')], 'Disappointment'

c.83/3, no. 1009

T0533 The fair Susanna bathing late
They might have gone a greater length.

[Thomas Hull]

c.528/58

T0534 The fair vermilion of your sav'ry lips,
Can no less praises of all mortals claim.

Sir Thomas Urquhart, 'To the Countess of [crossed
out]'

fb.217, p. 165

T0535 The fairest blossom of as fair a tree
Like unto these let Luknor be forgot.

b.197, p. 151

T0536 The fairest harbinger of spring,
Your smiles alone secure our love.

'The primrose'

c.89, p. 68

T0537 The fairest land that from her thrusts the rest,
A world within herself with wonders blest.

Samuel Daniel, 'Of this our land sings Samuel Daniel'
[3 lines quoted from Daniel in Camden's Remaines,
1657, p. 8]
[Crum T553]

b.208, p. 37

T0538 The fairy race, of tender frame,
A silver cordage drew.

'Translation of a Latin poem on the king of the fairies'

c.159, p. 207

T0539 The faithful wight doth need no colors brave
Without a cloak, to flatter, fain, and lie.

b.234, p. 311

T0540 The fall of man, his future bliss obtain'd,
While heav'n its god, with awful joy adores.

'On Milton'

c.159, p. 223

T0541 The famous deeds of courage, wit, and merry,
Sublimest glory, come far short of yours.

> Sir Thomas Urquhart, 'To the Earl of
> Northumberland'

fb.217, p. 91

T0542 The farm of Parnassus is beggar'd they say
To cleanse a foul brother, no fancy like Broom.

> Alexander Brome, 'On Mr Robert Napier a lawyer's
> kissing of my Lord John Butler's breech for a guinea,
> whom he beshit for his gains [i.e., pains?] at
> Orchard . . . 1665'

b.52/2, p. 127

T0543 The fastest friend the world affords
And all my bones be glad.

> [George Horne, bishop of Norwich], 'The friend by
> the same author'

Diggle Box: Poetry Box xi/48

T0544 The fatal effects of luxury are these
'Tis this—tho' man's a fool, yet God is wise.

> 'Medicina dietetica'

c.481, p. 59

T0545 The fates have to your little world allotted
The heav'ns continue your prosperity.

> Sir Thomas Urquhart, 'To the Earl of [crossed out]'

fb.217, p. 338

T0546 The fates, to dreaded Britain, gave
And rule beneath each sky.

> John Lockman, 'Translations, and imitations from
> Metastasio, and other Italian opera poets [21, by
> Signor Botarelli]'

c.267/4, p. 119

T0547 The father, son and spirit are
Thus must we join their Hallelujahs.

> [Edmund Wodehouse], 'Decr. 19 [1714]'

b.131, p. 118

T0548 The faults of our neighbors with freedom we blame,
Yet task not ourselves, though we practice the same.

c.378, p. 77

T0549 The faults of princes and of kings,
Blessed with those virtues, which will crown her end.

> 'The universal health, or a true union to the Q[ueen]
> and Princess [Mary]'
> [Crum T573]

b.204, p. 82

T0550 The fearful hares in troops forsake the lawn
Such are the mornings, are by me enjoy'd.

> [Abraham Cowley?], 'A scene of the morning'

File 3782/6

T0551 The fearful shepherd is fled the flock is blown astray
A left-legg'd halting independent beast.

> 'This is a true relation of something that passed
> between some informers and Presbyterians of
> Northwick [on learning that the meeting house called
> the Granera was to be let]'

File 13409

T0552 The feeling bosom mourns the widow's woe,
And you shall share the justice you denied.

> 'To the memory of John Hunt and Thomas Gilpin,
> who died exiles in Virginia 1778'

c.365, p. 155

T0553 The female who within this tomb is laid
I know of few so good who have but two.

> 'Epitaph on Mr. Bateman's dog at Old Windsor'
> [answered by 'Here I lie entomb'd . . .']

c.150, p. 38

T0554 The fence of a city, and heart of a wood
Is the name of the man, that's honest and good.

> 'A rebus on Sir Robert Walpole, Knt of the Garter'

c.360/1, p. 89

T0555 The festive board was met, the social band
Bring me women bring me wine.

> 'Song 162'

c.555, p. 247

T0556 The fête is past the punsters gone
Adieu! Believe me yours H. More.

> H[annah] More, 'The ramble'

c.341, p. 111

T0557 The fickle, vulgar, prostitute applause
Or but a blind idolatry at best.

> 'On popular applause'

c.360/2, no. 68

T0558 The fifth day of May, being airy and gay,
Of his brother, John Hedges.

> [John Hedges], 'A copy of a will in the Commons'
> [Crum T583]

c.83/1, no. 201; Poetry Box i/94; fc.51, p. 138; Diggle
Box: Poetry Box xi/43; c.81/1, no. 163; c.152, p. 44

T0559 The fifth of August, and the fifth
Into such books as are contriv'd.

    Jeffrey Neve, John Neve, Stowe Neve, 'Upon Prince
    Charles his arrival from Spain. Octob: 5, 1623'
    [Crum T584]

    b.197, p. 63

T0560 The finest lady that ever I saw
Yet none of 'em love to catch a fart.

    [Henry Neville], 'To the tune of Girls, girls, come out
    to play'

    Spence Papers, folder 108

T0561 The fire of love in youthful blood,
Yet is the heat as strong!

    [Charles Sackville, 6th earl of Dorset]
    [Crum T589]

    Spence Papers, folder 113 (2 copies)

T0562 The first a maid past twice fifteen
A good man in a friar's cape.

    'Six heads that will never be seen'

    c.356

T0563 The first and greatest, who betray'd long since
Then sum up all, and you may guess the third.

    'The three Olivers' [Cromwell, William III,
    George I]
    [Crum T593]

    fc.58, p. 13; c.570/1, p. 51

T0564 The first appears with an uneasy crown
And after these immortal crowns obtain.

    'The five monsters' [on William III and others]

    b.111, p. 439

T0565 The firstborn of the Egyptians all were slain
And from the womb w'are thine or else accurst.

    [Henry Phillipps]

    b.156, p. 27

T0566 The first day and the same,
I yielded up the ghost.

    'Mother Eve'

    c.536

T0567 The first day is not Sunday:
Those lamps 'gan first to shine.

    Sir Thomas Urquhart, 'Of Sunday, Monday, and
    Wednesday'

    fb.217, p. 211

T0568 The first day of this year
And then the tumult shall be ceas'd.

    'Sir Walter Raleigh's prognostication'

    b.356, p. 71

T0569 The first deceased; he for a little tried
To live without her, lik'd it not, then died.

    'An epitaph: on two lovers who being espoused died
    before they were married'

    b.197, p. 57; Poetry Box XII/65 ('she'); see also 'She first
    deceas'd/departed . . .'.

T0570 The first night Chloris did receive the favor
Befall them, that have taught you so great skill

    Sir Thomas Urquhart, 'How Chloris, the first night of
    her marriage, made her husband indirectly to know,
    that she was not a maid'

    fb.217, p. 321

T0571 The first of August ninety eight,
And champion of the flood!

    Alfred S. Powell, 'The battle of the Nile'

    Poetry Box V/105

T0572 The first of Hilary term shall be
The twenty eight[h] day of November.

    'A perfect rule for memory the terms of law to notify'

    b.234, p. 337

T0573 The first part of that [?] you observ'd
Your lust and belly with the mean(?) you had.

    [Sir Thomas Urquhart], 'Sell all that you have and
    give it to the poor'

    fb.217, p. 516

T0574 The first thing pretended was a strict union
For ten years still turns the chase.

    Poetry Box VIII/43

T0575 The first voice that e'er soothed mortal ear,
Since, by thy rival bow, the like is found.

    John Lockman, 'Writ under a mezzotinto, by
    Mr. Faber, from a portrait of Mr. Hibden, by
    Mr. Mercier . . . 1745'

    c.267/1, p. 30

T0576 The first word of an epitaph join to the same
Of a loyal old city that beat off the Scot.

    'A rebus'

    c.152, p. 71

T0577 The first's a name to female softness given,
Who goes to meeting church or mass.

    '[Enigma/Charade/Conundrum] 33' [sweetheart]

    c.389

T0578 The fish genteels comes ready drest,
Has ridicul'd ev'n ridicule.

> Rob[er]t Watts, 'The fish' [for the Lent Probation at
> the Merchant Taylor's School, 1700]
> [Crum T605]

Poetry Box VI/76

T0579 The fishes great devour the little fry:
So great rich men do poor men injury.

b.234, p. 27

T0580 The fleeting hours in circling race
Who now unwilling part.

> H[enry] Skrine, 'To Lady M—— and her party on
> their leaving Harrogate . . . Harrogate June 30 1785'

c.509, p. 71

T0581 The fleeting years fly swiftly by,
Than the rich pontiff's cup affords.

> John Belfour, 'For the Gazetteer no. 4 translation of
> the 14th ode of the second book of Horace . . .
> Wapping 20th Decr. 1766'

c.217, p. 16

T0582 The fleeting years, my friend, roll on apace,
Of Romish pamper'd prelates and luxurious priests.

> Ja[mes] Philips, 'Hor: lib 2: ode 14'

c.233, p. 104

T0583 The flowers of verse from quiet minds proceed;
All fear the muses fly (and court the shades of
                                                        peace).

c.346

T0584 The flow'rets fade before the northern blast
When bursting from the snow-clad mountain's side.

> Mrs. E. Diggle, 'Imitation of a French elegy on
> winter . . . 1787'

Diggle Box: Poetry Box XI/9

T0585 The folks of old were so nice
Of which I boats [boast?] his tub the type.

> 'Tobacco, a tale'

Poetry Box I/81

T0586 The fool in's heart is wont to say
To grace and love restore.

> 'Psalm 14'

c.264/1, p. 42

T0587 The fool, lacks wit: the envious, piety;
The fool, cannot: th'envious will not see.

> Sir Thomas Urquhart, 'Of the fool, and the envious'

fb.217, p. 74

T0588 The fool that is wealthy, is sure of a bride,
And I shall be rich, when I've you in my arms.

> 'Fools have fortune. May 9 . . . [17]82'

c.93; c.578, p. 8

T0589 The fool within his heart hath said
Blest Sion's King to praise.

> 'Psalm 53. Evening prayer'

c.264/2, p. 5

T0590 The foolish every new thing do despise
And envious folly new things sole to prize.

> 'Upon old and new fashions'

c.356

T0591 The foolish man deceived is
Is fraught with grief and strife.

b.234, p. 179

T0592 The force of music best is found
When soul subservient is to sound.

> 'On hearing a passage in Mr. Handel's late opera of
> Atalanta'
> [Crum T625]

c.94

T0593 The formal Christian's like a water mill
Of going till his wheels shall feel the stream.

> [Francis Quarles], 'On a formal Christian' [Divine
> fancies II, 90]

b.137, p. 191

T0594 The formal object of our mutual love
Is constant secret dealing: th'end's enjoyment.

> Sir Thomas Urquhart, 'To the quintessence of all
> perfection my well-beloved Aura'

fb.217, p. 281

T0595 The forward roses spread an infant bloom,
And purple honors crown the well-distinguish'd
                                                        year.

> [ ] Foxton, 'On primroses covered with snow'

c.244, p. 524

T0596 The Foundling Hospital we'll praise;
To worlds on high.

> John Lockman, 'National songs. The foundling
> hospital, in three parts . . . writ in 1753 . . .'

c.267/2, p. 58

T0597 The Fountain Tavern as the crystal clear,
Here more of water you will drink than wine.

c.53, fol. 23

T0598 The fourth more black than than [sic] fifth of
                                                November
And to the nation gives a greater blow.

> 'On the 4th November' [birthday of William III]
> [Crum T632]
>
> b.111, p. 419

T0599 The fowls have feathers: ev'ry sheep is fleec'd:
For he's less cold, the more, that he is naked.

> Sir Thomas Urquhart, 'The reason wherefore Cupid
> is painted without apparel'
>
> fb.217, p. 215

T0600 The fox and the cat as they travell'd one day
But tax not ourselves tho' we practice the same.

> [John Cunningham], 'The fox and cat—A fable'
>
> c.139, p. 56

T0601 The freeborn English generous and wise
To have enslav'd, but made this isle their friend.

> [Robert] Wolseley, 'The character of the English'
> [paraphrase of Tacitus' De vita agricola, 1680]
> [Crum T635]
>
> c.244, p. 290; b.54, p. 1196; fb.108, p. 367; c.94

T0602 The French are a-coming, as news writers say,
And your grand prospect vanish in smoke.

> John Lockman, 'The new Lilliburlero, to the old tune:
> On the threatened invasion from France, in the
> summer, 1759'
>
> c.267/2, p. 21

T0603 The French have taste in all they do,
Has only given us, gout.

> 'By a lady'
>
> c.378, p. 73; c.391, p. 83

T0604 The French, tho' beat, Te Deum sing
And make them cry—Oramus.

> 'On the French singing Te Deum at Paris after the
> Battle of Dettingen—fought on Thursday June 16.
> 1743'
>
> c.360/2, no. 14

T0605 The freshest rivers which the ocean greet,
Oft in the end proves bitter to the sense.

> Sir Thomas Urquhart, 'Of the unstayedness of venery'
>
> fb.217, p. 78

T0606 The friend demands—and I'll appear
Long may he hail you once a year!

> 'To Athenia. October 24. 1750'
>
> c.238, p. 37

The frost like fire hot shall burn   T0607
Forevermore in heaven may dwell. | Amen

> 'The nativity of our B[lessed] L[ord]. Septe. 8'
>
> a.30[31]

The fruit of tender maids   T0608
As plash'd against the walls.

> [Sir Thomas Urquhart], 'Young girls compared to that
> sort of fruit which in gardens groweth indifferently
> either at the side of a wall or upon beds'
>
> fb.217, p. 502

The fruit that soonest ripes doth soonest fade away, T0609
And that which slowly hath his time will not so
                                        soon decay.

> [Crum T646]
>
> c.339, p. 322 (ll. 1–2)

The fruitful earth carouses, and   T0610
Why may not we and all turn drinkers.

> [John Cleveland]
> [Crum T647]
>
> b.93, p. 1

The fruitful vine and virtuous wife,   T0611
The greatest even of kings.

> [Crum T650]
>
> b.227, p. 77

The fruits of autumn's rip'ning sun,   T0612
O give, I cried, a pair.

> c.591

The fruits of God's blest spirit are,   T0613
Thee to obey, adore, thy love t'acquire.

> [Edmund Wodehouse], 'Jan. 19 [1715] Galat[ian]s 5
> ch. 22.v'
>
> b.131, p. 145

The full dictatorship of Rome, when it   T0614
Skill to discern, our courage to mak't.

> Sir Thomas Urquhart, 'To the Earl of Strafford'
>
> fb.217, p. 255

The furniture that best do please   T0615
All superfluous are but these.

> [Jonathan] Swift, 'Dean Swift to a friend, who asked
> him what here his favorite furniture'
>
> c.94

The gallant looks and outward shows beguile,   T0616
And oft are cloaks to cogitations vile.

> c.339, p. 317

T0617 The garlands fade that spring so lately wove,
Ah! why has happiness—no second spring?

   Charlotte (Turner) Smith, 'Sonnet'

c.130, p. 92

T0618 The gates of heav'n it far surpasseth, whose
But hereat all men vivify their being.

   Sir Thomas Urquhart, 'The praise of a woman's
   quasimodo'

fb.217, p. 213

T0619 The gather'd coin of all the country comes
Which ne'er are dry: nor satiate the main.

   Sir Thomas Urquhart, 'Of the treasure of a king, or
   commonwealth'

fb.217, p. 175

T0620 The gay Fidelia view'd her face
And the false sex is caught with lies.

   'A tale of Fidelia's quarrel with her looking-glass'

c.188, p. 35; see also next.

T0621 The gay Olivia view'd her face,
But the fond sex is caught with lies.

   [William] Broome, 'The looking glass'

c.244, p. 487; see also previous.

T0622 The geese and the sturgeon divided must be
'Twixt Sister P. E. and Sister C. P.

   [Charles] Earle, 'On some sturgeon and two geese
   sent by . . . to his sisters Mrs. Philadelphia Earle and
   Mrs. Catharine Peard'

c.376

T0623 The generous Christian must as well improve
An ounce of serpent serves a pound of dove.

   [Francis Quarles], 'On the serpent, and the dove'

b.137, p. 192 (incomplete)

T0624 The genial day succeeds, that Anna gave,
Your silent triumphs Brunswick, are but mine.

   'On the 6th. of February' [1715]
   [Crum T656]

c.570/1, p. 10

T0625 The genius of th'Augustan age
That rots, and stinks, and is abhorr'd.

   [William Cowper], 'On the author of Letters of
   literature'

File 3794

T0626 The gentle dew distill'd from heav'n
Admits of no relief.

   'A soliloquy. By a lady'

c.83/1, no. 68

T0627 The gentle tailor could not choose, but please her
Then stitch'd her seam, and with his needle sew'd it.

   Sir Thomas Urquhart, 'Of a master fashioner, and his
   mistress'

fb.217, p. 315

T0628 The gently murm'ring, silver rill
Victorious, o'er opposing fate.

   John Lockman, 'Translations, and imitations from
   Metastasio, and other Italian opera poets [9]'

c.267/4, p. 99

T0629 The genuine grief, the sorrow void of art,
And what lost by thy death, by death regain.

   [ ] Lewis, 'On the death of Herbert Powell'

c.244, p. 459

T0630 The gifts indulgent, heav'n bestows,
Tomorrow may be fair.

   'To a friend in affliction'

c.391, p. 53

T0631 The girl that would know how to manage a man
Then let her say no if she can.

c.358, p. 130

T0632 The girls despise, th'enchanting fair,
Before life's latest sand is run.

   'Ode 11th. Anacreon, on his age'

c.94

T0633 The glasses crown'd, the absent female name
And by himself drink each forbidding toast.

   'The Tunbridge toasts—in the year—1713'

c.360/1, p. 81

T0634 The glitt'ring sun appears, sadness begone,
Vivat rex Carolus Secundus.

   John Maine, 'At the proclamation of our most royal
   sovereign Charles the 2d by the grace of God king of
   England, Scotland, France, and Ireland'

b.212, p. 220; see also 'And why such sudden . . .'.

T0635 The globe no land nor city can afford
A seat like this, nor palace such a lord.

   [W. F.], '[An elegant distichon etc.] The [English]
   version' [on Louis XIV]

Poetry Box VI/43

T0636 The globe of earth, on which we dwell, is tack't
                                          unto the poles;
Then why about one honest tack, do fools make
                                          such a pother.

   'The grand tack' [1705]
   [Crum T667, 'we move'; *POAS* VII.71]

b.90, p. 1; c.374 (var.)

T0637 The gloomy night is gathering fast,
Farewell the bonny banks of Ayr.

    R[obert] Burns, 'Sonnet written by . . . when
    preparing to go to the West Indies'

  c.142, p. 246

T0638 The glories of our birth, and state,
Smell sweet, and blossom in the dust.

    [James Shirley], 'The glittering shade' [on the earl of
    Orrery]
    [Crum T668]

  fb.107, p. 79; fb.66/11 (attr. Earl of Orrery); c.244,
  p. 289; b.54, p. 965 (with a supplement by J. Fuller);
  b.213, p. 148 (with extra lines?)

T0639 The glorious monarch, who fills the British throne,
None, but his whores, can tell he's flesh and blood.

    'On King G[eorge]'s statue in the 'Change'

  fc.58, p. 142

T0640 The glorious sun abroad did spread
To live in joy withouten end. | Amen

    'Of the presentation of our B[lessed] Lad[y]'
    [November 21]

  a.30[54]

T0641 The glory of the English arms retriev'd
To stamp his Q[ueen] and cuckold on one coin.

    'The medal. On one side the D: of M[arlboroug]h on
    horseback with this motto—Sine clade victor. On the
    reverse the Q[ueen]'
    [Crum T675]

  c.111, p. 74; Poetry Box IV/119

T0642 The glory of this world to Whigs are given,
Abjur'd their king and Barabbas did choose.

    'The English choice or the glory of the Whigs'
    [Crum T676]

  c.570/1, p. 163

T0643 The god of day, descending from above,
In verse immortal as thy gallery.

    [George Granville, 1st baron Lansdowne], 'The
    progress of beauty' [1694]
    [Crum T679]

  b.218, p. 48

T0644 The God of glory reigns supremely great
For if he frown ye perish all before him.

    P[hilip] Doddridge, 'God's universal dominion from
    Ps. LXVI 7'

  c.493, p. 55

T0645 The god of Indies now 'tis plain
Since greedy statemen rule the roost.

    'Some truths in plain English, occasioned by the
    arrival of the Spanish galleons'

  c.570/3, p. 64

T0646 The god of love appoints men mistresses
Thus money makes them love and be beloved.

    [Sir Thomas Urquhart], 'Of those who court young
    women for their beauty, and yet marry old wives for
    their riches'

  fb.217, p. 537

T0647 The God of love my shepherd is
So neither shall thy praise.

    [George Herbert], 'Poema pium or a holy hymn'
    [Psalm xxiii]
    [Crum T685]

  Poetry Box VI/41

T0648 The God of order did ordain
That faithful successors it never want.

    [Edward] Sparke, 'Poem 23th on St Matthias'

  b.137, p. 54

T0649 The god of verse provok'd to rage,
Ask'd pardon, and he gave—a nod.

    Abraham Oakes, 'The conclusion' [to 'Poetical
    essays']

  c.50, p. 161

T0650 The god who animates the lay,
Where genius, learning, sense are join'd.

    John Lockman, 'The complaint of poetry to Apollo.
    9th Sept: 1761'

  c.267/4, p. 364

T0651 The God who form'd you for supreme command,
And in his fear preserve you, thus we pray.

    W[illiam] Salmon, 'A poem to King William'

  c.166, p. 79

T0652 The god who Scarborough's far-fam'd urn supplies,
What can my springs without his healing art?

    John Lockman, 'Hearing that Dr. Shaw was invited to
    leave Scarborough; a little after part of the cliff had
    broke away'

  c.267/1, p. 164; c.268 (first part), p. 13

T0653 The goddess had her court display'd
Which glitter'd various colors far.

    'The rose and the lily'

  c.83/2, no. 396

T0654 The goddesses once, as the old poets tell us
The way through the stomach is the way to the
                                                    heart.

    [S. C., verses on a turkey from Mrs. Mattocks]
    [Crum T690]
Poetry Box v/28

T0655 The gods and Cato did in this divide,
The chose the conqu'ring, he the conquer'd side.

    'In Catonem'
c.81/1, no. 240

T0656 The gods and the goddesses lately did feast
For heaven was never true heaven till now.

    [Captain Alexander Radcliffe?], 'Upon a bowl of
    punch' [pr. 1713 (Foxon B336)]
    [Crum T692]
b.371, no. 24; c.555, p. 200 ('did meet'; incomplete)

T0657 The gods of love that sit above
My self to work your will withal.

'Braye Lute Book,' Music Ms. 13, fol. 55v

T0658 The gods on a day, when their worships were idle,
Her honor smelt worse than a stinking red herring.

    [mock-panegyric on Bacchus]
c.481, p. 271

T0659 The gods on thrones celestial seated,
I made Mount Edgecomb for you all.

    [George Lyttelton, 1st baron Lyttelton, but attr. David
    Garrick; answered by 'Leave, Garrick . . .']
Poetry Box v/31

T0660 The gods Pandora heaven's bright firmament,
Heaven shall clap hands, and give the *plaudite*.

    Charles Fitz-Geoffrey, 'On Sir Francis Drake'
b.356, p. 236

T0661 The gods, the gods have heard my prayers,
Thou'rt old upon record.

    [ ] Davys, of King's College Cambridge, 'Occasioned
    by a person's searching the registers for Molly Fowl's
    age and finding her born 1702'
fc.135

T0662 The gods to curse Pamelia with her prayers
She sighs, and is no duchess at the heart.

    'Wealth without content or the unhappy marriage'
c.186, p. 97

T0663 The gods, we are told, gave Pandora a box,
The grace of a saint to the meal of a sinner.

    [Charles Earle], 'To Justice S—— at Witheridge an
    extempore invitation to dinner, upon his fearing a visit
    after my touch of a fever'
c.376; see also 'Next Sunday by 10 . . .'.

T0664 The gods were pleas'd to choose the conqu'ring side,
But Cato thought he conquer'd when he died.

    'In Catonem . . . [no attribution]'
c.81/1, no. 240

T0665 The golden age is now at last restor'd
This day old Nol to judgment brought his king.

    'On the Thanksgiving Day' [20 March 1714/15, for
    George I's accession; printed, Foxon B284]
    [Crum T695]
fc.58, p. 122; c.570/1, p. 44

T0666 The golden beams that from the face,
Forever we may reign. | Amen

    'Of Saint Matthew. Sep. 27'
a.30[36]

T0667 The golden hair that Galla wears,
For I know where she bought it.

    'Epigram'
c.115; see also 'The goodly hair . . .'.

T0668 The golden rule to work exact
Like to your middle number in kind.

    [Mary Serjant], 'The golden rule'
fb.98, fol. 47

T0669 The golden sun, emerging from the main,
Float into air, and vanish in the sky.

    [Francis Fawkes], 'The death of the lark . . . 1739'
fc.21, p. 6

T0670 The good and prudent man whom Phoebus, when
He blames the bad, and crown[s] the good with
                                                    praise.

    [John Hobart?]
b.108, fol. 17

T0671 The good by praise is better, worse the bad,
The crafty craftier, the fool more mad.

    'An encomiastic'
c.356

T0672 The good folks at Bath, intending to raise
Of the man or the figure to tell which is which.

Poetry Box v/91

T0673 The good h'in three divides: yet what hath he:
Being foolish, sick, and poor, of all the three.

> Sir Thomas Urquhart, 'Of a certain philosophaster,
> teaching moral philosophy'
>
> fb.217, p. 347

T0674 The good man's aim the dart that wounds the curst
It ends all ills or is of all the worst.

> R[obert] Shirley, 1st earl of Ferrers, 'Audoeni Ep. J[?]
> 53: Ed: in 24. [?] death'
>
> c.347, p. 7

T0675 The good, the learn'd, the beauteous and the brave,
At once his weeping parents' grief and pride.

> Bonnell Thornton, 'In Cuddesden churchyard
> Oxfordshire on the son of Thos. Armborough, who
> died aged 21'
>
> c.240, p. 134

T0676 The good three children scorn a gilded god
No fire shall scorch where the angel is in place.

> 'Daniel the 3rd'
>
> b.206, p. 135

T0677 The goodly hair that Galla wears
For I know where she bought it.

> fb.69, p. 231; see also 'The golden hair . . .'.

T0678 The goods not spent, we keep, and what we save
We lose, only what we lose, not have.

> 'Riddle' [answering another riddle by Francis Quarles]
> [cf. Crum T702, 'The goods we spend we keep . . .']
>
> b.118, p. 225

T0679 The Gospel 'tis which streaks the morning bright,
Grace their last moments, nor desert their dust.

> 'On the Gospel'
>
> c.83/3, no. 813

T0680 The gracefullest of the Mnemosynids,
T'expede the better my intended course.

> Sir Thomas Urquhart, 'The invocation to Erato'
>
> fb.217, p. 226

T0681 The gracious Savior bow'd his head,
Proclaim that God is kind.

> 'Easter a poem'
>
> c.83/1, no. 142

T0682 The grammar school a long time taught I have
Yet all my skill could not decline the grave.

> 'On a schoolmaster'
>
> c.74

T0683 The Grampian provinces have scarce one corner,
To be the more angelically feasted.

> Sir Thomas Urquhart, 'Upon the Countess of [crossed
> out]'
>
> fb.217, p. 90

T0684 The Grand Commander of the Hospital
And doing it, you do yourself un-king.

> Sir John Strangways, 'A discourse between King
> Henry the Third and the prior of St. John's
> Hospital . . . 4to Decemb: 1646'
>
> b.304, p. 74

T0685 The grandsire, sire, and son, the gown all three
May honestly caress himself.

> [Sir Philip Wodehouse], 'Upon my neighbor
> Mr. Robert Long'
>
> b.131, back (no. 138)

T0686 The grateful cherish, for in them you'll find
When many(?) years to manhood have arriv'd.

> '[Greek:] Kalon insauron ketmene charis. Poet. min:'
>
> c.373, p. 63

T0687 The grateful tribute of these rural lays,
And growing always new, must always last.

> St[ephe]n Duck, 'The thresher's labor' [pr. in his
> Poems, 1730]
>
> c.165, p. 13; Poetry Box IV/188

T0688 The grave house of Commons by hook or by crook
But to throw out the bishops who threw out the bill.

> 'A ballad . . . 1680. Made upon casting the bill against
> the D. of York out of the House of Lords'
> [Crum T719-20; POAS II.375]
>
> b.54, p. 1194; Poetry Box VIII/37; Poetry Box VI/60

T0689 The grave is clos'd—the fairest star is dark,
Can ne'er efface, and little can alloy.

> c.340

T0690 The gravest author on my shelf,
Your most sincere obedient friend.

> [Isaac Freeman], 'The answer' [to 'Tomorrow,
> Sir . . .']
>
> fc.105

T0691 The gray-ey'd morn approach his friends drew near
Berkeley shall have their voices still.

> H[annah] More, 'On Mr. Berkeley's (afterward Lord
> Botetourt) being elected for Gloucestershire in 1754
> the author . . . being then ten years of age many pieces
> of hers in this book were wrote in her infant years'
>
> c.341, p. 102

T0692 The great Archpapist, learned Curio
And thou shalt be a privy counsellor.

'Religion ensnared by preferment' [on Henry
Howard, earl of Northampton, 1603/4]
[Crum T723]

b.200, p. 78; b.197, p. 65

T0693 The great Creator gave to brutes the light
That pardons sins, which from thy bounty grow.

[Sir Matthew Hale], 'A poem'

b.49, p. 21; fb.142, p. 41

T0694 The great design, the word becoming man,
Too much is that solemnity to pay.

'Christmas Day. 1666'

b.49, p. 11

T0695 The great good man, who fortune does displace,
And what they fail to raise, they will adore.

[Henry Hall, of Hereford? Or Daniel Kenrick?], 'The
great good man' [Bishop Ken? Or James II?]
[Crum T727]

c.244, p. 102

T0696 The great Jehovah bids his priests declaim
And to their rage shall fall a sacrifice.

b.90, p. 12

T0697 The great Jehovah from on high
In concert with th'angelic throng.

Henry Howard, 'A sacred rapture presented to the
Gentlemen's Soc[iety] at Spalding . . .'

c.229/1, fol. 24v

T0698 The great Messiah's name
On what his love has done.

T[homas] S[tevens], 'John 7.31'

c.259, p. 121

T0699 The great ones, from time immemorial enjoy
And in borrow'd plumes proudly they strut it away.

John Lockman, 'High and low life: tune, The lads of
Duna'

c.267/2, p. 149; c.268 (first part), p. 82

T0700 The greatest artist, that the world e'er saw
What great Apelles, sought in womankind.

[Thomas Hamilton, 6th earl of Haddington], 'Upon a
lady's picture'

c.458/2, p. 59

T0701 The greatest consequential apes
Their former fortunes to bewail.

S[tephen] Simpson, 'The servants a fable'

c.563

T0702 The greatest dignity and happiness
On which depends their honor and their life.

[Edmund Wodehouse], 'July 8 [1715]'

b.131, p. 229

T0703 The greatest gifts that nature can bestow,
It dies in rags, and scarce deserves a name.

[Thomas] Parnell, 'On poverty'

c.244, p. 525

T0704 The greatest power is to wise men due
Because they will not do but what they ought.

[Sir Thomas Urquhart], 'That wise men properly are
the most powerful men in the world'

fb.217, p. 522

T0705 The grief I bore was well repaid awhile,
And I submission write upon her grave.

'Epitaph on a girl of four years old in Cockermouth
churchyard'

c.139, p. 35

T0706 The groans of learning tell that Johnson dies,
And though you stain'd his spirit, spare his dust.

Anna Seward(?), 'Epitaph on Dr. Johnson'
[Crum T742 (attr. William Hayley)]

c.391, p. 119

T0707 The guide and tutor of my early youth,
From age to age, the honor'd name of Crisp!

[Charles Burney, the elder], 'Elegy on the death of an
old and dear friend'

c.33, p. 157 (last part crossed out)

T0708 The hand of him, here torpid lies
That saw the manners in the face.

[Samuel] Johnson, 'On [the death of Hogarth] by . . .
who bragged(?) that he could bring all that Garrick
had said into the compass of four lines'

c.504, p. 50

T0709 The hapless bird whose tender breast,
And O forgive him if he die.

[Robert Merry], 'To Chloe—in England written at
Florence'

Greathced Box/47

T0710 The happiest man on earth is he,
Raise our frail souls to the heav'nly throne.

[Edmund Wodehouse], 'Octr 1 [1715]'

b.131, p. 277

T0711 The happiest man that ever breath'd on earth
Content's a cordial that gives some relief.

    'To a man of quality and great riches, confined by the gout'

c.94

T0712 The happiest mortals once were we
Is to love and love in vain.

    [George Granville, 1st baron Lansdowne], 'Song 230'

c.555, p. 362

T0713 The happiness of all mankind,
To love, t'adore, sincerely obey.

    [Edmund Wodehouse], 'Apr. 24 [1715]'

b.131, p. 203

T0714 The happiness of her he hath embrac'd
He stirs her body neither night, nor day.

    Sir Thomas Urquhart, 'Of one, who was married with an old, and unuseful man'

fb.217, p. 290

T0715 The happy man on earth is he
Our joys to the same height would rise.

    [Edmund Wodehouse], '12 Sepr. 1715'

b.131, p. 263

T0716 The happy minute's come the nymph is laid
He throws himself and rifles all her charms.

    Sir W[illia]m Savage

c.229/1, fol. 55

T0717 The happy youth, whom strength of genius fires;
Nor quit the nymph till he obtain the clue.

    John Lockman, 'Writ under a mezzotinto, by Mr. Faber, representing a young man drawing'

c.267/1, p. 163

T0718 The hare and the hound shall first agree
And never do so to you again.

    Arthur Blanchindley
'Braye Lute Book,' Music Ms. 13, fol. 37

T0719 The heart of man, that iron door!
To part Thy face to see.

    T[homas] S[tevens], 'Christ knocking at the door of his people's hearts. Rev: 3.20. L. M.'

c.259, p. 127

T0720 The heart of the loaf, and the head of the spring
Is the name of the man, that beheaded the king.

    'A rebus on Oliver Cromwell'

c.360/1, p. 1

T0721 The hearth was clean, the fire clear,
Just so, to live and love.

    'The happy fireside'

c.83/2, no. 700

T0722 The heathen God are come into
Give thanks to thee, all honor, and all praise.

    Ja. Raynatt, 'Psalm 79'
    [Crum T763 ('Heathen Lord'; 'Jno. Rayment']

b.197, p. 106

T0723 The heav'nly angels, whom eternal fate
For all thou hast are but derivatives.

    J[ohn] R[obinson], 'Reges in ipsos imperium est Jovis'

c.370, fol. 50v

T0724 The heavenly lord who haughty heart doth hate,
Throws down the proud when sure they think their state.

c.339, p. 258, p. 312

T0725 The heav'ns conceive with man in generation
Whence though she heav'nly be, she's not divine.

    [Sir Thomas Urquhart], 'To one, whose mistress had manyer [more] heavenly qualities than good ones'

fb.217, p. 537

T0726 The heavens (my God) do silently proclaim—
O happiness secur'd.

    [Sir John Cotton, 'Hominus ad Deum']

fc.54, p. 39

T0727 The heav'ns still move: although the earth remain
Who's void of that terrestrial quality.

    Sir Thomas Urquhart

fb.217, p. 198

T0728 The heavens, whose vast extent we view,
My strength, and my salvation lies.

    Sam[ue]l Gay, of Ipswich, 'A version of the whole 19th. Psalm'

c.244, p. 1

T0729 The heav'ns declare thy glory, Lord,
Redemption is of Thee.

    'Psalm 19 Morning prayer 4 day'

c.264/1, p. 69

T0730 The heedless lover does not know
Inquires the name that has his heart.

    [Edmund] Waller, 'Waller to Van Dyck'

b.197, p. 250

T0731 The height of knowledge yieldeth to the pith
And are for sciences another Plato.

> Sir Thomas Urquhart, 'To Doctor William [crossed out] principal of the University of Aberdeen'
>
> fb.217, p. 102

T0732 The hermit's solace in his cell
The madman's sport; the wise man's pain.

> [Ambrose Philips?]
>
> c.189, p. 173

T0733 The hidden cause, I sacred muse repeat!
Must for a solo, invoke a Belcher's name.

> B[eaumont] Brenan, 'The grand secret found out, or Glasnevin the seat of the muses' [19 August 1751]
>
> File 1712

T0734 The highborn offspring of the best of men,
Implores your grace t'accept this worthless mite.

> 'To Charles Prince of Wales'
>
> fb.69, p. 115

T0735 The highest place at table she embrac'd
All day she rul'd him, her all night he guided.

> Sir Thomas Urquhart, 'In what manner a husband, and his wife did share their rooms betwixt them'
>
> fb.217, p. 321

T0736 The highest tides have lowest ebbs by kind
For men and women both by kind have fits.

> 'Her answer' [to 'So high a tide . . .']
>
> b.356, p. 103

T0737 The hinds how blest, who ne'er beguil'd
Beneath a flowery turf they sleep.

> [Thomas] Warton, 'The hamlet, written in Whichwood Forest'
>
> c.90

T0738 The hoary fool who many days
Tomorrow, till tonight, he's dead.

> c.362, p. 86

T0739 The holy brotherhood of zealous Scots
The Lord of heaven (we trust) will send them back.

> 'Upon the Scots. 1641'
> [Crum T792]
>
> b.54, p. 887

T0740 The holy spouse of Jesus Christ
To heaven may pave our way. | Amen

> 'S. Gregory Thaumaturgus. Nov. 17'
>
> a.30[53]

T0741 The holy wives of Edinburgh deface
The works they cherish inwardly unquarrel'd.

> Sir Thomas Urquhart, 'Of some puritan commers [sic] of Edinburgh'
>
> fb.217, p. 334

T0742 The hop, whose tendrils cling from pole to pole
Supports his age, and smooths the road to death!

> [Charles Burney, the elder], 'Eulogium on the hop plant. A fragment . . . Howlits, in Kent, 1778'
>
> c.33, p. 130 (crossed out)

T0743 The hopes we once did entertain
With all kind friendship else to you.

> E[lizabeth (Shirley)] C[ompton, countess of Northampton], 'Sept: 22d 1722'
>
> Accession 97.7.40

T0744 The hour conceal'd, and so remote the fear,
Death still draws nearer, never seeming near.

> 'In Brighthelmstone churchyard is the following excellent epitaph'
>
> c.240, p. 137

T0745 The hourglass thus, by love contriv'd,
And mourn his Daphne's loss in vain.

> [Thomas Hamilton, 6th earl of Haddington], 'The transformation of Daphne'
>
> c.458/2, p. 120

T0746 The hour must come, the last important hour;
And sing salvation to the lamb forever.

> [Elizabeth (Singer) Rowe], 'On death'
>
> fc.132/1, p. 29

T0747 The hours have wings to fly away,
H' has lively hopes to see God's face.

> [Edmund Wodehouse], 'Apr. 4 [1715]'
>
> b.131, p. 192

T0748 The House of Commons having lately sent
Embrace each other, and leave us content.

> [Crum T809]
>
> c.160, fol. 105; b.229, fol. 123 ('in their merriment')

T0749 The human fabric, each minutest part
As nature's self: great plastic, add thy wit.

> 'Verses I wrote 1719. on Monsieur de Nous's anatomical waxworks'
>
> c.371, fol. 70

To750 The humble petition of sorrowful Peter
I suppose (like the Scotch) on account of
connection.

'To the right honble Lady Cecilia Johnson from her
monkey, on his banishment'

c.157, p. 118

To751 The humbler that thou dost thyself a man behave
The more thou dost deserve the name of god to
have.

b.208, p. 124

To752 The husband is the head, as soon's h'unlocks
For he's not head, till she be cover'd by him.

Sir Thomas Urquhart, 'Why women go no longer
bareheaded after they be married'

fb.217, p. 341

To753 The h[ymn]s in scripture saith,
Work all thy will by love!

[Hymn]

c.180, p. 78

To754 The illegitimate Smectymnuan brat
God in his time those wicked men destroy.

'Upon the club-divines &c. 1662'

b.54, p. 937

To755 The image of our frailty, painted glass
The murderer himself weeps out his eyes.

[James Shirley?], 'On the martyrdom of St. Alban's,
painted in glass' [In the abbey church of St. Alban]
[Crum T819]

fb.143, p. 28

To756 The incendiary priests and friars
That you war and that we pray.

'['Couvre le feu you Huguenots . . .'] answered by a
nonconformist'

Poetry Box VI/17

To757 The Indian men have found a plant
I cannot yield nor ever will.

'Her answer' [to "There is a coal']

b.205, fol. 92v

To758 The Indian plant being withered quite
Thus think then drink | Tobacco.

[Crum T821, 'Indian weed']

b.205, fol. 2v

To759 The injur'd fair now sighs no more,
And with new luster shine.

'On the death of Mrs. Sa[rah] E[dwa]rds—an
unfortunate lady'

c.83/1, no. 130

To760 The injur'd love which now inspires my muse,
This said, he plung'd into the stream and died.

R. Meldrum, 'An elegy'

c.83/3, no. 909

To761 The inward pain
Well said the[y] say good will is all.

[R. M.]

Poetry Box VI/4

To762 The Jews (as we in sacred writ are told)
To keep up gold will even sell their God.

'Epigram'

c.115

To763 The jocund morn, in mantle gay,
And glorious Sol, lead on the joyous day!

'A morning serenade'

c.83/3, no. 864

To764 The joy of human life three things commend
All which she tantamounts—wit, wine, or friend.

[Sir Philip Wodehouse], 'Upon [Lady Mary
Wintour's] daughter Winifred Wintour'

b.131, back (no. 33)

To765 The judges are met—a terrible show!
'If moved—'tis nature; if surprised—'tis new.'

[William Parsons], 'Prologue to the tragedy of Don
Manuel'

Greatheed Box/55

To766 The judgment, which a painful education
By nature chiefly, to the height they're now in.

Sir Thomas Urquhart, 'To the Viscount of [crossed
out]'

fb.217, p. 283

To767 The King and the court, desirous to sport,
To preach before the King.

'Upon Dr. Corbett Dean of Christ's Church in
Oxford' [1624]
[Crum T844, with two more stanzas]

b.197, p. 220; b.200, p. 40 (incomplete)

To768 The King considering with gracious eyes
That very loyal body wanted learning.

[Joseph Trapp], 'On the King's sending a regiment of
soldiers to Oxon and giving [Bishop John Moore's]
books to Cambridge'
[cf. Crum T850, T853]

c.233, p. 83; see also 'The King observing . . .'.

To769 The King, (God bless him) let's all address him
He got from his Parliament.

c.360/1, p. 227

T0770　The King he rides to hunt
And this is England's knell.

　'England's knell'
　[cf. Crum T846, 'The King he hawks, and hunts']
　b.356, p. 304

T0771　The King in his council did order of late,
Calls down three persons from heaven to tack it.

　'On the clergy' [temp. George I]
　[Crum T847]
　c.570/1, p. 39

T0772　The King in his wisdom (it makes me quite frantic)
My rule shall be then to ask those who have raffled.

　'Advertisement . . . Mother Mack, Bath, Jan 4, 1781'
　Poetry Box II/32

T0773　The King in war, | To's foes by far
To a master as good as himself for his nose.

　'Mr. Upton's verses . . . thus paraphras'd'
　c.233, p. 113

T0774　The King my master your ally
And H—ce, shall with Fleury vie.

　'The speech of a certain ambassador to the King of
　France, on the birth of a dauphin versified'
　c.570/3, p. 75

T0775　The King observing with judicious eyes
How much that loyal body wanted learning.

　[Joseph Trapp], 'An epigram on King George the first
　sending a regiment to be quartered at Oxford and
　presenting the University of Cambridge with a library'
　[of Bishop John Moore, 1715; in answer to 'The king
　to Oxford', by Sir William Browne]
　[Crum T850]
　c.360/1, p. 163; Poetry Box VIII/69; see also 'The King
　considering . . .'.

T0776　The King of flow'rs, and lions did receive it:
And Leo Pope a Florentino gave it.

　Sir Thomas Urquhart, 'The title of defender of the
　faith, bestowed on Henry the Eighth, a descendent of
　the House of York, and king of England'
　fb.217, p. 304

T0777　The King of kings did once a thief forgive
To let him hang for this, he'll steal no more.

　'The traveller's answer' [reply to John Clavell's 'I that
　have robb'd . . .']
　b.200, p. 4; b.356, p. 70

T0778　The King of kings in heaven doth sit in state,
He sits triumphing in a glorious seat.

　'Another [on a spiritual King]'
　c.187, p. 21

T0779　The King of peace did cause the king of rest
To build a temple far above the best.

　[Robert Cottesford]
　b.144, p. 3

T0780　The King shall in thy strength exult
And sing glad songs to Thee.

　'Psalm 21'
　c.264/1, p. 77

T0781　The King the shepherd is, his people are
The [?] [?], who for physic get the law.

　[Sir Thomas Urquhart], 'Rex, grex, et lex'
　fb.217, p. 518

T0782　The King to Oxford sent a troop of horse
For Whigs admit no force but argument.

　[Sir William Browne; answered by 'The King
　observing . . .']
　Poetry Box VIII/69; Poetry Box X/167

T0783　The king whom fairyland obeys
To such commanding neatness due.

　[Phanuel Bacon], 'Accompanied with a crooked tester
　and put in Betty Trevor's shoe'
　c.237, fol. 74

T0784　The ladies he endeavors for to please,
He's primitive, slovenly, nasty, dirty Cob.

　[ ] Boles, of New College, Oxford, 'Verses spoke
　by . . . Terrae Filius in the year 1682, upon Mr. Jacob
　Allestry of Christ Church his brother Terrae Filius'
　fb.142, p. 21

T0785　The lads and the ladies were met on the green,
And may each have a husband before the next
　　　　　　　　　　　　　　year! | Derry down

　'Enigmas in The ladies' diary for the year 1747
　answered'
　c.241, p. 115

T0786　The lady that made the puzzling reply,
And the third son descended from their marriage
　　　　　　　　　　　　　　　　　bed.

　'Vauxhall and fiddler schoolmaster Jany. 3 1774'
　fc.85, fol. 80

T0787　The lamp of day with ill-presaging glare,
She said, and vanish'd with the sweeping blast.

　[Robert Burns], 'On the death of Sir James Hunter
　Blair'
　c.142, p. 281

T0788   The land was his, the land was his alone
To him, what death d'ye think's prepared for you?

    [Francis Quarles], 'On Ananias' [Divine
    fancies III, 82]

    b.137, p. 172

T0789   The landlord he looks very big
Come up my friend—and down it goes. | Oh good
                                  ale, &c.

    'Good ale thou art my darling' [9 Nov. 1797]

    Poetry Box x/131

T0790   The lands that long in darkness lay,
And reign to ages yet unknown.

    [Isaac Watts, Hymns and spiritual songs (1707), bk. I,
    Hymn 13]

    c.180, p. 23

T0791   The lark was up the morning gray
None can resist the British fair.

    'Song 179'

    c.555, p. 275

T0792   The lass of Bromhall Green
The landlord's hariot be.

    '25th song. The lass of Bromhall Green. To the tune of
    The lass of Patie's mill'

    Accession 97.7.40, p. 45

T0793   The lass of Patie's mill so bonny,
Should share the same wi' me.

    [Allan Ramsay]
    [Crum T867, 'Patty's']

    fc.61, p. 65

T0794   The lass whose legs, like silver bright
In silken hose bedight!

    R[ichard] V[ernon] S[adleir], 'To Miss —— with a
    present of silk stockings'

    c.106, p. 95

T0795   The last act of a jovial life is sad
And of a doleful(?) one the end is glad.

    [Sir Thomas Urquhart], 'How different the
    beginnings and catastrophes of man's [?] are'

    fb.217, p. 392

T0796   The last great age foretold by sacred rhymes,
And thro' the matted grass the liquid gold shall
                                  creep.

    'Christ will come to restore the world to its primitive
    splendor'

    c.83/1, no. 10

T0797   The last time Apelles' beamed hand
Thou needst not but for her t'have stopt.

    'Braye Lute Book,' Music Ms. 13, fol. 56v

T0798   The last time I came o'er the moor,
Before I cease to love her.

    [Allan Ramsay], 'A song' [pr. in Scots songs, 1718]
    [Crum T873]

    c.358, p. 25

T0799   The latest stage of life draws on apace,
No title's right, but that of heav'nly love.

    [Edmund Wodehouse], 'May 29 [1715]'

    b.131, p. 219

T0800   The latitude of virtues, which are hers
The hundredth part of her deserved praise.

    Sir Thomas Urquhart, 'Upon the Countess of [crossed
    out]'

    fb.217, p. 253

T0801   The laughing Zephyr thus the storm addrest:
'Unalterable nature drives me on.'

    [Georgiana Spencer Cavendish], duchess of
    Devonshire, 'Lines by the duchess of Devonshire'

    c.142, p. 545

T0802   The laurel we discard now Daniel's dead,
A man, of more beneficence of mind.

    Dr. [ ] Crane, 'On the death of S. Daniel, M. D.'

    c.83/3, no. 1061

T0803   The laurels now thou courts keep but thy ground
With them next year thy temples may be crown'd.

    'Nicolus Warrenus. Anagramma. Io nunc laurus serva.
    Epigramma . . . thus Englished'

    b.212, p. 83

T0804   The laurel's verdant still and free from blasting
Such be thy virtues fresh and everlasting.

    'Praemium. Laurea Apollinaris . . .'

    b.212, p. 73

T0805   The law from whence the covenanters draw
For none but dunces will be ruled by it.

    [Sir Thomas Urquhart], The puritans to justify their
    legal proceeding against the bishops say that they were
    justly expelled from Scotland which —— by the [?]
    of dunce law'

    fb.217, p. 387

T0806   The law is rough: the gospel mild and calm
That lanc'd the bile, and this pours in the balm.

    [Francis Quarles], 'On the law and the gospel'
    [Crum T876]

    b.137, p. 194

T0807 The law it is no rule of life at all
Laws they command, but love it acteth free.

    Mrs. M. B—y, 'On the law as a rule of life'

c.213

T0808 The lazy mist hangs from the brow of the hill,
For something beyond it poor man sure must live.

    [Robert Burns], 'The lazy mist'

c.142, p. 303

T0809 The learned arts at first are hard to see,
With trial oft they plain and easy be.

c.339, p. 319

T0810 The learned Tant-pis approach'd his patient's bed,
Had I prescrib'd, the patient had not died.

    'Les medicines from Fontaine'

c.89, p. 114

T0811 The length of days a blessing be,
Thus we take heav'n by violence.

    [Edmund Wodehouse], 'Novr. 22 [1714]'

b.131, p. 93

T0812 The less we speak the more we think,
For he sees most that seems to wink.

c.549, p. 118

T0813 The Levites the sev'nth day, sev'n times surrounded
The moon shines most, and least by the sun's rays.

    Sir Thomas Urquhart, 'Some covenanting preachers are compared here to the Levites'

fb.217, p. 189

T0814 The liar and the thief have one vocation
The first deceives by word the last by deed.

    [Francis Quarles], 'On the thief and the liar' [Divine fancies I, 73]

b.137, p. 186

T0815 The life of a Christian is running a race,
But that which survives wins the game.

    Abraham Oakes, 'Solution of enigma ['Tho' in the race Olympic . . .']

c.50, p. 160

T0816 The life of man hangs on a slender thread,
Weigh well the concerns of a future state.

    [John Robinson], 'Omnia sunt hominum tenui pendentia filo'

c.370, fol. 20v

T0817 The life of man, is like a game at dice
I'll fortune to correct, with honest art.

    [Sir Philip Wodehouse], 'Upon [Christopher Hatley's] son, Paul Hatley'

b.131, back (no. 159)

T0818 The line of Vere, so long renown'd in arms
They rose in valor, and in beauty set.

    [Charles Montagu], 'An epitaph on the Duchess of St. Albans'

c.360/1, p. 215

T0819 The lion in decline of age
The ass in silence, march'd along.

    'The theatrical brutes'

c.83/3, no. 957

T0820 The lion is the forest king,
Or grudges at Eliza's bliss.

    Joseph Hall, bp. of Norwich, 'On Queen Elizabeth's arms . . . Englished'
    [cf. Crum T899]

b.197, p. 59

T0821 The lion 'tis no matter how
The safe way's to be gone; when folks are for
                             hanging.

    'The lion's edict . . . Moral'

c.570/1, p. 81

T0822 The list'ning trees Amphion drew
And conquers all things like your eyes.

    'On a lady embroidering her aprons with arms and flowers'

c.172, p. 17

T0823 The little archer-god, who fondly flies,
O gentle Cupid! Change it for the heart.

    John Lockman, 'To a young lady: after stealing her pocket book . . . Feb. 1749/50'

c.267/1, p. 50

T0824 The little god of love I found
Him, fanning with his wings a wound of his own
                             making.

    J[ohn] H[oadly], 'Anacreon ode the 59'

c.176, p. 114

T0825 The lively bloom in Laura's cheeks
The pois'n'ous venom pierc'd her heart.

    'Art and nature'

Poetry Box IV/146

To826　The lives of men seem in two seas to swim
　　　　Death goes to young folks, and old go to him.

　　　　　'Death'
　　　　c.356

To827　The livid sun with stormlike hue
　　　　To [?] the [?] to the [?]some cave.

　　　　　[John Black], 'Woden and Mary' [rough draft]
　　　　fc.107, p. 16

To828　The living waters that revive
　　　　And over all, tho' weak, a Queen remains.

　　　　　Thomas Traherne
　　　　b.308, p. 219

To829　The lizard's eyes the face of man amazeth
　　　　Triumph o'er death, by him who conquer'd all.

　　　　　Jo. Binchy(?), 'May it please your Grace [James Duke
　　　　　of Ormonde] supposing the time of your departure
　　　　　drawing near . . .'
　　　　fb.228/35

To830　The loath of the stomach, and the word of disgrace
　　　　Is the gentleman's name with a brazen face.

　　　　　[Alexander Nowell], 'Noel [dean of St. Paul's] to
　　　　　Raleigh'
　　　　　[cf. Crum T1100, 'offence of the stomach']
　　　　b.356, p. 307

To831　The loaves of bread were five, the fishes two
　　　　Five were ordain'd by man, and two by heaven.

　　　　　[Francis Quarles], 'O[n] Rome's 7 sacraments' [Divine
　　　　　fancies I, 3]
　　　　b.137, p. 175; fb.69, p. 199; c.81/1, no. 105 ('The loaves
　　　　were five . . .')

To832　The lofty oak soon from its top
　　　　Nor drive me to despair.

　　　　　[John Black], 'The boat a ballad' [rough draft]
　　　　fc.107, p. 37

To833　The lofty pyramid that threats the skies,
　　　　My length of humble earth, and I'm content.

　　　　　[ ] Lewis, 'Thy pyramid'
　　　　c.244, p. 231

To834　The lofty tree with axe is overthrown
　　　　When bushes stand till storms be overblown.

　　　　c.339, p. 317

To835　The lonely muse from busy crowds retir'd,
　　　　While virtue warms his breast with gen'rous fires!

　　　　　'On solitude'
　　　　c.89, p. 10

To836　The long-neglected muse her aid denies
　　　　The kinder husband or the tenderer wife.

　　　　　C. Barrow [to a bride on her wedding morning]
　　　　Poetry Box x/56

To837　The longest day in time resigns to night
　　　　The raven dies, the eagle fails of flight.

　　　　　[Geffrey Whitney]
　　　　　[Crum T914]
　　　　c.339, p. 329

To838　The longest life's a winter's day
　　　　The longest life is, sup and go to bed.

　　　　　'A winter's thought'
　　　　c.186, p. 114; see also 'Man's life is like . . .'.

To839　The Lord a shepherd unto me
　　　　Thou best of shepherds unto me.

　　　　　John Black, 'XXIII. Psalm paraphrased'
　　　　fc.107, before p. 55

To840　The Lord and King whose presence doth surround
　　　　Silver, as owning Christ the only King.

　　　　　'Mat. 17.27'
　　　　c.160, fol. 53

To841　The Lord ascends his lofty throne
　　　　That I have wrought my God for thee.

　　　　　P[hilip] Doddridge, 'On Isaiah VI. 8'
　　　　c.493, p. 62

To842　The Lord doth reign; Messiah takes,
　　　　For holy is the Lord.

　　　　　'Psalm 99'
　　　　c.264/2, p. 110

To843　The Lord have mercy on the poet's head,
　　　　Thou'lt write an age, and not deserve a bit.

　　　　　[Robert Cholmeley], 'To Mr. Pattison Coll: Sid: who
　　　　　by a lampoon paid off a coffee house debt'
　　　　c.190, p. 63

To844　The Lord Himself, yea God the Lord,
　　　　Saith God, and my salvation see.

　　　　　'Psalm 50 Morning prayer 10 day'
　　　　c.264/1, p. 219

To845　The Lord how kind are all his ways
　　　　In thy much-injur'd grace.

　　　　　P[hilip] Doddridge, 'Backsliding sinners invited to
　　　　　return from Hos. II 6,7. And I would hedge up &c.'
　　　　c.493, p. 42

T0846　The Lord how kind are his returns
　　　　And long for you to share.

　　　　　T[homas] S[tevens], 'Same evening [4 January 1781]'

　　　　c.259, p. 110

T0847　The Lord is great, and greatly to be praised;
　　　　Will give us an eternity to sing.

　　　　　'Soliloquies [3]'

　　　　c.153, p. 153

T0848　The Lord is my shepherd my guardian my guide,
　　　　Be content all my life and resign'd at my death.

　　　　　[John Byrom]

　　　　c.362, p. 50

T0849　The Lord is only my support
　　　　My life forever spend.

　　　　　[William Whittingham], 'The 9 psalm for assurance
　　　　　of God's protection and guiding' [verses from
　　　　　Psalm 23]
　　　　　[Crum T941]

　　　　a.3, fol. 75v

T0850　The Lord is our defense and aid,
　　　　Build up thy walls and love it still.

　　　　　[John Hopkins and William Whittingham], 'The 20
　　　　　psalm for deliverance out of trouble and safety under
　　　　　providence' [verses from Psalms 46, 51]
　　　　　[cf. Crum T942]

　　　　a.3, fol. 95

T0851　The Lord mine innocence defends;
　　　　To sing thy mercy, love, and praise.

　　　　　[ ] C., 'Psalm the 23rd'

　　　　c.368, p. 108

T0852　The Lord my pasture shall prepare,
　　　　And streams shall murmur all around.

　　　　　[Joseph] Ad[dison? or Elizabeth Carter?], 'A steady
　　　　　reliance on God Almighty beautifully represented by
　　　　　David in his 23d psalm, and translated thus'

　　　　c.547, p. 153; c.259, p. 15; fc.132/1, p. 42; c.144, p. 133

T0853　The Lord of heaven and earth hath made a feast
　　　　T' have too much pepper, and too little salt.

　　　　　[Francis Quarles], 'On the spiritual feast'

　　　　b.137, p. 185

T0854　The lord of Houghton guideth me
　　　　My loit'ring place, shall be.

　　　　　'A Thanksgiving ode, addressed to the Lord of
　　　　　Houghton Hall [Robert Walpole] anno 1735 in the
　　　　　style and manner of Sternhold' [burlesque of
　　　　　Psalm 23]

　　　　Poetry Box x/34

T0855　The Lord Omnipotent doth reign
　　　　His truth, and former mercies sing.

　　　　　'Psalm 97'

　　　　c.264/2, p. 107

T0856　The Lord on me lifts up his light,
　　　　Thine heart! Confide in Him.

　　　　　'Psalm 27. Evening prayer'

　　　　c.264/1, p. 107

T0857　The Lord presides, great King of kings,
　　　　The justice of Thy reign.

　　　　　'Psalm 82 Evening prayer. 16 day'

　　　　c.264/2, p. 74

T0858　The Lord receives his highest praise
　　　　Unless that Grace has made him free?

　　　　　[William Cowper], 'A living and a dead faith'

　　　　c.141, p. 581

T0859　The Lord, the holy God thus spake
　　　　E'er he triumphant lift his head.

　　　　　'Psalm 110. Another meter morning prayer 23 day'

　　　　c.264/3, facing p. 35

T0860　The Lord the sovereign sends his summons forth,
　　　　Your trembling souls and no deliverers near.

　　　　　Isaac Watts, 'Psalm 50'

　　　　c.244, p. 176

T0861　The Lord was pleas'd to glorify himself;
　　　　God tried his patience further with a wife.

　　　　　R[obert] Shirley, 1st earl of Ferrers, 'Audoeni
　　　　　epigramma'

　　　　c.347, p. 49

T0862　The Lord will happiness divine
　　　　And heal it, if it be.

　　　　　[William] Cowper, 'The contrite heart'

　　　　c.141, p. 579

T0863　The lord you honor with your father's alliance
　　　　That both the Inds are not of greater value.

　　　　　Sir Thomas Urquhart, 'To the Countess of [crossed
　　　　　out]'

　　　　fb.217, p. 73

T0864　The Lord's almighty arm
　　　　To rest my weary head.

　　　　　'An evening hymn.—Praise the Lord likewise at
　　　　　evening. 1 Chron. 23—30th'

　　　　c.487, p. 120

T0865 The Lords and Commons having had their doom,
The Lords' vexation, and the King's by God.

> 'The character' [c. July 1679]
> [Crum T964; POAS II.135]
> b.54, p. 1140; b.371, no. 20 ('land's vexation')

T0866 The Lords craved all, and the Queen granted all
Without God's mercy the great devil will have all.

> 'The view of our late state under Queen Elizabeth'
> [Crum T965, 'The state of France . . . 1585']
> b.54, p. 881

T0867 The loss of goods I do lament,
Cannot be call'd again.

> b.234, p. 175

T0868 The loss of things I grieve but more of days,
Each stops that ill, but time for no man stays.

> R[obert] Shirley, 1st earl of Ferrers, 'Ep: ignota autore damna fleo rerum &c'
> c.347, p. 17

T0869 The loss of time all other loss exceeds,
And evermore it late repentance breeds.

> c.339, p. 321

T0870 The [?] lost years in slav'ry spent,
Blesses his God, and peaceful dies.

> John Lockman, 'To the King: on presenting His Majesty with newly arrived Shetland herrings. Sent from the Council of the Free British Fishery . . . Sept. 1761'
> c.267/1, p. 276

T0871 The loud wind roar'd, the rain fell fast,
Remembrance of the Negro's care.

> 'A Negro song'
> c.83/3, no. 1055

T0872 The love of God how oft do I name?
I'm sure, I want naught else to perfect bliss.

> [Edmund Wodehouse], 'July 30 [1715]'
> b.131, p. 237

T0873 The lovely owner of this book
And Sacharissa died unsung.

> 'Written in a lady's Waller'
> b.201, p. 141

T0874 The lovely Salmacis, the fountain own'd
And as they mingled souls their bodies join'd.

> [Charles Hopkins], 'The story of Salmacis and Hermaphroditus from the fourth book of Ovid's Metamorphoses'
> b.130, p. 99

T0875 The lowest shrubs have tops the ant her gall
They hear and see and sigh and then they break.

> [Sir Edward Dyer], 'On few words'
> [Crum T974]
> b.205, fol. 84v; see also 'The smallest trees . . .'.

T0876 The lowing herds in wild disorder lay,
A lasting monument of deathless fame.

> H[enry] Skrine, 'Prize poem at Batheaston Elegy on departed friends . . . Bath—March 25th 1779'
> c.509, p. 21

T0877 The lowland lads think they are fine
Our lowland lass and her highland laddie.

> [Allan Ramsay], 'The lowland laddie'
> [Crum T975]
> fc.61, p. 63 (incomplete?)

T0878 The lustful vigorous cock, that breeds well, pecks
And fit for business, then the hen necks him.

> 'Hen-pecked und: derivatur'
> c.81/1, no. 34

T0879 The maggot bites, I must begin;
For I'm a Goddikin already.

> Rup[ert] Barnesley, 'Vermin' [written for the Lent Probation at the Merchant Taylor's School, 1700]
> [Crum T979]
> Poetry Box VI/79

T0880 The magic muse in gothic days of yore
Approve your judgment and your taste commend.

> [( ) King], 'To the author of the Regent [Bertie Greatheed]'
> Greatheed Box/42

T0881 The maid is blest that will not hear
Shall rot in Drury Lane!

> A[lexander] Pope, 'A version of the first psalm for the use of a young lady' [pr. 1716 (Foxon P953)]
> c.74; c.265, p. 24

T0882 The maiden's secrets lock'd must be,
Unlock my secret if you dare—or can.

> 'Another [apology for the present fasion of the ladies' wearing keys on their breasts]'
> c.83/1, no. 140

T0883 The man, and wife before were two,
Which were but one.

> Sir Thomas Urquhart, 'The husband, the wife: the father, and the son'
> fb.217, p. 190

T0884   The man, dear Bret, that wears a condom,
And dare all foul diseases but the muggles.

> [Roger Boyle], 1st earl of Orrery, 'In praise of a
> condom'

c.189, p. 161

T0885   The man, dear Sir, whose spotless life is pure
The sweetly smiling sweetly speaking Lalage.

> '[Horace book 1 ode 22] by another hand'

c.578, p. 132

T0886   The man I choos'd to lie with me,
There riseth nothing on him.

> Sir Thomas Urquhart, 'The grievous complaint of a
> young lass, who had married an old man'

fb.217, p. 149

T0887   The man, (I mean not to deceive
As honest as his neighbor.

> 'Epitaph on a poor hard-working man'

c.487, p. 57

T0888   The man is blest who from the taint
To perish in their ways.

> 'Psalm 1. Morning prayer' [1st day]

c.264/1, p. 1

T0889   The man is blest who lives in fear
Whilst he, and his desires, decay.

> 'Psalm 112 Hallelujah'

c.264/3, p. 36

T0890   The man is blest whose wickedness
Be glad and eke rejoice.

> [Thomas Sternhold], 'The 12 psalm for remission of
> sins and release of sickness' [verses from Psalm 32]
> [Crum T989]

a.3, fol. 8ov

T0891   The man styl'd immortal in thirst after glory,
As the rabble have done shoes and stockings before.

> [on Louis XIV]

fb.68, p. 21

T0892   The man that careth not in youth
The vicious path refuse.

b.234, p. 28

T0893   The man that fell by faction's strife,
Of great St. Paul the second.

> 'St. Paul the second' [on the Jacobite William Paul; pr.
> 1716 (Foxon P571]

fc.58, p. 83

T0894   The man that good is, hardly will
Be seen it hardly to be so.

> Sir John Strangways, '22do Januarii 1646[/7]'

b.304, p. 71

T0895   The man that is drunk is void of all care,
And when I'm dead drunk, then I'll stagger away.

> 'Song 86'

c.555, p. 135

T0896   The man that puts his trust in God
Shall everlasting praises sing.

> 'Epitaph 1st [High Wycombe, Buckinghamshire]'

c.158, p. 83

T0897   The man that suffers, overcomes but then:
The suffering woman's overcome by men.

> 'Patience'

c.356

T0898   The man, that would know how a county to ride
You'll be certainly down in the mire.

> 'The lieutenant a most curious and diverting English
> ballad'

Poetry Box x/29

T0899   The man that's resolute and just,
By mean ignoble verse.

> [William] Walsh, [Horace, Odes III.iii, imitated; pr.
> 1706 (Foxon W33)]
> [Crum T1000]

fb.66/33; c.351, p. 89 (stanzas 1–4)

T0900   The man 'tis plain whoe'er maliciously
Backbites his friend, will do the same by thee.

c.361

T0901   The man to Jove did thus apply
Henceforth to me resign the rest.

> [Daniel Bellamy, the elder], 'The farmer and Jupiter.
> Fable 23rd' [from Æsop]

c.186, p. 71

T0902   The man who feels the dear disease
Molly you may believe him true.

> [Lady Mary Wortley Montagu], 'L'homme qui ne se
> trove point, et qui ne se trouvera jamais. By the same'

fc.51, p. 56

T0903   The man who first should heavenly things attain,
First undergoes the world with might and main.

c.339, p. 328

T0904 The man who walks in wisdom's ways
And by him shall be ever bless'd.

[Mary Pluret], 'Another by way of anagram to a friend [Thomas Young]'

c.354

T0905 The man who weds alone for gain,
Bad meals are better still, than none.

Frederick Corfield, 'Dick Dismal'

c.381/2

T0906 The man who would of friendship write,
No noisy court must know, nor guilty town.

'To Mrs. Belle Marrow with a sermon on friendship— 1719'

b.322, p. 36

T0907 The man whom falsehood guides, will find the dart
He venom'd shoots, transfix'd in his own heart.

'The moral' [to a prose fable, The shepherd's boy]

c.93

T0908 The man whom thou, Melpomene,
And if I please, O! Muse! I please thro' thee.

[William Popple, trans.], '[Horace] book 4th. Ode 3d. To Melpomene'

fc.104/2, p. 340

T0909 The man who's favored by almighty God
That makes a spring to be in barren land.

'Heb. 9.4'

c.160, fol. 55v

T0910 The man whose breast, no gentler passions fire,
Great source of being, light, and happiness!

'To a young lady'

c.89, p. 59

T0911 The man, whose conscious innocence
On sweetly smiling Lalage.

[William Mills], 'Odes of Horace translated. Book I. Ode XXII. To Aristius Fuscus'

c.472, p. 26

T0912 The man, whose days of youth and ease
And hates the world he made so bad.

'The hermitage'

fc.51, p. 258

T0913 The man whose life is innocent and plain,
And with fair peace attended, makes us bless'd.

'On innocence'

c.83/3, no. 942

T0914 The manly mean preserves its state
'Tween sordid and effeminate.

[John Hobart]

b.108, fol. 3

T0915 The man's authority is love
The holy writ's man's evidence.

[Sir Philip Wodehouse], 'Upon Dr. Taylor's warning'

b.131, p. 6

T0916 The many great favors I often have known
Dick Leveridge's play with your int'rest and vote. |
Derry down, down, down, derry down.

'A whimsical advertisement of Mr. Leveridge's The relapse (or virtue in danger) a comedy, written by Sir John Vanbrugh being to be acted at the Theater Royal in Covent Garden for his benefit—the tune—A cobbler there was, &c . . . Wednesday the 16th of April 1746'

c.360/2, no. 17

T0917 The masquerades were now begun
And then they went to bed.

[Elizabeth (Shirley) Compton, countess of Northampton], 'A ballad, to the tune of I'll tell thee Dick &c.'

Accession 97.7.40 (2 copies)

T0918 The master operator, now exclaims
And clears and lights at once the wat'ry way.

[James Mulcaster, sr.], 'A specimen of a poem upon refining'

c.118, p. 24

T0919 The match propos'd by you, (dear friend!)
To muse upon't—ev'n till I die.

John Lockman, 'Look before you leap, an epigram, by Mr. de Mauroix'

c.267/4, p. 147

T0920 The mayor of Harford in a rage
For thou shalt be a horse when he's no mare.

'Upon the mayor of Harford that [im]pounded a horse that cast his rider'

b.62, p. 118

T0921 The mayor's dead, rejoice ye scholars all
[?] will be cheap when such great calves do fall.

'On Mr. Perse Mayor of Cambridge'

b.356, p. 243

T0922 The meanest flower instruction does contain,
An emblem of her transient self in thee.

H[annah] More, 'The speech of a rose gathered by a gentleman at four in the morning and sent to a young woman who lay in bed late . . . June 28th 1767'

c.341, p. 27

T0923　The meditation of our dying day
They would say death were nothing but a dream.

　　　Sir John Strangways, 'Of the meditation of death. Or
　　　a preparation to death . . . 1647[/8] Feb. 14'

　　　b.304, p. 115

T0924　The meekest of creatures inheriting earth
Contending to clasp the fair nymph in his arms.

　　　'Rebus on Miss Lamborn of Hackney [later
　　　Brooksbank] 1741'

　　　c.360/1, p. 263 and 321 (incomplete)

T0925　The melancholious influence of Saturn
Christ being our light, our life, and prototype.

　　　Sir Thomas Urquhart, 'The several Sabbaths of the
　　　Christians, Turks, and Jews'

　　　fb.217, p. 87

T0926　The mem'ry of our dying Lord
But dwell at th'heavenly feast.

　　　[Isaac Watts, Hymns and spiritual songs (1707),
　　　bk. III, Hymn 15]

　　　c.180, p. 49

T0927　The memory of what hath been discloseth
Than yours, which none of them could yet make
　　　　　　　　　　　　　　　　　　　　　faulty.

　　　Sir Thomas Urquhart, 'To my Lady [crossed out]'

　　　fb.217, p. 244

T0928　The merchant Dick dilapidated hath
So that he hath no more to lose, but love.

　　　Sir Thomas Urquhart, 'Of a merchant, broke in his
　　　credit, and disdained of his mistress'

　　　fb.217, p. 124

T0929　The merchant in his dalliance was so bold,
Then measured by his yard the sticks thereof.

　　　Sir Thomas Urquhart

　　　fb.217, p. 272

T0930　The merchant wish the lawyers train,
But mind unstayed still discontent.

　　　[Sir Nicholas] Bacon, 'Against inconstancy'

　　　fa.8, fol. 164v

T0931　The mercies of the wicked cruel are
Mercies that shall forevermore endure.

　　　Sir John Strangways, 'De miserecordia Domine . . .
　　　24° Martii 1647[/8]'

　　　b.304, p. 126

T0932　The merry world did on a day
And then they have their answer home.

　　　George Herbert, 'The quip'
　　　[Crum T1023]

　　　c.139, p. 124

T0933　The midnight clock has toll'd, and hark the bell
Should be by all, or suffer'd, or enjoy'd.

　　　[William Mason], 'On the death of Lady Coventry'
　　　[1760]

　　　c.53, fol. 85; fc.132/1, p. 83; c.83/4, no. 2017 (ll. 1–36)

T0934　The midnight moon serenely smiles,
The music of the mind.

　　　[Elizabeth Carter], 'Inquiry after happiness'
　　　[Crum T1024]

　　　c.83/3, no. 827

T0935　The mighty difference of man from man,
For thereon do depend our real bliss.

　　　[Edmund Wodehouse], 'Octr. 20 1714'

　　　b.131, p. 63

T0936　The mighty great lamp from the rich sea will take
He might have given much more, with much more
　　　　　　　　　　　　　　　　　　　　　pleasure.

　　　[ ] Francis

　　　fb.23. p. 269

T0937　The mighty monarch of the British isle
Your souls to Rome but send the Pope to hell.

　　　'The deponents 88' [on the birth of the Old
　　　Pretender]
　　　[Crum T1031]

　　　File 17416

T0938　The mighty oak, that shrinks not with a blast,
With rage thereoft is broken down at last.

　　　c.339, p. 327

T0939　The mighty zeal which thou hast new put on,
Hereafter may take up the Whitsun ale!

　　　[Richard Corbett], 'To Mr [John] Hammond of
　　　Bewdley, for beating down the Maypole' [attr. John
　　　Harris]
　　　[Crum T1032]

　　　b.200, p. 238

T0940　The mildness of your countenance would soften
Which I may well admire, but not express.

　　　Sir Thomas Urquhart, 'To the Countess of [crossed
　　　out]'

　　　fb.217, p. 41

T0941 The ministers, (for the most part) of all
Heave shoulder, were the Levites' property.

> Sir Thomas Urquhart, 'The temporal felicity, which
> our Scots preachers enjoy, by having the jolliest
> dapper women to their wives, of all the parish and the
> best liquor in their houses, that the country can afford'
>
> fb.217, p. 243

T0942 The minstrel bards of Albion's elder days
Of old to valor and to beauty due.

> [Sir William Young?], 'London chronicle, April 25th
> 1778. On reading the second volume of Mr. Warton's
> History of English poetry just published'
>
> File 16591

T0943 The minstrels, (Ben alive,) in days of yore,
How whimsical a change in things is found!

> John Lockman, 'On the refusal of tickets to the poets,
> who write for the Academy of Music, in the Apollo
> (formerly Ben Jonson's room) in the Devil tavern . . .
> Jan. 1741/2'
>
> c.267/1, p. 26

T0944 The minutes, the hours, the days, and the year
For time can ne'er change, nor destroy.

> [John Hoadly], 'Song'
>
> c.241, p. 87

T0945 The miracles done
If religion proves worth a year's purchase.

> 'A song on the new bishops' [1691]
> [Crum T1035]
>
> b.111, p. 114; fb.207/3, p. 46; see also 'For the
> miracles . . .'.

T0946 The miser starts and trembling stares,
'Are blessings worthy of a god.'

> 'The miser and Plutus' [from Æsop, fable 6]
>
> c.186, p. 70

T0947 The mist so hinders objects from the eye
[?] [?] his tears and sigh at all he sighs.

> [John Black], 'To the rock of Roseneath on my
> return—Novr. 1797'
>
> fc.107, before p. 79

T0948 The modest snowdrop emblem of fair truth,
A warm reception in a gen'rous mind.

> Ann Murry, '. . . Modesty adds a grace to every other
> virtue'
>
> c.248

T0949 The modest water awed by power divine
Confess'd thee God, and blush'd itself to wine.

> 'On Christ's turning water into wine . . . per a scholar
> at Dr. Busby's'
> [Crum T1043]
>
> c.186, p. 48; c.81/1, no. 36

T0950 The modish wit's debauch't—fancy's debas't
To judge what's truly just, what's good, what's great.

> [Sir Philip Wodehouse], 'Upon his son Sr Francis
> North (now judge) Francis North Fancy r'enthrones'
>
> b.131, back (no. 6 [bis])

T0951 The monarch of Athina hath a stone
Flows from that jewel worth a world of treasure.

> [Sir Thomas Urquhart], How much more acceptable
> the king of Athina's stone would be to the lords and
> dames of this age than the philosopher's alchemistic
> one'
>
> fb.217, p. 388

T0952 The moon and woman in these points agree,
The moon but once a month, but woman every day.

> 'Epigramma [translated]'
>
> c.81/1, no. 86

T0953 The moon had climb'd the highest hill
Sweet Mary weep no more for me.

> [( ) Low, of New York], 'Mary's dream'
>
> c.140, p. 254

T0954 The moon was set, no stars in th' skies did shine,
A prince the most benign and debonair.

> 'On His Majesty's military sports at Windsor.
> London: printed for S.N.R.F. 1674'
>
> b.54, p. 905

T0955 The moonbeam rests on Kenmore heath;
To perish at his side.

> [Thomas] Gisborne, 'Orgil'
>
> File 5815

T0956 The moon's pale luster, and the lamp's dim ray
She's the selfsame dear charming still.

> c.186, p. 46

T0957 The more entirely we resign
That is, more favored by Thee.

> [Edmund Wodehouse], 'Ibidem [Epiphany, 1715]'
>
> b.131, p. 133

T0958 The more I praise them for the innate worth,
The countenancing of seditious factions.

> Sir Thomas Urquhart, 'Concerning the encomiums I
> bestow on covenanters'
>
> fb.217, p. 54

T0959 The more I think, the more I may
Shall call us to eternity.

    H[enry] C[olman], 'On death'
    [Crum T1047]

    b.2, p. 35

T0960 The more, that others you perceive to wallow
Of virtues, serving to adorn the soul.

    Sir Thomas Urquhart, 'To my Lady [crossed out]'

    fb.217, p. 70

T0961 The more, you give him, he's the more your friend:
The more, you trust him, he's the more unkind.

    Sir Thomas Urquhart, 'To a wealthy merchant
    concerning a bad debtor'

    fb.217, p. 206

T0962 The morn was clear, and the new-rising sun
Let this, Sir, be the bus'ness of today.

    [Joseph Spence], 'Thoughts for a birthday'

    Spence Papers, folder 155

T0963 The morning flowers display their sweets,
If firm the word of God remains.

    [ ] Lewis, 'Isaiah 40. 6. 8. verses paraphrased on the
    occasion of the death of a young lady'

    c.244, p. 191

T0964 The morning red did rise in sky
Prepare for us to heaven the way. | Amen

    'Of S. Michael. Sep. 29'

    a.30[40]

T0965 The morning smiles, the glorious sun is drest,
And may that standard happiness the world admire.

    Musgrave Heighington, 'To Richard Wallin esq. [on
    Ann Alethea's wedding] . . . Spalding August 15th.
    1751'

    c.229/2, fol. 73

T0966 The most aspiring spirits you embalm,
With courage, t'imitate your high deserts.

    Sir Thomas Urquhart, 'To my Lord [crossed out]'

    fb.217, p. 249

T0967 The most lascivious sparks of womankind
Which though required were refus'd to many.

    [Sir Thomas Urquhart]

    fb.217, p. 542

T0968 The moth so long with candle she doth play,
Till he consume them with his scourging rod.

    b.234, p. 26

T0969 The mother, lovely, tho' with grief opprest,
That death repented he had given the stroke.

    [John] Dryden, 'On the death of an infant'

    c.83/1, no. 119

T0970 The mountain Ætna (poets say)
Doth waste with angry fumes.

    'Dourte [Dort?] hand'

    b.234, p. 27, p. 122 ('Ætna with his flames')

T0971 The mountain lark day's herald, got on wing,
And nodding with her head he thus kept time.

    'The birds' consort'

    b.356, p. 121

T0972 The mournful silence of the quiet night
The morn appears and I must fly.

    [ ] Prigher, 'On the untimely death of Sidney Montagu
    esquire, who accompanying his noble kinsman the earl
    of Sandwich perished in the fight against the
    Dutch . . . 28 of May 1672'

    fb.68, p. 83

T0973 The moving heavens, the fixed stars contain:
But the fix'd earth, doth moving souls sustain.

    Sir Thomas Urquhart, 'Rest in motion, and motion on
    rest'

    fb.217, p. 190

T0974 The muse in haste has snatch'd her lyre
And heart hereafter meet your view.

    [Mary Cornwallis?], 'Written the morning of
    Caroline [Cornwallis]'s birthday July 12'

    fc.124, p. 113

T0975 The muse this morn, surpris'd to find
And wonder'd at the flame.

    'An answer to the foregoing ['Muse see thy
    favorite . . .', on Miss Betty Jeffreys; answered by 'To
    you my guide . . .' and 'Dear Betty leave . . .']

    c.360/1, p. 29

T0976 The muse who, in her infant days,
O! had [?] the royal youth.

    John Lockman, 'An ode to the Earl of Bute, with the
    following poem ['Truth: a vision. Most humbly
    addressed to the Prince of Wales: on his royal
    highness's birthday, June 4, 1758. Presented to his
    royal highness at Savile House'] . . . 2 June 1758'

    c.267/4, p. 10

T0977 The muse whom conscious virtue warms,
The flatt'ring portrait—show her you.

    'To [blank] with some satiric verses on Miss
    Chudleigh'

    c.89, p. 103

T0978 The muse whose sorrows darken'd Hagley's groves,
But leaves to mercy's God his final doom.

    'On the death of Lord Lyttelton a dissipated young
    man (son of the poet Lord L.) who died in February
    1780 [actually November 1779]'

    c.250

T0979 The muses all to Charlotte's choice pretend
And I half pleas'd and half affrighted woke.

    Ralph Broome, 'The dream of Ralph Broome esqr.'

    c.486, fol. 31v

T0980 The muses, grown sick of the nonsense of fools,
For naught can be worse than the plague of such
                                 rhymes!

    R[ichard] V[ernon] S[adleir], 'On hearing some
    copies of verses on several occasions'

    c.106, p. 126

T0981 The muses, on Parnassus Hill,
And shows them—all in one.

    John Lockman, 'To Mr. Champion: on his parallel (or
    imitations) of the most celebrated foreign writing
    masters . . . Sept. 1750'

    c.267/1, p. 53

T0982 The muses once esteem'd her beauty's boast
Obtain'd the chariot, set the world on fire.

    [Horace Walpole, 4th earl of Orford], 'D[uchess] of
    Queens[ber]ry' [d. 1777]
    [Crum T1066b]

    c.157, p. 67

T0983 The muses quite jaded with rhyming
To sing to the praise of Lepell.

    [Philip Dormer Stanhope, 4th earl of Chesterfield,
    'On Mrs. (Mary) Lepell' (baroness Hervey)]
    [Crum T1067]

    Poetry Box x/130

T0984 The muses were on Pindus met,
And plac'd it in lov'd Irby's hand.

    John Lockman, 'The muses, Mercury, and fame. On
    occasion of Sir William Irby's being enacted(?) Lord
    Boston [in Lincolnshire] . . . anno 1761'

    c.267/2, p. 314

T0985 The music of light-wafted sighs,
To envy we resign the rest.

    [Richard] Polwhele, 'To —— written at Manacan,
    1794'

    c.141, p. 559

T0986 The name of a game, that is [torn] in repute,
For what is much eate[n?] which you've to find out.

    'A rebus'

    c.360/3, no. 207

T0987 The name that you give to a garment not wore,
And the whole is the name of a sweet rural place.

    'A rebus'

    c.360/3, no. 89

T0988 The nature of death with horror strikes the soul,
Death in itself cannot afford much pain.

    'The following verses on death were spoke at a public
    scool in Edinburgh . . . 1732'

    c.160, fol. 69

T0989 The needle, which she oftest hath in hand
Through th'ocean of her water.

    Sir Thomas Urquhart, 'Of a lady, who had some skill
    in the art of navigation'

    fb.217, p. 239

T0990 The next in place, and punishment, are they
And, with nine circling streams, the captive souls
                                  enclose.

    [John] Dryden

    fc.14/10

T0991 The next that mounts the stage is the physician,
But kill they ne'er so oft, there's nothing said.

    'Of the physician' [Poor Robin's almanac]

    c.186, p. 140

T0992 The night-flood rakes upon the stony shore;
And shuns the eyes, that only wake to weep!

    [Charlotte (Turner) Smith], 'Sonnet written in a
    tempestuous night, on the coast of Sussex'

    c.141, p. 108

T0993 The night in sweet slumbers roll'd swiftly away
Their province is railing whilst ours is pleasure.

    Fanny Macartney, 'Fanny Macartney to Peggy Banks'

    fc.135; fc.51, p. 26

T0994 The night rush'd forth and with her brought,
You greatly rate the deed—as greatly then bestow.

    Anna Matilda, 'The chosen physician by . . . Paris
    March 15th 1789'

    c.344, p. 99

T0995 The night was calm, the flow'ry meadows gay,
Since far more solid pleasures are found here.

    Miss[ ] Jessop, 'A prospect from Tapton Hill'

    fc.61, p. 85

T0996 The night was dark, the wind blew cold;
Vain boy, to pierce my breast thine arrows are too
                                  weak.

    'Love and age'

    c.83/3, no. 888

T0997 The night was first: yet may I boldly say,
That the day's elder than the night b' a day.

> Sir Thomas Urquhart, 'Whether the night, or the day
> be of greatest age'

fb.217, p. 137

T0998 The nimble fairies on the grounds
It brushes off the wither[ed] leaves.

> John Black

fc.107, p. 19

T0999 The nineteenth of May recorded once did stand,
For God this country and their King.

> Mary Cornwallis, 'Song—the first of June . . . 1794'

fc.124, p. 115

T1000 The Ninevites believe the word
God reverst and chang'd his sentence.

c.158, p. 50

T1001 The noblest object in the works of art;
An ancient city that is much renown'd.

> [Anna Seward], 'A rebus'

c.157, p. 52; c.389

T1002 The noise of foreign wars
And make thee equal to the cradle of Jove.

> 'For her royal highness the Princess Anne of Denmark
> [later Queen Anne] on the birth of [William] the
> Duke of Gloucester sung at Hampton Court' [24 July
> 1689]

fb.108, p. 97

T1003 The noisy world complains of me,
And virtue stands the mark of universal spite.

> [Isaac] Watts, 'Solitude—addressed to Thomas
> Gunston esqr.'

c.244, p. 322

T1004 The noon was shady and soft airs
To him who gives me all.

> [William Cowper], 'The dog and the waterlily. No
> fable'

c.139, p. 520

T1005 The noontide hour is past, and toil is o'er
And mourn'd by such as they who weep for thee.

> C. Lipscomb, 'Elegy on the death of Dr. Warton . . .
> 1800'

c.495, p. 9

T1006 The northern man is fair the southern foul
Frolic the French, the Spaniard furious.

> [Robert Cottesford]

b.144, p. 10

T1007 The nurse of contemplation, night,
Give vigor to the mind.

> [John] Cunningham, 'The contemplatist: a night
> piece'

c.156, p. 221; see also 'The queen of contemplation . . .'.

T1008 The nurse—the doctor—and the midwife came!
And only had conceiv'd herself with child.

> 'A misconception'

c.81/1, no. 402

T1009 The nymph that cries, is much to blame
Weep out a brighter pair?

> [Robert Cholmeley], 'To a young lady crying for the
> loss of a pair of diamond earrings'

c.190, p. vi

T1010 The nymph that undoes me is fair and unkind,
Who sees her must love and who loves her must die.

> [Sir George Etherege], 'A song'
> [Crum T1098]

c.358, p. 2; fb.107, p. 15, p. 31(both incomplete); c.549,
p. 94

T1011 The objects which in spring are seen,
Enjoy your riches ere you die.

> 'An imitation of the 7th ode lib 4th of Horace'

c.233, p. 5

T1012 The Odysseys, and Iliads of Homer
And th'other shunn'd her paramour's embraces.

> Sir Thomas Urquhart, 'The paralleled renown of
> continency, and lubricity'

fb.217, p. 151

T1013 The ointments of your rare endowments favor
Sweeter than at the sugars of the east.

> Sir Thomas Urquhart, 'To the Earl of [crossed out]'

fb.217, p. 39

T1014 The old Egyptian[s] hid their wit
But folly's at full length.

> [Philip Dormer Stanhope, 4th earl of Chesterfield],
> 'Upon a whole length picture [by William Hoare] of
> Mr. Nash, placed between the busts of Sr Isaac
> Newton and Mr. Pope, in Lovelace's great room at
> Bath, placed so high that they are not well seen'
> [Crum T1101]

fc.51, p. 35; c.360/1, p. 131; see also 'Immortal
Newton . . .'.

T1015 The old game's again on trial,
Hark on the hawthorn-tree &c.

c.416

T1016 The old luxurious Romans vaunts did make
       If y' are not happy who the devil is?

    [Sir Aston Cokayne], 'To my brother in law Colonel
    Will Nevill'

    b.275, p. 58

T1017 The old Sicilian fox
       Before his side of Bacon.

    [on Sir Francis Bacon and Robert Cecil, earl of
    Salisbury]
    [Crum T1103a]

    b.197, p. 202

T1018 The one and twenty day of June
       John Fiddle went out of tune.

    'On John Fiddle'
    [Crum T1105a, 'John Fidler']

    b.356, p. 240

T1019 The one thing needful that good part
       And make me pure and clean within.

    'Hymn 8th'

    c.562, p. 9

T1020 The only wi[s]dom of a man
       That peace that ever shall endure.

    [Edmund Wodehouse], 'Feb. 11 [1715]'

    b.131, p. 164

T1021 The open heart, the polish'd mind,
       In the distressful struggle break!

    'Constantia—an elegy'

    c.140, p. 42

T1022 The optative is near the infinitive,
       For still ourselves we wish well, whilst we live.

    Sir Thomas Urquhart, 'Of endless desires'

    fb.217, p. 351

T1023 The other day at noon I stray'd,
       Those fatal eyes have pierc'd my heart.

    S. W., 'For the English chronicle, imitation of the 23d
    basium of Bonefonius'

    c.175, p. 85

T1024 The other day says Ned to Joe
       But then there's nothing in it.

    c.546, p. 20

T1025 The other morn at Phoebus rise
       Smiling I bade them both adieu.

    Miss [ ] Andrews, 'On seeing two young ladies making
    a bed'

    File 245/6

T1026 The overspreading reign of night
       And loud the eternal triumph sung.

    [Thomas Gibbons], 'The triumph of religion. A
    vision'

    c.139, p. 69

T1027 The painter brought the picture home;
       When thou art wither'd and decay'd.

    'The lady and her picture'

    c.83/3, no. 932

T1028 The painter, in whim as diverting as new,
       A dog when living, and a hare when dead.

    [Charles Earle], 'One side of a sign, wretchedly
    painted, a creature (instead of a hare hunted) appears
    like a dog: the other, the same creature (supposed to
    be killed) appears like an hare'

    c.376 (2 copies)

T1029 The painter's daring genius knows no laws
       Grasp at the bays, and try to sing like you.

    [Robert Cholmeley], 'To Mr. Drake AM lecturer'

    c.190, p. 75

T1030 The palace turn'd with ceaseless motion round
       Increasing as it goes from mouth to mouth.

    'The palace of fame imitated by Ovid and Chaucer'

    c.172, p. 40

T1031 The panting farewell spoke the adieu
       Nor her soft heart in chains of pearl been dy'd.

    '[From] yr grandson'

    File 13409

T1032 The papists cry up blind obedience
       They strive for truth, but from all peace depart.

    Sir John Strangways

    b.304, p. 33

T1033 The papists, God wot,
       Rid post in a cloud, to the Devil.

    'On the 5th of Novr.'
    [Crum T1117]

    c.233, p. 51

T1034 The Parliament sits with synod of wits
       . . . for Count Mansfield is come, | And lodged in
                                            her ladyship's bed.

    'Upon the Parliament. 1624'
    [Crum T1124]

    b.197, p. 201; b.356, p. 269

T1035 The parson and clerk one saint's day after pray'r
       But for my part I never once thought of the Lord.

    James Sellway, 'By . . . a parish clerk'

    Poetry Box III/61

T1036 The parson caught the crabfish
And my mistress['s] c—— together.

'The crabfish'
[Crum T1125]
Poetry Box IV/40

T1037 The parson long since join'd us two together
By far's the better joiner of the two!

[Phanuel Bacon], 'Epitaph on an old woman married
to a young man'
c.237, fol. 3

T1038 The parsons all keep whores
And good Queen Bess's days. | [A pox on all etc.]

'A new ballad to the tune of Chevy Chase'
[Crum T1127, with four more lines]
b.105, p. 392

T1039 The partial muse has, from my earliest hours,
If those paint sorrows best, who feel them most!

Charlotte (Turner) Smith, 'A sonnet wrote by . . . of
Bignor Park'
c.130, p. 79; c.504, p. 84

T1040 The parties, henpeck'd W[illia]m, are thy wives,
He without hair [heir], and thou without a crown.

[Sir Charles Sedley], 'The moral' [of a fable reflecting
on William III's struggle with the Whigs and Tories,
'In Æsop's tales . . .']
[Crum I1229, second part]
c.111, p. 12

T1041 The path of greatness do but slippery prove,
Full oft to those that do ambition love.

c.93

T1042 The paths to hell are s'easy, that the blind
Without a guide, the nearest way may find.

Sir Thomas Urquhart, 'The broad gate to destruction'
fb.217, p. 248

T1043 The patient bl[?], silent stole
Which [?] in the bays of men.

fc.76.iii/182

T1044 The pavement of the boundless main
Clear as the stream, deep as the sea.

'Rebus on Mr Sandford'
c.360/1, p. 89

T1045 The (pawns) have all the sport, and all their say
They have had sufficient checks, beware the mate.

[Thomas Middleton], '[Prologue and epilogue to]
The game at chess' [acted before the Prince of Wales,
March 1641/2]
[Crum T1132]
fb.106(1)

T1046 The peace is now proclaimed you know
For prelacy's but folly.

'Verses on the peace [16]68' [docket title]
Poetry Box VIII/17

T1047 The peace is sign'd, and Mars no more shall rage,
May they, like swans, first sing and then expire.

[Charles Darby], Upon the peace at Ryswick. 1697'
b.63, p. 86; see also ''Tis signed! . . .'.

T1048 The pealing thunders roll along the hill
I bid life's cares a lasting long adieu!

[Frances Burney d'Arblay], 'Sonnet. Written during a
storm'
c.486, fol. 15

T1049 The peasant must attend the painful plow,
And drain their money from them by degrees.

'The fatigues of a great man'
c.570/3, p. 98

T1050 The peasant's blest, who in his cot,
And may good deeds whene'er I die | Record my
fame.

'The peasant after the manner of Mr. Pope's Ode on
solutude'
[Crum T1134]
c.83/3, no. 1032

T1051 The pedantry of schools
With Gresset's parakeet!

R[ichard] V[ernon] S[adleir], 'To Miss Hamilton . . .
in answer to some verses addressed to me, too
flattering for me to copy in which she introduced an
elegy on her deceased goldfinch'
c.106, p. 104

T1052 The pencil's glowing lines, and vast command,
Till the piece sees the last great day, it paints.

[Nicholas] Amhurst, trans., 'On the resurrection as
painted by Mr. Fuller for an altarpiece at Magdelene
College in Oxon. Written in Latin by [Joseph]
Addison' [pr. 1718 (Foxon A204)]
[Crum T1136]
c.244, p. 431

T1053   The people called Quakers once decent and plain
The Lord will not us for his true people own.

> J. Fry, 'A lamentation of the grievous declension,
> amongst the people called Quakers' [1 Sept. 1742]
>
> c.517, fol. 25r

T1054   The people grumble all,
Or the devil take all.

> 'The libel'
>
> fb.140, p. 85

T1055   The people's zeal, makes pastors wealthy, 'nd fat:
The pious parent of a godless brat.

> Sir Thomas Urquhart, 'The pastor, and his people'
>
> fb.217, p. 47

T1056   The Persian finery I hate
I quaff in bowls the sparkling wine.

> 'The thirty-eight[h] ode of the first book of Horace
> imitated'
>
> Poetry Box I/113[3]

T1057   The philosophers, moralists, poets and those
And own this the method to fill up the span.

> 'Song 141'
>
> c.555, p. 194

T1058   The picture of a faithful friend
[?] earth a prelude to the joys of heaven.

> [William Hayley]
>
> File 6957

T1059   The picture of that fish behold in me,
The matchless beauties of the noble mind.

> William Dodd, [in answer to 'Vow'd at her Zephyran
> shrine', on the nautilus]
>
> c.229/2, fol. 72v

T1060   The piercing cold, the stormy wind,
Remember, time is on the wing.

> [Mary] Chandler, 'To the Revd. Dr. S—— —an
> invitation to a morning walk in the spring'
>
> c.351, p. 133

T1061   The piper said, now I begin
The meikel devil going wi' you, | Quod he.

> 'Of Peblis to the play' [from The piper of Peebles?]
>
> c.155, fol. 19v

T1062   The plague of satirists that brook [brood?] of
                           snake[s?]
Unto my prince, whilst I am Lauderdale.

> 'The commissioner's reply and defy both to satires
> and satirists'
>
> Poetry Box VIII/31

T1063   The planets' turqure [sic] colored pavilion,
Than that, which beautifies your lovely face.

> Sir Thomas Urquhart, 'To Lady [crossed out] now
> Lady [crossed out]'
>
> fb.217, p. 199

T1064   The play (great Sir) is done yet needs must fear
Scarce can it die more quickly then 'twas born.

> [Abraham Cowley], 'The epilogue [to The guardian,
> acted before Prince Charles at Cambridge March
> 1641/2]'
> [Crum T1149]
>
> fb.106(1)

T1065   The play is at an end, but where's the plot?
Pray let this prove a year of prose and sense.

> [George Villiers, 2nd] duke of Buck[ingham],
> 'Epilogue to The rehearsal Duke of Buck[ingham]'s
> play'
> [Crum T1148]
>
> b.52/2, p. 129

T1066   The play is done, though not begun you find:
Which none can poison but a popish king.

> 'The epilogue' [to Sir Richard Steele's 'The conscious
> lovers'?]
>
> Poetry Box x/10(5)

T1067   The play is over, and we now are come
Give but one parting clap, and let us go.

> 'An epilogue to Theodosius [a tragedy acted in
> Southwark in 1722] spoke by Theodosius, Leontine,
> Marcian, Atticus, and Pulcheria'
>
> c.360/2, no. 167

T1068   The play of love is now begun
The curtain falls—the play is done.

> 'The play of love'
>
> fc.61, p. 66

T1069   The play of your fingers we so much admire,
And charm'd, cry aloud—'Lo! An infant Apollo!'

> John Lockman, 'To Miss Cassandra Frederick, (ten
> years old,) after hearing her perform on the
> harpsichord'
>
> c.267/1, p. 54

T1070   The pleasant debauches of love are most sweet,
She's asleep when her husband would melt in her
                            arms.

> 'The city miss'
>
> fb.107, p. 48

T1071 The pleasure love's about
A child, that breaks it.

    Sir Thomas Urquhart, 'A parley betwixt Erastes and
    Despina, anent the lawfulness of love'

    fb.217, p. 56

T1072 The pleasure that we take in man
Is broken as her belly.

    Trumbull Box: Poetry Box XIII/84

T1073 The pleasures of the world are snares design'd,
She dwells in heav'nly charms array'd.

    'Thoughts on divine and moral subjects'

    c.83/2, no. 651

T1074 The pleasures preterite did often put her
That she desir'd so ardently t'enjoy it.

    Sir Thomas Urquhart, 'The inclination of a very kind
    woman, represented by the three times, the present,
    bypast, and to come'

    fb.217, p. 156

T1075 The poet Sir has offered to your sight
Till, Sir, that crown be given him by your hand.

    [Roger Boyle], 1st earl of Orrery, 'To the King'

    fb.66/9

T1076 The poets feign in music's praise
That can dispraise this noble art.

    'In commendation of music'
    [Crum T1157]

    b.197, p. 102

T1077 The poets say Chimaera's dire
For clear it is, I lead you by the nose.

    'Ignea vis'

    fc.76.iii/214

T1078 The points of your profession, if you show not,
But I'm for life, and death a covenanter.

    Sir Thomas Urquhart, 'To a very stout man for the
    covenant but an ignorant Christian'

    fb.217, p. 241

T1079 The polish'd arts, which, from the skies,
And, crown'd with roses, dance and sing.

    John Lockman, 'Song for Mr. Shipley's academy,
    Decr. 1760. Set to music by [blank]'

    c.267/2, p. 178

T1080 The poor are never strangers, where they come;
Being nowhere in exile: all where at home.

    Sir Thomas Urquhart, 'The advantage of poverty'

    fb.217, p. 79

T1081 The poor House of Commons by hook or by crook
For he headed the bishops that threw out the bill.

    'A ballad'

    b.327, f. 33v

T1082 The poor man toils and makes his shoulders bare
The rich to him gives food, and clothes to share.

    c.339, p. 313

T1083 The poor that strive with mighty are to blame
And sots that seek the learned to defame.

    c.339, p. 312

T1084 The poplars are fell'd, and adieu to the shade
Have a still shorter date, and die sooner than we.

    [William] Cowper, 'The poplars' [Gentleman's
    magazine, January 1785]
    [Crum T1170]

    c.142, p. 453; c.90

T1085 The pot and the pipe
Twice as in any more.

    'Song 5'
    [Crum T1171, 'pip']

    c.503, p. 60 [bis]

T1086 The pot-gun critic, who would raise a name
And shows that 'tis himself, not thou, art blind.

    John Lockman, 'Writ under a mezzotinto
    representing Mr. Pope . . . May 1744'

    c.267/1, p. 1

T1087 The power of kings (if rightly understood)
Who by their virtues, prove their right divine.

    [William] Somervile, 'Kings'

    c.244, p. 465

T1088 The power of Peter doth all power excel
Should Peter's successors mistake the key.

    [Francis Quarles], 'On Peter's keys' [Divine
    fancies I, 91]

    b.137, p. 174; fb.69, p. 207

T1089 The powers above deny
Admire all virtue in admiring she.

    'On a young gentlewoman'

    b.356, p. 257

T1090 The powers of invitation beam along,
Oh! come great gods, she cries and spreads her
                             arms.

    [Horace Walpole, 4th earl of Orford], 'Viscountess
    Townsh[en]d' [d.1770]
    [Crum T1175]

    c.157, p. 71

T1091 The pow'r that men o'er their own thoughts
On which that soul must soar to heav'nly things.

[Edmund Wodehouse], 'St. Stephen's Day [1714]'

b.131, p. 124

T1092 The pow'rs who rule the boundless deep
Nor meditate offensive praise.

'An ode occasioned by the Duke of Marlborough's
embarking for Ostend anno 1717'

c.73, p. 9

T1093 The presence of the God of grace
And guarded by Thy power.

T[homas] S[tevens]

c.259, p. 135

T1094 The presence of your younger years did grace
A better carriage, nor a choicer mind.

Sir Thomas Urquhart, 'To Sir [crossed out] Lord
[crossed out]'

fb.217, p. 242

T1095 The present time, the preterite, nor future
And by mere industry did's own enlarge.

Sir Thomas Urquhart, 'Upon the tutor of Cromarty,
my great grandfather's younger brother, and my
father's tutor'

fb.217, p. 105

T1096 The pride of ev'ry grove I chose,
The justice of thy Chloe's sorrow.

[Matthew Prior], 'The garland'

c.83/3, no. 978; c.163, p. 21

T1097 The pride of France is lily white
Successive, with sweet William's rich perfume.

'The sweet William written 1746' [on William Duke
of Cumberland]

c.360/2, no. 217

T1098 The prince of hea[l]th is love—the Stagyrite
Is both man's duty, and his dignity.

[Sir Philip Wodehouse], 'Upon my brother J. Cotton's
prose (?): Aristotle'

b.131, p. 19

T1099 The Prince of Heaven, from amidst the throng
Turns earth to Heaven, and makes a stall a throne.

'Christmas Day, 1665'

b.49, p. 17

T1100 The Prince of Wales with all his stately train
There he was found at first and there we leave him.

'On a masque acted before Prince Charles in Spain'
[1623]
[Crum T1189, 'royal train']

b.62, p. 73; b.200, p. 1

T1101 The Prince of Whigland swaggers in Whitehall
Tear the gilt paper use it when you shit.

'To the court'

b.113, p. 237

T1102 The prince, the poor, the prisoner and the slave,
They all at length are summon'd to their grave.

c.339, p. 315

T1103 The prince whom tatter'd subjects fear,
Else you may catch a Tartar.

John Lockman, 'British liberty or a fig for the French.
The music by Dr. Boyce; published during the heat of
the rebellion in 1745'

c.267/2, p. 9

T1104 The princes of the Earth prepare,
Of such as love His holy name.

'Psalm 29'

c.264/1, p. 115

T1105 The proctors being always much inclin'd
And scandal never blast a lady's joy.

'Prologue to the music speech at the commencement'
[Crum T1194b, 'much maligned']

fb.108, p. 321

T1106 The prologue's fill'd with such fine phrases,
Contrive to speak an epilogue.

'Epilogue [to Cato, presented at Leicester House,
spoken by] Lady Augusta' [daughter of Frederick,
prince of Wales, 1749]
[Crum T1198]

c.578, p. 62

T1107 The promise of my father's love
Made his own life the seal.

[Isaac Watts, Hymns and spiritual songs (1707),
bk. III, Hymn 3]

c.180, p. 37

T1108 The prophet did from those the ass exeem [sic],
The sons of David being to ride on him.

Sir Thomas Urquhart, 'Be not like the horse, and mule
which have no understanding. Psalm 32.10'

fb.217, p. 57

T1109 The prophet's vision that in several beasts
May own thee Lord, and find thee Savior.

> [Edward] Sparke, 'Poem 25th—upon the feast of St
> Mark'
>
> b.137, p. 56

T1110 The Protestant religion
Upon my coin it should be writ.

> Sir John Strangways, 'Upon the Oxford money coined
> [by] King Charles the First'
>
> b.304, p. 186

T1111 The proudest men in fear, or wars
Fell headlongs, in a ditch.

> Sir Thomas Urquhart, 'Against too much ambition'
>
> fb.217, p. 62

T1112 The proverb saith, one man is deemed none,
And life like death where man doth live alone.

> c.339, p. 313

T1113 The proverb saith, the bound must still obey,
Who serves must please, and hear what others say.

> c.339, p. 316

T1114 The proverb says, *Bis dat, qui cito?*
I beg, you send him thanks a million.

> 'To E[dward] Sheppard esqr. Decr. 19th 1758'
>
> c.484, p. 108

T1115 The proverb true, and ancient did grow,
That goods ill got away as ill will go.

> c.339, p. 321

T1116 The prudent cautious man that weds for gold,
But she'll turn whore and leave the fool to starve.

> 'Upon marriage'
>
> c.93

T1117 The purest air, and fire we cannot see:
But God, and angels are to us unknown.

> Sir Thomas Urquhart, 'What the eyes, and
> understanding of men may comprehend'
>
> fb.217, p. 101

T1118 The puritans still brag the purity
But 'tis so pure, it will exhale in fume.

> Sir Thomas Urquhart, 'Of the puritanical religion'
>
> fb.217, p. 148

T1119 The purity of your seraphic mind
Possessed with a judgment more celestial.

> Sir Thomas Urquhart, 'To Mistress Margaret [crossed
> out]'
>
> fb.217, p. 154

T1120 The Queen a message to the senate sent
At which her M[ajest]y and ['s] Gr[a]ce took snuff!

> [Sir Charles Hedges], 'The galleon' [on the refusal of
> the House of Commons to grant the Duke of
> Marlborough a pension, Dec. 1702]
> [Crum T1211]
>
> c.111, p. 60

T1121 The queen he follow'd as she moved along
And seemed to make a new Elysium here.

> [Francis Fawkes], 'A description of the goddess
> Calypso and her grotto . . . from Telemachus: book
> the first'
>
> fc.21, p. 20

T1122 The Queen (like heaven) shines equally on all
And then the Queen will see, as well as touch.

> [verses upon knighting Sir William Read and Sir
> Edward Hannes, July 1705]
> [Crum T1214]
>
> b.90, p. 1

T1123 The queen of contemplation, night,
Give vigor to the mind.

> [John Cunningham], 'The contemplatist. A
> night-piece'
>
> c.139, p. 36; see also 'The nurse of contemplation . . .'.

T1124 The Queen so greatly dies, the King so grieves
You'd think the hero dead, the woman lives.

> [on the death of Queen Mary]
> [Crum T1215, first two lines]
>
> Poetry Box VII/45

T1125 The Queen was brought by water to Whitehall,
Sh' had come by water had she come by land.

> 'Upon the removal of Queen Elizabeth's body from
> Richmond where she died to Whitehall, by water
> where she lay in state'
> [Crum T1217]
>
> c.152, p. 43; b.208, p. 57; c.81/1, no. 445; b.62, p. 42
> (incomplete; 'from Greenwich to Whitehall')

T1126 The queen wept sore, but was not mum,
Nothing but death made Dido-dumb.

> '[When Dido found . . .'] answered by a gentleman'
>
> Diggle Box: Poetry Box XI/69

T1127 The quick'ning sparkles of your matchless beauty,
As yours is fraughted with sublime perfection.

> Sir Thomas Urquhart, 'To the Countess of [crossed
> out]'
>
> fb.217, p. 66

T1128 The quiet of my wealth I will not trouble
Than by being poor, to be accounted such.

> Sir Thomas Urquhart, 'The speeches of one, whose
> humor inclined rather to be really rich without the
> reputation of being termed a liberal man . . .'
> fb.217, p. 349

T1129 The rabble hates, the gentry fear,
And thou the lumpish log.

> 'The present state of England. Oct.1680'
> [POAS II.342]
> b.54, p. 1159

T1130 The race of critics dull judicious rogues,
Let Nicolini act it if he can.

> 'Epilogue [to Edward Young's Busiris]. Spoken by
> Mr[s]. Oldfield'
> c.176, p. 64

T1131 The rage of rural sports, O goddess, sing,
Oh save my ros'ry, heaven, shall be thy last.

> 'A fragment of verses occasioned by the hounds
> running through the gardens at Denhill' [accompanied
> by printed prospectus of the sale of Denhill, the seat
> of Sir James Grey, sold at auction, 4 August 1773]
> Poetry Box IV/13

T1132 The raging torture of a slighted lover
My astral arts cannot to you discover.

> c.93

T1133 The rare divinities, and matchless luster
To make the rays of Phoebus the more bright.

> On my Lady Countess of [crossed out] lately
> deceased'
> fb.217, p. 115

T1134 The rarest object, that our eyes can find,
Being beauty; which breeds love; how's love blind?

> Sir Thomas Urquhart, 'That Cupid is not blind'
> fb.217, p. 100

T1135 The reason chiefly, why the teeth endure
All gluttons are tormented with in hell.

> Sir Thomas Urquhart, 'Upon the toothache'
> fb.217, p. 108

T1136 The reason is plain why honest Ned Hatton
Who married five wives would ne'er choose a fat one.

> 'The nearer the bone the sweeter the flesh'
> c.546, p. 23

T1137 The reason why a woman's best affections,
And women fancy not the female kind.

> Sir Thomas Urquhart, 'Why the greatest part of
> women, are not most taken with the best qualities of
> men'
> fb.217, p. 149

T1138 The reason why herself she doth not show,
When she is full.

> Sir Thomas Urquhart, 'Why a certain gentlewoman
> being with child was not to be seen in public'
> fb.217, p. 196

T1139 The reason why I ste'nd to leat
And what is worse I daub'd my coat!!

> [John Walker?], 'Hodge's disaster [an] epigram'
> fc.108, fol. 59

T1140 The reason why our orders in churches
Nothing but money will give them content.

> 'A song'
> b.197, p. 168

T1141 The reeling world turned poet, made a play,
I came to see't, dislik'd it, went my way.

> 'On an infant's death'
> [Crum T1230]
> b.200, p. 121

T1142 The reformers and drainers, without dread, or fear
Whilst full is the Ley, and bucks in the wood.

> [ ] Street, 'Mr. Street's verses about the draining of
> Slappen Ley' [answered by 'Finding these verses . . .']
> b.104, p. 1/2 (end of book)

T1143 The remembering of this day appeareth so
So serve thee I will not make the way a sin.

> Lady Jane Cavendish, 'On Good Friday'
> [Crum T1231]
> b.233, p. 37

T1144 The restless Whigs with their intrigues
When this was brought about man.

> 'The history of the skirmish or dance of Inverrery
> 23rd December 1745'
> c.275

T1145 The reverend Dean
He handled it more than his text.

> 'On Dr [Richard] Corbett [extracted from 'The King
> and the court . . .']
> [Crum T1233]
> b.200, p. 31

T1146   The reverend fools each other's faults expose,
For an estate which both have right to lose.

     fc.24, p. 6

T1147   The revolution is a blessed thing;
The metropolitan of all the three.

     'An encomium on the happy revolution by the
coherence of the years 1648 1688 and 1715'
[Crum T1235]

     c.570/1, p. 42

T1148   The rhetoricians whilst of old
From what? A *non regendo*.

     'Antiphrasis'

     c.81/1, no. 22

T1149   The rich men need no gifts and I give none
In giving and in taking prodigal.

     [Sir Thomas Urquhart], 'A certain honest man's
speech exceedingly eclipsed in his fortune to one
whose covetous humor did lead him by frequent
propines professing liberality toward those [who]
were wealthy . . .'

     fb.217, p. 512

T1150   The richest blessing life allows
(Although my body fail) shall never die.

     H[enry] C[olman], 'On health'

     b.2, p. 90

T1151   The riddle of riddles that dances and skips
But if money can buy it, it's not worth a groat.

     'A heart' [riddle]

     c.391; see also 'Pray tell me . . .'.

T1152   The ring he did present her on daylight,
T'encircle with her ring his longest finger.

     Sir Thomas Urquhart, 'Why a certain bride accepted
so cheerfully the ring from her bridegroom'

     fb.217, p. 316

T1153   The rites, and, worship are both old, but you
Commands a second sight, 'tis then first seen.

     [William Cartwright], 'A prologue to their
Ma[jes]t[ies] when it was acted by his Ma[jes]ty's
players at Hampton Court' [from The royal slave,
1636]
[Crum T1251]

     b.200, p. 154

T1154   The Roman fair, her father fix'd in chains,
Them that may claim a kindred seraph's tongue.

     John Lockman, 'Hearing Miss Davies, when but nine
years of age, practicing on the harpsichord and
german flute, preparatory to her benefit, 11 March,
1753'

     c.267/1, p. 70

T1155   The Roman priest, thinks not adultery;
Because he hath a wife, with whom to lie.

     Sir Thomas Urquhart, 'Why priests, and ministers
vary in their opinions, concerning the punishment of
adultery'

     fb.217, p. 183

T1156   The Roman worships God upon the wall.
The Turk, a false God: th'atheist, none at all.

     [Francis Quarles], 'On the Roman, Turk, and atheist'
[Crum T1254]

     b.137, p. 179

T1157   The Romans disciplin'd their youth in war;
Methinks, you make us somewhat more than men.

     T[homas] M[orell], 'An epilogue for the schoolboys at
Lowth, Linc. 1729'

     c.395, p. 28

T1158   The Romans in England, they once did sway
All come to be kings in their turn.

     'The chapter of kings'

     c.504, p. 194

T1159   The Romans sat, and saw with barbarous joy,
And royal pity pleads for godlike Caesar's grace.

     'Androcles and the lion'

     b.322, p. 46

T1160   The rope is old the jest is new
I'll take the jest, the rope take you.

     'The answer' [to 'That our loves may never alter . . .']
[second part of Crum T239]

     c.356; b.356, p. 305

T1161   The rose had been wash'd, just wash'd in a shower,
May be follow'd perhaps with a smile.

     [William Cowper], 'The rose had been washed'
[Crum T1258, 'was just washed']

     fc.57, p. 65; Poetry Box XII/73; c.391, p. 73; c.83/4,
no. 2009; c.90; c.504, p. 111; c.82, p. 6; see also 'I pluck'd
the sweet rose . . .'.

T1162   The rose in June is not half so sweet
As kisses when lovers meet.

     John [Rose]

     b.227, p. 36

T1163   The rose that weeps with morning dew
So bliss more brightly shines by woe.

     [Ann (Ward)] Radcliffe, 'Song'

     c.83/3, no. 855

T1164 The rose's age is but a day
It blows at morn, and fades at night!

[Ambrose] Philips, 'The rose' [parodied by Jonathan
Smedley, 'My age is not a moment's stay . . .']
[Crum T1259]

c.81/1, no. 325; c.549, p. 132

T1165 The roses, as good ancient authors write,
Our eyes pour down their briny showers, in vain.

T[homas] Rymer, 'To Lucasia overgone with green
sickness'

Poetry Box VI/98

T1166 The roses of the church excel
And win in heaven a joyful place. | Amen

'Of S. Sixtus. Aug. 6'

a.30[23]

T1167 The rosy morning streak'd the sky
Skimm'd with his load across the plain.

'The bee and butterfly, a fable'

c.186, p. 137

T1168 The routing the Earl of Mar's forces,
E'er he got to Midford again.

[Thomas Whittel], 'The Midford Galloway's ramble'

c.530, p. 101

T1169 The royal ghost rais'd from his peaceful urn,
And Woodstock once more boast a Rosamond.

[William Shippen?], 'Duke Humphrey's answer' [to
'When Sarah led by fancy . . .'; 1708]
[Crum T1263; POAS VII.334]

fc.24, p. 35

T1170 The rubies of your lips, and of your eyes
Surpass the treasures of the Indian traffic.

Sir Thomas Urquhart, 'To my Lady [crossed out]'

fb.217, p. 157

T1171 The ruling elders rays of zeal, exhale
On their assemblies down again in rains.

Sir Thomas Urquhart, 'The reason, why it rains so oft
at covenanting assemblies'

fb.217, p. 173

T1172 The sacred muses have made always claim
This present of my pains, it to defend.

[Edmund] Spenser, 'To the Rt Honble the Earl of
Northumbd'

b.150, p. 277

T1173 The sad defining(?) power of sin
But cleanse us Lord from every stain.

T[homas] S[tevens], 'Tuesday night Experience
Meeting August the 1. 1780 . . . the following sung'

c.259, p. 94

T1174 The sad unhappy merchant that beholds
None lives more faithful, or more bravely dies.

'Love terms'

fb.107, p. 62

T1175 The sages of old in prophecy told
This, this, is the honest brave fellow.

Poetry Box VII/5

T1176 The sailor oft with joy
The source from whence it rose.

[John Black]

fc.107, p. 80

T1177 The sailor sighs as sinks his native shore,
And clasps the maid he singled from the world.

[Samuel Rogers], 'The sailor—an elegy'
[Crum T1273]

c.355, p. 264; c.83/2, no. 570

T1178 The sailors when the sky grows dark
Leaving both clouds and winds behind.

c.416

T1179 The Salic law is grounded on that place,
T'invest a distaff with the arms of France.

Sir Thomas Urquhart, 'The reason of the Salic law'

fb.217, p. 139

T1180 The same as woman is, let me
But I make beggar great as king.

[Charles Earle], 'An another [thought] on [a
punch-ladle]'

c.376

T1181 The Saracen cares not for Abraham's bosom:
But in fair Sarah's gladly would repose him.

Sir Thomas Urquhart, 'Of Saracens'

fb.217, p. 291

T1182 The scene by Wilson's noble skill display'd
Proceed: and new elogiums will be thine.

John Lockman, 'To Mr. Woollet the engraver, on his
print of Niobe, from the painting of Mr. Richard
Wilson . . . Nov. 1761'

c.267/1, p. 312

T1183 The scene thus clos'd, no more remains of Rome;
We'll call this meeting, Cato's jubilee.

'Epilogue [to the Tragedy of Cato] spoken by Mr
Sutton senior'

Poetry Box x/154

T1184 The scent-strong swallow sweepeth to and fro
To benefactors never found ungrateful.

[Joshua Sylvester, trans. Guillaume de Salluste,
seigneur] Du Bartas, 'An excellent description of birds
and beasts and their admirable natures'

b.137, p. 97

T1185 The scepter and crown
That shall laugh at our trifling devices.

'The new policy'

Poetry Box VIII/32

T1186 The sceptics think, 'twas long ago,
'Tis all a wish, and all a ladle.

Mat[thew] Prior, 'The ladle'
[Crum T1282]

c.189, p. 129

T1187 The Scottish new pavement deserves well our praise
As that they have taken our posts all away.

'On the new pavement in London and removal of the
posts'

c.157, p. 53

T1188 The scourge of heaven, the prophet's lifted rod,
Look up ye slaves! Deliverance is nigh.

'The plagues of Nod' [Jacobite; pr. 1715 (Foxon
P469)]
[Crum T1287]

fc.58, p. 27; c.570/1, p. 46

T1189 The scribbling gentry ever frank and free
Ye beaux whose minds are flimsy as you stray.

'Prologue to the comedy of The school for rakes
[spoken] by Mr. King'

c.115

T1190 The scripture bids us fast from sin and pray
If you 'scape free from all your blood and plunder.

'These verses following were scattered in Leeds'
streets, upon a thanksgiving day'

c.160, fol. 103

T1191 The sea replies, she lies not in our deeps
From evil, is of virtue the most high.

'Query. Where is wisdom's habitation'

c.189, p. 35

T1192 The second reading, Sir! You say,
Is most ador'd by Patrick's Dean.

Abraham Oakes, 'Answer to a letter, in which
Mr. S[wift] said, he believed he was inspired. For he
found out the riddle, on the second reading'

c.50, p. 17

T1193 The secret cause of Ovid's sad mischance
Should [Cooke?] it be in a convenient place.

[Sir Aston Cokayne], 'Of Ovid's banishment'

b.275, p. 41

T1194 The seed of heav'nly life God's spirit sows,
The more its force, yet we more free still move.

[Edmund Wodehouse], 'Septr 14 [1715]'

b.131, p. 264

T1195 The seed of mustard is the smallest grain
With sugar 'tis a passing sauce for meat.

[Joshua Sylvester, trans. Guillaume de Salluste,
seigneur Du Bartas], 'Of mustard'

b.284, p. 52

T1196 The senate of almighty Jove
The fairest of the female train!

C[harles] B[urney], 'On the recovery of Miss Rachel
Wilcox from a dangerous illness. August. 1779'

c.38, p. 42

T1197 The senior fellows have a trick,
And so by whetting keep Nick out.

'In socios seniores Coll: Oxon: [5]'

c.81/1, no. 24

T1198 The setting sun had plung'd his weary steed,
And leave the dreary mansions of a tomb.

[ ] Roberts, of Eton, 'On the death of Mr. Keepe'

c.591

T1199 The setting sun, with dying gleam,
They clasp their child, who, smiling dies.

'The fugitive'

c.83/3, no. 1014

T1200 The seven first years of life, man's break of day,
Tir'd she stops short, and wishes all were past.

'Climacter'

c.81/1, no. 130

T1201 The shadowy cope of night was breaking fast
Nor needing fame if heav'n approve.

'A morning walk'

fc.53, p. 172

T1202 The shape and face let others prize
As the remorse of penitence!

Poetry Box XII/45

T1203 The sharpest wit being best, and memory,
The sharpest memory, and roundest wit.

Sir Thomas Urquhart, 'To a certain student, who had
very blunt, and shallow gifts for learning'

fb.217, p. 126

T1204 The shepherd Alexis as jolly a swain
If you frown, you will kill me, if you smile you will
cure.

[Thomas Hamilton, 6th earl of Haddington], 'A song'

c.458/2, p. 111

T1205 The shepherd leaves the rose
And let her beauties fade.

[John Black]

fc.107, p. 83

T1206 The shepherd Oliver, grown white with years,
And whose innocence teaches to die.

[John Walcot ('Peter Pindar')], 'Old Oliver or the
dying shepherd a cantata'

c.83/3, no. 778

T1207 The shepherd's plain life
Both lightnings and tempests assail.

[Crum T1304, with another stanza]

c.156, p. 109

T1208 The sheriff of Oxford late is grown so wise
The jury sat, and found it dead already.

[Benjamin Stone], 'On a courteous sheriff of Oxford'

b.62, p. 80; see also 'Fie, scholars, fie! . . .'.

T1209 The shining luster of your golden tresses
Being nothing mortal, they're of such perfection.

Sir Thomas Urquhart, 'To the matchless Aura'

fb.217, p. 37

T1210 The ship that now sails trim before the wind,
And then—their vows are ne'er remembered more.

'The seaman's vow'

c.503, p. 32

T1211 The shortest day, and longest night,
The brightest lightnings always fly.

'On Miss Charlotte Clayton's birthday, December
the 11'

c.360/3, no. 202

T1212 The shrew Xanthippe, fam'd of old,
That peals of thunder end in pain.

'What cannot be cured, must be endured'

c.53, fol. 1

T1213 The sickle [that] [is] [too] early [cannot] reap
[And] [ ] soon past are oft too late lamented.

'Temerarius amor quid sit'

b.205, fol. 14v

T1214 The sickness, with the man you take away,
You will not suffer him to be long sick.

Sir Thomas Urquhart, 'To a certain empiric, so
violent in his cures, that it was sudden death to the
person, who received them'

fb.217, p. 333

T1215 The siege is rais'd by Duc de Croy
And if I fail then *guardez toi.*

[1693?]
[Crum T1310b]

b.204, p. 2

T1216 The sight of Doctors Hare and Dick
The worst of maladies to cure.

Frederick Corfield, 'The doctors'

c.381/2

T1217 The sign of the sun you see it is I keep,
You know my mind—I say no more.

'Another [verse written on a sign] down in the west'

c.361

T1218 The silent river glided down the dale,
And curs'd his cruelty, and vainly mourn'd.

'Maria an elegy'

c.83/3, no. 758

T1219 The silent shade was always the retreat
Be clos'd and swallow'd in the joy of heav'n.

E[dmund] B[urke], 'To John Dame, esqr. By the same'

fc.46/3

T1220 The silver moon and all her starry train
Rich discontent is but a glorious hell.

'Grandeur no true happiness, or the pleasures of
retirement' [from Seneca]

c.186, p. 74; c.360/3, no. 164

T1221 The silver sound of music sweet
Cry hiss in the lungs of th' liquor.

'On a vicar'
[Crum T1315]

fb.143, p. 34

T1222 The silver swan, that, living, had no note,
More geese, than swans live now, more fools than
wise.

'Ætas nostra plures p[rae]tulit stultos'
[Crum T1316]

b.200, p. 99

T1223 The simple, unaffected lays,
'Tis Strephon, dear Strephon, alone bears the bell.

Poetry Box x/64

T1224 The simplest body, solid wits remark
With fear think when they're touch'd that they are
wounded.

[Sir Thomas Urquhart], 'That those who not being
unmov'd at matters of great consequence . . . [illeg.]'

fb.217, p. 521

T1225 The sins which Sodom overthrew
Shall praise thy glory in her songs.

T[homas] S[tevens]

c.259, p. 143

T1226 The sirens once deluded vainly charm'd
Condemn'd to perish by the slaughtering gun.

[George Granville, 1st baron] Lansdowne, 'To Mira
singing'

fc.60, p. 52

T1227 The sister graces, with a shining train,
Pointed to Delia, and the fair one crown'd.

John Lockman, 'Delia, at Mr. Hugford's ball . . . April
1758'

c.267/1, p. 103

T1228 The skillful artist first design'd the stone,
The founder's monument, but carv'd his own.

[from 'The amours of Alatheus and Eustathea']

c.379/1, p. 61

T1229 The skillful pilot, safe in port,
Must fly from love's destructive joy.

John Lockman, 'Translations, and imitations from
Metastasio, and other Italian opera poets [3]'

c.267/4, p. 95

T1230 The slanders foul and words like arrows keen,
Not virtue hurt, but turns her foes to [?].

c.339, p. 317

T1231 The sluggish morn as yet undrest
But left the sun her curate light.

[John Cleveland], 'Upon Phyllis walking before
sunrise'
[Crum T1330]

b.93, p. 25

T1232 The small birds rejoice in the green leaves returning,
Alas! can I make you no sweeter return!

[Robert Burns], 'The chevalier's lament'

c.142, p. 236

T1233 The smallest trees have tops, the ant her gall
They hear, and see, and sigh, and then they break.

[Sir Edward Dyer], 'The generality of love'

b.200, p. 80; see also 'The lowest shrubs . . .'.

T1234 The smiles of joy, the tears of woe,
There's nothing calm but heav'n.

fc.124, p. 71

T1235 The smiling morn leads on the day
And comfort to thy heart.

[Mary Cornwallis?], 'Written on the morning of
Caroline [Cornwallis]'s birthday the 12th of July'

fc.124, p. 118, p. 44 ('copied for E. C.')

T1236 The smiling morn, the breathing spring,
Adieu the berks of Endermay.

c.358, p. 168; Poetry Box I/71

T1237 The smiling spring again is seen,
And reign triumphant there.

Miss [ ] Craven, 'The spring. From Metastasio . . .
1795'

Greatheed Box/25

T1238 The smith to open through her door a way
Wherewith the springs of wedlock were made
patent.

Sir Thomas Urquhart, 'Of the bride and her
bridegroom who was a smith of his trade'

fb.217, p. 152

T1239 The smooth white fingers of the fair Italian
Which fredon'd [sic] on her Aphrodisian key.

Sir Thomas Urquhart, 'How an exceeding beautiful
Italian Donzella, tuned up her paramour's Cyprian kit,
to the harmony of an amorous dalliance'

fb.217, p. 284

T1240 The snow-crown'd thorn its shelt'ring verdure lost,
And seem to thrill his pensive elegy.

'The frozen red-breast's elegy'

c.83/2, no. 560

T1241 The snow dissolved from the Cambrian hills
With crystal streams the fertile valleys fills.

'Franciscus Leuvelineus. Anagramma. Fluvius nive
clarescens. Epigramma'

b.212, p. 87

T1242 The snow, dissolv'd, no more is seen;
Of fancy, reason, virtue, naught can me bereave.

[Samuel] Johnson, 'A translation from Horace
[book IV ode vii]'

c.83/2, no. 576

T1243 The snow goes off, the grass comes on
Or heal, or soothe his lasting pains.

'The seventh ode of the fourth book of Horace
translated'

Poetry Box I/113[6]

T1244 The snow which lately chill'd the fields
To free his dear Perithous from chains.

[John Hoadly], 'Horace Lib. IV ode vii'

c.176, p. 42

T1245 The snows all melt, the grass looks green
Somerset, Talbot, Hough are still no more.

'Horace book the 4th. ode the 7th'

Poetry Box I/138

T1246 The snows are fled; again the fields and trees
His dear Pirithous from the darksome grave.

[William Mills], 'Odes of Horace translated. Book IV.
Ode VII. To Torquatus'

c.472, p. 43

T1247 The snows are fled, verdure crowns the fields,
Lose Pirithous, from death's lasting chain.

[William Popple, trans.], '[Horace] book 4th. Ode
7th. To Manlius Torquatus'

fc.104/2, p. 356

T1248 The snows are melted all away,
Devouring fate, that spares nor old nor young.

Sir William Temple, 'Horace Lib. 4 ode 7'

b.150, p. 213

T1249 The snows are thaw'd, bleak winter's gone,
Could his Perithous restore.

[Thomas Hamilton, 6th earl of Haddington], 'Horace
ode 7th book 4th to Torquatus'
[cf. Crum T1335, T1336]

c.458/2, p. 100

T1250 The solemn death-bell (sad alarm) beats slow
In pray'rs for him who loves me not—she said |
                                          And breath'd no more.

'On the death of an unfortunate lady who died in
childbed of an illegitimate son'

c.91, p. 104

T1251 The solemn stillness of the night, invites
Or [Greek:] zon short, or [Greek:] kleos long.

'1792.—evening thoughts April 25th'

fc.124, p. 83

T1252 The solemn triumphs of the Persian court
Whene'er you go, great Sir, hearts will have eyes.

Will[iam] Cartwright, 'The epilogue to the King, and
Queen spoken by Cratander, the royal slave' [from
The royal slave, 1636]
[Crum T1344]

b.200, p. 152

T1253 The solitary bird of night,
Is vanity and woe.

[Elizabeth Carter], 'Ode to wisdom'

c.83/1, no. 100; Poetry Box X/111

T1254 The son of Kish, as head and shoulders taller
May mark how nature has o'ershot her mark.

'Verses on Mr. Henry Blacker who was shown at
London for his hight. 1751. being seven foot four
inches. A Sussex man, born in 1724' [cf. 'Amazing
man . . .']

c.360/3, no. 110

T1255 The son that doth in prudent acts delight
And fatal ruin through their offspring range.

[William Sandys?], 'Certain observations of moral
virtues, with their opposite vices: drawn out of the
proverbs of Solomon'

b.230, p. 55

T1256 The sonnet smooth let him compose
And matrimonial chiding.

H[enry] Skrine, 'To Dean D—— on his marriage . . .
July 8 1785'

c.509, p. 75

T1257 The sons of genius search thro' ev'ry age,
And judge like Englishmen—he asks no more.

[William Shirley], 'The prologue to the historical
tragedy of Edward the Black Prince'

c.578, p. 115

T1258 The sordid wretch who ne'er has known
Than share their boasted apathy.

'Ode to sensibility'

Poetry Box IV/140

T1259 The soul, alive to joy and woe
Suspend the tear, to dew my grave!

[Richard Polwhele], 'To the same'

c.141, p. 561

T1260 The soul being dear, we say dear friends: and here,
Wife's dear to man; because the flesh is dear.

    Sir Thomas Urquhart, 'Of friends, and wives'

fb.217, p. 336

T1261 The soul that feels for others' pains,
From heav'n its original proclaims.

c.93

T1262 The soul's interpreters, words only be,
But only that that holds a soul within.

    'Of the soul and body'

fb.69, p. 213

T1263 The sov'reign paraclete of the Olympic
Then would whole worlds of infidels convert.

    Sir Thomas Urquhart, 'To my Lord [crossed out]'

fb.217, p. 88

T1264 The spacious firmament on high,
The hand that made us is divine.

    [Joseph] Addison, 'Psalm 19th part of it paraphrased
    by . . .' [in Spectator 465]
    [Crum T1353]

c.244, p. 1; c.144, p. 134; c.547, p. 156; fc.132/1, p. 43

T1265 The span of my day's measured here I rest
The truth of all men argue here below.

    Sir Thomas Overbury, 'Sr. Thomas Overbury's
    epitaph on himself'

b.62, p. 1; b.356, p. 144

T1266 The Spaniard by repeated crimes made bold,
Wrongs to redress and losses to repair.

    '[Several copies of verses spoken at Westminster
    School on the anniversary of the defeat of the Spanish
    Armada] 6'

fc.24, p. 72

T1267 The Spaniards grandly teach in their politic schools
If princes swive loyal subjects of their own.

    'The whore of Babylon' [1678]
    [Crum T1355, 'gravely']

b.327, f. 32v

T1268 The Spaniards love the English, they them hate
Seeing 'tis known whole kingdoms love in vain.

    [Sir Aston Cokayne], 'Of the English, Spanish and
    French'

b.275, p. 84

T1269 The Spaniards say, a man who has
To think upon, the abbey's veil.

    [Thomas Hamilton, 6th earl of Haddington], 'The
    veil from Boccace'

c.458/2, p. 14

T1270 The spearmen heard the bugle sound
His jaws his fangs ran blood.

    William [Robert] Spencer, 'Beth Gelert or the grave
    of the greyhound'
    [Crum T1358]

Poetry Box IV/200 (incomplete)

T1271 The speeches of quaint youths ensnare the hearts,
Take Cupid's dart for Mercure's caducae.

    Sir Thomas Urquhart, 'That young damsels are much
    taken with eloquence, and fair words'

fb.217, p. 313

T1272 The spiders weave their cobwebs night and day
With hate(?) alarmed, which terrors do betoken.

b.208, p. 72

T1273 The spirit willing is the body weak,
We in his favor all that's good possess.

    [Edmund Wodehouse], 'Feb. 28 [1715]'

b.131, p. 173

T1274 The splendid hatchment, elegantly spread,
And there obtain the glorious prize.

    'On the death of Mr. Rich[ar]d Limbrey'

fc.85, fol. 86

T1275 The splendor of your reputation carries
Is that whereat posterity will aim.

    Sir Thomas Urquhart, 'To Sir [crossed out] Treasurer
    of the King's House and Secretary of State'

fb.217, p. 164

T1276 The sportsmen of Chatsworth, consulting which
                                  way
May with half of an eye kill whenever you please.

    David Garrick, 'By David Garrick esqr.'

Poetry Box X/134

T1277 The sprightly lark upon yond' eastern hill
Asham'd I lay it down, I've done so much, so ill.

    [George Daniel]

b.121, fol. 44

T1278 The spring appear'd, and hush'd was ev'ry wind,
With down more soft the the fam'd insect weaves.

    [John Lockman], 'The willow and the peach tree.
    From a Chinese tale'

c.268 (second part), p. 100; see also 'Fair spring
appear'd . . .'.

T1279 The spring compared is to infancy
To all degrees and sexes their estate.

    'Of the four quarters of the year'

b.234, p. 62

T1280 The spring, that paints with flow'rs th'enamell'd
                                                   ground
       Now beauty's in its bud!

          'Verses under the pictures of the four seasons; for
          Miss Herbert . . . spring'
       Spence Papers, folder 113

T1281 The spring was constant, and soft winds that blew
       And fruits were never out of season there.

          'The golden age'
       c.83/1, no. 9

T1282 The spring with fresh beauties hath drest up each
                                                   field,
       And when my nymph's kind, I will never forsake
                                                    her.

          'Love at a distance'
       fb.107, p. 60

T1283 The 'squire had din'd alone one day,
       'Tis men of sense, are men of worth.

          'The pepper-box and salt-cellar'
       c.83/2, no. 289

T1284 The stag did beat the horse out of the fields
       [torn]wth a little content cannot be . . . .

       b.53, p. 74 (incomplete)

T1285 The stage should be to life a faithful glass,
       Give your support, he asks no better friends.

          W[illiam] T[homas] Fitzgerald, 'The way to get
          married'
       c.175, p. 47

T1286 The stake's three crowns; four nations, gamesters
                                                    are,
       Though three men vie it, the fourth sets up his rest.

          'To the Parliament. Nov: 1640'
          [Crum T1372]
       b.54, p. 883

T1287 The star of the evening now bids thee retire
       O! had I been bless'd with thy beauties my fair.

          Charles James Fox, 'Lines written by . . . Annual
          register [17]89'
          [Crum T1373]
       c.344, p. 118

T1288 The star that sits in Charles his wain
       Then northern Charles look to thy wain.

          [Richard Corbett, bp. of Norwich, upon the blazing
          star of 1618, written in 1623 upon Charles' visit to
          Spain]
       b.197, p. 219

T1289 The star, whose radiant beams adorn
       What cares disturb the crowd below.

          R[ichard] Fitzpatrick, 'Inscribed in the temple of
          friendship at St. Anne's Hill'
       c.142, p. 518

T1290 The state and men's affairs are the best plays
       The bruised reed, nor quencheth the smoking flax.

          [Sir John Roe], 'An epistle to Mr. Ben. Jonson' [attr.
          John Donne]
          [Crum T1376]
       b.114, p. 144

T1291 The state lies sick, very sick in all haste
       A fast a Parliament fourteen heads.

          'Verses' [1640]
          [Crum T1377]
       b.229, fol. 125; b.200, p. 272 ('lay sick'); Poetry Box
       VIII/56

T1292 The state of France as it now stands
       Did leave from there and came my way.

          [Sir Walter Raleigh]
          [Crum T1378]
       fb.9, fol. 38v

T1293 The state wherein I stand is now so bad
       That was born free and hates to die a slave.

          Sir John Strangways
       b.304, p. 42

T1294 The stately oak, our safeguard of our pride
       Dating our progress from the kind applause.

          M[aurice] J[ohnson], 'An epilogue spoken at [Love for
          love] by Mr. M. Johnson . . . written by his father'
       c.229/2, fol. 51v

T1295 The stately stag when he his horns hath shed
       They both the loser, and the winner wound.

          'Not so strange as true'
       b.197, p. 168

T1296 The stepdame's self the artist formed, and so
       Forbid the milk i' th' bastard's mouth to flow.

          George Montagu, 'On a statue of Juno suckling
          Hercules'
       fc.135, p. 11

T1297 The stoe [sic] I blast not. 'Tis a noble stock
       As not to blast it by my life or love.

          [Sir Philip Wodehouse], 'Upon my brother Sr. J.
          Cotton's second wife . . . Elizabeth Cotton'
       b.131, back (no. 57)

T1298 The stoic common friendship doth compare,
Too fast, wants root; and in a moment dies.

[John Hobart], 'Of friendship'

b.108, fol. 15

T1299 The storm's dreadful genius is out,
And trembling acknowledge a God.

James M[ulcaste]r, sr., 'Written in a storm of snow'

c.118, p. 1

T1300 The story of King Arthur old
He made the dragon follow. | [Sing *Honi soit qui
mal y pense*]

[John Grubb], 'A ballad' [pr. 1707 (Foxon G303)]

fb.70, p. 119

T1301 The strait gate brings us to a large abode:
But to a narrow place, the way, that's broad.

Sir Thomas Urquhart, 'Of the paths to heaven, and
hell'

fb.217, p. 153

T1302 The streamlet that flow'd round her cot,
It reflected her back to the skies.

'Song'

c.250

T1303 The strong man, oft lacks wit: the good man, wealth:
The wise man, faith: and the devot[ed] man, health.

Sir Thomas Urquhart, 'The best things of any in this
transitory world have their own defects'

fb.217, p. 61

T1304 The sturdy ram, as fables tell of old,
Then shall be not your bishop be, but pope.

[( ) Garthwaite], 'A libel against [Samuel] Ward of
Ipswich' [answered by 'An odd northern tyke . . .']

b.197, p. 177

T1305 The style of Donna to their wives they give:
Although less pow'r than they, no women have.

Sir Thomas Urquhart, 'The name, which Italians
bestow on their wives, is merely titular'

fb.217, p. 317

T1306 The subject matters I propose,
He values nothing like our love.

[Edmund Wodehouse], 'Aug. 11 [1715]'

b.131, p. 244

T1307 The subjects' arms, the more their princes gave,
Not thank'd, but scorn'd, nor are they gifts, but
spoils.

fb.234, p. 65

T1308 The subtle serpent to G[eorg]e B—ke said
Usurpers must expect whene'er they come.

'The contract' [between George I and the devil; with
reference to Bolingbroke?]

c.570/2, p. 161

T1309 The sultans, by their laws are made
Are good for something when they please.

'On the Duchess of Norfolk and her company . . .
[dressing nineteen dishes without any attendant for
their dinner]'

c.150, p. 33; c.157, p. 95

T1310 The sum of fair behavior is
Be a peacock's, or a pigeon's nest.

[Sir Philip Wodehouse], 'Upon Livy's Ne sic arrogans
vel obnoxious . . .'

b.131, p. 22

T1311 The summer morn unveils her eyes,
And sing of thy almighty power!

'On the May morning'

c.578, p. 78

T1312 The summer's charms again withdrawn;
Tho' fortune frowns—and fates retard.

'Thoughts on the approach of winter 1776'

c.89, p. 106 (bis) (i.e., 108)

T1313 The sun, and world have motions quite contrary:
So man in's course of life from grace doth vary.

Sir Thomas Urquhart, 'The sun, and the world'

fb.217, p. 283

T1314 The sun from the East tips the mountains with gold,
And when tired abroad find contentment at home. |
With the sports, &c.

[Paul Whitehead], 'Song 69'

c.555, p. 104

T1315 The sun had clos'd the winter day
In light away.

[Robert Burns], 'The vision'

c.142, p. 249

T1316 The sun had just set and now evening comes on
And prove all your rules by the line and the square.

D. Drenham, 'The Bason guide'

c.364

T1317 The sun had long sunk in the west
So saying he plung'd in the wave.

'The negro's complaint' [signed Bertrand]

c.343, p. 13

T1318 The sun had purpled o'er the east
While Cynthia is her own.

'To C. W. B. esqr'
Poetry Box x/45, p. 29

T1319 The sun in splendor rides supreme,
That summer suns arise.

'The summer's day'
c.83/1, no. 21

T1320 The sun is swift; the hour is swifter tho',
But never could the hour have stopped so.

Sir Thomas Urquhart, 'Whether the sun or the hour
ought to be esteemed the speedier in course'
fb.217, p. 45

T1321 The sun just sinking shed a sickly ray
Nor reign in heaven more than in the grave.

[Frederick Corfield], 'Elegy'
c.381/1

T1322 The sun new risen in the eastern sky
Herself is now no more.

[ ] Ellison, 'The fishers: an ode . . . 1776'
Greatheed Box/30

T1323 The sun now darts fainter his ray;
To thee fam'd Elysium shall yield.

John Lockman, 'The adieu to Vauxhall Gardens. Set
to music by Dr. Boyes [William Boyce] . . . anno 1733'
c.267/2, p. 114; c.268 (first part), p. 52

T1324 The sun now shines by light of th' moon
If traitors were but at the bar.

b.213, p. 41

T1325 The sun obliquely shot a kindly ray
No nymph so graceful, virtuous, and so true.

'The resolution'
c.136, p. 47

T1326 The sun of righteousness when he arose
Accepted, and thy other wants supplies.

'Christmas Day 1665'
b.49, p. 3

T1327 The sun sets at night, and the stars shun the day
And thy son O Allinomook, shall never complain.

[Anne (Home)] Hunter, 'By a captive Indian while his
conquerors were preparing for his death'
c.391, p. 70; c.142, p. 368 ('Alknomock')

T1328 The sun (to use a classic notion)
But fix forever on a heart that's true.

'Novelty . . . Bath, Dec. 18. 1777'
Poetry Box II/56

T1329 The sun was just about to rise
Sweet Patty Bray.

H[enry] Lawman, 'Patty Bray'
Spence Papers, folder 97

T1330 The sun was sunk beneath the hill,
Who pays thy worth, must pay in love.

[John] Gay, 'A song by Mr. Gay'
[Crum T1412]
Trumbull Box: Poetry Box XIII/67b; fpc.31, fly leaf

T1331 The sunbeams in the east are spread
Tonight put on perfection and a woman's name.

[John Donne], 'Epithalamium on the marriage of the
La: Eli[zabeth, to Frederick V of Bohemia]'
[Crum T1415]
b.148, p. 24

T1332 The Sundays of man's life,
Of the eternal glorious king.

'The life of Mr. George Herbert'
c.160, fol. 51

T1333 The sun's eclipse is past, but not the fears
Driving his team; which sure doth signify . . . .

[William Lilly], 'A letter sent to a friend at London,
concerning the great eclipse of the sun. March 29.
1652'
[Crum T1417]
b.200, p. 301 (incomplete)

T1334 The sun's eclipse is rare: the moon's is common;
Thus man, is not so faulty, as the woman.

Sir Thomas Urquhart, 'Of man, and the sun: a
paradox in what concerneth the woman'
fb.217, p. 321

T1335 The sun's eclipse ne'er total is,
That doom so dismal to prevent.

[Edmund Wodehouse], 'Apr. 22 [1715] on the sun's
eclipse'
b.131, p. 202

T1336 The sun's not oft, the moon's oft in th'eclipse
So women are than men more prone to slips.

'Ever fall'
c.356

T1337 The superscription of an epigram,
That which is requisite for explication.

> Sir Thomas Urquhart, 'Of the lemma of an epigram'
>
> fb.217, p. 57

T1338 The surest state and best degree
Safety, quiet, and liberty.

> [Sir Nicholas] Bacon, 'In commendation of the mean estate'
>
> fa.8, fol. 162v

T1339 The swain who late at Paris sung
O'erjoy'd, the muse would spread their fame.

> John Lockman, 'Wilton House: a lyric poem . . . writ in the fields at Bemmerton, near Salisbury, in Aug. 1748'
>
> c.267/1, p. 331

T1340 The swallow, twittering, now proclaims the day
With piety to God, and love to all mankind.

> 'The dawn. A sonnet' [20 Sept. 1799]
>
> c.136, p. 165

T1341 The sweetbriar grows in the merry greenwood
Like the dew that flies over the mulberry tree.

> [William] Collins, 'The mulberry tree'
>
> Poetry Box IV/61

T1342 The sweet Emilia fairer to be seen
For with the rosy color strives her hue.

> [Horace Walpole, 4th earl of Orford], 'Count[ess] of Kildare'
> [Crum T1425]
>
> c.157, p. 68

T1343 The sweet rosy morning
As our sports crown the day.

> 'Song 40'
>
> c.555, p. 61

T1344 The sweetest flow'rs that grow, fair maid,
Shall snatch away our latest breath.

> Edward Sneyd, 'A love letter from Adam Tulip [gardener] to Dorothy Primrose [dairy maid]'
>
> c.214, p. 123

T1345 The sweetest wine makes vinegar most tart,
The more wit, the more wicked heart.

> [John Rose?]
>
> b.227, p. 36

T1346 The sweetness of your voice excels the sirens
Being quintessences of discourse and wit.

> [Sir Thomas Urquhart], 'To [blank]'
>
> fb.217, p. 527

T1347 The swift-wing'd hours, roll on the fatal day,
Receive that mercy sought in vain below.

> [William] Dodd, 'Elegy . . . he suffered June 27. 1777'
>
> c.83/1, no. 26

T1348 The tables of the covenanting lords
At Leith, the hazard of the entredeur.

> Sir Thomas Urquhart, 'Of some of the procedures of the green tables, against their northern adversaries'
>
> fb.217, p. 139

T1349 The table's spread and they—begin
A goodly capon and his gizzard.

> [John Cleveland], 'Upon Lee and Owens fencing, a Dr. Roan and a Jeffray'
>
> b.93, p. 23

T1350 The talk lately went
For sooner you cannot expect it.

> 'The stateholder's almanac . . . to the tune of Cold and raw the north [wind] did blow' [1688]
> [Crum T1431]
>
> fb.108, p. 199

T1351 [The] tallest pines are overblown
The highest hills are smitten down with
                                    thunder . . . .

> b.53, p. 67 (incomplete)

T1352 The task is blessed sure,
To rectify the mind, and learn again.

> Charles Atherton Allnutt, 'An effusion on hearing the Revd. Mr. Wills preach in the marketplace at Wallingford'
>
> c.112, p. 111

T1353 The tea dispatch'd, the cards are brought—
The rage for cards excludes it quite.

> 'The card table in the family way'
>
> c.83/2, no. 271

T1354 The teeming mother anxious for her race,
And hissing infamy proclaims the rest.

> S[amuel] Johnson, 'Advice to the fair sex'
>
> c.83/3, no. 780

T1355 The teeth of elephants, should raise a dread
The gods alone can throw and never lose.

> 'On dice'
>
> Poetry Box VII/5

T1356 The tenants of this spot, who, seiz'd with dread,
But acts, like those, court the meridian sun.

> John Lockman, 'Writ, whilst surveying the ruins of the fire in Exchange Alley . . . July 1748'
>
> c.267/1, p. 135

T1357 The tender pair, whom mutual favors bind
The lover that's forgotten will forget.

> [George] L[yttelton], 1st baron Lyttelton, 'Maxims in love' [no. 2]

> c.487, p. 28

T1358 The tender thing being very sick,
Than a poor agent of a crown.

> Sir Thomas Urquhart, 'Of a young lass, who feigned herself often to be not well in health, that so made free of other businesses, she might the better attend on lovely appointments'

> fb.217, p. 343

T1359 The tenth day of the winter month November
The widow's silver, I love silver well.

> Martha [(Dorsett) Prynne Thorogood] Moulsworth, 'November the 10th 1632 the memorandum of . . . widow'

> fb.150/6

T1360 The Thames flows proudly to the sea,
Among the friends of early days!

> [Robert Burns], 'The banks of Nith'

> c.142, p. 305; see also 'Yet, let me sigh . . .'.

T1361 The thief and slanderer are almost the same
T'one lives scorn['d], the other dies in shame.

> [Francis Quarles], 'On the thief and slanderer' [Divine fancies I, 67]

> b.137, p. 186

T1362 The thing that is useful to keep off the rain,
And I'll give you a bottle at old Sadler's Wells.

> 'A rebus'

> c.360/3, no. 214

T1363 The things that bring up true content,
And your last day, not wish nor fear.

> [William] Pattison, 'The farmer's ambition'

> c.244, p. 524

T1364 The things that make a virgin please
Not superstitious nor profane.

> K[atherine] P[hilips], 'The virgin' [Crum T1440]

> b.118, p. 55

T1365 The things that make this life to please
Death neither fear, nor wish to see.

> Sir R[ichard] Fanshawe, trans., 'Horace's ode of happy life to Martial [Martial, epigrams X.xlvii]' [Crum T1441]

> b.155, p. 63

T1366 The third of November Monsieur 'scap'd the water
The sixth of November was the next day after.

> [Ben Jonson?], 'On November' [cf. Crum T1442, 'Vandelin cross'd the water']

> b.356, p. 304

T1367 The thirteen of the month December
For now the Pricke doth lie beneath the stones.

> 'An epitaph on Mr. Pricke of Christ Coll[ege] in Cambridge'

> b.62, p. 46

T1368 The thresher Duck could o'er the Q[uee]n prevail
Thy toil is lessen'd and thy profits doubled.

> [Jonathan Swift], 'On Stephen Duck'

> fc.60, p. 46

T1369 The tigress of her young despoil'd,
Which, [?]-like, invade.

> John Lockman, 'Translations, and imitations from Metastasio, and other Italian opera poets [6]'

> c.267/4, p. 95

T1370 The time and place, hunger and hazard set,
The soldier got many a pound of Bacon.

> [ ] Pigg (pseud.?), 'Upon one Bacon robbed by a redcoat'

> c.170, p. 31

T1371 The time is now approaching
To choose an honest man. | And [a-voting we] &c.

> 'The honest voters'

> c.570/3, p. 6

T1372 The time we've here is but a little space
That we may never go astray.

> [Thomas Gurney], 'An anagram and epigram on the name of my loving brother Richd. Gurney . . . Run hard. Crying . . . 1739'

> c.213

T1373 The time will come as true as creed
To cause the Lord to cast this cruelty.

> 'These verses were found at Ixworth Abbey, between two stones in the altar' [Crum T1453]

> fb.7, fol. 5v

T1374 The times are so hard
And tints that cannot fade!

> R[ichard] V[ernon] S[adleir], 'To Colonel H—y—d and Mrs. Col—g—d on their marriage, who had desired me to write some verses on the subject—Sept. 1783'

> c.106, p. 91

T1375　The timid lover may repine,
　　　　We first deserve—then gain the fair.

　　　　　　Charles Burney, the younger, 'The soldier's joy . . .
　　　　　　1780'
　　　　c.35, p. 5

T1376　The tithes of Romney, now your great concern
　　　　Wave o'er the banks of Thames, and glad the swain.

　　　　　　'Horace's epistle to Iccius (ep.ii, lib. I) imitated'
　　　　fc.51, p. 183

T1377　The tokens of continual peace by present best are
　　　　　　　　　　　　　　　　　　　　　　　shown
　　　　That thousands have confirmed in war and
　　　　　　　　　　　　　　　　　millions left in woe.

　　　　　　'The boast of continual peace' [from 'Cecil's
　　　　　　commonwealth']
　　　　fb.40, p. 185

T1378　The tongue although it be a member small
　　　　Of man it is the best or worst of all.

　　　　b.234, p. 258; c.339, p. 313

T1379　The tongue was once a servant to the heart,
　　　　She makes the heart a servant to the tongue.

　　　　　　'Of the heart and tongue'
　　　　c.356

T1380　The topsails shiver in the wind
　　　　Our sails are full sweet girls adieu.

　　　　　　'Song 182'
　　　　c.555, p. 283

T1381　The Tories 'ad rat 'em
　　　　If a man should, for once, serve himself.

　　　　　　'An apology for Mr. Pitt Lloyd's evg. post Aug 18 1766'
　　　　c.157, p. 89

T1382　The tottering state of transitory things,
　　　　For if St. Giles were lame, how could he fly.

　　　　　　'Sir Giles Mompesson' [and Sir Francis Michell;
　　　　　　March 1621]
　　　　　　[Crum T1460]
　　　　b.197, p. 211

T1383　The town being full of confusion
　　　　They may rise, and you be De Witted.

　　　　　　'The Norfolk ballad' [on the Treaty of Vienna; pr. 1731
　　　　　　(Foxon N159)]
　　　　c.570/3, p. 113, p. 106 (var.)

T1384　The town reports the falsehood of my dear,
　　　　And let me rest contented in my shame.

　　　　c.549, p. 90

T1385　The tragic muse of all her charms bereft,
　　　　So with your leave, we'll now proceed—to Trial.

　　　　　　[Thomas] Panton, 'Prologue to Mr. Panton's opera
　　　　　　called The trial'
　　　　Smith Papers, folder 74/7

T1386　The treasures of your wit, and copious riches
　　　　Exceeding all the gold Peru brings forth.

　　　　　　Sir Thomas Urquhart, 'To the Earl of [crossed out]'
　　　　fb.217, p. 203

T1387　The tree a grace to Eden did appear
　　　　To try our duties to a rigid law.

　　　　　　[Sir Aston Cokayne], 'Of women'
　　　　b.275, p. 67

T1388　The trees have now hid at the edge of the hurst,
　　　　When ye let loose the demons of war.

　　　　　　[Charlotte (Turner) Smith], 'The forest boy'
　　　　c.141, p. 64

T1389　The tribute paid, O gracious King,
　　　　He calls forth plants and fruits and flow'rs.

　　　　　　John Lockman, 'On humbly presenting early Shetland
　　　　　　herrings to His Majesty, Aug. 1767, from the British
　　　　　　Fishing Society'
　　　　c.267/4, p. 385

T1390　The Trojan swain had judg'd the great dispute
　　　　By Mars himself that armor hath been tried.

　　　　　　[Matthew] Prior, 'Pallas and Venus. An epigram' [pr.
　　　　　　1706 (Foxon P1082)]
　　　　　　[Crum T1473]
　　　　fc.60, p. 47

T1391　The true elect, by true effectual faith,
　　　　On God's right hand for our poor souls to plead.

　　　　　　'Christ's love to man'
　　　　c.187, p. 44

T1392　The true messiah now appears
　　　　And pleads his wounded side.

　　　　　　[Isaac Watts, Hymns and spiritual songs (1707), bk II,
　　　　　　Hymn 12]
　　　　c.180, p. 30

T1393　The truest happiness of mankind is,
　　　　When it the body quits or in it reigns.

　　　　　　[Edmund Wodehouse], 'Feb. 5 [1715]'
　　　　b.131, p. 159

T1394 The trumpet sounds the judge's dread approach,
In the cold shelter of the silent tomb.

    H[enry] Skrine, 'Elegiac address to the Midland
    Circuit on the death of one of its members. In parody
    of Gray's elegy . . . 28 March 1786'

    c.509, p. 82

T1395 The tuneful throng was ever beauty's care,
Alike I'd scorn—your smiles are more than fame.

    [Soame Jenyns], 'To the right honble the Lady
    Margaret Cavendish Harley'

    c.147, p. 35

T1396 The turkey cock, as knows each feeder,
It hangs a red flag at his nose.

    'Why is Arabin like a turkey cock?'

    fc.76.iii/214

T1397 The twenty-eight[h] of May looks very dull
And we'll have him, or none.

    'The cart well lined'

    c.570/1, p. 125

T1398 The undeceived serpent did deceive
Who being deceived himself deceived him.

    [Sir Thomas Urquhart], 'Of the serpent Adam and
    Eve's active passive and mixed deceit'

    fb.217, p. 515

T1399 The unfill'd author, though he be assur'd
For you that made him live, may make him die.

    [William Cartwright], 'The epilogue to their
    Ma[jes]t[ies] at Hampton Court' [from The royal
    slave, 1636]

    b.200, p. 155

T1400 The universe methinks I see,
Father, brothers, for to see.

    Lady Jane Cavendish, 'Love's universe'
    [Crum T1489]

    b.233, p. 22

T1401 The upland shepherd, as reclin'd he lies
Ah! thus man spoils heav'n's glorious works with
                           blood!

    [Charlotte (Turner) Smith], 'Sonnet. The sea view . . .
    from the high down called the Beacon Hill, near
    Brighthelmstone'

    c.141, p. 140

T1402 The upright man that hath a conscience clear,
Doth constant stand and doth no perils fear.

    c.339, p. 313

T1403 The useful fan was first design'd
On things she dares not do.

    Frederick Corfield, 'Written on a lady's fan'

    c.381/2

T1404 The utmost grace the Greeks could show
Lull'd her asleep and then grew drunk.

    John Wilmot, 2nd earl of Rochester

    b.334, p. 177

T1405 The valiant actions of thy ancient line
But you fair charmer, do your friends destroy.

    [Thomas Hamilton, 6th earl of Haddington], 'To
    Lady Jean Douglas'

    c.458/2, p. 115

T1406 The valiant lion, when the vanquished
And beasts that are of less nobility.

    c.189, p. 26

T1407 The van of God, beheld the numerous train,
And equal show'rs their barns with plenty fill.

    'St. Matthew cap. 5'

    c.83/1, no. 183

T1408 The various change of things, and from what seeds
The greatest ills have great originals.

    [Joseph Spence], 'Syphilis: or the modern disease.
    from the Latin of Frascatorius'

    Spence Papers, folder 119

T1409 The various gifts of nature to mankind
To charm our senses and our reason too.

    'To the author of the following treatise' [Alexander
    Bayne]

    Music Ms. 3

T1410 The vast extent of the Olympic roof,
To what is good, surmounts our apprehension.

    Sir Thomas Urquhart, 'To the countess of [crossed
    out]'

    fb.217, p. 56

T1411 The vernal sun and rising juice
And fear each breath of wind like fate.

    'A riddle' [answered by 'I read your riddle . . .']

    c.578, p. 138

T1412 The verses, friend, which thou hast read, are mine,
But as thou read'st them, they may pass for thine.

    'Epigram'

    c.113/32

T1413 The very least refined thought, that harbors
Conform to th'inspirations of your talk.

> Sir Thomas Urquhart, 'To the Earl of [crossed out]'
> fb.217, p. 214

T1414 The very reverend Dean Smedley,
Return him beggar as he went!

> [Jonathan] Swift, 'Translation of a Latin inscription
> written by Dean Smedley (and engraved under his
> picture) on his departure for the East Indies'
> c.83/3, no. 905

T1415 The victor is no victor; if his game
Then life and safety of one friend to choose.

> 'Victoria truculenta victoria non est'
> b.205, fol. 11v

T1416 The village cock, with piercing notes,
For all my God! is full of thee.

> 'A morning rhapsody'
> c.83/1, no. 193

T1417 The violet is modesty
And bids th'admiring world adore.

> 'A nosegay'
> Diggle Box: Poetry Box XI/42

T1418 The Virgin Mary lived still a maid
Deservingly, as ev'ry Christian grants.

> Sir Thomas Urquhart, 'How it doth not argue any
> necessary consequence of unchastity in the child,
> whose parent on either side hath been procreatively
> conversant with several persons . . .'
> fb.217, p. 185

T1419 The virtues and graces once met on this morn
And bless me with her love three and thirty years
hence.

> J. B. D[ickinson], 'To M[artha] D[ickinson] 4. March
> 1791'
> c.391

T1420 The virtues which adorn a wife are these
The closed lips the third—the last the dove.

> 'Distich. Wrote under the figure of a woman standing
> upon a tortoise, a bunch of keys in her right hand, the
> forefinger of her left hand upon her lips, and a dove
> upon her shoulder . . . translations [9]'
> c.81/1, no. 70

T1421 The vizard now no longer need be wore
He that is once true Whig, is always devil.

> 'On occasional conformity'
> b.382(6)

T1422 The vocal nymph, this lovely huntsman view'd
Great is the moan yet is not echoless.

> [Charles Hopkins], 'The story of Narcissus and Echo
> from the third book of Ovid's Metamorphoses'
> b.130, p. 84

T1423 The voice of my beloved sounds
And leave all earthly loves behind.

> [Isaac Watts, Hymns and spiritual songs (1707), bk. I,
> Hymn 69]
> c.180, p. 66; c.259 (with extra lines?)

T1424 The voice said cry! He said, what shall I cry?
But the good word of God stands sure forever.

> Sir John Strangways, '8 Maii 1647'
> b.304, p. 96

T1425 The volumes great whoso doth still peruse,
Shoud have a care the fruit thereof to use.

> [Geffrey Whitney]
> [Crum T1505]
> c.339, p. 321

T1426 'The voyage life is longest made at home'
Calm in a crowd, 'mid armies unsubdued.

> 'To Cowley—in allusion to a poem of that author'
> fc.53, p. 37

T1427 The vulgar say, no lawyer blushes,
I find the blush on Julian's nose.

> 'More vulgar errors exploded by the same means
> [Arabin's nose]'
> fc.76.iii/214

T1428 The W. is double wealth
That I may once well married be.

> 'Responsio' to 'Upon a wife' ['The W. is double woe']
> [Crum T1510]
> b.205, fol. 45v; b.227, p. 70 (incomplete)

T1429 The W. is double woe
Good Lord deliver me from a wife.

> [John Sprint?], 'Upon a wife' [followed by
> 'Responsio', 'The W. is double wealth . . .']
> [Crum T1511]
> b.205, fol. 45v; b.227, p. 70 (incomplete); b.356, p. 71

T1430 The walls of Babel: the Coloss' of Rhodes:
But the eighth wonder is, that they are not.

> [Sir Thomas Urquhart], 'Of the seven wonders of the
> world'
> fb.217, p. 501

T1431   The wan moon seen with stormlike hue
And up he claspt the heavenly [?].

> [John Black], 'The time's at [?] | When all my bliss is
> o'er | When I of thee defend | And never [?] more'
>
> fc.107, p. 44

T1432   The wanton glance of thy beauty's eyes
Tells me all tales they tell of thee be lies.

> [Robert Cottesford]
>
> b.144, p. 3

T1433   The wanton troopers riding by
White as I can, though not as thee.

> Andrew Marvell, 'The nymph complaining for the
> death of her fawn'
>
> b.150, p. 208; c.391, p. 89

T1434   The wanton wife that loves a spark
And loves like him, a bet of old hat.

> [John Lockman], 'Tit for tat. Tune, Black joke'
>
> c.268 (first part), p. 88

T1435   The war's begun and will not end
I shall my dear Lord Jesus see.

> [Mary Pluret], 'Another on the proclamation of the
> war—think on the present state of things'
>
> c.354

T1436   The waves are all up
And higher to wash the face of the sun.

> [Sir William D'Avenant, 'Song. The winter storms,'
> ll. 3–6]
>
> fb.66/35

T1437   The wav'ring nymph, with pride and envy fir'd
And owns herself subdu'd by love's more potent
charms.

> c.549, p. 21

T1438   The way is made
And ride the faster.

> Sir Thomas Urquhart, 'A certain bridegroom . . .
> whilst he did but enter upon the consummation of his
> marriage, speaks thus to his bride'
>
> fb.217, p. 93

T1439   The way of sacred truth is hard to find
The calendar of time, with choicest place.

> [Edward] Sparke, 'Upon Christian solemnities in
> general, poem 1'
>
> b.137, p. 6

T1440   The way to heav'n, if you would know
The way from heav'n, came down to you.

> Sir Thomas Urquhart, 'To one, who was something
> doubtful, how to gain the kingdom of heaven'
>
> fb.217, p. 308

T1441   The way to make a Welshman hope for bliss
But place in heaven to feed upon the moon.

> [John Taylor], 'On a Welshman'
> [Crum T1521b]
>
> b.62, p. 111; b.205, fol. 44r

T1442   The way to virtue's hard, uneasy, bends
That always finds the plain and pleasant valleys.

> [Sir Thomas Urquhart], 'How difficult a thing it is to
> tread in paths of virtue'
>
> fb.217, p. 524

T1443   The way to write an epitaph
Hereunder lies fair Isabel.

> 'On fair Isabel'
>
> fb.143, p. 34; see also 'He who would write an
> epitaph . . .'.

T1444   The wealth of Europe now 'tis plain,
Whilst Alberoni rules the roost.

> 'Some truths in plain English'
>
> c.570/2, p. 31

T1445   The wealthy cit, grown old in trade
To stare about them, and to eat.

> 'The cit's country rose'
>
> c.83/2, no. 316

T1446   The weary sun had almost gone his round,
Than that—the seat of harmony and love.

> [ ] Tierney, 'An imitation of Strada's Philomelae and
> Indicinis certamen . . . Peterhouse College
> Cambridge'
>
> c.130, p. 32

T1447   The weary trav'ler lost in night
To serve my dearest Lord.

> 'Hymn 19th'
>
> c.562, p. 22

T1448   The wedding day appointed was
He sicken'd and he die did.

> 'Epitaph in Biddiford churchyard'
> [Crum T1529]
>
> c.250

T1449 The wench that says I will not do
Saying she will not when she will.

    'Cant: 15'
    [Crum T1531]
    b.4, fol. 10v (damaged)

T1450 The wheel of fortune does appear
Not as they ought, for heav'n aspire.

    [Edmund Wodehouse], 'Apr. 6 [1715] on the lottery'
    b.131, p. 193

T1451 The Whigs and Low Churchmen
Of so serious a thing.

    'The Anwick election'
    c.530, p. 139

T1452 The whim was strange your fancy hit
It has the most convincing ways.

    [Helen Craik], 'To a lady'
    c.375, p. 22

T1453 The whisp'ring of the town is now all spent
The bed is earnest, the incest but a jest.

    [William Strode], 'On a gentlewoman's marriage'
    b.205, fol. 66v

T1454 The whistling plowman hails the blushing dawn,
And shout to the sound of the horn.

    'Song 90'
    c.555, p. 138

T1455 The whitest lawn receives the deepest mole
Is with the greatest wickedness profaned.

    [Sir Thomas Urquhart], 'The busiest (?) being once
    depraved, become the most impious'
    fb.217, p. 498

T1456 The wicked men do quake at every blast,
And tempest rage doth make the world aghast.

    c.339, p. 314

T1457 The widow, she looks like a hag
And swears like any Hector.

    [Henry Neville], 'Ballad, on the serv[an]ts at
    Billingbear'
    Spence Papers, folder 108

T1458 The widows and maids
To delight my good lord and lady.

    [ballad, 1688. To the old tune, Taking of snuff]
    [Crum T1544; POAS IV.267]
    b.115, fol. 8v

T1459 The widow's weed does plainly show,
O that His Grace himself had been but there.

    'Upon the Queen 1708, dropped in St. James'
    b.90, p. 9

T1460 The wife of Vulcan was by Mars assaulted;
Because in Venus' games old Vulcan halted.

    Sir Thomas Urquhart, 'Why Vulcan could not escape
    from being a cuckold'
    fb.217, p. 60

T1461 The winds do rather sigh than blow,
Rise fair one, 'tis a lovely day.

    'A lover courting his lady to take the air'
    c.189, p. 27

T1462 The winds were loud, the clouds deep hung,
She'll scarce her duty pay.

    [ ] Markham, 'Written upon leaving a friend's
    house . . . Dodsley's collection Vol. 4th'
    c.221, p. 19

T1463 The wisdom that I beg is this,
As we employ this morning light.

    [Edmund Wodehouse], 'March 13 [1715]'
    b.131, p. 181

T1464 The wise Creator seldom breaks those laws
Deny his dear-bought love hath put off man.

    b.49, p. 1

T1465 The wise man loves the fools they are in love
Their objects the gayness of the rind.

    [Sir Philip Wodehouse], 'A frang. amabit sapiens . . .'
    b.131, p. 5

T1466 The wise the eloquent, the just
Is gone into eternal bliss.

    'Burgh under Stanemore Tho. Gebets esqr . . . Obit 25
    Martii . . . 1694'
    c.547, p. 329

T1467 The wisest men some follies are permitted(?)
Thus each man's foolish whilst: none still a fool.

    [Sir Thomas Urquhart], 'Folly is incident to all men:
    but to no man at all times'
    fb.217, p. 534

T1468 The wit hath long beholden been
Is now the sign of high degree.

    Will[iam] Strode, 'The caps'
    [Crum T1563]
    b.200, p. 355; b.213, p. 67 (ll. 1–81); b.4, fol. 23 (ll. 1–83)

T1469   The wit-inspiring ternaries of muses
        Hath from the dross of ignorance refin'd us.

> Sir Thomas Urquhart, 'Before there was any mention
> of a covenant, the church of Edinburgh meaned thus
> to Master [crossed out] now elect of [crossed out]'
>
> fb.217, p. 204

T1470   The wits and poets often tell the fair,
        Since a whole lock conspires to draw my love?

> 'On a lock of hair'
>
> c.233, p. 15

T1471   The woman's meat was surely standing corn
        That such a field was by a riverside.

> 'Another of the same' [1 Kings 17.16]
>
> c.160, fol. 55v

T1472   The woman's seed shall bruise the serpent's head,
        Nor would approve, nay endure, what some to her
                                                    say.

> [Edmund Wodehouse], 'Aug. 8 [1715]'
>
> b.131, p. 242

T1473   The women all tell me I'm false to my lass,
        Should you doubt what I say take a bumper and try.

> 'Song 33'
> [Crum T1570]
>
> c.555, p. 52

T1474   The wonder which we daily can't but find,
        In hopes of full felicity.

> [Edmund Wodehouse], 'Octr. 26 [1714]'
>
> b.131, p. 69

T1475   The wond'ring world inquires to know
        Would make the whole earth love him too.

> [Isaac Watts, Hymns and spiritual songs (1707), bk. I,
> Hymn 75]
>
> c.180, p. 26

T1476   The word of denial, and the letter of fifty
        Is the gentleman's name, yet would never be thrifty.

> [Sir Walter Raleigh], 'Raleigh to Noel [Alexander
> Nowell, dean of St. Paul's]'
> [Crum T1574]
>
> b.356, p. 307

T1477   The word of God is pure
        Nor clouds of darkness rise.

> T[homas] S[tevens]
>
> c.259, p. 111

T1478   The word transports of such import
        I should be so in t'other.

> 'A dialogue'
>
> c.546, p. 35

T1479   The world abounds with ills, no doubt,
        Supply fresh food to speculation . . . .

> [Charles Burney, the elder], 'The world as it goes'
>
> c.33, p. 214 (crossed out; incomplete)

T1480   The world alike hath wonders and wise men;
        For a wise man is wonderful to ken.

> Sir Thomas Urquhart, 'Of the seven wonders of the
> world, and the seven sages'
>
> fb.217, p. 51

T1481   The world and flesh and devil doth tempt
        In word, in deed . . . and thought. Amen.

> 'Of the three capital enemies of mankind'
>
> a.6, p. 28

T1482   The world cannot persevere to survive
        Will prove accomplish'd in your imitation.

> Sir Thomas Urquhart, 'To the Earl of [crossed out]'
>
> fb.217, p. 191

T1483   The world could not produce a man, so haughty,
        Upon the altar of his wounded heart.

> Sir Thomas Urquhart, 'On Lady Margaret [crossed
> out]'
>
> fb.217, p. 51

T1484   'The world how fair!'—But not to me so fair!
        When shall I greatly live and perfect peace obtain?

> 'On a fond attachment to the world'
>
> c.515, fol. 12r

T1485   The world is a city full of crooked streets
        The rich would live, the poor must surely die.

> 'An old epitaph in the churchyard at Stoke near to
> Guildford'
>
> c.360/1, p. 325

T1486   The world is bad! And 'tis God wot
        In Wales(?) thou may'st in quiet dwell.

> Sir John Strangways, 'Wouldst thou in quiet gladly
> dwell? Then do the things I here do tell . . . 22do
> Januarii 1646[/7]'
>
> b.304, p. 70

T1487   The world is but an inn for sickly man:
        And scorning vain life true life for to have.

> W[illiam] W[alker], 1599
>
> fpb.32, p. 199

T1488   The world is like a play, where every age
        Death speaks the epilogue and the play is done.

> 'On the shortness of life'
>
> b.62, p. 46

T1489   The world mistakes it was not Eve
        Thou! fairest child of Man.

    'A punning epigram on Miss Man'

Diggle Box: Poetry Box XI/68

T1490   The world must still wend in his common course,
        And then return unto his former fall.

    [Sir Francis Castillion], 'Gently always take, that
    ungently comes'

fb.69, p. 184

T1491   The world, says Shakespeare, is a stage,
        Sans sense, *sans* everything.

    Frederick Corfield

c.381/2

T1492   The world they say is full of holes
        Your nose will tell how they're inclined.

b.200, p. 380

T1493   The world would seem a wild and shapeless load,
        But He Himself was pleased man to frame.

    Dan[iel] Primerose, St. John's College, Oxford, 'Man'
    [written at the Merchant Taylor's School for the Lent
    Probation, 1700]
    [Crum T1590]

Poetry Box VI/73

T1494   The world's a bubble, and the life of man
        Not to be born, or being born, to die.

    Fran[cis] Bacon, 1st viscount St. Albans, 'On the
    world's vanity'
    [Crum T1591]

b.62, p. 134; b.356, p. 283

T1495   The world's a city, full of crooked street[s]
        The rich would always live, the poor alone would die.

    'Inscription on a gravestone in M. Romney
    churchyard'

c.373, p. 84

T1496   The world's a globe of state, our life a reign
        Never to die, or straight be born again.

    [parody of 'The world's a bubble . . .', by Sir Francis
    Bacon]
    [Crum T1595]

b.200, p. 299

T1497   The world's a school, wherein a general story
        And far off, makes the world young every year.

    [Joshua Sylvester, trans. Guillaume de Salluste,
    seigneur] Du Bartas, 'On the world: and what use we
    must make of God's works in it'

b.137, p. 86; b.144, p. 2 (incomplete)

T1498   The world's an inn; and I her guest
        Her lavish bills, and go my way.

    [Francis Quarles], 'On the world'
    [Crum T1604]

b.118, p. 224

T1499   The world's deceitful, and man's life at best
        Lord I may reign with thee eternally.

    H[enry] C[olman], 'On mortality'
    [Crum T1606]

b.2, p. 6

T1500   The world's four parks and all the various grass
        The center of fair friendship in the land.

    [Sir Aston Cokayne], 'To the same [Sir Andrew
    Knyveton] and his brothers'

b.275, p. 55.

T1501   The world's gay color that delights our eyes,
        Are clad with united rays of light.

    'The order of rays of color the first red, the second
    orange . . .'

c.83/1, no. 7

T1502   The world's great house cannot be masterless;
        For there's no house: but someone doth possess.

    Sir Thomas Urquhart, 'Against atheists'

fb.217, p. 196

T1503   The world's left part, the rightest faith doth breathe:
        The world's right part being left of saving faith.

    Sir Thomas Urquhart, 'Of right, and wrong faith'

fb.217, p. 233

T1504   The world's too much in debt though it may
        The poetry shall keep its own rent.

    [Thomas Carew], 'Carew to Ben Jonson'

b.356, p. 300

T1505   The worst is told, the best is hid
        He err'd but once, once, king, forgive.

    Mrs. [John] Hoskins(?), 'Mrs Hoskins to his M[ajes]ty
    for her husband'
    [Crum T1611]

b.200, p. 100

T1506   The wounds which time had thinly crusted o'er
        Where his dread sovereign is the God of gods.

    [( ) Bent], 'On the death of James Butler esqr of
    Downs in the County of Devon: who soon followed
    the author's father'

c.504, p. 62

T1507 The wretch alone hath all he hath; for he
The wretch alone lacks all, he doth possess.

Sir Thomas Urquhart, 'Of the avaricious man'
fb.217, p. 86

T1508 The wretch condemn'd with life to part,
Emits a brighter ray.

[Oliver] Goldsmith, 'Hope'
c.94; Poetry Box XII/96

T1509 The wretch (O love!) who trips thy smiles,
Beside a stream; and, plunging, dies.

John Lockman, 'Translations, and imitations from
Metastasio, and other Italian opera poets [17]'
c.267/4, p. 111

T1510 The wretch that today is o'erloaded with sorrow,
May soar above those, that oppress'd him tomorrow.

c.378, p. 77

T1511 The wretched victim of a quick decay,
Be yours the lesson—sad experience mine.

'The penitent prostitute, intended for her tombstone'
c.94

T1512 The wretch'dest father is most liberal
Th'estates of many to the hospital.

Sir Thomas Urquhart, 'On the covetous fathers of
spendthrift sons'
fb.217, p. 148

T1513 The year before
The reason's plain, the captains most were Tories.

[Sir Fleetwood] Sheppard, 'Mr Sheppard's remarks on
a late French prophecy [1691] . . . Remarks'
fb.70, p. 291

T1514 The year revolving now brings back the day,
Sweet to the world and seek its kindred skies.

[( ) H., jr.], 'To a young lady on her birthday'
Spence Papers, folder 113

T1515 The year revolving (sacred Fame!)
Where all the virtues sit enshrin'd.

John Lockman, 'The genius of Ireland to Fame. On
occasion of the long and auspicious administration of
his excellency George Lord Viscount Townshend. An
ode for New Year's Day, 1770'
c.267/4, p. 323

T1516 The years revolve, and every thing doth turn
And almanacs, as everything, must end.

[John Rose?]
b.227, p. 192

T1517 The years which gaily circle'd round,
My ev'ry step attend!

'Ode on the author's birthday—Apr. 19. [17]67'
c.89, p. 16

T1518 The yeoman all at Hackney met
Agreed 'twas very fine.

Poetry Box x/100

T1519 The young Bellario now in harmless toys
And he with perfect happiness be blest [May
young Bellario happily be blest.]

[Elizabeth (Shirley) Compton, countess of
Northampton]
Accession 97.7.40 (2 versions)

T1520 The young inexperienced maids admire
Break our sots' heads or damn our souls.

'Out of T. Brower's Latin'
c.416

T1521 The youth is tall to whom I inscribe my verse
And all the virtues crowded in his mind.

'Written on Peregrine Greatheed esqr in the time of
his life after his father's death'
Greatheed Box/95

T1522 The youth prepares for martial toils
And she present a race of new.

Dr. [ ] Earle, 'On the Prince of Orange's making a
campaign in Germany in 173[ ], while his princess was
pregnant with her first child'
c.360/2, no. 49

T1523 The youth was belov'd in the prime of his life,
Than thus to be hanged for cutting purse.

'A proper new ballad called Lamentable Lory. To the
tune of Youth, youth, thou had'st better be starved at
nurse' [on Lawrence Hyde, 3rd earl of Rochester,
Lord President of the Council, Aug. 1684; see 'Here
lies a creature . . .']
[Crum T1621, 'spring of youth']
fb.70, p. 195

T1524 The youth whose birth the sisters twain
They please from him alone.

Richard Berenger, 'Lib. 4 ode [3] of Horace, Quem tu
Melpomene, imitated'
fc.51, p. 312

T1525 The youth whose fortune the vast globe obey'd,
And let the good, the just, the brave prevail.

[Charles Sackville, 6th earl of Dorset], 'On the
assassination plot against King W[illia]m'
[Crum T1622]
c.244, p. 109 (attr. [George] Stepney)

T1526 The youths whose gentler souls have felt love's smart,
Yield to those gain'd o'er the mind.

    [John Lockman], 'Campaspe. A musical drama'

c.268 (second part), p. 53

T1527 Th'earth being below all things: the heav'ns 'bove
                    all;
Th'earth hath not, where: nor the heav'ns, whence
                    to fall.

    Sir Thomas Urquhart, 'Why neither the heavens nor
    the earth can fall naturally'

fb.217, p. 263

T1528 Th'earth stands says Solomon, and sits, quoth Ovid:
With violence, what doth it then? It lies.

    Sir Thomas Urquhart, 'Of the situation of the earth'

fb.217, p. 249

T1529 Th'earth's veins, are mines: bones, stones: her
                    skin's the crust:
Water, 's her blood: grass, hair: her flesh, is dust.

    Sir Thomas Urquhart, 'The heterogenial composition
    of the earth'

fb.217, p. 202

T1530 Thee, by what name shall I implore,
Safe from the herded sons of care.

    [ ] Ellison, 'Translation of Mr. Gray's ode made at the
    Grande Chartreuse'

Greatheed Box/35

T1531 Thee Flora's first and favorite child,
Shall lodge thee next his heart!

    'The violet'

c.83/1, no. 161

T1532 Thee God we praise, Thy name adore
As we trust in Thy name.

    'Te deum, or Song of Ambrose'

c.264/3, p. 127

T1533 Thee I forgive, repent thou honest man,
Because 'tis cordial, would 'twere in thy heart.

    'On a creditor'

b.200, p. 412; see also 'Not that in color . . .'.

T1534 Thee I love, and thee alone:
Or statesmen['s] pow'r—I love myself.

    'Soliloquy'

c.481, p. 126

T1535 Thee Jesus full of truth and grace,
The stamp of perfect love.

    'Hymn 74th'

c.562, p. 93

T1536 Thee, Lord, I love with my whole heart,
To sit on Israel's throne.

    'Psalm 18 Evening prayer'

c.264/1, p. 55

T1537 Thee! lucid arbiter 'twixt day and night,
Once lent to light me on my thorny way!

    [Charlotte (Turner) Smith], 'Sonnet to the morning
    star. Written near the sea'

c.141, p. 120

T1538 'Thee, Mary, with this ring I wed'—
And teach me all things—but repentance!

    [Samuel Bishop? or Edmund Burke?], 'Verses sent by
    a gentleman to his lady, with a ring, by the author of
    those with a knife'

c.391; c.175, p. 80

T1539 Thee, mighty God! we humbly praise,
Us ever hope in vain.

    'Te deum laudamus'

c.167, p. 5

T1540 Thee! Month benign, devoid of ills,
Among the blessings thou hast sent.

    [Charles Burney, the elder], 'June. Addressed to [Mrs.
    Thrale] on the birth of a daughter—the 21st of this
    month, 1778'

c.33, p. 124

T1541 Thee parent Nre form'd with beauteous face,
So may our mutual amity ne'er end.

    'Presented 3 Novr. 1755. with a print of Nre . . .
    Theophilus'

c.371, fol. 85

T1542 Thee, Stanley, thee, our gladden'd spirit hails
Diffus'd the blessings of her crystal shrine.

    [Anna Seward], 'Hoyle Lake . . . a poem written on
    that coast and addressed to its proprietor, Sir John
    Stanley'

c.141, p. 259

T1543 Thee to invite the great God sent a star
But like the day-star, only sets to rise.

    James I(?), 'King James on the death of Queen Anne'
    [March 1618/19]
    [Crum T1631]

b.200, p. 236; b.62, p. 1; fb.143, p. 25; b.356, p. 254

T1544 Thee will I laud my God and king
Forever shall accord.

    [Thomas Norton], 'A praise of God for his justice and
    mercy. Psal. 62' [verses from Psalm 145]
    [Crum T1635]

a.3, fol. 147

T1545 Thee will I praise Almighty Love,
Full harvests to eternity.

'Psalm 34'

c.264/1, p. 143

T1546 Thee will I praise my God and King,
To Him forevermore.

'Psalm 145 30 day'

c.264/3, p. 104

T1547 Thee will I praise my God, and sing
Above all blessing raise.

'Psalm 30—Morning prayer 6th day'

c.264/1, p. 117

T1548 Thee will I praise with my whole heart
Which Thy own hand did make.

[Thomas Norton], 'A thanks or praise of God for his
blessings. Psalm 58' [verses from Psalm 138]
[Crum T1638]

a.3, fol. 142v

T1549 Their branches the green willows wave,
And died, in pronouncing his name.

[Sophia (Raymond) Burrell Clay], 'Charlotte's
lamentation'

c.141, p. 526

T1550 Their care and pains the fair ones do bestow
They're only saints and angels in their look.

c.549, p. 46

T1551 Their crests well correspond, in their import
The other young and brisk in enterprise.

[Sir Philip Wodehouse], 'An additional armorial upon
[the Savage-Wodehouse marriage]'

b.131, p. 3 and back (after anagram 235)

T1552 Their habitations here is not their home
That's here on earth can give them full content.

[Mary Serjant]

fb.98, fol. 164

T1553 Their marriage bed is a new almanac
He may put Julie in the [?] of Winter.

[Sir Thomas Urquhart], 'Concerning Julius the
printer married to Master Winter'

fb.217, p. 388

T1554 Their mourning lasts but a morning
Set open doors to wicked doers.

'On women'

b.205, fol. 45

T1555 Their piety th'Egyptians show'd by art
Till its own ornament each grace become.

[Anne Finch, countess of Winchilsea], 'To Mrs. Belle
Marrow on the death of Lady Marrow, 1715'

b.322, p. 31

T1556 Their spirits in their arteries, and nerves
They from their vomit, fall to wine again.

Sir Thomas Urquhart, 'The custom of drunkards'

fb.217, p. 213

T1557 Their sweet conveyance in the saraband,
They grac'd their footing with the castanets.

Sir Thomas Urquhart, 'How a lover, and his mistress
danced the saraband together'

fb.217, p. 343

T1558 Their wives' defaults kind husbands will not see
Thus love not only blind but deaf appears.

'Blind love is deaf'

c.356

T1559 Then Altamont; accept this last adieu
Death shall divorce me from myself and thee.

'An epistle from Calista to Altamont' [Lady
Abergavenny to her lord]

c.53, fol. 53; see also 'To jealous love . . .'.

T1560 Then Deborah, with holy cries inspir'd,
Let them go out as th'sun in strongest might.

[William Sandys?], 'The song of Deborah and Barach
after the defeat of King Jabin the Canaanite's army
under the conduct of Sisera. Judges Chap: 5'

b.230, p. 23

T1561 Then drink of thy liquor and turn the glass over,
Seeing's believing, boys, all the world over.

'Another [drinking song] thus'

c.416

T1562 Then farewell! cruel Nancy!
Which bade me first pursue.

Poetry Box II/37

T1563 Then farewell my true-built wherry
With a sigh may cry, poor Tom.

'Poor Tom'

Poetry Box IV/50

T1564 Then forth my doubtful course I took,
The conflict was no more.

'Emma, who perished in her lover's arms from thirst
and fever'

c.83/2, no. 400

T1565 Then how should I believe you love me well,
Yet love is both when it is most extreme.

    'The enthusiast'

    fb.142, p. 38

T1566 Then Israel shall courage take
Shown his decree, which must forever stand.

    [William Sandys?], 'Israel triumphs over Babylon in
    the prophecy of Isaiah chap: 14: from ver: 4 to 24'

    b.230, p. 73

T1567 Then Judith the Bethulians' hearts doth raise:
And those with wares approach thy mercy seat.

    [William Sandys?], 'Judith's song after (by the death
    of Holifernes) she had delivered Bethulia chap: 16: to
    verse 17'

    b.230, p. 97

T1568 Then let it be said
No wonder the weapon is bloody.

    'On a lady who had a bloodshot eye'

    c.378, p. 5

T1569 Then let not winter's ragged hand deface
To be death's conquest, and make worms thy heir.

    [William] Shakespeare [Sonnet VI]

    c.94

T1570 Then let us boast of ancestors no more,
'Tis personal virtue only makes us truly great.

    'The conclusion' [of Defoe's The trueborn
    Englishman: 'Speak, satire . . .']

    fb.142, p. 18

T1571 Then, life of loveliness forbear
Thy shape and air without a fault!

    'To a lady in fears for the loss of her beauty, translated
    (with a small variation) from Anacreon by her
    husband'

    c.536

T1572 Then Moses and all Isr'el rais'd
Stood up, whilst Isr'el cross'd.

    'The song of Moses Exod: 15'

    c.264/3, p. 129

T1573 Then mourn we may not (as without hope) in vain
Even face to face, no glass between.

    'Verses consolatory'

    fc.61, p. 11, p. 137

T1574 Then Robert Stewart the second in that king
Daughter to Sr John Drummond of Globhall knight.

    '[Rulers of Scotland] 8'

    fa.4, fol. 28v

T1575 Then to the Lord, the vast triumphant throng
O'er the dry path, and trod the watery waste.

    [Christopher] Pitt, 'The song of mercy. Exodus 15'

    c.244, p. 512

T1576 Then vain honor was naught desired
Is turned. . . .

    [William Pulley?]

    b.134, p. 511 (incomplete)

T1577 Then what avails, since virtue now no more,
And for each good,—a star recording glows!

    'An elegiac ode, on the much lamented death of her
    grace the Duchess of Norfolk'

    c.90

T1578 Then Zacharias' loos'n'd tongue
And guide our feet, to paths of peace.

    'The song of Zacharias Luke 1. 68 and 79 inclus[ive]'

    c.264/3, p. 124

T1579 Th'engravers came out [?] and limners paint them:
But to the ear you lively represent them.

    [Sir Thomas Urquhart], 'Mendaciam dictam fictu
    pictim to Misaletes'

    fb.217, p. 513

T1580 Th'enliv'ning sun, bright orb of day,
It paves our way to heav'n.

    'Laura, by a young lady'

    c.83/2, no. 640

T1581 There are, I scarce can think it, but am told
My lords the judges laugh, and you're dismiss'd.

    Alex[ande]r Pope, 'A satire the 1st from the 2nd [book]
    of Horace in a dialogue between . . . and his learned
    council' [pr. 1733 (Foxon P886)]

    c.570/4, p. 92

T1582 There are that love the shades of life,
Guard thy emblematic flower.

    'The evening primrose'

    c.83/3, no. 995

T1583 There are—to whom my satires seem too bold,
And the poor plaintiff hang himself for grief.

    [William Popple, trans.], 'Horace book 2nd satire 1st
    imitated. (Dialogue between the poet and a friend)'

    fc.104/1, p. 191

T1584 There are you say, God bless the people!
As an *aurora borealis*.

    [William Hayley]

    File 6924

T1585 There being no possibility that men
And a good conscience shall be [?] wealth.

[Sir Thomas Urquhart], 'That our contentment while
we are upon earth resisteth more [?]not to be [illeg.]'
fb.217, p. 509

T1586 There constant love with equal ardor glows,
The feast or bath by day, and love by night.

[Alexander] Pope(?), 'Orrery's fling'
fc.14/10

T1587 There dwelt at Ephesus a noble dame
How the dead loss had climb'd the cross again.

W[illiam] S[mith], 'Dec. 24. 1800. The dame of
Ephesus translated from Petronius'
Smith Papers, folder 59

T1588 There dwelt sometimes in royal Rome
To heaven the perfect way. | Amen

'Of S. Alexius. July 17'
a.30[11]

T1589 There happened in the twilight of the day
Starts from his couch and bids the dame draw near.

'Sr. Edmundbury Godfrey's ghost. 1679'
b.54, p. 1085; see also 'It happened . . .'.

T1590 There, in gardens of eternal spring,
And every sense be lost in every joy.

'Mahomedan paradise. (Tenges[?])'
c.81/2, no. 579

T1591 There is a body without a heart
And loud doth speak and yet is dead.

'7. Enigma. Res. A bell'
b.205, fol. 99r

T1592 There is a bush fit for the nonce
They throw the empty skin away.

'A riddle on a gooseberry'
[Crum T1689]
b.62, p. 4

T1593 There is a coal that burns the more
Now yield in time or else I die.

'His 3 onset to move her to more pity' [answered by
'The Indian men . . .']
b.205, fol. 93r

T1594 There is a field thro' which I often pass,
(Live till tomorrow) will have pass'd away.

[William Cowper], 'The needless alarm. A tale'
c.140, p. 527

T1595 There is a God, all nature speaks,
And bow before Him, and adore.

'The voice of the Creator'
c.83/3, no. 899

T1596 There is a herb that men call lunary
Amen for charity.

[alchemical poem; see Brown-Robbins 1203]
fa.16, p. 40

T1597 There is a house, both new and fine,
To save a duck, to supper.

[Thomas Hamilton, 6th earl of Haddington], 'A song
made on a true story tune Chevy Chase'
c.458/1, p. 58

T1598 There is a House to be let for [the] steward has
swore
A long time kept shut up but paid for't at last.

'Set over the Parliament house'
b.327, f. 14; see also 'Here's a House . . .'.

T1599 There is a knack in doing many a thing,
I took the liberty to boil my peas!

[John Walcot(?) ('Peter Pindar')], 'The pilgrims and
the peas . . . Ode 6—1786'
c.355, p. 102

T1600 There is a land of pure delight
Fright back to Scotland's shore.

[Isaac Watts], '66 hymn 2d book Scotch version tune
Cambridge new'
fc.108, fol. 77v

T1601 There is a little thing, that's found in diverse lands
This is a famous riddle come, tell it, if you can.

[riddle on the letter M]
[Crum T1699]
Spence Papers, folder 113

T1602 There is a monster in this land
And many years will do the same again.

'Riddle' [Tyburn]
Poetry Box VII/49

T1603 There is a place by nature seemed designed
Our glory's to be free and render others so.

George Montagu, 'A description of Diana's temple at
Nismes and the prospect round about wrote 1737
by . . . and sent to Mr. Barrett now Lord Dacre'
fc.135, after p. 20 (2 copies)

T1604 There is a ship we understand
And haste away together.

'A merry new song in praise of lubberland'
File 17369

T1605 There is a standing jest you know
But am your friend sincere | J. W.

> J[ohn] W[alker], 'Poetical epistle to R. Waugh junior
> who went to Berwick'
>
> fc.108, fol. 60; see also 'My charming friend . . .'.

T1606 There is a thing it must be done
Cover the hole and shut the door.

> 'The one thing needful'
>
> c.546, p. 29

T1607 There is a thing that nothing is
Doth feed on nothing but itself.

> 'On jealousy'
> [Crum T1709]
>
> b.205, fol. 35r

T1608 There is a thing 'twixt head and foot
And some have none at all.

> 'A riddle'
>
> c.150, p. 150

T1609 There is a time when love no wish denies
That sense breaks short and when we taste, we die.

> c.546, p. 11

T1610 There is a tribe, O bless 'em
A bed of mud, and clay?

> 'A character common enough among the great vulgar'
>
> fc.53, p. 17

T1611 There is a virgin dead, but be it known
But 'tis enough that she is gone to heaven.

> 'On the death of Mrs Penelope Hanham'
>
> b.200, p. 225

T1612 There is an isle, I dare not name it,
Or faith ye souls are lost in air.

> 'Charade'
>
> c.389

T1613 There is no Christian, paynim, Jew nor Turk,
To be the better occupied thereby.

> Sir Thomas Urquhart, 'Of an extremely licentious
> woman'
>
> fb.217, p. 118

T1614 There is no difference death hath made
Is differenc'd or in heaven, or hell.

> 'A prolusion upon the emblem of the chapter being
> the last chapter'
>
> c.189, p. 75

T1615 There is no ill on earth which mortals fly
Lord, give me neither, give me but content.

> St[ephe]n Duck, 'On poverty'
>
> c.165, p. 24

T1616 There is no kind of a fragmental note
Nothing on earth should make a man repine.

> [John Byrom], 'The Italian bishop'
>
> c.139, p. 349

T1617 There is no reason, that his avarice,
For wealth is goods: and no more doth he seek.

> Sir Thomas Urquhart, 'Of covetousness a paradox.
> Upon a greedy churl'
>
> fb.217, p. 299

T1618 There is no scene of life I ween
Adieu! False shades—I'll look above.

> 'An abbreviated soliloquy'
>
> c.81/1, no. 10

T1619 There is not any lives below the spangled
It kills not, it is sure to overcome.

> Sir Thomas Urquhart, 'To Lady [crossed out]'
>
> fb.217, p. 80

T1620 There is not half so warm a fire
I pick a cabinet for a Bristol stone.

> [Zouch Towneley], 'On a lady in a veil'
> [Crum T1730]
>
> b.197, p. 22; fb.140, p. 140

T1621 There is not one below the azure cape,
The object of my verses, and affection.

> Sir Thomas Urquhart, 'To the elixir of beauty the
> every way accomplish'd Aura'
>
> fb.217, p. 210

T1622 There is one black and sullen hour
One minute of midnight is worth a whole day.

> [Thomas D'Urfey], 'Canto 113' [docket title; c. 1686?]
> [Crum T1731]
>
> File 19028

T1623 There is one thing my friends I must offer to you,
Export all the rest,—give the devil his due.

> 'Song 72'
>
> c.555, p. 109

T1624 There is scarce any other word that's Spanish,
The one from th'other, as their mortal foe.

> Sir Thomas Urquhart, 'Of no, and much'
>
> fb.217, p. 230

T1625   There lately into England came
Rather than want it will their presence buy.

     [ ] R., 'Riddle'

Poetry Box VII/49

T1626   Entry cancelled.
There liv'd long ago in a country place . . .

     See T1631.

T1627   There liv'd a bishop once upon a time,
Nothing on earth should make a man repine.

     [John] Byrom, of Manchester, 'The Italian bishop'

c.148, p. 9

T1628   There lived a gentleman, possest
His honor may his conscience clear.

     'The cobbler'

c.113/19

T1629   There lived a mouse in Balinocrazy
Stupid, stupid, aly, aly, croaker.

Poetry Box I/88

T1630   There liv'd in York, an age ago,
A wife by cheese—before he ties the noose.

     Captain Thompson, 'The choice of a wife by cheese'

fc.85, fol. 93v; Poetry Box X/130 (bis)

T1631   There liv'd long ago in a country place
For she scorn'd to be false for the lucre of gain.

     'A song'

c.536; Accession 97.7.40, p. 9

T1632   There lodgeth a lady of late
That Herbert goes down for a dainty.

     'Song'

fb.106(28)

T1633   There shall they shine like blazing stars
Peace, love, and joy to them and thee.

fb.234, p. 45

T1634   There should be no spectators, when we grope
(Lest we perceive them) when they're in conjunction.

     Sir Thomas Urquhart, 'That venery (how lawful
soever) should be practiced in secret'

fb.217, p. 60

T1635   There was a bonny blade
For to make a scolding wife hold her tongue.

     'The dumb maid'

c.503, p. 57

T1636   There was a cobbler, and he liv'd in a stall,
The cobbler he died and the knell it did toll.

     'Song'

c.503, p. 56; see also 'A cobbler there was . . .'.

T1637   There was a fair maid that liv'd under a hill
There may she live happy and finish her woe.

     'A ballad to the tune of Which nobody can deny'

Accession 97.7.40

T1638   There was a fine widow, a fine one indeed,
And when I'm of age take my doctor's degree.

     'The generous widow' [on Mrs. Jackson; to the tune
of The Archbishop of Canterbury]

fc.85, fol. 73

T1639   There was a great fleet, all they that did see't
For a wiser man to command.

     'Upon the English fleet set forth anno. 1625'

b.197, p. 226

T1640   There was a little man and he woo'd a little maid
She could have but the cat and her skin, skin, skin.

Poetry Box XII/58

T1641   There was a maid of Westmoreland
No creature's half so queer as he.

     'The maid of Westmoreland'

Poetry Box XII/99

T1642   There was a man, and he was *Semper Idem*,
She to requite him made him cuckold *gratis*.

     [on Sir Lionel Cranfield, later 1st earl of Middlesex,
Lord Treasurer]
     [Crum T1755]

fb.69, p. 224; see also 'There was a man whose
name . . .'.

T1643   There was a man bespoke a thing
Whether he had it, yea or no.

     'Riddle on a coffin'
     [Crum T1756]

c.360/1, p. 124; c.356; b.205, fol. 99v

T1644   There was a man called Job
The same case happen us.

     [Zacharie Boyd?]
     [Crum T1757]

b.232, p. 5; b.231, p. 6

T1645   There was a man whose name was *Semp[er] Idem*
She to requite him made him cuckold *gratis*.

     'Epigrams. 1. In cornutum jocosum' [on Sir Lionel
Cranfield, later 1st earl of Middlesex, Lord Treasurer]

b.205, fol. 97r; c.378, p. 5 (var.); see also 'There was a
man, and he . . .'.

T1646 There was a prudent grave physician
Custom and nature will prevail.

    [Sir Charles Sedley], 'The doctor and his patient'
    [Crum T1761]

    fb.68, p. 45; c.186, p. 49 (with extra lines?)

T1647 There was a thing on earth which scripture doth
                      record
Nor dwell in bliss, where blessed souls remain.

    'A riddle on the prophet Balaam's ass'

    c.360/1, p. 3

T1648 There was a thriving cobbling man
The cobbler Shrinky Hardscraes.

    'Shrinky Hardscraes. A ballad'

    File 13409

T1649 There was a time when Britain's daring sons
Brittania did, and will command the waves.

    'Past, present, and future' [General evening post,
    31 July 1777]

    c.157, p. 106

T1650 There was a time when on these plains
The memory of woman kind.

    'A song'
    [Crum T1763]

    b.207, p. 32

T1651 There was a time when that a certain teacher
E'er found this text there was a certain woman.

    'Quidam homo' [answered by 'That no man yet . . .']

    b.205, fol. 48r

T1652 There was a time when traitors to their king
And London reassume its ancient grace!

    'On city honors' [General evening post, 25 Aug. 1777]

    c.157, p. 106

T1653 There was a young, and valiant knight,
Beneath them, all is care.

    H[annah] More, 'Sir Eldred of the bower, a legendary
    tale'

    c.139, p. 364

T1654 There was an old man and tho' 'tis not common
Had he lived a day longer he'd been a day older.

    'The wonderful old man a song'

    fc.85, fol. 111; c.555, p. 213; see also T1656.

T1655 There was an old man in Northumberland
Can read as fast as you can run by the way, with a
                        toll de roll &c.

    'The north countryman's ramble'

    c.158, p. 468

T1656 There was an old man who liv'd on a common
Had he lived a day longer he'd have been a day
                   older. | Derry down [&c.].

    'The wonderful old man'

    c.179, p. 47; see also T1654.

T1657 There was an old prophecy found in a bog,
That we shall have again our old K[ing]. | Lero
              [lero . . . lilli bullero, bullen a la]

    'Song. To the tune of Lilliburlero'
    [Crum T1760, 'a prophecy'; POAS IV.312]

    fb.70, p. 265; b.209, p. 74 (ll. 1–4)

T1658 There was an old woman, as I've heard tell,
O, says the little woman, this is none of it. | Tiddle,
                    tiddle, etc.

    J[ohn] C[arter], 'The old woman and her little dog'

    c.488, p. 34

T1659 There was at court a lady of late,
There's passage for a Carr to ride.

    'On Sir Robert Carr [later earl of Somerset]'s wife'
    [Frances (Howard)]
    [Crum T1770]

    b.200, p. 409

T1660 There was lately a call,
Or sell all your souls for a song.

    'The holy week a Christmas tale'

    fc.85, fol. 84

T1661 There was once,—it is said
To the good folks of ev'ry profession. | Tol de rol &c.

    'Song 67'

    c.555, p. 96

T1662 There was so Chaucer hands the story down
That first he gave, and afterwards he taught.

    'The character of a good parson from Chaucer'

    c.83/2, no. 595

T1663 Thereon amongst his travels found,
And tread the Caesars in the dirt.

    [Isaac] Watts, 'The hero's school of mortality'
    [Crum T1774b]

    c.244, p. 308; c.360/2, no. 103

T1664 There's a place in this town to which all do repair
Which can conquer at once both the flesh and the
                    spirit.

    Poetry Box IV/149

T1665 There's an engine in optics enlarges each letter
What was made by her hand was ne'er destined to
age.

[Phanuel Bacon], 'The fly painted by a young lady on
the Revd. Doctor B——'s spectacles'
[Crum T1778]

c.237, fol. 5; c.94

T1666 There's mercy in each breath of air that mortal lips
e'er draw
There's mercy for each creeping thing, but man
has none for man.

[Matthew Gregory] Lewis

Diggle Box: Poetry Box XI/33

T1667 There's no such charm
Or shrill alarm.

[Sir Philip Wodehouse], 'Ann Armin Ann in arm'

b.131, back (no. 27/2)

T1668 There's no such hell as is a tortured mind,
Or else I beg my being may not be.

Lady Jane Cavendish, 'Love's torture'
[Crum T1783]

b.233, p. 14

T1669 There's no such thing as pleasure here,
Who said of pleasure, it is mad.

[Katherine Philips], 'Against pleasure'
[Crum T1785]

b.118, p. 73

T1670 There's no way to the world but one
Let Will still take his snuff.

'A defense of Wm. Patterson's taking snuff'

c.530, p. 151

T1671 There's none my beauty can deny—
Since both are partners of a crown.

[Phanuel Bacon], 'A riddle'
[Crum T1786]

c.237, fol. 19

T1672 There's none of your three sons resembleth either:
Though ev'ry one of them be like his father.

Sir Thomas Urquhart, 'To one, who was supposed to
be very uncertain of his children, whether they were
his, or not'

fb.217, p. 74

T1673 There's not a barber at Whitehall
G—— awake — and kill [t]his K——.

[William Popple, trans.], 'Horace book 1st satire 7th
imitated. M—— versus K——'

fc.104/1, p. 143

T1674 There's not a heath however rude
To love and call its own.

[Phanuel Bacon], 'Song'

c.237, fol. 81 [i.e., 101]

T1675 There's not a man of sense will prove,
And by possession must expire.

W[illiam Aliffe, 'Friendly advice'

fb.207/4, p. 30

T1676 There's not an echo round me,
Who fill a child with fear.

[William Cowper, trans.], 'Vol. 2. Cant. 144' [of
Jeanne Guion's 'Spiritual songs']

c.470 (autogr.)

T1677 There's not an evil, that we fly
What would we have? What want we more.

'Thoughts on poverty'

c.83/2, no. 287

T1678 There's not an ill on earth which mortals fly
Lord give me either give me but content.

Stephen Duck, 'On poverty'

c.547, p. 181

T1679 There's nothing more afflicts my grieved soul
All these I do invoke, to safe land you.

Lady Jane Cavendish, 'Passion's contemplation'
[Crum T1792]

b.233, p. 5

T1680 There's Orange Will with his long nose,
We shall send him to hell with his thund'ring Moll.

'On King William'

b.111, p. 416

T1681 There's pleasure sure in being cloth'd in green
When will tomorrow come?

[Sneyd Davies], 'Dr. Thirlby, Mr. Dodd and Whaley
after hunting: the scene Swallowfield'

c.157, p. 81

T1682 There's scarce a nobleman in all this nation,
Is more illustrious now, than it was ever.

Sir Thomas Urquhart, 'To the Earl of [crossed out]'

fb.217, p. 118

T1683 There's so great store of lunary 'mongst men:
That Cynthia rules the earth, as well's the main.

Sir Thomas Urquhart, 'Of Cynthia, the sovereign of
the sea'

fb.217, p. 318

T1684 There's some at court that would be critics call'd
And give good sport to those that hear him stutter.

[Sir Richard Bulstrode], 'Upon the court at St. Germain's'

fb.88, p. 115v

T1685 There's three, that with their fiery darts do level
Are three t' afflict, I'm but one, to bear.

[Francis Quarles], 'On man's three enemies' [Crum T1796]

b.137, p. 191

T1686 There's under sun as wisdom's self did show
Whatever subject unto human sense.

[Joshua Sylvester, trans. Guillaume de Salluste, seigneur] Du Bartas, 'Of the creation of man after God's Image and the excellency of his several parts'

b.137, p. 101

T1687 These awful walls for either bus'ness fit,
The cause resolv'd to like and to commend.

Timothy Neve, 'Prologue to Love for love as spoken by Mr. Richard Falkner who acted Nurse when played at the town hall of Spalding by the free school scholars of Spalding Decr. 1726'

c.229/2, fol. 50v

T1688 These delights if thou canst give
Mirth with thee we mean to live.

[John Milton], 'Chorus [5, with musical score for tenor and bass, from Handel's Il penseroso]'

Music MS. 534

T1689 These doting doctors in their books sore blame me
to be naught,
If want of stools doth make thee sick, cheese eaten
last will heal.

'In caseum' [translated from the Latin] [Crum T1801]

b.54, p. 877

T1690 These epigrams are few;
Were they ne'er so few.

Sir Thomas Urquhart, 'Why my epigrams are both short and few'

fb.217, p. 58

T1691 These epithets might suit an emperor,
Like to the place it hopes and makes for, heav'n.

[Sir Philip Wodehouse], 'Mr. Th[omas] Amyas' anagram upon my name with my own paraphrase Sir Philip Wodehouse wise old loved philosopher'

b.131, back (no. [234])

T1692 These fading trees shall soon again
To crown our blissful state.

'A thought on autumn—by a lady'

c.139, p. 403

T1693 These great names future ages will dwell on
Howe, Bridport, Vincent, Duncan and Nelson.

'On the British admirals'

c.546, p. 34

T1694 These hallowed stones an English heart enfold;
Pure as thy virtues as thy friendships true.

William Hayley

File 6969

T1695 These herrings, with a watermelon,
Till, like the sun, your faces shine.

John Lockman, 'I, Lockman, to the academicians: greeting (with a watermelon and some British herrings)'

c.267/1, p. 321

T1696 These lines had kissed your hands October last
But sets both hand and heart to this complaint.

[George Wither, preface to 'Vox ex lacrimae Anglorum'; before the parliament session, Feb. 1667/8] [Crum T1810]

File 16328

T1697 These lines (the product of a leisure hour)
In spite of sorrow, sickness, age, or pain.

'Verses to a lady with some of the above' ['Where can true happiness . . .']

c.135, p. 19

T1698 These lines with golden letters I have fill'd
Here lies the wife, whose husband's kindness kill'd.

'On a gentlewoman, written by her husband'

fb.143, p. 7, p. 28

T1699 These maidens all both great and small
But I will not say so.

'Braye Lute Book,' Music Ms. 13, fol. 39v

T1700 These pens which fair Euphilia gave
All are conjoined, all in one.

'To Euphilia on the gift of some pens'

c.90

T1701 These questions I ask of my heart,
Such feelings are virtuous, tho' strong.

'From Mrs. Gunnings' Mary'

c.83/2, no. 522

T1702 These sneerings at thy humble birth,
As all men have a spice.

John Lockman, 'To Sir Joseph Marby bart. 4th Jany 1768. on his being shamefully abused in the newspapers'

c.267/4, p. 396

T1703 These sprucely sauced cates whose relish'd taste
Which can digest a stone instead of flesh.

[Sir Thomas Urquhart], 'An expression of some gentlemen, who after they had come from hunting would needs exchange with a morsel of beef the feasary [sic] and curious junkets that were set down before them . . .'

fb.217, p. 504

T1704 These the twelve wonder[s] are of Hercules
Did pass in former time for veritable.

[Sir Thomas Urquhart], 'The exploits of Hercules, as they were set down by the ancient [?] and by the most part believed to be such as they were literally expressed'

fb.217, p. 504

T1705 These two things, bribes and anger both
And equity outface.

b.234, p. 147

T1706 These veins are nature's net
I hang and die in living pains.

[William Strode], 'On a necklace'
[Crum T1838]

b.197, p. 156 (ll. 1–8); b.205, fol. 31v (ll. 1–4; 'nature's, yet')

T1707 These works Menander claim our praise
Or nature wisely copied you.

B. Bellehot, of Trinity College, Cambridge

c.229/1, fol. 30v

T1708 Thespis is said to be the first found out
Lofty and grave; and in your buskins stalk.

c.361 (incomplete?)

T1709 Th'eternal center of my life and me,
I have observ'd, how vain all glories are.

K[atherine] P[hilips]

b.118, p. 42

T1710 Th'eternal God from his exalted throne
By sweet returns of everlasting love.

'To P . . . r M . . . r, Principal of the society of Dunkers (a religious sect) at Ephrata in North America—composed by a young gentleman of Philadelphia some years ago in consequence of a visit he made the above P.M. . . .'

c.487, p. 116

T1711 Th'eternal page of truth consigns
Forevermore, amen.

pc.97, back fly-leaf

T1712 Th'ethereal vigor is in all the same
And the pure ether of the soul remains.

[John Dryden], 'Virg. 6 Æn.'
Trumbull Box: Poetry Box XIII/32

T1713 Th'evangel's, and the law's beginning is
By Adam's, and our Savior's genesis.

Sir Thomas Urquhart, 'That Genesis is the first book both of the Old, and New Testament'

fb.217, p. 320

T1714 Th'exampl' of a good prince a rule imparts
By shunning he forbids, and bids by doing.

Sir Thomas Urquhart, 'Regis ad exemplum'

fb.217, p. 140

T1715 They are convertible in terms, as panthers,
All covenanters are not puritans.

Sir Thomas Urquhart, 'Lysimachus Nicanor, his collationing of covenanters, and puritans'

fb.217, p. 168

T1716 They are not alike, although th'alike appear;
Th'one fears for love, the other loves for fear.

'On filial love and servile'

b.118, p. 221

T1717 They are the tapers which preserve the fire
May burn it quickly to a living retour [sic].

[Sir Thomas Urquhart], 'Of the generative [?] of men'

fb.217, p. 542

T1718 They ate they drank and slept—what then?
That shook the earth with thund'ring tread. |
'Twas death

c.546

T1719 They both Cornelius are: yet differ thus,
That th'one, is Publius: th'other, Tacitus.

[Sir Thomas Urquhart], 'Concerning two Italian gentlemen of the family of Cornelius whose wives though equally dissolute conveyed not their actions with the like discretion'

fb.217, p. 503

T1720 They by aspiring both to the perfection
And crown'd the magisterium b'imbibition.

Sir Thomas Urquhart, 'How a gentleman with his mistress practiced their skill in alchemy'

fb.217, p. 134

T1721 They came to view our dark abode,
There souls, nor tempting world ensnare.

'On seven children of Mr. Butt'

c.362, p. 38

T1722 They come! Adorn'd with every grace,
In whom that virtue shines, which binds the chain!

[Charles Burney, the younger], 'Ode. Addressed to
Miss Rachel, and Miss Jessy Wilcox . . . Feb. 10. 1779'

c.38, p. 28

T1723 They did both Christ baptize, and circumcise:
Yet must we rest content with one of them.

Sir Thomas Urquhart, 'Of Christ, and us'

fb.217, p. 79

T1724 They differ thus: Eve sinned first, and then
They may sin with greater ease.

Sir Thomas Urquhart, 'The discrepance betwixt Eve,
and other women'

fb.217, p. 312

T1725 They idolize, who kneel to sovereigns,
For man's God's image; and the woman man's.

Sir Thomas Urquhart, 'Of reverence to kings and
queens a paradox'

fb.217, p. 346

T1726 They in prevention quarrel-like accurs't,
Scold, who being guilty | Yet will call whore first.

c.189, p. 34

T1727 They love the means which tendeth to the end
By shunning th'issue of a procreation.

[Sir Thomas Urquhart], 'What the most part of
whores do'

fb.217, p. 395

T1728 They may do what they will who think they may
Do naught but what they ought, and truth obey.

[Sir Philip Wodehouse], 'Upon [Sr John Potts's] son'

b.131, back (no. 169)

T1729 They say, as wholesome as a fish, and why?
(Save th'ark's sole guests) as, that did life enjoy.

Sir Thomas Urquhart, 'Of the English proverb, as
sound as a fish'

fb.217, p. 114

T1730 They seemed worn out with impotence and sloth
And to their motions all the world kept time.

[Enigma/Charade/Conundrum 68a]

c.389

T1731 They speak ill of thee. 'Tis not Ussher, Hall,
Who not for fierceness, but for custom bark.

[John Hobart], 'Against censure'

b.108, fol. 3

T1732 They tell me fortune thou wilt once be kind
For she that is content like me never need care for
more.

[Mrs. ( ) Feilding]

b.226, p. 6

T1733 They tell me gentlemen, 'tis now in vogue
To vie with any he that treads this stage.

[John Hoadly], 'Epilogue [to Constancy approved]'

c.176, p. 179

T1734 They tell ye that beauty soon fades
Accompany the strain.

[John Black]

fc.107, p. 24

T1735 They that in life opprest, and then bequeath
Their several actions send the like perfume.

[Francis Quarles], 'On pious uses' [Divine
fancies III, 83]

b.137, p. 193

T1736 They that in ships the sea explore,
And in my closet, speak Thy love.

'A hymn composed on the 13th Sept. 1797. in
commemoration of the author's deliverance from
shipwreck on that day 1780'

c.515, fol. 25v

T1737 They that lose goods gotten in wrong by might,
Do lose but that wherein they had no right.

c.339, p. 321

T1738 They told me, it was bleak and cold
A heart so warm'd, can ne'er grow chilly.

Miss [ ] Gwinson, 'Barons Court to the Marchioness
of Abercorn . . . impromptu'

c.340

T1739 They took so many bumpers in a hand,
And damps the passion she intends to raise.

[from Terrae Filius's speech, Oxford 1703]
[Crum T1863]

fc.24, p. 7

T1740 They touch'd the keys with lively strokes, most
quaintly
The soundboard echoing, as the start up brangled.

Sir Thomas Urquhart, 'The manner how a gentleman
with his mistress played on the virginals'

fb.217, p. 266

T1741   They who are happy find their life a span
One night's an age to the unhappy man.

> George Montagu, 'Translations of Greek epigrams at
> Eton school'

fc.135, p. 11

T1742   They, who though fall'n on a fastidious age,
And Doctor Joseph with Sir Joseph live!

> Joseph [Priestley], 'Dr. Joseph to Mr. Timothy
> [Priestley]'

c.83/3, no. 797

T1743   They wrong her much, that call her proud; for it's
And puts him in, as far's she can before her.

> Sir Thomas Urquhart, 'Of a very kind woman, who
> was reputed to be somewhat haughty'

fb.217, p. 180

T1744   They wrong their trust, who beauty misemploy,
Humble the proud—but spare the prostrate slave.

c.53, fol. 61

T1745   They're richer who diminish their desires
Have minds, that never will be satisfied.

> [Sir Thomas Urquhart], 'Those that have greatest
> means are not always wealthiest'

fb.217, p. 496

T1746   Thickest night o'erhang my dwelling!
But a world without a friend!

> [Robert Burns], 'Strathallan's lament'

c.142, p. 230

T1747   Th'immortal man serv'd church and court
How gloriously he was rewarded.

> 'The following lines were found written with charcoal
> on [Samuel] Butler's monument in Westminster
> Abbey'

c.360/2, no. 212

T1748   Th'industrious bee extracts from ev'ry flow'r,
Each mental sweet nor leave one vacant cell!

> Ann Murry, 'I recollect a few lines I wrote the other
> day on industry . . .'

c.248

T1749   Thine is the kingdom God of grace
And fill our blest eternity.

> T[homas] S[tevens]

c.259, p. 142

T1750   Thine, virtue! Thine is each persuasive charm
And joys that bloom'd more sweetly from the shade.

> 'On virtue'

c.83/3, no. 814

T1751   Things opposite in quality or kind,
The lofty thus contrasted by the low.

> 'Pope and Homer compared'

c.233, p. 103

T1752   Things seen, heard, tasted, touch'd and smell'd,
                         affect
Your senses, and their organs oft infect.

> Sir Thomas Urquhart, 'Of the five external senses to
> one very much addicted to sensual pleasure'

fb.217, p. 46

T1753   Things that be bitter, bitterer than gall,
Things oft help sick men, that do sound men kill.

> 'On women's tongues'

c.356

T1754   Things which *legere*, and trifling seem
Great Samson—in a with.

> [John] Winter, 'On the different things men take to
> make themselves agreeable'

c.74

T1755   Think dearest soul, let it thy study be
You there of pleasure then may eat your fill.

> Thomas Davis, 'Made by Thos. Davis'

c.213

T1756   Think how thy friend may live to be thy foe
Therefore thy tongue let not at random go.

c.339, p. 317

T1757   Think it not strange, that you're by fortune thrall'd;
For fortune's forehead's hoary: yours is bald.

> Sir Thomas Urquhart, 'To a certain bald man in
> misery'

fb.217, p. 215

T1758   Think man how that thy earthly stay will slide,
Do throw thee down, when sure thou thinkst thy
                            state.

b.234, p. 310

T1759   Think me not lost, for thee I heaven implore
Beyond all youth, all sense, and all desire.

> 'Epitaph in Salisbury churchyard'

c.391, p. 24

T1760   Think not by righteous judgment seiz'd,
And face the flash, which burns the ball.

> [Alexander Pope], 'An epitaph on John Hewit, and
> Sarah Dring who being contracted in order to
> marriage, were both one instant killed with a flash of
> lightning as they were at harvest-work in the year 1719'
> [Crum T1881, 'rigorous judgment', 'Sarah Drew']

c.244, p. 87

T1761   Think not 'cause men flattering say
Both bud and fade, both blow and wither.

> [Thomas Carew], 'An admonition to a coy
> acquaintance'
> [Crum T1882]

b.205, fol. 89r; b.356, p. 85

T1762   Think not dear girl in any book to find
Thy life surpass his best-drawn theory.

> Lady Lucas, 'Verses to Lady Bayham with Fordyce's
> sermons to young women'

c.504, p. 112

T1763   Think not dear love that I'll reveal
The world will see thy picture there.

> [Thomas Carew], 'To his m[ist]r[es]s'
> [Crum T1884]

b.205, fol. 27r; see also 'Fear not (dear love) . . .'.

T1764   Think not dear Sally to withdraw thy charms,
Since England's Venus from them turn'd her eyes.

> 'To [Miss Sally P—s] leaving Cheltenham July 9th.
> 1741'

c.221, p. 25

T1765   Think not good folks, because our play is done,
Who to an author's, joins a mother's fears.

> Lady [Elizabeth] Craven, 'Epilogue to Lady Craven's
> Arcadian pastoral'

c.83/1, no. 136

T1766   Think not, my friend, I insure those
Must live unknown, or cease to live.

> 'Apology for retirement . . . by a lady'

c.83/3, no. 803

T1767   Think not that he is niggardly inclin'd,
To feed his family with almost nothing.

> Sir Thomas Urquhart, 'The favorable censure that was
> desired to be made of a certain sparing man'

fb.217, p. 36

T1768   Think not the muse officious, mighty King,
And Britons pleas'd th' destin'd house obey.

> 'On the death of his late Majesty. Inscribed to his
> present [Majesty]'

c.503, p. 37

T1769   Think not this number of the ten of hearts,
Tho' ten, I send, on, only one I give.

> [J.] W[alke]r(?), of Eton, 'Upon sending a billet to a
> lady wrote on the ten of hearts'

c.591

T1770   Think not to court me from my dear retreat,
Envied by others, and as much dislik'd by me.

> [John] N[orris, of Bemerton], 'The refusal'

c.258

T1771   Think not to find one meant resemblance there;
So nature dictated what art has sought.

> 'Under Hogarth's modern midnight conversation'

c.74

T1772   Think not your friend Le Heup too free
To prove thyself true heir apparent.

> 'Le Heup's epistle to P. Frederick' [pr. 1727 (Foxon
> L94.8)]

c.570/3, p. 48

T1773   Think of the fate of auctioneers,
Death gives the blow and knocks me down.

> Bonnell Thornton

c.362, p. 32

T1774   Think O my charmer, if thy faithful slave
Her faithful slave, would leave this world with joy.

> [Thomas Hamilton, 6th earl of Haddington], 'To
> Florella epistle the eleventh'

c.458/1, p. 28

T1775   Think once, O man, how oft each circling year
Where angels raise their ever-happy voice.

> 'An elegy on the death of the late Revd. Francis
> Turner of Great Yarmouth'

c.94

T1776   Think! Says the vicar, with an angry frown;
Thank! For what? And knock'd the angel down.

> N. H., 'C. and the angel . . . in the v[icarage] house of
> K. the beam in the great chamber is supported by two
> angels with this motto—think and thank—one of the
> angels being lost, occasioned the following epig[ram]'

c.74

T1777   Think well or ill of him that slumber here
Oblige him, be a better man than he.

> 'Epitaph'

c.156, p. 74

T1778   Think what you will good sirs, at least agree,
Is at this time our only consolation.

> [David Garrick], 'Epilogue for Master Ernst'

Acquisition 92.3.1ff. (autogr.); see also 'Whate'er you
think . . .'.

T1779   Think you this paradox is strange
Non progredi—is retrograde.

> 'Epigramma . . . semper idem'

c.81/1, no. 257

T1780   Th'inkhorn w[?] h[?] he brought the pen
The characters of O. Y. P.

    [Sir Thomas Urquhart], 'The materials of Cupid's
    writing practiced betwixt a lover and his mistress'
    fb.217, p. 395

T1781   Thirty days hath September,
And all the rest have thirty and one.

    'A rule to know how many days every month in the
    year hath'
    c.339, p. 280

T1782   Thirty perfections, love, impart
Yet check the thought that seems to stray.

    [Phanuel Bacon], 'Thirty perfections'
    [Crum T1898]
    c.237, fol. 30

T1783   This ancient fabric deign t'accept
A hollow heart, in a deform'd outside.

    'To Lady Pembroke with the rind of a cheese'
    Poetry Box III/14

T1784   This babbling stream not uninstructing flows,
Who lets one precious moment run to waste.

    'Inscription under an hourglass in a grotto near the
    walk'
    c.83/3, no. 749; c.344, p. 4; see also 'This bubbling
    stream . . .'.

T1785   This ballad, though not honor'd to be sung
His weaker brains, against too hard a rock.

    George Reynolds, 'An answer unto the verses [by
    Mr. Street: 'The reformers and drainers . . .'] made
    upon the draining of Slappen Ley'
    b.104, p. 4 (end of book)

T1786   This bird beguil'd by Celia's eye
To all that I can guess or feign.

    'On a robin redbreast that in a stormy day flew in at a
    window and settled on a lady's breast, who cut off his
    tail and let him go'
    c.188, p. 45

T1787   This bottle's the sun of our table,
And shine as he goes round.

    'Song III'
    c.555, p. 163

T1788   This bracelet tho' a gaudy thing,
It most I prize—and give it you.

    'The bracelet'
    c.83/1, no. 186

T1789   This bubbling stream not uninstructive flows,
Who lets one precious moment run to waste.

    [ ] Graves(?), 'Written under an hourglass, in a grotto
    near the side of a river'
    fc.132/1, p. 166; see also 'This babbling stream . . .'.

T1790   This cause was giv'n to one, that was demanding
In woman a caparit', and conception.

    Sir Thomas Urquhart, 'The reason why it is a proper
    sort of speech, to say that Adam knew Eve'
    fb.217, p. 266

T1791   This comedy was written in those days
That is above, and this below our thoughts.

    'Prologue to [John Fletcher's] The loyal subject'
    Poetry Box I/111[13]

T1792   This cometh from your loving friend
Your loving coz: M. Montagu.

    Lady Frances (Scott) [Douglas, baroness Douglas],
    'Written by . . . in the name of Ly. Mary Montagu her
    niece, then about 11 years old. To Mary Countess of
    Courtown at Windsor. 13th of July 1780'
    Poetry Box III/48; File 3771

T1793   This Coriphaeus in his art
Holy hosannas to th'eternal King.

    [Sir Philip Wodehouse], 'Upon Mr. J[ohn] Jenkins the
    rare musician'
    b.131, back (no. 170)

T1794   This damnable tailor,
Alas, I've got a female Robespierre!

    M[ary (Derby)] R[obinson], [verse epistle to John
    Taylor, Salt Hill, 11 August 1794]
    File 12742

T1795   This Damon black is Aphrodisius hight
The beauty of the world's an honest man.

    [Sir Philip Wodehouse], 'Edmund Blackborn black
    Damon burn'd'
    b.131, back (no. 180)

T1796   This day a happy day for all on earth
My sins may never challenge me for bad.

    Lady Jane Cavendish, 'On Christmas Day to God'
    [Crum T1918]
    b.233, p. 37

T1797   This day allows Thy praise O Lord
Stay with me here or take me home.

    [John Norris, of Bemerton?], 'A poem of the fifth of
    November'
    c.548

T1798 This day as bridal of the earth and sky
Till all make up one hallelujah choir.

    [Edward] Sparke, 'Poem 3rd, on Christ's nativity'

b.137, p. 12

T1799 This day by commendable use design'd
Fill it with grace, and give it thee again.

    'Christmas Day 1668'

b.49, p. 13

T1800 This day devout enthusiasts greet
Long to preserve you what you are.

    [Henry Richard Vassall Fox, 3rd baron Holland], 'To a
    lady, on her birthday March 25th (Lady Day) 1800'

c.340

T1801 This day I did in perspective one view
So free herself from devil, hell, that's sad.

    Lady Jane Cavendish, 'The mind's salvation'
    [Crum T1922]

b.233, p. 39

T1802 This day I will my thanks sure now declare
And all my life in thanks a votary spend.

    Lady Jane Cavendish, 'On the 30th of June to God'
    [Crum T1923]

b.233, p. 38

T1803 This day my hourglass forth is run
Thy torch tomorrow may be done.

    'Epitaph'

c.360/3, no. 58

T1804 This day our prince our rising sun
This shall be our thanksgiving day.

    'On the Prince of Wales' first anniversary'

b.111, p. 21

T1805 This day shall happiness impart,
Enjoy their fruits, in blest eternity.

    'On the birthday of [the daughter of a lady] then 13 . . .
    July the 8th' [by the lady]

c.90

T1806 This day, the Deity to man has given
Each slight excuse, and needless journey shown.

    'On Sunday'

c.83/1, no. 221

T1807 This day the English and the French fleets met;
Thought they would fight next day more
                         handsomely.

    '28th July 1778'

c.81/1, no. 121

T1808 This day the festive board shall ring
A lesson to the virtuous mind.

    [ ] Crowfoot, 'On Diana [Burroughes]'s birthday—
    July 8th. 1778'

c.90

T1809 This day we praise Saint Austin's name
And so in heaven may have our place. | Amen

    'Of S. Austin. Aug. 28'

a.30[30]

T1810 This deep desire hath lastly moved me
Here in my travels-map I have revealed.

    'Verstegan's prefatory poem to his Restitution of
    decayed antiquities. London—1775'

c.311

T1811 This dismal morn when east winds blow,
The best elixir is my mind.

    'The hip. In a letter to W. C. esq.'

c.73, p. 13

T1812 This dog can fawn, bark, bite, rather than fail
But wants one dog's trick, dares not wag his tail.

    [William Breton, of Emmanuel College Cambaridge],
    'Anagram. [Gondomar] Roman dog'
    [Crum T1928, 'bark, bite, fawn']

File 19344

T1813 This dullness is improper to the day;
Why am I chok't? why am I stifled thus.

    [George Daniel]

b.121, fol. 77v

T1814 This evil from his inborn error springs
Is enough to offend a noble sense [and] quick.

    'Magnanimitas'

b.205, fol. 10r

T1815 This excellent man served church and state,
How gloriously he was rewarded.

    'On Butler's epitaph'

fc.24, p. 61

T1816 This fair young virgin for a bridal bed
Yet ere they bloom are kill'd by cruel frost.

    'In the Temple church London a white marble
    monument affixed to a column which supports the
    roof in memory of a daughter of the honorable Sr.
    Francis Gawdy a judge'

c.229/1, fol. 51

T1817 This faithful humble learned man of God,
His name, like precious ointment, sweetly smells.

    'An epitaph on the revd. Mr. Elcock who died 1630'

c.244, p. 208

T1818   This faithful servant will not feed until
They speed their master's work, they'll drink the
more.

[Francis Quarles], 'On Abraham's servant'
[Crum T1939]
b.137, p. 166

T1819   This fame reports fair Carteret of you
Who snatch'd me from destruction and the grave.

[Mary Barber?]
Poetry Box IV/131; see also 'Wearied with long
attendance . . .'.

T1820   This fever is like love
Instead of fever, favor may be put.

[Sir Philip Wodehouse], 'Mr. Francis Neave my honest
neighbor when he wooed Mrs. Ann Blackbourn his
now wife Nancy's fever'
b.131, back (no. 186)

T1821   This flame-expecting taper hath at length
My vain-aspiring thoughts! Lie down my puzzled
quill.

'Thoughts on the soul'
c.94

T1822   This flower but late, both fresh and green
And I ne'er give my love.

[Mrs. Christian Kerr], 'An answer to one who
reflected on the fading of a flower that he had
presented to him the night before'
c.102, p. 86 & 168

T1823   This flower, the damask in thy cheek displays;
And hence, to thee, this first-blown off'ring
brought.

John Lockman, 'To a young lady, with a natural rose
in her bosom, at the Lord Mayor's ball, on Easter
Monday, 1755'
c.267/1, p. 148

T1824   This garland, sent my fair one to adorn,
As these you flourish, and as these you'll fade.

M[aurice] Johnson, 'Mitto recens sertum pictumq . . .
Englished by . . . of [Eton]'
c.229/1, fol. 45

T1825   This gate hangs well
And cannot trust.

'Written under a sign at Wyas[t]on in Derbyshire the
sign of the gate'
c.361

T1826   This globe must perish, both of sea, and land;
For being divided, long it cannot stand.

Sir Thomas Urquhart, 'That the earth cannot endure
forever'
fb.217, p. 135

T1827   This goblin honor which the world adores
Ere they set footing in the nuptial bed.

[Thomas Carew], 'Then tell me why?' [ll. 1–3 from 'A
rapture'; attr. John Walton, 1662]
b.52/1, p. 120

T1828   This God is the God we adore
And trust him for all that's to come.

'Hymn 52d'
c.562, p. 61

T1829   This great Jehovah full of love
To joys that never end.

'An epitaph upon a child in Stilton C. Z.'
fb.142, p. 9 (second series)

T1830   This grotto seems for jolly shepherds made
So long your deathless honors shall remain.

John Mansell, 'A pastoral on the pleasures of the
country. Mopsus and Menaleus'
b.382(29)

T1831   This hair by time long blanch'd receive
Age has its spring, which ne'er decays.

'Translation of Vers de Madame la Maréchale de
Mirepoix . . . by a lady' [answered by 'On tresses
whiten'd . . .', by the Duc du Nivernais]
c.141, p. 536

T1832   This happy lord still loyal to the crown
Hath left an heir, heir to his renown.

fb.151/3

T1833   This hasty scribble to friend Doudle
Accept from your servant the Earl[e] of West-down.

[Charles Earle], 'To Mr. Doudle (if not married; | Old
Ling odd letter should be carried . . .'
c.376

T1834   This homely case a jewel doth contain
Enrich't, which beautifies the mind and face.

'On ——— P['s] wife'
fb.143, p. 35

T1835   This honest gentleman still dwells at home
If she love him—else both may roam.

[Sir Philip Wodehouse], 'Thomas Weld dwells at
home'
b.131, back (no. 214)

T1836   This humble grave, tho' no proud structure grace,
And holy friendship sits a mourner here.

> [David] Mallet, 'Epitaph'
> Poetry Box XII/97

T1837   This humble roof, this rustic court said he
But contemn wealth, and imitate a God.

> [Abraham Cowley], 'Taken out of Virgil . . .'
> b.118, p. 39

T1838   This if I live, I truly shall inherit
The benefits of Christ's soul-saving merit.

> Sir John Strangways [envoy to his translations of the Bible]
> b.304, p. 185

T1839   This Indian weed that's withered quite
That unto dust return we must | So think and drink tobacco.

> R. H.(?), 'Of tobacco R. H.' [first published in Thomas Jenner's The soul's solace, 1626]
> [cf. Crum T821, 'The Indian weed . . .']
> b.62, p. 150; Accession 97.7.40

T1840   This is a period that we all expect,
O heavenly advocate! Exalted nigh.

> 'Thoughts on death'
> c.515, fol. 8v

T1841   This is allow'd a fatal time
As well as save a deal of chink.

> 'Christmas time'
> c.115

T1842   This is in every timber
Come tell it if you can.

> 'A riddle'
> c.150, p. 143

T1843   This is my last will,
In the year seventy.

> W[illia]m Hickington, 'A singular will of . . . deceased; as proved in the Deanery Court of York'
> c.94

T1844   This is my oath Forever to despise
So far as conscience dictates It is good.

> 'The loyal subject's oath' [equivocal verses]
> b.111, p. 134

T1845   This is the best world that we live in
His the worst world that ever was known.

> 'Poetical anecdote on the world'
> c.361

T1846   This is the cause why he's not fortunate,
Having one only left he share her of it.

> [Sir Thomas Urquhart], 'Why a certain barber was unfortunate'
> fb.217, p. 537

T1847   This is the happy day,
To wish you happy days.

> [to Lady Anne Compton, sister-in-law of Elizabeth Compton, countess of Northumberland]
> Accession 97.7.40

T1848   This is the height the devil's arts can show,
To make man proud, because he is not so.

> 'On the devil's masterpiece'
> b.118, p. 222

T1849   This is the note that nobody wrote
To carry the note that nobody wrote.

> 'The note that nobody wrote' [parody of 'The house that Jack built'; on the 5th duke of Argyll]
> Poetry Box XII/35; Greatheed Box/80

T1850   This is the only way, to make a woman dumb,
To sit, and smile, and laugh her out, and not a word, but mum.

> [Sir Francis Castillion?]
> fb.69, p. 185

T1851   This is the rhetoric that Fisher Paganus
Come hither to Oxford to be thus derided.

> 'Upon the most loquent and somniforous declamatory lamentation of [James Ussher] Archbishop of Armagh's death by Pagan [Payne] Fisher Laureate . . . 1658' [satire]
> fb.140, p. 11

T1852   This is the sweet and pleasant month of May
Or else poor Field will burn in midst of May.

> 'On one Field suspected for too much familiarity with the Lady May'
> [Crum T1980]
> b.356, p. 131

T1853   This is the way to tramp on the lieges
But he is one extraordinary great.

> Poetry Box VIII/32

T1854   This is the wedding day, we are all fine and gay
Play up Tom Piper towdow and towdow and diddle diddle diddle dow.

> 'The merry wedding being a pretty old song to the tune of Long Laurence'
> c.158, p. 4

T1855 This is too much, but if I this abuse,
The fault which you create you must excuse.

  'Caesar to Cleopatra'

  c.189, p. 18

T1856 This is true love and worth commending
This is true love and worth commending.

  'The true lover's knot'

  c.158, p. viii

T1857 This is your bill of fare fall on and spare not,
Then as your stomach serves, fall on to either.

  'From an almanac—1745'

  c.93

T1858 This jolly adage soberly once meant
A royal one. And a paradise.

  [Sir Philip Wodehouse], 'My mind to me a kingdom is'

  b.131, p. 30

T1859 This joyful day did raise my muse
To wish you joy, long life, and happiness.

  [Sir William Trumbull], 'To the Right Hon[ora]ble
  the Lady Judith Trumbull on her birthday'

  Trumbull Box: Poetry Box XIII/30

T1860 This keeps my hand
From Cupid's band.

  [William Strode], in 'Posies for bracelets'
  [Crum T1988]

  b.205, fol. 55v

T1861 This knave by conscience and of law
Is made by much more fit to hang than draw.

  'On a vintner's boy'

  b.356, p. 306

T1862 This lady hath with fortune sympathy,
For fortune loves no dastards, neither she.

  Sir Thomas Urquhart, 'Of the disposition of a certain
  dame'

  fb.217, p. 191

T1863 This languishing head is at rest
And never shall flutter again.

  'On Richard Stevens (St. Lawrence)'

  c.546

T1864 This laurel chaplet on your brows we place
To crown the beauty of mind and face.

  'Praemium. Laurea Apollinaris . . .'

  b.212, p. 77

T1865 This letter's intended for telling
Where you and your Neptune may play.

  Ralph Broome, 'A letter from . . . to Miss Frances'

  c.486, fol. 32v

T1866 This life hath on earth no certain while
Pray unto God for mercy and grace.

  'On John, Mary and Oliver Stile'

  fb.143, p. 10

T1867 This life, with pain and pleasure intermix'd,
To raise the hero, and to mend the man.

  'The use of pain'

  c.83/2, no. 346; c.94

T1868 This life's a dance from infancy to age
The goodly [?] bird, of innocence.

  [Sir Philip Wodehouse], 'A sally Henry Earl of Dover
  (as delighting in country dancing) his fair honor led'

  b.131, back (no. 7/3)

T1869 This life's enfeebled, and with cares opprest
The joys seraphic of eternal day.

  S[tephen] Simpson, 'The almshouse an elegy in
  imitation of Jerningham's Magdalen and Nun'

  c.563

T1870 This life's like a cobweb as a body may say,
And death is the besom that sweeps us away.

  c.378, p. 7

T1871 This little babe into the world did peep
So fell asleep.

  'Epitaph'

  c.150, p. 39

T1872 This little Celsus ribbon blue!
To dub them noble Knight of Garter?

  [Charles Earle], 'To Miss Harris of Pickwell on
  finding a blue ribbon which she lost'

  c.376

T1873 This little garden little Jowett made,
He changed it to a little gravel walk.

  [William Lort Mansel? or Francis Wrangham?],
  'Epigram'

  c.116, p. 55

T1874 This little labor of my hand,
For its once tender father's sake.

  [Robert Cholmeley], 'To the book'

  c.190, p. 248

T1875 This little village serves to show
The cry is still a little more!

[Phanuel Bacon], 'Written in a window at Littlemore
near Oxford'

c.237, fol. 79

T1876 This magic wreath of blooming flowers
And merit shine with pleasure crown'd.

H[enry] Skrine, 'Presented to a very young lady with a
nosegay . . . July 6 1785'

c.509, p. 73

T1877 This making of bastards so great
May end their tricks in a string.

'Song. [Old Rowley the King] to the tune of Old
Simon the King' [1683]
[Crum T2001; POAS III.478]

Poetry Box VII/9

T1878 This man and he was of muckle might
And old Nab to a bishop's fine lady.

T[homas] M[orell], 'On the same [Stephen Duck's
taking orders]'

c.395, p. 73

T1879 This may be true—submitting still,
Are angels, just as kings are gods.

J[onathan] Swift, 'The function of a Viceroy (or Ld.
Lieut. of Ireland)' [excerpt from 'A libel on
Dr. Delaney']

c.144, p. 157

T1880 This minds me of great Williams whose miss
If hector'd by a whore.

P[hilip] W[odehouse], 'And this of mine in repartee to
the last of Acon'

b.131, p. 41

T1881 This modest stone what few vain marbles can
Thank'd heaven that he had lived—and that he died.

[Alexander Pope], 'Another on Mr. Congreve'
[actually on Elijah Fenton, d. 1730]

c.165, p. 54

T1882 This monitor, dear Chloe, shows
T'improve each moment of your time.

'For Miss S—nd—'s watch . . . 1760'

c.484, p. 60

T1883 This morn I gaily rang'd the wood
Which makes you good, though free and fair.

R[ichard] V[ernon] S[adleir], 'The pheasant—to Miss
[blank]'

c.106, p. 82

T1884 This morning betimes
In procuring the curate thulk's [sic] cloak.

'The cloak. To Mr. Edward Sheppard'

c.484, p. 97

T1885 This morning, dear Mother, as soon as 'twas light,
Who whistles his nags, while they stand in the river.

[Christopher Anstey], 'A description of bathing at
Bath from the Bath guide'

c.83/2, no. 286

T1886 This mystic knot includes two royal names,
Laurels on one, palms on the other wait.

'On a cipher of K[ing] James and K[ing] Louis'

b.111, p. 16

T1887 This new amazement made my limbs to shake,
My hair stood up, words my mouth forsake.

'One after an affright . . . English thus'

c.189, p. 33

T1888 This night's the day, I speak it with great sorrow
A cold frosty morning, I wish you all good nights.

'A bellman's blundering verses, spoke in the night
between the 4th and 5th of November'

c.360/2, no. 239

T1889 This nimble footman run away from death
And sent him out an errand to his grave.

[John Heath], 'On a footman'
[Crum T2015]

fb.143, p. 36

T1890 This no-bill-billed give unto ———
I'll send a bill—the Lord knows when.

[Charles Earle], 'J. H. esq. Of Pi—k—will sent J[ohn]
Scamp to Revd. Mr. Earle for his bill for tithe due to
him'

c.376

T1891 This only grant me, that my means may lie
Or in clouds hide them: I have lived today.

[Abraham] Cowley, 'These three odes were part of a
copy of verses wrote by Mr. A. Cowley at 13 years of
age'
[Crum T2020]

b.118, p. 30; b.135, p. 115

T1892 This only speaks her name—her quality
And birth is eminent—give *plaudites*.

[Sir Philip Wodehouse], 'Upon my cousin [Anne]
Paris—now Lady Colson'

b.131, back (no. 43)

T1893 This paper I stick on the wall
And send you to damnation.

'A paper stuck on the wall at St. Paul's, June 7, 1716 [on the Jacobite William Paul]'

fc.58, p. 53

T1894 This Parliament its business may have done
They'll only make false concords if they stay.

[Phanuel Bacon], 'Ut Cato Virgilius. (Spoken at school by a young gentleman of fortune)'

c.237, fol. 77

T1895 This pastoral could not own weak
Unto your judgment of pure wit.

[Elizabeth (Cavendish) Brackley, dedication of a pastoral to the Earl of Newcastle]
[Crum T2024]

b.233, p. 44

T1896 This peaceful tomb does now contain
Then robb'd us of the coming good.

[Abraham Cowley], 'Epitaph on a gentleman and his son' [Robert Huntington sr. and jr. of Stanton Harcourt]

c.360/3, no. 52

T1897 This picture was in former years
[Illegible] picture now.

[Phanuel Bacon], 'Wrote under his own picture'

c.237, fol. 84v

T1898 This pleasing sketch, by an ennobl'd fair,
No less from birth, pomp, titles or estate(?).

John Lockman, 'Writ under a landscape invented and drawn by the Countess of Strathmore, and presented to hier ladyship by the author . . . 11 Nov. 1768'

c.267/4, p. 394

T1899 This plume, as you wear it, will fully impart
But wavering and light as my own.

[Federick Howard, 5th earl of Carlisle], 'From a gentleman to his wife, with a plume of feathers'

Diggle Box: Poetry Box XI/69

T1900 This poem is no Sybil nor no prophet
Yet think it was Prince Arthur's Katherine.

'The gloss' [to 'The day was turned to starlight . . .'; on the Spanish match, 1623]

b.62, p. 63

T1901 This portico where, pleas'd, we take the air,
Fielding should take his broom, and sweep them
out.

John Lockman, 'Seeing the great piazza, in Covent Garden, strangely crowded every Sunday night . . . Feb. 1759'

c.267/1, p. 268

T1902 This posture, and these tears, that heav'n might
move,
The plaintive waters utter, as they flow.

'Lying at her feet'

c.189, p. 92

T1903 This preacher, silent, yet severe,
A joyful victor o'er the grave.

[( ) Stevenson, of Spalding], 'On seeing a skull'
[Crum T2029]

c.139, p. 64; c.186, p. 55; c.487, p. 78

T1904 This present time is so much beholden
That former ages never saw the like.

Sir Thomas Urquhart, 'To the paragon of her sex my angelic Aura'

fb.217, p. 318

T1905 This proud saloon, where art displays
And proves himself its warmest friend.

John Lockman, 'Writ on the back of a feast ticket, for the anniversary dinner of the governors &c. of the Middlesex Hospital, Thursday 19th May 1768. at the great room in Soho Square'

c.267/4, p. 372

T1906 This proverb is not general; for in
Before that man committed any sin.

Sir Thomas Urquhart, 'Ex malis moribus bonae leges'

fb.217, p. 186

T1907 This puts me in mind of Astley's elder crest—
They'll crown the scalps of such Andromaches.

[Sir Philip Wodehouse], A mantissa or kiss of friends, on the former'

b.131, p. 4 and back (after anagram 235)

T1908 This quatrain's last two lines afford us two
Whilst on, and in are proper to the male.

Sir Thomas Urquhart, 'Two rules of Despauter. Jung, to foemineis do go, and an in on maribus'

fb.217, p. 265

T1909 This register of friends when I survey
I first salute (with tears) your hallow'd dust.

[Thomas Stanley], 'A register of friends'

b.153, p. 1

T1910 This riddle dear Clara pray guess if you can
The youngest gives birth to the eldest of these.

'Another [riddle]'

Diggle Box: Poetry Box XI/71

T1911 This roof that rose by Caroline's command
So great in public or so great alone.

fc.135

T1912   This sage's works, the wonder of mankind!
Than these strong tints the features of his face.

[John Lockman], 'Written at Mr. Whood's under the picture of Dr. Halley'

c.268 (first part), p. 13

T1913   This said—a solemn silence breath'd around,
Still shouldst thou kiss the strings where he has play'd.

[ ] Pratt, 'Her brother's lyre to Mrs Sheridan by Mr Pratt' [answer to 'Sweet instrument . . .']

c.343, p. 94

T1914   This said, (though 'bout it authors vary)
And so Pythagoras—sav'd his bacon.

'Pythagoras's precept, abstine a fabis'

c.94

T1915   This say the spirit bless'd are they,
We may behold thy face.

P[hilip] Doddridge, 'The first resurrection Rev: XX. 6'

c.493, p. 71

T1916   This saying still has been allow'd by all;
Snow falls from heav'n yet its fall is light.

'Caelsa casu gravi ora . . .' ['On the fall of great things']

fb.142, p. 38

T1917   This scene, how different in its pristine state!
From useless things, things of noblest use.

'The forest of Anderida'

c.83/2, no. 724

T1918   This seems cross-heraldry, that the inferior
Their persons, their conditions, and their wit.

[Sir Philip Wodehouse], 'An animadversion upon the last distich' [of 'A cinquefoil marrying with a star . . .']

b.131, p. 3 and back (after anagram 235)

T1919   This shall be known when we are dead
And trust and praise the Lord.

'Transcribed from the almanac of my hon'd grandfather Mr. Philip Henry'

c.148, p. 7

T1920   This Sheffield rais'd, the sacred dust below
Was Dryden once, the rest who does not know.

A[lexander] Pope, 'The epitaph at first designed for Dryden's monument in Westminster Abbey erected by John Sheffield Duke of Buckingham'

c.360/1, p. 315

T1921   This [?] short(?) and bunch of feathers [?]
[?] fleeting light from [?] to be.

[Sir Thomas Urquhart], 'Of a [?] gentlewoman'

fb.217, p. 394

T1922   This sign doth William Norman's patron show,
By this the English him their K[ing] do know.

b.208, p. 130

T1923   This silent grave it doth embrace
Martha's care, and Mary's better part.

'Epitaph'

c.150, p. 13; see also 'Here lies interr'd . . .', 'She/The dame that takes . . .', 'She who here . . .'.

T1924   This silken wreath, which circles in mine arm
This makes my arm your prisoner, that my heart.

[Thomas] Carew, 'Upon a ribbon'
[Crum T2043]

b.225, p. 132; b.200, p. 116; b.62, p. 26

T1925   This song unto the Lord did David sing,
That they with me thy name may glorify.

[William Sandys?], 'David's song of thanksgiving after he had subdued the Philistines 2 Sam: 22'

b.230, p. 45

T1926   This spot in ev'ry vernal charm array'd;
Where shine the arts, and virtue reigns as queen.

John Lockman, 'Seeing lewd women refused admittance, into Vauxhall Gardens . . . published immediately after the first opening . . .'

c.267/1, p. 3; c.268 (first part), p. 3 (var.)

T1927   This spotless pattern of celestial love,
From every evil my beloved friend.

S[arah] Herd, 'Verses sent to B. Arthington with a print of Lady Jane Grey'

c.139, p. 464

T1928   This squire generous and free
Here lies a stinking fellow I mean knave.

'On one William Morrell alias Bowyer'

fb.143, p. 43

T1929   This stone doth tell the children | And the mother
Her life, for death | Will say, she did excel.

'Upon Eliz[abeth], the wife of Dan[iel] Caldwell esq.'

fb.143, p. 10

T1930 This strolling Presbyter from Scotland came
He, whom our servants scorned, does now command.

'The same [on Dr. Burnet] Englished' [translation of Latin verse, 1 July 1693]
[Crum T2048]

b.111, p. 159

T1931 This summer it chanced ere the rise of Aurora
And my hand seized a pen which their kindness inspir'd.

[William Hayley], 'In the summer's sweet prime as alert as Aurora . . .'

File 6949

T1932 This table you must have by heart,
Or to this work you need not start.

'Multiplication table. January 13th anno 1783'

c.93

T1933 This tender blossom of the opening year
Unfold its charms, and flourish in the skies.

'Another [epitaph on a child]'

c.83/3, no. 1021

T1934 This tender flow'ret, which so sweetly blows,
But to proclaim Sol's progress thro' the skies.

John Lockman, 'On occasion of the birth of a daughter, of which the Dauphiness [Marie-Josèph] was delivered [Oct. 1750]'

c.267/4, p. 167

T1935 This text considerately looked on
Where everlasting peace and glory is.

Thomas Cranley, 'A sermon preached in the King's Bench [21 Oct. 1638] by Mr. Andrew Wood. James the first, verse 27'

Poetry Box VII/21

T1936 This thousand and six hundred fortieth year,
The LorD Is With ye WhILst yoU be With hIM.

[Sir Thomas Urquhart], 'An encouragement to His Maj[esty] against the covenanters by way of a chronogram upon this present year of grace . . .'

fb.217, p. 395

T1937 This to my friend, whose heart for Britain glows;
Fourth, justly, the derision of the town.

John Lockman, 'A memento . . . July 1788'

c.267/1, p. 212

T1938 This, to the worthy Mrs. Mary,
You'll scarce find two such Mrs. Mary's.

John Lockman, 'To one of the Duchess of Buckingham's women . . . Paris, Oct. 1741'

c.267/2, p. 342

T1939 This tomb doth here enclose
Now naught but odor vile.

b.208, p. 156

T1940 This tomb encloses
One man and three noses.

'An epitaph on Sr Henry Cromwell'

b.197, p. 58

T1941 This town's my care, their bodies are my cure
I must not bind them both, in one degree.

[Sir Philip Wodehouse], 'Wilielmus Crop a surgeon of Norwich'

b.131, back (no. 206)

T1942 This trick of trimming is a fine thing
Sidney lets a fart and there's an end.

'The cushion dance at court. By way of mash to the tune of Joan Sanderson' [1683]
[Crum T2059]

b.113, p. 239

T1943 This village, sure! the happiest was,
Her like was nev'r before.

Abraham Oakes, 'A pastoral ditty: on the loss of Cuddy Clout'

c.50, p. 23

T1944 This was a high and active saint of heat,
For grace, so now for glory the complete.

[Edward] Sparke, 'Poem 30th on St. James'

b.137, p. 64

T1945 This was a man, who laboring hard
And broke his neck again.

'Epitaph . . . thus translated'

c.360/3, no. 117

T1946 This was my wish—a modest spot of ground,
And wealthier vales, and nobler bliss conferr'd.

[Thomas Hull]

c.20/5; c.21

T1947 This was the man, the glory of the gown,
To sit upon the clouds and judge mankind.

[Sir John Denham], 'An elegy upon Judge [Sir George] Crooke' [d. 16 Feb. 1641/2]
[Crum T2065]

fb.106(16)

T1948 This Wi[ld] said to Wa[lpole], make me undertaker
For as fast as they rob, they fill it again.

[Philip Wharton, 1st duke of Wharton], 'On robbing the Exchequer'

Trumbull Box: Poetry Box XIII/74; see also 'Quoth . . .'.

T1949   This window's like a mean estate
That women dying maids lead apes in hell.

    'Mary Crofts—Rachel Clutterbucke 1659'

b.52/2, p. 129

T1950   This work yclept the flower of medicine
Th'eleven thousandth year of Christ divine.

    [Philemon Holland, trans., introduction to Regimen
sanitatis salernitanum by John of Milan, ca.1650]

b.255

T1951   This world hath nothing pertinent, and this
World cannot stand because divided 'tis.

    'A kingdom divided'

c.356

T1952   This world is but a bubble
In misery soon to die.

    [Francis Bacon, 1st viscount St. Albans, 'Human life
characterised']
    [cf. Crum T1591, 'The world's a bubble . . .']

fb.88, p. 119

T1953   This world is like the sea, in it we're toss'd
Prize them so much, and to part with them fear.

    'On this world, comprehending this world's riches'

c.93

T1954   This world is not thy country, 'tis thy way
Unwelcome news to think upon a change.

    [Lady Ursula (Darcy) Wyvill]

b.222, p. 130

T1955   This world is the best, that we live in
It is the worst world, that ever was known.

    'On the world'

c.186, p. 47

T1956   This world presents few solid joys
Cry up today, whom next day load with shame.

    [Edmund Wodehouse], 'Feb. 3 [1715]'

b.131, p. 157

T1957   This world with all its pleasures are but vain
Guess at the rest then descant on the same.

    T[homas] G[urney], 'An acrostic on the name of my
esteemed friend Mr. Thos. Davis'

c.213

T1958   This world's God's church: the cross, the altar is:
Christ-man is both the priest and sacrifice.

    Sir Thomas Urquhart, 'A holy offering'

fb.217, p. 238

T1959   This world's the mode—good Mun then turn thy
                                coat
The wilderness and labyrinth of sin.

    [Sir Philip Wodehouse], 'Upon Mayor [Edmund]
Anguish'

b.131, back (no. 213)

T1960   This worthless tube of brittle clay,
Displays the state of all mankind.

    'Extempore. Pipe of tobacco'

c.81/1, no. 179; see also 'Thou worthless . . .'.

T1961   This worthy corpse, where shall we lay?
In Baxter's Saint's e'erlasting rest.

    'A new catch'

Poetry Box VII/13

T1962   This would be still my wish could I,
With fortunes that are low.

    [ ] Lewis, 'To a complaining friend . . . wrote on the
occasion of one who repined under his own
circumstances and admired those that had high spirits
though they were in low circumstances'

c.244, p. 448

T1963   Th'old mausoleum monuments of brass;
Gently fault, kind, Boreus, 'twill by thy glory.

    [J. A.], 'The transcriber upon the judicious author and
this his work'

fb.151/3 (end)

T1964   Th'old Roman words, and thoughts so seld' did vary,
Will scarce suffice to warrant their assertion.

    Sir Thomas Urquhart, 'A certain Spaniard's opinion,
why in the Latin speech, two negatives are equivalent
to one only affirmative . . . and that in the French
tongue, their must be at least, two negatives to make
up one sole negation . . .'

fb.217, p. 145

T1965   Thomas did once make my heart full glad
Yet Thomas I fear has betrayed the realm.

    [Captain Alexander Radcliffe], 'A song to the Scotch
tune: Zany: 1679' [on Thomas Osborne, earl of
Danby, later Duke of Leeds]
    [POAS II.110]

b.54, p. 1104

T1966   Thomas Warcup prepar'd this stone
Who me to save, Himself did die.

    'In [Wigton] churchyard [Cumberland] lies buried a
late vicar . . . obiit 1653'

c.547, p. 325

T1967   Thornhill whom doubly to my heart commend,
        When light shall unexpected bless thy eyes.

    [Nicholas] Rowe, 'Horace lib. 1. epis. 4 imitated and
    addressed to Esquire Thornhill'

    c.244, p. 180

T1968   Those arms, that oft have clasp'd thee close,
        Within thy mistress' heart.

    [Thomas Hull], 'Elegy'

    c.528/19

T1969   Those beasts which for the shambles are designed
        Serves but to fit them for the butcher's knife.

    c.189, p. 108

T1970   Those church-contemners, that can easily weigh
        If God in judgment should but give them heaven.

    [Francis Quarles], 'On church contemners' [Divine
    fancies I, 21]

    b.137, p. 180

T1971   Those glories that adorn'd thy father's throne,
        In humble adoration, humbly prays.

    [Thomas] Creech, '[Verses spoken in the theater] by
    Mr. [Philip] Bertie [son to the Earl of Lindsay] to the
    Duke [and Duchess] of York [and the Lady Anne].
    Great, good, and just' [Oxford, 21 May 1683]
    [Crum T2090]

    fb.142, p. 23

T1972   Those golden lines at your desire,
        T'have purified them.

    Sir Thomas Urquhart, 'Here one speaks to a friend of
    his, who had lent him some verses, which himself
    supposed to be good, that he might give his opinion of
    them'

    fb.217, p. 212

T1973   Those hours, that with gentle work did frame
        Lose but their show, their substance still live sweet.

    [William] Shakespeare [Sonnet v]

    c.94

T1974   Those ills the ancestors have done,
        (With all the pains we take) have skill enough to be.

    [Wentworth Dillon], 4th earl of Roscommon, 'The
    6th ode of the 3d book of Horace. Of the corruption
    of the times'
    [Crum T2093]

    b.201, p. 111; c.244, p. 83; c.351, p. 60

T1975   Those lamps of learning, which in former times
        Would say, they did deserve the name of doctor.

    Sir Thomas Urquhart, 'To Doctor [crossed out]
    Bishop of [crossed out]'

    fb.217, p. 140

T1976   Those many years our kingdom hath not seen
        Makes you both noble, beautiful, and good.

    Sir Thomas Urquhart, 'To the Countess of [crossed
    out; Wigton?]'

    fb.217, p. 195

T1977   Those men that have enough, and not contented
                                                    are,
        Time oft cuts off amid their cark and care.

    c.339, p. 325

T1978   Those men that help defer, when neighbors house
                                                    do burn,
        Are [?] with grief to see their own to cinders turn.

    c.339, p. 326

T1979   Those men that like all art that can be thought,
        Do comprehend not any as they ought.

    c.339, p. 313

T1980   Those men whose greedy minds, enough do think
                                                    too small,
        With more desire we wish the same to see.

    b.234, p. 325

T1981   Those stately lasses who not much confide
        Must have a fall, and it can fall no softer.

    [Sir Thomas Urquhart], 'Why the haughtiest women
    are subject to a venerian lapse'

    fb.217, p. 538

T1982   Those tears these eyes must shed for thee
        To others shall be dumb and blind.

    [Phanuel Bacon], 'A song'

    c.237, fol. 75

T1983   Those that have had the happiness to haunt
        Or less expos'd to vulgar ostentation.

    Sir Thomas Urquhart, 'To Sir Robert [crossed out] of
    that [ilk? Crossed out]

    fb.217, p. 212

T1984   Those that oppose themselves against the King,
        That up in arms against their sovereign are.

    Sir John Strangways, '30 Septr 1646'

    b.304, p. 57

T1985   Those that to pride are most inclin'd
        May learn its frailty to despise.

    R[obert] Shirley, 1st earl of Ferrers, 'On La Bruyere's
    picture—from Boileau'

    c.347, p. 31

T1986   Those that with you familiarly converse,
Can within its capacity admit.

      Sir Thomas Urquhart, 'To my Lord [crossed out]'
fb.217, p. 82

T1987   Those that would chose a pattern for a wife
Example for obedience youths to give.

      Lady Jane Cavendish, 'On a worthy friend'
      [Crum T2110b]
b.233, p. 24

T1988   Those things which are to me by fortune lent
Fetch them away again before my face.

      [Sir Thomas Urquhart], 'We should not be sorry at
      the loss of means'
fb.217, p. 499

T1989   Those tufted hillocks which thou passest by
That to the good—the grave's the way to bliss.

      [Phanuel Bacon], 'Epitaph for the son of Mrs. ———
      on the other side whose graves were close to each
      other'
c.237, fol. 81v [i.e., 101v]; see also 'Stop passenger . . .'.

T1990   Those unavailing rites he may receive,
These, after death, are all a God can give.

c.189, p. 87

T1991   Those well contend and those are captains good,
That win the field with shedding least of blood.

c.339, p. 324

T1992   Those who the various gifts of fortune gain,
Faithful friend from flatt'ring foe.

      'Sympathetic love, addressed to the nightingale'
c.83/1, no. 263

T1993   Those wicked imps, that lewdly run their race,
Are hailed back, at length to their deface.

c.339, p. 310

T1994   Those wonderful wise men, nicknam'd antiquaries,
To some, who too often, have kept them ruin.

      'A description of Holland'
b.111, p. 487

T1995   Those worthy Romans that scorn'd humble things
Which doth amaze the world, and strikes me mute.

      [Sir Aston Cokayne], 'To the truly noble Sir Arthur
      Gorges'
b.275, p. 53

T1996   Those zealous men make not so evident,
They have the greater hope to lose their pains.

      [Sir Thomas Urquhart]
fb.217, p. 541

T1997   Thou art a free good soul, of innocence
And so each one, may justly wish, for thee.

      Lady Jane Cavendish, 'On an acquaintance'
      [Crum T2124]
b.233, p. 19

T1998   Thou art a sinner, reader;—dost thou fly
The blood bought blessings of a Savior's love.

      Charles Atherton Allnutt, 'Epitaph on the late
      Mr. Cha[rle]s Pickman'
c.112, p. 129

T1999   Thou art gone to heaven we know full well,
For there's no Holidays in hell.

      'On Mr. Holiday'
      [Crum T266]
c.233, p. 67

T2000   Thou art my enemy I bear about me,
With thee I live not well, nor well without thee.

      'Ad carnem'
b.197, p. 173

T2001   Thou art not fair for all thy red and white
Embrace kiss and love me in despite.

      [Thomas Campion]
      [Crum T2133]
b.213, p. 17; b.4, fol. 24

T2002   Thou art so fair and cruel too,
That for thy sake I am accurst | I must and will
                                      adore.

      'A song'
b.54, p. 1163; c.158, p. 20

T2003   Thou art so pretty, young, and witty
Then, pretty, fair, and witty, to be kiss'd.

      Lady Jane Cavendish, 'The pert one, or otherwise, my
      sister Brackley'
      [Crum T2139]
b.233, p. 13

T2004   Thou at whose touch the snow-clad mountains
                                     smoke
His triumph over death!

      'God is love' [printed in Gentleman's magazine]
      [Crum T2141]
c.517, fol. 39r

T2005   Thou attractive charming one,
I'll drop my pen and so unfold.

c.93

T2006   Thou base, ungrateful, cunning, upstart thing!
Be agent still, but postmaster no more.

     'To D—r F—n'

fc.85, fol. 80

T2007   Thou blam'st the age, condemn'st the days of crimes
If thou wouldst mend thy faults, 'twould mend the
                                   times.

     [Francis Quarles], 'On Censorio' [Divine
     fancies IV, 42]

b.137, p. 183; b.118, p. 225

T2008   Thou blaster of thy own fair spreading fame
How wouldst thou shine by thy own folly's flame.

     'On the tearing out and burning the obscene pieces of
     the Earl of Rochester's works—in 1725'

c.360/2, no. 98

T2009   Thou blear-ey'd hag, whose vapid soul
The calm and leisure hour by mental pleasure
                                  grac'd.

     [Richard Hole], 'Ode to ignorance'

Diggle Box: Poetry Box XI/30

T2010   Thou blushing rose, within whose virgin leaves
Anticipating life, to hasten death.

     [Sir Richard Fanshawe]

b.150, p. 219

T2011   Thou bought'st a fool for twenty pounds, but I
Will not at such a price thee buy or buy.

     'To Hercinus'

c.356

T2012   Th[ou?] breath'st as the morn, or zephyr-wind
Inanimated with chaste piety.

     [Sir Philip Wodehouse], 'Sarai Sparrow another of my
     Lord Bish[op's lady]'

b.131, back (no. 122)

T2013   Thou cage full of foul birds and beasts
Devil take them all by bunches.

     'A dismal summons to the Doctors' Commons' [on
     Convocation, May 1640]
     [Crum T2147]

b.101, p. 88

T2014   Thou calmly snug, sequester'd seat
And wisdom's beam illumine ev'ry page.

     'Ode to a little-house'

c.382, p. 59

T2015   Thou caterpillar that devours
And when y'are drest, you're butterflies.

     'The lady and caterpillar'

c.489, p. 18

T2016   Thou cheat'st us Ford, makes one seem true by art
What is love's sacrifice, but a broken heart.

     [Richard Crashaw, on Ford's tragedies Love's force
     and The broken head]
     [Crum T2150]

b.356, p. 69

T2017   Thou common shore of this poetic town,
His mistress lost, and yet his pen's his sword.

     [George Villiers, 2nd duke of Buckingham?], 'A
     familiar epistle to Mr. [Robert] Julian Secretary of the
     Muses' [1677]
     [Crum T2152; POAS I.388]

b.105, p. 352; b.113, p. 43; b.54, p. 1184

T2018   Thou com'st in such a questionable guise,
Then tell ladies! Shall we read or burn?

     H[enry] W[illiams], 'The reader to the author—of
     The old maids (at that time unknown)'

Greatheed Box/61

T2019   Thou damned antipodes to common sense!
In the same strain thou writ'st thy comedy.

     Hen[ry] Savile(?), 'On Mr. Edw[ard] Howard upon
     his New utopia' [1669-1671]
     [Crum T2155; POAS I.340]

b.105, p. 189; b.371, no. 32 (ll. 1-38)

T2020   Thou dear inspirer of my happiest hours,
And crown with health and peace her future days.

     'To a friend'

c.90

T2021   Thou dear redeemer dying Lord
And Christ shall be our song.

     'Hymn 20'

c.562, p. 23

T2022   Thou dearest shade that waileth night and days
And to thy ashes make an offering.

     [Mrs. ( ) Feilding]

b.226, p. 9

T2023   Thou dear'st of all womankind
Durst plead with thee thyself to wrong.

     [Mrs. Christian Kerr], 'An answer' [to 'Cease, cease
     my friend . . .']

c.102, p. 95

T2024 Thou didst those creatures bless
Her instinct kindly guides them to't.

    Poetry Box VI/89 (incomplete)

T2025 Thou dome of death! By lonely musings led,
Consign'd with kindred shades in peace to rest.

    J[ohn] J[elliand], of Brundish, 'An elegy on a family
    tomb'

    c.130, p. 37; c.90

T2026 Thou dost deny me 'cause thou art a wife
You have two pallets and the best below.

    'Solicitation to a married woman'

    b.104, p. 114/2

T2027 Thou dost invite all wand'ring souls
To bring it to Heaven's rest.

    'An epitaph in Islip churchyard'

    c.240, p. 136

T2028 Thou everlasting tongue with brazen face,
King William's blemish, and King George's shame.

    'Reflections on a patent'

    Poetry Box IV/66

T2029 Thou fairest creature ever born,
Go ask papa—for he can tell—

    H[annah] More, 'An heroic epistle to Miss Sally
    Horne aged three years written in the blank leaves of
    Mother Bunch's tales and showing the superiority of
    those histories to most others'

    c.341, p. 24

T2030 Thou fairest, thou dearest of all womankind,
And the cold hand of death, soon extinguisht his
                        fire.

    [Thomas Hamilton, 6th earl of Haddington], 'Song to
    the tune of Auld Reb Morrice'

    c.458/1, p. 54

T2031 Thou filthy hypocrite of a dean!
Tell him the news—I'll see you often.,

    'A dialogue between the Lord Russell's ghost and the
    Dean [Tillotson] of Canterbury' [c. 1689]
    [Crum T2170]

    b.111, p. 135; fb.207/1, p. 31

T2032 Thou gentle nurse of pleasing woe!
Can never be secure.

    [Hester] Chapone(?), 'To solitude'

    c.130, p. 86; c.83/3, no. 980

T2033 Thou gentle, thou benignant pow'r
Sweet peace is lost and virtue dies.

    Miss [ ] Bradford, 'Ode to sensibility'

    c.504, p. 22

T2034 Thou God that hearest prayer
And take us to thy throne.

    'Hymn 11th'

    c.562, p. 12

T2035 Thou great and sacred Lord of all,
My trembling ghost prepare.

    [Mary Leapor], 'A request to the Divine being'

    c.487, p. 52

T2036 Thou great Creator of all human kind
Than live in this perpetual lethargy.

    [Mrs. ( ) Feilding]

    b.226, p. 88

T2037 Thou great Creator of this earth,
Return thee praises night and day.

    Margaret Oates, 'The husbandman's prayer'

    c.160, fol. 79

T2038 Thou happy Tuesday since that now I see
And so thyself will ever valued be.

    Lady Jane Cavendish, 'A recruited joy upon a letter
    from you Lo[rdshi]p'
    [Crum T2193]

    b.233, p. 29

T2039 Thou hast been savage on the martial stage
But thy Andromache at home assuage.

    [Sir Philip Wodehouse], 'Thomas Savage at home
    assuage'

    b.131, back (no. 141)

T2040 Thou hast, my friend, one female heir,
While ev'ry youth the danger flies.

    'Epistle IX. To Exelbee Lawford esqr.'

    fc.100, p. 39

T2041 Thou hast no lightnings O Thou just,
Than woe itself would be.

    [William Cowper, trans.], 'Divine justice amiable.
    Vol. 2. sonnet. 119' [of Jeanne Guion's 'Spiritual
    songs']

    c.470 (autogr.)

T2042 Thou hast not been so long neglected
A word's enough unto the wise.

    [Sir John Denham, on Sir William D'Avenant]

    pb.53, p. 13 (autogr.)

T2043 Thou hast O Lord, my secret soul descried
To dwell with thee in everlasting day.

    [Mary] Masters, 'Psalm 139'

    c.244, p. 246

T2044   Thou heard that Israel dost keep
And reign throughout the world.

     [John Hopkins], 'A thanksgiving for God's benefits.
     Psalm 33' [verses from Psalms 80, 83]

a.3, fol. 114v

T2045   Thou, heavenly maid, will grant the poor relief,
The mind forgets its bonds, if serving thee.

     'On humanity'

c.83/1, no. 84

T2046   Thou I invoke who grac'd the prophet's song
But stampt upon the heart, engraven on the mind.

     Tho[ma]s Stevenson, 'The charity school at Spalding,
     erected for learning and clothing thirty poor
     children . . . November 1750'

c.229/1, fol. 108

T2047   Thou in the fields, walk'st out thy supping hours
A salad worse than Spanish dieting.

     [John Donne], quatrain in 'The antiquary'
     [Crum T2202]

b.148, p. 56

T2048   Thou in whose name, a monument doth lie
Since we a plain Stone wisht to have thee.

     'On one Benjamin Stone'
     [Crum T2204]

b.356, p. 255

T2049   Thou kind, endearing, gladsome flame!
In pure seraphic sounds!

     [ ] Macaulay, 'An ode to hope. Attempted, from
     Macaulay's poems'

c.94 (incomplete?)

T2050   Thou kindest judge poor scribbler e'er could find,
Which loves not pain, yet makes not holy wars his
                          sport.

     'To Mr. Herring rector of Emington Oxfordshire'

b.322, p. 2

T2051   Thou knowest too well, how much thy form I prize
And yield with joy, to thee my youthful charms.

     [Daniel Bellamy], 'From The rival priests, or the
     female politicians'

c.186, p. 59

T2052   Thou last delight of fond parental care
To grieve is mortal—heavenly to adore.

     'Lines on the death of Miss B—go at Bristol'

c.83/2, no. 639

T2053   Thou learned Homer wanting coin
Than clowns which have much money.

b.234, p. 27

T2054   Thou lingering star, with less'ning ray,
Hear'st thou the groans that rend his breast?

     [Robert Burns], 'To Mary in heaven'

c.142, p. 232

T2055   Thou little monarch man small universe,
As thou art flesh, thou art a bait for worms.

     'To mankind'

c.189, p. 23

T2056   Thou little thing, thou once did sing
Forget the woes that's past.

     [E. S. J.], 'Julia and her dead robin'

Poetry Box x/55

T2057   Thou little wond'rous, miniature of man,
Or snatch her back to native nothing's gloom!

     Samuel Davies, 'Verses written by . . . President of the
     College of Princeton in New Jersey on the birth of his
     third son John Rogers Davies'

c.240, fol. 4

T2058   Thou lone companion of the specter'd night,
Destructive tyrant, I arrest thy pow'r.

     [John Wolcot] ('Peter Pindar'), 'To my candle'

c.343, p. 46

T2059   Thou look's[t] sweet boy, as if thou wouldest be,
Shall then convert your enemies' hearts to fears.

     Lady Jane Cavendish, 'On my sweet nephew Henry
     Harpur'
     [Crum T2210]

b.233, p. 12

T2060   Thou, Lord, be my defense and shield,
The just live in Thy sight.

     'Psalm 140'

c.264/3, p. 96

T2061   Thou Lord dost call me to draw near
She's quickly snatcht away.

     [Mary Pluret], 'Drawing near to God'

c.354

T2062   Thou Lord hast made us see that pious thoughts
Wilt on thy servant for his sake bestow.

     [Thomas Stanley], 'Meditat. I: Upon his Ma[jes]ty's
     calling this last Parliament'

b.152, p. 7

T2063   Thou Lord on him hast wrought a noble cure,
Which to Thy praise forever shall redound.

     [W. H.], 'Anagram. Caleb Vernon. An noble cure'

b.228, p. 75

T2064 Thou Lord on whom I still depend
God three in one and one in three.

'Hymn 88th'

c.562, p. 116

T2065 Thou Lord thro' ev'ry changing scene
Succeeding hymns of humble praise.

P[hilip] Doddridge, 'God the dwelling place of his people through all generations Ps. XC. 1'

c.493, p. 78

T2066 Thou Lord to me thy word hast given
Sit down and wond'ring say, Amen.

J[ohn?] C[halkhill?], 'A poetical meditation, wherein the usefulness, excellency, and several perfections of holy Scriptures are briefly hinted'

b.49, p. 28

T2067 Thou Lord who by thy wise decree,
Which to eternity shall last.

[Thomas Stanley], 'Meditat: XXI. Upon his Ma[jes]ty's letters taken and divulged'

b.152, p. 65

T2068 Thou lovely Bess, that art so plump and young,
And if so liked, we think them then well-penn'd.

Lady Jane Cavendish, 'On a chambermaid' [Crum T2215]

b.233, p. 18

T2069 Thou lovest not because thou art unkind,
By kind mind heart desert or anyone.

'Her answer' [to 'I love because it comes to me . . .']

c.356; b.197, p. 62; see also 'That if I do love . . .'.

T2070 Thou may'st in thy humility
Can't be a peacock's and a pigeon's nest.

[Sir Philip Wodehouse], 'Upon his learned and honest friend Mr John Whitefoot'

b.131, back (no. 157)

T2071 Thou must expire my soul, ordain'd to range,
Some strange hereafter or some hidden skies.

'On the departure of a soul'

c.391, p. 34, p.?

T2072 Thou nature's favorite! La Fontaine,
Thy charming fables, and thy tales.

John Lockman, 'Character of La Fontaine, by Voltaire'

c.267/4, p. 147

T2073 Thou need'st not say with mental sighs, O man!
And humbly in thy maker put thy truth.

'The internal monitor'

c.365, p. 27

T2074 Thou ne'er woot riddle neighbor John
Do take in great indudgeon.

Will[iam] Strode, 'A Devonshire song' [Crum T2225]

b.200, p. 181; see also 'Riddle, riddle, neighbor John . . .'.

T2075 Thou never-failing fountain O thou art
Let all my own desires be in me slain.

[Mary Serjant]

fb.98, fol. 165

T2076 Thou nothing sent'st thy nothing I repel,
Thou gav'st thyself I give thee back; farewell.

'P answer to Ph' [see 'How look'st . . .']

c.356

T2077 Thou, O rose, that scent'st the bushes,
Fearless of the ills between.

'Flora's moral lesson'

c.83/4, no. 1079

T2078 Thou old, yet still laborious, son of earth
So, when you please, to your delight adjourn.

[Thomas Morell], 'Boileau's epistle to his gardener, imitated'

c.395, p. 149

T2079 Thou on whose breast in early days
Free as the mountain wind thy pinions may be spread.

Edward Rushton, 'To a robin singing on a warehouse near the author's shop in Liverpool'

c.364

T2080 Thou on whose praises I delight to dwell!
Despis'd mean flatt'ry, and cherish'd truth.

John Lockman, 'Epistles. To a great lady [the late Duchess of Buckingham] with the Jesuit's travels [translated by the author]' [pr. 1743 (Foxon L223)]

c.267/2, p. 317

T2081 Thou, on whose rocks in savage grandeur pil'd,
From them, as lov'd companions, to depart.

Ed[ward] Hamley, 'Sonnet'

c.142, p. 147

T2082 Thou one-ey'd boy, whose sister of one mother
The queen of beauty, thou the god of love.

'On two beautiful infants who had each one eye' [Crum T2227]

c.81/1, no. 510; see also next, and 'An one-ey'd boy . . .'.

T2083 Thou one-eyed son, born of an half blind mother,
The queen of beauty—thou the god of love.

'On a beautiful lady and her son who had each but one eye'

c.378, p. 42; see also previous, and 'An one-ey'd boy . . .'.

T2084 Thou only object of my love,
Live, for I live alone for thee.

'Sonnet'

c.83/3, no. 764

T2085 Thou only pillar left of all the line
And pine(?), yet distant, consecrate thy own!

[William Hayley], 'Sonnet . . . Feb 10 [1800]'
File 6968

T2086 Thou passenger that shall have so much time,
Shall raise the remnant, bruise the serpent's seed.

'An epitaph composed by the Duke of Argyll himself, a little before his was beheaded 1695 [i.e., 1685]'

c.244, p. 288

T2087 Thou perverse, adverse Caleb D'anvers,
To your own works. Sign'd Caleb D'anvers.

[Nicholas Amhurst], 'On the treaty concluded at Seville'

c.570/3, p. 94

T2088 Thou pious shin'st in Latin spells thy name:
Thy life, in English, does make good the same.

[Sir Philip Wodehouse], 'Upon his wife's kinswoman Mrs. Lucia Repps'

b.131, back (no. 127, no. 227)

T2089 Thou plead'st, apostate, for thy silent lyre
Thou hidest in a sheepskin talents ten.

'Epigram on Mr. Eliot's apologetic verses for abjuring the Muses and commencing farmer'

Poetry Box x/11

T2090 Thou pow'r supreme! By whose command I live,
And take my soul expiring to thy arms.

[Elizabeth Carter], 'Wrote on her birthday'
[Crum T2236]

fc.132/1, p. 3; c.83/1, no. 101; c.193, p. 42; see also 'Wake O my soul . . .'.

T2091 Thou pretty little fluttering thing!
And smile upon my adverse day!

Miss P. Y[oung], 'Song by . . . addressed to her canary bird, when she was seized with lameness in the West Indies'
[Crum T2238, 'lively thing']

fc.124, p. 54

T2092 Thou pretty, wandering, flutt'ring thing!
With wit of thy own making.

[Matthew] Prior(?), 'Ditto ['Olius Adrianus . . . Animula, vagula, blandula . . . translation']

c.81/1, no. 219; see also 'Poor little, pretty . . .'.

T2093 Thou quick'ning power of genial life impart!
In sounds like mighty thunders cry Amen.

'A religious poem'

c.83/2, no. 373

T2094 Thou rare example in thy early prime
He yet shall be my guide and our reunion blest!

[William Hayley], 'Sonnet . . . Jan 21 [1800]'
File 6968

T2095 Thou restless fluctuating deep,
Shall fade beneath the gloom of spleen.

[Elizabeth Carter], 'Written extempore on the sea shore'

fc.132/1, p. 10

T2096 Thou righteous God that lovest right,
Thy face benign on me.

'Psalm 17'

c.264/1, p. 51

T2097 Thou rising sun, whose gladsome ray
Away to Orra, haste away.

'A Laplander's song'

c.186, p. 86

T2098 Thou robb'st my days of business and delight
Perish by turning everything to gold.

A[braham] C[owley], 'The thief'

c.258

T2099 Thou ruler of the sky, almighty name!
Conscious how impotent she is without thee.

[Elizabeth (Singer) Rowe], 'A short prayer to Christ in blank verse'

c.167, p. 25; fc.132/1, p. 81

T2100 Thou sapient bird unjustly styl'd a gull
And thou and those who gave thee to my bower.

[William Hayley], 'Sonnet'
File 6965

T2101 Thou say'st, it is a support, and it's fit
Fools act a sin, whilst they decline a vice.

[Francis Quarles], 'On non-conformists'

b.137, p. 181

T2102 Thou scoffing atheist that inquirest what
All those in one makes one eternal Trinity.

[Joshua Sylvester, trans. Guillaume de Salluste,
seigneur] Du Bartas, 'What God did before he made
the world'

b.137, p. 85

T2103 Thou sendest me prose and rhymes; I send for those
Being a maid begot his song of me.

[Thomas Woodward?]
[Crum T2246]

b.148, p. 88

T2104 Thou sent a message late
Love's Diana, that's you.

Lady Jane Cavendish, 'On a noble lady'
[Crum T2248]

b.233, p. 9

T2105 Thou sent'st to me a heart was crown'd [sound]
That so much honor'd thee.

[Sir Robert Ayton, 'To his mistress']
[Crum T2249]

b.213, p. 11; b.4, fol. 6v (damaged); b.197, p. 38; b.200,
p. 86

T2106 Thou setting sun, that calls my fair
A feeling heart, and constant mind.

'Inscribed to Miss ———'

c.83/2, no. 601

T2107 Thou shalt not laugh in this leaf (Muse) nor they
And dived near drowning, for what vanished.

[John Donne], 'Satira quinta'
[Crum T2252]

b.114, p. 43; b.148, p. 15

T2108 Thou shalt not steal, this law's for lawyers writ,
Thou shalt not kill, this for physicians fit.

'Thou shalt not kill thou shalt not steal'

c.356

T2109 Thou shepherd of Israel and mine
Eternally held in thy heart.

'Hymn 17th'

c.562, p. 19

T2110 Thou shepherd whose attentive eye
The world my sight since thee was hid.

[Aurelian Townshend]

b.213, p. 64

T2111 Thou shining metal, which in baleful hour,
On kinder shores to light her hallow'd fires.

S[arah] Herd, 'To gold'

c.141, p. 395

T2112 Thou silent moon, that look'st so pale,
He left thee, sickening, faint, and pale.

'To the moon from an old MS.'

b.150, p. 220

T2113 Thou smiling there thine image seems to smile,
But tho' thou speakest thine image speechless
                                                    proves.

'Of the picture in the looking glass'

c.356

T2114 Thou specter of terrific mien,
Till I may claim the hope, that shall not fade.

[Charlotte (Turner) Smith], 'Ode to despair'

c.83/3, no. 894

T2115 Thou still the same; forever blest
From bold blind zeal thy church defend.

[Thomas Stanley], 'Meditat: XVI. Upon the
ordinance against the Common Prayer Book'

b.152, p. 52

T2116 Thou stranger, which for Rome, in Rome here
                                                    seekest
And that is flitting, doth abide and stay.

[Edmund] Spenser, 'The ruins of old Rome by [Rene
du] Bellay, [baron de LaLande]—translated by . . .'

c.360/1, p. 145

T2117 Thou summer so lively and gay,
To welcome the season of love.

'Address to the summer'

c.83/2, no. 548

T2118 Thou sweetest rose that ever grew
Death calls, but finds he's not at home.

Edward Sneyd, 'An extempore on Miss G. F.
presenting me with a rose from her bosom'

c.214, p. 118

T2119 Thou tell'st me Cynthia that my sighs
Where ev'ry wish is full of thee.

[John Wolcot ('Peter Pindar')], 'Sonnet'

File 16344

T2120 Thou that alone art infinite
Yet shall no taint of fear my bright faith rust.

[Thomas Stanley], 'Meditat: XXIII. Upon the Scots
delivering the King to the English and his captivity at
Holmeby'

b.152, p. 70

T2121 Thou that fillest heaven and earth O King of kings
Have seen, in peace O let thy servant die.

    [Thomas Stanley], 'Meditat: XXVII. Upon death'

b.152, p. 89

T2122 Thou that hast neither shame nor sense
And still be Kitty's foe.

    'Answer to the author of the foregoing scurrilous
    rhymes' ['Chetwood as fame . . .']

c.360/1, p. 57

T2123 Thou that in want at rich man's door didst lie
For beggar here, in heaven thou art a king.

    'An epitaph on Lazarus'

c.189, p. 61

T2124 Thou that lovedst once, now love no more
She now'll sigh weep beg at thy door.

    [Sir Robert Ayton], 'An answer' [to 'I loved thee
    once . . .']
    [Crum T2273]

b.213, p. 26; b.197, p. 176

T2125 Thou that this little book dost take in hand,
At any time, He do as much for thee.

    'To the reader'

fb.69, p. 121

T2126 Thou, to whom the world unknown
And I, O fear, will dwell with thee!

    [William] Collins, 'Ode to fear'

c.351, p. 162

T2127 Thou, to whose eyes I bend, at whose command,
To her, who of mankind could love but thee alone.

    [Matthew Prior], 'Henry and Emma[.] To Chloe'
    [Crum T2284]

c.83/2, no. 337

T2128 Thou, to whose pow'r reluctantly we bend,
Still rule the conquer'd heart to life's remotest hour.

    'Lines written by a lady on observing some white hairs
    on her husband's head'

c.83/1, no. 163

T2129 Thou town of Woodstock double now thy pride
Britain the like ne'er had nor will have such.

    'Upon Blenheim the Duke of Marlborough's house at
    Woodstock'

c.158, p. 85

T2130 Thou unto others B[entle]y may
Let nothing now your praise prevent.

    [Mary Pluret, on William Bentley, her pastor]

c.354

T2131 Thou watchful taper, by whose silent light
From whose bright beams their being first arose.

    [William] Congreve, 'To a candle'

c.360/2, no. 121; c.138, p. 31

T2132 Thou wert the only piece of noble truth
That you a Talbot's greatness had, that's thee.

    Lady Jane Cavendish, 'On Gilbert earl of Shrewbury'
    [Crum T2290]

b.233, p. 33

T2133 Thou wert the prettiest thing that e'er I saw
A perfect handsome creature, I do swear.

    Lady Jane Cavendish, 'On an acquaintance'
    [Crum T2291]

b.233, p. 19

T2134 Thou, which art I, ('tis nothing to be so)
That though thy absence sterve me, I wish not thee.

    [John Donne], 'A storm. To Sir Basil [i.e.,
    Christopher] Brooke'
    [Crum T2295]

b.114, p. 221; b.148, p. 59

T2135 Thou who all souls all consciences doth sway
If thee I please, peace shall my foes allay.

    [Thomas Stanley], 'Meditat: XXII. Upon his
    Ma[jes]ty's leaving Oxford and going to the Scots'

b.152, p. 68

T2136 Thou who dost all my worldly thoughts employ,
And die, as I have liv'd, thy faithful wife.

    [Mary (Molesworth) Monck], 'A letter from a dying
    wife at Bath to her husband in London'
    [Crum T2301]

c.244, p. 108; c.481, p. 271 (incomplete); fc.132/1, p. 165;
b.197, p. 244; fc.51, p. 22; Poetry Box v/8

T2137 Thou who, in unseen state, thy tutelary reign
Of a gentle sway around.

    'Inter strepit anser olores. Genius of Lovington
    rejoice'

Poetry Box v/67

T2138 Thou, who in wit, in virtue didst excel
'Come; to thy father come again.'

    [ ] Ellison, 'Epitaph by Dr. Lowth, Bishop of London
    inscribed on a monument to the memory of his
    daughter . . . translation'

Greatheed Box/29

T2139   Thou, who not born wert snatch'd away by death!
Proud honor, spite of love, expell'd thee from it.

> John Lockman, 'The above sonnet ['O thou, whose
> eyes . . .'], translated almost literally [from Sieur D.
> Henault]'

c.267/4, p. 159; c.268 (second part), p. 91 ('Thou who
not born')

T2140   Thou, who within these hallowed walls shalt move,
And pity's stream shall soon o'erflow thine eyes!

> 'An epitaph in memory of Mrs. Margaret Robinson
> wife [of] Capt. [Robinson] who died March 22 1765
> buried St. Catharine's London'

c.58

T2141   Thou whom impassion'd truth and moral grace
New to his eye congenial to his heart.

> 'Epistles to [William] Hodges R. A . . . Epistle 1'

c.363, p. 1

T2142   Thou whom my soul admires above
Till my beloved lead me home.

> [Isaac Watts, Hymns and spiritual songs (1707), bk. I,
> Hymn 67]

c.180, p. 62

T2143   Thou! whom prosperity has always led
Mar the uncommon blessings of thy fate!

> [Charlotte (Turner) Smith], 'Sonnet to a querulous
> acquaintance'

c.141, p. 122

T2144   Thou whose great tremendous word
The yielding waves—O spare thy people; spare.

c.591

T2145   Thou, whose lank fortune heaven hath swell'd with
store
Will take thy part when all the world's against thee.

> [Francis Quarles, 'In prosperity', from Job militant,
> 1624]
> [cf. Crum T2308]

c.158, p. 30

T2146   Thou whose mercies know no bound
Truth my heart and actions knit.

> [Thomas Stanley], 'Meditat: II. Upon the Earl of
> Strafford's death'

b.152, p. 9

T2147   Thou whose sweet youth, and early hopes enhance
If well, the pain doth fade, the joy remain.

> [George] Herbert, 'The quatrains of [Guy du Faur de]
> Pibrac or pious exhortations for youth out of Du
> Bartas and Herbert's poems'
> [Crum T2310]

b.137, p. 76

T2148   Thou will not give but tak'st a kiss,
Knowing that taking one a giving is.

> 'Of Phyllis'

c.356

T2149   Thou, with hurried step advancing,
For if thy votary think—thy visions end.

> [( ) Smyth], 'Ode to mirth'

c.141, p. 13

T2150   Thou wither'd, lewd, lascivious wife
Till to the lees, drawn down.

> [William Popple, trans.], '[Horace] book 3rd. ode
> 15th. To Chloris'

fc.104/2, p. 260

T2151   Thou worst of flesh in superstition stew'd
That lubber'd wight into her palace pull.

> [on the Duke of York and the Queen, c. 1679]
> [Crum T2314]

b.371, no. iii (in back); b.54, p. 1229 (var.)

T2152   Thou worthless tube of brittle clay,
Displays the fate of all mankind.

> 'Extempore on a pipe of tobacco'

c.487, p. 71; see also 'This worthless . . .'.

T2153   Thou wretched man, why for a thousand year
Live close, why say'st not I shall one day die.

> 'On a covetous man'

c.356

T2154   Thou! To whom Amphion ow'd
Write—for thee, she gave up life.

> [William Popple, trans.], '[Horace] book 3rd. ode
> 11th. To Mercury'

fc.104/2, p. 244

T2155   Though a democracy of stars, at night
No other splendor will appear, but his one.

> Sir Thomas Urquhart, 'Of the King and covenanters,
> a prophecy'

fb.217, p. 100

T2156   Tho' a rogue we oft hide a frail nymph oft conceal
To be hung, drawn and quarter'd our lot.

> '[Enigma/Charade/Conundrum] 4' [curtains]

c.389

T2157   Though a young courtier said, against the stream
Should not a horse be plac'd before a mass.

> Sir Thomas Urquhart, 'To one, who taxed a certain
> gentleman of speaking improperly'

fb.217, p. 255

T2158   Tho' Albion's wishes did obstruct her way
       She pays for her William in losing her Gloucester.

       'An epitaph on the Duke of Gloucester' [1700]
       [Crum T2318]

       fb.207/1, p. 10

T2159   Though all earl's wives be countesses: yet whom
       His splendid orb, the moon irradiate.

       Sir Thomas Urquhart, 'Of earls and countesses'

       fb.217, p. 190

T2160   Though all some others do commit: yet few
       Without offence the truth of living men.

       [Sir Thomas Urquhart], 'How dangerous a thing it is
       to write of modern men'

       fb.217, p. 532

T2161   Tho' all that's charming deck the face,
       There honor braves the stealing hour.

       'To the fair'

       c.142, p. 426

T2162   Tho' all the world knows
       Her choice is to live in the pain.

       'An epigram on the death of Mrs. Bowes'

       c.188, p. 17; c.360/2, no. 78

T2163   Tho' all who see her, feel her piercing smart
       And at its cost, to wish her to be wise.

       [Sir Philip Wodehouse], 'Upon Mrs. Catharine
       Crompton a paragon of beauty'

       b.131, back (no. 72)

T2164   Tho' Artemesia talks by fits
       And wear a cleaner smock.

       [Alexander Pope], 'Female pedant'

       c.81/1, no. 331

T2165   Tho' Bacchus may boast of his care-killing bowl,
       That's mellow'd by friendship, and sweeten'd by
                                   love.

       Captain [Thomas] Morris, 'Song'

       c.391, p. 67; Poetry Box XII/3

T2166   Though beauties of inferior ray
       Admiring what I dare not praise.

       [John] Gay

       c.259, p. 146

T2167   Tho' beauties which adorn thy face
       When anger flashes from my eyes.

       John Lockman, 'Translations, and imitations from
       Metastasio, and other Italian opera poets [8]'

       c.267/4, p. 99

T2168   Tho' beauty did less prejudice receive
       And not pollute his glorious verse with mine.

       'Adam and Eve' [on Abraham Cowley]

       Poetry Box VI/111

T2169   Though beauty may charm the fond heart, with a
                                   smile,
       Were cherished by genius, and nurs'd with her tears.

       'Impromptu on Mr. Merry's marriage with Miss
       Brunton in consequence of her charming performance
       of Loriana in his tragedy of Lorenzo'

       c.391, p. 108

T2170   Tho' Boccace, Prior, and Fontaine
       Of her, the villain was to blame.

       [Thomas Hamilton, 6th earl of Haddington], 'The
       trap'

       c.458/2, p. 68

T2171   Though Boreas' blasts, and Neptune's waves, have
                                 tost me to and fro,
       Yet once again I must set sail our admiral Christ to
                                 meet.

       [epitaph in Stepney churchyard on Capt. John Dunch,
       1696, and at St. Michael's, Bristol, on James
       Muncaster, 12 Sept. 1713, and at Lyme]
       [Crum T2327]

       Poetry Box VII/55; c.546; see also 'The boist'rous
       winds . . .'.

T2172   Tho' Bruin's a beast that strikes men with dread
       He seeks for his safety in flight.

       c.546, p. 34

T2173   Though by her algebra she found equations,
       Of rooted quantity, annex'd into them.

       Sir Thomas Urquhart, 'How profoundly a certain
       woman was versed in the science of algebra'

       fb.217, p. 198

T2174   Though Constance(?) first advised me to contact
       T'enlarge her [?] before that I unpact(?) her.

       [Sir Thomas Urquhart], 'The expression of a certain
       gentleman, who did aim to have carnal dealing with
       the virgin he was to make chosen to be his wife before
       their wedding day [?] or they were affianced'

       fb.217, p. 518

T2175   Though Cupid blindlings hop in,
       The door is always open.

       Sir Thomas Urquhart, 'The chasteth woman that is,
       may at unawares be surprised'

       fb.217, p. 352

T2176 Tho' custom says, in every clime,
Oh may their offspring be delight.

    [William Hayley], 'To Wm Long 1777 with a picture
    of Cupid and Psyche'

File 6978

T2177 Tho' Damon's heart still opens to the fair,
But as he had by other swains been told.

    'Facit indignatio versum'

fb.142, p. 38

T2178 Though death of life did thee deprive
We'll say this happen'd once brave Savile died.

    'William Savile anagr. I am alive still'

Poetry Box VII/26

T2179 Though death to good men be the greatest boon
We might believe that spotless she had been.

    [William Strode], 'On the death of the lady Cæsar'
    [Anne, wife of Sir Charles Caesar, d. 13 Jan. 1625]
    [Crum T2343]

b.205, fol. 63r

T2180 Tho' Delia oft retires
Often finds the dose too much.

    [Isabella (Machell) Ingram], viscountess Irwin, 'Lady
    Irwin's answer' [to 'Why with Delia thus retire . . .']

fc.135

T2181 Tho' dim and ogling are the eyes
Since folly can't defend 'em.

    R[obert] Shirley, 1st earl of Ferrers, 'To Celia coquette
    and old and silly'

c.347, p. 31

T2182 Tho' distance parts my friend and me,
And lay my bones in Ballitore.

    [Mary (Shackleton) Leadbeater], 'Ballitore, a poem
    addressed to Rebecca Grubby(?)' [1778]

c.140, p. 225

T2183 Tho' dreadful storms and earthquakes toss
On heav'n itself make war.

    [Sir William Trumbull], 'Ps[alm] 73'

Trumbull Box: Poetry Box XIII/13; see also 'Tho'
tempests . . .'.

T2184 Though envious fortune which could ne'er have
                          while

My love in you began, in you shall end.

    'On a lover's departure'

b.197, p. 155

T2185 Tho' envy whisper malice round
Marriage, tho' freedoms I don't grudge | For auld
                            lang syne.

    [Mrs. Christian Kerr], 'A song to the tune of Auld
    lang syne'

c.102, p. 111

T2186 Tho' every action unto its end doth tend,
Yet life and love abominate their end.

    'Of life and love'

c.356

T2187 Tho' far from Chloe's face I rove
Which none but lovers know.

    [Robert Cholmeley], 'Absence. An ode to Chloe'

c.190, p. 8

T2188 Though fasts were instituted, that the flesh
Your spirit serve the flesh: and the flesh you.

    Sir Thomas Urquhart, 'To an epicurean, and
    licentious youth'

fb.217, p. 234

T2189 Though fear, the world with strange gods first did
                               load
The world hath now too little fear of God.

    Sir Thomas Urquhart, 'Against atheists, and paynims'

fb.217, p. 78

T2190 Though fire(?) the barren womb and [?] may(?)
                               give
He were to dig a grave within her belly.

    [Sir Thomas Urquhart], 'Of an aged man lately
    married with a young lascivious woman though
    barren'

fb.217, p. 387

T2191 Though for more perspicuity this little,
Is tied to make him all the world's commander.

    Sir Thomas Urquhart, 'The prologue [to Urquhart's
    epigrams]'

fb.217, p. 29

T2192 Though fortune both b'a goddess, and a queen:
Whilst wit, and valor are esteem'd of slightly.

    Sir Thomas Urquhart, 'Of fortune's lack of
    consideration'

fb.217, p. 201

T2193 Tho' fortune frown, remember friend,
For all are huddled in the grave.

    'All must die, 'tis so allotted. (In imitation of Horace)'

c.94

T2194 Tho' fortune frowns upon my just design
Than quitting purest gold for vilest brass.

[Mrs. Christian Kerr], 'Upon losing [to] a favorite
gentleman at cards' [answered by 'Blind fortune no
dominion . . .']

c.102, p. 94

T2195 Though frost, and snow lock'd from mine eyes
They cannot steal, thou giv'st so much.

Tho[mas] Carew, 'A gentleman on his entertainment
at Saxum in Kent'
[Crum T2348]

b.200, p. 232

T2196 Tho' (generous reader) now and then I write
They flow not from my heart, but from my pen.

[Sir Aston Cokayne], 'To the reader'

b.275, p. 33

T2197 Tho' George be gone over, yet to show his love
to us,
We must heartily pray, God would send home our
king. | Which nobody &c.

'A ballad in honor of the present regency'

c.570/2, p. 73

T2198 Though glasses and lasses be never so little
But pieces bring lasses to falling all under.

[Sir Thomas Urquhart], 'Of glasses and lasses and
lasses and glasses'

fb.217, p. 534

T2199 Tho' God all blessings do confer,
On them depends the eternal state.

[Edmund Wodehouse], 'Octr. 8 [1714]'

b.131, p. 55

T2200 Tho' God the King of kings vouchsafes to call
To whom that sacred name thus lent they owe.

[Edmund Wodehouse], 'St. John's Day [1714]'

b.131, p. 125

T2201 Though griev'd at the departure of my friend,
And help you lash the vices of the town.

[Isaac Watts?], 'The third satire of Juvenal'

File 17423

T2202 Tho' haste O youth should urge thy destin'd way,
Pursue thy road, and ever fare thee well.

'An epitaph by Marcus Pacuvius made for himself, he
was one of the earliest, as well as one of the most
celebrated dramatic poets in the year of Rome 590'

c.378, p. 74

T2203 Though hazarding my life in Amphitrite's jaws,
But by such sacred wings above the heavens fly.

Thomas Browne, 'Ala' [to his father Henry Browne]
Poetry Box VII/18

T2204 Though he b'a cuckold, yet
It was his wife, that did it.

Sir Thomas Urquhart, 'On Cornuto'

fb.217, p. 166

T2205 Though he for logic be more eminent
Entrap him headlong in a sophistry.

[Sir Thomas Urquhart], 'Of an exquisite logician who
was cuckolded by his wife'

fb.217, p. 498

T2206 Though he is dead, th'immortal name
No other head should wear the wreath.

[Sir John Denham], 'Elegy on Sr William D'Avenant'

pb.53, p. 26 (autogr.)

T2207 Though here in death thy relics lie,
In sorrow for a brother's doom.

[John Walcot ('Peter Pindar')], 'An epitaph on a
friend'

c.83/2, no. 582

T2208 Tho' here in death's cold arms I make my bed
Then I (with those that sleep in Christ) shall rise.

'On [his daughter's] grave in St. Peter's churchyard,
Alban's . . .'

c.517, fol. 14

T2209 Tho' here not martial trophies are,
When he approach'd, e'en heroes trembled.

'Epitaph to the memory of the Salop hangman'

c.90

T2210 Though hope, than fear b'a better quality:
I'd rather harbor fear, than hope, that way.

Sir Thomas Urquhart, 'That hope is not always so
acceptable as fear'

fb.217, p. 90

T2211 Though I am shut from friends, and pen, and ink
And by her freedom she is made my slave.

George Wither, 'George Withers close prisoner writ
with a coal on a wall, these verses'

b.197, p. 211

T2212 Tho' I be woe it is no wonder
A cruel lady she may—

'Braye Lute Book,' Music Ms. 13, fol. 46v

T2213 Though I explore
To mount Parnass'.

C[harles] B[urney], 'A Lilliputian ode, on my little
friend, Richard Burney, putting on breeches'

c.37, p. 51

T2214 Though I lie oft with a fair handsome lass
The beautiful Abishag, and ne'er knew her.

Sir Thomas Urquhart, 'Here an ancient man for
having another bedfellow of the female sex besides his
own married wife, excuseth himself thus'

fb.217, p. 309

T2215 Tho' I my real thoughts disguise
Then peaceful stagger'd up to bed.

S[tephen] Simpson, 'The happy triumvirate a tale'

c.563

T2216 Though I praise many, yet I praise not you;
In praises of yourself, you need not mine.

Sir Thomas Urquhart

fb.217, p. 69

T2217 Tho' I regret the absence of my friend,
Tho' cold the place, your satire to supply.

Samuel Derrick, 'May 27th 1754 . . . The third satire
of Juvenal'

c.475

T2218 Tho' in my days of youth and beauty
And lovers shall sigh at the feet of S. More.

'Mr. Printer'

c.341, at front

T2219 Tho' in the race Olympic, many
Who lags the most behind?

Abraham Oakes, 'Enigma'

c.50, p. 141

T2220 Tho' in their flame and passion cross'd
That please at once both your revenge and love.

'To R. S. upon the marriage of his mistress'

fb.142, p. 49

T2221 Tho' in this world, I've half a century been,
Tho' there Florella, doth my bosom warm.

[Thomas Hamilton, 6th earl of Haddington], 'To
Florella epistle the third'

c.458/1, p. 8

T2222 Tho' in your long illustrious race,
Nothing that you could grant or I receive.

[William Popple, trans.], 'Horace book 1st satire 6th
imitated. To His Grace the Duke of Newcastle'

fc.104/1, p. 123

T2223 Though in your presence I seem speechless, and
Who makes me as a rock, insensible.

Sir Thomas Urquhart, 'The words of a gentleman, to
one named Susanna, who did imagine, that he was
enamored with her'

fb.217, p. 187

T2224 Though it were true as husbands oft complain
Enjoy her fame, and happiness complete.

R[alph] Broome, 'Lines enclosed in a letter to
[Frances Burney] d'Arblay March 1st 1799'

c.486, fol. 39

T2225 Though languages dissent in diverse parts
But God, did first their varying tongues disperse.

Sir Thomas Urquhart, 'That the diversity of
languages amongst several nations, should not be a
motive to alienate their affections'

fb.217, p. 132

T2226 Tho' late in life, too early snatch'd away,
The Christian rose to heav'n—the mortal died.

'Epitaph'

c.83/2, no. 291

T2227 Though learned Homer come with all the Muses'
guard,
Yet if he nothing bring, must fast, and stand within
the yard.

c.339, p. 320

T2228 Though little be the god of love,
On Mars, than armies did before.

'Cupid's strength'

fb.107, p. 38

T2229 Though long the public on thy works has smil'd,
Are safely led to happiness complete.

[Charles Burney, the elder], 'To my daughter Fanny
(Mrs. d'Arblay) author of Evelina, Cecilia, and
Camilla . . . Jany. 1797'

c.33, p. 270

T2230 Tho' love be in choosing far better than gold
Let love come with somewhat the better to hold.

[James Rhodes?]

b.206, p. 151

T2231 Tho' love ne'er prattles at your eyes,
Or linger wretched if refus'd.

'To Celia'

c.83/3, no. 766

T2232 Tho' love t'your eyes b'an object of offence,
Paints lively hieroglyphics of fruition.

> Sir Thomas Urquhart, 'To an exceeding, stately,
> beautiful and chaste maid: but of a superlatively
> vigorous, and enamoring constitution of body'
>
> fb.217, p. 86

T2233 Tho' low, and humble is my birth
Before the close of day.

> 'Riddle . . . a coachman'
>
> c.391

T2234 Tho' low in earth, her beauteous frame decayed,
To bloom and triumph in eternal day.

> 'To the memory of John Camden esq. who died the
> 17th of October 1780 aged 57 and of his eldest
> daughter Elizabeth, wife of James Neild . . . who . . .
> died the 30th of June 1791 in her 36th year'
> [Crum T2369]
>
> c.83/4, no. 2030

T2235 Tho' Lyce, thou art in Scythia bred,
No side can always bear such wind.

> [William Popple, trans.], '[Horace] book 3rd. ode
> 10th. To Lyce'
>
> fc.104/2, p. 242 [bis]

T2236 Though marriage by most folks be reckon'd a curse,
And the third for a warming pan, doctor, and nurse.

> Thomas Bastard, 'Epigram. Thomas Bastard esqr:
> fellow of New College, 1588, wrote the following
> epigram on his three wives'
>
> c.81/2, no. 528

T2237 Tho' Mars, still friend to France,
And France must sue for peace. | For ocean's
empire, &c.

> John Lockman, 'Albion's maritime power. In honor of
> Admiral Hawke's victory over the French [14 Oct.
> 1747]. Set to music by Miss Gambarini, and sung, at
> Bath, for her benefit'
>
> c.267/2, p. 13

T2238 Though Mars, your body did o'erload with scars:
Strip'd Venus, harms you more, than armed Mars.

> Sir Thomas Urquhart, 'To a valiant, but very
> lecherous soldier'
>
> fb.217, p. 170

T2239 Tho' mean and humble be my birth,
Before the close of day.

> 'Another [riddle]'
>
> Diggle Box: Poetry Box XI/71

T2240 Tho' men by nature, often go astray,
Some men are honest many women true.

> [Thomas Hamilton, 6th earl of Haddington],
> 'Constancy rewarded from Boccace'
>
> c.458/2, p. 101

T2241 Though mine eyes distill no tears
And we will never part till death.

> 'Cant: 30 [bis]'
>
> b.4, fol. 26v

T2242 Though mirth's ordain'd to ease the cares of life
If they seem confin'd t'a certain measure.

> [Sir Thomas Urquhart], 'That our gladness be not
> excessive but a mediocrity to be kept therein'
>
> fb.217, p. 521

T2243 Tho' modest and a maid esteem'd
The height of human bliss.

> [William Hayley]
>
> File 6970

T2244 Tho' morning stars in agony expire
A glimmering light arising from the north.

> [Mrs. Christian Kerr], 'On the 10 of June 1719: being a
> cloudy morning'
>
> c.102, p. 100

T2245 Though music can each sense control
In this our polar star.

> R[ichard] V[ernon] S[adleir], 'The supper bell'
>
> c.106, p. 95

T2246 Tho' my first the rich miser is anxious to serve,
Is too thick for the moon's silver beams to pervade.

> '[Enigma/Charade/Conundrum] 51'
>
> c.389

T2247 Tho' my hairs fall away, and are silver'd by time,
Be rul'd by a friend—choose a juvenile swain.

> John Lockman, 'The rivals, or the virgin of Tafto: a
> musical dialogue, set by Mr. Worgan; and sung, in
> Vauxhall Gardens . . . May 1747'
>
> c.267/2, p. 90

T2248 Though my heart bleeds with pangs to think on you,
She lifts her head—and beauteous smiles again!

> 'Sonnet addressed to an unfortunate girl'
>
> c.83/2, no. 296

T2249 Tho' my wife is as honest as no woman born
We ne'er could get more than the sign of a son.

> [Phanuel Bacon]
>
> c.237, fol. 79v [i.e., 99v]

T2250   Though nature from each het'rogenian whole,
It could possess no better parts, than yours.

     Sir Thomas Urquhart, 'To the Countess of Airth'

fb.217, p. 328

T2251   Though naught in time be then the instant less,
So with the time, my love increaseth still.

     Sir Thomas Urquhart, 'The growth of love'

fb.217, p. 90

T2252   Though Nemesis on pleasure and venery
But Satan has bestirr'd his thoughts within.

     [Sir Thomas Urquhart], 'Who wares too much on
pleasure becomes a slave to pleasure'

fb.217, p. 522

T2253   Though night's unnumbered eyes, the world survey:
They see not all, so well's the day's one eye.

     Sir Thomas Urquhart, 'Of the sun, and the stars'

fb.217, p. 341

T2254   Though nine and fifty figures in a band
Come short of your good parts in calculation.

     Sir Thomas Urquhart, 'To the most excellent and
adorable Aura'

fb.217, p. 356

T2255   Though none can paint, or carve the meanest noise,
The echo utters a reflected voice.

     Sir Thomas Urquhart, 'The skill of the echo'

fb.217, p. 232

T2256   Tho' none can tell, how short their lives may be,
Who was Florella's faithful slave, and friend.

     [Thomas Hamilton, 6th earl of Haddington], 'To
Florella, epistle the fourteenth'

c.458/1, p. 46

T2257   Though none her sense of hearing can entire,
Who hath no ear for love, but in her belly.

     Sir Thomas Urquhart, 'Of a gentlewoman, who could
not endure to be courted with compliments, yet for all
that practiced in secret most cheerfully the intrinsical
effects of an amorous grant'

fb.217, p. 262

T2258   Tho' now Florella, rhyming gives me pain,
So fair a body, nor so rich a mind.

     [Thomas Hamilton, 6th earl of Haddington], 'To
Florella epistle the thirteenth'

c.458/1, p. 33

T2259   Tho' now no more, then like great cities, nam'd
To make on those th'impressing that they feel.

     [Abraham Cowley?], 'The vineyard'

File 3782/2

Tho' now to sickness, and to age a prey,   T2260
I have my wish, and ask no other praise.

     [Thomas Hamilton, 6th earl of Haddington], 'To
Florella'

c.458/2, p. 1

Though of love pranks unwillingly she hear: T2261
But to the touch, a perfect diapason.

     Sir Thomas Urquhart, 'Of a certain gentlewoman
concerning lascivious words, and deeds'

fb.217, p. 272

Though of your house no small account of old   T2262
May serve to raise it to a higher pitch.

     Sir Thomas Urquhart, 'To the Earl of [crossed out]'

fb.217, p. 236

Tho' oft we shiver'd to the gale   T2263
On the pale bud, the fainting flower!

     [Richard Polwhele], 'Verses—1736'

c.141, p. 569

Though oft with me the feats of love you've tried,   T2264
That gives me feasts of ambrosia, and nectar.

     Sir Thomas Urquhart, 'Sir Hector, and his mistress'

fb.217, p. 236

Though other light things nat'rally be seen   T2265
Their bringing up and fall the quicklier down.

     [Sir Thomas Urquhart], 'How different the
propensions of levity are in some women from all
other light things else'

fb.217, p. 392

Though our town be destroyed   T2266
Let wine be our tide.

     'A song: 1676'

b.54, p. 1035

Tho' Ovid has given so many relations   T2267
As they acted like boys they like boys should be
                 whipt. | Derry down &c.

     'On a certain knight [Sir Thomas Abney] appearing
on a late occasion' [Queen Caroline's funeral; pr. 1737
(Foxon E569)]
[Crum T2389]

b.382(22); Poetry Box I/124

Though paillard husbands 'gainst the divine laws   T2268
All horns are merely proper to the head.

     [Sir Thomas Urquhart], 'Why the wives of adulterous
husbands cannot properly be called cuckolds'

fb.217, p. 511

T2269 Tho' partial nature may have seem'd unkind
       Your heart wear fetters, tho' your tongue is bound.

           'By a young lady on a dumb gentleman'
           c.360/2, no. 108

T2270 Though Phoebus now indulgent strew
       And ev'ry real joy secure.

           'Written, on the absence of a friend—1776'

           c.90

T2271 Tho' plagued with algebraic lectures,
       He is a madman, if he feigns—

           [Edward Littleton], of King's College, Cambridge, 'A
           letter from Cambridge to a young gentleman [Henry
           Archer] at Eton school'
           [Crum T2391]

           c.176, p. 56; c.233, p. 52; c.416

T2272 Tho' poor, the victim, who to peace descends,
       And clos'd the curtains of the sightless eye.

           'On a village funeral'

           c.83/2, no. 505

T2273 Tho' Pope's fam'd numbers shine, from native fire;
       And what they see, and what they feel, adore.

           John Lockman, 'Seeing some lines, from Mr. Pope's
           Essay on man, beautifully transcribed by
           Mr. Champion . . . Decr. 1740'

           c.267/1, p. 155

T2274 Tho' prologues now like blackberries are plenty
       To pick up straws dropt from their harvest-home.

           [David] Garrick, 'Prologue to The spleen or Islington
           spa. Written by . . . spoken by Mr. King'

           c.68, p. 158

T2275 Though reason makes the man, heaven makes him
                                                    wise,
       How can his sorrows wish more fair relief.

           c.158, p. 30

T2276 Tho' religion's an idle law
       P. O. for fear of the worst.

           'Hobbes's ejaculations'

           b.371, no. 26

T2277 Tho' royal Sir you every act doth show
       None of our flatterers love us half so well.

           'Upon the late prorogation' [26 January 1678]
           [Crum T2396]

           b.371, no. 13; b.327, f. 22v

T2278 Tho' rude be my cottage, 'tis neat
       True pleasures in calmness abide.

           W. Gibson, 'The invitation to Delia in town—1767'

           c.90

T2279 Tho' self-description is a line
       Of Esther's having a sweet tooth.

           [Frederick Corfield], 'Mr. D. to Miss Fast'

           c.381/1

T2280 Though she be a comely creature to behold
       How can thou without some suppose to live.

           b.64, p. 15

T2281 Though she be noble beautiful, and wise,
       And gold is more substantial than perfection.

           Sir Thomas Urquhart, 'The despised condition of any
           gentlewoman, that hath not whereupon'

           fb.217, p. 72

T2282 Though she be white, and hath bright shining eyes,
       But she is hot, and moves us to lie down.

           Sir Thomas Urquhart, 'To a gentleman, who did
           compare the color of his mistress to the very snow:
           and the rays of her beauty to the sunbeams'

           fb.217, p. 281

T2283 Tho' slander follows wheresoe'er I go
       When their good name shall certain passwords
                                                    prove.

           'Masonic prologue'

       Poetry Box x/159

T2284 Though small the space that holds thy earthly frame
       Where the fair subject far exceeds all praise!

           'Verses by James the First, On the tomb af Laura at
           Avignon . . . Thus translated'

       Poetry Box XII/57

T2285 Tho' so lately disagreed
       Still stays to be pull'd by the nose.

           [Phanuel Bacon], 'St. Dunstan to St. Barnaby
           occasioned by the alteration of the style—and in
           answer to ['Next to that famous day of June . . .']'

           c.237, fol. 84

T2286 Tho' soft birds sing, not so my wayward fate;
       Scorn opposition, and still hope success.

           c.189, p. 48

T2287 Though sole Greece in one age bred these seven
                                                    sages
       The whole world scarce shows one now in seven
                                                    ages.

           [Sir Thomas Urquhart], 'How rare a thing it is to find
           a wise man nowadays'

           fb.217, p. 502

T2288 Tho' some would give Sir Bob no quarter
We'll freely vote to hang him then.

   'On Sir R[ober]t W[al]p[o]le'

c.570/2, p. 169

T2289 Tho' sorrowing friends deplore the stroke, that gave
The fruit will ripen in eternity.

   'Epitaph on a young lady, age 17.—copied from her
   monument, at Mr. Bacon's'

fc.132/1, p. 210

T2290 Tho' soul and body both must be
Their violence or flatteries.

   [Edmund Wodehouse], 'May 9 [1715]'

b.131, p. 209

T2291 Tho' strange it seems to our poor narrow sight,
Would gladly see you, Sir, behind the bar.

   T[homas] M[orell], 'To Mr Prince Gregory . . . on
   the death of his wife'

c.395, p. 115

T2292 Tho' sure this double office is but one
The owner's heart and tongue in one [agree?].

   [on the first Duke of Buckingham]

Poetry Box VI/29

T2293 Tho' surly wigs assembled in array
For every day shall be the tenth of June.

   [Mrs. Christian Kerr], 'on June the 11th for the 10th
   [1716] being Mrs Ford's birthday inscribed to her
   daughter Mrs Welch'

c.102, p. 103

T2294 Tho' tempests and fierce earthquake shake
On heav'n itself make war.

   [Sir William Trumbull], 'P[salm] 73' [rough draft]

Trumbull Box: Poetry Box XIII/14; see also 'Tho'
dreadful storms . . .'.

T2295 Tho' tempests rage and clouds of darkness hide
With her poor little dear in sweet content.

   [Mrs. Christian Kerr], 'To Astrea'

c.102, p. 93

T2296 Tho' the mountains and forests be cover'd with
                             snow,
Resolve to live happy in spite of the devil.

   Miss [ ] Jessop, 'A copy of verses wrote by . . . being
   stopped in her journey, by the great snows at
   Nottingham'

c.176, p. 71

T2297 Though the oak be the prince, and the pride of the
                             grove,
And birch, like the muses, immortal shall be.

   [T. Wilson], 'The birch'
   [Crum T2419]

Diggle Box: Poetry Box XI/54

T2298 Though the septemvirate of Dutch electors
H'is neither mighty, valiant wise nor rich.

   [Sir Thomas Urquhart], 'Who is not contented with
   his own fortune, how great soever it be is miserable'

fb.217, p. 501

T2299 Tho' the ungodly senate has decreed
He'll hear our plaints; as thou hast heard his own.

   'The vision. The 20 Psalm imitated from Buchanan'
   [pr. Edinburgh 1711 (Foxon T581)]

c.570/1, p. 38

T2300 Tho' the whole life should pass without a stain,
Its pride when living, and its grief when dead.

   'To the memory of Lady E. Mansell, true to the
   mother of Sr. Hervey Elwes'

c.83/2, no. 402; see also 'Beneath the cov'ring . . .'.

T2301 Though there be sundries wish you may survive
But it is a Platonic year.

   Sir Thomas Urquhart, 'To a friend'

fb.217, p. 290

T2302 Though there was never more ingrate man living:
For his diurnal progress to our God.

   [Sir Thomas Urquhart], 'To a liberal gentleman
   unthankfully acquit by the party obliged'

fb.217, p. 528

T2303 Tho' thou art gone from friendship, and from me
As thou wert his, so all his friends were thine.

   [Christopher] Smart, 'Epitaph on Mrs. Rolt'

c.83/2, no. 713

T2304 Tho' thousand torments men do here endure
And mourn the shortness of their hasty race.

   J[ohn] R[obinson], 'Nulla unquam de morte hominis
   cunctatio longa est'

c.370, fol. 23v

T2305 Tho' three years were spent in this nice calculation,
But they may in due time find the longitude out.

   'Curious calculation of the number of books, chapters,
   verses, words and letters &c. in the Old, and New
   Testament'

c.81/1, no. 204

T2306   Tho' time corroding quickly shall erase,
Her marble monument would not from grief
refrain.

     'An epitaph on Mrs. Ann Bryan who died 1723'
c.244, p. 286

T2307   Tho' 'tis by pray'r that I pretend,
Must owing to thy mercy be.

     [Edmund Wodehouse], 'May 14 [1715]'
b.131, p. 212

T2308   Tho' 'tis in vain to raise dead stones to her,
Till heaven again shall visit this rich dust.

     'An epitaph on Mrs. Merry(?)'
c.244, p. 285

T2309   Though 'tis ordain'd that once we all must die,
To God the Father, Son and Holy Ghost.

     'Character of the Revd. E. Armstrong'
c.83/3, no. 847

T2310   Tho' to the human eye I ne'er appear'd
Virgins you'll be and ever must remain.

     'Riddle on nothing'
c.360/1, p. 213

T2311   Though Venus follow in the heav'ns the sun:
She always on the earth the light doth shun.

     Sir Thomas Urquhart, 'Of Venus'
fb.217, p. 144

T2312   Though Venus was lame Vulcan's wife, and Jove
And married none; because there's no man wise.

     Sir Thomas Urquhart, 'Why the goddess of wisdom
was never married'
fb.217, p. 280

T2313   Though vice hath a path very broad
To dangers manyfold.

b.234, p. 26; see also 'Zeno our path . . .'.

T2314   Though virtue be her own reward and crown
And in your loyalty, securely smile.

     Sir Ph[ilip] Wodehouse, 'Upon Mary Lady
Townshend . . .'
b.131, back (no. 40)

T2315   Though want eclipse my liberality
For spending match a Caesar.

     Sir Thomas Urquhart, 'The regret of a certain
gentleman, whose fortune was not answerable to the
frankness of his disposition'
fb.217, p. 323

T2316   Tho' we a certain place don't know,
His presence makes a paradise.

     [Edmund Wodehouse], 'May 31 [1715]'
b.131, p. 220

T2317   Tho' we most firmly on God rely
Who most beg that felicity.

     [Edmund Wodehouse], 'Septr. 20 [1715]'
b.131, p. 268

T2318   Tho' wean'd from all those scandalous delights
Could brook the man her sister so betray'd.

     'A letter from Newmarket'
b.113, p. 111; b.327, f. 25; b.371, no. 10

T2319   Tho' wedlock by most men be deemed a curse
The third for a warming pan, doctress and nurse.

     Th[oma]s Bastard, 'On having three wives'
Poetry Box x/20

T2320   Tho' when whole and complete I no substance can
boast
'Tis the character of the Dutch nation.

     'Riddle'
Diggle Box: Poetry Box xi/71; c.389

T2321   Though wise and learned Epicure would needs
And this wherein we live, a world of words.

     [Sir Thomas Urquhart], 'A glance at the opinion of
ancient philosophers concerning the multiplicity of
worlds'
fb.217, p. 516

T2322   Though with my rapier, for the guerdon
Transpassions my revenge in mercy.

     Sir Thomas Urquhart, 'The generous speech of a
noble cavalier, after he had disarmed his adversary at
the single combat'
fb.217, p. 201

T2323   Though women's works by some is disrespected
Because presented in a purse that's black.

     [Mary Serjant]
fb.98, fol. 169

T2324   Though writings have no life: and words be *vive*:
Men's writings longer than their speeches live.

     Sir Thomas Urquhart, 'Of word, and write'
fb.217, p. 320

T2325   Though you be first among the earls of this
Since your minority, an oracle.

     Sir Thomas Urquhart, 'To the Earl of [crossed out]'
fb.217, p. 148

T2326   Though you be issu'd of a royal blood
But of an ev'ry way accomplish'd princess.

> Sir Thomas Urquhart, 'The first epigram to Princess
> Elizabeth of Palatine'
>
> fb.217, p. 260

T2327   Though you be not so strong as other men
Than who can with main force a lion bind.

> [Sir Thomas Urquhart]
>
> fb.217, p. 530

T2328   Though you derive on all sides your extraction
All men should consecrate their best affections.

> Sir Thomas Urquhart, 'To the Earl of [crossed out]'
>
> fb.217, p. 186

T2329   Though you Diana-like have lived still chaste
You were not made to look on . . . .

> [Sir John Suckling], 'Si sola es, nulla es'
>
> b.104, p. 121 (incomplete)

T2330   Though you doom all to die, who dare adore ye,
While others die of pain, I'll die of pleasure.

> 'The pleasant death'
>
> fb.107, p. 46

T2331   Tho' you flatter my gen'us, and praise what I write,
And the ladies till then, will with pleasure endure
'em.

> 'To Mr. S. upon his desiring his character to be
> painted by Miss Loggin'
>
> c.83/4, no. 2004

T2332   Tho' you in wealth abounded more,
They still want, what they seek for, peace.

> [William Popple, trans.], '[Horace] book 3rd. ode
> 24th'
>
> fc.104/2, p. 288

T2333   Though you ingrate receivers daily find
To give and lose so as to lose and give.

> [Sir Thomas Urquhart], 'The bad [?] of ingrate men
> should not deter us from being liberal'
>
> fb.217, p. 521

T2334   Though you more bless'd 'mongst women should
b'esteem'd,
But that you were a mother, we're redeem'd.

> Sir Thomas Urquhart, 'To the blessed Virgin'
>
> fb.217, p. 252

T2335   Tho' you, my Chloe, in some northern flood
With gloomy night, and black despair encompass'd
all around.

> c.549, p. 51

T2336   Tho' you to me the wreath decree
Rewarded and excell'd.

> [Phanuel Bacon], 'To a lady from whom the author
> receiv'd a crown of bays cut in paper'
>
> c.237, fol. 64

T2337   Tho' you were never passion's slave,
To cool their amorous tales.

> Frederick Corfield
>
> c.381/2

T2338   Tho' young he was
That sweeps us all away.

> 'Another [epitaph] upon an upright stone on the north
> side of the church of Town-malling in Kent'
>
> c.150, p. 39

T2339   Though young in riddling art, not twelve years old
So then your dark enigmas come to light.

> 'An answer' [to 'Or ere bright Sol . . .']
>
> c.578, p. 28

T2340   Tho' your commands most binding are
But hard to bring a name in rhyme.

> [to Elizabeth (Shirley) Compton, countess of
> Northampton]
>
> Accession 97.7.40

T2341   Tho' you're as cold as you are fair
And write it on the fair one's heart.

> [Phanuel Bacon], 'Written in a frosted pane of glass.
> To Mira'
> [Crum T2447]
>
> c.237, fol. 10

T2342   Though Zion sits in misery,
Unto their mother dear.

> [Thomas Stevens?], 'A meditation'
>
> c.259

T2343   Thoughts do not vex me while I sleep
At least leave off your scorning.

> 'A song'
> [Crum T2455]
>
> b.205, fol. 81v

T2344   Thou'rt gone, blest angel, with thy heav'nly lays,
Will lead with certainty to thee and God.

> 'On the death of a young child'
>
> c.83/4, no. 2020

T2345   Thou'rt in the midst: yet under all things liest:
So art thou virtue, of all things the highest.

> Sir Thomas Urquhart, 'A double mids: to the earth,
> and virtue'
>
> fb.217, p. 338

T2346 Thou'rt quintessence of beauty, goodness, truth,
May make a chaos, or all things to be.

> Lady Jane Cavendish, 'On my sweet sister Brackley'
> [Crum T2137]
>
> b.233, p. 13

T2347 Thou'st made a hopeful progress, keep thy ground
And as years ripen thou wilt be profound.

> 'Thomas Boundaius. Anagramma. Oh da tu bona
> musis. Epigramma'
>
> b.212, p. 97

T2348 Thou'st Nestor's tongue, O may'st thou reach his
                              years
And have thy jet turn'd into silver hairs.

> 'Wilielmus Coeleus. Anagramma. Melleus cluis, o
> viva. Epigramma . . . thus Englished'
>
> b.212, p. 81

T2349 Thracians quarrel in their wine,
Tho' their rage he could subdue.

> [William Popple, trans.], '[Horace] book 1st. ode 27.
> To his companions'
>
> fc.104/2, p. 76

T2350 Thraso picks quarrels when he's drunk at night
Drink not at night, or drink at morning too.

> [William Walsh], 'Epigram. Thraso'
>
> c.223, p. 77; see also 'Tharso . . .'.

T2351 Thrason in fight his rival kill'd though he
Without dissimulation double-hearted.

> [Sir Thomas Urquhart], 'Of a courageous gentleman,
> who was enamored of a lady that did not acquit him
> with the like respect'
>
> fb.217, p. 537

T2352 Three beggars once sat on a bank,
Bestow'd on mendicants.

> 'The sturdy beggars—a tale'
>
> c.344

T2353 Three bishops universal headship claim,
And this dead prophet over death shall reign.

> Roger Drake, 'Upon the sad loss of . . . William
> Taylor' [d. 7 September 1641]
>
> b.88, p. 3

T2354 Three children sliding on the ice,
Pray keep them all at home.

> 'The three children–a burlesque contrariety'
>
> c.360/3, no. 257; c.179, p. 51

T2355 Three cinquefoils lo—three roses wed
Those soldiers were with fighting Harry's grace.

> [Sir Philip Wodehouse], 'Upon [his father] Sir
> Thomas Wodehouse's marrying with Blanche Carey
> [his mother]—to John Lord Hunsdon'
>
> b.131, p. 2 and back (after anagram 235)

T2356 Three cinquefoils marry two—(each single ones)
Forth from their flow'ring beds sweet infants bring.

> [Sir Philip Wodehouse], 'An armorial toy upon Sr.
> Philip Watts (?) who bears three cinquefoils marrying
> his daughter Blanche to Sr. Jacob Astley . . .'
>
> b.131, p. 2 and back (after anagram 235)

T2357 Three days and nights, my Polly,
And now the charmer's mine.

> John Lockman, 'The serenade, or lovesick Polly; in
> imitation of Tre giorni sonchi Nina &c.: a celebrated
> Italian ballad'
>
> c.267/2, p. 101; c.267/4, p. 123 (var.)

T2358 Three different schemes philosophers assign
He only reasons, that believes a God.

> 'On chance and predestination' [1748]
> [Crum T2462]
>
> c.578, p. 36

T2359 Th[r]ee faithful worthies cast into the fire
They were extinguished by the glorious sun.

> 'Daniel 3.25'
>
> c.160, fol. 53

T2360 Three finer babes you ne'er see
And here they lies as dead as nits.

> 'Epitaph' [in Somersetshire]
> [Crum T2463]
>
> c.546, p. 15

T2361 Three genii, in three distant counties born,
Till the soft jew's harp joined the other two.

> John Lockman, 'A friendly hint, for the improvement
> of Mother Midnight's concert . . . Jany. 1751'
>
> c.267/1, p. 371

T2362 Three Kates, two Nans, and one dear Jane I wedded
One died in childbirth, and one me surviv'd.

> 'On K. Henry 8th' [and his wives]
>
> fb.143, p. 2

T2363 Three men of mettle, who did all things briskly
At Norwich city born, but liv'd at Bixley.

> 'Belonging to ['Grandfather, father and son . . .']'
>
> c.360/3, no. 120

T2364　Three merry lads met at the Rose
　　　　The matter's out, the nose is blown.

　　　'The nose'

　　　b.356, p. 285

T2365　Three mortal enemies remember
　　　　The Devil, Pretender and the Pope.

　　　'The triumvirate'

　　　c.546, p. 33

T2366　Three nations mighty Monarch crave
　　　　We must plunder; you may reign.

　　　'The true Whig's address' [to George I]
　　　[Crum T2470]

　　　c.570/1, p. 95

T2367　Three nymphs, as chaste as ever Venus bred,
　　　　And all my foes, such virtuous spouses get.

　　　'On the three late marriages'

　　　fb.70, p. 5

T2368　Three or four parsons full of October
　　　　Three or four Scots and the sessions is ended.

　　　'Description of a country sessions'

　　　c.487, p. 59; see also next.

T2369　Three or four parsons, three or four squires,
　　　　Three or four scolds and the sessions is ended.

　　　'Country quarter sessions'

　　　c.546, p. 8; see also previous.

T2370　Three Oxford gay schemers equipp'd for a ride—
　　　　And the devil a rat will frequent your house more!

　　　[Phanuel Bacon], 'Dedicoris pictiosus emptor'

　　　c.237, fol. 70 [i.e., 90]

T2371　Three Oxford gay sparks (you may fancy the names
　　　　With the backgammon table and candle in hand.

　　　[Phanuel Bacon]

　　　c.237, fol. 32v

T2372　Three persons sat down in a tavern to play
　　　　Who guesses this riddle is surely no ninny.

　　　'A riddle'

　　　c.150, p. 3; c.389

T2373　Three pints of wine the grave and wise
　　　　Transforms men into bears, or swine.

　　　'The rule of drinking, from the Greek of Eubulus'

　　　c.94

T2374　Three planets being above ye, three below:
　　　　The virtue in the midst from you doth flow.

　　　Sir Thomas Urquhart, 'To Phoebus'

　　　fb.217, p. 240

T2375　Three players in three different ages rose,
　　　　More than the former two conjoin'd in thee.

　　　'On three celebrated players [Betterton, Booth,
　　　Garrick] an imitation of ['Three poets in three distant
　　　ages . . .', by Dryden]'

　　　c.360/3, no. 239

T2376　Three poets in three distant ages born,
　　　　To make a third she join'd the former two.

　　　[John] Dryden, 'Epigram on Milton'

　　　c.360/3, no. 238

T2377　Three-pound-twelve pieces, are often call'd ports
　　　　Nor need I to say 'tis—Portsmouth.

　　　'Solution to [a rebus, 'To places where ships . . .']

　　　c.360/3, no. 218

T2378　Three powers in three different ages born
　　　　Keep then the last; and hang the former two.

　　　'Barons, Kings, and Commons. Or the progress of the
　　　English constitution by a Jacobin 1792' [epigram on a
　　　passage in Echard's History of England]

　　　Poetry Box II/25

T2379　Three properties are written in thy name
　　　　Fair, idle, blowse, and prove it back again.

　　　[Sir Philip Wodehouse], 'A toy in an anagram Sarah
　　　Blowfield'

　　　b.131, back (no. 117)

T2380　Three Richards liv'd in Brunswick['s] glorious
　　　　　　　　　　　　　　　　　　　　reign,
　　　　To make a third, she join'd the former two.

　　　'Verses in imitation of Mr. Dryden's upon Milton'

　　　c.73, p. 16

T2381　Three rival kings [subdued], three battles gained.
　　　　He gain'd the crown, got drunk, and was depos'd.

　　　'Advices from Mequinez, 1728'
　　　[Crum T2472]

　　　c.233, p. 114

T2382　Three sisters of one heav'nly parent born,
　　　　Approv'd, distinguish'd, near th'eternal throne.

　　　'1st Corinth[ians] chap. 12 ver: 13 paraphrased'

　　　c.83/1, no. 95; fc.132/1, p. 164

T2383　Three things there are that do delight my mind
　　　　For practice and for conversation.

　　　Sir John Strangways, 'Three good: three bad: ten
　　　happy things the author in these verses sings . . . 17mo
　　　Decembris 1646'

　　　b.304, p. 80

T2384 Three things there are that's counted faults in men,
These three things good, it is the world that's vain.

    'The vanity of the world'

c.187, p. 38

T2385 Three times five years my course has run
Where God, where Jesus reigns.

    'A birthday thought'

c.148, p. 10

T2386 Three trials past Serena says
I lose my triumphs if I read 'em.

    [Richard Brinsley Butler Sheridan], 'A fifth' [to
    William Hayley on his incomparably long poem
    entitled The triumphs of temper, c. 1781]

File 13565

T2387 Three virtues as by steps ascend int' heaven,
But charity to th' highest heaven and higher.

    'Heaven's ladder'

c.356

T2388 Three Wills with great and different talent born
Can stem the torment of the people's state.

    'On the three celebrated namesakes' [William
    Windham, William Shippen, William Pulteney]

c.570/3, p. 206

T2389 Three years of blood, of misery, and oppression
And car[eles]sly expend the heir's estate.

    'Upon the times' [c. 1715]

fc.58, p. 11

T2390 Thrice and above blest my soul's half art thou,
Not fear nor wish your dying day.

    [Robert] Herrick, 'Mr. Herrick's Country life' [cf.
    Martial, Epigrams x.xlvii]
    [Crum T2480]

b.197, p. 16

T2391 Thrice blest the modern muse that could inspire
And beg grim Death to spare my Bristol friend.

    S[tephen] Simpson, 'A complimentary poem'

c.563

T2392 Thrice had the circling earth, swift pacing, run,
Worthy, sacred Hyman! Thee.

    [ ] Fitz-Osborne, 'To Cleora, on her wedding day'

fc.132/1, p. 92

T2393 Thrice hail contentment! Blest heav'nborn kind,
And hence we'll speak thy praise.

    'On contentment. Aug. 24th anno Domini 1782'

c.93

T2394 Thrice happy book thou mayst securely go,
Phoebus himself should write on such a theme.

    '1728'

Trumbull Box: Poetry Box XIII/103, p. 9

T2395 Thrice happy calf, could'st thou divine
Fit for a knight or archbishop.

    'To a calf'

Poetry Box IV/190

T2396 Thrice happy Daniel and his wife,
I fear there's nothing done at night.

    'Epigram'

c.81/1, no. 371

T2397 Thrice happy day, when from the northern parts
They long by nature last, he ever lives by fame.

    [Thomas Robinson], 'Upon the happy beginning of
    our royal sovereign King James his reign'

fb.144, end

T2398 Thrice happy happy lives Who are from wedlock
                               free
Who does not them adore, Believe me he is wise.

    'A satire on wedlock and women' [equivocal verses]

fb.142, p. 20

T2399 Thrice happy he, and blessed from above
Who loyally does truth and honor love.

    [Sir Philip Wodehouse], 'Horatio Lord Townshend
    does truth and honor love'

b.131, back (no. 5)

T2400 Thrice happy he whose utmost wish enjoys
He patient waits to hope and death resign'd.

    S[tephen] Simpson, 'The degree below mediocrity'

c.563

T2401 Thrice happy is that pair, and more than so
And never part before they die.

    'Horace . . . lib. 1 car. 13'

c.489, p. 10

T2402 Thrice happy is that witty lord
They have prov'd it true there's none good, no not
                                      one.

    Rich[ard] Halley, 'Rich. Halley's answer to Lord
    Robert, asking if not mad'

c.489, p. 5

T2403 Thrice happy Job long liv'd in regal state,
Man was not made to question, but adore.

    [Edward Young], 'A paraphrase on the book of Job'
    [pr. 1719 (Foxon Y100)]

c.481, p. 71

T2404 Thrice happy John, who now must leave to rest
Who was without the straw to lay his head.

> [Sir Richard Bulstrode], 'Upon St. John's lying in
> Christ's bosom'

fb.88, p. 118

T2405 Thrice happy Lizzy! Blooming maid!
With tripping o'er the daisied green.

> John Lockman, 'Rural Lizzy. Set to music by Mr. de
> Fosch . . . writ in 1729'

c.267/2, p. 86; c.268 (first part), p. 60

T2406 Thrice happy man is he,
And bring him back unto his fold.

> Charles Atherton Allnutt, '5th Job 17 and 18 vs.—
> Behold, happy is the man . . .'

c.112, p. 77

T2407 Thrice happy man!—sure fortune ne'er was such—
No pain she suffer'd—thou art freed from much.

> [John] Winter, 'Spoken offhand by . . . on hearing a
> man's wife died in a moment'

c.74

T2408 Thrice happy pair: whom e'en a very crown
And come and curse they ever rebels were.

> 'To King William the 3d: and Queen Mary the 2d
> crown'd April the 11—1689'

c.360/1, p. 147

T2409 Thrice happy shirt, that doth with care protect
But in the relic, did the saint adore.

> [Thomas Hamilton, 6th earl of Haddington], 'To
> Florella's riding shirt'

c.458/1, p. 25

T2410 Thrice happy souls who borne from heav'n
Nor shall I fear my last.

> P[hilip] Doddridge, 'Of spending the day with God.
> Prov. XXIII. 17'

c.493, p. 27; c.562, p. 82

T2411 . . . Thrice happy they that equal move,
Till unkind death breaks the unwilling chain.

> [John Glanvill, excerpt from Ode XIII]

c.549, p. 86

T2412 Thrice happy times, that first on mortals smil'd,
And yellow harvest dropp'd from every bow.

> Henry Needler, 'Golden age from Ovid'
> [Metamorphoses, book 1]

c.244, p. 541

T2413 Thrice happy warblers, destin'd to the care
Be you convey'd, and chant his grateful tale.

> 'Written extempore by a gentleman on board the
> Revenge, in Anjengo Road, and sent to Mrs. W——
> with some feathered prisoners from the French prize'

fc.132/1, p. 82

T2414 Thrice happy William thou art truly great
Must serve your master tho' they damn your soul.

> 'An ironic satire on King William'
> [Crum T2500]

fb.207/3, p. 12

T2415 Thrice has my fate connubial fetters worn
The third I married purely to be nurs'd.

> 'Epigram'

Poetry Box x/23

T2416 Thrice have the muses wept: the tuneful train
Again smiles Phoebus, and a Stanhope reigns.

> Rev. [ ] Evelyn, 'Verses occasioned by the foregoing
> addressed to Adml. Boscawen'

fc.51, p. 228

T2417 Thrice honorable lady (for thy place,
When Mary laugh'd for joy, for sorrow wept.

> T[homas] Robinson, 'To his most honorable, and
> virtuous lady' [dedication of The life and death of
> Mary Magdalene]

fb.144, p. 2

T2418 Thrice honor'd pair whose mutual hearts and hands
New lovers fresh in blest Elysium.

> 'Congratulatory verses on the names and nuptials
> of . . . Sr Tho. Montpesson Kt . . . and the La.
> Bar[bara] Montpesson his most endeared consort'

Poetry Box VII/10

T2419 Thrice honor'd Sir arise now spur away
And own your humble servant to command.

> 'An invitation to Sir Matthew Wentworth to hasten
> out of Ireland into England . . .'

c.160, fol. 36

T2420 Thrice the doctors have been heard
And every one shall share the gains.

> 'Incantation for raising a phantom' [during the King's
> illness, 1679]
> [Crum T2503]

Poetry Box II/12

T2421 Thrice welcome hero from St. Malo's shore,
And prove that conquest still attends his name.

> John Lockman, 'Seeing Charles Duke of
> Marlborough, passing in his chariot, in Pall Mall . . .
> July 1758'

c.267/1, p. 284

T2422 Thrice welcome, hero! patriot! Ev'ry name
And, born to glory, shines in ev'ry voice.

John Lockman, 'To the honorable General
Townshend: on his arrival from Quebec . . . Decr.
1759'
c.267/2, p. 325

T2423 Thrice William, Richard, George, are royal names.
Whose troops victorious at the Boyne were found.

'Kings of England . . . Gazett[ee]r and new daily
advertiser Feb: 17. 1773'
c.157, p. 99

T2424 Thro' all our travails to reform mankind
Safe in their smiles, in their applauses great.

Timothy Neve, 'A prologue spoken to a play acted at
Spalding by Herbert's company on his wife's mother's
parting'
c.229/1, fol. 87v

T2425 Through all the changes of the day,
You'll find an Eden here.

[George] Horne, bishop of Norwich, 'The flowers' [in
several parts]
c.152, p. 74; see also 'The flow'r of innocence . . .'.

T2426 Thro' all the changes of the day
Alike—thy will be done.

[George] Horne, bishop [of Norwich], 'Short poems
by . . . The heliotrope' [first part of previous]
Diggle Box: Poetry Box XI/48

T2427 Thro' all the various shifting scenes
And fix'd my soul—my God! on Thee!

'An ode under affliction'
c.139, p. 497; fc.61, p. 121

T2428 Through every part of grief or mirth
Let others shine—but Garrick in his own.

[Christopher] Anstey, 'Letter from . . . to David
Garrick esqr. On meeting him at a friend's house'
c.68, p. 102; Poetry Box V/28

T2429 Through every period of my life
To utter all thy praise.

'The thanksgiving or the evening sacrifice'
c.186, p. 112; see also 'When all thy mercies . . .'.

T2430 Thro' flow'ry meads the muse delights to stray
But with your passionate and faithful friend.

M. Johnson, '27 March 1717'
fc.39/6

T2431 Through flow'ry paths may Time your footsteps
                                        guide
Your claims undoubted to the flitch of bacon!

[Charles Burney, the elder], 'Stanzas on the
anniversary of Mr. and Mrs. Thrale's wedding day'
c.33, p. 122 (crossed out)

T2432 Through freezing days you ask to bless your rooms
White in one vase eternal summer dwells.

[Anna] Seward, 'Receipt for an essence jar'
c.391

T2433 Through God my heart, undaunted, dares
For good success I hope.

[Nahum] Tate and [Nicholas] Brady, 'Ps[alm] 27 Tate
and Brady's version'
Poetry Box XIV/170

T2434 Through groves sequestered, dark, and still,
Nor honor's sanguinary palm.

[John] Hawkesworth, 'A moral thought'
[Crum T2511]
c.141, p. 152 (incomplete?)

T2435 Through human clouds thy rays
Forgive they know not what they do.

[Thomas Stanley], 'Meditat: IX. Upon the listing and
raising armies against the King'
b.152, p. 27

T2436 Through Jesu's watchful care
Defend me by thy grace.

'A morning hymn.—I will sing of thy mercy in the
morning. Ps. 59—16'
c.487, p. 119

T2437 Thro' many scenes, thro' many lands I've stray'd,
Bless'd be thy present hour, and bless'd thy future
                                          fate.

'Written on walking over Chester walls, after many
years' absence'
c.159, p. 229

T2438 Thro' me you pass to mourning's dark domain;
Ah guide, said I, hard sense is here contain'd.

[William Hayley, specimen of translation from
Dante's Inferno, Canto 3]
File 7050

T2439 Through neighbor woods the echoing report
Vouchsafe them leave to dance their roundelay.

Sir Francis Castillion, 'The masquing verses'
fb.69, p. 193

T2440 Thro' the close covert of a shady grove
Till they themselves like me, are turn'd to dust.

'A riddle'

fc.51, p. 143

T2441 Thro' the dim veil of evening's dusky shade,
Your best, your brightest fav'rite is no more.

[William Shenstone], 'Ophelia's urn'

c.149, p. 3

T2442 Thro' the tall pine which spreads its weight around,
Too soon thy music shall in death decay.

[ ] C., 'Theocritus Idyl: 1st Thyrsis and goatherd'

c.368, p. 38; Poetry Box 1/2 (var.); see also 'Begin, sweet muse . . .'.

T2443 Through the wide world, all hearts and tongues
Longer than time itself shall last.

[Sir William Trumbull], 'Ps[alm] 100. To the former tune'

Trumbull Box: Poetry Box XIII/18 & 19 (2 copies)

T2444 Through thee we now together came
O Jesus quickly come.

'Hymn 53d'

c.562, p. 62

T2445 Through thorns and briers the lily freshly blooms:
Among the bad so good men have their rooms.

c.339, p. 327

T2446 Through thy death and righteous merit
Dwells forever with my God.

'Hymn 23d'

c.562, p. 26

T2447 Thro' what strange turns of fortune have men gone,
So he defies even his greatest foes.

J[ohn] R[obinson], 'Misera est magni custodia census'

c.370, fol. 37

T2448 Throughout the world if it were sought
For why, their substance is but wind.

b.234, p. 26

T2449 Throughout the year the happiest day
Angels rejoice:—and so do I.

'Short paraphrase of a long speech Dies nolandus'

c.340

T2450 Throw an apple up a hill
Then shall nature cease to love.

'The force of love'

c.83/4, no. 2025

T2451 Throw away thy rod,
Throw away thy wrath.

George Herbert, 'Discipline'
[Crum T2522]

c.139, p. 138

T2452 Throw off, dear Hale in paradise,
To spoil your Adam's peeping.

D[avid] G[arrick], 'Upon Mrs. Hale calling Hampton paradise'

Acquisition 92.3.1ff. (autogr.)

T2453 Thursday farewell! Ah when again shall we
And live the joys of Thursday o'er again.

'Wilton, Dec. 1780'

Poetry Box III/32

T2454 Thus Adam look'd, when from the garden driven
His Eve went with him, mine I left behind.

[Sir William] Young, 'On quitting the garden where he had been sitting with two ladies, one of them, he was engaged to marry, a nobleman called upon him, that he did not like to go to, but the ladies made him' [Crum T2524]

c.378, p. 22; see also 'So the first man . . .'.

T2455 Thus all the day long we are frolic, and gay,
And to each pretty lass, we give a green-gown.

[Thomas Shadwell], 'Country pastime' [from The royal shepherdess, Act III]

fb.107, p. 8

T2456 Thus are mine eyes still captive to one sight
Since what I see think know, is all but you.

b.150, p. 191[insert]

T2457 Thus British Druids, as old bards rehearse,
Passing with age, itself appears more bright.

'Chyndonax Druid to Miriam Druidess 16 Oct. 1754. presented with schemes of the universe deduced from the dandelion seed globe'

c.371, fol. 81

T2458 Thus cited to a second night, we've here
Resume his former bonds, and be yours still.

Will[iam] Cartwright, 'The epilogue to the university, spoken by Arsamnes the Persian king' [from The royal slave, 1636] [Crum T2528]

b.200, p. 153

T2459 Thus could I fool away my time, in toys
Perhaps I may; farewell.

[George Daniel]

b.121, fol. 37

T2460 Thus death in all its gloomy pomp I see,
Nor is the cause the worse, when I am gone.

  'In Johannem Ashton' [translation of Latin poem; 1690]

  b.111, p. 86

T2461 Thus died the Prince of life thus he
Supports for th'utmost faith in Thee.

  [John Norris, of Bemerton?], 'On Christ's death and passion'

  c.548

T2462 Thus do the minutes fly away,
Tho' chiefly from our sense to banish night.

  [Edmund Wodehouse], 'March 14 [1715] on his custom to ask the minutes ere rising each morn'

  b.131, p. 181

T2463 Thus drinking round hath end; a fond delight!
And thus you have an end of an old story.

  'On the notable good fellow old Edward Story [of Gravely in the county of Cambridge]'
  [Crum T2535]

  b.104, p. 13

T2464 Thus fares the hen, in farmer's yard:
Jenny's resolv'd to marry me.

  'Lines sent to a rich miser, who had wasted his lungs in declaiming against marriage amongst the poorer class of people'

  c.83/2, no. 630 (bis)

T2465 Thus flows mankind, still day by day
At what they are so oft advis'd.

  [Edmund Wodehouse], 'Upon the death of my wife's mother [November 1714]'

  b.131, p. 92

T2466 Thus Habakkuk addrest his God, and said,
High as the heaven of heavens, in tuneful number raise.

  [Nathaniel Hamby], 'Habakkuk chapter the 3d. by the transcriber'

  c.244, p. 414

T2467 Thus have I blazon'd all estates
T'enjoy with him our best award.

  [John Taylor], 'The conclusion' [from 'The world turned upside down']

  fb.40, p. 406

T2468 Thus have I drawn the scheme my muse design'd
But kindred muses, and you shades farewell.

  [Abraham Cowley?], 'Epilogue' [to a series of poems on Camberwell]

  File 3782/8

T2469 Thus have I knit a virgin knot together
Is worth their pains, for they may see the court.

  'The epilogue'

  b.205, fol. 22r

T2470 Thus have I seen a barber and a collier fight
Till in the dust the combatants are lost.

  [Christopher] Smart

  c.546, p. 3

T2471 Thus have I seen a lion fell
That hinders not, but will permit.

  'A similitude'

  Poetry Box VIII/57

T2472 Thus have I seen a magpie in the street,
Peep knowingly into a marrow bone.

  [John Wolcot]('Peter Pindar'), 'A simile . . . on his present Majesty George 3d, describing the king when examining, or looking into a long pump when his Majesty visited Whitbread's brewery . . .'

  c.81/1, no. 249

T2473 Thus Holland spoke, as from the summit vast
In idle cheerfulness the muses' friend.

  'L[or]d H[olland] returning from Italy 1767'

  Poetry Box II/16

T2474 Thus I cheerful dance, and sing,
Seizeth all men, soon or late.

  'From [Anacreon's] Ode 39: on his drinking'

  c.94

T2475 Thus I to beauteous Delia pray'd
Her smiles too surely kill.

  'The fatal request'

  c.360/1, p. 125

T2476 Thus Jenny spoke—whilst in her eyes
And sack and toast dispell'd her grief.

  'Answer to [enigmas in The ladies' diary for 1741]'

  c.241, p. 122

T2477 Thus Juliet show, with irresistless charms,
All must gaze on thee with a Romeo's eye.

  John Lockman, 'To the new Juliet, after seeing her in the tragedy performed on Thursday 1st Decr 1768, at the Theater Royal in Covent Garden'

  c.267/4, p. 396

T2478 Thus Kitty beautiful and young,
And set the world on fire.

[Matthew Prior], '18th song Lady Kitty's petition' [on Catherine (Hyde) Douglas, duchess of Queensberry; pr. 1718 (Foxon P1093)]
[Crum T2548]

Accession 97.7.40, p. 30 (with separate copy)

T2479 Thus lamps expire, and darkness doth appear
When shall I celebrate with thee the blissful day.

Thomas Watson, 'Upon the death of . . . William Taylor' [d. 7 September 1641]

b.88, p. 4

T2480 Thus passeth time, (time fleeting stays for none,
And fleeting air, but nothing else beside.

'An hour is the 24th part of a day . . . a minute or moment is the fleeting part of an hour'

b.234, p. 57

T2481 Thus pleas'd rose Venus, in her blaze of charms:
Thus Mars smil'd o'er her, as she left his arms.

John Lockman, 'Seeing an officer, and his lady [the Duchess of Buckingham], the morning after their nuptials'

c.267/1, p. 62

T2482 Thus, reader, we have faithfully related,
You'll say, 'tis a mistake, and there's an end on't.

'From an almanac. By Merry Andrew professor of predictions by star-gazing at Tamtallon [sic]. 1745'

c.93

T2483 Thus said the Ruler of the skies,
The Savior and the king.

[Isaac Watts, Hymns and spiritual songs (1707), bk. II, Hymn 83]

c.180, p. 10

T2484 Thus Shakespeare wrote two hundred years ago
And give a sanction to our poor endeavor.

'An epilogue spoken by Miss Siddons in the character of Lady Townly'

Greatheed Box/72

T2485 Thus shall the son of Jesse said
And vanish in a blaze.

P[hilip] Doddridge, 'The last words of David. 2 Sam. 23 5–8'

c.493, p. 58

T2486 Thus spake the Lord from the thick cloud
The trumpet's sound, and thunder's noise.

'The Decalogue Exod. 20'

c.264/3, p. 120

T2487 Thus spoke to my lady, the knight full of care,
Give me but a barrack, a fig for the clergy.

[Jonathan Swift], 'The grand question debated, whether [J.] Hamilton's bawn shall be turned into a barrack or a malthouse' [pr. 1732 (Foxon S904)]

Poetry Box I/140

T2488 Thus Steele, who own'd what others writ
Withdrew, to starve and die in Wales.

[excerpt from 'A libel on Dr. Delany' by Jonathan Swift; answered by 'Granting he did . . .']

c.360/1, p. 279

T2489 Thus the perverseness of our fate is such,
She might be nearer—were she not so nigh.

'Epigram written by one who was desirous of marrying with his wife's sister'

c.74

T2490 Thus the sly priest with his ill-blended paint
All who dare doubt the miracles he works.

[William Hayley]

File 6971

T2491 Thus the young nightingale pours forth her lay;
Thou must depend, to make success thine own.

John Lockman, 'To Miss Formantel, after hearing her sing . . . Sept. 1756'

c.267/1, p. 112

T2492 Thus, thus, my boys, our anchors weigh'd,
Huzza, my souls, huzza. | For Neptune, &c.

'Song 82'

c.555, p. 129

T2493 Thus to be mock'd by ev'ry saucy billow,
And, without mercy, plunders friends and foes.

John Lockman, 'The shipwreck'd sailors: a mock-tragedy scene . . . this rhapsody was struck out in 1733, to ridicule the fustian; and the many unnatural similes and images with which some of our tragedies abound'

c.267/3, p. 373

T2494 Thus 'twas of old, when Israel felt the rod,
On standing pillars of immortal fame.

'To the haters of popery, by what names or titles soever distinguished' [1687]
[Crum T2574; POAS IV.178]

fb.155, p. 526

T2495 Thus virtues and the vices so confine
Must wait on prudence as their sovereign.

[Sir Philip Wodehouse], 'Virtutis et vitia sunt confinia . . .'

b.131, p. 14

T2496 Thus we deceive ourselves, and every day
Long Barnaby, was never half so gay.

[George Daniel]
b.121, fol. 45v

T2497 Thus when the poison'd shafts of death are sped,
On her own wound distills its charm in vain.

[Edward] Jerningham, 'Epitaph written by . . . on a
monument erected to the memory of Sir John Elliot
physician'
c.391, p. 72

T2498 Thus, where the Seine thro' realms of slavery strays
And still my friends and country share my heart.

[Francis] Atterbury, bishop of Rochester, 'Bp.
Atterbury's character of himself after his exile'
c.144, p. 153

T2499 Thus ye good powers, thus let me ever be
Sometimes by some cheap receipt their health
obtain.

[John] N[orris, of Bemerton], 'Sitting in an arbor'
c.258; c.547, p. 171

T2500 Thus young Achilles in Bythin[i]a's court
He writes a letter fill'd with words like these.

[Charles Hopkins], 'The parting of Achilles and
Deidamia'
b.130, p. 58

T2501 Thy ashes here, but in my mind
Forever Christ['s] which once were mine.

c.189, p. 103

T2502 Thy beard is long better it would thee fit,
To have a shorter beard and longer wit.

[Thomas Bastard], 'On a long beard'
c.356

T2503 Thy beard once black age hath made white, thy
mind
Once white's now black; once candid, now unkind.

'Of a certain old man'
c.356

T2504 Thy beauties Chambaud will not do for me
Would look with patience down a single page.

Miss [ ] Andrews, 'On Chambaud's grammar
addressed to Miss Howard'
File 245/12

T2505 Thy blessing (O Lord) give me and mine
That in life and death we may be thine.

b.234, p. 257

T2506 Thy breast, brain, reason, head, affections, heart,
Thy head completes thy heart with eminence.

'To Henry Prince of Wales'
c.356

T2507 Thy buckles O Garrick, thy friends may now use
But no mortal hereafter shall stand in thy shoes.

[Anna Laetitia (Aikin)] Barbauld, 'Epigram by . . . on
Mr. Garrick's presenting the buckles he wore the last
time he ever performed to Miss Hannah More'
c.341, p. 43

T2508 Thy Christian name spells Theodore
Set solemn orisons—lip-offerings.

[Sir Philip Wodehouse], 'Dorothea Bedingfield'
b.131, back (no. 96)

T2509 Thy daughter[,] Fox, in former days
Exulting cries, 'The day is mine!'

'The modern Quaker a parallel'
File 13409

T2510 Thy duty is a steady thing
While thou hast choice of two.

[William Cowper], 'On a Jacobite parson and poet to
the Revd. Dr. T.'
c.360/1, p. 303

T2511 Thy ev'ry limb and ev'ry feature,
Come cheer thy heart, and dry thy eyes.

c.536

T2512 Thy face, thy tongue, thy heart, are at a strife
Oh, (thou art proclaimed) a very effronted liar.

'Oh, a very effronted liar'
Poetry Box VIII/47

T2513 Thy feign'd and arbitrary farce I saw,
Thou art Drawcansir, thou art only Bayes.

'To the illustrious author his grace the Duke of
Buckingham upon his play called The rehearsal'
fb.140, p. 97

T2514 Thy fairing showed thyself to be
Wit's monkey that is thee.

Lady Jane Cavendish, 'Fairing's monkey'
[Crum T2596]
b.233, p. 23

T2515 Thy father all from thee, by his last will
Gave to the poor; thou hast good title still.

[John Donne], couplet in 'The antiquary'
[Crum T2597]
b.148, p. 56

T2516 Thy father digg'd a pit, and in it left
Only to bear her poor child company.

    [Sir. Thomas Jay], 'On an infant unborn, and a mother
    dying in labor'
    [Crum T2598]

    b.200, p. 137

T2517 Thy favor I my God to me,
Or live as Thou thinkst fit, with joy.

    [Edmund Wodehouse], 'Octr 1 [1715]'

    b.131, p. 277

T2518 Thy gen'rous birth and education claims
What's sown in virtue, shall heav'n's blessing reap.

    [Sir Philip Wodehouse], 'Upon [Sir John Knyvet's]
    son Colonel Thomas Knyvet'

    b.131, back (no. 134, no. 219)

T2519 Thy goodness O my God thy favor is
Itself entirely to thee to restore.

    [Edmund Wodehouse], 'May 3 [1715]'

    b.131, p. 208

T2520 Thy Grubstreet satire, poor empiric!
For thee and Satan I defy.

    [Stephen Barrett?], 'The challenge . . . Litera
    provocatoria' [on Colley Cibber]

    c.193, p. 30

T2521 Thy hand, O Lord, thro' rolling years
The labors of our hand.

    [Christopher] Pitt, 'Psalm 90'

    c.244, p. 505

T2522 Thy hands hath made me, all and every part
But well I know that it [is] so with thee.

    'Man's frailty and a description of our conception and
    being'

    b.137, p. 123

T2523 Thy hoarded gold, thy chests may quit,
And will be always so.

    [ ] Lewis, 'An epigram from Martial'

    c.244, p. 439

T2524 Thy horse does things by halves, like thee,
The King and constitution.

    'On a ballot in the House of Commons for seven
    commissioners to examine the public accounts, the
    following lines were put into one of the glosses instead
    of a list, occasioned by Mr. Pulteney's being thrown
    from his horse and very much bruised on Monday the
    24 May 1742'

    c.360/2, no. 64

T2525 Thy joyous blades with roses crown'd,
The earth wheel round with rapid pace.

    John Lockman, 'The earth's motion proved. Set to
    music by Mr. Leveridge'

    c.267/4, p. 83

T2526 Thy life on earth was grief, and thou art still
Will be content, in tilling his own ground.

    [Sir Richard Bulstrode], 'Afflictions of our Lord'

    fb.88, p. 117

T2527 Thy 'lov'd Northumberland
That envy may expire, | And guilt [?] cease!

    John Lockman, 'Song (in chorus) for the Duke of
    Northumberland's birthday, Friday 19 Decr. 1766. The
    tune, God save our noble king'

    c.267/2, p. 168

T2528 Thy loving-kindness, Lord, shall dwell
And Amens to Thy praises sing.

    'Psalm 89. Evening prayer'

    c.264/2, p. 85

T2529 Thy magic scenes I sing, lovely Torquay,
And chase each adverse cloud far, far away.

    'Torquay'

    Poetry Box XII/84, 121

T2530 Thy mercies Lord, ({hence in displeasure/to their
                         protection} fled)
Thy mercies are my trust thy wrath decline.

    [Thomas Stanley], 'Meditat: XII. Upon the rebellion
    and troubles in Ireland'

    b.152, p. 38

T2531 Thy mercy Lord to me extend,
And o'er the earth Thy glory bright.

    'Psalm 57'

    c.264/2, p. 12

T2532 Thy mind with art, and virtue thou hast guarded
And lo! thy pain is crown'd, thy hope rewarded.

    'Edward Hooper. Anagram. O hope rewarded.
    Epigram'

    b.212, p. 79

T2533 Thy nags (the leanest things alive)
It cost thee more in whips than hay.

    [Matthew] Prior, 'Another [epigram] hay less expense
    than whips'

    c.144, p. 79; c.115

T2534   Thy name denotes thee just and liberal
With prayer to Him, for room in Paradise.

    [Sir Philip Wodehouse], 'Rogerus Potitius Roger
    Potts'

    b.131, back (no. 210)

T2535   Thy name does bid thee highly dare
Thou fall'st with honor, and applause.

    [Sir Philip Wodehouse], 'Upon his noble kindred
    Fitz-Careys their surnames'

    b.131, back (no. 233)

T2536   Thy name does spell I never love
But stay. He lives | loves to love | live, his name
                               reprieve.

    [Sir Philip Wodehouse], 'Oliver Neve I never love O
    never live'

    b.131, back (no. 142)

T2537   Thy name in Greek, makes Eirenarch
Bred up for ornament of peace and truth.

    [Sir Philip Wodehouse], 'Richardus Neech my son
    John's tutor'

    b.131, back (no. 203)

T2538   Thy name O God I praise,
But worse, when hence we go.

    [Edmund Wodehouse], 'July 27 [1715]'

    b.131, p. 236

T2539   Thy name, thy noble nature does display
The richest, heav'nly store | I need not say no more.

    [Sir Philip Wodehouse], 'Upon Madam [Ann]
    Moseley eleemosyne'

    b.131, back (no. 124)

T2540   Thy name's a virtue—giv'n thee from above
Thou may't bestow't. Be this thy blessed doom.

    [Sir Philip Wodehouse], 'Upon his son Edmund's wife
    Mercy Wodehouse'

    b.131, back (no. 29)

T2541   Thy nature's only fit for Caesar's wife,
For monarchs for to wish they had but thee.

    Lady Jane Cavendish, 'On my sweet sister Brackley'
    [Crum T2637]

    b.233, p. 21

T2542   Thy numbers Pope, have giv'n immortal fame,
And crown their virtue with eternal life.

    [Mary] Cornwallis, 'Lucilla a true story . . . 1791'

    fc.124, p. 119

T2543   Thy parents fondly wish'd that thou
For years thou hast eternity.

    [M.] S[harpe], 'An epitaph by Mr S[harpe] intended
    for his daughter A[nna] S[harpe] whom he believed
    dying aged ten years, Sept 7th 1744'

    c.116, p. 27

T2544   Thy pedigree thus understood
You Prior are to all mankind.

    'The answer' [to 'Courtiers and heralds . . . ,' Matthew
    Prior's epitaph]
    [Crum c756, second part]

    fb.142, p. 69

T2545   Thy pregnant mother on this forth [fourth?] eve
Who hourly for thy absence still does mourn.

    [Mrs. Christian Kerr], 'On the 3 of D[ecember]'

    c.102, p. 84

T2546   Thy pregnant mother throbbing in her pain
Ere close of next thou's [thou'lt?] see a juster reign.

    [Mrs. Christian Kerr], 'Upon the birth of a friend D:
    4 D[ecember]'

    c.102, p. 84

T2547   Thy presence Mary, I with truth confess
Thus wert a crime to men, of looser sense.

    Lady Jane Cavendish, 'On a chambermaid'
    [Crum T2651]

    b.233, p. 28

T2548   Thy prime of youth is frozen with the faults:
And thus O Tichborne hath thy treason done.

    'The answer to the same' ['My prime of youth . . .']

    fb.9, fol. 30v

T2549   Thy proof is twofold, friend—no more enlarge,
And thy lines prove thee stranger to the muses.

    Charles Atherton Allnutt, 'In March 1795 a poem was
    published entitled The receding volunteers replete
    with sarcasm . . . which gave rise to the following
    epigrams—Epigram'

    c.112, p. 161

T2550   Thy relics, Rowe, to this fair shrine we trust
What a whole thankless land to his denies.

    A[lexander] Pope, 'The epitaph for Nicholas Rowe
    esqr. as at first designed . . . to be near the grave of
    Mr. Dryden . . .' [1718?]
    [Crum T2655]

    c.360/2, no. 188; see also next.

T2551 Thy relics Rowe, to this sad shrine we trust
That holds their ashes and expects her own.

> Alexander Pope, 'Another [epitaph] on Nicholas Rowe
> esq. [and his daughter Charlotte Rowe Fane, in
> Westminster Abbey; written 1743?]
> [Crum T2655]

fc.60, p. 118; c.360/2, no. 165 (ll. 1–10); see also previous,
and 'To this sad shrine . . .'.

T2552 Thy sacred will be done great God
If otherwise, to stoop, and kiss it.

> [Francis Quarles], 'A submission to God's will'
> [Crum T2656]

b.137, p. 194

T2553 Thy self-wrought sorrows Werther, which I view
That virtuous tears, alone, for virtuous sorrows flow.

> [Martha] Peckard, 'On reading The sorrows of
> Werther'
> [Crum T2661]

c.504, p. 13; c.83/2, no. 299 ('self-sought'); Diggle Box:
Poetry Box XI/8; Poetry Box III/41

T2554 Thy servant R—— Moone of late
'Tis yours—to let off—or to print.

> [Stephen Barrett], 'On a hint of my son-in-law,
> Edward Jer. Curteis [senior] that it would be a funny
> affair, if my servant, whose name was Moone should
> beget a Sun. Written in 1791'

c.193, p. 141

T2555 Thy shape and complexion how much I admire;
My pen's thy fair gift, well-employ'd in thy praise.

> Dr. [ ] Thompson, 'The bird's egg. An ode' [1797]

c.141, p. 349

T2556 Thy sins and hairs no man may equal call
For as thy sins increase thy hairs do fall.

> [John Donne], 'On a whoremaster'
> [Crum T2663]

b.62, p. 95; b.200, p. 409

T2557 Thy soothing strains unerring prove,
Receives the charm nor seeks the cause.

> 'On hearing a friend sing to the harp Thy fatal shafts
> unerring move'

c.504, p. 203

T2558 Thy statutes, Lord, upon the heart,
Praise God, Amen, Amen.

> 'Psalm 72'

c.264/2, p. 44

T2559 Thy strength'ning graces are the children's bread
But bread, I'm sure I shall have crumbs enow.

> [Francis Quarles], 'On the children's bread' [Divine
> fancies III, 76]

b.137, p. 172 and 193

T2560 Thy surname, spells thee blade
Thy Christian bids—beware thy head.

> [Sir Philip Wodehouse], 'Edoard Beadle blade!
> O dread'

b.131, back (no. 207)

T2561 Thy surname Thoroughgood, befitteth thee
Both of you through go and pass away.

> 'Upon Thoroughgood an unthrift'

b.197, p. 38

T2562 Thy taper shape, fine skin, and hair so bright
By how much other girls you far exceed.

> 'To Chloris—the poet's advice attempted in English
> by a member S[palding] G[rammar] S[chool]'

fc.39/6; c.229/2, fol. 57

T2563 Thy tongue thy heart interprets let thine heart
As the ambassador doth use his tongue.

> 'Of Battus'

c.356

T2564 Thy turtledoves O Lord to dragons turn
Shall clad thy wife and make her shine within.

> Thomas Traherne, [Meditation (second century)] 17'

b.308, p. 64

T2565 Thy venal tongue whose motion seems
Disgrace the Common Pleas.

> 'To Mr. Sergeant Nares on his failure in a motion
> made in the Court of Common Pleas for an
> attachment against the printer of the paper[.] From
> the Public advertiser'

File 1769

T2566 Thy verses are eternal, O my friend
For he that reads 'em, reads 'em to the end.

> 'Epigram'
> [Crum T2667, 'immortal . . . to no end']

c.360/1, p. 35

T2567 Thy virgin name is chang'd by marriage
And as thou liv'st and di'st, will be again.

> [Sir Philip Wodehouse], 'Upon a fair neighbor of his
> Maria Davy'

b.131, back (no. 61)

T2568 Thy warfare finish'd, ended thy career
Such as his life, such was his closing scene.

> Mrs. [ ] Walsingham, 'On the death of Henry Earl of Shannon, aged 80'

Poetry Box v/16

T2569 Thy will our God be done
As angels do in heaven.

> T[homas] S[tevens], 'Matt. 6.19 . . . March 11. 1781'

c.259, p. 131

T2570 Thy wish is half indulg'd; our senate hears;
And their brave phalanx check th'invading world.

> John Lockman, 'To the noble author C[harles] S[ackville, earl of Middlesex, later 2nd duke of Dorset] of a treatise concerning the militia . . . April 1756'

c.267/1, p. 116

T2571 Thy wit, and judgment in my verse to show,
I to thy wit and judgment mine submit.

> 'To [blank]'

c.356

T2572 Thy wit in vain the feeble critic gnaws
Forget thy body, to adorn thy soul.

> [Alexander] Pope(?), 'An epigram by . . .'

Poetry Box xiv/193

T2573 Thy word O Jesus we believe
And all its meaning good.

> [Thomas Stevens?], 'September the 10 Lord's day 1780'

c.259, p. 109

T2574 Thy works, my friend, are monuments of taste
That you be turn'd to marble with the thought.

> 'To Mr Roubiliac the sculptor on his marrying Miss Smart' [daughter of Dr. Smart of Chelsea, m. Jan. 1741/42]

c.360/1, p. 297

T2575 Thy world is ne'er from trouble free,
And who has that, the life of heav'n now live.

> [Edmund Wodehouse], 'Octr. 6 [1714]'

b.131, p. 54

T2576 Thy worth, O tea by tuneful nymphs be sung,
And let experience give their years the lie.

> 'My pipe and I'

c.94

T2577 Thy wounds bright maid (which heaven avert
All other wounds forget to smart.

> 'To Miranda enclosed with goldbeater's skin'

Poetry Box I/47

T2578 Thy zealous care to save thy God
Remains still tho' thy corpse lie here.

> 'On Mrs Dorcas Bentley wife of Jonathan Bentley citizen of London 1693'

fb.143, p. 24

T2579 Thyrsis, for nuptial joys prepare,
Rise with each joyful day, and crown each blissful
night.

> 'Epithalamion'

c.241, p. 123

T2580 Thyrsis lamenting o'er the cruel fate,
And pleasing thee form all my joy.

> John Lockman, 'To the Earl of Middlesex. Presented to his lordship on his birthday, 6 Feb. 1753. (O. S.)'

c.267/2, p. 186; see also 'Cupid and Hymen . . .'.

T2581 Thyrsis, the gayest one of all the swains
And when one nymph proves cruel find a new.

> [William Walsh], 'Eclogue. 2nd'

c.223, p. 85

T2582 Thyrsis when he left me swore
And spare the honor of my love.

> [Thomas] Gray, 'Lines by . . .' [answered by 'Thyrsis will return no more . . .']
> [Crum T2676]

c.340

T2583 Thyrsis will return no more
Trust and be deceived again.

> [Richard] Fitzpatrick, 'Answer by . . .' [to 'Thyrsis when he left me swore . . .']

c.340

T2584 Thyself a sacred Church, so each should look,
The style of virtue so all sex names thee.

> Lady Jane Cavendish, 'On a noble lady'
> [Crum T2659]

b.233, p. 8

T2585 Tiberius next comes on with blood and cruelty
And watch lost man Eden's fair garden to regain.

Poetry Box vi/93

T2586 Tie one end of a rope fast over a beam,
And leave all the rest of the work to the string.

> 'A receipt to cure a love fit which may indifferently serve for those that are tired of matrimony'

c.160, fol. 72

T2587 Till beauty, wit and softest strains
They cannot kill the dead.

> 'On Miss M. S. at Naples'

fc.51, p. 44

T2588 Till by Lucifer taught,
Bears the load of all France on his shoulders.

[Crum T2679]

b.111, p. 310

T2589 Till I have peace with thee, war other men
More glorious service, staying to make men.

[John Donne], 'Elegia quarta' [Love's wars]
[Crum T2681]

b.114, p. 79; b.205, fol. 82r ('with her'); b.148, p. 84

T2590 Till this morning I ha'n't had the least bit of time,
As you've hitherto done, to the end of your days.

Edward Sneyd, 'An epistle 2nd. To my niece Fanny
upon her going to be married May the 20th: 1773'

c.214, p. 14

T2591 Time breeds all things, and doth all things destroy
Time hath all things, and all things time enjoy.

Sir Thomas Urquhart, 'Of time, and things
temporary'

fb.217, p. 321

T2592 Time brings forth truth: and truth breeds hatred: so
That hate's the grandchild of old time, we know.

Sir Thomas Urquhart, 'Of time, truth, and hatred'

fb.217, p. 147

T2593 Time either moves too slow, or fast;
And crown your youth with pleasure.

[Frederick Corfield]

c.381/1

T2594 Time [I] ever must complain
And to Lethe sends him divining.

'To time a sonnet'

b.205, fol. 39r

T2595 Time is for all things made under the sun,
In spheres and orbs, where nature's courses run.

[John Rose?]

b.227, p. 1

T2596 Time, lovely Mira, time has been
And makes them ever gay.

[Phanuel Bacon], 'To Mira occasioned by her
presenting a firescreen worked with flowers'

c.237, fol. 52

T2597 Time may ambition's nest destroy
Till time is lost in endless night.

[Anne (Home)] Hunter, 'Time'

Diggle Box: Poetry Box XI/19

T2598 Time quick doth pass, no mortal can it stay,
For time once past, you nevermore will find.

'Lincup Hill 8th. August 1782 J[ohn] R[utherford]'

c.93

T2599 Time was I stood, when thou dost now
And others stand and look on thee.

'Epitaph on a gravestone in the ruins of an old church
near Boughton Green in Northamptonshire'

c.546, p. 15; c.360/3, no. 71

T2600 Time was when flatt'rers said that I
Her absence on the banks of Churn.

'To Mrs. Master of Cirencester February. 26. 1759'

c.484, p. 115

T2601 Time was, when many a cheerful thought
Like those of former days.

'On being desired to write something in Mrs. Crewe's
album . . . Crewe Hall, March 18th 1783'

Poetry Box II/43

T2602 Time was, gentle Venus, when in the wide field,
And Horace may yet make another campaign.

[William Popple, trans.], '[Horace] book 3rd. ode
26th. To Venus'

fc.104/2, p. 298

T2603 Time's iron hand plows furrows down my face,
And calm stern Caesar's too insatiate ire.

'Ovid's epistle to his wife from Pontus Book 1. Ep.4'

c.142, p. 409

T2604 Time's picture here invites your eyes
The times they fast in prison hold.

[William Strode], 'A watch string'
[Crum T2712]

b.205, fol. 55v

T2605 Tindal give o'er, thou ne'er wilt gain thy ends
Whilst cock and coney are the Church's friends.

'On Doctor Cockburn and Doctor Conybeare's
answers to Doctor Tindal's book wrote by a lady'

c.360/1, p. 231

T2606 Tir'd of continual roving
To travel the country round.

c.361

T2607 Tir'd with hoping and complaining
Here, expecting it I wait.

R[obert] Shirley, 1st earl of Ferrers, 'From the French.
La desperer &c.'

c.347, p. 14

T2608 Tired with the noisome follies of the age
Unthinking C[harles] ruled by unthinking thee.

    [Charles Sackville, 6th earl of Dorset?], 'Rochester's
    farewell' [1680]
    [Crum T2722; *POAS* II.218]

b.113, p. 79; b.52/2, p. 180; pb.52/12; see also 'Fill'd
with . . .'.

T2609 Tir'd with the sultry travels of the day
The better portion which her soul has chose.

    Tho[ma]s Gibbons, 'Our Savior's visit, Luke 10:38-42
    . . . from Juvenile poems'

    c.186, p. 28

T2610 Tir'd with their wilds; allur'd by Gallic gold;
And back, to their vile crannies, swiftly scour.

    John Lockman, 'The flight of the Highlanders: a
    simile . . . 11 Jan. 1746'

    c.267/1, p. 231

T2611 'Tis a fond mistake, my friend,
For his country or his friend.

    [William Popple, trans.], '[Horace] book 4th. Ode
    9th. To Lollius'

    fc.104/2, p. 366

T2612 'Tis a knot my dear John, that will bind you indeed!
Your blood was purloin'd by *furatque sacerdos*.

    Poetry Box XII/125[2]

T2613 'Tis an old maxim in the schools
Will condescend to take a bit.

    c.546

T2614 'Tis better slight, than earnestly desire
Such things as are impossible t'acquire.

    c.549, p. 44

T2615 'Tis bumpers lull all cares to rest,
And bumpers make us what we are.

    'Song 39'

    c.555, p. 60

T2616 'Tis but a frown I prithee let me die
And differ but in execution.

    b.213, p. 17

T2617 'Tis but a little space we have,
And neither wish, nor fear to die.

    'On life'

    c.83/1, no. 235

T2618 'Tis by fair expectation our spirit's kept up
To the Indus we sail by the Cape of Good Hope.

    [Phanuel Bacon], 'Spes est solamen miseris'

    c.237, fol. 71

T2619 'Tis by our spirits that we now,
O Father, Son and Spirit, One and Three!

    [Edmund Wodehouse], 'Jan. 17 [1715]'

b.131, p. 143

T2620 'Tis by the soul the body lives,
With those which true eternal be.

    [Edmund Wodehouse], 'Novr. 8 [1714]'

b.131, p. 80

T2621 'Tis certain dear Mall,
So you're sure of a man when you need one.

    'Love's maxim'

fb.107, p. 1

T2622 'Tis certain that each day we live,
All means whate'er our souls to him to raise.

    [Edmund Wodehouse], 'Iterum [1 December 1714]'

b.131, p. 101

T2623 'Tis cold (quoth Margery by William laid)
Then with the devil lie—sweet Margery.

    'Modern matrimony. An epigram' [names corrected
    from 'Emily' and 'Francis']

fc.53, p. 20

T2624 'Tis common, we know, for goblins to walk,
To make common dull prayers and duller reponses?

    'A dialogue betwixt the ghosts of [Lord] Russell and
    [Algernon] Sidney' [1689]
    [Crum T2747; *POAS* V.139]

fb.70, p. 295; b.111, p. 145

T2625 'Tis cruel Hymen to let sixty-five
A thing that's dead to what is all alive.

    'Epigram. 65 and 25'

c.81/1, no. 367

T2626 'Tis day: unfold thine arms
Displeasing to thy God.

    [Francis Quarles?]

b.156, p. 41 (incomplete)

T2627 'Tis done—he's crown'd, and one bright martyr
                         more,
But heaven his death in thunder groan'd aloud.

    'An epitaph on the Lord Russell beheaded by
    K. Ch[arles] 2d.' [1683]

c.244, p. 288

T2628 'Tis done—restor'd by thy immortal pen
Be still yourself the world can ask no more.

    [Charles Brinsden], 'To Mr. [Joseph] Spence on his
    essay on the Odyssey'

Spence Papers: Derby Anecdotes, p.xx +4.

T2629   'Tis done! Thou awful shade of Britain rise
Still has he honest been, still faithful just and true.

     'A copy of a paper dropped in the House of Commons
upon the excise scheme' [pr. 1733 (Foxon O203)]

     c.570/3, p. 214

T2630   'Tis doubtless, such is our access
Some taste of those full joys we can't conceive.

     [Edmund Wodehouse], 'Epiphany [1715]'

     b.131, p. 133

T2631   'Tis easy into hell to fall
But to get back from thence is all.

     [James Rhodes?]

     b.206, p. 149

T2632   'Tis enough—the hour is come
God of truth, and God of love!

     [James] Merrick, 'The Song of Simeon paraphrased'
[Luke II.29–32; Dodsley Collection]

     c.487, p. 128

T2633   'Tis fair Asteria's sweet employ,
O! let him wear a never-withering crown.

     [George Dyer], 'Asteria rocking the cradle'
[Crum T2759]

     c.142, p. 421

T2634   'Tis fit, cleric-podex
All's one, whose the breech is.

     Poetry Box I/131

T2635   'Tis folly all—let me no more be told
I plunge into that sea—, and there am lost.

     [William Cowper, trans.], 'The nativity. Vol. 4.32—
poeme heroique [in Jeanne Guion's 'Spiritual songs']

     c.470 (autogr.)

T2636   'Tis fortitude to dare, and to endure
And duty, so betrays his strength, to fear.

     [Sir Philip Wodehouse], 'Fortitude or valor'

     b.131, p. 12

T2637   'Tis friendship's pledge, my young, fair friend,
These joys could he improve.

     R[obert] Burns, 'Written by . . . in a blank leaf of a
copy . . . of his poems presented to Chloris'

     c.142, p. 296

T2638   'Tis God alone that I'll adore,
Oh how stupendous are its powers?

     [Edmund Wodehouse], 'Octr. 18 [1714]

     b.131, p. 60

T2639   'Tis God that gives this bower its awful gloom,
And yet avoid its dangers and its cares.

     'Extract from an ode to contentment'

     c.139, p. 7

T2640   'Tis good for me to bear the rod
While we in Mesheck dwell.

     T[homas] S[tevens], 'March 16. [17]80'

     c.259, p. 79

T2641   Tis good thou sov'reign all
My mansion in the sky.

     T[homas] S[tevens], 'Mr Jabez Brown preached in the
afternoon and evening ordinance day. 2 hymns sung in
evening before and after sermon'

     c.259, p. 94

T2642   'Tis good to give Jehovah thanks and sing
Injurious ill can be.

     'Psal: 92 another [version]'

     b.217, p. 55

T2643   'Tis good to thank the Lord
No injury in Him is seen.

     'Psal: 92'

     b.217, p. 53

T2644   'Tis hard my fair one, that I should be told
And heralds, must the ladies' charms decide.

     [Thomas Hamilton, 6th earl of Haddington], 'Copy
of an epistle to a friend under the name of Seraphina'

     c.458/1, p. 41

T2645   'Tis hard to raise the eye that drops with woe
Such virtues, matchless Adeline are thine.

     'On pity'

     c.83/1, no. 82

T2646   'Tis he that's happy, he alone
But sure what I have seiz'd already's all my own.

     [John Norris, of Bemerton]

     Diggle Box: Poetry Box XI/35

T2647   'Tis he; the lovely bloom of face,
Triumphant o'er the grave.

     T[homas] M[orell], 'For Mrs Barker, of the Grove, at
Chiswick; on seeing the picture of her nephew
[Viscount Deerhurst], copied by Zieman [Seeman],
sometime after his Lordship's death'

     c.395, p. 105

T2648   'Tis his deformity, that maketh her
So long's he was a satyr.

     Sir Thomas Urquhart, 'Of a pretty gentlewoman, who
     was enamored with one, that was none of the
     handsomest men'
     fb.217, p. 237

T2649   'Tis honesty which gives the noble end
In him, could seem enough to raise his wrath.

     [Sir Philip Wodehouse], '2 for honest end'
     b.131, p. 15

T2650   'Tis hope which softens want and woe,
In hope alone we live.

     'On hope'
     c.83/1, no. 118

T2651   'Tis I, Timon, not here, prithee, begone,
I ask no tears, only to be alone.

     George Montagu, 'On Timon the misanthrope'
     fc.135, p. 11

T2652   'Tis idle all, and ancient bards must dream,
Seen glitt'ring in the bath, expect a flame.

     John Lockman, 'Chloe in the King's bath . . . at Bath,
     Oct. 1747'
     c.267/1, p. 69

T2653   'Tis in the longest night, that the blind archer
Her hymen were hydropic.

     Sir Thomas Urquhart, 'The reason why in the longest
     night of all the year . . . after the sign of Sagittarius
     follows Capricorn'
     fb.217, p. 169

T2654   'Tis innocence and youth which makes
A marble one, so warm'd would speak.

     'On a young lady: playing with a snake'
     c.360/1, p. 179

T2655   'Tis long since wayward spring's invermeil'd prime
And leave the world to music, love, and thee!

     'Subject for the vase at Batheaston. December 3d'
     Poetry Box v/47

T2656   'Tis love breeds love in me; and cold disdain
Which never could to public tend.

     'Ben. Rudyerd' [answer to 'If her disdain . . .']
     [Crum T2778]
     b.148, p. 132

T2657   'Tis mercy and performing righteous things
To spring up, when the king first enter'd in.

     c.158, p. 49

T2658   'Tis merit in the muse to spare
You'd not think me your friend.

     [Frederick Corfield]
     c.381/1

T2659   'Tis midnight and Maria sits writing alone,
Pray, don't trouble yourself to return.

     [Matthew?] G[regory?] Lewis, 'Count Rollo's widow a
     ballad, founded on fact, and inscribed to H. R. and
     the Princess of Wales, by whose commands the tale
     was versified'
     c.340

T2660   'Tis midnight— black December rain
And night again with silence reign'd.

     Miss [ ] Bradford, 'An elegy written in an old house
     which had formerly been a nunnery'
     c.504, p. 42

T2661   'Tis mine to wound the gift of nature,
And guess my name the man who dare.

     [Dorothea Harris, sr.], 'A riddle'
     fc.124, p. 41

T2662   'Tis my true glory, thou Supreme!
Thro' endless ages, shall arise.

     'A hymn to the Deity'
     c.83/3, no. 1040

T2663   'Tis nature here bids pleasing scenes arise,
And proud for once adopts the work of man.

     Lady [Henrietta Knight] Luxborough, 'Verses written
     on a seat at the Leasowes [home of William
     Shenstone] (near Birmingham) in Dodsley's collection
     Vol. 4th'
     c.221, p. 19

T2664   'Tis neither fashionable nor fit they say,
Thus garter'd knights arose in Windsor's royal
                            bower.

     M[aurice] J[ohnson], 'Another epilogue by . . . spoken
     by Miss Dionysia Chalk'
     c.229/2, fol. 28

T2665   'Tis night, and now the flowers fresh odors send
And the ambitious joy of being once a god.

     George Montagu, 'Upon a lady singing to an echo.
     Wrote on Miss Molly Trevor at Glynd from
     Cambridge'
     fc.135, p. 18

T2666   'Tis night and on the hill of storms
For friends I lov'd so dear.

     'Colma's complaint' [signed Minossa Opium (?)]
     c.343, p. 77

T2667 'Tis no disparagement. A lady should
As before God and man she shineth bright.

[Sir Philip Wodehouse], 'Upon the Lady Anne
Bedingfield'

b.131, back (no. 77)

T2668 'Tis no dysanter [sic],
In the Capricorn.

Sir Thomas Urquhart, 'Some kind of comfort, to a
cuckold'

fb.217, p. 83

T2669 'Tis no fable that I feign,
Licking both thy legs and feet.

[William Popple, trans.], '[Horace] book 2nd. Ode
19th. On Bacchus. A rhapsody'

fc.104/2, p. 178

T2670 'Tis no new thing; but a worn maxim in
Of man, to see myself in my own heart.

[George Daniel]

b.121, fol. 83v

T2671 'Tis no strange thing that Walpole's tamed
As disaffected timber.

'The answer' [to 'What you said last . . .']

fc.58, p. 63; see also ''Tis not so strange . . .'.

T2672 'Tis noble to tell truth—to lie
Is baseness, and poor pedantry.

[Sir Philip Wodehouse], 'An Arabian proverb'

b.131, p. 32

T2673 'Tis not a coat of gray or shepherd's life
For men do often learn, when they do teach.

[Sir Henry Wotton, 'Against solitariness']
[Crum T2786]

b.148, p. 1 (attr. J[ohn] D[onne])

T2674 'Tis not a fast proclaim'd can countenance
Before you set on reformation.

Sir John Strangways, '7° Septr 1646'

b.304, p. 54

T2675 'Tis not a million of unpolish'd rhymes,
But 'tis a lion.

Sir Thomas Urquhart, 'A manifest difference put
betwixt many lines, and good ones'

fb.217, p. 247

T2676 'Tis not amiss, you cherish fornication;
Because you owe into it your generation.

Sir Thomas Urquhart, 'To a bastard lecherously
inclined'

fb.217, p. 146

T2677 'Tis not an easy matter for the rich
They have with angels their heav'ns here on earth.

[Sir Thomas Urquhart], 'The continuation of that
passage of Saint Luke against rich men'

fb.217, p. 497

T2678 'Tis not because this woman's virtue dies;
And now the poor cry—Hill'ry term is ended.

'An epitaph on Mrs. Ann Hillary who was buried in
the year 1653 in Beaminster Church in Dorsetshire'

c.487, p. 83

T2679 'Tis not because thy crimson cheeks doth stain
That made me first, and ever be a lover.

'To his mistress'

b.356, p. 145

T2680 'Tis not enough great gods! 'tis not enough
'Tis Caesar-like from many wounds a death to take.

'The hero'

fb.107, p. 17

T2681 'Tis not enough that the king's daughter should
With lives to men, as liv'd with hearts to God.

[Francis Quarles], 'On the Christian' [Divine
fancies IV, 109]

b.137, p. 185

T2682 'Tis not for us and our proud hearts
And make up one adoring choir.

[John Austin], 'Hym: 26' [Hymn xxiv, Devotions in
the ancient way of offices, 1672, p. 212]

c.178, p. 25

T2683 'Tis not for vulgar souls to feel
He cherishes the pensive sigh.

[Richard] Polwhele, 'On the susceptibility of the
poetical mind'

c.83/3, no. 792

T2684 'Tis not her foot, 'tis not her toe
That never puts me in the wrong.

'Parody on the foregoing' [''Tis not the liquid
brightness of her eyes . . .']

c.360/2, no. 72

T2685 'Tis not my care, but 'tis God's love,
This, this to do, I'll all my care apply.

[Edmund Wodehouse], 'May 1 [1715]'

b.131, p. 207

T2686 'Tis not my person, nor my play
Than Talbot was to France, or Drake to Spain.

[Barten Holiday?], 'Another' [answer to 'Brag on
proud Christ Church . . .']

b.200, p. 35

T2687 'Tis not my Tullus that I dread with thee
What anxious cares my anxious bosom rend.

'Propertius's sixth elegy in his first book'
Poetry Box I/31

T2688 'Tis not safe, tho' fair the breeze,
Reef in time the swelling sail.

[William Popple, trans.], '[Horace] book 2nd. Ode
10th. To Licinius Murena'
fc.104/2, p. 144

T2689 'Tis not so strange that Walp[o]l[e]'s tam'd
As disaffected timber.

'The Farnham maypole's reply' [to 'What you said
last . . .']
[Crum T2798]
c.570/1, p. 166; see also ''Tis no strange thing . . .'.

T2690 'Tis not strange, though they from their country
quit
In the republic of the old Athenians.

Sir Thomas Urquhart, 'Whom the covenanters have
persecuted need not to be ashamed of their exile'
fb.217, p. 58

T2691 'Tis not that I am weary grown
And be the mistress of mankind.

John Wilmot, 2nd earl of Rochester, '2. To Celia for
inconstancy. Song'
b.334, p. 182; b.105, p. 113

T2692 'Tis not the beauties of the face,
Whom all must equally admire.

c.174, p. 13

T2693 'Tis not the fear of death or smart
Whenever she's not there.

'An answer to a challenge'
[Crum T2803]
c.150, p. 167

T2694 'Tis not the knowledge of deep mysteries,
To thine and to our father for thy sake.

[Edmund Wodehouse], 'Novr. 16 [1714]'
b.131, p. 86

T2695 'Tis not the liquid brightness of those eyes
That thus have set my soul on fire!

[Joseph Spence], 'Sylvia's charms. May 30, 1745'
Spence Papers, folder 156; c.360/2, no. 71

T2696 'Tis not the quaffing off of healths, until
Drink shall make thee ever live.

H[enry] C[olman], 'Another' [on drunkenness]
[Crum T2805]
b.2, p. 40

T2697 'Tis not the threats of an enraged mob,
And triumph o'er the intrigues of factious men.

'The resolution'
b.111, p. 75

T2698 'Tis not to cry God mercy, and to sit
Confesses rather what he means to do.

[Francis Quarles], 'On repentance'
[Crum T2811]
b.137, p. 191

T2699 'Tis not to make a party; or to join
I am not wise enough to observe the time.

[George Daniel]
b.121, fol. 85v

T2700 'Tis not yon palace rais'd at your command
Nor ask for flattery's aid to raise thy fame.

W[illiam] S[mith], 'Epitaph on the late Sr. G. W.
Vannest bart . . . Jun. 5. 1791'
Smith Papers, folder 74

T2701 'Tis not your great look carries it away
And if he leaves you may put it in your eyes.

'Answer' [to I Eye . . .']
b.356, p. 118

T2702 'Tis now some years, if I have not forgot,
Or reprobates, or heretics in love.

[Thomas Hamilton, 6th earl of Haddington], 'Copy
of a second epistle to Seraphina'
c.458/1, p. 76

T2703 'Tis odd, I confess, but surprisingly true,
And shows by example what ladies should do.

'An epistle from the Countess of B—— at Tunbridge'
c.83/2, no. 513

T2704 'Tis odd that I great labor have bestow'd
Men are great boys and boys are little men!

W[illiam] P[arsons, to Bertie Greatheed]
Greatheed Box/11

T2705 'Tis on my God that I repose
Such is our share, our state of bliss.

[Edmund Wodehouse], 'Octr. 11 [1714]'
b.131, p. 57

T2706 'Tis one and twenty years, I've heard you say,
Wishing your first child may be a girl or a boy.

Nich[olas] Stirley, 'On Mr. Britt Bumbrige esq's
birthday'
Poetry Box IV/128

T2707 'Tis order guides and beautifies the world
Is not society but throng and crowd.

b.155, p. 62

T2708 'Tis over then: I give you joy,
And worthy them, from whom they sprung.

'To his royal highness the Elector Palatine [Karl
Theodor], at Manheim . . . Voltaire'

c.83/2, no. 690

T2709 'Tis past! Ah, calm thy cares to rest
And freedom to the slave.

'The following lines supposed to have been addressed
by an African Negro (condemned to be burnt for
attempting to regain his freedom) to his wife while he
was fastened to the stake and ready for execution'

c.391

T2710 'Tis past: another year forever gone
And lead my soul to peace—to bliss—to Thee!

'On the New Year'

c.83/1, no. 166

T2711 'Tis past—he's gone—the friendly struggle's o'er
There he remains, no more depriv'd of rest.

'Pompey's death'

c.91, p. 4

T2712 'Tis past: the iron north has spent his rage
Till the long night's gone, and the last morn rise.

[Michael Bruce], 'Elegy to spring'

c.139, p. 58; c.343, p. 98 (stanzas 16–23)

T2713 'Tis past! The sultry tyrant of the south
Unlock the glories of the world unknown.

[Anna Laetitia] (Aikin) [Barbauld], 'A summer
evening's meditations'

c.487, p. 5

T2714 'Tis pleasant safely to behold from shore,
Their beams abroad, and bring the darksome soul
to day.

[John] Dryden, trans., 'Lucretius a short fragment'
[from the beginning of Book II]
[Crum T2823]

c.244, p. 291

T2715 'Tis prayer that I desire, not praise,
Dare ev'n in that good purpose reap to himself
such end.

[Edmund Wodehouse], 'Novr. 7 [1714]'

b.131, p. 79

T2716 'Tis ruin to be caught! each jury shows
No gilding's dearer, than of c[u]ck[ol]d brows.

[Stephen Barrett], 'Kenionana. A friendly hint to all
modern adventurers in an extempore translation of a
line in Horace'

c.193, p. 149

T2717 'Tis rumor'd, the French will soon visit our coast,
Sheathe, sheathe thy sword, and give peace to the
world. | O the bold blades &c.

John Lockman, 'English bravery against French
invaders. Set to music by Mr. Worgan; and sung, by
Mr. Laws, Vauxhall Gardens, anno 1759 . . .'

c.267/2, p. 34

T2718 'Tis said a man is counted wise, so long,
If not O! take th'intention for the deed.

'An occasional prologue spoken at Newton Abbot by
C. Preyo esqr. on Tuesday Feb. the 18. 1786 to the
comedy of The beaux' strategem . . .'

c.382, p. 28

T2719 'Tis said dear Sir no poets please the town
I whisk into my coach and drive away.

Christopher Pitt, 'A l[ette]r from . . . to Mr. Robert
Lowth doing high honor to Ben Jonson poet laureate'

c.229/1, fol. 86

T2720 'Tis said for ev'ry common grief
Show Bath, like Tunbridge can inspire.

[Mary Barber?], 'To the Rt Honble the earl of Orrery'
[answered by 'Nor Bath . . .']

Poetry Box x/76

T2721 'Tis said that in Britain alone
Is he that's a slave to his passions.

W[illiam] S[mith], 'Liberty—a ballad'

Smith Papers, folder 73

T2722 'Tis said that Mercury, had once a mind
Into the bargain, I'll throw Mercury.

E[lizabeth (Shirley)] C[ompton, countess of
Northampton], 'Mercury and the carver'

Accession 97.7.40

T2723 'Tis said that our prince | Has a good deal of sense
To see all these but as they go.

'Song' [on the Lord Mayor's Day]
[Crum T2826]

fc.58, p. 45

T2724 'Tis said that our soldiers so lazy grow
Or a greater consumption of power.

'Epigram'

c.115; c.130, p. 31; c.360/1, p. 219

T2725 'Tis said when first resistless love
Of [sic] makes a man a goose.

    'Epigram'

c.360/3, no. 150

T2726 'Tis said when George did dragon slay
We'll throw up caps and loud will hollo.

    'A Westminster wedding or the town mouth' [on Sir
    George Jeffreys, June 1679]
    [Crum T2828; POAS II.351]

b.327, f. 31v

T2727 'Tis sign'd! And now no more shall martial rage,
May they (like swans) first sing and then expire.

    Charles Darby, 'On the peace of Ryswick anno. 1697'
    [Crum T2832]

fb.207/3, p. 22; see also 'The peace is sign'd . . .'.

T2728 'Tis sin to praise or weep, O let me vent
He is not cannon'd, no he's canonized.

    [Richard Love], 'An epitaph on the King of Sweden'
    [1632]
    [Crum T2833 ('pent'), with two more lines]

b.197, p. 24

T2729 'Tis so long since I took a ride
And sent them from the mount away.

    Frederick Corfield, 'The tumble'

c.381/2

T2730 'Tis sometimes best to put O before
Cupio: than spell it, I say no more.

    [Sir Francis Castillion]

fb.69, p. 191

T2731 'Tis strange that gentleman to all beholders
For sleeveless errands are his best employment.

    'Rochet [coat]s'
    [Crum T2838]

fb.106(5)

T2732 'Tis strange that he unborn ere he saw light
Grant me an honest life an happy death.

    [name cut away], 'Some experimental passages of her
    life with reflections upon Jacob's words[:] few and evil
    have the days of the years of my life been'

b.202, p. 91

T2733 'Tis strange that some people continue in vain
Let the devil lie warm and folks kiss their own
                                 ar[se]s.

    R[ichard] V[ernon] S[adleir], 'Epigram'

c.106, p. 61

T2734 'Tis strange to think, how love of riches
Because you heard, I kiss'd another.

    [Thomas Hamilton, 6th earl of Haddington], 'The
    Duke trap'

c.458/2, p. 112

T2735 'Tis strange what different thoughts inspire,
Regardless of his dying groans.

    'Desire, and possession'

c.481, p. 249

T2736 'Tis sweet to hear expiring summer's sigh
This filial token of a daughter's love.

    'Prologue'

c.340

T2737 'Tis sweet when whim and season hit
And frisk awhile on folly's tit.

    [Thomas Hull], 'Dulce est desirere in loco—
    Hor[ace]'

c.528/17

T2738 'Tis the Arabian bird alone
They would like doves and sparrows do.

    [John Wilmot], 2nd earl of Rochester(?), 'The
    encouragement'
    [Crum T2845]

c.189, p. 3; c.229/1, fol. 40

T2739 Tis the twenty-ninth of May
That they may rise, and Whigs may fall.

    'A new toast, or a ballad on the twenty-ninth of May.
    To the tune of Over the [hills and far away]' [pr. 1715
    (Foxon N233]
    [Crum T2848 (var.)]

c.570/1, p. 91

T2740 'Tis thought tall Richard first possest
Whom God grant long to reign.

    Abraham Cowley, 'The chronicle out of Cowley'

b.371, no. 30

T2741 'Tis thus I rove, 'tis thus complain,
I love, and I despair.

c.549, p. 2

T2742 'Tis to the press and pen, we mortals owe
And lov'd their native charms without your aid.

    'On the general advantage of reading and writing'

c.186, p. 91

T2743   'Tis to the vulgar death too harsh appears
And, tho' a tyrant, often liberty.

> [Sir Sameul Garth, from The dispensary (ll. 239-249
> of Canto III)]
> Trumbull Box: Poetry Box XIII/36; c.83/2, no. 710 (var.);
> c.549, p. 119

T2744   'Tis true, as some say, that to death from our birth,
With int'rest was paid by Mount Edgecombe to
                Garrick.

> [David Garrick], 'Good and evil by the same'
> Poetry Box v/119

T2745   'Tis true dear Ben thy just chastising hand
Than all men else, then thyself only less.

> [Thomas] Carew, 'Carew's answer to Ben Jonson's
> ode'
> [Crum T2857]
> b.356, p. 200

T2746   'Tis true, frail beauty, I did once resign
And gaze upon thy beatific face to all eternity.

> [John Norris, of Bemerton], 'Seraphic love'
> [Crum T2858, 'fair beauty']
> Poetry Box VII/52; c.258

T2747   'Tis true I call'd the doctor decent,
Proves him, or you without decorum.

> [William Carpenter], 'Another, on [a scurrilous ballad
> published in the General evening post]'
> c.247, p. 162

T2748   'Tis true I grant you by experience wise
The joys of wedlock I would gladly share.

> 'An epistle to Dr. D—ge in answer to me advising me
> to marry'
> Poetry Box I/68

T2749   'Tis true—in these well-polish'd lines
And our lov'd Sally now be your [own].

> 'Written in a lady's advice to a daughter'
> b.201, p. 140

T2750   'Tis true (my Phylanax) I once appear'd
Is (worse than atheism) theomachy.

> [Sir Philip Wodehouse], 'An answer prepared to your
> sense which he Philanax would have Hubert [John
> Hobart] assert'
> File 17713; c.259, p. 106

T2751   'Tis true my soul thy woes are great
And call the Lord, thy God.

> [Thomas Stevens?], 'Tuesday night at the conference
> following[:] the believer advising his soul to hope in
> God'
> c.259, p. 106

T2752   'Tis true my sufferings lately were complete,
And can with comfort boast another heart entire.

> 'Bri: Apol: fo. 45'
> c.549, p. 48

T2753   'Tis true of marriage bands I'm weary grown,
For there's a godlike liberty in love.

> c.189, p. 74

T2754   'Tis true, our life is but a long disease,
Ere we can call it ours.

> [Katherine Philips, 'Song to the tune of Adieu
> Phyllis']
> [Crum T2866]
> b.118, p. 81

T2755   'Tis true, some marry twice;
I ne'er shall find her peer.

> T[homas] M[orell], 'An epitaph . . . on the wife of the
> Rev: J. Mickleborough . . . translated in trimeters'
> c.395, p. 123

T2756   'Tis true 'tis break of day, what though it be?
Such wrong, as when a married man doth woo.

> [John Donne, in 'Break of day', following 'Stay O
> sweet . . .']
> [Crum T2871]
> fb.88, p. 120; b.205, fol. 25r ("Tis true 'tis day')

T2757   'Tis true to set oneself apart,
Whose heart the spirit sanctifies.

> [Edmund Wodehouse], 'Apr. 21 [1715]'
> b.131, p. 201

T2758   'Tis true unknowing of the distant coast
And be for once the gallant of the age.

> 'Sylvia's complaint to Cato' [on the South Seas bubble,
> c. 1720]
> c.360/1, p. 205

T2759   'Tis true, you o'er from Holland came,
Into a lump of tinder.

> 'Answer to riddle on page 54' ['With youth and
> perfect beauty . . .']
> c.578, p. 91

T2760   'Tis uncouth and ridiculous to see
Now it concerns them, to make peace with heav'n.

> [Sir Philip Wodehouse], 'Essay Charon de sequel
> (?) . . .'
> b.131, p. 27

T2761 'Tis vain to add a string or gem
Now tell me which the softer be.

    [William Strode], 'An ear string'
    [Crum T2876]

b.205, fol. 31v

T2762 'Tis vain to weep or in a rhyming spite
Of purer shadows lives the prince of ghosts.

    [William Cartwright?], 'On the death of King
    Charles his first son . . .' [May 1629]
    [Crum T2878]

b.62, p. 70

T2763 'Tis weak and worldly to conclude
All endless life when this is done.

    'On retirement'

c.83/2, no. 294

T2764 'Tis whisper'd, by a little fairy,
To 'scape these traps—my dear wife marry.

    John Lockman, 'Look sharp (the Lilliputian style) . . .
    March 1758'

c.267/1, p. 219

T2765 'Tis winter, cold, and rude
And where thy writings point thy action's guide.

    'What shall I read? An ode, 1780'

fc.53, p. 13

T2766 'Tis wisely done, you sons of Wadham,
Your punishment's the same.

    [Gloster Ridley]

Spence Papers, folder 127

T2767 'Tis—with reluctance I obey
How blest, for thee to die!

    Charles Burney, the younger, 'An epistle from Edwin
    to Angelina . . . December. 1779'

c.35, p. 7

T2768 'Tis written in thy name good Miss prepare
Christ make him henceforth thy heav'nly sovereign.

    [Sir Philip Wodehouse], 'Upon his neighbor [Mary
    Repps] 1680 at Easter being to receive'

b.131, back (no. 126, no. 226)

T2769 'Tis years one hundred thirty three,
'I bless my Fanny's natal day!'

    'To a young person on her birthday'

c.504, p. 214

T2770 'Tis you fair ladies I address,
Can tremble and adhere.

    'Another [rebus]'

Diggle Box: Poetry Box XI/71

'Tis you upholds the flourish of that stem
The famous crescent of that noble race.   T2771

    Sir Thomas Urquhart, 'To the Earl of Winton'

fb.217, p. 98

'Tis your request, my friend, that I the way
That the poor wretch may starve, who dares be just.   T2772

    'The art of thriving'

c.360/2, no. 132

Titus affronts Valerius—he straight   T2773
They both were saviors of each other's life.

    [Sir Philip Wodehouse], 'A romantic or Rhodamantic
    flash sent to Mr. J. Hob[ar]t and his return . . .'

b.131, p. 40

To a friend so sincere, to a comrade so gay   T2774
And green be the laurel that waves o'er his tomb.

    'On the death of a friend . . . Etonensis'

c.373, p. 59

To a king and no king, an uncle and father,   T2775
A health to my landlord his wife and his son Sir.

    'The royal health'

b.111, p. 35; fb.207/2, p. 45

To a rebellious house I'm sent from far   T2776
Have rent and torn the rebels hearts asunder.

    'The curate of Wickware [Mr. Sanderson]'

b.111, p. 118

To a sweet note the fowler's pipe is set   T2777
When he the bird, betrays into his net.

fb.151/3

To a thing much in use for winnowing corn,   T2778
Altho' charming in person, more charming in mind.

    'A rebus'

fc.85, fol. 108

To a weak and watery sun,   T2779
And then is swept away.

    [ ] Kingsman, 'Lines on the death of Miss L.
    Kingsman [a young lady aged 16] . . . set to music by
    Miss Kingsman—April 1791'

c.373, p. 64, 83

To all, and to singular, in this great meeting,   T2780
For assistance retire.

    'The inspirations'

fb.107, p. 66

T2781 To all clergy in this land
Pray give our service to your wives.

    'The pastoral' [pr. 1719 (Foxon P112, 'To all the
    clergy . . .')]

    c.570/2, p. 39

T2782 To all gen'rous Britons I sound this endeavor
Then swanlike will sing out my final adieu.

    'Old Leveridge the comedian of Covent Garden
    Theater's whimsical advertise[ment] 1751. On
    Wednesday April the 24 The city wives' confederacy
    will be acted for my benefit'

    c.360/3, no. 98

T2783 To all loyal subjects good tidings I bring
Shall be when govern'd by our lady.

    'A song to the tune of The black lady' [Jacobite; pr.
    1745? (Foxon E567)]

    c.275

T2784 To all our haunts I will repair
Whilst round thou didst enfold me.

    Peggy Trevor

    c.358, p. 142

T2785 To all our sisters now at Rome
You'll be welcome both to church and King.

    'An epistle from the ladies of Drury, to those at Rome'
    [temp. George I]
    [Crum T2890]

    c.570/2, p. 154

T2786 To all those liv'rymen of London,
As did these whelps, just so will you. | With &c.

    'Lord Wharton's puppies to the tune of To all ye
    ladies now at land' [pr. 1734 (Foxon L262)]

    c.570/4, p. 84

T2787 To all ye fair females that sometimes partake
For a saint might take part out without any blemish.

    'The Bath pudding a riddle'
    [Crum T2892]

    c.148, p. 6

T2788 To all ye ladies now at land
We have too much of that at sea.

    [Charles Sackville, 6th earl of Dorset]
    [Crum T2893]

    c.358, p. 173

T2789 To all ye men of sense in town
Shall look their fathers in the face. | With a fa la
                           de de.

    'The country lass's challenge. To the tune of To all ye
    ladies now at land'

    Poetry Box IV/93

T2790 To all ye merchants now at land
For Dunkirk's friends are Britain's foes.

    'The sailors' song, or, Dunkirk restored. To the tune
    of To ye ladies' [pr. 1730 (Foxon S16)]

    c.570/3, p. 97

T2791 To all ye Tories far from court,
So you're to blame if unprepared.

    'A song by the Earl of Dorset' [i.e., in imitation of his
    'To all ye ladies now at land'. Jacobite; pr.1714/15
    (Foxon N125)]
    [Crum T2894]

    fc.58, p. 72; Poetry Box x/50 ('All you'); c.570/1, p. 75

T2792 To an old ruin—desolate!
A penny sav'd's a penny got.

    [Phanuel Bacon], 'Cum deirit egenti as laquis pretium'

    c.237, fol. 81

T2793 To answer a letter it must be conceived [the first
                                      thing to do]
This word, 'tis an [FS]—and my [our] answer is
                                      finished.

    Lady F[rances](S[cott) Douglas, baroness Douglas]

    Poetry Box III/folder 21-30

T2794 To any, that inquires of your profession,
More from a Cath'lic faith, than love must flow.

    Sir Thomas Urquhart, 'To a certain woman, who was
    both of a Catholic religion, and carriage'

    fb.217, p. 350

T2795 To Apollo of old when young Phaeton came,
To prove none can rule like—the god of the day. |
                                  Fol, de, sol &c.

    Capt. [Charles] Morris, 'Capt. Morris's song made for
    Mr. Fox's birthday Jan. 24th'

    Smith Papers, folder 74

T2796 To Apollo, their king, at fam'd Helicon's court,
'Gainst the sons of true genius and friends of the
                                    Nine.

    [William Boscawen], 'Song. Sung [by Mr Sedgwick] at
    the anniversary dinner of the subscribers to the
    Literary Fund. 12 May 1796. Air—The sons of
    Anacreon.'

    fc.106, p. 29

T2797 To assume importance ev'ry Frenchman tries,
He's never half so empty or so foolish.

    [Charles Burney, the elder], 'From La Fontaine's fable
    of the mole and the elephant . . . translated'

    c.33, p. 138 (crossed out)

T2798 To atone for long absence, great ruler of day,
And shine forth this ev'ning, warm, cheerful and
fair.

'To the sun on shutting up Vauxhall Gardens
Thursday Sep. 14. 1752'
c.360/3, no. 231

T2799 To b'as Penelope, chaste, and religious,
Was once a proverb: but 'tis now prodigious.

Sir Thomas Urquhart, 'A Penelopean faith'
fb.217, p. 184

T2800 To be let on a lease for the term of my life
For further particulars pray inquire within.

'Advertisement'
c.81/1, no. 294

T2801 To be merry and wise, Mr. Fog,
And show the biter bit.

'To Fog. A ballad'
[Crum T2907 (var.)]
c.570/3, p. 128

T2802 To be of high birth, and of worthy fame,
Let his descent be mean, his worth's the more.

[John Rose?]
b.227, p. 77

T2803 To be surpassing good, you want but will:
And you lack naught but power to do ill.

Sir Thomas Urquhart, 'To a depravedly disposed man
of small authority'
fb.217, p. 189

T2804 To be the last of this first book of epigrams
That for their money they some laughter get.

[Sir Aston Cokayne], 'To his book'
b.275, p. 14

T2805 To be thought sweet what care Sir Fulsome shows
For the perfume dear knight you want within.

'To a very sweet knight'
fb.142, p. 58

T2806 To bear the labors of the war,
And blast the towering mind.

'The second ode of the third book of Horace . . . 1760'
fc.74, p. 5

T2807 To beat a poor whelp
And then lays a tax upon mum.

'On reading that the bill laws pass'd for granting
duties on malt—mum &c.'
Greatheed Box/102

T2808 To bed fair bride your happy groom
What heaven can give or lovers crave.

[Sir Aston Cokayne], 'On the Marriage of Mr. Francis
Shalcross, and Mrs Julia Boteler, my niece'
b.275, p. 75

T2809 To bed to bed sweet turtles now and write
Sport they never knew before.

'That which is wanting of the epithalamium in your
black book'
b.356, p. 228

T2810 To believe little is a fault, and such
As 'tis an error, to believe too much.

Sir Thomas Urquhart, 'Of faults, and errors in matters
of faith'
fb.217, p. 344

T2811 To bid the world a long farewell,
O shield from wrong their helpless age!

'Supposed to have been written by the late
unfortunate queen of France, the night before her
suffering'
c.83/2, no. 278

T2812 To black the soul by various strokes of dirt,
And learn to value what you buy so dear.

'Prologue, to be spoken by Mr. Russell at the opening
of his puppet show in Hugford's room. 1745'
fc.51, p. 71

T2813 To bless thy God, my soul, be thou inclin'd
Whilst breath doth last, thy goodness I'll repeat.

John Belcham, 'The following lines were composed
by . . . Clerk of Ribbenhall Chapel in Worcestershire,
who has been blind ever since he was a child of six
weeks old'
c.111, p. 168

T2814 To bounteous nature, sense and wit you owe;
Oh enter! And enjoy the promis'd land.

John Lockman, 'Writ in the blank leaf of a fourth
edition of Telemachus, prepared by my eldest daughter
and I. to Miss Nancy Jansson . . . Decr 1752'
c.267/1, p. 50

T2815 To bow before that sov'reign power,
Where sin and sorrow cease.

'An ode'
c.83/3, no. 913

T2816 To brave the danger, bear each toil,
And rule by seeming to obey.

'The sexes'
c.175, p. 72

T2817   To Britons dear, late may he fill the throne,
And noblest bards their high achievements sing.

> John Lockman, 'Frederick . . . 1749'

c.267/1, p. 255

T2818   To brush the cheeks of ladies fair
Amongst their loves and graces?

> [Christopher Anstey], 'To a lady who asked the author
> the reason why the men have left off weaving beards as
> they were used to do in former times'

File 17461

T2819   To call me traitor Liza,
It was before your face.

> Sir Thomas Urquhart, 'To one named Elizabeth, who
> had called him traitor, he having robbed her, as she
> alleged of her maidenhead'

fb.217, p. 355

T2820   To call the long past ages back to view,
And Charonea's fields at Oudenarde renew'd.

> John Whaley, 'An essay on painting: written ab[out]
> 1730 by . . . and printed with some explanatory notes
> [in] the first copy of the collection of his poems.
> Lond[o]n . . . 1732. To this transcript some additions
> are made, and more notes by M[aurice] Johnson . . .'

c.229/1, fol. 109

T2821   To care and trouble man is born
When they are turn'd to dust.

> 'An epitaph for Mr. Xxx'

Poetry Box I/46

T2822   To carve our loves in myrtle rinds
Where eyes do fail there souls begin.

b.213, p. 48

T2823   To celebrate the charms of May,
When quaffing from that silver spring.

> John Lockman, 'After drinking a glass of German spa,
> from Fiddes's mineral-water warehouse, in Tavistock
> Street, Covent Garden . . . May 1753'

c.267/1, p. 79

T2824   To celebrate thy praise, O Lord,
Our strength and Savior's rest. | Hallelujah.

> 'An hymn. Made by a young lady'

c.167, p. 13

T2825   To celebrate ('tis said) the best of men,
Who can it be but good Northumberland?

> John Lockman, 'Hearing the bells right, at the return
> of a nobleman from his seat in the country Sept. 2.
> 1766'

c.267/1, p. 394

T2826   To charity she lends a list'ning ear,
Cobblers and priests and priests and cobblers live.

> [Horace Walpole, 4th earl of Orford], 'C[ountes]s of
> Huntingd[o]n'

c.157, p. 68

T2827   To Charles: who is the example and the law
By whom the good are taught not kept in awe.

> [Sir William D'Avenant]

fb.66/34

T2828   To charming Celia's arms I flew
A runlet of night, Nancy.

> [Sir William Trumbull], 'Epi. 64 12 . . . Mar[tial]'

Trumbull Box: Poetry Box XIII/53 (stanzas 1–2), 40
(stanzas 3–5)

T2829   To cheat the public two contractors came
A rogue in spirit or a rogue in grain.

> 'On the two At[kinso]ns M. P. (one stood in the
> pillory for perjury on account of a contract he had
> with government for supplying wheat for the navy and
> the other took advantage of the minister in a large
> contract for rum)'
> [Crum T2918]

c.250

T2830   To choose the round, the square he did disdain;
For God made rounds: but squares were fram'd by
                                 men.

> Sir Thomas Urquhart, 'Of King Arthur's round table'

fb.217, p. 126

T2831   To Coleshill seat of noble peer
But of the court no more but mum!

> [Anne Finch, countess of Winchilsea, to Catherine
> Fleming at the Lord Digby's, Dec. 1718]
> [Crum T2923]

c.188, p. 63; Accession 97.7.40

T2832   To come down by one step's enough for any:
But to ascend at court you must need many.

> Sir Thomas Urquhart, 'The sale of promotion'

fb.217, p. 216

T2833   To court an humble shepherd came
Love moved him much | But more despair.

b.213, p. 111

T2834   To covet wealth I never was inclin'd
Upon and put my virtue(?) in exercise.

> [Sir Thomas Urquhart], 'The expression of a noble
> gentleman in how far he was affected with wealth'

fb.217, p. 523

T2835   To Cupid alone long penance I've done
Than all we can find in a Phyllis's arms.

> 'A song'

c.374

T2836   To curb our joys with vain pretense
When we, alas! shall cease to be.

> Captain Henry Berkeley, 'Translation of the regent's
> song L'austere philosophie'

fc.135

T2837   To Dagon's feast came the princes under whose
                         command
And many thousands died by the fall.

c.158, p. 31

T2838   To damn, or not—that is the question now,
Then hunt him, critics, he'll be noble game.

> [David] Garrick, 'Prologue to Eugenia, acted at Drury
> Lane Theater in February 1752. Written and spoken by
> Mr. Garrick'

c.360/3, no. 193

T2839   To dance after canons, like courtiers, hard fate!
And canons—to dine, I may—kiss your hare's foot.

> [Charles Earle], 'To a friend in the country, from
> Exeter, where I was long detained for an answer
> concerning a curacy. Extempore'

c.376

T2840   To dance or not to dance—that is the question:
Than dance to publish them.

> 'Written in a ballroom at Oxford 1779'

Diggle Box: Poetry Box XI/46

T2841   To death's dark regions paths unnumber'd lead,
And those whose satire wounds a fair one's name.

> John Lockman, 'Psyche's descent to the infernal
> regions' [translated from La Fontaine]

c.267/4, p. 251

T2842   To desert walls and lowly roofs confin'd
I wake and find my sorrow all renewed.

> 'To the same [Miranda]' [Ewelme, 31 Jan. 1735/6]

Poetry Box I/49

T2843   To die is nature's debt, and when
The captain's rapier or their art.

> [William Strode], 'On Mr [Francis] Lancaster run
> through by a captain'
> [Crum T2933]

b.205, fol. 29r

T2844   . . . To die within her arms in pleasure
But the de'il take me if e'er I do.

Poetry Box X/122 (incomplete; last lines of Poetry Box
X/44)

T2845   To dignities, as none should e'er ascend
Tho' silent I, all Cambridgeshire would tell.

> 'On Henry Bromley esqr [1st baron Montfort],
> member of Parliament for Cambridgeshire, being
> created a peer—1741'

c.360/1, p. 123

T2846   To Doric hymns lute let us raise
In his divinity divine.

> [Thomas Stanley], 'The hymns of Synesius. Hymn: I'

b.152, p. 123

T2847   To dote upon our hour is in vain;
Uncertain comforts, tho' time certain be.

> 'Lyncup Hill, 6th Aug. [17]82. J[oh]n Rutherford'

c.93

T2848   To drink of Clifton's healing spring,
And draw the arrow from my heart.

> John Lockman, 'Chloe at the Hot Well . . . 1749'

c.267/1, p. 69

T2849   To each thing its fit reason is assign'd
And so excuseless makes impiety.

> [John Taylor], 'The apology' [from 'The world
> turned upside down']

fb.40, p. 407

T2850   To earth, could our first parents reascend,
Think they, again, their darling Eden tread.

> John Lockman, 'Seeing the beautiful collection of
> birds &c: exhibiting at the great room, Spring
> Gardens'

c.267/1, p. 385

T2851   To ease affliction and to soothe distress
And what was Henry thus may George be now.

> W[illiam] Smith, 'Prologue to Henry 5th at the
> opening Covent Garden Theater after the death of his
> late Majesty George the 2nd . . . Nov. 17th 1760'

Smith Papers, folder 54

T2852   To ease thy mind, here I again restore
None will that purchase make, but at last pray'r.

> [Mrs. Christian Kerr], 'From a young lady upon
> restoring a ring that was put upon her finger in jest by
> way of a marriage ring' [answered by 'It eases not my
> mind . . .']

c.102, p. 93

T2853   To Egypt's fam'd book-room affix'd was the scroll
Who dispenses true physic and food for the mind.

> 'On newspapers. Written soon after Lord
> Mountstuart's Ad[mira]l Palliser's and General
> Burgoyne's letters. &c.'

c.89, p. 129

T2854   To Eliphaz thus answer'd Job and said
Cannot judge what's right and what is wrong?

> Sir John Strangways, 'The sixth chapter of Job
> translated into verse by J. S. 9no August: 1645'

b.304, p. 47

T2855   To emulate Amphion's praise
Being neither Buck nor Stone.

> 'The Opera House, built by Sir Jno. Vanbrugh, not at
> first succeeding induced the directors to send for
> Nicolini and Valentina, which occasioned the
> following epigram'

c.546, p. 1

T2856   To end I judge pleasure but scant
So good as a contented mind.

> [Sir Nicholas] Bacon, 'The conclusion'

fa.8, fol. 165

T2857   To enliven this circle you ask for a strain,
How may have what will soon make him how came
you so.

> 'Song 5'

c.555, p. 3

T2858   To ev'ry eye, that saw her, she was dainty,
In one, wherein no other good was seen.

> Sir Thomas Urquhart, 'On the Countess of [crossed
> out]'

fb.217, p. 239

T2859   To ev'ryone your merit so appears,
Sublime perfections in a riper age.

> Sir Thomas Urquhart, 'To the Earl of [crossed out]'

fb.217, p. 270

T2860   To factious malice virtue must give place
Whose charms can make a court why know [i.e.,
know why?] they shine.

> 'To the Duchess of Q—gh' [Queensberry]

c.188, p. 83.

T2861   To fairest looks trust not too far; nor yet to beauty
brave;
For hateful thoughts so finely mask'd, their deadly
poison have.

c.189, p. 28

T2862   To fame and to fortune adieu!
The richest on this side the grave!

> 'Birthday soliloquy'

Poetry Box XII/124

T2863   To fast for our sins, why it's decent enough
But I wish it would give us a stomach to fight.

c.150, p. 127

T2864   To Father, Son, and Spirit be,
And all blest saints in heav'n.

> 'The doxology'

c.264/3, p. 127

T2865   To feed on flesh is gluttony
With one light dish of smoke.

> 'Abstemiousness, the praise of tobacco'

b.200, p. 94

T2866   To fill an honest man is free
Restore me to my master.

> [John Rose?]

b.227, p. 99

T2867   To fill the measure of his widespread fame
Both starv'd the whole dramatic world to come.

> 'On hearing that Mr. Garrick intended to have played
> Hamlet this evening but revoked his design in order to
> give a benefit to an unfortunate person—impromptu'

c.341, p. 89

T2868   To find a poet, that is good, is rare:
Nor king, nor man, hath ever yet enjoyed.

> Sir Thomas Urquhart, 'To King James the Sixth'

fb.217, p. 94

T2869   To find out my first e'en Erskine would try,
And I heartily wish you to take it.

> [ ] Crabtree, '[Charade] 87 . . . by Mr. Cabtree—alias
> Crabtree' [pleasure]

c.389; see also 'To make out . . .'.

T2870   To five compositors I owe my frame
What the proud peer and peasant soon will be.

> 'Another [rebus]'

Diggle Box: Poetry Box XI/71

T2871   To follow nature wheresoe'er she leads,
And each soul glow with everlasting fire.

> Henry Baker, 'The duty of a poet'

c.244, p. 404

T2872 To foreign notes whilst others tune their lyre,
And give to jarring nations laws and peace.

> Miss [ ] Jones, 'To the Prince of Orange'
> Spence Papers, folder 113

T2873 To France, forbid it heav'n! O! wish no more
The gen'rous influence of Eliza's care.

> 'To Eliza, on her design of going to France July 1749'
> c.360/3, no. 49

T2874 To friend and foe
Then let not the charges dismay thee.

> 'Song 95'
> c.555, p. 143

T2875 To friendly Talman give, (indulgent fates!)
And vain, without it, were a monarch's wealth.

> John Lockman, 'A wish: to the reverend Mr. Talman
> of Salisbury . . . Dec. 1758'
> c.267/1, p. 219

T2876 To gain dishonor and immense disgrace
'Tis better to destroy than thus to build!

> H[enry] Hall, organist of Hereford Cathedral, 'To Sir
> Christopher Wren on his building St Paul's'
> c.233, p. 87

T2877 To gain the callous Walter's heart
And marriage worse than murder.

> 'Song 115'
> c.555, p. 166

T2878 To give a poignancy to taste,
And all the bear be done away!

> R[ichard] V[ernon] S[adleir], 'To a lady who
> presented me caviar and bears' tongues'
> c.106, p. 93

T2879 To give or take I use my right hand; why?
Lest what my right hand doth my left should spy.

> 'The right hand'
> c.356

T2880 To give such privilege to fools
'Tis to encourage bedlam's schools.

> [Edmund Wodehouse], 'June 28 [1715] on acceptance
> of Quakers' affirmation in lieu of an oath'
> b.131, p. 227

T2881 To give the last amendment to the bill
And the thin form their wand'ring eyes forsook.

> [Henry Hall, of Hereford? or Matthew Prior?], 'Et tu
> Brute?' [A consultation of the bishops concerning the
> bill on occasional conformity; 1703; pr. 1704? (Foxon
> E479)]
> [Crum T2961; POAS VI.510]
> c.111, p. 26; c.189, p. 150; b.204, p. 30

T2882 To give us empire o'er the sea,
Worthy their country and their king.

> John Lockman, 'A patriot toast, extempore . . . March
> 1757'
> c.267/1, p. 215

T2883 To God and Him alone,
And when he crieth God will hear.

> Charles Atherton Allnutt, '5 Job 8 v.—I would seek
> unto God and unto God would I commit my cause'
> c.112, p. 44

T2884 To God I'll ever seek to appear
And all that he commands, obey.

> [Edmund Wodehouse], 'Novr. 6 [1714]'
> b.131, p. 78

T2885 To God, my country and my friends I'm true
So in my name thrice honest written view.

> [Sir Philip Wodehouse], 'My epigram upon my cousin
> Coke's anagram Robertus Long . . .'
> b.131, back (no. 166)

T2886 To God our strength triumphing sing
They to satiety had eat.

> 'Psal: 81'
> b.217, p. 26

T2887 To God our strength your voices raise
When erst I brought a tide.

> 'Psalm 81 16 day'
> c.264/2, p. 72

T2888 To God supreme let everything
Before our maker and our King.

> Henry Baker, 'A hymn of praise'
> c.244, p. 404

T2889 To God the glory! peace on earth,
Most high forevermore!

> [Isaac Watts, Hymn]
> c.180, p. 38

T2890 To God, to prince, wife, kindred, friend, the poor
He that so liv'd, and so deceas'd, lies here.

'Proba Valeria Falconia a Roman matron (wife to
Adelphus Romanus Proconsul) writ on her husband's
tomb'

fb.143, p. 4

T2891 To God who guards me all the night
Th'almighty Maker's hand.

'Thoughts at first waking'

c.186, p. 37

T2892 To grace the Long Room the two sexes vie,
For balls, a palace: and for prayers—a stable!

John Lockman, 'Sundays, at the Hot Well, Bristol . . .
1747'

c.267/1, p. 65

T2893 To grow at once a doctor and a spouse
Before we enter, should our lives employ.

R[obert] Shirley, 1st earl of Ferrers, 'Upon a physician
that received a doctor's degree and a wife. From the
French'

c.347, p. 93

T2894 To H—— observes a certain friend
The poor too lose a dinner.

'On a gentleman who was always impatient of losing at
cards'

c.546, p. 20

T2895 To Hackfall's calm retreat where nature reigns
And bid this folly-fettered world adieu.

[Sir Walter] Scott, 'Hackfall an elegy to Neara'
Poetry Box v/6

T2896 To heal a wound a bee had made
The sting within my heart.

[Philip Dormer Stanhope], 4th earl of Chesterfield(?),
'Written by the late Ld. Chesterfield'
[Crum T2976]

Smith Papers, folder 74/19

T2897 To hear old Martha wheeze and cough,
And shams to give you pleasure.

c.83/2, no. 388

T2898 To hear thee, in a sweetly-solemn strain,
Kept back his sword, and sooth'd her piercing grief.

John Lockman, 'To Mr Beard: after hearing him sing,
in Mr. Hugford's great room, in David's lamentation
over Saul and Jonathan, writ by the author . . . Feb.
1741/2'

c.267/1, p. 188

T2899 To heaven and you repentant I confess
And furies snatch thee from the realms of light.

'The complaint—An epistle from a young lady'

c.83/3, no. 994

T2900 To help man, being the end of her creation,
Which never was accomplish'd yet without her.

Sir Thomas Urquhart, 'That the chief end of a
woman's being on earth, next to the glory of God, is
casual copulation. A paradox'

fb.217, p. 220

T2901 To him the sacred lyre they gave,
Add luster to thy country's name.

'The nature of genius by the muses . . . inscribed to
the members of the Royal Academy'

c.83/2, no. 503

T2902 To hope the best or fear the worst
That persuades the worst in all events.

[Sir Nicholas] Bacon, 'Of hope, fear, and persuasion'
fa.8, fol. 165v

T2903 To horse! To horse! Yourselves equip
Mine makes me sing, who never sung before.

'Dulce domum. In imitation of Mr. Pope's Ode on St.
Cecilia's Day'

c.241, p. 102

T2904 To horse, ye jolly sportsman
Revive the chase at night. | And a hunting &c.

'Song 26'

c.555, p. 32

T2905 To hug yourself in perfect ease
A longer or a shorter lease.

'Song 205'

c.555, p. 332

T2906 To hunt or not to hunt—that is the question,
Propitious smile, and vanish ev'ry doubt.

'Parody of the celebrated soliloquy in Shakespeare's
Hamlet'

c.360/3, no. 247; c.382, p. 58

T2907 To injured troops thus gallant Brunswick spoke,
Resolv'd to save her, or resolv'd to die.

'Speech of Prince Ferdinand of Brunswick to the
Hanoverian and Hessian troops' [battle of Minden,
1759 (?)]
[Crum T2994]

c.186, p. 53

T2908   To jealous love, and injur'd honor's ear
Death shall divorce me from myself and thee.

     [Charles Beckingham], 'Calista to Altamont . . .
     [Catharine Tatton Neville,] Lady Abergavenny to her
     lord' [printed 1729 (Foxon B135)]

     Poetry Box v/79; see also 'Then Altamont . . .'.

T2909   To John I ow'd great obligation
Sure John and I are more than quit.

     [Matthew] Prior, 'Epigram the obligation requited'
     [Crum T2996]

     c.144, p. 79

T2910   To keep a moderation in our diet
And feasts kill more than Galen ever cured.

     [Sir Thomas Urquhart], 'A temperate diet is the best
     physic'

     fb.217, p. 533

T2911   To keep ill-gotten goods strong houses cannot serve
For God can waste such pelf and make the owner
                               starve.

     c.339, p. 320

T2912   To keep my gentle Bessy
Of honey all the year.

     'Song 128'

     c.555, p. 183

T2913   To kneel with devotion, to vow, and to sigh,
And if this be not love—oh! I wonder what is.

     [Thomas Hull], 'Song 1st for Emily, in All in the
     right'

     c.528/14

T2914   To know a true dunghill this maxim prevails
For he's sure to have somewhere a Whitelock
                               about him.

     [Hester Lynch Thrale Piozzi], 'Epigram Genl
     W[hitelock]'

     fc.14/8

T2915   To lament me and mourn my sad case,
And well pretty Polly may sorrow.

     Mrs. [ ] Morgan, 'Mrs. Morgan to Mrs. Bentley with
     Miss Polly Parrot's compliments Stourfield House
     Oct. 29th, 1795'

     fc.40

T2916   To lampoon ladies thus for everything
And sav'd some virgins whom he never knew.

     'An answer, to the satire on Tunbridge Wells or, a
     whip, a whip, poor Pug lashed for spoiling the best
     parlor, 1680'

     b.54, p. 1131

T2917   To late old age from early youth,
At sixty than at thirty-nine.

     'To Stella. October 22. 1750'

     c.238, p. 1

T2918   To lay the soul that loves him low,
And make thee his delight.

     [William Cowper, trans.], 'God hides his people.
     Vol. 4. Son: 42' [of Jeanne Guion's 'Spiritual songs']

     c.470 (autogr.)

T2919   To learned Mead, thus Hanmer spoke
Snatch'd up a charcoal, and wrote.

     W[illia]m Murray, 'Epigram, on Shakespeare's
     pointing to a blank scroll on his monument [in
     Westminster Abbey]'

     c.360/1, p. 133

T2920   To Leicester House well-known of fame
And gave admittance to the dame.

     Poetry Box v/99

T2921   To Leonilla, Acon told his flame,
That both alike their equal pains should share.

     'Agens and patiens sunt simul. Translated from an
     epigram in Bourn's poems. The effects of matrimony'

     c.94

T2922   To little or no purpose I spent many days
I cannot deny what I know will undo me.

     [Sir George Etherege], 'The rambling lady' [song in
     She would if she could, v.i]
     [Crum T3004b]

     fb.107, p. 30

T2923   To live with ease, you must at virtue level
But dissolution full of pains and travail.

     [Sir Thomas Urquhart], 'That contentment reposeth
     nowhere but in virtue'

     fb.217, p. 512

T2924   To look like an angel the ladies believe
The blessings far greater to look like a Fury.

     'Epigram on a Miss Fury, a noted beauty'

     c.546, p. 1; c.391, p. 43

T2925   To love and social joys let's sing
Which as our sires their offspring must obey.

     M[aurice] J[ohnson], '1739. An ode for the celebration
     of the anniversary of the institution of the
     Gentlemen's Society in Spalding Lincolnshire
     composed by . . . founder and first secretary . . .'

     c.229/2, fol. 43

T2926 To Luke we must a double honor give
Greater by which so many learnt to die.

> [Robert Cholmeley], 'Epig., thus translated upon St Luke med. physician and evangelist'

c.190, p. 36

T2927 To madness, Swift bequeaths his whole estate,
Great wits to madness are most near allied.

> 'Epigram. Dean Swift intending his fortune to build a madhouse'

Poetry Box XIV/197

T2928 To make a fable keen and terse,
To scalp you all if you transgress.

> 'A love letter to the monthly reviewers published in the St James's chronicle'

Poetry Box IV/87

T2929 To make a rout or not, that is the question;
Card tables, plate, and candlesticks not my own.

> 'A soliloquy found among a lady's papers in Berks. D. Ad. to Winds. ladie[s]'

fc.85, fol. 83v

T2930 To make man wise, his age will not suffice;
For death o'ertakes him ere he can be wise.

> Sir Thomas Urquhart, 'Ars longa, vita brevis'

fb.217, p. 104

T2931 To make myself for that employment fit
None can so well instruct me as the Lord Mohun.

> 'Instructions to a young statesman'
> [Crum T3022]

fb.140, p. 138

T2932 To make new converts truly blest,
His convert launch'd beneath the ice.

> 'The monk and Jew. A tale'

fc.85, fol. 102

T2933 To make out my first, in Easter would try
And I heartily wish you to take it.

> [Four charades (2)]

Poetry Box II/42/2; see also 'To find out . . .'.

T2934 To make the doubt clear, that no woman's true
For though' tis got by chance 'tis kept by art.

> [John Donne], 'Elegy'
> [Crum T3023]

b.148, p. 90; b.197, p. 31 (ll. 1–68)

T2935 To make these numbers please thy tuneful ear,
The consort ended with his creature man.

> [Robert Cholmeley], 'The harmony of the Creation'

c.190, p. 196

T2936 To make this out, is somewhat hard
Makes ev'ry place, his habitation be.

> [Sir Philip Wodehouse], 'Upon Tom Reeve . . . ever's at home'

b.131, back (no. 174)

T2937 To man lewd lust bringeth these ills
A number of naughtiness to man it send.

> [Sir Nicholas] Bacon, 'Against lust'

fa.8, fol. 161

T2938 To me, had kind propitious heaven,
Why—e'en come here, and write a better.

> [Isaac Freeman], 'Epistle IIII. To Doctor MacKenzie from the Lazaretto at Leghorn'

fc.105

T2939 To me he is abhorred like death
Whose heart accords not with his breath.

> 'This is the poem of a very good author'

b.206, p. 133

T2940 To me it very odd appears,
I wish you well, at Aberdeen.

> [Thomas Hamilton, 6th earl of Haddington], 'The almanac from Boccace'

c.458/2, p. 1

T2941 To me, the vainest coxcomb then,
What's Phoebe's lyre without his skill.

> [David Garrick], 'Upon a golden pen'

File 19021

T2942 To mean self-interest ever blind,
Will, for thy faithless friends atone.

> John Lockman, 'The juncture . . . Feb. 20, 1761'

c.267/1, p. 320

T2943 To meditate on death, whilst well,
This may dispel all damps of fear.

> [Edmund Wodehouse], 'Apr. 20 [1715]'

b.131, p. 200

T2944 To meet her sweetheart at the fair
Or else the devil's in't—I swear.

> 'The inquiry'

c.241, p. 78

T2945 To Mister Newell—this with speed
Was hasting—hurrying—to her dinner.

> [Charles Earle?]

c.376

T2946　To mortal sight thy bended bow
　　　　'Tis lodg'd within my bleeding heart.

　　　　　'Lines on a young lady at a ball who wore a bow and
　　　　　arrow set in diamonds in her hair'

　　　　　c.546

T2947　To mourn, o'er thee, I['ll] not invoke the nine,
　　　　And heav'n's high arch with hallelujahs rung.

　　　　　John Lockman, 'To the manes of Mr. Handel on
　　　　　hearing the Messiah'

　　　　　c.267/1, p. 271

T2948　To mourn the much lamented friend whose virtue
　　　　　　　　　　　　　　　　　　　　　　　　　　truth
　　　　And joys that will remain, when time shall cease.

　　　　　'On the death of a much lamented friend who died in
　　　　　the 22nd year of his age'

　　　　　c.83/1, no. 80

T2949　To my B[ess] Sarney quintessence of beauty
　　　　Fold up thy clothes that I may kiss thy bumkin.

　　　　　Step[hen?] Loc[ket?], 'Step. Loc. to his Mistress B.
　　　　　Sarney'
　　　　　[Crum T3037]

　　　　　b.62, p. 103

T2950　To my best my friends are free;
　　　　When uneasy, free to go.

　　　　　'Inscription over the chimney of a gentleman's dining
　　　　　room near Bansley in Yorkshire—vive la liberte'

　　　　　c.139, p. 565; c.487, p. 30; c.94

T2951　To Neptune, Bacchus: Mars, t'Apollo join,
　　　　For learning tempers wars: as water wine.

　　　　　Sir Thomas Urquhart, 'That soldiers should be
　　　　　scholars'

　　　　　fb.217, p. 277

T2952　To Nev's a point of time he's wise
　　　　Ligh[t] airs, his ear's light sense, his soul reproves.

　　　　　[Sir Philip Wodehouse], 'An extemporanean of my
　　　　　cousin Newton . . .'

　　　　　b.131, back (no. 215)

T2953　To none the secret counsels of your mind
　　　　Those most who most resembles him will bless.

　　　　　[Mary Serjant]

　　　　　fb.98, fol. 153

T2954　To Norfolk House; lords, knights, and squires
　　　　　　　　　　　　　　　　　　　　　　　　　repair,
　　　　Bad is its head, but ten times worse its heart.

　　　　　[John] Hervey, baron Hervey of Ickworth, 'Norfolk
　　　　　House' [1738; answered by 'Malicious bard . . .']
　　　　　[Crum T3042]

　　　　　c.154, p. 9; Poetry Box V/12

T2955　To obey your commands my goodly Payne
　　　　The word can describe them, 'tis called perfection.

　　　　　Poetry Box II/17

T2956　To our monarch's return
　　　　Then both are at home.

　　　　　[Henry Hall, of Hereford], 'A health to the King's
　　　　　return'

　　　　　b.111, p. 36

T2957　To own a former error is no more
　　　　They eat the other end, but I eat this.

　　　　　'Ficti pravique tenax'

　　　　　c.139, p. 352

T2958　To paint in fancy's frolic page
　　　　Lest some rude breeze abroad should spoil it.

　　　　　H[enry] Skrine, 'The fate of a coxcomb . . . April 6th
　　　　　1780'

　　　　　c.509, p. 34

T2959　To paint thy worth if I did rightly know it,
　　　　Of all with me, to paint without digression, |
　　　　　　　　　　　　　　　　　　　　　　There's no expression.

　　　　　[Sir William] Burlase, 'Burlase the painter to B:
　　　　　J[onson] the poet' [answered by 'What though
　　　　　I be . . .']
　　　　　[Crum T3051]

　　　　　b.200, p. 247

T2960　To parents, sons should loving be and kind,
　　　　And during life that duty should them bind.

　　　　　c.339, p. 319

T2961　To pass an evening's hour away,
　　　　Got up in sober sadness.

　　　　　Frederick Corfield, 'The card table'

　　　　　c.381/2

T2962　To pay great Anson's sufferings on the main
　　　　Brave ev'ry hardship, and defy each storm?

　　　　　[Horace Walpole, 4th earl of Orford], 'Lady Ans[o]n'
　　　　　[Crum T3054]

　　　　　c.157, p. 71

T2963　To places where ships are safe from a storm
　　　　The name of a very brave place.

　　　　　'A rebus'

　　　　　c.360/3, no. 215

T2964　To plague mankind when Jove in anger rose
　　　　Nor could that box destroy as yours can save.

　　　　　H[ester Grenville] Pitt, countess of Chatham, 'To
　　　　　Mrs Mary Jones occasioned by some snuff' [answered
　　　　　by 'When poets uninspir'd . . .']

　　　　　c.233, p. 88

T2965 To play upon the viol if
But whilst the bow is running.

    'Advice to a virgin'

    fb.107, p. 64

T2966 To please her peevish child Nurse Lee
'Twas naughty nurse that lost it.

    'The nurse and the child. Sent in a letter to Edward
    Rudge 1753'

    c.360/3, no. 249

T2967 To please us is it? why then should we flout them
Or with them, or without them, never well.

    'On women'

    b.200, p. 45

T2968 To plow the wide ocean go we,
And are happy wherever we come.

    'The mariner'

    fb.107, p. 40

T2969 To plunge a world in misery and woe
Sooth'd and supported by thy gentle hand.

    Maria de Fleury, 'Redemption or paradise
    regained . . . unfinished'

    c.494

T2970 To poet's speech, that to the fields Elysian
Dark caves, he was in the Elysian fields.

    Sir Thomas Urquhart, 'Of Æneas his descent to the
    infernal valley'

    fb.217, p. 154

T2971 To pour [?] on friendship's lap
The happiest of creatures.

    [William Hayley], 'To sister Lucy in return for a
    nightcap of her work'

    File 6976

T2972 To practice hospitality,
Each guest believes that 'tis his own.

    John Lockman, 'Salisbury . . . June 1757'

    c.267/1, p. 215

T2973 To praise thy goodness we essay,
Oh, may we all be born again.

    Charles Atherton Allnutt, 'Collect for Christmas day'

    c.112, p. 56

T2974 To preach the gospel at Japan,
Do thou but kiss, and I'll repent.

    [Robert Cholmeley], 'The proselyte. A tale'

    c.190, p. 184

T2975 To preserve from my first
To enliven your care.

    'Charade [1]'

Diggle Box: Poetry Box XI/71

T2976 To print, or not to print—that is the question.
And lose the name of authors.

    [Richard] Jago, 'Hamlet's soliloquy, imitated'
    [Dodsley Collection]

    c.487, p. 135

T2977 To prosecute my journey, a good mounter,
One, who will ease you to your heart's desire.

    Sir Thomas Urquhart, 'Of a certain licentious woman,
    whose name was Kate, that offers herself indirectly to
    be enjoyed by a gentleman, who spoke thus'

    fb.217, p. 179

T2978 To prove and [?] the pangs of love
To love so fervently.

'Braye Lute Book,' Music Ms. 13, fol. 38v

T2979 To prove the charms of art, and nature join'd,
If equal merits challenge equal fame.

    John [or William?] Bunce, 'To Mr. Highmore the
    painter'

    c.244, p. 302; c.503, p. 29

T2980 To purchase kingdoms with a single vice,
And honors God by breaking of his laws.

    'The dear bargain'

    b.111, p. 506

T2981 To rack, and torture, thy unmeaning brain
For anything entirely but an ass.

    [John Wilmot, 2nd earl of Rochester], 'On the
    supposed author of a late poem in defense of satire'
    [by Sir Carr Scroope; answered by 'Rail on poor
    feeble scribbler . . .'; 1677]
    [POAS I.371]

    b.105, p. 102; b.54, p. 1021; see also 'To vex and
    torture . . .'.

T2982 To read your dream I left my play
Que je vous suis fort obligé.

    [Elizabeth (Shirley) Compton, countess of
    Northampton], 'To Mr. Davis . . . 1728/9' [in the name
    of her daughter Lady Jane Compton]

    Accession 97.7.40

T2983 To ready Scotland boys and girls are carried
Our follies sanction first, and then our vices.

    Poetry Box II/35; see also 'How arts improve . . .'.

T2984 To reckon up what nobles have
Nature's pride unnaturally.

[Thomas Mottershed, of Christ Church Oxford], 'On the Palsgrave [later Frederick V, king of Bohemia]'s eldest son [Prince Frederick Henry] drowning' [Crum T3069]

b.356, p. 30

T2985 To reconcile our scruples, it is fit
My faith in all things else to your belief.

Sir Thomas Urquhart, 'A Roman Catholic gentlewoman speaks thus to her husband, who was Protestant'

fb.217, p. 68

T2986 To represent, is but to personate,
He represents them best—who takes a bribe.

'Representative'

c.81/1, no. 107

T2987 To rhyme it again
My song of fair Hannah Todd.

T[homas] M[orell], 'Hannah Todd, of Lincolnshire, a ballad. 1728'

c.395, p. 39

T2988 To riches, beauty, pomp or pow'r,
No rose, without a thorn.

'To a friend on his birthday'

c.83/2, no. 512

T2989 To Richmond the folks of the very first mode
To see the cascade and Baddeley Squall?

[Frances Anne] (Greville) [Crewe], 'A party to Richmond'

Poetry Box v/27

T2990 To Robert Merry, count, and knight
From your true friend and servant W. P.

W[illiam] P[arsons]

Greatheed Box/13

T2991 To sail to farthest climes my wish, my vow,
To fall at home, inglorious by a knife!

John Lockman, 'Spanish cruelty: or the sufferings of Louis Leger, cook to Admiral (since Lord Anson) when going round the world—Leger supposed to be the author'

c.267/1, p. 119

T2992 To Saint Giles's I went
'Tis the lewdest in all the whole nation.

'St. Giles's Church' [St. Giles-in-the-Fields, temp. John Sharp, 1675/6-1691; answered by 'Hail Poet Laureate . . .']
[Crum T3076]

b.113, p. 205

T2993 To Saint Malo's was sent an express
And died of a leaden ball colic.

'Song 85'

c.555, p. 134

T2994 To save a maid, St. George a dragon slew
There was no George, pray God there be a maid.

'On St. George slaying a dragon'

b.356, p. 304; see also 'St. George and for a maid . . .'.

T2995 To save Hungaria's martial queen,
And factions cordially embrace.

John Lockman, 'Loyal songs. Writ for the chapel feast, after the battle of Dettingen . . . 1743'

c.267/2, p. 3

T2996 To save John Bull Pitt drains his skull
Of Holland, France and Spain.

c.546, p. 35

T2997 To say Clorinda tunes her warbling lays
Clorinda singeth as she occupies.

[Sir Thomas Urquhart], 'Wherewith most fitly the voice of Clorinda is unparallel'd deservingly to express, the excellency thereof'

fb.217, p. 394

T2998 To science sacred muse exalt thy lays;
A life celestial and begun in this.

[Henry Jones, bricklayer], 'Philosophy a poem' [pr. Dublin 1746 (Foxon J94)]

c.481, p. 149 (incomplete)

T2999 To screen me from too curious eyes
And in the reader lose a friend.

'An enigma in the manner of Dr. Swift'

Poetry Box I/13

T3000 To search after happiness surely were wise
When possest of the charms of the sweet Hannah More.

'On seeing Miss H[annah] More in the little page of the 2d. edition against the search after happiness a ballad'

c.341, p. 14

T3001 To see guid corn grow on the rigs,
Oh this would do mickle to wanton me.

'A [Jacobite] song'

fc.58, p. 125

T3002 To show a noise a wondrous thing may seem;
Before he utters it, in its due grace.

[Sir Philip Wodehouse], 'Upon Joshua Jones I show a noise'

b.131, back (no. 150)

T3003   To Shyrus' and Procrustes' fatal beds
        The amplest god t'a narrow commendation.

        [Sir Thomas Urquhart], 'That the reputation of the
        best wit(?) fashioned to the measure of a detractor's
        spleen suffers in the ears of the credulous most
        grievous [?]'

        fb.217, p. 517

T3004   To Sion's hills I lift mine eyes,
        Thy life from harm, thy soul from sin.

        'Psalm 121'

        c.264/3, p. 69

T3005   To Sion's mount my soul ascends
        His favor crowns with endless rest.

        'Psalm the 121st'

        c.481, p. 251

T3006   To slothful men the day, night, month, and year,
        Why of life's shortness do we then complain.

        'Life's length and shortness'

        c.356

T3007   To solemn grief and exquisite delight,
        Ransom'd souls! ere you give away to joy.

        'An ode on the nativity of Christ'

        c.166, p. 93

T3008   To soothe the sorrows of an anxious mind,
        Scarce can these sweets contentment's calm restore.

        [A. S.], 'Sonnet'

        c.139, p. 15

T3009   To soothe the soul, to humanize the heart,
        When Io's sweet voice bids latent merit rise.

        John Lockman, 'Writ to encourage the benefit of a
        fine musical performer, then little known'

        c.267/1, p. 80

T3010   To speak aright of your poor empty purse
        That neither good nor bad in it do enter.

        [Sir Thomas Urquhart], 'To one whose purse had an
        antipathy with money'

        fb.217, p. 536

T3011   To speak with drownded eyes, and mournful looks,
        I gather, there's a time to hold one's peace.

        'On the times'

        b.111, p. 460

T3012   To speak with freedom, dignity, and ease,
        But he is present—and I must forbear.

        'Prologue [to Cato, presented at Leicester House,
        1749] spoken by Prince George' [later George III]
        [Crum T3103]

        c.578, p. 62

T3013   To spin with skill, in ancient times, 'tis known,
        And each—and every one—be styl'd—a carder.

        [Gentleman's evening post, 16 July 1776]

        c.487, p. 98

T3014   To stand unmov'd, while a whole world's on fire!
        Will shave his head—look grave—and turn a friar.

        [Phanuel Bacon], 'To a young lady going into a
        nunnery . . .'

        c.237, fol. 50

T3015   To stay awhile the garlan[d]'d spring
        Then I'll give health | And I'll give fame.

        [Phanuel Bacon], 'To Mrs. Wimbleton aged 86 who
        made the most exquisite flowers with feathers'

        c.237, fol. 80 [i.e., 100]

T3016   To stop the current makes it swell the higher
        She'll still thereafter prove the more luxurious.

        [Sir Thomas Urquhart], Intimus in ventitum semper
        [?] in gun(?)'

        fb.217, p. 387

T3017   To stormy winds and raging seas
        Your aid and your sister's aid I claim.

        [William Mills], 'Odes of Horace translated. Book I.
        Ode XXVI. To his muse'

        c.472, p. 28

T3018   To supper calls the long-expected bell,
        I wish all hours would strike this grateful sound.

        c.53, fol. 22

T3019   To swear I love were now too late
        That in a breath can answer no and yea.

        'To a gentlewoman'

        b.205, fol. 5r

T3020   To take degrees by scraping, tho' of quick
        And learn before they run e'en how to creep.

        [Sir Richard Bulstrode], 'Against such as soon get
        honors, &c.'

        fb.88, p. 115v

T3021   To tame a shrew'd wife's tongue and haughty mind,
        A thirteenth labor Hercules would find.

        'A Herculean labor'

        c.356

T3022   To taste of fish none man alive can woo her
        Yet cares she not what flesh can do unto her.

        'An epigram on a woman'

        b.62, p. 77

T3023　To tax commissioners I make it known
Poor wife and I perchance might get a ride.

　　'1790'
fc.130, p. 51

T3024　To teach a lesson of uncertain life
Till death itself brings comfort and relief.

　　'Epitaph in the churchyard at Edgemere'
Poetry Box XII/59

T3025　To teach mankind how public blessings grow,
Such viceroys ever bid Hibernia smile.

　　'A prologue spoken at the theater in Dublin, in honor
　　of the Prince of Wales' birthday, Sunday May the 24
　　1752. He completes 14 years'
c.360/3, no. 213

T3026　To tell us why banks thus in Scotland obtain
Where there's plenty of rags, you'll have plenty of
　　　　　　　　　　　　　　　　　　　　　paper.

　　'On the bank and paper-credit of Scotland'
c.546, p. 1

T3027　To tell what gen'rals did or statesmen spoke,
To be more stupid is beyond your power.

　　'Epistle to the editors of the Antijacobin'
c.340

T3028　To temperance thou gift divine
And thy reward is happiness.

　　'Ode to temperance'
c.83/3, no. 952

T3029　To that place where the weary are at rest,
Replete with dangers, never free from strife.

　　I. H—t, 'Thoughts on the death of an infant niece'
c.118, p. 69

T3030　To the beloved vineyard tune your voice,
O great Jehovah! Let thine anger cease.

　　'Jehovah and his vineyard 2, 3, 4, 5. verses. From
　　[Isaiah] 27 chap.'
c.515, fol. 31v

T3031　To the dark and silent tomb,
That I hasted to the tomb.

　　[ ] Lewis, 'An epitaph on an infant'
c.244, p. 442; c.83/2, no. 720

T3032　To the Earl says the Countess—what makes you so
　　　　　　　　　　　　　　　　　　　　　dull
Had you been plain Madam, and I been plain Will.

　　'A dialogue, on William Pulteney esqr being created
　　Earl of Bath—1742'
c.360/1, p. 323

T3033　To the eternal on his throne,
Tho' worthless in itself, let thine his praise rehearse.

　　[Mary de la Rivière] Manley, 'Psalm 148'
c.244, p. 184

T3034　To the gay town where guilty pleasure reigns,
And to their foes the unfinish'd trophies yield.

　　'To Mr. Addison. Occasioned by his purchasing an
　　estate in Warwickshire'
c.73, p. 5

T3035　To the genius of this cell
Joys less simple are less true.

　　W[illiam] B[urke], 'Inscription for the rook-house
　　written on the spot'
File 2435

T3036　To the George Brown from Plymouth town
Yet subject some time to a storm.

　　Joh[n] Dayest [i.e., Day], 'From Plymouth: April 5 to
　　24: to the tune of Whoop do me no harm etc.'
b.197, p. 60

T3037　To the god of my love, in the morning, said she
Could have nothing more added, than what I
　　　　　　　　　　　　　　　　　　　　possess.

　　[John Byrom, of Manchester], 'Armelle Nicolas's
　　account of herself—from the French'
c.140, p. 47

T3038　To the good genius of each place alone
Then send us off with thunder every scene.

　　[Maurice Johnson], 'Est animus ulubris—a prologue
　　spoken at Spalding'
c.229/2, fol. 25v

T3039　To the graves, where sleep the dead,
How so poor a maiden died.

　　'Julia, an ancient ballad'
c.83/3, no. 936

T3040　To the great Earl of Warwick we next tune our lays
He [?]t no [?] birth our [?] quite empty.

　　W[illiam] S[mith]
Smith Papers, folder 73

T3041　To the hundreds of Drury I write
And teach 'em a new morris dance Sir.

　　'To.[the] hundred[s of] Drury'
c.503, p. 60

T3042　To the lords and ladies of both sexes,
'Tis wine not water that doth tope us.

　　'The title' [to 'Pulvis de novo . . .']
b.54, p. 934

T3043   To the name of a place where Spaniards of old
That will make you all laugh, from the clown to
the king.

     W[illiam] Smith, 'Charade'

Smith Papers, folder 73

T3044   To the Polwhele, in friendship's grateful lays,
And its own work assign'd to every day.

     'To the translator of Theocritus . . . 13 June [17]87
Gent[leman's] Mag[azine]'

c.382, p. 51

T3045   To the sweet bard who hopes bright pleasure's song
Nor disappointment mingle with thy train.

     'Lines by a young man written on Campbell's
Pleasures of hope'

c.83/4, no. 2029

T3046   To the things which in tilting our forefathers bold,
You'll find out the name of a town.

     'A rebus'

c.360/3, no. 206

T3047   To the wars I must alas!
Ch'ill [sic] kill a man he knows not how.

     'Song 197'

c.555, p. 316

T3048   To the waters we go
The doctors themselves will swear it.

     'The ladies' trip to Bath. Tune, The bright god of day'
[Crum T3128b]

c.233, p. 87; c.536

T3049   To thee Albinus! I rehearse
Extoll'd by fools in foreign courts.

     'The prodigal son a tale in a letter to Albinus'

fb.142, p. 69

T3050   To Thee all-glorious, ever-blessed power
To bless my sleep and sanctify my dreams.

     'A midnight hymn'

c.547, p. 207

T3051   To thee chaste Di, of antiquated maids
Receive the offering, and accept her vow!

     'An old maid's invocation' [1775]

Poetry Box III/38

T3052   To thee dear man, to thee I hither come,
Or sigh a whole eternity in vain.

     'To my lost and dearest husband'

c.83/2, no. 585

T3053   To thee, dear Tom, in verse I write,
Be sure at least, you have a troop.

     [Thomas Hamilton, 6th earl of Haddington], 'To the
Honble Thomas Leslie, an epistle'

c.458/2, p. 162

T3054   To Thee, great God, our hearts, our hands, our eyes
Thee, we adore for all.

     Henry Baker, 'A thankful hymn to God'

c.244, p. 396 (incomplete?)

T3055   To Thee I fly thou sole defense
May meet; this grant for thy dear Son.

     [Thomas Stanley], 'Meditat: IIII upon the insolency
of the tumults'

b.152, p. 13

T3056   To Thee is my uprightness known
Before the sons of men.

     [Thomas Stanley], 'Meditat: XVII. Of the difference
betweene the King and the two Houses in point of
church government'

b.152, p. 55

T3057   To Thee let my first off'rings rise
May well sustain my last.

     Isaac Watts(?), 'A morning hymn'

c.186, p. 26

T3058   To thee Machaon whose superior skill
Fame wealth and honor to the muse impart.

     [ ] Blackett, M. D.

File 1323

T3059   To thee my ever faithful Kitty
Blest in immortal arms since too divine for me.

     [Robert Cholmeley], 'To a gentleman who had met
with misfortune among the fair ladies of Dowry'

c.190, p. 157

T3060   To thee, my friend, permit me to impart
Flavia in thine, in mine be Stella press'd.

     'Epistle II. To Errato, on his being unfortunately in
love with two ladies at the same time'

fc.100, p. 5

T3061   To Thee my God I still appeal
Thy mercies may my suff'rings crown.

     [Thomas Stanley], 'Meditat: V. upon his Ma[jes]ty's
passing the bill for the triennial Parliament'

b.152, p. 15

T3062 To Thee, my God, though late, at last I turn
In the last hour, and at the day of doom!

Charles Hopkins, 'A hymn . . . wrote about an hour
before his death . . . first printed in The student, 1751'

c.94

T3063 To thee, my purse, thus troubl'd I complain,
Be heavy once again, or else I die.

'An extempore complaint'

c.578, p. 9

T3064 To Thee my solitary prayers I send
Relieving with their prayers my solitude.

[Thomas Stanley], 'Meditat. XXIV. Upon the denying
of his Ma[jes]ty the attendance of his chaplains'

b.152, p. 73

T3065 To thee, my truest, oldest friend,
Where not a nettle grows in vain.

Sir John Cullum, 'From a friend with a microscope'

c.90

T3066 To Thee, O generous God, my voice I raise,
Heal heal a broken heart, and let me live.

[Richard] Daniel, dean of Armagh, 'The happy
deceit—Psalm 34'

c.244, p. 353

T3067 To thee O gentle sleep alone
By thee our sorrows cease.

[William Smith]

Smith Papers, folder 73; c.83/1, no. 4 (var.)

T3068 To Thee O God do we give thanks
The horns of just men raise.

'Psal: 75'

b.217, p. 7

T3069 To Thee O God, I raise my fearful eyes;
Will give an exceeding weight of glory at last . . . .

A. B., 'Wrote in affliction'

c.116, p. 8 (incomplete)

T3070 To Thee O God we homage pay
On all his saints in endless day.

P[hilip] Doddridge, 'The sum of righteousness from
Mal. IV. 2'

c.493, p. 22

T3071 To Thee O God we thy just praises sing,
And face wide-gaping hell, and all its slighted
powers defy.

[John] Oldham, 'Te Deum paraphrased by . . .' [1680]
[Crum T3165]

c.244, p. 64

T3072 To Thee, O gracious Lord, I make my prayer,
That I may be with thee forever blest.

[ ] Newton, bishop [1789?]

File 6590

T3073 To thee, O Hanbury! the rural muse,
So long thy honor'd name her sons shall boast.

'To the R[everen]d Mr. Hanbury on his essay for
planting by a Warwickshire man'

c.186, p. 132

T3074 To thee O Jack a man of note
I rest your humble servant Henry Park.

[Henry] Park, 'Mr. Park's letter to a friend in London'

fc.61, p. 107

T3075 To Thee, O Lord, my Judge most just
And in thy praise unite.

'Psalm 26'

c.264/1, p. 103

T3076 To thee, O Molly, once my soul's delight
And Roger's peace cannot be greater curst.

Frederick Corfield, 'The fugitive'

c.381/2

T3077 To thee, sweet bard! my votive wreath I bring,
The guard of virtue, and to vice a foe.

Dr. [ ] Willowby, 'Sonnet to Wm Cowper esq.'

c.142, p. 505

T3078 To thee, sweet bird, the rustic muse is due
Rejoicing in the shades of liberty.

Dr. [ ] Thompson, 'The blackbird, an ode'

c.141, p. 353

T3079 To thee, sweet pleasing maid I bring
Fair, unaffected maid, can never fail to please.

'To a young lady with some flowers'

c.83/1, no. 160

T3080 To thee, the author of my pining care
Bless thy desires, and crown with joy thy youth.

Miss [ ] Poole, 'Verses supposd to be wrote by . . . and
addressed to Peter Delme esqr . . . 1724'

c.360/1, p. 309

T3081 To Thee, Thou great Supreme, all-knowing, yet
And naught appear, that dying I would blot.

'The poet's address, to the Supreme Being'

c.94

T3082   To thee, whose genuine science, modest worth,
And with exulting pride record a S—r's name.

> [William Boscawen], 'Epistle to a noble Earl with the printed account of the Literary Fund'
>
> fc.106, p. 84

T3083   To thee, whose tender love, and faithful care,
Read, Guillibeau, and mix thy drops with mine.

> [( ) Jones], 'To Mr. Guillibeau with verses on the death of Lord Compton' [son of the earl of Northampton; d. 1739]
> [Crum T3177]
>
> Accession 97.7.40

T3084   To these again whom death did wed,
Whose day shall never sleep in night.

> [Richard Crashaw], 'Upon a gentleman and his wife both buried together'
> [Crum T3180]
>
> fb.88, p. 114; see also 'Whilst thou, blest John . . .'.

T3085   To think well, to say well;
Will end well, when all's well; | So farewell.

> 'An epigram, by a gentleman aged 83. years'
>
> c.94

T3086   To this grandeur Sophronia might justly pretend,
For you're now, my small friend, like a pea in a
bladder.

> John Lockman, 'To a very little man, in a very great house . . . Nov. 1743'
>
> c.267/1, p. 34

T3087   To this great ship, which round the globe has run
To her in Oxford, and to him in heaven.

> Ab[raham] Cowley, 'On the chair made out of Sir Francis Drake's ship presented to the University Library of Oxford by John Davis of Deptford esqr.'
> [1662]
> [Crum T3184]
>
> c.360/2, no. 265

T3088   To this Lord Absalom but little spoke
Yet his great speakings no records express.

> b.199, back cover

T3089   To this moment a rebel, I throw down my arms,
At the thought of those joys, I should meet in her
arms!

> [John Wilmot, 2nd earl of Rochester], 'Song'
>
> b.105, p. 144; b.334, p. 187

T3090   To this sad shrine, whoe'er thou art! Draw near
And with a father's sorrows, mix his own.

> A[lexander] Pope, 'An epitaph at the church of Stanton-Harcourt in Oxfordshire on the honorable Simon Harcourt esqr. only son of the Lord Chancellor Harcourt . . . 1720'
>
> c.360/2, no. 201

T3091   To those so mourn'd in death, so lov'd in life,
That holds their ashes, and expects her own.

> [Alexander Pope], 'At the bottom [of the pedestal of the monument for Nicholas Rowe and his daughter Charlotte Rowe Fane, in Westminster Abbey]'
>
> c.360/2, no. 165; see also 'Thy relics, Rowe! . . .'.

T3092   To those who love in mirth to pass
To make poor Wat an ass.

> 'The doctor outwitted to the tune of Chevy-chase'
>
> Poetry Box x/33

T3093   To thy first stanza poetry laid by
In Grubstreet or Snowhill thy matches find.

> [Robert Wolseley], 'For Sr. Frivolous Insipid [Sir Harry Hubert]'
> [Crum T3186]
>
> b.219, p. 27

T3094   To titles I am born and with pride too I sing
That no mortal can live with or without me.

> 'A riddle' ['on a sirreverence given me . . .']
> [Crum T3188]
>
> c.150, p. 2

T3095   To toast the fair of Britain's isle
When dreadful youths like us pursue.

> 'Toasts for the English Committee . . . tune To all ye ladies [now at land]' [pr. 1731–35? (Foxon T404)]
>
> Poetry Box I/80

T3096   To trace great Nature's universal, awful sway,
Record his genius, and display your own.

> [William Boscawen], 'To the Honorable Mrs Boscawen on her erecting a seat, with inscriptions, to the memory of the poet Thomson, the former professor of her villa'
>
> fc.106, p. 11

T3097   To travel far as the wide world extends,
'If I'm once lost you'll never find me more.'

> [John Cunningham], 'Reputation, an allegory'
>
> c.139, p. 52

T3098　To Troy the fatal paragon of Greece,
　　　　You're gross, fat, as a grice, and full of grease.

> Sir Thomas Urquhart, 'To a very corpulent, and great-grown lady, who was sometime exceeding beautiful'
>
> fb.217, p. 263

T3099　To us and all the muses (O) how dear
　　　　Art thou thrice noble, and best worthy peer.

> 'Petrus Ebsworthy. Anagram. Best-worthy peer. Epigram'
>
> b.212, p. 77

T3100　To various turns and many shifts inured
　　　　And tho' I hold the reins I never guide.

> 'A riddle'
>
> c.150, p. 148

T3101　To vex and torture thy unmeaning brain
　　　　For anything entirely but an ass.

> John Wilmot, 2nd earl of Rochester, 'A poet [Sir Carr Scroope] who writ in the praise of satire'
> [Crum T3193]
>
> b.334, p. 167; see also 'To rack and torture . . .'.

T3102　To view Corinna's face,
　　　　Or if we see, we love.

> [Charles Earle], 'A song made years ago to the tune of Fanny blooming &c.'
>
> c.376

T3103　To wake at midnight from a mind replete
　　　　Friendship and love to your more earthly bliss.

> [William Hayley], 'Sonnet . . . Sept. 13 [1800]'
>
> File 6968

T3104　To wake the soul by tender strokes of art,
　　　　As Cato's self had not disdain'd to hear.

> [Alexander] Pope, 'Prologue to [Joseph Addison's] Cato' [pr. 1713, in The guardian, no. 33]
>
> c.163, p. 1

T3105　To want what I should have shall never make
　　　　To furnish in myself by not desiring.

> [Sir Thomas Urquhart], 'We should not be sorry to be destitute of anything so long as we have judgment to persuade [?] that we must minister and out[?] what we have not by not longing for it'
>
> fb.217, p. 522

T3106　To ware upon the counterfeit a peer,
　　　　Than half a crown.

> Sir Thomas Urquhart, 'To a man, that bought too dear the portrait of a courtesan'
>
> fb.217, p. 177

T3107　To wed, or not to wed—that is the question
　　　　I'll e'en like others run the risk, and thus resolve to
　　　　　　　　　　　　　　　　　　wed.

> 'On marriage, or a parody of Hamlet's soliloquy . . . July 94. Solwin'
> [Crum T3198]
>
> Poetry Box IV/176

T3108　To weep oft, still to flatter, sometimes spin,
　　　　Are properties women excel men in.

> [Robert Hayman], 'Women's properties'
> [Crum T3200]
>
> c.356

T3109　To weigh an airy sound—to scan a rhyme—
　　　　And feeling prove that reasoning can be wrong.

> 'Addressed to the reviewers by the author of The discarded spinster'
>
> c.83/3, no. 811

T3110　To what a cumbersome unwieldiness
　　　　And the game kill'd or lost, go talk or sleep.

> J[ohn] D[onne], 'Love's diet'
> [Crum T3201]
>
> b.148, p. 53; b.114, p. 264 (stanzas 1–2; 'unwieldy guess')

T3111　To what a height did infant Rome
　　　　Liv'd never equal or came nigh.

> 'Upon a rape'
>
> b.197, p. 245

T3112　To what a task am I assign'd
　　　　And an Ephesian matron prove.

> 'Epistle X. To Amanda'
>
> fc.100, p. 44

T3113　To William Callway now at Lyme,
　　　　Take notice. Lyme's in Dorsetshire.

> 'A superscription of a letter, put into a post office . . . 1737'
> [Crum T3211 ('Nov. 1. 1736']
>
> c.94

T3114　To wise men you seem foolish: and seem wise
　　　　To foolish men. What seem y' in your own eyes?

> Sir Thomas Urquhart, 'To a grave Stoic'
>
> fb.217, p. 182

T3115　To wish and will it is my part
　　　　With happiness to your life's end.

> b.27, fol. 40v

T3116 To woo, as Jacob did, displeaseth me:
Her servant fourteen years, before enjoyment.

Sir Thomas Urquhart, 'The speeches of a certain bachelor'

fb.217, p. 89

T3117 To you dear cuz I thus complain
Till when we bid you all adieu.

Dr. T. Stamper, 'Dr. Stamper's poetical epistle from Clapham to his Cosn. Bishop at London 6. Febr 1717'

b.155, p. 75

T3118 To you dear Tim whom music entertains,
To fret the bass, and punish me.

William Clark, 'A familiar epistle from the witty . . . F. G. S. to the Reverend Mr. Timothy Neve . . . on his inviting him to the concert'

c.229/2, fol. 46

T3119 To you dear wife, and all must grant
Whensoe'er you please, may see her too!

[Samuel] Bishop, 'To Mrs. Bishop with a pocket looking-glass by the late . . . master of Merchant Taylor's School'

c.83/2, no. 686; Greatheed Box/89; c.391, p. 76 ('dear girl')

T3120 To you Eliza be these lines consign'd
And trace the winding torrent's silver ways.

c.53, fol. 79

T3121 To you fair ladies now in town,
And every brighter charm disclose. | With a fa la
fa la

'An invitation into the country'
Accession 97.7.40, p. 1

T3122 To you fair nymph whom I adore
And ask his art to win her love.

'An address to a young lady'

c.172, p. 3

T3123 To you fine folks at Marlb'ro' house
And all our debts may then be paid. | With a fa la la

[Colonel ( ) G.], 'A new ballad—to the tune of To all ye ladies now at London' [pr. 1741? (Foxon N219)] [Crum T3226]

Accession 97.7.40 (2 copies)

T3124 To you German Sir, a petition I bring
For I've got all the world, when I've you in a string. |
Which nobody can deny.

'The petition [of Tyburn]' [Jacobite; pr. 1718? (Foxon P194)]
[Crum T3227, with sixteen more stanzas]

fc.58, p. 96; c.570/1, p. 180

T3125 To you great Earl of Delawarr
The best protection's want of charms.

'Answer to the Earl of Delawarr's farewell to the maids of honor'

Poetry Box v/14

T3126 To you great Sir the praise is due
If th'ark had fell where had they been.

[Thomas Gurney], 'To the ingenious gentleman who found out an answer to Warwick Church's letter, without saying if it should please the Lord to raise up an able minister. We will let him know of you and you of him'

c.213

T3127 To you great Sir whose power doth extend
It's time to have Don ——— your humble trout.

[John] Smallwood, 'A prologue of . . . when he was Tripos. Cant:'

b.115, fol. 33

T3128 To you kind mid-'s this poem I address
Because the poet's but a mid- himself.

'The cockpit' [addressed to the midshipmen]

Poetry Box x/52

T3129 To you, Lorenzo, I send these,
And show her what— 'tis happiness to know.

'To Lorenzo, an epistle, or arguments for a virtuous life drawn from a comparison of the happiness of the virtuous and vicious characters in life . . .'

c.136, p. 16

T3130 To you ——— who claim the privilege to sit
My heels will beat, to all I say and do.

[Frederick Corfield], 'The defense' [addressed to 'Mrs. Shawe']

c.381/1

T3131 To you my guide, tho' unknown friend
Fair fruit from out the rudest vine.

[Betty Jeffreys?], 'A supposed answer of . . . [to 'The muse this morn . . .']'

c.360/1, p. 29

T3132 To you my Lord whose unexperienc'd days
And emulating them, resolve to rise.

[Thomas] Cook, 'An epistle to Lord [George] Johnston'

c.156, p. 149

T3133 To you, Sir Ralph, I greeting send,
And meet you, be you there or no.

Mrs. [ ] Butson, 'Heroic epistle from . . . to Sir Ralph Payne'

Poetry Box II/15

T3134 To you that live possest great troubles do befall
You shall be brought to dust as —— is.

'Epitaph no. 1'
[Crum T3237, 'life possess']
c.158, p. 45

T3135 To you, whose toils in order spread
The olive branch of peace.

H[enry] Skrine, 'A peace-offering presented to a lady
on the writer's omitting to call for a purse which she
had promised him . . . Hambleden June 20 1783'
c.509, p. 63

T3136 To young Moggy the skipper old Bruno the canterer
Be lovely as Venus so prays your friend Bruno.

[William Hayley], 'An amorous heroic epistle'
File 6948

T3137 To your commands I own obedience due,
Within these walls such happiness resides: &c.

[Mary] Chandler, 'On Mr. B——'s garden—to Mrs.
S——'
c.351, p. 138

T3138 To your dear father (Sir) Job's self-report belong'd
Your father's guide be yours thus acting him below.

Poetry Box VI/123

T3139 To your lov'd bosom, pleas'd Marissa flies;
And in each other there eternally delight.

Lady [Mary] C[hudleigh], 'To Clorissa'
c.258

T3140 Tobacco, choicest, fragrant plant adieu!
And smoking cry, ah! puff! he'd gone.

'An epitaph upon a gentleman who killed himself by
excessive smoking said to have been written by
himself'
fb.142, p. 62

T3141 Tobacco is an Indian weed
Is but a puff | Think [of this and smoke tobacco].

fb.108, p. 195; b.227, p. 36 (var.); c.360/2, no. 185 ('is
but an')

T3142 Today a mighty hero comes to warm
At least he'll find some Cornish borough there.

[Sir Samuel] Garth, 'Prologue to Tamerlane . . .
representing the genius of England' [pr. Dublin, 1711
(Foxon G37)]
[Crum T2929]
Poetry Box IV/124

T3143 Today man's drest in gold and silver bright,
The present moment is the life of man.

'The difference between today and tomorrow'
[Crum T2930]
fc.130, p. 56

T3144 Today my tongue, the glory of my frame
Spend and be spent in service so divine.

'A meditation upon returning home after preaching.
Written by a clergyman now in Virginia . . . Sept. 16
1750'
c.148, p. 18

T3145 Today, says Dick, is April Day,
For you're a fool already made.

'The 1st of April'
c.81/2, no. 530

T3146 T'o'ercome or die, was erst the hero's boast,
In fame, was Wolfe's, who has accomplish'd each.

[James Mulcaster, sr.], 'On the death of
Major-General Wolfe'
c.118, p. 30

T3147 Toh! By my shoul thou art a beastly word
Thou'rt gone, Gad, thou stink'st too long to last.

'A satire against a fart written by an Irishman'
fc.24, p. 58

T3148 Tom and Will were shepherds twain
Let them go shake their ears.

Sidney Godolphin, earl of Godolphin, 'A song by . . .
on Tom Killigrew and Will Murrey [the disappointed
rivals]'
[Crum T3253]
b.201, p. 146; Poetry Box VII/58 (incomplete); Accession
97.7.40, p. 38 ('shepherd swains'; with a separate copy)

T3149 Tom Banks by native industry was taught
I'd rather you should choke than I should starve.

'The fisherman'
c.578, p. 42

T3150 Tom Drone and Jack Rant both preachers divine,
Or are toss'd by monsoons, in a tempest.

'The contrast. On a brace of modern preachers'
c.81/2, no. 540

T3151 Tom Fool, the tenant of this narrow space,
Point to his grave, and say—I lik'd the man.

D[avid] G[arrick], 'Epitaph for D[avid] G[arrick] who
chose to be buried in the grotto at Stourhead Augst
7th 1776'
Acquisition 92.3.1ff. (autogr.)

T3152 Tom Hooker did prognosticate
       Or the king enjoys his own again.

  'Song' [on the Old Pretender]

  fc.58, p. 59

T3153 Tom Jolly's nose I mean to abuse
       We despise it, and swear 'tis mine arse of a nose.

  'A drunken song. 1679'

  b.54, p. 1160

T3154 Tom loves Mary passing well
       That those you love may like you.

    'Cross-purposes an excellent new ballad to the tune of
    Betsy Bell'

  Poetry Box I/81 (2 copies)

T3155 Tom meets his friend and straight complains
       If not unto the Pole.

  c.546

T3156 Tom prais'd his friend who chang'd his state,
       'Twill be the end of mine.

    'Marriage the end of life . . . Nov. 16th 1797'

  c.113/30

T3157 Tom Ramble, a rake of true Catholic hope,
       One sneak'd to his gruel, and one to his punk.

    'The penitent rake a tale'

  c.241, p. 26

T3158 Tom, studious, all the morning thinks,
       Which can require such after drinking.

    'The tippling philosopher'

  c.94

T3159 Tom Tattle laughs in every place
       Show less of manners and of reason.

    [Robert Cholmeley], '[Catallus's Ineptus risus]
    translated'

  c.190, p. 65

T3160 Tom, who a thousand things had writ,
       Will feast, as well as on a rose.

    [Isaac Freeman], 'The balk. A quinigma [*sic*]'

  fc.105

T3161 Tomorrow didst thou say?
       Hold the dear angel fast, until he bless thee.

    [Nathaniel Cotton], 'Tomorrow'
    [Crum T3261]

  c.186, p. 125; fc.132/1, p. 171; fc.51, p. 269; Poetry Box
  IV/109

T3162 Tomorrow, I will live the fool does say,
       None ever yet made too much haste to live.

    [cf. Crum T3262]

  c.362, p. 86

T3163 Tomorrow Lord is thine
       In sudden endless night.

    P[hilip] Doddridge, 'The necessity of improving the
    proper time from the uncertainty of the future from
    Jam. IV. 13-15'

  c.493, p. 44

T3164 Tomorrow, Sir, the Mantuan pair,
       What finishes each friendly scroll.

    [Isaac Freeman], 'Extempore invitation to William
    Canvane esqr at Venice'

  fc.105

T3165 Tomorrow, Sir, you promised me you would
       To see you dead and rotting in your grave.

  c.546, p. 34

T3166 Tomorrow you will live you always say;
       Today itself's too late, the wise liv'd yesterday.

    [Abraham Cowley, trans.], 'Martial lib. 5, epigr. 59'
    [Crum T3262]

  b.118, p. 14; b.135, fol. 116v

T3167 Tom's coach and six!—whither in such haste going?
       But a short journey—to his own undoing.

    'Epigram'

  c.115

T3168 Tongue your shape you're naught but words I see,
       Tongue for the most part in the throat will lie.

    'Answer' [to 'Since thou to blare . . .']

  b.356, p. 117

T3169 Tonight—and not without a grateful tear,
       'Tis all I am, and all that you shall be.

    Emma Corbett

  c.83/1, no. 158

T3170 Tonight for our diversion we essay
       Were to divert ourselves, and please our friends.

    'A prologue to Theodosius a tragedy [by Nathaniel
    Lee] when it was acted in Southwark by some young
    gentlemen in the year 1722. Spoke by Leontine'

  c.360/2, no. 166

T3171 Tonight, grave Sir, both my poor house and I
       The liberty which we'll enjoy tonight!

    Ben Jonson, 'Ben Jonson's invitation of a gentleman to
    supper'

  b.356, p. 309

T3172 Tonight our shoving cronies meet
Believe me most sincerely yours.

> [Robert Cholmeley], 'To the honble Nicholas Leake
> esq. at St Johns College in Camb: sent upon the
> Coronation. October 13: 1727'

c.190, p. 236

T3173 Tonight usurping tyranny attend,
And rule with mercy by a right divine.

> 'A prologue to the tragedy of the Lady Jane Grey' [by
> Nicholas Rowe; acted at Drury Lane, 20 April 1715;
> Jacobite satire]
> [Crum T3265]

fc.58, p. 117; c.570/1, p. 2

T3174 Tonight's the day, I speak it with great sorrow,
'Tis a cold frosty morning, and so good night.

> '5th. [November] Irish bellman'

c.81/1, no. 295

T3175 Tony and Louisa upon a merry pin
They'll puff it out, and in and out, and in and out
again.

> 'A mock song on the K[ing] and Duch[ess] of
> Portsmouth Feb 1679'

b.54, p. 1157

T3176 Too curious, foolish, moth forbear,
Or, like the moth you'll be undone.

> 'The moth and the taper a fable'

Poetry Box VI/10

T3177 Too dearly had I bought my green and youthful
years
In woman's word but wisdom would mistrust it to
endure.

> 'Braye Lute Book,' Music Ms. 13, fol. 36

T3178 Too hasty night forbear; our praise
Ever attract, and crown our love.

> [John Austin], 'Hym: 40' [Hymn xxxix, Devotions in
> the ancient way of offices, 1672, p. 355]

c.178, p. 39

T3179 Too late for hope for my repose too soon,
Oh! I should ne'er have seen, or seen before.

c.549, p. 4

T3180 Too late I came into this room
Expect its prince to his native shore.

> 'This within written prophecy was found in
> Mr. Becket's room when dead, in Lancaster Castle,
> towards the latter end of Oates' plot, 26. or 27. years
> ago . . .' [c. 1710]
> [Crum T3276]

File 17422

T3181 Too long has hope on patience lean'd,
I'm orthodox you see again.

> [Helen Craik], 'To a gentleman . . . 1782'

c.375, p. 117

T3182 Too long hast thou dear cruel maid
How can you think to save your soul.

> [Mrs. Christian Kerr], 'To the young gentlewoman by
> her friend to persuade her to marry' [answered by
> 'Vain youth . . .']

c.102, p. 91

T3183 Too long, my masters, with unpatriot zeal
And may the devil bless what has been said.

> 'Epilogue to be spoken by Punch, the first night of
> Mr. Russell's puppet show' [1745]

fc.51, p. 73

T3184 Too long my muse in idle sports employ'd
Or else our lives are one continu'd lie.

> R[ichard] Shackleton, 'A copy of verses composed
> by . . . of Ballytare in Ireland'

c.517, fol. 18r

T3185 Too long, poetic maid, too long,
And in our Moses Virgil's majesty arise.

> Tho[mas] Scott, jr., 'To Mrs. Masters [of Norwich]'

c.244, p. 252

T3186 Too long the wise Commons have been in debate
Must be damn'd in the cup, like unworthy receivers.

> 'A satire' [sometimes attr. John Wilmot, 2nd earl of
> Rochester]
> [Crum T3281]

fb.140, p. 167

T3187 Too low my strains, too flat my artless song
When your eternal King inspires the song.

> [Elizabeth (Singer) Rowe], '[Soliloquies] (2)'

c.153, p. 149

T3188 Too much dreadful hail and snow,
Arms, or steeds, against us bring.

> [William Popple, trans.], '[Horace] book 1st. ode 2nd.
> To Augustus'

fc.104/2, p. 6

T3189 Too much thinking, gives us pain
New ones, every hour may grow.

> [Thomas Hamilton, 6th earl of Haddington], 'The
> translation of a French song'

c.458/2, p. 153

T3190 Too plain, dear youth, these tell-tale eyes
To fight with love, and you.

    [Soame Jenyns], 'Chloe to Strephon. A song'

c.147, p. 47; c.358, p. 35; c.360/1, p. 321; fc.132/1, p. 174

T3191 Too proud, too delicate to tell your wants
And what you must not write, you must not read.

    [Henry Fox, 1st baron Holland], 'With a china
    chamber pot to the Countess of Hillsborough'

Poetry Box II/55

T3192 Too soon alas into the ears of all
Since here th' are consummate but that made.

    [J. O.], 'On the death of the worthy princess the lady
    Arabella Seymour epicedium' [1615; followed by
    epitaph, 'Here lies she whom death befriended . . .']
    [Crum T3290]

b.197, p. 203

T3193 Too well these lines that fatal truth declare,
And though I like the lover quit the love.

    [John Hervey], baron Hervey [of Ickworth], 'An
    answer to the foregoing lines' ['O say thou dear
    possessor . . .']

c.130, p. 83; c.83/1, no. 114

T3194 Took Friandet to lead a joyful life
Although he was but thirty years of age.

    [Sir Thomas Urquhart]

fb.217, p. 541

T3195 Tormented by incessant pains
Admiring you, you pitying us.

    [Jonathan] Swift, 'To Stella'

c.83/1, no. 265

T3196 Torn from the arms of weeping love, here lies
Serving him, whose heart, now bleeds for her.

    [George] Lyttelton, 1st baron Lyttelton, 'Epitaph on
    Mrs. Rodney'

Poetry Box XII/8

T3197 Torn from those friends that were the most sincere
Nor aught but happiness in realms above!

    Cecilia B[urney], 'The travels of Orlando a tale . . .
    Cecelia B. aged 12 years'

c.486, fol. 36v

T3198 Torture fury rage despair
Die, presumptuous Acis, die.

    [John Gay, Alexander Pope, and/or John Hughes],
    'The flocks shall leave the mountains in [Handel's]
    Acis and Galatea' [with musical score for bass]

Music MS. 534

T3199 Tortur'd with pains enfeebled with disease,
Claps his glad plumes, and cleaves the airy way.

    Charles Atherton Allnutt, 'A poem supposed to be
    written in a hospital'

c.112, p. 157

T3200 Tossed in a troubled sea of griefs I float
Where it forever shall at anchor lie.

    [Thomas] Carew, 'To his mistress in absence a ship'
    [Crum T3295]

b.225, p. 130

T3201 Touch not your King the holy scripture teaches,
To see God's image on his Majesty.

    'Writ on the boards which encloses the church in
    Bloomsbury [with a statue of George I on its steeple]'

c.570/2, p. 162

T3202 Touch'd by your generous hearts, to spare the play,
And aid with generous hand, the music claim.

    'Prologue'

c.578, p. 72

T3203 Touching his life I nothing list to tell
When both conjoined, God shall be All in all.

fc.61, p. 137

T3204 Towards Ireland in haste her princes go,
May G[eorge] and W[illia]m O heavens the like
                        obtain.

    'On the King's expedition 1690'

fb.207/1, p. 40; see also 'In haste towards Ireland . . .'.

T3205 Town-wenches cries Rustic I've often been told
His deceit in their hearts and his sting in their tails.

c.546, p. 30

T3206 Towns, fields and churches, took from God and
                            men,
And Tirrell's arrow drink his guilty blood.

    'On the New Forest'

c.53, fol. 60

T3207 Toy with your books: and, as the various fits
And from prose to song.

    'A hint to readers'

c.94

T3208 Toys like these by rhyme protected
Glow with transport, mirth, and pleasure.

    H[enry] Skrine, 'To a lady with a weekly
    pocket-book . . . June 20 17[8-?]'

c.509, p. 64

T3209 Traitor to God, and rebel to thy pen,
May modestly believe transubstantiation.

  Tho[mas] Brown, 'To Mr. Dryden, on his conversion'
  [Crum T3300]

  c.189, p. 173; fc.24, p. 28

T3210 Transferring was my trade whilst I had breath
And purchase a long long annuity!

  'Epitaph on an eminent stock-jobber'

  fc.85, fol. 85

T3211 Transparent clouds receive the setting sun
And there repair lost beams, with cheerful fires.

  [Abraham Cowley?], 'Scene of the evening'

  File 3782/7

T3212 Transpierc'd with many a streaming wound,
Men feel who barter man for gold.

  Thomas Holcroft(?), 'The negro'

  c.141, p. 549

T3213 Transporting tidings which we hear
Tho' round their graves and near our own.

  P[hilip] Doddridge, 'Comf[ort from] the death of
  pious friends from 1 Thess. IV' [verses 13–14]

  c.493, p. 16

T3214 Travail thou must and undergo affliction
To think that pleasure gains such great renown.

  [Mary Serjant]

  fb.98, fol. 164

T3215 Trav'ler! If curious you would know
Himself the grand supreme in fame.

  'Epitaph on my dog'

  c.382, p. 48

T3216 Tread lightly, reader, I entreat thee,
Or else, by Jove, I'll rise and eat thee.

  'The glutton'

  c.233, p. 100

T3217 Treading alone the sacred dome
Nor wish to be in Eusden's place.

  'Request to his Grace the Duke of Chandos to erect a
  monument in Westminster Abbey to the memory of
  Milton . . . 1723' [Eusden was then Poet Laureate]

  c.360/2, no. 120

T3218 Treason doth never prosper, what's the reason
For if it prosper none dare call it treason.

  [Sir John Harington], 'On treason' [Epigrams,
  1618, IV]
  [Crum T3313]

  b.62, p. 96

T3219 Treason is like the basilisk his eye
First seeing kills, first being seen doth die.

  'Alter' [on treason]
  [Crum T3314]

  b.62, p. 96

T3220 Treast [sic] friends, I speak no ill of you, it is
Pick out, is that I am no puritan.

  Sir Thomas Urquhart, 'The author's apology to the
  puritans'

  fb.217, p. 53

T3221 Tremendous league, say where is now thy dread
Bellisle is taken, and the emperor dead.

  'An extempore on the death of the emperor Charles
  the 7th . . . 10—January 1744/5'

  c.360/1, p. 319

T3222 Tremendous sound I fear
Nor shall I be forsook.

  T[homas] S[tevens], 'Ez[e]k[ia]l 48'

  c.259, p. 121

T3223 Tridamians! Quadrigamians! Cleric too!
Nor can I find her peer, now she is gone.

  T[homas] M[orell], 'An epitaph . . . on the wife of the
  Rev. J. Mickleborough . . . translated . . . in
  pentameters'

  c.395, p. 122

T3224 Trifling mortal tell me why
When suns shall fade away.

  'Verses writ by a gentleman on finding an urn'

  c.547, p. 234; fc.85, fol. 22

T3225 Triple goddess! Woodland maid!
Each new year and bleed for thee.

  [William Popple, trans.], '[Horace] book 3rd. ode 22d.
  To Diana'

  fc.104/2, p. 284

T3226 Triptolemus did not in chariot sit:
Whilst steeds, and coaches go a broader way.

  Sir Thomas Urquhart, 'An encouragement to
  estaffiers, and lackeys'

  fb.217, p. 255

T3227 Triumphant and victorious he appears
I who most ready am, and mighty too to save.

  'Isa[iah] 63'

  c.148, p. 7

T3228 Troth lords I thought to've told you stories
When she's to knaves and fools so kind.

  Rob[ert] Watts, 'Westminster Hall'

  Poetry Box VI/103

T3229 True bounty springs from nobleness of mind,
On either hand these pinch those cast away.

> [Sir Philip Wodehouse], 'A cinquefoil of virtues with their bordering vices in their congruities and differences. Liberality or bounty'
>
> b.131, p. 12

T3230 True British hearts you are requir'd to pray
With one accord to render James his right.

> 'Verses thrown into houses on the tenth of June'
>
> c.570/1, p. 160

T3231 True courage was not understood by those
To come with ills is nobler than to fly.

> John Lockman, 'Against self-murder: from Madame Deshoulières'
>
> c.267/4, p. 163

T3232 True Englishmen, drink a good health to the miter:
As stout as our martyrs, and as just as our laws.

> 'A new catch in praise of the [seven] bishops' [1688] [Crum T3332; *POAS* IV.229]
>
> b.111, p. 108

T3233 True Englishmen ever approve yourselves loyal,
And pray that kind heaven may keep him from ill.

> 'Good advice'
>
> b.111, p. 596

T3234 True faith and wicked manners quarrel so,
Else when we talk of heav'n, we must dread hell.

> [Edmund Wodehouse], 'July 14 [1715] Dr. Scot of apostasy'
>
> b.131, p. 231

T3235 True love finds wit, but he whose wit doth move
Thinking to share the sport, but not the sin.

> [Sir John Roe], 'Elegia 15ta'
> [Crum T3336]
>
> b.114, p. 123 (attr. Donne); b.148, p. 96 (attr. J[ohn] D[onne])

T3236 True love, if there such a thing can be,
They scarce find heaven a more exalted state.

> c.158, p. 20

T3237 True modest worth with gentle manners join'd
From every eye the tribute of a tear.

> 'To the memory of Thos Lovell . . . who died . . . 8th of June 1762'
>
> Diggle Box: Poetry Box XI/44

T3238 True modesty is comeliness of mind
Yields things unfit, thro' more facility.

> [Sir Philip Wodehouse], 'Modesty or verecundia'
>
> b.131, p. 14

T3239 True passion has a force, too strong for art
Grasp thee thro' death—and be forever thine.

> 'Written on the right hand of Lord Petre's tomb' [in the Pensoroso]
>
> fc.51, p. 96

T3240 True to a patriot plan, [?] odious years,
And, from my scorn of riches, greater rise.

> John Lockman, 'The resolve . . . writ in April 1762, when vile practices were carrying on, in the [Herring Fishery] Society'
>
> c.267/1, p. 280

T3241 True to my trust, by night, by day,
Else not a knave of them I'd spare.

> John Lockman, 'Engraved on the collar of Lion, a faithful mastiff, at Buckingham House'
>
> c.267/1, p. 14

T3242 True to our sovereign, to the people just,
But who he is, not ev'n thyself shalt tell.

> 'On the mayoralty of Mr. Alderman Turner. 9 Nov. 1769 . . . Ignotus'
>
> c.267/4, p. 369

T3243 True wit is like the brilliant stone
And sparkles while it wounds.

> [Hester Lynch Thrale Piozzi], 'On wit written on a window at Mileham'
> [Crum T3344]
>
> c.360/1, p. 297; c.391, p. 47; fc.132/1, p. 47

T3244 True zeal and loyalty the poet warms
With thee Great Britain lives, without thee dies.

> 'The prologue' [to Sir Richard Steele's The conscious lovers(?); upon the perils of popery and the Pretender]
>
> Poetry Box X/10(4)

T3245 Truly, my soul, tho' sunk in grief,
To each man, as his work shall be.

> 'Psalm 62. Morning prayer 12 day'
>
> c.264/2, p. 20

T3246 Truly some men there be,
Sooner done, and shorter pain.

> 'Inscription in a schoolbook, in which is a border of naked women. Wyor. 1542'
>
> c.81/1, no. 58

T3247 Trumps ever rul'd the charming maid,
She married Tom the gardener.

> 'On a lady very fond of cards marrying her gardener'
>
> Diggle Box: Poetry Box XI/69

T3248 Trust me, Corvinus, when the rolling year
Forget the past and leave thy axe behind.

'Juvenal's twelfth satire. Natali corvine, die &c.'
fc.14/9

T3249 Trust me, Polly, 'tis a folly,
Nor deceiving nor deceiv'd!

[Heavily corrected]
Poetry Box IV/68

T3250 Trust Nan—for what she says she'll do.
Will bring thee a crown, of immortality.

[Sir Philip Wodehouse], 'Upon his pretty niece Anne
Strutt [later Samwell]'
b.131, back (no. 30)

T3251 Trust providence still
Whether we're Low Church—or High.

c.361

T3252 Trust to the winds you bark, but trust not Eve!
'Tis strange how bad for good should change its
                                          place.

'In faeminas . . . ditto [translation]'
c.81/1, no. 311

T3253 Trusting in God, with anxious care decay'd,
Unknown to all, known to myself, I die.

[Charles Earle], 'An epitaph on myself . . . Englished'
c.376 (two copies)

T3254 Truth is divine; for God is truth. It so
Truth is the tie of man's society.

[Sir Philip Wodehouse]
b.131, p. 32

T3255 Truth-telling fools speak things to be conceal'd,
Keeps four fools about him for their aid.

'Of Aulus a grandee'
c.356

T3256 Try all you can each one's good word to gain
As angels just, you still shall have a foe.

A[dam] S[mith], 'The best of friends oft turn the
worst of foes'
c.361

T3257 Try, heart, and reins, without, within,
That fills my heart with joy and love.

'The soul's request to God before the communion'
c.187, p. 53

T3258 Tune now yourselves my heart-strings high;
All glory now and ever be.

[John Austin], 'Hym. 25' [Hymn xxii, Devotions in
the ancient way of offices, 1672, p. 194]
c.178, p. 23

T3259 Tune your pipes ye jolly swains
Smil'd and blest, smil'd and blest | The happy pair.

'On King James' marriage. To the tune of Would fate
but make Belinda mine, &c.'
c.570/2, p. 92

T3260 Turn gentle hermit of the dale,
Shall break thy Edwin's too.

[Oliver] Goldsmith, 'The hermit. Or Edwin and
Angelina'
c.83/1, no. 15; c.156, p. 159; fc.132/1, p. 86; Poetry Box II/2
(stanzas 1–9)

T3261 Turn in my Lord, my heart's a homely place
Canst if thou wilt by saying give me take it.

[Sir Richard Bulstrode], 'The invitation to our Lord'
fb.88, p. 117

T3262 Turn not, O reader! from this humble stone,
On excellence alone, the tear bestows.

Lady [Mary] Sudley, viscountess, 'Epitaph in Weston
church yard by . . . in memory of her maid'
c.83/2, no. 634

T3263 Turn tame the [?] who Athens ruled
But ply thy soul until thy ardor cools.

[Sir Philip Wodehouse]
b.131, p. 4

T3264 Turn turn away Orlando dear
For refuge sought with thee?

'Lines addressed by a lady to her lover to whom she
had fled for protection from the tyranny of a father,
who expressed his alarm for her character'
c.546

T3265 T'ward Sicilus seated, to the welkin loftily peaking,
Void ye fro' these flamfews, quod the God, that
                                          begun work.

'The description of Liparen, expressed by Virgil . . .'
b.207, p. 11

T3266 'Twas at the gate of Calais Hogarth tells
Then scrubb'd himself, and thus bewail'd his case.

[Theodosius Forrest], 'The famed sorloin [sic]'
Poetry Box IV/58

T3267 'Twas at the hour, when evening's pall,
I'll seek my happy friend.

'Rodolpho, earl of Norfolk. A legendary tale'

c.83/3, no. 1064

T3268 'Twas at the royal feast, for Persia won,
She drew an angel down.

[John] Dryden, 'Alexander's feast'
[Crum T3369]

fc.132/1, p. 133

T3269 'Twas at the silent solemn hour
And word spoke never more.

[Sir Charles Hanbury Williams], 'William and
Margaret' [parody of David Mallet's 'When all was
wrapt . . .', against the Gin Act. Printed 1743 (Foxon
W503)]

c.179, p. 1; c.83/1, no. 238; Poetry Box 11/28

T3270 'Twas at the solemn midnight, silent hour
What Talbot's merit won, may fall to you.

[Sir John Rons], 'A dream'

c.130, p. 22

T3271 'Twas bright Augusta's nuptial morn
Scorns the feeble hand of art.

[John] Lockman, 'The sylph—a cantata, written
by . . . on the occasion of the marriage of her
Highness Augusta Princess of Saxe-Gotha with his
royal Highness Frederick, Prince of Wales, on
Tuesday April the 27—1736'

c.360/1, p. 141; c.268 (first part), p. 107 ('Bright
Lucinda's'); see also ''Twas fam'd Amanda's . . .'.

T3272 'Twas death alone could overcome
Once victor more, he'd only been translated!

'Proh dolor occubuit? . . .' [on the duke of
Marlborough]

Poetry Box XIV/176

T3273 'Twas early one morning in May
A demand, what each lady must take.

'Query division for the author's young accountants at
school'

c.91, p. 215

T3274 'Twas easy in her looks to trace
Was realiz'd at last.

[Helen Maria Williams], 'Edwin and Eltruda' [1782]

c.139, p. 523

T3275 'Twas evening, and the meager time drew near
He drops, and flutt'ring, yields his soul to air.

'Gallicidium' [cock-throwing]
[Crum T3374]

fb.142, p. 68

T3276 'Twas evening, when the feather'd choir,
Flutter'd his wings, sunk down, and died.

[Thomas Morell], 'The widowed swan'

c.395, p. 135

T3277 'Twas fam'd Amanda's nuptial morn,
And ev'ry charm will brighter grow.

John Lockman, 'Cantatas. The sylph: writ on occasion
of the nuptials of Augusta, Princess of Saxe-Gotha,
with his royal highness Frederick Prince of Wales . . .
anno 1736'

c.267/2, p. 181; see also ''Twas bright Augusta's . . .'.

T3278 'Twas fancy that made Delia fair
Narcissus and a pail of water.

'On fancy in love'

c.360/1, p. 267

T3279 'Twas in a vale where osiers grow
Unveil'd and unconfin'd.

[Isaac Watts], 'To Mr. N. Clark complaining of the
spleen and vapors'

c.349, fol. 2v

T3280 'Twas in heaven pronounc'd and 'twas mutter'd in
hell,
Ah! breathe on it softly—it dies in an hour!

'Sent to us by Lady Davy'

Greatheed Box/92

T3281 'Twas in mid-August, and at burning noon
To be thy special scribe and pimp and proctor.

'Written in August on a hot day in company, upon a
Deist (who greatly admired D. Hume) saying that
Dr. Johnson for his pride deserved to be the Devil's
secretary'

fc.53, p. 18

T3282 'Twas in sultry summer weather,
No more budget days may have.

'St James's chronicle a stroke at the budget by a
Madeley Wood colonel(?). Tune Jolly mortals fill your
glasses'

Poetry Box X/106

T3283 'Twas in the close recesses of a shade,
And darts as lightning thro' the cleaving skies.

[Elizabeth] (Singer) [Rowe], 'The vision'

c.244, p. 420

T3284 'Twas in the glad season of spring,
Resolves to have none of her own.

[William] Cowper, 'The morning dream; on the same
subject [the Negro's complaint]'

fc.132/1, p. 215

T3285 'Twas in the last college vacation
Join'd sweet pretty Kitty and me.

> Humphrey Senhouse, 'Humphrey Senhouse esquire
> verses—sweet pretty Kitty'
>
> fc.40

T3286 'Twas in the merry month of May
Than a whole Philistine army.

> 'Song'
>
> c.189, p. 176; see also next.

T3287 'Twas in the merry month of May
Or that which warns the cook.

> 'Enigmas in The ladies' diary for the year 1748
> answered'
>
> c.241, p. 117; see also previous.

T3288 'Twas in the seventeen hundred and ten
By men once call'd Whigs Swedes and Tories was
saved. | Which nobody can deny

> 'The historical ballad: which nobody can deny'
>
> Poetry Box XIV/177

T3289 'Twas in the summer's early pride,
Will cloud each future day.

> 'Lines which Vane put into Olivia's book'
>
> c.83/2, no. 403

T3290 'Twas in the town of London
And lead the mob to Hell, Sir.

> 'The mayor and the mob. To the tune of Royal race
> was Shinkin' [pr. 1742? (Foxon M154)]
>
> c.570/4, p. 57

T3291 'Twas June: and Cynthia's cloudless light
And take Minerva for your guide.

> John Lockman, 'Hymen and Cupid. A fable. On
> occasion of [blank]'s nuptials'
>
> c.267/2, p. 396

T3292 'Twas late, and cold, when with a mighty flame
I'll try this fancy fled, how to revive.

> [George Daniel]
>
> b.121, fol. 40v

T3293 'Twas L[ewi]s writ them we all know it
His beer has neither hops nor malt.

> 'In answer to ['The day! Is come . . .'] handed at
> [washed away]'
>
> c.74

T3294 'Twas mercy brought me from my pagan land
May be refin'd, and join the angelic train.

> P[hyllis] W[heatley], 'On being brought from Africa
> to America'
>
> c.259, p. 101

T3295 'Twas my purpose on a day,
'Twixt the bridegroom and his bride.

> [William Cowper, trans.], 'A figurative description of
> the procedure of divine love bringing a soul to the
> point of self-renunciation and absolute acquiescence.
> Vol. 2. Cant. 110' [of Jeanne Guion's 'Spiritual songs']
>
> c.470 (autogr.)

T3296 'Twas needless, Gough, to add two basses more:
Thy harmony was base enough before.

> [John Lockman], 'Upon Mr. Gough (of Marylebone
> Gardens) advertising that he would add the two
> deepest basses in England to his concert'
>
> c.268 (first part), p. 35; see also ''Twere . . .'.

T3297 'Twas night, when clinging on my breast,
And joy in thy disgrace?

> [William Popple, trans.], '[Horace, ep]ode 15th: to
> Neora'
>
> fc.104/2, p. 454

T3298 'Twas noon's meridian—summer's blaze
With a peculiar care.

> 'The hand of providence'
>
> c.91, p. 49

T3299 'Twas not his person nor his parts
But as he was before.

> b.213, p. 6

T3300 'Twas not you my Brute! that Caesar tried
And his Craterus, that Haephestion be.

> [Sir Philip Wodehouse], 'A true copy of his own
> prepared and sent immediately upon the tender of the
> former' [''Tis true (my Phylanax) . . .']
>
> File 17713

T3301 'Twas on a lofty vase's side
Nor all that glisters gold.

> [Thomas Gray], 'On a favorite cat called Selima that
> fell into a china tub with goldfishes in it and was
> drowned' [attr. John Gay]
> [Crum T3395]
>
> Poetry Box I/116; c.157, p. 44; fc.51, p. 231

T3302 'Twas on a mountain's airy spire
And meet on ev'ry blast a variegated ray.

> [Robert Merry], 'Extract from Diversity a poem'
>
> c.140, p. 167

T3303 'Twas on a river's verdant bank
And I with pleasure go.

> 'The dying swan'
> [Crum T3397, 'verdant side']
>
> c.186, p. 45; see also next, and ''Twas on a verdant . . .'.

T3304   'Twas on a river's verdant side
And it's a pain to live.

     'The swan—from The hive'
     [Crum T3396]
     c.244, p. 106; see also previous, and ''Twas on a
     verdant . . .'.

T3305   'Twas on a summer's day
And a shepherd all thy own.

     ''Twas on a summer's day. A ballad'
     Trumbull Box: Poetry Box XIII/70

T3306   'Twas on a verdant river's side
Soft scenes of happy love.

     'A song the dying swan'
     fb.68, p. 141 (incomplete); see also ''Twas on a
     river's . . .'.

T3307   'Twas on that dark, that doleful night,
The marriage supper of the lamb.

     [Isaac Watts, Hymns and spiritual songs (1707),
     bk. III, Hymn 1]
     c.180, p. 36

T3308   'Twas on that day, my friend, when from the brow
Thy country may rejoice in one true man.

     'An epistle to Edward Winnington esq. at Rome
     describing a journey of two days into N. Wales'
     fc.53, p. 57

T3309   'Twas on the day by Mansfield chosen
Bid thou put them all to rights.

     [George] H[owar]d, [6th earl of Carlisle], 'Parody of
     Dryden's ode occasioned by a strange alarm in
     Westminster Hall'
     c.197, p. 25

T3310   'Twas on the day, when sacred rest
And Christ the son of righteousness.

     Josh[ua] Williams, of Kidderminster, '(Saints shine
     with borrowed rays) On a journey Wednesday, July 22.
     1747'
     c.259, p. 114

T3311   'Twas on the evening of that day,
For my part I have done, and so goodnight.

     'Eucharisticon. Or an heroic poem upon the late
     Thanksgiving Day, which was the vigil or fast of St.
     Simon and St. Jude'
     b.111, p. 269

T3312   'Twas on the twentieth of September
Along with her good man.

     'Elegy of an honest country woman, on her husband
     who was killed by the wheels of a cart'
     c.391, p. 44

T3313   'Twas once my wish, nor did it aim too high—
Give me my farmhouse, and my beans and peas.

     [William Popple, trans.], 'Horace book 2nd satire 6th
     imitated. Inscribed to the R[ight] Honorable Sir
     Edward Walpole, knight'
     fc.104/1, p. 305

T3314   'Twas one May morning when the cloud undrawn
If all life's race, were wedding days like mine.

     'The wedding day'
     c.83/2, no. 380

T3315   'Twas post meridiem half past four
And to my throbbing heart press'd Nancy.

     'Sailor's journal' [Ferribridge, 31 August '97]
     Poetry Box V/66

T3316   'Twas said of late, the bragging lads of Spain
Pygmalion's sure ne'er to have news of them.

     'On Sir William Udall, who hid money in a church
     wall, and so lost it. 1608'
     b.200, p. 10

T3317   'Twas said of old, the Thracian's pow'rful song
Of fabled Orpheus and Eurydice.

     'On a beautiful lady with a fine voice'
     c.360/3, no. 45

T3318   'Twas somewhere in the southern climes of France
Provision for the convent at your cost.

     'Provision for a convent'
     c.53, fol. 81

T3319   'Twas spoke from heaven, the best of men must die
Forever praising God! Forever blest!

     Joseph Harris, 'A panagyrical elegy, on the much
     lamented death, of the right honorable the Earl of
     Thanet, &c.'
     fc.93

T3320   'Twas Sunday—long the bell had rung
This do in memory of me.

     [Helen Craik], 'To a gentleman . . . 1782'
     c.375, p. 25

T3321   'Twas that dread season of the year
And prove Thy glorious plan the happiest and the
                              best.

     William Warren Porter, 'Ode on Christmas Day
     by . . . St. John's Coll: Oxf.'
     c.373, p. 77

T3322　'Twas underneath a willow
Found death, a sure relief.

   [Thomas Hamilton, 6th earl of Haddington],
   'Tommy's complaint'

c.458/2, p. 149

T3323　'Twas when nor state nor crowds annoy
The vows (she cried) bestow'd at night revolving
                      day destroys.

   'The caliph . . . ordered each [poet] to compose a
   copy of verses . . . That of Abu Nowas was as follows'

c.326, p. 382

T3324　'Twas when the night in silent sable fled,
Or be to bless the nights my dreams like this.

   [Thomas Parnell], 'Piety or the vision'
   [Crum T3415]

File 11383, p. 14

T3325　'Twas when the rosy morn began to rise,
All o'er his limbs, and seal his eyes in sleep.

   [Stephen Barrett], 'The pleasures of a country life. A
   school exercise'

c.193, p. 60

T3326　'Twas when the seas were roaring,
She bow'd her head and died.

   [John Gay], 'A song' [from The comic farce, II.viii]
   [Crum T3416]

c.358, p. 86; Spence Papers, folder 113; Accession 97.7.40,
p. 23

T3327　'Twas when the sun's inspiring rays
Time, wisdom, glory, give the skies.

   John Lockman, 'Time, wisdom, and glory. Most
   humbly addressed to his royal highness, George Prince
   of Wales; in occasion of his birthday, June 4, 1759 . . .'

c.267/3, p. 93

T3328　'Twas wisely done to throw aside
The grandson of John Gunning.

   'On the Marquess of Clydesdale's baptism'

c.171, no. 14

T3329　Twenty lost years have stol'n their hours away,
Smile at discharge from care, and shut out life.

   Aaron Hill, 'Alone in an inn at Southampton. April
   the 25, 1787'

c.138, p. 35; c.83/2, no. 381

T3330　'Twere folly if ever | The Whigs should endeavor
'Twas lately found out by the prudent addressers.

   'A new ballad to the tune of the Irish jig' [1684; on the
   late plot, 1682–83, with reference to Dangerfield's
   Particular narrative, 1679]
   [Crum T3426; POAS III.506]

b.52/1, p. 3a

T3331　'Twere needless (Gough!) to add two basses more;
Thy harmony was base enough before.

   John Lockman, 'On Mr. Gough's advertising, that he
   would add two of the deepest basses in England, to his
   concert, in Marylebone Gardens'

c.267/1, p. 152; see also ''Twas . . .'.

T3332　Twice has the monitory clock
His gun never flash in the pan!

   R[ichard] V[ernon] S[adleir], 'To a friend who went
   shooting, forgetful of his appointment on business'

c.106, p. 30

T3333　Twice or thrice had I loved thee
'Twixt women's love, and men's will ever be.

   [John Donne], 'Angels and air'
   [Crum T3432]

b.114, p. 273; b.148, p. 108

T3334　Twice to my heart my wife true pleasure gave
Once in her bed, and once when in her grave.

   'An epigram'

fb.142, p. 32

T3335　Twice twelve years not fully told, a lifeless breath
That when death meets us we may be found ready.

   [on a gentleman of the Temple that died about the age
   of 24]
   [Crum T3434]

c.189, p. 106

T3336　Twice twenty days of lamentable Lent
Mourn for his belly, forty days in black.

   'Of wearing black in Lent'

b.62, p. 119

T3337　Twilight's soft dews steal o'er the village green,
Whose virtue triumphs, and her sons are blest!

   'The pleasures of memory'

c.355, p. 232

T3338　'Twixt footman John and Dr. Joe
'Twas footman versus Joeman.

   'An epigram'

Poetry Box XII/55

T3339　'Twixt ill and nothing being small differ John
Though you make many verses, you make none.

   Sir Thomas Urquhart, 'To a bad poet, whose name
   was John'

fb.217, p. 203

T3340   'Twixt our diseases there's no doubt
And I by taking't in.

    Sir Thomas Urquhart, 'The speeches of a maid, who
    had the green sickness, to a gentleman of her
    acquaintance oppressed with the toothache'

    fb.217, p. 173

T3341   'Twixt pounds and pence, two letters place,
'Twill show you something near His Grace.

    Diggle Box: Poetry Box XI/71

T3342   Entry cancelled. 'Two able physicians . . .' *See* next.

T3343   Two ancient physicians as e'er practic'd physic
For it was not my lord, but my lady, that p[i]st it.

    [Alexander] Pope(?), 'On Dr Mead and Sr Hans
    Sloane'

    c.74; c.81/1, no. 90 ('able physicians'); c.94 ('able
    physicians')

T3344   Two angels, on a shining cloud reclin'd,
And this kind [?] will complete the plan.

    John Lockman, 'On reading the advertisement, for the
    opera of Ezio, to be performed on Wednesday 24th
    April 1764; towards raising a sum, for adding a wing
    to the Middlesex Hospital'

    c.267/2, p. 397

T3345   Two bachelors meeting together today
With my compliments last, tho' they should have
                    been first.

    'A card compliment sent to a young lady'

    c.487, p. 65

T3346   Two bags are stolen or astray—
For fear of hanging, hang himself.

    [Charles Earle], 'A cry at West-down occasioned by
    the Revd. Mr. Earle having two bags stolen from his
    pantry window'

    c.376

T3347   Two blessings justly priz'd O God defend
To soothe their sufferings or increase their fame.

    [William Hayley], 'Sonnet . . . Feb 4 [1800]'

    File 6968

T3348   Two broom-men, drinking with each other,
'I steal them readymade.'

    'The broom-men. An epigram'

    Poetry Box IV/157

T3349   Two brothers drinking at a tavern, one
Our bottles hold, not much above a pint.

    'The difference ended'

    c.81/1, no. 351

Two brothers, fishers on the Thames,   T3350
'Twas one of them, brought me to crutches.

    [Thomas Hamilton, 6th earl of Haddington], 'The
    crutch'

    c.458/2, p. 107

Two bucks having lost their bamboos in a fray   T3351
The depth of his purse by the length of his cane.

    'Short canes'

    c.143, fol. 16

Two bulls there were of high renown,   T3352
Reel'd as they lov'd home to their lodgings.

    'The bull feast'

    c.176, p. 48

Two by themselves each other love and fear   T3353
Slain cruel friends by parting have joined here.

    [John Donne], 'Pyramus and Thisbe'
    [Crum T3443]

    b.148, p. 23

Two candles burning in a hall,   T3354
Barely to know the twilight of existence.

    'The two candles'

    c.83/2, no. 708

Two cats fell out and one another slew   T3355
But that they company so oft offend.

    [Sir Aston Cokayne], 'Of cats'

    b.275, p. 83

Two deities, (genius and art,)   T3356
Hark how she charms the shade!

    John Lockman, 'Writ in a blank leaf of Mr. Samuel
    Boyer's Poems . . . June 1757'

    c.267/1, p. 207

Two ears at a time are too many for use,   T3357
Be sure to be deaf of one ear.

    'Matrimonial deafness'

    c.94 (incomplete?)

Two English sailors strangers to the hyp   T3358
And leave the stable filthy as we found it.

    'On the HEALTH late in vogue: To the cleansing the
    Augean stable'

    Poetry Box XIV/175

Two Georges shine among the sons of men   T3359
One George defends, and one adorns the state.

    c.115

T3360 Two gibbets revers'd and the moon in full view
With pitchfork upright a cheese cut in two.

[on the name Lloyd]
[Crum T3455, 'gibbets dejected']
c.150, p. 8

T3361 Two gossips they luckily met
Should he for our sins be cut off.

'The gossip's toast, or the admiral' [ballad on Vernon's
capture of Porto Bello, Nov. 1739]
[Crum T3457]
Poetry Box I/100; c.555, p. 112 (incomplete?)

T3362 Two great physicians first
And then I died.

'Here lies the body of Molly Dickie the wife of Hall
Dickie, tailor . . . Cheltenham'
c.546; c.113/9

T3363 Two honest tradesmen meeting in the Strand,
Something that was as black, Sir, as a crow.

'A tale'
Diggle Box: Poetry Box XI/69

T3364 Two hopeful youths are sprung from G[eorge]'s
                                                loins
A prattling monkey, or a lump of lead.

[John Hervey, baron Hervey of Ickworth], 'The
brothers' [the Duke of Cumberland and the Prince of
Wales, 1738]
[Crum T3459]
c.154, p. 9; fc.58, p. 132; Poetry Box V/12

T3365 Two houses, now, are all the mode,
And rarely enter here.

John Lockman, 'The three houses . . . April 1742'
c.267/1, p. 115

T3366 Two hundred pence, what's that to thee, but say
O Judas that's the cause thou didst repine.

[Francis Quarles], 'On Judas, and the ointment'
b.137, p. 165

T3367 Two husbands two wives two sisters two brothers,
The son must be father, his wife her own mother.

'An epitaph . . . the answer'
c.83/1, no. 200

T3368 Two knights, six projectors, four squires and Tom
                                                Twitty,
And Packington's now taken in his own pound.

[William Walsh?], 'The Worcester cabal or a very new
ballad to a very old tune, called Packington's Pound.
The second edition with annotations and
amendments'
[POAS VI.313]
fb.70, p. 109

T3369 Two lovely nymphs desire my song
Be theirs the triumph, mine the pleasure.

C[olley] Cibber, 'To Miss Banks and Miss Howe'
c.360/2, no. 23

T3370 Two masters is a heavy yoke: yet we
Practic'd in sev'ral churches one devotion.

Sir Thomas Urquhart, 'Two masters, and two
mistresses'
fb.217, p. 169

T3371 Two maxims make most men mis-tread
The same fair and honest cozenage call.

Sir John Strangways, '1: Tanti valet . . . 2: Caveat
emptor . . . 12mo Octobris 1646'
b.304, p. 60

T3372 Two measures of the three your speeches bound;
Thy're long, and large enough: but not profound.

Sir Thomas Urquhart, 'To one, who spoke very much,
but exceedingly coarsely'
fb.217, p. 173

T3373 Two millers thin
That flesh and blood won't bear it.

[John Byrom, of Manchester], 'In the great scarcity of
corn two millers near Cambridge whose names
happened to be Skin and Bone became great
engrossers, which occasioned the following epigram'
c.74; see also 'Bone and Skin . . .'.

T3374 Two monsters Hercule in his cradle kill'd
In that which is most proper and [?]

[Sir Thomas Urquhart], 'The parallel of Zoroaster
who did laugh as soon as he was born: and of Hercules
who while he was lying in his cradle with his brother
Iphecles [killed two monsters]'
fb.217, p. 505

T3375 Two neighbors Clod and Toll, would married be,
We've beauty and a skillet more than they.

'The skillet'
c.578, p. 105

T3376 Two nymphs the most renown'd Sir
And stretch'd their lordship's ears.

'The compe[ti]tion, or the rival nymphs'
c.176, p. 153

T3377 Two nymphs with beauty's every charms,
When milder graces play.

John Head, 'Epigram'
c.341, p. 6

T3378 Two or three dears, and two or three sweets
Can never fail making a couple of fools.

'A receipt for courtship'
c.360/2, no. 155; c.233, p. 82 ('dearies'); c.489, p. 18;
Poetry Box XII/52; see also next.

T3379 Two or three sighs and two or three dears
And many a maid is took with the clue.

'Modern courtship'
c.83/1, no. 152; see also previous.

T3380 Two parliaments dissolved then let my heart,
That lambs feed on you? lions will come next.

'On the dissolution of the Parliament [5 May] 1640'
[Crum T3474]
Poetry Box VI/23

T3381 Two roses sprang in royal Rome
And everlasting light. | Amen

'S. Ruffina and Secunda. Ju[ly]. 10'
a.30[10]

T3382 Two score and nine odd years have I maintain'd
And with a longing (fiat) end her song.

Sir Fr[ancis] Hu[bert], 'The pilgrim's survey'
b.197, p. 221

T3383 Two songsters, Frazies of their kind
Pick up your crumbs, and hold your tongue.

'The robin and the canary birds a fable'
Poetry Box X/45, p. 17

T3384 Two steeds appointed were by Haman's hand
Of thine, first brought thee to thy journey's end.

[Francis Quarles], 'On Mordecai and Haman' [Divine
fancies II, 50]
b.137, p. 169

T3385 Two swains to win Corinna strove,
Is, conqueror, to save.

[William Carpenter], 'Imperet bellanto prior,
jacentem lenis in hostem'
c.247, p. 113

T3386 Two things have I requir'd before I die
Between the dearest husband and his wife.

Sir John Strangways, 'The 30 chapter of the proverbs
of Solomon beginning at the 7th verse—to the end
thereof . . . 1º Augusti 1647'
b.304, p. 113

T3387 Two things there are, to clean the room
In two verse ends, have told its name.

c.160, fol. 47

T3388 Two Toms, and a Nat, together sat
Will cover his dominion.

'The thanksgiving for the Queen's conception [of
James II's son, born 10 June 1688; to the tune of My
love is to Jamaica gone]'
[Crum T3489; POAS IV.240]
fb.108, p. 139; b.209, p. 78

T3389 Two vagrants as they hobbling stray,
And prove it thus: take each a shell.

John Lockman, 'The lawyer and the oyster: or the
blind and lame beggar'
c.267/3, p. 82

T3390 Two youths on whom Phoebus much wit had
bestow'd
Of what you confided to . . . . . and Helen.

[Helen Craik], 'The following lines were occasioned
by a humorous court-martial held and written by two
officers on some ladies who had disobliged them'
c.375, p. 70

T3391 'Twould seem a little strange, I must confess,
And none offended more than he could easily
forgive.

'A poem on the death of Thomas Cholmondeley of
Valeroyall esquire' [d. 26 Feb. 1701/2]
Poetry Box VII/24

T3392 Tyndarus attempting to kiss a fair lass with a long
nose
Hardly ye may kiss me, where no such gnomon
appeareth.

'Of Tyndarus that frumped a gentlewoman for having
a long nose delivered by Sr Thomas More in Latin'
b.207, p. 5

T3393 Tyrrell like Phillip's victor son
Can alter colors as create.

[Phanuel Bacon], 'To Belle Tyrrell upon a report that
she had changed her hair'
c.237, fol. 12

U

U0001 Ugly wretch, of horrid mien
And winter's snow incessant fall.

> [Thomas Hamilton, 6th earl of Haddington], 'To a lady in imitation of [Ambrose] Philips'

c.458/2, p. 129

U0002 Unaw'd by threats, unmov'd by force,
And sooth'd my soul to rest.

> 'Ode to patience'

c.83/3, no. 1076

U0003 Unblemish'd in his princely stem
This threefold purity does all resound his name.

> [Sir Philip Wodehouse], 'Princeps Rupertus'

b.131, back (no. 140)

U0004 Unblessed enthusiast! Fancy's darling child
And hails to Lethe's bank thy mis'ry-wasted form!

> [Anna Laetitia (Aikin) Barbauld], 'Sonnet on the death of Edmund Burke' [1797]

File 111

U0005 Unbounded learning, thoughts by genius fram'd,
Who, while the sage they honor'd, lov'd the friend.

> [Georgiana Spencer Cavendish], duchess of Devonshire, 'Lines on the death of Sir Wm. Jones'

c.83/4, no. 2036

U0006 Uncertain riches take their wings and flee
'Tis he on whom soul's care is hanged alone.

> 'Job 1'

c.160, fol. 57v

U0007 Uncivil death, that wouldst not once confer
Was fair (good Lord) to take his death 'twas so.

> 'An epitaph on the Lord Treasurer Buckhurst who died at the council table'
> [Crum U10, with six more lines]

b.197, p. 48; see also 'Discourteous death . . .'.

U0008 Unconquer'd hope, thou bane of fear,
Postpone our pain, and antedate our joy.

> 'Hope'

c.83/3, no. 772; c.116, p. 5 (var.)

U0009 Unconstant earth! Why do not mortals cease
At noon we flourish, and we fade at night.

> 'In Bampton churchyard Oxfordshire'

c.240, p. 133

U0010 Unconstant fortune various appears,
Whence hopes arise to me to thee but fears.

> 'Comfort for the poor. To the rich'

c.356

U0011 Unconstant world, 'tis plain to see
How variable thy actions be.

c.93

U0012 Uncouth is this moss-covered grotto of stone,
Then willow, wave all thy green tops to her song.

> [Richard Brinsley Butler] Sheridan, 'Mr. Sheridan meeting a Miss Linley now Mrs. Sheridan at the entrance of a grotto in the vicinity of Bath took the liberty of offering her some advice—with which apprehending that she was displeased he left the following lines in the grotto the next day'

c.341, p. 44; c.83/4, no. 2037; c.130, p. 42; c.139, p. 603 (stanzas 1–8); c.340; c.391, p. 1; Poetry Box XII/75

U0013 Under covert of a wood
Struck the poor lynx quite to the heart.

> William Warren Porter [verses written at the age of ten]

c.83/2, no. 531

U0014 Under fair shows such inward foes may lurk,
As when we trust, may our destruction wreak.

c.339, p. 314

U0015 Under five hundred kings three kingdoms groan
Making the people happy, monarch great.

> 'Upon the K[ing]'s dissolving the Parliament at Oxford 1681'
> [Crum U16; POAS II.411]

Poetry Box VII/83; c.171, p. 2 (ll. 1–18); c.189, p. 107 (ll. 1–18)

U0016 Under how hard a fate are women born,
And are besieg'd like frontier towns, if fair.

> E. C., 'Female fate'

c.360/3, no. 81, no. 203

U0017 Under that stone lies Gabriel John
If you please you may or let 'im alone. | 'Tis all one

c.160, fol. 85v; see also 'Under this stone . . .'.

U0018 Under the branches of a spreading tree,
And at last fall the trophies of honor, and love.

'The married life'

fb.107, p. 55

U0019 Under the broad seal of his Son's dear blood
God hath assur'd all riches grace and good.

[Robert Cottesford]

b.144, p. 3

U0020 Under the heaviest load of worldly woe
The sweets of life that can frail mortals cheer.

[Mrs. Christian Kerr], 'Astrea's answer' [to 'Tho'
tempests rage . . .']

c.102, p. 93

U0021 Under the notion of a play, you see,
'Tis that our play should be–at hide and seek.

'A prologue spoken by a boy seven years old at the
representation of a tragedy of Euripides'

c.360/3, no. 256

U0022 Under the rose bee's spoken you are she
You are the true Diana here in plaish [i.e., place?].

'Upon the pious work of the phoenix of the times
Dame Ursula Harvey' [acrostic on 'Ursula Harvey']

Poetry Box VI/109

U0023 Under this dust
In hopes that her paste shall be rais'd.

'An epitaph [on Moll Batchellor, an old piewoman at
Oxford]'

c.360/1, p. 161; see also 'Beneath this dust . . .', 'Here lies
Dick . . .', 'Beneath in the dust . . .'.

U0024 Under this marble lies a treasure,
His clients right, more than his fee!

'An epitaph on Mr. Alexander Rolle attorney at law'

c.244, p. 210

U0025 Under this marble stone do lie
When tree, and fruit shall spring again.

'On the death of of [sic] Rob: Huter, and his mother
that died at Winton 1632'

b.200, p. 227

U0026 Under this monument the relics lie
Until the resurrection of the just.

'An epitaph on William Banks, esquire'

c.244, p. 209

U0027 Under this sacred marble Newton lies,
He died—and helps attraction by his dust.

'On Sr Isaac Newton'

c.152, p. 16

U0028 Under this sacred urn doth lie entomb'd
In hopes to glorious resurrection rise.

'Epitaph'

Poetry Box x/3, p. 2

U0029 Under this same stone, here fast sleep the one
'Bout his heels to the ground.

'On a fat man'

fb.143, p. 29

U0030 Under this slate | Lies barren Kate
Under this stone | Lies one that has none.

c.233, p. 34

U0031 Under this stone doth lie | One born for victory
A man as great in war, as just in peace as he.

[George Villiers, 2nd duke of Buckingham], 'An
epitaph on Thomas, Lord Fairfax . . . 1676'
[Crum U35]

b.54, p. 1060; fc.61, p. 143; see also 'Fairfax! The
valiant! . . .'.

U0032 Under this stone, full five foot deep
Where will they meet with such a one?

Edward Sneyd, 'An epitaph upon a parish clerk'

c.214, p. 62

U0033 Under this stone here lies the dust
And if you don't they will impeach ye.

'An epitaph on Mr Dolben that manager against Mr
Sacheverell'

b.90, p. 20

U0034 Under this stone, his dust doth lie
His loss a public misery.

'An epitaph on Wil. Tothill of Peamont, esq.'

b.104, p. 2

U0035 Under this stone | Lies a reverend drone
As they led so he follow'd them all to the D[evi]l.

'On Mr Sam Smith late Ordinary of Newgate' [d.
1698; pr. Edinburgh 171-? (Foxon E441)]

fb.143, p. 12

U0036 Under this stone lies a woman
Till they laid her in this vale.

'Epitaph'

c.360/3, no. 143

U0037 Under this stone lies Katherine Gray
She in her shop may be again.

'Epitaph on a woman who sold earthenware'

c.150, p. 3; see also 'Beneath this stone . . .'.

U0038 Under this stone lies Gabriel John
Or let it alone, 'tis all one, 'tis all one.

'An epitaph and celebrated catch'

c.360/2, no. 193; see also 'Under that stone . . .'.

U0039 Under this stone lies Gilbert Nayle
Tho' Nayle is strucken to the head.

'Upon Gilbert Nayle'

b.208, p. 62

U0040 Under this stone lies John Day,
What old John? No. Young John? Aye.

c.233, p. 37; see also 'Underneath this stone lies here . . .'.

U0041 Under this stone lies Major Ralph
That he's the devil's Sergeant Major.

'Epitaph on an officer whose baptismal name was Ralph'

c.344

U0042 Under this stone my wife doth lie
Now she's at rest, and so am I.

'On a scold'

b.155, p. 64

U0043 Under this stone, reader, survey
Laid many a heavy load on thee.

[Abel Evans?], 'Sr. John Vanbrugh's epitaph'

c.176, p. 71; see also 'Reader beneath this stone . . .',
'Lie heavy on him . . .'.

U0044 Under this tomb the matchless Digby lies
His day of birth, of death, of victory.

'On Sr. Kenelm Digby' [d. 11 June 1665]
[Crum U48]

fb.143, p. 26

U0045 Under unhappy planets was I born
The world forsakes me and I'm left forlorn.

'Reflection'

c.360/3, no. 184

U0046 Underneath here
Our parents we both forgot.

'Epitaph on two children'

c.360/3, no. 122

U0047 Underneath lies Harry's clay
Tho' life indeed is but a jest.

Poetry Box x/91

U0048 Underneath this grassy clod,
Oh may we live eternally!

'The epitaph' [of John Wright, d. 1721; see 'No grief disturbs, no cares . . .']

c.244, p. 166

U0049 Underneath this marble hearse,
Time shall throw a dart at thee.

[William Browne of Tavistock?] 'An epitaph on Sr. Philip Sidney's sister'

c.244, p. 107 (ll. 1–6); c.360/2, no. 54 (ll. 1–6); c.481, p. 53 (ll. 1–6); c.481, p. 53 (ll. 1–6); c.547, p. 230 (ll. 1–6); see also next.

U0050 Underneath this sable hearse
Both thy mourner and thy tomb.

[William Browne of Tavistock?], 'An epitaph on the death of Mary Countess of Pembroke'
[Crum U59]

b.197, p. 219; b.356, p. 257; fb.143, p. 41; c.81/1, no. 291 (ll. 1–6); see also 'Underneath this marble . . .'.

U0051 Underneath this stone does lie
If she gets up I'll e'en lie still.

'An epitaph . . . Nov. 25th, 1797'

c.113/24; see also 'Underneath this turf . . .'.

U0052 Underneath this stone doth lie
I am sent for to receive a crown.

'Epitaph 8'

c.158, p. 48

U0053 Underneath this stone doth lie
To as much beauty as could live.

Ben Jonson, 'Epitaph on a lady [the Lady Elizabeth L.H.]'

c.360/1, p. 185; c.193, p. 48; c.244, p. 108; c.547, p. 231 ('as much virtue')

U0054 Underneath this stone is laid
And yet a maid, alas 'twas pity!

'On a chambermaid'
[Crum U62]

fb.143, p. 36

U0055 Underneath this stone lies here
What young John, aye, aye.

'Epitaph on a piper'

c.360/3, no. 123; see also 'Under this stone lies John Day . . .'.

U0056 Underneath this turf doth lie
If she gets up, I'll e'en be still.

'Epitaph'

c.81/1, no. 322; see also 'Underneath this stone . . .'.

U0057　Undone and plundered, waddling sad and slow
With thee her life, her love, her jointure, too she'll
share.

    [Elizabeth (Vassall) Fox], lady H[olland], 'Lady
    H[olland] to A.'

c.340

U0058　Undone undone the lawyers are
I would pull down Tyburn too.

    [Sir John Birkenhead], 'Ballad of Charing Cross'
    [Crum U63]

fb.106(11); b.213, p. 38

U0059　Uneasy under love's imperious reign
And smart severely 'cause I dar'd to rove.

    Maurice Johnson, '1705. Geo[rge] Buchanamis Scotus
    ad Neceram suam lib. 1 eleg. 9 . . . imitated'

c.229/2, fol. 34

U0060　Unenvied let inferior beauties boast
And makes a Whiteside captive to her charms.

    [David Stokes?], 'To Miss Debby Wrench' [1725]
    [Crum U64b]

c.233, p. 41

U0061　Unequal how shall I the search begin,
And undistinguish'd brightness charms the eye.

    [Judith (Cowper) Madan], 'The progress of poetry'

Poetry Box V/77

U0062　Unfeignedly I do not think that ever
That can eclipse the rays of estimation.

    Sir Thomas Urquhart, 'To Lady Margaret [crossed
    out]'

fb.217, p. 93

U0063　Unfold, Father Time, thy long records unfold,
That tears off thy chains, and bids millions be free!

    William Roscoe, 'Written in 1789'

c.142, p. 510

U0064　Ungallant youth! could royal Edward see
And pluck the star that beauty planted there.

    Captain [Thomas] Morris, 'Lines written by . . . upon
    the Prince of Wales who when dancing at a ball with
    Lady Salisbury, left her in the middle of the dance,
    upon seeing the Duchess of Devonshire enter the
    room'

Poetry Box XII/4

U0065　Ungirt unblest I never understood
In her blest path of life well-understood.

    [Sir Philip Wodehouse], 'Upon his fair kinswoman
    Elizabeth Gourdon . . .'

b.131, back (no. 108)

U0066　Ungrateful boy I will not call thee son
God's blood I'll send you to the rout below.

    'The K[in]g's answer to the Du. Of M[onmou]th's
    letter ['Disgrac'd, undone . . .]'
    [Crum U72; POAS II.255]

b.327, f. 15v; b.371, no. 12

U0067　Ungrateful were the lyric muse,
And the first nation in the world.

    John Lockman, 'To Signor Manzoli: after hearing him
    sing in the opera . . . May 1765'

c.267/1, p. 387

U0068　Ungrateful wretch! Can'st thou pretend a cause
His sword is steel; his god is but a wafer.

    'A dialogue: between a loyal addresser, and a blunt
    Whiggish clown'
    [Crum U74]

fb.108, p. 193

U0069　Ungrateful wretches that so soon forget
Too great indulgence is the seed of harm.

    'Copy of verses upon the [?] plot'

fb.228/40

U0070　Unhappy daughter of distress and woe
And weeping pity pays her debt to thee.

    Mary Young [or Mary Sewell?], 'On a young woman
    found dead in St. George's Fields'

fc.57, p. 43; fc.132/1, p. 211

U0071　Unhappy England, still in forty-one
And perish'd by a villain that he knew.

    [Sir Charles Hanbury Williams], 'On Sir Robert
    Walpole Knt. of the Garter, being obliged by the
    popular clamor, to resign the office of Prime
    Minister—in the year 1741'

c.360/1, p. 317; fc.135

U0072　Unhappy, erring man! not to the wise
As much may scheme, as little need despair!

    'To J. J. Rousseau'

Poetry Box X/125

U0073　Unhappy I run thou some other race
And breathe with her no more, that hath no merit.

    Sir Francis Castillion, '1618 . . . Threnodia'

fb.69, p. 197

U0074　Unhappy island, whose hard fate ordains
I've eas'd my mind and will securely smile.

    [Monmouth's rebellion, 1685]
    [Crum U83]

fb.70, p. 135

U0075 Unhappy isle! what made thy sons rebel?
And let th'indebted only pay.

'An expostulation' [on the Prince of Orange, 1688]
[Crum U84]

b.111, p. 503

U0076 Unhappy man, and born to suffer ills
Death soon this fine joy from our bosom tear.

[Sir William Trumbull], 'Milton Lat[in] poem
[Epitaphium Damonis]'

Trumbull Box: Poetry Box XIII/37

U0077 Unhappy man!—by nature made to sway
Here having felt one hell, they thought there was
no more.

[Thomas] Sprat, 'The plague of Athens' [pr. 1703
(Foxon S663)]

c.351, p. 99

U0078 Unhappy mortals, on how fine a thread
Therefore let's live merrily while we can.

'On the misery of mankind—[Flaminius] epigram 7th'

c.158, p. 133

U0079 Unhappy Tantalus, amidst the flood
In midst of endless treasures starves himself.

'Upon Tantalus. [Flaminius] Epigram 9'

c.158, p. 134

U0080 Unhappy they to whom God has not reveal'd
Of roots and herbs the wholesome luxury.

[Abraham Cowley], 'Taken out of Hesiod . . .'

b.118, p. 39

U0081 Unhappy tyrant! prithee stay
Should court thy destiny.

'An answer to No scornful beauty by a lady of quality.
1677'

b.54, p. 973

U0082 Unhappy West thy spring had promised fair
Of heaven had snatched him from his native land.

[George] H[owar]d, [6th earl of Carlisle],
'Occasioned by the thoughts of the death of Mr. West'

c.197, p. 8

U0083 Unhappy wretch! Who doom'd to certain death,
Which now in love's despite must cease in death.

R[obert] Shirley, 1st earl of Ferrers, 'Upon a lady that
being about to destroy her unborn child, thus
addresses herself to it. From the French, Toi qui
meurs &c.'

c.347, p. 78

U0084 Unhappy youth, the storm begins to low'r,
Falls unrewarded on the silent grave.

[George Howard, 6th earl of Carlisle], 'On the Earl of
Derwentwater's execution'

c.197, p. 12

U0085 Unhappy youths! On Camus sedgy wide
Not from the poet but the friend sincere.

c.364, p. 35

U0086 Unhurt untouch'd, I'm black and—blue
The labor of as many—hours.

[Mrs. ( ) Rudge?], 'A riddle on a slate given me by Mrs
Rudge'

c.360/1, p. 149

U0087 Unite, my roving thoughts, unite
To give its follies o'er.

[Thomas Stevens?], 'Hymn the 5th'

c.259

U0088 United force doth mightily prevail,
Where princes' powers with hate and discord quail.

c.339, p. 314

U0089 Unkind as you were to refuse one kind kiss
And what is more strange and more wonderful
still . . . .

'Esplanade Weymouth Septr. 1795'

Poetry Box XII/25 (incomplete)

U0090 Unknowing and unknown to fame,
Our heavenly Father will on us bestow.

[ ] Robertson, of York, 'Compassion and mercy
rewarded. A story by Ursinus Velius, paraphrased'

c.94

U0091 Unknown to all the folks he meets
But shows his littleness in great.

John Lockman, 'The picture. To a profligate young
heir . . . April 1744'

c.267/1, p. 91

U0092 Unknown to want from busy cares retir'd
Lorenzo calm'd, to peace retir'd anew.

S[tephen] Simpson, 'Lorenzo in imitation of Parnell's
Hermit'

c.563

U0093 Unlike Sir Thomas is my song
'Tis witty—and it is not long.

c.74

U0094 Unlike the triflers whose contracted view
Th'applause of angels, not the gaze of fools.

    [Elizabeth Carter], 'On a watch'
fc.132/1, p. 8

U0095 Unmark'd by sorrow, and unknown to care,
To seek those realms no pains or cares invade.

    'To Miss Cornwallis on her birthday July 28th [17]92'
fc.124, p. 87

U0096 Unmarkt by trophies of the great and vain
Yielding their souls to mansions of the just.

    'On a tomb in Brill churchyard Bucks where a man lies buried with sixteen of his children'
c.240, p. 135

U0097 Unmix'd be our wine, and pure let it flow,
Carousing melodious, we sing merry catches.

    'Leges bibendi . . . translation'
c.81/1, no. 101

U0098 Unmoved by death for Athens Codrus fought,
And public virtue's a forsaken way.

    'De Codro et Caesare . . . English'
c.368, p. 59

U0099 Unprologu'd plays are like I know not what
Proud if we gain the smallest share of praise.

    'Prologue to The orphan [by Thomas Otway]'
Poetry Box I/77 (cf. i/73)

U0100 Unquiet thoughts your cruel slaughter stint
Which burns thy eyes to flame thy thoughts to fire.

    'A lover's passion'
    [Crum U107, 'turn mine eyes to floods my thoughts']
b.356, p. 218

U0101 Unsatisfied with Earth
And in the grave forgotten lie.

    [George Daniel]
b.121, fol. 31v

U0102 Unseen associate whose mild voice I seem
Its guardian idol and its fav'rite guest!

    [William Hayley], '[Sonnet] June 8 [1800]'
File 6968

U0103 Unskill'd in art, thus Philomela sings:
And reigns th'unrivall'd minstrel of the groves.

    John Lockman, 'After hearing a song, from a very agreeable young lady in Salisbury'
    [Crum U114]
c.267/1, p. 22, p. 180

U0104 Unskill'd in Greek and Roman tongue,
But thee to join, in pleasure here.

    [William] Pattison, 'On a Latin ode written by Mr. Hedges'
c.244, p. 478

U0105 Untamed youth for want of good tuition
All delectable fruits the others bears.

    [Mary Serjant]
fb.98, fol. 153

U0106 Untaught of Venus, when she found
For shame,—to look some other way.

    'A hint'
c.94

U0107 Untaught, unskill'd we paint each noble sound
And the young mind for long duration close.

    'Riddle on the alphabet'
c.360/1, p. 117

U0108 Unthriftiness doth make men laugh'd to scorn
And bringeth want [beggary gives] to those, that
                         rich were [are] born.

c.339, p. 260, p. 310

U0109 Unthrifty loveliness,—why dost thou spend
Which used, lives th'executor to be.

    [William] Shakespeare, 'Magazine of beauty' [Sonnet IV]
c.94

U0110 Until someone Apelles I[?]it, in verse
There's none at full that can your praise rehearse.

b.62, p. 92

U0111 Untill'd, I sprung from Mother Earth
I'm the best jewel in the crown.

    'Riddle on tobacco'
c.360/2, no. 65

U0112 Untimely 'cause so late and late because
For if they both should meet they would fall out.

    'On John Lilburne' [d. 1657]
    [Crum U117]
fb.143, p. 35

U0113 Unto her lady she may well be said
With loving counsel, and all loyal will.

    [Sir Philip Wodehouse], 'Upon Mrs. Constantia Longland'
b.131, back (no. 128)

U0114 Unto Jehovah all the lands
From age to age descend.

'Psal: 100'

b.217, p. 70

U0115 Unto our names how many we trust
When I was Sands and now am dust.

'On one Sands'
[Crum U126, 'we must not trust']

b.356, p. 244

U0116 Unto Thee O God we will give thanks,
Set not your horns so high.

[Thomas Norton, Psalm lxxv]
[cf. Crum U135]

b.156, p. 29

U0117 Unto two kings he one allegiance pays,
Who has two gods to swear by more than we.

[Thomas Brown?], 'A satire on Doctor Sherlock . . .
Englished thus'
[Crum U141]

b.371, no. 42; fb.207/1, p. 13

U0118 Unto us a child is born
Wisdom to find a way to heaven.

'25 Dec. 1686. On Christmas Day'

Poetry Box VI/3

U0119 Unvanquish'd death inex'rable appears,
And to observ't, the surest guard from pain.

R[obert] Shirley, 1st earl of Ferrers, 'Upon death—
from Malherbe, La mortades rigneurs &c'

c.347, p. 25

U0120 Unwept, unworthy of tomorrow's sigh
The plan that forms the beauties of the mind.

'Upon a young lady of great merit'

c.53, fol. 16

U0121 Unwilling, dear Sir, that your lines so gallant,
And Keeper to Argus be join'd!

'Translated and sent with ['With hasty steps . . .']'

fc.124, p. 106

U0122 Unwise they are that flee abroad in hope to alter
kind
No foreign soil hath any force to change the
inward mind.

c.339, p. 322

Up and down, round about, all the streets I paraded,   U0123
And you all to please—be my constant endeavor. |
The pleasure &c.

'Jacob Gawky's ramble to Bath tune—Alley Croker'

c.382, p. 55

Up he rose,   U0124
Departed—as before.

'Doctor Jebb'

c.81/1, no. 275

Up my soul why slugg'st thou here?   U0125
Strive for to be innocent.

H[enry] C[olman], 'On immortality'
[Crum U149]

b.2, p. 11

Up, up, (my good lads!)—step forth vig'rous and   U0126
gay,
The blessings of harvest all hail.

John Lockman, 'Harvest home, or the farmer's song.
(August 1768) writ at the very friendly, James
Hugford's esqr. of Datchet, Bucks: for Mr. Bowry, of
Horton. The tune, O the roast beef of old
England &c.'

c.267/4, p. 309

Up, up wrong'd James's friends, what can you be   U0127
Take heed bold stars you set the world on fire.

'Now or never'
[cf. Crum U157, 'Charles's']

b.111, p. 42

Upbraid me not, capricious fair   U0128
When Ariadne's coy.

'A song'

c.358, p. 92

Upon a summer's day   U0129
Ere long for to make her to cry.

b.213, p. 108

Upon a sunshine summer's day   U0130
In tears to turn her wheel about.

[Thomas D'Urfey], 'Rural innocence betrayed'

c.360/1, p. 195

Upon a time the fairy elves   U0131
No shirt half so fine so fair.

[Edward Rawstorne]

b.209, p. 75

Upon a time there stroll'd to town   U0132
While there is pride you'll have A. Pope.

'An epigrammatical tale—on Alexander Pope esqr'

c.360/1, p. 273

U0133 Upon an holy day, when the nymphs had leave to play

And very very merry be.

'Songs [12]'

b.356, p. 290

U0134 Upon her stone write this, but dust here
At the name of stone she'll rise again I fear.

'Eundem' [on the Lady Penelope Rich]
[Crum H887]

b.62, p. 81

U0135 Upon high tow'ring waves did Peter go,
His wavering faith made him to waver too.

'Matthew 14.5.30'

c.160, fol. 51 [bis]

U0136 Upon that earth there is a hill
Adieu farewell all is forlorn.

[cf. Ashmole, Theatrum chemicum Britannicum, 1652, p. 378]

fa.16, p. 38

U0137 Upon the base of virtue you have grounded
To be attain'd unto by pious wits.

Sir Thomas Urquhart, 'To the Earl of [crossed out]'

fb.217, p. 351

U0138 Upon the earth thrive villainy and woe,
He liv'd and died within his mother's womb.

[ ] Alcroft, 'From Edinburgh 30 July 1724. At Gilmerton within 12 miles of this city, is the Cyclop's cave . . . over the entrance this inscription'

c.229/1, fol. 36; c.166, p. 238; c.360/2, no. 85

U0139 Upon the fruitful banks of Thame, whilst
mournfully I sat,
Then in a cloud of ambient air, this rev'rend form
withdrew.

[Edmond Stacy], 'Britannia's memorial . . . by the author of The blackbird's song' [pr. 1715 (Foxon S687)]

c.570/2, p. 25

U0140 Upon the pleasant, famous river's side
O Lord of Hosts, forever don't forget.

'The parable of the dove and the harpy'

b.111, p. 109

U0141 Upon the slippery tops of human state
Nor what he is, nor whither he's to go.

[Abraham Cowley, trans.], 'Seneca, ex Thyeste, Act 2. Chor.'
[Crum U179]

b.118, p. 13; b.54, p. 1214; b.63, p. 109; fb.142, p. 41

U0142 Upon the Thames I daily row'd
But lately as I pass'd I cried.

'On Lord Pembroke whitewashing the back of his house next the Thames'

c.115

U0143 Upon the twenty-seventh of September
Because poor P—k is laid beneath the stones.

'Epitaph on the death of Mr. P—k of Christ Church Cambridge'

fc.24, p. 69

U0144 Upon their backs they judge of elevations
From thence to'Aquarius, then to Capricorn.

Sir Thomas Urquhart, 'That lecherous women, such especially as are married, prove exquisite astronomers'

fb.217, p. 69

U0145 Upon these banks, our first archbishop stood
Whigs to their good old cause would bid adieu.

'Upon the Archbishop of York's coming to Richmond'

c.160, fol. 106

U0146 Upon this table you may faintly see,
You will only by his conversation find.

'Upon Dr. John Barefoot's effigies, letter carrier for Oxford'

fb.207/3, p. 4

U0147 Upon this tree you plainly see
The rest are all hobgoblins.

'Dream of advice for a Valentine: a tree bearing a number of shrivelled hearts, one plump one in the midst'

fc.124, p. 132

U0148 Upon your lyre, nothing so sweet as they,
Embrace a lasting peace, and fling by arms.

Barnaby Gouche, 'To Miss Lyon . . . upon hearing her play on the spinet'

c.229/2, fol. 27

U0149 Upon your salvation,
And prevent your damnation.

'The new oath' [c. 1715]

fc.58, p. 128

U0150 Urg'd by my hopes, check'd by my fears,
Believe me there's enough for two.

'To Mrs. Delaney on her 80 birthday 25 May 1780'

c.391, p. 69

U0151 Urg'd by the warmth of friendship's sacred flame,
To future times, and life in fame be thine.

> [Thomas Parnell], 'Dr. Parnell to Dr. Swift, on his
> birthday, Novr. 30. 1713'
>
> File 11383, p. 22

U0152 Urim was civil and not void of sense
A wretched scribbler or a rare buffoon.

> [Sir Samuel] Garth, 'The following lines were written
> by . . . on Doctor Francis Atterbury, Bishop of
> Rochester, long before he was a dignitary in the
> church'
>
> c.360/2, no. 106

U0153 Us who climb thy holy hill,
And to perfection grow.

> 'Hymn 101'
>
> c.562, p. 137

U0154 Use dunce, the helps that here you see
That art must recompense the wide defect.

> [Robert Cholmeley], 'Contrast to ['No more
> thyself . . .']'
>
> c.190, p. 27

U0155 Use labor still and leave thy slothful seat,
With sweat of brow see that thou get thy meat.

> [Geffrey Whitney]
> [Crum U194]
>
> c.339, p. 315

U0156 Usurping William now is very great
Will some shriek Master—no they go to Hell.

> [Sir Richard Bulstrode], 'Upon the Prince of Orange's
> invasion and his good success in these attempts'
>
> fb.88, p. 118; see also 'Invading William . . .'.

V

V0001   Vain are, much-injur'd queen! these artless lays,
To agonize again thy bleeding heart.

     'To the widowed mourner of a murdered king'
c.83/2, no. 391

V0002   Vain are the achievements of the sword
And Carteret with his prose.

     'The recorders. Publish'd July 13 1743'
c.360/2, no. 59

V0003   Vain as thou art say whence those airs arise,
In short the general ridicule of all.

     'Upon that vain conceited fop'
c.160, fol. 43

V0004   Vain Egypt, let thyself amazement cease
Yet might they all be found in Barbary.

     'On his mistress Barbary'
[Crum V2]
b.356, p. 89

V0005   Vain fops on glitt'ring follies set their minds
Eternal happiness contain'd in me.

     'Acrostic' [on virtue]
c.360/3, no. 70

V0006   Vain lyrist! Fair Ausonia's boast,
Hid by a laurel's echoing shade.

     John Lockman, 'Orpheus to Galuppi: on the opera of
Antigiono . . . 1746'
c.267/1, p. 183

V0007   Vain man! in grandeur given to gay attire?
Behold, what deeds of woe the locust can perform!

Diggle Box: Poetry Box XI/60

V0008   Vain man! Th'effect of sin's first cause we grieve,
Only by showing love when 'tis in vain.

     R[obert] Shirley, 1st earl of Ferrers, 'The folly of
lamenting a friend's death. March the 6th. 1710/11'
c.347, p. 72

V0009   Vain project vain for you to try
The haughty gown, presume to make a joke.

     Dr. [ ] Earle, 'To the dissenting ministers, preaching
against Popery'
c.360/1, p. 253

V0010   Vain thy disguise and all thy art
And place thy image there.

     T[homas] S[tevens], Job 27.8 . . . July 23. 1780'
c.259, p. 105

V0011   Vain 'twere in me, th'encomium to pretend,
Sure Wat, and twat, are very well acquainted!

     'In praise of a twat, by a fine lady's command: [with]
her answer' [Wat upon twat]
fb.66/6

V0012   Vain were the thought t'instruct the verse to flow
And life gush'd out, as he disclos'd the wound.

     'On the death of Queen Caroline 1737'
c.360/1, p. 97; Poetry Box I/122

V0013   Vain world adieu, your love I mean;
He'll cheerful make my exit day.

     [Edmund Wodehouse], 'Jan. 27 [1715]'
b.131, p. 151

V0014   Vain world farewell to you,
To see a smiling God.

     'An epitaph on Mrs. Ann Bowler'
c.244, p. 288

V0015   Vain youth you do accuse me wrong
No danger to my soul.

     [Mrs. Christian Kerr], 'The young gentlewoman's
answer' [to 'Too long hast thou . . .']
c.102, p. 92

V0016   Vainglory, honor, pleasure, pride,
So walk to Canaan's land.

     'The guides to heaven'
c.187, p. 29

V0017   Vainglory's emblem is a blazing taper
Where short-liv'd snuff ends in a noisome vapor.

     [John Rose?]
b.227, p. 76

V0018   Vainly now you strive to warm us,
Don't you think so, Mr. F[oot]e?

     'Tit for tat' [on the actor Samuel Foote]
c.578, p. 145

V0019   Valor's a virtue cardinal, wherein
The how and where, to venture or refrain.

     [Sir Philip Wodehouse], 'An expletive excursion or
     exigesis. 1. Virtue'

     b.131, p. 15

V0020   Valor's virtue which for honest end
Dares acts suffers undisturb'd in mind.

     [Sir Philip Wodehouse], 'An essay of fortitude'

     b.131, p. 15

V0021   Value thyself, fond youth, no more,
'Tis ten to one I cease to love her too.

     [William Walsh], 'Dialogue between a lover and his
     friend. (Irregular verse)'

     c.223, p. 68

V0022   Van Dyck had colors, softness, fire, and art
But she ne'er made a finish'd piece before.

     [Charles Montagu], 3rd earl of H[alifa]x, 'Verses
     written by . . . last summer at Althorp in a blank leaf
     of a Waller upon seeing Van Dyck's picture of the old
     Lady Sunderland'

     c.111, p. 30

V0023   Various the climate is in Britain's isle
Clos'd in with that the varied landscape ends.

     'On the moors'

     c.160, fol. 64

V0024   Varus, lose no time to plant
Shines like glass transparent through.

     [William Popple, trans.], '[Horace] book 1st. ode 18th.
     To Quintilius Varus'

     fc.104/2, p. 56

V0025   Veil bonnet j[i]gging festivals
Of English or outlandish.

     L. Whitakers

     b.197, p. 131

V0026   Vengeance will sit above our faults but till
Himself knows more.

     [John Donne, 'Of our sense of sin']
     [Crum V19]

     b.148, p. 93

V0027   Venus chanc't to love a boy,
When that time comes I shall be glad.

     'Venus, and Adonis'

     fb.107, p. 7

V0028   Venus O Venus thou goddess of love,
A pox of god confound you both.

     'A poetical fury'
     [Crum V25]

     b.197, p. 237

V0029   Venus was pleas'd to form the face;
And earth's inhabitants amaz'd.

     H[annah] More, 'On a gent[leman's] being vain of his
     person and understanding'

     c.341, p. 100

V0030   Verbs, nouns are thine and pronouns, yet alas!
Uxor you might, but Cornu you can't decline.

     Theophilus Hill, 'On Mr. Beavor an aged
     schoolmaster, who married a young lady of great
     fortune'

     c.546

V0031   Vernon, fam'd hero, with a slender train
Exult, Britannia! at thy growing fame!

     John Lockman, 'Upon the taking of Portobello, by
     Admiral Vernon. By Signor Nonci . . . 1741'

     c.267/4, p. 121

V0032   Versailles and Marly never did appear
Longing to see him next upon his throne.

     [Sir Richard Bulstrode], 'Upon her royal Highness
     [Louisa's] sickness at Versailles and upon her
     recovery' [c. 1708]

     fb.88, p. 116v

V0033   Verses I no more can make
Boy, or girl, with tuck'd-up hair.

     [William Popple, trans.], '[Horace, ep]ode 11th. To
     Pettius'

     fc.104/2, p. 438

V0034   Verses immortal as my bays I sing,
And seal their country's love with their departing.

     George Stepney, 'The 9th ode of the 4th book of
     Horace'

     c.351, p. 76

V0035   Vex not, (old friend!) suppress this dire alarm;
And stamp'd his robe with his own Tyrian dye.

     John Lockman, 'In excuse for my breaking a flask, the
     wine in which spoilt a gentleman's green damask
     nightgown . . . Jan. 1740/1'

     c.267/1, p. 240

V0036   Vex'd by the follies of the age
Eliza they must learn of you.

     'To Mrs. B[ernard]'

     Poetry Box x/45, p. 9

V0037 Vext with damn'd lawsuits all my abject life
For lawyers, doctors, and the bounds [i.e.,
hounds?] of hell.

    [Richard Burridge], 'Hell in an uproar or a scuffle
    between the lawyers and physicians' [pr. Dublin 1725
    (Foxon B586]

    c.158, p. 61

V0038 Vice common is yet nothing is more dear,
Virtue seems vice, yet rare it doth appear.

    'A paradox'

    c.356

V0039 Vice, depraver of the mind,
In heav'n—or some Elysian shade.

    'Axwell Park'

    c.93

V0040 Vice once with virtue did engage
Which thou canst ne'er enjoy.

    [Sir Charles Hanbury Williams?], 'The wife and the
    nurse, a ballad published in 1743' [Foxon W511]

    Poetry Box I/106

V0041 Victorious beauty, though your eyes
May steal a heart or two from you.

    [Aurelian Townshend, 'To the Countess of Salisbury']
    [Crum v31]

    b.148, p. 7

V0042 Victorious love! How uncontroll'd thy pow'r,
Stand at high noon, and shine divinely bright.

    'On our Savior's nativity'

    c.83/2, no. 564

V0043 Victorious men of earth, no more
Shall have the power to break a heart.

    [James Shirley], 'Death and his emissary' [in Cupid
    and Death, 1653]
    [Crum v33]

    fb.107, p. 44

V0044 Victory lies not in vainglorious hearts,
To crown with conquest whom [ ] loves.

    'Victoria dei donum'

    b.205, fol. 11r

V0045 View not with envy fretting in thy breast,
I never saw constrain'd to beg their bread.

    [Thomas Fitzgerald], 'Part of Psalm 37. paraphrased'

    c.244, p. 192 (attr. [ ] Lewis)

V0046 View we not virtue in a lovely light
By every tongue his worth and glory rais'd.

    [Maurice Johnson], 'From the Greek'

    c.229/2, fol. 14

V0047 Viewing the ranges of a library
And heaven on virtue show'rs rewards at last.

    c.189, p. 75

V0048 Viewless, through heav'n's vast vault your course ye
steer
I ask the still, sweet tear, that list'ning fancy weeps.

    [Ann (Ward)] Radcliffe, 'To the winds'

    c.83/3, no. 879

V0049 Views of ambition ne'er his hopes employ'd,
And prais'd his great Creator at his end.

    P[aul] Whitehead, 'Verses inscribed on Mr. Havard's
    tombstone'

    c.83/3, no. 738

V0050 Vile arms! Which fighting covertly
But they the stronger joints and safer hedge.

    [Sir Philip Wodehouse], 'Upon Mr. Andrew Marvell—
    a great Republican writer'

    b.131, back (no. 214 [bis])

V0051 Vile thing I am, as is on ground.
Whatever lives is mine.

    'A riddle'

    fc.74, p. 17

V0052 Vile weed, irascible! whene'er I view
Like thee, when firmly grasp'd, to native nothing
fall!

    'To the nettle'

    c.141, p. 305

V0053 Vincent Corbett, farther known
Whenas the son, and heir is griev'd.

    [Richard] Corbett, 'On Dr Corbett's father'

    b.200, p. 216; b.356, p. 260; b.197, p. 34 (with extra
    lines); fb.230

V0054 Vincent, the great comptroller of us all
The reason's surely this: those four be brothers.

    'Of Vincent doorkeeper at Haberdasher's Hall'

    b.52/2, p. 162

V0055 Vir, in the Latin yields of man th'expression:
If male, and female be not join'd together.

    Sir Thomas Urquhart, 'Of virginity'

    fb.217, p. 79

V0056 Virgil did treat of war and yet in Rome
What he did see being worse than what he wrote.

    [Sir Thomas Urquhart], 'That Ovid's Art of love was
    not the creation of his exile'

    fb.217, p. 535

V0057 Virginity's a narrow way; a broad,
Is wedlock, home most people ride the road.

'Of virginity and wedlock'
c.356

V0058 Virginity's a way so strait,
And of much less adventure.

Sir Thomas Urquhart, 'Why there be manier of those
who marry, than who lead a chaste life'
fb.217, p. 208

V0059 Virgins attend and let kind pity move,
On earthly blessings, heaven alone is just.

'Verses on an officer who lost his life at the Havana, by
a lady'
c.175, p. 61

V0060 Virgins if e'er by chance it prove,
No longer than tomorrow.

'The virgin's wish'
[Crum v50]
c.158, p. 19

V0061 Virgins must fear, loose looks to scatter
And is our good, or our evil angel, *semper*.

Sir F[rancis] C[astillion], 'Of a wife'
fb.69, p. 212, 258

V0062 Virgins should value nothing less,
At best; but for a golden ass.

'Advice to the ladies'
c.186, p. 103

V0063 Virtue alone, has that to give
And if we die, 'tis endless sorrow!

'The contrast'
c.487, p. 25; c.83/4, no. 2005; fc.132/1, p. 95

V0064 Virtue and fame the other day
'Tis Egremont!—go tell it fame.

[George] Lyttelton, 1st baron Lyttelton, 'On Lady
Egremont'
[Crum v53]
fc.51, p. 301; c.83/1, no. 24

V0065 Virtue and honor were at odds of late
(Wonder of women, mirror of your sex.)

'To the worthy author of a most heavenly and spiritual
work the virtuous and honored Lady Ursula Harvey
wife to that eminent pattern of religion Harcourt
Leighton esquire'
Poetry Box VI/110

V0066 Virtue, dear friend, needs no defense,
And dare all heat, but that of Celia's eyes.

[Wentworth Dillon], 4th earl of Roscommon, trans.,
'The 22nd ode of the 1st book of Horace'
b.201, p. 110; c.549, p. 81 (first four lines); c.351, p. 52;
differs from next.

V0067 Virtue dear friend needs no defense
They seem submissively to roar in ve[rse].

[Wentworth Dillon], 4th earl of Roscommon, 'To
Orinda' [Horace, book 1 ode 22, imitated]
b.218, p. 19; c.351, p. 53; Poetry Box IV/53; differs from
previous.

V0068 Virtue doth grow, where seed of vices spring:
And vices thrust at virtue all their sting.

c.339, p. 327

V0069 Virtue is free, and doth communicate
From lovely maids to charitable mothers.

[Sir Thomas Urquhart], 'Of two kind gentlewomen
the name of each which was Mistress Virtue'
fb.217, p. 539

V0070 Virtue is his proper and peculiar tomb
Outlasting marble, living till day's doom.

'In Penrith church on one William Dawson of York
who . . . died and was buried at Penrith Augt. 23 1632'
c.547, p. 333

V0071 Virtue is more lovely more acceptable
Proceeding from a personage amiable.

fb.151/3

V0072 Virtue no doubt hath her reward
Are followers at his back.

[backwards hand]
b.234, p. 27

V0073 Virtue not blood was thought of anciently
Not on our virtue but the blood of Jesus.

[Sir Thomas Urquhart], 'As it was a precept of
antiquity to lean more to virtue than to parentage, so
is it a tenet of Christianity(?) to repose more on the
blood of Christ, than our own merit'
fb.217, p. 516

V0074 Virtue rejoice, tho' heav'n may frown awhile,
Are those God loves, and who love God the best.

c.83/3, no. 812

V0075 Virtue sometimes doth grow
At virtue all her stings.

b.234, p. 28

V0076 Virtue sought where to dwell in you alone
Your joys I would but cannot well express.

'Madame, My bashful muse had thought long since to
tell | The world what matchless virtues in you dwell |
Dwell on them now my thoughts what eyes did see |
Speak tongue, tell what her speaking virtues be' [on
Dame Ursula Harvey]

Poetry Box VI/110

V0077 Virtue, sweeter than the light;
Heav'n shall guardian angels send.

'An encomium on virtue'

c.83/3, no. 1071

V0078 Virtue that's living revives the soul
Still seeking him that lasts forever.

[Mary Serjant]

fb.98, fol. 159

V0079 Virtue's the art of life—its theory
His virtue's still but in minority.

[Sir Philip Wodehouse], 'Upon Sir J[ohn] Knyvet . . .'

b.131, back (no. 133)

V0080 Vital spark of heavenly flame,
O death where is thy sting.

[Alexander Pope], 'The dying Christian'
[Crum v67]

c.362, p. 89

V0081 Vive motions, which Apelles could not paint:
Nor Phidias carve, a glass can represent.

Sir Thomas Urquhart, 'The virtue of a mirror'

fb.217, p. 264

V0082 Void of reproach, as void of fear,
This Bayard was a Knight of Malt-a?

c.340

V0083 Vouchsafe my God to lend a listening ear,
And strengthen thou the arm that strikes for thee.

[Richard] Daniel, dean of Armagh, 'The persecution.
Psalm 143'

c.244, p. 393

V0084 Vouchsafe my prisoner thus to be
He's faster bound that sent it thee.

[William Strode], in 'Posies for bracelets'
[Crum v70]

b.205, fol. 55v

V0085 Vouchsafe (O God) to hear the mournful cries
Loathing the freedom once thou gav'st before.

'A prayer for the nation. 1676'

b.54, p. 866

V0086 Vow'd at her Zephyran shrine, my shell I bring,
Whilst with great Egypt's queen, choice jewels
plac'd.

M[aurice] J[ohnson], 'On the nautilus or sailorfish
shell (the 5 epigram of Callimachus) . . . at the
instance of . . . Mr. W[illia]m Dodd of Clare Hall sent
him with a drawing of the nautilus'

c.229/2, fol. 72

V0087 Vows are desires resolv'd—'tis fervency
To thy vow'd sov'reign Dame Piety.

[Sir Philip Wodehouse], 'Upon his—Lucy
Wodehouse'

b.131, back (no. 24)

V0088 Vox populi, the lively voice of God
And sinners leaves without excuse, *vox populi.*

[John Taylor], 'The invocation' [from 'The world
turned upside down']

fb.40, p. 377

V0089 Vulcan [ ] leave [a] iron [and] [a] steel
Whilst they [do] sport on the Hyperean hill.

'The virgin's attraction'

b.205, fol. 17r

V0090 Vulcan, they say, made mighty arms for Mars,
Hammer'd out verses, and old iron too.

'On seeing some verses which were made by a certain
cutler and poesy-maker November 1723'

c.360/2, no. 242

V0091 Vulcan with armor Mars completel' adorns
Mars cuckolds him and gives for iron horns.

Sir Thomas Urquhart, 'Quid pro quo'

fb.217, p. 339

V0092 Vy! Vat Sir Watkin print and tell
When, for your betters bear a pair!

[Phanuel Bacon], 'Sir Watkin Lewis and Parson
Horne'

c.237, fol. 71v

W

W0001   W is the letter of the Christ-cross row
We find 'tis Wandsworth, where you choose to live.

     'Solution of the rebus no. 3 ['Take out a letter . . .']
c.360/3, no. 102

W0002   W—r to charm all womankind
Soar to his native skies.

     [William Carpenter], 'On a friend in the smallpox'
c.247, p. 111

W0003   Waft me to some soft [and] cooling breeze,
And bubbling springs refresh the glade.

     'The midsummer wish'
[Crum W4]
c.244, p. 102

W0004   Wail'd the sweet warbler to the lonely shade;
For me, who triumph in eternal years!

     [John Langhorne], 'Petrarch's 238th sonnet translated'
c.139, p. 563

W0005   Wake all my hopes, lift up your eyes,
Belov'd obey'd, ador'd.

     [John Austin], 'Hym: 39' [Hymn xxxvii, Devotions in the ancient way of offices, 1672, p. 339]
c.178, p. 38

W0006   Wake my Adonis do not die
A goddess am to grieve and not to die.

     [William Cartwright]
b.213, p. 130

W0007   Wake now my soul and humbly hear
Beyond the end of days.

     [John Austin], 'Hym: 3' [Hymn v, Devotions in the ancient way of offices, 1672, p. 49]
c.178, p. 3

W0008   Wake O my soul, address thyself to Him
And take my expiring soul into thy arms.

     'Written by a young lady on her birthday'
c.83/3, no. 900; see also 'Thou pow'r supreme . . .'.

W0009   Wake, O wake the noblest strain,
And pity dignifies delight.

     [William Boscawen], 'Ode for music'
fc.106, p. 39

W0010   Wake! rise! thy sleep of death is o'er,
Thy changing form—rise, rise—adieu!

     [( ) Smyth], 'The seraph'
c.141, p. 35

W0011   Wake the loud, ecstatic lay!
That His glory endureth forever!

     [Thomas Hull], 'Hymn from some passages in the 136th psalm'
c.528/12

W0012   Wake, ye nightingales, ah! wake
She could make a desert bloom.

     [Sir William Jones], 'Ode—by . . . to the nightingales of Bayley Wood, on the return of Miss Julianna S. . . . , to Oxford—in March—1779'
c.90

W0013   Walk in, Sir, and you shall see
Nuts and cakes with greeting Sir.

     Edward Sneyd, 'Wrote by the desire of Miss Grace Smith of Great Fenton who chose the subject [fairies] in the year 1777'
c.214, p. 100

W0014   Walk no more, in those sweet shades
We joy, or peace, or light, or pleasure call.

     [George Daniel]
b.121, fol. 73

W0015   Walking and meeting one not long ago,
But he that knows himself I never know.

     'Nosce teipsum'
c.356

W0016   Walking in a meadow fair
She would have one should mend it.

     'A wanton wench hath ne'er enough'
b.200, p. 370

W0017   Walking one day as chance my footsteps led
And left me to pursue my way at last.

     [William Popple, trans.], 'Horace book 1st satire 9th imitated'
fc.104/1, p. 159

W0018   Walking the park I to my horror there,
And penitence his suff'rings does atone.

     'On the colors at St. James's'
b.iii, p. 433

W0019   Waller! Blest poet of the British race,
To warm the natives of the frozen north.

     'To the Lady H[arpu]r reading her Ladyship's Waller'
b.322, p. 7

W0020   Waller, fond bard, 'twas nobly done,
And each thy Sacharissa's duplicate.

     'Give me but what this circle bound | Take all the rest the sun goes round—Waller'
Poetry Box II/47

W0021   Wan heralds of the sun and summer gale!
For fixt regret, and hopeless grief are mine.

     [Charlotte (Turner) Smith], 'Sonnet. Snow drops'
c.141, p. 132

W0022   Want is the badge of poverty, then he,
But as his wealth his wishes still increase.

c.158, p. 29

W0023   Want is the scorn of ev'ry wealthy fool,
And wit in rags is turn'd to ridicule.

c.536

W0024   Want we flesh skins young, dung, dice music-strings,
Wool, milk? One sheep supplies with all these things.

     'A sheep'
c.356

W0025   Wants he a grave whom heaven covers, was he
And then his requiem's sung by winged choirs.

     'On Felton hung in chains' [1628]
     [Crum w27]
b.62, p. 39

W0026   Warbling stranger! For a smile
Those who doubt, attend and hear.

     John Lockman, 'To Cuzzoni: on the benefit at Mr. Hugford's great room . . . 18 May 1750'
c.267/1, p. 184

W0027   Warm as the purple fluid flows,
For what is life without a friend?

     'To Miriam on her birthday, Sunday Novr. 3. 1754'
c.371, fol. 76

W0028   Warm from the heart and to the heart addresst,
The dead would but return to speak in vain.

     Mary [(Shackleton)] Leadbeater, 'The reply [to 'I marvel not . . .']'
c.303

W0029   Warm from the heart, my friend, receive
Ah! Then be theirs the fate of ancient Troy.

     C[harles] B[urney, the younger], 'To Mr. Francis'
c.37, p. 8

W0030   Warm from the heart, the truth-born lay
There blossoms, blooms, then fades, and dies.

     'To Stella. 1754'
c.238, p. 29

W0031   Warm meats and clothes this month are good,
Invite the poor, to sup, and dine.

     'Observations out of the alma[na]c how to order yourself every month in the year'
fb.69, p. 175

W0032   Warriors must have for instruments of death
To make a man though ne'er so valiant die.

     [Sir Thomas Urquhart], 'That judges are more dreadful than captains'
fb.217, p. 536

W0033   Was ever brow whereon once quiver'd sat
That handled crumbles into dust.

     'On his beauteous coy mistress'
b.356, p. 83

W0034   Was ever contract driven by better fate?
The married pair two realms, the sea the ring.

     [Ben Jonson], 'Upon the union of England and Scotland'
     [Crum w40]
b.197, p. 36

W0035   Was ever from matron
I must give up the ghost.

     [John Johnson], 'The lamentations of a wife'
File 17696

W0036   Was ever man so to himself unjust,
And that's too little for sweet Philomel.

     'A repentance for having shot the nightingale in Pantyoccyn [sic] Fields, 1673'
b.54, p. 936

W0037   Was ever such affection known
Is the highway of bliss to you.

     T[homas] S[tevens]
c.259, p. 144

W0038 Was hero fair? yes passing fair to see too
May live forevermore.

[R. M.]

Poetry Box VI/4

W0039 Was I deceived? Or did I late
And know to love my life again.

'At home, on my return after a short absence . . .
October 1774'

fc.74, p. 23

W0040 Was I not right–in spite of all their art,
If men were secret, women would be kind.

Susannah Maria Cibber, 'Epilogue. Spoken by . . . to
her own comedy, called the Oracle. First acted at the
Theater Royal in Covent Garden for her own benefit
after the tragedy of Macbeth on Tuesday March 17
1752'

c.360/3, no. 199

W0041 Was not Death a very gull
To leave Halfe Head without a skull.

'On one Halfe Head a Trinity College cook's scullion'

b.356, p. 246

W0042 Was Paris now to live again and prove
But to determine must divide the ball.

c.53, fol. 57

W0043 Was this the justice (Sir) you came to do?
These are the plagues that from rebellion springs!

'Plain dealing or a satire' [on William III]
[Crum w51]

fb.207/1, p. 19; see also 'What's this your justice . . .'.

W0044 Was this well done, amidst a later age
And your last efforts prove your strength divine.

'Complaint of the tragic poets, addressed to Doctor
Young on his tragedy of The brothers. 1753'

c.360/3, no. 248

W0045 Was ye not sadly frighten'd, honest Harry,
Yoi, sur, as lung as e'er I con, I will.

[John Byrom, of Manchester], 'A dialogue between Sir
John Jobson and Henry Homespun' [1745]

c.140, p. 15

W0046 Was you at church o' Sunday morning, John?
If onny comes I'll take it—John—good bye.

[John Byrom, of Manchester], 'A Lancashire dialogue'

c.140, p. 3

W0047 Was young Clorinda's sparkling eye
Can hang poor Jacob for his look.

[Robert Cholmeley], 'The fairest face not always the
most brains or the humble petition of Mr Jacob
Godley in behalf of his face'

c.190, p. 103

W0048 Was't ever seen before that a base quean
Gave (as she thought) the triple crown a buffet.

Sir Thomas Urquhart, 'Of Janie Muffet, who as it is
reported, was the first that offered violence to the
Bishop of Edinburgh in the church of St. Giles, at the
introduction of the service book in Scotland'

fb.217, p. 300

W0049 Wasters, are openhanded rhetoricians:
But niggards, are closehanded, as logicians.

Sir Thomas Urquhart, 'Zeno's comparison of logic,
and rhetoric'

fb.217, p. 155

W0050 Water drown'd th'other world for burning lust:
Fire for cold love, will bring this world to dust.

Sir Thomas Urquhart, 'Of the first world, and this'

fb.217, p. 255

W0051 Wave fancy, beauty's arched brow
Professor in seraphic love.

Richard Daniel, 'Cousin Richard Daniel to Mary . . .
Chamberlain, his wife'

b.52/2, p. 198

W0052 We address you today in a very new fashion
And 'tis easier to say as against France.

[Arthur Mainwaring?], 'The . . . address' [to Queen
Anne; pr. 1704 (Foxon A55)]
[POAS VI.619]

Poetry Box VI/83

W0053 We adore the rising sun as spring of day
Wherewith this lady does as Flora shine.

[Sir Philip Wodehouse], 'Upon the Lady Calthorpe in
her maiden name Dorothea Spring'

b.131, back (no. 55)

W0054 We all adore, she looks so well—
The binding's fine—but what's the book?

[Charles Burney, the younger], 'Bouts-rimes. Written
at Mr. Kirwan's Oct. 15. 1787—the words proposed by
Miss Betsy Kirwan, were, well she must look! Epigram
on a beautiful scold'

c.37, p. 70

W0055 We all are thee she-fool—who was stark blind
Our fancy, breeding, or complexion.

[Sir Philip Wodehouse], 'Excursus upon Caeca fatua'

b.131, p. 9

W0056   We all must die—the most insensible
Scarcely acquir'd, before we mourn their loss.

     'Death' [signed Mathilda]

     c.343, p. 44

W0057   We all salute you, on your own birthday,
That Lady Chatto long may with us stay.

     [Dr. ( ) Rutherford], 'On the return of the Lady
     Chatto's birthday August the 22: 1725'

     c.102, p. 130

W0058   We are a game at cards; the Cabal deal
We're cross, and why? Prerogative is trump.

     [Crum w70, 'council deal']

     b.54, p. 1213 [last line is last line of Crum T1383]

W0059   We are a garden wall'd around,
Demands more praise then tongues can give.

     [Isaac Watts, Hymns and spiritual songs (1707), bk. I,
     Hymn 74]

     c.180, p. 65

W0060   We are a score, nay something more
You will too quickly know us.

     'Enigma'

     Diggle Box: Poetry Box XI/71

W0061   We are agreed
My perfection.

     b.197, p. 152

W0062   We are all here but strangers that must flit,
The nearer home, the nearer to the pit.

     c.339, p. 328

W0063   We are deceiv'd; and fancy is not fit
Which if it be so I am happy here.

     [George Daniel]

     b.121, fol. 87

W0064   We are like bubbles that on waters rise
Or like the flowers, which the springtime dies.

     c.339, p. 327

W0065   We are little airy creatures,
It can never fly from you.

     [Jonathan Swift], '[Enigma/Charade/Conundrum] 60
     [vowels]'

     c.389

W0066   We are not blocks, we must not expect a call
Christ takes his spouse, by contract not by rape.

     [Francis Quarles], 'On man's cooperation' [Divine
     fancies III, 47]

     b.137, p. 192

We are told by the town, that a man of great note   W0067
To bail High Church one day and vote next for Low.

     [Tory ballad on Dr. William Lancaster, vicechancellor
     of Queens College Oxford, and the Oxfordshire
     election 1709/10; pr. 1710 (Foxon O279)]
     [Crum w76]

     b.90, p. 16; fc.24, p. 21; b.382(23r)

We are told the virtues taken are alone   W0068
A Vertue taken from a head of Whood?

     'Epigram on the head of the Revd Mr Joseph Spence
     engraved by Mr Vertue from a painting by Mr Whood
     and prefixed to his Polymetes'

     Spence Papers, folder 113

We are your betters, in a better sense   W0069
Would here conclude O vain logomachy.

     'The replication of John à Stile unto the comedians'
     answer, after whose rejoinder he will demur in law for
     the sufficiency of the plea'

     b.197, p. 83

We, as thy guards from outward harms are sent: W0070
And summon all their reason, at their need.

     'A dialogue between the angel Gabriel, and Adam in
     Paradise; concerning free will, and predestination'

     b.77, p. 74

We both are constant, (beauteous fair!)   W0071
To win your heart, or free my own.

     John Lockman, 'Phyllis: or the perplex'd lover'

     c.267/4, p. 151; c.268 (first part), p. 99

We both, so heav'n decrees, have lost our eyes,   W0072
Ev'n though we could not see without our
                                   spectacles.

     '[Voltaire] To Mad: du Pedan, a lady celebrated for
     her wit and understanding'

     c.83/2, no. 693

We cannot see the heav'ns for clouds: nor break   W0073
Hence have we little faith: less charity.

     Sir Thomas Urquhart, 'The cause, why in this world,
     there is so little faith, and love'

     fb.217, p. 251

We cannot see without the light: albeit   W0074
Nobody't be: th'air is: yet none can see it.

     Sir Thomas Urquhart, 'Of air, and light'

     fb.217, p. 345

W0075   We drink a health to the King, I mean the King in
                        the north
          From cobbling preachers, and heretical teachers |
                    By virtue [of the Protestation].

         'The Protestation protested, or an explanation of the
         Protestation' [May 1641]
         [cf. Crum 11097, 'I'll drink . . .']
         Poetry Box vi/35

W0076   We envy not the growth of Paestan fields,
          At once the ripe, the green, the bud, the blow.

         c.233, p. 34

W0077   We fasted, and then pray'd the war might cease;
          Could they but make an act there were no hell.

         'Upon the Parliamentary occurents &c. 1641' [upon
         John Pym]
         [Crum w91, 'Could Pym']
         b.54, p. 888

W0078   We Father Godden, Gregory, and all
          Or if you do, we can absolve you for't.

         'Advice to the testholders' [1687]
         [Crum w92; POAS iv.180]
         fb.108, p. 61; b.115, fol. 46 (ll. 1–54); Poetry Box vi/130

W0079   We first are young, after to age we yield,
          No wight so strong, but time doth mine the field.

         c.339, p. 320

W0080   We flit away as we had not been born,
          Yea wonders once are out of memory worn.

         c.339, p. 320

W0081   We gave abruptly off in middle
          Home, as a flock of sheep or drove of cows.

         c.519

W0082   We grieve our lost, blest soul, and might whole
                                    showers,
          Forbear, and only long to be with thee.

         'An epitaph on Mrs. Anne Hele 1654'
         c.244, p. 210

W0083   We hail the sacred board
          But all His will is done.

         T[homas] S[tevens], 'At the Lord's table Feb. 13. 1780'
         c.259, p. 76

W0084   We have a king but he is gone
          This realm to ruinate.

         'Tempora mutantur'
         b.111, p. 63

We have been young and strong yea valiant   W0085
                                       heretofore
Till crooke[d] age did hold us back, and bid us do
                                     no more.

         b.208, p. 71

We have long been employ'd   W0086
Of our worthies still hanging in chains.

         'A riddle on a seal'
         c.360/1, p. 5

We have no parent, but our God   W0087
And we are children of his dove.

         [William] Hayley, 'Hymn for the asylum'
         File 6943

We have not an high priest above   W0088
He bleeds the balm that makes us whole.

         [Benjamin Stillingfleet], 'Heb. 4. 15'
         Poetry Box x/166

We have plotted twenty years and more,   W0089
His tun of sack as French commodity.

         'To Mr. [William] Richards a lampoon 1689'
         fb.207/4, p. 12; see also 'We two have . . .'.

We have the promise of eternal truth,   W0090
Which no cessation knows.

         c.549, p. 18

We have two kings, the one is true,   W0091
Then judge who is Pretender.

         'The Pretender, to the tune of Daniel Cooper and his
         man' [Jacobite; pr. 1717/18 (Foxon P1042)]
         fc.58, p. 154

We hug, imprison, hang, and save   W0092
This foe, our friend, our Lord, our slave.

         [William Strode?], couplet beginning 'On a
         purse['s]-strings' [with 'While thus I hung . . .']
         [Crum w103]
         b.200, p. 121; b.205, fol. 56v

We invocate no gods nor call of thee   W0093
Express, and cannot[,] must be understood.

         'An elegy upon the death of the fair and virtuous lady
         the Lady Elizabeth Darell'
         Poetry Box vi/86

We justly when a meaner subject dies   W0094
(Great James) and turn thy tomb into a throne.

         [John] Ashburnham, 'On King James his death'
         b.197, p. 48

W0095   We know Charles Burney is a wit
As scholars please for dunce's bum!

    [William Parsons], 'Epigram on Dr. Charles Burney'
    [Crum W109]

    Greatheed Box/71

W0096   We learn to love, as it appears,
It enters in the heart.

    Sir Thomas Urquhart, 'Of the art of love'

    fb.217, p. 102

W0097   We live upon death's shore, our life's as near,
As earth and water one globe constitute.

    'One foot in the grave'

    c.356

W0098   We lived one and twenty year
Rending the clouds asunder.

    'Death of a wife, scold, by the husband'
    [Crum W114]

    c.81/1, no. 269; fb.143, p. 17; b.197, p. 33

W0099   We Mars, and Venus alike common find;
He being the common foe, and she the friend.

    Sir Thomas Urquhart, 'The soldier's expression
    concerning Mars, and Venus'

    fb.217, p. 123

W0100   We may boldly assert what no one denies,
Tom T—dman and Dr. live both by purgation. |
                     Which nobody can deny &c.

    'Song by a gentleman tune Which nobody can deny'

    c.361

W0101   We may hold them Christians, who contest
We're daily vexed with their protestations.

    Sir Thomas Urquhart, 'An antipuritan's opinion of the
    profession of covananters'

    fb.217, p. 45

W0102   We may not what we would: nor what we can,
Will we perform; s'irregular is man.

    Sir Thomas Urquhart, 'Of the will, and power of
    mankind'

    fb.217, p. 268

W0103   We men are not so fair as women nor
Who [?] their beauty with a glorious mind.

    [Sir Thomas Urquhart], 'To [blank]'

    fb.217, p. 522

W0104   We men in many faults abound,
Is naught in words and naught in deeds.

    [Samuel Rowlands], 'On women's faults'
    [Crum W122]

    c.356

W0105   We met a hundred of us met
Flew up and kick'd the beam.

    [John] Taylor (1750–1826), 'The vision' [enclosed in a
    letter to Michael Maurice, Norwich, 2 April 1794]

    File 16602 (autogr.)

W0106   We must confess and need we must allow,
That learning shall unto experience bow.

    c.339, p. 260, p. 309

W0107   We must have doves and serpents in our hearts
The dove can fly, the serpent only creep.

    [Francis Quarles], 'On doves and serpents' [Divine
    fancies III, 65]

    b.137, p. 172

W0108   We must not boast of fortune's dower
And friendship craves no second spring.

    'On receiving a [?] in October [17]79 from a friend'

    c.90

W0109   We never swear by love: but oft by faith;
Though faith have not a godhead, as love hath.

    Sir Thomas Urquhart, 'Of love and faith'

    fb.217, p. 88

W0110   We often read our blessed Savior wept
For us that sin so oft in mirth and sleep.

    [Francis Quarles], 'And Jesus wept'
    [Crum W133]

    b.137, p. 166

W0111   We pledge you son you've tattled long enough
Your wit is wooden, but your face we'll read.

    'Answer' to 'Does Bear . . .']

    b.356, p. 112

W0112   We praise thy name, O God,
And made us to rejoice. Alleluia. Alleluia.

    Hen[ry] Blaxton, '. . . Enemies to a song after yr per
    mo' [holograph? c. 1588; verses on the defeat of the
    Spanish armada]

    a.28, s. 2V8v

W0113   We pray'd for wars in time of peace
More fickle man than womankind.

    'Mutable man' [Suffolk Lanham, 31 Aug. 1744]

    c.157, p. 16

W0114   We prove by reason, there's a King of kings:
Thus faith's the work of reason in some things.

    Sir Thomas Urquhart, 'Of faith, and reason'

    fb.217, p. 305

W0115 We rail at Judas him that did betray
God knows some curse themselves in cursing him.

[Francis Quarles], 'On Judas Iscariot' [Divine
fancies I, 5, with two extra lines]

b.137, p. 165; b.118, p. 223

W0116 We rather should desire
To drown a thing divine.

Sir Thomas Urquhart, 'Against drunkenness'

fb.217, p. 36

W0117 We read, dear friend in ancient time,
Winter shall then as spring appear.

'September 1753. Printed in the London daily
advertiser, Friday Sept. 28. 1753'

c.371, fol. 71

W0118 We read in profane and sacred records
There's ten times more treason in brandy and ale.

[Andrew Marvell, 'A dialogue betwixt the brass horse
[of Charles I] at Charing Cross and the marble horse
[of Charles II] in Cheapside or Stocks Market' [1676]
[Crum W138; POAS I.275]

fb.106(19); fb.108, p. 13; b.327, f. 29 ('sacred and
profane')

W0119 We read of gods, and kings, that kindly took
That burn'd the temple where she was ador'd.

[Thomas Carew], 'A cruel mistress'
[Crum W140]

b.200, p. 114; b.356, p. 80 'kings and gods')

W0120 We read that once a noble dame,
With these thy saints in heaven may reign. | Amen

'Another of S. Katherine' [November 25]

a.30[58]

W0121 We read that things inanimate have mov'd
For British oak shall Briton's rights defend.

'The oak's address to Mr. Biddulph'
Poetry Box XII/125[1]

W0122 We sage Cartesians, who profess
'Tis loss of time to ply for you.

[Elijah] Fenton, 'The fair nun a tale, a poem'
c.166, p. 170

W0123 We scorn the threat'ning of the deep
The ropes and ring the bell there.

[John Walker?], 'The middle watch'
fc.108, fol. 79v

W0124 We see half heav'n: earth's thousand[th] part our
senses
Perceive not; being asham'd at our offences.

Sir Thomas Urquhart, 'Of heaven, and earth'

fb.217, p. 308

W0125 We see, no travel far, no coast, nor country strange,
Hath any force to alter kind, or nature's work to
change.

c.339, p. 322

W0126 We see that bitter fruit of mocking oft doth spring,
For scorners oft such mates do meet, that more
than serpents sting.

c.339, p. 318

W0127 We see that golden stars do shine
And get in heaven a dwelling place. | Amen

'S. Hierome. Septemb. 30'

a.30[42]

W0128 We should bring both those to a corner, mixt
They are not cover'd till they get the name.

Sir Thomas Urquhart, 'The equivocation of dames,
ladies, and such as are played with on a chessboard'

fb.217, p. 186

W0129 We should each one, to goodness every day
Still further pass, and not to turn nor stay.

c.339, p. 313

W0130 We should not faint for labor or for pain,
But still proceed, and hope at length to gain.

c.339, p. 319

W0131 We should pray rather, that it were diminish'd;
Nor with more perfidy, and wicked spleen.

Sir Thomas Urquhart, 'The Lord increase our faith'

fb.217, p. 175

W0132 We should relieve our parents in distress,
And reverence them that God our days may bless.

c.339, p. 319

W0133 We sin with joy and having sinn'd we mourn,
'Twixt our repentance, and profane desires.

[Sir Thomas Urquhart], 'That all our life is but a
notional curse and vicissitude of sinning and being
sorry for sin'

fb.217, p. 525

W0134 We sing the amazing deeds
His glory in the highest.

[Isaac Watts, Hymns and spiritual songs (1707),
bk. III, Hymn 17]

c.180, p. 48

W0135   We sing the wonders of our age
Whilst navigation is!

> 'To the Sheffield navigators their good neighbors the Doncaster navigators' greeting'

Poetry Box IV/180

W0136   We spirits who in airy throng
The sunshine of benevolence.

> Eliza Porter, 'The spirits of Abbots Langley, who often have enjoyed unseen, the pleasures and social comforts of the manor there . . .'

c.83/4, no. 2027

W0137   We talk of harvests. There are no such things,
And for their old acquaintance plead.

> [George] Herbert

c.259, p. 118

W0138   We, the maids of Exon city,
We pay most frequently for him.

> 'The Exeter maidens' petition, humbly addressed to the Hon. House of Commons'

c.382, p. 41

W0139   We three do furnish without grudging
Out of employment ne'er will throw us.

> [ ] R., 'Riddle [sheep, goose, etc.]'

Poetry Box VII/48

W0140   We to this place where Shakespeare dwelt of old,
And give for sterling money, sterling wit.

> [William] Somervile, 'Prologue—'

Poetry Box V/97

W0141   We two have plotted twenty years and more,
His tun of sack as French commodity.

> 'To William Richards'

b.111, p. 531; see also 'We have plotted . . .'.l

W0142   We use our God, as usurers do their bands:
Our bands are cancelled, and our God forsaken.

> [Francis Quarles], 'On man's behavior to God'
> [Crum W159]

b.137, p. 186

W0143   We weep, O nature, when the doom
Is fleeting as the rose.

> 'The rose: from rose of Ausonius—an ode' [10 Nov. 1799]

c.136, p. 170

W0144   We were not slain—but rais'd
Here we ten are one.

> 'Inscription on a tombstone in the churchyard of Christ Church in Hampshire inscribed to the memory of ten men who were killed by the earth of a pot falling in upon them as they were digging, in the year 1641'

c.361

W0145   We were two brothers and five sisters, now
An emulation shall in others move.

> [Sir Aston Cokayne], 'To my sister Mrs Katherine Weston'

b.275, p. 79

W0146   We, who your awful bulwarks steer,
Their rugged sides when stoutly mann'd.

> 'An address to his Majesty King George the Second from the seafaring men'

c.503, p. 18

W0147   We wisht for thee we wait for thee
We worship thee, we wait on thee.

b.208, p. 124

W0148   We yet are young, bold, strong, and ready to maintain
That quarrel still against all men, that on the earth remain.

b.208, p. 71

W0149   Weak crazy mortal why dost fear,
He may be said to take his leave at night.

> [Ann Shower?], 'On a short life'
> [Crum W173]

c.184, p. 79

W0150   Weak man! Who without reason aim
And leaves you all in happy hour.

> 'An essay on old maids'

c.83/1, no. 39

W0151   Wealth in the Hebrew language *hon* is named:
Gold's *or* in French: of those is honor framed.

> Sir Thomas Urquhart, 'The etymology of honor'

fb.217, p. 307

W0152   Wealth maketh many friends; but he that's poor
Yet their denials daily they renew.

> Sir John Strangways, '14° Octobris 1646'

b.304, p. 59

W0153   'Wealth may be bought too dear'—said those of old
Content with Britain's soil and Britain's weather.

> Lady Louisa Stuart

File 14615

W0154 Wear sable robes, sit mournful by her grave
My love enclos'd shall be, within my lonely heart.

> Sir Francis Castillion, 'An epitaph made upon the
> death of the Lady Castillion . . . 1603'
>
> fb.69, p. 192 and 196

W0155 Wear these, my little Mary Anne,
Her parents' joy may shine.

> [Mary (Shackleton) Leadbeater], 'To Mary Ann
> Coote, with a pair of gloves which had been Jane
> Leadbeater's'
>
> c.142, p. 128

W0156 Wearied with business and with care opprest
The infant by Christ is his new joy.

> 'The dream'
>
> File 17416

W0157 Wearied with earth and all below
We'll leave the sacred place.

> T[homas] S[tevens]
>
> c.259, p. 125

W0158 Wearied with long attendance on the court
Are now, O! sad reverse! my greatest dread.

> [Mary Barber?], 'The widow Gordon's petition to the
> R[igh]t Hon[ora]ble the Lady Carteret enclosed in the
> foregoing verses' [pr. 1725 (Foxon B80)]
>
> Poetry Box IV/133; File 13409 (var.); see also 'This fame
> reports . . .'.

W0159 Weary with business and opprest with care
The terror of a future punishment.

> 'A walk'
>
> b.216, p. 225

W0160 Weary with watching harmless sheep
For gods like men, grant all things to the fair.

> 'A pastoral. By the same hand' [as 'Tho' in their
> flame . . .']
>
> fb.142, p. 51

W0161 Wedding and hanging the destinies dispatch,
But hanging to some seems the better match.

> [John Davies, of Hereford], 'On marriage'
>
> c.356

W0162 Wedlock at first, indeed is vastly pleasant;
Sometimes a cuckoo—oft'ner a horn'd owl.

> 'Love and marriage [2]'
>
> c.81/1, no. 6

W0163 Wedlock I weigh'd with caution nice,
Egad I'll burn, before I'll marry.

> 'Epigram'
>
> c.81/1, no. 44

W0164 Wedlock to be the intolerablest yoke,
And saith no yoke like wedlock is so sweet.

> 'Of Alema'
>
> c.356

W0165 Wedlock's a lock, however large or thick,
Which every rascal has a key to pick.

> 'Love and marriage [3]'
>
> c.81/1, no. 6

W0166 Wedlock's a saucy, sad familiar state
Then puts his night-cap o'er his eyes and snores!

> 'Love and marriage [1]'
>
> c.81/1, no. 6

W0167 Weeds from the ground, instead of flowers upsprout
Then she had found no fruit, and we had known
                                          no sin.

> M. F., 'On a ruined garden'
>
> c.186, p. 69

W0168 Weep greatest island for thy mistress' death
On earth the chief, in heaven the second maid.

> 'On Q[ueen] Elizabeth'
> [Crum w187]
>
> b.62, p. 77; fb.143, p. 23; see also 'Weep little island . . .'.

W0169 Weep it thou, vain Muse, when blood-stained
                                    [chiefs] expire?
Unsullied virtue claims immortal joy.

> [William Boscawen], 'Stanzas to the memory of the
> Honorable Edward James Eliot'
>
> fc.106, p. 48

W0170 Weep little island, and for thy mistress' death
In earth the first, in heaven the second maid.

> 'Britain's lachrimae [on Queen Elizabeth] . . . Harl.
> MSS. No. 293. Fo. 94'
> [Crum w189]
>
> Poetry Box VII/78; see also 'Weep greatest island . . .'.

W0171 Weep, marble weep, so shall my pious eyes,
He gathered unto his people is.

> [Julius Glanvill], 'Verses on the funeral of ———'
> [John Bragge of Wadham College; Bragge and
> Glanvill matriculated March 1650/51]
> [Crum w191]
>
> b.263, fol. 18v

W0172 Weep no more my fond eyes, for the swain,
For I know what he says must be true.

> 'The flights' [first of 'Two pastoral ballads']
>
> Poetry Box IV/69

W0173   Weep not because this child hath died so young
They well are fitted both are but a span.

> [William Strode], 'On the death of Mris Mary
> Prideaux'
> [Crum W194]
>
> b.205, fol. 52v

W0174   Weep not, fond parent, that insatiate death
Spotless! may we, be ever so prepar'd!

> 'Sonnet'
>
> c.135, p. 27

W0175   Weep rocks weep mountains. Joy and mirth are fled
Young tender sucklings went the milky way.

> 'Herod's cruelty. Mat. 2. 16'
>
> c.160, fol. 57

W0176   Weep weep kind virgins; let those crystal [?]
How the bright cherubs sit and sing good praise |
                 In panegyric hallelujahs.

> 'A memorial of the virtuous and renowned lady Dame
> Jane wife of Sir Richard Heigham' [after 1623]
>
> File 17709

W0177   Weep, weep no more like those that vainly deem
And all its gilded pleasures only pain.

> 'An epitaph in Thames Ditton churchyard—Surrey'
>
> c.360/1, p. 281

W0178   Weep ye Clerenses, weep all about
He's gone but not Clere to Trinity Hall.

> 'On Mr. Newcomen of Clere Hall'
>
> c.74

W0179   Welcome abroad, O welcome from your bed
To one so school'd, and vers'd in martyrdom.

> [William Strode], 'To a gentleman [Mr. Rives]
> strangely cured by two chirurgeons'
> [Crum W210]
>
> b.200, p. 229

W0180   Welcome beauteous azure flowers
Fix thy root deep in my heart.

> 'On receiving a present of violets, by a young lady'
>
> c.83/1, no. 90

W0181   Welcome blest day of sweet repose
The wonders He hath done.

> 'Easter Day'
>
> c.83/3, no. 842

W0182   Welcome (dear sons) unto our court of Rome,
Help all you may to give the fatal blow.

> [John Taylor], 'A conference held at the Castle
> Angelo, between the Pope, the Emperor, and the
> K[ing] of Spain'
> [Crum W214]
>
> b.197, p. 214; b.101, p. 49 (with extra lines?)

W0183   Welcome, dear swallow! To thy well-known nest
And soothe with lullabies thy callow young!

> R[ichard] V[ernon] S[adleir], 'Lines written on seeing
> the first swallow in the spring 1790 and sent for the
> Gentleman's magazine, April'
>
> c.106, p. 133

W0184   Welcome, Elisa, to thy Esther's soul!
When time, and ages are no more, | To all eternity.

> W[illiam] C[arpenter, trans.], 'Esther a scripture
> tragedy from the French of Racine'
>
> c.247, p. 1

W0185   Welcome ever charming May,
Fill'd with sublime felicity.

> Henry Baker, 'On the month of May'
>
> c.244, p. 401

W0186   Welcome, fair princess, to the shore
Glad homage pay to thee.

> 'To her Highness, Augusta, Princess of Saxe Gotha on
> her landing at Greenwich, Sunday April the 25 1736'
>
> c.360/1, p. 139

W0187   Welcome fair scene;—welcome thou lov'd retreat,
Fix then, my heart, thy happiness is here.

> Robert Dodsley, 'Mrs. Pearse's salutation to her
> garden in the country'
>
> c.351, p. 144

W0188   Welcome great monarch to the throne we gave
Our purses, and our veins shall freely bleed.

> 'A congratulatory poem on his Ma[jes]ty's return
> from Ireland' [William III]
> [Crum W220]
>
> fb.68, p. 29; b.204, p. 77

W0189   Welcome great princess to this lovely place
Shall be the subject of all our loyal prayers.

> 'The bellman to the Princess Anne' [1692]
> [Crum W222 ('lonely place'); POAS v.340]
>
> b.111, p. 44

W0190   Welcome great shade to these amerc'd abodes
Have shown yourself most devil of the two.

> 'Dialogue between two usurpers in Hell'
>
> c.171, p. 9

W0191 Welcome great Sir, great both in name and deed,
Their mighty pow'rs with mighty virtues met.

[Edmund Wodehouse], 'Octr. 25 [1714] Address to King George'

b.131, p. 69

W0192 Welcome, illustrious peer!
Since to his love we owe | Northumberland.

John Lockman, 'Song. Sung at the arrival in Dublin, of his excellency the Earl of Northumberland Lord Lieutenant of Ireland. Set to music by Mr. Peter Valton'

c.267/2, p. 172

W0193 Welcome little helpless stranger,
And their fondest hopes fulfil.

[Anna Laetitia (Aikin)] Barbauld, 'On the birth of Dr Priestley's son'

c.130, p. 80

W0194 Welcome mighty King on shore
Tweedledum tweedle twee.

'The petition. &c.'

c.570/2, p. 97

W0195 Welcome, my friends, thrice welcome here this
night
Have in this temple just alighted.

F[rederick] Dickinson, 'Ware Dec: 27. 1782. written by . . . on our dance'

c.391

W0196 Welcome my health, physicians all adieu,
And let thy grace supply my want of wit.

[Sir Richard Bulstrode], 'A paradox, the worse the better'

fb.88, p. 114v

W0197 Welcome my honest long-expected friend
For none's so despicable as thy own.

[William Wharton], 'A familiar answer' [to Robert Wolseley]
[Crum w231]

b.219, p. 7; fb.108, p. 247

W0198 Welcome my lamp, awhile
The cock has summon'd day.

[George Daniel]

b.121, fol. 41v

W0199 Welcome once more, kind friends, to this our inn,
To gain your smiles and favors if we can.

William Smith, 'Copy of an occasional prologue written and spoken by . . . on the opening of Covent Garden Theater Sept. 1761'

Smith Papers, folder 53 (2 copies); c.115

W0200 Welcome peaceful calm retreat!
Till my latest sand falls down.

Dr. [ ] Brooks, 'The retirement'

c.481, p. 255

W0201 Welcome pleasing melancholy
Amend my mind, improve my heart.

S[tephen] Simpson, 'An address to melancholy'

c.563

W0202 Welcome sad night
In heaven's high court of parliament.

'Ode 2' [1640: answer to 'Go empty joys . . .']
[Crum G142, second part]

fb.106(10)

W0203 Welcome sun and southern show'rs
Drums and routs, adieu adieu.

'Sonnet by a young lady leaving town'

c.83/3, no. 931

W0204 Welcome, sweet season, when the wavy corn,
To labor ardent for the bread of life.

Charles Atherton Allnutt, 'Sonnet on harvest'

c.112, p. 147

W0205 Welcome sweet Titan, bridegroom of the year
Lift up their heads and now again revive.

[John Rose?], 'Of the spring quarter'

b.227, p. 166

W0206 Welcome the day antiquity enrolls
Should thus be sacrificed to ashes here.

[Edward] Sparke, 'Poem 9th, on the feast of Ash-Wednesday'

b.137, p. 22

W0207 Welcome the joys we cheaply buy!
And welcome those we cheaply buy.

c.83/1, no. 38

W0208 Welcome thou friendly earnest of fourscore
To entertain these well or ne'er come more.

[Elijah Fenton?], 'On the first fit of the gout' [pr. 1706 (Foxon F112)]
[Crum w242]

Poetry Box VII/17

W0209 Welcome thou modest sergeant of pale death,
Fully provided and insensibly.

[John Hobart], '[Præludia mortis.] Æt. 65. When his hand beg[a]n sometimes to shake—the welcome'

b.108, fol. 8

W0210 Welcome thou ne'er-to-be-forgotten day!
And Nassau's equitable blood.

'An ode. On the coronation of his Majesty King
William the Third'
Poetry Box VII/59 (incomplete?)

W0211 Welcome, thou presage of my certain doom.
And gain the plaudit of a smiling God.

[Mrs. ( ) Wakeford], 'The mourning ring'
c.153, p. 167

W0212 Welcome thou soft repose of busy care,
But by a zeal intense and fervent labors(?) dies.

Bay Ray, 'Upon sleep'
c.229/1, fol. 67

W0213 Welcome thrice welcome lovely sty!
Thou hold'st good Bacon now.

[Phanuel Bacon], 'On Dr. Bacon's taking shelter in a
pigsty in a hard storm'
c.237, fol. 54

W0214 Welcome to Scotia's plains [dear] injur'd youth
Now God, his King, and country all denies.

'Prince Charles his welcome to Scotland'
c.275

W0215 Welcome to this calm retreat,
But faint, and fainter, die away.

E. W., 'Addressed to S. P.'
Greatheed Box/96

W0216 Welcome, welcome again to thy wits
The way to cure madness is thus to be jolly.

'A song'
b.54, p. 1162

W0217 Welcome welcome brother debtor
Since there is nothing free but love.

[Wetenhall Wilkes], 'A song' [pr. 1748 (Foxon
W469)]
c.341, p. 41; c.358, p. 33 (attr. Sir John Fielding)

W0218 Welcome welcome from fatigue and drum,
A health and in that wish him on her. | Welcome
welcome &c.

'2 song'
fb.228/60

W0219 Welcome welcome little stranger
Have to guide your steps thro' life.

[John Walker?], 'On the birth of an infant'
fc.108, fol. 79

W0220 Welcome welcome rosy god!
And the tear that fills the eye.

[Robert Merry], 'Address to Bacchus a rant'
Greatheed Box/9

W0221 Welcome ye noble souls from the base seat
With oaths, and the plain truth itself defy.

'On the nonjurors in Norfolk'
[Crum w249]
b.111, p. 117

W0222 Well at last my dear aunt I'm set down to write
So I remain, with great truth, your affectionate
slave.

[William Lee], 'Oxon. Feb. 16, 1742/3'
Poetry Box I/142

W0223 Well! Be it so—sorrow, that streams not o'er,
And never pray thy will, but God's be done.

'The resignation'
c.83/2, no. 372

W0224 Well climb'd, Zaccheus; 'twas a stop well given,
From hence to the tree, and from the tree to
heaven.

[Francis Quarles], 'On Zaccheus'
[Crum w254]
b.118, p. 224

W0225 We'll consort with tempest, with earthquakes agree
And fuddle and fuddle like men.

'The drunkard's rant'
b.115, fol. 27v

W0226 Well did the Mantuan poet sing
Lewis [i.e., Love?] conquers, and all yield to love.

[Thomas Hamilton, 6th earl of Haddington], 'The
arbor from Boccace'
c.458/2, p. 49

W0227 Well do the am'rous sons of W[adha]m
And fear the punishment the same.

'On W[adha]m Coll[ege] being insured from fire'
c.241, p. 33

W0228 Well done Zelustus! god will scarce divide
An affectation from a secret pride.

[Francis Quarles, Divine fancies IV, 105]
b.137, p. 182

W0229 We'll drink and we'll never have done boys
And a fig for Sultan and Sophy.

'Song 219'
c.555, p. 346

W0230 Well fare those three, that when there was a dearth
Till we that wanted cups, now wanted drink.

> Geo[rge] Morley, 'On the drinking in the crown of an hat'
> [Crum W265]
> b.200, p. 242

W0231 Well for mankind had Adam been so dull
He by stupidity had sav'd his race.

> 'On Mr Jervoise refusing the Lady Sidley a breakfast at Bath'
> c.176, p. 26; c.360/1, p. 159

W0232 Well fortune, now (if e'er) you have shewn
Here's all thy gain, still to be thought more blind.

> [John] N[orris, of Bemerton], 'The defiance'
> c.258

W0233 Well has thy muse that charming hope display'd,
But heav'nly joys, to fill th'immortal mind.

> 'Ode to hope'
> c.83/2, no. 569

W0234 Well hast thou done my friend, to turn
For a court chaplain push in.

> T[homas] M[orell], 'To Stephen Duck, on his taking orders'
> c.395, p. 72

W0235 Well have I thought on't and I find
'Twill not be short because it's all my own.

> [John Norris, of Bemerton], 'The retirement'
> c.548; see also 'Well I have . . .'.

W0236 Well, here I am, I've managed matters rarely,
If you[r] kind plaudits tell me you are pleas'd.

> 'Occasional address spoken by Miss Fontinelle at the Theater Brighthelmston in the character of Maggy McGilpin'
> c.115

W0237 Well, I find my dear Ma'am you must have your
own way,
Keep the nag to yourself—we'll sit still and admire.

> 'Burton Head Monday night'
> Poetry Box III/33

W0238 Well! I have said it, and maintain it still,
Tho' 'tis not Pope's, it yet may stand the test.

> [William Popple, trans.], 'Horace book 1st satire 10th imitated. To the admirers of the late Mr. Pope'
> fc.104/1, p. 171

Well I have thought on't, and I find   W0239
'Twill not be short, because 'tis all my own.

> [John Norris, of Bemerton], 'An encomium upon a retired life'
> [Crum W274]
> c.160, fol. 96v; c.547, p. 169; see also 'Well have I . . .'.

Well I may now receive and die; my sin   W0240
(I hope esteem) my w[r]it canonical.

> [John Donne], 'Satira quarta [Against the court]'
> [Crum W275]
> b.114, p. 25; b.148, p. 17

Well, if affliction tends to make me wise   W0241
And the sweet prospects of immortal life.

> [Thomas Stevens?], 'On affliction'
> c.259

Well if I ever saw such another man since my   W0242
mother bound my head
And so I remain in a civil way your humble servant
to command.

> [Jonathan Swift], 'Mary the cookmaid's letter to Dr. Sheridan'
> fc.60, p. 55

Well Kitty, now I hope you are satisfied   W0243
And if we must repent be't in a coach and six.

> [David Garrick?], 'Epilogue to The lying valet'
> Poetry Box I/76

Well knows the artist where the earth contains   W0244
To fly from evil understanding sound.

> [J. M—tt], '28th chap. of Job'
> c.140, p. 509

Well, ladies, bless your stars that, nowadays,   W0245
We act from nature,—for we act for you.

> 'An occasional epilogue to The tragedy of the earl of Essex' [by Henry Jones; spoken Wednesday 13 Sept. 1775]
> c.136, p. 103

Well; let him climb for me, and stand, who will,   W0246
Who, known to all, himself not knowing, dies.

> [Thomas Morell], 'Stet qui cunq volet &c. Sen[eca] Thyestes—Act iii' [answered by 'Let him retire . . .']
> c.395, p. 34

We'll live and love and change no more   W0247
We'll die together in each other's arms.

> c.549, p. 56

W0248 Well may he rant—yes well he may!
Yet she too oft rebels, and hears not law.

   [Sir Philip Wodehouse], 'A rebustical concept of Sir William Rant (he married Mrs. Grey)'

   b.131, back (no. 193)

W0249 Well may Pulteney and Shippen rant, grumble, and rave,
But not one in the administration.

   'An epitaph on the busts in the Queen's grotto'

   c.233, p. 118

W0250 Well may suspicion shake its head,
Her very shoes—because they're fellows.

   'Suspicion'

   c.81/1, no. 281

W0251 Well may the human bosom sigh,
Hell bars th'eternal door.

   M. S., 'Another [thought on sickness]'

   c.156, p. 81

W0252 Well may the wicked die for fear
But waiting is thy part.

   '27 Psalm'

   c.124, no. 11

W0253 Well may ye, lovely nymphs, pursue
Nights still succeed of undisturb'd repose.

   C[harles] B[urney], 'Ode, written at Drumside, and addressed to the Miss Duncans . . . May 24. 1780'

   c.38, p. 49

W0254 Well met my faithful steward, where hast been?
They may say, thank the devil and the Pope.

   'A dialogue between the Pope and the devil. 1679'

   b.54, p. 1241

W0255 Well met, what cheer my messmate Sam
You might be happy as Sam and Joe.

   [John Walker?], 'The happy tars (tune When Sol descended to the deep)'

   fc.108, fol. 75

W0256 Well, my belov'd, from Paris am I come
Will teach you more than Hurd, or Markham knows.

   'Gallicia to Britannicus at Oxford'

   fc.53, p. 28

W0257 Well my prayers are now ended—the verses may go—
To toast a beefsteak on the hill.

   [Charles Burney, the younger], 'Sent with Edwin and Angelina to Lady Gordon and Mrs. Scott . . . Dec. 26. [17]79'

   c.37, p. 64

W0258 Well pleas'd with Pomfret's easy lines, I said,
I'll trust to heav'n for more substantial bliss.

   T[homas] M[orell], 'On conversation with the same [Miss Anne Barker, later his wife]'

   c.395, p. 58

W0259 Well Primrose! may our Godfrey's name on thee
Broke both the neck of Godfrey and the plot.

   'On Sr Edmundbury Godfrey's death' [murdered 12 Oct. 1678]

   fb.143, p. 29

W0260 Well she is dead, hear, envy, hear,
Obstructed glory's course.

   'On Lady Millar's death, to Miss Seward'

   fc.53, p. 54

W0261 Well Sir, 'tis granted, I said. Dryden's rhymes
Approve my sense I count their censure fame.

   John Wilmot, 2nd earl of Rochester, 'Satire, on the modern poets, an allusion to Horace, the 10th Satire of the 1st book' [1675]
   [Crum w289; POAS 1.358]

   b.334, p. 209; b.54, p. 974 ('Sirs')

W0262 Well Sirs, I guess, by what you'd seen tonight,
And place your merit in a brighter view.

   W[illiam] S[mith], 'Epilogue to The tempest performed at the Earl of Sandwich's at Hinchingbrook, spoke by Miss Courtenay who performed the part of Ariel'

   Smith Papers, folder 48

W0263 Well then; I now do plainly see,
That 'tis the way too thither.

   [Abraham Cowley], 'The wish'
   [Crum w291]

   b.135, fol. 111v; c.244, p. 213; see also 'Well then; now I . . .'.

W0264 Well then poor G[ay] lies underground
'Tis ten to one if he comes back.

   [Alexander Pope], 'Another [epigram]'

   fc.60, p. 50

W0265 Well then, Sir, you shall know how far extend
Let him not love that life that loves not me.

[Abraham Cowley], trans., 'Vota tui breviter.
Mart[ial], Epigram' [I.iv, 'A modest man's wish']
[Crum w292]

fb.142, p. 39; b.118, p. 9

W0266 Well then; now I do plainly see
And so make a city here.

A[braham] C[owley], 'The wish'

c.258; see also 'Well then; I now . . .'.

W0267 Well tho' these lower grounds afford
And fill with ardor all the way.

T[homas] S[tevens]

c.259, p. 146

W0268 Well, 'tis as Bickerstaff has guess'd,
As he himself could, when above.

[Jonathan Swift], 'A Grubstreet elegy on the supposed
death of Partridge the almanac maker. 1708'

c.265

W0269 Well! To our ball come twenty mile!
To greatness, but in vain allied? | Or who evol(?)?—

'To the gentlemen of the four in an assembly Waltham
Cross[.] A dialogue between the poet and his friend'

c.391, after p. 120 (incomplete)

W0270 Well, Tom! What think you of Gil Blas.
Tom shakes his head and cries—Alas.

'On the same [Gil Blas, by Edward Moore, acted for
nine nights at Drury Lane in Feb. 1750/1]

c.360/3, no. 86

W0271 Well Tunbridge I have seen thee thro' and thro'
And with the season, the dull farce complete.

'On Tunbridge Wells in Kent—1736'

c.360/1, p. 11

W0272 Well!—we have scal'd the precipice at last,
Retires confus'd, and will reveal no more.

Christopher Pitt, 'The masquerade'
[Crum w294]

c.244, p. 445

W0273 Well—what a night! Says angry Ned,
Ah! pox on both your houses.

'Epigram on the run of Shakespeare's tragedy of
Romeo and Juliet at the two theaters of Drury Lane
and Covent Garden which continued for 12 nights
from Sep. 28 to Octo. 11 1750'

c.360/3, no. 79

W0274 Well, what shall we say of this marriage so odd?
When 'tis long as 'tis broad, and broad as 'tis long.

'On the marriage of Mr. Long to Miss Broad'

c.81/1, no. 334; fc.85, fol. 86v

W0275 Well yesterday is pass'd, and cannot be
And all the host of heaven shall shout us welcome.

'Yesterday'

c.186, p. 126

W0276 Wench wholly martial, to whose inspiration
Character'd the impression of each line.

Sir Thomas Urquhart, 'The invocation to Clio'

fb.217, p. 65

W0277 We're all deluded, vainly searching ways,
That God conceals the happiness of death.

[Francis Quarles]
[Crum w301]

c.370, fol. 11 (attr. J[ohn] R[obinson])

W0278 Were Boreas' blasts, were Phoebus' burning ray
Ungrateful sounds, and at thy triumph swear.

John Lockman, 'To a brave admiral. In answer to
some detracting verses in a daily paper . . . 1747'

c.267/1, p. 25

W0279 We're born but one, and die a thousand ways:
Yet one health ends a thousand maladies.

Sir Thomas Urquhart, 'Of deaths, birth, health and
diseases'

fb.217, p. 319

W0280 Were both the Indies' treasures thine,
That wealth eternally remains.

'Relating to the second emblem'

c.189, p. 81

W0281 We're brutes by nature, and do know
In heavenly wisdom make me grow.

H[enry] C[olman], 'On wisdom'

b.2, p. 102

W0282 Were but my days imperfectly employ'd
Which his chief dignity chief glory is.

[Edmund Wodehouse], 'Decr. 14 [1714]'

b.131, p. 114

W0283 Were he a brother 'prentice that did write
And spread their nets fraught with preferment's
                                                    bait.

b.216, p. 190

W0284 Were I a priest, brave punch should be my text,
A poor man vastly rich, a rich man poor.

'In praise of punch'

c.578, p. 112

W0285 Were I invited to a nectar feast
Let who would meet the beauty of the sky.

'Sylvia'

c.176, p. 37

W0286 Were I so tall to reach the sky
The mind's the standard of the man.

'Anecdote of Dr. Watts'

c.487, p. 87; see also 'Mylo, forbear . . .'.

W0287 Were I to choose a mate for life—I'd have
Who would might take him for a row of pins.

'Enigmas in The ladies' diary for the year 1737,
answered—the maid's choice'

c.241, p. 124

W0288 Were I to choose what sort of shape I'd wear,
But a rare something of 'em all together.

'The answer' [to the Earl of Rochester's Satire on
mankind]
[Crum w313]

b.105, p. 22

W0289 Were I to cure the nation's fears,
But still reign monarch here.

'The loyal reformer' [Jacobite]
[Crum w315]

b.111, p. 55

W0290 Were I (who to my cost already am
Man differs more from man than man from beast.

[John Wilmot], 2nd E[arl] of R[ochester], 'A satire
against man'
[Crum w317]

b.105, p. 8; b.334, p. 153; b.369, p. 43; fb.140, p. 124 (ll. 1-
174); fb.66/42 (ll. 1-174); Poetry Box vi/68 (ll. 1-174);
b.369

W0291 We're ignorant, how soon, vain, mortal men
No more; but then, man's glass of life was run.

[John Rose?]

b.227, p. 192

W0292 Were my thoughts lovesick I could then compare
As to leave yours and make her hair a star.

'A hair bracelet sent by a gentlewoman to her friend
and to her sent back these verses'
[Crum w323]

b.205, fol. 91r

W0293 Were not my faith buoy'd up, I drown'd might'ly
You with the day may live to aftertimes.

[W[illia]m Newcourt, 'A panegyric on that Jesuitical
conspiracy revealed November the fifth. 1605'

b.212, p. 25

W0294 We're now become a fine cool shady walk
A welcome to a sad she-hermit's cave.

Lady Jane Cavendish, 'The first speech one woman
alone speaks from the rest' [in a pastoral]
[Crum w324]

b.233, p. 57

W0295 Were talents equal to our zeal,
How earnestly we wish you well.

[ ] Crowfoot, 'To Miss Diana Burroughes in answer to
an invitation given by her to Mr. and Miss Crowfoot,
to dine with her on her birthday—July the 8th. 1777'

c.90

W0296 Were there on earth, another voice like thine
And harmony recall thee from the grave.

[William Congreve], 'On the celebrated Miss Arabella
Hunt, who died on Wednesday the 26. of December in
the year 1705'

c.360/2, no. 50

W0297 Were women as little as they are good,
A peascod would make them a gown and a hood.

'On women'
[Crum w334]

c.356; c.74

W0298 Were you the zodiac, I would be the sun,
The limits of your Gnydian line each night.

Sir Thomas Urquhart, 'The speeches of an amorous
gentleman to his mistress'

fb.217, p. 350

W0299 Were't not for you I knew not how to live,
My Lord's returned, and add here you'll retain.

Lady Jane Cavendish, 'The quintessence of cordial'
[Crum w338]

b.233, p. 14

W0300 Westminster is a mill that grinds all causes,
The toll is oft made greater than the grist.

[Thomas Bastard], '[Epigrams.] 4. In aulam Westm.'

b.205, fol. 96v

W0301 Wet thro' to the skin, then confin'd half a day
And a whoremaster's punishment and three
                                        women's tongues.

Anthony Henley, 'Extempore compliment to Lady
Sebright Miss Green and Mistress Halsey in the grove
at Sr. W[illia]m Bucks bart. In Herefordshire . . . 1734'

c.229/1, fol. 25v

W0302 We've raised an army of lusty young fellows
Or else we shall sing but a sorrowful ditty.

'A song wrote about the time of . . . the French's being
landed in the Isle of Purbeck . . . 1678'

b.54, p. 1094

W0303 Wha' was ony like Willie Gairlace,
Whiskey's ill will skaith her maist!

Hector Macneill, 'The history o' Will and Jean'

c.142, p. 151

W0304 What a blockhead is he that's afraid to die poor!
My cash shall provide me whatever I please: | So
the matter is plain &c.

'Song 49'

c.555, p. 75

W0305 What—a book, and by Hogarth! 'Tis twenty to ten
He will publish—here goes, it's double or quit.

[Thomas Warton?], '. . . The following lines
whimsically enough describe [Hogarth's] feelings
[when discouraged by friends from writing about his
system]'

File 15773

W0306 What a chameleon? sure I think it is
And be what they pretend for Jesus' sake.

'On a Jesuit'

b.216, p. 157

W0307 What a cursed crew have we got
And he's welcome home.

'A [Jacobite] song' [pr. 1715? (Foxon N185)]

fc.58, p. 168; c.570/2, p. 62

W0308 What a dismal rough face winter lately put on,
Complacency, jollity, and peace.

John Lockman, 'For the Fraternity of the Grand
Khaibar. Sung at their general anniversary meeting,
Saturday 1 March 1740'

c.267/2, p. 249; c.268 (first part), p. 106

W0309 What a folly is riches, your gold what a jest?
They in happiness live, whiles contented in mind.

'Contentment'

c.578, p. 144

W0310 What a king call'd us all in a book once in fashion
You will conjure as well as the person I mean.

'An enigma'

c.154, p. 49

W0311 What a riddle is love if thought on aright
'Tis both the vexation and joy of one's heart.

c.549, p. 57, p. 14

W0312 What a rope ail these seamen so loudly to rail?
As to higgle for pay with so generous a king.

'A bob for the seamen' [satire; in mock-response to 'I
prithee, good Tommy' and 'Good people do but lend
an ear . . .']

b.111, p. 520

W0313 What a sentence of justice for misdoings past!
As the very same step helped us under before.

[Spencer] Madan, 'On an old apothecary who
mounted his horse on an inverted mortar'
[Crum w348]

Poetry Box x/135

W0314 What a stately appearance they make now they're
join'd,
They're safe in the front, as they are in the rear.

'Another' [on the fleet]

c.570/3, p. 70

W0315 What a strange moment will that be!
When one shall be variety.

[John] Norris, of Bemerton, 'The prospect'

c.244, p. 76

W0316 What a strange thing is man?
And diverse things, by the same name we call.

[George Daniel]

b.121, fol. 63v

W0317 What a whimsical change will be wrought in our
isle,
And waking all swore they had slept but one night.

'On the commencement of the new, or Gregorian
style throughout all the British dominions Sep. 1752'

c.360/3, no. 230

W0318 What accents from a lonely height
And each revolving year renew this festal day.

[William Boscawen], 'Ode. For the anniversary
meeting of subscribers to the Literary Fund. May 2nd
1799'

fc.106, p. 81

W0319 What ails the Scots I think the knaves are mad,
I see no help but knocks must end the fray.

b.101, p. 77

W0320 What ails thee, Jack, thou'rt grown so dull,
You'll be a gainer in the end.

'The nettle addressed to J—— R——, esq' [1751]

Poetry Box XIV/171

W0321 What ails thee so, that muffles up and shrouds
Ireland's terror here liveth under.

'An elegy upon the late renowned knight and
colonel Sr. Charles Coote . . . his epitaph'

fb.228/19

W0322 What? all the places full? pooh, nonsense, stuff!
We wish to raise no spirits here—but yours.

'Prologue spoken at Mr Le Ferier's'

Poetry Box x/155

W0323 What all women do, change the A for an E
Tells a maiden whose beauties no mortal can parry.

[Sir William Trumbull]

Trumbull Box: Poetry Box XIII/55

W0324 What and how great his virtue is, whose mind
He rides secure, who o'er the billows rides.

[William Popple, trans.], 'Horace book 2nd satire 2nd
imitated. inscribed to his friends'

fc.104/1, p. 205

W0325 What, and how great, the virtue and the art,
Let us be fix'd, and our own masters still.

[Alexander Pope], 'The 2nd. satire of the 2nd book of
Horace' [pr. 1734 (Foxon P893)]

c.570/4, p. 121

W0326 What anxious thoughts does grateful mind oppress
Yet God will act his will without control.

[Mrs. Christian Kerr], 'To an absent friend in
affliction describing the author's own sufferings by
dreams'

c.102, p. 122

W0327 What are Deucalion's days return'd, that we
When fishes leave the sea on hills to sport.

'On Mr Turbot who married Mris Hill'
[Crum w362]

b.205, fol. 46v

W0328 What? Are our *alma maters* barren grown?
Of studying language, manners, and good sense.

T[homas] M[orell], 'Another [epigram]'

c.395, p. 71

W0329 What are poor men but quickened lumps of earth?
His death a winter's night that finds no morrow.

'On man'

c.189, p. 104

What are the falling rills, and pendant shades   W0330
Inly she bleeds, and melts his [her] soul away.

[Alexander] Pope, 'On reading the foregoing lines' ['A
fit of spleen' by Benjamin Ibbot: 'Farewell vain
world!' . . .']

fc.51, p. 15; c.481, p. 33; fc.132/1, p. 79; Poetry Box 1/6

What are we come to? Gods! Shall Numps pretend   W0331
Ev'n Curll, to honesty make some pretense!

John Lockman, 'To a scribbler (a wretched
playwright,) who threatened to damn the
entertainments of Vauxhall Gardens, if a sum of
money were not given him . . . May 1735'

c.267/1, p. 260; c.268 (first part), p. 143 (var.)

What, are you not asham'd t'avow   W0332
A sempiternal rest.

Sir Thomas Urquhart, 'To one who was making very
heavy regrets for his wife's miscarriage'

fb.217, p. 88

What art thou death a silent empty shade   W0333
The world is trouble but the grave is peace.

'On death'

fc.60, p. 96; c.244, p. 610

What art thou doing, thou immortal part?   W0334
And taste, in thee, their dainties, knowledge,
                                        peace, and love.

'Set your affections on things above, not on things on
the earth for ye are dead and your life is hid &c.'
[March 1714]

fc.54, p. 60

What art thou? From what causes dost thou spring,   W0335
But either thou art heaven, or heav'n is thee.

'On divine music, taken from Cosgrove's news, and
then said to be done by a young gentleman of
Norwich'

c.244, p. 108

What art thou, memory of former days   W0336
This endless day whose sun shall never set.

'Ode'

c.140, p. 218

What art thou spleen that ev'rything dost ape?   W0337
And sunk beneath thy chain to a lamented grave.

[Anne Finch], countess of Winchilsea, 'A poem on the
spleen' [pr. 1709 (Foxon F141)]
[Crum w377]

c.229/1, fol. 58; Poetry Box x/54, p. 5; File 19023

W0338 What art thou Time? What shape or dress
I'll not complain of thy delay.

   'Absent from Eustathea. To Time' [from 'The amours
   of Alatheus and Eustathea']

c.379/2, p. 119

W0339 What art thou Wallingford? A baby pile,
As is the theme, her tongue essays to sing!

   Charles Atherton Allnutt, 'Wallingford a poem'

File 192

W0340 What artist's hand, dear Madam, yet was seen
Can ne'er be drawn but by a hand divine.

   'To Doctor Gardiner's lady, complaining of her
   picture drawn by Heins of Norwich 1732'

c.360/1, p. 103; see also 'Justly to copy . . .'.

W0341 What arts are tried, what various facts are shown
Our growing genius warm, and fan the kindling
                                  flame.

   'Prologue, spoke at the new little theater over against
   the Opera House in the Haymarket, near Charing
   Cross, on Thursday the 20th of February 1723/4'

c.360/2, no. 124

W0342 What asks the poet at Apollo's shrine,
Gild the bright ev'ning of my lengthen'd days.

   [William Mills], 'Odes of Horace translated. Book I.
   Ode XXXI. To Apollo'

c.472, p. 30

W0343 What awful silence! How these antique towers
That leaves an atom of it undefac'd!

   Horace Walpole, [4th earl of Orford], 'The
   mysterious mother a tragedy'

c.72, p. 1

W0344 What bard O Time discover,
Could picture thee with wings.

   [Richard Brinsley Butler Sheridan, song from The
   duenna]

Poetry Box XII/48

W0345 What base and unjust accusations we find,
To myself I subscribe your most dutiful son.

   [Christopher Anstey], 'A modern head-dress, with a
   little polite conversation, an epistle'

c.83/1, no. 151

W0346 What beauteous scenes enchant my sight
Their wonted tribute bring.

   'A song'

c.358, p. 152

W0347 What beauties does Flora disclose,
To steal an ambrosial kiss.

   'Charming Moggy'

Accession 97.7.40; c.358, p. 115; see also 'What
beauty . . .'.

W0348 What beauties with a grace may do;
What 'tis by all these what's I mean.

   'Enigma by a lady at Oxford' [answered by 'What
   every man of sense . . .']

c.157, p. 65 (incomplete?); c.150, p. 45; c.389; Diggle
Box: Poetry Box XI/33 ('beauty'), 71; Spence Papers,
folder 113 ('beauty')

W0349 What beauty does Flora disclose
I'd seal its ambrosial kiss.

   'Charming Molly'
   [Crum w381]

fc.61, p. 67 (incomplete); see also 'What beauties . . .'.

W0350 What better thing, in my heart can I bear?
Than this sound-soul word: *Deo gratias*.

   Sir John Strangways, '4to Januariii 1646'

b.304, p. 82

W0351 What better thought than think on God,
That ready are to starve.

   'Roman hand'

b.234, p. 31

W0352 What? Blanche which white denotes, now turn'd to
                                brown
Sh'has married him, and his complexion too.

   [Sir Philip Wodehouse], 'Upon Blanche Osbourn:
   Blanch? So brown?'

b.131, back (no. 37)

W0353 What blessings attend my dear Mother all those,
For I ne'er eat a better in all my born days.

   [Christopher Anstey], 'Description of a public
   breakfast at Bath in a letter from Mr. B—— to his
   mother'

c.83/2, no. 295

W0354 What bloody hand, what barbarous tiger's heart
May for thy sorrow mourn, be healed by thee.

   H[enry] C[olman], 'On Christ's wounded side and the
   soldier'
   [Crum w387]

b.2, p. 84

W0355 What bold magician dares presume
That time shall wait till you are gone.

   [ ] Balfour, 'Placed within the glass of a clock at a
   dance'

File 245/19

W0356 What boots it that my potent master sways
Of all her boasted treasure reaches Spain.

[James Mulcaster, sr.], 'Soliloquy: supposed to be
spoken by Gondomer, the Spanish ambassador in King
James the 1st's time, on the success of Sir Walter
Raleigh in the West Indies'

c.118, p. 27

W0357 What boots the favor of the greatest pow'r
All that the world can give, all that it has.

[Edmund Wodehouse], 'Decr. 16 [1714]'

b.131, p. 115

W0358 What born so late, and dead so soon 'tis true
The grave that next is open'd may be thine.

'On a young infant'

b.356, p. 265

W0359 What bounds, O Lord of all, confine thy sway?
Hail him of gods the God, the King of kings.

Thomas Cook, 'Psalm 97'

c.244, p. 577

W0360 What bow'ry dell, with fragrant breath,
Together o'er the mountains roam.

[Ann (Ward)] Radcliffe, 'The butterfly to his love'

c.83/3, no. 876

W0361 What brilliant gleam of golden light is yon
The heavens close, the imag'd visions from my
sight retire.

'The following lines are inscribed to the sacred
memory of that unfortunate and ever to be lamented
Princess Marie-Antoinette late Queen of France, the
recital of whose misfortunes must draw a sigh from
every heart capable of pity' [signed Edwin]

c.343, p. 29

W0362 What bringeth rust to iron smooth
By idleness be lost at length.

[Sir Nicholas] Bacon, 'Against idleness'

fa.8, fol. 162

W0363 What Briton can survey that heavenly face,
Each other, and restore Britannia's bliss.

'By a lady looking on the Chevalier's [the Old
Pretender's] picture'
[Crum w393 (var.)]

fc.58, p. 6; Poetry Box v/121 (incomplete); Poetry Box
x/39 (incomplete)

W0364 What busy, buzzing, dirty thing
Which idly barks, but ne'er can bite.

[William Hayley], 'The scoffer scoffed'

File 6922

W0365 What Caesar could not do, nor all his race,
O'er the whole isle diffus'd his father's reign.

'On his royal highness Duke William (otherwise)
William Duke of Cumberland, second son of His
Majesty King George the 2d, having defeated the
rebel army . . . 1746'

c.360/2, no. 180

W0366 What can be the mystery why Charing Cross
To behold every day such a court, such a son.

[Andrew Marvell], 'Upon the statue of brass of King
Charles the first . . . at Charing Cross' [1675]
[Crum w396; POAS I.270]

fb.106(18)

W0367 What can escape that form which all admire
And hold his freedom for another hour.

fb.68, p. 130

W0368 What can proud fortune give beyond content,
Just please the vain, and mock the miser's art.

'Sonnet . . . Yenda'

c.83/3, no. 784

W0369 What Cato advises
'Tis sunshine and summer with us the year round.

'Song 129'

c.555, p. 184

W0370 What certain judgment can the vulgar make
Above the present eye.

'[Elegy on] a remarkable inscription in Lavenstock
church Hants. Katherine the wife of Sr. Hugh
Stukeley . . . buried Nov. 7th 1679'

c.373, p. 65

W0371 What chance has brought thee into verse
So may they live full many a year.

'The female nine' [1690; wives or mistresses of
Carmaerthon, Devonshire, Dorset, Pembroke,
Nottingham, Monmouth, Marlborough, Lowther, and
Russell; answered by 'When Monmouth the
chaste . . .']
[Crum w408; POAS V.203]

b.111, p. 551

W0372 What cheerful sounds salute our ears,
But harvest crowns his toil.

'The triumph of Ceres or harvest home to the tune of
What beauteous scenes'

fc.85, fol. 117

W0373 What Chesterfield commend me? no, no, no
This answer I would send to you.

[N. Herbert]

Spence Papers, folder 91

W0374 What clamor's here about a dame
The duchess and the Hussey.

[Sir Charles Hanbury Williams], 'Ode addressed to
the author of The conquered duchess, in answer to
that celebrated performance' [pr. 1746 (Foxon
W486)]

c.241, p. 49

W0375 What clouds oppose the prospect of the mind?
For them's a gallows, me a cross design'd.

[David] Stokes

c.233, p. 41

W0376 What concerns your lovely daughter, Sir,
For Venus gives her graces with her humor.

Sir Thomas Urquhart, 'An excuse for a young girl's
lascivious humor, to her father'

fb.217, p. 214

W0377 What could luxurious woman wish for more
Secure your hearts; then—fool with what you will.

[Lady Mary Wortley Montagu], 'An epilogue to a new
play of Mary Queen of Scots, by the same'

fc.51, p. 64

W0378 What could our gracious king do more
Thus to lose what virtue gain'd.

'To the Duke of Argyll on his disgrace—May—1740'

c.360/1, p. 43; Spence Papers, folder 113

W0379 What cruel pains Corinna takes,
Her vassal should undo her.

[John Wilmot, 2nd earl of Rochester, 'Woman's
frailty. A] song'
[Crum w424]

b.105, p. 140; b.334, p. 185

W0380 What curst enticement has bewitch'd man's mind
And ne'er repents, till all his halcyon days are gone.

J[ohn] R[obinson], 'O superbiam inauditam in
facinore gloriari'

c.370, fol. 35

W0381 What Darby and Joan are most apt to differ in
                                        constitutes my first,
Up pops the pale head of my third and astonishes
                                        you quite.

[Sir Henry William Bunbury], 'Charade—4'

File 17066

W0382 What Dares made a knight! No don't be frighted,
He only lost his way, and was benighted.

'Ditto [on knighthood]'

c.81/1, no. 167

What day is this? What Belgic Boreas cloud   W0383
Tribute of praise on the usurper's day.

'On the fifth of November'

b.III, p. 420

What death commands no man can well withstand   W0384
And sought the seat of good where God is well.

Samuel Smithe, 'In obitu . . . dominae Okenor
carmina . . .' [20 March 1626]

Poetry Box VI/49

What decent time shall stay our tears   W0385
Resumes her long-deserted throne.

[ ] Lewis, 'A consolatory elegy . . . addressed to a
gentleman who had lately lost his father'

c.244, p. 456

What different effects does the laurel produce,   W0386
Let him drink of the juice, for profaning the bough.

'On [Colley] Cibber'
[Crum w428]

c.83/1, no. 83

What different follies govern human fate   W0387
Here vulgar fools prevail, here apes of state.

'[preface to] The court monkeys'

c.570/4, p. 17

What dismal sound is this that strikes my ear,   W0388
For angels only visit and away.

'On the death of Mrs Evera[r]d'

fb.142, p. 35

What distant sorrows o'er the stormy main   W0389
And strike with trembling hand the sounding shell.

[Anna] Seward

File 13378 (incomplete?)

What do I fright you? 'tis no wonder,   W0390
But always, always meet with me.

'Addressed to a gentleman'

c.389

What do scholars and bards and philosophers wise   W0391
For Richmond that night had lent her her face.

[Philip Dormer Stanhope], 4th earl of Chesterfield,
'On the Duchess of Richmond's supping with
Mr. Pulteney' [answered by 'His little heart . . .']
[Crum w435, 'poets and bards']

c.233, p. 81; c.53, fol. 53; c.188, p. 91

W0392 What do your thoughts begin in love to stray
Me, for to style, a lady for his mind.

> Lady Jane Cavendish, 'An answer to the verses
> Mr. Carey [Sir Thomas Carew] made to the Lady
> Carlisle'
> [Crum w436]
>
> b.233, p. 16

W0393 What does for death the best prepare,
And will at death, bring still more near.

> [Edmund Wodehouse], 'Septr 4 [1715] the old man's
> memento to coevals'
>
> b.131, p. 258

W0394 What does the poet's modest wish require?
And scorns whatever fate can give beside.

> [John Oldham], 'Paraphrase upon Horace book j. ode
> xxxj. Quid dedicatum poscit Apollinem vates? &c.'
>
> b.209, p. 45

W0395 What doleful cries are these that fright my sense,
Sad as his fate, and like his pictures, dumb.

> [Aphra] Behn, 'On the death of that most excellent
> painter, Mr. Greenhill'
>
> b.105, p. 221

W0396 What doleful sound approach my boding ear
His honor, worth, and loyalty proclaim.

> [Mrs. Christian Kerr], 'Elegy on the death and
> memory of the honored, pious, loyal, charitable,
> judicious, learned, and worthy gentleman Doctor
> Rutherford senior physician who departed this life,
> universally lamented at Eder the 8 of June 1730'
>
> c.102, p. 136

W0397 What doleful tidings 'cross th'Atlantic fly!
Completely holy, and completely blest!

> [Thomas Stevens?], 'An elegy on the late eminent and
> reverend George Whitefield . . . who . . . departed this
> life on the Lord's day, September 30, 1770 in the 56th
> year of his age'
>
> c.259, p. 72

W0398 What dost thou mean, death, thus to raise our fears
He took his living from him, you his life.

> S. T., 'Upon the death of . . . William Taylor' [d.
> 7 September 1641]
>
> b.88, p. 7

W0399 What duty bids we will resign
May now inspire delight.

> T[homas] S[tevens], 'Matthew the 6.1.2.3.4
> [21 January 1781]'
>
> c.259, p. 120

W0400 What energy, what strength of mind
He wrote—an elegy on shoes.

> 'Soliloquy. Poets are born, orators are taught'
> Poetry Box x/63

W0401 What equal honors shall we bring
And ev'ry creature say amen!

> [Isaac Watts, Hymns and spiritual songs (1707), bk. I,
> Hymn 63]
>
> c.180, p. 25

W0402 What every man of sense would do
By saying, doing—anything.

> 'Answer [to 'What beauties with a grace may do . . .']
> Gazetteer Apr 28 1759'
>
> c.157, p. 66

W0403 What eye hath seen, what ear hath heard,
Shall waft thee safe to realms above.

> Charles Atherton Allnutt, 'On the majesty of God . . .
> published in Theological miscellany for July 1788'
>
> c.112, p. 4

W0404 What! Fast and pray—
For unrepented sins, are ne'er forgiven.

> 'On the 30 of Janry' [1696; found on the church door
> at Whitehall]
> [Crum w449]
>
> c.570/1, p. 52

W0405 What fatal changes still increase
In Newgate put the nation.

> 'Worse, and worse'
> [Crum w450]
>
> c.570/1, p. 132

W0406 What folded up? The wretches then begin
Renounce them, and your sins, then as you were.

> 'Upon the pictures of Will. and Moll. being an
> imitation of a single sheet, hanging upon a deal
> wainscot the corners carelessly folding up'
>
> b.111, p. 410

W0407 What fool were you, to take a fair young wife,
To know that *cornu*'s indeclinable.

> Sir Thomas Urquhart, 'To the master of a grammar
> school, who though he was something old, did marry a
> young, and well-complexioned handsome lass'
>
> fb.217, p. 104

W0408 What form's illusive mocking sight
An angel smile illumin'd all her charms!

> R[ichard] V[ernon] S[adleir], 'The hermit's elegy'
>
> c.106, p. 62

W0409   What fortunes can there be in hell,
Who would not have the sickness for the cure!

     [William] Walsh, 'Cure of jealousy'

     c.351, p. 85

W0410   What from the bounty of the waves is due
Who gave one Venus, and have taken two?

     [Robert Cholmeley], 'An epigram upon two young
ladies drowned in the sea'

     c.190, p. 35

W0411   What from you love of me, you did impair,
Join thrice more now to that abstracted share.

     Sir Thomas Urquhart, 'In the second line of this
distich, are all the four species, of arithmetic. One to
his mistress'

     fb.217, p. 232

W0412   What fruit do I to myself propose
Their hearts, their souls to Thee, as th' ought.

     [Edmund Wodehouse], 'June 21 [1715]'

     b.131, p. 225

W0413   What fruit have grown upon the crop
Until you reach your home.

     T[homas] S[tevens], 'To Miss E. G. D. by . . . Sung at
the Exp: meet[in]g 17th Augt. [17]79'

     c.259, p. 4

W0414   What fury did these sudden broils engage,
And dangers of the angry waves increase.

     'Tryphena's speech for peace on board the ship of
Lycas'

     c.158, p. 142

W0415   What fury does disturb my rest?
To hate her makes me love her more.

     [William Walsh], 'Upon the same occasion [to a false
mistress]'

     c.223, p. 64

W0416   What Gallia's fleets could never do
Submits to your bright eyes.

     'On Sir W bowing to Miss Buncomb at Bath, 1736'

     c.360/1, p. 23

W0417   What genius can describe fair Anna's mind?
Her virtue nor her beauty stain'd with pride.

     'Anna's character'

     c.244, p. 623

W0418   What God is pleas'd to teach, man must believe,
And which is promis'd ev'n to this intent.

     [Edmund Wodehouse], 'Feb. 21 [1715]'

     b.131, p. 170

What God thinks proper to conceal,   W0419
To search where he's forbid to pry.

     Edward Sneyd, 'Romans the 11th: chapter and part of
the 33d verse . . .'

     c.214, p. 66

What god, what genius did the pencil move   W0420
And strong as Hercules.

     [Alexander Pope], 'To Sir Godfrey Kneller on his
painting for Mr. Pope, the statues of Apollo, Venus,
and Hercules'

     c.176, p. 70

What graceless wretch betrayed his gracious Lord?   W0421
His precious side; and for my sins he died.

     H[enry] C[olman], 'On Christ's passion'
[Crum w472]

     b.2, p. 12

What—gracious!—did you say you'd die?—oh dear!   W0422
Come, at her feet receive thy pardon here.

     'The conflict of passions'

   Poetry Box III/37

What great offence is this your squire hath made,   W0423
That he's s'abash'd, he dare not lift his head.

     Sir Thomas Urquhart, 'A bride the first night of her
marriage speaks thus to her husband, who was an old
man'

     fb.217, p. 87

What greater proofs can Romans give?   W0424
And humbly sue for peace.

     [William Popple, trans.], '[Horace] book 4. ode 14th.
To Augustus'

   fc.104/2, p. 376

What grievous weight soever be allowed   W0425
Though fortune force their bodies to succumb.

     [Sir Thomas Urquhart], 'How generous a thing it is in
adversity patiently to endure what cannot be [?]ed'

   fb.217, p. 523

What guards the city from the foe   W0426
The fairest fair one's name afford.

     'A rebus, on Miss Wallace'

   c.360/1, p. 89

What hand Florella or what art   W0427
Has paradise restored.

     'The fair architect or the artificial grove'

   c.186, p. 96

W0428 What hand, what skill can form the artful piece
And sell their country in a closer way.

> 'Advice to a painter [1698]'
> [*POAS* VI.15]
>
> b.204, p. 12; b.371, no. 40; Poetry Box VI/6 (ll. 1-101);
> Trumbull Box: Poetry Box XIII/58; fb.70, p. 177

W0429 What happiness the rural maid attends,
And health, not paint, the fading bloom repairs.

> 'Content alone is true happiness or the country lass'
>
> c.186, p. 95

W0430 What happy plant is this so lately sprung
Fill'd with succession of no other race.

> Tho[mas] May, 'Upon the birth of the prince May the
> 29. 1640 [*i.e.*, 1630?]'
>
> b.356, p. 204

W0431 What harm in so simple a token of love!
That granting a whisper is granting too much.

> [Thomas Hull], 'Wrote for Mrs. Pinto and sung by
> her at Navy Hall 1768'
>
> c.528/20

W0432 What has this bugbear Death that's worth our care,
'Tis nothing, Celia, but the losing thee.

> [William Walsh], 'Sonnet. Death'
>
> c.223, p. 61; c.351, p. 86

W0433 What has this life to make it worth our care?
And court the fancied tyrant for relief.

> 'The advice'
>
> b.218, p. 31

W0434 What has this world to fill my vast desires?
That ceaseless pants for God, its only rest.

> '[Soliloquies] (4)'
>
> c.153, p. 155

W0435 What hast thou done, grim death?
They only visit, vanish and away.

> 'An epitaph . . . of Mrs. Clough and her fair daughter
> Mrs. Susan . . . Feb. the 17. 1710/11'
>
> fb.142, p. 59

W0436 What hast thou done, thrice lovely maid?
Securely through thy windings wade.

> [ ] Williams, 'The journey of a female pilgrim from
> the isle of Anglesea of St. David's in Pembrokeshire'
>
> c.83/2, no. 520

W0437 What hath the world to equal this?
Bodies of eternal frame.

> 'Hymn 1st'
>
> c.562, p. 1

W0438 What have I learnt by my philosophy
He neither God, nor man, does rightly love.

> [Sir Philip Wodehouse], 'Sen—Quid pro philosophia
> meam didici . . .'
>
> b.131, p. 11

W0439 What have I seen? Whither is it gone;
There's still some joy laid up in fate for me.

> 'The wife of Pompey awakened out of her sleep, in
> which she dreamed she saw her husband's vision, who
> told her concerning her fortune fate'
>
> c.189, p. 25

W0440 What have the nine their Pegasaean tones
Let grief now cease, forevermore rejoice.

> W[illia]m Allen, 'On the unparalleled, and most
> execrable plot of the bloody-minded papists on the 5th
> of November'
>
> b.212, p. 15

W0441 What have we been, and what we are,
Which we have not conceiv'd or seen.

> 'The above ['Quod suit esse, quod est . . .']
> paraphrased in English'
>
> c.360/3, no. 136

W0442 What heart the tender sympathy can sway
T'alleviate every fellow mortal's woe.

> M[ary (Shackleton)] L[eadbeater], 'An elegy written
> at Purleigh . . . March 4th [17]88'
>
> c.303

W0443 What heat of learning kindled your desire
Had not there been by chance | As *in presenti*.

> [T. R.?], 'On the burning of a grammar school in
> Yorkshire' [Bridley? or Barkley?]
> [Crum w487]
>
> b.205, fol. 51v; b.62, p. 60; fb.142, p. 26

W0444 What hopes, what terrors does thy gift create,
Adorn Philander's head, or grace his tomb.

> S[amuel] Johnson, 'Lines at the request of a
> gentleman to whom a lady had given a sprig of myrtle'
>
> c.83/3, no. 781

W0445 What house is that much like unto a steeple
They feast their landlord, and so pay their rent.

> 'Riddle [hive of bees]'
>
> Poetry Box VII/47

W0446 What I am going to beneath,
In perfect charity with all mankind.

> 'The will of Nath. Lloyd esq.; Twickenham'
>
> fc.85, fol. 111v

W0447 What I believe to be the right
That they shall rule me, not my will.

    Sir John Strangways, '11 Septr 1646'

b.304, p. 56

W0448 What I shall leave thee none can tell,
As innocent as now thou art.

    [Richard] Corbett, 'To his son Vincent Corbett two
    years of age'

c.82, p. 29; c.83/3, no. 1036; b.150, p. 206

W0449 What I would bring
In a sad winter's night.

    [George Daniel]

b.121, fol. 44v

W0450 What I, a single man design,
Nor let a frown disgrace your brow.

    [William Popple, trans.], '[Horace] book 3rd. ode 8th.
    To Maecenas'

fc.104/2, p. 236

W0451 What ice becomes by heat of sun
Is given to soldiers by beat of drum.

    [Enigma/Charade/Conundrum 79b]

c.389

W0452 What if a day, or a month, or a year,
Both in mirth and mourning.

    [Thomas Campion], 'Sonnetto'
    [Crum w500]

Poetry Box VII/31, p. 4

W0453 What if a few by reading not refin'd
And walks sublime the first of virtue's train.

    'A theme from Lord Bacon's essays'

fc.53, p. 180

W0454 What if some wild capricious painter trace
New cast the lines uncouthly form'd before.

    'Horace's Art of poetry—last translation' [watermark
    1799]

fc.9, p. 1

W0455 What, if the stateliest buildings were thy own?
All happiness within, in this all glory lies.

    'Verses wrote on the gates of Bologna in Italy'

c.83/1, no. 269

W0456 What ill soever is upon thee brought
As fathers do their sons they best respect.

    Sir John Strangways, 'Comfort for an afflicted soul . . .
    20 July 1646'

b.304, p. 53

What innocence is said to wear
Speak her who of my heart is queen.

    'A rebus on Miss White'

c.360/1, p. 87

W0457

What irony has of late possess'd the brain!
The place shall live in song, and Claremont be the
                        name.

    Sir Samuel Garth, 'Claremont'

c.351, p. 63

W0458

What is a woman? Nature's oversight:
Cuckolds are of women's making.

    'On a woman, and a cuckold'

b.200, p. 411; b.62, p. 60

W0459

What is it brother Bucks, I pray,
Come, comrades, quickly push around | The bottle.

    'The bottle'

c.81/2, no. 527

W0460

What? is man confin'd
And what they want nightly, we give them by days.

    'The gallant'

fb.107, p. 32

W0461

What is man's form, but a bad mind, vain Will?
Th'efficient, and end, there reflect.

    'Four causes of man' [translation of John Owen]

c.356

W0462

What is our life? a play of passion:
Where we shall die in earnest, not in jest.

    [Sir Walter Raleigh], 'On man's life'
    [Crum w527]

b.200, p. 112; b.205, fol. 44r; b.208, p. 59; b.62, p. 46;
fb.69, p. 204

W0463

What is sure thus fleet thus transitory
Seems truly constant but inconstancy.

    'Nihil certum'

b.205, fol. 15v

W0464

What is termed Popery? To depose a king.
'Tis a French subject or—God save the King.

    'Interrogatories, or a dialogue between Whig and
    Tory'

b.111, p. 68

W0465

What is the blooming tincture of the skin
But these, these only, can that heart retain.

    'On the superiority of the beauties of the mind to
    those of the body'

c.487, p. 122

W0466

W0467 What is the cause, makes the bridegroom
B'a passive valor.

> Sir Thomas Urquhart, 'The parley of a certain
> gentleman's servants, who were present at the off-
> taking of his clothes, the first night of his
> marriage'

fb.217, p. 213

W0468 What is the cause the greedy man
But through desire mind discontent.

> [Sir Nicholas] Bacon, 'Against covetousness'

fa.8, fol. 164

W0469 What is the existence of man's life
And leaves no epilogue but death.

> [Henry] King, 'From Dr. King's very rare volume of
> poems, 1657'
> [Crum w538]

b.150, p. 275

W0470 What is the shining tincture of a skin
Yet, the other only can that heart maintain.

> 'For the ladies'

File 17485

W0471 What is the world a great exchange of ware,
Kill where they laugh and murder where they smile.

> [Francis Quarles, 'Fraus mundi', from Pentelogia,
> 1626]
> [Crum w546]

c.158, p. 34

W0472 What is the world where saints reside
In the bright worlds to which we go.

> T[homas] S[tevens], 'What is heaven'

c.259, p. 96

W0473 What? is the young Apollo grown of late
Ferry his soul to the Elysian shores.

> 'Epigramma' [on Dr. Whaly]

b.197, p. 157

W0474 What! Is there new a muse drinks stale?
One unmolested quart of sour small beer.

> 'In madidam (?) memoriam Jo[hn] Barrington e[s]q:
> [d. 24 June 1713]

c.416

W0475 What is this life that mortals idly crave?
And reach a height that ne'er was reach'd before.

> 'Picture of life . . . Newcastle upon Tyne, January 23d
> 1683'

c.93

What is this strange distemper of my mind?   W0476
That certain peace, which thou alone canst give.

> E. M., 'The spleen, or vapors'

Poetry Box IV/103

What is this world, Avarus cried,   W0477
Sprang upward to the realms of light.

> 'The discontented man and the angel'

c.83/2, no. 653

What is to come the prophet signifies   W0478
And poets oft of what is pass'd, tell lies.

> Sir Thomas Urquhart, 'Of poets, and prophets'

fb.217, p. 42

What is well done's ill done, if it be patent,   W0479
What's ill done, is well done, if it be latent.

> Sir Thomas Urquhart, 'A discrepance in opinion 'twixt
> theologs, and politicians'

fb.217, p. 117

What is't presumptious poets will not dare   W0480
As beggars brag of wealthy ancestors.

> 'Ut pictura poesis' [prologue to 'O Kneller . . .']

Poetry Box VI/46

What is't to love! 'Tis still to bear   W0481
Some flying spark should kindle love in you.

> 'To a lady who asked what love was'

c.360/3, no. 242

What is't to us who guides the state—   W0482
This moment and this glass is ours.

> John Howe, 'Horace. B: 2. Ode XI. Imitated'
> [Crum w556]

c.94

What joy! th'exulting tribes to hear!   W0483
Himself vouchsafes to dwell.

> 'Psalm 122'

c.264/3, p. 69

What joy, while thus I view the day,   W0484
And faith and hope farewell!

> [Theodor Zwinger], 'A parody on Psalm 122.
> Composed by . . . (of whom see an account in
> Thuanus) on his death-bed'

Poetry Box IV/21

What joys I feel what charms I see   W0485
Happy happy happy we.

> [John Gay, Alexander Pope, and/or John Hughes],
> 'Happy we 2nd chorus in [Handel's] Acis and Galatea'
> [with musical score for tenor and bass]

Music MS. 534

W0486   What labor's next, now Vide's taught to shine
And David's sacred warmth thy hallow'd notes
                                     inspire.

    [Joseph Spence], 'On Pitt's image'
Spence Papers, folder 157

W0487   What ladies love in a morning, what's good to
                 make punch with, and the spouse of a cow,
Is the name of a very fine lady, I vow.

    [Sir William Trumbull, riddle on Trumbull]
Trumbull Box: Poetry Box XIII/44

W0488   What lady but must praise this gallant dame
Sanction'd by virtue and enrich'd by love.

    [William Smith, epilogue to The dame of Ephesus,
    translated from Petronius]
Smith Papers, folder 59

W0489   What legions of fables, and whimsical tales,
So now we believe—in troth nothing at all.

    'On infidelity an epigram'
c.578, p. 1

W0490   What less than wit could be expected
Applause and love from every age!

    George Birch, 'From . . . on receiving a letter from
    Mr. [Richard Owen] Cambridge Jan 1782 . . .'
Poetry Box v/34

W0491   What! liberty of conscience, that's a change
Jure divino whip and spur again.

    'Dr Wild's ghost on liberty of conscience'
    [cf. Crum H1443, 'How liberty . . .']
fb.108, p. 91

W0492   What lies at the door to keep the house clean
Is what I've long wish'd for and so have you too.

    'Another [riddle]'
Poetry Box x/60

W0493   What lives are so happy as those of the fair
Such, such is the life of a belle.

    'The life of a belle'
Trumbull Box: Poetry Box XIII/51; see also 'How brimful
of nothing . . .'.

W0494   What lofty sound through echoing Albion rings!
A recompensing God will give the rest!

    'The triumph of benevolence'
File 17440

W0495   What love, what honor, thanks and praise,
To sing, and spread thy glorious fame.

    'On God's goodness and man's ingratitude'
c.83/3, no. 962

What luck had Peter, when he took a fish   W0496
There is not fishing to the sea—of Rome.

    [Francis Quarles], 'On Peter and the Pope' [Divine
    fancies IV, 11]
b.137, p. 174

What madmen are we of the versing trade?   W0497
For wit, beyond his argument.

    [George Daniel]
b.121, fol. 41v

What magic warblings to my ear   W0498
Nor will I quit thee at the grave.

    'Hope to the Duchess of Devonshire ode . . . May
    1781'
c.340

What magical charms   W0499
To Durham was just so.

    'The bishops defeated. A burlesque poem'
c.530, p. 237

What magistrates are these, that, spite of law   W0500
To swing themselves, since death's so easy made.

    'Upon the frequent executions in straw-effigy, at
    Aix-en-Provence'
Poetry Box x/21

What makes fond man the trifle life desire,   W0501
Open their eyes in everlasting day.

    Lady [Mary] C[hudleigh], 'On the vanities of this life.
    A Pindaric ode'
c.258

What makes so many women be unchaste?   W0502
It doth discover women's nakedness.

    Sir Thomas Urquhart, 'Of forbidden fruit a dialogue'
fb.217, p. 270

What makes the midst our feasts, and sports so   W0503
                                   swollen
Be merry blockhead: or the fiends confound thee.

    Sir Thomas Urquhart, 'To a certain bigot puritan
    hypocritically grave, that while others were most
    solatious, he was insupportably melancholious'
fb.217, p. 153

What makes thy face so fair and bright   W0504
A blooming contradiction.

c.150, p. 115

What makes your wife so pale and thin   W0505
And given her some Ferija's[?] balsam.

    'Question to R .P. Milton / R. P. W.'s [i.e.M.'s?]
    answer'
Poetry Box x/24

W0506   What man, almighty Lord! Wouldst thou
And glories has to come.

     [Charles Earle], 'Psalm XVth'

c.376

W0507   What man, can think on (without pain)
But you must teach us your receipt.

     [Thomas Hamilton, 6th earl of Haddington], 'The inquisition'

c.458/2, p. 156

W0508   What man in his wits had not rather be poor,
Let not even my enemy die.

     [ ] Lewis, 'The covetous bondsman'

c.244, p. 188

W0509   What man, who sees this glorious azure sky,
Could all these great, and beauteous works produce.

     [Henry] Needler, 'The Creator'

c.244, p. 560

W0510   What marts, in towns, expose,
And Mars, by guns, dispose.

     Sir Thomas Urquhart, 'Ars, Mars, marts'

fb.217, p. 246

W0511   What master is't rejoiceth in the hour,
So long as he's in prison.

     Sir Thomas Urquhart, 'A riddle'

fb.217, p. 172

W0512   What may those tongues deaf'ning who slanders
                                     spread,
Their mouths a mighty magazine of lies?

     John Lockman, 'A query: to a certain accountant . . . June 1758'

c.267/1, p. 99, p. 251

W0513   What mean our tapers to go out so fast
Whilst we below lament our loss in vain.

     R. T., 'An elegy to the memory of the reverend, and worthy Mr. John Sincklar minister of the gospel, who died at Delft March 24/April 3 . . . 1687'

Poetry Box VII/61

W0514   What mean you Sirs, with sharpen'd flints or knives
These being to both the happiest new year's gifts.

     [Edward] Sparke, 'Poem 7th, upon the circumcision of Christ'

b.137, p. 19

W0515   What means all these that sorrow's livery wear
Shall consecrate a never-dying fame.

     'On the death of Dr. Stubbins'

b.197, p. 158

W0516   What means all this sound
To live in content and enjoyment.

     'The medley of combats'

c.530, p. 120

W0517   What means compass? To put together! Well
Where Doric music sober anthems please.

     [Sir Philip Wodehouse], 'Another of the former James Cooper my musician compose air'

b.131, back (no. 198 [bis])

W0518   What means my muse that to prepare her wing
Make both the King and Church on nothing stand.

     'Verses on Lauderdale [16]70' [docket title]

Poetry Box VIII/20 (2 copies)

W0519   What means the funeral bell's tremendous sound
For what we feel, and what you have to fear.

     'Lines sent to Mrs. B[owdler?] on the death of her amiable daughter'

c.83/1, no. 66

W0520   What means the matter, can and old man fill
But something, when he passeth by.

     Sir Thomas Urquhart, 'To a young girl, who was very much taken up with the ceremonies used at the making of the mayor of London'

fb.217, p. 336

W0521   What means the sad silence around?
His own can best picture his praise.

     'To the memory of Mr. J. Cunningham'

c.83/3, no. 896

W0522   What means this house to make such ado,
What Ceasar said, by G— 'tis true.

     'Upon the floor of the H: of Commons . . . 1705/6'

b.90, p. 3

W0523   What means this mixture of disjointed things,
Go, seek some properer subject for thy wit.

     R[obert] Shirley, 1st earl of Ferrers, 'A satire against the clergy. From Boileau'

c.347, p. 50

W0524   What means this multitude, say what's the news
How feigned saints did use their real king.

     [Edward] Sparke, 'Poem 11th, on Palm Sunday'

b.137, p. 26

W0525 What means this quelling quir[e] and how comes
to pass
They'll find they've play'd the fool long ere
December.

'Another [satire against President Stair]'
Poetry Box VIII/32

W0526 What means this sadness? Why doth every eye
And mountains change into the smallest sand.

'In idem' [on the Gunpowder Plot]
b.212, p. 235

W0527 What means this strangeness now of late
The fairest of his game.

[Sir Robert Ayton]
[Crum w606]
b.213, p. 3

W0528 What means this sudden pang! This treacherous
sigh,
And grieve thy life till sorrow is no more.

S[tephen] Simpson, 'An elegy on the foregoing
melancholy subject [the death of R. S. B.] addressed to
T. Eyre'
c.563

W0529 What means this thrilling motion in my breast?
Remove the cause, or let the mourner die!

'Verses'
c.142, p. 393

W0530 What mean'st thou bride this company to keep
Thou leavest in him thy watchful eyes | Thy loving
heart.

'The bride's going to bed'
b.205, fol. 25r

W0531 What med'cine can soften the bosom's keen smart?
And Damon pretended to love.

[Charles Earle?]
c.376

W0532 What Melville said he would not tell
My leaky hogshead could not hold.

c.340

W0533 What more content can we have here below
With thankful soul, to walk thy sacred way.

[Francis Quarles], 'A meditation of God's creating all
things for man and man for himself'
b.137, p. 195

W0534 What more trouble yet? 'twas but an organist
Such foolish verses on a Holiday.

[William Meredith?], 'The answer' [to 'Christ
Church a marriage . . .']
[Crum w615–616, 'more anger']
b.62, p. 3; see also 'More trouble . . .'.

W0535 What mortal of the rhyming throng
And speak out my mind whenever I please.

'To Mrs Bernard' [all but B scratched out; 1767]
Poetry Box x/45, p. 21

W0536 What musing form by Cynthia's light
No more alas! to rise again.

[Helen Craik], 'The Indian maid—a tale—intended
for a companion to The harp'
c.375, p. 123

W0537 What must he do at Rome who can't employ
So all will there my company deny.

J[ohn] R[obinson], 'Quid Romae faciam! Mentiri
nescio'
c.370, fol. 31

W0538 What must I give my king? My state is small
The king must lose his own.

[Sir Philip Wodehouse], 'Edmundus Grei dem nudus
regi'
b.131, back (no. 185)

W0539 What, must our eyes melt too? waters oppress,
The barges now may come the carrier's way.

Dudley Digges, of All Souls, 'On the dissolution of
the great frost, and snow: 1634'
[Crum w620]
b.200, p. 27

W0540 What mystery is this, that I should find
Since, but by you, I have not blood to spill.

[William Strode], 'A gent: to his friend, whom kissing
at his departure, he left some sign of blood upon her'
[Crum w622]
b.200, p. 206; b.205, fol. 71v; b.356, p. 81

W0541 What Nanny o'er? And then give o'er
And 'twas Pitt that stole the prize.

[Robert Cholmeley], 'The kiss to Nanny'
c.190, p. 196

W0542 What need had we [a] care [for] bays
C—t and new clothes.

c.189, p. 117

W0543 What need of marble to preserve a name,
A virtuous daughter, an obedient wife.

'Bunhill burying place to the memory of Mrs.
Patience Briggs who deceased July 16. 1696'

Poetry Box VII/55

W0544 What needs you such
Doth ev'n as much.

Sir Thomas Urquhart, 'To a senator, whose bedfellow
was of a dissolute life'

fb.217, p. 269

W0545 What news abroad my friend today?
'Tis well 'tis neither I, nor U.

'Epigram'

Diggle Box: Poetry Box XI/69

W0546 What news today! O sad! Old woman, weep,
Why B[enson] for int'rest, and Saint P— for fear.

John Henley, 'Orator Henley's epitaph on Bishop
[Martin] Benson' [bp. of Gloucester, d. 30 August
1752]

c.360/3, no. 232

W0547 What news with Dagon; is thy shrine so hot
Not having head to plot, nor hand to fight.

[Francis Quarles], 'On Dagon and the ark' [Divine
fancies II, 8; 'strike' for 'fight']

b.137, p. 168

W0548 What nobler feelings marks th'illumin'd mind,
And dash to earth her tyrants and her chains.

[William Roscoe], 'Ode to the French nation—
imitated from a canzone of Petrarch'

c.139, p. 272

W0549 What Nostradame with all his art can guess
Under a female regency may rise.

John Dryden, 'The prologue to the new opera [by
Thomas Betterton] called The prophetess' [licenced
1683, 'spoken but once and after forbid by the Ld.
Chamberlain' (the earl of Mulgrave, later duke of
Buckingham and Normanby)]
[Crum W633]

b.111, p. 485; fb.70, p. 271; File 4629 (spoken by
Mr. Catterton)

W0550 What now presents? A cradle poor and mean!
Than palaces where eastern kings retire.

'The cradle'

c.515, fol. 2v

W0551 What numbers there are in the world of my name,
The lymph of the fountain, the juice of the vine.

'Enigma 92' [pipe]

c.389

W0552 What odd fantastic things we women do?
And every Lucia find a Cato's son.

[Sir Samuel] Garth, 'Epilogue to Cato'

c.163, p. 3

W0553 What of Phoebus shall the bard
Ease of mind and poetry.

[William Popple, trans.], '[Horace] book 1st. ode 30th
[i.e., 31st]. To Apollo'

fc.104/2, p. 86

W0554 What on earth deserves our trust;
What one moment calls again.

[Katherine Philips], 'The vanity of earthly things'

c.189, p. 23

W0555 What on the steeple's turn'd by wind
Gives name to her who's fair and kind.

'A rebus on the Lady Vane, wife of Lord Vane'

c.360/1, p. 89

W0556 What once the fox to the sick lion said
[torn] to the hole lean as at first he was.

b.53, p. 68

W0557 What only ser[v]'d to wrap up soap or plums
Thus with thyself fall victims to the flame.

'Epistola pastoralis flaminis sacra . . . thus made
English'

b.111, p. 161

W0558 What pains for other[s] the archpoet takes
Which from the feet takes off the power to stand.

[translation of lines from a dialogue between Guerno
and Pope Leo 10th]

c.81/2, no. 534

W0559 What part of man may that part be
Each marriage is made up or crost.

'2 Enigma resolutio Cor hominis'

b.205, fol. 99v

W0560 What passion now inflames my breast,
Service to friends around the Rekin.

'Carolina to Mr. J. M. occasioned by his last epistle'
['Fair mistress of the moving art . . .']

c.83/1, no. 256

W0561 What path is found to those sublime retreats,
For all the bright divinity is love.

'Where shall wisdom be found . . . who shall declare
his generation' [Job 28:12, Isaiah 53:8]

c.167, p. 36

W0562 What path of life by man is trod
Or not to live, or soon to die.

    [ ] Lewis, 'Life for it and against it'

    c.244, p. 190

W0563 What pictures are such poems ought to be,
By mutual turns attach'd, and terms express'd.

    [Maurice Johnson], 'Ut pictura poesis erit . . .'

    c.229/2, fol. 10v

W0564 What pity, (Handel!) that thy rapturous strains,
And wakes thy genius with returning day.

    John Lockman, 'Seeing Mr. Handel, when blind, had
    to play a concerto on the organ . . . March 1753'

    c.267/1, p. 69

W0565 What pity 'tis the heart should so debase
The blooming beauty of so fine a face.

    [ ] M., 'On the beautiful Mrs. B.'

    c.546, p. 7

W0566 What place doth the mill with two sh[?] grind
When you the mill and then the miller find?

    [Sir Thomas Urquhart], 'A riddle . . . this riddle may
    be easily read by those that haunt in the houses of
    Master Miller married to Jane Mill'

    fb.217, p. 388

W0567 What place is this? an universal school
What now thou art, and what thou soon wilt be.

    'At the entrance in the Pensoroso'

    fc.51, p. 93

W0568 What planet ruled at my unhappy birth
Love him that above all things seeks thy love.

    [Mrs. ( ) Feilding], 'Upon my Lady Desmond's
    reproaching of me wrongfully'

    b.226, p. 87

W0569 What pleasure I take
Than one that is faithful should die.

    'The melancholy virgin'

    fb.107, p. 17

W0570 What pleasures can the gaudy world afford?
Because they are unknowing, wild and rude.

    'The contemplation of vanity or decay of virtue'

    Spence Papers, folder 113

W0571 What poignant sorrows did her soul transfix
And bring yourself Tanetta back to life.

    [J. Knight], 'On the death of Tanetta, Miss F.
    Pettiward's favorite dormouse'

    c.150, p. 124

W0572 What poring over musty books
When folly all triumphant reigns.

    'Upon seeing Ld. [John] Percival [Egmont] often in a
    bookseller's shop at Bath'

    Poetry Box IV/131

W0573 What potent god, from Ayra's orient bow'r,
To warm, but not consume, his heart.

    Sir William Jones, 'A hymn'

    c.90

W0574 What praise dear parent, did thy life attend!
Whose youth was godly, and whose age was wise!

    C[harles] E[arle], 'Made on his father'

    c.376; see also 'Dear shade! . . .'.

W0575 What praise! What gratitude is due
Secures a never-dying fame!

    John Lockman, 'Verses, to His Majesty: on humbling
    receiving a mark of royal favor presented by the
    master of the [?] at St. James', 26 August 1767'

    c.267/4, p. 386

W0576 What precious moments we employ
I love thee Astrea dearly. | An' thou wad mine own
                thing . . . I would love thee, dearly.

    [Mrs. Christian Kerr], 'From a gentleman to a lady
    with whom he was innocently familiar to the tune of
    An' thou wad my own thing . . .' [answered by 'Why
    Damon do you thus complain . . .']

    c.102, p. 87

W0577 What print of fairy feet is here
Dissolve at once in air at Truth's resplendent day!

    'Morning on the seashore'

    c.83/3, no. 859

W0578 What progress does liberty make every week!
She has all she can wish—and she asks for no more.

    Richard Owen Cambridge, 'The progress of
    liberty . . . 1790'

    Poetry Box V/34; Poetry Box III/43

W0579 What puny elves are these which fight,
Folly is one, the other madness!

    'On a picture of two fighting Cupids mounted on
    goats'

    c.504, p. 93

W0580 What! Put our fav'rite playhouse down,
And see a play for nothing.

    'On turning the play[house] at Rich[mon]d into a
    Method[ist] mee[tinghouse]'

    fc.85, fol. 22

W0581   What radiant changes strike the astonish'd sight?
What terms of art can nature's powers display?

>[ ] Falconer, 'Beautiful coloring of the dolphin'
>
>c.81/2, no. 576

W0582   What rage provokes me thus to squabble
We'll keep the freedom nature gave us.

>'A reply to the former [the last three lines of Crum T2165, beginning 'In short a virtuous wife's a good estate'] by the author of the broadside against marriage'
>[Crum w655]
>
>b.54, p. 892

W0583   What railing still Deprecia? Fie! For shame!
For those who censure all are credited by—none!

>[Charles Earle?], 'An epigram'
>
>c.376

W0584   What raptures is the valiant warrior in,
Shield him some God, and let no shaft come near.

>'On His Majesty's King William's victory'
>
>fb.142, p. 28

W0585   What real grief, what pain of heart,
Eudocia is not here.

>'To Eudocia, absent on a tour into France written . . . Nov 19 1777 at Coventry, on my way to Birmingham'
>
>c.136, p. 119

W0586   What reason have I to complain
Should near [i.e., ne'er?] be stop't, a double death.

>'Dr. Bentley's verses on the death of the Duke of Gloucester . . . imitated in English, thus'
>
>c.111, p. 7

W0587   What rends the temple's veil? Where is day gone?
Nature must needs be sick, when God must die.

>[Thomas Randolph], 'On the passion'
>[Crum w656]
>
>c.81/1, no. 409

W0588   What rugged rock its lucid store retains?
Grief drank the offering ere it reach'd the eye.

>'Lines by ——— of whom it has been remarked that he had viewed the remains of a much loved and deeply lamented wife without shedding a tear'
>
>c.142, p. 430

W0589   What sacred hand now sways the regal rod,
The peaceful olive and the glorious bay.

>'On the coronation of King George the 2nd'
>
>b.197, p. 248

W0590   What sacred light is this, what glorious guest
And it embalms, as it away doth waste.

>[Robert Codrington], 'Funeral tears and consolations' [on Lady Winifred Fitzwilliam]
>
>b.87, p. 5

W0591   What sad? and to the muses dear!
That Lamia may survive in you.

>[Robert Cholmeley], 'Aliter'
>
>c.190, p. 183

W0592   What sad effects arise from fear
Jack was awhile a standing jest.

>'Epistle VIII. To W. Alexander Littlejohn on fear'
>
>fc.100, p. 34

W0593   What sage—but you dear Doctor can
Shall greater than Apollo's be.

>[Charles] Earle, 'From . . . to Dr. Aiton'
>
>c.376

W0594   What said he not one day
But see the maniac die.

>[John Black]
>
>fc.107, p. 80

W0595   What sailor is anxious great treasures to hoard?
Or I go to the bottom and so there's an end.

>'Song 30'
>
>c.555, p. 47

W0596   What say you? Stanhope praises sends,
Who prais'd of such a one the song | When he
                    would own it.

>[N.] Herbert, 'Sapphics'
>
>Spence Papers, folder 91

W0597   What says the prophet? Let the day be blest
Their answer to the call is—not at home.

>'On the Sabbath'
>
>c.83/3, no. 1063

W0598   What self-sufficiency and a false content
And only lives to know, he never can be blest.

>'The indolent' [Dodsley Collection]
>
>c.487, p. 127

W0599   What! shall a glorious nation be o'erthrown
And suck up all the fatness of the land.

>'The hypocritical Whig displayed'
>[Crum w666]
>
>b.111, p. 479

W0600 What shall a man desire in this world
She shall cease to be fair, and I will live to be true.

   Poetry Box VII/31, p. 1

W0601 What shall a tyrant thus usurp our crown
In triumph let him reign, and die in peace.

   'On the usurper' [George I]
   [Crum w667, 'thus possess our throne']

   c.570/1, p. 69

W0602 What shall be shall be, Bedford suits not thee
And once again endear a Russell's name.

   'On the motto of the Duke of Bedford. Che sera
   sera . . . January 4th 1796'

   c.115

W0603 What shall become of man so wise
Of what the knaves invent.

   'Of man'

   fb.207/4, p. 37

W0604 What shall I do? Or what shall I say,
Till the king enjoys his own again.

   'A song to the tune of The King shall enjoy his own
   again'

   b.111, p. 45

W0605 What shall I do to show how well I love her
Never had hero so glorious a death.

   [Thomas Betterton], 'For Mr. Sean Fleming esqr. at
   Rydell Hall near Ambleside' [song from The
   prophetess]
   [Crum w673]

   Poetry Box VI/82

W0606 What shall I do, ye gods! I cannot bear
Nor till by her condemn'd will I despair.

   c.416

W0607 What shall I for a lady wish
Whither her prayers incessant rise.

   John Lockman, 'To Mrs. Knight of Salisbury, after
   receiving the usual present from her . . . Christmas
   1760'

   c.267/2, p. 334

W0608 What shall I say! Oh how shall I appear!
And Britain ne'er shall want a patriot king.

   'Prologue'
   Poetry Box I/107

W0609 What shall I write upon wise Claudio said
For that will suit me when I go to sh—t.

   [Robert Merry], 'Extempore epigram'
   Greatheed Box/9

W0610 What? Shall the King the nation's genius raise,
But to deserve, and to receive the crown.

   Charles Montagu, 3rd earl of Halifax, 'An epistle to
   the Earl of Dorset, on the occasion of King William's
   victory at the Boyne'

   c.244, p. 260; b.204, p. 66

W0611 What shall we say when God doth so extend
Who is the Lord of lords and King of kings.

   [Mary Serjant]

   fb.98, fol. 162

W0612 What shepherd or nymph of the grove,
And the virtues all laid in her breast.

   [Anne Finch, countess of Winchilsea], 'The
   shepherd's complaint'

   c.83/1, no. 177

W0613 What shocking stuff after such puffing before,
If this be your writing, pray let's have no Mo[ore].

   'On the same de eodem' [Gil Blas, by Edward Moore,
   acted for nine nights at Drury Lane in Feb. 1750/1]

   c.360/3, no. 87

W0614 What should a man do with a very fine wife,
And ne'er be call'd cuckolds boys after we're gone.

   'Song'

   c.189, p. 170

W0615 What should I ask my friend? Which best would be
He left scorn'd Ammon to the vulgar rout.

   'Cato's answer to Labienus when he advised him to
   consult the oracle of Jupiter . . . [Lucan, ix.]'
   [Crum w683]

   Poetry Box x/81

W0616 What should they do or whither turn amaz'd
With Peyton to defraud them of their chase, and
                 chief delight.

   c.519

W0617 What signifies it, that you learning gain
The only ornament of all mankind.

   c.93

W0618 What signifies this world's in loud applause
Excite within the heart enlivening joys!

   [Edmund Wodehouse], 'Jan. 14 [1715]'

   b.131, p. 140

W0619 What silly fool, but Pope would e'er unfold
Instead of that has lost both praise and name.

   'Upon reading The dunciad [by Alexander Pope]'

   fb.142, p. 69

W0620   What simples can the hand of art
Beneath the burden [and] so conquer'd sinks.

     [Francis Lenton], 'Vis amoris insuperabilis'

     b.205, fol. 16r

W0621   What sinner, canst thou nothing see,
May now inspire delight.

     [Thomas Stevens?], 'Afternoon s[a]m[e] day Jany. 21.
[1781] Isaiah 53.2'

     c.259, p. 120

W0622   What sinner is thy present name
Now, and upon Mount Zion's hill.

     T[homas] S[tevens], 'Ruth 3, 14–18. March 12, [17]80'

     c.259, p. 78

W0623   What sits so heavy, Thyrsis, on your brow?
Inspired by Phoebus, and the sacred nine.

     [Stephen Barrett?], 'Corydon and Thyrsis. A pastoral.
A school exercise'

     c.193, p. 73

W0624   What sounds harmonious mingle with the storm?
Fix'd on basaltic columns stands thy fame!

     [William Parsons], 'Verses written [to Sir Joseph
Banks] in the Isle of Staffa. 6 August 1787'
[Crum w690]

     Greatheed Box/14

W0625   What state of life can be so blest,
Thou tyrant, tyrant of the mind.

     [John Dryden], 'On jealousy . . . Salisbury journal,
Decem. 4 [17]86'

     c.83/1, no. 115

W0626   What state or station God has thee assign'd
Is all His grace and pure gratuity.

     [Sir Philip Wodehouse], 'Persius' Quem te Deus essa'

     b.131, p. 23

W0627   What strange opposition in nature we find,
And it is not the fault of the man that is young.

     'The nature of youth'

     fb.107, p. 26

W0628   What strange thing's that whose whole is an half
And share both my bottle and bowl!

     R[ichard] V[ernon] S[adleir], 'Halfpenny [riddle]'

     c.106, p. 97

W0629   What strange unheard-of frenzy fills thy breast
Than this eternal nonsense of thy tongue!

     [William Parsons], 'Epigram' [on 'the Abbé L. having
mentioned fixed planets . . .']
[Crum w697]

     Greatheed Box/70

W0630   What strange unusual prodigy is here,
Disordered, and are sick, when God can die.

     H[enry] C[olman], 'On the strange apparitions at
Christ's death'
[Crum w698]

     b.2, p. 16

W0631   What stubborn still, base rebels take a view
Eternal laurels grown around his grave.

     'A poem on K[ing] J[ames] the 3d'

     c.570/2, p. 12

W0632   What sturdy storms, stupendious alarms
And wish well to King and good council.

     'A song to the tune of I love it, but I love it so &c
. . . .Feb. 13 1668'
[Crum w703]

     b.207, p. 38

W0633   What sudden chance hath darkt of late
Of Jack his son and Tom his man.

     'Upon Prince Charles and the D[uke] of
Buckingham's going into Spain' [1622/3]
[Crum w705]

     b.197, p. 104; b.101, p. 55; b.356, p. 142

W0634   What sudden crash! What complicated sound
Shalt then arise again to grace the hall!

     R[ichard] V[ernon] S[adleir], 'Soliloquy'

     c.106, p. 579

W0635   What sweet seraphic bliss they share
To shield them from the anger of their God.

     [Thomas Hull], 'Paraphrase of Psalm 1st'

     c.528/36

W0636   What sweet suffusion spread the face
And think at least of love and you!

     R[ichard] V[ernon] S[adleir], 'To Miss Frances
Graham, since Mrs. [blank]'

     c.106, p. 89

W0637   What talents thine, which with such ease,
Himself all tuneful birds, in one.

     John Lockman, 'Hearing Signora Galli, take off
Monticelli, in Lucio vero . . . Decr. 1747'

     c.267/1, p. 9

W0638   What thanks to God ought I to give?
When Thee I serve, myself I bless.

     [Edmund Wodehouse], 'Septr 21 1715'

     b.131, p. 270

W0639   What that the cruel Scythian queen did once
That by their infancy deserve the same.

     fb.228/2

W0640 What the devil ails our Parliament
Makes wretched speeches for the life | Of Thomas
earl of Danby.

[George Villiers, 2nd duke of Buckingham], 'A ballad
on the Earl of Danby'
[Crum w714]

b.327, f. 2; see also 'Zounds! What ails . . .'.

W0641 What the devil ye citizens keeps ye in London
Two rooms on a floor—but twelve guineas per week.

'O quam tempora or the complaint of the Brighton
horse-holders . . . .'

Diggle Box: Poetry Box XI/51

W0642 What! The friends of a Jervis the sons of a Grey,
Save a thief from the gallows, and he will hang you.

'A peep into the manager's box'

c.340

W0643 What! The Messias born, and shall a day
To the remembrance of this benefit.

'Christmas Day 1658'

b.49, p. 12

W0644 What then is breeding which alas! in vain,
That those who want them may appear more bright.

'On good breeding'

c.83/1, no. 12

W0645 What then O king of terrors, art thou come
Of clouds or storms, in everlasting day.

'An elegy on the death of the honorable John Gray of
Envield [sic] esqr., who died Feb. 14. 1708/9' [see
epitaph: 'Within this vault entomb'd doth lie . . .']

c.257

W0646 What thing is love a tyrant of the mind
Which sickness makes forlorn and time forgotten.

'Of love'

b.356, p. 76

W0647 What thing is that which is not felt nor seen,
That if some see't, 'twill make their hearts to bleed.

Will[iam] Strode, 'A kiss—riddle'
[Crum w729]

b.200, p. 190; b.205, fol. 98v

W0648 What think you, honest friend, if we
To raise their fines another year.

[Phanuel Bacon], 'Verses sent into the bursary at
Magdelen College Oxford by the junior fellows,
begging to partake of their good cheer at their great
audit, when the accounts of the whole year are settled,
according to custom'

c.237, fol. 98 [i.e., 118]

W0649 What this treaty will prove thou canst not divine,
His peace Robin holds. Prithee hold thine.

'To Caleb D'anvers esq.' [i.e., Nicholas Amhurst]

c.570/3, p. 103

W0650 What thou hast, spend not vainly
And what thou givest, give frankly.

b.234, p. 308

W0651 What tho', dear brother, genius sent from heav'n
For all may weep a brother buried here.

'A reflection by my brother's grave'

fc.53, p. 3

W0652 What though her sire be but a potter
Drink the juice and kiss the hold.

'A merry companion . . . taking up his jug made the
following droll'
[Crum w739]

b.104, p. 96

W0653 What though I be of a prodigious waist
To all posterity, I'd write Burlase.

[Ben Jonson], 'The poet to the painter [Sir William
Burlase]' [answer to 'To paint thy worth . . .']
[Crum w742]

b.200, p. 247

W0654 What tho' I guilty be of all these crimes
For me, to wash away my guilt he died.

H[enry] C[olman], 'The regenerate sinner's plea'
[Crum w743]

b.2, p. 25

W0655 What tho' my cheeks thy pallid liv'ry wear,
Her gentle influence thy pow'r suspends.

Maria Logan, 'Ode to sickness'

c.83/2, no. 397

W0656 What tho' my sins are of a crimson stain?
Will pardon all the ills that I have done.

c.153, p. 109

W0657 What tho' my strength, and spirits do decay,
While he has life, for thee to heaven shall send.

[Thomas Hamilton, 6th earl of Haddington], 'To
Florella epistle the eighth on her birthday April the
first 1732'

c.458/1, p. 22

W0658 What tho' my theme might well dispose
And worthy fame from thee.

'To be added to the verses on Lady Millar' [see 'Well
she is dead . . .']

fc.53, p. 45

W0659 What though night comes, though solar rays
Smile on my love, and hear my pray'r.

    Charles Burney, the younger, 'To Rosetta . . . Sept. 13.
    1782'

    c.35 (end)

W0660 What though no eastern virgin tries
And give up whole ages of praise.

    R[ichard] V[ernon] S[adleir], 'Billets written for a
    private ball given by General C. and so disposed that
    each gentleman was supposed to present one to his
    partner. 1768'

    c.106, p. 33

W0661 What tho' the body's laid in silent dust
And victory o'er death and grave for them will take.

    'Epitaph' [on Mary Pluret]

    c.354

W0662 What tho' the distance of the way
As much a purest gold surmounts the merest brass.

    [Edmund Burke], 'Spenser'

    fc.46/1

W0663 What tho' the sun withdraw his ray,
Shall wear the bloom of spring.

    'A winter thought'

    c.83/1, no. 111

W0664 What though they call me country lass
With a stand by—clear the way.

    [Henry Carey], 'The fine lady['s] life' [sung by Mrs.
    Cibber in The provoked husband]
    [Crum w756]

    fc.61, p. 65

W0665 What tho' this play a crowded audience drew
Gave praise to thee, and horror to the deed.

    'To Mr. Philips on his excellent tragedy of Humphrey
    Duke of Gloucester. Acted on Friday February the
    fifteenth, 1722/3 and had a run for several days, at the
    Theater Royal in Drury Lane . . .'

    c.360/2, no. 122

W0666 What! Tho' thou com'st in sable mantle clad,
Thou ask'st no more than he has power to give.

    'To winter'

    c.83/1, no. 198

W0667 What time, all-bounteous nature, blithe and gay,
The rapturous blessings of a virtuous love.

    [Charles Burney, the younger], 'Strephon and
    Monimia. A pastoral poem'

    c.37, p. 30

W0668 What time all creatures did by joint consent
Each to his mansion orderly resorted.

    [William Smith, allegory on time, c. 1600]

    a.21, fol. 2

W0669 What Timon, does old age begin t'approach
To drink bear-glass, and hear the Hectors roar.

    [John Wilmot, 2nd earl of Rochester], 'Satire by Sir
    Char[les] Sedley [sic]'

    b.105, p. 227

W0670 What to Queen Bess relates in least degree,
Nan like Queen Bess disdains a successor.

    c.233, p. 46; see also 'My lords and gentlemen . . .'.

W0671 What tortures can there be in hell
Who would no[t] have the sickness, for the cure?

    [William Walsh], 'Cure of jealousy'
    [Crum w770]

    c.223, p. 60

W0672 What tranquil road, unvex'd by strife
I'd never live, or quickly die.

    'Against life, from the Greek of Posidipus . . .
    Moschus'

    c.94 (incomplete?)

W0673 What trifle comes next! Spare the censure my
                friend,
From a youth, next to Shakespeare's, who honors
                thy grave.

    'Character and eulogium of Sterne'

    c.90

W0674 What! Trigamists! Quadrigamists! and parsons all,
And why? so good the first, she could not be
                surpass'd.

    T[homas] M[orell], 'An epitaph in Water-beach
    churchyard, Cambr. on the wife of the Rev. J.
    Mickleborough professor of chemistry at Cambridge.
    Translated in hexameters'

    c.395, p. 122

W0675 What troubles, Lord, what foes I have,
Thy special blessings send.

    'Psalm 3'

    c.264/1, p. 7

W0676 What turn'd a soldier Madam to oppose
Store of such ladies as theirs want of such.

    'Upon the work of the pious phoenix of the times
    Dame Ursula Harvey'

    Poetry Box VI/109

W0677 What! twice, thrice married! and again!
My first, a nonpareil, my last.

T[homas] M[orell], 'An epitaph . . . on the wife of the
Rev: J. Mickleborough . . . translated in tetrameters'
c.395, p. 123

W0678 What two-ey'd creature is it (Master Bell)
And have each, but one eye? I pray thee tell.

Sir Thomas Urquhart, 'A riddle to Master Bell'
fb.217, p. 153

W0679 What uncouth lethargy has thus possest
I'm still the same, the same I'll dying be.

W. F., 'A dream . . . 1660'
File 19231

W0680 What universal sadness glooms around?
Thus while we live th'allotted part to fill.

'On the death of the Revd. Dr Harrington of
Norwich'
c.83/3, no. 833

W0681 What urg'd thee, cross'd by hopeless love,
And arms her with the thorn.

'To a gentleman who behav'd rudely and indecently to
a young lady'
c.360/3, no. 229

W0682 What various charms can Celia boast
And charming when extended.

'On a lady sitting cross-legged for a gentleman at
cards'
c.546, p. 2; c.578, p. 100

W0683 What virtue or what mental grace
Or may my friend deceive me.

[William Cowper], 'Friendship'
c.470 (autogr.); Poetry Box v/104 (incomplete)

W0684 What vulgar people speak few be worse
As that they many attend and [be?] misleading.

[Sir Thomas Urquhart], 'That man if a solid wit will
neither be incensed by [?] nor [?] with [?]'
fb.217, p. 509

W0685 What wakes this new pain in my breast,
Alternate gives pleasure and smart. | What wakes
&c.

'What wakes this new pain in my breast'
Poetry Box IV/62

W0686 What want'st thou that thou art in this sad taking? |
A king.
Undone.

'An echo'
[Crum w777]
b.111, p. 529

W0687 What was the day, whereon our Laureston's eyes
Great Ormonde's glory, and his nobles' leal.

[ ] Davock, 'Mr. Davock's translation of Sr Rich.
Blake's verses'
fb.228/20

W0688 What we often make use of our thoughts to express
Is the name of a castle that Oliver won.

[Enigma/Charade/Conundrum 79d]
c.389

W0689 What will make joyful harvests when 'tis fit
Nor whips nor threats the foaming coursers hear.

[William Mills], 'The first book of the Georgics of
Virgil translated into blank verse'
c.472, p. 61

W0690 What! Will our clergy never cease
Advanc'd the work, of reformation.

[Thomas Hamilton, 6th earl of Haddington], 'The
opera'
c.458/2, p. 41

W0691 What woman could do, I have tried to be free,
Still—still he's the man.

[Colley Cibber?], '16th song the power of love'
Accession 97.7.40, p. 29

W0692 What wonders strike my eyes!
On what my hands can touch, and arms embrace?

'On a painted landscape'
c.244, p. 123

W0693 What wonders with each other vie,
They'll have no knowledge of your route.

[ ] Lawrence, jr., 'The air balloon'
c.83/1, no. 137

W0694 What words can paint what thoughts unfold the
breast,
And leave the world to mis'ry, and to me.

'On the death of Mrs. Cotes . . . Eto: S—ys.'
c.591

W0695 What! Write my name, when turned of sixty-five,
That neither ink, nor words should blab this truth.

[Josiah] Tucker
File 17450

W0696 What writings can the faults of women note
Whats'e'er it be, the ruffian being the pen.

> Sir Thomas Urquhart, 'Against the ordinary tenet that
> the husband wears the horns for the wife's
> licentiousness'
>
> fb.217, p. 113

W0697 What years betwixt Inachus, Codrus, have roll'd,
Keep up my old flame, and I with Glycera toy!

> [William Popple, trans.], '[Horace] book 3rd. ode
> 19th. To Telephus'
>
> fc.104/2, p. 274

W0698 What you give freely, your great love portends:
And what on credit, your great faith commends.

> Sir Thomas Urquhart, 'To a wealthy man very
> Christianly disposed, in applauding his faith, and
> charity'
>
> fb.217, p. 301

W0699 What you said last, we all allow
Be never saw'd for blocks.

> 'A letter from the Maypole in the Strand to the
> Maypole at Farnham, occasioned by an alteration
> made in certain persons, at the time of the last strange
> appearance in the clouds: March 6: 1715:16' [answered
> by ''Tis no strange thing . . .']
> [Crum w799]
>
> b.382(8); fb.7, fol. 7; c.570/1, p. 166; fc.58, p. 62

W0700 What you suspect I cannot tell
You weld the stern(?) of my relief.

> 'His 2 onset' [answered by 'How frames it . . .']
>
> b.205, fol. 93v

W0701 What you're afraid then?—'Yes I am you're right'
I'm not ashamed to own, I fear my God.

> 'Captn. ——['s] excuse for not fighting'
>
> c.378, p. 3

W0702 What? Ye great Syrius so far displac'd
By'r Lady they're compell'd to wear the horn.

> 'Syrius' [answered by 'Dog's very choleric . . .']
>
> b.356, p. 112

W0703 Whate'er man writes as man's, must ever be
Which honor owes the worthy, and the wise.

> 'On hypercriticism' [1781]
>
> fc.53, p. 1

W0704 Whate'er my brother will love me
That dooms us to eternity.

> [Edmund Wodehouse], 'June 19 [1715]'
>
> b.131, p. 224

W0705 Whate'er of praise, and of regret attend
To share the eternal triumph of the just.

> [Charlotte (Turner) Smith], 'Inscription on a stone in
> the churchyard at Boreham, in Essex raised by the
> honorable Elizabeth Olmins, to the memory of Ann
> Gardner'
>
> c.141, p. 144

W0706 Whate'er philosophers may chatter;
Give up that useful thing—a wife.

> 'Choose for yourself'
>
> c.83/2, no. 386

W0707 Whate'er the eye or judgment pleases
In one rich sparkling jewel shine.

> [Phanuel Bacon], 'To Miss Molly B—r'
>
> c.237, fol. 12

W0708 Whate'er thou art, thou excellence unknown!
Where thou art absent every place is hell!

> 'God unknown—Letters moral . . . said to be written
> by a Deist, reformed only from vice and debauchery'
>
> c.244, p. 580

W0709 Whate'er you think, good sirs, at least agree,
And get you too, was faith &c. .

> [David Garrick], 'Epilogue' [for Master Ernst]
>
> Acquisition 92.3.1ff. (autogr., incomplete); see also
> 'Think what you will . . .'

W0710 Whatever duties God requires,
And will vouchsafe us to behold his face.

> [Edmund Wodehouse], 'Jan. 10 [1715]'
>
> b.131, p. 137

W0711 Whatever in Philoclea the fair,
Which both myself, and you doth represent.

> [William Strode], 'A subscription on Sr Philip
> Sidney's Arcadia, sent for a token'
> [Crum w814]
>
> b.200, p. 123

W0712 Whatever in this war she got
But to the fisher let him go.

> [Charles Darby?], 'On the restitution of the French
> conquests . . . Englished' [1697]
> [Crum w815]
>
> fb.207/3, p. 23; see also 'Once in a ship . . .'.

W0713 'Whatever is, is right' tho' granted true,
And faith each caring impulse shall control.

> 'An epistle to Charissa'
>
> fc.53, p. 201

W0714 Whatever souls have been before or shall hereafter be
And there they shall keep holiday to all eternity.

c.158, p. 49

W0715 Whatever tends to general use
It argues strongly—my abuse.

[ ] Crowfoot, 'Enigma[:] he singing flies, and flying
sings'

c.90

W0716 What's a mortal and could know decay
Let my poor laurel give.

[Robert Cholmeley], 'To the memory of fair
Sacharissa who died in the twentieth year of her age'

c.190, p. 233

W0717 What's a Protector? 'tis a stately thing
From whom the King of kings protect us all.

[John Cleveland?], 'A Protector described' [pr.
Cleveland's works, 1687, p. 343]
[Crum w820]

b.108, fol. 16; Poetry Box vi/18 ('here's a stately . . .');
b.104, p. 10 (end of book); fb.140, p. 9; fb.228/28; see
also 'A Protector: what's that? . . .'.

W0718 What's black is still in darkness permanent
Therefore the devil must needs be black, not white.

[Sir Thomas Urquhart], 'Why the devil ought to be
printed black . . .'

fb.217, p. 520

W0719 What's forming in the womb of fate
But hold your virtue fast, for that alone you may.

[John Norris], 'The advice'

c.547, p. 165

W0720 What's friendship? 'Tis a pleasure:
Two minds, yet having both but one perfection.

H. R., 'On friendship'
[Crum w824]

b.200, p. 80; c.356 (''Tis a treasure | 'Tis a pleasure')

W0721 What's here! A vile cramp hand. I cannot see
And by the general voice will stand or fall.

'Prologue to The rivals, spoken by Mr. Woodward and
Mr. Quick'

c.68, p. 64

W0722 What's highest in the heav'ns: in earth, most low,
Profound: nor yet the heav'ns; they are so high.

Sir Thomas Urquhart, 'A certain student have this
following reason, why he could neither be a good
astrologian, nor naturalist'

fb.217, p. 70

W0723 What's human happiness? A word, a dream,
We meet the very ills we meant to shun.

[J. B.], 'Answer to this question, what's human
happiness? Partly taken from Doctor Young's estimate
of human happiness'

Poetry Box iv/155

W0724 What's innocence! a brighter gem,
This gem—'tis life for death, 'tis heav'n for hell.

M. S, 'On innocence'

c.156, p. 78; c.83/3, no. 997

W0725 What's love? why 'tis a fond desire
And all thy dictates doth obey.

'Love'

c.487, p. 57

W0726 What's new will soon be old; whence that shall
never
But whose new [?] ever it endless praise.

[Sir Thomas Urquhart], 'Showing how much
newfangled brains hunt after novelty'

fb.217, p. 519

W0727 What's salt, breeds thirst: the sea is salt; therefore
It drinks up of fresh waters so great store.

Sir Thomas Urquhart, 'Why rivers run into the
ocean. A syllogism'

fb.217, p. 151

W0728 What's sweet what's good—what's fair, in female sex
Here meet in her—may her no malice vex.

[Sir Philip Wodehouse], 'Upon [Alice Cotton] when
married to his nephew Humphrey Moneux'

b.131, back (no. 60)

W0729 What's that you call a maidenhead
'Tis kept but lost not had again.

'On a maidenhead'
[Crum w835]

b.205, fol. 22v

W0730 What's the matter England what's the cause
And from all other fears be sure abstain.

b.216, p. 150

W0731 What's this dull town to me,
Oh! I can ne'er forget Robin Adair.

[Robert Burns], 'Robin Adair'

Poetry Box xii/79

W0732 What's this I do not understand
Pure happiness without alloy.

'Itinerary with three notes explanatory'

Poetry Box x/42

W0733 What's this your justice Sir you come to do?
These are the plagues which from rebellion springs.

'The parley'

b.111, p. 385; see also 'Was this the justice . . .'.

W0734 What's worn on the head; and what makes a good
pudding,
Comes into the mind and goes out of a sudden.

'[Charade] 89' [caprice]

c.389

W0735 What's writ in's name is brave in gust
Nothing of interest, of love, or hate.

[Sir Philip Wodehouse], 'Upon Alderman Augustine
Briggs of Norwich'

b.131, back (no. 211)

W0736 Whats'ever in the world is most refin'd
Heav'n's [?] course, view'd a completer manual.

Sir Thomas Urquhart, 'To Lady [crossed out] of
[crossed out]'

fb.217, p. 85

W0737 Whelp'd on some Lars in ruefu' poortith bred
Without rehearing, and without appeal!

'Parsons versus Loughborough extracted from a
newspaper called the Courier'

Greatheed Box/74

W0738 When a bar of pure silver or ingot of gold
And unless you adorn it, a nausea follows.

[William Cowper], 'The flatting mill an illustration'

File 17718

W0739 When a Dutch monster with horns
And bring both wealth and peace.

'A prophecy' [of the return of 'James III']
[Crum w845, 'two horns']

c.570/1, p. 36

W0740 When a fam'd Fishery did begin,
My only aim's to get well out.

John Lockman, 'Strange vicissitude . . . Feb. 1758'

c.267/1, p. 211

W0741 When a German white horse is turn'd to an ass,
The man have his mare, and each rebel a rope.

'Prognostic'

c.570/2, p. 159

W0742 When a holy black Swede, the son of Bob,
Bury those carrots under a hill.

[Jonathan Swift], 'The Windsor prophecy . . . printed
in the year 1711' [Foxon S938; satire on Elizabeth
Seymour, duchess of Somerset]

b.204, p. 41

W0743 When a king or a queen
And as for the hoax—you'll excuse it.

[Joseph Jekyll], 'On the unsuccessful embassy of Ld.
Macartney' [to China; c. 1793]

File 17534

W0744 When a knight from the North is lopt in Axe Yard,
'Tis too late to repent sin on and be damned.

[Thomas Brown], 'The prophecy' [on Sir John
Fenwick; 'found in a football in Spittlefields by a
weaver'; 1697]
[Crum w847; POAS v.485]

c.171, p. 8; fb.207/3, p. 8

W0745 When a nymph at her toilet has spent the whole day,
And merit a love which no time shall remove.

'Little merit in being dressed fine'

c.83/2, no. 371

W0746 When a strange whelp shall rule a land,
The evils done to work this fall.

'A prophecy from Nostradamus' [of the return of the
Old Pretender]
[Crum w855]

c.570/1, p. 49

W0747 When a true friend may be best known
A sincere friend from a dissembled liar.

[Sir Thomas Urquhart], 'Poet and pot'

fb.217, p. 386

W0748 When a wall in a pool
Shall leave the man his own mare.

'A prophecy' [on Walpole and Bolingbroke, 1716]
[Crum w857]

c.570/1, p. 151

W0749 When a woman that's buxom a dotard does wed,
Proves a thief to himself, and a pimp to his wife.

'The mad marriage'

fb.107, p. 7

W0750 When Abel bade his fairest firstling bleed,
Fearful, lest envy should await reward.

Miss [ ] Priault, 'Epigram.—by . . . royal bounty! To
female genius' [on Queen Charlotte]

c.74

W0751 When Abr'am, full of sacred awe,
The God that heareth pray'r.

'On the fast for the war—by a young lady of 15'
[pr. Glasgow 174-? (Foxon H421)]

c.241, p. 82; c.303

W0752 When absence draws the curtain 'twixt mine eyes
A being whom old times laid in his grave.

Ed. Ch. [Edward Herbert, lord Herbert of
Cherbury?], 'On one's love. Ed. Ch.'
b.62, p. 108

W0753 When absent from the nymph, I love,
Who most deserve, the least obtain.

[Allan Ramsay], 'Song'
c.189, p. 175

W0754 When active days and amorous years began,
To nurse me then I took one partner more.

'On the Revd. Mr. Bastard'
c.362, p. 32

W0755 When Adam first his Eve did view
Than be a woman and not be a whore.

R[obert] Shirley, 1st earl of Ferrers, 'Adam and Eve.
From the French quand Adam vite [vide?] &c'
c.347, p. 12; see also next.

W0756 When Adam, first, his fair one view'd,
Like him I'd sell it for a kiss.

Frederick Corfield, 'To Miss Bright'
c.381/2; see also previous.

W0757 When Adrianus viewed well
To rest with you above the skies. | Amen

'Of S. Adrian. September. 8'
a.30[32]

W0758 When after dinner pipes and 'bacco come
And instantaneous by each pipe is lighted.

'The rule observed at the mansion house when Arabin
dines in the smoking parlor'
fc.76.iii/214

W0759 When age, all patient, and without regret
And each sad bosom heaves the sigh sincere.

[Francis Fawkes], 'On Philip Downes, son of
E. Downes esq. who died . . . 1743, aetat 15 in the
church of Thrighley in Cheshire'
[Crum w868]
fc.21, p. 25

W0760 When Albion owned Eliza's mild command
Whilst either lungs can breathe, or smoke ascend.

'[Several copies of verses spoken at Westminster
School on the anniversary of the defeat of the Spanish
Armada] 4'
fc.24, p. 71

When Alexis lay prest   W0761
The nymph died more quick, and the shepherd
                                               more slow.

'Love in fashion'
fb.107, p. 77

When all alone the other day,   W0762
Forget to be sincere.

'The reflection'
c.83/2, no. 731

When all our eyes are drawing straws   W0763
Informers we'll defy. | And a-gaping we will go
                                          will go. . . .

[Phanuel Bacon], 'Heigh-ho—to the tune of Begging
we will go'
c.237, fol. 16

When all the blandishments of life are gone   W0764
The coward creeps to death, the brave lives on.

'Suicide'
c.360/2, no. 186

When all the elements at once conspire   W0765
Call this success, Heaven's peculiar care.

'On raising the siege at Limerick' [1690]
[Crum w877-8]
b.111, p. 261; b.204, p. 58

When all thy mercies O my God   W0766
To utter all thy praise.

[Joseph Addison], 'A divine hymn. Spec[tator] 453'
[Crum w880]
c.144, p. 135; fc.132/1, p. 37; c.163, p. 13; c.547, p. 150;
c.244, p. 4; c.259, p. 18; see also 'Through every
period . . .'.

When all was wrapt in dark midnight,   W0767
And word spake nevermore.

[David Mallet], 'William—and Margaret' [pr. 1724
(Foxon M60)]
c.244, p. 103; c.341, p. 129; c.360/1, p. 241; Trumbull
Box: Poetry Box XIII/98

When all was wrapt in sable night   W0768
Farewell remember me.

'George and D—y or the injured'
c.116, p. 10

When ancient Bess was England's Queen   W0769
And push us into bed.

'Modern chastity. An epigram . . . [by] a bachelor'
c.487, p. 107

W0770 When ancient comedy became first known,
They dread the satire and the poets hate.

    fc.14/10

W0771 When angry Rowland fills the partial chair
Is all things friend king God that they adore.

    Poetry Box I/141; see also 'Whether on sad Avernus . . .'.

W0772 When angry storms roll o'er the boistrous main
Hither the vulgars' love or fear control.

    [Robert Cholmeley], 'Horace ode 16: lib 2: Otium
    divos rogat in patenti prensus agas'

    c.190, p. 98

W0773 When A[n]sl[e]y lay in nature's shelf,
Since losing it may lose his soul.

    'On J[oh]n A[n]sl[e]y. A poem'

    c.530, p. 308

W0774 When any dies, whose muse was rich in verse,
Others, are base and illegitimate.

    c.189, p. 78

W0775 When Arria pull'd the dagger from her side
I die by that which Paetus must receive.

    'Paetus and Arria' [Martial, ep. I.xiii]

    c.360/1, p. 241

W0776 When art in all her radiant pomp appears
Thy flow'ry shades, and Wilton's rev'rend towers.

    John Lockman, 'In 1730, the author began a poem on
    [Wilton House], addressed to the present Earl of
    Pembroke's grandfather . . . that poem opened in
    manner following'

    c.267/1, p. 339; c.268 (first part), p. 29 (incomplete?)

W0777 When Artimesia sings, my ravish'd ear
And with her sprightly wit, enslaves my heart.

    'Verses wrote at Tunbridge Wells—1733'

    c.360/1, p. 37

W0778 When as in Cornwall at Powlmaggon I
Able to feast the wandering deities.

    [Sir Aston Cokayne], 'To my cousin german Mrs
    Cordelia Harryes'

    b.275, p. 42

W0779 When Assheton to Kemble at first was promoted,
You may ask of the squire—or else the squire's wife.

    '1763 Le Couchon'

    c.484, p. 151

W0780 When at our house the servants brawl
And one scold makes another cease.

    [Nicholas Rowe], 'Verses made to a simile of
    Mr. Pope's'

    fc.60, p. 45

W0781 When at the Eternal's dread command
Till female beauty deign to crown the enchanting
                            scene.

    H. I. Dye, 'From the Critical review—introit from the
    poems of . . .'

    c.90

W0782 When at the full meridian height,
To stare against the day.

    [Robert Cholmeley], 'To Semun [Seeman] painting a
    young lady of nineteen years of age'

    c.190, p. 230

W0783 When at the patriarch's great command,
Nor doubt a fairer day.

    'Ode on the eclipse of the sun July 4th 1748'
    [Crum w903, 'July 14']

    c.578, p. 38

W0784 When Aurelia first I courted,
Kindle and maintain a flame.

    'Love in declension' [on Charles II and Barbara
    Villiers, duchess of Cleveland]
    [Crum w905]

    fb.107, p. 5; fb.140, p. 99; fb.66/8 (attr. Thomas
    Killigrew)

W0785 When Aureng-zebe usurp[ed] his father's chair
His title's good to reign as thine to write.

    'Aureng-zebe' [satire on William III, addressed to
    Thomas Shadwell]

    b.111, p. 343

W0786 When Bacchus jolly god invites
Still ev'ry glass is Chloe's health.

    'Song 232'

    c.555, p. 363

W0787 When banish'd Ovid bid to Rome adieu,
But oh! It ne'er rejoiced in that auspicious guest.

    'Travelling from Cambridge to Garesden Wilts.'

    b.322, p. 3

W0788 When bashful daylight once was gone,
Whether he were a fool or no.

    [Thomas Randolph], 'Upon six Cambridge lasses
    bathing themselves in a river, and espied by scholars'
    [Crum w910]

    b.54, p. 932

W0789   When beasts could speak, the learned say
How just it suits with humankind.

    [Jonathan Swift], 'The beasts' confession to the
    priest' [written 1732, pr. Dublin 1738 (Foxon S804)]

c.83/1, no. 51

W0790   When beating rains and piercing winds
And bless my social fire!

    'The social fire'

c.344, p. 52 [bis]

W0791   When beauteous Laura's gentle voice
Shines full upon the heart.

    W[illiam Robert] Spence[r?], 'On the Right Honble
    Lady Anne Ashley's hesitation in her speech'

Poetry Box XII/122; Spence Papers, folder 113 ('beauteous
Mira's')

W0792   When beauty drops untimely to the tomb,
And future triumphs in her ashes sleep.

    'An elegy on the death of a young lady'

c.83/1, no. 50

W0793   When beauty, sense and virtue chance to meet
The youth who gains her, gains a paraclete.

    'An extempore on a beautiful young lady'

c.360/3, no. 46

W0794   When beauty's soul attracting charms
All hail, sweet harmony, to thee!

    'Occasional ode performed at the Catch Club'

c.90

W0795   When Bibo thought fit from the world to retreat,
You may have forgot—you were drunk when you
                     died.

    [Matthew Prior], 'Song 100'

c.555, p. 152

W0796   When Biron's generous hand restores,
In the full force of beauty's charms!

    'On seeing Lady M. Fordyce, L[ad]y A. Lindsay, Mrs.
    Fitzherbert, Mrs. Lewis and Miss Bridgeman with the
    Maréchal Biron in his box at the opera in Paris'

Poetry Box II/39

W0797   When biting Boreas, fell and dour,
The most resembles God.

    [Robert Burns], 'A winter night'

c.139, p. 595

W0798   When blessed Mary did cast down her eye
'Twas once look up, 'tis now look down to heaven.

    [Sir Richard Bulstrode], 'Upon the Virgin Mary's
    being with child'

fb.88, p. 114v

When blooming beauties first appear   W0799
And sings without blushing to decenter measures.

fb.108, p. 287

When bold rebellion ranges o'er a land   W0800
Till time shall cease, and nature's self decay.

    John Freeman, 'A poem on His Majesty's intended act
    of grace'

Poetry Box X/10(2)

When born, in tears we saw thee drown'd,   W0801
And there in smiles be drest!

    J. D. Carlisle, 'To a friend on his birthday translated
    from the Arabic by . . . professor of Arabic at
    Cambridge'

c.83/4, no. 2039

When both the Scots, and English are   W0802
The English quaff a gallon.

    Sir Thomas Urquhart, 'Of the Scots, and English
    measure, in liquors, and their denomination of monies'

fb.217, p. 156

When bright Aurelia tripp'd the plain,   W0803
The more she loves her swain.

    '17th song. The bright Aurelia'
    [Crum W922 (var.)]

Accession 97.7.40, p. 29

When Britain first at Heaven's command   W0804
And manly hearts to guard the fair. |
            Rule Britannia [rule the waves |
               Britons never will be slaves].

    [James Thomson], 'Rule Britannia' [from David
    Mallet's Alfred]
    [Crum W924]

Poetry Box V/63; c.555, p. 160

When Britain heard the woeful news,   W0805
—And so she did, till she bepist her—.

    [Horace] Walpole, [4th earl of Orford], 'Ode 1766'

Poetry Box V/23 and 24

When Britain's Roscius on the stage appears,   W0806
When Garrick acts no passage seems perplext.

    [Mary Rogers], 'Written by a deaf pupil of
    Mr. Braidwood's without assistance or amendment . . .
    1768'

File 12780

When Briton bold of Spanish birth   W0807
As old a town as 'tis.

    'A prophecy lately found engraven on a plate of brass
    at Folkestone in Kent'
    [Crum W927]

b.52/1, p. 115

w0808   When Britons lay by foreigners oppress'd
James cures the fever and the evil too.

'The following lines were put up in the rooms of Bath'
fc.58, p. 170

w0809   When Bruno first embrac'd his wife in bed
And thrust her maidenhead beyond his reach.

'On Bruno'
[Crum w929]
b.200, p. 407

w0810   When Brute the answer of the Delphic maid
That those our Brutus give his mother sea.

[Phanuel Bacon], 'To Mr. Taunton'
c.237, fol. 75

w0811   When Burnet perceiv'd that the beautiful dames
The lady in gratitude grants him the favor.

[Arthur Mainwaring?], 'An excellent ballad [on building up the seats in St. James' Chapel] to the tune of Packington's Pound'
[Crum w934; POAS VI.40]
fb.70, p. 35

w0812   When bushes budded and trees did chip
Most generous town adieu.

[Samuel Colvill], 'Mock poem or Whigs' supplication part second' [pr. 1681 (Wing C5425)]
b.223

w0813   When Butler (needy wretch) was yet alive
He ask'd for bread, and he receiv'd a stone.

[Samuel Wesley, the younger], 'On Mr. [Samuel] Butler's bust erected in Westminster Abbey'
c.176, p. 39; see also 'While/Whilst Butler . . .'.

w0814   When, by a turn of wayward fate,
But, she return'd, he's doubly blest.

John Lockman, 'Translations, and imitations from Metastasio, and other Italian opera poets [15]'
c.267/4, p. 111

w0815   When by his falseness Phyllis dies
Can never break can never break in vain.

c.188, p. 69

w0816   When by inclemency of air,
Than marble stones, or golden letters are.

'An epitaph on Mr. John Green'
c.244, p. 86

w0817   When by the force of love['s] strong art
Then since thy wit resolve with me. | To sing &c.

'Cant: 29'
b.4, fol. 25

w0818   When by the sirens' coast Ulysses sail'd
Tho' sometimes ruffled still the same.

'To Delia'
Poetry Box I/38

w0819   When by thy scorn O murderess I am dead
Then by my threat'nings keep thee innocent.

J[ohn] D[onne], 'The apparition'
[Crum w942]
b.148, p. 53; b.150, p. 196

w0820   When Caesar died he brav'd each killing wound
Where blushes rose in scorn of human race.

[Anne Finch, countess of Winchilsea], 'Verses said to be wrote by Lady Anne Howard third daughter of Charles earl of Carlisle'
c.360/1, p. 151

w0821   When Caesar quitted Gaul, and marched home
From him in to pride, and craft, that's Caesar's mate.

[Sir Richard Bulstrode, translation of Latin poem]
fb.88, p. 118

w0822   When Caesar triumph'd o'er his Gallic foes
And vidi tells us all that he has done.

'Veni, vidi, vici'
c.373, p. 61

w0823   When call'd by Jove's command severe
Nor earth deserves, nor heav'n allows.

[ ] Mackenzie, M.D., 'In obitum. A. viri D ni Joha nis Davies M.D. Birminghamiensis . . . imitated in English'
fb.7, fol. 3v

w0824   When Carr in court at first a page began
He swell'd unto an earl and then he burst.

'On Sir Robert Carr earl of Somerset'
[Crum w947]
b.62, p. 42

w0825   When Celadon first from his cottage did stray,
'Twill signify nothing, for Roger's the man. |
           Derry down

'11th song Celadon's jug'
[Crum w949]
Accession 97.7.40, p. 18

w0826   When Celia first into my arms,
I meant—and not to you.

[I. W.], 'A song'
c.118, p. 68

wo827 When Celia her cordials sent briskly about
For that's my own water I made it today.

'My own water'
c.555, p. 56

wo828 When Celia, Phyllis, tread the stage,
We might mistake them for the graces.

John Lockman, 'Celia [Mrs. Garrick] and Phyllis
[Signora Nardi]: or the rival opera dancers . . . April
1746'
c.267/1, p. 179

wo829 When Celia sports her naked arms
Their beauties (while they hide) reveal.

'On the present prevailing nakedness of dress in
female fashion and the extreme indelicacy thereof'
Poetry Box XII/15

wo830 When chance or cruel business parts us two,
It sits and sings and so o'ercomes its rage.

A[braham] C[owley], 'Friendship in absence'
[Crum w951]
c.258

wo831 When Charley first my heart had gain'd
And ne'er deceive my bonny bonny lad.

[John Walker?], 'The bonny lad'
fc.108, fol. 19v

wo832 When, Chloe, I your charms survey,
I'll speak in terms most feeling.

'A song'
c.152, p. 12

wo833 When Chloe tried her virgin fires
That gave a charm to all.

[John] Hoadly, 'Lines by [the] late . . . [to Mrs. Joseph
Warton, 1776]'
[Crum w956]
c.83/1, no. 144

wo834 When Chloe's mute, methinks I Venus see
And when she sings, I hear Calliope.

'On Seigniora Elisabetta Du Parc detta La Francesina
1738'
c.360/2, no. 208; c.326, p. 183

wo835 When Chloe's picture was to Venus shown
Friend Howard's genius fancied all the rest.

[Matthew Prior], 'Venus mistaken'
fc.60, p. 29

wo836 When Christ, at Cana's feast, by pow'r divine
The bashful stream hath seen its God, and blush'd.

'First miracle [3]'
c.81/1, no. 36, no. 171 (bis)

When Christ hung 'twixt two thieves, I may assever, wo837
That virtue in the midst was then, or never.

Sir Thomas Urquhart, 'Of our Savior, and those that
were fixed upon the cross with him'
fb.217, p. 116

When Christ the Son of God most clear wo838
May evermore in joys remain. | Amen

'Of S. Peter. June. 30'
a.30[6]

When church on a hill to the Danube advances, wo839
By one that was lately in Packington's pound.

'A prophecy' [on Marlborough]
[cf. Crum w844, 'When a church']
c.111, p. 80

When Clarendon had discern'd beforehand wo840
He comes to be roasted next St. James' Fair.

[Andrew Marvell], 'Clarendon's housewarming'
[Crum w964; POAS I.88]
b.136, p. 43

When Clio ask'd to whose harmonious lays wo841
His own, his own—the heav'nly choir rung.

'On the death of that incomparable poet, Mr. Pope'
c.360/2, no. 257

When clouds drop fatness on the plains wo842
And laugh to scorn, the fear of God.

'On feeling an earthquake'
c.83/1, no. 110

When cock doth crow, methinks to me appears wo843
They'll make you pray upon the night.

'The crowing of the cock'
c.187, p. 3

When cold winter's withered brows, as pale and wo844
                                    white as sorrow,
Courting the day, for a longer stay, we may not be
                                    benighted.

Ed[ward] Hevell(?) [or Knightley Chetwood?], 'A
hunting song'
[Crum w968, attr. E. Bass]
fb.69, p. 191

When Colin's good dame, who long held him a tug, wo845
And whoever finds fault—I'll be shot—if I do.

[ ] H., 'True resignation . . . Dod[sley] Coll[ection]'
c.487, p. 126

wo846 When comes it, none is with their lot content
If your blear bard has robb'd Crispinus' desk.

'Horace lib. 1st satire 1st literally translated after
Dr. Bentley['s] edition'
Poetry Box I/115[2]

wo847 When comes that hour which brings with it relief
And puts an end to sorrow and to grief.

Petrarch
b.211, p. 60

wo848 When creatures first were form'd, they had by
                                   nature's laws,
Which makes the bold, the fierce, the swift, to
                                   stoop and plead for grace.

[Geffrey] Whitney, 'On the beauty of women, a
translation from the Latin take[n] from Whitney's
Emblems printed at Leiden, 1586'
[Crum w976]
c.360/2, no. 238

wo849 When Cupid blind god, once was stung by a bee,
Think, what pain he must feel whom you pierce to
                                   the heart.

'Cupid wounded'
c.83/3, no. 1026

wo850 When Cupid did his grandsire Jove entreat
Then call'd the happy composition Floyd.

[Jonathan Swift], 'To Mrs. Biddy Floyd. Anno 1708'
c.265, p. 13; fb.66/24

wo851 When Cupid had to go away
Lest it again should stray.

[John Black]
fc.107, p. 79

wo852 When Curtius plung'd, into the gaping grave,
The man that lov'd, and serv'd his king so well.

[Thomas Hamilton, 6th earl of Haddington], 'To the
Lord Viscount Townshend'
c.458/2, p. 150

wo853 When dames of Britain shall espouse
May hope to see a restoration.

'A prophecy' [Jacobite; pr. c. 1715 (Foxon P1136)]
fc.58, p. 125; c.570/1, p. 175

wo854 When Damon first his passion broke
Sinks down into the snare.

[Phanuel Bacon], 'A song'
[Crum w986]
c.237, fol. 18

wo855 When dangers seem'd to scorn resisting pow'r,
Your prudence, and magnificence admired.

Sir Thomas Urquhart, 'To my Lord [later earl]
Craven'
fb.217, p. 324

wo856 When daring Blood his rents to have regain'd
A bishop's cruelty, the crown had gone.

[Andrew Marvell], 'Upon Blood's stealing of the
crown out of the Tower of London' [9 May 1671]
[Crum w988; POAS I.178]
b.52/2, p. 159; b.54, p. 1158; fb.140, p. 136

wo857 When darkness long has veil'd my mind,
Be shame and self-abhorrence mine.

[William Cowper], 'Peace after a storm'
c.141, p. 583

wo858 When darkness wide expands her raven wing
Or where, at his command, the torrent's rage
                                   descends.

'The storm a sonnet to fancy'
c.142, p. 537

wo859 When deaf to every warning given
My God is reconciled to me.

[Thomas Stevens?], 'On the rainbow and covenant a
hymn . . . copied May. 1780'
c.259, p. 87

wo860 When dear Amanda bids me stay
O let them in to make up four?

R[ichard] V[ernon] S[adleir], 'Extempore lines when
one of two ladies with whom I was to pass the evening
was called away'
c.106, p. 115

wo861 When dearest I but think of thee
Which flows not every day but ever.

[Owen Felltham]
[Crum w990]
b.213, p. 105

wo862 When death doth call me to my bosom
While I am sleeping with my [heart's] delight.

[Elizabeth Burn?], 'Upon an upright stone close to the
wall near Bunhill . . . [on Richard Burn]'
Poetry Box VII/55

wo863 When Death gives his blast I'm resolv'd to be
                                   found,
Still staggering swear we'll outbrave it with scorn.

S[tephen] Simpson, 'A song written at school and then
revised by R[obert] L. R.'
c.563

wo864　When death shall part us from these kids,
So shall we smoothly pass away in sleep.

　　[Andrew Marvell], 'A sonnet set by Matt. Locke'
　　[Crum w995]

　　fb.142, p. 44; c.83/1, no. 73 (with extra lines?)

wo865　When Delia on the plain appears
Tell me, my heart, if this be love.

　　[George] Lyttelton, 1st baron Lyttelton, 'A song'
　　[Crum w1000]

　　Spence Papers, folder 101; c.358, p. 143; Accession
　　97.7.40, p. 43; c.152, p. 32

wo866　When Delme I impartially survey
The object both of envy and of love.

　　'The impartial judgment on reading the foregoing
　　verses ['At thy approach my quick'ning pulse . . .' and
　　'At thy approach my avarice . . .'] on Miss Delme'

　　c.360/2, no. 142

wo867　When Dian wearied from the chase
By showing charms too great to tell.

　　[Phanuel Bacon], 'The author sent to call Chloe to
　　breakfast finds her walking about her chambers in her
　　shift'
　　[Crum w1001]

　　c.237, fol. 33

wo868　When Dido found Æneas would not come,
She wept in silence and was Dido-dumb.

　　'Epigram on a lady' [answered by 'The Queen wept
　　sore . . .']

　　Diggle Box: Poetry Box XI/69

wo869　When Dioclesian o'er Rome bore sway,
And that religion be; which was a crime before.

　　'The Whig's idol, or the new-fashioned loyalty'

　　c.570/2, p. 44

wo870　When do the cruel beasts their kind devour!
Against each other daily whet their swords.

　　J[ohn] R[obinson], 'Cognatis maculis parcit fora'

　　c.370, fol. 21

wo871　When down the skies the sun his chariot drove,
And yet would any poet wish them less?

　　'Enjoyment'

　　c.111, p. 128

wo872　When dread convulsions shake this ball of earth,
Wicked or weak are all, who sneak away.

　　John Lockman, 'A word to the wise, and especially to
　　the [?], who are not yet run away from our metropolis'

　　c.267/1, p. 223

When duns were knocking at my door　　　　wo873
That you may all go home and spew as I did.

　　[Alexander Radcliffe], 'The ramble, writ in 1668'

b.54, p. 1234; see also 'Whilst . . .'.

When early the sun sinks in winter to bed,　　wo874
That bliss leads to woe, and then woe, leads to bliss.

　　'Written at an inn'

c.83/2, no. 620

When early youth and life's first kindling flame　wo875
And as the roses languish, so do I.

　　[ ] Robinson, 'Multa ferunt anni venientes commoda
　　secum, Multa recedentes adimunt. Horace . . . 1723'

c.190, p. 96

When ease, and sleep, the busy world hath husht　wo876
Of my own genius my purest rhyme | And poesy.

　　[George Daniel]

b.121, fol. 37

When Egypt's king, God's chosen tribe pursu'd　wo877
When seas can harden! And when rocks can flow.

　　'Epigram on the passage of the Israelites out of Egypt'

c.81/1, no. 394

When England shall her principles betray,　　wo878
Which cannot end, till Caesar has his due.

　　'An old prophecy made in the year 1297 by one Robert
　　de Cressy, a British astronomer, but found amongst
　　the manuscripts in Oxford in the year 1641'
　　[supposedly on George I]
　　[Crum w1006-8, 'De Cresly']

c.570/1, p. 27

When England's honor never had been lost,　　wo879
Nor cuckoldom so much in fashion then.

　　'The reverse of Sine clade victor' ['The glory of the
　　English arms . . .'; on Queen Anne and Marlborough]
　　[Crum w1009]

Poetry Box IV/119

When English no more shall be spoken at court　wo880
Come Luther, come Calvin, the devil and all.

　　'Woe to the church or an old prophecy new revived
　　[by Gilbert Burnet, Bishop of Sarum, 1714]'
　　[Crum w1011]

Poetry Box X/39; fc.58, p. 102

When envy does at Athens rise　　　　　　wo881
But being great and doing well.

　　Matthew Prior(?), 'On report of my Ld. Somers being
　　removed from [his office of] Ld.[High] Chancellor'
　　[1700]
　　[Crum w1012]

c.189, p. 175

w0882 When envy reigns there is no room for peace:
Instruct us Lord to entertain this guest.

Sir John Strangways, 'In invidum'

b.304, p. 40

w0883 When Europe's kings first couch'd the vengeful
lance
Confides her last, best hope on general peace.

Diggle Box: Poetry Box XI/63

w0884 When Eve the fruit had tasted
To eat it is no sin-a.

'On Dr. Sherlock's taking the oaths'

Poetry Box VII/5

w0885 When every bird begins to build and sing,
And sends the willing chief renew'd to war.

[Hester Lynch Thrale Piozzi]

Greatheed Box/16

w0886 When ev'ry want-wit, each mechanic slave
Me, to affect you with a chaster love.

'To a gentlewoman for her great discourtesy to her old
friend'

b.205, fol. 90v

w0887 When evil boils overwhelm a state
In spite of Shakespeare and of reason.

'Epistle IV. To the Rev. Mr. John Nenn on the
administration of Lieut. Governor M—er'

fc.100, p. 20

w0888 When exulting we tell how our fathers of yore,
And who robs man of these must offend the All-wise!

'Verses addressed to Englishmen'

c.140, p. 214

w0889 When fair Eliza seeks to know,
Believe the care it feels.

[William Boscawen], 'To a lady at Bath who had
consulted Mr Williams the fortune-teller'

fc.106

w0890 When fair Imperia's flatt'ring paramours
But she already hath produced fruit.

Sir Thomas Urquhart, 'Of Imperia, who was supposed
by some to be a virgin'

fb.217, p. 120

w0891 When Fairfax hath o'errun the land
May have free leave to plunder.

'A ballad to the tune of the fourth Psalm 1646 . . . the
whole indeed is imperfect'

b.54, p. 1010

w0892 When faithless senates venably [sic] betray
And he that violates its shade shall bleed.

Thomas Day, 'Stanzas written on the failure of the
application for an equal representation in
Parliament . . . by . . . Europ. Mag. June 1791'

File 14205

w0893 When fam'd Augusta, royal fair,
As pity's tear empearls thine eyes.

John Lockman, 'To the Countess of Middlesex: on
presenting her ladyship with Yarico, an American
pastoral drama; writ by the author, and set to music by
Mr. John Christopher Smith . . . anno 1750'

c.267/2, p. 242

w0894 When fam'd Pandora to the clouds withdrew,
Fire to the mind, and poison to the veins.

John Lockman, 'Label for a gin-bottle . . . [by] the
thunderer . . . Feb. 1751'

c.267/1, p. 192

w0895 When fam'd Pandora, to the earth,
Success must crown, what you befriend.

John Lockman, 'On occasion of the play, for the
benefit of the Middlesex Hospital, for sick and lame,
and lying-in women, on Wednesday the 16: Decr. 1761,
at the Theater Royal in Covent Garden'

c.267/1, p. 315

w0896 When famine spread over the land,
The judges do duly deplore.

'Charade 86' [message]

c.389

w0897 When fancied sorrows wake the players' art,
And each good actor prove an honest man.

[George?] Colman, 'On Mr. Powell written by . . . and
spoken by Mr. Holland. A prologue'

c.83/2, no. 717; c.341, p. 133

w0898 When Fanny blooming fair
May heaven and she refuse.

[Philip Dormer Stanhope, 4th earl of Chesterfield],
'6th song' [written on Lady Fanny Shirley]

Accession 97.7.40, p. 10; Poetry Box II/1 (applied to
Frances Payne, lady Lavington)

w0899 When Fanny first chants in the echoing grove,
To be sung by her ravishing voice.

'A pastoral song'

c.83/2, no. 282

w0900 When far off the night storm flies
Is but a point, compar'd to all.

[Robert Merry], 'To Anna Matilda an extract'

c.140, p. 166

[978]

W0901 When Farquhar's bold highwaymen met with a
                                                priest
They cry, hold my good folks, the church is our
                                                guide.
    W[illiam] S[mith], 'On the high price of butter. Some
    said and thought occasioned by a Revd. Dean's lady
    and the Revd. Hen: Heigham'
    Smith Papers, folder 71

W0902 When fate had decreed
Is restor'd million-fold, in a Gibbon.
    'The loss restored. An epigram to the fashionable
    admirers of a popular historian' [18 October 1788]
    Poetry Box III/8

W0903 When figures four set on their head,
The Turk, the Pope and's eldest son.
    [Sir Fleetwood Sheppard?], 'Prophecy, translated
    from the French'
    fb.70, p. 291

W0904 When fir'd by gold's destructive thirst,
Then smites you to the grave.
    John Lockman, 'Will Horse-Tail, on the mock
    anti-Gallican . . . Aug. 1750'
    c.267/1, p. 65

W0905 When first Columbus left his native shore
Now what I am, ingenious ladies say.
    'Another [rebus]'
    Diggle Box: Poetry Box XI/71

W0906 When first created things began
And from oblivion save.
    'An enigma'
    Poetry Box I/15

W0907 When first Florella I addrest,
With painful pleasure die.
    [William Carpenter], 'On Florella'
    c.247, p. 115

W0908 When first I did presume to come,
At glory's fire without being brent.
    [R. Williams]
    b.216, p. 151

W0909 When first I in this stage of life appear,
I am man's offspring, tho' I'm not a man.
    'A riddle' [answered by 'Suppose a picture . . .']
    c.578, p. 50

When first I past the happy night,   W0910
And make me sigh, and die for love, | Of thee, and
                                        only thee.
    'Another by the same hand' [as 'Tho' in their
    flame . . .']
    fb.142, p. 49

When first I saw thee graceful move,   W0911
In pity, O, forbear to hate.
    c.549, p. 11

When first I saw thee thou didst gently [sweetly]   W0912
                                        play
A fair sweet creature with a double heart.
    'To his Celia'
    [Crum W1035]
    b.205, fol. 46r; c.356 (with extra lines?)

When first I sought fair Celia's love,   W0913
Should I remember mine?
    [Soame Jenyns], 'A song'
    c.147, p. 46

When first I strove your virgin heart to gain,   W0914
Lead a happy life, and find a happy grave.
    R. S., 'To his mistress'
    fb.142, p. 30

When first I was bound out of Waterman's Hall   W0915
And steadily row my wherry.
    [John Walker?], 'The waterman'
    fc.108, fol. 69

When first, in fate's malignant hour,   W0916
Give one kiss more—and kill me quite.
    'To a young lady'
    c.487, p. 26

When first Lavinia to these waters came,   W0917
With chastity—she turn'd a prostitute.
    'Epigram. (Bade.) . . . imitation'
    c.81/1, no. 74

When first Lucinda here we came   W0918
Adieu the sweets of Arno's vale.
    [Jm. Richard Onely, trans.] 'A song' [by Lionel
    Cranfield, 1st duke of Dorset]
    c.358, p. 140; see also 'When here, Lucinda, first . . .'.

When first my eyes did behold thy fair feature,   W0919
I will let my laughter fly here disdain and coy
                                        cruelty.
    Poetry Box VII/76

W0920 When first my free heart,
I will seek for my cure.

'The platonic lover'

fb.107, p. 50

W0921 When first o'er Psyche's angel breast
Like meteors o'er the heav'n of beauty.

William [Robert] Spencer

Poetry Box XII/74

W0922 When first old Father Thames espied
The true and certain heir apparent of the crown.

'The same [a Latin poem entitled Theodoria] in
English'

fc.58, p. 160

W0923 When first simple Strephon perceiv'd that his heart
But boldly advance with a How do you do.

'How do you do'

fc.85, fol. 117v

W0924 When first Sir Loin his knighthood gain'd
I'll take upon Sir Reverence.

[Phanuel Bacon], 'Qui techno maritur brevis est
virum iste pirates qui descendit honor horridibus'

c.237, fols. 54, 68v ('Fictus honor brevis est . . .')

W0925 When first the duel reach'd the tender ear
Kiss'd her dear boy, and left him to repose.

'The Countess of Bristol to the Lord Hervey, after his
duel with Mr. Pulteney'

c.570/3, p. 109, p. 105 (first ten lines)

W0926 When first the early matrons run
On her hast'ning funeral.

'On a woman dying in childbed'

b.62, p. 30

W0927 When first the globe by Archimedes design'd
The more they search, the more our pow'r is known.

'Archimedes's globe'

c.94

W0928 When first the infant leaves the darksome space,
The pile forbid to raise its impious head.

'On language'

c.244, p. 628

W0929 When first the seals the good Lord King resign'd
His years no less may yield the world surprise.

'On Lord Hardwicke being appointed Lord High
Chancellor of Great Britain in the room of Lord
Talbot deceased'

c.360/1, p. 221

W0930 When first the Tatler to a mute was turn'd
'Tis the same sun that does himself succeed.

[Nahum] Tate, 'On the Spectator' [pr. 1712 (Foxon
T60)]
[Crum W1063]

c.391, p. 46

W0931 When first the widow's mournful case I read,
What is the widow's, son's, and daughter's share.

[arithmetic problem]

c.93

W0932 When first the world from the black chaos rose
Love join'd their souls and heav'n seal'd each heart.

[Sir Charles Sedley], 'Matrimonÿ pensitatio' [pr. 1702
(Foxon S193)]

fb.108, p. 43

W0933 When first this duel reached the tender ears
Kiss'd her dear boy and left him to repose.

'A great lady's speech to her son on her first seeing
him after his being wounded' [satire; supposedly the
Countess of Bristol to John lord Hervey after his duel
with William Pulteney]

Poetry Box X/126

W0934 When first this humble roof I knew,
The all of life is love.

General [John] Burgoyne, 'Love the all of life'

c.94

W0935 When first this infant world its form put on,
The faultless body, and the blameless mind.

[Nicholas] Rowe, 'The golden age'

c.244, p. 181

W0936 When first this mighty world began
Till death dissolves the union. | Till death dissolves
the union [&c.]

[John Walker?], 'The origin of foppery an anniversary
song'

fc.108, fol. 42v

W0937 When first th'omnific word with plastic call
Forever knowing ever yet unknown.

S[tephen] Simpson, 'Knowledge'

c.563

W0938 When first to Cambridge we do come
We may be parsons when we will.

'Song 225'

c.555, p. 356

W0939 When first unhappy Phaedra crown'd the stage
With tow'ring head, to meet his parent sun.

'Prologue spoken at the Theater Royal in Lincoln Inn Fields, 1722. on the revival of Phaedra and Hippolytus, a tragedy, written by Mr. Edmund Smith'

c.360/2, no. 122

W0940 When first we hear the boatswain bray,
Till charm'd by the song of heo hea heo.

'Song 10'

c.555, p. 14

W0941 When first with thoughtless look I view'd
And in the flame it dies.

'An ode on the same [to Miranda on her recovery]'

Poetry Box I/42 (cf. i/41)

W0942 When first you saw your husband and he you
The sick goddess fixed and wondrous kind.

[Sir Aston Cokayne], 'To Mrs Theophila Campbell my cousin german'

b.275, p. 100

W0943 When Flora deck'd the meadows gay,
Then hang me when I'm dead and rotten.

'The ladies washing'

c.530, p. 74

W0944 When Floro talks of Sacharissa's charms
You can doom thousands—you can bless but one.

'On the honorable Miss Mary Howe, maid of honor to her royal highness Caroline Princess of Wales—1722'

c.360/2, no. 95

W0945 When fly false Holland's ensigns now
And struck her flag to rise no more. | Rule
                                        Brittania &c.

W[illiam] Smith, 'Written during the play 18 Oct. 1797 on . . . Duncan['s] victory over the Dutch Oct. 11th . . . Wandering Jew'

Smith Papers, folder 73

W0946 When foes are o'ercome, we preserve them from
                                        slaughter
I'll maintain with my life, is heraldry good.

[Jonathan Swift], 'A poem on William Wood, brazier, tinker, hardware man, coiner, founder, and esquire. Writ in Ireland'

c.360/2, no. 134

W0947 When fond Clelia's maid to forego
Go poets and envy the tongue.

c.221

W0948 When foolish subjects banish kings before
They have their thanks and pay, in blood and gore.

c.189, p. 2

W0949 When Foote to George Colman his patent had sold
And I'll bet you ten pounds, that he'll yawn for a
                                        year.

'Friendly counsel'

Diggle Box: Poetry Box XI/69

W0950 When, for the loss of her, I [?] sigh,
And I remov'd to worlds, to man unknown.

John Lockman, 'Epitaph for Mrs. Mary Riddell, wife to James Riddell esq. Of Caistrin Norfolk, who died 12 April 1762, aged 27'

c.267/1, p. 393

W0951 When forc'd the dear fair one to leave,
Might assist to diminish my pain.

'Absence'

c.344, p. 87 (incomplete?)

W0952 When forced to part from those we love
Perhaps to part forever.

Poetry Box XII/95

W0953 When fortune smiles, ye favorites beware,
Your goddess is as fickle as she's fair.

'Fickle fortune'

c.360/3, no. 168

W0954 When fortune's kindest boons are drest
If Fancy—thou hast frown'd.

Poetry Box III/59

W0955 When forty winters shall besiege thy brow
And see thy blood warm when thou seest it cold.

[William Shakespeare], 'To one that would die a maid' [Sonnet 11]

b.205, fol. 54v; c.94

W0956 When fraud and faction, with united force,
Full of the joy a patriot deed inspires!

John Lockman, 'On the earl of Shaftesbury's going to Southwold, to forward there the outfit of the [Herring] Society's busses . . . June 1754'

c.267/1, p. 144

W0957 When [torn] fray begins
Then [?] the law.

'Another prophecy of Bede's exponed by Mother Shipton'

Poetry Box VIII/32

W0958 When friends shall shake their heads and say,
Persuade the world trouble me no more.

    [Thomas Flatman], 'Oh the sad day!'

fb.140, p. 101; see also 'Oh, the sad day! . . .'.

W0959 When friendship pants with anxious care,
Is little more than dross.

    [William Hayley]

File 7051

W0960 When, from the ark, the dove had flown her round,
May soon to all their ancient glory rise.

    John Lockman, 'Seeing the first barrel of herrings
    opened, sent hither from the British buss . . . July
    1750'

c.267/1, p. 175

W0961 When from the patriarch sent the curious maid
Nor dying Jacob scarce his sons forgive.

    'On Dinah'

File 13409

W0962 When from the virgin's birth a thousand years
And extreme grief shall be the common sum.

    'A prophecy that the world was either to be destroyed
    or in great desolation in the year 1588'

c.158, p. 114

W0963 When, from their long captivity God did recall
With joy, to bring his full-ear'd harvest home.

    J. B., 'Psalm 126 . . . Dec. 24. 1702'

b.63, p. 105, 108

W0964 When from your cherry lips I did receive
By cherries twain at length he perisht.

    'Upon two kisses'

b.205, fol. 42v

W0965 When Gabriel Archangel bright
Will evermore resound. | Amen

    'Of the visitation of our B[lessed] Lady. July. 2'

a.30[8]

W0966 When Gaby possession had got of the hall
For if Gaby don't like 'em, he'll pick out their eyes. |
                    Which nobody [can deny]

    [Herbert Beaver], 'On the master of a Hall in Oxford
    his picking out an I marked in a cushion: causing a U
    to be put in its place'
    [Crum W1094a]

fc.51, p. 33; c.241, p. 18

W0967 When 'gainst its sovereign, reason, it rebel
Who take the care of our soul's requiem.

    [Sir Philip Wodehouse], 'Upon Doctor William
    Smyth prebend . . .'

b.131, back (no. 152)

W0968 When Garrick rests, shall every Muse
A tear bedew his urn.

    [Charles Burney, the younger], 'Garrick'

c.37, p. 62

W0969 When gay in youthful bloom my power I try,
Or else ignobly in the jakes expire.

    'A riddle'

c.360/3, no. 220

W0970 When gay Philander fell a prize
And own Philander's lays are sweet.

    'A song'

c.358, p. 27

W0971 When General Monck unveils his hood,
Then on, and all shall cry God save the King.

c.160, fol. 102

W0972 When genius flourish'd and when Shakespeare wrote
And pour my praises, breathe my thanks to you.

    H[annah] More, 'A prologue'

c.341, p. 108

W0973 When gentle Thames rolls back her silver streams
And my poor suff'ring heart shall be at peace.

    Philip Wharton, 1st duke of Wharton(?), 'The duke
    of Wharton's Whens [sic] part 2nd' [1723; copied from
    Harl. 6933]
    [Crum W1095b (var.)]

c.468

W0974 When gentlefolks their sweethearts leave behind
When neither I can read, nor he can write.

    [John] Gay, 'Kitty Carrot—in Gay's What d'ye call it'

c.360/2, no. 161

W0975 When George, the great Elector of Hanover
They march'd away, and so the farce was done.

    'The Dutch embassy' [pr. 1714/15? (Foxon D558)]
    [Crum W1096]

fc.58, p. 112; c.570/1, p. 21

W0976 When George undutiful can prove
The same I'll be in years.

    George Bent, 'On his mother's expressing a distrust of
    his filial regard'

c.504, p. 59

W0977   When God Almighty had his palace fram'd
To add a place wanting in God's creation.

> [John Dunton, 'Stinking fish', pr. 1708 (Foxon D540)]
> [Crum W1098]
>
> c.188, p. 68

W0978   When God, contracted to humanity,
Die to the world, as he died for it then.

> K[atherine] P[hilips], ['2 Cor. 5 18. God was in Christ reconciling the world to himself']
> [Crum W1101]
>
> b.118, p. 45

W0979   When God hath stampt his image upon a mite
With joys eternal in Christ my only rest.

> 'A godly child's speech to it mourning parents after death'
>
> b.284, p. 59

W0980   When God himself as sacred stories tell
The soper [soprano] birds their treble voices raise.

> [Maurice Johnson], 'On the sovereignty of man, imperfect'
>
> c.229/2, fol. 10 (incomplete)

W0981   When God reveal'd his gracious name
And shout the blessings home.

> 'Hymn 31st'
>
> c.562, p. 36

W0982   When God vouchsafes me length of days,
This well perform'd partakes their (?) joy.

> [Edmund Wodehouse], 'March 28 [1715]'
>
> b.131, p. 189

W0983   When God vouchsafes us mortals leave
Thus join the saints, the blest above.

> [Edmund Wodehouse], 'Aug. 27 [1715]'
>
> b.131, p. 253

W0984   When God went forth before the world begun
To be conceiv'd by frail mortality.

> [Thomas Gurney], 'On the glorious work of the eternal Three'
>
> c.213

W0985   When godly Theodosius
Our happy way may take. | Amen

> 'Of the same day [St. Peter, August 1]'
>
> a.30[19]

W0986   When God's afflicting hand
Thus us'd for his eternal gain.

> Charles Atherton Allnutt, 'Now no chastening for the present seemeth to be joyous, but grievous . . . 12th Hebrews 11 verse'
>
> c.112, p. 27

W0987   When good King William ruled this land
'And leave her but fifteen!'

> 'Relic of ancient poetry'
>
> Poetry Box IV/172

W0988   When good men's corpse in graves enclosed lie,
Their famous art do pierce the azure sky.

> c.339, p. 324

W0989   When good queen Bess did rule this land
But here she'd rule alone.

> 'A new ballad to the tune of Chevy Chase' [comparing Queen Anne and Marlborough to Queen Elizabeth and Essex; pr. 1708 (Foxon N88)]
> [Crum W1113]
>
> b.90, p. 15

W0990   When Grafton that clown,
Had you fought me without steel bodies.

> 'On the Duke of Grafton's death'
>
> b.111, p. 142

W0991   When grateful nations bid their paeans rise
And fiery vengeance tinge the reddening sky.

> c.115

W0992   When grave divinity thought fit
His Lordship with a lady's mien.

> 'The review, or, the case fairly stated on both sides' [pr. 1734 (Foxon T324)]
>
> c.570/4, p. 44

W0993   When great Eliza Britain's scepter sway'd
He, first in science—thou, supreme in art.

> F. Pigott, 'To Mr. Bacon—upon his sculpture'
>
> Poetry Box IV/153

W0994   When great events occur, or only such
By him of light and glory with their maker.

> b.49, p. 9

W0995   When great Sir William, echo'd to the skies,
Not punish errors that proceed from love.

> 'On the marriage of Sir William Blacket, bart. with the Lady Barbara Villiers. A poem'
>
> c.530, p. 19

W0996 When greatness claims or merit gives
To have acted well thine own.

    'Occasioned by Mrs. Oldfield's being buried in
    Westminster Abbey'

    Poetry Box I/7

W0997 When Grecian Thespis in a barbarous age
Is to be heard most patiently by you.

    Henry James Leigh, 'Prologue written by . . . and
    spoken by himself before The tragedy of the
    distressed mother performed at Addlestrop by ladies
    and gentlemen'

    c.504, p. 124

W0998 When Grecians liv'd, auspicious time!
He call'd him soon from Teo's isle.

    [John Lockman], 'Stanzas'

    c.268 (first part), p. 43

W0999 When green with the renown of heroes ring,
Each varying impulse of the passive soul.

    John Lockman, 'To Miss Gambarini: after hearing her
    sing, and accompany, (on the harpsichord,) a piece of
    her own composing . . . Jany 1760'

    c.267/I, p. 280

W1000 When guilt distracts my lab'ring breast
And each in heaven of [i.e., or] hell appear.

    'The anchor set to music by a correspondent'

    c.91, p. 342

W1001 When Hamilton's grace, to obtain a green string,
The duke he was knighted, the earl bes[hi]t.

    [Thomas Hamilton, 6th earl of Haddington], 'The
    installation'

    c.458/2, p. 158

W1002 When haughty monarchs their proud state expose,
And where he found his refuge fix'd his shrine.

    [Simon] Harcourt, 1st viscount Harcourt, 'To the
    Queen at her coming to Christ C[hurch]'
    [Crum W1122]

    fc.24, p. 56

W1003 When haughty thoughts impuff thee, then
Both in the other world, and this.

    'Relating to the first emblem'

    c.189, p. 79

W1004 When he gives words for words, he's fain
Wherewith to weigh them.

    Sir Thomas Urquhart, 'Why a certain fool did draw
    out his speeches very leisurely'

    fb.217, p. 39

W1005 When he met with the poetess Panura,
To prosecute a Heliconian rapture.

    Sir Thomas Urquhart, 'An amorous contestation
    betwixt a poet, and a poetess'

    fb.217, p. 140

W1006 When he, who stirr'd(?) fam'd Julius, shook with
                         dread,
Proud of his charge, see Neptune smooths thy
                         way!

    John Lockman, 'To the duchess of Buckingham: writ
    in the passage between Dover and Calais . . . 20 June
    1741'

    c.267/I, p. 62

W1007 When heaven surrounded Britain by the main,
Who, bating but one blot, had been a saint!

    'The invasion' [1688]
    [Crum W1126]

    fb.70, p. 305; b.111, p. 495

W1008 When heav'nly Wigmore shows her moving charms
And may the poet grace thy nuptial bed.

    [Robert Cholmeley], 'To Mrs Elisa: Wigmore just
    after an acquaintance with her and just before going
    into the country'

    c.190, p. 125

W1009 When Helen fir'd the Asian world to arms
The hearts had flam'd, but not the walls of Troy.

    'To Mrs. Longe at court 1750'

    c.360/3, no. 80

W1010 When H.E.M.P.E. is spun,
England's done.

    [on Henry VIII, Edward VI, Mary I, Philip II,
    Elizabeth I]

    fb.69, p. 206

W1011 When Henry the Eighth pulled the Papacy down,
Sold altar and pews and transported the parson.

    'On selling the old church at Brentford by auction
    1763' [followed by 'When the parish of Brentford . . .']

    c.74

W1012 When Henry's fury first grew tame
As they go on we shall proceed.

    'Imitation of the first part of Hudibras'

    b.371, no. 29

W1013 When here, Lucinda, first we came,
Adieu the sweets of Arno's vale!

    J[m.] R[ichard] Onely, trans., 'Arno's vale by the late
    Duke of Dorset'

    Poetry Box IV/150; fc.135; Poetry Box II/37; see also
    'When first Lucinda here . . .'.

W1014   When heroes kings or noblemen
Then never fear what death can do.

     [John Walker?], 'Elegaic epistle on Tom Grimalkin a
     favorite large cat—to Miss Maria'

     fc.108, fol. 61

W1015   When high the greatest monarch's fame was blown
He only could command, but you inspire.

     'To Mrs Colt, at Tunbridge Wells 1713'

     c.360/1, p. 77

W1016   When his lov'd Germans George was forc'd to leave,
Each prince to govern, where he'll govern well.

     'On King George [I]' [pr. 1715 (Foxon L117)]
     [Crum W1137]

     c.570/1, p. 2

W1017   When Hobert's air, and captivating eyes
And quit the Mammon of unrighteousness.

     'Satire on Miss Reade [later Willis], late of Hackney,
     wrote at Bath—1741' [answered by 'Sure naught but
     disappointment . . .']
     [Crum W1139]

     c.360/1, p. 257

W1018   When Hodge had number'd up, how many score
His body fell, out fled his frighted soul.

     'Hodge's observations on the monument 1678[/9] . . .'
     [the Pyramid]
     [Crum W1141; POAS II.146]

     b.54, p. 1147

W1019   When holy scriptures mentions the rewarding
Of works we read not, for, but still according.

     [Francis Quarles], 'On reward' [Divine fancies III,
     100]

     b.137, p. 176; b.118, p. 220

W1020   When honest Thespis first a-strolling went
And may thy black-ey'd Susan still be chaste.

     [Joseph Spence], 'To Mr Andrews the comedian . . .
     Septr. 16, 1752'

     Spence Papers, folder 158; c.360/3, no. 236

W1021   When honor does the soldier call,
And glorious he dies.

     'The soldier—The hive'

     c.244, p. 105

W1022   When honor is conferred or friend to friend,
While maid, her father, husband when a wife.

     'Of genuflection, a problem'

     c.356

W1023   When hope lay hushed in silent night,
And died and lov'd too late.

     'William and Margaret, an ancient ballad'

     c.391, p. 96

W1024   When Horace worked his lyric strains,
And bids its beauties live.

     [William Boscawen], 'Verses to the ladies of
     Plainw[oo]d[?], near Llangollen, with the author's
     translation of the Odes of Horace'

     fc.106, p. 21

W1025   When horror seizes on my heart
My will at thy command.

     Joshua Toft

     c.517, fol. 1r

W1026   When Hulse for some trifling unorthodox jests
Now damn you (says he) who says I'm a fool.

     'On William Cheselden esqr, surgeon to the late
     Queen Caroline'

     c.360/1, p. 209

W1027   When I affirm, that of a thousand gallants,
Of lesser moment, on your commendation.

     Sir Thomas Urquhart, 'To my Lord [crossed out]'

     fb.217, p. 122

W1028   When I am dead, and doctors kn[ow] not why
Naked, you have odds enough of any man.

     J[ohn] D[onne], 'The damp'
     [Crum W1148]

     b.148, p. 2

W1029   When I am gone, and these of mine remain
My earth in atoms, men may read this verse.

     [George Daniel], 'Scattered fancies i'

     b.121, fol. 17

W1030   When I begin sadly to think upon
Will make a stall a court a *crêche* a throne.

     'On Christmas Day'

     Poetry Box x/13; see also 'But art thou come . . .'.

W1031   When I behold a woman rarely fair,
Divinely held betwixt her body and mind.

     [C. T.?] 'On the Lady An[ne] Cecil [later countess of
     Oxford], the Ld: Burleigh's daughter'
     [Crum W1155]

     b.200, p. 95

W1032   When I behold one fair
No matter what my outside be.

     H[enry] C[olman], 'On beauty'
     [Crum W1159]

     b.2, p. 44

W1033 When I can pay my parents, or my king
Begin with bribes, and finish with betraying.

> [Richard] Corbett, 'Dr. Corbett to the Duke of
> Buckingham'
> [Crum W1163]
>
> b.200, p. 215

W1034 When I can read my title clear
Across my peaceful breast.

> 'Hymn 68th'
>
> c.562, p. 81

W1035 When I collect all faculties I have,
For all things else are frail and vanity.

> 'No help in man'
>
> c.187, p. 37

W1036 When I consider, everything that grows
As he takes from you, I engraft you now.

> [William] Shakespeare [Sonnet XV]
>
> c.94

W1037 When I consider life 'tis all a cheat
Which fools us young and beggars us when old.

> [interlinear interpretation of the soliloquy in Dryden's
> Aureng-Zebe IV. i]
>
> Poetry Box V/3; c.83/3, no. 919 (var.); c.53, fol. 50 (var.;
> transcribed by Miss Glass on her sampler)

W1038 When I died last; and dear I die
But O, no man could hold it for 'twas thine.

> [John Donne], 'Canzone'
> [Crum W1165]
>
> b.114, p. 285; b.148, p. 79

W1039 When I do tell the clock, that tells the time,
Save breed,—to brave him when he takes thee hence.

> [William] Shakespeare
>
> c.94

W1040 When I first from my mother came
And part devoured be by hogs.

> [ ] R., 'Riddle [a wild fool]'
>
> Poetry Box VII/49

W1041 When I first the Lord Holdernesse saw
That woman won't always be kind.

> Miss [ ] Montagu, 'on the Earl of Holdernesse then
> about 15 years of age wrote by Miss Montagu daughter
> of Lady Mary Wortley Montagu a young lady about
> 14 years of age at Tunbridge Wells'
>
> c.360/1, p. 251

W1042 When I gaily fill the cheerful glass,
Social mirth our bumpers crown. | Hob or Nob &c.

> 'Song 35'
>
> c.555, p. 57

W1043 When I go musing all alone,
Naught so damn'd as melancholy.

> [Robert] Burton, 'Abstract upon melancholy'
>
> fb.142, p. 42

W1044 When I had seen two dear friends here lie dead:
I curs'd the cause, for which their blood was shed.

> Sir Thomas Urquhart, 'All the ten categories are
> comprehended in the first line of the distich'
>
> fb.217, p. 39

W1045 When I have wanted company sometimes
By whole book being a continual fault.

> [Sir Aston Cokayne], 'To my cousin Mr William
> Milward'
>
> b.275, p. 48

W1046 When I in court had spent my tender prime
To serve my Savior and the King of kings.

> 'On Mr. Charles Wrey' [aged 17; son to Sir William
> Wray; Ashbie Church, Lincolnshire]
> [Crum W1172]
>
> fb.143, p. 24

W1047 When I in prayer, pray God look on me
So let Christ's blood my soul clear wash from
                          shame.

> Lady Jane Cavendish
> [Crum W1173]
>
> b.233, p. 40

W1048 When I most fully am assur'd,
Thus highly tend to make us wise.

> [Edmund Wodehouse], 'June 9 [1715]'
>
> b.131, p. 222

W1049 When I my precious hours did vainly spend
That sweetens life and can perfume the grave.

> [John Norris, of Bemerton?], 'The young man's
> looking-glass Octr. 12 1711'
>
> c.548

W1050 When I pass'd Paul's and travell'd in the walk
Thou shalt not change deeds with him for his tomb.

> Richard Corbett, 'On Dr. Ravis, Bp. of London' [d.
> 1609]
> [Crum W1181]
>
> b.200, p. 243; b.205, fol. 80v

W1051   When I perceiv'd my hours were flying fast
When to appear before Him I presume.

     'Song of Hezekiah king of Judah, upon his recovery
from sickness. Isaiah 38 chap. from [Bishop Lowth's
version]'

c.515, fol. 32

W1052   When I protest I love you, straight you cry
I covet much, I fain would lie with you.

     'To his m[ist]r[es]s A: P:'

b.205, fol. 47r

W1053   When I recall the luckless night
How endless been my theme.

     [George] H[owar]d, [6th earl of Carlisle], 'Ovid'

c.197, p. 43

W1054   When I reflect, and human nature strip
But sink, and are forgotten, as a dream.

     'The folly, and uncertainty of life'

fc.54, p. 48

W1055   When I review these rude unfinish'd lays
And saves their rugged rhymes from Vulcan's pow'r.

     'Sonnet . . . 1784' [in reference to 'Guy an epic poem']

c.224, flyleaf

W1056   When I see the bright lies that my heart doth
                           enthrall,
So her folly makes whole whom her beauty doth
                           wound.

     [William Walsh], 'The antidote' [usual wording is
'bright nymph']

c.223, p. 65

W1057   When I shall feel the approach of my decease,
And love will raise the soul to the joys above.

     [Edmund Wodehouse], 'Novr. 4 1714'

b.131, p. 77

W1058   When I shall leave this world and cease to be
My epitaph be this here lies a sinner.

     'An epitaph'

b.356, p. 266

W1059   When I survey the bright design
To gain the promis'd coast!

     'An ode'

c.139, p. 507

W1060   When I survey the wondrous cross
Demands my soul, my life, my all.

     [Isaac Watts, Hymns and spiritual songs (1707),
bk. III, Hymn 7]

c.180, p. 18; c.58 (stanzas 1–2)

W1061   When I survey this mighty frame
Offending Thee no more.

     [William Meston], 'A sacred ode'

c.570/1, p. 159; Poetry Box IV/88

W1062   When I the human frame survey
A paradise create.

     'Moral reflections on man'

Poetry Box IV/157

W1063   When, I thro' love, a goddess make her
Descends, to nourish all below.

     [Phanuel Bacon], 'A song'

c.237, fol. 49

W1064   When I thy friend a boon from thee would borrow
Thou shalt have thanks tomorrow not today.

     'Of Paulinus'

c.356

W1065   When I to sleep address my mind
Then in return, I'll cry out, encore.

     'Song'
     [Crum W1191]

c.358, p. 82; b.382(11a)

W1066   When I unto the fameless Devia now
Her faith retracted, old, and overworn.

     [George Daniel]

b.121, fol. 35v

W1067   When I wake with painful brow,
And join with me in ha! ha! ha!

     'Crying, and laughing'

c.83/3, no. 966

W1068   When I was a freshman old age did appear
Is, that young people ought to know better.

     'The antiquity of man, a poem by Uncle James'

Poetry Box XII/103

W1069   When I was a young one, what girl was like me
I teach that to others, I once did myself.

     [Isaac Bickerstaffe], 'A song'; 'A song by Dorcas in
Tho[ma]s and Sally'

fc.85, fol. 77v

W1070   When I was to perfection brought
Such likeness can't be drawn by you.

     [Phanuel Bacon], 'A riddle'

c.237, fol. 78v

W1071   When I was young and debonair
The fairest girl to me, is Brown.

> George Lyttelton, 1st baron Lyttelton, 'Impromptu by . . . on Miss Brown'
> [Crum W1198]
>
> c.150, p. 120; c.378, p. 43

W1072   When I was young, and yet but Mary Sayer
But much good do him—he allow'd her such.

> [Sir Philip Wodehouse], 'Mary Burley may I ruler be'
>
> b.131, back (no. 69)

W1073   When I was young, I saw much life,
And say, pray do your worst Sir.

> 'The old man'
>
> Poetry Box IV/60

W1074   When I was younger, love cloy'd me,
Contract my stomach, or enlarge my diet.

> 'Wrote by a lady, who lamented the loss of youth'
>
> c.74; see also 'Coming a tender girl . . .'.

W1075   When I your face your legs and fingers praise
Think you I'm not the man I'd seem to be?

> R[obert] Shirley, 1st earl of Ferrers, 'To Galla. From Martial'
>
> c.347, p. 32

W1076   When I your heart my own could call,
Yet I would live and die with thee.

> 'Another dialogue between Strephon and Phyllis. By the same hand [as 'Grim death . . .']. A love quarrel. out of Horace'
>
> fb.142, p. 55

W1077   When in a convent guest, my thoughts did muse
When that's received well which was well meant.

> [Sir Richard Bulstrode], 'My first dedication of my poems in English, to the Princess [Louisa] of England' [between 1701 and 1711]
>
> fb.88, p. 117v

W1078   When in a gloomy temper o'er my tomb,
The paltry pleasures here, and look for those above.

> 'An epitaph on Mr. More'
>
> c.244, p. 285

W1079   When in a nymph's soft-heaving breast,
And all thy transports end in shame.

> [John Lockman], 'Advice to the fair'
>
> c.268 (first part), p. 87

W1080   When in a shade and all alone
Think then, O think my love is true.

> 'A shepherd to his nymph who told him he did not love her' [answered by 'When last alone . . .']
>
> fb.142, p. 54

W1081   When in heav'n we thunder hear,
Quitting ev'ry lesser care.

> [William Popple, trans.], '[Horace] book 3rd. ode 5th'
>
> fc.104/2, p. 218

W1082   When in learn'd Dummer's car I ride,
His chariot to the sky.

> John Lockman, 'To Jeremiah Dummer esqr., on his favoring me frequently, with the use of his chariot . . . June 1741'
>
> c.267/1, p. 156; c.268 (first part), p. 19

W1083   When in my troubles, on the Lord
Of peace, they war and bloodshed seek.

> 'Psalm 120. Morning prayer 27 day'
>
> c.264/3, p. 68

W1084   When in my younger years I had scarce pith
Of else the husband, I had first, to woo me.

> Sir Thomas Urquhart, 'The regrets of a gentlewoman in her second marriage'
>
> fb.217, p. 177

W1085   When in old times th'almighty Father sat
Nor he himself could bear, but as omnipotent.

> 'On the redemption of mankind by our ever blessed Lord and Savior Jesus Christ'
>
> c.186, p. 106

W1086   When in sad exile I complain'd
Then fiercer run to arms.

> [Sir William Trumbull], 'Ps[alm] 120'
>
> Trumbull Box: Poetry Box XIII/23

W1087   When in the cockpit all was grim,
Then growling up he goes.

> 'The midshipman'
>
> Poetry Box X/53

W1088   When in the garden God plac'd Eve
Our miseries from Eve.

> [Robert Cholmeley], 'The female miracle to Zelinda'
>
> c.190, p. 59

W1089   When in the grave my body lies,
That at my death he may my soul receive.

> [Edmund Wodehouse], 'Apr. 10 [1715]'
>
> b.131, p. 195

W1090   When in the night I muster up my wits,
So I commend thee to his helping hand.

    'To the reader'

    c.187, p. 1

W1091   When in thy cause O Lord, we fight,
Whose blood was first a martyr's styl'd.

    Charles Atherton Allnutt, 'Collect for Saint Stephen's
    day'

    c.112, p. 57

W1092   When in your pencil's matchless art
In polish'd arts of spotless fame.

    'To a lady on seeing some landscapes of her drawing'

    c.89, p. 104

W1093   When Irus on his deathbed lay
I'll bid him take his hog again.

    John Shackleton, 'Restitution a tale'

    c.241, p. 31

W1094   When Irus wanton'd in the pride of youth
And all thy virtue, live upon thy tomb.

    'The courtier'

    fc.60, p. 98; c.244, p. 602

W1095   When Islay to show his fine delicate taste
With a clump of Scotch firs by way of a screen.

    [Philip Dormer Stanhope, 4th earl of Chesterfield],
    'On Lord Islay's gardens on Hounslow Heath'

    Poetry Box x/120 and 121; see also 'Old Islay . . .'.

W1096   When Israel came from out a foreign land
To walk upon where none was e'er before.

    'Exodus 14.22'

    c.160, fol. 55

W1097   When Israel first provok'd the living Lord
Than little Jordan can compare to Thames.

    [Charles Sackville, 6th earl of Dorset], 'An epigram on
    King James the 2d. who abdicated the throne
    December the 23 anno Christi MDCLXXXVIII'

    c.360/1, p. 91; see also next.

W1098   When Israel first provok'd the living Lord
Much as B[isho]p Burnet did St. Paul.

    'Upon the thanksgiving for King G[eorge I]'s
    accession appointed at Dublin upon Shrove Tuesday'
    [imitation of Dorset's satire]
    [Crum W1220]

    fc.58, p. 106; c.570/1, p. 113; c.171, no. 9; see also
    previous.

W1099   When Israel freed from Pharaoh's hands
And fires and seas confess their Lord.

    [Joseph Addison], 'Psalm 114' [Spectator 461]

    c.186, p. 145; c.547, p. 185; c.144, p. 133; c.244, p. 137

W1100   When Israel's daughters mourn'd their past offenses
As decent to repent in as to sin in.

    [Alexander Pope], 'An epigram' [on the Richmond
    daughters]

    c.176, p. 35

W1101   When Isr'el out of Egypt came,
By his tremendous pow'r and rod.

    'Evening prayer Psalm 114 Hallelujah'

    c.264/3, p. 38

W1102   When J[ames] perceiv'd his P[rince] of W[ales]
How then shall such another.

    C[harles] D[arby], 'On [James II] taking the P[rince]
    of W[ales] with him to Italy'
    [Crum W1229]

    b.63, p. 89; fb.207/3, p. 24

W1103   When James the Third did first from Dunkirk sail
We soon shall answer [?] all objections.

    [Sir Richard Bulstrode], 'Upon the same subject by
    the same hand' [The Old Pretender's sailing from
    Dunkirk in 1708]

    fb.88, p. 117

W1104   When Jasper died, he knockt at heaven['s] gate,
What you quoth Peter? Sure you do but droll.

    'Prae foribus . . . English thus'

    c.189, p. 93

W1105   When Jeffrey's [soul] did to Hell come
Modestly rose and gave him place.

    'Jeffrey's welcome 1689'
    [Crum W1231]

    b.111, p. 141

W1106   When Jesus appeareth arrayed in light
But in the fruition shall be endless peace.

    [Mary Pluret], 'A song with a melodious tune'

    c.354

W1107   When Jesus Christ himself did preach
By which we must forever stand or fall.

    Sir John Strangways, 'The parable of the ten virgins:
    Matthew the 25th or take time whiles time serves . . .
    5to Novembris 1646'

    b.304, p. 69

W1108 When Jesus saw the multitude, he went
Ev'n as your father which in heaven is.

    Sir John Strangways, 'The fifth chapter of St.
    Matthew . . . 1665'

    b.304, p. 161

W1109 When John Bull was young and live[d] snug by
                            himself
But let the poor man have his ale.

    [John Walker?], 'The barrel of ale'

    fc.108, fol. 76v

W1110 When Jove in anger to the sons of earth,
And scatter roses round the silent tomb.

    [Charlotte (Turner) Smith], 'The origin of flattery'

    c.130, p. 70

W1111 When Jove incensed to see the human race,
Inseparably link'd, so gracious heaven ordain'd.

    'Love and hope'

    c.83/2, no. 546

W1112 When Jove lay blest in his Alcmaena's charms
As strong as Jove, she like Alcmaena fair.

    [Matthew Prior], 'The wedding night'

    c.189, p. 114

W1113 When Judas came with traitorous embrace
And where he'd wish a ribbon, place a rope!

    R[ichard] V[ernon] S[adleir], 'On some late
    appointments. 1782'

    c.106, p. 45

W1114 When Julius Caesar reigned king,
Pray kill me not for Caesar's sake.

    '. . . When Julius Caesar was here . . . he put a gold
    collar or ring about a stag's neck, on which was
    engraved the following petrastic'

    fc.78, fol. 5

W1115 When kings by republican maxims are made
Then Rome will submit to the Ottoman court.

    'The twelve impossibilities'

    c.570/2, p. 46

W1116 When kings from heav'n deserv'd their crowns,
With the fumes of a new reformation.

    'A song'

    c.570/1, p. 30

W1117 When laboring with excessive pain
Who rules the vaulted skies.

    A. Ford, 'A copy of verses written by . . .'

    c.517, fol. 1v

W1118 When last alone with you I was,
Then prithee what a fool were you.

    'Her answer' [to 'When in a shade . . .']

    fb.142, p. 54

W1119 When last we met, praising your beauty you
What privately I now but spake, your worth.

    b.197, p. 121

W1120 When late I attempted your pity to move,
But why did you kick me downstairs?

    [Isaac Bickerstaffe], 'The lover's expostulation to his
    mistress'

    c.378, p. 2

W1121 When late our senate held a strong debate
'Twould stop their building castles in the air.

    [Phanuel Bacon], 'Quae vos discordia cives?'

    c.237, fol. 77

W1122 When lately with some special friends,
And prove your friend is in the right.

    John Chichely, 'To Henry Bosseville esqr at his
    chambers in Lincoln's Inn'

    c.229/1, fol. 62

W1123 When latest autumn spreads her evening veil
And soothe the pensive visionary mind!

    Charlotte (Turner) Smith, 'Sonnet 32 . . . to
    melancholy written on the banks of the Arno October
    1785'

    c.504, p. 95

W1124 When lawless men their neighbors dispossess
If pillow slip aside, the monarch dies.

    [Arthur Mainwaring?], 'Suum cuique' [1689]
    [Crum W1257; POAS V.117]

    b.111, p. 401; fb.68, p. 93; Poetry Box VII/41

W1125 When laws are silenced and the noble gown
Since we will compare Justice Daylie meet.

    'Satire against Justice [Daylie?] in [?] for offering to
    imprison or fine an advocate and [one whether to be?]
    signet for some squabble betwixt them'

    Poetry Box VIII/32

W1126 When Lesbia first I saw so heav'nly fair
And what her eyes enthrall'd, her tongue unbound.

    W[illia]m Congreve, 'Song'
    [Crum W1261]

    c.189, p. 126

W1127 When life is past and death is come,
The well is he that well hath done.

    [John Rose?]

    b.227, p. 36

W1128 When life's tempestuous storms are o'er,
To him from whence I rose.

'The dying saint . . . Bombay 1777'
fc.132/1, p. 97; c.83/1, no. 267

W1129 When Liquorish Gravy, an old demure sinner,
Odzooks, John, quoth he, your beer's full of hops.

[Charles Burney, the younger], 'The glutton . . . 1773'
c.37, p. 68

W1130 When little Raymond shall acquire the art
And fools in thirty-eight grow wise in thirty-nine.

'A New Year's gift for the English at Paris 1739'
fc.135

W1131 When look on you then each should truly name
Wit's waggery, and that I swear is thee.

Lady Jane Cavendish, 'On an acquaintance'
[Crum w1272]
b.233, p. 8

W1132 When look on you, your face did teach one wealth
That so her labors they might justly take

Lady Jane Cavendish, 'On my grandmother the Lady Corbett'
[Crum w1273-4]
b.233, p. 32

W1133 When [Loughborough] by an English bench unaw'd,
But Satan, *bone fide*, bids for thee!

'From the same paper [the Courier]'
Greatheed Box/74

W1134 When Louis strove as all agree
A nun, oh fie, a nun, a nun.

'On the taking of Saint Maries [Puerto de Santa Maria, opposite Cadiz]. A poem' [pr. 1703, in Letters from the living (Foxon P643)]
c.481, p. 1

W1135 When love and friendship are in verse combin'd,
The soul collected in the ravish'd ear.

John Lockman, 'Hearing the sonata of love and friendship, set by Mr. de Fosch . . . March 1745'
c.267/1, p. 188

W1136 When love with unconfined wings
Enjoy such liberty.

Richard Lovelace, 'To Althea, from prison'
[Crum w1278]
b.150, p. 202; c.90; b.213, p. 58

When lovely Celia had resign'd   W1137
The wine and fruits—Ma'am Church and King.

[John Kidgell], 'Sir Joseph and his ladies at supper'
[pr. 1747 (Foxon K37)]
c.83/2, no. 718

When lovely Laura did from earth remove   W1138
For still, methinks, she bids me mend my pace.

[from Petrarch]
fb.66/21

When lovely nymphs, contending for the bays,   W1139
Swore each a Venus was—and pleas'd them all.

'The rival beauties. From Rufinus'
c.487, p. 103

When lovely Shelley condescends   W1140
And burn into a cinder!

R[ichard] V[ernon] S[adleir], 'To Lady Shelley at a first visit 1789—written with a pencil'
c.106, p. 90

When Lowin with coercive crack of whip   W1141
Reform and terrify from future crimes.

c.519

When Macerath liv'd 'mongst Arthur's crew   W1142
And proudly answers Nay-Bob.

'Epigram'
c.504, p. 113

When M[ada]m my hard fate shall part us two   W1143
When we shall meet again—till when—adieu.

[Maurice Johnson], 'To a young lady from her lover, on being to be absent from her written in 1709'
c.229/2, fol. 17

When man and woman die, as poets sing,   W1144
His heart's the last that stirs, of hers the tongue.

[Edward May], 'On man and woman'
c.356

When man had disobey'd his Lord,   W1145
In visions of eternal day.

'Ode on the nativity of the Messiah'
c.481, p. 252

When man was lost, Christ's pity walkt about   W1146
My want of tears with show(?) of precious blood.

[Sir Richard Bulstrode], 'Of sighs and tears'
fb.88, p. 114v

W1147 When marshall'd on the nightly plain,
The star!—the star of Bethlehem.

    H[enry] K[irke] White, 'The star of Bethlehem'

    File 17714

W1148 When Martin youth of noble race
In heaven with ye may have a place. | Amen

    'Of S. Martin another. Nove. 11'

    a.30[52]

W1149 When Mary's named, what life it gives
Great conquests gets, armies of rebels tame.

    Lady Jane Cavendish, 'On her most sacred Majesty'
    [Henrietta Maria]
    [Crum W1291]

    b.233, p. 11

W1150 When memory chill'd by absence shall decay
And whilst it proves my faith, recover thine.

    R[ichard] B[rinsley Butler] Sheridan, 'Lines sent with
    a picture'

    Poetry Box XII/95

W1151 When men dare censure church's head,
'Tis then you'll truly sing Te Deum.

    'To the Vice Chancellor of Cambridge'

    c.111, p. 105

W1152 When menac'd to be laid behind the fire;
What says th'unerring oracle? Retire.

    John Lockman, 'To a friend in jeopardy'

    c.267/1, p. 74

W1153 When midnight o'er the moonless skies
Since lifeless to my heart ye prove.

    [William Robert Spencer, 'The visionary']

    Diggle Box: Poetry Box XI/65; see also 'In Linden . . .'.

W1154 When mighty Persia and proud Chaldean
Their ruins to their ashes be an urn.

    [William Sandys?], 'A paraphrase upon the 137 psalm
    of David with some enlargement alluding to the
    present dangerous schisms of Presbytery and
    Independency . . . this writ in 1651 in Exeter jail'

    b.230, p. 110

W1155 When Mira, as the snowdrop fair,
To the fam'd pair from whom she sprung.

    John Lockman, 'Mira [Miss Kitty Cornwall] dancing
    [at the Sheriff's Ball, in Hereford, Aug. 1763]. Set to
    music by Mr. Valton'

    c.267/2, p. 119

W1156 When Mira talks, so elegant each phrase
Lest, pleasing others, she herself should wound!

    R[ichard] V[ernon] S[adleir], 'To Mrs. M[ood]y while
    at Gen[era]l M[ocher']s Enf[iel]d'

    c.106, p. 72

W1157 When monarch Adam, parent of mankind
The utmost heights of our forefather's love.

    J. N., 'Job. 8th 6th It is not good that man should be
    alone'

    b.204, p. 46

W1158 When Monmouth the chaste read those impudent
                          lines
With the want of true grammar, good English, on
                          [or] sense.

    [Charles Sackville, 6th earl of Dorset], 'An excellent
    new ballad . . . [on] a late famous poem . . . The
    female nine ['What chance has brought thee . . .'; on
    wives or mistresses of Carmaerthon, Devonshire,
    Dorset, Pembroke, Nottingham, Monmouth,
    Marlborough, Lowther, and Russell] to the tune
    Packington's Pound' [1690]
    [Crum W1312; POAS V.211]

    fb.70, p. 105; b.111, p. 548

W1159 When most of all your neighbors, out of awe
To testify a loyalty unstained.

    Sir Thomas Urquhart, 'To [crossed out]'

    fb.217, p. 67

W1160 When Mother Clud had rose from play
A mousetrap man, chief engineer.

    [Jonathan Swift], 'History of V[anbrugh']s house.
    1708'

    c.265, p. 20

W1161 When mountain asses bray, or horses snort,
When you shall sing and the bassoon shall sound.

    [Charles Burney, the younger], 'Epigrams. On the
    Shinfield singers'

    c.37, p. 56

W1162 When mournful evening's gradual vapors spread
Retain the love of liberty and truth.

    Rob[er]t Merry, 'The pains of memory'

    c.141, p. 197

W1163 When much-lov'd Frederick's death was known,
Whilst streams shall glide, or flow'rets blow.

    John Lockman, 'The change of mourning, for Prince
    Frederic, into colors'

    c.267/1, p. 279; c.267/2, p. 253

W1164 When music, heav'nly maid, was young,
Confirm the tales her sons relate.

   [William] Collins, 'The passions—an ode for music'
[Crum W1316]

c.363, p. 171

W1165 When musing on the banks of Lune
To meet thy great reward.

   M. P—ll, 'A soliloquy . . . Lancaster'

c.517, fol. 14v

W1166 When my breast labors with oppressive care,
Is he unwise? or, are ye less than they?

   [James Thomson], 'A paraphrase on the latter part of
the 6th chapter of St. Matthew'

c.139, p. 187; c.244, p. 634; fc.132/1, p. 1

W1167 When my Corydon, sits on a hill, making melody
My Phillida the golden ball.

   'Corydon, a song so called'

fb.69, p. 200

W1168 When my dear love sat on the flow'ry side
On journey thither and bring me to my home.

   Sir Chri[stopher] Wyvill, 3d bart., 'These verses was
made by my good brother upon his wife [Lady Ursula
(Darcy) Wyvill]'

b.222, p. 137

W1169 When my dear Strephon had resign'd his breath
And seem'd to like the place that it was settled in.

   [Mrs. ( ) Feilding]

b.226, p. 68

W1170 When my mind seems most engaged
You shall say ah well as I | That love hath wings: &c.

b.197, p. 108

W1171 When naked all, like Eve and Adam,
That dreadful thing—a gentleman.

   'John Ball's seditious text When Adam delv'd, and Eve
span | Who was then the gentleman?'

c.83/3, no. 1030

W1172 When Nassau ey'd his native coasts no more,
Bless future states, and nations yet unborn.

   [Joseph Spence], 'Verses, on the Prince of Orange's
coming over to marry the Princess Royal of England.
To a new tune'

Spence Papers, folder 42

W1173 When native goodness leaves these earthly plains,
With one accord show forth th'Almighty's praise.

   [J. Wilkinson], 'On the death of Isaac Wilson who
died the 18th of the 8th month 1785'

c.140, p. 55

W1174 When nature first inform'd the human soul,
Their youth with pleasure, and their age with wealth.

   [William Shenstone?], 'Mrs. Hull . . . Poetry
miscellaneous [?] by Shenstone' [docket]

c.528/53

W1175 When nature, in her earliest dress,
I mark thy power, and view thee there.

   'Extempore on her Maj[esty']s wedding day'

fc.85, fol. 118v

W1176 When nature lies in icy fetters bound,
From his example find the faith of heaven.

   'To the memory of Thos. Manning esqr. of Bungay—
Janry. 1787'

c.90

W1177 When nature Mira's works had seen
When all the world will think 'em mine!

   [Phanuel Bacon], 'To a lady who made flowers of
feathers'

c.237, fol. 66 [i.e., 86]

W1178 When nature of her wonted sharpness fails
And as he went a blockhead, so return'd a fool.

   [Robert Cholmeley], 'A tale—Horace'

c.190, p. 127

W1179 When nature pines beneath a hoary vest,
With heated fancies and distemper'd heads.

   'A village fireside'

c.94

W1180 When nature tired with thought, was sunk to rest
Than all the pangs and joys it had before.

   Lady [Elizabeth] Craven, 'By . . . a dialogue with her
heart'
[Crum W1334]

Poetry Box V/21

W1181 When nature's God for our offences died
And Judas' fate be your just destiny.

   'Verses upon the twelve judges of England eleven of
whom were of opinion the King could dispense with
the laws' [1686]
[POAS IV.93]

fb.207/2, p. 46

W1182 When Nebat's fam'd son undertook the old cause,
Made a calf o'th' high priest and himself the calf's
idol.

   'Another satire on the new Archbishop [Thomas
Tenison] &c.' [1696]
[Crum W1335; POAS V.469]

b.371, no. 43; fb.207/1, p. 8

W1183 When Ned said, that they were a thousand horses,
It being well known, that he was but an ass.

Sir Thomas Urquhart, 'Of an unpleasant loggerhead
whose name was Edward'

fb.217, p. 108

W1184 When Neptune's blasts, and Boreas' blazing storms
A rug'd gown's ribs are good to spur a horse.

'Nonsense'

b.197, p. 228

W1185 When Neville the stout Earl of Warwick lived here
He gives us some books and we read 'em.

David G[a]rr[ic]k, 'An inscription on the gateway . . .
on [the Earl of Warwick's] inviting some of his friends
to see his castle and take a family dinner'
[Crum W1338]

c.150, p. 31; c.160, fol. 41; Poetry Box IV/194

W1186 When night had o'er the earth her mantle spread,
And taste the rapt'rous sweets of pure celestial love!

'On the death of Amanda'

c.89, p. 1

W1187 When night her sable curtain draws around,
And bow, submissive, to this heartfelt blow.

'To the memory of my revered friend Lady Camply'

c.83/2, no. 532

W1188 When night is done, the gladsome day appears,
When storms be past, the varying weather clears.

c.339, p. 320

W1189 When night spreads her shadows around
And the wave shall send thee a tear.

'Lines'

c.83/3, no. 1004

W1190 When no one gave the cordial draught,
And innocence my shroud.

'Epitaph on an infant whose supposed parents were
vagrants'

c.83/1, no. 266

W1191 When nonresistance was run out of breath,
Thou art both rhyme and reason too to priest.

'Dr. [William] Sherlock's acknowledgment of the
royal bounty'

b.111, p. 201

W1192 When not the phalanx of great Rome, nor piles,
Proclaims both Haman's ruin and his guilt.

fb.234, p. 68

W1193 When now mature in classic knowledge,
And in pursuit alone it pleases.

[Thomas Warton], 'The progress of discontent. a
poem. Written at Oxford in the year 1746' [Dodsley
Collection]

c.487, p. 141

W1194 When now soft evening spreads her pleasing shade,
Sweet shall the numbers seem to friendship's ear.

'Elegy'

c.140, p. 201

W1195 When o'er the bark that Danaë bore
He said; and ocean was at peace.

[ ] Ellison, 'Danaë—from Simonides'

Greatheed Box/27

W1196 When o'er the moon a misty veil,
Supports the humble muleteer.

'The muleteer . . . M. Cot.'

c.83/2, no. 556

W1197 When o'er the Tuscan plain wild winter threw
My eyes are never closed.

[Robert Merry], 'Serenade'

Greatheed Box/45

W1198 When old Sir Gill had well perus'd
Whose treaties have undone ye.

'Sir Gilbert Heathcote's remarks on the treaty of
Seville'

c.360/2, no. 63

W1199 When on a trestle, pig was laid,
'He's gone and broke the cords asunder'.

'Verses on the situation of England and America in
the year 1779, in which England is described by Killpig
and America by Pig'

Poetry Box IV/181

W1200 When on increase of family,
My wife has got a chopping boy.

'Epigram. Equivoque. Entre nous'

c.81/1, no. 350

W1201 When on life's ever-changing stage,
And grasp'd her fast beneath the—water!

Charles Atherton Allnutt, 'A smile at a Baptist'

c.112, p. 182

W1202 When, on Mount Ida, Pan fix'd his choice,
He, on my Chloe had bestow'd the prize.

John Lockman, 'Chloe at Mr. Hugford's ball . . . April
1757'

c.267/1, p. 203

W1203   When on the bed of death outstretched I lie
And in the grave I've sworn the gift to hide.

> [Daniel King?], 'Lines written upon a locket which he constantly wore'
>
> Greatheed Box/78

W1204   When on the bed of loath'd disease,
The healing art of all mankind.

> Hugh Smithson, duke of Northumberland, 'By . . .'
>
> c.90

W1205   When on thy little finger look
And that is lovely each may see.

> Lady Jane Cavendish, 'On the least finger of her hand' [Crum w1354]
>
> b.233, p. 16

W1206   When on us heav'n show'r'd blessings down
Oh, the vile spawn of forty-one.

> 'Forty-one' [pr. 1719 (Foxon F207)]
>
> c.570/2, p. 41

W1207   When once th'Achaian virtue slept
For there's our Philopoemen.

> [by a student at King's School, Canterbury, 1760]
>
> c.169, p. 6

W1208   When once the doctor doth appear,
No other schemes we ever had in view.

> 'Of the apothecary' [Poor Robin's almanac]
>
> c.186, p. 141

W1209   When once the gods like us below
I want an overflowing bowl. | A flowing bowl, &c.

> 'Song 149'
>
> c.555, p. 207

W1210   When once the moon begets a sun;
There's been an act of grace in hell.

> [Stephen Barrett], 'The prophecy'
>
> c.193, p. 142

W1211   When once the presence of a friends is gone
To see our loved friends doth make our day.

> Lady Jane Cavendish [and Elizabeth Brackley (née Cavendish)], 'Song's Anthem' [in a pastoral] [Crum w1356]
>
> b.233, p. 69

W1212   When only fools and villains rule a state,
Or he'll unking thee; by heav'n it is his end.

> 'Advice'
>
> fb.70, p. 287

W1213   When Orange landed first upon our shore,
Pray was it not high time for to retire?

> 'The sham abdication'
>
> b.111, p. 452

W1214   When Orpheus, dying, sought his native skies,
And wond'ring Britons think they hear my lyre.

> John Lockman, 'Hearing that Signor Geminiani, was desired to play one of his own concertos, at the little theater in the Haymarket . . . March 1744/5'
>
> c.267/1, p. 184

W1215   When Orpheus went down to the regions below
Such merit had music in hell.

> [Thomas] Lisle, 'On the power of music, a sonnet composed by . . . of Magd. Coll. Oxford 1739 and set to music by Dr. Musgrave Heighington'
>
> c.229/2, fol. 44v; c.360/1, p. 39 ('such pow'r'); c.555, p. 152, p. 315; Accession 97.7.40 (with music)

W1216   When Orpheus went down to the regions you know
That she might be more happy in hell.

> Molly Green, '[When Orpheus went down to the regions below . . .'] answered by . . . to the same tune for Dr. Lisle'
>
> c.229/2, fol. 45v; c.360/1, p. 39; c.555, p. 316

W1217   When Orrery fam'd Pyrrha draws,
Born, nurs'd, and bred in Drury Lane.

> John Lockman, 'The two Pyrrhas. (Imitated from Horace book 1 ode 5) the one by the Earl of Orrery [now Earl of Cork], the other struck out by some insolent, dirty scribbler . . . Jany 1741/2'
>
> c.267/1, p. 21

W1218   When our first parents were in Eden plac'd,
Let us live well, and then not fear to die.

> 'Death a poem'
>
> c.83/2, no. 374

W1219   When our good God gave life unto my heart
But turned off, and yet left unrewarded.

> [Sir Richard Bulstrode], 'Upon myself, written in my old age at St. Germain's . . . 1710'
>
> fb.88, p. 116

W1220   When our gracious good Q[uee]n was brought
safely to bed,
Give your sons jockey milk, and they'll beat the
French hollow.

> 'On a late appointment of a nurse'
>
> c.116 (2 copies), loose page inserted in front & p. 65

W1221   When our Sappho appears she whose wit's so refin'd
Who'd think Mrs. Howard never thought it was she.

'In Miscellanies by Alexr. Pope esq [et al] printed . . .
London 1744 . . . pag. 49'

c.229/1, fol. 69v

W1222   When our tall ship her spreading sails unfurl'd,
Each hour to prove accumulating pain!

[ ] Thorne, 'The sorrows of separation'

c.83/2, no. 399

W1223   When paintings finely finished are display'd,
And none will here presume to follow you.

[John Walker?], 'A short commendatory poem on
Geo. Cremer's speaking Cary's Lecture upon
lectures[.] To Mr. George Cremer—Holborn'

fc.108, fol. 29

W1224   When Pallas saw the piece her pupils wrought,
Works so far superior to my own.

[Christopher Pitt], 'Verses on a flowered carpet
worked by the young ladies [the Misses Pitt] at
Kingston [Dorchester]'

File 11956; c.83/3, no. 1051

W1225   When pensive meditation loves to dwell
And give the sorrow momentary ease—a sigh.

[Erasmus Darwin], 'A rebus'

Poetry Box IV/192; see also 'Where . . .'.

W1226   When people are sending their histories forth
And we are closely connected you'll find in the end.

John Lee, 'A riddle . . . to William Lee Dec. 1757'

Poetry Box I/91; c.389

W1227   When people find their money's spent
With farthing candles lighted home before Sir.

[Thomas Brown?], 'The campaign. October 22nd.
1692'
[Crum W1380]

b.111, p. 293

W1228   When Persia's tyrant to th' Athenian coast
And reap their harvest, a triumphant peace.

[William Boscawen], 'Occasional prologue'

fc.106, p. 52

W1229   When Pharaoh's sins provok'd th'Almighty's hand
And doubly damned the monarch by a wife.

[Robert Cholmeley], 'The eighth plague of Egypt to
Leonora'

c.190, p. 59

W1230   When Philomel with Colin vied
Had call'd her back to life.

John Lockman, 'The warblings of a nightingale,
heard, one evening, in Vauxhall Gardens, while Miss
Brent was singing, suggested the following lines . . . Jn
1761'

c.267/1, p. 27

W1231   When Phoebus first did Daphne love,
To be a tree, if she could choose.

[Charles Rives?], 'Apollo's oath'
[Crum W1388]

b.200, p. 46

W1232   When Phoebus, harbinger of day,
And pleasure grace the charms of peace.

H[enry] Skrine, 'Epistle in answer to a gentleman at
Cambridge . . . Warley Octr 15 1785'

c.509, p. 67

W1233   When Phoebus, splendid god of day,
Art thou my lovely light.

'A Lapland ode'

Poetry Box IV/38

W1234   When Phyllis views my languid face,
Than I can yield to yours.

R[obert] Shirley, 1st earl of Ferrers, 'A stanza from
Malherbe'

c.347, p. 80

W1235   When Phyllis watcht the harmless sheep,
And in despair resolv'd to die.

[Sir George Etherege], 'The careful shepherdess' [in
The comical revenge, II.ii]

fb.107, p. 67

W1236   When pious frauds and holy pride no more
And art thou come? (the captive warrior cries).

Chr[istopher] Pitt, 'On the marriage of [Frederick
Louis] Prince of Wales' [1736]

File 17187

W1237   When Pix sought death armed with sword and
                         shield
I dare to say he'd rose and fought again.

'Upon Tho. Pix an old soldier, whose wife Florence
was a sutler'

c.229/1, fol. 35; see also 'When Vere . . .'.

W1238   When plac'd on guilt, then well may shame
That shot creates the pain.

[Thomas Hull]

c.528/46

W1239 When plac'd within the consecrated aisle,
Will from the priest require his people's blood.

'On hearing the Revd. Mr. R—d read the morning
service, and preach'

c.83/3, no. 977

W1240 When plate was at pawn, and fob at an ebb
And when nobody else quack *Vive le roi.*

[Andrew Marvell], 'A lampoon writ by the Lord
Buckhurst [*sic*]. 1667'
[Crum W1395]

b.54, p. 1015; see also 'When the plate . . .'.

W1241 When pleasure marks each hour that flies
To mark how few there yet remain?

[Hester Lynch Thrale Piozzi], 'On a watch'

File 19242

W1242 When poet Dryden's vitals stopt,
And too much wit will shorten half your days.

'A satire on the little illegitimates of Parnassus, who
durst presume to peep in the dark night of our
Laureate [Dryden]'s funeral' [1700]

fb.207/4, p. 15

W1243 When poets uninspir'd thus artful sing,
And they unrival'd claim'd our justest praise.

M[ary] Jones, 'Occasioned by the foregoing copies'
['To plague mankind . . .' and 'Now uninspir'd . . .']

c.233, p. 88

W1244 When potent Phrygia's king's good grace
To hit his folly in his dish.

[Phanuel Bacon], 'Votiqu paracti paenitet'

c.237, fol. 66

W1245 When pretty Gardener rul'd the town,
While she's the reigning beauty.

[Sir Edward Turner], 'The Oxford toasts. To the tune
of The vicar of Bray'
[Crum W1404]

Accession 97.7.40

W1246 When Prior sings of Chloe's potent charms,
And Henry's constancy shall yield to mine.

W. N., of Exeter College, Oxford, 'To Mrs. R—l H—
l—x'

c.233, p. 3

W1247 When Pritchard was Lord Mayor, I sadly found
Be happy with your murder'd, martyr'd friends.

Joshua Bowes, 'January the 14th 1701'

File 1596

W1248 When profit attends virtue we respect her
From honor have defrauded into gain.

[Sir Thomas Urquhart], 'Of the [?] and perverse [?] of
the greatest part of mankind'

fb.217, p. 509

W1249 When prudence declaims how time passes
'Tis *cent per cent* better to drink.

'Song 192'

c.555, p. 309

W1250 When prudent nature the new world had made
The noise of wakeful geese, saved falling Rome.

W[illiam] Browne, 'Birds' [written at Merchant
Taylors' school for the Lent Probation, 1700]
[Crum W1411]

Poetry Box VI/77

W1251 When public gratitude erects the bust,
A nation loves, a nation loves him still.

'Prologue spoken by Mr. Sheridan at the Theater
Royal in Dublin, to a play acted for the benefit of the
fund for erecting a monument to the memory of the
late Jonathan Swift, dean of St. Patrick's, etc. 1752'

c.360/3, no. 201

W1252 When Radcliffe fell, afflicted physic cried
She mourns with Radcliffe, but she dies with Friend.

S[amuel] Wesley, the younger, 'Epigram'

Poetry Box VIII/69

W1253 When rapid Julius drew his eager sword,
And his first step inverts the fate of war.

Spence Papers, folder 113

W1254 When reading authors, if you find
But put them down in black and white.

c.81/2, first leaf

W1255 When recent in the womb I lay,
Who stamp'd his image there.

[James] Merrick, 'A fragment' [Dodsley Collection]

c.487, p. 73

W1256 When reverend Austin did in Afric preach
Made hell for thee, O such audacious men.

[James Rhodes?]

b.206, p. 117

W1257 When Rhombus with his faction did ride out
The tub will be securer than the throne.

'Democracy rampant'

Poetry Box VI/72

W1258 When rising from the bed of death
       To make her pardon sure.

          [Joseph Addison], 'Serious thoughts by one in
          sickness . . . Spectator vol. 7'

       c.186, p. 36; c.244, p. 138; c.547, p. 162; fc.132/1, p. 41;
       Poetry Box VII/5

W1259 When Robin rul'd the British land,
       They will have cause to rue it.

          '[Isaac] Le Heup at Hanover, a song' [pr. 1727 (Foxon
          L94.3)]
          [Crum W1419]

       fc.135

W1260 When Rome had long enslav'd the nations more.
       Smiles at his woes, and triumphs in his chains.

          [Christopher Pitt], 'On the wedding' [of Frederick
          Louis, prince of Wales, and Augusta of Saxe-Gotha;
          in a letter to Joseph Spence, Blandford, 1 May 1736]

       File 17187; Poetry Box IV/44

W1261 When Rome her virtue lost and her piety
       And in a manger seek the King of kings.

          [Thomas Rymer]

       Poetry Box VI/101

W1262 When Rome of old; great Rome was all on fire
       And must till piety and right return.

          'On the late great fire in the city' [13 January 1715;
          George I attended a play]
          [Crum W1421]

       c.570/1, p. 45

W1263 When Rome's rough warriors conquer'd learned
                                              Greece
       Could not so well be tried, if we did need it less.

          'Prologue spoken by one of the Queen's Scholars of
          Westminster School who acted the part of Phormio in
          Terence, and afterwards played Scapin, in [Moliere's]
          Cheat of Scapin'

       c.111, p. 102

W1264 When rough Helvetia's hardy sons obey,
       Were dangers dreadful, or were toils severe.

          [John Langhorne], 'Caesar's dream before his invasion
          of Britain'

       c.139, p. 555

W1265 When royal Anna wore the British crown,
       Than be turned out, when J[ame]s shall claim his
                                              own.

          'The advice' [c. 1715]

       fc.58, p. 100

W1266 When royal Anne resigned her breath,
       George and his tribe went home again.

          '[The King's] speech paraphrased in plain English
          meter . . .' [March 1714/15; printed (Foxon M519)]
          [Crum W1424]

       fc.58, p. 15

W1267 When, royal youth, must we be blest again
       And consecrate with mirth his restoration day.

          'An imitation of Horace ode the 5th book the 4th to
          the King [the Old Pretender]' [pr. 1716–20
          (Foxon I21)]
          [Crum W1425]

       fc.58, p. 31; c.570/2, p. 53

W1268 When ruder blasts deform autumnal skies,
       And still was loyal in the pangs of death.

          'The apology upon being offered a chaplain's [?] in a
          marching regiment'

       c.221, p. 26

W1269 When sable clouds deform the skies,
       On the low vulgar's envious frown.

          [William Popple, trans.], '[Horace] book 2nd. Ode
          16th. To Grosphus'

       fc.104/2, p. 164

W1270 When sable night her gloomy veil diffus'd
       Her blot of horrors on the face of nature.

       c.519

W1271 When sad Britannia fear'd of late
       To hang up honest H[arley].

          'On Mr. Walpole's recovery' [1710]
          [Crum W1427]

       c.233, p. 10

W1272 When sage Prometheus form'd a man in clay,
       Since, with the form, they give the living fire.

          John Lockman, 'To Mr. Roubiliac, on viewing his
          Rape of Lucretia, and other models'

       c.267/1, p. 160; c.268 (first part), p. 18

W1273 When sages cry, how at your glass
       That he stood on a sandy foundation.

          'The laws to the sophister's class'
       Poetry Box IV/17

W1274 When Samson full of wrath devis'd
       Sufficient to destroy a nation!

          'Epigram'

       c.81/1, no. 451

W1275 When S[andwich] firm in fair religion's cause
True to his friend, and faithful to his God.

> [ ] Jackson, 'A tr[ue] character of L. E. of
> S[and]w[ic]h' [Oxford journal, 17 Dec. 1763]
>
> c.157, p. 72

W1276 When Sarah led by fancy, fate or scorn,
And Blenheim tower shall triumph o'er Whitehall.

> 'Upon the Duchess of Marlb[orough] visiting Duke
> Humphrey's tomb at St. Alban's' [1706]
> [Crum W1432]
>
> fc.24, p. 34

W1277 When Satan thought our Savior to betray
Satan had fled, and J[ame]s enjoy'd his own.

> 'On the same subject' [a contract between George I
> and the devil]
>
> c.570/2, p. 161

W1278 When satire strives to blast the fair one's fame
With equal ardor you proclaim that praise.

> 'To Richard Nash esqr. at Bath—1736'
>
> c.360/1, p. 31

W1279 When Saul receiv'd no answer down from heav'n,
How easy to be found's the way to the devil.

> 'On Saul's witch'
>
> b.118, p. 232

W1280 When savage Goths from Rhine return
For lo, her own Augustus reigns.

> 'A prophecy. By Merlin the famous British astronomer
> found written upon an old wall in Saxon characters.
> Dated the year 482 about the time of the restoration
> of King Vortigern to the British throne, faithfully
> transcribed from the original' [on George I; pr. 1718?
> (Foxon P1137)]
> [Crum W1435]
>
> c.570/1, p. 122

W1281 When Scotland's hundredth and ninth
                                    unconquered king
Through Scotland, England, Ireland, France and
                                                Spain.

> 'The prophecy of old Sybilla which secretly she told
> Tom Millay'
>
> b.101, p. 69

W1282 When seated on a blooming spray
Its greenest boughs in thee—?

> [Robert Cholmeley], 'To Mr Wilkinson A.B. Coll:
> Eman: Camb: occasioned by his resolutions to forsake
> the study of poetry for that of philosophy'
>
> c.190, p. 46

When Senefino breathes in vocal strains,
Thou, Senefino; or Apollo, he. W1283

> [John Lockman], 'To Mr. Roubiliac, on seeing a bust,
> carved by him, of Senefino'
>
> c.268 (first part), p. 4; c.267/1, p. 78

When Shakespeare flourish'd in Eliza's age W1284
And deathless fame, posterity repays.

> [Philip Yorke, 2nd earl of Hardwicke], 'A prologue,
> spoke by the Hon Mr Joseph Yorke, when The fall of
> Saguntum a tragedy was acted by the young
> gentlemen of Mr Newcome's School at Hackney,
> March the 18, 19, and 20—1740/41'
>
> c.360/1, p. 291

When Shakespeare, Jonson, Fletcher ruled the stage, W1285
Though by a different path, each goes astray.

> [Sir Carr Scroope], 'In defense of satire' [1677]
> [Crum W1441; POAS 1.364]
>
> b.105, p. 95; b.54, p. 1012

When shall I lay aside this case and be W1286
Of purity, as this life, will admit.

> 'In dominiae cena receptionem die d o: 5 die Apr:
> 1691. Euha sci Dunstani'
>
> b.127, p. 9

When shall I, my fair one, say, W1287
The winter's night, the summer's day.

> 'A love letter'
>
> c.83/2, no. 537

When shall I, with joy elate, W1288
Drink, and drown each care in wine.

> [William Popple, trans.], '[Horace, ep]ode 9th. To
> Maecenas'
>
> fc.104/2, p. 430

When shall the curtain fall, and these bless'd eyes W1289
Come cheering smiles, from the bright face of God!

> 'Death prayed for. Letters moral'
>
> c.244, p. 584

When shall the Savior's kingdom come W1290
Like as in heaven, in earth below.

> T[homas] S[tevens]
>
> c.259, p. 135

When shall we meet again? and have a taste W1291
Though you paid for th' ale, yet that paid me.

> 'The goodwife's ale' [attr. Ben Jonson]
> [Crum W1451]
>
> b.200, p. 172; b.205, fol. 72v; b.356, p. 302

W1292　When shall we see old England wise again Sir?
'Tis drawing on, then let it come, we'll pull and
　　　　　　　　　　　　　　　　　　　　　drink away.

　　　　'One and thirty loyal queries'
　　　b.111, p. 65

W1293　When shame for all my foolish youth had writ
Not going thither but new come from thence.

　　　　[Richard Duke], 'To Mr. Waller upon the last copy'
　　　fb.70, p. 165

W1294　When she was the church's daughter,
She's left the daughter in the lurch.

　　　　'Novelties 1705' [on Queen Anne]
　　　　[cf. Crum w887, 'When Anna . . .'; POAS VII.147]
　　　b.90, p. 1

W1295　When Sherwin shows his tricks with wondrous art,
This fellow, were he once in hell, would break him.

　　　　[David Stokes], 'On Sherwin the fire-eater'
　　　c.233, p. 41

W1296　When should men aim in honors to be greater
May strive with [?] in happiness.

　　　　[Sir Thomas Urquhart]
　　　fb.217, p. 499

W1297　When shrugging quacks about me wait
And leave her brats the world to range in.

　　　　'The Lord Wharton's will' [1715]
　　　　[Crum w1457]
　　　c.570/2, p. 134

W1298　When Sieur Tour
The one's turn'd coward, th'other a rank sot.

　　　　Sir Fleetwood Sheppard, 'The mock remarks' [1691]
　　　fb.70, p. 292

W1299　When Sion's God her sons redeem'd
With joy shall bring back weighty sheaves.

　　　　'Psalm 126. Evening prayer'
　　　c.264/3, p. 72

W1300　When Slander from her native hell
Far from the cheerful haunts of men.

　　　　R[ichard] V[ernon] S[adleir], 'Some very scandalous,
　　　　false and wicked anonymous letters having been
　　　　conveyed to some young gentlemen reproaching them
　　　　with a variety of criminal acts . . . occasioned the
　　　　following lines. 1792'
　　　c.106, p. 127

W1301　When sly Jemmy Twitcher had smugged up his face
Come buss me, I'll be Mrs. Twitcher myself.

　　　　[Thomas Gray], 'The university courtship' [written at
　　　　the time of Lord Sandwich's election for high steward
　　　　of the University of Cambridge; printed in
　　　　Gentleman's Magazine Jan. 1782]
　　　　[Crum w1466]
　　　Greatheed Box/37

W1302　When smiling autumn days are flown
May heaven increase and bless your store.

　　　　John Wolcot ('Peter Pindar'), 'Winter a poem of its
　　　　own kind . . . Scarborough 14th Decemb. 1695'
　　　Poetry Box IV/96

W1303　When smiling youth my days did bless,
Lash Chloe's pride.

　　　　'The 26th ode of the third book of Horace'
　　　Poetry Box I/113[5]

W1304　When snows descend and robe the fields,
Confirms the truth I sing.

　　　　[James Hervey], 'An ode' [imitation of Theocritus,
　　　　Idyll xxiii.28]
　　　　[Crum w1468]
　　　c.139, p. 410; c.140, p. 112; c.83/1, no. 204 (var.)

W1305　When Sol was at rest
And bless'd the kind aid of the stranger.

　　　　Colley Cibber, 'The fair ladies overthrown'
　　　fc.51, p. 250

W1306　When Sol's effulgence is from day withdrawn
Without my aid no comfort could be found.

　　　　'An enigma'
　　　Smith Papers, folder 74/20; see also 'Without my
　　　aid . . .'.

W1307　When some fair nymph, whose soul Apollo fires,
And prove you sister of the tuneful nine.

　　　　John Lockman, 'To a lady, author of Triumphant love;
　　　　when laboring under a grievous fit of sickness . . . Feb.
　　　　1732'
　　　c.267/2, p. 366

W1308　When some high monarch mingles with the dust
And universal goodness feels the shock.

　　　　'On the death of that celebrated poet Alexander Pope'
　　　c.360/2, no. 52

W1309　When some, long wish'd-for isle appears
And sometimes think of Granta and of me.

　　　　W. Davies, 'A valedictory ode to Macclesfield [School;
　　　　10 Sept. 1783]'
　　　Poetry Box XII/54

W1310   When some new piece is offer'd to the town
Will, if you smile in triumph crown the day.

'Prologue to the Tragedy of Cato . . . 1770. Spoken by
Mr. Coxe'

Poetry Box x/154

W1311   When songs of shepherds, in rustical roundelays,
What was conceited from hunting the hare.

'Song 83'

c.555, p. 130

W1312   When sorrow weeps, o'er virtue's sacred dust
Feels as a man, but as a Christian hears.

Charles Montagu, lord, 'Epitaph on Lady Charles
Montagu'

c.504, p. 6; c.546; c.341, p. 38

W1313   When sorrows agonize the heart
And He shall calm the troubled mind!

R[ichard] V[ernon] S[adleir], 'To Mrs. Sadleir on her
hearing of the death of Mrs. Rogers while at Gen[era]l
M[ocher]'s at Enfield'

c.106, p. 71

W1314   When sorrows rise and veil the sky
For Jesus' hand presents the crown.

T[homas] S[tevens]

c.259, p. 147

W1315   When sounds like thine attract the list'ning ear
And own him bless'd—because he fears the Lord.

'To the Revd Mr Rider on hearing his sermon on the
birth of a prince at St Luke's Old Street'

c.116, p. 41

W1316   When spleen's dull vapors crowd my brain,
For charity is all divine.

John Lockman, 'To Signor and Signora Paganini: on
reading the bill, for their benefit, for that of the
asylum, or house of refuge; and for that of Signor
Catarno, at the King's Theater in the Haymarket; on
Wednesday, 14 April 1762'

c.267/2, p. 393

W1317   When spring renews the flow'ry field,
Inspires new flames, revives extinguish'd lives.

'On the spring'

c.83/3, no. 1023

W1318   When storms blow highest, and the danger seems
And the great pearl possess, of a contented mind.

'Resignation'

fc.54, p. 45

W1319   When storms deterr'd the vulgar sons of law
'You carry Caesar and ——— his saddlebags.'

'On Counsellor Caesar B—w of the Munster circuit
crossing the ferry at Aberclaer, in a storm'

Diggle Box: Poetry Box xi/69

W1320   When stormy winds do blow
You may a pretty question find.

[acrostic: 'When may I lie with you?']
[cf. Crum w1478]

b.52/2, p. 178; see also 'When struggling/sturdy
storms . . .'.

W1321   When stormy winds in northern caverns sleep
Nor dreamt of other climes beyond their own.

[Henry] Needler, 'A sea piece—written at Portsmouth'

c.244, p. 545

W1322   When strangers stand and hear me tell
To dwell forever with my love.

[Isaac Watts, Hymns and spiritual songs (1707), bk. I,
Hymn 76]

c.180, p. 67

W1323   When Strephon tells his tender tale,
My tout ensemble's found.

'[Enigma/Charade/Conundrum] 35' [earring]

c.389

W1324   When struggling storms of strife are past
You shall herein a question find.

[acrostic: 'When may I lie with you?']
[cf. Crum w1478]

b.205, fol. 3r; see also next, and 'When stormy
winds . . .'.

W1325   When sturdy storms are past
You shall a secret question find.

[acrostic: 'When shall I lie with you?']
[cf. Crum w1478]

b.132, insert; b.227, p. 70 ('gone and past'); see also
previous, and 'When stormy winds do blow . . .'.

W1326   When subtle serpent did deceive
Then bliss we'll find forever.

'. . . Oh! Quoth I, the devil make hay of [Amy Price],
I know her . . . well enough, and thereupon wrote the
following lines, to the tune of, I love you more and
more each day'

fc.78, fol. 6

W1327   When sultry Sirius rages thro' the air
The same repeated hours can rarely please.

fc.39/6

W1328 When Taffy kept his birthday with cream cheese
He had for every guest, a cook that day.

[Maurice Johnson], 'Aude hospes contemnere
oper . . .'
c.229/2, fol. 9v

W1329 When Taplow walks the streets, the paviers cry
We thank you Sir and throw their rammers by.

[Abel Evans], 'On Mr. Taplow, a very fat gentleman'
c.176, p. 7; c.74

W1330 When teinding season draweth near
Being adapted only for teinding time.

'Gordonston teinding eve. A poem' [1789]
Poetry Box VIII/63

W1331 When that I came first to London town
It is a mile long or very near.

fb.106(14)

W1332 When that remnant of royalty Jemmy the Cully
While to William and Mary my crown I surrender.

fb.108, p. 151

W1333 When that the Monck pulls off his hood,
And Charles return from foreign coasts.

'An old prophecy'
b.104, p. 2 (end of book)

W1334 When the Almighty doth his firstborn bring
That wonders should attest and publish it.

'Christmas Day. 1657'
b.49, p. 6

W1335 When the Almighty wise and just
Then bless'd will be thy natal day.

'Thoughts on a birthday'
c.484, p. 101

W1336 When the archangel shakes the ground
In Hell they're still the same.

[Thomas Gurney], 'On the last judgment'
c.213

W1337 When the banners of war were unfurled in the
north,
Must give place to a *guerre de la russ*.

'Epigram'
c.81/2, no. 544

W1338 When the bells be merrily rung
Let them evermore thy mercy abide.

'Upon a merry and wealthy goldsmith of London at
St. Leonard's near Foster Lane'
[Crum W1502]
c.158, p. 105; fb.143, p. 19, p. 22 (incomplete; 'on Robert
Trappis')

W1339 When the bird like a swallow and beast like a horse
'Twas by a fox roasting a goose for an ass.

[Martin Moor], 'A prophecy found in a jackdaw nest
in an old gatehouse neare Latham in Lancashire'
Poetry Box VI/14

W1340 When the bold relics of the Trojan blood
And Anna's favor your success shall crown.

[ ] Bull, 'On the Congress at Utrecht' [1713]
c.170, p. 4

W1341 When the bright god of day
If you rashly approach to the sound.

'A song'
[Crum W1503]
c.536; see also 'O ye rovers beware . . .'.

W1342 When the bright sun his middle station held,
But with my joys transported woke and rose.

John Hoadly, 'To the ever sacred and immortal
memory of our late sovereign George the 1st'
c.176, p. 174

W1343 When the bright sun shone with vivific ray,
And wav'd their hands, while either was in view.

'Description of a journey of pleasure to the sea-houses
at Bourne in Sussex'
c.83/2, no. 654

W1344 When the brightest god of day
And Echo responded the song.

'A song'
c.358, p. 88

W1345 When the cool breezes mildly glide along,
And love for love with equal transport give.

S[tephen] Simpson, 'Absence to R[obert] L. R.'
c.563

W1346 When the crocus and snowdrop their white have
display'd
In her countenance revel, and laugh all the year!

[Charles Burney, the elder], 'To my daughter Susan,
on her recovery from the jaundice . . . London,
May 23d. 1776'
c.33, p. 95

W1347 When the curled billows, that impale
Then full of thoughts for his dear Charles retir'd.

'On Colonel Woogan'
fb.228/18

W1348 When the devil and George, went to it, to fight,
But if it comes to the push, your horns are the
longer.

'The combat'
[Crum W1510]
c.570/1, p. 157

W1349 When the dragon of Bow shall look over the Tower
Then hey for old England father Petre will cower.

'A short prophecy' [Bow = St. Mary le Bow]
fb.108, p. 114

W1350 When the effects of age me seize,
Thy mercy seeks to recover me.

[Edmund Wodehouse], 'June 7 [1715]'
b.131, p. 221

W1351 . . . When the eighth day was come
For to obey thy grace . . . .

'The triumph of our Lord Jesus Christ'
a.4, fol. 18 (incomplete)

W1352 When the eternal God designs
That's only in the Lord.

[Thomas Gurney], 'To Mrs. M. B[—y] on her poem
on the law not being a rule of life'
c.213

W1353 When the false perfidious swain
Grecian fires consume the town.

[William Popple, trans.], '[Horace] book 1st. ode 15th.
Nereus's song'
fc.104/2, p. 46

W1354 When the fam'd tints shall from the canvas fly,
And each great genius in thy transcript shine.

John Lockman, 'To Mr. Strange; on his engraving the
works of the principal Italian painters . . . March 1760'
c.267/1, p. 280

W1355 When the fierce north wind, with his airy force,
Whilst our hosannas all along the passage | Shout
the redeemer.

Isaac Watts, 'An ode. Attempted in English sapphics[.]
The day of judgment'
[Crum W1512]
c.186, p. 38; c.244, p. 299; see also 'When the north
wind . . .'.

W1356 When the first dawn of Celia's charms,
For love is virtue's gift alone.

[William Boscawen], 'The progress of affection'
fc.106, p. 11

W1357 When the first parents of our race
Speak thy deserved praise.

[Isaac Watts, Hymns and spiritual songs (1707), bk. II,
Hymn 78]
c.180, p. 7

W1358 When the goddesses strove
The apple had then been divided.

'On three sisters, equally fair, 1746'
c.360/2, no. 250

W1359 When the good man on any bed reclines,
Consolatory rays of penitence.

'A midnight thought'
c.83/3, no. 1058

W1360 When the great lamp of Heaven, the glorious sun
With his dear blood, the truth he had reveal'd.

'Christmas Day, 1663'
b.49, p. 5

W1361 When the immortal beauties of the skies
With Juno's aspect and Minerva's mind.

[John] Pomfret, 'Some lines of . . . in his Strephon's
love for Delia, justified'
c.360/2, no. 249 (ll. 43–49)

W1362 When the inspir'd preacher mounts the stool
But love to swallow down the slipp'ry bit.

'The prologue to the music speech spoken in the
Music School at Oxford in the time of the Act in the
year 1682'
fb.142, p. 20

W1363 When the joy of all hearts and desire of all eyes
But Orange shall reap the reward of his merit.

[Ralph Gray], '[The scamperers, to the tune of]
Packington's pound' [November 1688]
[POAS IV.327]
fb.108, p. 117

W1364 When the king came of late with his peers of state
The proctors and eke the taskers.

'A proper new song made of those that commenced
the King being at Cambridge December 1624 to the
tune of Whoop do me no harm'
[Crum W1519]
b.197, p. 53

W1365 When the king leaves off Sedley and sticks to the
                                                queen
That out of this nation it might not run.

  'The prophecy' [on Catharine Sedley, Countess of
  Dorchester]
  [Crum w1520]
  fb.108, p. 319

W1366 When the last [spring] I came to keel and found
The poor your lastingst epitaph will say.

  [Sir Aston Cokayne], 'To Noble Cousin Colonel
  Ralph Sneyde'
  b.275, p. 38

W1367 When the lone shepherd sees Sol's trembling rays
That I, once more, may feast upon her face!

  John Lockman, 'The lovesick shepherd, a song: from
  Petrarch'
  c.267/4, p. 131

W1368 When the lost glories of Lacana's charms
Lend fools thy aid once more, and give them brain.

  [Robert Cholmeley], 'To some particular gentlemen
  of the University who affirmed the foregoing copy to
  be scandalous'
  c.190, p. 30

W1369 When the loveliest expression to features is join'd
But love and love only the heart can inflame.

  Charles James Fox, 'Lines addressed to Mrs. Crewe'
  fc.57, p. 45; see also 'Where the loveliest . . .'.

W1370 When the monthly horned queen
And each did trip a fairy round.

  Sir Simeon Steward, 'King Oberon's apparel'
  [Crum w1527]
  b.197, p. 1; b.356, p. 1

W1371 When the most high from Teman came,
Increase my joys, thou art my peace!

  'Habakkuk. Ch. 3d. part. Poetical essays'
  c.244, p. 568

W1372 When the North Holland winds had froze the
                                          ground twice
They mangle themselves, as they did the D. Witts
            [Dutch?]. | Defend me [from Holland]

  b.115, fol. 23v

W1373 When the north wind with his airy forces
While our hosannas, all along the passage | Shout
                                        the Redeemer.

  [Isaac Watts], 'The day of judgment'
  c.176, p. 67; see also 'When the fierce . . .'.

When the number that stands next to that of the   W1374
                                              muses
You may swear contradictions are true and that
                                      Ten is one.

  'An ancient prophecy written in an old Saxon hand
  and found at the end of a manuscript in Lambeth
  Library' [construed to be about Thomas Tenison;
  1695]
  [cf. Crum w852, 'When a number . . .'; POAS v.468]
  Poetry Box VII/5; see also 'Where a number . . .'.

When the nymph had denied me with blushes and   W1375
                                              tears,
But tis you make us chaste by believing our lies.

  'The cunning lovers'
  fb.107, p. 1

When the parish of Brentford forsake holy Sion   W1376
The parson his bag, and the curate his cue [Kew].

  'A prophecy' [following 'When Henry the
  Eighth . . .']
  c.74

When the people of England had been so uncivil   W1377
Or no more than a text, 'twill go down with this age.

  [Thomas Morell], 'An epigram'
  c.395, p. 36

When the plate was at pawn, and the fob at an ebb,   W1378
And in their own language quack, *Vive le roi*.

  [Andrew Marvell], 'King Charles the second poor'
  [1670?]
  [Crum w1529; POAS I.159]
  fb.140, p. 18; b.52/1, p. 154, 155; see also 'When
  plate . . .'.

When the rose on the cheek, makes you dote on a   W1379
                                              fop,
Till the last hour of life, prove the last hour of love.

  [William Popple, trans.], '[Horace] book 1st. ode 13th.
  To Lydia'
  fc.104/2, p. 42

When the rosy bowl I drain,   W1380
Sad or merry, all must die.

  'Song 140'
  c.555, p. 192

When the rough hazards of the war are o'er   W1381
And justly own I'm overpaid in her.

  Z. D., 'Lines by . . . in Flanders'
  c.360/1, p. 325

W1382 When the rude, hostile Turks, with sword and fire,
And lay thy brightest lances at his feet.

John Lockman, 'To Signor Vinci of Florence, after
reading a proposal, for printing his works by
subscription . . . April 1741'

c.267/2, p. 345

W1383 When the soft tear steals silently down from the eye,
When the feelings alone sacrifice to the shrine.

'Stanzas'

c.142, p. 528

W1384 When the sun sets remember you must die
And when he riseth think on the last day.

[Sir Thomas Urquhart], 'A [?] advice concerning [?]
meditation'

fb.217, p. 393

W1385 When the sun shines out bright
Let me be blunt—heav'n only knows the way!

Poetry Box III/20

W1386 When the time of your going arriv'd
For the maid whom I saw at Roseneath.

[John Black], 'Palinodia or recantation'

fc.107, before p. 79

W1387 When the trees are all bare not a leaf to be seen
But such as each other may cure.

'Winter, a pastoral ballad'

c.186, p. 59

W1388 When the twenty brave pleaders cull'd out of the
throng
They went off with a hiss, but he with a hollo.

[verses on the trial of Dr. Sacheverell, copied by
Narcissus Luttrell 1710; printed (Foxon N98)]

File 9318

W1389 When the violet and lily, the woodbine and rose
Ye hate without reason and love. . . .

[Richard Vernon Sadleir?], 'Dialogue—written by
desire for V. H. and lengthened for the purpose of
being sung there 1769'

c.106, p. 46 (incomplete)

W1390 When Thetis roughly weened to entertain
Bid die true lovers all entombed together.

'The description of an Italian story'

Poetry Box VI/8

W1391 When things go cross, as oft they will,
On earth enjoys a heaven.

'On fortitude'

c.83/4, no. 2003

W1392 When this fly lived she used to play
Funeral, fame, tomb, obsequy.

Tho[mas] Carew, '. . . Something concerning a fly
which lay before him . . .'
[Crum W1557]

b.197, p. 52; b.205, fol. 28v; b.225, p. 133; b.356, p. 74

W1393 When Thou afflict'st me, Lord, if I repine,
I show myself to be my own, not thine.

[Francis Quarles], 'On affliction'
[Crum W1562]

b.137, p. 186; b.118, p. 219/2

W1394 When Thou art present with thy strength'ning
grace,
We either fall or stand.

'On the necessity of God's presence'

b.118, p. 233

W1395 When thou didst think I did not love
Men do not so.

[Sir Robert Ayton], 'Another to his unconstant
mistress'

b.356, p. 94

W1396 When Thou in glory dost appear
And to the world declare thy fame.

[Mary Pluret], 'In Febr. the year 1740 a song in the
night with a melodious tune'

c.354

W1397 When thou, my dear, amidst a train,
For you I'd go thro' all, and nothing fear.

[Mrs. Christian Kerr], 'Horace epode 1st imitated (7)'

c.102, p. 127

W1398 When thou wast taken out of this world's
house-room
They bade thee welcome to their cheer in hell.

'An epitaph on Dives'

c.189, p. 60

W1399 When thou wert weary, faint, distress'd,
This breast, to thee so gentle found?

'Song'

c.83/1, no. 8

W1400 When thousand hundreds six and forty two are
gone
And thee shall beneath great treasure see.

Anselm [of Canterbury](?), 'Shemang[sic] England'
[said to be a copy of a parchment found in an earthen
pot in a barrow in Derbyshire]
[Crum W1574]

fb.106(4)

W1401 When thus I hail thy natal day,
That life on which my own depends.

    [Elizabeth (Vassall) Fox], lady H[olland], 'To Lord
    Holland, on his birthday 21st Novr. 1799'

c.340

W1402 When thy sweet sonnets I peruse,
And speaks its language to the heart.

    'Addressed to Mrs. C[harlotte] Smith'

c.83/2, no. 527

W1403 When time's dark winter shall be o'er
But not like me to fade.

    [George Horne, bishop of Norwich], 'The primrose'

Diggle Box: Poetry Box XI/48

W1404 When 'tis night and the mid-watch is come
That her own true sailor, he was one.

    [Richard Brinsley Butler Sheridan]

Poetry Box XII/70

W1405 When titled statesmen render up their breath,
But this—to join with Floyer's praise, his name.

    Charles Burney, the younger, 'Epitaph . . . December.
    1777'

c.35, p. 41; c.37, p. 37

W1406 When to defy(?) your raging waves did well
Had not prepar'd her belly to receive him.

    [Sir Thomas Urquhart], 'Of one John Hus who had
    been hanged if Jean Whale had not approved him
    from his jailor to be her husband'

fb.217, p. 388

W1407 When to the Esquilian boundaries I come
And round my head, and fear my tortur'd end.

    'Hor. sat.'

fc.14/10

W1408 When to the great the suppliant muses press
Disrobe the pulpiteer, and strip the beau.

    E[lkanah] Settle, 'To the most renowned the president
    and the rest of the knights of the most noble order of
    the toast'
    [Crum w1581]

File 13339

W1409 When to the King I bid good morrow
And from that politic Gramont.

    [John Wilmot, 2nd earl of Rochester], 'Dialogue'
    [between Nell Gwyn and the Duchess of Portsmouth]
    [Crum w1582]

b.105, p. 396

W1410 When to the poor thou givest make speed the same
                            to do
Because one gift in time bestow'd is worth some
                           other two.

b.234, p. 30; c.339, p. 324

W1411 When to thy shop of charms Cadogan came
For see that void, I've kept it for the duke.

    [Robert Cholmeley], 'To Mr Richardson painting the
    Duke and Duchess of Richmond's picture in a piece'

c.190, p. 232

W1412 When Torrington to save our fleet,
Till you come back like Burnet.

    'The Lord Bolingbroke proved guilty of high treason'
    [upon his impeachment, June 1715; printed, Foxon
    L257]
    [Crum w1584]

fc.58, p. 29; c.570/1, p. 31

W1413 When Tottenham's temple, Sylvia's presence bless'd
Each little twinkling star presumes it shines.

    'On the marriage of Miss Sheldon of Tottenham,
    wrote by a gentleman of Oriel College—Oxon'

c.360/1, p. 115

W1414 When tragedy has shed tempestuous tears,
Her favor'd Britons—sick of being free!

    [William Hayley], 'Epilogue to Eudora'

File 6932

W1415 When treacherous Hermes, and adulterous Jove
The virgin hand, that drew the virgin face.

    W[illia]m T[aylo]r, 'On a copy painted by a young
    lady from Carlo Dolce's Madonna'

c.176, p. 68

W1416 When troubles come on every side
And as a martyr die.

    T[homas] S[tevens]

c.259, p. 141

W1417 When truth and loyalty are in disgrace
And future times shall reap the fruits of peace.

    'A prophecy by the Bishop of Worcester before the
    restoration of King Charles the Second'

c.570/1, p. 156

W1418 When tuneful Damon breathed
To please a better way.

    'A song'

c.374

W1419 When tuneful instruments appear
And we'll accord in heart and voice.

> 'To a young lady whose name was Organ on her return
> home after a few month's absence'
>
> c.83/3, no. 971

W1420 When tutor'd by mother she oftentimes said
For Jack is the lad that shall stick a pin there. |
                                    Stick a pin there &c.

> 'Song 243'
>
> c.555, p. 386

W1421 When undeserv'd report distains thy name
It shames not but perchance prevents a shame.

> [Francis Quarles], 'On slanders' [Divine
> fancies IV, 32]
>
> b.137, p. 193

W1422 When Venus had with tears survey'd
The instruments of his desires.

> George Montagu, 'The death of Adonis translated
> from Theocritus'
>
> fc.135, p. 3

W1423 When Venus on fam'd Ida's top
For friendship I give three.

> [Helen Craik], 'Intended to have been sent with a
> neck pin which was made with three golden balls'
>
> c.375, p. 13

W1424 When Venus sad, saw Philip Sidney slain
What had he done, if he had liv'd this while.

> James I, 'On the death of Sir Philip Sidney—1586.
> Written by King James the 6 of Scotland, and first of
> England'
> [Crum w1592]
>
> c.360/1, p. 217

W1425 When Venus saw her son's approaching fate,
T'have liv'd to grace the court, and not t'adorn the
                                                    green.

> 'To her Grace the Duchess of Leeds'
>
> Poetry Box v/82

W1426 When Venus saw the fair Adonis dead—
And burnt his tresses in the funeral flame.

> [Robert Cholmeley], 'Eis necron Adonin'
>
> c.190, p. 102

W1427 When Vere sought death armed with his sword and
                                                    shield
Death like a coward struck him and he died.

> 'On Sr Fra: Vere' [d. 28 Aug. 1609]
> [Crum w1594]
>
> fb.143, p. 25; see also 'When Pix . . .'.

W1428 When vice, or folly, overruns a state,
Long they have feasted—permit us now to eat.

> 'An occasional prologue spoken at Covent Garden
> Theater by Mr. Barry'
>
> c.578, p. 151

W1429 When vice prevail'd and impious discord reign'd
And Rome's great Cato yield to Britain's king.

> Frederick Montagu, 'Wrote by . . . at Eton School. He
> acted the part of Lucius with the Prince of Wales'
> children'
>
> fc.135

W1430 When virtue is the cause of love,
Nothing but death can it remove.

> [John Rose?]
>
> b.227, p. 75

W1431 When walking Peter was about to sink
And soundly follow'd, Peter has been drown'd.

> [Francis Quarles], 'On Peter's walking on the sea'
> [Divine fancies I, 28]
>
> b.137, p. 165

W1432 When was a contract better driven by fate
The 'spoused pair two realms, the sea the ring.

> Ben Jonson, 'On the union of England and Scotland'
> [Crum w1601]
>
> Diggle Box: Poetry Box xi/68 and 69

W1433 When we at Pembletons in Roster meet,
A knot of jovial blades and mighty drink.

> [Sir Aston Cokayne], 'To Mr John Adams'
>
> b.275, p. 92

W1434 When we can look within the veil
Will safe conduct me there.

> T[homas] S[tevens]
>
> c.259, p. 146

W1435 When we (dearest Nell!) shall be parted,
But come back quite brimful of love. | With
                        cannon by fate well directed &c.

> John Lockman, 'The Shadwell tar's farewell, when
> going against the French, under the brave Sir Edward
> Hawke [1759]. The tune: How gaily a sailor's life
> passes'
>
> c.267/2, p. 25

W1436 When we for age could neither read, nor write,
That stand upon the threshold of the new.

> [Edmund] Waller
> [Crum w1605]
>
> Trumbull Box: Poetry Box xiii/92; see also 'When we
> thro' . . .'.

W1437   When we our gracious God most praise,
Than by which others are gainsaid.

     [Edmund Wodehouse], 'Septr 23 [1715]'

b.131, p. 271

W1438   When we review our Britain's happy state
At home so merry, and abroad so wise.

     'State of Great Britain'

c.360/2, no. 58

W1439   When we strip off my first in most cases the art
That some strip my first from my second.

     'Charade [4]'

Greatheed Box/65

W1440   When we survey this mighty frame,
Offending Thee no more.

     'A holy ode, from Mount Alexander'

Poetry Box XIV/174

W1441   When we thro' age could neither read nor write
That stand upon the threshold of the new.

     [Edmund Waller], 'On the last poem in the book'

fb.70, p. 166; see also 'When we for . . .'.

W1442   When wearied wretches sink to sleep,
None but the whispering winds of heaven!

     T. Little, 'Elegaic stanzas'

c.142, p. 543

W1443   When whisp'ring strains do softly steal
And change his soul for harmony.

     [William Strode], 'A song in commendation of music
and song'
     [Crum W1613]

b.205, fol. 69r; b.200, p. 434

W1444   When Whitefield ev'ry nerve and sinew strains
What pathos! force! what energy is thine!

     '[Female characters.] 4.Urania, or the lively enthusiast'

Poetry Box IV/148

W1445   When wicked Dioclesian
Us thither for to bring. | Amen

     'S. Gorgomus and Dorotheus. Sep. 9'

a.30[33]

W1446   When wickedness condemned is
And lead the clean contrary way.

     Sir John Strangways, '30 Septr 1646'

b.304, p. 57

W1447   When Wilde, from King's Bench prison free,
And vilely turn themselves to brutes.

     [Phanuel Bacon?], 'On Wilde's enlargement and the
mob's attempting to draw his chariot'

c.237, fol. III [i.e., 131]

W1448   When will aspiring faction calm its pride
Led them to conquest, and their doubts remov'd.

     [ ] Norwood, 'On the death of the lions'

c.170, p. 33

W1449   When will audacious mortals cease to pry
Lest this Newmarket envoy spoil his flock.

     E. D., 'On Mr. Day's late unfortunate attempt at
Plymouth, under the auspices of Mr. B. . . . Chepstow
August 4, 1774'

fc.85, fol. 115v

W1450   When will you do yourself so great a right
To hear speaks the language of this isle.

     [Sir Aston Cokayne], 'To Mr Cassevilanc Burton'

b.275, p. 93

W1451   When William applied unto Susan to wed
But, both lying and rising the judge gets a curse.

     'Judge Buller's decree'

c.81/1, no. 139

W1452   When William's hand Oates with his lips approacht
Nor hand should grace those lips but only thine.

     'The hand and mouth' [translated from Latin, 1689]
     [Crum W1620]

b.111, p. 412 (incomplete?)

W1453   When winter ends comes in the pleasant spring,
When grief be gone, then joy doth make us sing.

c.339, p. 319

W1454   When wise Ulysses from his native coast
Own'd his returning lord—look'd up—and died.

     [Alexander] Pope, 'Argos: Ulysses' dog'
     [Crum W1626]

c.326, p. 170; c.176, p. 36

W1455   When wit and charming beauty meet
You first attack'd my passions, now my mind.

     'Song'

c.360/1, p. 267

W1456   When, with a Reaumur's skill, thy curious mind
And, with the swallow, wings the year away!

     S[amuel] Rogers, 'An epistle to a friend'

c.141, p. 439

W1457   When with attentive eye you view the page
And every modest virtue bloom around!

     'To a lady with Lady Rachel Russell's letter'

   c.89, p. 142

W1458   When with champagne the board is crown'd,
Glows in the cheek, and sparkles in the eye.

     John Lockman, 'No cosmetic like wine: a two-part
song, set by Dr. Green . . . 1732'

   c.267/2, p. 133; c.268 (first part), p. 56

W1459   When with politic sneer and with florid expression
Are laugh'd at, at once both for beggars and fools.

     'On the vote for the salt tax'

   c.570/3, p. 130

W1460   When with their plagues the gods equip't Pandora
Our box hath made atonement for the other.

     'Inscription on a tobacco box'

   Poetry Box VII/5

W1461   When wits with sportive malice aim
Become the love of praise.

     Hester Lynch Thrale Piozzi, 'In reply to some verses
of Dr. Burney on her charming and brilliant qualities'

   File 11943

W1462   When women weep in their dissembling art,
Their tears are sense, to their malicious heart.

     [Robert Hayman], 'Women's tears'

   c.356

W1463   When women's minds were undefil'd and chaste
They rise to show how easily they'll fall.

     'Epigram on the ladies' pads' [1793]

   c.344; c.250

W1464   When Woolstone, late his blasphemies profest,
And get it quite repeal'd next Parliament.

     'On breaking Mist's press'

   c.570/3, p. 58

W1465   When worthless grandeur fills th'embellish'd urn,
From earth to heaven, from blessing to be blest.

     [Hannah More], 'Sacred to the memory of Rev.
[Samuel] Love aged 29' [1773]
[Crum W1634]

   fc.85, fol. 88v; c.341, p. 88; see also 'Stranger, should
thou . . .'.

W1466   When wrongs and injuries augment,
By one of heaven, who is newly born.

     Charles Atherton Allnutt, 'On the forgiving injuries'

   c.112, p. 8

When York to heaven shall lift one solemn eye   W1467
And think on love and politics no more.

     Philip Wharton, 1st duke of Wharton(?), 'On the
bishops and judges. Giving the Duke's answer to a
gentleman who asked when his grace would leave off
love and politics'
[Crum W1638]

   c.468 (2 copies); c.570/2, p. 106; c.233, p. 38; c.176, p. 122;
see also 'At last sad proof . . .', 'When Young . . .'.

When York's fair Duchess first came here,   W1468
In the known greatness of her mind.

     'On the Duchess of York'

   c.83/2, no. 621

When York's name but nae the house   W1469
And Britons once more rule the main.

     [Sir George Lee], 'A Scotch prophecy'

   Poetry Box I/130

When you and I together meet   W1470
Then silly I can make but one.

     'Riddle'

   Poetry Box VII/47

When you awake, dull Britons! and behold   W1471
Shall still proclaim to your eternal praise.

     [William] Lewes, of Oriel Coll[ege](?), 'On the
displacing of Sr Francis Bacon Lord Chancello[r] of
England. 1621'
[Crum W1641]

   b.200, p. 19; b.197, p. 139; fb.23, p. 269

When you do preach of Mount Ararat   W1472
Your sermon bid with mountains drops a mouse.

     [Sir Aston Cokayne], 'To Parson Nameless'

   b.275, p. 92

When you embrace the ground of a just quarrel,   W1473
'Gainst the opposer, whosoe'er he be.

     Sir Thomas Urquhart, 'To Major [crossed out]
valiant, and judicious warrior'

   fb.217, p. 319

When you good ladies, bade me write   W1474
As in that day you'll not repent.

   c.83/3, no. 973

When you, my friend, recount the fears   W1475
We must be succored there.

     Charles Atherton Allnutt, 'To a friend—Mr. Edw[ar]d
Greenwood'

   c.112, p. 113

W1476   When you put on this little band
Think then I take you by the hand.

> [William Strode], 'Another' [following 'Posies for bracelets']
> [Crum w1646]
> b.205, fol. 56r

W1477   When you reduce observe this generally
You must divide or multiply the main.

> [Mary Serjant], 'Reduction of money'
> fb.98, fol. 33

W1478   When you sit down let me down too,
Then the house is dissolv'd and the members
                              adjourn.

> 'On a house of office' [comparing a privy to the House of Commons]
> Greatheed Box/83

W1479   When you to Carter's moral page attend,
Tho' who is nothing, fears not to be less.

> Hannah More, 'To Miss Bet Blandford 1762'
> c.341, p. 80

W1480   When you were got: your parents only drift,
That you owe not your birth, to either parent.

> Sir Thomas Urquhart, 'To one, who was begot betwixt a gentleman, and his mistress, in the greatest fervency of their reciprocal affection'
> fb.217, p. 319

W1481   When young Sabina's past her tender years
By providence, be blest, and fortunate [From
                     providence's hand, indulgent care.]

> [Elizabeth (Shirley) Compton, countess of Northampton]
> Accession 97.7.40 (2 versions)

W1482   When Young to prostitute his vote shall cease,
And Mislington shall speak one word of sense. |
                        Then will I &c.

> [Crum w1651]
> c.233, p. 53; Poetry Box v/20 (last line: 'And think of love . . .'); see also 'At last sad proof . . .', 'When York . . .'.

W1483   When [your] curiosity led you so far
Is the only favor your Lordship can hope. | Which
                        nobody can deny

> Philip Wharton, 1st duke of Wharton(?), 'An epistle from John Sheppard to the earl of Macclesfield'
> c.468; see also 'Since/Though your curiosity . . .'.

W1484   When youth begins his grand career,
In peace to rest his head.

> Frederick Corfield
> c.381/2

W1485   When youthful Betty first appeared
From second childhood now!

> 'The childhood of the drama'
> Diggle Box: Poetry Box XI/16

W1486   When youthful blood, swells every vein,
Can I then, with his sons comply?

> [Thomas Hamilton, 6th earl of Haddington], 'Turpe senex miles, turpe senilis amor'
> c.458/2, p. 165

W1487   When Zedechiah he whose hapless hand
That done, into the swift Euphrates threw it.

> [Francis Quarles]
> [Crum w1660]
> c.158, p. 35

W1488   Whenas a mask or vizard seems t'affright
Th'effects to last, and after that, to end.

> [John Rose?], 'Of the moon's eclipse'
> b.227, p. 168

W1489   Whenas astronomers pass by,
And stars dismount, again this Moon shall rise.

> Jos[eph] King, 'An epitaph on Jo: Moon sometime clerk of Modbury'
> c.189, p. 50

W1490   Whenas K[in]g G[eor]ge did rule this land
Brass to the treasury.

> 'Fair Rosamond's success'
> Poetry Box IV/48

W1491   Whenas K[ing] W[illia]m ruled this land
And plump-faced Madam Horn.

> 'A song on the D. Lord Albemarle and his prime Mrs. Squires' [to the tune of Chevy Chase; 1700]
> [Crum w894]
> Poetry Box v/1

W1492   Whenas our blessed Savior did undevil
They'll find you as y'are swine, if not as men.

> [Francis Quarles], 'On the possession of swine' [Divine fancies I, 11]
> b.137, p. 165

W1493   Whenas some children steal and come unto the
                             rope,
It often is the parents' fault that give them too
                             much scope.

> c.339, p. 318

W1494 Whenas the Egyptian lady did invite
Too sweet to serve so foul a master in.

    [Henry Phillipps]

b.156, p. 31

W1495 Whenas the generous man's drawn out and gone
As tailors do by turning upside down.

    'To the advocates that stayed behind'

Poetry Box VIII/32; see also 'As when . . .'.

W1496 Whenas the loud resounding trump [of] fame
And blest the tree which such fair fruit doth bring.

    'Upon the wished sight of two sisters'

b.205, fol. 43r

W1497 Whenas the night raven sung Pluto's matins
Frost, pond, and rivers glean. | Never did
                      incubus . . .

    [John Cleveland], 'Mock [song to Mark] Antony'
    [Crum w899]

b.93, p. 17

W1498 Whenas the nightingale chanted her vesper
With the fair Egyptian queen.

    [Samson Briggs? or John Cleveland?], 'Songs'
    [Crum w898]

b.356, p. 266

W1499 Whenas the sun his light seems for to lose
Are limited, as modern authors read.

    [John Rose?], 'Of the sun's eclipse'

b.227, p. 168

W1500 Whence are these cries, why all this heaviness,
Accept this mite, whilst others cast in treasure.

    [J. R.], 'From a young man that had read one of the
    first books of him. An epitaph on that pattern of piety,
    Caleb Vernon'

b.228, p. 3

W1501 Whence are these storms an angry poet cried
Rich as her verse, and radiant as her eyes.

    W[illiam] Hayley, 'On Miss Seward's visit to
    Eartham' [docket title]

Poetry Box V/62

W1502 Whence came I here? And what detains?
Where Jesus shows his bleeding heart.

    T[homas] S[tevens]

c.259, p. 140

W1503 Whence comes it, L—— that every fool,
Rose in a passion, and away he went.

    Robert Dodsley, 'Modern reasoning. An epistle to
    Mr. L——' [pr. 1734 (Foxon D385)]

c.351, p. 140

W1504 Whence comes it neighbor Dick,
As you have done before 'em. | Happy Dick

    'Song 17'
    [Crum w1668]

c.555, p. 23

W1505 Whence comes it that the haughty great,
Tho' homely, and in *deshabille*.

    John Lockman, 'The charms of deshabilles: or the
    humors of new Tunbridge Wells, Islington . . . writ in
    1733, and published in 1734'

c.267/1, p. 347; c.268 (second part), p. 1

W1506 Whence dear Sir Charles, and where so fast away?
Shou'd try each spring that may new pleasures give.

    [William Popple, trans.], 'Horace book 2nd satire 4th
    imitated. Interlocutors. Poet, Sir Ch—— M—— .'

fc.104/1, p. 277

W1507 Whence flow these copious streams of love
That grace may ever flourish there.

    Charles Atherton Allnutt, '8 [I] Esdras 78 V.—And
    now in some measure hath mercy been showed unto
    us from thee O Lord'

c.112, p. 57

W1508 Whence flow those cares
As well as grief.

    Sir Thomas Urquhart, 'The bridegroom going to bed,
    said to his bride, whom he perceived to be weeping'

fb.217, p. 276

W1509 Whence O! my friend, that sadly pensive sigh?
With the bright luster of her ancient days.

    'Reflections arising from well-known events' [25 Oct.
    1772]

c.517, fol. 35r

W1510 Whence rumbs proceed sailors they say are blind,
To great perfection in a little time.

    [George Fairfax?], 'Discursus histiodromicus'

b.323

W1511 Whence spring this wondrous art from heav'n
As those, whose semblance thou hast giv'n me here!

    [Thomas Hull]

c.528/40

W1512 Whence thunder comes is by the eagle shown
To act Jove's part by real thunder died.

    'To the Pope threatening to excommunicate the
    Spanish clergy that should not side with King Charles'

fc.73

W1513 Whence were the strains that gently on the sense
To chant, with artless grace, thy easy song?

'On some verses written by a lady to a sister before
marriage . . . 1772'

fc.74, p. 19

W1514 Whence without wound proceeds this horrid pain,
Such is the decree of Jove.

Gilbert West, 'The triumphs of the gout translated
from the Greek of Lucian'

c.103, p. 180; c.351, p. 10

W1515 Whene'er Chloe I begin
An holy day in heaven.

[Philip Dormer Stanhope, 4th earl of Chesterfield, on
Miss Diana Berke, afterwards Mrs. Williams]

c.144, p. 154; see also 'Whenever, Chloe . . .'.

W1516 Whene'er I meet my Celia's eyes,
A life of mutual love.

'Mutual love sung in Vauxhall Gardens by Mr. Lowe
1751'

c.360/3, no. 165

W1517 Whene'er I work, I'm always cloth'd
For, faith, I don't mind either.

'A riddle' [answered by 'I often read your riddle . . .']

c.578, p. 89; c.391

W1518 Whene'er in verse or flowery prose
But count the joys thou hast in store.

[John] Aikin, 'A wife's absence lamented'

c.355, p. 188

W1519 Whene'er the just, the gen'rous meet their doom
Follow his steps, and are what we admire.

'Elegy on the death of his Grace the Duke of
Norfolk . . . Ariadius'

Poetry Box v/112

W1520 Whene'er the waist makes too much haste
He quite undoes the owner too.

[William Strode], 'A girdle'
[Crum W1679]

b.205, fol. 55v

W1521 Whene'er those lovely eyes I view,
When heaven is kind, and pleas'd to save.

'Song'

fb.70, p. 91

W1522 Whene'er to pass the pensive hour,
To violate thy shade, to peace and wisdom dear.

Mary Cornwallis, 'The laurel bower. April 15th 1792'

fc.124, p. 82

W1523 Whene'er you call for ratafia
Where'er the parson is, am I.

[Riddles for Miss Coole: 2]

c.484, p. 69

W1524 Whene'er you invite me, dear Will, to a treat,
Invite whom you please—but strike me from the list.

c.83/2, no. 389

W1525 Whenever Chloe I begin
A holy day in heaven.

[Philip Dormer Stanhope], 4th earl of Chesterfield,
'On Miss Diana Berke, afterwards Mrs. Williams'
[Crum W1681]

Poetry Box v/19; c.233, p. 122; c.358, p. 162; c.360/3,
no. 72; see also 'Whene'er Chloe . . .'.

W1526 Whenever God erects a house of prayer
The latter has the greatest congregation.

[Thomas Stevens?]

c.259, p. 18

W1527 Whenever she appears, she treads on spoils
Our sex are vassals, and her own are foils.

'Written on a window at Richmond in Surrey 1746 on
pretty Mrs. Grimes, late Miss Black of Richmond'

c.360/2, no. 240

W1528 Whenever Solon 'mongst the crowd appear'd,
Bless the wise seer, and hail his golden rules.

'A necessary rule for conversation'

c.94

W1529 Where a number that stands next to that of the
muses
You may swear contradictions are not, and that
Ten is one.

[on Queen Mary and Archbishop Thomas Tenison]

Poetry Box VII/45; see also 'When the number . . .'.

W1530 Where am I? Oh what wonders I see!
And charm'd with visionary joys.

John Lockman, 'The enchantment: set to music by
Dr. Boyes [William Boyce]. (A person who had never
seen or heard of Vauxhall, is supposed to be carried
thither in his sleep; and being waked by the music
breaks into the following exclamation)'

c.267/2, p. 125

W1531 Where am I, or how came I here, hath death
Prepare, and fit me 'gainst the reck'ning day.

H[enry] C[olman], 'On Lazarus raised from death'
[Crum W1686]

b.2, p. 48

W1532 Where are my votaries? Venus cries,
To guard his favorite, Keeling.

[Miss ( ) Ives], 'Verses sent to Miss Keeling on
Valentine's day by . . . now Mrs. Drake'

c.391, p. 41, p.?

W1533 Where are, O Israel, thy glories fled?
And all the warlike weapons perished.

[William Sandys?], 'The lamentation of David upon
the death of Saul and Jonathan: 2 Sam: 1: verse 19 unto
the end'

b.230, p. 39

W1534 Where are the joys I have met in the morning
Enjoyment, I'll seek in my woe.

[Robert Burns], 'Time saw ye my father'

Poetry Box XII/27

W1535 Where are the muses? are there none to tell?
In praises of a just and loyal king.

'An elegy on Mr. [John] Ashton, March 7th. 1690[/1]'
[Crum w1688]

b.111, p. 89

W1536 Where are you now astrologers, that look
She aimed at two, and killed but half a child.

[William Strode], 'On the death of a twin'
[Crum w1691]

b.205, fol. 62v

W1537 Where art thou, happiness, O where
For happiness is but content.

'On happiness'

fc.51, p. 118

W1538 Where art thou, Mary, pure as fair,
But woes, and frenzy must be mine.

[Sir Samuel Egerton Brydges], 'From the novel of
Mary de Clifford' [pr. 1792]

c.83/2, no. 301

W1539 Where barbarous life deforms the human kind
Nor but for virtue wishes to be wise.

'On pride'

fc.53, p. 6

W1540 Where bright Aurora, smiling, paints the east;
And there rich sculptur'd fragments catch the eye.

John Lockman, 'The ant-hill' [translated from La
Fontaine]

c.267/4, p. 243

W1541 Where can true happiness be found?
He finds true happiness.

'On happiness'

c.135, p. 15

W1542 Where clust'ring roses vernal sweets combine,
Till friendship soothes the tear and bids it cease to
flow.

'The maternal shrine'

c.83/2, no. 555

W1543 Where Dee's pellucid water flows,
And bid me hope and live!

Charles Burney, the younger, 'The secret lover. A
song . . . Mar Lodge. Aug. 10. 1780'

c.35, p. 59

W1544 Where discord reigns in realm or town
The wicked win the chief renown.

b.208, p. 115

W1545 Where dost thou, Memory, thy seat maintain?
Be over-treasur'd there.

[William Mills], 'Ode to memory'

c.472, p. 11

W1546 Where Drake first found, there last, he lost his name
For who can say here lies Sir Francis Drake.

'On Sr Fran[cis] Drake'
[Crum w1702, 'his fame']

fb.143, p. 3

W1547 Where duty is, there's care. Each virtue assures
Is coronet o' th' head, in heav'n will set.

[Sir Philip Wodehouse], 'Upon [Lady Anne Carey's]
sister the Lady Judith Carey'

b.131, back (no. 21)

W1548 Where fate in angry mood has frown'd,
'Tis braver far to live.

'On suicide. (a thought from Martial)'

c.250

W1549 Where full in view Augusta['s] spires are seen,
Then torn with agonizing throes divide.

[William] Falconer, 'The shipwreck a poem'

c.156, p. 211

W1550 Where Garrick rests shall every muse
The nobly virtuous heart.

Charles Burney, the younger, 'Ode, to the memory of
David Garrick esq. . . . Feb. 8. 1779'

c.35, p. 57

W1551 Where gentle Thames thro' stately channels glides,
And in his own vile tatters stinks again.

[Joseph] Addison, 'Mr. Addison of Magd: [Oxford]'s
poem on the playhouse. 1699'
[Crum w1707]

b.201, p. 167

W1552 Where God doth bless in time abundance springs
And heaps are made of many little things.

    c.339, p. 315

W1553 Where God that all should keep an idol's mode
Darkness in light, madness in mirth abounding.

    [John Taylor], 'L'envoy, or the contents' [from 'The world turned upside down']

    fb.40, p. 379

W1554 Where harmony and conquering beauty reign,
And flames which vestals guard can ne'er expire.

    'Prologue to the music'

    c.111, p. 62

W1555 Where his forefathers pass'd their time away
The squire's life, one single day will do.

    T[homas] H[olland], of Jesus College, Oxford, 'Nativo habitans &c. carmina . . .' [Crum W1710]

    c.233, p. 1

W1556 Where is Apelles now to draw
This serves to light and warm our sphere.

    Patrick Neuterfield, 'Cant: 12. To the Lady Frances Weston'

    b.4, fol. 8v (damaged)

W1557 Where is he gone whom I adore?
Draw from my tender, bleeding heart.

    [Wentworth Dillon], 4th earl of R[oscommon], 'Song by my Ld R[oscommon]'

    b.201, p. 158

W1558 Where is my dearest Celia gone
To grace her nuptial day.

    'Written it is said by the Marquis of Montrose'

    c.171, no. 19

W1559 Where is my soul's delight, my guardian angel?
Till with her darling blest.

    John Lockman, 'The distressed virgin . . . set to music by the late Mr Lampi; and extracted from Zoroaster, an English opera, writ by the author'

    c.267/2, p. 97

W1560 Where is that fool philosophy
Pale death, and meet with triumph in the tomb.

    [William Habington], 'Deus deus meus'

    b.150, p. 270

W1561 Where is that hot fire which verse is said
As thou by coming near, keep'st it from me.

    J[ohn] D[onne], 'Sappho to Philenes' [Crum W1718]

    b.148, p. 112

W1562 Where is the blest memorial that insures
Which time may strew upon his sacred bust.

    [Richard Brinsley Butler] Sheridan, 'To the memory of Mr. Garrick'

    c.83/3, no. 740

W1563 Where is the cold you quak'd at, you that be
Our bones, each grave itself will prove a[n] urn.

    [Henry Coventry], 'On the hot summer following the great frost [of 1634], in imitation of the verses made upon it by W[illiam] C[artwright]' [Crum W1720]

    b.200, p. 191

W1564 Where is the sterling gold, Cadogan where?
And out there came—a calf!

    Charles Atherton Allnutt, 'Epigram' [on Jos. Eyre, 'a mere lecturer in morality']

    c.112, p. 171

W1565 Where is there faith or justice to be found,
Will dash your joys and make your glories fall.

    'Mene tekel' [on the confinement of the seven bishops in the Tower, 1688] [Crum W1721]

    b.111, p. 417; Poetry Box VIII/7 (var.)

W1566 Where late I sought to muse unseen
She lives admir'd by all, by all belov'd!

    R[ichard] V[ernon] S[adleir], 'On seeing a young lady show great dislike of her governess and treat her with rude haughtiness these lines were placed in her way as if by accident'

    c.106, p. 118

W1567 Where like a pillow on a bed
Small change when we are two bodies grown.

    [John Donne], 'The ecstasy' [Crum W1723]

    b.148, p. 8

W1568 Where moves the sun which sets without a cloud?
And though they feel but part, yet fear the whole.

    Diggle Box: Poetry Box XI/36

W1569 Where now is that sun of repose
May purchase my pardon above.

    'Written by a young lady that was at first seduced and afterwards betrayed by her lover—from Oxford' [Crum W1731, 'son']

    c.373, p. 45; c.83/1, no. 171

W1570 Where only one does guide and rule the ship
That Dux bears Crux and Crux not Dux again.

'Satire on Lauderdale' [last eight lines taken from a
satire against the first duke of Buckingham, 'Rex and
Grex have both one sound . . .']

Poetry Box VIII/32

W1571 Where pensive meditation loves to dwell
And give to sorrow momentary ease.

[Erasmus Darwin, 'A sigh']
[Crum W1734]

Poetry Box XII/71, 81; see also 'When . . .'.

W1572 Where pensive mem'ry might delight to rove,
My lov'd Augustus I shall meet in heav'n.

'The peaceful seclusion'

c.83/1, no. 85

W1573 Where pride and folly join their hands,
And let me feed with bards on air.

John Head, 'On two lovers Dr. T[i]bbs and Miss P.
B—b—h'

c.341, p. 1

W1574 Where proud Augusta rears her hundred spires
Love, beauty virtue all are ever mine.

'The lunatic'

c.244, p. 643

W1575 Where shall I fly? Where hide my impious head
Resent my folly and my loss deplore.

S[tephen] Simpson, 'To Aurelia written immediately
on perusal of Pope's Eloisa to Abelard'

c.563

W1576 Where shall perplex'd mortals fly to find
To wean from earth, and fit us for the skies.

'An epistle to a friend'

File 13409

W1577 Where shall the doubtful lover turn his eyes,
He is half cured who wishes for a cure.

Poetry Box IV/168

W1578 Where stands yon verdant grove of trembling trees,
And thus I'd share the sweets of solitude.

'Retirement'

c.83/3, no. 922

W1579 Where stray ye muses, in what hallow'd grove
His lays reflect the image of your mind!

'To a lady on Shenstone's poems'

c.89, p. 53

W1580 Where the broad pathway fronts yon ancient seat
Receiving misery is receiving thee.

[Edward Lovibond], 'On converting the late
Mr. Wooddesson's into a poorhouse and cutting down
the trees in front of it'

c.150, p. 64

W1581 Where the loveliest expression to features are join'd,
But love, and love only, our hearts can inflame!

[Charles James] Fox, 'To Mrs. Crewe'
[Crum W1752]

c.90; c.391, p. 11; c.83/1, no. 1; Files 5383, 5384; Poetry
Box X/135, p. 136 (var.); see also 'When the loveliest . . .'.

W1582 Where the Pacific deep in silence laves
Thy future triumphs o'er unnumber'd shores.

[Helen Maria Williams], 'Peru. A poem in six cantos'

c.140, p. 385

W1583 Where the smooth streams of famed Euphrates
stray,
And all her glories pink in everlasting shade?

[J. C.?], 'Psalm 137'

Spence Papers, folder 113

W1584 Where the steep mountain's flow'ry sides ascend
Alike may dare to live nor fear to die.

'To Mr. R——'

c.140, p. 197

W1585 Where the wild woods and pathless forests frown,
Then starting from his dream, he feels his woes
again!

[Charlotte (Turner) Smith], 'Sonnet'

c.141, p. 126

W1586 Where thy broad branches brave the bitter north,
And if he can't avert, endures the blast.

[Charlotte (Turner) Smith], 'Apostrophe to an old
tree'

c.141, p. 87

W1587 Where was the point of honor then, whereby
And got not so much as a challenge by it.

Sir Thomas Urquhart, 'All men are liars Psalm 116.1'

fb.217, p. 134

W1588 Where we have much received, again thence we,
To render, till my short life's lamp be spent.

Thomas Buckland, 'Lichfield from the Close' [30 Dec.
1628]

Poetry Box VI/26

W1589 Where, where resides content?
For to be free, with a hearth [heart?] innocent |
                    Is only true content.
    [George Daniel]
b.121, fol. 22

W1590 Where women are not handsome, chastity
Unworthy have been issu'd of a woman.
    Sir Thomas Urquhart, 'The opinion of a licentious
    man concerning continency and lubricity'
fb.217, p. 269

W1591 Where yon bleak mountain lifts its stormy brow,
Again he waited, the return of night.
    [Charles John] Fielding, 'Elegy'
c.130, p. 17

W1592 Where yonder cooing doves retire,
Then blissful call to disobey.
    John Lockman, 'Juliet set by Mr. de Fosch, and sung
    by Miss Faulkner, at her benefit, in Marylebone
    Gardens'
c.267/2, p. 107; File 9162

W1593 Whereas by misrepresentation
Than what you owe to old Queen Bess.
    [Charles Montagu, 3rd earl of Halifax?] 'The true and
    genuine explanation of one K: J.s his declaration'
    [POAS V.407]
fb.70, p. 113

W1594 Whereas notwithstanding I am in great pain
And be a true Whig while I'm not—in—game.
    'The speech'
    [POAS VII.530]
b.204, p. 34

W1595 Whereas our Oxford books, but only rules do give,
Th'examples of our fathers teach us how to live.
fb.151/3

W1596 Whereas the good do live amongst the bad
The wicked sort to wound the good and glad.
c.339, p. 327

W1597 Whereas, the Jacobites do brag,
Observe these orders as you please.
    'A proclamation. By Will and Moll a proclamation.
    Farther to gull the bubbled nation'
    [Crum W1768]
b.111, p. 379

W1598 Where'er my solitary steps I bend,
While crowding angels meet and hail their King.
    [Richard] Daniel, dean of Armagh, 'The Messiah—
    Psalm 16'
c.244, p. 346

W1599 Where'er the humble man of God
Non nobis Domini, non nobis!
    Charles Atherton Allnutt, 'Non nobis, non nobis'
c.112, p. 166

W1600 Wherefore do thy sad number[s] flow | So full of
                    woe?
Or blow my tears away or speak my death.
    [Thomas Carew], 'Grief engrossed'
    [Crum 1949]
b.225, p. 133

W1601 Wherefore was man thus form'd with eye sublime,
Gives to our lives a sweet vicissitude.
    'Ode written in a fit of the gout'
fc.51, p. 90

W1602 Where's faith? It's fled: what soul then may we trust?
All Souls' assenting needs must be the devil's.
    'On Hugh Halswell of All Souls and Frank Hyde
    Christ Church proctors' [1627]
    [Crum W1777, 'affecting needs']
b.200, p. 42

W1603 Where's happiness? Say all our sages,
And clasps the charmer to his breast.
    Elizabeth Griffith, 'Written extempore on passing a
    day at Mr. Garrick's villa near Hampton'
Poetry Box V/117

W1604 Where's now Othello's hairbreadth 'scapes
Britain's protector thro' the skies.
    Thomas Ash, 'To Lt. Col. Congreve on his courage
    on the continent'
Poetry Box X/139

W1605 Where's the conscience now so pure,
Like the charitable, faugh! faugh! faugh! | 'Tis
                    corporation all.
    John Lockman, 'Humorous songs. The modern
    world—the tune, Friar Bacon walks again . . . writ in
    1733'
c.267/2, p. 138; c.268 (first part), p. 74

W1606 Wherever fortune casts my lot
He let him go, what way he would.
    [Thomas Hamilton, 6th earl of Haddington], 'The
    porridge pot from Boccace'
c.458/2, p. 109

W1607 Wherever I am, and whatever I do,
I had rather love Phyllis, though false and unkind, |
   Than ever be [free from her power].

  [John Dryden], 'The cruel fair one' [from Almanzor
  and Almahide part I iv.2]

  fb.107, p. 12

W1608 Wherever knighthood went of yore
We wait to see her limping after.

  'On the King's making six city knights [Sir Daniel
  Lambert, Sir Robert Willimott, Sir Robert Westley,
  Sir Robert Ladbroke, Sir William Calvert, Sir Simon
  Urlin], Feb. 18 1743/4'

  c.360/2, no. 51

W1609 Wherever numerous parties meet,
Die, with four honors in their hands.

  'Sunday evening amusements (O horrid times)'

  c.83/3, no. 926

W1610 Whether affairs of policy or love
Than gave fresh matter, for his people's joy.

  'On Queen Caroline being left sole regent of the
  realm during the absence of his Majesty's King
  George the 2d: 1732'

  c.360/1, p. 121

W1611 Whether by faith we justified be
Or works, sole God doth both these justify.

  Sir Thomas Urquhart, 'Of justification'

  fb.217, p. 276

W1612 Whether first day God made you angels bright
T'avenge God's servants and procure their peace.

  [Joshua Sylvester, trans. Guillaume de Salluste,
  seigneur] Du Bartas, 'Of the creation of the angels,
  and the fall of the bad, and their subtlety and of the
  obedience of the good'

  b.137, p. 87

W1613 Whether I tales, or songs compose
I'm sure, the application's easy.

  [Thomas Hamilton, 6th earl of Haddington], 'To Mr
  [Gilbert] Burnet epistle 3d'

  c.458/2, p. 146

W1614 Whether in waking or in dream
And let them guard the throne.

  'To the Right Hon[ora]ble W[illia]m P[it]t' [on his
  resignation, October 1761]

  Poetry Box XIV/187

W1615 Whether it is from Eden's sacred plan
And be the subject of some future song.

  A. M., 'Hartwell Gardens. A poem humbly inscribed
  to Thomas Lee, bart., by A. M.'

  Poetry Box I/1

W1616 Whether my song you like, or like it not
At Tyburn where rabble will surely attend.

  'A new song on the [Popish] plot'

  c.171, p. 7

W1617 Whether on sad Avernus' banks thou dwell,
Is all things, friend, king, God, that they adore.

  'The capitade. A poem' [on Cambridge heads of
  houses; London evening post, 1 Nov. 1750]
  [Crum W1785]

  Poetry Box IV/125; see also 'When angry Rowland . . .'.

W1618 Whether sailor or not for a moment avast!
When he hears the last whistle, he'll jump upon
          deck.

  'Epitaph on a sailor'

  c.81/1, no. 103

W1619 Whether the fruitful Nile, or Tyrian shore,
And without stooping they may pass the gate.

  John Dryden, 'To the Earl of Roscommon on his
  excellent essay on translated verse'

  b.86, p. 45

W1620 Whether the 'graver did by this intend
But charmed with William's name march'd all away.

  'Upon a picture of King William's head upon Oliver
  Cromwell's body' [1690]
  [Crum W1789]

  b.111, p. 397

W1621 Whether thy choice or chance thee hither brings,
Go passenger and wail the hap of kings.

  F. D., 'An epitaph upon the heart of Henry the Third,
  late king of France and of Poland [slain 1589 by
  Jacques Clément, a Jacobin friar] . . . Englished'
  [Crum W1795]

  b.197, p. 218; fb.143, p. 27

W1622 Whether we mortals love or no,
Whilst for its want ye pine and lovers die.

  'Courtship'

  c.229/1, fol. 39

W1623 Whether you are of darkness, or of light
The child; being born in daytime: got at night.

  Sir Thomas Urquhart, 'To one that was begot at
  midnight, and born at noon. A problem'

  fb.217, p. 284

W1624 Which for your son would you allow,
Who follows nature follows God.

  [Charles Earle], 'On my road from Cullumpton, at
  Sylverton, made there for a schoolboy, to his parents,
  by his request'

  c.376

W1625 Which many thousands now can witness well,
Whose faults with woe, recanted are in hell.

'God as a revenger, follows at the heels of a sinner'
c.158, p. 112

W1626 Which of these three your names are listed under
Look in the book! Good payment is no plunder.

'Snaith [parish] register. Anno 1657 [2]'
c.81/1, no. 150

W1627 Which renowned seminary
His face most clearly shows a link on.

'The question answered'
fc.76.iii/214

W1628 Whig's the first letter of his odious name.
Noll's soul and Ireton's live within him yet.

[acrostic on Thomas, Lord Wharton; 1710]
[Crum W1807; POAS VII.488]
Poetry Box VII/5; b.90, p. 21

W1629 Whigs would Tories all devour
And the ills to come prevent.

'A song to the tune of Love's a dream'
Poetry Box IV/49

W1630 While all is feasting, mirth, illumination!
As you in happiness for both are one.

[David] Garrick, 'Mr. Garrick took his leave of the
public for the season on His Majesty's birthday with
the following address'
c.115

W1631 While amid the vocal cells | Amid . . .
They trace the thund'ring drum, and point the
slaughtious [sic] sword.

[Thomas Hull]
c.528/59

W1632 While at the helm of state you ride,
To take your humble servant lower.

Henry Fielding, 'A letter to Sir Robert Walpole'
[Dodsley Collection]
c.487, p. 138

W1633 While awful night in sable shades descends,
And feel ambitious thoughts first struggling in his
breast.

'Elegy upon the death of Capt. Charles Kellond
Courtenay, who was killed in the last campaign in
Germany, 1762'
Smith Papers, folder 74/21

W1634 While beauty and pleasure are now in their prime,
I'll bless the kind summons, and lie down and die.

[Hannah] More, 'Florella'
c.83/3, no. 769; fc.85, fol. 103

W1635 While birds salute the morn, and sing,
Nor in the evening fade.

'A May morning invitation to a young lady'
c.159, p. 219

W1636 While boroughs, and cities and counties still jar;
Keep glory's temple full in view.

John Lockman, 'A new ballad. For the election at
Guilford, of representatives for the county of Surrey,
Wednesday 30th March 1768. Tune, the Dorsetshire
march'
c.267/4, p. 377

W1637 While Britain, roused by Gallia's frantic pride
Unborrowed light, and luster all her own!

[George] Canning, 'At the D. of Portland's installation
at Oxford' [27 September 1792]
[Crum W1815]
File 2690; Poetry Box II/30

W1638 While Britons, securely, their blessings enjoy,
And long live the Prussian hero!

John Lockman, 'Frederick of Prussia: or the hero.
Writ for that monarch's birthday, 24th January 1757.
The tune O the roast beef of old England &c.'
c.267/2, p. 17

W1639 While bunters attending the archbishop's door
Concluded, 'twas plain they wanted his Grace.

[Crum W1817, 'bunkers']
c.546, p. 31

W1640 While Butler, needy wretch, was yet alive,
He ask'd for bread, and he received a stone.

Sam[ue]l Wesley, the younger, 'The following lines
were written by . . . upon the setting up of [Samuel]
Butler's monument in Westminster Abbey—Poems on
sevl. occasions 4to. 1736 page 62'
c.83/4, no. 2038; c.360/2, no. 210; see also 'When
Butler . . .', 'Whilst Butler . . .'.

W1641 While Caroline with soul serenely great
'Tis not for what I bear, but what you feel.

'On the operation performed on her late Majesty'
[Queen Caroline, d. 20 Nov. 1737]
fb.142, p. 66

W1642 While crowds officious to declare their joy
Auspicious era of the British state.

'On his Serene Highness the Prince of Orange his
marriage with the Princess Royal'
Poetry Box I/36

W1643 While Damon, you, in scenes of joy,
But something, sad as death, to part.

> John Lockman, 'Flavia to Damon . . . July 1740'
>
> c.267/1, p. 71

W1644 While death was freezing each exterior part,
And clos'd his many eyes, and dropp'd his honor'd
head.

> 'On hearing of the last words of the above
> ['T'o'ercome or die . . .' on the death of Wolfe]
>
> c.118, p. 30

W1645 While death's soft image seals my eyes
Prove nothing but a dream.

> [Robert Cholmeley], 'To a lady who after having
> discovered some inclination by telling me a dream
> pretended a cold to excuse herself from singing and
> talking'
>
> c.190, p. 58

W1646 While Denis' name to France shall sacred be
Thus you commanded and thus we obey'd.

> [Robert Cholmeley], 'The ceremonies of Staincoat
> Hole. Canto the Second'
>
> c.190, p. 140

W1647 While dissipation mars the age,
They need not pray to heaven for more!

> John Lockman, 'Business, pleasure and prudence. A
> fable. Inscribed to the right honble William Lord
> Boston'
>
> c.267/4, p. 315

W1648 While empty sounds incessant ring
Before the God he loved.

> Thomas Gisborne, 'Ode to the harp of Cowper.
> Written in 1798'
>
> Poetry Box v/113

W1649 While Europe's chiefs, in hostile arms,
These joys, will ever be your own.

> 'Christmas amusements to the British ladies'
>
> c.83/3, no. 763

W1650 While ev'ry lyre to fortune strung
And sail a nymph, or shine a star.

> 'Ad navem quae Carolum ad Angliam reduxit'
>
> c.416

W1651 While ev'ry shrub and ev'ry tree,
For hapless humankind.

> 'Written in the frost'
>
> c.83/1, no. 242

W1652 While fanatics and Papists and Quakers agree
And the Church in no matter of danger.

> 'The Church in no danger'
> [Crum w1829]
>
> b.382(10)

W1653 While fancied themes engage the sportive pen
Who lived to glory, and who died to fame.

> H[annah] M[ore], 'Elegy on Major More'
>
> c.341, p. 81

W1654 While far from toils your Damon sits secur'd,
Then haste, my Damon, haste, and come away.

> J[oshua] W[illiams, of Kidderminster], 'Pious
> friendship. Damon to Pythias . . . Pythias to Damon'
>
> c.259, p. 115

W1655 While festive mirth leads on the jocund hours
And here last parting glories gild her towers.

> H[annah] M[ore], 'An irregular ode to the Marquis of
> Worcester [later Duke of Beaufort] on his birthday
> Dec. 22 1780'
>
> c.341, p. 30

W1656 While fortune wraps the warm,
Lie there and rot.

> 'On fortune. Jan. 10th 1784'
>
> c.93

W1657 While from enamor'd Pan chaste Syrinx flew,
While soft approving sighs the shudd'ring reeds
return'd.

> 'The origin of the shepherd's pipe'
>
> c.83/3, no. 757

W1658 While from the skies the ruddy sun descends
He shall adorn my song and tune my voice to love.

> Elizabeth (Singer) Rowe, 'Love and friendship. A
> pastoral'
>
> fc.60, p. 81

W1659 While furious Balaam for the love of gold
He's more than ass the ass more man than he.

> 'Numb. 22.28'
>
> c.160, fol. 57v

W1660 While, 'gainst th'insulting foe, you lift the spear,
And fame reform'd them in immortal lays.

> John Lockman, 'The polite arts to Britannia: on
> occasion of his royal highness the Duke of
> Cumberland's repulsing the rebels from England, in
> 1746'
>
> c.267/2, p. 333

W1661 While gay young lords, put on their martial airs,
Doubly keen wit, the men who drop in fight.

[Thomas Hamilton, 6th earl of Haddington], 'To the King the petition of the ladies'

c.458/2, p. 161

W1662 While gen'ral spring with lavish grace,
Can make the objects please.

[J. B.], 'Song'

Poetry Box IV/155

W1663 While grass doth grow, the gallant steed doth
starve,

[?] seldom 'gainst the wisher's turn doth serve.

c.339, p. 311

W1664 While haughty Gallia's dames, that spread
And with unborrow'd blushes glow'd.

'Verses on Eliza's living at Paris'

c.360/3, no. 54

W1665 While heaven on me, some youth and health
bestow'd

That to the world, did first thy worth display.

[Thomas Hamilton, 6th earl of Haddington], 'To Florella epistle the seventeenth, on the first of April being her birthday 1733'

c.458/1, p. 71

W1666 While here entomb'd the virgin's ashes lies,
Their mourning mother rais'd thy marble frame.

'An epitaph on Mrs. May Browing who died aged 13 1/2 years'

c.244, p. 208

W1667 While I her wondrous charms survey'd,
Move slowly; when I'm absent, fly.

'Absent from Eustathea[.] To the hours' [from 'The amours of Alatheus and Eustathea']

c.379/1, p. 9

W1668 While I quaff the rosy wine
That common fate that waits us all.

'Song 247'

c.555, p. 397

W1669 While I unskill'd in oratory's lore
And now the bitterness of death is past.

Lord [ ] Russell, 'From . . . to Lord Cavendish'

File 245/26

W1670 While I was monarch of your heart
With you I climb to God and die.

[Wentworth Dillon, 4th earl of] R[oscommon], 'Out of Horace'

b.201, p. 125

W1671 While I was musing what was best
He's wise in all his ways.

[Mary Pluret], 'Another [song]'

c.354

W1672 While in full prospect to their dazzl'd eyes
Where social life, or culture never smil'd.

'The two lions and the mouse a fable'

Spence Papers, folder 113

W1673 While in the bower with beauty blest
Variety confusion.

[Leonard Welsted]
[Crum w1846]

c.549, p. 84

W1674 While in the kitchen with observant eye
And laugh beneath the patronizing dough.

[Phanuel Bacon], 'The apple-puff'

c.237, fol. 13

W1675 While joyful here we meet,
Forever may their line | The scepter sway.

John Lockman, 'Hymn. Composed for the anniversary toast of the governors of the smallpox and inoculation hospitals. Set to music by Lewis Granom esqr.: and sung, April 1762, in Draper's Hall . . .'

c.267/2, p. 175

W1676 While judgments speak, let Britons hear
Whose judgment's just begun.

[Thomas Stevens?], 'January the 16 meeting of prayer'

c.259, p. 113

W1677 While just ready for mirth, may I ask you to pause,
And the smile of consent is now beaming around.

Miss [ ] Andrews(?), 'Address intended to be spoken at the Richmond Theater by the daughter of Mrs. Benson'

File 245/28

W1678 While lark with little wing
What peace is there.

[Robert] Burns, 'Words for Robin Adair' ['Phyllis the fair']

Poetry Box XII/115

W1679 While London beaux to Hornsey Lane,
Have twenty yards to seek.

'Summer in the environs of London'

c.83/1, no. 22

W1680 While magazines expect th'impending load,
Than what all Europe knew as well before.

[Edward] Emily, 'Hymen, O hymenal . . . on the
King's marriage'

Poetry Box II/27

W1681 While martial sounds and softer strains proclaim
A new retirement sought, and fled to endless rest.

'Upon the death of the Revd. Mr. Modd, vice-master
of Trin: Coll: Camb: . . . he died Sept: 25. 1722'

b.382(4); see also 'Whilst . . .'.

W1682 While 'mid the sweet retreats of Stowe,
And at his call, retire.

'Lines to a friend'
[Crum W1853]

c.83/3, no. 839

W1683 While mighty Marlborough thunders your alarms
To you devoted are, nor shall they fail till dead.

Edward Griffin, 'Royal mercy. To the Queen' [1708]

b.382(20)

W1684 While monarchs in stern battle strove
To live, or love in peace.

[Anne Finch, countess of Winchilsea]

c.188, p. 24

W1685 While music invites to the grove
Still blesses his name with a tear.

T[homas] H[ull], 'Pastoral elegy to the memory of
W[illiam] S[henstone]'

c.528/26

W1686 While nations resound with the fate,
And pierce the fair enemy's heart.

[George?] Colman [the elder?], 'The country dance
militant. Occasioned by the ball Sept. the 16th 1760'

fc.51, p. 303

W1687 While night in solemn shade invests the pole,
The op'ning splendors of eternal day.

[Elizabeth Carter, 1796]
[Crum W1858]

fc.132/1, p. 7

W1688 While no attempts are plainly made,
And faction settle into peace.

Abraham Oakes, 'The faction: 1744'

c.50, p. 98

W1689 While numbers, to destructive pleasures prone,
By blest effects, his intervention shown.

John Lockman, 'The long-concealed promoter
[Stephen Theodore Jansson, afterwards member of
Parliament] of the cambric and tea-bills. Writ at the
close of the last session of Parliament . . . printed in
1746'

c.267/3, p. 1

W1690 While o'er the alpine cliff, I musing stray'd,
She wept, and folded in a cloud, withdrew.

[Helen Maria Williams], 'Verses . . . occasioned by a
note on the glaciers in Dr. Darwin's Botanic
garden &c.'

c.141, p. 466

W1691 While o'er the tomb of parents truly dear,
And hope to share your blissful heaven with you.

'On William Neame, aged 74, and his wife Jane
Neame aged 71 years' [in Birchington churchyard in
the Isle of Thanet, Kent]

c.240, p. 138

W1692 While oft from clime to clime I go,
Hail! Maker and preserver, hail!

'An hymn to God. By a person in foreign parts'

c.547, p. 201

W1693 While on my mount at early dawn I stood,
Now glittering to the rising sun.

'The vision of Hygeia—goddess of health'

fc.53, p. 173

W1694 While on the swelling surge I ride
For errors of my youth.

[Robert Cholmeley], 'Written by a gentleman sent to
sea for his follies to his sister in England'

c.190, p. 175

W1695 While on the winding banks of Thames I rove,
Excess of sorrow ill becomes the wise.

Thomas Cook, 'To Mr. Welsted on the death of his
only daughter'

c.244, p. 572

W1696 While on these lovely looks I gaze
The vanquisht dies with pleasure.

John Wilmot, 2nd earl of Rochester, '11. Song'

b.334, p. 191; b.105, p. 151

W1697 While Orpha kiss'd her mother and departed
If aught but death e'er make our bodies part.

[Thomas Gurney], 'An extempory poem done at the
request of Mr. J. P. from Ruth the 1. 16.17'

c.213

W1698 While other nymphs their silken snares devise
Strange! How she conquers all yet aims at none.

    'On Miss Evans Tunbridge Wells 1730'

    c.360/2, no. 115

W1699 While other wights present their pray'rs
Adds fragrance to the spicy gale!

    R[ichard] V[ernon] S[adleir], 'Lady Sh's having told
    me that her friend Miss B—h—n was coming to her
    on a visit and would rival her in my good opinion and
    affection occasioned this squib—1787'

    c.106, p. 113

W1700 While others, anxious to adorn
Then send him to Scotland, a civiliz'd bear!

    R[ichard] V[ernon] S[adleir], 'To Miss Hamilton with
    a ticket for the mas[te]r of ceremony's ball—Augt.
    1786'

    c.106, p. 112

W1701 While others are ensnaring hearts
The comely motions of her heaven's gate.

    'On Miss Cook'

    c.188, p. 43

W1702 While others, dreaming, in their cabins live,
And the Peruvian treasures had been ours.

    John Lockman, 'Extempore. Writ under a print,
    representing the [?] [?] to reinforce Admiral Vernon
    in the West Indies . . . 1740'

    c.267/1, p. 71

W1703 While others flatter conqu'ring chiefs and kings,
The Gauls shall mourn, and Corsica be free.

    [John M—r], 'Ode to General Paoli, the Corsican
    chief. Writ after his retreat to Leghorn' [1769]

    c.118, p. 76

W1704 While others fondly sad ambitions fire,
Inglorious, let me pass my peaceful days.

    [Henry] Needler, 'Retirement'

    c.244, p. 559

W1705 While others to the bosom rise
And murmuring bless that ——— of thine.

    'The shady bower'

    Poetry Box IV/39

W1706 While party rage still seems so high,
If you are innocent, you're mad.

    'Epistle XI to Exelbee Lawford esqr.'

    fc.100, p. 49

W1707 While past things vex, future perplex with care
Us men; beasts wiser, pleas'd with present are.

    'A beast'

    c.356

W1708 While pensions, places, are the sordid aim
Still framing plans to benefit mankind!

    John Lockman, 'On reading Sir John Fielding's
    humane proposal, relating to the providing for and
    properly employing, distressed, vagrant boys . . .
    14 Feb. 1769'

    c.267/4, p. 314

W1709 While pining anguish, wild despair,
While comfort glanc'd a healing ray.

    'On the death of a beloved wife written by her
    husband on her coffin'

    c.139, p. 609

W1710 While pious Sophron's mild discourse
'Examples teach where precepts fail!'

    'Extempore on seeing Miss ——— at Wells Cathedral'

    c.89, p. 94

W1711 While pleasing silence and the gloom of night
And my pale vision sickens with the day.

    [Robert Cholmeley], 'Upon the death of the honble
    ——— Sidney esq., brother of C[harles?] Montacute
    [Montagu?], killed by the Dutch in a sea engagement'

    c.190, p. 234

W1712 While pleasure's silken sons this day
And he's the lord of hosts.

    'A Lord's Day morning thought' [Gentleman's
    magazine, 1774]

    c.487, p. 114

W1713 While preparation's note with distant roar
To guard her fame, and vindicate her rights.

    [William Boscawen], 'Address to the subscribers of the
    Literary Fund at the anniversary meeting, 3 May 1798'

    fc.106, p. 54

W1714 While Prig of a lodging is taking survey
She archly replies I'm to be let alone.

    c.546, p. 25

W1715 While prime of youth us fireth within his flower,
Watch, write and read, and spend no idle hour.

    c.339, p. 321

W1716 While proud Goliath doth blaspheme in rage,
With this great beast disarms himself to fight.

    c.160, fol. 52v

W1717　While purchas'd grace by any is asserted
Th'unfeigned gift of the eternal Three.

　　[Thomas Gurney], '. . . You may as soon prove that
　　Christ purchased Hell for the reprobates as that he
　　purchased grace and the spirit for the elect . . . I will
　　repeat you a poem on this head'

　　c.213

W1718　While Ralph was wond'ring what his aunt
The undertaker's bill.

　　[Frederick Corfield]

　　c.381/1

W1719　While rich in brightest red the blushing rose
The warlike thistle's arms a sure defense for thee.

　　[Nicholas Rowe], 'An epigram on the union with
　　Scotland'

　　fc.60, p. 41

W1720　While Rome was wrapt in flames the learned say
When knaves and fools shall be remov'd, so be it.

　　'Remarks on the Council of Nine' [Carmarthen (later
　　duke of Leeds), Devonshire, Dorset, Bolton,
　　Nottingham, Peterborough, Marlborough, Lonsdale,
　　Orford; 1690]
　　[POAS v.214]

　　b.204, p. 75

W1721　While rosy health abounds in every breeze,
Our public father for the public weal.

　　[Francis Fawkes], 'To his Grace the Lord Archbishop
　　of Canterbury on his sickness and recovery, June 25,
　　1753'

　　fc.21, p. 15

W1722　While rotting here, a Protean miscreant lies,
Is ever grateful to th'eternal throne.

　　John Lockman, 'Epitaph (not a caricature) on a no
　　small sinner. Spoke in the person of Satan. 26 May
　　1762'

　　c.267/1, p. 305

W1723　While ruder bards their little wits employ,
And by rewarding merit—merit fame.

　　Poetry Box x/83

W1724　While sage Ulysses with his chosen band
But more of life he knows who lives at home.

　　[Robert Cholmeley], 'Plus habet hic vitae, plus habet
　　ille via.—Mart[ial]'

　　c.190, p. 66

W1725　While satire pleas'd and nothing else was writ
Not only what you wrote, but what you were.

　　Jeffrey Amherst, 1st baron Amherst, 'To the Earl of
　　Roscommon on his excellent essay on translated verse'

　　b.86, p. 51

W1726　While she her flames with blushes bold
I prithee love none but Jockey Nan.

　　b.213, p. 133

W1727　While she pretends to make the graces known
Is by her glass instructed how to write.

　　[Edmund] Waller, 'On a lady who writ in praise of
　　Mira'
　　[Crum w1875]

　　c.176, p. 124

W1728　While shepherds watch'd their flocks by night,
Begin and never cease.

　　[Nahum Tate], 'Christmas hymn'
　　[Crum w1876]

　　c.83/1, no. 167

W1729　While shrouded by an oak, in leafy state,
And feast three hours upon a single kiss.

　　John Lockman, 'Sonnet, from Goudeli[n], a famous
　　Gascon poem'

　　c.267/4, p. 87; see also 'Whilst . . .'.

W1730　While sinners, conscious of offence,
And wider spread the sacred flame!

　　R[ichard] V[ernon] S[adleir], 'On a lady sleeping
　　during part of divine service'

　　c.106, p. 90

W1731　While some pretty sonnets indite
In the lass with a masculine air.

　　'Song 235'

　　c.555, p. 372

W1732　While some to Bath's renewing springs repair
And gardens should be unto both resign'd.

　　[Abraham Cowley?], 'The comparison'

　　File 3782/1

W1733　While some with conscious guilt and boding fear
Blest in thy health, thy husband, and thy friends!

　　'Mrs B[ernard?] Augst 27 1767'

　　Poetry Box x/45, p. 35

W1734　While Spain's proud dons, beneath a woman's sway
And lead the van to humble Spain's proud queen.

　　John Hoadly, 'An epilogue, spoken by Mr Lacy in the
　　character of Candace—when the fall of Sagantum, a
　　tragedy was acted at Mr Newcome's School at
　　Hackney 1740/41'

　　c.360/1, p. 311

W1735　While strength and years permit, your work pursue
Ere stooping age steal unawares on you.

　　Poetry Box vi/114

W1736 While such as once have seen your beauty, dote
To bliss him with reciprocal affection.

    Sir Thomas Urquhart, 'To Lady Marie [crossed out]'
fb.217, p. 121

W1737 While sullen discord rears her snaky crest
To task the pleasures of a calm retreat.

    [Richard Vernon Sadleir?]
c.106, p. 55

W1738 While sympathy demands the tribute of a sigh,
Men will adore you, God forever bless.

    [R. H. C.], 'To ——— written after seeing The
    stranger [by Kotzebue]'
Poetry Box XII/61

W1739 While the air [is] mute so that [it] scarce [can] make
Then, and but then is a good master known.

    'Res adversa virtutes arguunt'
b.205, fol. 11r

W1740 While the dark world the sun's bright beams ascend,
As shadows bodies, when such things we see.

    'Feigned friendship'
c.356

W1741 While the distinguish'd orders of the state—
Prelude to fierce Culloden's deathless day.

    John Lockman, 'Verses: most humbly addressed to the
    Princess Dowager of Wales on her royal highness's
    birthday, 30 November 1757. Presented to her royal
    highness at Leicester House'
c.267/4, p. 29

W1742 While the lads of the village shall merrily ah!
Believe me thou'lt presently see. | While the lads &c.

    'The lads of the village'
Poetry Box IV/62

W1743 While the mongrel Calvinist boasts of his skill
I'd ha' all of a piece either Whitby or Gill.

    [Thomas Gurney], 'On the mongrel preacher. Written
    to his friend Mr. Thos. Brittain, a freewill Baptist
    minister'
c.213

W1744 While the saucy Frenchmen fluster,
They're of another style I hear.

    'The new lottery or eighty-seven blanks to a prize'
    [1756]
File 17488

W1745 While the way of the world is to keep all the best,
Give the thorn to yourself and the rose to your
                       friend.

    A[aron] Hill, 'To a lady who sent the top of a
    sweetbriar branch, and retained the worst end of it'
c.83/2, no. 716

W1746 While thee—dear Coote, thy fate removes
Which leadeth to thy fold of rest.

    [Mary (Shackleton) Leadbeater], 'To Charles Coote
    on leaving Ballitore School'
c.140, p. 84

W1747 While thee I seek protecting power,
That heart will rest on thee.

    'Address to the Deity'
c.391

W1748 While this gay toy attracts thy sight,
Secures an age in heav'n.

    Elizabeth Carter, 'On a watch addressed to a young
    lady'
    [Crum w1888]
fc.132/1, p. 2; File 13832

W1749 While those bright eyes subdue where'er you will
And more than all the muses can conspire.

    [William Walsh], 'Elegy. The power of verse to his
    mistress'
c.223, p. 54

W1750 While those who breathe Parnassus' air
To draw her heav'nly image at full length.

    'On pretty Sally the waiting maid at the sign of the
    Lamb . . . 1732'
c.360/1, p. 105

W1751 While through life's thorny road I go,
And for a chaplain I've God's grace.

    'The journey of life an allegoric elegy in the manner
    of Sir Walter Raleigh'
c.578, p. 23; c.83/1, no. 180

W1752 While thro' the slipp'ry paths of youth
And time shall be no more.

    [( ) Tomkins], 'Psalm 119, part 2d; paraphras'd'
Poetry Box IV/189

W1753 While thus I hang, you threaten'd see
The fate of him that stealeth me.

    [William Strode], couplet ending 'On a
    purse['s]-strings' [with 'We hug, imprison . . .']
    [Crum w1894]
b.200, p. 121; b.205, fol. 55v

W1754   While thus I wander, cheerless and unblest,
I only fly from doubt—to meet despair.

     C[harlotte (Turner)] Smith, 'Sonnet'

c.83/2, no. 715

W1755   While thy spouse is yet alive
Yet sorry I am that thou art gone.

     Cecilia [Burney], 'Lines addressed to Colonel
Leatherland . . . Cecelia aged 9 years'

c.486, fol. 35

W1756   While time advancing draws to nearer view,
For pleasures past my present misery.

Diggle Box: Poetry Box xi/64

W1757   While timid hope succceds well-grounded fears
Nor kill the maid of Enterkin again.

     [Helen Craik], 'To Captain Riddell'

c.375, p. 61

W1758   While to playhouses where comedians hear
And complaisant to feel and to be felt.

     [Sir Thomas Urquhart], 'Here is expressed an active
and passive example of all the five senses'

fb.217, p. 390

W1759   While tow'ring bards the fame of heroes sing
And all my suff'rings freely there impart.

     Edward Worlidge, 'The resurrection a poem' [pr. 1716
(Foxon W564)]

c.464

W1760   While W[olvese]y House neglected stands
Send down thy wife to sconce their diet!

     R[ichard] V[ernon] S[adleir], 'On a certain b[isho]p
[of Winchester] offering one of his [unfrequented]
episcopal palaces to be converted into a county
Bridewell'

c.106, p. 60, 75

W1761   While wandering oft near Dover's far-fam'd height,
Transmit that name whose luster gilds his own.

     [William Boscawen], 'Epistle to Mr Wm. Weller
Pepys, esquire, at Dover'

fc.106, p. 56

W1762   While weeping Albion does its loss bewail
And write a grief that ev'ry reader feels.

     [William Walsh], 'Funeral elegy upon the death of the
Queen, addressed to the Marquess of Normandy'

fc.61, p. 75

W1763   While winds frae off Ben Lomond blow,
His sweaty, wizen'd hide.

     [Robert Burns], 'Epistle to Davie' [1 Jan. 1787]

c.139, p. 586

W1764   While with a steady and a skillful hand
W'admire your conduct, and we hope for more.

     'To the Duke of Marlborough'

c.111, p. 89

W1765   While with fierce flames Whitehall was compast
                            round
To warn bold monarchs, and to grace this land.

     'Upon the burning of Whitehall, and preserving the
Banqueting House'

Poetry Box x/110; see also 'With the fierce flames . . .'.

W1766   While yet my poplar yields a doubtful shade,
And my soul bless thee in eternal night.

     [John Langhorne], 'Autumnal elegy, to ***'

c.139, p. 547

W1767   While you at ease in Tottridge Bowers
Bless all your valuable families.

     [Sir George Lee]

Poetry Box i/99; see also 'Whilst . . .'.

W1768   While you attack'd my work in prose
Rather than read, I fled the field.

     'From a celebrated author to a less celebrated critic'

Diggle Box: Poetry Box xi/69

W1769   While you, dear George, to pleasure true,
Mirth shall rule every day.

     [Charles Burney, the younger], 'To Mr. Grantham'

c.37, p. 13

W1770   While you dear Sir, inviting health and ease
And leave at home our countrymen to die.

     'An epistle to Richard Bentley esq. On the decline of
country innocence'

Poetry Box v/114 (incomplete?)

W1771   While you in cockpit, daily sat
So on the grass, I only lay.

     [Thomas Hamilton, 6th earl of Haddington], 'To the
Honble Mr Baillie an epistle'

c.458/2, p. 144

W1772   While you my fair one, sure to please,
No herb nor balm, can give me aid.

     'Love[.] Lines consisting entirely of monosyllables'

c.83/1, no. 218

W1773   While you my Lord the rural shades admire
And lines like Virgil's or like yours should praise.

     [Joseph] Addison, 'A letter from Italy, inscribed to the
Lord Halifax . . . 1701'

c.144, p. 49; c.244, p. 31

W1774 While you secure from noise and strife,
And wish you back to town again.

    'To Camilla'

c.153, p. 87

W1775 While you the circuit pleasures share,
And loudly I'll proclaim your merit.

    [Helen Craik], 'To Miss D——'

c.375, p. 74

W1776 While you, the flow'r of Yarrow, shine
To gable [gamble?] for the state!

    'Ode to Miss Mary Scott'

fc.51, p. 233

W1777 While you, with busy choice, and curious taste
The promise of his spring.

    'Ode to the author of the foregoing [Latin verse, on
    Milton's Paradise lost, by Timothy Thomas, of Christ
    Church, Oxford]'
    [Crum W1915]

c.241, p. 8

W1778 While you with more than Sapphic rage
To be admitted here again.

    'To Eliza [Bernard]'

Poetry Box x/45, p. 13

W1779 While young so turbulent the passions are
But oh! kind heav'n first teach me how to die.

    'A reflection'

c.487, p. 73

W1780 Whilom divided from the mainland stood
Whom it arising from the seas deters.

    [John Hepwith, 'The Caledonian forest']
    [Crum W1924]

b.5

W1781 Whilst a great many healths advance the stealth
For in a drunk out health, no health there is.

    Sir Thomas Urquhart, 'To one, whose too ardent
    comradeship in taverns was extremely prejudicial to
    his complexion'

fb.217, p. 121

W1782 Whilst Albion, to her rebel sons a prey
K[in]g J[ame]s she th[rone]d, as he did Charles
                      before.

    'On the 29th of May' [1715]

fc.58, p. 101

W1783 Whilst Albion's dauntless sons reap Gallic spoils;
Sly glaziers make tremendous conquests here.

    John Lockman, 'Writ whilst the mob were
    tumultuously calling out for lighted candles, and
    breaking windows, on account of the Battle of
    Dettingen . . . June 1743'

c.267/1, p. 33

W1784 Whilst all the town runs after Sally
Does far the puny Lamb exceed.

    'On Betty, the pretty maid at Dolly's beefsteak house
    at Butler's Head in Ivy Lane—London—1732'

c.360/2, no. 195

W1785 Whilst all your friends rejoicing say,
That I'm your friend, and so farewell.

    'Writ idly as an epistle to Bassett on his birthday
    June 2nd. [17]54 in the Easter holidays . . . April 19th.
    1754'

c.591

W1786 Whilst amo, and osculor she did begin
The active part, she made him a deponent.

    Sir Thomas Urquhart, 'An amorous trial betwixt a
    gentleman, and his mistress'

fb.217, p. 296

W1787 Whilst ancient dames and heroes in us live,
The memory of past actions great and good.

    [Benjamin Hoadley], 'Prologue to All for love, spoken
    to his grace the Duke of Marlborough'

c.176, p. 181 (attr. B. S.)

W1788 Whilst ancient fiction lends her magic aid,
And the true Jove maintain his envied sky?

    John Lockman, 'Writ during the rehearsal of the
    Italian drama, entitled La caduta di giganti, (The fall
    of the giants) performed at the opera house, after the
    expulsion of the rebels . . . Jany. 1745/6'

c.267/1, p. 176

W1789 Whilst at my house in Fleet Street once you lay
And live and died, dear Cob, with none but you.

    [Nicholas] Rowe, 'The reconcilement. A dialogue
    [between Jacob Tonson and William Congreve] in
    imitation of Hor. l. 3. od. 9 Donec gratus &c.'

Trumbull Box: Poetry Box XIII/69

W1790 Whilst at such distance from their native lands,
And check the Gallic pride, and humble haughty
                      Spain.

    'London, June 1740—on the three young lions
    whelped this month in the Tower'

c.94

W1791 Whilst Belgia's youth ambitious seeks to join
Be plung'd in Adria's depth to rise no more.

'Translation of an Alchaic [archaic?] ode prefixed . . .
by . . . Sr. Daniel Heinsius . . . counselor and
historiographer of Sweden to the old Elzivir ed[ition]
of Horace . . . 1629'

c.229/2, fol. 38

W1792 Whilst borne in sable state, Lorenzo's bier
Politian, master of th'Ausonian lyre.

[William Roscoe], trans., 'On the death of Politiano
by Cardinal Bembo' [from 'Lorenzo de Medici']

c.142, p. 108

W1793 Whilst Britain boast her empire o'er the deep,
And Spain still felt him when he breath'd no more.

[Edward Young], 'The epitaph on the monument in
Westminster Abbey erected in 1746 to the memory of
Lord Aubrey Beauclerk'

c.360/2, no. 147

W1794 Whilst Britain destitute of aid
Extracting gold from leaden brains.

'On Farinelli'

c.570/4, p. 167

W1795 Whilst Butler, needy wretch, was yet alive,
He ask'd for bread, and he received a stone.

[Samuel Wesley, the younger], 'Mr. Barber, an
alderman of the city of London, erected a monument
to the memory of Sam: Butler author of Hudibras,
several years since in Westminster Abbey. On which
occasion he wrote the following epigram'

c.83/2, no. 674; see also 'While . . .', 'When . . .'.

W1796 Whilst by invention's fancy-soothing aid,
'Where am I? 'tis the music of the spheres!'

John Lockman, 'Hearing Mr. Schuman perform on
the glasses . . . June 1761'

c.267/1, p. 311

W1797 Whilst cards, and drums(?), and dress the thoughts
engage,
And, from that culture, thou'lt sweet comforts find.

John Lockman, 'To a young lady, with my Epitome of
the history of England . . . June 1749'

c.267/1, p. 255

W1798 Whilst Cibber bard immortal crown'd with bays
To sing the day, and sing the nights | [With love,
wine and music &c.]

'Cantata for Mrs. Hope's birthday, Nov. 25th 1746 . . .
[music by] Handel: 'Twas at the royal feast . . .
recitative'

fc.51, p. 194

W1799 Whilst cities and boroughs, all keep such a pother
But the nation is living, tho' Sarah was dead.

[F. Pigott?], 'The poet's address To the Dis-honorable
W. P. esq.' [answered by 'Of envy you'll own . . .']

Poetry Box IV/152

W1800 Whilst crowding folks with strange ill faces,
That one mouse eats and t'other's starv'd.

[Matthew Prior?], 'To Fleetwood Sheppard'
[Crum W1933]

b.III, p. 534

W1801 Whilst cruel ague, thy dear health destroys
Heaven will relent, and all her joys restore.

[Thomas Hamilton, 6th earl of Haddington], 'To
Seraphine'

c.458/2, p. 171

W1802 Whilst Cupid, that he knew not's father,
Was any one more certain.

Sir Thomas Urquhart, 'The mother only knows
assuredly, who is the father of her child'

fb.217, p. 110

W1803 Whilst dauntless vice pursues its rapid way,
For Stonehouse lives what others only preach.

H[annah] More, 'The following lines were
wrote by . . .'

c.341, p. 160

W1804 Whilst duns were knocking at my door,
That you may all go home and spew | As I did.

Captain [Alexander] Radcliffe, 'Captain Radcliffe's
ramble'

b.105, p. 359; see also 'When duns . . .'.

W1805 Whilst early light springs from the skies,
Let those soft ties your hearts combine.

W[illiam] C[artwright], 'A wedding song'

b.200, p. 435

W1806 Whilst every bird upon the spray
Than on my native plains.

John Head, 'The native plains a song'

c.341, p. 4

W1807 Whilst ev'ry face, my lovely Charlotte, wears
And Erroll's blameless life a blest example prove.

Poetry Box II/4

W1808 Whilst Eyre with magic in his pious strains,
But empty sends good hearts, sound heads away.

    Charles Atherton Allnutt, 'The following epigram was
    addressed to the author of verses in the Reading paper,
    in praise of the revd. Jos. Eyre, a mere lecturer in
    morality . . .'

    c.112, p. 169

W1809 Whilst fame's hurried to diffuse,
And curs'd the twenty thousand pound.

    Trumbull Box: Poetry Box XIII/76

W1810 Whilst Fanny's native charms amaze
The other doth destroy.

    'The scornful beauty'

    c.94

W1811 Whilst Ferdinand the French is beating
Whether there hies a rogue like Wheton.

    [ ] Wheton, 'The surtout. To Mrs. Paul of Southfields
    Augt. the 25th 1759'

    c.484, p. 137

W1812 Whilst fierce Bellona threatn'd loud alarms,
For gold still brings its value from the mine.

    'A collection of state flowers' [pr. 1734 (Foxon C285)]

    c.570/4, p. 28

W1813 Whilst flatt'ring courtiers, on this gaudy day,
For all the rest, without a wish, are thine.

    John Lockman, 'To the Earl of Middlesex: New Year's
    Day, 1753'

    c.267/1, p. 218

W1814 Whilst, from the cloth, thou call'st the mimic life;
Throw rays round each, and mingle fire with fire!

    John Lockman, 'To Mr. Whood: when Mr. Handel
    was sitting for his picture . . . 1745'

    c.267/1, p. 163

W1815 Whilst from thy dreaded lovely light I flee
And pious visions gild the fleeting day.

    'Abelard to Eloisa writ by a young gentleman in
    answer to the celebrated Eloisa to Abelard written
    some years since by Mr. Pope'

    c.360/2, no. 144

W1816 Whilst Glaurus from a brawling chairman born
Whom they more fear than they admire his son.

    R[obert] Shirley, 1st earl of Ferrers, 'From [Boileau]'

    c.347, p. 90

W1817 Whilst grateful Britons chant the sacred lay,
And thunders its great fiat from the skies.

    John Lockman, 'After hearing Mr. Handel's God save
    the king, sung and played in Vauxhall Gardens, during
    violent thunder and lightning . . . 7 Sept. 1745'

    c.267/1, p. 264

W1818 Whilst half asleep my Chloe lies,
And think each precious moment flies too fast.

    [Soame Jenyns], 'Given to a lady with a watch which
    she borrowed to hang at her bed's head'

    c.147, p. 49

W1819 Whilst happy I, triumphant stood,
And of love's temple, keep the door.

    [Aphra] Behn, 'On a juniper tree now cut down to
    make busks'

    b.105, p. 214

W1820 Whilst happy in Clarinda's sight I live
Or language can declare how much I love.

    [Philip Doddridge], 'On forgetting Clarinda's
    birthday till it was too late to draw up a copy of verses
    which the author had intended upon that occasion.
    Oct. 1st 1729' [addressed to Miss Kitty Freeman]

    Poetry Box IV/45

W1821 Whilst he shaves one side of Luperius' face
Fresh hair grows up and fills the vacant place.

    R[obert] Shirley, 1st earl of Ferrers, 'To an ill barber.
    From [Martial]'

    c.347, p. 33

W1822 Whilst health and youth lead on the sprightly hours,
To fancy, friendship, harmony, and love.

    [William Roscoe], 'Verses written on the blank leaf of
    a book in which a lady had made a selection of poems'

    c.142, p. 512

W1823 Whilst heav'n protects us with a guardian hand
With wide-stretched faith believe thy damn'd
                                     infallibility.

    [ ] Archer, A. M., 'The fifth of November. AD 1725'

    c.190, p. 40

W1824 Whilst his sacred Majesty pays for my drink and
                                     my whore
And he rules his people,—by his own example.

    'To the tune of a country dance; then a good deal in
    fashion wrote early in Charles 2d's time'

    Spence Papers, folder 113

W1825 Whilst humble beings, to one lot confin'd,
Own how impartial are the laws of God.

    P. N. Shuttleworth, 'Non omnis moriar . . . 1800'

    c.495, p. 13

W1826   Whilst I gaze on Chloe trembling,
        Seldom meets with due repose.

        'A song'
        c.358, p. 76

W1827   Whilst I listen to thy voice
        Is that they sing, and that they love.

        [Edmund Waller]
        [Crum W1950]
        fb.66/27

W1828   Whilst I Maria's praise rehearse
        Give us joys unmix'd with pain.

        'An ode for Mrs. D—n—ll's birthday Feb. 27th 1737/8'
        Poetry Box I/62

W1829   Whilst I praise you, I neither lie, nor flatter
        So merit they most praise, can most despise it.

        Sir Thomas Urquhart, 'To my Lady [crossed out]'
        fb.217, p. 222

W1830   Whilst I was darling of your breast
        'Twill serve us two, to bowse in.

        'In imitation of the 9th ode of the 3d. book of Horace'
        [pr. 1719 (Foxon N304)]
        c.570/2, p. 64

W1831   Whilst I was lov'd by thee, and on thy breast
        Yet with my Horace would I live and die.

        'Horace lib. III ode ix'
        c.176, p. 46

W1832   Whilst in high jumping he could do no more,
        T'outstrip a measure of a greater length.

        Sir Thomas Urquhart, 'How a Scots gentleman did contest with his mistress in leaping upon heights'
        fb.217, p. 287

W1833   Whilst in the dark, on thy soft hand I hung,
        But when the candle enter'd, I was cur'd.

        'From Martial'
        b.197, p. 250

W1834   Whilst in your husband's dalliance you are bashful
        Your wit, and beauty, to crown his enjoying.

        Sir Thomas Urquhart, 'To the Countess of [crossed out]'
        fb.217, p. 234

W1835   Whilst it is day, you're th'object of my sight:
        But of my love, the subject, when 'tis night.

        Sir Thomas Urquhart, 'On speaks here to a fair gentlewoman with whom he had purchased leave, to be most intrinsically familiar'
        fb.217, p. 319

W1836   Whilst just faint-dawning in yon dappled east
        And love and carols blithe pass on the day.

        'On Bradfield'
        fc.61, p. 95

W1837   Whilst logically he reason'd with Despina
        T'infer a consequence in her mid-figue.

        Sir Thomas Urquhart, 'Of a logician, and his mistress Despina'
        fb.217, p. 20

W1838   Whilst martial sounds and loftier strains proclaim
        A new retirement sought and fled to endless rest.

        'On the death of the Revd Mr Modd Fellow of Trinity College soon after the death of the Duke of Marlborough' [1722?]
        Poetry Box X/72; see also 'While . . .'.

W1839   Whilst maudlin Whigs deplore their Cato's fate
        For this road leads directly to the heart.

        [Nicholas Rowe], 'An epigram on a lady who made water at seeing the tragedy of Cato'
        fc.60, p. 28

W1840   Whilst modern heroes, in pursuit of fame,
        Pomfret grac'd Oxford with these spoils of Rome.

        [William Carpenter], 'To Lady Pomfret on her visiting the University of Oxford, after having presented it with some valuable statues of antiquity'
        c.247, p. 132

W1841   Whilst nature did herself perplex
        But left him of the doubtful gender.

        [John] Taylor (1704–1766), 'An epigram upon a beautiful young man imitated from Ausonius by . . . and applied to Mr Lovell of St Johns Coll. Camb. Dum dubitat &c.' [answered by 'Lovell was of the doubtful gender . . .']
        c.190, p. 22

W1842   Whilst no repulse thy courage can abate
        These sad truths did appear.

        Bevill Higgons, 'Mr. Bevill Higgon's address to the Earl of Oxford, in the beginning of his poem on the late peace'
        c.570/1, p. 92

W1843   Whilst none more dear to Lydia's arms,
        With thee, I'd live and die.

        [William Popple, trans.], '[Horace] book 3rd. ode 9th. Dialogue between Horace and Lydia'
        fc.104/2, p. 240

W1844   Whilst o'er these moving lines which sweetly flow
        The plaintive verse to eternize your name.

        'To a young lady'
        c.130, p. 21

W1845　Whilst oft the coast of Shetland
Must swell the nation's wealth. | And a digging, &c.

　　John Lockman, 'The Welsh miners: the tune, And a
　　begging we will go &c'

　　c.267/2, p. 65

W1846　Whilst on the fam'd antiques intent we gaze,
Eclips'd the Grecian, by the Wilton Venus.

　　John Lockman, 'The busts, or the fair maid of
　　Wilton, the seat of the Earl of Pembroke . . . 1749'

　　c.267/1, p. 100

W1847　Whilst, on the Po's imperial stream,
But can't the fire of love.

　　[ ] Temple, 'Ode, wrote by . . . in his travels from
　　Naples'

　　fc.51, p. 43

W1848　Whilst on the verge of life I stand
To love and praise my Lord below.

　　[Philip] Doddridge, 'Lines wrote by . . . a few days
　　before his death'

　　c.487, p. 81

W1849　Whilst on thy bosom I recline
'Tis death to be disjoin'd.

　　'A sonnet wrote by a husband, but not a modern one'
　　File 17485

W1850　Whilst other princes tread th'ensanguin'd field,
And those shall crown thee with unenvied praise.

　　John Lockman, 'Writ under a print by Mr. Baron, by
　　his Majesty, when Prince of Wales, as governor of the
　　Herring Fishery . . . May 1755'

　　c.267/1, p. 147

W1851　Whilst others were to bolder action rous'd
Is to divine philosophy espous'd.

　　[Sir Philip Wodehouse?], 'Sir Philip Wodehouse
　　philosophy espous'd'

　　b.131, back (no. 17/1)

W1852　Whilst our great Moll bravely her breath resigns
Will should have knotted and Moll gone for
　　　　　　　　　　　　　　　　　　　　　Flanders.

　　[on the death of Queen Mary]
　　Poetry Box VII/45

W1853　Whilst petty offences, and felonies smart,
The muses, and graces, just make up a jury.

　　'Thrown into a young lady's lap, at a country assize'
　　c.378, p. 75

Whilst Phaon to the hothouse hies　　　　　　　W1854
But hang thyself and there's an end.

　　W. T., 'Sappho and Phaon by Sir C[ar]r Sc[roo]p[e]
　　done into burlesque'

　　b.371, no. 25

Whilst Phoebus shines on you, a shad' attends　　W1855
With your decaying fortune perisheth.

　　Sir Thomas Urquhart, 'To one, who was subject both
　　to change of fortune, and friends'

　　fb.217, p. 113

Whilst princes meet whence all rebellion springs,　W1856
And France's coffers must by Mons be filled.

　　'On the taking of Mons'
　　b.111, p. 262

Whilst Prior's ghost bewails his partial doom　　W1857
Thee live in him, as Prior lives in thee.

　　'To Mr. Le Hunt on his verses to the memory of
　　Matthew Prior esq; by Mr Rev[blotted]'

　　c.416

Whilst she was Peter's heart,　　　　　　　　　W1858
The horns being only Peter's.

　　Sir Thomas Urquhart, 'Of one too free of her body,
　　whose husband's name was Peter'

　　fb.217, p. 234

Whilst, shrouded by an oak, in leafy state,　　　W1859
And feast three hours upon a single kiss.

　　[John Lockman], 'Sonnet. From [Pierre] Goudelin,
　　celebrated Gascon poet'

　　c.268 (second part), p. 103; see also 'While . . .'.

Whilst silence gave new horror to the night,　　W1860
That all my doors, my Lord, were open left below.

　　'The apparition'
　　c.83/2, no. 366

Whilst sky-borne justice, mild, sagacious, clear,　W1861
And, like with incense, shall embalm thy name.

　　John Lockman, 'To his daughter Bennett, (when
　　under seven years of age,) whose evidence got the
　　author his damages, in a cause [Lockman vs. the
　　Salisbury coach owners] tried 18 June, 1745, in
　　Guildhall, before the Lord Chief Justice Willes'
　　[Crum W1977]

　　c.267/1, p. 167

Whilst some men honor raise from dust and sweat　W1862
Have lived, and may continue, as we here.

　　[George Daniel]
　　b.121, fol. 17

W1863 Whilst some the ancients, some the moderns praise
Thinking them gods, would sacrifice to men!

[Charles Earle], 'To Mr. John Drake of Barnstaple'

c.376

W1864 Whilst tasteless ministers, with pride attend
Their genius, maxims, all reviv'd in thee.

[John Lockman], 'To Mr. De Bussy, late envoy from
his Gallic Majesty'

c.268 (first part), p. 37; c.267/1, p. 259

W1865 Whilst that a silent poem on the wall
And this a speaking picture you may call.

M[aurice] J[ohnson], 'Dicitur haec—pictura loquens
selet illa vocari'

c.229/2, fol. 10v

W1866 Whilst that you may there treasure up your store,
Where without rust it lasts forevermore.

c.339, p. 328

W1867 Whilst the group of bright belles
Or are they three halfpence apiece.

'Made extempore upon a printed list of the
Scarborough beauties price three halfpence'

c.53, fol. 51

W1868 Whilst the lawn'd prelates crown the royal pair,
Seems, from on high, to bid the land rejoice.

John Lockman, 'A thought: on the sudden change in
the weather, from dark to beautiful, on the coronation
of their Majesties King George III. and Queen
Charlotte . . . 22 Sept. 1761'

c.267/1, p. 308

W1869 Whilst the mad rage of hostile foes
And science greatly thrives, and arts revive again.

Charles Atherton Allnutt, 'The happy state of Britain
contrasted with the misery of the belligerent powers
in the North'

c.112, p. 6

W1870 Whilst the magic force of mingled dyes,
And, close pursued, like desperados die.

John Lockman, 'A comparison: suggested by the grand
stage-battle, between the Macedonians and Indians, in
the opera of Alessandro with Indie . . . May 1746'

c.267/1, p. 42

W1871 Whilst the sad silence of the quiet night
My morning star of happiness appears.

[ ] Prigher, 'An ode in dialogue supposing the son
[Sidney Montagu, killed in battle 28 May 1672] to
comfort his mother in a dream'

fb.68, p. 83

W1872 Whilst the town's brimful of folly
Sing old songs as well as she.

'The prudential lover, set by Mr. Munro'

fc.61, p. 63

W1873 Whilst the weather-cock town veers to ev'rything
new,
When, prais'd by this voice, from my amorous lay.

John Lockman, 'To Chloe . . . Aug. 1750'

c.267/1, p. 220

W1874 Whilst the young poet's verses lie,
And makes immortal,—verse like mine.

[ ] Burges, 'Preface for a manuscript collection of
poems'

c.504, p. 1

W1875 Whilst thick to court transported Tories run
Forgive his father—not forget thine own.

'To the right honble. Earl of Oxford upon his not
appearing at court' [pr. 1727? (Foxon T392)]

c.570/3, p. 31

W1876 Whilst thieves, and robbers render what they catch:
Death naught restores: though she all mortals
snatch.

Sir Thomas Urquhart, 'Of the unsatiableness of death'

fb.217, p. 271

W1877 Whilst this bumper stands by me, brimful of
cider-o,
We'll be, as becomes us, exceeding drunk boys.

'An extempore catch on the Vigo expedition'

c.233, p. 99

W1878 Whilst thou blest John wert in thy mother's womb
Whose day shall never after sleep in night.

[Sir Richard Bulstrode], 'Upon St John Baptist['s] life
and death'

fb.88, p. 117v; see also 'To these again . . .'.

W1879 Whilst tho' absent all thy graces
Softest sighs shall tell the rest.

'To Stella'

Poetry Box I/39

W1880 Whilst thousands court fair Chloe's love
Than those, whene'er you fly.

[Soame Jenyns], 'To Chloe hunting'

c.147, p. 15

W1881 Whilst, thro' Her Grace's bounty, heaven bestows
Who poison all things with their filthy looks.

John Lockman, 'Writ at Berney, in France . . . 1741'

c.267/1, p. 62

w1882 Whilst tides of joy this day proclaim
And Trumbull shall again protect her state.

> [Sir William Trumbull, to his wife on the birth of their son?]
>
> Trumbull Box: Poetry Box XIII/99

w1883 Whilst timid bosoms sigh for Britain's fate,
Who labor more to make their country great.

> C. B., 'To Sr George Hay Lord of the Admiralty'
>
> c.74

w1884 Whilst to excess we drink, and live in ease,
Have not our work to do, when time is done.

> J[ohn] R[obinson], 'Dum bibimus, dum serta, unguenta, puella . . .'
>
> c.370, fol. 21v

w1885 Whilst treble brass thy harden'd brow defends
Can furnish halters to atone thy guilt.

> 'The reverse to Lord Oxford'
>
> c.570/1, p. 92

w1886 Whilst true religion is by thee embrac'd
Under the altar is thy safety plac'd.

> [Sir Philip Wodehouse], 'Jacobus Stuartus . . .'
>
> b.131, back (no. 3)

w1887 Whilst venal poets consecrate to fame
Unmixed, unchangeable, eternal joy.

> [John] Hervey, baron Hervey of Ickworth, 'Verses to the memory of my dearest sister Lady Barbara May'
>
> Poetry Box v/10

w1888 Whilst Venus plum'd his purple wings
Just as he freezes let her burn.

> M[aurice] J[ohnson], 'A song partly from Anacreon, partly from Catullus'
>
> c.229/2, fol. 18

w1889 Whilst we are blest with none but common joys,
And all around pleas'd Cupids clap their wings.

> [Thomas Creech], 'To the [Duke and] Duchess of York [and princess Anne, spoken] by Sir Thomas Trollope' [Oxford, 21 May 1683]
> [Crum w2004, 'were blest']
>
> fb.142, p. 24

w1890 Whilst weeping we inter this little form,
We may with him, blest favorite saint! be crowned.

> 'At the funeral of the Revd. Mr. Durande'
>
> Poetry Box XIV/185

w1891 Whilst well-wrote lines our wond'ring eyes command
To steal your hand, in hopes to steal your heart.

> [Soame Jenyns], 'To [a lady in town after leaving the country], in answer to a letter, wrote in a fine hand'
>
> c.147, p. 9

w1892 Whilst whores ruled Charles, those whores I rul'd
A friend at b[a]r shall send him home again.

> 'King John's reign Duke of Marlborough' [1714/15]
> [Crum w2006]
>
> fc.58, p. 104

w1893 Whilst William van Nassau with Bentinck bardasha
You shall hear of in prose and in verse.

> 'The reflection' [Jacobite satire on King William and Queen Mary, 1689]
> [Crum w2007; POAS v.60]
>
> b.111, p. 365; fb.207/2, p. 100; Spence Papers, folder 113

w1894 Whilst William's deeds and William's praise
And hang them on thy tomb.

> [Sir Charles Hanbury Williams], 'Ode to the right honorable Stephen Poyntz esqr. late preceptor to the Duke of Cumberland'
>
> c.241, p. 57

w1895 Whilst you at Chilcote live, and I at Pooley
To all our absent friends at every tale.

> [Sir Aston Cokayne], 'To my cousin, Mr W: Milward'
>
> b.275, p. 39

w1896 Whilst you at ease in Totteridge Bowers
Bless all your valuable families.

> [Sir George Lee], 'From Doctor's Commons Wednesday even | Decembris at the hour eleven'
>
> Poetry Box I/136; see also 'While . . .'.

w1897 Whilst you at your Stoke are enjoying your time,
And a night of sweet sleep crown'd a sweetly spent day.

> H[annah] M[ore], 'A trip to the Passage to Miss Blandford'
>
> c.341, p. 65

w1898 Whilst you content yourself in fold
I should much rather learn than teach.

> 'Horat. Epistol. lib. 1. epist. 10. Putney'
>
> Poetry Box I/133

w1899 Whilst you, dear friend, the rural sweets enjoy,
Perhaps delight me in a happier sphere.

> 'A letter from a gentleman in London to his friend at R—a in Monmouthshire'
>
> c.341, p. 54

W1900   Whilst you, dear maid, o'er thousands born to reign,
        Lost in eternal night, again she dies.

> [Soame Jenyns], 'To a lady in town soon after her
> leaving the country'

c.147, p. 3

W1901   Whilst you dear object of my care and joy,
        May you with greater luster be adorn'd.

> [Elizabeth (Shirley) Compton, countess of
> Northampton], 'To Lord Compton Aug: 31 1738'

Accession 97.7.40

W1902   Whilst you illumine Shakespeare's page,
        And leave to Heaven the rest.

> 'To Edmund Malone esq. . . . Sept 22. 1784' (Printed
> in GM January 1786)

c.343, p. 86

W1903   Whilst you, in black prunella gown,
        If so, dear Gibby, I rejoice.

> [Thomas Hamilton, 6th earl of Haddington], 'To
> Mr. [Gilbert] Burnet epistle 1st'

c.458/2, p. 123

W1904   Whilst you in mirth your Christmas spend
        And ever faithful friend | Pompey.

> 'Pompey's lamentation . . . this was written one year
> before his death'

c.91, p. 8

W1905   Whilst you in Rome about a twelvemonth stayed
        But what (without your leave) I shall not tell.

> [Sir Aston Cokayne], 'To my worthy friend Mr
> Richard Symmonds'

b.275, p. 100

W1906   Whilst you, my charming Nancy, reign
        They're conscious who 'twas libell'd you.

> [Robert] Downes, of Merton College, 'A ballad, to the
> tune of To you fair ladies now at land occasioned by a
> late copy of verses on Miss Brickenden's going to
> Newnham by water' ['From Isis's banks . . .']
> [Crum W2015]

Spence Papers, folder 113; Poetry Box IV/127

W1907   Whilst you my Lord with subtle tricks
        And love your country seat.

> [William] Pulteney, [earl of Bath], 'An epistle from
> Ld Lovel to Lord Chesterfield at Bath supposed to be
> wrote by . . .'

c.154, p. 17

W1908   Whilst you retir'd at Alsop in the Dale,
        You mix much pleasure with some easy cares.

> [Sir Aston Cokayne], 'To my cousin Mr Robert
> Milward'

b.275, p. 38

W1909   Whilst your fam'd works through the capacious
                                              earth
        Till judgment calls, it [?] ascends the skies.

> R[obert] Shirley, 1st earl of Ferrers, 'A translation of
> Cowley's epitaph—aurea dum &c.'

c.347, p. 7

W1910   Whilst you're below a man's enamor'd weight,
        Surmounts the burden in proportion.

> Sir Thomas Urquhart, 'That the burden of a gallant
> man in dalliance, maketh the woman so much the
> more sprightly, and lighter. To Sylvia'

fb.217, p. 200

W1911   Whilst youth doth last with lively sap and strength
        Then take thy rest, let younglings work and moil.

> [Geffrey Whitney]
> [Crum W2017]

b.234, p. 313

W1912   Whilst Zarah from the royal ground
        But her, that owns the wood.

> 'On the Duchess of Marlborough's cutting down the
> oak in her garden which was planted by King Charles
> the 2nd himself; from an acorn growing on the Royal
> Oak' [1708]
> [cf. Crum W1974, 'Whilst Sarah']

c.570/1, p. 61

W1913   Whirl'd through this rapid vortex, I
        Freed from the rigid gripe of care.

> [Charles Burney, the elder], 'Epistle, to Lady Hales,
> who had invited the author to her country house in
> Kent. Written in London. June. 1776'

c.33, p. 89

W1914   Whist is no cause for modern folks
        As sav'd his credit, and the game.

> [Maurice Johnson], 'To Wm. Noel in imitation of
> Monsr. Fontaine and Mr. Prior, on his behavior at
> Mr. Bayley's in Derby'

c.229/2, fol. 28v

W1915   W[hi]tb[rea]d a stranger like Bayard to fear
        Whoe'er in hatred did more good than harm.

c.340

W1916   White as her hand, fair Julia threw
        But with an equal fire.

> [Soame Jenyns], 'The snowball from Petronius
> Afranius'

c.147, p. 55

W1917 White maid, well met; what may I call thy name?
When purple robes do cover scarlet sins.

    Rob[ert] Davenport, 'They [policy and piety] meet
    and greet'

    b.52/2, p. 191

W1918 Whither are all her false oaths blown
That was so perjur'd in her love.

    [Robert Herrick], 'A complaint' [answered by 'Go
    perjur'd man . . .']
    [Crum w2023]

    b.205, fol. 73v

W1919 'Whither away, fair maid?' I cried,
And to each other grant us all.

    'Pious memory'

    c.83/3, no. 993

W1920 Whither Bacchus full of thee,
Ivy-crown'd, to follow thee.

    [William Popple, trans.], '[Horace] book 3rd. ode
    25th. To Bacchus'

    fc.104/2, p. 294

W1921 Whither fairest art thou running
I loathe the host I loathe the feast.

    [John Gay, Alexander Pope, and/or John Hughes],
    [chorus from Handel's Acis and Galatea, with musical
    score for bass]

    Music MS. 534

W1922 Whither O! whither flies the sleepy pow'r,
One gentle shepherd to thy wish unkind.

    Miss [ ] White, of Edgbaston, 'Elegy'

    c.532

W1923 Whither rush ye, foul with guilt?
Vengeance follow'd still his race.

    [William Popple, trans.], '[Horace ep]ode 7th. To the
    Roman people'

    fc.104/2, p. 424

W1924 Whither the three estates of this realm
Demonstrate us the way in peace, and wars.

    Sir Thomas Urquhart, 'To the Duke of Lenox'

    fb.217, p. 34

W1925 Whither thou son of Beor haste thou so,
Hath switch'd, and spurr'd him to eternal pain.

    H[enry] C[olman], 'On Balaam, and his ass'

    b.2, p. 97

W1926 Whither you impious Britons do you run?
Entails your curse and will confound you all.

    [Henry Hall, of Hereford], 'To the seventh epode of
    Horace'
    [Crum w2032]

    fb.207/3, p. 9; c.570/2, p. 131

W1927 Who are those mercenary elves
Why greedy fat churchwardens.

    'Churchwardens'

    c.360/3, no. 147

W1928 Who are wont to lie, their punishment is just
That when they speak a truth, they get no trust.

    [Sir Philip Wodehouse]

    b.131, p. 32

W1929 Who brought the marble to Praxiteles,
To him, that furnish'd Orpheus with the lute.

    Sir Thomas Urquhart, 'Concerning those who for
    affording the ground, whereon to build an epigram,
    ascribe to themselves the honor of the poesy: as if one,
    because he should have happened to say, that puritans
    are not charitable, would therefore allege, that the
    lines composed to that purpose, were his'

    fb.217, p. 322

W1930 Who but remembers yesterday
Adieu the hopes of Britain's isle.

    [Lionel Cranfield Sackville, 1st] duke of Dorset, 'On
    the death of Frederick Prince of Wales'
    [Crum w2040]

    Poetry Box IV/150; File 9162

W1931 Who can a verse to such a friend refuse?
Your hope's a crown great Sir a half-crown mine.

    [Phanuel Bacon], 'A schoolboy's first copy on the 10th
    of June who was promised half a crown for making it'

    c.237, fol. 11

W1932 Who can be silent or lukewarm, if he
We must be earnest, not impatient.

    [John Hobart], 'Advice to pray'

    b.108, fol. 3

W1933 Who can believe, with common sense,
Don't even signify a button.

    'A clergyman censured for wearing a button in his hat'
    [cf. Crum w2045, by Jonathan Swift]

    c.94

W1934 Who can deny the greatness of a man
But we will [?] you to drown out your [?].

    [( ) Forbes, laird of] Culloden, 'An epitaph on the
    Earl of Seaforth' [c. 1701]

    Poetry Box VIII/60

W1935 Who can doubt (Rice) to which eternal place
Which both should live by faith, and none by blood.

R[ichard] Corbett, 'On the death of Mr Rice, maniple of Ch[rist] Ch[urch]'
b.200, p. 211

W1936 Who can exalt their hearts above
Love towards all, such is the saints above.

[Edmund Wodehouse], 'Jan. 20 [1715]'
b.131, p. 146

W1937 Who can God's goodness show forth so,
And therefore our most real wisdom 'tis.

[Edmund Wodehouse], 'Iterum [21 April 1715]'
b.131, p. 202

W1938 Who can hide fire, if't be uncover'd, light,
If hid they're sighs, if open, they are words.

'Love inconcealable'
[Crum W2051]
c.360/3, no. 55

W1939 Who can on this picture look
Is whore in all things, but her face.

'On the Duchess of Portsmouth's picture'
[Crum W2053]
fb.140, p. 177

W1940 Who can the hardest task refuse
It must be from the deaf and blind.

[Mary Barber], 'To Lady [Elizabeth Brownlow] upon her desiring the author to send her some of her verses'
Poetry Box IV/132

W1941 Who can the joys discover?
And almost enjoy all over. | Who can &c.

'Song'
c.189, p. 117

W1942 Who can thy lady's name declare,
In what they all excel?

R[obert] Shirley, 1st earl of Ferrers, 'Upon an unknown beauty at the opera. From the French'
c.347, p. 40

W1943 Who can to thy bright character refuse
And bright like thine (dear shade) my sun go down.

'To the honored memory of Rebecca Smith'
c.517, fol. 6v

W1944 Who chooseth apples by their skin
And the French core in the other.

'Choice of a wife'
b.356, p. 102

W1945 Who could endure the reign
The highest sense of this great happiness.

[Sir William Trumbull], 'Mulb[erry] garden'
Trumbull Box: Poetry Box XIII/56

W1946 Who could have thought that Juliet e'er could prove
You then may claim her merit as your own.

'Prologue spoken by Mr. Barry in the character of Romeo at Covent Garden Theater on Mrs. Cibber's having left that house, and Miss Mary Nossiter commencing actress, being but in the 18th year of her age, and making her first appearance on the stage in the character of Juliet . . . Wednesday October the 10th 1753'
c.360/3, no. 255

W1947 Who could have thought that Rome's convert so near
For the honor of England to battle shall ride.

'A ballad on Ld. Sunder[land] coming to court. To Packington's pound'
[Crum W2061, with two more stanzas; POAS V.396]
b.204, p. 56; fb.70, p. 219; b.111, p. 541 ('thought of')

W1948 Who could have thought the rule of three
The graces are imprinted.

'Crewe Hall March 23rd 1783. On reading Mrs Crewe's little book of domestic laws'
Poetry Box II/43

W1949 Who could imagine that furious cutthroat Cromwell
And 'mongst bright angels, glorify your fames.

'A poem upon Cromwell, and his archtraitorous rabble . . .'
fb.228/27

W1950 Who could more happy, who more blest could live,
That fills me with excess of grief, this with excess of joy.

[William] Walsh, 'Jealousy'
c.351, p. 82; c.223, p. 56

W1951 Who counts the blades of grass that clothe the meads;
And there, 'mong fishes, won the regal title.

John Lockman, 'Herrings . . . Sept. 1751'
c.267/1, p. 107

W1952 Who dares affirm this is no pious age
The poet's wit than in the player's dressing.

[Jonathan] Swift, 'An epilogue wrote by . . . spoken at a benefit night for the poor weavers of Dublin' [pr. 1721 (Foxon S838)]
c.166, p. 214

W1953 Who does not extol our conquest marine?
Yet he triumphs at home and is victor by vote. |
Courage and conduct &c.

Poetry Box IV/97

W1954 Who does this glorious navy bring?
The suppliant world Protector else subdue!

[Katherine?] Philips, 'Upon his sacred Majesty's
Charles the Second's happy passage to England
May 29:th 1660'

b.207, p. 17

W1955 Who doth bad deeds with suff'rings will be crost,
Yet doth he still least ill, that suffers most.

Sir Thomas Urquhart, 'Action, and passion'

fb.217, p. 106

W1956 Who duly will consider each endowment,
To be compared with the least of them.

Sir Thomas Urquhart, 'To my Lord [crossed out]'

fb.217, p. 286

W1957 Who 'f naught made all, h'alone is all and aught,
That God of nothing made, that all is naught.

Sir Thomas Urquhart, 'The Creator and the
creatures'

fb.217, p. 297

W1958 Who fears a palsy doth the best death fear
Is sure mistaken and fears only death.

[John Hobart], '[Præludia mortis.] Æt. 60. The
choice'

b.108, fol. 7

W1959 Who first call'd letters to the wretch's aid?
Like thee they scrawl'd—but not like thee they sung.

Poetry Box III/2

W1960 Who from perennial streams shall bring,
O grief, beyond all other grief.

[William Roscoe], trans., 'Politiano on the death of
Lorenzo de Medici'

c.142, p. 104

W1961 Who gives to strumpets gold, his lust t'abate:
Buries his repentance at too dear a rate.

Sir Thomas Urquhart, 'Against expensive lechery'

fb.217, p. 333

W1962 Who governs his own course with heavy [steady]
hand

This I confess is a free man.

[Abraham Cowley]

b.118, p. 10

W1963 Who guiltless spend each fleeting hour,
May own and crown my toils!

'Horace, Book the 1st Ode 22d imitated'

c.135, p. 34

W1964 Who hapless, helpless, being! who
Which forfeit or secure your heav'n.

'Elegy on a poor idiot' [watermark 1797]

Poetry Box IV/46

W1965 Who has believ'd thy word,
And bore their sins, and died.

[Isaac Watts, Hymn]

c.180, p. 28

W1966 Who has e'er been at Woodhouse must needs
know the fair
Your view was confin'd to a foot and a half. | Derry
down down down derry

'Song' [imitation of Matthew Prior's 'Who has e'er
been at Paris . . .']
[cf. Crum w2082, W2083]

Poetry Box X/78

W1967 Who has lodg'd
To her last lodging here.

'An epitaph in Chipping Norton churchyard
Oxfordshire—Here lieth the body of Phyllis wife of
John Humphreys ratcatcher'

c.240, p. 133

W1968 Who hate declares, is sure of hate again:
Why is not love return'd with mutual love?

c.549, p. 23

W1969 Who hath of conscience a profound remorse
It being continued to a happy end.

[Sir Thomas Urquhart], 'The price of honest deeds
being in the doing the only true progress in a blessed
life'

fb.217, p. 529

W1970 Who haunts the playhouse but to please his ears
Not for the doctrine, but the music there.

b.155, p. 68

W1971 Who having what may fitly satisfy
The fault's not in the wealth, but in the mind.

[Sir Thomas Urquhart], 'He that hath that which is
necessary is not poor'

fb.217, p. 497

W1972 Who heartily loves God, is truly wise,
And therefore our more perfect wisdom is.

[Edmund Wodehouse], 'Feb. 12 [1715]'

b.131, p. 165

W1973 Who him envies with [?] [?] pays
       But who envies him not him he envies.

         [Sir Thomas Urquhart], 'An ambitious self-lover who
         puts his felicity in the fruition his aspiring [?], and to
         be honored with more than ordinary respect'

       fb.217, p. 518

W1974 Who honors kings doth honor God, for they
       Such as Maecenas did himself express.

         Robert Codrington, 'A welcome to London to the
         truly honorable Sir Robert Gordon knight and
         baronet'

       Poetry Box VIII/59

W1975 Who in this frantic strain to beauty's praise
       Flay'd by Apollo for a lesser crime.

         'To Mr. B—y on his ridiculous imitation of Paphos
         Britannica' [answer to 'From Troy Novant's
         northeastern gate . . .'; see also 'Begin the nine . . .']

       c.162, p. 17

W1976 Who in this synod bark like galley slaves
       And buy their stock to make a gleek of knaves.

       fb.70, p. 27

W1977 Who is a maid or not is so ambiguous
       To read the darkest secrets of the heart.

         [Sir Thomas Urquhart], 'How difficult a matter it is to
         know a real maid viricapable'

       fb.217, p. 498

W1978 Who is as the Christian great,
       Feasts forever on his love.

         'Hymn 48th'

       c.562, p. 56

W1979 Who is it gives thee thus to see
       That I would have it last forever.

         [Mary Serjant]

       fb.98, fol. 159

W1980 Who is not prompt to tell the wondrous things
       Exclaim'd with transport ''Tis the gate of heaven.'

         Charles Atherton Allnutt, 'Poverty a poem'

       c.112, p. 183

W1981 Who is the man that boldly dares
       That hated name shall fire festivity with rage.

         Charles Atherton Allnutt, 'Answer to lines in the
         Reading paper, extolling and vindicating [blank],
         against whom an impeachment for high crimes and
         misdemeanors are carrying on by the Lords and
         Commons'

       c.112, p. 80

W1982 Who is this that so beautiful
       You are the minister of it.

         [Mary Pluret], 'Anagram on Mr. W[illiam] B[entley]
         my pastor'

       c.354

W1983 Who is't that tames the raging of the seas,
       My fierce artillery in my time of war.

       c.158, p. 30

W1984 Who kill'd Kildare? Who dared Kildare to kill,
       Death says I kill'd Kildare, and dare kill whom I will.

         'Epitaph on the Bishop [or Earl] of Kildare'
         [Crum w2105]

       c.378, p. 46; c.259, p. 109; c.360/3, no. 179

W1985 Who killed poor Robin
       I said amen.

         Miss [ ] Townshend, 'On the death of General Robin
         Redbreast killed by Lafayette mistaking him for an
         Austrian general. Composed by a little daughter of
         Lord Townshend, only ten years old . . .'

       Poetry Box III/19

W1986 Who lies here? None; a body without name:
       And but the basest part of human frame.

         Sir Thomas Urquhart, 'Man, and woman's epitaph'

       fb.217, p. 55

W1987 Who looks for fruit when sterile mountains rise
       Humbled in dust tho' fruits my life adorn.

         Charles Atherton Allnutt, 'Lines adapted to the Revd.
         Mr. Pentycross's discourse on the 65th Psalm 13th v.
         20th Sept. 1795'

       c.112, p. 165

W1988 Who looks may leap and save his shins from knocks,
       He saves the steed that keeps him under locks.

         [Geffrey Whitney]
         [Crum w2122]

       c.339, p. 322

W1989 Who Lord in Sion with thee may
       In Sion's rest—the clangor sound.

         'Psalm 15. Morning prayer 3 day'

       c.264/1, p. 45

W1990 Who loves a glass without a G.
       Take L. away the rest is he.

         [G[iles] H[ayward?], 'On a wencher'

       b.62, p. 78

W1991   Who loves, obeys; and suff'reth Cupid's brands;
Who is belov'd, is active; and commands.

     Sir Thomas Urquhart, 'That amor is active, and amo
     passive'

     fb.217, p. 200

W1992   Who marries a fair girl, that loves him not
For a wise man would never hope t'avoid it.

     [Sir Thomas Urquhart], 'A ready way to have horns is
     to espouse a handsome woman who bears you no
     affection'

     fb.217, p. 532

W1993   Who measures poverty by nature's rules,
So long's we strain them to a higher pitch.

     [Sir Thomas Urquhart], 'What man it is that is truly
     wealthy'

     fb.217, p. 496

W1994   Who minds to bring his ship on happy shore
Than treasure great of gold or precious stone.

     b.234, p. 341

W1995   Who most to God devoted is,
To him that is to heav'nly bliss.

     [Edmund Wodehouse], 'July 1 [1715]'

     b.131, p. 227

W1996   Who mounts a Cyprian fort, and cannot tickle:
Transform'd himself, before he would assail her.

     Sir Thomas Urquhart, 'Of aged men lecherously
     disposed: though void of ability for the practice of
     venery'

     fb.217, p. 335

W1997   Who mourn Sol's absence; hail his rising fires?
The wond'ring Indian, and my old friend Tyers.

     John Lockman, 'The sun-worshipper . . . May, 1745'

     c.267/1, p. 1

W1998   Who names that lost thing love without a tear
The action love, the passion is forgot.

     c.549, p. 60

W1999   Who nature thro' her maze can trace?
And covet to be blind.

     [Robert Cholmeley], 'To Nicholas Saunderson, esq.,
     the blind professor of mathematics in the University
     of Cambridge'

     c.190, p. 220

W2000   Who ne'er saw death may death commend
Whoever lives in pleasure lives in fears.

     'On death'

     b.205, fol. 41r

W2001   Who nominative would to a woman prove
And to men's purses most times ablative.

     'In fœminam'

     b.205, fol. 49r

W2002   Who now his heart to God do raise,
In that eternal state, eternal place.

     [Edmund Wodehouse], 'Novr. 21 [1714]'

     b.131, p. 91

W2003   Who now shall grace our plains O hone O hone
Poor were thy sacrifice O hone O hone.

     'On the death of my Lord Francis Villiers' [1648]

     b.4, fol. 49v

W2004   Who of a little burden will complain
The stature of the body as the mind.

     [Sir Thomas Urquhart], 'A consolation to those that
     are of a little stature not to be sorry thereat'

     fb.217, p. 530

W2005   Who of his business makes a recreation
Then he that doth the body clothe and feed.

     [Mary Serjant]

     fb.98, fol. 154

W2006   Who place their hopes on silly schemes,
And all may see their scheme prevail.

     c.83/1, no. 107

W2007   Who read a chapter, when they rise,
But who drinks on, to hell may go.

     [George] Herbert, 'Divine charms and knots'
     [Crum W2144]

     b.137, p. 84

W2008   Who read your Laura, should thus praise your
                       spirit:
That you both Laura, and the laurel merit.

     Sir Thomas Urquhart, 'To Petrarch'

     fb.217, p. 81

W2009   Who rests you, is your slave: and he's Sylvester,
Your friend that pays: who pays you not, 's your
                       master.

     Sir Thomas Urquhart, 'Of good and bad debtors to
     Sylvester'

     fb.217, p. 217

W2010   Who said, that little nature did content:
Your nature thereby did not represent.

     Sir Thomas Urquhart, 'To a woman of a lecherous
     inclination'

     fb.217, p. 108

W2011   Who saith, or thinks no age did show
And magnify this swan's immortal praise.

     H[enry] C[olman], 'On the life of Christ. Allegoric'
[Crum w2145]

     b.2, p. 62

W2012   Who, save his own, all other faults espies,
Is to himself a fool: to others wise.

     Sir Thomas Urquhart, 'Of censurers'

     fb.217, p. 103

W2013   Who says he lies, which he tells truth he lies
In lying to speak truth, in speaking truth to lie.

     [Sir Philip Wodehouse], 'Chrysippi Qui dicit . . .'

     b.131, p. 32

W2014   Who says the times do learning disallow?
This comedy's acted by the heart.

     [Abraham Cowley], 'The prologue' [to The guardian,
acted before Prince Charles, 1641, Trinity College,
Cambridge]
[Crum w2149]

     fb.106(1)

W2015   Who says, this oratorio's all a hum—
[?] these choruses, and he'll be dumb.

     John Lockman, 'Extempore: while two young [?] were
saying, that the music of Gideon is not
Mr. Handel's . . . 18 Feb. 1769'

     c.267/4, p. 314

W2016   Who seeks much more his God to please
In God as on a rock he slights all these.

     [Edmund Wodehouse], 'May 7 [1715]'

     b.131, p. 209

W2017   Who seeks to quench by help of carnal friends
I will expect and trust no friend but Thee.

     [Francis Quarles], 'On carnal mirth' [Divine
fancies III, 55]

     b.137, p. 192

W2018   Who sees not his own faults, but others' spies,
Is wise unt' others, but t'himself unwise.

     'Self-love'

     c.356

W2019   Who sets his love on him whom the more he loves,
Celestial love of them's the antepart.

     [Edmund Wodehouse], 'Feb. 4 [1715] Ld. Ch[ief]
Just[ice] Hale's sense'

     b.131, p. 158

Who shall forbid the fond parental tear   W2020
And soothe the sorrows of a wounded heart.

     R[ichard] V[ernon] S[adleir], 'An apology to
condoling friends on the death of Miss Elisa Bayard at
Southampton in the 19 year of her age'

c.106, p. 143

Who shall pronounce thy fall, proud Bab'lon who?   W2021
Behold, the Lord: he hath desir'd it so.

     [William Sandys?], 'Inevitable plagues and desolation
threatened to Babylon and other place[s] Esdras lib: 2
chap: 16: to verse 35'

b.230, p. 93

Who shall rehearse   W2022
And set thy watch of angels on the place.

     [Sir William Trumbull]

Trumbull Box: Poetry Box XIII/28

Who shall say where friendship dwells   W2023
She lives within her feeling breast.

     Miss [ ] Andrews, 'On friendship'

File 245/13

Who shall this belull'd nation disabuse   W2024
Revenge the Pole and avarice the Dutch.

c.158, p. 52

Who strives to curb a woman in her nature   W2025
And water [?] must have its passage free.

     [Sir Thomas Urquhart], 'Of a quasimodo'

fb.217, p. 387

Who strive[s] to mount Parnassus hill   W2026
Great without patron, rich without South Sea.

     [Richard Bentley], 'A reply to a copy of verses sent by
Mr. Tit[ley] in the same measure and number of lines'
['He who would great in science . . .']
[Crum w2174a]

c.416; fc.135

Who takes a wife, he takes a Carey['s] fear   W2027
If to my house, her care she'll still neglect.

     [Sir Philip Wodehouse], 'A proverb dedicated to my
cousin Ma[ry] Car[ey]'

b.131, back (no. 231)

Who thinks that fortune cannot change her mind,   W2028
In peace provides fit arms against a war.

c.83/2, no. 323

Who tries may trust; else flatt'ring friends shall find,   W2029
Who speaks with heed may boldly speak his mind.

c.339, p. 323

W2030   Who uninspir'd can tread this sacred ground,
And from her lips acquires a new resistless grace.

    [Soame Jenyns], 'Written in the right honble the Earl
    of Oxford's library at Wimpole 1729'

    c.147, p. 27

W2031   Who vengeance on my wrongs hast shown
For them who on his death were bent.

    [Thomas Stanley], 'Meditat. VIII: Upon his
    Ma[jes]ty's repulse at Hull and the fates of the
    Hothams' [1645]

    b.152, p. 24

W2032   Who virtuously would settle his endeavors
Forgetting always bypast injuries.

    [Sir Thomas Urquhart], 'A ready way to goodness and
    true wisdom'

    fb.217, p. 512

W2033   Who was the man kiss'd Pat last night?
But her pouting lips who could deny? | Not I,
                                     not I, not I.

    'The kiss; hatched in four parts'

    c.487, p. 97

W2034   Who weareth horns, not knowing of it is
Is an ass cuckold, though his wife be best.

    [Sir Thomas Urquhart], 'Of three sorts of cuckolds
    and their wives'

    fb.217, p. 506

W2035   Who whilst she breath'd this mortal life, did see her
Nor will so long, as heav'ns, and earth appear.

    Sir Thomas Urquhart, 'Upon my Lady Marchioness
    of Huntly'

    fb.217, p. 188

W2036   Who will instruct me to endure
Their malice is—to let them talk.

    'On detraction'

    c.83/3, no. 887

W2037   Who wills for us our daily bread to plow,
Will not for naught eternal feasts bestow.

    Sir Thomas Urquhart, 'Paradise is not gained without
    great travail, and pains'

    fb.217, p. 80

W2038   Who with a deep consideration ponders
Was never wedded to so fair a face.

    Sir Thomas Urquhart, 'To the Duchess of Chevreuse'

    fb.217, p. 328

Who with affection hath possess'd his mind: W2039
Whence love must needs be no less deaf, than blind.

    Sir Thomas Urquhart, 'That Cupid neither sees, nor
    hears'

    fb.217, p. 324

Who woke the dormant muse from length'd rest,   W2040
And join our friend to separate no more.

    'Verses addressed to Catharine Payton, on the death
    of her companion and fellow laborer, Mary Piesly
    otherwise Neale'

    fc.79; c.517, fol. 3r

Who wonders, that the captain run   W2041
And the physicians are.

    'An officer making his escape from a highwayman,
    who was soon after shot dead by a physician, whom he
    likewise attempted to rob'

    c.94

Who woos a wife thinks wedded men do know   W2042
Than with this double woe to woo a wife.

    'In procos'

    c.356

Who would be truly wise must in all haste   W2043
And cannot dwell but in an empty place.

    [Sir Thomas Urquhart], 'How to be wise'

    fb.217, p. 498

Who would have thought but Damon's love   W2044
He sigh'd, he cried, he vow'd the same to her.

    'A song'

    b.54, p. 1162

Who would have thought my ruin was so near   W2045
Lo they be all as bad, as bad may be.

    'On William Lenthall speaker of the Long Parliament
    [removed from office April 1653]: acrostic . . . 1660'
    [Crum w2201]

    b.52/1, p. 149; fb.140, p. 4 (incomplete)

Who would have thought that Troy should fall   W2046
And woe-wan Somers rear his venerable head.

    'An ode on the melancholy state of public affairs an:
    Dom: 1781'

    fc.53, p. 8

Who would live in others' breath?   W2047
Sands I was but now I'm dust.

    [Thomas Bastard], "On a gentleman named Sands'
    [Crum w2204]

    fb.143, p. 7

W2048 Who would not be persuaded her t'embrace,
Than Tully had in's eloquence of old.

> Sir Thomas Urquhart, 'That a certain lady was of the
> more attractive comeliness, that she was daily painted.
> A paradox'
>
> fb.217, p. 329

W2049 Who would not fly, for help to such a one,
While ye consum'd, ye multiplied the more.

> 'Mark 6.38.44'
>
> c.160, fol. 51v [bis]

W2050 Who would not trust in God and never doubt
And cruse of oil did here aplenty deal.

> 'I Kings 17.16'
>
> c.160, fol. 55v

W2051 Who would Pindar emulate,
All the rest is red and gold.

> [William Popple, trans.], '[Horace] book 4th. Ode 2d.
> To Antonius Julius'
>
> fc.104/2, p. 332

W2052 Who writ this distich it is fit I tell
When (for his wit) Cambridge extold him so.

> [Sir Aston Cokayne], 'Of this. To Sir Robert Hilliard'
>
> b.275, p. 87

W2053 Who'd be the man lewd libels to indite
Those few unblemish'd are not meant in this.

> 'Satire unmuzzled' [after 24 November 1681]
> [Crum W2209; POAS II.209]
>
> b.113, p. 139

W2054 Who'd now a martial state embrace
Should say—Miss you're as bad as he.

> Edward Walpole, 'Augustam, amici, &c. Horatii
> ode II . . . li. 3 ad amicos'
>
> c.229/2, fol. 30

W2055 Whoe'er, by pride, or worldly pomp misled,
Rais'd, on the sands of guilt, by lawless pow'r.

> 'Sonnet, hung in a tent in a field'
>
> c.135, p. 29

W2056 Whoe'er excels in what we prize,
The pendant gets a mistress by it.

> 'Sympathetic love; or, fancy surpasses beauty'
> [Crum W2214, 'exceeds']
>
> c.186, p. 99

W2057 Whoe'er for pleasure plans a scheme,
And accident destroys the scheme.

> 'The milkmaid'
>
> c.83/3, no. 963

W2058 Whoe'er has money may securely sail;
For Jove himself's the treasure of his chest.

> 'On the power of God—3d [epigram, from Flaminius]'
>
> c.158, p. 130

W2059 Whoe'er he be that to a taste aspires
Is blockhead, coxcomb, puppy, fool and sot.

> [James Bramston], 'The man of taste' [pr. 1733 (Foxon
> B396)]
>
> c.570/4, p. 72

W2060 Whoe'er he is, whose senseless heart,
The crier said, I've found an ass.

> [Thomas Hamilton, 6th earl of Haddington], 'Man
> without love is a beast'
>
> c.458/2, p. 154

W2061 Whoe'er in Hymen's silken bands
Will render sweet the cup of life.

> 'On choosing a wife by a dish of tea'
>
> c.83/1, no. 149

W2062 Whoe'er like me, with trembling anguish brings,
And not to earth resign'd her, but to God.

> 'Epitaph on a lady, who died at the Hot Wells of a
> consumption'
>
> c.83/1, no. 79; c.546; Diggle Box: Poetry Box XI/52; c.116,
> p. 61 (attr. [ ] Mason); fc.132/1, p. 202 (attr. Hawkesworth)

W2063 Whoe'er surveys the face of thee, brave youth
But own thy triumph, and the Roman's lost.

> 'Written under James Sheppard's picture. He was
> born the 10th of June 1700. and was executed at
> Tyburn the 17. of March 1718'
>
> c.570/2, p. 13

W2064 Whoe'er thou art that durst with dying lays
And brings a sword as powerful as lines.

> 'A burlesque on Mrs. Digby'
>
> fc.73

W2065 Whoe'er thou art, that look'st upon
And set'st thy heart upon, is soonest lost.

> 'An epitaph on [Thomas] Flatman'
>
> c.244, p. 207; c.83/1, no. 92

W2066 Whoe'er thou art that tempts in such a strain
By several paths and none are in the right.

> [George Granville], 1st baron Lansdowne, 'A copy of
> verse, in answer to some that were sent to Lord
> Lansdowne ['Why Granville is thy life confin'd . . .']
> dissuading him from retiring in the country' [January
> 1711/12; printed, Foxon A54]
> [Crum W2225]
>
> fc.60, p. 30; c.244, p. 153; b.218, p. 10 ('art, who')

W2067 Whoe'er thou art these lines now reading,
And envy mine.

> [Matthew Gregory Lewis], 'Inscription in an
> hermitage'

c.83/3, no. 885; see also 'O breathe in gentle strains . . .'.

W2068 Whoe'er thou art, thy master see,
For such he was, is, or will be.

> John Lockman, 'Writ under a figure of Cupid,
> engraved by the ingenious Mr. Strange'

c.267/4, p. 147

W2069 Whoe'er thou art, whose soul's opprest with thirst,
Praise to the Lord our God, and praise his name
with joy.

> [Thomas Hamilton, 6th earl of Haddington], 'The 55
> chap: of Isaiah imitated'

c.458/2, p. 127

W2070 Whoe'er thou art, with rev'rence tread
For, know, thy Shenstone's dust lies here!

> 'On an urn erected to the memory of William
> Shenstone esqr. In Hales-Owen churchyard'

fc.132/1, p. 103

W2071 Whoe'er you are; friend, stranger, young, or old,
Inscribe his name;—and weep his last farewell.

> [Charles Earle], 'An epitaph on my dear friend W:
> K—lly'

c.376

W2072 Whoever be chief mourner at his hearse
As I may say to you old Agrippa's dead.

> Poetry Box VIII/52

W2073 Whoever comes to shroud me, do not harm
That since you would have none of me, I bury
some of you.

> J[ohn] D[onne], 'The funeral'
> [Crum W2236]

b.148, p. 51

W2074 Whoever guesses, thinks or dreams he knows
Nature beforehand hath out-cursed me.

> [John Donne], 'A curse'
> [Crum W2238]

b.114, p. 277; b.148, p. 116

W2075 Whoever hasn't any time
O'ercome by thee did die.

> [George] H[owar]d, [6th earl of Carlisle],
> 'Translation of the third epode in Horace'

c.197, p. 15

W2076 Whoever loves if he do not propose
As who by glisters [clysters] gave the stomach meat.

> [John Donne], 'Elegia undecima'
> [Crum W2241]

b.114, p. 106; b.148, p. 98

W2077 Whoever saw another such divine
That drank cold water when he might have wine.

> 'Upon Dr. Hancock's wonderfully comical liquid
> book'

c.489, p. 17

W2078 Whoever treadeth on this stone
Your honest friend Will Wheatley.

> 'Epitaphs in Stepney churchyard [1]'

c.487, p. 89; fb.143, p. 24; Poetry Box VII/55

W2079 Whole countries are protected by your grandeur,
Extends itself into the outmost Thule.

> Sir Thomas Urquhart, 'To the Earl of [crossed out]'

fb.217, p. 138

W2080 Whole stomach is so apt for meat,
And heat digesteth.

> Sir Thomas Urquhart, 'Of a wooer, who had a notable
> good appetite for his victuals'

fb.217, p. 44

W2081 Wholly on God do I depend,
Must of a cordial thanks to him partake.

> [Edmund Wodehouse], 'Novr. 2d [1714]'

b.131, p. 75

W2082 Whom all admir'd, whom [all] almost ador'd
Him [all] our ills [hath] slain by heaven's
displeasure.

> 'An epitaph . . . Joshua Sylvester'

b.205, fol. 9v

W2083 Whom chaste espousals by a sweet conjunction
Than can b'enjoy'd by bachelors, and freemen.

> Sir Thomas Urquhart, 'To my Lady [crossed out]'

fb.217, p. 208

W2084 Whom ev'ry man may on her back throw down,
For so she bears them up: nor cares how long.

> Sir Thomas Urquhart, 'Of a courtesan, who was
> surpassing able in body'

fb.217, p. 317

W2085 Whom fortune favor'd to be the domestic
Did ne'er produce a spir't more Amazonian.

> Sir Thomas Urquhart, 'To my Lady [crossed out]
> dowager'

fb.217, p. 228

W2086 Whom fortune vexeth if she turn her wheel,
For they, if fortune frown, are quickly lost.

J[ohn] R[obinson], 'Servis regna dabunt, captivis fata triumphos'

c.370, fol. 25v

W2087 Whom holy hope holds up, thrice happy he
He endless joys, inherits from above.

[Samuel?] Pepys, 'Mr Pepys' anagram upon him [Sir Philip Wodehouse] about the time of Sr G. Booth's defeat . . .'

b.131, back (no. 17/2)

W2088 Whom Hymenae obligeth to the duty
The parents, each, of others' progeny.

Sir Thomas Urquhart, 'To the Countess of [crossed out]'

fb.217, p. 307

W2089 Whom kind propitious fates do bless
Long in that torment may he live.

J[ohn] R[obinson], 'Vivat Pacuvius quaeso'

c.370, fol. 27v

W2090 Whom matrimony welcomes to the mansion,
That man should harbor in so heav'nl' a lodging.

Sir Thomas Urquhart, 'To Lady [crossed out]'

fb.217, p. 171

W2091 Whom opportunity allows to gaze
Transmits the object of so great delight.

Sir Thomas Urquhart, 'To Lady Jean Campbell'

fb.217, p. 339

W2092 Whom seek ye sinners Jesus? know that I
I am made clean from my impurity.

H[enry] C[olman], 'On Christ's passion' [Crum w2254]

b.2, p. 13

W2093 Whom will Clio choose today
Dart thy thunder from afar.

[William Popple, trans.], '[Horace] book 1st. ode 12th. To Augustus'

fc.104/2, p. 36

W2094 Whoop Holiday! why then 'twill ne'er be better
To write a Persean censure on his play.

[Peter Heylyn], 'On [Barten] Holiday's play [Technogamia: or the marriage of the arts] of Christ-Church acted before the king at Woodstock: 1621'
[Crum w2255]

b.200, p. 31

W2095 Who's rich? The wise: who's poor? The fool;
Then, if you be not rich, you are a fool.

Sir Thomas Urquhart, 'Of wisdom, and wealth' [translation of John Owen]

fb.217, p. 242

W2096 Who's Spence? a critic: what's a critic? Spence:
No—an exception to the gen'ral rule.

[N.] H[erbert], 'Epigram upon Mr Joseph Spence the critic'

Spence Papers, folder 91

W2097 Who's there? A Whig of quality,
You'll have sufficient force to keep your own.

'An account of what happened lately in Hell' [on Halifax, Burnet, and Wharton]
[Crum w2256b, 'Whig and one of']

c.570/1, p. 131

W2098 Who's this, that in the Stagyrite's despite,
Than the whole tribe of artists could before.

John Lockman, 'On reading some very rude criticisms, on Mr. Thomson's tragedy of Edward and Eleanora'

c.267/1, p. 159

W2099 Whose baddest fortune's past, he is twice happy:
Whose first good luck hath left him, twice unhappy.

Sir Thomas Urquhart, 'Of fortune, and misfortune'

fb.217, p. 353

W2100 Whose happy suns, without a cloud descend?
Where crown'd with glory glows thy ancient line!

John Wolcot ('Peter Pindar'), 'The Nymph of Tauris. Written on the death of Ann Trelawney sister to the late Governor Trelawney'

c.140, p. 122

W2101 Whose head befringed with bescattered tresses
Where beauty springs; and thus I kiss thy foot.

[Robert Herrick], 'The description of women' [Crum w2259]

b.197, p. 13

W2102 Whose imitating actions will not swerve
Which is conferr'd on men of estimation.

Sir Thomas Urquhart, 'To the Earl of [crossed out]'

fb.217, p. 295

W2103 Whose life's too joyful, have a grievous death:
Their death being joy, who've grieved whilst they breathe.

Sir Thomas Urquhart, 'Of the progress, and catastroph' of our life'

fb.217, p. 145

W2104 Whose mind with pride, and avarice doth flow
Leans most on hope, yields least to memory.

> [Sir Thomas Urquhart], 'Why [?] and too ambitious
> men prove not so thankful in the accounting of a
> gratuity'
>
> fb.217, p. 511

W2105 Whose rest is sleep, and Venus his delight,
Sleep kills the mind: and Venus kills the soul.

> Sir Thomas Urquhart, 'Of venery, and sleep'
>
> fb.217, p. 137

W2106 Whos'ever loves, with many fits is moved
And when belov'd must ardor them they move.

> [Sir Thomas Urquhart], 'Conceiving the passive case
> of lover, and the active of those that are beloved'
>
> fb.217, p. 526

W2107 Whoso hath seen, how one warm lump of wax
Because in one part they do symbolize.

> [Joshua Sylvester, trans. Guillaume de Salluste,
> seigneur] Du Bartas, 'Of the continual change of
> forms in the elements and their manner'
>
> b.137, p. 90

W2108 Whoso him bethought
All the world to win.

> 'This epitaph was written on marble in black-letter
> characters in the parish church of Feversham, Kent'
>
> c.240, p. 136

W2109 Whoso on the poor hath compassion,
God will increase his possession.

> b.234, p. 257

W2110 Whoso profanes with barbarous rage to scare
Be known her crimes: but let her memory die.

> 'On a satire written by a lady in 1761'
>
> fc.74, p. 9

W2111 Whoso their hopes entirely place
To him for all is due of all the praise.

> [Edmund Wodehouse], 'Iterum [12 February 1715]'
>
> b.131, p. 166

W2112 Who'th learn'd his grammar thorough in one year
May sure be styl'd ingenious and sincere.

> 'Johannes Scinnerus. Anagramma. In anno sincerus es.
> Epigramma . . . thus Englished'
>
> b.212, p. 93

W2113 Who've done good deeds, will follow on the same:
Who have done bad, their deeds will follow them.

> Sir Thomas Urquhart, 'Of good, and bad'
>
> fb.217, p. 208

W2114 Why Madam must I tell this idle tale
We met as lovers and we parted friends.

> 'The tale written to Mrs. —— at her request'
>
> c.150, p. 17

W2115 Why all these looks so solemn and so sad!
Praises and imitates Orinda best.

> 'On the death of Mrs. [Katherine] Philips, born 1631.
> at the desire of Lady Temple. By Sir Wm. [ ] not in his
> works'
>
> c.94

W2116 Why all this party noise
Darts brightest rays.

> James Saunders, 'Song by . . . 1 Jan. 1770. The new
> God bless great George our King, to the old tune.
> Writ (in imitation of the renowned Mr. Winman's
> Punch)'
>
> c.267/4, p. 368

W2117 Why all those tears ask not the cause
And got his full *quietus est*.

> 'An elegy upon Dr. Porter doctor of law'
>
> b.356, p. 225

W2118 Why am I loath to leave this earthly scene!
O aid me with thy help, Omnipotence divine!

> [Robert Burns], 'Stanzas on the prospect of death'
> [Crum w2274]
>
> c.142, p. 275

W2119 Why am I thus 'midst cares and fears,
Before I faint and die!

> Abraham Oakes, 'The expostulation: written when my
> wife was absent, and both my sons in Flanders. 1747'
>
> c.50, p. 134 (bis)

W2120 Why are all the muses mute?
Shall vanish together away.

> Poetry Box VII/43

W2121 Why are my eyes, Sir, like a sword
That, hence it bears the very name.

> [Phanuel Bacon], 'Conundrums [2]' [answer to 'I've
> thought, the fair Clarissa cries . . .']
>
> Poetry Box XIV/188

W2122 Why art thou Lord so long from us,
That hate Thee spitefully.

> [John Hopkins], 'Psalm: 30. A lamentation for the
> decay of true religion and godliness' [verses from
> Psalm 74]
> [Crum w2285, 'far from us']
>
> a.3, fol. 110v

W2123   Why art thou slow thou rest of trouble; death
In one short hour's delay is tyranny.

     'Song 46'

     b.4, fol. 37v

W2124   Why art thou thus with grief opprest,
Was to bestow diffusive bliss.

     [Henry] Needler, 'A hymn composed under a violent
     headache'

     c.244, p. 559

W2125   Why at thy christening did it rain, dear prince,
Earth was baptiz'd, and heaven the font would be.

     'On the Prince's christening' [Charles II; translated
     from the Latin 'In diem baptizationis . . .']
     [Crum w2288]

     b.200, p. 410

W2126   Why beats my heart, ah! more than tongue can tell
Then guard me heav'n, from madness and despair.

     'Spoken by an unhappy husband over the body of his
     wife who had destroyed herself'

     c.83/2, no. 633

W2127   Why boastest thou, thou tyrant, why!
Whereto thy saints agree.

     'Psalm 52'

     c.264/2, p. 3

W2128   Why, busy boys, why thus entwine,
For Care's disease is pleasure's birth.

     'Verses written on the tomb of Care, round which
     some boys were wreathing flowers, in a garden'

     c.391, p. 3

W2129   Why Celia, with that coy behavior
All but that hard heart of thine.

     c.549, p. 5

W2130   Why, Charles, when youth and love combine,
Nor time nor space thy fame confine.

     [William Roscoe], 'Stanzas from the Latin of Angelus
     Politianus'

     c.142, p. 516

W2131   Why, Clara, has thy muse so long
Nor proof against thy praise.

     'To Mrs. Sr. Hill'

     c.53, fol. 37

W2132   Why comes he not? Ah, whither, say,
Albert had slept abroad all night.

     'Albert absent'

     c.83/3, no. 785

W2133   Why court you sev'ral women with like passion
To make one key serveth use of many locks.

     [Sir Thomas Urquhart], 'To a certain suitor who
     would not refrain from his [?] of license [?]

     fb.217, p. 395

W2134   Why cruel death should honest Owen catch
Though Owen you have left the keys behind.

     [Benjamin Stone], 'Upon Owen the butler of Christ
     Church Oxoniae'
     [Crum w2296]

     b.205, fol. 44v; b.208, p. 60; see also 'That death should
     thus . . .'.

W2135   Why Damon do you this complain
And no more respect I'll bear thee. | An' thou [wad
                      my own thing, &c.]

     [Mrs. Christian Kerr], 'The lady's answer [to 'What
     precious moments . . .'] to the same tune' ['An' thou
     wad my own thing . . .']

     c.102, p. 88

W2136   Why did Ben Hyett tumults raise
Should take away your pay.

     Poetry Box x/35

W2137   Why did I leave my native Bangor's shore?
Abash'd the idol lay, and spake no more.

     [Sneyd Davies], 'Caducan and Dr. Milles'

     c.157, p. 78

W2138   Why did I wrong my judgment so
From her unconstancy expected.

     [Sir Robert Ayton], 'To his unconstant mistress'

     b.356, p. 93

W2139   Why did those cannibal-like wives ravage
To run like sows a-brimming after men.

     [Sir Thomas Urquhart], 'The reason why a little after
     the dissolving of the covenanter army at Dunslow(?)
     the women and wenches of Edinburgh pursued so
     fiercely my Lord of Aboyne his watch running from
     the castle to the abbey'

     fb.217, p. 387

W2140   Why did you bosom(?) that last sigh
But cannot take it in.

     b.213, p. 95

W2141   Why did you, Sir, the proof forego
And patriot mobs may bonfires make.

     'To I. Roberts esq.'

     fc.85, fol. 103v

W2142 Why dims this tear my melting eye
The best of women from the grave.

[Bertie Greatheed, on Lady Mary Greatheed]

Greatheed Box/38

W2143 Why do I wander through the lonesome grove
He sighs unheard, and he unpitied grieves.

'To the absent Dorinda—writ in 1724'

c.360/2, no. 97; c.549, p. 97

W2144 Why do my eyes behold the light
And bring his promis'd mercy near.

T[homas] S[tevens], 'Job 3rd. 23rd. Jany. 25th. [17]80'

c.259, p. 76

W2145 Why do not you take medicine from me?
Because as yet, I have no mind to die.

Sir Thomas Urquhart, 'The words of a bad physician
to a diseased gentlewoman, with the answer thereof'

fb.217, p. 351

W2146 Why do the heathen rage so loud,
On him; in him confide.

'Psalm 2'

c.264/1, p. 1

W2147 Why do the people rage and foam
Shall in short time be free.

'An hymn, to a psalm tune'

c.570/3, p. 200

W2148 Why do the preaching puritans take pleasure
The more they're certain, that the wares are coarse.

Sir Thomas Urquhart, 'Of puritan martyrs'

fb.217, p. 134

W2149 Why do the proud insult the poor?
But dwell forever near my God.

c.362, p. 45

W2150 Why do the strict-liv'd Catos of the age
And such lives the gods themselves possess.

'In defense of satire'

c.158, p. 142

W2151 Why do the tuneful choir attend
Recorded to posterity.

B[eaupré] Bell, '1720'

fc.39/6

W2152 Why do we seek felicity
Belov'd, obey'd, ador'd.

[John Austin], 'Hym. 2' [Hymn iii, Devotions in the
ancient way of offices, 1672, p. 33]

c.178, p. 2

W2153 Why do ye double in desire
Alas leave off and let me die.

'Braye Lute Book,' Music Ms. 13, fol. 20

W2154 Why do ye trifle thus your time away?
Mercy withdraws; Justice stops in her place | And
die he must.

[John Evelyn jr.], 'To such as stand idle in the market
places'

Poetry Box VI/114

W2155 Why do you harbor in your nuptial bed
Though they were four, and heretrixes all.

Sir Thomas Urquhart, 'To a certain lady, who though
her father's only child, did take to husband her nearest
kinsman'

fb.217, p. 119

W2156 Why do you not bestir your thighs
Made above that, which most reposeth.

Sir Thomas Urquhart, 'A parley betwixt a gallant, and
his mistress, in the interim of their dalliance'

fb.217, p. 109

W2157 Why do you toil, and vex your brain?
And end at once, your rhymes, and you.

[Thomas Hamilton, 6th earl of Haddington], 'To a
friend dissuading him from writing satire'

c.458/2, p. 130

W2158 Why do you with disdain refuse
As I have cause to love.

'To a lady more cruel than fair'

fb.66/13

W2159 Why does cruel nature sow
From the cradle to the grave!

[Charles Burney, the elder], 'On the propensity to evil
in some promising young persons'

c.33, p. 108

W2160 Why does the sun, dart forth his cheerful rays
For what is life, without the swain I love.

'The nymph's complaint, or the imprecation'

c.186, p. 108

W2161 Why does the tongue by slender efforts try,
Till closing life compel me to resign.

[ ] Harley, 'To ——— on her approaching visit to the
author in the country'

c.83/3, no. 791

W2162 Why don't your rival sister too expire!
If not; e'en drown thy self, dear John; that's all.

Poetry Box X/54, p. 11

W2163 Why dost thou ask, my charming creature,
He came, he saw, he lov'd.

> [Thomas Morell], 'To the same [Miss M. R—ds of
> Cambridge]'
>
> c.395, p. 2

W2164 Why dost thou grieve my dear Clorinda
And ev'ry night to pleasure thee.

> 'The answer' [to 'Go go O you most deceitful
> man . . .']
>
> c.374

W2165 Why dost thou heap up wealth, which thou must
quit,
Thy humble nest build on the ground.

> [Abraham Cowley, 'The vanity of heaping up riches']
> [Crum w2330]
>
> b.118, p. 5

W2166 Why dost thou root me up ungrateful hand,
To hang up traitors; or preserve a king.

> 'The murmurs of the oak' [cut down by the Duchess
> of Marlborough in 1708]
> [Crum w2332]
>
> c.570/1, p. 64

W2167 Why dost thou shun me, blest content? Ah why
The whole, 'the sad variety of woe'.

> [Frances Burney d'Arblay], 'Sonnet. To content'
>
> c.486, fol. 14

W2168 Why doth man's wit a woman's far exceed?
Because she's fram'd, not of the head, but side.

> Sir Thomas Urquhart, 'Of men and women a paradox'
>
> fb.217, p. 59

W2169 Why doth not golden Perseus wear the crown
Hard marble monuments of my renown.

> 'Perseus' [answered by 'Yes soon you must . . .']
>
> b.356, p. 107

W2170 Why doth one day another so excel
Order it; and, we stand bound to obey.

> Sir John Strangways, 'In defense of holy days . . .
> 13° Octobris 1646'
>
> b.304, p. 61

W2171 Why doth the man that hath a wife
But by lewd lust mind discontent.

> [Sir Nicholas] Bacon, 'Against lust'
>
> fa.8, fol. 164v

W2172 Why doth the son before the mother go,
That there's a doubt.

> Sir Thomas Urquhart, 'The reason, why in the
> manyest parts of the world, the son hath the
> precedency of his mother, and not of his father'
>
> fb.217, p. 155

W2173 Why doth the stubborn iron prove
I know, yet know not, why I love.

> [William] Habington, 'To Castara, inquiring why I
> love her'
>
> b.150, p. 264

W2174 Why doth thy passion lead thee blind
She's full, she'll fall even with a touch.

> 'Upon a virgin not marriageable'
>
> b.205, fol. 24r; see also 'Why should . . .', 'Would you
> have passion . . .'.

W2175 Why doth vain man with rash attempts desire,
And triumphs to be call'd the greatest one in hell.

> J[ohn] R[obinson], 'Noli amabo verberare lapidem, ne
> perdas manum'
>
> c.370, fol. 38

W2176 Why droop, my saddening heart, of joy forlorn;
And friendship fairest forms thy bliss complete.

> 'A sonnet written under the influence of a depression
> of spirits from the habitual headache' [Nuneaton,
> 12 Sept. 1789]
>
> c.136, p. 145

W2177 Why droops the downy wing of love?
In which I lov'd— nor thought of thee.

> 'To time'
>
> c.83/3, no. 1015

W2178 Why droops the head, why languishes the eye?
In every station say 'Thy will be done'.

> [Peter Pinnell?], 'Ps. 42.7. Why art thou so full of
> heaviness, O my soul . . .' [pr. Bristol? 174–? (Foxon
> H114, attr. Abraham Richard Hawksworth)]
> [Crum w2345]
>
> c.373, p. 67; c.504, p. 179; c.83/1, no. 2

W2179 Why excellent Corinna do you throw
You would appear unclouded of your smock.

> [Sir Aston Cokayne], 'To Corinna'
>
> b.275, p. 33

W2180 Why fair vow-breaker, hath thy sin thought fit
The third shall beg my curses be made true.

> [J. Vaughan?], 'An elegy on an invitation to a wedding'
> [Crum w2348]
>
> b.205, fol. 82v; b.52/2, p. 168

W2181 Why faith that Lusco he's a gentle man
And ever will, for that your father's deed.

   [R. M.]

Poetry Box VI/4

W2182 Why flow my tears? Why pensive do I stray?
And hail no unkind monitor in me.

   'In memory of Domville Poole esq. of Dane Bank
   Lyme near Warrington, who died at Bristol hot wells,
   19th of April (1795)'

c.82, p. 15

W2183 Why gracious God, am I so highly blest?
By doing all thy will—

   '[Soliloquies] (7)'

c.153, p. 163

W2184 Why, Granville, is thy life confin'd
She needs will love, and we shall have thee back
                                          again.

   [Elizabeth Higgons?], 'Verses sent by an unknown
   hand to Mr. G[eorge] Granville [Baron Lansdowne]
   in the country' [upon his retiring from court;
   answered by 'Whoe'er thou art . . .'; pr. 1712 (Foxon
   A54)]
   [Crum W2358]

b.218, p. 9

W2185 Why hang thy hopes on beauty's fading flower,
And waste their luster in the silent tomb.

   [ ] Giles, 'To a gentleman, captivated with the exterior
   charms of a young lady'

fc.132/1, p. 139

W2186 Why hangs my harp on willow tree so long?
But humbly hope, be still, and know thy God!

   M[ary (S[hackleton) Leadbeater], 'On the death of
   her aunt Deborah Carleton'

File 13409; c.140, p. 92

W2187 Why has Lord Egmont 'gainst this bill
And he has twice deserted.

   [Sir Charles Hanbury Williams], 'On Lord Egmont's
   opposing the mutiny and desertion bill 1748/9'

c.360/3, no. 148

W2188 Why heaves my fond bosom? Ah! What can it mean?
With compassion for him, who without thee must die.

   [1751?]
   [Crum W2360]

c.157, p. 57; c.358, p. 29

W2189 Why heaves the bosom with a tender sigh,
And as he yields, so may I yield my breath.

   Charles Atherton Allnutt, 'On the death of my friend
   Mr. Horton an eminent Christian'

c.112, p. 60

W2190 Why how can you tease me, and plague me to write?
Have it richly made up in the charms of your mind.

   [J. B.], 'To Miss Naper: often desiring the author to
   write a poem on her'

Poetry Box IV/155

W2191 Why how now bald pates will you never leave
Let it alone Sirs you are free to leave it.

b.216, p. 195 (incomplete)

W2192 Why how now Christ Church lads, what all amort,
'Tis said in Oxford that Breda is lost.

   'On the striving of Christ Church for the proctorship'
   [1625, when Mr. Payne stood]
   [Crum W2362]

b.200, p. 43

W2193 Why how now Pasquin since the last election
That four could lead four hundred by the nose.

   'A dialogue between Pasquin and Marforio two statues
   in Rome on w[hi]ch the reflections of the
   management of the public affairs are affixed' [pr. 1701?
   (Foxon D262)]

Poetry Box VI/1

W2194 Why in the left side rather than the right,
Is man's heart plac'd? To good cause opposite.

   'The heart'

c.356

W2195 Why is a woman than a man less wise?
Because Eve from man's rib, not head, did rise.

   'Of women's wit'

c.356

W2196 Why is Britannia thus in torture found
Italian tools or Frenchmen landing here.

   [Thomas Gurney], 'The rectifier written just after the
   breaking out of the rebellion—1745'

c.213

W2197 Why is each night on black both long, and shorter?
Grief would oppress her, or he could return.

   Sir Thomas Urquhart, 'A parley betwixt two, of the
   reason, why the night is overveiled with black'

fb.217, p. 291

W2198 Why is it now that men of [?] are
And mighty Ereuthalion wish'd appear.

   [Sir Thomas Urquhart], 'Of the privilege that old men
   have not to be enforced to enter in open arms against
   the enemy in an [?]sive way'

fb.217, p. 508

W2199 Why is it (worthy lord) that ever see the most
[?] we most mortal in their power, immortal in [?].

A[rchibald?] C[ampbell?], 'To the right honoble
Archibald earl of Argyll'

Poetry Box VIII/45

W2200 Why is man proud, who was conceiv'd in sin:
And from this life he needs must once depart.

b.234, p. 72

W2201 Why is man so thoughtless grown
Drops in the ditch, despairs and dies.

'To the Lord Cutts, at the siege of Namur'

c.360/1, p. 189

W2202 Why is my soul o'ercast with anxious fear?
He always hears them for he always loves.

'[Soliloquies] (8)'

c.153, p. 165

W2203 Why is not wit with beauty join'd?
And pierce my ear to wound my heart.

'Song'

c.111, p. 160

W2204 Why is our premier so unwilling
But tax all puppies in the nation.

'On the proposed dog-tax'

fc.130, p. 58

W2205 Why is't, that few men shall inhabitate
The heav'ns, they being so large? The way is strait.

Sir Thomas Urquhart, 'A question concerning the
salvation of mankind'

fb.217, p. 178

W2206 Why is the heart of man in his left side?
Because it to sinister things is tied.

Sir Thomas Urquhart, 'The depraved heart of man'

fb.217, p. 89

W2207 Why is the sun in sackcloth hid,
Heaven is rejoic'd and hell afraid.

[Thomas Stevens?], 'Thursday evening exposition
May 10. 1781 afterward sung the following hymn,
Mark 13.24.25.26.27. verses'

c.259, p. 145

W2208 Why is thy heart so full of grief?
And Jesus [?] thee to spare.

[Thomas Stevens?]

c.259, p. 88; see also next.

W2209 Why is your heart so full of grief?
And bid adieu to sin.

[Thomas Stevens?], 'Sent to a friend in great distress
of mind'

c.259, p. 60; see also previous.

W2210 Why joyful fireworks only in the park
Unless their lives the only winner.

'On an advertisement to prohibit the making of
fireworks'

c.186, p. 50

W2211 Why kinder you my thirsty soul to drink
Bid not a guest to dine that must not eat.

'To his coy mistress'

b.356, p. 80

W2212 Why knits my dear her angry brow?
You fairest, were the rest all fair.

'On jealousy, addressed to a young lady'

c.83/2, no. 369

W2213 Why like the rill from yonder fount that flows
Like night's pale specter at the blush of morn.

[John Wolcot ('Peter Pindar')], 'Persian sonnet'
[verses on Omar Khayyam]

File 17287

W2214 Why lovely boy, why fliest thou me
And thou shalt need no shade but I.

[Henry Rainolds], 'Puella ad juvenem' [answered by
'Black maid complain . . .']
[Crum W2373]

b.205, fol. 50r; b.62, p. 25

W2215 Why love's my flower, the sweetest flow'r
And lead oblivion into day.

[John Langhorne], 'The wallflower'
[Crum W2374]

c.140, p. 204 (incomplete?)

W2216 Why man! Dost thou so much delight in pride,
For all, thou hast, are but derivatives.

J[ohn] R[obinson], 'Qui sapit, in tucito gaudeat ille
sinu'

c.370, fol. 66

W2217 Why many tender most the marriage
Please widows, *ausa patet*.

Sir Thomas Urquhart, 'Of maids, and widows'

fb.217, p. 82

W2218 Why Martial's life so happy would you know
And death to wish as little for as fear.

[translation of Martial X.47]

Poetry Box x/10(11)

W2219 Why mourn so much your Pompey's fate,
Whose anguish wounds not mine.

'To the Misses —— on their concern for an
accident to a favorite dog'

c.89, p. 112

W2220 Why mourns my friend! Why weeps his downcast
eye?

From Jessy floating on her wat'ry bier!

[William] Shenstone, 'An elegy, describing the
melancholy event of a licentious amour'

fc.132/1, p. 98; c.83/1, no. 268

W2221 Why must the footman to his lady's pew
May rise from fashions void of common sense.

'A Sunday epigram' [1751]

Poetry Box XIV/171

W2222 Why noses should have such a prominent place
They have a firm hold by the knob of my nose.

[John Walker?]

fc.108, fol. 48

W2223 Why not the picture of our dying Lord
Within, tis th'object of our faith, not eyes.

[Francis Quarles], 'On a crucifix' [Divine
fancies III, 49]

b.137, p. 176

W2224 Why, not to underrate your muse,
England shall have my wishes still.

'Lady Augusta'

c.578, p. 64

W2225 Why on this day Sarcasmus cried,
Or George the Third began to reign?

R[ichard] V[ernon] S[adleir], 'Impromptu'

c.106, p. 130

W2226 Why, plaintive warbler! tell me why
The rapture of a single sigh!

'To the nightingale. Translation of the 15th ode of
Rousseau'

c.141, p. 553

W2227 Why pretty turtle, does thou mourn
Incessant sorrow will.

'A short epigrammatic dialogue between a passenger
and turtle dove written originally in French'

c.186, p. 78

W2228 Why Priapus? Aye, why? You're much to blame;
To shorten what is so much better long.

'Tu dicis Priapum . . . imitated'

c.221, p. 41

W2229 Why puritans reject all ceremonies,
Which bring instead of eight, ten in the hundred.

Sir Thomas Urquhart, 'Substance is better than
ceremonies'

fb.217, p. 203

W2230 Why shed we unavailing tears?
Dear youth! had been the same as thine?

[Stephen Barrett], 'On the death of Edward Jeremiah
Curteis j[unio]r . . . .in the fifth year of his age'

c.193, p. 148

W2231 Why should a man be confin'd,
'Tis advantage to make me the worse.

'The scolding wife'

fb.107, p. 68

W2232 Why should frail nature thus lament distress'd
And know your union seal'd by ties divine.

'To the memory of my valued friend Anthony Benezet
who died at Philadelphia in America . . . [5 May 1784]'

c.139, p. 601

W2233 Why should friends and kindred gravely make thee,
Suffers wealth to cuckold his affection.

'Love without money'

fb.107, p. 25

W2234 Why should honest men despair
God's justice or his power.

[to the tune of When I was a dame of honor]
[Crum w2394]

fc.58, p. 137; c.570/2, p. 34

W2235 Why should I fret me, or be cross,
By sin; then raging let my passion be.

H[enry] C[olman], 'On anger'
[Crum w2398]

b.2, p. 45

W2236 Why should I mourn my judgment so
From her inconstancy expected.

Sir Robert Atto. Scott

b.197, p. 46

W2237 Why should I shrink to dwell amongst the dead,
The vanity of what I was below.

'A dying reflection'

c.83/1, no. 146

W2238 Why should I sigh and shed a tear
To all eternity. Amen.

[Mary Pluret], 'Another [song]'

c.354

W2239 Why should man's sp'rit, the works of's flesh control;
Seeing that his body's elder than his soul.

> Sir Thomas Urquhart, 'Of the flesh, and the spirit. A problem'
>
> fb.217, p. 220

W2240 Why should men too much despise
That unto dust return we must | Thus think then
[drink tobacco].

> 'A meditation upon tobacco'
> [Crum w2401, 'so much']
>
> b.62, p. 114

W2241 Why should not pilgrims to thy body come
Is not enough a miracle to do .

> F[rancis] B[eaumont?]
> [Crum w2407]
>
> b.148, p. 150

W2242 Why should one blockhead's speech make such a
noise
And then like thee the mobile may cheat.

> 'On the speaking wooden head'
>
> fb.108, p. 137

W2243 Why should our joys transform to pain,
And wear the joyful chain.

> [Isaac] Watts, 'The Indian philosopher'
>
> c.244, p. 316; c.139, p. 30

W2244 Why should passion strike thee blind
That she will fall even with a touch.

> 'To his lovesick friend'
> [Crum w2408]
>
> b.356, p. 84; see also 'Why doth . . .', 'Would you have . . .', 'Why should thy . . .'.

W2245 Why should so much beauty fear?
You did their cunny tickle lust expel . . . .

> 'A song. 1670'
>
> b.54, p. 1199 (incomplete)

W2246 Why should tears forbear to flow?
What like patience softens grief.

> [William Popple, trans.], '[Horace] book 1st. ode 24th. To Virgil, on the death of Quintilius Varus'
>
> fc.104/2, p. 68

W2247 Why should the bells in merry peals thus roll
For Anna's virtue, shall in James survive.

> 'On the rejoicing on the 1st of Augst. Being the day of the Queen's death, and of G[eorg]e's accession to the throne' [pr. 1714 (Foxon O218)]
>
> c.570/1, p. 177

W2248 Why should thy passion lead thee blind
And make her taste and color sweeter.

> 'Upon one unmarriageable'
> [Crum w2414]
>
> b.62, p. 27; see also 'Why doth . . .', 'Would you have passion . . .', 'Why should passion . . .'.

W2249 Why should us blinded mortals think it strange
For tho' I'd lost my life, I'd pleas'd my sight.

> [Robert Cholmeley], 'Woman'
>
> c.190, p. 106

W2250 Why should we be asham'd to write in sheets
Paper with words than beds with deeds of lust.

> [Sir Thomas Urquhart], 'An apology for lascivious writing'
>
> fb.217, p. 532

W2251 Why should we not eat flesh on Friday, Ned?
'Tis Venus' day, who was 'mongst fishes bred.

> Sir Thomas Urquhart, 'Why on the Friday we ought to abstain from flesh. To Ned a problem'
>
> fb.217, p. 285

W2252 Why should we startle at th'approach of death,
When she's releas'd with gladness flies away.

> J. W., 'On death'
>
> c.258

W2253 Why should you in your sickness thus enrage
For if it leave not you you must leave it.

> [Sir Thomas Urquhart], 'An encouragement to an impatient man in an ague'
>
> fb.217, p. 528

W2254 Why should you say, that nature can admit
No vacuum: seeing your brains are void of wit.

> Sir Thomas Urquhart, 'To a fool, studying natural philosophy'
>
> fb.217, p. 157

W2255 Why should you shed so many brinish tears
And you shall find, that you have gained by it.

> [Sir Thomas Urquhart], 'Merchants should not be sore at the loss of wares'
>
> fb.217, p. 527

W2256 Why should you Strephon's love despise,
And labors only to be witty.

> 'Strephon's flames'
>
> fb.107, p. 73

W2257 Why sits my gentle Thyrsis thus forlorn?
And be attended with Cassandra's fate.

> 'A pastoral' [9 Sept. 1691]
>
> b.111, p. 77

W2258 Why sleep you mistress whilst it shines so bright?
Because I will be made t'awake this night.

    Sir Thomas Urquhart, 'To a bride, who was
    slumbering the first day of her marriage'

    fb.217, p. 187

W2259 Why slight thou her whom I approve
To love by judgment not by sense.

    [Henry King], 'A lover to one dispraising his mistress'
    [Crum w2425]

    b.62, p. 39

W2260 Why so far off, why hid'st thy face
And their oppression end.

    'Psalm 10'

    c.264/1, p. 31

W2261 Why so grave Harry? What's the matter pray?
At present, Sir, God bless ye, and farewell.

    [John Byrom, of Manchester], 'A dialogue between
    [Sir John Jobson and Harry Homespun]'

    c.140, p. 24

W2262 Why so pale and wan fond lover? | Prithee why so
                             pale?

Nothing can make her | The devil take her.

    [Sir John Suckling, song from Aglaura, IV.ii]
    [Crum w2428]

    b.213, p. 8

W2263 Why sounds the plain with sad complaint
And meet thy saint above.

    [Allan Ramsay], 'An ode sacred to the memory of her
    grace Anne, Duchess of Hamilton'

    c.360/2, no. 116

W2264 Why start! The case is yours—or will be soon;
Farewell, remember—lest you wake too late.

    'Lord's [skull]' [inscription for a skull in an alcove in
    the garden of Mr. Tyer's at Denbigh in Surrey]
    [Crum w2431]

    c.156, p. 59; c.83/1, no. 97 (var.)

W2265 Why stays my fair? See! The thick shades descend;
More sad, pursues the labor of the day.

    Philip Wharton, 1st duke of Wharton(?), 'Menalcas
    and Enosia. A pastoral dialogue'

    c.468

W2266 Why steals from my bosom the sigh?
The thought of her Colin pursue.

    [Henry Mackenzie], 'Lavinia. A pastoral—from The
    man of feeling'
    [Crum w2434]

    fc.132/1, p. 167

W2267 Why streams thy lovely downcast eye?
They speak, but to betray.

    'Lines to Miss L—— on seeing her in tears . . . Eliza'

    c.83/3, no. 755

W2268 Why study you in morals if you take
From any passion that you there may find.

    [Sir Thomas Urquhart], 'That virtue is of greater
    worth than knowledge'

    fb.217, p. 524

W2269 Why stun with fruitless pray'rs my ears?
Or failing my lost art deplore?

    [William Popple, trans.], 'Canidia's answer' [to 'I own,
    I own . . .'; Horace, epode 17]

    fc.104/2, p. 472

W2270 Why sure the necessary harms were framed
But happier; which to know them never care.

    'On women'

    c.356

W2271 Why sure you're married; take you the impression
To make one lock serve th'use of many keys.

    Sir Thomas Urquhart, 'To a certain courtesan, who,
    though lately wedded to a husband, could not for that
    abstain from her formerly accustomed liberty in
    prostitution'

    fb.217, p. 104

W2272 Why tailors cabbage, lawyers cheat
Truth loves no suits, no clothes it wears.

    [Phanuel Bacon], 'An epigram'

    c.237, fol. 49

W2273 Why tarries my love
For the pigeon that flutters and dies.

    'The dove a song'

    c.179, p. 19

W2274 Why tease thus, dear Peg! When you know all the
                             day,
Five hundred—there! There! I'm (by Neptune!) all
                             fire.

    John Lockman, 'John's answer' [to 'How dearly I love
    you . . .']

    c.267/1, p. 46

W2275 Why these I should sing
I am sure it can ne'er be a dry one.

    [ ] Kendall, 'On Dapper's chicks alias Anabaptists'

    c.170, p. 27

W2276 Why this day's shorter than the rest.
But lends his rays to Stella's eyes.

'On Miss Charlotte Clayton's birthday being the 11 of December'

c.360/3, no. 210

W2277 Why this long respite from the press my friend?
Some pity on a lesser madman take.

[William Popple, trans.], 'Horace book 2nd satire 3rd imitated. Dialogue between Dr L—n and the poet'

fc.104/1, p. 227

W2278 Why thus asleep, when justice bids ye rise,
And scourge these fruitless(?) knaves with more
than rhymes.

John Lockman, 'To the anti-Gallicans . . . Oct. 1749'

c.267/1, p. 183

W2279 Why, Thy own people, Lord, reject
And hate Thee more and more.

'Psalm 74'

c.264/2, p. 49

W2280 Why to our clay was life allowed, and breath?
Grant Lord once dead I rise to life again, | Amen.

H[enry] C[olman], 'Another' [on death]
[Crum w2440]

b.2, p. 37

W2281 Why to the west a golden sun
To match the lightnings of her eyes.

[John Wolcot ('Peter Pindar')], 'Sonnet'

File 16344

W2282 Why toils the world so eager after fame?
Low buried in the dust their honors lie.

'The vanity of mortal things'

c.94

W2283 Why treat me still with cold disdain?
For love alone, love's wounds can cure.

John Lockman, 'To Nancy: requesting her to visit Clifton, or Bristol Hot Well. Set by Dr. Boyes [William Boyce]'

c.267/2, p. 102

W2284 Why tries the gen'rous Thrale to make
By virtues, than by gifts.

[Charles Burney, the elder], 'To [Mrs. Thrale] on receiving from her a gold-headed cane, immediately after a severe fit of sickness'

c.33, p. 119 (crossed out)

W2285 Why veils the Queen of Isles her radiant brow?
And bring at last the welcome angel—peace.

Harriet Walker, 'Britannia . . . Thirsk, 4th March 1797'

c.175, p. 74

W2286 Why was I born, or why do I survive
True love for counterfeit, and gold for lead.

[John] Pomfret, 'A complaint'

c.360/2, no. 82 (ll. 21–32)

W2287 Why was it call'd the golden age, of old,
When Saturn liv'd, seeing then there was no gold.

Sir Thomas Urquhart, 'Of the golden age when there was no use of coin. A problem'

fb.217, p. 133

W2288 Why weep you here, and take this stone to be
Adds but more marble to this hallowed stone.

[Robert Codrington], 'Epitaph' [on the death of Lady Winifred Fitzwilliam]

b.87, p. 13

W2289 Why weep, Asterie, since the spring,
Be firm, and double ev'ry frown.

[William Popple, trans.], '[Horace] book 3rd. ode 7th. To Asterie'

fc.104/2, p. 232

W2290 Why weep'st thou, marble? is thy trust
A world compos'd of worth and wit.

'On Cornelius Agrippa'

fb.143, p. 32

W2291 Why, when the balm of sleep descends on man,
To want give affluence, and to slavery freedom.

[ ] Johnson

c.156, p. 233

W2292 Why will dear Amanda dwell
Haste, Amanda, come away!

R[ichard] V[ernon] S[adleir], 'To Lady Shelley, in lodgings near the churchyard of St. Mary—1787'

c.106, p. 100

W2293 Why will Delia thus retire
I believe the dose will [blank].

Lady Mary Wortley Montagu, 'To Lady [Isabella (Machell) Ingram] Irwin' [answered by 'Tho' Delia oft retires . . .']

fc.135 (incomplete)

W2294 Why will Florella when I gaze,
Tho' death attends them there.

> [Soame Jenyns]
> [Crum w2448]
>
> c.358, p. 163; c.83/1, no. 40

W2295 Why will my fair when I pursue her
You're now grown fit for lover's arms.

> 'To the same [Miranda] a translation of Horace ode
> [23] book the [1st]'
>
> Poetry Box I/48

W2296 Why will you strive to make the fair
Thy eloquence can fail.

> 'Verses made on Dr. Thomas Secker Bishop of Bristol
> giv[ing] advice to Miss Talbot, when at Bath—1736'
>
> c.360/1, p. 21

W2297 Why with such haste do thy affections roll
Which never can thee surfeit never cloy.

> [John Hobart]
>
> b.108, fol. 4

W2298 Why women love them best, who cull'd the favor
Most of the liquor, poured first into them.

> Sir Thomas Urquhart, 'The reason, why women for
> the most part carry greatest affection to those, that
> have enjoyed their maidenheads'
>
> fb.217, p. 337

W2299 Why would false Damon still amuse
Which she can ne'er regain.

> [Mrs. Christian Kerr]
>
> c.102, p. 135

W2300 Why would the knight a baron be
But by desire mind discontent.

> [Sir Nicholas] Bacon, 'Against ambition'
>
> fa.8, fol. 164

W2301 Why your name fits you, why not, would you know?
You're cold and black: you are and are not Snow.

> 'Upon Mrs. Snow'
>
> b.207, p. 5

W2302 Wife and servant are the same
You must be proud if you'd be wise.

> [Lady Mary Chudleigh]
> [Crum w2456, 'all the same']
>
> c.548; c.258

W2303 Wife take this child, and free me of his care;
Yet never did you leave me grudge thereat.

> [Sir Thomas Urquhart]
>
> fb.217, p. 540

W2304 Will Crambo, whom you know, the pretty
But view the charge that hangs behind.

> [Robert Cholmeley], '[Catallus] imitated and applied
> to the book'
>
> c.190, p. 64

W2305 Will it you[r] tempers, ladies, suit,
I'm not uncivil, nor unkind.

> C[harles] B[urney], 'Verses sent to the Miss Wilcox's,
> with some fruit. 1779'
>
> c.38, p. 37

W2306 Will mourns his wife whene'er he meets her mother
Then flies to say soft things at ———'s feet.

> R[ichard] V[ernon] S[adleir], 'Epigram'
>
> c.106, p. 83

W2307 Will my dear brother, and indulgent friend,
With lovely error crown my worthless lays.

> [Anna Laetitia (Aikin)] Barbauld, 'To Mr. J. Aikin of
> Warrington'
>
> c.364, p. 27

W2308 Will tells me, I'm grown monstrous proud,
Is, 'cause you ne'er could boast the like.

> John Lockman, 'The coxcomb . . . alluding to an
> epistle, of the author, to the [?] Duchess of
> Buckingham, prefixed to The Jesuit's travels. 1749'
>
> c.267/1, p. 5

W2309 Will the ladies permit me to offer before 'em
Shall these words be inscribed: ill to him who
                                          thinks ill.

> 'The origin of the Order of the Garter'
>
> c.115

W2310 Will thou stand fixt, and resolute (old Bully)
Makes answer and protests, my will the same.

> [Sir Philip Wodehouse], 'Upon an old Royalist
> William Hart . . .'
>
> b.131, back (no. 194)

W2311 Will was newly married, when
You had not Joan abed.

> R[obert] Shirley, 1st earl of Ferrers, 'The debt paid.
> From La Fontaine'
>
> c.347, p. 39

W2312 Will—with proviso-wills you testify,
Has made his will, but hath no will to die.

> 'An honest fellow's dying'
>
> c.74

W2313 Will you be guilty (Master) of this wrong
And shall we part now? No we'll hang together.

> [Henry Stonestreet], 'The old cloak's reply to The
> poet's farewell' [answer to 'Cloak (if I may so call
> thee . . .')]
> [Crum w2466]
> b.65, p. 194

W2314 Will you hear a Spanish lady
The like falls unto thy share. | Most fair lady!

> 'The English captain and Spanish lady'
> c.358, p. 181

W2315 Will you hear a strange thing never heard of before,
When the devil is divided against the devil. | With a
hey down &c.

> 'The House out of doors to the tune of Cook Lorell'
> [Crum w2469]
> Poetry Box VI/18, 65 (incomplete)

W2316 Will you hear a tender story?
And they sunk—to rise no more.

> 'Henry and Nancy an ancient ballad on two village
> lovers who drowned themselves in Whittlesea Moor'
> c.341, p. 48

W2317 Will you hear my good neighbors about a jackdaw
Quoth Jack flying off, I'll be sworn that's a lie.

> [Thomas Hull]
> c.528/47

W2318 Will you still lament and raise
Prevent your acts; peace guard this house.

> R[obert] H[errick?], 'Parkinson's shade to the house
> of Mr Palavicini taking his death ill'
> b.197, p. 10

W2319 William defends the lambs from cruel Satan's power
By love not force he's rais'd to power.

> Poetry Box VI/94

W2320 [?] William Duke of Normandy
Was [joyful?] due to England and France.

> 'Old verses upon the kings of England'
> [cf. Crum w2474]
> fa.14

W2321 William the Norman conquers England's state;
Lord of the ocean and his people's friend.

> 'A chronological history of England'
> c.504, p. 133

W2322 Will's wanton wife his waters watch'd so well
Flat in the fatal flood the fond fool fell!

> [Richard Vernon Sadleir?], 'Being asked the meaning
> of the word alliteration in poetry . . . William Flat the
> miller was drowned in his own stream'
> c.106, p. 132

W2323 Willy, a North British hallion,
Altho' they do oft meet, and clash.

> 'A song'
> c.530, p. 134

W2324 Wilt thou dear Jesus hear and help
What thou to me didst promise make.

> [Mary Pluret], 'Another [poem written on waste
> paper]'
> c.354

W2325 Wilt thou forsake me who in life's bright May
Where pity and remembrance bend and weep!

> [Charlotte (Turner) Smith], 'Sonnet to the muse'
> c.141, p. 142

W2326 Wilt thou hear what man can say
Than that it lived at all: farewell.

> B[en] Jonson, 'On the death of the Lady Eliz. Hobby'
> [Crum w2484]
> b.200, p. 100; fb.143, p. 34

W2327 Wilt thou nor cease but always strive to run
Each one upon thy VRNE shall read thee IOB.

> 'William Ioburne, anagramma I WILL Run me. A
> JCB.'
> b.62, p. 93

W2328 Wilt thou, so early skill'd in classic lore,
And long remember—'while we live, to live'.

> 'Sonnet to Dr. Sanden'
> c.89, p. 125

W2329 Wilt thou these little volumes then peruse?
Though mute, Janetta shall instruct mankind.

> [ ] G., 'From the Revd. Mr. G.'s lucubrations, on the
> poems and essays of a lady [Miss Bowdler] lately
> deceased at Bath'
> c.83/1, no. 64

W2330 Windsor at length be to your country just
For Anna ever to the Church was kind.

> 'Advice to the electors of the borough of New
> Windsor' [1715]
> [Crum w2489]
> c.570/1, p. 40

W2331 Wine from the brains steals man away, and lest
The sense perceive't, leaves in his place a beast.

> Sir Thomas Urquhart, 'That Bacchus is a thief'
>
> fb.217, p. 179

W2332 Wine is the oil of wit 'tis wine anoints
In satires it careers the while his pen's his lance.

> [Sir Philip Wodehouse], 'Epigram—an anacreontic . . .
> of wine'
>
> b.131, back (no. 87)

W2333 Wine Lot's, and Noah's secret parts made known
And Lot's exposed to his daughter's touch.

> [Sir Thomas Urquhart], 'How differently the children
> of Noah and Lot sinned in abusing that nakedness
> which both their fathers by too much drinking had
> discovered'
>
> fb.217, p. 501

W2334 Wine so imbrutes a man, it makes his brain
For it leaves you, ev'n as it finds y', a beast.

> Sir Thomas Urquhart, 'Here a blockish loggerhead for
> dispraising of wine, is roundly checked'
>
> fb.217, p. 165

W2335 Wine, vices, women, Vander Bruin!
Wine, vices, women were thy making.

> [Stephen Barrett?], 'Epigram on an extravagant son of
> a whore . . .' [in reference to Prior's 'Fire, water,
> women . . .']
>
> c.193, p. 104

W2336 Wine, wine alone is the brisk fountain of mirth,
Then glass after glass, my boys, let us pursue. | 'Tis
this, &c.

> 'Song 94'
>
> c.555, p. 142

W2337 Wing'd with pure joy, the peaceful moments flew,
They range secure, in the mansion of the blest.

> 'The underwritten inscription is wrote upon the
> tombstone that protects Caleb Ingham of Doncaster,
> and Margaret his wife . . .'
>
> c.175, p. 15

W2338 Winter and death, fell enemies
A Field amidst the skies.

> W[illia]m Jackson, 'To the memory of Miss Field an
> ode'
>
> c.229/1, fol. 74

W2339 Winter thy cruelty extend,
All taste we have of heav'nly joy.

> [Wentworth Dillon], 4th earl of Roscommon, 'Song
> on a young lady who sung finely, and was afraid of the
> cold'
>
> c.351, p. 57

W2340 Winter yields, now zephyr blows;
Who shall soon our virgins warm!

> [William Popple, trans.], '[Horace] book 1st. ode 4th.
> To Sestius'
>
> fc.104/2, p. 14

W2341 Wisdom and power with all their charms
At the first dawn of day.

> 'Love triumphant'
>
> c.186, p. 61

W2342 Wisdom I sing—what bearded sage can choose
('Tis all we ask) O teach us to be wise!

> [J. Wilkinson], 'Wisdom a poem'
>
> c.139, p. 321

W2343 Wisdom implies all that is good,
That wisdom is true happiness.

> [Edmund Wodehouse], 'March 20 [1715] Sophia
> Wodehouse'
>
> b.131, p. 184

W2344 Wisdom is chief and strength must come behind,
But both be good and gift from God assign'd.

> c.339, p. 320

W2345 Wisdom 'mongst us apocryphated lies:
But you're canonic, though you be not wise.

> Sir Thomas Urquhart, 'For a canon of a very shallow
> capacity'
>
> fb.217, p. 139

W2346 Wisdom (which is the worker of all things:
T'inflame prepared hearts with holy fires.

> [William Sandys?], 'A character of wisdom'
>
> b.230, p. 101

W2347 Wise men are wonders: but now wonders cease:
That wonders cease not, or that you're not wise.

> Sir Thomas Urquhart, 'To a senator-like man, who
> though he was very proud of the wit he had: being
> nevertheless, not very wise, is here subtly taxed for his
> folly'
>
> fb.217, p. 337

W2348 Wise men suffer good men grieve
Else knaves and fools will quite undo us.

> [Rev. ( ) Stevenson?], 'Short and sweet'
> [Crum w2513]
>
> b.111, p. 378; see also 'Good men suffer . . .', 'Wise men
> wonder / suffer . . .'.

W2349 Wise men, though wiser than the good, I prize
Less, than good men, who're better than the wise.

> Sir Thomas Urquhart, 'Of goodness, and wisdom'
>
> fb.217, p. 107

W2350 Wise men wonder, they honest grieve
Or knaves and fools, will soon undo us.

  b.103, p. 80; see also 'Wise/Good men suffer . . .'.

W2351 Wise Rochefoucault a maxim writ,
And get a hatband, scarf, and gloves.

  [Jonathan Swift], 'A life and character upon a maxim
  of Rochefoucault' [pr. 1733 (Foxon S884)]

  c.83/1, no. 52 (ll. 1–75)

W2352 Wise sentences who keepeth in his breast,
By proof shall find he harbors happy guests.

  c.339, p. 317; see also "Good sentences . . .'.

W2353 Wise Solon to the Lydian king:
And nothing but good nature flow.

  Abraham Oakes, 'A moral reflection on worldly
  happiness'

  c.50, p. 133

W2354 Wisely from man his maker has withheld
'They also serve who only stand and wait.'

  [William Hayley], 'Sonnet . . . August 31 [1800]'
  File 6968

W2355 Wish things as they are just what you see
So shall you never disappointed be.

  c.549, p. 26

W2356 Wit afterwards is like a shower of rain,
Which moists the soil, when withered is the grain.

  c.339, p. 260, p. 309

W2357 Wit had not learn'd to gloss and varnish crimes,
He advertises for a pregnant wife.

  [ ] Murphy, 'Seventeen hundred and ninety one . . . a
  picture of the times'

  c.83/4, no. 2023

W2358 Wit thy airy pinions spread
The lovely Caley holds me fast.

  Miss [ ] Andrews, 'Sent to Miss Mary Ann Caley'
  File 245/2

W2359 Wit, wisdom first wisdom, wit I do adore,
Wit goes before, but wisdom comes behind.

  'On wisdom, and wit'
  c.189, p. 46

W2360 With a damn'd and sullen fate let's no longer
                                        conspire,
'Tis love's the delight, and support of the world.

  'The atlas'
  fb.107, p. 67

W2361 With a grave look and courteous smile
That with one voice they cry well moved.

  'The opening of the sessions' [in the House of
  Commons, 1690]
  [Crum w2530, 'grave leg'; POAS v.260]

  b.111, p. 323; see also 'With grave leg . . .'.

W2362 With a new beard but lately trimm'd
O the King's new soldier.

  [William Strode?], 'The King's new soldier'
  [Crum w2533]

  fb.107, p. 71

W2363 With a Patten for wife, thro' the rough road of life
Nor the Foot find the Patten a clog.

  'On the marriage of Capt. E. W. Foot to Miss Patten'
  c.546

W2364 With a whirl of thought opprest,
I damn such fools—go—go—you're bit.

  [Jonathan] Swift, 'The day of judgment'
  c.362, p. 30

W2365 With aching head and languid mind
Whilst hope shows endless scenes of light.

  'The authoress was desired to write some verses'
  c.504, p. 149

W2366 With all instruction nobly fraught,
With all the just for Jesus' sake.

  Charles Atherton Allnutt, 'Lines address'd to a friend
  on returning him a book entitled Gataker's Joy of the
  just'

  c.112, p. 130

W2367 With all the powers my poor soul hath
To the eternal Trinity.

  [John Austin], 'Hym: 23' [Hymn xviii, Devotions in
  the ancient way of offices, 1672, p. 160]

  c.178, p. 21

W2368 With all the reverence and regard
With healing arts, and mortal song.

  [William Hayley]
  File 7052

W2369 With an honest old friend, and a merry old song,
For the more we are envied, the higher we rise.

  'Song 125'
  c.555, p. 179

W2370 With an old motley coat, and a malmsey nose,
And the Queen's old soldier.

  'The Queen's old soldier'
  fb.107, p. 69

W2371 With an old song made by an old ancient pate,
And the King's old courtier.

> [Mat. Trevenen?], 'The King's old courtier'
> [Crum W2541 or W2542]
>
> fb.107, p. 69; see also 'Here is an old song . . .'.

W2372 With anguish, that no force of words can tell,
And every doubting anxious thought control.

> 'Lady Jane Grey, to Lord Guilford Dudley'
>
> c.83/1, no. 168

W2373 With artful verse young Thyrsis you
I'll not protect a drone.

> [Sir Charles Keymes], 'The answer' [to 'In vain, my
> Chloe . . .', p. 22]
>
> c.233, p. 83

W2374 With avarice, a virtuous passion! fir'd,
More I received, yet More I still desir'd.

> B[enjamin] Kennicott, 'On Miss Hannah More
> leaving Christchurch, after a short visit'
>
> File 17453

W2375 With beauty nature has enrich'd thy face,
Bestudy them, thou'lt rise a finish'd fair.

> John Lockman, 'Writ in a blank leaf of my Amusing
> instructor, (English and Italian) when presented to
> Miss Kitty Cornwall . . . Feb. 1761'
>
> c.267/1, p. 311

W2376 With beauty, with pleasure surrounded, to
                                            languish—
They smile, but reply not—sure Delia can tell me!

> [Thomas Gray]
>
> c.83/3, no. 1069

W2377 With cautious, trembling step she steals;
Source whence unnumber'd blessings flow?

> John Lockman, 'Psyche awakes Cupid' [translated
> from La Fontaine]
>
> c.267/4, p. 215

W2378 With charming Cholmondeley well one might
My heart, my ease, my peace—adieu.

> 'Verses written upon some of the celebrated women
> who flourished in the year 1780'
>
> c.391, p. 35, 63 ('Female literati of 1780'); Poetry Box
> v/26

W2379 With Christian fortitude resigning,
Emits a feeble blaze, then dies.

> 'The dying Christian'
> [Crum W2548]
>
> c.83/2, no. 602

W2380 With clouted iron shoes, and sheepskin breeches,
Since for Sir Beelzebub, they'd do the same.

> 'His fine speech'
>
> fb.142, p. 17; fb.70, p. 101; c.158, p. 58 ('clouted shoes')

W2381 With dalliance once young Zephyr woos
And plenty load her ample horn.

> 'Ode 4th. The first of April'
>
> c.90

W2382 With deathless trophies, wreaths unfading crown'd
How bravely Dawnay for his country fell.

> 'On Henry Pleydell, Lord Viscount Downe who died
> of his wounds in Germany'
>
> c.81/1, no. 474

W2383 With decent pride, this am'rous walk survey,
Trees may have ears, and trees may not be dumb.

> 'Written over the entrance of a shady grove'
>
> c.487, p. 25

W2384 With Devon's girl so blithe and gay
Content to live and think with Crewe.

> C[harles] J[ames] Fox
>
> File 5386; Poetry Box v/26

W2385 With diligence and trust, most exemplary,
Art maketh some, but thus will nature all.

> [Thomas Randolph], 'Epitaph on William Lawrence
> prebendary' [d. 1621]
> [Crum W2551]
>
> c.360/3, no. 138; c.546, p. 23

W2386 With dogs five couple, in thick woods I roam:
What's caught I kill: what's not, I keep at home.

> 'An enigma . . . English' [on catching fleas]
>
> c.81/1, no. 362

W2387 With doubt—joy—apprehension—almost dumb,
'Tis for my King, and 'zounds I'll do my best.

> [David Garrick], 'Prologue to Much ado about
> nothing. Acted by command of His Majesty spoken by
> Mr. Garrick . . .' [14 November 1765]
> [Crum W2552]
>
> c.68, p. 143; c.115

W2388 With downcast eyes and folded arms,
Whose name he, yesterday, had flourished there.

> c.188, p. 71

W2389 With due respect E. Sneyd presents,
Heroic virtue never dies.

> E[dward] Sneyd, 'March 28th 1779. Epistle 18th: to
> Kirkman esqr. Cornet of Dragoons—belonging to his
> Royal Highness George Prince of Wales'
>
> c.214, p. 119

W2390 With duteous haste let all the muses come
And in fame's volume mold'ring time survive.

  'On the same [an epistle to Melissa]'
  [Crum W2555]
Poetry Box I/34

W2391 With early horn salute the morn,
All return to their 'livening sounds.

  'Song 36'
c.555, p. 58

W2392 With ecstasies of joy,
Is all in all.

  P[hilip] Doddridge, 'A hymn on 1 Pet II. 4, 6. . . .'
c.493, p. 35

W2393 With equal ardor, and bewitching passion
So choice a music they had ne'er deserted.

  Sir Thomas Urquhart, 'How a gentleman did play
  with his mistress upon the organs'
fb.217, p. 331

W2394 With ev'ry virtue, ev'ry grace possest
Fair without guilt, and as she's fair, serene.

  [Horace Walpole, 4th earl of Orford], 'D[uchess] of
  Hamilton'
c.157, p. 67

W2395 With eyes so bright and with that charming air
And what her eyes enthrall'd, her tongue unbound.

  'Fair and foolish'
c.229/1, fol. 73

W2396 With eyes unconstant to each fancy prone
But may be catched on the London road.

  'An advertisement on the hue and cry' [docket title:
  'Verses about Sr G. Mackenzie and the rest of the
  advocates (16)76']
Poetry Box VIII/29

W2397 With face, and fashion to be known
See a new teacher of the town, | Oh the town's, the
                  town's new teacher!

  [William Strode], 'The town's new teacher'
  [Crum W2558]
b.200, p. 365; b.213, p. 89

W2398 With Father coeternal Lord
Judge to his Judge and to all flesh.

  '[On God the Father Son and Holy Ghost from
  1: John 5:7: There be three that bear record in
  Heaven, and these three are one:] The Son'
b.137, p. 124

W2399 With favor and fortune fastidiously blest,
'Tis the cur-dog of Britain, and spaniel of Spain.

  [Jonathan Swift(?), on Sir Robert Walpole; translation
  of eight lines of French verse on Cardinal Fleury. Also
  attr. Samuel Wesley the younger; pr. 1731? (Foxon
  S830)]
fc.58, p. 133; c.570/3, p. 121

W2400 With fiery wings sublime thyself my sprite
But heaven gains keys(?) if each(?) comfort we take.

  [Richard Edes], The solace of the soul'
  [Crum W2560]
fb.29, fol. 7

W2401 With Frederick all the nation's joy lies dead,
But hold! Not all, since George is still our head.

  'On the death of his royal highness the Prince of
  Wales 1750/1'
c.360/3, no. 106

W2402 With gen'rous indignation fir'd,
Since he inspir'd thy lays.

Poetry Box III/folder 21-30

W2403 With gifts like these, the spoils of neighb'ring
                            shores,
With such a lovely nymph, in such a lovely bow'r.

  [Soame Jenyns], 'To Miss Caesar. Sent with a present
  of stones, and shells, designed for a grotto'
c.147, p. 23; c.83/3, no. 964

W2404 With God's good leave this is my last will
Seal'd and deliver'd in the presence of I. B.

  'Blacksmith's will' [25 July 1723]
c.150, p. 40

W2405 With grateful heart I write to thee
His respects would fain express.

  John Walter, 'Verses that were presented to Mrs.
  Hockley . . . Octr. 25 1791'
c.497, p. 8

W2406 With grateful heart my song I'll raise,
How apt the best to fail.

  'Hymn—the 17th of Jany. 1792'
fc.124, p. 74

W2407 With grave leg and courteous smile
That with one voice they cried well mov'd.

  'The opening of the session in the House of
  Commons' [1690]
  [cf. Crum W2530, 'With a grave leg'; POAS v.260]
fb.68, p. 1; c.111, p. 107; see also 'With a grave look . . .'.

W2408   With grief Alençon saw the leaders slain,
And every voice the warriors' praises sung

    'The death of the dukes of York and Alençon. From a
    manuscript poem on the battle of Agincourt' [signed
    Charles]

    c.343, p. 40

W2409   With grief, I am sure you will hear
Immur'd the fifteenth of September.

    [verse epistle to 'Dear Tinker']

    fc.40

W2410   With hair dishevell'd, drown'd in tears,
Shall guide thee safe to heav'n.

    [Dorothea Harris, sr.], 'On Mary Magdelene . . . 1778'

    fc.124, p. 39

W2411   With harden'd front I meet each night
I perish in a tear!

    R[ichard] V[ernon] S[adleir]

    c.106, p. 96

W2412   With hasty steps the shades of night advance;
Return, O happy Keeper to thy home!

    'Written by Monsieur Charles Simonde of Geneva,
    and returned with our dog Keeper who had followed
    him to Mr. Lettice's the beginning of May 1793 . . .
    translated'

    fc.124, p. 107

W2413   With haughty heart we no man should despise
But think how harm the simplest may devise.

    c.339, p. 313

W2414   With head upon his hand reposed
To write upon soft paper.

    [Robert Merry], 'Extempore another [epigram]'
    Greatheed Box/9

W2415   With heart and temper easy,
That best could ope her love.

    [Charles Burney, the younger], 'Buxom Het. An
    excellent new song to an old tune—A soldier, and a
    sailor, A tinker and a tailor &c. . . . Sept. 19th 1779'

    c.37, p. 57

W2416   With heart I do accord
Therefore praise ye His holy name.

    [Thomas Norton and William Kethe], 'A thanksgiving
    for God's merciful protection. Psal: 47' [verses from
    Psalms 111–113]
    [Crum W2578]

    a.3, fol. 125v

W2417   With her forever in woods I'd rest,
Where never human foot the ground hath prest.

    'On Miss M.'

    c.93

W2418   With his kind mother, who partakes thy woe
By miracles exceeding the power of man.

    [John Donne], '[Holy sonnets. La Corona] 4th'
    [Crum W2582a]

    b.114, p. 156

W2419   With honey mix'd cinquefoil doth cure the canker
And the stays the vomit, and the lase beside.

    [Joshua Sylvester, trans. Guillaume de Salluste,
    seigneur Du Bartas], 'Of cinquefoil'

    b.284, p. 52

W2420   With horns and with hounds I waken the day,
And Echo turns hunter and doubles the cry.

    'Song 142'

    c.555, p. 195

W2421   With humble pleasures Lord we trace
Bear and reflect th'immediate ray.

    P[hilip] Doddridge, 'On Moses' view of God's glory
    Exod. XXXIII. 18'

    c.493, p. 77

W2422   With instruments tun'd to Thy praise,
And the meek man that mourns.

    'Psalm 75 Morning prayer 15 day'

    c.264/2, p. 53

W2423   With Jaffier's woes still struggling in my breast
The blest effusions of fictitious woe.

    'An epilogue altered from one of Mr Sheridan's to
    Semiramis and spoken by Henry Heigham in the
    character of Jaffier Janry 12 and Decber 31st 1784 and
    Janry 5th 1785'

    c.130, p. 68

W2424   With joy, blest youth, we saw thee reach the goal,
Run to a fire, and crowd into a blaze.

    [Christopher] Pitt, 'On the death of a young
    gentleman'

    c.244, p. 499

W2425   With joy, sweet fair ones, I obey
Then use it—as the Greeks did Troy.

    C[harles] B[urney], 'Ode, sent to the Miss Gordons,
    with The good-natured man, a comedy, by
    Dr. Goldsmith . . . Feb. 6. 1779'

    c.38, p. 30

W2426   With joy the grateful nymphs thy name rehearse,
So shall eternal honors wait thy race.

> [Charles Burney, the younger], 'Fidelia. December 1.
> 1777' [printed in the Reading mercury]

c.37, p. 29

W2427   With joy unusual glow'd my breast,
To me it cheering luster lends.

> John Lockman, 'To the right honorable Arthur
> Onslow in the country on receiving a rose from that
> gentleman . . . 20 June, 1761'

c.267/1, p. 296

W2428   With joy we meditate the grace
In the distressing hour.

> 'Hymn 62d'

c.562, p. 75

W2429   With keenness trac'd, with nice attention tried
Give all men places, or resign your own.

> 'To the R. H. Sir Robt Walpole . . . [April] 1740'

Poetry Box IV/193

W2430   With lace hat cock'd, and peacock's air,
Ruin'd, his grandeur turns to smoke.

> John Lockman, 'Flirtillo. A vain worthless fellow, who
> came, unexpectedly, to a great fortune . . . 1744'

c.267/1, p. 13

W2431   With lifted hands and eyes
Shall celebrate thy fame.

> 'Psalm 142 Evening prayer'

c.264/3, p. 99

W2432   With little pleas'd I still lov'd to be poor,
To whom, who conquers all things all things else,
must bow.

c.146, p. 1

W2433   With longing cheer | The thirsty deer
One only God in vanity.

> 'A holy meditation of man's misery and God's mercy
> together with a devout prayer'

b.35, p. 51

W2434   With love, care, silence, she ne'er abroad trips
Who minds but the tortoise, the dove, keys, and lips.

> 'Distich. Wrote under the figure of a woman standing
> upon a tortoise, a bunch of keys in her right hand, the
> forefinger of her left hand upon her lips, and a dove
> upon her shoulder . . . translations [3]'

c.81/1, no. 70

W2435   With love tho' rude we crowd this hallow'd place,
And guard that goddess by whose care they grow.

> [Edmund Smith], 'To the Queen at supper spoke by
> Mr. [Heneage] Finch [later earl of Aylesford]'
> [Crum W2593]

fc.24, p. 57

W2436   With loyal heart I long have woo'd to be
Were in this room . . . .

b.216, p. 173 (incomplete)

W2437   With marble, snowy white, the walls were rear'd;
Which, as her form's reflected, brighter seem.

> John Lockman, 'Psyche's palace' [translated from La
> Fontaine]

c.267/4, p. 207

W2438   With me all women should this rule pursue,
Who thinks us false should never find us true.

c.549, p. 14

W2439   With me, the first and best of friends,
Who never will refuse, or lend?

> [Isaac Freeman], 'Primum est, ut praestes . . . Martial:
> Lib. 7. Epigr: 32'

fc.105, before p. 27

W2440   With mimic art to help the printer's skill
Should draw yourself, not give us but a part.

> 'To Lady Beaulieu's daughter who sent some dressed
> pictures 1769'

fc.135

W2441   With modest looks and downcast eye,
Unconscious shines in all the pomp of day.

> Charles Atherton Allnutt, 'Sonnet to godly simplicity'

c.112, p. 134

W2442   With monks and with hermits I chiefly reside
And when talk'd of, I am instantly fled.

> 'An enigma' [silence]

c.150, p. 138; c.389

W2443   With Monmouth-cap and cutlass by my side
You'll keep a wind as long as he did fight.

> [Sir Henry Sheeres], 'A long prologue to a short play:
> spoken by a woman at Oxford, dressed like a sea
> officer'
> [Crum W2596; POAS V.230]

fb.70, p. 253

W2444   With moral tale let ancient wisdom move,
She gave the horse, and gives the olive too.

> [Thomas Parnell], 'The horse and the olive, or war
> and peace' [pr. 1713 (Foxon P77)]

File 11383, p. 21

W2445 With my own milk unwittingly I nurse,
Kindness can't nature change, tho' it gains love.

> George Montagu, 'On a shepherdess suckling a young
> wolf'

fc.135, p. 11

W2446 With my whole heart I will give praise
What thine own hands have done.

> 'Psalm 138 28 day'

c.264/3, p. 90

W2447 With my whole heart, O Lord, to thee
That they but mortals were.

> 'Psalm 9. Morning prayer 2 day'

c.264/1, p. 25

W2448 With nature, Faber's art contends
And Faber in her eyes.

> 'On Mr. Faber's print of Mrs. Woffington the
> celebrated comedian'

c.360/2, no. 236

W2449 With neither care nor fear opprest
Becomes the fowler's prey.

> 'A moral song on fishing'

c.186, p. 72

W2450 With new translations Holland doth so fill us
That cobblers now translators termed be.

> 'In Doctorem Hollandum'

b.197, p. 109

W2451 With no poetic ardor fir'd,
When freedom is more dear than life.

> [Alexander] Pope, 'Verses left by . . . upon his lying in
> the same bed which Wilmot Earl of Rochester used at
> Atterbury a seat of the Duke of Argyle's in
> Oxfordshire July 9 1739'

c.531

W2452 With nor ivory nor gold,
Charon wafts them to their fate.

> [William Popple, trans.], '[Horace] book 2nd. Ode
> 18th'

fc.104/2, p. 174

W2453 With not one social virtue grac'd
But truth will give him none.

> 'An epigram'

c.360/3, no. 216

W2454 With our bones well fatigued, and our heads very
                                                 light

Ton tres obeisant obligé serviteur.

> H. B., '18 April' [verse epistle from Rome]

Poetry Box x/115

W2455 With patience forborne
Death would thou come a welcome thou shouldst
                                                 find.

b.64, p. 88

W2456 With patient Grizzel here's ado
What do you say to me?

> [Richard Brinsley Butler Sheridan], 'Another' [to
> William Hayley on his poem The triumphs of temper,
> c. 1781]

File 13565

W2457 With pleasing speech some promise and protest
When hateful hearts lie hidden in their breast.

c.339, p. 260, p. 311

W2458 With pleasure I read o'er your ladyship's letter
You'll still have a . . . . . to guard you from fear.

> [Helen Craik], 'To Lady ———'

c.375, p. 51

W2459 With pleasure I survey this shining pit
You'll soon pay t'other visit to the pump.

> 'An epilogue spoken at Bristol'

c.188, p. 49

W2460 With pompous splendor, and triumphal cars,
Ev'n Brunswick's self the cruel darts receiv'd.

> 'On the coronation of His Majesty King George the
> Second and his royal consort' [1727]

c.503, p. 52

W2461 With purple blushes glow'd the eastern skies,
When first to Stella's charms I fell a prey!

> [R. G. S.], 'Morning a pastoral'
> [Crum w2616]

c.89, p. 41

W2462 With radiance rose the morning sun,
Gives all thy virtues to the tomb.

> 'Lines supposed to have been spoken by a friend of the
> unfortunate Marie Antoinette, queen of France and
> Navarre'

c.343, p. 101

W2463 With ravish'd heart that crimson hail
Became like Sharon's rose.

> [George Horne, bishop of Norwich], 'The rose'

Diggle Box: Poetry Box xi/48

W2464 With ready joy O let me Lord agree
For short are impious joys and confidence.

> [Thomas Stanley], 'Meditat: XIX. Upon the various
> events of the war victories and defeats'

b.152, p. 61

W2465 With scorn and indignation fir'd
And will not trust him near the water.

> 'On Dr. Francis Atterbury bishop of Rochester when
> prisoner in the Tower of London 1722 for treason, and
> being removed from his apartment near the water to
> one more secure'
>
> c.360/2, no. 107

W2466 With sense unencumber'd, gay smirking and silly
Ever smiling to show his white teeth and his dimple.

> 'The beau'
>
> c.364, p. 67

W2467 With sickness, and a train of ills opprest,
The glories vanish'd, languish in the wild.

> John Lockman, 'Disappointment . . . 1735'
>
> c.267/1, p. 255

W2468 With social temper happy, and each art,
To pay their compliments, and crown thy night.

> John Lockman, 'On reading an advertisement, for
> Mr. Beard's benefit at Drury Lane theater, 9 April
> 1740, after a favor received'
>
> c.267/1, p. 232

W2469 With solemn nonsense tir'd, and knavish law,
The sun, by turns, must ev'ry region cheer.

> John Lockman, 'An epistolary prescription, humbly
> offer'd to the Duchess of Buckingham, when
> indisposed . . . March 1740/1'
>
> c.267/2, p. 341

W2470 With songs of joy all hail! The natal morn
So please his father and restore mankind.

> [Mary (Shackleton)] Leadbeater, 'Hymn for
> Christmas day'
>
> File 13409

W2471 With sorrow and repentance true,
And send him to me to confess.

> 'The confession'
>
> c.82, p. 20

W2472 With stage erected and set fast
A vo[tre] tres humble serviteur, | By John Punteg:
&c.

> [Francis?] Newman: Bras[enose] Col[lege, Oxford]
>
> b.200, p. 290

W2473 With strong aversion to heart-chilling ice,
With icy cream the owner's generous board.

> T[homas] M[orell], 'On seeing Mr Child's icehouse
> on fire at Osterley'
>
> c.395, p. 155

W2474 With such a sound discretion, full of pomp,
Inform a man, more proper for commanding.

> Sir Thomas Urquhart, 'To the Earl of [crossed out]'
>
> fb.217, p. 173

W2475 With sullen pomp, great Prince thy triumph pass,
The people's voice, like that of God's rose still.

> 'On the 20. of January' [1715]
> [Crum w2638, 'poor prince'; cf. Crum w2631, 'solemn
> pomp']
>
> c.570/1, p. 9

W2476 With supplication pray'r and praise
Praise ye the Lord alway.

> 'Psalm 105 Morning prayer 21 day'
>
> c.264/3, p. 15

W2477 With talents blest, which, wond'ring, we descry,
What pity so complete a wretch should live!

> John Lockman, 'William Smith executed at Tyburn,
> for forgery . . . Oct. 1750'
>
> c.267/1, p. 143

W2478 With tales of plunder in his head
Forbids your works to die.

> 'Impromptu' [on Matthew Gregory Lewis]
>
> Poetry Box x/32

W2479 With tenfold hoarseness! roll thy tide
Till happier seasons roll and realize my dreams.

> 'Ode'
>
> Poetry Box I/19

W2480 With the charms of Brighthelmston, what place
can compare
Only those who have grounds, lying near to the
Steine.

> 'A new ballad on the Steine' [addressed to Lady Payne]
>
> Poetry Box II/50

W2481 With the fierce flames W[hite]h[all] was compass'd
round
To warn bold monarchs and to grace the land.

> 'A satire on W[hite]h[all] . . .'
>
> Poetry Box VII/75; see also 'While with fierce
> flames . . .'.

W2482 With the muse whilst I agree,
Sing, and raise my Lamia's name.

> [William Popple, trans.], '[Horace] book 1st. ode
> 26th. To his Muse'
>
> fc.104/2, p. 74

W2483　With the three things, out of the twenty-four
　　　　That first and last are chang'd if there be seven.

　　　　　'Three things being given to many persons, how to
　　　　　know by 24 counters . . . whether the 3 former be
　　　　　exchanged or no, and if they be, who has each of them'
　　　　　b.63, p. 81

W2484　With thee forever [I] in woods could rest
　　　　And from a desert banish solitude.

　　　　　[Abraham Cowley]
　　　　　[Crum w2642]
　　　　　c.549, p. 115

W2485　With toil we happiness pursue,
　　　　In hopes of endless rest.

　　　　　'Ode to resignation'
　　　　　c.83/3, no. 843

W2486　With toilsome steps I pass thro' life's dull road
　　　　And mourn in prison when I keep the key?

　　　　　[Lady Mary Wortley Montagu], 'Addressed to ——
　　　　　by the same hand'
　　　　　fc.51, p. 49

W2487　With too much sun, too little rain,
　　　　But better wait, than live in endless care.

　　　　　[Thomas Hamilton, 6th earl of Haddington], 'A fable
　　　　　when it was believed E[ ] M[ ]t was to marry the C[ ]
　　　　　of E[ ]n'
　　　　　c.458/1, p. 68

W2488　With top of quality, and high-bred air,
　　　　The goddess' self receives fresh charms from you.

　　　　　'To Mrs. Abington on seeing her in the character of
　　　　　Lady Teazle'
　　　　　c.89, p. 126

W2489　With trembling artless hand again I strike,
　　　　Virtue's the base, of friendship and of love.

　　　　　'An epithalamium'
　　　　　c.481, p. 243

W2490　With truth if grave historians speak,
　　　　To help the Petworth navigation.

　　　　　'On a lady's purchase of a lot of utensils at a bishop's
　　　　　sale'
　　　　　Poetry Box v/115

W2491　With us alike each season suits,
　　　　We ask the gods no more.

　　　　　'A song'
　　　　　c.83/1, no. 98

W2492　With virtuous men be conversant
　　　　So men will judge of thee.

　　　　　b.234, p. 30, p. 82

With vital warmth to bed, the canvas glow,　　　　W2493
Transferr'd to native climes of endless day.

　　'To Mr. N——'
　c.140, p. 190

With what fond gaze my eye pursues　　　　　　　W2494
Stretch their black wings and fan the blaze.

　c.364, p. 53

With what rich offering shall I requite　　　　　　W2495
To my life's end, as every Christian should.

　　H[enry] C[olman], 'A vow'
　　[Crum w2656]
　b.2, p. 79

With what strange raptures would my soul be blest,　W2496
Who seiz'd it next, might do the same by me.

　　[William Walsh], 'Epigram. Written in a lady's table
　　book'
　　[Crum w2657]
　c.223, p. 53

With white distinguish'd let this day appear　　　W2497
To seats of endless joy, and peace, and rest.

　　Tho[ma]s Morell, 'To Miss A[nne] B[arker, later his
　　wife] of the Grove at Chiswick on her birthday,
　　March 25. 1735'
　c.395, p. 56

With wind and tide　　　　　　　　　　　　　W2498
Of England's commercial prosperity.

　　[ ] Porson
　Greatheed Box/94

With women and wine I defy ev'ry care　　　　　W2499
My bottle I'll break, and demolish my glass. | For
　　　　　　　　　　　　　　　　rather than forfeit &c.

　　'Song 34'
　c.555, p. 54

With you most noble Duke! I crave two words;　　W2500
Unless you wish to feel my tooth or claw!

　　'The lion in the tower and the Duke of Richmond'
　c.83/3, no. 801

With youth and perfect beauty blest　　　　　　W2501
Till it was brought to light.

　　'Riddle 1 [i.e., 55; tinder]
　c.389; c.578, p. 57; Accession 97.7.40

Withdrawn from all temptations that entice,　　　W2502
And call thee sister, savior, genius, friend!

　　'From Liberal opinions. Almeria or the penitent,
　　being a genuine epistle from an unfortunate daughter
　　in —— to her family in the country'
　c.83/1, no. 58; c.175, p. 17 (var.)

W2503 Within a close gloomy retreat,
And give me a Stuart again.

'A song. To the tune &c of Despairing beside a clear
stream'

c.570/2, p. 16

W2504 Within a fleece of silent waters drown'd
My last shall give me back to life again.

[William Browne of Tavistock], 'An epitaph upon one,
drowned in the snow'
[Crum w2664]

b.200, p. 219; b.54, p. 930; c.244, p. 212

W2505 Within a silent awful shade
Have faith in Christ and unto Him aspire.

J. Howell jr., 'A vision . . . Monday night 11 o'clock
29th Decr 1794'

c.303

W2506 Within my first to take the air
Now bravely toils now lolls at ease.

c.389

W2507 Within my heart I said! With heed
The silent grave descend.

'Psalm 39'

c.264/1, p. 173

W2508 Within my heart, my thoughts present
Nor foot against me lift the heel.

'Psalm 36'

c.264/1, p. 157

W2509 Within my mistress' garter
She loves not one, but any.

'Bonum, quo communio, eo melio. Admina, quo
communior, eo prior'
[Crum w2668]

b.200, p. 93

W2510 Within the magic circle of the arts,
Nor stop one instant, till they reach the center.

Charles Burney, the elder, 'The trial of Midas the
second, or congress of musicians. A poem in three
cantos'

c.40

W2511 Within the spacious compass of the azure
To hug within your arms, and marriage bed.

Sir Thomas Urquhart, 'To Lady [crossed out]'

fb.217, p. 250

W2512 Within the windings of a wood,
And finish'd, with his life, his moan.

'The honeysuckle and bee'

c.578, p. 34

W2513 Within this breast there ever shall
Bare one exemption whilst I live.

[Mrs. Christian Kerr], 'To a friend' [answered by 'But
oh! What arms . . .']

c.102, p. 96

W2514 Within this cavern rough there is
In which the King has often been.

'On the Hermitage at Richmond'

fc.135

W2515 Within this chest
Is now deceast.

'On John West'

fb.143, p. 34

W2516 Within this dormitory, lies,
Will think her better half alive.

'An epitaph'

c.83/1, no. 223

W2517 Within this drear and silent gloom
Shall drop unseen—a sainted tear.

[Mary (Derby)] Robinson, 'Louisa in a convent . . .
Vincenza'

c.83/2, no. 684

W2518 Within this everlasting tomb
T' have wed the church, that woo'd the hall.

'On a rich lawyer'
[Crum w2685]

fb.143, p. 36

W2519 Within this grave there is a grave entombed,
And keeps in travail till the day of doom.

William Browne of Tavistock(?), 'Upon an infant
unborn whose mother died in travail'
[Crum w2687]

b.200, p. 168

W2520 Within this house exempt from care and strife,
And left a silent, solitary cage.

J[oh]n Wingfield, 'An elegy on a canary bird by little
Master . . . of Tickencote'

c.229/1, fol. 73v

W2521 Within this house lives Justice Scroggs
Who hath killed more men then his father did hogs.

'Upon Sr George Wakeman's being acquitted July 18:
1679'

b.54, p. 1103

W2522 Within this house sit good men and true,
Who gave to Caesar, what was Caesar's due.

'The next day' [1705/6]

b.90, p. 3

W2523 Within this humble lonesome cell,
Survives, when marble molders into dust.

'The hermit'
[Crum w2689]

fb.207/4, p. 31

W2524 Within this marble casket lies
But show'd and then put up again.

'Epitaph on the Lady Sophia, youngest daughter of
King James the First, who died the day after birth'
[Crum w2690]

c.360/3, no. 63; b.62, p. 131; see also 'Reader, wonder . . .'.

W2525 Within this marble doth entombed lie
His *habeas corpus* at the grand Assize.

'On the E. of Warwick in whom the family was
extinct'

fb.143, p. 24

W2526 Within this sacred vault doth lie
Angels must limn it out or he.

'On K[ing] C[harles] martyr'

fb.143, p. 41

W2527 Within this tomb of marble fair
That Aire should die for want of breath.

'On Jarvas Aire'

b.356, p. 242

W2528 Within this vault entomb'd doth lie
And peace the fruit is of his prayer.

'An epitaph' [on John Gray of Enfield, d. 14 Feb.
1708/9; see 'What then O king of terrors . . .' for
elegy]

c.257

W2529 Within thy sacred temple Lord
Go home rejoicing in the Lord.

T[homas] S[tevens]

c.259, p. 135

W2530 Without a name forever senseless, dumb
'Tis all I am, and all that you must be.

'An epitaph in Gravesend churchyard 1723'
[Crum w2708]

c.360/2, no. 206

W2531 Without affectation, gay, youthful, and pretty
That none can admire, or praise them too much.

Henry Baker, 'Amanda's character'

c.244, p. 399

W2532 Without guilt, without strife,
With health and with quiet of heart.

'The shepherd's plain life'

c.83/3, no. 1027

W2533 Without my aid the drum would never beat
Without my aid no comfort could be found.

Smith Papers, folder 74/20; see also 'When Sol's
effulgence . . .'.

W2534 Without my first it is my real belief,
Tho' his friendship perhaps may be thought a
disgrace.

[Enigma]

c.389

W2535 Without preamble to my friend
Imprinted on my mind.

[Isabella Byron], Countess of Carlisle, 'Lady Carlisle's
answer to Mrs. Greville'

c.163, p. 18; fc.51, p. 309; Spence Papers, folder 113

W2536 Without some labor nothing's got
That industry's a treasure.

R[obert] Shirley, 1st earl of Ferrers, 'The farmer and
his children. From La Fontaine'

c.347, p. 48

W2537 Without the camp, see Achan die;
And brings the treasure down.

Charles Atherton Allnutt, 'The danger and
temptation of riches'

c.112, p. 154

W2538 Without the crabbed ribaldry of schools
In Britain's language ever in Huddesford's case.

[ ] Plumpton, 'Mr Plumpton to Mr. Huddesford'

c.181, p. 74

W2539 Without thy presence Lord
And bring my soul to God.

T[homas] S[tevens]

c.259, p. 139

W2540 Without your form we did design to pray,
And meet a Joab may vanquish Absolom.

'The subject's reply' [to 'New forms of prayers . . .']

b.111, p. 376

W2541 Witness thou my heart's kind ruler
Time alas will never cure.

[Thomas Hull]

c.528/49; see also 'Tell me thou . . .'

W2542 Wits have short memories—so proverbs cry:
For, sure as you've oblig'd, so sure you're bit.

John Lockman, 'The caution: on occasion of
ungenerous treatment from a supposed friend . . .
Oct. 1750'

c.267/1, p. 53

W2543 Wits there are in every town,
The sun that always makes them shine.

'The wits. A rhapsody'
c.81/1, no. 517

W2544 Wives (tho' most chaste) of th' doubtful are, o' th'
common
Are whores, o' th' feminine is every woman.

'Three genders'
c.356

W2545 Woe is me, for, I am, ev'n as when they,
The Lord shall be to me a glorious light.

Sir John Strangways, 'The 7th chapter of Micah
translated into verse the 6th of December 1646'
b.304, p. 75

W2546 Woe to the city Jesus cries
That every gospel fact is true.

T[homas] S[tevens], 'Sung Jany. 30. 1781'
c.259, p. 123

W2547 Wolfe, on the Plains of Abraham greatly fell!
England gave praise, and England's king a tear.

W. T., 'An epitaph on General Wolfe' [1765]
c.341, p. 158

W2548 Woman! The happiest pledge of heav'n's good will!
I would be man—to be by woman blest.

'On woman'
c.81/1, no. 77

W2549 Woman was once a rib (as truth hath said)
Of Adam's whirlebone [sic], when it was out of joint.

'Woman'
c.356

W2550 Women are dainty vessels, fine,
Because they bear so oft.

'On women'
[Crum w2750]
b.62, p. 2; b.356, p. 306

W2551 Women are govern'd by a stubborn fate,
Nor ill requital can efface their love.

Eliza (Fowler) Haywood, 'Advice to the female sex,
taken out of the Weekly journal or British gazetteer
Saturday June 1 1719'
c.158, p. vii

W2552 Women are like a book for they do go
Once press'd common to all: do not they so.

'On women'
[Crum w2752]
b.62, p. 80

W2553 Women be forgetful children be unkind
They answer God help me, he died a poor man.

[Crum w2754]
c.158, p. 47

W2554 Women in Eve were [?] of more perfection
With [?] women since men's [?] [?].

[Sir Thomas Urquhart]
fb.217, p. 387

W2555 . . . Women, like days are, some be far
But by as fair they have succeeded been.

c.549, p. 94

W2556 Women make us love, and love makes us sad,
Sadness makes us drink, and drinking makes us
mad.

'A catch'
b.54, p. 1133

W2557 Women talk of love for fashion;
Than they see the ghost of which they're talking.

'Tittletattle'
c.487, p. 58

W2558 Women think women far more constant be
Women are constant and most true in change.

'On women'
[Crum w2762]
c.356

W2559 Women's the center and the lines be men
But love gives leave to only one to enter.

'Jo. Lundsford . . . AD 1687' [but first printed 1640]
[Crum w2746]
Poetry Box VII/16

W2560 Wonder not, (Gascoyne!) that thy clear address,
And half the world holds transubstantiation.

John Lockman, 'After reading Sir Crisp[in]
Gascoyne's address to the liverymen of London, with
regard to the affair of Elizabeth Canning . . . July
1754'
c.267/1, p. 104, p. 140

W2561 Wonder not, Sir, you who instruct the town,
With sleep all night, and quiet all the day.

[Abraham Cowley, trans., 'Mart. lib. 2. ep. 90'
[Crum w2771]
b.118, p. 31

W2562 Wonder not though the gods do come
As rich to thee as Jason's fleece.

'The masque of Sir John Crofts at the King's being
entertained there'
b.197, p. 169

W2563 Wonder not why among so many of
And therefore all my friends must pardon me.

    [Sir Aston Cokayne], 'To Sir A[ndrew] Kny[veton]'

b.275, p. 54

W2564 Wonder of man what false delusive light
One moment drowns in an eternal sleep.

    Petrarch

b.211, p. 43

W2565 Wonderous machine! Interpreter of art!
Whence thy existence, say, or our surprise.

    [William] Pattison, 'The microscope'

c.244, p. 525

W2566 Woodford! Dear, delightful spot!
Will soon, alas! behold me die.

    [John Lockman], 'Vers tirez de L'Abbé de
    Chaulieu . . . [translated]'

c.268 (second part), p. 93; see also 'O Petersham . . .'.

W2567 Woods, where no light hath stream'd where every
                          trunk
Old time, and ev'n eternity would end.

    [ ] Ellison, 'On eternity; from Waller . . . March 1783'

Greatheed Box/32

W2568 Worldly rewards were not enough to raise
And Brett henceforth the Lion's Heart be call'd.

    [N.] H[erbert], 'Epigram upon the gallant behavior of
    Capn. Brett against the Elizabeth of the French in the
    late war'

Spence Papers, folder 91

W2569 Worn out with service Teague was grown
De pald-pate man instead of me.

    [Phanuel Bacon], 'Nil preter calvium doctus cantare.
    Hor[ace]'

c.237, fol. 78v [i.e., 98v]

W2570 Worse critic of bad poet made
That you've exhausted the profound.

    [Edmund Burke], 'On Dennis's turning critic'

Poetry Box v/41

W2571 Worth should determine every man his due,
Instead of hempen ones around the neck.

    'Epigram'

c.115

W2572 Worthy John Lovekyn, stockfishmonger of
                   London here is laid
His flesh to earth, his soul to God went straight.

    'Epitaph in St Michael's, Crooked Lane in old
    London'

c.360/1, p. 167

W2573 Would an Amazon were I!
If my beauty could not win.

    John Lockman, 'Translations, and imitations from
    Metastasio, and other Italian opera poets [12]'

c.267/4, p. 107

W2574 Would but indulgent fortune send
Nor once desire a happier state.

    [Lady Mary Chudleigh], 'The wish'

c.548

W2575 Would dear Bet Downs be taught to bless
In lovelier verdure rise.

    [Phanuel Bacon], 'To Miss Betty Downs of
    Hampshire'

c.237, fol. 48

W2576 Would Eva had been deaf, or Reseph mute,
That none man's fall might to their speech impute.

    Sir Thomas Urquhart, 'Of the pestiferous
    communication betwixt the serpent and Eva'

fb.217, p. 357

W2577 Would fate [to] me Belinda give
On the glories of a crown!

    'Song'

c.358, p. 153; c.160, fol. 86

W2578 Would full bags of guineas save
Rich I'll live, tho' poor I die.

    [Sir William Trumbull; alternate version: 'Would
    good store . . .']

Trumbull Box: Poetry Box XIII/88

W2579 Would golden fortune deign to be my friend
To endless transports and unfading days.

    'A wish'

Poetry Box X/112

W2580 Would good store of money save
And rich I'll live, tho' poor I die.

    [Sir William Trumbull; alternate version: 'Would full
    bags . . .']

Trumbull Box: Poetry Box XIII/88

W2581 Would heaven indulgent grant my wish,
I'd quit the world, nor wish a tear.

    Mary Chandler, 'The wish of . . .'

c.150, p. 14

W2582 Would heav'n propitious to my vows attend,
And close my eyes without a fear, in death.

    Thomas Cook, 'The choice of a friend'

c.244, p. 573

W2583 Would man take time to think, and calmly weigh
And doth no pity need, nor fear a frown.

    'On the instability of greatness' [from the Marquis of
    Granby's collection, c. 1760]

Poetry Box VII/81

W2584 Would some kind spirit inspire my muse,
And make thee, spite of thee, and their wild claws |
                     Make reparation.

c.239

W2585 Would they who have nine year looked sour
A commonwealth or else King James. | This is the
                              time.

    [Matthew Prior], 'A new answer to an argument
    against a standing army'

Poetry Box VII/1

W2586 Would thou hadst beauty less, or virtue more
For nothing's uglier than a pretty whore.

c.360/1, p. 91

W2587 Would ye preserve that heart-delighting joy
And fondness woo your husbands to your arms.

    John Lockman, 'To wives: a most useful recipe . . .
    Oct. 1756'

c.267/1, p. 212

W2588 Would you apply the cure, will make you well
Digesteth iron.

    Sir Thomas Urquhart, 'The counsel of a very
    dissolute youth to a maid heavily diseased of the green
    sickness'

fb.217, p. 353

W2589 Would you ask of love a blessing
Pox on all your bitter-sweets.

    'Mr. Nash'

fc.73

W2590 Would you be a man in favor?
Bishops will to Tyburn steer.

    'A song'
    [cf. Crum w2801]

b.111, p. 359; fb.108, p. 191 ('of favor')

W2591 Would you be a man in power
Can their k[ing] so neatly bubble.

    'Song to the tune of Men in fashion' [November 1688]
    [Crum w2801; POAS IV.303]

fb.108, p. 122

W2592 Would you be, Chloe, ever fair,
If cruel, freedom gain.

    'To Chloe'

pb.73, fly leaf

W2593 Would you be famous and renown'd in story
Make subjects love and enemies to quake. | This is
                         [the time].

    'Advice' [November 1688]
    [POAS IV.291]

fb.108, p. 317

W2594 Would you be famous t'after ages; vices
For Helen's known, as well's Penelope.

    Sir Thomas Urquhart, 'To a lady who was desirous,
    that her renown might reach to posterity'

fb.217, p. 339

W2595 Would you be free? 'Tis your chief wish, you say
The Persian King's a slave compar'd to thee.

    A[braham] C[owley], trans., 'Vis fieri liber?' ['The
    way to freedom,' Martial, Epigrams II.iiii]
    [Crum w2802]

fb.142, p. 38; fc.60, p. 80; b.118, p. 10

W2596 Would you be good you'll be't, do but will still;
For he can give the pow'r, that gave the will.

    Sir Thomas Urquhart, 'What efficacy is in the will of
    man, to one, that had a mind to thrive'

fb.217, p. 300

W2597 Would you be nice in any spot around?
Then like Theresa bid your friends adieu.

    'Theresa Tidy to her young female friends'

Poetry Box II/49

W2598 Would you be rid of each white hair of yours:
Keep inward kindness with all sorts of whores.

    Sir Thomas Urquhart, 'To one who was daily toiled,
    with causing [to] pull out every hair of his own, as it
    turned white'

fb.217, p. 55

W2599 Would you have passion lead me blind
That she'll fall even with a touch.

    'On a maid not marriageable'

b.200, p. 123; see also 'Why doth . . .', 'Why should . . .'.

W2600 Would you hope to gain my heart
Only teaches how to cheat.

    [ ] Johnson, 'Translation of song of Metastasio'

Diggle Box: Poetry Box XI/2

W2601 Would you in love succeed be brisk be gay—
Enjoys his wish, and well employs his time.

    Lord [ ] Altham[? or Charles Sackville, 6th duke of
    Dorset?], 'Advice to a young lover'

    c.229/1, fol. 45v

W2602 Would you know how we meet o'er our jolly full bowls
Love only remains our unquenchable fire.

    'Song'
    [Crum w2810]

    c.189, p. 158; fb.228/61 ('why we meet')

W2603 Would you know what's soft I dare
Name my mistress and 'tis done.

    [James Shirley]
    [Crum w2812]

    b.213, p. 2

W2604 Would you oblige to you a friend by giving
And when it is received yields delight.

    [Sir Thomas Urquhart], 'What benefits should be
    bestowed'

    fb.217, p. 498

W2605 Would you preach sermons that shall suit the taste,
And character; and cannot fail to please.

    'How to preach a sermon that shall please'

    c.83/2, no. 315

W2606 Would you see a man that slow,
And the last comer shall be Joe.

    'On a footman Joe proverbially slow and lazy in all his
    motions'

    Poetry Box IV/43

W2607 Would you see three nations bubbl'd
And drop plenty down in rain.

    'On King James the 2d'

    c.570/4, p. 14

W2608 Would you send Kate to Portugal
And once more make Charles king again. This is
    the time.

    'On the Chancellor's speech at the first meeting of this
    non-Parliament . . . this is the time . . . To the tune of
    Greensleeves and P[udding] pies' [1678/9]
    [Crum w2816; POAS II.293]

    Poetry Box IV/10; b.54, p. 1155 (with eight extra lines);
    Poetry Box VI/32; b.371, no. 38

W2609 Would you that Delville I describe,
There's nothing but yourself as great.

    Thomas Sheridan, 'A description of Dr. Delany's villa'

    c.83/1, no. 129

W2610 Would you the vicar please, my friend,
For says the proverb, like to like.

    [Thomas Morell], 'An epigram. 1731'

    c.395, p. 36

W2611 Would you think it, my Duck, for the fault I must
               own,
It begins with an M but I dare not say more.

    Jenny (H[a]m[i]lt[o]n) Moore, 'Miss Jenny
    H[a]m[i]lt[o]n [before her wedding to the poet
    Edward Moore, 4 Dec. 1749] to Miss Duck' [daughter
    to Stephen Duck]
    [Crum w2820]

    c.116, p. 35; fc.51, p. 289; c.157, p. 114

W2612 Would you to Orcus' shades descend
Nor ever think on love.

    'Epigram . . . Answer'

    c.94

W2613 Wouldst thou, Britannia! still reign ocean's queen,
Is your Palladium, and alone can save ye.

    John Lockman, 'A seasonable hint . . . London evening
    [post], Oct. 1751'

    c.267/1, p. 176

W2614 Wouldst thou from poverty exemption claim,
Room for his grace!—Merit, stand by and bow!

    'The advantages of flattery. From a MS copy'

    c.487, p. 108

W2615 Wouldst thou in grace to high perfection grow
And hadst not whereupon thy head to lay.

    [Sir Richard Bulstrode], 'In praise of humility and
    poverty'

    fb.88, p. 115v

W2616 Wouldst thou Mundano prove too great, too strong,
Heaven's aid, is far above the frowns of fortune.

    [Francis Quarles], 'Another [on Mundano]'
    [Crum w2831]

    b.118, p. 227

W2617 Wouldst thou my dearest Lesbia know,
Enough for my insatiate love.

    'To Lesbia' [Catullus, vii, 'Love insatiable']
    [Crum w2832]

    b.218, p. 22

W2618 Wouldst with a pleasing verse thy mistress court?
The dactyl measure best delights a woman.

    'Of a dactyl to a certain lover'

    c.356

W2619 Wounds set thee upright, he that dares be lame
Or halt by th'sword, know's how to lean on fame.

    T. Godfrey, 'Elegies on Sr. Horatio Vere'

b.52/2, p. 126

W2620 Wrapt in cold clay beneath this marble lies
And as they lov'd him living, mourn him dead.

    [Francis Fawkes], 'Intended for the Revd.
    Mr. Cookson Vicar of Leeds'

fc.21, p. 26

W2621 Wrapt in our sinful flesh, yet free from sin,
Blest be the donor, that such life doth give.

    [Elizabeth Middleton], 'The passion of our Savior
    Jesus Christ . . .' [1637?]
    [Crum w2838]

b.35, p. 1

W2622 Wrapt in sad silent night creation lay,
Accept endure absolve my lowly lays.

    'On Christmas Day'

c.362, p. 42

W2623 Wrath makes a man to sin courageously
Are sloven, filthy, villainous, and base.

    [Sir Thomas Urquhart], 'That lust and drunkenness
    are odious vices'

fb.217, p. 531

W2624 Wrath quickens dolts: and patience settleth ire:
As fire doth temper water: water fire.

    Sir Thomas Urquhart, 'Of anger, and patience'

fb.217, p. 348

W2625 Wrath sparkling fire, is born in scalding blood,
Whose horrid right hand knows no deed that's good.

    'Wrath'

c.189, p. 42

W2626 Wraye whom chaste wit and various arts adorn
Nor moved by fears nor hopes he lightens every care.

    'Sonnet in imitation of Milton, to Mr. Wraye'

Poetry Box I/119[2]

W2627 Wretch, whosoe'er thou art that longs for praise
And warns his comrades to repent, then dies.

    'Satire on the poets'
    [Crum w2842]

fb.108, p. 143

W2628 Wretched lovers fate has past
Hark how the thund'ring giant roars.

    [John Gay, Alexander Pope, and/or John Hughes], '3d
    chorus in [Handel's] Acis and Galatea' [with musical
    score for tenor]

Music MS. 534

W2629 Wretched mortals, why are you
Are exempt, or free from end.

    H[enry] C[olman], 'Another' [on mortality]
    [Crum w2844]

b.2, p. 9

W2630 Wretches give nothing till they cease to live:
And wasters after death have naught to give.

    Sir Thomas Urquhart, 'Niggards, and prodigals'

fb.217, p. 77

W2631 Write and pronounce it French, then spell it well
She has no peers, so is a Nonpariel.

    [Sir Philip Wodehouse], 'Upon his niece Sir Hugh
    Windham's daughter Blanche Naper'

b.131, back (no. 38)

W2632 Write for the Queen! It is a bold pretense
Th'eternal honors she vouchsafes to give.

    [Thomas Morell, on Queen Caroline]

c.395, p. 87

W2633 Writing of wits, most surely is the best,
Conscience for to regard i' th' least degree.

c.93

W2634 Wrong not, dear mistress of my heart,
May challenge double pity.

    [Sir Robert Ayton], 'To his mistress'
    [Crum w2846]

b.200, p. 78; b.197, p. 212 (attr. Lo. Wal.)

W2635 Wrong not my mold | I am as hot as cold
And give more for it than the world.

    'An answer' [to 'Mistake me not . . .']

b.213, p. 20

W2636 Wronged, yet not daring to express my pain
The shepherd hath thy death's record engraved.

    [Edmund Spenser], 'Virgiliana culex'

b.65, p. 37

X

X0001 Xenocrates the counsel gives,
And vicious things to flee.

    [Crum X1]

b.234, p. 33

X0002 Xerxes from a steep mountain's lofty brow
Few days dispatcht the business of an age.

    [Mary Serjant]

fb.98, fol. 154

Y

Y0001 Ye airy sprites, who oft as fancy calls,
A father's merits—still protect his child.

[William Roscoe], 'The following address occasioned
by the death of J. Palmer was spoken at the Theater
Liverpool. 1798'

c.141, p. 307

Y0002 Ye all remember well our Founder's Day
When epigrams for squibs and crackers fly.

c.233, p. 33

Y0003 Ye angels who 'round me do hover
From the beautiful Molly Dove.

'1728'

Trumbull Box: Poetry Box XIII/103, p. 1

Y0004 Ye bakers hear what I advise
Should put you in the oven.

'Advice to the bakers June 23th 1787'

fc.130, p. 48

Y0005 Ye bardlings twain, ye pair of poetasters
Let Speke ne'er write one line, nor Upton more
than two.

'To the Rev'd Mr. Speke and Mr. Upton on their
verses upon the death of the King. A D 1727'

c.233, p. 60

Y0006 Ye beaux and ye belles both in court and in city,
Then they'll never preach more, nor the court will
displease. | Derry down &c.

'The court sermon. A new ballad dedicated to the
Revd. Dr. Cobden' [pr. 1748 (Foxon C536)]

c.157, p. 46; fc.85, fol. 93

Y0007 Ye *beaux esprits*, say, what is grace?
To which at once we pay devotion.

[David] Garrick, 'Grace'

c.83/1, no. 89; Diggle Box: Poetry Box XI/4

Y0008 Ye belles and ye flirts and ye pert little things
But believe me you'll never be wives.

[Paul] Whitehead, 'Song for Ranelagh'

Poetry Box X/18

Y0009 Ye belles ye beaux, of whatsoe'er degree
I'll in the green-room wait for further orders.

'Prologue to The trip to Scotland spoken by Cupid'

c.68, p. 98

Y0010 Ye birds, whose tuneful warblings charm the grove,
Vanquish'd by sweeter sounds, we must retire.

[John Lockman], 'To the nightingales, on their going
to leave the spring gardens at Vauxhall'

c.268 (first part), p. 6

Y0011 Ye blithesome swains where Medway leads
From Medway's banks to Arno's vale!

Jm. Richard Onely, 'On the death of the late Duke of
Dorset'

Poetry Box IV/150

Y0012 Ye brave and fair who deign to grace our scenes
'Midst real beauty, worth, and innocence.

'A prologue spoken at the opening of Punch's Theater
at Bath'

c.188, p. 57

Y0013 Ye brave gen'rous Britons, who good works admire;
Till away, like a vision, the worlds round us pass.

John Lockman, 'Anniversary song: in honor of the
Middlesex Hospital and its noble founder. First sung,
27 March 1765, in the great room in Carlisle House,
Soho Square'

c.267/2, p. 179

Y0014 Ye British Jacobins attend,
Like Frenchmen they must fight or starve.

'Address to the British Jacobins'

c.83/2, no. 365

Y0015 Ye British youths with noble ardor fill'd
And never never see the world adieu.

'The Spanish lady made upon the old ballad so called'

Poetry Box XIV/183

Y0016 Ye Britons draw near
He's return'd—without killing—doubles.

[John] Winter, 'Blackguard ballad by . . . addressed to
A[dmira]l V[erno]n on his leaving a crown for the
relief of 24 debtors being apprised of the number'

c.74

Ye busses hail! Which to us send
And to the king of fishes.

> John Lockman, 'In honor of the true British busses,
> (the Pelham and Carberet,) which sent the first cargo
> of pickled herrings to London [1750]. The tune,
> When I was a dame of honor'
> [Crum Y15]

c.267/2, p. 70

Y0017

Ye c[al]ves of London would ye choose
Where Wilkes is not his drover.

> 'On choosing Bull a member'

fc.85, fol. 103v

Y0018

Ye candidates, who boast of honor dear
Alas! they've hobbled in the dark too long.

> [John Lockman], 'On the four candidates [Lord
> Sundon, Sir Charles Wager, Admiral Vernon, Charles
> Edwin] to represent the city of Westminster in
> Parliament—May—1741'

c.360/1, p. 305; c.267/1, p. 30

Y0019

Ye Catholic statesmen, and churchmen rejoice
For if this trick fail beware of your jacket.

> 'On the Queen's being with child'
> [cf. Crum Y242, 'You']

b.115, fol. 14v; see also 'You Catholic statesmen . . .'.

Y0020

Ye cider-land men,
Irradiate her entry; | A glorious train!

> John Lockman, 'Anniversary song. For the cider
> counties on the repeal of the Cider Act. (The tune,
> Bumper Squire Jones) . . . June 1766'

c.267/2, p. 163

Y0021

Ye cliffs I to your airy steep
To this ecstatic joy?

> [William Hayley]

Poetry Box v/50

Y0022

Ye commons and peers, pray lend me your ears
For, old bully, thy doctors are gone.

> [William] Congreve, 'Jack Frenchman's defeat to the
> tune of I'll tell the Dick' [battle of Oudenarde, 1708;
> printed, Foxon C269]
> [Crum Y24; POAS VII.341]

c.158, p. 85

Y0023

Ye country maids and rustic swains
To welcome harvest home.

> [John Walker?], 'Harvest home'

fc.108, fol. 45v

Y0024

Ye couples, who meet under love's smiling star,
And preserve your chaste flame from the smoke of
ennui.

> William Hayley, 'A charm for ennui—a ballad'

c.391, p. 56; c.130, p. 62

Y0025

Ye cruel gods what have ye done,
Or take that life which I do so much abhor.

> 'Corydon's loss lamented'

fb.107, p. 36

Y0026

Ye cruel gods! Why did not I
And that 'tis she must ease my woe.

> John Lockman, 'Translations, and imitations from
> Metastasio, and other Italian opera poets [10]'

c.267/4, p. 103

Y0027

Ye cuckolds all of fam'd Cheapside
Like eighty-eight, or forty-one.

> 'The reply to the fair prisoner [Sophia Dorothea,
> divorced wife of George I]'s doleful petition'
> [Crum Y27]

c.570/1, p. 102; fc.58, p. 81; see also 'You cuckolds . . .'.

Y0028

Ye darksome clouds, that big with teeming rain,
And no fell fears my quiet mind control.

> 'The shower to Eudora'

c.83/2, no. 632

Y0029

Ye dealers in riddles, who keep such a pother
A little, for these have their mouths in their tails.

> Dr. [ ] Wright, 'One morning I dreamed of a riddle,
> which was What is like a serpent, with its mouth at
> the tail' [1740]

c.360/1, p. 67

Y0030

Ye deities, who bear imperial sway,
From those great rules, brave Vaughan shall lead
the way.

> 'Upon the thesis, Omnia vincit amor [Virgil, Eclogue
> 10:69]. Given out by Mr. Vaughan'

c.530, p. 180

Y0031

Ye deities who rule mankind,
Let these in sweet effects, be shown.

> John Lockman, 'Translations, and imitations from
> Metastasio, and other Italian opera poets [19, by
> Signor Botarelli]'

c.267/4, p. 115

Y0032

Ye different sects, who all declare
Show me as Christians how we live.

c.546

Y0033

Y0034 Ye distant spires, ye antique towers,
'Tis folly to be wise.

[Thomas] Gray, 'Ode on a distant prospect of Eton
College' [pr. 1747 (Foxon G254)]
fc.132/1, p. 148; fc.51, p. 202

Y0035 Ye ever heedless beaus and belles
And show you have one pretense to taste.

c.188, p. 19

Y0036 Ye fair British beauties, the boast of the world,
And merit the praises of earth, and of heaven.

'An invocation to the fair sex' [General evening post,
19 July 1777]
c.157, p. 105

Y0037 Ye fair disclose the mystic theme,
And only serve in borrowed shapes.

'[Enigma/Charade/Conundrum] 5' [seal]
c.389

Y0038 Ye fair ladies of Old England
You'll be enslav'd, or him uncrown'd.

'The fair prisoner [Sophia Dorothea, divorced wife of
George I]'s doleful petition composed by Bob the
Sincere (for which he was disgraced at court) and
dropped by Zachariah at the meeting house. N.B. the
original is deposited in the Bibloth. Harliana'
c.570/1, p. 100; see also 'Ye/You ladies fair . . .'.

Y0039 Ye fair, who gild this gay, theatric round,
Each virgin merit Indiana's fame!

John Lockman, 'Epilogue on the same occasion [The
conscious lovers, in Covent Garden Theater, for the
benefit of the lying-in hospital in Aldersgate Street];
and intended to be spoke by Mrs. Hamilton . . .'
c.267/3, p. 126

Y0040 Ye fair who now flutter in life's busy throng,
By retiring subdues, and possesses the heart.

Miss [ ] Lock, 'Song'
c.83/2, no. 273

Y0041 Ye fair, whose prudence, cautious of deceit
Love, when it flatters most, is most sincere.

[George] L[yttelton], 1st baron Lyttelton, 'Maxims in
love' [no. 5]
c.487, p. 28

Y0042 Ye fairest muse! Assist a daring bard,
No skill is wanting from a foreign land.

[William Woty], 'Campanologia a poem in praise of
ringing, by the author of The shrubs of Parnassus,
1761'
c.481, p. 61

Y0043 Ye faithful souls who Jesus know,
Ye soon shall meet him in the skies.

'Hymn 100'
c.562, p. 136

Y0044 Ye fantastical fair ones, who constantly try,
But are kill'd with the vapors at home.

'Hints to the modern fine ladies'
Poetry Box IV/147

Y0045 Ye fearful hares, forsake your secret dens
For friendly death has broke old Roper's neck.

'On Mr. Roper of Eltham in Kent, a noted fox hunter
being killed by a fall from his horse, when he was
hunting 1722'
c.360/2, no. 83

Y0046 Ye fellows all
Of Mr. Muriall.

'On Mr. Muriall's horse'
b.356, p. 240

Y0047 Ye few who miss me if ye chance to come,
His prayer is heard—the grave that boon bestows.

[Daniel King?], 'Lines found among his papers'
Greatheed Box/78

Y0048 Ye fiends, and furies, come along,
He is so hot, he'd ravish her.

[Sir William D'Avenant], 'The furies' [song in The
unfortunate lover]
fb.107, p. 63

Y0049 Ye fools retire from Emma's charms
May cast a milder beam!

R[ichard] V[ernon] S[adleir], 'Miss F's mother, during
her pregnancy, happened to set her ruffle on fire by
which her arm was much burn'd and the daughter was
born with her right arm marked in the same state and
remains so at this day—and gave occasion to the
following stanzas . . .'
c.106, p. 68

Y0050 Ye freeholders most dear
And a fart for the sons of Apollo.

'A doleful complaint of Sr. H[umphre]y M[ackwor]th'
[on the loss of his election at Oxford]
c.111, p. 117; Poetry Box IV/113

Y0051 Ye friendly minds your imperfections known
To know my heart all feeling, like to his.

T[homas] S[tevens], 'Divine sympathy . . . Janry 26.
1781'
c.259, p. 133

Y0052 Ye friends to rural sports
'Twould scarce give half the round.

John Lockman, 'The diversions of Denby's [House,
opposite Box Hill in Surrey]. The tune, There was a
jovial beggar &c.'

c.267/2, p. 166

Y0053 Ye furious duelists who with the sword
He waited patiently the scythe of time.

'On duelling'

c.143, fol. 20

Y0054 Ye gay, and young, who, thoughtless of your doom,
For science—virtue—and for Small she mourns.

[Erasmus] Darwin, 'On a monument erected in
Mr. Bouton's garden to the memory of Dr. Small'

Poetry Box x/138; c.142, p. 140

Y0055 Ye gen'rous souls, whose steps pursue
To free our captive feet.

'Ode to virtue by Metastasio'

c.140, p. 114

Y0056 Ye gentle gales that fans [sic] the air
And what for her I undergo.

'2nd song'
[Crum Y51]

Accession 97.7.40, p. 4

Y0057 Ye gentle generous Whigs give ear,
English independent.

'The English independent'

Poetry Box x/79

Y0058 Ye giddy crowds who spend your hours in play
Will leave her virtue, to thy truth unpaid.

'On the death of my dear wife'

c.203

Y0059 Ye glades that just open, to greet the blue sky,
As the rose droops its head, when the sun fades away.

[Mary (Derby)] Robinson, 'Inscribed to a beloved
friend, when confined by indisposition'

c.83/2, no. 281

Y0060 Ye gloomy vault, ye heavy cells,
Which only unimpair'd can last.

T. S., 'Verses written on a brick in the ruins of the
holy abbey in Holy Island, near Berwick on Tweed'

fc.85, fol. 118

Y0061 Ye glorious Jove-born imps how you rejoice
Shall arm me 'gainst the rack, plague, sword, and
flame.

H[enry] C[olman], 'On the three children in the fiery
furnace'

b.2, p. 100

Y0062 Ye gods and men with presence and with praise
Make me the clerk, that I may say, amen.

Richard Corbie, 'Epithalamium for Ralph Asshton of
Middleton and Anne Asshton' [17 April 1651]

fc.61, p. 15

Y0063 Ye gods, are all my terrors vain,
Without a murmur, sink to rest.

[Charles Burney, the younger], 'Answer to The
shepherd's return ['At length, Catalio . . .'] . . . Janry.
13th 1780'

c.38, p. 9

Y0064 Ye gods of love
That I do now sustain.

'A sonnet'

b.356, p. 101

Y0065 Ye gods to whom my ardent pray'r,
And be no longer Payne.

'To Miss Payne, written by a boy at school'

c.83/1, no. 116

Y0066 Ye good fellows all,
Hark away to the claret a bumper | Squire Jones.

'Song 189'
[Crum Y60]

c.555, p. 300

Y0067 Ye good men of Middlesex, countrymen dear
Till thou soft'nest his heart and openest his ear.

'A ballad, called Peyton's downfall. To the tune of
Packington's pound; or Youth youth [in Bartholomew
fair]'
[Crum Y61 (var.)]

b.54, p. 1124; see also 'You good men . . .'.

Y0068 Ye good men of Surrey,
Have made Britannia weep. | Then for Onslow &c.

John Lockman, 'Onslow forever a song: on the
expected nomination (2d July 1765) of George Onslow
esqr. for one of the representatives of the county of
Surrey. The tune—There was a jovial beggar'

c.267/2, p. 52

Y0069 Ye great ones of the world your praise your blame
And share the blessings of his celestial palm.

[William Hayley], 'Sonnet . . . Sept. 11 [1800]'

File 6968

Y0070 Ye green-hair'd nymphs, whom Pan allows
When freedom fires the glowing patriot's tongue.

   [William Mason], 'Ode to a water-nymph'
Poetry Box I/83; Poetry Box v/76

Y0071 Ye groves where I oft with Rosina have stray'd,
'And let a low cottage and Henry be mine.'

   [Sophia (Raymond) Burrell Clay], 'Henry and Rosina'
c.141, p. 529

Y0072 Ye guardian spirits who with tender care
Fill the fond bard and satisfy his lyre.

   [William Hayley], 'Sonnet . . . May 13 [1800]'
File 6968

Y0073 Ye hallowed darlings of my thought whose praise
And to your fellowship exalt my soul.

   [William Hayley], 'Sonnet . . . Sept. 2 [1800]'
File 6968

Y0074 Ye heaven and earth now hear my declaration,
Heaven and earth judge not in words but action.

   'On the P[rince] of Orange's declaration'
b.III, p. 396

Y0075 Ye husbands and wives who both wish to see
And your skirmish be only the skirmish of bliss.

   [William] Hayley, 'Song by . . .'
Poetry Box x/19

Y0076 Ye husbands, who have gotten wives,
E'en take 'em as they're sent you!

   'Advice—to husbands, or bachelors'
c.94

Y0077 Ye hypocrites are these your pranks
Does God require thanks for murder.

   [Robert Burns], 'Stuck up in several places of the city
   on the day appointed for the Thanksgiving'
fc.58, p. 41

Y0078 Ye invalids and sickly tribe attend
Now took the business of an undertaker.

   'Dr Last to the public' [c. 1760]
Poetry Box x/96

Y0079 Ye Jacks of the town, and Whigs of renown
And the Queen, God be praised, din'd well. | With
                                            a hum, &c.

   'A humorous satire occasioned by a fart being let,
   while the Queen was at dinner'
c.III, p. 154

Y0080 Ye joyous youths, with roses crow[n]'d,
The earth wheel round with rapid pace.

   [John Lockman], 'The earth's motion proved. An ode.
   Set to music by Mr. Leveridge'
c.268 (first part), p. 105

Y0081 Ye judges of the earth do ye
The righteous will reward.

   'Psalm 58'
c.264/2, p. 14

Y0082 Ye knaves and ye fools, maids widows and wives,
Shall have their free choice to hang drown or break.

   'Britannia excised, part the second' [pr. 1733 (Foxon
   B462)]
   [Crum Y72]
c.570/3, p. 205

Y0083 Ye ladies fair of Britain's isles
When her mama can do the same.

   [pr. 1730 (Foxon A92)]
fc.135

Y0084 Ye ladies fair of old England
Or you enslav'd or he uncrowned. | With a fa la

   'The fair prisoner [Sophia Dorothea, divorced wife of
   George I]'s doleful petition' [to the English ladies;
   answered by 'You cuckolds all . . .']
   [Crum Y74]
Poetry Box IV/64; see also 'You ladies fair . . .', 'Ye fair
ladies . . .'.

Y0085 Ye ladies that in whist delight,
She'll turn a cat again.

   'The origin of old cats. Written at Tunbridge Wells
   1748 by Rowly Powly esq. A well-wisher to the
   mathematics'
fc.51, p. 76

Y0086 Ye ladies who with nicest care
A dram(?) is [?] the devil.

   [William Hayley]
File 6982

Y0087 Ye lads and ye lasses that live in Great Britain
You confounded French dogs have you got that
                              whore's trick. | Derry down &c.

   ['The pedlar' (Whig attack on Louis, duc d'Aumont);
   pr. 1713 (Foxon P139)]
Poetry Box IV/31

Y0088 Ye lads and ye lasses who hither resort,
So here I conclude with F, J, N, J, S. | Sing
                                       tantararara &c.

   'Song 23'
c.555, p. 27

Y0089   Ye lambkins that wantonly play,
Now his Corydon's bosom is cold.

    'Grief. A pastoral elegy'

c.83/1, no. 55

Y0090   Ye learned biographers whose leading aim
His works shall reach posterity's posteriors.

    The[ophilu]s Hill, 'On the biographical sketches of
Sir Jno. Hawkins'

c.546

Y0091   Ye learned doctors of the Smectymnuan creed
No crown of laurel, but an oaken ruff.

    'A rod for the fool's back, or an answer to a scurrilous
libel, called The changeling' ['Attend, good
people . . .']
[Crum Y76]

Poetry Box VIII (oversize), no. 4

Y0092   Ye learn'd of the age
He cures the disease of—a blood.

    'Song 200'

c.555, p. 322

Y0093   Ye leaves, whose hue yet undisguis'd by art—
Learn to be virtuous, and he must be great.

    'Written in George's pocket-book after his recovery'

c.340

Y0094   Ye lilies rise your sweets disclose
We weep below, but angels sing.

    'In the Stamford Mercury no. 524 July 15. 1742 . . .
[elegy on Mrs. Alice Horseman, d. 11 July 1742]'

c.229/1, fol. 66v

Y0095   Ye linnets, let us try beneath this grove,
I taste the sweets of truth—here only am secure.

    [William Cowper, trans.], 'Vol. 2. Cantique. 11' [of
Jeanne Guion's 'Spiritual songs']

c.470 (autogr.)

Y0096   Ye little chirpers of the grove,
Or yours upon the spray.

c.83/2, no. 587

Y0097   Ye little loves that round her wait
And haughty Strephon scorns to die.

    [Ambrose Philips], 'Freethinker no. [ ]'

c.549, p. 42

Y0098   Ye little strangers, say ah why,
In crystal drops you'll seem more bright.

    M[artha] Roberts, 'Written in a fall of snow 1790'

c.391, p. 115

Y0099   Ye living husbands, do my lays
To save her breath, gave up my own!

    [Charles Earle], 'An epitaph (made when I was a
schoolboy) on a certain husband who desired me to
make one on him'

c.376

Y0100   Ye liv'rymen brave, who justice revere,
To our chamberlain the glass, who such virtue has
                 shown, &c.

    John Lockman, 'London's glory: Chamberlain
Jansson's health. A ballad the tune, Heart of oak are
our ships, &c. 20th Jany 1765'

c.267/2, p. 51

Y0101   Ye liv'rymen! Who wish well to your king;
Be Jansson your choice, and our clarions shall
                 blow. | O the fam'd trade &c.

    John Lockman, 'Great Britain's glory, or trade
forever! Tune, O the roast beef of old England &c.'

c.267/2, p. 66

Y0102   Ye lofty towers, majestic in decay
The crush surrounding objects in the wreck.

    'To Craig Ellen Castle by Q. Ranie(?) sonnet'

c.344, p. 59

Y0103   Ye lords and ye lasses that live at Longleat,
He must first make a better or kiss my bum fiddle. |
                 Derry [derry down] &c.

    [Sir Henry Sheeres], 'A song. To the tune of the Abbot
of Canterbury' [on a gentleman's sitting on Lady
Weymouth's fiddle at Lord Weymouth's seat at
Longleat, 1708; pr. 1720 (Foxon B41)]

c.374; see also 'You lads . . .'.

Y0104   Ye lovely fair, who curious arts pursue
Can soon discover this strange creature's name.

    'A riddle'

c.241, p. 81

Y0105   Ye lovely nine—ye virgin train attend
But who gives their songs, or playbills credit.

    John Wolcot ('Peter Pindar'), 'The heroic poem'
[watermark 1794]

Poetry Box IV/96

Y0106   Ye lovely virgins, hear a swain,
And Emma who is fled.

    'On Emma's absence'

c.83/3, no. 985

Y0107 Ye lovers of your freedom,
To you we'll statues raise. | When a-fishing we have
gone. . . .

    John Lockman, 'Britannia's gold mine, or the Herring
    Fishery [Aug. 1750]: calculated for all jolly Christians'
    souls: and sung in Vauxhall and Cupr's [Cooper's?]
    Gardens; in Draper's Hall by the Antigallicans &c . . .
    the tune, There was a jovial beggar &c.'
    [Crum Y80]

c.267/2, p. 73

Y0108 Ye maids who Britain's court bedeck
Without one tender tear.

    [John West], earl of Delawarr, 'Verses by . . .
    Chamberlain to the Queen in his own handwriting'

Poetry Box IV/158

Y0109 Ye martial pow'rs, and all ye tuneful nine
With me, nor quit my regal roof again.

    Phyllis Wheatley, 'Goliah of Gath 1 Saml. 17
    chapter . . . a poem composed by . . . a Negro servant
    to Mr. John Wheatley of Boston, New England.
    Copied August 1780'

c.259

Y0110 Ye meaner beauties that combine
Whilst they retire away.

    'From the Leeds mercury'

c.139, p. 271

Y0111 Ye members of parliament all
But Lansdowne deliver'd a King. | Sing hey ding
ding a ding ding

    'On the falling of the sash window of the King's
    Gallery at the Chapel Royal' [1691]
    [Crum Y84; POAS V.152]

b.111, p. 413

Y0112 Ye men of art come bear a part
A body like great Carter.

    'Song'

Poetry Box XIV/186

Y0113 Ye men of letters, keepers of the seal,
Mind no mistake sirs, Newark upon Trent.

    'Another [superscription of a letter] . . . 1792'

c.94

Y0114 Ye men that live at home, and cannot brook the
flood,
Give praise to them that pass the waves to do their
country good.

c.339, p. 325

Y0115 Ye merry old nine
Why may you be served so all.

    H[enry] L[awman], 'Eighty four: a new song'
Spence Papers, folder 97

Y0116 Ye mighty princes, you oblations bring,
And crown our tribes with happiness and peace.

    [Christopher] Pitt, 'Psalm 29th'

c.244, p. 503

Y0117 Ye ministers what do ye think
Or faith they'll all beshit ye.

    'The good people of Eng[land]'s address to the
    ministry'
Trumbull Box: Poetry Box XIII/90

Y0118 Ye ministers who every hour
Who has not heard their treason tales . . . .

    'North Briton Extra. Feb 22d 1769'
Poetry Box X/105 (incomplete)

Y0119 Ye miter'd fathers of the land
We'll try a tug with Rome.

    'The sentiments to the bishops' [1688]
    [POAS IV.223]

fb.108, p. 85

Y0120 Ye miter'd members of the House of Peers,
And bring religion to its wonted splendor.

    Lewis Griffin, 'The ass's complaint against Balaam. Or
    the cry of the country against ignorant and scandalous
    ministers' [pr. 1661 (Wing G1981A); answered by 'You
    learned prelates . . .']

b.63, p. 49; b.104, p. 99

Y0121 Ye mortals who grieve for the loss of the sun,
We'll join in the triumph of Bacchus at night.

    'Song 109'

c.555, p. 161

Y0122 Ye muses aid me to congratulate
By all the blessings, that on earth are found.

c.150, p. 56

Y0123 Ye muses do not me deny
Whether with what nectar he feeds us.

    Edward Martin

pb.47, pl. 3

Y0124 Ye muses, graces, loves, O swift repair
Her face as fair, as she grant her mind.

    John Lockman, 'Miss Kitty Cornwall's birthday,
    Wednesday 15 Nov. 1769'

c.267/1, p. 396

Y0125 Ye muses nine, if you think fit
A little Will Castairs.

'Will Castairs described'

c.530, p. 95

Y0126 Ye nimble-footed measurers of time
You'll loiter for it, when again we meet.

[Thomas Morell], 'On the same [conversation with
Anne Barker, later his wife]'

c.395, p. 59

Y0127 Ye nymphs and silvan gods,
By following those, | That carry the milking pail?

[Thomas D'Urfey], 'The merry milkmaids a song'
[third song in the second act of Don Quixote, 1694]
[Crum Y99]

c.233, p. 14; File 19029

Y0128 Ye nymphs, be confident, that lover lies,
Whose tongue declares his love before his eyes.

[George] L[yttelton], 1st baron Lyttelton, 'Maxims in
love' [no. 3]

c.487, p. 28

Y0129 Ye nymphs, behold ambition fail,
Are all preferr'd before ye.

'Beware! Ye maidens'

c.94

Y0130 Ye nymphs of Albion! Begin the song
And factions strive who should applaud them most.

'Verses on the birth of the young Princess [Louisa,
later Queen of Denmark, d. 1751] dated from the
Inner Temple December the 8 1724'

c.360/2, no. 112

Y0131 Ye nymphs of Pindus the soft song attend:
Thus virtue be crown'd.

John Lockman, 'Rosalinda, [a musical drama]
performed, in two nights in 1740, at Mr. Hickford's
great room in Brewer Street . . . set to music by
Mr. John Christopher Smith, and inscribed to the
Duchess of Newcastle'

c.267/3, p. 162; c.268 (second part), p. 71

Y0132 Ye nymphs of Salem, who with hallow'd lays
And bids ye happy be more happy now.

[Walter Titley], 'An ode on Christmas Day—from the
Northampton mercury 1744'

c.167, p. 40; c.233, p. 48

Y0133 Ye nymphs of Solyma! Begin the song,
Thy realm forever lasts, thy own Messiah reigns.

[Alexander] Pope, 'Messiah. A sacred eclogue: written
in imitation of Virgil's Pollio' [in the fourth eclogue]
[Crum Y100]

fc.132/1, p. 34; c.83/2, no. 345

Y0134 Ye nymphs of the cloistered vale
And whisper fond shepherd I'm thine.

'Written in the mass house at Kirtlington park'

c.83/2, no. 600

Y0135 Ye nymphs who flaunt it up and down
In time will fall below it.

'Verses inscribed to the ladies'

fb.142, p. 62

Y0136 Ye pangs! that rend my aching heart,
And snatch me to the peaceful tomb.

John Lockman, 'Translations, and imitations from
Metastasio, and other Italian opera poets [7]'

c.267/4, p. 99

Y0137 Ye patriots, who so oft complain
Another Sandwich must be lost.

'On Commodore Griffith's ordering the ship Lord
Sandwich to be sunk in order to save Rhode Island'

c.89, p. 127

Y0138 Ye people clap your hands and sing,
Defends the earth for's own Name's sake.

'Psalm 47 Evening prayer'

c.264/1, p. 203

Y0139 Ye people who assembled are,
And thus I end my tale and verse.

'The last dying speech a confession of Dr. ———
T——r who was executed at Kensington Common
with three other convicts upon Wednesday the 14th
day of [?]. 1782'

File 17838

Y0140 Ye Persian maids! attend your poet's lays,
The shepherds lov'd, and Selim bless'd his song.

William Collins, 'Oriental eclogue[s]: eclogue first,
Selim; or, the shepherd's moral' [pr. 1742 (Foxon
C298)]

c.140, p. 126

Y0141 Ye phantoms what are ye
To see you dance, to hear your song.

'The masquerade'

Poetry Box I/105

Y0142 Ye poets take heed how ye trust to the muse
And so there's an end to a bob for the court.

[Nicholas Amhurst], 'An excellent new ballad called a
bob for the court to the tune of In the days of my
youth in The beggar's opera'

c.570/3, p. 46

Y0143 Ye pow'rs above, incline an ear;
       The lovelier person, found in thee!

         [Charles Earle], 'Made for a gentleman— by his
         request as a New Year's gift to his lady, born on New
         Year's Day'

       c.376

Y0144 Ye pow'r[s] who taught my artless sighs
       As paramount, as pure.

         [William] Hayley, 'To his wife after eight years'
         marriage'
         [Crum Y108]

       c.504, p. 5; Poetry Box v/49; Poetry Box x/19

Y0145 Ye prigs who are troubled by conscience's qualms
       Thus living I'm happy when dead I'm divine.

         'Song 154'

       c.555, p. 215

Y0146 Ye prudes, who ne'er such liberty could brook
       And all the prude now in the cat is seen.

         'The prude metamorphosed'

       Poetry Box IV/92; see also next.

Y0147 Ye prudes, who such a freedom scorn to brook,
       Our pow'r deny, and sacred laws disdain.

         'The Lewisham prude metamorphos'd into a cat'

       c.360/3, no. 74 (incomplete); see also previous.

Y0148 Ye puny sinners cease from tears
       We'll keep our mirth till better times.

         'Upon the general pardon'

       b.111, p. 525

Y0149 Ye rebussers in beauty's list enroll
       And wholly that which she can never be.

         'Rebus'

       Diggle Box: Poetry Box XI/71

Y0150 Ye righteous in the Lord rejoice,
       Do only trust in Thee.

         [John Hopkins], 'The 13 psalm a prayer of God's
         providence and power' [verses from Psalm 33]
         [Crum Y111]

       a.3, fol. 81

Y0151 Ye righteous in the Lord rejoice
       Whereon we did rely.

         'Psalm 33'

       c.264/1, p. 137

Y0152 Ye sacred bards of elder time,
       Assert its long-lost rights, and claim its native skies.

         [William Boscawen], 'Ode. For the anniversary
         meeting of the subscribers and friends to the Literary
         Fund, April 21, 1795'

       fc.106, p. 16

Y0153 Ye sacred nine lend all your aid,
       And friendship's holy flame.

         'The retired patriot'

       c.139, p. 34

Y0154 Ye sacred relics which that marble keep
       His pious widow consecrates this tomb.

         [John Dryden], 'On Sr Palmes Fairborne Kt. governor
         of Tangier . . . Oct. 24. 1680'

       fb.143, p. 26

Y0155 Ye sacred spirits! while your friends distress'd
       'Tis all a brother, all a son can give.

         'Epitaph'

       Poetry Box XII/67

Y0156 Ye sages of London, of state high and low,
       As always we used, we will zealously pray.

         'City justice or true equity exposed'
         [Crum Y117]

       b.111, p. 565

Y0157 Ye seats where oft in pensive rapture laid,
       Th'attending muse shall ne'er be long away.

         H[enry] J[ames] Pye, 'Sonnet on the residence of
         Thomson'

       c.142, p. 397

Y0158 Ye servants of the Lord bless ye
       Who ask'd a child in prayer.

         'Psalm 113. Hallelujah 23 day'

       c.264/3, p. 38

Y0159 Ye servants of the Lord, His name
       In Sion: He be prais'd. Hallelujah.

         'Psalm 135. Hallelujah'

       c.264/3, p. 82

Y0160 Ye she-Friends and he-Friends whoever inherit
       But all of them just as wise as they came.

         'The Quakers' ballad'

       b.54, p. 1189

Y0161 Ye sheep of Jesus hear his voice
       And we will cease to sigh or fear.

         T[homas] S[tevens]

       c.259, p. 147

Y0162 Ye shepherds so cheerful and gay,
Was faithless, and I am undone!

[William] Shenstone, 'A pastoral ballad, in four parts'

fc.132/1, p. 153; Poetry Box XII/28 (first part only)

Y0163 Ye shepherds your ill-tim'd amusements forego,
All mournfully slow to the village return'd.

[J. M—tt], 'Stanzas written during the illness of an
agreeable relation'

c.140, p. 368

Y0164 Ye solemn pedagogues, who teach
And blushing, glory is my choice.

[Richard] Cumberland, 'On Mrs. Herbert's marriage,
a daughter of Ld. George Sackville'

c.504, p. 7; c.391, p. 54

Y0165 Ye sons of art, where'er your *manes* rest
Alive, partake their skill; when dead, their fame.

T[homas] N[ewcomb], 'Verses to an eminent
physician; who attended the author in a late dangerous
sickness. Inscribed to Dr. Silvester'

File 10789

Y0166 Ye sons of Cona! on the heath
Ye sons of Sora, mourn your king.

[ ] Ellison, 'The death of Erragon; from [James
Macpherson's] Fingal'

Greatheed Box/28

Y0167 Ye sons of ease, who spread your sails,
To slumber, or to die.

Charles Burney, the younger, 'Epitaph . . . Jan. 11.
1786'

c.35, p. 42

Y0168 Ye sons of elegance, who truly taste
And weep the Christian, husband, father, friend.

William Mason, 'Epitaph on Mr. Lancelot Brown; the
celebrated landscape gardener'

fc.132/1, p. 212

Y0169 Ye sons of industry! Learn hence to know,
For know a good man's influence never dies.

'Epitaph on a gentleman, who became rich from a low
estate'

c.83/1, no. 202

Y0170 Ye sons of science, candidates for arts
A sober laic, than a graceless priest.

'To the students of Oxford who attended the meeting
of the people called Quakers on the 7th and 8th of 2nd
month 1759'

fc.79

Y0171 Ye sons of the cask
Let us join in the chorus | To the best lass in all
Christendom.

'Song 7'

c.555, p. 9

Y0172 Ye sons of Westminster who still retain
The monarch of this place is now a Friend.

'[Several copies of verses spoken at Westminster
School on the anniversary of the defeat of the Spanish
Armada] 2' [on John Friend]

fc.24, p. 71; c.233, p. 32

Y0173 Ye sots, whose *per annum* scarce last half a year
Be that as it will; he was born to good luck. |
Which nobody can deny.

T[homas] M[orell], 'The guinea a ballad'

c.395, p. 87

Y0174 Ye souls illustrious! That in days of yore
And just to public virtue, glory crown.

[George Huddesford], 'On the love of our country'

c.373, p. 51 (attr. [ ] Butson, of New College Oxford)

Y0175 Ye southern breezes gently blow
That sweets from ev'ry part may flow.

'Chorus [6, with musical score for tenor and bass,
claiming to be from Handel's Solomon (actually by
William Boyce?)]'

Music MS. 534

Y0176 Ye spacious rooms, ye folding doors
And snatch an envied joy.

[Richard Fitzpatrick], 'Ode in Almack's Assembly
Room. being a parody on Gray's Ode on a distant
prospect of Eton College'

Poetry Box X/137

Y0177 Ye sparks who flutter round the court,
We'll grant you brass, our age is gold.

'Merry Christmas. To the tune of—To you fair
ladies &c.'

Trumbull Box: Poetry Box XIII/96

Y0178 Ye sprightly sons of gaiety and mirth,
The scenes of care which open to the view.

'Spleen an elegy'

c.83/3, no. 762

Y0179 Ye sweet enchanters of this fav'rite grove,
And, with it, crown my Phyllis Queen of May.

John Lockman, 'To the nightingale of Vauxhall
Gardens, on the opening of the entertainment . . .
May 1756'

c.267/1, p. 100

Y0180　Ye sylvan scenes with artless beauty gay
　　　　How much the wife is dearer than the bride.

　　　　　　[George] Lyttelton, 1st baron Lyttelton, 'An irregular
　　　　　　ode wrote at Wickham in 1746'

　　　　　fc.51, p. 253

Y0181　Ye tender beaus and heedless belles
　　　　And prove you've one pretense to taste.

　　　　　　'Upon seeing Addison's Works, which were to be
　　　　　　raffled for want [of] two subscriptions to fill up the
　　　　　　number'

　　　　　Poetry Box IV/132

Y0182　Ye that are living now, and ye that after live,
　　　　Bear right your selves, when judgment ye do give.

　　　　　c.339, p. 311

Y0183　Ye that do sacred virtue love
　　　　I greatly you request.

　　　　　b.234, p. 36

Y0184　Ye that groan beneath the weight,
　　　　Come and taste tranquility.

　　　　　　'Tranquility'

　　　　　c.83/1, no. 45

Y0185　Ye thoughtless youth who, indiscreetly gay,
　　　　Forgive his faults, as you would be forgiven.

　　　　　　'On the death of Mr. Wm. Hunter of Hexham who
　　　　　　died in Dec. [17]82'

　　　　　c.93

Y0186　Ye townsmen of Oxford and scholars draw near
　　　　With three in his guard he departed for London.

　　　　　　'A ballad on the Duke of Monmouth's entertainment
　　　　　　at Oxford by the . . . mayor Mr. [Robert] Pauling . . .
　　　　　　to the tune of Packington's Pound' [16 Sept. 1680]
　　　　　　[Crum Y146; POAS II.262]

　　　　　fb.106(25) (ll. 1–151); Poetry Box VI/66 ('townsmen and
　　　　　scholars'; with two more lines)

Y0187　Ye tow'rs, which once contain'd the hardy knight,
　　　　In those which neither molder nor decay.

　　　　　　'Written among the ruins of an ancient castle'

　　　　　c.83/3, no. 761

Y0188　Ye trees, does your foliage delay
　　　　Which angels delighted will hear.

　　　　　　M[ary (Shackleton)] Leadbeater, 'The ruined cottage'

　　　　　c.142, p. 113

Y0189　Ye trueborn Englishmen proceed!
　　　　And all by your neglect.

　　　　　　[Daniel Defoe?], 'A satire dropt in our Parliament
　　　　　　April 20th at Westminster anno 1701' [printed, Foxon
　　　　　　B34]
　　　　　　[Crum Y147; POAS VI.321]

　　　　　fb.207/3, p. 25 (ll. 1–5); fb.207/4, p. 38 (ll. 1–5); see also
　　　　　'You trueborn . . .'.

Y0190　Ye two-legged dogs! Ye dogs with four,
　　　　O weep! For Bow-wow is no more.

　　　　　　John Lockman, 'To the memory of the incomparable
　　　　　　Bow-wow, a favorite dog in old Slaughter's
　　　　　　coffeehouse . . . July 1754'

　　　　　c.267/1, p. 243

Y0191　Ye vales and woods! fair scene of happier hours!
　　　　But the pale ashes, which her urn contains.

　　　　　　[Charlotte (Turner) Smith], 'Sonnet from [Petrarch]'

　　　　　c.343, p. 85

Y0192　Ye venerable walls! time-hallow'd towers!
　　　　And love, and guard, the good, their virtue won.

　　　　　　[ ] Ellison, 'Warwick Castle'

　　　　　Greatheed Box/36; fc.74, p. 11

Y0193　Ye vipers! from whose nest there springs
　　　　And rule you with a rod of iron.

　　　　　　[ ] B., 'To the inhabitants of Massachusetts Bay . . .
　　　　　　Jan. 27 [17]74'

　　　　　fc.85, fol. 22

Y0194　Ye virgin powers, defend my heart
　　　　The soonest is betray'd.

　　　　　　[Elizabeth Taylor], 'A song by a lady [mistrustful of
　　　　　　her own strength]'
　　　　　　[Crum Y151]

　　　　　b.201, p. 142

Y0195　Ye virgins! who love's raptures know,
　　　　The joy, the glory of mankind.

　　　　　　John Lockman, 'Translations, and imitations from
　　　　　　Metastasio, and other Italian opera poets [16]'

　　　　　c.267/4, p. 111

Y0196　Ye votaries of fashion who lavish your prime
　　　　That when once he is gone, he will never return.

　　　　　　'At a masked ball a person representing Time threw
　　　　　　scrolls of paper amongst the crowd in which the
　　　　　　following lines were written'

　　　　　c.83/2, no. 298

Y0197　Ye warbling nine! O animate my lyre!
Can thou, in all thy gen'rous plans, succeed.

> John Lockman, 'The congratulation of Ireland; on the happy arrival of his excellency the Earl of Halifax, in that kingdom. To be set to music by Lewis Granom esqr.'
> c.267/2, p. 278

Y0198　Ye warriors of highest heroical soul,
Scott the prince of her bards! Of her heroes the
Graeme!

> [William Hayley], 'An extempore triumphant song'
> File 6940

Y0199　Ye Warwickshire lads and ye lasses
And the thief of all thieves was a Warwickshire
thief.

> 'Song 234'
> c.555, p. 370

Y0200　Ye weavers all both far and near
Alone it is we will obey. | With a fa, la, &c.

> 'The weavers' ballad to the tune of, To you fair ladies now at land'
> Poetry Box IV/121

Y0201　Ye weeping muses, graces, virtues, tell
His inborn worth alone could Granville's deeds
inspire.

> [George Lyttelton, 1st baron Lyttelton], 'To the memory of Capt. Granville, who was slain on board the Defiance, in the engagement with the French fleet on the 3rd day of May 1747'
> [Crum Y154]
> fc.51, p. 221, p. 227; c.53, fol. 62 (var.)

Y0202　Ye Westminster men
Descends to the son. | For th'election prepare &c.

> John Lockman, 'Lord Warkworth [later duke of Northumberland]: or the Westminster election. A new toast. The tune: Heart of oak are our ships . . .'
> c.267/2, p. 59

Y0203　Ye Whigs and ye Tories | Repair to Whitehall,
And is led about | By republic Jack How.

> 'The female regency'
> b.111, p. 437

Y0204　Ye white-staff officers, ye golden keys!
What pygmies all compar'd to this great man!

> John Lockman, 'The truly great man: writ after seeing the Italian giant, at Mr. Cockerton's in the Poultry . . . July 1756'
> c.267/1, p. 111

Y0205　Ye, who come with hallow'd feet
'Tis peace, who bids you here be bless'd.

> [George Crabbe], 'Guy's cliff: an inscription'
> Greatheed Box/31 (attr. [ ] Ellison)

Y0206　Ye who dwell above the skies,
Oh how great! how excellent.

> George Sandys
> b.150, p. 222

Y0207　Ye, who lament the soldier's early death
Watchful to guard her from the fate of Rome.

> 'Sacred to the memory of Edward Hawke, esq., Lieutenant Colonel of the old regiment . . . parted this life, upon Dublin duty, October 2, 1773, aged 27'
> fc.85, fol. 36v

Y0208　Ye whose kind eyes these copious rhymes peruse
And yield to God the treasure of the heart.

> [William Hayley], 'Sonnet . . . Sept. 25 [1800]'
> File 6968

Y0209　Ye willing fair these precepts bear in mind,
Love, honor, and obey your sovereign lord.

> 'The happy marriage'
> c.503, p. 31

Y0210　Ye winds to which(?) Colin complains
And as constant a nymph I will prove.

> 'An answer to Colin's complaint'
> c.374

Y0211　Ye wise and ye witty,
Will lay it to Lord Chesterfield. | Will lay it, &c.

> [N.] Herbert, 'The noble monopolizer. A song' [on Lord Chesterfield]
> Spence Papers, folder 91

Y0212　Ye wives who are willing your husbands to please,
And never from home be addicted to roaming.

> 'Distich. Wrote under the figure of a woman standing upon a tortoise, a bunch of keys in her right hand, the forefinger of her left hand upon her lips, and a dove upon her shoulder . . . translations [8]'
> c.81/1, no. 70

Y0213　Ye women that do London love so well
Lest honest Adam pay for Eve's expense!

> 'Dr. Donne's counsel to the ladies and gentlewomen to depart the city according to the King's proclamation' [misattributed]
> [Crum Y168]
> b.356, p. 215; see also 'You women . . .'.

Y0214   Ye wood nymphs, while I touch the trembling string,
Her bosom emulate the Elysian grove.

> Charles Burney, the younger, 'Elegy on the death of a
> favorite canary bird'

c.35, p. 1

Y0215   Ye woods and wilds, receive me to your shade!
Our thoughts are lost in thy immortality.

> 'Walking in the woods and fields'

c.167, p. 33; c.244, p. 583; c.83/2, no. 566

Y0216   Ye woods and wilds serene and blest retreats
Faint images of those, which nature makes.

> [Charles Hopkins], 'A history of love a poem in a
> letter to a lady'

b.130, p. 1; c.360/1, p. 285 (var.)

Y0217   Ye woods and ye mountains unknown,
I feel till I see her again.

> 'The complaint'

c.83/3, no. 845

Y0218   Ye woods, ye groves, for weeping sorrow made,
A soul more pure, a brighter angel there!

> [ ] Walwyn, 'Elegy on the beautiful Mrs Walwyn of
> Longworth by her husband'

Poetry Box XII/13

Y0219   Ye works of God, on him alone,
In hymns of endless praise.

> [James] Merrick, 'The benedicite paraphrased'
> [Dodsley Collection]

c.487, p. 160

Y0220   Ye world of water wide that madly roar;
Convey the long-sought, wish'd-for stranger—rest.

> 'Sonnet 2. Despair'

c.341, p. 61

Y0221   Ye worthy patriots go on
Go home and look after your wives.

> [Daniel Defoe], 'An encomium upon a Parliament'
> [1699]
> [Crum Y171; POAS VI.49]

fb.68, p. 89

Y0222   Ye Yahoos mourn; for in this place,
Forever, ever, ever lost!

> 'An epitaph on Peter the wild youth—occasioned by a
> report of his death'

c.503, p. 20

Y0223   Ye youths and ye virgins, come list to my tale,
While you seek me you have me, when found I am
lost.

> [Anna Laetitia (Aikin)] Barbauld, 'Riddle by . . .'

Poetry Box V/71

Y0224   Ye youths licentious thro' the town
But liv'd to virtue as he ought.

> 'The gibbet a poem'

c.83/3, no. 1057

Y0225   Ye youths! Whose souls have felt love's pleasing
smart,
Yield to those gain'd in the mind.

> John Lockman, 'Campaspe. Musical drama. Writ in
> honor of painting'

c.267/3, p. 149

Y0226   Yea let them flow if tears can aught assuage
And with them peace and happiness return.

> [Sir Henry William Bunbury], 'On the death of Lady
> Granby'

Poetry Box IV/197 (incomplete?)

Y0227   Year after year roll fast away,
That must the true criterion be.

> [Edmund Wodehouse], 'Novr. 19 [1714]'

b.131, p. 88

Y0228   Yeohs! haste forward! Tally ho! Tally ho!
This splendid circle smiling round me here.

> 'The Cockney hunt or Easter Monday chase through
> Epping forest'

Poetry Box VI/9

Y0229   Yes, all the world must sure agree,
When once that love is past?

> [William Walsh], 'To his mistress against marriage'

c.223, p. 75

Y0230   Yes angels wonder at the scene
Which could not watch for Jesus' sake.

> T[homas] S[tevens], 'Mark 13. 37'

c.259, p. 98

Y0231   Yes, beauteous virgin yes, thy tears are just
To guard the weak, to waft the just to heaven.

> [Charles Miller], 'To Lady Horatia Waldegrave'

c.130, p. 1; Poetry Box XII/126

Y0232   Yes, Betsy too shall have her wish,
I shall rejoice to hear the news.

> T[homas] Stevens, 'Colchester. Feby. 15. 1780'

c.259, p. 71

Y0233 Yes—Britain seem'd to ruin doom'd
To magnify thy name.

    P[hilip] Doddridge, 'A hymn on the general fast
    Jan. 7. 1747 from Amos IV. 11 Ye were as a firebrand'

    c.493, p. 43

Y0234 Yes, charming nymphs! To you the muse
But let the sisters take, and share the prize.

    C[harles] B[urney], 'Ode, addressed to the Miss
    Urquharts Meldrum . . . July 6. 1780'

    c.38, p. 51

Y0235 Yes, every poet is a fool
Prove every fool to be a poet.

    [Matthew Prior], 'On a poet's being called a fool'
    [Crum Y178]

    fc.60, p. 41; c.144, p. 79

Y0236 Yes! Ev'ry day's experience proves
In Salem's, Sion's daughter's, gate.

    'Psalm 73. Here ends the second book of Psalms, or
    the prayers of David the son of Jesse. Evening prayer'

    c.264/2, p. 18

Y0237 Yes, fickle Cambridge, Perkin found this true
Of Sejanus' face made seven brass kettles.

    [George Stepney], 'Turba rhemi sequitur fortunam
    semper, et odit . . .' [on the burning of Monmouth's
    picture in Cambridge, 1685]
    [Crum Y179; POAS IV.41]

    fb.68, p. 87

Y0238 Yes, Herodorus, as good heav'n approves
Whate'er the good man meets with is success.

    [ ] Lewis, 'The virtuous man'

    c.244, p. 289

Y0239 Yes I could love, if I could find
Nor vain as to be pointed at.

    'A song: 1677'

    b.54, p. 1028

Y0240 Yes, my Alicia, you shall live
Of those who dwell above the spheres!

    R[ichard] V[ernon] S[adleir], 'To [Alice Hamilton] in
    answer to other verses written to me on her recovering
    from illness'

    c.106, p. 105

Y0241 Yes—Pollio!—Duty; friends; all bid me write,
Greatly enrich'd from art's exhaustless store.

    John Lockman, 'Menaleas's apology to Pollio [the
    Earl of Middlesex], for his not presuming to write at
    the ever-to-be lamented death of Frederick Prince of
    Wales'

    c.267/2, p. 346

Y0242 Yes she is gone—to memory dear!
And to heaven's roll did add another name?

    Charles Atherton Allnutt, 'Tribute to the memory of
    my much lamented [?] amiable friend the late Mrs.
    Blake'

    c.112, p. 125

Y0243 Yes soon you must be look'd to, do not think
And drown'd in cares put on his mourning weeds.

    'Answer' [to 'Why doth not golden . . .']

    b.356, p. 108

Y0244 Yes, Stella, I would always love
To follow her alone.

    H[annah] More, 'The following verses were translated
    from Voltaire by . . .'

    c.341, p. 114

Y0245 Yes! swift raise my voice in song
And thine own changeful heart.

    H[enry] K[irke] White, 'The broken heart'

    File 17714

Y0246 Yes the Redeemer rose
Beyond the skies.

    P[hilip] Doddridge, 'Christ's resurrection
    Luke XXIV 34'

    c.493, p. 17

Y0247 Yes thou art sure the queen of love
The world's in love with me.

    [Robert Merry], 'To Anna at Florence at the time the
    Emperor and King of Sweden were both there in 1783'

    Greatheed Box/45

Y0248 Yes, 'tis the time! I cried, impose the chain!
To take the only way to be forgiven.

    Alexander Pope(?), 'On the benefactions in the frost
    in the year 1740 . . . we ascribe this to Mr. Pope on the
    authority of the Gentleman's magazine in which it was
    published . . .'

    c.531

Y0249 Yes 'tis the voice of love divine
In silence swallows up my voice.

    P[hilip] Doddridge, 'The tender compassion and
    complacential love God bears to his church from
    Zeph. III. 16, 18'

    c.493, p. 57

Y0250 Yes—'twas the voice of grief—my Anna's tear
And with these purer spirits mix again!

    M[ary (S[hackleton] Leadbeater], 'On the death of
    Mary Nicholson addressed to Anne Shannon'

    File 13409

Y0251 Yes, we have liv'd—one pang, and then we part!
Yes! Says my country heav'n!! he said, and died!

[Alexander Pope], 'Dialogue. Doctor Francis
Atterbury was an exile at Paris during which time his
daughter went to visit him; he was extremely ill at the
time, and died in her arms'

c.81/1, no. 173

Y0252 Yes, yes I will go, and knowledge pursue
But to work and supply us with food.

T[homas] S[tevens], 'Going to school'

c.259, p. 76

Y0253 Yesterday morning about six o' clock
Into the street and died on the spot.

'A whim on a poor delirious woman who threw herself
out of a window on Monday November 10 1732'

c.360/2, no. 224

Y0254 Yet again attempt the sea—
Of the Cyclades beware.

[William Popple, trans.], '[Horace] book 1st. ode 14th.
To the ship in which his friends passed through the
Ægean sea'

fc.104/2, p. 44

Y0255 Yet do I live! Oh how shall I sustain
And in my cup of grief infuse one drop of joy.

Cuthbert Shaw, 'Monody on the death of a lady who
died in childbed. 1766'

c.140, p. 173

Y0256 Yet if I have not all thy love,
Groan there, dear I could have it all.

[John Donne]
[cf. Crum 11074]

b.114, p. 280 (incomplete)

Y0257 Yet, let me sigh, and think again,
Among the friends of early days.

Maria Riddell, 'The remembrance'

c.142, p. 520; see also 'The Thames flows proudly . . .'.

Y0258 Yet she ungrateful and obdurate still,
Still I complain and still I love her more.

c.549, p. 28

Y0259 Yet stay delusive thought sweet flatterer stay,
O'er aught the least that claims the name of love.

S[tephen] Simpson, 'A monody. In imitation of
Milton's Lycidas on the unfortunate death of R. S. B.'

c.563

Y0260 Yet were bidentals sacred, and the place
Are they, that will believe all he dares fear.

[John Eliot?], 'In laude[m] eiusem' [on the Duke of
Buckingham, 1628; printed in Eliot's Poems consisting
of epistles & epigrams, Wing S524A]
[Crum Y209]

b.200, p. 55; b.356, p. 99

Y0261 Yet while I hail thee sympathy divine
And principle for sentiment dethron'd.

Diggle Box: Poetry Box XI/13

Y0262 Yet while we live, what gratitude we owe,
Ere means, occasion, time, shall be no more.

'Written immediately after the second shock of an
earthquake, on the eighth of March. 1749'

c.547, p. 205

Y0263 Yet who can tell? But gracious heaven
These can his wonders tell.

[Thomas Stevens?], 'Another [hymn sung Tuesday
night 1 August 1780]'

c.259, p. 95

Y0264 Yet yet he lives! O yet kind heav'n spare
And is it thus our promis'd joys must end!

[William] Pattison, 'To a friend dangerously sick'

c.244, p. 531

Y0265 Yet you inflexible, obdurate prove,
These men much happier that can love thee less.

c.549, p. 47

Y0266 Yonder meadows and groves shall repeat my sad
moan,
For alas! my poor Celia how she lies all alone.

'A song'

b.54, p. 1162

Y0267 Yorkshire true sportsmen, in pursuit of hounds,
Run down whole kingdoms with a pack of curs.

'Yorkshire agt Norfolk, an epigram'

c.233, p. 117; c.570/3, p. 113

Y0268 You are a fool t'imagine with your rich,
Feed only upon man.

Sir Thomas Urquhart, 'To an old man who thought to
gain his mistress' favor by feasting'

fb.217, p. 305

Y0269 You are a husband just as one would wish,
A Brackley's truth I'll speak, and not in vain.

Lady Jane Cavendish, 'On the Lord Viscount
Brackley'
[Crum Y217]

b.233, p. 21

Y0270 You are by name an Hardman: yet I know
And y' are an heard man: and all this prov'd true.

  [Sir Aston Cokayne], 'To Mr Henry Hardman'
  b.275, p. 103

Y0271 You are endowed with a spirit from
The king, and commonwealth doth rejoice.

  [Sir Thomas Urquhart], 'To the Earl of Lewick'
  fb.217, p. 389

Y0272 You are his mistress, and you call me servant
Brings you a cockmate but me no co-rival.

  [Sir Thomas Urquhart], To a very handsome
  gentlewoman who was extremely in love with him at
  the arrival of another servant of hers'
  fb.217, p. 388

Y0273 You are indicted sinner (by the name
Confess, your guilt no other plea can show.

  H[enry] C[olman], 'The indictment'
  [Crum Y220-1]
  b.2, p. 23

Y0274 You are my patron and (my lord) I'll tell
And naughty wine does need a gallant bush.

  [Sir Aston Cokayne], To the right honorable Philip,
  Earl of Chesterfield, Baron of Shelford, my most
  honor'd uncle'
  b.275, p. 27

Y0275 You are so meritoriously religious
In whom to dwell together, but in you.

  Sir Thomas Urquhart, 'To the Countess of [crossed
  out] Dowager'
  fb.217, p. 335

Y0276 You are so universally scholastic
Proceeding from your skill in ev'ry science.

  Sir Thomas Urquhart, 'To Master [crossed out]
  preacher'
  fb.217, p. 340

Y0277 You are the academy of all truth,
'Tis Newcastle's excellence; none but he.

  Lady Jane Cavendish, 'The great example. To . . . my
  father, the Marquess of Newcastle'
  [Crum Y226]
  b.233, p. 3

Y0278 You are the trees, the bramble is the thing
Abimelech the scoff of Christendom.

  'The explanation' [of 'Soon as young Jotham . . .']
  c.570/2, p. 48, p. 140 (as last six lines of 'Go on brave
  Sirs . . .')

Y0279 You are too ample in your size,
Some larger, than at Paris.

  Sir Thomas Urquhart, 'The words of a Parisian
  bridegroom to his bride, who was a native of Saint
  Denis, the first night of their marriage'
  fb.217, p. 121

Y0280 You as the happy morning star, we'll sing
Withstanding powers o'ercome and reap the
                                    golden fruit.

  [Mrs. Christian Kerr], 'Addressed to an old lady who
  was born the same day' [10 June]
  c.102, p. 105

Y0281 You ask alas! why heaves the frequent sigh
But view well-pleas'd the tedious journey past.

  [Helen Craik], 'Helen—an epistle to a friend'
  c.375, p. 97

Y0282 You ask beauty? To a common whore
Both lure the gazers on to enter in.

  [Robert Cholmeley], 'To a lady of an indifferent
  character who asked me [?] beauty was'
  c.190, p. 184

Y0283 You ask, dear Harry, how my time I spend
We admire the first, but from the latter fly.

  'Bath 1730'
  c.392, p. 8

Y0284 You ask me, dear Mira, the man you should choose;
Beware of the man by a Chesterfield bred.

  'To Mira, extempore' [Middlesex journal and evening
  advertiser, 27 March 1777]
  c.157, p. 104

Y0285 You ask me, Emma, for a seal,
And stamp it there forever.

  'From a gentleman to a lady with a present of a seal'
  c.82, p. 19

Y0286 You ask, what death's: I were dead, could I show it:
When I'm dead then, come to m', if you would
                                    know it.

  Sir Thomas Urquhart, 'To one, who inquired what
  death was'
  fb.217, p. 266

Y0287 You beat your pate and fancy wit will come
Knock as you please there's nobody at home.

  [Alexander Pope], 'Another [epigram]'
  fc.60, p. 50

Y0288 You, beauteous songster of the winged kind
We find them oft canary birds in love?

[Mary] Leapor, 'On Mrs Diana Browning's canary
bird. By a lady'
Spence Papers, folder 113

Y0289 You being no more a virgin are unmask'd,
Through lack of sight (I'm sure) he knows you not.

Sir Thomas Urquhart, 'To a young gentlewoman,
about Whitehall, who had lost her maidenhead'
fb.217, p. 51

Y0290 You bid me Georgina, some verses to make
Tho' your love may be his—yet your friendship is
mine.

[Claude Champion de Crespigny]
File 17393

Y0291 You bid me my jovial companions forsake
May I always be drinking yet always be dry.

'Song 181'
c.555, p. 282

Y0292 You blessed spirits that bestow,
And like true swans, go singing to your death.

[Thomas Stanley], 'A paraphrase upon Psalm
CXLVIII'
b.152, p. 106

Y0293 You bliss your husband so with all the actions,
Of your fruition with a steadfast motion.

Sir Thomas Urquhart, 'To my Lady [crossed out]'
fb.217, p. 181

Y0294 You cannot love a virgin that is proud
For there is none of those things ready made.

[Sir Thomas Urquhart], 'To a bachelor who received a
wife endowed with meaner perfections than nature
readily allows'
fb.217, p. 536

Y0295 You cannot serve two masters well Sylvester;
Therefore you serve your mistress, not your master.

Sir Thomas Urquhart, 'Of service in matters of love.
To Sylvester'
fb.217, p. 236

Y0296 You can't conceive the reason why
Should in return present me yours.

[Isaac Freeman], 'Non donem tibi cur meos
libellos . . . Martial: Lib. 5. Epigr: 102'
fc.105, p. 35

Y0297 You Catholic statesmen and churchmen rejoice,
For if this trick fail then beware of your jacket.

'The miracle how the Duchess of Modena prayed to
the B[lessed] Virgin . . .' [on the birth of the Prince of
Wales 1688]
[Crum Y242]
Spence Papers, folder 113; Poetry Box VI/80; fb.108,
p. 277; see also 'Ye Catholic statesmen . . .'.

Y0298 You command me to write, and I wish to obey
And our fondness increase, as the wiser we grow.

'A letter to a lady'
fc.51, p. 110

Y0299 You complain, my good friend, that my lord, and
my lady,
For his errors apologies amply to find.

'To a friend'
fc.53, p. 158

Y0300 You counsel me to geld this book of some |
Lascivious epigrams:
But suchlike peers will not well become | The use
of gallant dames.

Sir Thomas Urquhart, 'To certain discreet, and
judicious ladies'
fb.217, p. 359

Y0301 You crag precipitously wild, where frown
The deep regard of ages be its claim!

[Richard Polwhele], 'St. Michael's Mount in
Cornwall' [1796]
c.141, p. 565

Y0302 You cuckolds all of fam'd Cheapside
Like eighty-eight or forty-one. | With a fa la

'The answer' [to 'Ye/You ladies fair of old
England . . .', on Sophia Dorothea, divorced wife of
George I]
[cf. Crum Y27, 'Ye cuckolds']
Poetry Box IV/64; see also 'Ye cuckolds . . .'.

Y0303 You did appear as if that black,
I love and kind shall be my pay.

Lady Jane Cavendish, 'On an acquaintance'
[Crum Y248a]
b.233, p. 19

Y0304 You do not us deceive,
And love is but a brat.

Sir Thomas Urquhart, 'To a gentlewoman, who gave it
out, that she disdained the charms of Cupid'
fb.217, p. 287

Y0305 You do swear by custom of confession
Of your own accord you do freely swear. . . .

'At a court baron of Sir Thomas May knt., holden at
Dunmow in the county of Essex, on Friday the [2]7th
of June 1701 . . . William Parsley a butcher and Jane
his wife . . . made oath of their mutuality love and
concord and claimed the flitch of bacon'
[Crum Y248b]

c.360/3, no. 154 (incomplete)

Y0306 You Englishmen all, that tender the curse
Not so soon from his wife, as his money is parted. |
Which nobody can deny.

'The divorce [of Henry Howard, duke of Norfolk,
from Lady Mary Mordaunt] . . . 9 April 1692'
[Crum Y251; *POAS* v.318]

fb.70, p. 59; b.111, p. 217 ('English folk all, that are under
the curse')

Y0307 You fair would travel and I know you may
England to know doth yield pre-eminence.

[Sir Aston Cokayne], 'To Mr Tho: Reppington his
brother'

b.275, p. 102

Y0308 You few that wisdom above treasure prize
With bodies, goods, and souls forevermore.

[Edward] Sparke, 'Poem 8th, on the Holy Epiphany'

b.137, p. 20

Y0309 You gallants of England of ev'ry degree
What the devil has caus'd the surrender of Varn.

'An excellent new ballad called Cornucopia or the
triumph of Count Horn to the tune of Youth, youth
thou hadst better been starved . . .'

Poetry Box VII/84

Y0310 You, George, with ev'ry social notion fraught,
I left the town, and left my friend behind.

[William Carpenter], 'To a friend'

c.247, p. 152

Y0311 You gloried to demolish all, and tread on
The workers of such antichristian deeds.

Sir Thomas Urquhart, 'To Master Knox, and others,
the overthrowers of the Scots churches'

fb.217, p. 115

Y0312 You good men of Middlesex countrymen dear
With thy own bro[ther] kid[der]s(?) and
burglaring fellows.

[ ] B., '[Sir Robert] Peyton's fate to the [tune] of
Youth youth . . . November the 13th 1679'

b.327, f. 4; fb.108, p. 313 (var.); see also 'Ye good
men . . .'.

Y0313 You, good Sir Beaumont! were by heav'n design'd
But simple as herself, and as your soul, serene.

[Thomas] Hooke, 'Fro[m] Mr Hooke's letter; Oct: 31,
1753. (after speak[in]g of gardening; at the Exchange)'
Spence Papers, folder 113

Y0314 You happier friend, in Barton's rural seat
And want no son, to mourn thy sacred bier.

J[effrey] Ekins, 'To Mr. Stevenson, who succeeded
upon the death of his father to the living of Barton'
c.157, p. 108; see also 'Go happier friend . . .'.

Y0315 You have approv'n your self 'gainst th'adversary
Nor ever was a stouter man a lord.

Sir Thomas Urquhart, 'To the Earl of [crossed out]'
fb.217, p. 80

Y0316 You have impoverished Darbyshire by giving
And for the loss then we may better bear it.

[Sir Aston Cokayne], 'To Mrs Anne Ellis, my cousin
germane'
b.275, p. 105

Y0317 You have in all your actions, such a relish
A quicker wit, or judgment less erroneous.

Sir Thomas Urquhart, 'To Lady [crossed out]'
fb.217, p. 78

Y0318 You have no cause to think it strange, that he
While life is but a journey into death.

[Sir Thomas Urquhart], 'To one lamenting the
decease of a friend of his'
fb.217, p. 525

Y0319 You have not such great cause to mourn,
His life rent could not choose but fall.

Sir Thomas Urquhart, 'Of a certain young gentleman,
who happened to decrease [decease] a just year after
his wife had made him cuckold to a friend of his
bewailing his death'
fb.217, p. 356

Y0320 You have of life and death a pow'r so divine,
The earth is open'd to unseal your [?].

[Sir Thomas Urquhart], 'To the bad physician'
fb.217, p. 518

Y0321 You have restor'd his kindness, if you owe
If not man would with empty hands be grateful.

[Sir Thomas Urquhart]
fb.217, p. 386

Y0322 You have two masters: but 'tis strange, I vow,
If you please both, or that they both please you.

   Sir Thomas Urquhart, 'To one, who had a couple of
   masters'
   fb.217, p. 286

Y0323 You having eight and twenty days: no other
Of all your brethren is so like your mother.

   Sir Thomas Urquhart, 'Of the month of February'
   fb.217, p. 299

Y0324 You heathen deities above,
The glory of our age.

   'Belly Thompson. A song'
   c.530, p. 80

Y0325 You Irish which do boast and say
Over the English graves.

   'Verses upon the breach of the peace in Ireland'
   fb.228/25

Y0326 You know my friends in former days
Grinn'd to see his lady hop.

   Miss [ ] Andrews, 'On Mrs. ———'
   File 245/11

Y0327 You know nothing, your knowledge is so small:
Nor know you, that you know nothing at all.

   Sir Thomas Urquhart, 'To a mere ignorant'
   fb.217, p. 40

Y0328 You know so perfectly, how to exoner,
Possession of them all, by your example.

   Sir Thomas Urquhart, 'To the Earl of [crossed out]'
   fb.217, p. 277

Y0329 You know where you slyly cheat,
Only let me feel a bit | You know where.

   R[obert] Shirley, 1st earl of Ferrers, 'Rondeau from
   Voiture'
   c.347, p. 89

Y0330 You ladies all of worth beware
The law is all mine arse.

   'Verses made on Lawyer Hoyle's trial for buggering of
   a boy'
   b.209, p. 74

Y0331 You, ladies fair of old England
His mien was great his robes were gay . . . .

   'The fair penitent [Sophia Dorothea, divorced wife of
   George I]'s doleful petition composed by Bob the
   sincere and dropped by Zachariah in a meeting house'
   [accession of George I]
   [Crum Y286]
   fc.58, p. 8 (incomplete); see also 'Ye ladies fair. .'.

Y0332 You ladies now perhaps would think it rude,
I caren't a rush, for I'm a married man.

   'The epilogue to the music speech' [at the Music
   School, Oxford, 1682]
   fb.142, p. 21

Y0333 You ladies of honor both wealthy and fair,
That no sooner he's in, but straight he comes out.

   'Four maids of honor'
   b.111, p. 557

Y0334 You ladies who ogle the prince and his train
And Lumley who from Argyll takes his cue.

   'A court ballad'
   c.570/1, p. 169

Y0335 You lads, and you lasses, that live at Longleat,
Let him first make a better, or kiss the bum-fiddle. |
                    D[er]ry down &c.

   [Sir Henry Sheeres], 'A ballad by Ld. Lansdowne'
   [false attribution; 'The disaster, or the fiddle's
   farewell, being an excellent new song to an admirable
   old tune, call'd King John, or the Abbot of
   Canterbury, composed by Sr. Henry Sheeres in a fit of
   the gout, at the Lord Weymouth's seat, called
   Longleat. 1706' [printed 1720 (Foxon B41)]
   Trumbull Box: Poetry Box XIII/65; c.176, p. 163; Poetry
   Box IV/2, iv/5; see also 'Ye lords . . .'.

Y0336 'You lead us by the nose,' you doughty pleader
Then hail, O Arabin! The circuit leader.

   'The poet's rejoinder and vale'
   fc.76.iii/214

Y0337 You learned prelates of the House of Peers
Thus kick Sir John, he'll quickly fling my lord.

   H. W., 'Balaam's reply to the ass, or the clergy's
   answer to the country's complaint' ['Ye miter'd
   members . . .']
   b.63, p. 53

Y0338 You like the ocean never are at rest
Always in bustle, to yourself a pest.

   'On Mr. H.'
   c.546, p. 19

Y0339 You little know the heart which you advise
To one great Being merciful and just.

   Lady Mary Wortley Montagu, 'Verses by . . .'
   [Crum Y289]
   fc.135; fc.51, p. 142

Y0340 You lords barons burghers and some earls—rejoice
Will have his pint in when the reckoning's paid.

    'The Scots jubilee or a g[r]ievous new ballad upon the
    redress of the grievances proclaimed March 25
    [16]74 . . . to the tune of Paddington's [Packington's]
    pound or Tunbridge . . .'

Poetry Box VIII/25

Y0341 You love the youth revere his name
And wishes from censure to preserve his fame.

    [Probably incomplete]

c.517, fol. 23v

Y0342 You mad-caps of England that soldiers would be,
And all that he'll say there lies a brave man.

    'An invitation to Ireland' [c. 1691]
    [Crum Y294]

b.111, p. 257

Y0343 You maidens, and wives, and young widows rejoice,
Their power of healing may never decay.

    [Thomas Head], 'The doctors of Tunbridge'
    [Crum Y295]

fb.107, p. 24; c.189, p. 122; Poetry Box I/90

Y0344 You make a viol speak: your nimble hand
How much your works mankind would delight.

    [Sir Aston Cokayne], 'To Mr Andrew Whitehall'

b.275, p. 82

Y0345 You marry, t'imitate the sacred lives
This, being a widow: and the first a whore.

    Sir Thomas Urquhart, 'To a certain churchman, twice
    married'

fb.217, p. 147

Y0346 You may do as you will but I'll fling away care
All the days of my life thus I'll frolic and laugh.

    'Song 204'

c.555, p. 330

Y0347 You may go to the combat without fear,
That you could like the meanest of them all.

    Sir Thomas Urquhart, 'An encouragement for the
    duel, to one, who was suspected to wear horns'

fb.217, p. 180

Y0348 You may observe this numeration table
That each three figures hundreds signify.

    [Mary Serjant], 'Numeration'

fb.98, fol. 5

Y0349 You may vow I'll not forget
My lips shall send a thousand back to you.

    [Robert] Herrick, 'Mr. Herrick to his mistress going a
    journey'

b.356, p. 42

Y0350 You meaner beauties of the night,
Th'eclipse and glory of her kind?

    Sir Henry Wotton, 'On his mistress the Queen of
    Bohemia'
    [Crum Y301]

b.150, p. 205; b.213, p. 28 (with extra lines?); see also
'Your meaner . . .'.

Y0351 You muses, we are your mournful weeds,
But wish if you may—ye blessed saints among.

fc.61, p. 132

Y0352 You must a little with her scorn dispense,
But she's my sister, give her humor vent.

    'Alexander [brother to Cleopatra] to his acquaintance'

c.189, p. 19

Y0353 You must in practice take the parts that are
How many parts your question do require.

    [Mary Serjant], 'Practice'

fb.98, fol. 92

Y0354 You my Lord Abbot, sit in state (I trow)
Forward and backward being both ways the same.

    'The same ['Abba sedes summus . . .'] Englished'

b.207, p. 8

Y0355 You need not care to know yourself Sir Volage;
But know that which is worthy of your knowledge.

    Sir Thomas Urquhart, 'That it is not always needful,
    nor for every person to study how to know themselves.
    A paradox. To one Sir Volage a man of no great
    consequence'

fb.217, p. 285

Y0356 You need not think it strange his face(?) should fail
To overthrow a stronger man than him.

    [Sir Thomas Urquhart], 'Of one [Jean] Lyon who in a
    three month's space had given the [?] to her husband'

fb.217, p. 388

Y0357 You need not wonder that her merit
Than which, no lighter thing can be.

    Sir Thomas Urquhart, 'Of a very wise, and judicious
    lady, who was something inconstant to a well-wisher
    of hers'

fb.217, p. 214

Y0358　You neighbors and friends I'll tell you what pains
In favors of his younger brother. | Fa la &c.

　　[Mrs. Christian Kerr], 'The quarrel, betwixt a country
　　esquire and his only son a ballad to the tune of You
　　Commons and peers'

　　c.102, p. 117

Y0359　You nurs'd me and burp'd me and hugg'd me 'tis true
A promise to make you a—martyr.

　　'The Duke of C[u]m[berlan]d's most gracious answer
　　to Lord Lovat['s] late address by way of [blot]
　　epigram'

　　b.54, p. 1243

Y0360　You oft to me have made your moan
I am with you, and you with me are still.

　　'A lover to [his] mistress'

　　b.62, p. 69

Y0361　You often have enquired where I have been
If for your satisfaction name the chief.

　　[Sir Aston Cokayne, 'To my son, Sir Thomas
　　Cokayne']

　　b.275, p. 108

Y0362　You often promise, but without effect
I'll e'en respect you, if you tell a lie.

　　'On a courtier'

　　c.546, p. 22

Y0363　You once did think to be a nun, but now
Under a vow you may lead out your life.

　　[Sir Aston Cokayne], 'To Mrs Frances Pegge my wife's
　　niece'

　　b.275, p. 78

Y0364　You ought not to intend his slaughter:
And fortitude's a virtue.

　　Sir Thomas Urquhart, 'To one who was about to kill
　　the man had ravished away, and forced his daughter'

　　fb.217, p. 238

Y0365　You ought to be Sir like the elephant,
As t'imitate the fashions of a beast.

　　Sir Thomas Urquhart, 'Here one reprehends her
　　husband for his licentiousness, and unsteadfast humor'

　　fb.217, p. 209

Y0366　You pay the man, to whom you rest not aught,
That of what you owe me, you may pay naught.

　　Sir Thomas Urquhart, 'To one who gave monies to a
　　lawyer, to suspend the payment of his just debts'

　　fb.217, p. 50

Y0367　You pensive souls, who lately by the cross
The living faith is chiefly comforted.

　　[Edward] Sparke, 'Poem 13th—on the resurrection'

　　b.137, p. 33

Y0368　You praise your mistress' charms, and swear,
And steals at once our eyes and heart.

　　'Epigram'

　　c.175, p. 88

Y0369　You pretty maidens all both great and small
Then maids take care of Mad Phyllis.

　　'Praise Capt. Maccan'

　　c.503, p. 64

Y0370　You rakes that are jolly, that never will marry,
Sweet Larry, my verses are added—are ended.

　　'Larry Grogan'

　　c.74

Y0371　You say I lie; I say you lie but choose whether
If we both lie then let us lie together.

　　'Answer' [to 'Say not you love . . .']
　　[Crum y336]

　　b.62, p. 16

Y0372　You say, my Fan! and seem to think it strange
The modest graces which to you belong.

　　'To Mrs. Crewe, when she was fifteen, on her saying,
　　no one had made verses on her'

　　Poetry Box 11/43

Y0373　You say, that in my lines you find
Will not perceive the light.

　　Sir Thomas Urquhart, 'To a critic'

　　fb.217, p. 114

Y0374　You say that some peculiar grace,
Is love of God, and love of man.

　　'A tale'

　　c.83/3, no. 1007

Y0375　You say that spite of all your zeal and art,
Shall join the choir, and heaven pronounce—Amen.

　　W[illia]m Dodd, 'An epistle to a lady by . . . chaplain
　　in ordinary to His Majesty [George III]' [Dodd was
　　executed in 1777 for forgery]

　　c.573

Y0376　You say the hare is not enough
You'd rather cut the cook than hare.

　　'Ecce nefas coctum . . .'

　　b.207, p. 11

Y0377 You say, the world is bad: yet by your means,
The world more badness daily entertains.

> Sir Thomas Urquhart, 'To a lewd man, who exclaimed
> much against wickedness'
>
> fb.217, p. 171

Y0378 You say, your lawyers travail make,
Have not her skill.

> Sir Thomas Urquhart, 'To a gentleman, whose
> bedfellow, and himself having several suits in law,
> employed but one, and the selfsame man, to prosecute
> their affairs'
>
> fb.217, p. 221

Y0379 You say, your left hand knows not what your right
Hand gives: it gives not aught: you say aright.

> Sir Thomas Urquhart, 'To one who was extolling
> himself, for being without ostentation charitable'
>
> fb.217, p. 243

Y0380 You scrapers that want a good fiddle well strung,
Young to play an old fiddle, and old to sell a new
song.

> 'Quibbling verses on John Young a maker of violins,
> and his son Talbot Young, a fine player on the violin'
>
> c.81/1, no. 499

Y0381 You shall not lie with me, unless that you
Subscribe it with the pen of procreation.

> Sir Thomas Urquhart, 'The speeches of a bride well
> affected to the covenant with her bridegroom's
> answer'
>
> fb.217, p. 197

Y0382 You shall not steal, 's enjoin'd to law practicians:
You shall not kill, to such as are physicians.

> Sir Thomas Urquhart, 'You shall not kill you shall not
> steal'
>
> fb.217, p. 270

Y0383 You should not for her lightness have disdained
The heav'n adorns, conjoineth with her after.

> Sir Thomas Urquhart, 'Here a gentleman is
> reprehended for withdrawing of his affection from a
> lady, by reason of her inconstancy'
>
> fb.217, p. 103

Y0384 You should not therefore slight at harmony;
Which both he spoke, and taught the Hebrew army.

> Sir Thomas Urquhart, 'To one who in his decaying
> years could not abide to hear music'
>
> fb.217, p. 166

You should not think her brutish in her love, Y0385
They daily move, that mankind may not perish: |
And so doth she.

> Sir Thomas Urquhart, 'An extenuating of the fault of
> venery, to one, who thought, that a certain wench of
> his acquaintance was too much addicted to it'
>
> fb.217, p. 217

You should perform more than you promise; for Y0386
As if you had two tongues, and but one hand.

> Sir Thomas Urquhart, 'To one rich in promise, and
> poor in performance'
>
> fb.217, p. 188

You sons of Sodom and Gomorrah Y0387
What shall become of men you need not fear.

> 'The battle of Libertoun fought by Jack Presbyter's
> viragos against Mr. James Dumbar's admission 7 Janr
> 1674'
>
> Poetry Box VIII/24

You speak no good: but ill of ev'ryone; Y0388
Hence no man pleaseth you: and you please none.

> Sir Thomas Urquhart, 'To a critic censurer, who could
> let nothing escape him uncarped at'
>
> fb.217, p. 301

You speak of love, you talk of cost Y0389
That enters there or ever shall.

> 'Her answer' [to an unidentified poem]
>
> b.205, fol. 95v

You stain your reputation Master Gilbert, Y0390
To throw away the shell.

> Sir Thomas Urquhart, 'To one named Master Gilbert
> who under promise of marriage, after he had
> depucelated [sic] a pretty handsome girl did care no
> more for her'
>
> fb.217, p. 77

You subjects of England pray listen awhile Y0391
I'll make thee my ranger of parks far and near.

> [temp. William III]
>
> fc.61, p. 61

You talk like simpletons: 'tis neither art Y0392
Have made them orators, and me a poet.

> William Middleton, 'Epilogue'
>
> b.210, p. 118

You talk of moderation! Sons of whores! Y0393
And shut your moderation out of doors!

> [Phanuel Bacon], 'Written on the outside door of a
> Presbyterian meeting house under Let your
> moderation be known unto all men'
>
> c.237, fol. 71

Y0394   You talk of reformation, desp'rate crew!
All, but the church, which, of all needs it least.

     'To the gent[lemen] at the Feather'
fc.85, fol. 81

Y0395   You tell me of a female pair;
Or else, say I, adieu! adieu!

     [George Legh], 'The clergyman's choice of a wife
delineated in a letter to Dr. C. in England, by a
foreign bishop, residing in Terra incognita' [pr. 1738
(Foxon L94)]
c.83/1, no. 251

Y0396   You tell me, Sir, you've got the gout
For I believe you cannot stand to't.

     [Phanuel Bacon], 'To —— who wrote me word that
his legs were wrapped up in flannel with a sore fit of
the gout'
c.237, fol. 84v

Y0397   You tell me the nation is all in a flame,
I'm sure I shall die in some eminent post.

     'Admiral Byng's answer to his friends who had s[ent]
an express to acquaint him of the public
resentment . . . June 10th 1756'
File 17486

Y0398   You that affright with lamentable notes
And tarries longer there and waits for us.

     [William Strode], 'On the death of Sr Tho[mas]
Leigh' [of Stonelly; d. 1 Feb. 1625/6?]
[Crum Y362]
b.205, fol. 63v

Y0399   You that are idle men, like me,
Had buried all the goose.

     'Michael Bowmer's stag turned goose, with some
account of the barbarous usage he met with upon his
changing sexes'
c.530, p. 65

Y0400   You that are she and you that are double she
Yet but of Judith, no such book as she.

     [John Donne], 'Elegy to the Lady Bedford'
[Crum Y366]
b.148, p. 75

Y0401   You that can grant or can refuse the pow'r,
Your chaplain then without your groats will pray.

     'A sea chaplain's petition to the lieutenants in the
wardroom, for the use of the quarter gallery by the
Revd. Mr. Tucker. In the manner of Swift'
c.382, p. 31

Y0402   You that can look through heaven and tell the stars,
I tread my fairest hopes, new born in grace.

     John Fletcher, ['Upon an honest man's fortune']
[Crum Y368]
b.197, p. 123

Y0403   You that have eyes now walk [i.e., wake] and weep,
James the peaceful and the just.

     Geo[rge] Morley, 'An epitaph on the death of King
James'
b.197, p. 51; see also 'All that have . . .', 'He that
hath . . .'.

Y0404   You that have seen within this ample table,
Which dost the match 'twixt Christ and us presage.

     [Joshua Sylvester, trans. Guillaume de Salluste,
seigneur] Du Bartas, 'Of the creation and comfort of
woman, marriage and epithalamy'
b.137, p. 105

Y0405   You that in punch and brandy take delight
And me as thy cups do now.

     [Anthony] Cumber, sr., of Tenterdon
c.158, p. 83

Y0406   You that love alehouses sing songs and tipple
And still maintain your old honored order. | Then
                          clergymen etc.

     'Upon the same [the restoration of St. Paul's] carmen
iconicum'
b.197, p. 184

Y0407   You that love mirth attend to my song
I'll see him hang'd up ere I'd serve him again.

     'Song 220'
c.555, p. 347

Y0408   You that profaned our windows, with a tongue
Know this was meant a poem not a tract.

     R[ichard] West[? or John Cleveland?], 'A poem in
defense of the decency of the Cathedral Church of
Christ in Oxford, occasioned by a Banbury brother,
who called us idolaters'
[Crum Y378]
b.200, p. 258

Y0409   You that think love can convey
Awake and see the rising sun.

     [Thomas Carew]
b.213, p. 2

Y0410   You that this horrid spectacle do see
Made an aunt's tongue the rope to hang himself.

     G[iles] H[ayward?], 'One upon himself, who pinned
this on his breast before he hung himself'
b.62, p. 93

Y0411 You that to write and judge are able
While she retains the softness of her own.

> [Matthew Prior?], 'A letter to Mr. [Fleetwood] Sheppard'
> [POAS V.107]

fb.70, p. 233; b.204, p. 73

Y0412 You that your face paint, may well nay must,
With Flaccus say, we shadows are and dust.

> 'Of painted ladies'

c.356

Y0413 You that your purse do shut, and doors do bar
(Heaven-citizen) as the good Hebrew did.

> [Francis Quarles], 'An exhortation to hospitality'

b.137, p. 195 and p. 121 (incomplete)

Y0414 You think him sure, who burns in his desire:
But he must needs be light, that is all fire.

> Sir Thomas Urquhart, 'That the ferventest lovers are not always the most constant. To Celia'

fb.217, p. 149

Y0415 You told me you lov'd me
For all lovers to see you to bleed.

> 'The dissembler'

fb.107, p. 30

Y0416 You Tories who the Whigs abhor
Or if 'tis right or wrong.

> 'On Whig, and Tory'

c.570/1, p. 167

Y0417 You trueborn Englishmen proceed
For we'll ne'er choose you more.

> [Daniel Defoe?, 'A satire dropt in our Parliament April 20th at Westminster anno 1701'; printed, Foxon B34]

Poetry Box IV/129; see also 'Ye trueborn . . .'.

Y0418 You tuneful birds, come teach my doleful quill,
Yet shall her love be 'tombed in my heart.

> [Sir Francis Castillion], 'Fancy in all is crossed . . . 17. Aug.'

fb.69, p. 236

Y0419 You want to know my dearest Tovey
Because you have a speckled belly.

> 'Epigram on Miss Tovey'

Poetry Box X/24

Y0420 You 'ware great cost, your vital thread to lengthen:
That, which you purposely debilitate.

> Sir Thomas Urquhart, 'To a lewd-living man, who bestowed much upon physic, that thereby he might better his constitution of body . . .'

fb.217, p. 119

Y0421 You were a Papist once, exceeding strict:
But now you're worse, for you are Catholic.

> Sir Thomas Urquhart, 'To a Roman Catholic gentlewoman, turned courtesan'

fb.217, p. 237

Y0422 You were on earth so exemplarly(?) modest
Than all the precepts of the godliest book.

> [Sir Thomas Urquhart], 'Lord [?]dale'

fb.217, p. 390

Y0423 You were the very magazine of rich
Thus his wise acts will ever him full speak.

> Lady Jane Cavendish, 'On my hon:ble grandmother, Elizabeth Countess of Shrewsbury'
> [Crum Y387]

b.233, p. 35

Y0424 You who o'er frozen Thames' smooth surface skate
Praise it, who pass it, I don't want it now.

c.53, fol. 22

Y0425 You who request this mournful lay
And most content when most retir'd.

> [Helen Craik], 'To Miss M. M.'

c.375, p. 83

Y0426 You, who shall stop where Thames' translucent wave
Who dare to love their country, and be poor.

> [Alexander Pope], 'On Mr. Pope's grotto [at Twickenham]'
> [Crum Y392]

Poetry Box VI/127

Y0427 You, who to forge lies think it graceful? Why
Hold you it disgraceful to receive the lie.

> Sir Thomas Urquhart, 'To vaingloriously talkative and quarrelsome soldiers'

fb.217, p. 44

Y0428 You, whom so oft, in early life,
Indulge the flow of soul.

> [William Boscawen], 'Horace ode 7. lib: 2. imitated . . . To Gen. Simcoe on his return from the government of St Domingo'

fc.106, p. 44

Y0429 You will wonder, my friend, why I stay here so long,
As was in beginning, is now, and shall be.

'The power of the fair. A familiar epistle'

c.382, p. 26

Y0430 You wily projectors why hang you the head?
When this come to pass God-a-mercy good Scot.

'God-a-mercy good Scot' [ballad upon the Parliament
and Scottish army, 1640; answered by 'Let
Englishmen sit . . .']
[Crum Y394]

b.229, fol. 131; b.101, p. 85; see also 'Come weavers . . .'.

Y0431 You wisely lurk: were't that you lurk, concealed:
But even, that you do lurk, it is revealed.

Sir Thomas Urquhart, 'To one, who all the time of
our civil wars, was obscure and not to be seen'

fb.217, p. 133

Y0432 You wives that are lately married,
Then the devil may have his right Sir.

'A song in the true blackguard taste. The blackamoor's
garland . . . a full and true account of an hundred and
thirty scolding wives carried away in one night's time
by a swarm of Indian blackamoors . . .' [pr. c. 1710
(Foxon J106)]

c.74

Y0433 You women that do London love so well
Lest honest Adam pay for Eve's offence.

'By King James' [counsel for ladies to depart the city
according to the King's proclamation, 10 Nov. 1622]
[Crum Y398]

b.197, p. 134

Y0434 You worms my rivals (when she was alive
Dead all her faults are in her forehead writ.

'On his mistress'

b.356, p. 264

Y0435 You would fain have me to be wise: but I
Should I desire to harbor her.

Sir Thomas Urquhart, 'One shows here to a friend of
his own the reason, why he studies not much for wit'

fb.217, p. 92

Y0436 You wrong heads, and strong heads, attend to my
                                              strains;
Tho' often mistaking the head for the tail. | Derry
                                              down &c.

'The heads: or, the year 1776'

c.487, p. 102

Y0437 You youthful charming ladies fair
Her death is our undoing.

'Historical ballad on Miss Susanna Holworthy 1721'

c.360/1, p. 233

Y0438 You'd have me say, here lies T: U.
And he's gone to receive it.

'Epitaph on an old covetous usurer'

c.360/1, p. 301

Y0439 You'll ask perhaps wherefore I stay
To wander far from you the center.

[Thomas Carew], 'To his mistress having stayed long
for her'
[Crum Y404]

b.62, p. 32; b.197, p. 237; b.205, fol. 45v

Y0440 You'll mind your life tomorrow, still you cry;
'Twill be both very old, and very dear.

c.93

Y0441 Young Bacchus when merry bestriding his sun
And himself most confoundedly drunk.

'Song 209'

c.555, p. 336

Y0442 Young, chaste, devote, rich, noble, fair | You are,
And wise: and if you be not proud | You're good!

Sir Thomas Urquhart, 'To a proper, comely, young
lady, whose endowments seemed to be starved with a
little haughtiness'

fb.217, p. 145

Y0443 Young Chloe whose slippery heart did ne'er prove
That ever must burn for her want of belief.

'Song'

Poetry Box I/111[7]

Y0444 Young Cleon was a sprightful swain,
And rallies smiles again.

'The conquest'

fb.107, p. 61

Y0445 Young Cupid I found
He like other puppies will drown.

'Song 22'

c.555, p. 27

Y0446 Young Damon once the happiest swain,
Our sex will e'er prove kind.

'10th song the timorous lover'

Accession 97.7.40, p. 16

Y0447 Young Dapperwit, a dull, unthinking soul,
The British church and throne.

'Verses made in answer to a copy in praise of Sr. Wm. M—ton'

c.530, p. 320

Y0448 Young Douglas was a parson's son
Broke her full heart and died.

W[illiam] S[mith], 'Young Douglas'

Smith Papers, folder 72

Y0449 Young Isaacs who lift up their eyes
Your great Creator mind.

Mrs. [ ] Vernon [on Caleb Vernon]

b.228, p. 56

Y0450 Young Jemmy was a lad
Poor Jemmy is undone.

[Aphra Behn], 'Upon the Duke of M——th supposed to be written by My Lady B. Felton'

b.105, p. 398

Y0451 Young Lubin was a shepherd boy,
Their common bed, the colder snow!

G[eorge] D[avies] Harley, 'Lubin and his dog Tray'

c.83/2, no. 631

Y0452 Young men fly when beauty['s] dart
Conquer love that run away.

[Thomas Carew, second verse of 'Ladies fly . . .'] [Crum Y428]

b.213, p. 2

Y0453 Young Orpheus ticked his harp so well
With her twinkum twatnum ranting canting
roaring ranting tongue.

'Song 159'

c.555, p. 242

Y0454 Young Paris was good Menelaus' friend
Cast Greece and Troy into decennial wars.

[Sir Philip Wodehouse], 'Paris and Helen'

b.131, p. 8

Y0455 Young rambling Cupid on a summer's day
Struck with love's bolts become his doting slaves.

[Robert Cholmeley], 'Death and Cupid'

c.190, p. 98

Y0456 Young Roger came tapping at Dolly's window
While Dolly's afraid, she must die an old maid. |
Mumpaty, mumpaty, mump.

'A song'
[Crum Y433]

c.536; c.555, p. 325

Y0457 Young Roger of the vale, one morning very soon
shouten
And who but thee and I | And who but thee and I.

'3rd song'

Accession 97.7.40, p. 5

Y0458 Young Strephon chief of shepherds and your pride,
True to our passion, to each other true!

'Noon a pastoral, to Miss *****'

c.89, p. 44

Y0459 Young Strephon, debonair and free
The pox ensu'd the grant.

'A more fatal request'

c.360/1, p. 125

Y0460 Young Thyrsis once the jolliest swain,
When all he sung and all he said, | Was *j'aime la liberté!*

'A song'

c.358, p. 149

Y0461 Youngest of our numerous race
And yield an heavenly crown.

F[rances] B[urney d'Arblay], 'On the birth of Amelia Maria Burney'

c.486, fol. 7

Y0462 Your Acon and Amyntas I confess
Fair/Foul farewell, and a chaste/curst conclusion.

Sir P[hilip] W[odehouse], 'My rejoinder'

b.131, p. 42

Y0463 Your admonitions will not break
T'a' belly without ears.

Sir Thomas Urquhart, 'Of the incorrigible humor of a drunkard. To a friend of his'

fb.217, p. 282

Y0464 Your aid (my Muse) this once I only ask
Here lies the only prince who left all evil ways.

'The man of no honor' [in praise of James II]

fb.108, p. 295

Y0465 Your anguish is infectious I confess
But know mankind would lose a friend in you.

'The reply' [to 'The answer by the Earl of Orrery': 'Nor Bath . . .']

Poetry Box x/76

Y0466 Your bane is pride for it alone you part
With peace, with comfort and a merry heart.

'On Mrs. H.'

c.546, p. 19

Y0467 Your Basford house you have adorned much
To both those Basfords you will show y'are heir.

    [Sir Aston Cokayne], 'To the same [Charles
    Cotton, jr.]'

    b.275, p. 89

Y0468 Your beauty engendered fame which breaking(?)
                                                  duty
Hath kill'd her mother your body fame your beauty.

    [Sir Thomas Urquhart]

    fb.217, p. 386

Y0469 Your beauty in your younger years did merit
The threats which fortune do to you menace.

    Sir Thomas Urquhart, 'The first epigram. To the
    Queen Mother of France, our Queen's mother'

    fb.217, p. 328

Y0470 Your beauty Phyllis like the sun,
That slaughter rates a victory.

    W[illiam] Aliffe, 'To Phyllis'

    fb.207/4, p. 29

Y0471 Your beauty tears the thoughts of men asunder
To join with you in bonds of matrimony.

    Sir Thomas Urquhart, 'To Lady Ann [crossed out]'

    fb.217, p. 248

Y0472 Your beauty'll not constrain us
Shines without heat.

    Sir Thomas Urquhart, 'To a comely aged woman, who
    was at all times desirous to be courted'

    fb.217, p. 307

Y0473 Your bed owes to my company
For I perceive, that he hath wept for it.

    Sir Thomas Urquhart, 'Dialogue betwixt a
    bridegroom and his bride the night of their marriage'

    fb.217, p. 366

Y0474 Your birthday past—unheeded too—
And even Dolben's natal day forgot.

    W[illiam] Smith, 'Copy of lines sent by . . . to late Sir
    Wm. Dolben bart.'

    Smith Papers, folder 73

Y0475 Your blessed self was even pure virtue's fame
So this mad chaos is for want of you.

    Lady Jane Cavendish, 'On my good aunt Jane
    Countess of Shrewsbury'
    [Crum Y441]

    b.233, p. 34

Y0476 Your boarding superiorly choice, and select
And what other blessings you mean to afford us.

    Ralph Broome, 'An advertisement in a newspaper:
    superiorly select boarding . . . the answer by Ralph
    Broome . . . X and his wife to YZ and his wife'

    c.486, fol. 33v

Y0477 Your body being at Dee constrain'd to die,
Their prince's statutes, whilst they live, obey.

    Sir Thomas Urquhart, 'To a kinsman of mine, the
    [crossed out] who was killed by the shot of a cannon at
    the bridge of Dee'

    fb.217, p. 313

Y0478 Your body being superlatively stored
At all times merit praise: and in all places.

    Sir Thomas Urquhart, 'To Lady Marie Stewart'

    fb.217, p. 343

Y0479 Your bold petition mortals I have seen
Unto the horrors of the alteration.

    'A gracious answer from the blessed saint to her
    whilom subjects' [to 'If saints in heaven . . .']
    [Crum Y444]

    b.197, p. 92 (incomplete?)

Y0480 Your breasts being hard, how is it, that
Below I'm beaten daily.

    Sir Thomas Urquhart, 'To a very lascivious woman,
    whose teats were in good case, and dainty'

    fb.217, p. 215

Y0481 Your calling is divine
Where lives the parson's wife?

    'Her answer' [to 'My calling is divine . . .']

    b.356, p. 309

Y0482 Your case is much the same as mine:
Trust God alone, for God is just.

    Edward Sneyd, 'Epistle 17th. To a friend, upon
    receiving a letter in which he complained on the
    coolness of his relations in supporting him with the
    common necessities of life, his spiritual preferment
    being small'

    c.214, p. 98

Y0483 Your censure of my rhymes, my hearing pierces:
As if you were the echo of my verses.

    Sir Thomas Urquhart, 'To a certain Momic taxer of
    my poesy, the sound of whose criticism, did but
    reflect, on the last syllable of the line'

    fb.217, p. 100

Y0484   Your charms, Camergo! dart delight,
       She, like the graces, skims the ground.

       John Lockman, 'On Mademoiselle Camergo, and
       Mademoiselle Salle dining together at the opera house
       in Paris . . . in 1734'
       [Crum Y448]

       c.267/4, p. 147; c.268 (second part), p. 99

Y0485   Your cheese we have eat, and a toast with it drank
       Jack Ketch do your duty, so tuck up the youth. |
                             Upon [Tyburn tree]

       'The Dutch bribe a ballad' [against John Cooper of
       Fife; printed, 17—? (Foxon D557)]

       Poetry Box IV/114

Y0486   Your compliments, dear lady, pray forbear,
       Give me but one, and burn the other nine.

       'To a lady who sent compliments to a clergyman upon
       the ten of hearts' [Dodsley Collection]

       c.487, p. 133; fc.130, p. 81

Y0487   Your conscience like the generous horse
       Secure, tho' dirty to your inn.

       'Hint to the scrupulous. An allegory'

       fc.51, p. 42

Y0488   Your counter's your fort and your surest plan,
       For from it you are more monkey than man.

       [ ] M., 'On Mr. B'

       c.546, p. 19

Y0489   Your courage, wit, and judgment this is true
       Example for great gallant souls that's thee.

       Lady Jane Cavendish, 'On my hon:ble aunt Mary
       Countess of Shrewsbury'
       [Crum Y452]

       b.233, p. 33

Y0490   Your crimes must needs be many 'nd capital,
       That in the sheriff's hand so oft you fall.

       Sir Thomas Urquhart, 'To the wife of a sheriff, who
       was a gallant gentleman'

       fb.217, p. 313

Y0491   Your dainty voice, and warbling breath
       When life's done, whither shall we go.

       'To his mistress'

       b.62, p. 77

Y0492   Your dalliance is so dear (upon my word)
       That ev'ry time, it stand you but a groat.

       Sir Thomas Urquhart, 'The regret of a certain
       nobleman, something struck in years, to his espoused
       bedfellow . . . together with her reply'

       fb.217, p. 206

Y0493   Your doctrine most sublime, and life but guile
       And walk before them, lest they go astray.

       Sir Thomas Urquhart, 'To Master [crossed out]'

       fb.217, p. 276

Y0494   Your every wish should fortune crown
       Who rais'd him up, to sink him lower.

       'Success and disappointment'

       c.83/2, no. 647

Y0495   Your face, and body's pale, and lean: so that,
       There's naught in you, save th'only spirit, fat.

       Sir Thomas Urquhart, 'To an extenuated fool'

       fb.217, p. 249

Y0496   Your face is a sweet mold for modesty,
       Thus you our nature's Bible, and the text.

       Lady Jane Cavendish, 'On my Lord, my father the
       Marquess of Newcastle'
       [Crum Y459]

       b.233, p. 4

Y0497   Your face the quintessence of modesty,
       Like lightning, will you charge upon his foe.

       Lady Jane Cavendish, 'On my sweet brother Charles'
       [Crum Y460]

       b.233, p. 4

Y0498   Your face, your tongue, your wit
       To serve, to trust, to fear.

       'An original piece'

       c.578, p. 85

Y0499   Your face's beauty is in tables drawn;
       And your worth out-Apollo represent.

       Sir Thomas Urquhart, 'To a young lady whose
       counterfeit by reason of her beauty was oft taken'

       fb.217, p. 271

Y0500   Your faculties heroic, so befit
       Did ever see a more accomplish'd woman.

       Sir Thomas Urquhart, 'To the Queen of Spain'

       fb.217, p. 191

Y0501   Your faith is not so great's to gain renown
       By miracles: nor to believe, what's done.

       Sir Thomas Urquhart, 'To a man of a weak faith'

       fb.217, p. 83

Y0502   Your fancy so substantially doth savor
       The one, no more, than th'other hath to give ye.

       Sir Thomas Urquhart, 'To a gallant woman, who
       without carrying affection to any did prostitute herself
       for gain'

       fb.217, p. 115

Y0503   Your favor being a paradise esteem'd,
Seeing you bar none, and daily lets in many.

     Sir Thomas Urquhart, 'To a very comely woman who
     was of too wenching a disposition'
    fb.217, p. 172

Y0504   Your fiery flame, your secret smart
Your love and you I both reject.

     'Her answer' [to "As flaming flakes . . .']
    b.205, fol. 94v

Y0505   Your first, was Clotho: your next, Lachisis:
But (sure) your Atropos, your last wife is.

     Sir Thomas Urquhart, 'To an old decrepit man in his
     third marriage, with a young, and able lady'
    fb.217, p. 297

Y0506   Your fortune? You are now too old,
The few red hairs, which deck your brow.

     'The gypsy'
    c.83/3, no. 884

Y0507   Your generosity and upright dealing
As almost kills the hope of imitation.

     Sir Thomas Urquhart, 'To the Earl of [crossed out]'
    fb.217, p. 86

Y0508   Your genius and your high descent,
Or lineal right inherit.

     'To the Prince of Wales upon his killing a wild boar'
    fb.68, p. 23 (incomplete)

Y0509   Your glorious virtues show that you inherit
Should be accounted, inconsiderate.

     Sir Thomas Urquhart, 'To my Lord [crossed out]'
    fb.217, p. 54

Y0510   Your goddess of the summer to adorn
Hymen, your flaming torch and hallow'd vest
                         prepare!

     'Verses under the pictures of the four seasons; for
     Miss Herbert . . . summer'
    Spence Papers, folder 113

Y0511   Your greatness is with clemency so mixed,
Cannot deny, but you are truly martial.

     Sir Thomas Urquhart, 'To the Earl Marischal of
     Scotland' [William Keith]
    fb.217, p. 305

Y0512   Your high descent, your virtue, beauty, stature,
Was never th'object of a man's affection.

     Sir Thomas Urquhart, 'To the Countess of [crossed
     out]'
    fb.217, p. 131

Y0513   Your high deserts made me peruse your name,
I could not choose, but end them with a King.

     Sir Thomas Urquhart, 'To General King' [later Lord
     Eythin]
    fb.217, p. 361

Y0514   Your husband claims your fondest care;
Fruits ever beauteous, ever new.

     John Lockman, 'To his dear daughter Bennett, with
     Boyer's dictionary . . . May 1755'
    c.267/1, p. 151

Y0515   Your husband gave to you a ring
A ring set round with hair.

     'Lady Tyrconnel's ring . . . World. 1788'
    c.81/1, no. 84

Y0516   Your inclination is so truly kind,
From the old bias of your constant virtue.

     Sir Thomas Urquhart, 'To my Lord [crossed out]'
    fb.217, p. 178

Y0517   Your industry the art to you hath given
And therefore never visit it within.

     [Sir Aston Cokayne], 'To astrologers'
    b.275, p. 77

Y0518   Your knowledge without virtue makes you proud
So leave to know the truth, and do the good!

     Sir Thomas Urquhart, 'A good scholar of a bad life'
    fb.217, p. 222

Y0519   Your leal for Mother Church is known,
Disgust us not with indolence.

     'An epistle 7th [to Edward Sneyd] from a lady at
     Birmingham who was reproved by the curate for
     stalking about the church in pattens in times of divine
     service'
    c.214, p. 24; see also 'Your zeal . . .'.

Y0520   Your learning, wisdom, action, piety
Nor more exactly doth the thing, he knows.

     Sir Thomas Urquhart, 'To the Bishop of [crossed out]
     a palindrome'
    fb.217, p. 76

Y0521   Your letter dear Pincher I duly received
So companions prepare for a rat which I smell. |
                           Anne Ashwell

     Miss [ ] Fleming, 'Miss Fleming's answer'
    fc.40

Y0522 Your letter I received
Where I did sit a Sunday.

[Lady ( ) Jacobs], 'Her answer' [to Sir John Hoskyn's
'O love whose power and might . . .']
[Crum Y471]

b.148, p. 6

Y0523 Your letter, Jemmy, full of wit
Shall be dear Jemmy ever thine.

Capt. [W.] Lushington, 'Epistle from . . . to Capt.
James [ ] . . . at Dublin'

fc.51, p. 276

Y0524 Your life and your actions, your nature degrade
And as for your beauty, soon it will fade.

'On Mrs. B.'

c.546, p. 19

Y0525 Your life is bad if you think't sweet, and dainty
But it is good, if it doth discontent ye.

Sir Thomas Urquhart, 'Of a good, and a bad life'

fb.217, p. 197

Y0526 Your life's the true example of a saint,
They would you crown on earth, and name you true.

Lady Jane Cavendish, 'On my noble uncle Sir Charles
Cavendish Knight'
[Crum Y472]

b.233, p. 5

Y0527 Your lines, poetic Sir, I read,
Convinc'd that you was fool or mad.

'From a lady to a gentleman in answer to a
complimentary copy of verses'

c.83/3, no. 965

Y0528 Your lips fair lady (if't be not to much
Rest in your midst where virtue doth consist.

'To his love'

b.205, fol. 3v

Y0529 Your looks are courage mixed with such sweetness,
For other name whatever would be thrall.

Lady Jane Cavendish, 'On her sacred Majesty'
[Catharine, queen of Charles II]
[Crum Y473]

b.233, p. 14

Y0530 Your looks contain the smiles of the Aurore,
Of all the world's most estimable pleasure.

Sir Thomas Urquhart, 'To the transcendent Aura'

fb.217, p. 71

Y0531 Your loss restor'd, exclaim no more!
Face—or else you'll lose again.

[Charles Earle], 'Advice given by me a conjuror, to a
person who had lost goods restored'

c.376

Y0532 Your meaner beauties of the night
As by the presence of the sun.

[Sir Henry Wotton], 'Song 49'

b.4, fol. 39; see also 'You meaner . . .'.

Y0533 Your memory a chronicle would make
That no man's pen, could ever praise too much.

Lady Jane Cavendish, 'On my noble grandfather Sr
Charles Cavendish'
[Crum Y477]

b.233, p. 30

Y0534 Your mind reposed, when of mighty towns
To trace in th'other a sublimer route.

Sir Thomas Urquhart, 'To a pilgrim who had
surceased from traveling, to employ his spirits upon
the composing of godly hymns'

fb.217, p. 170

Y0535 Your modern wits who call the world a star,
Will at last see to recompense her pain.

'To the same. The tears'

Poetry Box v/106

Y0536 Your Nottingham-ale, and Halifax-law
Oh Devil, I say, take Musgrave and Clarges!

['The Devil Tavern Club (1690)']
[Crum Y481; POAS V.166]

fb.70, p. 239

Y0537 Your nymph her temper keeps six cantos thro',
By God! It's more than half your readers do!

[Richard Brinsley Butler Sheridan], 'To Mr. [William]
H[ayle]y on his incomparably long poem entitled The
triumphs of temper' [c. 1781]

File 13565

Y0538 Your pedigree from princes is derived:
A subject, more superlatively loyal.

Sir Thomas Urquhart, 'To the [crossed out] of
[crossed out] when he traveled to publish the king's
proclamation against the covenant'

fb.217, p. 72

Y0539 Your pen with M[arlboroug]h's sword is much the
same:
Gold was his god of war, your god of verse.

[ ] Ham—n, 'To Mr. Pope on his second subscription
to Homer'
[Crum Y485]

c.233, p. 17

Y0540 Your person is too mean a cell,
But in the heav'n of beauty.

Sir Thomas Urquhart, 'To a woman, who though she
was still enamored with some one man, or other was
notwithstanding none of the handsomest'
fb.217, p. 211

Y0541 Your Phoebe return'd to her paces by rule,
Is learning abroad, and unlearning at home.

[Charles Earle], 'To Mr. Drake with his turnspit'
c.376

Y0542 Your picture fairest? why I ne'er believe
While Cupid thus hath drawn you in my heart.

'Upon a gentlewoman that would have her picture
drawn'
[Crum Y488]
b.205, fol. 28r

Y0543 Your precious time wisely today employ
For that will prove the best policy in the end.

[Mary Serjant]
fb.98, fol. 154

Y0544 Your present, dear Sir, came duly to hand
He will not forget when he sees London town.

'Answer' [to 'By the coach, I have . . .' ; London
magazine, Feb. 1776]
c.487, p. 90

Y0545 Your present to me, was so justly kind
Of comfort; that my father I shall see.

Lady Jane Cavendish, 'Thanks letter'
[Crum Y492]
b.233, p. 17

Y0546 Your Pulteney and Shippen, and such folks may rave
Tho' none in her administration.

'Wrote when Queen Caroline, was appointed Regent'
c.360/1, p. 17

Y0547 Your qualities are of such rare perfection,
Of all, that in the world besides, is best.

Sir Thomas Urquhart, 'To the Earl of [crossed out]'
fb.217, p. 355

Y0548 Your rebus good Sir is not hard to explain
To him I've resign'd the bottle I claim.

'Solution of [a rebus, 'The thing that is useful . . .']'
c.360/3, no. 217

Y0549 Your royal virtues in all men's opinions
Of greater worth, than all the Spains, and Inds.

Sir Thomas Urquhart, 'To the King of Spain'
fb.217, p. 223

Y0550 Your scoundrel rhymes (with much ado
Then I'm for you, and so good night.

'An answer to a copy of verses in Obse. re. 12:8 . . .
Oct. 23 1707'
b.90, p. 5

Y0551 Your second self enjoys the sweetest wishes,
Which cool the palpate of his burning passion.

Sir Thomas Urquhart, 'To the Countess of [crossed
out]'
fb.217, p. 346

Y0552 Your sermon preach'd at Bow
For shameless vice is want of sense.

[John James] Heidegger, 'Heidegger's letter to the
Bishop of London' [1724]
c.152, p. 23

Y0553 Your servant, kind masters, from bottom to top
Should you overturn him, you may overset me.

[David] Garrick, 'Prologue to Dr. Last in his chariot.
Written by . . . spoken by Mr. Foote'
c.68, p. 179

Y0554 Your servants now themselves to save
All day to give their characters of wit.

Lady Jane Cavendish, 'The charecter'
[Crum Y494]
b.233, p. 25

Y0555 Your ships are all taken, your merchants are stripp'd
Since no honor's now left in old England.

'A song to the tune of, Why should a blockhead have
'em so'
b.111, p. 510

Y0556 Your shutters no longer resound with the noise,
And prefer the young shoots of the tree.

[William Popple, trans.], '[Horace] book 1st. ode 25th.
To Lydia'
fc.104/2, p. 72

Y0557 Your sister Julia's married well and so
Sweetmeats (by the proverb) should have sour sauce.

[Sir Aston Cokayne], 'To my niece Mrs Isabella
Boteler'
b.275, p. 81

Y0558 Your sister virgins who your time improve
Must all the rest of womankind abase.

[Mrs. Christian Kerr], 'To two young ladies upon
their friendship'
c.102, p. 100

Y0559　Your skill is so superlative in grammar,
And parallels in prose the style of Varo.

　　Sir Thomas Urquhart, 'To Master [crossed out]'
fb.217, p. 83

Y0560　Your son's true worth (whom we lament as dead)
Perhaps needn't write twice more, before he die.

　　'To the Duchess of Ormonde'
fb.228/45

Y0561　Your sparkling wit in this champagne is seen;
The swain, possessing, and possess'd by thee!

　　John Lockman, 'To Chloe, in Vauxhall Gardens . . .
　　June 1754'
c.267/1, p. 148

Y0562　Your spirit should not be the more dejected,
To that which willingly you ought t'embrace.

　　[Sir Thomas Urquhart], 'That poverty is to be wished
　　for insofar as that we can hardly otherwise be
　　restrained from [?], [?] and [?]'
fb.217, p. 528

Y0563　Your steps to Langford Cottage bend,
But save the credit of the bard.

　　Dr. [ ] Crane, 'To a young lady on being desired to
　　describe the prospect from Mr. Whalley's villa'
c.83/2, no. 726

Y0564　Your strains in every breast such ardors raise
Or is the age with real Bevills blest?

　　'To Sr Richard Steele on his Conscious lovers, by a
　　young lady'
c.176, p. 44

Y0565　Your tale's absurd, quite out of modern taste
Since priests and females, prove there's no such
　　　　　　　　　　　　　　　　　　　　truth.

　　'Epigram to the author of Pamela . . . wrote 1741'
c.360/1, p. 93

Y0566　Your tender girls, when first their hands
Is always in our power to do.

　　'Upon marrying young by a woman'
c.158, p. 144

Y0567　Your thoughts in greatest plenty moderate,
That fortune may not find you unprepared.

　　[Sir Thomas Urquhart], 'It is the safest course to
　　entertain poverty in our greatest virtue'
fb.217, p. 525

Y0568　Your trickling tears (O friends) do now restrain
Tomorrow withers and doth fade away.

　　Cassibelan Burton, 'In obitum dominae Ouker
　　[Okenor] carmen funebre March 20. 1626'
Poetry Box VI/52

Y0569　Your valor promiseth the feats of Mars,
And the effects thereof, from none, but Wallace.

　　Sir Thomas Urquhart, 'To my Lord [crossed out]'
fb.217, p. 207

Y0570　Your valorous exploits rais'd from the ground
T'achieve hereafter things more memorable.

　　Sir Thomas Urquhart, 'To the French King'
fb.217, p. 291

Y0571　Your verses, complaisant, and smart,
Dote on a shadow, not on a swain.

　　'Carolina to Mr. J. M. on his verses addressed to her'
c.83/1, no. 254

Y0572　Your very childhood, t'all the parts and ends
You will augment the number of the nobles.

　　Sir Thomas Urquhart, 'The first epigram to the Duke
　　of York'
fb.217, p. 164

Y0573　Your virtue, meriteth a better place
Or in your traced footsteps will succeed ye.

　　Sir Thomas Urquhart, 'To the Countess of [crossed
　　out]'
fb.217, p. 131

Y0574　Your virtue notwithstanding the assaults
'Tis set upon by vice, it is the stronger.

　　Sir Thomas Urquhart, 'To the Countess of [crossed
　　out]'
fb.217, p. 260

Y0575　Your visage to mortality discovers
Are far more divine qualities enshrin'd.

　　Sir Thomas Urquhart, 'To my Lady [crossed out]'
fb.217, p. 110

Y0576　Your voices tune and raise them high
Sacred to harmony sacred to love.

　　[Newbergh Hamilton], 'Chorus Alexander feast'
　　[musical score for tenor and for bass]
Music MS. 534

Y0577　Your whimsical cradle,
Char: Earle, Cur——of Cull——.

　　Char[les] Earle, 'A fragment of a letter to my
　　b[rothe]r who had sent a dirty cradle (the size of a
　　basket) for Phil[adelphia Earle] . . .'
c.376

Y0578 Your wife doth paint herself so slovenly,
T'embrace an image, as did once Pygmalion.

> Sir Thomas Urquhart, 'To a gentleman, whose
> bedfellow was too often farded'
>
> fb.217, p. 40

Y0579 Your wife needs not for those horns have remorse,
Which is a virtue.

> Sir Thomas Urquhart, 'That a woman should not be
> sorry for giving of her husband horns. A paradox. To
> Cornuto'
>
> fb.217, p. 252

Y0580 Your wife on earth such pleasure hath received,
Because the Capricorn's a sign of heav'n.

> Sir Thomas Urquhart, 'His own good luck to come,
> and his wife's mishap. To a cuckold'
>
> fb.217, p. 344

Y0581 Your wife without command her will should have;
For she should not b'your mistress, nor your slave.

> Sir Thomas Urquhart, 'To a married man, how to
> govern his wife'
>
> fb.217, p. 165

Y0582 Your will did reason never yet abandon,
From all impurity of sin refin'd.

> Sir Thomas Urquhart, 'To my Lady [crossed out]'
>
> fb.217, p. 264

Y0583 Your wise philosophers aver
Tho' Lemuel is still the same.

> 'The comparison'
>
> c.172, p. 41

Y0584 Your worships, I beg you, (attend to my song
Backbiters and slanderers detected should be. |
Derry down.

> Poetry Box x/104

Y0585 Your worth is so deservingly enshrin'd
Wherewith to pencil out so rare a *mignon*.

> Sir Thomas Urquhart, 'To the Earl of Holland'
>
> fb.217, p. 219

Y0586 Your writing, your wit, little lady, is such
Will oblige your A[un]t P[e]a[r]d and your uncle.

> C[harles] E[arle], 'To his niece P[hiladelphia] E[arle]'
>
> c.376

Y0587 Your zeal for Mother Church is known,
Be questioned there about their pattens.

> Penelope P—e(?), 'The curate of ——— Church in
> Gloucestershire, who calls himself vice-rector, in the
> rector's absence took upon him to rebuke some . . . for
> coming to prayers in their pattens . . . Miss Penelope
> P—e . . . sent him the following epistle . . .'
>
> c.382, p. 36; see also 'Your leal . . .'.

Y0588 Your zealous ignorance doth oft dispraise
Where 'tis far worse to praise so much nonsense.

> [Sir Aston Cokayne], 'To Parson Dulman'
>
> b.275, p. 74

Y0589 You're fair of visage, in behavior gracious,
Than may suffice t'imparadise a king.

> Sir Thomas Urquhart, 'To Lady Jean [crossed out]
> before she was married to the Earl of Haddington'
>
> fb.217, p. 351

Y0590 You're married, Sir, from your abode
Your works will fail at home.

> 'On a rake who married a young wife'
>
> c.546, p. 22

Y0591 You're mightily deceiv'd, I swear,
May force th'imperious jilt to be his slave.

> 'On a happy life's consisting in virtue—[Flaminius,
> epigram] 5'
>
> c.158, p. 132

Y0592 You're old and ugly as a witch
When pleased you'll go without a spur.

> Poetry Box x/113 (incomplete?)

Y0593 You're the only child, that hath enriched, since
And is the glory of so tender years.

> Sir Thomas Urquhart, 'The first epigram. To the
> prince'
>
> fb.217, p. 98

Y0594 You're truly full of service this is true
Because each one, thy truth doth fully see.

> Lady Jane Cavendish [on a servant named John
> Procter]
> [Crum Y506]
>
> b.233, p. 26

Y0595 You're welcome from Craig's court
Hatch'd in our little nest | Dicky my dear.

> 'A new parody on Robin Adair from the first edition of
> Burn's poems, supposed . . . to be written by a young
> lady'
>
> Poetry Box XII/26

Y0596   You're welcome, my friend,
Nor e'er would she be | At the late coterie | [With]
a going [a going a going!]

[Thomas Hull], 'Pulpit and purchaser discovered in
auction . . . enter auctioneer'

c.528/16

Y0597   Yours I received. This comes to show
While t'other lies each month i'th' year.

[Thomas Gurney], 'In answer to a letter from Mrs.
M. B—y. Wherein she justifies the poem on the
mongrel preacher and desires to know who the person
is that is there fixed upon'

c.213

Y0598   Yours to begin in form in form received
At least have candor for a friend.

'To M. E—d T—le who desired me to write on the
following subject a letter from the same place
[Ewelme]'

Poetry Box I/50

Y0599   Yourself the only piece of nature's pride,
So all sex, cannot you, adore too much.

Lady Jane Cavendish, 'On my sweet brother Henry'
[Crum Y493]

b.233, p. 4

Y0600   Youth builds for age age builds for rest
But he that builds for heaven builds the best.

[epitaph, Peterborough Cathedral]
[Crum Y510]

c.158, p. 59

Y0601   Youth of the year, ah! who shall hail
And 'midst thy works remember thee!

S[arah] Herd, 'To spring, 1790'

c.141, p. 391

Youth's the season made for joy   Y0602
Life never knows the return of spring. | Let us
drink &c.

'Song 231'

c.555, p. 362

You've added hitherto, and multiplied: Y0603
But now t'express your zeal, abstract, divide.

Sir Thomas Urquhart, 'A counsel to a rich man
something skilled in arithmetic'

fb.217, p. 120

You've heard, no doubt, how all the globe   Y0604
And left the ark, like Noah, dry. | Tol de rol

'Song 134'

c.555, p. 188

You've heard of more than mortal jars,   Y0605
And end the conjuration.

[ ] Lewis, 'The masquerade'

c.244, p. 443

You've said my fair one, you would rather choose   Y0606
And dying saying, poor Celadon was true.

[Thomas Hamilton, 6th earl of Haddington], 'To
Florella epistle the sixth'

c.458/1, p. 17

You've so inflam'd his yard, that he may now   Y0607
Most justly say, he burns for love of you.

Sir Thomas Urquhart, 'To a courtesan of a favorite of
hers; on whom she had conferr'd the benefit of a
chaud'

fb.217, p. 273

Z

Z0001 Zadok the priest and Nathan the prophet
May the King live forever alleluia amen.

'Chorus [8, with musical score for tenor and bass,
from Handel's Zadok the priest]'
Music MS. 534

Z0002 Zealous for Britain, and to teach it sense,
Sent them back, cashless, to their native shore.

John Lockman, 'On the French players' opening, and
shutting up the same night, with a comedy entitled,
L'embarras des richesses'
c.267/1, p. 155; c.268 (first part), p. 19; c.360/1, p. 105

Z0003 Zealously practice what is good; and then,
Great will be thy reward in bliss. Amen.

'Lyncup Hill 12th Sepr. Anno Dom. 1782'
c.93

Z0004 Zelustus thinks his pains are worth his labor
Zelustus, that spend'st six, and keep'st but four.

[Francis Quarles, 'On Zelustus'; Divine
fancies IV, 91]
b.137, p. 182

Z0005 Zelustus wears his clothes as he were clod
Were nothing but a Christian out of fashion.

[Francis Quarles], 'On Zelustus' [Divine fancies IV,
103]
b.137, p. 181

Z0006 Zeno our paths to govern bide
To dangers manyfold.

'Chancery hand'
b.234, p. 37; see also 'Though vice hath . . .'.

Z0007 Zion enjoys a sacred rest
And sinners know the love of God.

T[homas] S[tevens], 'August 9. 1780 heard Mr. Sandys
preach from Acts ch. 9. ver. 31. (Wednesday)'
c.259, p. 99

Z0008 Zoilus, and Momus, with their numerous train,
These lines their author's monuments shall stand.

[John Rose?]
b.227, p. 190

Z0009 Zoilus doth grumble pray thee spare me not
Its men tie knots on ropes to make them hold.

[Sir Aston Cokayne], 'To Zoilus about a former
epigram'
b.275, p. 98

Z0010 'Zounds! Mrs. Reilly [Riley], what's come in your
head
The most successful—when we're pleasing you.

[Nicholas Rowe], 'Epilogue to Jane Shore'
Poetry Box x/156 and 157

Z0011 'Zounds what ailed our Parliament
And rogues like Tom of Danby.

[George Villiers], 2nd d[uke] of B[uckingham],
'Danby's corant to the tune of Black Jack. Wrote:
1678[/9] . . .'
[Crum z2, 'ails']
b.54, p. 1096; see also 'What the devil . . .'.

I. Index of Osborn Manuscripts Listed by Shelf-Marks

a.04, a.05, a.06, a.19, a.21, a.25, a.28, a.30

b.002, b.004, b.005, b.009, b.012, b.020, b.027, b.035, b.049, b.052, b.053, b.054, b.062, b.063, b.064, b.065, b.071, b.077, b.081, b.086, b.087, b.088, b.089, b.090, b.091, b.092, b.093, b.101, b.104, b.108, b.111, b.113, b.114, b.115, b.118, b.121, b.125, b.126, b.127, b.130, b.131, b.132, b.134, b.135, b.136, b.137, b.138, b.139, b.141, b.144, b.148, b.150, b.152, b.153, b.154, b.155, b.156, b.169, b.173, b.177, b.186, b.195, b.197, b.199, b.200, b.201, b.202, b.203, b.204, b.205, b.206, b.207, b.208, b.209, b.210, b.211, b.212, b.213, b.214, b.215, b.216, b.217, b.218, b.219, b.220, b.221, b.222, b.223, b.224, b.225, b.226, b.227, b.228, b.229, b.230, b.231, b.232, b.233, b.234, b.245, b.255, b.259, b.263, b.275, b.284, b.304, b.308, b.322, b.323, b.327, b.333, b.334, b.356, b.371, b.372, b.377, b.382, b.389

c.020, c.021, c.033, c.035, c.037, c.038, c.040, c.050, c.053, c.058, c.068, c.072, c.073, c.074, c.081, c.082, c.083, c.089, c.090, c.091, c.093, c.094, c.102, c.103, c.106, c.111, c.112, c.113, c.115, c.116, c.118, c.124, c.130, c.135, c.136, c.138, c.139, c.140, c.141, c.142, c.143, c.144, c.146, c.147, c.148, c.149, c.150, c.151, c.152, c.153, c.154, c.155, c.156, c.157, c.158, c.159, c.160, c.161, c.162, c.163, c.164, c.165, c.166, c.167, c.168, c.169, c.170, c.171, c.172, c.174, c.175, c.176, c.178, c.179, c.180, c.181, c.184, c.186, c.187, c.188, c.189, c.190, c.193, c.194, c.197, c.203, c.213, c.214, c.217, c.221, c.223, c.224, c.229, c.230, c.233, c.237, c.238, c.239, c.240, c.241, c.244, c.245, c.247, c.248, c.250, c.257, c.258, c.259, c.264, c.265, c.266, c.267, c.268, c.275, c.303, c.310, c.311, c.323, c.326, c.328, c.339, c.340, c.341, c.342, c.343, c.344, c.345, c.346, c.347, c.349, c.351, c.352, c.354, c.355, c.356, c.358, c.360, c.361, c.362, c.363, c.364, c.365, c.368, c.369, c.370, c.371, c.372, c.373, c.374, c.375, c.376, c.378, c.379, c.381, c.382, c.389, c.391, c.392, c.395, c.402, c.416, c.458, c.464, c.468, c.470, c.472, c.475, c.481, c.484, c.486, c.487, c.488, c.489, c.493, c.494, c.495, c.497, c.503, c.504, c.509, c.515, c.517, c.519, c.528, c.530, c.531, c.532, c.536, c.540, c.546, c.547, c.548, c.549, c.551, c.553, c.555, c.562, c.563, c.570, c.573, c.578

fa.04, fa.08, fa.14, fa.16, fa.19

fb.007, fb.009, fb.023, fb.029, fb.040, fb.064, fb.066, fb.068, fb.069, fb.070, fb.088, fb.098, fb.100, fb.106, fb.107, fb.108, fb.138, fb.139, fb.140, fb.142, fb.143, fb.144, fb.150, fb.151, fb.155, fb.206, fb.207, fb.217, fb.228, fb.230, fb.234

fc.009, fc.014, fc.021, fc.024, fc.039, fc.040, fc.046, fc.051, fc.053, fc.054, fc.055, fc.057, fc.058, fc.059, fc.060, fc.061, fc.073, fc.074, fc.076, fc.078, fc.079, fc.085, fc.093, fc.100, fc.104, fc.105, fc.106, fc.107, fc.108, fc.109, fc.124, fc.130, fc.132, fc.135, fc.156, fc.179

fpb.27, fpb.32

fpc.31

pb.47, pb.52, pb.53, pb.73, pc.55

pc.97

Files 00111, 00192, 00245, 00274, 00294, 00295, 01040, 01323, 01596, 01712, 01769, 01927, 01965, 02233, 02234, 02435, 02690, 02763, 03245, 03561, 03744, 03771, 03782, 03783, 03793, 03794, 03945, 04043, 04050, 04314, 04315, 04316, 04317, 04322, 04328, 04629, 05080, 05154, 05380, 05385, 05386, 05610, 05611, 05612, 05815, 06565, 06590, 06922, 06924, 06925, 06926, 06929, 06930, 06931, 06932, 06935, 06936, 06937, 06940, 06941, 06942, 06943, 06947, 06948, 06949, 06950, 06951, 06952, 06953, 06954, 06956, 06957, 06958, 06959, 06960, 06961, 06962, 06963, 06965, 06968, 06969, 06970, 06971, 06972, 06973, 06974, 06975, 06976, 06977, 06978, 06979, 06982, 07048, 07048, 07048, 07049, 07050, 07050, 07051, 07052, 07052, 07201, 07202, 07714, 07764, 07846, 09162, 09162, 09162, 09318, 09519, 10577, 10789, 10820, 11119, 11383, 11696, 11943, 11955, 11956, 11957, 12108, 12118, 12742, 12780, 13119, 13339, 13370, 13371, 13372, 13375, 13376, 13377, 13378, 13409, 13565, 13832, 13884, 13885, 14024, 14205, 14207, 14214, 14215, 14451, 14615, 15773, 16328, 16328, 16328, 16343, 16344, 16346, 16591, 16592, 16602, 16683, 16819, 16887, 16934, 16945, 16982, 16983, 17066, 17071, 17187, 17190, 17287, 17323, 17369, 17375, 17383, 17392, 17393, 17394, 17395, 17396, 17397, 17398, 17399, 17416, 17421, 17422, 17423, 17440, 17441, 17448, 17449, 17450, 17452, 17453, 17460, 17461, 17462, 17474, 17481, 17482, 17483, 17484, 17485, 17486, 17487, 17488, 17513, 17534, 17579, 17635, 17696, 17706, 17707, 17709, 17710, 17711, 17712, 17713, 17714, 17718, 17727, 17838, 17839, 17867, 17923, 17951, 17952, 17988, 18061, 18072, 19009, 19017, 19019, 19020, 19021, 19022, 19023, 19024, 19025, 19028, 19029, 19030, 19031, 19032, 19033, 19035, 19231, 19242, 19344, 19405, 19415

Music MSS. 003, 008, 013, 016, 534

Greatheed Box

Poetry Box I

Poetry Box II

Poetry Box III

Poetry Box IV

Poetry Box V

Poetry Box VI

Poetry Box VII

Poetry Box VIII

Poetry Box X

Diggle Box: Poetry Box XI

Poetry Box XII

Trumbull Box: Poetry Box XIII

Poetry Box XIV

Smith Papers

Spence Papers

Stair Papers

Accession 92.3.1ff., Accession 97.7.40 (not yet catalogued)

II. Index of Authors

A., [ ]: I1310, N0469
A., C.: I1194
A., J.: T1963
A., P.: D0072
A., W.: C0023
Abbotts, Henry, of Gloucester: G0320
Addison, Joseph, 1673–1719: H1167, K0058, S0547, T0852,
    T1264, W0766, W1099, W1258, W1551, W1773
Aikin, John, 1747–1822: A1026, F0556, F0704, I0685,
    I1566, O0315, P0182, W1518
Akenside, Mark, 1721–1770: H1437, S0168
Alcroft, [ ]: U0138
Aldrich, Henry: I0498
Aliffe, William: H1283, S0183, T1675, Y0470
Allen, William: W0440
Allnutt, Charles Atherton, 1767–1850: A0271, A0328,
    A0692, A1067, A1172, A1346, A1600, B0118, B0164, B0168,
    B0311, B0323, C0160, C0496, D0234, E0055, E0117, E0133,
    F0192, F0420, F0555, F0779, G0033, G0089, G0105, G0397,
    H0230, H0290, H0305, H0571, H1113, H1313, H1397, I0383,
    I0470, J0139, L0243, L0456, L0503, L0560, M0190,
    M0279, M0311, N0401, N0490, N0501, O0144, O0317,
    O0641, O0654, O0655, O0738, O0773, P0157, P0306, R0111,
    S0123, S0335, S0403, S0488, S1185, S1248, T1352, T1998,
    T2406, T2549, T2883, T2973, T3199, W0204, W0339,
    W0403, W0986, W1091, W1201, W1466, W1475, W1507,
    W1564, W1599, W1808, W1869, W1980, W1981, W1987,
    W2189, W2366, W2441, W2537, Y0242
Alsop, Ann: A1315
Alsop, George, 1625–1673: L0101
Altham, [ ], lord: W2601
Ambler, Mary: I0199
Amherst, Elizabeth: A1845, J0109
Amherst, Jeffrey, 1st baron,1717–1797: W1725
Amhurst, Nicholas, 1697–1742: A1826, H0115, H1453,
    L0046, O0182, S0709, T1052, T2087, Y0142
Andrewes, Francis: A0227
Andrews, Miss [ ]: A0279, A0590, A0838, A1285, C0331,
    F0166, F0390, F0469, H0341, I0035, I0380, O0310, O0622,
    O0743, P0048, S0752, T1025, T2504, W1677, W2023,
    W2358, Y0326
Andrews, Petit, d. 1711: F0248, G0154, G0193, H0325,
    S0827
Anselm of Canterbury, c. 1033–1109: W1400
Anstey, Christopher, 1724–1805: D0135, K0005, O0194,
    T1885, T2428, T2818, W0345, W0353
Apsley, Allen Algernon, viscount, 1616–1683: M0665
Arbuthnot, John, 1667–1734: G0027, H1446
Archdall, Richard: B0365
Archer, [ ], A. M.: W1823
Arden, Rev. [ ]: I1603
Armyns, Mary: F0585
Arscall, Henry: H0323
Arundel, Philip Howard, 23rd earl, 1557–1595: O0821

Ash, Thomas: W1604
Ashburnham, John, 1603–1671: W0094
Ashmore, John: H0389
Ashton, Edmund: A1696
Aston, Thomas: A0352
Aston, Walter Aston, baron, 1660?–1748: T0281
Atterbury, Francis, bishop, 1662–1734: F0316, T2498
Atwood, [ ]: I1135
Austin, John, 1613–1669: A1188, A1221, A1223, A1225,
    A1925, A1930, B0209, B0380, C0346, C0347, C0364, C0365,
    C0389, C0404, C0419, D0107, D0346, F0007, H1234,
    J0043, J0044, L0140, L0235, L0493, L0606, L0617,
    M0540, M0554, M0703, O0006, O1056, S1318, T0117,
    T2682, T3178, T3258, W0005, W0007, W2152, W2367
Austin, William, 1587–1634: H0973, O0830, S0392
Author, John: H0016, L0568
Ayloffe, John, d. 1685: F0724
Ayton, Sir Robert, 1570–1638: D0183, D0310, I0262,
    L0652, L0697, M0474, N0189, T0096, T2105, T2124,
    W0527, W1395, W2138, W2634

B., [ ]: H1399, Y0193, Y0312
B., A.: B0435, T3069
B., C.: L0552, O0688, S1255, W1883
B., Mrs. E. M.: S0633
B., F.: P0061
B., G: S0390, C0530, H0808
B., H.: W2454
B., J.: A0130, A0201, A0485, A0812, A1075, A1690, B0656,
    E0065, H0024, H1287, I0843, L0053, O0758, T0392,
    W0723, W0963, W1662, W2190
B., J. W.: N0339
B., R.: T0167
B., S.: A1077
B., T.: P0254
B., W.: A1796, I0002
B———, capt.: S0595
B——k, earl: A0035
B——ly, [ ]: F0750
B——y, Mrs. M.: S0982, T0807
B——y, N.: A0086
Bacon, Dr. [ ]: T0329
Bacon, Sir Nicholas, 1509–1579: A0293, A1379, A1427,
    A1684, I0738, I0740, K0071, L0318, L0368, L0557, L0558,
    N0375, O0104, T0523, T0930, T1338, T2856, T2902,
    T2937, W0362, W0468, W2171, W2300
Bacon, Phanuel, 1700–1783: A0006, A0102, A0103, A0156,
    A0174, A0195, A0200, A0280, A0331, A0340, A0483,
    A0566, A1065, A1137, A1271, A1491, A1606, A1639, A1773,
    A1778, A1847, B0005, B0232, B0639, B0662, C0166, C0533,
    D0110, F0313, F0526, F0595, G0039, H0513, H0604,
    H1064, H1204, I0404, I0622, I0660, I0739, I0845, I1270,
    I1447, I1615, J0130, K0026, L0094, L0166, L0173, L0190,
    L0264, L0641, M0278, M0653, N0038, N0042, N0116,

Bacon, Phanuel (*continued*)
O0735, O1004, O1005, O1139, O1147, P0080, P0309, P0351,
R0047, S0211, S0615, S0641, S0699, S0706, S0888, S1061,
S1134, T0049, T0063, T0195, T0249, T0305, T0783,
T1037, T1665, T1671, T1674, T1782, T1875, T1894, T1897,
T1982, T1989, T2249, T2285, T2336, T2341, T2370, T2371,
T2596, T2618, T2792, T3014, T3015, T3393, V0092,
W0213, W0648, W0707, W0763, W0810, W0854, W0867,
W0924, W1063, W1070, W1121, W1177, W1244, W1447,
W1674, W1931, W2121, W2272, W2569, W2575, Y0393,
Y0396

Baker, Daniel, 1654–1723: A0592, B0615, O0150, T2051

Baker, G.: S1124

Baker, Henry, 1698–1774: D0216, G0095, G0359, H0490,
H1450, I0799, M0555, T2871, T2888, T3054, W0185,
W2531

Baker, Sir James: A1640, B0157

Baker, Thomas, fl. 1700–1709: N0056

Baker, William: I0894

Balfour, [ ]: A1028, I0684, W0355

Balon, Dr. [ ]: L0066

Bankes, J.: H1157

Barbauld, Anna Laetitia (Aikin), 1743–1825: A1928,
F0507, G0228, G0393, H0492, H0581, H1179, J0026,
O0095, O0145, O0240, O0397, O0715, P0249, S0124,
S0277, S1300, T2507, T2713, U0004, W0193, W2307, Y0223

Barber, Mary, 1690?–1757: A0316, A1160, D0145, E0129,
F0035, I1353, M0016, S0660, S0816, T1819, T2720, W0158,
W1940, N0293

Barford, R.: N0521

Barker, Dr. [ ]: S0265

Barlowe, William: C0305

Barnard, Thomas, 1728–1806: G0285

Barnes, Joshua, 1654–1712: M0017

Barnett, Nehemiah: M0043

Barnseley, Rupert, b. 1683: O0011, T0879

Barrett, Stephen, 1718–1801: A1881, B0621, C0068, C0295,
D0106, F0755, I0901, L0682, M0435, O0023, P0129, R0158,
S0596, S0664, S1286, S1334, T2520, T2554, T2716, T3325,
W0623, W1210, W2230, W2335

Barrett, William: B0317

Barrington, [ ]: D0302

Barrington, George, b. 1755: F0634

Barrow, C.: T0836

Barwick, [ ], sr.: H0359

Basse, William, 1585–1653: M0333, R0134

Bastard, Thomas, 1566–1618: H0729, T2236, T2319,
T2502, W0300, W2047

Bath, William Pulteney, earl, 1684–1764: M0028,
M0188, M0361, O0408, R0102, W1907

Bayley, [ ]: A1761

Beattie, James, 1735–1803: A0320, A0804, A1781, A1851

Beaumont, Francis, 1584–1616: A0641, A1687, G0305,
I0266, S0627, W2241

Beaver, Herbert: B0270, S0991, W0966

Beckingham, Charles, 1699–1731: T2908

Bedford, Lucy Harington, countess, 1581–1627: D0200

Bedford, Wriothsley Russell, 3rd duke, 1708–1732:
S1387

Bedingfield, Edward: T0184

Behn, Aphra, 1640–1689: W0395, W1819, Y0450

Belcham, John: T2813

Belfour, John, 1746?–1805: A1563, A1580, F0710, I0338,
N0353, T0581

Bell, Beaupré: B0076, W2151

Bell, Betsy: A1023

Bell, Henry, capt.: R0213

Bell, Jane: A1023

Bell, Peter: A1023

Bellamy, Daniel, the elder, b. 1687: A1385, T0901, T0946

Bellehot, B.: T1707

Bent, [ ]: T1506

Bent, George: W0976

Bentley, Mrs. [ ]: O1164

Bentley, Richard, 1662–1742: W2026

Berenger, Richard, d. 1782: T1524

Berkeley, Henry, capt.: T2836

Best, Charles: E0050

Betterton, Thomas, 1635?–1710: A1871, W0605

Bickerstaffe, Isaac, c. 1735–c. 1812: T0514, W1069, W1120

Biddle, Henry: M0014

Bidlake, [ ]: I1443

Binchy, Jo.: T0829

Birch, [ ]: A0690, A0708, A1229, H1034, L0488

Birch, George: W0490

Birkenhead, Sir John, 1616–1669: U0058, N0471

Birkett, M.: H0170

Bishop, Samuel, 1732–1795: A0202, T1538, T3119

Bittleston, Thomas: D0086

Black, John: A0646, A0801, A1228, A1660, B0016, D0307,
G0146, L0280, N0526, O0922, T0827, T0832, T0839,
T0947, T0998, T1176, T1205, T1431, T1734, W0594,
W0851, W1386

Blackett, [ ], M. D.: T3058

Blackwell, Isaac, fl. 1674–1687: S0249

Blair, Robert: S0101

Blanchindley, Arthur: T0718

Blaney, [ ], lord: A0981

Blaxton, Henry: H0023, W0112

Blount, Charles, 1654–1693: I0630, N0249

Blyth, John, b. 1682: C0076, S1049

Bold, Henry, 1627–1683: C0181

Boles, [ ], of New College, Oxford: H1118, T0784

Booth, Barton: S1280

Boothby, Brook: O0174

Boringdon, John Parker, 2nd lord, 1772–1840: O0190

Borlase, Edmund, d. 1682: B0577

Boscawen, Frances Glanville, d. 1805: D0057

Boscawen, William, 1752–1811: B0445, B0637, C0134,
C0371, G0257, H0553, I0786, I0865, I1232, M0146, N0534,
O0030, O0177, P0035, P0149, S0879, T2796, T3082,
T3096, W0009, W0169, W0318, W0889, W1024, W1228,
W1356, W1713, W1761, Y0152, Y0428

Bosseville, Henry: M0623

Bostock, George, of Churton: G0418

Bourchier, Sir H.: A0547

Bowden, John, d. 1750: C0528, S1336

Bowden, Samuel, fl. 1753–1761: L0172, S0093, T0158

Bowes, Joshua: W1247

Bowles, [ ]: A0972

Bowles, William Lisle, 1762–1850: A1560, O0229, O0759

Box, [ ]: A0972

Box, Stephen: S1158

Boyd, Hugh, 1746–1794: H0523

Boyd, Zacharie, 1585–1653: A0588, T1644

Boyle, Robert, 1627–1691: N0016

Boyse, Samuel: F0581

Brackley, Elizabeth (Cavendish), 1626–1663: I0170, M0611, T1895, W1211

Bradford, [ ]: I0946

Bradford, Miss [ ]: A1937, D0266, L0511, M0053, O0362, S0003, T2033, T2660

Bradley, A.: G0051

Brady, Nicholas, 1659–1726: T2433

Bramston, [ ]: H0814

Bramston, James, 1694?–1744: W2059

Brand, Sir Thomas, c. 1669–1761: I0793, O0701

Bransby, Arthur: A1014

Brathwaite, Richard, 1588–1673: B0448, D0198, D0246

Brenan, Beaumont: T0733

Breton, William, of Emmanuel College Cambridge: T1812

Brett, Col. [ ]: K0015

Briggs, Samson, fellow of King's College Cambridge (1633–1643): W1498

Brinsden, Charles: T2628

Brisco, E.: I1177

Brittain, Thomas: R0189

Brockhurst, [ ]: H0710

Brome, Alexander, 1620–1666: I0315, M0159, M0287, N0063, N0522, N0524, T0542

Brome, Richard, 1590?–1652: N0305, S0473

Brooks, Dr. [ ]: W0200

Broome, Charlotte Ann: A1650

Broome, Ralph, 1743–1805: C0020, C0127, F0378, H0019, H0160, I0645, P0119, T0233, T0979, T1865, T2224, Y0476

Broome, William, 1689–1745: A0652, A1715, A1938, B0075, S1258, T0620, T0621

Brown, [ ]: H0918

Brown, George: A1865

Brown, Littleton: B0358

Brown, Rev. [ ]: A1825, G0403

Brown, Thomas, 1663–1704: A0299, A0864, A1197, A1200, A1535, B0048, B0680, C0177, C0451, F0603, I0640, I1021, I1144, L0278, M0021, M0055, O0816, T3209, U0117, W0744, W1227

Browne, Edward, 1644–1708: A1414

Browne, Isaac Hawkins, 1706–1760: B0407, C0567, L0417, O0694

Browne, Joseph, fl. 1700–1721: B0069

Browne, Moses, 1704–1787: S0744

Browne, Thomas: T2203

Browne, Sir William, 1692–1774: S0469, T0782

Browne, William, 1590–1645: N0035, U0049, U0050, W2504, W2519

Browne, William, b. 1682: W1250

Bruce, Michael, 1746–1767: T2712

Brydges, Sir Samuel Egerton, 1762–1837: W1538

Buckingham and Normanby, John Sheffield, 1st duke, 1648–1721: A0482, F0608, G0307, H1231, I1275, I1302, O0975, S0593, S1205

Buckingham, George Villiers, 2nd duke, 1628–1687: C0590, F0281, F0512, G0307, S0787, T1065, T2017, U0031, W0640, Z0011

Buckland, Thomas: W1588

Bull, [ ]: W1340

Buller, W.: E0075

Bulstrode, Sir Richard, 1610–1711: A0079, B0059, B0677, C0345, G0347, H0394, H1310, H1465, I0326, I0399, I1425, L0049, L0163, L0327, M0684, M0729, O0478, O1041, S1182, T0363, T1684, T2404, T2526, T3020, T3261, U0156, V0032, W0196, W0798, W0821, W1077, W1103, W1146, W1219, W1878, W2615

Bunbury, Sir Henry William, 1750–1811: A1605, B0652, I0538, S1357, W0381, Y0226

Bunce, John: I1552, T2979

Bunce, William: T2979

Burges, [ ]: W1874

Burghe, Nicholas: K0049

Burgoyne, Frances (Montagu), lady, d. 1788: A1566, S0449

Burgoyne, John, general, 1722–1792: W0934

Burke, Edmund, 1729–1797: A1711, B0303, H1309, O0388, S0189, S0990, T1219, T1538, W0662, W2570

Burke, William: T3035

Burlase, Sir William: T2959

Burn, Elizabeth: W0862

Burney, C. C.: F0133

Burney, Cecelia: D0367, I1258, O0294, O0407, S0651, T3197, W1755

Burney, Charles, 1726–1814: A1162, A1181, B0651, C0152, C0153, C0174, C0320, D0021, D0139, E0024, F0156, F0569, H0088, H1132, H1243, H1298, H1395, I0527, I0991, L0250, L0708, M0534, M0535, M0638, N0169, N0345, O0945, P0260, R0066, R0136, S0019, S0804, S1137, T0163, T0206, T0352, T0707, T0742, T1479, T1540, T2229, T2431, T2797, W1346, W1913, W2159, W2284, W2510

Burney, Charles, 1757–1817: A0618, A0655, A0710, A0758, A0774, A0779, A0783, A1424, A1815, B0013, B0159, B0398, B0571, B0583, C0325, C0575, F0568, F0621, F0780, G0127, G0138, G0140, I0543, I1388, L0124, L0268, M0131, M0189, N0299, O0283, O0289, O0323, O0471, O0602, O0796, O1067, P0075, P0293, R0093, S0068, S0071, S0236, S0368, S0585, S0606, S0913, S1140, T0124, T0166, T1196, T1375, T1722, T2213, T2767, W0029, W0054, W0253, W0257, W0659, W0667, W0968, W1129, W1161, W1405, W1543, W1550, W1769, W2305, W2415, W2425, W2426, Y0063, Y0167, Y0214, Y0234

Burney, E. F.: N0043, T0111

Burney, N.: B0244, C0587

Burney, S. E.: E0044

Burney, Sarah Harriet: P0029

Burns, Robert, 1759–1796: A0694, A1470, E0041, F0739, H0956, H0976, H1486, I0361, I1469, K0004, L0332, M0408, M0442, M0622, N0241, O0237, O0459, O0472, O0700, O0719, O0955, R0023, S0333, S0666, S0768, T0637, T0787, T0808, T1232, T1315, T1360, T1746, T2054, T2637, W0731, W0797, W1534, W1678, W1763, W2118, Y0077

Burrell, [ ], lady: A1311, L0286

Burridge, Richard, b. 1670: V0037

Burton, Cassibelan, 1609–1682: Y0568

Burton, Robert, 1577–1640: W1043

Butler, Samuel, 1612–1680: S1192

Butler, Thomas Hamly, 1762–1823: B0470
Butson, Mrs. [ ]: T3133
Byrom, John, 1692–1763: A0045, B0447, B0493, C0420,
    C0520, D0131, G0196, I0190, M0720, O0386, O0663,
    S0895, S0948, T0848, T1616, T1627, T3037, T3373,
    W0045, W0046, W2261

C., [ ]: B0134, T0851, T2442
C., [ ], of Kings College, Cambridge: L0133
C., A.: B0646
C., Miss A.: D0019
C., C. H.: I0841
C., E.: G0016, O0680, U0016
C., G.: D0171
C., J.: B0084, C0492, F0363, M0464, N0538, W1583
C., R.: A1459
C., R. H.: W1738
C., S.: B0281, T0654
C., W.: H0375, I1547
C———, [ ]: C0327
Cambridge, Richard Owen, 1717–1802: W0578
Campbell, [ ]: A1863, I0857
Campbell, Archibald: W2199
Campbell, Thomas, 1777–1844: I1133
Campion, Thomas, 1567–1620: B0356, I0616, L0507,
    N0096, T2001, W0452
Canning, George, 1770–1827: A1231, H0214, W1637
Care, Henry, 1646–1688: D0275
Carew, Thomas, 1595–1639: A0657, A1748, B0485, D0194,
    F0025, F0077, F0225, F0364, G0184, H0270, H0436,
    H0517, I0189, I0801, I0867, I1016, I1163, I1253, I1376,
    I1460, K0063, L0007, L0151, L0365, M0139, M0141,
    M0415, N0203, N0502, O0321, O0553, S0800, T0198,
    T1504, T1761, T1763, T1827, T1924, T2195, T2745, T3200,
    W0119, W1392, W1600, Y0409, Y0439, Y0452
Carey, Henry, 1687?–1743: A0988, A1942, F0323, O0440,
    S0776, W0664
Carleton, Joshua: I1056
Carlisle, Charles Howard, 3rd earl, 1674–1738: I0778
Carlisle, Frederick Howard, 5th earl, 1748–1825: T1899
Carlisle, George Howard, 6th earl, 1773–1848: A0389,
    A0825, A1323, A1335, A1794, B0433, C0009, D0273, E0001,
    F0489, H0133, H0155, I0690, L0713, M0663, N0235,
    O0764, O1154, S0064, S0312, T0409, T3309, U0082,
    U0084, W1053, W2075
Carlisle, Isabella Byron, countess, 1721–1795: W2535
Carlisle, J. D.: W0801
Carpenter, William, b. 1736: A0852, C0463, C0504,
    D0051, F0326, F0464, F0684, L0553, N0076, S0830,
    T0446, T2747, T3385, W0002, W0184, W0907, W1840,
    Y0310
Carter, Elizabeth, 1717–1806: C0388, H1426, H1454,
    I1179, L0130, S1118, T0934, T2090, T2095, U0094,
    W1687, W1748, T1253, S1302, T0852
Carter, John: I0368, S0601, T1658
Cartwright, William, 1611–1643: A0377, A0675, C0316,
    C0403, C0410, F0682, I1466, N0473, S0489, T0097, T1153,
    T1252, T1399, T2458, T2762, W0006, W1805
Cary, Thomas: F0155
Castillion, Sir Francis, 1561–1638: F0170, F0242, F0351,
    G0197, H0027, H0677, I0133, I0627, L0112, O1073, R0195,

T1490, T1850, T2439, T2730, U0073, V0061, W0154,
    Y0418
Cavendish, Lady Jane, 1621–1669: A0143, A0447, A0681,
    A1098, D0287, E0015, F0255, F0394, F0523, G0468, G0470,
    H1054, I0084, I0085, I0105, I0106, I0150, I0176, I0226,
    I0459, I0469, I0887, L0545, M0008, M0015, M0022,
    M0040, M0052, M0182, M0360, M0433, M0565, M0605,
    M0613, N0023, N0443, N0464, O1085, S0055, S0344,
    S0734, T0475, T1143, T1400, T1668, T1679, T1796,
    T1801, T1802, T1987, T1997, T2003, T2038, T2059,
    T2068, T2104, T2132, T2133, T2346, T2514, T2541, T2547,
    T2584, W0294, W0299, W0392, W1047, W1131, W1132,
    W1149, W1205, W1211, Y0269, Y0277, Y0303, Y0423,
    Y0475, Y0489, Y0496, Y0497, Y0526, Y0529, Y0533,
    Y0545, Y0554, Y0594, Y0599
Cellier, Elizabeth, fl. 1680: C0146
Centlivre, Susanna (Carroll), 1667–1723: A0583, S0270
Chalkhill, John, fl. 1600: T2066
Chamberlaine, Walter, d. before 1708: A0168
Champion de Crespigny, Claude, 1734–1818: B0528,
    Y0290
Chandler, Mary, 1687–1745: A1066, F0144, F0591, H1202,
    T1060, T3137, W2581
Chapone, Hester, 1727–1801: T2032
Chares, [ ]: I0540
Charles I, king of England, 1600–1649: L0623
Charles II, king of England, 1630–1685: N0240
Chatham, Hester (Grenville) Pitt, countess, 1721–1803:
    B0603, T2964
Chatham, William Pitt, 1st earl, 1708–1788: L0086,
    S0388
Chaucer, Geoffrey, 1340–1400: F0344, I1320
Checke, [ ], lady: T0248
Cheek, Thomas: L0690
Chesterfield, Philip Dormer Stanhope, 4th earl, 1694–
    1773: A0360, A0949, A1766, C0099, H0500, H0875,
    I0005, I0009, I0942, I1075, L0252, M0289, N0412, O0856,
    T0983, T1014, T2896, W0391, W0898, W1095, W1515,
    W1525
Chetwood, Knightley, 1650–1720: A1243, A1702, W0844
Cheyne, George, 1671–1743: D0362, M0713
Chichely, John: W1122
Cholmeley, Robert, b. 1706: A0385, A1154, A1418, A1433,
    A1439, A1568, A1599, A1608, A1646, A1725, A1898, A1949,
    B0100, B0105, B0385, B0561, B0624, B0638, C0038,
    C0074, C0179, C0467, C0521, C0534, C0540, C0541,
    D0009, D0105, D0148, F0105, F0304, F0360, F0401,
    F0606, F0627, F0729, F0767, F0778, F0782, G0432, G0458,
    H0042, H0124, H0783, H1151, H1323, I0408, I0428, I0699,
    I0721, I0723, I0741, I0750, I0882, I0948, I1030, I1385,
    I1508, J0036, L0055, L0059, L0246, L0248, L0431, L0678,
    M0031, M0194, M0424, M0589, N0067, N0215, N0217,
    N0226, O0962, P0097, P0311, P0330, P0343, R0096,
    R0234, S0051, S0104, S0244, S0362, S0543, S0563, S0626,
    S0657, S0683, S0705, S0801, S1129, S1229, T0142, T0325,
    T0501, T0843, T1009, T1029, T1874, T2187, T2926,
    T2935, T2974, T3059, T3159, T3172, U0154, W0047,
    W0410, W0541, W0591, W0716, W0772, W0782, W1008,
    W1088, W1178, W1229, W1282, W1368, W1411, W1426,
    W1645, W1646, W1694, W1711, W1724, W1999, W2249,
    W2304, Y0282, Y0455

Cholmley, Sir Henry, 1609-1666: H0970
Chudleigh, Lady Mary, 1656-1710: C0307, H0193,
    H0386, N0255, T3139, W0501, W2302, W2574
Churchill, Charles, 1731-1764: H0491
Cibber, Colley, 1671-1757: N0529, O0071, O0610, O0978,
    T3369, W0691, W1305
Cibber, Susannah Maria (Arne), 1714-1766: W0040
Clancy, Michael: A1351
Clark, Miss [ ]: I0100
Clark, P. [or E.]: I0194
Clark, William: T3118
Clavell, John, of Brasenose College, Oxford: I0393
Clay, Sophia Raymond Burrell, 1750-1802: A0866,
    C0321, T1549, Y0071
Cleggate, William, 1646-1688: F0547
Cleveland, John, 1613-1658: A1245, A1772, B0029, B0360,
    C0335, F0234, H0880, H0983, H1383, I0151, I0234, I0276,
    I0926, I1529, L0304, N0049, N0108, N0162, N0172,
    N0308, O0647, P0064, P0197, P0326, R0163, S0251,
    S0634, S0707, S0716, S0775, S1048, S1085, T0610, T1231,
    T1349, W0717, W1497, W1498
Clever, William, bp., 1742-1815: H0602
Cliff, Jeremy: B0015
Cobbold, Elizabeth (Knipe), 1767-1824: A0412
Codrington, Robert, d. 1665: W0590, W1974, W2288
Cokayne, Sir Aston, 1608-1684: A0104, A0363, A0489,
    A0554, A0678, A1042, A1086, A1283, A1630, B0020,
    B0086, B0108, B0111, B0410, C0017, C0509, C0554, C0582,
    D0038, D0082, F0111, F0189, F0476, G0059, G0449,
    H0278, H0300, H0628, H0641, H0681, H0689, H0716,
    H0742, H0779, H0920, H1102, I0282, I0309, I0405, I0746,
    I0826, I1116, I1172, I1595, K0003, L0220, M0030, M0059,
    M0167, M0173, M0306, M0356, M0600, M0610, N0088,
    O0073, O0085, O0162, O0953, O1093, O1137, P0021, P0120,
    P0270, Q0004, S0359, S0688, S0695, S0700, S0719, S0731,
    S0820, S0890, S1074, S1077, S1232, S1337, T0052, T0314,
    T0341, T1016, T1193, T1268, T1387, T1500, T1995, T2196,
    T2804, T2808, T3355, W0145, W0778, W0942, W1045,
    W1366, W1433, W1450, W1472, W1895, W1905, W1908,
    W2052, W2179, W2563, Y0270, Y0274, Y0307, Y0316,
    Y0344, Y0361, Y0363, Y0467, Y0517, Y0557, Y0588, Z0009
Coke, Sir Edward, 1552-1634: S0747
Coleridge, Samuel Taylor, 1772-1834: A1171, H0516
Colladon, Sir Theodore, fl. 1700: A1319
College, Stephen, d. 1681: A0034, L0260
Collins, William, 1721-1759: F0158, H0949, H1409, I0521,
    I1066, I1090, I1213, O0687, O0714, O0731, O0878, T1341,
    T2126, W1164, Y0140
Colman, George, 1732-1794: A0265, B0520, C0568,
    F0190, W0897, W1686
Colman, Henry: A1344, B0163, B0187, C0033, C0043,
    C0202, C0207, C0545, D0432, E0128, F0231, F0520, H0101,
    H1109, H1223, H1259, H1311, H1329, H1433, H1475, H1488,
    I0044, I0202, I0468, I1349, K0068, L0117, L0463, M0140,
    M0154, M0345, M0426, N0018, N0354, O0170, O1165,
    P0302, S0453, S0496, S0661, T0351, T0959, T1150, T1499,
    T2696, U0125, W0281, W0354, W0421, W0630, W0654,
    W1032, W1531, W1925, W2011, W2092, W2235, W2280,
    W2495, W2629, Y0061, Y0273
Colton, Dr. [ ]: I1363, O0098, R0095
Colvill, Samuel, fl. 1640-1680: A0671, W0812

Combes, William: A0802, A1891, S1309
Compton, Katharine: F0332
Concannon, L.: A0644, N0333
Congreve, William, 1670-1729: A0318, A0766, G0353,
    N0406, O0624, P0078, P0141, S0314, S0659, S0853, T2131,
    W0296, W1126, Y0023
Constable, Henry, 1562-1613: I1235
Conway, Gen. [ ]: S0636, S0639
Conyers, Rev. [ ]: L0465
Cook, Thomas, 1744-1818: A1588, M0023, N0048, N0377,
    O0931, T3132, W0359, W1695, W2582
Cooper, Dr. [ ]: L0460
Corbett, Emma: T3169
Corbett, Richard, bishop, 1582-1635: A0463, B0030,
    B0341, D0039, D0115, E0150, F0524, H0041, H0340,
    H1224, I0316, I0581, I1535, I1538, I1601, I1609, L0013,
    L0388, M0257, N0224, N0303, T0121, T0939, T1288,
    V0053, W0448, W1033, W1050, W1935
Corbie, Richard, fl. 1651: Y0062
Corfield, Frederick, fl. 1794: A0262, A0266, A0291,
    A0478, A0760, A0967, B0191, D0177, E0153, E0182,
    G0408, H0015, H0038, H1398, I0940, I0993, L0039,
    L0098, L0549, M0148, M0401, O0065, O0812, O0957,
    S0147, T0437, T0905, T1216, T1321, T1403, T1491, T2279,
    T2337, T2593, T2658, T2729, T2961, T3076, T3130,
    W0756, W1484, W1718
Cornwallis, Mary: A1912, F0604, I0545, I1341, M0434,
    S0993, T0974, T0999, T1235, T2542, W1522
Cornwallis, Sarah: O0944
Corwallis, Sir Jedd: H1274
Cottesford, Robert: E0034, G0215, O0566, O0768, R0081,
    S0792, T0779, T1006, T1432, U0019
Cotton, Charles, 1630-1687: H0538, H1043, H1180
Cotton, Sir John, 1621-1701: T0726
Cotton, Nathaniel, 1705-1788: D0062, M0469, T3161
Courtier, Peter Lionel: O0245
Coventry, Henry, 1618-1686: W1563
Cowell, John, 1554-1611: T0276
Cowley, Abraham, 1618-1667: A0300, A0586, A1301,
    A1302, A1576, A1856, B0098, B0390, B0602, C0303, C0471,
    D0327, E0083, E0163, F0267, F0301, F0311, F0432, F0444,
    F0657, F0670, G0049, G0150, H0119, H0195, H0225,
    H0489, H0568, H1008, H1129, H1144, H1145, I0069,
    I0123, I0231, I0547, I0561, I1475, I1518, I1520, I1561, I1596,
    L0486, M0208, N0257, O0175, O0281, O0470, S0546,
    S0864, S0937, T0062, T0550, T1064, T1837, T1891,
    T1896, T2098, T2259, T2468, T2740, T3087, T3166,
    T3211, U0080, U0141, W0263, W0265, W0266, W0830,
    W1732, W1962, W2014, W2165, W2484, W2561, W2595
Cowper, William, 1731-1800: A0189, A0778, A0871,
    A1192, B0227, B0273, B0413, B0560, F0478, F0744, H0479,
    H1278, I0021, I0023, I0026, I0299, I0320, I0350, I1202,
    I1352, J0016, J0094, L0639, L0657, M0005, M0169,
    M0573, M0689, M0708, O0005, O0514, O0516, O0664,
    O0686, P0054, P0066, P0139, R0215, S0406, S0580, S1013,
    T0153, T0356, T0412, T0625, T0858, T0862, T1004,
    T1084, T1161, T1594, T1676, T2041, T2510, T2635,
    T2918, T3284, T3295, W0683, W0738, W0857, Y0095
Cowslade, Thomas: A1251
Coyte, William: O1109
Crabbe, George, 1754-1832: S0381, Y0205

Crabtree, [ ]: T2869

Craik, Helen, 1750?-1824: A0578, A1818, E0114, E0173,
F0577, F0601, F0665, F0732, F0746, H0829, H0913, H0921,
I1040, J0114, M0199, N0411, O0092, O0921, P0040,
P0198, S0078, T0229, T0263, T0335, T0443, T1452,
T3181, T3320, T3390, W0536, W1423, W1757, W1775,
W2458, Y0281, Y0425

Crane, Dr. [ ]: A1142, T0802, Y0563

Crane, J.: S0999

Cranley, [ ]: S0925

Cranley, Thomas, fl. 1638: T1935

Crashaw, Richard, 1612?-1649: C0266, H1141, L0614,
T2016, T3084

Craven, Miss [ ]: T0156, T1237

Craven, Elizabeth, lady, 1750-1828: T1765, W1180

Crawford, W.: H0508

Creech, Thomas, 1659-1700: B0593, H0442, T1971,
W1889

Crewe, Frances Anne (Greville), baroness, d. 1818:
O0193, T2989

Crop, Thomas, jr.: O0618

Cross, Thomas, fl. 1632-1682: O0652

Crosse, Edward: M0532

Crowe, William: I1063, M0212

Crowfoot, [ ]: T1808, W0295, W0715

Croyland, Thomas Orby Hunter, lord, b. c. 1714:
I0864

Culloden, [ ] Forbes, laird: W1934

Cullum, Sir John: S0416, T3065

Cumber, Anthony, of Tenterdon, fl. 1704: N0206,
Y0405

Cumberland, Richard, 1732-1811: I0688, L0538, O0585,
P0334, S0891, Y0164

Cunningham, John, 1729-1773: C0422, F0423, I1237,
N0499, O0022, P0065, S1335, T0600, T1007, T1123, T3097

Cusacke, John, fl. 1615-1621: I0599

Cutts, Col. [ ]: H0076

D., E.: W1449

D., F.: W1621

D., H. F.: A1752

D., R.: F0165

D., W.: A0891

D., Z.: W1381

D——e, Mrs. [ ]: F0216

Daniel, George, 1616-1657: A0088, A0126, A1227, A1296,
A1305, A1306, A1910, A1944, B0042, B0043, B0051, C0031,
C0140, C0228, C0358, C0398, C0401, C0494, D0330,
D0431, E0005, F0008, F0123, F0310, G0084, G0098, G0132,
G0158, G0395, H1160, H1358, H1482, I0029, I0033, I0078,
I0109, I0110, I0147, I0208, I0337, I0881, I1523, I1537,
L0381, L0459, L0479, L0534, M0091, M0225, M0332,
M0461, N0057, N0095, N0176, N0184, N0210, N0211,
N0222, N0352, N0376, N0410, N0510, O0222, O0274,
O0277, O0426, O0434, O1118, P0143, P0192, P0195, P0213,
R0011, R0016, R0138, R0204, S0098, S0220, S0369, S0370,
S0765, S0786, S0840, S0846, S0861, T0064, T0420,
T0457, T0507, T1277, T1813, T2459, T2496, T2670,
T2699, T3292, U0101, W0004, W0063, W0198, W0316,
W0449, W0497, W0876, W1029, W1066, W1589, W1862

Daniel, Richard: R0190, W0051

Daniel, Richard, dean of Armagh, d. 1739: A0606,
A0731, A1318, B0406, B0551, F0708, F0723, G0399, G0405,
G0483, H0496, H0509, H1288, L0404, M0698, O0172,
T3066, V0083, W1598

Daniel, Samuel, 1562-1619: T0537

D'Arblay, Frances (Burney), 1752-1840: A0959, A1901,
B0152, C0328, C0426, D0022, F0719, F0727, G0107,
H0064, H0077, H0103, H0125, N0214, O0029, O0328,
O0453, O0705, S0142, T1048, W2167, Y0461

Darby, Charles, c. 1635-1709: O0965, T1047, T2727,
W0712, W1102

Darby, Charles, of Kediton in Suffolk: A1021

Dart, John: L0071

Darwin, Erasmus, 1731-1802: D0268, D0407, F0563,
N0491, W1225, W1571, Y0054

D'Avenant, Sir William, 1606-1668: A1655, A1714,
F0011, G0147, M0033, M0567, M0599, N0233, R0224,
S1022, T1436, T2827, Y0048

Davenport, Robert, fl. 1623: C0098, H1079, W1917

Davies, Dr. [ ]: A0947

Davies, Sir John, 1569-1626: A0207, A1378, M0353, S0959,
T0692, W0161

Davies, Samuel: T2057

Davies, Sneyd, 1709-1769: A0687, F0205, T1681, W2137

Davies, W.: W1309

Davis, [ ]: A0408

Davis, Thomas: T1755

Davis, William: B0279

Davison, Francis, 1575-1619: A1303, L0638

Davock, [ ]: W0687

Davys, [ ]: T0661

Dawkins, Caroline: T0323

Day, John, fl. 1637: T3036

Day, Thomas: B0339, W0892

De Fleury, Maria, fl. 1773-1791: T2969

Defoe, Daniel, 1660?-1731: S1021, S1199, Y0189, Y0221,
Y0417

Dekker, Thomas, 1570?-1632: T1125

Delany, Patrick, 1685?-1768: A0215, I1243

Delawarr, John West, earl, 1693-1766: Y0108

Denham, Sir John, 1615-1669: A0677, A0679, A0922,
A1456, A1529, B0596, D0263, G0455, H0007, I0037,
N0482, O0037, O0255, O0844, O1129, R0006, R0221,
S0730, S1263, T1947, T2042, T2206

Denn, Dr. [ ], of Trinity College: F0202

Dennis, John, 1657-1734: F0572

Dennis, William: I0836, I1225, N0423, S0011, S0818

Dering, Catherine: F0632

Derrick, Samuel: T2217

Devonshire, Georgiana Spencer Cavendish, duchess,
1757-1806: B0408, B0514, H0919, T0801, U0005

Devonshire, William Cavendish, 1st duke, 1640-1707:
C0016

Diaper, William, d. 1717: F0445, H0194

Dibdin, Charles, 1768-1833: G0166, S1243

Dickinson, Frederick: A0484, B0062, C0079, H0322,
L0497, W0195

Dickinson, Frederick, sr.: H0157

Dickinson, J. B.: A1918, B0668, E0094, F0781, I1322,
M0205, M0628, P0212, T1419

Dickinson, Jonathan: M0732

Dickinson, M.: I1613, S0239

Dickinson, Martha: S1130

Digges, Dudley, fellow of All Souls: W0539

Diggle, Mrs. E.: T0584

Diggs, Col. [ ]: I1340

Dixie, Willoughby: I0446

Dobbins, Joseph: L0480

Dobyns, Robert, b. 1665: L0240, S0545

Dodd, William, 1727–1777: I1278, T1059, T1347, Y0375

Doddridge, Philip, 1702–1751: A0607, A0830, A1059,
A1242, A1316, A1321, A1883, A1915, B0167, B0176, B0182,
B0193, B0213, E0124, E0134, F0209, F0211, G0431, G0450,
G0452, H0063, H0156, H0285, H0293, H0367, H1047,
H1257, H1261, H1388, I1186, I1421, J0057, J0069, L0423,
L0585, L0605, M0143, M0539, N0458, N0459, O0347,
O0442, O0826, O1055, O1088, O1135, S0223, S0260, S0347,
S0446, S0670, S0671, S0796, S1015, T0644, T0841,
T0845, T1915, T2065, T2410, T2485, T3070, T3163,
T3213, W1820, W1848, W2392, W2421, Y0233, Y0246,
Y0249

Dodsley, Robert, 1703–1754: I1359, M0105, S1329, W0187,
W1503

Done, Maria: A0911, A1153, D0155, D0410, R0153

Donne, John, 1573–1631: A0904, A0927, A1044, A1663,
A1691, A1836, A1948, B0120, B0362, B0461, B0559, B0642,
B0650, C0378, C0386, D0118, D0207, D0243, F0055,
F0206, F0368, F0387, F0395, F0412, G0124, G0129, G0340,
H0048, H0385, H0670, H0912, H0958, H0977, H1002,
H1408, I0051, I0052, I0072, I0079, I0136, I0166, I0240,
I0339, I0460, I0621, I0820, I0883, I0886, I0936, I0939,
I1456, K0033, L0034, L0177, L0362, L0377, L0630, M0003,
M0080, M0083, M0135, M0161, M0303, M0642, N0051,
N0252, N0359, N0517, O0275, O0462, O0720, O0951,
O1140, S0043, S0044, S0330, S0332, S0542, S0609, S0704,
S0721, S0851, S0923, S0958, S1007, S1053, S1072, S1364,
T0023, T0055, T1331, T2047, T2107, T2134, T2515, T2556,
T2589, T2756, T2934, T3110, T3333, T3353, V0026,
W0240, W0819, W1028, W1038, W1561, W1567, W2073,
W2074, W2076, W2418, Y0256, Y0400

Dormer, Robert: G0317

Dorset, Charles Sackville, 6th earl, 1638–1706: A0686,
A0722, A1389, A1833, C0222, C0412, C0599, D0014, F0270,
F0285, F0393, I1098, I1403, M0197, M0639, O0078, P0125,
P0127, P0130, S0484, T0081, T0561, T2608, T2788,
W1097, W1158, W2601, D0378, T1525, H0646, I1351,
N0003, W1930

Doughty, Miss [ ]: O0111

Douglas, Anne Capell Ingram, d. 1764: M0719

Douglas, Frances (Scott) Douglas, baroness,
1750–1817: F0188, H0071, N0106, T1792, T2793

Dowett, Edward: O1133

Downes, Robert, of Merton College: W1906

Drake, Roger, 1608–1669: T2353

Drayton, Michael, 1563–1631: G0293, H1346, I0304

Drenham, D.: T1316

Drew, Major [ ], of Exeter: N0208

Drummond, Francis: H1350

Drummond, Henry, of Balloch: C0143

Drummond, William, 1585–1649: F0713, I0220, M0625,
S0758

Dryden, John, 1631–1700: A0063, A0343, A0365, A0683,

A0915, A1551, A1708, B0248, B0418, B0573, C0014, C0092,
C0158, C0562, F0037, F0154, F0176, H1055, H1443, I0131,
I0426, L0547, O0094, O0456, S0749, S0793, S0863,
T0969, T0990, T1712, T2376, T2714, T3268, W0549,
W0625, W1607, W1619, Y0154

Du Bois, Lady Dorothea: S1173

Duck, Stephen, 1705–1756: A1377, B0429, D0244, I0163,
I0791, S0076, T0687, T1615, T1678

Duffett, Thomas, fl. 1674–1678: L0307, S0539

Duke, Richard, 1658–1711: A0685, W1293

Dunbar, William, 1460?–1520?: I1206

Duncombe, William, 1690–1769: N0182

Dunlop, [ ], of Glasgow: H0738

Dunton, John, 1659–1733: W0977

Duppa, Brian, 1588–1662: H0747, H0860

D'Urfey, Thomas, 1653–1723: A0926, A1313, C0249, E0155,
G0419, I0139, I0983, J0084, L0123, R0222, T1622, U0130,
Y0127

Dye, H. I.: W0781

Dyer, George, 1755–1841: C0382, H0559, T2633

Dyer, Sir Edward, 1543–1607: M0633, T0875, T1233

Dyer, John, 1700?–1758: C0269, S0518

E., [ ], lord: A0450, B0053, I0007, M0366, O0091, P0151

E., J.: B0280, C0005, P0180

Earle, Charles: A0092, A0308, A0410, A0420, A0596,
A0989, A1076, A1322, A1636, B0027, B0046, B0386,
B0676, D0024, D0074, D0142, D0157, D0160, D0161,
D0162, D0166, D0168, D0374, D0436, F0422, F0479,
G0284, G0391, H0906, H1191, H1318, I0059, I0065, I0092,
I0362, I0704, I1043, I1151, L0505, M0037, M0259, M0314,
N0112, N0113, N0115, N0340, O0942, P0018, P0085, P0140,
P0154, Q0001, S0703, S0733, T0622, T0663, T1028, T1180,
T1833, T1872, T1890, T2839, T2945, T3102, T3253, T3346,
W0506, W0531, W0574, W0583, W0593, W1624, W1863,
W2071, Y0099, Y0143, Y0531, Y0541, Y0577, Y0586

Earle, Dr. [ ]: T1522, V0009

Earle, William Benson: P0337

Earles, John, 1601–1665: D0304, O0820

Eckersall, James: I0633

Edes, Richard, 1555–1604: W2400

Edwards, Bryan, 1743–1800: S0161

Edwards, Samuel: I1598

Edwards, Thomas, 1699–1757: S1155

Edwin, [ ]: I0056

Egremont, Charles Windham, 2nd earl, 1710–1763:
B0127

Ekins, Jeffrey, d. 1791: E0172, G0141, Y0314

Eliot, John, poet: Y0260

Elizabeth I, queen of England, 1533–1603: C0201, I0146,
I1580, O0311

Ellis, George, 1753–1815: I1019

Ellison, [ ]: A0322, A1016, A1511, D0032, H0975, I1577,
O0633, O0661, T1322, T1530, T2138, W1195, W2567,
Y0166, Y0192

Emily, Edward, 1617–1657: W1680

Erskine, Henry, 1746–1817: S0080

Erskine, Ralph, 1685–1752: H0260, I1108

Essex, Robert Devereux, 2nd earl, 1566–1601: H0247,
I1579

Estrice, [ ]: A0981

Etherege, Sir George, 1635?-1691: A0668, A0718, A0769, H1148, H1240, I0613, I0700, I1533, L0674, S0549, S0583, S1362, T0085, T1010, T2922, W1235

Evans, Dr. [ ]: H0766

Evans, Abel, 1679-1737: L0320, R0043, U0043, W1329

Evelyn, Rev. [ ]: A1616, T2416

Evelyn, John, jr., 1655-1699: W2154

Eyers, [ ]: A1768, I0716, L0508

Eyre, George: A0040, A1740

F., E.: I1216

F., Is.: A1189

F., J.: I0668

F., M.: S0550, W0167

F., W.: F0548, H0111, I1122, N0135, T0635, W0679

Fahie, Anthony: O0888

Fairfax, George: W1510

Fairfax, Thomas Fairfax, 3rd baron, 1612-1671: H0024

Falconer, [ ] (= William?): W0581

Falconer, William, 1732-1769: W1549

Fanshawe, Sir Richard, 1608-1666: T1365, T2010

Farmer, Dr. [ ]: H1417

Farnham, John Newson: J0144

Farnham, Richard: B0567

Farquhar, George, 1677-1707: A0497

Farrell, [ ]: J0131

Faulconer, Dr. [ ] (= William Falconer?): B0346

Favel, John: A1274

Fawkes, Francis, 1720-1777: A1729, B0252, B0504, C0443, C0531, D0179, F0204, H0212, I0557, I0652, M0027, M0284, M0678, O0064, O0239, O0469, P0072, S0079, T0076, T0669, T1121, W0759, W1721, W2620

Feilding, Mrs. [ ]: A0429, C0053, G0398, H1242, H1448, I0082, I0086, I0544, L0359, N0396, O0595, P0189, P0219, T0074, T1732, T2022, T2036, W0568, W1169

Felltham, Owen, 1602?-1668: I0020, L0504, W0861

Fenton, Elijah, 1683-1730: A1063, M0427, N0430, W0122, W0208

Ferrers, Robert Shirley, 1st earl, 1650-1717: A0046, A0303, A0454, A0546, A0794, A0865, A0872, A0970, A1125, A1127, A1155, A1434, A1572, A1843, C0002, C0103, C0105, C0107, C0108, C0110, C0216, C0598, D0184, E0006, E0028, E0175, F0012, F0022, F0066, F0236, F0467, F0617, G0175, G0382, G0423, H0114, H0622, H0698, H1000, H1138, I0191, I0344, I0583, I0771, I1004, I1026, I1082, I1083, I1338, L0040, L0041, L0462, L0512, L0513, L0629, M0070, M0570, N0089, N0167, N0418, O0304, O0877, O1038, P0023, P0131, P0188, P0208, P0259, R0216, S0694, S1381, T0253, T0674, T0861, T0868, T1985, T2181, T2607, T2893, U0083, U0119, V0008, W0523, W0755, W1075, W1234, W1816, W1821, W1909, W1942, W2311, W2536, Y0329

Ferrers, Charlotte (Compton) Ferrers, baroness, 1729-1770: F0332

Ferrers, Laurence Shirley, 4th earl, 1720-1760: I1042

Fielding, Charles John: H0524, I1463, W1591

Fielding, Henry, 1707-1754: D0113, W1632

Fitz-Geoffrey, Charles: T0660

Fitzgerald, Thomas, 1695?-1752: G0476, I1293, N0155, N0223, V0045

Fitzgerald, William Thomas: T1285

Fitz-Osborne, [ ]: T2392

Fitzpatrick, Mrs. [ ]: F0460

Fitzpatrick, Richard, 1747-1813: A0351, A1276, A1627, T1289, T2583, Y0176

Flatman, Thomas, 1637-1688: A0242, A1569, O0675, P0077, W0958

Fleming, Miss [ ]: Y0521

Fletcher, Giles, 1549-1611: R0069

Fletcher, John, 1570-1625: A0641, C0136, H0552, Y0402, L0546

Fletcher, Phineas, 1582-1650: A1486

Ford, A.: W1117

Fordyce, [ ]: T0480

Forrest, Theodosius: C0329, T3266

Fosbroke, Thomas Dudley, 1770-1842: A0755, D0056

Fowler, William, 1560-1612: I0803

Fownes, Sir William, d. 1735: M0725

Fox, Charles James, 1749-1806: A1234, H0476, I0573, K0038, M0294, O0586, S0754, T1287, W1369, W1581, W2384

Foxton, [ ]: T0595

Francis, [ ]: T0936

Frasert, James: S1080

Frederick, Mrs. L.: D0083

Free, J.: K0064

Freeman, Isaac, 1712-1764?: A0663, B0012, B0633, D0033, D0080, E0137, H0062, H0074, H0144, H1013, I0064, I0414, I0559, I0973, I1499, M0317, M0710, P0095, T0092, T0690, T2938, T3160, T3164, W0800, W2439, Y0296

Freeman, Thomas: A0061

Freke, John, b. 1652: C0144

Fry, J.: A0934, A1730, S0645, T1053

Fuller, Dr. [ ]: S0960

Fuller, Thomas, 1608-1661: A0030

G., [ ]: W2329

G., [ ], colonel: T3123

G., D.: A1404

G., E.: S0718

G., J.: F0635, H0295

G., R.: O0802

G., W., jr.: T0377

G——, [ ], lord: F0483

Gainsborough, Baptist Noel, 4th earl, 1708-1751: O0097

Gainsford, John: A1667

Gardiner, [ ]: I0681

Gardiner, [ ], junior: S0925

Gardner, E.: S1305, S1331

Garrick, David, 1717-1779: A0024, A0122, A0194, A0476, A0577, A1168, A1484, A1502, A1509, A1779, B0530, B0609, C0466, D0008, E0170, F0127, F0160, F0490, F0671, G0061, H0118, H0648, I0431, I0634, I0770, I0784, I1318, I1454, J0120, K0054, M0044, M0324, M0357, N0068, N0126, P0042, P0228, Q0019, Q0027, S0082, S0588, S0955, S1241, T0279, T1276, T1778, T2274, T2452, T2744, T2838, T2941, T3151, W0243, W0709, W1185, W1630, W2387, Y0007, Y0553

Garth, Sir Samuel, 1661-1719: C0085, P0011, T2743, T3142, U0152, W0458, W0552

Garthwaite, [ ]: T1304

Gataker, Thomas, d. 1654: I0401

Gay, John, 1685-1732: A0921, C0035, C0077, C0086, E0111,
G0012, G0171, H1115, I0318, I0523, I1064, I1173, L0326,
L0669, L0687, M0373, O0053, O0584, O0600, O0674,
O0988, R0127, S0145, S0896, T1330, T2166, T3198, T3326,
W0485, W0974, W1921, W2628

Gay, Samuel, of Ipswich: T0728

Gibbons, Thomas, 1720-1785: E0125, T1026, T2609

Gibson, W.: S1103, T2278

Giles, [ ]: W2185

Gill, Alexander, the younger: I1478

Gilpin, Joseph: O0747

Gisborne, Thomas, 1758-1846: T0955, W1648

Glanvill, John, 1664?-1735: R0010, T2411

Glanvill, Julius: W0171

Glover, Richard, 1712-1785: A1549

Goad, George: H0927

Goddard, [ ], of St. John's, Cambridge: A0543

Godfrey, John: H0741

Godfrey, T.: W2619

Godolphin, Sidney Godolphin, earl, 1645-1712: T3148

Godwin, Edward: T0517

Goldsmith, Oliver, 1728-1774: T1508, H0633, H0727,
O0126, O0540, T3260

Goodwyn, Thomas, 1586?-1642: I0068, I0425

Gouche, Barnaby: H1440, L0415, S0442, U0148

Gough, James, 1712-1780: A0137, S0586

Gough, Richard: I0332, I1171

Gowland, Thomas, of Bryanston Street: T0434

Graham, Henry: H0636

Grange, John, fl. 1577: B0415, S0527

Grantham, Henry d'Auverquerque, earl, 1672?-1754:
C0341, C0375

Graves, [ ]: T1789

Gray, [ ]: A0880

Gray, Ralph: W1363

Gray, Thomas, 1716-1771: A1906, D0034, H0937, I1013,
N0507, O0840, O1156, R0238, T0441, T2582, T3301,
W1301, W2376, Y0034

Greatheed, Bertie, 1759-1826: W2142

Greatheed, Peregrine: A1591, C0069

Green, Molly: W1216

Green, Rev. [ ]: O1087

Green, T.: O0344

Greenwood, Dr. [ ]: O0265

Gregory, James, 1753-1821: O0744

Grenville-Temple, Hester Temple, countess,
c. 1685-1752: A1270

Griffin, Edward: W1683

Griffin, Lewis, d. 1676?: A1903, R0002, Y0120

Griffith, Elizabeth: W1603

Griffith, J.: M0048

Grogan, [ ], lady: B0606

Grove, [ ]: I0061, O0270

Grubb, John, c. 1645-1697: T1300

Gurney, Thomas, 1705-1770: A1718, A1738, A1947, B0124,
B0166, B0622, C0067, G0445, H0302, H1023, H1478,
I0502, I0530, I0664, I0794, I0840, J0129, M0084, M0186,
M0364, P0217, R0055, R0064, R0229, S0902, T1372,
T1957, T3126, W0984, W1336, W1352, W1697, W1717,
W1743, W2196, Y0597

Guyon, Captain [ ], fl. 1757: R0167

Gwinson, Miss [ ]: T1738

Gwyn, George: O0934

H., [ ]: W0845

H., [ ], jr.: T1514

H., A.: B0364

H., H.: I0511

H., J.: O0146, Q0008

H., M.: H1439

H., Miss M.: S1016

H., N.: T1776

H., R.: I0821, T1839

H., W.: T2063

H———, A.: I0922

H———, James: T0154

H——t, I.: T3029

Habington, William, 1605-1654: B0412, C0063, F0501,
N0200, O0797, T0376, W1560, W2173

Hackett, [ ]: A0811

Haddington, Thomas Hamilton, 6th earl, 1680-1735:
A0056, A0107, A0152, A0272, A0282, A0341, A0430,
A0438, A0442, A0518, A0827, A1035, A1148, A1304, A1398,
A1564, A1570, A1679, A1808, B0231, C0026, C0028, C0133,
D0055, D0158, D0339, F0153, H1353, H1474, I0272, I0546,
I0584, I0607, I0647, I0749, I0762, I0975, I1076, I1334,
L0514, L0518, L0528, L0529, L0694, M0165, M0211,
M0437, N0342, O0041, O0048, O0054, O0058, O0326,
O0346, O0976, O1058, O1059, R0177, S0592, S0629, S0648,
S0773, S0994, T0060, T0118, T0700, T0745, T1204,
T1249, T1269, T1405, T1597, T1774, T2030, T2170, T2221,
T2240, T2256, T2258, T2260, T2409, T2644, T2702,
T2734, T2940, T3053, T3189, T3322, T3350, U0001,
W0226, W0507, W0657, W0690, W0852, W1001, W1486,
W1606, W1613, W1661, W1665, W1771, W1801, W1903,
W2060, W2069, W2157, W2487, Y0606

Haddington, Thomas Hamilton, 7th earl, 1720?-1794:
F0484

Haines, Joseph, d. 1701: A0999, F0146, H1119, I0880

Hale, Sir Matthew, 1609-1676: B0564, L0162, L0283,
P0069, T0693

Halford, Jane: L0418

Halifax, Charles Montagu, 3rd earl, 1661-1715: A1409,
A1550, H0167, H0631, N0317, V0022, W0610, W1593

Halked, N. B., b. 1745: H0065

Hall, Dr. [ ]: L0609

Hall, Henry, of Hereford, fl. 1720: C0274, H0863,
H0863, M0024, T0695, T2876, T2881, T2956, W1926

Hall, Joseph, bishop, 1574-1656: S0795, T0820

Halley, Richard: T2402

Ham——n, [ ]: Y0539

Hamby, Nathaniel: G0066, T0336, T2466

Hamilton, Newbergh: Y0576

Hamilton, William: A0493

Hamley, Edward, 1764-1834: S0185, T2081

Hammond, Anthony, 1668-1738: H0141

Hammond, James, 1710-1742: C0435, G0148, H0473,
L0218, O0609, T0140

Hanbury Williams, Sir Charles, 1708-1759: A1300,
A1844, C0235, G0392, M0460, O0765, P0216, S0192, S1135,
T3269, U0071, V0040, W0374, W1894, W2187

Harcourt, Simon Harcourt, 1st viscount, 1661?-1727: W1002

Harding, [ ]: B0275

Harding, Nicholas: F0618

Harding, Thomas: F0576

Hardwicke, Philip Yorke, 2nd earl, 1720-1790: F0098, O0445, W1284

Harington, Sir John, 1561-1612: A0141, A0405, A0477, A0509, A1134, G0252, H0330, I1057, I1167, S0746, T3218

Harley, [ ]: W2161

Harley, George Davies, d. 1811: Y0451

Harper, [ ]: P0276

Harris, Dorothea, sr.: O0141, T2661, W2410

Harris, Joseph: T3319

Harris, William: H0190

Harrison, William, 1685-1713: F0461, H0140, L0119, M0283

Hart, J.: S0989

Harte, Walter, 1709-1744: A1927, F0121, H0201, M0335

Harvey, Anne (Montagu), lady: T0009

Harvey, Christopher, 1597-1663: A0842, F0083

Harvey, John, capt., 1740-1794: I0667

Hastings, Warren, 1732-1818: F0385

Hawes, [ ], the younger: O0940

Hawkesworth, John, 1719-1773: T2434

Hawkesworth, Lydia: S0508

Hay, [ ]: H0273

Hayley, William, 1745-1820: A0666, A0897, A1088, A1136, A1253, A1254, A1333, A1374, A1397, B0181, B0208, B0212, B0243, B0355, B0387, B0397, C0318, C0556, D0040, D0048, D0081, D0084, D0137, D0147, D0154, D0167, D0193, D0222, D0289, E0062, E0085, E0095, F0045, F0118, F0318, F0335, F0497, G0047, G0136, G0469, H0058, H0095, H0161, H0162, H0318, H1065, H1136, H1230, I0137, I0186, I0862, I1047, I1060, I1080, I1259, I1268, I1405, I1415, I1544, I1559, K0022, K0027, L0072, L0155, L0350, L0451, L0686, M0202, M0216, M0268, M0300, M0305, M0336, M0416, M0480, M0727, N0006, N0008, N0021, O0055, O0153, O0466, O0538, P0050, P0070, P0074, P0301, R0026, R0104, R0168, S0337, S0343, S0472, S0835, S1330, S1347, T0043, T0485, T1058, T1584, T1694, T1931, T2085, T2094, T2100, T2176, T2243, T2438, T2490, T2971, T3103, T3136, T3347, U0102, W0087, W0364, W0959, W1414, W1501, W2354, W2368, Y0022, Y0025, Y0069, Y0072, Y0073, Y0075, Y0086, Y0144, Y0198, Y0208

Hayman, Robert, 1575-1628: G0286, T3108, W1462

Hayward, Giles, fl. 1636-1641: C0041, I0081, I0824, I1223, O0465, W1990, Y0410

Haywood, Eliza (Fowler), 1693-1756: E0009, H1147, W2551

Head, John: P0290, T3377, W1573, W1806

Head, Thomas: A0729, Y0343

Headley, Henry, 1765-1788: S0498

Heappe, John: A1180

Hearne, Thomas, 1678-1735: S0647

Heath, John: T1889

Heathcote, Enesor: H0521

Hedges, Sir Charles, 1650?-1714: T1120

Hedges, John, d. 1737: T0558

Heidegger, John James, 1659?-1749: Y0552

Heighington, Musgrave: T0965

Hemings, William, b. 1602?: H0872

Henderson, J., 1747-1785: B0396

Henley, Anthony: W0301

Henley, John, 1692-1759: W0546

Henry, [ ]: A1436

Hepwith, John: W1780

Herbert of Cherbury, Edward Herbert, lord, 1583-1648: I0838, M0243, M0410, W0752

Herbert, George, 1593-1633: A0853, B0586, C0015, C0046, C0405, H0600, H1463, J0039, K0044, L0596, M0082, P0201, P0257, R0110, S1366, T0061, T0647, T0932, T2147, T2451, W0137, W2007

Herbert, N., b. 1688: A0701, A1618, A1635, D0077, D0100, F0633, F0691, H0590, I0288, I0410, I0930, I1545, L0457, M0582, N0498, O0086, O0627, O0959, O0967, P0289, S1379, W0373, W0596, W2096, W2568, Y0211

Herbert, Newcomen: N0496, T0280

Herbert, William: O1045

Herd, Sarah: B0427, I0138, L0301, L0380, N0147, O0723, P0009, T1927, T2111, Y0601

Herrick, Robert, 1591-1674: A0240, A0776, A1104, A1750, C0137, E0103, F0177, F0775, G0126, G0167, G0186, G0292, I0164, L0024, S0320, S0852, S0858, T2390, W1918, W2101, W2318, Y0349

Hertford, [ ], lady: P0224

Hervey of Ickworth, John Hervey, baron, 1696-1743: B0269, F0468, F0471, S0530, S0578, T2954, T3193, T3364, W1887

Hervey, James, 1714-1758: W1304

Hesse, J. A.: H1044

Hevell, Edward: W0844

Heylyn, Peter, 1599-1662: H1345, I1182, W2094

Heywood, Thomas, d. 1641: I0661, I1185, S0614

Hickes, Thomas, 1599-1634: S0510

Hickington, William: T1843

Hicks, [ ], of Christ Church, Oxford: F0615

Higden, Henry: B0023

Higgons, Bevil, 1670-1735: I1195, W1842

Higgons, Elizabeth: W2184

Hill, Aaron, 1685-1750: H1146, S0172, T0274, T3329, W1745

Hill, Theophilus, 1682-1746: A0536, V0030, Y0090

Hilton, [ ], of Gloucestershire: I1412

Hitchcock, Robert, d. 1809: I1549

Hoadley, Benjamin, 1676-1761: W1787

Hoadly, John, 1711-1776: A1462, A1595, C0070, G0072, I0931, L0407, T0824, T0944, T1244, T1733, W0833, W1342, W1734

Hobart, John, d. 1683: A0109, A0628, C0040, G0376, H1487, I0289, I0775, I1572, M0271, M0693, M0740, N0275, S0170, S0617, S0931, T0670, T0914, T1298, T1731, W0209, W1932, W1958, W2297

Holcroft, Thomas, 1745-1809: T3212

Hole, Richard, 1746-1803: O0717, T2009

Holiday, Barten, 1593-1661: T2686

Holland, Elizabeth (Vassall) Fox, lady, 1770-1845: U0057, W1401

Holland, Henry Fox, 1st baron, 1705-1744: F0026, O0793, T3191

Holland, Henry Richard Vassall Fox, 3rd baron, 1773-1840: T1800

Holland, Philemon, 1552-1637: A0948, T1950

Holland, Thomas, of Jesus College, Oxford: A1521, B0087, F0494, H0088, H0717, M0297, N0324, O0035, W1555

Hooke, Thomas: Y0313

Hoole, John, 1727-1803: H0045

Hopkins, Charles, 1664?-1700?: A0492, F0622, H1053, H1438, P0338, R0034, S0812, S1094, T0874, T1422, T2500, T3062, Y0216

Hopkins, John, d. 1570: A0930, B0404, G0078, G0109, G0244, G0480, H0342, H0345, H1476, I0416, I0458, J0122, L0554, L0592, M0696, O0250, O0336, O0355, O0496, O0498, O0621, P0361, R0094, S0059, S0673, T0039, T0850, T2044, W2122, Y0150

Horne, George, bishop, 1730-1792: A0253, E0054, M0398, T0372, T0543, T2425, T2426, W1403, W2463

Horsley, [ ]: N0131

Hoskins, John, 1566- 1638: M0166, A0589, D0390, O0515, P0352, Q0029, R0051, R0056, S1287

Hoskins, Mrs. [John]: T1505

How, John: D0317

Howard, [ ]: F0628

Howard, Anne: I1198

Howard, Henry: A0159, I1052, T0697

Howard, Sir Robert: A1872, I1368, S0528

Howard, Samuel: C0214

Howe, John: B0025, W0482

Howe, John Grubham, 1629-1703: L0047

Howell, J.: H0073

Howell, J., jr.: W2505

Howell, James, 1594?-1666: A1623

Howson, John: G0118

Hubert, Sir Francis, d. 1629: I0379, T3382

Hubert, Sir Harry: S1041, T0264

Huddesford, [ ]: A1507, B0304, F0380

Huddesford, George, 1749-1809: N0466, Y0174

Hughes, [ ]: O0266

Hughes, Henry: H0550, I0317, O0569, S0245, T0022

Hughes, Jabez, 1685-1731: F0642

Hughes, John, 1677-1720: C0077, C0086, G0012, I0318, I1395, L0687, M0373, O0600, O0674, T3198, W0485, W1921, W2628

Hull, Thomas, 1728-1808: A0021, A0387, A0585, A0649, A1277, B0067, B0276, B0643, C0247, C0319, C0421, D0232, D0241, F0096, G0116, H0495, H0567, H0974, H1123, H1498, I1204, I1323, I1464, L0442, L0526, N0476, O0379, O1000, P0016, P0354, R0037, S0065, S0279, S0877, S1065, S1361, T0109, T0126, T0344, T0533, T1946, T1968, T2737, T2913, W0011, W0431, W0635, W1238, W1511, W1631, W1685, W2317, W2541, Y0596

Humphreys, David: A0899

Hunter, Anne (Home), 1742-1821: I0352, T1327, T2597

Huntington, Robert, d. 1701: O1001

Hurd, Dr. [ ]: B0058

Hutton, Hugh: S1159

Hutton, James: H0452

Hynard, Mrs. [ ]: I1607

I., [ ]: F0132

Ibbot, Benjamin, 1680-1725: F0182

Instry, G.: M0291

Irwin, Isabella (Machell) Ingram, viscountess, 1670-1764: B0617, I0513, T2180

Irye, [ ]: S1035

Ives, Miss [ ]: W1532

Ives, Simon, 1600-1662: S0346

J., E.: L0520

J., E. S.: L0351, T2056

Jackett, William: I0144

Jackson, [ ]: A0043, W1275

Jackson, William, 1730-1803: A1579, B0171, B0260, F0688, W2338

Jacobs, [ ]: A0247, A1367

Jacobs, [ ], lady: Y0522

Jago, Richard, 1715-1781: T2976

James I, king of England, 1566-1621: O0631, T1543, W1424, S0252

Jay, Sir Thomas: T2516

Jeffery, Samuel: R0053

Jeffreys, Betty: T3131

Jeffreys, George: S1228

Jekyll, Elizabeth: D0212, F0229, L0242

Jekyll, Joseph, d. 1837: W0743

Jelliand, John, of Brundish: T2025

Jenyns, Soame,1704-1787: A1252, C0507, F0063, F0426, F0453, H0014, H0811, I1033, I1045, J0137, M0417, O0946, P0207, S0630, T1395, T3190, W0913, W1818, W1880, W1891, W1900, W1916, W2030, W2294, W2403

Jephson, [ ]: B0670

Jerningham, Edward, 1727-1812: E0066, I1428, L0449, M0144, O0615, T2497

Jersey, Edward Villiers, 1st earl, 1656?-1711: A1577

Jessop, Miss [ ]: T0995, T2296

Johnson, [ ]: R0090, W2291, W2600

Johnson, Esther, 1683-1728: O0617

Johnson, J.: O0083

Johnson, John: I1610, W0035

Johnson, M.: T2430

Johnson, Maurice, 1688-1755: A0080, A0364, A1012, A1510, A1638, B0089, B0497, D0347, F0728, G0028, I0196, I0285, I0649, L0501, M0204, N0019, N0310, N0537, O0651, O0729, S0323, S0331, S0790, S0843, S0849, S0917, S1018, T0020, T1294, T1824, T2664, T2925, T3038, U0059, V0046, V0086, W0563, W0980, W1143, W1328, W1865, W1888, W1914

Johnson, Samuel, 1709-1784: B0160, C0462, F0589, H0810, H1015, H1413, I0237, I1007, L0681, O0013, O0018, P0111, S0034, T0708, T1242, T1354, W0444

Jones, [ ]: T3083

Jones, Miss [ ]: T2872

Jones, Christopher: L0464

Jones, Henry, bricklayer, 1721-1770: I1288, T2998

Jones, J., of Balliol: F0664

Jones, Mary: W1243

Jones, Molly: C0170

Jones, Sir William, 1746-1794: A0714, F0060, H0504, O0914, S0349, S1324, W0012, W0573

Jonson, Ben, 1573?-1637: C0112, C0397, C0502, D0343, D0386, F0406, H0185, H0355, H0734, I0173, I0609, M0224, N0421, O0276, Q0002, R0147, S0100, S0253,

Jonson, Ben (*continued*)

    S0739, S1093, S1123, T1366, T3171, U0053, W0034, W0653, W1432, W2326

Jordan, Thomas, 1612?–1685?: C0237, L0291

K., J.: F0474

K., M.: S0109

K., R.: A1523

K——lly, Mrs. [ ]: G0466

Kempt, Joseph: H1444

Ken, Thomas, 1637–1711: A1923

Kendall, [ ]: W2275

Kendel, [ ]: S0763, S1030

Kennedy, Elizabeth: I0354

Kennick, [ ]: L0467

Kennicott, Benjamin: W2374

Kenrick, Daniel: T0695

Kerr, John, of Frogden: F0005

Kerr, Mrs. Christian, b. 1679: A0067, A0513, A0839, A1109, A1895, B0417, B0501, B0574, C0071, C0129, C0257, F0334, G0019, H1210, H1221, H1289, H1467, I0451, I0551, I1332, I1498, I1588, I1589, L0403, M0288, N0263, O0889, O0909, O0949, S0272, S0622, S0655, S1209, S1252, T1822, T2023, T2185, T2194, T2244, T2293, T2295, T2545, T2546, T2852, T3182, U0020, V0015, W0326, W0396, W0576, W1397, W2135, W2299, W2513, Y0280, Y0358, Y0558

Kethe, William, d. 1608?: G0109, O0495, W2416

Keymes, Sir Charles, 1651–1702: W2373

Kidgell, John, b. 1722: H0006, W1137

King, [ ]: T0880

King, Dr. [ ]: F0570

King, Daniel: I0167, J0014, W1203, Y0047

King, Henry, 1592–1669: A0621, B0351, B0580, F0157, G0407, I0858, L0191, L0354, L0392, S0009, T0093, T0123, W0469, W2259

King, Joseph: W1489

King, William, D. C. L., 1663–1712: F0672

Kingsman, [ ]: N0301, T2779

Kinwelmarsh, Francis, d. 1580?: O0402

Knight, Miss [ ]: A0296

Knight, Ellis Cornelia, 1757–1837: O0189

Knight, J.: W0571

Knowles, Mary, 1733–1807: D0030

Kynaston, [ ]: O0138

L, W., jr.: O0836

L., A.: C0427

L., G. W., jr.: I0969

Lacke, Mrs. [ ]: H0968

Lackington, [ ]: L0017

Lakes, William: A0004, R0169

Laney, [ ]: A1393

Langham, Sir James, 2nd bart., 1620–1699: A1008

Langhorne, John, 1735–1779: A0480, A1411, C0159, D0138, F0574, L0233, L0405, P0031, R0015, R0075, S1327, S1339, W0004, W1264, W1766, W2215

Lansdowne, George Granville, 1st baron, 1667–1735: A0023, A1387, A1820, B0228, B0500, C0178, C0232, E0081, F0371, M0001, O0293, P0287, S0850, T0643, T0712, T1226, W2066

Lapworth, Edward, 1574–1636: R0239

Lavington, Frances (Kolbel) Payne, baroness, d. 1830: I0737, S0612

Lavington, Ralph Payne, 1st baron, 1737?–1807: O0531

Law, Thomas: S0729

Lawes, William, 1602–1645: B0047

Lawman, Henry: T1329, Y0115

Lawrence, [ ], jr.: W0693

Lea, Sir Henry: M0559

Leadbeater, Mary (Shackleton), 1758–1826: A1211, C0446, D0392, H0153, O0439, O0699, O0972, S1260, S1314, T2182, W0028, W0155, W0442, W1746, W2186, W2470, Y0188, Y0250

Leapor, Mary, 1722–1746: F0299, I0407, I0950, M0019, T2035, Y0288

Lee, Sir George, 1700–1758: W1469, W1767, W1896

Lee, J. W.: A0595

Lee, John: W1226

Lee, Nathaniel, 1653–1692: A0725

Lee, William, d. 1778: W0222

Legh, George, 1694–1776: Y0395

Leigh, Henry James: W0997

Leigh, Thomas: A1203

Lely, Richard, fl. 1727: B0201, P0329, S0868

Lenton, Francis, fl. 1630–1640: A0413, H1005, I1154, N0237, N0349, N0362, R0188, W0620

Lepipre, Mary: I1203, I1612

Lesley, [ ]: I1200

L'Estrange, Sir Roger, 1616–1704: B0080

Lettice, John, 1737–1832: D0274

Lewes, William, of Oriel College: B0562, H0414, K0060, W1471

Lewis, [ ]: A0310, A0854, F0006, F0392, F0757, G0114, I0436, I0577, I1085, I1149, O0894, S0514, S0526, T0629, T0833, T0963, T1962, T2523, T3031, W0385, W0508, W0562, Y0238, Y0605

Lewis, David, 1683?–1760: F0485

Lewis, Matthew Gregory, 1775–1818: A0515, N0389, O0526, S0075, T1666, T2659, W2067

Lewis, William Thomas, 1748–1811: I0334

Lewkenor, Sir Edward, d. 1618: O0164

Liddiard, Thomas: B0401, I1329, N0402, O0186, S0581, S0637

Lightfoote, Josiah: O0269

Lightfoote, Samuel: D0202

Lilly, William, 1602–1681: T1333

Lipscome, C.: T1005

Lisle, Thomas, of Magdalen College, Oxford: I1193, M0640, W1215

Lithgow, William, 1582–1645: S0240

Little, T.: W1442

Littleton, Edward, of King's College, Cambridge: A1348, T2271

Lock, Miss [ ]: Y0040

Locket, Stephen: T2949

Lockman, John, 1698–1771: A0029, A0058, A0062, A0112, A0119, A0150, A0157, A0170, A0288, A0335, A0339, A0407, A0469, A0479, A0593, A0602, A0604, A0610, A0612, A0636, A0642, A0775, A0820, A0887, A0905, A0916, A0917, A0990, A1020, A1025, A1060, A1064, A1069, A1081, A1090, A1100, A1187, A1217, A1267, A1268, A1290,

A1308, A1327, A1370, A1383, A1391, A1417, A1430, A1445,
A1450, A1490, A1514, A1527, A1533, A1543, A1567, A1584,
A1587, A1637, A1658, A1666, A1688, A1703, A1758, A1759,
A1760, A1762, A1890, A1933, A1952, B0017, B0022, B0035,
B0116, B0170, B0210, B0236, B0308, B0345, B0361, B0403,
B0409, B0420, B0421, B0438, B0440, B0453, B0481,
B0495, B0499, B0506, B0527, B0529, B0532, B0536, B0541,
B0620, B0627, B0645, C0011, C0060, C0062, C0064,
C0066, C0131, C0139, C0171, C0188, C0313, C0349, C0390,
C0505, C0511, C0512, C0514, C0537, C0577, C0583, C0589,
C0600, D0004, D0010, D0018, D0065, D0133, D0176,
D0182, D0189, D0235, D0236, D0242, D0247, D0250,
D0254, D0269, D0406, D0425, E0002, E0030, E0059,
E0068, E0086, E0115, E0156, E0160, E0161, E0165, E0180,
F0044, F0052, F0054, F0057, F0088, F0103, F0104, F0106,
F0107, F0108, F0110, F0143, F0162, F0219, F0251, F0275,
F0277, F0278, F0305, F0321, F0324, F0325, F0327, F0330,
F0336, F0357, F0365, F0396, F0419, F0441, F0499, F0500,
F0519, F0530, F0551, F0600, F0625, F0706, F0730, F0741,
F0787, G0005, G0007, G0010, G0011, G0015, G0017,
G0060, G0117, G0254, G0344, G0366, G0390, G0414,
G0435, G0437, G0460, G0464, G0484, G0486, H0008,
H0020, H0069, H0098, H0135, H0172, H0177, H0228,
H0239, H0245, H0248, H0255, H0287, H0292, H0315,
H0499, H0512, H0532, H0623, H0909, H0962, H1083,
H1108, H1111, H1114, H1196, H1199, H1200, H1216, H1218,
H1220, H1247, H1294, H1326, H1352, H1374, H1411, H1419,
H1422, H1430, H1456, H1484, H1494, I0132, I0268, I0273,
I0328, I0384, I0481, I0493, I0518, I0522, I0524, I0534,
I0680, I0691, I0701, I0757, I0765, I0781, I0806, I0900,
I0937, I0956, I0957, I0974, I1059, I1089, I1095, I1110,
I1118, I1208, I1217, I1234, I1266, I1291, I1300, I1316, I1324
J0045, J0135, J0143, K0025, K0061, L0018, L0021, L0091,
L0105, L0372, L0379, L0383, L0432, L0454, L0466, L0470,
L0481, L0490, L0491, L0620, L0621, L0705, L0707,
M0038, M0076, M0128, M0192, M0318, M0319, M0392,
M0430, M0441, M0583, M0598, M0731, N0001, N0072,
N0171, N0202, N0218, N0278, N0292, N0313, N0314,
N0327, N0358, N0467, N0495, N0505, O0034, O0045,
O0127, O0168, O0176, O0196, O0197, O0198, O0228, O0271,
O0288, O0302, O0390, O0393, O0415, O0416, O0428,
O0431, O0432, O0433, O0441, O0444, O0452, O0464,
O0525, O0547, O0568, O0578, O0582, O0583, O0611,
O0638, O0672, O0673, O0691, O0740, O0757, O0776,
O0807, O0808, O0813, O0814, O0832, O0885, O0907,
O0913, O0936, O0970, O0994, O1051, O1117, O1163, P0001,
P0006, P0033, P0044, P0086, P0183, P0184, P0185,
P0202, P0308, P0310, P0325, P0365, Q0020, R0007, R0086,
R0132, R0182, R0197, R0211, R0232, R0235, S0001, S0002,
S0012, S0016, S0116, S0119, S0129, S0130, S0136, S0139,
S0150, S0155, S0156, S0157, S0181, S0184, S0193, S0199,
S0201, S0205, S0230, S0232, S0234, S0235, S0241, S0242,
S0274, S0275, S0281, S0282, S0334, S0354, S0404, S0463,
S0567, S0604, S0613, S0620, S0681, S0712, S0736, S0767,
S0777, S0783, S0799, S0894, S0926, S0951, S1004, S1033,
S1036, S1047, S1100, S1144, S1145, S1146, S1152, S1177,
S1236, S1239, S1240, S1250, S1265, S1278, S1332, S1342,
S1344, S1353, S1367, S1382, S1389, T0116, T0144, T0164,
T0175, T0252, T0257, T0304, T0380, T0427, T0438,
T0470, T0492, T0511, T0546, T0575, T0596, T0602,
T0628, T0650, T0652, T0699, T0717, T0823, T0870,

T0919, T0943, T0976, T0981, T0984, T1069, T1079,
T1086, T1103, T1154, T1182, T1227, T1229, T1278, T1323,
T1339, T1356, T1369, T1389, T1434, T1509, T1515, T1526,
T1695, T1702, T1823, T1898, T1901, T1905, T1912, T1926,
T1934, T1937, T1938, T2072, T2080, T2139, T2167, T2237,
T2247, T2273, T2357, T2361, T2405, T2421, T2422, T2477,
T2481, T2491, T2493, T2525, T2527, T2570, T2580,
T2610, T2652, T2717, T2764, T2814, T2817, T2823,
T2825, T2841, T2848, T2850, T2875, T2882, T2892,
T2898, T2942, T2947, T2972, T2991, T2995, T3009,
T3086, T3231, T3240, T3241, T3271, T3277, T3291, T3296,
T3327, T3331, T3344, T3356, T3365, T3389, U0067, U0091,
U0103, U0126, V0006, V0031, V0035, W0026, W0071,
W0192, W0278, W0308, W0331, W0512, W0564, W0575,
W0607, W0637, W0740, W0776, W0814, W0828, W0872,
W0893, W0894, W0895, W0904, W0950, W0956,
W0960, W0998, W0999, W1006, W1079, W1082, W1135,
W1152, W1155, W1163, W1202, W1214, W1217, W1230,
W1272, W1283, W1307, W1316, W1354, W1367, W1382,
W1435, W1458, W1505, W1530, W1540, W1559, W1592,
W1605, W1636, W1638, W1643, W1647, W1660, W1675,
W1689, W1702, W1708, W1722, W1729, W1741, W1783,
W1788, W1796, W1797, W1813, W1814, W1817, W1845,
W1846, W1850, W1859, W1861, W1864, W1868, W1870,
W1873, W1881, W1951, W1997, W2015, W2068, W2098,
W2274, W2278, W2283, W2308, W2375, W2377, W2427,
W2430, W2437, W2467, W2468, W2469, W2477, W2542,
W2560, W2566, W2573, W2587, W2613, Y0010, Y0013,
Y0017, Y0019, Y0021, Y0027, Y0032, Y0039, Y0052,
Y0068, Y0080, Y0100, Y0101, Y0107, Y0124, Y0131, Y0136,
Y0179, Y0190, Y0195, Y0197, Y0202, Y0204, Y0225,
Y0241, Y0484, Y0514, Y0561, Z0002

Lockyer, Francis: G0319, I0228
Loddington, Rev. [ ]: H0876
Lofft, Capel, 1751-1824: G0025, S1341
Logan, Maria: I0116, W0655
Lort, Michael, 1725-1790: I1586
Love, [ ]: S1349
Love, Richard, 1596-1661: T2728
Lovel, Peter: T0151
Lovelace, Richard, 1618-1658: W1136
Lovell, Joseph: A1622, D0428
Lovibond, Edward, 1724-1775: W1580
Low, [ ], of New York: T0953
Lowth, Robert, 1710-1787: A1837, B0570, N0425
Lucas, [ ], lady: T1762
Lucas, Sir [ ]: O0026
Lullay, Richard: B0334
Lumley, P.: H0450
Lushington, W., capt.: Y0523
Luttrell, Henry, 1765-1851: A0005, H0943
Luxborough, Henrietta (St. John) Knight, lady,
    1699-1756: T2663
Luyd, R.: A0312
Lyly, John, 1554?-1606: C0578
Lytler, Thomas: I1406
Lyttelton, George Lyttelton, 1st baron, 1709-1773:
    A0257, A0302, A1664, A1817, B0452, F0221, I1229, M0046,
    M0255, N0291, O0741, O0990, P0026, S1282, T0120,
    T0423, T0659, T1357, T3196, V0064, W0865, W1071,
    Y0041, Y0128, Y0180, Y0201

M., Dr. [ ], of Emmanual College, Cambridge: 11445
M****, M.: H0275
M., [ ]: I0582, T0185, W0565, Y0488
M., A.: W1615
M., C.: L0092
M., E.: W0476
M., G.: S0638
M., J.: C0036, F0041, I0998, O0886
M., R.: 11576, S0374, T0761, W0038, W2181
M———, T.: B0247
M——r, John: A1009, B0419, W1703
M——tt, J.: A0753, F0128, O0474, O0709, W0244, Y0163
Macartney, Fanny: T0993
Macaulay, [ ]: T2049
Mackenzie, [ ], M. D.: W0823
Mackenzie, Henry, 1745–1831: L0524, W2266
Mackereth, John, fl. 1778: A0264, I0411, S0398
Macneill, Hector, 1746–1818: H1455, O0646, R0105,
    S1128, W0303
Madan, Judith (Cowper), 1702–1781: A1212, A1935, I1159,
    L0715, O0708, O0726, R0108, R0227, U0061
Madan, Martin, 1725–1790: R0038
Madan, Spencer, 1758–1836: W0313
Maine, John: T0634
Mainwaring, Arthur, 1668–1712: A0971, G0194, I0371,
    I1317, W0052, W0811, W1124
Mallet, David, 1705?–1765: D0332, F0136, T1836,
    W0767
Man, Henry: H0094
Man, William: O0971
Manisty, Edward: K0051
Manley, Mary de la Riviere, 1663–1724: T3033
Manners, Catherine Rebecca ( ), lady, 1767?–1852:
    B0424, C0497
Mansel, William Lort, 1753–1820: H0036, T1873
Mansell, John: T1830
Marckant, John, fl. 1559–1581: O0325, O0589
Markham, [ ]: T1462
Markham, Robert: A1726
Marlowe, Christopher, 1564–1593: C0379, L0424
Marriott, William: F0495
Marten, Henry, 1602–1680: H0928
Martin, Edward: Y0123
Marvell, Andrew, 1621–1678: A0688, A1388, G0434,
    H0867, I0885, I0947, K0016, N0061, O0151, P0004,
    S0047, S0810, T0364, T1433, W0118, W0366, W0840,
    W0856, W0864, W1240, W1378
Mary Stuart, queen of Scots, 1524–1587: F0737
Mason, William, 1725–1797: A0715, C0245, F0120, G0363,
    H0562, H0951, I0554, M0370, S0122, T0028, T0933,
    Y0070, Y0168
Masser, [ ]: H1106
Masters, Mary, 1694?–1771: L0496, T0455, T2043
Matilda, Anna: T0994
Matthew, Sir Tobie, 1577–1655: S0067
Matthews, [ ]: C0299
Mawby, Sir Joseph: A0768
Maxwell, John, fl. 1740–1761: A1260
May, Edward: I0058, W1144
May, Thomas, 1595–1660: S0327, W0430
Mayne, Jasper, 1604–1672: M0272

Melcombe, George Bubb Dodington, lord,
    1691?–1762: L0672
Meldrum, R.: T0760
Melmoth, William: A0564
Melmurth, [ ]: O0730
Mennes, Sir John, 1599–1671: S0698, H1365
Meredith, William, organist at New College, Oxford:
    C0191, M0326, W0534
Merrick, James, 1720–1769: B0215, G0227, O0192, S1076,
    S1089, T2632, W1255, Y0219
Merry, Robert, 1755–1798: A0487, A1119, A1861, C0162,
    H0629, I0209, I1604, O0770, T0709, T3302, W0220,
    W0609, W0900, W1162, W1197, W2414, Y0247
Meston, William, 1688?–1745: F0656, I0903, W1061
Middleton, Elizabeth: W2621
Middleton, Thomas, c. 1580–1627: T1045
Middleton, William: Y0392
Miller, Charles: Y0231
Miller, Jessy: S0658
Mills, Rev. [ ]: K0020, S1190
Mills, William: A0843, B0173, B0457, F0382, F0452, F0470,
    H0235, L0679, M0047, M0051, M0529, O0382, T0911,
    T1246, T3017, W0342, W0689, W1545
Milner, Frances: B0062
Milton, John, 1608–1674: B0126, P0229, S1301, T1688
Monck, Mary (Molesworth), c. 1677–1715: O0032, T2136
Montagu, Miss [ ], b. 1719: W1041
Montagu, Charles: A0940, T0818
Montagu, Charles, lord: W1312
Montagu, Edward, lt. col.: 11354
Montagu, Frederick, 1733–1800: I0807, S1189, W1429
Montagu, George, 1751–1815: A1463, A1877, B0083,
    B0516, C0338, H0196, I0423, I1540, L0167, L0366, M0536,
    N0180, S0226, S1114, T1296, T1603, T1741, T2651, T2665,
    W1422, W2445
Montagu, Lady Mary (Pierrepoint) Wortley, 1689–
    1762: A1813, D0066, F0462, G0090, G0306, H0087,
    H1295, I0497, I1448, R0029, S0388, S1113, T0902, W0377,
    W2293, W2486, Y0339
Montrose, James Graham, 1st marquis, 1612–1650:
    G0406
Moody, Elizabeth, d. 1814: A0307, G0020, O0924
Moor, Martin: W1339
Moore, [ ]: T0225
Moore, Betty: L0691
Moore, Edward, 1712–1757: F0733, O0778, T0299
Moore, J.: C0115
Moore, Jenny (Hamilton): W2611
Moore, Rev. [ ], of Cornwall: S1179
Mordaunt, Major [ ]: G0155
More, Hannah, 1745–1833: A0597, A0617, A1193, A1396,
    B0451, D0096, D0373, E0126, F0130, F0295, F0701,
    H0046, H0097, I0500, I0569, I0658, I0994, L0016, L0033,
    M0215, M0465, N0261, O0258, O0272, O0374, O0697,
    O0954, P0073, P0137, P0348, R0109, S0050, S0197, S0513,
    S0886, S0995, S1350, T0361, T0556, T0691, T0922, T1653,
    T2029, V0029, W0972, W1465, W1479, W1634, W1653,
    W1655, W1803, W1897, Y0244
More, Sarah: A1024, D0191
Morell, Thomas, 1703–1784: A1215, A1257, A1380, A1394,
    A1517, A1716, B0315, C0306, C0393, D0017, D0073, F0179,

F0284, F0492, H0271, H1285, I0308, I0666, I1254, I1437,
K0055, L0161, L0425, L0426, L0427, M0560, M0658,
N0058, N0144, O0204, O0739, O1021, O1061, P0222,
S0138, S0231, S0556, S0924, T0094, T0104, T1157, T1878,
T2078, T2291, T2647, T2755, T2987, T3223, T3276,
W0234, W0246, W0258, W0328, W0674, W0677, W1377,
W2163, W2473, W2497, W2610, W2632, Y0126, Y0173

Morgan, [ ], lady: T0355

Morgan, Mrs. [ ]: O1159, T2915

Morice, Sir William: A0336, N0073

Morley, George, bishop of Worcester, 1597-1681:
A0950, F0451, H0426, M0596, W0230, Y0403

Morpeth, [ ], lord: F0337

Morris, Mrs. [ ]: M0295

Morris, Charles, capt.: T2795

Morris, Thomas, capt., b. 1732: H1075, I1137, T2165,
U0064

Moss, Robert, 1666-1729: M0566

Mottershed, Thomas, of Christ Church, Oxford:
T2984

Motteux, Peter, 1663-1718: L0680

Moulsworth, Martha (Dorsett) Prynne Througood,
1577?-1632 or later: T1359

Mulcaster, James, sr.: A0031, A1887, C0251, H1491, M0219,
P0277, T0918, T1299, T3146, W0356

Mundy, F. N. B.: L0446

Mundy, J. W.: N0083

Murphy, [ ]: A0359, W2357

Murphy, Arthur, 1727-1805: H1051

Murray, [ ]: B0393

Murray, Christian: T0095

Murray, William: T2919

Murry, Ann, fl. 1778-1792: E0162, G0161, H0075, H0082,
H0563, O0004, T0948, T1748

N., J.: A1542, D0136, W1157

N., W., of Exeter College, Oxford: R0074, W1246

Nane, Col. [ ]: T0346

Nares, Rev. [ ]: A0931, O1072

Nash, [ ]: C0224, L0396, T0339

Needham, [ ]: O0079

Needler, Henry, 1690-1718: A0849, A0936, A1314, C0538,
D0412, D0413, G0453, H0072, I1176, N0039, O0358,
P0340, S0221, S0548, S0590, S1170, T2412, W0509, W1321,
W1704, W2124

Neuterfield, Patrick: W1556

Neve, Jeffrey: T0559

Neve, John: T0559

Neve, Stowe: T0559

Neve, Timothy: T1687, T2424

Nevil, [ ]: H0298

Neville, Christopher: N0097

Neville, Henry, 1620-1694: A1444, H0180, I0642,
K0050, S0160, T0560, T1457

Newcastle, William Cavendish, duke, 1592-1676: I0118,
I0249

Newcomb, Thomas: Y0165

Newcourt, William: W0293

Newman, Francis, c. 1604-1649: W2472

Newton, [ ]: I0638

Newton, [ ], bp.: T3072

Newton, John: S0063

Nichols, Dr. [ ], chancellor of Carlisle: N0246, N0306

Nixson, John, d. 1818: H0357

Noel, Mrs. [ ]: I0422

Norris, John, 1657-1711: A1214, B0321, B0486, D0067,
H1222, H1334, I0062, I0108, I0236, I1550, L0506, M0745,
N0166, N0360, S0066, T0046, T1770, T1797, T2461,
T2499, T2646, T2746, W0232, W0235, W0239, W0315,
W0719, W1049

North, [ ]: I1028

Northampton, Elizabeth (Shirley) Compton,
countess, 1694-1741: A0237, A1573, A1574, F0033,
F0624, I0391, I0917, J0141, L0412, O0036, O0642, O0985,
P0092, P0316, T0743, T0917, T1519, T2722, T2982,
W1481, W1901

Northampton, James Compton, 5th earl, 1687-1754:
I1184, L0509

Northcote, James: S0204

Northcote, N. A.: P0317

Northumberland, Hugh Smithson, duke, 1742-1817:
H0408, W1204

Norton, Thomas, 1532-1584: G0106, G0109, I0251, L0593,
N0367, O0398, O0499, O0508, P0253, S0672, T1544,
T1548, U0116, W2416

Norwich, Edward Denny, 1st earl, 1569-1630: H1012

Norwood, [ ]: W1448

Nourse, [ ]: L0284

Nowell, Alexander, 1507?-1602: T0830

Nugent, [ ]: H1149

Nugent, Robert Nugent, earl, 1702-1788: R0130

O., Miss [ ]: A1261

O., J.: T3192

Oakes, Abraham, c. 1686-1756: A0241, A1120, B0458,
B0641, C0254, D0400, F0543, F0786, H0432, H0462,
H1299, H1336, H1500, I0342, I1534, L0469, M0050,
M0239, M0309, M0453, O0114, O0249, O0929, P0047,
P0053, S0004, S0203, S0250, S0365, S0943, S0964, S1273,
T0649, T0815, T1192, T1943, T2219, W1688, W2119,
W2353

Oakes, John Jacob: A1515, A1919

Oates, Margaret: T2037

O'Brian, William, d. 1815: A0024

Ogle, Dr. [ ]: N0070

Ogle, Sir Thomas: A0981

Oldham, John, 1653-1683: A0818, F0122, I0182, L0051,
M0654, N0243, N0404, P0238, T0071, T3071, W0394

Olding, Ann: M0477

Oldisworth, Nicholas, 1612-1645: D0314

Oldisworth, William, 1680-1734: N0343

Oldnow, Gregory: M0450, N0395

Oldys, William, 1696-1761: B0558

Olgivie, James: A1593

Oliver, Thomas: B0082, C0117, C0203, H1357

O'Neill, Henrietta, 1758-1793: N0329

Onely, Jm. Richard: W0918, W1013, Y0011

Opie, Amelia Alderson, 1769-1853: S1068

Oram, [ ]: I0225

Orford, Horace Walpole, 4th earl, 1717-1797: A0012,
A0523, A0648, A1727, A1955, B0198, B0511, B0519, C0453,
D0282, E0027, E0132, E0138, F0397, G0036, G0481, H0584,

Orford, Horace Walpole(*continued*)
  H1162, I1188, L0371, O0377, O0518, O1014, O1053, P0115,
  S0210, S0339, T0382, T0436, T0982, T1090, T1342,
  T2826, T2962, W0343, W0805, W2394
Orrery, John Boyle, 5th earl, 1707-1762: E0090, N0266,
  N0293
Orrery, Roger Boyle, 1st earl, 1621-1679: O1150, T0241,
  T0884, T1075
Otway, Thomas, 1652-1685: I1226, O1096
Overbury, Sir Thomas, 1581-1613: T1265
Owen, Richard, 1606-1683: A0114, H0961, N0194

P., [ ]: G0348
P., Miss [ ]: R0173
P., J.: T0328
P., M.: A0571, B0634, H0907, H1407, L0519, O0257
P., R. K. C.: M0407
P., S.: A0914, C0006, D0225, H0382
P., T.: D0059
P——e, Penelope: Y0587
P——ll, M.: W1165
Paget, Thomas Catesby Paget, baron, 1689-1742:
  P0159
Painter, Richard, 1615-: M0280
Palmer, Francis, fl. 1631-1646: H1137
Paman, Clement, d. 1695: H0880
Panton, Thomas, 1731-1808: T1385
Park, Henry, d. 1704: T3074
Parker, W.: I0323
Parnell, Thomas, 1679-1718: A1369, B0659, C0457, F0134,
  F0717, L0684, N0408, P0088, R0106, R0131, S0264,
  T0703, T3324, U0151, W2444
Parrot, Henry, fl. 1606-1626: A0524, M0127, P0296, T0190
Parsons, [ ]: H0145, P0186
Parsons, Thomas: H0232
Parsons, William, fl. 1785-1807: A0028, A1199, A1619,
  A1621, D0049, D0393, H1046, H1489, I1384, L0273,
  L0342, M0207, N0363, N0533, O0016, O0080, S1315,
  T0343, T0765, T2704, T2990, W0095, W0624, W0629
Paterson, John: S1066
Patrick, Simon, 1616-1707: F0212, G0287, J0068, J0140
Pattison, John, jr., 1758-1782: P0169, T0310
Pattison, William, 1706-1727: A0901, A1269, A1467,
  A1489, B0185, C0087, F0302, H1150, L0408, N0302, T1363,
  U0104, W2565, Y0264
Pauncefort, Robert: H0470
Payne, George William: M0458
Pearce, William, fl. 1785-1796: F0386
Pearson, [ ]: F0014, I1131
Pebham, Mrs. [ ]: G0131
Peckard, Martha: B0289, T2553
Peeris, William, fl. 1520: B0122, C0209
Pennecuik, Alexander, 1652-1722: M0677
Pennington, Miss [ ], of Huntingdon, 1734-1759:
  H0134
Penny, Anne (Christian): S0873
Pepys, Samuel, 1633-1703: W2087
Percy, Thomas, 1729-1811: S0893
Perne, Chester: S0696
Peterborough and Monmouth, Charles Mordaunt, 3rd
  earl, 1658-1735: I0329

Peterson, Dr. [ ]: S0049
Petty, Mrs. [ ]: S0531
Petty, Sir William, 1623-1687: T0350
Philips, Ambrose, 1675-1749: A0015, B0384, F0650,
  G0052, H1312, I1205, L0414, O0381, O0763, P0332, S0889,
  T0732, T1164, Y0097
Philips, James: T0582
Philips, John, 1676-1709: F0675, H0229
Philips, Katherine, 1631-1664: A0065, A0422, A0832,
  A1493, A1713, B0037, C0473, C0490, F0668, G0178,
  H0554, H1381, H1389, H1459, I0601, I0605, M0462,
  N0025, O0007, O1063, T1364, T1669, T1709, T2754,
  W0554, W0978, W1954
Phillipps, Henry, fl. 1655: A0352, A0354, C0004, F0773,
  H0411, I1161, L0210, O0528, S0916, T0565, W1494
Phillips, [ ]: A0611
Phillips, Edward, 1630-1696?: C0314
Phillips, John, 1631-1706: C0413, T0068
Phillips, Samuel, of St. John's College, Oxford: I0575
Phipps, S.: A0244
Pick, Samuel, fl. 1639: H0847, I1555
Pierson, [ ]: A0844, C0301, H0551, H1442, I0215, I1481,
  I1482, I1483, I1484, L0563, M0585, M0680, O0305, O0662,
  O1110, P0284, T0150
Pigg, [ ]: T1370
Pigott, F.: W0993, W1799
Pilkington, Laetitia (Van Lewen), 1712?-1750: I0961,
  O0628, S1096
Pilon, Frederick: B0129
Pinnell, Peter: P0007, W2178
Piozzi, Hester Lynch Thrale, 1741-1821: I1236, I1410,
  O0928, S0432, T2914, T3243, W0885, W1241, W1461
Pitt, [ ], of New College, Oxford: H0933
Pitt, Christopher, 1699-1748: A1074, C0517, F0119, H1165,
  M0687, N0204, O0279, O0451, O0895, O0935, T1575,
  T2521, T2719, W0272, W1224, W1236, W1260, W2424,
  Y0116
Pittis, William, 1674-1724: A0097
Pixell, [ ]: M0709
Plaistow, William: M0354
Plaxton, William: F0561
Playford, John, 1623-1686?: D0322
Plumer, Thomas: I1215
Plumpton, [ ]: W2538
Pluret, Mary, 1713-1741: A0163, A1312, B0172, C0368,
  C0406, C0430, D0108, H1236, I0415, I0424, I0856, I1067,
  I1387, L0561, L0589, L0619, M0045, M0119, M0142,
  M0387, M0542, M0576, M0660, M0702, M0744, O0375,
  O0447, P0242, S0992, S1110, S1285, S1319, S1320, T0904,
  T1435, T2061, T2130, W1106, W1396, W1671, W1982,
  W2238, W2324
Polwhele, Richard, 1760-1838: A0800, O0178, O0549,
  T0487, T0985, T1259, T2263, T2683, Y0301
Pomfret, John, 1667-1702: A1631, I0593, N0285, S0643,
  W1361, W2286
Poole, Miss [ ]: T3080
Poole, Walton: I0702
Pooly, [ ]: D0180
Pope, Alexander, 1688-1744: A0167, A0358, A1921, B0140,
  B0576, B0591, C0077, C0086, C0424, D0272, D0298,
  D0379, F0203, F0247, F0331, G0002, G0134, H0222, H0533,

H0627, H0711, H0935, H0980, H1360, I0318, I0514, I1148,
I1273, I1276, I1371, K0056, L0637, L0687, M0361, M0373,
M0607, N0022, N0382, O0047, O0096, O0113, O0224,
O0290, O0600, O0674, P0034, P0103, P0138, S0267,
S0491, S0507, S0687, S0906, S1058, S1231, T0006, T0881,
T1581, T1586, T1760, T1881, T1920, T2164, T2550, T2551,
T2572, T3090, T3091, T3104, T3198, T3343, V0080,
W0264, W0325, W0330, W0420, W0485, W1100, W1454,
W1921, W2451, W2628, Y0133, Y0248, Y0251, Y0287,
Y0426

Pope, Walter, d. 1714: I0611, O0607

Popple, William, 1701-1764: A0313, A0691, A0867, A1182,
A1263, A1329, A1601, A1645, A1731, A1735, B0001, B0190,
B0343, B0383, B0449, B0455, B0607, B0674, C0090,
C0219, C0231, D0143, D0156, D0416, E0092, F0046,
F0071, F0194, F0218, F0249, F0250, F0353, F0722, F0738,
G0253, G0421, G0475, H0569, H1039, H1107, H1470, I0122,
I0296, I0474, I0507, I0679, I0758, I0814, I1594, J0015,
K0017, L0227, L0267, L0277, L0293, L0296, L0352, L0382,
L0714, M0234, M0330, N0059, N0094, O0299, O0313,
O0815, O0880, O0911, O0920, O0968, O0991, O1024,
P0055, P0181, P0225, P0315, Q0006, R0142, S0077, S0229,
S0278, S0492, S0635, S0692, S1014, S1039, S1057, S1261,
T0077, T0079, T0089, T0125, T0141, T0908, T1247,
T1583, T1673, T2150, T2154, T2222, T2235, T2332, T2349,
T2602, T2611, T2669, T2688, T3188, T3225, T3297, T3313,
V0024, V0033, W0017, W0238, W0324, W0424, W0450,
W0553, W0697, W1081, W1269, W1288, W1353, W1379,
W1506, W1843, W1920, W1923, W2051, W2093, W2246,
W2269, W2277, W2289, W2340, W2452, W2482, Y0254,
Y0556

Porson, [ ]: W2498
Porter, [ ]: C0527, S0750
Porter, Eliza: W0136
Porter, Thomas, 1636-1680: A1057
Porter, William Warren, 1776-1804: A0600, H1264,
S0165, T3321, U0013
Potter, James: L0516
Pounceforth, [ ]: O0594
Powell, Alfred S.: T0571
Powell, George, 1658?-1714: O0574
Powys, [ ]: D0144
Pratt, [ ] (= Samuel Jackson Pratt?): T1913
Priault, Miss [ ]: W0750
Price, Daniel, 1581-1631: S0862
Price, H.: M0468
Price, Henry: N0109
Priestley, Joseph, 1733-1804: T1742
Priestley, Timothy: A0745
Prigher, [ ]: I1214, T0972, W1871
Primerose, Daniel, 1681-1761: T1493
Prior, Matthew, 1644-1721: A0863, A1084, A1102, A1357,
A1384, A1405, A1648, A1787, A1828, B0145, B0256, B0394,
C0100, D0061, D0173, D0185, D0306, F0058, F0276,
F0491, F0673, F0698, H0187, H0543, H0611, H0778,
H1198, I0808, I0888, I1420, M0213, M0608, N0221,
N0276, O0987, P0211, S0072, S0536, S1059, S1181, T0290,
T1096, T1186, T1390, T2092, T2127, T2533, T2909,
W0795, W0835, W0881, W1112, W1800, W2585, Y0235,
Y0411, C0553, I0976, T2478, T2881
Pritchard, Mrs. [ ]: T0444

Pulley, William: O0446, T1576
Pye, Henry James, 1745-1813: L0712, Y0157
Pyne, John: H0179

Quarles, Francis, 1592-1644: A0829, A0878, A1295,
A1343, A1839, B0049, B0513, B0647, C0025, C0111, D0299,
D0354, D0424, E0042, E0119, E0177, F0056, F0082,
F0262, F0265, F0307, F0514, F0788, G0202, G0248, G0267,
H0050, H0313, H0314, H0383, H0454, H1029, H1070,
H1096, H1158, H1209, H1380, H1464, I0097, I0217, I0223,
I0594, I0693, I0763, I0769, I0897, I0902, I0986, I1187,
I1522, J0032, J0125, J0126, K0067, L0070, L0390, L0567,
L0573, L0574, L0704, M0114, M0145, M0246, M0252,
M0676, N0086, N0193, N0197, N0198, N0251, N0350,
N0472, O0039, O0429, O0430, O0711, O0753, O0790,
O0810, O1089, O1090, O1111, O1131, O1145, P0108, P0152,
P0163, P0331, R0176, S0018, S0521, S0677, S0915, S0950,
S1212, T0135, T0226, T0338, T0369, T0413, T0439, T0505,
T0593, T0623, T0788, T0806, T0814, T0831, T0853,
T1088, T1156, T1361, T1498, T1685, T1735, T1818, T1970,
T2007, T2101, T2145, T2552, T2559, T2626, T2681,
T2698, T3366, T3384, W0066, W0107, W0110, W0115,
W0142, W0224, W0228, W0277, W0471, W0496, W0533,
W0547, W1019, W1393, W1421, W1431, W1487, W1492,
W2017, W2223, W2616, Y0413, Z0004, Z0005

Quick, Thomas: A1247, A1720

R., [ ]: A0510, A0868, F0647, I0174, I1032, I1166, T1625,
W0139, W1040
R., A.: A0858, F0217, I1344
R., D.: B0286
R., F.: A0568
R., H.: W0720
R., J.: A0767, F0437, H0536, I1035, L0028, S0390, W1500
R., R.: H0548
R., T.: G0053, M0414, W0443
R., W.: A0290, I0812
Rack, Edmund, 1735?-1787: A1835
Radcliffe, Alexander, fl. 1669-1696: A0371, A1118, R0021,
T0656, T1965, W1804
Radcliffe, Ann (Ward), 1764-1823: A0759, C0155, D0391,
H1376, H1414, H1423, H1432, I1267, L0043, L0340, M0328,
N0392, O0019, O0195, O0301, O0392, O0571, S0878, S0882,
S0885, S1028, S1284, T1163, V0048, W0360
Radney, Sir George: F0690
Rainolds, Henry: F0016, W2214
Raleigh, Sir Walter, 1552?-1618: C0012, E0151, G0094,
G0180, H0649, H0748, I0074, L0373, P0043, S0099,
S0448, T1292, T1476, W0463
Ramsay, Allan, 1686-1758: A1643, A1846, C0516, F0180,
F0279, F0308, H0591, I0980, I1003, O0227, S0456, S0735,
T0793, T0798, T0877, W0753, W2263
Ramsey, Miss [ ]: C0323
Randolph, Thomas, 1605-1635: A1324, A1575, B0092,
B0200, D0117, D0221, D0226, F0090, F0763, G0179,
H0510, I0090, L0031, M0404, N0239, P0240, S1019,
W0587, W0788, W2385, I0790
Rantzove, Henry: A1287
Rawson, Joseph, c. 1665-1719: D0300
Rawstorne, Edward: U0131
Ray, Bay: W0212

Raymond, Samuel: A0822, T0145

Raynatt, Ja.: T0722

Reade, Henry, of Queens College, Cambridge: C0572

Reader, William, jr., 1782–1852: F0027

Reynolds, George, fl. 1628: T1785

Rhodes, James: C0546, L0002, L0389, T2230, T2631, W1256

Rich, Charles: I0923

Rich, Thomas: E0040

Riddell, Maria (Woodley), 1772–1808: Y0257

Ridley, Gloster, 1702–1774: H0399, T2766

Rigby, Joseph, d. 1671: A0108

Rives, Charles: W1231

Roberts, [ ], of Eton: T1198

Roberts, Martha: I0866, T0269, Y0098

Robertson, [ ], of York: U0090

Robinson, [ ]: L0174, L0436, W0875

Robinson, John: A0980, B0367, C0549, D0385, H0202, H0472, H0477, H1225, H1250, H1348, H1349, I1210, I1230, I1358, L0062, L0453, M0221, N0219, O0998, R0165, S0167, S0178, S0325, S0358, S1204, S1206, S1267, T0099, T0723, T0816, T2304, T2447, W0380, W0537, W0870, W1884, W2086, W2089, W2175, W2216

Robinson, Mary (Derby), 1758?–1800: A0797, A1594, D0025, G0176, H0534, I0250, I0520, I0965, T1794, W2517, Y0059

Robinson, Thomas, fl. 1616–1619: A0614, A1216, H0736, T0468, T2397, T2417

Roche, [ ]: A0903, H0080

Rochester, Elizabeth Wilmot, countess, d. 1684: N0373

Rochester, John Wilmot, 2nd earl, 1647–1680: A0203, A0344, A0591, A0670, A0705, A0937, A0975, A1117, A1173, A1174, A1615, A1799, B0556, C0104, C0169, C0571, D0085, D0089, F0023, G0092, H0806, H0908, H1120, H1182, H1284, H1436, I0185, I0385, I0692, I0853, I1256, I1409, K0035, L0631, M0389, M0413, N0002, N0383, O0512, P0123, P0318, Q0030, S0083, S0619, S1166, T1404, T2691, T2738, T2981, T3089, T3101, W0261, W0290, W0379, W0669, W1409, W1696

Roderick, Richard, d. 1756: P0116

Roe, Sir John, 1581–1606: C0310, D0116, I0587, M0232, S0375, S0755, T0069, T1290, T3235

Roe, Sir Thomas, 1581?–1644: C0081, S0311, S1084

Rogers, Miss [ ]: H0598

Rogers, Mary: W0806

Rogers, Samuel, 1763–1855: M0270, O0809, O0933, T1177, W1456

Rogers, Thomas, 1574?–1610?: G0385, I0395

Rolle, Edward, 1703–1791: A1544, M0526

Rons, Sir John: T3270

Roper, Miss [ ]: S1276

Roper, William, 1496–1578: E0181

Roscoe, William, 1753–1831: A0623, A0772, A0831, A1435, A1557, A1673, A1757, F0417, G0163, M0331, N0242, N0331, O0173, O0804, R0076, S0309, S1027, U0063, W0548, W1792, W1822, W1960, W2130, Y0001

Roscommon, Wentworth Dillon, 4th earl, 1633?–1685: A0737, A0954, B0142, C0469, F0629, H0209, I0134, M0557, O0219, O0552, S0400, S1310, T0456, T1974, V0066, V0067, W1557, W1670, W2339

Rose, Aquila: I0373

Rose, John, b. 1754: A0026, A1281, A1338, A1442, C0252, C0605, E0142, F0042, F0139, F0312, F0352, H0199, I0028, I0625, I1158, L0645, M0063, N0187, N0338, N0447, N0479, O0437, P0089, P0090, P0117, P0162, R0123, S0901, T1162, T1345, T1516, T2595, T2802, T2866, V0017, W0205, W0291, W1127, W1430, W1488, W1499, Z0008

Ross, William Stewart: S1172

Roussignac, Peter: A1364, S0179

Routh, G.: D0338

Rowe, Elizabeth (Singer), 1674–1737: A1031, B0088, B0399, G0115, G0428, I1365, N0372, S1351, T0746, T2099, T3187, T3283, W1658

Rowe, Nicholas, 1674–1718: D0280, D0350, F0296, I0096, S1062, T1967, W0780, W0935, W1719, W1789, W1839, Z0010

Rowlands, Samuel: W0104

Rowley, William, 1585?–1642?: A1339

Rudge, Mrs. [ ]: U0086

Rule, Joseph: A0181

Rushton, Edward, 1756–1814: I0954, T2079

Russell, [ ], lord: W1669

Russell, Thomas, 1762–1788: C0542

Rutherford, Dr. [ ], d. 1730: W0057

Rutherford, John: I0953, J0101

Rymer, Thomas, 1641–1713: L0085, O0060, S0007, T0520, T1165, W1261

S., A.: T3008

S., J.: C0054, I1192, S0985

S., L.: G0408

S., M.: A0446, C0037, H0021, L0022, W0251, W0724

S., R.: W0914

S., R. G.: W2461

S., T.: Y0060

S——, Lady Mary: O0246

Sacheverell, George: M0359

Sadleir, Richard Vernon: A0603, A0840, A1386, B0335, B0456, B0679, C0048, C0075, C0089, C0125, C0472, C0536, D0101, D0128, D0237, D0368, E0048, E0053, F0049, F0070, G0001, G0043, H0029, H0099, H0169, H0319, H0321, H0916, H1128, I0490, I0703, I0709, I1346, J0007, J0083, L0150, L0199, L0429, M0383, M0636, N0209, O0372, O0373, O0722, O0861, O0902, O0950, O1162, P0096, S0056, S0097, S0256, S0259, S0389, S0632, S0939, S1029, S1121, T0794, T0980, T1051, T1374, T1883, T2245, T2733, T2878, T3332, W0183, W0408, W0628, W0634, W0636, W0660, W0860, W1113, W1140, W1156, W1300, W1313, W1389, W1566, W1699, W1700, W1730, W1737, W1760, W2020, W2225, W2292, W2306, W2322, W2411, Y0049, Y0240

Salmon, William, 1644–1713: T0651

Salter, James, 1650–1718: A0380

Saltier, Nathaniel: S0572

Sandford, [ ]: G0032

Sandly, Paul: A0041

Sandwich, Edward Montagu, 3rd earl, d. 1729: A1550

Sandys, George, 1578–1644: F0200, Y0206

Sandys, William: A1210, B0174, H0186, H1017, H1228, H1302, I0049, J0110, M0308, M0662, T1255, T1560, T1566, T1567, T1925, W1154, W1533, W2021, W2346

Saunders, James: W2116

Savage, Sir William: T0716

Savidge, John: I0503

Savile, Henry, 1642–1687: G0387, S1034, T2019

Schone, [ ]: F0745

Scott, Job: A1831, I0264, M0452

Scott, Sir Robert Atto.: W2236

Scott, Thomas, jr.: F0582, I1039, L0345, L0458, M0549, O0502, O0898, T3185

Scott, Sir Walter, 1771–1832: I0964, O0412, T2895

Scroope, Sir Carr, 1649–1680: A1362, C0243, I0076, R0004, W1285

Seares, John: P0304

Sedley, Sir Charles, 1639?–1701: A0721, C0182, F0226, I0976, L0079, P0160, P0323, S1192, T0102, T0152, T1040, T1646, W0932

Sellway, James: T1035

Senhouse, Humphrey: T3285

Senhouse, Richard, d. 1626: I0175

Serjant, Mary, b. 1673: A0098, A0635, A0662, A1233, A1325, B0363, C0227, C0491, D0229, D0341, E0063, E0127, E0149, F0341, F0456, G0349, G0380, G0411, H0017, H0203, I0602, I0696, I0849, I1081, I1374, I1377, I1455, I1467, I1472, K0070, L0184, M0062, M0262, N0381, O0280, O0409, O0520, P0234, P0244, Q0017, R0164, S0383, S0386, S0597, S0909, S1187, S1188, S1235, T0192, T0668, T1552, T2075, T2323, T2953, T3214, U0105, V0078, W0611, W1477, W1979, W2005, X0002, Y0348, Y0353, Y0543

Settle, Elkanah, 1648–1724: I0644, W1408

Sewal, Dr. [ ]: P0027

Seward, Anna, 1742–1809: A0601, A1129, A1332, B0175, F0243, F0663, F0748, H0095, I0257, I1407, L0056, L0711, M0176, N0531, O0616, O0882, P0344, R0157, S0262, S0502, S0544, S0905, S1325, T0525, T0706, T1001, T1542, T2432, W0389

Seward, Thomas, 1708–1790: F0612

Sewell, Mary: U0070

Sexton, John: H0842

Shackleton, John: F0762, W1093

Shackleton, Richard, 1728–1792: H1309, S0039, T0078, T3184

Shadwell, Thomas, 1642?–1692: A0421, I0958, T0472, T2455

Shakespeare, William, 1564–1616: A1420, B0426, C0558, F0427, F0564, F0643, G0296, I0747, I1441, I1562, L0447, L0541, M0405, N0330, O0667, S0175, T0114, T0132, T0244, T1569, T1973, U0109, W0955, W1036, W1039

Sharpe, M.: A0388, H1490, T2543

Shaw, Cuthbert, 1739–1771: S1290, Y0255

Sheeres, Sir Henry, d. 1710: W2443, Y0103, Y0335

Sheldon, Captain [ ]: H0673

Shenstone, William, 1714–1763: A0756, A1689, C0431, C0432, C0584, G0187, H0493, H0660, I1014, I1295, O0394, O0460, O0539, O0835, S0151, S0450, S0726, S1390, T2441, W1174, W2220, Y0162

Shepherd, William, 1768–1847: A1598, H0174

Sheppard, Sir Fleetwood, 1634–1698: F0644, H0701, M0071, O0216, O1080, T1513, W0903, W1298

Sheridan, Elizabeth Ann (Linley), 1754–1792: I0550, I1333, S1313

Sheridan, Richard Brinsley Butler, 1751–1816: B0235, C0149, C0163, C0529, D0329, F0454, G0077, H1169, H1486, I0159, I0278, I0565, I1183, L0411, M0147, N0066,

S0162, T0119, T2386, U0012, W0344, W1150, W1404, W1562, W2456, Y0537

Sheridan, Thomas, 1719–1788: I0292, W2609

Sherwill, Abraham: I1434

Shippen, William, 1673–1743: I1397, T1169

Shirley, James, 1596–1666: H0832, L0401, T0638, T0755, V0043, W2603

Shirley, William, fl. 1739–1780: A0704, T1257

Shower, Ann: W0149

Shuttleworth, P. N.: O0989, W1825

Siddons, T.: O0253

Sidney, Sir Charles: A0981

Sidney, Sir Philip, 1554–1586: A1272, H1058

Sillon, Joseph: I0184

Simcoe, [ ], general: F0571

Simpson, Richard: H0947

Simpson, Stephen, fl. 1773–1776: A0037, A0465, A0660, A0939, C0059, H1315, H1321, I0222, I1174, M0714, P0175, P0339, T0394, T0701, T1869, T2215, T2391, T2400, U0092, W0201, W0528, W0863, W0937, W1345, W1575, Y0259

Skinner, John, 1721–1807: O0803

Skipwith, Thomas, 1619–1694: E0070

Skrine, Henry, 1755–1803: A0498, A0569, A1512, A1812, B0271, B0298, B0467, C0001, D0123, G0236, H0561, H0638, I1301, I1367, L0226, L0265, L0410, O0033, P0271, S0872, T0287, T0580, T0876, T1256, T1394, T1876, T2958, T3135, T3208, W1232

Smallwood, John, fl. 1705: A0684, T3127

Smart, Christopher, 1722–1770: H0404, H0570, I0938, O0842, T2303, T2470, A0002

Smedley, Jonathan, 1671–1729: I1570, M0422

Smith, [ ], of University College, Oxford: I0201

Smith, Miss [ ]: S0874

Smith, Adam: T3256

Smith, Charlotte (Turner), 1749–1806: A0698, A0739, A0814, A0815, A1497, C0118, C0248, D0023, D0169, F0084, F0185, G0159, G0463, H0393, H0644, I0255, I0874, I1048, I1099, I1298, I1468, L0358, M0419, N0388, N0535, O0005, O0414, O0580, P0214, Q0010, S0479, S0760, S0774, S1343, S1370, T0398, T0617, T0992, T1039, T1388, T1401, T1537, T2114, T2143, W0021, W0705, W1110, W1123, W1585, W1586, W1754, W2325, Y0191

Smith, Edmund, 1672–1710: J0013, W2435

Smith, John, fl. 1713: H0932

Smith, John, of Magdalen College, Oxford, 1662–1717: A0223

Smith, Thomas, of University College, Oxford: A0672

Smith, William, 1730–1819: A0095, A1158, C0286, C0508, C0526, F0168, F0181, I0624, I0822, I1416, P0294, S0111, S0501, S1321, T1587, T2700, T2721, T2851, T3040, T3043, T3067, W0199, W0262, W0488, W0901, W0945, Y0448, Y0474

Smith, William, fl. 1596: W0668

Smithe, Samuel: W0384

Smyth, [ ]: A0696, H0303, S1156, T0497, T2149, W0010

Smyth, Aaron: A1770

Smyth, William: H0034

Snelling, Anna: G0031

Sneyd, Edward, 1734–1795: A1508, A1744, D0047, D0050, D0129, D0140, D0163, F0129, H1122, I0370, I0483, I0654,

Sneyd, Edward(*continued*)
    M0049, M0241, M0399, M0463, M0466, O1029, S0481,
    S0574, S1233, T0207, T1344, T2118, T2590, U0032, W0013,
    W0419, W2389, Y0482
Snoade, Henry: M0440
Snook, [ ]: C0213
Snow, Gorstello: I0656
Soame, Master [ ]: A1953
Soame, Henry Francis Robert: A1328
Soame, James: S1132
Soaper, Miss [ ]: A0874, A0889
Somervile, William, 1675–1742: I0753, I0754, I1023,
    O0102, O0364, O0746, T1087, W0140
Sone, R.: T0157
Sotheby, William, 1757–1833: A1055, C0034
South, Dr. [ ]: O1097
Southcott, Joanna, 1750–1814: A0254
Southey, Robert, 1774–1843: A1294, H1172, I1382, I1565, J0099
Southwell, Robert, 1561–1595: B0180
Sparke, Edward, 1613?–1692: A1699, A1717, B0443, C0095,
    C0280, E0185, H0917, H1016, H1466, I0588, I1197, I1281,
    L0102, L0478, M0338, O0070, P0037, S0037, S0213, S0384,
    S0397, S0805, S0813, T0405, T0648, T1109, T1439, T1798,
    T1944, W0206, W0514, W0524, Y0308, Y0367
Sparrow, Joseph: D0419
Spatter, [ ]: I1012
Speed, John, 1552–1629: S1071
Speed, Robert, fl. 1647: L0258
Spence, [ ]: M0274
Spence, Joseph, 1699–1768: A0539, A0877, A1647, F0342,
    G0086, H0702, H1271, I0562, I0727, I1339, M0078, S0836,
    S1023, T0962, T1408, T2695, W0486, W1020, W1172
Spencer, William Robert, 1769–1834: F0753, T1270,
    W0791, W0921, W1153
Spenser, Edmund, 1552?–1599: A1130, I1575, R0099,
    T1172, T2116, W2636
Spinage, Anthony: A1709
Sprat, Thomas, bp., 1635–1713: U0077
Springthorpe, [ ]: I0036
Sprint, John: T1429
St. Albans, Francis Bacon, 1st viscount, 1561–1626:
    T1494, T1952
Stacy, Edmond, fl. 1710–1715: U0139
Stamper, Dr. T.: G0335, O1079, T3117
Standish, Francis: P0295
Stanley, Thomas, 1625–1678: B0471, E0136, G0427, H0122,
    H0132, H0183, I0443, I1485, L0570, L0595, L0599, L0600,
    L0601, L0677, M0547, M0645, M0646, M0723, O0132,
    O0503, O0556, O1119, S0455, T1909, T2062, T2067, T2115,
    T2120, T2121, T2135, T2146, T2435, T2530, T2846, T3055,
    T3056, T3061, T3064, W2031, W2464, Y0292
Steele, Sir Richard, 1672–1729: F0696, H0189, H1270,
    H1301, L0201, L0499, N0440, O0854, O1023
Steer, William, jr., rector of Whiston, fl. 1738: A0083
Stennet, [ ]: T0112
Stepney, George, 1663–1707: A1785, B0508, D0134,
    V0034, Y0237
Sterne, Laurence, 1713–1768: H0280, O0244
Sternhold, Thomas, d. 1549: B0373, H0343, H0345, H1338,
    H1476, I0232, I0439, I1383, J0122, L0554, L0580, M0686,
    O0336, O0338, O0342, O0350, O0476, O0495, T0890

Stevens, George Alexander, 1710–1784: C0084, I0970,
    O0852, O1012, S0831
Stevens, Thomas, Baptist minister: A0066, A0406,
    A0834, A0841, A0855, A1053, B0161, B0177, B0214, B0268,
    B0441, B0584, C0361, C0478, C0563, D0238, D0265,
    D0285, D0301, D0369, D0384, D0402, E0035, E0047,
    E0064, E0135, E0178, F0210, F0637, F0659, G0120, G0302,
    G0402, G0479, H0090, H0176, H0192, H0236, H0258,
    H0281, H0366, H0539, H1159, H1213, H1226, H1241, H1254,
    H1304, H1368, H1434, H1451, I0148, I0377, I0466, I1212,
    I1486, J0019, J0047, J0049, J0056, J0060, J0063,
    J0066, J0074, J0076, J0078, K0039, L0500, L0502,
    L0594, L0611, L0618, M0550, M0644, M0706, N0082,
    N0145, N0321, N0346, N0465, O0330, O0345, O0436,
    O0581, O0603, O0658, O0823, O1057, O1105, P0032, P0250,
    P0274, P0278, P0285, P0314, R0087, S0061, S0115, S0460,
    S0676, S0785, S0825, S0839, S1026, S1279, T0053, T0127,
    T0256, T0698, T0719, T0846, T1093, T1173, T1225,
    T1477, T1749, T2342, T2569, T2573, T2640, T2641,
    T2751, T3222, U0087, V0010, W0037, W0083, W0157,
    W0241, W0267, W0397, W0399, W0413, W0472, W0621,
    W0622, W0859, W1290, W1314, W1416, W1434, W1502,
    W1526, W1676, W2144, W2207, W2208, W2209, W2529,
    W2539, W2546, Y0051, Y0161, Y0230, Y0232, Y0252,
    Y0263, Z0007
Stevenson, [ ], of Spalding: T1903
Stevenson, Rev. [ ]: G0311, W2348, W2350
Stevenson, Thomas: T2046
Steward, Sir Simeon: W1370
Stewart, C. E.: M0185
Stillingfleet, Benjamin, 1702–1771: O0732, W0088
Stirley, Nicholas: T2706
Stockdale, Percival, 1736–1811: M0147
Stokes, David: B0070, U0060, W0375, W1295
Stone, [ ], dean: S1119
Stone, Benjamin, of New College Oxford
    (1605–1609): F0263, J0037, T0190, T1208, W2134
Stonestreet, Henry: W2313
Straight, John: A0632
Strangways, Sir John, 1584–1666: A0206, A0268, A0433,
    A0495, A0659, A0956, A1017, A1330, B0106, B0347, B0542,
    B0618, E0046, F0079, F0224, F0533, G0389, H0405,
    H0421, H0429, H0447, I0004, I0040, I0107, I0321, I0529,
    I1091, I1308, I1309, I1519, J0123, K0007, L0316, L0565,
    M0656, N0163, N0304, O0353, O1054, S0114, S0466,
    S0566, S0690, S0724, S1143, T0026, T0684, T0894,
    T0923, T0931, T1032, T1110, T1293, T1424, T1486,
    T1838, T1984, T2383, T2674, T2854, T3371, T3386,
    W0152, W0350, W0447, W0456, W0882, W1107, W1108,
    W1446, W2170, W2545
Street, [ ]: T1142
Strode, William, 1602–1645: A0014, A0123, A0511, A1464,
    A1469, A1613, B0056, B0203, C0024, C0151, C0292, C0519,
    F0061, G0022, G0125, G0142, G0149, G0283, H0333, H0339,
    H0588, H1193, I0043, I0195, I0216, I0333, I0477, I0539,
    I0598, I0726, I0894, I1307, I1436, I1504, K0010, L0391,
    L0393, L0452, L0540, L0652, L0697, M0087, M0619,
    N0195, N0506, O0461, O0643, O1032, P0082, P0279,
    R0160, R0186, S0225, S0520, S0691, S1069, T0018, T1453,
    T1468, T1706, T1860, T2074, T2179, T2604, T2761,
    T2843, V0084, W0092, W0173, W0179, W0540, W0647,

W0711, W1443, W1476, W1520, W1536, W1753, W2362, W2397, Y0398

Strutt, Benjamin, 1754–1827: M0256

Strutt, Joseph: N0405

Stuart, Lady Louisa: W0153

Stukeley, William, 1687–1765: A1698, B0411, H1499, O0716, P0071, S0329

Suckling, Sir John, 1609–1642: D0382, H1131, I0317, I0802, I0884, L0654, L0671, O1155, T2329, W2262

Sudley, Mary, viscountess: T3262

Suffolk and Berkshire, Henry Howard, earl, 1739–1779: H0301

Sunbury, [ ], lord: A1732

Swayne, Arthur, 1609–1644: I0178

Swift, Jonathan, 1667–1745: A0435, A0689, A0894, A1170, A1471, A1530, A1596, A1873, C0057, C0284, D0043, D0170, D0313, H0091, H0296, I0263, I0933, I0997, I1313, I1563, L0591, M0726, N0428, O0817, O0983, P0100, Q0026, R0225, T0222, T0615, T1368, T1414, T1879, T2487, T2488, T3195, W0065, W0242, W0268, W0742, W0789, W0850, W0946, W1160, W1952, W2351, W2364, W2399

Sylvester, Joshua, 1563–1618: A0706, A1144, A1354, B0332, B0585, C0226, C0484, E0057, I1072, I1196, I1513, L0282, M0244, O0546, R0236, S0017, T0509, T0510, T1184, T1195, T1497, T1686, T2102, W1612, W2107, W2419, Y0404

Symonds, John, sr.: I0080

T., C.: W1031

T., G.: L0319

T., R.: W0513

T., S.: W0398

T., S. T.: A1587

T., W.: W1854, W2547

T——n, Lady F.: I0603

Talbot. [ ]: I0689

Tankerville, [ ], lady: N0146

Tanner, Paul: H0089

Tarlton, Richard: O0260

Tate, Nahum, 1652–1715: C0348, I1356, N0064, T2433, W0930, W1728

Taylor, Elizabeth: Y0194

Taylor, J., of Norwich: N0437

Taylor, John, 1580–1653: F0013, G0401, L0439, M0307, M0380, T1441, T2467, T2849, V0088, W0182, W1553

Taylor, John, 1704–1766: W1841

Taylor, John, 1750–1826: W0105

Taylor, William: A0039, A0198, A0273, A1297, H0240, H1134, H1418, I1492, I1542, M0368, Q0025, T0522, W1415

Tebbit, John: H1416

Temple, [ ]: W1847

Temple, Sir William, 1628–1698: T1248

Templeman, Dr. [ ]: B0282

Terrent, Jeremiah: C0260

Thomas, Captain [ ]: C0433

Thomas, Crook: I1327, I1337

Thompson, Captain [ ]: T1630

Thompson, Dr. [ ]: C0573, F0015, F0028, T2555, T3078

Thompson, Mrs. [ ]: P0094

Thompson, Ed.: A1520

Thompson, William: J0082

Thomson, [ ]: A1208, G0299, P0106

Thomson, James, 1700–1748: A0749, A0793, A1668, C0322, F0482, H0061, H1032, O0748, S0782, S1348, S1354, S1355, W0804, W1166

Thorne, [ ]: W1222

Thornton, Bonnell, 1724–1768: T0675, T1773

Thurston, Joseph: B0151

Thurston, Katherine: H1469

Tichborne, Chidiock, c. 1558–1586: M0661

Tickell, Thomas, 1686–1740: C0042, H0044, H1152, O0309

Tierney, [ ], of Peterhouse College, Cambridge: T1446

Tierney, George, 1761–1830: O0736

Tipping, Thomas, 1686–1752: D0214

Titley, Walter, 1700–1768: D0099, H0482, Y0132

Toft, Joshua: W1025

Tollett, Elizabeth, 1694–1754: I1345, O0853

Tomkins, [ ]: W1752

Tooke, Charles: B0115

Toplady, [ ]: F0201

Touchet, Lady Amy: M0690

Towneley, Zouch: E0078, I1493, T1620

Townshend, Miss [ ]: W1985

Townshend, Aurelian, fl. 1601–1643: B0006, L0209, T2110, V0041

Traherne, Thomas, 1636–1674: A1222, D0423, F0187, I0495, M0569, O0620, T0828, T2564

Trap, Dr. [ ]: D0217

Trapp, Joseph, 1679–1747: B0121, B0131, T0768, T0775

Trell, Mrs. [ ]: M0470

Trevenen, Mat.: W2371

Trevor, Peggy: O0555, T2784

Trim, Marjorie, pseud.: H1211

Trotter, Dr. [ ]: T0458

Trumbull, Sir William, 1639–1716: A1649, A1693, B0128, B0430, C0391, D0366, F0614, G0420, G0439, H0136, H0233, H0234, H0373, H0583, H1452, I0183, L0571, M0556, M0685, M0700, M0704, N0093, O0361, O0468, O0481, O0597, O1017, O1020, S1219, S1245, T0403, T1859, T2183, T2294, T2443, T2828, U0076, W0323, W0487, W1086, W1882, W1945, W2022, W2578, W2580

Truth, Rebecca, pseud.: F0252

Tucker, Josiah: W0695

Tunstall, William: F0677

Turberville, George, 1540–1610: A1273

Turner, Sir Edward, 1719–1770: W1245

Turner, J.: H0682

Turningham, [ ]: C0097

Tutchin, John, 1661?–1707: I0397, L0531

Tweddell, John: B0342, T0115

Urquhart, Sir Thomas, 1611–1660: A0044, A0051, A0085, A0106, A0111, A0128, A0135, A0142, A0144, A0145, A0153, A0154, A0155, A0175, A0182, A0184, A0193, A0209, A0217, A0219, A0226, A0229, A0270, A0297, A0327, A0381, A0382, A0383, A0396, A0397, A0425, A0427, A0455, A0460, A0470, A0472, A0488, A0504, A0527, A0530, A0552, A0553, A0582, A0624, A0630, A0656, A0782, A0869, A0881, A0883, A0886, A0924, A0952, A0963, A0969, A0978, A0979, A0982, A0983, A1034, A1037, A1039, A1041, A1046, A1047, A1048, A1049, A1050, A1051,

Urquhart, Sir Thomas, (*continued*)

A1080, A1099, A1101, A1103, A1139, A1163, A1166, A1235,
A1278, A1291, A1359, A1366, A1373, A1392, A1431, A1447,
A1499, A1500, A1501, A1516, A1528, A1534, A1537, A1546,
A1583, A1589, A1607, A1610, A1614, A1629, A1642, A1653,
A1654, A1661, A1674, A1685, A1686, A1710, A1723, A1728,
A1737, A1739, A1741, A1742, A1763, A1776, A1782, A1802,
A1811, A1850, A1854, A1950, B0010, B0011, B0024, B0044,
B0077, B0079, B0109, B0110, B0112, B0113, B0217, B0218,
B0220, B0221, B0222, B0225, B0226, B0314, B0316, B0318,
B0320, B0330, B0331, B0357, B0371, B0459, B0462, B0463,
B0464, B0465, B0487, B0565, B0604, B0608, B0625,
B0635, B0657, B0658, B0678, C0030, C0189, C0190,
C0192, C0195, C0198, C0208, C0211, C0220, C0449, C0495,
C0500, C0501, C0515, C0532, C0569, C0581, C0609,
D0088, D0097, D0152, D0197, D0201, D0213, D0220,
D0256, D0260, D0261, D0262, D0295, D0342, D0348,
D0353, E0010, E0011, E0013, E0018, E0020, E0021, E0022,
E0023, E0029, E0079, E0098, E0100, E0113, E0122, E0143,
E0144, F0068, F0081, F0195, F0198, F0199, F0244, F0245,
F0254, F0272, F0309, F0366, F0374, F0377, F0383, F0398,
F0399, F0407, F0410, F0413, F0424, F0431, F0465, F0517,
F0518, F0536, F0540, F0560, F0578, F0580, F0588, F0609,
F0652, F0674, F0718, F0731, F0766, G0009, G0023, G0067,
G0192, G0198, G0201, G0205, G0211, G0220, G0222, G0223,
G0277, G0278, G0338, G0339, G0360, G0371, G0377, G0412,
G0426, G0441, G0465, H0003, H0011, H0022, H0032,
H0035, H0039, H0182, H0297, H0329, H0332, H0356,
H0362, H0370, H0376, H0377, H0379, H0380, H0384,
H0387, H0388, H0390, H0397, H0398, H0400, H0401,
H0402, H0410, H0463, H0468, H0487, H0515, H0529,
H0549, H0575, H0577, H0582, H0587, H0589, H0593,
H0595, H0596, H0597, H0599, H0603, H0605, H0610,
H0612, H0613, H0978, H0985, H1018, H1019, H1020,
H1021, H1028, H1033, H1038, H1059, H1063, H1067,
H1068, H1069, H1073, H1076, H1080, H1081, H1084,
H1085, H1090, H1092, H1093, H1094, H1097, H1103,
H1143, H1188, H1192, H1195, H1316, H1367, I0019, I0088,
I0093, I0095, I0114, I0115, I0119, I0128, I0135, I0177,
I0192, I0200, I0235, I0244, I0256, I0269, I0270, I0271,
I0280, I0281, I0287, I0310, I0325, I0398, I0400, I0402,
I0438, I0440, I0441, I0442, I0447, I0450, I0456, I0464,
I0467, I0471, J0006, J0017, J0107, J0112, J0115, J0121,
J0128, K0001, K0002, K0006, K0037, K0042, K0045,
L0035, L0060, L0063, L0064, L0107, L0115, L0139, L0142,
L0170, L0185, L0186, L0196, L0212, L0225, L0262, L0285,
L0306, L0311, L0376, L0385, L0399, L0468, L0633, L0640,
L0650, L0651, L0653, L0655, L0666, L0675, L0688,
L0689, L0693, L0696, L0709, L0710, M0004, M0054,
M0072, M0074, M0075, M0077, M0085, M0086, M0092,
M0107, M0112, M0118, M0120, M0162, M0223, M0227,
M0228, M0229, M0230, M0249, M0250, M0298, M0310,
M0312, M0320, M0323, M0327, M0341, M0343, M0350,
M0362, M0363, M0367, M0391, M0429, M0431, M0447,
M0571, M0575, M0577, M0581, M0612, M0627, M0634,
M0666, M0694, M0707, N0040, N0041, N0045, N0047,
N0101, N0117, N0132, N0134, N0141, N0148, N0157,
N0159, N0160, N0164, N0165, N0170, N0186, N0190,
N0227, N0229, N0234, N0247, N0260, N0262, N0270,
N0279, N0281, N0283, N0284, N0288, N0290, N0319,
N0336, N0348, N0369, N0385, N0399, N0451, N0500,

N0532, O0043, O0082, O0130, O0133, O0136, O0143,
O0148, O0156, O0163, O0167, O0169, O0201, O0378,
O0614, O0884, O0999, O1019, O1022, O1046, O1066,
O1075, O1077, O1084, O1108, O1120, O1122, O1126, O1134,
O1143, P0039, P0059, P0098, P0135, P0174, P0209, P0215,
P0236, P0243, P0298, P0305, P0336, P0349, P0358, P0364,
Q0003, Q0011, R0077, R0088, R0098, R0135, R0141,
R0174, S0022, S0028, S0173, S0182, S0286, S0287, S0288,
S0289, S0290, S0291, S0292, S0293, S0294, S0295, S0296,
S0297, S0298, S0299, S0300, S0301, S0302, S0303, S0304,
S0305, S0306, S0307, S0308, S0317, S0318, S0322, S0405,
S0408, S0412, S0413, S0414, S0418, S0420, S0424, S0426,
S0427, S0428, S0429, S0431, S0435, S0439, S0444, S0459,
S0465, S0482, S0524, S0591, S0674, S0682, S0693, S0701,
S0708, S0732, S0789, S0802, S0817, S0819, S0821, S0823,
S0844, S0859, S0897, S0908, S0910, S0911, S0912, S0918,
S0921, S0922, S0928, S0940, S0942, S0944, S0945, S0962,
S0967, S0969, S0976, S0977, S0978, S0979, S1024, S1025,
S1043, S1175, S1193, S1194, S1202, S1208, S1214, S1215,
S1216, S1218, S1220, S1246, S1374, T0029, T0035, T0054,
T0056, T0059, T0066, T0138, T0148, T0168, T0171,
T0172, T0173, T0174, T0176, T0178, T0180, T0186,
T0196, T0197, T0199, T0200, T0204, T0205, T0210,
T0211, T0212, T0214, T0215, T0217, T0219, T0224,
T0228, T0230, T0231, T0234, T0235, T0243, T0250,
T0251, T0255, T0259, T0260, T0261, T0267, T0271,
T0277, T0278, T0282, T0285, T0291, T0293, T0294,
T0295, T0297, T0298, T0300, T0301, T0302, T0312,
T0324, T0326, T0327, T0332, T0345, T0349, T0371,
T0390, T0391, T0396, T0399, T0404, T0406, T0421,
T0430, T0435, T0462, T0467, T0474, T0482, T0483,
T0494, T0506, T0513, T0515, T0519, T0531, T0534,
T0541, T0545, T0567, T0570, T0573, T0587, T0594,
T0599, T0605, T0608, T0614, T0618, T0619, T0627,
T0646, T0673, T0680, T0683, T0704, T0714, T0725,
T0727, T0731, T0735, T0741, T0752, T0766, T0776,
T0781, T0795, T0800, T0805, T0813, T0863, T0883,
T0886, T0925, T0927, T0928, T0929, T0940, T0941,
T0951, T0958, T0960, T0961, T0966, T0967, T0973,
T0989, T0997, T1012, T1013, T1022, T1042, T1055,
T1063, T1071, T1074, T1078, T1080, T1094, T1095,
T1108, T1111, T1117, T1118, T1119, T1127, T1128, T1133,
T1134, T1135, T1137, T1138, T1149, T1152, T1155, T1170,
T1171, T1179, T1181, T1203, T1209, T1214, T1224, T1238,
T1239, T1260, T1263, T1271, T1275, T1301, T1303, T1305,
T1313, T1320, T1334, T1337, T1346, T1348, T1358, T1386,
T1398, T1410, T1413, T1418, T1430, T1438, T1440,
T1442, T1455, T1460, T1467, T1469, T1480, T1482,
T1483, T1502, T1503, T1507, T1512, T1527, T1528, T1529,
T1553, T1556, T1557, T1579, T1585, T1613, T1617, T1619,
T1621, T1624, T1634, T1672, T1682, T1683, T1690,
T1703, T1704, T1713, T1714, T1715, T1717, T1719, T1720,
T1723, T1724, T1725, T1727, T1729, T1740, T1743, T1745,
T1752, T1757, T1767, T1780, T1790, T1826, T1846, T1862,
T1904, T1906, T1908, T1921, T1936, T1958, T1964,
T1972, T1975, T1976, T1981, T1983, T1986, T1988,
T1996, T2155, T2157, T2159, T2160, T2173, T2174, T2175,
T2188, T2189, T2190, T2191, T2192, T2198, T2204, T2205,
T2210, T2214, T2216, T2223, T2225, T2232, T2238, T2242,
T2250, T2251, T2252, T2253, T2254, T2255, T2257, T2261,
T2262, T2264, T2265, T2268, T2281, T2282, T2287,

T2298, T2301, T2302, T2311, T2312, T2315, T2321, T2322,
T2324, T2325, T2326, T2327, T2328, T2333, T2334, T2345,
T2351, T2374, T2591, T2592, T2648, T2653, T2668,
T2675, T2676, T2677, T2690, T2771, T2794, T2799,
T2803, T2810, T2819, T2830, T2832, T2834, T2858,
T2859, T2868, T2900, T2910, T2923, T2930, T2951,
T2970, T2977, T2985, T2997, T3003, T3010, T3016,
T3098, T3105, T3106, T3114, T3116, T3194, T3220, T3226,
T3339, T3340, T3370, T3372, T3374, U0062, U0137,
U0144, V0055, V0056, V0058, V0069, V0073, V0081,
V0091, W0032, W0048, W0049, W0050, W0073, W0074,
W0096, W0099, W0101, W0102, W0103, W0109, W0114,
W0116, W0124, W0128, W0131, W0133, W0151, W0276,
W0279, W0298, W0332, W0376, W0407, W0411, W0423,
W0425, W0467, W0478, W0479, W0502, W0503, W0510,
W0511, W0520, W0544, W0566, W0678, W0684, W0696,
W0698, W0718, W0722, W0726, W0727, W0736, W0747,
W0802, W0837, W0855, W0890, W1004, W1005, W1027,
W1044, W1084, W1159, W1183, W1248, W1296, W1384,
W1406, W1473, W1480, W1508, W1587, W1590, W1611,
W1623, W1736, W1758, W1781, W1786, W1802, W1829,
W1832, W1834, W1835, W1837, W1855, W1858, W1876,
W1910, W1924, W1929, W1955, W1956, W1957, W1961,
W1969, W1971, W1973, W1977, W1986, W1991, W1992,
W1993, W1996, W2004, W2008, W2009, W2010, W2012,
W2025, W2032, W2034, W2035, W2037, W2038, W2039,
W2043, W2048, W2079, W2080, W2083, W2084, W2085,
W2088, W2090, W2091, W2095, W2099, W2102, W2103,
W2104, W2105, W2106, W2113, W2133, W2139, W2145,
W2148, W2155, W2156, W2168, W2172, W2197, W2198,
W2205, W2206, W2217, W2229, W2239, W2250, W2251,
W2253, W2254, W2255, W2258, W2268, W2271, W2287,
W2298, W2303, W2331, W2333, W2334, W2345, W2347,
W2349, W2393, W2474, W2511, W2554, W2576, W2588,
W2594, W2596, W2598, W2604, W2623, W2624, W2630,
Y0268, Y0271, Y0272, Y0275, Y0276, Y0279, Y0286,
Y0289, Y0293, Y0294, Y0295, Y0300, Y0304, Y0311,
Y0315, Y0317, Y0318, Y0319, Y0320, Y0321, Y0322, Y0323,
Y0327, Y0328, Y0345, Y0347, Y0355, Y0356, Y0357, Y0364,
Y0365, Y0366, Y0373, Y0377, Y0378, Y0379, Y0381, Y0382,
Y0383, Y0384, Y0385, Y0386, Y0388, Y0390, Y0414,
Y0420, Y0421, Y0422, Y0427, Y0431, Y0435, Y0442,
Y0463, Y0468, Y0469, Y0471, Y0472, Y0473, Y0477,
Y0478, Y0480, Y0483, Y0490, Y0492, Y0493, Y0495,
Y0499, Y0500, Y0501, Y0502, Y0503, Y0505, Y0507,
Y0509, Y0511, Y0512, Y0513, Y0516, Y0518, Y0520, Y0525,
Y0530, Y0534, Y0538, Y0540, Y0547, Y0549, Y0551,
Y0559, Y0562, Y0567, Y0569, Y0570, Y0572, Y0573,
Y0574, Y0575, Y0578, Y0579, Y0580, Y0581, Y0582,
Y0585, Y0589, Y0593, Y0603, Y0607

Vanbrugh, Sir John, 1664-1726: O0068
Vanhomrigh, Esther, 1690-1723: H0051
Vaughan, J.: W2180
Veel, Robert: H1232
Vernon, Mrs. [ ]: Y0449
Vernon, John: A0326, C0010
Vintner, Henry: L0234

W., [ ], of Eton: R0085
W., E.: N0511, W0215

W., H.: Y0337
W., I.: N0419, W0826
W., J.: F0472, H0274, H0865, L0658, S0283, W2252
W., R.: C0083, H0773
W., S.: M0614, T1023
W., T.: M0632
W., W.: O0423
W———, Eliza: A1547
W——n, Dr. [ ]: H0731
Wakefield, G.: F0567
Wakeford, Mrs. [ ]: W0211
Waker, James: C0056
Waldo, [ ]: I0246
Waldron, Dr. [ ]: S0534
Walker, Edward: S1169
Walker, [ ]: I1132
Walker, Harriet: W2285
Walker, J., of Eton: L0489, T1769
Walker, John, 1692-1741: A0124, A0499, A0500, A0966,
A1525, D0146, D0376, E0112, G0014, G0295, G0304, G0313,
H0070, H0188, H0614, H0616, I0018, I0381, I0606, I0911,
I0919, I1299, L0048, L0050, L0533, M0164, M0436,
M0451, M0479, M0564, M0650, M0737, N0081, O0009,
O0775, O0980, O0996, S0540, S0589, T0491, T1139,
T1605, W0123, W0219, W0255, W0831, W0915, W0936,
W1014, W1109, W1223, W2222, Y0024
Walker, William, fl. 1599: T1487
Waller, Edmund, 1606-1687: A1603, B0312, B0545, C0180,
C0185, C0187, C0215, F0002, F0031, F0282, G0157, L0378,
N0105, N0378, N0414, P0063, S1200, T0288, T0730,
W1436, W1441, W1727, W1827
Walpole, Catherine (Shorter), lady, 1682-1737: B0036
Walpole, Edward: W2054
Walsh, William, 1663-1700: A0719, A0763, A0910, A1320,
B0141, C0106, C0109, C0173, C0510, D0333, G0151, G0172,
I0211, I1465, L0263, N0477, R0178, S0494, S0495, T0169,
T0899, T2350, T2581, T3368, V0021, W0409, W0415,
W0432, W0671, W1056, W1749, W1762, W1950, W2496,
Y0229
Walsingham, Mrs. [ ]: I0140, I1130, S1099, T2568
Walsingham, William De Grey, baron, 1719-1781: L0171
Walter, John: W2405
Walters, John: B0554
Walwyn, [ ]: Y0218
Wander, J.: A1939
Ward, Edward, 1667-1731: D0320, G0332, H0944, I1139,
I1366
Ward, James: D0239, H0926
Ward, Samuel, 1577-1640: A1161, O0565
Warmestry, Gervase: T0334
Warmestry, Thomas, 1610-1665: K0066
Warner, [ ]: C0585
Warton, [ ]: A0909
Warton, Joseph, 1722-1800: H0110, H0564, O0363, O0576
Warton, Thomas, 1728-1790: A0284, B0266, B0302,
G0343, L0701, T0381, T0411, T0737, W0305, W1193
Wastell, [ ]: F0376
Watkins, Anne: C0477
Watson, John: M0602
Watson, Thomas, d. 1686: T2479
Watson-Taylor, George, d. 1841: M0177

Watts, Isaac, 1674–1748: A0826, A0935, A1022, A1224,
A1258, A1869, A1917, B0078, B0178, B0183, B0184, B0195,
B0197, B0274, B0422, C0256, C0360, C0362, C0414,
D0037, D0192, E0043, E0110, E0131, F0214, H0282,
H0289, H1153, H1154, H1166, H1208, H1386, H1391, I0030,
I0158, I0205, I0224, I0358, I0553, I1400, I1401, I1503,
J0058, J0059, J0073, J0077, J0079, K0011, K0028, L0113,
L0160, L0271, L0279, L0290, L0338, L0422, L0455, L0566,
L0604, M0029, M0138, M0670, M0741, N0046, N0316,
N0413, N0446, N0454, N0456, N0520, O0669, O0801,
O1138, O1152, P0165, S0008, S0090, S0340, S0452, S0741,
S1148, S1369, T0790, T0860, T0926, T1003, T1107, T1392,
T1423, T1475, T1600, T1663, T2142, T2201, T2483,
T2889, T3057, T3279, T3307, W0059, W0134, W0401,
W1060, W1322, W1355, W1357, W1373, W1965, W2243
Watts, Robert, 1683–1726: T0578, T3228
Wd., J.: I0844
Weaver, Thomas, 1616–1663: A1004, D0172, N0230
Web, [ ]: L0537
Webb, [ ]: A1559, L0214, O0941
Webb, Arnold: F0286
Weever, [ ]: M0448
Welce, W.: M0475
Weldon, John, 1676–1736: I1372
Wells, John, 1623–1676: S1126
Welsted, Leonard, 1688–1714: O0049, O0238, A1954,
C0561, W1673
Wesley, Samuel, 1662–1735: A1899, B0259, O0573
Wesley, Samuel, 1691–1739: C0376, I0889, L0430, O0125,
P0218, S0710, S0920, W0813, W1252, W1640, W1795
West, Mrs. [ ]: E0091, M0592
West, Gilbert, 1703–1756: A1426, B0277, N0065, O0761,
S1291, W1514
West, Richard, fl. 1606–1619: I0847, Y0408
Westmorland, Mildmay Fane, 2nd earl, c. 1600–1666:
C0018
Weston, Gilbert: B0597
Weston, Nat.: H0327
Whaley, [ ]: Q0036
Whaley, John, 1710–1745: T2820
Wharton, Philip Wharton, 1st duke, 1698–1731: A1558,
A1791, D0114, F0714, G0232, H0128, I1064, L0203, O0988,
P0355, Q0039, S0106, S0656, T1948, W0973, W1467,
W1483, W2265
Wharton, Thomas Wharton, 1st marquis, 1648–1715:
H1110, I0013, O1095
Wharton, William, d. 1697: W0197
Wheatley, Phyllis, 1753–1784: H0092, M0299, T3294,
Y0109
Wheeler, Dr. [ ]: D0031
Wheton, [ ]: W1811
Whitakers, L.: V0025
White, Miss [ ], of Edgbaston: A0806, B0211, C0395,
H0001, H1324, I1272, L0287, M0681, O0395, O0683,
S0996, W1922
White, Henry Kirke, 1785–1806: W1147, Y0245
Whitehead, [ ]: L0298
Whitehead, George, 1636–1723: P0322
Whitehead, Paul, 1710–1774: T1314, V0049, Y0008
Whitehead, William, 1715–1785: A0176, B0537, H0945,
M0266, O0564, P0041

Whitehouse, [ ]: S0880
Whitney, Geffrey, 1548?–1601?: A0638, O0087, O0128,
T0837, T1425, U0155, W0848, W1911, W1988
Whittel, Thomas: T1168
Whittell, [ ]: G0312
Whittell, Mrs. [ ]: A0803
Whittingham, William, d. 1579: B0370, G0480, O0495,
T0849, T0850
Whittington, [ ]: E0003
Whyte, Laurence: H1400
Wild, Robert, 1609–1679: A1177, A1340, A1880, C0448,
E0087, F0598, G0190, G0345, G0442, H0703, H0845,
I0130, I0813, I1578, L0082, L0551, N0060, N0416, N0528,
R0046, R0067, S0680, S1125, T0130, T0453
Wilkes, John, 1727–1797: A1958
Wilkes, Wetenhall, d. 1751: W0217
Wilkinson, Dr. [ ]: I0960
Wilkinson, Henry, 1616–1690: O0154
Wilkinson, J.: G0099, W1173, W2342
Wilkinson, Thomas, 1751–1836: N0527
Williams, [ ]: F0238, W0436
Williams, Helen Maria, 1762–1827: C0560, R0203,
T3274, W1582, W1690
Williams, Henry: O0559, T2018
Williams, Joshua, of Kidderminster: B0233, O0692,
T3310, W1654
Williams, Maria: M0439
Williams, R.: W0908
Willowby, Dr.: T3077
Wilson, Cuthbert: H0307
Wilson, John: C0409, O0242
Wilson, T.: T2297
Wilson, Thomas: O1009
Winchilsea, Anne Finch, countess, 1661–1720: B0391,
G0045, H1255, H1317, T1555, T2831, W0337, W0612,
W0820, W1684
Wingfield, John: W2520
Winter, John: C0175, D0076, I0907, J0035, L0542, T0084,
T1754, T2407, Y0016
Wither, George, 1588–1667: B0563, F0095, G0249, I0558,
L0597, M0524, M0683, R0133, S0378, T1696, T2211
Wodehouse, Edmund: A0059, A0120, A0134, A0140,
A0171, A0424, A0622, A0625, A0709, A0938, A0961,
A1128, A1255, A1259, A1382, A1400, A1423, A1432, A1440,
A1586, A1675, A1694, A1733, A1788, B0623, D0204,
D0206, D0208, D0227, D0231, D0335, D0389, D0411,
E0007, E0147, E0148, E0183, F0223, F0232, F0240, F0241,
F0683, G0208, G0209, G0214, G0216, G0217, G0224, G0231,
G0259, G0261, G0262, G0264, G0266, G0268, G0269,
G0271, G0272, G0274, G0275, G0276, G0280, G0281,
G0294, G0303, G0352, G0355, G0356, G0357, G0361, G0362,
G0413, H0210, H0243, H0363, H0409, H0413, H0418,
H0419, H0427, H0430, H0431, H0433, H0434, H0435,
H0441, H0446, H0449, H0458, H0464, H0537, H1030,
H1227, H1262, H1263, H1266, H1277, H1344, H1351, H1355,
H1359, H1361, H1362, H1373, H1390, H1406, H1412, I0060,
I0218, I0388, I0491, I0499, I0509, I0515, I0516, I0585,
I0610, I0675, I0797, I0861, I1107, K0048, L0126, L0127,
L0176, L0333, M0100, M0124, M0187, M0438, M0444,
M0541, M0543, M0544, M0545, M0552, M0574, M0587,
M0648, M0651, M0659, M0717, M0724, N0053, N0138,

N0140, N0185, N0280, N0379, N0497, O0084, O0233, O0298, O0332, O0337, O0341, O0354, O0359, O0410, O0411, O0533, O0534, O0557, O0649, O0650, O0656, O0657, O0659, O0665, O0666, O0676, O0777, O0783, O0837, O0838, O0893, O0896, O1070, O1071, O1074, O1081, O1091, O1092, O1113, O1114, O1132, R0180, S0399, S0402, S0500, S0753, S0927, S1109, T0002, T0003, T0004, T0005, T0183, T0191, T0193, T0202, T0246, T0266, T0272, T0275, T0289, T0317, T0416, T0418, T0547, T0613, T0702, T0710, T0713, T0715, T0747, T0799, T0811, T0872, T0935, T0957, T1020, T1091, T1194, T1273, T1306, T1335, T1393, T1450, T1463, T1472, T1474, T1956, T2199, T2200, T2290, T2307, T2316, T2317, T2462, T2465, T2517, T2519, T2538, T2575, T2619, T2620, T2622, T2630, T2638, T2685, T2694, T2705, T2715, T2757, T2880, T2884, T2943, T3234, V0013, W0191, W0282, W0357, W0393, W0412, W0418, W0618, W0638, W0704, W0710, W0982, W0983, W1048, W1057, W1089, W1350, W1437, W1936, W1937, W1972, W1995, W2002, W2016, W2019, W2081, W2111, W2343, Y0227

Wodehouse, Sir Philip, 1608-1681: A0019, A0020, A0068, A0069, A0089, A0099, A0105, A0125, A0151, A0179, A0180, A0187, A0204, A0221, A0228, A0236, A0239, A0317, A0414, A0415, A0432, A0464, A0475, A0491, A0507, A0556, A0658, A0744, A0833, A0870, A0943, A0986, A1113, A1116, A1122, A1133, A1141, A1220, A1239, A1345, A1415, A1453, A1487, A1526, B0055, B0085, B0091, B0102, B0103, B0144, B0219, B0241, B0354, B0477, B0655, C0197, C0557, D0383, D0408, E0049, E0123, F0091, F0113, F0259, F0261, F0545, F0546, G0087, G0112, G0119, G0122, G0203, G0204, G0263, G0288, G0301, G0341, H0231, H0304, H0361, H0368, H0474, H0475, H0485, H0527, H0528, H0585, H0601, H0607, H0608, H0619, H1024, H1025, H1026, H1045, H1057, H1086, H1087, H1098, H1161, I0003, I0032, I0039, I0071, I0098, I0197, I0221, I0267, I0274, I0322, I0349, I0482, I0719, I0760, I0819, I0921, I1006, I1126, I1128, I1289, I1297, I1422, I1459, I1476, I1488, I1496, J0117, L0157, L0204, L0230, L0231, L0317, L0353, L0433, L0445, L0636, L0644, L0703, M0006, M0060, M0258, M0329, M0449, M0558, M0584, M0643, M0712, N0004, N0010, N0033, N0084, N0098, N0188, N0236, N0265, N0289, N0294, O0207, O0235, O0606, O0626, O0839, O1064, O1124, O1148, P0014, P0081, P0084, P0099, P0112, P0113, P0226, P0251, P0273, R0012, R0013, R0072, R0137, R0192, R0207, S0057, S0215, S0372, S0409, S0415, S0422, S0440, S0568, S0571, S0608, S0727, S0847, S0865, S0953, S0956, S1001, S1056, S1201, S1213, S1358, T0001, T0057, T0170, T0188, T0417, T0685, T0764, T0817, T0915, T0950, T1098, T1297, T1310, T1465, T1551, T1667, T1691, T1728, T1793, T1795, T1820, T1835, T1858, T1868, T1880, T1892, T1907, T1918, T1941, T1959, T2012, T2039, T2070, T2088, T2163, T2314, T2355, T2356, T2379, T2399, T2495, T2508, T2518, T2534, T2535, T2536, T2537, T2539, T2540, T2560,

T2567, T2636, T2649, T2667, T2672, T2750, T2760, T2768, T2773, T2885, T2936, T2952, T3002, T3229, T3238, T3250, T3254, T3263, T3300, U0003, U0065, U0113, V0019, V0020, V0050, V0079, V0087, W0053, W0055, W0248, W0352, W0438, W0517, W0538, W0626, W0728, W0735, W0967, W1072, W1547, W1851, W1886, W1928, W2013, W2027, W2310, W2332, W2631, Y0454, Y0462

Wolcot, John ('Peter Pindar'), 1738-1819: A0027, A0362, A0437, A0512, A0790, A1519, A1582, B0045, D0035, E0051, F0050, F0257, F0314, F0315, F0661, G0191, H0952, H1168, H1214, H1217, H1246, I0083, I0286, I1271, L0473, L0474, M0601, O0200, O0220, O0319, O0513, O0545, O0745, O0755, P0350, S0085, S0105, S0120, S1316, S1326, S1333, S1359, T0532, T1206, T1599, T2058, T2119, T2207, T2472, W1302, W2100, W2213, W2281, Y0105

Wolseley, Robert, 1649-1697: D0001, F0274, H0310, R0187, T0601, T3093

Wolthers, [ ]: G0396

Woodd, George: G0057

Woodhouse, James, 1735-1820: A0786, L0217

Woodward, Thomas: T2103

Worlidge, Edward: S0248, W1759

Worseley, [ ]: A0735

Wotton, Sir Henry, 1568-1639: F0184, H1286, O0292, R0200, S0411, T2673, Y0350, Y0532

Woty, William, 1731?-1791: A0647, H0059, Y0042

Wrangham, Francis, 1769-1842: T1873

Wren, Matthew, 1585-1667: G0121

Wright, [ ]: S0054

Wright, Dr. [ ]: Y0030

Wright, W.: H1393

Wycherley, William, 1633-1688: A0535, A1628, S0644

Wyvill, Sir Christopher, 3rd bart., 1614-1672?: W1168

Wyvill, Ursula (Darcy), lady, 1619-1672: C0380, L0581, L0612, L0615, M0578, M0701, O0742, T1954

Yalden, Thomas, 1670-1736: D0029

Yates, Dr. [ ]: G0182

Yates, William: M0254

Yearsley, [ ]: I1471

Yorke, Charles: I1444, I1556

Young, Edward, 1683?-1765: A0594, A1206, L0408, M0344, S1306, T2403, W1793

Young, H.: S0367

Young, Mary: U0070

Young, Miss P.: T2091

Young, Sir William (=Yonge?): B0036, G0306, S0860, T2454

Young, Sir William, 1749-1815: M0402, S0187, T0942

Zappi, Faustina Marratti: O0572

Zouch, Richard, 1590-1661: H0982, O1078

Zwinger, Theodor, 1533-1588: W0484

III. Index of Names Mentioned

A., [ ]: U0057

A., [ ], lord: I1150

A., Mrs. [ ]: S0849

A., E.: L0501

A., S.: A1315

A———, Rev. [ ]: D0400

A———, Sir A———: A1380

A——ds, Miss [ ]: A0420

à Preen, Richard: *See* Preen, Richard à

Abbey, William, d. 1772: R0038

Abbot, Mordecai: H0615

Abelard, Peter, 1079–1142: I1159, I1276

Abercorn, Cecil (Hamilton) Hamilton, marchioness, 1770–1819: T0355, T1738

Abergavenny, Catharine Tatton Neville, d. 1729: S0388, T1559, T2908

Abingdon, Anna Maria (Collins) Bertie, countess, d. 1763: D0182

Abingdon, Henry: H0893

Abington, Frances, 1737–1815: A1484, C0032, C0466, F0490, W2488

Abney, Sir Thomas, 1691–1750: T2267

Aboyne, James Gordon, viscount, d. 1648: I0984, W2139

Adams, John: W1433

Adams, Sir William: A1526

Addington, [ ]: I0488

Addison, Joseph, 1672–1719: A1689, I1417, W0930, F0656, H0659, I1233, K0057, O0763, S0267, T3034, T3104, Y0181

Aiken, Dr. [ ]: N0177

Aiken, R.: M0622

Aikin, John, of Warrington, brother of Mrs. Barbauld: W2307

Aire, Jarvas: W2527

Aires, Mary: N0297

Airth, Agnes (Gray) Graham, countess: T2250

Aislabie, Mrs. [ ] (1779–80): B0271, H0561

Aislabie, William, d. 1781: O0146

Aiton, Dr. [ ]: W0593

Albemarle, Christopher Monck, 2nd duke, 1653–1688: A1769, N0069

Albemarle, George Monck, 1st duke, 1608–1670: A0661, H1327, I0979, R0156, T0453, W0971, W1333, W1491

Alberoni, Giulio, 1664–1752: A0988, T1444

Aldrich, Thomas: P0113

Aldworth, Mrs. [ ]: I0942

Alençon, Jean, duke, 1385–1415: W2408

Alford, [ ], lady, d. 1636: S0098

Alford, Sir William, d. 1642: I0029

Alfred, of Beverley, fl. 1143: A0519

Algarotti, Francesco, 1712–1764: H1013

Allen, Mother [ ]: H0717

Allen, Elizabeth: A1181

Allen, Simon, vicar of Bray, 1540–1588: A0491, I1017, I1018, I1096

Allen, Thomas, of Bath: N0143

Allestry, Jacob, 1653–1686: H1118, T0784

Allibond, Bridget: H0920

Allibond, Peter: H0628

Allinomook [Alknomock?], Cherokee: T1327

Allnutt, Charles: C0496

Allott, [ ] (1750): M0357

Almack, William, 1741–1781: I0481, Y0176

Alsop, Judith: A0117, S1377

Altham, Dr. [ ]: I0089

Altyre, [ ], lord, d. 1748: G0459

Ambler, Anne (Paxton): B0315

Ambler, Mary, d. 1725: I1052

Ambrose, Eleanor. *See* Palmer, Eleanor (Ambrose), lady.

Amelia Sophia Eleanora Hanover, princess, 1711–1786: A1066, S0110

Amherst, Jeffrey Amherst, baron, 1717–1797: I0132

Amhurst, Nicholas, 1697–1742: H0352, I0279, R0102, W0649

Amyas, Thomas: A1453

Ancaster, Mary (Panton) Bertie, duchess, d. 1793: G0036

Ancrum, Robert Ker, 1st earl, 1578–1654: C0220

André, John, major, 1750–1780: I0865

Andrews, [ ], comedian (1752): W1020

Andrews, Miss [ ]: H0534

Angell, Anne: A1262

Anglesey, Arthur Annesley, 1st earl, 1614–1686: A0983

Anguish, [ ], of Corpus Christi College, Oxford: S0968

Anguish, Ann: N0004

Anguish, Dolly: I1113

Anguish, Edmund: T1959

Anguish, John, capt.: S1358

Annabella Drummond, queen consort of Robert III, king of Scotland, d. 1401: T1574

Anne, queen of Great Britain, 1665–1714: A0049, A1494, B0009, B0154, B0450, B0593, D0375, D0409, H0130, H1310, I0946, I1038, I1244, I1247, I1342, L0269, L0292, L0515, M0026, M0028, M0206, M0615, N0077, O0140, O0210, O0217, O0218, O0592, O0729, P0011, P0017, R0008, S1199, T0402, T0624, T0641, T1002, T1120, T1122, T1459, T1971, W0052, W0189, W0670, W0879, W0989, W1002, W1265, W1266, W1294, W1340, W1683, W1762, W1889, W2247, W2435, Y0079, F0525

Anne, queen consort of James I, 1574–1619: G0436, H0736, M0130, N0224, N0295, S0252, T1543

Anne Boleyn, queen consort of Henry VIII, king of England, 1502–1536: T2362, H0813

Anne Hanover, of Great Britain, consort of William

IV, prince of Orange, 1709-1759: B0480, F0051, O0383, T1522, W1172, W1642

Anne of Austria, queen consort of Louis XIII, king of France, 1602-1666: T0173, Y0469

Anne of Cleves, queen consort of Henry VIII, king of England, 1515-1557: T2362

Ansley, John: W0773

Anson, Elizabeth (Yorke), lady, 1725-1760: T2962

Anson, George Anson, lord admiral, 1697-1762: L0105, L0490, T2962, T2991

Anson, Thomas, 1695-1773: A0687

Anstey, Christopher, 1724-1805: A1509

Anstruther, Lady Margaret: I0980

Ap Rees, Hugh: H1483

Appleby, [ ], lady: P0088

Apthorp, Sophia: I0453

Arabin, [ ]: A1091, A1289, D0251, H0403, J0090, O0074, P0062, S1293, T1396, T1427, W0758, Y0336

Arbuthnot, John, 1667-1734: S0491

Archer, Betty: S1354

Archer, Henry, of Eton School, c. 1716: T2271

Arden, Judith: I1154

Aretino, Pietro, 1492-1556: H0620, H0621, H0622, H0625

Arglass, [ ], lord: M0600

Argyll, [ ]: Y0334

Argyll, Archibald Campbell, 8th earl, 1598-1661: S0190, W2199

Argyll, Archibald Campbell, 9th earl, 1629-1685: P0167, T2086

Argyll, Archibald Campbell, 3rd duke, and 1st earl of Islay, 1682-1761: O0856, W1095

Argyll, Elizabeth (Gunning) Douglas-Hamilton Campbell, duchess, 1733-1790: A1754

Argyll, John Campbell, 2nd duke, 1678-1743: W0378

Argyll, John Campbell, 4th duke, c. 1693-1770: W2451

Argyll, John Campbell, 5th duke, 1723-1806: T1849

Arlington, Henry Bennet, 1st earl, 1618-1685: A1682, F0281, G0325

Armborough, [ ]: T0675

Armborough, Thomas: T0675

Armin, Ann: A1141, T1667

Armstrong, [ ]: R0172, S1264

Armstrong, Archibald, d. 1672: M0390, N0323

Armstrong, E.: T2309

Armstrong, Sir Thomas, 1624-1684: H0040

Arne, Mrs. [ ]: A1514, O0176

Arne, Thomas, 1710-1778: A1514, B0527, A1020

Arthington, B.: T1927

Artis, Mrs. [ ] (Pearse) (1741): N0161

Arundel, Thomas Howard, 21st earl, 1586-1644: H0039

Asberry, Rev. [ ]: L0228

Ashbrook, Elizabeth (Tatton) Flower, viscountess, d.1759: T0040

Ashbury, Joseph, 1638-1720: A1425

Ashenhurst, Dr. [ ]: F0340

Ashley, Lady Anne: W0791

Ashton, John, d.1691: A1745, B0189, H1027, L0116, T2460, W1535

Assheton, [ ]: W0779

Asshton, Anne (m. 1751): Y0062

Asshton, Ralph (m. 1751): Y0062

Astley, Dr. [ ]: A0068, T1918

Astley, Mrs. [ ] (Hobarts): A0068, T1918

Astley, Blanche (Watts): M0060, T2356

Astley, Elizabeth: S1056

Astley, Herbert: A0228

Astley, Sir Jacob: G0288, S1056, T1907, T2356

Atkins, John, of Plaistow, Essex (1756-57): A0602, I0518

Atkinson, [ ], [ ]: T2829

Atterbury, Francis, bp. of Rochester, 1662-1732: A0923, A1558, A1791, C0376, I0890, M0213, O0209, U0152, W2465, Y0251

Augusta Hanover, daughter of Frederick Louis, prince of Wales, 1737-1813: T1106, W2224

Augusta of Saxe-Gotha, Princess of Wales, 1719-1772: F0651, G0018, I0513, L0190, O0205, O0433, T3271, T3277, W0186, W1260, W1741

Aumont, Louis, duc d', 1667-1723: Y0087

Aylesford, Charlotte (Seymour) Finch, countess, d. 1805: T0014

Aylesford, Heneage Finch, 1st earl, 1649-1719: W2435

Ayliffe, John, 1676-1732: A1958

B., [ ]: B0669, C0079, Y0488

B., [ ] (1774): W1449

B., Miss [ ]: I0806, I1350

B., Mrs. [ ]: W0565, Y0524

B., B.: I1456

B., C. W.: T1318

B., Catharine: H0073

B., I. (1723): W2404

B., L.: H0071

B., Miss M.: I0158

B., O.: D0089

B., R. S.: W0528

B., S.: O0720

B., Miss S.: I0064

B., Z. (1773): A0799

B———, [ ]: T0307, T3137

B———, [ ], countess: T2703

B———, Rev. [ ]: T1665

B———, Mrs. [ ]: A0620, W0353

B———, Miss [ ] (1764): H0137

B———b———h, Miss P.: W1573

B———df———d, S. (1782): P0073

B———go, Miss [ ]: T2052

B———h———n, Miss [ ] (1787): W1699

B———ks———n, [ ], lady: S1121

B———m, [ ]: G0043, S0056

B———m, Miss Hy.: G0156

B———n, Miss [ ]: A0378, H0916

B———r, Molly: W0707

B———so———n, [ ], justice: D0157

B———ss———t, Mrs. [ ]: B0335

B———t, [ ]: B0543

B———w, Caesar: W1319

B———y, [ ]: W1975

B———y, Mrs. M.: B0622, W1352, Y0597

Baber, Sir John, physician, 1625-1704: T0130

Bacon, [ ]: T1370, T2289

Bacon, Dr. [ ]: W0213

Bacon, Sir Edward: H0601

Bacon, Elizabeth, lady: H0601
Bacon, Sir Francis: *See* St. Albans, Francis Bacon, 1st viscount
Bacon, John, 1740–1799: W0993
Bacon, Roger, 1214–1292: R0209, W1605
Baddison, John, capt.: A1274
Badger, [ ]: B0013
Bagot, Sir Edward, 1616–1673: I1547
Bagot, Sir Harvey, 1590–1660: H0375
Bagot, Lewis, bishop of Norwich (1783–1790): D0056
Bailey, Richard, president of St. John's College, Oxford: S0031
Baillie, George, d. 1738?: W1771
Bajazid I, sultan of Turkey, 1347–1403: A0325
Baker, Mrs. [ ]: A1904
Baker, Ann: C0074
Baker, Anthony: H0835
Baker, John: H0761
Baker, Thomas, 1656–1740: F0401, I0721
Baker, William: F0729
Baldock, Sir Robert, d. 1691: R0207
Bale, John, 1495–1563: S0808
Bales, William, colonel (2): S0820
Ball, Jo., weaver of Spittlefields: H0899
Ball, John, d. 1381: W1171
Balliol, John, king of Scotland, d. 1269: J0087
Balmerino, Arthur Elphinstone, 6th baron, 1688–1746: A1866
Bambridge, Dr. [ ]: A0173, A1209, H0565, I1070
Bampfield, Thomas, d.1693: A0699
Bancroft, Richard, abp., d. 1619: A0227
Bancroft, Thomas, fl. 1633–1658: A0104, S0695
Banknot, Anne: H0877
Banknot, William: H0877
Banks, [ ]: C0022
Banks, Miss [ ] (1745): A0149, B0517, B0518, C0213, D0149, T3369
Banks, Sir Joseph, 1743–1820: W0624
Banks, Peggy: T0993
Banks, William: U0026
Bannister, W.: N0201
Barbauld, Rev. [ ] (1778): H1179
Barber, [ ]: W1795
Barefoot, John: U0146
Barkeley, Sir Charles: S0571
Barker, Mrs. [ ]: T2647
Barker, Benjamin: A0663
Barker, Isabel: H0278
Barker, William: C0164
Barlow, Thomas, 1607–1691: P0268
Barnard, Mrs. [ ]: C0008
Barnard, Gilbert Vane, 2nd lord, 1678–1753: A0862
Barnard, Jane (1738): A0665
Barnard, Sir John, lord mayor of London, 1685?–1764: A0665
Barnard, Thomas, bp. of Killaloe (1780–1794): C0008
Barnard, William, bp. of Derry (1747–1768): C0008
Barnes, John: A0040
Barnes, Joshua, d. 1712: K0019
Barnwell, Dr. [ ]: S0696
Baron, Bernard, 1696–1762: W1850

Barrett, [ ] (1747): K0025
Barrett, Miss [ ] (1787): R0158
Barrett, Deborah: H0528
Barrett, Mary: S1286
Barrett, Stephen, 1718–1801?: H0307
Barrington, John, d. 1713: W0474
Barrow, Maurice: H1057
Barry, Spranger, 1717?–1777: W1428, W1946
Barsanti, Jane, actress, d. 1795: A0774, O0118
Bartlet, Barbara, c. 1721–1741: T0527
Barton, Joshua: A1007
Barwick, Thomas, colonel, 1621–1648: S1078
Barwise, Richard, d. 1648: B0246
Bass, E.: W0844
Basset, William, of Blore, Staffordshire: A0143
Bassett, [ ]: W1785
Bastard, Rev. [ ]: W0754
Bastwick, John, 1593–1654: A1080
Batchellor, Elinor (or Moll): B0263, B0270, U0023
Bate, [ ] (1781): M0459
Bateman, [ ]: T0553
Bateman, William Bateman, viscount, 1695?–1744: H0624
Batereau, John, colonel (1742–48): C0433
Bates, Henry, d. 1774: F0036
Bath, Anna Maria (Gumley), countess, c.1693–1758: T3032
Bath, John Grenville, earl, 1628–1701: A0547
Bath, William Pulteney, 1st earl, 1684–1764: F0256, F0409, G0392, I1045, L0046, L0427, R0130, S0192, T2388, T2524, T3032, W0249, W0391, W0925, W0933, Y0546
Bathurst, Allen Bathurst, 1st earl, 1684–1775: H1295, I1273
Battie, William 1704–1776: N0058
Baxter, Richard, 1615–1691: T1961
Bayard, [ ]: O0101, O0841, V0082, W1915
Bayard, Elisa: W2020
Bayham, Frances (Molesworth), viscountess, d. 1829: T1762
Bayley, [ ]: W1914
Bayne, Alexander, d.1737: T1409
Beach, Mary: H0782
Beadle, Edward: T2560
Beal, Miss [ ]: A1644
Bean, [ ]: O0225
Beard, [ ] (1740–42): T2898, W2468
Beattie, Dr. [ ]: H0154
Beattie, Sir James, 1735–1803: A0783
Beauclerk, Aubrey Beauclerk, lord, 1711–1740: W1793
Beaufort, Henry Charles Somerset, 6th duke, and marquess of Worcester, 1766–1835: W1655
Beaufort, Henry Somerset, 2nd duke, 1684–1714: H0557
Beaulieu, Edward Hussey (later Montagu), earl, d. 1802: C0235, S1135, W0374
Beaulieu, Isabelle Montagu Hussey-Montagu, countess, c. 1708–1786: C0235, W0374, W2440
Beaumont, Francis, 1584–1616: H0727
Beauvoir, Osmond: A0609
Beavor, [ ]: A0536, V0030
Becket, [ ]: T3180

Beckford, [ ], alderman (1768): C0514

Bede, the venerable, 673–735: W0957

Bedel, Isabella: B0241

Bedford, Francis Russell, 5th duke, 1765–1802: W0602

Bedford, Gertrude (Leveson-Gower), duchess, 1719–1794: O0368, O1053

Bedford, John Russell, 4th duke, 1710–1771: G0243

Bedford, Lucy (Harington), countess, 1581–1627: F0055, Y0400

Bedingfield, Lady Anne: T2667

Bedingfield, Christopher: B0219

Bedingfield, Dorothea: T2508

Bedingfield, Sir Henry, 1614–1685: I0032

Bedloe, William, captain, 1650–1680: B0156, S0529

Behn, Aphra (Johnson), 1640–1689: H0707, I0512

Beighton, Rev. [ ], of Edgham: N0068

Belasyse, Susan Armyne, baroness, d. 1713: W0371, W1158

Belingham, Dimple: D0433

Bell, [ ]: B0077, B0242, W0678

Bell, Bessie, d. 1645?: F0005, O0227

Bell, John: J0088

Bellamy, Daniel, d. 1788: F0284, O0204

Bellamy, George Anne, 1731?–1788: A0549

Bellarmino, Roberto, 1542–1621: O0073

Belville, [ ], lord: L0555

Bendbow, [ ], lady: I0074

Bendish, Mrs. [ ]: M0029

Benedict XIV, pope, 1675–1758: T2365

Benezet, Anthony, 1713–1784: W2232

Benn, Sir Anthony, recorder of London, d. 1618: I1109

Bennet, [ ]: R0041

Bennet, Elizabeth: F0005

Bennett, Mrs. [ ] (Lockman), b. 1738: W1861, Y0514

Benson, Mrs. [ ]: W1677

Benson, Francis, d. 1570: H0885

Benson, Martin, bp. of Gloucester, d. 1752: W0546

Benson, William: H0959

Bentinck, [ ]: *See* Portland, William Bentinck, 1st earl

Bentivoglio, Guido, 1579–1644: D0038

Bent, John: H0521

Bentham, Dr. [ ], Regius Professor at Oxford: A0071

Bentley, [ ], captain (1794): O1164

Bentley, Mrs. [ ] (1795): O1159, T2915

Bentley, Betty: M0720

Bentley, Dorcas, d. 1693: T2578

Bentley, Jonathan: T2578

Bentley, Richard, 1708–1782: T0184

Bentley, Richard, D. D., 1662–1742: H0482, M0720, W0846, W1770

Bentley, William: T2130, W1982

Berkeley, Lady Betty, 1680–1769: O0983

Berkeley, Charles: C0124

Berkeley, Sir Robert, d. 1616: H0461

Bernard, saint, 1090–1153: I1211

Bernard, Mlle. [ ]: S0694

Bernard, Eliza (1767): L0662, P0056, V0036, W0535, W1733, W1778

Bertie, Mrs. [ ]: A1207

Bertie, Philip (1683): B0593, T1971

Berwick, James Fitzjames, duke, 1670–1734: L0421

Bethell, Slingsby, lord mayor of London (1755): A1666, N0327, T1823

Bethell, W.: B0323

Betterton, Thomas, 1635?–1710: W0549, T2375

Bevan, I. G.: A1315

Bever, [ ], colonel, d. 1758: T0104

Bever, Samuel: T0104

Beveridge, [ ]: I1369

Beveridge, William, bp., 1637–1708: C0452

Bewly, Betty: T0362

Biarley, Mrs. [ ]: G0122

Bickley, Sir Francis: G0301, M0258

Bickley, Mary: M0258

Biddulph, [ ]: W0121

Billingsley, [ ]: A1054

Bincks, Miss [ ]: I1217

Bing, [ ]: M0563

Binning, [ ], lord: S0612

Birch, [ ]: B0317

Birch, Mrs. [ ]: A0690

Birch, John, colonel, 1616–1691: H1215

Birch, Peter, 1652–1710?: A1085

Bird, [ ]: B0348

Bird, Miss [ ]: D0128

Birdee, Peter: M0314

Birkbeck, Morris (m. 1776): O0972

Birkbeck, Sarah (Hall) (m. 1776): O0972

Birmingham, [ ], lady: A1744

Biron, Louis-Antoine de Gontaut, duc de, maréchal de France, 1700–1788: W0796

Bishop, [ ], cousin of T. Stamper (1717): T3117

Bishop, Mrs. [ ]: T3119

Bl———, Sir R———d: B0048

Blackborn, Edmund: T1795

Blackbourn, Ann: I1459

Blackbourne, Lancelot, abp. of York, 1658–1743: B0353, L0057, N0124, W1467

Blackburman, [ ]: B0354

Blacker, Henry, b. 1724: T1254

Blacket, Barbara (Villiers), lady, d. 1761: I0563, O0897, W0995

Blacket, Sir William, d. 1728: D0267, I0563, S0728, W0995

Blackett, Sir Walter: D0215

Blackhood, [ ]: C0508

Blackmore, Sir Richard, 1650–1729: B0521, D0413

Blacow, Richard: H0626

Bladen, Thomas: F0250

Blair, Sir James Hunter, 1741–1787: T0787

Blake, Mrs. [ ]: Y0242

Blake, William, 1757–1827: B0355

Blakeney, William Blakeney, baron, 1672–1761: I1545, O0086

Blandford, Elizabeth, d. 1788: M0215, O0272, W1479, W1897

Blandford, T., d. 1771: I0569

Blandy, Miss [ ]: A1140

Blandy, Mary: G0008

Blank, Sir Thomas, c. 1515–1588: H0693

Bleau, Willem Jansz, 1571–1638: S0906

Blin de Sainmore, Adrien-Michel, 1733–1807: T0159

Block, Ben: B0250

Blood, Thomas, colonel, 1618?-1680: B0423, W0856

Blount, Mrs. E., d. 1754: S0261

Blount, Martha, 1690-1762: C0223

Blowfield, Sarah: T2379

Bly, [ ] (1768): I0701

Blythe, [ ]: H0272

Boccaccio, Giovanni, 1313-1375: T2170

Bogan, Ellen: E0040

Bogan, Zachary, 1625-1659: A1798

Bold, Henry, of New College, Oxford: G0238

Boline, Henry: I0581

Bolingbroke, Henry St. John, 1st viscount, 1678-1751: A0944, A1669, B0436, T1308, W0748, W1412

Bolton, Charles Paulet, 6th marquis of Winchester and 1st duke, d. 1699: A0482, H0646, W1720

Bolton, Henrietta (Crofts) Paulet, duchess, d. 1730: C0085

Bonaparte, Napoleon, 1769-1821: I1271

Bond, Dennis, d. 1658: N0528

Bond, W. Daniel: P0354

Bone, [ ]: B0447, T3373

Bonevant, Richard, d. 1459: P0275

Bonfoy, Thomas, b. 1711: S0801

Bonner, B.: M0395

Bononcini, Giovanni, 1670-1747: S0184, S0948

Bonsar, John (1798): J0089

Boole, Thomas (1797): D0098

Booth, Barton, 1681-1733: T2375

Boothy, Elizabeth: A1189

Boscawen, Edward, admiral, 1711-1761: H1258, T2416

Boscawen, Francis (Glanville), d. 1805: A0597, D0083, F0217, I1344, T3096

Boscawen, Hugo (c. 1693): O1080

Bosseville, Henry: W1122

Boston, Christiana (Methuen) Irby, lady (1761): S0181

Boston, William Irby, 1st baron, cr. 1761: T0984, W1647

Boswell, [ ]: B0421

Boswell, James, 1740-1795: A0629

Boteler, Mrs. [ ]: H1202

Boteler, Isabella: Y0557

Botetourt, Norborne Berkeley, lord, 1717-1770: N0366, T0691

Bothell, [ ], candidate for Parliament (1747): O0444

Bothmer, Johann Kaspar von, count, 1656-1732: B0466

Bouillon, Godefroi-Charles-Henri de la Tour, duc de, 1728-1792: M0260

Boulstrede, Cecilia, d. 1609: D0207, L0034, M0243, S0375, S1093

Boulton, Matthew, 1728-1809: F0563

Bounds(?), Thomas: T2347

Bourchier, Elizabeth: B0325

Bourdois, [ ]: S0651

Bouton, [ ]: Y0054

Bowden, Samuel, fl. 1733-1761: T0151

Bowdler, Mrs. [ ]: W0519

Bowdler, Jane, 1743-1784: W0519, W2329

Bower, [ ]: H0100

Bowes, Miss [ ] (1757): I0765

Bowes, Mrs. [ ], d. 1724: H0087, H0128, H1173, T2162

Bowes, George, d. 1760: F0162, H0087, H1173, T2162

Bowes, Joshua: H1269

Bowler, Ann: V0014

Bowline, Tom: H0614

Bowman, [ ]: A1576, B0471

Bowman, Mrs. [ ]: A1576

Bowman, William, vicar of Dewsbury (1730-44): O0862

Bowmer, [ ]: M0579

Bowmer, Michael: Y0399

Bowry, [ ]: U0126

Bowtell, [ ]: J0106

Bowyer, A.: O0778

Bowyer, William, 1699-1777: A0792

Boyce, William, 1711-1779: A1658

Boyer, Abel, 1667-1729: P0086, Y0514

Boyer, Samuel (1757): T3356

Boyle, Miss [ ] (1779): O0615

Bracciano, [ ]: O1158

Brace, Alice (1752): A1089

Bracegirdle, Anne, 1663?-1748: D0350

Brackley, [ ], viscount: *See* Bridgewater, John Egerton, 1st earl

Brackley, Elizabeth: *See* Bridgewater, Elizabeth (Cavendish) Egerton, countess

Bradford, Francis Newport, 1st earl, 1619-1708: N0005

Bradpeace, Mrs. [ ], singer: F0653

Bragge, John, of Wadham College Oxford (matr. 1651): W0171

Brahe, Tycho, 1546-1601: G0457

Braidwood, [ ], schoolmaster (1768): W0806

Braithwait, Dr. [ ]: A0972

Bramston, James, 1694?-1744: O0856

Bray, Patty: T1329

Breckin, Johnny: H0526

Brent, Miss [ ], singer (1761): W1230

Brett, Sir Piercy, 1709-1781: W2568

Bretterg, Catherine: H1384

Bretton, Mrs. [ ]: R0068

Bretton, Francis: G0365

Brickenden, Nancy (m. 1767): D0290, F0664, W1906

Bridgeman, K.: A1708

Bridgeman, Miss [ ]: W0796

Bridges, [ ], lady: A0078

Bridges, Mrs. [ ]: A1336

Bridgewater, [ ], countess: A0913

Bridgewater, Elizabeth (Cavendish) Egerton, countess: L0545, M0182, T2003, T2346, T2541

Bridgewater, John Egerton, 1st earl, d. 1649: B0126

Bridgewater, John Egerton, 2nd earl, and 3rd viscount Brackley, d. 1686: Y0269

Bridgman, [ ]: O1032

Bridport, Alexander Hood, 1st viscount, 1726-1814: T1693

Briggs, Augustine: W0735

Briggs, Patience, d. 1696: W0543

Bright, Miss [ ]: W0756

Brindley, James: A1508, F0129

Brine, [ ]: L0066

Briscoe, Mrs. [ ] (1713): A1421

Bristol, Elizabeth (Felton) Hervey, countess, 1676-1741: W0925, W0933

Brittain, Thomas: W1743
Broad, Miss [ ]: W0274
Brockitwell, John: A0957
Bromley, [ ]: H0962
Bromley, William, 1663–1732: L0269, H0028
Brooke, [ ]: A1806
Brooke, Sir Basil: T2134
Brooke, Christopher: T2134
Brooke, William, M. D. (1740): H0212
Brookes, Mrs. [ ] (1713): A1705
Brooksbank, Mrs. [ ] (Lamborn) (1741): L0683, T0924
Broome, Charlotte Ann (Burney) Francis, 1761–1838:
    C0020, H0019, N0169, T0979
Broughton, [ ]: H1037
Browing, May: W1666
Brown, Dr. [ ]: A0020, F0179
Brown, Miss [ ]: W1071
Brown, Mrs. [ ], d. 1729: F0179
Brown, Barbara: I1289
Brown, Jabez: J0060, T2641
Brown, John, 1715–1766: I1454
Brown, Lancelot ('Capability'), 1716–1783: Y0168
Brown, Samuel: A0846
Brown, Thomas, 1663–1704: D0378, I0976, S0484
Browne, [ ]: S0534
Browne, Henry: T2203
Browning, Diana: Y0288
Brownlow, Lady Elizabeth: W1940
Broxholme, Noel, 1689?–1748: S0331
Brunswick, [ ]: T2380, W2460
Bryan, Ann, d. 1723: T2306
Bryant, [ ]: O0775
Bryant, Mrs. [ ]: O0775
Buckhurst, [ ], lord: *See* Dorset, Charles Sackville, 6th
    earl, and 1st earl of Middlesex
Buckhurst, Thomas Sackville, 1st baron, 1536–1608:
    D0325, H0694, U0007
Buckingham: *See also* Buckingham and Normanby
Buckingham, George Villiers, 1st duke, 1592–1628:
    A0201, A1180, A1236, A1249, A1326, A1682, A1841, E0078,
    F0092, H0414, H0531, H0683, H0777, H0832, H0872,
    H0970, I0054, I0394, I0620, I1601, I1609, N0233, N0460,
    O0413, O0448, P0357, R0050, R0063, R0175, S0026,
    T2292, W0025, W0633, W1033, W1570, Y0260
Buckingham, George Villiers, 2nd duke, 1628–1687:
    A1770, B0544, C0503, F0599, H0483, I0054, I0376, I1273,
    I1371, N0462, Q0031, T2513
Buckingham and Normanby, Catherine Phipps,
    duchess, d. 1742?: A1703, D0425, F0365, F0551, H1220,
    I0524, L0481, O0415, T1938, T2080, T2481, W1006,
    W2308, W2469
Buckingham and Normanby, Edmund Sheffield, 2nd
    duke, d. 1735: A1933, O0416
Buckingham and Normanby, John Sheffield, 1st duke,
    1648–1721: A0685, B0556, D0085, F0389, F0433, H0189,
    H1240, H1270, I0185, I0290, I0853, O0573, T1920, W0549,
    W1762
Bucks, Mrs. [ ]: I1546
Bucks, Sir William (1734): W0301
Budgell, Eustace, 1686–1737: A1267
Buford, [ ]: B0546

Bull, [ ]: S1338, Y0018
Buller, [ ]: S0050
Buller, [ ], judge: W1451
Bumbrige, Britt: T2706
Bunbury, Lady Sarah: A0194
Bunce, John: I1557
Bunch, Mother [ ]: H1001
Buncomb, Miss [ ]: W0416
Bunyan, [ ] (1741): L0018
Burbage, Richard, 1567?–1619: S0954
Burchell, Miss [ ], singer (1751): H0292, O0938
Burdsyards, [ ]: L0524
Burgess, Daniel, 1645–1713: I1426
Burgess, Donald: D0374
Burgoyne, Frances (Montagu), lady, d. 1788: B0435
Burgoyne, John, general, 1722–1792: T2853
Burgundy, [ ], duc de: G0076
Burke, Edmund, 1729?–1797: A0445, F0537, G0393,
    M0185, M0618, U0004
Burke, Richard, 1758–1794: M0185
Burlase, Sir William: W0653
Burlasy, Anne: A0833
Burleigh, [ ]: G0093
Burleigh, William Cecil, 1st baron, 1520–1598: B0552,
    W1031
Burley, Mary (Sayer): W1072
Burlington, Dorothy (Savile) Boyle, countess,
    1699–1758: M0607, T0184
Burlington, Richard Boyle, 3d earl, and 4th earl of
    Cork, 1695–1753: I0514, M0607
Burn, Richard: W0862
Burnet, [ ], judge: M0188
Burnet, Alexander (1780): C0325
Burnet, Gilbert, bp. of Salisbury, 1643–1715: A0097,
    A0379, A0440, A0531, A1095, A1304, B0553, F0717, H0161,
    H0944, I0595, O0211, P0268, Q0028, S0265, T0479,
    T1930, W0811, W0880, W1098, W1412, W1613, W1903,
    W2097
Burnett, [ ], M. D.: B0317
Burnett, Dr. [ ]: I0700
Burnett, Elizabeth, of Monboddo, 1766–1790: L0332
Burney, Miss [ ] (1779): A0774
Burney, Mrs. [ ]: S0142
Burney, Amelia Maria: Y0461
Burney, Cecilia: B0554
Burney, Charles, 1726–1814: B0554, W0095, W1461
Burney, Charles, 1757–1817: S0658
Burney, Charlotte: *See* Broome, Charlotte Ann
    (Burney) Francis
Burney, Richard Gustavus, d. 1791: S1035, T2213
Burney, Sarah: T0352
Burney, Thomas Frederick, d. 1784: A0747
Burns, Robert, 1759–1796: B0588, F0732, H0921, M0419,
    R0076
Burroughes, Diana (1777–1778): T1808, W0295
Burroughs, Sir John, d. 1627: O0820
Burton, Cassevilane: W1450
Burton, John: N0236
Burton, Richard, printer in Smithfield (1641): S0036
Busby, Richard, 1606–1695: T0949
Bute, John Stuart, 3rd earl, 1713–1794: A1958, T0976

Butler, [ ]: T1815
Butler, Dr. [ ]: H0862
Butler, James, of Downs, Devon: T1506
Butler, John, lord (1665): T0542
Butler, Joseph, bishop of Durham, 1692–1752: H1022
Butler, Samuel, 1612–1680: H0932, I0943, O0052, R0144, T1747, W0813, W1640, W1795
Butson, [ ], of New College Oxford: Y0174
Butt, [ ]: T1721
Button, [ ], mayor of Chester: G0418
Button, John: C0574, H0763, O0404
Buxton, William: S0535
Bxxx, [ ], countess: O0905
Byde, Eleanor: E0094
Byng, John, admiral, 1704–1757: A0701, B0230, D0164, I1545, Y0397
Byrkes, Margaret: H1472
Byrkes, Robert: H1472
Byron, Mrs. George: C0439

C., [ ]: F0131, F0247, H0882, I0087
C., [ ], general (1768): W0660
C., Dr. [ ]: Y0395
C., Miss [ ]: F0131
C., E.: O0609, T1235
C., Sir H. D.: S0348
C., J., of the Middle Temple: N0415
C., Robert: G0153
C., V.: E0082
C., W.: F0559, T1811
C———, [ ]: I1390
C———, [ ], lord: M0601
C———, Dr. [ ]: A1557
C———, Mrs. [ ] (1782): T0287
C———, J——— (1710): L0512
C——e, [ ]: I0122
C——ford, Humphrey: S0688
C——l, Samuel: P0320
C——r, Maria: A0852
C——x, Mrs. [ ]: H0914
C——y, M———: O0050
Ca——ns, [ ], lady: A0186
Cade, [ ]: G0080
Cadogan, [ ]: W1564
Cadogan, William, 1st earl, d. 1726: A1640
Caesar, Miss [ ]: W2403
Caesar, Mrs. [ ] (1741): P0310
Caesar, Anne, lady, d. 1625?: T2179
Caithness, James Sinclair, 12th earl, 1766–1823: E0114
Cajanus, Daniel, d. 1749: A1061
Calamy, Edmund, 1600–1666: M0359
Caldwell, [ ], captain: N0097
Caldwell, Daniel: T1929
Caldwell, Elizabeth: T1929
Caldwell, Florence: E0037
Caley, Miss [ ]: P0048
Caley, Mrs. [ ]: C0331, O0622
Caley, Mary Ann: W2358
Calfe, Sir John, lord mayor of York: A0879, H0823, O0260
Callway, William, of Lyme: T3113

Calthorpe, Sir Christopher: A0658, I1476
Calthorpe, Dorothea (Spring), lady: W0053
Calvert, Sir William, lord mayor of London (1741), knighted 1744: W1608
Calvin, John, 1509–1564: A1077, J0098, W0880, W1743
Calybute, Frances: F0545
Calzo, [ ] (1749): L0621
Cambridge, James Stuart, duke, 1663–1667: K0016
Cambridge, Richard Owen, 1717–1802: W0490
Camden, [ ]: N0068
Camden, Charles Pratt, 1st earl, 1714–1794: A0138, F0205
Camden, John, 1723–1780: T2234
Camden, William, 1551–1623: C0018, F0205, H0745, H0884, H0895, T0537
Camergo, Mlle. [ ], dancer (1734): Y0484
Cameron, Jenny (1745): P0294
Campbell, Caroline: S0636, S0639
Campbell, Lady Jean: W2091
Campbell, Theophila: W0942
Campbell, Thomas, 1777–1844: T3045
Campbell, William, lord: S0639
Campden, Baptist Noel, 3rd viscount, 1612–1682: R0057
Camperdown, Adam Duncan, 1st viscount, 1731–1804: T1693
Camply, [ ], lady: W1187
Candish, Sir William (= Cavendish?): M0334
Canning, Elizabeth, b. 1735: W2560
Canning, George, 1770–1827: C0009, F0489, I0690
Cannock, Ann (1776): M0463
Canvane, William: T3164
Capel, Arthur Capel, 1st baron, of Hadham, 1610?–1649: H0972
Capell, Nan: N0005
Caporali, [ ] (1754): I0534
Care, [ ]: W2128
Carew, Thomas, 1595–1639: G0147, W0392
Carey, [ ], lady: H0977
Carey, Mrs. [ ]: D0236
Carey, Lady Anne: S0440, W1547
Carey, Henry, 1687?–1743: D0236
Carey, Lady Judith: W1547
Carey, Mary: G0087, L0230, T0001, W2027
Carey, Lady Philadelphia: P0112
Carleton, Deborah: W2186
Carlie, [ ] (1762): C0060
Carlisle, [ ] Howard, countess: T1899
Carlisle, Charles Howard, 1st earl (third creation), 1629–1685: D0246, W0820
Carlisle, Isabella (Byron) Howard, countess, 1721–1795: E0132, O0193
Carlisle, James Hay, 2nd earl (second creation), 1612–1660: T0324
Carlisle, Lucy (Percy) Hay, countess, 1599–1660: W0392
Carmarthen, [ ], marquess: *See* Leeds, Thomas Osborne, 1st duke
Carmarthen, Anne (Seymour), marchioness, d. 1722: F0063
Carnegie, John: J0104

Caroline Amelia of Brunswick, second wife of George
   IV, 1768–1821: T2659
Caroline Mathilde, queen of Denmark, 1751–1775:
   A1818
Caroline, queen consort of George II of Great
   Britain, 1683–1737: A0862, A1398, B0169, F0484, F0558,
   G0348, G0435, H0754, H0774, H0775, H0875, I0729,
   M0375, N0144, O0238, P0332, Q0034, R0061, S0554,
   S0776, S0791, S1158, S1177, T2267, V0012, W0944, W1026,
   W1610, W1641, W2632, Y0108, Y0546
Carr, Maria: H0662
Carrington, Miss [ ] (1745): C0039
Carson, Mrs. [ ]: L0190
Carstairs, William: Y0125
Carter, [ ]: Y0112
Carter, Elizabeth, 1717–1806: A1438, W1479
Carter, George, provost of Oriel College Oxford,
   d. 1727: N0110
Carter, J.: J0094
Carter, Sir Laurence: Q0036
Carteret. [ ], lord: *See* Granville, John Carteret, 1st
   earl
Carver, Francis: H0368
Castalion, Sir Balthazar: H1052
Castalion, Hyppolyta Taurella, lady: H1052
Castillion, Elizabeth St. John, d. 1603: I0627, V0061,
   W0154
Castle, Elizabeth: S0215
Castlehaven, Anne (Stanley) Touchet, countess,
   1580–1647: I0277
Castlehaven, George Touchet, 1st earl, 1550–1617:
   M0690
Castlehaven, Mervyn Touchet (Lord Audley), 2nd
   earl, 1592?–1631: I0277, I1593, R0214
Catarno, [ ] (1762): W1316
Cathcart, Jean (Hamilton) Cathcart, baroness,
   1726–1771: F0492
Catherine Howard, queen consort of Henry VIII,
   king of England, 1521?–1542: T2362
Catherine of Aragon, queen consort of Henry VIII,
   king of England, 1485–1536: T2362
Catherine of Braganza, queen consort of Charles II,
   1638–1705: R0092, T2151, W2608, Y0529
Catherine Parr, queen consort of Henry VIII, king of
   England, 1512–1548: T2362
Catlin, Elizabeth (Houghton): I0349
Catterton, [ ], actor (1683): W0549
Cavan, Richard Ford William Lambart, 4th earl,
   major general, 1763–1836: H1471
Cave, Miss [ ]: P0137
Cave, Edward, 1691–1754: C0295
Cavendish, [ ], lord: W1669
Cavendish, [ ], lady: O0042
Cavendish, Catherine (baroness Ogle): M0565
Cavendish, Sir Charles, d. 1617: M0565
Cavendish, Sir Charles, 1591–1654: Y0526, Y0533
Cavendish, Frances, d. 1678: A1098, N0023
Cavendish, Lady Jane, 1621–1669: M0009
Caxton, William, 1422–1491: P0327
Cecil, [ ]: G0407
Centlivre, Susanna, 1667?–1723: I1159, S0588

Chalk, Dionysia, actress: T2664
Chalran, [ ]: H1218
Chambaud, Louis, d. 1776: T2504
Chamberlain, Anne, b. 1738: N0038
Chamberlain, John: J0042
Chambers, John: J0091
Chambers, Sir William, 1726–1796: H0158
Champion, [ ], writingmaster (1740–50): N0358, T0981,
   T2273
Chance, Jack: O0910
Chandler, Mary, 1687–1745: O0617
Chandler, Samuel: F0144
Chandos, Anne (Wells) Jeffries Brydges, duchess,
   d. 1759: G0481
Chandos, Henry Brydges, 2nd duke, 1708–1771: G0481
Chandos, James Brydges, 1st duke, and marquis of
   Carnarvon, 1674–1744: C0062, T3217
Charles Edward Stuart, the Young Pretender, 1720–
   1788: A1029, E0180, H0093, H0302, L0159, N0403, P0289,
   T2365, W0214
Charles I, king of England, 1600–1649: A0201, A0785,
   A1201, B0165, B0602, C0042, C0293, E0136, F0003, F0175,
   F0682, G0318, G0367, G0386, G0406, G0425, G0426,
   H0034, H0630, H0725, H0956, I0492, I0537, I0699,
   I0982, K0066, L0599, L0600, L0633, M0360, M0547,
   N0135, N0355, O0132, O0306, O0503, O0556, O0573,
   O0997, O1083, O1119, S0164, S0358, S0795, S1042, T0242,
   T0459, T0559, T1034, T1100, T1110, T1153, T1252, T1288,
   T1399, T1900, T1936, T2062, T2067, T2120, T2135,
   T2435, T3056, T3061, T3064, W0118, W0366, W0633,
   W1512, W1680, W2031, W2526, W0075, A0374
Charles II, king of England, 1630–1685: A0429, A0463,
   A0688, A1245, A1247, A1388, A1468, A1485, A1492, A1577,
   A1898, B0080, B0471, B0545, C0123, C0144, C0244,
   C0590, D0028, D0328, D0398, D0401, F0270, F0282,
   F0534, G0292, G0318, G0387, G0442, G0443, G0446,
   H0113, H0349, H0806, H0908, H0956, H0995, H1120,
   H1274, I0010, I0297, I0682, I0699, I0947, I1017, I1018,
   I1096, I1256, I1414, I1506, I1560, L0436, M0313, N0504,
   O0012, O0138, O0286, O0552, O0997, O1128, P0239, P0341,
   R0163, S0475, S0734, S0810, T0009, T0286, T0634,
   T0734, T0865, T0954, T1045, T1064, T1075, T1129,
   T1598, T1877, T1965, T2277, T2420, T2827, T3175, U0015,
   U0066, W0118, W0366, W0430, W0632, W0784, W0971,
   W1333, W1365, W1378, W1409, W1417, W1650, W1782,
   W1824, W1954, W2014, W2125, W2608
Charles III, king of Spain, 1685–1740: A0616, B0009,
   H0104, M0456, P0011
Charles James Stuart, duke of Cornwall, 1629–1629:
   T2762
Charles Louis, elector Palatine, c. 1610–1680: I0629
Charles VI, Holy Roman Emperor, 1685–1740: O0152
Charles VII, Holy Roman Emperor, 1697–1745: T3221
Charles XII, king of Sweden, 1682–1718: O0799
Charles, [ ]: J0139
Charleton, [ ], capt.: M0025
Charlotte, queen consort of George III, 1744–1818:
   G0035, S0241, T0164, W0750, W1220, W1868
Chatham, William Pitt, 1st earl, 1708–1778: A0047,
   H1258, J0124, K0031, L0470, O0579, P0042, S0116, S0148,
   S0361, T1381, W0486, W0541, W1614

Chatto, [ ], lady: L0403, W0057

Chaucer, Geoffrey, 1343?-1400: A1012, I0727, O0844, O1093, S0369, T1662, G0093

Chaworth, Lady Sophia: R0013

Cheselden, William, 1688-1752: W1026

Chesterfield, Philip Dormer Stanhope, 4th earl, 1694-1773: A0594, F0317, H0055, H1328, N0146, O0408, P0181, S0419, S0780, S1250, T2416, W0373, W0596, W1907, Y0211

Chesterfield, Philip Stanhope, 1st earl, d. 1656: Y0274

Chetwood, Knightley, 1650-1720: C0150, T2122

Chetwynd, Miss [ ]: K0022

Chevers, Anne: R0045

Chevers, John: R0045

Chevers, Thomas: R0045

Chevreuse, Marie de Rohan, duchess, 1600-1679: W2038

Cheyne, George, 1673-1743: T0084

Chichely, John: M0623

Child, [ ]: W2473

Cholmeley, Rebecca: R0096

Cholmondeley, [ ], colonel (1741): N0161

Cholmondeley, [ ], lady (1780): W2378

Cholmondeley, Catherine (Stanhope), d. 1657: P0342

Cholmondeley, Charles, 1684-1759: I1598

Cholmondeley, Mary (Holford), lady, d. 1625: I1406

Cholmondeley, Thomas, 1627-1702: A1752, T3391

Chowne, Betty (1741): E0141, M0179

Christian VII, king of Denmark, 1749-1809: H0499

Chubb, Philippa: F0315

Chudleigh, Miss [ ]: C0210, G0018, T0977

Churchill, [ ], general: See Marlborough, John Churchill, 1st duke

Churchill, Charles, 1731-1764: N0353

Churchill, George, 1653-1716: S0494

Churchyard, Thomas, 1520?-1604: C0255

Chute, Sir Walter, b. 1577: T0422

Cibber, Colley, 1671-1757: A0149, A0157, A1271, C0022, C0213, C0214, C0253, G0234, I1148, O1102, T2520, W0386, W1798

Cibber, Susannah Maria (Arne), 1714-1766: M0160, O0440, W0664, W1946

Clairien, Françoise, actress, 1753-1815: I0328

Clancy, Dr. [ ] (1744): A1450

Clapham, Ann: C0446

Clarendon, Edward Hyde, 1st earl, 1609-1674: C0222, H0161, H0793, H0867, I0642, K0016, M0746, P0300, W0840

Clarges, Sir Thomas, 1618?-1695: Y0536

Clark, [ ]: I0163

Clark, N.: T3279

Clarke, Eliza (1749): A0506, H0217

Clarke, Henry (1727): F0488

Clarke, Samuel, 1675-1729: S1158

Clasper, Jane: S0946

Clavell, John, of Brasenose College, Oxford: T0777

Claxton, John, 1740-1790: J0092

Clayton, Charlotte: T1211, W2276

Clayton, Sir Robert, 1629-1707: F0599

Clement XIV, pope, 1705-1774: S0625

Clément, Jacques, 1567-1589: W1621

Clench, Thomasina: C0557

Cleve, Thomas, d. 1545: N0312

Cleveland, Anne Pulteney, duchess, 1663-1746: C0235

Cleveland, Barbara (Villiers) Palmer, duchess, 1641-1709: C0233, D0264, Q0030, W0784

Cleveland, John, secretary of the Admiralty, d. 1763: B0230, D0164

Clifford of Chudleigh, Thomas Clifford, baron, 1630-1673: A1682, G0325

Clifford, [ ]: F0493

Clifford, Rosamond, c. 1140-c. 1176: R0030, R0223, T1169, W1490

Clifford, Thomas, d. 1671: I0812

Clifton, Penelope [ ], lady: S0627

Clive, Catherine (Raftor), 1711-1785: C0150, C0236, F0038, H0673, H1187, I0860, T2122

Clive, Robert Clive, baron, 1725-1774: I1234

Cloncorry, [ ]: C0240

Clough, Mrs. [ ], d. 1711: W0435

Clough, Susan, d. 1711: W0435

Clutterbucke, Rachel: T1949

Clydesdale, [ ], marquess: See Hamilton, James George Douglas-Hamilton, 7th duke

Cobden, Edward, 1684-1764: Y0006

Cobham, Richard Temple, 1st viscount, 1679-1749: F0641, S0659

Cockburn, Dr. [ ]: T2605

Cockburne, Jean: D0006

Cockerton, [ ] (1746): Y0204

Cockman, Thomas, 1674-1745: F0159

Cocks, Elizabeth (Cholmley) lady, d. 1749: A0851

Cokayne, Mary: B0108

Cokayne, Thomas, son of Sir Aston Cokayne: L0220, Y0361

Coke, [ ]: T2885

Coke, Sir Edward, 1552-1634: O0708, O0726

Coke, Elizabeth: I0098

Coke, Jane: I0322

Coker, Thomas, b. c.1670: D0300

Cole, Thomas: H0871

Cole, William: D0388, T2348

Colinaeus, Michael, 1608-1635: S0906

Colleton, Miss [ ]: O0097

Collier, [ ]: A0008

Collier, Mrs. [ ]: I1038

Collins, Pandolfo (1757): D0182

Colman, George, 1732-1794: H1122, O0118, W0949

Colson, Anne (Paris), lady: T1892

Colston, Mrs. [ ]: M0023

Colt, Mrs. [ ] (1713): G0058, W1015

Colt, Harry: O1107

Colt, Nan: I0746

Combe, [ ]: T0132

Comber, [ ], earl: I0686

Comber, Harriet [ ], countess: I0686

Comer, [ ]: F0284

Compton, Lady Anne, 1693-1766: F0624, P0092, P0316, T1847, I0917

Compton, Charlotte, lady: See Ferrers, Charlotte (Compton) Ferrers, baroness

Compton, Henry, bp. of London, 1632-1713: A1506

Compton, Lord James, 1723-1739: A0408, F0332, I0391, O0188, T3083

Compton, Lady Jane, d. 1749: T2982
Conder, [ ]: H0854
Conflanu, [ ]: C0468
Congreve, Charles Walter, c. 1707-1777: W1604
Congreve, William, 1670-1729: N0441, N0529, T1881, W1789
Constable, Lady W. M.: I1040
Conti, Louise Élizabeth (Condé), princess, 1693-1775: A0299
Conway, [ ]: B0519
Conybeare, John, bp. of Bristol, 1692-1755: T2605
Cook, Miss [ ]: W1701
Cook, Thomas: S1082
Cookson, Rev. [ ]: W2620
Coole, Miss [ ]: D0078, M0525, W1523
Cooling, Richard, d. 1697: I0494
Cooper, [ ]: O0708
Cooper, James: A0475, W0517
Cooper, John Gilbert, 1723-1769: A1945
Cooper, Thomas: O0867
Coote, Sir Charles, colonel, d. 1642: S0628, W0321
Coote, Charles: W1746
Coote, Mary Ann: W0155
Coram, Thomas, capt., 1668?-1751: F0625
Corbet, Emma: A0771
Corbett, [ ], lady: W1132
Corbett, Elizabeth: H0935
Corbett, Richard, bishop, 1582-1635: A0401, A0884, C0260, F0092, I0333, L0191, S0862, T0767, T1145
Corbett, Vincent, b. 1627: W0448
Corbett, Vincent, d. 1619: I0173, V0053
Cordier, Mathurin, 1480?-1564: S0119
Corelli, Arcangelo, 1653-1713: C0506, O1020
Coretti, Dr. [ ]: A1187
Cork and Orrery, John Boyle, 5th earl, 1706-1762: W1217
Corneille, Pierre, 1606-1684: M0260
Cornlay, [ ]: H0501
Cornwall, Mrs. [ ] (1752): S0155
Cornwall, Kitty (1752-69): H0135, O0288, S0155, W1155, W2375, Y0124
Cornwall, Velters (1764-68): C0511, C0512, F0106, H0512, S0354, S0567
Cornwallis, Miss [ ] (1791-92): H0163, U0095
Cornwallis, Caroline Frances (1797): D0358, M0434, S0993, T0974, T1235
Cornwallis, Charles Cornwallis, 1st marquis, 1738-1805: M0171
Cornwallis, William, b. 1752: A1232
Corsley, M.: O0992
Cortez, Hernando, 1485-1547: P0261
Cosgrove, [ ]: W0335
Cot., M.: W1196
Cotes, Mrs. [ ]: W0694
Cotton, Charles, 1630-1684: D0038, I1116, P0021, S1232, Y0467
Cotton, Elizabeth: T1297
Cotton, J.: T1098
Cotton, Sir John, 1621-1701: O1020, T1297
Cotton, Kitty: M0469
Cotton, Nell: A0232

Cotton, Phoebe: M0469
Cottrell, Jane: I0183
Courtenay, Miss [ ], actress, fl. 1777: W0262
Courtenay, Catharina (Stapleton): B0227, S0406
Courtenay, Charles Kellond, captain, d. 1762: W1633
Courtenay, George: B0227
Courtenay, John, 1741-1816: A0629
Courtown, Mary (Powys) Stopford, countess, d. 1810: N0106, T1792
Covel, John: S0956
Coventry, Sir John, d. 1682: I0357, K0032
Coventry, Maria (Gunning) Coventry, countess, 1730-1760: B0198, T0933
Cowley, [ ]: S0239
Cowley, Abraham, 1618-1667: A0847, O0844, O1150, T1426, T2168
Cowper, Ashley, d. 1788: O0726
Cowper, George Nassau, 3rd earl, 1738-1789: H0629
Cowper, Spencer Cowper, 1669-1728: A1212
Cowper, William Cowper, 1st earl, 1664?-1723: A1954, B0069, S0350
Cowper, William, 1731-1800: A1205, B0181, C0556, D0167, D0193, H1136, M0147, M0336, N0021, T3077, W1648
Coxe, [ ], actor (1770): W1310
Coxe, Miss [ ] (c. 1759): M0035
Coxe, Betty: E0025
Crabb, [ ]: B0440
Craddock, Elizabeth: A0020
Craggs, James, 1686-1721: S1058
Craker, [ ]: H0797
Cramer, [ ], singer (1794): N0333
Crashaw, [ ]: S1127
Craven, Mrs. [ ]: I1531
Craven, Elizabeth Craven, baroness, 1750-1828: C0163
Craven, William Craven, earl, 1606-1697: W0855
Crawford, Betty: M0236
Crayle, Ann, d. 1754: G0182
Creak, Ralph: H0042
Creech, [ ]: A1393
Creed, [ ]: T0187
Creitton, Robert: A1086
Cremer, George: W1223
Cretio, Thomas: L0633
Crew, Ann (Wodehouse): N0098
Crewe, [ ]: O0629
Crewe, Frances Anne (Greville), baroness, d. 1818: A1192, I1019, T0119, T2601, W1369, W1581, W1948, W2384, W2535, Y0372
Crewe, Nathaniel Crewe, 3rd baron, bp. of Durham, 1633-1721: T0359, T3388
Crews, Robert, c. 1670-1731: H0466
Criegton, John: I0204
Crisp, Samuel: R0066
Crockett, [ ] (1795): M0291
Croft, Herbert, bp. of Hereford, 1603-1691: H1215
Crofte, [ ], lord: D0263
Croftes, Cicely: H1005
Crofts, Sir John: M0584, W2562
Crofts, Mary: T1949
Cromarty, [ ], laird: R0135
Crompton, Catharine: T2163

Cromwell, Sir Henry: T1940
Cromwell, Oliver, 1599-1658: A0390, A0563, A1743, C0045, C0407, E0121, F0480, G0318, H0786, I1501, I1520, K0057, N0528, O0863, S0706, T0563, T0665, T0720, W0717, W1620, W1628, W1949
Cromwell, Richard, 1626-1712: N0522, N0524, W1954
Crooke, Sir George, 1560-1642: T1947
Crooke, Sir John: D0390, P0352
Crooker, John: H0764
Crop, William: T1941
Crosthwait, Thomas, d. 1710: S0534
Crowder, [ ]: T0187
Crowfoot, Miss [ ]: W0295
Crownfeild, C. (1726): G0432
Croxall, Samuel, d. 1752: I0492
Croy, [ ], duc de: T1215
Croza, Dr. [ ] (1748-49): I0956, O0994
Cubit, [ ]: S0631
Cufand, Simeon, d. 1638: G0461
Cumber, Mrs. [ ]: H0756
Cumber, Anthony: H0756
Cumberland, Dennison, 1705-1774: H0633
Cumberland, William Augustus, duke, 1721-1765: F0492, F0691, I0901, I1419, O0967, S0363, S0664, S0943, T1097, W0365, W1894, O0464, W1660, F0706, Y0359, T3364
Cummings, Dr. [ ]: G0039, S0641
Cundall, [ ], surgeon (1777): A0618, C0575
Cunningham, J.: W0521
Curll, Edmund, 1675-1747: C0600, W0331
Currier, [ ]: R0076
Curteis, Edward Jeremiah, jr.: W2230
Curteis, Edward Jeremiah, sr. (1791): T2554
Cutts, John Cutts, baron, 1661-1707?: W2201
Cuzzoni, Francesca, c. 1700-1770: L0414, W0026

D., [ ]: A0760, T2279
D., Dr. [ ]: G0364
D., Miss E. G. (1779): W0413
D., Miss M. R.: H1304
D., Sir R.: H0861
D———, [ ]: E0173, T0229
D———, [ ], dean (m. 1785): T1256
D———, Miss [ ]: E0114, W1775
D———n, Miss [ ]: C0101
D——ge, Dr. [ ]: T2748
D——n——ll, Miss [ ] (1738): P0291
D——n——ll, Mrs. Maria (1738): W1828
Dacre, Thomas Barrett-Lennard, 17th baron, 1717-1786: T1603
Dacres, [ ], lady: L0087
Dalby, [ ] (1752): O1139
Dalmon, Miss [ ]: I1014
Dame, John: T1219
Dance, [ ]: L0001
Dancer, [ ]: B0286, C0083, D0019, F0474, H0808
D'Ancre, Concino Concini, maréchal, d. 1617: E0106
Dangerfield, Thomas, 1650?-1685: T3330
Daniel, Mary (Chamberlain): W0051
Daniel, S., M. D.: T0802
Dante Alleghieri, 1265-1321: A0595

D'Arblay, Frances (Burney), 1752-1840: A0710, B0554, H0160, P0119, T1865, T2224, T2229
Darby, [ ]: A1021
Darcy, Lady Elizabeth: M0030
Darell, Lady Elizabeth: W0093
Darey, Jane, lady: I0071
Darnell, [ ]: B0023
Darner, Mrs. [ ]: B0433
Darwin, Erasmus, 1731-1802: W1690
Dashe, Thomas: H0870
Dashwood, Emma, d. 1779: C0435, O0609
D'Avenant, Sir William, 1606-1668: A0679, A1456, A1529, D0263, I0037, O0037, R0006, R0221, S0730, T2042, T2206
D'Avila, Henrico Caterino, 1576-1631: D0038
Davenport, R. (1796): O0245
Davidson, Alexander, lieut.: I0165
Davidson, Harriet: I0165
Davies, [ ], actor (after 1695): G0013
Davies, Miss [ ], b. 1744: M0400, T1154
Davies, John Rogers: T2057
Davies, John, M.D.: W0823
Davis, Elizabeth: M0532
Davis, George: G0053
Davis, John, d. 1721: A1947
Davis, Joseph, d. 1739: A1947
Davis, Mary: B0279
Davis, Thomas, d. 1733: A1947, T1957
Davison, [ ]: H1271
Davy, [ ], lady: T3280
Davy, Maria: T2567
Davy, Maud: P0262
Davy, Richard: P0262
Dawson, John, butler of Christ Church Oxford, d. 1622: D0039
Dawson, Nancy: O0051
Dawson, William, d. 1632: V0070
Day, [ ] (1774): W1449
Day, Miss [ ]: C0536
Day, John: U0040
Day, John, poet: H0923
Day, Miss Merrill: L0431
Day, Ro.: T0188
Daye, Mary: I0824
Daylie, [ ], justice: W1125
De Bussy, [ ], French envoy: W1864
De Clifford, Mary, 1416?-1478: W1538
De la Clu, [ ]: C0468
De Mauroix, [ ]: T0919
De Nous, [ ] (1719): T0749
De Rosier, Pilatre, d. 1785: S0988
De Veil, Sir Thomas, d. 1746: S0720
De Winter, Jan Willem, admiral, 1750-1812: I0582, T0185
De Witt, [ ]: T1383
de Worde, Wynken, d. 1535: P0327
Dearden, Miss [ ]: F0147, F0147
Death, John: H0765
Deerhurst, Catherine (Henley) Coventry, viscountess, d. 1779: P0231
Deerhurst, Thomas Henry Coventry, Viscount, 1721-1744: T2647

Delamere, George Booth, 1st baron, 1621–1684: W2087

Delaney, Mrs. [ ], b. 1700: U0150

Delany, Patrick, dean of Down, 1695?–1768: H0091, T1879, T2488, W2609

Delawarr, John West, earl, 1693–1766: T3125

Delbo, [ ]: D0249

Delme, Miss [ ] (1730): A1867, A1868, W0866

Delme, Peter (1724): T3080

Denby, [ ] (1740): L0705, Y0052

Denham, [ ], lord (= Sir John Denham, 1615–1669?): A1151

Denham, Sir John, 1615–1669: A1190, D0401, G0434, P0005, S0047

Denham, Margaret (Brooke), d. 1666: A1479, D0264, K0016

Dennis, John, 1657–1734: I0279, O0872, W2570

Dennis, William: H1309

Derby, Mary: S0442

Dering, Sir Edward, 1625–1684: T0009

Derrick, [ ]: N0012

Derwentwater, James Radcliffe, 3rd earl, d. 1716: H0864, H1357, S1055, U0084

Des Cageaux, [ ], poet (1751): A0604

Descartes, René, 1596–1650: L0149

Desmond, Bridget (Stanhope) Feilding, countess, c. 1615–1665: W0568

Despauter, Johannes, d. 1520: T1908

d'Estrées, Gabrielle, 1573–1599: T0159

Devonshire, [ ], earl: *See* Hartington, William Cavendish, marquis, and earl of Devonshire

Devonshire, Christiana Cavendish, countess, d. 1675: A1293

Devonshire, Edward de Courtenay, earl, 1363?–1419: H1112

Devonshire, Georgiana (Spencer) Cavendish, duchess, 1757–1806: T0014, U0064, W0498

Devonshire, Mary (Butler) Cavendish, duchess, 1646–1710: W0371, W1158

Devonshire, Maud (de Camoys) de Courtenay, countess, b. c. 1398: H1112

Devonshire, William Cavendish, 1st duke, 1640–1707: A0040, A0482, I1130, S0351, W1720

Dew, Mrs. [ ]: M0125

Dew, Sir John: O0541

D'hu, Ian: M0747

Dicey, [ ], d. 1776: O0697

Dickie, Hall: T3362

Dickie, Molly: T3362

Dickinson, Ann (1791): A0484, F0781, I1613

Dickinson, J. Baron: T0269

Dickinson, Martha (1788–91): A1918, H0494, L0520, T1419

Dickson, Neal: D0086

Dickson, Robert, d. 1674: A0643, O0772, S1153

Digby, [ ], lord: B0055, G0134

Digby, Mrs. [ ]: H0557, W2064

Digby, Mrs. M., d. 1729: A1611

Digby, Mary, d. 1727: G0134

Digby, Sir Kenelm, 1603–1665: E0065, S1151, U0044

Digby, Rachel (Windham): B0055

Digby, Robert, d. 1726: G0134

Digby, Venetia (Stanley), lady, 1600–1633: B0092, D0226, S0739

Digby, William Digby, 5th baron, 1661–1752: T2831

Dillon, Sir John Talbot, c. 1740–1805: H1127

Diodati, [ ]: T0051

Dobson, Anne: F0087

Dod, Mrs. [ ]: M0282

Dodd, [ ]: T1681

Dodd, William: V0086

Dodsley, Robert, 1703–1754: I1193, A0039, A0114, A0632, A1404, C0432, G0306, H0295, I0923, I1492, J0137, M0368, O0688, S0151, T1462, T2632, T2663, T2976, W0598, W0845, W1193, W1255, W1632, Y0219, Y0486

Dodson, Mrs. [ ]: A1246

Doe, J.: D0364

Doe, Martin: D0364

Dolben, John, 1662–1710: G0310, U0033

Dolben, Sir William, 1727–1814: S0111, Y0474

Dolce, Carlo, 1616–1686: W1415

Donglay, [ ], marquis: B0462

Donne, John, 1572–1631: C0310, F0184, M0007, M0232, I0266, I0587, I0609, R0239, S0375, S0755, S1232, T0069, T1290, T2673, T3235, Y0213

Dorchester, Catherine Sedley, countess, 1657–1717: D0378, T0081, W1365

Dorset, Charles Sackville, 2nd duke, and earl of Middlesex, 1711–1769: F0054, H0702, I1110, M0192, O0441, O0583, O0913, P0184, P0325, R0182, S0001, S1004, S1119, T2570, T2580, W1813, Y0241

Dorset, Charles Sackville, 6th earl, and 1st earl of Middlesex, 1638–1706: A0482, D0379, I0678, L0694, O0216, S0355, S0551, T0290, W0610, W1240, W1720

Dorset, Elizabeth (Colyear) Sackville, duchess, and countess of Middlesex, d. 1768: B0453, O0691, W0893

Dorset, Grace (Boyle) Sackville, duchess, and countess of Middlesex, d. 1763: C0400, T0374

Dorset, Lionel Cranfield Sackville, 1st duke, and earl of Middlesex, 1688–1765: F0650, G0476, L0591, N0423, O0691, S0001, S0829, T0374, Y0011

Dorset, Mary (Compton) Sackville, countess, 1669–1691: W0371, W1158

Dorset, Mary [or Elizabeth?] (Bagot) Berkeley, countess, d. 1679: I0678

Dorset, Richard Sackville, 3rd earl, 1590–1624: L0191, R0188

Doudle, [ ]: T1833

Douff family: C0257, L0403

Douglas, [ ]: Y0448

Douglas, [ ], capt., d. 1667: O0151

Douglas, Dr. [ ]: H0036

Douglas, Lady Jane, 1698–1753: T1405

Dove, Mary: H0755

Dove, Molly (1728): Y0003

Dover, Henry Carey, 1st earl, 1580?–1666: H1025, H1026, T1868

Dover, Henry Jermyn, baron, 1636–1708: M0245

Dowdeswell, William, 1721–1775: C0512

Downe, Henry Pleydell Dawnay, 3rd viscount, 1727–1760: W2382

Downes, E.: W0759

Downes, Philip, d. 1743: W0759

Downing, [ ]: D0397
Downs, Betty: W2575
Doyly, [ ] (Hadly), lady: A0204
Drake, [ ]: A0410, Y0541
Drake, [ ], A. M.: T1029
Drake, Dr. [ ]: G0391
Drake, Miss [ ]: S0076
Drake, Mrs. [ ] (Keeling): W1532
Drake, Sir Francis, 1540?–1596: A1108, L0142, O0899,
    S0685, T2686, T3087, W1546
Drake, John: W1863
Drayton, Michael, 1563–1631: D0354, S1232
Drelincourt, Peter, 1644–1722: S1228
Dring, Sarah, d. 1719: T1760
Dromgold, [ ]: O0127
Drummond, Miss [ ]: H0562, H0951
Drummond, Mrs. G. (Harley): I0432
Drummond, John: D0420
Drummond, May: O0744
Drummond, Sir Henry: H1350
Drummond, Robert Hay, abp. of York, 1709–1776: H0562
Drummond, William, 1585–1649: S0782
Drury, Robert, 1587–1623: K0065
Dry, John: H0839
Dryden, John, 1631–1700: A0977, A1328, A1787, B0142,
    B0400, D0016, H0127, H0310, H0394, I0205, I1113, I1266,
    N0509, P0268, S0787, S1241, T0286, T0364, T1586,
    T1920, T2513, T2550, T3209, W0261, W1242, W1787
Du Bartas, Guillaume de Salluste, seigneur,
    1544–1590: T2147
Du Bocage, Anne Marie: I0433
Du Missy, Rev. [ ], m. 1754: S1353
Du Missy, Mrs. [ ] (Amproux), m. 1754: S1353
Du Parc, Elisabetta, d. 1778: W0834
Du Pedan, Mme. [ ]: W0072
Du Vall, [ ]: H0733
Dubos, Jean Baptiste, abbé, 1670–1742: H1411
Duck, Miss [ ], daughter of Stephen Duck: W2611
Duck, Stephen, 1705–1756: D0426, I1437, L0091, I1368,
    T1878, W0234
Dudley, Charles (1799): A1622, D0428
Dudley, Guilford, lord: W2372
Duelly, [ ]: A1219
Dum., [ ], lord: A1737
Dumbar, James: Y0387
Dumbelow, Richard: D0042, H0734
Dummer, Jeremiah (1741): W1082
Duncan, Adam Duncan, 1st viscount, admiral,
    1731–1804: W0945
Duncan, Misses [ ], [ ] (1780): W0253
Dunch, John, captain, d. 1696: T2171
Duncombe, [ ]: A1801
Duncombe, Sir Charles, d. 1711: A0583, T0449
Duncombe, Lewis, d. 1730: I1552
Duncombe, William, 1690–1769: F0642, I1552
Dundee, John Graham, 1st viscount, 1649?–1689:
    F0176, H0853, O0456, O0612
Duns Scotus, John, c. 1266–1308: B0130, D0436
Dunstan, saint, 924–988: I1030
Dunton, Elizabeth: S0005
Durande, Rev. [ ]: W1890

Durant, Elizabeth: R0190
Durastanti, Margherita, fl. 1700–1734: G0027
D'Urfey, Thomas, 1653–1723: O0106
Dursley, [ ]: O0106
Dyer, Samuel: D0080
Dysart, Grace (Carteret) Tollemache, countess,
    1713–1755: A0648, F0035

E., Colonel F. P.: M0176
E[ ]n, [ ], countess?: W2487
Earl, Ralph: M0643
Earle, [ ]: A0092
Earle, Mrs. [ ]: A0092
Earle, Ferdinand: H0641
Earle, Giles, 1678?–1758: M0460
Earle, Philadelphia: D0142, D0166, T0622, Y0577, Y0586
Earle, Rev. [ ]: T3346
Earth, Roger, d. 1634: F0638
Ebsworthy, Peter: T3099
Eccles, Rev. [ ]: B0300
Ecclestone, Mrs. [ ] (Jacomb), m. 1746: H1239
Ecclestone, Theophilus, m. 1746: H1239
Echard, Laurence, 1670?–1730: T2378
Eckardt, [ ], painter (1746): D0282
Edgcumbe, Richard Edgcumbe, 1st baron, 1680–1758:
    S0350
Edgeworth, Honora Sneyd, d. 1780: L0056
Edward Hanover, son of Frederick Louis, prince of
    Wales, 1739–1767: G0055, I1058
Edward I, king of England, 1239–1307: R0238
Edward II, king of England, 1284–1327: I0379
Edward III, king of England, 1327–1377: I1309
Edward IV, king of England, 1442–1483: O0284
Edward VI, king of England, 1537–1553: A0099, W1010
Edward, prince of Wales (the Black Prince),
    1330–1376: A0704, T1257
Edwards, [ ]: F0637
Edwards, Dennis, Oxford University vergerer
    (1642–43): N0250
Edwards, Jo.: S1095
Edwards, Sarah: T0759
Edwin, Charles: Y0019
Edwin, Sir Humphrey, 1642–1707: I0041
Egbert, king of England, c. 784–838: M0421
Egerton, Lady Alice: I0084
Egmont, John Percival, 1st earl, 1683–1748: S0110
Egmont, John Percival, 2nd earl, 1711–1770: W0572,
    W2187
Egremont, Alicia Maria (Carpenter) Wyndham,
    countess, d. 1794: V0064
Ekins, Anna: E0172
Elcock, Rev. [ ]: T1817
Eld, George, lt. col., d. 1793: A0762
Elderton, William, d. 1592?: H0668
Elforde, [ ]: N0092
Eliot, [ ], poet and farmer: T2089
Eliot, Mrs. [ ] (1792): F0663
Eliot, Edward James: W0169
Elizabeth I, queen of England, 1533–1603: A0099,
    A0122, A0505, B0271, C0379, E0050, F0737, H0746, H0855,
    H1178, I0695, I0697, I1375, K0049, L0009, L0083, M0386,

M0421, M0615, N0133, P0011, R0010, R0025, T0260,
T0820, T0866, T1038, T1125, W0168, W0170, W0670,
W0769, W0989, W0993, W1010, W1284, W1593

Elizabeth of England, consort of Frederick, king of
Bohemia, 1596-1662: H0048, T1331, Y0350

Elizabeth of Palatine, princess, 1618-1680: T2326

Elizabeth, princess, 1635-1650: A1772, M0320

Ellesmere, Thomas Egerton, baron, 1540?-1617: S1007

Elliot, George Augustus: *See* Heathfield, George
Augustus Elliot, 1st baron

Elliot, Sir John, physician, 1736-1786: T2497

Ellis, Ann (1781): O0561, S0939

Ellis, Anne: Y0316

Ellison, [ ]: Y0205

Eltinbrode, Martin: H0676, H0904

Elton, Miss [ ]: S0094

Elton, Sir Abraham: G0162

Elton, Rebecca (Berry), d. 1696: C0355

Elton, Thomas: C0355

Elwes, Mrs. D. (Ewer), d. 1768: O1021

Elwes, Sir Hervey, 1683-1763: T2300

Elwes, John: H0964

Emerson, William: H0878

Empson, Miss [ ], d. 1732: O0915

English, Anna Christiana: S0832

English, Annabella: R0033

Erasmus, Desiderius, 1466-1536: E0100, H1327

Ernley, Sir John: T0009

Ernst, Master [ ]: T1778, W0709

Erroll, Charlotte(?): W1807

Erskine, [ ]: T2869

Essex, Arthur Capell, 1st earl, 1632-1683: T0009

Essex, Frances (Hanbury), countess, d. 1759: E0027

Essex, Robert Devereux, 3rd earl, 1591-1646: A1177,
E0121, W0989

Essex, Walter Devereux, 1st earl, 1541?-1576: O0402

Ethelfleda, d. 198?: O0284

Etherege, Sir George, 1635?-1691: F0226, I0853, T0152

Eusden, Laurence, 1688-1730: T3217

Euston, Charles Fitzroy, earl, 1683-1757: L0214

Evans, [ ]: H0999

Evans, Dr. [ ]: H0730

Evans, Miss [ ] (1730): W1698

Evelyn, John, 1620-1706: H0195

Evelyn, Julia: I1344

Everard, Mrs. [ ]: W0388

Every, Alexander, d. 1588: I1143

Ewen, Mrs. [ ]: H0180

Ewer, [ ] (1742): O1021

Exeter, [ ], earl: G0270

Eyles, Sir John, lord mayor of London (1688): F0446

Eyre, Joseph: M0279, W1564, W1808

Eyre, T.: H1315, I1174, M0714, W0528

Eyres, Mary Anne: M0264

Eythin, James King, 1st baron, 1589-1652: Y0513

F., Miss A.: H1171, I0483

F., C.: I1207

F., Miss G.: T2118

F., M.: H0780

F——, [ ], cornet: I1203

F——h, [ ]: O0075

F——kes, Mrs. [ ]: T0388

F——n, D——r: T2006

F——r, [ ], lady: A0035

F——t——r, Miss [ ]: H1128

Faber, John, the younger, 1695-1756: C0139, C0171,
D0010, O0196, T0575, T0717, W2448

Fabian, Robert, d. 1513: L0364

Fairborne, Sir Palmes, 1644-1680: Y0154

Fairfax, Thomas Fairfax, 3rd baron, 1612-1671: F0078,
U0031, W0891

Fairfax, Sir William, 1609-1644: H0122

Falkland, Lucius Henry Cary, 6th viscount,
1687-1730: O0293

Falkner, Richard, actor (1726): T1687

Falmouth, Charles Berkeley, 1st earl, d. 1665: I0678

Fane, Charlotte (Rowe), 1718-1739: T2551, T3091

Fane, I.: B0279

Fanshawe, Miss F—— (1776): G0031

Far, John (1730): I1611

Farinelli (Carolos Broschi), 1705-1782: A1567, L0476,
W1794

Farquhar, George, 1678-1707: T2718, W0901

Farquharson, Dr. [ ]: S0049

Farrell, William, ensign (1740): B0435

Farwell, [ ]: M0166

Fast, Miss [ ]: A0760, T2279

Faulcon, [ ], lady: C0400

Faulkner, Miss [ ], singer: W1592

Faulkner, George, 1699-1725: I0964

Felton, Elizabeth (Howard), lady, 1656?-1681: D0399,
O0042, Y0450

Felton, John, 1595?-1628: A1236, E0078, H0970, I0054,
W0025

Fénelon, François de Selignac de la Mothe, archbishop
of Cambray, 1651-1715: C0016

Fenton, Elijah, 1683-1730: A0231, B0392, T1881

Fenton, Roger, 1565-1616: B0562

Fenwick, Sir John, 1645?-1797: H0863, W0744

Ferdinand VI, king of Spain, 1713-1759: W1811

Ferdinand, prince of Brunswick, 1721-1792: T2907

Ferguson, Robert, 1750-1774: N0241

Fermin, Peter: P0101

Fermor, Minny: P0097

Ferrari, [ ]: H1168

Ferrer, E.: S0848

Ferrers of Tamworth, Washington Shirley, earl,
1672-1729: H0931

Ferrers, Charlotte (Compton) Ferrers, baroness,
1729-1770: D0127, I0455, T0157

Ferrers, Sir John [Sir Thomas?]: G0283, I1504

Ferrers, Laurence Shirley, 4th earl, 1720-1760: L0075

Fiddes, [ ] (1753): T2823

Field, Miss [ ]: W2338

Fielding, Sir John, 1721-1780: A0119, J0143, K0061, S0193,
S0653, S1239, T0257, T1901, W0217, W1708

Finch, [ ] (1701): N0267

Finch, Lady Charlotte: A0296, A1771

Finch, Sir John Finch, baron, 1584-1660: H0517

Findlater, James Ogilvy, 4th earl, and 1st earl of
Seafield, 1664-1730: A0430, W1001

Fisher, Mrs. [ ], actress (1777): L0008
Fisher, Caroline: F0017
Fisher, Clement: S0359
Fisher, Payne, 1616-1693: T1851
Fisher, W. (1772): I1323
Fitter, Miss [ ]: G0043, S0056, Y0049
Fitzherbert, Mrs. [ ]: W0796
Fitzherbert, Basil: B0020
Fitzherbert, Jane (Cotton): B0020
Fitzherbert, Margaret: N0328
Fitzherbert, Lady Mary: H1180
Fitzherbert, Ralph: C0509
Fitzroy, Misses [ ] [ ]: S1321
Fitzroy, Lady Caroline: B0519
Fitzwilliam, Lady Winifred, d. 1597: W0590, W2288
Fizgerald, Sir Thomas: O1115
Flamand, Miss [ ], actress (1745): B0645
Flat, William: W2322
Flatman, Thomas, 1637-1688: W2065
Flaxman, [ ]: F0318
Flecknoe, Richard, c. 1620-1678: A0915
Fleetwood, [ ], lady: S0614
Fleetwood, Sir Thomas, 6th bart., 1748-1802: S0497
Fleming, [ ]: H0383
Fleming, [ ], lady: A1739
Fleming, [ ], of Stanmore, d. 1635: N0273
Fleming, Catherine (1718): T2831
Fleming, Sean: W0605
Fletcher, Cumberland (1768): A0029
Fletcher, John, 1579-1625: T1791, W1285
Fleury, Andre-Hercule de, cardinal, 1653-1742: C0011,
    E0160, T0774, W2399
Flower, Jane: S0063
Floyd, Biddy (1708): W0850
Folkes, Martin, 1690-1754: D0131
Folkestone, Jacob de Bouverie, 1st viscount,
    1694-1761: E0161
Fon——r——can, Mrs. [ ]: B0679
Fontayne, Mrs. [ ] (Whichcot), 1731-1750: I0557, I1350
Fontayne, John, dean of York: I0557, I1350
Fontinelle, Miss [ ]: W0236
Foot, [ ]: H0801
Foot, E. W., capt.: W2363
Foot, John: R0058
Foote, Samuel, 1720-1777: A0476, A1590, F0357, F0528,
    I1318, N0075, T0077, T0419, V0018, W0949, Y0553
Ford, Mrs. [ ] (1716): T2293
Ford, John, c. 1586-1640: T2016
Fordyce, James, 1720-1796: O0197, T1762
Fordyce, Lady M.: W0796
Foreman, [ ]: L0524
Formantel, Miss [ ], singer (1756): T2491
Forster, [ ]: F0502
Fortery, James: J0105
Fortery, Mary: J0105
Fortescue, Anne Campbell, lady, d. 1812: S0339
Fortescue, Elizabeth: I0482
Fortinbras, Thomas: S0833
Fortune, Miss [ ] (c. 1759): M0035
Foster, James, 1697-1753: T0489
Fothergill, Dr. [ ]: L0301

Fothergill, John: O0315
Fothergill, Samuel, 1715-1782: F0151, I1156, I1381, L0030
Fourbin, Claude de, comte, 1656-1733: L0049
Fowl, Molly, b. 1702: T0661
Fowler, Madam [ ]: G0305
Fox, [ ]: B0079
Fox, Charles James, 1749-1806: A0351, F0537, H0919,
    K0031, T2795
Fox, George, 1624-1691: A0922, T2509
Fox, James, d. 1754?: P0072
Fox, Lady M———: S0754
Fox, Stephen: F0471
Fox, W.: R0014
Foxe, John, 1516-1587: H0671
Frampton, Robert, bp. of Gloucester, 1622-1708:
    C0441, G0330
Francis II, king of France, 1544-1560: I1145
Francis, Charlotte (Burney): See Broome, Charlotte
    Ann (Burney) Francis
Francis, Charlottine (1795): D0276, M0638
Francis, Clement (m. 1786): N0169, W0029
Francis, James: M0189
Francis, Polly: P0293
Francis, William: T0124
Francklin, Frances: I1157
Franklin, Benjamin, 1706-1790: F0660
Frazer, Betty: H0586
Frazie, [ ], singer: T3383
Frazier, [ ] (= Carey Fraser, later countess of
    Peterborough and Monmouth?): A1428
Frazier, Dr. [ ]: I0396, I0437
Frederica Charlotte of Prussia, duchess of York,
    1767-1820: W1468
Frederick Augustus, duke of York and Albany,
    1763-1827: A0060, A1816
Frederick Henry, son of Frederick V, king of Bohemia,
    1614-1629: T2984
Frederick II, king of Prussia, 1712-1786: G0011, G0396,
    I1181, P0332, W1638
Frederick Louis, prince of Wales, 1701-1751: G0464,
    W1429, A0862, C0518, E0165, F0054, F0691, G0195,
    H0291, I1058, O0433, O0967, P0006, P0325, S0856,
    T0976, T1106, T1772, T2817, T3271, T3277, T3364,
    W1163, W1236, W1260, W1930, W2401, Y0241
Frederick V, king of Bohemia, 1597?-1632?: H0048,
    S1084, T1331, T2984
Frederick William II, king of Prussia, 1744-1797: S1173
Frederick, Miss [ ] (1733): A0941
Frederick, Cassandra: T1069
Frederick, Charles (1748): D0057
Freeman, [ ]: A0663
Freeman, Kitty (1729): W1820
Freke, John, surgeon (1743-1754): H1114, H1419
Freron, Elie Catherine, 1719-1776: F0557
Friandet, [ ]: T3194
Friend, [ ]: W1252
Friend, John, 1675-1728: Y0172
Friend, Robert, 1667-1751: I0791
Frodsham, John, capt., 1729-1783: H1088
Frowd, Sarah: S0050
Fry, J.: A0137

Fuller, [ ], barrister: I0144
Fuller, [ ], painter (1718): T1052
Fuller, Dr. [ ]: H0712
Fuller, Mrs. [ ]: H0712, S0960
Fuller, J.: T0638
Fury, Miss [ ]: T2924
Fuseli, Henry, 1741-1825: S1027
Fyndall, [ ]: F0789

G., M.: D0089
G., Sir W.: P0040, S0078
G——h, [ ]: G0060
G——s, [ ]: A0544
Gabets, Thomas, d. 1694: T1466
Gabriel, John: I0941
Gadbury, John, 1627-1704: C0413
Gallagher, James, bishop of Kildare and Leighlin, 1681-1751: W1984
Galli, Signora [ ] (1747): W0637
Galuppi, Baldassare, 1706-1785: V0006
Gambarini, Elizabetta de, b. 1731: W0999
Gardener, Miss [ ]: W1245
Gardiner, Colonel [ ]: H0293
Gardiner, Dr. [ ] (1732): W0340
Gardiner, Mrs. [ ] (1732): W0340
Gardiner, Francis, alderman of Norwich: F0546
Gardner, Ann: W0705
Garnier, [ ]: Q0027
Garrett, Sir Thomas, deputy lieutenant: T0057
Garrick, David, 1717-1779: A1448, D0073, D0356, G0015, G0016, H0524, H0727, I0328, I0334, L0086, O0629, P0337, T0659, T0708, T2375, T2428, T2507, T2867, W0806, W0968, W1550, W1562, W1603
Garrick, Eva Maria (Veigel), 1724-1822: A1865, S0955, W0828
Garth, Sir Samuel, 1661-1719: G0307, M0001
Garthwaite, [ ]: A1161
Gascoigne, Richard, d. 1716: H0645
Gascoyne, [ ]: L0425
Gascoyne, Sir Crisp, 1700-1761: W2560
Gataker, [ ]: W2366
Gauden, John, 1605-1662: H0003
Gawdy, Miss [ ]: T1816
Gawdy, Anne: H0541
Gawdy, Sir Francis, 1532-1606: T1816
Gay, John, 1685-1732: A0835, E0090, O0041, O0113, T0232, T3301, W0264
Gayland, [ ]: A0572
Gayland, Mrs. [ ] (Darby): A0572
Geminiani, Francesco, 1680?-1762: C0537, O0808, W1214
George I, king of Great Britain, 1660-1727: A0466, A1165, A1439, A1553, A1604, A1626, A1805, A1825, B0154, B0466, B0526, B0582, C0278, C0297, F0433, F0636, G0052, G0056, H0254, H0537, H0953, I0013, I0053, I0258, I0895, I0945, I0955, I1017, K0057, L0145, M0393, M0448, M0616, O0081, O0794, O1036, O1094, P0093, P0286, S0268, S0350, S0474, S0562, S0618, S0834, T0400, T0479, T0563, T0639, T0665, T0768, T0771, T0773, T0775, T0782, T1308, T1768, T2028, T2197, T2366, T2785, T3124, T3201, W0091, W0191, W0601, W0800, W0878, W0975, W1016, W1098, W1266, W1277, W1280, W1342, W1348, W1782, W2247, W2475, Y0005, Y0038, Y0084, Y0302, Y0331, W1262
George II, king of Great Britain, 1683-1760: A0315, A1074, A1165, A1317, A1365, A1398, A1608, A1729, B0210, F0103, F0484, G0241, H0347, I0741, L0057, L0276, L0527, M0274, M0349, M0354, M0445, O0139, O0599, O0701, O0825, O0978, O1102, Q0034, S0027, S0201, S0242, S0341, S0554, S0560, S0776, S0791, T0400, T0769, T1768, T2197, T2851, W0146, W0194, W0214, W0365, W0378, W0589, W1137, W1490, W1608, W1610, W1661, W1850, W2401, W2460
George III, king of Great Britain, 1738-1820: A1547, A1816, B0535, D0247, F0103, G0195, G0396, G0435, H0081, H0133, I0320, I0513, I0900, K0038, L0454, O0034, O0302, O0328, O0449, O0452, O0453, O0464, O0561, O0721, P0001, S0105, S0239, S0367, S1389, T0164, T0412, T0772, T0870, T1389, T2423, T2472, T3012, T3025, T3327, T3359, W0575, W1868, W2116, W2225, W2387, Y0004, Y0006
George IV, king of Great Britain, 1762-1830: F0519, T2659, T3359, U0064
George William Hanover, prince, 1717-1718: A1804, G0241, T0400
George, prince of Denmark, consort of Queen Anne, 1653-1708: A0049, I1102, I1244, T3204
George, Rev. [ ] (1715): G0303
Gibbon, Edward, 1731-1794: F0497, K0038, S0367, W0902
Gibbons, Thomas: R0128
Gibson, [ ]: A1136
Gibson, Edmund, bishop of London, 1669-1748: G0062, Y0552
Gibson, Richard, 1615-1690: S0047
Gibson, Thomas: S1369
Gibson, William, 1713-1771: G0061, R0037
Gilbert, [ ]: Y0390
Gill, Adam: B0294
Gill, John, 1697-1771: C0067, I0502, I0664, I0794, I0840, J0129, W1743
Gillespie, Patrick: G0314
Gilpin, Thomas, d. 1778: T0552
Giordeni, [ ] (1750): M0357
Giornovich, [ ], singer (1794): N0333
Girard, Miss [ ]: O0323
Gisborne, Mrs. [ ], of Stavely: F0709
Glanville, Joseph, 1636-1680: H1332, I1487
Glass, Miss [ ]: W1037
Glean, [ ], lady: A1122
Glean, Sir Peter: P0099
Glenbervie, Sylvester Douglas, baron, 1743-1823: A1333
Gloucester and Hertford, Richard de Clare, 5th earl, 1222-1262: C0141
Goad, Dr. Thomas: G0121
Godden, Thomas, 1624-1688: I0396, I0437, W0078
Godfrey, Anna: I0274
Godfrey, Sir Edmund Berry, 1621-1678: A0179, I1506, T1589, W0259
Godfrey, Minuna: L0074
Godfrey, Thomas: I1320
Godley, Jacob: W0047
Godolphin, Francis Godolphin, 2nd earl, 1678-1766: G0258

Godolphin, Sidney Godolphin, 1st earl, 1645–1712:
T0009

Goethe, Johann Wolfgang von, 1749–1832: A0850,
F0601, T2553

Goldsmith, Oliver, 1728–1774: A0647, G0285, H1413

Gondomar, Diego, 1567?–1626: T1812, W0356, O0413

Goodman, Joan: H0759

Goodman, William: H0879

Goodrick, Athelina: A1517

Goodwin, William, d. 1620: I1452

Goodwood, [ ]: I1097

Goodyear, Sir Henry, of Polesworth: A1156

Gordon, [ ], capt.: A0988

Gordon, [ ], count: O0814

Gordon, [ ], general?: D0099

Gordon, Miss [ ] (1779): W2425

Gordon, Mrs. [ ], d. 1744: I0937

Gordon, Harriet (Finch Hatton), lady, 1752–1821:
W0257

Gordon, Mary, widow (1725): E0129, F0035, T1819,
W0158

Gordon, Nancy (1779): S0068, S0236, W2425

Gordon, Sir Robert, 1580–1666: W1974

Gordon, Thomas (1744): I0937

Gordon, William Gordon, lord (1755): A1641, I1608

Gordonstoun, Elizabeth Farquhar, lady, d. 1663: S1080

Gore, Miss [ ]: L0429

Gorges, Sir Arthur: T1995

Goring, George Goring, baron, 1608–1657: H1274, I0154

Gosling, Humphrey: H0751, H0890

Gouch, Rev. [ ] (1780): O0536

Goudelin, Pierre, 1579–1649: W1729

Gough, [ ], choirmaster, of Marylebone Gardens
(1738): G0344, T3296, T3331

Gould, Robert, d. 1709: P0172

Gourdon, Elizabeth: U0065

Gower, John Leveson-Gower, 1st earl, 1695–1754:
S0158

Grafton, [ ], duke: C0059

Grafton, Augustus Henry Fitzroy, 3d duke, 1735–1811:
A0942

Grafton, Charles Fitzroy, 2nd duke, 1683–1757: D0170,
H0631, I1570

Grafton, Elizabeth (Wrottesley) Fitzroy, duchess,
1745–1822: P0115

Grafton, Henry Fitzroy, 1st duke, 1663–1690: B0306,
H0701, W0990

Grafton, Hugh, d. 1743: F0239

Grafton, Isabella (Bennet) Fitzroy, duchess,
1667?–1723: H0631

Graham, [ ]: A1445, G0408, S1055

Graham, Frances: W0636

Gramont, Philibert, comte de, 1621–1707: W1409

Granby, Frances (Seymour), marchioness, 1728–1761:
Y0226

Granby, John Manners, marquis, 1721–1770: F0423,
W2583

Grange, John: F0077

Grantham, George: W1769

Grantham, Henrietta (Butler), countess, d. 1724:
P0022

Grantham, Vincent (1729): T0094

Granville, Frances (Worsley) Carteret, countess,
1694–1743: A0215, T1819, W0158

Granville, John Carteret, 1st earl, 1690–1763: A1052,
C0453, D0350, M0725, M0726, S0463, S0467, V0002

Granville, Thomas, capt., d. 1747: Y0201

Gray, [ ]: M0564

Gray, Andrew: H0905

Gray, John, of Enfield, d. 1709: W0645, W2528

Gray, Katherine: B0296, U0037

Gray, Mary, d. 1645?: O0227

Gray, Thomas, 1716–1771: F0623, T0184

Greatheed, Bertie, 1759–1826: A1119, A1939, D0049,
M0207, N0533, O0369, T0880, T2704

Greatheed, Mary (Bertie), lady, d. 1774: W2142

Greatheed, Peregrine: T1521

Greber, Jacob (c. 1702): H0167

Green, [ ]: I0575

Green, Clement: A0069

Green, Jn. (1745): B0260

Green, John: W0816

Green, Rev. [ ]: M0560, S0138

Green, Miss [ ] (1734): W0301

Green, Mrs. [ ]: I0575, S0323

Green, Molly: I0754

Green, Ruth: M0407

Green, Thomas: H1087

Green, William: S0140

Greenhill, John, 1644?–1676: W0395

Greenville, Sir Richard, d. 1595: H1101

Greenwood, Mrs. [ ]: O0265

Greenwood, Edward: W1475

Gregg, Henry (1796): P0035, P0149

Gregory, Mrs. [ ]: T2291

Gregory, Francis, 1625?–1707: F0085, W0078

Gregory, Prince: T2291

Grenville, Capt. [ ], d.1747: H0467

Greville, Fulke, b. 1717?: O0945

Grey, [ ]: W0642

Grey, Arthur: R0029

Grey, Edmund: W0538

Grey, Sir James (1773): T1131

Grey, Lady Jane, 1537–1554: N0516, T1927, T3173, W2372

Griffith, Walter, commodore, d. 1779: Y0137

Grimes, [ ], colonel: P0216

Grimes, Mrs. [ ] (Black) (1746): W1527

Grimstone, [ ], 1714–1671: B0249

Grogan, Larry: Y0370

Grogan, Patrick, d. 1721: K0062, P0199

Grubby, Rebecca (1778): T2182

Guerno, [ ]: W0558

Guicciardini, Francesco, 1483–1640: D0038

Guilford, Francis North, 1st baron, 1637–1685: G0373,
T0950

Guilford, Frederick North, 2nd earl, 1732–1792: D0031,
L0108

Guillibeau, [ ]: I3083

Guise, Miss [ ]: E0025

Gunning, Betty: *See* Argyll, Elizabeth (Gunning)
Douglas-Hamilton Campbell, duchess

Gunning, John, colonel: T3328

Gunning, Misses [ ], [ ] (1751): B0503

Gunning, Peter, bishop of Chichester, 1614-1684: I1433

Gunnings, Mrs. [ ]: T1701

Gunston, Thomas: T1003

Gurney, Richard (1739): T1372

Gustaf III, king of Sweden, 1746-1792: Y0247

Gustavus Adolphus II, king of Sweden, 1594-1632:
    C0024, C0081, G0396, G0417, G0457, I0075, I1355, L0354,
    O0465, S0311, S1084, T2728

Gutenberg, Johann, c. 1400-1468: F0198

Guy of Warwick, Sir, 14th c.: O0316

Gwatkin, Miss [ ]: D0096

Gwatkin, Robert Lovewell (1778): A1024

Gwin, John, bp. of St. David's: B0666

Gwyn, Eleanor, 1650-1687: I0369, I0700, I1505, O0159,
    O0401, W1409

Gwyn, Madam [ ]: I0369

Gwynedd ap Gruffydd, Owen, d. 1169: O1156

Gwynn, Edward: I0511

Gybon, Francis: N0294

Gybs, Thomas: A0317

H., [ ]: Y0338

H., Mrs. [ ]: Y0466

H., B.: A1196

H., Betty: N0081

H., Mrs. E.: S0647

H., Lady Elizabeth L.: U0053

H., Elizabeth: B0317

H., J.: T1890

H., Mrs. M., d. 1779: H1213

H., N.: B0410

H., T.: P0198

H., V. (1769): W1389

H———, [ ]: O0788, T0307

H———, [ ], earl: M0255

H———, Dr. [ ]: H0179

H——l——x, Mrs. R——l: W1246

H——re, [ ]: P0166

H——ry, [ ]: S0105

H——t, [ ]: H1480

H——y, Mrs. [ ]: I1048

H——y——d, [ ], colonel, m. 1783: T1374

H——y——d, Mrs. ( ) Col——g——d, m. 1783:
    T1374

Habington, Lucy (Herbert), b. 1608: B0412, C0063,
    F0501, T0376, W2173

Hackett, Dr. [ ]: D0419

Hackett, Mrs. [ ]: D0419

Hackman, James, d. 1779: T0443

Haddington, Jean (Gordon) Hamilton, countess,
    d. 1655: Y0589

Haddington, Elizabeth [ ], lady, d. 1618: D0115

Haddington, Thomas Hamilton, 2nd earl, 1600-1640:
    Y0589

Haddock, Sir Richard, 1629-1746: S0938

Hadly, [ ]: A0204

Haines, John: C0041

Hale, Miss [ ]: O0373

Hale, Barnard: F0671

Hale, Bernard, colonel: J0120, Q0019

Hale, Mary Ann, d. 1805: T2452

Hale, Sacheverel, d. 1746: D0236

Hales, [ ], lady: W1913

Hales, Matthew: H1086

Hales, Dr. Stephen, of Cambridge (1702): S1005

Halifax, Charles Montagu, 1st earl, 1661-1715: G0300,
    I1100, T0013, W1773, W2097

Halifax, George Montagu-Dunk, 2nd earl, 1716-1771:
    I0807, S1189, Y0197

Hall, John: H0767, J0095

Hall, John, 1627-1656: M0645

Hall, John, d. 1716: D0340, S0737

Hall, Joseph, bp., 1574-1656: T1731

Haller, [ ]: A0817

Halley, Edmond, 1656-1742: T1912

Halsey, Mrs. [ ] (1734): W0301

Halswell, Hugh, proctor of All Souls, Oxford (1627):
    W1602

Haly, Sir Christopher: M0025

Ham, [ ], d. 1715: H1351

Hamilton, [ ]: W1001

Hamilton, [ ] (1793): A0041

Hamilton, [ ], lady (1747): T0380

Hamilton, Alice, b. 1776: L0199, T1051, W1700, Y0240

Hamilton, Anne (Cochran) Hamilton, duchess,
    d. 1724: S0456, W2263

Hamilton, Anne (Spencer) Douglas-Hamilton,
    duchess, d. 1771: A1860, W2394

Hamilton, Dorothy (Haws), lady: F0616

Hamilton, Douglas Douglas-Hamilton, 8th duke,
    1756-1799: H0738

Hamilton, Esther, d. 1787: Y0039

Hamilton, Lady Harriet: A1751

Hamilton, J., fl. 1609: T2487

Hamilton, James Douglas, 4th duke, 1702-1743: D0284

Hamilton, James Douglas-Hamilton, 6th duke,
    1724-1758: A1754

Hamilton, James George Douglas-Hamilton, 7th
    duke, 1755-1769: T3328

Hamilton, James Hamilton, 1st duke, 1606-1649:
    A0368, A0397

Hamilton, Rev. [ ], of Ireland: L0199

Hamilton, Sir David, 1663-1721: F0639

Hamilton, William, lord: F0616

Hamilton, Sir William: G0306

Hammond, [ ] (1704): N0206

Hammond, John: T0939

Hammond, Thomas: B0660

Hammond, William, 1614-1685: H0183

Hampden, John, 1594-1643: A1004, B0596, G0159

Hampton, Elizabeth: E0080

Hanbury, [ ]: O0615

Hanbury, William, 1725-1778: T3073

Hanbury Williams, Sir Charles, 1708-1759: F0426,
    P0125

Hancocke, John, physician, d. 1728: W2077

Handel, George Friedrich, 1685-1759: B0656, D0406,
    F0108, H1044, O0547, R0007, R0211, S1177, T0252, T0492,
    T0592, T2947, W0564, W1814, W1817, W2015, Y0175

Handson, Edward: H1075

Hanger, [ ]: A1892

Hanger, Elizabeth (Bond), m. 1737: O0527
Hanger, Gabriel, m. 1737: O0527
Hanham, Penelope: T1611
Hanmer, Lady Catherine: C0400
Hanmer, Thomas Hanmer, 4th baron, 1677-1746: T2919
Hannes, Sir Edward, c. 1664-1710: T1122
Hanway, Jonas: A1238
Hanway, Louisa: I0520
Harcourt, Simon Harcourt, 1st viscount, c. 1661-1727: T3090
Harcourt, Simon Harcourt, 2nd viscount, 1714-1777: H0945
Harcourt, Simon, 1684-1720: T3090
Hardcastle, Mrs. [ ]: I1546
Hardman, Mrs. [ ]: I0282
Hardman, Henry: Y0270
Hardwick, [ ]: I0203
Hardwicke, earls of: S1155
Hardwicke, Margaret (Cocks), countess, d. 1761: I1188
Hardwicke, Philip Yorke, 1st earl, 1690-1764: W0929
Hardwicke, Philip Yorke, 2nd earl, 1720-1790: F0426
Hare, Elizabeth: A0464
Hare, Sir L.: R0012
Hare, Sir Ralph: A0464
Harington, John Harington, 2nd baron, d. 1614: F0055
Harley, [ ]: See Oxford, Robert Harley, 1st earl
Harley, Margaret Cavendish, lady, d. 1785: T1395
Harley, Thomas (1775): S1154
Harper, Miss [ ], singer: T0109
Harpur, [ ] (Cavendish), lady: A0447
Harpur, [ ], lady: A0172, W0019
Harpur, Crew, d. 1725: O1106
Harpur, Henry: T2059
Harpur, Master [ ]: A0172
Harpur, Mr. [ ]: T0213
Harrington, Caroline (Fitzroy) Stanhope, countess, 1722-1784: A0012
Harrington, Rev. [ ]: W0680
Harris, Miss [ ]: G0284, T1872
Harris, Frances: T0222
Harris, John: T0939
Harrison, George: G0054
Harrison, Thomas, 1555-1631: I0790
Harryes, Cordelia: W0778
Hart, William: W2310
Hartington, William Cavendish, marquis, and earl of Devonshire, 1641-1707: H1124
Hartop, John: L0422
Harvey, John: I0012
Harvey, Margaret: S1294
Harvey, Samuel, d. 1729: H0865
Harvey, Dame Ursula: See Leighton, Ursula (Harvey), lady
Harvey, William, 1578-1657: A1403, I1561
Haslam, Miss A.: D0092
Hasse, Johann Adolph, 1699-1783: A0593, A1584
Hastings, Warren, 1732-1818: F0537
Hatley, Andrew: H0475
Hatley, Christopher: H0527, T0817
Hatley, Paul: T0817

Hatton, [ ], lady: F0258
Hatton, Edward: T1136
Havard, William, 1710-1778: B0021, V0049
Hawes, [ ], sr.: A1872, O0940
Hawke, [ ], singer: S0985
Hawke, Edward Hawke, 1st baron, admiral, 1705-1781: B0210, F0321, H1258, T2237, W1435
Hawke, Edward, lieutenant colonel, 1746-1773: Y0207
Hawkesworth, Abraham Richard, d. 1769?: W2062, W2178
Hawkins, Sir John, 1719-1789: I0991, Y0090
Hawkins, William: O1148
Hay, [ ], musician (1764-1767): F0305, O0393
Hay, Miss [ ]: C0300, T0037
Hay, Abigail (Holland), lady: H0361
Hay, Lady Anne, daughter of John Hay, 1st earl of Carlisle: I0189
Hay, John, lord (1767): A0320
Hay, Sir George, 1715-1778: W1883
Hayley, Ann: T0485
Hayley, Eliza (Ball), 1750-1797: E0095, M0727, S0259, Y0144
Hayley, Lucy: T2971
Hayley, William, 1745-1820: A0601, D0101, F0454, I0565, I1183, R0215, T2386, W2456, Y0537
Hayman, Francis, 1708-1776: A0917, H0008
Hays, Peggy: A1587
Hayward, Rev. [ ], d. 1757: I1212
Head, Halfe: W0041
Hearne, Thomas, 1678-1735: S0647
Heathcote, Sir Gilbert, 1651-1733: F0525, W1198
Heathfield, George Augustus Elliot, 1st baron, 1717-1790: G0394
Hedges, [ ]: S0362, U0104
Hedges, John: S0917
Heidegger, John James, 1659?-1749: F0104
Heigham, Dame Jane, d. 1623?: W0176
Heigham, Henry, actor (1784-85): W2423
Heigham, Rev. Henry: W0901
Heigham, Sir Richard: W0176
Heins, John Theodore, sr., 1697-1756: W0340
Hele, Anne, d. 1654: W0082
Héloïse, c. 1101-1164: I1159, I1276
Henley, John, 1692-1759: I0279, S0136
Henri III, king of France, 1551-1589: W1621
Henri IV, king of France, 1553-1610: F0476, T0159, T0284
Henrietta Maria, queen consort of Charles I, king of England, 1609-1669: F0011, F0682, I0090, L0595, L0623, M0033, M0567, S0821, T0242, T1153, T1252, W1149
Henry Frederick, prince of Wales, 1594-1612: D0310, H0732, H1477, I0175, I1198, M0410, R0069, T2506
Henry I, king of England, 1068-1135: I0445
Henry II, king of England, 1133-1189: R0030
Henry III, king of England, 1207-1272: F0736, O0682, T0684
Henry V, king of England, 1387-1422: T2851
Henry VIII, king of England, 1491-1547: I0560, O0968, S0164, S1091, T0241, T0776, T2362, W1010, W1011, W1376
Henry, Philip: T1919
Hensham, John: H0833

Herbert, [ ]: B0242, Y0164

Herbert, [ ], actor (1761): P0094, S0831, T2424

Herbert, Miss [ ]: F0322, N0449, T1280, Y0510

Herbert, Mrs. [ ] (Sackville): Y0164

Herbert, Mrs. [ ], actress (1761): F0034, P0094, S0831

Herbert, Lady Charlotte: B0283

Herbert, George, 1593–1633: T1332

Herbert of Cherbury, Edward Herbert, 1st baron,
    1583–1648: M0080, T0241

Heriot, [ ]: T0196

Heron, Dorothy: B0103

Herring, Rev. [ ], of Emington: T2050

Herring, Mrs. [ ], wife of Thomas, archbishop of
    Canterbury: M0027

Herring, Thomas, abp. of Canterbury, 1693–1757:
    B0504, M0027, W1721

Hertford, Arabella (Stuart) Seymour, countess,
    1575–1615: F0690, H0821, H1224, T3192

Hertford, [ ], lady: Q0007

Hervey, Miss [ ]: L0408

Hervey, James, 1714–1758: A1593

Hervey, Mary (Lepell) Hervey, baroness, 1700–1768:
    A1955, F0033, I0096, L0054, S1009, T0983

Hervey of Ickworth, John Hervey, baron, 1696–1743:
    A1955, F0221, L0408, P0138, W0925, W0933

Hesilrige, Arthur Hesilrige, 2nd baron, 1601–1661:
    A1004

Hesketh, Harriet (Cowper), lady, 1733–1807: I0320,
    T0356

Hesketh, Thomas: R0070

Heveningham, Lady Mary: G0112

Hewett, Richard: H0816

Hewit, John, 1614–1658: S0564

Hewit, John, d. 1719: T1760

Hewit, Robin: I0263

Heydon, Belle: K0050

Heydon, Sir John, d. 1653: K0050

Heywood, Mrs. [ ]: S0905

Hibden, [ ] (1745): T0575

Hickford, James, jr. (1759–68): S0274, U0126

Hickford, James, sr., dancing master (1742–1759):
    A1268, A1383, F0305, H1247, H1422, I1089, N0202, O0673,
    S1036, T1227, T2812, T2898, W0026, W1202, Y0131

Hicks, Dr. [ ] (1715): H1373

Highman, Joseph, d. 1780: A1347

Highmore, Joseph, 1692–1780: T2979

Hill, Dr. [ ], jr.: F0421

Hill, Mrs. [ ]: W0327

Hill, Mrs. [ ], sr.: W2131

Hill, John, 1716?–1775: H0208, I0634, I0770

Hill, Richard: J0136

Hill, Robert, 1699–1777: M0582

Hill, Mrs. Robert (1759): M0582

Hill, Sir Rowland, 1492?–1561: A0136

Hillary, Ann, d. 1653: T2678

Hilles, John: J0106

Hilliard, Sir Robert: W2052

Hillsborough, Mary (Stalwell) Hill, countess,
    1726–1780: T3191

Hilton, Rev. [ ], of St. Nicholas, Gloucestershire: O0644

Hivers, Henry: I0356

Hoadley, Benjamin, bp. of Winchester, 1676–1761:
    A1084, A1102, B0251, I0506, N0436

Hoare, William, d. 1779: T1014

Hobart, Barbara: R0072

Hobart, Lady Frances: P0226

Hobart, John, d. 1683: A1239, G0203, N0033, T2750, T2773

Hobbes, Thomas, 1588–1679: L0508, P0304, S1205, T2276

Hobbs, Richard, d. 1561: H0818

Hobby, Elizabeth, lady: W2326

Hobert, [ ]: S1257, W1017

Hobson, [ ]: H0651

Hobson, Thomas, d. 1631: C0135, H0650, H1116, H1117

Hockley, Mrs. [ ] (1791): W2405

Hodges, William, R. A., 1744–1787: T2141

Hodgson, [ ], m. 1764: H0065

Hodgson, Dr. [ ]: A1216, I1177

Hodgson, Mrs. [ ] (Ranger), m. 1764: H0065

Hodman, Thomas: L0415

Hog, Joan: I0313

Hogarth, William, 1697–1764: B0620, F0160, G0060,
    H0008, H1200, I0781, T0708, T1771, T3266, W0305

Hogg, Robin: A0190

Hogg, Roger: H0900

Holberg, Ludvig, baron, 1684–1754: S0783

Holdernesse, Robert Darcy, 4th earl, 1718–1778: W1041

Holiday, [ ]: T1999

Holiday, Barten, 1593–1661: A1780, B0476, C0191, M0326,
    N0307, W0534, W2094

Holland, Abigail: O0235

Holland, Charles, 1733–1769: D0073, N0353, W0897

Holland, Elizabeth (Vassall) Fox, lady, 1770–1845:
    I1310

Holland, Henry Fox, 1st baron, 1705–1744: C0235,
    A0351, A1958, I0573, O0840, T2473

Holland, Henry Rich, 1st earl, 1590–1649: B0675, Y0585

Holland, Henry Vassall Fox, 3rd baron, 1773–1840:
    A1276, W1401

Holland, Jo.: A0232

Holland, Sir John: A0236

Holland, Philemon, 1552–1637: W2450

Holles, Denzil Holles, 1st baron, 1599–1680: A1004

Holt, Mrs. [ ]: M0293

Holt, Christopher: O1104

Holworthy, Susanna (1721): Y0437

Home, [ ], countess: M0612

Home, [ ], painter (1768): F0110

Home, John, 1722–1808: A1779, F0490

Hood, Isabel: H0278

Hooker, Thomas: T3152

Hooper, Edward: T2532

Hooper, Sarah (Ashton): O0207

Hope, Mrs. [ ] (1746): W1798

Hopkins, [ ]: A1445

Hopkins, [ ], prompter (1765): N0055

Hopkins, Miss [ ], b. 1759: N0055

Hopkins, Mrs. [ ], actress (1765): N0055

Hopkins, Alice: A0328

Horn, Madam [ ]: W1491

Horn, Charles Edward, 1786–1849: F0027

Hornblow, Rev. [ ], ordained 1779: T0328

Horne, Rev. [ ]: V0092

Horne, Sally: T2029

Horseman, Alice, d. 1742: Y0094

Horseman, Peggy: C0540, F0767

Horsley, Samuel, bp. of Rochester, 1733-1806: D0393

Horsman, Andrew, c. 1592-c. 1661: A0767, A0822, F0437, I0615, I1434, S0390, T0145

Hort, Josiah, bp. of Kilmore, 1674?-1751: L0591

Horton, [ ]: W2189

Hosier, Sir Francis, vice-admiral, 1673-1727: A1549, A1550

Hoskins, Ann: A1203

Hoskins, Benjamin: S1287

Hoskins, John, 1566-1638: T0422, T1505, Y0522

Hotham, Miss [ ]: H1162

Hotham, Sir John, 1589-1645: W2031

Hotham, John, 1610-1645: W2031

Hough, [ ]: T1245

Houghton, Lydia: S0409

Hovill, Mrs. [ ] (Lilly): I0003

Hovill, Sir William: I0003

How, [ ]: C0022

How, Miss [ ]: O1026

Howard, [ ]: W0835

Howard, [ ], lord marshall: L0231

Howard, Miss [ ]: S0752, T2504

Howard, Mrs. [ ]: W1221

Howard, Lady Anne: W0820

Howard, Britannia, d. 1732: F0290

Howard, Dorothy, wife of Francis, governor of Carlisle: N0306

Howard, Edward, playwright (1669): A1696, C0412, T2019

Howard, Eliza: F0469

Howard, Elizabeth: N0362

Howard, Elizabeth (Vere), 1712-1746: E0184

Howard, Frances: See Somerset, Frances (Howard) Carr, countess

Howard, Francis, governor of Carlisle: N0246

Howard, John, 1726?-1790: F0699, I1415

Howard, Thomas. L0231

Howe, Miss [ ] (1745): A0149, A0575, H0592, T3369

Howe, Miss [ ], of Somerset House: S0388

Howe, John Grubham, 1657-1722: F0693

Howe, Mary (1722-23): I0854, W0944

Howe, Richard Howe, 1st earl, 1726-1799: T1693

Howe, Sophia (1726): S0578

Howes, Lucy: L0361

Howkins, Richard: H0819

Howlit, [ ]: H1478

Hoyle, [ ]: Y0330

Hubberton, John: H0768

Hubert, Sir Harry: R0187, T3093

Huddesford, [ ]: L0066, W2538

Huddesford, Misses [ ], [ ], [ ]: B0304

Huddesford, Eliza, d. 1768: H0522, N0466

Huddesford, John (1754): F0380

Huett, [ ]: A1801

Hugford. See Hickford

Hughes, John, 1677-1720: A1297, A1954, R0227

Hull, Mrs. [ ]: W1174

Hulse, Sir Edward, 1st bart., 1682-1759: W1026

Humberstone, Matthew, 1705-1736: F0179

Humble, Richard: L0390

Hume, Sir Abraham, 1749-1838: F0570

Hume, David, 1711-1776: H0161, O0139, T3281

Humfreys, Miss [ ]: M0014

Humfreys, Sir William, lord mayor of London (1714): T2723

Humphrey, duke of Gloucester, 1390-1447: T1169, W0665, W1276

Humphreys, John: W1967

Humphreys, Phyllis: W1967

Humphreys, Rev. [ ] (1737): O0527

Hungate, [ ]: L0157

Hunsdon, John Hunsdon, lord: T2355

Hunt, Arabella, d. 1705: W0296

Hunt, John, d. 1778: T0552

Hunt, Martha: M0186

Hunter, William, of Hexham: Y0185

Huntingdon, Henry Hastings, 5th earl, 1586-1643: P0295

Huntingdon, Selina (Shirley) Hastings, countess, 1707-1791: T0281, T2826

Huntington, [ ], apothecary: A1904

Huntly, Mary (Grant) Gordon, marchioness: W2035

Hurd, [ ]: W0256

Hus, John: W1406

Husbands, S.: T0329

Hussey, [ ]: See Beaulieu, Edward Hussey (later Montagu), earl

Hussey, Harriet, b. 1759: B0621, L0682

Hutchinson, Miss [ ]: T0115

Huter, Robert, d. 1662: U0025

Hyde, Hon. Edward, 1645-1665: H0793

Hyde, Francis, proctor of Christ Church Oxford (1627): W1602

Hyde, Lady Katherine: A1433, C0038

Hyett, Ben: W2136

I——d, [ ]: I0427

I——e, [ ]: I0122

Ibbot, Benjamin, 1680-1725: W0330

Ibbott, Sarah, fl. 1750-1825: L0009

Ignatius of Loyola, 1491-1556: J0098

Illson, [ ]: M0450

Ince, Richard: O0815

Inge, Miss [ ] (1785): A0601

Ingham, Caleb: W2337

Ingham, Margaret: W2337

Ingram, Hastings: K0064

Innocent X, pope, 1574-1655: P0227

Innocent XI, pope, 1611-1689: L0109, A0323, A0864, C0450, D0387, F0765, W0254

Ireton, Henry, 1611-1651: W1628

Irwin, Isabella (Machell) Ingram, lady, 1670-1764: M0719, W2293

Iseham or Isham, Sir Justinian, 2nd bart., 1610-1674: I1485

Islay: See Argyll, Archibald Campbell, 3rd duke, and 1st earl of Islay

J., [ ]: I0817

J., Mrs. [ ]: M0013

J——n, Mrs. [ ]: 11448
J——ys, Peg: S0947
Jackson, [ ], artist: H1456
Jackson, [ ], d. 1766: H1083
Jackson, [ ], musician: F0499
Jackson, Mrs. [ ]: T1638
Jackson, William: 10845
Jacob, Jenny: D0106
Jacobs, [ ], lady: O0515
James I, king of England, 1566-1621: G0385, H0731,
    A0386, A0950, A0955, A1326, A1378, C0024, C0191, D0219,
    D0310, D0325, F0080, F0451, F0713, H0334, H0426,
    H0694, H0956, I1538, N0037, N0421, O0413, O0631,
    O0756, O0857, O1121, O1136, S0028, S0269, T0767, T1034,
    T1505, T2397, T2868, W0094, W0356, W1364, Y0403,
    Y0433
James I, king of Scotland, 1394-1437: J0010
James II, king of England, 1633-1701: A0640, A1197,
    A1334, A1388, A1409, A1478, A1479, A1480, A1553, A1770,
    B0329, B0466, B0479, C0279, C0372, C0411, C0452, C0593,
    D0286, D0398, E0130, F0282, F0435, F0631, G0345,
    G0444, H0084, H0956, H1104, H1251, I0239, I0494,
    I0630, I0788, I1392, K0016, L0141, L0175, L0312, M0313,
    M0522, N0480, O0012, O0183, O0202, O0859, O0965,
    R0001, S0603, S0961, S1034, S1269, T0358, T0516, T0688,
    T0695, T1040, T1886, T1971, T2151, T2956, T3388,
    U0127, W0018, W0084, W0289, W0383, W0604, W1097,
    W1102, W1181, W1213, W1332, W1535, W1593, W1782,
    W1886, W1889, W2585, W2607, Y0464, Y0572
James II, king of Scotland, 1430-1460: J0011
James III, king of Scotland, 1452?-1488: J0012
James IV, king of Scotland, 1473-1513: J0012
James IV, king of Scotland, 1473-1513: K0041
James V, king of Scotland, 1512-1542: A1213, K0040
James, Prince of Wales, the Old Pretender, 1688-1766:
    A0461, A0902, A1251, A1279, A1310, A1480, A1842, A1911,
    B0450, B0482, B0524, B0526, C0278, C0311, D0150, E0157,
    G0052, H0018, H0251, H0324, H0365, H0990, H0992,
    H0994, I0397, L0049, L0121, L0299, M0196, O0577,
    O0867, O0876, P0353, S0268, S0391, T0937, T1188, T1804,
    T2723, T3152, T3230, T3259, T3388, W0091, W0307,
    W0363, W0631, W0739, W0746, W0808, W1102, W1103,
    W1265, W1267, W1277, W2247, W2503, Y0297
James, Sir William, 1721-1783: R0009
Jane Seymour, queen consort of Henry VIII, king of
    England, 1505-1537: T2362
Jane, [ ]: L0268
Jansson, [ ], alderman (1752): M0038
Jansson, [ ], candidate for Parliament (1747): O0444
Jansson, [ ], chamberlain (1765): Y0100
Jansson, [ ], liveryman: Y0101
Jansson, [ ], sheriff (1749): M0430
Jansson, Mrs. [ ] (1752): M0038
Jansson, Nancy (1752): T2814
Jansson, Stephen Theodore (1746): W1689
Jansson, William (1754): S0012
Jaques, Christopher, d. 1699: O0021
Jarrot, [ ], d. 1626: S0904
Jebb, Dr. [ ]: U0124
Jeffray, [ ]: T1349
Jeffreys, Betty (1736): D0052, M0396, T0975

Jeffreys, Frances (1736): F0010, O0730
Jeffreys, George Jeffreys, 1st baron, judge, 1648-1689:
    A0481, T2726, W1105
Jeffreys, George, 1678-1755: J0142
Jekyll, Elizabeth, d. 1652: D0212
Jellicoe, Miss [ ] (1776): F0328
Jener, John: M0406
Jenkins, John: T1793
Jenyns, Soame, 1704-1787: O0445
Jepson, Sarah: L0380
Jernegan, Sir Henry, d. 1571: J0048
Jersey, William Villiers, 2nd earl, d. 1721: O0897
Jervis, [ ]: W0642
Jervoise, [ ]: W0231
Jesser, Myrtilla (1777): H0159
Jesson, [ ]: A0906
Joan of Arc, 1412-1431: B0579, H0760, I1600
Jobson, Colin: C0254
Jobson, Sir John (1745): W0045, W2261
Jobson, Mopsa: C0254
Joburne, William: W2327
Jocelyn, Robert (1747): 10836
Johannot, [ ]: L0608
John, Gabriel, d. 1001: U0017, U0038
John, king of England, 1199-1216: A0122, J0099
Johnes, Miss [ ]: A1598
Johnson, [ ]: S0696
Johnson, Mrs. [ ] (A.): O0651
Johnson, Lady Cecilia: T0750
Johnson, Esther, 1683-1728: O0617
Johnson, Henry: M0213
Johnson, John: A1014, O0010
Johnson, Julian (1709): B0251
Johnson, M.: T1294
Johnson, Martin: C0282, I0575
Johnson, Maurice, 1688-1774: I0199, I0656, T2820
Johnson, Maurice, sr.: B0171, O0010
Johnson, Samuel, 1709-1784: A0629, C0295, H0811,
    I0949, T0706, T3281
Johnson, Shadrach, d. 1741: S0357
Johnston, [ ]: I1042
Johnston, Arthur: 10804
Johnston, George, lord: N0048, T3132
Johnston, Sir James: P0273
Johnston, James, 1655-1737: M0211
Jones, [ ] (1745): C0039
Jones, Henry, 1721-1770: S1250, W0245
Jones, Joanna: T0366
Jones, John: H0769
Jones, Joshua: T3002
Jones, Mary: N0521, T2964
Jones, Michael: A1230
Jones, Sir William, 1746-1794: S0729, U0005
Jonson, [ ], son of Ben Jonson: R0147
Jonson, Ben, 1573?-1637: B0042, G0252, G0395, H0013,
    H0727, I0587, I0958, I1478, I1493, S1287, T0943, T1290,
    T1504, T2719, T2745, T2959, W1285, D0314, H0772,
    T0075, W1291
Jope, John: O0652
Jope, Samuel, d. 1660: O0652
Jordan, Dorothea, 1762-1816: H0103, S1357

Jordan, Thomas, 1612?-1685?: O1090
Joseph II, emperor of Germany, 1741-1790: Y0247
Jowett, [ ]: T1873
Juggins, Thomas, d. 1719: J0130
Julian, [ ] (1775): I0841
Julian, Robert, fl. 1677-1684: D0091, D0111, F0725,
    G0103, J0132, J0133, S0328, T0110, T2017
Julius II, pope, 1433-1513: H1094
Juxon, William, bishop of London and High
    Treasurer of England, 1582-1663: I0175, N0134

K., Miss E. (1791): S1011
K., Mrs. E.: G0125
K——lly, W.: G0466, W2071
Karl Theodor of Sulzbach, elector Palatine,
    1724-1799: T2708
Kauffman, Angelica, 1741-1807: H1034
Kaye, Sir John, bart., ktd. 1662: A1218, S0842
Keate, George (1781): N0209, O0372
Keepe, [ ]: T1198
Keith, William, 7th earl marischal of Scotland,
    c. 1627-1661: Y0511
Kelly, [ ]: H0727
Kelynge, [ ]: K0015
Kemble, [ ]: W0779
Kempe, Lady Mary: A1133
Ken, Thomas, bp. of Bath and Wells, 1637-1711: C0441,
    G0330, H0173, L0131, P0046, T0695, T3232, W1565
Kendal, Charles Stuart, duke, 1666-1667: K0016
Kendal, Ehrengarde Melusina (von Schulenberg),
    duchess, 1667-1743: A0315, A0466, M0393
Kennedy, [ ]: A1337
Kennedy, Margaret (Farrell), d. 1793: A0549
Kennicott, Benjamin: M0398
Kensington, [ ], earl (1637): I0154
Kent, Frances, d. 1677: H0984
Kent, William, 1684-1748: M0175
Keppel, Augustus Keppel, viscount, 1725-1786: A1024
Kerr, [ ], of Chatto, b. 1649. H1467, S0655
Kerr, John, of Frogden: A0064
Kerr, Mrs. Christian, b. 1679: A0064, N0371, S0652,
    W0057
Ketch, Jack, fl. 1678-1686: G0337, S0128, Y0485
Kettlewell, John, 1653-1695: S1229
Key, Margareta: A0621
Keyes, [ ], lord: A0226
Kildare, Emilia (Lennox), countess, d. 1832: T1342
Kildare, Robert Fitzgerald, earl, 1675-1744: W1984
Killigrew, Thomas, 1612-1683: D0180, T3148, W0784
Kilmarnock, William [ ], earl, d. 1746: A1866
Kinderton, Frances (Cholmondeley) Venables, lady:
    M0384
Kinderton, Peter Venables, baron, 1605-1679: M0384
King, Anne (Berkeley), d. 1624: A0621
King, Anne, daughter of John King, bishop of
    London: M0272
King, Edward, d. 1637: I0234
King, John, bishop of London, 1559-1621: I0858, S0009
King, Thomas, 1730-1805: A0122, A0892, A1168, A1627,
    B0442, C0163, F0190, I0822, N0107, T1189, T2274
Kingham, [ ] (1704): G0317

Kingsman, Miss [ ], d. 1800: N0301
Kingsman, Miss L., 1775-1791: T2779
Kingston, [ ], lady: C0178
Kingston, Elizabeth Chudleigh, duchess, 1720-1788:
    C0210
Kingston, Evelyn Pierrepont, 2nd duke, 1711-1773:
    A1365
Kinnier, Paul, surgeon: D0078
Kirk, Mary: M0178
Kirkby, Mrs. [ ] (1757): D0124
Kirkman, [ ], cornet (1779): W2389
Kirwan, [ ] (1787): W0054
Kirwan, Elizabeth (1787): W0054
Kitchen, [ ]: H0802, K0053
Knapp, [ ]: B0070
Knapp, Belinda: B0070
Kneller, Sir Godfrey, 1646-1723: A0854, F0315, I1100,
    K0056, K0057, K0058, O0455, T1029, W0420, W0480
Knight, Mrs. [ ], of Salisbury (1745-1760): A1762,
    W0607
Knight, Daniel, 1695-1756: H0898
Knight, John: O0290
Knight, Mall, mistress of Charles II: I0700, Q0030
Knight, Sir William: G0375
Knowles, Thomas: H0886
Knox, John, 1505-1572: Y0311
Knyvet, Sir John: T2518, V0079
Knyvet, Thomas, colonel: T2518
Knyveton, [ ] [ ]: T1500
Knyveton, Sir Andrew: T1500, W2563
Knyveton, Gilbert: P0270
Knyveton, Thomas: P0270
Königsmarck, Philipp Christoph von, count,
    1665-1694: G0384, W0742
Kosciuszko, Tadeusz, 1752-1817: H0303
Kotzebue, Augustus von, 1761-1817: W1738

L, [ ], abbé: W0629
L, [ ], Dr.: S0647
L., G. S. (1724): O0224
L——, [ ]: F0163
L——, [ ] (1734): W1503
L——, Miss [ ]: W2267
L——, Miss [ ] (1782): T0287
L——de, I——s: H0250
L——dl——w, [ ]: S0256, S0259
L——ge, [ ]: O0112
L——l, [ ]: I0122
L——n, Dr. [ ]: W2277
L——n, [ ], laureate: N0017
La Boneille, Rev. [ ]: P0023
La Bruyere, Jean de, 1645-1696: T1985
La Fontaine, Jean de, 1621-1695: T2072, T2170
La Lande, René du Bellay, baron de, d. 1606: T2116
La Rochefoucauld, François, duc de, 1613-1680: A1596,
    W2351
La Sabliere, Margeurite de, c. 1640-1693: I1431
Lacke, [ ]: H0968
Lackington, Mrs. [ ]: L0017
Lacy, [ ], of Mr. Newcome's School (1741): W1734
Lacy, Willoughby: M0044

Ladbroke, Sir Robert, 1713?–1773: W1608

Lafayette, Marie Joseph Gilbert, marquis de, 1757–1834: W1985

Lake, John, bp. of Chichester, 1624–1689: C0441, G0330, H0173, L0131, P0046, P0067, T3232, W1565

Lake, Mary (Ryder), lady, d. 1643: H0844

Lake, Sir Thomas, 1567?–1630: H0844

Lamb, [ ]: B0079, N0399

Lamb, Dr. [ ]: H0634, I0592, L0029

Lamb, Penelope: P0081

Lambe, [ ]: A1477

Lambert, Dr. [ ], of St. John's College Cambridge: I1292

Lambert, Mme. [ ]: E0095

Lambert, Sir Daniel, alderman of London, knighted 1744: W1608

Lambertini, [ ], principessa (1785): S0432

Lampasse, [ ], lord: H0948

Lancaster, [ ], duke: C0374

Lancaster, Francis: T2843

Lancaster, William, vicechancellor of Queen's College Oxford, d. 1717: W0067

Landen, Thomas: C0142

Lane, George: G0342

Lang, Willy: I1015

Langham, Elizabeth, d. 1639: I0810

Langham, Mary (Ashton), d. 1660: A1008

Langhorne, John, 1735–1779: L0033

Lansdowne, Charles Granville, viscount, 1661–1701: Y0111

Lansdowne, George Granville, 1st baron, 1667–1735: O0367, W2184, Y0335

Lansdowne, Henry Petty-Fitzmaurice, 3rd marquess, 1780–1863: L0564

Last, Dr. [ ]: Y0078, Y0553

Laud, William, abp. of Canterbury, 1573–1645: F0424, I0276, I0932, M0597, O1076, P0193

Lauderdale, Elizabeth (Murray), duchess, d. 1698: F0152

Lauderdale, John Maitland, 1st duke, 1616–1682: A1682, D0429, F0152, M0313, W0518, W1570

Laughton, [ ]: P0204

Laureston, [ ]: W0687

Lavington, Frances (Kolbel) Payne, baroness, d. 1830: A1352, F0463, M0295, M0458, O0531, R0032, S0367, T2955, W0898, W2480

Lavington, Ralph Payne, 1st baron, 1737?–1807: I0737, T2955, T3133, W0898

Law, Thomas: A0714

Lawford, Exelbee: T2040, W1706

Lawrence, [ ], general: B0451

Lawrence, Miss [ ]: A1761

Lawrence, William, d. 1621: W2385

Laws, [ ], singer (1759): H0287, T2717

Laycock, [ ]: I0652

Layton, Susannah: N0277

Le Brosse, [ ] (1762): A0522

Le Compte, [ ]: D0125

Le Couchon, [ ] (1763): W0779

Le Ferier, [ ]: W0322

Le Heup, Isaac, 1685?–1747: T1772, W1259

Le Hunt, [ ]: W1857

Lea, Caroline: A0239

Leadbeater, Jane: W0155

Leadbeater, Mary (Shackleton), 1758–1826: D0059, I0264

Leadbeater, William (1798): H0153

Leah, James (1750): H0617

Leake, Nicholas, of St. John's College, Cambridge (1727): T3172

Leatherland, [ ], colonel: W1755

Leaver, Dorothy: F0495

Lee Boo, prince: C0392

Lee, [ ]: I0994, S0211, T1349

Lee, Elizabeth (Dyke): H1495

Lee, Sir George, 1700–1758: A0595

Lee, Katherine: S1129

Lee, Nathaniel, 1653–1692: T3170

Lee, Sir Thomas, d. 1749: W1615

Lee, William, d. 1778: H1495, W1226

Leeds, Bridget (Bertie) Osborne, duchess, and marchioness of Carmarthen, 1629–1704: W0371, W1158

Leeds, Mary (Godolphin) Osborne, duchess, 1723–1764: I0193, W1425

Leeds, Peregrine Hyde Osborne, 3rd duke, 1691–1731: T0499

Leeds, Thomas Osborne, 1st duke, 1631–1712: A0482, B0310, C0061, F0726, I0885, I1362, S0140, T1965, W0640, W1720, Z0011

Leg, [ ]: P0080, P0351

Leger, Louis: T2991

Legg, [ ]: S1264

Leicester, Philip Sydney, earl, 1619–1698: L0079

Leicester, Robert Dudley, earl, 1533–1588: G0385, H0869, I0395

Leicester, Thomas Coke, earl, 1697–1759: O0408

Leigh, Andrew: H0618

Leigh, Rev. Archer (1793): L0341

Leigh, Sir Harry: H0637, H0851

Leigh, Henrietta, 1778–1793: L0341

Leigh, Peter: H0618

Leigh, Sir Thomas, of Stonelly, d. 1626: Y0398

Leighton, Harcourt: V0065

Leighton, Ursula (Harvey), lady: M0043, U0022, V0065, V0076, W0676

Lenthall, William, 1591–1662: G0318, W2045

Lenton, Francis, fl. 1630–1640: S0700

Leo X, pope, 1475–1521: T0776, W0558

L'Epine, (Francesca) Margherita, 1680?–1746: H0167

Leslie, Sir Alexander, c. 1582–1661: S0173, S0174

Leslie, Charles, d. 1722: O0903

Leslie, Thomas: A1035, T3053

L'Estrange, Hamon, 1605–1660: B0080

L'Estrange, Sir Roger, 1616–1704: A1880, F0626, L0109, S1046

Lettice, [ ] (1793): W2412

Lettice, Miss [ ]: O0262

Lettice, John: A0997, J0096

Leveridge, Richard, 1670–1758: B0481, M0430, T0916, T2782

Leveson-Gower, Granville, lord, 1773–1846: O0190

Levet, Robert: C0462

Lewick, [ ], earl: Y0271
Lewis, [ ]: S0518, T0454, T3293, V0045
Lewis, Mrs. [ ]: O0304, W0796
Lewis, Anne: H1161, N0010, S0422
Lewis, John: G0227
Lewis, Matthew Gregory, 1775-1818: M0177, W2478
Lewis, Sir Watkin: V0092
Lewood, Thomas (1739): F0645
Leycester, Edward: A0570
Licet, Mrs. [ ], of Mallow, Ireland: A1690
Lightwood, Thomas: S0719
Lilburne, John, 1614-1657: I1450, U0112
Lilly, William, 1602-1681: F0776
Limbrey, Richard: T1274
Lincoln, Catherine (Pelham), countess, d. 1760: E0138
Lindsey, Ms. [ ]: C0044
Lindsay, Lady A.: W0796
Lindsey, Robert Bertie, 1st earl, and 12th lord
    Willoughby of Eresby: S1218
Lindsey, Robert Bertie, 3rd earl: T1971
Ling, [ ]: T1833
Lingo, Sir Edmund: S0691
Linley, Mary: L0411
Linley, Thomas, 1756-1778: S1313
Linley, Thomas, sr.: F0117
Linois, Charles Durand, compte de, admiral,
    1761-1848: I1271
Lintot, Bernard, 1675-1736: S0906
Lisle, Thomas, of Magdalen College, Oxford: W1216
Little, Mrs. [ ]: O0258
Littlejohn, W. Alexander: W0592
Littleton, Anne: H0822, H0946
Littleton, Sir Edward, sr.: H0679
Littleton, Sir Edward, jr.: H0679
Littleton, Sir Edward III: H0679
Littleton, Edward: H0822
Littleton, Sir Thomas, d. 1481: H0822, O0708, O0726
Llewellyn, Francis: T1241
Lloyd, [ ]: D0114
Lloyd, Nath.: W0446
Lloyd, William, bp. of Norwich, 1637-1710: C0441,
    G0330, H0173, L0131, P0046, T3232, W1565, I0653
Lochermaker, [ ], lady: F0258
Locke, John, 1632-1704: S1158
Lockman, Miss [ ], daughter of John Lockman
    (1744-52): N0495, T2814
Lockman, Misses [ ], [ ], daughters of John Lockman
    (1765): I0680
Lockman, Mrs. [ ], mother of John Lockman, d. 1742:
    B0499
Lockman, Mrs. [ ], wife of John Lockman (1744):
    N0495
Lockman, Elizabeth, daughter of John Lockman,
    d. 1742: L0432
Lockman, John, 1698-1771: A1351, K0015, O0802
Lockman, Jonathan, son of John Lockman, d. 1736:
    F0500
Lockman, Molly, daughter of John Lockman, d. 1731:
    S0275
Loggan, Thomas, fan-painter (1748): H0006, P0007
Loggerhead, [ ]: H0612

Loggin, Miss [ ]: T2331
Loneretti, [ ] (1754): I0534
Long, [ ]: W0274
Long, Miss [ ]: L0525
Long, Helen (Gournay): A0187, B0085
Long, Robert: T0685, T2885
Long, William (1777): T2176
Longe, Mrs. [ ] (1750): W1009
Longland, Constantia: U0113
Longville, Henry: M0167
Lonsdale, James Lowther, 1st earl, 1736-1802: F0257
Lonsdale, John Lowther, 1st viscount, 1655-1700:
    A0482, W1720
Lonsdale, Katherine (Thynne) Lowther, countess,
    d. 1713 or earlier: W0371, W1158
Lorraine, Charles Leopold, duc de, 1643-1690: R0218
Lorraine, Stanislas Leszczynski, duc de, 1677-1766:
    B0480, F0051
Lottisham, Jane: F0268
Loughborough, Alexander Wedderburn, 1st earl,
    1733-1805: W0737, W1133
Louis XIII, king of France, 1601-1643: E0106, Y0570
Louis XIV, king of France, 1638-1715: I0099, I1256,
    A1197, A1721, C0553, F0379, F0544, F0673, H0166, H0611,
    I0145, I0397, I1591, L0495, N0206, N0276, S1059, T0173,
    T0428, T0635, T0891, T1886, W1102, W1134, W1856,
    Y0023
Louis XV, king of France, 1710-1774: H0302
Louis XVI, king of France, 1754-1793: G0014
Louis, dauphin of France, 1785-1795?: A1070
Louisa Maria Theresa, daughter of James II, king of
    England, 1692-1712: W1077, G0128, V0032
Louisa, daughter of George I, queen of Denmark,
    1724-1751: Y0130
Louisbourg, [ ]: B0495
Lovat, Simon Fraser, 12th baron, 1667?-1747: Y0359
Love, Christopher, 1618-1651: N0416
Love, Samuel, 1744-1773: F0140, W1465
Loveday, [ ]: L0066
Lovegrove, Robert: O0144, P0306
Lovekyn, John, c. 1368: W2572
Lovel, [ ], lord: I0129, W1907
Lovel, Peter (1747): T0158
Lovelace of Hurley, John Lovelace, 3rd baron,
    1638?-1693: A0223, A1375
Lovelace of Hurley, Nevill Lovelace, baron,
    1708-1736: I1033
Lovelace, [ ]: T1014
Lovelace, Richard, 1618-1658: I0884, L0677
Lovell, Edith, d. 1781: O0699
Lovell, Edward, b. 1707: L0678, S0801, W1841
Lovell, Thomas, c. 1731-1762: T3237
Lovet, Thomasin: S0953
Low, [ ]: S0241
Lowe, [ ], singer (1751): W1516
Lowell, Sir Thomas, d. 1524: A0987
Lower, Richard, 1631-1691: F0726
Lowin, [ ]: W1141
Lowman, [ ] (1741): I0633
Lowth, Robert, bp. of London, 1710-1787: D0188,
    T2719

Lowther, Miss [ ]: S0088
Lowther, Anthony (1726): S0578
Lucar, Elizabeth, d. 1537: E0154, S0443
Lucar, Emanual: E0154, S0443
Lucas, John, lord, d. 1649: F0720
Lumber, Hugh: I1023
Lumley, [ ]: Y0334
Lundsford, Jo.: W2559
Lundy, Mrs. [ ]: H0778
Lunn, Sally: N0208
Luther, Anne, d. 1680: H0680
Luther, Martin, 1483–1546: W0880
Luttrell, Narcissus, 1657–1732: W1388
Luxembourg, François Henri de Montmorency, duc
    de, 1628–1694: A0334
Lyddal, Henry: L0714
Lynch, Dr. [ ]: I1353, S0816
Lynch, Miss [ ]: S1302
Lynch, John, dean of Canterbury Cathedral: I0787
Lyon, Miss [ ]: U0148
Lyon, Mrs. [ ]: N0399
Lyon, Jean: I1557, Y0356
Lyttelton, Elizabeth (Rich), baroness, d. 1795: O0377
Lyttelton, George Lyttelton, 1st baron, 1709–1773:
    B0277, F0098, F0623, F0655, H0161, H0482, L0086,
    N0065, O0377, O0778, O0834, T0978
Lyttelton, Lucy (Fortescue), baroness, 1718–1747:
    A1817, B0452, F0655, M0046, O0377
Lyttelton, Thomas Lyttelton, 2nd baron, 1744–1779:
    T0978

M., [ ]: H0913
M., Miss [ ]: H0579, W2417
M., Mrs. [ ]: B0456
M., G.: S0630
M., J.: L0519, W0560, Y0571
M., Miss M.: Y0425
M———, [ ]: I1333
M———, [ ], lady (1785): T0580
M———, Mrs. [ ]: H0505, N0415, S0596
M———, Sir Charles: W1506
M[ ]t, E.: W2487
M——be, Mrs. [ ] (1782): L0511
M——er, [ ], lieut. gov.: W0887
M——r, P——r: T1710
M——r——n, [ ]: N0078
M——ton, Sir William: Y0447
M——y, [ ]: H1000
Macartney, George Macartney, 1st earl, 1737–1806:
    I1225, W0743
Macaulay, Catharine (Sawbridge), 1731–1791: A1193,
    I0454
Maccan, [ ], captain: Y0369
Macclesfield, Anne (Mason) Gerard, countess,
    1666?–1753: H1146
Macclesfield, Thomas Parker, 1st earl, 1666?–1732:
    L0274, S0656, W1483
Macdonald, Simon, ensign (1779): L0124
Macdougal, [ ]: D0121
Mackenzie, Dr. [ ]: O0746, T2938
Mackenzie, Sir George, advocate, 1636–1691: W2396

Mackerel, James: Q0036
Mackett, Miss [ ]: I1346
Mackland, Sir Charles: H0381
Macklin, Charles, 1699?–1797: F0705, P0203
Mackworth, Sir Humphrey, 1657–1727: Y0050
Maddox, [ ], actor (1705): F0728
Maddox, Isaac Price, c. 1740–1757: S0231
Maddox, Isaac, bp. of Worcester, 1697–1759: S0231
Maidston, Elizabeth: A0986
Maintenon, Mme. Françoise (d'Aubigne), 1635–1719:
    I0099, O0816, T0428
Mallet, Mrs. [ ]: H0340
Mallet, David, 1705?–1765: G0484, W0804
Malone, Edmund, 1741–1812: W1902
Man, Miss [ ]: T1489
Manchester, [ ], duchess: M0016. *See also* Beaulieu,
    Isabelle Montagu Hussey-Montagu, countess
Manchester, Edward Montagu, 2nd earl (formerly
    Lord Kimbolton), 1602–1672: A1004, O0647
Manchester, Harriet (Dunch) Montagu, duchess,
    d. 1755: F0397
Mander, Dr. [ ], master of Balliol (1703): A1602
Mandeville, Sir John, fl. c. 1500: A1002
Manifold, Isabel: A1630, H0278
Manley, Mary (de la Riviere), 1663–1724: H1255, M0204
Manning, Thomas, d. 1787: W1176
Mansell, Lady Elizabeth: B0269, T2300
Mansfeld, Ernst, graf von, 1580–1626: T1034
Mansfield, [ ]: T3309
Mansfield, Charles Cavendish, viscount, 1627–1659:
    Y0497
Mansfield, William Murray, 1st earl, 1705–1793: A1311
Manzoli, [ ], opera singer (1765): U0067
Mar, John Erskine, 6th or 11th earl, 1675–1732: T1168
Marby, Sir Joseph, bart. (1768): T1702
Marguerite, queen consort of Henri II, king of
    Navarre, 1492–1549: H1162
Maria Anne Fitzherbert, first wife of George IV,
    1756–1837: T2659
Mariana of Austria, queen consort of Philip IV of
    Spain, 1634–1696: Y0500
Marie Anne (Hapsburg), infanta of Spain, 1606–1646:
    G0367, T0459, T1900
Marie Antoinette, queen consort of Louis XVI, king
    of France, 1755–1793: B0033, S0198, W0361, W2462
Marie de Medici, queen consort of Henri VI, king of
    France, 1573–1642: E0106
Marie-Josèph de Saxe, wife of Louis, dauphin of
    France, 1731–1767: T1934
Markham, [ ]: W0256
Markham, [ ] (Harrington), lady, d. 1609: A1687,
    D0200, M0083
Marlborough, Charles Churchill, 3rd duke, 1706–1758:
    A1365, C0188, T2421
Marlborough, Elizabeth (Trevor), duchess, d. 1761:
    S0210
Marlborough, Henrietta (Churchill) Godolphin, 2nd
    duchess, 1681–1733: G0258
Marlborough, John Churchill, 1st duke, 1650–1722:
    A0482, A0616, A0631, A0805, A1721, A1827, A1954,
    B0444, D0277, F0308, G0058, G0258, G0423, H0584,

Marlborough, John Churchill, 1st duke, (*continued*) H0766, H0944, H0944, I0053, I0889, L0145, M0149, O0293, O0765, P0026, Q0028, R0103, S1113, T0379, T0641, T1092, T1120, T2129, T3272, W0839, W0879, W0989, W1683, W1720, W1764, W1787, W1838, W1892, Y0539

Marlborough, Sarah (Jennings) Churchill, duchess, 1660-1744: B0028, B0403, F0308, H0766, N0271, N0477, T0095, T1169, W0371, W1158, W1276, W1912, W2166

Marsin, Ferdinand de, comte, maréchal, 1656-1706: B0444

Martin, [ ]: M0166

Martin, Mrs. [ ]: B0353

Martin, Cornelius: B0353

Martin, Roger: L0090

Martins, John: F0425

Marvell, Andrew, 1621-1678: F0724, V0050

Mary I, queen of England, 1516-1558: A0099, A0355, C0201, I1580, S0707, W1010

Mary II, queen of England, 1662-1694: A0049, A1313, A1371, A1603, A1784, A1828, B0613, B0629, C0121, C0548, F0631, G0330, H0031, H0639, H0795, I1264, I1342, I1480, L0143, L0144, M0172, O0183, O0202, O0455, S0584, T0549, T1124, T1680, T2408, W0406, W1332, W1529, W1597, W1852, W1893

Mary Hanover, daughter of George II, 1723-1772: P0332

Mary of Lorraine, queen consort of James V, king of Scotland, later Regent of Scotland, 1515-1580: A1213

Mary of Modena, queen consort of James II, king of England, 1658-1718: A1480, H1310, L0175, T1971, T3388, W1889, Y0020, Y0297

Mary Stuart, daughter of James I, 1605-1607: A1378

Mary Stuart, queen of Scots, 1524-1587: B0289, F0732, I0352, I1145, S1220, W0377

Masham, Abigail (Hill) Masham, baroness, d. 1734: A0971, A0976, D0375, N0477, P0052

Masham, Samuel Masham, 1st baron, 1679?-1758: P0052

Mason, [ ]: W2062

Mason, Mary (Sherman), d. 1767: T0028

Mason, Richard, of Morborn, d. 1723: S1117

Mason, Sally: P0363

Massinger, Philip, 1583-1640: S1232

Master, [ ]: F0585

Master, Mrs. [ ], of Cirencester (1759): A0605, T2600

Masters, [ ]: W1191

Masters, Mrs. [ ], of Norwich: T3185

Masters, Mary: T0455

Mathew, Tobias, archbishop of York, 1546-1628: A1244

Mattei, Seignora [ ] (1758-60): A1890, O0271

Matthias, Holy Roman Emperor, 1557-1619: W0182

Mattocks, Isabella (Hallam), 1746-1826: L0538, T0654

Maurice, Michael (1794): W0105

Maxwell, William, styled, Lord Maxwell, d. 1776: A0261

May, Barbara (Hervey), lady: W1887

May, Sir Thomas (1701): Y0305

Maynard, Elizabeth: T0170

Maynard, Francis, capt.: I1284

Maynard, Mary: T0170

Mayson, Peter: P0061

Mazarin, Hortense Mancini, duchess, 1646-1699: C0244, J0133

Mazarin, Jules, cardinal, 1602-1661: H0773

McLaren, William, 1772-1832: H0476

Mead, [ ]: Q0027

Mead, Richard, 1673-1754: S1145, T2919, T3343

Meadows, Sarah: H1170

Meare, Mary: M0210

Mears, Dr. [ ]: F0461, L0699

Mears, Margaret: F0461, L0699

Medici, Lorenzo de, 1449-1492: A0772, A0831, A1435, A1757, G0163, N0331, S0309, W1792, W1960

Melcombe, George Bubb Dodington, baron, 1691-1762: M0460

Melville, Henry Dundas, 1st earl, 1742-1811: C0370, E0102, S0565, W0532

Mercer, James, major, d. after 1797: A1333

Mercer, Katherine, d. after 1797: A1333

Mercier, Philip, 1689-1760: D0010, T0575

Meredith, William, d. 1637: H0894, N0307

Merrion, Jo.: F0685

Merrion, Mary, d. 1693: F0685

Merry, [ ]: T2169

Merry, Mrs. [ ]: T2308

Merry, Mrs. [ ] (Brunton): T2169

Merry, Robert, 1755-1798: T2990

Metastasio, Pietro, 1698-1782: F0330, Y0032

Meyer, Jeremiah, 1735-1789: R0168

Mezeray, François Eudes de, 1610-1683: B0385

Michals, Lucy: C0526

Michell, Sir Francis, 1556-1628 or later: T1382

Mickleborough, Mrs. [ ]: O1061, S0924, T2755, T3223, W0674, W0677

Mickleborough, John: O1061, S0924, T2755, T3223, W0674, W0677

Micoe, Samuel: H0653

Middlesex, Lionel Cranfield, 1st earl, 1575-1645: T1642, T1645

Middleton, Alan Brodrick, viscount, 1660-1728: O0960

Middleton, Charles Middleton, 2nd earl, 1640?-1719: S0583

Middleton, Conyers, 1683-1750: B0641

Milford, John: J0144

Mill, Jane: W0566

Millar, Andrew, jr., d. 1650: A1043

Millar, Andrew, sr.: A1043

Millay, Thomas: W1281

Miller, [ ]: W0566

Miller, Anna (Riggs), lady, 1741-1781: D0123, W0260, W0658

Miller, Miss Jessy: S0606

Milles, Dr. [ ]: W2137

Milles, Walter: H0891

Millicent, [ ]: M0306

Mills, William, fl. 1780: R0031

Milner, Frances: H0322

Milton, John, 1608-1674: C0533, F0750, H0650, H0930, I0848, I1257, R0007, S1027, T0540, T2376, T2380, T3217, W1777

Milton, R. P.: W0505

Milward, John: O0162

Milward, Robert: W1908

Milward, William: W1045, W1895

Mingotti, Signora [ ] (1757): F0107

Mirepoix, [ ], maréchale: O0639, O0939

Mislington, [ ]: W1482

Mist, Nathaniel, d. 1737: I1453, W1464

Mitchell, Miss [ ]: I1388

Mocher, [ ], general: H1128, I0490, W1156, W1313

Mocher, Mrs. [ ]: I0490, O0722

Modd, George, d. 1722: W1681, W1838

Mohun of Okehampton, Warwick Mohun, 2nd baron, 1620–1665: M0610

Moira, Francis Rawdon-Hastings, 2nd earl, 1754–1826: I0445, S0133

Molesworth, Robert Molesworth, 1st viscount, 1656–1725: O0032

Molière (Jean Baptiste Poquelin), 1622–1673: F0275, W1263

Mompesson, Sir Giles, 1584–1651?: T1382

Monaghan, Dermot: H0616

Monboddo, James Burnett, lord, 1714–1799: L0332

Monck, [ ]: *See* Albemarle, George Monck, 1st duke

Monck, George, d. 1715 or later: T2136

Moneux, Alice (Cotton): A0556, W0728

Moneux, Humphrey: W0728

Monmouth: *See also* Peterborough and Monmouth

Monmouth, James Scott, duke, 1649–1685: A1769, D0328, I0357, K0032, M0313, N0069, O1128, P0164, S0400, S0536, S1141, T1877, U0066, U0074, Y0186, Y0237, Y0450

Montagu, [ ], lady: W1312

Montagu, Mrs. [ ]: M0294

Montagu, Charles: W1711

Montagu, Elizabeth (Robinson), 1720–1800: T0356

Montagu, George: *See* Halifax, George Montagu-Dunk, 2nd earl

Montagu, John Montagu, 2nd duke, 1690–1749: A1698, G0101

Montagu, Mary (Churchill) Montagu, duchess, 1694–1745: M0150

Montagu, Lady Mary (Pierrepont) Wortley, 1689–1762: A1387, G0306, T2180, W1041

Montagu, Mary, b. 1769: T1792

Montagu, Ralph Montagu, 1st duke, 1638?–1709: C0124

Montagu, Sidney, d. 1672: I1214, T0972, W1871

Montesquieu, Charles-Louis de Secondat, baron de, 1689–1755: A1267

Montezuma, c. 1480–1520: I0426, P0261

Montfort, Henry Bromley, 1st baron, of Horseheath, 1705–1755: T2845

Montgomery, [ ], countess: H1012

Monthermer, [ ], lady: F0615

Monticelli, [ ] (1747): W0637

Montpesson, Barbara ( ), lady, d. 1676: T2418

Montpesson, Sir Thomas, fl. c. 1662: T2418

Montrose, James Graham, 1st marquis, 1612–1650: W1558

Montrose, Lucy (Manners): H1149

Moody, [ ]: A0307, G0020, G0312

Moody, Mrs. [ ]: F0064, W1156

Moon, Cicely: D0294

Moon, Jo.: W1489

Moone, R———: T2554

Moore, Edward, 1712–1757: I0295, S1191, W0270, W0613, W2611

Moore, John, abp. of Canterbury (1783–1805): F0165

Moore, John, apothecary: H1360

Moore, John, bp. of Ely, d. 1714: A0920, T0768, T0775

Moore, Juliana: I0811

Moore, Mary: F0165

Moore, Rev. John: O0102

More, [ ]: W1078

More, [ ], major: W1653

More, Miss B.: A0617

More, Hannah, 1745–1833: A0480, D0151, F0127, I1200, M0398, O0549, T2507, T3000, W2374

More, I., d. 1715: D0204

More, S.: T2218

More, Sarah: R0015

Morell, Anne (Barker): A1215, L0426, O0739, W0258, W2497, Y0126

Morell, Thomas, 1703–1784: H1469

Moreton, [ ]: S0615

Morgan, [ ], b. 1748: H0981

Morgan, Miss [ ]: H1191, N0113

Morgan, Luce: H0740

Morgan, Sir William, of Tredegar, 1710–1731: H0500

Morrell, William, alias Bowyer: T1928

Morrell, William, mayor of Oxford: N0462

Morris, John, d. 1682: F0599

Morris, Mary, b. 1694 or 1695: I0605

Morrow, [ ], lady, d. 1715: T1555

Morrow, Belle: T0906, T1555

Morton, Anne (Villiers), lady, d. 1654: N0105

Moseley, Mrs. [ ]: O0189

Moseley, Ann: T2539

Motteaux, Peter Anthony, 1660–1718: H0925

Mountain, [ ], lord: H1265

Mountstuart, John Stuart, viscount, 1744–1794: T2853

Mouther, [ ], captain: I1595

Mudd, Catherine (Wheeler), m. 1790: L0624

Mudd, Richard, surgeon, m. 1790: L0624

Muffet, Jane: W0048

Muggot, Maria, d. 1743: B0264

Mugridge, Mrs. [ ], 1719–1755: H0704

Mugridge, Emanual: H0704

Mulgrave, [ ], lord: *See* Buckingham and Normanby, John Sheffield, 1st duke

Muncaster, James, d. 1713: T2171

Munday, [ ]: D0351

Muriall, [ ]: Y0046

Murray, Eliza Anne, b. 1786: B0393

Murray, Grisell (Baillie), 1692–1759: R0029

Murrey, William: T3148

Musgrave, Dr. [ ]: T2925

Musgrave, Sir Christopher, c. 1631–1704: Y0536

Musgrove, Lady Elizabeth: E0049

Musket, [ ]: M0166

N., [ ]: H0792

N———, [ ]: W2493

N———le, [ ]: A1554

Naper, Miss [ ]: W2190

Napier, Blanche (Windham): W2631
Napier, Robert, 1611–1686: T0542
Napier, Sarah (Lennox), d. 1826 (formerly Lady
    Bunbury): S0040
Nardi, Signora [ ], dancer (1746): W0828
Nares, [ ], sergeant: T2565
Nares, Robert, 1753–1829: P0035
Nash, [ ]: W2589
Nash, Richard ('Beau Nash'), 1674–1761: I0942, N0012,
    T1014, W1278
Nayle, Gilbert: U0039
Nayler, James, 1617?–1660: A0922
Neal, Miss [ ]: M0465
Neale, Ann (1741): S0458
Neale, John: H1444
Neale, Thomas: H1444
Neame, William: W1691
Neave, Ann (Blackbourn): T1820
Neave, Francis: T1820
Neech, [ ]: H1161, N0010
Neech, Richard: T2537
Neech, Thomasin: B0655
Needham, Elizabeth: A1613
Neild, Elizabeth (Camden): T2234
Neild, James: T2234
Nelson, Horatio Nelson, 1st viscount, 1758–1805:
    C0286, K0030, L0314, T1693
Nelson, Robert (1713): A0899
Nenn, John: W0887
Neve, Oliver: T2536
Neve, Timothy: T3118
Nevill, Elizabeth: I0826
Nevill, William, colonel: T1016
Neville, Anne (Heydon): K0050
Neville, Sir Henry, 1564–1615: T0422
Neville, Richard, colonel, 1615–1676: K0050
Nevison, Sir Roger: H0826
New, Mary: S0434
Newburgh, [ ]: F0388
Newbury, Master [ ]: H0570
Newby, Sally: S0244
Newcastle, [ ], duke: B0546
Newcastle, Elizabeth (Bassett) Howard Cavendish,
    countess, d. 1643: I0150
Newcastle, Harriet (Godolphin) Pelham-Holles,
    duchess, d. 1776: G0258, S1096, Y0131
Newcastle, Henry Cavendish, 2nd duke, 1630–1691:
    Y0599
Newcastle, Thomas Pelham-Holles, duke, 1693–1768:
    O0869, T2222
Newcastle, William Cavendish, duke, 1592–1676:
    A0681, F0255, M0605, M0611, T1895, T2038, Y0277,
    Y0496
Newcombe, [ ]: T0522
Newcome, [ ]: O0854
Newcome, Peter, d. 1797: W1284
Newcomen, [ ]: W0178
Newell, [ ]: T2945
Newland, Abraham, 1730–1807: N0087
Newman, Goody [ ]: H0820
Newman, Mrs. [ ]: H0896

Newnham, [ ], lord: C0533
Newton, [ ]: I1006, T2952
Newton, Dr. [ ]: N0110
Newton, Abigail: I1006
Newton, Sir Iaaac, 1642–1727: A1286, H0922, K0069,
    M0325, N0022, N0111, R0143, S1238, U0027, I0942, L0149,
    N0109, O0827, S1158, T1014
Newtown, Robert: H0796
Nichol, Miss [ ]: L0166, O0735
Nichols, John, 1745–1826: A0792
Nicholson, Joseph (1793): I0264
Nicholson, Mary: Y0250
Nicke, Anthony: H0619
Nicksbody, Thomas: H0873
Nicolini (Nicolino Grimaldi), 1673–1732: T1130, T2855
Nivernais, Louis-Jules Mancini-Mazarini, duc de,
    1716–1798: B0204, T1831
Noailles, Adrien Maurice, duc de, maréchal,
    1715–1766: I0242, P0281
Noel, Bridget: M0017
Noel, William: W1914
Nolms, [ ], [ ] (1757): P0202
Nonci, [ ]: V0031
Norfolk, Henry Howard, 6th duke, 1628–1684: I0197
Norfolk, Henry Howard, 7th duke, 1654–1701: W1519,
    Y0306
Norfolk, John Howard, 1st duke, 1430?–1485: I0045,
    J0005
Norfolk, Mary (Mordaunt) Howard, duchess,
    1659–1705: T1309, T1577, Y0306
Norman, Anna: S0394
Norris, [ ], of Canterbury cathedral: I0787
Norris, Mrs. [ ]: I0787
Norris, Richard: D0293
North, Brownlow, bishop of Worcester (1774–1781)
    and Winchester (1781–1820): C0148, W1760
North, Dudley [ ], lord: H1024
North, Sir Francis: *See* Guilford, Francis North, 1st
    baron
North, Mrs. Peregrine: N0084
North, Thomasin: F0547
North, William (1790): F0576
Northampton, Elizabeth (Shirley) Compton,
    countess, 1694–1741: I1184, L0509, T2340
Northampton, Henry Howard, 1st earl, 1540–1614:
    T0692
Northampton, James Compton, 5th earl, 1687–1754:
    O0188, W1901
Northcote, Sir Stafford Henry, 7th bart., 1762–1851:
    H1082
Northumberland, Algernon Percy, 10th earl,
    1602–1668: T0541
Northumberland, Elizabeth (Seymour) Percy,
    countess, 1716–1776: A0905, T0436
Northumberland, Henry Percy, 9th earl, 1564–1632:
    T1172
Northumberland, Hugh Percy, 1st earl [later duke],
    c. 1714–1786: A0905, A1069, G0029, H0499, N0313,
    N0314, S0282, T0511, T2527, T2825, W0192
Northumberland, Hugh Percy, 2nd duke, 1742–1817:
    A1527, G0460, Y0202

Norton, [ ]: A0169
Nostradamus, 1503–1566: A0584, T0364, W0549, W0746
Not, Peg: L0443
Nott, Mrs. [ ]: N0322, N0386, N0387
Nott, Randolph: O0594
Nottingham, Anne (Hatton) Finch, countess, d. 1743:
    W0371, W1158
Nottingham, Daniel Finch, 2nd earl, 1647–1730:
    A0482, A1170, W1720
Nottingham, Heneage Finch, 1st earl, 1621–1682:
    W2608
Noverre, [ ]: L0339
Nowell, Alexander, 1507?–1602: T1476
Nugent, Robert Nugent, earl, 1702–1788: S0192
Nuneham, Elizabeth (Venables Vernon) Harcourt,
    viscountess, 1746–1826: M0266
Nutting, Mrs. Elizabeth: I0428
Nuttings, Misses [ ], [ ]: C0038
Nyon, Mrs. [ ]: I1136

O., R.: T0263
O., Walter: A1336
O——n, Dr. [ ]: N0129
Oakes, Abraham, c. 1686–1756: A1515, A1919, S0718
Oakes, John Jacob: O0929
Oates, Titus, 1648–1705: A0907, B0251, D0383, T3180,
    W1452
O'Brian, Larry: O0009
Ogie, Katherine: A1692
Ogilby, Alexander: G0329
Ogle, [ ], lady: *See* Cavendish, Catherine (baroness
    Ogle)
Ogle, Anna: N0265
Ogle, Dorothy: G0119
Ogle, Henry: S0344
O'Keeffe, John, 1747–1833: A0129
Okenor, [ ], lady, d. 1626: D0202, O0269, W0384, Y0568
Oldfield, Anne, 1683–1730: B0645, N0440, S0556, T1130,
    W0996
Oldham, John, 1653–1683: I0205, L0430
Oldmixon, John, 1673–1742: A1268, F0572
Olmins, Elizabeth: W0705
Om——ch, Catherine: C0534
Omar Khayyam, 1073?–1123: W2213
Onslow, Arthur, 1691–1768: A0612, M0175, O1051, W2427
Onslow, George (1765): Y0068
Orford, Edward Russell, earl (first creation),
    1653–1727: A0482, S0385, W1720
Orford, Horace Walpole, 4th earl, 1717–1797: O1115,
    S0350, T0007, T0774
Orford, Maria (Skerrett) Walpole, countess,
    c. 1702–1738: A1813
Orford, Robert Walpole, 1st earl, 1676–1745: A0404,
    A0409, A0929, A0944, A0949, A1317, A1813, B0440,
    D0114, G0162, G0333, G0388, H0115, H0244, I0492, I1034,
    I1542, L0046, M0340, O0069, O0869, O1115, P0320,
    Q0026, Q0039, S0192, S0350, S0710, S0711, S0712, S0713,
    S0714, S0715, T0554, T0854, T1948, T2288, T2671,
    T2689, U0071, W0748, W1259, W1271, W2399, W2429
Organ, Miss [ ]: W1419
Orgen, Helen: A1477

Orgen, John: A1477
Orléans, Philip II, duc d', 1674–1723: H1446, T2836
Ormonde, Elizabeth (Preston) Butler, duchess,
    d. 1685: Y0560
Ormonde, James Butler, 1st duke, 1610–1695: A0785,
    A1457, I0413, L0213, M0602, N0432, S0624, T0829,
    W0687
Ormonde, James Butler, 2nd duke and earl of Ossory,
    1665–1745: A1243, A1425, G0342, L0121
Ormonde, Mary (Somerset) Butler, d. 1733: M0036
Orrery, John Boyle, 5th earl, 1707–1762: A0453, L0228,
    T1586, T2720, Y0465
Orrery, Roger Boyle, 1st earl, 1621–1689: A0179, T0638
Osborn, Edward: A0414
Osborne, [ ]: S0254
Osborne, Penelope (Verney), lady (1688): M0020
Osbourn, Blanche: W0352
Ossory, Thomas Butler, earl, 1634–1680: T0350, Y0560
Otway, Thomas, 1652–1685: I0057, I1229, U0099
Overbury, Sir Thomas, 1581–1613: H0041, H0362
Overbury, Walter: M0558
Overton, [ ]: H0784
Owen, [ ], butler of Christ Church Oxford: T0190,
    W2134
Owens, [ ]: T1349
Oxborough, [ ] Bedingfield, count: C0088
Oxford, Anne (Cecil) de Vere, countess, d. 1588: W1031
Oxford, Edward Harley, 2nd earl, 1689–1741: W1875,
    W2030
Oxford, Robert Harley, 1st earl, 1661–1724: A0926,
    A0971, A0976, C0590, H0296, H1361, I0376, I1247, N0477,
    Q0028, S0350, S1231, W1271, W1842, W1875, W1885

P., [ ]: T1834
P., Miss [ ]: G0057
P., Mrs. A.: W1052
P., G. F.: G0001
P., J.: W1697
P., Mrs. R.: S1066
P., S.: W0215
P., W.: W1799
P., W. (1778): M0209
P——k, [ ], of Christ Church Cambridge: U0143
P——s, Sally (1741): A1905, B0431, B0628, T1764
P——y, Dr. [ ]: A0378
Paganini, [ ] (1762): W1316
Paganini, Signora [ ] (1762): W1316
Page, [ ]: F0618
Page, Misses [ ], [ ]: I1049
Page, T.: N0498
Paine, Miss [ ]: P0190, P0237
Paine, Thomas, 1737–1809: C0371, D0035
Palavicini, [ ]: W2318
Palavicini, Mme. [ ]: M0025
Palfreyman, John: J0097
Palliser, Sir Hugh, admiral, 1723–1796: A1024, T2853
Palmer, [ ], of Oxford: P0013
Palmer, Eleanor (Ambrose), lady, 1720–1818: C0099,
    F0317, I1075, S0419, S0780
Palmer, John, 1742?–1798: B0616, G0164, Y0001
Palmer, Thomas (1709): H0194

Palmerston, Frances (Poole) Temple, viscountess, d. 1769: H0945
Palmes, Lady Mary: P0014
Paoli, Pasquale, 1725-1807: W1703
Parker, Dorothy: O1064
Parker, Eliza, d. 1793: D0218
Parker, Matthew, abp. of Canterbury, 1540-1575: M0180
Parker, Sir Peter, 1721?-1811: I0600
Parker, Samuel, bishop of Oxford, 1640-1688: H0955
Parker, Sir Thomas, 1695?-1784: P0280
Parkinson, [ ]: W2318
Parkyns, Sir Thomas, d. 1741: H0963
Parrot, Simon, proctor of Magdelen College Oxford (1545/6): A0473
Parry, Dr. [ ], m. 1778: H1179, I1099, F0507, N0437
Parry, Mrs. [ ] (1759): M0735
Parry, Mrs. [ ] (Rigby), m. 1778: F0507, N0437
Parsley, Jane (1701): Y0305
Parsley, William (1701): Y0305
Parsons, [ ]: W0737
Parsons, Robert, organist of Westminster Abbey, d. 1623: D0221
Parsons, William, 1736-1795: H0929
Parsons, William, fl. 1785-1807: A1119, P0035
Partridge, John, 1644-1715: W0268
Paston, Margaret: S0793
Paston, Sir William: I0039, S0727
Pater, [ ] (1754): F0479
Patrick, Simon, 1626-1707: A0943, B0329
Patten, Miss [ ]: W2363
Patterson, William: T1670
Pattison, William, 1706-1727: S0362, T0843
Paul V, pope, 1605-1621: W0182
Paul, Miss [ ], of Southfields (c. 1759): M0035
Paul, Mrs. [ ], of Southfields (1757-59): M0035, M0039, W1811
Paul, William, 1678-1716: D0340, S0737, T0893, T1893
Pauling, Robert, mayor of Oxford (1679/80): Y0186
Pawley, Miss [ ]: S0096
Pawley, Mrs. [ ]: S0096
Payne: See also Lavington
Payne, Miss [ ]: Y0065
Payne, Robert, of Christ Church Oxford (matr. 1611): W2192
Payne, Susanna: A1345
Payton, Catharine: W2040
Peacock, Mary: H0282
Pearce, Belle: D0191
Pearce, Zachary, bishop of Bangor and dean of Westminster, 1690-1774: A1874, F0604
Peard, [ ]: A1322
Peard, Catherine: D0168, T0622
Peard, Mrs. [ ]: Y0586
Peard, Miss Su.: L0505
Pearse, Mrs. [ ]: W0187
Peasley, Mary: F0148
Peck, [ ]: H0700
Peckham, Miss [ ]: C0213, C0214
Pegge, Mrs. [ ] (Cokayne): A1042
Pegge, Frances: Y0363

Peirse, Dr. [ ], of Caius College, Cambridge: D0363, T0133
Pelham, Miss [ ]: T0382
Pelham, Henry, 1695?-1754: O0869, P0080, P0351, T0299
Pelling, Edward, d. 1718: R0170
Pembroke and Montgomery, Philip Herbert, 4th earl, 1584-1650: I0597
Pembroke, [ ], countess: A1265
Pembroke, [ ], lady: A1761, T1783
Pembroke, Elizabeth (Spencer) Herbert, countess, d. 1794: H0584
Pembroke, George Augustus, 11th earl, 1759-1827: U0142
Pembroke, Henry Herbert, 9th earl, 1689?-1750: W1846
Pembroke, Henry Herbert, 10th earl, 1734-1794: W0776
Pembroke, Margaret (Sawyer) Herbert, countess, d. 1706: W0371, W1158
Pembroke, Mary (Howe) Herbert, countess, d. 1749: F0026
Pembroke, Mary (Sidney) Herbert, countess, 1561-1621: S0708, U0049, U0050
Pembroke, Thomas Herbert, 8th earl, 1656?-1733: W0776
Pembroke, William Herbert, 3rd earl, 1580-1630: D0304
Pengrowze, [ ]: P0083
Penistone, Thomas, clerk of the Council to Queen Elizabeth: L0083
Penn, Jemmy: M0016
Penn, William, 1644-1718: F0635, N0317
Penny, Dr. [ ], dean of Lichfield: I0667
Pentreath, Dolly: O0847
Pentycross, Rev. [ ] (1795): N0501, W1987
Pepusch, [ ], son of Johann Cristoph Pepusch: A0062
Pepusch, Johann Christoph, 1667-1752: A0062
Pepys, Sir William Weller, 1758-1825: W1761
Percy family: B0122, C0209
Percy, [ ] (1768): M0731
Percy, Thomas, 1729-1811: A1945, D0135, C0314, F0727
Perry, Micajah (1741): I0783
Perse, [ ], mayor of Cambridge: T0921
Peterborough and Monmouth, Carey (Fraser) Mordaunt, countess, d. 1709: W0371, W1158
Peterborough and Monmouth, Charles Mordaunt, 3rd earl, 1658-1735: A0482, W1158, W1720
Petrarca, Francesco, 1304-1374: P0231, W2008
Petre, Father Edward, 1631-1699: B0466, W1349
Petre, Robert James, 8th baron, 1713-1742: S1227, T3239
Pettat, [ ], capt.: D0125
Pettat, Mrs. [ ]: D0125
Pettiward, Miss F.: W0571
Petty, Henry, lord: See Lansdowne, Henry Petty-Fitzmaurice, 3rd marquess
Petty, Sir William, 1623-1687: N0061
Peyton, [ ]: W0616
Peyton, Miss [ ] (1733): A1581, D0305
Peyton, Mrs. [ ]: A1145
Peyton, Sir Robert (1679-80): Y0067, Y0312
Philip II, king of Spain, 1527-1598: A0355, S0707, W1010

Philip III, king of Spain, 1578-1621: W0182

Philip IV, king of Spain, 1605-1665: F0734, Y0549

Philipps, [ ], of St. John's College Oxford (1706): S0843

Philipps, Bridget, d. 1734: B0555

Philipps, Sir Robert: H0309

Philips, Ambrose, 1675-1749: A0988, N0003, N0011, O0096, T0442, W0665

Philips, Claude, d. 1732: P0111

Philips, Hector: W0554

Philips, Katherine, 1631-1664: A0242, O1065, W2115

Philips, [ ]. lady: M0640

Philips, Teresia Constantia, d. 1765: I1001

Philips, William, 1675-1734: N0390

Phillips, G.: C0170

Phillips, Susan Elizabeth (Burney), 1755-1800: C0153, M0535, N0214, W1346

Pickman, Charles: T1998

Pico della Mirandola, Giovanni, 1463-1494: H0783

Pierce, Lucy: S0608

Pierson, Isaac, 1723-1736: A0844, I1481, I1482, I1483, I1484, M0680

Piesly, Mary [Neale]: W2040

Pighburgh, [ ]: B0582

Pigott, Rev. F.: O0083

Pilkington, Laetitia (Van Lewen), 1712-1750: C0300, I1001, T0037

Pinchbeck, Christopher, 1710?- 1783: O0033

Pinery, Prince: N0397

Pinto, Mrs. [ ], singer (1768): S0877, W0431

Piozzi, Hester Lynch (Salusbury) Thrale, 1741-1821: A1119, H1015, H1132, I0527, N0345, S0142, S0804, T1540, T2431, W2284

Pitt, Misses [ ], [ ]: O0935, W1224

Pitt, William, the elder: *See* Chatham, William Pitt, 1st earl

Pitt, William, the younger, 1759-1806: A0047, H0064, O0532, S0209, T2996

Pius VI, pope, 1717-1799: I1312, T0216

Pix, Thomas: W1237

Platen, Sophia Charlotte Kielmansegge, countess, b. 1673?: B0582

Plumpton, Mrs. [ ]: A1507

Pluret, Mary: A1204, W0661

Plymouth, Catherine Archer, countess, d. 1790: A1727

Pocklington, Roger: B0510

Polivicini, Sir Horatio: D0228

Poliziano, Angelo, 1454-1494: A1757, W1792

Polwhele, Richard, 1760-1838: T3044

Pomfret, Henrietta (Jeffreys) Fermor, 1700?-1761: W1840

Pomfret, John, 1667-1702: W0258

Ponis, [ ]: S1076

Poole, [ ]: I1239

Poole, Lady Anne (1655): B0567

Poole, Beatrice (Brydges): I0702

Poole, Domville, d. 1795: W2182

Poole, Sir Harry: Q0029

Pope, [ ]: I1043

Pope, Alexander, 1688-1744: A0233, A0835, A1611, B0617, B0621, C0600, D0239, D0315, E0061, E0082, E0090, F0182, F0315, G0485, H0091, H0926, H1013, H1446, H1500, I0279, I0848, I0942, I1159, I1290, I1359, N0109, O0046, O0134, P0211, S0176, S0389, S0828, T1014, T1086, T1751, T2273, T2542, T2628, U0132, W0238, W0619, W0713, W0841, W1221, W1308, W1575, W1815, Y0539

Pope, Anne: S0269

Pope, Elizabeth (Watson): S0269

Pope, Sir William: S0269

Popham, Alexander: H1323

Porter, [ ]: I1012

Porter, Dr. [ ], LLD: H1462, W2117

Porter, Miss [ ]: A0337

Porter, Endymion, 1587-1649: G0147

Porter, Isabella: R0137

Porter, Olivia (Boteler), d. 1663: G0147

Portland, William Bentinck, 1st earl, 1649-1709: B0310, C0333, W1893, A1365

Portland, William Henry Cavendish Bentinck, 3rd duke, 1738-1809: I1063, W1637

Portman, Sir John, d. 1624: I1436

Portmore, Charles Colyear, 2nd earl, 1700-1785: T0499

Portmore, Juliana (Hele) Osborne, countess, c. 1705-1794: T0499

Portsmouth, Louise Renée de Kéroualle, duchess, 1649-1734: A1389, C0244, D0264, F0270, H0030, I1505, T3175, W1409, W1939

Pory, [ ], capt.: B0675

Postlethwait, Malachi (1758): A0610

Potter, [ ]: A0906, B0348

Potts, [ ]: T1728

Potts, Elizabeth: S0372

Potts, Roger: T2534

Potts, Sir John: M0449, T1728

Poulter, Richard: S1061, T0249

Powell, [ ]: B0520, W0897

Powell, Mrs. [ ]: I0500, O0954

Powell, George, jr., d. 1714?: D0120

Powell, Herbert: T0629

Powell, Mary: M0237

Powell, William: C0074

Power, Mrs. [ ]: H0841

Powis, [ ] (1701): N0267

Powys, Sir Thomas, 1649-1719: A0584

Poyntz, Stephen, 1685-1750: O0741, W1894

Pratier, Dr. [ ]: D0398

Pratt, [ ], m. 1786: D0144

Pratt, Mrs. [ ] (Molesworth), m. 1786: D0144

Preen, John à: H0838

Preen, Richard à, d. 1589: H0817

Preston, Robert, 1703-1730: B0008

Prettyman, Catherine: H0883

Preyo, C., actor (1786): O0827, T2718

Price, [ ], attorney (1731): G0486

Price, Dr. [ ]: A1285

Price, Amy: W1326

Price, Daniel, 1581-1631: E0150, N0303

Price, Eliza: H1492

Price, Mary (1744): M0468

Price, Thomas, capt. (1748): C0433

Prichard, Richard: H0635

Pricke, Edmund, d. 1618: T1367
Prideaux, Anne: N0035
Prideaux, John, bp. of Worcester, 1578–1650: G0381
Prideaux, John, Regius Professor at Oxford: N0035
Prideaux, Mary: W0173
Priestley, [ ], son of Joseph Priestley: W0193
Priestley, Joseph, 1733–1804: A0745, A1346, O0397, W0193
Priestley, Timothy, 1734–1814: T1742
Primer, Richard: H0729
Prince, Sir Francis, knighted 1611: M0293
Pring, John: S0212
Pring, Sarah: S0212
Pringe, Martin: H1089
Pringles, [ ]: I0864
Prior, Matthew, 1644–1721: D0002, A0490, A0835, A1433,
     A1587, B0385, B0651, C0091, C0540, O0733, P0310, P0311,
     S0563, T2170, T2544, W1246, W1857, W2335
Prior, Thomas, 1682?–1751: S0561
Pritchard, Miss [ ]: P0348
Pritchard, Hannah (Vaughan), 1709–1768: O0071
Pritchard, Sir William, lord mayor of London (1682),
     1632?–1705: W1247
Pritchard, William, 1708–1763: H1077
Proby, Frances: R0192
Proby, Sir Thomas: R0192
Procter, John: Y0594
Proctor, [ ]: A0308
Prynne, William, 1600–1669: H0848, N0484
Pulham, Grace (1753): L0491
Pullam, Tom: F0561
Pulteney, William: *See* Bath, William Pulteney, 1st
     earl
Punteg, John: W2472
Punto, Aurea, d. 1746: H0843
Purcell, Henry, 1659–1695: F0678
Putterkin, [ ]: A0080
Pym, John, 1584–1643: A1004, W0077

Quarles, Francis, 1592–1644: S0164, T0678
Queensberry, Catherine (Hyde) Douglas, duchess,
     1700–1777: D0298, S1096, T0982, T2478, T2860
Quested, Master [ ]: H1454
Quick, John, 1748–1831: N0485, W0721
Quin, James, 1693–1766: A1590, P0228, T0279

R., Miss [ ]: F0486
R., Miss A. (1713): M0205
R., Miss M. (1713): M0205
R., Robert L.: I0222, W0863, W1345
R., W.: D0087
R———, [ ]: W1584
R———, [ ], duchess: O0537
R———, John (1751): W0320
R———, Miss S———: A0898
R——d, Rev. [ ]: W1239
R——dd, Betsy: D0051
R——ds, Miss M. (1722): H0271, W2163
Rabbets, Thomas: I0002
Rabelais, François, c. 1490–1553?: P0168
Racine, Jean, 1639–1699: T0442
Radcliff, Sir George, 1593?–1657: I1479

Radcliffe, [ ]: W1252
Radcliffe, Miss [ ]: F0340
Rainwell, John: C0217
Raleigh, Sir Walter, 1552?–1618: C0379, G0165, G0407,
     I0718, I0987, T0568, T0830, W0356
Ramsay, [ ], capt.: T0323
Ramsay, Allan, 1713–1784: A1009, S1390
Ramsbottom, Abraham: D0146
Rancliffe, Elizabeth (James), lady: R0009
Randal, [ ]: P0344
Randal, [ ], justice: G0252
Randal, Peter: H0814
Randolph, [ ], servant of Queen Elizabeth: R0010
Randolph, Dr.: H0450
Randolph, Thomas, 1606–1635: P0326, S0707
Ranelagh, Richard Jones, 3rd viscount and 1st earl,
     1636?–1712: P0266
Ranie, Q.: Y0102
Rant, [ ] (Grey), lady: W0248
Rant, Sir William: W0248
Ranzini, [ ]: S1326
Raphael, [ ]: H0933
Rapin, René, 1621–1687: H0161
Rathbone, Joseph, d. 1790: L0241
Ravenscroft, James: I0285
Ravenscroft, Magdalein: H0608
Ravis, Thomas, bishop of London, 1560–1609: W1050
Rawlet, John: R0024
Ray, Rev. Bay (1747): F0688
Rayment, John: T0722
Raymond, Sir Jemmet, formerly of St. Edmund Hall
     Oxford: S0991
Raymond, Robert Raymond, 1st baron, 1673–1733:
     N0003, W1130
Read, Sir William, d. 1715: T1122
Reade, Miss [ ] (1741): S1257, W1017
Reaumur, René Antoine Ferchault de, 1683–1757: W1456
Reay, Martha, d. 1779: T0443
Redman, Thomas: B0599
Ree, Walter: A0072
Reeve, Thomas: T2936
Reignolds, John, 1549–1607: B0158, C0315
Remmett, Robert: A0754
Reppington, Sir John: I0309
Reppington, Letitia: S1337
Reppington, Marie: S1337
Reppington, Seabright: S0731
Reppington, Thomas: Y0307
Repps, Ann: P0084
Repps, Lucia: F0545, T2088
Repps, Mary: T2768
Reresford, [ ]: F0729
Reynolds, Mrs. [ ]: M0301
Reynolds, Edward, bishop of Norwich, 1599–1676:
     A1116, C0197, L0082, L0551, R0067
Reynolds, Elizabeth: H0735
Reynolds, John: I1182
Reynolds, Sir Joshua, 1723–1792: B0303, F0156, I0406
Reynolds, Thomas: H0735
Reynolds, William: I1182
Rice, [ ]: W1935

Rich, Sir Edwin, d. 1675: S0854

Rich, Mrs. Essex (afterwards Lady Cheke): H0977

Rich, Ms. Honor: I1077

Rich, John, 1682?-1761: D0017

Rich, Penelope (Devereux), lady, 1562-1607: H0798,
   H0807, U0134

Richard III, king of England, 1452-1485: I0703, J0005,
   T2423

Richards, [ ]: L0004

Richards, Mrs. [ ]: M0036

Richards, William: W0089, W0141

Richardson, Jonathan, 1665-1745: W1411

Richardson, Samuel, 1689-1761: S0604, Y0565

Richelieu, Armand-Jean du Plessis, cardinal,
   1585-1642: S1090

Richmond and Lennox, dukes of: D0302

Richmond and Lennox, Charles Lennox, 2nd duke,
   1701-1750: W1411

Richmond and Lennox, Charles Lennox, 3rd duke,
   1735-1806: W2500, A0060

Richmond and Lennox, James Stuart, 1st duke,
   1612-1655: W1924

Richmond and Lennox, Mary (Bruce) Lennox,
   duchess, d. 1796: O0518

Richmond and Lennox, Mary (Villiers) Stuart,
   duchess, 1622?-1685: N0378

Richmond and Lennox, Sarah (Cadogan) Lennox,
   duchess, 1706-1751: W0391, W1411

Richmond, Ludovic Stuart, 1st duke, 1574-1624: A1292

Richmond, Misses [ ], [ ]: W1100

Riddell, [ ], capt.: O0921, W1757

Riddell, Frances (Marsham), lady, 1778-1868: H0029

Riddell, James (1762): W0950

Riddell, Mary, 1735-1762: W0950

Rider, Rev. [ ]: W1315

Ridley, Nicholas, 1500?-1555: R0027

Rigby, Miss [ ]: H1179

Rigby, Mrs. [ ] (1794): A0644, N0333

Rigby, Joseph, c. 1683-1732: H0697

Riggs, [ ]: A0169

Riggs, Ann: H0724

Riggs, Catherine: H0724

Riggs, Mary: H0724

Right, Henry: H0300

Rinsdale, [ ], d. 1740: A1158

Rinsdale, William, capt. (1740): A1158

Rivers, Anne: H0805

Rivers, Mary: H0805

Rivers, Thomas: H0805

Rives, [ ]: W0179

Rizzio, David, 1533-1566: O0296

Ro——e, [ ]: I1477

Roan, Dr. [ ]: T1349

Rob——ts, Miss [ ]: B0679

Robert II, king of Scotland, 1316-1390: T1574

Robert III, king of Scotland, 1340?-1406: T1574

Roberts, [ ]: B0102

Roberts, [ ], lord: B0102, D0403

Roberts, I.: W2141

Roberts, Martha: M0628

Roberts, Mary: T0001

Roberts, Sarah: B0102

Robespierre, Maximilien Marie Isidore, 1758-1794:
   O0866, T1794

Robinson, [ ]: M0604

Robinson, [ ], capt.: T2140

Robinson, Mrs. [ ]: T2417

Robinson, Ellen: D0009, F0767, H0042, N0226

Robinson, Fanny: H0573

Robinson, John: W0277

Robinson, John, bishop of Bristol, 1650-1723: O0729,
   W0742

Robinson, Margaret (Jenkins), d. 1765: T2140

Robinson, Sir Thomas: M0534

Robinson, William, 1575-1626: A0614, T0468

Rochester, John Wilmot, 2nd earl, 1647-1680: A1569,
   B0019, C0123, C0144, F0270, F0725, H0586, I1581, R0004,
   T0071, T2008, T2608, T3186, W0288, W2451

Rochester, Laurence Hyde, 1st earl, 1641-1711: C0599,
   H0686, H0910, T0009, T1523

Rochford, Lucy (Young) Nassau, countess, d. 1773:
   A0523

Rodney, Jane (Compton), 1730-1757: T3196

Roe, Sir Thomas, 1581?-1644: T0069

Rogers, [ ]: H0943, O0809

Rogers, [ ], of Pilton: S0703

Rogers, [ ], of Gloucestershire: O0094

Rogers, Mrs. [ ]: W1313

Rogers, Charles, d. 1746: F0138

Rogers, Edward, d. 1795: M0331

Rogers, John, d. 1676: N0173

Rolle, Alexander: U0024

Rollin, [ ], d. 1741: C0131

Rolt, Mrs. [ ]: T2303

Romney, George, 1734-1802: R0215

Romney, Henry Sidney, earl, 1641-1704: N0426

Rook, Mrs. [ ]: H0188

Rooke, Sir George, 1650-1709: T0373

Roper, [ ], d. 1722: Y0045

Roper, Samuel, colonel: M0059

Roscoe, [ ]: A1153

Roscommon, Wentworth Dillon, 4th earl, 1633?-1685:
   A1702, H0141, S0643, W1619, W1725

Rose, Mrs. [ ]: B0318, H0605

Rose, Mrs. [ ], of Banff: N0299

Ross, Thomas, d. 1675: S0400

Roubiliac, Mrs. [ ] (Smart), m. 1742: T2574

Roubiliac, Louis François, 1695-1762: D0406, F0108,
   T0252, T2574, W1272, W1283

Rous, Elizabeth: A0415

Rous, Sir John: A0151

Rousseau Burney, [ ], b. 1777: P0260

Rousseau Burney, [ ], b. 1789: D0139

Rousseau Burney, Esther (Burney): D0139, P0260

Rousseau, Jean-Jacques, 1712-1778: H0674, I0350,
   L0244, O0174, U0072

Routh, J.: D0338

Routh, M.: D0338

Rowe, Elizabeth (Singer), 1674-1737: A0615, O0930,
   S1222

Rowe, Nicholas, 1674-1718: S0270, T2550, T2551, T3091,
   T3173

Rowe, Thomas, 1687-1715: I1365

Rowland, [ ]: W0771

Rowland, John, 1606-1660: N0522, N0524

Rudd, [ ], of St. Johns College Cambridge: S0543

Rudge, Edward (1753): T2966

Rudyerd, Benjamin, 1572-1658: T2656

Ruggle, George, 1575-1622: F0080, N0400, R0169, I1149

Rupert, prince, count Palatine, 1619-1682: I0734, O0647, U0003

Russell, [ ], puppeteer (1745): T2812, T3183

Russell, Edward: *See* Orford, Edward Russell, earl (first creation)

Russell, John, c. 1689-1735: G0473

Russell, Lady Rachel: W1457

Russell, Samuel (1743): H0228

Russell, William Russell, lord, 1639-1683: T2031, T2624, T2627

Rutherford, Dr. [ ], d. 1730: S0652, W0396

Rutherford, John: M0473, N0201, R0124, T0384, T2598, T2847

Rutland, Elizabeth (Sidney), countess, d. 1612: I0266

S., [ ]: O0114, T2331

S., Rev. [ ]: T1060

S., Mrs. [ ]: S0259

S., Anna (1754): A1261

S., B.: O0677, W1787

S., Ch.: M0415

S., Dr.: H0357

S., Eliza: H1398

S., F. (1705): J0013

S., Lord G.: L0075

S., H.: I0922

S., Julianna (1779): W0012

S., L.: F0715

S., Miss M.: T2587

S., R.: D0275, T2220

S., Susannah: O0957

S., T.: B0196

S———, [ ], justice: A0596, T0663

S———, Miss [ ]: S1234

S———, Mrs. [ ]: T3137

S———, Mrs. E———n: H0829

S———l, [ ]: S1255

S———nd———, Miss [ ] (1760): T1882

S———nore, Miss [ ]: O0769

S———r, [ ]: T3082

S———ter, Miss [ ]: S0091

Sabine, Mrs. [ ]: F0492

Sacheverell, Henry, 1674?-1724: A1084, A1102, A1393, F0372, F0428, G0310, H1004, L0515, O0217, O0592, S0547, T0208, U0033, W1388

Sacket, [ ]: T0368

Sackville, George Sackville, 1st viscount, 1716-1785: Y0164

Sader, Thomas: I0899

Sadleir, Mrs. [ ], d. 1793: H0099, O0950, W1313

Sadleir, Sir Ralph, 1507-1587: S1029

Sadler, Richard: R0145

Saffin, Thomas, c. 1664-1687: H0960

St. Albans, Charles Beauclerk, 2nd duke, 1696-1751: A1365

St. Albans, Diana (de Vere), duchess, d. 1742: T0818

St. Albans, Francis Bacon, 1st viscount, 1561-1626: G0484, T1017, W0993, W1471

St. Clair, John, capt.: O0439

St. John, [ ]: S0029

St. Leger, Sir Warham, d. 1631: S1223

Salisbury, Catharine (Howard) Cecil, d. 1673: V0041

Salisbury, Hester Maria (Cotton), d. 1773: A0359

Salisbury, James Cecil, 3rd earl, d. 1683: C0503, H0483, S0607

Salisbury, James Cecil, 4th earl, 1666-1694: D0399

Salisbury, Mary Amelia (Hill) Cecil, countess, 1750-1835: U0064

Salisbury, Robert Cecil, 1st earl, 1563-1612: A1175, H0649, H0748, H0869, N0259, T1017, T1377

Salisbury, William Longsword, earl, d. 1226: R0233

Salkeld, Sir Richard, knighted 1487: H0825

Salle, Mlle. [ ], dancer (1734): Y0484

Salmon, Thomas, 1648-1706: H0132

Salter, Humphrey: H0752

Salton, [ ], lord: T0176

Salusbury, Robert: A0572

Sambourne, Sir Henry, sheriff of Oxford: F0263, T1208

Samwell, Anne (Strutt): A1487, I1297, T3250

Samwell, William: A1487, I1297

Sancroft, William, abp. of Canterbury, 1617-1693: C0441, G0330, H0173, H1325, L0131, P0046, T3232, W1565

Sanden, Dr. [ ]: I1049, W2328

Sanderson, [ ]: N0102

Sanderson, [ ], curate of Wickware: T2776

Sanderson, Joan: T1942

Sandford, [ ]: T1044

Sandford, Mrs. [ ]: D0367

Sandford, Robert: B0439

Sands, [ ]: U0115, W2047

Sands, Miss [ ]: I0464

Sandwich, Edward Montagu, 1st earl, 1625-1672: G0434, I1214, S0047, T0972, W1275, Y0137

Sandwich, John Montagu, 4th earl, 1718-1792: W0262, W1301

Sandys of Ombersley, Samuel Sandys, 1st baron, 1695?-1770: I1542

Sandys, [ ] (1768): M0731

Sandys, George, 1578-1644: P0020

Sandys, Rev. [ ] (1780): Z0007

Sapworth, Dr. [ ]: A0463

Sarney, Bess: T2949

Satter, William: H0876

Saul, Daniel: H0837

Saumarez, Sir James, admiral, 1757-1826: I1271

Saunders, Valentine: I0819

Saunderson, Nicholas, 1682-1739: W1999

Saurin, Jacques, 1677-1730: I1200

Savage, [ ]: L0433, S0057, T1551

Savage, Dr. [ ] (1760): P0276

Savage, Margaret (Wodehouse): S0057, T1551

Savage, Richard, 1648-1743: H1146

Savage, Thomas: T2039

Savile, William: T2178

Saville, Sir Thomas, knighted 1617: T0018

Savoy, Victor Amadeus II, duke, 1675-1730: L0495

Scamp, John: T1890

Scarborough, Richard Lumley, 1st earl, 1650?-1721: S0351

Scargill, Daniel: F0091

Scarron, Paul, 1610-1660: O0126

Scarsdale, Nicholas Leake, 4th earl: D0350

Schaub, Marguerite de Ligonier du Buisson, lady, d. 1793: I1013

Schomberg, [ ], baroness de: N0339

Schomberg, Frédéric Armand de, 1615-1690: G0440

Schuman, [ ] (1761): W1796

Schwarz, Berthold: F0198

Scoch, John, 1685-1707: A0992

Scot, Dr. [ ] (1715): T3234

Scot, Grace: H0455

Scot, Margaret, d. 1728 (=Marion Scott, d. 1727?): S1133

Scot, Thomas: H0455, I1209

Scott, [ ]: S0020

Scott, Major [ ]: D0273

Scott, Mrs. [ ] (1779): W0257

Scott, Mrs. [ ] (Kempe): H0828

Scott, Lady Helen (1725): S0652

Scott, Marion, d. 1727 (=Margaret Scot, d. 1728?): S1079

Scott, Mary: W1776

Scott, Sir Thomas, d. 1594: H0828

Scott, Sir Walter, 1771-1832: Y0198

Scott, Thomas, 1705-1775: L0496

Scroggs, Sir William, 1623?-1683: A0034, H0911, O0632, W2521

Scroope, Sir Carr, 1649-1680: A1428, C0571, O1129, T2981, T3101

Scudamore, Frances (Digby) Scudamore, viscountess: H0520

Scudamore, James Scudamore, 3rd viscount, 1684-1716: H0520

Seaforth, Kenneth Mackenzie, 4th earl, 1661-1701: W1934

Sebright, Henrietta (Dashwood), lady, d. 1772: W0301

Secker, Thomas, abp. of Canterbury, 1693-1768: W2296

Sedgwick, [ ], singer (1796): T2796

Sedley, Sir Charles, 1639?-1701: L0674, W0669

Seeman, Enoch, 1694-1744: T2647, W0782

Selkirk, Alexander, 1676-1721: I0026

Sellar, Abednego, 1646-1705: L0118

Selwyn, Mrs. [ ]: O1023

Selwyn, George Augustus, 1719-1791: T0079

Selwyn, John: P0055

Senefino, [ ]: W1283

Serafina, [ ], singer: A1584

Sergeant, John, 1622-1707: A0432

Seton, Sir Andrew, castellan of Berwick castle (1333): I1309

Settle, Elkanah, 1648-1724: S0619

Seward, Anna, 1749-1809: A1374, H1127, O0466, O0749, S1347, W0260, W1501

Seward, Percy: S0282

Seward, Thomas, 1708-1790: B0397

Sewell, Mary: U0070

Sexton, Sarah: H0842

Seymour, [ ], lady: I0689

Seymour, Arabella: *See* Hertford, Arabella (Stuart) Seymour, countess

Seymour, Lady Caroline, d. 1773: B0192, H0629

Seymour, Dorothy: A0413

Sh[ ], [ ], lady (1787): W1699

Sh———, [ ]: A1609

Sh———y, [ ]: D0368

Shackleton, Elizabeth (Carleton), 1726-1804: S1294

Shackleton, Richard, 1728-1792: N0496, T0280

Shackleton, Sarah: S0039

Shadwell, Thomas, 1641?-1692: A0915, T0142, W0785

Shaftesbury, Anthony Ashley Cooper, 1st earl, 1621-1683: A1443, A1682, C0503, H0483, W0956

Shakespeare, William, 1564-1616: A0387, A0676, B0609, F0065, G0015, G0296, I0703, I0931, I1444, N0353, O0827, O0853, O0963, R0134, S0359, S0373, T2484, T2851, T2919, W0140, W0262, W0273, W1284, W1285, W1604, W1902

Shalcross, Francis: T2808

Shalcross, Julia (Boteler): T2808

Shannon, Anne: Y0250

Shannon, Henry Boyle, earl, 1682-1764: T2568

Shard, Sir Abraham (1745): A0055

Sharp, John, archbishop of York, 1643-1714: T2992

Sharpe, Dr. [ ], d. 1782: N0154

Sharpe, Anna, b. 1734: T2543

Sharpe, Gregory, 1713-1771: S0404, S0783

Shaw, Dr. [ ]: T0652

Shaw, Mrs. [ ] (Spooner), m. 1757: I1393

Shaw, Peter, m. 1757: I1393

Shaw, Thomas, principal of St. Edmund Hall Oxford, d. 1751: S0991

Shawe, Mrs. [ ]: T3130

Sheldon, Miss [ ]: W1413

Sheldon, Gilbert, abp. of Canterbury, 1598-1677: F0695, T0358

Shelley, Elizabeth (Pilford) Shelley, lady, b. c. 1763: I0709, N0070, W1140, W2292

Shelton, [ ]: S1213

Shelton, Martha (Appleton): S1213

Shelton, Mary: B0133

Shenstone, William, 1714-1763: A0786, C0422, M0709, T2663, W1579, W1685, W2070

Sheppard, Mrs. [ ] (1738): M0018

Sheppard, Edward (1758): T1114, T1884

Sheppard, Sir Fleetwood, 1634-1698: A0490, I0494, T0103, W1800, Y0411

Sheppard, James, 1700-1718: W2063

Sheppard, John, 1702-1724: S0454, S0656, W1483

Sheppard, Samuel: B0439, G0337

Sherburne, Sir Edward, 1618-1702: S0455

Sheridan, Elizabeth Ann (Linley), 1754-1792: B0470, F0117, T1913, U0012

Sheridan, Frances (Chamberlaine), 1724-1766: G0140

Sheridan, Richard Brinsley Butler, 1751-1816: A0243, A1171, A1538, F0537, H1331, I0658, I0822, O0736

Sheridan, Thomas, 1687?-1738: W0242, W1251

Sherlock, Elizabeth (Gardner): A0392

Sherlock, William, 1641?-1707: A0097, A0392, A1535, D0422, F0491, H0776, M0289, N0146, P0045, U0117, W0884, W1191

Sherman, John, archdeacon of Salisbury, d. 1667: A1709

Sherwin, [ ]: W1295

Sheward, Miss [ ] (1754): I0534

Shields, Jane, 1723-1638: A0170

Shipley, [ ], schoolmaster (1760): T1079

Shippen, William, 1673-1743: T2388, W0249, Y0546

Shipsquire, Sir John: H0824

Shipton, Ursula, 1488-1561: W0957

Shirley, Lady Frances, 1706?-1778: A1766, W0898

Shirley, James, 1596-1666: M0646

Shirley, Lewis: F0617

Shore, [ ] (1701): N0267

Shore, Jane, d. 1527?: H1485, Z0010

Shoringham, [ ], d. 1715: T0193

Short, William: A0744

Shovell, [ ]: F0772

Shovell, Sir Cloudsley, c. 1650-1707: A1506

Shrewsbury, Adelaide (Paleotti) Talbot, duchess, d. 1726: H0166, O1158

Shrewsbury, Anna Maria (Brudenell) Talbot, countess, 1642-1702: Q0031

Shrewsbury, Charles Talbot, 1st duke, 1660-1718: H0166, O1158, T2686

Shrewsbury, Elizabeth (Hardwick) Cavendish, countess, 1525?-1608: Y0423

Shrewsbury, Gilbert Talbot, 7th earl, 1552-1616: T2132

Shrewsbury, Jane (Ogle) Talbot, countess, 1540?-1597: Y0475

Shrewsbury, Mary (Cavendish) Talbot, countess, 1556-1632: Y0489

Shrider, Christopher, c. 1680-1751: H0941

Shrow, John, d. 1589: F0169

Shuter, Edward, 1728?-1776: B0247, O0322

Siddons, Sarah (Kemble), 1755-1831: S0501, S0502, T2484

Sidley, [ ], lady: W0231

Sidney, Algernon, 1622-1683: A0864, R0054, T1942, T2624

Sidney, Sir Philip, 1554-1586: E0072, G0159, H0298, S0708, U0049, W0711, W1424

Sillion, John: I0184

Silvester, Dr. [ ]: Y0165

Simcoe, John Graves, general, 1752-1806: Y0428

Simons, Malachi: R0149

Simons, Mary, c. 1627-1677: R0149

Simpson, Mrs. [ ], actress: I1132

Simpson, Sarah (Leaper): M0714, P0339

Sincklar, John, d. 1687: W0513

Sinclair, Alexander, d. 1721: I1584

Singleton, Jemmy: F0561

Singleton, Lady Mary: M0171

Skin, [ ]: B0447, T3373

Skinner, John: W2112

Skipworth, [ ]: N0027

Slaughter, [ ], owner of coffeehouse: Y0190

Sloane, Sir Hans, 1660-1753: S0647, T3343

Small, William, 1734-1775: B0339, Y0054

Smart, Dr. [ ], of Chelsea (1742): T2574

Smart, Christopher, 1722-1771: A1060, E0086, G0010, G0015

Smedley, Jonathan, 1671-1729: D0170

Smith, [ ]: F0376

Smith, Miss [ ]: N0113

Smith, Mrs. [ ]: F0251

Smith, Anne: S0441

Smith, Charlotte (Turner), 1749-1806: N0329, W1402

Smith, Edmund: W0939

Smith, Grace: I0654, W0013

Smith, Jane: S1075

Smith, John, servant: D0175

Smith, John, speaker of the House of Commons (1705): H0028

Smith, John, tailor: S0441

Smith, Joseph: B0325

Smith, Sir Nicholas: S0755

Smith, Rebecca: W1943

Smith, Samuel, ordinary of Newgate, 1620-1698: U0035

Smith, Stephen: D0086

Smith, William, d. 1750: W2477

Smith, William, 1730?-1819: K0020

Smyth, [ ], surgeon, d. 1791: I1471

Smyth, Miss [ ]: G0040

Smyth, Mark, M. D.: S0015

Smyth, William: W0967

Sneyd, Edward, 1734-1795: Y0519

Sneyde, Ralph, colonel: H0681, W1366

Snook, [ ]: C0214

Snow, [ ]: B0348

Snow, Mrs. [ ]: W2301

Soame, [ ]: O0776

Soame, Stephen, d. 1771: S1132

Sobieski, [ ], princess: *See* Stuart, Maria Clementina (Sobieski), wife of James Edward ('Old Pretender')

Somers of Evesham, John Somers, baron, 1651-1716: B0069, B0430, S0351, W0881

Somers, [ ]: W2046

Somerset, [ ]: T1245

Somerset, [ ], duke: I0689

Somerset, Algernon Percy Seymour, 7th duke, and earl of Hertford, 1684-1750: P0224

Somerset, Charles Seymour, 6th duke, 1662-1743: B0069, S0351

Somerset, Elizabeth (Percy) Seymour, duchess, 1670-1722: W0742

Somerset, Frances [ ], duchess: G0306

Somerset, Frances (Howard) Carr, countess, 1593-1632: T1659

Somerset, Francis Seymour, 5th duke, 1658-1678: A1769, N0069

Somerset, Robert Carr, earl, 1587?-1645: T1659, W0824

Somes, Sir Steven: H0827

Sommerton, John, scrivener: A0490

Soosly, Ann: L0325

Soosly, Dorothy: L0325

Soosly, Sarah: L0325

Sophia Charlotte, queen consort of George III, 1744-1818: H0133, P0308

Sophia Dorothea, princess of Brunswick, divorced wife of George I, 1666-1726: T0624, T2380, W2460, Y0028, Y0038, Y0084, Y0302, Y0331, W2460

Sophia, princess, daughter of James I, d. 1606: W2524

Sorres, [ ], sieur: A1112

Sotheby, [ ]: A0840
Sound, [ ]: H0799
South, Robert, 1634-1716: A0097
Southcott, [ ], lady: O0598
Southerne, Thomas, 1660-1746: P0258
Southwell, Miss [ ] (1745): C0039
Sowden, Samuel: S1016
Sparges, Father [ ]: H0884
Sparke, Edward, d. 1692: A0030
Sparrow, Anthony, bishop of Norwich, 1612-1685:
   C0197, O0626, P0251, T2012
Sparrow, Joseph: O0699
Sparrow, Sarai: T2012
Sparrow, Susan: P0251
Speed, Harriet: I1013
Speke, Rev. [ ]: Y0005
Spelman, Rev. [ ]: H1395
Spelman, Mrs. [ ] (Harwin): H1395
Spence, Joseph, 1699-1768: B0099, B0275, I0288, I0930,
   I1607, M0526, N0144, O0627, O1013, S1379, T2628,
   W0068, W1260, W2096
Spencer, Lady Caroline, b. 1762: C0134
Spencer, Lady Diana: M0016
Spencer, Lady Elizabeth, 1771-1812: O0190
Spencer, George Spencer, 2nd earl, 1758-1834: I1603
Spencer, John Spencer, 1st earl, 1734-1783: I0555
Spencer, Polly: A1888
Spencer, William Robert, 1769-1834: I1133
Spenser, Edmund, 1552?-1599: A1789, O1137, R0134
Spier, Anthony: F0208
Spilsbury, Miss [ ]: C0075
Spinke, [ ]: I0127
Spottiswoode, John, archbishop of St. Andrews,
   1565-1639: T0404
Spr——g, J.: C0302
Sprat, Jo.: B0299
Sprat, Thomas, bishop of Rochester, 1635-1713: T3388
Squires, Mrs. [ ]: W1491
St——ne, [ ], countess: A0107
Stable, E.: C0375
Stafford, William Howard, 1st viscount, 1614-1680:
   I1474
Staines, Dr. [ ]: I0117
Stair, James Dalrymple, 1st viscount, 1619-1695: R0126,
   W0525
Stamford, Edward, colonel: G0449
Stanhope, [ ], lord: A1198
Stanhope, Ferdinand: C0554
Stanhope, John: C0554
Stanley, [ ]: S1055
Stanley, [ ], secretary of the Customs: O0629
Stanley, Sir John: T1542
Stanton, Daniel: I0275
Stanton, Matthew: I0921
Star, Richard: D0294
Starkey, William: A0099
Steavens, Thomas: D0033, I0559, I1499, M0710, T0092
Stebbing, Henry, 1687-1763: S1095, T0489
Steel, Edward: I1054
Steele, Sir Richard, 1672-1729: G0364, G0454, I0998,
   L0480, T1066, T2488, T3244, W0930, Y0564

Steele, Thomas: C0318
Steevens, George, 1736-1800: P0074
Stephen, king of England, 1096-1154: I1036
Stephens, Mrs. [ ]: A1507
Stephens, Ann, d. 1741: S0458
Stepney, George, 1663-1707: T1525
Sterling, William Alexander, 1st earl of Sterling,
   1567-1640: I1305
Sterne, Laurence, 1713-1768: L0429, S1107, W0673
Sternhold, Thomas, d. 1549: I1101
Stevens, [ ]: I1217
Stevens, [ ], esq.: I0356
Stevens, John: A1525
Stevens, Richard: T1863
Stevenson, [ ]: Y0314
Stevenson, Miss [ ]: C0505
Steward, Misses [ ], [ ]: H1218
Stewart, Lady Marie: Y0478
Stiffy, [ ]: H1003, M0064
Stile, John, 1582-1583: T1866
Stile, Mary, 1583-1585: T1866
Stile, Oliver, 1584-1585: T1866
Stiles, John: F0080, R0169, W0069
Stillingfleet, Edward, bp. of Worcester, 1635-1699:
   C0222, P0268
Stirling, Judith (Lee) Alexander, countess,
   b. c. 1642-1681: N0093
Stitch, Samuel: A0967
Stockdale, Percival, 1736-1811: G0127, M0148, S0389
Stone, Benjamin, of New College Oxford
   (1605-1609): H0982, T2048
Stone, Thomas, capt.: A1652
Stonehouse, Rev. Dr. [ ]: I1200, W1803
Stonehouse, Mrs. [ ], d. 1788: D0373
Storges, [ ]: N0357
Story, Edward, of Gravely, Cambridge: T2463
Stout, Sarah, d. 1699: A1212
Stow, Maria: H0157
Strafford, Mrs. [ ]: N0351
Strafford, Thomas Wentworth, 1st earl, 1593-1641:
   G0455, H0880, P0223, R0199, S0251, T0422, T0614, T2146
Strafford, Thomas Wentworth, 3rd earl, 1672-1739:
   A0944
Strange, [ ]: H0696
Strange, Sir Robert, 1721-1792: P0365, W1354, W2068
Strangman, Ann: S1314
Strathmore, Mary Eleanor (Bowes) Lyon, countess,
   1749-1800: A1548, D0046, T1898
Street, [ ]: F0273, T1785
Street, Agnes, d. 1400: S1195
Street, Simon, d. 1400: S1195
Strode, William, 1599-1646: A1004, L0365
Stuart, James, elector of Edinburgh: T0087
Stuart, Maria Clementina (Sobieski), wife of James
   Edward ('Old Pretender'), 1702-1735: A0902, H0276,
   H0990, T3259
Stubbins, Dr. [ ]: W0515
Stukeley, Sir Hugh: W0370
Stukeley, Katherine, lady, d. 1679: W0370
Stukeley, Sir Lewis, d. 1620: I0987
Stumpy, [ ]: M0064

Suckling, Charles: L0703

Suckling, Lucy: L0703

Suckling, Sir John, 1609–1642: S0698, S1232

Suffolk, Henrietta (Howard), countess, 1688–1767: I0210, I0329

Sullivan, [ ]: L0490

Summers, William: S1091

Sunderland, [ ], of Clare Hall, Cambridge: L0298

Sunderland, Anne (Churchill) Spencer, duchess, 1682/3–1715: H0002

Sunderland, Charles Spencer, 3rd earl, 1674–1722: F0525, S0350, S0351

Sunderland, Dorothy Spencer, countess, 1617–1684: C0085, I1100, V0022

Sunderland, Elizabeth (Trevor) Spencer, countess, d. 1761: A0940

Sunderland, Robert Spencer, 2nd earl, 1641–1702: H0360, H0852, W1947

Sundon of Ardagh, William Clayton, baron, 1672?–1752: Y0019

Sunnybank, [ ] (1545/6): A0473

Surflen, Miss [ ]: B0322

Sutherland, [ ], countess: H1447

Sutherland, [ ], earl: H1447

Sutherland, John Gordon, 14th earl, 1609–1679: S0529

Sutton, [ ], sr., actor: T1183

Swift, [ ]: H0897

Swift, David: A0254

Swift, Edmund: O0833

Swift, Jonathan, 1667–1745: A0215, A0453, A0835, B0612, D0045, G0364, H1400, H1446, I0964, I0976, I1243, I1570, M0273, M0422, M0725, O0134, O0617, P0034, P0103, S0132, S0687, S0951, T0006, T0463, T0464, T1192, T2927, U0151, W1251, Y0222

Swift, Robert: S0847

Sydenham, [ ]: D0160, D0161, D0162, N0115

Sydney, [ ]: G0144

Sylvester, Miss [ ]: I0335

Sylvester, Joshua, 1563–1618: W2082

Symmonds, Richard: W1905

Symms, Richard: L0498

Symon, [ ]: S1389

Symonds, John: M0297

Symons, Richard: F0106

T., Miss [ ]: F0486, F0559

T., Mrs. E., d. 1659: I1578, R0046

T., Joseph, D. D.: T2510

T., M.: I0649

T——, Miss D——: S0089

T——dman, Thomas: W0100

T——le, E——d: Y0598

T——r, Dr. [ ]: Y0139

Tagg, Sally: M0344, M0402, S0187

Talbot, [ ]: T1245, T1657, T2132, T3270

Talbot, Catherine, 1721–1770: F0754, O0628, W2296

Talbot, Charles Talbot, of Hensol, 1685–1737: W0929

Tallard, Camille d'Hostun de la Baume, duc de, maréchal, 1652–1728: B0444

Talman, [ ]: T2875

Tamworth, [ ], lord: See Ferrers of Tamworth, Washington Shirley, earl

Tanket, Mlle. Catan: J0083, S0259

Taplow, [ ]: W1329

Tart, Thomas: G0320

Tate, Nahum, 1652–1715: S0164

Taunton, [ ]: W0810

Tavernier, Jean-Baptiste, 1605–1689: F0617

Tavistock, Elizabeth (Keppel), marchioness, 1739–1768: S0065

Taylor, [ ]: A0901, S1387

Taylor, [ ], fellow of St. Johns, Cambridge: S0362

Taylor, Dr. [ ]: A1711, T0915

Taylor, Miss [ ]: M0446

Taylor, Abraham: M0364

Taylor, Ann: A0221

Taylor, John, 1704–1766: D0105, I0723

Taylor, John (1794): T1794

Taylor, William, pastor of Stephen's, Coleman Street, d. 1641: A1077, D0171, O0154, S1126, T2353, T2479, W0398

Temple, [ ], lady: W2115

Temple, Richard Grenville-Temple, 1st earl, 1711–1779: M0048

Tenison, Thomas, abp. of Canterbury, 1636–1715: W1182, W1374, W1529

Terrent, Jer.: B0030

Th——g, [ ], lady: D0368

Thanet, Thomas Tufton, 6th earl, 1644–1729: T3319

Thirlby, Dr. [ ]: T1681

Thoe, Miss [ ]: B0510

Thomas, [ ]: D0152

Thomas, Betsy: L0169

Thomas, Timothy: W1777

Thomas(?), William: A0234

Thompson, Belly: Y0324

Thompson, Benjamin: I0159

Thompson, John: B0298

Thompson, John, B. D.: J0102

Thompson, Joseph: O0695

Thompson, Sally: F0028

Thomson, Dr. [ ], d. 1677: H0881, M0409

Thomson, James, 1700–1748: A1555, A1716, H0571, T3096, W2098, Y0157

Thomson, Joan: H0515

Thornhill, [ ]: T1967

Thornhill, Sir James, 1676–1734: S0454

Thornton, Richard, of Leeds, d. 1710: A0645

Thorold, Katherine: S1085

Thoroughgood, [ ]: T2561

Thou, Jacques-Auguste de, 1553–1617: W0484

Thrale, Miss [ ], b. 1778: T1540

Thrale, Mrs. [ ]: See Piozzi, Hester Lynch (Salusbury) Thrale

Thrale, Henry, d. 1781: T2431

Thumb, Christopher: O0635

Thurot, François, captain, 1727–1760: C0468

Thurlow, Edward Thurlow, baron, 1731–1806: S1302

Thwaites, William, d. 1693: L0530

Thynne, Thomas, 1648–1682: M0413

Tibbs, Dr. [ ]: P0290, W1573

Tichborne, Chidiock, 1558?-1586: T2548

Tickell, Mary (Linley), 1756?-1787: F0117

Tickell, Thomas, 1685-1740: E0129

Tillotson, John, 1630-1694: I1399, T2031

Timperan, Thomas: L0416

Tindal, Matthew, 1653?-1733: H0731, T2605

Tinker, [ ]: D0070, W2409

Tirrell, [ ]: T3206

Tissey, John, d. 1732: B0278, H0391, M0240

Titley, Walter, 1700-1768: S0362, W2026

Titus, Mrs. [ ]: D0175

Titus, Silius, 1623?-1704: A1409

Todd, Hannah: T2987

Toft, Mary: M0361

Tollett, George: O0853

Tomkinson, Thomas: T0697

Tomlinson, Kellom: M0188

Tonson, Jacob, 1656?-1736: W1789

Topham, [ ], serjeant to the House of Commons:
    M0220

Torrington, Arthur Herbert, earl, 1647-1716: W1412,
    S1044

Tothill, William: U0034

Toulouse, Louis-Alexandre de Bourbon, comte de,
    1678-1737: T0373

Tour, [ ], Sieur: W1298

Tovey, Miss [ ]: Y0419

Townley, Charles, 1737-1805?: T0201

Townsend, John: J0103

Townshend, Charles Townshend, 2nd viscount,
    1674-1738: D0316, M0604, S0350, S0351, S0917, W0852

Townshend, Charlotte (Compton) Townshend,
    viscountess, d. 1770: T1090

Townshend, George Townshend, 4th viscount,
    1724-1807: I0406, I1316, M0598, T1515, T2422, W1985

Townshend, Horatio Townshend, 1st viscount,
    1630-1687: R0012, T2399

Townshend, Mary ( ), lady: T2314

Trafford, Sir Clement: I0818

Traine, Miss [ ]: C0530

Trancker, [ ]: H0452

Trappis, Robert: W1338

Trelawny, Ann: W2100

Trelawny, Sir Jonathan, bp. of Winchester, 1650-1721:
    H0173, L0131, P0046, T3232, W1565

Trelawny, Sir William, governor of Jamaica, d. 1772:
    W2100

Trench, [ ]: M0604

Trevor, Betty: T0783

Trevor, Sir John, 1637-1717: S0684

Trevor, Molly: T2665

Trice, [ ]: B0660

Trollope, Sir Thomas, 3rd bart., d. 1729: W1889

Tromp, Maarten Harpertszoon, admiral, 1597-1653:
    B0206

Trueman, Joan: H0726, H0758

Trumbull family: W0487

Trumbull, Catharine (Cotterell), lady, d. 1704: O1020

Trumbull, Judith (Alexander), lady, 1681-1742: W1882

Trumbull, Lady Judith, d. 1724: T1859

Trumbull, Sir William, 1639-1716: A0358, T2743

Trumbull, William, d. 1760: W1882

Tryon, Samuel: B0280

Tucker, Rev. [ ], sea chaplain: Y0401

Tudway, Thomas, d. 1726: P0200

Tufton, [ ]: N0302

Tufton, Lady Mary: I0523

Tully, [ ], capt.: H0836

Turbot, [ ]: W0327

Turner, [ ], alderman: T3242

Turner, Miss [ ]: O0673

Turner, Sir Edward: D0408

Turner, Francis, bp. of Ely, 1638?-1700: C0441, G0330,
    H0173, L0131, P0046, T3232, W1565

Turner, Rev. Francis, of Great Yarmouth: T1775

Turner, J.: H0704

Turner, Mary: D0278, M0134

Turner, William: A1525

Turville, Henry: M0356

Tutchin, John, 1661?-1707: S0054

Tweeddale, [ ], earl: I1530

Twining, Thomas, 1735-1804: A1162, C0152, F0569,
    M0534

Twistleton, John: S0568

Twitty, Thomas, 1660?-1728: T3368

Tyers, Jonathan, 1702-1767: B0432, S0799, W1997, W2264

Tyler, Wat, d. 1381: O0867

Tyrconnel, [ ] Carpenter, lady: E0097, Y0515

Tyrconnel, Richard Talbot, earl, 1630-1691: T1657

Tyrer, Ralph, d. 1727: L0471

Tyrrell, Belle: T3393

U., T.: Y0438

Udall, Sir William, fl. 1608: T3316

Underwood, John: A0726

Unwin, Mary (Cawthorne): M0169

Upton, James, 1670-1749: Y0005

Urban VIII, pope, 1568-1644: K0065

Urlin, Sir Simon, recorder of London (1742-1746),
    knighted 1744: W1608

Urquhart, Misses [ ], [ ]: Y0234

Urry, John, 1666-1715: F0344

Ussher, James, bp., 1581-1656: T1731, T1851

Valentia, Lucy (Lyttelton) Annesley, viscountess,
    1743-1783: A0808

Valentina, la (Caterina Azzolini), opera singer:
    T2855

Valentine, bishop of Interamna, d. 270: H0048

Valvine, [ ], canon of Canterbury Cathedral: I0787

Van Dyck, Sir Anthony, 1599-1641: I1100, S1387, T0730,
    V0022

Van Haacken, [ ], artist: A1081, O0045

Vanbrugh, Sir John, 1664-1726: I1313, L0320, T0916,
    T2855, U0043, W1160

Vane, [ ]: T3289

Vane, Frances (Hawes) Hamilton Vane, c. 1715-1788:
    I1001, L0371, W0555

Vane, Hon. Anne, 1705-1736: A0862

Vane, William Holles Vane, 2nd viscount, 1714-1789:
    W0555

Vanneck, Sir Gerard William, 1743?-1791: T2700

Varrio, [ ]: G0093
Vaughan, [ ]: I0144, Y0031
Vaughan, Madam [ ]: D0121
Vaughan, Richard: H0172, H0245
Vaughan, Sir William, d. 1649: G0373
Vere, [ ], lady, B0284
Vere, Miss [ ]: O0067
Vere, Charles: I0338
Vere, Horace Vere, baron, 1565–1635: B0577, H1137,
    I0847, M0280, T0346, W2619
Vere, Sir Francis, 1560–1609: W1427
Vere, Thomas: E0184
Vernell, Peter, d. 1671: A1769, N0069
Vernon, Miss [ ]: M0266
Vernon, Caleb, 1653–1665: A0326, A0891, A0914, B0646,
    C0006, C0010, C0023, D0225, H0382, I0080, I0540,
    T2063, W1500, Y0449
Vernon, Edward, admiral, 1684–1757: E0108, T3361,
    V0031, W1702, Y0016, Y0019
Vernon, Sir Titus: S0723
Vertue, George, 1684–1756: I0840, W0068
Villette, Charles de, marquis, 1736–1793: H1244
Villiers, Lady Barbara: See Blacket, Barbara (Villiers),
    lady
Villiers, Catherine: D0433
Villiers, Eleanor: N0237
Villiers, Lord Francis, 1629–1648: W2003
Villiers, Francis (1683): J0133, L0090, O0042
Villiers, George, colonel, d. 1703: S0072
Vincent, [ ], doorkeeper of Haberdasher's Hall: V0054
Vincent, John Jervis, earl, 1735–1823: T1693
Vinci, Leonardo, 1690–1730: W1382
Viner, Sir Robert, 1631–1688: A1388, W0366
Vines, Dr. Richard, d. 1656: A1340
Visconti, [ ], singer: A1584
Vise, Mrs. [ ]: D0076
Voisenon, Claude Henry de Fusee, abbé de, 1708–1775:
    I0149
Voltaire (François-Marie Arouet), 1694–1778: L0466,
    O0198
Vyse, [ ], archdeacon: D0104

W., Sir [ ]: W0416
W., H.: O0677
W., T.: A0904, F0087
W——, [ ]: O0602
W——, Miss [ ]: I1301, O0187, S1200
W——, Mrs. [ ]: T2413
W——, Charlotte: S0097
W——, Rev. W——: Y0587
W——n, Miss [ ]: A1681
W——r, [ ]: W0002
W——r——t——n, [ ] (1781): M0459
Waddington, Edward, bishop of Chichester,
    1670?–1731: R0042
Wade, [ ]: S0616
Wager, Sir Charles, 1666?–1743: Y0019
Wagg, Madam [ ]: H0781
Wait, Mrs. [ ], of Broad Somerford: A0008
Wakeman, Sir George, fl. 1668–1685: A0034, W2521
Walcot, [ ]: F0038

Waldegrave, Anne Horatia, lady, 1759–1801: Y0231
Waldegrave, Marie Walpole, countess, 1736–1807:
    B0511
Waldgrave, Jemmonia: L0024
Wale, Miss [ ]: S1176
Walgrave, Nicolas: L0445
Walker, [ ]: O1162
Walker, Josiah: A1631
Walker, Obadiah, 1616–1699: F0607
Wall, Tobias: O0888
Wallace, Miss [ ]: W0426
Wallace, Craigie: F0145
Wallaston, F. J. H.: A0779
Waller, Edmund, 1606–1687: A1190, F0155, H0216, I1257,
    T0873, V0022, W0019, W0020, W1293
Wallin, Ann Alethea: T0965
Wallin, Richard: C0481, T0965
Walpole, Anne: A1415
Walpole, Sir Edward, 1706–1784: T3313
Walpole, Horace: See Orford, Horace Walpole, 4th earl
Walpole, Mary (Burwell): S1201
Walpole, Robert: See Orford, Robert Walpole, 1st earl
Walsingham, [ ]: S0254
Walsingham, Mrs. B.: A0619
Walsingham, Sir Francis, 1530?–1590: B0552
Walsingham, Petronella Melusina (de Schulemberg),
    countess, 1693?–1778: M0289
Walter, John: O0180
Walton, [ ], lord: W2634
Walton, Izaak, 1593–1683: H0538
Walton, John, fl. 1640: T1827
Walworth, Sir William, d. 1385: B0484, H1010
Walwyn, [ ], prebendary of Canterbury: I1179
Walwyn, Mrs. [ ], of Longworth: Y0218
Warburton, Mrs. [ ]: B0619
Warburton, William, bishop of Gloucester,
    1698–1779: B0621, H0491, S1095
Warcup, Thomas: T1966
Ward, [ ]: T0414
Ward, Miss [ ], of Dublin: E0065
Ward, Samuel, 1577–1640: T1304
Ward, Sir Edward, sr.: G0351
Ward, Sir Edward, jr.: G0351
Ward, Sir Edward III: G0351
Ward, Thomas: M0712
Warner, Richard: O0885
Warner, Vere (1794): A0644, N0333
Warre, [ ]: M0166
Warren, [ ]: I1277
Warren, Audrey: L0003
Warren, Nicholas: T0803
Warren, Sir Peter, admiral, 1703–1752: L0490
Warrington, Henry Booth, 1st earl, and 1st baron
    Delamere, 1652–1694: I0371, S0650
Warton, Charlotte (Nicholas), d. 1809: W0833
Warton, Joseph, 1722–1800: S0879, T1005
Warton, Thomas, 1728–1790: O0902, T0942
Warwick, [ ], earl: T3040, W2525
Warwick, [ ], lady: F0458
Warwick, Francis Greville, 1st earl, and 1st earl
    Brooke, 1719–1773: S0955, W1185

Warwick, Richard Neville, earl, 1428–1471: A0126, R0138, W1185

Washington, George, 1732–1799: I0967, P0182

Washington, Thomas, d. 1623: H0311, K0060

Watts, Mrs. [ ], mother of Isaac Watts: E0043

Watts, Isaac, 1674–1748: G0479, W0286

Watts, Mrs. M., d. 1693: I0224

Watts, Sir Philip: T2356

Waugh, R., jr.: T1605

Webster, John, 1580?–1625?: A1339

Wedgwood, [ ]: D0163

Weekes, John: A0776, H1365

Welby, Selina: M0031

Welch, Mrs. [ ] (Ford) (1716): T2293

Weld, Thomas: T1835

Wells, Edward, jr.: O0654

Welsted, Leonard, 1688–1747: F0331, I1199, W1695

Wentworth, [ ]: B0348

Wentworth, Lady A. ., (c. 1635): H0517

Wentworth, Sir Matthew: T2419

Wesley, Mrs. [ ]: I1228

Wesley, Samuel, 1662–1735: S0265

Wesley, Samuel, 1691–1739: W2399

West, [ ]: U0082

West, [ ] (1793): A0041

West, Miss [ ]: O1087

West, James: S0138

West, John: W2515

West, Ned: H0794

Westley, Sir Robert, lord mayor of London (1743), knighted 1744: W1608

Westmorland, John Fane, 7th earl, 1682?–1762: B0277, H0301, N0065, S1291

Weston, Lady Frances: W1556

Weston, Katherine: W0145

Weston, Mary: F0148

Weston, Thomas, 1637–1776: D0293, H1051, I0906

Weymouth, Frances (Finch) Thynne, lady, 1650–1712: Y0103, Y0335

Weymouth, Thomas Thynne, 1st viscount, 1640–1714: Y0103, Y0335

Whale, Jean: W1406

Whaley, [ ]: T1681

Whalley, [ ]: Y0563

Whaly, Dr. [ ]: G0369, W0473

Wharton, Lady Mary: I0267

Wharton, Philip Wharton, 1st duke, 1698–1731: S0702, B0544, C0503, H0483

Wharton, Thomas Wharton, 1st marquis, 1648–1715: A0531, B0553, G0300, I1397, O0592, Q0028, S0351, T2786, W1297, W1628, W2097

Wharton, William, d. 1697: D0001, F0274, O0078

Wheatley, John: Y0109

Wheatley, William, c. 1625–1683: W2078

Wheeler, Eliza (Mrs. Molloy), d. 1794: I1463

Whichcot, Thomas: I0557

Whinney, Jenny: L0667

Whiston, William, 1667–1752: B0641, O0137

Whitaker, Jeremiah, 1599–1654: I0813, N0060

Whitbread, Samuel, 1720–1796: S0045, T2472, W1915

Whitby, Daniel, 1638–1726: W1743

White, [ ]: B0352, O0315

White, [ ], esq., of Tattingston Hall: S0020

White, Miss [ ]: W0457

White, Francis, fl. 1693–1733: T0187

White, John: H0691, O0860

White, Robert: C0441, O0883

White, Thomas, bp. of Peterborough, 1628–1689: C0441, G0330, H0173, L0131, P0046, T3388, T3232

Whitefield, George, 1714–1770: G0445, H0092, I0907, W0397, W1444

Whitefoot, [ ]: A1345

Whitefoot, John: T2070

Whitehall, Andrew: Y0344

Whitehead, [ ]: N0014

Whitehead, William, 1715–1785: A0498

Whitelocke, John, 1757–1833: T2914

Whiteside, [ ]: U0060

Whitfield, Henry: L0370

Whitfield, Martha, 1697–1753: L0370

Whood, Isaac, 1689–1752: H0909, S1387, T1912, W0068, W1814

Whyniard, Robert, capt., d. 1671: A1505

Wi———, [ ]: T1948

Wiggins, Joseph: H1219

Wigham, Mabel: B0396

Wigmore, Eliza: A1418, A1433, W1008

Wigton, Jean (Drummond) Fleming, countess, d. 1658 or later: T1976

Wilcox, Jessy (1779): G0140, O0289, O0796, T1722, W2305

Wilcox, Rachel (1779): G0140, O0289, T1196, T1722, W2305

Wild, Jonathan, c. 1682–1725: A1725, Q0039, T1948

Wild, Robert, 1609–1679: M0359, N0225, W0491

Wildbore, [ ], capt.: H0723

Wilde, [ ]: W1447

Wilkes, [ ]: Y0018

Wilkinson, [ ], of Emmanuel College Cambridge: W1282

Willes, Polly: A1886

William I, king of England, 1027–1087: I0445, I1031, T0136, T1922, W0987, W2320, W2321

William III, king of England, 1650–1702: A0049, A0358, A0440, A1334, A1371, A1472, A1485, A1603, A1828, B0274, B0479, B0613, B0629, C0553, D0013, F0285, F0544, F0631, F0726, F0751, F0761, G0235, G0240, G0322, G0326, G0330, G0332, H0360, H0611, H0989, H0991, I0073, I0630, I0788, I0903, I0976, I1102, I1195, I1425, I1480, I1591, K0046, K0047, L0143, L0144, L0194, L0272, L0299, L0421, L0484, M0191, M0376, M0617, M0647, N0213, N0276, N0408, O0161, O0420, O0455, O0558, O0696, P0353, Q0033, R0202, S0008, S0194, S0961, S1005, S1059, S1199, T0161, T0179, T0516, T0563, T0564, T0598, T0651, T1040, T1124, T1525, T1680, T2028, T2158, T2408, T2414, T2423, T2775, T3204, U0075, U0156, W0043, W0188, W0210, W0312, W0383, W0406, W0584, W0610, W0785, W1213, W1332, W1363, W1452, W1491, W1597, W1620, W1852, W1856, W1893, Y0074, Y0111, Y0391

William IV, prince of Orange, 1711–1751: O0383, O0787, T1522, T2872, W1172, W1642

William of Wickham, 1324–1404: L0055

William, duke of Gloucester, 1689-1700: F0393, T1002, T2158, W0586, Y0508
Williams, [ ]: T1880, W0889
Williams, Miss [ ]: A1380, F0045
Williams, Andrew: H0850
Williams, Anthony: T0083
Williams, Dela: M0423
Williams, Diana (Berke): W1515, W1525
Williams, John, abp. of York, 1582-1650: H0983, L0441
Williams, Sally: O0559, S0041
Williamson, J., of Balliol College Oxford: F0756
Willimott, Sir Robert, lord mayor of London (1742), knighted 1744: W1608
Willis, Mrs. [ ]: A1111
Willis, Jane: S0415
Willis, John: H1098
Willis, Maria (Savage): L0433
Willis, Sir Thomas: H1098
Wills, Dr. [ ], d. 1630: H0902
Wills, Rev. [ ]: T1352
Wilmot, Miss [ ]: N0126
Wilson, Cuthbert: O0023
Wilson, Isaac, d. 1785: W1173
Wilson, Richard, 1714-1782: T1182, B0129
Wilton, [ ]: M0254
Wilton, Nicolas: G0341
Wimbleton, Mrs. [ ]: T3015
Winch, John: N0265
Windebank, Sir Francis, 1582-1646: A1741
Windham, Sir Hugh: B0055, W2631
Windham, William: T2388
Wingerworth, [ ]: I1310
Wingfield, Eliz. (Oldfield): H0327
Wingfield, John: H0327, S0899
Winnington, Edward: T3308
Winter, [ ]: T1553
Winter, John: D0362, M0713
Winter, Julie: T1553
Winton, George Seton, 3rd earl, 1584-1650: T2771
Wintour, Lady Mary: M0006, T0764
Wintour, Winifred: T0764
Winwood, Master [ ]: I1424
Winwood, Sir Ralph, 1563-1617: I1424
Wise, [ ], alderman: L0321
Withers, Henry, general, d. 1727: H0980
Withye, Richard: M0094
Wivell, Mar.: A0678
Wodehouse, Ann: A0105
Wodehouse, Blanche (Carey): G0263, T2355
Wodehouse, Edmund: I1422, T2540
Wodehouse, John: T2537
Wodehouse, Lucy: M0060, V0087
Wodehouse, Margaret: H0607
Wodehouse, Mercy: E0049, T2540
Wodehouse, Sir Philip, 1609-1681: I0775, W2087
Wodehouse, Sophia: W2343
Wodehouse, Sir Thomas: T2355
Woffington, Margaret, 1714?-1760: P0148, T0374, W2448
Wogan, Sir Charles, ca. 1698-ca. 1752: F0677
Wolcot, John ('Peter Pindar'), 1738-1819: C0082, S0601

Wolfe, James, general, 1727-1759: I0967, L0192, T3146, W1644, W2547
Wolfe, Mall: A0173, A1209, H0565, I1070
Wollaston, Charles: F0621
Wollaston, Francis, 1694-1774: A1892
Wollaston, William, 1659-1724: S1158
Wolseley, Robert, 1649-1697: D0317, O0078, S1041, T0264, W0197
Wolsey, Thomas, cardinal, 1475?-1530: B0143
Wolston, [ ]: M0352
Wom——, Miss [ ]: C0536
Wood, [ ], lieutenant general, d. 1712: H0478
Wood, Andrew: T1935
Wood, William, 1671-1730: W0946
Woodcock, Sir John, d. 1405: H1036
Woodcock, Martin, 1603-1646: A0922
Woodd, George: R0173
Wooddesson, [ ]: W1580
Woodhouse, John Chappel, b. 1749: C0119, C0120, F0771
Woods, William, 1749-1802: A1424
Woodward, Miss [ ]: S1385
Woodward, Henry, 1714-1777: D0008, E0170, O0322, W0721
Woodward, Sir Rowland, 1573-1637: L0377
Woogan, [ ], colonel: W1347
Woollet, William, engraver: T1182
Woolsey, [ ], cardinal: H1453
Woolstone, [ ]: W1464
Wotton, Sir Henry, 1568-1639: K0013, S0704
Wotton, Sir Thomas: L0087
Wray, William: H0903
Wraye, [ ]: W2626
Wren, Sir Christopher, 1632-1723: L0457, T2876
Wren, Sir Thomas: A1360
Wrench, Deborah (1725): U0060
Wrey, Mrs. [ ] (Thresher): S0232
Wrey, Charles: W1046
Wrey, Sir Bourchier, 1715?-1784: S0232
Wrey, Sir William: W1046
Wright, [ ]: B0157
Wright, [ ], capt.: I0862
Wright, [ ], writingmaster: E0045
Wright, Mrs. [ ]: F0324
Wright, John, d. 1721: N0158, U0048
Wright, John, hymnwriter: R0055
Wroth, Lady Mary, 1587?-1651?: H1012
Wyvill, Ursula (Darcy), lady, 1619-1672?: W1168

Y——, Mrs. [ ]: A0814
Yallop, Dorothea: H0585
Yarborough, Mrs. [ ]: S0980
Yarmouth, Amelia Sophia de Walmoden (von Wendt), countess, 1704-1765: O1102, S0341
Yartie, [ ]: A1892
Yates, Mary Ann, actress (1776): D0329
Yerrow, Thomas: B0168
Yonge, Sir William, 1693?-1755: D0066
York, Anne (Hyde), duchess, 1637-1671: A1784, K0016
York, Edward, duke, 1373?-1415: W2408
York, John: I1603
Yorke, Joseph: W1284

Young, [ ]: W1482
Young, Miss [ ]: A0793
Young, Edward, 1683–1765: I0848, L0672, T1130, W0044
Young, Eliza: M0436
Young, John: O0871, Y0380

Young, Talbot: O0871, Y0380
Young, Thomas: T0904
Young, William: M0344

Z., C.: T1829
Zamparini, [ ], actress (1768): F0110

IV. Index of Authors of Works Translated, Paraphrased, or Imitated

Abu Nowas: T3323
Addison, Joseph, 1672–1719: O0934, T1052
Æsop, Fable 6: T0946
    Fable 7: A1385, T1040
    Fable 23: T0901
    See also A0371, A0430, A0442, I0975, I0976
Akenside, Mark, 1721–1770, 'Pleasures of the
    imagination': A0858
Alabaster, William, 1567–1640: I1182
Amalteo, Giovanni Battista, 1525?–1573, 'Lumine Acon
    dextro . . .': O0771
Amalteo, Girolamo, 1507–1574, 'De gemellis . . .':
    A0627
Amyas, Thomas: T1691
Anacreon, Ode 1: I0410
    Ode 2: N0031
    Ode 3: A1563, A1787, I1577
    Ode 8: A1462
    Ode 9: L0681, P0292
    Ode 10: H0196
    Ode 11: T0632
    Ode 13: I0743
    Ode 16: C0070
    Ode 25: A0960
    Ode 30: C0580
    Ode 36: H0148
    Ode 39: T2474
    Ode 40: L0407
    Ode 59: T0824
    See also A1463, A1722, B0083, C0338, C0524, Q0015,
        S0581, T0247, T1571, W1888
Apostle's creed: I1091, I1092
Aratus: B0076
Arbuthnot, John, 1667–1734: P0355
Ariosto, Satire 5: I0285
Aripheon: D0102
Aristotle, Nichomachian ethics IV.3: H0485
Arrianus, Flavius: N0289
Augustine, St., Confessions I.2: G0204
    Epistle 52: L0636
Ausonius, Decimus Magnus, Epigram 78: H0588
    See also W0143, W1841
Avienus: A0371

Bacchylides: I0543, P0075, P0169
Behn, Aphra, 1640–1685: N0019
Bentley, Richard, 1662–1742: W0586
Betterton, Thomas, 1635?–1710, 'The prophetess':
    L0274
Bembo, Pietro, 1470–1547: W1792

Beys, Charles, 1610–1659, 'Le jovissance imparfaite':
    A0668
Bible, Genesis: A1210, C0160, I1528, M0539
    Exodus: A1017, A1883, H1017, M0339, M0566, O0443,
        O1016, T1572, T1575, T2108, T2486, W1096, W2421
    Leviticus: L0225
    Numbers: W1659
    Joshua: C0550
    Judges: S0997, T1560
    Ruth: W0622
    1 Samuel: A0818, H0186, O0898, O0931, T0336, Y0109
    2 Samuel: T1925, T2485, W1533
    1 Kings: O0823, T1471, W2050
    1 Chronicles: T0864
    Judith: T1567
    Job: B0193, B0425, C0052, E0135, H0306, I0470, J0082,
        L0270, O0131, T2403, T2406, T2854, T2883, U0006,
        V0010, W0244, W0561, W2144
    Psalm 1: B0406, H0233, H0442, T0881, T0888, W0635
    Psalm 2: I0377, W2146
    Psalm 3: A0731, W0675
    Psalm 3–4: O0350
    Psalm 4: C0391, H0519, O0481, O0597
    Psalm 4, 12, 37, 73, 94, 97: B0404
    Psalm 5: I1383, O0506
    Psalm 6: H0509, L0577, O0483
    Psalm 6–7: L0580
    Psalm 7: G0229, O1088
    Psalm 8: E0126, G0399, O0451, O0490
    Psalm 9: S0670, W2447
    Psalm 9, 11: H0343
    Psalm 10: W2260
    Psalm 11: I1094
    Psalm 12: S0058
    Psalm 13: H1339, Y0150
    Psalm 13, 16: H1338
    Psalm 14: T0586
    Psalm 15: W0506, W1989
    Psalm 16: L0590, W1598
    Psalm 17: O0476, T2096
    Psalm 18: O0342, T1536
    Psalm 19: O0327, T0728, T0729
    Psalm 20: H0496, I0981, T2299
    Psalm 21: T0780
    Psalm 22: M0546, O0338, T0039
    Psalm 23: G0230, T0647, T0839, T0849, T0851, T0852,
        T0854
    Psalm 24: F0119, T0503
    Psalm 25: H0236, I0232, I0319
    Psalm 26: T3075
    Psalm 26–28: L0554

Psalm 27: T0856, T2433, W0252

Psalm 28: O0486

Psalm 29: A1318, B0516, T1104, T1264, Y0116

Psalm 30: T1547, W2122

Psalm 30–31: A0930

Psalm 31: I1274, M0556, O0479, O1135

Psalm 32: B0378, H1288, T0890, T1108

Psalm 33: Y0151

Psalm 34: I0439, I1005, T1545, T3066

Psalm 35: L0592, P0155

Psalm 36: W2508

Psalm 36–37: G0480

Psalm 37: G0303, M0685, M0691, V0045

Psalm 38: O0491, P0361

Psalm 39: H1335, W2507

Psalm 39–40: I0416

Psalm 40: I1069

Psalm 41: B0377

Psalm 41–43: J0122

Psalm 42: A1649, A1656, A1660, C0138, L0366, O0621, W2178

Psalm 43: M0606

Psalm 44: O0349

Psalm 45: M0572

Psalm 46: B0067, G0218, O0894, O0895

Psalm 46, 51: T0850

Psalm 47: Y0138

Psalm 48: G0219, G0483

Psalm 49: L0404, O0399

Psalm 50: F0708, T0844, T0860

Psalm 51: B0128, G0405, H0344, S0486

Psalm 52: W2127

Psalm 53: T0589

Psalm 54: L0556

Psalm 54–55: G0244

Psalm 55: O0489, S1245

Psalm 56: H0342, L0578

Psalm 57: G0420, T2531

Psalm 58: Y0081

Psalm 59: M0538, T2436

Psalm 60: O0504

Psalm 60–62: O0498

Psalm 61: L0584, O0508, R0094

Psalm 62: T3245

Psalm 63: O0345, O0352

Psalm 63–66: O0336

Psalm 64: L0613

Psalm 65: N0258, W1987

Psalm 66: L0500, O0214, T0644

Psalm 67: E0134, I1178

Psalm 67–68: H0345

Psalm 68: G0066, L0579

Psalm 69: S0059, S0060

Psalm 70: H0326

Psalm 70–71: O0355

Psalm 71: O0482

Psalm 72: A0606, T2558

Psalm 72–73: H1476

Psalm 73: T2183, T2294, Y0236

Psalm 74: W2279

Psalm 75: T3068, U0116, W2422

Psalm 76: A0607, I1123, I1124

Psalm 77: I0444, I0458, M0728

Psalm 78: G0073, M0655

Psalm 79: O0351, O0496, O0497, T0722

Psalm 80: G0075, S0446

Psalm 80, 83: T2044

Psalm 81: T2886, T2887

Psalm 82: G0212, T0857

Psalm 83: K0009, O0343

Psalm 84: H1341, O0488

Psalm 85: L0603, O0348

Psalm 86: J0018, O0505

Psalm 87: A1071, F0521

Psalm 88: H0543, J0020, L0562

Psalm 89: J0031, L0585, T2528

Psalm 90: G0439, J0029, L0598, O0475, T2065, T2521

Psalm 91: H0373, H0428, H0457, I0767

Psalm 92: G0453, H1319, T2642, T2643

Psalm 93: J0024, J0027

Psalm 94: O0334, O0356

Psalm 95: C0437, O0250, O0251, O0252

Psalm 96: L0246, O0754, S0669

Psalm 96–97: S0673

Psalm 97: I1540, J0025, T0855, W0359

Psalm 98: S0667, S0668

Psalm 99: A1316, J0028, T0842

Psalm 100: H1498, O0212, O0213, R0201, T2443, U0114

Psalm 101: I0206, I0877, O0115

Psalm 102: F0723, H0502, J0021, O0398, O0658

Psalm 103: L0605, M0686, M0695, M0697, M0698, M0700, O0230

Psalm 104: A1927, B0131, G0116, L0345, M0662, M0682, M0690, O0172

Psalm 105: O0324, W2476

Psalm 105–106: G0106

Psalm 106: F0614, O0588, P0252

Psalm 107: M0335, O0596

Psalm 107–109: G0109

Psalm 108: O0340

Psalm 109: L0583

Psalm 110: T0146, T0859

Psalm 111: A1010

Psalm 111–113: W2416

Psalm 112: H0234, T0889

Psalm 113: Y0158

Psalm 114: W1099, W1101

Psalm 115: N0367, N0368

Psalm 116: G0452, I0252, W1587

Psalm 116–117: I0251

Psalm 117: L0148, O0215

Psalm 118: O0325, O0645

Psalm 119: B0370, B0375, I1135, W1752

Psalm 120: W1083, W1086

Psalm 120–121, 123–125: O0495

Psalm 121: T3004, T3005

Psalm 122: O0758, W0483, W0484

Psalm 123: O0480

Psalm 124: H0024, H0025

Psalm 125: S1197

Psalm 126: W0963, W1299

Psalm 127: E0167, E0168

Bible (*continued*)

Psalm 128: O0231

Psalm 128-130, 134: B0373

Psalm 129: F0783

Psalm 130: B0551, F0676

Psalm 131: L0571, L0602, O0485

Psalm 132: O0492

Psalm 133: H1377

Psalm 134: S0280

Psalm 135: O0589, Y0159

Psalm 136: G0108, W0011

Psalm 137: A1370, A1588, A1693, A1695, B0610, F0122,
  S0279, W1154, W1583

Psalm 138: T1548, W2446

Psalm 139: G0427, O0279, O0499, O0500, O0501, O0502,
  T2043

Psalm 140: T2060

Psalm 140-143: L0593

Psalm 141: O0510

Psalm 142: W2431

Psalm 143: H0518, V0083

Psalm 144: M0687, O0232

Psalm 145: T1544, T1546

Psalm 146: I1176, M0696, M0704, P0246, P0247

Psalm 147: O0587, P0253

Psalm 148: G0078, H0181, T3033, Y0292

Psalm 149: O0591, P0256

Psalm 149-150: S0672

Psalm 150: P0245, P0255

Proverbs: H0470, H0474, H1257, I0321, L0216, M0679,
  N0459, O0273, T1255, T2410, T3386

Ecclesiastes: L0458, M0678

Song of Solomon: A1312, D0108, M0387, O0447, O0748

Ecclesiasticus: N0205

Isaiah: A1059, B0167, B0213, H0260, H0514, H1303,
  J0030, J0082, M0143, N0430, S0671, T0841, T0963,
  T1566, T3030, T3227, W0561, W0621, W1051, W2069

Jeremiah: B0176, G0431, H1408

Lamentations: H1228

Ezekial: G0450, H1261, T3222

Daniel: I1567, T2359

Hosea: T0845

Amos: S0676, Y0233

Jonah: J0110

Micah: M0311, W2545

Habakkuk: A1038, T2466, W1371

Zephaniah: Y0249

Zechariah: H0063, P0314, S1015

Malachi: T3070

Matthew: A0830, A1321, B0372, B0379, C0461, F0209,
  H1254, I0466, I1486, J0047, J0123, L0249, S0223,
  S0886, T0026, T0387, T0840, T1407, T2569, U0135,
  W0175, W0399, W1107, W1108, W1166

Mark: A1915, J0069, W2049, W2207

Luke: A0613, A1013, A1015, A1018, A1185, B0034, B0369,
  D0265, D0336, F0204, H0285, H0367, H1047, I1146,
  L0611, N0518, O0259, O0530, T0134, T1578, T2609,
  T2632, T2677, T2926, Y0246

John, st.: A1458, C0196, C0199, I1186, L0502, M0590,
  S1026, T0698

Acts: D0234, S0123, Z0007

Romans: A1242, C0368, O0655, W0419

1 Corinthians: D0306, G0458, H0016, N0321, T2382

Ephesians: D0060

Colossians: H0156

1 Thessalonians: T3213

1 Timothy: O0826

Hebrews: E0124

Hebrews: F0211, O0347, S0347, S0796, T0909, W0088,
  W0986

James: A0433, B0182, T3163

1 Peter: H1388, J0057, W2392

1 John: A1030, T0415, W2398

Revelation: B0177, H0293, O0442, S0260, T0719, T1915

1 Esdras: W1507

2 Esdras: B0174, W2021

Bion: A0576, I0414, N0151

Blake, Sir Richard, d. 1663: W0687

Boccaccio, Giovanni, 1313-1375: H1353, I0647, I1076,
  I1334, O0048, O0058, T2240, T2940, W0226, W1606

Boileau-Despréaux, Nicolas, 1636-1711, Lutrin: G0307

Satire 7: F0467

Satire 9: D0184

See also A0865, A0970, A1843, B0046, F0617, H1138,
  I0191, I1083, I1338, L0462, N0167, S0619, T1985,
  T2078, W0523, W1816

Bonnefons, Joannes, 1554-1614, Basium 11: M0417

Basium 23: T1023

Botarelli, Giovan Gualberto: C0349, F0330, L0620,
  T0546, Y0032

Bourn, [ ]: T2921

Boyd, Zacharie, 1585-1653: A1208, G0299, P0106

Brower, T.: T1520

Broxholme, Noel, 1689?-1748: S0917

Buchanan, George, 1506-1582: 'In rusticum . . .':
  A0079

Elegies 1.9: U0059

See also R0010, T2299

Buckingham and Normanby, John Sheffield, 1st duke,
  1648-1721: O0181

Bürger, Gottfried Augustus, 1748-1794: E0032, F0753

Burns, Robert, 1759-1796, 'Robin Adair': Y0595

Burton, Robert, 1577-1640, 'Abstract upon
  melancholy': M0304

Butler, Samuel, 1612-1680, 'Hudibras': M0359, W1012

Callimachus, Epigram 5: V0086, I0196

Callistratus: A0322

Carew, Thomas, 1595-1639, 'Ask me no more . . .':
  A1746, A1747

Carphyllides: M0722, O0633

Cartwright, William, 1611-1643, 'On the great frost.
  1634': W1563

Catullus, 'Ad Lesbiam': C0266

'Ineptus risus . . .': T3159

Carmen nupt. 63: A1616

Ode 29: S1363

See also C0572, I0712, I1465, R0205, W1888, W2304

Chaucer, Geoffrey, 1343-1400, 'House of fame': T1030

'Prologue to the Canterbury tales': A0070, A0343, N0114

'Reeve's tale': A1871

See also A0544, F0121, F0346, F0778, F0784, R0195

Chaulieu, Guillaume Amfrye de, 1639–1720: O0578, W2566

Chesterfield, Philip Dormer Stanhope, 4th earl, 1694–1773: C0210

Chrysippus: W2013

Claudius Claudianus: B0212, B0402, M0070

Cleanthes: O0761

Congreve, William, 1670–1729, 'The mourning bride': M0401, M0402

Cornelius Gallus: A1848, M0557

Corsi, Gioseffo: A1621

Cowley, Abraham, 1618–1667: W1909

Cowper, William, 1731–1800, 'John Gilpin': G0236

Crashaw, Richard, 1613–1650, 'I sing the name . . .': A1929

Cunningham, John, 1729–1773: N0511

Dante Alighieri, 1265–1321, Inferno, Canto 1: I1259
    Inferno, Canto 3: T2438

De Cressy, Robert (1297): W0878

Della Casa, Giovanni, 1503–1556: L0532

Deloney, Thomas, 1543?–1600, 'Garland of good will': A1736

Denham, Sir John, 1615–1669, 'Cooper's hill': F0331

Deshoulières, Antoinette, 1638–1694: T3231

Despériers, Bonaventure, 1500?–1544: H1162

Dies irae: T0456

Donne, John, 1573–1631, Satire 3: C0457

Dorrington, Theophilus, d. 1715: A1912

Dorset, Charles Sackville, 6th earl, and 1st earl of Middlesex, 1638–1706: W1098, W0918, W1013

Doxology: T2864

Dryden, John, 1631–1700, 'Alexander's feast': T3309
    'Aurung-Zebe': W1037
    'Three poets in three different ages . . .': I1266, T2375, T2380
    See also H1013

Du Bartas, Guillaume de Salluste, seigneur, 1544–1590, 'Weeks and works': A0706, A1144, A1354, B0585, C0226, C0484, E0057, I1072, I1196, I1513, L0282, M0244, O0546, R0236, S0017, T0509, T0510, T1184, T1195, T1497, T1686, T2102, W1612, W2107, W2419, Y0404

Eubolus: T2373

Eupolis: A1899, S0892

Euripides, 'Hippolytus': O0450

Farnaby, [ ]: H0197

Fénelon, François de Salignac de la Mothe-, 1651–1715, Les aventures de Télémaque, book i: T1121

Flaminius: A0540, C0177, C0451, H0316, U0078, U0079, W2058, Y0591, Y0592

Fontanelle, Bernard le Bovier de, 1657–1757: P0211

Frascatoro, Girolamo, 1483–1553: T1408

Frederick Louis, prince of Wales, 1701–1751: C0400

Galen, De alimentorum facultatibus: H0111

Gay, John, 1685–1732: A1257

Gibbon, John, 1629–1718: R0018

Glover, Richard, 1712–1785, 'Admiral Hosier's ghost': A1550

Goudelin, Pierre, 1550–1619: W1859, W1729

Gower, John, 1325–1428: I1191

Gray, Thomas, 1716–1771, 'Elegy in a country churchyard': H0938, S0035, T1394
    'Ode on a distant prospect of Eton College': Y0176
    Latin ode at the Grande Chartreuse: O0318, O0737, T1530

Greek anthologia, Book 7: H0544, A0127

Greek epigrams: I0423, M0536, T1741

Greek idyllium: B0508

Grotius, Hugo, 1583–1645: N0039

Guarini, Giovanni Battista, 1537–1612, 'Pastor Fido': M0721
    I.i: N0469
    I.iv: A1490
    II.v: A0737

Guion, Jeanne Marie Bouvier de la Motte, 1648–1717, 'Spiritual songs': A0778, A0871, B0413, F0744, H1278, I0021, I0299, I1352, J0016, L0639, L0657, M0005, M0573, M0708, O0514, O0516, O0686, P0066, S0580, S1013, T1676, T2041, T2635, T2918, T3295, Y0095

Hadrian, 'Animula vagula blandula . . .': P0211, T2092

Hafia, 1325?–1389?: S1324

Hale, Sir Matthew, 1609–1676, 'On Christmas day': T0319, W2019

Hall, Joseph, bishop, 1574–1656: E0046, S0724

Hedges, John: S0331

Heinsius, Daniel, 1580–1655: W1791

Henault, Sieur D.: O0740, T2139

Henry of Avranches, fl. 1232: I0755

Hesiod: U0080

Homer, Iliad: N0406, S0853
    Odyssey: O0454, W1454
    See also N0477

Horace, Ars poetica: W0454
    V.43: H0068
    Epistle 1.1: O0815
    Epistle 1.2: L0714, T1376
    Epistle 1.3: S0659
    Epistle 1.4: P0035, T1967
    Epistle 1.5: S0735
    Epistle 1.7: H0296
    Epistle 1.10: H0489, W1898
    Epistle 1.11: S1119
    Epistle 1.16: I1293
    Epode 1: O0920, W1397
    Epode 2: B0383
    Epode 3: I0507, W2075
    Epode 4: A1640, A1731
    Epode 5: B0607
    Epode 6: S0077
    Epode 7: W1923, W1926
    Epode 8: A1182
    Epode 9: W1288
    Epode 10: L0461, S1261
    Epode 11: V0033
    Epode 12: O0299
    Epode 13: T0125
    Epode 14: K0017
    Epode 15: T3297

Horace, Ars poetica: (*continued*)

    Epode 16: A1263, F0089

    Epode 17: I0296, W2269

    Ode 1.1: B0449, M0049, M0050, M0051

    Ode 1.2: T3188

    Ode 1.3: D0158, F0046, S0826

    Ode 1.4: C0469, F0710, L0453, W2340

    Ode 1.5: F0462, O0880, W1217

    Ode 1.6: I0408, L0296

    Ode 1.7: F0716, L0227

    Ode 1.8: L0685, S0040, T0089

    Ode 1.9: S0229

    Ode 1.10: M0234

    Ode 1.11: F0470, N0094

    Ode 1.12: W2093

    Ode 1.13: T2401, W1379

    Ode 1.14: M0528, Y0254

    Ode 1.15: W1353

    Ode 1.16: F0071

    Ode 1.17: L0352

    Ode 1.18: V0024

    Ode 1.19: A0693, B0001, B0173, L0668

    Ode 1.20: P0149, P0225

    Ode 1.21: T0141

    Ode 1.22: A1149, A1329, T0885, T0911, V0066, V0067, W1963

    Ode 1.23: L0382, W2295

    Ode 1.24: W2246

    Ode 1.25: Y0556

    Ode 1.26: T3017, W2482

    Ode 1.27: T2349

    Ode 1.28: B0190, S0072

    Ode 1.29: E0092

    Ode 1.30: O0765, Q0006, S0312

    Ode 1.31: W0342, W0394, W0553

    Ode 1.32: I0814

    Ode 1.33: G0475

    Ode 1.34: B0674

    Ode 1.35: F0249

    Ode 1.36: H1107

    Ode 1.37: D0416

    Ode 1.38: T1056

    Ode 2.1: C0219

    Ode 2.2: H1039, N0235

    Ode 2.3: B0025, M0330, M0529, R0119

    Ode 2.4: A0766, A0828, A0843, C0547, D0350, N0059

    Ode 2.5: A1735

    Ode 2.6: D0156

    Ode 2.7: D0143, Y0428

    Ode 2.8: I0758

    Ode 2.9: L0267

    Ode 2.10: I0659, L0319, T2688

    Ode 2.11: B0539, C0090, L0269, W0482

    Ode 2.12: B0343

    Ode 2.13: F0194

    Ode 2.14: A0827, F0353, T0581, T0582

    Ode 2.15: S1057

    Ode 2.16: A0241, F0385, F0392, F0426, I1045, I1226, I1395, W0772, W1269

    Ode 2.17: S1014

    Ode 2.18: F0409, W2452

    Ode 2.19: T2669

    Ode 2.20: B0458, O0911

    Ode 3.1: H0568, H0569

    Ode 3.2: F0566, H0482, L0293, T2806, W2054

    Ode 3.3: H0471, N0332, O0991, T0899

    Ode 3.4: F0738, T0434

    Ode 3.5: W1081

    Ode 3.6: B0523, F0722, T1974

    Ode 3.7: D0134, W2289

    Ode 3.8: W0450

    Ode 3.9: A0763, H1151, H1181, W1789, W1830, W1831, W1843

    Ode 3.10: S1221, T2235

    Ode 3.11: T2154

    Ode 3.12: H1470

    Ode 3.13: C0231

    Ode 3.14: O1102, S0278

    Ode 3.15: T2150

    Ode 3.16: S0492

    Ode 3.17: A0867

    Ode 3.18: F0218

    Ode 3.19: A1601

    Ode 3.20: W0697

    Ode 3.21: J0015

    Ode 3.22: T3225

    Ode 3.23: I0679, I0685

    Ode 3.24: T2332

    Ode 3.25: W1920

    Ode 3.26: O0961, T2602, W1303

    Ode 3.27: A1639, L0277

    Ode 3.28: S0635

    Ode 3.29: C0005, F0512, M0047, S0964, S1039

    Ode 3.30: A0313

    Ode 4.1: A0691, A1809

    Ode 4.2: W2051

    Ode 4.3: T0908, T1524

    Ode 4.4: A1645, A1664

    Ode 4.5: B0455, W1267

    Ode 4.6: G0253

    Ode 4.7: T1011, T1242, T1243, T1244, T1245, T1246, T1247, T1248, T1249

    Ode 4.8: I0474

    Ode 4.9: T2611, V0034

    Ode 4.10: O0313

    Ode 4.11: I1594

    Ode 4.14: W0424

    Ode 4.15: R0142

    Satire 1.1: F0755, I0123, P0055, W0846

    Satire 1.2: B0023, T0079

    Satire 1.3: F0250

    Satire 1.4: P0181

    Satire 1.5: I0122

    Satire 1.6: T2222

    Satire 1.7: T1673

    Satire 1.8: O0968

    Satire 1.9: W0017

    Satire 1.10: W0238, W0261

    Satire 2.1: T1581, T1583

    Satire 2.2: W0324, W0325

    Satire 2.3: W2277

    Satire 2.4: W1506

Satire 2.5: O1024
Satire 2.6: A1856
Satire 2.6: T3313
Satire 2.7: S0692
Satire 2.8: T0077
Satires: W1407
Secular poem: G0421
To his boy: P0315
See also A0385, A1186, C0175, C0455, F0704, F0711,
    H0424, P0138, S0999, S1375, T2193, T2716, W1076,
    W1178, W1670
House that Jack built, The: T1849
Hudfield, [ ]: M0636

James I, king of England, 1566-1621: N0460, T2284
Jerningham, Edward, 1737?-1812, 'Magdalen and Nun':
    T1869
John of Milan, Regimen sanitatis salernitanum: A0948,
    T1950
Jonson, Ben, 1573?-1637, 'Bartholomew fair': M0630
Jortin, John, 1698-1770, Lusus poetici: O0661
Juvenal, Satire 1: M0413, S0362
    Satire 3: T2217
    Satires 6, 9: S0749
    Satire 9: B0573, S1237
    Satire 10: L0547
    Satire 12: T3248
    Satires: R0079

Kethe, William, d. 1608?: A0945

La Fontaine, Jean de, 1621-1695: A0056, A0335, A0872,
    A1125, A1127, A1155, A1391, A1572, D0004, D0005, F0052,
    G0390, H0098, H0187, H0623, H1200, H1430, I1059,
    I1095, I1357, I1431, M0317, N0089, N0218, O0428, O0816,
    O0993, P0033, P0207, S0894, S1265, S1278, T0116, T0118,
    T0810, T2797, T2841, W1540, W1914, W2311, W2377,
    W2437, W2536
Leibniz, Gottfried Wilhelm, 1646-1716: M0138
Livy, Ab urbe condita, books 21-22: H0631
Lowth, Robert, bishop of London, 1710-1787: H1303,
    J0030, T2138, W1051
Lucan, Pharsalia, book 9: H0530, S1224, W0615
    See also S0327
Lucian: W1514
Lucretius, De rerum natura, book 2: T2714
    See also O0438

Macpherson, James, 1736-1796, 'Fingal': Y0166
Malherbe, François de, 1555-1628: C0105, C0108, F0066,
    G0382, T0253, U0119, W1234
Mallet, David, 1705?-1765, 'William and Margaret':
    T3269
Mallevile, Claude de, 1597-1647: T0470
Manilius: A1184
Mantuanus, Baptista, 1447-1516, Eclogue 3: A0001
Marcus Pacuvius: T2202
Marlowe, Christopher, 1564-1593: C0378
Marot, Clément, 1496-1544: A1533
Martial, 'In pessimos conjugas . . .': S0657
    'Pauper videm . . .': B0354

'To Galla': W1075
Epigrams: C0002, T2523
Epigram 1.4: A1529, W0265
Epigram 1.13: W0775
Epigram 1.40: L0425, L0426
Epigram 1.56: S0590
Epigram 2.4: W2595
Epigram 2.90: W2561
Epigram 4.29: S0563
Epigram 4.77: M0658
Epigram 5.59: T3166
Epigram 5.102: Y0296
Epigram 7.32: W2439
Epigram 8.95: I0973
Epigram 10.47: S0545, S0546, S0548, T1365, T2390,
    W2218
Epigram 10.96: M0208
Epigram 12.12: P0049
Epigram 12.64: T2828
See also C0107, C0216, H1129, I0547, I0583, I0614, L0128,
    S0705, W1548, W1821, W1833
Mary, queen of Scots, 1542-1587: B0600, B0601, O0693
Masters, [ ], of New College, Oxford: E0083
Medici, Lorenzo de, 1449-1492: A0772, A0831, A1435,
    N0331, S0309
Mesihi, 1470-1512: H0504
Metastasio, Pietro, 1698-1782: D0274, F0044, H1294,
    I0522, O0432, P0116, R0132, R0232, S1344, T0628, T1229,
    T1237, T1369, T1509, T2167, T2357, W0814, W2573,
    W2600, Y0027, Y0032, Y0055, Y0136, Y0195
Metredorus: M0102
Milton, John, 1608-1674, 'Ad patrem': R0093
    'L'allegro', 'Il penseroso': L0446
    'L'allegro': H0561
    'Epitaphium Damonis': U0076
    'On his blindness': W2354
    'Paradise lost': B0252
    'Lycidas': Y0259
    See also A1014, H0229, O0732, T0068, W2626
Mirepoix, [ ], maréchale: B0204, T1831
Molière (Jean-Baptiste Poquelin), 1622-1673: B0064
More, Sir Thomas, 1478-1535: F0283, H0893, L0398,
    T3126
Musaeus, Grammaticus: S0665, T0365

Neville, Henry, 1620-1694: A1428
Nicolas, Armelle, 1606-1671: T3037
Nivernais, Louis-Jules Mancini-Mazarini, duc de,
    1716-1798: O0639, O0939

Ovid, Amores 2.9: O0512
    Amores 3.11: I0182
    Ars amatoria: N0131
    Heroides: R0034
    Metamorphoses, book 1: T2412
    Metamorphoses, book 3: T1422
    Metamorphoses, book 4: F0382, T0874
    Metamorphoses, book 8: A0492, I0997
    Metamorphoses, book 10: F0619, H1053, H1438, P0338,
        S0812
    Metamorphoses, book 13: S0051

Ovid (*continued*)
    Pontus 1.4: T2603
    See also F0248, S1310, T1030, W1053
Owen, John, 1560-1622: F0197, H0376, I0447, I0771,
    M0570, M0571, O1044, O1134, P0188, T0674, T0861,
    W0462, W2095

Parnell, Thomas, 1679-1718, Hermit: U0092
Pathelin, Pierre (c. 1465): F0278
Persius, Satire 1: I0279
See also W0626
Petrarca, Francesco, 1304-1374: A1319, D0205, D0223,
    E0159, F0562, I0048, I1288, L0335, N0339, N0486, O0376,
    O0580, S1268, W0004, W0548, W0847, W1138, W1367,
    W2564, Y0191
Petronius Afranius: W1916
Petronius Arbiter, Satyricon: T1587, W0488
Phaedrus: A0371, A1488
Philips, Ambrose, 1675-1749: L0408, L0417, M0422,
    U0001
Pibrac, Guy du Faur, seigneur de, 1529-1584: T2147
Pindar: A0640, B0597, C0598, E0017, E0130, G0014, G0128,
    H1027, H1440, I0901, I0948, L0120, L0272, R0238
Pitcairne, Alexander, 1652-1713: F0176, O0456, S1181
Plato: F0445, T0042
Pliny the elder, Natural history, book 10: A1530
Poliziano, Angelo, 1454-1494, 'Ambra': G0163, W1960,
    W2130
Pope, Alexander, 1688-1744, 'Epitaph intended for Sir
    Isaac Newton': K0069, N0109
    'Ode on St. Cecilia's day': D0273, T2903
    'Solitude: an ode': T1050
    See also B0407, H0936, H1105, I0721, W0780
Pope, Walter, 1630-1714, 'The old man's wish': S0570
Posedipus: W0672
Prior, Matthew, 1664-1721, 'Alma': A1678
    'Epitaph on himself': J0104
    'Erle Robert's mice': F0778
    'Who has e'er been at Paris . . .': W1966
    See also D0069, D0122, I1030, W1914
Propertius, Sexti Propertiae elegiae, Book 1.6: T2687
Prudentius: F0212, G0287, J0068, J0140
Pythagoras, Golden verses: B0066, F0296, M0061

Quarles, Francis, 1592-1644, 'Our life's a journey . . .':
    O1109

Racine, Jean, 1639-1699, Esther: W0184
    Esther, Act IV: D0417
Raleigh, Sir Walter, 1552?-1618: W1751
Randolph, Thomas, 1605-1635, 'On importunate
    duns': I1185
Rochester, John Wilmot, 2nd earl, 1647-1680, 'On
    nothing': S0507
Rousseau, Jean Jacques, 1712-1778, Ode 15: A1635,
    W2226
Rudel, Jaufre, before 1125-1148: S0007, T0520

Saint-Evremond (Charles de Saint-Denis), 1613-1703:
    F0673, I0545, I1341, L0553, O0944
Sappho: C0596, H0140, W1355

Sarbiewski, Mathias Casimir, 1595-1649, Ode 2:
    A1949
Saul, [ ], A. M.: F0105
Saumazarius: B0497
Scroope, Sir Carr, 1649-1680, 'Sappho and Phaeon':
    W1854
Seneca, Cleanthes: F0201
    Ep. 101: S0779
    Hippolytus, Act 3: B0624
    Oedipus: F0200
    Serenus: S0323
    Thyestes, Act 2: L0162, L0163, L0240, U0141
    Thyestes, Act 3: W0246
    Troas, Act 2: A0670
    See also A0936, L0283, O0839, T0487, T1220
Shakespeare, William, 1564-1616, 'As you like it':
    T1491
    'Hamlet': T2840, T2906, T2976, T3107
    'Macbeth': I0301
    'Othello': I0307
    'Romeo and Juliet': I0113
    See also A0966, A1858, C0270, F0182, H1331, N0253,
    S1022
Shenstone, William, 1714-1763, 'Poet and dun': I1261
    'Shepherd, wouldst thou here . . .': P0354
    'Ye shepherds so cheerful . . .': M0425
    See also C0247
Sheridan, Richard Brinsley Butler, 1751-1816,
    'Semiramis': W2423
Sidaine, [ ], Epistle: T0163
Silius Italicus, Punica, book XV: B0255
Simonde, Charles: W2412
Simonides: H0057, I1356, N0377, W1195
Smedley, Jonathan, 1671-1729: T1414
Spenser, Edmund, 1552?-1599: A1394, A1716, B0211,
    R0195
St. Albans, Francis Bacon, viscount, 1561-1626: B0144,
    T1496, W0453
Sterne, Laurence, 1713-1768, 'Sentimental journey':
    D0155
Sternhold, Thomas, d. 1549, 23: T0854
Strada, Famiano, 1572-1649: N0489, N0506, T1446
Suckling, Sir John, 1609-1642, 'I'll tell thee, Dick . . .':
    I0885, L0027
Suetonius: A0664
Swift, Jonathan, 1667-1745, 'Mordanto': G0394
    See also L0487, T2999, W1933, Y0401
Synesius, Hymn 1: T2846

Tacitus, De vita agricola: T0601
Tansillo, Luigi, 1510-1568: A0623
Tarfat Jo'n al Abad: M0218
Tasso, Torquato, 1544-1595, 'Jerusalem delivered':
    T0530, L0559, S0226
Te deum: P0025, T1532, T3071
Teresa, saint, 1515-1582: S0163
Theocritus, Idyllium 1: T2442
    Idyllium 19: C0585, C0588
    Idyllium 23: W1304
    See also A1877, B0134, W1422
Thomson, James, 1700-1748: O0694

Tibullus, Elegy 1: L0222
    Elegy 3.2: H0473
    See also L0218
Tremellius, Immanuel, 1510–1580: H1408

Upton, James, 1670–1749: T0773
Ursinus Velius: U0090

Veni Creator Spiritus: C0344, C0345, C0346, C0347, C0562
'Vicar of Bray, The': I1018
Vincenzio da Filicaia, 1642–1707: B0211
Virgil, Æneid: S1087
    Æneid, book 4: B0602, N0122
    Æneid, book 6: T1712
    Eclogue 3: A1848
    Eclogue 4: Y0133
    Eclogue 6: I0134
    Eclogue 8: A1320
    Eclogue 10.69: N0310
    Georgic 1: D0394, W0689
    Georgic 2: O0382, O0388
    Georgic 4: F0452, S0494
    See also B0276, C0394, H1106, T1837, T3265, W2636

Voiture, Vincent, 1597–1648, 'Sonnet to Urania': H1148
    See also B0089, F0012, F0022, L0041, Y0329
Voltaire (François-Marie Arouet), 1694–1778,
    Adelaide, Act 2: I1442
    Alzira, III.4: I1458
    Maid of Orleans, Canto 1: B0257
    See also G0017, I1181, M0260, T0051, T0159, T0311,
        T2072, T2708, W0072, Y0244

Waller, Edmund, 1606–1687, 'Directions to a painter': N0061
    See also I1046, S0790, W2567
Waring, Robert, of Christ Church, Oxford: P0180
Whitehead, William, 1715–1785, 'Ode to the New Year 1774': P0040
Wieland, Christophe Martin, 1733–1813, 'Oberon': A1055, C0034
Wilcox, Thomas, 1622–1687, 'Guide to eternal glory': B0584
Wild, Robert, 1609–1679: H0704
Wotton, Sir Henry, 1568–1639: F0454

Xenophon: I1315

Young, Edward, 1683–1765: A1700, C0567, O0564, W0723

V. Index of References to Composers of Settings and of Tunes Named or Quoted

'A cobbler there was': T0916
'A health to Betty': C0334, L0090
'A noble race of Shinkin': Q0037
'A pudding': G0322
'A reverend dean': I1501
'A soldier and a sailor': W2415
'A very pretty fancy': A1952
'A young man and a maid': H1352
'Abbot of Canterbury, The': C0369, C0374, Y0103
'A-begging we will go': I0005, I0013, W0763, W1845
'Adieu Phyllis': T2754
'Alexis shunned his fellow swains': O0642
'Ally Croker': F0785, T1629, U0123
'An old man is a bedful of bones': G0103, I0962
'An' thou wad my own thing': W0576, W2135
'Archbishop of Canterbury, The': I0890, T1638
Arnold, Samuel, 1740-1802: C0313, H1083, O0228
'Arthur of Bradley': S0730
'As Cupid one day': A0157
'As near Portobello lying': A1554
'Auld lang syne': S0475, T2185
'Auld Reb Morrice': T2030
'Away to the Downs': C0447

Bach, Johann Christian, 1735-1782: F0088
'Beggar of Hull, The': O0036
'Beggar wench of Hull, The': I1509
'Betsy Bell': T3154
'Black jack': Z0011
'Black joke': T1434
'Black lady, The': T2783
'Blacksmith, The': A0298, I0365
Blow, John, 1648-1708: A1571
'Bonny Nell': I1535
'Bow bow': A0966
Boyce, William, 1711-1779: B0541, F0052, F0325, L0481,
    N0072, O0428, O0525, O0852, S0201, T0116, T1103, T1323,
    W1530, W2283, Y0175
'Bright god of day, The': T3048
'Britain's new health': G0384
'Britons strike home': P0286
'Broom of Cowden knows, The': F0153, H0252
'Broom, The': H0251
'Bumper Squire Jones': M0430, M0731, O0913, Y0021
Burrell, [ ], composer: L0308

'Cambridge new': T1600
Campion, Thomas, 1567-1620: I0616

'Caron': D0397, H1116
'Cavallilly man': F0626
'Chevy Chase': A0920, G0235, G0238, G0239, G0240,
    G0241, G0242, G0243, J0094, O0904, R0225, T1038,
    T1597, T3092, W0989, W1491
'Children in the wood, The': M0448
Cocchi, Gioacchino, b. c. 1720: O0271
'Cold and raw the north wind did blow': T1350
'Colin's complaint': A0993
'Come buy my greens and flowers fine': P0185
'Commons and Peers, The': A1805, A1878
'Cook Lorell': W2315
'Couragio': C0290
'Cuckolds all a-row': N0462
'Cutpurse, The': C0445, O0983

'Dainty Davie': A0513
'Damask rose, The': C0047
'Daniel Cooper and his man': W0091
De Fosch, [ ], composer (1729-1745): A1064, T2405,
    W1135, W1592
'Dear Catholic brother': P0263
'Derry down': A0041
'Despairing beside a clear stream': B0664, W2503
'Doctor Faustus': A1880
'Dorsetshire march, The': W1636
'Down derry down': S0354
'Down the burn Davie': A1564
'Dragon of Wantley, The': I1591
'Duke of Lorraine's march, The': R0218
'Dumb &c.': T0425
Dupuis, Thomas Sanders, 1733-1796: I1110, S0199
'Dursley [D'Urfey?]'s fart': O0106
'Eckey's mare': I1015

'Fair lady lay your costly robes aside': F0441
'Fairest isle': C0268
'Fanny blooming': T3102
Festing, John, composer (1730): H1196
'First came my Lord Scroope': O1129
'Forsaken maid, The': N0073
'Fortune my foe': O0037
'Fourth Psalm': R0001, W0891
'Friar Bacon walks again': W1605

Gambarini, Elizabetta, 1731-1765: T2237
'Gather your rosebuds': K0012
'Gilding of the devil': O0598

'Girls, girls, come out to play': T0560
Gladwin, [ ], composer, d. 1740 or earlier: D0133
'God bless great George our king': W2116
'God prosper long our noble King': I0494
'God save great George our king': S1389
'God save our noble king': S0242, T2527
Granom, Lewis, composer (1729–62): G0007, L0490,
    N0505, O0611, W1675, Y0197
Green, Dr. [ ], composer (1732): W1458
'Greensleeves and pudding pies': W2608

Handel, George Friedrich, 1685–1759: C0077, C0086,
    G0012, I0318, L0687, M0373, O0600, O0674, S1010, T1688,
    T3198, W0485, W1798, W1921, W2628, Y0576, Z0001
Hayes, William, 1708–1777: D0031
Haym, Nicola Francesco, 1678–1729: A0335
'Heart of oak are our ships': Y0100, Y0202
Heighington, Musgrave, 1679–1764: A1638, W1215
'Help Lords and Commons': N0463
'High-mettled racer': I0969
Holcombe, Henry, c. 1693–c. 1750: B0497
'Hosier's ghost': A1554
'How gaily a sailor's life passes': W1435
'How now comes on': C0278
Howard, Samuel, 1710–1782: D0250, S1033

'I love it, but I love it so': W0632
'I love you more and more each day': W1326
'Ianthe the lovely': J0023
'If a body see a body': I0488
'I'll make thee, fair, to follow me': A0990
'I'll range around the shady bowers': F0178
'I'll tell thee Dick': C0298, T0917, Y0023
'In Crete day': M0633
'In the days of my youth': Y0142
'Irish jig, The': T3330

'Jama both ragged and bound': K0032
'Jamaica': A0107
'Joan Sanderson': T1942
'Jolly mortals fill your glasses': T3282
'Jovial beggar, The': I0009

'Katherine Moggy': B0473, L0180
'Katherine Ogie': A1692
'King and the cobbler, The': A0994
'King John and the Abbot of Canterbury': A1626,
    C0370, I0329, Y0335
'King of France with forty thousand men': H0350
'King shall enjoy his own again, The': W0664
Kingsman, Miss [ ], composer (1791): T2779

'Lads of Duna, The': T0699
'Lady lie near me': M0064
'Lady's fall, The': G0194
Lampi, [ ], composer: W1559
'Lass of Patie's mill, The': T0792
'Last time I came o'er the moor, The': M0288
Le Grange, [ ], composer (1677): N0240
'Let ambition fill thy mind': B0532
Leveridge, Richard, 1670–1758: T2525, Y0080

'Lilliburlero': I1247, T0602, T1657
Locke, Matthew, 1629–1677: W0864
'Long Laurence': T1854
'Louvre, the': A0928
'Love's a dream': W1629
'Loyal tinker, The': A0923
'Lud what's come to my mother': L0707

'Men in fashion': W2591
Munro, John, composer: W1872
'My love is to Jamaica gone': T3122

'Nancy Dawson': O0051

'Oak stick, The': I0919
'Of noble race was Shinkin': H0500, O0794, T3290
'Oh the charming month of May': O0672
'Oh the roast beef of old England': A0029, B0210, B0481,
    F0321, U0126, W1638, Y0101
'Old Simon the king': T1877
'Old stories tell how Heracles': G0289
'One evening having lost': L0288
'Over the hills and far away': T2739

'Packington's pound': A1845, B0613, C0372, D0277, L0143,
    L0147, M0617, M0630, O1115, R0102, T3368, W0811,
    W1158, W1363, Y0067, Y0186, Y0340
Palma, P., composer (1751): H1494
Pepusch, Johann Christoph, 1667–1752: S0208
'Play of love, The': M0278
'Poor Shon': S0036
'Pretty parrot, say': P0319
'Princess royal': F0051
'Profitez bien jeunes fillettes': I0493
Purcell, Henry, 1659–1695: A1313, H0317, N0253, O0574,
    S0175

Riesh, [ ], composer: A1069
'Rise up Randall': O1121
'Roast beef of old England, The': C0371, C0514, S0601
'Robin had a horse, and Jenny had a mare': A1688
'Roslin's castle': A1937
Rossetti, [ ]: I0616

'Sage leaf': I0376
'Saint Martin's Lane': E0112
'Sally': E0118
'Scotch haymakers': I1054
Smith, John Christopher, 1712–1795: A1064, B0420,
    F0219, F0251, O0590, W0893, Y0151

'Taking of snuff': T1458
'There was a jovial beggar': Y0052, Y0068, Y0107
'There was an old woman and she sold puddings and
    pies': A1428
'To all ye ladies now at land': S0350, T2786, T2788,
    T2790, T3095, T2789, T2791
'To all ye ladies now at London': T3123
'To you fair ladies now at land': W1906, Y0177, Y0200
'Tom o' Bedlam': A1004
'Tom Tyler': N0462

'Townsman's cap, The': L0114
'Trip to Marylebone': O0168
''Twas early one morning': I0892

'Under the greenwood tree': C0341, C0375

Valton, Peter, composer (1763): W0192, W1155
'Vicar of Bray, The': I1017, I1018, I1096, W1245
Vincent, R., composer (1738): D0017, I1324
'Walsingham': A1456

Weldon, John, 1676–1736: F0653
'What beauteous scenes': W0372
'What is greater joy or pleasure': L0481
'When fair Aurelia': L0203
'When I was a dame of honor': W2234, Y0017
'When Orpheus went down to the regions below':
    W1216
'When Sol descended to the deep': W0255

'When the weather is cold and raw': A0016
'Wherry Whigs a woman': N0403
'Which nobody can deny': F0304, P0266, T1637, W0100
'Whoop do me no harm': O1083, T3036, W1364
'Why should a blockhead have 'em so': Y0555
'Widow's song, The': R0195
'Windsor Tarras': D0375
Worgan, John, 1724–1790: C0505, H0287, I0132, T2247,
    T2717
'World's past, The': G0329
'Would fate but make Belinda mine': T3259

'Ye beaux of pleasure': O0473
'Ye Commons and Peers': F0381, Y0358
'Yeoman of Kent, The': O0970
'Youth youth thou hadst better been starved': T1523,
    Y0309, Y0312

'Zany': T1965
'Zephyrs gently court': A1494